## Index of Categories



Turn first to the Index of Categories for an overview of all the subjects.
OR

Look up your idea word in the Key Word Index (see back endpapers).
OR

# THE INTERNATIONAL THESAURUS OF QUOTATIONS

# The INTERNATIONAL THESAURUS of QUOTATIONS

compiled by

*Rhoda Thomas Tripp*

*London*

GEORGE ALLEN & UNWIN LTD

RUSKIN HOUSE · MUSEUM STREET

First Published in Great Britain in 1973

Second impression 1974



ISBN 0 04 808013 6

Printed in Great Britain

by Unwin Brothers Limited, Gresham Press, Old Woking, Surrey

## ACKNOWLEDGMENTS

Grateful acknowledgment is made to the following for permission to reprint selections included in this book:

George Allen & Unwin Ltd.: quotations from *The Ethics of Aristotle*, translated by J. A. K. Thomson; from the *Panchatantra*, translated by Franklin Edgerton; from *The Revolt of the Masses* by José Ortega y Gasset; from *The Conquest of Happiness* and *Unpopular Essays* by Bertrand Russell.

Beacon Press: quotations from *Notes of a Native Son*, reprinted by permission of the Beacon Press, copyright © 1955 by James Baldwin. The Bobbs-Merrill Company, Inc.: quotations from Epicurus, *Letters, Principal Doctrines and Vatican Sayings*, translated by Russel M. Geer, copyright © 1964 by The Bobbs-Merrill Company, Inc., reprinted by permission of The Liberal Arts Press Division; from *Company Manners*, copyright 1951, 1953, 1954 by Louis Kronenberger, reprinted by permission of the publishers, The Bobbs-Merrill Company, Inc. The Bodley Head: quotations from *The Crack-Up* by F. Scott Fitzgerald (*The Bodley Head Scott Fitzgerald*, Vol. III). George Braziller, Inc.: quotations from *Music from Inside Out* by Ned Rorem, reprinted with the permission of the publisher, copyright © 1967 by Ned Rorem. Curtis Brown, Ltd.: quotations from *The Passionate State of Mind* by Eric Hoffer, reprinted by permission of Curtis Brown, Ltd., copyright 1954, 1955 by Eric Hoffer.

Calder and Boyars, Ltd.: quotations from *Silence* by John Cage; from *The Art of Love* by Ovid, translated by Rolfe Humphries. Chandler Publishing Company: quotations from *Three Plays on Justice* by Ugo Betti. Chatto and Windus and Mrs. Laura Huxley: quotations from *Collected Essays* by Aldous Huxley. Constable Publishers: quotations from *Dialogues in Limbo* by George Santayana. Cornell University Press: quotations from Plato's *Apology*, translated by Lane Cooper.

Joan Daves: quotations from *Strength to Love* by Martin Luther King, reprinted by permission of Joan Daves, copyright © 1963 by Martin Luther King, Jr. Dodd, Mead & Company: 500 quotations from *The Home Book of Quotations* by Burton Stevenson. Doubleday & Company, Inc.: quotations from *The Summing Up* by W. Somerset Maugham, copyright 1938 by W. Somerset Maugham, reprinted by permission of Doubleday & Company, Inc. E. P. Dutton & Co., Inc.: quotations from *And Even Now* and *A Christmas Garland* by Max Beerbohm, Dutton Paperback Edition (1960), reprinted by permission of E. P. Dutton & Co., Inc.; from *Naked Masks: Five Plays* by Luigi Pirandello, edited by Eric Bentley, copyright 1922, 1952 by E. P. Dutton & Co., Inc., renewal, 1950, in the names of Stefano, Fausto and Lietta Pirandello, reprinted by permission of the publishers.

Norma Millay Ellis: lines from *Collected Poems* by Edna St. Vincent Millay.

Faber and Faber Ltd.: quotations from *Markings* by Dag Hammarskjöld, translated by Leif Sjöberg and W. H. Auden, reprinted by permission of Faber and Faber Ltd. John Farquharson Ltd.: quotations from *Notes of a Native Son* by James Baldwin. Farrar, Straus & Giroux, Inc.: quotations, reprinted with the permission of Farrar, Straus & Giroux, Inc., from *Against Interpretation* by Susan Sontag, copyright © 1961, 1962, 1963, 1964, 1965, 1966 by Susan Sontag; from *Earthly Paradise* by Robert Phelps, copyright © 1966 by Farrar, Straus & Giroux, Inc.

Hamish Hamilton Ltd.: quotations from *The Unquiet Grave* by Cyril Connolly; from *Carnets (Notebooks)* by Albert Camus, copyright © 1966, Hamish Hamilton Ltd., London. Harcourt, Brace & World, Inc.: quotations from *The Modern Temper* by Joseph Wood Krutch; from *Flight to Arras* by Antoine de Saint-Exupéry, translated by Lewis Galantière, copyright, 1942, by Harcourt, Brace & World, Inc. and reprinted with their permission; from *Wind, Sand and Stars* by Antoine de Saint-Exupéry, translated by Lewis Galantière, copyright, 1939, by Antoine de Saint-Exupéry, copyright, 1967, by Lewis Galantière, reprinted by permission of Harcourt, Brace & World, Inc.; from *The Wisdom of the Sands* by Antoine de Saint-Exupéry, translated by Stuart Gilbert, copyright, 1950, by Harcourt, Brace & World, Inc. and reprinted with their permission; from *Complete Poems* of Carl Sandburg; from *Poems 1923–1954* by E. E. Cummings; from *The People, Yes* by Carl Sandburg, copyright, 1936, by Harcourt, Brace & World, Inc., copyright, 1964, by Carl Sandburg, reprinted by permission of the publisher. Harper & Row, Publishers, Inc.: quotations from *The Passionate State of Mind* by Eric Hoffer, Harper, 1955; from *The True Believer* by Eric Hoffer, Harper, 1951; from *The Ordeal of Change* by Eric Hoffer, Harper & Row, 1963; from *The Colby Essays* by Frank Moore Colby, edited by Clarence Day, Jr., Harper, 1926; from *The Unquiet Grave* by Palinurus (Cyril Connolly), Harper, 1945; from *Mark Twain's Notebook*, with comments by Albert Bigelow Paine, Harper, 1935; from *Collected Essays* by Aldous Huxley, Harper, 1959; from *Strength to Love* (Pocket Books edition) by Martin Luther King, Jr., Harper & Row, 1963. Harvard University Press: lines from *The Poems of Emily Dickinson*, edited by Thomas H. Johnson, reprinted by permission of the publishers and the Trustees of Amherst College, The Belknap Press of Harvard University Press, copyright, 1951, 1955, by The President and Fellows of Harvard College, Cambridge, Mass. Piet Hein: lines from *Grooks*, 1966. William Heinemann Ltd.: quotations from *And Even Now* and *A Christmas Garland* by Max Beerbohm; and from *The Summing Up* by W. Somerset Maugham. Hill and Wang, Inc.: quotations from *Mark Twain on the Damned Human Race*, edited by Janet Smith. Holt, Rinehart and Winston, Inc.: quotations from *Complete Poems of Robert Frost*, copyright 1923, 1928, 1930, 1939 by Holt, Rinehart and Winston, Inc., copyright 1936, 1951, © 1956, 1958 by Robert Frost, copyright © 1964, 1967 by Lesley Frost Ballantine; from *Selected Prose of Robert Frost*, edited by Hyde Cox and Edward Connery Lathem, copyright 1946 by Robert Frost, reprinted by permission of Holt, Rinehart and Winston, Inc. Houghton Mifflin Company: quotations from *The Autobiography of Will Rogers*, selected and edited by Donald Day, 1949.

Indiana University Press: quotations from *The Art of Love* by Ovid, translated by Rolfe Humphries. The International Copyright Bureau Ltd.: quotations from *Naked Masks: Five Plays* by Luigi Pirandello, edited by Eric Bentley.

Louis Kronenberger: quotations from *Company Manners*, 1954.

Max Lerner: quotations from *Actions and Passions*, 1949, and from *The Unfinished Country*, 1959. J. B. Lippincott Company: quotations from *Sundial of the Seasons* by Hal Borland; and from *More in Anger* by Marya Mannes. Little, Brown and Company: lines from *Verses from 1929 On* by Ogden Nash, copyright 1931, 1932, 1933, 1934, 1935, 1936, 1937, 1938, 1939, 1940, 1941, 1942, 1943, 1944, 1945, 1946, 1947, 1948, 1949, 1950, 1951, 1952, 1953, 1954, 1955, © 1956, 1957, 1959, by Ogden Nash; from *The Complete Poems of Emily Dickinson*, ed. by Thomas H. Johnson, copyright 1890, 1891, 1896 by Roberts Brothers, copyright 1914, 1918, 1919, 1924, 1929, 1930, 1932, 1935, 1937, 1942 by Martha Dickinson Bianchi, © copyright 1951, 1955 by the President and Fellows of Harvard College, copyright 1952 by Alfred Leete Hampson, copyright © 1957, 1958, 1960 by Mary L. Hampson. Liveright Publishing Corporation: quotations from *The Conquest of Happiness* by Bertrand Russell, permission by Liveright, Publishers, New York, copyright ® 1958 by Bertrand Russell.

MacGibbon & Kee Ltd.: lines from *Paterson*, Book III, and from *Pictures from Brueghel and Other Poems* by William Carlos Williams. W. Somerset Maugham: quotations from *The Summing Up*. William Morrow & Company, Inc.: quotations from *The Twelve Seasons* by Joseph Wood Krutch, copyright 1949, Apollo edition. John Murray (Publishers) Ltd.: proverbs from *Burmese Proverbs*, translated by Hla Pe, copyright 1962, Wisdom of the East series.

New Directions Publishing Corp.: quotations from *The Crack-Up* by F. Scott Fitzgerald, copyright 1934, 1935 by Esquire Publications, Inc., 1945 by New Directions Publishing Corporation; from *The Wisdom of the Heart*, copyright 1941 by New Directions Publishing Corporation; from *Paterson*, Book III, copyright 1949 by William Carlos Williams; from *Pictures from Brueghel and Other Poems*, copyright 1955 by William Carlos Williams; all quotations reprinted by permission of New Directions Publishing Corporation. W. W. Norton & Company, Inc.: quotations from *The Revolt of the Masses* by José Ortega y Gasset, copyright 1932 by W. W. Norton & Company, Inc., copyright renewed © 1960 by Teresa Carey.

Penguin Books Ltd.: quotations from *Meditations* by Marcus Aurelius, translated by Maxwell Staniforth; from *The Misanthrope and Other Plays* by Molière, translated by John Wood. Peter Pauper Press, Inc.: proverbs from *African Proverbs*, compiled by Charlotte and Wolf Leslau. Laurence Pollinger Limited: quotations from *The Wisdom of the Heart* by Henry Miller. Antonio Porchia, D. J. Vogelmann, and *Harper's Bazaar:* quotations from *Voces* by Antonio Porchia. Princeton University Press: quotations from *Heraclitus*, translated by Philip Wheelwright, copyright © 1959 by Princeton University Press.

Random House, Inc. Alfred A. Knopf, Inc.: quotations from *The Divine Comedy* by Dante, translated by Lawrence Grant White, copyright 1948 by Pantheon Books, Inc., reprinted by permission of Random House, Inc.; from *Beyond Good and Evil* by Friedrich Nietzsche, translated by Walter Kaufmann, copyright © 1966 by Random House, Inc., reprinted by permission; from *The Journals of André Gide*, vols. I & II, translated by Justin O'Brien, copyright 1947 and 1948 by Alfred A. Knopf, Inc., reprinted by permission of the publisher; from *The Counterfeiters* by André Gide, translated by Dorothy Bussy and Justin O'Brien, copyright, 1927, 1951, 1955 by Alfred A. Knopf, Inc., reprinted by permission of the publisher; from *Markings* by Dag Hammarskjöld, translated by Leif Sjöberg and W. H. Auden, copyright © 1964 by Alfred A. Knopf, Inc. and Faber and Faber, Ltd., reprinted by permission of the publisher; from *Notebooks* by Albert Camus, translated by Philip Thody, copyright © 1963 by Hamish Hamilton Ltd. and Alfred A. Knopf, Inc., reprinted by permission of the publisher; from *The Prophet* by Kahlil Gibran, reprinted with permission of the publisher, Alfred A. Knopf, Inc., copyright 1923 by Kahlil Gibran, renewal copyright 1951 by Administrators C.T.A. of Kahlil Gibran Estate, and Mary G. Gibran; from *Minority Report* by H. L. Mencken, reprinted by permission of the publisher, copyright © 1956 by Alfred A. Knopf, Inc.; from the *Prejudices* series by H. L. Mencken, reprinted by permission of the publisher, copyright 1919, 1920, 1922, 1924, 1926, 1927 by Alfred A. Knopf, Inc., renewed 1947, 1948, 1950, 1954, 1955 by H. L. Mencken; from *The Cart and the Horse*, by Louis Kronenberger, copyright © 1957, 1958, 1961, 1963, 1964 by Louis Kronenberger, reprinted by permission of Alfred A. Knopf, Inc.

St. Martin's Press, Inc.: quotations from *Unkempt Thoughts* by Stanislaw Lec. Leah Salisbury, Inc.: quotations from *Once Around the Sun* by Brooks Atkinson, copyright © 1951, reprinted by permission of Brooks Atkinson. Schocken Books Inc.: proverbs from *Yiddish Proverbs*, edited by Hanan J. Ayalti, copyright © 1949 by Schocken Books Inc. Charles Scribner's Sons: quotations from *Dialogues in Limbo* by George Santayana, used by permission of Charles Scribner's Sons; from *Reflections on America* by Jacques Maritain, pages 20, 37, 44, 97, 134, 140, 153, 166, 190, 196, used by permission of Charles Scribner's Sons. Martin Secker & Warburg Limited: quotations from *Earthly Paradise* by Colette, edited by Robert Phelps; from *Writers at Work*, The *Paris Review* Interviews, vol. I, edited by Malcolm Cowley. Sidgwick & Jackson Ltd.: quotations from *The Ordeal of Change* by Eric Hoffer. Simon and Schuster, Inc.: quotations from *Actions and Passions* by Max Lerner, copyright 1949; from *Unpopular Essays* by Bertrand Russell, copyright 1950.

Mrs. James Thurber: quotations from *Lanterns and Lances*, copyright © 1960 by James Thurber, published by Harper & Row, New York.

University Books Inc.: quotations from *The Sacred Books of Confucius*, edited and translated by Ch'u Chai and Winberg Chai. University of California Press: quotations from *Juan de Mairena* by Antonio Machado, translated by Ben Belitt. The University of Chicago Press: lines from *The Odes of Pindar*, translated by Richmond Lattimore, copyright 1947 by The University of Chicago; from Homer's *Iliad*, translated by Richmond Lattimore, copyright 1951 by The University of Chicago; from The Complete Greek Tragedies, edited by David Grene and Richmond Lattimore, as follows: *Aeschylus*, vol. 1, copyright 1942 by The University of Chicago and vol. 2, copyright © 1956; *Sophocles*, vol 1, copyright 1941 by Harcourt, Brace & World, Inc., copyright 1942, 1954 by The University of Chicago and vol. 2, copyright © 1957 by The University of Chicago Press; *Euripides*, vol. 1, copyright © 1942, 1955, 1956 by The University of Chicago, vol. 2, copyright © 1956, 1958 by The University of Chicago, and vol. 3, copyright © 1958, 1959 by The University of Chicago.

Vanguard Press, Inc.: quotations from *The Mechanical Bride* by Marshall McLuhan, 1951. The Viking Press, Inc.: quotations from *The Portable Dorothy Parker*, copyright 1926, 1954 by Dorothy Parker, reprinted by permission of The Viking Press, Inc.; from *The Province of the Heart* by Phyllis McGinley, copyright 1949, 1951, 1952, 1954, 1956, © 1958, 1959 by Phyllis McGinley, reprinted by permission of The Viking Press, Inc.; from *Writers at Work*, The *Paris Review* Interviews, edited by Malcolm Cowley, copyright © 1957, 1958 by The Paris Review, Inc., reprinted by permission of The Viking Press, Inc.; from *Thus Spoke Zarathustra* by Friedrich Nietzsche, translated and edited by Walter Kaufmann.

A. P. Watt & Son: quotations from *The Summing Up* by W. Somerset Maugham, reprinted by permission of the Literary Executor of W. Somerset Maugham and William Heinemann Ltd. Wesleyan University Press: quotations from *Silence* by John Cage, copyright © 1939, 1944, 1949, 1952, 1954, 1955, 1957, 1958, 1959, 1961 by John Cage. World's Work Ltd.: quotations from *The Province of the Heart* by Phyllis McGinley.

# CONTENTS

# PUBLISHER'S PREFACE

Over a century ago Peter Mark Roget invented a method of classifying words by meaning and called the collection that he made a "thesaurus." His book quickly proved to be the most precise and useful compendium of synonyms ever devised. Frequently revised to keep pace with a changing language, it has long held a place beside the dictionary as a basic tool for speakers and writers.

In *The International Thesaurus of Quotations*, we have tried to create a book that performs with quotations the same service that *Roget's International Thesaurus* performs with words and phrases. This new reference book, compiled at our request by Mrs. Tripp, is primarily intended for those who want to use quotations, rather than simply to read them or recall them to mind. Like its model, it is for persons who have an idea and who are looking for the means to express it exactly and effectively. Although its indexes offer the key to finding half-remembered quotations, it is particularly designed for a generation that seldom memorizes literary passages. Its users will very likely turn to it less often to recall a familiar saying than to find fresh words that eloquently express and enlarge ideas of their own.

In order to make the contents of this book readily accessible to that purpose, we have adopted the basic principles of Roget's *Thesaurus*. Certain features of his classification scheme, however, are not suited to the cataloguing of quotations. An alphabetical arrangement of subject headings, for example, provides readier access to quotations than any adaptation that we might have made of Roget's synopsis of categories. At the same time, we have found it advantageous to remain faithful to those qualities of Roget's book which, in our estimation, account for the effectiveness with which it achieves its objectives. These qualities are comprehensiveness, timeliness, and precision, which together add up to utility.

The criterion of utility demanded that we make our thesaurus of quotations as much a practical tool as Roget's *Thesaurus*. Since both books are primarily intended for the convenience of speakers and writers, we had to decide at the outset what kinds of quotations would be most used today in writing and formal speech. Almost any quotation might, of course, find some occasion for use, but a book intended for quick and frequent reference must be kept to a handy size. It was evident that, although comprehensiveness was to be one of our goals, we must find a stricter definition for it than mere inclusiveness.

Examination of the larger standard anthologies was helpful in showing us that we could well do without whole classes of material, such as slogans, titles of books and songs, and old saws. Much more reluctantly we decided to eliminate phrases in favor of quotations in complete sentences. Although this decision was dictated mainly by considerations of space, we felt that familiar phrases, however colorful or apt, quickly degenerate into clichés that tend to ossify speech rather than enliven it. Omitting phrases enabled us to include sixteen thousand quotations, each of which makes a complete, though concise, statement of a point of view about some aspect of life.

Another characteristic of utility that we hoped to achieve in this book was timeliness, in its broad sense of relevance to the concerns of present-day users. Our thesaurus, if it were to be useful to a wide range of speakers and writers in a generation preoccupied with the present moment, would have to give full attention to its own age without being obsessed by it. More than a third of the quotations in this book come from our own century. Many of the book's most contemporary-sounding observations were, however, made by men of other centuries, some as far back as the time of Solon. Scores of penetrating and pungent comments have been gathered from figures who are represented in most anthologies only by pious sentiments. Nevertheless, piety has its spokesmen here, as does every shade of opinion on philosophical, political, and social topics. And we have retained the thousands of familiar quotations that have something to say to our time.

In keeping with the global awareness of the reading public today, we have included quotations, both old and new, from the literatures of many countries. Where up-to-date translations were not available, we asked translators to supply them. In addition to quotations, there are proverbs from many peoples, some not previously represented in standard books of quotations.

An important aspect of timeliness in a modern book of quotations is, simply, time. Because time is a scarce and highly valued commodity among today's readers and audiences, writers and speakers must perforce be sparing in the demands that they make upon it. Lengthy quotations, therefore, are not in favor, and we have included none in this thesaurus. There are very few that exceed fifty words in length, and most are considerably shorter. In order to insure, however, that users of the quotations can check them if they wish against their original context, we have given a full citation of the source in every case where that source could be discovered.

The third characteristic of utility in which we hoped to match Roget's *Thesaurus* was precision. The key to the success of the Roget system is the exactness with which it classified words by subject. Since our thesaurus is intended primarily to aid those who in searching for quotations can best find them through subject categories, it was essential that we classify each quotation strictly by its meaning. This seemed an obvious aim for any collection of quotations arranged by subject, but investigation of other topically arranged anthologies showed us that their quotations were often included under subject headings that reflected key words rather than the meanings of the quotations as a whole. (For example, the well-known proverb "In the country of the blind the one-eyed man is king" is usually placed under the heading Blindness, though the proverb is obviously not concerned with physical affliction.) We tried to avoid this pitfall by examining the basic sense of each quotation apart from its apparent subject matter, which is often quite different. Many of the greatest sayings, however, do not have absolute meanings. They owe their universality to their ambiguity, their capacity to hold different meanings for different people and ages. Inevitably, users of this thesaurus will quarrel with our decisions in categorizing certain quotations. We hope that the profusion of cross-references we have made between categories will enable them to find every quotation that bears any relation to a given subject. The indexes of key words and authors should lead users to familiar quotations.

A word should be said about our solution to the problem of quotations that have more than one source. The origin of most proverbs is, by their nature, untraceable. We have generally cited the earliest sources of which we are aware, but we have not hesitated to choose later versions of the same ideas when they seemed more felicitously worded. We followed this same practice with sayings attributed to individuals.

As we have said, our intention has been to construct a reference book for speakers and writers that would worthily complement *Roget's International Thesaurus.* In so doing we have deliberately focused our attention on a somewhat strictly defined goal. Happily, the acute perceptions and lively words of thoughtful and witty men and women have a life of their own that refuses to be confined by lexicographic theories. We hope that users of this book will find it as helpful as we have tried to make it. We would be disappointed, however, if they could not take equal satisfaction in browsing through its pages for the casual pleasures they will find there.

Mrs. Tripp was aided by the persons listed below in gathering, indexing, and classifying the quotations in this book. We extend our thanks to them. In most instances where translators are not specified, French translations are by Miss Holder or Mrs. Hatvary, Latin translations by Miss Vaughan.

Geraldyne Addison
Ernestine Samuels Austen
Joan Cenedella
Arlene Donly
George Flynn
Michael Gelber
Zachary Goodyear
Maureen Grice
Roy Harris
Bertha Hatvary
Walter Hayward
Maryse Holder
Gloria Jordan
Geraldine Koepke
Margaret Miner
Samuel Mitnick
Robert Nero
Charles North
Gail Quinn
Michael Rose
Richard Schlesinger
Sharon Schlesinger
William Schwartz
Susan Simon
Victoria Simons
William Stern
Anne Vaughan
Lewis Warsh

James B. Simpson's *Contemporary Quotations*, published by the Thomas Y. Crowell Company in 1964, was used as a source for some of the quotations dated 1950 and later.

# INTERNATIONAL THESAURUS OF QUOTATIONS

# INTERNATIONAL THESAURUS OF QUOTATIONS

## A

### 1. ABILITY

**See also 309. Excellence; 956. Talent; 1029. Vocations**

1. Natural abilities are like natural plants, that need pruning by study; and studies themselves do give forth directions too much at large, except they be bounded in by experience. FRANCIS BACON, "Of Studies," *Essays* (1625).

2. Knowledge may give weight, but accomplishments give lustre, and many more people see than weigh. LORD CHESTERFIELD, *Letters*, May 8, 1750.

3. History repeats itself, but the special call of an art which has passed away is never reproduced. It is as utterly gone out of the world as the song of a destroyed wild bird. JOSEPH CONRAD, *The Mirror of the Sea* (1906), 8.

4. As many languages as he has, as many friends, as many arts and trades, so many times is he a man. EMERSON, "Culture," *The Conduct of Life* (1860).

5. Everyone must row with the oars he has. ENGLISH PROVERB.

6. The same man cannot well be skilled / in everything; each has his special excellence. EURIPIDES, *Rhesus* (c. 455–441 B.C.), tr. Richmond Lattimore.

7. In a world as empirical as ours, a youngster who does not know what he is good *at* will not be sure what he is good *for*. EDGAR Z. FRIEDENBERG, "Emotional Development in Adolescence," *The Vanishing Adolescent* (1959).

8. 'Tis skill, not strength, that governs a ship. THOMAS FULLER, M.D., *Gnomologia* (1732), 5116.

9. The winds and waves are always on the side of the ablest navigators. EDWARD GIBBON, *Decline and Fall of the Roman Empire* (1776), 68.

10. Most do violence to their natural aptitude, and thus attain superiority in nothing. BALTASAR GRACIÁN, *The Art of Worldly Wisdom* (1647), 24, tr. Joseph Jacobs.

11. Skill and confidence are an unconquered army. GEORGE HERBERT, *Jacula Prudentum* (1651).

12. One should stick to the sort of thing for which one was made; / I tried to be an herbalist, / Whereas I should keep to the butcher's trade. LA FONTAINE, "The Horse and the Wolf," *Fables* (1668–94), tr. Marianne Moore.

13. It is easier to appear worthy of positions that we have not got, than of those that we have. LA ROCHEFOUCAULD, *Maxims* (1665), tr. Kenneth Pratt.

14. Our vanity desires that what we do best should be considered what is hardest for us. NIETZSCHE, *Beyond Good and Evil* (1886), 143, tr. Walter Kaufmann.

15. Skills vary with the man. We must tread a straight path and strive by that which is born in us. PINDAR, *Odes* (5th c. B.C.), Nemea 1, tr. Richmond Lattimore.

16. He is the best sailor who can steer within fewest points of the wind, and exact a motive power out of the greatest obstacles. THOREAU, "Friday," *A Week on the Concord and Merrimack Rivers* (1849).

### 2. ABSENCE

**See also 666. Parting**

1. The heart may think it knows better: the senses know that absence blots people

out. We have really no absent friends. ELIZABETH BOWEN, *The Death of the Heart* (1938), 2.2.

2. Our hours in love have wings; in absence crutches. COLLEY CIBBER, *Xerxes* (1699), 4.3.

3. It takes time for the absent to assume their true shape in our thoughts. After death they take on a firmer outline and then cease to change. COLETTE, "The Captain," *Earthly Paradise* (1966), 1, ed. Robert Phelps.

4. How great love is, presence best trial makes, / But absence tries how long this love will be. JOHN DONNE, "Valediction: Of the Book," *Songs and Sonnets* (1633).

5. Those who are absent are always wrong. ENGLISH PROVERB.

6. Absence sharpens love, presence strengthens it. THOMAS FULLER, M.D., *Gnomologia* (1732), 755.

7. When you part from your friend, you grieve not; / For that which you love most in him may be clearer in his absence, as the mountain to the climber is clearer from the plain. KAHLIL GIBRAN, "On Friendship," *The Prophet* (1923).

8. Sometimes, when one person is missing, the whole world seems depopulated. LAMARTINE, *Premières méditations poétiques* (1820), 1.

9. Absence lessens ordinary passions and augments great ones, as the wind blows out a candle and makes a fire blaze. LA ROCHEFOUCAULD, *Maxims* (1665), tr. Kenneth Pratt.

10. The absent shall not be made heir. LATIN PROVERB.

11. The fabric of my faithful love / No power shall dim or ravel / Whilst I stay here,—but oh, my dear, / If I should ever travel! EDNA ST. VINCENT MILLAY, "To the Not Impossible Him."

12. Absences are a good influence in love and keep it bright and delicate. ROBERT LOUIS STEVENSON, title essay, 1, *Virginibus Puerisque* (1881).

13. Greater things are believed of those who are absent. TACITUS, *Histories* (A.D. 104–109), 2.83.

## ABSTINENCE

**See 859. Self-denial**

## 3. THE ABSURD

**See also 4. Absurdity; 30. Alienation; 315. Existentialism; 569. Meaning**

1. If life must not be taken too seriously—then so neither must death. SAMUEL BUTLER (d. 1902), "Death," *Note-Books* (1912).

2. The absurd is born of the confrontation between the human call and the unreasonable silence of the world. ALBERT CAMUS, *The Myth of Sisyphus* (1942).

3. The absurd is sin without God. ALBERT CAMUS, "An Absurd Reasoning," *The Myth of Sisyphus* (1942), tr. Justin O'Brien.

4. Man is able to do what he is unable to imagine. His head trails a wake through the galaxy of the absurd. RENÉ CHAR, *Leaves of Hypnos*, 227, in *Hypnos Waking* (1956), tr. Jackson Mathews and others.

5. In a world where everything is ridiculous, nothing can be ridiculed. You cannot unmask a mask. G. K. CHESTERTON, "On the Comic Spirit," *Generally Speaking* (1928).

6. Life is a jest, and all things show it; / I thought so once, but now I know it. JOHN GAY, "My Own Epitaph," *Fables* (1727–38).

7. Unextinguished laughter shakes the skies. HOMER, *Iliad* (9th c. B.C.), 1.771, tr. Alexander Pope.

8. Life has to be given a meaning because of the obvious fact that it has no meaning. HENRY MILLER, "Creative Death," *The Wisdom of the Heart* (1941).

9. Now humanity does not know where to go because no one is waiting for it: not even God. ANTONIO PORCHIA, *Voces* (1968), tr. W. S. Merwin.

10. Man's "progress" is but a gradual discovery that his questions have no meaning. SAINT-EXUPÉRY, *The Wisdom of the Sands* (1948), 39, tr. Stuart Gilbert.

11. The more absurd life is, the more insupportable death is. JEAN-PAUL SARTRE, *The Words* (1964), 1.

12. God made everything out of the void, but the void shows through. PAUL VALÉRY, *Mauvaises pensées et autres* (1941).

## 4. ABSURDITY

**See also 3. The Absurd; 814. Ridicule**

1. There is no idea, no fact, which could not be vulgarized and presented in a ludi-

crous light. DOSTOEVSKY, "Mr. —bov and the Question of Art," *Polnoye Sobraniye Sochinyeni (Complete Collected Works*, 1895), v. 9.

2. Few men, I believe, are much worth loving, in whom there is not something well worth laughing at. JULIUS CHARLES HARE and AUGUSTUS WILLIAM HARE, *Guesses at Truth* (1827).

3. The privilege of absurdity; to which no living creature is subject but man only. THOMAS HOBBES, *Leviathan* (1651), 1.5.

4. There is but one step from the sublime to the ridiculous. Attributed to NAPOLEON I, after the retreat from Russia, December 1812.

5. Life is full of infinite absurdities, which, strangely enough, do not even need to appear plausible, since they are true. LUIGI PIRANDELLO, *Six Characters in Search of an Author* (1921), 1, tr. Edward Storer.

6. Look for the ridiculous in everything and you will find it. JULES RENARD, *Journal*, February 1890, ed. and tr. Louise Bogan and Elizabeth Roget.

7. No one is laughable who laughs at himself. SENECA, *De Constantia Sapientis* (1st c.).

## ACCIDENT
**See 114. Chance**

## ACCOMPLISHMENT
**See 1. Ability; 6. Achievement**

## 5. ACCUSATION
**See also 203. Criticism; 513. Judging Others; 898. Slander**

1. When a man points a finger at someone else, he should remember that three of his fingers are pointing at himself. Author unidentified.

2. Accusing is proving, where Malice and Force sit judges. THOMAS FULLER, M.D., *Gnomologia* (1732), 758.

3. Even doubtful accusations leave a stain behind them. THOMAS FULLER, M.D., *Gnomologia* (1732), 1395.

4. It is honorable to be accused by those who deserve to be accused. LATIN PROVERB.

## 6. ACHIEVEMENT
**See also 33. Ambition; 55. Aspiration; 938. Success**

1. It is not the going out of port, but the coming in, that determines the success of a voyage. HENRY WARD BEECHER, *Proverbs from Plymouth Pulpit* (1887).

2. Who cares about great marks left behind? We have one life, rigidly defined. Just one. Our life. We have nothing else. UGO BETTI, *The Inquiry* (1944–45), 2.2, ed. Gino Rizzo.

3. By their fruits ye shall know them. *Bible*, Matthew 7:20.

4. Achievement, n. The death of endeavor and the birth of disgust. AMBROSE BIERCE, *The Devil's Dictionary* (1881–1911).

5. That low man seeks a little thing to do, / Sees it and does it: / This high man, with a great thing to pursue, / Dies ere he knows it. ROBERT BROWNING, "A Grammarian's Funeral," *Men and Women* (1855).

6. To know a man, observe how he wins his object, rather than how he loses it; for when we fail our pride supports us, when we succeed, it betrays us. CHARLES CALEB COLTON, *Lacon* (1825), 1.265.

7. The house praises the carpenter. EMERSON, *Journals*, 1836.

8. The reward of a thing well done is to have done it. EMERSON, "New England Reformers," *Essays: Second Series* (1844).

9. If you tell [count] every step, you will make a long journey of it. THOMAS FULLER, M.D., *Gnomologia* (1732), 2793.

10. Who begins too much accomplishes little. GERMAN PROVERB.

11. Back of every achievement is a proud wife and a surprised mother-in-law. BROOKS HAYS, *New York Herald Tribune*, Dec. 2, 1961.

12. When you feel how depressingly / slowly you climb, / it's well to remember that / Things Take Time. PIET HEIN, "T.T.T.," *Grooks* (1966).

13. A man dies still if he has done nothing, as one who has done much. HOMER, *Iliad* (9th c. B.C.), 9.320, tr. Richmond Lattimore.

14. It is not enough to aim, you must hit. ITALIAN PROVERB.

15. Something attempted, something done, / Has earned a night's repose. LONGFELLOW, "The Village Blacksmith" (1839), 7.

16. The heights by great men reached and kept / Were not attained by sudden flight, / But they, while their companions slept, / Were toiling upward in the night. LONGFELLOW, "The Ladder of Saint Augustine" (1858), 10.

17. Since it is not granted us to live long, let us transmit to posterity some memorial that we have at least lived. PLINY THE YOUNGER, *Letters* (c. 97–110), 3.7, tr. William Melmoth and W. M. L. Hutchinson.

18. Mighty rivers can easily be leaped at their source. PUBLILIUS SYRUS, *Moral Sayings* (1st c. B.C.), 442, tr. Darius Lyman.

19. Let the end try the man. SHAKESPEARE, *2 Henry IV* (1597–98), 2.2.50.

20. Thou shalt ever joy at eventide if thou spend the day fruitfully. THOMAS À KEMPIS, *The Imitation of Christ* (1426), 1.25.

21. The awareness of the ambiguity of one's highest achievements (as well as one's deepest failures) is a definite symptom of maturity. PAUL TILLICH, *Time*, May 17, 1963.

22. To achieve great things we must live as though we were never going to die. VAUVENARGUES, *Reflections and Maxims* (1746), 142, tr. F. G. Stevens.

## 7. ACQUAINTANCES

**See also 151. Company; 363. Friendship**

1. Like driftwood spars, which meet and pass / Upon the boundless ocean-plain, / So on the sea of life, alas! / Man meets man—meets and quits again. MATTHEW ARNOLD, "Switzerland," 7, *Empedocles on Etna, and Other Poems* (1852).

2. Acquaintance, n. A person whom we know well enough to borrow from, but not well enough to lend to. AMBROSE BIERCE, *The Devil's Dictionary* (1881–1911).

3. How casually and unobservedly we make all our most valued acquaintances. EMERSON, *Journals*, 1833.

4. There is a scarcity of friendship, but not of friends. THOMAS FULLER, M.D., *Gnomologia* (1732), 4880.

5. If a man does not make new acquaintance as he advances through life, he will soon find himself left alone. A man, Sir, should keep his friendship in constant repair. SAMUEL JOHNSON, quoted in Boswell's *Life of Samuel Johnson*, April 1775.

6. What causes us to like new acquaintances is not so much weariness of our old ones, or the pleasure of change, as disgust at not being sufficiently admired by those who know us too well, and the hope of being admired more by those who do not know so much about us. LA ROCHEFOUCAULD, *Maxims* (1665), tr. Kenneth Pratt.

## 8. ACQUISITION

**See also 401. Greed; 596. Money; 710. Possession; 740. Property**

1. Seek not proud riches, but such as thou mayest get justly, use soberly, distribute cheerfully, and leave contentedly. FRANCIS BACON, "Of Riches," *Essays* (1625).

2. Hand, n. A singular instrument worn at the end of a human arm and commonly thrust into somebody's pocket. AMBROSE BIERCE, *The Devil's Dictionary* (1881–1911).

3. It is easy to get everything you want, provided you first learn to do without the things you can not get. ELBERT HUBBARD, *The Note Book* (1927).

4. I glory / More in the cunning purchase of my wealth / Than in the glad possession. BEN JONSON, *Volpone* (1605), 1.1.

5. With the catching end the pleasures of the chase. ABRAHAM LINCOLN, speech, Jan. 27, 1838.

6. The collector walks with blinders on; he sees nothing but the prize. In fact, the acquisitive instinct is incompatible with true appreciation of beauty. ANNE MORROW LINDBERGH, "A Few Shells," *Gift from the Sea* (1955).

7. People find gold in fields, veins, river beds and pockets. Whichever, it takes work to get it out. ART LINKLETTER, *A Child's Garden of Misinformation* (1965), 7.

8. In the race for money some men may come first, but man comes last. MARYA MANNES, in *Life*, June 12, 1964.

9. I should describe the human race / as a strange species of bipeds / who cannot run fast enough / to collect the money / which they owe themselves. DON MARQUIS,

"quote and only man is vile quote," *Archy's Life of Mehitabel* (1933).

10. An end to our gettings is the only end to our losses. PUBLILIUS SYRUS, *Moral Sayings* (1st c. B.C.), 661, tr. Darius Lyman.

11. How could there be any question of acquiring or possessing, when the one thing needful for a man is to *become*—to *be* at last, and to die in the fullness of his being. SAINT-EXUPÉRY, *The Wisdom of the Sands* (1948), 38, tr. Stuart Gilbert.

12. Accursed greed for gold, / To what dost thou not drive the heart of man? VERGIL, *Aeneid* (30–19 B.C.), 3.56, tr. T. H. Delabere-May.

## 9. ACTION

**See also 10. Activity; 224. Deeds; 502. Involvement; 967. Theory**

1. Effective action is always unjust. JEAN ANOUILH, *Catch As Catch Can* (1960), tr. Lucienne Hill.

2. In the arena of human life the honours and rewards fall to those who show their good qualities in action. ARISTOTLE, *Nicomachean Ethics* (4th c. B.C.), 1.8, tr. J. A. K. Thomson.

3. A thought which does not result in an action is nothing much, and an action which does not proceed from a thought is nothing at all. GEORGES BERNANOS, "France Before the World of Tomorrow," *The Last Essays of Georges Bernanos* (1955), tr. Joan and Barry Ulanov.

4. Action should culminate in wisdom. *Bhagavadgita*, 4, tr. P. Lal.

5. Unreal is action without discipline, charity without sympathy, ritual without devotion. *Bhagavadgita*, 17, tr. P. Lal.

6. Action springs not from thought, but from a readiness for responsibility. DIETRICH BONHOEFFER, "Thoughts on Baptism," *Letters and Papers from Prison* (1953), tr. Eberhard Bethge.

7. We often do not know ourselves the grounds / On which we act, though plain to others. BERTOLT BRECHT, *Roundheads and Peakheads* (1933), 4, tr. N. Goold-Verschoyle.

8. It's all right to hesitate if you then go ahead. BERTOLT BRECHT, prologue, *The Good Woman of Setzuan* (1938–40), tr. Bentley and Apelman.

9. What hand and brain went ever paired? / What heart alike conceived and dared? / What act proved all its thought had been? ROBERT BROWNING, "The Last Ride Together," *Men and Women* (1855), 6.

10. . . . "Men of action," whose minds are too busy with the day's work to see beyond it. They are essential men, we cannot do without them, and yet we must not allow all our vision to be bound by the limitations of "men of action." PEARL S. BUCK, *What America Means to Me* (1943), 4.

11. Think'st thou existence doth depend on time? / It doth; but actions are our epochs. BYRON, *Manfred* (1817), 2.1.

12. He that has done nothing has known nothing. THOMAS CARLYLE, "Corn-Law Rhymes" (1832).

13. Once turn to practice, error and truth will no longer consort together. THOMAS CARLYLE, "Corn-Law Rhymes" (1832).

14. There can be no acting or doing of any kind, till it be recognized that there is a thing to be done; the thing once recognized, doing in a thousand shapes becomes possible. THOMAS CARLYLE, *Chartism* (1839), 6.

15. In action, be primitive; in foresight, a strategist. RENÉ CHAR, *Leaves of Hypnos*, 72, in *Hypnos Waking* (1956), tr. Jackson Mathews and others.

16. A man's most open actions have a secret side to them. JOSEPH CONRAD, *Under Western Eyes* (1911), 1.2.

17. One starts an action / Simply because one must do *something*. T. S. ELIOT, *The Elder Statesman* (1958), 2.

18. Begin and proceed on a settled and not-to-be-shaken conviction that but little is permitted to any man to do or to know, and if he complies with the first grand laws, he shall do well. EMERSON, *Journals*, 1832.

19. People who know how to act are never preachers. EMERSON, *Journals*, 1844.

20. No matter how much faculty of idle seeing a man has, the step from knowing to doing is rarely taken. EMERSON, "Power," *The Conduct of Life* (1860).

21. The materials of action are variable, but the use we make of them should be constant. EPICTETUS, *Discourses* (2nd c.), 2.5, tr. Thomas W. Higginson.

22. Most men are in a coma when they are at rest and mad when they act. EPICURUS, "Vatican Sayings" (3rd c. B.C.), 11, in

*Letters, Principal Doctrines, and Vatican Sayings*, tr. Russel M. Geer.

23. Action is the proper fruit of knowledge. THOMAS FULLER, M.D., *Gnomologia* (1732), 760.

24. Act quickly, think slowly. GREEK PROVERB.

25. In our era, the road to holiness necessarily passes through the world of action. DAG HAMMARSKJÖLD, "1955," *Markings* (1964), tr. Leif Sjoberg and W. H. Auden.

26. Life is made up of constant calls to action, and we seldom have time for more than hastily contrived answers. LEARNED HAND, speech, New York City, Jan. 27, 1952.

27. A life of action and danger moderates the dread of death. It not only gives us fortitude to bear pain, but teaches us at every step the precarious tenure on which we hold our present being. WILLIAM HAZLITT, "On the Fear of Death," *Table Talk* (1821–22).

28. To dispose a soul to action we must upset its equilibrium. ERIC HOFFER, *The Ordeal of Change* (1964), 5.

29. Action is thought tempered by illusion. ELBERT HUBBARD, *The Philistine* (1895–1915).

30. The great end of life is not knowledge but action. THOMAS HENRY HUXLEY, "Technical Education" (1877).

31. Act only on that maxim whereby you can at the same time will that it should become a universal law. IMMANUEL KANT, *Critique of Practical Reason* (1788).

32. Action [is] the great business of mankind, and the whole matter about which all laws are conversant. JOHN LOCKE, *An Essay Concerning Human Understanding* (1690), 2.22.10.

33. Lust and force are the source of all our actions; lust causes voluntary actions, force involuntary ones. PASCAL, *Pensées* (1670), 334, tr. W. F. Trotter.

34. The test of any man lies in action. PINDAR, *Odes* (5th c. B.C.), Olympia 4, tr. Richmond Lattimore.

35. We cannot withdraw our cards from the game. Were we as silent and as mute as stones, our very passivity would be an act. JEAN-PAUL SARTRE, "Présentation des 'Temps Modernes,' " *Situations* (1947–49), v. 2.

36. "I am ashamed of my emptiness," said the Word to the Work. / "I know how poor I am when I see you," said the Work to the Word. RABINDRANATH TAGORE, *Stray Birds* (1916), 138.

37. Action will remove the doubt that theory cannot solve. TEHYI HSIEH, *Chinese Epigrams Inside Out and Proverbs* (1948), 1.

38. I myself must mix with action, lest I wither by despair. ALFRED, LORD TENNYSON, "Locksley Hall" (1842).

39. Against Nature's silence I use action / In the vast indifference I invent a meaning / I don't watch unmoved I intervene / and say that this and this are wrong / and I work to alter them and improve them. PETER WEISS, *Marat/Sade* (1964), 1.13, tr. Geoffrey Skelton and Adrian Mitchell.

40. From the moment of birth we are immersed in action, and can only fitfully guide it by taking thought. ALFRED NORTH WHITEHEAD, *Science and the Modern World* (1925), 12.

41. Action is transitory—a step, a blow, / The motion of a muscle—this way or that— / 'Tis done, and in the after-vacancy / We wonder at ourselves like men betrayed. WILLIAM WORDSWORTH, *The Borderers* (1795–96).

## 10. ACTIVITY

**See also 9. Action; 161. Compulsiveness; 409. Haste; 444. Idleness; 502. Involvement; 530. Leisure; 806. Restlessness**

1. The quality of a life is determined by its activities. ARISTOTLE, *Nicomachean Ethics* (4th c. B.C.), 1.10, tr. J. A. K. Thomson.

2. To represent some party, / Busy-ness, / Travelling to, and from, / Is the distinguishing stamp of a world / Which does not see well. GOTTFRIED BENN, "Poems That Stand Still," *Statische Gedichte* (1948).

3. Renunciation and activity both liberate, / but to work is better than to renounce. *Bhagavadgita*, 5, tr. P. Lal.

4. One cannot manage too many affairs: like pumpkins in the water, one pops up while you try to hold down the other. CHINESE PROVERB.

5. It is better to wear out than to rust out. RICHARD CUMBERLAND, quoted in George Horne's *Sermon on the Duty of Contending for the Truth* (1730–92).

6. The worshipper of energy is too physi-

cally energetic to see that he cannot explore certain higher fields until he is still. CLARENCE DAY, *This Simian World* (1920), 5.

7. The most active lives have so much routine as to preclude progress almost equally with the most inactive. EMERSON, *Journals*, 1833.

8. He that is everywhere is nowhere. THOMAS FULLER, M.D., *Gnomologia* (1732), 2176.

9. What is the use of running when we are not on the right road? GERMAN PROVERB.

10. The majority prove their worth by keeping busy. A busy life is the nearest thing to a purposeful life. ERIC HOFFER, *The Ordeal of Change* (1964), 5.

11. A really busy person never knows how much he weighs. EDGAR WATSON HOWE, *Country Town Sayings* (1911).

12. If you want work well done, select a busy man: the other kind has no time. ELBERT HUBBARD, *The Note Book* (1927).

13. Determine never to be idle. No person will have occasion to complain of the want of time who never loses any. It is wonderful how much may be done if we are always doing. THOMAS JEFFERSON, letter to Martha Jefferson, May 5, 1787.

14. There is no kind of idleness by which we are so easily seduced as that which dignifies itself by the appearance of business. SAMUEL JOHNSON, *The Idler* (1758–60), 48.

15. Travel, trouble, music, art, / A kiss, a frock, a rhyme,— / I never said they feed my heart, / But still, they pass my time. DOROTHY PARKER, "Faute de Mieux," *Enough Rope* (1926), 2.

16. Our nature consists in motion; complete rest is death. PASCAL, *Pensées* (1670), 129, tr. W. F. Trotter.

17. There are people who want to be everywhere at once and they seem to get nowhere. CARL SANDBURG, "Anywhere and Everywhere People," *Complete Poems* (1950).

18. Men need some kind of external activity, because they are inactive within. SCHOPENHAUER, "Further Psychological Observations," *Parerga and Paralipomena* (1851), tr. T. Bailey Saunders.

19. Every one has time if he likes. Business runs after nobody: people cling to it of their own free will and think that to be busy is a proof of happiness. SENECA, *Letters to Lucilius* (1st c.), 106.1, tr. E. Phillips Barker.

20. Better to be eaten to death with a rust than to be scoured to nothing with perpetual motion. SHAKESPEARE, *2 Henry IV* (1597–98), 1.2.245.

21. Where most of us end up there is no knowing, but the hellbent get where they are going. JAMES THURBER, "The Wolf Who Went Places," *Further Fables for Our Time* (1956).

## 11. ACTORS

**See also 59. Audience; 143. Comedians; 965. Theater**

1. For an actress to be a success she must have the face of Venus, the brains of Minerva, the grace of Terpsichore, the memory of Macaulay, the figure of Juno, and the hide of a rhinoceros. ETHEL BARRYMORE, quoted in George Jean Nathan's *The Theatre in the Fifties* (1953).

2. The movie actor, like the sacred king of primitive tribes, is a god in captivity. ALEXANDER CHASE, *Perspectives* (1966).

3. Good actors are good because of the things they can tell us without talking. When they are talking, they are the servants of the dramatist. It is what they can show the audience when they are not talking that reveals the fine actor. CEDRIC HARDWICKE, *Theatre Arts*, February 1958.

4. Players, Sir! I look on them as no better than creatures set upon tables and joint stools to make faces and produce laughter, like dancing dogs. SAMUEL JOHNSON, quoted in Boswell's *Life of Samuel Johnson*, 1775.

5. An actor can remember his briefest notice well into senescence and long after he has forgotten his phone number and where he lives. JEAN KERR, "One Half of Two on the Aisle," *Please Don't Eat the Daisies* (1957).

6. By the time an actor knows how to act any sort of part he is often too old to act any but a few. W. SOMERSET MAUGHAM, *The Summing Up* (1938), 31.

7. O, it offends me to the soul to hear a robustious periwig-pated fellow tear a passion to tatters, to very rags, to split the ears of the groundlings. SHAKESPEARE, *Hamlet* (1600), 3.2.9.

8. Every actor in his heart believes ev-

erything bad that's printed about him. ORSON WELLES, news reports, Jan. 13, 1956.

## ADAPTATION
See 12. Adjustment

## 12. ADJUSTMENT
See also 168. Conformity; 630. Normality

1. A life will be successful or not according as the power of accommodation is equal to or unequal to the strain of fusing and adjusting internal and external changes. SAMUEL BUTLER (d. 1902), *The Way of All Flesh* (1903), 69.

2. It is not necessarily those lands which are the most fertile or most favoured in climate that seem to me the happiest, but those in which a long struggle of adaptation between man and his environment has brought out the best qualities of both. T. S. ELIOT, "After Strange Gods" (1934).

3. The best / Thing we can do is to make wherever we're lost in / Look as much like home as we can. CHRISTOPHER FRY, *The Lady's Not for Burning* (1949), 3.

4. Every new adjustment is a crisis in self-esteem. ERIC HOFFER, *The Ordeal of Change* (1963).

5. We are all sentenced to capital punishment for the crime of living, and though the condemned cell of our earthly existence is but a narrow and bare dwelling-place, we have adjusted ourselves to it, and made it tolerably comfortable for the little while we are to be confined in it. OLIVER WENDELL HOLMES, SR., *Over the Teacups* (1891), 2.

6. All conditioning aims at that: making people like their inescapable social destiny. ALDOUS HUXLEY, *Brave New World* (1932).

7. Since the house is on fire let us warm ourselves. ITALIAN PROVERB.

8. Ours must be the first age whose great goal, on a nonmaterial plane, is not fulfillment but adjustment; and perhaps just such a goal has served as maladjustment's weapon. LOUIS KRONENBERGER, *Company Manners* (1954), 1.4.

9. Adjustment, that synonym for conformity that comes more easily to the modern tongue, is the theme of our swan song, the piper's tune to which we dance on the brink of the abyss, the siren's melody that destroys our senses and paralyzes our wills. ROBERT LINDNER, title essay, *Must You Conform?* (1956).

10. The supple, well-adjusted man is the one who has learned to hop into the meat-grinder while humming a hit-parade tune. MARSHALL MC LUHAN, "Education," *The Mechanical Bride* (1951).

11. I dance to the tune that is played. SPANISH PROVERB.

12. There are no conditions to which a man cannot become accustomed, especially if he sees that all those around him live in the same way. LEO TOLSTOY, *Anna Karenina* (1873–76), 7.13.

13. Adapt or perish, now as ever, is Nature's inexorable imperative. H. G. WELLS, *Mind at the End of Its Tether* (1946), 19.

## 13. ADMINISTRATION
See also 313. Executives

1. An administration, like a machine, does not create. It carries on. SAINT-EXUPÉRY, *Flight to Arras* (1942), 10, tr. Lewis Galantière.

2. Bad administration, to be sure, can destroy good policy; but good administration can never save bad policy. ADLAI STEVENSON, speech, Los Angeles, Sept. 11, 1952.

## 14. ADMIRATION
See also 49. Approval; 350. Following; 424. Honors; 706. Popularity; 802. Respect; 1061. Worship

1. Admiration is a very short-lived passion that immediately decays upon growing familiar with its object, unless it be still fed with fresh discoveries, and kept alive by a new perpetual succession of miracles rising up to its view. JOSEPH ADDISON, *The Spectator* (1711–12), 256.

2. Admiration involves a glorious obliquity of vision. MAX BEERBOHM, "Some Damnable Errors About Christmas," *A Christmas Garland* (1895).

3. Admiration, n. Our polite recognition of another's resemblance to ourselves. AMBROSE BIERCE, *The Devil's Dictionary* (1881–1911).

4. Always we like those who admire us, but we do not always like those whom we

admire. LA ROCHEFOUCAULD, *Maxims* (1665), tr. Kenneth Pratt.

5. Fools admire, but men of sense approve. ALEXANDER POPE, *An Essay on Criticism* (1711), 2.190.

### ADOLESCENCE
**See 1064. Youth**

### ADULTERY
**See 470. Infidelity**

### 15. ADVANTAGE
**See also 152. Comparison; 153. Compensation; 546. Losers**

1. Unto every one that hath shall be given, and he shall have abundance: but from him that hath not shall be taken away even that which he hath. *Bible*, Matthew 25:29.

2. It's them as take advantage that get advantage i' this world. GEORGE ELIOT, *Adam Bede* (1859), 32.

3. Every advantage has its tax. EMERSON, "Compensation," *Essays: First Series* (1841).

4. He that has one eye is a prince among those that have none. THOMAS FULLER, M.D., *Gnomologia* (1732), 2137.

5. Against great advantages in another, there are no means of defending ourselves except love. GOETHE, *Elective Affinities* (1809), 23.

6. Fortune turns everything to the advantage of those she favours. LA ROCHEFOUCAULD, *Maxims* (1665), tr. Kenneth Pratt.

7. The concessions of the privileged to the unprivileged are seldom brought about by any better motive than the power of the unprivileged to extort them. JOHN STUART MILL, *The Subjugation of Women* (1869), 3.

8. When Fortune is on our side, popular favor bears her company. PUBLILIUS SYRUS, *Moral Sayings* (1st. c. B.C.), 275, tr. Darius Lyman.

9. Men who possess all the advantages of life are in a state where there are many accidents to disorder and discompose, but few to please them. JONATHAN SWIFT, *Thoughts on Various Subjects* (1711).

### 16. ADVENTURE
**See also 213. Danger; 311. Excitement**

1. An adventure is only an inconvenience rightly considered. An inconvenience is only an adventure wrongly considered. G. K. CHESTERTON, "On Running After One's Hat," *All Things Considered* (1908).

2. It is only in adventure that some people succeed in knowing themselves—in finding themselves. ANDRÉ GIDE, *Journals*, Oct. 26, 1924, tr. Justin O'Brien.

3. Give me the storm and tempest of thought and action, rather than the dead calm of ignorance and faith! ROBERT G. INGERSOLL, *The Gods* (1872).

4. Life is either a daring adventure or nothing. To keep our faces toward change and behave like free spirits in the presence of fate is strength undefeatable. HELEN KELLER, *Let Us Have Faith* (1940).

5. Adventure does not exist. It exists only in the mind of the man who pursues it, and as soon as his fingers graze it, it vanishes to appear much further off, in another form, at the limits of the imagination. PIERRE MAC ORLAN, *Petit manuel du parfait aventurier* (1920), 2.

6. They sicken of the calm, who know the storm. DOROTHY PARKER, "Fair Weather," *Sunset Gun* (1928).

7. A life without adventure is likely to be unsatisfying, but a life in which adventure is allowed to take whatever form it will is sure to be short. BERTRAND RUSSELL, "Social Cohesion and Human Nature," *Authority and the Individual* (1949).

8. A race preserves its vigour so long as it harbours a real contrast between what has been and what may be; and so long as it is nerved by the vigour to adventure beyond the safeties of the past. Without adventure civilisation is in full decay. ALFRED NORTH WHITEHEAD, *Adventures in Ideas* (1933), 19.

9. If we didn't live venturously, plucking the wild goat by the beard, and trembling over precipices, we should never be depressed, I've no doubt; but already should be faded, fatalistic and aged. VIRGINIA WOOLF, *A Writer's Diary*, May 26, 1924.

## 17. ADVERSITY

See also 152. Comparison; 153. Compensation; 156. Complaint; 177. Consolations; 225. Defeat; 243. Difficulty; 285. Endurance; 327. Failure; 546. Losers; 547. Loss; 745. Prosperity and Adversity; 939. Suffering

1. Misfortune / wandering the same track lights now upon one / and now upon another. AESCHYLUS, *Prometheus Bound* (c. 478 B.C.), tr. David Grene.

2. Better be wise by the misfortunes of others than by your own. AESOP, "The Lion, the Ass and the Fox Hunting," *Fables* (6th c. B.C.), tr. Thomas James.

3. A high heart ought to bear calamities and not flee them, since in bearing them appears the grandeur of the mind and in fleeing them the cowardice of the heart. PIETRO ARETINO, letter to the King of France, April 24, 1525, tr. Samuel Putnam.

4. The beauty of the soul shines out when a man bears with composure one heavy mischance after another, not because he does not feel them, but because he is a man of high and heroic temper. ARISTOTLE, *Nicomachean Ethics* (4th c. B.C.), 1.10, tr. J. A. K. Thomson.

5. Calamity is man's true touchstone. BEAUMONT and FLETCHER, *Four Plays in One: The Triumph of Honour* (1647), 1.

6. Even when things go well, they're still going poorly. If nothing else, because we grow old. UGO BETTI, *The Inquiry* (1944–45), 1.10, ed. Gino Rizzo.

7. Man is born unto trouble, as the sparks fly upward. *Bible*, Job 5:7.

8. Calamity, n. ... Calamities are of two kinds: misfortune to ourselves, and good fortune to others. AMBROSE BIERCE, *The Devil's Dictionary* (1881–1911).

9. To be unable to bear an ill is itself a great ill. BION (2nd c. B.C.?), quoted in Diogenes Laertius' *Lives and Opinions of Eminent Philosophers* (3rd c. A.D.), tr. R. D. Hicks.

10. In every kind of adversity, the bitterest part of a man's affliction is to remember that he once was happy. BOETHIUS, *The Consolation of Philosophy* (A.D. 524), 2.

11. Affliction smarts most in the most happy state. SIR THOMAS BROWNE, *Christian Morals* (1716), 2.

12. Welcome each rebuff / That turns earth's smoothness rough, / Each sting that bids nor sit nor stand but go! ROBERT BROWNING, "Rabbi Ben Ezra," *Dramatis Personae* (1864), 6.

13. Public calamity is a mighty leveller. EDMUND BURKE, speech, "On Conciliation with the American Colonies," March 22, 1775.

14. Adversity, if a man is set down to it by degrees, is more supportable with equanimity by most people than any great prosperity arrived at in a single lifetime. SAMUEL BUTLER (d. 1902), *The Way of All Flesh* (1903), 5.

15. Adversity is the first path to Truth. BYRON, *Don Juan* (1819–24), 12.50.

16. He that has never suffered extreme adversity, knows not the full extent of his own depravation. CHARLES CALEB COLTON, *Lacon* (1825), 1.19.

17. There are three modes of bearing the ills of life: by indifference, by philosophy, and by religion. CHARLES CALEB COLTON, *Lacon* (1825), 1.95

18. He deposes Doom / Who hath suffered him—. EMILY DICKINSON, poem (c. 1862).

19. The memory of man is as old as misfortune. LAWRENCE DURRELL, *Balthazar* (1958), 4.12.

20. Every calamity is a spur and valuable hint. EMERSON, "Fate," *The Conduct of Life* (1860).

21. Misfortunes when asleep are not to be awakened. ENGLISH PROVERB.

22. The misfortune of the wise is better than the prosperity of the fool. EPICURUS (3rd c. B.C.), quoted in Diogenes Laertius' *Lives and Opinions of Eminent Philosophers* (3rd c. A.D.), tr. R. D. Hicks.

23. Disaster appears, to crush / one man now, but afterward another. EURIPIDES, *Alcestis* (438 B.C.), tr. Richmond Lattimore.

24. Human misery must somewhere have a stop: / there is no wind that always blows a storm. EURIPIDES, *Heracles* (c. 422 B.C.), tr. William Arrowsmith.

25. In misfortune, what friend remains a friend? EURIPIDES, *Heracles* (c. 422 B.C.), tr. William Arrowsmith.

26. Ignorance of one's misfortunes is clear gain. EURIPIDES, *Antiope* (c. 408 B.C.), 204, tr. M. H. Morgan.

27. If afflictions refine some, they consume others. THOMAS FULLER, M.D., *Gnomologia* (1732), 2666.

28. The worse the passage the more wel-

come the port. THOMAS FULLER, M.D., *Gnomologia* (1732), 4848.

29. Greater dooms win greater destinies. HERACLITUS, *Fragments* (c. 500 B.C.), 70, tr. Philip Wheelwright.

30. When an elephant is in trouble, even a frog will kick him. HINDU PROVERB.

31. No man can smile in the face of adversity and mean it. EDGAR WATSON HOWE, *Country Town Sayings* (1911).

32. It is the first shower that wets. ITALIAN PROVERB.

33. If a man talks of his misfortunes there is something in them that is not disagreeable to him; for where there is nothing but pure misery there never is any recourse to the mention of it. SAMUEL JOHNSON, quoted in Boswell's *Life of Samuel Johnson*, 1780.

34. He knows not his own strength that hath not met adversity. BEN JONSON, "Explorata," *Timber* (1640).

35. Philosophy triumphs easily over past evils and future evils; but present evils triumph over it. LA ROCHEFOUCAULD, *Maxims* (1665).

36. Let us be of good cheer, however, remembering that the misfortunes hardest to bear are those which never come. JAMES RUSSELL LOWELL, "Democracy," *Democracy and Other Addresses* (1887).

37. People don't ever seem to realize that doing what's right's no guarantee against misfortune. WILLIAM MC FEE, *Casuals of the Sea* (1916), 2.1.6.

38. man is a queer looking gink / who uses what brains he has / to get himself into trouble with / and then blames it on the fates. DON MARQUIS, "quote and only man is vile quote," *Archy's Life of Mehitabel* (1933).

39. there is always / a comforting thought / in time of trouble when / it is not our trouble. DON MARQUIS, "comforting thoughts," *Archy Does His Part* (1935).

40. The world is quickly bored by the recital of misfortune, and willingly avoids the sight of distress. W. SOMERSET MAUGHAM, *The Moon and Sixpence* (1919), 16.

41. The oldest and best known evil was ever more supportable than one that was new and untried. MONTAIGNE, "Of vanity," *Essays* (1580–88), tr. Charles Cotton and W. C. Hazlitt.

42. People could survive their natural / trouble all right if it weren't for the trouble they make for themselves. OGDEN NASH, "Little Miss Muffet Sat on a Prophet—And Quite Right, Too!" *I'm a Stranger Here Myself* (1938).

43. The only incurable troubles of the rich are the troubles that money can't cure, / Which is a kind of trouble that is even more troublesome if you are poor. OGDEN NASH, "The Terrible People," *Verses from 1929 On* (1959).

44. That which does not kill me makes me stronger. NIETZSCHE, "Maxims and Missiles," 8, *Twilight of the Idols* (1888), tr. Anthony M. Ludovici.

45. The drowning man is not troubled by rain. PERSIAN PROVERB.

46. If fortune turns against you, even jelly breaks your tooth. PERSIAN PROVERB.

47. With man, most of his misfortunes are occasioned by man. PLINY THE ELDER, *Natural History* (1st. c.), 7.5, tr. J. Bostock and H. T. Riley.

48. I never knew any man in my life who could not bear another's misfortunes perfectly like a Christian. ALEXANDER POPE, *Thoughts on Various Subjects* (1727).

49. Learn to see in another's calamity the ills which you should avoid. PUBLILIUS SYRUS, *Moral Sayings* (1st. c. B.C.), 120, tr. Darius Lyman.

50. To be brave in misfortune is to be worthy of manhood; to be wise in misfortune is to conquer fate. AGNES REPPLIER, "Strayed Sympathies," *Under Dispute* (1924).

51. Take warning by the mischance of others, that others may not take warning by thine. SA'DI, *Gulistan* (1258), 8.105, tr. James Ross.

52. Light troubles speak; the weighty are struck dumb. SENECA, *Hippolytus* (1st c.), 607, tr. Frank Justus Miller.

53. Fire is the test of gold; adversity, of strong men. SENECA, *On Providence* (1st c.), 5.9.

54. Sweet are the uses of adversity, / Which, like the toad, ugly and venomous, / Wears yet a precious jewel in his head. SHAKESPEARE, *As You Like It* (1599–1600), 2.1.12.

55. The worst is not / So long as we can say "This is the worst." SHAKESPEARE, *King Lear* (1605–06), 4.1.27.

56. Misery acquaints a man with strange bedfellows. SHAKESPEARE, *The Tempest* (1611–12), 2.2.43.

57. An earthquake achieves what the law promises but does not in practice maintain —the equality of all men. IGNAZIO SILONE, "Why I Became a Socialist," in *The God That Failed* (1949), ed. Richard Crossman.

58. It is a painful thing / To look at your own trouble and know / That you yourself and no one else has made it. SOPHOCLES, *Ajax* (c. 447 B.C.), tr. John Moore.

59. One's own escape from troubles makes one glad; / but bringing friends to trouble is hard grief. SOPHOCLES, *Antigone* (442–41 B.C.), tr. Elizabeth Wyckoff.

60. God gives almonds to those who have no teeth. SPANISH PROVERB.

61. There is no man in this world without some manner of tribulation or anguish, though he be king or pope. THOMAS À KEMPIS, *The Imitation of Christ* (1426), 1.22.

62. By trying we can easily learn to endure adversity. Another man's, I mean. MARK TWAIN, "Pudd'nhead Wilson's New Calendar," *Following the Equator* (1897), 2.3.

63. Individual misfortunes give rise to the general good; so that the more individual misfortunes exist, the more all is fine. VOLTAIRE, *Candide* (1759), 10.

64. Trouble will come soon enough, and when he does come receive him as pleasantly as possible. Like the tax-collector, he is a disagreeable chap to have in one's house, but the more amiably you greet him the sooner he will go away. ARTEMUS WARD, "Hunting Trouble," *Artemus Ward in London* (1872).

65. When you are down and out, something always turns up—and it is usually the noses of your friends. ORSON WELLES, *The New York Times*, April 1, 1962.

## 18. ADVERTISING

**See also 102. Business and Commerce; 103. Buying and Selling; 739. Propaganda; 754. Publicity**

1. The advertisements in a newspaper are more full of knowledge in respect to what is going on in a state or community than the editorial columns are. HENRY WARD BEECHER, *Proverbs from Plymouth Pulpit* (1887).

2. The deeper problems connected with advertising come less from the unscrupulousness of our "deceivers" than from our pleasure in being deceived, less from the desire to seduce than from the desire to be seduced. DANIEL J. BOORSTIN, *The Image* (1962), 5.3.

3. Doing business without advertising is like winking at a girl in the dark. You know what you are doing, but nobody else does. STEUART HENDERSON BRITT, *New York Herald Tribune*, Oct. 30, 1956.

4. Advertisements are now so numerous that they are very negligently perused, and it is therefore become necessary to gain attention by magnificence of promises, and by eloquences sometimes sublime and sometimes pathetic. SAMUEL JOHNSON, *The Idler* (1758–60), 40.

5. Promise, large promise, is the soul of an advertisement. SAMUEL JOHNSON, *The Idler* (1758–60), 41.

6. The trouble with us in America isn't that the poetry of life has turned to prose, but that it has turned to advertising copy. LOUIS KRONENBERGER, "The Spirit of the Age," *Company Manners* (1954).

7. [The advertiser] is the overrewarded court jester and court pander at the democratic court. JOSEPH WOOD KRUTCH, "Permissive Exploitation," *Human Nature and the Human Condition* (1959).

8. The modern Little Red Riding Hood, reared on singing commercials, has no objection to being eaten by the wolf. MARSHALL MC LUHAN, "Book of the Hour," *The Mechanical Bride* (1951).

9. I think that I shall never see / A billboard lovely as a tree. / Indeed, unless the billboards fall / I'll never see a tree at all. OGDEN NASH, "Song of the Open Road," *Verses from 1929 On* (1959).

10. Advertising in the final analysis should be news. If it is not news it is worthless. ADOLPH S. OCHS, *The New York Times Magazine*, March 9, 1958.

11. One Ad is worth more to a paper than forty Editorials. WILL ROGERS, "Well, Who Is Prunes?" *The Illiterate Digest* (1924).

## 19. ADVICE

**See also 229. Deliberation**

1. There is nothing which we receive with so much reluctance as advice. JOSEPH

ADDISON, *The Spectator* (1711–12), 512.

2. It is an easy thing for one whose foot / is on the outside of calamity / to give advice and to rebuke the sufferer. AESCHYLUS, *Prometheus Bound* (c. 478 B.C.), tr. David Grene.

3. Never trust the advice of a man in difficulties. AESOP, "The Fox and the Goat," *Fables* (6th c. B.C.?), tr. Joseph Jacobs.

4. Distrust interested advice. AESOP, "The Fox Without a Tail," *Fables* (6th c. B.C.?), tr. Joseph Jacobs.

5. The light that a man receiveth by counsel from another is drier and purer than that which cometh from his own understanding and judgment, which is ever infused and drenched in his affections and customs. FRANCIS BACON, "Of Friendship," *Essays* (1625).

6. In the multitude of counsellors there is safety. *Bible*, Proverbs 11:14 and 24:6.

7. Advice, n. The smallest current coin. AMBROSE BIERCE, *The Devil's Dictionary* (1881–1911).

8. Who cannot give good counsel? 'Tis cheap, it costs them nothing. ROBERT BURTON, *The Anatomy of Melancholy* (1621), 2.2.3.

9. We ask advice, but we mean approbation. CHARLES CALEB COLTON, *Lacon* (1825), 1.190.

10. When we feel a strong desire to thrust our advice upon others, it is usually because we suspect their weakness; but we ought rather to suspect our own. CHARLES CALEB COLTON, *Lacon* (1825), 2.91.

11. Advice after injury is like medicine after death. DANISH PROVERB.

12. He who builds to every man's advice will have a crooked house. DANISH PROVERB.

13. We are all wise for other people, none for himself. EMERSON, *Journals*, 1834.

14. A woman's advice is no great thing, but he who won't take it is a fool. ENGLISH PROVERB.

15. Everybody knows good counsel except him that has need of it. GERMAN PROVERB.

16. Do people conform to the instructions of us old ones? Each thinks he must know best about himself, and thus many are lost entirely. GOETHE, quoted in Johann Peter Eckermann's *Conversations with Goethe*, Sept. 18, 1823.

17. The advice of the elders to young men is very apt to be as unreal as a list of the hundred best books. OLIVER WENDELL HOLMES, JR., speech, Boston, Jan. 8, 1897.

18. When a man asks your advice, he usually tells you just how he expects you to decide. EDGAR WATSON HOWE, *Country Town Sayings* (1911).

19. Teeth placed before the tongue give good advice. ITALIAN PROVERB.

20. It is not often that any man can have so much knowledge of another, as is necessary to make instruction useful. SAMUEL JOHNSON, *The Rambler* (1750–52), 87.

21. The toad beneath the harrow knows / Exactly where each tooth-point goes; / The butterfly upon the road / Preaches contentment to that toad. RUDYARD KIPLING, "Pagett, M.P." *Departmental Ditties* (1886).

22. We give nothing so freely as advice. LA ROCHEFOUCAULD, *Maxims* (1665), tr. Kenneth Pratt.

23. We may give advice, but we cannot inspire conduct. LA ROCHEFOUCAULD, *Maxims* (1665).

24. You will always find some Eskimos ready to instruct the Congolese on how to cope with heat waves. STANISLAW LEC, *Unkempt Thoughts* (1962), tr. Jacek Galazka.

25. This is the gist of what I know: / Give advice and buy a foe. PHYLLIS MC GINLEY, "A Garland of Precepts," *The Love Letters of Phyllis McGinley* (1954).

26. Advice is a stranger; if welcome he stays for the night; if not welcome he returns home the same day. MALAGASY PROVERB.

27. A hundred sage counsels are lost upon one who cannot take advice; a hundred bits of wisdom are lost upon the unintelligent. *Panchatantra* (c. 5th c.), 1, tr. Franklin Edgerton.

28. Where's the man who counsel can bestow, / Still pleased to teach, and yet not proud to know? ALEXANDER POPE, *An Essay on Criticism* (1711), 3.72.

29. Though men give you their advice gratis, you will often be cheated if you take it. GEORGE DENNISON PRENTICE, *Prenticeana* (1860).

30. Many receive advice, few profit by it. PUBLILIUS SYRUS, *Moral Sayings* (1st c. B.C.), 149, tr. Darius Lyman.

31. We are so happy to advise others that occasionally we even do it in their inter-

est. JULES RENARD, *Journal* (1887–1910).

32. It is wrong to follow the advice of an adversary; nevertheless it is right to hear it, that you may do the contrary; and this is the essence of good policy. SA'DI, *Gulistan* (1258), 8.18, tr. James Ross.

33. Friendly counsel cuts off many foes. SHAKESPEARE, *1 Henry VI* (1591–92), 3.1. 184.

34. In giving advice seek to help, not to please, your friend. SOLON (7th–6th c. B.C.), quoted in Diogenes Laertius' *Lives and Opinions of Eminent Philosophers* (3rd c. A.D.), tr. R. D. Hicks.

35. It can be no dishonor / to learn from others when they speak good sense. SOPHOCLES, *Antigone* (442–41 B.C.), tr. Elizabeth Wyckoff.

36. No enemy is worse than bad advice. SOPHOCLES, *Electra* (c. 418–14 B.C.), tr. David Grene.

37. The counsels of old age give light without heat, like the sun in winter. VAUVENARGUES, *Reflections and Maxims* (1746), 159.

## 20. AESTHETICS

**See also 53. Art and Artists; 70. Beauty; 204. Criticism, Professional; 607. Music; 702. Poetry and Poets; 1062. Writing and Writers**

1. Pleasure is by no means an infallible critical guide, but it is the least fallible. W. H. AUDEN, "Reading," *The Dyer's Hand* (1962).

2. The eye is the painter and the ear the singer. EMERSON, *Journals*, 1836.

3. Pay attention only to the form; emotion will come spontaneously to inhabit it. A perfect dwelling always finds an inhabitant. ANDRÉ GIDE, "Portraits and Aphorisms," *Pretexts* (1903), tr. Angelo P. Bertocci and others.

4. Aesthetics is for the artist like ornithology is for the birds. BARNETT NEWMAN, quoted in "Speaking of Books," *The New York Times Book Review*, Feb. 18, 1968.

5. Tomes of aesthetic criticism hang on a few moments of real delight and intuition. GEORGE SANTAYANA, *The Life of Reason: Reason in Art* (1905–06), 10.

6. Oh who can tell the range of joy / Or set the bounds of beauty? SARA TEASDALE, "A Winter Bluejay," *Rivers to the Sea* (1915).

7. Ethics, like natural selection, make existence possible. Aesthetics, like sexual selection, make life lovely and wonderful, fill it with new forms, and give it progress, and variety and change. OSCAR WILDE, "The Critic as Artist," *Intentions* (1891).

## AFFECTATION

**See 45. Appearance; 726. Pretension**

## 21. AFFECTION

**See also 22. Affinity; 282. Emotions; 363. Friendship; 548. Love**

1. Most people would rather get than give affection. ARISTOTLE, *Nicomachean Ethics* (4th c. B.C.), 8.8, tr. J. A. K. Thomson.

2. We are uneasy with an affectionate man, for we are positive he wants something of us, particularly our love. EDWARD DAHLBERG, "On Love and Friendship," *Reasons of the Heart* (1965).

3. The affections cannot keep their youth any more than men. EMERSON, *Journals*, 1831.

4. One must not be mean with affections; what is spent of the funds is renewed in the spending itself. Left untouched for too long, they diminish imperceptibly or the lock gets rusty; they are there all right but one cannot make use of them. SIGMUND FREUD, letter to Martha Bernays, Aug. 18, 1882.

5. Whatever pretext we may give for our affections, often it is only interest and vanity which cause them. LA ROCHEFOUCAULD, *Maxims* (1665), tr. Kenneth Pratt.

6. Talk not of wasted affection, affection never was wasted; / If it enrich not the heart of another, its waters, returning / Back to their springs, like the rain, shall fill them full of refreshment; / That which the fountain sends forth returns again to the fountain. LONGFELLOW, *Evangeline* (1847), 2.1.

7. Affection is created by habit, community of interests, convenience and the desire of companionship. It is a comfort rather than an exhilaration. W. SOMERSET MAUGHAM, *The Summing Up* (1938), 77.

8. A mixture of admiration and pity is

one of the surest recipes for affection. ANDRÉ MAUROIS, *Ariel* (1923).

9. Most affections are habits or duties we lack the courage to end. HENRY DE MONTHERLANT, *Queen After Death* (1942), 2.3.

10. Human nature is so constructed that it gives affection most readily to those who seem least to demand it. BERTRAND RUSSELL, *The Conquest of Happiness* (1930), 12.

11. Praise is well, compliment is well, but affection—that is the last and final and most precious reward that any man can win, whether by character or achievement. MARK TWAIN, "When in Doubt, Tell the Truth," *Speeches* (1923), ed. A. B. Paine.

## 22. AFFINITY

**See also 57. Association**

1. There can be little liking where there is no likeness. AESOP, "The Collier and the Fuller," *Fables* (6th c. B.C.?), tr. Thomas James.

2. Greybeard finds greybeard's tongue sweetest, / Child child's, and woman consorts with woman; / Invalid suits invalid, and a man woebegone / Is charmed by a fellow-sufferer. Anonymous quotation in PLUTARCH's "Flattery and Friendship," *Moralia* (c. A.D. 100), tr. Moses Hadas.

3. A fellow-feeling makes one wondrous kind. DAVID GARRICK, "On Quitting the Stage," prologue to Henry Fielding's *The Fathers* (1776–77).

4. The profoundest affinities are those most readily felt. GEORGE SANTAYANA, *The Life of Reason: Reason and Society* (1905–06), 1.

5. When elderly invalids meet with fellow-victims of their own ailments, then at last real conversation begins, and life is delicious. LOGAN PEARSALL SMITH, *Afterthoughts* (1931), 2.

## 23. AFRICA AND AFRICANS

1. The African race is an india-rubber ball: the harder you dash it to the ground, the higher it will rise. AFRICAN PROVERB.

2. A jungle is only a place that's heavily vegetated—the soil is so rich and the climate is so good that everything grows, and it doesn't grow in season—it grows all the time. MALCOLM X, *Malcolm X Speaks* (1965), 10.

## AFTERLIFE

**See 412. Heaven; 414. Hell; 452. Immortality**

## 24. AFTERTHOUGHT

1. Second thoughts are ever wiser. EURIPIDES, *Hippolytus* (428 B.C.), 436, tr. M. H. Morgan.

2. Afterthought makes the first resolve a liar. SOPHOCLES, *Antigone* (442–41 B.C.), tr. Elizabeth Wyckoff.

## AGE

**See 296. Era; 580. Middle Age; 646. Old Age; 1064. Youth**

## 25. AGENTS

**See also 102. Business and Commerce; 103. Buying and Selling**

1. It is well known what a middle man is: he is a man who bamboozles one party and plunders the other. BENJAMIN DISRAELI, speech, Maynooth, April 11, 1845.

2. Little by little, the pimps have taken over the world. They don't do anything, they don't make anything—they just stand there and take their cut. JEAN GIRAUDOUX, *The Madwoman of Chaillot* (1945), 1, adapted by Maurice Valency.

## AGGRAVATION

**See 506. Irritations**

## 26. AGGRESSION

**See also 154. Competition; 354. Force; 853. Self-assertion; 1024. Violence; 1035. War**

1. At worst, is not this an unjust world, full of nothing but beasts of prey, four-footed or two-footed? THOMAS CARLYLE, "Count Cagliostro" (1833).

2. Attack is the reaction. I never think I

have hit hard unless it rebounds. SAMUEL JOHNSON, quoted in Boswell's *Life of Samuel Johnson*, April 2, 1775.

3. No absolute is going to make the lion lie down with the lamb: unless the lamb is inside. D. H. LAWRENCE, *The Later D. H. Lawrence* (1952).

4. man eats the big fish / the big fish eat the / little fish / the little fish / eat insects / in the water / the water insects / eat the water plants / the water plants / eat mud / mud eats man. DON MARQUIS, "archy's song," *Archy's Life of Mehitabel* (1933).

5. It is unfair to blame man too fiercely for being pugnacious; he learned the habit from Nature. CHRISTOPHER MORLEY, *Inward Ho!* (1923), 8.

6. If aggressors are wrong above, they are right here below. NAPOLEON I, *Maxims* (1804–15).

7. To knock a thing down, especially if it is cocked at an arrogant angle, is a deep delight to the blood. GEORGE SANTAYANA, *The Life of Reason: Reason in Society* (1905–06), 3.

8. In solitude it is possible to love mankind; in the world, for one who knows the world, there can be nothing but secret or open war. GEORGE SANTAYANA, "The Latin School," *Persons and Places: The Background of My Life* (1944).

9. Men must have corrupted nature a little, for they were not born wolves, and they have become wolves. VOLTAIRE, *Candide* (1759), 4.

## AGNOSTICISM

See 263. Doubt, Religious; 897. Skepticism; 997. Unbelief

## 27. AGREEMENT

See also 46. Appeasement; 51. Argument; 160. Compromise; 164. Conciliation; 250. Discord; 766. Quarreling; 987. Treaties

1. It is by universal misunderstanding that all agree. For if, by ill luck, people understood each other, they would never agree. CHARLES BAUDELAIRE, *Intimate Journals* (1887), 99, tr. Christopher Isherwood.

2. Minds do not act together in public; they simply stick together; and when their private activities are resumed, they fly apart again. FRANK MOORE COLBY, "Simple Simon," *The Colby Essays* (1926), v. 1.

3. We are more inclined to hate one another for points on which we differ, than to love one another for points on which we agree. CHARLES CALEB COLTON, *Lacon* (1825), 2.127.

4. Insofar as it represents a genuine reconciliation of differences, a consensus is a fine thing; insofar as it represents a concealment of differences, it is a miscarriage of democratic procedure. J. WILLIAM FULBRIGHT, speech, U.S. Senate, Oct. 22, 1965.

5. Three may keep counsel, if two be away. JOHN HEYWOOD, *Proverbs* (1546), 2.5.

6. Men . . . are not agreed about any one thing, not even that heaven is over our heads. MONTAIGNE, "Apology for Raimond de Sebonde," *Essays* (1580–88), tr. Charles Cotton and W. C. Hazlitt.

7. Nobody agrees with anybody else anyhow, but adults conceal / it and infants show it. OGDEN NASH, "Birdies, Don't Make Me Laugh," *Verses from 1929 On* (1959).

8. Agreement is made more precious by disagreement. PUBLILIUS SYRUS, *Moral Sayings* (1st c. B.C.), 151.

9. Friends are generally of the same sex, for when men and women agree, it is only in their conclusions; their reasons are always different. GEORGE SANTAYANA, *The Life of Reason: Reason in Society* (1905–06), 6.

10. If all pulled in one direction, the world would keel over. *Yiddish Proverbs* (1949), ed. Hanan J. Ayalti.

## AGRICULTURE

See 334. Farms and Farming

## AID

See 56. Assistance

## AIM

See 284. Ends; 765. Purpose

## 28. AIRPLANES

See also 984. Transportation

1. Lovers of air travel find it exhilarating to hang poised between the illusion of immortality and the fact of death. ALEXANDER CHASE, *Perspectives* (1966).

2. The airplane has unveiled for us the true face of the earth. SAINT-EXUPÉRY, *Wind, Sand, and Stars* (1939), 5, tr. Lewis Galantière.

### 29. AIR POLLUTION

1. I durst not laugh, for fear of opening my lips and receiving the bad air. SHAKESPEARE, *Julius Caesar* (1599–1600), 1.2.250.

### 30. ALIENATION

**See also 3. The Absurd; 216. Deadness, Spiritual; 288. Ennui; 298. Escape; 464. Indifference; 908. Solitude**

1. When you're all alienated together, you're not really lonely. Anonymous college student, quoted by Spencer Brown in *The New York Times Book Review*, Nov. 27, 1966.

2. One is better off seated than standing, lying than seated, asleep than awake, and dead than alive. ARABIC PROVERB.

3. When one realizes that his life is worthless he either commits suicide or travels. EDWARD DAHLBERG, "On Futility," *Reasons of the Heart* (1965).

4. The man who regards his own life and that of his fellow-creatures as meaningless is not merely unfortunate but almost disqualified for life. EINSTEIN, "The Meaning of Life," *The World As I See It* (1934), tr. Alan Harris.

5. Everything intercepts us from ourselves. EMERSON, *Journals*, 1833.

6. Alienation ends where yours begins. Graffito written during French student revolt, May 1968.

7. As this is the simple truth—that to live is to feel oneself lost—he who accepts it has already begun to find himself, to be on firm ground. JOSÉ ORTEGA Y GASSET, *The Revolt of the Masses* (1930), 14.

8. Peace dies when the framework is ripped apart. When there is no longer a place that is yours in the world. When you know no longer where your friend is to be found. SAINT-EXUPÉRY, *Flight to Arras* (1942), 13, tr. Lewis Galantière.

### 31. ALOOFNESS

**See also 141. Coldness; 976. Togetherness**

1. Retirement accords with the tone of my mind: / I will not descend to a world I despise. BYRON, "Lines," *Hours of Idleness* (1806), 1.

2. A man's profundity may keep him from opening on a first interview, and his caution on a second; but I should suspect his emptiness if he carried on his reserve to a third. CHARLES CALEB COLTON, *Lacon* (1825), 2.81.

3. Anonymity represents for many people a liberating even more than a threatening phenomenon. HARVEY COX, *The Secular City* (1966), 2.

4. To spare oneself from grief at all cost can be achieved only at the price of total detachment, which excludes the ability to experience happiness. ERICH FROMM, *Man for Himself* (1947), 4.

5. Before I built a wall I'd ask to know / What I was walling in or walling out, / And to whom I was like to give offence. ROBERT FROST, "Mending Wall," *North of Boston* (1914).

6. By keeping men off, you keep them on. JOHN GAY, *The Beggar's Opera* (1728), 1.8, air 9.

7. Reserve is an artificial quality that is developed in most of us but as the result of innumerable rebuffs. W. SOMERSET MAUGHAM, *The Summing Up* (1938), 19.

8. The main motive for "non-attachment" is a desire to escape from the pain of living, and above all from love, which, sexual or non-sexual, is hard work. GEORGE ORWELL, "Reflections on Ghandi," *Shooting an Elephant* (1950).

9. If a man makes me keep my distance, the comfort is, he keeps his at the same time. JONATHAN SWIFT, *Thoughts on Various Subjects* (1711).

10. For an impenetrable shield, stand inside yourself. THOREAU, *Journal*, June 27, 1840.

### 32. ALTERNATION

1. What's my turn today may be thine tomorrow. THOMAS FULLER, M.D., *Gnomologia* (1732), 5513.

ALTRUISM
See 430. Humanitarianism

## 33. AMBITION

See also 6. Achievement; 55. Aspiration; 289. Enterprise; 938. Success

1. Never soar aloft on an enemy's pinions. AESOP, "The Tortoise and the Birds," *Fables* (6th c. B.C.?), tr. Joseph Jacobs.

2. What shall it profit a man, if he shall gain the whole world, and lose his own soul? *Bible*, Mark 8:36.

3. No bird soars too high, if he soars with his own wings. WILLIAM BLAKE, "Proverbs of Hell," *The Marriage of Heaven and Hell* (1790).

4. If you take big paces you leave big spaces. *Burmese Proverbs* (1962), 100, ed. Hla Pe.

5. He who would rise in the world should veil his ambition with the forms of humanity. CHINESE PROVERB.

6. All ambitions are lawful except those which climb upward on the miseries or credulities of mankind. JOSEPH CONRAD, "A Familiar Preface," *A Personal Record* (1912).

7. He who would leap high must take a long run. DANISH PROVERB.

8. Wild Ambition loves to slide, not stand, / And Fortune's ice prefers to Virtue's land. JOHN DRYDEN, *Absalom and Achitophel* (1681), 1.198.

9. A feeble man can see the farms that are fenced and tilled, the houses that are built. The strong man sees the possible houses and farms. His eye makes estates as fast as the sun breeds clouds. EMERSON, "Power," *The Conduct of Life* (1860).

10. Who never climbed high never fell low. THOMAS FULLER, M.D., *Gnomologia* (1732), 5713.

11. Nothing arouses ambition so much in the heart as the trumpet-clang of another's fame. BALTASAR GRACIÁN, *The Art of Worldly Wisdom* (1647), 75, tr. Joseph Jacobs.

12. The true way is the middle one, halfway between deserving a place and pushing oneself into it. BALTASAR GRACIÁN, *The Art of Worldly Wisdom* (1647), 199, tr. Joseph Jacobs.

13. Nothing is so common-place as to wish to be remarkable. OLIVER WENDELL HOLMES, SR., *The Autocrat of the Breakfast Table* (1858), 12.

14. Ambition is only vanity ennobled. JEROME K. JEROME, "On Vanity and Vanities," *The Idle Thoughts of an Idle Fellow* (1889).

15. Ambition makes more trusty slaves than need. BEN JONSON, *Sejanus His Fall* (1603), 1.1.

16. A wise man is cured of ambition by ambition itself; his aim is so exalted that riches, office, fortune, and favour cannot satisfy him. LA BRUYÈRE, *Characters* (1688), 2.43, tr. Henri Van Laun.

17. A slave has but one master; an ambitious man has as many masters as there are people who may be useful in bettering his position. LA BRUYÈRE, *Characters* (1688), 8.70, tr. Henri Van Laun.

18. Ambition does not see the earth she treads on: the rock and the herbage are of one substance to her. WALTER SAVAGE LANDOR, "Tiberius and Vipsania," *Imaginary Conversations* (1824–53).

19. We often pass from love to ambition, but we hardly ever return from ambition to love. LA ROCHEFOUCAULD, *Maxims* (1665), tr. Kenneth Pratt.

20. What appears to be generosity is often only ambition disguised, which despises small interests to pursue great ones. LA ROCHEFOUCAULD, *Maxims* (1665), tr. Kenneth Pratt.

21. Most people would succeed in small things, if they were not troubled with great ambitions. LONGFELLOW, "Table-Talk," *Driftwood* (1857).

22. An upstart is a sparrow eager to be betrothed to a hornbill. MALAY PROVERB.

23. A man's worth is no greater than the worth of his ambitions. MARCUS AURELIUS, *Meditations* (2nd c.), 7.3, tr. Maxwell Staniforth.

24. Be wise; / Soar not too high to fall; but stoop to rise. PHILIP MASSINGER, *The Duke of Milan* (1620), 1.2.

25. He who does not hope to win has already lost. JOSÉ JOAQUÍN OLMEDO, quoted in *Reader's Digest*, June 1968.

26. People Who Do Things exceed my

endurance; / God, for a man that solicits insurance! DOROTHY PARKER, "Bohemia," *Sunset Gun* (1928).

27. All sins have their origin in a sense of inferiority, otherwise called ambition. CESARE PAVESE, *The Burning Brand* (1961).

28. The tallest trees are most in the power of the winds, and ambitious men of the blasts of fortune. WILLIAM PENN, *Some Fruits of Solitude* (1693), 2.97.

29. There is a mortal breed most full of futility. / In contempt of what is at hand, they strain into the future, / hunting impossibilities on the wings of ineffectual hopes. PINDAR, *Odes* (5th c. B.C.), Pythia 3, tr. Richmond Lattimore.

30. He is much to be dreaded who stands in dread of poverty. PUBLILIUS SYRUS, *Moral Sayings* (1st c. B.C.), 933, tr. Darius Lyman.

31. Though ambition may be a fault in itself, it is often the mother of virtues. QUINTILIAN, *Institutio Oratoria* (c. A.D. 95), 1.2, tr. Clyde Murley.

32. Ambition often puts men upon doing the meanest offices; so climbing is performed in the same posture with creeping. JONATHAN SWIFT, *Thoughts on Various Subjects* (1711).

33. In private enterprises men may advance or recede, whereas they who aim at empire have no alternative between the highest success and utter downfall. TACITUS, *Histories* (A.D. 104–109), 2.74, tr. Alfred J. Church and William J. Brodribb.

34. This is the posture of fortune's slave: one foot in the gravy, one foot in the grave. JAMES THURBER, "The Mouse and the Money," *Further Fables for Our Time* (1956).

35. The greatest evil which fortune can inflict on men is to endow them with small talents and great ambition. VAUVENARGUES, *Reflections and Maxims* (1746), 562, tr. F. G. Stevens.

## AMBIVALENCE

**See 167. Conflict, Inner**

## 34. AMERICA AND AMERICANS

**See also 104. California; 105. Canada; 419. Hollywood; 621. New England; 625. New York; 1037. Washington, D.C.**

1. We [Americans] cheerfully assume that in some mystic way love conquers all, that good outweighs evil in the just balances of the universe and that at the eleventh hour something gloriously triumphant will prevent the worst before it happens. BROOKS ATKINSON, "January," *Once Around the Sun* (1951).

2. It is a sad fact about our culture that a poet can earn much more money writing or talking about his art than he can by practicing it. W. H. AUDEN, foreword, *The Dyer's Hand* (1962).

3. The making of an American begins at that point where he himself rejects all other ties, any other history, and himself adopts the vesture of his adopted land. JAMES BALDWIN, "Many Thousands Gone" (1951), *Notes of a Native Son* (1955).

4. American muse, whose strong and diverse heart / So many men have tried to understand / But only made it smaller with their art, / Because you are as various as your land. STEPHEN VINCENT BENÉT, "Invocation," *John Brown's Body* (1928).

5. Never have people been more the masters of their environment. Yet never has a people felt more deceived and disappointed. For never has a people expected so much more than the world could offer. DANIEL J. BOORSTIN, introduction to *The Image* (1962).

6. [Americans] expect to eat and stay thin, to be constantly on the move and ever more neighborly . . . to revere God and be God. DANIEL J. BOORSTIN, *Newsweek*, Feb. 26, 1962.

7. These are the gardens of the Desert, these / The unshorn fields, boundless and beautiful, / For which the speech of England has no name— / The Prairies. WILLIAM CULLEN BRYANT, "The Prairies" (1832).

8. We are not a nation, but a union, a confederacy of equal and sovereign states. JOHN C. CALHOUN, letter to Oliver Dyer, Jan. 1, 1849.

9. There is nothing the matter with Americans except their ideals. The real American is all right; it is the ideal American who is all wrong. G. K. CHESTERTON, quoted in *The New York Times*, Feb. 1, 1931.

10. Americans think of themselves collectively as a huge rescue squad on twenty-four-hour call to any spot on the globe where dispute and conflict may erupt. ELDRIDGE CLEAVER, "Rallying Round the Flag," *Soul on Ice* (1968).

11. Little of beauty has America given the world save the rude grandeur God himself stamped on her bosom; the human spirit in this new world has expressed itself in vigor and ingenuity rather than in beauty. W. E. B. DU BOIS, *The Souls of Black Folk* (1903), 14.

12. Behold [America], th' land iv freedom, where ivry man's as good as ivry other man, on'y th' other man don't know it. FINLEY PETER DUNNE, "The New York Custom House," *Mr. Dooley's Opinions* (1901).

13. Whatever America hopes to bring to pass in the world must first come to pass in the heart of America. DWIGHT D. EISENHOWER, Inaugural Address, Jan. 20, 1953.

14. When American life is most American it is apt to be most theatrical. RALPH ELLISON, *Shadow & Act* (1964).

15. The Yankee is one who, if he once gets his teeth set on a thing, all creation can't make him let go. EMERSON, *Journals*, 1842.

16. In America nature is autocratic, saying, "I am not arguing, I am telling you." ERIK H. ERIKSON, *Childhood and Society* (1950), 8.

17. America is so vast that almost everything said about it is likely to be true, and the opposite is probably equally true. JAMES T. FARRELL, introduction to H. L. Mencken's *Prejudices: A Selection* (1958).

18. We [Americans] are an obsessively moral people, but our morality is a team morality. EDGAR Z. FRIEDENBERG, "The Impact of the School," *The Vanishing Adolescent* (1959).

19. So much of learning to be an American is learning not to let your individuality become a nuisance. EDGAR Z. FRIEDENBERG, "The Impact of the School," *The Vanishing Adolescent* (1959).

20. The growing American characteristically defends himself against anxiety by learning not to become too involved. EDGAR Z. FRIEDENBERG, "The Vanishing Adolescent," *The Vanishing Adolescent* (1959).

21. In the modern world, we Americans are the old inhabitants. We first had political freedom, high industrial production, an economy of abundance. PAUL GOODMAN, *Growing Up Absurd* (1960), 7.2.

22. The organization of American society is an interlocking system of semi-monopolies notoriously venal, an electorate notoriously unenlightened, misled by mass media notoriously phony. PAUL GOODMAN, *The Community of Scholars* (1962).

23. In America, with all of its evils and faults, you can still reach through the forest and see the sun. But we don't know yet whether that sun is rising or setting for our country. DICK GREGORY, "One Less Door," *Nigger* (1964).

24. Our affluent [American] society contains those of talent and insight who are driven to prefer poverty, to choose it, rather than to submit to the desolation of an empty abundance. MICHAEL HARRINGTON, *The Other America* (1962), 5.1

25. Thou, O my country, hast thy foolish ways, / Too apt to purr at every stranger's praise! OLIVER WENDELL HOLMES, SR., "An After-Dinner Poem" (1843).

26. The Americans burn incense before it [democracy], but they are themselves ruled by the Boss and the Trust. WILLIAM RALPH INGE, "Our Present Discontents," *Outspoken Essays: First Series* (1919).

27. I tremble for my country when I reflect that God is just. THOMAS JEFFERSON, *Notes on the State of Virginia* (1784–85), 18.

28. When a great ship cuts through the sea, the waters are always stirred and troubled. And our ship is moving—moving through troubled new waters, toward new and better shores. LYNDON B. JOHNSON, State of the Union Message, Jan. 17, 1968.

29. The American, by nature, is optimistic. He is experimental, an inventor and a builder who builds best when called upon to build greatly. JOHN F. KENNEDY, address, Washington, D.C., Jan. 1, 1960.

30. I look forward to a great future for America—a future in which our country will match its military strength with our moral restraint, its wealth with our wisdom, its power with our purpose. JOHN F. KENNEDY, address, Amherst College, Mass., Oct. 26, 1963.

31. The compelling fact about art in America is that it is not organic. It has almost no share in shaping our life; it offers,

rather, compensation for the shapelessness. LOUIS KRONENBERGER, *Company Manners* (1954), 1.1.

32. The American Way is so restlessly creative as to be essentially destructive; the American Way is to carry common sense itself almost to the point of madness. LOUIS KRONENBERGER, "Last Thoughts," *Company Manners* (1954).

33. The typical American believes that no necessity of the soul is free and that there are precious few, if any, which cannot be bought. JOSEPH WOOD KRUTCH, "The European Visitor," *If You Don't Mind My Saying So* (1964).

34. America is a passionate idea or it is nothing. America is a human brotherhood or it is a chaos. MAX LERNER, "The United States as Exclusive Hotel," *Actions and Passions* (1949).

35. Action, swiftness, violence, power: these are native, homegrown American qualities, derived from the vast continent that has been ours to open up, and the big prizes that have made our economy into a jungle where the law is eat or be eaten. MAX LERNER, "Violence Without Meaning," *Actions and Passions* (1949).

36. If destruction be our lot we must ourselves be its author and finisher. As a nation of free men we must live through all time, or die by suicide. ABRAHAM LINCOLN, speech, Springfield, Ill., Jan. 27, 1838.

37. America, which has the most glorious present still existing in the world today, hardly stops to enjoy it, in her insatiable appetite for the future. ANNE MORROW LINDBERGH, "The Beach at My Back," *Gift from the Sea* (1955).

38. We live in a welfare state which seeks to put a floor below which no one sinks but builds no ceiling to prevent man from rising. HENRY CABOT LODGE, JR., news reports, Sept. 18, 1959.

39. This is America, / This vast, confused beauty, / This staring, restless speed of loveliness, / Mighty, overwhelming, crude, of all forms,/ Making grandeur out of profusion, / Afraid of no incongruities, / Sublime in its audacity, / Bizarre breaker of moulds. AMY LOWELL, "The Congressional Liberty," *What's O'Clock* (1925).

40. We are a nation of twenty million bathrooms, with a humanist in every tub. MARY MC CARTHY, "America the Beautiful: The Humanist in the Bathtub," *On the Contrary* (1961).

41. The American character looks always as if it had just had a rather bad haircut, which gives it, in our eyes at any rate, a greater humanity than the European, which even among its beggars has an all too professional air. MARY MC CARTHY, "America the Beautiful: The Humanist in the Bathtub," *On the Contrary* (1961).

42. The happy ending is our national belief. MARY MC CARTHY, "America the Beautiful: The Humanist in the Bathtub," *On the Contrary* (1961).

43. American youth attributes much more importance to arriving at driver's-license age than at voting age. MARSHALL MC LUHAN, *Understanding Media* (1964), 22.

44. Sitting at the table doesn't make you a diner, unless you eat some of what's on that plate. Being here in America doesn't make you an American. Being born here in America doesn't make you an American. MALCOLM X, *Malcolm X Speaks* (1965), 3.

45. An American who can make money, invoke God, and be no better than his neighbor, has nothing to fear but truth itself. MARYA MANNES, *More in Anger* (1958), 1.2.

46. If American men are obsessed with money, American women are obsessed with weight. The men talk of gain, the women talk of loss, and I do not know which talk is the more boring. MARYA MANNES, *More in Anger* (1958), 1.3.

47. Americans seem sometimes to believe that if you are a thinker you must be a frowning bore, because thinking is so damn serious. JACQUES MARITAIN, *Reflections on America* (1958), 15.

48. The great and admirable strength of America consists in this, that America is truly the American people. JACQUES MARITAIN, *Reflections on America* (1958), 20.

49. The American people, taking one with another, constitute the most timorous, sniveling, poltroonish, ignominious mob of serfs and goose-steppers ever gathered under one flag in Christendom since the end of the Middle Ages. H. L. MENCKEN, *Prejudices: Third Series* (1922), 1.

50. I have never been able to look upon America as young and vital but rather as prematurely old, as a fruit which rotted

before it had a chance to ripen. HENRY MILLER, "Dr. Souchon: Surgeon-Painter," *The Air-Conditioned Nightmare* (1945).

51. The word which gives the key to the national [American] vice is waste. HENRY MILLER, "Dr. Souchon: Surgeon-Painter," *The Air-Conditioned Nightmare* (1945).

52. It isn't the oceans which cut us off from the world—it's the American way of looking at things. HENRY MILLER, "Letter to Lafayette," *The Air-Conditioned Nightmare* (1945).

53. In America there are no ladies, except salesladies. LANGDON MITCHELL, *The New York Idea* (1907), 2.

54. America is still a government of the naïve, for the naïve, and by the naïve. He who does not know this, nor relish it, has no inkling of the nature of his country. CHRISTOPHER MORLEY, *Inward Ho!* (1923), 5.

55. The pursuit of happiness, which American citizens are obliged to undertake, tends to involve them in trying to perpetuate the moods, tastes and aptitudes of youth. MALCOLM MUGGERIDGE, "Women of America," *The Most of Malcolm Muggeridge* (1966).

56. If we ever pass out as a great nation we ought to put on our tombstone "America died from a delusion that she had moral leadership." WILL ROGERS, *The Autobiography of Will Rogers* (1949), 16.

57. I sometimes think that the saving grace of America lies in the fact that the overwhelming majority of Americans are possessed of two great qualities—a sense of humor and a sense of proportion. FRANKLIN D. ROOSEVELT, address, Savannah, Ga., Nov. 18, 1933.

58. Self-help and self-control are the essence of the American tradition. FRANKLIN D. ROOSEVELT, State of the Union Message, Jan. 3, 1934.

59. From the very beginning our people have markedly combined practical capacity for affairs with power of devotion to an ideal. The lack of either quality would have rendered the other of small value. THEODORE ROOSEVELT, speech, Philadelphia, Nov. 22, 1902.

60. Frustrate a Frenchman, he will drink himself to death; an Irishman, he will die of angry hypertension; a Dane, he will shoot himself; an American, he will get drunk, shoot you, then establish a million dollar aid program for your relatives. Then he will die of an ulcer. STANLEY RUDIN, *The New York Times*, Aug. 22, 1963.

61. America is the greatest of opportunities and the worst of influences. GEORGE SANTAYANA, *The Last Puritan* (1935), 14.

62. It's complicated, being an American, / Having the money and the bad conscience, both at the same time. LOUIS SIMPSON, "On the Lawn at the Villa," *Selected Poems* (1965).

63. With the supermarket as our temple and the singing commercial as our litany, are we likely to fire the world with an irresistible vision of America's exalted purpose and inspiring way of life? ADLAI STEVENSON, *Wall Street Journal*, June 1, 1960.

64. The patriots are those who love America enough to see her as a model to mankind. ADLAI STEVENSON, "The Hard Kind of Patriotism," *Harper's Magazine*, July 1963.

65. We [America] are a nation that has always gone in for the loud laugh, the wow, the belly laugh and the dozen other labels for the roll-'em-in-the-aisles gagerissimo. JAMES THURBER, "The Quality of Mirth," *The New York Times*, Feb. 21, 1960.

66. If an American were condemned to confine his activity to his own affairs, he would be robbed of one half of his existence. ALEXIS DE TOCQUEVILLE, *Democracy in America* (1835–39), 1.14.

67. The aspect of American society is animated, because men and things are always changing; but it is monotonous, because all these changes are alike. ALEXIS DE TOCQUEVILLE, *Democracy in America* (1835–39), 2.3.17.

68. America is a large, friendly dog in a very small room. Every time it wags its tail, it knocks over a chair. ARNOLD TOYNBEE, news summaries, July 14, 1954.

69. There isn't a single human characteristic that can be safely labeled as "American." MARK TWAIN, "What Paul Bourget Thinks of Us" (1895).

70. We [Americans] are the lavishest and showiest and most luxury-loving people on the earth; and at our masthead we fly one true and honest symbol, the gaudiest flag the world has ever seen. MARK TWAIN, "Diplomatic Pay and Clothes" (1899).

71. We Americans worship the almighty dollar! Well, it is a worthier god than Heredity Privilege. MARK TWAIN, *Notebook* (1935).

72. What is it that distinguishes the American Man from his counterparts in other climes; what *is* it that makes him so special? He is quietly affirmative. He is trustworthy, loyal, helpful, friendly, courteous, kind, obedient, cheerful, thrifty, brave, clean, and reverent. JOHN UPDIKE, "Anywhere Is Where You Hang Your Hat," *Assorted Prose* (1965).

73. Whatever else an American believes or disbelieves about himself, he is absolutely sure he has a sense of humor. E. B. WHITE, "Some Remarks on Humor," *The Second Tree from the Corner* (1954).

74. In nothing is there more evolution than the American mind. WALT WHITMAN, "Foundation Stages—Then Others," *Notes Left Over* (1881).

75. It is possible to believe in progress as a fact without believing in progress as an ethical principle; but in the catechism of many Americans, the one goes with the other. NORBERT WIENER, *The Human Use of Human Beings* (1954), 2.

76. In America the President reigns for four years, and Journalism governs for ever and ever. OSCAR WILDE, *The Soul of Man Under Socialism* (1891).

77. The youth of America is their oldest tradition. OSCAR WILDE, *A Woman of No Importance* (1893), 1.

78. If the American dream is for Americans only, it will remain our dream and never be our destiny. RENÉ DE VISME WILLIAMSON, *Christianity Today*, June 19, 1961.

79. We [Americans] have a great ardor for gain; but we have a deep passion for the rights of man. WOODROW WILSON, speech, New York, Dec. 6, 1911.

80. America was established not to create wealth but to realize a vision, to realize an ideal—to discover and maintain liberty among men. WOODROW WILSON, address, Chicago, Feb. 12, 1912.

81. Just what is it that America stands for? If she stands for one thing more than another it is for the sovereignty of self-governing people. WOODROW WILSON, speech, Pittsburgh, Pa., Jan. 29, 1916.

82. The thing that impresses me most about America is the way parents obey their children. DUKE OF WINDSOR, *Look*, March 5, 1957.

## AMUSEMENT

See 290. Entertainment; 434. Humor; 523. Laughter

## 35. ANALOGY

See also 521. Language

1. Though analogy is often misleading, it is the least misleading thing we have. SAMUEL BUTLER (d. 1902), "Lord, What Is Man?" *Note-Books* (1912).

2. Analogies, it is true, decide nothing, but they can make one feel more at home. SIGMUND FREUD, "The Dissection of the Psychical Personality," *New Introductory Lectures on Psychoanalysis* (1933), tr. James Strachey.

3. The metaphor is perhaps one of man's most fruitful potentialities. Its efficacy verges on magic, and it seems a tool for creation which God forgot inside one of His creatures when He made him. JOSÉ ORTEGA Y GASSET, *The Dehumanization of Art* (1925).

4. All perception of truth is the detection of an analogy. THOREAU, *Journal*, Sept. 5, 1851.

## 36. ANARCHY

See also 393. Government; 906. Society

1. It is not honest inquiry that makes anarchy; but it is error, insincerity, half-belief and untruth that make it. THOMAS CARLYLE, *On Heroes, Hero-Worship and the Heroic in History* (1841), 4.

2. During the time men live without a common power to keep them in awe, they are in that condition which is called war; and such a war as is of every man against every man. THOMAS HOBBES, *Leviathan* (1651), 1.8.

3. Anarchy is the stepping stone to absolute power. NAPOLEON I, *Maxims* (1804–15).

## 37. ANCESTRY

**See also 81. Birth; 306. Evolution**

1. There are many kinds of conceit, but the chief one is to let people know what a very ancient and gifted family one descends from. BENVENUTO CELLINI, *Autobiography* (1558–66), tr. George Bull.

2. To forget one's ancestors is to be a brook without a source, a tree without a root. CHINESE PROVERB.

3. The pride of ancestry is a superstructure of the most imposing height, but resting on the most flimsy foundation. CHARLES CALEB COLTON, *Lacon* (1825), 2.272.

4. Noble and common blood is of the same color. GERMAN PROVERB.

5. I can trace my ancestry back to a protoplasmal primordial atomic globule. Consequently, my family pride is something in-conceivable. I can't help it. I was born sneering. W. S. GILBERT, *The Mikado* (1885), 1.

6. Happy the man who can recall his fathers / With joy, who with their deeds and greatness can / Regale a hearer, and with quiet pleasure / Beholds himself at the close of that fair / Succession. GOETHE, *Iphigenia in Tauris* (1787), 1, tr. Charles E. Passage.

7. I am the family face; / Flesh perishes, I live on, / Projecting trait and trace / Through time to times anon, / And leaping from place to place / Over oblivion. THOMAS HARDY, "Heredity," *Moments of Vision* (1917).

8. High birth is a poor dish at table. ITALIAN PROVERB.

9. Birth is nothing without virtue, and we have no claim to share in the glory of our ancestors unless we strive to resemble them. MOLIÈRE, *Don Juan* (1665), 4.2, tr. John Wood.

10. Good birth is a fine thing, but the merit is our ancestors'. PLUTARCH, "The Education of Children," *Moralia* (c. A.D. 100), tr. Moses Hadas.

11. Pride thyself on what virtue thou hast, and not on thy parentage. SA'DI, *Gulistan* (1258), 8.60, tr. James Ross.

12. A man who prides himself on his ancestry is like the potato plant, the best part of which is under ground. SPANISH PROVERB.

13. Each has his own tree of ancestors, but at the top of all sits Probably Arboreal. ROBERT LOUIS STEVENSON, *Memories and Portraits* (1887), 6.

14. The stream is brightest at its spring, / And blood is not like wine; / Nor honored less than he who heirs / Is he who founds a line. JOHN GREENLEAF WHITTIER, *Amy Wentworth* (1862), 2.

## 38. ANGELS

**See also 412. Heaven**

1. An angel is a spiritual being, created by God without a body, for the service of Christendom and the Church. MARTIN LUTHER, *Table Talk* (1569), 569.

2. It is not known precisely where angels dwell—whether in the air, the void, or the planets. It has not been God's pleasure that we should be informed of their abode. VOLTAIRE, "Angels," *Philosophical Dictionary* (1764).

## 39. ANGER

**See also 209. Cursing; 465. Indignation; 961. Temper, Bad**

1. Anger represents a certain power, when a great mind, prevented from executing its own generous desires, is moved by it. PIETRO ARETINO, letter to Girolamo Quirini, Nov. 21, 1537, tr. Samuel Putnam.

2. Angry men are blind and foolish, for reason at such a time takes flight and, in her absence, wrath plunders all the riches of the intellect, while the judgment remains the prisoner of its own pride. PIETRO ARETINO, letter to Girolamo Quirini, Nov. 21, 1537, tr. Samuel Putnam.

3. It is easy to fly into a passion—anybody can do that—but to be angry with the right person to the right extent and at the right time and with the right object and in the right way—that is not easy, and it is not everyone who can do it. ARISTOTLE, *Nicomachean Ethics* (4th c. B.C.), 2.9, tr. J. A. K. Thomson.

4. No man is angry that feels not himself hurt. FRANCIS BACON, "Of Anger," *Essays* (1625).

5. Rage can only with difficulty, and never entirely, be brought under the domination of the intelligence and is therefore not susceptible to any arguments whatever. JAMES BALDWIN, "Stranger in the Village"

(1953), *Notes of a Native Son* (1955).

6. A man that does not know how to be angry does not know how to be good. HENRY WARD BEECHER, *Proverbs from Plymouth Pulpit* (1887).

7. He that is slow to anger is better than the mighty; and he that ruleth his spirit than he that taketh a city. *Bible*, Proverbs 16:32.

8. Let not the sun go down upon your wrath. *Bible*, Ephesians 4:26.

9. The tigers of wrath are wiser than the horses of instruction. WILLIAM BLAKE, "Proverbs of Hell," *The Marriage of Heaven and Hell* (1790).

10. A background of wrath, which can be stirred up to the murderous infernal pitch, does lie in every man. THOMAS CARLYLE, "Two Hundred and Fifty Years Ago" (1850).

11. I know of no more disagreeable situation than to be left feeling generally angry without anybody in particular to be angry at. FRANK MOORE COLBY, "The Literature of Malicious Exposure," *The Colby Essays* (1926), v. 1.

12. Many people lose their tempers merely from seeing you keep yours. FRANK MOORE COLBY, "Trials of an Encyclopedist," *The Colby Essays* (1926), v. 1.

13. Life is thorny; and youth is vain; / And to be wroth with one we love / Doth work like madness in the brain. SAMUEL TAYLOR COLERIDGE, *Christabel* (1816), 2.410.

14. Anger as soon as fed is dead— / 'Tis starving makes it fat—. EMILY DICKINSON, poem (c. 1881).

15. Th' next pleasantest feelin' in th' wurruld to bein' perfectly happy is bein' perfectly cross. FINLEY PETER DUNNE, "On Golf," *Mr. Dooley On Making a Will* (1919).

16. A sharp-tempered woman, or, for that matter, a man, / Is easier to deal with than the clever type / Who holds her tongue. EURIPIDES, *Medea* (431 B.C.), tr. Rex Warner.

17. Anger is one of the sinews of the soul; he that wants [lacks] it hath a maimed mind. THOMAS FULLER, D.D., "Of Anger," *The Holy State and the Profane State* (1642).

18. A man in a passion rides a horse that runs away with him. THOMAS FULLER, M.D., *Gnomologia* (1732), 283.

19. Anger without power is folly. GERMAN PROVERB.

20. He who has been angry becomes cool again. GREEK PROVERB.

21. Anger may be foolish and absurd, and one may be irritated when in the wrong; but a man never feels outraged unless in some respect he is at bottom right. VICTOR HUGO, "Fantine," *Les Misérables* (1862), 2.7, tr. Charles E. Wilbour.

22. A tall man is never his own man till he be angry. BEN JONSON, *Every Man in His Humour* (1598), 4.8.

23. Usually when people are sad, they don't do anything. They just cry over their condition. But when they get angry, they bring about a change. MALCOLM X, *Malcolm X Speaks* (1965), 9.

24. He who doesn't know anger doesn't know anything. He doesn't know the immediate. HENRI MICHAUX, *Selected Writings* (1952), tr. Richard Ellman.

25. How often, being moved under a false cause, if the person offending makes a good defense and presents us with a just excuse, are we angry against truth and innocence itself? MONTAIGNE, "Of anger," *Essays* (1580–88), tr. Charles Cotton and W. C. Hazlitt.

26. Nothing on earth consumes a man more quickly than the passion of resentment. NIETZSCHE, *Ecce Homo* (1888), tr. Anthony M. Ludovici.

27. To be angry is to revenge the fault of others upon ourselves. ALEXANDER POPE, *Thoughts on Various Subjects* (1727).

28. The bare recollection of anger kindles anger. PUBLILIUS SYRUS, *Moral Sayings* (1st c. B.C.), 125, tr. Darius Lyman.

29. Always shun whatever may make you angry. PUBLILIUS SYRUS, *Moral Sayings* (1st c. B.C.), 879, tr. Darius Lyman.

30. Anger would inflict punishment on another; meanwhile, it tortures itself. PUBLILIUS SYRUS, *Moral Sayings* (1st c. B.C.), 1009, tr. Darius Lyman.

31. The brain may devise laws for the blood, but a hot temper leaps o'er a cold decree. SHAKESPEARE, *The Merchant of Venice* (1596–97), 1.2.19.

32. There is no old age for a man's anger, / Only death. SOPHOCLES, *Oedipus at Colonus* (401 B.C.), tr. Robert Fitzgerald.

33. When angry, count four; when very angry, swear. MARK TWAIN, "Pudd'nhead Wilson's Calendar," *Pudd'nhead Wilson* (1894), 10.

## 40. ANGLO-SAXONS

1. An Anglo-Saxon, Hinnissy, is a German that's forgot who was his parents. FINLEY PETER DUNNE, "On the Anglo-Saxon," *Mr. Dooley in Peace and in War* (1898).

2. Most of us, Anglo-Saxons, tremble before a tear when we might fearlessly beard a tiger. DAVID GRAYSON, *Adventures in Contentment* (1907), 4.

## 41. ANIMALS

**See also 80. Birds; 344. Fish; 479. Insects; 484. Instinct**

1. Is it not wonderful, that the love of the [animal] parent should be so violent while it last and that it should last no longer than is necessary for the preservation of the young? JOSEPH ADDISON, *The Spectator* (1711–12), 120.

2. The dog was created specially for children. He is the god of frolic. HENRY WARD BEECHER, *Proverbs from Plymouth Pulpit* (1887).

3. The Llama is a woolly sort of fleecy hairy goat, / With an indolent expression and an undulating throat / Like an unsuccessful literary man. HILAIRE BELLOC, "The Llama," *More Beasts for Worse Children* (1897).

4. [Animals] are not brethren, they are not underlings; they are other nations, caught with ourselves in the net of life and time. HENRY BESTON, "Autumn, Ocean, and Birds," *The Outermost House* (1928).

5. Cat, n. A soft, indestructible automaton provided by nature to be kicked when things go wrong in the domestic circle. AMBROSE BIERCE, *The Devil's Dictionary* (1881–1911).

6. The great pleasure of a dog is that you may make a fool of yourself with him and not only will he not scold you, but he will make a fool of himself too. SAMUEL BUTLER (d. 1902), "Higgledy-Piggledy," *Note-Books* (1912).

7. Dogs have more love than integrity. They've been true to us, yes, but they haven't been true to themselves. CLARENCE DAY, *This Simian World* (1920), 7.

8. Elephants suffer from too much patience. Their exhibitions of it may seem superb,—such power and such restraint, combined, are noble,—but a quality carried to excess defeats itself. CLARENCE DAY, *This Simian World* (1920), 7.

9. 'Orses and dorgs is some men's fancy. They're wittles and drink to me—lodging, wife, and children—reading, writing, and 'rithmetic—snuff, tobacker, and sleep. CHARLES DICKENS, *David Copperfield* (1849–50), 19.

10. The Bat is dun, with wrinkled Wings — / Like fallow Article— / And not a song pervade his Lips— / Or none perceptible. EMILY DICKINSON, poem (c. 1876).

11. Animals are such agreeable friends —they ask no questions, they pass no criticisms. GEORGE ELIOT, "Mr. Gilfil's Love-Story," *Scenes of Clerical Life* (1857), 7.

12. The Latin proverb, *homo homini lupus*—man is a wolf to man— . . . is a libel on the wolf, which is a gentle animal with other wolves. GEOFFREY GORER, *The New York Times Magazine*, Nov. 27, 1966.

13. One must remember that both wild things and men are animals, but wild things are not people. HELEN HOOVER, "The Resident Birds," *The Long-Shadowed Forest* (1963).

14. We have enslaved the rest of the animal creation, and have treated our distant cousins in fur and feathers so badly that beyond doubt, if they were able to formulate a religion, they would depict the Devil in human form. WILLIAM RALPH INGE, "The Idea of Progress," *Outspoken Essays: Second Series* (1922).

15. If animals are deprived of hope (as well as of fear), they are compensated by being given an almost endless patience for enduring, or simply for waiting. JOSEPH WOOD KRUTCH, "February," *The Twelve Seasons* (1949).

16. Cats seem to go on the principle that it never does any harm to ask for what you want. JOSEPH WOOD KRUTCH, "February," *The Twelve Seasons* (1949).

17. Cats are rather delicate creatures and they are subject to a good many different ailments, but I never heard of one who suffered from insomnia. JOSEPH WOOD KRUTCH, "February," *The Twelve Seasons* (1949).

18. Cats, like men, are flatterers. WALTER SAVAGE LANDOR, "La Fontaine and De La Rochefoucault," *Imaginary Conversations* (1824–53).

19. There is no faith which has never yet been broken, except that of a truly faithful dog. KONRAD Z. LORENZ, *King Solomon's Ring* (1952), 10, tr. Marjorie Kerr Wilson.

20. A dog's best friend is his illiteracy. OGDEN NASH, title poem, *The Private Dining Room* (1953).

21. The trouble with a kitten is / That / Eventually it becomes a / Cat. OGDEN NASH, "The Kitten," *Verses from 1929 On* (1959).

22. Our dogs will love and admire the meanest of us, and feed our colossal vanity with their uncritical homage. AGNES REPPLIER, "The Idolatrous Dog," *Under Dispute* (1924).

23. A real dog, beloved and therefore pampered by his mistress, is a lamentable spectacle. He suffers from fatty degeneration of his moral being. AGNES REPPLIER, "The Idolatrous Dog," *Under Dispute* (1924).

24. G stands for goat and also / For genius. If you are one, / Learn from the other, for he / Combines domestication, / Venery, and independence. KENNETH REXROTH, "A Bestiary," *Natural Numbers* (1956).

25. A dog will never forget the crumb thou gavest him, though thou mayst afterwards throw a hundred stones at his head. SA'DI, *Gulistan* (1258), 8.99, tr. James Ross.

26. There is one respect in which brutes show real wisdom when compared with us —I mean their quiet, placid enjoyment of the present moment. SCHOPENHAUER, "On the Sufferings of the World," *Parerga and Paralipomena* (1851), tr. T. Bailey Saunders.

27. Dogs live with man as courtiers round a monarch, steeped in the flattery of his notice and enriched with sinecures. To push their favor in this world of pickings and caresses is, perhaps, the business of their lives; and their joys may lie outside. ROBERT LOUIS STEVENSON, "The Character of Dogs" (1883).

28. Those who wish to pet and baby wild animals, "love" them. But those who respect their natures and wish to let them live normal lives, love them more. EDWIN WAY TEALE, "April 28," *Circle of the Seasons* (1953).

29. Of all God's creatures there is only one that cannot be made the slave of the lash. That one is the cat. If man could be crossed with the cat it would improve man, but it would deteriorate the cat. MARK TWAIN, *Notebook* (1935).

30. Let dogs delight to bark and bite, / For God hath made them so; / Let bears and lions growl and fight, / For 'tis their nature too. ISAAC WATTS, *Divine Songs for Children* (1720), 16.

31. They say a reasonable amount o' fleas is good fer a dog—keeps him from broodin' over *bein'* a dog, mebbe. EDWARD NOYES WESTCOTT, *David Harum* (1898), 32.

32. The cow crunching with depressed head surpasses any statue, / And a mouse is miracle enough to stagger sextillions of infidels. WALT WHITMAN, "Song of Myself," *Leaves of Grass* (1855–92).

33. The best thing about animals is that they don't talk much. THORNTON WILDER, *The Skin of Our Teeth* (1942), 1.

## ANSWER

See 478. Inquiry

## ANTICIPATION

See 316. Expectation; 1033. Waiting

## 42. ANTIQUITY

See also 134. Classics; 400. Greece, Ancient; 417. History and Historians; 669. Past; 979. Tradition

1. What is a ruin but Time easing itself of endurance? DJUNA BARNES, *Nightwood* (1937).

2. An archeologist is the best husband any woman can have: the older she gets, the more interested he is in her. AGATHA CHRISTIE, news reports, March 9, 1954.

3. If we look backwards to antiquity, it should be as those that are winning a race. CHARLES CALEB COLTON, *Lacon* (1825), 2.148.

4. When eras die, their legacies / Are left to strange police. / Professors in New England guard / The glory that was Greece. CLARENCE DAY, "Thoughts on Deaths," *Thoughts Without Words* (1928).

5. There's a fascination frantic / In a ruin that's romantic. W. S. GILBERT, *The Mikado* (1855), 2.

6. Antiquity was perhaps created to provide professors with their bread and butter.

EDMOND and JULES DE GONCOURT, *Journal*, Jan. 6, 1866.

7. Had the Greeks held novelty in such disdain as we, what work of ancient date would now exist? HORACE, *Epistles* (20–c. 8 B.C.), 2.1.

8. Antiquity is full of the praises of another antiquity still more remote. VOLTAIRE, "Ancients and Moderns," *Philosophical Dictionary* (1764).

## ANTS
See 479. Insects

## 43. ANXIETY
See also 340. Fear; 480. Insecurity; 861. Self-doubt

1. We poison our lives with fear of burglary and shipwreck and, ask anyone, the house is never burgled and the ship never goes down. JEAN ANOUILH, *The Rehearsal* (1950), 2, tr. Lucienne Hill.

2. Jealousy and anger shorten life, and anxiety brings on old age too soon. *Apocrypha*, Ecclesiasticus 30:24.

3. As a rule, what is out of sight disturbs men's minds more seriously than what they see. JULIUS CAESAR, *Gallic War* (58–52 B.C.), tr. H. J. Edwards.

4. Stupidity is without anxiety. GOETHE, quoted in Johann Peter Eckermann's *Conversations with Goethe*, Aug. 16, 1824.

5. How much pain have cost us the evils which have never happened. THOMAS JEFFERSON, letter to Thomas Jefferson Smith, Feb. 21, 1825.

6. This is, I think, very much the Age of Anxiety, the age of the neurosis, because along with so much that weighs on our minds there is perhaps even more that grates on our nerves. LOUIS KRONENBERGER, "The Spirit of the Age," *Company Manners* (1954).

7. Joy, interrupted now and again by pain and terminated ultimately by death, seems the normal course of life in Nature. Anxiety and distress, interrupted occasionally by pleasure, is the normal course of man's existence. JOSEPH WOOD KRUTCH, "May," *The Twelve Seasons* (1949).

8. Fear, born of the stern matron Responsibility, sits on one's shoulders like some heavy imp of darkness, and one is preoccupied and, possibly, cantankerous. WILLIAM MC FEE, "The Crusaders," *Harbours of Memory* (1921).

9. Grief has limits, whereas apprehension has none. For we grieve only for what we know has happened, but we fear all that possibly may happen. PLINY THE YOUNGER, *Letters* (c. 97–110), 8.17, tr. William Melmoth and W. M. L. Hutchinson.

10. We are more often frightened than hurt: our troubles spring more often from fancy than reality. SENECA, *Letters to Lucilius* (1st c.), 13, tr. E. Phillips Barker.

11. Care is no cure, but rather corrosive, / For things that are not to be remedied. SHAKESPEARE, *1 Henry VI* (1591–92), 3.3.3.

12. Tenterhooks are the upholstery of the anxious seat. ROBERT SHERWOOD, news reports, Nov. 15, 1955.

13. Anxiety and conscience are a powerful pair of dynamos. Between them, they have ensured that I shall work hard, but they cannot ensure that one shall work at anything worthwhile. ARNOLD J. TOYNBEE, "Why and How I Work," *Saturday Review*, April 5, 1969.

14. My apprehensions come in crowds; / I dread the rustling of the grass; / The very shadows of the clouds / Have power to shake me as they pass: / I question things and do not find / One that will answer to my mind; / And all the world appears unkind. WILLIAM WORDSWORTH, "The Affliction of Margaret——" (1804), 10.

15. Worries go down better with soup than without. *Yiddish Proverbs* (1949), ed. Hanan J. Ayalti.

## APATHY
See 216. Deadness, Spiritual; 464. Indifference

## 44. APOLOGY
See also 785. Regret; 793. Repentance

1. Apologies only account for that which they do not alter. BENJAMIN DISRAELI, speech, July 28, 1871.

2. To no kind of begging are people so averse, as to begging pardon; that is, when there is any serious ground for doing so. JULIUS CHARLES HARE and AUGUSTUS WIL-

LIAM HARE, *Guesses at Truth* (1827).

3. Apology is only egotism wrong side out. OLIVER WENDELL HOLMES, SR., *The Professor at the Breakfast Table* (1860), 6.

4. "Excuse me, pray." Without that excuse I would not have known there was anything amiss. PASCAL, *Pensées* (1670), 58, tr. W. F. Trotter.

## 45. APPEARANCE

**See also 54. Artificiality; 189. Cosmetics; 265. Dress; 335. Fashion; 405. Hair; 442. Identity; 726. Pretension; 819. Role-playing**

1. Outside show is a poor substitute for inner worth. AESOP, "The Fox and the Mask," *Fables* (6th c. B.C.?), tr. Joseph Jacobs.

2. The Lord seeth not as man seeth; for man looketh on the outward appearance, but the Lord looketh on the heart. *Bible*, 1 Samuel 16:7.

3. Fine words and an insinuating appearance are seldom associated with true virtue. CONFUCIUS, *Analects* (6th c. B.C.), 1.3, tr. James Legge.

4. Always scorn appearances and you always may. EMERSON, "Self-Reliance," *Essays: First Series* (1841).

5. They are not all saints who use holy water. ENGLISH PROVERB.

6. A good presence is letters of recommendation. THOMAS FULLER, M.D., *Gnomologia* (1732), 170.

7. By the husk you may guess at the nut. THOMAS FULLER, M.D., *Gnomologia* (1732), 1044.

8. 'Tis not the habit that makes the monk. THOMAS FULLER, M.D., *Gnomologia* (1732), 5104.

9. Things are seldom what they seem, / Skim milk masquerades as cream. W. S. GILBERT, *H. M. S. Pinafore* (1878), 2.

10. What is not seen is as if it was not. Even the Right does not receive proper consideration if it does not seem right. BALTASAR GRACIÁN, *The Art of Worldly Wisdom* (1647), 130, tr. Joseph Jacobs.

11. Personal appearance is looking the best you can for the money. VIRGINIA CARY HUDSON, *O Ye Jigs & Juleps!* (1962).

12. We love good looks rather than what is practical, / Though good looks may prove destructive. LA FONTAINE, "The Stag and His Reflection," *Fables* (1668–94), tr. Marianne Moore.

13. A man, in order to establish himself in the world, does everything he can to appear established there. LA ROCHEFOUCAULD, *Maxims* (1665), tr. Kenneth Pratt.

14. An ox with long horns, even if he does not butt, will be accused of butting. MALAY PROVERB.

15. Be content to seem what you really are. MARTIAL, *Epigrams* (A.D. 86), 10.83.

16. It is easy to be beautiful; it is difficult to appear so. FRANK O'HARA, title poem, *Meditations in an Emergency* (1967).

17. Long whiskers cannot take the place of brains. RUSSIAN PROVERB.

18. Many is the gracious form that is covered with a veil; but on withdrawing this thou discoverest a grandmother. SA'DI, *Gulistan* (1258), 8.44, tr. James Ross.

19. It is only shallow people who do not judge by appearances. The true mystery of the world is the visible, not the invisible. OSCAR WILDE, *The Picture of Dorian Gray* (1891), 2.

## 46. APPEASEMENT

**See also 27. Agreement; 160. Compromise; 164. Conciliation; 987. Treaties**

1. Yield to all and you will soon have nothing to yield. AESOP, "The Man and His Two Wives," *Fables* (6th c. B.C.?), tr. Joseph Jacobs.

2. An appeaser is one who feeds a crocodile—hoping it will eat him last. SIR WINSTON CHURCHILL, *Reader's Digest*, December 1954.

3. If once you have paid him the Danegeld / You never get rid of the Dane. RUDYARD KIPLING, "Dane-Geld" (1910).

4. No man can tame a tiger into a kitten by stroking it. There can be no appeasement with ruthlessness. There can be no reasoning with an incendiary bomb. FRANKLIN D. ROOSEVELT, Fireside Chat, Dec. 29, 1940.

5. A really great people, proud and high-spirited, would face all the disasters of war rather than purchase that base prosperity which is bought at the price of national honor. THEODORE ROOSEVELT, speech, Harvard University, Feb. 23, 1907.

6. No man can sit down and withhold his hands from the warfare against wrong and get peace from his acquiescence. WOODROW WILSON, address, Denver, Colo., May 7, 1911.

APPETITE
See 236. Desires; 401. Greed; 435. Hunger; 492. Intemperance; 963. Temperance

## 47. APPRECIATION

See also 48. Appreciation, Lack of; 49. Approval; 397. Gratitude; 716. Praise; 1019. Value

1. Wise men appreciate all men, for they see the good in each and know how hard it is to make anything good. BALTASAR GRACIÁN, *The Art of Worldly Wisdom* (1647), 195, tr. Joseph Jacobs.

2. I would rather be able to appreciate things I can not have than to have things I am not able to appreciate. ELBERT HUBBARD, *The Note Book* (1927).

3. Do not expect to be acknowledged for what you are, much less for what you would be; since no one can well measure a great man but upon the bier. WALTER SAVAGE LANDOR, "Lucullus and Caesar," *Imaginary Conversations* (1824–53).

## 48. APPRECIATION, LACK OF

See also 47. Appreciation; 473. Ingratitude

1. Neither cast ye pearls before swine, lest they trample them under their feet, and turn again and rend you. *Bible*, Matthew 7: 6.

2. Futility: playing a harp before a buffalo. *Burmese Proverbs* (1962), 28, ed. Hla Pe.

3. It is folly to sing twice to a deaf man. ENGLISH PROVERB.

4. What is the voice of song, when the world lacks the ear of taste? NATHANIEL HAWTHORNE, "Canterbury Pilgrims," *The Snow Image* (1851).

5. The greatest humiliation in life, is to work hard on something from which you expect great appreciation, and then fail to get it. EDGAR WATSON HOWE, *Ventures in Common Sense* (1919), 32.65.

6. Fleas do not know whether they are upon the body of a giant or upon one of ordinary stature. WALTER SAVAGE LANDOR, "Southey and Porson," *Imaginary Conversations* (1824–53).

7. Hay is more acceptable to an ass than gold. LATIN PROVERB.

8. A frog would leap from a throne of gold into a puddle. PUBLILIUS SYRUS, *Moral Sayings* (1st c. B.C.), 821, tr. Darius Lyman.

9. One good deed dying tongueless / Slaughters a thousand waiting upon that. SHAKESPEARE, *The Winter's Tale* (1610–11), 1.2.92.

10. Ignorant men / Don't know what good they hold in their hands until / They've flung it away. SOPHOCLES, *Ajax* (c. 447 B.C.), tr. John Moore.

APPROPRIATENESS
See 942. Suitability

## 49. APPROVAL

See also 14. Admiration; 47. Appreciation; 472. Ingratiation; 706. Popularity; 716. Praise

1. He only is a great man who can neglect the applause of the multitude and enjoy himself independent of its favour. JOSEPH ADDISON, *The Spectator* (1711–12), 172.

2. Lean too much upon the approval of people, and it becomes a bed of thorns. TEHYI HSIEH, *Chinese Epigrams Inside Out and Proverbs* (1948), 14.

APRIL
See 848. Seasons

APTITUDE
See 1. Ability; 374. Genius; 956. Talent

## 50. ARCHITECTURE

See also 53. Art and Artists; 235. Design; 428. Houses

1. Architect, n. One who drafts a plan of your house, and plans a draft of your money. AMBROSE BIERCE, *The Devil's Dictionary* (1881–1911).

2. Architecture is inhabited sculpture. CONSTANTIN BRANCUSI, quoted in Igor Stravinsky's *Themes and Episodes* (1966).

3. We shape our buildings: thereafter they shape us. SIR WINSTON CHURCHILL, *Time*, Sept. 12, 1960.

4. The Gothic cathedral is a blossoming in stone subdued by the insatiable demand of harmony in man. EMERSON, "History," *Essays: First Series* (1841).

5. The brevity of human life gives a melancholy to the profession of the architect. EMERSON, *Journals*, 1842.

6. Light, God's eldest daughter, is a principal beauty in a building. THOMAS FULLER, D.D., "Of Building," *The Holy State and the Profane State* (1642).

7. I call architecture "petrified music." Really there is something in this; the tone of mind produced by architecture approaches the effect of music. GOETHE, quoted in Johann Peter Eckermann's *Conversations with Goethe*, March 23, 1829.

8. An arch never sleeps. HINDUSTANI PROVERB.

9. The genius of architecture seems to have shed its maledictions over this land. THOMAS JEFFERSON, *Notes on the State of Virginia* (1784–85), 15.

10. Of all forms of visible otherworldliness, it seems to me, the Gothic is at once the most logical and the most beautiful. It reaches up magnificently—and a good half of it is palpably useless. H. L. MENCKEN, "The New Architecture," *The American Mercury*, February 1931.

11. In architecture the pride of man, his triumph over gravitation, his will to power, assume a visible form. Architecture is a sort of oratory of power by means of forms. NIETZSCHE, "Skirmishes in a War with the Age," *Twilight of the Idols* (1888), tr. Anthony M. Ludovici.

12. If the design of the building be originally bad, the only virtue it can ever possess will be signs of antiquity. JOHN RUSKIN, *Modern Painters* (1843–60), v. 1, 2.1.7.26.

13. When we build, let us think that we build for ever. JOHN RUSKIN, *The Seven Lamps of Architecture* (1849), 5.

14. No architecture is so haughty as that which is simple. JOHN RUSKIN, *The Stones of Venice* (1851–53), v. 2, 6.78.

15. No person who is not a great sculptor or painter can be an architect. If he is not a sculptor or painter, he can only be a builder. JOHN RUSKIN, *Lectures on Architecture and Painting* (1853), no. 61.

16. Lovely promise and quick ruin are seen nowhere better than in Gothic architecture. GEORGE SANTAYANA, "Avila," *Persons and Places: The Background of My Life* (1944).

## 51. ARGUMENT

**See also 250. Discord; 256. Dissent; 649. Opinion; 683. Persuasion; 766. Quarreling; 778. Reason**

1. There is nothing that a New-Englander so nearly worships as an argument. HENRY WARD BEECHER, *Proverbs from Plymouth Pulpit* (1887).

2. Positive, adj. Mistaken at the top of one's voice. AMBROSE BIERCE, *The Devil's Dictionary* (1881–1911).

3. In all disputes, so much as there is of passion, so much there is of nothing to the purpose; for then reason, like a bad hound, spends upon a false scent, and forsakes the question first started. SIR THOMAS BROWNE, *Religio Medici* (1642), 2.

4. Yea, even amongst wiser militants, how many wounds have been given, and credits slain, for the poor victory of an opinion, or beggarly conquest of a distinction! SIR THOMAS BROWNE, *Religio Medici* (1642), 2.

5. When an argument is over, how many weighty reasons does a man recollect which his heat and violence made him utterly forget? EUSTACE BUDGELL in *The Spectator* (1711–12), 197.

6. It is not he who gains the exact point in dispute who scores most in controversy, but he who has shown the most forbearance and the better temper. SAMUEL BUTLER (d. 1902), "Reconciliation," *Note-Books* (1912).

7. Somebody has to have the last word. If not, every argument could be opposed by another and we'd never be done with it. ALBERT CAMUS, *The Fall* (1956).

8. If you would convince others, seem open to conviction yourself. LORD CHESTERFIELD, *Letters to His Son*, Feb. 22, 1748.

9. A majority is always the best repartee. BENJAMIN DISRAELI, *Tancred* (1847), 14.

10. In a philosophical dispute, he gains

most who is defeated, since he learns most. EPICURUS, "Vatican Sayings" (3rd c. B.C.), 74, in *Letters, Principal Doctrines, and Vatican Sayings*, tr. Russel M. Geer.

11. Argument seldom convinces anyone contrary to his inclinations. THOMAS FULLER, M.D., *Gnomologia* (1732), 812.

12. One may be confuted and yet not convinced. THOMAS FULLER, M.D., *Gnomologia* (1732), 3771.

13. The best way I know of to win an argument is to start by being in the right. LORD HAILSHAM, *The New York Times*, Oct. 16, 1960.

14. There is no such thing as a convincing argument, although every man thinks he has one. EDGAR WATSON HOWE, *Country Town Sayings* (1911).

15. To make arguments in my study and confute them is easy, where I answer myself, not an adversary. BEN JONSON, "Explorata," *Timber* (1640).

16. The aim of argument, or of discussion, should not be victory, but progress. JOSEPH JOUBERT, *Pensées* (1842), 7.31, tr. Katharine Lyttelton.

17. If in argument we can make a man angry with us, we have drawn him from his vantage ground and overcome him. WALTER SAVAGE LANDOR, "Marcus Tullius and Quinctus Cicero," *Imaginary Conversations* (1824–53).

18. Anyone who in discussion relies upon authority uses, not his understanding, but rather his memory. LEONARDO DA VINCI, *Notebooks* (c. 1500), tr. Jean Paul Richter.

19. In arguing of the shadow, we forgo the substance. JOHN LYLY, *Euphues: The Anatomy of Wit* (1579).

20. When we wish to correct with advantage, and to show another that he errs, we must notice from what side he views the matter, for on that side it is usually true. PASCAL, *Pensées* (1670), 9, tr. W. F. Trotter.

21. A disputant no more cares for the truth than the sportsman for the hare. ALEXANDER POPE, *Thoughts on Various Subjects* (1727).

22. True disputants are like true sportsmen; their whole delight is in the pursuit. ALEXANDER POPE, *Thoughts on Various Subjects* (1727).

23. The most savage controversies are those about matters as to which there is no good evidence either way. BERTRAND RUSSELL, "An Outline of Intellectual Rubbish," *Unpopular Essays* (1950).

24. A wise man will not dispute with one that is hasty. SA'DI, *Gulistan* (1258), 4.5, tr. James Ross.

25. Arguments that make their point by means of similarities are imposters, and, unless you are on your guard against them, will quite readily deceive you. SIMMIAS, in Plato's *Phaedo* (4th–3rd c. B.C.), tr. Lane Cooper.

26. The partisan, when he is engaged in a dispute, cares nothing about the rights of the question, but is anxious only to convince his hearers of his own assertions. SOCRATES, in Plato's *Phaedo* (4th–3rd c. B.C.), tr. Benjamin Jowett.

27. Arguments only confirm people in their own opinions. BOOTH TARKINGTON, *Looking Forward to the Great Adventure* (1926).

28. It is difficult to be emphatic when no one is emphatic on the other side. CHARLES DUDLEY WARNER, "Thirteenth Week," *My Summer in a Garden* (1871).

29. In formal logic, a contradiction is the signal of a defeat: but in the evolution of real knowledge it marks the first step in progress towards a victory. This is one great reason for the utmost toleration of variety of opinion. ALFRED NORTH WHITEHEAD, *Science and the Modern World* (1925), 12.

30. Arguments are to be avoided; they are always vulgar and often convincing. OSCAR WILDE, *The Importance of Being Earnest* (1895), 2.

## 52. ARISTOCRACY

**See also 133. Class; 582. Middle Class; 675. The People; 773. Rank; 906. Society**

1. There is a natural aristocracy among men. The grounds of this are virtue and talent. THOMAS JEFFERSON, letter to John Adams, Oct. 28, 1813.

2. High people, Sir, are the best; take a hundred ladies of quality, you'll find them better wives, better mothers, more willing to sacrifice their own pleasures to their children, than a hundred other women. SAMUEL JOHNSON, quoted in Boswell's *Life of Samuel Johnson*, May 14, 1778.

3. The true policy of a government is to make use of aristocracy, but under the

forms and in the spirit of democracy. NAPOLEON I, *Maxims* (1804–15).

4. There is no stronger craving in the world than that of the rich for titles, except that of the titled for riches. HESKETH PEARSON, *The Marrying Americans* (1961).

### ARITHMETIC

See 566. Mathematics

### ARMS

See 226. Defense; 582. The Military; 633. Nuclear Power; 1035. War; 1042. Weapons

### ARMY

See 582. The Military

### 53. ART AND ARTISTS

See also 20. Aesthetics; 50. Architecture; 198. Creation and Creativity; 235. Design; 607. Music; 659. Painting; 965. Theater; 1062. Writing and Writers

1. Art is in love with luck, and luck with art. AGATHON, quoted in Aristotle's *Nicomachean Ethics* (4th c. B.C.), 6.4, tr. J. A. K. Thomson.

2. True art selects and paraphrases, but seldom gives a verbatim translation. THOMAS BAILEY ALDRICH, "Leaves from a Notebook," *Ponkapog Papers* (1903).

3. There is no comfort in adversity / More sweet than Art affords. The studious mind / Poising in meditation, there is fixed, / And sails beyond its troubles unperceiving. AMPHIS (4th c. B.C.).

4. Life is very nice, but it lacks form. It's the aim of art to give it some. JEAN ANOUILH, *The Rehearsal* (1950), 1.2, tr. Lucienne Hill.

5. The business of every art is to bring something into existence, and the practice of an art involves the study of how to bring into existence something which is capable of having such an existence and has its efficient cause in the maker and not in itself. ARISTOTLE, *Nicomachean Ethics* (4th c. B.C.), 6.4, tr. J. A. K. Thomson.

6. Nobody is fully alive who cannot apply to art as much discrimination and appreciation as he applies to the work by which he earns his living. BROOKS ATKINSON, "March 12," *Once Around the Sun* (1951).

7. All art is a kind of confession, more or less oblique. All artists, if they are to survive, are forced, at last, to tell the whole story, to vomit the anguish up. JAMES BALDWIN, "The Northern Protestant," *Nobody Knows My Name* (1961).

8. The artist's morality lies in the force and truth of his description. JULES BARBEY D'AUREVILLY, introduction to *Une vieille maîtresse* (1851).

9. Art distills sensation and embodies it with enhanced meaning in memorable form – or else it is not art. JACQUES BARZUN, *The House of Intellect* (1959), 6.

10. I wonder whether art has a higher function than to make me feel, appreciate, and enjoy natural objects for their art value? BERNARD BERENSON, *Time*, April 25, 1955.

11. The ultimate function of art is to make men do what they want to do, as it is to make them recognize what they know. MAURICE BLONDEL, introduction, *L'Action* (1893), 5.

12. What is more natural in a democratic age than that we should begin to measure the stature of a work of art – especially of a painting – by how widely and how well it is reproduced? DANIEL J. BOORSTIN, *The Image* (1962), 4.1.

13. Art is meant to disturb. Science reassures. GEORGES BRAQUE, *Pensées sur l'art*.

14. The artist has never been a dictator, since he understands better than anybody else the variations in human personality. HEYWOOD BROUN, "Bring on the Artist," *New York World Telegram*, Jan. 19, 1933.

15. One may do whate'er one likes / In Art: the only thing is, to make sure / That one does like it. ROBERT BROWNING, "Noon," *Pippa Passes* (1841).

16. Every man's work, whether it be literature or music or pictures or architecture or anything else, is always a portrait of himself, and the more he tries to conceal himself the more clearly will his character appear in spite of him. SAMUEL BUTLER (d. 1902), *The Way of All Flesh* (1903), 14.

17. The youth of an art is, like the youth of anything else, its most interesting period. SAMUEL BUTLER (d. 1902), "A Painter's Views on Painting," *Note-Books* (1912).

18. When we separate music from life we

get art. JOHN CAGE, "Composition as Process," *Silence* (1961), 3.

19. An artist conscientiously moves in a direction which for some good reason he takes, putting one work in front of the other with the hope he'll arrive before death overtakes him. JOHN CAGE, "Erik Satie," *Silence* (1961).

20. The responsibility of the artist consists in perfecting his work so that it may become attractively disinteresting. JOHN CAGE, "Forerunners of Modern Music," *Silence* (1961).

21. The problem in art is a problem of translation. Bad authors are those who write with reference to an inner context which the reader cannot know. ALBERT CAMUS, *Notebooks 1935–1942* (1962), 3, tr. Philip Thody.

22. I know with certainty that a man's work is nothing but the long journey to recover, through the detours of art, the two or three simple and great images which first gained access to his heart. ALBERT CAMUS, *The New York Times*, Jan. 24, 1960.

23. The dignity of the artist lies in his duty of keeping awake the sense of wonder in the world. In this long vigil he often has to vary his methods of stimulation; but in this long vigil he is also himself striving against a continual tendency to sleep. G. K. CHESTERTON, "On Maltreating Words," *Generally Speaking* (1928).

24. An artist carries on throughout his life a mysterious, uninterrupted conversation with his public. MAURICE CHEVALIER, *Holiday*, September 1956.

25. Without tradition, art is a flock of sheep without a shepherd. Without innovation, it is a corpse. SIR WINSTON CHURCHILL, *Time*, May 11, 1953.

26. An artist cannot speak about his art any more than a plant can discuss horticulture. JEAN COCTEAU, *Newsweek*, May 16, 1955.

27. The true work of art is the one which the seventh wave of genius throws up the beach where the under-tow of time cannot drag it back. CYRIL CONNOLLY, *The Unquiet Grave* (1945), 3.

28. An artist is a man of action, whether he creates a personality, invents an expedient, or finds the issue of a complicated situation. JOSEPH CONRAD, *The Mirror of the Sea* (1906), 9.

29. The artistic impulse seems not to wish to produce finished work. It certainly deserts us half-way, after the idea is born; and if we go on, art is labor. CLARENCE DAY, *This Simian World* (1920), 6.

30. The attitude that nature is chaotic and that the artist puts order into it is a very absurd point of view, I think. All that we can hope for is to put some order into ourselves. WILLEM DE KOONING, in *trans/formation*, 1951.

31. Life, the raw material, is only lived *in potentia* until the artist deploys it in his work. LAWRENCE DURRELL, *Justine* (1957), 1.

32. For us artists there waits the joyous compromise through art with all that wounded or defeated us in daily life. LAWRENCE DURRELL, *Justine* (1957), 1.

33. The artist's work constitutes the only satisfactory relationship he can have with his fellow men since he seeks his real friends among the dead and the unborn. LAWRENCE DURRELL, *Mountolive* (1959), 1.

34. An artist is only someone unrolling and digging out and excavating the areas normally accessible to normal people everywhere, and exhibiting them as a sort of scarecrow to show people what can be done with themselves. LAWRENCE DURRELL, interview, *Writers at Work: Second Series* (1963).

35. There is no progress in art. ILYA EHRENBURG, "What I Have Learned," *Saturday Review*, Sept. 30, 1967.

36. Every master knows that the material teaches the artist. ILYA EHRENBURG, "What I Have Learned," *Saturday Review*, Sept. 30, 1967.

37. Man is apt to be more moved by the art of his own period, not because it is more perfect, but because it is organically related to him. ILYA EHRENBURG, "What I Have Learned," *Saturday Review*, Sept. 30, 1967.

38. No poet, no artist of any art, has his complete meaning alone. His significance, his appreciation is the appreciation of his relation to the dead poets and artists. T. S. ELIOT, "Tradition and the Individual Talent" (1919).

39. No generation is interested in art in quite the same way as any other; each generation, like each individual, brings to the contemplation of art its own categories of appreciation, makes its own demands upon

art, and has its own uses for art. T. S. ELIOT, "The Use of Poetry and the Use of Criticism" (1933).

40. Every artist writes his own autobiography. HAVELOCK ELLIS, *The New Spirit* (1890).

41. Life is as the sea, art a ship in which man conquers life's crushing formlessness, reducing it to a course, a series of swells, tides and wind currents inscribed on a chart. RALPH ELLISON, *Shadow & Act* (1964).

42. It depends little on the object, much on the mood, in art. EMERSON, *Journals*, 1836.

43. Picture and sculpture are the celebrations and festivities of form. EMERSON, "Art," *Essays: First Series* (1841).

44. Art is a jealous mistress. EMERSON, "Wealth," *The Conduct of Life* (1860).

45. By artist I mean of course everyone who has tried to create something which was not here before him, with no other tools and material than the uncommerciable ones of the human spirit. WILLIAM FAULKNER, address, New York City, Jan. 25, 1955.

46. The aim of every artist is to arrest motion, which is life, by artificial means and hold it fixed so that a hundred years later, when a stranger looks at it, it moves again since it is life. WILLIAM FAULKNER, interview, *Writers at Work: First Series* (1958).

47. An artist is a creature driven by demons. He don't know why they choose him and he's usually too busy to wonder why. WILLIAM FAULKNER, interview, *Writers at Work: First Series* (1958).

48. To make us feel small in the right way is a function of art; men can only make us feel small in the wrong way. E. M. FORSTER, "A Book That Influenced Me," *Two Cheers for Democracy* (1951).

49. In art, as in love, instinct is enough. ANATOLE FRANCE, *Le Jardin d'Epicure* (1895).

50. Art helps nature, and experience art. THOMAS FULLER, M.D., *Gnomologia* (1732), 814.

51. The work of art is the exaggeration of an idea. ANDRÉ GIDE, *Journals* (1896), tr. Justin O'Brien.

52. The artist cannot get along without a public; and when the public is absent, what does he do? He invents it, and turning his back on his age, he looks toward the future for what the present denies. ANDRÉ GIDE, "The Importance of the Public," *Pretexts* (1903), tr. Angelo P. Bertocci and others.

53. The work of art is a part of nature seen through a temperament. ANDRÉ GIDE, "The Limits of Art," *Pretexts* (1903), tr. Angelo P. Bertocci and others.

54. Being impressed in art is worth nothing unless it yields at once to emotion; and most often it stands in the way of emotion. ANDRÉ GIDE, *Journals*, June 3, 1921, tr. Justin O'Brien.

55. There is no better deliverance from the world than through art; and a man can form no surer bond with it than through art. GOETHE, *Elective Affinities* (1809), 23.

56. Nature scarcely ever gives us the very best; for that we must have recourse to art. BALTASAR GRACIÁN, *The Art of Worldly Wisdom* (1647), 12, tr. Joseph Jacobs.

57. Nobody, I think, ought to read poetry, or look at pictures or statues, who cannot find a great deal more in them than the poet or artist has actually expressed. NATHANIEL HAWTHORNE, *The Marble Faun* (1860), 41.

58. Wonder at the first sight of works of art may be the effect of ignorance and novelty; but real admiration and permanent delight in them are the growth of taste and knowledge. WILLIAM HAZLITT, "On the Pleasure of Painting," *Table Talk* (1821–22).

59. The genuine artist is as much a dissatisfied person as the revolutionary, yet how diametrically opposed are the products each distills from his dissatisfaction. ERIC HOFFER, *The Passionate State of Mind* (1954), 17.

60. Art and science create a balance to material life and enlarge the world of living experience. Art leads to a more profound concept of life, because art itself is a profound expression of feeling. HANS HOFMANN, *Search for the Real* (1967).

61. If you would have me weep, you must first of all feel grief yourself. HORACE, *Ars Poetica* (13–8 B.C.).

62. He is the true enchanter, whose spell operates, not upon the senses, but upon the imagination and the heart. WASHINGTON IRVING, "Stratford on Avon," *The Sketch Book of Geoffrey Crayon, Gent.* (1819–20).

63. The moment you cheat for the sake of beauty, you know you're an artist. MAX JACOB, *Art poétique* (1922).

64. The first prerogative of an artist in any medium is to make a fool of himself. PAULINE KAEL, "Is There a Cure for Film Criticism?" *I Lost It at the Movies* (1965).

65. Art changes all the time, but it never "improves." It may go down, or up, but it never improves as technology and medicine improve. ALFRED KAZIN, "Art on Trial," *Harper's Magazine*, October 1967.

66. If art is to nourish the roots of our culture, society must set the artist free to follow his vision wherever it takes him. JOHN F. KENNEDY, address, Amherst College, Amherst, Mass., Oct. 26, 1963.

67. We must never forget that art is not a form of propaganda; it is a form of truth. JOHN F. KENNEDY, address, Amherst College, Amherst, Mass., Oct. 26, 1963.

68. Art does not reproduce the visible; rather, it makes visible. PAUL KLEE, *The Inward Vision* (1959).

69. The more minimal the art, the more maximum the explanation. HILTON KRAMER, quoted in Marilyn Bender's *The Beautiful People* (1967).

70. Art, for most Americans, is a very queer fish – it can't be reasoned with, it can't be bribed, it can't be doped out or duplicated; above all, it can't be cashed in on. LOUIS KRONENBERGER, *Company Manners* (1954), 1.1.

71. In art, there are tears that do often lie too deep for thoughts. LOUIS KRONENBERGER, *Company Manners* (1954), 1.1.

72. Art enlarges experience by admitting us to the inner life of others. WALTER LIPPMANN, "The Golden Rule and After," *A Preface to Politics* (1914).

73. The artist in his teens who is happy is a charlatan. Life comes bursting in all around us too suddenly, too crudely, too cruelly, for happiness. WILLIAM MC FEE, "Dedication," *Harbours of Memory* (1921).

74. The artist isn't particularly keen on getting a thing done, as you call it. He gets his pleasure out of doing it, playing with it, fooling with it, if you like. The mere completion of it is an incident. WILLIAM MC FEE, "The Shining Hour," *Harbours of Memory* (1921).

75. With the pride of the artist, you must blow against the walls of every power that exists, the small trumpet of your defiance. NORMAN MAILER, *The Deer Park* (1955), 28.

76. The only domain where the divine is visible is that of art, whatever name we choose to call it. ANDRÉ MALRAUX, *Les Métamorphoses des dieux* (1957), 2.1.

77. There is a way of being an artist that goes so deep and is so much a matter of origins and destinies that no longing seems to it sweeter and more worth knowing than longing after the bliss of the commonplace. THOMAS MANN, "Tonio Kröger" (1903), *Death in Venice*, tr. H. T. Lowe-Porter.

78. Thought that can merge wholly into feeling, feeling that can merge wholly into thought – these are the artist's highest joy. THOMAS MANN, title story (1913), *Death in Venice*, tr. H. T. Lowe-Porter.

79. The world of sight is still limitless. It is the artist who limits vision to the cramped dimensions of his own ego. MARYA MANNES, *More in Anger* (1958), 3.2.

80. Art should be appreciated with passion and violence, not with a tepid, deprecating elegance that fears the censoriousness of a common room. W. SOMERSET MAUGHAM, *The Summing Up* (1938), 24.

81. To the artist the communication he offers is a by-product. W. SOMERSET MAUGHAM, *The Summing Up* (1938), 49.

82. The artist's egoism is outrageous: it must be; he is by nature a solipsist and the world exists only for him to exercise upon it his powers of creation. W. SOMERSET MAUGHAM, *The Summing Up* (1938), 61.

83. An art is only great and significant if it is one that all may enjoy. The art of a clique is but a plaything. W. SOMERSET MAUGHAM, *The Summing Up* (1938), 76.

84. The grandeur of man lies in song, not in thought. FRANÇOIS MAURIAC, "The Poet's Pride," *Second Thoughts* (1961), tr. Adrienne Foulke.

85. Art teaches nothing, except the significance of life. HENRY MILLER, "Reflections on Writing," *The Wisdom of the Heart* (1941).

86. An artist is primarily one who has faith in himself. He does not respond to the normal stimuli: he is neither a drudge nor a parasite. He lives to express himself and in so doing enriches the world. HENRY MILLER, "Dr. Souchon: Surgeon-Painter," *The Air-Conditioned Nightmare* (1945).

87. I feel that America is essentially against the artist, that the enemy of America is the artist, because he stands for individu-

ality and creativeness, and that's *un*-American somehow. HENRY MILLER, interview, *Writers at Work: Second Series* (1963).

88. To speak of morals in art is to speak of legislature in sex. Art is the sex of the imagination. GEORGE JEAN NATHAN, "Art," *American Mercury*, July 1926.

89. Art raises its head where creeds relax. NIETZSCHE, *Human, All Too Human* (1878), 150, tr. Helen Zimmern.

90. Art is essentially the affirmation, the blessing, and the deification of existence. NIETZSCHE, *The Will to Power* (1888), 821, tr. Anthony M. Ludovici.

91. Being an artist means ceasing to take seriously that very serious person we are when we are not an artist. JOSÉ ORTEGA Y GASSET, *The Dehumanization of Art* (1925).

92. Were art to redeem man, it could do so only by saving him from the seriousness of life and restoring him to an unexpected boyishness. JOSÉ ORTEGA Y GASSET, *The Dehumanization of Art* (1925).

93. The trend toward pure art betrays not arrogance, as is often thought, but modesty. Art that has rid itself of human pathos is a thing without consequence—just art with no other pretenses. JOSÉ ORTEGA Y GASSET, *The Dehumanization of Art* (1925).

94. All art constantly aspires towards the condition of music. WALTER PATER, "Giorgione," *Studies in the History of the Renaissance* (1873).

95. Art comes to you proposing frankly to give nothing but the highest quality to your moments as they pass. WALTER PATER, "Conclusion," *Studies in the History of the Renaissance* (1873).

96. The classical artist can be recognized by his sincerity, the romantic by his laborious insincerity. CHARLES PÉGUY, preface to Jean Hugues' *La Grève*.

97. Art is a lie that makes us realize the truth. PABLO PICASSO, *Quote*, Sept. 21, 1958.

98. As to the artists, do we not know that he only of them whom love inspires has the light of fame?—he whom love touches not walks in darkness. PLATO, *The Symposium* (4th c. B.C.), tr. Benjamin Jowett.

99. Ods life! must one swear to the truth of a song? MATTHEW PRIOR, "A Better Answer" (1718).

100. Less disappointing than life is, great works of art do not begin by giving us all their best. MARCEL PROUST, *Remembrance of Things Past: Within a Budding Grove* (1913–27), tr. C. K. Scott-Moncrieff.

101. Thanks to art, instead of seeing one world, our own, we see it multiplied and as many original artists as there are, so many worlds are at our disposal. MARCEL PROUST, *Remembrance of Things Past: The Past Recaptured* (1913–27), tr. Stephen Hudson.

102. Art is never didactic, does not take kindly to facts, is helpless to grapple with theories, and is killed outright by a sermon. AGNES REPPLIER, "Fiction in the Pulpit," *Points of View* (1891).

103. Most events are inexpressible, taking place in a realm which no word has ever entered, and more inexpressible than all else are works of art, mysterious existences, the life of which, while ours passes away, endures. RAINER MARIA RILKE, *Letters to a Young Poet*, Feb. 17, 1903, tr. M. D. Herter Norton.

104. The expressionist, that inner-man become explosive, who pours the lava of his boiling mood over all things, to insist that the chance form in which the crust hardens is the new, the coming, the valid outline of existence, is simply a desperate man. RAINER MARIA RILKE, letter to Anni Mewes, Sept. 12, 1919, in *Wartime Letters*, tr. M. D. Herter Norton.

105. Artists—by definition innocent—don't steal. But they do borrow without giving back. NED ROREM, "Anatomy of Two Songs," *Music from Inside Out* (1967).

106. An artist doesn't necessarily have deeper feelings than other people, but he can express these feelings. He is like everyone else—only more so! He speaks with a Formal Sigh. NED ROREM, "Four Questions Answered," *Music from Inside Out* (1967).

107. Artists don't seek reasons. They are all by definition children, and vice versa. NED ROREM, "Random Notes from a Diary," *Music from Inside Out* (1967).

108. To follow art for the sake of being a great man, and therefore to cast about continually for some means of achieving position or attracting admiration, is the surest way of ending in total extinction. JOHN RUSKIN, *Modern Painters* (1843–60), v. 3, 4.3.3.

109. Great art is precisely that which never was, nor will be taught, it is preeminently and finally the expression of the spirits of great men. JOHN RUSKIN, *Mod-*

*ern Painters* (1843–60), v. 3, 4.3.28.

110. Greater completion marks the progress of art, absolute completion usually its decline. JOHN RUSKIN, *The Seven Lamps of Architecture* (1849), 4.30.

111. An artist should be well read in the best books, and thoroughly high bred, both in heart and bearing. In a word, he should be fit for the best society, *and should keep out of it.* JOHN RUSKIN, *The Stones of Venice* (1851–53), v. 3, 2.13.

112. Fine art is that in which the hand, the head, and the heart of man go together. JOHN RUSKIN, *The Two Paths* (1859), 2.

113. Art must take reality by surprise. It takes those moments which are for us merely a moment, plus a moment, plus another moment, and arbitrarily transforms them into a special series of moments held together by a major emotion. FRANÇOISE SAGAN, interview, *Writers at Work: First Series* (1958).

114. We must not subject him who creates to the desires of the multitude. It is, rather, his creation that must become the multitude's desire. SAINT-EXUPÉRY, *The Wisdom of the Sands* (1948), 23, tr. Stuart Gilbert.

115. The arts must study their occasions; they must stand modestly aside until they can slip in fitly into the interstices of life. GEORGE SANTAYANA, *The Sense of Beauty* (1896), 2.

116. Art is the response to the demand for entertainment, for the stimulation of our senses and imagination, and truth enters into it only as it subserves these ends. GEORGE SANTAYANA, *The Sense of Beauty* (1896), 2.

117. Art, like life, should be free, since both are experimental. GEORGE SANTAYANA, *The Life of Reason: Reason in Art* (1905–06), 9.

118. The man who would emancipate art from discipline and reason is trying to elude rationality, not merely in art, but in all existence. GEORGE SANTAYANA, *The Life of Reason: Reason in Art* (1905–06), 9.

119. Art is the right hand of nature. The latter only gave us being, but the former made us men. SCHILLER, *Fiesco* (1783), 2.17.

120. The artist is the child of his time; but woe to him if he is also its disciple, or even its favorite. SCHILLER, *On the Aesthetic Education of Man* (1795), 9, tr. Reginald Snell.

121. Art almost always has its ingredient of impudence, its flouting of established authority, so that it may substitute its own authority and its own enlightenment. BEN SHAHN, "Artists in Colleges," *The Shape of Content* (1957).

122. The true artist will let his wife starve, his children go barefoot, his mother drudge for his living at seventy, sooner than work at anything but his art. GEORGE BERNARD SHAW, *Man and Superman* (1903), 1.

123. You use a glass mirror to see your face: you use works of art to see your soul. GEORGE BERNARD SHAW, *Back to Methuselah* (1921), 5.

124. Without art, the crudeness of reality would make the world unbearable. GEORGE BERNARD SHAW, *Back to Methuselah* (1921), 5.

125. Poets, not otherwise than philosophers, painters, sculptors, and musicians, are, in one sense, the creators, and, in another, the creations, of their age. SHELLEY, preface, *Prometheus Unbound* (1818–19).

126. The basic unit for contemporary art is not the idea, but the analysis of and extension of sensations. SUSAN SONTAG, "One Culture and the New Sensibility," *Against Interpretation* (1961).

127. The moral pleasure in art, as well as the moral service that art performs, consists in the intelligent gratification of consciousness. SUSAN SONTAG, "On Style," *Against Interpretation* (1961).

128. Art postulates communion, and the artist has an imperative need to make others share the joy which he experiences himself. IGOR STRAVINSKY, *An Autobiography* (1936), 10.

129. The artist is the lover of Nature, therefore he is her slave and her master. RABINDRANATH TAGORE, *Stray Birds* (1916), 85.

130. What marks the artist is his power to shape the material of pain we all have. LIONEL TRILLING, "Art and Neurosis," *The Liberal Imagination* (1950).

131. Art is like baby shoes. When you coat them with gold, they can no longer be worn. JOHN UPDIKE, "Alphonse Peintre," *Assorted Prose* (1965).

132. Art imitates Nature in this: not to

dare is to dwindle. JOHN UPDIKE, "Beerbohm and Others," *Assorted Prose* (1965).

133. The refusal to rest content, the willingness to risk excess on behalf of one's obsessions, is what distinguishes artists from entertainers, and what makes some artists adventurers on behalf of us all. JOHN UPDIKE, "Franny and Zooey," *Assorted Prose* (1965).

134. Fertilisation of the soul is the reason for the necessity of art. ALFRED NORTH WHITEHEAD, *Science and the Modern World* (1925), 13.

135. No great artist ever sees things as they really are. If he did he would cease to be an artist. OSCAR WILDE, "The Decay of Lying," *Intentions* (1891).

136. All art is at once surface and symbol. Those who go beneath the surface do so at their peril. OSCAR WILDE, preface, *The Picture of Dorian Gray* (1891).

137. To reveal art and conceal the artist is art's aim. OSCAR WILDE, preface, *The Picture of Dorian Gray* (1891).

138. Good artists exist simply in what they make, and consequently are perfectly uninteresting in what they are. OSCAR WILDE, *The Picture of Dorian Gray* (1891), 4.

139. This is the artist, then—life's hungry man, the glutton of eternity, beauty's miser, glory's slave. THOMAS WOLFE, *Of Time and the River* (1935), 62.

140. I see as realism whatever is genuinely begotten by life and moves the human spirit, even if there are no images of people, houses, and trees. YEVGENY YEVTUSHENKO, *A Precocious Autobiography* (1963), tr. Andrew R. MacAndrew.

141. If you ask me what I came to do in this world, I, an artist, I will answer you: "I am here to live out loud." ÉMILE ZOLA, *Mes haines* (1866).

## 54. ARTIFICIALITY

**See also 45. Appearance; 60. Authenticity; 726. Pretension; 944. Superficiality**

1. Ours is the age of substitutes: instead of language, we have jargon; instead of principles, slogans; and, instead of genuine ideas, Bright ideas. ERIC BENTLEY, *The Dramatic Event* (1954).

2. To know only artificial night is as absurd and evil as to know only artificial day. HENRY BESTON, "Night on the Great Beach," *The Outermost House* (1928).

3. To whiten ivory with dye is to spoil nature by art. LATIN PROVERB.

4. Natural beauty is essentially temporary and sad; hence the impression of obscene mockery which artificial flowers give us. JOHN UPDIKE, "Rhyming Max," *Assorted Prose* (1965).

5. A cynic might suggest as the motto of modern life this simple legend—"Just as good as the real." CHARLES DUDLEY WARNER, "First Study," *Backlog Studies* (1873).

6. The first duty in life is to be as artificial as possible. What the second duty is no one has yet discovered. OSCAR WILDE, "Phrases and Philosophies for the Use of the Young" (1891).

## ASCETICISM

**See 859. Self-denial**

## 55. ASPIRATION

**See also 6. Achievement; 33. Ambition; 938. Success**

1. What you are must always displease you, if you would attain to that which you are not. ST. AUGUSTINE, *Sermons* (5th c.), 150.

2. Ah, but a man's reach should exceed his grasp, / Or what's a heaven for? ROBERT BROWNING, "Andrea Del Sarto," *Men and Women* (1855).

3. 'Tis not what man Does which exalts him, but what man Would do! ROBERT BROWNING, "Saul," *Men and Women* (1855), 18.

4. If you aspire to the highest place, it is no disgrace to stop at the second, or even the third, place. CICERO, *On Oratory* (55 B.C.).

5. Every man believes that he has a greater possibility. EMERSON, "Circles," *Essays: First Series* (1841).

6. First, say to yourself what you would be; and then do what you have to do. EPICTETUS, *Discourses* (2nd c.), 3.23, tr. Thomas W. Higginson.

7. Slight not what's near through aiming at what's far. EURIPIDES, *Rhesus* (c. 455–41 B.C.), 482, tr. M. H. Morgan.

8. Just as a cautious businessman avoids tying up all his capital in one concern, so, perhaps, worldly wisdom will advise us not to look for the whole of our satisfaction from a single aspiration. SIGMUND FREUD, *Civilization and Its Discontents* (1930), 2, tr. James Strachey.

9. One may miss the mark by aiming too high as too low. THOMAS FULLER, M.D., *Gnomologia* (1732), 3769.

10. I drink the wine of aspiration and the drug of illusion. Thus I am never dull. JOHN GALSWORTHY, *The Wine Horn Mountain.*

11. It takes a certain level of aspiration before one can take advantage of opportunities that are clearly offered. MICHAEL HARRINGTON, *The Other America* (1962), 8.2.

12. People are always neglecting something they can do in trying to do something they can't do. EDGAR WATSON HOWE, *Country Town Sayings* (1911).

13. He who stands on tiptoe does not stand firm. LAOTSE, *The Character of Tao* (6th. c. B.C.), 24, tr. Lin Yutang.

14. If you would hit the mark, you must aim a little above it; / Every arrow that flies feels the attraction of earth. LONGFELLOW, "Elegiac Verse" (1881).

15. Not failure, but low aim, is crime. JAMES RUSSELL LOWELL, "For an Autograph," *Under the Willows and Other Poems* (1868).

16. Life is a petty thing unless it is moved by the indomitable urge to extend its boundaries. Only in proportion as we are desirous of living more do we really live. JOSÉ ORTEGA Y GASSET, *The Dehumanization of Art* (1925).

17. May God grant me love for that which has splendor; / but in this time of my life let me strive for attainable things. PINDAR, *Odes* (5th c. B.C.), Pythia 11, tr. Richmond Lattimore.

18. He who bears in his heart a cathedral to be built is already victorious. He who seeks to become sexton of a finished cathedral is already defeated. SAINT-EXUPÉRY, *Flight to Arras* (1942), 22, tr. Lewis Galantière.

19. Ever a man seeks after what is weightiest in him; and not for happiness. SAINT-EXUPÉRY, *The Wisdom of the Sands* (1948), 55, tr. Stuart Gilbert.

20. 'Tis but a base, ignoble mind / That mounts no higher than a bird can soar. SHAKESPEARE, *2 Henry VI* (1590–91), 2.1.

21. An aspiration is a joy for ever, a possession as solid as a landed estate, a fortune which we can never exhaust and which gives us year by year a revenue of pleasurable activity. ROBERT LOUIS STEVENSON, "El Dorado," *Virginibus Puerisque* (1881).

22. In the long run men hit only what they aim at. Therefore, though they should fail immediately, they had better aim at something high. THOREAU, "Economy," *Walden* (1854).

23. It is only the fools who keep straining at high C all their lives. CHARLES DUDLEY WARNER, "Third Study," *Backlog Studies* (1873).

24. We are all in the gutter, but some of us are looking at the stars. OSCAR WILDE, *Lady Windermere's Fan* (1892), 3.

25. Too low they build, who build beneath the stars. EDWARD YOUNG, *Night Thoughts* (1742–46), 8.215.

## ASSERTION

**See 853. Self-assertion**

## 56. ASSISTANCE

**See also 118. Charity; 233. Dependence; 382. Gifts and Giving; 430. Humanitarianism; 880. Service; 1016. Usefulness**

1. If the sailors become too numerous, the ship sinks. ARABIC PROVERB.

2. It is hideous and coarse to assume that we can do something for others—and it is vile not to endeavor to do it. EDWARD DAHLBERG, *Because I Was Flesh* (1963).

3. The aid we can give each other is only incidental, lateral, and sympathetic. EMERSON, *Journals*, 1836.

4. It is not necessary to light a candle to the sun. ENGLISH PROVERB.

5. Often we can help each other most by leaving each other alone; at other times we need the hand-grasp and the word of cheer. ELBERT HUBBARD, *The Note Book* (1927).

6. With so many roosters crowing, the sun never comes up. ITALIAN PROVERB.

7. Too many boatmen will run the boat up to the top of a mountain. JAPANESE PROVERB.

8. Kick away the ladder and one's feet are left dangling. MALAY PROVERB.

9. We are doubly willing to jump into the water after some one who has fallen in, if there are people present who have not the courage to do so. NIETZSCHE, *Human, All Too Human* (1878), 325, tr. Helen Zimmern.

10. In about the same degree as you are helpful, you will be happy. KARL REILAND, *New York Herald Tribune*, Nov. 6, 1961.

11. At bottom, and just in the deepest and most important things, we are unutterably alone, and for one person to be able to advise or even help another, a lot must happen, a lot must go well, a whole constellation of things must come right in order once to succeed. RAINER MARIA RILKE, *Letters to a Young Poet*, April 5, 1903, tr. M. D. Herter Norton.

12. 'Tis not enough to help the feeble up, / But to support him after. SHAKESPEARE, *Timon of Athens* (1607–08), 1.1.107.

13. The bird thinks it is an act of kindness to give the fish a lift in the air. RABINDRANATH TAGORE, *Stray Birds* (1916), 123.

14. Knowing sorrow well, I learn the way to succor the distressed. VERGIL, *Aeneid* (30–19 B.C.), 1.630, tr. T. H. Delabere-May.

15. It is one of the beautiful compensations of this life that no one can sincerely try to help another without helping himself. CHARLES DUDLEY WARNER, "Fifth Study," *Backlog Studies* (1873).

## 57. ASSOCIATION

**See also 22. Affinity; 151. Company; 331. Familiarity; 798. Reputation**

1. The strong and the weak cannot keep company. AESOP, "The Two Pots," *Fables* (6th c. B.C.?), tr. Joseph Jacobs.

2. Whoever touches pitch will be defiled. *Apocrypha*, Ecclesiasticus 13:1.

3. A wise man associating with the vicious becomes an idiot; a dog traveling with good men becomes a rational being. ARABIC PROVERB.

4. Can a man take fire in his bosom, and his clothes not be burned? *Bible*, Proverbs 6:27.

5. A man is known by the company he organizes. AMBROSE BIERCE, "Saw," *The Devil's Dictionary* (1881–1911).

6. Tell me thy company, and I'll tell thee what thou art. CERVANTES, *Don Quixote* (1605–15), 2.3.23, tr. Peter Motteux and John Ozell.

7. Bad company is as instructive as debauchery: one is indemnified for the loss of innocence by the loss of prejudice. DENIS DIDEROT, *Rameau's Nephew* (1762), tr. Jacques Barzun and Ralph H. Bowen.

8. The sun visits cesspools without being defiled. DIOGENES THE CYNIC (4th c. B.C.), quoted in Diogenes Laertius' *Lives and Opinions of Eminent Philosophers* (3rd c. A.D.), tr. R. D. Hicks.

9. As, when there is sympathy, there needs but one wise man in a company and all are wise, so, a blockhead makes a blockhead of his companion. EMERSON, "Considerations by the Way," *The Conduct of Life* (1860).

10. He that takes the Devil into his boat must carry him over the sound. ENGLISH PROVERB.

11. Every man is like the company he is wont to keep. EURIPIDES, *Phoenix* (c. 425 B.C.), 809, tr. M. H. Morgan.

12. A wise man may look ridiculous in the company of fools. THOMAS FULLER, M.D., *Gnomologia* (1732), 474.

13. Better fare hard with good men than feast it with bad. THOMAS FULLER, M.D., *Gnomologia* (1732), 893.

14. He that lies down with dogs shall rise up with fleas. LATIN PROVERB.

15. The lion is ashamed, it's true, when he / Hunts with the fox:—of foxes, not of guile. GOTTHOLD EPHRAIM LESSING, *Nathan the Wise* (1779), 3.5, tr. Bayard Quincy Morgan.

16. By associating with good and evil persons a man acquires the virtues and vices which they possess, even as the wind blowing over different places takes along good and bad odours. *Panchatantra* (c. 5th c.), 1, tr. Franklin Edgerton.

17. If you live with a cripple, you will learn to limp. PLUTARCH, "The Education of Children," *Moralia* (c. A.D. 100), tr. Moses Hadas.

18. To take refuge with an inferior is to betray one's self. PUBLILIUS SYRUS, *Moral Sayings* (1st c. B.C.), 667, tr. Darius Lyman.

19. Court the society of a superior, and make much of the opportunity; for in the company of an equal thy good fortune must

decline. SA'DI, *Gulistan* (1258), 6.2, tr. James Ross.

20. Let me have men about me that are fat, / Sleek-headed men, and such as sleep-a-nights. / Yond Cassius has a lean and hungry look. / He thinks too much. Such men are dangerous. SHAKESPEARE, *Julius Caesar* (1599–1600), 1.2.192.

21. It is better to weep with wise men than to laugh with fools. SPANISH PROVERB.

22. Ill company is like a dog, who dirts those most whom he loves best. JONATHAN SWIFT, *Thoughts on Various Subjects* (1711).

23. Satan's friendship reaches to the prison door. TURKISH PROVERB.

## ASSURANCE

**See 113. Certainty; 854. Self-confidence**

## ASTRONOMY

**See 413. The Heavens; 843. Science**

## ATHEISM

**See 997. Unbelief**

## ATOM

**See 633. Nuclear Power**

## 58. ATTITUDE

**See also 682. Perspective**

1. If you look at life one way, there is always cause for alarm. ELIZABETH BOWEN, *The Death of the Heart* (1938), 3.6.

2. There is no object on earth which cannot be looked at from a cosmic point of view. DOSTOEVSKY, "Critical Articles: Introduction," *Polnoye Sobraniye Sochinyeni* (*Complete Collected Works*, 1895), v. 9.

3. There are no ugly loves nor handsome prisons. BENJAMIN FRANKLIN, *Poor Richard's Almanack* (1732–57).

4. It is the disposition of the thought that altereth the nature of the thing. JOHN LYLY, *Euphues: The Anatomy of Wit* (1579).

5. All seems infected that the infected spy, / As all looks yellow to the jaundiced eye. ALEXANDER POPE, *An Essay on Criticism* (1711), 2.358.

6. The eye of the master fattens the steed. SPANISH PROVERB.

7. Every man will speak of the fair as his own market has gone in it. LAURENCE STERNE, *Tristram Shandy* (1759–67), 1.5.

8. The important thing / is to pull yourself up by your own hair / to turn yourself inside out / and see the whole world with fresh eyes. PETER WEISS, *Marat/Sade* (1964), 1.13, tr. Geoffrey Skelton and Adrian Mitchell.

## AUDACITY

**See 90. Boldness**

## 59. AUDIENCE

**See also 11. Actors; 642. Observation; 965. Theater**

1. Actors should be overheard, not listened to, and the audience is fifty percent of the performance. SHIRLEY BOOTH, news summaries, Dec. 13, 1954.

2. Attention is like a narrow-mouthed vessel; pour into it what you have to say cautiously, and, as it were, drop by drop. JOSEPH JOUBERT, *Pensées* (1842), 21.45, tr. Katharine Lyttelton.

3. If one talks to more than four people, it is an audience; and one cannot really think or exchange thoughts with an audience. ANNE MORROW LINDBERGH, "The Paper and String of Life," *North to the Orient* (1935).

4. The audience is a very curious animal. It is shrewd rather than intelligent. Its mental capacity is less than that of its most intellectual members. W. SOMERSET MAUGHAM, *The Summing Up* (1938), 36.

5. The audience is not the least important actor in the play and if it will not do its allotted share the play falls to pieces. The dramatist then is in the position of a tennis player who is left on the court with nobody to play with. W. SOMERSET MAUGHAM, *The Summing Up* (1938), 36.

6. It's the admirer and the watcher who provoke us to all the insanities we commit. SENECA, *Letters to Lucilius* (1st c.), 94.71, tr. E. Phillips Barker.

7. An audience is an abstraction; it has no taste. It must depend on the only person who has (pardon, should have), the conduc-

tor. IGOR STRAVINSKY, *Conversations with Igor Stravinsky* (1959).

8. To have great poets, there must be great audiences too. WALT WHITMAN, "Ventures on an Old Theme," *Notes Left Over* (1881).

### 60. AUTHENTICITY

See also 54. Artificiality

1. Men often applaud an imitation and hiss the real thing. AESOP, "The Buffoon and the Countryman," *Fables* (6th c. B.C.?), tr. Joseph Jacobs.

2. True eloquence makes light of eloquence, true morality makes light of morality. PASCAL, *Pensées* (1670), 4, tr. W. F. Trotter.

### 61. AUTHORITY

See also 528. Leadership; 636. Obedience; 713. Power; 825. Rulers

1. If your heart is quite set upon a crown, make and put on one of roses, for it will make the prettier appearance. EPICTETUS, *Discourses* (2nd c.), 1.19, tr. Thomas W. Higginson.

2. New faces / Have more authority than accustomed ones. EURIPIDES, *Andromache* (c. 426 B.C.), tr. John F. Nims.

3. Authority is never without hate. EURIPIDES, *Ion* (c. 421–408 B.C.), tr. Ronald F. Willetts.

4. Lawful and settled authority is very seldom resisted when it is well employed. SAMUEL JOHNSON, *The Rambler* (1750–52), 50.

5. Authority has every reason to fear the skeptic, for authority can rarely survive in the face of doubt. ROBERT LINDNER, "Education for Maturity," *Must You Conform?* (1956).

6. Most men, after a little freedom, have preferred authority with the consoling assurances and the economy of effort which it brings. WALTER LIPPMANN, *A Preface to Morals* (1929), 1.1.3.

7. People who are masters in their own house are never tyrants. NAPOLEON I, *Maxims* (1804–15).

8. Jurisdiction is not given for the sake of the judge, but for that of the litigant. PASCAL, *Pensées* (1670), 878, tr. W. F. Trotter.

9. The man who says to one, go, and he goeth, and to another, come, and he cometh, has, in most cases, more sense of restraint and difficulty than the man who obeys him. JOHN RUSKIN, "The Nature of Gothic," *The Stones of Venice* (1851–53), v. 2, 6.

10. Man, proud man, / Drest in a little brief authority, / Most ignorant of what he's most assured. SHAKESPEARE, *Measure for Measure* (1604–05), 2.2.117.

### AUTHORS

See 1062. Writing and Writers

### 62. AUTOBIOGRAPHY

See also 79. Biography

1. When writing of oneself one should show no mercy. Yet why at the first attempt to discover one's own truth does all inner strength seem to melt away in floods of self-pity and tenderness and rising tears? GEORGES BERNANOS, *The Diary of a Country Priest* (1936), 1, tr. Pamela Morris.

2. Diary, n. A daily record of that part of one's life, which he can relate to himself without blushing. AMBROSE BIERCE, *The Devil's Dictionary* (1881–1911).

3. Autobiography is now as common as adultery, and hardly less reprehensible. JOHN GRIGG, *Sunday Times*, London, Feb. 28, 1962.

4. When you put down the good things you ought to have done, and leave out the bad ones you did do—well, that's Memoirs. WILL ROGERS, *The Autobiography of Will Rogers* (1949), 16.

5. There aint nothing that breaks up homes, country, and nations like somebody publishing their memoirs. WILL ROGERS, *The Autobiography of Will Rogers* (1949), 19.

6. To start writing about your life is, from one standpoint, to stop living it. You must avoid adventures today so as to make time for registering those of yesterday. NED ROREM, "Random Notes from a Diary," *Music from Inside Out* (1967).

7. What pursuit is more elegant than that of collecting the ignominies of our nature and transfixing them for show, each on the

bright pin of a polished phrase? LOGAN PEARSALL SMITH, *Afterthoughts* (1931), 6.

8. I always say, keep a diary and someday it'll keep you. MAE WEST, in *Every Day's a Holiday* (1937).

### AUTOMATION
See 960. Technology

### 63. AUTOMOBILES
See also 984. Transportation

1. The automobile is technologically more sophisticated than the bundling board, but the human motives in their uses are sometimes the same. CHARLES M. ALLEN, "Unity in a University," speech at Wake Forest University, Winston-Salem, N.C., April 25, 1967.

2. Except the American woman, nothing interests the eye of American man more than the automobile, or seems so important to him as an object of esthetic appreciation. A. H. BARR, JR., on displaying "pop art" that incorporated pieces of old automobiles, 1963.

3. After all, what is a pedestrian? He is a man who has two cars—one being driven by his wife, the other by one of his children. ROBERT BRADBURY, *The New York Times*, Sept. 5, 1962.

4. The automobile has not merely taken over the street, it has dissolved the living tissue of the city. Its appetite for space is absolutely insatiable; moving and parked, it devours urban land, leaving the buildings as mere islands of habitable space in a sea of dangerous and ugly traffic. JAMES MARSTON FITCH, *The New York Times*, May 1, 1960.

5. The car has become a secular sanctuary for the individual, his shrine to the self, his mobile Walden Pond. EDWARD MC DONAGH, *Time*, May 10, 1963.

6. The car has become an article of dress without which we feel uncertain, unclad, and incomplete. MARSHALL MC LUHAN, *Understanding Media* (1964), 22.

7. People on horses look better than they are. People in cars look worse than they are. MARYA MANNES, *More in Anger* (1958), 1.4.

8. Our national flower is the concrete cloverleaf. LEWIS MUMFORD, *Quote*, Oct. 8, 1961.

9. Beneath this slab / John Brown is stowed. / He watched the ads, / And not the road. OGDEN NASH, "Lather As You Go," *Good Intentions* (1943).

10. The only way to solve the Traffic problems of the Country is to pass a law that only paid-for Cars are allowed to use the Highways. That would make traffic so scarce we could use our Boulevards for Children's play grounds. WILL ROGERS, *The Autobiography of Will Rogers* (1949), 9.

11. Everything in life is somewhere else, and you get there in a car. E. B. WHITE, "Fro-Joy," *One Man's Meat* (1944).

### AUTONOMY
See 860. Self-determination; 873. Self-sufficiency

### AUTUMN
See 848. Seasons

### AVARICE
See 401. Greed

### AWARENESS
See 172. Consciousness; 876. Sensibility

## B

### 64. BABIES
See also 121. Children

1. There are one hundred and fifty-two distinctly different ways of holding a baby—and all are right. HEYWOOD BROUN, "Holding a Baby," *Seeing Things at Night* (1921).

2. Men profess a total lack of ability to wash baby's face simply because they believe there's no great fun in the business, at either end of the sponge. HEYWOOD BROUN, "Holding a Baby," *Seeing Things at Night* (1921).

3. Babies are unreasonable; they expect far too much of existence. Each new generation that comes takes one look at the world, thinks wildly, "Is *this* all they've done to it?" and bursts into tears. CLARENCE DAY, "Odd Countries," *The Crow's Nest* (1921).

4. Tender are a mother's dreams, / But her babe's not what he seems. / See him plotting in his mind / To grow up some other kind. CLARENCE DAY, "Thoughts on Peculiar Dawns," *Thoughts Without Words* (1928).

5. Every baby born into the world is a finer one than the last. CHARLES DICKENS, *Nicholas Nickleby* (1838-39), 36.

6. Infancy conforms to nobody; all conform to it. EMERSON, "Self-Reliance," *Essays: First Series* (1841).

7. A baby is an angel whose wings decrease as his legs increase. FRENCH PROVERB.

8. Adam and Eve had many advantages, but the principal one was that they escaped teething. MARK TWAIN, "Pudd'nhead Wilson's Calendar," *Pudd'nhead Wilson* (1894), 4.

## 65. BACHELORS

1. It is a truth universally acknowledged, that a single man in possession of a good fortune, must be in want of a wife. JANE AUSTEN, *Pride and Prejudice* (1813), 1.

2. I would be married, but I'd have no wife, / I would be married to a single life. RICHARD CRASHAW, "On Marriage," *The Delights of the Muses* (1646).

3. There is no character in the comedy of human life more difficult to play well than that of an old bachelor. WASHINGTON IRVING, "Bachelors," *Bracebridge Hall* (1822).

4. Marriage has many pains, but celibacy has no pleasures. SAMUEL JOHNSON, *Rasselas* (1759), 26.

5. The bachelor's admired freedom is often a yoke, for the freer a man is to himself the greater slave he often is to the whims of others. GEORGE JEAN NATHAN, *The Bachelor Life* (1941).

6. The fear of women is the basis of good health. SPANISH PROVERB.

7. Bachelor's fare: bread and cheese and kisses. JONATHAN SWIFT, *Polite Conversation* (1738), 1.

8. The happy marrid man dies in good stile at home, surrounded by his weeping wife and children. The old bachelor don't die at all—he sort of rots away, like a pollywog's tail. ARTEMUS WARD, "Draft in Baldinsville," *Artemus Ward, His Book* (1862).

## 66. BACKGROUND

**See also 292. Environment**

1. The background reveals the true being and state of being of the man or thing. If I do not possess the background, I make the man transparent, the thing transparent. JUAN RAMÓN JIMÉNEZ, "José Martí," *Selected Writings* (1957), tr. H. R. Hays.

## BADNESS

**See 305. Evil; 1048. Wickedness; 1063. Wrongdoing**

## BAD TEMPER

**See 961. Temper, Bad**

## 67. BANALITY

**See also 93. Bores**

1. Men are seldom more commonplace than on supreme occasions. SAMUEL BUTLER (d. 1902), "Material for a Projected Sequel to *Alps and Sanctuaries*," *Note-Books* (1912).

2. The banalities of a great man pass for wit. ALEXANDER CHASE, *Perspectives* (1966).

3. In modern life nothing produces such an effect as a good platitude. It makes the whole world kin. OSCAR WILDE, *An Ideal Husband* (1895), 1.

## 68. BANKING

**See also 102. Business and Commerce**

1. Put not your trust in money, but put your money in trust. OLIVER WENDELL HOLMES, SR., *The Autocrat of the Breakfast Table* (1858), 2.

2. A bank is a place that will lend you money if you can prove that you don't need it. BOB HOPE, quoted in Alan Harrington's "The Tyranny of Forms," *Life in the Crystal Palace* (1959).

3. Bankers Are Just Like Anybody Else, Except Richer. OGDEN NASH, verse title, *I'm a Stranger Here Myself* (1938).

## 69. BARBARISM
See also 131. Civilization

1. To most people a savage nation is wan that doesn't wear oncomf'rtable clothes. FINLEY PETER DUNNE, "Casual Observations," *Mr. Dooley's Philosophy* (1900).

2. Wherein does barbarism consist, unless in not appreciating what is excellent. GOETHE, quoted in Johann Peter Eckermann's *Conversations with Goethe*, March 22, 1831.

3. Savagery is necessary every four or five hundred years in order to bring the world back to life. Otherwise the world would die of civilization. EDMOND and JULES DE GONCOURT, *Journal*, Sept. 3, 1855, tr. Robert Baldick.

4. Men have been barbarians much longer than they have been civilized. They are only precariously civilized, and within us there is the propensity, persistent as the force of gravity, to revert under stress and strain, under neglect or temptation, to our first natures. WALTER LIPPMANN, *The Public Philosophy* (1955), 7.5.

5. Barbarism is the absence of standards to which appeal can be made. JOSÉ ORTEGA Y GASSET, *The Revolt of the Masses* (1930), 8.

6. Since barbarism has its pleasures it naturally has its apologists. GEORGE SANTAYANA, *The Life of Reason: Reason in Society* (1905–06), 3.

7. The existence of the soldier, next to capital punishment, is the most grievous vestige of barbarism which survives among men. ALFRED DE VIGNY, *Servitude et grandeur militaires* (1835), 1.2.

## BASHFULNESS
See 973. Timidity

## BATHING
See 135. Cleanliness

## 70. BEAUTY
See also 119. Charm; 189. Cosmetics; 394. Grace; 996. Ugliness

1. Things are beautiful if you love them. JEAN ANOUILH, *Mademoiselle Colombe* (1950), 2.2., tr. Louis Kronenberger.

2. Beauty, real beauty, is something very grave. If there is a God, He must be partly that. JEAN ANOUILH, *The Rehearsal* (1950), 2, tr. Lucienne Hill.

3. Beauty is one of the rare things that do not lead to doubt of God. JEAN ANOUILH, *Becket* (1959), 1.

4. Personal beauty requires that one should be tall; little people may have charm and elegance, but beauty—no. ARISTOTLE, *Nicomachean Ethics* (4th c. B.C.), 4.3, tr. J. A. K. Thomson.

5. Beauty is a greater recommendation than any letter of introduction. ARISTOTLE (4th c. B.C.), quoted in Diogenes Laertius' *Lives and Opinions of Eminent Philosophers* (3rd c.), tr. R. D. Hicks.

6. Beauty, n. The power by which a woman charms a lover and terrifies a husband. AMBROSE BIERCE, *The Devil's Dictionary* (1881–1911).

7. Beauty being the best of all we know / Sums up the unsearchable and secret aims / Of Nature. ROBERT BRIDGES, *The Growth of Love* (1876), 8.

8. Where does beauty begin and where does it end? Where it ends is where the artist begins. JOHN CAGE, "Lecture on Nothing," *Silence* (1961).

9. Beauty is unbearable, drives us to despair, offering us for a minute the glimpse of an eternity that we should like to stretch out over the whole of time. ALBERT CAMUS, *Notebooks 1935–1942* (1962), 1, tr. Philip Thody.

10. There is in true beauty, as in courage, somewhat which narrow souls cannot dare to admire. WILLIAM CONGREVE, *The Old Bachelor* (1693), 4.4.

11. Beauty—be not caused—It Is— / Chase it, and it ceases— / Chase it not, and it abides—. EMILY DICKINSON, poem (c. 1862).

12. He who loveliness within / Hath found, all outward loathes, / For he who color loves, and skin, / Loves but their oldest clothes. JOHN DONNE, "The Undertaking," *Songs and Sonnets* (1633).

13. We fly to Beauty as an asylum from the terrors of finite nature. EMERSON, *Journals*, 1836.

14. The beautiful rests on the foundations of the necessary. EMERSON, "The Poet," *Essays: Second Series* (1844).

15. Beauty without expression tires. EMERSON, "Beauty," *The Conduct of Life* (1860).

16. Things are pretty, graceful, rich, elegant, handsome, but, until they speak to the imagination, not yet beautiful. EMERSON, "Beauty," *The Conduct of Life* (1860).

17. Any extraordinary degree of beauty in man or woman involves a moral charm. EMERSON, "Worship," *The Conduct of Life* (1860).

18. If eyes were made for seeing, / Then Beauty is its own excuse for being. EMERSON, "The Rhodora," *May Day and Other Pieces* (1867).

19. Oh, what a vileness human beauty is, / corroding, corrupting everything it touches! EURIPIDES, *Orestes* (408 B.C.), tr. William Arrowsmith.

20. Beauty is a primeval phenomenon, which itself never makes its appearance, but the reflection of which is visible in a thousand different utterances of the creative mind, and is as various as nature herself. GOETHE, quoted in Johann Peter Eckermann's *Conversations with Goethe*, April 18, 1827.

21. Beauty is not for sharing; he who has mastered her / Would rather slay her, with a curse on love that's shared. GOETHE, "Before the Palace of Menelaus in Sparta," *Faust: Part II* (1832), tr. Philip Wayne.

22. She who is born a beauty is born betrothed. ITALIAN PROVERB.

23. A thing of beauty is a joy for ever: / Its loveliness increases; it will never / Pass into nothingness. JOHN KEATS, *Endymion* (1817), 1.1.

24. Beauty is truth, truth beauty,—that is all / Ye know on earth, and all ye need to know. JOHN KEATS, "Ode on a Grecian Urn" (1819).

25. He was the mightiest of Puritans no less than of philistines who first insisted that beauty is only skin deep. LOUIS KRONENBERGER, *Company Manners* (1954), 1.1.

26. Beauty hath no true glass, except it be / In the sweet privacy of loving eyes. JAMES RUSSELL LOWELL, "A Chippewa Legend" (1843).

27. Thou seest no beauty save thou make it first; / Man, Woman, Nature each is but a glass / Where the soul sees the image of herself, / Visible echoes, offsprings of herself. JAMES RUSSELL LOWELL, "For an Autograph," *Under the Willows and Other Poems* (1868).

28. Anything in any way beautiful derives its beauty from itself, and asks nothing beyond itself. Praise is no part of it, for nothing is made worse or better by praise. MARCUS AURELIUS, *Meditations* (2nd c.), 4.20, tr. Maxwell Staniforth.

29. beauty gets the best of it / in this world. DON MARQUIS, "unjust," *Archy and Mehitabel* (1927).

30. Beauty is an ecstasy; it is as simple as hunger. There is really nothing to be said about it. W. SOMERSET MAUGHAM, *Cakes and Ale* (1930), 11.

31. We find things beautiful because we recognize them and contrariwise we find things beautiful because their novelty surprises us. W. SOMERSET MAUGHAM, *The Summing Up* (1938), 76.

32. Beauty in all things—no, we cannot hope for that; but some place set apart for it. EDNA ST. VINCENT MILLAY, "Invocation to the Muses," *Make Bright the Arrows* (1940).

33. Beauty is Nature's coin, must not be hoarded, / But must be current, and the good thereof / Consists in mutual and partaken bliss. MILTON, *Comus* (1634), 739.

34. Beauty, though injurious, hath strange power, / After offence returning, to regain / Love once possessed. MILTON, *Samson Agonistes* (1671), 1003.

35. Beauty is everlasting / and dust is for a time. MARIANNE MOORE, "In Distrust of Merits," *Collected Poems* (1951).

36. Truth is the strong compost in which beauty may sometimes germinate. CHRISTOPHER MORLEY, *Inward Ho!* (1923), 2.

37. Take the advice of light when you're looking at linens or jewels; / Looking at faces or forms, take the advice of the day. OVID, *The Art of Love* (c. A.D. 8), 1, tr. Rolfe Humphries.

38. Judgment of beauty can err, what with the wine and the dark. OVID, *The Art of Love* (c. A.D. 8), 1, tr. Rolfe Humphries.

39. 'Tis not a lip or eye we beauty call, / But the joint force and full result of all. ALEXANDER POPE, *An Essay on Criticism* (1711), 2.45.

40. Beauty deprived of its proper foils and adjuncts ceases to be enjoyed as beauty, just as light deprived of all shadow ceases to

be enjoyed as light. JOHN RUSKIN, *Modern Painters* (1843–60), v. 3, 4.3.14.

41. Remember that the most beautiful things in the world are the most useless: peacocks and lilies, for instance. JOHN RUSKIN, *The Stones of Venice* (1851–53), v. 1, 2.17.

42. A little beauty is preferable to much wealth. SA'DI, *Gulistan* (1258), 3.28, tr. James Ross.

43. To keep beauty in its place is to make all things beautiful. GEORGE SANTAYANA, *The Life of Reason: Reason in Art* (1905–06), 9.

44. All beauties are to be honored, but only one embraced. GEORGE SANTAYANA, "No. 302 Beacon Street," *Persons and Places: The Background of My Life* (1944).

45. Outstanding beauty, like outstanding gifts of any kind, tends to get in the way of normal emotional development, and thus of that particular success in life which we call happiness. MILTON R. SAPIRSTEIN, *Paradoxes of Everyday Life* (1955), 4.

46. Beauty itself doth of itself persuade / The eyes of men without an orator. SHAKESPEARE, *The Rape of Lucrece* (1594), 29.

47. Beauty provoketh thieves sooner than gold. SHAKESPEARE, *As You Like It* (1599–1600), 1.3.112.

48. Beauty is nothing other than the promise of happiness. STENDHAL, *On Love* (1822), 17.

49. Beauty is not immortal. In a day / Blossom and June and rapture pass away. ARTHUR STRINGER, "A Fragile Thing Is Beauty."

50. O Beauty, find thyself in love, not in the flattery of thy mirror. RABINDRANATH TAGORE, *Stray Birds* (1916), 28.

51. Beauty is truth's smile / when she beholds her own face / in a perfect mirror. RABINDRANATH TAGORE, *Fireflies* (1928).

52. Beauty more than bitterness / Makes the heart break. SARA TEASDALE, "Vignettes Overseas," *Rivers to the Sea* (1915).

53. Spend all you have for loveliness, / Buy it and never count the cost; / For one white singing hour of peace / Count many a year of strife well lost, / And for a breath of ecstasy / Give all you have been, or could be. SARA TEASDALE, "Barter," *Love Songs* (1917).

54. Forever / Seek for Beauty, she only / Fights with man against Death! SARA TEASDALE, "The Voice," *Flame and Shadow* (1920).

55. Look for a lovely thing and you will find it, / It is not far— / It never will be far. SARA TEASDALE, "Night," *Stars To-night* (1930).

56. And is there any moral shut / Within the bosom of the rose? ALFRED, LORD TENNYSON, "Moral," *The Day-Dream* (1835).

57. Loveliness / Needs not the foreign aid of ornament, / But is when unadorned adorned the most. JAMES THOMSON, "Autumn," *The Seasons* (1726–30), 204.

58. Such is beauty ever,—neither here nor there, now nor then,—neither in Rome nor in Athens, but wherever there is a soul to admire. THOREAU, *Journal*, Jan. 21, 1838.

59. Ask a toad what is beauty . . . ; he will answer that it is a female with two great round eyes coming out of her little head, a large flat mouth, a yellow belly and a brown back. VOLTAIRE, "Beauty," *Philosophical Dictionary* (1764).

60. It is not sufficient to see and to know the beauty of a work. We must feel and be affected by it. VOLTAIRE, "Taste," *Philosophical Dictionary* (1764).

61. They are the elect to whom beautiful things mean only Beauty. OSCAR WILDE, preface, *The Picture of Dorian Gray* (1891).

62. Beauty is feared / more than death. WILLIAM CARLOS WILLIAMS, *Paterson* (1948), 3.1.

## 71. BED

**See also 599. Morning; 626. Night; 899. Sleep**

1. The fate of the worm refutes the pretended ethical teaching of the proverb, which assumes to illustrate the advantage of early rising and does so by showing how extremely dangerous it is. THOMAS BAILEY ALDRICH, "Asides: Writers and Talkers," *Ponkapog Papers* (1903).

2. When I lie down, I say, When shall I arise, and the night be gone? and I am full of tossings to and fro unto the dawning of the day. *Bible*, Job 7:4.

3. Bed is a bundle of paradoxes: we go to it with reluctance, yet we quit it with regret. CHARLES CALEB COLTON, *Lacon* (1825), 2.262.

4. He that riseth late must trot all day.

BENJAMIN FRANKLIN, *Poor Richard's Almanack* (1732–57).

5. Age and wedlock bring a man to his nightcap. THOMAS FULLER, M.D., *Gnomologia* (1732), 778.

6. The average, healthy, well-adjusted adult gets up at seven-thirty in the morning feeling just plain terrible. JEAN KERR, "Where Did You Put the Aspirin?" *Please Don't Eat the Daisies* (1957).

7. The best thing about lying in bed late is that you learn to distinguish between first things and trivia, for whatever presses on you has to prove its importance before it makes you move. MAX LERNER, "Lying in Bed Late," *The Unfinished Country* (1959), 1.

8. Was it for this I uttered prayers, / And sobbed and cursed and kicked the stairs, / That now, domestic as a plate, / I should retire at half-past eight? EDNA ST. VINCENT MILLAY, "Grown-up," *A Few Figs From Thistles* (1920).

9. 'Tis very warm weather when one's in bed. JONATHAN SWIFT, *Journal to Stella*, Nov. 8, 1710.

10. A man's bed is his cradle, but a woman's is often her rack. JAMES THURBER, "The Chipmunk and His Mate," *Further Fables for Our Time* (1956).

## BEES

See 479. Insects

## 72. BEGGARS

See also 382. Gifts and Giving; 712. Poverty

1. The strong demand, contend, prevail; the beggar is a fool! GEORGIA DOUGLAS JOHNSON, "The Suppliant," *Bronze* (1922).

2. The poor man commands respect; the beggar must always excite anger. NAPOLEON I, *Maxims* (1804–15).

3. Beggars should be abolished entirely! Verily, it is annoying to give to them and it is annoying not to give to them. NIETZSCHE, "On the Pitying," *Thus Spoke Zarathustra* (1883–92), 2, tr. Walter Kaufmann.

## 73. BEGINNING

See also 74. Beginning and Ending; 283. Ending

1. A journey of a thousand miles must begin with a single step. CHINESE PROVERB.

2. The merit belongs to the beginner should his successor do even better. EGYPTIAN PROVERB.

3. The great majority of men are bundles of beginnings. EMERSON, *Journals*, 1828.

4. It is better to begin in the evening than not at all. ENGLISH PROVERB.

5. Once begun, / A task is easy; half the work is done. HORACE, *Epistles* (20–c. 8 B.C.), 1.2.

6. The births of all things are weak and tender, and therefore we should have our eyes intent on beginnings. MONTAIGNE, "Of managing the will," *Essays* (1580–88), tr. Charles Cotton and W. C. Hazlitt.

7. Nothing is more expensive than a start. NIETZSCHE, *The Will to Power* (1888), 731, tr. Anthony M. Ludovici.

## 74. BEGINNING AND ENDING

See also 73. Beginning; 283. Ending

1. Men perish because they cannot join the beginning with the end. ALCMAEON (c. 500 B.C.), quoted in Philip Wheelwright's *Heraclitus*.

2. Better is the end of a thing than the beginning thereof. *Bible*, Ecclesiastes 7:8.

3. A good beginning makes a good ending. ENGLISH PROVERB.

4. You begin well in nothing except you end well. THOMAS FULLER, M.D., *Gnomologia* (1732), 5863.

5. Life never presents us with anything which may not be looked upon as a fresh starting point, no less than as a termination. ANDRÉ GIDE, *The Counterfeiters* (1925), 3.13, tr. Dorothy Bussy.

6. Do, and have done. The former is far the easiest. JULIUS CHARLES HARE and AUGUSTUS WILLIAM HARE, *Guesses at Truth* (1827).

7. A hard beginning maketh a good ending. JOHN HEYWOOD, *Proverbs* (1546), 1.4.

8. He who begins many things finishes but few. ITALIAN PROVERB.

9. The truth is that the beginning of anything and its end are alike touching. YOSHIDA KENKŌ, "Life Frail and Fleeting,"

*The Harvest of Leisure (Tsure-Zure Gusa,* c. 1330–35), tr. Ryukichi Kurata.

10. Great is the art of beginning, but greater the art is of ending. LONGFELLOW, "Elegiac Verse" (1881).

11. The world is round and the place which may seem like the end may also be only the beginning. IVY BAKER PRIEST, *Parade,* Feb. 16, 1958.

12. Every exit is an entry somewhere else. TOM STOPPARD, *Rosencrantz & Guildenstern Are Dead* (1967).

## 75. BEHAVIOR

See also 210. Custom; 559. Manners; 598. Morality

1. A man's behavior is the index of the man, and his discourse is the index of his understanding. ALI IBN-ABI-TALIB, *Sentences* (7th c.), 7, tr. Simon Ockley.

2. Conduct is three-fourths of our life and its largest concern. MATTHEW ARNOLD, *Literature and Dogma* (1873), 1.

3. Behavior, n. Conduct, as determined, not by principle, but by breeding. AMBROSE BIERCE, *The Devil's Dictionary* (1881–1911).

4. In great matters, men behave as they are expected to; in little ones, as they would naturally. CHAMFORT, *Maximes et pensées* (1805), 52.

5. A beautiful behavior is better than a beautiful form; it gives a higher pleasure than statues or pictures; it is the finest of the fine arts. EMERSON, "Manners," *Essays: Second Series* (1844).

6. Sympathy of manners maketh conjunction of minds. THOMAS FULLER, M.D., *Gnomologia* (1732), 4300.

7. Behavior is a mirror in which every one displays his own image. GOETHE, *Elective Affinities* (1809), 23.

8. When, in the present world, men behave well, that is no doubt sometimes because they are creatures of habit as well as, sometimes, because they are reasonable. JOSEPH WOOD KRUTCH, "Ignoble Utopias," *The Measure of Man* (1954).

9. The conduct of our lives is the true mirror of our doctrine. MONTAIGNE, "Of the education of children," *Essays* (1580–88), tr. Charles Cotton and W. C. Hazlitt.

10. Right conduct can never, except by some rare accident, be promoted by ignorance or hindered by knowledge. BERTRAND RUSSELL, "The Taboo on Sex Knowledge," *Marriage and Morals* (1929).

11. Every attempt to explain human behavior, especially the irrational, must as a matter of course end in simplification. MORTON IRVING SEIDEN, *The Paradox of Hate: A Study in Ritual Murder* (1967), 14.

12. Fine conduct is always spontaneous. SENECA, *Letters to Lucilius* (1st c.), 66.16, tr. E. Phillips Barker.

## BEING

See 314. Existence

## 76. BELIEF

See also 199. Credulity; 263. Doubt, Religious; 328. Faith; 897. Skepticism; 947. Superstition; 997. Unbelief; 998. Uncertainty

1. When you want to believe in something you also have to believe in everything that's necessary for believing in it. UGO BETTI, *Struggle Till Dawn* (1949), 2, tr. G. H. McWilliam.

2. Everything possible to be believed is an image of truth. WILLIAM BLAKE, *The Marriage of Heaven and Hell* (1790).

3. A firm belief atthracts facts. They come out iv holes in th' ground an' cracks in th' wall to support belief, but they run away fr'm doubt. FINLEY PETER DUNNE, "Things Spiritual," *Mr. Dooley Says* (1910).

4. He does not believe that does not live according to his belief. THOMAS FULLER, M.D., *Gnomologia* (1732), 1838.

5. Through fear of resembling one another, through horror at having to submit, through uncertainty as well, through skepticism and complexity, there is a multitude of individual little beliefs for the triumph of strange little individuals. ANDRÉ GIDE, "Concerning Influence in Literature," *Pretexts* (1903), tr. Angelo P. Bertocci and others.

6. The belief that becomes truth for me . . . is that which allows me the best use of my strength, the best means of putting my virtues into action. ANDRÉ GIDE, *The Counterfeiters* (1925), 2.4, tr. Dorothy Bussy.

7. We are so constituted that we believe the most incredible things; and, once they are engraved upon the memory, woe to him who would endeavor to erase them. GOETHE, *The Sorrows of Young Werther* (1774), 1, Aug. 15, 1771, tr. Victor Lange.

8. Loving is half of believing. VICTOR HUGO, *Les Chants du crépuscule* (1835), 38.

9. Believe that life *is* worth living, and your belief will help create the fact. WILLIAM JAMES, "Is Life Worth Living?" *The Will to Believe* (1896).

10. First there is a time when we believe everything without reasons, then for a little while we believe with discrimination, then we believe nothing whatever, and then we believe everything again—and, moreover, give reasons why we believe everything. GEORG CHRISTOPH LICHTENBERG, *Aphorisms* (1764–99), tr. J. P. Stern.

11. Under all that we think, lives all we believe, like the ultimate veil of our spirits. ANTONIO MACHADO, *Jaun de Mairena* (1943), 33, tr. Ben Belitt.

12. Nothing is so firmly believed, as what we least know. MONTAIGNE, "That a man is soberly to judge of the divine ordinances," *Essays* (1580–88), tr. Charles Cotton and W. C. Hazlitt.

13. You're not free / until you've been made captive by / supreme belief. MARIANNE MOORE, "Spenser's Ireland," *Collected Poems* (1951).

14. Convictions are more dangerous enemies of truth than lies. NIETZSCHE, *Human, All Too Human* (1878), 483, tr. Helen Zimmern.

15. It is natural for the mind to believe, and for the will to love; so that, for want of true objects, they must attach themselves to false. PASCAL, *Pensées* (1670), 81, tr. W. F. Trotter.

16. Mix a conviction with a man and something happens! ADAM CLAYTON POWELL, "Minimum Living—Minimum Religion," *Keep the Faith, Baby!* (1967).

17. It is desire that engenders belief and if we fail as a rule to take this into account, it is because most of the desires that create beliefs end . . . only with our own life. MARCEL PROUST, *Remembrance of Things Past: The Sweet Cheat Gone* (1913–27), tr. C. K. Scott-Moncrieff.

18. Man makes holy what he believes as he makes beautiful what he loves. ERNEST RENAN, "La Tentation du Christ," *Etudes d'histoire religieuse* (1857).

19. The fact that an opinion has been widely held is no evidence whatever that it is not utterly absurd; indeed in view of the silliness of the majority of mankind, a widespread belief is more likely to be foolish than sensible. BERTRAND RUSSELL, "Christian Ethics," *Marriage and Morals* (1929).

20. Man is a credulous animal, and must believe *something;* in the absence of good grounds for belief, he will be satisfied with bad ones. BERTRAND RUSSELL, "An Outline of Intellectual Rubbish," *Unpopular Essays* (1950).

21. To know is not to prove, nor to explain. It is to accede to vision. SAINT-EXUPÉRY, *Flight to Arras* (1942), 5, tr. Lewis Galantière.

22. Of what worth are convictions that bring not suffering? SAINT-EXUPÉRY, *The Wisdom of the Sands* (1948), 29, tr. Stuart Gilbert.

23. To believe with certainty we must begin with doubting. STANISLAUS I OF POLAND, *Maxims* (c. 18th c.), 61.

24. That which has been believed by everyone, always and everywhere, has every chance of being false. PAUL VALÉRY, *Tel quel I* (1943).

25. Man can believe the impossible, but man can never believe the improbable. OSCAR WILDE, "The Decay of Lying," *Intentions* (1891).

## BENEVOLENCE

**See 430. Humanitarianism; 517. Kindness**

## 77. BETRAYAL

**See also 986. Treason**

1. They talk of a man betraying his country, his friends, his sweetheart. There must be a moral bond first. All a man can betray is his conscience. JOSEPH CONRAD, *Under Western Eyes* (1911), 1.2.

2. If I had to choose between betraying my country and betraying my friend, I hope I should have the guts to betray my country. E. M. FORSTER, "What I Believe," *Two Cheers for Democracy* (1951).

3. Why is betrayal the only truth that sticks? ARTHUR MILLER, *After the Fall* (1964).

4. To betray you must first belong. HAROLD PHILBY, *The New York Times*, Dec. 19, 1967.

5. Though those that are betrayed / Do feel the treason sharply, yet the traitor / Stands in worse case of woe. SHAKESPEARE, *Cymbeline* (1609–10), 3.4.87.

## 78. BIBLE

1. Thy word is a lamp unto my feet, and a light unto my path. *Bible*, Psalms 119:105.

2. Christian, n. One who believes that the New Testament is a divinely inspired book admirably suited to the spiritual needs of his neighbor. AMBROSE BIERCE, *The Devil's Dictionary* (1881–1911).

3. Those who talk of the Bible as a "monument of English prose" are merely admiring it as a monument over the grave of Christianity. T. S. ELIOT, "Religion and Literature" (1935).

4. The English Bible—a book which if everything else in our language should perish, would alone suffice to show the whole extent of its beauty and power. THOMAS BABINGTON MACAULAY, "On John Dryden" (1828).

5. It was subtle of God to learn Greek when he wished to become an author—and not to learn it better. NIETZSCHE, *Beyond Good and Evil* (1886), 121, tr. Walter Kaufmann.

6. The Scripture in time of disputes is like an open town in time of war, which serves indifferently the occasions of both parties. ALEXANDER POPE, *Thoughts on Various Subjects* (1727).

7. We pick out a text here and there to make it serve our turn; whereas, if we take it all together, and considered what went before and what followed after, we should find it meant no such thing. JOHN SELDEN, "The Scriptures," *Table Talk* (1689).

8. Maybe the Bible don't read as lively as the scratch sheet, but it is at least twice as accurate. JO SWERLING, ABE BURROWS, and FRANK LOESSER, *Guys and Dolls* (1951), 2.3.

9. The Christian's Bible is a drug store. Its contents remain the same, but the medical practice changes. MARK TWAIN, "Bible Teaching and Religious Practice" (1923).

## BIGOTRY

**See 262. Dogmatism; 333. Fanaticism; 498. Intolerance; 720. Prejudices**

## 79. BIOGRAPHY

**See also 62. Autobiography; 91. Books and Reading; 1062. Writing and Writers**

1. In writing biography, fact and fiction shouldn't be mixed. And if they are, the fiction parts should be printed in red ink, the fact parts in black ink. CATHERINE DRINKER BOWEN, *Publishers' Weekly*, March 24, 1958.

2. A well-written Life is almost as rare as a well-spent one. THOMAS CARLYLE, "Richter," *Edinburgh Review* (1827).

3. How inexpressibly comfortable to know our fellow-creature; to see into him, understand his goings-forth, decipher the whole heart of his mystery: nay, not only to see into him, but even to see out of him, to view the world altogether as he views it. THOMAS CARLYLE, "Biography" (1832).

4. Read no history: nothing but biography, for that is life without theory. BENJAMIN DISRAELI, *Contarini Fleming* (1844), 1.23.

5. Biography broadens the vision and allows us to live a thousand lives in one. ELBERT HUBBARD, *The Note Book* (1927).

6. Nobody can write the life of a man but those who have eaten and drunk and lived in social intercourse with him. SAMUEL JOHNSON, quoted in Boswell's *Life of Samuel Johnson*, March 31, 1772.

7. What I fear is not being forgotten after my death, but, rather, not being enough forgotten. As we were saying, it is not our books that survive, but our poor lives that linger in the histories. FRANÇOIS MAURIAC, interview, *Writers at Work: First Series* (1958).

8. Biographies are but the clothes and buttons of the man—the biography of the man himself cannot be written. MARK TWAIN, *Autobiography* (1924), v. 1, ed. A. B. Paine.

9. Just how difficult it is to write biography can be reckoned by anybody who sits down and considers just how many people know the real truth about his or her love affairs. REBECCA WEST, "The Art of Skepticism," *Vogue*, Nov. 1, 1952.

## 80. BIRDS

1. Nothing wholly admirable ever happens in this country except the migration of birds. BROOKS ATKINSON, "March 23," *Once Around the Sun* (1951).

2. The wild goose comes north with the voice of freedom and adventure. He is more than a big, far-ranging bird; he is the epitome of wanderlust, limitless horizons and distant travel. He is the yearning and the dream, the search and the wonder, the unfettered foot and the wind's-will wing. HAL BORLAND, "Wild Goose—April 8," *Sundial of the Seasons* (1964).

3. The owl, that bird of onomatopoetic name, is a repetitious question wrapped in feathery insulation especially for Winter delivery. HAL BORLAND, "Questioner—December 27," *Sundial of the Seasons* (1964).

4. That's the wise thrush; he sings each song twice over, / Lest you should think he never could recapture / The first fine careless rapture! ROBERT BROWNING, "Home-thoughts, from Abroad," *Dramatic Romances and Lyrics* (1845), 2.

5. No ladder needs the bird but skies / To situate its wings, / Nor any leader's grim baton / Arraigns it as it sings. EMILY DICKINSON, poem (1883?).

6. Cheerfulness is proper to the cock, which rejoices over every little thing, and crows with varied and lively movements. LEONARDO DA VINCI, *Notebooks* (c. 1500), tr. Jean Paul Richter.

7. He [the eagle] clasps the crag with crooked hands; / Close to the sun in lonely lands, / Ringed with the azure world, he stands. / The wrinkled sea beneath him crawls; / He watches from his mountain walls, / And like a thunderbolt he falls. ALFRED, LORD TENNYSON, "The Eagle" (1851).

8. It's hard to tell the purpose of a bird; / for relevance it does not seem to try. / No line can trace, no flute exemplify / its traveling; it darts without the word. / Who wills devoutly to absorb, contain, / birds give him pain. RICHARD WILBUR, "In a Bird Sanctuary," *The Beautiful Changes* (1947).

## 81. BIRTH

**See also 37. Ancestry; 73. Beginning; 218. Death; 536. Life**

1. The best thing for a man to do is to be born and, being born, to die at once. PIETRO ARETINO, letter to Pietro Trivisano dai Crocicchieri, Dec. 18, 1537, tr. Samuel Putnam.

2. We brought nothing into this world, and it is certain we can carry nothing out. *Bible*, 1 Timothy 6:7.

3. The egg it is the source of all. / 'Tis everyone's ancestral hall. / The bravest chief that ever fought, / The lowest thief that e'er was caught, / The harlot's lip, the maiden's leg, / They each and all came from an egg. CLARENCE DAY, "Thoughts on Peculiar Dawns," *Thoughts Without Words* (1928).

4. The day of our birth is one day's advance towards our death. THOMAS FULLER, M.D., *Gnomologia* (1732), 4466.

5. There is nothing like a start, and being born, however pessimistic one may become in later years, is undeniably a start. WILLIAM MC FEE, "Lost Adventures," *Harbours of Memory* (1921).

6. One must mourn not the death of men, but their birth. MONTESQUIEU, *Lettres persanes* (1721), 40.

7. Where, unwilling, dies the rose / Buds the new, another year. DOROTHY PARKER, "Recurrence," *Enough Rope* (1926), 1.

8. The hour which gives us life begins to take it away. SENECA, *Hercules Furens* (1st c.), 1.874.

9. Our birth is nothing but our death begun. EDWARD YOUNG, *Night Thoughts* (1742–46), 5.718.

## 82. BIRTH CONTROL

**See also 707. Population; 796. Reproduction**

1. A small family is soon provided for. ENGLISH PROVERB.

2. No woman can call herself free who does not own and control her body. No woman can call herself free until she can choose consciously whether she will or will not be a mother. MARGARET SANGER, *Parade*, Dec. 1, 1963.

## 83. BLACKS

See also 585. Minorities; 769. Racial Prejudice; 1047. Whites

1. It is only in his music, which Americans are able to admire because a protective sentimentality limits their understanding of it, that the Negro in America has been able to tell his story. JAMES BALDWIN, "Many Thousands Gone" (1951), *Notes of a Native Son* (1955).

2. Aunt Jemima and Uncle Tom are dead, their places taken by a group of amazingly well-adjusted young men and women, almost as dark, but ferociously literate, well-dressed and scrubbed, who are never laughed at. JAMES BALDWIN, "Many Thousands Gone" (1951), *Notes of a Native Son* (1955).

3. Our dehumanization of the Negro then is indivisible from our dehumanization of ourselves; the loss of our own identity is the price we pay for our annulment of his. JAMES BALDWIN, "Many Thousands Gone" (1951), *Notes of a Native Son* (1955).

4. The Negro is superior to the white race. If the latter do not forget their pride of race and color, and amalgamate with the purer and richer blood of the blacks, they will die out and wither away in unprolific skinniness. HENRY WARD BEECHER, speech, New York City, 1866.

5. It is not healthy when a nation lives within a nation, as colored Americans are living inside America. A nation cannot live confident of its tomorrow if its refugees are among its own citizens. PEARL S. BUCK, *What America Means to Me* (1943), 1.

6. The Negro revolt is not aimed at winning friends but at winning freedom, not interpersonal warmth but institutional justice. HARVEY COX, *The Secular City* (1966), 6.

7. Having despised us, it is not strange that Americans should seek to render us despicable; having enslaved us, it is natural that they should strive to prove us unfit for freedom; having denounced us as indolent, it is not strange that they should cripple our enterprises. FREDERICK DOUGLASS, *Proceedings of the Colored National Convention*, Rochester, New York, July 6–8, 1853.

8. Just being a Negro doesn't qualify you to understand the race situation any more than being sick makes you an expert on medicine. DICK GREGORY, ". . . and they didn't even have what I wanted," *Nigger* (1964).

9. To be a Negro is to participate in a culture of poverty and fear that goes far deeper than any law for or against discrimination. MICHAEL HARRINGTON, *The Other America* (1962), 4.

10. Because my mouth / Is wide with laughter / And my throat / Is deep with song, / You do not think / I suffer after / I have held my pain / So long? / Because my mouth / Is wide with laughter, / You do not hear / My inner cry? / Because my feet / Are gay with dancing, / You do not know / I die? LANGSTON HUGHES, "In Love with Harlem," *Freedomways*, Summer 1963.

11. If you are black the only roads into the mainland of American life are through subservience, cowardice, and loss of manhood. These are the white man's roads. LE ROI JONES, "Black Is a Country," *Home* (1966).

12. It is a measure of the Negro's circumstance that, in America, the smallest things usually take him so very long, and that, by the time he wins them, they are no longer little things: they are miracles. MURRAY KEMPTON, "George," *Part of Our Time* (1955).

13. Only in the case of the Negro has the melting pot failed to bring a minority into the full stream of American life. JOHN F. KENNEDY, *A Nation of Immigrants* (1958).

14. We will not be satisfied until justice rolls down like waters and righteousness like a mighty stream. MARTIN LUTHER KING, JR., speech, Washington, D.C., June 15, 1963.

15. A young white boy's badness is simply the overflowing of young animal spirits; the black boy's badness is badness, pure and simple. Letter from a Negro mother, *The Independent*, Sept. 18, 1902.

16. The black man continues on his way. He plods wearily no longer—he is striding freedom road with the knowledge that if he hasn't got the world in a jug, at least he has the stopper in his hand. ADAM CLAYTON POWELL, "Black Power: A Form of Godly Power," *Keep the Faith, Baby!* (1967).

17. Treat us like men, and there is no danger but we will all live in peace and happiness together. For we are not like you, hard hearted, unmerciful, and unforgiving. What a happy country this will be, if the

whites will listen. DAVID WALKER, *Walker's Appeal* (Sept. 28, 1829).

## BLAME

See 203. Criticism; 403. Guilt; 797. Reproof; 841. Scapegoat

## BLASPHEMY

See 439. Iconoclasm; 504. Irreverence; 950. Swearing

## 84. BLINDNESS, PHYSICAL

See also 875. Senses; 890. Sight

1. There is a budding morrow in midnight; / There is a triple sight in blindness keen. JOHN KEATS, "To Homer" (1818).

2. As they say of the blind, / Sounds are the things I see. SOPHOCLES, *Oedipus at Colonus* (401 B.C.), tr. Robert Fitzgerald.

3. Last night I dreamed of a small consolation enjoyed only by the blind: Nobody knows the trouble I've *not* seen! JAMES THURBER, *Newsweek*, June 16, 1958.

## 85. BLINDNESS, SPIRITUAL

See also 481. Insensitivity; 676. Perception; 1000. Understanding; 1027. Vision

1. They are ill discoverers that think there is no land, when they see nothing but sea. FRANCIS BACON, *The Advancement of Learning* (1605), 2.7.5.

2. People who shut their eyes to reality simply invite their own destruction, and anyone who insists on remaining in a state of innocence long after that innocence is dead turns himself into a monster. JAMES BALDWIN, "Stranger in the Village" (1953), *Notes of a Native Son* (1955).

3. It is we that are blind, not Fortune. SIR THOMAS BROWNE, *Religio Medici* (1642), 1.

4. He has the greatest blind side who thinks he has none. DUTCH PROVERB.

5. There are none so blind as they that won't see. ENGLISH PROVERB.

6. A blind man will not thank you for a looking-glass. THOMAS FULLER, M.D., *Gnomologia* (1732), 18.

7. All men are the same. They take no notice of the stag in the thicket because they're already chasing the hare. JEAN GIRAUDOUX, *Tiger at the Gates* (1935), 2, tr. Christopher Fry.

8. Most people do not take heed of the things they encounter, nor do they grasp them even when they have learned about them, although they suppose they do. HERACLITUS, *Fragments* (c. 500 B.C.), 57, tr. Philip Wheelwright.

9. He does not weep who does not see. VICTOR HUGO, "Jean Valjean," *Les Misérables* (1862), 1.16, tr. Charles E. Wilbour.

10. One may have good eyes and see nothing. ITALIAN PROVERB.

11. We run carelessly to the precipice, after we have put something before us to prevent us seeing it. PASCAL, *Pensées* (1670), 183, tr. W. F. Trotter.

12. A blind man who sees is better than a seeing man who is blind. PERSIAN PROVERB.

## 86. BLUNDER

See also 297. Error

1. Half of our mistakes in life arise from feeling where we ought to think, and thinking where we ought to feel. JOHN CHURTON COLLINS, (1848–1908), aphorism.

2. He who is shipwrecked the second time cannot lay the blame on Neptune. ENGLISH PROVERB.

3. It is worse than a crime: it is a blunder. JOSEPH FOUCHÉ, comment on the execution of the Duc d'Enghien, March 21, 1804. Attributed also to Boulay de la Meurthe and Talleyrand.

4. A stumble may prevent a fall. THOMAS FULLER, M.D., *Gnomologia* (1732), 424.

5. I hate all bungling like sin, but most of all bungling in state affairs, which produces nothing but mischief to thousands and millions. GOETHE, quoted in Johann Peter Eckermann's *Conversations with Goethe*, March 1832.

6. Great blunders are often made, like large ropes, of a multitude of fibres. VICTOR HUGO, "Cosette," *Les Misérables* (1862), 5.10, tr. Charles E. Wilbour.

7. He that has much to do will do something wrong. SAMUEL JOHNSON, *Rasselas* (1759), 27.

8. The man who makes no mistakes does not usually make anything. WILLIAM CONNOR MAGEE, sermon, 1868.

9. The body pays for a slip of the foot and gold pays for a slip of the tongue. MALAY PROVERB.

10. It's not the tragedies that kill us, it's the messes. DOROTHY PARKER, interview, *Writers at Work: First Series* (1958).

11. The pain others give passes away in their later kindness, but that of our own blunders, especially when they hurt our vanity, never passes away. WILLIAM BUTLER YEATS, *Dramatis Personae* (1896–1902).

12. Better to trip with the feet than with the tongue. ZENO OF CITIUM (c. 300 B.C.), quoted in Diogenes Laertius' *Lives and Opinions of Eminent Philosophers* (3rd c. A.D.), tr. R. D. Hicks.

### BLUSHING
See 886. Shame

### 87. BOASTING
See also 163. Conceit

1. He who killeth a lion when absent feareth a mouse when present. ENGLISH PROVERB.

2. The noisiest drum has nothing in it but air. ENGLISH PROVERB.

3. You must stir it and stump it, / And blow your own trumpet, / Or trust me, you haven't a chance. W. S. GILBERT, *Ruddigore* (1887), 1.

4. Do not make yourself so big, you are not so small. JEWISH PROVERB.

5. Nothing ought more to humiliate men who have merited great praise than the care they still take to boast of little things. LA ROCHEFOUCAULD, *Maxims* (1665), tr. Kenneth Pratt.

6. The big drum beats fast but does not realize its hollowness. MALAY PROVERB.

### BOATS
See 888. Ships and Boats

### 88. BODY
See also 411. Health; 584. Mind and Body

1. Poor body, time and the long years were the first tailors to teach you the merciful use of clothes! Though some scold to-day because you are too much seen, to my mind, you are not seen fully enough or often enough when you are beautiful. HENRY BESTON, "The Year at High Tide," *The Outermost House* (1928).

2. Only death reveals what a nothing the body of man is. JUVENAL, *Satires* (c. 100), 10.172, tr. Hubert Creekmore.

3. Skin is like wax paper that holds everything in without dripping. ART LINKLETTER, *A Child's Garden of Misinformation* (1965), 5.

4. Body am I entirely, and nothing else; and soul is only a word for something about the body. NIETZSCHE, "On the Despisers of the Body," *Thus Spoke Zarathustra* (1883–92), tr. Walter Kaufmann.

5. The abdomen is the reason why man does not easily take himself for a god. NIETZSCHE, *Beyond Good and Evil* (1886), 141, tr. Walter Kaufmann.

6. Though it be disfigured by many defects, to whom is his own body not dear? *Panchatantra* (c. 5th c.), 1, tr. Franklin Edgerton.

7. What is more important in life than our bodies or in the world than what we look like? GEORGE SANTAYANA, "My Sister Susana," *Persons and Places: The Background of My Life* (1944).

8. He will be the slave of many masters who is his body's slave. SENECA, *Letters to Lucilius* (1st c.), 14.1, tr. E. Phillips Barker.

9. This is a world of bodies / each body pushing with a terrible power / each body alone racked with its own unrest. PETER WEISS, *Marat/Sade* (1964), 2.30, tr. Geoffrey Skelton and Adrian Mitchell.

10. If any thing is sacred the human body is sacred. WALT WHITMAN, *I Sing the Body Electric* (1855–81), 8.

### BODY AND SOUL
See 584. Mind and Body

### 89. BOHEMIANS
See also 168. Conformity; 466. Individualism

1. The hippies have usurped the prerogatives of children—to dress up and be irresponsible. Anonymous, quoted in Mark Harris' "The Flowering of the Hippies,"

*The Atlantic Monthly*, September 1967.

2. The importance of the Beats is twofold: first, they act out a critique of the organized system that everybody in some sense agrees with. But second—and more important in the long run—they are a kind of major pilot study of the use of leisure in an economy of abundance. PAUL GOODMAN, *Growing Up Absurd* (1960), 9.1.

3. Bohemia is nothing more than the little country in which you do not live. If you try to obtain citizenship in it, at once the court and retinue pack the royal archives and treasure and move away beyond the hills. O. HENRY, "The Country of Elusion," *The Trimmed Lamp* (1907).

4. Hip is the sophistication of the wise primitive in a giant jungle. NORMAN MAILER, "The White Negro," *Advertisements for Myself* (1959).

5. It is not difficult to be unconventional in the eyes of the world when your unconventionality is but the convention of your set. W. SOMERSET MAUGHAM, *The Moon and Sixpence* (1919), 14.

6. In almost any society, I think, the quality of the nonconformists is likely to be just as good as and no better than that of the conformists. MARGARET MEAD, *Redbook*, January 1961.

7. Bohemia is a state of mind inhabited by those who, whether or not they are creative or particularly intellectual, like to stand on the margins and scoff at the babbitts. VANCE PACKARD, *The Status Seekers* (1959), 1.3.

## 90. BOLDNESS

**See also 26. Aggression; 192. Courage; 853. Self-assertion; 973. Timidity**

1. Tact in audacity is knowing how far you can go without going too far. JEAN COCTEAU, "Le Coq et l'Arlequin," *Le Rappel à l'ordre* (1926).

2. Boldness, without the rules of propriety, becomes insubordination. CONFUCIUS, *Analects* (6th c. B.C.), 8.2, tr. James Legge.

3. The people I respect most behave as if they were immortal and as if society was eternal. E. M. FORSTER, "What I Believe," *Two Cheers for Democracy* (1951).

4. Better hazard once than always be in fear. THOMAS FULLER, M.D., *Gnomologia*, (1732), 906.

5. It had need to be / A wily mouse that should breed in the cat's ear. JOHN HEYWOOD, *Proverbs* (1546), 2.5.

6. Tender-handed stroke a nettle, / And it stings you for your pains; / Grasp it like a man of mettle, / And it soft as silk remains. AARON HILL, *Verses Written on a Window in Scotland* (1794).

7. A decent boldness ever meets with friends. HOMER, *Odyssey* (9th c. B.C.), 7.67, tr. Alexander Pope.

8. It is the bold man who every time does best, at home or abroad. HOMER, *Odyssey* (9th c. B.C.), 7, tr. E. V. Rieu.

9. Unless you enter the tiger's den you cannot take the cubs. JAPANESE PROVERB.

10. In difficult situations when hope seems feeble, the boldest plans are safest. LIVY, *Ab Urbe Condita* (c. 29 B.C.), 25.28.

11. The best mask for demoralization is daring. LUCAN, *On the Civil War* (1st c.), tr. Robert Graves.

12. With audacity one can undertake anything, but not do everything. NAPOLEON I, *Maxims* (1804–15).

13. I love the valiant; but it is not enough to wield a broadsword, one must also know against whom. NIETZSCHE, "On Old and New Tablets," *Thus Spoke Zarathustra* (1883–92), 3, tr. Walter Kaufmann.

14. When the mouse laughs at the cat, there is a hole nearby. NIGERIAN PROVERB.

15. Audacity augments courage; hesitation, fear. PUBLILIUS SYRUS, *Moral Sayings* (1st c. B.C.), 63, tr. Darius Lyman.

16. Yield not thy neck / To fortune's yoke, but let thy dauntless mind / Still ride in triumph over all mischance. SHAKESPEARE, *3 Henry VI* (1590–91), 3.3.16.

## BOMB, ATOM

**See 633. Nuclear Power**

## 91. BOOKS AND READING

**See also 62. Autobiography; 79. Biography; 134. Classics; 242. Dictionaries; 341. Fiction; 535. Libraries; 542. Literature; 1057. Words; 1062. Writing and Writers**

1. I have observed, that a reader seldom peruses a book with pleasure, 'till he knows

whether the writer of it be a black or a fair man, of a mild or choleric disposition, married or a bachelor, with other particulars of the like nature, that conduce very much to the right understanding of an author. JOSEPH ADDISON, *The Spectator* (1711–12), 1.

2. A man is known by the company his mind keeps. THOMAS BAILEY ALDRICH, "Leaves from a Notebook," *Ponkapog Papers* (1903).

3. Some books are undeservedly forgotten; none are undeservedly remembered. W. H. AUDEN, "Reading," *The Dyer's Hand* (1962).

4. Books will speak plain when counselors blanch. FRANCIS BACON, "Of Counsel," *Essays* (1625).

5. Some books are to be tasted, others to be swallowed, and some few to be chewed and digested. FRANCIS BACON, "Of Studies," *Essays* (1625).

6. A book is good company. It is full of conversation without loquacity. It comes to your longing with full instruction, but pursues you never. HENRY WARD BEECHER, *Proverbs from Plymouth Pulpit* (1887).

7. Thank God for books! And yet thank God that the great realm of truth lies yet outside of books, too vast to be mastered by types or imprisoned in libraries. HENRY WARD BEECHER, *Proverbs from Plymouth Pulpit* (1887).

8. Of making many books there is no end; and much study is a weariness of the flesh. *Bible*, Ecclesiastes 12:12.

9. Best-sellerism is the star system of the book world. A "best seller" is a celebrity among books. It is a book known primarily (sometimes exclusively) for its well-knownness. DANIEL J. BOORSTIN, *The Image* (1962), 4.8.

10. Books succeed, / And lives fail. ELIZABETH BARRETT BROWNING, *Aurora Leigh* (1856), 7.705.

11. The adult relation to books is one of absorbing rather than being absorbed. ANTHONY BURGESS, "The Book Is Not for Reading," *The New York Times Book Review*, Dec. 4, 1966.

12. The possession of a book becomes a substitute for reading it. ANTHONY BURGESS, "The Book Is Not for Reading," *The New York Times Book Review*, Dec. 4, 1966.

13. How much there is in books that one does not want to know, that it would be a mere weariness and burden to the spirit to know. JOHN BURROUGHS, *Indoor Studies* (1889).

14. In books lies the soul of the whole past time. THOMAS CARLYLE, *On Heroes, Hero-Worship and the Heroic in History* (1841), 5.

15. "What is the use of a book," thought Alice, "without pictures or conversations?" LEWIS CARROLL, *Alice's Adventures in Wonderland* (1865), 1.

16. Most of today's books have an air of having been written in one day from books read the night before. CHAMFORT, *Maximes et pensées* (1805), 6.

17. What is responsible for the success of many works is the rapport between the mediocrity of the author's ideas and the mediocrity of the public's. CHAMFORT, *Maximes et pensées* (1805), 6.

18. The easiest books are generally the best; for, whatever author is obscure and difficult in his own language, certainly does not think clearly. LORD CHESTERFIELD, *Letters to His Son*, Feb. 8, 1750.

19. When one can read, can penetrate the enchanted realm of books, why write? COLETTE, "The Footwarmer," *Earthly Paradise* (1966), 1, ed. Robert Phelps.

20. Some read to think—these are rare; some to write, these are common; and some read to talk, and these form the great majority. CHARLES CALEB COLTON, *Lacon* (1825), 1.554.

21. Many books require no thought from those who read them, and for a very simple reason—they made no such demand upon those who wrote them. CHARLES CALEB COLTON, *Lacon* (1825), 2.248.

22. While thought exists, words are alive and literature becomes an escape, not from, but into living. CYRIL CONNOLLY, *The Unquiet Grave* (1945), 3.

23. The man who reads only for improvement is beyond the hope of much improvement before he begins. JONATHAN DANIELS, *Three Presidents and Their Books*, (1956).

24. The reading of all good books is like conversation with the finest men of past centuries. DESCARTES, *Discourse on Method* (1639), 1.

25. A precious—mouldering pleasure—'tis— / To meet an Antique Book— / In just the Dress his Century wore— / A privilege

–I think–. EMILY DICKINSON, poem (c. 1862).

26. A book, like a landscape, is a state of consciousness varying with readers. ERNEST DIMNET, *The Art of Thinking* (1928), 3.8.

27. Reading, to most people, means an ashamed way of killing time disguised under a dignified name. ERNEST DIMNET, *The Art of Thinking* (1928), 3.8.

28. A book is not harmless merely because no one is consciously offended by it. T. S. ELIOT, "Religion and Literature" (1935).

29. What can we see, read, acquire, but ourselves. Take the book, my friend, and read your eyes out, you will never find there what I find. EMERSON, *Journals*, 1832.

30. Books take their place according to their specific gravity as surely as potatoes in a tub. EMERSON, *Journals*, 1834.

31. What's a book? Everything or nothing. The eye that sees it is all. EMERSON, *Journals*, 1834.

32. We are too civil to books. For a few golden sentences we will turn over and actually read a volume of four or five hundred pages. EMERSON, *Journals*, 1841.

33. The modernness of all good books seems to give me an existence as wide as man. EMERSON, "Nominalist and Realist," *Essays: Second Series* (1844).

34. For the most part, our novel-reading is a passion for results. EMERSON, "In Praise of Books," *The Conduct of Life* (1860).

35. I should as soon think of swimming across Charles River, when I wish to go to Boston, as of reading all my books in originals, when I have them rendered for me in my mother tongue. EMERSON, "In Praise of Books," *The Conduct of Life* (1860).

36. A wicked book is the wickeder because it cannot repent. ENGLISH PROVERB.

37. I suggest that the only books that influence us are those for which we are ready, and which have gone a little farther down our particular path than we have yet got ourselves. E. M. FORSTER, "A Book That Influenced Me," *Two Cheers for Democracy* (1951).

38. Learning hath gained most by those books by which the printers have lost. THOMAS FULLER, D.D., "Of Books," *The Holy State and the Profane State* (1642).

39. To read a writer is for me not merely to get an idea of what he says, but to go off with him, and travel in his company. ANDRÉ GIDE, "Third Imaginary Interview," *Pretexts* (1903), tr. Angelo P. Bertocci and others.

40. I know every book of mine by its scent, and I have but to put my nose between the pages to be reminded of all sorts of things. GEORGE GISSING, "Spring," *The Private Papers of Henry Ryecroft* (1903).

41. How our life has been warped by books! We are not contented with realities: we crave conclusions. DAVID GRAYSON, *Adventures in Contentment* (1907), 9.

42. What a convenient and delightful world is this world of books!–if you bring to it not the obligations of the student, or look upon it as an opiate for idleness, but enter it rather with the enthusiasm of the adventurer! DAVID GRAYSON, *Adventures in Contentment* (1907), 12.

43. Few books have more than one thought: the generality indeed have not quite so many. JULIUS CHARLES HARE and AUGUSTUS WILLIAM HARE, *Guesses at Truth* (1827).

44. Books give not wisdom where was none before, / But where some is, there reading makes it more. SIR JOHN HARINGTON, *Epigrams* (1615), 1.2.

45. The book-worm wraps himself up in his web of verbal generalities, and sees only the glimmering shadows of things reflected from the minds of others. WILLIAM HAZLITT, "On the Ignorance of the Learned," *Table Talk* (1821–22).

46. What refuge is there for the victim who is oppressed with the feeling that there are a thousand new books he ought to read, while life is only long enough for him to attempt to read a hundred? OLIVER WENDELL HOLMES, SR., *Over the Teacups* (1891), 7.

47. When I get hold of a book I particularly admire, I am so enthusiastic that I loan it to some one who never brings it back. EDGAR WATSON HOWE, *Country Town Sayings* (1911).

48. A book on cheap paper does not convince. It is not prized, it is like a wheezy doctor with pigtail tobacco breath, who needs a manicure. ELBERT HUBBARD, *The Philistine* (1895–1915).

49. A bad book is as much of a labour to write as a good one; it comes as sincerely from the author's soul. ALDOUS HUXLEY, *Point Counter Point* (1928), 13.

50. One of the amusements of idleness is reading without the fatigue of close attention; and the world, therefore, swarms with writers whose wish is not to be studied, but to be read. SAMUEL JOHNSON, *The Idler* (1758–60), 31.

51. A man ought to read just as inclination leads him, for what he reads as a task will do him little good. SAMUEL JOHNSON, quoted in Boswell's *Life of Samuel Johnson*, July 14, 1763.

52. We find little in a book but what we put there. But in great books, the mind finds room to put many things. JOSEPH JOUBERT, *Pensées* (1842), 22.98, tr. Katharine Lyttelton.

53. We read fine things but never feel them to the full until we have gone the same steps as the author. JOHN KEATS, letter to John Hamilton Reynolds, May 3, 1818.

54. There is as much trickery required to grow rich by a stupid book as there is folly in buying it. LA BRUYÈRE, *Characters* (1688), 1.46, tr. Henri Van Laun.

55. I love to lose myself in other men's minds. When I am not walking, I am reading; I cannot sit and think. Books think for me. CHARLES LAMB, "Detached Thoughts on Books and Reading," *Last Essays of Elia* (1833).

56. In some respects the better a book is, the less it demands from binding. CHARLES LAMB, "Detached Thoughts on Books and Reading," *Last Essays of Elia* (1833).

57. What is reading but silent conversation? WALTER SAVAGE LANDOR, "Aristoteles and Callisthenes," *Imaginary Conversations* (1824–53).

58. A book is a mirror: if an ass peers into it, you can't expect an apostle to look out. GEORG CHRISTOPH LICHTENBERG, *Aphorisms* (1764–99), tr. J. P. Stern.

59. To read means to borrow; to create out of one's readings is paying off one's debts. GEORG CHRISTOPH LICHTENBERG, *Aphorisms* (1764–99), tr. F. H. Mautner and H. Hatfield.

60. Reading furnishes the mind only with materials of knowledge; it is thinking makes what we read ours. JOHN LOCKE, *Of the Conduct of the Understanding* (1706), 20.

61. Endless volumes, larger, fatter, / Prove man's intellectual climb, / But in essence it's a matter / Just of having lots of time. "Endless Volumes," editorial, *The London Times Literary Supplement*, Dec. 28, 1967.

62. There are favorable hours for reading a book, as for writing it. LONGFELLOW, "Table-Talk," *Driftwood* (1857).

63. All books are either dreams or swords. AMY LOWELL, "Sword Blades and Poppy Seeds," *Sword Blades and Poppy Seeds* (1914).

64. Make him [the reader] laugh and he will think you a trivial fellow, but bore him in the right way and your reputation is assured. W. SOMERSET MAUGHAM, *The Gentleman in the Parlour* (1930).

65. The only important thing in a book is the meaning it has for you. W. SOMERSET MAUGHAM, *The Summing Up* (1938), 26.

66. Who kills a man kills a reasonable creature, God's image; but he who destroys a good book kills reason itself. MILTON, *Areopagitica* (1644).

67. Books are not absolutely dead things, but do contain a potency of life in them to be as active as that soul was whose progeny they are; nay they do preserve as in a vial the purest efficacy and extraction of that living intellect that bred them. MILTON, *Tractate of Education* (1644).

68. He that I am reading seems always to have the most force. MONTAIGNE, "Apology for Raimond de Sebonde," *Essays* (1580–88), tr. Charles Cotton and W. C. Hazlitt.

69. Every abridgement of a good book is a stupid abridgement. MONTAIGNE, "Of the art of conference," *Essays* (1580–88).

70. I seek in the reading of books, only to please myself, by an honest diversion. MONTAIGNE, "Of books," *Essays* (1580–88), tr. Charles Cotton and W. C. Hazlitt.

71. I have never known any distress that an hour's reading did not relieve. MONTESQUIEU, *Pensées diverses* (1899).

72. A book is made better by good readers and clearer by good opponents. NIETZSCHE, *Miscellaneous Maxims and Opinions* (1879), 2153, tr. Paul V. Cohn.

73. Books for all the world are always foul-smelling books: the smell of small people clings to them. NIETZSCHE, *Beyond Good and Evil* (1886), 30, tr. Walter Kaufmann.

74. When we read too fast or too slowly, we understand nothing. PASCAL, *Pensées* (1670), 69, tr. W. F. Trotter.

75. How many good books suffer neglect through the inefficiency of their beginnings! EDGAR ALLAN POE, *Marginalia* (1844–49), 1.

76. In reading some books we occupy ourselves chiefly with the thoughts of the author; in perusing others, exclusively with our own. EDGAR ALLAN POE, *Marginalia* (1844–49), 2.

77. No man understands a deep book until he has seen and lived at least part of its contents. EZRA POUND, *The ABC of Reading* (1934).

78. There is no reason why the same man should like the same books at eighteen and forty-eight. EZRA POUND, *The ABC of Reading* (1934), 8.

79. No book, any more than helpful word, can do anything decisive if the person concerned is not already prepared through quite invisible influences for a deeper receptivity and absorption, if his hour of self-communion has not come anyway. RAINER MARIA RILKE, letter to Ilse Blumenthal-Weiss, Dec. 28, 1921, in *Wartime Letters*, tr. M. D. Herter Norton.

80. All books are divisible into two classes: the books of the hour, and the books of all time. JOHN RUSKIN, *Sesame and Lilies* (1865), 1.8.

81. A best-seller is the gilded tomb of a mediocre talent. LOGAN PEARSALL SMITH, *Afterthoughts* (1931), 5.

82. People say that life is the thing, but I prefer reading. LOGAN PEARSALL SMITH, *Afterthoughts* (1931), 6.

83. No furniture so charming as books. SYDNEY SMITH, quoted in Lady S. Holland's *Memoir* (1855), v. 1.9.

84. Hard-covered books break up friendships. You loan a hard-covered book to a friend and when he doesn't return it you get mad at him. It makes you mean and petty. But twenty-five-cent books are different. JOHN STEINBECK, news summaries, April 25, 1954.

85. In anything fit to be called by the name of reading, the process itself should be absorbing and voluptuous; we should gloat over a book, be rapt clean out of ourselves. ROBERT LOUIS STEVENSON, "A Gossip on Romance" (1882).

86. A great book should leave you with many experiences, and slightly exhausted at the end. You live several lives while reading it. WILLIAM STYRON, interview, *Writers at Work: First Series* (1958).

87. Books, like proverbs, receive their chief value from the stamp and esteem of ages through which they have passed. SIR WILLIAM TEMPLE, "Of Ancient and Modern Learning," *Miscellanea* (1692), v. 2.

88. How many a man has dated a new era in his life from the reading of a book! THOREAU, "Reading," *Walden* (1854).

89. Books must be read as deliberately and reservedly as they are written. THOREAU, "Reading," *Walden* (1854).

90. It is with books as with men—a very small number play a great part; the rest are lost in the multitude. VOLTAIRE, "Books," *Philosophical Dictionary* (1764).

91. Have you any right to read, especially novels, until you have exhausted the best part of the day in some employment that is called practical? CHARLES DUDLEY WARNER, "First Study," *Backlog Studies* (1873).

92. There is no such thing as a moral or an immoral book. Books are well written, or badly written. That is all. OSCAR WILDE, preface, *The Picture of Dorian Gray* (1891).

93. Up! up! my Friend, and quit your books; / Or surely you'll grow double. / Up! up! my Friend, and clear your looks; / Why all this toil and trouble? WILLIAM WORDSWORTH, "The Tables Turned" (1798).

## 92. BOREDOM

**See also 93. Bores; 268. Dullness; 288. Ennui**

1. Passions are less mischievous than boredom, for passions tend to diminish, boredom to increase. JULES BARBEY D'AUREVILLY, *Une vieille maîtresse* (1851), 2.

2. Society is now one polished horde, / Formed of two mighty tribes, the *Bores* and *Bored.* BYRON, *Don Juan* (1819–24), 13.95.

3. Man is the only animal that can be bored. ERICH FROMM, *The Sane Society* (1955), 3.

4. The prospect of being pleased tomorrow will never console me for the boredom of today. Graffito written during French student revolt, May 1968.

5. If we examine well the diverse effects of boredom, we shall find that it causes us to

neglect more duties than does interest. LA ROCHEFOUCAULD, *Maxims* (1665), tr. Kenneth Pratt.

6. A nap, my friend, is a brief period of sleep which overtakes superannuated persons when they endeavour to entertain unwelcome visitors or to listen to scientific lectures. GEORGE BERNARD SHAW, *Back to Methuselah* (1921), 4.1.

7. One can be bored until boredom becomes the most sublime of all emotions. LOGAN PEARSALL SMITH, *Afterthoughts* (1931), 4.

8. One must choose in life between boredom and torment. MME DE STAËL, letter to Claude Rochet, 1800.

9. Boredom: the desire for desires. LEO TOLSTOY, *Anna Karenina* (1873–76), 5.8.

## 93. BORES

**See also 67. Banality; 92. Boredom; 268. Dullness**

1. The man who suspects his own tediousness is yet to be born. THOMAS BAILEY ALDRICH, "Leaves from a Notebook," *Ponkapog Papers* (1903).

2. Bore, n. A person who talks when you wish him to listen. AMBROSE BIERCE, *The Devil's Dictionary* (1881–1911).

3. Each man reserves to himself alone the right of being tedious. EMERSON, *Journals*, 1843.

4. It is the peculiarity of the bore that he is the last person to find himself out. OLIVER WENDELL HOLMES, SR., *Over the Teacups* (1891), 4.

5. If the best company is that which we leave feeling most satisfied with ourselves, it follows that it is the company we leave most bored. GIACOMO LEOPARDI, *Pensieri* (1834–37), 21, tr. William Fense Weaver.

6. What things are sure this side of paradise: / Death, taxes, and the counsel of the bore. / Though we outwit the tithe, make death our friend, / Bores we have with us even to the end. PHYLLIS MC GINLEY, "A Choice of Weapons," *The Love Letters of Phyllis McGinley* (1954).

7. A healthy male adult bore consumes each year one and a half times his own weight in other people's patience. JOHN UPDIKE, "Confessions of a Wild Bore," *Assorted Prose* (1965).

8. The secret of being a bore is to tell everything. VOLTAIRE, *Sept discours en vers sur l'homme* (1738), 2.

## 94. BORROWING AND LENDING

**See also 219. Debt; 639. Obligation**

1. A borrowed cloak does not keep one warm. ARABIC PROVERB.

2. The borrower is servant to the lender. *Bible*, Proverbs 22:7.

3. Me timp'rature is normal save whin I'm asked f'r money. FINLEY PETER DUNNE, "Thanksgiving," *Mr. Dooley's Opinions* (1901).

4. The human species, according to the best theory I can form of it, is composed of two distinct races, the men who borrow, and the men who lend. CHARLES LAMB, "The Two Races of Men," *Essays of Elia* (1823).

5. I *don't* believe in princerple, / But, oh, I *du* in interest. JAMES RUSSELL LOWELL, *The Biglow Papers: First Series* (1848), 6.

6. Neither a borrower nor a lender be; / For loan oft loses both itself and friend. SHAKESPEARE, *Hamlet* (1600), 1.3.75.

7. The person whom you favoured with a loan, if he be a good man, will think himself in your debt after he has paid you. RICHARD STEELE, *The Spectator* (1711–12), 346.

8. Have a horse of your own and you may borrow another's. WELSH PROVERB.

## BOURGEOISIE

**See 581. Middle Class**

## 95. BOYS

**See also 121. Children; 909. Sons; 1064. Youth**

1. Boys naturally look on all force as an enemy. HENRY ADAMS, *The Education of Henry Adams* (1907), 1.

2. A boy is a piece of existence quite separate from all things else, and deserves separate chapters in the natural history of men. HENRY WARD BEECHER, *Proverbs from Plymouth Pulpit* (1887).

3. A lazy boy and a warm bed are difficult to part. DANISH PROVERB.

4. A boy becomes an adult three years

before his parents think he does, and about two years after he thinks he does. GENERAL LEWIS B. HERSHEY, news summaries, Dec. 31, 1951.

5. The truly passionate are little boys. MURRAY KEMPTON, "Monkey on His Back," *America Comes of Middle Age* (1963).

6. Boys are capital fellows in their own way, among their mates; but they are unwholesome companions for grown people. CHARLES LAMB, "The Old and the New Schoolmaster," *Essays of Elia* (1823).

7. A boy's will is the wind's will, / And the thoughts of youth are long, long thoughts. LONGFELLOW, "My Lost Youth" (1858).

8. Schoolboys have no fear of facing life. They champ at the bit. The jealousies, the trials, the sorrows of the life of man do not intimidate the schoolboy. SAINT-EXUPÉRY, *Flight to Arras* (1942), 1, tr. Lewis Galantière.

### BRAVERY
**See 192. Courage**

### BREEDING
**See 37. Ancestry; 389. Good Breeding; 796. Reproduction**

### 96. BREVITY
**See also 916. Speaking**

1. Let thy speech be short, comprehending much in few words. *Apocrypha*, Ecclesiasticus 32:8.

2. Least said is soonest disavowed. AMBROSE BIERCE, "Saw," *The Devil's Dictionary* (1881–1911).

3. Brevity is very good, / When we are, or are not understood. SAMUEL BUTLER (d. 1680), *Hudibras* (1663), 1.1.

4. Promise is most given when the least is said. GEORGE CHAPMAN, *Hero and Leander* (1598), tr. from a poem by Musæus.

5. Men are born with two eyes, but with one tongue, in order that they should see twice as much as they say. CHARLES CALEB COLTON, *Lacon* (1825), 1.112.

6. Yes and No are soon said, but give much to think over. BALTASAR GRACIÁN, *The Art of Worldly Wisdom* (1647), 70, tr. Joseph Jacobs.

7. When I struggle to be terse, I end by being obscure. HORACE, *Ars Poetica* (13–8 B.C.).

8. Half a brain is enough for him who says little. ITALIAN PROVERB.

9. To be brief is almost a condition of being inspired. GEORGE SANTAYANA, *Little Essays* (1920), 57, ed. Logan Pearsall Smith.

10. Men of few words are the best men. SHAKESPEARE, *Henry V* (1598–99), 3.2.40.

11. All pleasantry should be short; and it might even be as well were the serious short also. VOLTAIRE, "Prior, Butler, and Swift," *Philosophical Dictionary* (1764).

### 97. BRIBERY
**See also 188. Corruption; 964. Temptation**

1. Many a man has been dined out of his religion, and his politics, and his manhood, almost. HENRY WARD BEECHER, *Proverbs from Plymouth Pulpit* (1887).

2. He refuseth the bribe but putteth forth his hand. ENGLISH PROVERB.

3. They say the gods themselves / Are moved by gifts, and gold does more with men than words. EURIPIDES, *Medea* (431 B.C.), tr. Rex Warner.

4. A friend that you buy with presents will be bought from you. THOMAS FULLER, M.D., *Gnomologia* (1732), 121.

5. He that bringeth a present findeth the door open. THOMAS FULLER, M.D., *Gnomologia* (1732), 2052.

6. A conscience which has been bought once will be bought twice. NORBERT WIENER, *The Human Use of Human Beings* (1954), 7.

### BROAD-MINDEDNESS
**See 977. Tolerance**

### 98. BROTHERHOOD
**See also 150. Community; 496. International Relations; 619. Neighbors; 1009. Unity**

1. Have we not all one father? hath not one God created us? *Bible*, Malachi 2:10.

2. While there is a lower class I am in it, while there is a criminal element I am of it;

while there is a soul in prison, I am not free. EUGENE V. DEBS, speech, Cleveland, Ohio, Sept. 9, 1917.

3. There is the sky, which is all men's together, there / is the world to live in, fill with houses of our own / nor hold another's, nor tear it from his hands by force. EURIPIDES, *Helen* (412 B.C.), tr. Richmond Lattimore.

4. I ought not to fear to survive my own people so long as there are men in the world; for there are always some whom one can love. ANATOLE FRANCE, *The Crime of Sylvestre Bonnard* (1881), 2, tr. Lafcadio Hearn.

5. It is easy enough to be friendly to one's friends. But to befriend the one who regards himself as your enemy is the quintessence of true religion. The other is mere business. MOHANDAS K. GANDHI, *Non-Violence in Peace and War* (1948), 2.248.

6. My country is the world; my countrymen are mankind. WILLIAM LLOYD GARRISON, prospectus for *The Liberator* (1803).

7. A low capacity for getting along with those near us often goes hand in hand with a high receptivity to the idea of the brotherhood of men. ERIC HOFFER, *The Ordeal of Change* (1964), 11.

8. There is always a type of man who says he loves his fellow men, and expects to make a living at it. EDGAR WATSON HOWE, *Ventures in Common Sense* (1919), 2.5.

9. A man may have strong humanitarian and democratic principles; but if he happens to have been brought up as a bath-taking, shirt-changing lover of fresh air, he will have to overcome certain physical repugnances before he can bring himself to put those principles into practice. ALDOUS HUXLEY, *Jesting Pilate* (1926), 1.

10. We are so bound together that no man can labor for himself alone. Each blow he strikes in his own behalf helps to mold the universe. JEROME K. JEROME, "On Getting On in the World," *The Idle Thoughts of an Idle Fellow* (1889).

11. As man increases his knowledge of the heavens, why should he fear the unknown on earth? As man draws nearer to the stars, why should he not also draw nearer to his neighbor? LYNDON B. JOHNSON, news conference, Johnson City, Texas, Aug. 29, 1965.

12. We seek not the worldwide victory of one nation or system but a worldwide victory of men. JOHN F. KENNEDY, State of the Union Message, Jan. 14, 1963.

13. Our most basic common link is that we all inhibit this planet. We all breathe the same air. We all cherish our children's future. And we are all mortal. JOHN F. KENNEDY, address, The American University, Washington, D.C., June 10, 1963.

14. The supreme reality of our time is our indivisibility as children of God and the common vulnerability of this planet. JOHN F. KENNEDY, address to Irish Parliament, Dublin, June 28, 1963.

15. There is neither East nor West, Border, nor Breed, nor Birth, / When two strong men stand face to face, though they come from the ends of the earth! RUDYARD KIPLING, "The Ballad of East and West" (1899).

16. Either men will learn to live like brothers, or they will die like beasts. MAX LERNER, "The Gifts of the Magi," *Actions and Passions* (1949).

17. Adapt yourself to the environment in which your lot has been cast, and show true love to the fellow-mortals with whom destiny has surrounded you. MARCUS AURELIUS, *Meditations* (2nd c.), 6.39, tr. Maxwell Staniforth.

18. There is a destiny which makes us brothers; / None goes his way alone. EDWIN MARKHAM, "A Creed" (1900).

19. Every experience proves that the real problem of our existence lies in the fact that we ought to love one another, but do not. REINHOLD NIEBUHR, *Christian Realism and Political Problems* (1953), 8.

20. Those who love not their fellow-beings live unfruitful lives, and prepare for their old age a miserable grave. SHELLEY, preface, *Alastor* (1815).

21. The universal brotherhood of man is our most precious possession, what there is of it. MARK TWAIN, "Pudd'nhead Wilson's New Calendar," *Following the Equator* (1897), 1.27.

22. Our true nationality is mankind. H. G. WELLS, *The Outline of History* (1920, 1921), 40.1.

23. A "fraternity" is the antithesis of *fraternity*. The first (that is, the order of organization) is predicated on the idea of exclusion; the second (that is, the abstract thing) is based on a feeling of total equality.

E. B. WHITE, "Intimations," *One Man's Meat* (1944).

### BROTHERS
See 332. Family

### 99. BUDGET
See also 220. Debt, National; 275. Economics; 958. Taxes

1. As quickly as you start spending federal money in large amounts, it looks like free money. DWIGHT D. EISENHOWER, Feb. 9, 1955.

2. The Federal Government is the people and the budget is a reflection of their need. JOHN F. KENNEDY, address, American Society of Newspaper Editors, Washington, D.C., April 19, 1963.

3. A minister of finance is a legally authorized pickpocket. PAUL RAMADIER, *Quote*, Oct. 7, 1956.

4. The budget is a mythical bean bag. Congress votes mythical beans into it, and then tries to reach in and pull real beans out. WILL ROGERS, *The Autobiography of Will Rogers* (1949), 18.

5. In general, the art of government consists in taking as much money as possible from one part of the citizens to give to the other. VOLTAIRE, "Money," *Philosophical Dictionary* (1764).

### BUGS
See 479. Insects

### 100. BUREAUCRACY
See also 645. Officialism; 925. Statistics

1. The perfect bureaucrat everywhere is the man who manages to make no decisions and escape all responsibility. BROOKS ATKINSON, "September 9," *Once Around the Sun* (1951).

2. Bureaucracies are designed to perform public business. But as soon as a bureaucracy is established, it develops an autonomous spiritual life and comes to regard the public as its enemy. BROOKS ATKINSON, "September 9," *Once Around the Sun* (1951).

3. Large organization is loose organization. Nay, it would be almost as true to say that organization is always disorganization. G. K. CHESTERTON, "The Bluff of the Big Shops," *Outline of Sanity* (1926).

4. Government defines the physical aspects of man by means of The Printed Form, so that for every man in the flesh there is an exactly corresponding man on paper. JEAN GIRAUDOUX, *The Enchanted* (1933), 3, adapted by Maurice Valency.

5. It's all papers and forms, the entire Civil Service is like a fortress made of papers, forms and red tape. ALEXANDER OSTROVSKY, *The Diary of a Scoundrel* (1868).

6. There is something about a bureaucrat that does not like a poem. GORE VIDAL, preface to *Sex, Death and Money* (1968).

### 101. BURIAL
See also 218. Death; 365. Funerals; 603. Mourning

1. Nature is honest, we aren't; we embalm our dead. UGO BETTI, *Goat Island* (1946), 2, 3, ed. Gino Rizzo.

2. Epitaph, n. An inscription on a tomb, showing that virtues acquired by death have a retroactive effect. AMBROSE BIERCE, *The Devil's Dictionary* (1881–1911).

3. As well a well-wrought urn becomes / The greatest ashes, as half-acre tombs. JOHN DONNE, "The Canonization," *Songs and Sonnets* (1633).

4. It makes small difference to the dead, if they / are buried in the tokens of luxury. All this / is an empty glorification left for those who live. EURIPIDES, *The Trojan Women* (415 B.C.), tr. Richmond Lattimore.

5. "Let the dead bury the dead." There is not a single word of Christ to which the so-called Christian religion has paid less attention. ANDRÉ GIDE, *Journals*, July 13, 1930, tr. Justin O'Brien.

6. The marble keeps merely a cold and sad memory of a man who would else be forgotten. No man who needs a monument ever ought to have one. NATHANIEL HAWTHORNE, *English Note-Books*, Nov. 12, 1857.

7. Dust to dust, ashes to ashes, and the cremains to a memorial park. All this is supposed to maintain the dignity of death. Or is it the dignity of undertakers? JOSEPH WOOD KRUTCH, title essay, 1, *If You Don't Mind My Saying So* (1964).

8. A cemetery saddens us because it is the only place of the world in which we do not meet our dead again. FRANÇOIS MAURIAC, "All Souls' Day," *Cain, Where Is Your Brother?* (1962).

9. Heap not on this mound / Roses that she loved so well; / Why bewilder her with roses, / That she cannot see or smell? EDNA ST. VINCENT MILLAY, "Epitaph," *Second April* (1921).

## 102. BUSINESS AND COMMERCE

See also 18. Advertising; 25. Agents; 68. Banking; 103. Buying and Selling; 106. Capitalism; 275. Economics; 313. Executives; 487. Insurance; 501. Investment; 732. Profiteering

1. Live together like brothers and do business like strangers. ARABIC PROVERB.

2. Time is the measure of business. FRANCIS BACON, "Of Dispatch," *Essays* (1625).

3. For the merchant, even honesty is a financial speculation. CHARLES BAUDELAIRE, *Intimate Journals* (1887), 97, tr. Christopher Isherwood.

4. That's the definition of business, something goes through, something else doesn't. Make use of one, forget the other. HENRY BECQUE, *Woman of Paris* (1885), 2, tr. Jacques Barzun.

5. No matter who reigns, the merchant reigns. HENRY WARD BEECHER, *Proverbs from Plymouth Pulpit* (1887).

6. The commerce of the world is conducted by the strong, and usually it operates against the weak. HENRY WARD BEECHER, *Proverbs from Plymouth Pulpit* (1887).

7. Corporation, n. An ingenious device for obtaining individual profit without individual responsibility. AMBROSE BIERCE, *The Devil's Dictionary* (1881–1911).

8. Dispatch is the soul of business, and nothing contributes more to Dispatch than Method. LORD CHESTERFIELD, *Letters to His Son*, Feb. 5, 1750.

9. Fuel is not sold in a forest, nor fish on a lake. CHINESE PROVERB.

10. The business of America is business. CALVIN COOLIDGE, address, Society of Newspaper Editors, Jan. 17, 1925.

11. Here's the rule for bargains: "Do other men, for they would do you." That's the true business precept. CHARLES DICKENS, *Martin Chuzzlewit* (1844), 11.

12. Keep thy shop, and thy shop will keep thee. ENGLISH PROVERB.

13. Light gains make heavy purses. ENGLISH PROVERB.

14. The customer is an object to be manipulated, not a concrete person whose aims the businessman is interested to satisfy. ERICH FROMM, *Escape from Freedom* (1941), 4.

15. Boldness in business is the first, second, and third thing. THOMAS FULLER, M.D., *Gnomologia* (1732), 1006.

16. The usual trade and commerce is cheating all round by consent. THOMAS FULLER, M.D., *Gnomologia* (1732), 4814.

17. Production only fills a void that it has itself created. JOHN KENNETH GALBRAITH, *The Affluent Society* (1958), 11.1.

18. It is difficult but not impossible to conduct strictly honest business. What is true is that honesty is incompatible with the amassing of a large fortune. MOHANDAS K. GANDHI, *Non-Violence in Peace and War* (1948), 2.127.

19. Everything which is properly *business* we must keep carefully separate from *life*. Business requires earnestness and method; life must have a freer handling. GOETHE, *Elective Affinities* (1809), 4.

20. Honour sinks where commerce long prevails. OLIVER GOLDSMITH, *The Traveller* (1765), 91.

21. Commerce is the art of exploiting the need or desire someone has for something. EDMOND and JULES DE GONCOURT, *Journal*, July 1864.

22. American society has tried so hard and so ably to defend the practice and theory of production for profit and not primarily for use that now it has succeeded in making its jobs and products profitable and useless. PAUL GOODMAN, *Growing Up Absurd* (1960), 1.1.

23. Merchants have no country. The mere spot they stand on does not constitute so strong an attachment as that from which they draw their gains. THOMAS JEFFERSON, letter to Horatio G. Spafford, March 17, 1814.

24. Ours is not so much an age of vulgarity as of vulgarization; everything is tampered with or touched up, or adulterated or

watered down, in an effort to make it palatable, in an effort to make it pay. LOUIS KRONENBERGER, "The Spirit of the Age," *Company Manners* (1954).

25. It is true that America produces and consumes more cars, soap, and bathtubs than any other nation, but we live among these objects rather than by them. MARY MC CARTHY, "America the Beautiful: The Humanist in the Bathtub," *On the Contrary* (1961).

26. A corporation is an artificial being, invisible, intangible, and existing only in contemplation of law. JOHN MARSHALL, *Trustees of Dartmouth College v. Woodward* (1819).

27. It takes no more actual sagacity to carry on the everyday hawking and haggling of the world, or to ladle out its normal doses of bad medicine and worse law, than it takes to operate a taxicab or fry a pan of fish. H. L. MENCKEN, "The Feminine Mind," *In Defense of Women* (1922).

28. A man in business must put up many affronts if he loves his own quiet. WILLIAM PENN, *Some Fruits of Solitude* (1693), 1.182.

29. A man who is always ready to believe what is told him will never do well, especially a businessman. PETRONIUS, *Satyricon* (1st c.), tr. M. Heseltine.

30. If you can build a business up big enough, it's respectable. WILL ROGERS, *The Autobiography of Will Rogers* (1949), 13.

31. There are two fools in every market: one asks too little, one asks too much. RUSSIAN PROVERB.

32. People of the same trade seldom meet together, even for merriment and diversion, but the conversation ends in a conspiracy against the public, or in some contrivance to raise prices. ADAM SMITH, *The Wealth of Nations* (1776), 1.10.

33. You never expected justice from a company, did you? They have neither a soul to lose, nor a body to kick. SYDNEY SMITH, quoted in Lady S. Holland's *Memoir* (1855), v. 1.11.

34. Perpetual devotion to what a man calls his business, is only to be sustained by perpetual neglect of many other things. ROBERT LOUIS STEVENSON, "An Apology for Idlers," *Virginibus Puerisque* (1881).

35. In democracies, nothing is more great or more brilliant than commerce: it attracts the attention of the public, and fills the imagination of the multitude; all energetic passions are directed towards it. ALEXIS DE TOCQUEVILLE, *Democracy in America* (1835–39), 2.2.19.

36. The bonus is really one of the great give-aways in business enterprise. It is the annual salve applied to the conscience of the rich and the wounds of the poor. E. B. WHITE, "Control," *One Man's Meat* (1944).

37. What is good for the country is good for General Motors, and vice versa. CHARLES E. WILSON, news reports, Jan. 23, 1953.

38. Big business is not dangerous because it is big, but because its bigness is an unwholesome inflation created by privileges and exemptions which it ought not to enjoy. WOODROW WILSON, acceptance speech, Democratic National Convention, July 7, 1912.

39. The world is too much with us; late and soon, / Getting and spending, we lay waste our powers: / Little we see in Nature that is ours; / We have given our hearts away, a sordid boon! WILLIAM WORDSWORTH, "The World Is Too Much With Us" (1807).

## BUSYNESS

See 10. Activity

## 103. BUYING AND SELLING

See also 8. Acquisition; 18. Advertising; 25. Agents; 102. Business and Commerce; 106. Capitalism; 740. Property

1. Men go shopping just as men go out fishing or hunting, to see how large a fish may be caught with the smallest hook. HENRY WARD BEECHER, *Proverbs from Plymouth Pulpit* (1887).

2. How many pretenses men that sell goods weave! What poor articles, with what a good face, do they palm off on their customers! HENRY WARD BEECHER, *Proverbs from Plymouth Pulpit* (1887).

3. A false balance is abomination to the Lord: but a just weight is his delight. *Bible*, Proverbs 11:1.

4. Auctioneer, n. The man who proclaims with a hammer that he has picked a pocket with his tongue. AMBROSE BIERCE, *The Devil's Dictionary* (1881–1911).

5. A man without a smiling face must not open a shop. CHINESE PROVERB.

6. He that speaks ill of the mare will buy her. BENJAMIN FRANKLIN, *Poor Richard's Almanack* (1732–57).

7. Man does not only sell commodities, he sells himself and feels himself to be a commodity. ERICH FROMM, *Escape from Freedom* (1941), 4.

8. He who findeth fault meaneth to buy. THOMAS FULLER, M.D., *Gnomologia* (1732), 2383.

9. The urge to consume is fathered by the value system which emphasizes the ability of the society to produce. JOHN KENNETH GALBRAITH, *The Affluent Society* (1958), 11.2.

10. Try novelties for salesman's bait, / For novelty wins everyone. GOETHE, "Martha's Garden," *Faust: Part I* (1808), tr. Philip Wayne.

11. Looking at bargains from a purely commercial point of view, someone is always cheated, but looked at with the simple eye both seller and buyer always win. DAVID GRAYSON, *Adventures in Contentment* (1907), 2.

12. A miser and a liar bargain quickly. GREEK PROVERB.

13. The buyer needs a hundred eyes, the seller not one. GEORGE HERBERT, *Jacula Prudentum* (1651).

14. Pleasing ware is half sold. GEORGE HERBERT, *Jacula Prudentum* (1651).

15. When a man is trying to sell you something, don't imagine he is that polite all the time. EDGAR WATSON HOWE, *Country Town Sayings* (1911).

16. He would sell even his share of the sun. ITALIAN PROVERB.

17. Never buy what you do not want because it is cheap; it will be dear [costly] to you. THOMAS JEFFERSON, letter to Thomas Jefferson Smith, Feb. 21, 1825.

18. Ours is the country where, in order to sell your product, you don't so much point out its merits as you first work like hell to sell yourself. LOUIS KRONENBERGER, *Company Manners* (1954), 3.3.

19. "Scorn not the common man," says the age of abundance. "He may have no soul; his personality may be exactly the same as his neighbor's; and he may not produce anything worth having. But thank God, he consumes." JOSEPH WOOD KRUTCH, "The Condition Called Prosperity," *Human Nature and the Human Condition* (1959).

20. If you don't want prosperity to falter, then Buy, Buy, Buy—on credit, of course. In other words, the surest way of bringing on a rainy day is to prepare for it. JOSEPH WOOD KRUTCH, "The Twentieth Century: Dawn or Twilight?" *Human Nature and the Human Condition* (1959).

21. The consumer today is the victim of the manufacturer who launches on him a regiment of products for which he must make room in his soul. MARY MC CARTHY, "America the Beautiful: The Humanist in the Bathtub," *On the Contrary* (1961).

22. When producers want to know what the public wants, they graph it as curves. When they want to tell the public what to get, they say it in curves. MARSHALL MC LUHAN, "Eye Appeal," *The Mechanical Bride* (1951).

23. Production goes up and up because high pressure advertising and salesmanship constantly create new needs that must be satisfied: this is *Admass*—a consumer's race with donkeys chasing an electric carrot. J. B. PRIESTLEY, "The Writer in a Changing Society," *Thoughts in the Wilderness* (1957).

24. Today the future occupation of all moppets is to be skilled consumers. DAVID RIESMAN, "A Jury of Their Peers," *The Lonely Crowd* (1950).

25. Cheat me in price, but not in the goods I purchase. SPANISH PROVERB.

26. Forgive us for frantic buying and selling; for advertising the unnecessary and coveting the extravagant, and calling it good business when it is not good for you. UNITED PRESBYTERIAN CHURCH, *Litany for Holy Communion* (1968).

27. Conspicuous consumption of valuable goods is a means of reputability to the gentleman of leisure. THORSTEIN VEBLEN, *The Theory of the Leisure Class* (1899), 4.

# C

## CALAMITY

See 17. Adversity

## 104. CALIFORNIA

1. California, that advance post of our

civilisation, with its huge aircraft factories, TV and film studios, automobile way of life . . . , its flavourless cosmopolitanism, its charlatan philosophies and religions, its lack of anything old and well-tried, rooted in tradition and character. J. B. PRIESTLEY, "They Come from Inner Space," *Thoughts in the Wilderness* (1957).

### CALMNESS

**See 159. Composure; 982. Tranquility**

### CALUMNY

**See 898. Slander**

### 105. CANADA

1. Geography has made us [America and Canada] neighbors. History has made us friends. Economics has made us partners. And necessity has made us allies. Those whom nature hath so joined together, let no man put asunder. JOHN F. KENNEDY, address to Canadian Parliament, Ottawa, May 17, 1961.

### CANDOR

**See 360. Frankness**

### 106. CAPITALISM

**See also 102. Business and Commerce; 103. Buying and Selling; 710. Possession; 732. Profiteering; 740. Property**

1. There is a good deal of solemn cant about the common interests of capital and labor. As matters stand, their only common interest is that of cutting each other's throat. BROOKS ATKINSON, "September 7," *Once Around the Sun* (1951).

2. One beats the bush, another catches the bird. GERMAN PROVERB.

3. If you mean by capitalism the God-given right of a few big corporations to make all the decisions that will affect millions of workers and consumers and to exclude everyone else from discussing and examining those decisions, then the unions are threatening capitalism. MAX LERNER, "A Look at the Books and a Share of the Pie," *Actions and Passions* (1949).

4. It was all prices to them: they never looked at it: why should they look at the land? they were Empire Builders: it was all in the bid and the asked and the ink on their books. ARCHIBALD MAC LEISH, "Wildwest," *Collected Poems, 1917–1952* (1952).

5. You show me a capitalist, I'll show you a bloodsucker. MALCOLM X, *Malcolm X Speaks* (1965), 10.

6. Landlords, like all other men, love to reap where they never sowed. KARL MARX, "First Manuscript" (1884), *Early Writings*, ed. T. B. Bottomore.

7. The trouble with the profit system has always been that it was highly unprofitable to most people. E. B. WHITE, "Control," *One Man's Meat* (1944).

### CAPITAL PUNISHMENT

**See 761. Punishment, Capital**

### 107. CAPTIVITY

**See also 729. Prison; 882. Servitude**

1. Fetters of gold are still fetters, and silken cords pinch. ENGLISH PROVERB.

2. The narrower the cage, the sweeter the liberty. GERMAN PROVERB.

3. A cat pent up becomes a lion. ITALIAN PROVERB.

4. If men and women are in chains, anywhere in the world, then freedom is endangered everywhere. JOHN F. KENNEDY, campaign statement, Washington, D.C., Pulaski Day, Oct. 2, 1960.

5. I don't want the cheese, I just want to get out of the trap. LATIN AMERICAN PROVERB.

6. Familiarize yourself with the chains of bondage and you prepare your own limbs to wear them. ABRAHAM LINCOLN, speech, Edwardsville, Ill., Sept. 11, 1858.

7. A deer with a chain of gold, if she escape, will run off to the forest to eat grass. MALAY PROVERB.

8. Man is born free; and everywhere he is in chains. ROUSSEAU, *The Social Contract* (1762), 1.1, tr. G. D. H. Cole.

9. He who is conceived in a cage / yearns for the cage. YEVGENY YEVTUSHENKO,

"Monologue of a Blue Fox on an Alaskan Animal Farm," quoted in *The New York Times*, Jan. 18, 1968.

### CARD-PLAYING

See 367. Gambling

### CAREFULNESS

See 110. Cautiousness; 722. Preparedness; 749. Prudence

### CATHOLICISM

See 123. Christianity

### CATS

See 41. Animals

## 108. CAUSE AND EFFECT

See also 114. Chance; 173. Consequences; 238. Destiny; 809. Retribution

1. Take away the cause, and the effect ceases; what the eye ne'er sees, the heart ne'er rues. CERVANTES, *Don Quixote* (1605–15), 2.4.67, tr. Peter Motteux and John Ozell.

2. The secret of the world is the tie between person and event. Person makes event and event person. EMERSON, "Fate," *The Conduct of Life* (1860).

3. Shallow men believe in luck. . . . Strong men believe in cause and effect. EMERSON, "Worship," *The Conduct of Life* (1860).

4. Nothing comes from nothing. LUCRETIUS, *On the Nature of Things* (1st c. B.C.), 1.

5. Every why hath a wherefore. SHAKESPEARE, *The Comedy of Errors* (1592–93), 2.2.45.

6. Our least deed, like the young of the land crab, wends its way to the sea of cause and effect as soon as born, and makes a drop there to eternity. THOREAU, *Journal*, March 14, 1838.

7. There's no limit to how complicated things can get, on account of one thing always leading to another. E. B. WHITE, title chapter, *Quo Vadimus?* (1939).

## 109. CAUSES

See also 443. Ideology; 564. Mass Movements; 667. Partisanship

1. Obstinacy in a bad cause is but constancy in a good. SIR THOMAS BROWNE, *Religio Medici* (1642), 1.

2. When great causes are on the move in the world, stirring all men's souls, drawing them from their firesides, casting aside comfort, wealth and the pursuit of happiness in response to impulses at once awe-striking and irresistible, we learn that we are spirits, not animals. SIR WINSTON CHURCHILL, radio broadcast, June 16, 1941.

3. If a cause be good, the most violent attack of its enemies will not injure it so much as an injudicious defense of it by its friends. CHARLES CALEB COLTON, *Lacon* (1825), 1.475.

4. A just cause is not ruined by a few mistakes. DOSTOEVSKY, "Critical Articles: Introduction," *Polnoye Sobraniye Sochinyeni* (*Complete Collected Works*, 1895), v. 9.

5. The best cause requires a good pleader. DUTCH PROVERB.

6. Those who serve the greater cause may make the cause serve them. T. S. ELIOT, *Murder in the Cathedral* (1935), 1.

7. Those whose cause is just will never lack / good arguments. EURIPIDES, *Hecuba* (c. 425 B.C.), tr. William Arrowsmith.

8. A good cause and a good tongue: and yet money must carry it. THOMAS FULLER, M.D., *Gnomologia* (1732), 139.

9. A good cause makes a stout heart and a strong arm. THOMAS FULLER, M.D., *Gnomologia* (1732), 140.

10. He that hath the worst cause makes the most noise. THOMAS FULLER, M.D., *Gnomologia* (1732), 2153.

11. Truth never damages a cause that is just. MOHANDAS K. GANDHI, *Non-Violence in Peace and War* (1948), 2.162.

12. Faith in a holy cause is to a considerable extent a substitute for the lost faith in ourselves. ERIC HOFFER, *The True Believer* (1951), 1.2.8.

13. We can be satisfied with moderate confidence in ourselves and with a moderately good opinion of ourselves, but the faith we have in a holy cause has to be extravagant and uncompromising. ERIC HOFFER, *The Ordeal of Change* (1964), 1.

14. It is characteristic of all movements and crusades that the psychopathic element rises to the top. ROBERT LINDNER, "Political Creed and Character," *Must You Conform?* (1956).

15. In a just cause the weak will beat the strong. SOPHOCLES, *Oedipus at Colonus* (401 B.C.), tr. Robert Fitzgerald.

## 110. CAUTIOUSNESS

**See also 749. Prudence**

1. He that observeth the wind shall not sow; and he that regardeth the clouds shall not reap. *Bible*, Ecclesiastes 11:4.

2. When a man feels the difficulty of doing, can he be other than cautious and slow in speaking? CONFUCIUS, *Analects* (6th c. B.C.), 12.3, tr. James Legge.

3. He that will not sail till all dangers are over must never put to sea. THOMAS FULLER, M.D., *Gnomologia* (1732), 2353.

4. Avoiding danger is no safer in the long run than outright exposure. The fearful are caught as often as the bold. HELEN KELLER, *Let Us Have Faith* (1940).

5. Fear to let fall a drop and you spill a lot. MALAY PROVERB.

6. The torment of precautions often exceeds the dangers to be avoided. It is sometimes better to abandon one's self to destiny. NAPOLEON I, *Maxims* (1804–15).

7. Measure a thousand times and cut once. TURKISH PROVERB.

## CELEBRITY

**See 330. Fame**

## CELIBACY

**See 120. Chastity; 595. Monasticism**

## 111. CENSORSHIP

**See also 725. Press, Freedom of the; 817. Rights**

1. As we see censorship it is a stupid giant traffic policeman answering "Yes" to "Am I my brother's copper?" He guards a one-way street and his semaphore has four signs, all marked "STOP." FRANKLIN P. ADAMS, *Nods and Becks* (1944).

2. We are willing enough to praise freedom when she is safely tucked away in the past and cannot be a nuisance. In the present, amidst dangers whose outcome we cannot foresee, we get nervous about her, and admit censorship. E. M. FORSTER, "The Tercentenary of the 'Areopagitica,'" *Two Cheers for Democracy* (1951).

3. Where there is official censorship it is a sign that speech is serious. Where there is none, it is pretty certain that the official spokesmen have all the loud-speakers. PAUL GOODMAN, *Growing Up Absurd* (1960), 2.2.

4. Persons who undertake to pry into, or cleanse out all the filth of a common sewer, either cannot have very nice noses, or will soon lose them. WILLIAM HAZLITT, "On the Clerical Character," *Political Essays* (1819).

5. No government ought to be without censors; and where the press is free, no one ever will. THOMAS JEFFERSON, letter to George Washington, Sept. 9, 1792.

6. A respectable minority is useful as censors. THOMAS JEFFERSON, letter to Joel Barlow, May 3, 1802.

7. The problem of freedom in America is that of maintaining a competition of ideas, and you do not achieve that by silencing one brand of idea. MAX LERNER, "The Muzzling of the Movies," *Actions and Passions* (1949).

8. Men in earnest have no time to waste / In patching fig-leaves for the naked truth. JAMES RUSSELL LOWELL, "A Glance Behind the Curtain" (1843).

9. Censorship may be useful for the preservation of morality, but can never be so for its restoration. ROUSSEAU, *The Social Contract* (1762), 4.7, tr. G. D. H. Cole.

10. Assassination is the extreme form of censorship. GEORGE BERNARD SHAW, *The Rejected Statement*, 1.

## CENSURE

**See 203. Criticism; 797. Reproof**

## 112. CEREMONY

**See also 194. Courtesy; 559. Manners; 743. Propriety**

1. Ritualism, n. A Dutch Garden of God where He may walk in rectilinear freedom,

keeping off the grass. AMBROSE BIERCE, *The Devil's Dictionary* (1881–1911).

2. Ceremony is the smoke of friendship. CHINESE PROVERB.

3. Friendship should be surrounded with ceremonies and respects, and not crushed into corners. EMERSON, "Behavior," *The Conduct of Life* (1860).

4. Feasts must be solemn and rare, or else they cease to be feasts. ALDOUS HUXLEY, *Do What You Will* (1929).

5. It is superstition to put one's hope in formalities; but it is pride to be unwilling to submit to them. PASCAL, *Pensées* (1670), 249, tr. W. F. Trotter.

6. Ceremony was but devised at first / To set a gloss on faint deeds, hollow welcomes, / Recanting goodness, sorry ere 'tis shown; / But where there is true friendship, there needs none. SHAKESPEARE, *Timon of Athens* (1607–08), 1.2.15.

## 113. CERTAINTY

**See also 262. Dogmatism; 850. Security; 998. Uncertainty**

1. Oh! let us never, never doubt / What nobody is sure about! HILAIRE BELLOC, "The Microbe," *More Beasts for Worse Children* (1897).

2. There is one thing certain, namely, that we can have nothing certain; therefore it is not certain that we can have nothing certain. SAMUEL BUTLER (d. 1902), "First Principles," *Note-Books* (1912).

3. Life is the art of drawing sufficient conclusions from insufficient premises. SAMUEL BUTLER (d. 1902), "Lord, What Is Man?" *Note-Books* (1912).

4. To have his path made clear for him is the aspiration of every human being in our beclouded and tempestuous existence. JOSEPH CONRAD, *The Mirror of the Sea* (1906), 27.

5. We can be absolutely certain only about things we do not understand. ERIC HOFFER, *The True Believer* (1951), 3.13.57.

6. Certainty generally is illusion, and repose is not the destiny of man. OLIVER WENDELL HOLMES, JR., speech, Boston University School of Law, Jan. 8, 1897.

7. A reasonable probability is the only certainty. EDGAR WATSON HOWE, *Country Town Sayings* (1911).

8. Every area of trouble gives out a ray of hope, and the one unchangeable certainty is that nothing is certain or unchangeable. JOHN F. KENNEDY, State of the Union Message, Jan. 11, 1962.

9. There is only one thing about which I am certain, and this is that there is very little about which one can be certain. W. SOMERSET MAUGHAM, *The Summing Up* (1938), 5.

10. It is the dull man who is always sure, and the sure man who is always dull. The more a man dreams, the less he believes. H. L. MENCKEN, *Prejudices: Second Series* (1920), 1.

11. Confidence is a plant of slow growth in an aged bosom; youth is the season of credulity. WILLIAM PITT THE ELDER, speech in the House of Commons, Jan. 14, 1766.

12. Certainties are arrived at only on foot. ANTONIO PORCHIA, *Voces* (1968), tr. W. S. Merwin.

13. He who knows nothing doubts nothing. SPANISH PROVERB.

## 114. CHANCE

**See also 127. Circumstance; 337. Fate; 358. Fortune**

1. Accident counts for much in companionship as in marriage. HENRY ADAMS, *The Education of Henry Adams* (1907), 4.

2. Life is full of chances and changes, and the most prosperous of men may in the evening of his days meet with great misfortunes. ARISTOTLE, *Nicomachean Ethics* (4th c. B.C.), 1.9, tr. J. A. K. Thomson.

3. They, believe me, who await / No gifts from chance, have conquered fate. MATTHEW ARNOLD, "Resignation," *The Strayed Reveller, and Other Poems* (1849).

4. What is the use of working out chances? There are no chances against God. GEORGES BERNANOS, *The Diary of a Country Priest* (1936), 1, tr. Pamela Morris.

5. We cannot bear to regard ourselves simply as playthings of blind chance; we cannot admit to feeling ourselves abandoned. UGO BETTI, *Struggle Till Dawn* (1949), 2, tr. G. H. McWilliam.

6. Chance, to be precise, is a leap, provides a leap out of reach of one's own grasp of oneself. JOHN CAGE, "45′ for a Speaker," *Silence* (1961).

7. They who lose today may win tomorrow. CERVANTES, *Don Quixote* (1605–15), 1.1.7, tr. Peter Motteux and John Ozell.

8. It is not Justice the servant of men, but accident, hazard, Fortune—the ally of patient Time—that holds an even and scrupulous balance. JOSEPH CONRAD, *Lord Jim* (1900), 34.

9. We are ruled by chance but never have enough patience to accept its despotism. EDWARD DAHLBERG, "On Futility," *Reasons of the Heart* (1965).

10. Enjoy yourself, drink, call the life you live today / your own, but only that, the rest belongs to chance. EURIPIDES, *Alcestis* (438 B.C.), tr. Richmond Lattimore.

11. A wise man turns chance into good fortune. THOMAS FULLER, M.D., *Gnomologia* (1732), 475.

12. There is an ambush everywhere from the army of accidents; therefore the rider of life runs with loosened reins. HĀFIZ, ghazals from the *Divan* (14th c.), 84, tr. Justin Huntly McCarthy.

13. Fortune and humour govern the world. LA ROCHEFOUCAULD, *Maxims* (1665), tr. Kenneth Pratt.

14. There is many a slip 'twixt the cup and the lip. PALLADAS (fl. A.D. 400), in *The Greek Anthology* (7th c. B.C.–10th c. A.D.), 10.32.

15. Chance gives rise to thoughts, and chance removes them; no art can keep or acquire them. PASCAL, *Pensées* (1670), 370, tr. W. F. Trotter.

16. What the reason of the ant laboriously drags into a heap, the wind of accident will collect in one breath. SCHILLER, *Fiesco* (1783), 2.4.

17. Every possession and every happiness is but lent by chance for an uncertain time, and may therefore be demanded back the next hour. SCHOPENHAUER, *The World as Will and Idea* (1819), 1.

18. Chance makes a football of man's life. SENECA, *Letters to Lucilius* (1st c.), 16.5, tr. E. Phillips Barker.

19. Why should man fear since chance is all in all / for him, and he can clearly foreknow nothing? / Best to live lightly, as one can, unthinkingly. SOPHOCLES, *Oedipus the King* (c. 430 B.C.), tr. David Grene.

## 115. CHANGE

**See also 116. Changelessness; 176. Consistency; 347. Flexibility; 462. Inconsistency; 477. Innovation; 632. Novelty; 647. Open-mindedness; 735. Progress; 794. Repetition; 983. Transience**

1. For what wears out the life of mortal men? / 'Tis that from change to change their being rolls; / 'Tis that repeated shocks, again, again, / Exhaust the energy of strongest souls / And numb the elastic powers. MATTHEW ARNOLD, "The Scholar-Gipsy," *Poems* (1853).

2. The absurd man is he who never changes. AUGUSTE BARTHÉLÉMY, *Ma justification* (1830–31).

3. Great cultural changes begin in affectation and end in routine. JACQUES BARZUN, *The House of Intellect* (1959).

4. Each new season grows from the leftovers from the past. That is the essence of change, and change is the basic law. HAL BORLAND, "Autumn's Clutter—November 3," *Sundial of the Seasons* (1964).

5. The mill wheel turns, it turns forever, / Though what is uppermost remains not so. BERTOLT BRECHT, *Roundheads and Peakheads* (1933), 8, tr. N. Goold-Verschoyle.

6. Weep not that the world changes—did it keep / A stable, changeless state, 'twere cause indeed to weep. WILLIAM CULLEN BRYANT, "Mutation" (1824).

7. The interval between the decay of the old and the formation and the establishment of the new, constitutes a period of transition, which must always necessarily be one of uncertainty, confusion, error, and wild and fierce fanaticism. JOHN C. CALHOUN, *A Disquisition on Government* (1850).

8. To remain young one must change. The perpetual campus hero is not a young man but an old boy. ALEXANDER CHASE, *Perspectives* (1966).

9. The world's a scene of changes, and to be / Constant, in Nature were inconstancy. ABRAHAM COWLEY, "Inconstancy" (1647).

10. Change as change is mere flux and lapse; it insults intelligence. Genuinely to know is to grasp a permanent end that real-

izes itself through changes. JOHN DEWEY, "The Influence of Darwinism on Philosophy" (1909).

11. Life is not a static thing. The only people who do not change their minds are incompetents in asylums, who can't, and those in cemeteries. EVERETT M. DIRKSEN, press conference, Washington, D.C., Jan. 1, 1965.

12. In the life of one man, never / The same time returns. T. S. ELIOT, *Murder in the Cathedral* (1935), 1.

13. We cannot remain consistent with the world save by growing inconsistent with our past selves. HAVELOCK ELLIS, preface, *The Dance of Life* (1923).

14. All is change; all yields its place and goes. EURIPIDES, *Heracles* (c. 422 B.C.), tr. William Arrowsmith.

15. There is something in the pang of change / More than the heart can bear, / Unhappiness remembering happiness. EURIPIDES, *Iphigenia in Tauris* (c. 414–12 B.C.), tr. Witter Bynner.

16. All changes, even the most longed for, have their melancholy; for what we leave behind us is a part of ourselves; we must die to one life before we can enter into another! ANATOLE FRANCE, *The Crime of Sylvestre Bonnard* (1881), 2, tr. Lafcadio Hearn.

17. Most of the change we think we see in life / Is due to truths being in and out of favor. ROBERT FROST, "The Black Cottage," *North of Boston* (1914).

18. Through loyalty to the past, our mind refuses to realize that tomorrow's joy is possible only if today's makes way for it; that each wave owes the beauty of its line only to the withdrawal of the preceding one. ANDRÉ GIDE, *Journals*, 1928, tr. Justin O'Brien.

19. What is more enthralling to the human mind than this splendid, boundless, colored mutability!—life in the making? DAVID GRAYSON, *Adventures in Contentment* (1907), 9.

20. We accept the verdict of the past until the need for change cries out loudly enough to force upon us a choice between the comforts of further inertia and the irksomeness of action. LEARNED HAND, address, Supreme Judicial Court of Massachusetts, Nov. 21, 1942.

21. You cannot step twice into the same river, for other waters are continually flowing in. HERACLITUS, *Fragments* (c. 500 B.C.), 21, tr. Philip Wheelwright.

22. Nothing is permanent but change. HERACLITUS (fl. c. 500 B.C.), quoted in Diogenes Laertius' *Lives and Opinions of Eminent Philosophers* (3rd c. A.D.).

23. Even in slight things the experience of the new is rarely without some stirring of foreboding. ERIC HOFFER, *The Ordeal of Change* (1964), 1.

24. There is a certain relief in change, even though it be from bad to worse. WASHINGTON IRVING, "To the Reader," *Tales of a Traveller* (1824).

25. The more things change, the more they remain the same. ALPHONSE KARR, *Les Guêpes*, January 1849.

26. Change is the law of life. And those who look only to the past or the present are certain to miss the future. JOHN F. KENNEDY, address, Frankfurt, West Germany, June 25, 1963.

27. Progress is a nice word. But change is its motivator. And change has its enemies. ROBERT F. KENNEDY, "Federal Power and Local Poverty," *The Pursuit of Justice* (1964).

28. For young people today things move so *fast* there is no problem of adjustment. Before you can adjust to A, B has appeared leading C by the hand, and with D in the distance. LOUIS KRONENBERGER, "Reflections and Complaints of Late Middle Age," *The Cart and the Horse* (1964), 3.

29. Whenever a thing changes and quits its proper limits, this change is at once the death of that which was before. LUCRETIUS, *On the Nature of Things* (1st c. B.C.), 3, tr. H. A. J. Munro.

30. Continuity in everything is unpleasant. Cold is agreeable, that we may get warm. PASCAL, *Pensées* (1670), 355, tr. W. F. Trotter.

31. Time, in the turning-over of days, works change for better or worse. PINDAR, *Odes* (5th c. B.C.), Isthmia 3, tr. Richmond Lattimore.

32. The pace of events is moving so fast that unless we can find some way to keep our sights on tomorrow, we cannot expect to be in touch with today. DEAN RUSK, *Time*, Dec. 6, 1963.

33. "Change" is scientific, "progress" is ethical; change is indubitable, whereas

progress is a matter of controversy. BERTRAND RUSSELL, "Philosophy and Politics," *Unpopular Essays* (1950).

34. Man's yesterday may ne'er be like his morrow; / Nought may endure but Mutability. SHELLEY, "Mutability" (1816).

35. The felt unreliability of human experience brought about by the inhuman acceleration of historical change has led every sensitive modern mind to the recording of some kind of nausea, of intellectual vertigo. SUSAN SONTAG, "The Anthropologist as Hero," *Against Interpretation* (1961).

36. When old words die out on the tongue, new melodies break forth from the heart; and where the old tracks are lost, new country is revealed with its wonders. RABINDRANATH TAGORE, *Gitanjali* (1912), 37.

37. The old order changeth yielding place to new, / And God fulfills himself in many ways, / Lest one good custom should corrupt the world. ALFRED, LORD TENNYSON, "The Passing of Arthur," *Idylls of the King* (1869).

38. In every age of well-marked transition there is the pattern of habitual dumb practice and emotion which is passing, and there is oncoming a new complex of habit. ALFRED NORTH WHITEHEAD, *Adventures of Ideas* (1933), 1.

39. There is a time for departure even when there's no certain place to go. TENNESSEE WILLIAMS, *Camino Real* (1953), 8.

## 116. CHANGELESSNESS

See also 115. Change

1. Wood may remain ten years in the water, but it will never become a crocodile. CONGOLESE PROVERB.

2. It is a long lane that has no turning. ENGLISH PROVERB.

3. Happiness is never really so welcome as changelessness. GRAHAM GREENE, *The Heart of the Matter* (1948), 3.3.

4. Men very seldom change; try though we will, beneath the shifts of exterior doctrine, our hearts so often remain what they were. MURRAY KEMPTON, "O'er Moor and Fen," *Part of Our Time* (1955).

5. Everything that has been is eternal: the sea will wash it up again. NIETZSCHE, *The Will to Power* (1888), 1065, tr. Anthony M. Ludovici.

6. Me this unchartered freedom tires; / I feel the weight of chance-desires: / My hopes no more must change their name, / I long for a repose that ever is the same. WILLIAM WORDSWORTH, "Ode to Duty" (1805).

## CHAOS

See 255. Disorder

## 117. CHARACTER

See also 442. Identity; 489. Integrity; 680. Personality

1. Character is tested by true sentiments more than by conduct. A man is seldom better than his word. LORD ACTON, postscript, letter to Mandell Creighton, April 5, 1887.

2. Happiness is not the end of life: character is. HENRY WARD BEECHER, *Life Thoughts* (1858).

3. As he thinketh in his heart, so is he. *Bible*, Proverbs 23:7.

4. When a person lacks character, he is badly in need of a method. ALBERT CAMUS, *The Fall* (1956).

5. The more peculiarly his own a man's character is, the better it fits him. CICERO, *De Officiis* (44 B.C.), 1.31.113.

6. I know sage, wormwood, and hyssop, but I can't smell character unless it stinks. EDWARD DAHLBERG, "On Human Nature," *Reasons of the Heart* (1965).

7. If you act, you show character; if you sit still, you show it; if you sleep [you show it]. EMERSON, *Journals* (1836).

8. Nature magically suits the man to his fortunes, by making these the fruit of his character. EMERSON, "Fate," *The Conduct of Life* (1860).

9. Men are what their mothers made them. EMERSON, "Fate," *The Conduct of Life* (1860).

10. People seem not to see that their opinion of the world is also a confession of character. EMERSON, "Worship," *The Conduct of Life* (1860).

11. As if they were our own handiwork, we place a high value on our characters. EPICURUS, "Vatican Sayings" (3rd c. B.C.), 15, in *Letters, Principal Doctrines, and Vatican Sayings*, tr. Russel M. Geer.

12. Old age and sickness bring out the es-

sential characteristics of a man. FELIX FRANKFURTER, *Felix Frankfurter Reminisces* (1960), 2.

13. Genius is formed in quiet, character in the stream of human life. GOETHE, *Torquato Tasso* (1790), 1.2.

14. A man's character is his guardian divinity. HERACLITUS, *Fragments* (c. 500 B.C.), 69, tr. Philip Wheelwright.

15. Character cannot be developed in ease and quiet. Only through experience of trial and suffering can the soul be strengthened, vision cleared, ambition inspired, and success achieved. HELEN KELLER, *Helen Keller's Journal* (1938).

16. Between ourselves and our real natures we interpose that wax figure of idealizations and selections which we call our character. WALTER LIPPMANN, "Some Necessary Iconoclasm," *A Preface to Politics* (1914).

17. A lost wife can be replaced, but the loss of character spells ruin. MALAY PROVERB.

18. Listen to a man's words and look at the pupil of his eye. How can a man conceal his character? MENCIUS, *Works* (4th–3rd c. B.C.), 4, tr. Charles A. Wong.

19. No man can climb out beyond the limitations of his own character. JOHN MORLEY, "Robespierre," *Critical Miscellanies* (1871–1908).

20. When the character's right, looks are a greater delight. OVID, *The Art of Beauty* (c. A.D. 8), tr. Rolfe Humphries.

21. Character is much easier kept than recovered. THOMAS PAINE, *The American Crisis* (1776–83), 13.

22. Character is inured habit. PLUTARCH, "The Education of Children," *Moralia* (c. A.D. 100), tr. Moses Hadas.

23. His own character is the arbiter of every one's fortune. PUBLILIUS SYRUS, *Moral Sayings* (1st c. B.C.), 283, tr. Darius Lyman.

24. The things that really move liking in human beings are the gnarled nodosities of character, vagrant humours, freaks of generosity, some little unextinguishable spark of the aboriginal savage, some little sweet savour of the old Adam. ALEXANDER SMITH, "On Vagabonds," *Dreamthorp* (1863).

25. Not on the stage alone, in the world also, a man's real character comes out best in his asides. ALEXANDER SMITH, "William Dunbar," *Dreamthorp* (1863).

26. Every cask smells of the wine it contains. SPANISH PROVERB.

27. No one is ignorant that our character and turn of mind are intimately connected with the water-closet. VOLTAIRE, "Slow Bellies," *Philosophical Dictionary* (1764).

28. Character begins to form at the first pinch of anxiety about ourselves. YEVGENY YEVTUSHENKO, "There's Something I Often Notice: (To M. Roshchin)," *The New Russian Poets: 1953 to 1966* (1966), tr. George Reavey.

29. The man that makes a character makes foes. EDWARD YOUNG, *To Mr. Pope* (1730), 1.28.

## 118. CHARITY

**See also 382. Gifts and Giving; 430. Humanitarianism; 517. Kindness; 548. Love; 977. Tolerance**

1. In necessary things, unity; in doubtful things, liberty; in all things, charity. RICHARD BAXTER (1615–1691), motto.

2. Then gently scan your brother man, / Still gentler sister woman; / Tho' they may gang a kennin wrang, / To step aside is human. ROBERT BURNS, "Address to the Unco Guid" (1787).

3. Did universal charity prevail, earth would be a heaven, and hell a fable. CHARLES CALEB COLTON, *Lacon* (1825), 1.160.

4. He that has no charity deserves no mercy. ENGLISH PROVERB.

5. Charity begins at home, but should not end there. THOMAS FULLER, M.D., *Gnomologia* (1732), 1085.

6. To think ill of mankind, and not wish ill to them, is perhaps the highest wisdom and virtue. WILLIAM HAZLITT, *Characteristics* (1823), 241.

7. I as little fear that God will damn a man that has charity, as I hope that the priests can save one who has not. ALEXANDER POPE, *Thoughts on Various Subjects* (1727).

8. In faith and hope the world will disagree, / But all mankind's concern is charity. ALEXANDER POPE, *An Essay on Man* (1733–34), 3.303.

9. The robbed that smiles steals something from the thief. SHAKESPEARE, *Othello* (1604–05), 1.3.208.

10. The silver ore of pure charity is an expensive article in the catalogue of a man's good qualities. RICHARD BRINSLEY SHERIDAN, *The School for Scandal* (1777), 5.2.

11. Charity and personal force are the only investments worth anything. WALT WHITMAN, "Song of Prudence," *Leaves of Grass* (1855–92).

## 119. CHARM

1. Charm: that quality in others of making us more satisfied with ourselves. HENRI FRÉDÉRIC AMIEL, *Journal* (1882–84).

2. It's [charm] a sort of bloom on a woman. If you have it, you don't need to have anything else; and if you don't have it, it doesn't much matter what else you have. J. M. BARRIE, *What Every Woman Knows* (1908), 1.

3. Charm is a glow within a woman that casts a most becoming light on others. JOHN MASON BROWN, *Vogue*, Nov. 15, 1956.

4. Corporeal charms may indeed gain admirers, but there must be mental ones to retain them. CHARLES CALEB COLTON, *Lacon* (1825), 2.96.

5. Charm is a product of the unexpected. JOSÉ MARTÍ, *Granos de oro: pensamientos seleccionados en las Obras de José Martí* (1942).

6. Charming people live up to the very edge of their charm, and behave just as outrageously as the world will let them. LOGAN PEARSALL SMITH, *Afterthoughts* (1931), 3.

7. A beauty is a woman you notice; a charmer is one who notices you. ADLAI STEVENSON, *The Stevenson Wit* (1966).

8. It's absurd to divide people into good and bad. People are either charming or tedious. OSCAR WILDE, *Lady Windermere's Fan* (1892).

9. All charming people, I fancy, are spoiled. It is the secret of their attraction. OSCAR WILDE, *The Portrait of Mr. W. H.* (1901).

## 120. CHASTITY

See also 595. Monasticism; 764. Purity; 859. Self-denial

1. Give me chastity and continence, but not just now. ST. AUGUSTINE, *Confessions* (5th c.), 8.7.

2. The essence of chastity is not the suppression of lust, but the total orientation of one's life towards a goal. DIETRICH BONHOEFFER, "Miscellaneous Thoughts," *Letters and Papers from Prison* (1953), tr. Eberhard Bethge.

3. Be warm, but pure; be amorous, but be chaste. BYRON, *English Bards and Scotch Reviewers* (1809).

4. Filth and old age, I'm sure you will agree, / Are powerful wardens upon chastity. CHAUCER, "The Wife of Bath's Tale," *The Canterbury Tales* (c. 1387–1400), tr. Nevill Coghill.

5. Chastity is not chastity in an old man, but a disability to be unchaste. JOHN DONNE, *Sermons*, No. 5, 1619.

6. Too chaste an adolescence makes for a dissolute old age. It is doubtless easier to give up something one has known than something one imagines. ANDRÉ GIDE, *Journals*, Jan. 21, 1929, tr. Justin O'Brien.

7. Chastity more rarely follows fear, or a resolution, or a vow, than it is the mere effect of lack of appetite and, sometimes even, of distaste. ANDRÉ GIDE, *Journals*, March 12, 1938, tr. Justin O'Brien.

8. A woman's chastity consists, like an onion, of a series of coats. NATHANIEL HAWTHORNE, *Journals*, March 16, 1854.

9. I will find you twenty lascivious turtles ere one chaste man. SHAKESPEARE, *The Merry Wives of Windsor* (1597), 2.1.82.

10. If you cannot be chaste, be cautious. SPANISH PROVERB.

11. The only chaste woman is the one who has not been asked. SPANISH PROVERB.

12. Chastity is a wealth that comes from the abundance of love. RABINDRANATH TAGORE, *Stray Birds* (1916), 73.

## CHEERFULNESS

See 390. Good Nature

## 121. CHILDREN

See also 64. Babies; 95. Boys; 215. Daughters; 332. Family; 383. Girls; 663. Parenthood; 909. Sons

1. Blessed be childhood, which brings down something of heaven into the midst of our rough earthliness. HENRI FRÉDÉRIC AMIEL, *Journal*, Jan. 26, 1868, tr. Mrs. Humphry Ward.

2. The life of children, as much as that of intemperate men, is wholly governed by their desires. ARISTOTLE, *Nicomachean Ethics* (4th c. B.C.), 3.12, tr. J. A. K. Thomson.

3. Children have never been very good at listening to their elders, but they have never failed to imitate them. JAMES BALDWIN, "Fifth Avenue, Uptown," *Nobody Knows My Name* (1961).

4. That energy which makes a child hard to manage is the energy which afterward makes him a manager of life. HENRY WARD BEECHER, *Proverbs from Plymouth Pulpit* (1887).

5. One always hopes that the children—that things will turn out better for them. That's what children are. UGO BETTI, *Goat Island* (1946), 3.2, ed. Gino Rizzo.

6. There is no end to the violations committed by children on children, quietly talking alone. ELIZABETH BOWEN, *The House in Paris* (1935), 1.2.

7. Childish fantasy, like the sheath over the bud, not only protects but curbs the terrible budding spirit, protects not only innocence from the world, but the world from the power of innocence. ELIZABETH BOWEN, *The Death of the Heart* (1938), 3.5.

8. Boys like romantic tales; but babies like realistic tales—because they find them romantic. G. K. CHESTERTON, "The Logic of Elfland," *Orthodoxy* (1908).

9. Who takes the child by the hand, takes the mother by the heart. DANISH PROVERB.

10. In the little world in which children have their existence, whosoever brings them up, there is nothing so finely perceived and so finely felt, as injustice. CHARLES DICKENS, *Great Expectations* (1860–61), 8.

11. There never was child so lovely but his mother was glad to get him asleep. EMERSON, *Journals*, 1836.

12. As soon as a child has left the room his strewn toys become affecting. EMERSON, *Journals*, 1839.

13. We find delight in the beauty and happiness of children that makes the heart too big for the body. EMERSON, "Illusions," *The Conduct of Life* (1860).

14. Children are poor men's riches. ENGLISH PROVERB.

15. How delicate the skin, how sweet the breath of children! EURIPIDES, *Medea* (431 B.C.), tr. Rex Warner.

16. That child whose mother has never smiled upon him is worthy neither of the table of the gods nor the couch of the goddesses. ANATOLE FRANCE, *The Crime of Sylvestre Bonnard* (1881), 1, tr. Lafcadio Hearn.

17. Children are completely egoistic; they feel their needs intensely and strive ruthlessly to satisfy them. SIGMUND FREUD, "Dreams of the Death of Beloved Persons," *The Interpretation of Dreams* (1899), tr. James Strachey.

18. Juvenile appraisals of other juveniles make up in clarity what they lack in charity. EDGAR Z. FRIEDENBERG, "Emotional Development in Adolescence," *The Vanishing Adolescent* (1959).

19. What children hear at home soon flies abroad. THOMAS FULLER, M.D., *Gnomologia* (1732), 5482.

20. Your children are not your children. / They are the sons and daughters of Life's longing for itself. KAHLIL GIBRAN, "On Children," *The Prophet* (1923).

21. One of the greatest pleasures of childhood is found in the mysteries which it hides from the skepticism of the elders, and works up into small mythologies of its own. OLIVER WENDELL HOLMES, SR., *The Poet at the Breakfast Table* (1872), 1.

22. A little girl without a doll is almost as unfortunate and quite as impossible as a woman without children. VICTOR HUGO, "Cosette," *Les Misérables* (1862), 3.8, tr. Charles E. Wilbour.

23. Children are remarkable for their intelligence and ardor, for their curiosity, their intolerance of shams, the clarity and ruthlessness of their vision. ALDOUS HUXLEY, "Vulgarity in Literature," *Music at Night* (1931).

24. Children need models rather than critics. JOSEPH JOUBERT, *Pensées* (1842), 18.1, tr. Katharine Lyttelton.

25. Children are the true connoisseurs. What's precious to them has no price—only value. BEL KAUFMAN, television interview, 1967.

26. A child's nature is too serious a thing to admit of its being regarded as a mere appendage to another being. CHARLES LAMB,

"A Bachelor's Complaint of the Behaviour of Married People," *Essays of Elia* (1823).

27. A sweet child is the sweetest thing in nature. CHARLES LAMB, "A Bachelor's Complaint of the Behaviour of Married People," *Essays of Elia* (1823).

28. Thou, straggler into loving arms, / Young climber up of knees, / When I forget thy thousand ways, / Then life and all shall cease. MARY LAMB, "Parental Recollections," *Poetry for Children* (1809).

29. A torn jacket is soon mended; but hard words bruise the heart of a child. LONGFELLOW, "Table-Talk," *Driftwood* (1857).

30. Children are God's apostles, day by day / Sent forth to preach of love, and hope, and peace. JAMES RUSSELL LOWELL, "On the Death of a Friend's Child" (1844).

31. Children know the grace of God / Better than most of us. They see the world / The way the morning brings it back to them, / New and born and fresh and wonderful. ARCHIBALD MAC LEISH, *JB* (1958), 1.

32. Childhood is the kingdom where nobody dies. EDNA ST. VINCENT MILLAY, "Childhood Is the Kingdom Where Nobody Dies," *Wine From These Grapes* (1934).

33. We find ourselves more taken with the running up and down, the games, and puerile simplicities of our children, than we do, afterward, with their most complete actions; as if we had loved them for our sport, like monkeys, and not as men. MONTAIGNE, "Of the affections of fathers to their children," *Essays* (1580–88), tr. Charles Cotton and W. C. Hazlitt.

34. Children, when they are little, they make parents fools; when great, mad. JOHN RAY, *English Proverbs* (1670).

35. Children pick up words as pigeons peas / And utter them again as God shall please. JOHN RAY, *English Proverbs* (1670).

36. Children are entitled to their otherness, as anyone is; and when we reach them, as we sometimes do, it is generally on a point of sheer delight, to us so astonishing, but to them so natural. ALASTAIR REID, *Places, Poems, Preoccupations* (1963).

37. Give a little love to a child, and you get a great deal back. JOHN RUSKIN, *The Crown of Wild Olive* (1866), 2.

38. Children, after being limbs of Satan in traditional theology and mystically illuminated angels in the minds of educational reformers, have reverted to being little devils—not theological demons inspired by the Evil One, but scientific Freudian abominations inspired by the Unconscious. BERTRAND RUSSELL, "The Virtue of the Oppressed," *Unpopular Essays* (1950).

39. A child is not frightened at the thought of being patiently transmuted into an old man. SAINT-EXUPÉRY, *Flight to Arras* (1942), 4, tr. Lewis Galantière.

40. Children are natural mythologists: they beg to be told tales, and love not only to invent but to enact falsehoods. GEORGE SANTAYANA, *Dialogues in Limbo* (1925), 5.

41. Making terms with reality, with things as they are, is a full-time business for the child. MILTON R. SAPIRSTEIN, *Paradoxes of Everyday Life* (1955), 2.

42. A child hasn't a grown-up person's appetite for affection. A little of it goes a long way with them; and they like a good imitation of it better than the real thing, as every nurse knows. GEORGE BERNARD SHAW, *Getting Married* (1911).

43. Children are the anchors that hold a mother to life. SOPHOCLES, *Phaedra* (c. 435–29 B.C.), tr. M. H. Morgan.

44. Perhaps a child who is fussed over gets a feeling of destiny, he thinks he is in the world for something important and it gives him drive and confidence. BENJAMIN SPOCK, *New York Sunday News*, May 11, 1958.

45. A child should always say what's true, / And speak when he is spoken to, / And behave mannerly at table: / At least as far as he is able. ROBERT LOUIS STEVENSON, "Whole Duty of Children," *A Child's Garden of Verses* (1885).

46. Life's aspirations come / in the guise of children. RABINDRANATH TAGORE, *Fireflies* (1928).

47. If men do not keep on speaking terms with children, they cease to be men, and become merely machines for eating and for earning money. JOHN UPDIKE, "A Foreword for Younger Readers," *Assorted Prose* (1965).

48. The difference between a childhood and a boyhood must be this: our childhood is what we alone have had; our boyhood is what any boy in our environment would have had. JOHN UPDIKE, "Environment," *Assorted Prose* (1965).

49. It is true that a child is always hungry all over; but he is also curious all over, and his curiosity is excited about as early as his hunger. CHARLES DUDLEY WARNER, "Seventeenth Week," *My Summer in a Garden* (1871).

50. Children begin by loving their parents. After a time they judge them. Rarely, if ever, do they forgive them. OSCAR WILDE, *A Woman of No Importance* (1893), 2.

51. A simple Child, / That lightly draws its breath, / And feels its life in every limb, / What should it know of death? WILLIAM WORDSWORTH, "We Are Seven" (1798).

## 122. CHOICE

**See also 719. Preference; 1049. Will**

1. Alternatives, and particularly desirable alternatives, grow only on imaginary trees. SAUL BELLOW, *Dangling Man* (1944).

2. What man wants is simply *independent* choice, whatever that independence may cost and wherever it may lead. DOSTOEVSKY, *Notes from Underground* (1864), 1.7, tr. Constance Garnett.

3. As a man thinketh so is he, and as a man chooseth so is he. EMERSON, "Spiritual Laws," *Essays: First Series* (1841).

4. It is your own conviction which compels you; that is, choice compels choice. EPICTETUS, *Discourses* (2nd c.), 1.17, tr. Thomas W. Higginson.

5. Some of necessity go astray, because for them there is no such thing as a right path. THOMAS MANN, "Tonio Kröger" (1903), *Death in Venice*, tr. H. T. Lowe-Porter.

6. The difficulty in life is the choice. GEORGE MOORE, *The Bending of the Bough* (1900), 4.

7. We often experience more regret over the part we have left, than pleasure over the part we have preferred. JOSEPH ROUX, *Meditations of a Parish Priest* (1886), 5.26, tr. Isabel F. Hapgood.

## CHRIST

**See 509. Jesus**

## 123. CHRISTIANITY

**See also 78. Bible; 124. Church; 136. Clergy; 328. Faith; 509. Jesus; 561. Martyrs and Martyrdom; 590. Missionaries; 595. Monasticism; 763. Puritans and Puritanism; 790. Religion; 829. Sabbath; 830. Sacrament; 834. Saints and Sainthood; 835. Salvation**

1. The glory of Christianity is to conquer by forgiveness. WILLIAM BLAKE, "To the Deists," *Jerusalem* (1804–20).

2. I fear that Christians who stand with only one leg upon earth also stand with only one leg in heaven. DIETRICH BONHOEFFER, letter to his fiancée, Aug. 12, 1943.

3. Christians have burnt each other, quite persuaded / That all the Apostles would have done as they did. BYRON, *Don Juan* (1819–24), 1.83.

4. Those of us who were brought up as Christians and who have lost our faith have retained the Christian sense of sin without the saving belief in redemption. This poisons our thought and so paralyses us in action. CYRIL CONNOLLY, *The Unquiet Grave* (1945), 1.

5. Christ beats his drum, but he does not press men; Christ is served with voluntaries. JOHN DONNE, *Sermons*, No. 39, 1626.

6. Instead of making Christianity a vehicle of truth, you make truth only a horse for Christianity. EMERSON, *Journals*, 1832.

7. Every stoic was a stoic; but in Christendom where is the Christian? EMERSON, "Self-Reliance," *Essays: First Series* (1841).

8. It is curious that Christianity, which is idealism, is sturdily defended by the brokers, and steadily attacked by the idealists. EMERSON, *Journals*, 1853.

9. By the irresistible maturing of the general mind, the Christian traditions have lost their hold. EMERSON, "Worship," *The Conduct of Life* (1860).

10. No one is without Christianity, if we agree on what we mean by the word. It is every individual's individual code of behavior by means of which he makes himself a better human being than his nature wants to be, if he followed his nature only. WILLIAM FAULKNER, interview, *Writers at Work: First Series* (1958).

11. Christianity, above all, consoles; but there are naturally happy souls who do not need consolation. Consequently Christianity begins by making such souls unhappy, for otherwise it would have no power over

them. ANDRÉ GIDE, *Journals*, Oct. 10, 1893, tr. Justin O'Brien.

12. The difficulty comes from this, that Christianity (Christian orthodoxy) is exclusive and that belief in *its* truth excludes belief in any other truth. It does not absorb; it repulses. ANDRÉ GIDE, *Journals*, June 14, 1926, tr. Justin O'Brien.

13. Almost every sect of Christianity is a perversion of its essence, to accommodate it to the prejudices of the world. WILLIAM HAZLITT, "On the Causes of Methodism," *The Round Table* (1817).

14. The Papacy is not other than the Ghost of the deceased Roman Empire, sitting crowned upon the grave thereof. THOMAS HOBBES, *Leviathan* (1651), 4.47.

15. Christianity supplies a Hell for the people who disagree with you and a Heaven for your friends. ELBERT HUBBARD, *The Note Book* (1927).

16. The Christian religion not only was at first attended with miracles, but even at this day cannot be believed by any reasonable person without one. DAVID HUME, *On Miracles*, 2.

17. The most important thing about me is that I am a Catholic. It's a superstructure within which you can work, like a sonnet. JEAN KERR, *Time*, April 14, 1961.

18. No man is a Christian who cheats his fellows, perverts the truth, or speaks of a "clean bomb," yet he will be the first to make public his faith in God. MARYA MANNES, *More in Anger* (1958), 4.6.

19. The chief contribution of Protestantism to human thought is its massive proof that God is a bore. H. L. MENCKEN, *Minority Report* (1956), 309.

20. 'Tis faith alone that vividly and certainly comprehends the deep mysteries of our religion. MONTAIGNE, "Apology for Raimond de Sebonde," *Essays* (1580–88), tr. Charles Cotton and W. C. Hazlitt.

21. No kingdom has ever suffered as many civil wars as Christ's. MONTESQUIEU, *Lettres persanes* (1721), 29.

22. Christianity in particular should be dubbed a great treasure-chamber of ingenious consolations, such a store of refreshing, soothing, deadening drugs has it accumulated within itself. NIETZSCHE, *The Genealogy of Morals* (1887), 3.17, tr. Horace B. Samuel.

23. The Catholic must adopt the decision handed down to him; the Protestant must learn to decide for himself. ROUSSEAU, *Les Confessions* (1766–70).

24. The true Christian is in all countries a pilgrim and a stranger. GEORGE SANTAYANA, *Winds of Doctrine* (1913).

25. If a Jew is fascinated by Christians it is not because of their virtues, which he values little, but because they represent anonymity, humanity without race. JEAN-PAUL SARTRE, *Anti-Semite and Jew* (1948).

26. The strange fate of Christianity in its modern dress is precisely that it has reduced man to the futility of idly gossiping about God. GABRIEL VAHANIAN, *The Death of God* (1962), 1.

27. We live in a post-Christian era because Christianity has sunk into religiosity. GABRIEL VAHANIAN, afterword, *The Death of God* (1962).

28. How else but through a broken heart / May Lord Christ enter in? OSCAR WILDE, *The Ballad of Reading Gaol* (1898), 5.14.

## CHRISTMAS

**See 418. Holidays**

## 124. CHURCH

**See also 123. Christianity; 125. Church and State; 126. Churchgoing; 136. Clergy; 561. Martyrs and Martyrdom; 590. Missionaries; 595. Monasticism; 718. Preaching and Preachers; 790. Religion; 830. Sacrament; 834. Saints and Sainthood**

1. Every church must put its treasures into a safe-deposit box and issue common money, a common money of love, which we need so much. ATHENAGORAS I, *Time*, July 5, 1963.

2. I have no objections to churches so long as they do not interfere with God's work. BROOKS ATKINSON, "November 10," *Once Around the Sun* (1951).

3. Except the Lord build the house, they labour in vain that build it. *Bible*, Psalms 127:1.

4. The real ecumenical crisis today is not between Catholics and Protestants but between traditional and experimental forms of church life. HARVEY COX, *The Secular City* (1966), 7.

5. If I should go out of church whenever

I hear a false sentiment, I could never stay there five minutes. EMERSON, *Journals*, 1841.

6. God builds his temple in the heart on the ruins of churches and religions. EMERSON, "Worship," *The Conduct of Life* (1860).

7. He who is near the Church is often far from God. FRENCH PROVERB.

8. In the visible church the true Christians are invisible. GERMAN PROVERB.

9. Perhaps the Church is trying to lock the stable door after the Messiah has been stolen. CHRISTOPHER MORLEY, *Inward Ho!* (1923), 1.

10. My own mind is my own church. THOMAS PAINE, *The Age of Reason* (1794, 1796), 1.

11. All things are God's already: we can give him no right by consecrating any that he had not before. JOHN SELDEN, "Consecrated Places," *Table Talk* (1689).

12. While God waits for His temple to be built of love, / men bring stones. RABINDRANATH TAGORE, *Fireflies* (1928).

13. The chiefest sanctity of a temple is that it is a place to which men go to weep in common. MIGUEL DE UNAMUNO, "The Man of Flesh and Bone," *Tragic Sense of Life* (1913), tr. J. E. Crawford Flitch.

14. The itch of disputation will prove the scab of the Church. SIR HENRY WOTTON, *Panegyric of King Charles* (1649).

## 125. CHURCH AND STATE

**See also 124. Church; 923. State**

1. Render to Caesar the things that are Caesar's, and to God the things that are God's. *Bible*, Mark 12:17.

2. All religions united with government are more or less inimical to liberty. All separated from government are compatible with liberty. HENRY CLAY, speech, U.S. House of Representatives, March 24, 1818.

3. History reveals the Church and the State as a pair of indispensable Molochs. They protect their worshiping subjects, only to enslave and destroy them. ALDOUS HUXLEY, "Variations on a Philosopher," *Themes and Variations* (1950).

4. In all ages, hypocrites, called priests, have put crowns upon the heads of thieves, called kings. ROBERT G. INGERSOLL, *Prose-Poems and Selections* (1884).

5. The church must be reminded that it is not the master or the servant of the state, but rather the conscience of the state. MARTIN LUTHER KING, JR., *Strength to Love* (1963), 6.3.

6. Two orders of mankind are the enemies of church and state; the king without clemency, and the holy man without learning. SA'DI, *Gulistan* (1258), 8.20, tr. James Ross.

## 126. CHURCHGOING

**See also 124. Church; 718. Preaching and Preachers**

1. How beautiful to have the church always open, so that every tired wayfaring man may come in and be soothed by all that art can suggest of a better world when he is weary with this. EMERSON, *Journals*, 1833.

2. The idea of God ends in a paltry Methodist meeting-house. EMERSON, *Journals*, 1850.

3. No temple can still the personal griefs and strifes in the breasts of its visitors. MARGARET FULLER, *Summer on the Lakes* (1844), 1.

4. Many come to bring their clothes to church rather than themselves. THOMAS FULLER, M.D., *Gnomologia* (1732), 3342.

5. God attributes to place / No sanctity, if none be thither brought / By men who there frequent, or therein dwell. MILTON, *Paradise Lost* (1667), 10.836.

6. The eleven o'clock hour on Sunday is the most segregated hour in American life. JAMES A. PIKE, *U.S. News & World Report*, May 16, 1960.

7. Our hymn-books resound with a melodious cursing of God and enduring Him forever. THOREAU, "Economy," *Walden* (1854).

8. Forgive us for turning our churches into private clubs; for loving familiar hymns and religious feelings more than we love You; for pasting stained glass on our eyes and our ears to shut out the cry of the hungry and the hurt of the world. UNITED PRESBYTERIAN CHURCH, *Litany for Holy Communion* (1968).

9. One of the advantages of pure congregational singing is that you can join in the singing whether you have a voice or not.

The disadvantage is, that your neighbor can do the same. CHARLES DUDLEY WARNER, "Seventh Study," *Backlog Studies* (1873).

## CINEMA
**See 604. Movies**

## 127. CIRCUMSTANCE
**See also 114. Chance; 303. Events; 617. Necessity**

1. It is futile to rail at circumstances / For they are indifferent. He shall fare well / Who confronts circumstances aright. Anonymous quotation in PLUTARCH's "Contentment," *Moralia* (c. A.D. 100), tr. Moses Hadas.

2. Man is not the creature of circumstances. Circumstances are the creatures of men. BENJAMIN DISRAELI, *Vivian Grey* (1826–27), 6.7.

3. The Circumstance is Nature. Nature is what you may do. There is much you may not. EMERSON, "Fate," *The Conduct of Life* (1860).

4. Our first mistake is the belief that the circumstance gives the joy which we give to the circumstance. EMERSON, "Illusions," *The Conduct of Life* (1860).

5. None of us can help the things life has done to us. They're done before you realize it, and once they're done they make you do other things until at last everything comes between you and what you'd like to be, and you've lost your true self forever. EUGENE O'NEILL, *Long Day's Journey into Night* (1956), 2.1.

6. I am myself plus my circumstance and if I do not save it, I cannot save myself. JOSÉ ORTEGA Y GASSET, "To the Reader," *Meditations on Quixote* (1914).

7. If all our happiness is bound up entirely in our personal circumstances it is difficult not to demand of life more than it has to give. BERTRAND RUSSELL, *The Conquest of Happiness* (1930), 10.

8. The people who get on in this world are the people who get up and look for the circumstances they want, and, if they can't find them, make them. GEORGE BERNARD SHAW, *Mrs. Warren's Profession* (1898), 2.

9. What a man is depends on his character; but what he does, and what we think of what he does, depends on his circumstances. GEORGE BERNARD SHAW, preface, *Major Barbara* (1905).

10. I make the most of all that comes, / And the least of all that goes. SARA TEASDALE, "The Philosopher."

## 128. CIRCUS

1. Circus, n. A place where horses, ponies and elephants are permitted to see men, women and children acting the fool. AMBROSE BIERCE, *The Devil's Dictionary* (1881–1911).

## 129. CITIES
**See also 191. The Country; 543. London; 625. New York; 664. Paris; 937. Suburbs; 1022. Venice; 1037. Washington, D.C.**

1. A great city is not to be confounded with a populous one. ARISTOTLE, *Politics* (4th c. B.C.), 7.4, tr. Benjamin Jowett.

2. A very populous city can rarely, if ever, be well governed. ARISTOTLE, *Politics* (4th c. B.C.), 7.4, tr. Benjamin Jowett.

3. In a great town friends are scattered; so that there is not that fellowship, for the most part, which is in less neighborhoods. FRANCIS BACON, "Of Friendship," *Essays* (1625).

4. A ghetto can be improved in one way only: out of existence. JAMES BALDWIN, "Fifth Avenue, Uptown," *Nobody Knows My Name* (1961).

5. A quiet city is a contradiction in terms. It is a thing uncanny, spectral. MAX BEERBOHM, "Advertisements," *Mainly On the Air* (1946).

6. The silence of a shut park does not sound like country silence: it is tense and confined. ELIZABETH BOWEN, *The Death of the Heart* (1938), 1.6.

7. I live not in myself, but I become / Portion of that around me; and to me / High mountains are a feeling, but the hum / Of human cities torture. BYRON, *Childe Harold's Pilgrimage* (1812–18), 3.72.

8. If a large city can, after intense intellectual efforts, choose for its mayor a man who merely will not steal from it, we consider it a triumph of the suffrage. FRANK

MOORE COLBY, "On Seeing Ten Bad Plays," *The Colby Essays* (1926), v. 1.

9. If you would be known, and not know, vegetate in a village; if you would know, and not be known, live in a city. CHARLES CALEB COLTON, *Lacon* (1825), 1.334.

10. In great cities men are more callous both to the happiness and the misery of others, than in the country; for they are constantly in the habit of seeing both extremes. CHARLES CALEB COLTON, *Lacon* (1825), 2.94.

11. No city should be too large for a man to walk out of in a morning. CYRIL CONNOLLY, *The Unquiet Grave* (1945), 1.

12. God the first garden made, and the first city Cain. ABRAHAM COWLEY, "The Garden" (1666).

13. The real illness of the American city today, and especially of the deprived groups within it, is voicelessness. HARVEY COX, *The Secular City* (1966), 6.

14. Cities degrade us by magnifying trifles. EMERSON, "Culture," *The Conduct of Life* (1860).

15. What is the city in which we sit here, but an aggregate of incongruous materials, which have obeyed the will of some man? EMERSON, "Fate," *The Conduct of Life* (1860).

16. A great city—a great solitude. ENGLISH PROVERB.

17. 'Tis the men, not the houses, that make the city. THOMAS FULLER, M.D., *Gnomologia* (1732), 5121.

18. Parks are but pavement disguised with a growth of grass. GEORGE GISSING, "Spring," *The Private Papers of Henry Ryecroft* (1903).

19. What we get in the city is not life, but what someone else tells us about life. DAVID GRAYSON, *Adventures in Contentment* (1907), 13.

20. In the Big City a man will disappear with the suddenness and completeness of the flame of a candle that is blown out. O. HENRY, "The Sleuths," *Sixes and Sevens* (1911).

21. Farmers worry only during the growing season, but town people worry all the year 'round. EDGAR WATSON HOWE, *Country Town Sayings* (1911).

22. Cities produce ferocious men, because they produce corrupt men; the mountains, the forest, and the sea, render men savage; they develop the fierce, but yet do not destroy the human. VICTOR HUGO, "Fantine," *Les Misérables* (1862), 2.6, tr. Charles E. Wilbour.

23. The modern town-dweller has no God and no Devil; he lives without awe, without admiration, without fear. WILLIAM RALPH INGE, "Our Present Discontents," *Outspoken Essays: First Series* (1919).

24. Great cities are not like towns, only larger. They differ from towns and suburbs in basic ways, and one of these is that cities are, by definition, full of strangers. JANE JACOBS, *The Death and Life of Great American Cities* (1961), 1.2.

25. The urban man is an uprooted tree, he can put out leaves, flowers and grow fruit but what a nostalgia his leaf, flower, and fruit will always have for mother earth! JUAN RAMÓN JIMÉNEZ, "Aristocracy and Democracy," *Selected Writings* (1957), tr. H. R. Hays.

26. A neighborhood is where, when you go out of it, you get beat up. MURRAY KEMPTON, quoting Puerto Rican Labor Office worker, "Group Dynamics," *America Comes of Middle Age* (1963).

27. We will neglect our cities to our peril, for in neglecting them we neglect the nation. JOHN F. KENNEDY, message to U.S. Congress, Jan. 30, 1962.

28. Peace and freedom walk together. In too many of our cities today, the peace is not secure because freedom is incomplete. JOHN F. KENNEDY, commencement address, American University, Washington, D.C., June 10, 1963.

29. The sweetest souls, like the sweetest flowers, soon canker in cities, and no purity is rarer there than the purity of delight. WALTER SAVAGE LANDOR, "La Fontaine and De La Rochefoucault," *Imaginary Conversations* (1824–53).

30. To say the least, a town life makes one more tolerant and liberal in one's judgment of others. LONGFELLOW, *Hyperion* (1839), 2.10.

31. I have an affection for a great city. I feel safe in the neighborhood of man, and enjoy the sweet security of streets. LONGFELLOW, "The Great Metropolis," *Driftwood* (1857).

32. The city is squalid and sinister, / With the silver-barred street in the midst, / Slow-moving, / A river leading nowhere.

AMY LOWELL, "A London Thoroughfare. 2 A.M.," *Sword Blades and Poppy Seeds* (1914).

33. Cities rob men of eyes and hands and feet, / Patching one hole of many incomplete; / The general preys upon the individual mind, / And each alone is helpless as the wind. JAMES RUSSELL LOWELL, "The Pioneer" (1847).

34. In great cities men are like a lot of stones thrown together in a bag; their jagged corners are rubbed off till in the end they are as smooth as marbles. W. SOMERSET MAUGHAM, *The Summing Up* (1938), 53.

35. A sample of the country does the city good; a sample of the city does the country good. JOSEPH ROUX, *Meditations of a Parish Priest* (1886), 7.16, tr. Isabel F. Hapgood.

36. What is the city but the people? SHAKESPEARE, *Coriolanus* (1607–08), 3.1. 199.

37. The city man, in his neon-and-mazda glare, knows nothing of nature's midnight. His electric lamps surround him with synthetic sunshine. They push back the dark. They defend him from the realities of the age-old night. EDWIN WAY TEALE, *North with the Spring* (1951), 15.

38. Forgive us when we deplore violence in our cities if we live in suburbs, where lawns are clipped and churches enlarge, or in green villages where there are too many steeples. UNITED PRESBYTERIAN CHURCH, *Litany for Holy Communion* (1968).

39. The thing generally raised on city land is taxes. CHARLES DUDLEY WARNER, "Sixteenth Week," *My Summer in a Garden* (1871).

40. Commuters give the city its tidal restlessness; natives give it solidity and continuity; but the settlers give it passion. E. B. WHITE, "Here Is New York," *Holiday*, April 1949.

41. A great city is that which has the greatest men and women. WALT WHITMAN, "Song of the Broad-Axe," 4, *Leaves of Grass* (1855-92).

42. Oh, blank confusion! true epitome / Of what the mighty City is herself, / To thousands upon thousands of her sons, / Living amid the same perpetual whirl / Of trivial objects, melted and reduced / To one identity. WILLIAM WORDSWORTH, *The Prelude* (1799–1805), 7.

## 130. CITIZENS

**See also 393. Government; 923. State; 1030. Voting**

1. It is not always the same thing to be a good man and a good citizen. ARISTOTLE, *Nicomachean Ethics* (4th c. B.C.), 5.2, tr. J. A. K. Thomson.

2. Man exists for his own sake and not to add a laborer to the State. EMERSON, *Journals*, 1839.

3. Those self-important fathers of their country / Think they're above the people. Why they're nothing! / The citizen is infinitely wiser. EURIPIDES, *Andromache* (c. 426 B.C.), tr. John F. Nims.

4. To educate the masses politically is to make the totality of the nation a reality to each citizen. It is to make the history of the nation part of the personal experience of each of its citizens. FRANTZ FANON, "The Pitfalls of National Consciousness," *The Wretched of the Earth* (1961), tr. Constance Farrington.

5. The citizen is a variety of man; whether a degenerate or a primitive variety, he is to man what an alley-cat is to a jungle cat. RÉMY DE GOURMONT, "Paradoxes sur le citoyen," *Epilogues* (1895–1912).

6. In America there must be only citizens, not divided by grade, first and second, but citizens, east, west, north, and south. JOHN F. KENNEDY, campaign address, National Conference on Constitutional Rights and American Freedom, New York City, Oct. 12, 1960.

7. The citizen is influenced by principle in direct proportion to his distance from the political situation. MILTON RAKOVE, *The Virginia Quarterly Review*, Summer 1965.

8. The first requisite of a good citizen in this republic of ours is that he shall be able and willing to pull his weight. THEODORE ROOSEVELT, address, New York City, Nov. 11, 1902.

9. Every subject's duty is the King's, but every subject's soul is his own. SHAKESPEARE, *Henry V* (1598–99), 4.1.185.

10. All the citizens of a state cannot be equally powerful, but they may be equally free. VOLTAIRE, "Government," *Philosophical Dictionary* (1764).

11. Citizenship *is* man's basic right for it is nothing less than the right to have rights. Remove this priceless possession and there

remains a stateless person, disgraced and degraded in the eyes of his countrymen. CHIEF JUSTICE EARL WARREN, dissent, *Perez v. Brownell* (1958).

12. Whatever makes men good Christians, makes them good citizens. DANIEL WEBSTER, speech, Plymouth, Mass., Dec. 22, 1820.

## 131. CIVILIZATION

**See also 69. Barbarism; 207. Culture; 735. Progress; 906. Society**

1. Civilization is the lamb's skin in which barbarism masquerades. THOMAS BAILEY ALDRICH, "Leaves from a Notebook," *Ponkapog Papers* (1903).

2. The crimes of extreme civilization are probably worse than those of extreme barbarism, because of their refinement, the corruption they presuppose, and their superior degree of intellectuality. JULES BARBEY D'AUREVILLY, "La vengeance d'une femme," *Les Diaboliques* (1874).

3. The true savage is a slave, and is always talking about what he must do; the true civilised man is a free man, and is always talking about what he may do. G. K. CHESTERTON, "Humanitarianism and Strength," *All Things Considered* (1908).

4. A good civilization spreads over us freely like a tree, varying and yielding because it is alive. A bad civilization stands up and sticks out above us like an umbrella—artificial, mathematical in shape; not merely universal, but uniform. G. K. CHESTERTON, "Cheese," *Alarms and Discursions* (1910).

5. Averageness is a quality we must put up with. Men march toward civilization in column formation, and by the time the van has learned to admire the masters the rear is drawing reluctantly away from the totem pole. FRANK MOORE COLBY, "The Reading Public," *The Colby Essays* (1926), v. 1.

6. Civilization is an active deposit which is formed by the combustion of the Present with the Past. Neither in countries without a Present nor in those without a Past is it to be discovered. CYRIL CONNOLLY, *The Unquiet Grave* (1945), 2.

7. The civilization of one epoch becomes the manure of the next. CYRIL CONNOLLY, *The Unquiet Grave* (1945), 2.

8. Increased means and increased leisure are the two civilisers of man. BENJAMIN DISRAELI, "Conservative Principles," speech, April 3, 1872.

9. Th' fav'rite pastime iv civilized man is croolty to other civilized man. FINLEY PETER DUNNE, "Corporal Punishment," *Dissertations by Mr. Dooley* (1906).

10. There is held to be no surer test of civilisation than the increase per head of the consumption of alcohol and tobacco. Yet alcohol and tobacco are recognisably poisons, so that their consumption has only to be carried far enough to destroy civilisation altogether. HAVELOCK ELLIS, *The Dance of Life* (1923), 7.

11. The true test of civilization is, not the census, nor the size of cities, nor the crops—no, but the kind of man the country turns out. EMERSON, "Civilization," *Society and Solitude* (1870).

12. The civilized man is a larger mind but a more imperfect nature than the savage. MARGARET FULLER, *Summer on the Lakes* (1844), 6.

13. The social moulds civilization fits us into have no more relation to our actual shapes than the conventional shapes of the constellations have to real star patterns. THOMAS HARDY, *Jude the Obscure* (1895), 4.1.

14. In a state of nature, the weakest go to the wall; in a state of over-refinement, both the weak and the strong go to the gutter. ELBERT HUBBARD, *The Philistine* (1895–1915).

15. A nation advances in civilisation by increasing in wealth and population, and by multiplying the accessories and paraphernalia of life. WILLIAM RALPH INGE, "Our Present Discontents," *Outspoken Essays: First Series* (1919).

16. Civilizations die from philosophical calm, irony, and the sense of fair play quite as surely as they die of debauchery. JOSEPH WOOD KRUTCH, "The Paradox of Humanism," *The Modern Temper* (1929).

17. In the dust where we have buried the silent races and their abominations we have buried so much of the delicate magic of life. D. H. LAWRENCE, quoted in Stewart L. Udall's *The Quiet Crisis* (1963), 1.

18. Human history, if you read it right, is the record of the efforts to tame Father.

Next to striking of fire and the discovery of the wheel, the greatest triumph of what we call civilization was the domestication of the human male. MAX LERNER, "The Revolt of the American Father," *The Unfinished Country* (1959), 2.

19. Why build these cities glorious / If man unbuilded goes? / In vain we build the world, unless / The builder also grows. EDWIN MARKHAM, "Man-Making" (1920).

20. Civilization does everything for the mind and favors it entirely at the expense of the body. NAPOLEON I, *Maxims* (1804–15).

21. We don't cut our nails to disarm ourselves, Maurizio. On the contrary: just to make us look more civilized, so we can hold our own in a far more desperate struggle than the one our ancestors fought with nothing but their claws. LUIGI PIRANDELLO, *The Pleasure of Honesty* (1917), 1, tr. William Murray.

22. You can't say civilization dont advance, . . . for in every war they kill you a new way. WILL ROGERS, *The Autobiography of Will Rogers* (1949), 14.

23. The passage from the state of nature to the civil state produces a very remarkable change in man, by substituting justice for instinct in his conduct. ROUSSEAU, *The Social Contract* (1762), 1.8, tr. G. D. H. Cole.

24. Civilization is the making of civil persons. JOHN RUSKIN, *The Crown of Wild Olive* (1866).

25. Every advance in civilization has been denounced as unnatural while it was recent. BERTRAND RUSSELL, "An Outline of Intellectual Rubbish," *Unpopular Essays* (1950).

26. The more we realize our minuteness and our impotence in the face of cosmic forces, the more astonishing becomes what human beings have achieved. BERTRAND RUSSELL, *New Hopes for a Changing World* (1951).

27. A civilization that is really strong fills man to the brim, though he never stir. SAINT-EXUPÉRY, *Flight to Arras* (1942), 12, tr. Lewis Galantière.

28. A civilization is built on what is required of men, not on that which is provided for them. SAINT-EXUPÉRY, *The Wisdom of the Sands* (1948), 9, tr. Stuart Gilbert.

29. Civilization is a movement and not a condition, a voyage and not a harbor. ARNOLD TOYNBEE, *Reader's Digest*, October 1958.

30. Soap and education are not as sudden as a massacre, but they are more deadly in the long run. MARK TWAIN, "The Facts Concerning the Recent Resignation," *Sketches New and Old* (1900).

31. Nature is rarely allowed to enter the sacred portals of civilized society. HENDRIK WILLEM VAN LOON, *Multiple Man* (1928).

32. A few suits of clothes, some money in the bank, and a new kind of fear constitute the main differences between the average American today and the hairy men with clubs who accompanied Attila to the city of Rome. PHILIP WYLIE, *Generation of Vipers* (1942), 1.

## CIVIL RIGHTS

See 817. Rights

## 132. CLARITY

1. What is conceived well is expressed clearly, / And the words to say it with arrive with ease. NICOLAS BOILEAU, *L'Art poétique* (1674), 1.

2. A man does not know what he is saying until he knows what he is not saying. G. K. CHESTERTON, "About Impenitence," *As I Was Saying* (1936).

3. Every man speaks and writes with intent to be understood; and it can seldom happen but he that understands himself might convey his notions to another, if, content to be understood, he did not seek to be admired. SAMUEL JOHNSON, *The Idler* (1758–60), 36.

4. A matter that becomes clear ceases to concern us. NIETZSCHE, *Beyond Good and Evil* (1886), 80, tr. Walter Kaufmann.

5. Clarity is the politeness of the man of letters. JULES RENARD, *Journal*, 1892.

6. There is a poignancy in all things clear, / In the stare of the deer, in the ring of a hammer in the morning. / Seeing a bucket of perfectly lucid water / We fall to imagining prodigious honesties. RICHARD WILBUR, "Clearness," *Ceremony* (1950).

### 133. CLASS

**See also 52. Aristocracy; 231. Democracy; 295. Equality; 581. Middle Class; 675. The People; 773. Rank; 903. Snobbery; 906. Society; 926. Status**

1. I was told that the Privileged and the People formed two nations. BENJAMIN DISRAELI, *Sybil* (1845), 4.8.

2. In class society everyone lives as a member of a particular class, and every kind of thinking, without exception, is stamped with the brand of a class. MAO TSE-TUNG, *Quotations from Chairman Mao Tse-tung* (1966), 2.

3. It is no longer clear which way is up even if one wants to rise. DAVID RIESMAN, "From Morality to Morals," *The Lonely Crowd* (1950).

4. The diminution of the reality of class, however socially desirable in many respects, seems to have the practical effect of diminishing our ability to see people in their difference and specialness. LIONEL TRILLING, "Art and Fortune," *The Liberal Imagination* (1950).

### 134. CLASSICS

**See also 42. Antiquity; 91. Books and Reading; 979. Tradition**

1. Books that have become classics—books that have had their day and now get more praise than perusal—always remind me of retired colonels and majors and captains who, having reached the age limit, find themselves retired on half pay. THOMAS BAILEY ALDRICH, "Leaves from a Notebook," *Ponkapog Papers* (1903).

2. Speak of the moderns without contempt and of the ancients without idolatry; judge them all by their merits, but not by their age. LORD CHESTERFIELD, *Letters to His Son*, Feb. 22, 1748.

3. A great classic means a man whom one can praise without having read. G. K. CHESTERTON, "Tom Jones and Morality," *All Things Considered* (1908).

4. The praise of ancient authors proceeds not from the reverence of the dead, but from the competition and mutual envy of the living. THOMAS HOBBES, "A Review and Conclusion," *Leviathan* (1651).

5. What a sense of security in an old book which Time has criticized for us! JAMES RUSSELL LOWELL, "Library of Old Authors," *Literary Essays* (1864–90).

6. There is but one way left to save a classic: to give up revering him and use him for our own salvation. JOSÉ ORTEGA Y GASSET, "In Search of Goethe from Within, Letter to a German," *Partisan Review*, December 1949, tr. Willard R. Trask.

7. *"Classic."* A book which people praise and don't read. MARK TWAIN, "Pudd'nhead Wilson's New Calendar," *Following the Equator* (1897), 1.25.

8. A classic is something that everybody wants to have read and nobody wants to read. MARK TWAIN, speech, "The Disappearance of Literature," New York, Nov. 20, 1900.

9. In Art, the public accept what has been, because they cannot alter it, not because they appreciate it. They swallow their classics whole, and never taste them. OSCAR WILDE, *The Soul of Man Under Socialism* (1891).

### 135. CLEANLINESS

**See also 246. Dirtiness; 411. Health**

1. Cleanliness is not next to godliness nowadays, for cleanliness is made an essential and godliness is regarded as an offence. G. K. CHESTERTON, "On Lying in Bed," *Tremendous Trifles* (1909).

2. Man does not live by soap alone; and hygiene, or even health, is not much good unless you can take a healthy view of it—or, better still, feel a healthy indifference to it. G. K. CHESTERTON, "On St. George Revivified," *All I Survey* (1933).

3. The graveyards are full of women whose houses were so spotless you could eat off the floor. Remember the second wife always has a maid. HELOISE CRUSE, *Saturday Evening Post*, March 2, 1963.

4. People who wash much have a high mind about it, and talk down to those who wash little. EMERSON, *Journals*, 1847.

5. Hygiene is the corruption of medicine by morality. H. L. MENCKEN, *Prejudices: Third Series* (1922), 14.

6. Man and other civilized animals are the only creatures that ever become dirty. JOHN MUIR, *A Thousand-Mile Walk to the Gulf* (1916), 5.

7. I test my bath before I sit, / And I'm

always moved to wonderment / That what chills the finger not a bit / Is so frigid upon the fundament. OGDEN NASH, "Samson Agonistes," *Good Intentions* (1943).

8. What separates two people most profoundly is a different sense and degree of cleanliness. NIETZSCHE, *Beyond Good and Evil* (1886), 271, tr. Walter Kaufmann.

## 136. CLERGY

**See also 123. Christianity; 124. Church; 590. Missionaries; 595. Monasticism; 718. Preaching and Preachers**

1. Clergyman, n. A man who undertakes the management of our spiritual affairs as a method of bettering his temporal ones. AMBROSE BIERCE, *The Devil's Dictionary* (1881–1911).

2. The clergyman is expected to be a kind of human Sunday. SAMUEL BUTLER (d. 1902), *The Way of All Flesh* (1903), 26.

3. Parsons as well as other folks must live:— / From rage he rails not, rather say from dread, / He does not speak for Virtue, but for bread. BYRON, "Soliloquy of a Bard in the Country" (1806).

4. Clergy are men as well as other folks. HENRY FIELDING, *Joseph Andrews* (1742), 2.6.

5. A broad hat does not always cover a venerable head. THOMAS FULLER, M.D., *Gnomologia* (1732), 26.

6. In times of death and famine, reason is on the side of the priests—who have their own kind of logic which cries for miracles and, on occasion, invents them. JEAN GIRAUDOUX, *Judith* (1931), 1, tr. John K. Savacool.

7. As Pastor X steps out of bed / he slips a neat disguise on: / that halo round his priestly head / is really his horizon. PIET HEIN, "Circumscripture," *Grooks* (1966).

8. Priests are no more necessary to religion than politicians to patriotism. JOHN HAYNES HOLMES, *The Sensible Man's View of Religion* (1933).

9. The minister is coming down every generation nearer and nearer to the common level of the useful citizen,—no oracle at all, but a man of more than average moral instincts, who, if he know anything, knows how little he knows. OLIVER WENDELL HOLMES, SR., *The Poet at the Breakfast Table* (1872), 5.

10. A man who is good enough to go to heaven is good enough to be a clergyman. SAMUEL JOHNSON, quoted in Boswell's *Life of Samuel Johnson*, April 5, 1772.

11. I have always considered a clergyman as the father of a larger family than he is able to maintain. SAMUEL JOHNSON, quoted in Boswell's *Life of Samuel Johnson*, April 1778.

12. Hood an ass with reverend purple, / So you can hide his two ambitious ears, / And he shall pass for a cathedral doctor. BEN JONSON, *Volpone* (1605), 1.2.

13. An orator preaches to get a bishopric, an apostle to save souls; the latter deserves what the other aims at. LA BRUYÈRE, *Characters* (1688), 15.21, tr. Henri Van Laun.

14. The priest is the first form of the more delicate animal that scorns more easily than it hates. NIETZSCHE, *The Genealogy of Morals* (1887), 3.15, tr. Horace B. Samuel.

15. The clergy would have us believe them against our own reason, as the woman would have her husband against his own eyes. JOHN SELDEN, "Clergy," *Table Talk* (1689).

16. How can a bishop marry? How can he flirt? The most he can say is, "I will see you in the vestry after service." SYDNEY SMITH, quoted in Lady S. Holland's *Memoir* (1855), v. 1.9.

17. There are three sexes—men, women, and clergymen. SYDNEY SMITH, quoted in Lady S. Holland's *Memoir* (1855), v. 1.9.

## 137. CLEVERNESS

**See also 197. Craftiness; 491. Intelligence; 936. Subtlety; 1054. Wit**

1. An ounce of mother wit is worth a pound of clergy. JOHN ADAMS, letter to Abigail Adams, Oct. 29, 1775.

2. It is a / profitable thing, if one is wise, to seem foolish. AESCHYLUS, *Prometheus Bound* (c. 478 B.C.), tr. David Grene.

3. Sharp men, like sharp needles, break easy, though they pierce quick. HENRY WARD BEECHER, *Proverbs from Plymouth Pulpit* (1887).

4. All clever men are birds of prey. ENGLISH PROVERB.

5. The bold are helpless without cleverness. EURIPIDES, *Helen* (412 B.C.), tr. Richmond Lattimore.

6. It is not strength, but art, obtains the

prize, / And to be swift is less than to be wise. HOMER, *Iliad* (9th c. B.C.), 23.383, tr. Alexander Pope.

7. The world must be rather a rough place for clever people. Ordinary folk dislike them, and as for themselves, they hate each other most cordially. JEROME K. JEROME, "On Cats and Dogs," *The Idle Thoughts of an Idle Fellow* (1889).

8. The desire of appearing clever often prevents our becoming so. LA ROCHEFOUCAULD, *Maxims* (1665), tr. Kenneth Pratt.

9. We are clever,—we are as clever as monkeys; and some of us / Have intellect, which is our danger, for we lack intelligence / And have forgotten instinct. EDNA ST. VINCENT MILLAY, untitled poem, *Make Bright the Arrows* (1940).

10. Here's a good rule of thumb: / Too clever is dumb. OGDEN NASH, "Reflection on Ingenuity," *Verses from 1929 On* (1959).

11. Some people will never learn any thing, for this reason, because they understand every thing too soon. ALEXANDER POPE, *Thoughts on Various Subjects* (1727).

12. The devil can cite Scripture for his purpose. SHAKESPEARE, *The Merchant of Venice* (1596–97), 1.3.99.

13. If all the good people were clever, / And all clever people were good, / The world would be nicer than ever / We thought that it possibly could. ELIZABETH WORDSWORTH, "The Clever and the Good," *St. Christopher and Other Poems* (1890).

14. When luck joins in the game, cleverness scores double. *Yiddish Proverbs* (1949), ed. Hanan J. Ayalti.

## 138. CLIMATE

See also 943. Sun; 1043. Weather

1. What men call gallantry, and gods adultery, / Is much more common where the climate's sultry. BYRON, *Don Juan* (1819–24), 1.63.

2. In all countries where nature does the most, man does the least. CHARLES CALEB COLTON, *Lacon* (1825), 1.67.

3. Men born in hot countries love the night because it refreshes them and have a horror of light because it burns them; and therefore they are of the color of night, that is black. And in cold countries it is just the contrary. LEONARDO DA VINCI, *Notebooks* (c. 1500), tr. Jean Paul Richter.

4. Bright and fierce and fickle is the South, / And dark and true and tender is the North. ALFRED, LORD TENNYSON, "The Princess; A Medley" (1851), 4.

## CLIQUES

See 903. Snobbery

## CLOTHING

See 265. Dress; 335. Fashion

## 139. COARSENESS

See also 1031. Vulgarity

1. A certain crudity makes people interesting just as much as a certain cultivation: in many ways, the next best thing to what Harvard represents is what the school of hard knocks does. LOUIS KRONENBERGER, *Company Manners* (1954), 3.1.

2. People who lack a coarse streak, I have discovered, almost always possess a cruel one. LOUIS KRONENBERGER, "Conformity's Cultured Sister," *The Cart and the Horse* (1964), 4.

3. To endeavour to work upon the vulgar with fine sense is like attempting to hew blocks with a razor. ALEXANDER POPE, *Thoughts on Various Subjects* (1727).

## COCKTAIL PARTY

See 665. Parties

## 140. COFFEE

1. The morning cup of coffee has an exhilaration about it which the cheering influence of the afternoon or evening cup of tea cannot be expected to reproduce. OLIVER WENDELL HOLMES, SR., *Over the Teacups* (1891), 1.

2. Coffee, which makes the politician wise, / And see thro' all things with his half-shut eyes. ALEXANDER POPE, *The Rape of the Lock* (1712), 3.117.

3. Coffee should be black as Hell, strong as death, and sweet as love. TURKISH PROVERB.

## 141. COLDNESS

**See also 31. Aloofness**

1. The cold in clime are cold in blood, / Their love can scarce deserve the name. BYRON, *The Giaour* (1813).

2. Are you then unable to recognize a sob unless it has the same sound as yours? ANDRÉ GIDE, *Journals*, 1922, tr. Justin O'Brien.

3. Men of cold passions have quick eyes. NATHANIEL HAWTHORNE, *Journals*, 1837.

4. Every heart has its secret sorrows which the world knows not, and oftentimes we call a man cold, when he is only sad. LONGFELLOW, *Hyperion* (1839), 3.4.

5. You do not see the river of mourning because it lacks one tear of your own. ANTONIO PORCHIA, *Voces* (1968), tr. W. S. Merwin.

6. What makes people hard-hearted is this, that each man has, or fancies he has, as much as he can bear in his own troubles. SCHOPENHAUER, "Further Psychological Observations," *Parerga and Paralipomena* (1851), tr. T. Bailey Saunders.

## COLONIALISM

**See 456. Imperialism**

## 142. COLOR

1. Colors speak all languages. JOSEPH ADDISON, *The Spectator* (1711–12), 416.

2. Grey is a colour that always seems on the eve of changing to some other colour. G. K. CHESTERTON, "The Glory of Grey," *Alarms and Discursions* (1910).

3. The purest and most thoughtful minds are those which love colour the most. JOHN RUSKIN, *The Stones of Venice* (1851–53), v. 2, 5.30.

## 143. COMEDIANS

**See also 144. Comedy; 290. Entertainment; 434. Humor**

1. All that the comedian has to show for his years of work and aggravation is the echo of forgotten laughter. FRED ALLEN, *Treadmill to Oblivion* (1954).

2. Who are a little wise, the best fools be. JOHN DONNE, "The Triple Fool," *Songs and Sonnets* (1633).

3. The art of the clown is more profound than we think; it is neither tragic nor comic. It is the comic mirror of tragedy and the tragic mirror of comedy. ANDRÉ SUARÈS, "Essai sur le clown," *Remarques* (1917–18), 1.

## 144. COMEDY

**See also 143. Comedians; 290. Entertainment; 434. Humor; 838. Satire; 965. Theater; 980. Tragedy; 1054. Wit**

1. Like dreams, farces show the disguised fulfillment of repressed wishes. ERIC BENTLEY, "The Psychology of Farce," introduction to *Let's Get a Divorce and Other Plays* (1958).

2. All tragedies are finished by a death, / All comedies are ended by a marriage. BYRON, *Don Juan* (1819–24), 3.9.

3. It is very difficult to be wholly joyous or wholly sad on this earth. The comic, when it is human, soon takes upon itself the face of pain. JOSEPH CONRAD, "A Familiar Preface," *A Personal Record* (1912).

4. Comedy is an escape, not from the truth but from despair; a narrow escape into faith. CHRISTOPHER FRY, *Time*, Nov. 20, 1950.

5. In black comedy, you murder your grandmother by shoving her off a high cliff in a wheelchair; in sick comedy, you do precisely the same thing, but she is already dying of cancer, and you know it. BRENDAN GILL, *The New Yorker*, Jan. 28, 1968.

6. Comedy naturally wears itself out – destroys the very food on which it lives; and by constantly and successfully exposing the follies and weaknesses of mankind to ridicule, in the end leaves itself nothing worth laughing at. WILLIAM HAZLITT, "On Modern Comedy," *The Round Table* (1817).

7. Comedy appeals to the collective mind of the audience and this grows fatigued; while farce appeals to a more robust organ, their collective belly. W. SOMERSET MAUGHAM, *The Summing Up* (1938), 39.

8. The test of a real comedian is whether you laugh at him before he opens his mouth. GEORGE JEAN NATHAN, "Test of a Comedian," *American Mercury*, September 1929.

9. If tragedy is an experience of hyperinvolvement, comedy is an experience of underinvolvement, of detachment. SUSAN SONTAG, "Notes on Camp," *Against Interpretation* (1961).

10. The only rules comedy can tolerate are those of taste, and the only limitations those of libel. JAMES THURBER, "The Duchess and the Bugs," *Lanterns and Lances* (1961).

11. Comedy has ceased to be a challenge to the mental processes. It has become a therapy of relaxation, a kind of tranquilizing drug. JAMES THURBER, "Magical Lady," *Lanterns and Lances* (1961).

12. The perfect tribute to perfection in comedy is not immediate laughter, but a curious and instantaneous tendency of the eyes to fill. JAMES THURBER, "Magical Lady," *Lanterns and Lances* (1961).

## COMMAND

See 61. Authority; 528. Leadership

## COMMERCE

See 102. Business and Commerce; 103. Buying and Selling; 732. Profiteering

## 145. COMMITMENT

See also 109. Causes; 502. Involvement

1. Something must happen—that explains most human commitments. Something must happen, even servitude without love, even war, or death. ALBERT CAMUS, *The Fall* (1956).

2. He is poor indeed that can promise nothing. THOMAS FULLER, M.D., *Gnomologia* (1732), 1941.

3. The beauty of a strong, lasting commitment is often best understood by a man incapable of it. MURRAY KEMPTON, "O'er Moor and Fen," *Part of Our Time* (1955).

4. The need for devotion to something outside ourselves is even more profound than the need for companionship. If we are not to go to pieces or wither away, we all must have some purpose in life; for no man can live for himself alone. ROSS PARMENTER, "The Doctor and the Cleaning Woman," *The Plant in My Window* (1949).

## 146. COMMITTEES

See also 229. Deliberation

1. A committee is a group that keeps the minutes and loses hours. MILTON BERLE, news summaries, July 1, 1954.

2. We always carry out by committee anything in which any one of us alone would be too reasonable to persist. FRANK MOORE COLBY, "Subsidizing Authors," *The Colby Essays* (1926), v. 1.

3. What is a committee? A group of the unwilling, picked from the unfit, to do the unnecessary. RICHARD HARKNESS, *New York Herald Tribune*, June 15, 1960.

4. Committees are to get everybody together and homogenize their thinking. ART LINKLETTER, *A Child's Garden of Misinformation* (1965), 12.

## COMMON MAN

See 675. The People

## 147. COMMON SENSE

See also 714. Practicality; 749. Prudence

1. Pedantry prides herself on being wrong by rules; while common sense is contented to be right without them. CHARLES CALEB COLTON, *Lacon* (1825), 1.48.

2. Common sense is the most fairly distributed thing in the world, for each one thinks he is so well-endowed with it that even those who are hardest to satisfy in all other matters are not in the habit of desiring more of it than they already have. DESCARTES, *Discourse on Method* (1639), 1.

3. Poverty, Frost, Famine, Rain, Disease, are the beadles and guardsmen that hold us to Common Sense. EMERSON, *Journals*, 1836.

4. Nothing astonishes men so much as common sense and plain dealing. EMERSON, "Art," *Essays: First Series* (1841).

5. Common sense is as rare as genius. EMERSON, "Experience," *Essays: Second Series* (1844).

6. The best prophet is common sense, our native wit. EURIPIDES, *Helen* (412 B.C.), tr. Richmond Lattimore.

7. Logic is one thing and commonsense another. ELBERT HUBBARD, *The Note Book* (1927).

8. Good intentions are useless in the absence of common sense. JAMI, "The Camel and the Rat," *Baharistan* (15th c.).

9. Fine sense and exalted sense are not half so useful as common sense. ALEXANDER POPE, *Thoughts on Various Subjects* (1727).

10. A man of great common sense and good taste—meaning thereby a man without originality or moral courage. GEORGE BERNARD SHAW, "Notes: Julius Caesar," *Caesar and Cleopatra* (1906).

11. Why level downward to our dullest perception always, and praise that as common sense? The commonest sense is the sense of men asleep, which they express by snoring. THOREAU, "Conclusion," *Walden* (1854).

12. Most people die of a sort of creeping common sense, and discover when it is too late that the only things one never regrets are one's mistakes. OSCAR WILDE, *The Picture of Dorian Gray* (1891), 3.

## 148. COMMUNICATION

**See also 132. Clarity; 185. Conversation; 640. Obscurantism; 916. Speaking; 1062. Writing and Writers**

1. You cannot speak of ocean to a well-frog,—the creature of a narrower sphere. You cannot speak of ice to a summer insect,—the creature of a season. CHUANG TZU, "Autumn Floods" (4th–3rd c. B.C.), tr. Herbert A. Giles.

2. Speech is one symptom of Affection / And Silence one— / The perfectest communication / Is heard of none—. EMILY DICKINSON, *Poems* (c. 1862–86).

3. Much unhappiness has come into the world because of bewilderment and things left unsaid. DOSTOEVSKY, "Critical Articles: Introduction," *Polnoye Sobraniye Sochinyeni* (*Complete Collected Works*, 1895), v. 9.

4. When the eyes say one thing, and the tongue another, a practised man relies on the language of the first. EMERSON, "Behavior," *The Conduct of Life* (1860).

5. Use what language you will, you can never say anything but what you are. EMERSON, "Worship," *The Conduct of Life* (1860).

6. No one would talk much in society, if he only knew how often he misunderstands others. GOETHE, *Elective Affinities* (1809), 22.

7. To think justly, we must understand what others mean: to know the value of our thoughts, we must try their effect on other minds. WILLIAM HAZLITT, "On People of Sense," *The Plain Speaker* (1826).

8. The dumbness in the eyes of animals is more touching than the speech of men, but the dumbness in the speech of men is more agonizing than the eyes of animals. HINDUSTANI PROVERB.

9. Good communication is stimulating as black coffee, and just as hard to sleep after. ANNE MORROW LINDBERGH, "Argonauta," *Gift from the Sea* (1955).

10. We seek pitifully to convey to others the treasures of our heart, but they have not the power to accept them, and so we go lonely, side by side but not together, unable to know our fellows and unknown by them. W. SOMERSET MAUGHAM, *The Moon and Sixpence* (1919), 41.

11. The attempt to speak without speaking any particular language is not more hopeless than the attempt to have a religion that shall be no religion in particular. GEORGE SANTAYANA, *The Life of Reason: Reason in Religion* (1905–06), 1.

12. In this world we must either institute conventional forms of expression or else pretend that we have nothing to express; the choice lies between a mask and a fig-leaf. GEORGE SANTAYANA, "Carnival," *Soliloquies in England* (1922).

13. I distrust the incommunicable; it is the source of all violence. JEAN-PAUL SARTRE, *What Is Literature* (1950), tr. Bernard Frechtman.

14. The articulate voice is more distracting than mere noise. SENECA, *Letters to Lucilius* (1st c.), 56, tr. E. Phillips Barker.

15. Precision of communication is important, more important than ever, in our era of hair-trigger balances, when a false, or misunderstood word may create as much disaster as a sudden thoughtless act. JAMES THURBER, "Friends, Romans, Countrymen, Lend Me Your Ear Muffs," *Lanterns and Lances* (1961).

## COMMUNICATIONS

**See 563. Mass Media**

## 149. COMMUNISM

**See also 393. Government; 887. Sharing; 905. Socialism**

1. In dealing with the Communists, remember that in their mind what is secret is serious, and what is public is merely propaganda. CHARLES E. BOHLEN, quoted by James Reston in *The New York Times*, Jan. 2, 1966.

2. There is not one single social or economic principle or concept in the philosophy of the Russian Bolshevik which has not been realized, carried into action, and enshrined in immutable laws a million years ago by the white ant. SIR WINSTON CHURCHILL, "Politics," *The Churchill Wit* (1965), ed. Bill Adler.

3. One strength of the communist system of the East is that it has some of the character of a religion and inspires the emotions of a religion. EINSTEIN, *Out of My Later Life* (1950), 31.

4. What is a communist? One who hath yearnings / For equal division of unequal earnings. EBENEZER ELLIOTT, "Epigram," *Poetical Works* (1840).

5. Let us beware of those who want to apply Communism coldly, of those who want, at whatever cost, to plow straight furrows on a curving field, of those who prefer to each man the idea they have formed of humanity. ANDRÉ GIDE, *Journals*, 1937, tr. Justin O'Brien.

6. Communists have committed great crimes, but at least they have not stood aside, like an established society, and been indifferent. I would rather have blood on my hands than water like Pilate. GRAHAM GREENE, *The Comedians* (1966).

7. What is the difference between Capitalism and Communism? Capitalism is the exploitation of man by man; Communism is the reverse. Joke reported from Warsaw.

8. The Communists offer one precious, fatal boon: they take away the sense of sin. MURRAY KEMPTON, "The Sheltered Life," *Part of Our Time* (1955).

9. As an organized political group, the Communists have done nothing to damage our society a fraction as much as what their enemies have done in the name of defending us against subversion. MURRAY KEMPTON, "What Harvey Did," *America Comes of Middle Age* (1963).

10. Communism has sometimes succeeded as a scavenger, but never as a leader. It has never come to power in any country that was not disrupted by war or internal corruption or both. JOHN F. KENNEDY, address, North Atlantic Treaty Organization headquarters, Naples, Italy, July 3, 1963.

11. Far from being a classless society, Communism is governed by an elite as steadfast in its determination to maintain its prerogatives as any oligarchy known to history. ROBERT F. KENNEDY, "Berlin East and West," *The Pursuit of Justice* (1964).

12. We should not wonder at the success of communism, for so much of its success is rather that of religion. ROBERT LINDNER, "Political Creed and Character," *Must You Conform?* (1956).

13. We Communists are like seeds and the people are like the soil. Wherever we go, we must unite with the people, take root and blossom among them. MAO TSE-TUNG, *Quotations from Chairman Mao Tse-tung* (1966), 28.

14. The objection to a Communist always resolves itself into the fact that he is not a gentleman. H. L. MENCKEN, *Minority Report* (1956), 15.

15. Leave the fear of red to horned animals. Poster during the French student riots, June 1968.

16. Communism is like Prohibition, it's a good idea but it won't work. WILL ROGERS, *The Autobiography of Will Rogers* (1949), 12.

17. Cow of many – well milked and badly fed. SPANISH PROVERB.

18. Communism is the corruption of a dream of justice. ADLAI STEVENSON, speech, Urbana, Ill., 1951.

## 150. COMMUNITY

**See also 98. Brotherhood; 976. Togetherness; 1009. Unity**

1. Rain does not fall on one roof alone. CAMEROONIAN PROVERB.

2. When the head aches, all the members partake of the pain. CERVANTES, *Don Quixote* (1605–15), 2.3.2, tr. Peter Motteux and John Ozell.

3. No man is an island, entire of itself; every man is a piece of the continent. JOHN DONNE, *Devotions* (1624), 17.

4. Life is lived in common, but not in community. MICHAEL HARRINGTON, *The Other America* (1962), 7.4.

5. Your own safety is at stake when your neighbor's wall is ablaze. HORACE, *Epistles* (20–c. 8 B.C.), 1.18.

6. What is not good for the swarm is not good for the bee. MARCUS AURELIUS, *Meditations* (2nd c.), 6.54, tr. Morris Hickey Morgan.

7. Mankind has become so much one family that we cannot insure our own prosperity except by insuring that of everyone else. If you wish to be happy yourself, you must resign yourself to seeing others also happy. BERTRAND RUSSELL, "The Science to Save Us from Science," *The New York Times Magazine*, March 19, 1950.

8. Man ceases to be concerned with himself: he recognizes of a sudden what he forms part of. If he should die, he would not be cutting himself off from his kind, but making himself one with them. SAINT-EXUPÉRY, *Flight to Arras* (1942), 19, tr. Lewis Galantière.

9. An isolated individual does not exist. He who is sad, saddens others. SAINT-EXUPÉRY, *Flight to Arras* (1942), 23, tr. Lewis Galantière.

10. I am a part of all that I have met. ALFRED, LORD TENNYSON, "Ulysses" (1842).

## 151. COMPANY

See also 7. Acquaintances; 57. Association; 363. Friendship; 426. Hospitality; 494. Interestingness; 787. Relationships, Human; 907. Society, Polite; 976. Togetherness

1. With three or more people there is something bold in the air: direct things get said which would frighten two people alone and conscious of each inch of their nearness to one another. To be three is to be in public, you feel safe. ELIZABETH BOWEN, *The House in Paris* (1935), 2.6.

2. Not only is there no question of solitude, but in the long run we may not choose our company. ELIZABETH BOWEN, *The Death of the Heart* (1938), 2.4.

3. He who must needs have company, must needs have sometimes bad company. SIR THOMAS BROWNE, *Christian Morals* (1716), 3.

4. The social, friendly, honest man, / Whate'er he be, / 'Tis he fulfils great Nature's plan, / And none but he! ROBERT BURNS, "Epistle to John Lapraik No. 2" (1786).

5. We do not mind our not arriving anywhere nearly so much as our not having any company on the way. FRANK MOORE COLBY, "Thinking It Through in Haste," *The Margin of Hesitation* (1921).

6. What is the odds so long as the fire of soul is kindled at the taper of conwiviality, and the wing of friendship never moults a feather? CHARLES DICKENS, *The Old Curiosity Shop* (1840), 2.

7. Now I grow sure, that if a man would have / Good company, his entry is a grave. JOHN DONNE, "Obsequies to the Lord Harrington, Brother to the Lady Lucy, Countess of Bedford" (c. 1614).

8. How many times go we to comedies, to masques, to places of great and noble resort, nay even to church only to see the company? JOHN DONNE, *Sermons*, No. 16, 1622.

9. No man can have society upon his own terms. If he seek it, he must serve it too. EMERSON, *Journals*, 1833.

10. To be social is to be forgiving. ROBERT FROST, "The Star-Splitter," *New Hampshire* (1923).

11. No man is much pleased with a companion who does not increase, in some respect, his fondness of himself. SAMUEL JOHNSON, *The Rambler* (1750–52), 104.

12. I live in the crowd of jollity, not so much to enjoy company as to shun myself. SAMUEL JOHNSON, *Rasselas* (1759), 16.

13. In general, American social life constitutes an evasion of talking to people. Most Americans don't, in any vital sense, get together; they only do things together. LOUIS KRONENBERGER, *Company Manners* (1954).

14. While you are alone you are entirely your own master and if you have one companion you are but half your own, and the less so in proportion to the indiscretion of his behavior. LEONARDO DA VINCI, *Notebooks* (c. 1500), tr. Jean Paul Richter.

15. Infinitely often it is clear that we appreciate, even respect—not a multitude—but ten people gathered in a room, each of whom, taken by himself, we consider of no account. GIACOMO LEOPARDI, *Pensieri* (1834–37), 83, tr. William Fense Weaver.

16. Man loves company even if only that

of a small burning candle. GEORG CHRISTOPH LICHTENBERG, *Aphorisms* (1764–99), tr. F. H. Mautner and H. Hatfield.

17. Hating the crowd, where gregarious men / Lead lonely lives, I love society. JAMES RUSSELL LOWELL, title poem, *Under the Willows and Other Poems* (1868).

18. "Love or perish" we are told and we tell ourselves. The phrase is true enough so long as we do not interpret it as "Mingle or be a failure." PHYLLIS MC GINLEY, "A Lost Privilege," *The Province of the Heart* (1959).

19. An ancient father says that a dog we know is better company than a man whose language we do not understand. MONTAIGNE, "Of liars," *Essays* (1580–88), tr. Charles Cotton and W. C. Hazlitt.

20. At the heart of our friendly or purely social relations, there lurks a hostility momentarily cured but recurring by fits and starts. MARCEL PROUST, *Remembrance of Things Past: Cities of the Plain* (1913–27), tr. C. K. Scott-Moncrieff.

21. An agreeable companion on a journey is as good as a carriage. PUBLILIUS SYRUS, *Moral Sayings* (1st c. B.C.), 143, tr. Darius Lyman.

22. Society in shipwreck is a comfort to all. PUBLILIUS SYRUS, *Moral Sayings* (1st c. B.C.), 144, tr. Darius Lyman.

23. To have the universe bear one company would be a great consolation in death. PUBLILIUS SYRUS, *Moral Sayings* (1st c. B.C.), 894, tr. Darius Lyman.

24. Society is no comfort / To one not sociable. SHAKESPEARE, *Cymbeline* (1609–10), 4.2.12.

25. The American has dwindled into an Odd Fellow,—one who may be known by the development of his organ of gregariousness. THOREAU, *Civil Disobedience* (1849).

26. What men call social virtues, good fellowship, is commonly but the virtue of pigs in a litter, which lie close together to keep each other warm. THOREAU, *Journal*, Oct. 23, 1851.

27. Society is commonly too cheap. We meet at very short intervals, not having had time to acquire any new value for each other. We meet at meals three times a day, and give each other a new taste of that old musty cheese that we are. THOREAU, "Solitude," *Walden* (1854).

28. Good company and good discourse are the very sinews of virtue. IZAAK WALTON, *The Compleat Angler* (1653), 1.2.

## 152. COMPARISON

**See also 15. Advantage; 17. Adversity; 153. Compensation; 177. Consolations; 184. Contrast; 788. Relativeness**

1. Comparison, more than reality, makes men happy or wretched. THOMAS FULLER, M.D., *Gnomologia* (1732), 1133.

2. Nothing is good or bad but by comparison. THOMAS FULLER, M.D., *Gnomologia* (1732), 3966.

3. Instead of comparing our lot with that of those who are more fortunate than we are, we should compare it with the lot of the great majority of our fellow men. It then appears that we are among the privileged. HELEN KELLER, *We Bereaved* (1929).

4. I murmured because I had no shoes, until I met a man who had no feet. PERSIAN PROVERB.

5. The man with toothache thinks everyone happy whose teeth are sound. The poverty stricken man makes the same mistake about the rich man. GEORGE BERNARD SHAW, "Maxims for Revolutionists," *Man and Superman* (1903).

## COMPASSION

**See 577. Mercy; 692. Pity**

## 153. COMPENSATION

**See also 15. Advantage; 152. Comparison; 177. Consolations; 745. Prosperity and Adversity**

1. Every sweet hath its sour; every evil its good. EMERSON, "Compensation," *Essays: First Series* (1841).

## 154. COMPETITION

**See also 26. Aggression; 33. Ambition**

1. Competitions are for horses, not artists. BÉLA BARTÓK, *Saturday Review*, Aug. 25, 1962.

2. It is in the blood of genius to love play for its own sake, and whether one uses one's skill on thrones or women, swords or pens,

gold or fame, the game's the thing. GELETT BURGESS, "April Essays," *The Romance of the Commonplace* (1916).

3. One barber shaves not so close but another finds work. ENGLISH PROVERB.

4. When two souls compose a single song, / The muse fans / Livid wrath before long. EURIPIDES, *Andromache* (c. 426 B.C.), tr. John F. Nims.

5. He may well win the race that runs by himself. BENJAMIN FRANKLIN, *Poor Richard's Almanack* (1732–57).

6. Life should be a humane / undertaking. I know. I / undertook it. Yet have found / that in every move / I prevent someone / from stepping where I step. THOM GUNN, *Positives* (1967).

7. Potter is potter's enemy, and craftsman is craftsman's / rival; tramp is jealous of tramp, and singer of singer. HESIOD, *Works and Days* (8th c. B.C.), 25, tr. Richmond Lattimore.

8. Man is a gaming animal. He must be always trying to get the better in something or other. CHARLES LAMB, "Mrs. Battle's Opinions on Whist," *Essays of Elia* (1823).

9. The world is but a school of inquisition: it is not who shall enter the ring, but who shall run the best courses. MONTAIGNE, "Of the art of conference," *Essays* (1580–88), tr. Charles Cotton and W. C. Hazlitt.

10. A horse never runs so fast as when he has other horses to catch up and outpace. OVID, *The Art of Love* (c. A.D. 8), 3, tr. J. Lewis May.

11. The combative instinct is a savage prompting by which one man's good is found in another's evil. GEORGE SANTAYANA, *The Life of Reason: Reason in Society* (1905–06), 3.

12. We learn not for life but for the debating-room. SENECA, *Letters to Lucilius* (1st c.), 106.12, tr. E. Phillips Barker.

13. Do as adversaries do in law— / Strive mightily, but eat and drink as friends. SHAKESPEARE, *The Taming of the Shrew* (1593–94), 1.2.278.

## 155. COMPLACENCY

**See also 163. Conceit; 727. Pride; 902. Smugness**

1. Comfort, n. A state of mind produced by contemplation of a neighbor's uneasiness. AMBROSE BIERCE, *The Devil's Dictionary* (1881–1911).

2. The seat of perfect contentment is in the head; for every individual is thoroughly satisfied with his own proportion of brains. CHARLES CALEB COLTON, *Lacon* (1825), 1.163.

3. If happiness in self-content is placed, / The wise are wretched, and fools only blessed. WILLIAM CONGREVE, *The Double-Dealer* (1694), 3.3.

4. He that is too secure is not safe. THOMAS FULLER, M.D., *Gnomologia* (1732), 2195.

5. The man who thinks his wife, his baby, his house, his horse, his dog, and himself severally unequalled, is almost sure to be a good-humored person, though liable to be tedious at times. OLIVER WENDELL HOLMES, SR., *The Autocrat of the Breakfast Table* (1858), 1.

6. Most human beings have an almost infinite capacity for taking things for granted. ALDOUS HUXLEY, "Variations on a Philosopher," *Themes and Variations* (1950).

7. We cannot be satisfied with things as they are. We cannot be satisfied to drift, to rest on our oars, to glide over a sea whose depths are shaken by subterranean upheavals. JOHN F. KENNEDY, campaign address, Syracuse, N.Y., Sept. 29, 1960.

8. Complacency is the enemy of study. We cannot really learn anything until we rid ourselves of complacency. MAO TSE-TUNG, *Quotations from Chairman Mao Tse-tung* (1966), 33.

9. The form most contradictory to human life that can appear among the human species is the "self-satisfied man." JOSÉ ORTEGA Y GASSET, *The Revolt of the Masses* (1930), 11.

10. The path is smooth that leadeth on to danger. SHAKESPEARE, *Venus and Adonis* (1593), 788.

## 156. COMPLAINT

1. To make wail and lament for one's ill fortune, when one will win a tear from the audience, is well worthwhile. AESCHYLUS, *Prometheus Bound* (c. 478 B.C.), tr. David Grene.

2. The dogs bark, but the caravan moves on. ARABIC PROVERB.

3. Such is the historical importance of "griping" in this country that a man, to stand on his own feet in a powerfully changing world, must keep himself up by his own gripes. ERIK H. ERIKSON, *Childhood and Society* (1950), 8.

4. Howsoever every man may complain occasionally of the hardships of his condition, he is seldom willing to change it for any other on the same level. SAMUEL JOHNSON, *The Rambler* (1750–52), 2.

5. When people cease to complain, they cease to think. NAPOLEON I, *Maxims* (1804–15).

6. He that falls by himself never cries. TURKISH PROVERB.

## COMPLETION

See 283. Ending

## 157. COMPLIANCE

See also 683. Persuasion

1. He that complies against his will, / Is of his own opinion still. SAMUEL BUTLER (d. 1680), *Hudibras* (1663), 3.3.

2. Much compliance, much craft. THOMAS FULLER, M.D., *Gnomologia* (1732), 3479.

## 158. COMPLIMENTS

See also 346. Flattery

1. Compliments cost nothing, yet many pay dear for them. GERMAN PROVERB.

2. A compliment is something like a kiss through a veil. VICTOR HUGO, "Saint Denis," *Les Misérables* (1862), 8.1, tr. Charles E. Wilbour.

3. To say a compliment well is a high art and few possess it. MARK TWAIN, letter to John Brisben Walker, Oct. 19, 1909.

4. There is nothing you can say in answer to a compliment. I have been complimented myself a great many times, and they always embarrass me—I always feel that they have not said enough. MARK TWAIN, "Fulton Day, Jamestown," *Speeches* (1923), ed. A. B. Paine.

5. When you cannot get a compliment in any other way pay yourself one. MARK TWAIN, *Notebook* (1935).

6. Ah, now-a-days we are all of us so hard up, that the only pleasant things to pay are compliments. They're the only things we *can* pay. OSCAR WILDE, *Lady Windermere's Fan* (1892), 1.

## 159. COMPOSURE

See also 982. Tranquility

1. Calmness is always Godlike. EMERSON, *Journals*, 1840.

2. To bear all naked truths, / And to envisage circumstance, all calm, / That is the top of sovereignty. JOHN KEATS, "Hyperion" (1820), 2.

3. Everyone knows that in most people's estimation, to do anything coolly is to do it genteelly. HERMAN MELVILLE, *Moby Dick* (1851), 5.

4. He is a first-rate collector who can, upon all occasions, collect his wits. GEORGE DENNISON PRENTICE, *Prenticeana* (1860).

5. Nothing is so aggravating as calmness. There is something positively brutal about the good temper of most modern men. OSCAR WILDE, *A Woman of No Importance* (1893), 2.

## COMPREHENSION

See 1000. Understanding

## 160. COMPROMISE

See also 27. Agreement; 46. Appeasement; 164. Conciliation; 987. Treaties

1. Compromise, n. Such an adjustment of conflicting interests as gives each adversary the satisfaction of thinking he has got what he ought not to have, and is deprived of nothing except what was justly his due. AMBROSE BIERCE, *The Devil's Dictionary* (1881–1911).

2. All government,—indeed, every human benefit and enjoyment, every virtue and every prudent act,—is founded on compromise and barter. EDMUND BURKE, speech, "On Conciliation with the Ameri-

can Colonies," March 22, 1775.

3. If one could recover the uncompromising spirit of one's youth, one's greatest indignation would be for what one has become. ANDRÉ GIDE, *The Counterfeiters* (1925), 1.18, tr. Dorothy Bussy.

4. A lean compromise is better than a fat lawsuit. GEORGE HERBERT, *Jacula Prudentum* (1651).

5. It is better to lose the saddle than the horse. ITALIAN PROVERB.

6. If you cannot catch a bird of paradise, better take a wet hen. NIKITA KHRUSHCHEV, quoted in *Time*, Jan. 6, 1958.

7. Compromise, if not the spice of life, is its solidity. PHYLLIS MC GINLEY, "Suburbia, of Thee I Sing," *The Province of the Heart* (1959).

## 161. COMPULSIVENESS

**See also 10. Activity; 620. Neurosis; 643. Obsession**

1. They must needs go whom the Devil drives. CERVANTES, *Don Quixote* (1605–15), 1.4.4, tr. Peter Motteux and John Ozell.

## 162. CONCEALMENT

**See also 197. Craftiness; 438. Hypocrisy**

1. Do not reveal your thoughts to everyone, lest you drive away your good luck. *Apocrypha*, Ecclesiasticus 8:19.

2. The power of hiding ourselves from one another is mercifully given, for men are wild beasts, and would devour one another but for this protection. HENRY WARD BEECHER, *Proverbs from Plymouth Pulpit* (1887).

3. There is nothing that gives more assurance than a mask. COLETTE, "Literary Apprenticeship: 'Claudine,'" *Earthly Paradise* (1966), 2, ed. Robert Phelps.

4. It is most absurdly said, in popular language, of any man, that he is disguised in liquor; for, on the contrary, most men are disguised by sobriety. THOMAS DE QUINCEY, *Confessions of an English Opium-Eater* (1821–56).

5. He who conceals his disease cannot expect to be cured. ETHIOPIAN PROVERB.

6. From your confessor, lawyer and physician, / Hide not your case on no condition. SIR JOHN HARINGTON, *The Metamorphosis of Ajax* (1596), 98.

7. No man, for any considerable period, can wear one face to himself, and another to the multitude, without finally getting bewildered as to which may be the true. NATHANIEL HAWTHORNE, *The Scarlet Letter* (1850), 20.

8. Our greatest pretenses are built up not to hide the evil and the ugly in us, but our emptiness. The hardest thing to hide is something that is not there. ERIC HOFFER, *The Passionate State of Mind* (1954), 217.

9. Have an open face, but conceal your thoughts. ITALIAN PROVERB.

10. A man had rather have a hundred lies told of him than one truth which he does not wish should be told. SAMUEL JOHNSON, quoted in Boswell's *Life of Samuel Johnson*, April 15, 1773.

11. Wolves can't catch what dogs do not expose. LA FONTAINE, "The Dog with Cropped Ears," *Fables* (1668–94), tr. Marianne Moore.

12. We are so accustomed to disguise ourselves to others, that in the end we become disguised to ourselves. LA ROCHEFOUCAULD, *Maxims* (1665), tr. Kenneth Pratt.

13. Customary use of artifice is the sign of a small mind, and it almost always happens that he who uses it to cover one spot uncovers himself in another. LA ROCHEFOUCAULD, *Maxims* (1665), tr. Kenneth Pratt.

14. The surest way of concealing from others the boundaries of one's own knowledge is not to overstep them. GIACOMO LEOPARDI, *Pensieri* (1834–37), 86, tr. William Fense Weaver.

15. It is the bright, the bold, the transparent who are cleverest among those who are silent: their ground is down so deep that even the brightest water does not betray it. NIETZSCHE, "Upon the Mount of Olives," *Thus Spoke Zarathustra* (1883–92), 3, tr. Walter Kaufmann.

16. Talking about oneself can also be a means to conceal oneself. NIETZSCHE, *Beyond Good and Evil* (1886), 169, tr. Walter Kaufmann.

17. Woe to him who doesn't know how to wear his mask, be he king or Pope! LUIGI PIRANDELLO, *Henry IV* (1922), 1, tr. Edward Storer.

18. Concealment is equated, unknow-

ingly to ourselves, with individuality: the more we conceal the more it seems we are asserting our very personality, resisting a somewhat repellent, unwelcome intrusion of other things into ourselves. ELI SIEGEL, "The Ordinary Doom," *A Book of Nonfiction* (1960).

19. The bad are frequently good enough to let you see how bad they are, but the good as frequently endeavor to get between you and themselves. THOREAU, *Journal*, Dec. 2, 1851.

20. Everyone is a moon and has a dark side which he never shows to anybody. MARK TWAIN, *Notebook* (1935).

21. A mask tells us more than a face. OSCAR WILDE, "Pen, Pencil and Poison," *Intentions* (1891).

## 163. CONCEIT

**See also 87. Boasting; 155. Complacency; 433. Humility; 727. Pride; 869. Self-love; 1020. Vanity**

1. The smaller the mind the greater the conceit. AESOP, "The Gnat and the Bull," *Fables* (6th c. B.C.?), tr. Thomas James.

2. Why do men seek honour? Surely in order to confirm the favourable opinion they have formed of themselves. ARISTOTLE, *Nicomachean Ethics* (4th c. B.C.), 1.5, tr. J. A. K. Thomson.

3. To say that a man is vain means merely that he is pleased with the effect he produces on other people. A conceited man is satisfied with the effect he produces on himself. MAX BEERBOHM, "Quia Imperfectum," *And Even Now* (1920).

4. There has never been a poet or orator who thought another better than himself. CICERO, *Ad Atticum* (1st c. B.C.), 14.

5. Those who know the least of others think the highest of themselves. CHARLES CALEB COLTON, *Lacon* (1825), 1.443.

6. I've never any pity for conceited people, because I think they carry their comfort about with them. GEORGE ELIOT, *The Mill on the Floss* (1860), 5.4.

7. What is the first business of philosophy? To part with self-conceit. For it is impossible for any one to begin to learn what he thinks that he already knows. EPICTETUS, *Discourses* (2nd c.), 2.17, tr. Thomas W. Higginson.

8. Conceit is vanity driven from all other shifts, and forced to appeal to itself for admiration. WILLIAM HAZLITT, *Characteristics* (1823), 110.

9. Talk about conceit as much as you like, it is to human character what salt is to the ocean; it keeps it sweet, and renders it endurable. OLIVER WENDELL HOLMES, SR., *The Autocrat of the Breakfast Table* (1858), 1.

10. Conceit is the finest armour a man can wear. JEROME K. JEROME, "On Being Shy," *The Idle Thoughts of an Idle Fellow* (1889).

11. Whenever Nature leaves a hole in a person's mind, she generally plasters it over with a thick coat of self-conceit. LONGFELLOW, "Intellect," *The Blank-Book of a Country Schoolmaster* (1857).

12. The bigger a man's head, the worse his headache. PERSIAN PROVERB.

13. Conceit may puff a man up, but never prop him up. JOHN RUSKIN, *Pre-Raphaelitism* (1851), 7.

14. Every person thinks his own intellect perfect, and his own child handsome. SA'DI, *Gulistan* (1258), 8.31, tr. James Ross.

## CONCENTRATION

**See 896. Single-mindedness**

## 164. CONCILIATION

**See also 46. Appeasement; 160. Compromise; 987. Treaties**

1. A soft answer turneth away wrath. *Bible*, Proverbs 15:1.

2. Blessed are the peacemakers: for they shall be called the children of God. *Bible*, Matthew 5:9.

3. Be swift to hear, slow to speak, slow to wrath. *Bible*, James 1:19.

4. Blessed are the peacemakers, / For they have freed themselves from sinful wrath. DANTE, "Purgatorio," 17, *The Divine Comedy* (c. 1300–21), tr. Lawrence Grant White.

5. Not by a radiant jewel, not by the sun nor by fire, but by conciliation alone is dis-

pelled the darkness born of enmity. *Panchatantra* (c. 5th c.), 1, tr. Franklin Edgerton.

6. Your If is the only peacemaker. Much virtue in If. SHAKESPEARE, *As You Like It* (1599–1600), 5.4.107.

7. It behooves a prudent person to make trial of everything before arms. TERENCE, *The Eunuch* (161 B.C.), 4.7.19, tr. Henry Thomas Riley.

8. Settlements may be temporary, but the action of the nations in the interest of peace and justice must be permanent. We can set up permanent processes. We may not be able to set up permanent decisions. WOODROW WILSON, address, Paris, Jan. 25, 1919.

## CONDOLENCE
See 953. Sympathy

## CONDUCT
See 75. Behavior

## 165. CONFESSION

1. A generous confession disarms slander. THOMAS FULLER, M.D., *Gnomologia* (1732), 126.

2. We acknowledge our faults in order to repair by our sincerity the damage they have done us in the eyes of others. LA ROCHEFOUCAULD, *Maxims* (1665), tr. Kenneth Pratt.

3. The confession of one man humbles all. ANTONIO PORCHIA, *Voces* (1968), tr. W. S. Merwin.

4. Confession of our faults is the next thing to innocence. PUBLILIUS SYRUS, *Moral Sayings* (1st c. B.C.), 1060, tr. Darius Lyman.

5. It is not the criminal things which are hardest to confess, but the ridiculous and shameful. ROUSSEAU, *Confessions* (1766–70), 1.1.

## CONFIDENCE
See 113. Certainty; 657. Overconfidence; 849. Secrets; 854. Self-confidence

## 166. CONFIDENCES
See also 849. Secrets

1. No receipt [recipe] openeth the heart, but a true friend, to whom you may impart griefs, joys, fears, hopes, suspicions, counsels, and whatsoever lieth upon the heart to oppress it. FRANCIS BACON, "Of Friendship," *Essays* (1625).

2. We rarely confide in those who are better than we are. ALBERT CAMUS, *The Fall* (1956).

3. Shyness has laws: you can only give yourself, tragically, to those who least understand. LAWRENCE DURRELL, *Justine* (1957), 2.

4. Doubtless a good general rule for close friendships, where confidences are freely exchanged, is that what one is not informed about one may not inquire about. LOUIS KRONENBERGER, *Company Manners* (1954), 2.2.

5. It is so much easier to tell intimate things in the dark. WILLIAM MC FEE, *Casuals of the Sea* (1916), 1.1.4.

6. If thou tellest the sorrows of thy heart, let it be to him in whose countenance thou mayst be assured of prompt consolation. SA'DI, *Gulistan* (1258), 3.13, tr. James Ross.

7. A healthy ear can stand hearing sick words. SENEGALESE PROVERB.

8. To whom you tell your secrets, to him you resign your liberty. SPANISH PROVERB.

## 167. CONFLICT, INNER
See also 495. Interests, Divided; 684. Perverseness

1. When the fight begins within himself, / A man's worth something. ROBERT BROWNING, "Bishop Blougram's Apology," *Men and Women* (1855).

2. I hate and love. You ask, perhaps, how that can be? / I know not, but I feel the agony. CATULLUS, *Poems* (1st c. B.C.), 85, tr. Gilbert Highet.

3. We are sure to be losers when we quarrel with ourselves; it is a civil war, and in all such contentions, triumphs are defeats. CHARLES CALEB COLTON, *Lacon* (1825), 1.439.

4. What man knows is everywhere at war with what he wants. JOSEPH WOOD KRUTCH, "The Genesis of a Mood," *The Modern Temper* (1929).

## 168. CONFORMITY

**See also 12. Adjustment; 89. Bohemians; 466. Individualism; 630. Normality; 926. Status; 928. Stereotypes**

1. Abnormal, adj. Not conforming to standard. In matters of thought and conduct, to be independent is to be abnormal, to be abnormal is to be detested. AMBROSE BIERCE, *The Devil's Dictionary* (1881–1911).

2. It isn't difficult to keep alive, friends—just don't *make* trouble—or if you must make trouble, make the sort of trouble that's expected. ROBERT BOLT, *A Man for All Seasons* (1962), 2.

3. Conformity is the ape of harmony. EMERSON, *Journals*, 1840.

4. The great majority of men grow up and grow old in seeming and following. EMERSON, *Journals*, 1841.

5. No man on earth is truly free, / All are slaves of money or necessity. / Public opinion or fear of prosecution / forces each one, against his conscience, to conform. EURIPIDES, *Hecuba* (c. 425 B.C.), tr. William Arrowsmith.

6. People are always talking about originality, but what do they mean? As soon as we are born, the world begins to work upon us, and this goes on to the end. GOETHE, quoted in Johann Peter Eckermann's *Conversations with Goethe*, May 12, 1825.

7. Try not to beat back the current, yet be not drowned in its waters; / Speak with the speech of the world, think with the thoughts of the few. JOHN HAY, "Distichs" (1871?), 17.

8. Conformity is the jailer of freedom and the enemy of growth. JOHN F. KENNEDY, address to United Nations General Assembly, Sept. 25, 1961.

9. Success, recognition, and conformity are the bywords of the modern world where everyone seems to crave the anesthetizing security of being identified with the majority. MARTIN LUTHER KING, JR., *Strength to Love* (1963), 2.

10. One of the saddest things about conformity is the ghastly sort of non-conformity it breeds: the noisy protesting, the aggressive rebelliousness, the rigid counterfetishism. LOUIS KRONENBERGER, *Company Manners* (1954), 3.3.

11. Conformity, humility, acceptance—with these coins we are to pay our fares to paradise. ROBERT LINDNER, title essay, *Must You Conform?* (1956).

12. How protean are the devices available to human intelligence when it lends itself to the persistence of the conformist error. ROBERT LINDNER, "Homosexuality and the Contemporary Scene," *Must You Conform?* (1956).

13. Trumpet in a herd of elephants; / Crow in the company of cocks; / Bleat in a flock of goats. MALAY PROVERB.

14. No reason makes it right /To shun accepted ways from stubborn spite; / And we may better join the foolish crowd / Than cling to wisdom, lonely though unbowed. MOLIÈRE, *The School for Husbands* (1661), 1.2, tr. Donald M. Frame.

15. Men are created different; they lose their social freedom and their individual autonomy in seeking to become like each other. DAVID RIESMAN, "Autonomy and Utopia," *The Lonely Crowd* (1950).

16. "Queuemania" is an ailment that afflicts people with a compulsive urge to line up behind someone or something, even a lamp-post. THOMAS P. RONAN, *The New York Times*, Aug. 23, 1955.

17. We are half ruined by conformity, but we should be wholly ruined without it. CHARLES DUDLEY WARNER, "Eighteenth Week," *My Summer in a Garden* (1871).

18. We arrange our lives—even the best and boldest men and women that exist, just as much as the most limited—with reference to what society conventionally rules and makes right. WALT WHITMAN, "Ventures, on an Old Theme," *Notes Left Over* (1881).

## CONFUSION

**See 255. Disorder**

## 169. CONGRESS

**See also 393. Government; 705. Politics and Politicians; 755. Public Office**

1. Of representative assemblies may not this good be said: That contending parties in a country do thereby ascertain one another's strength? They fight there, since fight they must, by petition, parliamentary eloquence, not by sword, bayonet and bursts of military cannon. THOMAS CARLYLE, *Chartism* (1839), 8.

2. He who is free and blessed has his twenty-thousandth part of a master of tongue-fence in National Palaver; whosoever is not blessed but unhappy, the ailment of him is that he has it not. THOMAS CARLYLE, *Chartism* (1839), 9.

3. Congress—these, for the most part, illiterate hacks whose fancy vests are spotted with gravy, and whose speeches, hypocritical, unctuous, and slovenly, are spotted also with the gravy of political patronage. MARY MC CARTHY, "America the Beautiful: The Humanist in the Bathtub," *On the Contrary* (1961).

4. Large legislative bodies resolve themselves into coteries, and coteries into jealousies. NAPOLEON I, *Maxims* (1804–15).

5. The way to judge a good Comedy is by how long it will last and have people talk about it. Now Congress has turned out some that have lived for years and people are still laughing about them. WILL ROGERS, *The Autobiography of Will Rogers* (1949), 8.

6. A Congressman is never any better than his roads, and sometimes worse. WILL ROGERS, *The Autobiography of Will Rogers* (1949), 19.

7. It is the duty of the President to propose and it is the privilege of the Congress to dispose. FRANKLIN D. ROOSEVELT, press conference, July 23, 1937.

8. It could probably be shown by facts and figures that there is no distinctly native American criminal class except Congress. MARK TWAIN, "Pudd'nhead Wilson's New Calendar," *Following the Equator* (1897), 1.8.

## 170. CONQUEST

**See also 938. Success; 1035. War**

1. When you have gained a victory, do not push it too far; 'tis sufficient to let the company and your adversary see 'tis in your power but that you are too generous to make use of it. EUSTACE BUDGELL in *The Spectator* (1711–12), 197.

2. Victory at all costs, victory in spite of all terror, victory however long and hard the road may be; for without victory there is no survival. SIR WINSTON CHURCHILL, House of Commons, May 13, 1940.

3. The problems of victory are more agreeable than those of defeat, but they are no less difficult. SIR WINSTON CHURCHILL, speech, House of Commons, Nov. 11, 1942.

4. He that has gone so far as to cut the claws of the lion, will not feel himself quite secure until he has also drawn his teeth. CHARLES CALEB COLTON, *Lacon* (1825), 1.43.

5. The god of Victory is said to be one-handed, but Peace gives victory to both sides. EMERSON, *Journals*, 1867.

6. Dead men have no victory. EURIPIDES, *The Phoenician Women* (c. 411–409 B.C.), tr. Elizabeth Wyckoff.

7. One completely overcomes only what one assimilates. ANDRÉ GIDE, *Journals*, 1922, tr. Justin O'Brien.

8. All victories breed hate, and that over your superior is foolish or fatal. BALTASAR GRACIÁN, *The Art of Worldly Wisdom* (1647), 7, tr. Joseph Jacobs.

9. He that is taken and put into prison or chains is not conquered, though overcome; for he is still an enemy. THOMAS HOBBES, "A Review and Conclusion," *Leviathan* (1651).

10. 'Tis man's to fight, but Heaven's to give success. HOMER, *Iliad* (9th c. B.C.), 6.427, tr. Alexander Pope.

11. When in doubt, win the trick. EDMOND HOYLE, "Twenty-four Short Rules for Learners," *Hoyle's Games: Whist* (1742).

12. In human history a moral victory is always a disaster, for it debauches and degrades both the victor and the vanquished. H. L. MENCKEN, "The Calamity of Appomattox," *The American Mercury*, September 1930.

13. Triumph cannot help being cruel. JOSÉ ORTEGA Y GASSET, *Notes on the Novel* (1925).

14. There is no pain in the wound received in the moment of victory. PUBLILIUS SYRUS, *Moral Sayings* (1st c. B.C.), 1077, tr. Darius Lyman.

15. The right of conquest has no foundation other than the right of the strongest. ROUSSEAU, *The Social Contract* (1762), 1.4, tr. G. D. H. Cole.

16. You win the victory when you yield to friends. SOPHOCLES, *Ajax* (c. 447 B.C.), tr. John Moore.

17. Minds are conquered not by arms, but by love and magnanimity. SPINOZA, *Ethics* (1677), 4, tr. Andrew Boyle.

18. War will of itself discover and lay open the hidden and rankling wounds of

the victorious party. TACITUS, *Histories* (A.D. 104–109), 2.77, tr. Alfred J. Church and William J. Brodribb.

19. To conquer with arms is to make only a temporary conquest; to conquer the world by earning its esteem is to make a permanent conquest. WOODROW WILSON, address to Congress, Nov. 11, 1918.

## 171. CONSCIENCE

**See also 403. Guilt; 598. Morality; 816. Right; 1063. Wrongdoing**

1. Conscience is the frame of character, and love is the covering for it. HENRY WARD BEECHER, *Proverbs from Plymouth Pulpit* (1887).

2. Conscience is thoroughly well-bred and soon leaves off talking to those who do not wish to hear it. SAMUEL BUTLER (d. 1902), *Note-Books* (1912).

3. In many walks of life, a conscience is a more expensive encumbrance than a wife or a carriage. THOMAS DE QUINCEY, "Preliminary Confessions," *Confessions of an English Opium-Eater* (1821–56).

4. Nothing but man of all invenomed things / Doth work upon itself, with inborne stings. JOHN DONNE, "Elegy on the Lady Marckham" (1609).

5. God has delegated himself to a million deputies. EMERSON, "Worship," *The Conduct of Life* (1860).

6. A guilty conscience needs no accuser. ENGLISH PROVERB.

7. A quiet conscience sleeps in thunder. ENGLISH PROVERB.

8. The fact that human conscience remains partially infantile throughout life is the core of human tragedy. ERIK H. ERIKSON, *Childhood and Society* (1950), 7.

9. There is one thing alone / that stands the brunt of life throughout its course, / a quiet conscience. EURIPIDES, *Hippolytus* (428 B.C.), tr. David Grene.

10. A good conscience is the best divinity. THOMAS FULLER, M.D., *Gnomologia* (1732), 141.

11. Conscience is a just but a weak judge. Weakness leaves it powerless to execute its judgment. KAHLIL GIBRAN, "A Story of a Friend," *Thoughts and Meditations* (1960), tr. Anthony R. Ferris.

12. Conscience is a coward, and those faults it has not strength enough to prevent it seldom has justice enough to accuse. OLIVER GOLDSMITH, *The Vicar of Wakefield* (1766), 13.

13. If we cannot be powerful and happy and prey on others, we invent conscience and prey on ourselves. ELBERT HUBBARD, *The Philistine* (1895–1915).

14. Our conscience is not the vessel of eternal verities. It grows with our social life, and a new social condition means a radical change in conscience. WALTER LIPPMANN, "Some Necessary Iconoclasm," *A Preface to Politics* (1914).

15. A state of conscience is higher than a state of innocence. THOMAS MANN, in *I Believe* (1939), ed. Clifton Fadiman.

16. Conscience is the guardian in the individual of the rules which the community has evolved for its own preservation. W. SOMERSET MAUGHAM, *The Moon and Sixpence* (1919), 14.

17. Conscience is the inner voice which warns us that someone may be looking. H. L. MENCKEN, "Sententiae," *A Book of Burlesques* (1920).

18. The laws of conscience, which we pretend to be derived from nature, proceed from custom. MONTAIGNE, "Of custom," *Essays* (1580–88), tr. Charles Cotton and W. C. Hazlitt.

19. There is only one way to achieve happiness on this terrestrial ball, / And that is to have either a clear conscience, or none at all. OGDEN NASH, "Inter-Office Memorandum," *I'm a Stranger Here Myself* (1938).

20. It is only because man believes himself to be free, not because he is free, that he experiences remorse and pricks of conscience. NIETZSCHE, *Human, All Too Human* (1878), 39, tr. Helen Zimmern.

21. The bite of conscience teaches men to bite. NIETZSCHE, "On the Pitying," *Thus Spoke Zarathustra* (1883–92), 2, tr. Walter Kaufmann.

22. Don't you see that that blessed conscience of yours is nothing but other people inside you? LUIGI PIRANDELLO, *Each in His Own Way* (1924), 1, tr. Arthur Livingston.

23. We believe that humanness consists in what we call conscience, in that courage, if you wish, which we have shown on one single occasion rather than in the cowardice which on many occasions has counselled

prudence. LUIGI PIRANDELLO, *Each in His Own Way* (1924), 2, tr. Arthur Livingston.

24. Even when there is no law, there is conscience. PUBLILIUS SYRUS, *Moral Sayings* (1st c. B.C.), 237, tr. Darius Lyman.

25. An evil conscience is often quiet, but never secure. PUBLILIUS SYRUS, *Moral Sayings* (1st c. B.C.), 1084, tr. Darius Lyman.

26. The strongest feelings assigned to the conscience are not moral feelings at all; they express merely physical antipathies. GEORGE SANTAYANA, *The Life of Reason: Reason in Science* (1905–06), 9.

27. My conscience hath a thousand several tongues, / And every tongue brings in a several tale, / And every tale condemns me for a villain. SHAKESPEARE, *Richard III* (1592–93), 5.3.194.

28. Conscience does make cowards of us all. SHAKESPEARE, *Hamlet* (1600), 3.1.83.

29. A peace above all earthly dignities, / A still and quiet conscience. SHAKESPEARE, *Henry VIII* (1612–13), 3.2.379.

30. Trust that man in nothing who has not a conscience in everything. LAURENCE STERNE, *Sermons* (1760–69), 27.

31. The glory of good men is in their conscience and not in the mouths of men. THOMAS À KEMPIS, *The Imitation of Christ* (1426), 2.6.

32. The more estimable the offender, the greater the torment. VOLTAIRE, *Sémiramis* (1748), 5.8.

33. Conscience and cowardice are really the same things. Conscience is the trade name of the firm. OSCAR WILDE, *The Picture of Dorian Gray* (1891), 1.

## 172. CONSCIOUSNESS

**See also 876. Sensibility; 999. Unconsciousness**

1. A sub-clerk in the post office is the equal of a conqueror if consciousness is common to them. ALBERT CAMUS, "The Absurd Man," *The Myth of Sisyphus* (1942), tr. Justin O'Brien.

2. I do not know the man so bold / He dare in lonely Place / That awful stranger Consciousness / Deliberately face—. EMILY DICKINSON, poem (c. 1874).

3. To be too conscious is an illness—a real thorough-going illness. DOSTOEVSKY, *Notes from Underground* (1864), 1.2, tr. Constance Garnett.

4. The ultimate gift of conscious life is a sense of the mystery that encompasses it. LEWIS MUMFORD, "Orientation to Life," *The Conduct of Life* (1951).

5. If I were to begin life again, I should want it as it was. I would only open my eyes a little more. JULES RENARD, *Journal*, March 1906, ed. and tr. Louise Bogan and Elizabeth Roget.

## 173. CONSEQUENCES

**See also 108. Cause and Effect; 337. Fate; 505. Irrevocableness; 809. Retribution**

1. Quite often good things have hurtful consequences. There are instances of men who have been ruined by their money or killed by their courage. ARISTOTLE, *Nicomachean Ethics* (4th c. B.C.), 1.3, tr. J. A. K. Thomson.

2. How great a matter a little fire kindleth! *Bible*, James 3:5.

3. All systems of morality are based on the idea that an action has consequences that legitimize or cancel it. A mind imbued with the absurd merely judges that those consequences must be considered calmly. ALBERT CAMUS, "The Absurd Man," *The Myth of Sisyphus* (1942), tr. Justin O'Brien.

4. A mighty flame followeth a tiny spark. DANTE, "Paradiso," 1, *The Divine Comedy* (c. 1300–21), tr. J. A. Carlyle and P. H. Wicksteed.

5. The sower may mistake and sow his peas crookedly: the peas make no mistake, but come up and show his line. EMERSON, *Journals*, 1843.

6. A bad beginning makes a bad ending. EURIPIDES, *Aeolus* (c. 423 B.C.), 32, tr. M. H. Morgan.

7. Everything we do has a result. But that which is right and prudent does not always lead to good, nor the contrary to what is bad. GOETHE, quoted in Johann Peter Eckermann's *Conversations with Goethe*, Dec. 25, 1825.

8. Logical consequences are the scarecrows of fools and the beacons of wise men. THOMAS HENRY HUXLEY, "Animal Automatism" (1874).

9. The consequences of our actions take hold of us quite indifferent to our claim that meanwhile we have "improved." NIETZ-

SCHE, *Beyond Good and Evil* (1886), 179, tr. Walter Kaufmann.

10. In each action we must look beyond the action at our past, present, and future state, and at others whom it affects, and see the relations of all those things. And then we shall be very cautious. PASCAL, *Pensées* (1670), 505, tr. W. F. Trotter.

11. Half of the results of a good intention are evil; half the results of an evil intention are good. MARK TWAIN, "The Dervish and the Offensive Stranger," *Europe and Elsewhere* (1923).

## 174. CONSERVATION

**See also 29. Air Pollution; 292. Environment; 988. Trees**

1. The world to-day is sick to its thin blood for lack of elemental things, for fire before the hands, for water welling from the earth, for air, for dear earth itself underfoot. HENRY BESTON, "The Beach," *The Outermost House* (1928).

2. Do no dishonour to the earth lest you dishonour the spirit of man. HENRY BESTON, "Orion Rises on the Dunes," *The Outermost House* (1928).

3. [Man] thinks of himself as a creator instead of a user, and this delusion is robbing him, not only of his natural heritage, but perhaps of his future. HELEN HOOVER, "The Waiting Hills," *The Long-Shadowed Forest* (1963).

4. We abuse land because we regard it as a commodity belonging to us. When we see land as a community to which we belong, we may begin to use it with love and respect. ALDO LEOPOLD, quoted in Stewart L. Udall's *The Quiet Crisis* (1963), 14.

5. The earth we abuse and the living things we kill will, in the end, take their revenge; for in exploiting their presence we are diminishing our future. MARYA MANNES, *More in Anger* (1958), 1.5.

6. The nation that destroys its soil destroys itself. FRANKLIN D. ROOSEVELT, letter to the governors urging uniform soil conservation laws, Feb. 26, 1937.

7. Everything is perfect coming from the hands of the Creator; everything degenerates in the hands of man. ROUSSEAU, *Émile* (1762), 1.

8. The long fight to save wild beauty represents democracy at its best. It requires citizens to practice the hardest of virtues—self-restraint. EDWIN WAY TEALE, "February 2," *Circle of the Seasons* (1953).

9. America today stands poised on a pinnacle of wealth and power, yet we live in a land of vanishing beauty, of increasing ugliness, of shrinking open space, and of an over-all environment that is diminished daily by pollution and noise and blight. STEWART L. UDALL, foreword to *The Quiet Crisis* (1963).

10. The more we get out of the world the less we leave, and in the long run we shall have to pay our debts at a time that may be very inconvenient for our own survival. NORBERT WIENER, *The Human Use of Human Beings* (1954), 2.

## 175. CONSERVATISM

**See also 533. Liberalism; 704. Political Parties; 770. Radicalism**

1. When a nation's young men are conservative, its funeral bell is already rung. HENRY WARD BEECHER, *Proverbs from Plymouth Pulpit* (1887).

2. Conservative, n. A statesman who is enamored of existing evils, as distinguished from the Liberal, who wishes to replace them with others. AMBROSE BIERCE, *The Devil's Dictionary* (1881–1911).

3. The healthy stomach is nothing if not conservative. Few radicals have good digestions. SAMUEL BUTLER (d. 1902), "Mind and Matter," *Note-Books* (1912).

4. A conservative government is an organised hypocrisy. BENJAMIN DISRAELI, speech, "Agricultural Distress," March 17, 1845.

5. All conservatives are such from personal defects. They have been effeminated by position or nature . . . and can only, like invalids, act on the defensive. EMERSON, "Fate," *The Conduct of Life* (1860).

6. Conservatism, ever more timorous and narrow, disgusts the children, and drives them for a mouthful of fresh air into radicalism. EMERSON, "Power," *The Conduct of Life* (1860).

7. A man who is determined never to move out of the beaten road cannot lose his

way. WILLIAM HAZLITT, "Character of the Late Mr. Pitt," *The Round Table* (1817).

8. A mellowing rigorist is always a much pleasanter object to contemplate than a tightening liberal, as a cold day warming up to 32° Fahrenheit is much more agreeable than a warm one chilling down to the same temperature. OLIVER WENDELL HOLMES, SR., *The Poet at the Breakfast Table* (1872), 1.

9. Orthodoxy: That peculiar condition where the patient can neither eliminate an old idea nor absorb a new one. ELBERT HUBBARD, *The Note Book* (1927).

10. The reason men oppose progress is not that they hate progress, but that they love inertia. ELBERT HUBBARD, *The Note Book* (1927).

11. The sickly, weakly, timid man fears the people, and is a Tory by nature. THOMAS JEFFERSON, letter to Lafayette, Nov. 4, 1823.

12. Ribbons a-flutter and orchids a-tremble, / Yearly the vigilant Daughters assemble, / Affirming in fervid and firm resolutions / Their permanent veto on all revolutions. MARYA MANNES, "D. A. R. Wants Atoms-for-Peace Project Abandoned," *Subverse: Rhymes for Our Times* (1959).

13. All reactionaries are paper tigers. MAO TSE-TUNG, *Quotations from Chairman Mao Tse-tung* (1966), 6.

14. The true conservative is the man who has a real concern for injustices and takes thought against the day of reckoning. FRANKLIN D. ROOSEVELT, speech, Syracuse, N.Y., Sept. 29, 1936.

15. A conservative is a man with two perfectly good legs who, however, has never learned to walk forward. FRANKLIN D. ROOSEVELT, radio address, Oct. 26, 1939.

16. A reactionary is a somnambulist walking backwards. FRANKLIN D. ROOSEVELT, radio address, Oct. 26, 1939.

17. The radical invents the views. When he has worn them out the conservative adopts them. MARK TWAIN, *Notebook* (1935).

18. The only reactionaries are those who find themselves at home in the present. MIGUEL DE UNAMUNO, "Don Quixote Today," *Tragic Sense of Life* (1913), tr. J. E. Crawford Flitch.

## 176. CONSISTENCY

**See also 115. Change; 462. Inconsistency**

1. A foolish consistency is the hobgoblin of little minds, adored by little statesmen and philosophers and divines. EMERSON, "Self-Reliance," *Essays: First Series* (1841).

2. The consistent thinker, the consistently moral man, is either a walking mummy or else, if he has not succeeded in stifling all his vitality, a fanatical monomaniac. ALDOUS HUXLEY, *Do What You Will* (1929).

3. It is not best to swap horses while crossing the river. ABRAHAM LINCOLN, reply to the National Union League, June 9, 1864.

4. To hold the same views at forty as we held at twenty is to have been stupefied for a score of years and to take rank, not as a prophet, but as an unteachable brat, well birched and none the wiser. ROBERT LOUIS STEVENSON, "Crabbed Age and Youth," *Virginibus Puerisque* (1881).

5. A man finds it almost as difficult to be inconsistent in his language as to be consistent in his conduct. ALEXIS DE TOCQUEVILLE, introduction, *Democracy in America* (1835–39).

6. There are those who would misteach us that to stick in a rut is consistency—and a virtue, and that to climb out of the rut is inconsistency—and a vice. MARK TWAIN, "Consistency" (1923).

## 177. CONSOLATIONS

**See also 17. Adversity; 153. Compensation; 791. Remedies**

1. Perhaps the greatest consolation of the oppressed is to consider themselves superior to their tyrants. JULIEN GREEN, *Adrienne Mesurat* (1927), 1.9.

2. The kind of solace that arises from having company in misery is spiteful. SENECA, *Ad Marciam de Consolatione* (1st c.).

3. There is nothing so bitter that a patient mind cannot find some solace for it. SENECA, "On Peace of Mind," *Moral Essays* (1st c.), 10.

4. Many a green isle needs must be / In the deep wide sea of Misery, / Or the mariner, worn and wan, / Never thus could voy-

age on. SHELLEY, "Lines Written Among the Euganean Hills" (1818).

## 178. CONSTANCY AND INCONSTANCY

**See also 489. Integrity; 470. Infidelity; 553. Loyalty**

1. Nothing that is not a real crime makes a man appear so contemptible and little in the eyes of the world as inconstancy. JOSEPH ADDISON, *The Spectator* (1711–12), 162.

2. We should measure affection, not like youngsters by the ardor of its passion, but by its strength and constancy. CICERO, *De Officiis* (44 B.C.), 1.15.47.

3. One man; two loves. No good ever comes of that. EURIPIDES, *Andromache* (c. 426 B.C.), tr. John F. Nims.

4. Only the person who has faith in himself is able to be faithful to others. ERICH FROMM, *The Art of Loving* (1956), 4.

5. A faithful woman looks to the spring, a good book, perfume, earthquakes, and divine revelation for the experience others find in a lover. They deceive their husbands, so to speak, with the entire world, men excepted. JEAN GIRAUDOUX, *Amphitryon 38* (1929), 1, tr. Phyllis La Farge with Peter H. Judd.

6. Faithful woman are all alike. They think only of their fidelity and never of their husbands. JEAN GIRAUDOUX, *Amphitryon 38* (1929), 3, tr. Phyllis La Farge with Peter H. Judd.

7. To be capable of steady friendship or lasting love, are the two greatest proofs, not only of goodness of heart, but of strength of mind. WILLIAM HAZLITT, *Characteristics* (1823), 235.

8. It is as foolish to make experiments upon the constancy of a friend, as upon the chastity of a wife. SAMUEL JOHNSON, quoted in Boswell's *Life of Samuel Johnson*, Sept. 9, 1779.

9. There are two sorts of constancy in love; the one comes from the constant discovery in our beloved of new grounds for love, and the other comes from making it a point of honour to be constant. LA ROCHEFOUCAULD, *Maxims* (1665), tr. Kenneth Pratt.

10. Constancy in love is a perpetual inconstancy, which makes the heart attach itself successively to all the qualities of the person we love, giving preference now to one and presently to another. LA ROCHEFOUCAULD, *Maxims* (1665), tr. Kenneth Pratt.

11. The violence we do to ourselves in order to remain faithful to the one we love is hardly better than an act of infidelity. LA ROCHEFOUCAULD, *Maxims* (1665).

12. The heart grows weary after a little / Of what it loved for a little while. EDNA ST. VINCENT MILLAY, "Three Songs from 'The Lamp and the Bell,'" 2, *The Harp-Weaver* (1923).

13. Parrots, tortoises and redwoods / Live a longer life than men do, / Men a longer life than dogs do, / Dogs a longer life than loves does. EDNA ST. VINCENT MILLAY, "Pretty Love, I Must Outlive You," *Huntsman, What Quarry?* (1939).

14. O heaven, were man / But constant, he were perfect! SHAKESPEARE, *The Two Gentlemen of Verona* (1594–95), 5.4.110.

15. He wears his faith but as the fashion of his hat. SHAKESPEARE, *Much Ado About Nothing* (1598–99), 1.1.75.

16. Men's minds are given to change in hate and friendship. SOPHOCLES, *Ajax* (c. 447 B.C.), tr. John Moore.

17. Out upon it, I have loved / Three whole days together; / And am like to love three more, / If it prove fair weather. SIR JOHN SUCKLING, "A Poem with the Answer," *Fragmenta Aurea* (1646).

18. There is nothing in this world constant but inconstancy. JONATHAN SWIFT, *A Tritical Essay Upon the Faculties of the Mind* (1707).

19. Faithfulness is to the emotional life what consistency is to the life of the intellect—simply a confession of failures. OSCAR WILDE, *The Picture of Dorian Gray* (1891), 4.

## 179. CONSTITUTIONS

**See also 393. Government**

1. The Constitution of the United States is a law for rulers and people, equally in war and peace, and covers with the shield of its protection all classes of men, at all times, and under all circumstances. JUSTICE DAVID DAVIS, *Ex Parte Milligan* (1866).

2. Though written constitutions may be violated in moments of passion or delusion, yet they furnish a text to which those who are watchful may again rally and recall the people; they fix too for the people the principles of their political creed. THOMAS JEFFERSON, letter to Joseph Priestley, June 19, 1802.

3. Some men look at constitutions with sanctimonious reverence, and deem them like the ark of the covenant, too sacred to be touched. THOMAS JEFFERSON, letter to Samuel Kercheval, July 12, 1816.

4. Our Constitution is founded on the principle that all men are equal as citizens, and entitled to the same rights, whether they achieved citizenship by birth, or after coming here as immigrants, seeking to find in America new freedom and new opportunities. JOHN F. KENNEDY, campaign statement on Citizenship Day, Washington, D.C., Sept. 17, 1960.

5. Constitutions are good only as we make progress under them. NAPOLEON I, *Maxims* (1804–15).

6. Constitutions are checks upon the hasty action of the majority. They are the self-imposed restraints of a whole people upon a majority of them to secure sober action and a respect for the rights of the minority. WILLIAM HOWARD TAFT, veto of Arizona Enabling Act, Aug. 22, 1911.

## CONSUMERS

See 103. Buying and Selling

## 180. CONTEMPLATION

See also 717. Prayer; 868. Self-knowledge; 920. Spirituality

1. I neglect God and his angels for the noise of a fly, for the rattling of a coach, for the whining of a door. JOHN DONNE, *Sermons*, No. 80, 1626.

2. Nowhere can man find a quieter or more untroubled retreat than in his own soul. MARCUS AURELIUS, *Meditations* (2nd c.), 4.3, tr. Maxwell Staniforth.

3. If thou may not continually gather thyself together, do it some time at least once a day, morning or evening. THOMAS À KEMPIS, *The Imitation of Christ* (1426), 1.19.

## 181. CONTEMPORANEOUSNESS

See also 296. Era; 372. Generations; 593. Modernity

1. Men are more like the time they live in than they are like their fathers. ALI IBN-ABI-TALIB, *Sentences* (7th c.), 79, tr. Simon Ockley.

2. The men who come on the stage at one period are all found to be related to each other. Certain ideas are in the air. EMERSON, "Fate," *The Conduct of Life* (1860).

3. Let me stand in my age with all its waters flowing round me. If they sometimes subdue, they must finally upbear me, for I seek the universal—and that must be the best. MARGARET FULLER, *Summer on the Lakes* (1844), 5.

4. Woe to these people who have no appetite for the very dish that their age serves up. ANDRÉ GIDE, "Second Imaginary Interview," *Pretexts* (1903), tr. Angelo P. Bertocci and others.

5. We are connected with our own age if we recognize ourselves in relation to outside events; and we have grasped its spirit when we influence the future. HANS HOFMANN, *Search for the Real* (1967).

6. A man lives not only his personal life, as an individual, but also, consciously or unconsciously, the life of his epoch and his contemporaries. THOMAS MANN, *The Magic Mountain* (1924), 2.2, tr. H. T. Lowe-Porter.

7. We changed with the times, so we cant blame the children for just joining the times, without even having to change. WILL ROGERS, *The Autobiography of Will Rogers* (1949), 14.

8. The man who thinks only of his own generation is born for few. SENECA, *Letters to Lucilius* (1st c.), 79.17, tr. E. Phillips Barker.

9. All our affirmations are mere matters of chronology; and even our bad taste is nothing more than the bad taste of the age we live in. LOGAN PEARSALL SMITH, *Afterthoughts* (1931), 5.

10. A man is wise with the wisdom of his time only, and ignorant with its ignorance. Observe how the greatest minds yield in

some degree to the superstitions of their age. THOREAU, *Journal*, Jan. 31, 1853.

11. We are obliged to place ourselves on the level of our age before we can rise above it. VOLTAIRE, "Buffoonery," *Philosophical Dictionary* (1764).

## 182. CONTEMPT

See also 913. Sour Grapes

1. Contempt, n. The feeling of a prudent man for an enemy who is too formidable safely to be opposed. AMBROSE BIERCE, *The Devil's Dictionary* (1881–1911).

2. There is no fate that cannot be surmounted by scorn. ALBERT CAMUS, title essay, *The Myth of Sisyphus* (1942), tr. Justin O'Brien.

3. Many can bear adversity, but few contempt. THOMAS FULLER, M.D., *Gnomologia* (1732), 3340.

4. Whenever we pretend, on all occasions, a mighty contempt for any thing, it is a pretty clear sign that we feel ourselves very nearly on a level with it. WILLIAM HAZLITT, "On Vulgarity and Affectation," *Table Talk* (1821–22).

5. Men more quickly learn and more gladly recall what they deride than what they approve and esteem. HORACE, *Epistles* (20–c. 8 B.C.), 2.1.

6. There is no being so poor and so contemptible, who does not think there is somebody still poorer, and still more contemptible. SAMUEL JOHNSON, quoted in Boswell's *Life of Samuel Johnson*, Feb. 15, 1766.

7. The great despisers are the great reverers. NIETZSCHE, "On the Higher Man," *Thus Spoke Zarathustra* (1883–92), 4, tr. Walter Kaufmann.

8. Moral contempt is a far greater indignity and insult than any kind of crime. NIETZSCHE, *The Will to Power* (1888), 740, tr. Anthony M. Ludovici.

9. Who can refute a sneer? WILLIAM PALEY, *Principles of Moral and Political Philosophy* (1785), v, 2, 5.9.

10. Only a small mind traffics in scorn; a mind whose truth accords no place to others'. SAINT-EXUPÉRY, *The Wisdom of the Sands* (1948), 32, tr. Stuart Gilbert.

11. Silence is the most perfect expression of scorn. GEORGE BERNARD SHAW, *Back to Methuselah* (1921), 5.

12. Everything can be borne except contempt. VOLTAIRE, "Philosopher," *Philosophical Dictionary* (1764).

## 183. CONTENTMENT

See also 155. Complacency; 249. Discontent; 407. Happiness; 695. Plain Living; 839. Satisfaction; 982. Tranquility

1. Be content with your lot; one cannot be first in everything. AESOP, "The Peacock and Juno," *Fables* (6th c. B.C.?), tr. Joseph Jacobs.

2. I have learned, in whatsoever state I am, therewith to be content. *Bible*, Philippians 4:11.

3. Who is content with nothing possesses all things. NICOLAS BOILEAU, letter to M. de Guilleragues, *Epîtres* (1669), 5.

4. Content may dwell in all stations. To be low, but above contempt, may be high enough to be happy. SIR THOMAS BROWNE, *Christian Morals* (1716), 1.

5. True contentment is a thing as active as agriculture. It is the power of getting out of any situation all that there is in it. It is arduous and it is rare. G. K. CHESTERTON, "The Contented Man," *A Miscellany of Men* (1912).

6. If you would know contentment, let your deeds be few. DEMOCRITUS (5th–4th c. B.C.), quoted in Marcus Aurelius' *Meditations* (2nd c. A.D.), 4.24.

7. Do not spoil what you have by desiring what you have not; but remember that what you now have was once among the things only hoped for. EPICURUS, "Vatican Sayings" (3rd c. B.C.), 35, in *Letters, Principal Doctrines, and Vatican Sayings*, tr. Russel M. Geer.

8. That man is happiest / who lives from day to day and asks no more, / garnering the simple goodness of a life. EURIPIDES, *Hecuba* (c. 425 B.C.), tr. William Arrowsmith.

9. Better a little fire to warm us than a great one to burn us. THOMAS FULLER, M.D., *Gnomologia* (1732), 865.

10. Fat hens lay few eggs. GERMAN PROVERB.

11. Oh, don't the days seem lank and long, / When all goes right and nothing goes wrong / And isn't your life extremely flat / With nothing whatever to grumble at! W. S. GILBERT, *Princess Ida* (1884), 3.

12. Nothing will content him who is not

content with a little. GREEK PROVERB.

13. Be content with what thou hast received, and smooth thy frowning forehead, for the door of choice is not open either to thee or me. HĀFIZ, ghazals from the *Divan* (14th c.), 12, tr. Justin Huntly McCarthy.

14. He is poor who does not feel content. JAPANESE PROVERB.

15. I have not a word to say against contented people so long as they keep quiet. But do not, for goodness' sake, let them go strutting about, as they are so fond of doing, crying out that they are the true models for the whole species. JEROME K. JEROME, "On Getting On in the World," *The Idle Thoughts of an Idle Fellow* (1889).

16. If you are foolish enough to be contented, don't show it, but grumble with the rest. JEROME K. JEROME, "On Getting On in the World," *The Idle Thoughts of an Idle Fellow* (1889).

17. He who is contented is rich. LAOTSE, *The Character of Tao* (6th c. B.C.), 33, tr. Lin Yutang.

18. Contentment is a warm sty for the eaters and sleepers. EUGENE O'NEILL, *Marco Millions* (1928), 2.2.

19. All fortune belongs to him who has a contented mind. Is not the whole earth covered with leather for him whose feet are encased in shoes? *Panchatantra* (c. 5th c.), 2, tr. Franklin Edgerton.

20. If thou covetest riches, ask not but for contentment, which is an immense treasure. SA'DI, *Gulistan* (1258), 2.27, tr. James Ross.

21. My crown is called content; / A crown it is that seldom kings enjoy. SHAKESPEARE, *3 Henry VI* (1590–91), 3.1.64.

22. Poor and content is rich, and rich enough. SHAKESPEARE, *Othello* (1604–05), 3.3.172.

23. Good friends, good books and a sleepy conscience: this is the ideal life. MARK TWAIN, *Notebook* (1935).

24. Well-being is attained by little and little, and nevertheless it is no little thing itself. ZENO OF CITIUM (c. 300 B.C.), quoted in Diogenes Laertius' *Lives and Opinions of Eminent Philosophers* (3rd c. A.D.), tr. R. D. Hicks.

## CONTRADICTION

**See 462. Inconsistency**

## 184. CONTRAST

**See also 152. Comparison**

1. 'Tis Opposites—entice— / Deformed Men—ponder Grace— / Bright fires—the Blanketless— / The Lost—Day's face— / The Blind—esteem it be / Enough Estate—to see—. EMILY DICKINSON, poem (c. 1862).

2. We are so made that we can derive intense enjoyment only from a contrast and very little from a state of things. SIGMUND FREUD, *Civilization and Its Discontents* (1930), 2, tr. James Strachey.

3. It is by disease that health is pleasant; by evil that good is pleasant; by hunger, satiety; by weariness, rest. HERACLITUS, *Fragments* (c. 500 B.C.), 99, tr. Philip Wheelwright.

4. Sleep, riches, and health, to be truly enjoyed, must be interrupted. JEAN PAUL RICHTER, *Flower, Fruit, and Thorn* (1796–97), 8.

## CONTROVERSY

**See 51. Argument; 250. Discord; 766. Quarreling**

## CONVALESCENCE

**See 889. Sickness**

## 185. CONVERSATION

**See also 148. Communication; 540. Listening; 916. Speaking**

1. Good-nature is more agreeable in conversation than wit, and gives a certain air to the countenance which is more amiable than beauty. JOSEPH ADDISON, *The Spectator* (1711–12), 169.

2. For parlor use the vague generality is a life-saver. GEORGE ADE, "The Wise Piker," *Forty Modern Fables* (1901).

3. Conversation, n. A fair for the display of the minor mental commodities, each exhibitor being too intent upon the arrangement of his own wares to observe those of his neighbor. AMBROSE BIERCE, *The Devil's Dictionary* (1881–1911).

4. A free conversation will no more bear

a dictator than a free government will. LORD CHESTERFIELD, *Letters to His Godson,* Dec. 18, 1765.

5. Too much agreement kills a chat. ELDRIDGE CLEAVER, "A Day in Folsom Prison," *Soul on Ice* (1968).

6. Talk ought always to run obliquely, not nose to nose with no chance of mental escape. FRANK MOORE COLBY, "Simple Simon," *The Colby Essays* (1926), v. 1.

7. Private, accidental, confidential conversation breeds thought. Clubs produce oftener words. EMERSON, *Journals,* 1836.

8. The art of conversation, or the qualification for a good companion, is a certain self-control, which now holds the subject, now lets it go, with a respect for the emergencies of the moment. EMERSON, *Journals,* 1854.

9. The best of life is conversation, and the greatest success is confidence, or perfect understanding between sincere people. EMERSON, "Behavior," *The Conduct of Life* (1860).

10. Conversation is an art in which a man has all mankind for his competitors, for it is that which all are practising every day while they live. EMERSON, "Considerations by the Way," *The Conduct of Life* (1860).

11. Reading makes a full man, meditation a profound man, discourse a clear man. BENJAMIN FRANKLIN, *Poor Richard's Almanack* (1732–57).

12. Never speak of yourself to others; make them talk about themselves instead: therein lies the whole art of pleasing. Everyone knows it and everyone forgets it. EDMOND and JULES DE GONCOURT, *Idées et sensations* (1866).

13. If to talk to oneself when alone is folly, it must be doubly unwise to listen to oneself in the presence of others. BALTASAR GRACIÁN, *The Art of Worldly Wisdom* (1647), 141, tr. Joseph Jacobs.

14. In conversation discretion is more important than eloquence. BALTASAR GRACIÁN, *The Art of Worldly Wisdom* (1647), 148, tr. Joseph Jacobs.

15. A person who talks with equal vivacity on every subject, excites no interest in any. Repose is as necessary in conversation as in a picture. WILLIAM HAZLITT, *Characteristics* (1823).

16. The art of conversation is the art of hearing as well as of being heard. WILLIAM HAZLITT, "On the Conversation of Authors," *The Plain Speaker* (1826).

17. That is the happiest conversation where there is no competition, no vanity, but a calm quiet interchange of sentiments. SAMUEL JOHNSON, quoted in Boswell's *Life of Samuel Johnson,* April 14, 1775.

18. Conversation is not a search after knowledge, but an endeavour at effect. JOHN KEATS, letter to Benjamin Robert Haydon, May 10–11, 1817.

19. A gossip is one who talks to you about others; a bore is one who talks to you about himself; and a brilliant conversationalist is one who talks to you about yourself. LISA KIRK, *New York Journal-American,* March 9, 1954.

20. The success of conversation consists less in being witty than in bringing out wit in others; the man who leaves after talking with you, pleased with himself and his own wit, is perfectly pleased with you. LA BRUYÈRE, *Characters* (1688), 5.16.

21. A man may do very well with a very little knowledge, and scarce be found out, in mixed company; every body is so much more ready to produce his own, than to call for a display of your acquisitions. But in a *tête-à-tête* there is no shuffling. CHARLES LAMB, "The Old and the New Schoolmaster," *Essays of Elia* (1823).

22. To listen closely and reply well is the highest perfection we are able to attain in the art of conversation. LA ROCHEFOUCAULD, *Maxims* (1665), tr. Kenneth Pratt.

23. Confidence contributes more to conversation than wit. LA ROCHEFOUCAULD, *Maxims* (1665), tr. Kenneth Pratt.

24. Do you know that conversation is one of the greatest pleasures in life? But it wants leisure. W. SOMERSET MAUGHAM, "The Fall of Edward Barnard," *The Trembling of a Leaf* (1921).

25. We do not talk—we bludgeon one another with facts and theories gleaned from cursory readings of newspapers, magazines and digests. HENRY MILLER, "The Shadows," *The Air-Conditioned Nightmare* (1945).

26. For table-talk, I prefer the pleasant and witty before the learned and the grave; in bed, beauty before goodness. MONTAIGNE, "Of friendship," *Essays* (1580–88), tr. Charles Cotton and W. C. Hazlitt.

27. The more the pleasures of the body

fade away, the greater to me is the pleasure and charm of conversation. PLATO, *The Republic* (4th c. B.C.), 1, tr. Benjamin Jowett.

28. Wit in conversation is only a readiness of thought and a facility of expression, or (in the midwives' phrase) a quick conception, and an easy delivery. ALEXANDER POPE, *Thoughts on Various Subjects* (1727).

29. It is not what we learn in conversation that enriches us. It is the elation that comes of swift contact with tingling currents of thought. AGNES REPPLIER, "The Luxury of Conversation," *Compromises* (1904).

30. Whoever interrupts the conversation of others to make a display of his fund of knowledge, makes notorious his own stock of ignorance. SA'DI, *Gulistan* (1258), 8.95, tr. James Ross.

31. It is a secret known but to few, yet of no small use in the conduct of life, that when you fall into a man's conversation, the first thing you should consider is, whether he has a greater inclination to hear you, or that you should hear him. RICHARD STEELE, *The Spectator* (1711–12), 49.

32. It is a wonderful thing that so many, and they not reckoned absurd, shall entertain those with whom they converse by giving them the history of their pains and aches and imagine such narrations their quota of conversation. RICHARD STEELE, *The Spectator* (1711–12), 100.

33. It is an impertinent and unreasonable fault in conversation for one man to take up all the discourse. RICHARD STEELE, *The Spectator* (1711–12), 428.

34. Is there anything more terrible than a "call"? It affords an occasion for the exchange of the most threadbare commonplaces. Calls and the theatre are the two great centers for the propagation of platitudes. MIGUEL DE UNAMUNO, "Large and Small Towns," *Essays and Soliloquies* (1924), tr. J. E. Crawford Flitch.

35. The necessity of saying something, the embarrassment produced by the consciousness of having nothing to say, and the desire to exhibit ability, are three things sufficient to render even a great man ridiculous. VOLTAIRE, "Society of London, and Academies," *Philosophical Dictionary* (1764).

36. That talk must be very well in hand, and under great headway, that an anecdote thrown in front of will not pitch off the track and wreck. CHARLES DUDLEY WARNER, "Third Study," *Backlog Studies* (1873).

37. Learned conversation is either the affectation of the ignorant or the profession of the mentally unemployed. OSCAR WILDE, "The Critic as Artist," *Intentions* (1891).

38. When people talk to us about others they are usually dull. When they talk to us about themselves they are nearly always interesting. OSCAR WILDE, "The Critic as Artist," *Intentions* (1891).

## 186. COOKS AND COOKING

**See also 272. Eating; 352. Food**

1. The discovery of a new dish does more for the happiness of mankind than the discovery of a star. ANTHELME BRILLAT-SAVARIN, *Physiologie du goût* (1825), 9.

2. Cookery has become an art, a noble science; cooks are gentlemen. ROBERT BURTON, *The Anatomy of Melancholy* (1621), 1.2.2.2.

3. God sends meat and the Devil sends cooks. ENGLISH PROVERB.

4. An ill cook should have a good cleaver. ENGLISH PROVERB.

5. Our God is great and the cook is his prophet. JEROME K. JEROME, "On Eating and Drinking," *The Idle Thoughts of an Idle Fellow* (1889).

6. Condiments are like old friends—highly thought of, but often taken for granted. MARILYN KAYTOR, "Condiments: the Tastemakers," *Look*, Jan. 29, 1963.

7. A good cook is the peculiar gift of the gods. He must be a perfect creature from the brain to the palate, from the palate to the finger's end. WALTER SAVAGE LANDOR, "Anacreon and Polycrates," *Imaginary Conversations* (1824–53).

8. Men do not have to cook their food; they do so for symbolic reasons to show they are men and not beasts. EDMUND LEACH, "Brain-Twister," *New York Review of Books*, Oct. 12, 1967.

9. Bad cooks—and the utter lack of reason in the kitchen—have delayed human development longest and impaired it most. NIETZSCHE, *Beyond Good and Evil* (1886), 234, tr. Walter Kaufmann.

10. Let onions lurk within the bowl /

And, scarce-suspected, animate the whole. SYDNEY SMITH, "Recipe for Salad," quoted in Lady S. Holland's *Memoir* (1855), v. 1.11.

11. Cooking is like love. It should be entered into with abandon or not at all. HARRIET VAN HORNE, *Vogue*, Oct. 15, 1956.

12. A good cook is a certain slow poisoner, if you are not temperate. VOLTAIRE, "Poisonings," *Philosophical Dictionary* (1764).

13. Lettuce, like conversation, requires a good deal of oil, to avoid friction, and keep the company smooth. CHARLES DUDLEY WARNER, "Ninth Week," *My Summer in a Garden* (1871).

14. There is no dignity in the bean. Corn, with no affectation of superiority, is, however, the child of song. It waves in all literature. But mix it with beans, and its high tone is gone. Succotash is vulgar. CHARLES DUDLEY WARNER, "Ninth Week," *My Summer in a Garden* (1871).

## COOLNESS

See 141. Coldness; 159. Composure

## 187. COOPERATION

See also 1009. Unity

1. Where two people are writing the same book, each believes he gets all the worries and only half the royalties. AGATHA CHRISTIE, news summaries, March 15, 1955.

2. Joint undertakings stand a better chance / When they benefit both sides. EURIPIDES, *Iphigenia in Tauris* (c. 414–12 B.C.), tr. Witter Bynner.

3. Clapping with the right hand only will not produce a noise. MALAY PROVERB.

4. One man may hit the mark, another blunder; but heed not these distinctions. Only from the alliance of the one, working with and through the other, are great things born. SAINT-EXUPÉRY, *The Wisdom of the Sands* (1948), tr. Stuart Gilbert.

## COQUETRY

See 348. Flirtation

## 188. CORRUPTION

See also 97. Bribery; 305. Evil; 893. Sin; 927. Stealing; 964. Temptation; 1048. Wickedness

1. If the camel once get his nose in the tent, his body will soon follow. ARABIC PROVERB.

2. Where God hath a temple, the Devil will have a chapel. ROBERT BURTON, *The Anatomy of Melancholy* (1621), 3.4.1.1.

3. Corruption is like a ball of snow: whence once set a-rolling it must increase. CHARLES CALEB COLTON, *Lacon* (1825), 2.6.

4. Countries are like fruit—the worms are always inside. JEAN GIRAUDOUX, *Siegfried* (1928), 1, tr. Phyllis La Farge with Peter H. Judd.

5. Power corrupts the few, while weakness corrupts the many. ERIC HOFFER, *The Passionate State of Mind* (1954), 41.

6. Public money is like holy water; everyone helps himself to it. ITALIAN PROVERB.

7. No man is worthy of unlimited reliance—his treason, at best, only waits for sufficient temptation. H. L. MENCKEN, "The Skeptic," *The Smart Set*, May 1919.

8. The American way is to seduce a man by bribery and make a prostitute of him. Or else to ignore him, starve him into submission and make a hack out of him. HENRY MILLER, "Letter to Lafayette," *The Air-Conditioned Nightmare* (1945).

9. What more oft in nations grown corrupt, / And by their vices brought to servitude, / Than to love bondage more than liberty, / bondage with ease than strenuous liberty. MILTON, *Samson Agonistes* (1671), 268.

10. The corruption of the age is made up by the particular contribution of every individual man; some contribute treachery, others injustice, irreligion, tyranny, avarice, cruelty, according to their power. MONTAIGNE, "Of vanity," *Essays* (1580–88), tr. Charles Cotton and W. C. Hazlitt.

11. The corruption of every government begins nearly always with that of principles. MONTESQUIEU, *L'Esprit des lois* (1748), 1.

12. There is something in corruption which, like a jaundiced eye, transfers the color of itself to the object it looks upon, and sees everything stained and impure. THOMAS PAINE, *The American Crisis* (1776–83), 6.

13. Lilies that fester smell far worse than

weeds. SHAKESPEARE, *Sonnets* (1609), 94.14.

14. Corruption wins not more than honesty. SHAKESPEARE, *Henry VIII* (1612–13), 3.2.444.

15. There is no odor so bad as that which arises from goodness tainted. THOREAU, "Economy," *Walden* (1854).

16. The first gold star a child gets in school for the mere performance of a needful task is its first lesson in graft. PHILIP WYLIE, *Generation of Vipers* (1942), 7.

## 189. COSMETICS

**See also 324. Face; 678. Perfume**

1. Most women are not so young as they are painted. MAX BEERBOHM, "In Defense of Cosmetics" (1922).

2. Darling, at the Beautician's you buy / Your [a] hair / [b] complexion / [c] lips / [d] dimples, & / [e] teeth. / For a like amount you could just as well buy a face. *Greek Anthology* (7th c. B.C.–10th c. A.D.), 11.310, tr. Dudley Fitts.

3. God hath given you one face, and you make yourselves another. SHAKESPEARE, *Hamlet* (1600), 3.1.149.

## 190. COSMOPOLITANISM

**See also 496. International Relations; 910. Sophistication**

1. All good men are international. Nearly all bad men are cosmopolitan. If we are to be international we must be national. G. K. CHESTERTON, "French and English," *All Things Considered* (1908).

2. I am a citizen of the world. DIOGENES THE CYNIC (4th c. B.C.), quoted in Diogenes Laertius' *Lives and Opinions of Eminent Philosophers* (3rd c. A.D.), tr. R. D. Hicks.

3. To be really cosmopolitan, a man must be at home even in his own country. THOMAS WENTWORTH HIGGINSON, "Henry James," *Short Studies of American Authors* (1906).

4. A man's feet must be planted in his country, but his eyes should survey the world. GEORGE SANTAYANA, *The Life of Reason: Reason in Society* (1905–06), 7.

5. That man's the best cosmopolite / Who loves his native country best. ALFRED, LORD TENNYSON, "Hands All Round" (1885).

## COST

**See 1019. Value**

## COUNSEL

**See 19. Advice; 229. Deliberation**

## 191. THE COUNTRY

**See also 129. Cities; 334. Farms and Farming; 349. Flowers; 369. Gardening; 937. Suburbs**

1. To sit in the shade on a fine day and look upon verdure is the most perfect refreshment. JANE AUSTEN, *Mansfield Park* (1814), 9.

2. It is only in the country that we can get to know a person or a book. CYRIL CONNOLLY, *The Unquiet Grave* (1945), 3.

3. Nor rural sights alone, but rural sounds, / Exhilarate the spirit, and restore / The tone of languid Nature. WILLIAM COWPER, "The Sofa," *The Task* (1785), 182.

4. God made the country, and man made the town. WILLIAM COWPER, "The Sofa," *The Task* (1785), 749.

5. The lowest and vilest alleys of London do not present a more dreadful record of sin than does the smiling and beautiful countryside. SIR ARTHUR CONAN DOYLE, "Copper Beeches," *The Adventures of Sherlock Holmes* (1891).

6. I lived in solitude in the country and noticed how the monotony of a quiet life stimulates the creative mind. EINSTEIN, *Out of My Later Years* (1950), 24.

7. A man's soul may be buried and perish under a dungheap or in a furrow of the field, just as well as under a pile of money. NATHANIEL HAWTHORNE, *Journals*, June 1, 1841.

8. In the country we forget the town, and in town we despise the country. WILLIAM HAZLITT, "On Going a Journey," *Table Talk* (1821–22).

9. To one who has been long in city pent, / 'Tis very sweet to look into the fair / And open face of heaven. JOHN KEATS, "To One Who Has Been Long in City Pent" (1816).

10. The good thing about the country is . . . that we don't have there any bad

weather at all—only a number of different kinds of good. JOSEPH WOOD KRUTCH, "June," *The Twelve Seasons* (1949).

11. The city has a face, the country a soul. JACQUES DE LACRETELLE, "Les Paysages hérités," *Idées dans un chapeau* (1946).

12. A man must be of a very quiet and happy nature, who can long endure the country; and, moreover, very well contented with his own insignificant person. LONGFELLOW, *Hyperion* (1839), 2.10.

13. Why one day in the country / Is worth a month in town; / Is worth a day and a year / Of the dusty, musty, lag-last fashion / That days drone elsewhere. CHRISTINA ROSSETTI, "Summer" (1862).

14. I love all waste / And solitary places; where we taste the pleasure of believing what we see / Is boundless, as we wish our souls to be. SHELLEY, "Julian and Maddalo" (1818–19).

15. Flat country seems to give the sky such a chance. DODIE SMITH, *I Capture the Castle* (1948), 3.

16. I have no relish for the country; it is a kind of healthy grave. SYDNEY SMITH, letter to Miss G. Harcourt, 1838.

17. The country has its charms—cheapness for one. ROBERT SMITH SURTEES, *Hillingdon Hill* (1845), 5.

## 192. COURAGE

**See also 90. Boldness; 196. Cowardice; 237. Despair; 340. Fear; 933. Strength; 973. Timidity**

1. It is easy to be brave from a safe distance. AESOP, "The Wolf and the Kid," *Fables* (6th c. B.C.?), tr. Joseph Jacobs.

2. Until the day of his death, no man can be sure of his courage. JEAN ANOUILH, *Becket* (1959), 1.

3. The coward calls the brave man rash, the rash man calls him a coward. ARISTOTLE, *Nicomachean Ethics* (4th c. B.C.), 2.8, tr. J. A. K. Thomson.

4. All bravery stands upon comparisons. FRANCIS BACON, "Of Vain-Glory," *Essays* (1625).

5. Courage is the thing. All goes if courage goes. J. M. BARRIE, Rectorial Address, St. Andrew's, May 3, 1922.

6. It is a brave act of valour to contemn [despise] death; but where life is more terrible than death, it is then the truest valour to dare to live. SIR THOMAS BROWNE, *Religio Medici* (1642), 1.

7. The stout heart is also a warm and kind one; affection dwells with danger, all the holier and the lovelier for such stern environment. THOMAS CARLYLE, "Corn-Law Rhymes" (1832).

8. Valour lies just half way between rashness and cowheartedness. CERVANTES, *Don Quixote* (1605–15), 2.3.4, tr. Peter Motteux and John Ozell.

9. The paradox of courage is that a man must be a little careless of his life even in order to keep it. G. K. CHESTERTON, "The Methuselahite," *All Things Considered* (1908).

10. Between cowardice and despair, valour is gendred. JOHN DONNE, *Paradoxes, Problems, and Essays* (1633), 3.

11. None but the brave deserves the fair. JOHN DRYDEN, "Alexander's Feast" (1687), 15.

12. Every man has his own courage, and is betrayed because he seeks in himself the courage of other persons. EMERSON, *Journals*, 1847.

13. A great part of courage is the courage of having done the thing before. EMERSON, "Wealth," *The Conduct of Life* (1860).

14. This is courage in a man: / to bear unflinchingly what heaven sends. EURIPIDES, *Heracles* (c. 422 B.C.), tr. William Arrowsmith.

15. A coward turns away but a brave man's choice / Is danger. EURIPIDES, *Iphigenia in Tauris* (c. 414–12 B.C.), tr. Witter Bynner.

16. Without justice, courage is weak. BENJAMIN FRANKLIN, *Poor Richard's Almanack* (1732–57).

17. Life only demands from you the strength you possess. Only one feat is possible—not to have run away. DAG HAMMARSKJÖLD, "1925–1930," *Markings* (1964), tr. Leif Sjoberg and W. H. Auden.

18. People with courage and character always seem sinister to the rest. HERMANN HESSE, *Demian* (1919), 2, tr. Michael Roloff and Michael Lebeck.

19. If you knew how cowardly your enemy is, you would slap him. Bravery is knowledge of the cowardice in the enemy. EDGAR WATSON HOWE, *Country Town Sayings* (1911).

20. There is plenty of courage among us for the abstract but not for the concrete. HELEN KELLER, *Let Us Have Faith* (1940).

21. Love of fame, fear of disgrace, schemes for advancement, desire to make life comfortable and pleasant, and the urge to humiliate others are often at the root of the valour men hold in such high esteem. LA ROCHEFOUCAULD, *Maxims* (1665).

22. No one can answer for his courage when he has never been in danger. LA ROCHEFOUCAULD, *Maxims* (1665), tr. Kenneth Pratt.

23. Perfect valour consists in doing without witnesses that which we would be capable of doing before everyone. LA ROCHEFOUCAULD, *Maxims* (1665), tr. Kenneth Pratt.

24. Hidden valor is as bad as cowardice. LATIN PROVERB.

25. Fate loves the fearless; / Fools, when their roof-tree / Falls, think it doomsday; / Firm stands the sky. JAMES RUSSELL LOWELL, "The Voyage to Vinland," *Under the Willows and Other Poems* (1868), 3.

26. Valor is stability, not of legs and arms, but of the courage and the soul. MONTAIGNE, "Of cannibals," *Essays* (1580–88), tr. Charles Cotton and W. C. Hazlitt.

27. Courage is like love; it must have hope for nourishment. NAPOLEON I, *Maxims* (1804–15).

28. Everyone becomes brave when he observes one who despairs. NIETZSCHE, "The Welcome," *Thus Spoke Zarathustra* (1883–92), 4, tr. Walter Kaufmann.

29. Even the pluckiest among us has but seldom the courage of what he really knows. NIETZSCHE, "Maxims and Missiles," 2, *Twilight of the Idols* (1888), tr. Anthony M. Ludovici.

30. Courage is a kind of salvation. PLATO, *The Republic* (4th c. B.C.), 4, tr. Benjamin Jowett.

31. That man is not truly brave who is afraid either to seem to be, or to be, when it suits him, a coward. EDGAR ALLAN POE, *Marginalia* (1844–49), 8.

32. That is at bottom the only courage demanded of us: to have courage for the most strange, the most singular and the most inexplicable that we may encounter. RAINER MARIA RILKE, *Letters to a Young Poet*, Aug. 12, 1904, tr. M. D. Herter Norton.

33. Courage does not always march to airs blown by a bugle: is not always wrought out of the fabric ostentation wears. FRANCES RODMAN, "For a Six-Year-Old," *The New York Times*, May 13, 1961.

34. Valor is a gift. Those having it never know for sure whether they have it till the test comes. And those having it in one test never know for sure if they will have it when the next test comes. CARL SANDBURG, news reports, Dec. 14, 1954.

35. Life without the courage for death is slavery. SENECA, *Letters to Lucilius* (1st c.), 77.15, tr. E. Phillips Barker.

36. Sometimes even to live is an act of courage. SENECA, *Letters to Lucilius* (1st c.), 78.3, tr. E. Phillips Barker.

37. Courage mounteth with occasion. SHAKESPEARE, *King John* (1596–97), 2.1.82.

38. It is courage, courage, courage, that raises the blood of life to crimson splendor. GEORGE BERNARD SHAW, *Back to Methuselah* (1921), 1.2.

39. They are surely to be esteemed the bravest spirits who, having the clearest sense of both the pains and pleasures of life, do not on that account shrink from danger. THUCYDIDES, *The Peloponnesian War* (c. 400 B.C.) 2.40, tr. Benjamin Jowett.

40. Courage is resistance to fear, mastery of fear–not absence of fear. Except a creature be part coward it is not a compliment to say it is brave. MARK TWAIN, "Pudd'nhead Wilson's Calendar," *Pudd'nhead Wilson* (1894), 12.

## 193. COURT, ROYAL

See also 518. Kings; 823. Royalty

1. The ability to stand is meritorious among courtiers; and all courtiers believe that blessedness after death must comprise permission to sit. NIETZSCHE, "On Old and New Tablets," *Thus Spoke Zarathustra* (1883–92), 3, tr. Walter Kaufmann.

2. The art o' th' court, / As hard to leave as keep, whose top to climb / Is certain falling, or so slipp'ry that / The fear's as bad as falling. SHAKESPEARE, *Cymbeline* (1609–10), 3.3.46.

3. The two maxims of any great man at court are, always to keep his countenance, and never to keep his word. JONATHAN SWIFT, *Thoughts on Various Subjects* (1711).

## COURT OF LAW

See 515. Justice; 525. Law and Lawyers

## 194. COURTESY

See also 112. Ceremony; 376. Gentlemen; 389. Good Breeding; 559. Manners; 743. Propriety; 824. Rudeness

1. Politeness, n. The most acceptable hypocrisy. AMBROSE BIERCE, *The Devil's Dictionary* (1881–1911).

2. Courtesy is the due of man to man; not of suit-of-clothes to suit-of-clothes. THOMAS CARLYLE, "Corn-Law Rhymes" (1832).

3. It is wise to apply the oil of refined politeness to the mechanism of friendship. COLETTE, "The Pure and the Impure," *Earthly Paradise* (1966), 5, ed. Robert Phelps.

4. The first point of courtesy must always be truth. EMERSON, "Manners," *Essays: Second Series* (1844).

5. We must be as courteous to a man as we are to a picture, which we are willing to give the advantage of a good light. EMERSON, "Behavior," *The Conduct of Life* (1860).

6. All doors open to courtesy. THOMAS FULLER, M.D., *Gnomologia* (1732), 512.

7. There is a courtesy of the heart. It is akin to love. Out of it arises the purest courtesy in the outward behavior. GOETHE, *Elective Affinities* (1809), 23.

8. Courtesy is the politic witchery of great personages. BALTASAR GRACIÁN, *The Art of Worldly Wisdom* (1647), 40, tr. Joseph Jacobs.

9. Politeness is the outward garment of goodwill. But many are the nutshells, in which, if you crack them, nothing like a kernel is to be found. JULIUS CHARLES HARE and AUGUSTUS WILLIAM HARE, *Guesses at Truth* (1827).

10. Everyone has to think to be polite; the first impulse is to be impolite. EDGAR WATSON HOWE, *Country Town Sayings* (1911).

11. In truth, politeness is artificial good humor, it covers the natural want of it, and ends by rendering habitual a substitute nearly equivalent to the real virtue. THOMAS JEFFERSON, letter to Thomas Jefferson Randolph, Nov. 24, 1808.

12. There can be no defence like elaborate courtesy. E. V. LUCAS, *Reading, Writing, and Remembering* (1932).

13. The knowledge of courtesy and good manners is a very necessary study. It is, like grace and beauty, that which begets liking and an inclination to love one another at the first sight. MONTAIGNE, "The ceremony of the interview of princes," *Essays* (1580–88), tr. Charles Cotton and W. C. Hazlitt.

14. Politeness is to human nature what warmth is to wax. SCHOPENHAUER, "The Wisdom of Life," *Parerga and Paralipomena* (1851).

15. The greater man the greater courtesy. ALFRED, LORD TENNYSON, "The Last Tournament," *Idylls of the King* (1871).

## 195. COURTSHIP

See also 348. Flirtation; 548. Love; 560. Marriage; 820. Romance; 851. Seduction

1. Those marriages generally abound most with love and constancy that are preceded by a long courtship. The passion should strike root and gather strength before marriage be grafted on it. JOSEPH ADDISON, *The Spectator* (1711–12), 261.

2. Better be courted and jilted / Than never be courted at all. THOMAS CAMPBELL, "The Jilted Nymph."

3. If you cannot inspire a woman with love of you, fill her above the brim with love of herself—all that runs over will be yours. CHARLES CALEB COLTON, *Lacon* (1825), 2.89.

4. Courtship to marriage is as a very witty prologue to a very dull play. WILLIAM CONGREVE, *The Old Bachelor* (1693), 5.4.

5. Let men tremble to win the hand of woman, unless thy win along with it the utmost passion of her heart! NATHANIEL HAWTHORNE, *The Scarlet Letter* (1850), 15.

6. Do not let any sweet-talking woman beguile your good sense / with the fascinations of her shape. It's your barn she's after. HESIOD, *Works and Days* (8th c. B.C.), 373, tr. Richmond Lattimore.

7. A woman might as well propose: her husband will claim she did. EDGAR WATSON HOWE, *Country Town Sayings* (1911).

8. Men are always doomed to be duped,

not so much by the arts of the [other] sex as by their own imaginations. They are always wooing goddesses, and marrying mere mortals. WASHINGTON IRVING, "Wives," *Bracebridge Hall* (1822).

9. Either you have a rival or you don't. If you have one, you must please in order to be preferred to him, and if you don't you must still please—in order to avoid having one. PIERRE CHODERLOS DE LACLOS, Letter 152, *Les Liaisons dangereuses* (1782).

10. When once the young heart of a maiden is stolen, / The maiden herself will steal after it soon. THOMAS MOORE, "Omens," *Irish Melodies* (1807–35).

11. I flee who chases me, and chase who flees me. OVID, *The Loves* (c. A.D. 8), 2.19, tr. J. Lewis May.

12. She will never win him, whose / Words had shown she feared to lose. DOROTHY PARKER, "The Lady's Reward," *Death and Taxes* (1931).

13. This swift business / I must uneasy make, lest too light winning / Make the prize light. SHAKESPEARE, *The Tempest* (1611–12), 1.2.450.

14. Courtesy wins woman all as well / As valor may, but he that closes both / Is perfect. ALFRED, LORD TENNYSON, "The Last Tournament," *Idylls of the King* (1871).

## 196. COWARDICE

**See also 192. Courage; 298. Escape; 302. Evasion; 340. Fear; 973. Timidity**

1. Cowards never use their might, / But against such as will not fight. SAMUEL BUTLER (d. 1680), *Hudibras* (1663), 1.3.

2. A man's acts are slavish, not true but specious; his very thoughts are false, he thinks too as a slave and coward, till he have got Fear under his feet. THOMAS CARLYLE, *On Heroes, Hero-Worship and the Heroic in History* (1841), 1.

3. That cowardice is incorrigible which the love of power cannot overcome. CHARLES CALEB COLTON, *Lacon* (1825), 1.44.

4. Optimism and self-pity are the positive and negative poles of modern cowardice. CYRIL CONNOLLY, *The Unquiet Grave* (1945), 1.

5. No man gains credit for his cowardly courtesies. EMERSON, *Journals*, 1832.

6. Many would be cowards if they had courage enough. THOMAS FULLER, M.D., *Gnomologia* (1732), 3366.

7. Cowardice, as distinguished from panic, is almost always simply a lack of ability to suspend the functioning of the imagination. ERNEST HEMINGWAY, introduction to *Men at War* (1942).

8. Between two cowards, he has the advantage who first detects the other. ITALIAN PROVERB.

9. The most mortifying infirmity in human nature, to feel in ourselves, or to contemplate in another, is, perhaps, cowardice. CHARLES LAMB, "Stage Illusion," *Last Essays of Elia* (1833).

10. Perfect courage and utter cowardice are two extremes which rarely occur. LA ROCHEFOUCAULD, *Maxims* (1655), tr. Kenneth Pratt.

11. Let us be wary of ready-made ideas about cowardice and courage: the same burden weighs infinitely more heavily on some shoulders than on others. FRANÇOIS MAURIAC, "Solitude during the War," *Second Thoughts* (1961), tr. Adrienne Foulke.

12. Cowards die many times before their deaths; / The valiant never taste of death but once. SHAKESPEARE, *Julius Caesar* (1599–1600), 2.2.32.

13. The human race is a race of cowards: and I am not only marching in that procession but carrying a banner. MARK TWAIN, "Reflections on Being the Delight of God," *Mark Twain in Eruption* (1940), ed. Bernard De Voto.

## 197. CRAFTINESS

**See also 137. Cleverness; 162. Concealment; 936. Subtlety**

1. The weak in courage is strong in cunning. WILLIAM BLAKE, "Proverbs of Hell," *The Marriage of Heaven and Hell* (1790).

2. With foxes we must play the fox. THOMAS FULLER, M.D., *Gnomologia* (1732), 5797.

3. Every man wishes to be wise, and they who cannot be wise are almost always cunning. SAMUEL JOHNSON, *The Idler* (1758–60), 92.

4. A man has made great progress in cunning when he does not seem too clever to others. LA BRUYÈRE, *Characters* (1688), 8.85.

5. There is great ability in knowing how to conceal one's ability. LA ROCHEFOUCAULD, *Maxims* (1665).

6. If men are only shrewd enough, they may even serve kings, eat poison, and dally with women. *Panchatantra* (c. 5th c.), 1, tr. Franklin Edgerton.

7. The fox knows many tricks, but the hedgehog's one trick is the best of all. Attributed by Zenobius to PIGRES, *Margites* (6th c. B.C.?).

8. He can best avoid a snare who knows how to set one. PUBLILIUS SYRUS, *Moral Sayings* (1st c. B.C.), 573, tr. Darius Lyman.

9. The greatest cunning is to have none at all. CARL SANDBURG, *The People, Yes* (1936).

## 198. CREATION AND CREATIVITY

See also 53. Art and Artists; 239. Destruction; 483. Inspiration; 702. Poetry and Poets; 863. Self-expression; 1062. Writing and Writers

1. The noblest works and foundations have proceeded from childless men, which have sought to express the images of their minds, where those of their bodies have failed. FRANCIS BACON, "Of Parents and Children," *Essays* (1625).

2. The creative person is both more primitive and more cultivated, more destructive, a lot madder and a lot saner, than the average person. FRANK BARRON, *Think*, November–December 1962.

3. Men are like trees: each one must put forth the leaf that is created in him. HENRY WARD BEECHER, *Proverbs from Plymouth Pulpit* (1887).

4. Except a corn of wheat fall into the ground and die, it abideth alone; but if it die, it bringeth forth much fruit. *Bible*, John 12:24.

5. God was satisfied with his own work, and that is fatal. SAMUEL BUTLER (d. 1902), *Note-Books* (1912).

6. For good and evil, man is a free creative spirit. This produces the very queer world we live in, a world in continous creation and therefore continuous change and insecurity. JOYCE CARY, interview, *Writers at Work: First Series* (1958).

7. Every production must resemble its author. CERVANTES, author's preface, *Don Quixote* (1605–15), tr. Peter Motteux and John Ozell.

8. With the offspring of genius, the law of parturition is reversed: the throes are in the conception, the pleasure in the birth. CHARLES CALEB COLTON, *Lacon* (1825), 2.17.

9. Our inventions mirror our secret wishes. LAWRENCE DURRELL, *Mountolive* (1959), 7.

10. Nature is a rag merchant, who works up every shred and ort and end into new creations. EMERSON, "Considerations by the Way," *The Conduct of Life* (1860).

11. Creativity varies inversely with the number of cooks involved in the broth. BERNICE FITZ-GIBBON, *Macy's, Gimbel's and Me* (1967).

12. Think before you speak is criticism's motto; speak before you think creation's. E. M. FORSTER, "The Raison d'Etre of Criticism in the Arts," *Two Cheers for Democracy* (1951).

13. Creative minds always have been known to survive any kind of bad training. ANNA FREUD, 1968 annual Freud lecture to N. Y. Psychoanalytic Society.

14. Man's main task in life is to give birth to himself. ERICH FROMM, *Man for Himself* (1947), 4.

15. Man unites himself with the world in the process of creation. ERICH FROMM, *The Art of Loving* (1956), 2.

16. All men are creative but few are artists. PAUL GOODMAN, *Growing Up Absurd* (1960), 9.3.

17. The most gifted members of the human species are at their creative best when they cannot have their way. ERIC HOFFER, *The Ordeal of Change* (1964), 6.

18. Man, like Deity, creates in his own image. ELBERT HUBBARD, *The Note Book* (1927).

19. To build is to be robbed. SAMUEL JOHNSON, *The Idler* (1758–60), 62.

20. He that, building, stays at one / Floor, or the second, hath erected none. BEN JONSON, *Catiline His Conspiracy* (1611), 1.1.

21. We can invent only with memory. ALPHONSE KARR, *Les Guêpes*, April 1841.

22. Human salvation lies in the hands of the creatively maladjusted. MARTIN LUTHER KING, JR., *Strength to Love* (1963), 2.3.

23. Let a human being throw the ener-

gies of his soul into the making of something, and the instinct of workmanship will take care of his honesty. WALTER LIPPMANN, "The Changing Focus," *A Preface to Politics* (1914).

24. In creating, the only hard thing's to begin; / A grass blade's no easier to make than an oak. JAMES RUSSELL LOWELL, *A Fable for Critics* (1848).

25. Generalization is necessary to the advancement of knowledge; but particularity is indispensable to the creations of the imagination. THOMAS BABINGTON MACAULAY, "Milton" (1825).

26. One must die to life in order to be utterly a creator. THOMAS MANN, "Tonio Kröger" (1903), *Death in Venice*, tr. H. T. Lowe-Porter.

27. The artist produces for the liberation of his soul. It is his nature to create as it is the nature of water to run down hill. W. SOMERSET MAUGHAM, *The Summing Up* (1938), 49.

28. One must still have chaos in oneself to be able to give birth to a dancing star. NIETZSCHE, "Zarathustra's Prologue," *Thus Spoke Zarathustra* (1883–92), 1, tr. Walter Kaufmann.

29. Creation—that is the great redemption from suffering, and life's growing light. But that the creator may be, suffering is needed and much change. NIETZSCHE, "Upon the Blessed Isles," *Thus Spoke Zarathustra* (1883–92), 2, tr. Walter Kaufmann.

30. We live at a time when man believes himself fabulously capable of creation, but he does not know what to create. JOSÉ ORTEGA Y GASSET, *The Revolt of the Masses* (1930), 4.

31. In life it is more necessary to lose than to gain. A seed will only germinate if it dies. BORIS PASTERNAK, *I Remember* (1959).

32. I will work out the divinity that is busy within my mind / and tend the means that are mine. PINDAR, *Odes* (5th c. B.C.), Pythia 3, tr. Richmond Lattimore.

33. He who does not know how to create should not know. ANTONIO PORCHIA, *Voces* (1968), tr. W. S. Merwin.

34. Man is, above all, he who creates. And theirs alone is brotherhood who work together. SAINT-EXUPÉRY, *The Wisdom of the Sands* (1948), 9, tr. Stuart Gilbert.

35. Such is man that he rejoices only in what he himself builds up, and, to enjoy the poem, he needs must undergo the toil of its ascent. SAINT-EXUPÉRY, *The Wisdom of the Sands* (1948), 35, tr. Stuart Gilbert.

36. The artist finds a greater pleasure in painting than in having completed the picture. SENECA, *Letters to Lucilius* (1st c.), 9.7, tr. E. Phillips Barker.

37. If I bind the future I bind my will. If I bind my will I strangle creation. GEORGE BERNARD SHAW, *Back to Methuselah* (1921), 1.1.

38. A creative artist works on his next composition because he was not satisfied with his previous one. DMITRI SHOSTAKOVICH, *The New York Times*, Oct. 25, 1959.

39. In order to create there must be a dynamic force, and what force is more potent than love? IGOR STRAVINSKY, *An Autobiography* (1936), 5.

40. The art of creation / is older than the art of killing. ANDREY VOZNESENSKY, "Poem with a Footnote," *The New York Times Review of Books*, May 19, 1967.

41. The imagination imitates. It is the critical spirit that creates. OSCAR WILDE, *Intentions* (1891).

## 199. CREDULITY

**See also 76. Belief; 611. Naïveté; 948. Surprise; 1056. Wonder**

1. People everywhere enjoy believing things that they know are not true. It spares them the ordeal of thinking for themselves and taking responsibility for what they know. BROOKS ATKINSON, "February 2," *Once Around the Sun* (1951).

2. The most imaginative people are the most credulous, for to them everything is possible. ALEXANDER CHASE, *Perspectives* (1966).

3. Precisely in proportion to our own intellectual weakness will be our credulity as to those mysterious powers assumed by others. CHARLES CALEB COLTON, *Lacon* (1825), 2.86.

4. Our credulity is greatest concerning the things we know least about. And since we know least about ourselves, we are ready to believe all that is said about us. Hence the mysterious power of both flattery and calumny. ERIC HOFFER, *The Passionate State of Mind* (1955).

5. Each believes easily what he fears and what he desires. LA FONTAINE, "The Wolf and the Fox," *Fables* (1668–94).

6. Credulity is the man's weakness, but the child's strength. CHARLES LAMB, "Witches, and Other Night-Fears," *Essays of Elia* (1823).

7. There is no crime in the cynical American calendar more humiliating than to be a sucker. MAX LERNER, "How Grateful Should Europe Be?" *Actions and Passions* (1949).

8. People can be induced to swallow anything, provided it is sufficiently seasoned with praise. MOLIÈRE, *The Miser* (1668), 1, tr. John Wood.

## 200. CREEDS

See also 262. Dogmatism; 328. Faith; 443. Ideology; 790. Religion

1. There lies at the back of every creed something terrible and hard for which the worshipper may one day be required to suffer. E. M. FORSTER, "What I Believe," *Two Cheers for Democracy* (1951).

2. A creed is an ossified metaphor. ELBERT HUBBARD, *The Note Book* (1927).

3. It is only in the lonely emergencies of life that our creed is tested: then routine maxims fail, and we fall back on our gods. WILLIAM JAMES, "The Sentiment of Rationality," *The Will to Believe* (1896).

4. There is no doctrine will do good where nature is wanting. BEN JONSON, "Of the Diversity of Wits," *Timber* (1640).

5. The test, surely, of a creed is not the ability of those who accept it to announce their faith; its test is its ability to change their behavior in the ordinary round of daily life. Judged by that test, I know no religion that has a moral claim upon the allegiance of men. HAROLD J. LASKI, in *I Believe* (1939), ed. Clifton Fadiman.

6. I know that a creed is the shell of a lie. AMY LOWELL, "Evelyn Ray," *What's O'Clock* (1925).

7. If you have embraced a creed which appears to be free from the ordinary dirtiness of politics—a creed from which you yourself cannot expect to draw any material advantage—surely that proves that you are in the right? GEORGE ORWELL, "Lear, Tolstoy and the Fool," *Shooting an Elephant* (1950).

## 201. CRIME

See also 305. Evil; 446. Illegality; 516. Killing; 893. Sin; 927. Stealing; 1023. Vice; 1063. Wrongdoing

1. There exists among the intolerably degraded the perverse and powerful desire to force into the arena of the actual those fantastic crimes of which they have been accused, achieving their vengeance and their own destruction through making the nightmare real. JAMES BALDWIN, "Many Thousands Gone" (1951), *Notes of a Native Son* (1955).

2. The great thieves lead away the little thief. DIOGENES THE CYNIC (4th c. B.C.), quoted in Diogenes Laertius' *Lives and Opinions of Eminent Philosophers* (3rd c. A.D.), tr. R. D. Hicks.

3. We / live in an earth of well-dressed gangs. EDWARD DORN, "The Biggest Killing," *A Controversy of Poets* (1965), ed. Paris Leary and Robert Kelly.

4. The more featureless and commonplace a crime is, the more difficult it is to bring it home. SIR ARTHUR CONAN DOYLE, "The Boscombe Valley Mystery," *The Adventures of Sherlock Holmes* (1891).

5. The chief problem in any community cursed with crime is not the punishment of the criminals, but the preventing of the young from being trained to crime. W. E. B. DU BOIS, *The Souls of Black Folk* (1903), 9.

6. Commit a crime, and the earth is made of glass. There is no such thing as concealment. EMERSON, "Compensation," *Essays: First Series* (1841).

7. Juvenile delinquency serves many purposes, including that of providing sadistic adults with fantasies suited to their special tastes. EDGAR Z. FRIEDENBERG, "The Impact of the School," *The Vanishing Adolescent* (1959).

8. The number of malefactors authorizes not the crime. THOMAS FULLER, M.D., *Gnomologia* (1732), 4687.

9. He who holds the ladder is as bad as the thief. GERMAN PROVERB.

10. When a felon's not engaged in his employment, / Or maturing his felonious little plans, / His capacity for innocent enjoyment / Is just as great as any honest man's.

W. S. GILBERT, *The Pirates of Penzance* (1879), 2.

11. Crime leaves a trail like a water-beetle; / Like a snail, it leaves its shine; / Like a horse-mango it leaves its reek. MALAY PROVERB.

12. it takes all sorts of / people to make an / underworld. DON MARQUIS, "mehitabel again," *Archy's Life of Mehitabel* (1933).

13. Nothing is worse than a naked robber. MARTIAL, *Epigrams* (A.D. 86), 12.63, tr. Walter C. A. Ker.

14. The study of crime begins with the knowledge of oneself. HENRY MILLER, "The Soul of Anaesthesia," *The Air-Conditioned Nightmare* (1945).

15. Collective crimes incriminate no one. NAPOLEON I, *Maxims* (1804–15).

16. Great crimes come never singly; they are linked / To sins that went before. RACINE, *Phaedra* (1677), 4, tr. Robert Henderson.

17. Most men only commit great crimes because of their scruples about petty ones. CARDINAL DE RETZ, *Mémoires* (1718).

18. Crime is a logical extension of the sort of behavior that is often considered perfectly respectable in legitimate business. ROBERT RICE, *The Business of Crime* (1956).

19. Successful and fortunate crime is called virtue. SENECA, *Hercules Furens* (1st c.), 255.

20. Between the acting of a dreadful thing / And the first motion, all the interim is / Like a phantasma or a hideous dream. / The genius and the mortal instruments / Are then in council, and the state of man, / Like to a little kingdom, suffers then / The nature of an insurrection. SHAKESPEARE, *Julius Caesar* (1599–1600), 2.1.63.

21. Fear succeeds crime – it is its punishment. VOLTAIRE, *Sémiramis* (1748), 5.1.

22. The faculties for getting into jail seem to be ample. We want more organizations for keeping people out. CHARLES DUDLEY WARNER, "Eighth Study," *Backlog Studies* (1873).

## 202. CRISES

**See also 17. Adversity**

1. We learn geology the morning after the earthquake. EMERSON, "Considerations by the Way," *The Conduct of Life* (1860).

2. For an extraordinary situation, extraordinary measures, and sacrifices in proportion. Graffito written during French student revolt, May 1968.

3. Great crises produce great men and great deeds of courage. JOHN F. KENNEDY, *Profiles in Courage* (1956).

4. When written in Chinese, the word "crisis" is composed of two characters – one represents danger and the other represents opportunity. JOHN F. KENNEDY, address, United Negro College Fund Convocation, Indianapolis, Ind., April 12, 1959.

5. If you can keep your head when all about you are losing theirs, it's just possible you haven't grasped the situation. JEAN KERR, introduction, *Please Don't Eat the Daisies* (1957).

6. I don't see America as a mainland, but as a sea, a big ocean. Sometimes a storm arises, a formidable current develops, and it seems it will engulf everything. Wait a moment, another current will appear and bring the first one to naught. JACQUES MARITAIN, *Reflections on America* (1958), 4.

7. Nationwide thinking, nationwide planning and nationwide action are the three great essentials to prevent nationwide crises for future generations to struggle through. FRANKLIN D. ROOSEVELT, speech, New York City, April 25, 1936.

## 203. CRITICISM

**See also 5. Accusation; 204. Criticism, Professional; 339. Faults; 513. Judging Others; 797. Reproof; 857. Self-criticism**

1. The blow of a whip raises a welt, but a blow of the tongue crushes bones. *Apocrypha*, Ecclesiasticus 28:17.

2. No man can tell another his faults so as to benefit him, unless he loves him. HENRY WARD BEECHER, *Proberbs from Plymouth Pulpit* (1887).

3. Judge not, that ye be not judged. *Bible*, Matthew 7:1.

4. Wherein thou judgest another, thou condemnest thyself. *Bible*, Romans 2:1.

5. If a man is devout, we accuse him of hypocrisy; if he is not, of impiety; if he is humble, we look on his humility as a weak-

ness; if he is generous, we call his courage pride. LOUIS BOURDALOUE, "Sur le jugement téméraire" (1822–26).

6. I do not resent criticism, even when, for the sake of emphasis, it parts for the time with reality. SIR WINSTON CHURCHILL, speech, House of Commons, Jan. 22, 1941.

7. Never join with your friend when he abuses his horse or his wife, unless the one is about to be sold, and the other to be buried. CHARLES CALEB COLTON, *Lacon* (1825), 1.376.

8. When certain persons abuse us, let us ask ourselves what description of characters it is that they admire; we shall often find this a very consolatory question. CHARLES CALEB COLTON, *Lacon* (1825), 2.28.

9. It is much easier to be critical than to be correct. BENJAMIN DISRAELI, speech, Jan. 24, 1860.

10. One must first learn to live oneself before one blames others. DOSTOEVSKY, *Notes from Underground* (1864), 2.4, tr. Constance Garnett.

11. Criticism should not be querulous and wasting, all knife and root-puller, but guiding, instructive, inspiring, a south wind, not an east wind. EMERSON, *Journals*, 1847.

12. The frying-pan says to the kettle, "Avaunt, black brows." ENGLISH PROVERB.

13. It is easier to discover a deficiency in individuals, in states, and in Providence, than to see their real import and value. HEGEL, introduction to *Philosophy of History* (1832), tr. John Sibree.

14. There is so much good in the worst of us, / And so much bad in the best of us, / That it hardly behooves any of us / To talk about the rest of us. Attributed to EDWARD WALLIS HOCH (1849–1925).

15. You may scold a carpenter who has made you a bad table, though you cannot make a table. It is not your trade to make tables. SAMUEL JOHNSON, quoted in Boswell's *Life of Samuel Johnson*, June 15, 1763.

16. Men are ready to suffer anything from others or from heaven itself, provided that, when it comes to words, they are untouched. GIACOMO LEOPARDI, *Pensieri* (1834–37), 1, tr. William Fense Weaver.

17. I have never found, in a long experience of politics, that criticism is ever inhibited by ignorance. HAROLD MACMILLAN, *Wall Street Journal*, Aug. 13, 1963.

18. He can see a louse as far away as China but is unconscious of an elephant on his nose. MALAY PROVERB.

19. People ask you for criticism, but they only want praise. W. SOMERSET MAUGHAM, *Of Human Bondage* (1915), 50.

20. The greater one's love for a person the less room for flattery. The proof of true love is to be unsparing in criticism. MOLIÈRE, *The Misanthrope* (1666), 2, tr. John Wood.

21. We every day and every hour say things of another that we might more properly say of ourselves, could we but apply our observations to our own concerns. MONTAIGNE, "Of the affections of fathers to their children," *Essays* (1580–88), tr. Charles Cotton and W. C. Hazlitt.

22. I don't care how unkind the things people say about me so / long as they don't say them to my face. OGDEN NASH, "Hush, Here They Come," *Verses from 1929 On* (1959).

23. We find fault with perfection itself. PASCAL, *Pensées* (1670), 357, tr. W. F. Trotter.

24. We are apt to be very pert at censuring others, where we will not endure advice ourselves. WILLIAM PENN, *Some Fruits of Solitude* (1693), 1.41.

25. They have a right to censure that have a heart to help. WILLIAM PENN, *Some Fruits of Solitude* (1693), 1.46.

26. It is folly to censure him whom all the world adores. PUBLILIUS SYRUS, *Moral Sayings* (1st c. B.C.), tr. Darius Lyman.

27. Next to the joy of the egotist is the joy of the detractor. AGNES REPPLIER, "Writing an Autobiography," *Under Dispute* (1924).

28. Many a man will have the courage to die gallantly, but will not have the courage to say, or even to think, that the cause for which he is asked to die is an unworthy one. Obloquy is, to most men, more painful than death. BERTRAND RUSSELL, "An Outline of Intellectual Rubbish," *Unpopular Essays* (1950).

29. Expose not the secret failings of mankind, otherwise you must verily bring scandal upon them and distrust upon yourself. SA'DI, *Gulistan* (1258), 8.41, tr. James Ross.

30. Take each man's censure, but reserve thy judgment. SHAKESPEARE, *Hamlet* (1600), 1.3.69.

31. Censure is the tax a man pays to the public for being eminent. JONATHAN SWIFT, *Thoughts on Various Subjects* (1711).

32. I am sorry to think that you do not get a man's most effective criticism until you provoke him. THOREAU, *Journal*, March 15, 1854.

33. If you're out to beat a dog, you're sure to find a stick. *Yiddish Proverbs* (1949), ed. Hanan J. Ayalti.

## 204. CRITICISM, PROFESSIONAL

See also 20. Aesthetics

1. They who are to be judges must also be performers. ARISTOTLE, *Politics* (4th c. B.C.), 8.6, tr. Benjamin Jowett.

2. There should be a dash of the amateur in criticism. For the amateur is a man of enthusiasm who has not settled down and is not habit-bound. BROOKS ATKINSON, "July 8," *Once Around the Sun* (1951).

3. One cannot review a bad book without showing off. W. H. AUDEN, "Reading," *The Dyer's Hand* (1962).

4. Critics are like brushers of noblemen's clothes. FRANCIS BACON, *Apothegms* (1625), 64.

5. The critic who justly admires all kinds of things simultaneously cannot love any one of them. MAX BEERBOHM, "George Moore," *Mainly On the Air* (1946).

6. A good writer is not *per se* a good book critic. No more than a good drunk is automatically a good bartender. JIM BISHOP, *New York Journal-American*, Nov. 26, 1957.

7. Posterity is as likely to be wrong as anybody else. HEYWOOD BROUN, "The Last Review," *Sitting on the World* (1924).

8. A man must serve his time to every trade / Save Censure—Critics all are ready made. BYRON, *English Bards and Scotch Reviewers* (1809).

9. As soon / Seek roses in December—ice in June; / Hope constancy in wind, or corn in chaff, / Believe a woman or an epitaph, / Or any other thing that's false, before / You trust in Critics. BYRON, *English Bards and Scotch Reviewers* (1809).

10. 'Tis strange the mind, that very fiery particle, / Should let itself be snuffed out by an article. BYRON, *Don Juan* (1819–24), 11.60.

11. Criticism is like champagne: nothing more execrable if bad, nothing more excellent if good. CHARLES CALEB COLTON, *Lacon* (1825), 2.122.

12. Only paper flowers are afraid of the rain. We are not afraid of the noble rain of criticism because with it will flourish the magnificent garden of music. KONSTANTIN DANKEVICH, *The New York Times*, Nov. 19, 1959.

13. Criticism is easy, art is difficult. PHILIPPE DESTOUCHES, *Le Glorieux* (1732), 2.5.

14. You know who critics are?—the men who have failed in literature and art. BENJAMIN DISRAELI, *Lothair* (1870), 28.

15. Every nation, every race, has not only its own creative, but its own critical turn of mind; and is even more oblivious of the shortcomings and limitations of its critical habits than of those of its creative genius. T. S. ELIOT, "Tradition and the Individual Talent" (1919).

16. No man can be criticised but by a greater than he. Do not, then, read the reviews. EMERSON, *Journals*, 1842.

17. Taking to pieces is the trade of those who cannot construct. EMERSON, *Journals*, 1858.

18. Great is paint; nay God is the painter; and we rightly accuse the critic who destroys too many illusions. EMERSON, "Illusions," *The Conduct of Life* (1860).

19. The artist is a cut above the critic, for the artist is writing something which will move the critic. The critic is writing something which will move everybody but the artist. WILLIAM FAULKNER, interview, *Writers at Work: First Series* (1958).

20. Now, in reality, the world have paid too great a compliment to critics, and have imagined them men of much greater profundity than they really are. HENRY FIELDING, *Tom Jones* (1749), 5.1.

21. A man is a critic when he cannot be an artist, in the same way that a man becomes an informer when he cannot be a soldier. FLAUBERT, *Correspondance, à Louise Colet*, October 1846.

22. A good critic is the man who describes his adventures among masterpieces. ANATOLE FRANCE, preface to *La Vie littéraire* (1883–92), 1.

23. The real connoisseurs in art are those who make people accept as beautiful something everybody used to consider ugly, by

revealing and resuscitating the beauty in it. EDMOND and JULES DE GONCOURT, *Journal*, June 30, 1881, tr. Robert Baldick.

24. The Stones that Critics hurl with Harsh Intent / A Man may use to build his Monument. ARTHUR GUITERMAN, *A Poet's Proverbs* (1924).

25. When a man says he sees nothing in a book, he very often means that he does not see himself in it: which, if it is not a comedy or a satire, is likely enough. JULIUS CHARLES HARE and AUGUSTUS WILLIAM HARE, *Guesses at Truth* (1827).

26. What a blessed thing it is, that Nature, when she invented, manufactured, and patented her authors, contrived to make critics out of the chips that were left! OLIVER WENDELL HOLMES, SR., *The Professor at the Breakfast Table* (1860), 1.

27. What the mulberry leaf is to the silkworm, the author's book, treatise, essay, poem, is to the critical larvae that feed upon it. It furnishes them with food and clothing. OLIVER WENDELL HOLMES, SR., *Over the Teacups* (1891), 2.

28. There is one gratification an old author can afford a certain class of critics: that, namely, of comparing him as he is with what he was. It is a pleasure to mediocrity to have its superiors brought within range. OLIVER WENDELL HOLMES, SR., *Over the Teacups* (1891), 2.

29. The slanders of the pen pierce to the heart; they rankle longest in the noblest spirits; they dwell ever present in the mind and render it morbidly sensitive to the most trifling collision. WASHINGTON IRVING, "English Writers on America," *The Sketch Book of Geoffrey Crayon, Gent.* (1819–20).

30. The ambition of superior sensibility and superior eloquence disposes the lovers of arts to receive rapture at one time, and communicate it at another; and each labours first to impose upon himself, and then to propagate the imposture. SAMUEL JOHNSON, *The Idler* (1758–60), 50.

31. He who first praises a book becomingly is next in merit to the author. WALTER SAVAGE LANDOR, "Alfieri and Salomon," *Imaginary Conversations* (1824–53).

32. Nature fits all her children with something to do, / He who would write and can't write can surely review. JAMES RUSSELL LOWELL, *A Fable for Critics* (1848).

33. A good critic is the sorcerer who makes some hidden spring gush forth unexpectedly under our feet. FRANÇOIS MAURIAC, "A Critique of Criticism," *Second Thoughts* (1961), tr. Adrienne Foulke.

34. The critic, to interpret his artist, even to understand his artist, must be able to get into the mind of his artist; he must feel and comprehend the vast pressure of the creative passion. H. L. MENCKEN, *Prejudices: First Series* (1919), 1.

35. There is no reward so delightful, no pleasure so exquisite, as having one's work known and acclaimed by those whose applause confers honour. MOLIÈRE, *The Would-be Gentleman* (1670), 1, tr. John Wood.

36. There is no fate more distressing for an artist than to have to show himself off before fools, to see his work exposed to the criticism of the vulgar and ignorant. MOLIÈRE, *The Would-be Gentleman* (1670), 2, tr. John Wood.

37. Every place swarms with commentaries; of authors there is great scarcity. MONTAIGNE, "Of experience," *Essays* (1580–88), tr. Charles Cotton and W. C. Hazlitt.

38. There is more ado to interpret interpretations than to interpret things, and more books upon books than upon any other subject; we do nothing but comment upon one another. MONTAIGNE, "Of experience," *Essays* (1580–88), tr. Charles Cotton and W. C. Hazlitt.

39. Scarcely any literature is so entirely unprofitable as the so-called criticism that overlays a pithy text with a windy sermon. JOHN MORLEY, "Emerson," *Critical Miscellanies* (1871–1908).

40. Criticism is the windows and chandeliers of art: it illuminates the enveloping darkness in which art might otherwise rest only vaguely discernible, and perhaps altogether unseen. GEORGE JEAN NATHAN, *The Critic and the Drama* (1922), 1.

41. Insects sting, not from malice, but because they want to live. It is the same with critics—they desire our blood, not our pain. NIETZSCHE, *Miscellaneous Maxims and Opinions* (1879), 164, tr. Paul V. Cohn.

42. Let such teach others who themselves excel, / And censure freely who have written well. ALEXANDER POPE, *An Essay on Criticism* (1711), 1.15.

43. Some judge of authors' names, not works, and then / Nor praise nor blame the

writings, but the men. ALEXANDER POPE, *An Essay on Criticism* (1711), 2.212.

44. Works of art are of an infinite loneliness and with nothing so little to be reached as with criticism. RAINER MARIA RILKE, *Letters to a Young Poet*, April 23, 1903, tr. M. D. Herter Norton.

45. The hardest of all the arts to speak of is music, because music has no meaning to speak of. NED ROREM, "Random Notes from a Diary," *Music from Inside Out* (1967).

46. To substitute judgments of fact for judgments of value, is a sign of pedantic and borrowed criticism. GEORGE SANTAYANA, *The Sense of Beauty* (1896), 2.

47. With an artist no sane man quarrels, any more than with the colour of a child's eyes. GEORGE SANTAYANA, *The Life of Reason: Reason in Art* (1905–06), 9.

48. A drama critic is a man who leaves no turn unstoned. GEORGE BERNARD SHAW, *The New York Times*, Nov. 5, 1950.

49. If certain Critics were as clear-sighted as they are malignant, how great would be the benefit to be derived from their writings! SHELLEY, preface, *The Revolt of Islam* (1817).

50. I never read a book before reviewing it; it prejudices a man so. SYDNEY SMITH, quoted in H. Pearson's *The Smith of Smiths* (1934), 3.

51. In a culture whose already classical dilemma is the hypertrophy of the intellect at the expense of energy and sensual capability, interpretation is the revenge of the intellect upon art. SUSAN SONTAG, title essay, *Against Interpretation* (1961).

52. Real art has the capacity to make us nervous. By reducing the work of art to its content and then interpreting *that*, one tames the work of art. SUSAN SONTAG, title essay, *Against Interpretation* (1961).

53. He that can carp in the most eloquent or acute manner at the weakness of the human mind is held by his fellows as almost divine. SPINOZA, *Ethics* (1677), 3, tr. Andrew Boyle.

54. Of all the cants which are canted in this canting world, though the cant of hypocrites may be the worst, the cant of criticism is the most tormenting. LAURENCE STERNE, *Tristram Shandy* (1759–67), 3.12.

55. If the men of wit and genius would resolve never to complain in their works of critics and detractors, the next age would not know that they ever had any. JONATHAN SWIFT, *Thoughts on Various Subjects* (1711).

56. A critic is a man who knows the way but can't drive the car. KENNETH TYNAN, *The New York Times Magazine*, Jan. 9, 1966.

57. When critics disagree, the artist is in accord with himself. OSCAR WILDE, preface, *The Picture of Dorian Gray* (1891).

58. Has anybody ever seen a dramatic critic in the daytime? Of course not. They come out after dark, up to no good. P. G. WODEHOUSE, *New York Mirror*, May 27, 1955.

## 205. CROWDS

**See also 591. Mob; 707. Population**

1. A man has his distinctive personal scent which his wife, his children and his dog can recognize. A crowd has a generalized stink. The public is odorless. W. H. AUDEN, "The Poet and the City," *The Dyer's Hand* (1962).

2. Observe any meetings of people, and you will always find their eagerness and impetuosity rise or fall in proportion to their numbers. LORD CHESTERFIELD, *Letters to His Son*, Sept. 13, 1748.

3. I do not believe that any human being is fundamentally happier for being finally lost in a crowd, even if it is called a crowd of comrades. G. K. CHESTERTON, "About the Workers," *As I Was Saying* (1936).

4. As crowds increase we build our forts of inattention, and the more we talk the easier it is to mean little and listen not at all. FRANK MOORE COLBY, "Simple Simon," *The Colby Essays* (1926), v. 1.

5. Away with this hurrah of masses, and let us have the considerate vote of single men. EMERSON, "Considerations by the Way," *The Conduct of Life* (1860).

6. In the crowd, herd, or gang, it is a mass-mind that operates—which is to say, a mind without subtlety, a mind without compassion, a mind, finally, uncivilized. ROBERT LINDNER, "The Mutiny of the Young," *Must You Conform?* (1956).

7. Nothing is so uncertain or unpredictable as the feelings of a crowd. LIVY, *Ab Urbe Condita* (c. 29 B.C.), 31.34.

8. He who goes into a crowd must now go one way and then another, keep his elbows close, retire, or advance, and quit the straight way, according to what he encounters. MONTAIGNE, "Of vanity," *Essays* (1580–88), tr. Charles Cotton and W. C. Hazlitt.

9. In the hateful, hostile mob (O strange vagary!) / My only port and refuge can I find, / Such is my fear to find myself alone. PETRARCH, "Laura Living," *Canzoniere* (1360), 198.

10. Man goes into the noisy crowd to drown his own clamour of silence. RABINDRANATH TAGORE, *Stray Birds* (1916), 110.

11. I would rather sit on a pumpkin and have it all to myself than be crowded on a velvet cushion. THOREAU, "Economy," *Walden* (1854).

## 206. CRUELTY

See also 832. Sadism; 1011. Unkindness

1. Man is subject to innumerable pains and sorrows by the very condition of humanity, and yet, as if nature had not sown evils enough in life, we are continually adding grief to grief and aggravating the common calamity by our cruel treatment of one another. JOSEPH ADDISON, *The Spectator* (1711–12), 169.

2. Cruelty ever proceeds from a vile mind, and often from a cowardly heart. LODOVICO ARIOSTO, *Orlando Furioso* (1516), 36, notes, tr. Sir John Harington.

3. Man's inhumanity to man / Makes countless thousands mourn. ROBERT BURNS, "Man Was Made to Mourn" (1786).

4. Cruelty is, perhaps, the worst kind of sin. Intellectual cruelty is certainly the worst kind of cruelty. G. K. CHESTERTON, "Conceit and Caricature," *All Things Considered* (1908).

5. One's cruelty is one's power; and when one parts with one's cruelty, one parts with one's power; and when one has parted with that, I fancy one's old and ugly. WILLIAM CONGREVE, *The Way of the World* (1700), 2.2.

6. Cruelty is a tyrant that is always attended by fear. ENGLISH PROVERB.

7. All the world will beat the man whom fortune buffets. THOMAS FULLER, M.D., *Gnomologia* (1732), 559.

8. Cruelty is the law pervading all nature and society; and we can't get out of it if we would. THOMAS HARDY, *Jude the Obscure* (1895), 5.8.

9. Pity is not natural to man. Children always are cruel. Savages are always cruel. SAMUEL JOHNSON, quoted in Boswell's *Life of Samuel Johnson*, July 20, 1763.

10. Today there's more fellowship among snakes than among mankind. / Wild beasts spare those with similar markings. JUVENAL, *Satires* (c. 100), 15.159, tr. Hubert Creekmore.

11. When men are inhuman, take care not to feel towards them as they do towards other humans. MARCUS AURELIUS, *Meditations* (2nd c.), 7.65, tr. Maxwell Staniforth.

12. Nature has, herself, I fear, imprinted in man a kind of instinct to inhumanity. MONTAIGNE, "Of cruelty," *Essays* (1580–88), tr. Charles Cotton and W. C. Hazlitt.

13. Man is the cruelest animal. At tragedies, bullfights, and crucifixions he has so far felt best on earth; and when he invented hell for himself, behold, that was his heaven on earth. NIETZSCHE, "The Convalescent," *Thus Spoke Zarathustra* (1883–92), 3, tr. Walter Kaufmann.

14. Opinions which justify cruelty are inspired by cruel impulses. BERTRAND RUSSELL, "Ideas That Have Harmed Mankind," *Unpopular Essays* (1950).

15. There is in man a specific lust for cruelty which infects even his passion of pity and makes it savage. GEORGE BERNARD SHAW, "Preface on Doctors: The Scientific Investigation of Cruelty," *The Doctor's Dilemma* (1913).

16. Man is worse than an animal when he is an animal. RABINDRANATH TAGORE, *Stray Birds* (1916), 248.

17. The vast majority of the race, whether savage or civilized, are secretly kind-hearted and shrink from inflicting pain, but in the presence of the aggressive and pitiless minority they don't dare to assert themselves. MARK TWAIN, *The Mysterious Stranger* (1916).

## 207. CULTURE

See also 131. Civilization; 485. Institutions; 906. Society

1. Culture, the acquainting ourselves with the best that has been known and said

in the world, and thus with the history of the human spirit. MATTHEW ARNOLD, preface, *Literature and Dogma* (1873).

2. Culture is the one thing that we cannot deliberately aim at. It is the product of a variety of more or less harmonious activities, each pursued for its own sake. T. S. ELIOT, *Notes Towards the Definition of Culture* (1948).

3. Culture opens the sense of beauty. EMERSON, "Culture." *The Conduct of Life* (1860).

4. A cheerful, intelligent face is the end of culture. EMERSON, "Culture," *The Conduct of Life* (1860).

5. A cultivated man, wise to know and bold to perform, is the end to which nature works. EMERSON, "Power," *The Conduct of Life* (1860).

6. Culture has never the translucidity of custom; it abhors all simplification. In its essence it is opposed to custom, for custom is always the deterioration of culture. FRANTZ FANON, "On National Culture," *The Wretched of the Earth* (1961), tr. Constance Farrington.

7. If you're anxious for to shine in the high aesthetic line as a man of culture rare, / You must get up all the germs of the transcendental terms, and plant them everywhere. W. S. GILBERT, *Patience* (1881), 1.

8. Man is born a barbarian, and only raises himself above the beast by culture. BALTASAR GRACIÁN, *The Art of Worldly Wisdom* (1647), 87, tr. Joseph Jacobs.

9. Human life is reduced to real suffering, to hell, only when two ages, two cultures and religions overlap. HERMANN HESSE, preface to *Der Steppenwolf* (1927), tr. Basil Creighton, rev. Walter Sorell.

10. Of the significant and pleasurable experiences of life only the simplest are open indiscriminately to all. The rest cannot be had except by those who have undergone a suitable training. ALDOUS HUXLEY, "Beliefs," *Ends and Means* (1937).

11. Culture is simply how one lives and is connected to history by habit. LE ROI JONES, "The Legacy of Malcolm X," *Home* (1966).

12. Prig and philistine, Ph.D. and C.P.A., despot of English 218c and big shot of the Kiwanis Club—how much, at bottom, they both hate Art, and how hard it is to know which of them hates it the more. LOUIS KRONENBERGER, *Company Manners* (1954), 1.4.

13. Educated people do indeed speak the same languages; cultivated ones need not speak at all. LOUIS KRONENBERGER, "Overture," *The Cart and the Horse* (1964), 1.

14. The value of culture is its effect on character. It avails nothing unless it ennobles and strengthens that. Its use is for life. Its aim is not beauty but goodness. W. SOMERSET MAUGHAM, *The Summing Up* (1938), 24.

15. Learning is nothing without cultivated manners, but when the two are combined in a woman, you have one of the most exquisite products of civilization. ANDRÉ MAUROIS, *Ariel* (1924), 16, tr. Ella D'Arcy.

16. Culture itself is neither education nor law-making: it is an atmosphere and a heritage. H. L. MENCKEN, *Minority Report* (1956), 360.

17. Culture is half-way to heaven. GEORGE MEREDITH, *The Ordeal of Richard Feverel* (1859), 12.

18. Experience and understanding are our rather abstract god-figures, and ignorance and stupidity will make them angry. Our schools and universities are our religious training centres, our libraries, museums, art galleries, theatres, concert halls and sports arenas are our places of communal worship. DESMOND MORRIS, *The Naked Ape* (1967), 5.

19. The Law of Raspberry Jam: The wider any culture is spread, the thinner it gets. ALVIN TOFFLER, *The Culture Consumers* (1964).

20. Culture is an instrument wielded by professors to manufacture professors, who when their turn comes will manufacture professors. SIMONE WEIL, *The Need for Roots* (1949).

## CURES

See 791. Remedies

## 208. CURIOSITY

See also 478. Inquiry

1. One shouldn't be too inquisitive in life / Either about God's secrets or one's wife. CHAUCER, "Words Between the Host and

the Miller," *The Canterbury Tales* (c. 1387–1400), tr. Nevill Coghill.

2. Curiosity is free-wheeling intelligence. ... It endows the people who have it with a generosity in argument and a serenity in their own mode of life which spring from the cheerful willingness to let life take the forms it will. ALISTAIR COOKE, "The Art of Curiosity," *Vogue*, January 1953.

3. Creatures whose mainspring is curiosity will enjoy the accumulating of facts, far more than the pausing at times to reflect on those facts. CLARENCE DAY, *This Simian World* (1920), 9.

4. Some people have an unconquerable love of riddles. They may have the chance of listening to plain sense, or to such wisdom as explains life; but no, they must go and work their brains over a riddle, just because they do not understand what it means. ISAK DINESEN, "The Deluge at Norderney," *Seven Gothic Tales* (1934).

5. Only that mind draws me which I cannot read. EMERSON, *Journals*, 1847.

6. Enquire not what boils in another's pot. THOMAS FULLER, M.D., *Gnomologia* (1732), 1373.

7. Curiosity is one of the permanent and certain characteristics of a vigorous intellect. SAMUEL JOHNSON, *The Rambler* (1750–52), 103.

8. There are various sorts of curiosity; one is from interest, which makes us desire to know that which may be useful to us; and the other, from pride which comes from the wish to know what others are ignorant of. LA ROCHEFOUCAULD, *Maxims* (1665), tr. Kenneth Pratt.

9. Glory and curiosity are the two scourges of the soul; the last prompts us to thrust our noses into everything, the other forbids us to leave anything doubtful and undecided. MONTAIGNE, "That it is folly to measure truth and error by our own capacity," *Essays* (1580–88), tr. Charles Cotton and W. C. Hazlitt.

10. He that breaks a thing to find out what it is has left the path of wisdom. J. R. R. TOLKIEN, *The Fellowship of the Ring* (1954), 2.2.

11. A man should live if only to satisfy his curiosity. *Yiddish Proverbs* (1949), ed. Hanan J. Ayalti.

## 209. CURSING

See also 950. Swearing

1. A thousand curses never tore a shirt. ARABIC PROVERB.

## 210. CUSTOM

See also 75. Behavior; 404. Habit; 979. Tradition

1. Since custom is the principal magistrate of man's life, let men by all means endeavor to obtain good customs. FRANCIS BACON, "Of Custom and Education," *Essays* (1625).

2. Customs represent the experience of mankind. HENRY WARD BEECHER, *Proverbs from Plymouth Pulpit* (1887).

3. An old custom is so sacred when it is bad! HECTOR BERLIOZ, letter to Desmarest, Berlin, 1843.

4. Custom reconciles us to everything. EDMUND BURKE, *A Philosophical Inquiry into the Origin of Our Ideas of the Sublime and Beautiful* (1756), 18.

5. Innumerable are the illusions and legerdemain-tricks of custom: but of all of these, perhaps the cleverest is her knack of persuading us that the miraculous, by simple repetition, ceases to be miraculous. THOMAS CARLYLE, *Sartor Resartus* (1833–34), 3.4.

6. Custom looks to things that are past, and fashion to things that are present, but both of them are somewhat blind as to things that are to come. CHARLES CALEB COLTON, *Lacon* (1825), 1.547.

7. Custom is the guide of the ignorant. ENGLISH PROVERB.

8. A bad custom is like a good cake, better broken than kept. ENGLISH PROVERB.

9. What men call civilization is the condition of present customs; what they call barbarism, the condition of past ones. ANATOLE FRANCE, *Sur la pierre blanche* (1903), 4.

10. Custom makes all things easy. THOMAS FULLER, M.D., *Gnomologia* (1732), 1225.

11. Old custom without truth is but an old error. THOMAS FULLER, M.D., *Gnomologia* (1732), 3710.

12. Most of the things we do, we do for no better reason than that our fathers have

done them or our neighbors do them, and the same is true of a larger part than what we suspect of what we think. OLIVER WENDELL HOLMES, JR., speech, Boston, Jan. 8, 1897.

13. There is no conceivable human action which custom has not at one time justified and at another condemned. JOSEPH WOOD KRUTCH, "The Genesis of a Mood," *The Modern Temper* (1929).

14. What humanity abhors, custom reconciles and recommends to us. JOHN LOCKE, *Some Thoughts Concerning Education* (1693), 116.

15. To almost all men the state of things under which they have been used to live seems to be the necessary state of things. THOMAS BABINGTON MACAULAY, "Southey's Colloquies" (1830).

16. Customs are made for customary circumstances, and customary characters. JOHN STUART MILL, *On Liberty* (1859), 3.

17. He who does anything because it is the custom, makes no choice. JOHN STUART MILL, *On Liberty* (1859), 3.

18. There is nothing so extreme that is not allowed by the custom of some nation or other. MONTAIGNE, "Apology for Raimond de Sebonde," *Essays* (1580–88), tr. Charles Cotton and W. C. Hazlitt.

19. Custom is a second nature, and no less powerful. MONTAIGNE, "Of managing the will," *Essays* (1580–88), tr. Charles Cotton and W. C. Hazlitt.

20. When one wants to change manners and customs, one should not do so by changing the laws. MONTESQUIEU, *L'Esprit des lois* (1748), 19.16.

21. There are a lot of people who must have the table laid in the usual fashion or they will not enjoy the dinner. CHRISTOPHER MORLEY, *Inward Ho!* (1923), 9.

22. Custom creates the whole of equity, for the simple reason that it is accepted. PASCAL, *Pensées* (1670), 294, tr. W. F. Trotter.

23. Custom determines what is agreeable. PASCAL, *Pensées* (1670), 309, tr. W. F. Trotter.

24. We are more sensible of what is done against custom than against nature. PLUTARCH, "Of Eating Flesh," *Moralia* (c. A.D. 100).

25. The universality of a custom is pledge of its worth. AGNES REPPLIER, "The Pilgrim's Staff," *Compromises* (1904).

26. There is nothing sacred about convention: there is nothing sacred about primitive passions or whims; but the fact that a convention exists indicates that a way of living has been devised capable of maintaining itself. GEORGE SANTAYANA, *Persons and Places: The Middle Span* (1945), 3.

27. Assume a virtue, if you have it not. / That monster, custom, who all sense doth eat / Of habits evil, is angel yet in this, / That to the use of actions fair and good / He likewise gives a frock or livery, / That aptly is put on. SHAKESPEARE, *Hamlet* (1600), 3.4.160.

28. How many things, both just and unjust, are sanctioned by custom! TERENCE, *The Self-Tormentor* (163 B.C.), 4.7.11, tr. Henry Thomas Riley.

29. Old custom is hard to break and scarce any man will be led otherwise than seemeth good unto himself. THOMAS À KEMPIS, *The Imitation of Christ* (1426), 1.14.

30. Often a quite assified remark becomes sanctified by use and petrified by custom; it is then a permanency, its term of activity a geologic period. MARK TWAIN, "Does the Race of Man Love a Lord?" *North American Review*, April 1902.

31. It does not matter what men say in words, so long as their activities are controlled by settled instincts. The words may ultimately destroy the instincts. But until this has occurred, words do not count. ALFRED NORTH WHITEHEAD, *Science and the Modern World* (1925), 1.

## 211. CYNICISM

1. A cynic is not merely one who reads bitter lessons from the past; he is one who is prematurely disappointed in the future. SYDNEY J. HARRIS, *On the Contrary* (1962), 7.

2. It is only the cynicism that is born of success that is penetrating and valid. GEORGE JEAN NATHAN, "Cynicism," *Monks Are Monks* (1929).

3. The cynic, a parasite of civilisation, lives by denying it, for the very reason that he is convinced that it will not fail. JOSÉ ORTEGA Y GASSET, *The Revolt of the Masses* (1930), 11.

4. What is a cynic? A man who knows the price of everything, and the value of nothing. OSCAR WILDE, *Lady Windermere's Fan* (1892), 3.

# D

## 212. DANCING

1. A good education is usually harmful to a dancer. A good calf is better than a good head. AGNES DE MILLE, news summaries, Feb. 1, 1954.

2. Modern dancers give a sinister portent about our times. The dancers don't even look at one another. They are just a lot of isolated individuals jiggling in a kind of self-hypnosis and dancing with others only to remind themselves that we are not completely alone in this world. AGNES DE MILLE, *The New York Times*, June 10, 1963.

3. Dancing is the loftiest, the most moving, the most beautiful of the arts, because it is no mere translation or abstraction from life; it is life itself. HAVELOCK ELLIS, *The Dance of Life* (1923), 2.

4. Dancing is a very crude attempt to get into the rhythm of life. GEORGE BERNARD SHAW, *Back to Methuselah* (1921), 5.

5. Dance is the only art of which we ourselves are the stuff of which it is made. TED SHAWN, *Time*, July 25, 1955.

## 213. DANGER

See also 16. Adventure; 90. Boldness; 192. Courage; 311. Excitement; 969. Threat

1. Who will pity a snake charmer bitten by a serpent, or any who go near wild beasts? *Apocrypha*, Ecclesiasticus 12:13.

2. Perils commonly ask to be paid in pleasures. FRANCIS BACON, "Of Love," *Essays* (1625).

3. Dangers, by being despised, grow great. EDMUND BURKE, speech, "On the Petition of the Unitarians," 1792.

4. Those who'll play with cats must expect to be scratched. CERVANTES, *Don Quixote* (1605–15), 1.3.8, tr. Peter Motteux and John Ozell.

5. Mystery magnifies danger as the fog the sun. CHARLES CALEB COLTON, *Lacon* (1825), 1.359.

6. However well organized the foundations of life may be, life must always be full of risks. HAVELOCK ELLIS, *On Life and Sex: Essays of Love and Virtue* (1937), 1.

7. The wise man in the storm prays God, not for safety from danger, but for deliverance from fear. EMERSON, *Journals*, 1833.

8. Danger and delight grow on one stalk. ENGLISH PROVERB.

9. A man who has been in danger / When he comes out of it forgets his fears, / And sometimes he forgets his promises. EURIPIDES, *Iphigenia in Tauris* (c. 414–12 B.C.), tr. Witter Bynner.

10. Danger past, God is forgotten. THOMAS FULLER, M.D., *Gnomologia* (1732), 1234.

11. In comradeship is danger countered best. GOETHE, "On the Lower Peneus," *Faust: Part II* (1832), tr. Philip Wayne.

12. Great perils have this beauty, that they bring to light the fraternity of strangers. VICTOR HUGO, "Saint Denis," *Les Misérables* (1862), 12.4, tr. Charles E. Wilbour.

13. Any danger spot is tenable if men—brave men—will make it so. JOHN F. KENNEDY, address to the nation, July 25, 1961.

14. It is pleasurable, when winds disturb the waves of a great sea, to gaze out from land upon the great trials of another. LUCRETIUS, *On the Nature of Things* (1st c. B.C.), 2.

15. To be alive at all involves some risk. HAROLD MACMILLAN, quoted in *The New York Times*, Dec. 30, 1959.

16. Every man has a right to risk his own life in order to preserve it. Has it ever been said that a man who throws himself out of the window to escape from a fire is guilty of suicide? ROUSSEAU, *The Social Contract* (1762), 2.5, tr. G. D. H. Cole.

17. So long as money can answer, it were wrong in any business to put the life in danger. SA'DI, *Gulistan* (1258), 8.15, tr. James Ross.

18. Wise men say nothing in dangerous times. JOHN SELDEN, "Wisdom," *Table Talk* (1689).

19. He that stands upon a slippery place / Makes nice of no vile hold to stay him up. SHAKESPEARE, *King John* (1596–97), 3.4.137.

20. Everything is sweetened by risk. ALEXANDER SMITH, "Of Death and the Fear of Dying," *Dreamthorp* (1863).

21. When tremendous dangers are involved, no one can be blamed for looking to his own interest. THUCYDIDES, *The Peloponnesian War* (c. 400 B.C.), 1.6, tr. Rex Warner.

## 214. DARKNESS

See also 626. Night

1. There is, indeed, no such thing in life as absolute darkness; one's eyes revolt and hasten to fill the vacuum by floating in sparks, dream-patterns, figures whimsical and figures grotesque, shifting, clad in complementary colors, to appease the indignant cups and rods of the retina. GELETT BURGESS, "Confessions of an Ignoramus," *The Romance of the Commonplace* (1916).

2. In darkness one may be / ashamed of what one does, without the shame of disgrace. SOPHOCLES, *The Women of Trachis* (c. 413 B.C.), tr. Michael Jameson.

3. The darkness of night, like pain, is dumb, / the darkness of dawn, like peace, is silent. RABINDRANATH TAGORE, *Fireflies* (1928).

## 215. DAUGHTERS

See also 383. Girls; 663. Parenthood

1. To an old father, nothing is more sweet / Than a daughter. Boys are more spirited, but their ways / Are not so tender. EURIPIDES, *The Suppliant Women* (c. 421 B.C.), tr. Frank W. Jones.

2. Trust not your daughters' minds / By what you see them act. SHAKESPEARE, *Othello* (1604–05), 1.1.171.

3. A fluent tongue is the only thing a mother don't like her daughter to resemble her in. RICHARD BRINSLEY SHERIDAN, *St. Patrick's Day* (1775), 1.2.

4. He who has daughters is always a shepherd. SPANISH PROVERB.

5. The Mother weeps / At that white funeral of the single life, / Her maiden daughter's marriage; and her tears / Are half of pleasure, half of pain. ALFRED, LORD TENNYSON, "To H.R.H. Princess Beatrice" (1843).

## DAWN

See 599. Morning

## DAYDREAMS

See 687. Phantasy

## 216. DEADNESS, SPIRITUAL

See also 30. Alienation; 464. Indifference; 502. Involvement

1. It's extraordinary how we go through life with eyes half shut, with dull ears, with dormant thoughts. Perhaps it's just as well; and it may be that it is this very dullness that makes life to the incalculable majority so supportable and so welcome. JOSEPH CONRAD, *Lord Jim* (1900), 13.

2. It takes so many years / To learn that one is dead. T. S. ELIOT, *The Family Reunion* (1939), 2.3.

3. In the nineteenth century the problem was that God is dead; in the twentieth century the problem is that man is dead. ERICH FROMM, *The Sane Society* (1955), 9.

4. Most persons have died before they expire—died to all earthly longings, so that the last breath is only, as it were, the locking of the door of the already deserted mansion. OLIVER WENDELL HOLMES, SR., *The Professor at the Breakfast Table* (1860), 11.

5. It is nothing to die; it is frightful not to live. VICTOR HUGO, "Jean Valjean," *Les Misérables* (1862), 9.5, tr. Charles E. Wilbour.

6. Science may have found a cure for most evils; but it has found no remedy for the worst of them all—the apathy of human beings. HELEN KELLER, *My Religion* (1927).

7. Shame on the soul, to falter on the road of life while the body still perseveres. MARCUS AURELIUS, *Meditations* (2nd c.), 6.29, tr. Maxwell Staniforth.

8. The only true infidelity is for a live man to vote himself dead. HERMAN MELVILLE, *Mardi and a Voyage Thither* (1849), 13.

9. To live a life half dead, a living death. MILTON, *Samson Agonistes* (1671), 100.

10. To fear love is to fear life, and those who fear life are already three parts dead.

BERTRAND RUSSELL, "Sex and Individual Well-Being," *Marriage and Morals* (1929).

11. The worst evil of all is to leave the ranks of the living before one dies. SENECA, "On Peace of Mind," *Morals Essays* (1st c.), tr. Aubrey Stewart.

## 217. DEAFNESS

1. None so deaf as he that will not hear. THOMAS FULLER, M.D., *Gnomologia* (1732), 3657.

## 218. DEATH

**See also 81. Birth; 101. Burial; 300. Eternity; 365. Funerals; 452. Immortality; 536. Life; 538. Life and Death; 600. Mortality; 603. Mourning; 761. Punishment, Capital; 941. Suicide**

1. The end of a man's life is often compared to the winding up of a well-written play, where the principal persons still act in character, whatever the fate is which they undergo. JOSEPH ADDISON, *The Spectator* (1711–12), 349.

2. Pain lays not its touch / Upon a corpse. AESCHYLUS, *Fragments* (525–456 B.C.), 250, tr. Edward H. Plumptre.

3. The descent to Hades is much the same from whatever place we start. ANAXAGORAS (6th c. B.C.), quoted in Diogenes Laertius' *Lives and Opinions of Eminent Philosophers* (3rd c. A.D.), tr. R. D. Hicks.

4. Death cancels everything but truth. Anonymous.

5. Death has to be waiting at the end of the ride before you truly see the earth, and feel your heart, and love the world. JEAN ANOUILH, *The Lark* (1955), 2, adapted by Lillian Hellman.

6. Man dies when he wants, as he wants, of what he chooses. JEAN ANOUILH, *Catch As Catch Can* (1960), tr. Lucienne Hill.

7. Do not rejoice over anyone's death; remember that we all must die. *Apocrypha*, Ecclesiasticus 7:7.

8. Hardest of deaths to a mortal / Is the death he sees ahead. BACCHYLIDES, *Croesus* (5th c. B.C.), 3.15.

9. Men fear death, as children fear to go in the dark; and as that natural fear in children is increased with tales, so is the other. FRANCIS BACON, "Of Death," *Essays* (1625).

10. It is as natural to die as to be born. FRANCIS BACON, "Of Death," *Essays* (1625).

11. Every tiny part of us cries out against the idea of dying, and hopes to live forever. UGO BETTI, *Struggle Till Dawn* (1949), 2, tr. G. H. McWilliam.

12. Your teeth chatter from the cold. Faint shadows that you are, how wrong it was to go to the trouble of giving you separate names. Your dying breath barely tarnishes the air, and yet you imagine it as your spirit "returning unto God who gave it." UGO BETTI, *The Fugitive* (1953), 3, tr. G. H. McWilliam.

13. Dust thou art, and unto dust shalt thou return. *Bible*, Genesis 3:19.

14. We must needs die, and are as water spilt on the ground, which cannot be gathered up again. *Bible*, 2 Samuel 14:14.

15. Even at our birth, death does but stand aside a little. And every day he looks towards us and muses somewhat to himself whether that day or the next he will draw nigh. ROBERT BOLT, *A Man for All Seasons* (1962), 2.

16. Death is the supreme festival on the road to freedom. DIETRICH BONHOEFFER, "Miscellaneous Thoughts," *Letters and Papers from Prison* (1953), tr. Eberhard Bethge.

17. Could the Devil work my belief to imagine I could never die, I would not outlive that very thought. SIR THOMAS BROWNE, *Religio Medici* (1642), 1.

18. Though it be in the power of the weakest arm to take away life, it is not in the strongest to deprive us of death. SIR THOMAS BROWNE, *Religio Medici* (1642), 1.

19. We all labour against our own cure, for death is the cure of all diseases. SIR THOMAS BROWNE, *Religio Medici* (1642), 2.

20. You never know what life means till you die; / Even throughout life, 'tis death that makes life live, / Gives it whatever the significance. ROBERT BROWNING, *The Ring and the Book* (1868–69), 11.

21. Sustained and soothed / By an unfaltering trust, approach thy grave, / Like one who wraps the drapery of his couch / About him, and lies down to pleasant dreams. WILLIAM CULLEN BRYANT, "Thanatopsis" (1811).

22. [Death,] Thou dost avenge, / In thy

good time, the wrongs of those who know / No other friend. WILLIAM CULLEN BRYANT, "Hymn to Death" (1820).

23. Everything on earth fades fast / Death will take us all at last, / That's a truth we know won't pass. GEORG BÜCHNER, *Woyzeck* (1836), 4, tr. Theodore Hoffman.

24. To die is to leave off dying and do the thing once for all. SAMUEL BUTLER (d. 1902), *Note-Books* (1912).

25. To die completely, a person must not only forget but be forgotten, and he who is not forgotten is not dead. SAMUEL BUTLER (d. 1902), "Death," *Note-Books* (1912).

26. Our own death is a premium which we must pay for the far greater benefit we have derived from the fact that so many people have not only lived but also died before us. SAMUEL BUTLER (d. 1902), "Unprofessional Sermons," *Note-Books* (1912).

27. What is this Death?—a quiet of the heart? / The whole of that of which we are a part? BYRON, "A Fragment" (1816).

28. Death, so called, is a thing which makes men weep, / And yet a third of Life is passed in sleep. BYRON, *Don Juan* (1819–24), 14.3.

29. Do you know why we are more fair and just toward the dead? . . . We are not obliged to them, we can take our time, fit in the paying of respects between a cocktail party and an affectionate mistress, in our spare time. ALBERT CAMUS, *The Fall* (1956).

30. Men are convinced of your arguments, your sincerity, and the seriousness of your efforts only by your death. ALBERT CAMUS, *The Fall* (1956).

31. The dead are all holy, even they that were base and wicked while alive. Their baseness and wickedness was not they, was but the heavy and unmanageable environment that lay round them. THOMAS CARLYLE, "Biography" (1832).

32. Death eats up all things, both the young lamb and old sheep. CERVANTES, *Don Quixote* (1605–15), 2.3.20, tr. Peter Motteux and John Ozell.

33. Death does not blow a trumpet. DANISH PROVERB.

34. You'll find it—when you try to die— / The Easier to let go— / For recollecting such as went— / You could not spare—you know. EMILY DICKINSON, poem (c. 1862).

35. The distance that the dead have gone / Does not at first appear— / Their coming back seems possible / For many an ardent year. EMILY DICKINSON, *Poems* (c. 1862–86).

36. Death is the supple Suitor / That wins at last— / It is a stealthy Wooing / Conducted first / By pallid innuendoes / And dim approach / But brave at last with Bugles. EMILY DICKINSON, poem (c. 1878).

37. We never know we go when we are going— / We jest and shut the Door— / Fate—following—behind us bolts it— / And we accost no more—. EMILY DICKINSON, poem (c. 1881).

38. God himself took a day to rest in, and a good man's grave is his Sabbath. JOHN DONNE, *Sermons*, No. 12, 1622.

39. Any man's death diminishes me, because I am involved in mankind; and therefore never send to know for whom the bell tolls; it tolls for thee. JOHN DONNE, *Devotions* (1624), 17.

40. Death in itself is nothing; but we fear / To be we know not what, we know not where. JOHN DRYDEN, *Aurengzebe* (1676), 4.1.

41. All human things are subject to decay, / And when fate summons, monarchs must obey. JOHN DRYDEN, *Mac Flecknoe* (1682), 11.1.

42. I have seen the eternal Footman hold my coat, and snicker. T. S. ELIOT, "The Love Song of J. Alfred Prufrock" (1915).

43. Our fear of death is like our fear that summer will be short, but when we have had our swing of pleasure, our fill of fruit, and our swelter of heat, we say we have had our day. EMERSON, *Journals*, 1855.

44. Death always comes too early or too late. ENGLISH PROVERB.

45. Why, do you not know, then, that the origin of all human evils, and of baseness, and cowardice, is not death, but rather the fear of death? EPICTETUS, *Discourses* (2nd c.), 3.26, tr. Thomas W. Higginson.

46. Death, the most dreaded of evils, is therefore of no concern to us; for while we exist death is not present, and when death is present we no longer exist. EPICURUS, Letter to Menoeceus (3rd c. B.C.), in *Letters, Principal Doctrines, and Vatican Sayings*, tr. Russel M. Geer.

47. It is possible to provide security against other ills, but as far as death is concerned, we men all live in a city without

walls. EPICURUS, "Vatican Sayings" (3rd c. B.C.), 36, in *Letters, Principal Doctrines, and Vatican Sayings*, tr. Russel M. Geer.

48. To die with glory, if one has to die at all, / is still, I think, pain for the dier. EURIPIDES, *Rhesus* (c. 455–441 B.C.), tr. Richmond Lattimore.

49. What greater pain could mortals have than this: / To see their children dead before their eyes? EURIPIDES, *The Suppliant Women* (c. 421 B.C.), tr. Frank W. Jones.

50. What good can come from meeting death with tears? ... If a man / Is sorry for himself, he doubles death. EURIPIDES, *Iphigenia in Tauris* (c. 414–12 B.C.), tr. Witter Bynner.

51. It hath often been said, that it is not death, but dying, which is terrible. HENRY FIELDING, *Amelia* (1751), 3.4.

52. Death is never sweet, not even if it is suffered for the highest ideal. ERICH FROMM, *Escape from Freedom* (1941), 7.

53. To die is poignantly bitter, but the idea of having to die without having lived is unbearable. ERICH FROMM, *Man for Himself* (1947), 4.

54. The nearest friends can go / With anyone to death, comes so far short / They might as well not try to go at all. ROBERT FROST, "Home Burial," *North of Boston* (1914).

55. Time gives the promise of time in every death, / Not of any ceasing. CHRISTOPHER FRY, *A Sleep of Prisoners* (1956).

56. Death surprises us in the midst of our hopes. THOMAS FULLER, M.D., *Gnomologia* (1732), 1254.

57. He hath lived ill that knows not how to die well. THOMAS FULLER, M.D., *Gnomologia* (1732), 1890.

58. Is life a boon? / If so, it must befall / That Death, whene'er he call, / Must call too soon. W. S. GILBERT, *The Yeoman of the Guard* (1888), 1.

59. Death holds no horrors. It is simply the ultimate horror of life. JEAN GIRAUDOUX, *The Enchanted* (1933), 2, adapted by Maurice Valency.

60. Death is the next step after the pension—it's perpetual retirement without pay. JEAN GIRAUDOUX, *The Enchanted* (1933), 3, adapted by Maurice Valency.

61. Few are wholly dead: / Blow on a dead man's embers / And a live flame will start. ROBERT GRAVES, "To Bring the Dead to Life," *Collected Poems* (1961).

62. Death borders upon our birth, and our cradle stands in the grave. JOSEPH HALL, *Epistles* (1608), 3.2.

63. Do not seek death. Death will find you. But seek the road which makes death a fulfillment. DAG HAMMARSKJÖLD, "1957," *Markings* (1964), tr. Leif Sjoberg and W. H. Auden.

64. We dread life's termination as the close, not of enjoyment, but of hope. WILLIAM HAZLITT, "On the Love of Life," *The Round Table* (1817).

65. Our repugnance to death increases in proportion to our consciousness of having lived in vain. WILLIAM HAZLITT, "On the Love of Life," *The Round Table* (1817).

66. There was a time when we were not: this gives us no concern—why then should it trouble us that a time will come when we shall cease to be? WILLIAM HAZLITT, "On the Fear of Death," *Table Talk* (1821–22).

67. To die is to go into the Collective Unconscious, to lose oneself in order to be transformed into form, pure form. HERMANN HESSE, quoted in Miguel Serrano's *C. G. Jung and Hermann Hesse* (1966), tr. Frank MacShane.

68. Man is the only animal that contemplates death, and also the only animal that shows any sign of doubt of its finality. WILLIAM ERNEST HOCKING, *The Meaning of Immortality in Human Experience* (1957).

69. There is need for some kind of make-believe in order to face death unflinchingly. To our real, naked selves there is not a thing on earth or in heaven worth dying for. ERIC HOFFER, *The True Believer* (1951), 3.13.47.

70. Death has but one terror, that it has no tomorrow. ERIC HOFFER, *The Passionate State of Mind* (1954), 206.

71. Death's dark way / Must needs be trodden once, however we pause. HORACE, *Odes* (23–c. 15 B.C.), 1.28.

72. One thing is sure, there are just two respectable ways to die. One is of old age, and the other is by accident. ELBERT HUBBARD, *The Philistine* (1895–1915).

73. A belief in hell and the knowledge that every ambition is doomed to frustration at the hands of a skeleton have never prevented the majority of human beings from behaving as though death were no more than an unfounded rumor, and survival a

thing beyond the bounds of possibility. ALDOUS HUXLEY, "Variations on a Baroque Tomb," *Themes and Variations* (1950).

74. Our last garment is made without pockets. ITALIAN PROVERB.

75. Those most like the dead are those most loath to die. LA FONTAINE, "Death and the Dying," *Fables* (1688–94), tr. Marianne Moore.

76. Neither the sun nor death can be looked at steadily. LA ROCHEFOUCAULD, *Maxims* (1665), tr. Kenneth Pratt.

77. Not all the preaching since Adam / Has made Death other than Death. JAMES RUSSELL LOWELL, "After the Burial," *Under the Willows and Other Poems* (1868).

78. You may complete as many generations as you please during your life; none the less will that everlasting death await you. LUCRETIUS, *On the Nature of Things* (1st c. B.C.), 3, tr. H. A. J. Munro.

79. I have asked for death. Begged for it. Prayed for it. Then the worst thing can't be death. ARCHIBALD MAC LEISH, *JB* (1958), 10.

80. It is death that is the guide of our life, and our life has no goal but death. MAURICE MAETERLINCK, "The Pre-Destined," *The Treasure of the Humble* (1896), tr. Alfred Sutro.

81. Flowers and buds fall, and the old and ripe fall. MALAY PROVERB.

82. A man's dying is more the survivors' affair than his own. THOMAS MANN, *The Magic Mountain* (1924), 6.8, tr. H. T. Lowe-Porter.

83. One cannot live with the dead; either we die with them or we make them live again. Or else we forget them. LOUIS MARTIN-CHAUFFIER, *L'Homme et la bête* (1947), 1.

84. The grave's a fine and private place, / But none, I think, do there embrace. ANDREW MARVELL, "To His Coy Mistress" (1650).

85. Death hath a thousand doors to let out life. PHILIP MASSINGER, *A Very Woman* (1655), 5.4.

86. Blessed be Death, that cuts in marble / What would have sunk to dust! EDNA ST. VINCENT MILLAY, "Keen," *The Harp-Weaver* (1923).

87. Even Rome cannot grant us a dispensation from death. MOLIÈRE, *L'Etourdi* (1665), 2.4.

88. God is favorable to those whom he makes to die by degrees; 'tis the only benefit of old age. The last death will be so much the less painful: it will kill but a quarter of a man or but half a one at most. MONTAIGNE, "Of experience," *Essays* (1580–88), tr. Charles Cotton and W. C. Hazlitt.

89. The premeditation of death is the premeditation of liberty; he who has learned to die has unlearned to serve. MONTAIGNE, "That to study philosophy is to learn to die," *Essays* (1580–88), tr. Charles Cotton and W. C. Hazlitt.

90. The perpetual work of your life is but to lay the foundation of death. MONTAIGNE, "That to study philosophy is to learn to die," *Essays* (1580–88), tr. Charles Cotton and W. C. Hazlitt.

91. There is only one way to be prepared for death: to be sated. In the soul, in the heart, in the spirit, in the flesh. To the brim. HENRY DE MONTHERLANT, "Explicit Mysterium," *Mors et Vita* (1932).

92. One should part from life as Odysseus parted from Nausicaa—blessing it rather than in love with it. NIETZSCHE, *Beyond Good and Evil* (1886), 96, tr. Walter Kaufmann.

93. One should die proudly when it is no longer possible to live proudly. NIETZSCHE, "Skirmishes in a War with the Age," 36, *Twilight of the Idols* (1888), tr. Anthony M. Ludovici.

94. Dust into Dust, and under Dust to lie, / Sans Wine, sans Song, sans Singer, and—sans End! OMAR KHAYYÁM, *Rubáiyát* (11th–12th c.), tr. Edward FitzGerald, 4th ed., 24.

95. Strange, is it not? that of the myriads who / Before us passed the door of Darkness through, / Not one returns to tell us of the Road, / Which to discover we must travel too. OMAR KHAYYÁM, *Rubáiyát* (11th–12th c.), tr. Edward FitzGerald, 4th ed., 64.

96. Death will not see me flinch; the heart is bold / That pain has made incapable of pain. DOROTHY PARKER, "Testament," *Enough Rope* (1926), 1.

97. It costs me never a stab nor squirm / To tread by chance upon a worm. / "Aha, my little dear," I say, / "Your clan will pay me back one day." DOROTHY PARKER, "Thought for a Sunshiny Morning," *Sunset Gun* (1928).

98. All I know is that I must soon die, but what I know least is this very death which I cannot escape. PASCAL, *Pensées* (1670), 194, tr. W. F. Trotter.

99. The last act is tragic, however happy all the rest of the play is; at the last a little earth is thrown upon our head, and that is the end for ever. PASCAL, *Pensées* (1670), 210, tr. W. F. Trotter.

100. Death is a camel that lies down at every door. PERSIAN PROVERB.

101. Rich man and poor move side by side toward the limit / of death. PINDAR, *Odes* (5th c. B.C.), Nemea 7, tr. Richmond Lattimore.

102. As men, we are all equal in the presence of death. PUBLILIUS SYRUS, *Moral Sayings* (1st c. B.C.), 1, tr. Darius Lyman.

103. Death is a thing of grandeur. It brings instantly into being a whole new network of relations between you and the ideas, the desires, the habits of the man now dead. It is a rearrangement of the world. SAINT-EXUPÉRY, *Flight to Arras* (1942), 2, tr. Lewis Galantière.

104. Man imagines that it is death he fears; but what he fears is the unforeseen, the explosion. What man fears is himself, not death. SAINT-EXUPÉRY, *Flight to Arras* (1942), 19, tr. Lewis Galantière.

105. He who has gone, so we but cherish his memory, abides with us, more potent, nay, more present, than the living man. SAINT-EXUPÉRY, *The Wisdom of the Sands* (1948), 2, tr. Stuart Gilbert.

106. Death is stronger than all the governments because the governments are men and men die and then death laughs: now you see 'em, now you don't. CARL SANDBURG, "Death Snips Proud Men," *Complete Poems* (1950).

107. Death either destroys or unhusks us. If it means liberation, better things await us when our burden's gone: if destruction, nothing at all awaits us; blessings and curses are abolished. SENECA, *Letters to Lucilius* (1st c.), 24.18, tr. E. Phillips Barker.

108. Death takes us piecemeal, not at a gulp. SENECA, *Letters to Lucilius* (1st c.), 120.18, tr. E. Phillips Barker.

109. There is nothing after death, and death itself is nothing. SENECA, *The Trojan Women* (1st c.), 397, tr. Frank Justus Miller.

110. The tongues of dying men / Enforce attention like deep harmony. SHAKESPEARE, *Richard II* (1595–96), 2.1.5.

111. This fell sergeant, Death, / Is strict in his arrest. SHAKESPEARE, *Hamlet* (1600), 5.2.347.

112. The sense of death is most in apprehension, / And the poor beetle that we tread upon, / In corporal sufferance finds a pang as great / As when a giant dies. SHAKESPEARE, *Measure for Measure* (1604–05), 3.1.78.

113. Men must endure / Their going hence, even as their coming hither. SHAKESPEARE, *King Lear* (1605–06), 5.2.9.

114. He that dies pays all debts. SHAKESPEARE, *The Tempest* (1611–12), 3.2.140.

115. Life levels all men: death reveals the eminent. GEORGE BERNARD SHAW, "Maxims for Revolutionists," *Man and Superman* (1903).

116. It is a modest creed, and yet / Pleasant if one considers it, / To own that death itself must be, / Like all the rest, a mockery. SHELLEY, "The Sensitive Plant" (1820).

117. When the lamp is shattered / The light in the dust lies dead— / When the cloud is scattered / The rainbow's glory is shed. / When the lute is broken, / Sweet tones are remembered not; / When the lips have spoken, / Loved accents are soon forgot. SHELLEY, "When the Lamp Is Shattered" (1822), 1.

118. How little room / Do we take up in death, that, living, know / No bounds! JAMES SHIRLEY, *The Wedding* (1626), 4.4.

119. Death takes away the commonplace of life. ALEXANDER SMITH, "Of Death and the Fear of Dying," *Dreamthorp* (1863).

120. Nobody knows, in fact, what death is, nor whether to man it is not perchance the greatest of all blessings; yet people fear it as if they surely knew it to be the worst of evils. SOCRATES, in Plato's *Apology* (4th c. B.C.), tr. Lane Cooper.

121. Even the bold will fly when they see Death / drawing in close enough to end their life. SOPHOCLES, *Antigone* (442–41 B.C.), tr. Elizabeth Wyckoff.

122. For the dead there are no more toils. SOPHOCLES, *The Women of Trachis* (c. 413 B.C.), tr. Michael Jameson.

123. Death is not anything . . . death is not . . . It's the absence of presence, nothing more . . . the endless time of never coming back . . . a gap you can't see, and when the wind blows through it, it makes no sound.

TOM STOPPARD, *Rosencrantz & Guildenstern Are Dead* (1967), 3.

124. There is no God found stronger than death; and death is a sleep. ALGERNON CHARLES SWINBURNE, "Hymn to Proserpine," *Poems and Ballads: First Series* (1866).

125. Old men must die, or the world would grow mouldy, would only breed the past again. ALFRED, LORD TENNYSON, prologue, *Becket* (1884).

126. Sunset and evening star, / And one clear call for me! / And may there be no moaning of the bar, / When I put out to sea. ALFRED, LORD TENNYSON, "Crossing the Bar" (1889).

127. When we are dead / Rugs are no richer than a quick-thorn bed. THEOGNIS (6th c. B.C.).

128. Do not go gentle into that good night, / Old age should burn and rave at close of day; / Rage, rage against the dying of the light. DYLAN THOMAS, "Do Not Go Gentle into That Good Night," *Collected Poems* (1953).

129. The end of all is death and man's life passeth away suddenly as a shadow. THOMAS À KEMPIS, *The Imitation of Christ* (1426), 1.23.

130. In the depth of the anxiety of having to die is the anxiety of being eternally forgotten. PAUL TILLICH, *The Eternal Now* (1963), 1.2.3.

131. Death is like a fisherman who catches fish in his net and leaves them for a while in the water; the fish is still swimming but the net is around him, and the fisherman will draw him up—when he thinks fit. IVAN TURGENEV, *On the Eve* (1860), 35, tr. Constance Garnett.

132. Let us endeavour so to live that when we come to die even the undertaker will be sorry. MARK TWAIN, "Pudd'nhead Wilson's Calendar," *Pudd'nhead Wilson* (1894), 6.

133. The world so quickly readjusts itself after any loss, that the return of the departed would nearly always throw it, even the circle most interested, into confusion. CHARLES DUDLEY WARNER, "Ninth Study," *Backlog Studies* (1873).

134. Every death even the cruellest death / drowns in the total indifference of Nature / Nature herself would watch unmoved / if we destroyed the entire human race. PETER WEISS, *Marat/Sade* (1964), 1.12, tr. Geoffrey Skelton and Adrian Mitchell.

135. To die is different from what any one supposed, and luckier. WALT WHITMAN, "Song of Myself," *Leaves of Grass* (1855–92)

136. A man, when he burns, leaves only a handful of ashes. No woman can hold him. The wind must blow him away. TENNESSEE WILLIAMS, *The Rose Tattoo* (1951), 3.3.

## DEBATE

See 51. Argument

## DEBAUCHERY

See 733. Profligacy

## 219. DEBT

See also 94. Borrowing and Lending; 99. Budget; 220. Debt, National; 639. Obligation

1. Interest works night and day, in fair weather and in foul. It gnaws at a man's substance with invisible teeth. HENRY WARD BEECHER, *Proverbs from Plymouth Pulpit* (1887).

2. There are but two ways of paying debt: increase of industry in raising income, increase of thrift in laying out. THOMAS CARLYLE, "Government," *Past and Present* (1843).

3. It is hard to pay for bread that has been eaten. DANISH PROVERB.

4. Say nothing of my debts unless you mean to pay them. ENGLISH PROVERB.

5. Creditors are a superstitious sect, great observers of set days and times. BENJAMIN FRANKLIN, *Poor Richard's Almanack* (1732–57).

6. A poor man's debt makes a great noise. THOMAS FULLER, M.D., *Gnomologia* (1732), 355.

7. Debt is the worst poverty. THOMAS FULLER, M.D., *Gnomologia* (1732), 1258.

8. Let us live in as small a circle as we will, we are either debtors or creditors before we have had time to look round. GOETHE, *Elective Affinities* (1809), 22.

9. A creditor is worse than a master; for a master owns only your person, a creditor owns your dignity and can belabour that.

VICTOR HUGO, "Marius," *Les Misérables* (1862), 5.2, tr. Charles E. Wilbour.

10. If thy debtor be honest and capable, thou hast thy money again, if not with increase, with praise; if he prove insolvent, don't ruin him to get that which it will not ruin thee to lose, for thou art but a steward. WILLIAM PENN, *Some Fruits of Solitude* (1693), 1.48.

11. A small loan makes a debtor; a great one, an enemy. PUBLILIUS SYRUS, *Moral Sayings* (1st c. B.C.), 12, tr. Darius Lyman.

12. It's not politics that is worrying this Country; it's the Second Payment. WILL ROGERS, *The Autobiography of Will Rogers* (1949), 9.

13. First payments is what made us think we were prosperous, and the other nineteen is what showed us we were broke. WILL ROGERS, *The Autobiography of Will Rogers* (1949), 15.

14. Words pay no debts. SHAKESPEARE, *Troilus and Cressida* (1601–02), 3.2.58.

15. If a man owes you money and he is unable to pay, do not pass before him. Haggadah, *Palestinian Talmud* (4th c.).

## 220. DEBT, NATIONAL

See also 99. Budget

1. A national debt, if it is not excessive, will be to us a national blessing. ALEXANDER HAMILTON, letter to Robert Morris, Apr. 30, 1781.

2. No nation ought to be without a debt. A national debt is a national bond; and when it bears no interest, is in no case a grievance. THOMAS PAINE, "Of the Present Ability of America," *Common Sense* (1776).

3. Our national debt after all is an internal debt owed not only *by* the nation but *to* the nation. If our children have to pay interest on it they will pay that interest to *themselves*. FRANKLIN D. ROOSEVELT, speech before the American Retail Foundation, Washington, May 22, 1939.

## DECADENCE

See 188. Corruption; 223. Decline; 554. Luxury

## DECEIT

See 221. Deception

## DECENCY

See 743. Propriety

## 221. DECEPTION

See also 162. Concealment; 329. Falsehood; 438. Hypocrisy; 858. Self-deception

1. Dishonesty is the raw material not of quacks only, but also in great part of dupes. THOMAS CARLYLE, "Count Cagliostro" (1833).

2. Without some dissimulation no business can be carried on at all. LORD CHESTERFIELD, *Letters to His Son*, May 22, 1749.

3. There are some frauds so well conducted that it would be stupidity not to be deceived by them. CHARLES CALEB COLTON, *Lacon* (1825), 1.96.

4. No mask like open truth to cover lies, / As to go naked is the best disguise. WILLIAM CONGREVE, *Love for Love* (1695), 5.4.

5. A clean glove often hides a dirty hand. ENGLISH PROVERB.

6. Man is practised in disguise; / He cheats the most discerning eyes. JOHN GAY, introduction to *Fables* (1727–38).

7. Who will not be deceived must have as many eyes as hairs on his head. GERMAN PROVERB.

8. One deceit needs many others, and so the whole house is built in the air and must soon come to the ground. BALTASAR GRACIÁN, *The Art of Worldly Wisdom* (1647), 175, tr. Joseph Jacobs.

9. Deceive not thy physician, confessor, nor lawyer. GEORGE HERBERT, *Jacula Prudentum* (1651).

10. It holds for good polity ever, to have that outwardly in vilest estimation, that inwardly is most dear to us. BEN JONSON, *Every Man in His Humour* (1598), 2.3.

11. What renders us so bitter against those who trick us is that they believe themselves to be more clever than we are. LA ROCHEFOUCAULD, *Maxims* (1665), tr. Kenneth Pratt.

12. We are never so easily deceived as when we imagine we are deceiving others. LA ROCHEFOUCAULD, *Maxims* (1665), tr. Kenneth Pratt.

13. It is vain to find fault with those arts

of deceiving wherein men find pleasure to be deceived. JOHN LOCKE, *An Essay Concerning Human Understanding* (1690), 3.11.34.

14. It is with a pious fraud as with a bad action; it begets a calamitous necessity of going on. THOMAS PAINE, *The Age of Reason* (1704, 1796), 1.

15. Whoever has even once become notorious by base fraud, even if he speaks the truth, gains no belief. PHAEDRUS, *Fables* (1st c.), 1.10.1, tr. H. T. Riley.

16. If any man thinks to swindle / God, he is wrong. PINDAR, *Odes* (5th c. B.C.), Olympia 1, tr. Richmond Lattimore.

17. To blow and swallow at the same moment is not easy. PLAUTUS, *The Haunted House* (200–194 B.C.), 3.2.104, tr. Henry Thomas Riley.

18. It is more tolerable to be refused than deceived. PUBLILIUS SYRUS, *Moral Sayings* (1st c. B.C.), 836, tr. Darius Lyman.

19. He who digs a hole for another may fall in himself. RUSSIAN PROVERB.

20. I like not fair terms and a villain's mind. SHAKESPEARE, *The Merchant of Venice* (1596–97), 1.3.180.

21. One may smile, and smile, and be a villain. SHAKESPEARE, *Hamlet* (1600), 1.5.108.

22. You can fool too many of the people too much of the time. JAMES THURBER, "The Owl Who Was God," *The Thurber Carnival* (1945).

23. Hatred of dishonesty generally arises from fear of being deceived. VAUVENARGUES, *Reflections and Maxims* (1746), 523, tr. F. G. Stevens.

24. People always overdo the matter when they attempt deception. CHARLES DUDLEY WARNER, "Tenth Week," *My Summer in a Garden* (1871).

## 222. DECISION

**See also 24. Afterthought; 229. Deliberation; 463. Indecision; 801. Resolution**

1. To be always ready a man must be able to cut a knot, for everything cannot be untied. HENRI FRÉDÉRIC AMIEL, *Journal*, June 16, 1851, tr. Mrs. Humphry Ward.

2. Decisiveness is often the art of timely cruelty. HENRY BECQUE, "Notes d'album," *Oeuvres complètes* (1924–26), v. 7.

3. Decide, v. i. To succumb to the preponderance of one set of influences over another set. AMBROSE BIERCE, *The Devil's Dictionary* (1881–1911).

4. It is the characteristic excellence of the strong man that he can bring momentous issues to the fore and make a decision about them. The weak are always forced to decide between alternatives they have not chosen themselves. DIETRICH BONHOEFFER, "Miscellaneous Thoughts," *Letters and Papers from Prison* (1953), tr. Eberhard Bethge.

5. In a minute there is time / For decisions and revisions which a minute will reverse. T. S. ELIOT, "The Love Song of J. Alfred Prufrock" (1915).

6. Nothing is more difficult, and therefore more precious, than to be able to decide. NAPOLEON I, *Maxims* (1804–15).

7. It is always thus, impelled by a state of mind which is destined not to last, that we make our irrevocable decisions. MARCEL PROUST, *Remembrance of Things Past: Within a Budding Grove* (1913–27), tr. C. K. Scott-Moncrieff.

## 223. DECLINE

**See also 327. Failure; 646. Old Age**

1. There is not a more unhappy being than a superannuated idol. JOSEPH ADDISON, *The Spectator* (1711–12), 73.

2. Statesmen and beauties are very rarely sensible of the gradations of their decay. LORD CHESTERFIELD, *Letters to His Son*, Feb. 26, 1754.

3. He should be envied / Who when his strength is spent lays down his life. / Old age reserves a melancholy fate / For noble souls before their life is done. CORNEILLE, *The Cid* (1636), 2.8, tr. Paul Landis.

4. The passing years steal from us one thing after another. HORACE, *Epistles* (20–c. 8 B.C.), 2.2.

5. As favour and riches forsake a man, we discover in him the foolishness they concealed, and which no one perceived before. LA BRUYÈRE, *Characters* (1688), 6.4, tr. Henri Van Laun.

6. How many worthy men have we known to survive their own reputation, who have seen and suffered the honor and glory

most justly acquired in their youth, extinguished in their own presence? MONTAIGNE, "Of glory," *Essays* (1580–88), tr. Charles Cotton and W. C. Hazlitt.

7. The Wine of Life keeps oozing drop by drop, / The Leaves of Life keep falling one by one. OMAR KHAYYÁM, *Rubáiyát* (11th–12th c.), tr. Edward FitzGerald, 4th ed., 8.

8. He who survives his reputation, lives out of despite of himself, like a man listening to his own reproach. THOMAS PAINE, *The American Crisis* (1776–83), 5.

9. When the snake is old, the frog will tease him. PERSIAN PROVERB.

10. Apples taste sweetest when they're going. SENECA, *Letters to Lucilius* (1st c.), 12.4, tr. E. Phillips Barker.

11. Men shut their doors against a setting sun. SHAKESPEARE, *Timon of Athens* (1607–08), 1.2.150.

12. The wolf loses his teeth, but not his inclinations. SPANISH PROVERB.

13. Authority forgets a dying king, / Laid widowed of the power in his eye / That bowed the will. ALFRED, LORD TENNYSON, "The Passing of Arthur," *Idylls of the King* (1869).

14. When the ox stumbles, all whet their knives. *Yiddish Proverbs* (1949), ed. Hanan J. Ayalti.

15. Like our shadows, / Our wishes lengthen as our sun declines. EDWARD YOUNG, *Night Thoughts* (1742–46), 5.627.

## 224. DEEDS

**See also 9. Action; 173. Consequences; 386. Golden Rule; 391. Goodness; 430. Humanitarianism; 880. Service; 881. Services; 1063. Wrongdoing**

1. We become just by performing just actions, temperate by performing temperate actions, brave by performing brave actions. ARISTOTLE, *Nicomachean Ethics* (4th c. B.C.), 2.1, tr. J. A. K. Thomson.

2. We do not what we ought, / What we ought not, we do, / And lean upon the thought / That chance will bring us through; / But our own acts, for good or ill, are mightier powers. MATTHEW ARNOLD, *Empedocles on Etna* (1852), 1.2.

3. Anything that is worth doing has been done frequently. Things hitherto undone should be given, I suspect, a wide berth. MAX BEERBOHM, "From Bloomsbury to Bayswater," *Mainly On the Air* (1946).

4. Whatsoever thy hand findeth to do, do it with thy might. *Bible*, Ecclesiastes 9:10.

5. Great actions are not always true sons / Of great and mighty resolutions. SAMUEL BUTLER (d. 1680), *Hudibras* (1663), 1.1.

6. Urgent necessity prompts many to do things, at the very thoughts of which they perhaps would start at other times. CERVANTES, *Don Quixote* (1605–15), 1.3.9, tr. Peter Motteux and John Ozell.

7. Time often serves to justify a deed / Which seems at first unjustifiable. CORNEILLE, *The Cid* (1636), 5.7, tr. Paul Landis.

8. Our deeds determine us, as much as we determine our deeds. GEORGE ELIOT, *Adam Bede* (1859), 29.

9. What I must do is all that concerns me, not what the people think. EMERSON, "Self-Reliance," *Essays: First Series* (1841).

10. Our acts our angels are, or good or ill, / Our fatal shadows that walk by us still. JOHN FLETCHER, verses on *An Honest Man's Fortune* (1613).

11. A man is not good or bad for one action. THOMAS FULLER, M.D., *Gnomologia* (1732), 280.

12. He that returns a good for evil obtains the victory. THOMAS FULLER, M.D., *Gnomologia* (1732), 2268.

13. The most decisive actions of our life —I mean those that are most likely to decide the whole course of our future—are, more often than not, unconsidered. ANDRÉ GIDE, *The Counterfeiters* (1925), 3.16, tr. Dorothy Bussy.

14. The greatest pleasure I know is to do a good action by stealth, and to have it found out by accident. CHARLES LAMB, "The Athenaeum," Jan. 4, 1834.

15. Though men pride themselves on their great actions, often they are not the result of any great design but of chance. LA ROCHEFOUCAULD, *Maxims* (1665), tr. Kenneth Pratt.

16. All the beautiful sentiments in the world weigh less than a single lovely action. JAMES RUSSELL LOWELL, *Rousseau and the Sentimentalists* (1870).

17. Is it really so difficult to tell a good action from a bad one? I think one usually knows right away or a moment afterward, in a horrid flash of regret. MARY MC CARTHY,

"My Confession," *On the Contrary* (1961).

18. A man makes no noise over a good deed, but passes on to another as a vine to bear grapes again in season. MARCUS AURELIUS, *Meditations* (2nd c.), 5.16, tr. Morris Hickey Morgan.

19. To treat of human actions is to deal wholly with second causes. HERMAN MELVILLE, Supplement to *Battlepieces and Aspects of the War* (1866).

20. Boast not of what thou would'st have done, but do / What then thou would'st. MILTON, *Samson Agonistes* (1671), 1104.

21. Men are all alike in their promises. It is only in their deeds that they differ. MOLIÈRE, *The Miser* (1668), 1, tr. John Wood.

22. Saying is one thing and doing is another; we are to consider the sermon and the preacher distinctly and apart. MONTAIGNE, "Of anger," *Essays* (1580–88), tr. Charles Cotton and W. C. Hazlitt.

23. The majority of men are more capable of great actions than of good ones. MONTESQUIEU, *Variétés*.

24. The truth is, men are very hard to know, and yet, not to be deceived, we must judge them by their present actions, but for the present only. NAPOLEON I, *Maxims* (1804–15).

25. One will seldom go wrong if one attributes extreme actions to vanity, average ones to habit, and petty ones to fear. NIETZSCHE, *Human, All Too Human* (1878), 74, tr. Helen Zimmern.

26. We immoralists have the suspicion that the decisive value of an action lies precisely in what is unintentional in it. NIETZSCHE, *Beyond Good and Evil* (1886), 32, tr. Walter Kaufmann.

27. Whatever is done for love always occurs beyond good and evil. NIETZSCHE, *Beyond Good and Evil* (1886), 153, tr. Walter Kaufmann.

28. Noble deeds are most estimable when hidden. PASCAL, *Pensées* (1670), 159, tr. W. F. Trotter.

29. Not always actions show the man; we find / Who does a kindness is not therefore kind. ALEXANDER POPE, *Moral Essays* (1731–35), 1.109.

30. The stellar universe is not so difficult of comprehension as the real actions of other people. MARCEL PROUST, *Remembrance of Things Past: The Captive* (1913–27), tr. C. K. Scott-Moncrieff.

31. It is no profit to have learned well, if you neglect to do well. PUBLILIUS SYRUS, *Moral Sayings* (1st c. B.C.), 1043, tr. Darius Lyman.

32. Not all of those to whom we do good love us, neither do all those to whom we do evil hate us. JOSEPH ROUX, *Meditations of a Parish Priest* (1886), 9.41, tr. Isabel F. Hapgood.

33. It is in your act that you exist, not in your body. Your act is yourself, and there is no other you. SAINT-EXUPÉRY, *Flight to Arras* (1942), 19, tr. Lewis Galantière.

34. The profit on a good action is to have done it. SENECA, *Letters to Lucilius* (1st c.), 81.20, tr. E. Phillips Barker.

35. Only the actions of the just / Smell sweet, and blossom in their dust. JAMES SHIRLEY, *The Contention of Ajax and Ulysses* (1659), 1.3.

36. Ugly deeds are taught by ugly deeds. SOPHOCLES, *Electra* (c. 418–14 B.C.), tr. David Grene.

37. Every great action is extreme when it is undertaken. Only after it has been accomplished does it seem possible to those creatures of more common stuff. STENDHAL, *The Red and the Black* (1830), 2.11.

38. What old people say you cannot do, you try and find that you can. Old deeds for old people, and new deeds for new. THOREAU, "Economy," *Walden* (1854).

39. What to do is just a shadow of what we want to do. PETER WEISS, *Marat/Sade* (1964), 1.15, tr. Geoffrey Skelton and Adrian Mitchell.

40. Each little thing that we do passes into the great machine of life which may grind our virtues to powder and make them worthless, or transform our sins into elements of a new civilisation, more marvellous and more splendid than any that has gone before. OSCAR WILDE, "The Critic as Artist," *Intentions* (1891).

## 225. DEFEAT

**See also 17. Adversity; 170. Conquest; 327. Failure**

1. Defeat is a school in which truth always grows strong. HENRY WARD BEECHER, *Proverbs from Plymouth Pulpit* (1887).

2. Who, apart / From ourselves, can see

any difference between / Our victories and our defeats? CHRISTOPHER FRY, *Thor, with Angels* (1948).

3. There are defeats more triumphant than victories. MONTAIGNE, "Of cannibals," *Essays* (1580–88), tr. Charles Cotton and W. C. Hazlitt.

4. Defeat is a thing of weariness, of incoherence, of boredom. And above all futility. SAINT-EXUPÉRY, *Flight to Arras* (1942), 1, tr. Lewis Galantière.

5. One safety the vanquished have, to hope for none. VERGIL, *Aeneid* (30–19 B.C.), 2.354, tr. H. R. Fairclough.

## 226. DEFENSE

See also 850. Security; 949. Survival

1. It may well be that we shall by a process of sublime irony have reached a state in this story where safety will be the sturdy child of terror, and survival the twin brother of annihilation. SIR WINSTON CHURCHILL, speech, House of Commons, March 1, 1955.

2. No nation ever had an army large enough to guarantee it against attack in time of peace or insure it victory in time of war. CALVIN COOLIDGE, address, Oct. 6, 1925.

3. Be as beneficent as the sun or the sea, but if your rights as a rational being are trenched on, die on the first inch of your territory. EMERSON, *Journals*, 1832.

4. In International / Consequences / the players must reckon / to reap what they've sown. / We have a defense / against other defenses, / But what's to defend us / against our own? PIET HEIN, "Defense Wanted," *Grooks* (1966).

5. The only defense / that is more than pretense / is to act on the fact / that there is no defense. PIET HEIN, "The True Defense," *Grooks* (1966).

6. One sword keeps another in the sheath. GEORGE HERBERT, *Jacula Prudentum* (1651).

7. The guns and the bombs, the rockets and the warships, are all symbols of human failure. They are necessary symbols. They protect what we cherish. But they are witness to human folly. LYNDON B. JOHNSON, address, The Johns Hopkins University, April 7, 1965.

8. It is an unfortunate fact that we can secure peace only by preparing for war. JOHN F. KENNEDY, campaign address, Seattle, Wash., Sept. 6, 1960.

9. Diplomacy and defense are not substitutes for one another. Either alone would fail. JOHN F. KENNEDY, address, University of Washington, Seattle, Nov. 16, 1961.

10. Stretch a bow to the very full, / And you will wish you had stopped in time. LAOTSE, *The Character of Tao* (6th c. B.C.), 9, tr. Lin Yutang.

11. It is not the armed forces which can protect our democracy. It is the moral strength of democracy which alone can give any meaning to the efforts at military security. MAX LERNER, "The Negroes and the Draft," *Actions and Passions* (1949).

12. The price of eternal vigilance is indifference. MARSHALL MC LUHAN, *Understanding Media* (1964), 2.

13. What boots it at one gate to make defence, / And at another to let in the foe? MILTON, *Samson Agonistes* (1671), 560.

14. Isn't the best defense always a good attack? OVID, *The Loves* (c. A.D. 8), 1.7, tr. Rolfe Humphries.

15. Peace with a cudgel in hand is war. PORTUGUESE PROVERB.

16. Our security is not a matter of weapons alone. The arm that wields them must be strong, the eye that guides them clear, the will that directs them indomitable. FRANKLIN D. ROOSEVELT, message to Congress, May 16, 1940.

17. The core of our defense is the faith we have in the institutions we defend. FRANKLIN D. ROOSEVELT, speech, Dayton, Ohio, Oct. 12, 1940.

18. If the sky fall, hold up your hands. SPANISH PROVERB.

19. The arms race is based on an optimistic view of technology and a pessimistic view of man. It assumes there is no limit to the ingenuity of science and no limit to the deviltry of human beings. I. F. STONE, "Nixon and the Arms Race," *The New York Review of Books*, March 27, 1969.

20. To be prepared for war is one of the most effectual means of preserving peace. GEORGE WASHINGTON, speech to both houses of Congress, Jan. 8, 1790.

## DEFERENCE

See 802. Respect

## 227. DEFINITION

**See also 132. Clarity; 242. Dictionaries; 1057. Words**

1. Definitions are a kind of scratching and generally leave a sore place more sore than it was before. SAMUEL BUTLER (d. 1902), "Higgledy-Piggledy," *Note-Books* (1912).

2. A definition is the enclosing a wilderness of idea within a wall of words. SAMUEL BUTLER (d. 1902), "Higgledy-Piggledy," *Note-Books* (1912).

3. Every definition is dangerous. ERASMUS, *Adagia* (1500).

4. Define, define, well-educated infant. SHAKESPEARE, *Love's Labour's Lost* (1594–95), 1.2.99.

## 228. DELAY

**See also 463. Indecision; 721. Prematureness; 759. Punctuality; 900. Slowness; 972. Timeliness**

1. Delay always breeds danger and to protract a great design is often to ruin it. CERVANTES, *Don Quixote* (1605–15), 1.4.2, tr. Peter Motteux and John Ozell.

2. Defer not till to-morrow to be wise, / To-morrow's sun to thee may never rise. WILLIAM CONGREVE, *Letter to Cobham.*

3. And dilly-dalliers never yet / Have at the proper moment sallied / To where they were supposed to get. COUNTEE CULLEN, "The-Snake-That-Walked-Upon-His-Tail," *On These I Stand* (1947).

4. We are always getting ready to live, but never living. EMERSON, *Journals*, 1834.

5. One of these days is none of these days. ENGLISH PROVERB.

6. What may be done at any time will be done at no time. THOMAS FULLER, M.D., *Gnomologia* (1732), 5500.

7. There is a time when the word "eventually" has the soothing effect of a promise, and a time when the word evokes in us bitterness and scorn. ERIC HOFFER, *The Passionate State of Mind* (1954), 163.

8. Between saying and doing many a pair of shoes is worn out. ITALIAN PROVERB.

9. Delay is preferable to error. THOMAS JEFFERSON, letter to George Washington, May 16, 1792.

10. procrastination is the / art of keeping up with yesterday. DON MARQUIS, "certain maxims of archy," *Archy and Mehitabel* (1927).

11. Life, as it is called, is for most of us one long postponement. HENRY MILLER, "The Enormous Womb," *The Wisdom of the Heart* (1941).

12. By-and-by is easily said. SHAKESPEARE, *Hamlet* (1600), 3.2.404.

13. Procrastination is the thief of time. EDWARD YOUNG, *Night Thoughts* (1742–46), 1.393.

## 229. DELIBERATION

**See also 146. Committees**

1. What takes place after dinner must never be taken as counsel. PHILIPPE DE COMMYNES, *Mémoires* (1524), 2.2.

2. No grand idea was ever born in a conference, but a lot of foolish ideas have died there. F. SCOTT FITZGERALD, "Note-Books," *The Crack-Up* (1945).

3. As a bamboo conduit makes a round jet of water / So taking counsel together rounds men to one mind. MALAY PROVERB.

4. The length of a meeting rises with the square of the number of people present. EILEEN SHANAHAN, quoted by Harold Faber in *The New York Times Magazine*, March 17, 1968.

## 230. DEMAGOGUERY

**See also 564. Mass Movements; 705. Politics and Politicians; 757. Public Speaking**

1. Where the laws are not supreme, there demagogues spring up. ARISTOTLE, *Politics* (4th c. B.C.), 4.4, tr. Benjamin Jowett.

2. The people are capable of good judgment when they do not listen to demagogues. NAPOLEON I, *Maxims* (1804–15).

3. Demagogy enters at the moment when, for want of a common denominator, the principle of equality degenerates into a principle of identity. SAINT-EXUPÉRY, *Flight to Arras* (1942), 23, tr. Lewis Galantière.

## 231. DEMOCRACY

**See also 133. Class; 295. Equality; 361. Freedom, Individual; 393. Government; 534. Liberty; 585. Minorities; 906. Society; 1030. Voting**

1. The masses are the material of democracy, but its form—that is to say, the laws which express the general reason, justice, and utility—can only be rightly shaped by wisdom, which is by no means a universal property. HENRI FRÉDÉRIC AMIEL, *Journal*, Feb. 16, 1874, tr. Mrs. Humphry Ward.

2. Democracy is the form of government in which the free are rulers. ARISTOTLE, *Politics* (4th c. B.C.), 4.4, tr. Benjamin Jowett.

3. If liberty and equality, as is thought by some, are chiefly to be found in democracy, they will be best attained when all persons alike share in the government to the utmost. ARISTOTLE, *Politics* (4th c. B.C.), 4.4, tr. Benjamin Jowett.

4. Democracy means government by discussion but it is only effective if you can stop people talking. CLEMENT ATTLEE, *Anatomy of Britain* (1962).

5. The real democratic American idea is, not that every man shall be on a level with every other man, but that every man shall have liberty to be what God made him, without hindrance. HENRY WARD BEECHER, *Proverbs from Plymouth Pulpit* (1887).

6. In a democracy the general good is furthered only when the special interests of competing minorities accidentally coincide—or cancel each other out. ALEXANDER CHASE, *Perspectives* (1966).

7. It has been said that Democracy is the worst form of government except all those other forms that have been tried from time to time. SIR WINSTON CHURCHILL, speech, House of Commons, November 1947.

8. Though reconciled to the future of democracy, including that of the people in the subway, I cannot be sanguine about it. FRANK MOORE COLBY, "Trolley-Cars and Democratic Raptures," *The Margin of Hesitation* (1921).

9. The most may err as grossly as the few. JOHN DRYDEN, *Absalom and Achitophel* (1681), 1.782.

10. The evils of popular government appear greater than they are; there is compensation for them in the spirit and energy it awakens. EMERSON, "Power," *Conduct of Life* (1860).

11. Democracy is the name we give to the people each time we need them. ROBERT DE FLERS, *L'Habit vert* (1912), 1.2.

12. Two Cheers for Democracy: one because it admits variety and two because it permits criticism. Two cheers are quite enough: there is no occasion to give three. E. M. FORSTER, "What I Believe," *Two Cheers for Democracy* (1951).

13. My notion of democracy is that under it the weakest should have the same opportunity as the strongest. This can never happen except through non-violence. MOHANDAS K. GANDHI, *Non-Violence in Peace and War* (1948), 1.269.

14. You cannot possibly have a broader basis for any government than that which includes all the people, with all their rights in their hands, and with an equal power to maintain their rights. WILLIAM LLOYD GARRISON, *Life* (1885–89), v. 4.

15. Even though counting heads is not an ideal way to govern, at least it is better than breaking them. LEARNED HAND, speech, Federal Bar Association, March 8, 1932.

16. Modesty and reverence are no less virtues of freemen than the democratic feeling which will submit neither to arrogance nor to servility. OLIVER WENDELL HOLMES, JR., speech, Harvard Law School Association, Nov. 5, 1886.

17. Democracy is a form of government which may be rationally defended, not as being good, but as being less bad than any other. WILLIAM RALPH INGE, "Our Present Discontents," *Outspoken Essays: First Series* (1919).

18. Every government degenerates when trusted to the rulers of the people alone. The people themselves therefore are its only safe depositories. THOMAS JEFFERSON, *Notes on the State of Virginia* (1784–85), 14.

19. I know no safe depository of the ultimate powers of the society but the people themselves; and if we think them not enlightened enough to exercise their control with a wholesome discretion, the remedy is not to take it from them, but to inform their discretion by education. THOMAS JEFFERSON, letter to William C. Jarvis, Sept. 28, 1820.

20. Democracy is the superior form of government, because it is based on a respect for man as a reasonable being. JOHN F. KENNEDY, *Why England Slept* (1940).

21. A democracy is the most difficult kind of government to operate. It represents the last flowering, really, of the human experience. JOHN F. KENNEDY, campaign address, Pocatello, Idaho, Sept. 6, 1960.

22. Self-government requires qualities of self-denial and restraint. JOHN F. KENNEDY, campaign address, Washington, D.C., Sept. 20, 1960.

23. Democracy is never a final achievement. It is a call to untiring effort, to continual sacrifice and to the willingness, if necessary, to die in its defense. JOHN F. KENNEDY, address at El Bosque housing project, San José, Costa Rica, March 19, 1963.

24. The grand paradox of our society is this: we magnify man's rights but we minimize his capacities. JOSEPH WOOD KRUTCH, "The Function of Discourse," *The Measure of Man* (1954).

25. A democracy is a state which recognizes the subjection of the minority to the majority, that is, an organization for the systematic use of violence by one class against the other, by one part of the population against another. LENIN, *The State and the Revolution* (1917).

26. The taste of democracy becomes a bitter taste when the fullness of democracy is denied. MAX LERNER, "The Negroes and the Draft," *Actions and Passions* (1949).

27. This country, with its institutions, belongs to the people who inhabit it. Whenever they shall grow weary of the existing government, they can exercise their constitutional right of amending it, or their revolutionary right to dismember or overthrow it. ABRAHAM LINCOLN, First Inaugural Address, March 4, 1861.

28. "The consent of the governed" is more than a safeguard against ignorant tyrants: it is an insurance against benevolent despots as well. WALTER LIPPMANN, "The Golden Rule and After," *A Preface to Politics* (1914).

29. No amount of charters, direct primaries, or short ballots will make a democracy out of an illiterate people. WALTER LIPPMANN, "Revolution and Culture," *A Preface to Politics* (1914).

30. This is one of the paradoxes of the democratic movement—that it loves a crowd and fears the individuals who compose it—that the religion of humanity should have no faith in human beings. WALTER LIPPMANN, "Routineer and Inventor," *A Preface to Politics* (1914).

31. The tragedy of modern democracies is that they have not yet succeeded in effecting democracy. JACQUES MARITAIN, "La Tragédie de la démocratie," *Christianisme et démocratie* (1940).

32. Democracy is the theory that the common people know what they want, and deserve to get it good and hard. H. L. MENCKEN, "Sententiae," *A Book of Burlesques* (1920).

33. What democracy needs most of all is a party that will separate the good that is in it theoretically from the evils that beset it practically, and then try to erect that good into a workable system. H. L. MENCKEN, "A Glance Ahead," *Notes on Democracy* (1926).

34. The blind lead the blind. It's the democratic way. HENRY MILLER, "With Edgar Varèse in the Gobi Desert," *The Air-Conditioned Nightmare* (1945).

35. Republican despotism is more fertile in acts of tyranny, because everyone has a hand in it. NAPOLEON I, *Maxims* (1804–15).

36. Democracy is good. I say this because other systems are worse. JAWAHARLAL NEHRU, *The New York Times*, Jan. 25, 1961.

37. Democracy represents the disbelief in all great men and in all élite societies: everybody is everybody's equal. NIETZSCHE, *The Will to Power* (1888), 752, tr. Anthony M. Ludovici.

38. The majority is the best way, because it is visible, and has strength to make itself obeyed. Yet it is the opinion of the least able. PASCAL, *Pensées* (1670), 877, tr. W. F. Trotter.

39. Let the people think they govern and they will be governed. WILLIAM PENN, *Some Fruits of Solitude* (1693), 1.337.

40. Democracy . . . is a charming form of government, full of variety and disorder, and dispensing a sort of equality to equals and unequals alike. PLATO, *The Republic* (4th c. B.C.), 8, tr. Benjamin Jowett.

41. One of the evils of democracy is, you have to put up with the man you elect whether you want him or not. WILL ROGERS, *The Autobiography of Will Rogers* (1949), 17.

42. Democracy is not a static thing. It is

an everlasting march. FRANKLIN D. ROOSEVELT, speech, Los Angeles, Oct. 1, 1935.

43. Democracy, the practice of self-government, is a covenant among free men to respect the rights and liberties of their fellows. FRANKLIN D. ROOSEVELT, State of the Union message, Jan. 4, 1939.

44. Were there a people of gods, their government would be democratic. So perfect a government is not for men. ROUSSEAU, *The Social Contract* (1762), 3.5, tr. G. D. H. Cole.

45. Envy is the basis of democracy. BERTRAND RUSSELL, *The Conquest of Happiness* (1930), 6.

46. If one man offers you democracy and another offers you a bag of grain, at what stage of starvation will you prefer the grain to the vote? BERTRAND RUSSELL, *Silhouettes in Satire* (1958).

47. The republic is a dream. / Nothing happens unless first a dream. CARL SANDBURG, "Washington Monument by Night," *Complete Poems* (1950).

48. If Despotism failed only for want of a capable benevolent despot, what chance has Democracy, which requires a whole population of capable voters. GEORGE BERNARD SHAW, "Epistle Dedicatory," *Man and Superman* (1903).

49. Democracy substitutes election by the incompetent many for appointment by the corrupt few. GEORGE BERNARD SHAW, "Maxims for Revolutionists," *Man and Superman* (1903).

50. Self-criticism is the secret weapon of democracy, and candor and confession are good for the political soul. ADLAI STEVENSON, address, Democratic National Convention, July 21, 1952.

51. The essence of a republican government is not command. It is consent. ADLAI STEVENSON, speech, Springfield, Ill., Aug. 14, 1952.

52. We are called a democracy, for the administration is in the hands of the many and not of the few. THUCYDIDES, *The Peloponnesian War* (c. 400 B.C.), 2.37, tr. Benjamin Jowett.

53. When the people rule, they must be rendered happy, or they will overturn the state. ALEXIS DE TOCQUEVILLE, *Democracy in America* (1835–39), 1.17.

54. Democratic nations care but little for what has been, but they are haunted by visions of what will be. ALEXIS DE TOCQUEVILLE, *Democracy in America* (1835–39), 2.1.17.

55. Democratic institutions generally give men a lofty notion of their country and themselves. ALEXIS DE TOCQUEVILLE, *Democracy in America* (1835–39), 2.3.3.

56. That a peasant may become king does not render the kingdom democratic. WOODROW WILSON, address, Chattanooga, Tenn., Aug. 31, 1910.

57. The world must be made safe for democracy. Its peace must be planted on the tested foundations of political liberty. WOODROW WILSON, address to Congress, April 2, 1917.

## DEMOCRATS

See 704. Political Parties

## 232. DENTISTS

1. Dentist, n. A prestidigitator who, putting metal into your mouth, pulls coins out of your pocket. AMBROSE BIERCE, *The Devil's Dictionary* (1881–1911).

## 233. DEPENDENCE

See also 56. Assistance; 873. Self-sufficiency

1. Nothing is more desirable than to be released from an affliction, but nothing is more frightening than to be divested of a crutch. JAMES BALDWIN, introduction, *Nobody Knows My Name* (1961).

2. To be obliged to beg our daily happiness from others bespeaks a more lamentable poverty than that of him who begs his daily bread. CHARLES CALEB COLTON, *Lacon* (1825), 1.445.

3. There is not a soul who does not have to beg alms of another, either a smile, a handshake, or a fond eye. EDWARD DAHLBERG, "On Love and Friendship," *Reasons of the Heart* (1965).

4. We often have to put up with most from those on whom we most depend. BALTASAR GRACIÁN, *The Art of Worldly Wisdom* (1647), 159, tr. Joseph Jacobs.

5. A dwarf on a giant's shoulders sees farther of the two. GEORGE HERBERT, *Jacula Prudentum* (1651).

6. Every man expects somebody or something to help him. And when he finds he must help himself, he says he lacks liberty and justice. EDGAR WATSON HOWE, *Ventures in Common Sense* (1919), 4.3.

7. Life for most of us is full of steep stairs to go puffing up and, later, of shaky stairs to totter down; and very early in the history of stairs must have come the invention of banisters. LOUIS KRONENBERGER, "Unbrave New World," *The Cart and the Horse* (1964), 2.

8. To depend on one's own child is blindness in one eye; to depend on a stranger, blindness in both eyes. MALAY PROVERB.

9. He who is being carried does not realize how far the town is. NIGERIAN PROVERB.

10. The only person who does his own will is he who has no need of another's arm to lengthen his own. ROUSSEAU, *Émile* (1762), 2.

11. Independence? That's middle class blasphemy. We are all dependent on one another, every soul of us on earth. GEORGE BERNARD SHAW, *Pygmalion* (1913), 5.

12. Sometimes a good crutch is often better than a bad foot. TEHYI HSIEH, *Chinese Epigrams Inside Out and Proverbs* (1948), 233.

## 234. DEPRIVATION

See also 547. Loss; 618. Need; 712. Poverty

1. Men cannot bear to be deprived long together of anything they are used to; not even of their fears. WALTER SAVAGE LANDOR, "Lucullus and Caesar," *Imaginary Conversations* (1824–53).

2. We know well only what we are deprived of. FRANÇOIS MAURIAC, "G. Flaubert," *Trois grands hommes devant Dieu* (1930).

3. Little privations are easily endured when the heart is better treated than the body. ROUSSEAU, *Reveries of a Solitary Walker* (1782), 9.

4. To be without some of the things you want is an indispensable part of happiness. BERTRAND RUSSELL, *The Conquest of Happiness* (1930), 2.

## 235. DESIGN

See also 53. Art and Artists

1. Always design a thing by considering it in its next larger context – a chair in a room, a room in a house, a house in an environment, an environment in a city plan. ELIEL SAARINEN, *Time*, July 2, 1956.

## 236. DESIRES

See also 364. Frustration; 668. Passion; 839. Satisfaction

1. The desire for imaginary benefits often involves the loss of present blessings. AESOP, "The Kites and the Swans," *Fables* (6th c. B.C.?), tr. George Fyler Townsend.

2. We would often be sorry if our wishes were gratified. AESOP, "The Old Man and Death," *Fables* (6th c. B.C.?), tr. Joseph Jacobs.

3. Make us, not fly to dreams, but moderate desire. MATTHEW ARNOLD, *Empedocles on Etna* (1852), 1.2.

4. Men have a thousand desires to a bushel of choices. HENRY WARD BEECHER, *Proverbs from Plymouth Pulpit* (1887).

5. He who desires but acts not, breeds pestilence. WILLIAM BLAKE, "Proverbs of Hell," *The Marriage of Heaven and Hell* (1790).

6. Great desire obtains little. *Burmese Proverbs* (1962), 466, ed. Hla Pe.

7. Mankind, why do ye set your hearts on things / That, of necessity, may not be shared? DANTE, "Purgatorio," 14, *The Divine Comedy* (c. 1300–21), tr. Lawrence Grant White.

8. What the eye sees not, the heart craves not. DUTCH PROVERB.

9. Those desires that do not bring pain if they are not satisfied are not necessary; and they are easily thrust aside whenever to satisfy them appears difficult or likely to cause injury. EPICURUS, "Principal Doctrines" (3rd c. B.C.), 26, in *Letters, Principal Doctrines, and Vatican Sayings*, tr. Russel M. Geer.

10. If you desire many things, many things will seem but a few. BENJAMIN FRANKLIN, *Poor Richard's Almanack* (1732–57).

11. Modern man lives under the illusion that he knows what he wants, while he actually wants what he is supposed to want.

ERICH FROMM, *Escape from Freedom* (1941), 7.

12. Our desires, once realized, haunt us again less readily. MARGARET FULLER, *Summer on the Lakes* (1844), 1.

13. Other people's appetites easily appear excessive when one doesn't share them. ANDRÉ GIDE, *The Counterfeiters* (1925), 3.1, tr. Dorothy Bussy.

14. We are never further from our wishes than when we imagine that we possess what we have desired. GOETHE, *Elective Affinities* (1809), 23.

15. When desire dies, fear is born. BALTASAR GRACIÁN, *The Art of Worldly Wisdom* (1647), 200, tr. Joseph Jacobs.

16. How few are our real wants! and how easy is it to satisfy them! Our imaginary ones are boundless and insatiable. JULIUS CHARLES HARE and AUGUSTUS WILLIAM HARE, *Guesses at Truth* (1827).

17. A strong passion for any object will ensure success, for the desire of the end will point out the means. WILLIAM HAZLITT, "On Manner," *The Round Table* (1817).

18. The wretched are in this respect fortunate, that they have the strongest yearnings after happiness; and to desire is in some sense to enjoy. WILLIAM HAZLITT, *Characteristics* (1823).

19. It is hard to fight against impulsive desire; whatever it wants it will buy at the cost of the soul. HERACLITUS, *Fragments* (c. 500 B.C.), 51, tr. Philip Wheelwright.

20. It would not be better if things happened to men just as they wish. HERACLITUS, *Fragments* (c. 500 B.C.), 52, tr. Philip Wheelwright.

21. We are less dissatisfied when we lack many things than when we seem to lack but one thing. ERIC HOFFER, *The True Believer* (1951), 2.5.23.

22. Often, the thing we pursue most passionately is but a substitute for the one thing we really want and cannot have. ERIC HOFFER, *The Passionate State of Mind* (1954), 3.

23. Some desire is necessary to keep life in motion, and he whose real wants are supplied must admit those of fancy. SAMUEL JOHNSON, *Rasselas* (1759), 8.

24. Life is a progress from want to want, not from enjoyment to enjoyment. SAMUEL JOHNSON, quoted in Boswell's *Life of Samuel Johnson*, May 1776.

25. There are certain people who so ardently and passionately desire a thing, that from dread of losing it they leave nothing undone to make them lose it. LA BRUYÈRE, *Characters* (1688), 4.61, tr. Henri Van Laun.

26. We do not wish ardently for what we desire only through reason. LA ROCHEFOUCAULD, *Maxims* (1665), tr. Kenneth Pratt.

27. It is very much easier to extinguish a first desire than to satisfy those which follow it. LA ROCHEFOUCAULD, *Maxims* (1665), tr. Kenneth Pratt.

28. We should scarcely desire things ardently if we were perfectly acquainted with what we desire. LA ROCHEFOUCAULD, *Maxims* (1665), tr. Kenneth Pratt.

29. It is impossible to abolish either with a law or an axe the desires of men. WALTER LIPPMANN, "The Taboo," *A Preface to Politics* (1914).

30. We know that it is possible to harness desire to many interests, that evil is one form of a desire, and not the nature of it. WALTER LIPPMANN, "The Taboo," *A Preface to Politics* (1914).

31. At any moment in our lives we desire only those objects which we are then capable of desiring and in the way we are then capable of desiring them. WALTER LIPPMANN, *A Preface to Morals* (1929), 2.9.6.

32. Granting our wish one of Fate's saddest jokes is! JAMES RUSSELL LOWELL, "Two Scenes from the Life of Blondel, Autumn, 1863," *Under the Willows and Other Poems* (1868), 2.2.

33. The ordinary life of men is like that of the saints. They all seek their satisfaction, and differ only in the object in which they place it; they call those their enemies who hinder them. PASCAL, *Pensées* (1670), 642, tr. W. F. Trotter.

34. We do not succeed in changing things according to our desire, but gradually our desire changes. MARCEL PROUST, *Remembrance of Things Past: The Sweet Cheat Gone* (1913–27), tr. C. K. Scott-Moncrieff.

35. I look at what I have not and think myself unhappy; others look at what I have and think me happy. JOSEPH ROUX, *Meditations of a Parish Priest* (1886), 5.38, tr. Isabel F. Hapgood.

36. The superiority of the distant over

the present is only due to the mass and variety of the pleasures that can be suggested, compared with the poverty of those that can at any time be felt. GEORGE SANTAYANA, *Little Essays* (1920), 97, ed. Logan Pearsall Smith.

37. No one can have all he wants, but a man can refrain from wanting what he has not, and cheerfully make the best of a bird in the hand. SENECA, *Letters to Lucilius* (1st c.), 123.3, tr. E. Phillips Barker.

38. All impediments in fancy's course / Are motives of more fancy. SHAKESPEARE, *All's Well That Ends Well* (1602–03), 5.3.214.

39. There are two tragedies in life. One is to lose your heart's desire. The other is to gain it. GEORGE BERNARD SHAW, *Man and Superman* (1903), 4.

## 237. DESPAIR

**See also 192. Courage; 251. Discouragement; 425. Hope**

1. You may not know it, but at the far end of despair, there is a white clearing where one is almost happy. JEAN ANOUILH, *Restless Heart* (1934), 3, tr. Lucienne Hill.

2. Because thou must not dream, thou need'st not then despair! MATTHEW ARNOLD, *Empedocles on Etna* (1852), 1.2.

3. There's something so showy about desperation, it takes hard wits to see it's a grandiose form of funk. ELIZABETH BOWEN, *The Death of the Heart* (1938), 3.6.

4. To eat bread without hope is still slowly to starve to death. PEARL S. BUCK, "To the Young," *To My Daughters, With Love* (1967).

5. Safe Despair it is that raves— / Agony is frugal. / Puts itself severe away / For its own perusal. EMILY DICKINSON, poem (c. 1873).

6. In despair there are the most intense enjoyments, especially when one is very acutely conscious of the hopelessness of one's position. DOSTOEVSKY, *Notes from Underground* (1864), 1.2, tr. Constance Garnett.

7. In a real dark night of the soul it is always three o'clock in the morning, day after day. F. SCOTT FITZGERALD, "The Crack-Up," *The Crack-Up* (1945).

8. Despair is the price one pays for setting oneself an impossible aim. GRAHAM GREENE, *The Heart of the Matter* (1948), 2.4.

9. Where there is no hope there can be no endeavour. SAMUEL JOHNSON, *The Rambler* (1750–52), 110.

10. When water covers the head, a hundred fathoms are as one. PERSIAN PROVERB.

11. If clearness about things produces a fundamental despair, a fundamental despair in turn produces a remarkable clearness or even playfulness about ordinary matters. GEORGE SANTAYANA, "My Mother," *Persons and Places: The Background of My Life* (1944).

12. I was much further out than you thought / And not waving but drowning. STEVIE SMITH, "Not Waving but Drowning," *Selected Poems* (1964).

13. The mass of men lead lives of quiet desperation. What is called resignation is confirmed desperation. From the desperate city you go into the desperate country, and have to console yourself with the bravery of minks and muskrats. THOREAU, "Economy," *Walden* (1854).

14. Lord save us all from old age and broken health and a hope tree that has lost the faculty of putting out blossoms. MARK TWAIN, letter to Joe T. Goodman, April 1891.

## DESPOTISM

**See 995. Tyranny**

## 238. DESTINY

**See also 337. Fate; 358. Fortune; 617. Necessity**

1. Thy lot or portion of life is seeking after thee; therefore be at rest from seeking after it. ALI IBN-ABI-TALIB (7th c.), quoted in Emerson's "Self-Reliance," *Essays: First Series*.

2. How true it is that our destinies are decided by nothings and that a small imprudence helped by some insignificant accident, as an acorn is fertilized by a drop of rain, may raise the trees on which perhaps we and others shall be crucified. HENRI FRÉDÉRIC AMIEL, *Journal*, Apr. 9, 1856, tr. Mrs. Humphry Ward.

3. Destiny, n. A tyrant's authority for crime and a fool's excuse for failure. AM-

BROSE BIERCE, *The Devil's Dictionary* (1881–1911).

4. It is a mistake to look too far ahead. Only one link of the chain of destiny can be handled at a time. SIR WINSTON CHURCHILL, speech, House of Commons, Feb. 27, 1945.

5. If thou follow thy star, thou canst not fail of glorious heaven. DANTE, "Purgatorio," 3, *The Divine Comedy* (c. 1300–21), tr. Charles Eliot Norton.

6. How easy 'tis, when Destiny proves kind, / With full-spread sails to run before the wind! JOHN DRYDEN, *Astraea Redux* (1660), 11.63.

7. What we seek we shall find; what we flee from flees from us. EMERSON, "Fate," *The Conduct of Life* (1860).

8. As we are, so we do; and as we do, so is it done to us; we are the builders of our fortunes. EMERSON, "Worship," *The Conduct of Life* (1860).

9. [Destiny] is simply the relentless logic of each day we live. JEAN GIRAUDOUX, *Tiger at the Gates* (1935), 1, tr. Christopher Fry.

10. Destiny grants us our wishes, but in its own way, in order to give us something beyond our wishes. GOETHE, *Elective Affinities* (1809), 28.

11. We are not permitted to choose the frame of our destiny. But what we put into it is ours. DAG HAMMARSKJÖLD, "1945–1949: Towards new shores—?" *Markings* (1964), tr. Leif Sjoberg and W. H. Auden.

12. To go in search of destiny—what is this but to seek all the sorrows of man? MAURICE MAETERLINCK, "The Star," *The Treasure of the Humble* (1896), tr. Alfred Sutro.

13. It is the fate of the coconut husk to float, for the stone to sink. MALAY PROVERB.

14. Love nothing but that which comes to you woven in the pattern of your destiny. For what could more aptly fit your needs? MARCUS AURELIUS, *Meditations* (2nd c.), 7.57, tr. Maxwell Staniforth.

15. Our destiny rules over us, even when we are not yet aware of it; it is the future that makes laws for our to-day. NIETZSCHE, *Human, All Too Human* (1878), tr. Helen Zimmern.

16. 'Tis all a Chequer-board of Nights and Days / Where Destiny with Men for Pieces plays: / Hither and thither moves, and mates, and slays, / And one by one back in the Closet lays. OMAR KHAYYÁM, *Rubáiyát* (11th–12th c.), tr. Edward FitzGerald, 1st ed., 49.

17. Everything comes gradually and at its appointed hour. OVID, *The Art of Love* (c. A.D. 8), 1, tr. J. Lewis May.

18. Where destiny blunders, human prudence will not avail. PUBLILIUS SYRUS, *Moral Sayings* (1st c. B.C.), 943, tr. Darius Lyman.

19. There's a divinity that shapes our ends, / Rough-hew them how we will. SHAKESPEARE, *Hamlet* (1600), 5.2.10.

20. Whatever God has brought about / Is to be borne with courage. SOPHOCLES, *Oedipus at Colonus* (401 B.C.), tr. Robert Fitzgerald.

21. Man's destiny lies half within himself, half without. To advance in either half at the expense of the other is literally insane. PHILIP WYLIE, *Generation of Vipers* (1942), 7.

## 239. DESTRUCTION

**See also 439. Iconoclasm; 1024. Violence**

1. When one builds and another tears down, what do they gain but toil? APOCRYPHA, Ecclesiasticus 34:23.

2. All destruction, by violent revolution or however it be, is but new creation on a wider scale. THOMAS CARLYLE, *On Heroes, Hero-Worship and the Heroic in History* (1841), 4.

3. One minute gives invention to destroy; / What to rebuild, will a whole age employ. WILLIAM CONGREVE, *The Double-Dealer* (1694), 1.3.

4. There is nothing we value and hunt and cultivate and strive to draw to us, but in some hour we turn and rend it. EMERSON, *Journals*, 1836.

5. Breaking and building / In the progression of this world go hand in hand. CHRISTOPHER FRY, *The Boy with a Cart* (1945).

6. The passion for destruction is a creative joy. Graffito written during French student revolt, May 1968.

7. To be able to destroy with good conscience, to be able to behave badly and call your bad behavior "righteous indignation"—this is the height of psychological luxury,

the most delicious of moral treats. ALDOUS HUXLEY, *Crome Yellow* (1921).

8. The impulse to mar and to destroy is as ancient and almost as nearly universal as the impulse to create. The one is an easier way than the other of demonstrating power. JOSEPH WOOD KRUTCH, *The Best of Two Worlds* (1950).

9. It is not science that has destroyed the world, despite all the gloomy forebodings of the earlier prophets. It is man who has destroyed man. MAX LERNER, "The Human Heart and the Human Will," *Actions and Passions* (1949).

10. Let not him who is houseless pull down the house of another, but let him work diligently and build one for himself, thus by his example assuring that his own shall be safe from violence when built. ABRAHAM LINCOLN, reply to the New York Workingmen's Association, March 21, 1864.

11. After all, to make a beautiful omelet, you have to break an egg. SPANISH PROVERB.

### DEVELOPMENT

See 402. Growth and Development; 567. Maturity

### 240. DEVIL

See also 385. God; 414. Hell

1. Be sober, be vigilant; because your adversary the devil, as a roaring lion, walketh about, seeking whom he may devour. *Bible*, 1 Peter 5:8.

2. An apology for the Devil: It must be remembered that we have only heard one side of the case. God has written all the books. SAMUEL BUTLER (d. 1902), "Higgledy-Piggledy," *Note-Books* (1912).

3. The snake, it is known, is the animal monkeys most dread. Hence when men give their devil a definite form they make him a snake. A race of super-chickens would have pictured their devil a hawk. CLARENCE DAY, *This Simian World* (1920), 16.

4. One is always wrong to open a conversation with the devil, for, however he goes about it, he always insists upon having the last word. ANDRÉ GIDE, *Journals*, 1917, tr. Justin O'Brien.

5. The Devil was a great loss in the preternatural world. He was always something to fear and to hate; he supplied the antagonist powers of the imagination, and the arch of true religion hardly stands firm without him. WILLIAM HAZLITT, "Commonplaces," *The Round Table* (1817), 77.

6. Why should the Devil have all the good tunes? Ascribed to ROWLAND HILL (1795–1879).

7. The devil is merely a fallen angel, and when God lost Satan he lost one of his best lieutenants. WALTER LIPPMANN, "The Red Herring," *A Preface to Politics* (1914).

8. The serpent subtlest beast of all the field, / Of huge extent sometimes, with brazen eyes / And hairy mane terrific. MILTON, *Paradise Lost* (1667), 7.495.

9. Sometimes / The Devil is a gentleman. SHELLEY, "Peter Bell the Third" (1819), 2.2.

10. God seeks comrades and claims love, / the Devil seeks slaves and claims obedience. RABINDRANATH TAGORE, *Fireflies* (1928).

11. We may not pay Satan reverence, for that would be indiscreet, but we can at least respect his talents. MARK TWAIN, "Concerning the Jews," *Harper's Magazine*, September 1899.

12. A person [Satan] who has during all time maintained the imposing position of spiritual head of four-fifths of the human race, and political head of the whole of it, must be granted the possession of executive abilities of the loftiest order. MARK TWAIN, "Concerning the Jews," *Harper's Magazine*, September 1899.

### DEVOTION

See 1061. Worship

### 241. DIAGNOSIS

See also 791. Remedies

1. A disease known is half cured. THOMAS FULLER, M.D., *Gnomologia* (1732), 75.

### DICTATORSHIP

See 995. Tyranny

## 242. DICTIONARIES

See also 227. Definition; 1057. Words

1. Lexicographer, n. A pestilent fellow who, under the pretense of recording some particular stage in the development of a language, does what he can to arrest its growth, stiffen its flexibility and mechanize its methods. AMBROSE BIERCE, *The Devil's Dictionary* (1881–1911).

2. Neither is a dictionary a bad book to read. There is no cant in it, no excess of explanation, and it is full of suggestion, – the raw material of possible poems and histories. EMERSON, "In Praise of Books," *The Conduct of Life* (1860).

3. When I feel inclined to read poetry I take down my Dictionary. The poetry of words is quite as beautiful as that of sentences. The author may arrange the gems effectively, but their shape and lustre have been given by the attrition of ages. OLIVER WENDELL HOLMES, SR., "The Autocrat's Autobiography," *The Autocrat of the Breakfast Table* (1858), 1.

4. Lexicographer: a writer of dictionaries, a harmless drudge. SAMUEL JOHNSON, quoted in Boswell's *Life of Samuel Johnson*, 1755.

5. Dictionaries are like watches; the worst is better than none, and the best cannot be expected to go quite true. SAMUEL JOHNSON, quoted in Hester Lynch Piozzi's *Anecdotes of Samuel Johnson* (1786).

## 243. DIFFICULTY

See also 17. Adversity; 156. Complaint; 279. Effort; 325. Facility; 579. Method; 679. Perseverance

1. It is hard to keep a secret, to employ leisure well, and to be able to bear an injury. CHILON (6th c. B.C.), quoted in Diogenes Laertius' *Lives and Opinions of Eminent Philosophers* (3rd c. A.D.), tr. R. D. Hicks.

2. A smooth sea never made a skillful mariner. ENGLISH PROVERB.

3. Every path has its puddle. ENGLISH PROVERB.

4. Difficulties are things that show what men are. EPICTETUS, *Discourses* (2nd c.), 1.24, tr. Thomas W. Higginson.

5. All things are difficult before they are easy. THOMAS FULLER, M.D., *Gnomologia* (1732), 560.

6. Nothing is easy to the unwilling. THOMAS FULLER, M.D., *Gnomologia* (1732), 3663.

7. Our energy is in proportion to the resistance it meets. We can attempt nothing great, but from a sense of the difficulties we have to encounter. WILLIAM HAZLITT, *Characteristics* (1823), 156.

8. Many things difficult to design prove easy to performance. SAMUEL JOHNSON, *Rasselas* (1759), 13.

9. If at times our actions seem to make life difficult for others, it is only because history has made life difficult for us all. JOHN F. KENNEDY, State of the Union Message, Jan. 14, 1963.

10. What's too hard for a man must be worth looking into. KENYAN PROVERB.

11. I walk firmer and more secure up hill than down. MONTAIGNE, "Of the education of children," *Essays* (1580–88), tr. Charles Cotton and W. C. Hazlitt.

12. Difficulty gives all things their estimation. MONTAIGNE, "That our desires are augmented by difficulty," *Essays* (1580–88), tr. Charles Cotton and W. C. Hazlitt.

13. In the difficult are the friendly forces, the hands that work on us. RAINER MARIA RILKE, *Letters* (1892–1910; 1910–26), tr. Jane Barnard Greene and M. D. Herter Norton.

14. Set a stout heart to a steep hillside. SCOTTISH PROVERB.

15. Have the courage to face a difficulty lest it kick you harder than you bargain for. STANISLAUS I OF POLAND, *Maxims* (c. 18th c.).

## 244. DIGNITY

1. What is dignity without honesty? CICERO, *Ad Atticum* (1st c. B.C.), 7.

2. Let not a man guard his dignity, but let his dignity guard him. EMERSON, *Journals*, 1836.

3. The only kind of dignity which is genuine is that which is not diminished by the indifference of others. DAG HAMMARSKJÖLD, "1955," *Markings* (1964), tr. Leif Sjoberg and W. H. Auden.

4. Dignity is a matter which concerns only mankind. LIVY, *Ab Urbe Condita* (c. 29 B.C.), 6.41.

5. Our dignity is not in what we do, but in what we understand. GEORGE SANTAYANA, *Winds of Doctrine* (1913).

6. By dignity, I mean the high place attained only when the heart and mind are lifted, equally at once, by the creative union of perception and grace. JAMES THURBER, "Magical Lady," *Lanterns and Lances* (1961).

**DILIGENCE**
**See 279. Effort**

## 245. DIPLOMATS AND DIPLOMACY

**See also 496. International Relations; 987. Treaties**

1. The ambassadors of peace shall weep bitterly. *Bible*, Isaiah 33:7.

2. Consul, n. In American politics, a person who having failed to secure an office from the people is given one by the Administration on conditon that he leave the country. AMBROSE BIERCE, *The Devil's Dictionary* (1881–1911).

3. No government could survive without champagne. Champagne in the throat of our diplomatic people is like oil in the wheels of an engine. JOSEPH DARGENT, *New York Herald Tribune*, July 21, 1955.

4. Diplomats are useful only in fair weather. As soon as it rains they drown in every drop. CHARLES de GAULLE, *Newsweek*, Oct. 1, 1962.

5. There are three species of creatures who when they seem coming are going, / When they seem going they come: Diplomats, women, and crabs. JOHN HAY, "Distichs" (1871?), 2.

6. Lofty words cannot construct an alliance or maintain it; only concrete deeds can do that. JOHN F. KENNEDY, address, Frankfurt, West Germany, June 25, 1963.

7. A diplomat should be yielding and supple as a liana that can be bent but not broken. MALAY PROVERB.

8. Diplomacy is the police in grand costume. NAPOLEON I, *Maxims* (1804–15).

9. Foreign relations are like human relations. They are endless. The solution of one problem usually leads to another. JAMES RESTON, *Sketches in the Sand* (1967).

10. Diplomats write Notes, because they wouldent have the nerve to tell the same thing to each other's face. WILL ROGERS, *The Autobiography of Will Rogers* (1949), 12.

11. The only real diplomacy ever performed by a diplomat is in deceiving their own people after their dumbness has got them into a war. WILL ROGERS, *The Autobiography of Will Rogers* (1949), 16.

12. My advice to any diplomat who wants to have a good press is to have two or three kids and a dog. CARL ROWAN, *New Yorker*, Dec. 7, 1963.

13. A diplomat is a person who can tell you to go to hell in such a way that you actually look forward to the trip. CASKIE STINNETT, *Out of the Red* (1960).

14. Diplomacy is the lowest form of politeness because it misquotes the greatest number of people. A nation, like an individual, if it has anything to say, should simply say it. E. B. WHITE, "Compost," *One Man's Meat* (1944).

15. An ambassador is an honest man sent to lie abroad for the commonwealth. SIR HENRY WOTTON, witticism written in the autograph album of Christopher Fleckmore (1604), published in *Reliquiae Wottonianae* (1651).

## 246. DIRTINESS

**See also 135. Cleanliness**

1. Mud-pies gratify one of our first and best instincts. So long as we are dirty, we are pure. CHARLES DUDLEY WARNER, "Preliminary," *My Summer in a Garden* (1871).

**DISADVANTAGE**
**See 15. Advantage; 546. Losers**

**DISAGREEMENT**
**See 27. Agreement; 256. Dissent; 651. Opposition**

## 247. DISAPPOINTMENT

**See also 252. Disillusionment; 316. Expectation; 913. Sour Grapes**

1. The world hath failed to impart / The joy our youth forbodes, / Failed to fill up the

void which in our breasts we bear. MATTHEW ARNOLD, *Empedocles on Etna* (1852), 1.2.

2. Disappointment tears the bearable film of life. ELIZABETH BOWEN, *The House in Paris* (1935), 2.1.

3. Are you angry that others disappoint you? remember you cannot depend upon yourself. BENJAMIN FRANKLIN, *Poor Richard's Almanack* (1732–57).

4. A good salad may be the prologue to a bad supper. THOMAS FULLER, M.D., *Gnomologia* (1732), 174.

5. All things that are / Are with more spirit chased than enjoyed. SHAKESPEARE, *The Merchant of Venice* (1596–97), 2.6.12.

## DISASTER

See 17. Adversity

## DISCIPLES

See 350. Following

## 248. DISCIPLINE

See also 468. Indulgence; 760. Punishment; 856. Self-control; 981. Training

1. He who requires much from himself and little from others, will keep himself from being the object of resentment. CONFUCIUS, *Analects* (6th c. B.C.), 15.14, tr. James Legge.

2. Life is always a discipline, for the lower animals as well as for men; it is so dangerous that only by submitting to some sort of discipline can we become equipped to live in any true sense at all. HAVELOCK ELLIS, *On Life and Sex: Essays of Love and Virtue* (1937), 2.3

3. Do not consider painful what is good for you. EURIPIDES, *Medea* (431 B.C.), tr. Rex Warner.

4. If men live decently it is because / discipline saves their very lives for them. SOPHOCLES, *Antigone* (442–41 B.C.), tr. Elizabeth Wyckoff.

5. It is not the whip that makes men, but the lure of things that are worthy to be loved. WOODROW WILSON, address, Cleveland, Ohio, May 19, 1906.

## 249. DISCONTENT

See also 183. Contentment; 1004. Unhappiness

1. He that is discontented in one place will seldom be happy in another. AESOP, "The Ass and His Masters," *Fables* (6th c. B.C.?), tr. Thomas James.

2. What a miserable thing life is: you're living in clover, only the clover isn't good enough. BERTOLT BRECHT, *Jungle of Cities* (1924), 5, tr. Anselm Hollo.

3. It is not irritating to be where one is. It is only irritating to think one would like to be somewhere else. JOHN CAGE, "Lecture on Nothing," *Silence* (1961).

4. Man is fond of counting his troubles, but he does not count his joys. If he counted them up as he ought to, he would see that every lot has enough happiness provided for it. DOSTOEVSKY, *Notes from Underground* (1864), 2.4, tr. Constance Garnett.

5. To have a grievance is to have a purpose in life. ERIC HOFFER, *The Passionate State of Mind* (1954), 166.

6. When you are in Rome you long to be in the country, and when you are in the country you praise the distant town to the skies. HORACE, *Satires* (35–30 B.C.), 2.7.

7. The average man is rich enough when he has a little more than he has got, and not till then. WILLIAM RALPH INGE, "Patriotism," *Outspoken Essays: First Series* (1919).

8. It is a flaw / In happiness, to see beyond our bourn,— / It forces us in summer skies to mourn, / It spoils the singing of the nightingale. JOHN KEATS, "Epistle to John Hamilton Reynolds" (1818).

9. Wealth . . . and poverty: the one is the parent of luxury and indolence, and the other of meanness and viciousness, and both of discontent. PLATO, *The Republic* (4th c. B.C.), 4, tr. Benjamin Jowett.

10. Discontent is the first step in the progress of a man or a nation. OSCAR WILDE, *A Woman of No Importance* (1893), 2.

## 250. DISCORD

See also 27. Agreement; 51. Argument; 256. Dissent; 342. Fighting; 651. Opposition; 766. Quarreling; 1035. War

1. He who incites to strife is worse than he who takes part in it. AESOP, "The Trum-

peter Taken Prisoner," *Fables* (6th c. B.C.?), tr. Thomas James.

2. In any assembly the simplest way to stop the transacting of business and split the ranks is to appeal to a principle. JACQUES BARZUN, *The House of Intellect* (1959).

3. Where no wood is, there the fire goeth out: so where there is no tale-bearer, the strife ceaseth. *Bible*, Proverbs 26:20.

4. All men who reflect on controversial matters should be free from hatred, friendship, anger, and pity. JULIUS CAESAR, quoted in Sallust's *Conspiracy of Catiline* (1st c. B.C.), 51.

5. Wars of opinion, as they have been the most destructive, are also the most disgraceful of conflicts, being appeals from right to might and from argument to artillery. CHARLES CALEB COLTON, *Lacon* (1825), 1.534.

6. There are fearful excitements on any side. / Any side can accuse the other / And feel virtuous without the hardships of virtue. CHRISTOPHER FRY, *The Dark Is Light Enough* (1954), 1.

7. The unity of freedom has never relied on uniformity of opinion. JOHN F. KENNEDY, State of the Union Message, Jan. 14, 1963.

8. The ultimate measure of a man is not where he stands in moments of comfort and convenience, but where he stands at times of challenge and controversy. MARTIN LUTHER KING, JR., *Strength to Love* (1963), 3.2.

9. There is no squabbling so violent as that between people who accepted an idea yesterday and those who will accept the same idea tomorrow. CHRISTOPHER MORLEY, *Religio Journalistici* (1924).

10. Dissension, well directed, may divide even the true-hearted, as a mighty stream of waters divides mountains of solid rock. *Panchatantra* (c. 5th c.), 1, tr. Franklin Edgerton.

11. Discord gives a relish for concord. PUBLILIUS SYRUS, *Moral Sayings* (1st c. B.C.), 198, tr. Darius Lyman.

12. What sets men at variance is but the treachery of language, for always they desire the same things. SAINT-EXUPÉRY, *The Wisdom of the Sands* (1948), 17, tr. Stuart Gilbert.

13. Civil dissension is a viperous worm / That gnaws the bowels of the commonwealth. SHAKESPEARE, *1 Henry VI* (1591–92), 3.1.72.

## 251. DISCOURAGEMENT

**See also 237. Despair**

1. Don't let life discourage you; everyone who got where he is had to begin where he was. RICHARD L. EVANS, *Time*, July 26, 1963.

2. Trouble has no necessary connection with discouragement—discouragement has a germ of its own, as different from trouble as arthritis is different from a stiff joint. F. SCOTT FITZGERALD, "The Crack-Up," *The Crack-Up* (1945).

## DISCOVERY

**See 477. Innovation**

## DISCRETION

**See 749. Prudence**

## DISHONESTY

**See 188. Corruption; 221. Deception; 329. Falsehood; 927. Stealing**

## 252. DISILLUSIONMENT

**See also 247. Disappointment**

1. Disillusion can become itself an illusion / If we rest in it. T. S. ELIOT, *The Cocktail Party* (1949), 2.

2. The flowers of life are but illusions. How many fade away and leave no trace; how few yield any fruit; and the fruit itself, how rarely does it ripen! GOETHE, *The Sorrows of Young Werther* (1774), 1, Aug. 30, 1771, tr. Victor Lange.

3. Every real object must cease to be what it seemed, and none could ever be what the whole soul desired. GEORGE SANTAYANA, *The Life of Reason: Reason in Society* (1905–06), 1.

4. Things sweet to taste prove in digestion sour. SHAKESPEARE, *Richard II* (1595–96), 1.3.236.

5. Our bitterest wine is always drained

from crushed ideals. ARTHUR STRINGER, *The Devastator* (1944).

6. The youth gets together his materials to build a bridge to the moon, or, perchance, a palace or temple on the earth, and, at length, the middle-aged man concludes to build a woodshed with them. THOREAU, *Journal*, July 14, 1852.

7. Hope is the only good thing that disillusion respects. VAUVENARGUES, *Reflections and Maxims* (1746), 690, tr. F. G. Stevens.

## 253. DISLIKE

See also 286. Enemies; 299. Estrangement; 410. Hatred; 588. Misanthropy

1. Rejection is a form of self-assertion. You have only to look back upon yourself as a person who hates this or that to discover what it is that you secretly love. GEORGE SANTAYANA, "My Father," *Persons and Places: The Background of My Life* (1944).

2. Dark and distorting are the minds of people who dislike us; and when we meet them, we make dismal reflections. LOGAN PEARSALL SMITH, *Afterthoughts* (1931), 3.

## 254. DISOBEDIENCE

See also 636. Obedience; 770. Rebellion

1. Disobedience, the rarest and most courageous of virtues, is seldom distinguished from neglect, the laziest and commonest of the vices. GEORGE BERNARD SHAW, "Maxims for Revolutionists," *Man and Superman* (1903).

2. Disobedience, in the eyes of any one who has read history, is man's original virtue. It is through disobedience that progress has been made, through disobedience and through rebellion. OSCAR WILDE, *The Soul of Man Under Socialism* (1891).

## 255. DISORDER

See also 654. Order

1. Chaos often breeds life, when order breeds habit. HENRY ADAMS, *The Education of Henry Adams* (1907), 16.

2. Chaos stamped with a seal becomes rightful order. UGO BETTI, *The Gambler* (1950), 3.2, tr. Gino Rizzo.

3. Confusion is a word we have invented for an order which is not understood. HENRY MILLER, "Interlude," *Tropic of Capricorn* (1938).

4. Have a place for everything and keep the thing somewhere else. This is not advice, it is merely custom. MARK TWAIN, *Notebook* (1935).

## DISPOSITION

See 390. Good Nature; 961. Temper, Bad; 962. Temperament

## DISPUTE

See 51. Argument; 766. Quarreling

## 256. DISSENT

See also 51. Argument; 250. Discord; 254. Disobedience; 362. Free Speech; 651. Opposition; 725. Press, Freedom of the; 747. Protest; 766. Quarreling; 779. Rebellion; 813. Revolution; 1024. Violence

1. The essence of a heretic, that is, of someone who has a particular opinion, is that he clings to his own ideas. JACQUES-BÉNIGNE BOSSUET, *Histoire des variations* (1688), 29.

2. We owe almost all our knowledge not to those who have agreed, but to those who have differed. CHARLES CALEB COLTON, *Lacon* (1825), 2.121.

3. Assent—and you are sane— / Demure—you're straightway dangerous— / And handled with a Chain—. EMILY DICKINSON, poem (c. 1862).

4. They that approve a private opinion, call it opinion; but they that mislike it, heresy, and yet heresy signifies no more than private opinion. THOMAS HOBBES, *Leviathan* (1651), 1.11.

5. A heresy can spring only from a system that is in full vigor. ERIC HOFFER, *The Ordeal of Change* (1964), 5.

6. Freedom to differ is not limited to things that do not matter much. That would be a mere shadow of freedom. The test of its substance is the right to differ as to things that touch the heart of the existing order.

JUSTICE ROBERT JACKSON, *West Virginia State Board. v. Barnette* (1943).

7. The heresy of one age becomes the orthodoxy of the next. HELEN KELLER, *Optimism* (1903), 2.

8. Let us not be afraid of debate or dissent—let us encourage it. For if we should ever abandon these basic American traditions in the name of fighting Communism, what would it profit us to win the whole world when we have lost our soul? JOHN F. KENNEDY, address, National Civil Liberties Conference, Washington, D.C., April 16, 1959.

9. It is more often from pride than from defective understanding that people oppose established opinions: they find the best places taken in the good party and are reluctant to accept inferior ones. LA ROCHEFOUCAULD, *Maxims* (1665), tr. Kenneth Pratt.

10. In a dead religion there are no more heresies. ANDRÉ SUARÈS, *Péguy* (1912), 4.

11. Say, Not so, and you will outcircle the philosophers. THOREAU, *Journal*, June 26, 1840.

12. Discussion in America means dissent. JAMES THURBER, "The Duchess and the Bugs," *Lanterns and Lances* (1961).

## 257. DISTRUST

**See also 77. Betrayal; 990. Trust**

1. He who is too much afraid of being duped has lost the power of being magnanimous. HENRI FRÉDÉRIC AMIEL, *Journal*, Dec. 26, 1868, tr. Mrs. Humphry Ward.

2. There is nothing makes a man suspect much, more than to know little. FRANCIS BACON, "Of Suspicion," *Essays* (1625).

3. Suspicion is a thing very few people can entertain without letting the hypothesis turn, in their minds, into fact. DAVID CORT, *Social Astonishments* (1963).

4. What loneliness is more lonely than distrust? GEORGE ELIOT, *Middlemarch* (1871–72), 5.44.

5. At the gate which suspicion enters, love goes out. THOMAS FULLER, M.D., *Gnomologia* (1732), 828.

6. Trust the friends of to-day as if they will be enemies to-morrow. BALTASAR GRACIÁN, *The Art of Worldly Wisdom* (1647), 217, tr. Joseph Jacobs.

7. I had rather take my chance that some traitors will escape detection than spread abroad a spirit of general suspicion and distrust, which accepts rumor and gossip in place of undismayed and unintimidated inquiry. LEARNED HAND, speech, New York State University, Oct. 24, 1952.

8. It is a matter of regret that many low, mean suspicions turn out to be well founded. EDGAR WATSON HOWE, *Ventures in Common Sense* (1919), 32.28.

9. When you grow suspicious of a person and begin a system of espionage upon him, your punishment will be that you will find your suspicions true. ELBERT HUBBARD, *The Note Book* (1927).

10. Suspicion on one side breeds suspicion on the other, and new weapons beget counterweapons. JOHN F. KENNEDY, address, The American University, Washington, D.C., June 10, 1963.

11. It is more shameful to mistrust one's friends than to be deceived by them. LA ROCHEFOUCAULD, *Maxims* (1665), tr. Kenneth Pratt.

12. Our distrust justifies the deceit of others. LA ROCHEFOUCAULD, *Maxims* (1665), tr. Kenneth Pratt.

13. Made wary by impostors, men look for something wrong even in the righteous. *Panchatantra* (c. 5th c.), 1, tr. Franklin Edgerton.

14. Trust in God, but tie your camel. PERSIAN PROVERB.

15. Suspicion begets suspicion. PUBLILIUS SYRUS, *Moral Sayings* (1st c. B.C.), 928, tr. Darius Lyman.

16. The most mistrustful are often the greatest dupes. CARDINAL DE RETZ, *Mémoires* (1718).

17. I hold it cowardice / To rest mistrustful where a noble heart / Hath pawned an open hand in sign of love. SHAKESPEARE, *3 Henry VI* (1590–91), 4.2.7.

18. O father Abram, what these Christians are, / Whose own hard dealing teaches them suspect / The thoughts of others! SHAKESPEARE, *The Merchant of Venice* (1596–97), 1.3.161.

19. I fear the Greeks even when they bring gifts. VERGIL, *Aeneid* (30–19 B.C.), 2.49.

20. We have to distrust each other. It is our only defense against betrayal. TENNESSEE WILLIAMS, *Camino Real* (1953), 10.

## 258. DIVERSITY
**See also 467. Individuality; 1007. Uniqueness; 1009. Unity**

1. Them which is of other naturs thinks different. CHARLES DICKENS, *Martin Chuzzlewit* (1844), 19.

2. There are no elements so diverse that they cannot be joined in the heart of a man. JEAN GIRAUDOUX, *Siegfried* (1928), 4, tr. Phyllis La Farge with Peter H. Judd.

3. There never were, in the world, two opinions alike, no more than two hairs, or two grains; the most universal quality is diversity. MONTAIGNE, "Of the resemblance of children to their fathers," *Essays* (1580–88), tr. Charles Cotton and W. C. Hazlitt.

## DIVIDED INTERESTS
**See 167. Conflict, Inner; 495. Interests, Divided**

## DIVINE REVELATION
**See 810. Revelation, Divine**

## 259. DIVINITY
**See also 385. God; 429. Humanism**

1. There is surely a piece of divinity in us, something that was before the elements, and owes no homage unto the sun. SIR THOMAS BROWNE, *Religio Medici* (1642), 2.

2. Earth's crammed with heaven, / And every common bush afire with God. ELIZABETH BARRETT BROWNING, *Aurora Leigh* (1856), 7.821.

3. The mystery of a person, indeed, is ever divine to him that has a sense for the godlike. THOMAS CARLYLE, *Sartor Resartus* (1833–34), 2.4.

4. If we meet no gods, it is because we harbor none. If there is grandeur in you, you will find grandeur in porters and sweeps. EMERSON, "Worship," *The Conduct of Life* (1860).

5. What is divine escapes men's notice because of their incredulity. HERACLITUS, *Fragments* (c. 500 B.C.), 63, tr. Philip Wheelwright.

6. Man is God by his faculty for thought. LAMARTINE, première préface, *Les Premières méditations* (1820).

7. The indwelling ideal lends all the gods their divinity. GEORGE SANTAYANA, *The Life of Reason: Reason in Religion* (1905–06), 10.

8. I found Him in the shining of the stars, / I marked Him in the flowering of His fields, / But in His ways with men I find Him not. ALFRED, LORD TENNYSON, "The Passing of Arthur," *Idylls of the King* (1869).

## 260. DIVORCE
**See also 560. Marriage**

1. I read about divorce, and I can't see why two people can't get along together in harmony, and I see two people and I can't see how either of them can live with the other. FRANKLIN P. ADAMS, *Nods and Becks* (1944).

2. What therefore God hath joined together, let not man put asunder. *Bible*, Matthew 19:6.

3. The only solid and lasting peace between a man and his wife is, doubtless, a separation. LORD CHESTERFIELD, *Letters to His Son*, Sept. 1, 1763.

4. Our marriage is dead, when the pleasure is fled: / 'Twas pleasure first made it an oath. JOHN DRYDEN, *Songs* (1673), 25.7.

5. Better a tooth out than always aching. THOMAS FULLER, M.D., *Gnomologia* (1732), 869.

6. Alimony—The ransom that the happy pay to the devil. H. L. MENCKEN, "Sententiae," *A Book of Burlesques* (1920).

7. There are four minds in the bed of a divorced man who marries a divorced woman. Haggadah, *Palestinian Talmud* (4th c.).

8. Divorce is probably of nearly the same date as marriage. I believe, however, that marriage is some weeks more ancient. VOLTAIRE, "Divorce," *Philosophical Dictionary* (1764).

## 261. DOCTORS
**See also 232. Dentists; 572. Medicine; 751. Psychiatry**

1. Keep away from physicians. It is all probing and guessing and pretending with

them. They leave it to Nature to cure in her own time, but they take the credit. As well as very fat fees. ANTHONY BURGESS, "1592–1599," *Nothing Like the Sun* (1964), 8.

2. Physicians must discover the weaknesses of the human mind, and even condescend to humour them, or they will never be called in to cure the infirmities of the body. CHARLES CALEB COLTON, *Lacon* (1825), 1.482.

3. A patient in th' hands iv a doctor is like a hero in th' hands iv a story writer. He's goin' to suffer a good dale, but he's goin' to come out all right in th' end. FINLEY PETER DUNNE, "Going to See the Doctor," *Mr. Dooley On Making a Will* (1919).

4. The best surgeon is he that hath been hacked himself. ENGLISH PROVERB.

5. Every physician almost hath his favourite disease. HENRY FIELDING, *Tom Jones* (1749), 2.9.

6. God heals, and the doctor takes the fees. BENJAMIN FRANKLIN, *Poor Richard's Almanack* (1732–57).

7. Yesterday Dr Marcus went to see the statue of / Zeus. / Though Zeus, / & though marble, / We're burying the statue today. *Greek Anthology* (7th c. B.C.–10th c. A.D.), 11.113, tr. Dudley Fitts.

8. Doctors cut, burn, and torture the sick, and then demand of them an undeserved fee for such services. HERACLITUS, *Fragments* (c. 500 B.C.), 107, tr. Philip Wheelwright.

9. The physician must have at his command a certain ready wit, as dourness is repulsive both to the healthy and the sick. HIPPOCRATES, *Decorum* (c. 400 B.C.), 7, tr. W. H. S. Jones.

10. The dignity of a physician requires that he should look healthy, and as plump as nature intended him to be; for the common crowd consider those who are not of this excellent bodily condition to be unable to take care of themselves. HIPPOCRATES, *The Physician* (c. 400 B.C.), tr. W. H. S. Jones.

11. As long as men are liable to die and are desirous to live, a physician will be made fun of, but he will be well paid. LA BRUYÈRE, *Characters* (1688), 14.65, tr. Henri Van Laun.

12. Remember how many physicians are dead after puckering up their brows so often over their patients. MARCUS AURELIUS, *Meditations* (2nd c.), 4.48.

13. There's a sort of decency among the dead, a remarkable discretion: you never find them making any complaint against the doctor who killed them! MOLIÈRE, *A Doctor in Spite of Himself* (1666), 3, tr. John Wood.

14. Who ever saw one physician approve of another's prescription, without taking something away, or adding something to it? MONTAIGNE, "Of the resemblance of children to their fathers," *Essays* (1580–88), tr. Charles Cotton and W. C. Hazlitt.

15. A physician can sometimes parry the scythe of death, but has no power over the sand in the hourglass. HESTER LYNCH PIOZZI, letter to Fanny Burney, Nov. 12, 1781.

16. The best doctor in the world is the Veterinarian. He can't ask his patients what is the matter–he's got to just know. WILL ROGERS, *The Autobiography of Will Rogers* (1949), 12.

17. Only a fool will make a doctor his heir. RUSSIAN PROVERB.

18. Let no one suppose that the words doctor and patient can disguise from the parties the fact that they are employer and employee. GEORGE BERNARD SHAW, "Preface on Doctors: The Future of Private Practice," *The Doctor's Dilemma* (1913).

19. There is no better surgeon than one with many scars. SPANISH PROVERB.

20. There are worse occupations in this world than feeling a woman's pulse. LAURENCE STERNE, "The Pulse," *A Sentimental Journey* (1768).

21. The best doctors in the world are Doctor Diet, Doctor Quiet, and Doctor Merryman. JONATHAN SWIFT, *Polite Conversation* (1738), 2.

22. To preserve a man alive in the midst of so many chances and hostilities, is as great a miracle as to create him. JEREMY TAYLOR, *The Rule and Exercise of Holy Dying* (1651), 1.

23. Men who are occupied in the restoration of health to other men, by the joint exertion of skill and humanity, are above all the great of the earth. They even partake of divinity, since to preserve and renew is almost as noble as to create. VOLTAIRE, "Physicians," *Philosophical Dictionary* (1764).

24. Physicians are like kings— / They brook no contradiction. JOHN WEBSTER, *The Duchess of Malfi* (c. 1613), 5.2.

### DOCTRINE

See 966. Theology

### 262. DOGMATISM

See also 113. Certainty; 200. Creeds; 333. Fanaticism; 443. Ideology; 498. Intolerance; 613. Narrowness; 720. Prejudices; 872. Self-righteousness

1. Bigot, n. One who is obstinately and zealously attached to an opinion that you do not entertain. AMBROSE BIERCE, *The Devil's Dictionary* (1881–1911).

2. The man who never alters his opinion is like standing water, and breeds reptiles of the mind. WILLIAM BLAKE, "A Memorable Fancy," *The Marriage of Heaven and Hell* (1790).

3. It is in the uncompromisingness with which dogma is held and not in the dogma or want of dogma that the danger lies. SAMUEL BUTLER (d. 1902), *The Way of All Flesh* (1903), 68.

4. We call a man a bigot or a slave of dogma because he is a thinker who has thought thoroughly and to a definite end. G. K. CHESTERTON, "The Error of Impartiality," *All Things Considered* (1908).

5. There are two kinds of people in the world: the conscious dogmatists and the unconscious dogmatists. I have always found myself that the unconscious dogmatists were by far the most dogmatic. G. K. CHESTERTON, "On Europe and Asia," *Generally Speaking* (1928).

6. We ought not to extract pernicious honey from poison-blossoms of misrepresentation and mendacious half truth, to pamper the coarse appetite of bigotry and self-love. SAMUEL TAYLOR COLERIDGE, "Preliminary Observations," *Aids to Reflection* (1825).

7. Religion is as effectually destroyed by bigotry as by indifference. EMERSON, *Journals*, 1831.

8. Bigotry is the sacred disease. HERACLITUS, *Fragments* (c. 500 B.C.), 56, tr. Philip Wheelwright.

9. We are least open to precise knowledge concerning the things we are most vehement about. ERIC HOFFER, *The Passionate State of Mind* (1954), 60.

10. The implacable stand is directed more against the doubt within than the assailant without. ERIC HOFFER, *The Passionate State of Mind* (1954), 63.

11. No man should dogmatize except on the subject of theology. Here he can take his stand, and by throwing the burden of proof on the opposition, he is invincible. We have to die to find out whether he is right. ELBERT HUBBARD, *The Note Book* (1927).

12. Profound ignorance makes a man dogmatic. The man who knows nothing thinks he is teaching others what he has just learned himself; the man who knows a great deal can't imagine that what he is saying is not common knowledge, and speaks more indifferently. LA BRUYÈRE, *Characters* (1688), 5.76.

13. How strange it is to see with how much passion / People see things only in their own fashion! MOLIÈRE, *The School for Wives* (1662), 1.2, tr. Donald M. Frame.

14. I am Sir Oracle, / And when I ope my lips, let no dog bark! SHAKESPEARE, *The Merchant of Venice* (1596–97), 1.1.93.

15. The most positive men are the most credulous. JONATHAN SWIFT, *Thoughts on Various Subjects* (1711).

16. Bigotry tries to keep truth safe in its hand / with a grip that kills it. RABINDRANATH TAGORE, *Fireflies* (1928).

### DOGS

See 41. Animals

### DOING

See 6. Achievement; 9. Action; 10. Activity; 224. Deeds

### DOUBT

See 263. Doubt, Religious; 897. Skepticism; 998. Uncertainty

### 263. DOUBT, RELIGIOUS

See also 328. Faith; 897. Skepticism; 997. Unbelief; 998. Uncertainty

1. The more of doubt, the stronger faith, I say, / If faith o'ercomes doubt. ROBERT BROWNING, "Bishop Blougram's Apology," *Men and Women* (1855).

2. Do we, holding that the gods exist, / deceive ourselves with unsubstantial

dreams / and lies, while random careless chance and change / alone control the world? EURIPIDES, *Hecuba* (c. 425 B.C.), tr. William Arrowsmith.

3. Wilt Thou not take the doubt of Thy children whom the time commands to try all things in the place of the unquestioning faith of earlier generations? OLIVER WENDELL HOLMES, SR., *The Poet at the Breakfast Table* (1872), 7.

4. Question with boldness even the existence of a God; because, if there be one, he must more approve of the homage of reason, than that of blindfolded fear. THOMAS JEFFERSON, letter to Peter Carr, Aug. 10, 1787.

5. Ten thousand difficulties do not make one doubt. JOHN HENRY NEWMAN, *Apologia pro Vita Sua* (1864).

6. O Lord, if there is a Lord, save my soul, if I have a soul. ERNEST RENAN, *Prière d'un sceptique.*

7. I am afraid I shall not find Him [God]: but I shall still look for Him, if He exists. He may be appreciative of my efforts. JULES RENARD, *Journal*, September 1903, ed. and tr. Louise Bogan and Elizabeth Roget.

8. Doubt is faith in the main: but faith, on the whole, is doubt: / We cannot believe by proof: but could we believe without? ALGERNON CHARLES SWINBURNE, "The Higher Pantheism in a Nutshell," *The Heptalogia* (1880).

9. There lives more faith in honest doubt, / Believe me, than in half the creeds. ALFRED, LORD TENNYSON, "In Memoriam A. H. H." (1850), 96.

10. A faith which does not doubt is a dead faith. MIGUEL DE UNAMUNO, *The Agony of Christianity* (1925).

11. In the present age doubt has become immune to faith and faith has dissociated itself from doubt. GABRIEL VAHANIAN, *The Death of God* (1962), 1.

**DRAMA**
See 965. Theater

## 264. DREAMS

See also 440. Idealism; 447. Illusion; 687. Phantasy; 899. Sleep

1. Dreaming men are haunted men. STEPHEN VINCENT BENÉT, *John Brown's Body* (1928), 1.

2. One of the characteristics of the dream is that nothing surprises us in it. With no regret, we agree to live in it with strangers, completely cut off from our habits and friends. JEAN COCTEAU, "Du rêve," *La Difficulté d'être* (1947).

3. Dreaming permits each and every one of us to be quietly and safely insane every night of our lives. WILLIAM DEMENT, *Newsweek*, Nov. 30, 1959.

4. Judge of your natural character by what you do in your dreams. EMERSON, *Journals*, 1833.

5. The net of the sleeper catches fish. GREEK PROVERB.

6. We are not hypocrites in our sleep. WILLIAM HAZLITT, "On Dreams," *The Plain Speaker* (1826).

7. We often forget our dreams so speedily: if we cannot catch them as they are passing out at the door, we never set eyes on them again. WILLIAM HAZLITT, "On Dreams," *The Plain Speaker* (1826).

8. The waking have one world in common; sleepers have each a private world of his own. HERACLITUS, *Fragments* (c. 500 B.C.), 15, tr. Philip Wheelwright.

9. Dreams are faithful interpreters of our inclinations; but there is art required to sort and understand them. MONTAIGNE, "Of experience," *Essays* (1580–88), tr. Charles Cotton and W. C. Hazlitt.

10. Dreams, which, beneath the hovering shades of night, / Sport with the ever-restless minds of men, / Descend not from the gods. Each busy brain / Creates its own. THOMAS LOVE PEACOCK, "Dreams," *Petronius Arbiter* (1806).

11. In bed my real love has always been the sleep that rescued me by allowing me to dream. LUIGI PIRANDELLO, *The Rules of the Game* (1918), 2, tr. William Murray.

12. There is a prodigious selfishness in dreams: they live perfectly deaf and invulnerable amid the cries of the real world. GEORGE SANTAYANA, *The Life of Reason: Reason in Common Sense* (1905–06), 10.

13. I talk of dreams; / Which are the children of an idle brain, / Begot of nothing but vain fantasy. SHAKESPEARE, *Romeo and Juliet* (1594–95), 1.4.96.

14. In the drowsy dark cave of the mind / dreams build their nest with fragments / dropped from day's caravan. RABINDRANATH TAGORE, *Fireflies* (1928).

15. Dreams are true while they last, and do we not live in dreams? ALFRED, LORD TENNYSON, "The Higher Pantheism" (1869).

## 265. DRESS

See also 45. Appearance; 335. Fashion; 634. Nudity

1. Clothes and manners do not make the man; but, when he is made, they greatly improve his appearance. HENRY WARD BEECHER, *Proverbs from Plymouth Pulpit* (1887).

2. From the cradle to the coffin underwear comes first. BERTOLT BRECHT, *The Threepenny Opera* (1928), 2.2, tr. Desmond Vesey and Eric Bentley.

3. *We* know, Mr. Weller—we, who are men of the world—that a good uniform must work its way with the women, sooner or later. CHARLES DICKENS, *Pickwick Papers* (1836–37), 7.

4. Any man may be in good spirits and good temper when he's well dressed. There an't much credit in that. CHARLES DICKENS, *Martin Chuzzlewit* (1844), 5.

5. Probably every new and eagerly expected garment ever put on since clothes came in, fell a trifle short of the wearer's expectation. CHARLES DICKENS, *Great Expectations* (1860–61), 19.

6. Know, first, who you are; and then adorn yourself accordingly. EPICTETUS, *Discourses* (2nd c.), 3.1, tr. Thomas W. Higginson.

7. Good clothes open all doors. THOMAS FULLER, M.D., *Gnomologia* (1732), 1705.

8. A man has his clothes made to fit him; a woman makes herself fit her clothes. EDGAR WATSON HOWE, *Country Town Sayings* (1911).

9. A man with a good coat upon his back meets with a better reception than he who has a bad one. SAMUEL JOHNSON, quoted in Boswell's *Life of Samuel Johnson*, July 20, 1763.

10. Fine clothes are good only as they supply the want of other means of procuring respect. SAMUEL JOHNSON, quoted in Boswell's *Life of Samuel Johnson*, March 27, 1776.

11. In a world of moral nudism, wearing clothes doesn't just mean that you're prudish; it suggests that you may have something to hide. LOUIS KRONENBERGER, *Company Manners* (1954), 2.2

12. In clothes as well as speech, the man of sense / Will shun all these extremes that give offense, / Dress unaffectedly, and, without haste, / Follow the changes in the current taste. MOLIÈRE, *The School for Husbands* (1661), 1.2, tr. Donald M. Frame.

13. A man becomes the creature of his uniform. NAPOLEON I, *Maxims* (1804–15).

14. A lady wants to be dressed exactly like everybody else but she gets pretty up- / set if she sees anybody else dressed exactly like / her. OGDEN NASH, "Thoughts Thought on an Avenue," *Marriage Lines* (1964).

15. The most loyal and faithful woman indulges her imagination in a hypothetical liaison whenever she dons a new street frock for the first time. GEORGE JEAN NATHAN, "General Conclusions About the Coarse Sex," *The Theatre, the Drama, the Girls* (1921).

16. Contentment preserves one even from catching a cold. Has a woman who knew she was well-dressed ever caught cold? NIETZSCHE, "Maxims and Missiles," 25, *Twilight of the Idols* (1888), tr. Anthony M. Ludovici.

17. Where's the man could ease a heart / Like a satin gown? DOROTHY PARKER, "The Satin Dress," *Enough Rope* (1926), 1.

18. Costly thy habit as thy purse can buy, / But not expressed in fancy; rich, not gaudy. SHAKESPEARE, *Hamlet* (1600), 1.3.70.

19. The apparel oft proclaims the man. SHAKESPEARE, *Hamlet* (1600), 1.3.72.

20. To call a fashion wearable is the kiss of death. No new fashion worth its salt is ever wearable. EUGENIA SHEPPARD, *New York Herald Tribune*, Jan. 13, 1960.

21. A hat is the difference between wearing clothes and wearing a costume; it's the difference between being dressed—and being dressed up; it's the difference between looking adequate and looking your best. MARTHA SLITER, *Advertising Age*, April 13, 1959.

22. A man cannot dress, but his ideas get clothed at the same time. LAURENCE STERNE, *Tristram Shandy* (1759–67), 9.13.

23. No one knows how ungentlemanly he

can look, until he has seen himself in a shocking bad hat. ROBERT SMITH SURTEES, *Mr. Facey Romford's Hounds* (1865), 9.

24. Beware of all enterprises that require new clothes, and not rather a new wearer of clothes. THOREAU, "Economy," *Walden* (1854).

25. She's adorned / Amply that in her husband's eye looks lovely. JOHN TOBIN, *The Honeymoon* (1805), 3.4.

26. The rush of power to the head is not as becoming as a new hat. HELEN VAN SLYKE, *The New York Times*, Aug. 28, 1963.

27. A cheap coat makes a cheap man. THORSTEIN VEBLEN, quoting a contemporary, *The Theory of the Leisure Class* (1899), 6.

28. The corset is, in economic theory, substantially a mutilation, undergone for the purpose of lowering the subject's vitality and rendering her permanently and obviously unfit for work. THORSTEIN VEBLEN, *The Theory of the Leisure Class* (1899), 7.

29. Let me be dressed fine as I will, / Flies, worms, and flowers, exceed me still. ISAAC WATTS, *Divine Songs for Children* (1720), 22.

30. With an evening coat and a white tie, anybody, even a stockbroker, can gain a reputation for being civilized. OSCAR WILDE, *The Picture of Dorian Gray* (1891), 1.

## 266. DRINKING

**See also 140. Coffee**

1. Bronze is the mirror of the form; wine, of the heart. AESCHYLUS, *Fragments* (525–456 B.C.), 384, tr. M. H. Morgan.

2. The vine bears three kinds of grapes: the first of pleasure, the next of intoxication, and the third of disgust. ANACHARSIS (c. 600 B.C.), quoted in Diogenes Laertius' *Lives and Opinions of Eminent Philosophers* (3rd. c. A.D.), tr. R. D. Hicks.

3. When the cock is drunk, he forgets about the hawk. ASHANTI PROVERB.

4. Man, being reasonable, must get drunk; / The best of Life is but intoxication. BYRON, *Don Juan* (1819–24), 2.179.

5. Under a bad cloak there is often a good drinker. CERVANTES, *Don Quixote* (1605–15), 2.3.33.

6. Drink moderately, for drunkenness neither keeps a secret, nor observes a promise. CERVANTES, *Don Quixote* (1605–15), 2.4.43, tr. Peter Motteux and John Ozell.

7. Wine, to a gifted bard, / Is a mount that merrily races; / From watered wits / No good has ever grown. CRATINUS (6th–5th c. B.C.), quoted by Nicaenetus (fl. 280 B.C.).

8. What the sober man has in his heart, the drunken man has on his lips. DANISH PROVERB.

9. Then trust me, there's nothing like drinking / So pleasant on this side the grave; / It keeps the unhappy from thinking, / And makes e'en the valiant more brave. CHARLES DIBDIN (1745–1814), "Nothing Like Grog."

10. There is wan thing an' on'y wan thing to be said in favor iv dhrink, an' that is that it has caused manny a lady to be loved that otherwise might've died single. FINLEY PETER DUNNE, "The Army Canteen," *Mr. Dooley Says* (1910).

11. Dhrink niver made a man betther, but it has made manny a man think he was betther. FINLEY PETER DUNNE, "The Army Canteen," *Mr. Dooley Says* (1910).

12. Intemperance is the only vulgarity. EMERSON, *Journals*, 1841.

13. The secret of drunkenness is, that it insulates us in thought, whilst it unites us in feeling. EMERSON, *Journals*, 1857.

14. It's the wise man who stays home when he's drunk. EURIPIDES, *The Cyclops* (c. 425 B.C.), tr. William Arrowsmith.

15. Drink to-day, and drown all sorrow; / You shall perhaps not do it to-morrow. FLETCHER and MASSINGER, *The Bloody Brother* (c. 1616), 2.2.

16. He that will to bed go sober / Falls with leaf still in October. FLETCHER and MASSINGER, *The Bloody Brother* (c. 1616), 2.2.

17. There are more old drunkards than old doctors. FRENCH PROVERB.

18. It is only the first bottle that is expensive. FRENCH PROVERB.

19. Bacchus hath drowned more men than Neptune. THOMAS FULLER, M.D., *Gnomologia* (1732), 830.

20. From wine what sudden friendship springs! JOHN GAY, "The Squire and his Cur," *Fables* (1727–38).

21. Brandy is lead in the morning, silver at noon, gold at night. GERMAN PROVERB.

22. Drunkenness is never anything but a

substitute for happiness. It amounts to buying the dream of a thing when you haven't money enough to buy the dreamed-of thing materially. ANDRÉ GIDE, *Journals*, 1896, tr. Justin O'Brien.

23. Remember Euboulos the sober, you who pass by, / And drink: there is one Hadês for all men. *Greek Anthology* (7th c. B.C.–10th c. A.D.), 7.452, tr. Dudley Fitts.

24. I fear the man who drinks water / And so remembers this morning what the rest of us said last night. *Greek Anthology* (7th c. B.C.–10th c. A.D.), 11.31, tr. Dudley Fitts

25. Wine is like rain: when it falls on the mire it but makes it the fouler, / But when it strikes the good soil wakes it to beauty and bloom. JOHN HAY, "Distichs" (1871?), 7.

26. Although it is better to hide our ignorance, this is hard to do when we relax over wine. HERACLITUS, *Fragments* (c. 500 B.C.), 53, tr. Philip Wheelwright.

27. Drink not the third glass, which thou canst not tame, / When once it is within thee. GEORGE HERBERT, "The Church Porch," 5, *The Temple* (1633).

28. There is in all men a demand for the superlative, so much so that the poor devil who has no other way of reaching it attains it by getting drunk. OLIVER WENDELL HOLMES, JR., "Natural Law," *Harvard Law Review* (1918), v. 32.

29. Wine can of their wits the wise beguile, / Make the sage frolic, and the serious smile. HOMER, *Odyssey* (9th c. B.C.), 14.520, tr. Alexander Pope.

30. Who, after wine, talks of war's hardships or of poverty? HORACE, *Odes* (23 B.C.), 1.18.5.

31. What does drunkenness not accomplish? It unlocks secrets, confirms our hopes, urges the indolent into battle, lifts the burden from anxious minds, teaches new arts. HORACE, *Epistles* (20–c. 8 B.C.), 1.5.16.

32. Malt does more than Milton can, / To justify God's ways to man. A. E. HOUSMAN *A Shropshire Lad* (1896), 62.

33. God made only water, but man made wine. VICTOR HUGO, "La Fête chez Thérèse," *Les Contemplations* (1856).

34. We drink one another's healths and spoil our own. JEROME K. JEROME, "On Eating and Drinking," *The Idle Thoughts of an Idle Fellow* (1889).

35. Wine gives a man nothing. It neither gives him knowledge nor wit; it only animates a man, and enables him to bring out what a dread of the company has repressed. SAMUEL JOHNSON, quoted in Boswell's *Life of Samuel Johnson*, April 28, 1778.

36. Claret is the liquor for boys; port for men; but he who aspires to be a hero must drink brandy. SAMUEL JOHNSON, quoted in Boswell's *Life of Samuel Johnson*, April 7, 1779.

37. Wine is only sweet to happy men. JOHN KEATS, "To— [Fanny Brawne]" (1819).

38. The drinking man is never less himself than during his sober intervals. CHARLES LAMB, "Confessions of a Drunkard," *Last Essays of Elia* (1833).

39. When thirsty grief in wine we steep, / When healths and draughts go free, / Fishes, that tipple in the deep, / Know no such liberty. RICHARD LOVELACE, "To Althea from Prison" (1649), 2.

40. Long quaffing maketh a short life. JOHN LYLY, *Euphues: The Anatomy of Wit* (1579).

41. an old stomach / reforms more whiskey drinkers / than a new resolve. DON MARQUIS, "archy on this and that," *Archy Does His Part* (1935).

42. I drank at every vine. / The last was like the first. / I came upon no wine / So wonderful as thirst. EDNA ST. VINCENT MILLAY, "Feast," *The Harp-Weaver* (1923).

43. Candy / Is dandy / But liquor / Is quicker. OGDEN NASH, "Reflections on Ice-Breaking," *Verses From 1929 On* (1959).

44. Drink! for you know not whence you came, nor why: / Drink! for you know not why you go, nor where. OMAR KHAYYÁM, *Rubáiyát* (11th–12th c.), tr. Edward FitzGerald, 4th ed., 74.

45. I wonder often what the Vintners buy / One half so precious as the stuff they sell. OMAR KHAYYÁM, *Rubáiyát* (11th–12th c.), tr. Edward FitzGerald, 4th ed., 95.

46. The drunken man's happiness is blind. Like everything in the world it has a cause, the alcohol; but it has no motive. JOSÉ ORTEGA Y GASSET, *The Dehumanization of Art* (1925).

47. When there is plenty of wine, sorrow and worry take wing. OVID, *The Art of Love* (c. A.D. 8), 1, tr. Rolfe Humphries.

48. Too much and too little wine. Give him none, he cannot find truth; give him too

much, the same. PASCAL, *Pensées* (1670), 71, tr. W. F. Trotter.

49. There are two reasons for drinking: one is, when you are thirsty, to cure it; the other, when you are not thirsty, to prevent it. THOMAS LOVE PEACOCK, *Melincourt* (1817), 16.

50. In wine there is truth. PLINY THE ELDER, *Natural History* (1st c.), 14.141, tr. J. Bostock and H. T. Riley.

51. To dispute with a drunkard is to debate with an empty house. PUBLILIUS SYRUS, *Moral Sayings* (1st c. B.C.), 4, tr. Darius Lyman.

52. If a man be discreet enough to take to hard drinking in his youth, before his general emptiness in ascertained, his friends invariably credit him with a host of shining qualities which, we are given to understand, lie balked and frustrated by his one unfortunate weakness. AGNES REPPLIER, "A Plea for Humor," *Points of View* (1891).

53. The sober man's secret is the drunken man's speech. RUSSIAN PROVERB.

54. Drunkenness doesn't create vices, but it brings them to the fore. SENECA, *Letters to Lucilius* (1st c.), 83.20, tr. E. Phillips Barker.

55. O God, that men should put an enemy in their mouths to steal away their brains! that we should with joy, pleasance, revel, and applause tranform ourselves into beasts! SHAKESPEARE, *Othello* (1604–05), 2.3.291.

56. Good wine is a good familiar creature if it be well used. SHAKESPEARE, *Othello* (1604–05), 2.3.313.

57. Lechery, sir, it [drink] provokes, and unprovokes: it provokes the desire, but it takes away the performance. SHAKESPEARE, *Macbeth* (1605–06), 2.3.32.

58. A bumper of good liquor / Will end a contest quicker / Than justice, judge, or vicar. RICHARD BRINSLEY SHERIDAN, *The Duenna* (1775), 2.3.

59. For a bad night, a mattress of wine. SPANISH PROVERB.

60. Wine is wont to show the mind of man. THEOGNIS, *Maxims* (6th c. B.C.), 500.

61. Water taken in moderation cannot hurt anybody. MARK TWAIN, *Notebook* (1935).

62. What marriage is to morality, a properly conducted licensed liquor traffic is to sobriety. MARK TWAIN, *Notebook* (1935).

63. A drinking man's someone who wants to forget he isn't still young an' believing. TENNESSEE WILLIAMS, *Cat on a Hot Tin Roof* (1955), 2.

64. Over the bottle many a friend is found. *Yiddish Proverbs* (1949), ed. Hanan J. Ayalti.

## DRUDGERY

See 1058. Work

## 267. DRUGS

1. Opiate, n. An unlocked door in the prison of Identity. It leads into the jail yard. AMBROSE BIERCE, *The Devil's Dictionary* (1881–1911).

2. The spirit of the world, the great calm presence of the creator, comes not forth to the sorceries of opium or of wine. EMERSON, "The Poet," *Essays: Second Series* (1844).

3. Science and art are only too often a superior kind of dope, possessing this advantage over booze and morphia: that they can be indulged in with a good conscience and with the conviction that, in the process of indulging, one is leading the "higher life." ALDOUS HUXLEY, "Beliefs," *Ends and Means* (1937).

4. What is dangerous about the tranquilizers is that whatever peace of mind they bring is a packaged peace of mind. Where you buy a pill and buy peace with it, you get conditioned to cheap solutions instead of deep ones. MAX LERNER, "The Assault on the Mind," *The Unfinished Country* (1959), 2.

## DRUNKENNESS

See 266. Drinking

## 268. DULLNESS

See also 92. Boredom; 93. Bores; 445. Ignorance; 934. Stupidity

1. I have never met an author who admitted that people did not buy his book because it was dull. W. SOMERSET MAUGHAM, *The Summing Up* (1938), 46.

2. There is no law of right which conse-

crates dulness. JOHN RUSKIN, *Edinburgh Lectures* (1853), v. 1.

3. Dullness is the coming of age of seriousness. OSCAR WILDE, "Phrases and Philosophies for the Use of the Young" (1891).

## 269. DUTY

**See also 639. Obligation; 804. Responsibility**

1. Our duty is to be useful, not according to our desires but according to our powers. HENRI FRÉDÉRIC AMIEL, *Journal*, Dec. 17, 1856, tr. Mrs. Humphry Ward.

2. Rich men are to bear the infirmities of the poor. Wise men are to bear the mistakes of the ignorant. HENRY WARD BEECHER, *Proverbs from Plymouth Pulpit* (1887).

3. Nobody is bound by any obligation unless it has first been freely accepted. UGO BETTI, *The Fugitive* (1953), 3, tr. G. H. McWilliam.

4. In practice it is seldom very hard to do one's duty when one knows what it is, but it is sometimes exceedingly difficult to find this out. SAMUEL BUTLER (d. 1902), "First Principles," *Note-Books* (1912).

5. If all experiences are indifferent, that of duty is as legitimate as any other. ALBERT CAMUS, "The Absurd Man," *The Myth of Sisyphus* (1942), tr. Justin O'Brien.

6. Duty, honor! We make these words say whatever we want, the same as we do with parrots. ALFRED CAPUS, *Mariage bourgeois* (1898), 2.10.

7. The path of duty lies in the thing that is nearby, but men seek it in things far off. CHINESE PROVERB.

8. Do your duty, and leave the rest to the gods. CORNEILLE, *Horace* (1640), 2.8.

9. must's a schoolroom in the month of may. E. E. CUMMINGS, "nothing false and possible is love," *100 Selected Poems* (1959).

10. You will always find those who think they know what is your duty better than you know it. EMERSON, "Self-Reliance," *Essays: First Series* (1841).

11. Duty largely consists of pretending that the trivial is critical. JOHN FOWLES, *The Magus* (1965), 18.

12. If you are willing to forget that there is an element of duty in love and of love in duty, then it's easy to choose between the two. JEAN GIRAUDOUX, *Siegfried* (1928), 3, tr. Phyllis La Farge with Peter H. Judd.

13. What, then, is your duty? What the day demands. GOETHE, *Sprüche in Prosa*, 3.151.

14. The last pleasure in life is the sense of discharging our duty. WILLIAM HAZLITT, *Characteristics* (1823), 409.

15. The burning conviction that we have a holy duty toward others is often a way of attaching our drowning selves to a passing raft. ERIC HOFFER, *The True Believer* (1951), 1.2.11.

16. When habit has strengthened our sense of duties, they leave us no time for other things; but when young we neglect them and this gives us time for anything. THOMAS JEFFERSON, letter to Abigail Adams, Aug. 22, 1813.

17. Without duty, life is soft and boneless; it cannot hold itself together. JOSEPH JOUBERT, *Pensées* (1842), 8.52, tr. Katharine Lyttelton.

18. What is the use of such terrible diligence as many tire themselves out with, if they always postpone their exchange of smiles with Beauty and Joy to cling to irksome duties and relations? HELEN KELLER, *My Religion* (1927).

19. God obligeth no man to more than he hath given him ability to perform. *Koran* (6th and 7th c.), 65.

20. Whilst weakness and timidity keep us to our duty, virtue has often all the honour for it. LA ROCHEFOUCAULD, *Maxims* (1665), tr. Kenneth Pratt.

21. Duty then is the sublimest word in our language. Do your duty in all things. You cannot do more. You should never wish to do less. ROBERT E. LEE (1807–70), inscription beneath his bust in the Hall of Fame for Great Americans, New York University.

22. New occasions teach new duties. JAMES RUSSELL LOWELL, "The Present Crisis" (1844).

23. The cradle is rocked but the baby is pinched. MALAY PROVERB.

24. When Duty comes a-knocking at your gate, / Welcome him in; for if you bid him wait, / He will depart only to come once more / And bring seven other duties to your door. EDWIN MARKHAM, "Duty" (1922).

25. If a sense of duty tortures a man, it also enables him to achieve prodigies. H. L. MENCKEN, *Prejudices: First Series* (1919).

26. To an honest man, it is an honor to have remembered his duty. PLAUTUS, *The Three-Penny Day* (c. 194 B.C.), 3.2.

27. Conscientious men are, almost everywhere, less encouraged than tolerated. JOSEPH ROUX, *Meditations of a Parish Priest* (1886), 4.80, tr. Isabel F. Hapgood.

28. A sense of duty is useful in work, but offensive in personal relations. People wish to be liked, not to be endured with patient resignation. BERTRAND RUSSELL, *The Conquest of Happiness* (1930), 10.

29. There is no growth except in the fulfillment of obligations. SAINT-EXUPÉRY, *Flight to Arras* (1942), 20, tr. Lewis Galantière.

30. Alas! when duty grows thy law, enjoyment fades away. SCHILLER, "The Playing Boy" (1795).

31. The words of Mercury are harsh after the songs of Apollo. SHAKESPEARE, *Love's Labour's Lost* (1594–95), 5.2.40.

32. When a stupid man is doing something he is ashamed of, he always declares that it is his duty. GEORGE BERNARD SHAW, *Caesar and Cleopatra* (1906), 3.

33. There is no duty we so much underrate as the duty of being happy. ROBERT LOUIS STEVENSON, "An Apology for Idlers," *Virginibus Puerisque* (1881).

34. The paths of glory at least lead to the Grave, but the paths of duty may not get you Anywhere. JAMES THURBER, "The Patient Bloodhound," *Fables for Our Time* (1943).

35. There's life alone in duty done, / And rest alone in striving. JOHN GREENLEAF WHITTIER, "The Drovers" (1847).

36. Duty is what one expects from others, it is not what one does one's self. OSCAR WILDE, *A Woman of No Importance* (1893), 2.

# E

## EARNESTNESS
See 879. Seriousness

## 270. EARTH
See also 174. Conservation; 413. The Heavens; 616. Nature; 1060. World

1. Touch the earth, love the earth, honour the earth, her plains, her valleys, her hills, and her seas; rest your spirit in her solitary places. HENRY BESTON, "Orion Rises on the Dunes," *The Outermost House* (1928).

2. Earth being so good, would Heaven seem best? ROBERT BROWNING, "The Last Ride Together," *Men and Women* (1855), 9.

3. Earth, with her thousand voices, praises God. SAMUEL TAYLOR COLERIDGE, "Hymn Before Sunrise" (1802).

4. We are so often ashamed of the Earth —the soil of it, the sweat of it, the good common coarseness of it. To us in our fine raiment and soft manners, it seems indelicate. DAVID GRAYSON, *Adventures in Contentment* (1907), 6.

5. Let me enjoy the earth no less / Because the all-enacting Might / That fashioned forth its loveliness / Had other aims than my delight. THOMAS HARDY, "Let Me Enjoy," *Time's Laughingstocks and Other Verses* (1909).

6. The earth is given as a common stock for man to labor and live on. THOMAS JEFFERSON, letter to James Madison, 1785.

7. That the sky is brighter than the earth means little unless the earth itself is appreciated and enjoyed. Its beauty loved gives the right to aspire to the radiance of the sunrise and the stars. HELEN KELLER, *My Religion* (1927).

8. The earth is like the breasts of a woman: useful as well as pleasing. NIETZSCHE, "On Old and New Tablets," *Thus Spoke Zarathustra* (1883–92), 3, tr. Walter Kaufmann.

## EASE
See 325. Facility; 530. Leisure

## 271. EAST AND WEST
See also 496. International Relations

1. The main barrier between East and West today is that the white man is not willing to give up his superiority and the colored man is no longer willing to endure his inferiority. PEARL S. BUCK, *What America Means to Me* (1943), 2.

2. Oh, East is East, and West is West, and never the twain shall meet, / Till Earth and Sky stand presently at God's great Judgment Seat. RUDYARD KIPLING, "The Ballad of East and West" (1899).

3. The West can teach the East how to

get a living, but the East must eventually be asked to show the West how to live. TEHYI HSIEH, *Chinese Epigrams Inside Out and Proverbs* (1948), 588.

### EASTER

See 418. Holidays

### 272. EATING

See also 186. Cooks and Cooking; 352. Food; 401. Greed; 435. Hunger; 637. Obesity; 974. Tipping; 1021. Vegetarianism

1. Every man should eat and drink, and enjoy the good of all his labour, it is the gift of God. *Bible*, Ecclesiastes 3:13.

2. Tell me what you eat and I will tell you who you are. ANTHELME BRILLAT-SAVARIN, *Physiologie du goût* (1825), 4.

3. A full gut supports moral precepts. BURMESE PROVERBS (1962), 109, ed. Hla Pe.

4. Man is the only animal that can remain on friendly terms with the victims he intends to eat until he eats them. SAMUEL BUTLER (d. 1902), "Mind and Matter," *Note-Books* (1912).

5. All eating is a kind of proselytising—a kind of dogmatising—a maintaining that the eater's way of looking at things is better than the eatee's. SAMUEL BUTLER (d. 1902), "Mind and Matter," *Note-Books* (1912).

6. That all-softening, overpowering knell, / The Tocsin of the Soul—the dinner-bell. BYRON, *Don Juan* (1819–24), 5.49.

7. Spread the table and contention will cease. ENGLISH PROVERB.

8. The glutton digs his grave with his teeth. ENGLISH PROVERB.

9. When a man's stomach is full it makes no difference whether he is rich or poor. EURIPIDES, *Electra* (413 B.C.), tr. Emily Townsend Vermeule.

10. A good meal ought to begin with hunger. FRENCH PROVERB.

11. To eat well is no whoredom, and to starve is no gentility. THOMAS FULLER, M.D., *Gnomologia* (1732), 5159.

12. I have known many meat eaters to be far more non-violent than vegetarians. MOHANDAS K. GANDHI, *Non-Violence in Peace and War* (1948), 1.323.

13. A gourmet is just a glutton with brains. PHILLIP W. HABERMAN, JR., "How To Be a Calorie Chiseler," *Vogue*, Jan. 15, 1961.

14. Life, within doors, has few pleasanter prospects than a neatly arranged and well-provisioned breakfast-table. NATHANIEL HAWTHORNE, *The House of the Seven Gables* (1851), 7.

15. Where the guests at a gathering are well-acquainted, they eat 20 per cent more than they otherwise would. EDGAR WATSON HOWE, *Country Town Sayings* (1911).

16. A man may be a pessimistic determinist before lunch and an optimistic believer in the will's freedom after it. ALDOUS HUXLEY, "Pascal," *Do What You Will* (1929).

17. The whole of nature, as has been said, is a conjugation of the verb to eat, in the active and passive. WILLIAM RALPH INGE, "Confessio Fidei," *Outspoken Essays: Second Series* (1922).

18. A man seldom thinks with more earnestness of anything than he does of his dinner. SAMUEL JOHNSON, quoted by Hester Lynch Piozzi in *Anecdotes of Samuel Johnson* (1786).

19. A man is in general better pleased when he has a good dinner upon his table, than when his wife talks Greek. SAMUEL JOHNSON, quoted in Birkbeck Hill's *Johnsonian Miscellanies* (1897), v. 2.

20. If you have formed the habit of checking on every new diet that comes along, you will find that, mercifully, they all blur together, leaving you with only one definite piece of information: french-fried potatoes are out. JEAN KERR, "Aunt Jean's Marshmallow Fudge Diet," *Please Don't Eat the Daisies* (1957).

21. I hate a man who swallows [his food], affecting not to know what he is eating. I suspect his taste in higher matters. CHARLES LAMB, "Grace before Meat," *Essays of Elia* (1823).

22. He that eateth well, drinketh well; he that drinketh well, sleepeth well; he that sleepeth well, sinneth not; he that sinneth not goeth straight through Purgatory to Paradise. WILLIAM LITHGOW, *Rare Adventures* (1614).

23. Americans can eat garbage, provided you sprinkle it liberally with ketchup, mustard, chili sauce, tobasco sauce, cayenne pepper, or any other condiment which destroys the original flavor of the dish. HENRY

MILLER, "The Staff of Life," *Remember to Remember* (1947).

24. The art of dining well is no slight art, the pleasure not a slight pleasure. MONTAIGNE, "Of experience," *Essays* (1580–88), tr. Charles Cotton and W. C. Hazlitt.

25. Strange to see how a good dinner and feasting reconciles everybody. SAMUEL PEPYS, *Diary*, Nov. 9, 1665.

26. For two nights the glutton cannot sleep for thinking, first on an empty, and next on a sated stomach. SA'DI, *Gulistan* (1258), 8.54, tr. James Ross.

27. There is nothing to which men, while they have food and drink, cannot reconcile themselves. GEORGE SANTAYANA, *Interpretations of Poetry and Religion* (1900).

28. A dinner lubricates business. WILLIAM SCOTT, quoted in James Boswell's *Life of Samuel Johnson* (1791), 8.

29. Serenely full, the epicure would say, / Fate cannot harm me, I have dined today. SYDNEY SMITH, quoted in Lady S. Holland's *Memoir* (1855), v. 1.11.

30. He who distinguishes the true savor of his food can never be a glutton; he who does not cannot be otherwise. THOREAU, "Higher Laws," *Walden* (1854).

31. Seeing is deceiving. It's eating that's believing. JAMES THURBER, *Further Fables for Our Time* (1956).

32. One cannot think well, love well, sleep well, if one has not dined well. VIRGINIA WOOLF, *A Room of One's Own* (1929), 1.

## 273. EAVESDROPPING

1. Listeners ne'er hear good of themselves. JOHN RAY, *English Proverbs* (1670).

## 274. ECCENTRICITY

See also 467. Individuality; 655. Originality

1. We might define an eccentric as a man who is a law unto himself, and a crank as one who, having determined what the law is, insists on laying it down to others. LOUIS KRONENBERGER, *Company Manners* (1954), 3.3.

2. Eccentricity has always abounded when and where strength of character has abounded; and the amount of eccentricity in a society has generally been proportional to the amount of genius, mental vigor, and moral courage which it contained. JOHN STUART MILL, *On Liberty* (1859), 3.

3. More cranks take up unfashionable errors than unfashionable truths. BERTRAND RUSSELL, "An Outline of Intellectual Rubbish," *Unpopular Essays* (1950).

## 275. ECONOMICS

See also 99. Budget; 102. Business and Commerce; 958. Taxes

1. I don't think you can spend yourself rich. GEORGE HUMPHREY, news summaries, Jan. 28, 1957.

2. I do not believe that Washington should do for the people what they can do for themselves through local and private effort. JOHN F. KENNEDY, campaign address, Associated Business Publications Conference, New York City, Oct. 12, 1960.

3. Economic growth without social progress lets the great majority of the people remain in poverty, while a privileged few reap the benefits of rising abundance. JOHN F. KENNEDY, message to Congress on the Inter-American Fund for Social Progress, March 14, 1961.

4. Just as men cannot now escape taking on collective responsibility for peace, neither can they escape taking on collective responsibility for economic plenty. MAX LERNER, "The Consequences of the Atom," *Actions and Passions* (1949).

5. If being a communist or being a capitalist or being a socialist is a crime, first you have to study which of those systems is the most criminal. And then you'll be slow to say which one should be in jail. MALCOLM X, *Malcolm X Speaks* (1965), 10.

6. the high cost of / living isnt so bad if you / dont have to pay for it. DON MARQUIS, "the merry flea," *Archy and Mehitabel* (1927).

7. It is not possible for this nation to be at once politically internationalist and economically isolationist. This is just as insane as asking one Siamese twin to high dive while the other plays the piano. ADLAI STEVENSON, speech, New Orleans, La., Oct. 10, 1952.

8. With the exception of the instinct of self-preservation, the propensity for emulation is probably the strongest and most alert and persistent of the economic motives proper. THORSTEIN VEBLEN, *The Theory of the Leisure Class* (1899), 5.

## ECONOMY

See 275. Economics; 970. Thrift

## 276. ECSTASY

See also 407. Happiness; 609. Mysticism

1. Take all away from me, but leave me Ecstasy, / And I am richer then than all my Fellow Men—. EMILY DICKINSON, poem (c. 1885).

2. To be bewitched is not to be saved, though all the magicians and aesthetes in the world should pronounce it to be so. GEORGE SANTAYANA, *The Life of Reason: Reason in Art* (1905–06), 9.

## EDITORS AND EDITING

See 758. Publishing

## 277. EDUCATION

See also 520. Knowledge;
529. Learning; 566. Mathematics;
842. Scholars and Scholarship;
959. Teaching; 981. Training

1. Nothing in education is so astonishing as the amount of ignorance it accumulates in the form of inert facts. HENRY ADAMS, *The Education of Henry Adams* (1907), 25.

2. Education makes a greater difference between man and man than nature has made between man and brute. JOHN ADAMS, letter to Abigail Adams, Oct. 29, 1776.

3. Education is an ornament in prosperity and a refuge in adversity. ARISTOTLE (4th c. B.C.), quoted in Diogenes Laertius' *Lives and Opinions of Eminent Philosophers* (3rd c. A.D.), tr. R. D. Hicks.

4. The roots of education are bitter, but the fruit is sweet. ARISTOTLE (4th c. B.C.), quoted in Diogenes Laertius' *Lives and Opinions of Eminent Philosophers* (3rd c. A.D.), tr. R. D. Hicks.

5. It takes most men five years to recover from a college education, and to learn that poetry is as vital to thinking as knowledge. BROOKS ATKINSON, "August 31," *Once Around the Sun* (1951).

6. The test and the use of man's education is that he finds pleasure in the exercise of his mind. JACQUES BARZUN, "Science vs. the Humanities: A Truce to the Nonsense on Both Sides," *Saturday Evening Post*, May 3, 1958.

7. Education, n. That which discloses to the wise and disguises from the foolish their lack of understanding. AMBROSE BIERCE, *The Devil's Dictionary* (1881–1911).

8. Education makes a people easy to lead, but difficult to drive; easy to govern, but impossible to enslave. LORD BROUGHAM, speech, House of Commons, Jan. 29, 1828.

9. There's a new tribunal now / Higher than God's—the educated man's! ROBERT BROWNING, "The Pope," *The Ring and the Book* (1868–69).

10. The grand result of schooling is a mind with just vision to discern, with free force to do: the grand schoolmaster is Practice. THOMAS CARLYLE, "Corn-Law Rhymes" (1832).

11. By nature all men are alike, but by education widely different. CHINESE PROVERB.

12. Children have to be educated, but they have also to be left to educate themselves. ERNEST DIMNET, *The Art of Thinking* (1928), 2.5.

13. A school is a place through which you have to pass before entering life, but where the teaching proper does not prepare you for life. ERNEST DIMNET, *The Art of Thinking* (1928), 2.5.

14. The function of the university is not simply to teach bread-winning, or to furnish teachers for the public schools or to be a centre of polite society; it is, above all, to be the organ of that fine adjustment between real life and the growing knowledge of life, an adjustment which forms the secret of civilization. W. E. B. DU BOIS, *The Souls of Black Folk* (1903), 5.

15. How is it that little children are so intelligent and men so stupid? It must be education that does it. ALEXANDRE DUMAS FILS, quoted in L. Treich's *L'Esprit d'Alexandre Dumas*.

16. Degrees is good things because they

livils all ranks. FINLEY PETER DUNNE, "Colleges and Degrees," *Mr. Dooley's Opinions* (1901).

17. Idjacation is something that a man has to fight f'r an' pull out iv its hole by th' hair iv its head. FINLEY PETER DUNNE, "Mr. Carnegie's Gift," *Mr. Dooley's Opinions* (1901).

18. Ye can lade a man up to th' university, but ye can't make him think. FINLEY PETER DUNNE, "Mr. Carnegie's Gift," *Mr. Dooley's Opinions* (1901).

19. Knowledge has outstripped character development, and the young today are given an education rather than an upbringing. ILYA EHRENBURG, "What I Have Learned," *Saturday Review*, Sept. 30, 1967.

20. The things taught in colleges and schools are not an education, but the means of education. EMERSON, *Journals*, 1831.

21. Meek young men grow up in colleges and believe it is their duty to accept the views which books have given, and grow up slaves. EMERSON, *Journals*, 1836.

22. We are shut up in schools and college recitation rooms for ten or fifteen years, and come out at last with a bellyful of words and do not know a thing. EMERSON, *Journals*, 1839.

23. What we do not call education is more precious than that which we call so. EMERSON, "Spiritual Laws," *Essays: First Series* (1841).

24. Only the educated are free. EPICTETUS, *Discourses* (2nd c.), 2.1.

25. Whoso neglects learning in his youth, loses the past and is dead for the future. EURIPIDES, *Phrixus* (c. 412 B.C.), 927, tr. M. H. Morgan.

26. An education which does not cultivate the will is an education that depraves the mind. ANATOLE FRANCE, *The Crime of Sylvestre Bonnard* (1881), 2, tr. Lafcadio Hearn.

27. Education is the ability to listen to almost anything without losing your temper or your self-confidence. ROBERT FROST, *Reader's Digest*, April 1960.

28. Education doesn't change life much. It just lifts trouble to a higher plane of regard. ROBERT FROST, *Quote*, July 9, 1961.

29. Learning makes a man fit company for himself. THOMAS FULLER, MD., *Gnomologia* (1732), 3163.

30. I'm very good at integral and differential calculus; / I know the scientific names of beings animalculous. W. S. GILBERT, *The Pirates of Penzance* (1879), 1.

31. Education makes us more stupid than the brutes. A thousand voices call to us on every hand, but our ears are stopped with wisdom. JEAN GIRAUDOUX, *The Enchanted* (1933), 2, adapted by Maurice Valency.

32. They teach in academies far too many things, and far too much that is useless. GOETHE, quoted in Johann Peter Eckermann's *Conversations with Goethe*, Feb. 24, 1824.

33. If you feel that you have both feet planted on level ground, then the university has failed you. ROBERT GOHEEN, *Time*, June 23, 1961.

34. There *is* only one curriculum, no matter what the method of education: what is basic and universal in human experience and practice, the underlying structure of culture. PAUL GOODMAN, *Growing Up Absurd* (1960), 4.6.

35. The philosophic aim of education must be to get each one out of his isolated class and into the one humanity. PAUL GOODMAN, *Compulsory Mis-education* (1964).

36. It is better to be able neither to read nor write than to be able to do nothing else. WILLIAM HAZLITT, "On the Ignorance of the Learned," *Table Talk* (1821–22).

37. That which any one has been long learning unwillingly, he unlearns with proportionable eagerness and haste. WILLIAM HAZLITT, "On Personal Character," *The Plain Speaker* (1826).

38. Much learning does not teach understanding. HERACLITUS, *Fragments* (c. 500 B.C.), 6, tr. Philip Wheelwright.

39. The main part of intellectual education is not the acquisition of facts but learning how to make facts live. OLIVER WENDELL HOLMES, JR., speech, Harvard Law School Association, Nov. 5, 1886.

40. Education is what you learn in books, and nobody knows you know it but your teacher. VIRGINIA CARY HUDSON, *O Ye Jigs & Juleps!* (1962).

41. That man, I think, has had a liberal education, who has been so trained in youth that his body is the ready servant of his will. THOMAS HENRY HUXLEY, "A Liberal Education" (1868).

42. Colleges are places where pebbles

are polished and diamonds are dimmed. ROBERT G. INGERSOLL, *Prose-Poems and Selections* (1884).

43. State a moral case to a ploughman and a professor. The former will decide it as well, and often better than the latter, because he has not been led astray by artificial rules. THOMAS JEFFERSON, letter to Peter Carr, Aug. 10, 1787.

44. Education is not a *product:* mark, diploma, job, money—in that order; it is a *process*, a never-ending one. BEL KAUFMAN, television interview, 1967.

45. The goal of education is the advancement of knowledge and the dissemination of truth. JOHN F. KENNEDY, address, Harvard University, Cambridge, Mass., 1956.

46. I find the three major administrative problems on a campus are sex for the students, athletics for the alumni, and parking for the faculty. CLARK KERR, *Time*, Nov. 17, 1958.

47. Our schools have become vast factories for the manufacture of robots. We no longer send our young to them primarily to be taught and given the tools of thought, no longer primarily to be informed and acquire knowledge; but to be "socialized." ROBERT LINDNER, title essay, *Must You Conform?* (1956).

48. A single conversation across the table with a wise man is better than ten years' mere study of books. LONGFELLOW, *Hyperion* (1839), 1.7.

49. The world no doubt is the best or most serviceable schoolmaster; but the world's curriculum does not include Latin and Greek. E. V. LUCAS, *Reading, Writing, and Remembering* (1932), 3.

50. Education in a technological world of replaceable and expendable parts is neuter. MARSHALL MC LUHAN, "Co-Education," *The Mechanical Bride* (1951).

51. Education then, beyond all other devices of human origin, is a great equalizer of the conditions of men,—the balance wheel of the social machinery. HORACE MANN, report as Secretary of Massachusetts State Board of Education, 1848.

52. School days, I believe, are the unhappiest in the whole span of human existence. They are full of dull, unintelligible tasks, new and unpleasant ordinances, brutal violations of common sense and common decency. H. L. MENCKEN, "Travail," *The Baltimore Evening Sun*, Oct. 8, 1928.

53. Human nature is not a machine to be built after a model, and set to do exactly the work prescribed for it, but a tree, which requires to grow and develop itself on all sides, according to the tendency of the inward forces which make it a living thing. JOHN STUART MILL, *On Liberty* (1859), 3.

54. Oh, children, growing up to be / Adventurers into sophistry, / Forbear, forbear to be of those / That read the rood to learn the rose. EDNA ST. VINCENT MILLAY, untitled poem, *Mine the Harvest* (1954).

55. The aim of the college, for the individual student, is to eliminate the need in his life for the college; the task is to help him become a self-educating man. C. WRIGHT MILLS, "Mass Society and Liberal Education," *Power, Politics and People* (1963).

56. Once you have the cap and gown all you need do is open your mouth. Whatever nonsense you talk becomes wisdom and all the rubbish, good sense. MOLIÈRE, *The Imaginary Invalid* (1673), 3, tr. John Wood.

57. We only labor to stuff the memory, and leave the conscience and the understanding unfurnished and void. MONTAIGNE, "Of pedantry," *Essays* (1580–88), tr. Charles Cotton and W. C. Hazlitt.

58. A man must always study, but he must not always go to school: what a contemptible thing is an old abecedarian! MONTAIGNE, "All things have their season," *Essays* (1580–88), tr. Charles Cotton and W. C. Hazlitt.

59. Higher education is booming in the United States; the Gross National Mind is mounting along with the Gross National Product. MALCOLM MUGGERIDGE, "The Gross National Mind," *The Most of Malcolm Muggeridge* (1966).

60. Education produces natural intuitions, and natural intuitions are erased by education. PASCAL, *Pensées* (1670), 95, tr. W. F. Trotter.

61. The direction in which education starts a man, will determine his future life. PLATO, *The Republic* (4th c. B.C.), 4, tr. Benjamin Jowett.

62. Knowledge which is acquired under compulsion obtains no hold on the mind. PLATO, *The Republic* (4th c. B.C.), 7, tr. Benjamin Jowett.

63. Nature without learning is blind,

learning apart from nature is fractional, and practice in the absence of both is aimless. PLUTARCH, "The Education of Children," *Moralia* (c. A.D. 100), tr. Moses Hadas.

64. It is only the ignorant who despise education. PUBLILIUS SYRUS, *Moral Sayings* (1st c. B.C.), 571, tr. Darius Lyman.

65. There is nothing so stupid as an educated man, if you get off the thing that he was educated in. WILL ROGERS, quoted in Will Durant's *On the Meaning of Life* (1932).

66. The vine that has been made to bear fruit in the spring, withers and dies before autumn. ROUSSEAU, *Émile* (1762), 4.

67. Education, properly understood, is that which teaches discernment. JOSEPH ROUX, *Meditations of a Parish Priest* (1886), 7.7, tr. Isabel F. Hapgood.

68. Education is the leading human souls to what is best, and making what is best out of them; and these two objects are always attainable together, and by the same means; the training which makes men happiest in themselves also makes them most serviceable to others. JOHN RUSKIN, *The Stones of Venice* (1851–53), 3.

69. Education, which was at first made universal in order that all might be able to read and write, has been found capable of serving quite other purposes. By instilling nonsense it unifies populations and generates collective enthusiasm. BERTRAND RUSSELL, "An Outline of Intellectual Rubbish," *Unpopular Essays* (1950).

70. The great difficulty in education is to get experience out of ideas. GEORGE SANTAYANA, *The Life of Reason: Reason in Common Sense* (1905–06).

71. Education, like neurosis, begins at home. MILTON R. SAPIRSTEIN, *Paradoxes of Everyday Life* (1955), 2.

72. What we call education and culture is for the most part nothing but the substitution of reading for experience, of literature for life, of the obsolete fictitious for the contemporary real. GEORGE BERNARD SHAW, "Epistle Dedicatory," *Man and Superman* (1903).

73. One by one the solid scholars / Get the degrees, the jobs, the dollars. W. D. SNODGRASS, "April Inventory" (1959).

74. I have learned much from my teachers, and from my colleagues more than from my teachers, and from my students more than from all. Haggadah, *Palestinian Talmud* (4th c.).

75. The schools of the country are its future in miniature. TEHYI HSIEH, *Chinese Epigrams Inside Out and Proverbs* (1948), 22.

76. What does education often do? It makes a straight-cut ditch of a free, meandering brook. THOREAU, *Journal*, 1850.

77. In the first place God made idiots. This was for practice. Then he made school boards. MARK TWAIN, "Pudd'nhead Wilson's New Calendar," *Following the Equator* (1897), 2.25.

78. Education consists mainly in what we have unlearned. MARK TWAIN, *Notebook* (1935).

79. Genius lasts longer than Beauty. That accounts for the fact that we all take such pains to overeducate ourselves. OSCAR WILDE, *The Picture of Dorian Gray* (1891), 1.

## EFFECT

See 108. Cause and Effect

## 278. EFFICIENCY

See also 579. Method

1. A new broom is good for three days. ITALIAN PROVERB.

2. Superfluous branches / We lop away, that bearing boughs may live. SHAKESPEARE, *Richard II* (1595–96), 3.4.63.

## 279. EFFORT

See also 243. Difficulty; 289. Enterprise; 679. Perseverance; 1058. Work

1. They that sow in tears shall reap in joy. *Bible*, Psalms 126:5.

2. By labor fire is got out of a stone. DUTCH PROVERB.

3. The bitter and the sweet come from the outside, the hard from within, from one's own efforts. EINSTEIN, *Out of My Later Years* (1950), 2.

4. Elbow-grease is the best polish. ENGLISH PROVERB.

5. Nothing is got without pain but dirt and long nails. ENGLISH PROVERB.

6. Try first thyself, and after call in God; /

For to the worker God himself lends aid. EURIPIDES, *Hippolytus* (428 B.C.), 435, tr. M. H. Morgan.

7. Much effort, much prosperity. EURIPIDES, *The Suppliant Women* (c. 421 B.C.), tr. Frank W. Jones.

8. Care and diligence bring luck. THOMAS FULLER, M.D., *Gnomologia* (1732), 1057.

9. He that would have the fruit must climb the tree. THOMAS FULLER, M.D., *Gnomologia* (1732), 2366.

10. To win one's joy through struggle is better than to yield to melancholy. ANDRÉ GIDE, *Journals*, May 12, 1927, tr. Justin O'Brien.

11. Few things are impossible to diligence and skill. SAMUEL JOHNSON, *Rasselas* (1759), 12.

12. When we do the best that we can, we never know what miracle is wrought in our life, or in the life of another. HELEN KELLER, *Out of the Dark* (1913).

13. Few things are of themselves impossible, and we lack the application to make them a success rather than the means. LA ROCHEFOUCAULD, *Maxims* (1665), tr. Kenneth Pratt.

14. He who limps is still walking. STANISLAW LEC, *Unkempt Thoughts* (1962), tr. Jacek Galazka.

15. Despite the success cult, men are most deeply moved not by the reaching of the goal but by the grandness of effort involved in getting there—or failing to get there. MAX LERNER, "Man's Belief in Himself," *The Unfinished Country* (1959), 5.

16. We seldom break our leg so long as life continues a toilsome upward climb. The danger comes when we begin to take things easily and choose the convenient paths. NIETZSCHE, *Miscellaneous Maxims and Opinions* (1879), 266, tr. Paul V. Cohn.

17. Effort is only effort when it begins to hurt. JOSÉ ORTEGA Y GASSET, "In Search of Goethe from Within, Letter to a German," *Partisan Review*, December 1949, tr. William R. Trask.

18. The struggle alone pleases us, not the victory. PASCAL, *Pensées* (1670), 135, tr. W. F. Trotter.

19. Life has not taught me to expect nothing, but she has taught me not to expect success to be the inevitable result of my endeavors. She taught me to seek sustenance from the endeavor itself, but to leave the result to God. ALAN PATON, "The Challenge of Fear," *Saturday Review*, Sept. 9, 1967.

20. No one knows what he can do till he tries. PUBLILIUS SYRUS, *Moral Sayings* (1st c. B.C.), 786, tr. Darius Lyman.

21. Nothing can come of nothing. SHAKESPEARE, *King Lear* (1605–06), 1.1.91.

22. To travel hopefully is a better thing than to arrive, and the true success is to labor. ROBERT LOUIS STEVENSON, "El Dorado," *Virginibus Puerisque* (1881).

## EGOTISM

**See 865. Self-importance**

## ELECTIONS

**See 1030. Voting**

## 280. ELEGANCE

**See also 335. Fashion; 935. Style; 957. Taste**

1. Elegance is good taste *plus* a dash of daring. CARMEL SNOW, *The World of Carmel Snow* (1962).

2. The only real elegance is in the mind; if you've got that, the rest really comes from it. DIANA VREELAND, *Newsweek*, Dec. 10, 1962.

## 281. ELOQUENCE

**See also 683. Persuasion; 757. Public Speaking; 916. Speaking**

1. Everything that steel achieves in war can be won in politics by eloquence. DEMETRIUS (4th–3rd c. B.C.), quoted in Diogenes Laertius' *Lives and Opinions of Eminent Philosophers* (3rd c. A.D.), tr. R. D. Hicks.

2. The eloquent man is he who is no beautiful speaker, but who is inwardly and desperately drunk with a certain belief. EMERSON, *Journals*, 1845.

3. He that has no silver in his purse should have silver on his tongue. THOMAS FULLER, M.D., *Gnomologia* (1732), 2149.

4. There is no more sovereign eloquence

than the truth in indignation. VICTOR HUGO, "Marius," *Les Misérables* (1862), 4.1, tr. Charles E. Wilbour.

5. True eloquence consists in saying all that should be said, and that only. LA ROCHEFOUCAULD, *Maxims* (1665), tr. Kenneth Pratt.

6. Eloquence lies as much in the tone of the voice, in the eyes, and in the speaker's manner, as in his choice of words. LA ROCHEFOUCAULD, *Maxims* (1665), tr. Kenneth Pratt.

7. Today it is not the classroom nor the classics which are the models of eloquence, but the ad agencies. MARSHALL MC LUHAN, "Plain Talk," *The Mechanical Bride* (1951).

8. Eloquence.—It requires the pleasant and the real; but the pleasant must itself be drawn from the true. PASCAL, *Pensées* (1670), 25, tr. W. F. Trotter.

9. Continous eloquence wearies. PASCAL, *Pensées* (1670), 355, tr. W. F. Trotter.

10. A thing said walks in immortality / if it has been said well. PINDAR, *Odes* (5th c. B.C.), Isthmia 4, tr. Richmond Lattimore.

11. Eloquence is a republican art, as conversation is an aristocratic one. GEORGE SANTAYANA, *Character and Opinion in the United States* (1921), 1.

12. Eloquence wins its great and enduring fame quite as much from the benches of our opponents as from those of our friends. TACITUS, *A Dialogue on Oratory* (c. A.D. 81), 34, tr. Alfred J. Church and William J. Brodribb.

## EMBARRASSMENT

**See 886. Shame**

## EMINENCE

**See 330. Fame; 384. Glory; 938. Success**

## 282. EMOTIONS

**See also 21. Affection; 167. Conflict, Inner; 410. Hatred; 548. Love; 668. Passion; 876. Sensibility; 962. Temperament**

1. A man's heart changes his countenance, either for good or for evil. *Apocrypha*, Ecclesiasticus 13:25.

2. We are adhering to life now with our last muscle—the heart. DJUNA BARNES, *Nightwood* (1937).

3. No emotion, any more than a wave, can long retain its own individual form. HENRY WARD BEECHER, *Proverbs from Plymouth Pulpit* (1887).

4. It is not our exalted feelings, it is our sentiments that build the necessary home. ELIZABETH BOWEN, *The Death of the Heart* (1938), 2.2.

5. Men live but by intervals of reason under the sovereignty of humour [caprice] and passion. SIR THOMAS BROWNE, *A Letter to a Friend* (1690).

6. We have hearts within, / Warm, live, improvident, indecent hearts. ELIZABETH BARRETT BROWNING, *Aurora Leigh* (1856), 3.461.

7. Where the heart lies, let the brain lie also. ROBERT BROWNING, "One Word More," *Men and Women* (1855), 1.

8. Man is, and was always, a block-head and dullard; much readier to feel and digest, than to think and consider. THOMAS CARLYLE, *Sartor Resartus* (1833–34), 1.8.

9. The heart has such an influence over the understanding that it is worth while to engage it in our interest. LORD CHESTERFIELD, *Letters to His Son*, March 9, 1748.

10. Men, as well as women, are much oftener led by their hearts than by their understandings. LORD CHESTERFIELD, *Letters to His Son*, June 21, 1748.

11. It is as healthy to enjoy sentiment as to enjoy jam. G. K. CHESTERTON, "On Sentiment," *Generally Speaking* (1928).

12. Let my heart be wise. / It is the gods' best gift. EURIPIDES, *Medea* (431 B.C.), tr. Rex Warner.

13. The emotions may be endless. The more we express them, the more we may have to express. E. M. FORSTER, "Notes on the English Character," *Abinger Harvest* (1936).

14. The heart errs like the head; its errors are not any the less fatal, and we have more trouble getting free of them because of their sweetness. ANATOLE FRANCE, *Little Pierre* (1918), 5.

15. Seeing's believing, but feeling's the truth. THOMAS FULLER, M.D., *Gnomologia* (1732), 4087.

16. The important thing is being capable of emotions, but to experience only *one's*

*own* would be a sorry limitation. ANDRÉ GIDE, *Journals*, May 12, 1892, tr. Justin O'Brien.

17. All the knowledge I possess everyone else can acquire, but my heart is all my own. GOETHE, *The Sorrows of Young Werther* (1774), 2, May 9, 1772, tr. Victor Lange.

18. Every person's feelings have a front-door and a side-door by which they may be entered. OLIVER WENDELL HOLMES, SR., *The Autocrat of the Breakfast Table* (1858), 6.

19. Emotion is always new and the word has always served; therein lies the difficulty of expressing emotion. VICTOR HUGO, *Les Travailleurs de la mer* (1866), 3.1.2.

20. Blossoms are scattered by the wind and the wind cares nothing, but the blossoms of the heart no wind can touch. YOSHIDA KENKŌ, "The Inevitable Way," *The Harvest of Leisure (Tsure-Zure Gusa*, c. 1330–35), tr. Ryukichi Kurata.

21. The head does not know how to play the part of the heart for long. LA ROCHEFOUCAULD, *Maxims* (1665), tr. Kenneth Pratt.

22. The human heart is like a ship on a stormy sea driven about by winds blowing from all four corners of heaven. MARTIN LUTHER, preface to his translation of the *Psalms* (1534).

23. Time cools, time clarifies; no mood can be maintained quite unaltered through the course of hours. THOMAS MANN, *The Magic Mountain* (1924), 7.9, tr. H. T. Lowe-Porter.

24. Pity me that the heart is slow to learn / What the swift mind beholds at every turn. EDNA ST. VINCENT MILLAY, *Sonnets* (1941), 29.

25. One ought to hold on to one's heart; for if one lets it go, one soon loses control of the head too. NIETZSCHE, "On the Pitying," *Thus Spoke Zarathustra* (1883–92), 2, tr. Walter Kaufmann.

26. The heart has its reasons which reason does not know. PASCAL, *Pensées* (1670), 277.

27. The direct speech of feeling is allegorical and cannot be replaced by anything. BORIS PASTERNAK, *Safe Conduct* (1931), 2.7, tr. Beatrice Scott.

28. In a full heart there is room for everything, and in an empty heart there is room for nothing. ANTONIO PORCHIA, *Voces* (1968), tr. W. S. Merwin.

29. All emotions are pure which gather you and lift you up; that emotion is impure which seizes only *one* side of your being and so distorts you. RAINER MARIA RILKE, *Letters to a Young Poet*, Nov. 4, 1904, tr. M. D. Herter Norton.

30. Reason guides but a small part of man, and that the least interesting. The rest obeys feeling, true or false, and passion, good or bad. JOSEPH ROUX, *Meditations of a Parish Priest* (1886), 4.95, tr. Isabel F. Hapgood.

31. Nothing vivifies, and nothing kills, like the emotions. JOSEPH ROUX, *Meditations of a Parish Priest* (1886), 5.2, tr. Isabel F. Hapgood.

32. We know too much and feel too little. At least we feel too little of those creative emotions from which a good life springs. BERTRAND RUSSELL, "The Role of Individuality," *Authority and the Individual* (1949).

33. Whatever makes an impression on the heart seems lovely in the eye. SA'DI, *Gulistan* (1258), 5.1, tr. James Ross.

34. It is only with the heart that one can see rightly; what is essential is invisible to the eye. SAINT-EXUPÉRY, *The Little Prince* (1943), 21, tr. Katherine Woods.

35. Though in itself emotion counts for little, processes of mind must make good through emotion. SAINT-EXUPÉRY, *The Wisdom of the Sands* (1948), 23, tr. Stuart Gilbert.

36. Emotion is primarily about nothing, and much of it remains about nothing to the end. GEORGE SANTAYANA, *The Life of Reason: Reason in Art* (1905–06), 4.

37. The heart is forever inexperienced. THOREAU, "Rumors from an Aeolian Harp," *A Week on the Concord and Merrimack Rivers* (1849).

38. Emotion has taught mankind to reason. VAUVENARGUES, *Reflections and Maxims* (1746), 154, tr. F. G. Stevens.

39. Life is the enjoyment of emotion, derived from the past and aimed at the future. ALFRED NORTH WHITEHEAD, *Modes of Thought* (1938).

40. The secret of life is never to have an emotion that is unbecoming. OSCAR WILDE, *A Woman of No Importance* (1893), 3.

41. The heart is half a prophet. *Yiddish Proverbs* (1949), ed. Hanan J. Ayalti.

**EMPATHY**
See 953. Sympathy;
1001. Understanding Others

**EMULATION**
See 449. Imitation

**ENDEAVOR**
See 279. Effort

## 283. ENDING
See also 73. Beginning;
74. Beginning and Ending;
284. Ends; 570. Means and Ends

1. The unfinished is nothing. HENRI FRÉDÉRIC AMIEL, *Journal*, Nov. 25, 1861.

2. A finished product is one that has already seen its better days. ART LINKLETTER, *A Child's Garden of Misinformation* (1965), 9.

3. God alone can finish. JOHN RUSKIN, *Modern Painters* (1843–60), v. 3, 4.9.4.

4. It's the job that's never started as takes longest to finish. J. R. R. TOLKIEN, *The Fellowship of the Ring* (1954), 2.7.

## 284. ENDS
See also 283. Ending; 570. Means and Ends;
601. Motives; 765. Purpose

1. Whatsoever thou takest in hand, remember the end, and thou shalt never do amiss. *Apocrypha*, Ecclesiasticus 7:36.

2. Men achieve a certain greatness unawares, when working to another aim. EMERSON, "Considerations by the Way," *The Conduct of Life* (1860).

3. Not every end is the goal. The end of a melody is not its goal, and yet if a melody has not reached its end, it has not reached its goal. A parable. NIETZSCHE, *The Wanderer and His Shadow* (1880), 204, tr. Paul V. Cohn.

4. What is there more of in the world than anything else? Ends. CARL SANDBURG, *The People, Yes* (1936).

## 285. ENDURANCE
See also 670. Patience; 679. Perseverance;
800. Resignation; 930. Stoicism;
949. Survival

1. People are too durable, that's their main trouble. They can do too much to themselves, they last too long. BERTOLT BRECHT, *Jungle of Cities* (1924), 9, tr. Anselm Hollo.

2. To bear is to conquer our fate. THOMAS CAMPBELL, "On Visiting a Scene in Argyleshire."

3. The man who sticks it out against his fate / shows spirit, but the spirit of a fool. EURIPIDES, *Heracles* (c. 422 B.C.), tr. William Arrowsmith.

4. 'Tis as manlike to bear extremities as godlike to forgive. JOHN FORD, *'Tis Pity She's a Whore* (1633), 4.3.

5. To endure what is unendurable is true endurance. JAPANESE PROVERB.

6. Sorrow and silence are strong, and patient endurance is godlike. LONGFELLOW, *Evangeline* (1847), 2.1.

7. Endurance is the crowning quality, / And patience all the passion of great hearts. JAMES RUSSELL LOWELL, "Columbus" (1844).

8. To bear lightly the neck's yoke / brings strength; but kicking / against the goads is the way / of failure. PINDAR, *Odes* (5th c. B.C.), Pythia 2, tr. Richmond Lattimore.

9. Many can brook the weather that love not the wind. SHAKESPEARE, *Love's Labour's Lost* (1594–95), 4.2.34.

10. We may be masters of our every lot / By bearing it. VERGIL, *Aeneid* (30–19 B.C.), 5.710, tr. T. H. Delabere-May.

11. He that can't endure the bad, will not live to see the good. *Yiddish Proverbs* (1949), ed. Hanan J. Ayalti.

## 286. ENEMIES
See also 299. Estrangement; 410. Hatred;
474. Injury; 658. Pacifism; 811. Revenge

1. You will only injure yourself if you take notice of despicable enemies. AESOP, "The Bald Man and the Fly," *Fables* (6th c. B.C.?), tr. Joseph Jacobs.

2. Enemies' promises were made to be broken. AESOP, "The Nurse and the Wolf," *Fables* (6th c. B.C.?), tr. Joseph Jacobs.

3. He who has a thousand friends has not a friend to spare, / And he who has one

enemy shall meet him everywhere. ALI IBN-ABI-TALIB (7th c.), quoted in Emerson's *Conduct of Life*, 7.

4. Pay attention to your enemies, for they are the first to discover your mistakes. ANTISTHENES (5th–4th c. B.C.), quoted in Diogenes Laertius' *Lives and Opinions of Eminent Philosophers* (3rd c. A.D.), tr. R. D. Hicks.

5. Never ascribe to an opponent motives meaner than your own. J. M. BARRIE, rectorial address, St. Andrew's, May 3, 1922.

6. If thine enemy hunger, feed him; if he thirst, give him drink: for in so doing thou shalt heap coals of fire on his head. *Bible*, Proverbs 25:21 and Romans 12:20.

7. You shall judge of a man by his foes as well as by his friends. JOSEPH CONRAD, *Lord Jim* (1900), 34.

8. A strong foe is better than a weak friend. EDWARD DAHLBERG, *The Sorrows of Priapus* (1957).

9. Life'd not be worth livin' if we didn't keep our inimies. FINLEY PETER DUNNE, "New Year's Resolutions," *Mr. Dooley in Peace and in War* (1898).

10. There's nothing like the sight / Of an old enemy down on his luck. EURIPIDES, *Herakleidai* (c. 429–27 B.C.), tr. Ralph Gladstone.

11. Your worst enemy / Becomes your best friend, once he's underground. EURIPIDES, *Herakleidai* (c. 429–27 B.C.), tr. Ralph Gladstone.

12. There is no little enemy. FRENCH PROVERB.

13. If we are bound to forgive an enemy, we are not bound to trust him. THOMAS FULLER, M.D., *Gnomologia* (1732), 2728.

14. A wise man gets more use from his enemies than a fool from his friends. BALTASAR GRACIÁN, *The Art of Wordly Wisdom* (1647), 84, tr. Joseph Jacobs.

15. Invite your friend to dinner; have nothing to do with your enemy. HESIOD, *Works and Days* (8th c. B.C.), 342, tr. Richmond Lattimore.

16. It is your enemies who keep you straight. For real use one active, sneering enemy is worth two ordinary friends. EDGAR WATSON HOWE, *Country Town Sayings* (1911).

17. Our enemies approach nearer to truth in their judgments of us than we do ourselves. LA ROCHEFOUCAULD, *Maxims* (1665), tr. Kenneth Pratt.

18. If we could read the secret history of our enemies, we should find in each man's life sorrow and suffering enough to disarm all hostility. LONGFELLOW, "Table-Talk," *Driftwood* (1857).

19. The real enemy can always be met and conquered, or won over. Real antagonism is based on love, a love which has not recognized itself. HENRY MILLER, "Stieglitz and Marin," *The Air-Conditioned Nightmare* (1945).

20. He who lives by fighting with an enemy has an interest in the preservation of the enemy's life. NIETZSCHE, *Human, All Too Human* (1878), 531, tr. Helen Zimmern.

21. If you have an enemy, do not requite him evil with good, for that would put him to shame. Rather prove that he did you some good. NIETZSCHE, "On the Adder's Bite," *Thus Spoke Zarathustra* (1883–92), 1, tr. Walter Kaufmann.

22. There is no safety in regaining the favor of an enemy. PUBLILIUS SYRUS, *Moral Sayings* (1st c. B.C.), 174, tr. Darius Lyman.

23. Shun an angry man for a moment—your enemy forever. PUBLILIUS SYRUS, *Moral Sayings* (1st c. B.C.), 396, tr. Darius Lyman.

24. Whenever thy hand can reach it, tear out thy foe's brain, for such an opportunity washes anger from the mind. SA'DI, *Gulistan* (1258), 3.28, tr. James Ross.

25. Have I not learned this, / Only so much to hate my enemy / As though he might again become my friend, / And so much good to wish to do my friend, / As knowing he may yet become my foe? SOPHOCLES, *Ajax* (c. 447 B.C.), tr. John Moore.

26. He makes no friend who never made a foe. ALFRED, LORD TENNYSON, "Lancelot and Elaine," *Idylls of the King* (1859).

27. Be thine enemy an ant, see in him an elephant. TURKISH PROVERB.

## ENERGY

See 279. Effort; 1028. Vitality

## 287. ENGLAND AND ENGLISHMEN

See also 543. London

1. I think the British have the distinction above all other nations of being able to put

new wine into old bottles without bursting them. CLEMENT ATTLEE, *Time*, Nov. 6, 1950.

2. The English may not like music, but they absolutely love the noise it makes. SIR THOMAS BEECHAM, *New York Herald Tribune*, March 9, 1961.

3. It is a part of English hypocrisy—or English reserve—that, whilst we are fluent enough in grumbling about small inconveniences, we insist on making light of any great difficulties or griefs that may beset us. MAX BEERBOHM, "Books Within Books," *And Even Now* (1920).

4. The House of Lords is the British Outer Mongolia for retired politicians. ANTHONY WEDGWOOD BENN, *The New York Times*, Feb. 11, 1962.

5. The English have a scornful insular way / Of calling the French light. ELIZABETH BARRETT BROWNING, *Aurora Leigh* (1856), 6.1.

6. The English winter—ending in July, / To recommence in August. BYRON, *Don Juan* (1819–24), 13.42.

7. The maxim of the British people is "Business as usual." SIR WINSTON CHURCHILL, speech, Guildhall, Nov. 9, 1914.

8. An Irishman fights before he reasons, a Scotchman reasons before he fights, an Englishman is not particular as to the order of precedence, but will do either to accommodate his customers. CHARLES CALEB COLTON, *Lacon* (1825), 1.274.

9. "It is in bad taste," is the most formidable word an Englishman can pronounce. EMERSON, *Journals*, 1839.

10. It is not that the Englishman can't feel—it is that he is afraid to feel. He has been taught at his public school that feeling is bad form. He must not express great joy or sorrow, or even open his mouth too wide when he talks—his pipe might fall out if he did. E. M. FORSTER, "Notes on the English Character," *Abinger Harvest* (1936).

11. The Englishman walks before the law like a trained horse in the circus. He has the sense of legality in his bones, in his muscles. MAXIM GORKY, *Enemies* (1906), 1.

12. The difference between the vanity of a Frenchman and an Englishman seems to be this: the one thinks everything right that is French, the other thinks everything wrong that is not English. WILLIAM HAZLITT, *Characteristics* (1823), 334.

13. The Englishman is too apt to neglect the present good in preparing against the possible evil. WASHINGTON IRVING, "English and French Character," *Wolfert's Roost* (1855).

14. An Englishman is never so natural as when he's holding his tongue. HENRY JAMES, *The Portrait of a Lady* (1881), 10.

15. An Englishman never takes his collar off when he is writing. How can you expect him to show you his soul? WILLIAM MC FEE, "Reviewing Books," *Harbours of Memory* (1921).

16. One matter Englishmen don't think in the least funny is their happy consciousness of possessing a deep sense of humor. MARSHALL MC LUHAN, "The Ballet Luce," *The Mechanical Bride* (1951).

17. It is good to be on your guard against an Englishman who speaks French perfectly; he is very likely to be a card-sharper or an attaché in the diplomatic service. W. SOMERSET MAUGHAM, *The Summing Up* (1938), 29.

18. The Englishman, be it noted, seldom resorts to violence; when he is sufficiently goaded he simply opens up, like the oyster, and devours his adversary. HENRY MILLER, "Raimu," *The Wisdom of the Heart* (1941).

19. Humor is practically the only thing about which the English are utterly serious. MALCOLM MUGGERIDGE, "Tread Softly For You Tread on My Jokes," *The Most of Malcolm Muggeridge* (1966).

20. In the end it may well be that Britain will be honored by the historians more for the way she disposed of an empire than for the way in which she acquired it. DAVID ORMSBY GORE, *The New York Times*, Oct. 28, 1962.

21. But Lord! To see the absurd nature of Englishmen that cannot forbear laughing and jeering at everything that looks strange. SAMUEL PEPYS, *Diary*, Nov. 27, 1662.

22. England is the paradise of individuality, eccentricity, heresy, anomalies, hobbies, and humours. GEORGE SANTAYANA, "The British Character," *Soliloquies in England* (1922).

23. An Englishman thinks he is moral when he is only uncomfortable. GEORGE BERNARD SHAW, *Man and Superman* (1930), 3.

24. There is nothing so bad or so good that you will not find Englishmen doing it; but you will never find an Englishman in the wrong. He does everything on principle. GEORGE BERNARD SHAW, *The Man of Destiny* (1907).

25. Go anywhere in England, where there are natural, wholesome, contented, and really nice English people; and what do you always find? That the stables are the real centre of the household. GEORGE BERNARD SHAW, *Heartbreak House* (1920), 1.

26. The English, generally remarkable for doing very good things in a very bad manner, seem to have reserved the maturity and plenitude of their awkwardness for the pulpit. SYDNEY SMITH, quoted in Lady S. Holland's *Memoir* (1855), v. 1.3.

27. What two ideas are more inseparable than Beer and Britannia? SYDNEY SMITH, quoted in H. Pearson's *The Smith of Smiths* (1934), 11.

28. An English home—gray twilight poured / On dewy pastures, dewy trees, / Softer than sleep—all things in order stored, / A haunt of ancient Peace. ALFRED, LORD TENNYSON, "The Palace of Art" (1842).

29. The way to ensure summer in England is to have it framed and glazed in a comfortable room. HORACE WALPOLE, letter to William Cole, May 28, 1774.

## ENGLISH

See 287. England and Englishmen; 521. Language

## ENJOYMENT

See 698. Pleasure

## 288. ENNUI

See also 30. Alienation; 92. Boredom

1. Ennui has made more gamblers than avarice, more drunkards than thirst, and perhaps as many suicides as despair. CHARLES CALEB COLTON, *Lacon* (1825), 1.259.

2. The flesh is sad, alas, and I've read all the books. STÉPHANE MALLARMÉ, "Brise marine," *Poésies complètes* (1887).

## ENOUGH

See 940. Sufficiency

## 289. ENTERPRISE

See also 33. Ambition; 279. Effort; 650. Opportunity; 873. Self-sufficiency

1. None will improve your lot / If you yourselves do not. BERTOLT BRECHT, *Roundheads and Peakheads* (1933), 3, tr. N. Goold-Verschoyle.

2. Neither a wise man nor a brave man lies down on the tracks of history to wait for the train of the future to run over him. DWIGHT D. EISENHOWER, campaign speech, *Time*, Oct. 6, 1952.

3. On the neck of the young man sparkles no gem so gracious as enterprise. HĀFIZ, quoted by Emerson in "Power," *The Conduct of Life* (1860).

4. The passion to get ahead is sometimes born of the fear lest we be left behind. ERIC HOFFER, *The Passionate State of Mind* (1954), 257.

5. Nothing will ever be attempted, if all possible objections must be first overcome. SAMUEL JOHNSON, *Rasselas* (1759), 6.

6. Roasted pigeons will not fly into one's mouth. PENNSYLVANIA DUTCH PROVERB.

7. Go and wake up your luck. PERSIAN PROVERB.

8. If you don't crack the shell, you can't eat the nut. RUSSIAN PROVERB.

9. To avoid an occasion for our virtues is a worse degree of failure than to push forward pluckily and make a fall. ROBERT LOUIS STEVENSON, title essay, 2, *Virginibus Puerisque* (1881).

## 290. ENTERTAINMENT

See also 128. Circus; 143. Comedians; 144. Comedy; 563. Mass Media; 607. Music; 697. Play; 965. Theater

1. For what do we live, but to make sport for our neighbours, and laugh at them in our turn? JANE AUSTEN, *Pride and Prejudice* (1813), 57.

2. The mass production of distraction is now as much a part of the American way of life as the mass production of automobiles. C. WRIGHT MILLS, "The Unity of Work and Leisure," *Power, Politics and People* (1963).

3. When I play with my cat, who knows whether I do not make her more sport than she makes me? We mutually divert one another with our monkey-tricks. MONTAIGNE, "Apology for Raimond de Sebonde," *Essays* (1580–88), tr. Charles Cotton and W. C. Hazlitt.

4. Entertainment confirms rather than challenges. NED ROREM, "Song and Singer," *Music from Inside Out* (1967).

## 291. ENTHUSIASM

**See also 333. Fanaticism; 511. Joie de vivre; 921. Spontaneity; 1028. Vitality; 1066. Zeal**

1. He too serves a certain purpose who only stands and cheers. HENRY ADAMS, *The Education of Henry Adams* (1907), 24.

2. In things pertaining to enthusiasm, no man is sane who does not know how to be insane on proper occasions. HENRY WARD BEECHER, *Proverbs from Plymouth Pulpit* (1887).

3. Enthusiasm, n. A distemper of youth, curable by small doses of repentance in connection with outward applications of experience. AMBROSE BIERCE, *The Devil's Dictionary* (1881–1911).

4. You can't sweep other people off their feet, if you can't be swept off your own. CLARENCE DAY, "A Wild Polish Hero," *The Crow's Nest* (1921).

5. Nothing great was ever achieved without enthusiasm. EMERSON, "Circles," *Essays: First Series* (1841).

6. The world belongs to the enthusiast who keeps cool. WILLIAM MC FEE, *Casuals of the Sea* (1916), 1.

7. The measure of an enthusiasm must be taken between interesting events. It is between bites that the lukewarm angler loses heart. EDWIN WAY TEALE, "September 16," *Circle of the Seasons* (1953).

8. Man never rises to great truths without enthusiasm. VAUVENARGUES, *Reflections and Maxims* (1746), 335, tr. F. G. Stevens.

## 292. ENVIRONMENT

**See also 66. Background; 174. Conservation; 368. Garbage**

1. When the Pleiades and the wind in the grass are no longer a part of the human spirit, a part of very flesh and bone, man becomes, as it were, a kind of cosmic outlaw, having neither the completeness and integrity of the animal nor the birthright of a true humanity. HENRY BESTON, foreword to *The Outermost House* (1928).

2. Men are like plants; the goodness and flavour of the fruit proceeds from the peculiar soil and exposition in which they grow. MICHEL GUILLAUME JEAN DE CRÈVECOEUR, *Letters from an American Farmer* (1782), 3.

3. Many people live in ugly wastelands, but in the absence of imaginative standards, most of them do not even know it. C. WRIGHT MILLS, "The Big City: Private Troubles and Public Issues," *Power, Politics and People* (1963).

4. In remaking the world in the likeness of a steam-heated, air-conditioned metropolis of apartment buildings we have violated one of our essential attributes—our kinship with nature. ROSS PARMENTER, "Inward Sign," *The Plant in My Window* (1949).

5. A grateful environment is a substitute for happiness. It can quicken us from without as a fixed hope and affection, or the consciousness of a right life, can quicken us from within. GEORGE SANTAYANA, *The Sense of Beauty* (1896), 26.

6. Since the individual's desire to dominate his environment is not a desirable trait in a society which every day grows more and more confining, the average man must take to daydreaming. GORE VIDAL, "Tarzan Revisited," *Esquire*, December 1963.

## 293. ENVY

**See also 557. Malice**

1. In few men is it part of nature to respect / a friend's prosperity without begrudging him. AESCHYLUS, *Agamemnon* (458 B.C.), tr. Richmond Lattimore.

2. He who goes unenvied shall not be admired. AESCHYLUS, *Agamemnon* (458 B.C.), tr. Richmond Lattimore.

3. As iron is eaten away by rust, so the envious are consumed by their own passion. ANTISTHENES (5th–4th c. B.C.), quoted in Diogenes Laertius' *Lives and Opinions of Eminent Philosophers* (3rd c. A.D.), tr. R. D. Hicks.

4. He that cannot possibly mend his own case will do what he can to impair another's. FRANCIS BACON, "Of Envy," *Essays* (1625).

5. Let age, not envy, draw wrinkles on thy cheeks. SIR THOMAS BROWNE, *A Letter to a Friend* (1690).

6. For one man who sincerely pities our misfortunes, there are a thousand who sincerely hate our success. CHARLES CALEB COLTON, *Lacon* (1825), 1.507.

7. If envy were a fever, all the world would be ill. DANISH PROVERB.

8. Envy is everywhere. / Who is without envy? And most people / Are unaware or unashamed of being envious. T. S. ELIOT, *The Elder Statesman* (1958), 1.

9. Envy is the tax which all distinction must pay. EMERSON, *Journals*, 1824.

10. Some folks rail against other folks, because other folks have what some folks would be glad of. HENRY FIELDING, *Joseph Andrews* (1742), 4.6.

11. It is only at the tree loaded with fruit that the people throw stones. FRENCH PROVERB.

12. Nothing sharpens sight like envy. THOMAS FULLER, M.D., *Gnomologia* (1732), 3674.

13. Envy's a sharper spur than pay. JOHN GAY, "The Elephant and the Bookseller," *Fables* (1727–38).

14. The envious die not once, but as oft as the envied win applause. BALTASAR GRACIÁN, *The Art of Worldly Wisdom* (1647), 162, tr. Joseph Jacobs.

15. Envy is a littleness of soul, which cannot see beyond a certain point, and if it does not occupy the whole space feels itself excluded. WILLIAM HAZLITT, *Characteristics* (1823), 23.

16. How much better a thing it is to be envied than to be pitied. HERODOTUS, *The Histories* (5th c. B.C.), 3.52, tr. A. D. Godley.

17. The envious man grows lean when his neighbor waxes fat. HORACE, *Epistles* (20–c. 8 B.C.), 1.2.

18. All envy is proportionate to desire; we are uneasy at the attainments of another, according as we think our own happiness would be advanced by the addition of that which he withholds from us. SAMUEL JOHNSON, *The Rambler* (1750–52), 17.

19. Those who speak against the great do not usually speak from morality, but from envy. WALTER SAVAGE LANDOR, "Diogenes and Plato," *Imaginary Conversations* (1824–53).

20. Envy is more irreconcilable than hatred. LA ROCHEFOUCAULD, *Maxims* (1665), tr. Kenneth Pratt.

21. Envy is destroyed by true friendship, as coquetry by true love. LA ROCHEFOUCAULD, *Maxims* (1665), tr. Kenneth Pratt.

22. Our envy always lasts much longer than the happiness of those we envy. LA ROCHEFOUCAULD, *Maxims* (1665), tr. Kenneth Pratt.

23. Even success softens not the heart of the envious. PINDAR, *Odes* (5th c. B.C.), Pythia 2, tr. Richmond Lattimore.

24. Our nature holds so much envy and malice that our pleasure in our own advantages is not so great as our distress at others'. PLUTARCH, "Contentment," *Moralia* (c. A.D. 100), tr. Moses Hadas.

25. A brave man or a fortunate one is able to bear envy. PUBLILIUS SYRUS, *Moral Sayings* (1st c. B.C.).

26. Envy . . . is one form of a vice, partly moral, partly intellectual, which consists in seeing things never in themselves but only in their relations. BERTRAND RUSSELL, *The Conquest of Happiness* (1930), 6.

27. There is not a passion so strongly rooted in the human heart as envy. RICHARD BRINSLEY SHERIDAN, *The Critic* (1779), 1.1.

28. Man will do many things to get himself loved; he will do all things to get himself envied. MARK TWAIN, "Pudd'nhead Wilson's New Calendar," *Following the Equator* (1897), 1.21.

29. I can endure my own despair, / But not another's hope. WILLIAM WALSH, "Song: Of All the Torments" (1692?).

30. A show of envy is an insult to oneself. YEVGENY YEVTUSHENKO, "People Were Laughing Behind a Wall," *The Poetry of Yevgeny Yevtushenko: 1953–1965* (1965), tr. George Reavey.

## 294. EPIGRAMS

**See also 568. Maxims; 767. Quotations**

1. What is an epigram? A dwarfish whole, / Its body brevity, and wit its soul. SAMUEL TAYLOR COLERIDGE, "An Epigram" (1802).

2. The epigram has been compared to a scorpion, because as the sting of the scor-

pion lieth in the tail, the force of the epigram is in the conclusion. LILIUS GYRALDUS, *De Poetica Historia* (1545), 10.

3. Epigrams need no crier, but are content with their own tongue. MARTIAL, *Epigrams* (A.D. 86), 2, "Valerius Martialis to His Decianus Sends Greetings," tr. Walter C. A. Ker.

4. Such is epigram, requiring / Wit, occasion, and good luck. CHRISTOPHER MORLEY, "The Epigram" (1927).

5. Somewhere in the world there is an epigram for every dilemma. HENDRIK WILLEM VAN LOON, *Tolerance* (1925).

## EPOCH

See 296. Era

## 295. EQUALITY

See also 133. Class; 231. Democracy; 469. Inequality; 817. Rights

1. When quarrels and complaints arise, it is when people who are equal have not got equal shares, or *vice versa*. ARISTOTLE, *Nicomachean Ethics* (4th c. B.C.), 5.3, tr. J. A. K. Thomson.

2. The democrats think that as they are equal they ought to be equal in all things. ARISTOTLE, *Politics* (4th c. B.C.), 5.1, tr. Benjamin Jowett.

3. Equality consists in the same treatment of similar persons. ARISTOTLE, *Politics* (4th c. B.C.), 7.14, tr. Benjamin Jowett.

4. Intellect has nothing to do with equality except to respect it as a sublime convention. JACQUES BARZUN, *The House of Intellect* (1959).

5. Naked I came into the world, naked I shall go out of it! And a very good thing too, for it reminds me that I am naked under my shirt, whatever its colour. E. M. FORSTER, "What I Believe," *Two Cheers for Democracy* (1951).

6. Just as modern mass production requires the standardization of commodities, so the social process requires standardization of man, and this standardization is called equality. ERICH FROMM, *The Art of Loving* (1956), 2.

7. Equality is a mortuary word. CHRISTOPHER FRY, *Venus Observed* (1950), 1.

8. There can be no truer principle than this—that every individual of the community at large has an equal right to the protection of government. ALEXANDER HAMILTON, address, Constitutional Convention, June 29, 1787.

9. I am proud up to the point of equality: everything above or below that appears to me arrant impertinence or abject meanness. WILLIAM HAZLITT, "Commonplaces," *The Round Table* (1817), 10.

10. When all candles be out, all cats be gray. JOHN HEYWOOD, *Proverbs* (1546), 1.5.

11. We clamor for equality chiefly in matters in which we ourselves cannot hope to obtain excellence. ERIC HOFFER, *The Passionate State of Mind* (1954), 198.

12. The man who insists he is as good as anybody, believes he is better. EDGAR WATSON HOWE, *Country Town Sayings* (1911).

13. We hold these truths to be self-evident, that all men are created equal, that they are endowed by their creator with certain unalienable Rights, that among these are Life, Liberty and the pursuit of happiness. THOMAS JEFFERSON, *Declaration of Independence*, July 4, 1776.

14. It is better that some should be unhappy than that none should be happy, which would be the case in a general state of equality. SAMUEL JOHNSON, quoted in Boswell's *Life of Samuel Johnson*, April 7, 1776.

15. All of us do not have equal talent, but all of us should have an equal opportunity to develop our talents. JOHN F. KENNEDY, address, San Diego State College, San Diego, Calif., June 6, 1963.

16. It is the American vice, the democratic disease which expresses its tyranny by reducing everything unique to the level of the herd. HENRY MILLER, "Raimu," *The Wisdom of the Heart* (1941).

17. Weariness is the shortest path to equality and fraternity—and finally liberty is bestowed by sleep. NIETZSCHE, *The Wanderer and His Shadow* (1880), 263, tr. Paul V. Cohn.

18. Where there are no distinctions there can be no superiority; perfect equality affords no temptation. THOMAS PAINE, "Thoughts on the Present State of American Affairs," *Common Sense* (1776).

19. Unless man is committed to the belief that all of mankind are his brothers, then he labors in vain and hypocritically in the

vineyards of equality. ADAM CLAYTON POWELL, "Black Power: A Form of Godly Power," *Keep the Faith, Baby!* (1967).

20. The Lord so constituted everybody that no matter what color you are you require the same amount of nourishment. WILL ROGERS, *The Autobiography of Will Rogers* (1949), 12.

21. Inside the polling booth every American man and woman stands as the equal of every other American man and woman. There they have no superiors. There they have no masters save their own minds and consciences. FRANKLIN D. ROOSEVELT, speech, Worcester, Mass., Oct. 21, 1936.

22. In America everybody is of opinion that he has no social superiors, since all men are equal, but he does not admit that he has no social inferiors. BERTRAND RUSSELL, "Ideas That Have Harmed Mankind," *Unpopular Essays* (1950).

23. It was the contemplation of God that created men who were equal, for it was in God that they were equal. SAINT-EXUPÉRY, *Flight to Arras* (1942), 23, tr. Lewis Galantière.

24. When none but the wealthy had watches, they were almost all very good ones: few are now made which are worth much, but everybody has one in his pocket. ALEXIS DE TOCQUEVILLE, *Democracy in America* (1835–39), 2.1.11.

25. The principle of equality does not destroy the imagination, but lowers its flight to the level of the earth. ALEXIS DE TOCQUEVILLE, *Democracy in America* (1835–39), 2.3.11.

## 296. ERA

**See also 181. Contemporaneousness; 372. Generations; 593. Modernity; 633. Nuclear Power; 669. Past; 994. Twentieth Century**

1. In every age "the good old days" were a myth. No one ever thought they were good at the time. For every age has consisted of crises that seemed intolerable to the people who lived through them. BROOKS ATKINSON, "February 8," *Once Around the Sun* (1951).

2. Every age has its pleasures, its style of wit, and its own ways. NICOLAS BOILEAU, *L'Art poétique* (1674), 3.374.

3. 'Tis hard to find a whole age to imitate, or what century to propose for example. SIR THOMAS BROWNE, *Christian Morals* (1716), 3.

4. Every age, / Through being beheld too close, is ill-discerned / By those who have not lived past it. ELIZABETH BARRETT BROWNING, *Aurora Leigh* (1856), 5.167.

5. The "good old times"—all times when old are good— / Are gone. BYRON, *The Age of Bronze* (1823).

6. How strange it is that we of the present day are constantly praising that past age which our fathers abused, and as constantly abusing that present age, which our children will praise. CHARLES CALEB COLTON, *Lacon* (1825), 2.101.

7. The "times," "the age," what is that, but a few profound persons and a few active persons who epitomize the times? EMERSON, "Fate," *The Conduct of Life* (1860).

8. The golden age was never the present age. ENGLISH PROVERB.

9. Accusing the times is but excusing ourselves. THOMAS FULLER, M.D., *Gnomologia* (1732), 759.

10. Every age confutes old errors and begets new. THOMAS FULLER, M.D., *Gnomologia* (1732), 1403.

11. Time is a strange thing. It is a whimsical tyrant, which in every century has a different face for all that one says and does. GOETHE, quoted in Johann Peter Eckermann's *Conversations with Goethe*, Feb. 25, 1824.

12. The reason for the sadness of this modern age and the men who live in it is that it looks for the truth in everything and finds it. EDMOND and JULES DE GONCOURT, *Journal*, Oct. 23, 1864, tr. Robert Baldick.

13. The golden age was the age in which gold did not reign. The golden calf is still made of mud. Graffito written during French student revolt, May 1968.

14. Every age thinks its battle the most important of all. HEINRICH HEINE, "Don't Laugh, Later Reader . . . ," *Heinrich Heine, Works of Prose* (1943), tr. E. B. Ashton.

15. If it is the great delusion of moralists to suppose that all previous ages were less sinful than their own, then it is the great delusion of intellectuals to suppose that all previous ages were less sick. LOUIS KRONENBERGER, "The Spirit of the Age," *Company Manners* (1954).

16. In history as it comes to be written, there is usually some Spirit of the Age which historians can define, but the shape of things is seldom so clear to those who live them. To most thoughtful men it has generally seemed that theirs was an Age of Confusion. JOSEPH WOOD KRUTCH, "The Loss of Confidence," *The Measure of Man* (1954).

17. Every age has a keyhole to which its eye is pasted. MARY MC CARTHY, "My Confession," *On the Contrary* (1961).

18. At each epoch of history the world was in a hopeless state, and at each epoch of history the world muddled through; at each epoch the world was lost, and at each epoch it was saved. JACQUES MARITAIN, *Reflections on America* (1958), 19.4.

19. All thoughts are always ready, potentially if not actually. Each age selects and assimilates the philosophy that is most apt for its wants. JOHN MORLEY, "Emerson," *Critical Miscellanies* (1871–1908).

20. These are the times that try men's souls. THOMAS PAINE, *The American Crisis* (1776–83), 1.

21. Even though a god, I have learned to obey the times. PALLADAS (fl. A.D. 400), "On a Statue of Heracles," in *The Greek Anthology* (7th c. B.C.–10th c. A.D.), 9.441.

22. Every epoch, under names more or less specious, has deified its peculiar errors. SHELLEY, *A Defence of Poetry* (1821).

23. The altar cloth of one aeon is the doormat of the next. MARK TWAIN, *Notebook* (1935).

24. Each age has its choice of the death it will die. CHARLES DUDLEY WARNER, "Second Study," *Backlog Studies* (1873).

25. Every epoch has its character determined by the way its population re-act to the material events which they encounter. ALFRED NORTH WHITEHEAD, *Adventures in Ideas* (1933), 6.

## 297. ERROR

**See also 86. Blunder; 329. Falsehood; 455. Imperfection; 462. Inconsistency; 677. Perfection; 992. Truth and Falsehood**

1. The errors of young men are the ruin of business, but the errors of aged men amount to this, that more might have been done, or sooner. FRANCIS BACON, "Of Youth and Age," *Essays* (1625).

2. The Errors of a Wise Man make your Rule / Rather than the Perfections of a Fool. WILLIAM BLAKE, "English Encouragement of Art: Cromek's Opinions Put into Rhyme" (1808–11).

3. Intelligence is not to make no mistakes / But quickly to see how to make them good. BERTOLT BRECHT, *The Measures Taken* (1930), 3, tr. Eric Bentley.

4. Truth, crushed to earth, shall rise again; / The eternal years of God are hers; / But Error, wounded, writhes in pain, / And dies among his worshippers. WILLIAM CULLEN BRYANT, "The Battle-Field" (1837).

5. Every great mistake has a halfway moment, a split second when it can be recalled and perhaps remedied. PEARL S. BUCK, *What America Means to Me* (1943), 10.

6. There is no such source of error as the pursuit of absolute truth. SAMUEL BUTLER (d. 1902), "Truth and Convenience," *Note-Books* (1912).

7. I do not mind lying, but I hate inaccuracy. SAMUEL BUTLER (d. 1902), "Truth and Convenience," *Note-Books* (1912).

8. An error is simply a failure to adjust immediately from a preconception to an actuality. JOHN CAGE, "45′ for a Speaker," *Silence* (1961).

9. Any man can make mistakes, but only an idiot persists in his error. CICERO, *Philippics* (44–43 B.C.), 6.

10. Truth is a good dog; but beware of barking too close to the heels of an error, lest you get your brains kicked out. SAMUEL TAYLOR COLERIDGE, *Table Talk*, June 7, 1830.

11. Ignorance is a blank sheet, on which we may write; but error is a scribbled one, on which we must first erase. CHARLES CALEB COLTON, *Lacon* (1825), 1.1.

12. may i be wrong / for whenever men are right they are not young. E. E. CUMMINGS, "may my heart always be open to little," *100 Selected Poems* (1959).

13. Who has enough credit in this world to pay for his mistakes? EDWARD DAHLBERG, "On Wisdom and Folly," *Reasons of the Heart* (1965).

14. This is a hard and precarious world, where every mistake and infirmity must be paid for in full. CLARENCE DAY, *This Simian World* (1920), 19.

15. No doubt about it: error is the rule, truth is the accident of error. GEORGES

DUHAMEL, "Avant-propos," *Le Notaire du Havre* (1933).

16. He who is wrong fights against himself. EGYPTIAN PROVERB.

17. People seldom learn from the mistakes of others—not because they deny the value of the past, but because they are faced with new problems. ILYA EHRENBURG, "What I Have Learned," *Saturday Review*, Sept. 30, 1967.

18. Error is always in haste. THOMAS FULLER, M.D., *Gnomologia* (1732), 1382.

19. Man must strive, and striving he must err. GOETHE, "Prologue in Heaven," *Faust: Part I* (1808), tr. Philip Wayne.

20. The greatest mistake you can make in life is to be continually fearing you will make one. ELBERT HUBBARD, *The Note Book* (1927).

21. Error of opinion may be tolerated where reason is left free to combat it. THOMAS JEFFERSON, first inaugural address, March 4, 1801.

22. When everyone is wrong, everyone is right. PIERRE-CLAUDE NIVELLE DE LA CHAUSSÉE, *La Gouvernante* (1744), 1.3.

23. It is one thing to show a man that he is in error, and another to put him in possession of truth. JOHN LOCKE, *An Essay Concerning Human Understanding* (1690), 4.7.11.

24. All men are liable to error; and most men are, in many points, by passion or interest, under temptation to it. JOHN LOCKE, *An Essay Concerning Human Understanding* (1690), 4.20.17.

25. Were half the power that fills the world with terror, / Were half the wealth bestowed on camps and courts, / Given to redeem the human mind from error, / There were no need of arsenals or forts. LONGFELLOW, "The Arsenal at Springfield" (1845).

26. The errors of great men are venerable because they are more fruitful than the truths of little men. NIETZSCHE, "Fragment of a Critique of Schopenhauer" (1867), in *The Portable Nietzsche*, tr. Walter Kaufmann.

27. The most powerful cause of error is the war existing between the senses and reason. PASCAL, *Pensées* (1670), 82, tr. W. F. Trotter.

28. The man who can own up to his error is greater than he who merely knows how to avoid making it. CARDINAL DE RETZ, *Mémoires* (1718).

29. We are more conscious that a person is in the wrong when the wrong concerns ourselves. JOSEPH ROUX, *Meditations of a Parish Priest* (1886), 4.25, tr. Isabel F. Hapgood.

30. Truth lies within a little and certain compass, but error is immense. HENRY ST. JOHN, *Reflections upon Exile* (1716).

31. A life spent in making mistakes is not only more honorable but more useful than a life spent doing nothing. GEORGE BERNARD SHAW, "Preface on Doctors: The Technical Problem," *The Doctor's Dilemma* (1913).

32. All error, not merely verbal, is a strong way of stating that the current truth is incomplete. ROBERT LOUIS STEVENSON, "Crabbed Age and Youth," *Virginibus Puerisque* (1881).

33. A man should never be ashamed to own he has been in the wrong, which is but saying, in other words, that he is wiser today than he was yesterday. JONATHAN SWIFT, *Thoughts on Various Subjects* (1711).

34. Who can deny that all men are violent lovers of truth, when we see them so positive in their errors, which they will maintain out of their zeal to truth, although they contradict themselves every day of their lives? JONATHAN SWIFT, *Thoughts on Various Subjects* (1711).

35. If you shut your door to all errors truth will be shut out. RABINDRANATH TAGORE, *Stray Birds* (1916), 130.

36. Mistakes live in the neighbourhood of truth / and therefore delude us. RABINDRANATH TAGORE, *Fireflies* (1928).

37. Life's errors cry for the merciful beauty / that can modulate their isolation / into a harmony with the whole. RABINDRANATH TAGORE, *Fireflies* (1928).

38. All erroneous ideas would perish of their own accord if given clear expression. VAUVENARGUES, *Reflections and Maxims* (1746), 6, tr. F. G. Stevens.

39. Love truth, but pardon error. VOLTAIRE, *Sept Discours en vers sur l'homme* (1738), 3.

40. Error flies from mouth to mouth, from pen to pen, and to destroy it takes ages.

VOLTAIRE, "Assassin," *Philosophical Dictionary* (1764).

41. The progress of rivers to the ocean is not so rapid as that of man to error. VOLTAIRE, "Rivers," *Philosophical Dictionary* (1764).

## 298. ESCAPE

**See also 196. Cowardice; 302. Evasion; 340. Fear; 447. Illusion**

1. Oh that I had wings like a dove! for then would I fly away, and be at rest. *Bible*, Psalms 55:6.

2. Those that fly, may fight again, / Which he can never do that's slain. / Hence timely running's no mean part / Of conduct, in the martial art. SAMUEL BUTLER (d. 1680), *Hudibras* (1663), 3.3.

3. The efforts which we make to escape from our destiny only serve to lead us into it. EMERSON, "Fate," *The Conduct of Life* (1860).

4. The best way out is always through. ROBERT FROST, "A Servant to Servants," *North of Boston* (1914).

5. In running away from ourselves we either fall on our neighbor's shoulder or fly at his throat. ERIC HOFFER, *The True Believer* (1951), 1.2.10.

6. The man does better who runs from disaster than he who is caught by it. HOMER, *Iliad* (9th c. B.C.), 14.81, tr. Richmond Lattimore.

7. A man trying to escape never thinks himself sufficiently concealed. VICTOR HUGO, "Cosette," *Les Misérables* (1862), 5.6, tr. Charles E. Wilbour.

8. A runaway monk never speaks well of his monastery. ITALIAN PROVERB.

9. There is no need of spurs when the horse is running away. PUBLILIUS SYRUS, *Moral Sayings* (1st c. B.C.), 216, tr. Darius Lyman.

10. Flight is lawful, when one flies from tyrants. RACINE, *Phaedra* (1677), 5, tr. Robert Henderson.

11. It is always fair sailing, when you escape evil. SOPHOCLES, *Philoctetes* (409 B.C.), tr. David Grene.

12. He who flees will fight again. TERTULLIAN, *De Fuga in Persecutione* (3rd c.), 10.

## ESTABLISHMENT

**See 485. Institutions**

## ESTEEM

**See 716. Praise; 802. Respect; 862. Self-esteem**

## 299. ESTRANGEMENT

**See also 253. Dislike; 549. Love, Loss of**

1. At best, the renewal of broken relations is a nervous matter. HENRY ADAMS, *The Education of Henry Adams* (1907), 16.

2. A broken friendship may be soldered, but will never be sound. THOMAS FULLER, M.D., *Gnomologia* (1732), 27.

3. It is a proof of little friendship not to perceive any cooling in the warmth of that of our friends. LA ROCHEFOUCAULD, *Maxims* (1665), tr. Kenneth Pratt.

4. The surest sign of the estrangement of the opinions of two persons is when they both say something ironical to each other and neither of them feels the irony. NIETZSCHE, *Human, All Too Human* (1878), 331, tr. Helen Zimmern.

## 300. ETERNITY

**See also 452. Immortality; 971. Time; 983. Transience**

1. The sand of the sea, the drops of rain, and the days of eternity—who can count them? *Apocrypha*, Ecclesiasticus 1:2.

2. Reversion to destiny is called eternity. LAOTSE, *The Character of Tao* (6th c. B.C.), 16, tr. Ch'u Ta-Kao.

3. The One remains, the many change and pass; / Heaven's light forever shines, Earth's shadows fly; / Life, like a dome of many-coloured glass, / Stains the white radiance of Eternity, / Until Death tramples it to fragments. SHELLEY, *Adonais* (1821), 52.

4. Eternity is a terrible thought. I mean, where's it going to end? TOM STOPPARD, *Rosencrantz & Guildenstern Are Dead* (1967), 2.

## ETHICS

**See 598. Morality**

### ETIQUETTE
See 559. Manners

### 301. EUROPE

1. Europe has what we do not have yet, a sense of the mysterious and inexorable limits of life, a sense, in a word, of tragedy. And we [Americans] have what they sorely need: a sense of life's possibilities. JAMES BALDWIN, "The Discovery of What It Means to Be an American," *Nobody Knows My Name* (1961).

2. We go to Europe to be Americanized. EMERSON, "Culture," *The Conduct of Life* (1860).

3. The immense popularity of American movies abroad demonstrates that Europe is the unfinished negative of which America is the proof. MARY MC CARTHY, "America the Beautiful: The Humanist in the Bathtub," *On the Contrary* (1961).

4. That Europe is nothin' on earth but a great big auction. TENNESSEE WILLIAMS, *Cat on a Hot Tin Roof* (1955), 2.

### 302. EVASION
See also 298. Escape; 776. Realism

1. Without health and courage we cannot face the present or the germ of the future in the present, and we take refuge in evasion. CYRIL CONNOLLY, *The Unquiet Grave* (1945), 3.

2. It is the wise man's part / to leave in darkness everything that is ugly. EURIPIDES, *Hippolytus* (428 B.C.), tr. David Grene.

3. Many people today don't want honest answers insofar as honest means unpleasant or disturbing. They want a soft answer that turneth away anxiety. LOUIS KRONENBERGER, "Unbrave New World," *The Cart and the Horse* (1964), 2.

4. Who shrinks from knowledge of his calamities but aggravates his fear; troubles half seen do torture all the more. SENECA, *Agamemnon* (1st c.), 419, tr. Frank Justus Miller.

### 303. EVENTS
See also 127. Circumstance

1. Often do the spirits / Of great events stride on before the events, / And in today already walks tomorrow. SAMUEL TAYLOR COLERIDGE, *Wallenstein* (1800), 1.5.1.

2. People to whom nothing has ever happened / Cannot understand the unimportance of events. T. S. ELIOT, *The Family Reunion* (1939), 1.1.

3. Events expand with the character. EMERSON, "Fate," *The Conduct of Life* (1860).

4. The soul contains the event that shall befall it, for the event is only the actualization of its thoughts; and what we pray to ourselves for is always granted. EMERSON, *The Conduct of Life* (1860).

5. The enemy of the conventional wisdom is not ideas but the march of events. JOHN KENNETH GALBRAITH, *The Affluent Society* (1958), 2.4.

6. There are no events so disastrous that adroit men do not draw some advantage from them, nor any so fortunate that the imprudent cannot turn to their own prejudice. LA ROCHEFOUCAULD, *Maxims* (1665), tr. Kenneth Pratt.

7. Nothing befalls us that is not of the nature of ourselves. There comes no adventure but wears to our soul the shape of our everyday thoughts. MAURICE MAETERLINCK, *Wisdom and Destiny* (1898), 10, tr. Alfred Sutro.

8. The greatest events—they are not our loudest but our stillest hours. NIETZSCHE, "On Great Events," *Thus Spoke Zarathustra* (1883–92), 2, tr. Walter Kaufmann.

9. It is one thing to be moved by events; it is another to be mastered by them. RALPH W. SOCKMAN, bulletin of Fourth Presbyterian Church, Chicago, Nov. 17, 1957.

### 304. EVIDENCE
See also 709. Portent; 738. Proof

1. By a small sample we may judge of the whole piece. CERVANTES, *Don Quixote* (1605–15), 1.1.4, tr. Peter Motteux and John Ozell.

2. Some circumstantial evidence is very strong, as when you find a trout in the milk. THOREAU, *Journal*, Nov. 11, 1850.

## 305. EVIL

**See also 188. Corruption; 201. Crime; 387. The Good; 388. Good and Evil; 391. Goodness; 893. Sin; 1048. Wickedness; 1063. Wrongdoing**

1. Destroy the seed of evil, or it will grow up to your ruin. AESOP, "The Swallow and the Other Birds," *Fables* (6th c. B.C.?), tr. Joseph Jacobs.

2. No notice is taken of a little evil, but when it increases it strikes the eye. ARISTOTLE, *Politics* (4th c. B.C.), 6.4, tr. Benjamin Jowett.

3. Some men wish evil and accomplish it / But most men, when they work in that machine, / Just let it happen somewhere in the wheels. / The fault is no decisive, villainous knife / But the dull saw that is the routine mind. STEPHEN VINCENT BENÉT, *John Brown's Body* (1928), 5.

4. Sufficient unto the day is the evil thereof. *Bible*, Matthew 6:34.

5. Those who would extirpate evil from the world know little of human nature. As well might punch be palatable without souring as existence agreeable without care. JAMES BOSWELL, *London Journal*, July 5, 1763.

6. There is this of good in real evils; they deliver us, while they last, from the petty despotism of all that were imaginary. CHARLES CALEB COLTON, *Lacon* (1825), 2.219.

7. Evils in the journey of life are like the hills which alarm travellers upon their road; they both appear great at a distance, but when we approach them we find that they are far less insurmountable than we had conceived. CHARLES CALEB COLTON, *Lacon* (1825), 2.241.

8. All evils are equal when they are extreme. CORNEILLE, *Horace* (1640), 1.3.

9. Man's evil love / Makes the crooked path seem straight. DANTE, "Purgatorio," 10, *The Divine Comedy* (c. 1300–21), tr. Lawrence Grant White.

10. God may still be in His Heaven, but there is more than sufficient evidence that all is not right with the world. IRWIN EDMAN, "How to Be Sweet Though Sophisticated," *Adam, the Baby, and the Man from Mars* (1929).

11. Every evil to which we do not succumb is a benefactor. EMERSON, "Compensation," *Essays: First Series* (1841).

12. Good is a good doctor, but Bad is sometimes a better. EMERSON, "Considerations by the Way," *The Conduct of Life* (1860).

13. Evil enters like a needle and spreads like an oak tree. ETHIOPIAN PROVERB.

14. Evil men by their own nature cannot ever prosper. EURIPIDES, *Ion* (c. 421–408 B.C.), tr. Ronald F. Willetts.

15. The Devil gets up to the belfry by the vicar's skirts. THOMAS FULLER, M.D., *Gnomologia* (1732), 4476.

16. Must I do all the evil I can before I learn to shun it? Is it not enough to know the evil to shun it? If not, we should be sincere enough to admit that we love evil too well to give it up. MOHANDAS K. GANDHI, *Non-Violence in Peace and War* (1948), 2.74.

17. There are two infinities in this world: God up above, and down below, human baseness. EDMOND and JULES DE GONCOURT, *Journal*, Nov. 23, 1862, tr. Robert Baldick.

18. There is no evil unless your conscience or that of others says that there is. Graffito written during French student revolt, May 1968.

19. He who does evil that good may come, pays a toll to the devil to let him into heaven. JULIUS CHARLES HARE and AUGUSTUS WILLIAM HARE, *Guesses at Truth* (1827).

20. The man who does evil to another does evil to himself, / and the evil counsel is most evil for him who counsels it. HESIOD, *Works and Days* (8th c. B.C.), 265, tr. Richmond Lattimore.

21. It is by its promise of a sense of power that evil often attracts the weak. ERIC HOFFER, *The Passionate State of Mind* (1954), 91.

22. What we most want to ask of our Maker is an unfolding of the divine purpose in putting human beings into conditions in which such numbers of them would be sure to go wrong. OLIVER WENDELL HOLMES, SR., *Over the Teacups* (1891), 10.

23. He who passively accepts evil is as much involved in it as he who helps to perpetrate it. He who accepts evil without protesting against it is really cooperating with it. MARTIN LUTHER KING, JR., *Stride Toward Freedom* (1958).

24. Badness is accidental, like disease.

We find more tempers good than bad, where proper care is taken in proper time. WALTER SAVAGE LANDOR, "La Fontaine and De La Rochefoucault," *Imaginary Conversations* (1824–53).

25. When you choose the lesser of two evils, always remember that it is still an evil. MAX LERNER, "Politics and the Connective Tissue," *Actions and Passions* (1949).

26. When evil acts in the world it always manages to find instruments who believe that what they do is not evil but honorable. MAX LERNER, "The Case of the Wolf Whistle," *The Unfinished Country* (1959), 4.

27. It is the evil that lies in ourselves that is ever least tolerant of the evil that dwells within others. MAURICE MAETERLINCK, *Wisdom and Destiny* (1898), 108, tr. Alfred Sutro.

28. There is no explanation for evil. It must be looked upon as a necessary part of the order of the universe. To ignore it is childish; to bewail it senseless. W. SOMERSET MAUGHAM, *The Summing Up* (1938), 73.

29. Evil alone has oil for every wheel. EDNA ST. VINCENT MILLAY, untitled poem, *Mine the Harvest* (1954).

30. The great epochs of our life come when we gain the courage to rechristen our evil as what is best in us. NIETZSCHE, *Beyond Good and Evil* (1886), 116, tr. Walter Kaufmann.

31. Submit to the present evil, lest a greater one befall you. PHAEDRUS, *Fables* (1st c.), 1.2.31, tr. H. T. Riley.

32. Our greatest evils flow from ourselves. ROUSSEAU, *Émile* (1762), 1.

33. Much the most important evils that mankind have to consider are those which they inflict upon each other through stupidity or malevolence or both. BERTRAND RUSSELL, "Ideas That Have Harmed Mankind," *Unpopular Essays* (1950).

34. Shall I tell you what the real evil is? To cringe to the things that are called evils, to surrender to them our freedom, in defiance of which we ought to face any suffering. SENECA, *Letters to Lucilius* (1st c.), 85.28, tr. E. Phillips Barker.

35. If you expect the wise man to be as angry as the baseness of crimes requires, then he must not only be angry but go insane. SENECA, *On Anger* (1st c.).

36. There's small choice in rotten apples. SHAKESPEARE, *The Taming of the Shrew* (1593–94), 1.1.138.

37. There is some soul of goodness in things evil, / Would men observingly distil it out. SHAKESPEARE, *Henry V* (1598–99), 4.1.4.

38. Men's evil manners live in brass; their virtues / We write in water. SHAKESPEARE, *Henry VIII* (1612–13), 4.2.45.

39. It is among people who think no evil that Evil can flourish without fear. LOGAN PEARSALL SMITH, *Afterthoughts* (1931), 3.

40. Between two evils, I always pick the one I never tried before. MAE WEST, in *Klondike Annie* (1936).

## 306. EVOLUTION

See also 37. Ancestry; 735. Progress

1. Progress is / The law of life, man is not man as yet. ROBERT BROWNING, *Paracelsus* (1835), 5.

2. From the war of nature, from famine and death, the most exalted object which we are capable of conceiving, namely, the production of the higher animals, directly follows. CHARLES DARWIN, "Conclusion," *The Origin of Species* (1859).

3. As to modesty and decency, if we are simians we have done well, considering: but if we are something else – fallen angels – we have indeed fallen far. CLARENCE DAY, *This Simian World* (1920), 13.

4. It's more comfortable to feel that we're a slight improvement on a monkey thin such a fallin' off fr'm th' angels. FINLEY PETER DUNNE, "On the Descent of Man," *Mr. Dooley On Making a Will* (1919).

5. Darwinian Man, though well-behaved, / At best is only a monkey shaved! W. S. GILBERT, *Princess Ida* (1884), 2.

6. It is an error to imagine that evolution signifies a constant tendency to increased perfection. That process undoubtedly involves a constant remodeling of the organism in adaptation to new conditions; but it depends on the nature of those conditions whether the direction of the modifications effected shall be upward or downward. THOMAS HENRY HUXLEY, *The Struggle for Existence in Human Society* (1888).

7. The tide of evolution carries everything before it, thoughts no less than bodies, and persons no less than nations. GEORGE

SANTAYANA, *Little Essays* (1920), 44, ed. Logan Pearsall Smith.

8. So careful of the type she [nature] seems, / So careless of the single life. ALFRED, LORD TENNYSON, "In Memoriam A. H. H." (1850), 54.

9. I believe that our Heavenly Father invented man because he was disappointed in the monkey. MARK TWAIN, *Mark Twain in Eruption* (1940), ed. Bernard De Voto.

## 307. EXAGGERATION

1. The temptation to vivify the tale and make it walk abroad on its own legs is hard to deny. GELETT BURGESS, "Sub Rosa," *The Romance of the Commonplace* (1916).

2. Exaggeration is a prodigality of the judgment which shows the narrowness of one's knowledge or one's taste. BALTASAR GRACIÁN, *The Art of Worldly Wisdom* (1647), 41, tr. Joseph Jacobs.

3. To exaggerate is to begin to invent. Graffito written during French student revolt, May 1968.

4. To exaggerate is to weaken. JEAN-FRANÇOIS DE LA HARPE, *Mélanie* (1770), 1.1.

5. By speaking, by thinking, we undertake to clarify things, and that forces us to exacerbate them, dislocate them, schematize them. Every concept is in itself an exaggeration. JOSÉ ORTEGA Y GASSET, "In Search of Goethe from Within, Letter to a German," *Partisan Review*, December 1949, tr. Willard R. Trask.

6. Camp is a vision of the world in terms of style – but a particular style. It is the love of the exaggerated. SUSAN SONTAG, "Notes on Camp," *Against Interpretation* (1961).

7. Exaggeration, the inseparable companion of greatness. VOLTAIRE, "Solomon," *Philosophical Dictionary* (1764).

## 308. EXAMPLE

1. Example is the best precept. AESOP, "The Two Crabs," *Fables* (6th c. B.C.?), tr. Joseph Jacobs.

2. Example is better than following it. AMBROSE BIERCE, "Saw," *The Devil's Dictionary* (1881–1911).

3. The example of good men is visible philosophy. ENGLISH PROVERB.

4. He teaches me to be good that does me good. THOMAS FULLER, M.D., *Gnomologia* (1732), 2034.

5. The crab instructs its young, "Walk straight ahead – like me." HINDUSTANI PROVERB.

6. We need someone, I say, on whom our character may mould itself: you'll never make the crooked straight without a ruler. SENECA, *Letters to Lucilius* (1st c.), 11.10, tr. E. Phillips Barker.

7. Few things are harder to put up with than the annoyance of a good example. MARK TWAIN, "Pudd'nhead Wilson's Calendar," *Pudd'nhead Wilson* (1894), 19.

## 309. EXCELLENCE

**See also 1. Ability; 374. Genius; 578. Merit; 945. Superiority; 956. Talent; 1029. Vocations**

1. What is well done is done soon enough. SEIGNEUR DU BARTAS, *Divine Weekes and Workes* (1578), 1.1.

2. Human excellence means nothing / Unless it works with the consent of God. EURIPIDES, *The Suppliant Women* (c. 421 B.C.), tr. Frank W. Jones.

3. There is none who cannot teach somebody something, and there is none so excellent but he is excelled. BALTASAR GRACIÁN, *The Art of Worldly Wisdom* (1647), 195, tr. Joseph Jacobs.

4. Either dance well or quit the ballroom. GREEK PROVERB.

5. One shining quality lends a lustre to another, or hides some glaring defect. WILLIAM HAZLITT, *Characteristics* (1823), 162.

6. Men of genius do not excel in any profession because they labour in it, but they labour in it because they excel. WILLIAM HAZLITT, *Characteristics* (1823), 416.

7. It is not sufficiently considered in the hour of exultation, that all human excellence is comparative; that no man performs much but in proportion to what others accomplish, or to the time and opportunities which have been allowed him. SAMUEL JOHNSON, *The Rambler* (1750–52), 127.

8. Consider first, that great / Or bright infers not excellence. MILTON, *Paradise Lost* (1667), 8.90.

9. The heart of man does not tolerate an absence of the excellent and supreme. JOSÉ

ORTEGA Y GASSET, "Preliminary Meditation," *Meditations on Quixote* (1914).

10. We measure the excellency of other men by some excellency we conceive to be in ourselves. JOHN SELDEN, "Measure of Things," *Table Talk* (1689).

11. Life's like a play: it's not the length, but the excellence of the acting that matters. SENECA, *Letters to Lucilius* (1st c.), 77.20, tr. E. Phillips Barker.

12. What is our praise or pride / But to imagine excellence, and try to make it? / What does it say over the door of Heaven / But *homo fecit?* RICHARD WILBUR, "For the New Railway Station in Rome," *Things of This World* (1956).

13. All excellence is equally difficult. THORNTON WILDER, interview, *Writers at Work: First Series* (1958), ed. Malcolm Cowley.

## 310. EXCESS

**See also 307. Exaggeration; 322. Extravagance; 401. Greed; 468. Indulgence; 492. Intemperance; 554. Luxury; 592. Moderation; 940. Sufficiency; 963. Temperance**

1. The road of excess leads to the palace of wisdom. WILLIAM BLAKE, "Proverbs of Hell," *The Marriage of Heaven and Hell* (1790).

2. To go beyond is as wrong as to fall short. CONFUCIUS, *Analects* (6th c. B.C.), 11.15, tr. James Legge.

3. The best of things, beyond their measure, cloy. HOMER, *Iliad* (9th c. B.C.), 13.795, tr. Alexander Pope.

4. The dinosaur's eloquent lesson is that if some bigness is good, an overabundance of bigness is not necessarily better. ERIC JOHNSTON, *Quote*, Feb. 23, 1958.

5. Too much work and too much energy kill a man just as effectively as too much assorted vice or too much drink. RUDYARD KIPLING, "Thrown Away," *Plain Tales from the Hills* (1888).

6. Excess on occasion is exhilarating. It prevents moderation from acquiring the deadening effect of a habit. W. SOMERSET MAUGHAM, *The Summing Up* (1938), 15.

7. The archer that shoots over, misses as much as he that falls short. MONTAIGNE, "Of moderation," *Essays* (1580–88), tr. Charles Cotton and W. C. Hazlitt.

8. They are as sick that surfeit with too much as they that starve with nothing. SHAKESPEARE, *The Merchant of Venice* (1596–97), 1.2.6.

9. It's just as unpleasant to get more than you bargain for as to get less. GEORGE BERNARD SHAW, *Getting Married* (1911).

10. Excesses accomplish nothing. Disorder immediately defeats itself. WOODROW WILSON, address to Congress, Nov. 11, 1918.

## 311. EXCITEMENT

**See also 16. Adventure; 213. Danger**

1. People's sympathies seem generally to be with the fire so long as no one is in danger of being burned. SAMUEL BUTLER (d. 1902), "Written Sketches," *Note-Books* (1912).

2. Where Life becomes a Spasm, / And History a Whiz: / If that is not Sensation, / I don't know what it is. LEWIS CARROLL, "Poeta Fit, Non Nascitur" (1869).

3. There is a pleasure in being in a ship beaten about by a storm, when we are sure that it will not founder. PASCAL, *Pensées* (1670), 858, tr. W. F. Trotter.

## 312. EXCUSES

**See also 320. Explanation; 339. Faults; 775. Rationalization**

1. With the help of an "if" you might put Paris into a bottle. FRENCH PROVERB.

2. Bad excuses are worse than none. THOMAS FULLER, M.D., *Gnomologia* (1732), 833.

3. One unable to dance blames the unevenness of the floor. MALAY PROVERB.

4. One of man's greatest failings is that he looks almost always for an excuse, in the misfortune that befalls him through his own fault, before looking for a remedy—which means he often finds the remedy too late. CARDINAL DE RETZ, *Mémoires* (1718).

5. Oftentimes excusing of a fault / Doth make the fault the worse by the excuse. SHAKESPEARE, *King John* (1596–97), 4.2.30.

## 313. EXECUTIVES

**See also 13. Administration**

1. What is worth doing is worth the trouble of asking somebody to do it. AMBROSE BIERCE, "Saw," *The Devil's Dictionary* (1881–1911).

2. Some men owe most of their greatness to the ability of detecting in those they destine for their tools the exact quality of strength that matters for their work. JOSEPH CONRAD, *Lord Jim* (1900), 42.

3. He is the rich man who can avail himself of all men's faculties. EMERSON, "Wealth," *The Conduct of Life* (1860).

4. Damn the great executives, the men of measured merriment, damn the men with careful smiles, damn the men that run the shops, oh, damn their measured merriment. SINCLAIR LEWIS, *Arrowsmith* (1925), 25.

5. A decision is the action an executive must take when he has information so incomplete that the answer does not suggest itself. ARTHUR WILLIAM RADFORD, *Time*, Feb. 25, 1957.

6. Nothing is impossible for the man who doesn't have to do it himself. A. H. WEILER, in a privately circulated memorandum of *The New York Times*.

## EXILE

**See 421. Homeland**

## 314. EXISTENCE

**See also 315. Existentialism; 442. Identity; 536. Life**

1. At a given moment I open my eyes and exist. And before that, during all eternity, what was there? Nothing. UGO BETTI, *The Inquiry* (1944–45), 2.2, ed. Gino Rizzo.

2. To be alive – is Power – / Existence – in itself – / Without a further function – / Omnipotence – Enough –. EMILY DICKINSON, poem (c. 1863).

3. As long as any man exists, there is some need of him; let him fight for his own. EMERSON, "Nominalist and Realist," *Essays: Second Series* (1844).

4. Man is the only animal for whom his own existence is a problem which he has to solve. ERICH FROMM, *Man for Himself* (1947), 3.

5. The individual who has to justify his existence by his own efforts is in eternal bondage to himself. ERIC HOFFER, *The Ordeal of Change* (1964), 5.

6. Every life is its own excuse for being. ELBERT HUBBARD, *The Note Book* (1927).

7. An atom tossed in a chaos made / Of yeasting worlds, which bubble and foam. / Whence have I come? / What would be home? / I hear no answer. I am afraid! AMY LOWELL, "The Last Quarter of the Moon," *Sword Blades and Poppy Seeds* (1914).

8. All life is the struggle, the effort to be itself. JOSÉ ORTEGA Y GASSET, *The Revolt of the Masses* (1930), 11.

9. We spend our lives talking about this mystery: our life. JULES RENARD, *Journal*, April 1894, ed. and tr. Louise Bogan and Elizabeth Roget.

10. A sanctity hangs about the sources of our being, whether physical, social, or imaginary. GEORGE SANTAYANA, *The Life of Reason: Reason in Society* (1905–06), 7.

11. That I exist is a perpetual surprise which is life. RABINDRANATH TAGORE, *Stray Birds* (1916), 22.

12. Being is the great explainer. THOREAU, *Journal*, Feb. 26, 1841.

## 315. EXISTENTIALISM

**See also 3. The Absurd; 314. Existence**

1. Man is nothing else but what he makes of himself. Such is the first principle of existentialism. JEAN-PAUL SARTRE, *Existentialism* (1947).

2. Existentialism is possible only in a world where God is dead or a luxury, and where Christianity is dead. GABRIEL VAHANIAN, *The Death of God* (1962), 9.

## 316. EXPECTATION

**See also 247. Disappointment; 366. Future; 425. Hope; 1033. Waiting**

1. For people who live on expectations, to face up to their realisation is something of an ordeal. ELIZABETH BOWEN, *The Death of the Heart* (1938), 2.5.

2. Nothing is so good as it seems beforehand. GEORGE ELIOT, *Silas Marner* (1861).

3. Prospect is often better than possession. THOMAS FULLER, M.D., *Gnomologia* (1732), 3958.

4. The hours we pass with happy prospects in view are more pleasing than those crowned with fruition. OLIVER GOLDSMITH, *The Hermit* (1764), 10.

5. The best part of our lives we pass in counting on what is to come. WILLIAM HAZLITT, "On Novelty and Familiarity," *The Plain Speaker* (1826).

6. Lighten grief with hopes of a brighter morrow; / Temper joy, in fear of a change of fortune. HORACE, *Odes* (23–c. 15 B.C.), 2.10.

7. If pleasures are greatest in anticipation, just remember that this is also true of trouble. ELBERT HUBBARD, *The Note Book* (1927).

8. It seems to be the fate of man to seek all his consolations in futurity. The time present is seldom able to fill desire or imagination with immediate enjoyment, and we are forced to supply its deficiencies by recollection or anticipation. SAMUEL JOHNSON, *The Rambler* (1750–52), 203.

9. Blessed is he who expects nothing, for he shall never be disappointed. ALEXANDER POPE, letter to John Gay, Oct. 6, 1727.

10. Even if it is to be, what end do you serve by running to meet distress? SENECA, *Letters to Lucilius* (1st c.), 13, tr. E. Phillips Barker.

11. Oft expectation fails and most oft there / Where most it promises, and oft it hits / Where hope is coldest and despair most fits. SHAKESPEARE, *All's Well That Ends Well* (1602-03), 2.1.145.

12. 'Tis expectation makes a blessing dear; / Heaven were not heaven if we knew what it were. SIR JOHN SUCKLING, "Against Fruition," *Fragmenta Aurea* (1646), 4.

13. It is only because we are ill informed that anything surprises us; and we are disappointed because we expect that for which we have not provided. CHARLES DUDLEY WARNER, "Eighteenth Week," *My Summer in a Garden* (1871).

## 317. EXPEDIENCY

See also 570. Means and Ends

1. In practice, such trifles as contradictions in principle are easily set aside; the faculty of ignoring them makes the practical man. HENRY ADAMS, *The Education of Henry Adams* (1907), 3.

2. We do what we must, and call it by the best names. EMERSON, "Considerations by the Way," *The Conduct of Life* (1860).

3. Philanthropic and religious bodies do not commonly make their executive officers out of saints. EMERSON, "Power," *The Conduct of Life* (1860).

4. a certain / alloy of expediency improves the / gold of morality and makes / it wear all the longer. DON MARQUIS, "clarence the ghost," *Archy and Mehitabel* (1927).

5. Policy sits above conscience. SHAKESPEARE, *Timon of Athens* (1607–08), 3.2.94.

6. In every sort of danger there are various ways of winning through, if one is ready to do and say anything whatever. SOCRATES, in Plato's *Apology* (4th c. B.C.), tr. Lane Cooper.

7. Custom adapts itself to expediency. TACITUS, *Annals* (A.D. 115–117?), 12.6, tr. Alfred J. Church and William J. Brodribb.

## 318. EXPENDABILITY

See also 1005. Unimportance

1. A man overboard, a mouth the less. DUTCH PROVERB.

2. Every man is wanted, and no man is wanted much. EMERSON, "Nominalist and Realist," *Essays: Second Series* (1844).

3. In the world I fill up a place, which may be better supplied when I have made it empty. SHAKESPEARE, *As You Like It* (1599–1600), 1.2.203.

## 319. EXPERIENCE

See also 502. Involvement; 529. Learning; 536. Life; 910. Sophistication

1. Only when you have crossed the river can you say the crocodile has a lump on his snout. ASHANTI PROVERB.

2. A man that is young in years may be old in hours if he have lost no time. FRANCIS BACON, "Of Youth and Age," *Essays* (1625).

3. Experience isn't interesting until it begins to repeat itself—in fact, till it does that, it hardly *is* experience. ELIZABETH BOWEN, *The Death of the Heart* (1938), 1.1.

4. We do but learn to-day what our better advanced judgements will unteach us to-morrow. SIR THOMAS BROWNE, *Religio Medici* (1642), 2.

5. You cannot create experience. You

must undergo it. ALBERT CAMUS, *Notebooks 1935–1942* (1962), 1, tr. Philip Thody.

6. The authentic insight and experience of any human soul, were it but insight and experience in hewing of wood and drawing of water, is real knowledge, a real possession and acquirement. THOMAS CARLYLE, "Corn-Law Rhymes" (1832).

7. The knowledge of the world is only to be acquired in the world, and not in a closet. LORD CHESTERFIELD, *Letters to His Son*, Oct. 4, 1746.

8. When you have really exhausted an experience you always reverence and love it. G. K. CHESTERTON, "The Contented Man," *A Miscellany of Men* (1912).

9. Experience which was once claimed by the aged is now claimed exclusively by the young. G. K. CHESTERTON, "On Experience," *All Is Grist* (1931).

10. Experience is a comb which nature gives us when we are bald. CHINESE PROVERB.

11. To most men, experience is like the stern lights of a ship, which illumine only the track it has passed. SAMUEL TAYLOR COLERIDGE, *Table Talk* (1835).

12. It is far better to borrow experience than to buy it. CHARLES CALEB COLTON, *Lacon* (1825), 1.33.

13. No one over thirty-five is worth meeting who has not something to teach us,—something more than we could learn ourselves, from a book. CYRIL CONNOLLY, *The Unquiet Grave* (1945), 1.

14. Life is a succession of lessons enforced by immediate reward, or, oftener, by immediate chastisement. ERNEST DIMNET, *The Art of Thinking* (1928), 2.6.

15. I have no fund of tears to weep / For happenings that undeceive. PAUL LAWRENCE DUNBAR, "After the Quarrel," *The Complete Poems* (1962).

16. If ye live enough befure thirty ye won't care to live at all afther fifty. FINLEY PETER DUNNE, "Casual Observations," *Mr. Dooley's Philosophy* (1900).

17. Experience is the only teacher, and we get his lesson indifferently in any school. EMERSON, *Journals*, 1845.

18. Life is a succession of lessons which must be lived to be understood. EMERSON, "Illusions," *The Conduct of Life* (1860).

19. Only the wearer knows where the shoe pinches. ENGLISH PROVERB.

20. Experience, travel— / These are an education in themselves. EURIPIDES, *Andromache* (c. 426 B.C.), tr. John F. Nims.

21. I know by my own pot how the others boil. FRENCH PROVERB.

22. Scalded cats fear even cold water. THOMAS FULLER, M.D., *Gnomologia* (1732), 4075.

23. He who has once burnt his mouth always blows his soup. GERMAN PROVERB.

24. An experience teaches only the good observer; but far from seeking a lesson in it, everyone looks for an argument in experience, and everyone interprets the conclusion in his own way. ANDRÉ GIDE, *Journals*, 1922, tr. Justin O'Brien.

25. You know more of a road by having travelled it than by all the conjectures and descriptions in the world. WILLIAM HAZLITT, "On the Conduct of Life," *Literary Remains* (1836).

26. I have but one lamp by which my feet are guided, and that is the lamp of experience. I know of no way of judging of the future but by the past. PATRICK HENRY, speech, Virginia Convention, March 23, 1775.

27. The fool knows after he's suffered. HESIOD, *Works and Days* (8th c. B.C.), 218, tr. Richmond Lattimore.

28. Experience is not what happens to you; it is what you do with what happens to you. ALDOUS HUXLEY, *Reader's Digest*, March 1956.

29. From their own experience or from the recorded experience of others (history), men learn only what their passions and their metaphysical prejudices allow them to learn. ALDOUS HUXLEY, *Collected Essays* (1959).

30. What does not poison, fattens. ITALIAN PROVERB.

31. A man should have the fine point of his soul taken off to become fit for this world. JOHN KEATS, letter to John Hamilton Reynolds, Nov. 22, 1817.

32. Many people know so little about what is beyond their short range of experience. They look within themselves—and find nothing! Therefore they conclude that there is nothing outside themselves, either. HELEN KELLER, *The World I Live In* (1908).

33. We arrive at the various stages of life quite as novices. LA ROCHEFOUCAULD, *Maxims* (1665), tr. Kenneth Pratt.

34. Experience does not err; only your judgments err by expecting from her what is not in her power. LEONARDO DA VINCI, *Notebooks* (c. 1500), tr. Jean Paul Richter.

35. He who neglects to drink of the spring of experience is likely to die of thirst in the desert of ignorance. LING PO, epigram.

36. No man's knowledge here can go beyond his experience. JOHN LOCKE, *An Essay Concerning Human Understanding* (1690), 2.1.19.

37. One thorn of experience is worth a whole wilderness of warning. JAMES RUSSELL LOWELL, "Shakespeare Once More," *Among My Books* (1870).

38. The finest edge is made with the blunt whetstone. JOHN LYLY, *Euphues: The Anatomy of Wit* (1579).

39. No one can shed light on vices he does not have or afflictions he has never experienced. ANTONIO MACHADO, *Juan de Mairena* (1943), 13, tr. Ben Belitt.

40. No man alive can say, This shall not happen to me. MENANDER (4th–3rd c. B.C.), quoted in Plutarch's "Contentment," *Moralia* (c. A.D. 100), tr. Moses Hadas.

41. Nothing has happened to you unless you make much of it. MENANDER (4th–3rd c. B.C.), quoted in Plutarch's "Contentment," *Moralia* (c. A.D. 100), tr. Moses Hadas.

42. Not sense data or atoms or electrons or packets of energy, but purposes, interests, and meanings, constitute the underlying facts of human experience. LEWIS MUMFORD, "Orientation to Life," *The Conduct of Life* (1951).

43. The burnt child, urged by rankling ire, / Can hardly wait to get back at the fire. OGDEN NASH, "Experience to Let," *I'm a Stranger Here Myself* (1938).

44. Men use a new lesson or experience later on as a ploughshare or perhaps also as a weapon; women at once make it into an ornament. NIETZSCHE, *Miscellaneous Maxims and Opinions* (1879), 290, tr. Paul V. Cohn.

45. When one has finished building one's house, one suddenly realizes that in the process one has learned something that one really needed to know in the worst way—before one began. NIETZSCHE, *Beyond Good and Evil* (1886), 277, tr. Walter Kaufmann.

46. A strong and well-constituted man digests his experiences (deeds and misdeeds) just as he digests his meats, even when he has some tough morsels to swallow. NIETZSCHE, *The Genealogy of Morals* (1887), 3.16, tr. Horace B. Samuel.

47. He who has been bitten by a snake fears a piece of string. PERSIAN PROVERB.

48. Our whole knowledge of the world hangs on this very slender thread: the re-gu-la-ri-ty of our experiences. LUIGI PIRANDELLO, *The Pleasure of Honesty* (1917), 1, tr. William Murray.

49. That which we have not been forced to decipher, to clarify by our own personal effort, that which was made clear before, is not ours. MARCEL PROUST, *Remembrance of Things Past: The Sweet Cheat Gone* (1913–27), tr. C. K. Scott-Moncrieff.

50. We are forced to participate in the games of life before we can possibly learn how to use the options in the rules governing them. PHILIP RIEFF, "Conflict and Character," *Freud: The Mind of the Moralist* (1959).

51. What is experience? A poor little hut constructed from the ruins of the palace of gold and marble called our illusions. JOSEPH ROUX, *Meditations of a Parish Priest* (1886), 4.15, tr. Isabel F. Hapgood.

52. Experience seems to most of us to lead to conclusions, but empiricism has sworn never to draw them. GEORGE SANTAYANA, *Character and Opinion in the United States* (1921), 3.

53. Men are wise in proportion, not to their experience, but to their capacity for experience. GEORGE BERNARD SHAW, "Maxims for Revolutionists," *Man and Superman* (1903).

54. Everything happens to everybody sooner or later if there is time enough. GEORGE BERNARD SHAW, *Back to Methuselah* (1921), 4.

55. If we shake hands with icy fingers, it is because we have burnt them so horribly before. LOGAN PEARSALL SMITH, *Afterthoughts* (1931), 2.

56. He who was first an acolyte, and afterwards an abbot or curate, knows what the boys do behind the altar. SPANISH PROVERB.

57. Doubtless the world is quite right in a million ways; but you have to be kicked

about a little to convince you of the fact. ROBERT LOUIS STEVENSON, "Crabbed Age and Youth," *Virginibus Puerisque* (1881).

58. It is strange how often a heart must be broken / Before the years can make it wise. SARA TEASDALE, "Dust," *Flame and Shadow* (1920).

59. All experience is an arch wherethrough / Gleams that untravelled world whose margin fades / For ever and for ever when I move. ALFRED, LORD TENNYSON, "Ulysses" (1842).

60. Others' follies teach us not / Nor much their wisdom teaches; / And most, of sterling worth, is what / Our own experience preaches. ALFRED, LORD TENNYSON, "Will Waterproof's Lyrical Monologue" (1842).

61. There's nothing in the world so unfair as a man who has no experience of life; he thinks nothing is done right except what he's doing himself. TERENCE, *The Brothers* (160 B.C.), tr. William A. Oldfather.

62. Experience is in the fingers and head. The heart is inexperienced. THOREAU, *Journal*, April 3, 1841.

63. The difference between ancients and moderns is that the ancients asked what have we experienced, and moderns asked what can we experience. ALFRED NORTH WHITEHEAD, *Adventures in Ideas* (1933), 15.

64. Experience is the name everyone gives to their mistakes. OSCAR WILDE, *Lady Windermere's Fan* (1892), 3.

65. To regret one's own experiences is to arrest one's own development. To deny one's own experiences is to put a lie into the lips of one's life. It is no less than a denial of the soul. OSCAR WILDE, *De Profundis* (1905).

## EXPERTS

See 917. Specialists

## 320. EXPLANATION

See also 312. Excuses; 775. Rationalization

1. There is no waste of time in life like that of making explanations. BENJAMIN DISRAELI, speech, "University Education Bill (Ireland)," March 11, 1873.

2. Ah! how different it is to render an account to ourselves of ourselves and to render account to the public of ourselves. EMERSON, *Journals*, 1844.

3. Never explain. Your friends do not need it and your enemies will not believe you anyway. ELBERT HUBBARD, *The Note Book* (1927).

4. An idle reason lessens the weight of the good ones you gave before. JONATHAN SWIFT, *Thoughts on Various Subjects* (1711).

## 321. EXPLOITATION

1. If you allow men to use you for your own purposes, they will use you for theirs. AESOP, "The Horse, Hunter, and Stag," *Fables* (6th c. B.C.?), tr. Joseph Jacobs.

2. Being creative is having something to sell, or knowing how to sell something, or having sold something. It has taken over what we used to mean by being "wised-up," knowing the tricks, the shortcuts. PAULINE KAEL, "The Creative Business," *Kiss Kiss Bang Bang* (1968).

3. The human being as a commodity is the disease of our age. MAX LERNER, "The Assault on the Mind," *The Unfinished Country* (1959), 2.

## 322. EXTRAVAGANCE

See also 310. Excess; 554. Luxury; 592. Moderation; 970. Thrift

1. We deny that it is fun to be saving. It is fun to be prodigal. Go to the butterfly, thou parsimonious sluggard; consider her ways and get wise. FRANKLIN P. ADAMS, *Nods and Becks* (1944).

2. Delight in splendor is / No more than happiness with little: for both / Have their appeal. EURIPIDES, *Ion* (c. 421–408 B.C.), tr. Ronald F. Willetts.

3. Dry happiness is like dry bread. We eat, but we do not dine. I wish for the superfluous, for the useless, for the extravagant, for the too much, for that which is not good for anything. VICTOR HUGO, "Jean Valjean," *Les Misérables* (1862), 5.6, tr. Charles E. Wilbour.

## EXTREMISM

See 333. Fanaticism

## 323. EYES

See also 324. Face; 875. Senses; 890. Sight; 918. Spectacles

1. The eyes indicate the antiquity of the soul. EMERSON, "Behavior," *The Conduct of Life* (1860).

2. Eyes, you know, are the great intruders. ERVING GOFFMAN, interview, *The New York Times*, Feb. 12, 1969.

3. The eyes have one language everywhere. GEORGE HERBERT, *Jacula Prudentum* (1651).

4. I dislike an eye that twinkles like a star. Those only are beautiful which, like the planets, have a steady, lambent light, are luminous, but not sparkling. LONGFELLOW, *Hyperion* (1839), 3.4.

# F

## 324. FACE

See also 148. Communication; 189. Cosmetics; 323. Eyes; 875. Senses

1. There are mystically in our faces certain characters which carry in them the motto of our souls, wherein he that cannot read A,B,C may read our natures. SIR THOMAS BROWNE, *Religio Medici* (1642), 2.

2. There is a case for keeping wrinkles. They are the long-service stripes earned in the hard campaign of life. *Daily Mail*, London, editorial, "In Praise of Wrinkles," Jan. 20, 1961.

3. The eyebrows form but a small part of the face, and yet they can darken the whole of life by the scorn they express. DEMETRIUS (4th–3rd c. B.C.), quoted in Diogenes Laertius' *Lives and Opinions of Eminent Philosophers* (3rd c. A.D.), tr. R. D. Hicks.

4. A man finds room in the few square inches of his face for the traits of all his ancestors; for the expression of all his history, and his wants. EMERSON, "Behavior," *The Conduct of Life* (1860).

5. Not only does beauty fade, but it leaves a record upon the face as to what became of it. ELBERT HUBBARD, *The Note Book* (1927).

6. The features of our face are hardly more than gestures which have become permanent. MARCEL PROUST, *Remembrance of Things Past: Within a Budding Grove* (1913–27), tr. C. K. Scott-Moncrieff.

7. If the eyes are sometimes the organ through which our intelligence is revealed, the nose is generally the organ in which stupidity is most readily displayed. MARCEL PROUST, *Remembrance of Things Past: Cities of the Plain* (1913–27), tr. C. K. Scott-Moncrieff.

8. There are quantities of human beings, but there are many more faces, for each person has several. RAINER MARIA RILKE, *The Notebooks of Malte Laurids Brigge* (1910), tr. M. D. Herter Norton.

9. A great nose indicates a great man— / Genial, courteous, intellectual, / Virile, courageous. EDMOND ROSTAND, *Cyrano de Bergerac* (1879), 1, tr. Brian Hooker.

10. A lovely face is the solace of wounded hearts and the key of locked-up gates. SA'DI, *Gulistan* (1258), 3.28, tr. James Ross.

## 325. FACILITY

See also 243. Difficulty

1. A bald head is soon shaven. ENGLISH PROVERB.

2. He who accounts all things easy will have many difficulties. LAOTSE, *The Simple Way* (6th c. B.C.).

3. For easy things, that may be got at will, / Most sorts of men do set but little store. EDMUND SPENSER, *Amoretti* (1595), 51.

## 326. FACTS

See also 777. Reality; 925. Statistics; 967. Theory

1. You can't make the Duchess of Windsor into Rebecca of Sunnybrook Farm. The facts of life are very stubborn things. CLEVELAND AMORY, news reports, Oct. 6, 1955.

2. Thank God, except at its one moment there's never any such thing as a bare fact. Ten minutes later, half an hour later, one's begun to gloze the fact over with a deposit of some sort. ELIZABETH BOWEN, *The Death of the Heart* (1938), 3.2.

3. Conclusive facts are inseparable from

inconclusive except by a head that already understands and knows. THOMAS CARLYLE, *Chartism* (1839), 2.

4. The grand aim of all science is to cover the greatest number of empirical facts by logical deduction from the smallest number of hypotheses or axioms. EINSTEIN, *Life*, Jan. 9, 1950.

5. Time dissipates to shining ether the solid angularity of facts. EMERSON, "History," *Essays: First Series* (1841).

6. If a man will kick a fact out of the window, when he comes back he finds it again in the chimney corner. EMERSON, *Journals*, 1842.

7. The chief value of the new fact, is to enhance the great and constant fact of life. EMERSON, "The Poet," *Essays: Second Series* (1844).

8. All generous minds have a horror of what are commonly called "facts." They are the brute beasts of the intellectual domain. OLIVER WENDELL HOLMES, SR., *The Autocrat of the Breakfast Table* (1858), 1.

9. A wise man recognizes the convenience of a general statement, but he bows to the authority of a particular fact. OLIVER WENDELL HOLMES, SR., *The Poet at the Breakfast Table* (1872), 10.

10. Particulars, as everyone knows, make for virtue and happiness; generalities are intellectually necessary evils. Not philosophers but fret-sawyers and stamp collectors compose the backbone of society. ALDOUS HUXLEY, *Brave New World* (1932), 1.

11. Contemporary philosophers, even rationalistically minded ones, have on the whole agreed that no one has intelligibly banished the mystery of *fact*. WILLIAM JAMES, "The Problem of Being," *Some Problems of Philosophy* (1911).

12. Though we face the facts of sex we are more reluctant than ever to face the fact of death or the crueler facts of life, either biological or social. JOSEPH WOOD KRUTCH, title essay, 1, *If You Don't Mind My Saying So* (1964).

13. The facts are to blame, my friend. We are all imprisoned by facts: I was born, I exist. LUIGI PIRANDELLO, *The Rules of the Game* (1918), 1, tr. William Murray.

14. A fact is like a sack which won't stand up when it is empty. In order that it may stand up, one has to put into it the reason and sentiment which have caused it to exist. LUIGI PIRANDELLO, *Six Characters in Search of an Author* (1921), 1, tr. Edward Storer.

15. When you have duly arrayed your "facts" in logical order, lo, it is like an oil-lamp that you have made, filled and trimmed, but which sheds no light unless first you light it. SAINT-EXUPÉRY, *The Wisdom of the Sands* (1948), 43, tr. Stuart Gilbert.

16. Facts are all accidents. They all might have been different. They all may become different. They all may collapse altogether. GEORGE SANTAYANA, *Persons and Places: My Host the World* (1953), 2.

17. Consciousness of a fact is not knowing it: if it were, the fish would know more of the sea than the geographers and the naturalists. GEORGE BERNARD SHAW, *Back to Methuselah* (1921), 4.1.

18. You will find that the truth is often unpopular and the contest between agreeable fancy and disagreeable fact is unequal. For, in the vernacular, we Americans are suckers for good news. ADLAI STEVENSON, commencement address, Michigan State University, June 8, 1958.

19. It is the spirit of the age to believe that any fact, no matter how suspect, is superior to any imaginative exercise, no matter how true. GORE VIDAL, "French Letters: Theories of the New Novel," *Encounter*, December 1967.

## 327. FAILURE

**See also 17. Adversity; 223. Decline; 225. Defeat; 546. Losers; 547. Loss; 938. Success**

1. There is much to be said for failure. It is more interesting than success. MAX BEERBOHM, "A Small Boy Seeing Giants," *Mainly On the Air* (1946).

2. Woe to him that is alone when he falleth; for he hath not another to help him up. *Bible*, Ecclesiastes 4:10.

3. The tragedy of life is not that man loses but that he almost wins. HEYWOOD BROUN, "Sport for Art's Sake," *Pieces of Hate, and Other Enthusiasms* (1922).

4. Fail I alone, in words and deeds?/ Why, all men strive and who succeeds? ROBERT BROWNING, "The Last Ride Together," *Men and Women* (1855), 5.

5. What I aspired to be, / And was not, comforts me: / A brute I might have been, but would not sink i' the scale. ROBERT BROWNING, "Rabbi Ben Ezra," *Dramatis Personae* (1864), 7.

6. All men that are ruined, are ruined on the side of their natural propensities. EDMUND BURKE, *Letters on a Regicide Peace* (1795–97), 1.

7. I am bored with dying of a broken heart. Everything I timidly start fails with a boldness before unknown. JOHN CAGE, "Erik Satie," *Silence* (1961).

8. Doing is overrated, and success undesirable, but the bitterness of failure even more so. CYRIL CONNOLLY, *The Unquiet Grave* (1945), 4.

9. O human race! Born to ascend on wings, / Why do ye fall at such a little wind? DANTE, "Purgatorio," 12, *The Divine Comedy* (c. 1300–21), tr. Lawrence Grant White.

10. Nothing more aggravates ill success than the near approach to good. HENRY FIELDING, *Tom Jones* (1749), 13.2.

11. One is always more vexed at losing a game of any sort by a single hole or ace, than if one has never had a chance of winning it. WILLIAM HAZLITT, "On Great and Little Things," *Literary Remains* (1836).

12. There is no loneliness greater than the loneliness of a failure. The failure is a stranger in his own house. ERIC HOFFER, *The Passionate State of Mind* (1954), 223.

13. There is no failure except in no longer trying. ELBERT HUBBARD, *The Note Book* (1927).

14. The line between failure and success is so fine that we scarcely know when we pass it: so fine that we are often on the line and do not know it. ELBERT HUBBARD, *The Note Book* (1927).

15. There is the greatest practical benefit in making a few failures early in life. THOMAS HENRY HUXLEY, "On Medical Education" (1870).

16. There is not a fiercer hell than the failure in a great object. JOHN KEATS. preface, *Endymion* (1818).

17. We are neurotically haunted today by the imminence, and by the ignominy, of failure. We know at how frightening a cost one *succeeds:* to fail is something too awful to think about. LOUIS KRONENBERGER, "Our Unhappy Happy Endings," *The Cart and the Horse* (1964), 2.

18. Men fall from great fortune because of the same shortcomings that led to their rise. LA BRUYÈRE, *Characters* (1688), 8.34.

19. Man can muff his / Life as badly as his lines and louder. / In it or out of it he's ham. ARCHIBALD MAC LEISH, *JB* (1958), 7.

20. We may stop ourselves when going up, never when coming down. NAPOLEON I, *Maxims* (1804–15).

21. Failure is lovable and what is lovable is commercial. V. S. PRITCHETT, "Quixote's Translators," *The Living Novel & Later Appreciations* (1964).

22. Flops are a part of life's menu and I've never been a girl to miss out on any of the courses. ROSALIND RUSSELL, *New York Herald Tribune*, April 11, 1957.

23. I would prefer even to fail with honor than win by cheating. SOPHOCLES, *Philoctetes* (409 B.C.), tr. David Grene.

24. Do we move ourselves, or are moved by an unseen hand at a game / That pushes us off from the board, and others ever succeed? ALFRED, LORD TENNYSON, "Maud; A Monodrama" (1856), 4.5.

25. We women adore failures. They lean on us. OSCAR WILDE, *A Woman of No Importance* (1893), 1.

26. He that lies on the ground cannot fall. *Yiddish Proverbs* (1949), ed. Hanan J. Ayalti.

## 328. FAITH

**See also 76. Belief; 200. Creeds; 263. Doubt, Religious; 897. Skepticism; 997. Unbelief**

1. The relation of faith between subject and object is unique in every case. Hundreds may believe, but each has to believe by himself. W. H. AUDEN, "Genius and Apostle," *The Dyer's Hand* (1962).

2. Faith is to believe what you do not yet see; the reward for this faith is to see what you believe. ST. AUGUSTINE, *Sermons* (5th c.), 43.

3. A man consists of the faith that is in him. Whatever his faith is, he is. *Bhagavadgita*, 17, tr. Swami Prabhavananda and Christopher Isherwood.

4. Faith is the substance of things hoped for, the evidence of things not seen. *Bible*, Hebrews 11:1.

5. Faith without works is dead. *Bible*, James 2:26.

6. Faith, n. Belief without evidence in what is told by one who speaks without knowledge, of things without parallel. AMBROSE BIERCE, *The Devil's Dictionary* (1881–1911).

7. He's a Blockhead who wants a proof of what he can't Perceive, / And he's a Fool who tries to make such a Blockhead believe. WILLIAM BLAKE, "To Flaxman" (1808–11).

8. To believe only possibilities is not faith, but mere philosophy. SIR THOMAS BROWNE, *Religio Medici* (1642), 1.

9. What is faith but a kind of betting or a speculation after all? SAMUEL BUTLER (d. 1902), *Note-Books* (1912).

10. You can do very little with faith, but you can do nothing without it. SAMUEL BUTLER (d. 1902), "Rebelliousness," *Note-Books* (1912).

11. Faith—is the Pierless Bridge / Supporting what We see / Unto the Scene that We do not—. EMILY DICKINSON, poem (c. 1864).

12. As he that fears God fears nothing else, so, he that sees God sees every thing else. JOHN DONNE, *Sermons*, No. 7, c. 1620.

13. No faith is our own that we have not arduously won. HAVELOCK ELLIS, *The Dance of Life* (1923), 4.

14. A believer, a mind whose faith is consciousness, is never disturbed because other persons do not yet see the fact which he sees. EMERSON, *Journals*, 1836.

15. The care of God for us is a great thing, / if a man believe it at heart: / it plucks the burden of sorrow from him. EURIPIDES, *Hippolytus* (428 B.C.), tr. David Grene.

16. Faith, to my mind, is a stiffening process, a sort of mental starch, which ought to be applied as sparingly as possible. E. M. FORSTER, "What I Believe," *Two Cheers for Democracy* (1951).

17. If you have abandoned one faith, do not abandon all faith. There is always an alternative to the faith we lose. Or is it the same faith under another mask? GRAHAM GREENE, *The Comedians* (1966).

18. A faith that sets bounds to itself, that will believe so much and no more, that will trust thus far and no further, is none. JULIUS CHARLES HARE and AUGUSTUS WILLIAM HARE, *Guesses at Truth* (1827).

19. Faith always implies the disbelief of a lesser fact in favor of a greater. A little mind often sees the unbelief, without seeing the belief of a large one. OLIVER WENDELL HOLMES, SR., *The Professor at the Breakfast Table* (1860), 5.

20. If your faith is opposed to experience, to human learning and investigation, it is not worth the breath used in giving it expression. EDGAR WATSON HOWE, *Ventures in Common Sense* (1919), 3.7.

21. Faith is not a formula which is agreed to if the weight of evidence favors it. WALTER LIPPMANN, *A Preface to Morals* (1929), 1.4.2.

22. Faith is a living and unshakeable confidence, a belief in the grace of God so assured that a man would die a thousand deaths for its sake. MARTIN LUTHER, preface to his translation of St. Paul's epistle to the Romans (1522).

23. Faith, like a jackal, feeds among the tombs, and even from these dead doubts she gathers her most vital hope. HERMAN MELVILLE, *Moby Dick* (1851), 7.

24. The terrors of truth and dart of death / To faith alike are vain. HERMAN MELVILLE, "The Conflict of Convictions," *Battlepieces and Aspects of the War* (1866).

25. The most satisfying and ecstatic faith is almost purely agnostic. It trusts absolutely without professing to know at all. H. L. MENCKEN, "Quid Est Veritas?" *Damn! A Book of Calumny* (1918).

26. Faith may be defined briefly as an illogical belief in the occurrence of the improbable. H. L. MENCKEN, *Prejudices: Third Series* (1922), 14.

27. Not Truth, but Faith, it is / That keeps the world alive. EDNA ST. VINCENT MILLAY, "Interim," *Renascence* (1917).

28. And what is faith, love, virtue unassayed / Alone, without exterior help sustained? MILTON, *Paradise Lost* (1667), 9.335.

29. Let none henceforth seek needless cause to approve / The faith they owe; when earnestly they seek / Such proof, conclude, they then begin to fail. MILTON, *Paradise Lost* (1667), 9.1140.

30. Faith, fanatic Faith, once wedded fast / To some dear falsehood, hugs it to the last. THOMAS MOORE, "The Veiled Prophet of Khorassan," *Lalla Rookh* (1817).

31. And this I know: whether the one True Light / Kindle to Love, or Wrath consume me quite, / One Flash of It within the

Tavern caught / Better than in the Temple lost outright. OMAR KHAYYÁM, *Rubáiyát* (11th–12th c.), tr. Edward FitzGerald, 4th ed., 77.

32. It is your own assent to yourself, and the constant voice of your own reason, and not of others, that should make you believe. PASCAL, *Pensées* (1670), 260, tr. W. F. Trotter.

33. Console thyself, thou wouldst not seek Me, if thou hadst not found Me. PASCAL, *Pensées* (1670), 552, tr. W. F. Trotter.

34. Faith embraces many truths which seem to contradict each other. PASCAL, *Pensées* (1670), 861, tr. W. F. Trotter.

35. Proofs are the last thing looked for by a truly religious mind which feels the imaginative fitness of its faith. GEORGE SANTAYANA, *Interpretations of Poetry and Religion* (1900).

36. Hope looks for unqualified success; but Faith counts certainly on failure, and takes honorable defeat to be a form of victory. ROBERT LOUIS STEVENSON, title essay, 2, *Virginibus Puerisque* (1881).

37. Faith speaks when hope dissembles: / Faith lives when hope dies dead. ALGERNON CHARLES SWINBURNE, "Jacobite Song," *Astrophel and Other Poems* (1894).

38. How sweet to have a common faith! / To hold a common scorn of death! ALFRED, LORD TENNYSON, "Supposed Confessions" (1830).

39. Cleave ever to the sunnier side of doubt, / And cling to Faith beyond the forms of Faith. ALFRED, LORD TENNYSON, "The Ancient Sage" (1885).

40. Faith is the state of being ultimately concerned. PAUL TILLICH, *Dynamics of Faith* (1957), 1.

41. Faith embraces itself and the doubt about itself. PAUL TILLICH, *The New York Times*, May 5, 1963.

42. Faith is believing what you know ain't so. MARK TWAIN, "Pudd'nhead Wilson's New Calendar," *Following the Equator* (1897), 1.12.

43. Faith is, before all and above all, wishing God may exist. MIGUEL DE UNAMUNO, "Faith, Hope, and Charity," *Tragic Sense of Life* (1913), tr. J. E. Crawford Flitch.

44. Faith consists in believing not what seems true, but what seems false to our understanding. VOLTAIRE, "Faith," *Philosophical Dictionary* (1764).

## FAITHFULNESS

**See 178. Constancy; 470. Infidelity**

## FALL

**See 848. Seasons**

## FALLING

**See 327. Failure**

## 329. FALSEHOOD

**See also 221. Deception; 858. Self-deception; 991. Truth; 992. Truth and Falsehood; 993. Truthfulness**

1. A liar will not be believed, even when he speaks the truth. AESOP, "The Shepherd's Boy," *Fables* (6th c. B.C.?), tr. Joseph Jacobs.

2. One falsehood spoils a thousand truths. ASHANTI PROVERB.

3. A lie faces God and shrinks from man. FRANCIS BACON, "Of Truth," *Essays* (1625).

4. Man can certainly keep on lying (and does so), but he cannot make truth falsehood. KARL BARTH, quoted in his obituary, *The New York Times*, Dec. 11, 1968.

5. A lie always needs a truth for a handle to it. HENRY WARD BEECHER, *Proverbs from Plymouth Pulpit* (1887).

6. Never to lie is to have no lock to your door, you are never wholly alone. ELIZABETH BOWEN, *The House in Paris* (1935), 2.8.

7. There's a real love of a lie, / Liars find ready-made for lies they make, / As hand for glove, or tongue for sugar-plum. ROBERT BROWNING, "Mr. Sludge, The Medium," *Dramatis Personae* (1864).

8. The best liar is he who makes the smallest amount of lying go the longest way. SAMUEL BUTLER (d. 1902), *The Way of All Flesh* (1903), 39.

9. Any fool can tell the truth, but it requires a man of some sense to know how to tell a lie well. SAMUEL BUTLER (d. 1902), "Truth and Convenience," *Note-Books* (1912).

10. Lying has a kind of respect and rever-

ence with it. We pay a person the compliment of acknowledging his superiority whenever we lie to him. SAMUEL BUTLER (d. 1902), "Truth and Convenience," *Note-Books* (1912).

11. And, after all, what is a lie? 'Tis but / The truth in masquerade; and I defy / Historians—heroes—lawyers—priests, to put / A fact without some leaven of a lie. BYRON, *Don Juan* (1819–24), 11.37.

12. A falsehood is, in one sense, a dead thing; but too often it moves about, galvanized by self-will, and pushes the living out of their seats. SAMUEL TAYLOR COLERIDGE, "Preliminary Observations," *Aids to Reflection* (1825).

13. Falsehood is often rocked by truth, but she soon outgrows her cradle and discards her nurse. CHARLES CALEB COLTON, *Lacon* (1825), 1.550.

14. A train of thought is never false. The falsehood lies deep in the necessities of existence, in secret fears and half-formed ambitions, in the secret confidence combined with a secret mistrust of ourselves, in the love of hope and the dread of uncertain days. JOSEPH CONRAD, *Under Western Eyes* (1911), 1.2.

15. I think a lie with a purpose is wan iv th' worst kind an' th' mos' profitable. FINLEY PETER DUNNE, "On Lying," *Mr. Dooley's Opinions* (1901).

16. Every violation of truth is not only a sort of suicide in the liar, but is a stab at the health of human society. EMERSON, "Prudence," *Essays: First Series* (1841).

17. Without lies humanity would perish of despair and boredom. ANATOLE FRANCE, afterword to *The Bloom of Life* (1922).

18. Falsehood is the jockey of misfortune. JEAN GIRAUDOUX, *Siegfried* (1928), 2, tr. Phyllis La Farge with Peter H. Judd.

19. You know what it's like when you find out a friend is a liar? Whatever he says, after that, sounds false, however true it may be. JEAN GIRAUDOUX, *Tiger at the Gates* (1935), 1, tr. Christopher Fry.

20. A single lie destroys a whole reputation for integrity. BALTASAR GRACIÁN, *The Art of Worldly Wisdom* (1647), 181, tr. Joseph Jacobs.

21. The most mischievous liars are those who keep sliding on the verge of truth. JULIUS CHARLES HARE and AUGUSTUS WILLIAM HARE, *Guesses at Truth* (1827).

22. As hypocrisy is said to be the highest compliment to virtue, the art of lying is the strongest acknowledgment of the force of truth. WILLIAM HAZLITT, "On Patronage and Puffing," *Table Talk* (1821–22).

23. The great masses of the people . . . will more easily fall victims to a big lie than to a small one. ADOLF HITLER, *Mein Kampf* (1924), 1.10.

24. You never need think you can turn over any old falsehood without a terrible squirming and scattering of the horrid little population that dwells under it. OLIVER WENDELL HOLMES, SR., *The Autocrat of the Breakfast Table* (1858), 5.

25. Sin has many tools, but a lie is the handle which fits them all. OLIVER WENDELL HOLMES, SR., *The Autocrat of the Breakfast Table* (1858), 6.

26. Americans detest all lies except lies spoken in public or printed lies. EDGAR WATSON HOWE, *Ventures in Common Sense* (1919), 2.6.

27. Life is a system of half-truths and lies, / Opportunistic, convenient evasion. LANGSTON HUGHES, "Elderly Politicians," *The Langston Hughes Reader* (1958).

28. If we live all our lives under lies, it becomes difficult to see *anything* if it does not have anything to do with these lies. LE ROI JONES, "Cuba Libre," *Home* (1966).

29. If there were no falsehood in the world, there would be no doubt; if there were no doubt, there would be no inquiry; if no inquiry, no wisdom, no knowledge, no genius; and Fancy herself would lie muffled up in her robe, inactive, pale, and bloated. WALTER SAVAGE LANDOR, "Epicurus, Leontion, and Ternissa," *Imaginary Conversations* (1824–53).

30. Lying is not only excusable; it is not only innocent, and instinctive; it is, above all, necessary and unavoidable. Without the ameliorations that it offers life would become a mere syllogism, and hence too metallic to be borne. H. L. MENCKEN, *Prejudices: Fourth Series* (1924), 15.

31. In plain truth, lying is an accursed vice. We are not men, nor have other tie upon one another, but by our word. MONTAIGNE, "Of liars," *Essays* (1580–88), tr. Charles Cotton and W. C. Hazlitt.

32. I do myself a greater injury in lying than I do him of whom I tell a lie. MONTAIGNE, "Of presumption," *Essays*

(1580–88), tr. Charles Cotton and W. C. Hazlitt.

33. That lies should be necessary to life is part and parcel of the terrible and questionable character of existence. NIETZSCHE, *The Will to Power* (1888), 853, tr. Anthony M. Ludovici.

34. A liar should have a good memory. QUINTILIAN, *Institutio Oratoria* (c. A.D. 95), 4.2, tr. H. E. Butler.

35. Repetition does not transform a lie into a truth. FRANKLIN D. ROOSEVELT, radio address, Oct. 26, 1939.

36. To tell a falsehood is like the cut of a sabre; for though the wound may heal, the scar of it will remain. SA'DI, *Gulistan* (1258), 8.98, tr. James Ross.

37. People lie because they don't remember clear what they saw. / People lie because they can't help making a story better than it was the way it happened. CARL SANDBURG, *The People, Yes* (1936).

38. A liar goes in fine clothes, / A liar goes in rags. / A liar is a liar, clothes or no clothes. CARL SANDBURG, "The Liars," *Complete Poems* (1950).

39. The devil can cite Scripture for his purpose. / An evil soul producing holy witness / Is like a villain with smiling cheek, / A goodly apple rotten at the heart. SHAKESPEARE, *The Merchant of Venice* (1596–97), 1.3.99.

40. O, what a goodly outside falsehood hath! SHAKESPEARE, *The Merchant of Venice* (1596–97), 1.3.103.

41. False words are not only evil in themselves, but they infect the soul with evil. SOCRATES, in Plato's *Phaedo* (4th–3rd c. B.C.), tr. Benjamin Jowett.

42. A lie is troublesome, and sets a man's invention upon the rack, and one trick needs a great many more to make it good. RICHARD STEELE, *The Spectator* (1711–12), 352.

43. A lie is an abomination unto the Lord, and a very present help in trouble. ADLAI STEVENSON, speech, Springfield, Ill., January 1951.

44. The cruellest lies are often told in silence. ROBERT LOUIS STEVENSON, title essay, 4, *Virginibus Puerisque* (1881).

45. A lie which is half a truth is ever the blackest of lies. ALFRED, LORD TENNYSON, "The Grandmother" (1864), 8.

46. One man lies in his words, and gets a bad reputation; another in his manners, and enjoys a good one. THOREAU, *Journal*, June 25, 1851.

47. One of the most striking differences between a cat and a lie is that a cat has only nine lives. MARK TWAIN, "Pudd'nhead Wilson's Calendar," *Pudd'nhead Wilson* (1894), 7.

48. It is often the case that a man who can't tell a lie thinks that he is the best judge of one. MARK TWAIN, *Notebook* (1935).

49. Mendacity is a system that we live in. Liquor is one way out an' death's the other. TENNESSEE WILLIAMS, *Cat on a Hot Tin Roof* (1955), 2.

## 330. FAME

**See also 350. Following; 384. Glory; 416. Heroes and Heroism; 424. Honors; 578. Merit; 641. Obscurity; 798. Reputation; 1061. Worship**

1. No public character has ever stood the revelation of private utterance and correspondence. LORD ACTON, postscript, letter to Mandell Creighton, April 5, 1887.

2. If men of eminence are exposed to censure on one hand, they are as much liable to flattery on the other. If they receive reproaches which are not due to them, they likewise receive praises which they do not deserve. JOSEPH ADDISON, *The Spectator* (1711–12), 101.

3. A celebrity is a person who works hard all his life to become known, then wears dark glasses to avoid being recognized. FRED ALLEN, *Treadmill to Oblivion* (1954).

4. Fame is the stepmother of death and ambition the excrement of glory. PIETRO ARETINO, letter to Lionardo Parpaglioni, Dec. 2, 1537, tr. Samuel Putnam.

5. Fame is like a river, that beareth up things light and swollen, and drowns things weighty and solid. FRANCIS BACON, "Of Ceremonies and Respects," *Essays* (1625).

6. You canna expect to be baith grand and comfortable. J. M. BARRIE, *The Little Minister* (1891), 10.

7. Public men are bees working in a glass hive; and curious spectators enjoy themselves in watching every secret movement, as if it were a study in natural history. HENRY WARD BEECHER, *Proverbs from Plymouth Pulpit* (1887).

8. Men prominent in life are mostly hard to converse with. They lack small-talk, and at the same time one doesn't like to confront them with their own great themes. MAX BEERBOHM, "T. Fenning Dodworth," *Mainly On the Air* (1946).

9. A sign of a celebrity is often that his name is worth more than his services. DANIEL J. BOORSTIN, *The Image* (1962), 5.4.

10. The top of a pinnacle now, fire-wood soon. *Burmese Proverbs* (1962), 266, ed. Hla Pe.

11. Celebrity: the advantage of being known by those who don't know you. CHAMFORT, *Maximes et pensées* (1805), 1.

12. There are many paths to the top of the mountain, but the view is always the same. CHINESE PROVERB.

13. Celebrity: I picture myself as a marble bust with legs to run everywhere. JEAN COCTEAU, "Des beaux-arts considérés comme un assassinat," *Essai de critique indirecte* (1932).

14. Fill an author with a titanic fame and you do not make him titanic; you often merely burst him. FRANK MOORE COLBY, "Literary War Losses," *The Margin of Hesitation* (1921).

15. A man's renown is like the hue of grass, / Which comes and goes. DANTE, "Purgatorio," 11, *The Divine Comedy* (c. 1300–21), tr. Lawrence Grant White.

16. Worldly renown is but a breath of wind / Coming first from here and then from there, / And changes name because it changes quarter. DANTE, "Purgatorio," 11, *The Divine Comedy* (c. 1300–21), tr. Lawrence Grant White.

17. How dreary—to be—Somebody! / How public—like a Frog— / To tell your name—the livelong June— / To an admiring Bog! EMILY DICKINSON, poem (c. 1861).

18. Fame is a bee. / It has a song— / It has a sting— / Ah, too, it has a wing. EMILY DICKINSON, *Poems* (c. 1862–86).

19. Fame is a magnifying glass. ENGLISH PROVERB.

20. People that seem so glorious are all show; / Underneath they're like anybody else. EURIPIDES, *Andromache* (c. 426 B.C.), tr. John F. Nims.

21. Fame sometimes hath created something of nothing. THOMAS FULLER, D.D., "Of Fame," *The Holy State and the Profane State* (1642).

22. All fame is dangerous: good bringeth envy; bad, shame. THOMAS FULLER, M.D., *Gnomologia* (1732), 513.

23. We imagine that the admiration of the works of celebrated men has become common, because the admiration of their names has become so. WILLIAM HAZLITT, "Why the Arts Are Not Progressive," *Round Table* (1817).

24. Fame usually comes to those who are thinking about something else. OLIVER WENDELL HOLMES, SR., *The Autocrat of the Breakfast Table* (1858), 12.

25. How vain, without the merit, is the name. HOMER, *Iliad* (9th c. B.C.), 17.158, tr. Alexander Pope.

26. Men have a solicitude about fame; and the greater share they have of it, the more afraid they are of losing it. SAMUEL JOHNSON, quoted in Boswell's *Life of Samuel Johnson*, July 21, 1763.

27. On any morning these days whole segments of the population wake up to find themselves famous, while, to keep matters shipshape, whole contingents of celebrities wake up to find themselves forgotten. LOUIS KRONENBERGER, "The Spirit of the Age," *Company Manners* (1954).

28. There is no business in this world so troublesome as the pursuit of fame: life is over before you have hardly begun your work. LA BRUYÈRE, *Characters* (1688), 2.9, tr. Henri Van Laun.

29. The renown of great men should always be measured by the means which they have used to acquire it. LA ROCHEFOUCAULD, *Maxims* (1665), tr. Kenneth Pratt.

30. When I hear a man applauded by the mob I always feel a pang of pity for him. All he has to do to be hissed is to live long enough. H. L. MENCKEN, *Minority Report* (1956), 351.

31. Fame is the spur that the clear spirit doth raise / (That last infirmity of noble mind) / To scorn delights, and live laborious days. MILTON, *Lycidas* (1637).

32. We are all clever enough at envying a famous man while he is yet alive, and at praising him when he is dead. MIMNERMUS, extant fragment (7th c. B.C.).

33. The dispersing and scattering our names into many mouths, we call making them more great. MONTAIGNE, "Of glory," *Essays* (1580–88), tr. Charles Cotton and W. C. Hazlitt.

34. We are more solicitous that men speak of us, than how they speak. MONTAIGNE, "Of glory," *Essays* (1580–88), tr. Charles Cotton and W. C. Hazlitt.

35. Put a rogue in the limelight and he will act like an honest man. NAPOLEON I, *Maxims* (1804–15).

36. False is the praise which says that men's eminence comes from their noble qualities; for the people of this world as a rule do not care about a man's true nature. *Panchatantra* (c. 5th c.), 1, tr. Franklin Edgerton.

37. The charm of fame is so great that we like every object to which it is attached, even death. PASCAL, *Pensées* (1670), 158, tr. W. F. Trotter.

38. Unblemished let me live, or die unknown; / O grant an honest fame, or grant me none! ALEXANDER POPE, *The Temple of Fame* (1711), 523.

39. Would you be known by everybody? Then you know nobody. PUBLILIUS SYRUS, *Moral Sayings* (1st c. B.C.), 979, tr. Darius Lyman.

40. Fame is a constant effort. JULES RENARD, *Journal*, 1887, ed. and tr. Louise Bogan and Elizabeth Roget.

41. Fame, that public destruction of one in process of becoming, into whose building-ground the mob breaks, displacing his stones. RAINER MARIA RILKE, *The Notebooks of Malte Laurids Brigge* (1910), tr. M. D. Herter Norton.

42. He lives in fame that died in virtue's cause. SHAKESPEARE, *Titus Andronicus* (1592–93), 1.1.390.

43. Fame is but an inscription on a grave, and glory the melancholy blazon on a coffin lid. ALEXANDER SMITH, "On the Writing of Essays," *Dreamthorp* (1863).

44. People before the public live an imagined life in the thought of others, and flourish or feel faint as their self outside themselves grows bright or dwindles in that mirror. LOGAN PEARSALL SMITH, *Afterthoughts* (1931), 3.

45. Fame has also this great drawback, that if we pursue it we must direct our lives in such a way as to please the fancy of men, avoiding what they dislike and seeking what is pleasing to them. SPINOZA, *On the Correction of the Understanding* (1677), 1, tr. Andrew Boyle.

46. A plague on eminence! I hardly dare cross the street any more without a convoy, and I am stared at wherever I go like an idiot member of a royal family or an animal in a zoo; and zoo animals have been known to die from stares. IGOR STRAVINSKY, "Stravinsky on the Musical Scene and Other Matters," *The New York Review of Books* (May 12, 1966).

47. Blessed is he whose fame does not outshine his truth. RABINDRANATH TAGORE, *Stray Birds* (1916), 295.

48. The whole earth is the sepulchre of famous men. THUCYDIDES, *The Peloponnesian War* (c. 400 B.C.), 2.43, tr. Benjamin Jowett.

49. He who seeks fame by the practice of virtue asks only for what he deserves. VAUVENARGUES, *Reflections and Maxims* (1746), 295, tr. F. G. Stevens.

50. If you wish to obtain a great name or to found an establishment, be completely mad; but be sure that your madness corresponds with the turn and temper of your age. VOLTAIRE, "Ignatius Loyola," *Philosophical Dictionary* (1764).

51. The modern world is not given to uncritical admiration. It expects its idols to have feet of clay, and can be reasonably sure that press and camera will report their exact dimensions. BARBARA WARD, *Saturday Review*, Sept. 30, 1961.

52. You must be as clearsighted when you are loved as when you are hated. This love is only an advance payment for what they expect of you. YEVGENY YEVTUSHENKO, *A Precocious Autobiography* (1963), tr. Andrew R. MacAndrew.

## 331. FAMILIARITY

**See also 497. Intimacy; 605. The Mundane**

1. Familiarity breeds contentment. GEORGE ADE, "The Uplift That Moved Sideways," *Hand-Made Fables* (1920).

2. When we know exactly all a man's views and how he comes to speak and act so and so, we lose any respect for him, though we may love and admire him. JAMES BOSWELL, *London Journal*, Feb. 3, 1763.

3. That song is best esteemed with which our ears are most acquainted. WILLIAM BYRD, preface to *Psalmes, Songs, and Sonnets* (1611).

4. A shocking occurrence ceases to be shocking when it occurs daily. ALEXANDER CHASE, *Perspectives* (1966).

5. No man is a hayro to his undertaker. FINLEY PETER DUNNE, "The End of Things," *Observations by Mr. Dooley* (1902).

6. The hues of the opal, the light of the diamond, are not to be seen if the eye is too near. EMERSON, "Friendship," *Essays: First Series* (1841).

7. Every ship is a romantic object, except that we sail in. EMERSON, "Experience," *Essays: Second Series* (1844).

8. Though familiarity may not breed contempt, it takes off the edge of admiration. WILLIAM HAZLITT, *Characteristics* (1823), 2.

9. Where's the cheek that doth not fade, / Too much gazed at? JOHN KEATS, "Fancy" (1818).

10. Great men lose somewhat of their greatness by being near us; ordinary men gain much. WALTER SAVAGE LANDOR, "Aeschines and Phocion," *Imaginary Conversations* (1824–53).

11. Though the familiar use of things about us take off our wonder, yet it cures not our ignorance. JOHN LOCKE, *An Essay Concerning Human Understanding* (1690), 3.6.9.

12. Sweets grown common lose their dear delight. SHAKESPEARE, *Sonnets* (1609), 102.12.

13. Familiar acts are beautiful through love. SHELLEY, *Prometheus Unbound* (1818–19), 4.

14. A rose too often smelled loses its fragrance. SPANISH PROVERB.

15. Familiarity breeds contempt—and children. MARK TWAIN, *Notebook* (1935).

## 332. FAMILY

**See also 37. Ancestry; 64. Babies; 121. Children; 215. Daughters; 420. Home; 560. Marriage; 663. Parenthood; 789. Relatives; 909. Sons**

1. When brothers agree, no fortress is so strong as their common life. ANTISTHENES (5th–4th c. B.C.), quoted in Diogenes Laertius' *Lives and Opinions of Eminent Philosophers* (3rd c. A.D.), tr. R. D. Hicks.

2. The family is the association established by nature for the supply of man's everyday wants. ARISTOTLE, *Politics* (4th c. B.C.), 1.2, tr. Benjamin Jowett.

3. Cruel is the strife of brothers. ARISTOTLE, *Politics* (4th c. B.C.), 7.7, tr. Benjamin Jowett.

4. He that hath wife and children hath given hostages to fortune; for they are impediments to great enterprises, either of virtue or mischief. FRANCIS BACON, "Of Marriage and Single Life," *Essays* (1625).

5. I think the family is the place where the most ridiculous and least respectable things in the world go on. UGO BETTI, *The Inquiry* (1944–45), 1.8, ed. Gino Rizzo.

6. Sisterly love is, of all sentiments, the most abstract. Nature does not grant it any functions. UGO BETTI, *The Gambler* (1950), 2.2, ed. Gino Rizzo.

7. If woman is to recapture the lost companionship with man and child, she must once more forget herself, as she did in the old pioneer days, and follow them into the world. PEARL S. BUCK, "Man, Woman and Child," *To My Daughters, With Love* (1967).

8. To make a happy fire-side clime / To weans and wife, / That's the true pathos and sublime / Of human life. ROBERT BURNS, "To Dr. Blacklock" (1789).

9. I believe that more unhappiness comes from this source [the family] than from any other—I mean from the attempt to prolong family connections unduly and to make people hang together artificially who would never naturally do so. SAMUEL BUTLER (d. 1902), "Elementary Morality," *Note-Books* (1912).

10. The family is the test of freedom; because the family is the only thing that the free man makes for himself and by himself. G. K. CHESTERTON, "Dramatic Unities," *Fancies versus Fads* (1923).

11. Govern a family as you would cook a small fish—very gently. CHINESE PROVERB.

12. Are there any brothers who do not criticize a bit and make fun of the fiancé who is stealing a sister from them? COLETTE, "Wedding Day," *Earthly Paradise* (1966), 2, ed. Robert Phelps.

13. The parents' age must be remembered, both for joy and anxiety. CONFUCIUS, *Analects* (6th c. B.C.), 4.21, tr. Ch'u Chai and Winberg Chai.

14. Accidents will happen in the best-regulated families. CHARLES DICKENS, *David Copperfield* (1849–50), 28.

15. As states subsist in part by keeping their weaknesses from being known, so is it the quiet of families to have their chancery and their parliament within doors, and to compose and determine all emergent differences there. JOHN DONNE, *Sermons*, No. 32, 1625.

16. There's no vocabulary / For love within a family, love that's lived in / But not looked at, love within the light of which / All else is seen, the love within which / All other love finds speech. / This love is silent. T. S. ELIOT, *The Elder Statesman* (1958), 2.

17. Families break up when people take hints you don't intend and miss hints you do intend. ROBERT FROST, interview, *Writers at Work: Second Series*. (1963).

18. Natural affection is a prejudice: for though we have cause to love our nearest connections better than others, we have no reason to think them better than others. WILLIAM HAZLITT, "On Prejudice," *Sketches and Essays* (1839).

19. When you deal with your brother, be pleasant, but get a witness. HESIOD, *Works and Days* (8th c. B.C.), 371, tr. Richmond Lattimore.

20. A man's women folk, whatever their outward show of respect for his merit and authority, always regard him secretly as an ass, and with something akin to pity. H. L. MENCKEN, "The Feminine Mind," *In Defense of Women* (1922).

21. There is little less trouble in governing a private family than a whole kingdom. MONTAIGNE, "Of solitude," *Essays* (1580–88), tr. Charles Cotton and W. C. Hazlitt.

22. One would be in less danger / From the wiles of the stranger / If one's own kin and kith / Were more fun to be with. OGDEN NASH, "Family Court," *Verses From 1929 On* (1959).

23. A family is but too often a commonwealth of malignants. ALEXANDER POPE, *Thoughts on Various Subjects* (1717).

24. Bringing up a family should be an adventure, not an anxious discipline in which everybody is constantly graded for performance. MILTON R. SAPIRSTEIN, *Paradoxes of Everyday Life* (1955), 3.

25. Big sisters are the crab grass in the lawn of life. CHARLES M. SCHULZ, *Peanuts* (1952).

26. An ounce of blood is worth more than a pound of friendship. SPANISH PROVERB.

27. Between brothers, two witnesses and a notary. SPANISH PROVERB.

28. The Family! Home of all social evils, a charitable institution for indolent women, a prison workshop for the slaving breadwinner, and a hell for children. AUGUST STRINDBERG, *The Son of a Servant* (1886).

29. Sacred family! . . . The supposed home of all the virtues, where innocent children are tortured into their first falsehoods, where wills are broken by parental tyranny, and self-respect smothered by crowded, jostling egos. AUGUST STRINDBERG, *The Son of a Servant* (1886).

30. He that loves not his wife and children, feeds a lioness at home and broods a nest of sorrows. JEREMY TAYLOR, "Married Love," *Sermons* (1651–53).

31. Happy families are all alike; every unhappy family is unhappy in its own way. LEO TOLSTOY, *Anna Karenina* (1873–76), 1.1, tr. Constance Garnett.

32. Though men are brothers their pockets are not sisters. TURKISH PROVERB.

## 333. FANATICISM

See also 262. Dogmatism; 291. Enthusiasm; 498. Intolerance; 720. Prejudices; 1066. Zeal

1. Just as every conviction begins as a whim so does every emancipator serve his apprenticeship as a crank. A fanatic is a great leader who is just entering the room. HEYWOOD BROUN, "Whims," *New York World*, Feb. 6, 1928.

2. A fanatic is one who can't change his mind and won't change the subject. SIR WINSTON CHURCHILL, quoted in *The New York Times*, July 5, 1954.

3. A fanatic is a man that does what he thinks th' Lord wud do if He knew th' facts iv th' case. FINLEY PETER DUNNE, "Casual Observations," *Mr. Dooley's Philosophy* (1900).

4. He that rides his hobby gently must always give way to him that rides his hobby hard. EMERSON, *Journals*, 1832.

5. There is no strong performance without a little fanaticism in the performer. EMERSON, *Journals*, 1859.

6. Political extremism involves two prime

ingredients: an excessively simple diagnosis of the world's ills and a conviction that there are identifiable villains back of it all. JOHN W. GARDNER, *No Easy Victories* (1968), 2.

7. I would remind you that extremism in the defense of liberty is no vice. And let me remind you also that moderation in the pursuit of justice is no virtue. BARRY GOLDWATER, acceptance speech, Republican National Convention, July 16, 1964.

8. There is no fury like that against one who, we fear, may succeed in making us disloyal to beliefs we hold with passion, but have not really won. LEARNED HAND, address, Harvard University, June 22, 1932.

9. The less justified a man is in claiming excellence for his own self, the more ready is he to claim all excellence for his nation, his religion, his race or his holy cause. ERIC HOFFER, *The True Believer* (1951), 1.2.9.

10. If there is anything more dangerous to the life of the mind than having no independent commitment to ideas, it is having an excess of commitment to some special and constricting idea. RICHARD HOFSTADTER, *Anti-Intellectualism in American Life* (1963), 1.2.

11. At least two thirds of our miseries spring from human stupidity, human malice and those great motivators and justifiers of malice and stupidity, idealism, dogmatism and proselytizing zeal on behalf of religious or political idols. ALDOUS HUXLEY, *Tomorrow and Tomorrow and Tomorrow* (1956).

12. Fanatics have their dreams, wherewith they weave / A paradise for a sect. JOHN KEATS, "The Fall of Hyperion" (1819), 1.

13. What is objectionable, what is dangerous about extremists is not that they are extreme, but that they are intolerant. The evil is not what they say about their cause, but what they say about their opponents. ROBERT F. KENNEDY, "Extremism, Left and Right," *The Pursuit of Justice* (1964).

14. There is no arguing with the pretenders to a divine knowledge and to a divine mission. They are possessed with the sin of pride, they have yielded to the perennial temptation. WALTER LIPPMANN, *The Public Philosophy* (1955), 7.5.

15. The moral powers of the vegetarian, the pacifist, and the nationalist have been so refined away from the source of much power—infantile violence—that their moral powers exhibit a leanness, a keenness, and total ferocity which can only hint at worlds given up. NORMAN MAILER, *Miami and the Siege of Chicago* (1968), 2.2.

16. The true inquisitor is a creature of policy, not a man of blood by taste. JOHN MORLEY, "Robespierre," *Critical Miscellanies* (1871–1908).

17. There is no place in a fanatic's head where reason can enter. NAPOLEON I, *Maxims* (1804–15).

18. Belief in a Divine mission is one of the many forms of certainty that have afflicted the human race. BERTRAND RUSSELL, "Ideas That Have Harmed Mankind," *Unpopular Essays* (1950).

19. Fanaticism consists in redoubling your effort when you have forgotten your aim. GEORGE SANTAYANA, introduction, *The Life of Reason: Reason in Common Sense* (1905–06).

20. There is nobody as enslaved as the fanatic, the person in whom one impulse, one value, has assumed ascendency over all others. MILTON R. SAPIRSTEIN, *Paradoxes of Everyday Life* (1955), 8.

21. An infallible method of making fanatics is to persuade before you instruct. VOLTAIRE, "Oracles," *Philosophical Dictionary* (1764).

## FANTASY

See 448. Imagination; 687. Phantasy

## 334. FARMS AND FARMING

1. Burn down your cities and leave our farms, and your cities will spring up again as if by magic; but destroy our farms and the grass will grow in the streets of every city in the country. WILLIAM JENNINGS BRYAN, "Cross of Gold" speech, July 8, 1896.

2. It is thus with farming: if you do one thing late, you will be late in all your work. CATO THE ELDER, *De Agri Cultura* (2nd c. B.C.).

3. Farming looks mighty easy when your plow is a pencil, and you're a thousand miles from the corn field. DWIGHT D. EISENHOWER, address, Peoria, Ill., Sept. 25, 1956.

4. Remote though your farm may be, / It's something to be the lord of one green

lizard—and free. JUVENAL, *Satires* (c. 100), 3.230, tr. Hubert Creekmore.

5. The farmer is the only man in our economy who buys everything he buys at retail, sells everything he sells at wholesale, and pays the freight both ways. JOHN F. KENNEDY, campaign address, national plowing contest, Sioux Falls, S.D., Sept. 22, 1960.

6. Blessed be agriculture! if one does not have too much of it. CHARLES DUDLEY WARNER, "Preliminary," *My Summer in a Garden* (1871).

7. There is life in the ground: it goes into the seeds; and it also, when it is stirred up, goes into the man who stirs it. CHARLES DUDLEY WARNER, "Preliminary," *My Summer in a Garden* (1871).

8. When tillage begins, other arts follow. The farmers therefore are the founders of human civilization. DANIEL WEBSTER, remarks on agriculture, Jan. 13, 1840.

9. A good farmer is nothing more nor less than a handy man with a sense of humus. E. B. WHITE, "The Practical Farmer," *One Man's Meat* (1944).

10. Farming is not really a business; it is an occupation. WILLIAM E. WOODWARD, *Money for Tomorrow* (1932).

## 335. FASHION

**See also 45. Appearance; 265. Dress; 280. Elegance; 405. Hair; 632. Novelty**

1. Nothing is thought rare / Which is not new, and followed; yet we know / That what was worn some twenty years ago / Comes into grace again. BEAUMONT and FLETCHER, prologue to *The Noble Gentleman* (1647), 4.

2. Fashion, which elevates the bad to the level of the good, subsequently turns its back on bad and good alike. ERIC BENTLEY, introduction to *Naked Masks: Five Plays by Luigi Pirandello* (1952).

3. Fashion, n. A despot whom the wise ridicule and obey. AMBROSE BIERCE, *The Devil's Dictionary* (1881–1911).

4. He is only fantastical that is not in fashion. ROBERT BURTON, *The Anatomy of Melancholy* (1621), 3.2.2.3.

5. Fashion is made to become unfashionable. COCO CHANEL, *Life*, Aug. 19, 1957.

6. There's never a new fashion but it's old. CHAUCER, "The Knight's Tale," *The Canterbury Tales* (c. 1387–1400), tr. Nevill Coghill.

7. If you are not in fashion, you are nobody. LORD CHESTERFIELD, *Letters to His Son*, April 30, 1750.

8. One had as good be out of the world, as out of the fashion. COLLEY CIBBER, *Love's Last Shift* (1696), 2.

9. Art produces ugly things which frequently become beautiful with time. Fashion, on the other hand, produces beautiful things which always become ugly with time. JEAN COCTEAU, *New York World-Telegram & Sun*, Aug. 21, 1960.

10. [Fashion's] smile has given wit to dullness and grace to deformity, and has brought everything into vogue, by turns, but virtue. CHARLES CALEB COLTON, *Lacon* (1825), 1.547.

11. Ladies of Fashion starve their happiness to feed their vanity, and their love to feed their pride. CHARLES CALEB COLTON, *Lacon* (1825), 2.217.

12. The present fashion is always handsome. THOMAS FULLER, M.D., *Gnomologia* (1732), 4718.

13. Even knowledge has to be in the fashion, and where it is not, it is wise to affect ignorance. BALTASAR GRACIÁN, *The Art of Worldly Wisdom* (1647), 120, tr. Joseph Jacobs.

14. Fashion is gentility running away from vulgarity and afraid of being overtaken. WILLIAM HAZLITT, *The Conversations of James Northcote* (1830).

15. Fashion is the abortive issue of vain ostentation and exclusive egotism: it is haughty, trifling, affected, servile, despotic, mean and ambitious, precise and fantastical, all in a breath—tied to no rule, and bound to conform to every whim of the minute. WILLIAM HAZLITT, "On Fashion," *Sketches and Essays* (1839).

16. The fear of becoming a "has been" keeps some people from becoming anything. ERIC HOFFER, *The Passionate State of Mind* (1954), 231.

17. Fashion is only the attempt to realize Art in living forms and social intercourse. OLIVER WENDELL HOLMES, SR., *The Professor at the Breakfast Table* (1860), 6.

18. The greater part of mankind judge of men only by their fashionableness or their

fortune. LA ROCHEFOUCAULD, *Maxims* (1665), tr. Kenneth Pratt.

19. Some people resemble popular songs which are sung only for a certain time. LA ROCHEFOUCAULD, *Maxims* (1665), tr. Kenneth Pratt.

20. Fashion is more powerful than any tyrant. LATIN PROVERB.

21. Fashion condemns us to many follies; the greatest is to make oneself its slave. NAPOLEON I, *Maxims* (1804–15).

22. I cannot keep track of all the vagaries of fashion, / Every day, so it seems, brings in a different style. OVID, *The Art of Love* (c. A.D. 8), 3, tr. Rolfe Humphries.

23. Be not the first by whom the new are tried, / Nor yet the last to lay the old aside. ALEXANDER POPE, *An Essay on Criticism* (1711), 2.133.

24. The fashion wears out more apparel than the man. SHAKESPEARE, *Much Ado About Nothing* (1598–99), 3.3.148.

25. New customs, / Though they be never so ridiculous / (Nay, let 'em be unmanly), yet are followed. SHAKESPEARE, *Henry VIII* (1612–13), 1.2.2.

26. Fashions, after all, are only induced epidemics. GEORGE BERNARD SHAW, "Preface on Doctors: Fashions and Epidemics," *The Doctor's Dilemma* (1913).

27. Nothing is so hideous as an obsolete fashion. STENDHAL, *On Love* (1822), 19, tr. H. B. V., under direction of C. K. Scott-Moncrieff.

28. Conformism is so hot on the heels of the mass-produced avant gardes that the "ins" and the "outs" change places with the speed of Mach III. IGOR STRAVINSKY, "Stravinsky on the Musical Scene and Other Matters," *The New York Review of Books*, May 12, 1966.

29. Every generation laughs at the old fashions, but follows religiously the new. THOREAU, *Walden* (1854), 1.

30. The first thing the first couple did after committing the first sin was to get dressed. Thus Adam and Eve started the world of fashion, and styles have been changing ever since. "Gilding the Lily," *Time*, Nov. 8, 1963.

31. When seen in the perspective of half-a-dozen years or more, the best of our fashions strike us as grotesque, if not unsightly. THORSTEIN VEBLEN, *The Theory of the Leisure Class* (1899), 7.

32. It is fancy rather than taste which produces so many new fashions. VOLTAIRE, "Taste," *Philosophical Dictionary* (1764).

## 336. FASTIDIOUSNESS

1. It is not only a troublesome but slavish thing to be nice [fastidious]. WILLIAM PENN, *Some Fruits of Solitude* (1693), 2.136.

2. A nice man is a man of nasty ideas. JONATHAN SWIFT, *Thoughts on Various Subjects* (1711).

## 337. FATE

**See also 114. Chance; 238. Destiny; 358. Fortune; 617. Necessity; 748. Providence; 930. Stoicism**

1. Fate is not an eagle, it creeps like a rat. ELIZABETH BOWEN, *The House in Paris* (1935), 2.2.

2. These struggling tides of life that seem / In wayward, aimless course to tend, / Are eddies of the mighty stream / That rolls to its appointed end. WILLIAM CULLEN BRYANT, "The Crowded Street" (1843).

3. Whatsoe'er we perpetrate, / We do but row, we are steered by fate. SAMUEL BUTLER (d. 1680), *Hudibras* (1663), 1.1.

4. By the side of fate, set up resistance to fate. You will know strange heights. RENÉ CHAR, "Bulletin from Les Baux," *Le Poème pulvérisé* in *Hypnos Waking* (1956), tr. Jackson Mathews and others.

5. I do not believe in a fate that falls on men however they act; but I do believe in a fate that falls on them unless they act. G. K. CHESTERTON, "On Holland," *Generally Speaking* (1928).

6. Superiority to Fate / Is difficult to gain / 'Tis not conferred of Any / But possible to earn. EMILY DICKINSON, poem (c. 1866).

7. Whatever limits us, we call Fate. EMERSON, "Fate," *The Conduct of Life* (1860).

8. We stand against Fate, as children stand up against the wall in their father's house, and notch their height from year to year. But when the boy grows to man, and is master of the house, he pulls down that wall and builds a new and bigger. EMERSON, "Fate," *The Conduct of Life* (1860).

9. Fate . . . is a name for facts not yet

passed under the fire of thought—for causes which are unpenetrated. EMERSON, "Fate," *The Conduct of Life* (1860).

10. Necessity is harsh. / Fate has no reprieve. EURIPIDES, *Hecuba* (c. 425 B.C.), tr. William Arrowsmith.

11. Failure or success seem to have been allotted to men by their stars. But they retain the power of wriggling, of fighting with their star or against it, and in the whole universe the only really interesting movement is this wriggle. E. M. FORSTER, "Our Diversions," *Abinger Harvest* (1936).

12. See how the Fates their gifts allot, / For A is happy – B is not. / Yet B is worthy, I dare say, / Of more prosperity than A. W. S. GILBERT, *The Mikado* (1885), 2.

13. Even-handed fate / Hath but one law for small and great: / That ample urn holds all men's names. HORACE, *Odes* (23–c. 15 B.C.), 3.1.

14. If fate means you to lose, give him a good fight anyhow. WILLIAM MC FEE, *Casuals of the Sea* (1916), 2.1.2.

15. Fate has to do with events in history that are the summary and unintended results of innumerable decisions of innumerable men. C. WRIGHT MILLS, "Culture and Politics," *Power, Politics and People* (1963).

16. The Moving Finger writes; and, having writ, / Moves on: nor all your Piety nor Wit / Shall lure it back to cancel half a Line, / Nor all your Tears wash out a Word of it. OMAR KHAYYÁM, *Rubáiyát* (11th–12th c.), tr. Edward Fitzgerald, 4th ed., 71.

17. Fate leads the willing, and drags along the reluctant. SENECA, *Letters to Lucilius* (1st c.).

18. What fates impose, that men must needs abide; / It boots not to resist both wind and tide. SHAKESPEARE, *3 Henry VI* (1590–91), 4.3.58.

19. There is no armour against fate; / Death lays his icy hands on kings. JAMES SHIRLEY, *The Contention of Ajax and Ulysses* (1659), 3.

20. Fate has terrible power. / You cannot escape it by wealth or war. / No fort will keep it out, no ships outrun it. SOPHOCLES, *Antigone* (442–41 B.C.), tr. Elizabeth Wyckoff.

## FATHERS

**See 663. Parenthood**

## 338. FATIGUE

1. Life is one long process of getting tired. SAMUEL BUTLER (d. 1902), "Lord, What Is Man?" *Note-Books* (1912).

2. The young feel tired at the end of an action,— / The old, at the beginning. T. S. ELIOT, *The Family Reunion* (1939), 2.2.

3. In the morning a man walks with his whole body; in the evening, only with his legs. EMERSON, *Journals*, 1836.

4. The feeling of sleepiness when you are not in bed, and can't get there, is the meanest feeling in the world. EDGAR WATSON HOWE, *Country Town Sayings* (1911).

5. The strongest have their moments of fatigue. NIETZSCHE, *The Will to Power* (1888), tr. Anthony M. Ludovici.

## FATNESS

**See 637. Obesity**

## 339. FAULTS

**See also 165. Confession; 203. Criticism; 312. Excuses; 351. Folly; 455. Imperfection; 539. Limitations; 677. Perfection; 797. Reproof; 1040. Weakness**

1. It is easier to confess a defect than to claim a quality. MAX BEERBOHM, "Hosts and Guests," *And Even Now* (1920).

2. The greatest of faults, I should say, is to be conscious of none. THOMAS CARLYLE, *On Heroes, Hero-Worship and the Heroic in History* (1841), 2.

3. A man without faults is a mountain without crevasses. He is of no interest to me. RENÉ CHAR, *Leaves of Hypnos*, 4, in *Hypnos Waking* (1956), tr. Jackson Mathews and others.

4. The real fault is to have faults and not to amend them. CONFUCIUS, *Analects* (6th c. B.C.), 15.29, tr. Ch'u Chai and Winberg Chai.

5. I have no confidence in a man whose faults you cannot see. EDWARD DAHLBERG, "On Human Nature," *Reasons of the Heart* (1965).

6. Our faults are not seen, / But past us; neither felt, but only in / The punishment. JOHN DONNE, "Ode: Of Our Sense of Sin," *Divine Poems* (1607).

7. A man must thank his defects, and stand in some terror of his talents. EMERSON, "Fate," *The Conduct of Life* (1860).

8. He is lifeless that is faultless. ENGLISH PROVERB.

9. Rich men's faults are covered with money and physicians' with earth. ENGLISH PROVERB.

10. Worse / than a true evil is it to bear the burden of faults that are not truly yours. EURIPIDES, *Helen* (412 B.C.), tr. Richmond Lattimore.

11. A benevolent man should allow a few faults in himself, to keep his friends in countenance. BENJAMIN FRANKLIN, *Autobiography* (1791), 1.

12. Small faults indulged are little thieves that let in greater. THOMAS FULLER, M.D., *Gnomologia* (1732), 4191.

13. Those see nothing but faults that seek for nothing else. THOMAS FULLER, M.D., *Gnomologia* (1732), 5021.

14. Each day the worst of our faults, our deficiencies, our crimes, the truth of our lives, is stifled under a triple layer of forgetfulness, death and the ordinary course of justice. JEAN GIRAUDOUX, *Electra* (1937), 1, tr. Phyllis La Farge with Peter H. Judd.

15. People will allow their faults to be shown them; they will let themselves be punished for them; they will patiently endure many things because of them; they only become impatient when they have to lay them aside. GOETHE, *Elective Affinities* (1809), 22.

16. Certain defects are necessary for the existence of individuality. GOETHE, *Elective Affinities* (1809), 22.

17. It is well that there is no one without a fault; for he would not have a friend in the world. WILLIAM HAZLITT, *Characteristics* (1823).

18. It is too bad how thoughtlessly we set up harsh and unkind rules against ourselves. No one is born without faults. That man is best who has fewest. HORACE, *Satires* (35–30 B.C.), 1.3.

19. It is in our faults and failings, not in our virtues, that we touch one another and find sympathy. JEROME K. JEROME, "On Vanity and Vanities," *The Idle Thoughts of an Idle Fellow* (1889).

20. There exists scarcely any man so accomplished, or so necessary to his own family, but he has some failing which will diminish their regret at his loss. LA BRUYÈRE, *Characters* (1688), 2.35, tr. Henri Van Laun.

21. We only admit to minor faults to persuade ourselves that we have no major ones. LA ROCHEFOUCAULD, *Maxims* (1665).

22. If we had no faults, we would not take so much pleasure in noticing them in others. LA ROCHEFOUCAULD, *Maxims* (1665).

23. We have scarcely any faults which are not more pardonable than the shifts we make to hide them. LA ROCHEFOUCAULD, *Maxims* (1665), tr. Kenneth Pratt.

24. We forget our faults easily when they are known to ourselves alone. LA ROCHEFOUCAULD, *Maxims* (1665), tr. Kenneth Pratt.

25. Faults shared are comfortable as bedroom slippers and as easy to slip into. PHYLLIS MC GINLEY, "How to Get Along with Men," *The Province of the Heart* (1959).

26. A good man does not spy around for the black spots in others, but presses unswervingly on towards his mark. MARCUS AURELIUS, *Meditations* (2nd c.), 4.18, tr. Maxwell Staniforth.

27. The defects of human nature afford us opportunities of exercising our philosophy, the best employment of our virtues. If all men were righteous, all hearts true and frank and loyal, what use would our virtues be? MOLIÈRE, *The Misanthrope* (1666), 5, tr. John Wood.

28. Our shortcomings are the eyes with which we see the ideal. NIETZSCHE, *Miscellaneous Maxims and Opinions* (1879), 86, tr. Paul V. Cohn.

29. Truly it is an evil to be full of faults; but it is a still greater evil to be full of them, and to be unwilling to recognise them. PASCAL, *Pensées* (1670), 100, tr. W. F. Trotter.

30. Whoe'er he be / That tells my faults, I hate him mortally. ALEXANDER POPE, *Prologue to the Wife of Bath's Tale* (c. 1709).

31. When the defects of others are perceived with so much clarity, it is because one possesses them oneself. JULES RENARD, *Journal*, October 1908, ed. and tr. Louise Bogan and Elizabeth Roget.

32. Whoever is aware of his own failing will not find fault with the failings of other men. SA'DI, *Gulistan* (1258), 5.19, tr. James Ross.

33. Whatever folly men commit, be their shortcomings or their vices what they may, let us exercise forbearance; remember that

when these faults appear in others it is our follies and vices that we behold. SCHOPENHAUER, "On the Sufferings of the World," *Parerga and Paralipomena* (1851), tr. T. Bailey Saunders.

34. They say best men are moulded out of faults, / And, for the most, become much more the better / For being a little bad. SHAKESPEARE, *Measure for Measure* (1604–05), 5.1.444.

35. More faults are often committed while we are trying to oblige than while we are giving offense. TACITUS, *Annals* (A.D. 115–117?), 15.21, tr. Alfred J. Church and William J. Brodribb.

36. Gladly we desire to make other men perfect but we will not amend our own fault. THOMAS À KEMPIS, *The Imitation of Christ* (1426), 1.16.

37. The faultfinder will find faults even in paradise. THOREAU, "Conclusion," *Walden* (1854).

38. Our failings sometimes bind us to one another as closely as could virtue itself. VAUVENARGUES, *Reflections and Maxims* (1746), 176, tr. F. G. Stevens.

39. None of us can stand other people having the same faults as ourselves. OSCAR WILDE, *The Picture of Dorian Gray* (1891), 1.

40. Misfortunes one can endure—they come from outside, they are accidents. But to suffer for one's own faults—ah! there is the sting of life. OSCAR WILDE, *Lady Windermere's Fan* (1892), 1.

## FAVORS

See 881. Services

## 340. FEAR

See also 43. Anxiety; 192. Courage; 196. Cowardice; 298. Escape; 302. Evasion; 973. Timidity

1. Fear is stronger than arms. AESCHYLUS, *Seven Against Thebes* (468–67 B.C.), tr. David Grene.

2. Excessive fear is always powerless. AESCHYLUS, *The Suppliant Maidens* (463 B.C.), tr. Seth G. Bernardete.

3. There are times when fear is good. / It must keep its watchful place / at the heart's controls. There is / advantage in the wisdom won from pain. AESCHYLUS, *The Eumenides* (458 B.C.), tr. Richmond Lattimore.

4. God! Is there anything uglier than a frightened man! JEAN ANOUILH, *Antigone* (1942), tr. Lewis Galantière.

5. Behind everything we feel, there is always a sense of fear. UGO BETTI, *Struggle Till Dawn* (1949), 1, tr. G. H. McWilliam.

6. No passion so effectually robs the mind of all its powers of acting and reasoning as fear. EDMUND BURKE, *A Philosophical Inquiry into the Origin of Our Ideas of the Sublime and Beautiful* (1756), 2.2.

7. Men as resolute appear / With too much, as too little fear. SAMUEL BUTLER (d. 1680), *Hudibras* (1663), 3.3.

8. Fear is sharp-sighted, and can see things under ground, and much more in the skies. CERVANTES, *Don Quixote* (1605–15), 1.3.6, tr. Peter Motteux and John Ozell.

9. We are all / dangerous till our fears grow thoughtful. JOHN CIARDI, "Incident," *This Strangest Everything* (1966).

10. How does one kill fear, I wonder? How do you shoot a spectre through the heart, slash off its spectral head, take it by its spectral throat? JOSEPH CONRAD, *Lord Jim* (1900), 33.

11. The difference between Despair / And Fear—is like the One / Between the instant of a Wreck— / And when the Wreck has been. EMILY DICKINSON, poem (c. 1862).

12. Fear is an instructor of great sagacity and the herald of all revolutions. EMERSON, "Compensation," *Essays: First Series* (1841).

13. It is not death or pain that is to be dreaded, but the fear of pain or death. EPICTETUS, *Discourses* (2nd c.), 2.1, tr. Thomas W. Higginson.

14. Any device whatever by which one frees himself from the fear of others is a natural good. EPICURUS, "Principal Doctrines" (3rd c. B.C.), 6, in *Letters, Principal Doctrines, and Vatican Sayings*, tr. Russel M. Geer.

15. He that fears you present will hate you absent. THOMAS FULLER, M.D., *Gnomologia* (1732), 2101.

16. Fear comes from uncertainty. When we are absoutely certain, whether of our worth or worthlessness, we are almost impervious to fear. Thus a feeling of utter unworthiness can be a source of courage. ERIC

HOFFER, *The Passionate State of Mind* (1954), 87.

17. A good scare is worth more to a man than good advice. EDGAR WATSON HOWE, *Country Town Sayings* (1911).

18. God is good, there is no devil but fear. ELBERT HUBBARD, *The Note Book* (1927).

19. Evil is uncertain in the same degree as good, and for the reason that we ought not to hope too securely, we ought not to fear with too much dejection. SAMUEL JOHNSON, *The Rambler* (1750–52), 30.

20. Oh / How vain and vile a passion is this fear! / What base uncomely things it makes men do. BEN JONSON, *Sejanus His Fall* (1603), 5.6.

21. Just as courage imperils life, fear protects it. LEONARDO DA VINCI, *Notebooks* (c. 1500), tr. Jean Paul Richter.

22. Fear has the largest eyes of all. BORIS PASTERNAK, "Hoarfrost," *The Poetry of Boris Pasternak* (1959), ed., tr. George Reavey.

23. When men are ruled by fear, they strive to prevent the very changes that will abate it. ALAN PATON, "The Challenge of Fear," *Saturday Review*, Sept. 9, 1967.

24. What we fear comes to pass more speedily than what we hope. PUBLILIUS SYRUS, *Moral Sayings* (1st c. B.C.), 805, tr. Darius Lyman.

25. Of all the passions, fear weakens judgment most. CARDINAL DE RETZ, *Mémoires* (1718).

26. The only thing we have to fear is fear itself—nameless, unreasoning, unjustified terror which paralyzes needed efforts to convert retreat into advance. FRANKLIN D. ROOSEVELT, first Inaugural Address, March 4, 1933.

27. Fear is the main source of superstition, and one of the main sources of cruelty. BERTRAND RUSSELL, "An Outline of Intellectual Rubbish," *Unpopular Essays* (1950).

28. Neither a man nor a crowd nor a nation can be trusted to act humanely or to think sanely under the influence of a great fear. BERTRAND RUSSELL, "An Outline of Intellectual Rubbish," *Unpopular Essays* (1950).

29. Were the diver to think on the jaws of the shark he would never lay hands on the precious pearl. SA'DI, *Gulistan* (1258), 3.28, tr. James Ross.

30. Where fear is, happiness is not. SENECA, *Letters to Lucilius* (1st c.), 74.5, tr. E. Phillips Barker.

31. He who fears from near at hand often fears less. SENECA, *The Trojan Women* (1st c.), 516.

32. Present fears / Are less than horrible imaginings. SHAKESPEARE, *Macbeth* (1605–06), 1.3.137.

33. Fear betrays unworthy souls. VERGIL, *Aeneid* (30–19 B.C.), 4.13.

34. Fear could never make virtue. VOLTAIRE, "Socrates," *Philosophical Dictionary* (1764).

35. The terror of society, which is the basis of morals, the terror of God, which is the secret of religion—these are the two things that govern us. OSCAR WILDE, *The Picture of Dorian Gray* (1891), 2.

### FEBRUARY
See 848. Seasons

### FEELINGS
See 282. Emotions

### FELLOWSHIP
See 151. Company

## 341. FICTION
See also 931. Storytelling; 1062. Writing and Writers

1. Fiction is not a dream. Nor is it guess work. It is imagining based on facts, and the facts must be accurate or the work of imagining will not stand up. MARGARET CULKIN BANNING, *The Writer*, March 1960.

2. What, in fact, is a novel but a universe in which action is endowed with form, where final words are pronounced, where people possess one another completely, and where life assumes the aspect of destiny? ALBERT CAMUS, "Rebellion and the Novel," *The Rebel* (1951), tr. Anthony Bower.

3. What is a novel if not a conviction of our fellow-men's existence strong enough to take upon itself a form of imagined life clearer than reality and whose accumulated verisimilitude of selected episodes puts to shame the pride of documentary history?

JOSEPH CONRAD, *A Personal Record* (1912), 1.

4. All novels are about certain minorities: the individual is a minority. RALPH ELLISON, interview, *Writers at Work: Second Series* (1963).

5. Good fiction is made of that which is real, and reality is difficult to come by. RALPH ELLISON, *Shadow & Act* (1964).

6. The love of novels is the preference of sentiment to the senses. EMERSON, *Journals*, 1831.

7. Don't make a novel to establish a principle of political economy. You will spoil both. EMERSON, *Journals*, 1857.

8. I can find my biography in every fable that I read. EMERSON, *Journals*, 1866.

9. The final test for a novel will be our affection for it, as it is the test of our friends, and of anything else which we cannot define. E. M. FORSTER, "Introductory," *Aspects of the Novel* (1927).

10. History is a novel which did take place; a novel is history that could take place. EDMOND AND JULES DE GONCOURT, *Idées et sensations* (1866).

11. Journalism allows its readers to witness history; fiction gives its readers an opportunity to live it. JOHN HERSEY, *Time*, March 13, 1950.

12. Readers of novels are a strange folk, upon whose probable or even possible tastes no wise book-maker would ever venture to bet. E. V. LUCAS, *Reading, Writing, and Remembering* (1932), 14.

13. Just as the painter thinks with his brush and paints the novelist thinks with his story. W. SOMERSET MAUGHAM, *The Summing Up* (1938), 5.

14. Stories, like whiskey, must be allowed to mature in the cask. SEAN O'FAOLAIN, *Atlantic Monthly*, December 1956.

15. When the characters are really alive before their author, the latter does nothing but follow them in their action, in their words, in the situations which they suggest to him. LUIGI PIRANDELLO, *Six Characters in Search of an Author* (1921), 3, tr. Edward Storer.

16. The principle of procrastinated rape is said to be the ruling one in all the great bestsellers. V. S. PRITCHETT, "Clarissa," *The Living Novel & Later Appreciations* (1964).

17. Fiction is to the grown man what play is to the child: it is there that he changes the atmosphere and tenor of his life. ROBERT LOUIS STEVENSON, "A Gossip on Romance" (1882).

18. Novels are sweets. All people with healthy literary appetites love them—almost all women; a vast number of clever, hard-headed men. WILLIAM MAKEPEACE THACKERAY, "On a Lazy, Idle Boy," *The Roundabout Papers* (1863).

19. History is the recital of facts represented as true. Fable, on the other hand, is the recital of facts represented as fiction. VOLTAIRE, "History," *Philosophical Dictionary* (1764).

20. Plots are no more exhausted than men are. Every man is a new creation, and combinations are simply endless. CHARLES DUDLEY WARNER, "Sixth Study," *Backlog Studies* (1873).

21. All fiction for me is a kind of magic and trickery—a confidence trick, trying to make people believe something is true that isn't. ANGUS WILSON, interview, *Writers at Work: First Series* (1958).

22. Fiction is like a spider's web, attached ever so slightly perhaps, but still attached to life at all four corners. VIRGINIA WOOLF, *A Room of One's Own* (1929), 3.

## FIDELITY

**See 178. Constancy; 470. Infidelity**

## 342. FIGHTING

**See also 250. Discord; 766. Quarreling; 1035. War**

1. People seem to fight about things very unsuitable for fighting. They make a frightful noise in support of very quiet things. They knock each other about in the name of very fragile things. G. K. CHESTERTON, "On Changes in Taste," *Generally Speaking* (1928).

2. What counts is not necessarily the size of the dog in the fight—it's the size of the fight in the dog. DWIGHT D. EISENHOWER, address to Republican National Committee, Jan. 31, 1958.

3. Never contend with a man who has nothing to lose. BALTASAR GRACIÁN, *The Art of Worldy Wisdom* (1647), 172, tr. Joseph Jacobs.

4. There are not fifty ways of fighting, there is only one: to be the conqueror. ANDRÉ MALRAUX, *L'Espoir* (1937), 2.2.12.

5. In a fight the rich man tries to save his face, the poor man his coat. RUSSIAN PROVERB.

6. Whoever contends with the great sheds his own blood. SA'DI, *Gulistan* (1258), 8.47, tr. James Ross.

7. To fight is a radical instinct; if men have nothing else to fight over they will fight over words, fancies, or women, or they will fight because they dislike each other's looks, or because they have met walking in opposite directions. GEORGE SANTAYANA, *The Life of Reason: Reason in Society* (1905–06), 3.

## FINISHING

See 283. Ending

## 343. FIRE

1. Fire is the most tolerable third party. THOREAU, *Journal*, Jan. 2, 1853.

## 344. FISH

See also 345. Fishing

1. Fish die belly-upward and rise to the surface; it is their way of falling. ANDRÉ GIDE, *Journals*, May 18, 1930, tr. Justin O' Brien.

2. No human being, however great, or powerful, was ever so free as a fish. JOHN RUSKIN, *The Two Paths* (1859), 5.

## 345. FISHING

See also 344. Fish

1. The gods do not deduct from man's allotted span the hours spent in fishing. BABYLONIAN PROVERB, often quoted by Herbert Hoover.

2. Overwork, n. A dangerous disorder affecting high public functionaries who want to go fishing. AMBROSE BIERCE, *The Devil's Dictionary* (1881–1911).

3. Fly fishing may be a very pleasant amusement; but angling or float fishing I can only compare to a stick and a string, with a worm at one end and a fool at the other. Attributed to SAMUEL JOHNSON.

4. As no man is born an artist, so no man is born an angler. IZAAK WALTON, "Epistle to the Reader," *The Compleat Angler* (1653).

5. Angling may be said to be so like the mathematics that it can never be fully learnt. IZAAK WALTON, "Epistle to the Reader," *The Compleat Angler* (1653).

## FLAG

See 671. Patriotism

## 346. FLATTERY

See also 158. Compliments

1. There is no food more satiating than milk and honey; and just as such foods produce disgust for the palate, so perfumed and gallant words make our ears belch. PIETRO ARETINO, letter to Gianfrancesco Pocopanno, Nov. 24, 1537, tr. Samuel Putnam.

2. Mountains of gold would not seduce some men, yet flattery would break them down. HENRY WARD BEECHER, *Proverbs from Plymouth Pulpit* (1887).

3. The flattery of posterity is not worth much more than contemporary flattery, which is worth nothing. JORGE LUIS BORGES, "Dead Men's Dialogue," *Dreamtigers* (1964), tr. Mildred Boyer.

4. Flattery is a juggler, and no kin unto sincerity. SIR THOMAS BROWNE, *Christian Morals* (1716), 1.

5. Some indeed there are who profess to despise all flattery, but even these are nevertheless to be flattered, by being told that they do despise it. CHARLES CALEB COLTON, *Lacon* (1825), 1.444.

6. We must be careful how we flatter fools too little, or wise men too much, for the flatterer must act the very reverse of the physician, and administer the strongest dose only to the weakest patient. CHARLES CALEB COLTON, *Lacon* (1825), 2.198.

7. If a man is vain, flatter. If timid, flatter. If boastful, flatter. In all history, too much flattery never lost a gentleman. KATHRYN CRAVENS, *Pursuit of Gentlemen* (1952).

8. We love flattery, even though we are not deceived by it, because it shows that we are of importance enough to be courted.

EMERSON, "Gifts," *Essays: Second Series* (1844).

9. Flattery sits in the parlour when plain dealing is kicked out of doors. THOMAS FULLER, M.D., *Gnomologia* (1732), 1552.

10. Roughness may turn one's humour, but flattery one's stomach. THOMAS FULLER, M.D., *Gnomologia* (1732), 4061.

11. It is necessary to the success of flattery, that it be accommodated to particular circumstances or characters, and enter the heart on that side where the passions are ready to receive it. SAMUEL JOHNSON, *The Rambler* (1750–52), 106.

12. Flattery pleases very generally. In the first place, the flatterer may think what he says to be true; but, in the second place, whether he thinks so or not, he certainly thinks those whom he flatters of consequence enough to be flattered. SAMUEL JOHNSON, quoted in Boswell's *Life of Samuel Johnson*, April 11, 1775.

13. Of all wild beasts preserve me from a tyrant; / And of all tame, a flatterer. BEN JONSON, *Sejanus His Fall* (1603), 1.1.

14. Learn that every flatterer / Lives at the flattered listener's cost. LA FONTAINE, "The Fox and the Crow," *Fables* (1668–94), tr. Marianne Moore.

15. Flattery is a base coin which is current only through our vanity. LA ROCHEFOUCAULD, *Maxims* (1665), tr. Kenneth Pratt.

16. If we did not flatter ourselves, the flattery of others would not hurt us. LA ROCHEFOUCAULD, *Maxims* (1665), tr. Kenneth Pratt.

17. We imagine sometimes that we hate flattery, but it is only the manner of flattering which we hate. LA ROCHEFOUCAULD, *Maxims* (1665), tr. Kenneth Pratt.

18. He who knows how to flatter also knows how to slander. NAPOLEON I, *Maxims* (1804–15).

19. The world is grown so full of dissimulation and compliment, that men's words are hardly any signification of their thoughts. RICHARD STEELE, *The Spectator* (1711–12), 103.

20. Flattery is all right—if you don't inhale. ADLAI STEVENSON, speech, Feb. 1, 1961.

21. Love of flattery, in most men, proceeds from the mean opinion they have of themselves; in women, from the contrary. JONATHAN SWIFT, *Thoughts on Various Subjects* (1711).

22. We despise no source that can pay us a pleasing attention. MARK TWAIN, "Does the Race of Man Love a Lord?" *North American Review*, April 1902.

## 347. FLEXIBILITY

See also 115. Change; 644. Obstinacy; 647. Open-mindedness; 649. Opinion

1. The hearts of the great can be changed. HOMER, *Iliad* (9th c. B.C.), 15.203, tr. Richmond Lattimore.

2. My opinion is a view I hold until—well–until I find out something that changes it. LUIGI PIRANDELLO, *Each in His Own Way* (1924), 1, tr. Arthur Livingston.

3. Docility is the observable half of reason. GEORGE SANTAYANA, *The Life of Reason: Reason in Common Sense* (1905–06), 9.

4. A wise man changes his mind, a fool never will. SPANISH PROVERB.

## FLIES

See 479. Insects

## FLIGHT

See 28. Airplanes; 298. Escape

## 348. FLIRTATION

See also 195. Courtship; 548. Love; 736. Promiscuity; 851. Seduction

1. Life is not long enough for a coquette to play all her tricks in. JOSEPH ADDISON, *The Spectator* (1711–12), 89.

2. She who trifles with all / Is less likely to fall / Than she who but trifles with one. JOHN GAY, "The Coquet Mother and the Coquet Daughter" (1727).

3. When you see a woman who can go nowhere without a staff of admirers, it is not so much because they think she is beautiful, it is because she has told them they are handsome. JEAN GIRAUDOUX, *The Apollo of Bellac* (1942), adapted by Maurice Valency.

4. He who wins a thousand common hearts is entitled to some renown; but he who keeps undisputed sway over the heart of a coquette is indeed a hero. WASHING-

TON IRVING, "The Legend of Sleepy Hollow," *The Sketch Book of Geoffrey Crayon, Gent.* (1819–20).

5. Love's greatest miracle is the curing of coquetry. LA ROCHEFOUCAULD, *Maxims* (1665), tr. Kenneth Pratt.

6. Flirtation is merely an expression of considered desire coupled with an admission of its impracticability. MARYA MANNES, "A Plea for Flirtation," *But Will It Sell?* (1955–64).

7. One must cease letting oneself be eaten when one tastes best: that is known to those who want to be loved long. NIETZSCHE, "On Free Death," *Thus Spoke Zarathustra* (1883–92), 1, tr. Walter Kaufmann.

8. Venus favors the bold. OVID, *The Art of Love* (c. A.D. 8), 1, tr. Rolfe Humphries.

9. Whether a pretty woman grants or withholds her favours, she always likes to be asked for them. OVID, *The Art of Love* (c. A.D. 8), 1, tr. J. Lewis May.

10. Whoever loves above all the approach of love will never know the joy of attaining it. SAINT-EXUPÉRY, *The Wisdom of the Sands* (1948), 2, tr. Stuart Gilbert.

11. Conscience has no more to do with gallantry than it has with politics. RICHARD BRINSLEY SHERIDAN, *The Duenna* (1775), 2.4.

## 349. FLOWERS

1. Any nose / May ravage with impunity a rose. ROBERT BROWNING, *Sordello* (1840), 6.

2. The Dandelion's pallid tube / Astonishes the Grass, / And Winter instantly becomes / An infinite Alas—. EMILY DICKINSON, poem (c. 1881).

3. The flower is the poetry of reproduction. It is an example of the eternal seductiveness of life. JEAN GIRAUDOUX, *The Enchanted* (1933), 1, adapted by Maurice Valency.

4. Break not the rose; its fragrance and beauty are surely sufficient: / Resting contented with these, never a thorn shall you feel. JOHN HAY, "Distichs" (1871?), 8.

5. Reign endless, Rose! for fair you are, / Nor heaven reserves a fairer thing. HERMAN MELVILLE, "A Rose or Two," *Weeds and Wildings Chiefly: with A Rose or Two* (1924).

6. There is that in the glance of a flower which may at times control the greatest of creation's braggart lords. JOHN MUIR, *A Thousand-Mile Walk to the Gulf* (1916), 5.

7. Flower in the crannied wall, / I pluck you out of the crannies, / I hold you here, root and all, in my hand, / Little flower—but *if* I could understand / What you are, root and all, and all in all, / I should know what God and man is. ALFRED, LORD TENNYSON, "Flower in the Crannied Wall" (1869).

8. To me the meanest flower that blows can give / Thoughts that do often lie too deep for tears. WILLIAM WORDSWORTH, "Ode: Intimations of Immortality from Recollections of Early Childhood" (1803), 11.

## FOG

See 1043. Weather

## 350. FOLLOWING

See also 14. Admiration; 528. Leadership; 564. Mass Movements; 1061. Worship

1. People, like sheep, tend to follow a leader—occasionally in the right direction. ALEXANDER CHASE, *Perspectives* (1966).

2. Having disciples is in the end like having children, only not with love but with self-love preeminent. LOUIS KRONENBERGER, "Reflections and Complaints of Late Middle Age," *The Cart and the Horse* (1964), 3.

3. Every master has but one disciple, and that one becomes unfaithful to him, for he too is destined for mastership. NIETZSCHE, *Mixed Opinions and Maxims* (1879), 357, in *The Portable Nietzsche*, tr. Walter Kaufmann.

4. The followers of a great man often put their eyes out, so that they may be the better able to sing his praise. NIETZSCHE, *Miscellaneous Maxims and Opinions* (1879), 390, tr. Paul V. Cohn.

## 351. FOLLY

See also 339. Faults; 353. Fools; 774. Rashness; 934. Stupidity

1. The folly of one man is the fortune of another. FRANCIS BACON, "Of Fortune," *Essays* (1625).

2. If others had not been foolish, we should be so. WILLIAM BLAKE, "Proverbs of Hell," *The Marriage of Heaven and Hell* (1790).

3. Folly loves the martyrdom of Fame. BYRON, "Monody on the Death of R. B. Sheridan" (1816).

4. If we're not foolish young, we're foolish old. CHAUCER, "The Knight's Tale," *The Canterbury Tales* (c. 1387–1400), tr. Nevill Coghill.

5. Those who realize their folly are not true fools. CHUANG TZU, *Works* (4th–3rd c. B.C.), 20.2, tr. Lin Yutang.

6. It is folly to drown on dry land. ENGLISH PROVERB.

7. How ugly, seen near beauty's pride, is ugliness. / How foolish, seen at wisdom's side, is foolishness. GOETHE, "Before the Palace of Menelaus in Sparta," *Faust: Part II* (1832), tr. Philip Wayne.

8. Fools rush in through the door; for folly is always bold. BALTASAR GRACIÁN, *The Art of Worldly Wisdom* (1647), 78, tr. Joseph Jacobs.

9. It is the folly of the world, constantly, which confounds its wisdom. Not only out of the mouths of babes and sucklings, but out of the mouths of fools and cheats, we may often get our truest lessons. OLIVER WENDELL HOLMES, SR., *The Professor at the Breakfast Table* (1860), 1.

10. Wisdom at times is found in folly. HORACE, *Odes* (23–c. 15 B.C.), 4.12.

11. He who lives without folly is not so wise as he believes. LA ROCHEFOUCAULD, *Maxims* (1665), tr. Kenneth Pratt.

12. Folly pursues us at all periods of our lives. If someone seems wise it is only because his follies are proportionate to his age and fortune. LA ROCHEFOUCAULD, *Maxims* (1665), tr. Kenneth Pratt.

13. The folly which we might have ourselves committed is the one which we are least ready to pardon in another. JOSEPH ROUX, *Meditations of a Parish Priest* (1886), 4.84, tr. Isabel F. Hapgood.

14. Folly is perennial and yet the human race has survived. BERTRAND RUSSELL, "An Outline of Intellectual Rubbish," *Unpopular Essays* (1950).

15. Tell him to be a fool every so often / and to have no shame over having been a fool / yet learning something over every folly. CARL SANDBURG, *The People, Yes* (1936).

16. A way foolishness has of revenging itself is to excommunicate the world. GEORGE SANTAYANA, *The Life of Reason: Reason in Art* (1905–06), 9.

17. Do you think that the things people make fools of themselves about are any less real and true than the things they behave sensibly about? GEORGE BERNARD SHAW, *Candida* (1903), 1.

18. What is life but a series of inspired follies? The difficulty is to find them to do. GEORGE BERNARD SHAW, *Pygmalion* (1913), 2.

19. If you think my acts are foolishness / the foolishness may be in a fool's eye. SOPHOCLES, *Antigone* (442–41 B.C.), tr. Elizabeth Wyckoff.

20. Give me the young man who has brains enough to make a fool of himself! ROBERT LOUIS STEVENSON, "Crabbed Age and Youth," *Virginibus Puerisque* (1881).

21. Men are contented to be laughed at for their wit, but not for their folly. JONATHAN SWIFT, *Thoughts on Various Subjects* (1711).

22. Wisdom loves the children of men, but she prefers those who come through foolishness to wisdom. PAUL TILLICH, *The Eternal Now* (1963), 3.15.3.

23. What use is wisdom when folly reigns? *Yiddish Proverbs* (1949), ed. Hanan J. Ayalti.

## 352. FOOD

**See also 186. Cooks and Cooking; 272. Eating; 435. Hunger; 1021. Vegetarianism**

1. The French fried potato has become an inescapable horror in almost every public eating place in the country. "French fries," say the menus, but they are not French fries any longer. They are a furry-textured substance with the taste of plastic wood. RUSSELL BAKER, "Observer," *The New York Times*, Feb. 22, 1968.

2. I doubt whether the world holds for any one a more soul-stirring surprise than the first adventure with ice-cream. HEYWOOD BROUN, "Holding a Baby," *Seeing Things at Night* (1921).

3. Food, one assumes, provides nourish-

ment; but Americans eat it fully aware that small amounts of poison have been added to improve its appearance and delay its putrefaction. JOHN CAGE, "Indeterminacy," *Silence* (1961).

4. Cheese—milk's leap toward immortality. CLIFTON FADIMAN, *Any Number Can Play* (1957).

5. Talk of joy: there may be things better than beef stew and baked potatoes and home-made bread—there may be. DAVID GRAYSON, *Adventures in Contentment* (1907), 6.

6. A cucumber should be well sliced, and dressed with pepper and vinegar, and then thrown out as good for nothing. SAMUEL JOHNSON, quoted in Boswell's *Journal of a Tour to the Hebrides with Samuel Johnson*, Oct. 5, 1773.

7. You can travel fifty thousand miles in America without once tasting a piece of good bread. HENRY MILLER, "The Staff of Life," *Remember to Remember* (1947).

8. A depraved taste in food is gratified with that which disgusts other people: it is a species of disease. VOLTAIRE, "Taste," *Philosophical Dictionary* (1764).

9. Happy is said to be the family which can eat onions together. They are, for the time being, separate from the world, and have a harmony of aspiration. CHARLES DUDLEY WARNER, "Eighteenth Week," *My Summer in a Garden* (1871).

## 353. FOOLS

See also 351. Folly; 774. Rashness; 934. Stupidity

1. A prosperous fool is a grievous burden. AESCHYLUS, *Fragments* (525–456 B.C.), 383, tr. M. H. Morgan.

2. Fine clothes may disguise, but foolish words will disclose a fool. AESOP, "The Ass in the Lion's Skin," *Fables* (6th c. B.C.?), tr. Joseph Jacobs.

3. Weep for the dead, for he lacks the light; and weep for the fool, for he lacks intelligence; weep less bitterly for the dead, for he has attained rest; but the life of the fool is worse than death. *Apocrypha*, Ecclesiasticus 22:11.

4. Even a fool, when he holdeth his peace, is counted wise. *Bible*, Proverbs 17:28.

5. Answer a fool according to his folly. *Bible*, Proverbs 26:5.

6. The Fool shall not enter into Heaven let him be ever so Holy. WILLIAM BLAKE, *A Vision of the Last Judgment* (1810).

7. A wise man may be duped as well as a fool; but the fool publishes the triumph of the deceiver. CHARLES CALEB COLTON, *Lacon* (1825), 1.96.

8. There is no need to fasten a bell to a fool. DANISH PROVERB.

9. A fool's head never whitens. ENGLISH PROVERB.

10. There are bearded fools. ENGLISH PROVERB.

11. Talk sense to a fool / and he calls you foolish. EURIPIDES, *The Bacchae* (c. 405 B.C.), tr. William Arrowsmith.

12. Wise men . . . learn by others' harms, fools scarcely by their own. BENJAMIN FRANKLIN, "The Way to Wealth" (July 7, 1757).

13. Every man hath a fool in his sleeve. THOMAS FULLER, M.D., *Gnomologia* (1732), 1424.

14. 'Tis wisdom sometimes to seem a fool. THOMAS FULLER, M.D., *Gnomologia* (1732), 5125.

15. A fool's bolt is soon shot. JOHN HEYWOOD, *Proverbs* (1546), 2.3.

16. If the fools do not control the world, it isn't because they are not in the majority. EDGAR WATSON HOWE, *Country Town Sayings* (1911).

17. The fool is not the man who merely does foolish things. The fool is the man who does not know enough to cash in on his foolishness. ELBERT HUBBARD, *The Note Book* (1927).

18. The silliest woman can manage a clever man; but it needs a very clever woman to manage a fool. RUDYARD KIPLING, "Three and—an Extra," *Plain Tales from the Hills* (1888).

19. A fool must follow his natural bent / (Even as you and I!). RUDYARD KIPLING, "The Vampire" (1897).

20. Old fools are more foolish than young ones. LA ROCHEFOUCAULD, *Maxims* (1665), tr. Kenneth Pratt.

21. A learned fool is sillier than an ignorant one. MOLIÈRE, *Les Femmes savantes* (1672), 4.3.

22. The fool has one great advantage over a man of sense—he is always satisfied with

himself. NAPOLEON I, *Maxims* (1804–15).

23. Fools rush in where angels fear to tread. ALEXANDER POPE, *An Essay on Criticism* (1711), 3.66.

24. No creature smarts so little as a fool. ALEXANDER POPE, *Prologue to the Satires* (1735), 84.

25. To never see a fool you lock yourself in your room and smash the looking-glass. CARL SANDBURG, *The People, Yes* (1936).

26. How ill white hairs become a fool and jester! SHAKESPEARE, *2 Henry IV* (1597–98), 5.5.52.

27. Always the dulness of the fool is the whetstone of the wits. SHAKESPEARE, *As You Like It* (1599–1600), 1.2.58.

28. There are four types of men in the world: lovers, opportunists, lookers-on, and imbeciles. The happiest are the imbeciles. HIPPOLYTE TAINE, *Vie et opinions de Thomas Graingorge* (1867).

29. Let us be thankful for the fools. But for them the rest of us could not succeed. MARK TWAIN, "Pudd'nhead Wilson's New Calendar," *Following the Equator* (1897), 1.28.

30. If every fool wore a crown, we should all be kings. WELSH PROVERB.

## 354. FORCE

**See also 26. Aggression; 157. Compliance; 377. Gentleness; 658. Pacifism; 713. Power; 795. Repression; 933. Strength; 1024. Violence**

1. Let the sword decide after stratagem has failed. ARABIC PROVERB.

2. Forcible ways make not an end of evil, but leave hatred and malice behind them. SIR THOMAS BROWNE, *Christian Morals* (1716), 3.

3. The use of force alone is temporary. It may subdue for a moment, but it does not remove the necessity of subduing again: and a nation is not governed which is perpetually to be conquered. EDMUND BURKE, speech, "On Conciliation with the American Colonies," March 22, 1775.

4. Fraud is the homage that force pays to reason. CHARLES P. CURTIS, *A Commonplace Book* (1957).

5. Where might is master, justice is servant. GERMAN PROVERB.

6. Every act of submission to an exterior force rots me standing; I am dead before being buried by the legitimate gravediggers of the establishment. Graffito written during French student revolt, May 1968.

7. The one means that wins the easiest victory over reason: terror and force. ADOLF HITLER, *Mein Kampf* (1924), 1.2.

8. Force without reason falls of its own weight. HORACE, *Odes* (23–c. 15 B.C.), 3.4.

9. A man may build himself a throne of bayonets, but he cannot sit on it. WILLIAM RALPH INGE, quoted in Marchant's *Wit and Wisdom of Dean Inge* (1927).

10. When a fact can be demonstrated, force is unnecessary; when it cannot be demonstrated, force is infamous. ROBERT G. INGERSOLL, *Prose-Poems and Selections* (1884).

11. Force works on servile natures, not the free. BEN JONSON, *Every Man in His Humour* (1598), 1.2.

12. When one by force subdues men, they do not submit to him in heart. They submit because their strength is not adequate to resist. MENCIUS, *Works* (4th–3rd c. B.C.), 4, tr. Charles A. Wong.

13. Whatever needs to be maintained through force is doomed. HENRY MILLER, "The Absolute Collective," *The Wisdom of the Heart* (1941).

14. Who overcomes / By force, hath overcome but half his foe. MILTON, *Paradise Lost* (1667), 1.648.

15. There is no real force without justice. NAPOLEON I, *Maxims* (1804–15).

16. Justice without force is impotent, force without justice is tyranny. . . . Not being able to make what is just strong, we make what was strong just. PASCAL, *Pensées* (1670), 298.

17. Do not expect justice where might is right. PHAEDRUS, "The Cow, the Goat, the Sheep and the Lion," *Fables* (1st c.), tr. Thomas James.

18. Where there is no might right loses itself. PORTUGUESE PROVERB.

19. Against naked force the only possible defense is naked force. The aggressor makes the rules for such a war; the defenders have no alternative but matching destruction with more destruction, slaughter with greater slaughter. FRANKLIN D. ROOSEVELT, message to Young Democrats Convention, Louisville, Ky., Aug. 21, 1941.

20. Not hammer-strokes, but dance of the

water sings the pebbles into perfection. RABINDRANATH TAGORE, *Stray Birds* (1916), 126.

## 355. FOREIGNERS AND FOREIGNNESS

1. Everyone's quick to blame the alien. AESCHYLUS, *The Suppliant Maidens* (463 B.C.), tr. Seth G. Bernardete.

2. Everything foreign is respected, partly because it comes from afar, partly because it is ready made and perfect. BALTASAR GRACIÁN, *The Art of Worldly Wisdom* (1647), 198, tr. Joseph Jacobs.

3. Admiration for ourselves and our institutions is too often measured by our contempt and dislike for foreigners. WILLIAM RALPH INGE, "Patriotism," *Outspoken Essays: First Series* (1919).

4. America shudders at anything alien, and when it wants to shut its mind against any man's ideas it calls him a foreigner. MAX LERNER, "America in the Sunlight," *Actions and Passions* (1949).

5. That which is close to home afflicts all alike, / but a heart soon goes free of grief / over a stranger's unhappiness. PINDAR, *Odes* (5th c. B.C.), Nemea 1, tr. Richmond Lattimore.

6. Man is not man, but a wolf, to those he does not know. PLAUTUS, *The Comedy of Asses* (3rd c. B.C.).

7. Ants and savages put strangers to death. BERTRAND RUSSELL, "The Functions of a Teacher," *Unpopular Essays* (1950).

8. The tears of strangers are only water. RUSSIAN PROVERB.

9. The stranger has no friend, unless it be a stranger. SA'DI, *Gulistan* (1258), 3.28, tr. James Ross.

10. He will deal harshly by a stranger who has not been himself often a traveller and stranger. SA'DI, *Gulistan* (1258), 3.28, tr. James Ross.

11. Whoever live at a different end of the town from me, I look upon as persons out of the world, and only myself and the scene about me to be in it. JONATHAN SWIFT, *Thoughts on Various Subjects* (1711).

## FOREIGN RELATIONS

**See 496. International Relations**

## 356. FORETHOUGHT

**See 110. Cautiousness; 722. Preparedness; 749. Prudence; 1027. Vision**

1. Affairs are easier of entrance than of exit; and it is but common prudence to see our way out before we venture in. AESOP, "The Sick Lion," *Fables* (6th c. B.C.?), tr. Thomas James.

2. The arrow seen before cometh less rudely. DANTE, "Paradiso," 17, *The Divine Comedy* (c. 1300–21), tr. J. A. Carlyle and P. H. Wicksteed.

3. In every affair consider what precedes and follows, and then undertake it. EPICTETUS, *Discourses* (2nd c.), 3.15, tr. Thomas W. Higginson.

4. The man who knows when not to act / Is wise. To my mind, bravery is forethought. EURIPIDES, *The Suppliant Women* (c. 421 B.C.), tr. Frank W. Jones.

5. A danger foreseen is half avoided. THOMAS FULLER, M.D., *Gnomologia* (1732), 67.

6. The time to repair the roof is when the sun is shining. JOHN F. KENNEDY, State of the Union Message, Jan. 11, 1962.

7. Forethought and Ready-wit both prosper in peace; Come-what-will perishes. *Panchatantra* (c. 5th c.), 1, tr. Franklin Edgerton.

8. You can't hatch chickens from fried eggs. PENNSYLVANIA DUTCH PROVERB.

9. The wise man avoids evil by anticipating it. PUBLILIUS SYRUS, *Moral Sayings* (1st c. B.C.), 878, tr. Darius Lyman.

10. Nothing in the world can one imagine beforehand, not the least thing. Everything is made up of so many unique particulars that cannot be foreseen. RAINER MARIA RILKE, *The Notebooks of Malte Laurids Brigge* (1910), tr. M. D. Herter Norton.

11. To fear the worst oft cures the worse. SHAKESPEARE, *Troilus and Cressida* (1601–02), 3.2.78.

12. Only those who get into scrapes with their eyes open can find the safe way out. LOGAN PEARSALL SMITH, *Afterthoughts* (1931), 1.

13. Look to the end, no matter what it is you are considering. Often enough God gives a man a glimpse of happiness, and then utterly ruins him. SOLON (7th–6th c.

B.C.), quoted in Herodotus' *Histories* (5th c. B.C.), 1.32, tr. Aubrey de Sélincourt.

### FORGETTING
See 574. Memory

### 357. FORGIVENESS
See also 577. Mercy

1. Forgive us our debts, as we forgive our debtors. *Bible*, Matthew 6:12.

2. Be ye kind one to another, tenderhearted, forgiving one another, even as God for Christ's sake hath forgiven you. *Bible*, Ephesians 4:32.

3. It is easier to forgive an enemy than to forgive a friend. WILLIAM BLAKE, "What God Is," *Jerusalem* (1804–20).

4. We all like to forgive, and we all love best not those who offend us least, nor those who have done most for us, but those who make it most easy for us to forgive them. SAMUEL BUTLER (d. 1902), "Reconciliation," *Note-Books* (1912).

5. Forgiveness to the injured does belong; / For they ne'er pardon who have done the wrong. JOHN DRYDEN, *The Conquest of Granada* (1670–71), 2.1.2.

6. Reason to rule but mercy to forgive: / The first is law, the last prerogative. JOHN DRYDEN, *The Hind and the Panther* (1687), 1.261.

7. Forgotten is forgiven. F. SCOTT FITZGERALD, "Note-Books," *The Crack-Up* (1945).

8. The worst of men are those who will not forgive. THOMAS FULLER, M.D., *Gnomologia* (1732), 4849.

9. Amnesty: an act by which sovereigns commonly pardon injustices committed by themselves. Graffito written during French student revolt, May 1968.

10. Forgiveness is the answer to the child's dream of a miracle by which what is broken is made whole again, what is soiled is again made clean. DAG HAMMARSKJÖLD, "1956," *Markings* (1964), tr. Leif Sjoberg and W. H. Auden.

11. The offender never pardons. GEORGE HERBERT, *Jacula Prudentum* (1651).

12. The ineffable joy of forgiving and being forgiven forms an ecstasy that might well arouse the envy of the gods. ELBERT HUBBARD, *The Note Book* (1927).

13. We pardon as long as we love. LA ROCHEFOUCAULD, *Maxims* (1665), tr. Kenneth Pratt.

14. Did man e'er live / Saw priest or woman yet forgive? JAMES RUSSELL LOWELL, "Villa France, 1859," *Under the Willows and Other Poems* (1868).

15. If there is something to pardon in everything, there is also something to condemn. NIETZSCHE, *The Will to Power* (1888), tr. Anthony M. Ludovici.

16. To err is human, to forgive divine. ALEXANDER POPE, *An Essay on Criticism* (1711), 2.325.

17. Forgiving presupposes remembering. PAUL TILLICH, *The Eternal Now* (1963), 1.2.2.

18. What power has love but forgiveness? / In other words / by its intervention / what has been done / can be undone. / What good is it otherwise? WILLIAM CARLOS WILLIAMS, "Asphodel, That Greeny Flower," *Pictures from Brueghel* (1962), 3.

### FORM
See 654. Order

### 358. FORTUNE
See also 15. Advantage; 114. Chance; 546. Losers; 745. Prosperity and Adversity; 1041. Wealth

1. Fortune is like the market, where many times, if you can stay a little, the price will fall. FRANCIS BACON, "Of Delay," *Essays* (1625).

2. Who has good luck is good, / Who has bad luck is bad. BERTOLT BRECHT, *The Exception and the Rule* (1937), 6, tr. Eric Bentley.

3. Let everyone witness how many different cards fortune has up her sleeve when she wants to ruin a man. BENVENUTO CELLINI, *Autobiography* (1558–66), tr. George Bull.

4. Heaven's help is better than early rising. CERVANTES, *Don Quixote* (1605–15), 2.4.34, tr. Peter Motteux and John Ozell.

5. Good fortune leads one to the highest glory, / But to renounce it calls for equal courage. CORNEILLE, *Cinna* (1639), 2.1, tr. Paul Landis.

6. Luck is not chance— / It's Toil— / Fortune's expensive smile / Is earned—. EMILY DICKINSON, poem (c. 1875).

7. To believe in luck, if it were not a solecism so to use the word *believe*, is skepticism. EMERSON, *Journals*, 1841.

8. Don't envy men / Because they seem to have a run of luck, / Since luck's a nine day's wonder. Wait their end. EURIPIDES, *Herakleidai* (c. 429–27 B.C.), tr. Ralph Gladstone.

9. Fortune always will confer an aura / Of worth, unworthily; and in this world / The lucky person passes for a genius. EURIPIDES, *Herakleidai* (c. 429–27 B.C.), tr. Ralph Gladstone.

10. The man who glories in his luck / May be overthrown by destiny. EURIPIDES, *The Suppliant Women* (c. 421 B.C.), tr. Frank W. Jones.

11. There is in the worst of fortune the best of chances for a happy change. EURIPIDES, *Iphigenia in Tauris* (c. 414–12 B.C.), 721, tr. M. H. Morgan.

12. None can hold fortune still and make it last. EURIPIDES, *Helen* (412 B.C.), tr. Richmond Lattimore.

13. He who is not lucky, let him not go a-fishing. THOMAS FULLER, M.D., *Gnomologia* (1732), 2392.

14. Industry is Fortune's right hand, and frugality her left. THOMAS FULLER, M.D., *Gnomologia* (1732), 3092.

15. It is a great piece of skill to know how to guide your luck even while waiting for it. BALTASAR GRACIÁN, *The Art of Worldly Wisdom* (1647), 26, tr. Joseph Jacobs.

16. When you find Fortune favorable, stride boldly forward, for she favors the bold, and being a woman, the young. BALTASAR GRACIÁN, *The Art of Worldly Wisdom* (1647), 26, tr. Joseph Jacobs.

17. Fortune pays you sometimes for the intensity of her favors by the shortness of their duration. She soon tires of carrying any one long on her shoulders. BALTASAR GRACIÁN, *The Art of Worldly Wisdom* (1647), 28, tr. Joseph Jacobs.

18. Some folk want their luck buttered. THOMAS HARDY, *The Mayor of Casterbridge* (1886), 13.

19. Fortune, men say, doth give too much to many, / But yet she never gave enough to any. SIR JOHN HARINGTON, "Of Fortune," *Epigrams* (1615).

20. Ah Fortune, what god is more cruel to us than thou! How thou delightest ever to make sport of human life! HORACE, *Satires* (35–30 B.C.), 2.7.

21. Have but luck, and you will have the rest; be fortunate, and you will be thought great. VICTOR HUGO, "Fantine," *Les Misérables* (1862), 1.12, tr. Charles E. Wilbour.

22. Very few live by choice. Every man is placed in his present condition by causes which acted without his foresight, and with which he did not always willingly cooperate; and therefore you will rarely meet one who does not think the lot of his neighbor better than his own. SAMUEL JOHNSON, *Rasselas* (1759), 16.

23. Fortune, thou hadst no deity, if men / Had wisdom. BEN JONSON, *Sejanus His Fall* (1603), 5.10.

24. Ill fortune never crushed that man whom good fortune deceived not. BEN JONSON, "Explorata," *Timber* (1640).

25. Good or bad fortune usually comes to those who have more of the one than the other. LA ROCHEFOUCAULD, *Maxims* (1665), tr. Kenneth Pratt.

26. Fortune never appears so blind as to those to whom she does no good. LA ROCHEFOUCAULD, *Maxims* (1665), tr. Kenneth Pratt.

27. Fortunate persons hardly ever amend their ways: they always imagine that they are in the right when fortune upholds their bad conduct. LA ROCHEFOUCAULD, *Maxims* (1665), tr. Kenneth Pratt.

28. When Fortune comes, seize her in front with a sure hand, because behind she is bald. LEONARDO DA VINCI, *Notebooks* (c. 1500), tr. Jean Paul Richter.

29. What men call luck / Is the prerogative of valiant souls, / The fealty life pays its rightful kings. JAMES RUSSELL LOWELL, "A Glance Behind the Curtain" (1843).

30. now and then / there is a person born / who is so unlucky / that he runs into accidents / which started out to happen to somebody else. DON MARQUIS, "archy says," *Archy's Life of Mehitabel* (1933).

31. Whatever the benefits of fortune are, they yet require a palate fit to relish them. 'Tis fruition, and not possession that renders us happy. MONTAIGNE, "Of the inequality among us," *Essays* (1580–88), tr. Charles Cotton and W. C. Hazlitt.

32. When a man is a favorite of Fortune

she never takes him unawares, and, however astonishing her favors may be, she finds him ready. NAPOLEON I, *Maxims* (1804–15).

33. When the fountain has gone up, it comes down. PERSIAN PROVERB.

34. We must master our good fortune, or it will master us. PUBLILIUS SYRUS, *Moral Sayings* (1st c. B.C.), 109, tr. Darius Lyman.

35. Fortune makes a fool of him whom she favors too much. PUBLILIUS SYRUS, *Moral Sayings* (1st c. B.C.), 271, tr. Darius Lyman.

36. When Fortune flatters, she does it to betray. PUBLILIUS SYRUS, *Moral Sayings* (1st c. B.C.), 277, tr. Darius Lyman.

37. It is more easy to get a favor from fortune than to keep it. PUBLILIUS SYRUS, *Moral Sayings* (1st c. B.C.), 282, tr. Darius Lyman.

38. Fortune's not content with knocking a man down; she sends him spinning head over heels, crash upon crash. SENECA, *Letters to Lucilius* (1st c.), 8.5, tr. E. Phillips Barker.

39. Luck never made a man wise. SENECA, *Letters to Lucilius* (1st c.), 76.6, tr. E. Phillips Barker.

40. Fortune brings in some boats that are not steered. SHAKESPEARE, *Cymbeline* (1609–10), 4.3.46.

41. Fortune is not on the side of the faint-hearted. SOPHOCLES, *Phaedra* (c. 435–29 B.C.), tr. M. H. Morgan.

42. Look how men live, always precariously / balanced between good and bad fortune. SOPHOCLES, *Philoctetes* (409 B.C.), tr. David Grene.

43. I must complain the cards are ill shuffled, till I have a good hand. JONATHAN SWIFT, *Thoughts on Various Subjects* (1711).

44. The power of fortune is confessed only by the miserable, for the happy impute all their success to prudence or merit. JONATHAN SWIFT, *Thoughts on Various Subjects* (1711).

45. Fortune favors the brave. TERENCE, *Phormio* (161 B.C.), tr. William A. Oldfather.

46. Fortune sides with him who dares. VERGIL, *Aeneid* (30–19 B.C.), 10.284, tr. T. H. Delabere-May.

47. Fortune's a right whore: / If she give ought, she deals it in small parcels, / That she may take away all at one swoop. JOHN WEBSTER, *The White Devil* (1612), 1.1.

48. 'Tis better to be fortunate than wise. JOHN WEBSTER, *The White Devil* (1612), 5.6.

49. Luck is not something you can mention in the presence of self-made men. E. B. WHITE, "Control," *One Man's Meat* (1944).

50. Not a man alive / Has so much luck that he can play with it. WILLIAM BUTLER YEATS, *The Land of Heart's Desire* (1894).

## 359. FRANCE AND FRENCHMEN

See also 664. Paris

1. Everything ends this way in France—everything. Weddings, christenings, duels, burials, swindlings, diplomatic affairs—everything is a pretext for a good dinner. JEAN ANOUILH, *Cécile* (1949), tr. Luce and Arthur Klein.

2. Political thought in France is either nostalgic or utopian. RAYMOND ARON, *The Opium of the Intellectual* (1957).

3. How can you be expected to govern a country that has two hundred and forty-six kinds of cheese? CHARLES DE GAULLE, *Newsweek*, Oct. 1, 1962.

4. A Frenchman must be always talking, whether he knows anything of the matter or not; an Englishman is content to say nothing, when he has nothing to say. SAMUEL JOHNSON, quoted in Boswell's *Life of Samuel Johnson*, 1780.

5. The Frenchman is first and foremost a *man*. He is likeable often just because of his weaknesses, which are always thoroughly human, even if despicable. HENRY MILLER, "Raimu," *The Wisdom of the Heart* (1941).

6. Frenchmen have an unlimited capacity for gallantry and indulge it on every occasion. MOLIÈRE, *The Sicilian* (1666), 2, tr. John Wood.

7. Who can help loving the land that has taught us / Six hundred and eighty-five ways to dress eggs? THOMAS MOORE, *The Fudge Family in Paris* (1818), 8.64.

8. The French complain of everything, and always. NAPOLEON I, *Maxims* (1804–15).

9. The French are highly individualistic and ungovernable and the extraordinary thing is that, although they project great leaders about once a century, those leaders rule effectively but bequeath chaos. C. L.

SULZBERGER, editorial, *The New York Times*, April 30, 1969.

10. France has neither winter nor summer nor morals—apart from these drawbacks it is a fine country. MARK TWAIN, *Notebook* (1935).

## 360. FRANKNESS

See also 423. Honesty; 894. Sincerity; 993. Truthfulness

1. If people would dare to speak to one another unreservedly, there would be a good deal less sorrow in the world a hundred years hence. SAMUEL BUTLER (d. 1902), *The Way of All Flesh* (1903), 44.

2. Of all plagues, good Heaven, thy wrath can send, / Save, save, oh save me from the candid friend! GEORGE CANNING, *New Morality* (1798), 36.207.

3. Straightforwardness, without the rules of propriety, becomes rudeness. CONFUCIUS, *Analects* (6th C. B.C.), 8.2, tr. James Legge.

4. People tell me to be frank, but how can I be whin I don't dare to know mesilf? FINLEY PETER DUNNE, "Casual Observations," *Mr. Dooley's Philosophy* (1900).

5. Plain dealing is a jewel, but they that wear it are out of fashion. THOMAS FULLER, M.D., *Gnomologia* (1732), 3878.

6. Praise, of course, is best: plain speech breeds hate. / But ah the Attic honey / Of telling a man exactly what you think of him! *Greek Anthology* (7th C. B.C.–10th C. A.D.), 11.340, tr. Dudley Fitts.

7. Honesty and wisdom are such a delightful pastime, at another person's expense! NATHANIEL HAWTHORNE, *The Blithedale Romance* (1852), 16.

8. Lies kill love, it's been said. Well, what about frankness, then. ABEL HERMANT, *Éloge du mensonge* (1925).

9. Be yourself and speak your mind today, though it contradict all you have said before. ELBERT HUBBARD, *The Note Book* (1927).

10. It is the weak and confused who worship the pseudosimplicities of brutal directness. MARSHALL MC LUHAN, "The Tough as Narcissus," *The Mechanical Bride* (1951).

11. One open way of speaking introduces another open way of speaking, and draws out discoveries, like wine and love. MONTAIGNE, "Of profit and honesty," *Essays* (1580–88), tr. Charles Cotton and W. C. Hazlitt.

12. Not every sheer truth / is the better for showing her face. Silence also / many times is the wisest thing for a man to have in his mind. PINDAR, *Odes* (5th C. B.C.), Nemea 5, tr. Richmond Lattimore.

13. To be outspoken is easy when you do not wait to speak the complete truth. RABINDRANATH TAGORE, *Stray Birds* (1916), 128.

14. All faults may be forgiven of him who has perfect candor. WALT WHITMAN, preface to *Leaves of Grass* (1855).

15. All cruel people describe themselves as paragons of frankness. TENNESSEE WILLIAMS, *The Milk Train Doesn't Stop Here Anymore* (1963), 1.

## FRAUD

See 221. Deception

## 361. FREEDOM, INDIVIDUAL

See also 107. Captivity; 362. Free Speech; 534. Liberty; 817. Rights; 873. Self-sufficiency; 882. Servitude

1. Better starve free than be a fat slave. AESOP, "The Dog and the Wolf," *Fables* (6th C. B.C.? ), tr. Joseph Jacobs.

2. Freedom is not something that anybody can be given; freedom is something people take and people are as free as they want to be. JAMES BALDWIN, "Notes for a Hypothetical Novel," *Nobody Knows My Name* (1961).

3. The misfortune which befalls man from his once having been a child is that his liberty was at first concealed from him, and all his life he will retain the nostalgia for a time when he was ignorant of its exigencies. SIMONE DE BEAUVOIR, *Pour une morale de l'ambiguïté* (1947), 2.

4. Absolute freedom mocks at justice. Absolute justice denies freedom. ALBERT CAMUS, "Historical Murder," *The Rebel* (1951), tr. Anthony Bower.

5. Freedom suppressed and again regained bites with keener fangs than freedom never endangered. CICERO, *De Officiis* (44 B.C.), 2.7.24.

6. Freedom has a thousand charms to show, / That slaves, howe'er contented, never know. WILLIAM COWPER, *Table Talk* (1782), 260.

7. I only ask to be free. The butterflies are free. CHARLES DICKENS, *Bleak House* (1852), 6.

8. Everything that is really great and inspiring is created by the individual who can labor in freedom. EINSTEIN, *Out of My Later Years* (1950), 7.

9. Liberty is a different kind of pain from prison. T. S. ELIOT, *The Family Reunion* (1939), 2.2.

10. If you cannot be free, be as free as you can. EMERSON, *Journals*, 1836.

11. Though we love goodness and not stealing, yet also we love freedom and not preaching. EMERSON, *Journals*, 1842.

12. A part of Fate is the freedom of man. Forever wells up the impulse of choosing and acting in his soul. EMERSON, "Fate," *The Conduct of Life* (1860).

13. Wild liberty breeds iron conscience; natures with great impulses have great resources, and return from far. EMERSON, "Power," *The Conduct of Life* (1860).

14. What is it that every man seeks? To be secure, to be happy, to do what he pleases without restraint and without compulsion. EPICTETUS, *Discourses* (2nd c.), 4.1, tr. Thomas W. Higginson.

15. Freedom is the greatest fruit of self-sufficiency. EPICURUS, "Vatican Sayings" (3rd c. B.C.), 77, in *Letters, Principal Doctrines, and Vatican Sayings*, tr. Russel M. Geer.

16. The American feels so rich in his opportunities for free expression that he often no longer knows what he is free from. Neither does he know where he is not free; he does not recognize his native autocrats when he sees them. ERIK H. ERIKSON, *Childhood and Society* (1950), 8.

17. Whilst we strive / To live most free, we're caught in our own toils. JOHN FORD, *The Lover's Melancholy* (1629), 1.3.

18. The moment the slave resolves that he will no longer be a slave, his fetters fall. He frees himself and shows the way to others. Freedom and slavery are mental states. MOHANDAS K. GANDHI, *Non-Violence in Peace and War* (1948), 2.10.

19. Your freedom when it loses its fetters becomes itself the fetter of a greater freedom. KAHLIL GIBRAN, "On Freedom," *The Prophet* (1923).

20. To know how to free oneself is nothing; the arduous thing is to know what to do with one's freedom. ANDRÉ GIDE, *The Immoralist* (1902), 1.1, tr. Dorothy Bussy.

21. He only earns his freedom and existence who daily conquers them anew. GOETHE, *Faust* (1832), 2.

22. The liberty of others extends mine to infinity. Graffito written during French student revolt, May 1968.

23. We prate of freedom; we are in deadly fear of life. LEARNED HAND, speech, Harvard Law School, March 20, 1930.

24. Liberty is the only true riches: of all the rest we are at once the masters and the slaves. WILLIAM HAZLITT, "Commonplaces," *The Round Table* (1817), 2.

25. The history of the world is none other than the progress of the consciousness of freedom. HEGEL, introduction to *Philosophy of History* (1832), tr. John Sibree.

26. Unless a man has the talents to make something of himself, freedom is an irksome burden. ERIC HOFFER, *The True Believer* (1951), 2.5.26.

27. There can be no real freedom without the freedom to fail. ERIC HOFFER, *The Ordeal of Change* (1964), 12.

28. Freedom is a condition of mind, and the best way to secure it is to breed it. ELBERT HUBBARD, *The Note Book* (1927).

29. Freedom is the supreme good—freedom from self-imposed limitation. ELBERT HUBBARD, *The Note Book* (1927).

30. It is better to die on your feet than to live on your knees. DOLORES IBARRURI, speech in Paris, Sept. 3, 1936.

31. What does any man *want*? To be left alone with his life, and have some hope of making that life what he wants it to be. LE ROI JONES, "LeRoi Jones Talking," *Home* (1966).

32. A man is either free or he is not. There cannot be any apprenticeship for freedom. LE ROI JONES, "Tokenism: 300 Years for Five Cents," *Home* (1966).

33. The most powerful single force in the world today is neither Communism nor capitalism, neither the H-bomb nor the guided missile—it is man's eternal desire to be free and independent. JOHN F. KENNEDY, address, Washington, D.C., July 2, 1957.

34. The free way of life proposes ends, but it does not prescribe means. ROBERT F. KENNEDY, "Berlin East and West," *The Pursuit of Justice* (1964).

35. Freedom is a very great reality. But it means, above all things, freedom from lies. D. H. LAWRENCE, *Pornography and Obscenity* (1930).

36. Man is a masterpiece of creation, if only because no amount of determinism can prevent him from believing that he acts as a free being. GEORG CHRISTOPH LICHTENBERG, *Aphorisms* (1764–99), tr. J. P. Stern.

37. True freedom is to share / All the chains our brothers wear, / And, with heart and hand, to be / Earnest to make others free! JAMES RUSSELL LOWELL, "Stanzas on Freedom" (1843), 3.

38. You can't separate peace from freedom because no one can be at peace unless he has his freedom. MALCOLM X, *Malcolm X Speaks* (1965), 12.

39. The dagger plunged in the name of Freedom is plunged into the breast of Freedom. JOSÉ MARTÍ, *Granos de oro: pensamientos seleccionados en las Obras de José Martí* (1942).

40. The liberty of the individual must be thus far limited: he must not make himself a nuisance to other people. JOHN STUART MILL, *On Liberty* (1859), 3.

41. Let us forget such words, and all they mean, / as Hatred, Bitterness and Rancor, Greed, / Intolerance, Bigotry; let us renew / our faith and pledge to Man, his right to be / Himself, and free. EDNA ST. VINCENT MILLAY, "Poem and Prayer for an Invading Army," *Make Bright the Arrows* (1940).

42. Freedom is the will to be responsible to ourselves. NIETZSCHE, "Skirmishes in a War with the Age," 36, *Twilight of the Idols* (1888), tr. Anthony M. Ludovici.

43. True individual freedom cannot exist without economic security and independence. People who are hungry and out of a job are the stuff of which dictatorships are made. FRANKLIN D. ROOSEVELT, message to Congress, Jan. 11, 1944.

44. Man's estate is as a citadel: he may throw down the walls to gain what he calls freedom, but then nothing of him remains save a dismantled fortress, open to the stars. And then begins the anguish of not-being. SAINT-EXUPÉRY, *The Wisdom of the Sands* (1948), 2, tr. Stuart Gilbert.

45. Freedom is baffling: / men having it often / know not they have it / till it is gone and / they no longer have it. CARL SANDBURG, "Freedom Is a Habit," *Complete Poems* (1950).

46. Freedom can't be bought for nothing. If you hold her precious, you must hold all else of little worth. SENECA, *Letters to Lucilius* (1st c.), 104.34, tr. E. Phillips Barker.

47. When a prisoner sees the door of his dungeon open, he dashes for it without stopping to think where he shall get his dinner outside. GEORGE BERNARD SHAW, preface to *Back to Methuselah* (1921).

48. The virtue of a free man appears equally great in refusing to face difficulties as in overcoming them. SPINOZA, *Ethics* (1677), 4, tr. Andrew Boyle.

49. We have confused the free with the free and easy. ADLAI STEVENSON, *Putting First Things First* (1960).

50. We gain freedom when we have paid the full price / for our right to live. RABINDRANATH TAGORE, *Fireflies* (1928).

51. Emancipation from the bondage of the soil / is no freedom for the tree. RABINDRANATH TAGORE, *Fireflies* (1928).

52. As long as possible live free and uncommitted. It makes but little difference whether you are committed to a farm or the county jail. THOREAU, "Where I Lived, and What I Lived For," *Walden* (1854).

## FREEDOM OF THE PRESS

See 725. Press, Freedom of the

## 362. FREE SPEECH

See also 256. Dissent;
361. Freedom, Individual;
534. Liberty; 623. Newspapers;
725. Press, Freedom of the; 758. Publishing

1. Freedom of speech means that you shall not do something to people either for the views they have, or the views they express, or the words they speak or write. HUGO BLACK, *One Man's Stand for Freedom* (1963).

2. Free speech is about as good a cause as the world has ever known. But, like the poor, it is always with us and gets shoved

aside in favor of things which seem at some given moment more vital. HEYWOOD BROUN, "The Miracle of Debs," *New York World*, Oct. 23, 1926.

3. Almost nobody means precisely what he says when he makes the declaration, "I'm in favor of free speech." HEYWOOD BROUN, "The Miracle of Debs," *New York World*, Oct. 23, 1926.

4. Everyone is in favour of free speech. Hardly a day passes without its being extolled, but some people's idea of it is that they are free to say what they like, but if anyone says anything back, that is an outrage. SIR WINSTON CHURCHILL, speech, House of Commons, Oct. 13, 1943.

5. The very aim and end of our institutions is just this: that we may think what we like and say what we think. OLIVER WENDELL HOLMES, SR., *The Professor at the Breakfast Table* (1860), 5.

6. The right to be heard does not automatically include the right to be taken seriously. HUBERT H. HUMPHREY, speech to National Student Association, Madison, Wis., Aug. 23, 1965.

7. Let no one ever think for a moment that national debate means national division. LYNDON B. JOHNSON, commencement address, National Cathedral School for Girls, Washington, D.C., June 1, 1965.

8. If all mankind, minus one, were of one opinion, and only one person were of the contrary opinion, mankind would be no more justified in silencing that one person, than he, if he had the power, would be justified in silencing mankind. JOHN STUART MILL, *On Liberty* (1859), 2.

9. A people which is able to say everything becomes able to do everything. NAPOLEON I, *Maxims* (1804–15).

10. The sound of tireless voices is the price we pay for the right to hear the music of our own opinions. ADLAI STEVENSON, speech, New York City, Aug. 28, 1952.

## FREE WILL

**See 361. Freedom, Individual; 860. Self-determination**

## FRIENDLINESS

**See 151. Company**

## 363. FRIENDSHIP

**See also 7. Acquaintances; 57. Association; 151. Company; 166. Confidences; 178. Constancy and Inconstancy; 299. Estrangement; 497. Intimacy; 544. Loneliness; 736. Promiscuity; 787. Relationships, Human; 908. Solitude**

1. Friends are born, not made. HENRY ADAMS, *The Education of Henry Adams* (1907), 7.

2. Friendship needs a certain parallelism of life, a community of thought, a rivalry of aim. HENRY ADAMS, *The Education of Henry Adams* (1907), 20.

3. One friend in a lifetime is much; two are many; three are hardly possible. HENRY ADAMS, *The Education of Henry Adams* (1907), 20.

4. A doubtful friend is worse than a certain enemy. Let a man be one thing or the other, and we then know how to meet him. AESOP, "The Hound and the Hare," *Fables* (6th c. B.C.?), tr. Thomas James.

5. That man travels the longest journey that undertakes it in search of a sincere friend. ALI IBN-ABI-TALIB, *Sentences* (7th c.), 160, tr. Simon Ockley.

6. Forsake not an old friend, for a new one does not compare with him. *Apocrypha*, Ecclesiasticus 9:10.

7. A new friend is like new wine; when it has aged you will drink it with pleasure. *Apocrypha*, Ecclesiasticus 9:10.

8. I keep my friends as misers do their treasure, because, of all the things granted us by wisdom, none is greater or better than friendship. PIETRO ARETINO, letter to Giovanni Pollastra, July 7, 1537, tr. Samuel Putnam.

9. Between friends there is no need of justice. ARISTOTLE, *Nicomachean Ethics* (4th c. B.C.), 8.1, tr. J. A. K. Thomson.

10. Wishing to be friends is quick work, but friendship is a slow-ripening fruit. ARISTOTLE, *Nicomachean Ethics* (4th c. B.C.), 8.3, tr. J. A. K. Thomson.

11. My best friend is the man who in wishing me well wishes it for my sake. ARISTOTLE, *Nicomachean Ethics* (4th c. B.C.), 9.8, tr. J. A. K. Thomson.

12. Friendship is a single soul dwelling in two bodies. ARISTOTLE (4th c. B.C.), quoted in Diogenes Laertius' *Lives and Opinions of Eminent Philosophers* (3rd c. A.D.), tr. R. D. Hicks.

13. Business, you know, may bring money, but friendship hardly ever does. JANE AUSTEN, *Emma* (1816), 34.

14. There is little friendship in the world, and least of all between equals. FRANCIS BACON, "Of Followers and Friends," *Essays* (1625).

15. This communicating of a man's self to his friend works two contrary effects; for it redoubleth joys, and cutteth griefs in half. FRANCIS BACON, "Of Friendship," *Essays* (1625).

16. There's nothing worth the wear of winning, / But laughter and the love of friends. HILAIRE BELLOC, "Dedicatory Ode," *Verses* (1910).

17. The first temptation, upon meeting an old friend after many years, is always to—look the other way. UGO BETTI, *The Inquiry* (1944–45), 2.2, ed. Gino Rizzo.

18. Love your friends as if they would some day hate you. BIAS (6th c. B.C.), quoted in Diogenes Laertius' *Lives and Opinions of Eminent Philosophers* (3rd c. A.D.), tr. R. D. Hicks.

19. Faithful are the wounds of a friend; but the kisses of an enemy are deceitful. *Bible*, Proverbs 27:6.

20. Friendship, n. A ship big enough to carry two in fair weather, but only one in foul. AMBROSE BIERCE, *The Devil's Dictionary* (1881–1911).

21. A companion loves some agreeable qualities which a man may possess, but a friend loves the man himself. JAMES BOSWELL, *London Journal*, July 7, 1763.

22. Let him have the key of thy heart, who hath the lock of his own. SIR THOMAS BROWNE, *Christian Morals* (1716), 3.

23. Friendship is a strong and habitual inclination in two persons to promote the good and happiness of one another. EUSTACE BUDGELL in *The Spectator* (1711–12), 385.

24. Old friends, we say, are best, when some sudden disillusionment shakes our faith in a new comrade. GELETT BURGESS, "Old Friends and New," *The Romance of the Commonplace* (1916).

25. Friendship is like money, easier made than kept. SAMUEL BUTLER (d. 1902), *Note-Books* (1912).

26. Friendship is Love without his wings! BYRON, "L'Amitié est L'Amour Sans Ailes" (1806).

27. Don't believe your friends when they ask you to be honest with them. All they really want is to be maintained in the good opinion they have of themselves. ALBERT CAMUS, *The Fall* (1956).

28. A man must eat a peck of salt with his friend before he knows him. CERVANTES, *Don Quixote* (1605–15), 1.3.1, tr. Peter Motteux and John Ozell.

29. Friendship makes prosperity more brilliant, and lightens adversity by dividing and sharing it. CICERO, *De Amicitia* (44 B.C.).

30. What a delight it is to make friends with someone you have despised! COLETTE, "Sido and I," *Earthly Paradise* (1966), 1, ed. Robert Phelps.

31. The firmest friendships have been formed in mutual adversity, as iron is most strongly united by the fiercest flame. CHARLES CALEB COLTON, *Lacon* (1825), 1.365.

32. True friendship is like sound health; the value of it is seldom known until it be lost. CHARLES CALEB COLTON, *Lacon* (1825), 2.3.

33. The friendships which last are those wherein each friend respects the other's dignity to the point of not really wanting anything from him. CYRIL CONNOLLY, *The Unquiet Grave* (1945), 1.

34. Acquaintance I would have, but when't depends / Not on the number, but the choice of friends. ABRAHAM COWLEY, "Of Myself" (17th c.).

35. The real friendships among men are so rare that when they occur they are famous. CLARENCE DAY, *This Simian World* (1920), 6.

36. Friendships begin with liking or gratitude—roots that can be pulled up. GEORGE ELIOT, *Daniel Deronda* (1874–76), 4.32.

37. Endurance of friendship does not depend / Upon ourselves, but upon circumstance. / But circumstance is not undetermined. T. S. ELIOT, *Murder in the Cathedral* (1935), 1.

38. It is one of the blessings of old friends that you can afford to be stupid with them. EMERSON, *Journals*, 1836.

39. Every man passes his life in the search after friendship. EMERSON, "Friendship," *Essays: First Series* (1841).

40. A friend may well be reckoned the masterpiece of nature. EMERSON, "Friendship," *Essays: First Series* (1841).

41. The only way to have a friend is to be one. EMERSON, "Friendship," *Essays: First Series* (1841).

42. The condition which high friendship demands is ability to do without it. EMERSON, "Friendship," *Essays: First Series* (1841).

43. We do not so much need the help of our friends as the confidence of their help in need. EPICURUS, "Vatican Sayings" (3rd c. B.C.), 34, in *Letters, Principal Doctrines, and Vatican Sayings*, tr. Russel M. Geer.

44. Real friendship is shown in times of trouble; / prosperity is full of friends. EURIPIDES, *Hecuba* (c. 425 B.C.), tr. William Arrowsmith.

45. I loathe a friend whose gratitude grows old, / a friend who takes his friend's prosperity / but will not voyage with him in his grief. EURIPIDES, *Heracles* (c. 422 B.C.), tr. William Arrowsmith.

46. I would / Prefer as friend a good man ignorant / Than one more clever who is evil too. EURIPIDES, *Ion* (c. 421–408 B.C.), tr. Ronald F. Willetts.

47. Friends show their love / in times of trouble, not in happiness. EURIPIDES, *Orestes* (408 B.C.), tr. William Arrowsmith.

48. One loyal friend is worth ten thousand relatives. EURIPIDES, *Orestes* (408 B.C.), tr. William Arrowsmith.

49. It is in the thirties that we want friends. In the forties we know they won't save us any more than love did. F. SCOTT FITZGERALD, "Note-Books," *The Crack-Up* (1945).

50. A good friend is my nearest relation. THOMAS FULLER, M.D., *Gnomologia* (1732), 151.

51. Few there are that will endure a true friend. THOMAS FULLER, M.D., *Gnomologia* (1732), 1529.

52. Friendship that flames goes out in a flash. THOMAS FULLER, M.D., *Gnomologia* (1732), 1623.

53. Have friends. 'Tis a second existence. BALTASAR GRACIÁN, *The Art of Worldly Wisdom* (1647), 111, tr. Joseph Jacobs.

54. Few are the friends of a man's self, most those of his circumstances. BALTASAR GRACIÁN, *The Art of Worldly Wisdom* (1647), 156, tr. Joseph Jacobs.

55. Friendship multiplies the good of life and divides the evil. 'Tis the sole remedy against misfortune, the very ventilation of the soul. BALTASAR GRACIÁN, *The Art of Worldly Wisdom* (1647), 158, tr. Joseph Jacobs.

56. Friends provoked become the bitterest of enemies. BALTASAR GRACIÁN, *The Art of Worldly Wisdom* (1647), 257, tr. Joseph Jacobs.

57. No real friendship is ever made without an initial clashing which discloses the metal of each to each. DAVID GRAYSON, *Adventures in Contentment* (1907), 2.

58. Nobody who is afraid of laughing, and heartily too, at his friend, can be said to have a true and thorough love for him. JULIUS CHARLES HARE and AUGUSTUS WILLIAM HARE, *Guesses at Truth* (1827).

59. Make all good men your well-wishers, and then, in the years' steady sifting, / Some of them turn into friends. Friends are the sunshine of life. JOHN HAY, "Distichs" (1871?), 18.

60. We often choose a friend as we do a mistress—for no particular excellence in themselves, but merely from some circumstance that flatters our self-love. WILLIAM HAZLITT, *Characteristics* (1823), 58.

61. True friendship is self-love at second-hand. WILLIAM HAZLITT, "On the Spirit of Obligations," *The Plain Speaker* (1826).

62. Neither make thy friend equal to a brother; but if thou shalt have made him so, be not the first to do him wrong. HESIOD, *Works and Days* (8th c. B.C.), 707, tr. J. Banks.

63. One cannot help using his early friends as the seaman uses the log, to mark his progress. OLIVER WENDELL HOLMES, SR., *The Autocrat of the Breakfast Table* (1858), 4.

64. A sympathetic friend can be quite as dear as a brother. HOMER, *Odyssey* (9th c. B.C.), 8, tr. E. V. Rieu.

65. Your friend is the man who knows all about you, and still likes you. ELBERT HUBBARD, *The Note Book* (1927).

66. Friendship, like credit, is highest where it is not used. ELBERT HUBBARD, *The Note Book* (1927).

67. One of the principal functions of a friend is to suffer (in a milder and symbolic form) the punishments that we should like, but are unable, to inflict upon our enemies. ALDOUS HUXLEY, *Brave New World* (1932).

68. Friends are to be feared, not so much for what they make us do as for what they keep us from doing. HENRIK IBSEN, quoted in André Gide's *Journals*, 1917, tr. Justin O'Brien.

69. Friendship is seldom lasting but between equals, or where the superiority on one side is reduced by some equivalent advantage on the other. SAMUEL JOHNSON, *The Rambler* (1750–52), 64.

70. That friendship may be at once fond and lasting, there must not only be equal virtue on each part, but virtue of the same kind; not only the same end must be proposed, but the same means must be approved by both. SAMUEL JOHNSON, *The Rambler* (1750–52), 64.

71. When my friends are one-eyed, I look at them in profile. JOSEPH JOUBERT, *Pensées* (1842), titre préliminaire.

72. Friendship may sometimes step a few paces in advance of truth; and who would check her? WALTER SAVAGE LANDOR, "Milton and Marvel," *Imaginary Conversations* (1824–53).

73. Friendship is only a reciprocal conciliation of interests, and an exchange of good offices; it is a species of commerce out of which self-love always expects to gain something. LA ROCHEFOUCAULD, *Maxims* (1665).

74. However rare true love may be, it is less so than true friendship. LA ROCHEFOUCAULD, *Maxims* (1665), tr. Kenneth Pratt.

75. A true friend is the greatest of all blessings, and that which we take the least care of all to acquire. LA ROCHEFOUCAULD, *Maxims* (1665), tr. Kenneth Pratt.

76. We do not regret the loss of our friends by reasons of their merit, but because of our needs and for the good opinion that we believed them to have held of us. LA ROCHEFOUCAULD, *Maxims* (1665), tr. Kenneth Pratt.

77. It's no good trying to keep up old friendships. It's painful for both sides. The fact is, one grows out of people, and the only thing is to face it. W. SOMERSET MAUGHAM, *Cakes and Ale* (1930), 1.

78. We know our friends by their defects rather than by their merits. W. SOMERSET MAUGHAM, *The Summing Up* (1938), 57.

79. A man of active and resilient mind outwears his friendships just as certainly as he outwears his love affairs, his politics and his epistemology. H. L. MENCKEN, *Prejudices: Third Series* (1922), 14.

80. If a man should importune me to give a reason why I loved him, I find it could no otherwise be expressed, than by making answer: because it was he, because it was I. MONTAIGNE, "Of friendship," *Essays* (1580–88), tr. Charles Cotton and W. C. Hazlitt.

81. What we commonly call friendships are nothing but acquaintance and familiarities, either occasionally contracted or upon some design, by means of which there happens some little intercourse between our souls. MONTAIGNE, "Of friendship," *Essays* (1580–88), tr. Charles Cotton and W. C. Hazlitt.

82. Friendship is a contract in which we render small services in expectation of big ones. MONTESQUIEU, *Pensées et jugements* (1899).

83. Love demands infinitely less than friendship. GEORGE JEAN NATHAN, "Attitude toward Love and Marriage," *The Autobiography of an Attitude* (1925).

84. Women can form a friendship with a man very well; but to preserve it—to that end a slight physical antipathy must probably help. NIETZSCHE, *Human, All Too Human* (1878), 390, in *The Portable Nietzsche*, tr. Walter Kaufmann.

85. A friend should be a master at guessing and keeping still. NIETZSCHE, "On the Friend," *Thus Spoke Zarathustra* (1883–92), 1, tr. Walter Kaufmann.

86. Hold a true friend with both your hands. NIGERIAN PROVERB.

87. Love is rarer than genius itself. And friendship is rarer than love. CHARLES PÉGUY, "The Search for Truth," *Basic Verities* (1943), tr. Ann and Julian Green.

88. God save me from my friends—I can protect myself from my enemies. PROVERB common in many languages.

89. Friendship either finds or makes equals. PUBLILIUS SYRUS, *Moral Sayings* (1st c. B.C.), 32, tr. Darius Lyman.

90. We die as often as we lose a friend. PUBLILIUS SYRUS, *Moral Sayings* (1st c. B.C.), 323, tr. Darius Lyman.

91. The friendship that can come to an end, never really began. PUBLILIUS SYRUS, *Moral Sayings* (1st c. B.C.), 719, tr. Darius Lyman.

92. A friendship from which the every-day disappears becomes an allegory. JULES ROMAINS, *Les Hommes de bonne volonté* (1932–47), v. 24.17.

93. Sooner or later you've heard all your best friends have to say. Then comes the tolerance of real love. NED ROREM, "Random Notes from a Diary," *Music from Inside Out* (1967).

94. Friendship admits of difference of character, as love does that of sex. JOSEPH ROUX, *Meditations of a Parish Priest* (1886), 9.24, tr. Isabel F. Hapgood.

95. To like and dislike the same things, this is what makes a solid friendship. SALLUST, *Conspiracy of Catiline* (1st c. B.C.), 20.

96. Friendship is almost always the union of a part of one mind with a part of another; people are friends in spots. GEORGE SANTAYANA, "Friendships," *Soliloquies in England* (1922).

97. To cement a new friendship, especially between foreigners or persons of a different social world, a spark with which both were secretly charged must fly from person to person, and cut across the accidents of place and time. GEORGE SANTAYANA, *Persons and Places: The Middle Span* (1945), 2.

98. It is characteristic of spontaneous friendship to take on first, without enquiry and almost at first sight, the unseen doings and unspoken sentiments of our friends; the parts known give us evidence enough that the unknown parts cannot be much amiss. GEORGE SANTAYANA, *Persons and Places: My Host the World* (1953), 6.

99. One who's our friend is fond of us: one who's fond of us isn't necessarily our friend. SENECA, *Letters to Lucilius* (1st c.), 35.1, tr. E. Phillips Barker.

100. Great friendship is never without anxiety. MARQUISE DE SÉVIGNÉ, letter to Mme de Grignan, Sept. 10, 1671.

101. Friendship is constant in all other things / Save in the office and affairs of love. SHAKESPEARE, *Much Ado About Nothing* (1598–99), 2.1.182.

102. A friend should bear his friend's infirmities. SHAKESPEARE, *Julius Caesar* (1599–1600), 4.3.86.

103. We need new friends; some of us are cannibals who have eaten their old friends up; others must have ever-renewed audiences before whom to re-enact the ideal version of their lives. LOGAN PEARSALL SMITH, *Afterthoughts* (1931), 3.

104. I cannot love a friend whose love is words. SOPHOCLES, *Antigone* (442–41 B.C.), tr. Elizabeth Wyckoff.

105. To throw away / an honest friend is, as it were, to throw / your life away. SOPHOCLES, *Oedipus the King* (c. 430 B.C.), tr. David Grene.

106. It is good to have friends, even in hell. SPANISH PROVERB.

107. Life is partly what we make it, and partly what it is made by the friends whom we choose. TEHYI HSIEH, *Chinese Epigrams Inside Out and Proverbs* (1948), 66.

108. How often we find ourselves turning our backs on our actual Friends, that we may go and meet their ideal cousins. THOREAU, "The Atlantides," *A Week on the Concord and Merrimack Rivers* (1849).

109. A man cannot be said to succeed in this life who does not satisfy one friend. THOREAU, *Journal*, Feb. 19, 1857.

110. Friendship is a furrow in the sand. TONGAN PROVERB.

111. The holy passion of Friendship is of so sweet and steady and loyal and enduring a nature that it will last through a whole lifetime, if not asked to lend money. MARK TWAIN, Pudd'nhead Wilson's Calendar," *Pudd'nhead Wilson* (1894), 8.

112. The proper office of a friend is to side with you when you are in the wrong. Nearly anybody will side with you when you are in the right. MARK TWAIN, *Notebook* (1935).

113. Friendship is the marriage of the soul, and this marriage is liable to divorce. VOLTAIRE, "Friendship," *Philosophical Dictionary* (1764).

114. You cannot be friends upon any other terms than upon the terms of equality. WOODROW WILSON, speech, Oct. 27, 1913.

## FRUGALITY

**See 695. Plain Living; 970. Thrift**

## 364. FRUSTRATION

**See also 236. Desires; 425. Hope; 457. Impotence; 1003. Unfulfillment**

1. Not to get what you have set your heart on is almost as bad as getting nothing at all.

ARISTOTLE, *Nicomachean Ethics* (4th c. B.C.), 9.1, tr. J. A. K. Thomson.

2. The worst things: / To be in bed and sleep not, / To want for one who comes not, / To try to please and please not. EGYPTIAN PROVERB.

3. We desire truth, and find within ourselves only uncertainty. We seek happiness, and find only misery and death. PASCAL, *Pensées* (1670), 437, tr. W. F. Trotter.

## FULFILLMENT

**See 502. Involvement; 711. Potential; 1003. Unfulfillment**

## 365. FUNERALS

**See also 101. Burial; 218. Death; 603. Mourning**

1. Spare me the whispering, crowded room, / The friends who come and gape and go, / The ceremonious air of gloom— / All, which makes death a hideous show. MATTHEW ARNOLD, "A Wish" (1867).

2. Funeral, n. A pageant whereby we attest our respect for the dead by enriching the undertaker, and strengthen our grief by an expenditure that deepens our groans and doubles our tears. AMBROSE BIERCE, *The Devil's Dictionary* (1881–1911).

3. Those who bequeath unto themselves a pompous funeral, are at just so much expense to inform the world of something that had much better be concealed; namely, that their vanity has survived themselves. CHARLES CALEB COLTON, *Lacon* (1825), 1.510.

4. 'Tis a good thing fun'ral sermons ar-re not composed in th' confissional. FINLEY PETER DUNNE, "Casual Observations," *Mr. Dooley's Philosophy* (1900).

5. The chief mourner does not always attend the funeral. EMERSON, *Journals*, 1832.

6. No American is prepared to attend his own funeral without the services of highly skilled cosmeticians. Part of the American dream, after all, is to live long and die young. EDGAR Z. FRIEDENBERG, "Adult Imagery and Feeling," *The Vanishing Adolescent* (1959).

7. After sixty years the stern sentence of the burial service seems to have a meaning that one did not notice in former years. There begins to be something personal about it. OLIVER WENDELL HOLMES, SR., *Over the Teacups* (1891), 2.

8. The pomp of funerals has more regard to the vanity of the living than the honour of the dead. LA ROCHEFOUCAULD, *Maxims* (1665), tr. Kenneth Pratt.

9. One ought to go to a funeral instead of to church when one feels the need of being uplifted. People have on good black clothes, and they take off their hats and look at the coffin, and behave serious and reverent, and nobody dares to make a bad joke. THOMAS MANN, *The Magic Mountain* (1924), 4.3, tr. H. T. Lowe-Porter.

10. We simply rob ourselves when we make presents to the dead. PUBLILIUS SYRUS, *Moral Sayings* (1st c. B.C.), 1034, tr. Darius Lyman.

11. Funerals are pretty compared to death. TENNESSEE WILLIAMS, *A Streetcar Named Desire* (1947), 1.

## 366. FUTURE

**See also 238. Destiny; 316. Expectation; 669. Past; 723. Present**

1. The future / you shall know when it has come; before then, forget it. AESCHYLUS, *Agamemnon* (458 B.C.), tr. Richmond Lattimore.

2. The future is like heaven—everyone exalts it but no one wants to go there now. JAMES BALDWIN, "A Fly in Buttermilk," *Nobody Knows My Name* (1961).

3. We steal if we touch tomorrow. It is God's. HENRY WARD BEECHER, *Proverbs from Plymouth Pulpit* (1887).

4. Future, n. That period of time in which our affairs prosper, our friends are true and our happiness is assured. AMBROSE BIERCE, *The Devil's Dictionary* (1881–1911).

5. The future is an opaque mirror. Anyone who tries to look into it sees nothing but the dim outlines of an old and worried face. JIM BISHOP, *New York Journal-American*, March 14, 1959.

6. You can never plan the future by the past. EDMUND BURKE, *Letter to a Member of the National Assembly* (1791).

7. The future is the only transcendental value for men without God. ALBERT

CAMUS, "The Fastidious Assassins," *The Rebel* (1951), tr. Anthony Bower.

8. If a man carefully examine his thoughts he will be surprised to find how much he lives in the future. His well-being is always ahead. Such a creature is probably immortal. EMERSON, *Journals*, 1827.

9. Remember that the future is neither ours nor wholly not ours, so that we may neither count on it as sure to come nor abandon hope of it as certain not to be. EPICURUS, Letter to Menoeceus (3rd c. B.C.), in *Letters, Principal Doctrines, and Vatican Sayings*, tr. Russel M. Geer.

10. The man least dependent upon the morrow goes to meet the morrow most cheerfully. EPICURUS (3rd. c. B.C.), quoted in Plutarch's "Contentment," *Moralia* (c. A.D. 100), tr. Moses Hadas.

11. What we look for does not come to pass; / God finds a way for what none foresaw. EURIPIDES, *Alcestis* (438 B.C.), tr. Richmond Lattimore.

12. He that fears not the future may enjoy the present. THOMAS FULLER, M.D., *Gnomologia* (1732), 2100.

13. Only mothers can think of the future —because they give birth to it in their children. MAXIM GORKY, *Vassa Zheleznova* (1910), tr. Alexander Bakshy.

14. A preoccupation with the future not only prevents us from seeing the present as it is but often prompts us to rearrange the past. ERIC HOFFER, *The Passionate State of Mind* (1954), 75.

15. The only way to predict the future is to have power to shape the future. ERIC HOFFER, *The Passionate State of Mind* (1954), 78.

16. There is nothing like dream to create the future. Utopia to-day, flesh and blood tomorrow. VICTOR HUGO, "Marius," *Les Misérables* (1862), 4.1, tr. Charles E. Wilbour.

17. Yesterday is not ours to recover, but tomorrow is ours to win or to lose. LYNDON B. JOHNSON, address to the nation, Nov. 28, 1963.

18. The most prevalent opinion among our so confused contemporaries seems to be that tomorrow will be wonderful—that is, unless it is indescribably terrible, or unless indeed there just isn't any. JOSEPH WOOD KRUTCH, "The Twentieth Century: Dawn or Twilight?" *Human Nature and the Human Condition* (1959).

19. Life is an irreversible process and for that reason its future can never be a repetition of the past. WALTER LIPPMANN, "Revolution and Culture," *A Preface to Politics* (1914).

20. Do we not all spend the greater part of our lives under the shadow of an event that has not yet come to pass? MAURICE MAETERLINCK, "The Pre-Destined," *The Treasure of the Humble* (1896), tr. Alfred Sutro.

21. Never let the future disturb you. You will meet it, if you have to, with the same weapons of reason which today arm you against the present. MARCUS AURELIUS, *Meditations* (2nd c.), 7.8, tr. Maxwell Staniforth.

22. We are never present with, but always beyond ourselves; fear, desire, hope, still push us on toward the future. MONTAIGNE, "That our affections carry themselves beyond us," *Essays* (1580–88), tr. Charles Cotton and W. C. Hazlitt.

23. People live for the morrow, because the day-after-to-morrow is doubtful. NIETZSCHE, *The Will to Power* (1888), tr. Anthony M. Ludovici.

24. The struggle with the past is not a hand-to-hand fight. The future overcomes it by swallowing it. If it leaves anything outside it is lost. JOSÉ ORTEGA Y GASSET, *The Revolt of the Masses* (1930), 10.

25. I believe the future is only the past again, entered through another gate. SIR ARTHUR WING PINERO, *The Second Mrs. Tanqueray* (1893), 4.

26. The future struggles that it may not become the past. PUBLILIUS SYRUS, *Moral Sayings* (1st c. B.C.), 290, tr. Darius Lyman.

27. The future enters into us in order to transform itself in us long before it happens. RAINER MARIA RILKE, *Letters to a Young Poet*, Aug. 12, 1904, tr. M. D. Herter Norton.

28. As for the Future, your task is not to foresee, but to enable it. SAINT-EXUPÉRY, *The Wisdom of the Sands* (1948), 50, tr. Stuart Gilbert.

29. O that a man might know / The end of this day's business ere it come! SHAKESPEARE, *Julius Caesar* (1599–1600), 5.1.122.

30. We know what we are, but know not what we may be. SHAKESPEARE, *Hamlet* (1600), 4.5.42.

31. What men have seen they know; / But what shall come hereafter / No man before the event can see, / Nor what end

waits for him. SOPHOCLES, *Ajax* (c. 447 B.C.), tr. John Moore.

32. The future has waited long enough; if we do not grasp it, other hands, grasping hard and bloody, will. ADLAI STEVENSON, quoted in Murray Kempton's *America Comes of Middle Age* (1963).

33. The future is called "perhaps," which is the only possible thing to call the future. And the important thing is not to allow that to scare you. TENNESSEE WILLIAMS, "The Past, Present, and Perhaps," *Orpheus Descending* (1957).

# G

## 367. GAMBLING

1. Whoever plays deep must necessarily lose his money or his character. LORD CHESTERFIELD, *Letters to His Godson*, 1773.

2. A man's idee in a card game is war—crool, devastatin', an' pitiless. A lady's idee iv it is a combynation iv larceny, embezzlement, an' burglary. FINLEY PETER DUNNE, "On the Game of Cards," *Mr. Dooley On Making a Will* (1919).

3. I've seen a game iv cards start among frinds, but I niver see frinds in a game iv cards. FINLEY PETER DUNNE, "On the Game of Cards," *Mr. Dooley On Making a Will* (1919).

4. The best throw of the dice is to throw them away. ENGLISH PROVERB.

5. Gambling is the great leveller. All men are equal—at cards. NIKOLAI GOGOL, *Gamblers* (1842).

6. True luck consists not in holding the best of the cards at the table: / Luckiest he who knows just when to rise and go home. JOHN HAY, "Distichs" (1871?), 15.

7. I am sorry I have not learnt to play at cards. It is very useful in life: it generates kindness and consolidates society. SAMUEL JOHNSON, quoted in Boswell's *Journal of a Tour to the Hebrides with Samuel Johnson*, Nov. 21, 1773.

8. Cards are war, in disguise of a sport. CHARLES LAMB, "Mrs. Battle's Opinions on Whist," *Essays of Elia* (1823).

9. Adventure upon all the tickets in the lottery, and you lose for certain; and the greater the number of your tickets the nearer you approach to this certainty. ADAM SMITH, *The Wealth of Nations* (1776), 1.10.

## GAMES

See 367. Gambling; 697. Play; 922. Sports

## 368. GARBAGE

1. We live in an environment whose principal product is garbage. The shined shoe in such a society is a hypocritical statement because it promotes the lie that we can thrive on garbage without being dirtied by it. RUSSELL BAKER, "Observer," *The New York Times*, Feb. 22, 1968.

2. The cockroach and the bird were both here long before we were. Both could get along very well without us, although it is perhaps significant that of the two the cockroach would miss us more. JOSEPH WOOD KRUTCH, "November," *The Twelve Seasons* (1949).

## 369. GARDENING

1. You fight dandelions all week end, and late Monday afternoon there they are, pert as all get out, in full and gorgeous bloom, pretty as can be, thriving as only dandelions can in the face of adversity. HAL BORLAND, "Dandelions—May 10," *Sundial of the Seasons* (1964).

2. A weed is no more than a flower in disguise, / Which is seen through at once, if love give a man eyes. JAMES RUSSELL LOWELL, *A Fable for Critics* (1848).

3. To own a bit of ground, to scratch it with a hoe, to plant seeds, and watch their renewal of life,—this is the commonest delight of the race, the most satisfactory thing a man can do. CHARLES DUDLEY WARNER, "Preliminary," *My Summer in a Garden* (1871).

4. What a man needs in gardening is a cast-iron back, with a hinge in it. CHARLES DUDLEY WARNER, "Third Week," *My Summer in a Garden* (1871).

## 370. GAUCHERIE

See also 394. Grace

1. God may forgive sins, but awkwardness has no forgiveness in heaven or earth.

EMERSON, title essay, *Society and Solitude* (1876).

2. It is a great misfortune not to possess sufficient wit to speak well, nor sufficient judgment to keep silent. LA BRUYÈRE, *Characters* (1688), 5.18.

## 371. GENERALIZATION

1. All generalizations are false, including this one. ALEXANDER CHASE, *Perspectives* (1966).

2. The cause of all human evils is the not being able to apply general principles to special cases. EPICTETUS, *Discourses* (2nd c.), 4.1, tr. Thomas W. Higginson.

3. Any general statement is like a checque drawn on a bank. Its value depends on what is there to meet it. EZRA POUND, *The ABC of Reading* (1934), 1.1.

4. Intellectual generalities are always interesting, but generalities in morals mean absolutely nothing. OSCAR WILDE, *A Woman of No Importance* (1893), 2.

## 372. GENERATIONS

See also 181. Contemporaneousness; 296. Era

1. It is always self-defeating to pretend to the style of a generation younger than your own; it simply erases your own experience in history. RENATA ADLER, "What's So Funny?" *The New York Times*, July 7, 1968.

2. Each generation must out of relative obscurity discover its mission, fulfill it, or betray it. FRANTZ FANON, "On National Culture," *The Wretched of the Earth* (1961), tr. Constance Farrington.

3. It is mere childishness to expect men to believe as their fathers did; that is, if they have any minds of their own. The world is a whole generation older and wiser than when the father was of his son's age. OLIVER WENDELL HOLMES, SR., *Over the Teacups* (1891), 10.

4. Like leaves on trees the race of man is found,— / Now green in youth, now withering on the ground; / Another race the following spring supplies: / They fall successive, and successive rise. HOMER, *Iliad* (9th c. B.C.), 6.181, tr. Alexander Pope.

5. Each generation takes a special pleasure in removing the household gods of its parents from their pedestals, and consigning them to the cupboard. WILLIAM RALPH INGE, "The Victorian Age," *Outspoken Essays: Second Series* (1922).

6. Every old man complains of the growing depravity of the world, of the petulance and insolence of the rising generation. SAMUEL JOHNSON, *The Rambler* (1750–52), 50.

7. We have to hate our immediate predecessors to get free of their authority. D. H. LAWRENCE, quoted in Henry Miller's "Creative Death," *The Wisdom of the Heart* (1941).

8. Our strife pertains to ourselves—to the passing generations of men—and it can without convulsion be hushed forever with the passing of one generation. ABRAHAM LINCOLN, message to Congress, Dec. 1, 1862.

9. In a brief space the generations of living beings are changed and like runners pass on the torches of life. LUCRETIUS, *On the Nature of Things* (1st c. B.C.), 2.

10. Every generation revolts against its fathers and makes friends with its grandfathers. LEWIS MUMFORD, *The Brown Decades* (1931).

11. Every age and generation must be as free to act for itself in all cases as the ages and generations which preceded it. The vanity and presumption of governing beyond the grave is the most ridiculous and insolent of all tyrannies. THOMAS PAINE, *The Rights of Man* (1791), 1.

12. We think our fathers fools, so wise we grow; / Our wiser sons, no doubt, will think us so. ALEXANDER POPE, *An Essay on Criticism* (1711), 2.237.

13. The weeks slide by like a funeral procession, but generations pass like a snowstorm. NED ROREM, "Listening and Hearing," *Music from Inside Out* (1967).

14. Nothing so dates a man as to decry the younger generation. ADLAI STEVENSON, speech, University of Wisconsin, Madison, Oct. 8, 1952.

15. It is one of nature's ways that we often feel closer to distant generations than to the generation immediately preceding us. IGOR STRAVINSKY, *Conversations with Igor Stravinsky* (1959).

16. Amongst democratic nations, each new generation is a new people. ALEXIS DE TOCQUEVILLE, *Democracy in America* (1834–39), 2.1.13.

17. It is fortunate that each generation does not comprehend its own ignorance. We are thus enabled to call our ancestors barbarous. CHARLES DUDLEY WARNER, "Second Study," *Backlog Studies* (1873).

18. Each generation criticises the unconscious assumptions made by its parent. It may assent to them, but it brings them out in the open. ALFRED NORTH WHITEHEAD, *Science and the Modern World* (1925), 2.

### 373. GENEROSITY

**See also 56. Assistance; 382. Gifts and Giving; 430. Humanitarianism; 522. Largeness; 881. Services; 1014. Unselfishness**

1. Cast thy bread upon the waters: for thou shalt find it after many days. *Bible*, Ecclesiastes 11:1.

2. If a man is prodigal, he cannot be truly generous. JAMES BOSWELL, *London Journal*, Feb. 9, 1763.

3. If riches increase, let thy mind hold pace with them; and think it not enough to be liberal, but munificent. SIR THOMAS BROWNE, *A Letter to a Friend* (1690).

4. Lavishness is not generosity. THOMAS FULLER, M.D., *Gnomologia* (1732), 3147.

5. People who think they're generous to a fault usually think that's their only fault. SYDNEY J. HARRIS, *On the Contrary* (1962), 7.

6. Generosity is the flower of justice. NATHANIEL HAWTHORNE, *American Note-Books*, Dec. 19, 1850.

7. Of all virtues, magnanimity is the rarest. There are a hundred persons of merit for one who willingly acknowledges it in another. WILLIAM HAZLITT, *Characteristics* (1823), 1.

8. The hand of liberality is stronger than the arm of power. SA'DI, *Gulistan* (1258), 2.48, tr. James Ross.

9. Magnanimity will not consider the prudence of its motives. VAUVENARGUES, *Reflections and Maxims* (1746), 130, tr. F. G. Stevens.

10. Generosity gives assistance, rather than advice. VAUVENARGUES, *Reflections and Maxims* (1746), 491, tr. F. G. Stevens.

### 374. GENIUS

**See also 309. Excellence; 375. Genius vs. Talent; 399. Greatness; 945. Superiority**

1. Genius is sorrow's child. JOHN ADAMS, letter to Benjamin Waterhouse, May 21, 1821.

2. The function of genius is to furnish cretins with ideas twenty years later. LOUIS ARAGON, "Le Porte-Plume," *Traité du style* (1928).

3. No great genius has ever been without some madness. ARISTOTLE (4th c. B.C.), quoted in Seneca's "On Peace of Mind," *Moral Essays* (1st c. A.D.).

4. Geniuses are the luckiest of mortals because what they must do is the same as what they most want to do. W. H. AUDEN, foreword to Dag Hammarskjöld's *Markings* (1964).

5. If men of genius only knew what love their works inspire! HECTOR BERLIOZ, letter to Desmarest, Berlin, 1843.

6. Genius is but a greater aptitude for patience. Attributed to GEORGES BUFFON.

7. Genius in one grand particular is like life. We know nothing of either but by their effects. CHARLES CALEB COLTON, *Lacon* (1825), 2.133.

8. The first thing the world does to a genius is to make him lose all his youth. CLARENCE DAY, "The Seamy Side of Fabre," *The Crow's Nest* (1921).

9. You cannot create genius. All you can do is nurture it. NINETTE de VALOIS, *Time*, Sept. 26, 1960.

10. Too often we forget that genius, too, depends upon the data within its reach, that even Archimedes could not have devised Edison's inventions. ERNEST DIMNET, *The Art of Thinking* (1928), 4.

11. Patience is a necessary ingredient of genius. BENJAMIN DISRAELI, *Contarini Fleming* (1832), 4.5.

12. Sensibility alters from generation to generation in everybody, whether we will or no; but expression is only altered by a man of genius. T. S. ELIOT, introductory essay (1930) to Samuel Johnson's *London: A Poem and The Vanity of Human Wishes.*

13. Genius seems to consist merely in trueness of sight, in using such words as show that the man was an eye-witness, and not a repeater of what was told. EMERSON, *Journals*, 1834.

14. Genius always finds itself a century too early. EMERSON, *Journals*, 1840.

15. The young man reveres men of genius, because, to speak truly, they are more himself than he is. EMERSON, "The Poet," *Essays: Second Series* (1844).

16. Genius is the ability to put into effect what is in your mind. F. SCOTT FITZGERALD, "The Note-Books," *The Crack-Up* (1945).

17. Genius goes around the world in its youth incessantly apologizing for having large feet. What wonder that later in life it should be inclined to raise those feet too swiftly to fools and bores. F. SCOTT FITZGERALD, "The Note-Books," *The Crack-Up* (1945).

18. He whose genius appears deepest and truest excels his fellows in nothing save the knack of expression; he throws out occasionally a lucky hint at truths of which every human soul is profoundly though unutterably conscious. NATHANIEL HAWTHORNE, "The Procession of Life," *Mosses from an Old Manse* (1846).

19. Genius is a native to the soil where it grows—is fed by the air, and warmed by the sun; and is not a hothouse plant or an exotic. WILLIAM HAZLITT, "Commonplaces," *The Round Table* (1817), 27.

20. The definition of genius is that it acts unconsciously; and those who have produced immortal works have done so without knowing how or why. WILLIAM HAZLITT, "Whether Genius Is Conscious of Its Powers?" *The Plain Speaker* (1826).

21. Genius is gifted with a vitality which is expended in the enrichment of life through the discovery of new worlds of feeling. HANS HOFMANN, *Search for the Real* (1967).

22. Unpretending mediocrity is good, and genius is glorious; but a weak flavor of genius in an essentially common person is detestable. It spoils the grand neutrality of a commonplace character, as the rinsings of an unwashed wineglass spoil a draught of fair water. OLIVER WENDELL HOLMES, SR., *The Autocrat of the Breakfast Table* (1858), 1.

23. A person of genius should marry a person of character. Genius does not herd with genius. OLIVER WENDELL HOLMES, SR., *The Professor at the Breakfast Table* (1860), 11.

24. Ever since the habitations of men were reared two stories high has the garret been the nursery of genius. JEROME K. JEROME, "On Furnished Apartments," *The Idle Thoughts of an Idle Fellow* (1889).

25. The true genius is a mind of large general powers, accidentally determined to some particular direction. SAMUEL JOHNSON, *Lives of the Poets: Cowley* (1779–81).

26. Everyone is a genius at least once a year. The real geniuses simply have their bright ideas closer together. GEORG CHRISTOPH LICHTENBERG, *Aphorisms* (1764–99), tr. F. H. Mautner and H. Hatfield.

27. Towering genius disdains a beaten path. It seeks regions hitherto unexplored. ABRAHAM LINCOLN, speech, Springfield, Ill., Jan. 27, 1838.

28. A genius is a man who does unique things of which nobody would expect him to be capable. E. V. LUCAS, *Reading, Writing, and Remembering* (1932), 5.

29. Genius can only breathe freely in an *atmosphere* of freedom. JOHN STUART MILL, *On Liberty* (1859), 3.

30. There are two types of genius: one which above all begets and wants to beget, and another which prefers being fertilized and giving birth. NIETZSCHE, *Beyond Good and Evil* (1886), 248, tr. Walter Kaufmann.

31. The genius—in work and in deed—is necessarily a squanderer: the fact that he spends himself constitutes his greatness. NIETZSCHE, "Skirmishes in a War with the Age," 44, *Twilight of the Idols* (1888), tr. Anthony M. Ludovici.

32. Better beware of notions like genius and inspiration; they are a sort of magic wand and should be used sparingly by anybody who wants to see things clearly. JOSÉ ORTEGA Y GASSET, *Notes on the Novel* (1925).

33. Men of genius are far more abundant than is supposed. In fact, to appreciate thoroughly the work of what we call genius, is to possess all the genius by which the work was produced. EDGAR ALLAN POE, *Marginalia* (1844–49), 3.

34. The true genius shudders at incom-

pleteness—and usually prefers silence to saying the something which is not every thing that should be said. EDGAR ALLAN POE, *Marginalia* (1844–49), 9.

35. The concept of genius as akin to madness has been carefully fostered by the inferiority complex of the public. EZRA POUND, *The ABC of Reading* (1934), 8.

36. We should like to have some towering geniuses, to reveal us to ourselves in colour and fire, but of course they would have to fit into the pattern of our society and be able to take orders from sound administrative types. J. B. PRIESTLEY, "Candles Burning Low," *Thoughts in the Wilderness* (1957).

37. Men who produce works of genius are not those who live in the most delicate atmosphere, whose conversation is most brilliant or their culture broadest, but those who have had the power, ceasing in a moment to live only for themselves, to make use of their personality as of a mirror. MARCEL PROUST, *Remembrance of Things Past: Within a Budding Grove* (1913–27), tr. C. K. Scott-Moncrieff.

38. The deep waters of time will flow over us: only a few men of genius will lift a head above the surface, and though doomed eventually to pass into the same silence, will fight against oblivion and for a long time hold their own. SENECA, *Letters to Lucilius* (1st c.), 21.5, tr. E. Phillips Barker.

39. Genius has never been accepted without a measure of condonement. SENECA, *Letters to Lucilius* (1st c.), 114.12, tr. E. Phillips Barker.

40. When a true genius appears in the world, you may know him by this sign, that the dunces are all in confederacy against him. JONATHAN SWIFT, *Thoughts on Various Subjects* (1711).

41. The persecution of genius fosters its influence. TACITUS, *Annals* (A.D. 115–117?), 4.35, tr. Alfred J. Church and William J. Brodribb.

42. We wish genius and morality were affectionate companions, but it is a fact that they are often bitter enemies. They don't necessarily coalesce any more than oil and water do. ARTEMUS WARD, "Morality and Genius," *Artemus Ward in London* (1872).

43. Genius is more often found in a cracked pot than in a whole one. E. B. WHITE, "Lime," *One Man's Meat* (1944).

44. The public is wonderfully tolerant. It forgives everything except genius. OSCAR WILDE, "The Critic as Artist," *Intentions* (1891).

## 375. GENIUS VS. TALENT

See also 374. Genius

1. To do easily what is difficult for others is the mark of talent. To do what is impossible for talent is the mark of genius. HENRI FRÉDÉRIC AMIEL, *Journal*, Dec. 17, 1856, tr. Mrs. Humphry Ward.

2. Coffee is good for talent, but genius wants prayer. EMERSON, *Journals*, 1841.

3. Genius is sacrificed to talent every day. EMERSON, *Journals*, 1841.

4. The difference between Talent and Genius is, that Talent says things which he has never heard but once, and Genius things which he has never heard. EMERSON, *Journals*, 1843.

5. Genius is power; talent is applicability. EMERSON, *Journals*, 1843.

6. The world is always ready to receive talent with open arms. Very often it does not know what to do with genius. OLIVER WENDELL HOLMES, SR., "Iris, Her Book," *The Professor at the Breakfast Table* (1860).

7. Talent is often to be envied, and genius very commonly to be pitied. It stands twice the chance of the other of dying in a hospital, in jail, in debt, in bad repute. OLIVER WENDELL HOLMES, SR., "Iris, Her Book," *The Professor at the Breakfast Table* (1860).

8. Talent is a very common family trait; genius belongs rather to individuals—just as you find one giant or one dwarf in a family, but rarely a whole brood of either. OLIVER WENDELL HOLMES, SR., "Iris, Her Book," *The Professor at the Breakfast Table* (1860).

9. Talent is that which is in a man's power; genius is that in whose power a man is. JAMES RUSSELL LOWELL, *Rousseau and the Sentimentalists* (1870).

## GENTILITY

See 389. Good Breeding; 803. Respectability

## 376. GENTLEMEN

**See also 194. Courtesy; 389. Good Breeding; 559. Manners**

1. As the dog becomes thoroughbred in the laws of clan and caste—obedient, fraternal, loyal—so is a man who accepts the Gentleman's Code. GELETT BURGESS, "The Gentleman's Code," *The Romance of the Commonplace* (1916).

2. Repose and cheerfulness are the badge of the gentleman,—repose in energy. EMERSON, "Culture," *The Conduct of Life* (1860).

3. To be a gentleman is to be oneself, all of a seam, on camera and off. MURRAY KEMPTON, "The Party's Over," *America Comes of Middle Age* (1963).

4. It is almost a definition of a gentleman to say he is one who never inflicts pain. JOHN HENRY NEWMAN, *The Idea of a University* (1853–58), 1.8.10.

5. Anyone can be heroic from time to time, but a gentleman is something you have to be all the time. Which isn't easy. LUIGI PIRANDELLO, *The Pleasure of Honesty* (1917), 1, tr. William Murray.

6. The gentle minde by gentle deeds is knowne. EDMUND SPENSER, *The Faerie Queene* (1596), 6.3.1.

## 377. GENTLENESS

**See also 354. Force; 517. Kindness**

1. When a man is made up wholly of the dove, without the least grain of the serpent in his composition, he becomes ridiculous in many circumstances of life, and very often discredits his best actions. JOSEPH ADDISON, *The Spectator* (1711–12), 245.

2. The great mind knows the power of gentleness, / Only tries force, because persuasion fails. ROBERT BROWNING, "Herakles" (1871).

3. Fair and softly goes far. CERVANTES, *Don Quixote* (1605–15), 1.3.2, tr. Peter Motteux and John Ozell.

4. The cat in gloves catches no mice. ENGLISH PROVERB.

5. Use a sweet tongue, courtesy, and gentleness, and thou mayst manage to guide an elephant with a hair. SA'DI, *Gulistan* (1258), 3.28, tr. James Ross.

6. Nothing is so strong as gentleness, and nothing is so gentle as real strength. RALPH W. SOCKMAN, *New York Mirror*, June 8, 1952.

## 378. GEOGRAPHY

**See also 138. Climate**

1. Boundary, n. In political geography, an imaginary line between two nations, separating the imaginary rights of one from the imaginary rights of the other. AMBROSE BIERCE, *The Devil's Dictionary* (1881–1911).

2. Mountains interposed / Make enemies of nations who had else, / Like kindred drops, been mingled into one. WILLIAM COWPER, "The Timepiece," *The Task* (1785), 1.

3. The importance of geology to geography is that, without geology, geography would have no place to put itself. ART LINKLETTER, *A Child's Garden of Misinformation* (1965), 7.

## 379. GERMANS

1. We Germans fear God, but nothing else in the world. OTTO VON BISMARCK, speech in the Reichstag, Feb. 6, 1888.

2. The German's wit is in his fingers. GEORGE HERBERT, *Jacula Prudentum* (1651).

3. Everything ponderous, viscous, and solemnly clumsy, all long-winded and boring types of style are developed in profuse variety among Germans. NIETZSCHE, *Beyond Good and Evil* (1886), 28, tr. Walter Kaufmann.

4. Whenever the literary German dives into a sentence, that is the last you are going to see of him till he emerges on the other side of his Atlantic with his verb in his mouth. MARK TWAIN, *A Connecticut Yankee in King Arthur's Court* (1889), 22.

5. The great virtues of the German people have created more evils than idleness ever did vices. PAUL VALÉRY, "La Crise de l'esprit, 1re lettre," *Variété* (1924–44) V. 1.

## 380. GERMS

1. Microbes is a vigitable, an' ivry man is like a conservatory full iv millyons iv these potted plants. FINLEY PETER DUNNE, "Christian Science," *Mr. Dooley's Opinions* (1901).

## 381. GHOSTS

**See also 447. Illusion; 687. Phantasy; 946. Supernatural**

1. Ghost, n. The outward and visible sign of an inward fear. AMBROSE BIERCE, *The Devil's Dictionary* (1881–1911).

2. I'm inclined to think we are all ghosts —every one of us. It's not just what we inherit from our mothers and fathers that haunts us. It's all kinds of old defunct theories, all sorts of old defunct beliefs, and things like that. HENRIK IBSEN, *Ghosts* (1881).

3. Ghosts remind me of men's smart crack about women, you can't live with them and can't live without them. EUGENE O'NEILL, *Strange Interlude* (1928), 3.

4. Phantoms in general are nothing more than trifling disorders of the spirit: images we cannot contain within the bounds of sleep. LUIGI PIRANDELLO, *Henry IV* (1922), 2, tr. Edward Storer.

5. He who does not fill his world with phantoms remains alone. ANTONIO PORCHIA, *Voces* (1968), tr. W. S. Merwin.

## 382. GIFTS AND GIVING

**See also 72. Beggars; 373. Generosity; 430. Humanitarianism; 517. Kindness; 589. Misers; 639. Obligation; 780. Receiving; 881. Services; 887. Sharing; 929. Stinginess**

1. What you get free costs too much. JEAN ANOUILH, *The Lark* (1955), 1, adapted by Lillian Hellman.

2. To give and then not feel that one has given is the very best of all ways of giving. MAX BEERBOHM, "Hosts and Guests," *And Even Now* (1920).

3. It is more blessed to give than to receive. *Bible*, Acts 20:35.

4. Every good gift and every perfect gift is from above. *Bible*, James 1:17.

5. A man whose leg has been cut off does not value a present of shoes. CHUANG TZU, *Works* (4th–3rd c. B.C.), 55.1, tr. Lin Yutang.

6. Riches may enable us to confer favours, but to confer them with propriety and grace requires a something that riches cannot give. CHARLES CALEB COLTON, *Lacon* (1825), 1.455.

7. How painful to give a gift to any person of sensibility, or of equality! It is next worst to receiving one. EMERSON, *Journals*, 1836.

8. We do not quite forgive a giver. The hand that feeds us is in some danger of being bitten. EMERSON, "Gifts," *Essays: Second Series* (1844).

9. The only gift is a portion of thyself. EMERSON, "Gifts," *Essays: Second Series* (1844).

10. There is no benefit in the gifts of a bad man. EURIPIDES, *Medea* (431 B.C.), tr. Rex Warner.

11. A gift, with a kind countenance, is a double present. THOMAS FULLER, M.D., *Gnomologia* (1732), 131.

12. He that gives to be seen would never relieve a man in the dark. THOMAS FULLER, M.D., *Gnomologia* (1732), 2115.

13. That is the bitterness of a gift, that it deprives us of our liberty. THOMAS FULLER, M.D., *Gnomologia* (1732), 4359.

14. Avarice hoards itself poor; charity gives itself rich. GERMAN PROVERB.

15. It is well to give when asked, but it is better to give unasked, through understanding. KAHLIL GIBRAN, "On Giving," *The Prophet* (1923).

16. We are thankful for good-will rather than for services, for the motive than the quantum of favour received. WILLIAM HAZLITT, "On the Spirit of Obligations," *The Plain Speaker* (1826).

17. We probably have a greater love for those we support than those who support us. Our vanity carries more weight than our self-interest. ERIC HOFFER, *The Passionate State of Mind* (1954), 202.

18. There is sublime thieving in all giving. Someone gives us all he has and we are his. ERIC HOFFER, *The Passionate State of Mind* (1954), 236.

19. What with your friend you nobly share, / At least you rescue from your heir. HORACE, *Odes* (23–c. 15 B.C.), 4.7.

20. Let him that desires to see others happy, make haste to give while his gift can be enjoyed, and remember that every moment of delay takes away something from the value of his benefaction. SAMUEL JOHNSON, *The Idler* (1758–60), 43.

21. Bounty always receives part of its value from the manner in which it is bestowed. SAMUEL JOHNSON, letter to the earl of Bute, July 20, 1762, quoted in Boswell's *Life of Samuel Johnson*.

22. Presents, I often say, endear absents. CHARLES LAMB, "A Dissertation upon Roast Pig," *Essays of Elia* (1823).

23. Some people have a knack of putting upon you gifts of no real value, to engage you to substantial gratitude. We thank them for nothing. CHARLES LAMB, "Popular Fallacies, 11," *Last Essays of Elia* (1833).

24. We are better pleased to see those on whom we confer benefits than those from whom we receive them. LA ROCHEFOUCAULD, *Maxims* (1665), tr. Kenneth Pratt.

25. He gives only the worthless gold / Who gives from a sense of duty. JAMES RUSSELL LOWELL, "The Vision of Sir Launfal" (1848), 1.6.

26. Gifts are like hooks. MARTIAL, *Epigrams* (A.D. 86), 5.18, tr. Walter C. A. Ker.

27. This is what is hardest: to close the open hand because one loves. NIETZSCHE, "The Child with the Mirror," *Thus Spoke Zarathustra* (1883–92), 2, tr. Walter Kaufmann.

28. The heart and hand of those who always mete out become callous from always meting out. NIETZSCHE, "The Night Song," *Thus Spoke Zarathustra* (1883–92), 2, tr. Walter Kaufmann.

29. You can't give it to everywan offen provides an excuse to give it to no-wan. SEAN O'CASEY, *Nannie's Night Out* (1924).

30. Presents, believe me, seduce both men and gods. OVID, *The Art of Love* (c. A.D. 8), 3, tr. J. Lewis May.

31. I know what I have given you. I do not know what you have received. ANTONIO PORCHIA, *Voces* (1968), tr. W. S. Merwin.

32. A gift in season is a double favor to the needy. PUBLILIUS SYRUS, *Moral Sayings* (1st c. B.C.), 90, tr. Darius Lyman.

33. The spirit in which a thing is given determines that in which the debt is acknowledged; it's the intention, not the face-value of the gift, that's weighed. SENECA, *Letters to Lucilius* (1st c.), 81.6, tr. E. Phillips Barker.

34. Rich gifts wax poor when givers prove unkind. SHAKESPEARE, *Hamlet* (1600), 3.1.101.

35. You pay a great deal too dear for what's given freely. SHAKESPEARE, *The Winter's Tale* (1610–11), 1.1.18.

36. An enemy's gift is ruinous and no gift. SOPHOCLES, *Ajax* (c. 447 B.C.), tr. John Moore.

37. Leave out my name from the gift / if it be a burden, / but keep my song. RABINDRANATH TAGORE, *Fireflies* (1928).

38. Man discovers his own wealth / when God comes to ask gifts of him. RABINDRANATH TAGORE, *Fireflies* (1928).

39. Surely great loving-kindness yet may go / With a little gift: all's dear that comes from friends. THEOCRITUS, *Idyll* 28 (3rd c. B.C.).

40. The excellence of a gift lies in its appropriateness rather than in its value. CHARLES DUDLEY WARNER, "Eleventh Study," *Backlog Studies* (1873).

41. When I give I give myself. WALT WHITMAN, "Song of Myself," 40, *Leaves of Grass* (1855–92).

42. Give all thou canst; high Heaven rejects the lore / Of nicely-calculated less or more. WILLIAM WORDSWORTH, "Inside of King's College Chapel Cambridge" (1821).

## 383. GIRLS

See also 1064. Youth

1. Young girls like the excess of any quality. Without knowing, they want to suffer, to suffer they must exaggerate; they like to have loud chords struck on them. ELIZABETH BOWEN, *The House in Paris* (1935), 2.5.

2. There is no need to waste pity on young girls who are having their moments of disillusionment, for in another moment they will recover their illusion. COLETTE, "Wedding Day," *Earthly Paradise* (1966), 2, ed. Robert Phelps.

3. Young girls are the chatelaines of truth; they must see that it is protected, that the guilty lead the life of the guilty, even if the world rocks on its foundations. JEAN GIRAUDOUX, *Electra* (1937), 1, tr. Phyllis La Farge with Peter H. Judd.

4. There is nothing so difficult to support imperturbably as the head of a lovely girl, except her grief. WALTER SAVAGE LANDOR, "Aesop and Rhodope," *Imaginary Conversations* (1824–53).

5. Dear to the heart of a girl is her own beauty and charm. OVID, *The Art of Beauty* (c. A.D. 8), tr. Rolfe Humphries.

## GIVING

See 382. Gifts and Giving

## GLASSES

See 918. Spectacles

## 384. GLORY

See also 330. Fame; 424. Honors; 716. Praise; 798. Reputation

1. It may be a fire—tomorrow it will be ashes. ARABIC PROVERB.

2. Thou shalt confess the vain pursuit / Of human glory yields no fruit / But an untimely grave. THOMAS CAREW, "On the Duke of Buckingham," *Poems* (1640).

3. Achilles exists only by the grace of Homer. Take away the art of writing from this world and you will probably take away its glory. CHATEAUBRIAND, préface, *Les Natchez* (1826).

4. We are all motivated by a keen desire for praise, and the better a man is, the more he is inspired by glory. The very philosophers themselves, even in those books which they write on contempt of glory, inscribe their names. CICERO, *Pro Archia* (62 B.C.).

5. Glory is that bright tragic thing / That for an instant / Means Dominion— / Warms some poor name / That never felt the Sun, / Gently replacing / In oblivion—. EMILY DICKINSON, *Poems* (c. 1862–86).

6. Humility must always be the portion of any man who receives acclaim earned in the blood of his followers and the sacrifices of his friends. DWIGHT D. EISENHOWER, address, London, June 12, 1945.

7. Glory comes from the unchanging din-din-din of one supreme gift. F. SCOTT FITZGERALD, "The Note-Books," *The Crack-Up* (1945).

8. When glory comes, memory departs. FRENCH PROVERB.

9. Hasty glory goes out in a snuff. THOMAS FULLER, M.D., *Gnomologia* (1732).

10. The paths of glory lead but to the grave. THOMAS GRAY, "Elegy Written in a Country Churchyard," (1742?–50), 9.

11. Glory is largely a theatrical concept. There is no striving for glory without a vivid awareness of an audience. ERIC HOFFER, *The True Believer* (1951), 3.13.47.

12. Do we want laurels for ourselves most, / Or most that no one else shall have any? AMY LOWELL, "La Ronde du Diable," *What's O'Clock* (1925).

13. To the ashes of the dead glory comes too late. MARTIAL, *Epigrams* (A.D. 86), 1.25, tr. Walter C. A. Ker.

14. The shortest way to arrive at glory would be to do that for conscience which we do for glory. MONTAIGNE, "Of repentance," *Essays* (1580–88), tr. Charles Cotton and W. C. Hazlitt.

15. Glory and repose are things that cannot possibly inhabit in one and the same place. MONTAIGNE, "Of solitude," *Essays* (1580–88), tr. Charles Cotton and W. C. Hazlitt.

16. Glory ought to be the consequence, not the motive of our actions. PLINY THE YOUNGER, *Letters* (c. 97–110), 1.8, tr. William Melmoth and W. M. L. Hutchison.

17. One crowded hour of glorious life / Is worth an age without a name. SIR WALTER SCOTT, *Old Mortality* (1816), 34.

18. Glory is like a circle in the water, / Which never ceaseth to enlarge itself / Till by broad spreading it disperse to naught. SHAKESPEARE, *1 Henry VI* (1591–92), 1.2.133.

19. Avoid shame, but do not seek glory,—nothing so expensive as glory. SYDNEY SMITH, quoted in Lady S. Holland's *Memoir* (1855), v.1.4.

20. The nearest way to glory—a short cut, as it were—is to strive to be what you wish to be thought to be. SOCRATES (5th–4th c. B.C.), quoted in Cicero's *De Officiis* (44 B.C.), 2.12.43, tr. Walter Miller.

21. The desire of glory is the last infirmity cast off even by the wise. TACITUS, *Histories* (A.D. 104–109), 4.6, tr. Alfred J. Church and William J. Brodribb.

22. Glories, like glow-worms, afar off shine bright, / But iooked to near, have neither heat nor light. JOHN WEBSTER, *The Duchess of Malfi* (c. 1613), 4.2.

## GLUTTONY

See 272. Eating; 401. Greed

## GOALS

See 284. Ends; 765. Purpose

## 385. GOD

**See also 240. Devil; 259. Divinity; 748. Providence; 790. Religion; 810. Revelation, Divine; 966. Theology; 1012. The Unknown**

1. The power that holds the sky's majesty wins our worship. AESCHYLUS, *The Libation Bearers* (458 B.C.), tr. Richmond Lattimore.

2. Every man thinks God is on his side. The rich and powerful know He is. JEAN ANOUILH, *The Lark* (1955), 1, adapted by Lillian Hellman.

3. You cannot plumb the depths of the human heart, nor find out what a man is thinking; how do you expect to search out God, who made all these things, and find out his mind or comprehend his thoughts? *Apocrypha*, Judith 8:14.

4. We, peopling the void air, / Make Gods to whom to impute / The ills we ought to bear; / With God and Fate to rail at, suffering easily. MATTHEW ARNOLD, *Empedocles on Etna* (1852), 1.2.

5. Canst thou by searching find out God? *Bible*, Job 11:7.

6. God is our refuge and strength, a very present help in trouble. *Bible*, Psalms 46:1.

7. If I ascend up into heaven, thou [God] art there: if I make my bed in hell, behold, thou art there. *Bible*, Psalms 139:8.

8. We should find God in what we do know, not in what we don't; not in outstanding problems, but in those we have already solved. DIETRICH BONHOEFFER, *Letters and Papers from Prison*, May 25, 1944, tr. Eberhard Bethge.

9. God is the Celebrity-Author of the World's Best Seller. We have made God into the biggest celebrity of all, to contain our own emptiness. DANIEL J. BOORSTIN, *The Image* (1962), 5.

10. God is the perfect poet, / Who in his person acts his own creations. ROBERT BROWNING, *Paracelsus* (1835), 2.

11. God is seen God / In the star, in the stone, in the flesh, in the soul and the clod. ROBERT BROWNING, "Saul," *Men and Women* (1855), 17.

12. He who, from zone to zone, / Guides through the boundless sky thy certain flight, / In the long way that I must tread alone, / Will lead my steps aright. WILLIAM CULLEN BRYANT, "To a Waterfowl" (1818).

13. God without the devil is dead, being alone. SAMUEL BUTLER (d. 1902), "Elementary Morality," *Note-Books* (1912).

14. God's merits are so transcendent that it is not surprising his faults should be in reasonable proportion. SAMUEL BUTLER (d. 1902), "Rebelliousness," *Note-Books* (1912).

15. Theist and Atheist: The fight between them is as to whether God shall be called God or shall have some other name. SAMUEL BUTLER (d. 1902), "Rebelliousness," *Note-Books* (1912).

16. The certainty of a God giving meaning to life far surpasses in attractiveness the ability to behave badly with impunity. ALBERT CAMUS, "The Absurd Man," *The Myth of Sisyphus* (1942), tr. Justin O'Brien

17. Is there no God, then, but at best an absentee God, sitting idle, ever since the first Sabbath, at the outside of his Universe? THOMAS CARLYLE, *Sartor Resartus* (1833–34), 2.7.

18. Though God's attributes are equal, yet his mercy is more attractive and pleasing in our eyes than his justice. CERVANTES, *Don Quixote* (1605–15), 2.4.42, tr. Peter Motteux and John Ozell.

19. Man appoints, and God disappoints. CERVANTES, *Don Quixote* (1605–15), 2.4.55, tr. Peter Motteux and John Ozell.

20. There cannot be a personal God without a pessimistic religion. As soon as there is a personal God he is a disappointing God. CYRIL CONNOLLY, *The Unquiet Grave* (1945), 1.

21. God is for men and religion for women. JOSEPH CONRAD, *Nostromo* (1904).

22. His will, that binds our own, is peace to us. DANTE, "Paradiso," 3, *The Divine Comedy* (c. 1300–21), tr. Lawrence Grant White.

23. God is indeed a jealous God— / He cannot bear to see / That we had rather not with Him / But with each other play. EMILY DICKINSON, *Poems* (c. 1862–86).

24. If every gnat that flies were an archangel, all that could but tell me that there is a God; and the poorest worm that creeps tells me that. JOHN DONNE, *Sermons*, No. 57, 1628.

25. Do not speak of God much. After a very little conversation on the highest nature, thought deserts us and we run into formalism. EMERSON, *Journals*, 1836.

26. God is our name for the last generalization to which we can arrive. EMERSON,

*Journals*, 1836.

27. The only money of God is God. He pays never with any thing less, or any thing else. EMERSON, "Friendship," *Essays: First Series* (1841).

28. Heaven always bears some proportion to earth. The god of the cannibal will be a cannibal, of the crusaders a crusader, and of the merchants a merchant. EMERSON, "Worship," *The Conduct of Life* (1860).

29. If god is truly god, he is perfect, / lacking nothing. EURIPIDES, *Heracles* (c. 422 B.C.), tr. William Arrowsmith.

30. The way of God is complex, he is hard / for us to predict. He moves the pieces and they come / somehow into a kind of order. EURIPIDES, *Helen* (412 B.C.), tr. Richmond Lattimore.

31. I am waiting / for them to prove / that God is really American. LAWRENCE FERLINGHETTI, "I Am Waiting," *A Coney Island of the Mind* (1958).

32. The skirts of the gods / Drag in our mud. We feel the touch / And take it to be a kiss. CHRISTOPHER FRY, *Thor, with Angels* (1948).

33. No one has the capacity to judge God. We are drops in that limitless ocean of mercy. MOHANDAS K. GANDHI, *Non-Violence in Peace and War* (1948), 2.321.

34. That which Love begets, / That which Rebellion creates, / That which Freedom rears, / Are three manifestations of God. / And God is the expression / Of the intelligent Universe. KAHLIL GIBRAN, "Vision," *Thoughts and Meditations* (1960), tr. Anthony R. Ferris.

35. God lies ahead. I convince myself and constantly repeat to myself that: He depends on us. It is through us that God is achieved. ANDRÉ GIDE, *Journals*, 1947, tr. Justin O'Brien.

36. I believe in the gods. Or rather I believe that I believe in the gods. But I don't believe that they are great brooding presences watching over us; I believe they are completely absent-minded. JEAN GIRAUDOUX, *Electra* (1937), 1, tr. Phyllis La Farge with Peter H. Judd.

37. Everyone, whether he is self-denying or self-indulgent, is seeking after the Beloved. Every place may be the shrine of love, whether it be mosque or synagogue. HĀFIZ, ghazals from the *Divan* (14th c.), 8, tr. Justin Huntly McCarthy.

38. The First Cause worked automatically like a somnambulist, and not reflectively like a sage. THOMAS HARDY, *Jude the Obscure* (1895), 6.3.

39. God is day and night, winter and summer, war and peace, satiety and want. HERACLITUS, *Fragments* (c. 500 B.C.), 121, tr. Philip Wheelwright.

40. If any man obeys the gods, they listen to him also. HOMER, *Iliad* (9th c. B.C.), 1.218, tr. Richmond Lattimore.

41. To see so much misery everywhere, I suspect that God is not rich. He keeps up appearances, it is true, but I feel the pinch. He gives a revolution as a merchant, whose credit is low, gives a ball. VICTOR HUGO, "Saint Denis," *Les Misérables* (1862), 12.2, tr. Charles E. Wilbour.

42. An honest God is the noblest work of man. ROBERT G. INGERSOLL, *The Gods* (1872).

43. God has been replaced, as he has all over the West, with respectability and air conditioning. LE ROI JONES, "What Does Nonviolence Mean?" *Home* (1966).

44. God is but a word invented to explain the world. LAMARTINE, "Le Tombeau d'une mère," *Nouvelles harmonies poétiques et religieuses* (1832).

45. God is what man finds that is divine in himself. God is the best way man can behave in the ordinary occasions of life, and the farthest point to which man can stretch himself. MAX LERNER, "Seekers and Losers," *The Unfinished Country* (1959), 5.

46. 'Tis heaven alone that is given away, / 'Tis only God may be had for the asking. JAMES RUSSELL LOWELL, prelude to part 1, "The Vision of Sir Launfal" (1848).

47. If God is Will / And Will is well / Then what is ill? / God still? / Dew tell! ARCHIBALD MAC LEISH, *JB* (1958), 5.

48. God is the immemorial refuge of the incompetent, the helpless, the miserable. They find not only sanctuary in His arms, but also a kind of superiority, soothing to their macerated egos; He will set them above their betters. H. L. MENCKEN, *Minority Report* (1956), 35.

49. It takes a long while for a naturally trustful person to reconcile himself to the idea that after all God will not help him. H. L. MENCKEN, *Minority Report* (1956), 194.

50. Only this I know, / That one celestial

father gives to all. MILTON, *Paradise Lost* (1667), 5.402.

51. Just are the ways of God, / And justifiable to men; / Unless there be who think not God at all. MILTON, *Samson Agonistes* (1671), 293.

52. If triangles had a god, he would have three sides. MONTESQUIEU, *Lettres persanes* (1721), 59.

53. God is a thought that makes crooked all that is straight. NIETZSCHE, "Upon the Blessed Isles," *Thus Spoke Zarathustra* (1883–92), 2, tr. Walter Kaufmann.

54. One is most dishonest to one's god: he is not *allowed* to sin. NIETZSCHE, *Beyond Good and Evil* (1886), 65a, tr. Walter Kaufmann.

55. When men make gods, there is no God. EUGENE O'NEILL, *Lazarus Laughed* (1927), 2.2.

56. Let us weigh the gain and the loss, in wagering that God is. Consider these alternatives: if you win, you win all; if you lose, you lose nothing. Do not hesitate, then, to wager that He is. PASCAL, *Pensées* (1670), 233.

57. It is the heart which experiences God, and not the reason. PASCAL, *Pensées* (1670), 278, tr. W. F. Trotter.

58. If there were only one religion, God would indeed be manifest. PASCAL, *Pensées* (1670), 584, tr. W. F. Trotter.

59. It is fear that first brought gods into the world. PETRONIUS, *Satyricon* (1st c.).

60. One on God's side is a majority. WENDELL PHILLIPS, speech, Nov. 1, 1859.

61. It is God that accomplishes all term to hopes, / God, who overtakes the flying eagle, outpasses the dolphin / in the sea; who bends under his strength the man with thoughts too high. PINDAR, *Odes* (5th c. B.C.), Pythia 2, tr. Richmond Lattimore.

62. God, he whom everyone knows, by name. JULES RENARD, *Journal*, April 1894, ed. and tr. Louise Bogan and Elizabeth Roget.

63. The existence of a world without God seems to me less absurd than the presence of a God, existing in all his perfection, creating an imperfect man in order to make him run the risk of Hell. ARMAND SALACROU, "Certitudes et incertitudes," *Théâtre* (1943), 6.

64. No religion has ever given a picture of deity which men could have imitated without the grossest immorality. GEORGE SANTAYANA, *The Life of Reason: Reason in Art* (1905–06), 9.

65. Nothing can be lower or more wholly instrumental than the substance and cause of all things. GEORGE SANTAYANA, *Little Essays* (1920), 26, ed. Logan Pearsall Smith.

66. Respectable society believed in God in order to avoid having to speak about him. JEAN-PAUL SARTRE, *The Words* (1964), 1.

67. We have been born under a monarchy; to obey God is freedom. SENECA, "On a Happy Life," *Moral Sayings* (1st c.), tr. Aubrey Stewart.

68. As flies to wanton boys are we to the gods. / They kill us for their sport. SHAKESPEARE, *King Lear* (1605–06), 4.1.36.

69. Our love for God is tested by the question of whether we seek Him or His gifts. RALPH W. SOCKMAN, interview with James B. Simpson, 1961.

70. God is the indwelling and not the transient cause of all things. SPINOZA, *Ethics* (1677), 1, tr. Andrew Boyle.

71. Your idol is shattered in the dust to prove that God's dust is greater than your idol. RABINDRANATH TAGORE, *Stray Birds* (1916), 51.

72. Closer is He than breathing, and nearer than hands and feet. ALFRED, LORD TENNYSON, "The Higher Pantheism" (1869).

73. There is strife between God's ways and human ways; damned by you, we are absolved by God. TERTULLIAN, *Apology* (3rd c.), 50.

74. Short arm needs man to reach to Heaven, / So ready is Heaven to stoop to him. FRANCIS THOMPSON, "Grace of the Way" (1897).

75. If God were not a necessary Being of Himself, He might seem to be made for the use and benefit of men. JOHN TILLOTSON, *Sermons* (1695–1704), 93.

76. We need God, not in order to understand the *why*, but in order to feel and sustain the ultimate *wherefore*, to give a meaning to the Universe. MIGUEL DE UNAMUNO, "Love, Suffering, Pity, and Personality," *Tragic Sense of Life* (1913), tr. J. E. Crawford Flitch.

77. If God created us in his own image, we have more than reciprocated. VOLTAIRE, *Le Sottisier*, 32.

78. If God did not exist, he would have to be invented. VOLTAIRE, *Épitre CIV à*

*l'auteur du livre des trois imposteurs* (1769).

79. No reason can be given for the nature of God, because that nature is the ground of rationality. ALFRED NORTH WHITEHEAD, *Science and the Modern World* (1925), 11.

80. All your Western theologies, the whole mythology of them, are based on the concept of God as a senile delinquent. TENNESSEE WILLIAMS, *The Night of the Iguana* (1961), 2.

81. A God all mercy is a God unjust. EDWARD YOUNG, *Night Thoughts* (1742–46), 4.233.

## GOLDEN AGE

See 296. Era

## 386. GOLDEN RULE

See also 224. Deeds

1. Do unto yourself as your neighbors do unto themselves and look pleasant. GEORGE ADE, "The Lingering Thirst," *Hand-Made Fables* (1920).

2. All things whatsoever ye would that men should do to you, do ye even so to them: for this is the law and the prophets. *Bible*, Matthew 7:12.

3. What you do not want done to yourself, do not do to others. CONFUCIUS, *Analects* (6th c. B.C.), 15.23, tr. James Legge.

4. Do not do unto others as you would that they should do unto you. Their tastes may not be the same. GEORGE BERNARD SHAW, "Maxims for Revolutionists," *Man and Superman* (1903).

5. Do unto the other feller the way he'd like to do unto you an' do it fust. EDWARD NOYES WESTCOTT, *David Harum* (1898), 20.

## GOLF

See 922. Sports

## 387. THE GOOD

See also 305. Evil; 388. Good and Evil; 391. Goodness; 816. Right

1. Whatever befalls in accordance with nature should be accounted good. CICERO, *De Senectute* (44 B.C.), 19.71.

2. We know the good, we apprehend it clearly. / But we can't bring it to achievement. EURIPIDES, *Hippolytus* (428 B.C.), tr. David Grene.

3. We look for good on earth and cannot recognize it / when met. EURIPIDES, *Electra* (413 B.C.), tr. Emily Townsend Vermeule.

4. Nothing is good for everyone, but only relatively to some people. ANDRÉ GIDE, *The Counterfeiters* (1925), 2.4, tr. Dorothy Bussy.

5. Good things, when short, are twice as good. BALTASAR GRACIÁN, *The Art of Worldly Wisdom* (1647), 105, tr. Joseph Jacobs.

6. The good things of life are not to be had singly, but come to us with a mixture; like a schoolboy's holiday, with a task affixed to the tail of it. CHARLES LAMB, "Popular Fallacies, 13," *Last Essays of Elia* (1833).

7. To know the good is to react against the bad. Indifference is the mark of deprivation. MARYA MANNES, "Introducing Myself," *More in Anger* (1958).

8. We must take the good with the bad; / For the good when it's good, is so very good / That the bad when it's bad can't be bad! MOLIÈRE, second intermission of *The Imaginary Invalid* (1673), tr. Mildred Marmur.

9. The good is, like nature, an immense landscape in which man advances through centuries of exploration. JOSÉ ORTEGA Y GASSET, "To the Reader," *Meditations on Quixote* (1914).

10. It is good to be tired and wearied by the vain search after the true good, that we may stretch out our arms to the Redeemer. PASCAL, *Pensées* (1670), 422, tr. W. F. Trotter.

11. Our will is always for our own good, but we do not always see what that is. ROUSSEAU, *The Social Contract* (1762), 2.3, tr. G. D. H. Cole.

12. Men always love what is good or what they find good; it is in judging what is good that they go wrong. ROUSSEAU, *The Social Contract* (1762), 4.7, tr. G. D. H. Cole.

13. Happiness is not best achieved by those who seek it directly; and it would seem that the same is true of the good. BERTRAND RUSSELL, title essay, *Mysticism and Logic* (1917).

14. There is nothing either good or bad but thinking makes it so. SHAKESPEARE, *Hamlet* (1600), 2.2.255.

15. Beauty, Good, and Knowledge are three sisters / That doat upon each other, friends to man, / Living together under the same roof, / And never can be sundered without tears. ALFRED, LORD TENNYSON, "To—" (1832).

16. Everyone places his good where he can and has as much of it as he can, in his own way. VOLTAIRE, "Good," *Philosophical Dictionary* (1764).

17. A good is never productive of evil but when it is carried to a culpable excess, in which case it completely ceases to be a good. VOLTAIRE, "Property," *Philosophical Dictionary* (1764).

## 388. GOOD AND EVIL

See also 305. Evil; 387. The Good; 391. Goodness

1. Good and evil lie close together. Seek no artistic unity in character. LORD ACTON, postscript, letter to Mandell Creighton, April 5, 1887.

2. It's wiser being good than bad; / It's safer being meek than fierce: / It's fitter being sane than mad. ROBERT BROWNING, "Apparent Failure," *Dramatis Personae* (1864), 7.

3. White shall not neutralize the black, nor good / Compensate bad in man, absolve him so: / Life's business being just the terrible choice. ROBERT BROWNING, "The Pope," *The Ring and the Book* (1868–69).

4. Let no man presume to think that he can devise any plan of extensive good, unalloyed and unadulterated with evil. CHARLES CALEB COLTON, *Lacon* (1825), 1.7.

5. The meaning of good and bad, of better and worse, is simply helping or hurting. EMERSON, *Journals*, 1836.

6. Good and bad may not be dissevered; / There is, as there should be, a commingling. EURIPIDES, quoted in Plutarch's "Contentment," *Moralia* (c. A.D.100), tr. Moses Hadas.

7. Even as the holy and the righteous cannot rise beyond the highest which is in each one of you, so the wicked and the weak cannot fall lower than the lowest which is in you also. KAHLIL GIBRAN, "On Crime and Punishment," *The Prophet* (1923).

8. Nothing is good for him for whom nothing is bad. BALTASAR GRACIÁN, *The Art of Worldly Wisdom* (1647), 250, tr. Joseph Jacobs.

9. There is no such thing in man's nature as a settled and full resolve either for good or evil, except at the very moment of execution. NATHANIEL HAWTHORNE, "Fancy's Show Box," *Twice-Told Tales* (1837).

10. Goodness without wisdom always accomplishes evil. ROBERT A. HEINLEIN, *Stranger in a Strange Land* (1961), 36.

11. Jove weighs affairs of earth in dubious scales, / And the good suffers while the bad prevails. HOMER, *Odyssey* (9th c. B.C.), 6.229, tr. Alexander Pope.

12. Almost all the moral good which is left among us is the apparent effect of physical evil. SAMUEL JOHNSON, *The Idler* (1758–60), 89.

13. We cannot freely and wisely choose the right way for ourselves unless we know both good and evil. HELEN KELLER, *My Religion* (1927).

14. We often do good in order to accomplish evil with impunity. LA ROCHEFOUCAULD, *Maxims* (1665), tr. Kenneth Pratt.

15. The betrothed of good is evil, / The betrothed of life is death, / The betrothed of love is divorce. MALAY PROVERB.

16. Evil can be condoned only if in the beyond it is compensated by good and God himself needs immortality to vindicate his ways to man. W. SOMERSET MAUGHAM, *The Summing Up* (1938), 70.

17. Life in itself is neither good nor evil; it is the scene of good or evil, as you make it. MONTAIGNE, "That to study philosophy is to learn to die," *Essays* (1580–88), tr. Charles Cotton and W. C. Hazlitt.

18. One should seek for the salutary in the unpleasant; if it is there, it is after all nectar. One should seek for the deceitful in the pleasant; if it is there, it is after all poison. *Panchatantra* (c. 5th c.), 1, tr. Franklin Edgerton.

19. If we could see all the evil that may spring from good, what should we do? LUIGI PIRANDELLO, *Six Characters in Search of an Author* (1921), 1, tr. Edward Storer.

20. The omission of good is no less reprehensible than the commission of evil. PLUTARCH, "Contentment," *Moralia* (c. A.D. 100), tr. Moses Hadas.

21. Saints cannot arise where there have

been no warriors, nor philosophers where a prying beast does not remain hidden in the depths. GEORGE SANTAYANA, *The Life of Reason: Reason in Science* (1905–06), 9.

22. The apprehension of the good / Gives but the greater feeling to the worse. SHAKESPEARE, *Richard II* (1595–96), 1.3.300.

23. The evil that men do lives after them; / The good is oft interred with their bones. SHAKESPEARE, *Julius Caesar* (1599–1600), 3.2.81.

24. A good thing which prevents us from enjoying a greater good is in truth an evil. SPINOZA, *Ethics* (1677), 4, tr. Andrew Boyle.

25. Good and evil . . . are not what vulgar opinion accounts them; many who seem to be struggling with adversity are happy; many, amid great affluence, are utterly miserable. TACITUS, *Annals* (A.D. 115–117?), 6.22, tr. Alfred J. Church and William J. Brodribb.

26. This truth within thy mind rehearse, / That in a boundless universe / Is boundless better, boundless worse. ALFRED, LORD TENNYSON, "The Two Voices" (1833), 9.

27. O, yet we trust that somehow good / Will be the final goal of ill. ALFRED, LORD TENNYSON, "In Memoriam A. H. H." (1850), 54.

28. The character of human life, like the character of the human condition, like the character of all life, is "ambiguity": the inseparable mixture of good and evil, the true and false, the creative and destructive forces—both individual and social. PAUL TILLICH, *Time*, May 17, 1963.

29. The question of good and evil remains in irremediable chaos for those who seek to fathom it in reality. It is a mere mental sport to the disputants, who are captives that play with their chains. VOLTAIRE, "Optimism," *Philosophical Dictionary* (1764).

## 389. GOOD BREEDING

**See also 194. Courtesy; 376. Gentlemen; 559. Manners; 743. Propriety**

1. There is no society or conversation to be kept up in the world without good-nature, or something which must bear its appearance and supply its place. For this reason mankind have been forced to invent a kind of artificial humanity, which is what we express by the word Good-Breeding. JOSEPH ADDISON, *The Spectator* (1711–12), 169.

2. With fowls, the pedigree; with men, breeding. *Burmese Proverbs* (1962), 1, ed. Hla Pe.

3. It is good breeding alone that can prepossess people in your favor at first sight, more time being necessary to discover greater talents. LORD CHESTERFIELD, *Letters to His Son*, c. 1741.

4. The scholar without good breeding is a pedant; the philosopher, a cynic. LORD CHESTERFIELD, *Letters to His Son*, Oct. 9, 1747.

5. There is no creature perfectly civil but a husband. For in a little time he grows only rude to his wife, and this is the highest good breeding, for it begets his civility to other people. WILLIAM CONGREVE, *Love for Love* (1695), 1.1.

6. Good breeding, a union of kindness and independence. EMERSON, "Manners," *Essays: Second Series* (1844).

7. The whole essence of true gentle-breeding (one does not like to say gentility) lies in the wish and the art to be agreeable. Good-breeding is surface-Christianity. OLIVER WENDELL HOLMES, SR., *The Professor at the Breakfast Table* (1860), 6.

8. The test of a man or woman's breeding is how they behave in a quarrel. GEORGE BERNARD SHAW, *The Philanderer* (1893), 4.

9. Good breeding consists in concealing how much we think of ourselves and how little we think of other persons. MARK TWAIN, *Notebook* (1935).

## 390. GOOD NATURE

**See also 961. Temper, Bad**

1. I have always preferred cheerfulness to mirth. The latter I consider as an act, the former as an habit of mind. Mirth is short and transient, cheerfulness fixed and permanent. JOSEPH ADDISON, *The Spectator* (1711–12), 381.

2. Good nature is worth more than knowledge, more than money, more than honor, to the persons who possess it. HENRY WARD BEECHER, *Proverbs from Plymouth Pulpit* (1887).

3. The teeth are smiling, but is the heart? CONGOLESE PROVERB.

4. The best part of health is fine disposition. EMERSON, "Considerations by the Way," *The Conduct of Life* (1860).

5. Of cheerfulness, or a good temper—the more it is spent, the more of it remains. EMERSON, "Considerations by the Way," *The Conduct of Life* (1860).

6. If you would be tasted for old wine, be in the mouth a pleasant grape. JOHN LYLY, *Euphues: The Anatomy of Wit* (1579).

7. Good-fellowship, unflagging, is the prime requisite for success in our society, and the man or woman who smiles only for reasons of humor or pleasure is a deviate. MARYA MANNES, *More in Anger* (1958), 1.2.

8. Affability contains no hatred of men, but for that very reason too much contempt for men. NIETZSCHE, *Beyond Good and Evil* (1886), 93, tr. Walter Kaufmann.

9. A good disposition is a virtue in itself, and it is lasting; the burden of the years cannot depress it, and love that is founded on it endures to the end. OVID, *The Art of Beauty* (c. A.D. 8), tr. J. Lewis May.

10. A good-natured man has the whole world to be happy out of. ALEXANDER POPE, *Thoughts on Various Subjects* (1727).

11. Good-humor is a philosophic state of mind; it seems to say to Nature that we take her no more seriously than she takes us. ERNEST RENAN, *Feuillès détachées* (c. 1880).

12. Discussion without asperity, sympathy with fusion, gayety unracked by too abundant jests, mental ease in approaching one another,—these are the things which give a pleasant smoothness to the rough edge of life. AGNES REPPLIER, "The Luxury of Conversation," *Compromises* (1904).

13. Mutual good humour is a dress we ought to appear in wherever we meet, and we should make no mention of what concerns our selves, without it be of matters wherein our friends ought to rejoice. RICHARD STEELE, *The Spectator* (1711–12), 100.

14. Few are qualified to shine in company, but it is in most men's power to be agreeable. JONATHAN SWIFT, *Thoughts on Various Subjects* (1711).

## 391. GOODNESS

**See also 188. Corruption; 224. Deeds; 305. Evil; 387. The Good; 388. Good and Evil; 430. Humanitarianism; 598. Morality; 691. Piety; 816. Right; 1025. Virtue**

1. To make one good action succeed another, is the perfection of goodness. ALI IBN-ABI-TALIB, *Sentences* (7th c.), 75, tr. Simon Ockley.

2. It is easy to perform a good action, but not easy to acquire a settled habit of performing such actions. ARISTOTLE, *Nicomachean Ethics* (4th c. B.C.), 5.9, tr. J. A. K. Thomson.

3. Goodness is easier to recognize than to define. W. H. AUDEN, in *I Believe* (1939), ed. Clifton Fadiman.

4. Good men are not those who now and then do a good act, but men who join one good act to another. HENRY WARD BEECHER, *Proverbs from Plymouth Pulpit* (1887).

5. Goodness is achieved not in a vacuum, but in the company of other men, attended by love. SAUL BELLOW, *Dangling Man* (1944).

6. A man is only as good as what he loves. SAUL BELLOW, *Seize the Day* (1956), 1.

7. Be not overcome of evil, but overcome evil with good. *Bible*, Romans 12:21.

8. No one can be good for long if goodness is not in demand. BERTOLT BRECHT, *The Good Woman of Setzuan* (1938–40), 1-a, tr. Eric Bentley and Maja Apelman.

9. May the good God pardon all good men. ELIZABETH BARRETT BROWNING, *Aurora Leigh* (1856), 4.506.

10. The only fault's with time; / All men become good creatures: but so slow! ROBERT BROWNING, *Luria* (1846), 5.

11. They're only truly great who are truly good. GEORGE CHAPMAN, *Revenge for Honour* (1654), 5.2.

12. Good is not good, unless / A thousand it possess, / But doth waste with greediness. JOHN DONNE, "Confined Love," *Songs and Sonnets* (1633).

13. It must be a good thing to be good or ivrybody wudden't be pretendin' he was. FINLEY PETER DUNNE, "Hypocrisy," *Observations by Mr. Dooley* (1902).

14. It is very hard to be simple enough to be good. EMERSON, *Journals*, 1836.

15. Goodness that preaches undoes itself. EMERSON, *Journals*, 1836.

16. Every actual State is corrupt. Good men must not obey the laws too well.

EMERSON, "Politics," *Essays: Second Series* (1844).

17. Seek not good from without: seek it within yourselves, or you will never find it. EPICTETUS, *Discourses* (2nd c.), 3.24, tr. Thomas W. Higginson.

18. A good man has more hope in his death than a wicked man in his life. THOMAS FULLER, M.D., *Gnomologia* (1732), 159.

19. The Devil himself is good when he is pleased. THOMAS FULLER, M.D., *Gnomologia* (1732), 4478.

20. A good man isn't good for everything. JOHN W. GARDNER, *No Easy Victories* (1968), 22.

21. Jail doesn't teach anyone to do good, nor Siberia, but a man—yes! A man can teach another man to do good—believe me! MAXIM GORKY, *The Lower Depths* (1903), 3, tr. Alexander Bakshy.

22. Goodness is uneventful. It does not flash, it glows. DAVID GRAYSON, *Adventures in Contentment* (1907), 11.

23. Few persons have courage enough to appear as good as they really are. JULIUS CHARLES HARE and AUGUSTUS WILLIAM HARE, *Guesses at Truth* (1827).

24. Do well and right, and let the world sink. GEORGE HERBERT, *A Priest to the Temple* (1652).

25. It is a hard thing for a man / to be righteous, if the unrighteous man is to have the greater right. HESIOD, *Works and Days* (8th c. B.C.), 271, tr. Richmond Lattimore.

26. All men are good when free from passion, interest, or error. EUGENIO MARÍA de HOSTOS, "Hombres e ideas," *Obras* (1939–54), 14.

27. As I know more of mankind I expect less of them, and am ready now to call a man a good man upon easier terms than I was formerly. SAMUEL JOHNSON, quoted in Boswell's *Life of Samuel Johnson*, September 1783.

28. Good men are the stars, the planets of the ages wherein they live, and illustrate the times. BEN JONSON, "Explorata," *Timber* (1640).

29. Be good, sweet maid, and let who will be clever. CHARLES KINGSLEY, "A Farewell."

30. Goodness does not more certainly make men happy than happiness makes them good. WALTER SAVAGE LANDOR, "Lord Brooke and Sir Philip Sidney," *Imaginary Conversations* (1824–53).

31. Nobody deserves to be praised for his goodness if he has not the power to be wicked. All other goodness is often only weakness and impotence of the will. LA ROCHEFOUCAULD, *Maxims* (1665), tr. Kenneth Pratt.

32. It's easier to swoon in pious dreams / Than do good actions. GOTTHOLD EPHRAIM LESSING, *Nathan the Wise* (1779), 1.3, tr. Bayard Quincy Morgan.

33. It is from reason that justice springs, but goodness is born of wisdom. MAURICE MAETERLINCK, *Wisdom and Destiny* (1898), 29, tr. Alfred Sutro.

34. Live not as though there were a thousand years ahead of you. Fate is at your elbow; make yourself good while life and power are still yours. MARCUS AURELIUS, *Meditations* (2nd c.), 4.17, tr. Maxwell Staniforth.

35. Waste no more time arguing what a good man should be. Be one. MARCUS AURELIUS, *Meditations* (2nd c.), 10.16, tr. Maxwell Staniforth.

36. Loving-kindness is the better part of goodness. It lends grace to the sterner qualities of which this consists. W. SOMERSET MAUGHAM, *The Summing Up* (1938), 77.

37. Goodness thinks no ill / Where no ill seems. MILTON, *Paradise Lost* (1667), 3.668.

38. Good, the more / Communicated, more abundant grows. MILTON, *Paradise Lost* (1667), 5.71.

39. There is no man so good, who, were he to submit all his thoughts and actions to the laws, would not deserve hanging ten times in his life. MONTAIGNE, "Of vanity," *Essays* (1580–88), tr. Charles Cotton and W. C. Hazlitt.

40. To become a good man, one must have faithful friends, or outright enemies. NAPOLEON I, *Maxims* (1804–15).

41. Whatever harm the evil may do, the harm done by the good is the most harmful harm. NIETZSCHE, "On Old and New Tablets," *Thus Spoke Zarathustra* (1883–92), 3, tr. Walter Kaufmann.

42. Do good by stealth, and blush to find it fame. ALEXANDER POPE, *Epilogue to the Satires* (1738), 1.136.

43. Yes, that is what good is: to forgive evil. There is no other good. ANTONIO PORCHIA, *Voces* (1968), tr. W. S. Merwin.

44. It is his nature, not his standing, that makes the good man. PUBLILIUS SYRUS, *Moral Sayings* (1st c. B.C.), 977, tr. Darius Lyman.

45. The good life, as I conceive it, is a happy life. I do not mean that if you are good you will be happy; I mean that if you are happy you will be good. BERTRAND RUSSELL, *New Hopes for a Changing World* (1951).

46. Be thou good thyself, and let people speak evil of thee; it is better than to be wicked, and that they should consider thee as good. SA'DI, *Gulistan* (1258), 2.22, tr. James Ross.

47. Good people are good because they've come to wisdom through failure. WILLIAM SAROYAN, *New York Journal-American*, Aug. 23, 1961.

48. If to do were as easy as to know what were good to do, chapels had been churches, and poor men's cottages princes' palaces. SHAKESPEARE, *The Merchant of Venice* (1596–97), 1.2.13.

49. Living or dead, to a good man there can come no evil. SOCRATES, in Plato's *Apology* (4th c. B.C.), tr. Lane Cooper.

50. The good befriend themselves. SOPHOCLES, *Oedipus at Colonus* (401 B.C.), tr. Robert Fitzgerald.

51. A good man's pedigree is little hunted up. SPANISH PROVERB.

52. He who does good comes to the temple gate, / he who loves reaches the shrine. RABINDRANATH TAGORE, *Fireflies* (1928).

53. Profit smiles on goodness / when the good is profitable. RABINDRANATH TAGORE, *Fireflies* (1928).

54. Goodness is the only investment that never fails. THOREAU, "Higher Laws," *Walden* (1854).

55. To be good is noble; but to show others how to be good is nobler and no trouble. MARK TWAIN, "Pudd'nhead Wilson's New Calendar," *Following the Equator* (1897), 1.

56. I am afraid that good people do a great deal of harm in this world. Certainly the greatest harm they do is that they make badness of such extraordinary importance. OSCAR WILDE, *Lady Windermere's Fan* (1892), 1.

## 392. GOSSIP

**See also 571. Meddling; 686. Pettiness; 827. Rumors; 840. Scandal; 898. Slander**

1. He that repeateth a matter separateth very friends. *Bible*, Proverbs 17:9.

2. A woman and a mouse, they carry a tale wherever they go. GELETT BURGESS, *The Maxims of Methuselah* (1907), 10.

3. Out of some little thing, too free a tongue / Can make an outrageous wrangle. EURIPIDES, *Andromache* (c. 426 B.C.), tr. John F. Nims.

4. He's my friend that speaks well of me behind my back. THOMAS FULLER, M.D., *Gnomologia* (1732), 2465.

5. The best loved man or maid in the town would perish with anguish / Could they hear all that their friends say in the course of a day. JOHN HAY, "Distichs" (1871?), 14.

6. To create an unfavourable impression, it is not necessary that certain things should be true, but that they have been said. WILLIAM HAZLITT, *Characteristics* (1823).

7. If you say a bad thing, you may soon hear a worse thing said about you. HESIOD, *Works and Days* (8th c. B.C.), 721, tr. Richmond Lattimore.

8. Gossip is an evil thing by nature, she's a light weight to lift up, / oh very easy, but heavy to carry, and hard to put down again. HESIOD, *Works and Days* (8th c. B.C.), 761, tr. Richmond Lattimore.

9. In the old days of barbarism, the people fought with hatchets. Civilized men buried the hatchet, and now fight with gossip. EDGAR WATSON HOWE, *Country Town Sayings* (1911).

10. Someone who gossips well has a reputation for being good company or even a wit, never for being a gossip. LOUIS KRONENBERGER, *Company Manners* (1954), 3.1.

11. Another good thing about gossip is that it is within / everybody's reach, / And it is much more interesting than any / other form of speech. OGDEN NASH, "I Have It on Good Authority," *I'm a Stranger Here Myself* (1938).

12. Count not him among your friends who will retail your privacies to the world. PUBLILIUS SYRUS, *Moral Sayings* (1st c. B.C.), 1038, tr. Darius Lyman.

13. Gossip needs no carriage. RUSSIAN PROVERB.

14. Whoever gossips to you will gossip about you. SPANISH PROVERB.

15. There is only one thing in the world worse than being talked about, and that is not being talked about. OSCAR WILDE, *The Picture of Dorian Gray* (1891), 1.

## 393. GOVERNMENT

See also 36. Anarchy; 99. Budget; 100. Bureaucracy; 106. Capitalism; 130. Citizens; 149. Communism; 169. Congress; 231. Democracy; 518. Kings; 675. The People; 724. Presidency; 825. Rulers; 905. Socialism; 906. Society; 923. State; 924. Statesmen and Statesmanship; 958. Taxes; 978. Totalitarianism; 1030. Voting

1. Some insomniacs take this or that potion. Our favorite soporific is the announcement by some official that this or that department will be run without regard to politics. FRANKLIN P. ADAMS, *Nods and Becks* (1944).

2. As the happiness of the people is the sole end of government, so the consent of the people is the only foundation of it. JOHN ADAMS, proclamation (1774).

3. The divine science of government is the science of social happiness, and the blessings of society depend entirely on the constitutions of government. JOHN ADAMS, *Thoughts on Government* (1776).

4. The essence of a free government consists in an effectual control of rivalries. JOHN ADAMS, *Discourses on Davila* (1789), 4.

5. A monarchy is a merchantman, which sails well, but will sometimes strike on a rock and go to the bottom; whilst a republic is a raft, which would never sink, but then your feet are always in water. FISHER AMES, quoted in Emerson's "Politics," *Essays: Second Series* (1844).

6. That rule is the better which is exercised over better subjects. ARISTOTLE, *Politics* (4th c. B.C.), 1.5, tr. Benjamin Jowett.

7. We need supermen to rule us—the job is so vast and the need for wise judgment is so urgent. But, alas, there are no supermen. BROOKS ATKINSON, "January 27," *Once Around the Sun* (1951).

8. You talk about capitalism and communism and all that sort of thing, but the important thing is the struggle everybody is engaged in to get better living conditions, and they are not interested too much in the form of government. BERNARD M. BARUCH, in a press conference in New York City, Aug. 18, 1964.

9. The worst thing in this world, next to anarchy, is government. HENRY WARD BEECHER, *Proverbs from Plymouth Pulpit* (1887).

10. It is for men to choose whether they will govern themselves or be governed. HENRY WARD BEECHER, *Proverbs from Plymouth Pulpit* (1887).

11. Administration, n. An ingenious abstraction in politics, designed to receive the kicks and cuffs due to the premier or president. AMBROSE BIERCE, *The Devil's Dictionary* (1881–1911).

12. Government is a contrivance of human wisdom to provide for human wants. EDMUND BURKE, *Reflections on the Revolution in France* (1790).

13. In the long-run every government is the exact symbol of its people, with their wisdom and unwisdom. THOMAS CARLYLE, *Past and Present* (1843), 4.4.

14. Government is a trust, and the officers of the government are trustees; and both the trust and the trustees are created for the benefit of the people. HENRY CLAY, speech, Lexington, Ky., May 16, 1829.

15. The requisites of government are that there be sufficiency of food, sufficiency of military equipment, and the confidence of the people in their ruler. CONFUCIUS, *Analects* (6th c. B.C.), 12.7, tr. James Legge.

16. Nations it may be have fashioned their Governments, but the Governments have paid them back in the same coin. JOSEPH CONRAD, *Under Western Eyes* (1911), 1.1.

17. Every time the government attempts to handle our affairs, it costs more and the results are worse than if we had handled them ourselves. BENJAMIN CONSTANT, *Cours de politique constitutionnelle* (1818–20).

18. Th' modhren idee iv governmint is "Snub th' people, buy th' people, jaw th' people." FINLEY PETER DUNNE, "Casual Observations," *Mr. Dooley's Philosophy* (1900).

19. In a healthy nation there is a kind of dramatic balance between the will of the people and the government, which pre-

vents its degeneration into tyranny. EINSTEIN, *Out of My Later Life* (1950), 27.

20. Only one in command: that's the way in the home / And the way in the state when it must find / Measures best for mankind. EURIPIDES, *Andromache* (c. 426 B.C.), tr. John F. Nims.

21. Those who govern, having much business on their hands, do not generally like to take the trouble of considering and carrying into execution new projects. The best public measures are therefore seldom adopted from previous wisdom, but forced by the occasion. BENJAMIN FRANKLIN, *Autobiography* (1791), 2.

22. A government that is big enough to give you all you want is big enough to take it all away. BARRY GOLDWATER, speech, West Chester, Pa., Oct. 21, 1964.

23. Even to observe neutrality you must have a strong government. ALEXANDER HAMILTON, address, Constitutional Convention, June 29, 1787.

24. No matter how noble the objectives of a government, if it blurs decency and kindness, cheapens human life, and breeds ill will and suspicion—it is an evil government. ERIC HOFFER, *The Passionate State of Mind* (1954), 147.

25. Chaos and ineptitude are anti-human; but so too is a superlatively efficient government, equipped with all the products of a highly developed technology. ALDOUS HUXLEY, *Tomorrow and Tomorrow and Tomorrow* (1956).

26. If the perpetual oscillation of nations between anarchy and despotism is to be replaced by the steady march of self-restraining freedom, it will be because men will gradually bring themselves to deal with political, as they now deal with scientific questions. THOMAS HENRY HUXLEY, "Science and Culture" (1880).

27. A good government remains the greatest of human blessings, and no nation has ever enjoyed it. WILLIAM RALPH INGE, "The State, Visible and Invisible," *Outspoken Essays: Second Series* (1922).

28. There are no necessary evils in government. Its evils exist only in its abuses. ANDREW JACKSON, veto of the Bank Bill, July 10, 1832.

29. The only orthodox object of the institution of government is to secure the greatest degree of happiness possible to the general mass of those associated under it. THOMAS JEFFERSON, letter to F. A. Van Der Kemp, March 22, 1812.

30. A compassionate government keeps faith with the trust of the people and cherishes the future of their children. Through compassion for the plight of one individual, government fulfills its purpose as the servant of all the people. LYNDON B. JOHNSON, *My Hope for America* (1964).

31. I would not give half a guinea to live under one form of government rather than another. It is of no moment to the happiness of an individual. SAMUEL JOHNSON, quoted in Boswell's *Life of Samuel Johnson*, March 31, 1772.

32. Too often our Washington reflex is to discover a problem and then throw money at it, hoping it will somehow go away. KENNETH B. KEATING, *The New York Times*, Dec. 24, 1961.

33. It is a function of government to invent philosophies to explain the demands of its own convenience. MURRAY KEMPTON, "Academic Pride," *America Comes of Middle Age* (1963).

34. Any system of government will work when everything is going well. It's the system that functions in the pinches that survives. JOHN F. KENNEDY, *Why England Slept* (1940).

35. No government is better than the men who compose it. JOHN F. KENNEDY, campaign address, Wittenberg College Stadium, Springfield, Ohio, Oct. 17, 1960.

36. The basis of effective government is public confidence. JOHN F. KENNEDY, message to Congress on ethical conduct in government, April 27, 1961.

37. No man is good enough to govern another man without that other's consent. ABRAHAM LINCOLN, speech, Oct. 16, 1854.

38. It is safe to assert that no government proper ever had a provision in its organic law for its own termination. ABRAHAM LINCOLN, first Inaugural Address, March 4, 1861.

39. It is perfectly true that that government is best which governs least. It is equally true that that government is best which provides most. WALTER LIPPMANN, "The Red Herring," *A Preface to Politics* (1914).

40. The invisible government [bosses] is malign. But the evil doesn't come from the

fact that it plays horse with the Newtonian theory of the constitution. What is dangerous about it is that we do not see it, cannot use it, and are compelled to submit to it. WALTER LIPPMANN, "Routineer and Inventor," *A Preface to Politics* (1914).

41. Popular government has not yet been proved to guarantee, always and everywhere, good government. WALTER LIPPMANN, *The Public Philosophy* (1955), 1.2.

42. no form of government / matters nearly as much / as the spirit and intelligence / brought to the administration / of any form of government. DON MARQUIS, "archy's newest deal," *Archy Does His Part* (1935).

43. It must be that to govern a nation you need a specific talent and that this may very well exist without general ability. W. SOMERSET MAUGHAM, *The Summing Up* (1938), 1.

44. Virtue alone is not sufficient for the exercise of government; laws alone cannot carry themselves into practice. MENCIUS, *Works* (4th–3rd c. B.C.), 4, tr. Charles A. Wong.

45. It is very easy to accuse a government of imperfection, for all mortal things are full of it. MONTAIGNE, "Of presumption," *Essays* (1580–88), tr. Charles Cotton and W. C. Hazlitt.

46. The art of governing consists in not letting men grow old in their jobs. NAPOLEON I, *Maxims* (1804–15).

47. Society in every state is a blessing, but government, even in its best state, is but a necessary evil; in its worst state an intolerable one. THOMAS PAINE, "On the Origin and Design of Government," *Common Sense* (1776).

48. Society is produced by our wants and government by our wickedness. THOMAS PAINE, "On the Origin and Design of Government," *Common Sense* (1776).

49. The guilt of a government is the crime of a whole country. THOMAS PAINE, *The American Crisis* (1776–83), 12.

50. Governments arise either out of the people or over the people. THOMAS PAINE, *The Rights of Man* (1791), 1.

51. Everybody knows that government never began anything. It is the whole world that thinks and governs. WENDELL PHILLIPS, lecture, "Idols," Boston, Oct. 4, 1859.

52. Governments exist to protect the rights of minorities. The loved and the rich need no protection: they have many friends and few enemies. WENDELL PHILLIPS, speech, Boston, Dec. 21, 1860.

53. Nothing is as dangerous for the state as those who would govern kingdoms with maxims found in books. CARDINAL RICHELIEU, *Political Testament* (1687), 1.8.

54. It is the purpose of the government to see that not only the legitimate interests of the few are protected but that the welfare and rights of the many are conserved. FRANKLIN D. ROOSEVELT, speech, Portland, Ore., Sept. 21, 1932.

55. The body politic, as well as the human body, begins to die as soon as it is born, and carries in itself the causes of its destruction. ROUSSEAU, *The Social Contract* (1762), 3.11, tr. G. D. H. Cole.

56. Government and co-operation are in all things the laws of life; anarchy and competition the laws of death. JOHN RUSKIN, *Unto This Last* (1862), 3.54.

57. In our complex world, there cannot be fruitful initiative without government, but unfortunately there can be government without initiative. BERTRAND RUSSELL, "Control and Initiative," *Authority and the Individual* (1949).

58. Government is the political representative of a natural equilibrium, of custom, of inertia; it is by no means a representative of reason. GEORGE SANTAYANA, *The Life of Reason: Reason in Society* (1905–06), 3.

59. Government among us is certainly not an art, but a fatality. In so far as it is not a matter of mere tradition and routine, it results from contrary purposes and parties pulling against each other in a tug-of-war, for the sake of office or of some immediate reform or relief. GEORGE SANTAYANA, *Dialogues in Limbo* (1925), 6.

60. Government cannot be stronger or more tough-minded than its people. It cannot be more inflexibly committed to the task than they. ADLAI STEVENSON, speech, Chicago, Sept. 29, 1952.

61. Government is at best but an expedient; but most governments are usually, and all governments are sometimes, inexpedient. THOREAU, *Civil Disobedience* (1849).

62. Every central government worships uniformity: uniformity relieves it from inquiry into an infinity of details, which must be attended to if rules have to be adapted to

different men, instead of indiscriminately subjecting all men to the same rule. ALEXIS DE TOCQUEVILLE, *Democracy in America* (1835–39), 2.4.3.

63. Whenever you have an efficient government you have a dictatorship. HARRY S. TRUMAN, lecture, Columbia University, April 28, 1959.

64. That government is not best which best secures mere life and property—there is a more valuable thing—manhood. MARK TWAIN, *Notebook* (1935).

65. The pleasure of governing must certainly be exquisite, if we may judge from the vast numbers who are eager to be concerned with it. VOLTAIRE, "Government," *Philosophical Dictionary* (1764).

66. Governments are best classified by considering who are the "somebodies" they are in fact endeavoring to satisfy. ALFRED NORTH WHITEHEAD, *Adventures in Ideas* (1933), 4.

67. Man is about the same, in the main, whether with despotism, or whether with freedom. WALT WHITMAN, "Democracy in the New World," *Notes Left Over* (1881).

68. Government expands to absorb revenue and then some. TOM WICKER, quoted by Harold Faber in *The New York Times Magazine*, March 17, 1968.

69. The firm basis of government is justice, not pity. WOODROW WILSON, Inaugural Address, March 4, 1912.

70. No government has ever been beneficent when the attitude of government was that it was taking care of the people. The only freedom consists in the people taking care of the government. WOODROW WILSON, address, Sept. 4, 1912.

## 394. GRACE

**See also 370. Gaucherie**

1. Those graces which from their presumed facility encourage all to attempt an imitation of them, are usually the most inimitable. CHARLES CALEB COLTON, *Lacon* (1825), 1.584.

2. Without grace beauty is an unbaited hook. FRENCH PROVERB.

3. Merit is not enough unless supported by grace. BALTASAR GRACIÁN, *The Art of Worldly Wisdom* (1647), 274, tr. Joseph Jacobs.

4. Grace is the absence of everything that indicates pain or difficulty, hesitation or incongruity. WILLIAM HAZLITT, "On Beauty," *The Round Table* (1817).

5. Gracefulness is to the body what understanding is to the mind. LA ROCHEFOUCAULD, *Maxims* (1665), tr. Kenneth Pratt.

6. If we cannot be decent, let us endeavor to be graceful. If we can't be moral, at least we can avoid being vulgar. LANGDON MITCHELL, *The New York Idea* (1907), 2.

## 395. GRAFFITI

1. A white wall is the fool's paper. FRENCH PROVERB.

## 396. GRAMMAR

**See also 521. Language; 1057. Words**

1. Grammar, n. A system of pitfalls thoughtfully prepared for the feet of the self-made man, along the path by which he advances to distinction. AMBROSE BIERCE, *The Devil's Dictionary* (1881–1911).

2. The adjective is the banana peel of the parts of speech. CLIFTON FADIMAN, *Reader's Digest*, September 1956.

3. It is well to remember that grammar is common speech formulated. W. SOMERSET MAUGHAM, *The Summing Up* (1938), 13.

4. Damn the subjunctive. It brings all our writers to shame. MARK TWAIN, *Notebook* (1935).

5. Why care for grammar as long as we are good? ARTEMUS WARD, "Pyrotechny," *Artemus Ward in London* (1872).

6. A writer who can't write in a grammerly manner better shut up shop. ARTEMUS WARD, "Science and Natural History," *Artemus Ward in London* (1872).

7. English usage is sometimes more than mere taste, judgment, and education—sometimes it's sheer luck, like getting across a street. E. B. WHITE, "Shop Talk," *The Second Tree from the Corner* (1954).

## 397. GRATITUDE

**See also 47. Appreciation; 473. Ingratitude; 639. Obligation**

1. Next to ingratitude, the most painful thing to bear is gratitude. HENRY WARD

BEECHER, *Proverbs from Plymouth Pulpit* (1887).

2. God give you pardon from gratitude / and other mild forms of servitude. ROBERT CREELEY, "Song," *For Love* (1962).

3. Be thankful f'r what ye have not, Hinnissy—'tis th' on'y safe rule. FINLEY PETER DUNNE, "Thanksgiving," *Mr. Dooley's Opinions* (1901).

4. Gratefulness is the poor man's payment. ENGLISH PROVERB.

5. When I'm not thanked at all, I'm thanked enough, / I've done my duty, and I've done no more. HENRY FIELDING, *Tom Thumb the Great* (1730), 1.3.

6. Revenge is profitable, gratitude is expensive. EDWARD GIBBON, *Decline and Fall of the Roman Empire* (1776), 11.

7. In the majority of men gratitude is only a veiled desire of receiving greater benefaction. LA ROCHEFOUCAULD, *Maxims* (1665), tr. Kenneth Pratt.

8. We seldom find people ungrateful so long as we are in a position to be beneficial. LA ROCHEFOUCAULD, *Maxims* (1665), tr. Kenneth Pratt.

9. Gratitude is the most exquisite form of courtesy. JACQUES MARITAIN, *Reflections on America* (1958), 17.

10. A grateful mind / By owing owes not, but still pays, at once / Indebted and discharged. MILTON, *Paradise Lost* (1667), 4.55.

11. Evermore thanks, the exchequer of the poor. SHAKESPEARE, *Richard II* (1595–96), 2.3.65.

12. Bees sip honey from flowers and hum their thanks when they leave. / The gaudy butterfly is sure that the flowers owe thanks to him. RABINDRANATH TAGORE, *Stray Birds* (1916), 127.

13. Gratitude is a debt which usually goes on accumulating like blackmail; the more you pay, the more is exacted. MARK TWAIN, *Autobiography* (1924), v. 1, ed. A. B. Paine.

## 398. GREAT AND SMALL

**See also 399. Greatness; 641. Obscurity; 901. Smallness; 1005. Unimportance**

1. You may share the labours of the great, but you will not share the spoil. AESOP, "The Lion's Share," *Fables* (6th c. B.C.?), tr. Joseph Jacobs.

2. When the house of a great one collapses / Many little ones are slain. BERTOLT BRECHT, *The Caucasian Chalk Circle* (1944–45), 1.1, tr. Eric Bentley and Maja Apelman.

3. We find great things are made of little things, / And little things go lessening till at last / Comes God behind them. ROBERT BROWNING, "Mr. Sludge, 'The Medium,'" *Dramatis Personae* (1864).

4. No man is so tall that he need never stretch and none so small that he need never stoop. DANISH PROVERB.

5. A great man stands on God. A small man stands on a great man. EMERSON, *Journals*, 1839.

6. Great engines turn on small pivots. ENGLISH PROVERB.

7. A small leak will sink a great ship. THOMAS FULLER, M.D., *Gnomologia* (1732), 407.

8. The privilege and pleasure / That we treasure beyond measure / Is to run on little errands for the Ministers of State. W. S. GILBERT, *The Gondoliers* (1889), 2.

9. From the height from which the great look down on the world all the rest of mankind seem equal. WILLIAM HAZLITT, "Commonplaces," *The Round Table* (1817), 23.

10. An ant hole may collapse an embankment. JAPANESE PROVERB.

11. Great men too often have greater faults than little men can find room for. WALTER SAVAGE LANDOR, "Diogenes and Plato," *Imaginary Conversations* (1824–53).

12. However big the whale may be, the tiny harpoon can rob him of life. MALAY PROVERB.

13. When a dead tree falls, the woodpeckers share in its death. MALAY PROVERB.

14. The great man is too often all of a piece; it is the little man that is a bundle of contradictory elements. He is inexhaustible. You never come to the end of the surprises he has in store for you. W. SOMERSET MAUGHAM, *The Summing Up* (1938), 2.

15. The herd seek out the great, not for their sake but for their influence; and the

great welcome them out of vanity or need. NAPOLEON I, *Maxims* (1804–15).

16. I will be small in small things, great among great. PINDAR, *Odes* (5th c. B.C.), Pythia 3, tr. Richmond Lattimore.

17. To vilify a great man is the readiest way in which a little man can himself attain greatness. EDGAR ALLAN POE, *Marginalia* (1844–49), 14.

18. If a little tree grows in the shade of a larger tree, it will die small. SENEGALESE PROVERB.

## 399. GREATNESS

See also 398. Great and Small; 416. Heroes and Heroism; 522. Largeness; 641. Obscurity; 1005. Unimportance

1. Men in great places are thrice servants: servants of the sovereign or state, servants of fame, and servants of business. FRANCIS BACON, "Of Great Place," *Essays* (1625).

2. Every man has a house-broken heart except the great man. DJUNA BARNES, *Nightwood* (1937).

3. Great men are but life-sized. Most of them, indeed, are rather short. MAX BEERBOHM, "A Point to Be Remembered by Very Eminent Men," *And Even Now* (1920).

4. All your youth you want to have your greatness taken for granted; when you find it taken for granted, you are unnerved. ELIZABETH BOWEN, *The House in Paris* (1935), 2.2.

5. Be substantially great in thyself, and more than thou appearest unto others. SIR THOMAS BROWNE, *Christian Morals* (1716), 1.

6. He is greatest who is most often in men's good thoughts. SAMUEL BUTLER (d. 1902), "Higgledy-Piggledy," *Note-Books* (1912).

7. All great deeds and all great thoughts have a ridiculous beginning. ALBERT CAMUS, "An Absurd Reasoning," *The Myth of Sisyphus* (1942), tr. Justin O'Brien.

8. Are not our greatest men as good as lost? The men that walk daily among us, warming us, feeding us, walk shrouded in darkness, mere mythic men. THOMAS CARLYLE, *Chartism* (1839), 8.

9. Men worship the shows of great men; the most disbelieve that there is any reality of great men to worship. THOMAS CARLYLE, *On Heroes, Hero-Worship and the Heroic in History* (1841), 3.

10. The loftiest towers rise from the ground. CHINESE PROVERB.

11. Greatness and goodness are not means, but ends. SAMUEL TAYLOR COLERIDGE, "The Good Great Man" (1802).

12. Great men, like comets, are eccentric in their courses, and formed to do extensive good by modes unintelligible to vulgar minds. CHARLES CALEB COLTON, *Lacon* (1825), 1.252.

13. Great offices will have great talents. WILLIAM COWPER, "The Winter Evening," *The Task* (1785), 788.

14. The greatest spirits are capable of the greatest vices as well as of the greatest virtues. DESCARTES, *Discourse on Method* (1639) 1.

15. Desire of greatness is a godlike sin. JOHN DRYDEN, *Absalom and Achitophel* (1681), 1.372.

16. 'Tis a good sign whin people acknowledge that other people ar-re gr-great. It shows self-resthraint. It's far aisier to say no man was gr-reat. FINLEY PETER DUNNE, "Famous Men," *Mr. Dooley On Making a Will* (1919).

17. To be great is to be misunderstood. EMERSON, "Self Reliance," *Essays: First Series* (1941).

18. Let him be great, and love shall follow him. EMERSON, "Spiritual Laws," *Essays: First Series* (1841).

19. When nature removes a great man, people explore the horizon for a successor; but none comes, and none will. His class is extinguished with him. In some other and quite different field, the next man will appear. EMERSON, "Uses of Great Men," *Representative Men* (1850).

20. The measure of a master is his success in bringing all men round to his opinion twenty years later. EMERSON, "Culture," *The Conduct of Life* (1860).

21. No great thing is created suddenly. EPICTETUS, *Discourses* (2nd c.), 1.15, tr. Thomas W. Higginson.

22. Greatness brings no profit to people. / God indeed, when in anger, brings / greater ruin to great men's houses. EURIPIDES, *Medea* (431 B.C.), tr. Rex Warner.

23. I distrust Great Men. They produce a desert of uniformity around them and often

a pool of blood too, and I always feel a little man's pleasure when they come a cropper. E. M. FORSTER, "What I Believe," *Two Cheers for Democracy* (1951).

24. All great expression, which on a superficial survey seems so easy as well as so simple, furnishes after a while, to the faithful observer, its own standard by which to appreciate it. MARGARET FULLER, *Summer on the Lakes* (1844), 1.

25. All greatness affects different minds, each in "its own particular kind," and the variations of testimony mark the truth of feeling. MARGARET FULLER, *Summer on the Lakes* (1844), 1.

26. Great and good are seldom the same man. THOMAS FULLER, M.D., *Gnomologia* (1732), 1752.

27. A great man's failures to understand define him. ANDRÉ GIDE, "Concerning Influence in Literature," *Pretexts* (1903), tr. Angelo P. Bertocci and others.

28. Great minds tend toward banality. It is the noblest effort of individualism. But it implies a sort of modesty, which is so rare that it is scarcely found except in the greatest, or in beggars. ANDRÉ GIDE, "Portraits and Aphorisms," *Pretexts* (1903), tr. Angelo P. Bertocci and others.

29. The privilege of the great is to see catastrophes from a terrace. JEAN GIRAUDOUX, *Tiger at the Gates* (1935), 2.13.

30. To make an epoch in the world, two conditions are manifestly essential—a good head and a great inheritance. GOETHE, quoted in Johann Peter Eckermann's *Conversations with Goethe*, May 2, 1824.

31. Few great men could pass Personnel. PAUL GOODMAN, *Growing Up Absurd* (1960), 7.6.

32. Great men have to be lifted upon the shoulders of the whole world, in order to conceive their great ideas, or perform their great deeds. NATHANIEL HAWTHORNE, *Journals*, May 7, 1850.

33. No man is truly great who is great only in his lifetime. The test of greatness is the page of history. WILLIAM HAZLITT, "The Indian Jugglers," *Table Talk* (1821–22).

34. He who comes up to his own idea of greatness must always have had a very low standard of it in his mind. WILLIAM HAZLITT, "Whether Genius Is Conscious of Its Powers?" *The Plain Speaker* (1826).

35. No really great man ever thought himself so. WILLIAM HAZLITT, "Whether Genius Is Conscious of Its Powers?" *The Plain Speaker* (1826).

36. A great man's greatest good luck is to die at the right time. ERIC HOFFER, *The Passionate State of Mind* (1954), 276.

37. A great man represents a great ganglion in the nerves of society, or, to vary the figure, a strategic point in the campaign of history, and part of his greatness consists in his being *there*. OLIVER WENDELL HOLMES, JR., speech on John Marshall, Feb. 4, 1901.

38. To know the great men dead is compensation for having to live with the mediocre. ELBERT HUBBARD, *The Note Book* (1927).

39. No man was ever great by imitation. SAMUEL JOHNSON, *Rasselas* (1759), 10.

40. He ne'er is crowned / With immortality, who fears to follow / Where airy voices lead. JOHN KEATS, *Endymion* (1817), 2.

41. I would sooner fail than not be among the greatest. JOHN KEATS, letter to James Augustus Hessey, Oct. 8, 1818.

42. To be a great man it is necessary to know how to profit by the whole of our good fortune. LA ROCHEFOUCAULD, *Maxims* (1665), tr. Kenneth Pratt.

43. Great men too make mistakes, and many among them do it so often that one is almost tempted to call them little men. GEORG CHRISTOPH LICHTENBERG, *Aphorisms* (1764–99), tr. J. P. Stern.

44. Lives of great men all remind us / We can make our lives sublime, / And, departing, leave behind us / Footprints on the sands of time. LONGFELLOW, "A Psalm of Life" (1839), 7.

45. Every great man inevitably resents a partner in greatness. LUCAN, *On the Civil War* (1st c.), tr. Robert Graves.

46. Though a tree grow ever so high, the falling leaves return to the root. MALAY PROVERB.

47. Men are like the stars: some generate their own light while others reflect the brilliance they receive. JOSÉ MARTÍ, *Granos de oro: pensamientos seleccionados en las Obras de José Martí* (1942).

48. Because a man can write great works he is none the less a man. W. SOMERSET MAUGHAM, *The Summing Up* (1938), 16.

49. Conceit and presumption have not been any more fatal to the world, than the

waste which comes of great men failing in their hearts to recognise how great they are. JOHN MORLEY, "Byron," *Critical Miscellanies* (1871–1908).

50. In a narrow sphere great men are blunderers. NAPOLEON I, *Maxims* (1804–15).

51. It is the privilege of greatness to confer intense happiness with insignificant gifts. NIETZSCHE, *Human, All Too Human* (1878), 496, tr. Helen Zimmern.

52. A great man does not lose his self-possession when he is afflicted; the ocean is not made muddy by the falling in of its banks. *Panchatantra* (c. 5th c.), 1, tr. Franklin Edgerton.

53. Do not despise the bottom rungs in the ascent to greatness. PUBLILIUS SYRUS, *Moral Sayings* (1st c. B.C.), 579.

54. Greatness is not the effect of which inspiration is the cause. We are all inspired, but we are all not great. NED ROREM, "Four Questions Answered," *Music from Inside Out* (1967).

55. The Great don't innovate, they fertilize seeds planted by lackeys, then leave to others the inhaling of the flowers whose roots they've manured. A deceptive memory may be the key to their originality. NED ROREM, "Random Notes from a Diary," *Music from Inside Out* (1967).

56. All great books contain boring portions, and all great lives have contained uninteresting stretches. BERTRAND RUSSELL, *The Conquest of Happiness* (1930), 4.

57. The loftiest edifices need the deepest foundations. GEORGE SANTAYANA, *The Life of Reason: Reason in Society* (1905–06), 1.

58. A great man need not be virtuous, nor his opinions right, but he must have a firm mind, a distinctive luminous character. GEORGE SANTAYANA, *Winds of Doctrine* (1913).

59. They that stand high have many blasts to shake them. SHAKESPEARE, *Richard III* (1592–93), 1.3.259.

60. Some are born great, some achieve greatness, and some have greatness thrust upon 'em. SHAKESPEARE, *Twelfth Night* (1599–1600), 2.5.157.

61. Great men hallow a whole people, and lift up all who live in their time. SYDNEY SMITH, quoted in Lady S. Holland's *Memoir* (1855), v. 1.7.

62. Nothing is likely about masterpieces, least of all whether there will be any. IGOR STRAVINSKY, *Conversations with Igor Stravinsky* (1959).

63. Great things are accomplished by men who are not conscious of the impotence of man. Such insensitiveness is precious. PAUL VALÉRY, "Fluctuations on Liberty," *Reflections on the World Today* (1931), tr. Francis Scarfe.

64. Great men have all been formed either before academies or independent of them. VOLTAIRE, "Society of London, and Academies," *Philosophical Dictionary* (1764).

65. A man is not as big as his belief in himself; he is as big as the number of persons who believe in him. WOODROW WILSON, speech, Oct. 3, 1912.

66. Masterpieces are not single and solitary births; they are the outcome of many years of thinking in common, of thinking by the body of the people, so that the experience of the mass is behind the single voice. VIRGINIA WOOLF, *A Room of One's Own* (1929), 4.

67. Great men with great truths have seldom had much support from their associates. PHILIP WYLIE, *Generation of Vipers* (1942), 10.

68. None think the great unhappy but the great. EDWARD YOUNG, *Love of Fame* (1728), 1.238.

## 400. GREECE, ANCIENT

**See also 42. Antiquity**

1. The spirit of Greece, passing through and ascending above the world, hath so animated universal nature, that the very rocks and woods, the very torrents and wilds burst forth with it. WALTER SAVAGE LANDOR, "Scipio, Polybius, and Panaetius," *Imaginary Conversations* (1824–53).

2. Except the blind forces of Nature, nothing moves in this world which is not Greek in its origin. SIR HENRY JAMES MAIN, Cambridge Rede Lecture, 1875, *Village Communities in the East and West.*

3. We [Greeks] are lovers of the beautiful, yet simple in our tastes, and we cultivate the mind without loss of manliness. THUCYDIDES, *The Peloponnesian War* (c. 400 B.C.), 2.40, tr. Benjamin Jowett.

## 401. GREED

See also 8. Acquisition; 310. Excess; 589. Misers

1. A covetous man's penny is a stone. ALI IBN-ABI-TALIB, *Sentences* (7th c.), 8, tr. Simon Ockley.

2. It is not greedy to enjoy a good dinner, any more than it is greedy to enjoy a good concert. But I do think there is something greedy about trying to enjoy the dinner and the concert at the same time. G. K. CHESTERTON, "On Pleasure-Seeking," *Generally Speaking* (1928).

3. The avarice of the miser may be termed the grand sepulchre of all his other passions, as they successively decay. CHARLES CALEB COLTON, *Lacon* (1825), 1.24.

4. Avarice is a fine, absorbin' passion, an' manny an ol' fellow is as happy with his arm around his bank account as he was sleigh ridin' with his first girl. FINLEY PETER DUNNE, "On Old Age," *Mr. Dooley On Making a Will* (1919).

5. Want is a growing giant whom the coat of Have was never large enough to cover. EMERSON, "Wealth," *The Conduct of Life* (1860).

6. He is better with a rake than a fork. ENGLISH PROVERB.

7. The belly overreaches the head. FRENCH PROVERB.

8. When all other sins are old, avarice is still young. FRENCH PROVERB.

9. Greed is a bottomless pit which exhausts the person in an endless effort to satisfy the need without ever reaching satisfaction. ERICH FROMM, *Escape from Freedom* (1941), 4.

10. He is not poor that hath not much, but he that craves much. THOMAS FULLER, M.D., *Gnomologia* (1732), 1937.

11. If your desires be endless, your cares and fears will be so too. THOMAS FULLER, M.D., *Gnomologia* (1732), 2803.

12. Riches have made more covetous men than covetousness hath made rich men. THOMAS FULLER, M.D., *Gnomologia* (1732), 4044.

13. Nothing in the world is so incontinent as a man's accursed appetite. HOMER, *Odyssey* (9th c. B.C.), 7, tr. E. V. Rieu.

14. Care clings to wealth: the thirst for more / Grows as our fortunes grow. HORACE, *Odes* (23–c. 15 B.C.), 3.16.

15. Big mouthfuls often choke. ITALIAN PROVERB.

16. Extreme avarice misapprehends itself almost always; there is no passion which more often misses its aim, nor upon which the present has so much influence to the prejudice of the future. LA ROCHEFOUCAULD, *Maxims* (1665), tr. Kenneth Pratt.

17. Avarice is a cursed vice: offer a man enough gold, and he will part with his own small hoard of food, however great his hunger. LUCAN, *On the Civil War* (1st c.), tr. Robert Graves.

18. People who are greedy have extraordinary capacities for waste—they must, they take in too much. NORMAN MAILER, *Miami and the Siege of Chicago* (1968), 2.2.

19. The covetous man fares worse with his passion than the poor, and the jealous man than the cuckold. MONTAIGNE, "Of presumption," *Essays* (1580–88), tr. Charles Cotton and W. C. Hazlitt.

20. I could not possibly count the golddigging ruses of women, / Not if I had ten mouths, not if I had ten tongues. OVID, *The Art of Love* (c. A.D. 8), 1, tr. Rolfe Humphries.

21. Though avarice will prevent a man from being necessitously poor, it generally makes him too timorous to be wealthy. THOMAS PAINE, "Of Monarchy and Hereditary Succession," *Common Sense* (1776).

22. To hazard much to get much has more of avarice than wisdom. WILLIAM PENN, *Some Fruits of Solitude* (1693), 1.247.

23. Avarice is as destitute of what it has, as poverty of what it has not. PUBLILIUS SYRUS, *Moral Sayings* (1st c. B.C.), 1079, tr. Darius Lyman.

24. The greedy man is incontinent with a whole world set before him. SA'DI, *Gulistan* (1258), 8.32, tr. James Ross.

25. For greed all nature is too little. SENECA, *Hercules Oetaeus* (1st c.), 631, tr. Frank Justus Miller.

26. Greed's worst point is its ingratitude. SENECA, *Letters to Lucilius* (1st c.), 73.3, tr. E. Phillips Barker.

27. Though statisticians in our time have never kept the score, Man wants a great deal here below and Woman even more. JAMES THURBER, "The Godfather and His Godchild," *Further Fables for Our Time* (1956).

28. Men hate the individual whom they call avaricious only because nothing can be gained from him. VOLTAIRE, "Avarice," *Philosophical Dictionary* (1764).

29. A poor man's roast and a rich man's death are sniffed far off. *Yiddish Proverbs* (1949), ed. Hanan J. Ayalti.

## GRIEF

See 911. Sorrow

## GROUP

See 151. Company; 205. Crowds; 591. Mob

## 402. GROWTH AND DEVELOPMENT

See also 450. Immaturity; 529. Learning; 567. Maturity; 647. Open-mindedness; 711. Potential; 981. Training

1. Some people are molded by their admirations, others by their hostilities. ELIZABETH BOWEN, *The Death of the Heart* (1938), 2.2.

2. Growth itself contains the germ of happiness. PEARL S. BUCK, "To the Young," *To My Daughters, With Love* (1967).

3. Every one should keep a mental wastepaper basket and the older he grows the more things he will consign to it—torn up to irrecoverable tatters. SAMUEL BUTLER (d. 1902), "Higgledy-Piggledy," *Note-Books* (1912).

4. There are few successful adults who were not first successful children. ALEXANDER CHASE, *Perspectives* (1966).

5. The strongest principle of growth lies in human choice. GEORGE ELIOT, *Daniel Deronda* (1874–76), 6.42.

6. A man's growth is seen in the successive choirs of his friends. EMERSON, "Circles," *Essays: First Series* (1841).

7. Man always dies before he is fully born. ERICH FROMM, *Man for Himself* (1947), 3.

8. A child-like man is not a man whose development has been arrested; on the contrary, he is a man who has given himself a chance of continuing to develop long after most adults have muffled themselves in the cocoon of middle-aged habit and convention. ALDOUS HUXLEY, "Vulgarity in Literature," *Music at Night* (1931).

9. Whatever is formed for long duration arrives slowly to its maturity. SAMUEL JOHNSON, *The Rambler* (1750–52), 169.

10. Just as we outgrow a pair of trousers, we outgrow acquaintances, libraries, principles, etc., at times before they're worn out and at times—and this is the worst of all—before we have new ones. GEORG CHRISTOPH LICHTENBERG, *Aphorisms* (1764–99), tr. F. H. Mautner and H. Hatfield.

11. All growth is a leap in the dark, a spontaneous, unpremeditated act without benefit of experience. HENRY MILLER, "The Absolute Collective," *The Wisdom of the Heart* (1941).

12. Growth is the only evidence of life. JOHN HENRY NEWMAN, *Apologia pro Vita Sua* (1864).

13. He who would learn to fly one day must first learn to stand and walk and run and climb and dance: one cannot fly into flying. NIETZSCHE, "On the Spirit of Gravity," *Thus Spoke Zarathustra* (1883–92), 3, tr. Walter Kaufmann.

14. One must be thrust out of a finished cycle in life, and that leap [is] the most difficult to make—to part with one's faith, one's love, when one would prefer to renew the faith and recreate the passion. ANAÏS NIN, *The Diary of Anaïs Nin*, November 1932.

15. Stretch your foot to the length of your blanket. PERSIAN PROVERB.

16. Not to go back is somewhat to advance, / And men must walk, at least, before they dance. ALEXANDER POPE, *Epilogue to the Satires* (1738), 1.1.53.

17. Some people seem as if they can never have been children, and others seem as if they could never be anything else. GEORGE DENNISON PRENTICE, *Prenticeana* (1860).

18. There is no fruit which is not bitter before it is ripe. PUBLILIUS SYRUS, *Moral Sayings* (1st c. B.C.), 561, tr. Darius Lyman.

19. Life is cut to allow for growth . . . one may vigorously put on weight before one fills it out entirely. RAINER MARIA RILKE, letter to Alfred Walther von Heymel, Oct. 12, 1941, in *Wartime Letters*, tr. M. D. Herter Norton.

20. No single event can awaken within us a stranger totally unknown to us. To live is to be slowly born. SAINT-EXUPÉRY, *Flight to Arras* (1942), 8, tr. Lewis Galantière.

21. Manhood and sagacity ripen of themselves; it suffices not to repress or distort them. GEORGE SANTAYANA, *Character and Opinion in the United States* (1921), 2.

22. It is the highest creatures who take the longest to mature, and are the most helpless during their immaturity. GEORGE BERNARD SHAW, *Back to Methuselah* (1921), 3.

23. Every man's road in life is marked by the graves of his personal likings. ALEXANDER SMITH, "On the Importance of a Man to Himself," *Dreamthorp* (1863).

24. Man is a born child, his power is the power of growth. RABINDRANATH TAGORE, *Stray Birds* (1916), 25.

25. A road that does not lead to other roads always has to be retraced, unless the traveller chooses to rust at the end of it. TEHYI HSIEH, *Chinese Epigrams Inside Out and Proverbs* (1948), 144.

26. The shell must break before the bird can fly. ALFRED, LORD TENNYSON, "The Ancient Sage" (1885).

27. The Child is father of the Man. WILLIAM WORDSWORTH, "My Heart Leaps Up When I Behold" (1802).

## GUESTS

**See 426. Hospitality**

## 403. GUILT

**See also 171. Conscience; 841. Scapegoat; 886. Shame**

1. Everyone in daily life carries such a heavy, mixed burden on his own conscience that he is reluctant to penalize those who have been caught. BROOKS ATKINSON, "February 28," *Once Around the Sun* (1951).

2. The wicked flee when no man pursueth; but the righteous are bold as a lion. *Bible*, Proverbs 28:1.

3. There may be responsible persons, but there are no guilty ones. ALBERT CAMUS, "The Absurd Man," *The Myth of Sisyphus* (1942), tr. Justin O'Brien.

4. We are all exceptional cases . . . . Each man insists on being innocent, even if it means accusing the whole human race, and heaven. ALBERT CAMUS, *The Fall* (1956).

5. The guilty think all talk is of themselves. CHAUCER, "The Canon's Yeoman's Prologue," *The Canterbury Tales* (c. 1387–1400), tr. Nevill Coghill.

6. Guilt is ever at a loss, and confusion waits upon it; when innocence and bold truth are always ready for expression. WILLIAM CONGREVE, *The Double-Dealer* (1694), 4.5.

7. Guilt always hurries towards its complement, punishment: only there does its satisfaction lie. LAWRENCE DURRELL, *Justine* (1957), 3.

8. He declares himself guilty who justifies himself before accusation. THOMAS FULLER, M.D., *Gnomologia* (1732), 1833.

9. They who feel guilty are afraid, and they who are afraid somehow feel guilty. To the onlooker, too, the fearful seem guilty. ERIC HOFFER, *The Passionate State of Mind* (1954), 183.

10. Where guilt is, rage and courage doth abound. BEN JONSON, *Sejanus His Fall* (1602), 2.2.

11. This is his first punishment, that by the verdict of his own heart no guilty man is acquitted. JUVENAL, *Satires* (c. 100), 13.2.

12. We have no choice but to be guilty. / God is unthinkable if we are innocent. ARCHIBALD MAC LEISH, *JB* (1958), 8.

13. Without guilt / What is a man? An animal, isn't he? / A wolf forgiven at his meat, / A beetle innocent in his copulation. ARCHIBALD MAC LEISH, *JB* (1958), 9.

14. There is a sort of man who pays no attention to his good actions, but is tormented by his bad ones. This is the type that most often writes about himself. W. SOMERSET MAUGHAM, *The Summing Up* (1938), 4.

15. Each of us when he appears before his fellows is clothed in a certain dignity. But every man knows what unconfessable things pass within the secrecy of his own heart. LUIGI PIRANDELLO, *Six Characters in Search of an Author* (1921), 1, tr. Edward Storer.

16. How unhappy is he who cannot forgive himself. PUBLILIUS SYRUS, *Moral Sayings* (1st c. B.C.), 729, tr. Darius Lyman.

17. It is only too easy to compel a sensitive human being to feel guilty about anything. MORTON IRVING SEIDEN, *The Paradox of Hate: A Study in Ritual Murder* (1967), 13.

18. Suspicion always haunts the guilty

mind; / The thief doth fear each bush an officer. SHAKESPEARE, *3 Henry VI* (1590–91), 5.4.11.

19. So full of artless jealousy is guilt / It spills itself in fearing to be spilt. SHAKESPEARE, *Hamlet* (1600), 4.5.19.

20. To deny all is to confess all. SPANISH PROVERB.

21. Nothing more unqualifies a man to act with prudence than a misfortune that is attended with shame and guilt. JONATHAN SWIFT, *Thoughts on Various Subjects* (1711).

# H

## 404. HABIT

See also 210. Custom; 822. Routine

1. To learn new habits is everything, for it is to reach the substance of life. Life is but a tissue of habits. HENRI FRÉDÉRIC AMIEL, *Journal*, Dec. 30, 1850, tr. Mrs. Humphry Ward.

2. Habit, n. A shackle for the free. AMBROSE BIERCE, *The Devil's Dictionary* (1881–1911).

3. Habit is not mere subjugation, it is a tender tie; when one remembers habit it seems to have been happiness. ELIZABETH BOWEN, *The Death of the Heart* (1938), 2.2.

4. Habit will reconcile us to everything but change. CHARLES CALEB COLTON, *Lacon* (1825), 1.558.

5. The evolution from happiness to habit is one of death's best weapons. JULIO CORTÁZAR, *The Winners* (1960), 14, tr. Elaine Kerrigan.

6. Man like every other animal is by nature indolent. If nothing spurs him on, then he will hardly think, and will behave from habit like an automaton. EINSTEIN, *Out of My Later Years* (1950), 24.

7. Habit, my friend, is practice long pursued, / That at the last becomes the man himself. EVENUS (5th c. B.C.), quoted in Aristotle's *Nicomachean Ethics* (4th c. B.C.), 7.10, tr. J. A. K. Thomson.

8. An old dog can't alter his way of barking. THOMAS FULLER, M.D., *Gnomologia* (1732), 643.

9. It is unpleasant to miss even the most trifling thing to which we have been accustomed. GOETHE, *Elective Affinities* (1809), 17.

10. Wise living consists perhaps less in acquiring good habits than in acquiring as few habits as possible. ERIC HOFFER, *The Passionate State of Mind* (1954), 265.

11. Habituation is a falling asleep or fatiguing of the sense of time; which explains why young years pass slowly, while later life flings itself faster and faster upon its course. THOMAS MANN, *The Magic Mountain* (1924), 4.2, tr. H. T. Lowe-Porter.

12. Habit creates the appearance of justice; progress has no greater enemy than habit. JOSÉ MARTÍ, *Granos de oro: pensamientos seleccionados en las Obras de José Martí* (1942).

13. A man's habit clings / And he will wear tomorrow what today he wears. EDNA ST. VINCENT MILLAY, untitled poem, *Mine the Harvest* (1954).

14. Ill habits gather by unseen degrees,— / As brooks make rivers, rivers run to seas. OVID, *Metamorphoses* (c. A.D. 8) 15.155, tr. John Dryden.

15. Habit is a second nature which prevents us from knowing the first, of which it has neither the cruelties nor the enchantments. MARCEL PROUST, *Remembrance of Things Past: Cities of the Plain* (1913–27).

16. It is not in novelty but in habit that we find the greatest pleasure. RAYMOND RADIGUET, *Le Diable au corps* (1923).

17. Habit is stronger than reason. GEORGE SANTAYANA, *Interpretations of Poetry and Religion* (1900).

18. Laws are never as effective as habits. ADLAI STEVENSON, speech, New York City, Aug. 28, 1952.

19. Habit is habit, and not to be flung out of the window by any man, but coaxed downstairs a step at a time. MARK TWAIN, "Pudd'nhead Wilson's Calendar," *Pudd'nhead Wilson* (1894), 6.

## 405. HAIR

1. There is not so variable a thing in nature as a lady's headdress: within my own memory I have known it rise and fall above thirty degrees. JOSEPH ADDISON, *The Spectator* (1711–12), 98.

2. A haircut is a metaphysical operation. JULIO CORTÁZAR, *The Winners* (1960), 33, tr. Elaine Kerrigan.

3. 'Tis not the beard that makes the philosopher. THOMAS FULLER, M.D., *Gnomologia* (1732), 5102.

4. Fair tresses man's imperial race insnare, / And beauty draws us with a single hair. ALEXANDER POPE, *The Rape of the Lock* (1712), 2.27.

## 406. HANDSHAKE

1. I hate the giving of the hand unless the whole man accompanies it. EMERSON, *Journals*, 1839.

## 407. HAPPINESS

**See also 183. Contentment; 276. Ecstasy; 698. Pleasure; 744. Prosperity; 1004. Unhappiness**

1. True happiness is of a retired nature, and an enemy to pomp and noise; it arises, in the first place, from the enjoyment of one's self, and, in the next, from the friendship and conversation of a few select companions. JOSEPH ADDISON, *The Spectator* (1711–12), 15.

2. Gladness of heart is the life of man, and the rejoicing of a man is length of days. *Apocrypha*, Ecclesiasticus 30:22.

3. Happiness is an expression of the soul in considered actions. ARISTOTLE, *Nicomachean Ethics* (4th c. B.C.), 1.8, tr. J. A. K. Thomson.

4. Happiness depends upon ourselves. ARISTOTLE, *Nicomachean Ethics* (4th c. B.C.), 1.9, tr. J. A. K. Thomson.

5. Different men seek after happiness in different ways and by different means, and so make for themselves different modes of life and forms of government. ARISTOTLE, *Politics* (4th c. B.C.), 7.8, tr. Benjamin Jowett.

6. Indeed, man wishes to be happy even when he so lives as to make happiness impossible. ST. AUGUSTINE, *The City of God* (426), 14.

7. Happy men are grave. They carry their happiness cautiously, as they would a glass filled to the brim which the slightest movement could cause to spill over, or break. JULES BARBEY D'AUREVILLY, "Le Bonheur dans le crime," *Les Diaboliques* (1874).

8. In this world, full often, our joys are only the tender shadows which our sorrows cast. HENRY WARD BEECHER, *Proverbs from Plymouth Pulpit* (1887).

9. The greatest happiness of the greatest number is the foundation of morals and legislation. JEREMY BENTHAM, "Elogia," *Commonplace Books* (1781–85).

10. Joy is hard for being pure and delicate, but no less hard for having its feet on the ground. It is bliss without otherworldliness. It lies tantalizingly in between the extremes of beatitude and bestiality which are increasingly the postulates of our world. ERIC BENTLEY, introduction to *Naked Masks: Five Plays by Luigi Pirandello* (1952).

11. When we are not rich enough to be able to purchase happiness, we must not approach too near and gaze on it in shop windows. TRISTAN BERNARD, *Le Danseur inconnu* (1907).

12. The bird of paradise alights only upon the hand that does not grasp. JOHN BERRY, *Flight of White Crows* (1961).

13. He that is of a merry heart hath a continual feast. *Bible*, Proverbs 15:15.

14. A merry heart doeth good like a medicine. *Bible*, Proverbs 17:22.

15. Happiness, n. An agreeable sensation arising from contemplating the misery of another. AMBROSE BIERCE, *The Devil's Dictionary* (1881–1911).

16. He who binds to himself a joy / Does the winged life destroy; / But he who kisses the joy as it flies / Lives in eternity's sun rise. WILLIAM BLAKE, "Eternity" (1793–99).

17. Whose happiness is so firmly established that he has no quarrel from any side with his estate of life? BOETHIUS, *The Consolation of Philosophy* (A.D. 524), 2, tr. W. V. Cooper.

18. The right to happiness is fundamental: / Men live so little time and die alone. BERTOLT BRECHT, *The Threepenny Opera* (1928), 1.3, tr. Desmond Vesey and Eric Bentley.

19. What's a joy to the one is a nightmare to the other. / That's how it is today, that's how it'll be forever. BERTOLT BRECHT, *Salzburg Dance of Death* (1963), 5, tr. Eric Bentley.

20. All who joy would win / Must share it,—Happiness was born a Twin. BYRON, *Don Juan* (1819–24), 2.172.

21. One moment may with bliss repay / Unnumbered hours of pain. THOMAS CAMPBELL, "The Ritter Bann" (1824).

22. To be happy, we must not be too concerned with others. ALBERT CAMUS, *The Fall* (1956).

23. You are forgiven for your happiness and your successes only if you generously consent to share them. ALBERT CAMUS, *The Fall* (1956).

24. It seldom happens that any felicity comes so pure as not to be tempered and allayed by some mixture of sorrow. CERVANTES, *Don Quixote* (1605–15), 1.4.14, tr. Peter Motteux and John Ozell.

25. Happiness is like a sunbeam, which the least shadow intercepts. CHINESE PROVERB.

26. Can you learn to live? Yes, if you are not happy. There is no virtue in felicity. COLETTE, "Literary Apprenticeship: 'Claudine,'" *Earthly Paradise* (1966), 2, ed. Robert Phelps.

27. Happiness, that grand mistress of the ceremonies in the dance of life, impels us through all its mazes and meanderings, but leads none of us by the same route. CHARLES CALEB COLTON, *Lacon* (1825), 2.109.

28. Happiness lies in the fulfillment of the spirit through the body. CYRIL CONNOLLY, *The Unquiet Grave* (1945), 1.

29. Happiness depends, as Nature shows, / Less on exterior things than most suppose. WILLIAM COWPER, *Table Talk* (1782), 246.

30. Illusory joy is often worth more than genuine sorrow. DESCARTES, *Traité des passions de l'âme* (1650).

31. Eden is that old-fashioned House / We dwell in every day / Without suspecting our abode / Until we drive away. EMILY DICKINSON, *Poems* (c. 1862–86).

32. True joy is the earnest which we have of heaven, it is the treasure of the soul, and therefore should be laid in a safe place, and nothing in this world is safe to place it in. JOHN DONNE, *Sermons*, No. 28, (1624–25?).

33. Happiness does not lie in happiness, but in the achievement of it. DOSTOEVSKY, *A Diary of a Writer* (1876), 3, January.

34. Present joys are more to flesh and blood, / Than a dull prospect of a distant good. JOHN DRYDEN, *The Hind and the Panther* (1687), 11.1658.

35. To fill the hour,—that is happiness; to fill the hour, and leave no crevice for a repentance or an approval. EMERSON, "Experience," *Essays: Second Series* (1844).

36. It is impossible to live a pleasant life without living wisely and well and justly, and it is impossible to live wisely and well and justly without living pleasantly. EPICURUS (3rd c. B.C.), quoted in Diogenes Laertius' *Lives and Opinions of Eminent Philosophers* (3rd c. A.D.), tr. R. D. Hicks.

37. Of mortals there is no one who is happy. / If wealth flows in upon one, one may be perhaps / Luckier than one's neighbor, but still not happy. EURIPIDES, *Medea* (431 B.C.), tr. Rex Warner.

38. Happiness is brief. / It will not stay. / God batters at its sails. EURIPIDES, *Orestes* (408 B.C.), tr. William Arrowsmith.

39. These kind of hair-breadth missings of happiness look like the insults of Fortune. HENRY FIELDING, *Tom Jones* (1749), 13.2.

40. A great obstacle to happiness is to anticipate too great a happiness. FONTENELLE, *Du Bonheur* (1687).

41. Human felicity is produced not so much by great pieces of good fortune that seldom happen as by little advantages that occur every day. BENJAMIN FRANKLIN, *Autobiography* (1791), 2.

42. What we call happiness in the strictest sense comes from the (preferably sudden) satisfaction of needs which have been dammed up to a high degree. SIGMUND FREUD, *Civilization and Its Discontents* (1930), 2, tr. James Strachey.

43. Modern man's happiness consists in the thrill of looking at the shop windows, and in buying all that he can afford to buy, either for cash or on installments. ERICH FROMM, *The Art of Loving* (1956), 1.

44. Happiness makes up in height for what it lacks in length. ROBERT FROST, poem title (1942).

45. He is happy that knoweth not himself to be otherwise. THOMAS FULLER, M.D., *Gnomologia* (1732), 1918.

46. No man can be happy without a friend, nor be sure of his friend till he is unhappy. THOMAS FULLER, M.D., *Gnomologia* (1732), 3593.

47. Your joy is your sorrow unmasked. / And the selfsame well from which your laughter rises was oftentimes filled with your tears. KAHLIL GIBRAN, "On Joy and

Sorrow," *The Prophet* (1923).

48. Nothing is more fatal to happiness than the remembrance of happiness. ANDRÉ GIDE, *The Immoralist* (1902), 1.8, tr. Dorothy Bussy.

49. I have the happiness of the passing moment, and what more can mortal ask? GEORGE GISSING, "Spring," *The Private Papers of Henry Ryecroft* (1903).

50. [Happiness] always looks small while you hold it in your hands, but let it go, and you learn at once how big and precious it is. MAXIM GORKY, *The Zykovs* (1914), 4.

51. The happy man's without a shirt. JOHN HEYWOOD, *Be Merry Friends* (16th c.).

52. The search for happiness is one of the chief sources of unhappiness. ERIC HOFFER, *The Passionate State of Mind* (1954), 280.

53. One can bear grief, but it takes two to be glad. ELBERT HUBBARD, *The Note Book* (1927).

54. Happiness is a thing of gravity. It seeks for hearts of bronze, and carves itself there slowly; pleasure startles it away by tossing flowers to it. Joy's smile is much more close to tears than it is to laughter. VICTOR HUGO, *Hernani* (1830), 5.3.

55. Universal happiness keeps the wheels steadily turning; truth and beauty can't. ALDOUS HUXLEY, *Brave New World* (1932).

56. It is neither wealth nor splendor, but tranquility and occupation, which give happiness. THOMAS JEFFERSON, letter to Mrs. A. S. Marks, 1788.

57. Happiness is enjoyed only in proportion as it is known; and such is the state or folly of man, that it is known only by experience of its contrary. SAMUEL JOHNSON, *The Adventurer* (1753), 67.

58. We are long before we are convinced that happiness is never to be found, and each believes it possessed by others, to keep alive the hope of obtaining it for himself. SAMUEL JOHNSON, *Rasselas* (1759), 16.

59. A peasant and a philosopher may be equally satisfied, but not equally happy. Happiness consists in the multiplicity of agreeable consciousness. SAMUEL JOHNSON, quoted in Boswell's *Life of Samuel Johnson*, February 1766.

60. Happiness is composed of misfortunes avoided. ALPHONSE KARR, *Les Guêpes*, January 1842.

61. Wherein lies happiness? In that which becks / Our ready minds to fellowship divine, / A fellowship with essence; till we shine, / Full alchemized, and free of space. Behold / The clear religion of heaven! JOHN KEATS, *Endymion* (1817), 1.777.

62. No matter how dull, or how mean, or how wise a man is, he feels that happiness is his indisputable right. HELEN KELLER, *Optimism* (1903), 1.

63. When one door of happiness closes, another opens; but often we look so long at the closed door that we do not see the one which has been opened for us. HELEN KELLER, *We Bereaved* (1929).

64. Happiness is itself a kind of gratitude. JOSEPH WOOD KRUTCH, "October," *The Twelve Seasons* (1949).

65. What is good cheer / Which death threats can disrupt? LA FONTAINE, "The Town Rat and the Country Rat," *Fables* (1668–94), tr. Marianne Moore.

66. We are never so happy nor so unhappy as we imagine. LA ROCHEFOUCAULD, *Maxims* (1665), tr. Kenneth Pratt.

67. Happiness is in the taste, and not in the things. LA ROCHEFOUCAULD, *Maxims* (1665), tr. Kenneth Pratt.

68. When you jump for joy, beware that no one moves the ground from beneath your feet. STANISLAW LEC, *Unkempt Thoughts* (1962), tr. Jacek Galazka.

69. I am happy and content because I think I am. ALAIN-RENÉ LESAGE, *Histoire de Gil Blas de Santillane* (1715–35), 7.7.

70. Happiness, to some, elation; / Is, to others, mere stagnation. / Days of passive somnolence, / At its wildest, indolence. AMY LOWELL, "Happiness," *Sword Blades and Poppy Seeds* (1914).

71. Happiness to me is wine, / Effervescent, superfine. / Full of tang and fiery pleasure, / Far too hot to leave me leisure / For a single thought beyond it. AMY LOWELL, "Happiness," *Sword Blades and Poppy Seeds* (1914).

72. We possess only the happiness we are able to understand. MAURICE MAETERLINCK, *Wisdom and Destiny* (1898), 13.

73. The joy that is dead weighs heavy, and bids fair to crush us, if we cause it to be with us for ever. MAURICE MAETERLINCK, *Wisdom and Destiny* (1898), 101, tr. Alfred Sutro.

74. Happiness is fun and food / Kodachromed for later view. MARYA MANNES,

"Controverse," *But Will It Sell?* (1955–64).

75. A man's happiness,—to do the things proper to man. MARCUS AURELIUS, *Meditations* (2nd c.), 8.26, tr. Morris Hickey Morgan.

76. it is better to be happy / for a moment / and be burned up with beauty / than to live a long time / and be bored all the while. DON MARQUIS, "the lesson of the moth," *Archy and Mehitabel* (1927).

77. Unquestionably, it is possible to do without happiness; it is done involuntarily by nineteen-twentieths of mankind. JOHN STUART MILL, *Utilitarianism* (1863), 2.

78. Ask yourself whether you are happy, and you cease to be so. JOHN STUART MILL, *Autobiography* (1873), 2.

79. That thou art happy, owe to God; / That thou continuest such, owe to thyself, / That is, to thy obedience. MILTON, *Paradise Lost* (1667), 5.520.

80. One cannot but mistrust a prospect of felicity: one must enjoy it before one can believe in it. MOLIÈRE, *Tartuffe* (1664), 4, tr. John Wood.

81. There is some shadow of delight and delicacy which smiles upon and flatters us even in the very lap of melancholy. MONTAIGNE, "That we taste nothing pure," *Essays* (1580–88), tr. Charles Cotton and W. C. Hazlitt.

82. We should consider every day lost on which we have not danced at least once. And we should call every truth false which was not accompanied by at least one laugh. NIETZSCHE, "On Old and New Tablets," *Thus Spoke Zarathustra* (1883–92), 3, tr. Walter Kaufmann.

83. There are many roads / to happiness, if the gods assent. PINDAR, *Odes* (5th c. B.C.), Olympia 8, tr. Richmond Lattimore.

84. When [man] is happy, he takes his happiness as it comes and doesn't analyze it, just as if happiness were his right. LUIGI PIRANDELLO, *Six Characters in Search of an Author* (1921), 3, tr. Edward Storer.

85. Man's real life is happy, chiefly because he is ever expecting that it soon will be so. EDGAR ALLAN POE, *Marginalia* (1844–49), 2.

86. No man is happy who does not think himself so. PUBLILIUS SYRUS, *Moral Sayings* (1st c. B.C.), 584, tr. Darius Lyman.

87. The happy man is not he who seems thus to others, but who seems thus to himself. PUBLILIUS SYRUS, *Moral Sayings* (1st c. B.C.), 1010, tr. Darius Lyman.

88. It is not enough to be happy, it is also necessary that others not be. JULES RENARD, *Journal* (1887–1910).

89. Happiness is indeed a Eurydice, vanishing as soon as gazed upon. It can exist only in *acceptance*, and succumbs as soon as it is laid claim to. DENIS DE ROUGEMONT, *Love in the Western World* (1939), 7.4, tr. Montgomery Belgion.

90. The happiest is he who suffers the least pain; the most miserable, he who enjoys the least pleasure. ROUSSEAU, *Émile* (1762), 2.

91. The happiness which is lacking makes one think even the happiness one has unbearable. JOSEPH ROUX, *Meditations of a Parish Priest* (1886), 5.37, tr. Isabel F. Hapgood.

92. Most people ask for happiness on condition. Happiness can only be felt if you don't set any condition. ARTUR RUBINSTEIN, news reports, Feb. 5, 1956.

93. Man needs, for his happiness, not only the enjoyment of this or that, but hope and enterprise and change. BERTRAND RUSSELL, "Philosophy and Politics," *Unpopular Essays* (1950).

94. Happiness is the only sanction of life; where happiness fails, existence remains a mad lamentable experiment. GEORGE SANTAYANA, *The Life of Reason: Reason in Common Sense* (1905–06), 10.

95. A string of excited, fugitive, miscellaneous pleasures is not happiness; happiness resides in imaginative reflection and judgment, when the *picture* of one's life, or of human life, as it truly has been or is, satisfies the will, and is gladly accepted. GEORGE SANTAYANA, *Persons and Places: The Middle Span* (1945), 1.

96. The greatest happiness you can have is knowing that you do not necessarily require happiness. WILLIAM SAROYAN, news summaries, Dec. 16, 1957.

97. Happiness of any given life is to be measured, not by its joys and pleasures, but by the extent to which it has been free from suffering—from positive evil. SCHOPENHAUER, "On the Sufferings of the World," *Parerga and Paralipomena* (1851), tr. T. Bailey Saunders.

98. Unhappy is the man, though he rule the world, who doesn't consider himself su-

premely blest. SENECA, *Letters to Lucilius* (1st c.), 9.21, tr. E. Phillips Barker.

99. Silence is the perfectest herald of joy. I were but little happy if I could say how much. SHAKESPEARE, *Much Ado About Nothing* (1598–99), 2.1.316.

100. How bitter a thing it is to look into happiness through another man's eyes! SHAKESPEARE, *As You Like It* (1599–1600), 5.2.47.

101. A merry heart goes all the day, / Your sad tires in a mile-a. SHAKESPEARE, *The Winter's Tale* (1610–11), 4.3.134.

102. We have no more right to consume happiness without producing it than to consume wealth without producing it. GEORGE BERNARD SHAW, *Candida* (1903), 1.

103. It is God's giving if we laugh or weep. SOPHOCLES, *Ajax* (c. 447 B.C.), tr. John Moore.

104. Our happiness depends / on wisdom all the way. SOPHOCLES, *Antigone* (442–41 B.C.), tr. Elizabeth Wyckoff.

105. We live in an ascending scale when we live happily, one thing leading to another in an endless series. ROBERT LOUIS STEVENSON, "El Dorado," *Virginibus Puerisque* (1881).

106. I find my joy of living in the fierce and ruthless battles of life, and my pleasure comes from learning something. AUGUST STRINDBERG, preface to *Miss Julie* (1888).

107. So long as we can lose any happiness, we possess some. BOOTH TARKINGTON, *Looking Forward to the Great Adventure* (1926).

108. Those undeserved joys which come uncalled and make us more pleased than grateful are they that sing. THOREAU, *Journal*, Feb. 28, 1842.

109. A wise man sings his joy in the closet of his heart. TIBULLUS, *Elegies* (1st c. B.C.), 3.19, tr. Hubert Creekmore.

110. Every man's happiness is built on the unhappiness of another. IVAN TURGENEV, *On the Eve* (1860), 33, tr. Constance Garnett.

111. There are people who can do all fine and heroic things but one—keep from telling their happiness to the unhappy. MARK TWAIN, *Notebook* (1935).

112. The satisfied, the happy, do not love; they fall asleep in habit, near neighbor to annihilation. MIGUEL DE UNAMUNO, "Faith, Hope, and Charity," *Tragic Sense of Life* (1913), tr. J. E. Crawford Flitch.

## HARM

See 474. Injury

## 408. HARMONY

See also 654. Order; 742. Proportion

1. How much finer things are in composition than alone. EMERSON, *Journals*, 1833.

2. The hidden harmony is better than the obvious. HERACLITUS, *Fragments* (c. 500 B.C.), 116, tr. Philip Wheelwright.

3. It is indeed from the experience of beauty and happiness, from the occasional harmony between our nature and our environment, that we draw our conception of the divine life. GEORGE SANTAYANA, introduction, *The Sense of Beauty* (1896).

4. The movement of life has its rest in its own music. RABINDRANATH TAGORE, *Stray Birds* (1916), 227.

5. Harmony would lose its attractiveness if it did not have a background of discord. TEHYI HSIEH, *Chinese Epigrams Inside Out and Proverbs* (1948), 292.

## 409. HASTE

See also 10. Activity; 454. Impatience; 900. Slowness; 919. Speed

1. We can outrun the wind and the storm, but we cannot outrun the demon of Hurry. JOHN BURROUGHS, *Indoor Studies* (1889).

2. Ther n' is no werkman whatever he be / That may both werken wel and hastily. CHAUCER, "The Merchant's Tale," *The Canterbury Tales* (1387–1400), 585, ed. Thomas Tyrwhitt.

3. Whoever is in a hurry shows that the thing he is about is too big for him. LORD CHESTERFIELD, *Letters to His Son*, Aug. 10, 1749.

4. One of the great disadvantages of hurry is that it takes such a long time. G. K. CHESTERTON, "The Case for the Ephemeral," *All Things Considered* (1908).

5. Desire to have things done quickly prevents their being done thoroughly. CONFUCIUS, *Analects* (6th c. B.C.), 13.17, tr. James Legge.

6. Do nothing hastily but catching of

fleas. THOMAS FULLER, M.D., *Gnomologia* (1732), 1309.

7. People in a hurry cannot think, cannot grow, nor can they decay. They are preserved in a state of perpetual puerility. ERIC HOFFER, *The Passionate State of Mind* (1954), 172.

8. The greatest assassin of life is haste, the desire to reach things before the right time which means overreaching them. JUAN RAMÓN JIMÉNEZ, "Heroic Reason," *Selected Writings* (1957), tr. H. R. Hays.

9. One of the most pernicious effects of haste is obscurity. SAMUEL JOHNSON, *The Rambler* (1750–52), 169.

10. Along with being forever on the move, one is forever in a hurry, leaving things inadvertently behind—friend or fishing tackle, old raincoat or old allegiance. LOUIS KRONENBERGER, "Reflections and Complaints of Late Middle Age," *The Cart and the Horse* (1964), 3.

11. Nothing can be done at once hastily and prudently. PUBLILIUS SYRUS, *Moral Sayings* (1st c. B.C.), 557, tr. Darius Lyman.

12. Whatever is produced in haste goes hastily to waste. SA'DI, *Gulistan* (1258), 8.36, tr. James Ross.

13. Wisely, and slow. They stumble that run fast. SHAKESPEARE, *Romeo and Juliet* (1594–95), 2.3.94.

14. Too swift arrives as tardy as too slow. SHAKESPEARE, *Romeo and Juliet* (1594–95), 2.6.15.

15. Hurry, hurry has no blessing. SWAHILI PROVERB.

## 410. HATRED

**See also 253. Dislike; 286. Enemies; 548. Love; 551. Love and Hate; 588. Misanthropy**

1. All mourning fears its end and thinks with terror of the day when its pain will subside. In the same way, hate fears above all to be delivered of itself. Once more, it grips its tail between its teeth. HERVÉ BAZIN, *La Mort du petit cheval*, 19.

2. Even hatred of vileness / Distorts a man's features. BERTOLT BRECHT, "To Posterity" (1938), tr. Michael Hamburger.

3. Now Hatred is by far the longest pleasure; / Men love in haste, but they detest at leisure. BYRON, *Don Juan* (1819–24), 13.6.

4. The price of hating other human beings is loving oneself less. ELDRIDGE CLEAVER, "On Becoming," *Soul on Ice* (1968).

5. Pity is a thing often avowed, seldom felt; hatred is a thing often felt, seldom avowed. CHARLES CALEB COLTON, *Lacon* (1825), 1.478.

6. Hate is the consequence of fear; we fear something before we hate it; a child who fears noises becomes a man who hates noise. CYRIL CONNOLLY, *The Unquiet Grave* (1945), 3.

7. The fires of hate, compressed within the heart, / Burn fiercer and will break at last in flame. CORNEILLE, *The Cid* (1636), 2.3, tr. Paul Landis.

8. Pure good soon grows insipid, wants variety and spirit. Pain is a bitter-sweet, which never surfeits. Love turns, with a little indulgence, to indifference or disgust; hatred alone is immortal. WILLIAM HAZLITT, "On the Pleasure of Hating," *The Plain Speaker* (1826).

9. The pleasure of hating, like a poisonous mineral, eats into the heart of religion, and turns it to rankling spleen and bigotry; it makes patriotism an excuse for carrying fire, pestilence, and famine into other lands: it leaves to virtue nothing but the spirit of censoriousness. WILLIAM HAZLITT, "On the Pleasure of Hating," *The Plain Speaker* (1826).

10. If you hate a person, you hate something in him that is part of yourself. What isn't part of ourselves doesn't disturb us. HERMANN HESSE, *Demian* (1919), 6, tr. Michael Roloff and Michael Lebeck.

11. To wrong those we hate is to add fuel to our hatred. Conversely, to treat an enemy with magnanimity is to blunt our hatred for him. ERIC HOFFER, *The True Believer* (1951), 3.14.70.

12. The man that is once hated, both his good and his evil deeds oppress him. BEN JONSON, "Explorata," *Timber* (1640).

13. Hatred is so lasting and stubborn, that reconciliation on a sickbed certainly forebodes death. LA BRUYÈRE, *Characters* (1688), 11.108, tr. Henri Van Laun.

14. When our hatred is too keen it puts us beneath those whom we hate. LA ROCHEFOUCAULD, *Maxims* (1665), tr. Kenneth Pratt.

15. To put more faith in lies and hate /

Than truth and love is the true atheism. JAMES RUSSELL LOWELL, "Sonnet 17" (1842).

16. One does not hate as long as one still despises, but only those whom one esteems equal or higher. NIETZSCHE, *Beyond Good and Evil* (1886), 173, tr. Walter Kaufmann.

17. Hatred is a feeling which leads to the extinction of values. JOSÉ ORTEGA Y GASSET, "To the Reader," *Meditations on Quixote* (1914).

18. He whose anger is due to a cause will surely be appeased when the cause is removed. But if his mind harbours groundless hate, how shall another appease him? *Panchatantra* (c. 5th c.), 1, tr. Franklin Edgerton.

19. All men naturally hate one another. They employ lust as far as possible in the service of the public weal. But this is only a pretence and a false image of love; for at bottom it is only hate. PASCAL, *Pensées* (1670), 451, tr. W. F. Trotter.

20. Great hatred can be concealed in the countenance, and much in a kiss. PUBLILIUS SYRUS, *Moral Sayings* (1st c. B.C.), 1036, tr. Darius Lyman.

21. The human heart as modern civilization has made it is more prone to hatred than to friendship. And it is prone to hatred because it is dissatisfied. BERTRAND RUSSELL, *The Conquest of Happiness* (1930), 6.

22. To the eye of enmity virtue appears the ugliest blemish. SA'DI, *Gulistan* (1258), 4.1, tr. James Ross.

23. It is enough that one man hate another for hate to gain, little by little, all mankind. JEAN-PAUL SARTRE, *The Devil and the Good Lord* (1951), 1, third tableau, scene 6.

24. Hatred is the coward's revenge for being intimidated. GEORGE BERNARD SHAW, *Major Barbara* (1905), 3.

25. You want to hate somebody, if you can, just to keep your powers of discrimination bright, and to save yourself from becoming a mere mush of good-nature. CHARLES DUDLEY WARNER, "Ninth Study," *Backlog Studies* (1873).

## HAVES AND HAVE NOTS

**See 15. Advantage; 546. Losers; 1004. Unhappiness**

## 411. HEALTH

**See also 88. Body; 135. Cleanliness; 572. Medicine; 584. Mind and Body; 690. Physical Fitness; 836. Sanity; 889. Sickness**

1. Digestion exists for health, and health exists for life, and life exists for the love of music or beautiful things. G. K. CHESTERTON, "On Misunderstanding," *Generally Speaking* (1928).

2. The trouble about always trying to preserve the health of the body is that it is so difficult to do without destroying the health of the mind. G. K. CHESTERTON, "On the Classics," *Come to Think of It* (1930).

3. The sense of wellbeing! It's often with us / When we are young, but then it's not noticed; / And by the time one has grown to consciousness / It comes less often. T. S. ELIOT, *The Elder Statesman* (1958), 2.

4. Health and appetite impart the sweetness to sugar, bread, and meat. EMERSON, "Illusions," *The Conduct of Life* (1860).

5. The first wealth is health. EMERSON, "Power," *The Conduct of Life* (1860).

6. Sickness is felt, but health not at all. THOMAS FULLER, M.D., *Gnomologia* (1732), 4160.

7. There is a certain state of health that does not allow us to understand everything; and perhaps illness shuts us off from certain truths; but health shuts us off just as effectively from others. ANDRÉ GIDE, *Journals*, July 25, 1930, tr. Justin O'Brien.

8. If you mean to keep as well as possible, the less you think about your health the better. OLIVER WENDELL HOLMES, SR., *Over the Teacups* (1891), 8.

9. We should pray for a sane mind in a sound body. JUVENAL, *Satires* (c. 100), 10.356.

10. Preserving the health by too severe a rule is a wearisome malady. LA ROCHEFOUCAULD, *Maxims* (1665), tr. Kenneth Pratt.

11. A sound mind in a sound body, is a short but full description of a happy state in this world. JOHN LOCKE, *Some Thoughts Concerning Education* (1693), 1.

12. Life is not living, but living in health. MARTIAL, *Epigrams* (A.D. 86), 6.70, tr. Walter C. A. Ker.

13. We are not sensible of the most perfect health, as we are of the least sickness.

MONTAIGNE, "Apology for Raimond de Sebonde," *Essays* (1580–88), tr. Charles Cotton and W. C. Hazlitt.

14. Health is a precious thing, and the only one, in truth, meriting that a man should lay out, not only his time, sweat, labor and goods, but also his life itself to obtain it. MONTAIGNE, "Of the resemblance of children to their fathers," *Essays* (1580–88), tr. Charles Cotton and W. C. Hazlitt.

15. What some call health, if purchased by perpetual anxiety about diet, isn't much better than tedious disease. GEORGE DENNISON PRENTICE, *Prenticeana* (1860).

16. The wish for healing has ever been the half of health. SENECA, *Hippolytus* (1st c.), 249, tr. Frank Justus Miller.

17. Use your health, even to the point of wearing it out. That is what it is for. Spend all you have before you die; and do not outlive yourself. GEORGE BERNARD SHAW, "Preface on Doctors: The Latest Theories," *The Doctor's Dilemma* (1913).

18. If you would live in health, be old early. SPANISH PROVERB.

19. Since we cannot promise our selves constant health, let us endeavour at such temper as may be our best support in the decay of it. RICHARD STEELE, *The Spectator* (1711–12), 143.

20. When we are well, we all have good advice for those who are ill. TERENCE, *The Woman of Andros* (166 B.C.).

21. Health is the vital principle of bliss, / And exercise of health. JAMES THOMSON, *The Castle of Indolence* (1748), 2.57.

22. Look to your health; and if you have it, praise God, and value it next to a good conscience; for health is the second blessing that we mortals are capable of; a blessing that money cannot buy. IZAAK WALTON, *The Compleat Angler* (1653), 1.21.

## HEART

See 282. Emotions

## 412. HEAVEN

See also 38. Angels; 414. Hell

1. This world cannot explain its own difficulties without the assistance of another. CHARLES CALEB COLTON, *Lacon* (1825), 1.540.

2. Heaven is large, and affords space for all modes of love and fortitude. EMERSON, "Spiritual Laws," *Essays: First Series* (1841).

3. Modern man, if he dared to be articulate about his concept of heaven, would describe a vision which would look like the biggest department store in the world, showing new things and gadgets, and himself having plenty of money with which to buy them. ERICH FROMM, *The Sane Society* (1955), 5.

4. Those who have had none of the cares of this life to harass and disturb them, have been obliged to have recourse to the hopes and fears of the next to vary the prospect before them. WILLIAM HAZLITT, "On a Sun-dial," *Sketches and Essays* (1839).

5. A good man in an exclusive heaven would be in hell. ELBERT HUBBARD, *The Philistine* (1895–1915).

6. With the indifference of happiness, with the contempt of bliss, heaven barely glances at the miseries of earth. ROBERT G. INGERSOLL, *Prose-Poems and Selections* (1884).

7. Do not ask God the way to heaven; he will show you the hardest way. STANISLAW LEC, *Unkempt Thoughts* (1962), tr. Jacek Galazka.

8. The heaven of each is but what each desires. THOMAS MOORE, "The Veiled Prophet of Khorassan," *Lalla Rookh* (1817).

9. Paradise is a center whither the souls of all men are proceeding, each sect in its particular road. NAPOLEON I, *Maxims* (1804–15).

10. And that inverted Bowl they call the Sky, / Whereunder crawling cooped we live and die, / Lift not your hands to It for help —for it / As impotently moves as you or I. OMAR KHAYYÁM, *Rubáiyát* (11th–12th c.), tr. Edward FitzGerald, 4th ed., 72.

11. Heaven is equally distant everywhere. PETRONIUS, *Satyricon* (1st c.), tr. William Burnaby.

12. Believe in something for another World, but dont be too set on what it is, and then you wont start out that life with a disappointment. WILL ROGERS, *The Autobiography of Will Rogers* (1949), 16.

13. Men have feverishly conceived a heaven only to find it insipid, and a hell to find it ridiculous. GEORGE SANTAYANA, *The Life of Reason: Reason in Art* (1905–06), 9.

14. What they do in heaven we are ignorant of; what they do not we are told expressly, that they neither marry, nor are given in marriage. JONATHAN SWIFT, *Thoughts on Various Subjects* (1711).

15. All we know / Of what they do above, / Is that they happy are, and that they love. EDMUND WALLER, "Upon the Death of My Lady Rich" (1645).

16. Heaven-gates are not so highly arched / As princes' palaces; they that enter there / Must go upon their knees. JOHN WEBSTER, *The Duchess of Malfi* (c. 1613), 4.2.

## 413. THE HEAVENS

**See also 270. Earth; 597. Moon; 914. Space; 943. Sun; 1010. Universe**

1. The heavens declare the glory of God; and the firmament showeth his handiwork. *Bible*, Psalms 19:1.

2. For rich people, the sky is just an extra, a gift of nature. The poor, on the other hand, can see it as it really is: an infinite grace. ALBERT CAMUS, *Notebooks 1935–1942* (1962), 1, tr. Philip Thody.

3. The heavens call to you, and circle around you, displaying to you their eternal splendours, and your eye gazes only to earth. DANTE, "Purgatorio," 14, *The Divine Comedy* (c. 1300–21), tr. J. A. Carlyle and P. H. Wicksteed.

4. Overhead the sanctities of the stars shine forevermore, . . . pouring satire on the pompous business of the day which they close, and making the generations of men show slight and evanescent. EMERSON, *Journals*, 1836.

5. They cannot scare me with their empty spaces / Between stars—on stars where no human race is. / I have it in me so much nearer home / To scare myself with my own desert places. ROBERT FROST, "Desert Places," *A Further Range* (1936).

6. Comets are the nearest thing to nothing that anything can be and still be something. National Geographic Society, press release, March 31, 1955.

7. Before the days of Kepler the heavens declared the glory of the Lord. GEORGE SANTAYANA, *The Sense of Beauty* (1896).

8. If we could count the stars, we should not weep before them. GEORGE SANTAYANA, *Little Essays* (1920), 112, ed. Logan Pearsall Smith.

9. It is easier to accept the message of the stars than the message of the salt desert. The stars speak of man's insignificance in the long eternity of time; the desert speaks of his insignificance right now. EDWIN WAY TEALE, *Autumn Across America* (1956), 19.

## HEDONISM

**See 698. Pleasure; 700. Pleasure-seeking**

## 414. HELL

**See also 240. Devil; 412. Heaven**

1. Hell, madame, is to love no longer. GEORGES BERNANOS, *The Dairy of a Country Priest* (1936), 2.

2. Hell has three gates: lust, anger, and greed. *Bhagavadgita*, 16, tr. P. Lal.

3. Believing in Hell must distort every judgement on this life. CYRIL CONNOLLY, *The Unquiet Grave* (1945), 1.

4. He is the coward who, outfaced in this, / Fears the false goblins of another life. PAUL LAURENCE DUNBAR, "The Right to Die," *The Complete Poems* (1962).

5. What is hell? Hell is oneself, / Hell is alone, the other figures in it / Merely projections. T. S. ELIOT, *The Cocktail Party* (1949), 1.3.

6. Hell is the bloodcurdling mansion of time, in whose profoundest circle Satan himself waits, winding a gargantuan watch in his hand. ANTONIO MACHADO, *Juan de Mairena* (1943), 7, tr. Ben Belitt.

7. Hell hath no limits, nor is circumscribed / In one self place; but where we are is hell, / And where hell is, there must we ever be. CHRISTOPHER MARLOWE, *Doctor Faustus* (c. 1588), 2.2.

8. Which way I fly is hell; myself am hell; / And in the lowest deep a lower deep / Still threatening to devour me opens wide, / To which the hell I suffer seems a heaven. MILTON, *Paradise Lost* (1667), 4.75.

9. The merit of Mahomet is that he founded a religion without an inferno. NAPOLEON I, *Maxims* (1804–15).

10. To work hard, to live hard, to die hard, and then to go to hell after all would be too damned hard. CARL SANDBURG, *The People, Yes* (1936).

11. Hell is others. JEAN-PAUL SARTRE, *No Exit* (1944), 5.

12. Hell is a city much like London – / A populous and smoky city. SHELLEY, "Peter Bell the Third" (1819), 3.1.

13. There is a dreadful Hell, / And everlasting pains; / There sinners must with devils dwell / In darkness, fire, and chains. ISAAC WATTS, *Divine Songs for Children* (1720), 11.

## HELPING

See 56. Assistance; 118. Charity; 382. Gifts and Giving; 430. Humanitarianism

## 415. HEREDITY

See also 663. Parenthood; 796. Reproduction

1. That which comes of a cat will catch mice. ENGLISH PROVERB.

2. Deep in the cavern of the infant's breast / The father's nature lurks, and lives anew. HORACE, *Odes* (23–c. 15 B.C.), 4.4.

3. With him for a sire and her for a dam, / What should I be but just what I am? EDNA ST. VINCENT MILLAY, "The Singing-Woman from the Wood's Edge," *A Few Figs from Thistles* (1920).

4. The whelp of a wolf must prove a wolf at last, notwithstanding he may be brought up by a man. SA'DI, *Gulistan* (1258), 1.4, tr. James Ross.

5. The seed of the cedar will become cedar. The seed of the bramble can only become bramble. SAINT-EXUPÉRY, *Flight to Arras* (1942), 22, tr. Lewis Galantière.

## HERESY

See 256. Dissent

## 416. HEROES AND HEROISM

See also 330. Fame; 384. Glory; 399. Greatness

1. Heroes are very human, most of them; very easily touched by praise. MAX BEERBOHM, "A Point to Be Remembered by Very Eminent Men," *And Even Now* (1920).

2. The hero was distinguished by his achievement; the celebrity by his image or trademark. The hero created himself; the celebrity is created by the media. The hero was a big man; the celebrity is a big name. DANIEL J. BOORSTIN, *The Image* (1962), 2.4.

3. Every hero becomes a bore at last. EMERSON, "Uses of Great Men," *Representative Men* (1850).

4. The hero is suffered to be himself. EMERSON, "Behavior," *The Conduct of Life* (1860).

5. Show me a hero and I will write you a tragedy. F. SCOTT FITZGERALD, "The Note-Books," *The Crack-Up* (1945).

6. An efficiency-regime cannot be run without a few heroes stuck about it to carry off the dullness – much as plums have to be put into a bad pudding to make it palatable. E. M. FORSTER, "What I Believe," *Two Cheers for Democracy* (1951).

7. In war-time a man is called a hero. It doesn't make him any braver, and he runs for his life. But at least it's a hero who is running away. JEAN GIRAUDOUX, *Tiger at the Gates* (1935), 1, tr. Christopher Fry.

8. A hero cannot be a hero unless in an heroic world. NATHANIEL HAWTHORNE, *Journals*, May 7, 1850.

9. The greatest obstacle to being heroic, is the doubt whether one may not be going to prove one's self a fool; the truest heroism is to resist the doubt, and the profoundest wisdom to know when it ought to be resisted, and when to be obeyed. NATHANIEL HAWTHORNE, *The Blithdale Romance* (1852), 2.

10. Heroism does not require spiritual maturity. ABEL HERMANT, *Xavier ou les entretiens sur la grammaire française* (1923), 1.

11. The heroic man does not pose; he leaves that for the man who wishes to be thought heroic. ELBERT HUBBARD, *The Note Book* (1927).

12. Life, misfortunes, isolation, abandonment, poverty, are battlefields which have their heroes; obscure heroes, sometimes greater than the illustrious heroes. VICTOR HUGO, "Marius," *Les Misérables* (1862), 5.1, tr. Charles E. Wilbour.

13. Posterity attributes to a hero it knows by name the great deeds of others it doesn't know, and to an immortal genius the innovations of forgotten creatures. MAX JACOB, "Hamletism," *Art poétique* (1922), tr. Wallace Fowlie.

14. However great the advantages given us by nature, it is not she alone, but fortune

with her, which makes heroes. LA ROCHEFOUCAULD, *Maxims* (1665), tr. Kenneth Pratt.

15. We moderns do not believe in demigods, but our smallest hero we expect to feel and act as a demigod. GOTTHOLD EPHRAIM LESSING, *Laocoön* (1766), 4, tr. W. A. Steel.

16. Deeds of heroism are but offered to those who, for many long years, have been heroes in obscurity and silence. MAURICE MAETERLINCK, *Wisdom and Destiny* (1898), 10, tr. Alfred Sutro.

17. No hero to me is the man who, by easy shedding of his blood, purchases fame: my hero is he who, without death, can win praise. MARTIAL, *Epigrams* (A.D. 86), 1.8, tr. Walter C. A. Ker.

18. The chief business of the nation, as a nation, is the setting up of heroes, mainly bogus. H. L. MENCKEN, *Prejudices: Third Series* (1922), 1.

19. The epic disappeared along with the age of personal heroism; there can be no epic with artillery. ERNEST RENAN, "Probabilités," *Dialogues et fragments philosophiques* (1876).

20. This thing of being a hero, about the main thing to do is to know when to die. Prolonged life has ruined more men than it ever made. WILL ROGERS, *The Autobiography of Will Rogers* (1949), 13.

21. A hero is a man who does what he can. ROMAIN ROLLAND, "L'Adolescent," *Jean Christophe* (1904–12), 3.

22. Though thou art able to tear the scalp off an elephant, if deficient in humanity, thou art no hero. SA'DI, *Gulistan* (1258), 2.42, tr. James Ross.

23. Heroism has no model. LOUIS ANTOINE LÉON DE SAINT-JUST, *Discours à la convention*, April 15, 1794.

24. Better not be a hero than work oneself up into heroism by shouting lies. GEORGE SANTAYANA, *Dialogues in Limbo* (1925), 2.

25. Every hero is a Samson. The strong man succumbs to the intrigues of the weak and the many; and if in the end he loses all patience he crushes both them and himself. SCHOPENHAUER, "A Few Parables," *Parerga and Paralipomena* (1851), tr. T. Bailey Saunders.

26. The savage bows down to idols of wood and stone: the civilized man to idols of flesh and blood. GEORGE BERNARD SHAW, "Maxims for Revolutionists," *Man and Superman* (1903).

## HESITATION

See 228. Delay; 463. Indecision

## HIDING

See 162. Concealment

## 417. HISTORY AND HISTORIANS

See also 296. Era; 669. Past; 979. Tradition

1. History provides neither compensation for suffering nor penalties for wrong. LORD ACTON, postscript, letter to Mandell Creighton, April 5, 1887.

2. History is a tangled skein that one may take up at any point, and break when one has unravelled enough. HENRY ADAMS, *The Education of Henry Adams* (1907), 20.

3. The historian must not try to know what is truth, if he values his honesty; for, if he cares for his truths, he is certain to falsify his facts. HENRY ADAMS, *The Education of Henry Adams* (1907), 31.

4. The only lesson history has taught us is that man has not yet learned anything from history. Anonymous.

5. People are trapped in history and history is trapped in them. JAMES BALDWIN, "Stranger in the Village" (1953), *Notes of a Native Son* (1955).

6. More history's made by secret handshakes than by battles, bills, and proclamations. JOHN BARTH, *The Sot-Weed Factor* (1960), 2.1.

7. History, n. An account mostly false, of events mostly unimportant, which are brought about by rulers mostly knaves, and soldiers mostly fools. AMBROSE BIERCE, *The Devil's Dictionary* (1881–1911).

8. What makes a good writer of history is a guy who is suspicious. Suspicion marks the real difference between the man who wants to write honest history and the one who'd rather write a good story. JIM BISHOP, *The New York Times*, Feb. 5, 1955.

9. History is unpainful, memory does not cloud it; you join the emphatic lives of the long dead. ELIZABETH BOWEN, *The House in Paris* (1935), 2.8.

10. World history would be different if humanity did more sitting on its rear. BERTOLT BRECHT, *Drums in the Night* (1922), 2, tr. Frank Jones.

11. History is largely concerned with arranging good entrances for people; and later exits not always quite so good. HEYWOOD BROUN, "Sport for Art's Sake," *Pieces of Hate, and Other Enthusiasms* (1922).

12. The history of the world is the record of the weakness, frailty and death of public opinion. SAMUEL BUTLER (d. 1902), "Pictures and Books," *Note-Books* (1912).

13. History, with all her volumes vast, / Hath but one page. BYRON, *Childe Harold's Pilgrimage* (1812–18), 4.108.

14. History is the essence of innumerable biographies. THOMAS CARLYLE, "On History" (1830).

15. The disadvantage of men not knowing the past is that they do not know the present. History is a hill or high point of vantage, from which alone men see the town in which they live or the age in which they are living. G. K. CHESTERTON, "On St. George Revivified," *All I Survey* (1933).

16. To be ignorant of what occurred before you were born is to remain always a child. For what is the worth of human life, unless it is woven into the life of our ancestors by the records of history? CICERO, *Orator* (46 B.C.)

17. What is history after all? History is facts which become lies in the end; legends are lies which become history in the end. JEAN COCTEAU, *The Observer*, Sept. 22, 1957.

18. The more we know of History, the less shall we esteem the subjects of it, and to despise our species is the price we must too often pay for our knowledge of it. CHARLES CALEB COLTON, *Lacon* (1825), 2.157.

19. The history of free men is never really written by chance but by choice—their choice. DWIGHT D. EISENHOWER, address, Pittsburgh, Pa., Oct. 9, 1956.

20. The historical sense involves a perception, not only of the pastness of the past, but of its presence. T. S. ELIOT, "Tradition and the Individual Talent" (1919).

21. There is no history; only biography. EMERSON, *Journals*, 1839.

22. History is the action and reaction of these two, nature and thought—two boys pushing each other on the curbstone of the pavement. EMERSON, "Fate," *The Conduct of Life* (1860).

23. It is pleasant to be transferred from an office where one is afraid of a sergeant-major into an office where one can intimidate generals, and perhaps this is why History is so attractive to the more timid among us. We can recover self-confidence by snubbing the dead. E. M. FORSTER, "The Consolations of History," *Abinger Harvest* (1936).

24. Historians relate not so much what is done as what they would have believed. BENJAMIN FRANKLIN, *Poor Richard's Almanack* (1732–57).

25. Man himself is the most important creation and achievement of the continuous human effort, the record of which we call history. ERICH FROMM, *Escape from Freedom* (1941), 1.

26. History never looks like history when you are living through it. It always looks confusing and messy, and it always feels uncomfortable. JOHN W. GARDNER, *No Easy Victories* (1968), 27.

27. There are only two great currents in the history of mankind: the baseness which makes conservatives and the envy which makes revolutionaries. EDMOND and JULES DE GONCOURT, *Journal*, July 12, 1867, tr. Robert Baldick.

28. Peoples and governments never have learned anything from history, or acted on principles deduced from it. HEGEL, introduction to *Philosophy of History* (1832), tr. John Sibree.

29. The game of history is usually played by the best and the worst over the heads of the majority in the middle. ERIC HOFFER, *The True Believer* (1951), 2.4.18.

30. That men do not learn very much from the lessons of history is the most important of all the lessons that history has to teach. ALDOUS HUXLEY, *Collected Essays* (1959).

31. Truth is a totality, the sum of many overlapping partial images. History, on the other hand, sacrifices totality in the interest of continuity. EDMUND LEACH, "Brain-Twister," *New York Review of Books*, Oct. 12, 1967.

32. Old events have modern meanings; only that survives / Of past history which finds kindred in all hearts and lives. JAMES RUSSELL LOWELL, "Mahmood the Image-

Breaker," *Under the Willows and Other Poems* (1868).

33. The mark of the historic is the nonchalance with which it picks up an individual and deposits him in a trend, like a house playfully moved in a tornado. MARY MC CARTHY, "My Confession," *On the Contrary* (1961).

34. The history of the world is the history of a privileged few. HENRY MILLER, *Sunday after the War* (1944).

35. The middle sort of historians, of which the most part are, they spoil all; they will chew our meat for us. MONTAIGNE, "Of books," *Essays* (1580–88), tr. Charles Cotton and W. C. Hazlitt.

36. Every fact and every work exercises a fresh persuasion over every age and every new species of man. History always enunciates new truths. NIETZSCHE, *The Will to Power* (1888), 974, tr. Anthony M. Ludovici.

37. We have need of history in its entirety, not to fall back into it, but to see if we can escape from it. JOSÉ ORTEGA Y GASSET, *The Revolt of the Masses* (1930), 10.

38. It is impossible to write ancient history because we lack source materials, and impossible to write modern history because we have far too many. CHARLES PÉGUY, *Clio* (1917).

39. There is no history of mankind, there are only many histories of all kinds of aspects of human life. And one of these is the history of political power. This is elevated into the history of the world. SIR KARL R. POPPER, *The Open Society and Its Enemies* (1950).

40. The talent of historians lies in their creating a true ensemble out of facts which are but half-true. ERNEST RENAN, preface to 13th edition of *La Vie de Jésus* (1863).

41. History, if thoroughly comprehended, furnishes something of the experience which a man would acquire who should be a contemporary of all ages and a fellow-citizen of all peoples. JOSEPH ROUX, *Meditations of a Parish Priest* (1886), 3.1, tr. Isabel F. Hapgood.

42. History says, if it pleases, Excuse me, I beg your pardon, it will never happen again if I can help it. CARL SANDBURG, "Good Morning, America," *Complete Poems* (1950).

43. We can chart our future clearly and wisely only when we know the path which has led to the present. ADLAI STEVENSON, speech, Richmond, Va., Sept. 20, 1952.

44. Wherever men have lived there is a story to be told, and it depends chiefly on the story-teller or historian whether that is interesting or not. THOREAU, *Journal*, March 18, 1860.

45. The very ink with which all history is written is merely fluid prejudice. MARK TWAIN, "Pudd'nhead Wilson's New Calendar," *Following the Equator* (1897), 2.33.

46. History justifies whatever we want it to. It teaches absolutely nothing, for it contains everything and gives examples of everything. PAUL VALÉRY, "De l'histoire," *Regards sur le monde actuel* (1931).

47. Regrets are idle; yet history is one long regret. Everything might have turned out so differently! CHARLES DUDLEY WARNER, "Eighteenth Week," *My Summer in a Garden* (1871).

48. History is all explained by geography. ROBERT PENN WARREN, interview, *Writers at Work: First Series* (1958).

49. Human history becomes more and more a race between education and catastrophe. H. G. WELLS, *The Outline of History* (1920, 1921), 40.4.

50. As soon as histories are properly told there is no more need of romances. WALT WHITMAN, preface to *Leaves of Grass* (1855–92).

51. Our history is every human history; a black and gory business, with more scoundrels than wise men at the lead, and more louts than both put together to cheer and follow. PHILIP WYLIE, *Generation of Vipers* (1942), 7.

## 418. HOLIDAYS

**See also 624. The New Year; 660. Parades**

1. From the sepulcher at sunrise to the fashion parade on Fifth Avenue is the boorish measure of our denial of Christ—from innocent wonder to cynical worldliness. BROOKS ATKINSON, "March 28," *Once Around the Sun* (1951).

2. [Thanksgiving] as founded be th' Puritans to give thanks f'r bein' presarved fr'm th' Indyans, an' we keep it to give thanks we are presarved fr'm th' Puritans. FINLEY PETER DUNNE, "Thanksgiving," *Mr. Dooley's Opinions* (1901).

3. Th' Turkey bur-rd's th' rale cause iv Thanksgivin'. He's th' naytional air. Abolish th' Turkey an' ye destroy th' tie that binds us as wan people. FINLEY PETER DUNNE, "Thanksgiving," *Mr. Dooley's Opinions* (1901).

4. How many observe Christ's birthday! How few, his precepts! O! 'tis easier to keep holidays than commandments. BENJAMIN FRANKLIN, *Poor Richard's Almanack* (1732–57).

5. Holidays / Have no pity. EUGENIO MONTALE, "Eastbourne," *Selected Poems* (1965), tr. G. S. Fraser.

6. People can't concentrate properly on blowing other / people to pieces properly if their minds are poisoned / by thoughts suitable to the twenty-fifth of De- / cember. OGDEN NASH, "Merry Christmas, Nearly Everybody!" *I'm a Stranger Here Myself* (1938).

7. Labor Day symbolizes our determination to achieve an economic freedom for the average man which will give his political freedom reality. FRANKLIN D. ROOSEVELT, Fireside Chat, Sept. 6, 1936.

8. If all the year were playing holidays, / To sport would be as tedious as to work. SHAKESPEARE, *I Henry IV* (1597–98), 1.2.228.

9. *April 1*. This is the day upon which we are reminded of what we are on the other three hundred and sixty-four. MARK TWAIN, "Pudd'nhead Wilson's Calendar," *Pudd'nhead Wilson* (1894), 21.

## 419. HOLLYWOOD

See also 604. Movies

1. Hollywood is a place where there is no definition of your worth earlier than your last picture. MURRAY KEMPTON, "The Day of the Locust," *Part of Our Time* (1955).

2. Hollywood money isn't money. It's congealed snow, melts in your hand, and there you are. DOROTHY PARKER, interview, *Writers at Work: First Series* (1958).

## 420. HOME

See also 332. Family; 421. Homeland; 426. Hospitality; 428. Houses

1. Be it ever so humble, there's no place like home for wearing what you like. GEORGE ADE. "The Good Fairy of the Eighth Ward," *Forty Modern Fables* (1901).

2. It's hard for women, you know, / To get away. There's so much to do. / Husbands to be patted and put in good tempers: / Servants to be poked out: children washed / Or soothed with lullays or fed with mouthfuls of pap. ARISTOPHANES, *Lysistrata* (411 B.C.), tr. Jack Lindsay.

3. Whoever makes home seem to the young dearer and more happy, is a public benefactor. HENRY WARD BEECHER, *Proverbs from Plymouth Pulpit* (1887).

4. To know after absence the familiar street and road and village and house is to know again the satisfaction of home. HAL BORLAND, "Homecoming—August 29," *Sundial of the Seasons* (1964).

5. You are a king by your own fire-side, as much as any monarch in his throne. CERVANTES, author's preface, *Don Quixote* (1605–15), tr. Peter Motteux and John Ozell.

6. A man's home is his wife's castle. ALEXANDER CHASE, *Perspectives* (1966).

7. In love of home, the love of country has its rise. CHARLES DICKENS, *The Old Curiosity Shop* (1840), 38.

8. Where Thou art—that—is Home. EMILY DICKINSON, poem (c. 1863).

9. Let a man behave in his own house as a guest. EMERSON, *Journals*, 1836.

10. Every roof is agreeable to the eye, until it is lifted; then we find tragedy and moaning women, and hard-eyed husbands. EMERSON, "Experience," *Essays: Second Series* (1844).

11. The ornament of a house is the friends who frequent it. EMERSON, "Domestic Life," *Society and Solitude* (1870).

12. Home is the place where, when you have to go there, / They have to take you in. ROBERT FROST, "The Death of the Hired Man," *North of Boston* (1914).

13. The most fortunate of men, / Be he a king or commoner, is he / Whose welfare is assured in his own home. GOETHE, *Iphigenia in Tauris* (1787), 1, tr. Charles E. Passage.

14. Daughter am I in my mother's house, / But mistress in my own. RUDYARD KIPLING, "Our Lady of the Snows" (1897).

15. Stay, stay at home, my heart, and rest; / Home-keeping hearts are happiest. LONGFELLOW, "Song" (1877).

16. A home is not a mere transient shel-

ter: its essence lies in its permanence, in its capacity for accretion and solidification, in its quality of representing, in all its details, the personalities of the people who live in it. H. L. MENCKEN, *Prejudices: Fifth Series* (1926), 11.

17. A man's house is his castle; and whilst he is quiet, he is well guarded as a prince in his castle. JAMES OTIS, speech against the writs of assistance, Feb. 24, 1761.

18. The dog is a lion in his own house. PERSIAN PROVERB.

19. Happy the man whose wish and care / A few paternal acres bound, / Content to breathe his native air, / In his own ground. ALEXANDER POPE, *Ode on Solitude* (1699), 1.

20. Plasticity loves new moulds because it can fill them, but for a man of sluggish mind and bad manners there is decidedly no place like home. GEORGE SANTAYANA, *The Life of Reason: Reason in Society* (1905–06), 6.

21. Home-keeping youth have ever homely wits. SHAKESPEARE, *The Two Gentlemen of Verona* (1594–95), 1.1.2.

22. 'Tis ever common / That men are merriest when they are from home. SHAKESPEARE, *Henry V* (1598–99), 1.2.271.

23. Everybody's always talking about people breaking into houses . . . but there are more people in the world who want to break out of houses. THORNTON WILDER, *The Matchmaker* (1955), 4.

## 421. HOMELAND

See also 671. Patriotism

1. Each blade of grass has its spot on earth whence it draws its life, its strength; and so is man rooted to the land from which he draws his faith together with his life. JOSEPH CONRAD, *Lord Jim* (1900), 21.

2. There is no sorrow above / The loss of a native land. EURIPIDES, *Medea* (431 B.C.), tr. Rex Warner.

3. I, for one, know of no sweeter sight for a man's eyes than his own country. HOMER, *Odyssey* (9th c. B.C.), 9, tr. E. V. Rieu.

4. Every man has a lurking wish to appear considerable in his native place. SAMUEL JOHNSON, quoted in Boswell's *Life of Samuel Johnson*, July 17, 1771.

5. Though it rain gold and silver in a foreign land and daggers and spears at home, yet it is better to be at home. MALAY PROVERB.

6. It is right to prefer our own country to all others, because we are children and citizens before we can be travellers or philosophers. GEORGE SANTAYANA, *The Life of Reason: Reason in Religion* (1905–06), 10.

7. Breathes there the man, with soul so dead, / Who never to himself hath said, / This is my own, my native land! SIR WALTER SCOTT, *The Lay of the Last Minstrel* (1805), 6.1.

## 422. HOMOSEXUALITY

1. Homosexuality is a sickness, just as are baby-rape or wanting to become head of General Motors. ELDRIDGE CLEAVER, "Notes on a Native Son," *Soul on Ice* (1968).

2. Fairies: Nature's attempt to get rid of soft boys by sterilizing them. F. SCOTT FITZGERALD, "The Note-Books," *The Crack-Up* (1945).

3. There is probably no sensitive heterosexual alive who is not preoccupied with his latent homosexuality. NORMAN MAILER, "The Homosexual Villain," *Advertisements for Myself* (1959).

## 423. HONESTY

See also 329. Falsehood; 360. Frankness; 489. Integrity; 894. Sincerity; 993. Truthfulness

1. An honest man's word is as good as his bond. CERVANTES, *Don Quixote* (1605–15), 2.4.34, tr. Peter Motteux and John Ozell.

2. Who cannot open an honest mind / No friend will he be of mine. EURIPIDES, *Medea* (431 B.C.), tr. Rex Warner.

3. No such thing as a man willing to be honest—that would be like a blind man willing to see. F. SCOTT FITZGERALD, "The Note-Books," *The Crack-Up* (1945).

4. He that resolves to deal with none but honest men must leave off dealing. THOMAS FULLER, M.D., *Gnomologia* (1732), 2267.

5. There is no well-defined boundary line between honesty and dishonesty. The frontiers of one blend with the outside limits of the other, and he who attempts to

tread this dangerous ground may be sometimes in the one domain and sometimes in the other. O. HENRY, "Bexar Scrip No. 2692," *Rolling Stones* (1912).

6. I have no idea what the mind of a low-life scoundrel is like, but I know what the mind of an honest man is like: it is terrifying. ABEL HERMANT, *Le Bourgeois* (1906), 4.

7. Honesty is largely a matter of information, of knowing that dishonesty is a mistake. Principle is not as powerful in keeping people straight as a policeman. EDGAR WATSON HOWE, *Ventures in Common Sense* (1919), 16.10.

8. Honesty's praised, then left to freeze. JUVENAL, *Satires* (c. 100), 1.75, tr. Hubert Creekmore.

9. To state the facts frankly is not to despair for the future nor indict the past. JOHN F. KENNEDY, State of the Union Message, Jan. 29, 1961.

10. A show of a certain amount of honesty is in any profession or business the surest way of growing rich. LA BRUYÈRE, *Characters* (1688), 6.44, tr. Henri Van Laun.

11. honesty is a good / thing but / it is not profitable to / its possessor / unless it is / kept under control / if you are not / honest at all / everybody hates you / and if you are / absolutely honest / you get martyred. DON MARQUIS, "archygrams," *Archy's Life of Mehitabel* (1933).

12. The surest way to remain poor is to be an honest man. NAPOLEON I, *Maxims* (1804–15).

13. The life of an honest man must be a perpetual infidelity. CHARLES PÉGUY, "The Search for Truth," *Basic Verities* (1943), tr. Ann and Julian Green.

14. Honesty is for the most part less profitable than dishonesty. PLATO, *The Republic* (4th c. B.C.), 2, tr. Benjamin Jowett.

15. An honest man's the noblest work of God. ALEXANDER POPE, *An Essay on Man* (1733–34), 4.247.

16. God looks at the clean hands, not the full ones. PUBLILIUS SYRUS, *Moral Sayings* (1st c. B.C.), 715, tr. Darius Lyman.

17. To make your children capable of honesty is the beginning of education. JOHN RUSKIN, *Time and Tide* (1867), 8.

18. No legacy is so rich as honesty. SHAKESPEARE, *All's Well That Ends Well* (1602–03), 3.5.13.

19. I hope I shall always possess firmness and virtue enough to maintain what I consider the most enviable of all titles, the character of an "Honest Man." GEORGE WASHINGTON (1732–1799), maxim.

## HONOR

See 489. Integrity

## 424. HONORS

See also 330. Fame; 384. Glory

1. Some are born great, some achieve greatness, and others have it pinned on them. GEORGE ADE, "The Rise and Flight of the Winged Insect," *Hand-Made Fables* (1920).

2. A prophet is not without honour, save in his own country. *Bible*, Matthew 13:57.

3. A medal glitters, but it also casts a shadow. SIR WINSTON CHURCHILL, speech, House of Commons, March 22, 1944.

4. The honor paid to a wise man is a great good for those who honor him. EPICURUS, "Vatican Sayings" (3rd c. B.C.), 32, in *Letters, Principal Doctrines, and Vatican Sayings*, tr. Russel M. Geer.

5. High honors are sweet / To a man's heart, but ever / They stand close to the brink of grief. EURIPIDES, *Iphigenia in Aulis* (c. 405 B.C.), tr. Charles R. Walker.

6. In lapidary inscriptions a man is not upon oath. SAMUEL JOHNSON, quoted in Boswell's *Life of Samuel Johnson*, 1775.

7. Great honours are great burdens, but on whom / They are cast with envy, he doth bear two loads. BEN JONSON, *Catiline His Conspiracy* (1611), 3.1.

8. Great power, which incites / Great envy, hurls some men to destruction; they are drowned / In a long, splendid stream of honors. JUVENAL, *Satires* (c. 100), 10.56, tr. Hubert Creekmore.

9. My slumber broken and my doublet torn, / I find the laurel also bears a thorn. WALTER SAVAGE LANDOR, "Lately Our Poets" (1863).

10. It is sure that those are most desirous of honour or glory who cry out loudest of its abuse and the vanity of the world. SPINOZA, *Ethics* (1677), 5, tr. Andrew Boyle.

## 425. HOPE

**See also 237. Despair; 316. Expectation; 1033. Waiting**

1. Hope is a waking dream. ARISTOTLE (4th c. B.C.), quoted in Diogenes Laertius' *Lives and Opinions of Eminent Philosophers* (3rd c. A.D.), tr. R. D. Hicks.

2. Hope is a risk that must be run. GEORGES BERNANOS, "Why Freedom?" *The Last Essays of Georges Bernanos* (1955), tr. Joan and Barry Ulanov.

3. Hope deferred maketh the heart sick. *Bible*, Proverbs 13:12.

4. Hope not sunshine ev'ry hour, / Fear not clouds will always lour. ROBERT BURNS, "Written in Friars Carse Hermitage" (1793).

5. Hope is a prodigal young heir, and Experience is his banker. CHARLES CALEB COLTON, *Lacon* (1825), 1.108.

6. Hope is a strange invention— / A Patent of the Heart— / In unremitting action / Yet never wearing out—. EMILY DICKINSON, poem (c. 1877).

7. The reason of idleness and of crime is the deferring of our hopes. EMERSON, "Nominalist and Realist," *Essays: Second Series* (1844).

8. Ten thousand men possess ten thousand hopes. / —A few bear fruit in happiness; the others go awry. EURIPIDES, *The Bacchae* (c. 405 B.C.), tr. William Arrowsmith.

9. He that lives upon hope will die fasting. BENJAMIN FRANKLIN, "The Way to Wealth" (July 7, 1757).

10. He fishes on who catches one. FRENCH PROVERB.

11. If it were not for hopes, the heart would break. THOMAS FULLER, M.D., *Gnomologia* (1732), 2689.

12. There are situations in which hope and fear run together, in which they mutually destroy one another, and lose themselves in a dull indifference. GOETHE, *Elective Affinities* (1809), 22.

13. Hope is a great falsifier of truth. BALTASAR GRACIÁN, *The Art of Worldly Wisdom* (1647), 19, tr. Joseph Jacobs.

14. In the time of trouble avert not thy face from hope, for the soft marrow abideth in the hard bone. HĀFIZ, ghazals from the *Divan* (14th c.), 107, tr. Justin Huntly McCarthy.

15. Hope is the best possession. None are completely wretched but those who are without hope, and few are reduced so low as that. WILLIAM HAZLITT, *Characteristics* (1823), 33.

16. Death is the greatest evil, because it cuts off hope. WILLIAM HAZLITT, *Characteristics* (1823), 35.

17. It is natural to man to indulge in the illusion of hope. We are apt to shut our eyes against a painful truth, and listen to the song of that siren, till she transforms us into beasts. PATRICK HENRY, speech, Virginia Convention, March 23, 1775.

18. It is the around-the-corner brand of hope that prompts people to action, while the distant hope acts as an opiate. ERIC HOFFER, *The Ordeal of Change* (1964), 10.

19. The short span of life forbids us to take on far-reaching hopes. HORACE, *Odes* (23–c. 15 B.C.), 1.4.

20. There is nothing so well known as that we should not expect something for nothing—but we all do and call it Hope. EDGAR WATSON HOWE, *Country Town Sayings* (1911).

21. Hope is necessary in every condition. The miseries of poverty, sickness, of captivity, would, without this comfort, be insupportable. SAMUEL JOHNSON, *The Rambler* (1750–52), 67.

22. We should not let our fears hold us back from pursuing our hopes. JOHN F. KENNEDY, address, Washington, D.C., Dec. 11, 1959.

23. In the history of thought and culture the dark nights have perhaps in some ways cost mankind less grief than the false dawns, the prison houses in which hope persists less grief than the Promised Lands where hope expires. LOUIS KRONENBERGER, *Company Manners* (1954), 1.1.

24. Hope, deceitful as it is, serves at least to lead us to the end of our lives by an agreeable route. LA ROCHEFOUCAULD, *Maxims* (1665), tr. Kenneth Pratt.

25. Hope has as many lives as a cat or a king. LONGFELLOW, *Hyperion* (1839), 3.9.

26. the only way boss / to keep hope in the world / is to keep changing its / population frequently. DON MARQUIS, "archy and the old un," *Archy's Life of Mehitabel* (1933).

27. Oh, what a valiant faculty is hope, that in a mortal subject, and in a moment, makes nothing of usurping infinity, immen-

sity, eternity, and of supplying its master's indigence, at its pleasure, with all things he can imagine or desire! MONTAIGNE, "Of names," *Essays* (1580–88), tr. Charles Cotton and W. C. Hazlitt.

28. Hope in reality is the worst of all evils, because it prolongs the torments of man. NIETZSCHE, *Human, All Too Human* (1878), 71, tr. Helen Zimmern.

29. Strong hope is a much greater stimulant of life than any single realised joy could be. NIETZSCHE, *The Antichrist* (1888), 23, tr. Anthony M. Ludovici.

30. Never give out while there is hope; but hope not beyond reason, for that shows more desire than judgment. WILLIAM PENN, *Some Fruits of Solitude* (1693), 1.235.

31. Just as dumb creatures are snared by food, human beings would not be caught unless they had a nibble of hope. PETRONIUS, *Satyricon* (1st c.), tr. M. Heseltine.

32. Even now I am full of hope, but the end lies in God. PINDAR, *Odes* (5th c. B.C.), Olympia 13, tr. Richmond Lattimore.

33. Hope springs eternal in the human breast: / Man never is, but always to be blest. ALEXANDER POPE, *An Essay on Man* (1733–34), 1.95.

34. At first we hope too much, later on, not enough. JOSEPH ROUX, *Meditations of a Parish Priest* (1886), 5.8, tr. Isabel F. Hapgood.

35. Extreme hopes are born of extreme misery. BERTRAND RUSSELL, "The Future of Mankind," *Unpopular Essays* (1950).

36. Hope is an echo, hope ties itself yonder, yonder. CARL SANDBURG, *The People, Yes* (1936).

37. Hope is brightest when it dawns from fears. SIR WALTER SCOTT, *The Lady of the Lake* (1810), 4.1.

38. True hope is swift and flies with swallow's wings; / Kings it makes gods, and meaner creatures kings. SHAKESPEARE, *Richard III* (1592–93), 5.2.23.

39. The miserable have no other medicine / But only hope. SHAKESPEARE, *Measure for Measure* (1604–05), 3.1.2.

40. If Winter comes, can Spring be far behind? SHELLEY, "Ode to the West Wind" (1819), 5.

41. Hope deceives more men than cunning does. VAUVENARGUES, *Reflections and Maxims* (1746), 569.

42. Hope should no more be a virtue than fear; we fear and we hope, according to what is promised or threatened us. VOLTAIRE, "Virtue," *Philosophical Dictionary* (1764).

## HORSEMANSHIP

**See 815. Riding**

## HORSE-RACING

**See 922. Sports**

## 426. HOSPITALITY

**See also 355. Foreigners and Foreignness**

1. What is there / more kindly than the feeling between host and guest? AESCHYLUS, *The Libation Bearers* (458 B.C.), tr. Richmond Lattimore.

2. It is nothing won to admit men with an open door, and to receive them with a shut and reserved countenance. FRANCIS BACON, "Civil Knowledge," *The Advancement of Learning* (1605), 3.

3. Humility is a virtue, and it is a virtue innate in guests. MAX BEERBOHM, "Hosts and Guests," *And Even Now* (1920).

4. When hospitality becomes an art, it loses its very soul. MAX BEERBOHM, "Hosts and Guests," *And Even Now* (1920).

5. The hospitable instinct is not wholly altruistic. There is pride and egoism mixed up with it. MAX BEERBOHM, "Hosts and Guests," *And Even Now* (1920).

6. Withdraw thy foot from thy neighbor's house; lest he be weary of thee, and so hate thee. *Bible*, Proverbs 25:17.

7. Seven days is the length of a guest's life. BURMESE PROVERBS (1962), 444, ed. Hla Pe.

8. A house may draw visitors, but it is the possessor alone that can detain them. CHARLES CALEB COLTON, *Lacon* (1825), 1.30.

9. Fish and guests smell at three days old. DANISH PROVERB.

10. Happy the man who never puts on a face, but receives every visitor with that countenance he has on. EMERSON, *Journals*, 1833.

11. My evening visitors, if they cannot see the clock should find the time in my face. EMERSON, *Journals*, 1842.

12. Friendship increases in visiting friends, but in visiting them seldom. THOMAS FULLER, M.D., *Gnomologia* (1732), 1618.

13. Welcome is the best cheer. THOMAS FULLER, M.D., *Gnomologia* (1732), 5470.

14. A guest never forgets the host who had treated him kindly. HOMER, *Odyssey* (9th c. B.C.), 15, tr. E. V. Rieu.

15. It is equally offensive to speed a guest who would like to stay and to detain one who is anxious to leave. HOMER, *Odyssey* (9th c. B.C.), 15, tr. E. V. Rieu.

16. To be an ideal guest, stay at home. EDGAR WATSON HOWE, *Country Town Sayings* (1911).

17. I will gladly lecture for fifty dollars, but I'll not be a guest for less than a hundred. ELBERT HUBBARD, *The Philistine* (1895–1915).

18. Not many sounds in life, and I include all urban and all rural sounds, exceed in interest a knock at the door. CHARLES LAMB, "Valentine's Day," *Essays of Elia* (1823).

19. One of the main conveniences of marriage is to be able to pass a visitor whom one can't stand along to one's wife. GEORG CHRISTOPH LICHTENBERG, *Aphorisms* (1764–99), tr. F. H. Mautner and H. Hatfield.

20. A guest sees more in an hour than the host in a year. POLISH PROVERB.

21. Unbidden guests / Are often welcomest when they are gone. SHAKESPEARE, *I Henry VI* (1591–92), 2.2.55.

## HOSPITALS

See 889. Sickness

## 427. HOTELS

1. The great advantage of a hotel is that it's a refuge from home life. GEORGE BERNARD SHAW, *You Never Can Tell* (1898), 2.

2. All saints can do miracles, but few of them can keep a hotel. MARK TWAIN, *Notebook* (1935).

## 428. HOUSES

See also 50. Architecture; 420. Home; 740. Property

1. There is much virtue in a window. It is to a human being as a frame is to a painting, as a proscenium to a play, as "form" to literature. It strongly defines its content. MAX BEERBOHM, "Fenestralia," *Mainly On the Air* (1946).

2. A man builds a fine house; and now he has a master, and a task for life; he is to furnish, watch, show it, and keep it in repair the rest of his days. EMERSON, "Works and Days," *Society and Solitude* (1870).

3. The worst of a modern stylish mansion is, that it has no place for ghosts. OLIVER WENDELL HOLMES, SR., *The Poet at the Breakfast Table* (1872), 1.

4. Small rooms or dwellings discipline the mind, large ones weaken it. LEONARDO DA VINCI, *Notebooks* (c. 1500), tr. Jean Paul Richter.

5. The surroundings householders crave are glorified autobiographies ghost-written by willing architects and interior designers who, like their clients, want to show off. T. H. ROBSJOHN-GIBBINGS, "Robsjohn-Gibbings Names the Biggest Bore," *Town and Country*, January 1961.

6. Some women marry houses. / It's another kind of skin; it has a heart, / a mouth, a liver and bowel movements. ANNE SEXTON, "Housewife," *All My Pretty Ones* (1962).

7. A man's house is his stage. Others walk on to play their bit parts. Now and again a soliloquy, a birth, an adultery. KARL SHAPIRO, *The Bourgeois Poet* (1964), 1.29.

8. Our houses are such unwieldy property that we are often imprisoned rather than housed in them. THOREAU, "Economy," *Walden* (1854).

## 429. HUMANISM

See also 259. Divinity

1. What the world needs is not redemption from sin but redemption from hunger and oppression; it has no need to pin its hopes upon Heaven, it has everything to hope for from this earth. FRIEDRICH DÜRRENMATT, *The Marriage of Mr. Mississippi* (1952), 1, tr. Michael Bullock.

2. From the failure of the humanist tradition to participate fully or to act decisively, civilizations may perhaps crumble or perish at the hands of barbarians. But unless the humanist tradition itself in some form sur-

vives, there can really be no civilization at all. LOUIS KRONENBERGER, *Company Manners* (1954), 1.1.

3. When men can no longer be theists, they must, if they are civilized, become humanists. WALTER LIPPMANN, *A Preface to Morals* (1929), 1.7.7.

4. In all humanism there is an element of weakness, which in some circumstances may be its ruin, connected with its contempt of fanaticism, its patience, its love of scepticism; in short, its natural goodness. THOMAS MANN, "Europe, Beware," *The Thomas Mann Reader* (1950), tr. H. T. Lowe-Porter.

5. Dead are all the Gods: now do we desire the Superman to live. NIETZSCHE, "The Bestowing Virtue," *Thus Spoke Zarathustra* (1883–92), 3, tr. Thomas Common.

6. We now no longer camp as for a night, but have settled down on earth and forgotten heaven. THOREAU, "Economy," *Walden* (1854).

## 430. HUMANITARIANISM

**See also 56. Assistance; 72. Beggars; 118. Charity; 224. Deeds; 382. Gifts and Giving; 391. Goodness; 588. Misanthropy; 783. Reform; 880. Service; 1014. Unselfishness**

1. Do not give, as many rich men do, like a hen that lays her egg and then cackles. HENRY WARD BEECHER, *Proverbs from Plymouth Pulpit* (1887).

2. When thou doest alms, let not thy left hand know what thy right doeth. *Bible*, Matthew 6:3.

3. Inasmuch as ye have done it unto one of the least of these my brethren, ye have done it unto me. *Bible*, Matthew 25:40.

4. Let us not be weary in well doing: for in due season we shall reap, if we faint not. *Bible*, Galatians 6:9.

5. Too many have dispensed with generosity to practice charity. ALBERT CAMUS, *The Fall* (1956).

6. Social work is a band-aid on the festering wounds of society. ALEXANDER CHASE, *Perspectives* (1966).

7. It is better to light a candle than to curse the darkness. CHINESE PROVERB. Motto of the Christophers.

8. A man of humanity is one who, in seeking to establish himself, finds a foothold for others and who, desiring attainment for himself, helps others to attain. CONFUCIUS, *Analects* (6th c. B.C.), 6.28, tr. Ch'u Chai and Winberg Chai.

9. If I am virtuous and worthy, for whom should I not maintain a proper concern? CONFUCIUS, *Analects* (6th c. B.C.), 19.3, tr. Ch'u Chai and Winberg Chai.

10. Isn't it better to have men being ungrateful than to miss a chance to do good? DENIS DIDEROT, *Discours sur la poésie dramatique* (1773–78).

11. The rich have no more of the kingdom of heaven than they have purchased of the poor by their alms. JOHN DONNE, *Sermons*, No. 59, 1628.

12. In abstract love of humanity one almost always only loves oneself. DOSTOEVSKY, *The Idiot* (1868), 3.10, tr. David Magarshack.

13. As often as we do good we sacrifice. THOMAS FULLER, M.D., *Gnomologia* (1732), 721.

14. He that gives his heart will not deny his money. THOMAS FULLER, M.D., *Gnomologia* (1732), 2111.

15. By Jove the stranger and the poor are sent, / And what to those we give, to Jove is lent. HOMER, *Odyssey* (9th c. B.C.), 6.247, tr. Alexander Pope.

16. That action is best which procures the greatest happiness for the greatest numbers. FRANCIS HUTCHESON, *Inquiry Concerning Moral Good and Evil* (1720), 3.

17. A decent provision for the poor is the true test of civilization. SAMUEL JOHNSON, quoted in Boswell's *Life of Samuel Johnson*, 1770.

18. Men that talk of their own benefits are not believed to talk of them because they have done them, but to have done them because they might talk of them. BEN JONSON, "Explorata," *Timber* (1640).

19. Philanthropy is commendable, but it must not cause the philanthropist to overlook the circumstances of economic injustice which make philanthropy necessary. MARTIN LUTHER KING, JR., *Strength to Love* (1963), 3.2.

20. A large part of altruism, even when it is perfectly honest, is grounded upon the fact that it is uncomfortable to have un-

happy people about one. H. L. MENCKEN, *Prejudices: Fourth Series* (1924), 11.

21. High-toned humanitarians constantly overestimate the sufferings of those they sympathize with. H. L. MENCKEN, *Minority Report* (1956), 226.

22. It is not enough to do good; one must do it in the right way. JOHN MORLEY, *On Compromise* (1874).

23. If all alms were given only from pity, all beggars would have starved long ago. NIETZSCHE, *The Wanderer and His Shadow* (1880), 239, in *The Portable Nietzsche*, tr. Walter Kaufmann.

24. I give no alms. For that I am not poor enough. NIETZSCHE, "Zarathustra's Prologue," *Thus Spoke Zarathustra* (1883–92), 1, tr. Walter Kaufmann.

25. The humanitarian wishes to be a prime mover in the lives of others. He cannot admit either the divine or the natural order, by which men have the power to help themselves. The humanitarian puts himself in the place of God. ISABEL PATERSON, *The God of the Machine* (1943).

26. When you say you are in love with humanity, you are satisfied with yourself! LUIGI PIRANDELLO, *Each in His Own Way* (1924), 1, tr. Arthur Livingston.

27. Philanthropy and friendship seldom exist together in the same bosom. The heart that stretches from pole to pole is apt to spurn all intermediate ties. GEORGE DENNISON PRENTICE, *Prenticeana* (1860).

28. Human altruism which is not egoism, is sterile. MARCEL PROUST, *Remembrance of Things Past: The Past Recaptured* (1913–27), tr. Stephen Hudson.

29. Do good even to the wicked; it is as well to shut a dog's mouth with a crumb. SA'DI, *Gulistan* (1258), 1.33, tr. James Ross.

30. The dignity of the individual demands that he be not reduced to vassalage by the largesse of others. SAINT-EXUPÉRY, *Flight to Arras* (1942), 23, tr. Lewis Galantière.

31. How far that little candle throws his beams! / So shines a good deed in a naughty world. SHAKESPEARE, *The Merchant of Venice* (1596–97), 5.1.90.

32. He who wants to do good knocks at the gate; he who loves finds the gate open. RABINDRANATH TAGORE, *Stray Birds* (1916), 83.

33. He who is too busy doing good finds no time to be good. RABINDRANATH TAGORE, *Stray Birds* (1916), 184.

34. Philanthropy is almost the only virtue which is sufficiently appreciated by mankind. THOREAU, *Walden* (1854), 1.

35. Benevolence doesn't consist in those who are prosperous pitying and helping those who are not. Benevolence consists in fellow feeling that puts you upon actually the same level with the fellow who suffers. WOODROW WILSON, speech, Oct. 28, 1912.

36. If charity cost no money and benevolence caused no heartache, the world would be full of philanthropists. *Yiddish Proverbs* (1949), ed. Hanan J. Ayalti.

## 431. HUMAN NATURE

**See also 484. Instinct; 558. Mankind**

1. In a different time, in a different place, it is always some other side of our common human nature that has been developing itself. The actual true is the sum of all these. THOMAS CARLYLE, *On Heroes, Hero-Worship and the Heroic in History* (1841), 1.

2. Human nature is the same everywhere; the modes only are different. LORD CHESTERFIELD, *Letters to His Godson*, 1773.

3. Never can custom conquer nature, for she is ever unconquered. CICERO, *Tusculanae Disputationes* (44 B.C.), 5.27.78.

4. By nature, men are nearly alike; by practice, they get to be wide apart. CONFUCIUS, *Analects* (6th c. B.C.), 17.2, tr. James Legge.

5. It's a burden to us even to be human beings—men with our own real body and blood; we are ashamed of it, we think it a disgrace and try to contrive to be some sort of impossible generalized man. DOSTOEVSKY, *Notes from Underground* (1864), 2.10, tr. Constance Garnett.

6. Could we perfect human nature, we might also expect a perfect state of things. GOETHE, quoted in Johann Peter Eckermann's *Conversations with Goethe*, Feb. 25, 1824.

7. It is to the credit of human nature, that, except where its selfishness is brought into play, it loves more readily than it hates. NATHANIEL HAWTHORNE, *The*

*Scarlet Letter* (1850), 13.

8. The perfect joys of heaven do not satisfy the cravings of nature. WILLIAM HAZLITT, "On the Literary Character," *The Round Table* (1817).

9. Man's chief goal in life is still to become and stay human, and defend his achievements against the encroachment of nature. ERIC HOFFER, "The Return of Nature," *The Temper of Our Time* (1967), 5.

10. Drive Nature from your door with a pitchfork, and she will return again and again. HORACE, *Epistles* (20–c. 8 B.C.), 1.10.

11. The thief and the murderer follow nature just as much as the philanthropist. THOMAS HENRY HUXLEY, "Evolution and Ethics" (1893).

12. Beneath the dingy uniformity of international fashions in dress, man remains what he has always been—a splendid fighting animal, a self-sacrificing hero, and a bloodthirsty savage. WILLIAM RALPH INGE, "Our Present Discontents," *Outspoken Essays: First Series* (1919).

13. Scenery is fine—but human nature is finer. JOHN KEATS, letter to Benjamin Bailey, March 13, 1818.

14. Whenever man forgets that man is an animal, the result is always to make him less humane. JOSEPH WOOD KRUTCH, "March," *The Twelve Seasons* (1949).

15. Before Man made us citizens, great Nature made us men. JAMES RUSSELL LOWELL, "On the Capture of Fugitive Slaves near Washington" (1845), 2.

16. That a thing is unnatural . . . is no argument for its being blamable; since the most criminal actions are, to a being like man, not more unnatural than most of the virtues. JOHN STUART MILL, "Nature," *Three Essays on Religion* (1874).

17. It disturbs me no more to find men base, unjust, or selfish than to see apes mischievous, wolves savage, or the vulture ravenous for its prey. MOLIÈRE, *The Misanthrope* (1666), 1, tr. John Wood.

18. To be natural means to dare to be as immoral as Nature is. NIETZSCHE, *The Will to Power* (1888), tr. Anthony M. Ludovici.

19. The essence of being human is that one does not seek perfection. GEORGE ORWELL, "Reflections on Gandhi," *Shooting an Elephant* (1950).

20. We ride through life on the beast within us. Beat the animal, but you can't make it think. LUIGI PIRANDELLO, *The Pleasure of Honesty* (1917), 1, tr. William Murray.

21. What does reason demand of a man? A very easy thing—to live in accord with his own nature. SENECA, *Letters to Lucilius* (1st c.), 41, tr. E. Phillips Barker.

22. Nature her custom holds, / Let shame say what it will. SHAKESPEARE, *Hamlet* (1600), 4.7.189.

23. One touch of nature makes the whole world kin. SHAKESPEARE, *Troilus and Cressida* (1601–02), 3.3.175.

24. All is disgust when one leaves his own nature / and does things that misfit it. SOPHOCLES, *Philoctetes* (409 B.C.), tr. David Grene.

25. It is usually the case with most men that their nature is so constituted that they pity those who fare badly and envy those who fare well. SPINOZA, *Ethics* (1677), 3, tr. Andrew Boyle.

26. The human being says that the beast in him has been aroused, when what he actually means is that the human being in him has been aroused. JAMES THURBER, "The Trouble with Man Is Man," *Lanterns and Lances* (1961).

27. Nature has always had more power than education. VOLTAIRE, *Vie de Molière* (1739).

28. I guess the' 's about as much human nature in some folks as the' is in others, if not more. EDWARD NOYES WESTCOTT, *David Harum* (1898), 28.

## 432. HUMILIATION

See also 814. Ridicule; 886. Shame

1. It is a bitter dose to be taught obedience after you have learned to rule. PUBLILIUS SYRUS, *Moral Sayings* (1st c. B.C.), 1019, tr. Darius Lyman.

2. Better a quiet death than a public misfortune. SPANISH PROVERB.

## 433. HUMILITY

See also 163. Conceit; 594. Modesty; 727. Pride

1. Meekness, n. Uncommon patience in planning a revenge that is worth while. AMBROSE BIERCE, *The Devil's Dictionary* (1881–1911).

2. The eagle never lost so much time as when he submitted to learn of the crow. WILLIAM BLAKE, "Proverbs of Hell," *The Marriage of Heaven and Hell* (1790).

3. They are proud in humility; proud in that they are not proud. ROBERT BURTON, *The Anatomy of Melancholy* (1621), 1.2.3.14.

4. Humility has its origin in an awareness of unworthiness, and sometimes too in a dazzled awareness of saintliness. COLETTE, "Lady of Letters," *Earthly Paradise* (1966), 4, ed. Robert Phelps.

5. Nothing is beneath you if it is in the direction of your life. EMERSON, "Wealth," *The Conduct of Life* (1860).

6. A poor spirit is poorer than a poor purse. THOMAS FULLER, M.D., *Gnomologia* (1732), 358.

7. Humility is just as much the opposite of self-abasement as it is of self-exaltation. DAG HAMMARSKJÖLD, "1959," *Markings* (1964), tr. Leif Sjoberg and W. H. Auden.

8. Humility is not renunciation of pride but the substitution of one pride for another. ERIC HOFFER, *The Passionate State of Mind* (1954), 212.

9. Humility is the first of the virtues—for other people. OLIVER WENDELL HOLMES, SR., *The Professor at the Breakfast Table* (1860), 5.

10. Meekness is the mask of malice. ROBERT G. INGERSOLL, *Prose-Poems and Selections* (1884).

11. Plenty of people wish to become devout, but no one wishes to be humble. LA ROCHEFOUCAULD, *Maxims* (1665), tr. Kenneth Pratt.

12. Humility is often only feigned submission which people use to render others submissive. It is a subterfuge of pride which lowers itself in order to rise. LA ROCHEFOUCAULD, *Maxims* (1665), tr. Kenneth Pratt.

13. A man who has humility will have acquired in the last reaches of his beliefs the saving doubt of his own certainty. WALTER LIPPMANN, *The Public Philosophy* (1955), 10.4.

14. The fuller the ear is of rice-grain, the lower it bends; empty of grain, it grows taller and taller. MALAY PROVERB.

15. One may be humble out of pride. MONTAIGNE, "Of presumption," *Essays* (1580–88), tr. Charles Cotton and W. C. Hazlitt.

16. He that humbleth himself wishes to be exalted. NIETZSCHE, *Human, All Too Human* (1878), 87, tr. Helen Zimmern.

17. Humility has the toughest hide. NIETZSCHE, "The Stillest Hour," *Thus Spoke Zarathustra* (1883–92), 2, tr. Walter Kaufmann.

18. There must be feelings of humility, not from nature, but from penitence, not to rest in them, but to go on to greatness. PASCAL, *Pensées* (1670), 524, tr. W. F. Trotter.

19. Who builds a church to God and not to fame, / Will never mark the marble with his name. ALEXANDER POPE, *Moral Essays* (1731–35), 3.285.

20. Humility neither falls far, nor heavily. PUBLILIUS SYRUS, *Moral Sayings* (1st c. B.C.), 334, tr. Darius Lyman.

21. There is no humiliation for humility. JOSEPH ROUX, *Meditations of a Parish Priest* (1886), 4.5, tr. Isabel F. Hapgood.

22. The first test of a truly great man is his humility. JOHN RUSKIN, *Modern Painters* (1843–60), v. 3, 4.16.24.

23. The sons of Adam are formed from dust; if not humble as the dust, they fall short of being men. SA'DI, *Gulistan* (1258), 2.42, tr. James Ross.

24. Humility is a virtue all preach, none practice, and yet everybody is content to hear. JOHN SELDEN, "Humility," *Table Talk* (1689).

25. Those who are believed to be most abject and humble are usually most ambitious and envious. SPINOZA, *Ethics* (1677), 3, tr. Andrew Boyle.

26. We come nearest to the great when we are great in humility. RABINDRANATH TAGORE, *Stray Birds* (1916), 57.

27. Man was created on the sixth day so that he could not be boastful, since he came after the flea in the order of creation. Haggadah, *Palestinian Talmud* (4th c.).

28. If thou have any good things believe better things of others that thou may keep thy meekness. THOMAS À KEMPIS, *The Imitation of Christ* (1426), 1.7.

29. Do not seek so anxiously to be developed, to subject yourself to many influences to be played on; it is all dissipation. Humility like darkness reveals the heavenly lights. THOREAU, "Conclusion," *Walden* (1854).

30. Too humble is half proud. *Yiddish Proverbs* (1949), ed. Hanan J. Ayalti.

## 434. HUMOR

See also 143. Comedians; 144. Comedy; 523. Laughter; 762. Puns; 814. Ridicule; 874. Sense and Nonsense; 879. Seriousness; 1054. Wit

1. Clumsy jesting is no joke. AESOP, "The Ass and the Lapdog," *Fables* (6th c. B.C.?), tr. Joseph Jacobs.

2. Humor is a delicate shrub, with the passing hectic flush of its time. The current topic variety is especially subject to early frosts, as is also the dialectic species. THOMAS BAILEY ALDRICH, "Leaves from a Notebook," *Ponkapog Papers* (1903).

3. Men will let you abuse them if only you will make them laugh. HENRY WARD BEECHER, *Proverbs from Plymouth Pulpit* (1887).

4. Humor is falling downstairs if you do it while in the act of warning your wife not to. KENNETH BIRD, news summaries, May 3, 1954.

5. A sense of humor keen enough to show a man his own absurdities, as well as those of other people, will keep him from the commission of all sins, or nearly all, save those that are worth committing. SAMUEL BUTLER (d. 1902), "Lord, What Is Man?" *Note-Books* (1912).

6. Mirth resting on earnestness and sadness, as the rainbow on black tempest: only a right valiant heart is capable of that. THOMAS CARLYLE, *On Heroes, Hero-Worship and the Heroic in History* (1841), 1.

7. When once you have got hold of a vulgar joke, you may be certain that you have got hold of a subtle and spiritual idea. G. K. CHESTERTON, "Cockneys and Their Jokes," *All Things Considered* (1908).

8. Men will confess to treason, murder, arson, false teeth, or a wig. How many of them will own up to a lack of humor? FRANK MOORE COLBY, "Satire and Teeth," *The Colby Essays* (1926), V. 1.

9. Th' las' man that makes a joke owns it. FINLEY PETER DUNNE, "On the Midway," *Mr. Dooley's Opinions* (1901).

10. A difference of taste in jokes is a great strain on the affections. GEORGE ELIOT, *Daniel Deronda* (1874–76), 2.15.

11. Better lose a jest than a friend. THOMAS FULLER, M.D., *Gnomologia* (1732), 915.

12. Humor is an affirmation of dignity, a declaration of man's superiority to all that befalls him. ROMAIN GARY, *Promise at Dawn* (1961).

13. A jest often decides matters of importance more effectually and happily than seriousness. HORACE, *Satires* (35–30 B.C.), 1.10.

14. The free mind must have one policeman, Irony. ELBERT HUBBARD, *The Philistine* (1895–1915).

15. He that jokes confesses. ITALIAN PROVERB.

16. Of all the griefs that harass the distressed, / Sure the most bitter is a scornful jest. SAMUEL JOHNSON, *London* (1738).

17. Humor simultaneously wounds and heals, indicts and pardons, diminishes and enlarges; it constitutes inner growth at the expense of outer gain, and those who possess and honestly practice it make themselves more through a willingness to make themselves less. LOUIS KRONENBERGER, *Company Manners* (1954), 3.2.

18. The teller of a mirthful tale has latitude allowed him. We are content with less than absolute truth. CHARLES LAMB, "Stage Illusion," *Last Essays of Elia* (1833).

19. The humorist has a good eye for the humbug; he does not always recognize the saint. W. SOMERSET MAUGHAM, *The Summing Up* (1938), 20.

20. Good taste and humor are a contradiction in terms, like a chaste whore. MALCOLM MUGGERIDGE, *Time*, Sept. 14, 1953.

21. Gentle Dulness ever loves a joke. ALEXANDER POPE, *The Dunciad* (1743), 2.34.

22. The profoundly humorous writers are humorous because they are responsive to the hopeless, uncouth concatenations of life. V. S. PRITCHETT, "The Minor Dostoevsky," *The Living Novel & Later Appreciations* (1964).

23. Everything is funny as long as it is happening to somebody else. WILL ROGERS, "Warning to Jokers: Lay Off the Prince," *The Illiterate Digest* (1942).

24. Fun is a good thing but only when it spoils nothing better GEORGE SANTAYANA, "The Comic," *The Sense of Beauty* (1896).

25. A jest's prosperity lies in the ear / Of him that hears it, never in the tongue / Of him that makes it. SHAKESPEARE, *Love's Labour's Lost* (1594–95), 5.2.70.

26. For every ten jokes, thou hast got an hundred enemies. LAURENCE STERNE, *Tristram Shandy* (1759–67), 1.12.

27. Humor is emotional chaos remembered in tranquility. JAMES THURBER, *New York Post*, Feb. 29, 1960.

28. As brevity is the soul of wit, form, it seems to me, is the heart of humor and the salvation of comedy. JAMES THURBER, "The Case for Comedy," *Lanterns and Lances* (1961).

29. The secret source of humor is not joy but sorrow. There is no humor in heaven. MARK TWAIN, "Pudd'nhead Wilson's New Calendar," *Following the Equator* (1897), 1.10.

30. Pleasantry is never good on serious points, because it always regards subjects in that point of view in which it is not the purpose to consider them. VOLTAIRE, "Style," *Philosophical Dictionary* (1764).

31. The world likes humor, but it treats it patronizingly. It decorates its serious artists with laurel, and its wags with Brussels sprouts. E. B. WHITE, "Some Remarks on Humor," *The Second Tree from the Corner* (1954).

32. Humour is the first of the gifts to perish in a foreign tongue. VIRGINIA WOOLF, "On Not Knowing Greek," *The Common Reader: First Series* (1925).

## 435. HUNGER

See also 272. Eating

1. Appetite, n. An instinct thoughtfully implanted by Providence as a solution to the labor question. AMBROSE BIERCE, *The Devil's Dictionary* (1881–1911).

2. There's no sauce in the world like hunger. CERVANTES, *Don Quixote* (1605–15), 2.3.5, tr. Peter Motteux and John Ozell.

3. All's good in a famine. THOMAS FULLER, M.D., *Gnomologia* (1732), 545.

4. Hunger can explain many acts. It can be said that all vile acts are done to satisfy hunger. MAXIM GORKY, *Enemies* (1906), 1.

5. Love and business and family and religion and art and patriotism are nothing but shadows of words when a man's starving. O. HENRY, "Cupid à la Carte," *Heart of the West* (1907).

6. A hungry stomach has no ears. LA FONTAINE, "The Kite and the Nightingale," *Fables* (1668–94).

7. It has been well said that a hungry man is more interested in four sandwiches than four freedoms. HENRY CABOT LODGE, JR., news reports, March 29, 1955.

8. Hunger is the teacher of the arts and the bestower of invention. PERSIUS, prologue to the *Satires* (1st c.), 10.

9. The belly is ungrateful—it always forgets we already gave it something. RUSSIAN PROVERB.

10. To him who is stinted of food a boiled turnip will relish like a roast fowl. SA'DI, *Gulistan* (1258), 3.19, tr. James Ross.

11. An empty stomach will not listen to anything. SPANISH PROVERB.

12. A hungry man is not a free man. ADLAI STEVENSON, speech, Kasson, Minn., Sept. 6, 1952.

13. Hunger does not breed reform; it breeds madness and all the ugly distempers that make an ordered life impossible. WOODROW WILSON, address to Congress, Nov. 11, 1918.

## 436. HUNTING

1. The creatures that want to live a life of their own, we call wild. If wild, then no matter how harmless, we treat them as outlaws, and those of us who are specially well brought up shoot them for fun. CLARENCE DAY, *This Simian World* (1920), 7.

2. There is a passion for hunting something deeply implanted in the human breast. CHARLES DICKENS, *Oliver Twist* (1837–39), 10.

3. It is very strange, and very melancholy, that the paucity of human pleasures should persuade us ever to call hunting one of them. SAMUEL JOHNSON, quoted in Birkbeck Hill's *Johnsonian Miscellanies* (1897), v. 1.

4. The fox, when caught, is worth nothing: he is followed for the pleasure of following. SYDNEY SMITH, quoted in Lady S. Holland's *Memoir* (1855), v. 1.6.

5. The English country gentleman galloping after a fox—the unspeakable in full pursuit of the uneatable. OSCAR WILDE, *A Woman of No Importance* (1893), 1.

## HURRY

See 409. Haste; 919. Speed

## 437. HYPOCHONDRIA

See also 889. Sickness

1. Hypochondriacs squander large sums of time in search of nostrums by which they vainly hope they may get more time to squander. CHARLES CALEB COLTON, *Lacon* (1825), 2.70.

2. An imaginary ailment is worse than a disease. *Yiddish Proverbs* (1949), ed. Hanan J. Ayalti.

## 438. HYPOCRISY

See also 221. Deception; 681. Personality, Dual; 894. Sincerity

1. Many among men are they who set high / the show of honor, yet break justice. AESCHYLUS, *Agamemnon* (458 B.C.), tr. Richmond Lattimore.

2. We are always making God our accomplice, that so we may legalize our own iniquities. Every successful massacre is consecrated by a Te Deum, and the clergy have never been wanting in benedictions for any victorious enormity. HENRI FRÉDÉRIC AMIEL, *Journal*, Oct. 6, 1866, tr. Mrs. Humphry Ward.

3. Occident, n. The part of the world lying west (or east) of the Orient. It is largely inhabited by Christians, a powerful subtribe of the Hypocrites, whose principal industries are murder and cheating, which they are pleased to call "war" and "commerce." These, also, are the principal industries of the Orient. AMBROSE BIERCE, *The Devil's Dictionary* (1881–1911).

4. Of lies, false modesty is the most decent. CHAMFORT, *Maximes et pensées* (1805), 1.

5. It is easier to pretend to be what you are not than to hide what you really are; but he that can accomplish both has little to learn in hypocrisy. CHARLES CALEB COLTON, *Lacon* (1825), 1.315.

6. Among men, Hinnissy, wet eye manes dhry heart. FINLEY PETER DUNNE, "Casual Observations," *Mr. Dooley's Philosophy* (1900).

7. The child is sincere, and the man when he is alone, if he be not a writer; but on the entrance of the second person, hypocrisy begins. EMERSON, *Journals*, 1834.

8. The hater of property and of government takes care to have his warranty deed recorded; and the book written against fame and learning has the author's name on the title-page. EMERSON, *Journals*, 1857.

9. Do as the maids do, say no and take it. ENGLISH PROVERB.

10. Often a noble face hides filthy ways. EURIPIDES, *Electra* (413 B.C.), tr. Emily Townsend Vermeule.

11. The true hypocrite is the one who ceases to perceive his deception, the one who lies with sincerity. ANDRÉ GIDE, *Journal of "The Counterfeiters,"* Second Notebook, August 1921, tr. Justin O'Brien.

12. He is a hypocrite who professes what he does not believe; not he who does not practise all he wishes or approves. WILLIAM HAZLITT, "On Cant and Hypocrisy," *Sketches and Essays* (1839).

13. I detest that man, who / hides one thing in the depths of his heart, and speaks forth another. HOMER, *Iliad* (9th c. B.C.), 9.312, tr. Richmond Lattimore.

14. Most people have seen worse things in private than they pretend to be shocked at in public. EDGAR WATSON HOWE, *Country Town Sayings* (1911).

15. It is not uncommon to charge the difference between promise and performance, between profession and reality, upon deep design and studied deceit; but the truth is, that there is very little hypocrisy in the world. SAMUEL JOHNSON, *The Idler* (1758–60), 27.

16. Spread yourself upon his bosom publicly, whose heart you would eat in private. BEN JONSON, *Every Man Out of His Humour* (1599), 3.1.

17. How ready we all are with our praises when a cake is to be divided,—if it is not ours! WALTER SAVAGE LANDOR, "Diogenes and Plato,' *Imaginary Conversations* (1824–53).

18. Hypocrisy is the homage which vice pays to virtue. LA ROCHEFOUCAULD, *Maxims* (1665), tr. Kenneth Pratt.

19. In the mouths of many men soft words are like roses that soldiers put into the muzzles of their muskets on holidays. LONGFELLOW, "Table-Talk," *Driftwood* (1857).

20. I mean not to run with the hare and hold with the hound. JOHN LYLY, *Euphues: The Anatomy of Wit* (1579).

21. Hypocrisy is a fashionable vice, and all fashionable vices pass for virtues. MOLIÈRE, *Don Juan* (1665), 5.2, tr. Donald M. Frame.

22. The hypocrite who always plays one and the same part ceases at last to be a hypocrite. NIETZSCHE, *Human, All Too Human* (1878), 51, tr. Helen Zimmern.

23. That character in conversation which commonly passes for agreeable is made up of civility and falsehood. ALEXANDER POPE, *Thoughts on Various Subjects* (1727).

24. With devotion's visage / And pious action we do sugar o'er / The devil himself. SHAKESPEARE, *Hamlet* (1600), 3.1.47.

25. To show an unfelt sorrow is an office / Which the false man does easy. SHAKESPEARE, *Macbeth* (1605–06), 2.3.142.

26. Hypocrisy in anything whatever may deceive the cleverest and most penetrating man, but the least wide-awake of children recognizes it, and is revolted by it, however ingeniously it may be disguised. LEO TOLSTOY, *Anna Karenina* (1873–76), 3.9, tr. Constance Garnett.

27. Men use thought only as authority for their injustice, and employ speech only to conceal their thoughts. VOLTAIRE, Dialogue 14, "Le Chapon et la poularde" (1763), 14.

28. He who lives more lives than one / More deaths than one must die. OSCAR WILDE, *The Ballad of Reading Gaol* (1898), 3.37.

# I

## 439. ICONOCLASM

**See also 239. Destruction; 504. Irreverence; 813. Revolution; 979. Tradition**

1. These, if ever, are the brave free days of destroyed landmarks, while the ingenious minds are busy inventing the forms of the new beacons which, it is consoling to think, will be set up presently in the old places. JOSEPH CONRAD, *A Personal Record* (1912), 5.

2. By despising all that has preceded us, we teach others to despise ourselves. WILLIAM HAZLITT, "On Reading New Books," *Sketches and Essays* (1839).

3. Rough work, iconoclasm, – but the only way to get at truth. OLIVER WENDELL HOLMES, SR., *The Professor at the Breakfast Table* (1860), 5.

4. We must not roughly smash other people's idols because we know, or think we know, that they are of cheap human manufacture. OLIVER WENDELL HOLMES, SR., *The Poet at the Breakfast Table* (1872), 11.

5. When smashing monuments, save the pedestals – they always come in handy. STANISLAW LEC, *Unkempt Thoughts* (1962), tr. Jacek Galazka.

## 440. IDEALISM

**See also 252. Disillusionment; 443. Ideology; 783. Reform; 1018. Utopia**

1. Idealism springs from deep feelings, but feelings are nothing without the formulated idea that keeps them whole. JACQUES BARZUN, *The House of Intellect* (1959), 6.

2. Our bodies can be mobilized by law and police and men with guns, if necessary – but where shall we find that which will make us believe in what we must do, so that we can fight through to victory? PEARL S. BUCK, *What America Means to Me* (1943), 5.

3. If two or three persons should come with a high spiritual aim and with great powers, the world would fall into their hands like a ripe peach. EMERSON, *Journals*, 1844.

4. Don't make your will before dying for an ideal: make a kid who will be worthy of his father. Graffito written during French student revolt, May 1968.

5. Never look down to test the ground before taking your next step: only he who keeps his eye fixed on the far horizon will find his right road. DAG HAMMARSKJÖLD, "1925–1930," *Markings* (1964), tr. Leif Sjoberg and W. H. Auden.

6. All men are prepared to accomplish the incredible if their ideals are threatened. HERMANN HESSE, *Demian* (1919), 7, tr. Michael Roloff and Michael Lebeck.

7. That at the core of every idealist there reigns a demon of cruelty, a monster thirsty for blood – no one must admit this as a universal law, else Time, the suave impostor, could not go on with Life, his miracle-force.

ELBERT HUBBARD, *The Philistine* (1895–1915).

8. Idealism is the noble toga that political gentlemen drape over their will to power. ALDOUS HUXLEY, *New York Herald Tribune*, Nov. 25, 1963.

9. Don't use that foreign word "ideals." We have that excellent native word "lies." HENRIK IBSEN, *The Wild Duck* (1884), 5.

10. Ideals are an imaginative understanding of that which is desirable in that which is possible. WALTER LIPPMANN, *A Preface to Morals* (1929), 3.12.7.

11. God, when he makes the prophet, does not unmake the man. JOHN LOCKE, quoted in Emerson's *Representative Men: Swedenborg* (1850).

12. An idealist is one who, on noticing that a rose smells better than a cabbage, concludes that it will also make better soup. H. L. MENCKEN, "Sententiae," *A Book of Burlesques* (1920).

13. It is not materialism that is the chief curse of the world, as pastors teach, but idealism. Men get into trouble by taking their visions and hallucinations too seriously. H. L. MENCKEN, *Minority Report* (1956), 305.

14. The visionary denies the truth to himself, the liar only to others. NIETZSCHE, *Miscellaneous Maxims and Opinions* (1879), 6, tr. Paul V. Cohn.

15. The idealist is incorrigible: if he be thrown out of his Heaven, he makes himself a suitable ideal out of Hell. NIETZSCHE, *Miscellaneous Maxims and Opinions* (1879), 23, tr. Paul V. Cohn.

16. Man is an animal who lifts his head to the sky and does not see the spiders on his ceiling. JULES RENARD, *Journal*, April 1894, ed. and tr. Louise Bogan and Elizabeth Roget.

17. It is only in marriage with the world that our ideals can bear fruit: divorced from it, they remain barren. BERTRAND RUSSELL, title essay, *Mysticism and Logic* (1917).

18. It seems to be the fate of idealists to obtain what they have struggled for in a form which destroys their ideals. BERTRAND RUSSELL, "The Liberation of Women," *Marriage and Morals* (1929).

19. The toe of the star-gazer is often stubbed. RUSSIAN PROVERB.

20. The vital straining towards an ideal, definite but latent, when it dominates a whole life, may express that ideal more fully than could the best-chosen words. GEORGE SANTAYANA, *Little Essays* (1920), 57, ed. Logan Pearsall Smith.

21. A man gazing on the stars is proverbially at the mercy of the puddles in the road. ALEXANDER SMITH, "Men of Letters," *Dreamthorp* (1863).

## 441. IDEAS

See also 649. Opinion; 968. Thought

1. Nothing is more dangerous than an idea, when it is the only idea we have. ALAIN, *Libres-propos* (1908–14).

2. Every man with an idea has at least two or three followers. BROOKS ATKINSON, "January 2," *Once Around the Sun* (1951).

3. Defeat is a fact and victory can be a fact. If the idea is good, it will survive defeat, it may even survive the victory. STEPHEN VINCENT BENÉT, *John Brown's Body* (1928), 2.

4. Those ideas which are least our own are the ones most easily expressed in language. HENRI BERGSON, *Essai sur les données immédiates de la conscience* (1889).

5. It's unpleasant to be able to turn certain ideas over in your mind that nobody suspects you of having. UGO BETTI, *Struggle Till Dawn* (1949), 2, tr. G. H. McWilliam.

6. A new idea is delicate. It can be killed by a sneer or a yawn; it can be stabbed to death by a quip and worried to death by a frown on the right man's brow. CHARLES BROWER, *Advertising Age*, Aug. 10, 1959.

7. Hang ideas! They are tramps, vagabonds, knocking at the back-door of your mind, each taking a little of your substance, each carrying away some crumb of that belief in a few simple notions you must cling to if you want to live decently and would like to die easy! JOSEPH CONRAD, *Lord Jim* (1900), 5.

8. Old ideas give way slowly; for they are more than abstract logical forms and categories. They are habits, predispositions, deeply ingrained attitudes of aversion and preference. JOHN DEWEY, "The Influence of Darwinism on Philosophy" (1909).

9. Black are the brooding clouds and troubled the deep waters, when the Sea of Thought, first heaving from a calm, gives up its Dead. CHARLES DICKENS, "Third Quarter," *The Chimes* (1844).

10. Ideas are fatal to caste. E. M. FORSTER, *A Passage to India* (1924), 1.7.

11. The idea is the old age of the spirit and the disease of the mind. EDMOND and JULES DE GONCOURT, *Journal*, Dec. 10, 1858, tr. Robert Baldick.

12. The only sure weapon against bad ideas is better ideas. WHITNEY GRISWOLD, *The New York Times*, Feb. 24, 1959.

13. Any new formula which suddenly emerges in our consciousness has its roots in long trains of thought; it is virtually old when it first makes its appearance among the recognized growths of our intellect. OLIVER WENDELL HOLMES, SR., *The Autocrat of the Breakfast Table* (1858), 2.

14. There never was an idea started that woke up men out of their stupid indifference but its originator was spoken of as a crank. OLIVER WENDELL HOLMES, SR., *Over the Teacups* (1891), 7.

15. Ideas are born, they struggle, triumph, change, and they are transformed; but is there a dead idea which in the end does not live on, transformed into a broader and clearer goal? EUGENIO MARÍA DE HOSTOS, "Hombres e ideas," *Obras* (1939–54), 14.

16. To say that an idea is fashionable is to say, I think, that it has been adulterated to a point where it is hardly an idea at all. MURRAY KEMPTON, "The Day of the Locust," *Part of Our Time* (1955).

17. A man may die, nations may rise and fall, but an idea lives on. Ideas have endurance without death. JOHN F. KENNEDY, address, Greenville, N. C., Feb. 8, 1963.

18. The thinker dies, but his thoughts are beyond the reach of destruction. Men are mortal; but ideas are immortal. WALTER LIPPMANN, *A Preface to Morals* (1929), 1.3.2.

19. A young man must let his ideas grow, not be continually rooting them up to see how they are getting on. WILLIAM MC FEE, "The Idea," *Harbours of Memory* (1921).

20. In the matter of ideas he who meditates is lost. WILLIAM MC FEE, "The Idea," *Harbours of Memory* (1921).

21. Just as our eyes need light in order to see, our minds need ideas in order to conceive. NICOLAS MALEBRANCHE, *Recherche de la vérité* (1674–75), 6.

22. If you are possessed by an idea, you find it expressed everywhere, you even *smell* it. THOMAS MANN, "Tonio Kröger" (1903), *Death in Venice*, tr. H. T. Lowe-Porter.

23. A single idea, if it is right, saves us the labor of an infinity of experiences. JACQUES MARITAIN, *Reflections on America* (1958), 12.

24. One has to be a lowbrow, a bit of a murderer, to be a politician, ready and willing to see people sacrificed, slaughtered, for the sake of an idea, whether a good one or a bad one. HENRY MILLER, interview, *Writers at Work: Second Series* (1963).

25. Great ideas are not charitable. HENRY DE MONTHERLANT, *Le Maître de Santiago* (1947), 1.4.

26. It is one thing to study historically the ideas which have influenced our predecessors, and another thing to seek in them an influence fruitful for ourselves. JOHN MORLEY, "Carlyle," *Critical Miscellanies* (1871–1908).

27. You cannot put a rope around the neck of an idea; you cannot put an idea up against a barrack-square wall and riddle it with bullets; you cannot confine it in the strongest prison cell that your slaves could ever build. SEAN O'CASEY, *Death of Thomas Ashe* (1918), 4.

28. An idea is a putting truth in checkmate. JOSÉ ORTEGA Y GASSET, *The Revolt of the Masses* (1930), 8.

29. The secret of living is to find a pivot, the pivot of a concept on which you can make your stand. LUIGI PIRANDELLO, *The Rules of the Game* (1918), 1, tr. William Murray.

30. One should operate by dissociation, and not by association, of ideas. An association is almost always commonplace. Dissociation decomposes, and uncovers latent affinities. JULES RENARD, *Journal*, January 1890, ed. and tr. Louise Bogan and Elizabeth Roget.

31. General and abstract ideas are the source of the greatest errors of mankind. ROUSSEAU, *Émile* (1762), 4.

32. Man is a fighting animal; his thoughts are his banners, and it is a failure of nerve in him if they are only thoughts. GEORGE SANTAYANA, *Dialogues in Limbo* (1925), 2.

33. In the abstracting of an idea one may lose the very intimate humanity of it. BEN SHAHN, "The Biography of a Painting," *The Shape of Content* (1957).

34. The slowness of one section of the world about adopting the valuable ideas of another section of it is a curious thing and unaccountable. MARK TWAIN, "Some National Stupidities" (1923).

35. An idea does not pass from one language to another without change. MIGUEL DE UNAMUNO, preface, *Tragic Sense of Life* (1913), tr. J. E. Crawford Flitch.

36. No man can establish title to an idea —at the most he can only claim possession. The stream of thought that irrigates the mind of each of us is a confluent of the intellectual river that drains the whole of the living universe. MAURICE VALENCY, introduction to *Jean Giraudoux: Four Plays* (1958).

37. Human life is driven forward by its dim apprehension of notions too general for its existing language. ALFRED NORTH WHITEHEAD, *Adventures in Ideas* (1933), 2.

38. All great ideas are dangerous. OSCAR WILDE, *De Profundis* (1905).

## 442. IDENTITY

**See also 45. Appearance; 117. Character; 314. Existence; 467. Individuality; 587. Mirrors; 612. Names; 681. Personality, Dual; 852. Self; 868. Self-knowledge**

1. He that is neither one thing nor the other has no friends. AESOP, "The Bat, the Birds, and the Beasts," *Fables* (6th c. B.C.?), tr. Joseph Jacobs.

2. To its own impulse every creature stirs; / Live by thy light, and earth will live by hers! MATTHEW ARNOLD, "Religious Isolation," *The Strayed Reveller, and Other Poems* (1849).

3. Resolve to be thyself: and know, that he / Who finds himself, loses his misery. MATTHEW ARNOLD, "Self-Dependence" (1852).

4. Rain beats a leopard's skin, but it does not wash out the spots. ASHANTI PROVERB.

5. A strong sense of identity gives man an idea he can do no wrong; too little accomplishes the same. DJUNA BARNES, *Nightwood* (1937).

6. We wander but in the end there is always a certain peace in being what one is, in being that completely. The condemned man has that joy. UGO BETTI, *Goat Island* (1946), 3.2, ed. Gino Rizzo.

7. Can the Ethiopian change his skin, or the leopard his spots? *Bible*, Jeremiah 13:23.

8. People remain what they are, even when their faces fall to pieces. BERTOLT BRECHT, *Jungle of Cities* (1924), 9, tr. Anselm Hollo.

9. To be nobody-but-myself—in a world which is doing its best, night and day, to make you everybody else—means to fight the hardest battle which any human being can fight, and never stop fighting. E. E. CUMMINGS, quoted in Charles Norman's *The Magic-Maker* (1958).

10. Our [American] culture impedes the clear definition of any faithful self-image—indeed, of any clear image whatever. We do not break images; there are few iconoclasts among us. Instead, we blur and soften them. EDGAR Z. FRIEDENBERG, "The Vanishing Adolescent," *The Vanishing Adolescent* (1959).

11. You are, when all is done—just what you are. GOETHE, "Faust's Study," *Faust: Part I* (1808), tr. Philip Wayne.

12. Be what you are. This is the first step toward becoming better than you are. JULIUS CHARLES HARE and AUGUSTUS WILLIAM HARE, *Guesses at Truth* (1827).

13. It is thus with most of us; we are what other people say we are. We know ourselves chiefly by hearsay. ERIC HOFFER, *The Passionate State of Mind* (1954), 129.

14. While you cannot resolve what you are, at last you will be nothing. MARTIAL, *Epigrams* (A.D. 86), 2.64, tr. Walter C. A. Ker.

15. [Philosophy] forms us for ourselves, not for others; to be, not to seem. MONTAIGNE, "Of the resemblance of children to their fathers," *Essays* (1580–88), tr. Charles Cotton and W. C. Hazlitt.

16. Not one of us can lie or pretend. We're all fixed in good faith in a certain concept of ourselves. LUIGI PIRANDELLO, *Henry IV* (1922), 1, tr. Edward Storer.

17. It matters not what you are thought to be, but what you are. PUBLILIUS SYRUS, *Moral Sayings* (1st c. B.C.), 785, tr. Darius Lyman.

18. No matter how much you feed a wolf he will always return to the forest. RUSSIAN PROVERB.

19. Freedom and constraint are two as-

pects of the same necessity, the necessity of being the man you are and not another. You are free to be that man, but not free to be another. SAINT-EXUPÉRY, *The Wisdom of the Sands* (1948), 43, tr. Stuart Gilbert.

20. We only become what we are by the radical and deep-seated refusal of that which others have made of us. JEAN-PAUL SARTRE, preface to Frantz Fanon's *The Wretched of the Earth* (1961), tr. Constance Farrington.

21. Rose is a rose is a rose is a rose. GERTRUDE STEIN, "Sacred Emily," *Geography and Plays* (1922).

22. What thou art, that thou art; that God knoweth thee to be and thou canst be said to be no greater. THOMAS À KEMPIS, *The Imitation of Christ* (1426), 2.6.

23. There is no ache more / Deadly than the striving to be oneself. YEVGENIY VINOKUROV, "I," *The New Russian Poets: 1953 to 1966* (1966), tr. George Reavey.

24. At every single moment of one's life one is what one is going to be no less than what one has been. OSCAR WILDE, *De Profundis* (1905).

25. Men can starve from a lack of self-realization as much as they can from a lack of bread. RICHARD WRIGHT, *Native Son* (1940), 3.

## 443. IDEOLOGY

**See also 109. Causes; 200. Creeds; 262. Dogmatism; 441. Ideas; 564. Mass Movements**

1. All truly historical peoples have an idea they must realize, and when they have sufficiently exploited it at home, they export it, in a certain way, by war; they make it tour the world. VICTOR COUSIN, *Cours de philosophie moderne* (1841–46).

2. Everything starts as a mystique and ends as politics. Graffito written during French student revolt, May 1968.

3. We are now again in an epoch of wars of religion, but a religion is now called an "ideology." BERTRAND RUSSELL, "Philosophy and Politics," *Unpopular Essays* (1950).

4. Ideology is not the product of thought; it is the habit or the ritual of showing respect for certain formulas to which, for various reasons having to do with emotional safety, we have very strong ties of whose meaning and consequences in actuality we have no clear understanding. LIONEL TRILLING, "The Meaning of a Literary Idea," *The Liberal Imagination* (1950).

## 444. IDLENESS

**See also 10. Activity; 527. Laziness; 530. Leisure; 805. Rest; 807. Retirement**

1. Consider the lilies of the field, how they grow; they toil not, neither do they spin: And yet I say unto you, That even Solomon in all his glory was not arrayed like one of these. *Bible*, Matthew 6:28–29.

2. Expect poison from the standing water. WILLIAM BLAKE, "Proverbs of Hell," *The Marriage of Heaven and Hell* (1790).

3. It is because artists do not practise, patrons do not patronize, crowds do not assemble to reverently worship the great work of Doing Nothing, that the world has lost its philosophy and even failed to invent a new religion. G. K. CHESTERTON, "On Leisure," *Generally Speaking* (1928).

4. Absence of occupation is not rest, / A mind quite vacant is a mind distressed. WILLIAM COWPER, *Retirement* (1782), 623.

5. Idleness and pride tax with a heavier hand than kings and parliaments. BENJAMIN FRANKLIN, letter on the Stamp Act, July 1, 1765.

6. Rust wastes more than use. FRENCH PROVERB.

7. He is idle that might be better employed. THOMAS FULLER, M.D., *Gnomologia* (1732), 1919.

8. Idleness is a mother. She has a son, robbery, and a daughter, hunger. VICTOR HUGO, "Saint Denis," *Les Misérables* (1862), 7.1, tr. Charles E. Wilbour.

9. No man is so methodical as a complete idler, and none so scrupulous in measuring out his time as he whose time is worth nothing. WASHINGTON IRVING, "My French Neighbor," *Wolfert's Roost* (1855).

10. Idleness, like kisses, to be sweet must be stolen. JEROME K. JEROME, "On Being Idle," *The Idle Thoughts of an Idle Fellow* (1889).

11. If you are idle, be not solitary; if you are solitary, be not idle. SAMUEL JOHNSON, letter to James Boswell, Oct. 27, 1779, quoted in Boswell's *Life of Samuel Johnson*.

12. By too much sitting still the body becomes unhealthy; and soon the mind. LONGFELLOW, *Hyperion* (1839), 1.7.

13. Love is born of idleness and, once born, by idleness is fostered. OVID, *Love's Cure* (c. A.D. 8), tr. J. Lewis May.

14. If a soldier or labourer complain of the hardship of his lot, set him to do nothing. PASCAL, *Pensées* (1670), 130, tr. W. F. Trotter.

15. A faculty for idleness implies a catholic appetite and a strong sense of personal identity. ROBERT LOUIS STEVENSON, "An Apology for Idlers," *Virginibus Puerisque* (1881).

16. It is better to have loafed and lost than never to have loafed at all. JAMES THURBER, "The Courtship of Arthur and Al," *Fables for Our Time* (1943).

17. The devil tempts all other men, but idle men tempt the devil. TURKISH PROVERB.

18. To do nothing at all is the most difficult thing in the world, the most difficult and the most intellectual. OSCAR WILDE, "The Critic as Artist," *Intentions* (1891).

19. The hardest work is to go idle. *Yiddish Proverbs* (1949), ed. Hanan J. Ayalti.

## IDOLATRY

See 1061. Worship

## 445. IGNORANCE

See also 268. Dullness; 520. Knowledge; 611. Naïveté; 934. Stupidity

1. Ignorance is the womb of monsters. HENRY WARD BEECHER, *Proverbs from Plymouth Pulpit* (1887).

2. Wisdom is prevented by ignorance, and delusion is the result. *Bhagavadgita*, 5, tr. P. Lal.

3. If the blind lead the blind, both shall fall into the ditch. *Bible*, Matthew 15:14.

4. Ignoramus, n. A person unacquainted with certain kinds of knowledge familiar to yourself, and having certain other kinds that you know nothing about. AMBROSE BIERCE, *The Devil's Dictionary* (1881–1911).

5. Ignorance is always ready to admire itself, / Procure yourself critical friends. NICOLAS BOILEAU, *L'Art poétique* (1674), 1.

6. Ignorance is not innocence but sin. ROBERT BROWNING, *The Inn Album* (1875), 5.

7. An ignorant man is insignificant and contemptible; nobody cares for his company, and he can just be said to live, and that is all. LORD CHESTERFIELD, *Letters to His Son*, 1739.

8. The whole family of pride and ignorance are incestuous, and mutually beget each other. CHARLES CALEB COLTON, *Lacon* (1825), 1.443.

9. all ignorance toboggans into know / and trudges up to ignorance again. E. E. CUMMINGS, "all ignorance toboggans into know," *100 Selected Poems* (1959).

10. To be conscious that you are ignorant is a great step to knowledge. BENJAMIN DISRAELI, *Sybil* (1845), 5.

11. Ignorance and incuriosity are two very soft pillows. FRENCH PROVERB.

12. He that knows least commonly presumes most. THOMAS FULLER, M.D., *Gnomologia* (1732), 2208.

13. He that knows little often repeats it. THOMAS FULLER, M.D., *Gnomologia* (1732), 2209.

14. Better an empty purse than an empty head. GERMAN PROVERB.

15. Where ignorance is bliss, / 'Tis folly to be wise. THOMAS GRAY, "On a Distant Prospect of Eton College" (1747), 10.

16. The little I know, I owe to my ignorance. SACHA GUITRY, *Toutes réflexions faites* (1947), 5.

17. Far more crucial than what we know or do not know is what we do not want to know. ERIC HOFFER, *The Passionate State of Mind* (1954), 58.

18. Ignorance is preferable to error; and he is less remote from the truth who believes nothing, than he who believes what is wrong. THOMAS JEFFERSON, *Notes on the State of Virginia* (1784–85), 6.

19. A man must have a certain amount of intelligent ignorance to get anywhere. CHARLES F. KETTERING, remark on his seventieth birthday, Aug. 29, 1946.

20. Nothing in all the world is more dangerous than sincere ignorance and conscientious stupidity. MARTIN LUTHER KING, JR., *Strength to Love* (1963), 4.3.

21. He who would be cured of ignorance must confess it. MONTAIGNE, "Of cripples," *Essays* (1580–88).

22. He that had never seen a river, imagined the first he met with to be the sea. MONTAIGNE, "That it is folly to measure truth and error by our own capacity," *Es-*

*says* (1580–88), tr. Charles Cotton and W. C. Hazlitt.

23. Genuine victories, the sole conquests yielding no remorse, are those gained over ignorance. NAPOLEON I, *Maxims* (1804–15).

24. Not to know is bad; not to wish to know is worse. NIGERIAN PROVERB.

25. It is admirable to consider how many millions of people come into, and go out of, the world, ignorant of themselves and of the world they have lived in. WILLIAM PENN, *Some Fruits of Solitude* (1693), 1.1.

26. From ignorance our comfort flows, / The only wretched are the wise. MATTHEW PRIOR, "To the Hon. Charles Montague" (1692), 9.

27. Better to be ignorant of a matter than half know it. PUBLILIUS SYRUS, *Moral Sayings* (1st c. B.C.), 865, tr. Darius Lyman.

28. Nothing is so good for an ignorant man as silence, and if he knew this he would no longer be ignorant. SA'DI, *Gulistan* (1258), 8.38, tr. James Ross.

29. There is no dunce like a mature dunce. GEORGE SANTAYANA, *Character and Opinion in the United States* (1921), 2.

30. Uncultivated minds are not full of wild flowers, like uncultivated fields. Villainous weeds grow in them and they are the haunt of toads. LOGAN PEARSALL SMITH, *Afterthoughts* (1931), 3.

31. If ignorance is indeed bliss, it is a very low grade of the article. TEHYI HSIEH, *Chinese Epigrams Inside Out and Proverbs* (1948), 95.

32. Blind and naked Ignorance / Delivers brawling judgments, unashamed, / On all things all day long. ALFRED, LORD TENNYSON, "Merlin and Vivien," *Idylls of the King* (1859).

33. There is that indescribable freshness and unconsciousness about an illiterate person that humbles and mocks the power of the noblest expressive genius. WALT WHITMAN, preface to *Leaves of Grass* (1855).

34. Ignorance is not bliss—it is oblivion. PHILIP WYLIE, *Generation of Vipers* (1942), 4.

## 446. ILLEGALITY

**See also 201. Crime; 893. Sin**

1. Stolen waters are sweet, and bread eaten in secret is pleasant. *Bible*, Proverbs 9:17.

2. Stolen sweets are best. COLLEY CIBBER, *The Rival Fools* (1709), 1.

## ILLNESS

**See 889. Sickness**

## 447. ILLUSION

**See also 264. Dreams; 298. Escape; 381. Ghosts; 610. Myth; 687. Phantasy; 777. Reality**

1. Beware lest you lose the substance by grasping at the shadow. AESOP, "The Dog and the Shadow," *Fables* (6th c. B.C.?), tr. Joseph Jacobs.

2. We [Americans] suffer primarily not from our vices or our weaknesses, but from our illusions. We are haunted, not by reality, but by those images we have put in place of reality. DANIEL J. BOORSTIN, introduction to *The Image* (1962).

3. Illusions are art, for the feeling person, and it is by art that we live, if we do. ELIZABETH BOWEN, *The Death of the Heart* (1938), 1.7.

4. Time strips our illusions of their hue, / And one by one in turn, some grand mistake / Casts off its bright skin yearly like the snake. BYRON, *Don Juan* (1819–24), 5.21.

5. We must select the illusion which appeals to our temperament, and embrace it with passion, if we want to be happy. CYRIL CONNOLLY, *The Unquiet Grave* (1945), 3.

6. A man that is born falls into a dream like a man who falls into the sea. If he tries to climb out into the air as inexperienced people endeavour to do, he drowns. JOSEPH CONRAD, *Lord Jim* (1900), 20.

7. Every age is fed on illusions, lest men should renounce life early and the human race come to an end. JOSEPH CONRAD, *Victory* (1915), 2.3.

8. We wake from one dream into another dream. EMERSON, "Illusions," *The Conduct of Life* (1860).

9. Life is the art of being well deceived; and in order that the deception may succeed it must be habitual and uninterrupted. WILLIAM HAZLITT, "On Pedantry," *The Round Table* (1817).

10. Rob the average man of his life-illusion and you rob him of his happiness at

one stroke. HENRIK IBSEN, *The Wild Duck* (1884), 5.

11. The most important part of our lives—our sensations, emotions, desires, and aspirations—takes place in a universe of illusions which science can attenuate or destroy, but which it is powerless to enrich. JOSEPH WOOD KRUTCH, "The Disillusion with the Laboratory," *The Modern Temper* (1929).

12. Man has always sacrificed truth to his vanity, comfort and advantage. He lives not by truth but by make-believe. W. SOMERSET MAUGHAM, *The Summing Up* (1938), 75.

13. The notion that as man grows older his illusions leave him is not quite true. What is true is that his early illusions are supplanted by new and, to him, equally convincing illusions. GEORGE JEAN NATHAN, "General Conclusions about the Coarse Sex," *The Theatre, the Drama, the Girls* (1921).

14. Obsessed by a fairy tale, we spend our lives searching for a magic door and a lost kingdom of peace. EUGENE O'NEILL, *More Stately Mansions* (1964), 3.2.

15. Our experience is composed rather of illusions lost than of wisdom acquired. JOSEPH ROUX, *Meditations of a Parish Priest* (1886), 4.28, tr. Isabel F. Hapgood.

16. If you prefer illusions to realities, it is only because all decent realities have eluded you and left you in the lurch; or else your contempt for the world is mere hypocrisy and funk. GEORGE SANTAYANA, *Dialogues in Limbo* (1925), 5.

## 448. IMAGINATION

**See also 583. Mind; 687. Phantasy; 812. Reverie**

1. The imagination is the secret and marrow of civilization. It is the very eye of faith. HENRY WARD BEECHER, *Proverbs from Plymouth Pulpit* (1887).

2. Imagination, n. A warehouse of facts, with poet and liar in joint ownership. AMBROSE BIERCE, *The Devil's Dictionary* (1881–1911).

3. Imagination is like a lofty building reared to meet the sky—fancy is a balloon that soars at the wind's will. GELETT BURGESS, "Where Is Fancy Bred?" *The Romance of the Commonplace* (1916).

4. People can die of mere imagination. CHAUCER, "The Miller's Tale," *The Canterbury Tales* (c. 1387–1400), tr. Nevill Coghill.

5. The power which makes a man able to entertain a good impulse is the same as that which enables him to make a good gun; it is imagination. G. K. CHESTERTON, "Humanitarianism and Strength," *All Things Considered* (1908).

6. Fairyland is nothing but the sunny country of common sense. G. K. CHESTERTON, "The Logic of Elfland," *Orthodoxy* (1908).

7. Imagination = nostalgia for the past, the absent; it is the liquid solution in which art develops the snapshots of reality. CYRIL CONNOLLY, *The Unquiet Grave* (1945), 2.

8. Only in men's imagination does every truth find an effective and undeniable existence. Imagination, not invention, is the supreme master of art as of life. JOSEPH CONRAD, *A Personal Record* (1912), 1.

9. Imagination, that dost so abstract us / That we are not aware, not even when / A thousand trumpets sound about our ears! DANTE, "Purgatorio," 17, *The Divine Comedy* (c. 1300–21), tr. Lawrence Grant White.

10. The Possible's slow fuse is lit / By the Imagination. EMILY DICKINSON, *Poems* (c. 1862–86).

11. I imagine, therefore I belong and am free. LAWRENCE DURRELL, *Justine* (1957), 2.

12. The imagination and the senses cannot be gratified at the same time. EMERSON, "Beauty," *The Conduct of Life* (1860).

13. There are no days in life so memorable as those which vibrated to some stroke of the imagination. EMERSON, "Beauty," *The Conduct of Life* (1860).

14. Were it not for imagination a man would be as happy in the arms of a chambermaid as of a duchess. SAMUEL JOHNSON, quoted in Boswell's *Life of Samuel Johnson*, May 9, 1778.

15. Almost any man may like the spider spin from his own inwards his own airy citadel. KEATS, letter to John Hamilton Reynolds, Feb. 19, 1818.

16. Heard melodies are sweet, but those unheard / Are sweeter. KEATS, "Ode on a Grecian Urn" (1819).

17. The problems of the world cannot

possibly be solved by skeptics or cynics whose horizons are limited by the obvious realities. We need men who can dream of things that never were. JOHN F. KENNEDY, address, Dublin, Ireland, June 28, 1963.

18. The more we see the more we must be able to imagine; and the more we imagine, the more we must think we see. GOTTHOLD EPHRAIM LESSING, *Laocoön* (1766), 3, tr. W. A. Steel.

19. To give reason for fancy were to weigh the fire, and measure the wind. JOHN LYLY, *Euphues: The Anatomy of Wit* (1579).

20. Imagination is the mad boarder. NICOLAS MALEBRANCHE, preface to *Recherche de la vérité* (1674–75).

21. Imagination grows by exercise and contrary to common belief is more powerful in the mature than in the young. W. SOMERSET MAUGHAM, *The Summing Up* (1938), 43.

22. Imagination.—It is that deceitful part in man, that mistress of error and falsity, the more deceptive that she is not always so; for she would be an infallible rule of truth, if she were an infallible rule of falsehood. PASCAL, *Pensées* (1670), 82, tr. W. F. Trotter.

23. The eyes are not responsible when the mind does the seeing. PUBLILIUS SYRUS, *Moral Sayings* (1st c. B.C.), 562, tr. Darius Lyman.

24. That which we know is but little; that which we have a presentiment of is immense; it is in this direction that the poet outruns the learned man. JOSEPH ROUX, *Meditations of a Parish Priest* (1886), 1.17, tr. Isabel F. Hapgood.

25. I have imagination, and nothing that is real is alien to me. GEORGE SANTAYANA, *Little Essays* (1920), 42, ed. Logan Pearsall Smith.

26. Imagination is potentially infinite. Though actually we are limited to the types of experience for which we possess organs, those organs are somewhat plastic. Opportunity will change their scope and even their centre. GEORGE SANTAYANA, *Persons and Places: My Host the World* (1953), 3.

27. Such tricks hath strong imagination, / That, if it would but apprehend some joy, / It comprehends some bringer of that joy; / Or in the night, imagining some fear, / How easy is a bush supposed a bear! SHAKESPEARE, *A Midsummer Night's Dream* (1595–96), 5.1.18.

28. Reason respects the differences, and imagination the similitudes of things. SHELLEY, *A Defence of Poetry* (1821).

29. You can't depend on your judgment when your imagination is out of focus. MARK TWAIN, *Notebook* (1935).

30. Imagination is more robust in proportion as reasoning power is weak. GIAMBATTISTA VICO, *The New Science* (1725–44), 1.2.

31. Woe to the man / who tries to stretch the imagination of man / He shall be mocked he shall be scourged / by the blinkered guardians of morality. PETER WEISS, *Marat/Sade* (1964), 1.26, tr. Geoffrey Skelton and Adrian Mitchell.

32. Society often forgives the criminal; it never forgives the dreamer. OSCAR WILDE, "The Critic as Artist," *Intentions* (1891).

33. The instant / trivial as it is / is all we have / unless—unless / things the imagination feeds upon, / the scent of the rose, / startle us anew. WILLIAM CARLOS WILLIAMS, "Shadows," *Pictures from Brueghel* (1962).

## 449. IMITATION

**See also 694. Plagiarism; 726. Pretension**

1. Sparrows who emulate peacocks are likely to break a thigh. *Burmese Proverbs* (1962), 96, ed. Hla Pe.

2. We are, in truth, more than half what we are by imitation. LORD CHESTERFIELD, *Letters to His Son*, Jan. 18, 1750.

3. Imitation is the sincerest flattery. CHARLES CALEB COLTON, *Lacon* (1825).

4. When people are free to do as they please, they usually imitate each other. ERIC HOFFER, *The Passionate State of Mind* (1955).

5. The sense of inferiority inherent in the act of imitation breeds resentment. The impulse of the imitators is to overcome the model they imitate. ERIC HOFFER, *The Ordeal of Change* (1964), 4.

6. No living person is sunk so low as not to be imitated by somebody. WILLIAM JAMES, "The Gospel of Relaxation," *Talks to Teachers and to Students* (1899).

7. The crow that mimics a cormorant gets drowned. JAPANESE PROVERB.

8. Almost all absurdity of conduct arises from the imitation of those whom we cannot

resemble. SAMUEL JOHNSON, *The Rambler* (1750–52), 135.

9. To refrain from imitation is the best revenge. MARCUS AURELIUS, *Meditations* (2nd c.), 6.6, tr. Maxwell Staniforth.

10. When the bad imitate the good, there is no knowing what mischief is intended. PUBLILIUS SYRUS, *Moral Sayings* (1st c. B.C.), 551, tr. Darius Lyman.

11. Imitation is a necessity of nature; when young, we imitate others; when old, ourselves. JOSEPH ROUX, *Meditations of a Parish Priest* (1886), 4.40, tr. Isabel F. Hapgood.

## 450. IMMATURITY

**See also 402. Growth and Development; 567. Maturity**

1. We are like thistle-down blown about by the wind—up and down, here and there—but not one in a thousand ever getting beyond seed-hood. SAMUEL BUTLER (d. 1902), "Lord, What Is Man?" *Note-Books* (1912).

2. The wisest man is just a boy / who grieves that he's grown up. VINCENZO CARDARELLI, "Adolescent," *Poesie* (1943).

3. There are cases in which the blade springs, but the plant does not go on to flower. There are cases where it flowers, but no fruit is subsequently produced. CONFUCIUS, *Analects* (6th c. B.C.), 9.21, tr. James Legge.

4. Is life so wretched? Isn't it rather your hands which are too small, your vision which is muddied? You are the one who must grow up. DAG HAMMARSKJÖLD, "1945–1949: Towards new shores—?" *Markings* (1964), tr. Leif Sjoberg and W. H. Auden.

5. How many really capable men are children more than once during the day! NAPOLEON I, *Maxims* (1804–15).

6. How shall one who is so weak in his childhood become really strong when he grows older? We only change our fancies. PASCAL, *Pensées* (1670), 88, tr. W. F. Trotter.

## 451. IMMIGRATION

1. A nation, like a tree, does not thrive well till it is engraffed with a foreign stock. EMERSON, *Journals*, 1823.

2. The great social adventure of America is no longer the conquest of the wilderness but the absorption of fifty different peoples. WALTER LIPPMANN, "Some Necessary Iconoclasm," *A Preface to Politics* (1914).

## IMMORALITY

**See 305. Evil; 598. Morality; 1023. Vice; 1048. Wickedness; 1063. Wrongdoing**

## 452. IMMORTALITY

**See also 300. Eternity; 600. Mortality**

1. To live in hearts we leave / Is not to die. THOMAS CAMPBELL, "Hallowed Ground" (1825).

2. Should this my firm persuasion of the soul's immortality prove to be a mere delusion, it is at least a pleasing delusion, and I will cherish it to my latest breath. CICERO, *De Senectute* (44 B.C.).

3. Death be not proud, though some have called thee / Mighty and dreadful, for thou art not so, / For those whom thou think'st thou dost overthrow, / Die not, poor death, nor yet canst thou kill me. JOHN DONNE, Sonnet 10, *Divine Poems* (1607).

4. A man has only one way of being immortal on this earth: he has to forget he is a mortal. JEAN GIRAUDOUX, *Tiger at the Gates* (1935), 1, tr. Christopher Fry.

5. Let him who believes in immortality enjoy his happiness in silence; he has no reason to give himself airs about it. GOETHE, quoted in Johann Peter Eckermann's *Conversations with Goethe*, Feb. 25, 1824.

6. Our Creator would never have made such lovely days, and have given us the deep hearts to enjoy them, unless we were meant to be immortal. NATHANIEL HAWTHORNE, "The Old Manse," *Mosses from an Old Manse* (1846).

7. To occupy an inch of dusty shelf—to have the title of their works read now and then in a future age by some drowsy churchman or casual straggler, and in another age to be lost, even to remembrance. Such is the amount of boasted immortality. WASHINGTON IRVING, "The Mutability of Literature," *The Sketch Book of Geoffrey Crayon, Gent.* (1819–20).

8. If life were eternal all interest and anticipation would vanish. It is uncertainty

which lends its fascination. YOSHIDA KENKŌ, "Man the Ephemera," *The Harvest of Leisure (Tsure-Zure Gusa*, c. 1330–35), tr. Ryukichi Kurata.

9. A syllogism: other men die; but I / Am not another; therefore I'll not die. VLADIMIR NABOKOV, *Pale Fire* (1962), 2.213.

10. The mortal nature is seeking as far as is possible to be everlasting and immortal: and this is only to be attained by generation, because the new is always left in the place of the old. PLATO, *The Symposium* (4th c. B.C.), tr. Benjamin Jowett.

11. I have good hope that there is something after death. PLATO, *Phaedo* (4th–3rd c. B.C.), tr. Lane Cooper.

12. The soldier is convinced that a certain interval of time, capable of being indefinitely prolonged, will be allowed him before the bullet finds him, the thief before he is taken, men in general before they have to die. MARCEL PROUST, *Remembrance of Things Past: Within a Budding Grove* (1913–27), tr. C. K. Scott-Moncrieff.

13. Man's life is short; and therefore an honorable death is his immortality. PUBLILIUS SYRUS, *Moral Sayings* (1st c. B.C.), 1087, tr. Darius Lyman.

14. If you question any candid person who is no longer young, he is very likely to tell you that, having tasted life in this world, he has no wish to begin again as a "new boy" in another. BERTRAND RUSSELL, "Ideas That Have Harmed Mankind," *Unpopular Essays* (1950).

15. All the doctrines that have flourished in the world about immortality have hardly affected men's natural sentiment in the face of death. GEORGE SANTAYANA, *The Life of Reason: Reason in Religion* (1905–06), 4.

16. Death is the veil which those who live call life: / They sleep, and it is lifted. SHELLEY, *Prometheus Unbound* (1818–19), 3.3.

17. We feel and know that we are eternal. SPINOZA, *Ethics* (1677), 5, tr. Andrew Boyle.

18. Thou madest man, he knows not why, / He thinks he was not made to die. ALFRED, LORD TENNYSON, "In Memoriam A. H. H." (1850).

19. All men think all men mortal but themselves. EDWARD YOUNG, *Night Thoughts* (1742–46), 1.424.

## 453. IMPARTIALITY

**See also 515. Justice; 667. Partisanship**

1. What people call impartiality may simply mean indifference, and what people call partiality may simply mean mental activity. G. K. CHESTERTON, "The Error of Impartiality," *All Things Considered* (1908).

2. He is not good himself who speaks well of everybody alike. THOMAS FULLER, M.D., *Gnomologia* (1732), 1935.

3. The tree casts its shade upon all, even upon the woodcutter. HINDUSTANI PROVERB.

4. He who treats his friends and enemies alike, has neither love nor justice. ROBERT G. INGERSOLL, *Prose-Poems and Selections* (1884).

5. In times like the present, one who desires to be impartially just in the expression of his views, moves as among swordpoints presented on every side. HERMAN MELVILLE, Supplement to *Battlepieces and Aspects of the War* (1866).

6. Neutrality consists in having the same weights and measures for each. NAPOLEON I, *Maxims* (1804–15).

7. "Pity for all" would be hardness and tyranny toward *you*, my dear neighbor. NIETZSCHE, *Beyond Good and Evil* (1886), 82, tr. Walter Kaufmann.

8. A friend to everybody and to nobody is the same thing. SPANISH PROVERB.

## 454. IMPATIENCE

**See also 409. Haste; 670. Patience; 806. Restlessness; 1033. Waiting**

1. Though we seem grieved at the shortness of life in general, we are wishing every period of it at an end. JOSEPH ADDISON, *The Spectator* (1711–12), 93.

2. Impatience is the mark of independence, / not of bondage. MARIANNE MOORE, "Marriage," *Collected Poems* (1951).

## 455. IMPERFECTION

**See also 297. Error; 339. Faults; 539. Limitations; 677. Perfection**

1. A good garden may have some weeds. THOMAS FULLER, M.D., *Gnomologia* (1732), 152.

2. The best brewer sometimes makes bad beer. GERMAN PROVERB.

3. What day is so festal it fails to reveal some theft? JUVENAL, *Satires* (c. 100), 13.23, tr. Hubert Creekmore.

4. When the curry is good, the rice is half-cooked; when the rice is good, the curry is half-cooked. MALAY PROVERB.

5. All things are literally better, lovelier, and more beloved for the imperfections which have been divinely appointed, that the law of human life may be effort, and the law of human judgment, mercy. JOHN RUSKIN, *The Stones of Venice* (1851–53), v. 2, 6.25.

6. People are crying up the rich and variegated plumage of the peacock, and he is himself blushing at the sight of his ugly feet. SA'DI, *Gulistan* (1258), 2.8, tr. James Ross.

7. The habit of looking for beauty in everything makes us notice the shortcomings of things; our sense, hungry for complete satisfaction, misses the perfection it demands. GEORGE SANTAYANA, *The Sense of Beauty* (1896), 30.

8. The Fates, like an absent-minded printer, seldom allow a single line to stand perfect and unmarred. GEORGE SANTAYANA, *The Life of Reason: Reason in Society* (1905–06), 1.

9. O me! for why is all around us here / As if some lesser god had made the world, / But had not force to shape it as he would? ALFRED, LORD TENNYSON, "The Passing of Arthur," *Idylls of the King* (1859–85), 13.

10. The visible imperfections of handwrought goods, being honorific, are accounted marks of superiority in point of beauty, or serviceability, or both. THORSTEIN VEBLEN, *The Theory of the Leisure Class* (1899), 6.

11. There is no beauty like that which was spoiled by an accident; no accomplishments and graces are so to be envied as those that circumstances rudely hindered the development of. CHARLES DUDLEY WARNER, "Third Study," *Backlog Studies* (1873).

12. There is no deformity / But saves us from a dream. WILLIAM BUTLER YEATS, "The Phases of the Moon," *The Wild Swans at Coole* (1919).

## 456. IMPERIALISM

**See also 995. Tyranny**

1. It is natural anywhere that people like their own kind, but it is not necessarily natural that their fondness for their own kind should lead them to the subjection of whole groups of other people not like them. PEARL S. BUCK, *What America Means to Me* (1943), 2.

2. In imperialism nothing fails like success. If the conqueror oppresses his subjects, they will become fanatical patriots, and sooner or later have their revenge; if he treats them well, and "governs them for their good," they will multiply faster than their rulers, till they claim their independence. WILLIAM RALPH INGE, "Patriotism," *Outspoken Essays: First Series* (1919).

3. It's easy to become a satellite today without even being aware of it. This country can seduce God. Yes, it has that seductive power—the power of dollarism. MALCOLM X, *Malcolm X Speaks* (1965), 15.

4. In the eyes of empire builders men are not men, but instruments. NAPOLEON I, *Maxims* (1804–15).

5. Shall we go on conferring our Civilization upon the peoples that sit in darkness, or shall we give those poor things a rest? MARK TWAIN, "To the Person Sitting in the Darkness' (1901).

## IMPERMANENCE

**See 115. Change; 983. Transience**

## IMPIETY

**See 439. Iconoclasm; 504. Irreverence**

## IMPORTANCE

**See 865. Self-importance**

## 457. IMPOTENCE

**See also 364. Frustration; 713. Power; 1040. Weakness**

1. Powerlessness frustrates; absolute powerlessness frustrates absolutely. Absolute frustration is a dangerous emotion to run a world with. RUSSELL BAKER, "Observer," *The New York Times*, May 1, 1969.

2. The worst pain a man can have is to know much and be impotent to act. HERODOTUS, *The Histories* (5th c. B.C.), 9.16, tr. Aubrey de Sélincourt.

3. We look for some reward of our endeavors and are disappointed; not success, not happiness, not even peace of conscience, crowns our ineffectual efforts to do well. Our frailties are invincible, our virtues barren; the battle goes sore against us to the going down of the sun. ROBERT LOUIS STEVENSON, "Pulvis et Umbra" (1888).

4. We've travelled too far, and our momentum has taken over; we move idly towards eternity, without possibility of reprieve or hope of explanation. TOM STOPPARD, *Rosencrantz & Guildenstern Are Dead* (1967), 3.

5. Asks the Possible of the Impossible, "Where is your dwelling-place?" / "In the dreams of the Impotent," comes the answer. RABINDRANATH TAGORE, *Stray Birds* (1916), 129.

6. But what am I? / An infant crying in the night; / An infant crying for the light, / And with no language but a cry. ALFRED, LORD TENNYSON, "In Memoriam A. H. H." (1850), 54.

7. We all live in a house on fire, no fire department to call; no way out, just the upstairs window to look out of while the fire burns the house down with us trapped, locked in it. TENNESSEE WILLIAMS, *The Milk Train Doesn't Stop Here Anymore* (1963), 6.

8. Our thought has been "Let every man look out for himself, let every generation look out for itself," while we reared giant machinery which made it impossible that any but those who stood at the levers of control should have a chance to look out for themselves. WOODROW WILSON, first Inaugural Address, March 4, 1913.

### 458. IMPROVEMENT

See also 711. Potential; 783. Reform; 801. Resolution

1. Improvement makes straight roads; but the crooked roads without improvement are roads of genius. WILLIAM BLAKE, "Proverbs of Hell," *The Marriage of Heaven and Hell* (1790).

2. Old houses mended, / Cost little less than new, before they're ended. COLLEY CIBBER, prologue to *The Double Gallant* (1707).

3. Every man contemplates an angel in his future self. EMERSON, *Journals*, 1829.

4. If way to the Better there be, it exacts a full look at the Worst. THOMAS HARDY, "In Tenebris II," *Poems of the Past and Present* (1901).

5. Happy are they that hear their detractions and can put them to mending. SHAKESPEARE, *Much Ado About Nothing* (1598–99), 2.3.237.

6. Have therefore first zeal to better thyself and then mayst thou have zeal to thy neighbour. THOMAS À KEMPIS, *The Imitation of Christ* (1426), 2.3.

7. Poets lose half the praise they should have got, / Could it be known what they discreetly blot. EDMUND WALLER, "Upon the Earl of Roscommon's Translation of Horace" (1680).

### IMPROVISATION

See 921. Spontaneity

### 459. IMPULSIVENESS

See also 921. Spontaneity; 1046. Whim

1. If men as individuals surrender to the call of their elementary instincts, avoiding pain and seeking satisfaction only for their own selves, the result for them all taken together must be a state of insecurity, of fear, and of promiscuous misery. EINSTEIN, *Out of My Later Years* (1950), 7.

2. If you believed more in life you would fling yourselves less to the moment. NIETZSCHE, "On the Preachers of Death," *Thus Spoke Zarathustra* (1883–92), 1, tr. Walter Kaufmann.

3. In order to do certain crazy things, it is necessary to behave like a coachman who has let go of the reins and fallen asleep. JULES RENARD, *Journal*, November 1888, ed. and tr. Louise Bogan and Elizabeth Roget.

### 460. INADEQUACY

See also 461. Incompetence; 539. Limitations

1. That is a bad bridge which is shorter than the stream. GERMAN PROVERB.

## 461. INCOMPETENCE
See also 460. Inadequacy

1. A bad workman quarrels with the man who calls him that. AMBROSE BIERCE, "Saw," *The Devil's Dictionary* (1881–1911).

2. The worse the carpenter, the more the chips. DUTCH PROVERB.

3. A bad workman never gets a good tool. THOMAS FULLER, M.D., *Gnomologia* (1732), 5.

4. O thrice unhappy home / Whose master doesn't know the difference between a watt and an ohm! OGDEN NASH, "Up from the Wheelbarrow," *I'm a Stranger Here Myself* (1938).

5. This world is a round gulf, and he who cannot swim must go to the bottom. SPANISH PROVERB.

6. The girl who can't dance says the band can't play. *Yiddish Proverbs* (1949), ed. Hanan J. Ayalti.

## INCOMPLETION
See 283. Ending

## 462. INCONSISTENCY
See also 115. Change; 176. Consistency; 684. Perverseness

1. When the man you like switches from what he said a year ago, or four years ago, he is a broadminded person who has courage enough to change his mind with changing conditions. When a man you don't like does it, he is a liar who has broken his promises. FRANKLIN P. ADAMS, *Nods and Becks* (1944).

2. I wish to say what I think and feel today, with the proviso that tomorrow perhaps I shall contradict it all. EMERSON, *Journals*, 1839.

3. Speak what you think today in words as hard as cannon balls, and tomorrow speak what tomorrow thinks in hard words again, though it contradict everything you said today. EMERSON, "Self-Reliance," *Essays: First Series* (1841).

4. People who honestly mean to be true really contradict themselves much more rarely than those who try to be "consistent." OLIVER WENDELL HOLMES, SR., *The Professor at the Breakfast Table* (1860), 2.

5. If anyone accuses me of contradicting myself, I reply: Because I have been wrong once, or oftener, I do not aspire to be always wrong. VAUVENARGUES, *Reflections and Maxims* (1746), 643, tr. F. G. Stevens.

6. Do I contradict myself? / Very well then I contradict myself, / (I am large, I contain multitudes). WALT WHITMAN, "Song of Myself," 51, *Leaves of Grass* (1855–92).

## INCONSTANCY
See 178. Constancy and Inconstancy; 470. Infidelity

## 463. INDECISION
See also 222. Decision; 228. Delay; 765. Purpose; 998. Uncertainty

1. Between two stools one sits on the ground. FRENCH PROVERB.

2. Half the failures in life arise from pulling in one's horse as he is leaping. JULIUS CHARLES HARE and AUGUSTUS WILLIAM HARE, *Guesses at Truth* (1827).

3. There is no more miserable human being than one in whom nothing is habitual but indecision. WILLIAM JAMES, *The Principles of Psychology* (1892), 10.

4. Indecision is like the stepchild: if he doesn't wash his hands, he is called dirty; if he does, he is wasting the water. MADAGASCAN PROVERB.

5. No wind serves him who addresses his voyage to no certain port. MONTAIGNE, "Of the inconstancy of our actions," *Essays* (1580–88), tr. Charles Cotton and W. C. Hazlitt.

6. It is human nature to stand in the middle of a thing. MARIANNE MOORE, "A Grave," *Collected Poems* (1951).

7. He who hesitates is sometimes saved. JAMES THURBER, "The Glass in the Field," *The Thurber Carnival* (1945).

8. He became an infidel hesitating between two mosques. TURKISH PROVERB.

## INDEPENDENCE

See 361. Freedom, Individual; 534. Liberty; 873. Self-sufficiency

## 464. INDIFFERENCE

See also 30. Alienation; 216. Deadness, Spiritual

1. We play make believe, pretend to take ourselves and each other seriously—to love each other, hate each other—but then—it isn't true! It isn't true, we don't care at all! UGO BETTI, *The Inquiry* (1944–45), 3.4, ed. Gino Rizzo.

2. O, if thou car'st not whom I love / Alas, thou lov'st not me. JOHN DONNE, "A Hymn to Christ, at the Author's Last Going into Germany," *Divine Poems* (1607).

3. Most people go on living their everyday life: half-frightened, half indifferent, they behold the ghostly tragi-comedy that is being performed on the international stage before the eyes and ears of the world. EINSTEIN, *Out of My Later Life* (1950), 33.

4. He injures a fair lady that beholds her not. THOMAS FULLER, M.D., *Gnomologia* (1732), 1904.

5. Nothing is more conducive to peace of mind than not having any opinion at all. GEORG CHRISTOPH LICHTENBERG, *Aphorisms* (1764–99), tr. J. P. Stern.

6. I know I am but summer to your heart, / And not the full four seasons of the year. EDNA ST. VINCENT MILLAY, "Two Seasons."

7. To try may be to die, but not to care is never to be born. WILLIAM REDFIELD, "One Might Have Played Hamlet, the Other Did," *The New York Times*, Jan. 15, 1968.

8. The worst sin towards our fellow creatures is not to hate them, but to be indifferent to them: that's the essence of inhumanity. GEORGE BERNARD SHAW, *The Devil's Disciple* (1897), 2.

9. He who has never hoped can never despair. GEORGE BERNARD SHAW, *Caesar and Cleopatra* (1906), 4.

## 465. INDIGNATION

See also 39. Anger

1. A good indignation brings out all one's powers. EMERSON, *Journals*, 1841.

2. There is perhaps no phenomenon which contains so much destructive feeling as "moral indignation," which permits envy or hate to be acted out under the guise of virtue. ERICH FROMM, *Man for Himself* (1947), 4.

3. Indignation does no good unless it is backed with a club of sufficient size to awe the opposition. EDGAR WATSON HOWE, *Ventures in Common Sense* (1919), 32.9.

4. Indignation is the seducer of thought. No man can think clearly when his fists are clenched. GEORGE JEAN NATHAN, "Indignation," *The World in Falseface* (1923).

5. No one lies as much as the indignant do. NIETZSCHE, *Beyond Good and Evil* (1886), 26, tr. Walter Kaufmann.

## INDISCRIMINATENESS

See 736. Promiscuity

## 466. INDIVIDUALISM

See also 89. Bohemians; 168. Conformity; 442. Identity; 467. Individuality

1. Let those who would affect singularity with success first determine to be very virtuous, and they will be sure to be very singular. CHARLES CALEB COLTON, *Lacon* (1825), 1.460.

2. Individualism is rather like innocence; there must be something unconscious about it. LOUIS KRONENBERGER, *Company Manners* (1954), 3.3.

3. True individualists tend to be quite unobservant; it is the snob, the would-be sophisticate, the frightened conformist, who keeps a fascinated or worried eye on what is in the wind. LOUIS KRONENBERGER, *Company Manners* (1954), 3.3.

4. Non-conformism is the major, perhaps the only, sin of our time. ROBERT LINDNER, "Homosexuality and the Contemporary Scene," *Must You Conform?* (1956).

5. We need the faith to go a path untrod, / The power to be alone and vote with God. EDWIN MARKHAM (1852–1940), "The Need of the Hour."

6. The man who walks alone is soon trailed by the F.B.I. WRIGHT MORRIS, *A Bill of Rites, A Bill of Wrongs, A Bill of Goods* (1967), 7.

7. They will say that you are on the wrong road, if it is your own. ANTONIO PORCHIA, *Voces* (1968), tr. W. S. Merwin.

8. If a man does not keep pace with his companions, perhaps it is because he hears a different drummer. Let him step to the music he hears, however measured or far away. THOREAU, "Conclusion," *Walden* (1854).

9. Art is the most intense mode of individualism that the world has known. OSCAR WILDE, *The Soul of Man Under Socialism* (1891).

## 467. INDIVIDUALITY

See also 258. Diversity; 274. Eccentricity; 442. Identity; 466. Individualism; 655. Originality; 852. Self; 1007. Uniqueness

1. The absolutely banal—my sense of my own uniqueness. W. H. AUDEN, "Hic et Ille," *The Dyer's Hand* (1962).

2. Meeting people unlike oneself does not enlarge one's outlook; it only confirms one's idea that one is unique. ELIZABETH BOWEN, *The House in Paris* (1935), 2.3.

3. One man means as much to me as a multitude, and a multitude only as much as one man. DEMOCRITUS, *Fragments* (5th c. B.C.), 302.

4. Every man is an infinitely repelling orb, and holds his individual being on that condition. EMERSON, *Journals*, 1836.

5. We fancy men are individuals; so are pumpkins; but every pumpkin in the field goes through every point of pumpkin history. EMERSON, "Nominalist and Realist," *Essays: Second Series* (1844).

6. Every individual strives to grow and exclude and to exclude and grow, to the extremities of the universe, and to impose the law of its being on every other creature. EMERSON, "Uses of Great Men," *Representative Men* (1850).

7. Singularity is dangerous in everything. FÉNELON, *Les Aventures de Télémaque, fils d'Ulysse* (1699), 19.

8. Anybody who is any good is different from anybody else. FELIX FRANKFURTER, *Felix Frankfurter Reminisces* (1960), 2.

9. Men are born equal but they are also born different. ERICH FROMM, *Escape from Freedom* (1941), 7.

10. It is the individual man / In his individual freedom who can mature / With his warm spirit the unripe world. CHRISTOPHER FRY, *The Firstborn* (1946), 1.1.

11. A whole bushel of wheat is made up of single grains. THOMAS FULLER, M.D., *Gnomologia* (1732), 456.

12. The individual man tries to escape the race. And as soon as he ceases to represent the race, he represents man. ANDRÉ GIDE, *Journals*, 1896, tr. Justin O'Brien.

13. Man is more interesting than men. God made him and not them in his image. Each one is more precious than all. ANDRÉ GIDE, *Journals*, 1896, tr. Justin O'Brien.

14. Every one must form himself as a particular being, seeking, however, to attain that general idea of which all mankind are constituents. GOETHE, quoted in Johann Peter Eckermann's *Conversations with Goethe*, April 20, 1825.

15. If individuality has no play, society does not advance; if individuality breaks out of all bounds, society perishes. THOMAS HENRY HUXLEY, "Administrative Nihilism" (1871).

16. The man whom God wills to slay in the struggle of life He first individualizes. HENRIK IBSEN, *Brand* (1866), 5.

17. Though all men be made of one metal, yet they be not cast all in one mold. JOHN LYLY, *Euphues: The Anatomy of Wit* (1579).

18. When two do the same thing, it is not the same thing after all. PUBLILIUS SYRUS, *Moral Sayings* (1st c. B.C.), 338, tr. Darius Lyman.

19. The flower you single out is a rejection of all other flowers; nevertheless, only on these terms is it beautiful. SAINT-EXUPÉRY, *The Wisdom of the Sands* (1948), 6, tr. Stuart Gilbert.

20. You have to go the rounds from individual to individual in order to gather the totality of the race. SCHILLER, *On the Aesthetic Education of Man* (1795), 6, tr. Reginald Snell.

21. As many men, so many minds; every one his own way. TERENCE, *Phormio* (161 B.C.), 2.4.14, tr. Henry Thomas Riley.

22. None but himself can be his parallel. LEWIS THEOBALD, *The Double Falsehood* (1727).

## 468. INDULGENCE

**See also 248. Discipline; 310. Excess; 531. Leniency**

1. If we had to tolerate in others all that we permit in ourselves, life would become completely unbearable. GEORGES COURTELINE, *La Philosophie de G. Courteline* (1917).

2. Indulgences, not fulfillment, is what the world / Permits us. CHRISTOPHER FRY, *A Phoenix Too Frequent* (1950).

3. Excessive indulgence to others, especially to children is in fact only self-indulgence under an alias. JULIUS CHARLES HARE and AUGUSTUS WILLIAM HARE, *Guesses at Truth* (1827).

4. The more you let yourself go, the less others let you go. NIETZSCHE, *Miscellaneous Maxims and Opinions* (1879), 82, tr. Paul V. Cohn.

## 469. INEQUALITY

**See also 295. Equality**

1. Couldn't we even argue that it is because men are unequal that they have that much more need to be brothers? CHARLES DU BOS, *Journal*, Feb. 27, 1918.

2. We are all Adam's children, but silk makes the difference. THOMAS FULLER, M.D., *Gnomologia* (1732), 5425.

3. That's part of American greatness, is discrimination. Yes, sir. Inequality, I think, breeds freedom and gives a man opportunity. LESTER MADDOX, quoted in *The New York Times Magazine*, Nov. 6, 1966.

4. Whatever may be the general endeavor of a community to render its members equal and alike, the personal pride of individuals will always seek to rise above the line, and to form somewhere an inequality to their own advantage. ALEXIS DE TOCQUEVILLE, *Democracy in America* (1835–39), 2.3.13.

## 470. INFIDELITY

**See also 178. Constancy and Inconstancy; 736. Promiscuity**

1. Maidens' hearts are always soft: / Would that men's were truer! WILLIAM CULLEN BRYANT, "Song—Dost Thou Idly Ask to Hear."

2. It is the fear of middle-age in the young, of old-age in the middle-aged, which is the prime cause of infidelity, that infallible rejuvenator. CYRIL CONNOLLY, *The Unquiet Grave* (1945), 2.

3. It is natural / For a woman to be wild with her husband when he / Goes in for secret love. EURIPIDES, *Medea* (431 B.C.), tr. Rex Warner.

4. When cheated, wife or husband feels the same. EURIPIDES, *Andromache* (c. 426 B.C.), tr. John F. Nims.

5. Where there's marriage without love, / there will be love without marriage. BENJAMIN FRANKLIN, *Poor Richard's Almanack* (1732–57).

6. When a man steals your wife, there is no better revenge than to let him keep her. SACHA GUITRY, *Elles et toi* (1948).

7. Inconstancy no sin will prove / If we consider that we love / But the same beauty in another face, / Like the same body in another place. EDWARD HERBERT, "Inconstancy" (c. 1610).

8. Wives invariably flourish when deserted; . . . it is the deserting male, the reckless idealist rushing about the world seeking a non-existent felicity, who often ends in disaster. WILLIAM MC FEE, "Knights and Turcopoliers," *Harbours of Memory* (1921).

9. Adultery is the application of democracy to love. H. L. MENCKEN, "Sententiae," *A Book of Burlesques* (1920).

10. 'Tis sweet to think, that, where'er we rove, / We are sure to find something blissful and dear, / And that, when we're far from the lips we love, / We've but to make love to the lips we are near. THOMAS MOORE, " 'Tis Sweet to Think," *Irish Melodies* (1807–35).

11. The fickleness of the women I love is only equalled by the infernal constancy of the women who love me. GEORGE BERNARD SHAW, *The Philanderer* (1893), 4.

12. No woman is capable of being beautiful who is not incapable of being false. RICHARD STEELE, *The Spectator* (1711–12), 33.

13. Old love, old love, / How can I be true? / Shall I be faithless to myself / Or to you? SARA TEASDALE, "New Love and Old," *Rivers to the Sea* (1915).

14. No man worth having is true to his wife, or can be true to his wife, or ever was, or ever will be so. SIR JOHN VANBRUGH, *The Relapse* (1697), 3.2.

15. Adultery is an evil only inasmuch as it is a theft; but we do not steal that which is given to us. VOLTAIRE, "Adultery," *Philosophical Dictionary* (1764).

16. Those who are faithful know only the trivial side of love; it is the faithless who know love's tragedies. OSCAR WILDE, *The Picture of Dorian Gray* (1891), 1.

17. Young men want to be faithful, and are not; old men want to be faithless, and cannot. OSCAR WILDE, *The Picture of Dorian Gray* (1891), 2.

## 471. INFLUENCE

1. Let the wise beware / Lest they bewilder / The minds of the ignorant / Hungry for action. *Bhagavadgita*, 3, tr. Swami Prabhavananda and Christopher Isherwood.

2. Evil communications corrupt good manners. *Bible*, 1 Corinthians 15:33.

3. People exercise an unconscious selection in being influenced. T. S. ELIOT, "Religion and Literature" (1935).

4. The best effect of fine persons is felt after we have left their presence. EMERSON, *Journals*, 1839.

5. Our chief want in life is somebody who shall make us do what we can. EMERSON, "Considerations by the Way," *The Conduct of Life* (1860).

6. Influence is neither good nor bad in an absolute manner, but only in relation to the one who experiences it. ANDRÉ GIDE, "Concerning Influence in Literature," *Pretexts* (1903), tr. Angelo P. Bertocci and others.

7. No one is a light unto himself, not even the sun. ANTONIO PORCHIA, *Voces* (1968), tr. W. S. Merwin.

8. Of all the pulpits from which human voice is ever sent forth, there is none from which it reaches so far as from the grave. JOHN RUSKIN, *The Seven Lamps of Architecture* (1849), 6.9.

9. Half our standards come from our first masters, and the other half from our first loves. GEORGE SANTAYANA, *The Life of Reason: Reason in Art* (1905–06), 10.

10. Every hair makes its shadow on the ground. SPANISH PROVERB.

11. If we imagine any one to love, desire, or hate anything which we ourselves love, hate, or desire, by that very fact we shall love, hate, or desire it the more. SPINOZA, *Ethics* (1677), 3, tr. Andrew Boyle.

## 472. INGRATIATION

**See also 49. Approval; 706. Popularity**

1. Please all, and you will please none. AESOP, "The Man, the Boy, and the Donkey," *Fables* (6th c. B.C.?), tr. Joseph Jacobs.

2. When we want to please in the world, we must resign ourselves to learning many things from people who are ignorant of them. CHAMFORT, *Maximes et pensées* (1805), 2.

3. How I like to be liked, and what I do to be liked! CHARLES LAMB, letter to Dorothy Wordsworth, Jan. 8, 1821.

4. Take here the grand secret—if not of pleasing all, yet of displeasing none—court mediocrity, avoid originality, and sacrifice to fashion. JOHANN KASPAR LAVATER, *Aphorisms on Man* (1788).

5. It is in vain to hope to please all alike. Let a man stand with his face in what direction he will, he must necessarily turn his back on one half of the world. GEORGE DENNISON PRENTICE, *Prenticeana* (1860).

6. Words calculated to catch everyone may catch no one. ADLAI STEVENSON, address, Democratic National Convention, Chicago, July 21, 1952.

## 473. INGRATITUDE

**See also 397. Gratitude; 639. Obligation**

1. Wan raison people ar-re not grateful is because they're proud iv thimsilves an' they niver feel they get half what they desarve. Another raison is they know ye've had all th' fun ye're entitled to whin ye do annything f'r annybody. FINLEY PETER DUNNE, "Gratitude," *Observations by Mr. Dooley* (1902).

2. A wretched child / Is he who does not return his parents' care. EURIPIDES, *The Suppliant Women* (c. 421 B.C.), tr. Frank W. Jones.

3. Eaten bread is forgotten. THOMAS FULLER, M.D., *Gnomologia* (1732), 1358.

4. We should hear little of ingratitude,

unless we were so apt to exaggerate the worth of our better deeds, and to look for a return in proportion to our own exorbitant estimate. JULIUS CHARLES HARE and AUGUSTUS WILLIAM HARE, *Guesses at Truth* (1827).

5. A man is very apt to complain of the ingratitude of those who have risen far above him. SAMUEL JOHNSON, quoted in Boswell's *Life of Samuel Johnson*, March 28, 1776.

6. Men are slower to recognize blessings than evils. LIVY, *Ab Urbe Condita* (c. 29 B.C.), 30.21.

7. There are far fewer ungrateful men than we believe, for there are far fewer generous men than we think. SAINT-ÉVREMOND, *Sur les ingrats* (1705).

8. Blow, blow, thou winter wind, / Thou art not so unkind / As man's ingratitude. SHAKESPEARE, *As You Like It* (1599–1600), 2.7.174.

9. How sharper than a serpent's tooth it is / To have a thankless child! SHAKESPEARE, *King Lear* (1605–06), 1.4.310.

10. If you pick up a starving dog and make him prosperous, he will not bite you. This is the principal difference between a dog and a man. MARK TWAIN, "Pudd'nhead Wilson's Calendar," *Pudd'nhead Wilson* (1894), 16.

## INHERITANCE

**See 1051. Wills and Inheritance**

## INITIATIVE

**See 289. Enterprise**

## 474. INJURY

**See also 286. Enemies; 475. Injustice; 486. Insult; 658. Pacifism; 782. Recompense; 811. Revenge; 866. Self-injury; 939. Suffering**

1. Injuries may be forgiven, but not forgotten. AESOP, "The Man and the Serpent," *Fables* (6th c. B.C.?), tr. Joseph Jacobs.

2. Wounds cannot be cured without searching. FRANCIS BACON, "Of Expense," *Essays* (1625).

3. An injury is much sooner forgotten than an insult. LORD CHESTERFIELD, *Letters to His Son*, Oct. 9, 1746.

4. I will not be revenged, and this I owe to my enemy; but I will remember, and this I owe to myself. CHARLES CALEB COLTON, *Lacon* (1825), 1.35.

5. Men are apt to offend ('tis true) where they find most goodness to forgive. WILLIAM CONGREVE, *The Old Bachelor* (1693), 4.4.

6. He that does you a very ill turn will never forgive you. ENGLISH PROVERB.

7. Forgetting of a wrong is a mild revenge. THOMAS FULLER, M.D., *Gnomologia* (1732), 1592.

8. 'Tis better to suffer wrong than do it. THOMAS FULLER, M.D., *Gnomologia* (1732), 5068.

9. Everyone suffers wrongs for which there is no remedy. EDGAR WATSON HOWE, *Country Town Sayings* (1911).

10. Who offends writes on sand, who is offended on marble. ITALIAN PROVERB.

11. He threatens many that hath injured one. BEN JONSON, *Sejanus His Fall* (1603), 2.3.

12. Wounds heal and become scars. But scars grow with us. STANISLAW LEC, *Unkempt Thoughts* (1962), tr. Jacek Galazka.

13. To deaden yourself against any hurt is to deaden yourself also against the hurt of others. MAX LERNER, "An Element of Blank," *The Unfinished Country* (1959), 5.

14. There are some men whom a staggering emotional shock, so far from making them mental invalids for life, seems, on the other hand, to awaken, to galvanize, to arouse into an almost incredible activity of soul. WILLIAM MCFEE, "On a Balcony," *Harbours of Memory* (1921).

15. Reject your sense of injury and the injury itself disappears. MARCUS AURELIUS, *Meditations* (2nd c.), 4.7, tr. Maxwell Staniforth.

16. Nothing may help or heal / While Amor incensed remembers wrong. HERMAN MELVILLE, "After the Pleasure Party," *John Marr and Other Sailors* (1888).

17. It is far pleasanter to injure and afterwards beg forgiveness than to be injured and grant forgiveness. He who does the former gives evidence of power and afterwards of kindness of character. NIETZSCHE, *Human, All Too Human* (1878), 348, tr. Helen Zimmern.

18. A brave man thinks no one his superior who does him an injury; for he has it

then in his power to make himself superior to the other by forgiving it. ALEXANDER POPE, *Thoughts on Various Subjects* (1727).

19. In all the ills which befall us, we look more at the intention than the effect. A tile which falls from the house may hurt more, but does not vex us so much as a stone thrown designedly by an ill-natured hand. ROUSSEAU, *Reveries of a Solitary Walker* (1782), 8.

20. That which deceives us and does us harm also undeceives us and does us good. JOSEPH ROUX, *Meditations of a Parish Priest* (1886), 5.53, tr. Isabel F. Hapgood.

21. If you have given a person serious cause of offence, and should afterwards do him a hundred kind offices, rest not secure against his revenge of that one offence; for the dart may be extracted from the wound, yet the smart of it will rankle in the heart. SA'DI, *Gulistan* (1258), 3.28, tr. James Ross.

22. Those whom men have injured they despise. SENECA, *On Anger* (1st c.).

23. Since I wronged you, I have never liked you. SPANISH PROVERB.

24. It belongs to human nature to hate those you have injured. TACITUS, *Agricola* (c. A.D. 98), 42.

25. He that wrongs his friend / Wrongs himself more, and ever bears about / A silent court of justice in his breast, / Himself the judge and jury, and himself / The prisoner at the bar, ever condemned. ALFRED, LORD TENNYSON, "Aylmer's Field" (1864).

26. There are offences given and offences not given but taken. IZAAK WALTON, "Epistle to the Reader," *The Compleat Angler* (1653).

## 475. INJUSTICE

See also 474. Injury; 515. Justice; 531. Leniency; 783. Reform

1. Justice is my being allowed to do whatever I like. Injustice is whatever prevents my doing so. SAMUEL BUTLER (d. 1902), *Note-Books* (1912).

2. No man at bottom means injustice; it is always for some obscure distorted image of a right that he contends: an obscure image diffracted, exaggerated, in the wonderfulest way, by natural dimness and selfishness; getting tenfold more diffracted by exasperation of contest, till at length it become all but irrecognisable. THOMAS CARLYLE, *Chartism* (1839), 1.

3. It is the feeling of injustice that is insupportable to all men. THOMAS CARLYLE, *Chartism* (1839), 5.

4. We must believe in the gods no longer if injustice is to prevail over justice. EURIPIDES, *Electra* (413 B.C.), tr. Moses Hadas and John McLean.

5. A grievance is most poignant when almost redressed. ERIC HOFFER, *The True Believer* (1951), 2.5.22.

6. Injustice, swift, erect, and unconfined, / Sweeps the wide earth, and tramples o'er mankind. HOMER, *Iliad* (9th c. B.C.), 9.628, tr. Alexander Pope.

7. Abuse a man unjustly, and you will make friends for him. EDGAR WATSON HOWE, *Country Town Sayings* (1911).

8. Nothing is absolutely unjust. There is no real equity, no total grandeur, no pure vice, no absolute crime. JULIEN OFFROY DE LA METTRIE, "Discours préliminaire," *Oeuvres philosophiques* (1754).

9. I'm willin' a man should go tollable strong / Agin wrong in the abstract, fer that kind o' wrong / Is ollers unpop'lar an' never gits pitied, / Because it's a crime no one never committed. JAMES RUSSELL LOWELL, *The Biglow Papers: First Series* (1848), 4.

10. An unrectified case of injustice has a terrible way of lingering, restlessly, in the social atmosphere like an unfinished question. MARY MC CARTHY, "My Confession," *On the Contrary* (1961).

11. There is no social evil, no form of injustice whether of the feudal or the capitalist order which has not been sanctified in some way or other by religious sentiment and thereby rendered more impervious to change. REINHOLD NIEBUHR, *Christian Realism and Political Problems* (1953), 8.

12. Injustice all around is justice. PERSIAN PROVERB.

13. Mankind censure injustice, fearing that they may be victims of it and not because they shrink from committing it. PLATO, *The Republic* (4th c. B.C.), 1, tr. Benjamin Jowett.

14. When innocence trembles, it condemns the judge. PUBLILIUS SYRUS, *Moral Sayings* (1st c. B.C.), 944, tr. Darius Lyman.

15. Injustice in this world is not something comparative; the wrong is deep, clear,

and absolute in each private fate. GEORGE SANTAYANA, *Little Essays* (1920), 71, ed. Logan Pearsall Smith.

16. Injustice which lasts for three long centuries and which exists among millions of people over thousands of square miles of territory, is injustice no longer; it is an accomplished fact of life. RICHARD WRIGHT, *Native Son* (1940), 3.

## 476. INNOCENCE

See also **611. Naïveté; 764. Purity; 892. Simplicity**

1. 'Tis e'er the lot of the innocent in the world, to fly to the wolf for succor from the lion. JOHN BARTH, *The Sot-Weed Factor* (1960), 3.11.

2. Innocence dwells with Wisdom, but never with Ignorance. WILLIAM BLAKE, annotations, *The Four Zoas* (c. 1795–1804).

3. The innocent is the person who explains nothing. ALBERT CAMUS, *Notebooks 1935–1942* (1962), 2, tr. Philip Thody.

4. A man is not to aim at innocence, any more than he is to aim at hair; but he is to keep it. EMERSON, *Journals*, 1855.

5. Those who are incapable of committing great crimes do not readily suspect them in others. LA ROCHEFOUCAULD, *Maxims* (1665), tr. Kenneth Pratt.

6. The great man is he who does not lose his child's-heart. MENCIUS, *Works* (4th–3rd c. B.C.), 4, tr. Charles A. Wong.

7. Whoever would become as a child must overcome his youth too. NIETZSCHE, "The Stillest Hour," *Thus Spoke Zarathustra* (1883–92), 2, tr. Walter Kaufmann.

8. It is innocence that is full and experience that is empty. It is innocence that wins and experience that loses. CHARLES PÉGUY, "Innocence and Experience," *Basic Verities* (1943), tr. Ann and Julian Green.

9. He's armed without that's innocent within. ALEXANDER POPE, *Epilogue to the Satires* (1738), 1.1.94.

10. If you would live innocently, seek solitude. PUBLILIUS SYRUS, *Moral Sayings* (1st c. B.C.), 1078, tr. Darius Lyman.

11. Whoever blushes is already guilty; true innocence is ashamed of nothing. ROUSSEAU, *Émile* (1762), 4.

12. Thrice happy state again to be / The trustful infant on the knee, / Who lets his rosy fingers play / About his mother's neck, and knows / Nothing beyond his mother's eyes! ALFRED, LORD TENNYSON, "Supposed Confessions" (1830).

13. Through our own recovered innocence we discern the innocence of our neighbors. THOREAU, "Spring," *Walden* (1854).

## 477. INNOVATION

See also **115. Change; 500. Invention; 632. Novelty**

1. Time is the greatest innovator. FRANCIS BACON, "Of Innovations," *Essays* (1625).

2. We ought not to be over-anxious to encourage innovation in cases of doubtful improvement, for an old system must ever have two advantages over a new one; it is established, and it is understood. CHARLES CALEB COLTON, *Lacon* (1825), 1.521.

3. Inventors and men of genius have almost always been regarded as fools at the beginning (and very often at the end) of their careers. DOSTOEVSKY, *The Idiot* (1868), 3.1, tr. David Magarshack.

4. One doesn't discover new lands without consenting to lose sight of the shore for a very long time. ANDRÉ GIDE, *The Counterfeiters* (1925), 3.15, tr. Dorothy Bussy.

5. We are more ready to try the untried when what we do is inconsequential. Hence the remarkable fact that many inventions had their birth as toys. ERIC HOFFER, *The Ordeal of Change* (1964), 14.

6. Out of every ten innovations attempted, all very splendid, nine will end up in silliness; the tenth and the last, though it escape the preposterous, will show little that is new in the end. ANTONIO MACHADO, *Juan de Mairena* (1943), 21, tr. Ben Belitt.

7. The new always carries with it the sense of violation, of sacrilege. What is dead is sacred; what is new, that is, *different*, is evil, dangerous, or subversive. HENRY MILLER, "With Edgar Varèse in the Gobi Desert," *The Air-Conditioned Nightmare* (1945).

8. Let no one say that I have said nothing new; the arrangement of the subject is new. PASCAL, *Pensées* (1670), 22, tr. W. F. Trotter.

9. The vitality of a new movement in art or letters can be pretty accurately gauged

by the fury it arouses. LOGAN PEARSALL SMITH, *Afterthoughts* (1931), 5.

10. The rude beginnings of every art acquire a greater celebrity than the art in perfection; he who first played the fiddle was looked upon as a demigod. VOLTAIRE, "Amplification," *Philosophical Dictionary* (1764).

11. However hard we try to bring in the new / it comes into being only / in the midst of clumsy deals. PETER WEISS, *Marat / Sade* (1964), 1.15, tr. Geoffrey Skelton and Adrian Mitchell.

## 478. INQUIRY

See also 208. Curiosity

1. A sudden, bold, and unexpected question doth many times surprise a man and lay him open. FRANCIS BACON, "Of Cunning," *Essays* (1625).

2. He who asks questions cannot avoid the answers. CAMEROONIAN PROVERB.

3. Clever people seem not to feel the natural pleasure of bewilderment, and are always answering questions when the chief relish of a life is to go on asking them. FRANK MOORE COLBY, "Simple Simon," *The Colby Essays* (1926), v. 1.

4. Examinations are formidable even to the best prepared, for the greatest fool may ask more than the wisest man can answer. CHARLES CALEB COLTON, *Lacon* (1825), 1.322.

5. Better ask twice than lose your way once. DANISH PROVERB.

6. The sun shines and warms and lights us and we have no curiosity to know why this is so; but we ask the reason of all evil, of pain, and hunger, and mosquitoes and silly people. EMERSON, *Journals*, 1830.

7. Many a profound genius, I suppose, who fills the world with fame of his exploding renowned errors, is yet every day posed [baffled] by trivial questions at his own supper-table. EMERSON, *Journals*, 1832.

8. An answer is always a form of death. JOHN FOWLES, *The Magus* (1965), 75.

9. I know of no inquiry which the impulses of man suggests that is forbidden to the resolution of man to pursue. MARGARET FULLER, *Summer on the Lakes* (1844), 5.

10. 'Tis not every question that deserves an answer. THOMAS FULLER, M.D., *Gnomologia* (1732), 5094.

11. To question a wise man is the beginning of wisdom. GERMAN PROVERB.

12. More trouble is caused in the world by indiscreet answers than by indiscreet questions. SYDNEY J. HARRIS, *Chicago Daily News*, March 27, 1958.

13. Questions show the mind's range, and answers its subtlety. JOSEPH JOUBERT, *Pensées* (1842), 3.21, tr. Katharine Lyttelton.

14. I keep six honest serving-men / (They taught me all I knew); / Their names are What and Why and When / And How and Where and Who. RUDYARD KIPLING, "The Elephant's Child," *Just-So Stories* (1902).

15. There is frequently more to be learned from the unexpected questions of a child than the discourses of men, who talk in a road, according to the notions they have borrowed and the prejudices of their education. JOHN LOCKE, *Some Thoughts Concerning Education* (1693), 120.

16. The great pleasure of ignorance is the pleasure of asking questions. The man who has lost this pleasure or exchanged it for the pleasure of dogma, which is the pleasure of answering, is already beginning to stiffen. ROBERT LYND, "The Pleasures of Ignorance," in *I Was Just Thinking* (1959), ed. Elinor Parker.

17. There aren't any embarrassing questions—just embarrassing answers. CARL ROWAN, *New Yorker*, Dec. 7, 1963.

18. It is better to ask some of the questions than to know all of the answers. JAMES THURBER, "The Scotty Who Knew Too Much," *The Thurber Carnival* (1945).

## INSANITY

See 555. Madness

## 479. INSECTS

1. Ants are good citizens: they place group interest first. But they carry it so far, they have few or no political rights. An ant doesn't have the vote, apparently: he just has his duties. CLARENCE DAY, *This Simian World* (1920), 5.

2. The Spider as an Artist / Has never been employed— / Though his surpassing

Merit / Is freely certified. EMILY DICKINSON, poem (c. 1873).

3. Where's the state beneath the firmament / That doth excel the bees for government? SEIGNEUR DU BARTAS, *Divine Weekes and Workes* (1578), 1.5.1.

4. Two-legged creatures we are supposed to love as well as we love ourselves. The four-legged, also, can come to seem pretty important. But six legs are too many from the human standpoint. JOSEPH WOOD KRUTCH, "August," *The Twelve Seasons* (1949).

5. insects have / their own point / of view about / civilization / a man / thinks he amounts / to a great deal / but to a / flea or a / mosquito a / human being is / merely something / good to eat. DON MARQUIS, "certain maxims of archy," *Archy and Mehitabel* (1927).

6. Is there a polity better ordered, the offices better distributed, and more inviolably observed and maintained, than that of bees? MONTAIGNE, "Apology for Raimond de Sebonde," *Essays* (1580–88), tr. Charles Cotton and W. C. Hazlitt.

7. God in His wisdom made the fly / And then forgot to tell us why. OGDEN NASH, "The Fly," *Good Intentions* (1943).

8. The fly ought to be used as the symbol of impertinence and audacity; for whilst all other animals shun man more than anything else, and run away even before he comes near them, the fly lights upon his very nose. SCHOPENHAUER, "A Few Parables," *Parerga and Paralipomena* (1851), tr. T. Bailey Saunders.

9. How doth the little busy bee / Improve each shining hour, / And gather honey all the day / From every opening flower! ISAAC WATTS, *Divine Songs for Children* (1720), 20.

## 480. INSECURITY

**See also 43. Anxiety; 850. Security; 861. Self-doubt; 998. Uncertainty**

1. Is not man himself the most unsettled of all the creatures of the earth? What is this trembling sensation that is intensified with each ascending step in the natural order? UGO BETTI, *The Fugitive* (1953), 3, tr. G. H. McWilliam.

2. Suspense—is Hostiler than Death— / Death—tho'soever Broad, / Is just Death, and cannot increase— / Suspense—does not conclude—. EMILY DICKINSON, poem (c. 1863).

3. People wish to be settled: only as far as they are unsettled is there any hope for them. EMERSON, "Circles," *Essays: First Series* (1841).

4. What can we take on trust / in this uncertain life? Happiness, greatness, / pride—nothing is secure, nothing keeps. EURIPIDES, *Hecuba* (c. 425 B.C.), tr. William Arrowsmith.

5. How can a man learn navigation / Where there's no rudder? CHRISTOPHER FRY, *A Sleep of Prisoners* (1951).

6. We are reassured almost as foolishly as we are alarmed; human nature is so constituted. VICTOR HUGO, "Saint Denis," *Les Misérables* (1862), 15.1, tr. Charles E. Wilbour.

7. The mind leaps, and leaps perhaps with a sort of elation, through the immensities of space, but the spirit, frightened and cold, longs to have once more above its head the inverted bowl beyond which may lie whatever paradise its desires may create. JOSEPH WOOD KRUTCH, "The Genesis of a Mood," *The Modern Temper* (1929).

## 481. INSENSITIVITY

**See also 85. Blindness, Spiritual; 876. Sensibility**

1. It is useless attacking the insensible. AESOP, "The Serpent and the File," *Fables* (6th c. B.C.?), tr. Joseph Jacobs.

2. But we, we have no sense of direction; impetus / Is all we have; we do not proceed, we only / Roll down the mountain, / Like disbalanced boulders, crushing before us many / Delicate springing things, whose plan it was to grow. EDNA ST. VINCENT MILLAY, untitled poem, *Make Bright the Arrows* (1940).

3. O, what men dare do! what men may do! what men daily do, not knowing what they do! SHAKESPEARE, *Much Ado About Nothing* (1598–99), 4.1.19.

## INSIGHT

**See 499. Intuition; 1000. Understanding; 1001. Understanding Others**

## INSIGNIFICANCE
**See 1005. Unimportance**

## 482. INSINCERITY
**See also 438. Hypocrisy; 726. Pretension; 894. Sincerity**

1. The ring of a false coin is not more recognizable than that of a rhyme setting forth a false sorrow. THOMAS BAILEY ALDRICH, "Asides: On a Certain Affectation," *Ponkapog Papers* (1903).

2. Artlessness, n. A certain engaging quality to which women attain by long study and severe practice upon the admiring male, who is pleased to fancy it resembles the candid simplicity of his young. AMBROSE BIERCE, *The Devil's Dictionary* (1881–1911).

3. A false friend and a shadow attend only while the sun shines. BENJAMIN FRANKLIN, *Poor Richard's Almanack* (1732–57).

4. The most exhausting thing in life, I have discovered, is being insincere. ANNE MORROW LINDBERGH, "Channelled Whelk," *Gift from the Sea* (1955).

5. Is insincerity such a terrible thing? I think not. It is merely a method by which we can multiply our personalities. OSCAR WILDE, *The Picture of Dorian Gray* (1891), 11.

## INSOMNIA
**See 71. Bed**

## 483. INSPIRATION
**See also 198. Creation and Creativity**

1. Commonsense is the wick of the candle. EMERSON, *Journals*, 1845.

2. There is no wide road which leads to the Muses. PROPERTIUS, *Elegies* (c. 28–c. 16 B.C.), 3.1.14.

3. Inspiration could be called inhaling the memory of an act never experienced. NED ROREM, "Four Questions Answered," *Music from Inside Out* (1967).

4. Divine fires do not blaze each day, but an artist functions in their afterglow hoping for their recurrence. NED ROREM, "Four Questions Answered," *Music from Inside Out* (1967).

5. Just as appetite comes by eating, so work brings inspiration, if inspiration is not discernible at the beginning. IGOR STRAVINSKY, *An Autobiography* (1936), 10.

## 484. INSTINCT
**See also 431. Human Nature**

1. Trust the instinct to the end, though you can render no reason. EMERSON, "Intellect," *Essays: First Series* (1841).

2. Be a good animal, true to your animal instincts. D. H. LAWRENCE, *The White Peacock* (1911), 2.2.

3. *Instinct.* When the house burns one forgets even lunch. Yes, but one eats it later in the ashes. NIETZSCHE, *Beyond Good and Evil* (1886), 83, tr. Walter Kaufmann.

4. A dog reasons the way he sniffs, and / the smells that he gets are for him. CESARE PAVESE, "Instinct," *Modern European Poetry* (1966), ed. Willis Barnstone.

5. None of us can estimate what we do when we do it from instinct. LUIGI PIRANDELLO, *Henry IV* (1922), 1, tr. Edward Storer.

6. Well-bred instinct meets reason halfway. GEORGE SANTAYANA, *The Life of Reason: Reason in Society* (1905–06), 1.

## 485. INSTITUTIONS
**See also 100. Bureaucracy**

1. The test of every religious, political, or educational system, is the man which it forms. If a system injures the intelligence it is bad. If it injures the character it is vicious, if it injures the conscience it is criminal. HENRI FRÉDÉRIC AMIEL, *Journal*, June 17, 1852, tr. Mrs. Humphry Ward.

2. Individualities may form communities, but it is institutions alone that can create a nation. BENJAMIN DISRAELI, speech, Manchester, 1866.

3. The test of political institutions is the condition of the country whose future they regulate. BENJAMIN DISRAELI, speech, "Conservative Principles," April 3, 1872.

4. We do not make a world of our own,

but fall into institutions already made, and have to accommodate ourselves to them to be useful at all. EMERSON, *Journals*, 1832.

5. An institution is the lengthened shadow of one man. EMERSON, "Self-Reliance," *Essays: First Series* (1841).

6. Every institution not only carries within it the seeds of its own dissolution, but prepares the way for its most hated rival. WILLIAM RALPH INGE, "The Victorian Age," *Outspoken Essays: Second Series* (1922).

7. Wise and prudent men—intelligent conservatives—have long known that in a changing world worthy institutions can be conserved only by adjusting them to the changing time. FRANKLIN D. ROOSEVELT, speech, Syracuse, N.Y., Sept. 29, 1936.

8. A kingdom is embellished by the wise, and religion rendered illustrious by the pious. SA'DI, *Gulistan* (1258), 8.6, tr. James Ross.

9. The more rational an institution is the less it suffers by making concessions to others. GEORGE SANTAYANA, *The Life of Reason: Reason in Science* (1905–06), 9.

10. Catastrophes come when some dominant institution, swollen like a soap-bubble and still standing without foundations, suddenly crumbles at the touch of what may seem a word or an idea, but is really some stronger material force. GEORGE SANTAYANA, *Persons and Places: The Middle Span* (1945), 8.

## 486. INSULT

See also 474. Injury; 824. Rudeness

1. Young men soon give, and soon forget, affronts; / Old age is slow in both. JOSEPH ADDISON, *Cato* (1713), 2.5.

2. No one can be as calculatedly rude as the British, which amazes Americans, who do not understand studied insult and can only offer abuse as a substitute. PAUL GALLICO, *The New York Times*, Jan. 14, 1962.

3. A wise man is superior to any insults which can be put upon him, and the best reply to unseemly behavior is patience and moderation. MOLIÈRE, *The Would-be Gentleman* (1670), 2, tr. John Wood.

4. Insults should be well avenged or well endured. SPANISH PROVERB.

## 487. INSURANCE

1. Insurance, n. An ingenious modern game of chance in which the player is permitted to enjoy the comfortable conviction that he is beating the man who keeps the table. AMBROSE BIERCE, *The Devil's Dictionary* (1881–1911).

2. When the praying does no good, insurance does help. BERTOLT BRECHT, *The Mother* (1932), 11, tr. Lee Baxandall.

3. 'Tis said that persons living on annuities / Are longer lived than others. BYRON, *Don Juan* (1819–24), 2.65.

4. Buy an annuity cheap, and make your life interesting to yourself and everybody else that watches the speculation. CHARLES DICKENS, *Martin Chuzzlewit* (1844), 18.

## 488. THE INTANGIBLE

See also 920. Spirituality

1. Clocks ar-re habichool liars, an' so ar-re scales. As soon as annything gets good enough to weigh ye can't weigh it. FINLEY PETER DUNNE, "Things Spiritual," *Mr. Dooley Says* (1910).

## 489. INTEGRITY

See also 117. Character; 178. Constancy and Inconstancy; 423. Honesty; 553. Loyalty; 598. Morality; 628. Nobility; 728. Principle; 894. Sincerity; 933. Strength; 1025. Virtue

1. Let us be true: this is the highest maxim of art and of life, the secret of eloquence and of virtue, and of all moral authority. HENRI FRÉDÉRIC AMIEL, *Journal*, Dec. 17, 1854, tr. Mrs. Humphry Ward.

2. A man who permits his honor to be taken, permits his life to be taken. PIETRO ARETINO, letter to Giambattista Castaldo, Mar. 25, 1537, tr. Samuel Putnam.

3. He that is faithful in that which is least is faithful also in much; and he that is unjust in the least is unjust also in much. *Bible*, Luke 16:10.

4. Honor is like a steep island without a shore: one cannot return once one is outside. NICOLAS BOILEAU, *Satires* (1666), 10.

5. Nothing so completely baffles one who is full of trick and duplicity himself, than straightforward and simple integrity in another. CHARLES CALEB COLTON, *Lacon* (1825), 2.140.

6. Morality regulates the acts of man as a private individual; honor, his acts as a public man. ESTEBAN ECHEVERRÍA, *Dogma Socialista.*

7. Nothing is at last sacred but the integrity of our own mind. Absolve you to yourself, and you shall have the suffrage of the world. EMERSON, "Self-Reliance," *Essays: First Series* (1841).

8. Honour, / How much we fight with weakness to preserve thee! JOHN FORD, *The Broken Heart* (1633), 2.3.

9. Would that the simple maxim, that honesty is the best policy, might be laid to heart; that a sense of the true aim of life might elevate the tone of politics and trade till public and private honor became identical. MARGARET FULLER, *Summer on the Lakes* (1844), 4.

10. A man of honor should never forget what he is because he sees what others are. BALTASAR GRACIÁN, *The Art of Worldly Wisdom* (1647), 280, tr. Joseph Jacobs.

11. Wisdom and virtue are like the two wheels of a cart. JAPANESE PROVERB.

12. Integrity without knowledge is weak and useless, and knowledge without integrity is dangerous and dreadful. SAMUEL JOHNSON, *Rasselas* (1759), 41.

13. Hold it the greatest wrong to prefer life to honor and for the sake of life to lose the reason for living. JUVENAL, *Satires* (c. 100), 8.83.

14. To be individually righteous is the first of all duties, come what may to one's self, to one's country, to society, and to civilization itself. JOSEPH WOOD KRUTCH, title essay, 6, *If You Don't Mind My Saying So* (1964).

15. The just man, O Xerxes, walks humbly in the presence of his God, but walks fearlessly. WALTER SAVAGE LANDOR, "Xerxes and Artabanus," *Imaginary Conversations* (1824–53).

16. He has honor if he holds himself to an ideal of conduct though it is inconvenient, unprofitable, or dangerous to do so. WALTER LIPPMANN, *A Preface to Morals* (1929), 3.11.3.

17. I could not love thee, dear, so much, / Loved I not honour more. RICHARD LOVELACE, "To Lucasta, on Going to the Wars" (1649), 3.

18. You cannot throw words like heroism and sacrifice and nobility and honor away without abandoning the qualities they express. MARYA MANNES, *More in Anger* (1958), 3.2.

19. The courage of all one really knows comes but late in life. NIETZSCHE, *The Will to Power* (1888), tr. Anthony M. Ludovici.

20. Honour and shame from no condition rise; / Act well your part, there all the honour lies. ALEXANDER POPE, *An Essay on Man* (1733–34), 4.193.

21. Without money, honor is a malady. RACINE, *Les Plaideurs* (1668), 1.1.

22. You cannot drive straight on a twisting lane. RUSSIAN PROVERB.

23. This above all: to thine own self be true, / And it must follow, as the night the day, / Thou canst not then be false to any man. SHAKESPEARE, *Hamlet* (1600), 1.3.78.

24. Rightly to be great / Is not to stir without great argument, / But greatly to find quarrel in a straw / When honour's at the stake. SHAKESPEARE, *Hamlet* (1600), 4.4.53.

25. Honour travels in a strait so narrow / Where one but goes abreast. SHAKESPEARE, *Troilus and Cressida* (1601–02), 3.3.154.

26. The truth is, hardly any of us have ethical energy enough for more than one really inflexible point of honor. GEORGE BERNARD SHAW, "Preface on Doctors: The Psychology of Self-Respect in Surgeons," *The Doctor's Dilemma* (1913).

27. It is an endless and frivolous pursuit to act by any other rule than the care of satisfying our own minds in what we do. RICHARD STEELE, *The Spectator* (1711–12), 4.

28. Even honor and virtue make enemies, condemning, as they do, their opposites by too close a contrast. TACITUS, *Annals* (A.D.115–117?), 4.33, tr. Alfred J. Church and William J. Brodribb.

29. Where there are no men, strive thou to be a man. Haggadah, *Palestinian Talmud* (4th c.).

30. When faith is lost, when honor dies, / The man is dead. JOHN GREENLEAF WHITTIER, "Ichabod" (1850), 8.

31. How happy is he born and taught, / That serveth not another's will; / Whose armour is his honest thought, / And simple

truth his utmost skill. SIR HENRY WOTTON, "The Character of a Happy Life" (1651), 1.

### 490. INTELLECTUALS AND INTELLECTUALISM

**See also 491. Intelligence; 583. Mind**

1. The intellectuals' chief cause of anguish are one another's works. JACQUES BARZUN, *The House of Intellect* (1959), 1.

2. An intellectual is someone whose mind watches itself. ALBERT CAMUS, *Notebooks 1935–1942* (1962), I, tr. Philip Thody.

3. It is always the task of the intellectual to "think otherwise." This is not just a perverse idiosyncrasy. It is an absolutely essential feature of a society. HARVEY COX, *The Secular City* (1966), 10.

4. Only those who know the supremacy of the intellectual life – the life which has a seed of ennobling thought and purpose within it – can understand the grief of one who falls from that serene activity into the absorbing soul wasting struggle with worldly annoyances. GEORGE ELIOT, *Middlemarch* (1871–72), 73.

5. A man known to us only as a celebrity in politics or in trade, gains largely in our esteem if we discover that he has some intellectual taste or skill. EMERSON, "Culture," *The Conduct of Life* (1860).

6. An "egghead" is one who stands firmly on both feet in mid-air on both sides of an issue. HOMER FERGUSON, news summaries, May 28, 1954.

7. Intellectualism, though by no means confined to doubters, is often the sole piety of the skeptic. RICHARD HOFSTADTER, *Anti-Intellectualism in American Life* (1963), 1.2.

8. The intellectual is *engagé* – he is pledged, committed, enlisted. What everyone else is willing to admit, namely that ideas and abstractions are of signal importance in human life, he imperatively feels. RICHARD HOFSTADTER, *Anti-Intellectualism in American Life* (1963), 1.2.

9. The intellectual is constantly betrayed by his vanity. God-like, he blandly assumes that he can express everything in words; whereas the things one loves, lives, and dies for are not, in the last analysis, completely expressible in words. ANNE MORROW LINDBERGH, *The Wave of the Future* (1940).

10. On the heights it is warmer than people in the valley suppose, especially in winter. The thinker recognizes the full import of this simile. NIETZSCHE, *Miscellaneous Maxims and Opinions* (1879), 335, tr. Paul V. Cohn.

### 491. INTELLIGENCE

**See also 137. Cleverness; 583. Mind; 778. Reason; 934. Stupidity; 1000. Understanding; 1053. Wisdom**

1. Intelligence is characterized by a natural incomprehension of life. HENRI BERGSON, *L'Évolution créatrice* (1907).

2. Men are admitted into Heaven not because they have curbed and governed their Passions or have No Passions, but because they have Cultivated their Understandings. WILLIAM BLAKE, *A Vision of the Last Judgment* (1810).

3. Intelligence in chains loses in lucidity what it gains in intensity. ALBERT CAMUS, "Absolute Negation," *The Rebel* (1951), tr. Anthony Bower.

4. A superior man may be made to go to the well, but he cannot be made to go down into it. He may be imposed upon, but he cannot be fooled. CONFUCIUS, *Analects* (6th c. B.C.), 6.24, tr. James Legge.

5. It is not enough to have a good mind; the main thing is to use it well. DESCARTES, *Discourse on Method* (1639), 1.

6. To the dull mind all nature is leaden. To the illumined mind the whole world burns and sparkles with light. EMERSON, *Journals*, 1831.

7. We pay / a high price for being intelligent. Wisdom hurts. EURIPIDES, *Electra* (413 B.C.), tr. Emily Townsend Vermeule.

8. The test of a first-rate intelligence is the ability to hold two opposed ideas in the mind at the same time, and still retain the ability to function. F. SCOTT FITZGERALD, "The Crack-Up," *The Crack-Up* (1945).

9. Reason is man's faculty for grasping the world by thought, in contradiction to intelligence, which is man's ability to manipulate the world with the help of thought. ERICH FROMM, *The Sane Society* (1955), 3.

10. One good head is better than a hundred strong hands. THOMAS FULLER, M.D., *Gnomologia* (1732), 3753.

11. Generally among intelligent people are found nothing but paralytics and among

men of action nothing but fools. ANDRÉ GIDE, "Portraits and Aphorisms," *Pretexts* (1903), tr. Angelo P. Bertocci and others.

12. The greatest intelligence is precisely the one that suffers most from its own limitations. ANDRÉ GIDE, *The Counterfeiters* (1925), 3.7, tr. Dorothy Bussy.

13. Little-minded people's thoughts move in such small circles that five minutes' conversation gives you an arc long enough to determine their whole curve. An arc in the movement of a large intellect does not sensibly differ from a straight line. OLIVER WENDELL HOLMES, SR., *The Autocrat of the Breakfast Table* (1858), 1.

14. All fact-collectors, who have no aim beyond their facts, are one-story men. Two-story men compare, reason, generalize, using the labors of the fact-collectors as well as their own. Three-story men idealize, imagine, predict; their best illumination comes from above, through the skylight. OLIVER WENDELL HOLMES, SR., *The Poet at the Breakfast Table* (1872), 2.

15. No man is smart, except by comparison with others who know less; the smartest man who ever lived has reason to be ashamed of himself. EDGAR WATSON HOWE, *Ventures in Common Sense* (1919), 4.22.

16. An honest heart being the first blessing, a knowing head is the second. THOMAS JEFFERSON, letter to Peter Carr, Aug. 19, 1785.

17. The true, strong, and sound mind is the mind that can embrace equally great things and small. SAMUEL JOHNSON, quoted in Boswell's *Life of Samuel Johnson*, April 29, 1778.

18. Everyone speaks well of his heart, but no one dares to say it of his head. LA ROCHEFOUCAULD, *Maxims* (1665), tr. Kenneth Pratt.

19. The sign of an intelligent people is their ability to control emotions by the application of reason. MARYA MANNES, *More in Anger* (1958), 3.1.

20. 'Tis the sharpness of our mind that gives the edge to our pains and pleasures. MONTAIGNE, "That the relish of good and evil depends in a great measure upon the opinion we have of them," *Essays* (1580–88), tr. Charles Cotton and W. C. Hazlitt.

21. If the human intellect functions, it is actually in order to solve the problems which the man's inner destiny sets it. JOSÉ ORTEGA Y GASSET, "In Search of Goethe from Within, Letter to a German," *Partisan Review*, December 1949, tr. Willard R. Trask.

22. The first mark of intelligence, to be sure, is not to start things; the second mark of intelligence is to pursue to the end what you have started. *Panchatantra* (c. 5th c.), 3, tr. Franklin Edgerton.

23. The greater intellect one has, the more originality one finds in men. Ordinary persons find no difference between men. PASCAL, *Pensées* (1670), 7, tr. W. F. Trotter.

24. Intellect, without firmness, is craft and chicanery; and firmness, without intellect, perverseness and obstinacy. SA'DI, *Gulistan* (1258), 8.65, tr. James Ross.

25. The intelligent man known to history flourishes within a dullard and holds a lunatic in leash. GEORGE SANTAYANA, *The Life of Reason: Reason in Common Sense* (1905–06), 2.

26. Intelligence is quickness in seeing things as they are. GEORGE SANTAYANA, *Little Essays* (1920), 62, ed. Logan Pearsall Smith.

27. A good mind possesses a kingdom. SENECA, *Thyestes* (1st c.), 380.

28. It's not a man's great frame / Or breadth of shoulders makes his manhood count: / A man of sense has always the advantage. SOPHOCLES, *Ajax* (c. 447 B.C.), tr. John Moore.

29. Many complain of their looks, but none of their brains. *Yiddish Proverbs* (1949), ed. Hanan J. Ayalti.

## 492. INTEMPERANCE

**See also 266. Drinking; 310. Excess; 733. Profligacy; 963. Temperance**

1. The impulses of an incontinent man carry him in the opposite direction from that towards which he was aiming. ARISTOTLE, *Nicomachean Ethics* (4th c. B.C.), 1.13, tr. J. A. K. Thomson.

2. Debauchee, n. One who has so earnestly pursued pleasure that he has had the misfortune to overtake it. AMBROSE BIERCE, *The Devil's Dictionary* (1881–1911).

3. If the things that produce the pleasures of the dissolute were able to drive away from their minds their fears about

what is above them and about death and pain, and to teach them the limit of desires, we would have no reason to find fault with the dissolute. EPICURUS, "Principal Doctrines" (3rd c. B.C.), 10, in *Letters, Principal Doctrines, and Vatican Sayings*, tr. Russel M. Geer.

4. Since the creation of the world there has been no tyrant like Intemperance, and no slaves so cruelly treated as his. WILLIAM LLOYD GARRISON, *Life* (1885–89), v. 1.

5. Intemperance is the plague of sensuality, and temperance is not its bane but its seasoning. MONTAIGNE, "Of experience," *Essays* (1580–88).

6. When a man has been intemperate so long that shame no longer paints a blush upon his cheek, his liquor generally does it instead. GEORGE DENNISON PRENTICE, *Prenticeana* (1860).

7. Intemperance is the physician's provider. PUBLILIUS SYRUS, *Moral Sayings* (1st c. B.C.), 483, tr. Darius Lyman.

## INTENTION

See 765. Purpose

## 493. INTEREST

See also 867. Selfishness

1. Hungry hatred / Will not strive against intelligent self-interest. T. S. ELIOT, *Murder in the Cathedral* (1935), 1.

2. The laundress washeth her own smock first. ENGLISH PROVERB.

3. Men are not against you; they are merely for themselves. GENE FOWLER, *Skyline* (1961).

4. Every man's affairs, however little, are important to himself. SAMUEL JOHNSON, letter to the earl of Bute, Nov. 3, 1762, quoted in Boswell's *Life of Samuel Johnson.*

5. Principles do not mainly influence even the principled; we talk on principle, but we act on interest. WALTER SAVAGE LANDOR, "Banos and Alpuente," *Imaginary Conversations* (1824–54).

6. Interest speaks all sorts of tongues, and plays all sorts of parts, even that of disinterestedness. LA ROCHEFOUCAULD, *Maxims* (1665).

7. Do not confuse your vested interests with ethics. Do not identify the enemies of your privilege with the enemies of humanity. MAX LERNER, "Politics and the Connective Tissue," *Actions and Passions* (1949).

8. A man will fight harder for his interests than his rights. NAPOLEON I, *Maxims* (1804–15).

9. It is common to forget a man and slight him if his good will cannot help you. PLAUTUS, *The Captives* (3rd c. B.C.).

10. A world of vested interests is not a world which welcomes the disruptive force of candour. AGNES REPPLIER, "Are Americans Timid?" *Under Dispute* (1924).

## 494. INTERESTINGNESS

1. A man who can be entertaining for a full day will be in his grave by night-fall. EDWARD DAHLBERG, "On Time and Death," *Reasons of the Heart* (1965).

2. If men would avoid that general language and general manner in which they strive to hide all that is peculiar, and would say only what was uppermost in their own minds, after their own individual manner, every man would be interesting. EMERSON, *Journals*, 1827.

3. The test of interesting people is that subject matter doesn't matter. LOUIS KRONENBERGER, *Company Manners* (1954), 3.1.

4. The fascinating necessarily tends to call a certain attention to itself; the interesting need not. An evening spent with a fascinating person leaves vivid memories; one spent with interesting people has merely a sort of bouquet. LOUIS KRONENBERGER, *Company Manners* (1954), 3.1.

5. To know when one's self is interested, is the first condition of interesting other people. WALTER PATER, *Marius the Epicurian* (1885), 6.

## 495. INTERESTS, DIVIDED

See also 167. Conflict, Inner

1. No man can serve two masters: for either he will hate the one, and love the other; or else he will hold to the one, and despise the other. *Bible*, Matthew 6:24.

2. The perplexity of life arises from there being too many interesting things in it for us to be interested properly in any of them.

G. K. CHESTERTON, "The Secret of a Train," *Tremendous Trifles* (1909).

3. If you run after two hares, you will catch neither. THOMAS FULLER, M.D., *Gnomologia* (1732), 2782.

4. He who serves two masters has to lie to one. PORTUGUESE PROVERB.

5. Those who set out to serve both God and Mammon soon discover that there is no God. LOGAN PEARSALL SMITH, *Afterthoughts* (1931), 3.

## 496. INTERNATIONAL RELATIONS

See also 98. Brotherhood; 190. Cosmopolitanism; 245. Diplomats and Diplomacy; 271. East and West; 456. Imperialism; 615. Nationalism; 987. Treaties; 1008. United Nations

1. Alliance, n. In international politics, the union of two thieves who have their hands so deeply inserted in each other's pocket that they cannot separately plunder a third. AMBROSE BIERCE, *The Devil's Dictionary* (1881–1911).

2. I do not know the method of drawing up an indictment against a whole people. EDMUND BURKE, speech, "On Conciliation with the American Colonies," March 22, 1775.

3. An ally need not own the land he helps. EURIPIDES, *Ion* (c. 421–408 B.C.), tr. Ronald F. Willetts.

4. Conferences at the top level are always courteous. Name-calling is left to the foreign ministers. W. AVERELL HARRIMAN, news summaries, Aug. 1, 1955.

5. We shall be judged more by what we do at home than what we preach abroad. JOHN F. KENNEDY, State of the Union Message, Jan. 14, 1963.

6. World peace, like community peace, does not require that each man love his neighbor—it requires only that they live together with mutual tolerance, submitting their disputes to a just and peaceful settlement. JOHN F. KENNEDY, commencement address, American University, Washington, D.C., June 10, 1963.

7. That expression "positive neutrality" is a contradiction in terms. There can be no more positive neutrality than there can be a vegetarian tiger. V. K. KRISHNA MENON, *The New York Times*, Oct. 18, 1960.

8. Some of the more fatuous flag-waving Americans are in danger of forgetting that you can't extract gratitude as you would extract a tooth; that unless friendship is freely given, it means nothing and less than nothing. MAX LERNER, "How Grateful Should Europe Be?" *Actions and Passions* (1949).

9. In aid, the proper attitude / Is one omitting gratitude. MARYA MANNES, "Strings," *Subverse: Rhymes for Our Times* (1959).

10. Amity itself can only be maintained by reciprocal respect, and true friends are punctilious equals. HERMAN MELVILLE, Supplement to *Battlepieces and Aspects of the War* (1866).

11. International incidents should not govern foreign policy, but foreign policy, incidents. NAPOLEON I, *Maxims* (1804–15).

12. In a world shaped and coloured more and more by politicians, the nations meet politically—and hardly any other way—to settle their differences. J. B. PRIESTLEY, "Sacred White Elephants," *Thoughts in the Wilderness* (1957).

13. The friendships of nations, built on common interests, cannot survive the mutability of those interests. AGNES REPPLIER, "Allies," *Under Dispute* (1924).

14. This is the devilish thing about foreign affairs: they are foreign and will not always conform to our whim. JAMES RESTON, *The New York Times*, Dec. 16, 1964.

15. International crises have their advantages. They frighten the weak but stir and inspire the strong. JAMES RESTON, *Sketches in the Sand* (1967).

16. More than an end to war, we want an end to the beginning of all wars—yes, an end to this brutal, inhuman and thoroughly impractical method of settling the differences between governments. FRANKLIN D. ROOSEVELT, message for Jefferson Day, April 13, 1945.

17. I asked Tom if countries always apologized when they had done wrong, and he says: "Yes; the little ones does." MARK TWAIN, *Tom Sawyer Abroad* (1894).

18. Our interests are those of the open door—a door of friendship and mutual advantage. This is the only door we care to enter. WOODROW WILSON, statement, March 19, 1913.

19. Interest does not tie nations together;

it sometimes separates them. But sympathy and understanding does unite them. WOODROW WILSON, speech, Oct. 27, 1913.

20. There must be, not a balance of power, but a community of power; not organized rivalries, but an organized peace. WOODROW WILSON, address to U.S. Senate, Jan. 22, 1917.

## 497. INTIMACY

**See also 57. Association; 331. Familiarity; 976. Togetherness**

1. If ever a man and his wife, or a man and his mistress, who pass nights as well as days together, absolutely lay aside all good-breeding, their intimacy will soon degenerate into a coarse familiarity, infallibly productive of contempt or disgust. LORD CHESTERFIELD, *Letters to His Son*, Nov. 3, 1749.

2. A man knows his companion in a long journey and a little inn. THOMAS FULLER, M.D., *Gnomologia* (1732), 284.

3. No stranger can get a great many notes of torture out of a human soul; it takes one that knows it well,—parent, child, brother, sister, intimate. OLIVER WENDELL HOLMES, SR., *The Autocrat of the Breakfast Table* (1858), 6.

4. When married people don't get on they can separate, but if they're not married it's impossible. It's a tie that only death can sever. W. SOMERSET MAUGHAM, *The Circle* (1921), 3.

5. Housekeeping in common is for women the acid test. ANDRÉ MAUROIS, *Ariel* (1924), 35, tr. Ella D'Arcy.

## INTIMIDATION

**See 340. Fear; 354. Force; 969. Threat**

## 498. INTOLERANCE

**See also 262. Dogmatism; 333. Fanaticism; 613. Narrowness; 720. Prejudices; 769. Racial Prejudice; 977. Tolerance**

1. He has the courage of his conviction and the intolerance of his courage. He is opposed to the death penalty for murder, but he would willingly have anyone electrocuted who disagreed with him on the subject. THOMAS BAILEY ALDRICH, "Leaves from a Notebook," *Ponkapog Papers* (1903).

2. Intolerance is the "Do Not Touch" sign on something that cannot bear touching. We do not mind having our hair ruffled, but we will not tolerate any familiarity with the toupée that covers our baldness. ERIC HOFFER, *The Passionate State of Mind* (1954), 62.

3. No loss by flood and lightning, no destruction of cities and temples by the hostile forces of nature, has deprived man of so many noble lives and impulses as those which his intolerance has destroyed. HELEN KELLER, *Optimism* (1903), 2.

## INTROSPECTION

**See 752. Psychoanalysis; 868. Self-knowledge**

## 499. INTUITION

**See also 282. Emotions; 676. Perception; 876. Sensibility**

1. It is the heart always that sees, before the head can see. THOMAS CARLYLE, *Chartism* (1839), 5.

2. Women, as most susceptible, are the best index of the coming hour. EMERSON, "Fate," *The Conduct of Life* (1860).

3. Intuition attracts those who wish to be spiritual without any bother, because it promises a heaven where the intuitions of others can be ignored. E. M. FORSTER, "Roger Fry," *Abinger Harvest* (1936).

## 500. INVENTION

**See also 198. Creation and Creativity; 477. Innovation; 960. Technology**

1. Inventor, n. A person who makes an ingenious arrangement of wheels, levers and springs, and believes it civilization. AMBROSE BIERCE, *The Devil's Dictionary* (1881–1911).

2. Name the greatest of all the inventors. Accident. MARK TWAIN, *Notebook* (1935).

3. It must be confessed that the inventors of the mechanical arts have been much more useful to men than the inventors of syllogisms. VOLTAIRE, "Philosophy," *Philosophical Dictionary* (1764).

## 501. INVESTMENT

See also 102. Business and Commerce

1. If a little does not go, much cash will not come. CHINESE PROVERB.

2. 'Tis sweet to know that stocks will stand / When we with daisies lie, / That commerce will continue, / And trades as briskly fly. EMILY DICKINSON, *Poems* (c. 1862–86).

3. A nimble sixpence is better than a slow shilling. ENGLISH PROVERB.

4. 'Tis money that begets money. THOMAS FULLER, M.D., *Gnomologia* (1732), 5091.

5. There is nothing like the ticker tape except a woman—nothing that promises, hour after hour, day after day, such sudden developments; nothing that disappoints so often or occasionally fulfills with such unbelievable, passionate magnificence. WALTER KNOWLETON GUTMAN, *Coronet*, March 1960.

6. Speculation is the romance of trade, and casts contempt upon all its sober realities. It renders the stock-jobber a magician, and the exchange a region of enchantment. WASHINGTON IRVING, "A Time of Unexampled Prosperity," *Wolfert's Roost* (1855).

7. Let Wall Street have a nightmare and the whole country has to help get them back in bed again. WILL ROGERS, *The Autobiography of Will Rogers* (1949), 14.

8. There are two times in a man's life when he should not speculate: when he can't afford it, and when he can. MARK TWAIN, "Pudd'nhead Wilson's New Calendar," *Following the Equator* (1897), 2.20.

## 502. INVOLVEMENT

See also 10. Activity; 145. Commitment; 216. Deadness, Spiritual; 319. Experience; 511. Joie de vivre

1. To say yes, you have to sweat and roll up your sleeves and plunge both hands into life up to the elbows. It is easy to say no, even if saying no means death. JEAN ANOUILH, *Antigone* (1942), tr. Lewis Galantière.

2. Is it so small a thing / To have enjoyed the sun, / To have lived light in the spring, / To have loved, to have thought, to have done? MATTHEW ARNOLD, *Empedocles on Etna* (1852), 1.2.

3. Say "Yes" to the seedlings and a giant forest cleaves the sky. Say "Yes" to the universe and the planets become your neighbors. Say "Yes" to dreams of love and freedom. It is the password to utopia. BROOKS ATKINSON, "March 19," *Once Around the Sun* (1951).

4. Do not fear death so much, but rather the inadequate life. BERTOLT BRECHT, *The Mother* (1932), 11, tr. Lee Baxandall.

5. Let the fruition of things bless the possession of them, and take no satisfaction in dying but living rich. SIR THOMAS BROWNE, *A Letter to a Friend* (1690).

6. The wise find pleasure in water; the virtuous find pleasure in hills. The wise are active; the virtuous are tranquil. The wise are joyful; the virtuous are long-lived. CONFUCIUS, *Analects* (6th c. B.C.), 6.21, tr. James Legge.

7. The civilized are those who get more out of life than the uncivilized, and for this the uncivilized have not forgiven them. CYRIL CONNOLLY, *The Unquiet Grave* (1945), 2.

8. Be a football to Time and Chance, the more kicks, the better, so that you inspect the whole game and know its utmost law. EMERSON, *Journals*, 1836.

9. To finish the moment, to find the journey's end in every step of the road, to live the greatest number of good hours, is wisdom. EMERSON, "Experience," *Essays: Second Series* (1844).

10. The kind of relatedness to the world may be noble or trivial, but even being related to the basest kind of pattern is immensely preferable to being alone. ERICH FROMM, *Escape from Freedom* (1941), 1.

11. Strongly spent is synonymous with kept. ROBERT FROST, *The Constant Symbol* (1946).

12. It is by losing himself in the objective, in inquiry, creation, and craft, that a man becomes something. PAUL GOODMAN, *The Community of Scholars* (1962).

13. The joy of life is to put out one's power in some natural and useful or harmless way. There is no other. And the real misery is not to do this. OLIVER WENDELL

HOLMES, JR., speech, Boston Bar Association, March 7, 1900.

14. Life without absorbing occupation is hell—joy consists in forgetting life. ELBERT HUBBARD, *The Note Book* (1927).

15. Live all you can; it's a mistake not to. It doesn't so much matter what you do in particular, so long as you have your life. If you haven't had that, what have you had? HENRY JAMES, *The Ambassadors* (1903), 11.

16. There is certainly no greater happiness than to be able to look back on a life usefully and virtuously employed, to trace our own progress in existence, by such tokens as excite neither shame nor sorrow. SAMUEL JOHNSON, *The Rambler* (1750–52), 41.

17. A piece of incense may be as large as the knee but, unless burnt, emits no fragrance. MALAY PROVERB.

18. The moment one is on the side of life "peace and security" drop out of consciousness. The only peace, the only security, is in fulfillment. HENRY MILLER, "The Absolute Collective," *The Wisdom of the Heart* (1941).

19. My trade and art is to live. MONTAIGNE, "Use makes perfect," *Essays* (1580–88), tr. Charles Cotton and W. C. Hazlitt.

20. To do all that one is able to do, is to be a man; to do all that one would like to do, is to be a god. NAPOLEON I, *Maxims* (1804–15).

21. I postpone death by living, by suffering, by error, by risking, by giving, by losing. ANAÏS NIN, *The Diary of Anaïs Nin*, March 1933.

22. Better be left by twenty dears / Than lie in a loveless bed; / Better a loaf that's wet with tears, / Than cold, unsalted bread. DOROTHY PARKER, "The Whistling Girl," *Sunset Gun* (1928).

23. Love, children, and work are the great sources of fertilizing contact between the individual and the rest of the world. BERTRAND RUSSELL, "The Place of Love in Human Life," *Marriage and Morals* (1929).

24. The notion of looking on at life has always been hateful to me. What am I if I am not a participant? In order to be, I must participate. SAINT-EXUPÉRY, *Flight to Arras* (1942), 20, tr. Lewis Galantière.

25. Life finds its wealth by the claims of the world, and its worth by the claims of love. RABINDRANATH TAGORE, *Stray Birds* (1916), 33.

26. However mean your life is, meet it and live it; do not shun it and call it hard names. It is not so bad as you are. THOREAU, "Conclusion," *Walden* (1854).

27. It is easier to stay out than get out. MARK TWAIN, "Pudd'nhead Wilson's New Calendar," *Following the Equator* (1897), 1.18.

## 503. IRELAND AND IRISHMEN

1. The Irish are a fair people; they never speak well of one another. SAMUEL JOHNSON, quoted in Boswell's *Life of Samuel Johnson*, February 1775.

2. Where there are Irish there's loving and fighting, / And when we stop either, it's Ireland no more! RUDYARD KIPLING, "The Irish Guards" (1918).

## IRONY

See 434. Humor

## IRRATIONALITY

See 1013. Unreason

## 504. IRREVERENCE

See also 439. Iconoclasm; 1061. Worship

1. Impiety, n. Your irreverence toward my deity. AMBROSE BIERCE, *The Devil's Dictionary* (1881–1911).

2. Genuine blasphemy, genuine in spirit and not purely verbal, is the product of partial belief, and is as impossible to the complete atheist as to the perfect Christian. T. S. ELIOT, "Baudelaire" (1930).

3. Beware of the community in which blasphemy does not exist: underneath, atheism runs rampant. ANTONIO MACHADO, *Juan de Mairena* (1943), 1, tr. Ben Belitt.

4. All great truths begin as blasphemies. GEORGE BERNARD SHAW, *Annajanska* (1919).

5. Irreverence is the champion of liberty and its only sure defense. MARK TWAIN, *Notebook* (1935).

## 505. IRREVOCABLENESS

See also 173. Consequences; 337. Fate; 617. Necessity; 669. Past; 800. Resignation

1. You can't unscramble scrambled eggs. AMERICAN PROVERB.

2. What's said is said and goes upon its way, / Like it or not, repent it as you may. CHAUCER, "The Manciple's Tale," *The Canterbury Tales* (c. 1387–1400), tr. Nevill Coghill.

3. Of this I am quite sure, that if we open a quarrel between the past and the present, we shall find we have lost the future. SIR WINSTON CHURCHILL, speech, House of Commons, June 18, 1940.

4. It's over, and can't be helped, and that's one consolation, as they say in Turkey, ven they cuts the wrong man's head off. CHARLES DICKENS, *Pickwick Papers* (1836–37), 23.

5. The book of Nature is the book of Fate. She turns the gigantic pages—leaf after leaf—never re-turning one. EMERSON, "Fate," *The Conduct of Life* (1860).

6. What is done, is done: / Spend not the time in tears, but seek for justice. JOHN FORD, *'Tis Pity She's a Whore* (1633), 3.9.

7. A word and a stone let go cannot be called back. THOMAS FULLER, M.D., *Gnomologia* (1732), 485.

8. Time flies, and what is past is done. GOETHE, "Martha's Garden," *Faust: Part I* (1808), tr. Philip Wayne.

9. The mill cannot grind with water that's past. GEORGE HERBERT, *Jacula Prudentum* (1651).

10. A statement once let loose cannot be caught by four horses. JAPANESE PROVERB.

11. The arrow that has left the bow never returns. PERSIAN PROVERB.

12. What's gone and what's past help / Should be past grief. SHAKESPEARE, *The Winter's Tale* (1630–11), 3.2.223.

13. Of all sad words of tongue or pen, / The saddest are these: "It might have been!" JOHN GREENLEAF WHITTIER, "Maud Muller" (1854), 53.

## 506. IRRITATIONS

1. Men often bear little grievances with less courage than they do large misfortunes. AESOP, "The Ass and the Frogs," *Fables* (6th c. B.C.?), tr. George Fyler Townsend.

2. To great evils we submit; we resent little provocations. WILLIAM HAZLITT, "On Great and Little Things," *Literary Remains* (1836).

3. Continual dripping wears away a stone. LUCRETIUS, *On the Nature of Things* (1st c. B.C.), 1.313.

4. The mass of men live lives of quiet exasperation. PHYLLIS MC GINLEY, "Pipeline and Sinker," *The Province of the Heart* (1959).

5. too many creatures / both insects and humans / estimate their own value / by the amount of minor irritation / they are able to cause / to greater personalities than themselves. DON MARQUIS, "pride," *Archy Does His Part* (1935).

## ISOLATION

See 30. Alienation; 31. Aloofness; 908. Solitude

## 507. ITALY

See also 1022. Venice

1. A man who has not been in Italy is always conscious of an inferiority. SAMUEL JOHNSON, quoted in Boswell's *Life of Samuel Johnson*, April 11, 1776.

## ITCH

See 846. Scratching

# J

## JANUARY

See 848. Seasons

## 508. JEALOUSY

See also 293. Envy

1. Jealousy is that pain which a man feels from the apprehension that he is not equally beloved by the person whom he entirely loves. JOSEPH ADDISON, *The Spectator* (1711–12), 170.

2. A jealous man is very quick in his application: he knows how to find a double edge in an invective, and to draw a satire on himself out of a panegyrick on another. JO-

SEPH ADDISON, *The Spectator* (1711–12), 170.

3. A jealous ear hears all things. *Apocrypha*, Wisdom of Solomon 1:10.

4. Shall I tell you the opinion of a famous economist on jealousy? Jealousy is just the fact of being deprived. Nothing more. HENRY BECQUE, *Woman of Paris* (1885), 3, tr. Jacques Barzun.

5. Love is strong as death; jealousy is cruel as the grave. *Bible*, Song of Solomon 8:6.

6. Jealousy is no more than feeling alone against smiling enemies. ELIZABETH BOWEN, *The House in Paris* (1935), 2.8.

7. Jealousy dislikes the world to know it. BYRON, *Don Juan* (1819–24), 1.65.

8. Jealousy is beautiful only on a young and ardent face. After the first wrinkles, trust must return. ALFRED CAPUS, *Les Passagères* (1906), 1.4.

9. Jealousy is not at all low, but it catches us humbled and bowed down, at first sight. COLETTE, "The Pure and the Impure," *Earthly Paradise* (1966), 5, ed. Robert Phelps.

10. Of all the passions, jealousy is that which exacts the hardest service and pays the bitterest wages. Its service is to watch the success of our enemy; its wages, to be sure of it. CHARLES CALEB COLTON, *Lacon* (1825), 1.47.

11. Jealousy's a proof of love, / But 'tis a weak and unavailing medicine; / It puts out the disease and makes it show, / But has no power to cure. JOHN DRYDEN, *All for Love* (1678), 4.

12. It is not love that is blind, but jealousy. LAWRENCE DURRELL, *Justine* (1957), 3.

13. Jealousy: that dragon which slays love under the pretense of keeping it alive. HAVELOCK ELLIS, *On Life and Sex: Essays of Love and Virtue* (1937), 1.

14. Where there is no jealousy there is no love. GERMAN PROVERB.

15. Jealousy feeds upon suspicion, and it turns into fury or it ends as soon as we pass from suspicion to certainty. LA ROCHEFOUCAULD, *Maxims* (1665).

16. In jealousy there is more of self-love than love. LA ROCHEFOUCAULD, *Maxims* (1665), tr. Kenneth Pratt.

17. Jealousy is always born with love, but does not always die with it. LA ROCHEFOUCAULD, *Maxims* (1665), tr. Kenneth Pratt.

18. Jealousy is the greatest of all evils, and the one which arouses the least pity in the person who causes it. LA ROCHEFOUCAULD, *Maxims* (1665), tr. Kenneth Pratt.

19. Love that is fed by jealousy dies hard. OVID, *Love's Cure* (c. A.D. 8), tr. J. Lewis May.

20. The jealous are troublesome to others, but a torment to themselves. WILLIAM PENN, *Some Fruits of Solitude* (1693), 2.190.

21. To jealousy, nothing is more frightful than laughter. FRANÇOISE SAGAN, *La Chamade* (1966).

22. Trifles light as air / Are to the jealous confirmations strong / As proofs of holy writ. SHAKESPEARE, *Othello* (1604–05), 3.3.322.

## 509. JESUS

1. [Jesus], a man who was completely innocent, offered himself as a sacrifice for the good of others, including his enemies, and became the ransom of the world. It was a perfect act. MOHANDAS K. GANDHI, *Non-Violence in Peace and War* (1948), 2.166.

2. Thou hast conquered, O pale Galilean; the world has grown grey from thy breath. ALGERNON CHARLES SWINBURNE, "Hymn to Proserpine," *Poems and Ballads: First Series* (1866).

## 510. JEWS

1. To the Christian the Jew is the incomprehensibly obdurate man, who declines to see what has happened; and to the Jew the Christian is the incomprehensibly daring man, who affirms in an unredeemed world that its redemption has been accomplished. MARTIN BUBER, *Paths in Utopia* (1949).

2. From the beginning, the Christian was the theorizing Jew; consequently, the Jew is the practical Christian. KARL MARX, "The capacity of the present-day Jews and Christians to become free" (1884), *Early Writings*, ed. T. B. Bottomore.

3. A Jewish man with parents alive is a fifteen-year-old boy, and will remain a fifteen-year-boy till they die. PHILIP ROTH, *Portnoy's Complaint* (1969).

4. I am a Jew. Hath not a Jew eyes? Hath not a Jew hands, organs, dimensions, senses, affections, passions? SHAKESPEARE, *The Merchant of Venice* (1596–97), 3.1.61.

5. The Jews generally give value. They make you pay; but they deliver the goods. In my experience the men who want something for nothing are invariably Christians. GEORGE BERNARD SHAW, *Saint Joan* (1923), 4.

## 511. JOIE DE VIVRE

See also 291. Enthusiasm; 502. Involvement; 698. Pleasure; 1028. Vitality

1. Exuberance is Beauty. WILLIAM BLAKE, "Proverbs of Hell," *The Marriage of Heaven and Hell* (1790).

2. Zest is the secret of all beauty. There is no beauty that is attractive without zest. CHRISTIAN DIOR, *Ladies' Home Journal*, April 1956.

3. Let us live while we live. PHILIP DODDRIDGE, quoted in Job Orton's *Life of Doddridge* (1764).

4. Exuberance is better than taste. FLAUBERT, *Sentimental Education* (1869), 4, tr. Robert Baldick.

5. Live thy life as it were spoil and pluck the joys that fly. MARTIAL, *Epigrams* (A.D. 86), 7.47, tr. Walter C. A. Ker.

6. My candle burns at both ends; / It will not last the night; / But ah, my foes, and oh, my friends— / It gives a lovely light! EDNA ST. VINCENT MILLAY, "First Fig," *A Few Figs from Thistles* (1920).

7. The gayety of life, like the beauty and the moral worth of life, is a saving grace, which to ignore is folly, and to destroy is crime. There is no more than we need,—there is barely enough to go round. AGNES REPPLIER, "The Gayety of Life," *Compromises* (1904).

8. What hunger is in relation to food, zest is in relation to life. BERTRAND RUSSELL, *The Conquest of Happiness* (1930), 10.

9. Where people drink, they spill. ANDREY VOZNESENSKY, "Wedding," *The New Russian Poets: 1953 to 1966* (1966), tr. George Reavey.

## JOKES

See 434. Humor; 1054. Wit

## JOURNALISM

See 622. News; 623. Newspapers

## JOY

See 276. Ecstasy; 407. Happiness; 698. Pleasure

## 512. JUDGES

See also 515. Justice; 525. Law and Lawyers

1. That judges of important causes should hold office for life is a disputable thing, for the mind grows old as well as the body. ARISTOTLE, *Politics* (4th c. B.C.), 2.9, tr. Benjamin Jowett.

2. Judges must beware of hard constructions and strained inferences, for there is no worse torture than the torture of laws. FRANCIS BACON, "Of Judicature," *Essays* (1625).

3. Take all the robes of all the good judges that have ever lived on the face of the earth, and they would not be large enough to cover the iniquity of one corrupt judge. HENRY WARD BEECHER, *Proverbs from Plymouth Pulpit* (1887).

4. To an incompetent judge I must not lie, but I may be silent; to a competent I must answer. JOHN DONNE, *Sermons*, No. 67, 1630.

5. I have gr-reat respect f'r th' joodicyary, as fine a lot iv cross an' indignant men as ye'll find annywhere. FINLEY PETER DUNNE, "The Big Fine," *Mr. Dooley Says* (1910).

6. The Law is the true embodiment / Of everything that's excellent. / It has no kind of fault or flaw, / And I, my Lords, embody the Law. W. S. GILBERT, *Iolanthe* (1882), 1.

7. Judges commonly are elderly men, and are more likely to hate at sight any analysis to which they are not accustomed, and which disturbs repose of mind, than to fall in love with novelties. OLIVER WENDELL HOLMES, JR., address, New York State Bar Association, Jan. 17, 1899.

8. The judge should not be young; he should have learned to know evil, not from his own soul, but from late and long observation of the nature of evil in others. PLATO, *The Republic* (4th c. B.C.), 3, tr. Benjamin Jowett.

9. He who the sword of heaven will bear / Should be as holy as severe. SHAKESPEARE, *Measure for Measure* (1604–05), 3.2.275.

10. The worthy administrators of justice are like a cat set to take care of a cheese, lest it should be gnawed by the mice. One bite of the cat does more damage to the cheese than twenty mice can do. VOLTAIRE, "Allegory," *Philosophical Dictionary* (1764).

## 513. JUDGING OTHERS

**See also 203. Criticism; 656. Others**

1. Don't judge any man until you have walked two moons in his moccasins. AMERICAN INDIAN PROVERB.

2. It's a good thing to have people size ye up wrong; whin they've got ye'er measure ye'er in danger. FINLEY PETER DUNNE, "On St. Patrick's Day," *Mr. Dooley On Making a Will* (1919).

3. Every man is entitled to be valued by his best moment. EMERSON, "Beauty," *The Conduct of Life* (1860).

4. Don't hear one and judge two. GREEK PROVERB.

5. To judge a man means nothing more than to ask: What content does he give to the form of humanity? What concept should we have of humanity if he were its only representative? WILHELM VON HUMBOLDT, *Über den Geist der Menschheit* (1797).

6. Do not measure another's coat on your own body. MALAY PROVERB.

7. When we come to judge others it is not by ourselves as we really are that we judge them, but by an image that we have formed of ourselves from which we have left out everything that offends our vanity or would discredit us in the eyes of the world. W. SOMERSET MAUGHAM, *The Summing Up* (1938), 16.

8. Our natural egoism leads us to judge people by their relations to ourselves. We want them to be certain things to us, and for us that is what they are; because the rest of them is no good to us, we ignore it. W. SOMERSET MAUGHAM, *The Summing Up* (1938), 20.

9. Do not judge, and you will never be mistaken. ROUSSEAU, *Émile* (1762), 3.

10. I do not judge men by anything they can do. Their greatest deed is the impression they make on me. THOREAU, *Journal*, Feb. 18, 1841.

## 514. JUDGMENT

**See also 453. Impartiality**

1. Nothing, it appears to me, is of greater value in a man than the power of judgment; and the man who has it may be compared to a chest filled with books, for he is the son of nature and the father of art. PIETRO ARETINO, letter to Fausto Longiano, Dec. 17, 1537, tr. Samuel Putnam.

2. For all right judgment of any man or thing it is useful, nay, essential, to see his good qualities before pronouncing on his bad. THOMAS CARLYLE, "Goethe," *Edinburgh Review*, 1828.

3. In judgement be ye not too confident, / Even as a man who will appraise his corn / When standing in a field, ere it is ripe. DANTE, "Paradiso," 13, *The Divine Comedy* (c. 1300–21), tr. Lawrence Grant White.

4. Most people suspend their judgement till somebody else has expressed his own and then they repeat it. ERNEST DIMNET, *The Art of Thinking* (1928), 3.8.

5. Rightness of judgment is bitterness to the heart. EURIPIDES, *Hippolytus* (428 B.C.), tr. David Grene.

6. He hath a good judgment that relieth not wholly on his own. THOMAS FULLER, M.D., *Gnomologia* (1732), 1882.

7. In order to judge properly, one must get away somewhat from what one is judging, after having loved it. ANDRÉ GIDE, "Portraits and Aphorisms," *Pretexts* (1903), tr. Angelo P. Bertocci and others.

8. Our judgments about things vary according to the time left us to live—that we think is left us to live. ANDRÉ GIDE, *Journals*, Dec. 19, 1930, tr. Justin O'Brien.

9. Familiarity confounds all traits of distinction: interest and prejudice take away the power of judging. WILLIAM HAZLITT, "On the Knowledge of Character," *Table Talk* (1821–22).

10. A mistake in judgment isn't fatal, but too much anxiety about judgment is. PAULINE KAEL, "Zeitgeist and Poltergeist," *I Lost It at the Movies* (1965).

11. Everyone complains of his memory,

but no one complains of his judgment. LA ROCHEFOUCAULD, *Maxims* (1665), tr. Kenneth Pratt.

12. We are mistaken in believing the mind and the judgment two separate things; judgment is only the extent of the mind's illumination. LA ROCHEFOUCAULD, *Maxims* (1665), tr. Kenneth Pratt.

13. He that judges without informing himself to the utmost that he is capable, cannot acquit himself of judging amiss. JOHN LOCKE, *An Essay Concerning Human Understanding* (1690), 2.21.

14. The ultimate cynicism is to suspend judgment so that you are not judged. MARYA MANNES, "Introducing Myself," *More in Anger* (1958).

15. The judgment is an utensil proper for all subjects, and will have an oar in everything. MONTAIGNE, "Of Democritus and Heraclitus," *Essays* (1580–88), tr. Charles Cotton and W. C. Hazlitt.

16. We easily enough confess in others an advantage of courage, strength, experience, activity, and beauty; but an advantage in judgment we yield to none. MONTAIGNE, "Of presumption," *Essays* (1580–88), tr. Charles Cotton and W. C. Hazlitt.

17. We praise or blame as one or the other affords more opportunity for exhibiting our power of judgement. NIETZSCHE, *Human, All Too Human* (1878), 86, tr. Helen Zimmern.

18. Knowledge is the treasure, but judgment the treasurer of a wise man. WILLIAM PENN, *Some Fruits of Solitude* (1693), 1.162.

19. 'Tis with our judgements as our watches, none / Go just alike, yet each believes his own. ALEXANDER POPE, *An Essay on Criticism* (1711), 1.9.

20. A hasty judgment is a first step to recantation. PUBLILIUS SYRUS, *Moral Sayings* (1st c. B.C.), 8, tr. Darius Lyman.

21. It is one thing to lack a heart and another to possess eyes and a just imagination. GEORGE SANTAYANA, *The Life of Reason: Reason in Religion* (1905–06), 10.

22. Reason wishes that the judgment it gives be just; anger wishes that the judgment it has given seem to be just. SENECA, *On Anger* (1st c.).

23. Such as every man is inwardly so he judgeth outwardly. THOMAS À KEMPIS, *The Imitation of Christ* (1426), 2.4.

24. Men, generally going with the stream, seldom judge for themselves, and purity of taste is almost as rare as talent. VOLTAIRE, "Amplification," *Philosophical Dictionary* (1764).

## 515. JUSTICE

**See also 453. Impartiality; 475. Injustice; 512. Judges; 531. Leniency**

1. All virtue is summed up in dealing justly. ARISTOTLE, *Nicomachean Ethics* (4th c. B.C.), 5.1, tr. J. A. K. Thomson.

2. Somehow, our sense of justice never turns in its sleep till long after the sense of injustice in others has been thoroughly aroused. MAX BEERBOHM, "Servants," *And Even Now* (1920).

3. It's perfectly obvious that somebody's responsible and somebody's innocent. Otherwise it [justice] makes no sense at all. UGO BETTI, *Landscape* (1936), 3, tr. G. H. McWilliam.

4. Justice! Custodian of the world! But since the world errs, justice must be custodian of the world's errors. UGO BETTI, *The Gambler* (1950), 3.2, tr. Gino Rizzo.

5. There is a difference between justice and consideration in one's relations to one's fellow men. It is the function of justice not to do wrong to one's fellow men; of considerateness, not to wound their feelings. CICERO, *De Officiis* (44 B.C.), 1.28.99.

6. The victim to too severe a law is considered as a martyr rather than a criminal. CHARLES CALEB COLTON, *Lacon* (1825), 2.139.

7. Men are too unstable to be just; they are crabbed because they have not passed water at the usual time, or testy because they have not been stroked or praised. EDWARD DAHLBERG, *The Sorrows of Priapus* (1957).

8. Many have justice in their hearts, but slowly it is let fly, for it comes not without council to the bow. DANTE, "Purgatorio," 6, *The Divine Comedy* (c. 1300–21), tr. J. A. Carlyle and P. H. Wicksteed.

9. Justice is always violent to the party offending, for every man is innocent in his own eyes. DANIEL DEFOE, *The Shortest Way with the Dissenters* (1702).

10. I tell ye Hogan's r-right whin he says: "Justice is blind." Blind she is, an' deef an' dumb an' has a wooden leg! FINLEY PETER

DUNNE, "Cross-examinations," *Mr. Dooley's Opinions* (1901).

11. In this counthry [America] a man is presoomed to be guilty ontil he's proved guilty an' afther that he's presoomed to be innocent. FINLEY PETER DUNNE, "On Criminal Trials," *Mr. Dooley On Making a Will* (1919).

12. Justice is not a mincing-machine but a compromise. FRIEDRICH DÜRRENMATT, *The Marriage of Mr. Mississippi* (1952), 1, tr. Michael Bullock.

13. There is no such thing as justice in the abstract; it is merely a compact between men. EPICURUS, "Principal Doctrines" (3rd c. B.C.), 33, in *Letters, Principal Doctrines, and Vatican Sayings*, tr. Russel M. Geer.

14. Keep alive the light of justice, / And much that men say in blame will pass you by. EURIPIDES, *The Suppliant Women* (c. 421 B.C.), tr. Frank W. Jones.

15. Justice will not condemn even the Devil himself wrongfully. THOMAS FULLER, M.D., *Gnomologia* (1732), 3116.

16. Rigid justice is the greatest injustice. THOMAS FULLER, M.D., *Gnomologia* (1732), 4055.

17. That trial is not fair where affection is judge. THOMAS FULLER, M.D., *Gnomologia* (1732), 4373.

18. A great deal may be done by severity, more by love, but most by clear discernment and impartial justice. GOETHE, quoted in Johann Peter Eckermann's *Conversations with Goethe*, March 22, 1825.

19. If a man destroy the eye of another man, they shall destroy his eye. HAMMURABI, *Code* (c. 2030 B.C.).

20. What makes it so difficult to do justice to others is, that we are hardly sensible of merit, unless it falls in with our own views and line of pursuit; and where this is the case, it interferes with our own pretensions. WILLIAM HAZLITT, *Characteristics* (1823).

21. If you study the history and records of the world you must admit that the source of justice was the fear of injustice. HORACE, *Satires* (35–30 B.C.), 1.3.

22. When you cannot be just through virtue, be so through pride. EUGENIO MARÍA DE HOSTOS, "Hombres e ideas," *Obras* (1939–54), 14.

23. Justice should remove the bandage from her eyes long enough to distinguish between the vicious and the unfortunate. ROBERT G. INGERSOLL, *Prose-Poems and Selections* (1884).

24. The triumph of justice is the only peace. ROBERT G. INGERSOLL, *Prose-Poems and Selections* (1884).

25. Every one loves justice in the affairs of another. ITALIAN PROVERB.

26. Justice is the right of the weakest. JOSEPH JOUBERT, *Pensées* (1842), 15.17.

27. Justice is truth in action. JOSEPH JOUBERT, *Pensées* (1842). Quoted by Benjamin Disraeli in a speech, "Agricultural Distress," Feb. 11, 1851.

28. Justice delayed is democracy denied. ROBERT F. KENNEDY, "To Secure These Rights," *The Pursuit of Justice* (1964).

29. Justice is the very last thing of all wherewith the universe concerns itself. It is equilibrium that absorbs its attention. MAURICE MAETERLINCK, *Wisdom and Destiny* (1898), 79, tr. Alfred Sutro.

30. Even, it [justice] is as the sun on a flat plain; uneven, it strikes like the sun on a thicket. MALAY PROVERB.

31. Injustice is relatively easy to bear; what stings is justice. H. L. MENCKEN, *Prejudices: Third Series* (1922), 3.

32. For one crime which is expiated in prison ten thousand are committed thoughtlessly by those who condemn. HENRY MILLER, "The Soul of Anaesthesia," *The Air-Conditioned Nightmare* (1945).

33. Even the laws of justice themselves cannot subsist without mixture of injustice. MONTAIGNE, "That we taste nothing pure," *Essays* (1580–88), tr. Charles Cotton and W. C. Hazlitt.

34. In matters of government, justice means force as well as virtue. NAPOLEON I, *Maxims* (1804–15).

35. We see neither justice nor injustice which does not change its nature with change in climate. Three degrees of latitude reverse all jurisprudence; a meridian decides the truth. PASCAL, *Pensées* (1670), 294, tr. W. F. Trotter.

36. Everywhere there is one principle of justice, which is the interest of the stronger. PLATO, *The Republic* (4th c. B.C.), 1, tr. Benjamin Jowett.

37. The judge is condemned when the criminal is acquitted. PUBLILIUS SYRUS, *Moral Sayings* (1st c. B.C.), 407, tr. Darius Lyman.

38. No one should be judge in his own

cause. PUBLILIUS SYRUS, *Moral Sayings* (1st c. B.C.), 545, tr. Darius Lyman.

39. Extreme justice is often unjust. RACINE, *The Thebaid* (1664), 4.3.

40. There is a justice, but we do not always see it. Discreet, smiling, it is there, at one side, a little behind injustice, which makes a big noise. JULES RENARD, *Journal*, December 1906, ed. and tr. Louise Bogan and Elizabeth Roget.

41. We love justice greatly, and just men but little. JOSEPH ROUX, *Meditations of a Parish Priest* (1886), 4.10, tr. Isabel F. Hapgood.

42. It is impossible to be just if one is not generous. JOSEPH ROUX, *Meditations of a Parish Priest* (1886), 4.109, tr. Isabel F. Hapgood.

43. Use every man after his desert, and who should scape whipping? SHAKESPEARE, *Hamlet* (1600), 2.2.555.

44. The jury, passing on the prisoner's life, / May in the sworn twelve have a thief or two / Guiltier than him they try. SHAKESPEARE, *Measure for Measure* (1604–05), 2.1.19.

45. Justice is impartiality. Only strangers are impartial. GEORGE BERNARD SHAW, *Back to Methuselah* (1921), 3.

46. Be just before you're generous. RICHARD BRINSLEY SHERIDAN, *The School for Scandal* (1777), 4.1.

47. A man who deals in fairness with his own, / he can make manifest justice in the state. SOPHOCLES, *Antigone* (442–41 B.C.), tr. Elizabeth Wyckoff.

48. There are times when even justice brings harm with it. SOPHOCLES, *Electra* (c. 418–14 B.C.), tr. David Grene.

49. If they are just, they are better than clever. SOPHOCLES, *Philoctetes* (409 B.C.), tr. David Grene.

50. It is better to risk saving a guilty man than to condemn an innocent one. VOLTAIRE, *Zadig* (1747), 6.

51. Justice is / reason enough for anything ugly. It balances the beauty in the world. DIANE WAKOSKI, "Justice is reason enough," quoted in Paris Leary and Robert Kelly's *A Controversy of Poets* (1965).

52. Justice is the great interest of man on earth. DANIEL WEBSTER, on Mr. Justice Story, Sept. 12, 1845.

53. No man can be just who is not free. WOODROW WILSON, acceptance speech, Democratic National Convention, July 7, 1912.

54. Justice is like a train that's nearly always late. YEVGENY YEVTUSHENKO, *A Precocious Autobiography* (1963), tr. Andrew R. MacAndrew.

## JUVENILE DELINQUENCY

See 201. Crime

# K

## 516. KILLING

See also 1024. Violence; 1035. War

1. Human blood is heavy; the man that has shed it cannot run away. AFRICAN PROVERB.

2. Murderers, in general, are people who are consistent, people who are obsessed with one idea and nothing else. UGO BETTI, *Struggle Till Dawn* (1949), 1, tr. G. H. McWilliam.

3. The worst thing that can be said of the most powerful is that they can take your life; but the same thing can be said of the most weak. CHARLES CALEB COLTON, *Lacon* (1825), 1.456.

4. Assassination has never changed the history of the world. BENJAMIN DISRAELI, speech, May 1865.

5. What can you do by killing? Nothing. You kill one dog, the master buys another—that's all there is to it. MAXIM GORKY, *Enemies* (1906), 2.

6. We kill everybody, my dear. Some with bullets, some with words, and everybody with our deeds. We drive people into their graves, and neither see it nor feel it. MAXIM GORKY, *Enemies* (1906), 2.

7. Whom man kills, him God restoreth to life. VICTOR HUGO, "Fantine," *Les Misérables* (1862), 1.4, tr. Charles E. Wilbour.

8. The overfaithful sword returns the user / His heart's desire at price of his heart's blood. RUDYARD KIPLING, "The Pro-Consuls (Lord Milner)" (1905).

9. To live without killing is a thought which could electrify the world, if men were only capable of staying awake long enough to let the idea soak in. HENRY MILLER, "Reunion in Brooklyn," *The Henry Miller Reader* (1959).

10. Must we kill to prevent there being any wicked? This is to make both parties wicked instead of one. PASCAL, *Pensées* (1670), 910, tr. W. F. Trotter.

11. One kills a man, one is an assassin; one kills millions, one is a conqueror; one kills everybody, one is a god. JEAN ROSTAND, *Pensées d'un biologiste* (1939).

12. A sword never kills anybody; it's a tool in the killer's hand. SENECA, *Letters to Lucilius* (1st c.), 87.30, tr. E. Phillips Barker.

13. There is no sure foundation set on blood, / No certain life achieved by others' death. SHAKESPEARE, *King John* (1596–97), 4.2.104.

14. It hath the primal eldest curse upon't, A brother's murder! SHAKESPEARE, *Hamlet* (1600), 3.3.37.

15. It is long and hard and painful to create life: it is short and easy to steal the life others have made. GEORGE BERNARD SHAW, *Back to Methuselah* (1921), 1.2.

16. He who bears the brand of Cain shall rule the earth. GEORGE BERNARD SHAW, *Back to Methuselah* (1921), 1.2.

17. No humane being, past the thoughtless age of boyhood, will wantonly murder any creature which holds its life by the same tenure that he does. THOREAU, "Higher Laws," *Walden* (1854).

18. It is forbidden to kill; therefore all murderers are punished who kill not in large companies, and to the sound of trumpets. VOLTAIRE, "Rights," *Philosophical Dictionary* (1764).

## 517. KINDNESS

**See also 118. Charity; 377. Gentleness; 382. Gifts and Giving; 1011. Unkindness**

1. There is no sickness worse / for me than words that to be kind must lie. AESCHYLUS, *Prometheus Bound* (c. 478 B.C.), tr. David Grene.

2. Everyone, / To those weaker than themselves, is kind. AESCHYLUS, *The Suppliant Maidens* (463 B.C.), tr. Seth G. Bernardete.

3. Kindness effects more than severity. AESOP, "The Wind and the Sun," *Fables* (6th c. B.C.?), tr. Joseph Jacobs.

4. The unfortunate need people who will be kind to them; the prosperous need people to be kind to. ARISTOTLE, *Nicomachean Ethics* (4th c. B.C.), 9.9, tr. J. A. K. Thomson.

5. Kindness, n. A brief preface to ten volumes of exaction. AMBROSE BIERCE, *The Devil's Dictionary* (1881–1911).

6. The drying up a single tear has more / Of honest fame, than shedding seas of gore. BYRON, *Don Juan* (1819–24), 8.3.

7. Kindness acts / Not always as you think; a hated hand / Renders it odious. CORNEILLE, *Cinna* (1639), 1.2, tr. Paul Landis.

8. By Chivalries as tiny, / A Blossom, or a Book, / The seeds of smiles are planted– / Which Blossom in the dark. EMILY DICKINSON, poem (c. 1858).

9. There is no beautifier of complexion, or form, or behavior, like the wish to scatter joy and not pain around us. EMERSON, "Behavior," *The Conduct of Life* (1860).

10. Unseasonable kindness gets no thanks. THOMAS FULLER, M.D., *Gnomologia* (1732), 5407.

11. True kindness presupposes the faculty of imagining as one's own the suffering and joys of others. ANDRÉ GIDE, "Portraits and Aphorisms," *Pretexts* (1903), tr. Angelo P. Bertocci and others.

12. Kindness can become its own motive. We are made kind by being kind. ERIC HOFFER, *The Passionate State of Mind* (1954), 123.

13. Always set a high value on spontaneous kindness. He whose inclination prompts him to cultivate your friendship of his own accord, will love you more than one whom you have been at pains to attach to you. SAMUEL JOHNSON, quoted in Boswell's *Life of Samuel Johnson*, c. May 1781.

14. Nature, in giving tears to man, confessed that he / Had a tender heart; this is our noblest quality. JUVENAL, *Satires* (c. 100), 15.132, tr. Hubert Creekmore.

15. You can accomplish by kindness what you cannot do by force. PUBLILIUS SYRUS, *Moral Sayings* (1st c. B.C.), 971, tr. Darius Lyman.

16. Do not ask me to be kind; just ask me to act as though I were. JULES RENARD, *Journal*, April 1898, ed. and tr. Louise Bogan and Elizabeth Roget.

17. Human kindness has never weakened the stamina or softened the fiber of a free people. A nation does not have to be cruel to be tough. FRANKLIN D. ROOSEVELT, radio address, Oct. 13, 1940.

18. A word of kindness is better than a fat pie. RUSSIAN PROVERB.

19. Give nobody's heart pain so long as thou canst avoid it, for one sigh may set a whole world into a flame. SA'DI, *Gulistan* (1258), 1.26, tr. James Ross.

20. Kindness it is that brings forth kindness always. SOPHOCLES, *Ajax* (c. 447 B.C.), tr. John Moore.

21. One who knows how to show and to accept kindness / will be a friend better than any possession. SOPHOCLES, *Philoctetes* (409 B.C.), tr. David Grene.

22. Men are cruel, but Man is kind. RABINDRANATH TAGORE, *Stray Birds* (1916), 219.

23. Kind hearts are more than coronets, / And simple faith than Norman blood. ALFRED, LORD TENNYSON, *Lady Clara Vere de Vere* (1833), 7.

24. Benevolence is the characteristic element of humanity, and the great exercise of it is in loving relatives. TZE-SZE, *The Doctrine of the Mean* (5th c. B.C.), 20.5, tr. James Legge.

25. That best portion of a good man's life, / His little, nameless, unremembered acts / Of kindness and of love. WILLIAM WORDSWORTH, "Lines Composed a Few Miles Above Tintern Abbey" (1798).

## 518. KINGS

**See also 193. Court, Royal; 393. Government; 823. Royalty; 825. Rulers**

1. Fear created gods; audacity created kings. PROSPER JOLYOT CRÉBILLON, *Xerxès* (1714), 1.1.

2. A king nowadays is no more thin a hitchin' post f'r wan pollytician afther another. He ain't allowed to move himsilf, but anny crazy pollytician that ties up to him is apt to pull him out be th' roots. FINLEY PETER DUNNE, "King Edward's Coronation," *Observations by Mr. Dooley* (1902).

3. In a few years there will be only five kings in the world—the King of England and the four kings in a pack of cards. KING FAROUK I OF EGYPT, *Life*, April 10, 1950.

4. It is no bad thing to be a king—to see one's house enriched and one's authority enhanced. HOMER, *Odyssey* (9th c. B.C.), 1, tr. E. V. Rieu.

5. A monarch frequently represents his subjects better than an elected assembly; and if he is a good judge of character he is likely to have more capable and loyal advisers. WILLIAM RALPH INGE, "Our Present Discontents," *Outspoken Essays: First Series* (1919).

6. What are kings, when regiment is gone, / But perfect shadows in a sunshine day? CHRISTOPHER MARLOWE, *Edward II* (c. 1593), 5.1.

7. A king can stand people's fighting but he can't last long if people start thinking. WILL ROGERS, *The Autobiography of Will Rogers* (1949), 8.

8. Kings stand more in need of the company of the intelligent than the intelligent do of the society of kings. SA'DI, *Gulistan* (1258), 8.6, tr. James Ross.

9. The foremost art of kings is the power to endure hatred. SENECA, *Hercules Furens* (1st c.), 353.

10. A king is he who has laid fear aside and the base longings of an evil heart; whom ambition unrestrained and the fickle favor of the reckless mob move not. SENECA, *Thyestes* (1st c.), 348, tr. Frank Justus Miller.

11. Not all the water in the rough rude sea / Can wash the balm off from an anointed king. SHAKESPEARE, *King Richard II* (1595–96), 3.2.54.

12. Kings are like stars—they rise and set, they have / The worship of the world, but no repose. SHELLEY, *Hellas* (1821).

13. All kings is mostly rapscallions. MARK TWAIN, *The Adventures of Huckleberry Finn* (1884), 1.

14. The kingly office is entitled to no respect. It was originally procured by the highwayman's methods; it remains a perpetuated crime, can never be anything but the symbol of a crime. It is no more entitled to respect than is the flag of a pirate. MARK TWAIN, *Notebook* (1935).

15. The first who was king was a fortunate soldier. VOLTAIRE, *Mérope* (1743), 1.3.

## 519. KISSING

1. kisses are a better fate / than wisdom. E. E. CUMMINGS, "since feeling is first," *100 Selected Poems* (1959).

2. The kiss originated when the first male

reptile licked the first female reptile, implying in a subtle, complimentary way that she was as succulent as the small reptile he had for dinner the night before. F. SCOTT FITZGERALD, "The Note-Books," *The Crack-Up* (1945).

3. When a rogue kisses you, count your teeth. HEBREW PROVERB.

4. Kissing don't last: cookery do! GEORGE MEREDITH, *The Ordeal of Richard Feverel* (1859), 28.

5. A kiss can be a comma, a question mark or an exclamation point. That's basic spelling that every woman ought to know. MISTINGUETT, *Theatre Arts*, December 1955.

6. A kiss, when all is said, what is it? / An oath that's given closer than before; / A promise more precise; the sealing of / Confessions that till then were barely breathed; / A rosy dot placed on the i in loving. EDMOND ROSTAND, *Cyrano de Bergerac* (1897), 3.10, tr. Charles Renauld.

7. Though I know he loves me, / Tonight my heart is sad; / His kiss was not so wonderful / As all the dreams I had. SARA TEASDALE, "The Kiss," *Helen of Troy* (1911).

## 520. KNOWLEDGE

**See also 445. Ignorance; 529. Learning; 842. Scholars and Scholarship; 1000. Understanding; 1012. The Unknown**

1. Knowledge is power. FRANCIS BACON, "De Haeresibus," *Meditationes Sacrae* (1597).

2. Knowledge is not an abstract homogeneous good, of which there cannot be enough. Beyond the last flutter of actual or possible significance, pedantry begins. JACQUES BARZUN, *The House of Intellect* (1959), 9.

3. Many men are stored full of unused knowledge. Like loaded guns that are never fired off, or military magazines in times of peace, they are stuffed with useless ammunition. HENRY WARD BEECHER, *Proverbs from Plymouth Pulpit* (1887).

4. The raft of knowledge ferries the worst sinner to safety. *Bhagavadgita*, 4, tr. P. Lal.

5. He that increaseth knowledge increaseth sorrow. *Bible*, Ecclesiastes 1:18.

6. Learning, n. The kind of ignorance distinguishing the studious. AMBROSE BIERCE, *The Devil's Dictionary* (1881–1911).

7. To know a little of anything gives neither satisfaction nor credit, but often brings disgrace or ridicule. LORD CHESTERFIELD, *Letters to His Son*, Oct. 4, 1746.

8. Knowledge is a comfortable and necessary retreat and shelter for us in an advanced age; and if we do not plant it while young, it will give us no shade when we grow old. LORD CHESTERFIELD, *Letters to His Son*, Dec. 11, 1747.

9. That knowledge which stops at what it does not know, is the highest knowledge. CHUANG TZU, "The Music of Heaven and Earth" (4th–3rd c. B.C.), tr. Herbert A. Giles.

10. Knowledge is two-fold, and consists not only in an affirmation of what is true, but in the negation of that which is false. CHARLES CALEB COLTON, *Lacon* (1825), 1.181.

11. Learning without thought is labour lost; thought without learning is perilous. CONFUCIUS, *Analects* (6th c. B.C.), 2.15, tr. James Legge.

12. When you know a thing, to hold that you know it, and when you do not know a thing, to allow that you do not know it: this is knowledge. CONFUCIUS, *Analects* (6th c. B.C.), 2.17, tr. James Legge.

13. Knowledge is power. Unfortunate dupes of this saying will keep on reading, ambitiously, till they have stunned their native initiative, and made their thoughts weak. CLARENCE DAY, *This Simian World* (1920), 9.

14. Information's pretty thin stuff, unless mixed with experience. CLARENCE DAY, "The Three Tigers," *The Crow's Nest* (1921).

15. It is knowledge that influences and equalizes the social condition of man; that gives to all, however different their political position, passions which are in common, and enjoyments which are universal. BENJAMIN DISRAELI, speech, "The Value of Literature to Men of Business," Oct. 23, 1844.

16. There is no subject so old that something new cannot be said about it. DOSTOEVSKY, *A Diary of a Writer* (1876), 3, July–August.

17. A man should keep his little brain attic stocked with all the furniture that he is likely to use, and the rest he can put away in the lumber-room of his library, where he can get it if he wants it. SIR ARTHUR CONAN

DOYLE, "Five Orange Pips," *The Adventures of Sherlock Holmes* (1891).

18. If you would know what nobody knows, read what everybody reads, just one year afterwards. EMERSON, *Journals*, 1834.

19. If I cannot brag of knowing something, then I brag of not knowing it. EMERSON, *Journals*, 1866.

20. Why / do we make so much of knowledge, struggle so hard / to get some little skill not worth the effort? EURIPIDES, *Hecuba* (c. 425 B.C.), tr. William Arrowsmith.

21. In order that knowledge be properly digested, it must have been swallowed with a good appetite. ANATOLE FRANCE, *The Crime of Sylvestre Bonnard* (1881), 2, tr. Lafcadio Hearn.

22. To be proud of knowledge is to be blind with light. BENJAMIN FRANKLIN, *Poor Richard's Almanack* (1732–57).

23. 'Tis not knowing much, but what is useful, that makes a wise man. THOMAS FULLER, M.D., *Gnomologia* (1732), 5097.

24. We live by information, not by sight. BALTASAR GRACIÁN, *The Art of Worldly Wisdom* (1647), 80, tr. Joseph Jacobs.

25. Knowing what / thou knowest not / is in a sense / omniscience. PIET HEIN, "Omniscience," *Grooks* (1966).

26. Knowledge and timber shouldn't be much used till they are seasoned. OLIVER WENDELL HOLMES, SR., *The Autocrat of the Breakfast Table* (1858), 6.

27. To be master of any branch of knowledge, you must master those which lie next to it; and thus to know anything you must know all. OLIVER WENDELL HOLMES, JR., lecture, Harvard University, Feb. 17, 1886.

28. If a little knowledge is dangerous, where is the man who has so much as to be out of danger? THOMAS HENRY HUXLEY, "On Elemental Instruction in Physiology" (1877).

29. The fruit of the tree of knowledge always drives man from some paradise or other; and even the paradise of fools is not an unpleasant abode while it is habitable. WILLIAM RALPH INGE, "The Idea of Progress," *Outspoken Essays: Second Series* (1922).

30. There are no national frontiers to learning. JAPANESE PROVERB.

31. Man is not weak, knowledge is more than equivalent to force. The master of mechanics laughs at strength. SAMUEL JOHNSON, *Rasselas* (1759), 13.

32. A desire of knowledge is the natural feeling of mankind; and every human being, whose mind is not debauched, will be willing to give all that he has to get knowledge. SAMUEL JOHNSON, quoted in Boswell's *Life of Samuel Johnson*, July 30, 1763.

33. All knowledge is of itself of some value. There is nothing so minute or inconsiderable, that I would not rather know it than not. SAMUEL JOHNSON, quoted in Boswell's *Life of Samuel Johnson*, April 10, 1775.

34. Knowledge is of two kinds: we know a subject ourselves, or we know where we can find information upon it. SAMUEL JOHNSON, quoted in Boswell's *Life of Samuel Johnson*, April 18, 1775.

35. An extensive knowledge is needful to thinking people – it takes away the heat and fever; and helps, by widening speculation, to ease the burden of the mystery. JOHN KEATS, letter to John Hamilton Reynolds, May 3, 1818.

36. The greater our knowledge increases, the greater our ignorance unfolds. JOHN F. KENNEDY, address, Rice University, Houston, Texas, Sept. 12, 1962.

37. Liberty without learning is always in peril, and learning without liberty is always in vain. JOHN F. KENNEDY, address, Vanderbilt University, Nashville, Tenn., May 18, 1963.

38. He who does not know one thing knows another. KENYAN PROVERB.

39. To know things well, we must know them in detail; but as that is almost endless, our knowledge is always superficial and imperfect. LA ROCHEFOUCAULD, *Maxims* (1665), tr. Kenneth Pratt.

40. Learning acquired in youth arrests the evil of old age; and if you understand that old age has wisdom for its food, you will so conduct yourself in youth that your old age will not lack for nourishment. LEONARDO DA VINCI, *Notebooks* (c. 1500), tr. Jean Paul Richter.

41. Every step by which men add to their knowledge and skills is a step also by which they can control other men. MAX LERNER, "Manipulating Life," in the *New York Post*, Jan. 24, 1968.

42. A reading-machine, always wound up

and going, / He mastered whatever was not worth the knowing. JAMES RUSSELL LOWELL, *A Fable for Critics* (1848).

43. There is no more merit in being able to attach a correct description to a picture than in being able to find out what is wrong with a stalled motorcar. In each case it is special knowledge. W. SOMERSET MAUGHAM, *The Summing Up* (1938), 24.

44. Sin, guilt, neurosis—they are one and the same, the fruit of the tree of knowledge. HENRY MILLER, "Creative Death," *The Wisdom of the Heart* (1941).

45. In expanding the field of knowledge we but increase the horizon of ignorance. HENRY MILLER, "The Wisdom of the Heart," *The Wisdom of the Heart* (1941).

46. The first and wisest of them all professed / To know this only, that he nothing knew. MILTON, *Paradise Regained* (1671), 4.293.

47. Without knowledge, life is no more than the shadow of death. MOLIÈRE, *The Would-be Gentleman* (1670), 2, tr. John Wood.

48. Such is the constitution of the human mind, that any kind of knowledge, if it be really such, is its own reward. JOHN HENRY NEWMAN, *The Idea of a University* (1853–58), 1.5.2.

49. Rather know nothing than half-know much. NIETZSCHE, "The Leech," *Thus Spoke Zarathustra* (1883–92), 4, tr. Walter Kaufmann.

50. Wisdom sets bounds even to knowledge. NIETZSCHE, "Maxims and Missiles," 5, *Twilight of the Idols* (1888), tr. Anthony M. Ludovici.

51. Learning, the destroyer of arrogance, begets arrogance in fools; even as light, that illumines the eye, makes owls blind. *Panchatantra* (c. 5th c.), 1, tr. Franklin Edgerton.

52. Knowledge is the true organ of sight, not the eyes. *Panchatantra* (c. 5th c.), 2, tr. Franklin Edgerton.

53. Since we cannot be universal and know all that is to be known of everything, we ought to know a little about everything. PASCAL, *Pensées* (1670), 37, tr. W. F. Trotter.

54. Most people affirm pleasure to be the good, but the finer sort of wits say it is knowledge. PLATO, *The Republic* (4th c. B.C.), 6, tr. Benjamin Jowett.

55. All knowledge that is divorced from justice must be called cunning. PLATO (5th–4th c. B.C.), quoted in Cicero's *De Officiis* (44 B.C.), 1.19.62, tr. Walter Miller.

56. A little learning is a dangerous thing; / Drink deep, or taste not the Pierian spring: / There shallow draughts intoxicate the brain, / And drinking largely sobers us again. ALEXANDER POPE, *An Essay on Criticism* (1711), 2.15.

57. What harm in getting knowledge even from a sot, a pot, a fool, a mitten, or an old slipper? RABELAIS, *Gargantua and Pantagruel* (1532–64), 3.

58. Knowledge—that is, education in its true sense—is our best protection against unreasoning prejudice and panic-making fear, whether engendered by special interest, illiberal minorities, or panic-stricken leaders. FRANKLIN D. ROOSEVELT, speech, Boston, Oct. 31, 1932.

59. Whoever acquires knowledge and does not practise it resembles him who ploughs his land and leaves it unsown. SA'DI, *Gulistan* (1258), 8.42, tr. James Ross.

60. Knowledge is recognition of something absent; it is a salutation, not an embrace. GEORGE SANTAYANA, *The Life of Reason: Reason in Common Sense* (1905–06), 3.

61. Learning is but an adjunct to ourself, / And where we are our learning likewise is. SHAKESPEARE, *Love's Labour's Lost* (1594–95), 4.3.314.

62. The right to know is like the right to live. If is fundamental and unconditional in its assumption that knowledge, like life, is a desirable thing. GEORGE BERNARD SHAW, "Preface on Doctors: The Flaw in the Argument," *The Doctor's Dilemma* (1913).

63. The desire of knowledge, like the thirst of riches, increases ever with the acquisition of it. LAURENCE STERNE, *Tristram Shandy* (1759–67), 2.3.

64. If we value the pursuit of knowledge, we must be free to follow wherever that search may lead us. The free mind is no barking dog, to be tethered on a ten-foot chain. ADLAI STEVENSON, speech, University of Wisconsin, Madison, Oct. 8, 1952.

65. Forasmuch as many people study more to have knowledge than to live well therefore ofttimes they err and bring forth little fruit or none. THOMAS À KEMPIS, *The Imitation of Christ* (1426), 1.3.

66. So much has already been written about everything that you can't find out anything about it. JAMES THURBER, "The New Vocabularianism," *Lanterns and Lances* (1961).

67. Any piece of knowledge I acquire today has a value at this moment exactly proportioned to my skill to deal with it. Tomorrow, when I know more, I recall that piece of knowledge and use it better. MARK VAN DOREN, *Liberal Education* (1960).

68. The things we know best are the things we haven't been taught. VAUVENARGUES, *Reflections and Maxims* (1746), 479.

69. The more I read, the more I meditate; and the more I acquire, the more I am enabled to affirm that I know nothing. VOLTAIRE, "Occult Qualities," *Philosophical Dictionary* (1764).

70. Knowledge, in truth, is the great sun in the firmament. Life and power are scattered with all its beams. DANIEL WEBSTER, address on laying the cornerstone of the Bunker Hill Monument, Boston, Mass., June 17, 1825.

71. Knowledge is the only fountain both of the love and the principles of human liberty. DANIEL WEBSTER, on completion of the Bunker Hill Monument, Boston, Mass., June 17, 1843.

72. Knowledge is always accompanied with accessories of emotion and purpose. ALFRED NORTH WHITEHEAD, *Adventures of Ideas* (1933), 1.

73. To live effectively is to live with adequate information. NORBERT WIENER, *The Human Use of Human Beings* (1954), 1.

74. Education is an admirable thing, but it is well to remember from time to time that nothing that is worth knowing can be taught. OSCAR WILDE, "The Critic as Artist," *Intentions* (1891).

75. I am still of the opinion that only two topics can be of the least interest to a serious and studious mind—sex and the dead. WILLIAM BUTLER YEATS, letter to Olivia Shakespear, October 1927.

# L

## LABOR

**See 1006. Unions; 1058. Work**

## LABOR DAY

**See 418. Holidays**

## LACK

**See 234. Deprivation; 618. Need**

## LAND

**See 334. Farms and Farming; 740. Property**

## 521. LANGUAGE

**See also 35. Analogy; 132. Clarity; 227. Definition; 396. Grammar; 916. Speaking; 935. Style; 1057. Words; 1062. Writing and Writers**

1. Dialect tempered with slang is an admirable medium of communication between persons who have nothing to say and persons who would not care for anything properly said. THOMAS BAILEY ALDRICH, "Leaves from a Notebook," *Ponkapog Papers* (1903).

2. By its very looseness, by its way of evoking rather than defining, suggesting rather than saying, English is a magnificent vehicle for emotional poetry. MAX BEERBOHM, "On Speaking French," *And Even Now* (1920).

3. If language be not in accordance with the truth of things, affairs cannot be carried on to success. CONFUCIUS, *Analects* (6th c. B.C.), 13.5, tr. James Legge.

4. To a teacher of languages there comes a time when the world is but a place of many words and man appears a mere talking animal not much more wonderful than a parrot. JOSEPH CONRAD, prologue to Part 1, *Under Western Eyes* (1911).

5. Correct English is the slang of prigs who write history and essays. And the strongest slang of all is the slang of poets. GEORGE ELIOT, *Middlemarch* (1871–72), 2.

6. Poetry should help, not only to refine the language of the time, but to prevent it from changing too rapidly. T. S. ELIOT, "Milton" (1947).

7. Language is the archives of history. EMERSON, "The Poet," *Essays: Second Series* (1844).

8. Language, —human language, —after

all is but little better than the croak and cackle of fowls, and other utterances of brute nature,—sometimes not so adequate. NATHANIEL HAWTHORNE, *American Note-Books*, July 14, 1850.

9. Language, if it throws a veil over our ideas, adds a softness and refinement to them, like that which the atmosphere gives to naked objects. WILLIAM HAZLITT, "On Classical Education," *The Round Table* (1817).

10. The tongue of man is a twisty thing, there are plenty of words there / of every kind, the range of words is wide, and their variance. HOMER, *Iliad* (9th c. B.C.), 20.248, tr. Richmond Lattimore.

11. Language is by its very nature a communal thing; that is, it expresses never the exact thing but a compromise—that which is common to you, me and everybody. THOMAS ERNEST HULME, "Romanticism and Classicism," *Speculations* (1923).

12. I am always sorry when any language is lost, because languages are the pedigree of nations. SAMUEL JOHNSON, quoted in Boswell's *Journal of a Tour to the Hebrides with Samuel Johnson*, Sept. 18, 1773.

13. Next in criminality to him who violates the laws of his country, is he who violates the language. WALTER SAVAGE LANDOR, "Archdeacon Hare and Walter Landor," *Imaginary Conversations* (1824–53).

14. The habitude of pleasing by flattery makes a language soft; the fear of offending by truth makes it circuitous and conventional. WALTER SAVAGE LANDOR, "Demosthenes and Eubulides," *Imaginary Conversations* (1824–53).

15. The only living language is the language in which we think and have our being. ANTONIO MACHADO, *Juan de Mairena* (1943), 30, tr. Ben Belitt.

16. Slang is a poor-man's poetry. JOHN MOORE, *You English Words* (1962).

17. What is most difficult to render from one language into another is the tempo of its style. NIETZSCHE, *Beyond Good and Evil* (1886), 28, tr. Walter Kaufmann.

18. The great enemy of clear language is insincerity. When there is a gap between one's real and one's declared aims, one turns as it were instinctively to long words and exhausted idioms, like a cuttlefish squirting out ink. GEORGE ORWELL, "Politics and the English Language," *Shooting an Elephant* (1950).

19. The sum of human wisdom is not contained in any one language, and no single language is CAPABLE of expressing all forms and degrees of human comprehension. EZRA POUND, *The ABC of Reading* (1934), 1.3.

20. The art of translation lies less in knowing the other language than in knowing your own. NED ROREM, "Random Notes from a Diary," *Music from Inside Out* (1967).

21. To grasp the meaning of the world of today we use a language created to express the world of yesterday. The life of the past seems to us nearer our true natures, but only for the reason that it is nearer our language. SAINT-EXUPÉRY, *Wind, Sand, and Stars* (1939), 3, tr. Lewis Galantière.

22. Slang is a language that rolls up its sleeves, spits on its hands and goes to work. CARL SANDBURG, *The New York Times*, Feb. 13, 1959.

23. It were as wise to cast a violet into a crucible that you might discover the formal principle of its colour and odour, as seek to transfuse from one language into another the creations of a poet. SHELLEY, *A Defence of Poetry* (1821).

24. Where shall we look for standard English, but to the words of a standard man? THOREAU, "Sunday," *A Week on the Concord and Merrimack Rivers* (1849).

25. Ours is a precarious language, as every writer knows, in which the merest shadow line often separates affirmation from negation, sense from nonsense, and one sex from the other. JAMES THURBER, "Such a Phrase as Drifts Through Dreams," *Lanterns and Lances* (1961).

26. English orthography satisfies all the requirements of the canons of reputability under the law of conspicuous waste. It is archaic, cumbrous, and ineffective; its acquisition consumes much time and effort; failure to acquire it is easy of detection. THORSTEIN VEBLEN, *The Theory of the Leisure Class* (1899), 14.

27. A child, when it begins to speak, learns what it is that it knows. JOHN HALL WHEELOCK, "A True Poem Is a Way of Knowing," *What Is Poetry?* (1963).

### 522. LARGENESS

See also 373. Generosity; 399. Greatness; 901. Smallness

1. Grains of rice counted – / Can any one so spend life? / Be spacious and wise. AMY LOWELL, "The Anniversary," *What's O'Clock* (1925).

2. All spaciousness, as in life – also the inner – is in the last analysis a question of proportion. RAINER MARIA RILKE, letter to Countess M., June 25, 1920, in *Wartime Letters*, tr. M. D. Herter Norton.

### 523. LAUGHTER

See also 290. Entertainment; 434. Humor; 524. Laughter and Tears; 814. Ridicule; 1045. Weeping; 1054. Wit

1. Even in laughter the heart is sorrowful; and the end of mirth is heaviness. *Bible*, Proverbs 14:13.

2. Laughter, n. An interior convulsion, producing a distortion of the features and accompanied by inarticulate noises. AMBROSE BIERCE, *The Devil's Dictionary* (1881–1911).

3. The man who cannot laugh is not only fit for treasons, stratagems, and spoils; but his whole life is already a treason and a stratagem. THOMAS CARLYLE, *Sartor Resartus* (1833–34), 1.4.

4. No man who has once heartily and wholly laughed can be altogether irreclaimably bad. THOMAS CARLYLE, *Sartor Resartus* (1833–34), 1.4.

5. The most wasted day is that in which we have not laughed. CHAMFORT, *Maximes et pensées* (1805), 1.

6. Mirth is the Mail of Anguish. EMILY DICKINSON, poem (c. 1860).

7. One can know a man from his laugh, and if you like a man's laugh before you know anything of him, you may confidently say that he is a good man. DOSTOEVSKY, *The House of the Dead* (1862), 1.3, tr. Constance Garnett.

8. A human being should beware how he laughs, for then he shows all his faults. EMERSON, *Journals*, 1836.

9. He is not laughed at that laughs at himself first. THOMAS FULLER, M.D., *Gnomologia* (1732), 1936.

10. There is nothing in which people more betray their character than in what they laugh at. GOETHE, *Elective Affinities* (1809), 22.

11. Sudden glory is the passion which maketh those grimaces called laughter. THOMAS HOBBES, *Leviathan* (1651), 1.6.

12. Pain is deeper than all thought; laughter is higher than all pain. ELBERT HUBBARD, *The Philistine* (1895–1915).

13. We must laugh before we are happy from fear of dying without ever having laughed at all. LA BRUYÈRE, *Characters* (1688), 4.63.

14. Anything awful makes me laugh. I misbehaved once at a funeral. CHARLES LAMB, letter to Robert Southey, Aug. 9, 1815.

15. You are not angry with people when you laugh at them. Humour teaches tolerance. W. SOMERSET MAUGHAM, *The Summing Up* (1938), 20.

16. A laugh's the wisest, easiest answer to all that's queer. HERMAN MELVILLE, *Moby Dick* (1851), 39.

17. One horse-laugh is worth ten thousand syllogisms. It is not only more effective; it is also vastly more intelligent. H. L. MENCKEN, *Prejudices: Fourth Series* (1924), 7.

18. Not by wrath does one kill but by laughter. NIETZSCHE, "On Reading and Writing," *Thus Spoke Zarathustra* (1883–92), 1, tr. Walter Kaufmann.

19. In laughter all that is evil comes together, but is pronounced holy and absolved by its own bliss. NIETZSCHE, "The Seven Seals," *Thus Spoke Zarathustra* (1883–92), 3, tr. Walter Kaufmann.

20. He who laughs best to-day, will also laugh last. NIETZSCHE, "Maxims and Missiles," 43, *Twilight of the Idols* (1888), tr. Anthony M. Ludovici.

21. One inch of joy surmounts of grief a span, / Because to laugh is proper to the man. RABELAIS, "To the Reader," *Gargantua and Pantagruel* (1532–64), 1.

22. We are in the world to laugh. In purgatory or in hell we shall no longer be able to do so. And in heaven it would not be proper. JULES RENARD, *Journal*, June 1907, ed. and tr. Louise Bogan and Elizabeth Roget.

23. What monstrous absurdities and paradoxes have resisted whole batteries of seri-

ous arguments, and then crumbled swiftly into dust before the ringing death-knell of a laugh! AGNES REPPLIER, "A Plea for Humor," *Points of View* (1891).

24. No one is more profoundly sad than he who laughs too much. JEAN PAUL RICHTER, *Hesperus* (1795).

25. Our sincerest laughter / With some pain is fraught: / Our sweetest songs are those that tell of saddest thought. SHELLEY, "To a Skylark" (1820).

26. The world loved man when he smiled. The world became afraid of him when he laughed. RABINDRANATH TAGORE, *Stray Birds* (1916), 297.

27. Laughter is not at all a bad beginning for a friendship, and it is far the best ending for one. OSCAR WILDE, *The Picture of Dorian Gray* (1891), 1.

## 524. LAUGHTER AND TEARS

See also 523. Laughter; 1045. Weeping

1. Excess of sorrow laughs. Excess of joy weeps. WILLIAM BLAKE, "Proverbs of Hell," *The Marriage of Heaven and Hell* (1790).

2. And if I laugh at any mortal thing, / 'Tis that I may not weep. BYRON, *Don Juan* (1819–24), 4.4.

3. Those who weep recover more quickly than those who smile. JEAN GIRAUDOUX, *Amphitryon 38* (1929), 1, tr. Phyllis La Farge with Peter H. Judd.

4. Between the laughing and the weeping philosopher there is no opposition: *the same facts* that make one laugh make one weep. GEORGE SANTAYANA, "The Latin School," *Persons and Places: The Background of My Life* (1944).

5. We laugh and laugh. Then cry and cry— / Then feebler laugh, Then die. MARK TWAIN, *Notebook* (1935).

6. Laugh, and the world laughs with you; / Weep, and you weep alone; / For the sad old earth must borrow its mirth, / But has trouble enough of its own. ELLA WHEELER WILCOX, "Solitude," *Collected Poems* (1917).

## 525. LAW AND LAWYERS

See also 475. Injustice; 512. Judges; 515. Justice; 526. Law and Order; 531. Leniency

1. Wrong must not win by technicalities. AESCHYLUS, *The Eumenides* (458 B.C.), tr. Richmond Lattimore.

2. Nobody has a more sacred obligation to obey the law than those who make the law. JEAN ANOUILH, *Antigone* (1942), tr. Lewis Galantière.

3. Whereas the law is passionless, passion must ever sway the heart of man. ARISTOTLE, *Politics* (4th c. B.C.), 3.15, tr. Benjamin Jowett.

4. Good laws, if they are not obeyed, do not constitute good government. ARISTOTLE, *Politics* (4th c. B.C.), 4.8, tr. Benjamin Jowett.

5. Riches without law are more dangerous than is poverty without law. HENRY WARD BEECHER, *Proverbs from Plymouth Pulpit* (1887).

6. It usually takes a hundred years to make a law, and then, after it has done its work, it usually takes a hundred years to get rid of it. HENRY WARD BEECHER, *Proverbs from Plymouth Pulpit* (1887).

7. The law is good, if a man use it lawfully. *Bible*, 1 Timothy 1:8.

8. Litigant, n. A person about to give up his skin for the hope of retaining his bones. AMBROSE BIERCE, *The Devil's Dictionary* (1881–1911).

9. The law is a causeway upon which, so long as he keeps to it, a citizen may walk safely. ROBERT BOLT, *A Man for All Seasons* (1962), 2.

10. The law is simply and solely made for the exploitation of those who do not understand it or of those who, for naked need, cannot obey it. BERTOLT BRECHT, *The Threepenny Opera* (1928), 3.1, tr. Desmond Vesey and Eric Bentley.

11. A legal broom's a moral chimney-sweeper, / And that's the reason he himself's so dirty. BYRON, *Don Juan* (1819–24), 10.15.

12. All bad precedents began as justifiable measures. JULIUS CAESAR, quoted in Sallust's *Conspiracy of Catiline* (1st c. B.C.), 51.

13. Laws that only threaten, and are not kept, become like the log that was given to the frogs to be their king, which they feared at first, but soon scorned and trampled on. CERVANTES, *Don Quixote* (1605–15), 2.4.51,

tr. Peter Motteux and John Ozell.

14. We do not get good laws to restrain bad people. We get good people to restrain bad laws. G. K. CHESTERTON, "Thoughts Around Koepenick," *All Things Considered* (1908).

15. The science of legislation is like that of medicine in one respect: that it is far more easy to point out what will do harm than what will do good. CHARLES CALEB COLTON, *Lacon* (1825), 1.529.

16. Lawyers and painters can soon change white to black. DANISH PROVERB.

17. If there were no bad people there would be no good lawyers. CHARLES DICKENS, *The Old Curiosity Shop* (1840), 56.

18. Anyone who takes it upon himself, on his private authority, to break a bad law, thereby authorizes everyone else to break the good ones. DENIS DIDEROT, *Supplement to Bougainville's "Voyage"* (1796).

19. No matter whether th' constitution follows th' flag or not, th' supreme coort follows th' iliction returns. FINLEY PETER DUNNE, "The Supreme Court's Decisions," *Mr. Dooley's Opinions* (1901).

20. People say law but they mean wealth. EMERSON, *Journals*, 1841.

21. Our statute is a currency which we stamp with our own portrait. EMERSON, "Politics," *Essays: Second Series* (1844).

22. A just cause needs no interpreting. / It carries its own case. But the unjust argument / since it is sick, needs clever medicine. EURIPIDES, *The Phoenician Women* (c. 411–409 B.C.), tr. Elizabeth Wyckoff.

23. Give a wise man an honest brief to plead / and his eloquence is no remarkable achievement. EURIPIDES, *The Bacchae* (c. 405 B.C.), tr. William Arrowsmith.

24. If there isn't a law, there will be. HAROLD FABER, *The New York Times Magazine*, March 17, 1968.

25. Fragile as reason is and limited as law is as the institutionalized medium of reason, that's all we have standing between us and the tyranny of mere will and the cruelty of unbridled, undisciplined feeling. FELIX FRANKFURTER, *Felix Frankfurter Reminisces* (1960), 19.

26. God works wonders now and then: / Behold! a lawyer, an honest man! BENJAMIN FRANKLIN, *Poor Richard's Almanack* (1732–57).

27. Laws too gentle are seldom obeyed; too severe, seldom executed. BENJAMIN FRANKLIN, *Poor Richard's Almanack* (1732–57).

28. Law cannot persuade where it cannot punish. THOMAS FULLER, M.D., *Gnomologia* (1732), 3148.

29. The more laws, the more offenders. THOMAS FULLER, M.D., *Gnomologia* (1732), 4663.

30. The law is what it is—a majestic edifice, sheltering all of us, each stone of which rests on another. JOHN GALSWORTHY, *Justice* (1910), 2.

31. An unjust law is itself a species of violence. Arrest for its breach is more so. MOHANDAS K. GANDHI, *Non-Violence in Peace and War* (1948), 2.150.

32. The more laws, the less justice. GERMAN PROVERB.

33. There's no better way of exercising the imagination than the study of law. No poet ever interpreted nature as freely as a lawyer interprets truth. JEAN GIRAUDOUX, *Tiger at the Gates* (1935), 2, tr. Christopher Fry.

34. You're an attorney. It's your duty to lie, conceal and distort everything, and slander everybody. JEAN GIRAUDOUX, *The Madwoman of Chaillot* (1945), 2, adapted by Maurice Valency.

35. Laws grind the poor, and rich men rule the law. OLIVER GOLDSMITH, *The Traveller* (1765), 386.

36. Every new time will give its law. MAXIM GORKY, *The Lower Depths* (1903), 4, tr. Alexander Bakshy.

37. Laws are to govern all alike—those opposed as well as those who favor them. I know of no method to repeal of bad or obnoxious laws so effective as their stringent execution. ULYSSES S. GRANT, first Inaugural Address, March 4, 1869.

38. There is something monstrous in commands couched in invented and unfamiliar language; an alien master is the worst of all. The language of the law must not be foreign to the ears of those who are to obey it. LEARNED HAND, speech, Washington, D.C., May 11, 1929.

39. The people should fight for their law as for their city wall. HERACLITUS, *Fragments* (c. 500 B.C.), 82, tr. Philip Wheelwright.

40. Those who are too lazy and comfortable to think for themselves and be their

own judges obey the laws. Others sense their own laws within them. HERMANN HESSE, *Demian* (1919), 3, tr. Michael Roloff and Michael Lebeck.

41. The law is the witness and external deposit of our moral life. Its history is the history of the moral development of the race. OLIVER WENDELL HOLMES, JR., speech, Boston, Jan. 8, 1897.

42. Great cases like hard cases make bad law. OLIVER WENDELL HOLMES, JR., opinion, *Northern Securities Company v. United States* (1904).

43. There are not enough jails, not enough policemen, not enough courts to enforce a law not supported by the people. HUBERT H. HUMPHREY, speech, Williamsburg, Va., May 1, 1965.

44. Laws and institutions must go hand in hand with the progress of the human mind. THOMAS JEFFERSON, letter to Samuel Kercheval, July 12, 1816.

45. The law is the last result of human wisdom acting upon human experience for the benefit of the public. SAMUEL JOHNSON, quoted in Hester Lynch Piozzi's *Anecdotes of Samuel Johnson* (1786).

46. Our nation is founded on the principle that observance of the law is the eternal safeguard of liberty and defiance of the law is the surest road to tyranny. JOHN F. KENNEDY, television address appealing for peaceful compliance with Federal court order admitting James Meredith to University of Mississippi, Sept. 30, 1962.

47. Morality cannot be legislated, but behavior can be regulated. Judicial decrees may not change the heart, but they can restrain the heartless. MARTIN LUTHER KING, JR., *Strength to Love* (1963), 3.3.

48. Many laws as certainly make bad men, as bad men make many laws. WALTER SAVAGE LANDOR, "Diogenes and Plato," *Imaginary Conversations* (1824–53).

49. Ignore what a man desires and you ignore the very source of his power; run against the grain of a nation's genius and see where you get with your laws. WALTER LIPPMANN, "The Making of Creeds," *A Preface to Politics* (1914).

50. No law is quite appropriate for all. LIVY, *Ab Urbe Condita* (c. 29 B.C.), 34.3.

51. Wherever law ends, tyranny begins. JOHN LOCKE, *Two Treatises on Government* (1690), 2.

52. Useless laws weaken necessary ones. MONTESQUIEU, *L'Esprit des lois* (1748), 14.

53. Law was once introduced without reason, and has become reasonable. PASCAL, *Pensées* (1670), 294, tr. W. F. Trotter.

54. The best use of good laws is to teach men to trample bad laws under their feet. WENDELL PHILLIPS, speech, April 12, 1852.

55. Law is experience developed by reason and applied continually to further experience. ROSCOE POUND, *Christian Science Monitor*, April 24, 1963.

56. No man is above the law and no man is below it; nor do we ask any man's permission when we ask him to obey it. THEODORE ROOSEVELT, address, January 1904.

57. Good laws lead to the making of better ones; bad ones bring about worse. ROUSSEAU, *The Social Contract* (1762), 3.15, tr. G. D. H. Cole.

58. Government can easily exist without law, but law cannot exist without government. BERTRAND RUSSELL, "Ideas That Have Helped Mankind," *Unpopular Essays* (1950).

59. One can always legislate against specific acts of human wickedness; but one can never legislate against the irrational itself. MORTON IRVING SEIDEN, *The Paradox of Hate: A Study in Ritual Murder* (1967), 15.

60. Certain laws have not been written, but they are more fixed than all the written laws. SENECA THE ELDER, *Controversiae* (1st c. A.D.), 1.

61. In law, what plea so tainted and corrupt / But, being seasoned with a gracious voice, / Obscures the show of evil. SHAKESPEARE, *The Merchant of Venice* (1596–97), 3.2.75.

62. We must not make a scarecrow of the law, / Setting it up to fear the birds of prey, / And let it keep one shape till custom make it / Their perch, and not their terror. SHAKESPEARE, *Measure for Measure* (1604–05), 2.1.1.

63. Laws are like spider's webs which, if anything small falls into them they ensnare it, but large things break through and escape. SOLON (7th–6th c. B.C.), quoted in Diogenes Laertius' *Lives and Opinions of Eminent Philosophers* (3rd c. A.D.), tr. R. D. Hicks.

64. Rigorous law is often rigorous injustice. TERENCE, *The Self-Tormentor* (163 B.C.), 4.5.48, tr. Henry Thomas Riley.

65. The lawyer's truth is not Truth, but consistency or a consistent expediency. THOREAU, *Civil Disobedience* (1849).

66. The man for whom law exists—the man of forms, the conservative—is a tame man. THOREAU, *Journal*, March 30, 1851.

67. The certitude of laws is an obscurity of judgment backed only by authority. GIAMBATTISTA VICO, *The New Science* (1725–44), 1.2.

68. Let all the laws be clear, uniform, and precise; to interpret laws is almost always to corrupt them. VOLTAIRE, *Philosophical Dictionary* (1764).

69. The opinion of all lawyers, the unanimous cry of the nation, and the good of the state, are in themselves a law. VOLTAIRE, "Privilege—Privileged Cases," *Philosophical Dictionary* (1764).

70. It ain't no sin if you crack a few laws now and then, just so long as you don't break any. MAE WEST, in *Every Day's a Holiday* (1937).

71. The world is shocked, or amused, by the sight of saintly old people hindering in the name of morality the removal of obvious brutalities from a legal system. ALFRED NORTH WHITEHEAD, *Adventures in Ideas* (1933), 20.

## 526. LAW AND ORDER

**See also 525. Law and Lawyers; 654. Order; 703. Police**

1. Today there's law and order in everything. You can't beat anybody for nothing. If you do beat anyone, it's got to be for the sake of order. MAXIM GORKY, *The Lower Depths* (1903), 1, tr. Alexander Bakshy.

2. A man's respect for law and order exists in precise relationship to the size of his paycheck. ADAM CLAYTON POWELL, "Black Power: A Form of Godly Power," *Keep the Faith, Baby!* (1967).

3. Revolt and terror pay a price. / Order and law have a cost. CARL SANDBURG, *The People, Yes* (1936).

## 527. LAZINESS

**See also 444. Idleness**

1. Flee laziness, which, while it produces an immediate delight, ends in the sorrow of repentance. And know that nature without exercise is a seed shut up in the pod, and art without practice is nothing. PIETRO ARETINO, letter to Antonio Gallo, Aug. 6, 1537, tr. Samuel Putnam.

2. Go to the ant, thou sluggard; consider her ways and be wise: / Which having no guide, overseer, or ruler, / Provideth her meat in the summer, and gathereth her food in the harvest. *Bible*, Proverbs 6:6–8.

3. Laziness travels so slowly that poverty soon overtakes him. BENJAMIN FRANKLIN, "The Way to Wealth" (July 7, 1757), 1.

4. Indolence is a delightful but distressing state: we must be doing something to be happy. WILLIAM HAZLITT, "On the Pleasure of Painting," *Table Talk* (1821–22).

5. Don't yield to that alluring witch, Laziness, or else be prepared to surrender all that you have won in your better moments. HORACE, *Satires* (35–30 B.C.), 2.3.

6. It is the just doom of laziness and gluttony to be inactive without ease and drowsy without tranquility. SAMUEL JOHNSON, *The Adventurer* (1753), 39.

7. Only the game fish swims upstream, / But the sensible fish swims down. OGDEN NASH, "When You Say That, Smile! Or All Right Then, Don't Smile," *Verses from 1929 On* (1959).

8. Failure is not our only punishment for laziness: there is also the success of others. JULES RENARD, *Journal*, January 1898, ed. and tr. Louise Bogan and Elizabeth Roget.

9. The lazy are always wanting to do something. VAUVENARGUES, *Reflections and Maxims* (1746), 458.

10. What use is a good head if the legs won't carry it? *Yiddish Proverbs* (1949), ed. Hanan J. Ayalti.

## 528. LEADERSHIP

**See also 61. Authority; 313. Executives; 350. Following; 636. Obedience; 825. Rulers**

1. He who has never learned to obey cannot be a good commander. ARISTOTLE, *Politics* (4th c. B.C.), 3.4, tr. Benjamin Jowett.

2. I see it said that leaders should keep their ears to the ground. All I can say is that the British nation will find it very hard to look up to the leaders who are detected in that somewhat ungainly posture. SIR WIN-

STON CHURCHILL, speech, House of Commons, September 1941.

3. The man who commands efficiently must have obeyed others in the past, and the man who obeys dutifully is worthy of being some day a commander. CICERO, *De Legibus* (c. 52 B.C.), 3.2.5.

4. The superior man is easy to serve and difficult to please. CONFUCIUS, *Analects* (6th c. B.C.), 13.25, tr. James Legge.

5. Men are of no importance. What counts is who commands. CHARLES DE GAULLE, quoted in *The New York Times Magazine*, May 12, 1968.

6. There are men, who, by their sympathetic attractions, carry nations with them, and lead the activity of the human race. EMERSON, "Power," *The Conduct of Life* (1860).

7. For the most part our leaders are merely following out in front; they do but marshal us the way that we are going. BERGEN EVANS, *The Spoor of Spooks and Other Nonsense* (1954).

8. If you command wisely, you'll be obeyed cheerfully. THOMAS FULLER, M.D., *Gnomologia* (1732), 2746.

9. The leader, mingling with the vulgar host, / Is in the common mass of matter lost. HOMER, *Odyssey* (9th c. B.C.), 4.397, tr. Alexander Pope.

10. The weaknesses of the many make the leader possible. ELBERT HUBBARD, *The Note Book* (1927).

11. The final test of a leader is that he leaves behind him in other men the conviction and the will to carry on. WALTER LIPPMANN, "Roosevelt Has Gone," *New York Herald Tribune*, April 14, 1945.

12. To lead means to direct and to exact, and no man dare do either. He might be unpopular. What authority we are given now is a trinity: the grin, the generality, and God (the word). MARYA MANNES, "Introducing Myself," *More in Anger* (1958).

13. No man is great enough or wise enough for any of us to surrender our destiny to. The only way in which any one can lead us is to restore to us the belief in our own guidance. HENRY MILLER, "The Alcoholic Veteran with the Washboard Cranium," *The Wisdom of the Heart* (1941).

14. The real leader has no need to lead—he is content to point the way. HENRY MILLER, "The Wisdom of the Heart," *The Wisdom of the Heart* (1941).

15. A leader is a dealer in hope. NAPOLEON I, *Maxims* (1804–15).

16. The inevitable end of multiple chiefs is that they fade and disappear for lack of unity. NAPOLEON I, *Maxims* (1804–15).

17. To do great things is difficult; but to command great things is more difficult. NIETZSCHE, "The Stillest Hour," *Thus Spoke Zarathustra* (1883–92), 2, tr. Walter Kaufmann.

18. Any one can hold the helm when the sea is calm. PUBLILIUS SYRUS, *Moral Sayings* (1st c. B.C.), 358, tr. Darius Lyman.

19. The leader must know, must know that he knows, and must be able to make it abundantly clear to those about him that he knows. CLARENCE B. RANDALL, *Making Good in Management* (1964).

20. A chief is a man who assumes responsibility. He says, "I was beaten." He does not say, "My men were beaten." Thus speaks a real man. SAINT-EXUPÉRY, *Flight to Arras* (1942), 23, tr. Lewis Galantière.

21. We cannot all be masters, nor all masters / Cannot be truly followed. SHAKESPEARE, *Othello* (1604–05), 1.1.43.

22. What you cannot enforce, / Do not command. SOPHOCLES, *Oedipus at Colonus* (401 B.C.), tr. Robert Fitzgerald.

23. What a man dislikes in his superiors, let him not display in the treatment of his inferiors. TSANG SIN, *The Great Learning* (5th c. B.C.), 10.2, tr. James Legge.

## 529. LEARNING

**See also 277. Education; 319. Experience; 402. Growth and Development; 520. Knowledge; 715. Practice; 842. Scholars and Scholarship**

1. What one knows is, in youth, of little moment; they know enough who know how to learn. HENRY ADAMS, *The Education of Henry Adams* (1907), 21.

2. To learn is a natural pleasure, not confined to philosophers, but common to all men. ARISTOTLE, *Poetics* (4th c. B.C.), 1.5, tr. Thomas Twining.

3. Never believe on faith, / see for yourself! / What you yourself don't learn / you don't know. BERTOLT BRECHT, *The Mother* (1932), 6, tr. Lee Baxandall.

4. The great poem and the deep theorem

are new to every reader, and yet are his own experiences, because he himself re-creates them. JACOB BRONOWSKI, "The Creative Mind," *Science and Human Values* (1956).

5. They do most by books, who could do much without them, and he that chiefly owes himself unto himself is the substantial man. SIR THOMAS BROWNE, *Christian Morals* (1716), 2.

6. Learn as though you would never be able to master it; hold it as though you would be in fear of losing it. CONFUCIUS, *Analects* (6th c. B.C.), 8.17, tr. Ch'u Chai and Winberg Chai.

7. Everywhere, we learn only from those whom we love. GOETHE, quoted in Johann Peter Eckermann's *Conversations with Goethe*, May 12, 1825.

8. Make your friends your teachers and mingle the pleasures of conversation with the advantages of instruction. BALTASAR GRACIÁN, *The Art of Worldly Wisdom* (1647), 11, tr. Joseph Jacobs.

9. Learning is its own exceeding great reward. WILLIAM HAZLITT, "On Old English Writers and Speakers," *The Plain Speaker* (1826).

10. Just as eating against one's will is injurious to health, so study without a liking for it spoils the memory, and it retains nothing it takes in. LEONARDO DA VINCI, *Notebooks* (c. 1500), tr. Jean Paul Richter.

11. As turning the logs will make a dull fire burn, so change of studies a dull brain. LONGFELLOW, "Table-Talk," *Driftwood* (1857).

12. a man who is so dull / that he can learn only by personal experience / is too dull to learn / anything important by experience. DON MARQUIS, "archy on this and that," *Archy Does His Part* (1935).

13. A man has no ears for that to which experience has given him no access. NIETZSCHE, *Ecce Homo* (1888), tr. Anthony M. Ludovici.

14. Trees and fields tell me nothing; men are my teachers. PLATO, *Phaedrus* (4th c. B.C.).

15. Freedom to learn is the first necessity of guaranteeing that man himself shall be self-reliant enough to be free. FRANKLIN D. ROOSEVELT, speech, New York City, June 30, 1938.

16. The learning of books that you do not make your own wisdom is money in the hands of another in time of need. SANSKRIT PROVERB.

17. You have learnt something. That always feels at first as if you had lost something. GEORGE BERNARD SHAW, *Major Barbara* (1905), 3.

18. A man, though wise, should never be ashamed / of learning more, and must unbend his mind. SOPHOCLES, *Antigone* (442–41 B.C.), tr. Elizabeth Wyckoff.

19. I have learned throughout my life as a composer chiefly through my mistakes and pursuits of false assumptions, not by my exposure to founts of wisdom and knowledge. IGOR STRAVINSKY, "Contingencies," *Themes and Episodes* (1966).

20. To be fond of learning is to be near to knowledge. TZE-SZE, *The Doctrine of the Mean* (5th c. B.C.), 20.10, tr. James Legge.

21. The thirst to know and understand, / A large and liberal discontent; / These are the goods in life's rich hand, / The things that are more excellent. SIR WILLIAM WATSON, "Things That Are More Excellent," *Collected Poems* (1905).

## LEGACY

See 1051. Wills and Inheritance

## 530. LEISURE

See also 10. Activity; 444. Idleness; 697. Play; 805. Rest; 807. Retirement

1. There can be no high civilization where there is not ample leisure. HENRY WARD BEECHER, *Proverbs from Plymouth Pulpit* (1887).

2. When a man's busy, why leisure / Strikes him as wonderful pleasure: / 'Faith, and at leisure once is he? / Straightway he wants to be busy. ROBERT BROWNING, "The Glove," *Dramatic Romances and Lyrics* (1845).

3. What is this life if, full of care, / We have no time to stand and stare? W. H. DAVIES, "Leisure," *Songs of Joy* (1911).

4. Friendship requires more time than poor busy men can usually command. EMERSON, "Behavior," *The Conduct of Life* (1860).

5. It takes application, a fine sense of value, and a powerful community-spirit for a people to have serious leisure, and this has

not been the genius of the Americans. PAUL GOODMAN, *Growing Up Absurd* (1960), 1.8.

6. To be at ease is better than to be at business. Nothing really belongs to us but time, which even he has who has nothing else. BALTASAR GRACIÁN, *The Art of Worldly Wisdom* (1647), 247, tr. Joseph Jacobs.

7. More free time means more time to waste. The worker who used to have only a little time in which to get drunk and beat his wife now has time to get drunk, beat his wife—and watch TV. ROBERT HUTCHINS, news summaries, Jan. 2, 1954.

8. Leisure and curiosity might soon make great advances in useful knowledge, were they not diverted by minute emulation and laborious trifles. SAMUEL JOHNSON, *The Rambler* (1750–52), 177.

9. Lie down and listen to the crabgrass grow, / The faucet leak, and learn to leave them so. MARYA MANNES, "Controverse," *But Will It Sell?* (1955–64).

10. Freedom from worries and surcease from strain are illusions that always inhabit the distance. EDWIN WAY TEALE, "April 3," *Circle of the Seasons* (1953).

11. The highest pleasure to be got out of freedom, and having nothing to do, is labor. MARK TWAIN, letter to Mr. Burrough of St. Louis, Nov. 1, 1876.

12. In itself and in its consequences the life of leisure is beautiful and ennobling in all civilised men's eyes. THORSTEIN VEBLEN, *The Theory of the Leisure Class* (1899), 3.

## LENDING

See 94. Borrowing and Lending

## 531. LENIENCY

See also 468. Indulgence; 475. Injustice; 515. Justice; 577. Mercy; 760. Punishment; 883. Severity

1. He that spares the bad injures the good. THOMAS FULLER, M.D., *Gnomologia* (1732), 2308.

2. Pardon one offence, and you encourage the commission of many. PUBLILIUS SYRUS, *Moral Sayings* (1st c. B.C.), 750, tr. Darius Lyman.

3. Whoever has his foe at his mercy, and does not kill him, is his own enemy. SA'DI, *Gulistan* (1258), 8.56, tr. James Ross.

4. He who forbids not sin when he may, commands it. SENECA, *The Trojan Women* (1st c.), 291.

## 532. LETTERS

See also 556. Mailmen

1. Sir, more than kisses, letters mingle souls; / For, thus friends absent speak. JOHN DONNE, "To Sir Henry Wotton" (1633).

2. We lay aside letters never to read them again, and at last we destroy them out of discretion, and so disappears the most beautiful, the most immediate breath of life, irrecoverably for ourselves and for others. GOETHE, *Elective Affinities* (1809), 27.

3. A woman seldom writes her mind but in her postscript. RICHARD STEELE, *The Spectator* (1711–12), 79.

4. Those who are absent, by its means become present; it [mail] is the consolation of life. VOLTAIRE, "Post," *Philosophical Dictionary* (1764).

## LEXICOGRAPHY

See 227. Definition; 242. Dictionaries

## 533. LIBERALISM

See also 175. Conservatism; 704. Political Parties; 770. Radicalism

1. A rich man told me recently that a liberal is a man who tells other people what to do with their money. LE ROI JONES, "Tokenism: 300 years for five cents," *Home* (1966).

2. Liberal institutions straightway cease from being liberal the moment they are soundly established. NIETZSCHE, "Skirmishes in a War with the Age," *Twilight of the Idols* (1888), tr. Anthony M. Ludovici.

3. A Liberal is a man who uses his legs and his hands at the behest—at the command—of his head. FRANKLIN D. ROOSEVELT, radio address, Oct. 26, 1939.

4. The essence of the Liberal outlook lies not in *what* opinions are held, but in *how* they are held: instead of being held dogmatically, they are held tentatively, and with a consciousness that new evidence may at any moment lead to their abandon-

ment. BERTRAND RUSSELL, "Philosophy and Politics," *Unpopular Essays* (1950).

### LIBERALITY

See 373. Generosity

### LIBERTINISM

See 733. Profligacy

## 534. LIBERTY

See also 107. Captivity; 231. Democracy; 361. Freedom, Individual; 817. Rights; 882. Servitude

1. Liberty, next to religion, has been the motive of good deeds and the common pretext of crime. LORD ACTON, address, "The History of Freedom in Antiquity," Feb. 26, 1877.

2. Liberty is not a means to a higher political end. It is itself the highest political end. LORD ACTON, address, "The History of Freedom in Antiquity," Feb. 26, 1877.

3. Despotism accomplishes great things illegally; liberty doesn't even go to the trouble of accomplishing small things legally. BALZAC, *La Peau de chagrin* (1831), 1.

4. Liberty is the soul's right to breathe, and, when it can not take a long breath, laws are girdled too tight. HENRY WARD BEECHER, *Proverbs from Plymouth Pulpit* (1887).

5. Liberty, n. One of Imagination's most precious possessions. AMBROSE BIERCE, *The Devil's Dictionary* (1881–1911).

6. None who have always been free can understand the terrible fascinating power of the hope of freedom to those who are not free. PEARL S. BUCK, *What America Means to Me* (1943), 4.

7. Hereditary Bondsmen! know ye not / Who would be free themselves must strike the blow? BYRON, *Childe Harold's Pilgrimage* (1812–18), 2.76.

8. Liberty may be of no more use / Than stirring up the flame of civil wars; / Then, by disorder fatal to the world, / One wants no king, the other wants no equal. CORNEILLE, *Cinna* (1639), 2.1, tr. Paul Landis.

9. Eternal vigilance is the price of liberty. JOHN PHILPOT CURRAN, speech on the Right of Election of the Lord Mayor of Dublin, July 10, 1790.

10. The hungry and the homeless don't care about liberty any more than they care about cultural heritage. To pretend that they do care is cant. E. M. FORSTER, "Liberty in England," *Abinger Harvest* (1936).

11. The ultimate foundation of a free society is the binding tie of cohesive sentiment. FELIX FRANKFURTER, *Minersville School District v. Gobitis* (1940).

12. Lean liberty is better than fat slavery. THOMAS FULLER, M.D., *Gnomologia* (1732), 3158.

13. The cause of liberty becomes a mockery if the price to be paid is the wholesale destruction of those who are to enjoy liberty. MOHANDAS K. GANDHI, *Non-Violence in Peace and War* (1948), 1.272.

14. Liberty is necessity's conscience. Graffito written during French student revolt, May 1968.

15. Liberty is so much latitude as the powerful choose to accord to the weak. LEARNED HAND, speech, University of Pennsylvania Law School, June 1930.

16. The spirit of liberty is the spirit which is not too sure it is right. LEARNED HAND, speech, New York City, May 21, 1944.

17. Is life so dear or peace so sweet, as to be purchased at the price of chains and slavery? Forbid it, Almighty God! I know not what course others may take, but as for me, give me liberty or give me death! PATRICK HENRY, speech, Virginia Convention, March 23, 1775.

18. Liberation is not deliverance. VICTOR HUGO, "Fantine," *Les Misérables* (1862), 2.9, tr. Charles E. Wilbour.

19. My fellow citizens of the world: ask not what America will do for you, but what together we can do for the freedom of man. JOHN F. KENNEDY, Inaugural Address, Jan. 20, 1961.

20. Let every nation know, whether it wishes us well or ill, that we shall pay any price, bear any burden, meet any hardship, support any friend, oppose any foe, in order to assure the survival and the success of liberty. JOHN F. KENNEDY, Inaugural Address, Jan. 20, 1961.

21. If the self-discipline of the free cannot match the iron discipline of the mailed fist, in economic, political, scientific, and all the other kinds of struggles, as well as the

military, then the peril to freedom will continue to rise. JOHN F. KENNEDY, address, American Society of Newspaper Editors, Washington, D.C., April 20, 1961.

22. We stand for freedom. That is our conviction for ourselves; that is our only commitment to others. JOHN F. KENNEDY, message to Congress, May 25, 1961.

23. The shepherd drives the wolf from the sheep's throat, for which the sheep thanks the shepherd as his liberator, while the wolf denounces him for the same act, as the destroyer of liberty, especially as the sheep was a black one. ABRAHAM LINCOLN, speech, Baltimore, April 18, 1864.

24. We've a war, an' a debt, an' a flag; an' ef this / Ain't to be inderpendunt, why, wut on airth is? JAMES RUSSELL LOWELL, *The Biglow Papers: Second Series* (1867), 4.

25. Martyred many times must be / Who would keep his country free. EDNA ST. VINCENT MILLAY, "To the Maid of Orleans," *Make Bright the Arrows* (1940).

26. Liberty is the right to do what the laws permit. MONTESQUIEU, *L'Esprit des lois* (1748), 11.3.

27. The word liberty has often served for the destruction of the substance of liberty. JOSÉ MARÍA LUIS MORA, *Obras sueltas*, v. 2, p. 78.

28. In order that a people may be free, it is necessary that the governed be sages, and those who govern, gods. NAPOLEON I, *Maxims* (1804–15).

29. People demand freedom only when they have no power. NIETZSCHE, *The Will to Power* (1888), 784, tr. Anthony M. Ludovici.

30. Those who expect to reap the blessings of freedom must, like men, undergo the fatigue of supporting it. THOMAS PAINE, *The American Crisis* (1776–83), 4.

31. He that would make his own liberty secure must guard even his enemy from oppression. THOMAS PAINE, *Dissertation on First Principles of Government* (1795).

32. Tyranny is always better organized than freedom. CHARLES PÉGUY, "War and Peace," *Basic Verities* (1943), tr. Ann and Julian Green.

33. Whether in chains or in laurels, liberty knows nothing but victories. WENDELL PHILLIPS, speech, Nov. 1, 1859.

34. Liberty don't work as good in practice as it does in Speech. WILL ROGERS, *There's Not a Bathing Suit in Russia* (1927), 5.

35. A Country can get more real joy out of just Hollering for their Freedom than they can if they get it. WILL ROGERS, *The Autobiography of Will Rogers* (1949), 17.

36. Oh liberty, what crimes are committed in your name! Attributed to MADAME ROLAND: last words before her execution, Nov. 8, 1793.

37. In the truest sense freedom cannot be bestowed, it must be achieved. FRANKLIN D. ROOSEVELT, greeting on 74th anniversary of the Emancipation Proclamation, Sept. 16, 1936.

38. Our government is based on the belief that a people can be both strong and free, that civilized men need no restraint but that imposed by themselves against abuse of freedom. FRANKLIN D. ROOSEVELT, address, Harvard University, Cambridge, Mass., Sept. 18, 1936.

39. To renounce liberty is to renounce being a man, to surrender the rights of humanity and even its duties. ROUSSEAU, *The Social Contract* (1762), 1.4, tr. G. D. H. Cole.

40. Too little liberty brings stagnation, and too much brings chaos. BERTRAND RUSSELL, "The Role of Individuality," *Authority and the Individual* (1949).

41. Liberty plucks justice by the nose; / The baby beats the nurse, and quite athwart / Goes all decorum. SHAKESPEARE, *Measure for Measure* (1604–05), 1.3.29.

42. Liberty means responsibility. That is why most men dread it. GEORGE BERNARD SHAW, "Maxims for Revolutionists," *Man and Superman* (1903).

43. A nation has character only when it is free. MME DE STAËL, *De la littérature* (1800), 1.5.

44. Carelessness about our security is dangerous; carelessness about our freedom is also dangerous. ADLAI STEVENSON, speech, Detroit, Mich., Oct. 7, 1952.

45. If the world knew how to use freedom without abusing it, tyranny would not exist. TEHYI HSIEH, *Chinese Epigrams Inside Out and Proverbs* (1948), 293.

46. It is by the goodness of God that in our country we have those three unspeakably precious things: freedom of speech, freedom of conscience, and the prudence never to practice either of them. MARK

TWAIN, "Pudd'nhead Wilson's New Calendar," *Following the Equator* (1897), 1.20.

47. It is a worthy thing to fight for one's freedom; it is another sight finer to fight for another man's. MARK TWAIN, letter to the Reverend Joseph Twichell, 1898.

48. It must be admitted that liberty is the hardest test that one can inflict on a people. To know how to be free is not given equally to all men and all nations. PAUL VALÉRY, "On the Subject of Dictatorship," *Reflections on the World Today* (1931), tr. Francis Scarfe.

49. The true charter of liberty is independence, maintained by force. VOLTAIRE, "Venice. And, Incidentally, of Liberty," *Philosophical Dictionary* (1764).

50. Liberty exists in proportion to wholesome restraint. DANIEL WEBSTER, speech at the Charleston Bar Dinner, May 10, 1847.

51. Liberty is never out of bounds or off limits; it spreads wherever it can capture the imagination of men. E. B. WHITE, "Letter from the West," *The Points of My Compass* (1960).

52. The shallow consider liberty a release from all law, from every constraint. The wise see in it, on the contrary, the potent Law of Laws. WALT WHITMAN, "Freedom," *Notes Left Over* (1881).

53. The history of liberty is a history of limitation of government power, not the increase of it. WOODROW WILSON, address, New York City, Sept. 9, 1912.

54. Liberty is its own reward. WOODROW WILSON, address, Sept. 12, 1912.

55. You cannot tear up ancient rootages and safely plant the tree of liberty in soil that is not native to it. WOODROW WILSON, speech, Sept. 25, 1912.

56. Liberty does not consist in mere general declarations of the rights of men. It consists in the translation of those declarations into definite action. WOODROW WILSON, speech, Philadelphia, July 4, 1914.

57. If liberty has any meaning it means freedom to improve. PHILIP WYLIE, introduction, *Generation of Vipers* (1942).

## 535. LIBRARIES

**See also 91. Books and Reading**

1. The true university of these days is a collection of books. THOMAS CARLYLE, *On Heroes, Hero-Worship and the Heroic in History* (1841), 5.

2. Th' first thing to have in a libry is a shelf. Fr'm time to time this can be decorated with lithrachure. But th' shelf is th' main thing. FINLEY PETER DUNNE, "Books," *Mr. Dooley Says* (1910).

3. A man's library is a sort of harem. EMERSON, "In Praise of Books," *The Conduct of Life* (1860).

4. A company of the wisest and wittiest men that could be picked out of all civil countries, in a thousand years, have set in best order the results of their learning and wisdom. EMERSON, "In Praise of Books," *The Conduct of Life* (1860).

5. My experience with public libraries is that the first volume of the book I inquire for is out, unless I happen to want the second, when *that* is out. OLIVER WENDELL HOLMES, SR., *The Poet at the Breakfast Table* (1872), 7.

6. No place affords a more striking conviction of the vanity of human hopes, than a public library. SAMUEL JOHNSON, *The Rambler* (1750–52), 106.

7. Borrowers of books—those mutilators of collections, spoilers of the symmetry of shelves, and creators of odd volumes. CHARLES LAMB, "The Two Races of Men," *Essays of Elia* (1823).

## LIES

**See 329. Falsehood**

## 536. LIFE

**See also 3. The Absurd; 81. Birth; 218. Death; 314. Existence; 502. Involvement; 537. Life, Stages of; 538. Life and Death; 545. Longevity; 569. Meaning; 600. Mortality; 983. Transience; 1012. The Unknown; 1060. World**

1. Life is a wonderful thing to talk about, or to read about in history books—but it is terrible when one has to live it. JEAN ANOUILH, *Time Remembered* (1939), 2.1, tr. Patricia Moyes.

2. Life has a way of setting things in order and leaving them be. Very tidy, is life. JEAN ANOUILH, *The Rehearsal* (1950), 2, tr. Lucienne Hill.

3. Life is a toy made of glass; it appears to be of inestimable price, but in reality it is very cheap. PIETRO ARETINO, letter to Bernardo Tassò, Sept. 26, 1537, tr. Samuel Putnam.

4. Men cling to life even at the cost of enduring great misfortune. ARISTOTLE, *Politics* (4th c. B.C.), 3.6, tr. Benjamin Jowett.

5. Life is seldom as unendurable as, to judge by the facts, it logically ought to be. BROOKS ATKINSON, "December 22," *Once Around the Sun* (1951).

6. Life, the permission to know death. DJUNA BARNES, *Nightwood* (1937).

7. The life of every man is a diary in which he means to write one story, and writes another; and his humblest hour is when he compares the volume as it is with what he vowed to make it. J. M. BARRIE, *The Little Minister* (1891), 1.

8. Life backs up life. Nobody loves creditors and dead men. UGO BETTI, *The Gambler* (1950), 3.2, ed. Gino Rizzo.

9. Life is one vast tangled conglomeration, inflamed with passion. UGO BETTI, *The Fugitive* (1953), 1, tr. G. H. McWilliam.

10. Can't you see that life itself is the biggest mistake of all, that life is the agent of your sufferings? UGO BETTI, *The Fugitive* (1953), 3, tr. G. H. McWilliam.

11. A living dog is better than a dead lion. *Bible*, Ecclesiastes 9:4.

12. I count life just a stuff / To try the soul's strength on. ROBERT BROWNING, "In a Balcony," *Men and Women* (1855).

13. We mortals cross the ocean of this world / Each in his average cabin of a life; / The best's not big, the worst yields elbow-room. ROBERT BROWNING, "Bishop Blougram's Apology," *Men and Women* (1855), 99.

14. How good is man's life, the mere living! how fit to employ / All the heart and the soul and the senses forever in joy! ROBERT BROWNING, "Saul," *Men and Women* (1855), 9.

15. To live is like to love—all reason is against it, and all healthy instinct for it. SAMUEL BUTLER (d. 1902), "Higgledy-Piggledy," *Note-Books* (1912).

16. Life is not so much a riddle to be read as a Gordian knot that will get cut sooner or later. SAMUEL BUTLER (d. 1902), "Lord, What Is Man?" *Note-Books* (1912).

17. We are involved in a life that passes understanding and our highest business is our daily life. JOHN CAGE, "Where Are We Going? And What Are We Doing?" *Silence* (1961).

18. Men must live and create. Live to the point of tears. ALBERT CAMUS, *Notebooks 1935–1942* (1962), 1, tr. Philip Thody.

19. In living and in seeing other men, the heart must break or become as bronze. CHAMFORT, *Caractères et anecdotes* (1771), 164.

20. Life is fleeting—and therefore endurable. ALEXANDER CHASE, *Perspectives* (1966).

21. Life is a maze in which we take the wrong turning before we have learnt to walk. CYRIL CONNOLLY, *The Unquiet Grave* (1945), 1.

22. There are men here and there to whom the whole of life is like an after-dinner hour with a cigar; easy, pleasant, empty, perhaps enlivened by some fable of strife to be forgotten before the end is told. JOSEPH CONRAD, *Lord Jim* (1900), 5.

23. Life is an incurable disease. ABRAHAM COWLEY, "To Dr. Scarborough" (1656), 6.

24. Man pines to live but cannot endure the days of his life. EDWARD DAHLBERG, *The Sorrows of Priapus* (1957).

25. Life is like a B-picture script. It is that corny. If I had my life story offered to me to film, I'd turn it down. KIRK DOUGLAS, *Look*, Oct. 4, 1955.

26. When I consider life, 'tis all a cheat. / Yet fooled with hope, men favour the deceit. JOHN DRYDEN, *Aurengzebe* (1676), 4.1.

27. A minute to smile and an hour to weep in, / A pint of joy to a peck of trouble, / And never a laugh but the moans come double; / And that is life! PAUL LAURENCE DUNBAR, "Life," *The Complete Poems* (1962).

28. Birth, and copulation, and death. / That's all the facts when you come to brass tacks. T. S. ELIOT, "Fragment of an Agon," *Sweeney Agonistes* (1926).

29. It has always been difficult for man to realize that his life is all an art. It has been more difficult to conceive it so than to act it so. HAVELOCK ELLIS, *The Dance of Life* (1923), 1.

30. Life only avails, not the having lived.

EMERSON, "Self-Reliance," *Essays: First Series* (1841).

31. We do not live an equal life, but one of contrasts and patchwork; now a little joy, then a sorrow, now a sin, then a generous or brave action. EMERSON, *Journals*, 1845.

32. Life consists in what a man is thinking of all day. EMERSON, *Journals*, 1847.

33. Life is a short affair; / We should try to make it smooth, and free from strife. EURIPIDES, *The Suppliant Women* (c. 421 B.C.), tr. Frank W. Jones.

34. Alas!—but why Alas? / It is the lot of mortality we experience. EURIPIDES (5th c. B.C.), quoted in Plutarch's "Contentment," *Moralia* (c. A.D. 100), tr. Moses Hadas.

35. Irony and pity are two good counselors: one, in smiling, makes life pleasurable; the other, who cries, makes it sacred. ANATOLE FRANCE, *Le Jardin d'Épicure* (1895).

36. Life is half spent before one knows what life is. FRENCH PROVERB.

37. Life is like an onion, which one peels crying. FRENCH PROVERB.

38. There is only one meaning of life: the act of living itself. ERICH FROMM, *Escape from Freedom* (1941), 7.

39. We are born crying, live complaining, and die disappointed. THOMAS FULLER, M.D., *Gnomologia* (1732), 5427.

40. Life's a pudding full of plums. W. S. GILBERT, *The Gondoliers* (1889), 1.

41. Life's perhaps the only riddle / That we shrink from giving up. W. S. GILBERT, *The Gondoliers* (1889), 1.

42. A just conception of life is too large a thing to grasp during the short interval of passing through it. THOMAS HARDY, *A Pair of Blue Eyes* (1873), 19.

43. Life is made up of marble and mud. NATHANIEL HAWTHORNE, *The House of the Seven Gables* (1851), 2.

44. The art of life is to know how to enjoy a little and to endure much. WILLIAM HAZLITT, "Commonplaces," *The Round Table* (1817), 1.

45. Life is a continued struggle to be what we are not, and to do what we cannot. WILLIAM HAZLITT, "Disappointment," *Lectures on the Dramatic Literature of the Age of Elizabeth* (1820).

46. Life has a value only when it has something valuable as its object. HEGEL, introduction to *Philosophy of History* (1832), tr. John Sibree.

47. I'd like to know / what this whole show / is all about / before it's out. PIET HEIN, "I'd Like—," *Grooks* (1966).

48. Life is made up of sobs, sniffles, and smiles, with sniffles predominating. O. HENRY, "The Gift of the Magi," *The Four Million* (1906).

49. There is a saying that no man has tasted the full flavor of life until he has known poverty, love, and war. O. HENRY, "The Complete Life of John Hopkins," *The Voice of the City* (1908).

50. Life is a fatal complaint, and an eminently contagious one. OLIVER WENDELL HOLMES, SR., *The Poet at the Breakfast Table* (1872), 12.

51. Life is an end in itself, and the only question as to whether it is worth living is whether you have enough of it. OLIVER WENDELL HOLMES, JR., speech, Boston Bar Association, March 7, 1900.

52. Life seems to me like a Japanese picture which our imagination does not allow to end in the margin. OLIVER WENDELL HOLMES, JR., speech, Federal Bar Association, Feb. 29, 1932.

53. To live is to climb the Andes: the more one climbs, the steeper become the precipices. EUGENIO MARÍA DE HOSTOS, "Hombres e ideas," *Obras* (1939–54), 14.

54. So long as we do not blow our brains out, we have decided life is worth living. EDGAR WATSON HOWE, *Ventures in Common Sense* (1919), 32.23.

55. The best way to prepare for life is to begin to live. ELBERT HUBBARD, *The Note Book* (1927).

56. Life is simply one damned thing after another. Ascribed to ELBERT HUBBARD (1856–1915).

57. The earth belongs to the living, not to the dead. THOMAS JEFFERSON, letter to John W. Eppes, June 24, 1813.

58. I do not cut my life up into days but my days into lives, each day, each hour, an entire life. JUAN RAMÓN JIMÉNEZ, "Heroic Reason," *Selected Writings* (1957), tr. H. R. Hays.

59. Life is a pill which none of us can bear to swallow without gilding. SAMUEL JOHNSON, quoted in Hester Lynch Piozzi's *Anecdotes of Samuel Johnson* (1786).

60. A man's life of any worth is a continual allegory—and very few eyes can see the mystery of his life—a life like the scrip-

tures, figurative. JOHN KEATS, letter to George and Georgiana Keats, Feb. 14–May 3, 1819.

61. For men must work and women must weep, / And the sooner it's over, the sooner to sleep. CHARLES KINGSLEY, "The Three Fishers."

62. There is no easy path leading out of life, and few are the easy ones that lie within it. WALTER SAVAGE LANDOR, "Epicurus, Leontion, and Ternissa," *Imaginary Conversations* (1824–53).

63. What a rotten writer of detective stories life is! NATHAN LEOPOLD, *Life Plus 99 Years* (1958).

64. Life for the European is a career; for the American, it is a hazard. MARY MC CARTHY, "America the Beautiful: The Humanist in the Bathtub," *On the Contrary* (1961).

65. Life is what despairs in death / And, desperate, is life still. ARCHIBALD MAC LEISH, *JB* (1958), 6.

66. Deem not life a thing of consequence. For look at the yawning void of the future, and at that other limitless space, the past. MARCUS AURELIUS, *Meditations* (2nd c.), 4.50, tr. Morris Hickey Morgan.

67. The art of living is more like wrestling than dancing. MARCUS AURELIUS, *Meditations* (2nd c.), 7.61, tr. Morris Hickey Morgan.

68. No man is quick enough to enjoy life. MARTIAL, *Epigrams* (A. D. 86), 2.90, tr. Walter C. A. Ker.

69. It takes life to love Life. EDGAR LEE MASTERS, "Lucinda Matlock," *Spoon River Anthology* (1915).

70. The life force is vigorous. The delight that accompanies it counter-balances all the pains and hardships that confront men. It makes life worth living. W. SOMERSET MAUGHAM, *The Summing Up* (1938), 73.

71. The basic fact about human existence is not that it is a tragedy, but that it is a bore. It is not so much a war as an endless standing in line. H. L. MENCKEN, *Prejudices: Sixth Series* (1927), 3.

72. It is not true that life is one damn thing after another—it's one damn thing over and over. EDNA ST. VINCENT MILLAY, *Letters of Edna St. Vincent Millay* (1952), ed. A. R. Macdougal.

73. The aim of life is to live, and to live means to be aware, joyously, drunkenly, serenely, divinely aware. HENRY MILLER, "Creative Death," *The Wisdom of the Heart* (1941).

74. Nor love thy life, nor hate; but what thou liv'st / Live well; how long or short permit to Heaven. MILTON, *Paradise Lost* (1667), 11.553.

75. Of all human foibles love of living is the most powerful. MOLIÈRE, *Love's the Best Doctor* (1665), 3, tr. John Wood.

76. There is nothing so fine and legitimate as well and duly to play the man; nor science so arduous as well and naturally to know how to live this life. MONTAIGNE, "Of experience," *Essays* (1580–88), tr. Charles Cotton and W. C. Hazlitt.

77. The great business of life is to be, to do, to do without, and to depart. JOHN MORLEY, address on aphorisms, Edinburgh, 1887.

78. Life is the only art that we are required to practice without preparation, and without being allowed the preliminary trials, the failures and botches, that are essential for the training of a mere beginner. LEWIS MUMFORD, "The Way and the Life," *The Conduct of Life* (1951).

79. Human life is but a series of footnotes to a vast obscure unfinished masterpiece. VLADIMIR NABOKOV, "Commentary," *Pale Fire* (1962), 939.

80. Life is strewn with so many dangers, and can be the source of so many misfortunes, that death is not the greatest of them. NAPOLEON I, *Maxims* (1804–15).

81. Life is not having been told that the man has just waxed the floor. OGDEN NASH, "You and Me and P. B. Shelley," *Good Intentions* (1943).

82. We love life, not because we are used to living but because we are used to loving. NIETZSCHE, "On Reading and Writing," *Thus Spoke Zarathustra* (1883–92), 1, tr. Walter Kaufmann.

83. Life is perhaps most wisely regarded as a bad dream between two awakenings, and every day is a life in miniature. EUGENE O'NEILL, *Marco Millions* (1928), 2.2.

84. Our lives are merely strange dark interludes in the electric display of God the Father. EUGENE O'NEILL, *Strange Interlude* (1928), 9.

85. Life is the external text, the burning bush by the edge of the path from which God speaks. JOSÉ ORTEGA Y GASSET,

"Preliminary Meditation," *Meditations on Quixote* (1914).

86. In order to master the unruly torrent of life the learned man meditates, the poet quivers, and the political hero erects the fortress of his will. JOSÉ ORTEGA Y GASSET, "Preliminary Meditation," *Meditations on Quixote* (1914).

87. To say that we live is the same as saying that we find ourselves in an atmosphere of definite possibilities. JOSÉ ORTEGA Y GASSET, *The Revolt of the Masses* (1930), 4.

88. We never live, but we hope to live; and, as we are always preparing to be happy, it is inevitable we should never be so. PASCAL, *Pensées* (1670), 172, tr. W. F. Trotter.

89. Between us and heaven or hell there is only life, which is the frailest thing in the world. PASCAL, *Pensées* (1670), 213, tr. W. F. Trotter.

90. The art of living is the art of knowing how to believe lies. CESARE PAVESE, *The Burning Brand* (1961).

91. Life is little more than a loan shark: it exacts a very high rate of interest for the few pleasures it concedes. LUIGI PIRANDELLO, *The Pleasure of Honesty* (1917), 1, tr. William Murray.

92. Every true man, sir, who is a little above the level of the beasts and plants does not live for the sake of living, without knowing how to live; but he lives so as to give a meaning and a value of his own to life. LUIGI PIRANDELLO, *Six Characters in Search of an Author* (1921), 3, tr. Edward Storer.

93. One lives in the hope of becoming a memory. ANTONIO PORCHIA, *Voces* (1968), tr. W. S. Merwin.

94. Life is short, but its ills make it seem long. PUBLILIUS SYRUS, *Moral Sayings* (1st c. B.C.), 124, tr. Darius Lyman.

95. I ask you, what is human life? Is it not a maimed happiness—care and weariness, weariness and care, with the baseless expectation, the strange cozenage of a brighter tomorrow? ERNEST RENAN, *Feuilles détachées* (c. 1880).

96. I don't understand life at all, but I don't say it is impossible that God may understand it a little. JULES RENARD, *Journal*, March 1910, ed. and tr. Louise Bogan and Elizabeth Roget.

97. Fate loves to invent patterns and designs. Its difficulty lies in complexity. But life itself is difficult because of its simplicity. It has only a few things of a grandeur not fit for us. RAINER MARIA RILKE, *The Notebooks of Malte Laurids Brigge* (1910), tr. M. D. Herter Norton.

98. "Does the road wind up-hill all the way?" / "Yes, to the very end." / "Will the day's journey take the whole long day?" / "From morn to night, my friend." CHRISTINA ROSSETTI, "Up-Hill" (1861).

99. From the first moment of life, men ought to begin learning to deserve to live. ROUSSEAU, *A Discourse on Political Economy* (1758), tr. G. D. H. Cole.

100. There is no wealth but life. JOHN RUSKIN, *Unto This Last* (1862), 4.77.

101. Real life is, to most men, a long second-best, a perpetual compromise between the ideal and the possible. BERTRAND RUSSELL, "The Study of Mathematics," *Mysticism and Logic* (1917).

102. Life stands on the verge of a single breath; and this world is an existence between two nonentities. SA'DI, *Gulistan* (1258), 8.34, tr. James Ross.

103. Life has a meaning only if one barters it day by day for something other than itself. SAINT-EXUPÉRY, *The Wisdom of the Sands* (1948), 5, tr. Stuart Gilbert.

104. It is the acme of life to understand life. GEORGE SANTAYANA, *Little Essays* (1920), 57, ed. Logan Pearsall Smith.

105. There is no cure for birth and death save to enjoy the interval. GEORGE SANTAYANA, "War Shrines," *Soliloquies in England* (1922).

106. Life is a task to be done. It is a fine thing to say *defunctus est;* it means that the man has done his task. SCHOPENHAUER, "On the Sufferings of the World," *Parerga and Paralipomena* (1851), tr. T. Bailey Saunders.

107. It is only in the microscope that our life looks so big. It is an indivisible point, drawn out and magnified by the powerful lenses of Time and Space. SCHOPENHAUER, "The Vanity of Existence," *Parerga and Paralipomena* (1851), tr. T. Bailey Saunders.

108. The scenes of our life are like pictures done in rough mosaic. Looked at close, they produce no effect. There is nothing beautiful to be found in them, unless you stand some distance off. SCHOPENHAUER, "The Vanity of Existence," *Parerga and Paralipomena* (1851), tr. T. Bailey Saunders.

109. Nothing is so false as human life,

nothing so treacherous. God knows no one would have accepted it as a gift, if it had not been given without our knowledge. SENECA, *Ad Marciam de Consolatione* (1st c.).

110. Life's neither a good nor an evil: it's a field for good and evil. SENECA, *Letters to Lucilius* (1st c.), 99.12, tr. E. Phillips Barker.

111. It is more fitting for a man to laugh at life than to lament over it. SENECA, "On Peace of Mind," *Moral Essays* (1st c.).

112. Life is as tedious as a twice-told tale / Vexing the dull ear of a drowsy man. SHAKESPEARE, *King John* (1596–97), 3.4.108.

113. The time of life is short! / To spend that shortness basely were too long. SHAKESPEARE, *1 Henry IV* (1597–98), 5.2.82.

114. The web of our life is of a mingled yarn, good and ill together. SHAKESPEARE, *All's Well That Ends Well* (1602–03), 4.3.83.

115. Life's but a walking shadow, a poor player, / That struts and frets his hour upon the stage / And then is heard no more. It is a tale / Told by an idiot, full of sound and fury, / Signifying nothing. SHAKESPEARE, *Macbeth* (1605–06), 5.5.24.

116. Life is too short for men to take it seriously. GEORGE BERNARD SHAW, *Back to Methuselah* (1921), 2.

117. Living well and beautifully and justly are all one thing. SOCRATES, in Plato's *Crito* (4th c. B.C.), tr. Lane Cooper.

118. What most counts is not to live, but to live aright. SOCRATES, in Plato's *Crito* (4th c. B.C.), tr. Lane Cooper.

119. You cannot know a man's life before the man / has died, then only can you call it good or bad. SOPHOCLES, *The Women of Trachis* (c. 413 B.C.), tr. Michael Jameson.

120. What is the life of man! Is it not to shift from side to side?—from sorrow to sorrow?—to button up one cause of vexation!—and unbutton another! LAURENCE STERNE, *Tristram Shandy* (1759–67), 4.31.

121. Everyday life is a stimulating mixture of order and haphazardry. The sun rises and sets on schedule but the wind bloweth where it listeth. ROBERT LOUIS STEVENSON, "Pan's Pipes," *Virginibus Puerisque* (1881).

122. Life is a gamble, at terrible odds—if it was a bet you wouldn't take it. TOM STOPPARD, *Rosencrantz & Guildenstern Are Dead* (1967), 3.

123. Life is a tragedy wherein we sit as spectators for a while and then act our part in it. JONATHAN SWIFT, *Thoughts on Various Subjects* (1711).

124. Life is given to us, we earn it by giving it. RABINDRANATH TAGORE, *Stray Birds* (1916), 56.

125. Life, like a child, laughs, shaking its rattle of death as it runs. RABINDRANATH TAGORE, *Lover's Gift* (1918), 42.

126. Better a thousand times even a swiftly fading, ephemeral moment of life than the epoch-long unconsciousness of the stone. EDWIN WAY TEALE, *Autumn Across America* (1956), 8.

127. Life is a frail moth flying / Caught in the web of the years that pass. SARA TEASDALE, "Come," *Rivers to the Sea* (1915).

128. Now at last I have come to see what life is, / Nothing is ever ended, everything only begun, / And the brave victories that seem so splendid / Are never really won. SARA TEASDALE, "At Midnight," *Flame and Shadow* (1920).

129. Children, who play life, discern its true law and relations more clearly than men, who fail to live it worthily, but who think that they are wiser by experience, that is, by failure. THOREAU, "Where I Lived, and What I Lived For," *Walden* (1854).

130. Each person is born to one possession which outvalues all his others—his last breath. MARK TWAIN, "Pudd'nhead Wilson's New Calendar," *Following the Equator* (1897), 2.6.

131. The shortness of life cannot dissuade us from its pleasures, nor console us for its pains. VAUVENARGUES, *Reflections and Maxims* (1746), 324, tr. F. G. Stevens.

132. What is a great life if not a youthful idea executed by the man of mature years? ALFRED DE VIGNY, *Cinq-Mars* (1826), 20.

133. Whoever is not in his coffin and the dark grave let him know he has enough. WALT WHITMAN, "The Sleepers," 2, *Leaves of Grass* (1855–92).

134. Life imitates art far more than art imitates life. OSCAR WILDE, "The Decay of Lying," *Intentions* (1891).

135. Life is not governed by will or intention. Life is a question of nerves, and fibers, and slowly built-up cells in which thought hides itself and passion has its dreams. OSCAR WILDE, *The Picture of Dorian Gray* (1891), 19.

136. Life is an unanswered question, but

let's still believe in the dignity and importance of the question. TENNESSEE WILLIAMS, *Camino Real* (1953).

137. Most people's lives—what are they but trails of debris, each day more debris, more debris, long, long trails of debris with nothing to clean it all up but, finally, death. TENNESSEE WILLIAMS, *Suddenly Last Summer* (1958), 1.

138. Life is the greatest bargain; we get it for nothing. *Yiddish Proverbs* (1949), ed. Hanan J. Ayalti.

## 537. LIFE, STAGES OF

**See also 536. Life; 567. Maturity; 646. Old Age; 1064. Youth; 1065. Youth and Age**

1. Life is a child playing around your feet, a tool you hold firmly in your grip, a bench you sit down upon in the evening, in your garden. JEAN ANOUILH, *Antigone* (1942), tr. Lewis Galantière.

2. In the morning, we carry the world like Atlas; at noon, we stoop and bend beneath it; and at night, it crushes us flat to the ground. HENRY WARD BEECHER, *Proverbs from Plymouth Pulpit* (1887).

3. Man arrives as a novice at each age of his life. CHAMFORT, *Caractères et anecdotes* (1771), 576.

4. Every stage of human life, except the last, is marked out by certain and defined limits; old age alone has no precise and determinate boundary. CICERO, *De Senectute* (44 B.C.).

5. Youth is a blunder; manhood a struggle; old age a regret. BENJAMIN DISRAELI, *Coningsby* (1844), 3.1.

6. At twenty man is a peacock, at thirty a lion, at forty a camel, at fifty a serpent, at sixty a dog, at seventy an ape, at eighty nothing at all. BALTASAR GRACIÁN, *The Art of Worldly Wisdom* (1647), 276, tr. Joseph Jacobs.

7. At twenty the will rules; at thirty the intellect; at forty the judgment. BALTASAR GRACIÁN, *The Art of Worldly Wisdom* (1647), 298, tr. Joseph Jacobs.

8. There are but three events which concern men: birth, life, and death. They are unconscious of their birth, they suffer when they die, and they neglect to live. LA BRUYÈRE, *Characters* (1688), 11.48, tr. Henri Van Laun.

9. In the morn of life we are alert, we are heated in its noon, and only in its decline do we repose. WALTER SAVAGE LANDOR, "Menander and Epicurus," *Imaginary Conversations* (1824–53).

10. The four stages of man are infancy, childhood, adolescence and obsolescence. ART LINKLETTER, *A Child's Garden of Misinformation* (1965), 8.

11. As an infant, man is wrapped in his mother's womb; grown up, he is wrapped in custom; dead, he is wrapped in earth. MALAY PROVERB.

12. For the complete life, the perfect pattern includes old age as well as youth and maturity. W. SOMERSET MAUGHAM, *The Summing Up* (1938), 73.

13. We do not have a childhood, a maturity, an old age: several times during our lives we have our seasons, but their course is not well known: it is not clearly laid out. JULES RENARD, *Journal*, October 1905, ed. and tr. Louise Bogan and Elizabeth Roget.

14. Life is a disease; and the only difference between one man and another is the stage of the disease at which he lives. GEORGE BERNARD SHAW, *Back to Methuselah* (1921), 2.

## 538. LIFE AND DEATH

**See also 218. Death; 536. Life**

1. In the midst of life we are in death. The Order for the Burial of the Dead, *The Book of Common Prayer* (1549, 1789, 1928).

2. If a man know not life which he hath seen, how shall he know death, which he hath not seen? SAMUEL BUTLER (d. 1902), "Death," *Note-Books* (1912).

3. What is called a reason for living is also an excellent reason for dying. ALBERT CAMUS, "An Absurd Reasoning," *The Myth of Sisyphus* (1942), tr. Justin O'Brien.

4. Whatever lives is granted breath / But by the grace and sufferance of Death. COUNTEE CULLEN, "Song Dialogue," *On These I Stand* (1947).

5. All our life is but a going out to the place of execution, to death. JOHN DONNE, *Sermons*, No. 4, 1619.

6. The endless part of disintegration / Is that it will build again. RICHARD EBERHART, "The Wisdom of Insecurity," *Selected Poems 1930–1965* (1965).

7. The art of living well and the art of dying well are one. EPICURUS, Letter to Menoeceus (3rd c. B.C.), in *Letters, Principal Doctrines, and Vatican Sayings*, tr. Russel M. Geer.

8. Healthy children will not fear life if their elders have integrity enough not to fear death. ERIK H. ERIKSON, *Childhood and Society* (1950), 7.

9. Death is what men want when the anguish of living / is more than they can bear. EURIPIDES, *Hecuba* (c. 425 B.C.), tr. William Arrowsmith.

10. It is better that we live ever so / Miserably than die in glory. EURIPIDES, *Iphigenia in Aulis* (c. 405 B.C.), tr. Charles R. Walker.

11. Our final experience, like our first, is conjectural. We move between two darknesses. E. M. FORSTER, "People," *Aspects of the Novel* (1927).

12. The whole life of instinct serves the one end of bringing about death. SIGMUND FREUD, *Beyond the Pleasure Principle* (1920), tr. C. J. M. Hubback.

13. Life and death / Is cat and dog in this double bed of a world. CHRISTOPHER FRY, *A Phoenix Too Frequent* (1950).

14. Dying is as natural as living. THOMAS FULLER, M.D., *Gnomologia* (1732), 1348.

15. A good life fears not life nor death. THOMAS FULLER, M.D., *Gnomologia* (1732), 157.

16. I'm not afraid of death. It's the stake one puts up in order to play the game of life. JEAN GIRAUDOUX, *Amphitryon 38* (1929), 2, tr. Phyllis La Farge with Peter H. Judd.

17. Grieve not; though the journey of life be bitter, and the end unseen, there is no road which does not lead to an end. HĀFIZ, ghazals from the *Divan* (14th c.), 18, tr. Justin Huntly McCarthy.

18. Some people seem to think that death is the only reality in life. Others, happier and rightlier minded, see and feel that life is the true reality in death. JULIUS CHARLES HARE and AUGUSTUS WILLIAM HARE, *Guesses at Truth* (1827).

19. The most rational cure after all for the inordinate fear of death is to set a just value on life. WILLIAM HAZLITT, "On the Fear of Death," *Table Talk* (1821–22).

20. It matters not how a man dies but how he lives. The act of dying is not of importance, it lasts so short a time. SAMUEL JOHNSON, quoted in Boswell's *Life of Samuel Johnson*, Oct. 26, 1769.

21. Life and death appear more certainly ours than whatsoever else: and yet hardly can that be called ours, which comes without our knowledge, and goes without it. WALTER SAVAGE LANDOR, "Marcus Tullius and Quinctus Cicero," *Imaginary Conversations* (1824–53).

22. Our life is made by the death of others. LEONARDO DA VINCI, *Notebooks* (c. 1500), tr. Jean Paul Richter.

23. In the attempt to defeat death man has been inevitably obliged to defeat life, for the two are inextricably related. Life moves on to death, and to deny one is to deny the other. HENRY MILLER, "Creative Death," *The Wisdom of the Heart* (1941).

24. Long life, and short, are by death made all one; for there is no long, nor short, to things that are no more. MONTAIGNE, "That to study philosophy is to learn to die," *Essays* (1580–88), tr. Charles Cotton and W. C. Hazlitt.

25. Who that hath ever been / Could bear to be no more? / Yet who would tread again the scene / He trod through life before? JAMES MONTGOMERY, *The Falling Leaf* (1825).

26. Life is a great surprise. I do not see why death should not be an even greater one. VLADIMIR NABOKOV, "Commentary," *Pale Fire* (1962), 549.

27. A dead man is nothing more than a dead man, and a living man of the slightest pretensions is stronger than the dead man's memory. NAPOLEON I, *Maxims* (1804–15).

28. One wants to live, of course, indeed one only stays alive by virtue of the fear of death. GEORGE ORWELL, "How the Poor Die," *Shooting an Elephant* (1950).

29. The whole motley confusion of acts, omissions, regrets and hopes which is the life of each one of us finds in death, not meaning or explanation, but an end. OCTAVIO PAZ, *The Labyrinth of Solitude* (1950).

30. Death then, being the way and condition of life, we cannot love to live if we cannot bear to die. WILLIAM PENN, *Some Fruits of Solitude* (1693), 1.505.

31. There is silence that saith, "Ah me!" / There is silence that nothing saith; / One is the silence of life forlorn, / One the silence of death; / One is, and the other shall be. CHRISTINA ROSSETTI, "Golden Silences" (1882).

32. Death is but an instant, life a long torment. BERNARD JOSEPH SAURIN, *Beverlei* (1768), 5.5.

33. We are wrong in looking forward to death: in great measure it's past already. SENECA, *Letters to Lucilius* (1st c.), 1.2, tr. E. Phillips Barker.

34. You will die not because you're ill, but because you're alive. SENECA, *Letters to Lucilius* (1st c.), 78.6, tr. E. Phillips Barker.

35. One must take all one's life to learn how to live, and, what will perhaps make you wonder more, one must take all one's life to learn how to die. SENECA, *On the Shortness of Life* (1st c.).

36. The weariest and most loathed worldly life / That age, ache, penury, and imprisonment / Can lay on nature is a paradise / To what we fear of death. SHAKESPEARE, *Measure for Measure* (1604–05), 3.1.129.

37. Life does not cease to be funny when people die any more than it ceases to be serious when people laugh. GEORGE BERNARD SHAW, *The Doctor's Dilemma* (1913), 5.

38. Death is given in a kiss; the dearest kindnesses are fatal; and into this life, where one thing preys upon another, the child too often makes its entrance from the mother's corpse. ROBERT LOUIS STEVENSON, "Pan's Pipes" (1878).

39. Death's stamp gives value to the coin of life; making it possible to buy with life what is truly precious. RABINDRANATH TAGORE, *Stray Birds* (1916), 99.

40. Life is a coquetry / Of Death, which wearies me, / Too sure / Of the amour. FRANCIS THOMPSON, "To the Dead Cardinal of Westminster" (1892).

41. Whoever has lived long enough to find out what life is, knows how deep a debt of gratitude we owe to Adam, the first great benefactor of our race. He brought death into the world. MARK TWAIN, "Pudd'nhead Wilson's Calendar," *Pudd'nhead Wilson* (1894), 3.

42. Why is it that we rejoice at a birth and grieve at a funeral? It is because we are not the person involved. MARK TWAIN, "Pudd'nhead Wilson's Calendar," *Pudd'nhead Wilson* (1894), 9.

43. Pity is for the living, envy is for the dead. MARK TWAIN, "Pudd'nhead Wilson's New Calendar," *Following the Equator* (1897), 1.19.

44. Oh Death where is thy sting! It has none. But life has. MARK TWAIN, *Notebook* (1935).

45. Science says: "We must live," and seeks the means of prolonging, increasing, facilitating and amplifying life, of making it tolerable and acceptable; wisdom says: "We must die," and seeks how to make us die well. MIGUEL DE UNAMUNO, "Arbitrary Reflections," *Essays and Soliloquies* (1924), tr. J. E. Crawford Flitch.

46. Man has given a false importance to death / Any animal plant or man who dies / adds to Nature's compost heap / becomes the manure without which / nothing could grow nothing could be created / Death is simply part of the process. PETER WEISS, *Marat/Sade* (1964), 1.12, tr. Geoffrey Skelton and Adrian Mitchell.

47. Death is one moment, and life is so many of them. TENNESSEE WILLIAMS, *The Milk Train Doesn't Stop Here Anymore* (1963), 5.

### LIKING

**See 21. Affection; 22. Affinity; 719. Preference**

### 539. LIMITATIONS

**See also 339. Faults; 450. Immaturity; 455. Imperfection; 460. Inadequacy; 1040. Weakness**

1. Each of us has a day, more or less sad, more or less distant, when he has to accept, finally, the fact that he is a man. JEAN ANOUILH, *Antigone* (1942).

2. The humorous man recognizes that absolute purity, absolute justice, absolute logic and perfection are beyond human achievement and that men have been able to live happily for thousands of years in a state of genial frailty. BROOKS ATKINSON, "April 4," *Once Around the Sun* (1951).

3. Who ever is adequate? We all create situations each other can't live up to, then break our hearts at them because they

don't. ELIZABETH BOWEN, *The Death of the Heart* (1938), 3.1.

4. The common problem, yours, mine, every one's / Is—not to fancy what were fair in life / Provided it could be,—but, finding first / What may be, then find how to make it fair / Up to our means: a very different thing! ROBERT BROWNING, "Bishop Blougram's Apology," *Men and Women* (1855), 87.

5. A bird can roost but on one branch. A mouse can drink no more than its fill from a river. CHINESE PROVERB.

6. Men cease to interest us when we find their limitations. EMERSON, "Circles," *Essays: First Series* (1841).

7. I am not eternity, but a man; a part of the whole, as an hour is of the day. EPICTETUS, *Discourses* (2nd c.), 2.5, tr. Thomas W. Higginson.

8. Our accepting what we are must always inhibit our being what we ought to be. JOHN FOWLES, *The Magus* (1965), 27.

9. A good marksman may miss. THOMAS FULLER, M.D., *Gnomologia* (1732), 163.

10. The thing I am most aware of is my limits. And this is natural; for I never, or almost never, occupy the middle of my cage; my whole being surges toward the bars. ANDRÉ GIDE, *Journals*, Aug. 4, 1930, tr. Justin O'Brien.

11. We expect more of ourselves than we have any right to, in virtue of our endowments. OLIVER WENDELL HOLMES, SR., *Over the Teacups* (1891), 12.

12. We cannot all hope to combine the pleasing qualities of good looks, brains, and eloquence. HOMER, *Odyssey* (9th c. B.C.), 8, tr. E. V. Rieu.

13. It is of great use to the sailor to know the length of his line, though he cannot with it fathom all the depths of the ocean. JOHN LOCKE, *An Essay Concerning Human Understanding* (1690), 1.1.6.

14. O my soul, do not aspire to immortal life, but exhaust the limits of the possible. PINDAR, *Odes* (5th c. B.C.), Pythia 3.61.

15. A bull does not enjoy fame in two herds. RHODESIAN PROVERB.

16. Knowledge of what is possible is the beginning of happiness. GEORGE SANTAYANA, *Little Essays* (1920), 105, ed. Logan Pearsall Smith.

17. The best country is the one which has most. It is the same with people: no man is ever self-sufficient—there is sure to be something missing. SOLON (7th–6th c. B.C.), quoted in Herodotus' *Histories* (5th c. B.C.), 1.32, tr. Aubrey de Sélincourt.

18. Perhaps nobody ever accomplishes all that he feels lies in him to do; but nearly every one who tries his powers touches the walls of his being occasionally, and learns about how far to attempt to spring. CHARLES DUDLEY WARNER, "Third Study," *Backlog Studies* (1873).

## LIQUOR
See 266. Drinking

## 540. LISTENING
See also 185. Conversation; 273. Eavesdropping; 916. Speaking

1. The hearing ear is always found close to the speaking tongue. EMERSON, "Race," *English Traits* (1856).

2. We only consult the ear because the heart is wanting. PASCAL, *Pensées* (1670), 30, tr. W. F. Trotter.

3. A man who listens because he has nothing to say can hardly be a source of inspiration. The only listening that counts is that of the talker who alternately absorbs and expresses ideas. AGNES REPPLIER, "The Luxury of Conversation," *Compromises* (1904).

4. Give every man thine ear, but few thy voice. SHAKESPEARE, *Hamlet* (1600), 1.3.68.

5. The reason why we have two ears and only one mouth is that we may listen the more and talk the less. ZENO OF CITIUM (c. 300 B.C.), quoted in Diogenes Laertius' *Lives and Opinions of Eminent Philosophers* (3rd c. A.D.), tr. R. D. Hicks.

## 541. LITERALNESS

1. The letter killeth, but the spirit giveth life. *Bible*, 2 Corinthians 3:6.

## 542. LITERATURE
See also 91. Books and Reading; 1062. Writing and Writers

1. The unusual is only found in a very small percentage, except in literary crea-

tions, and that is exactly what makes literature. JULIO CORTÁZAR, *The Winners* (1960), 31, tr. Elaine Kerrigan.

2. The "greatness" of literature cannot be determined solely by literary standards though we must remember that whether it is literature or not can be determined only by literary standards. T. S. ELIOT, "Religion and Literature" (1935).

3. What is so wonderful about great literature is that it transforms the man who reads it towards the condition of the man who wrote, and brings to birth in us also the creative impulse. E. M. FORSTER, "Anonymity: An Enquiry," *Two Cheers for Democracy* (1951).

4. Reality is not an inspiration for literature. At its best, literature is an inspiration for reality. ROMAIN GARY, *New York Herald Tribune*, Jan. 13, 1960.

5. It is with noble sentiments that bad literature gets written. ANDRÉ GIDE, *Journal*, Sept. 2, 1940.

6. Literature flourishes best when it is half a trade and half an art. WILLIAM RALPH INGE, "The Victorian Age," *Outspoken Essays: Second Series* (1922).

7. The literary world is made up of little confederacies, each looking upon its own members as the lights of the universe; and considering all others as mere transient meteors, doomed soon to fall and be forgotten, while its own luminaries are to shine steadily on to immortality. WASHINGTON IRVING, "Literary Life," *Tales of a Traveller* (1824).

8. The land of literature is a fairy land to those who view it at a distance, but, like all other landscapes, the charm fades on a nearer approach, and the thorns and briars become visible. WASHINGTON IRVING, "Notoriety," *Tales of a Traveller* (1824).

9. The existence of good bad literature—the fact that one can be amused or excited or even moved by a book that one's intellect simply refuses to take seriously—is a reminder that art is not the same thing as cerebration. GEORGE ORWELL, "Good Bad Books," *Shooting an Elephant* (1950).

10. Literature was formerly an art and finance a trade: today it is the reverse. JOSEPH ROUX, *Meditations of a Parish Priest* (1886), 1.65, tr. Isabel F. Hapgood.

11. The illusion of art is to make one believe that great literature is very close to life, but exactly the opposite is true. Life is amorphous, literature is formal. FRANÇOISE SAGAN, interview, *Writers at Work: First Series* (1958).

12. The literary sensibility is geared to the timeless, that is, to the now only as an avenue by which all time can be reached. JOHN SIMON, "Should Albee Have Said 'No Thanks'?" *The New York Times*, Aug. 20, 1967.

13. Perversity is the muse of modern literature. SUSAN SONTAG, "Camus' Notebooks," *Against Interpretation* (1961).

14. No human being ever spoke of scenery for above two minutes at a time, which makes me suspect that we hear too much of it in literature. ROBERT LOUIS STEVENSON, "Talk and Talkers" (1882), 1.

15. Literature is the human activity that takes the fullest and most precise account of variousness, possibility, complexity, and difficulty. LIONEL TRILLING, preface, *The Liberal Imagination* (1950).

16. It is in literature that the concrete outlook of humanity receives its expression. ALFRED NORTH WHITEHEAD, *Science and the Modern World* (1925), 5.

17. Literature is the orchestration of platitudes. THORNTON WILDER, *Time*, Jan. 12, 1953.

## LOAN

See 94. Borrowing and Lending; 219. Debt

## LOGIC

See 778. Reason

## 543. LONDON

See also 287. England and Englishmen

1. London, that great cesspool into which all the loungers of the Empire are irresistibly drained. SIR ARTHUR CONAN DOYLE, *A Study in Scarlet* (1887).

2. When a man is tired of London, he is tired of life; for there is in London all that life can afford. SAMUEL JOHNSON, quoted in Boswell's *Life of Samuel Johnson*, Sept. 20, 1777.

3. Nursed amid her [London's] noise, her crowds, her beloved smoke—what have I been doing all my life, if I have not lent out

my heart with usury to such scenes? CHARLES LAMB, letter to Thomas Manning, Feb. 15, 1802.

## 544. LONELINESS

**See also 908. Solitude**

1. No one would choose a friendless existence on condition of having all the other things in the world. ARISTOTLE, *Nicomachean Ethics* (4th c. B.C.), 8.1, tr. J. A. K. Thomson.

2. Only in a house where one has learnt to be lonely does one have this solicitude for *things*. One's relation to them, the daily seeing or touching, begins to become love, and to lay one open to pain. ELIZABETH BOWEN, *The Death of the Heart* (1938), 2.2.

3. Who knows what true loneliness is—not the conventional word but the naked terror? To the lonely themselves it wears a mask. The most miserable outcast hugs some memory or some illusion. JOSEPH CONRAD, *Under Western Eyes* (1911), 1.2.

4. Whom the heart of man shuts out, / Sometimes the heart of God takes in, / And fences them all round about / With silence mid the world's loud din. JAMES RUSSELL LOWELL, "The Forlorn" (1842).

5. The most I ever did for you was to outlive you. / But that is much. EDNA ST. VINCENT MILLAY, untitled poem, *Make Bright the Arrows* (1940).

6. In solitude the lonely man is eaten up by himself, among crowds by the many. NIETZSCHE, *Miscellaneous Maxims and Opinions* (1879), 348, tr. Paul V. Cohn.

7. The lonely one offers his hand too quickly to whomever he encounters. NIETZSCHE, "On the Way of the Creator," *Thus Spoke Zarathustra* (1883–92), 1, tr. Walter Kaufmann.

8. Man's loneliness is but his fear of life. EUGENE O'NEILL, *Lazarus Laughed* (1927), 3.2.

9. Loneliness is bred of a mind that has grown earthbound. For the spirit has its homeland, which is the realm of the meaning of things. SAINT-EXUPÉRY, *The Wisdom of the Sands* (1948), 79, tr. Stuart Gilbert.

10. The body is a house of many windows: there we all sit, showing ourselves and crying on the passers-by to come and love us. ROBERT LOUIS STEVENSON, title essay, 4, *Virginibus Puerisque* (1881).

## 545. LONGEVITY

**See also 646. Old Age**

1. It isn't how long you stick around but what you put over while you are here. GEORGE ADE, "The Ripe Persimmon," *Hand-Made Fables* (1920).

2. Often a man who is very old in years has nothing beyond his age by which he can prove that he has lived a long time. ATHENODORUS (1st c. B.C.), quoted in Seneca's "On Peace of Mind," *Moral Essays* (1st c. A.D.), tr. Aubrey Stewart.

3. 'Tis very certain the desire of life / Prolongs it. BYRON, *Don Juan* (1819–24), 2.64.

4. Measurement of life should be proportioned rather to the intensity of the experience than to its actual length. THOMAS HARDY, *A Pair of Blue Eyes* (1873), 27.

5. Life protracted is protracted woe. SAMUEL JOHNSON, *The Vanity of Human Wishes* (1749).

6. The longest-lived and the shortest-lived man, when they come to die, lose one and the same thing. MARCUS AURELIUS, *Meditations* (2nd c.), 2.14, tr. Morris Hickey Morgan.

7. The wise man lives as long as he ought, not so long as he can. MONTAIGNE, "A custom of the Isle of Cea," *Essays* (1580–88), tr. Charles Cotton and W. C. Hazlitt.

8. They live ill who expect to live always. PUBLILIUS SYRUS, *Moral Sayings* (1st c. B.C.), 457, tr. Darius Lyman.

9. The man who has lived the longest is not he who has spent the greatest number of years, but he who has had the greatest sensibility of life. ROUSSEAU, *Émile* (1762), 1.

10. Nothing can be meaner than the anxiety to live on, to live on anyhow and in any shape. GEORGE SANTAYANA, *Winds of Doctrine* (1913).

11. Not a soul takes thought how well he may live—only how long: yet a good life might be everybody's, a long one can be nobody's. SENECA, *Letters to Lucilius* (1st c.), 22.17, tr. E. Phillips Barker.

12. It is not the years in your life but the life in your years that counts! ADLAI STEVENSON, "If I Were Twenty-One," *Coronet*, December 1955.

13. Every man desires to live long, but no man would be old. JONATHAN SWIFT, *Thoughts on Various Subjects* (1711).

14. It is vanity to desire a long life and to take no heed of a good life. THOMAS À KEMPIS, *The Imitation of Christ* (1426), 1.1.

## 546. LOSERS

See also 15. Advantage; 17. Adversity; 327. Failure

1. In a game, just losing is almost as satisfying as just winning. . . . In life the loser's score is always zero. W. H. AUDEN, "Postscript: The Frivolous and the Earnest," *The Dyer's Hand* (1962).

2. Those who had no share in the good fortunes of the mighty / Often have a share in their misfortunes. BERTOLT BRECHT, *The Caucasian Chalk Circle* (1944–45), 1.1, tr. Eric Bentley and Maja Apelman.

3. If a man once fall, all will tread upon him. THOMAS FULLER, M.D., *Gnomologia* (1732), 2662.

4. Some people are so fond of ill-luck that they run half-way to meet it. DOUGLAS JERROLD, "Meeting Troubles Half-way," *Wit and Opinions of Douglas Jerrold* (1859).

5. Nobody ever chooses the already unfortunate as objects of his loyal friendship. LUCAN, *On the Civil War* (1st c.), tr. Robert Graves.

6. When the world has once begun to use us ill, it afterwards continues the same treatment with less scruple or ceremony, as men do to a whore. JONATHAN SWIFT, *Thoughts on Various Subjects* (1711).

7. The shlemiehl lands on his back and bruises his nose. *Yiddish Proverbs* (1949), ed. Hanan J. Ayalti.

## 547. LOSS

See also 17. Adversity; 234. Deprivation; 327. Failure; 549. Love, Loss of; 631. Nostalgia

1. It is the image in the mind that binds us to our lost treasures, but it is the loss that shapes the image. COLETTE, "Literary Apprenticeship: 'Claudine,'" *Earthly Paradise* (1966), 2, ed. Robert Phelps.

2. He loseth nothing that keepeth God for his friend. THOMAS FULLER, M.D., *Gnomologia* (1732), 1976.

3. You must lose a fly to catch a trout. GEORGE HERBERT, *Jacula Prudentum* (1651).

4. A good man should and must / Sit rather down with loss than rise unjust. BEN JONSON, *Sejanus His Fall* (1603), 4.3.

5. Loss is nothing else but change, and change is Nature's delight. MARCUS AURELIUS, *Meditations* (2nd c.), 9.35, tr. Maxwell Staniforth.

6. Alack our life, so beautiful to see, / With how much ease life losest, in a day, / What many years with pain and toil amassed! PETRARCH, "Laura Dead," *Canzoniere* (1360), 229.

7. There are occasions when it is undoubtedly better to incur loss than to make gain. PLAUTUS, *The Captives* (3rd c. B.C.), 2.2.77, tr. Henry Thomas Riley.

8. That's a miserable and cursed word, to say I *had*, when what I have is nothing. PLAUTUS, *Rope* (3rd c. B.C.).

9. The loss which is unknown is no loss at all. PUBLILIUS SYRUS, *Moral Sayings* (1st c. B.C.), 38, tr. Darius Lyman.

10. Whatever you can lose, reckon of no account. PUBLILIUS SYRUS, *Moral Sayings* (1st c. B.C.), 191, tr. Darius Lyman.

11. He that is robbed, not wanting what is stol'n, / Let him not know't, and he's not robbed at all. SHAKESPEARE, *Othello* (1604–05), 3.3.342.

12. No man can lose what he never had. IZAAK WALTON, *The Compleat Angler* (1653), 1.5.

13. How blessings brighten as they take their flight! EDWARD YOUNG, *Night Thoughts* (1742–46), 2.602.

## 548. LOVE

See also 21. Affection; 22. Affinity; 118. Charity; 178. Constancy and Inconstancy; 195. Courtship; 282. Emotions; 348. Flirtation; 497. Intimacy; 508. Jealousy; 519. Kissing; 549. Love, Loss of; 550. Love, Unrequited; 551. Love and Hate; 552. Lovers; 668. Passion; 820. Romance; 851. Seduction; 885. Sex

1. Oh, love is real enough; you will find it someday, but it has one archenemy—and

that is life. JEAN ANOUILH, *Ardèle* (1948), 1, tr. Lucienne Hill.

2. Love is, above all, the gift of oneself. JEAN ANOUILH, *Ardèle* (1948), 2, tr. Lucienne Hill.

3. I think the only reason one loves, monsieur, is for his own pleasure. JEAN ANOUILH, *Cécile* (1949), tr. Luce and Arthur Klein.

4. I don't want people to love me. It makes for obligations. JEAN ANOUILH, *The Lark* (1955), 2, adapted by Lillian Hellman.

5. Among those whom I like or admire, I can find no common denominator, but among those whom I love, I can: all of them make me laugh. W. H. AUDEN, "Notes on the Comic," *The Dyer's Hand* (1962).

6. It is impossible to love and be wise. FRANCIS BACON, "Of Love," *Essays* (1625).

7. To love without criticism is to be betrayed. DJUNA BARNES, *Nightwood* (1937).

8. It's so difficult to know what the people we love really need. UGO BETTI, *Struggle Till Dawn* (1949), 1, tr. G. H. McWilliam.

9. Many waters cannot quench love, neither can floods drown it. *Bible*, Song of Solomon 8:7.

10. There is no fear in love; but perfect love casteth out fear. *Bible*, 1 John 4:18.

11. Who would give a law to lovers? / Love is unto itself a higher law. BOETHIUS, *The Consolation of Philosophy* (A.D. 524), 3.

12. To fall in love is to create a religion that has a fallible god. JORGE LUIS BORGES, "The Meeting in a Dream," *Other Inquisitions* (1952), tr. R. L. Simms.

13. There is only one way to be happy by means of the heart—to have none. PAUL BOURGET, *La Physiologie de l'amour moderne* (1890).

14. First love, with its frantic haughty imagination, swings its object clear of the everyday, over the rut of living, making him all looks, silences, gestures, attitudes, a burning phrase with no context. ELIZABETH BOWEN, *The House in Paris* (1935), 2.5.

15. When you love someone all your saved-up wishes start coming out. ELIZABETH BOWEN, *The Death of the Heart* (1938), 1.9.

16. The wish to lead out one's lover must be a tribal feeling; the wish to be seen as loved is part of one's self-respect. ELIZABETH BOWEN, *The Death of the Heart* (1938), 2.4.

17. Love is also like a coconut which is good while it's fresh, but you have to spit it out when the juice is gone, what's left tastes bitter. BERTOLT BRECHT, *Baal* (1926), 2, tr. Eric Bentley and Martin Esslin.

18. Whoso loves / Believes the impossible. ELIZABETH BARRETT BROWNING, *Aurora Leigh* (1856), 5.409.

19. O Lyric Love, half angel and half bird, / And all a wonder and a wild desire. ROBERT BROWNING, *The Ring and the Book* (1868–69), 1.

20. Eternal Love doth keep / In his complacent arms, the earth, the air, the deep. WILLIAM CULLEN BRYANT, "The Ages" (1821).

21. Love dies only when growth stops. PEARL S. BUCK, "What Shall I Tell My Daughter," *To My Daughters, With Love* (1967).

22. The more violent the love, the more violent the anger. *Burmese Proverbs* (1962), 453, ed. Hla Pe.

23. 'Tis sweet to know there is an eye will mark / Our coming, and look brighter when we come. BYRON, *Don Juan* (1819–24), 1.123.

24. Who hath not owned, with rapture-smitten frame, / The power of grace, the magic of a name? THOMAS CAMPBELL, *The Pleasures of Hope* (1799), 2.5.

25. Then fly betimes, for only they / Conquer Love that run away. THOMAS CAREW, "Conquest by Flight," *Poems* (1640).

26. Love is Nature's second sun. GEORGE CHAPMAN, *All Fools* (c. 1599), 1.1.

27. All thoughts, all passions, all delights, / Whatever stirs this mortal frame, / All are ministers of Love, / And feed his sacred flame. SAMUEL TAYLOR COLERIDGE, "Love" (1799).

28. Love is the admiration and cherishing of the amiable qualities of the beloved person, upon the condition of yourself being the object of their action. SAMUEL TAYLOR COLERIDGE, *Table Talk*, June 24, 1827.

29. Sympathy constitutes friendship; but in love there is a sort of antipathy, or opposing passion. Each strives to be the other, and both together make up one whole. SAMUEL TAYLOR COLERIDGE, *Table Talk*, Sept. 27, 1830.

30. Friendship often ends in love; but love in friendship—never. CHARLES CALEB COLTON, *Lacon* (1825), 2.83.

31. To love a thing means wanting it to live. CONFUCIUS, *Analects* (6th c. B.C.), 12.10, tr. Ch'u Chai and Winberg Chai.

32. Words are the weak support of cold indifference; love has no language to be heard. WILLIAM CONGREVE, *The Double-Dealer* (1694), 4.5.

33. If there's delight in love, 'tis when I see / That heart which others bleed for, bleed for me. WILLIAM CONGREVE, *The Way of the World* (1700), 3.12.

34. The object of Loving is to end Love. We achieve this through a series of unhappy love affairs or, without a death-rattle, through one that is happy. CYRIL CONNOLLY, *The Unquiet Grave* (1945), 1.

35. Love is a tyrant sparing none. CORNEILLE, *The Cid* (1636), 1.2, tr. Paul Landis.

36. Love lives on hope, and dies when hope is dead; / It is a flame which sinks for lack of fuel. CORNEILLE, *The Cid* (1636), 1.2, tr. Paul Landis.

37. Never love with all your heart, / It only ends in aching. COUNTEE CULLEN, "Song in Spite of Myself," *On These I Stand* (1947).

38. No man may be so cursed by priest or pope / but what the Eternal Love may still return / while any thread of green lives on in hope. DANTE, "Purgatorio," 3, *The Divine Comedy* (c. 1300–21), tr. John Ciardi.

39. Love alone / is the true seed of every merit in you, / and of all acts for which you must atone. DANTE, "Purgatorio," 17, *The Divine Comedy* (1300–21), tr. John Ciardi.

40. Unable are the Loved to die / For Love is Immortality. EMILY DICKINSON, poem (c. 1864).

41. Behold this little Bane— / The Boon of all alive— / As common as it is unknown / The name of it is Love. EMILY DICKINSON, poem (c. 1878).

42. Love is done when Love's begun, / Sages say, / But have Sages known? EMILY DICKINSON, poem (c. 1880).

43. Love, with very young people, is a heartless business. We drink at that age from thirst, or to get drunk; it is only later in life that we occupy ourselves with the individuality of our wine. ISAK DINESEN, "The Old Chevalier," *Seven Gothic Tales* (1934).

44. Without outward declarations, who can conclude an inward love? JOHN DONNE, *Sermons*, No. 21, 1623.

45. Love all love of other sights controls, / And makes one little room an everywhere. JOHN DONNE, "The Good-Morrow" (1633).

46. Love is a growing, or full constant light; / And his first minute, after noon, is night. JOHN DONNE, "A Lecture upon the Shadow," *Songs and Sonnets* (1633).

47. Love, all alike, no season knows, nor clime, / Nor hours, age, months, which are the rags of time. JOHN DONNE, "The Sun Rising," *Songs and Sonnets* (1633).

48. I am two fools, I know, for loving, and for saying so. JOHN DONNE, "The Triple Fool," *Songs and Sonnets* (1633).

49. Love built on beauty, soon as beauty, dies. JOHN DONNE, Elegy 2, "The Anagram" (1635).

50. Being got it [love] is a treasure sweet, / Which to defend, is harder than to get: / And ought not be profaned on either part, / For though 'tis got by chance, 'tis kept by art. JOHN DONNE, Elegy 17, "The Expostulation" (1635).

51. Where there is no love there is no sense either. DOSTOEVSKY, *Notes from Underground* (1864), 2.4, tr. Constance Garnett.

52. With love one can live even without happiness. DOSTOEVSKY, *Notes from Underground* (1864), 2.4, tr. Constance Garnett.

53. In order to love simply, it is necessary to know how to show love. DOSTOEVSKY, "Bookishness and Literacy," *Polnoye Sobraniye Sochinyeni (Complete Collected Works*, 1895), v. 9.

54. Pains of love be sweeter far / Than all other pleasures are. JOHN DRYDEN, *Tyrannic Love* (1669), 4.1.

55. Heaven be thanked, we live in such an age, / When no man dies for love, but on the stage. JOHN DRYDEN, Epilogue to *Mithridates* (1678).

56. Love reckons hours for months, and days for years; / And every little absence is an age. JOHN DRYDEN, *Amphitryon* (1690), 3.1.

57. Love, love, love. All th' wurruld is love. Soft an' sweet an' sticky it covers th' globe. FINLEY PETER DUNNE, "On the Power of Music," *Mr. Dooley On Making a Will* (1919).

58. The richest love is that which submits to the arbitration of time. LAWRENCE DURRELL, *Clea* (1960), 3.2.

59. Love compels cruelty / To those who do not understand love. T. S. ELIOT, *The Family Reunion* (1939), 2.2.

60. No love can be bound by oath or covenant to secure it against a higher love. EMERSON, "Circles," *Essays: First Series* (1841).

61. He that loveth maketh his own the grandeur he loves. EMERSON, "Compensation," *Essays: First Series* (1841).

62. Love is the bright foreigner, the foreign self. EMERSON, *Journals*, 1849.

63. They love too much that die for love. ENGLISH PROVERB.

64. Love must not touch the marrow of the soul. / Our affections must be breakable chains that we / can cast them off or tighten them. EURIPIDES, *Hippolytus* (428 B.C.), tr. David Grene.

65. Love is all we have, the only way / that each can help the other. EURIPIDES, *Orestes* (408 B.C.), tr. William Arrowsmith.

66. To love nothing is not to live; to love but feebly is to languish rather than live. FÉNELON, *À un homme du monde* (1699).

67. Pleasure of love lasts but a moment, / Pain of love lasts a lifetime. JEAN PIERRE CLARIS DE FLORIAN, *Célestine* (1842).

68. Love is a tyrant, / Resisted. JOHN FORD, *The Lover's Melancholy* (1629), 1.3.

69. Love is a great force in private life; it is indeed the greatest of all things; but love in public affairs does not work. E. M. FORSTER, "Tolerance," *Two Cheers for Democracy* (1951).

70. Love makes the time pass. Time makes love pass. FRENCH PROVERB.

71. Try to reason about love, and you will lose your reason. FRENCH PROVERB.

72. Erotic love begins with separateness, and ends in oneness. Motherly love begins with oneness, and leads to separateness. ERICH FROMM, *The Sane Society* (1955), 3.

73. Love is union with somebody, or something, outside oneself, under the condition of retaining the separateness and integrity of one's own self. ERICH FROMM, *The Sane Society* (1955), 3.

74. Love is often nothing but a favorable exchange between two people who get the most of what they can expect, considering their value on the personality market. ERICH FROMM, *The Sane Society* (1955), 5.

75. There is hardly any activity, any enterprise, which is started with such tremendous hopes and expectations, and yet which fails so regularly, as love. ERICH FROMM, *The Art of Loving* (1956), 1.

76. Immature love says: "I love you because I need you." Mature love says: "I need you because I love you." ERICH FROMM, *The Art of Loving* (1956), 2.

77. It seems that it is madder never to abandon one's self than often to be infatuated; better to be wounded, a captive and a slave, than always to walk in armor. MARGARET FULLER, *Summer on the Lakes* (1844), 5.

78. Love, the itch, and a cough cannot be hid. THOMAS FULLER, M.D., *Gnomologia* (1732), 3298.

79. There is more pleasure in loving than in being beloved. THOMAS FULLER, M.D., *Gnomologia* (1732), 4900.

80. What we call love is the desire to awaken and to keep awake in another's body, heart and mind, the responsibility of flattering, in our place, the self of which we are not very sure. PAUL GÉRALDY, *L'Homme et l'amour* (1951).

81. We must resemble each other a little in order to understand each other, but we must be a little different to love each other. PAUL GÉRALDY, *L'Homme et l'amour* (1951).

82. Love knows hidden paths. GERMAN PROVERB.

83. Even as love crowns you so shall he crucify you. Even as he is for your growth so is he for your pruning. KAHLIL GIBRAN, "On Love," *The Prophet* (1923).

84. Love is the irresistible desire to be desired irresistibly. LOUIS GINSBERG, reading at St. Mark's in the Bowery, April 1, 1968.

85. Agreement is never reached in love. The life of a wife and husband who love each other is never at rest. Whether the marriage is true or false, the marriage portion is the same: elemental discord. JEAN GIRAUDOUX, *Tiger at the Gates* (1935), 2, tr. Christopher Fry.

86. A life without love, without the presence of the beloved, is nothing but a mere magic-lantern show. We draw out slide after slide, swiftly tiring of each, and pushing it back to make haste for the next. GOETHE, *Elective Affinities* (1809), 27.

87. Friendship is a disinterested commerce between equals; love, an object intercourse between tyrants and slaves. OLIVER GOLDSMITH, *The Good-Natured Man* (1768), 1.

88. When one loves somebody, everything is clear—where to go, what to do—it all takes care of itself and one doesn't have to ask anybody about anything. MAXIM GORKY, *The Zykovs* (1914), 4.

89. 'Tis much to gain universal admiration; more, universal love. BALTASAR GRACIÁN, *The Art of Worldly Wisdom* (1647), 40, tr. Joseph Jacobs.

90. Love is a universal migraine, / A bright stain on the vision, / Blotting out reason. ROBERT GRAVES, "Symptoms of Love," *Collected Poems* (1961).

91. Words have no language which can utter the secrets of love; and beyond the limits of expression is the expounding of desire. HĀFIZ, ghazals from the *Divan* (14th c.), 46, tr. Justin Huntly McCarthy.

92. What is first love worth, except to prepare for a second? / What does second love bring? Only regret for the first. JOHN HAY, "Distichs" (1871?), 5.

93. Love is that condition in which the happiness of another person is essential to your own. ROBERT A. HEINLEIN, *Stranger in a Strange Land* (1961), 34.

94. Love is the true price of love. GEORGE HERBERT, *Jacula Prudentum* (1651).

95. The love we give away is the only love we keep. ELBERT HUBBARD, *The Note Book* (1927).

96. The supreme happiness of life is the conviction that we are loved. VICTOR HUGO, "Fantine," *Les Misérables* (1862), 5.4, tr. Charles E. Wilbour.

97. The word "love" bridges for us those chasms of momentary indifference and boredom which gape from time to time between even the most ardent lovers. ALDOUS HUXLEY, *The Olive Tree* (1937).

98. Love is an excuse for its own faults. ITALIAN PROVERB.

99. Love is like the measles; we all have to go through it. Also like the measles we take it only once. JEROME K. JEROME, "On Being in Love," *The Idle Thoughts of an Idle Fellow* (1889).

100. Love is too pure a light to burn long among the noisome gases that we breathe, but before it is choked out we may use it as a torch to ignite the cozy fire of affection. JEROME K. JEROME, "On Being in Love," *The Idle Thoughts of an Idle Fellow* (1889).

101. Love is the wisdom of the fool and the folly of the wise. SAMUEL JOHNSON, quoted in Birkbeck Hill's *Johnsonian Miscellanies* (1897), v. 2.

102. As selfishness and complaint pervert and cloud the mind, so love with its joy clears and sharpens the vision. HELEN KELLER, *My Religion* (1927).

103. Though a man excels in everything, unless he has been a lover his life is lonely, and he may be likened to a jewelled cup which can contain no wine. YOSHIDA KENKŌ, "The Consideration of Women," *The Harvest of Leisure (Tsure-Zure Gusa*, c. 1330–35), tr. Ryukichi Kurata.

104. Time, which strengthens friendship, weakens love. LA BRUYÈRE, *Characters* (1688), 4.4.

105. We perceive when love begins and when it declines by our embarrassment when alone together. LA BRUYÈRE, *Characters* (1688), 4.33, tr. Henri Van Laun.

106. Where love finds the soul he neglects the body, and only turns to it in his idleness as to an afterthought. Its best allurements are but the nuts and figs of the divine repast. WALTER SAVAGE LANDOR, "Scipio, Polybius, and Panaetius," *Imaginary Conversations* (1824–53).

107. True love is like ghosts, which everybody talks about and few have seen. LA ROCHEFOUCAULD, *Maxims* (1665).

108. When we are in love we often doubt that which we most believe. LA ROCHEFOUCAULD, *Maxims* (1665), tr. Kenneth Pratt.

109. The pleasure of love is in loving, and we are made happier by the passion that we experience than by that which we inspire. LA ROCHEFOUCAULD, *Maxims* (1665), tr. Kenneth Pratt.

110. There is no disguise which can hide love for long where it exists, or simulate it where it does not. LA ROCHEFOUCAULD, *Maxims* (1665), tr. Kenneth Pratt.

111. The restraints we impose on ourselves to refrain from loving are often more cruel than the severities of our beloved. LA ROCHEFOUCAULD, *Maxims* (1665), tr. Kenneth Pratt.

112. What the bloom is on fruit, the charm of novelty is to love; it imparts a

lustre which is easily effaced and which never returns. LA ROCHEFOUCAULD, *Maxims* (1665), tr. Kenneth Pratt.

113. Love, like fire, cannot subsist without constant impulse; it ceases to live from the moment it ceases to hope or to fear. LA ROCHEFOUCAULD, *Maxims* (1665), tr. Kenneth Pratt.

114. Love, all agreeable as it is, charms more by the fashion in which it displays itself, than by its own true merit. LA ROCHEFOUCAULD, *Maxims* (1665), tr. Kenneth Pratt.

115. The truest comparison we can make of love is to liken it to a fever; we have no more power over the one than the other, either as to its violence or duration. LA ROCHEFOUCAULD, *Maxims* (1665), tr. Kenneth Pratt.

116. In love deceit nearly always goes further than mistrust. LA ROCHEFOUCAULD, *Maxims* (1665), tr. Kenneth Pratt.

117. Sometimes we are less unhappy in being deceived by those we love, than in being undeceived by them. LA ROCHEFOUCAULD, *Maxims* (1665), tr. Kenneth Pratt.

118. Love should be practiced like Lent, secretly and dumbly. PARIS LEARY, "Onan," *A Controversy of Poets* (1965), ed. Paris Leary and Robert Kelly.

119. Him that I love, I wish to be / Free— / Even from me. ANNE MORROW LINDBERGH, "Even—," *The Unicorn and Other Poems, 1935–55* (1956).

120. There is no harvest for the heart alone; / The seed of love must be / Eternally / Resown. ANNE MORROW LINDBERGH, "Second Sowing," *The Unicorn and Other Poems, 1935–1955* (1956).

121. True love is but a humble, low-born thing, / And hath its food served up in earthen ware. JAMES RUSSELL LOWELL, "Love" (1840).

122. That love for one, from which there doth not spring / Wide love for all, is but a worthless thing. JAMES RUSSELL LOWELL, "Sonnet 3" (1840).

123. I am of this mind, that both might and malice, deceit and treachery, all perjury, any impiety may lawfully be committed in love, which is lawless. JOHN LYLY, *Euphues: The Anatomy of Wit* (1579).

124. For all who move / In the mortal sun / Know halfway warm / Is better than freezing, / As half a love / Is better than none. PHYLLIS MC GINLEY, "Lesson for Beginners," *The Love Letters of Phyllis McGinley* (1954).

125. The souls of all our brethren are ever hovering about us, craving for a caress, and only waiting for the signal. MAURICE MAETERLINCK, "The Invisible Goodness," *The Treasure of the Humble* (1896), tr. Alfred Sutro.

126. Love is simple to understand if you haven't got a mind soft and full of holes. It's a crutch, that's all, and there isn't a one of us doesn't need a crutch. NORMAN MAILER, *Barbary Shore* (1951), 19.

127. He who loves the more is the inferior and must suffer. THOMAS MANN, "Tonio Kröger" (1903), *Death in Venice*, tr. H. T. Lowe-Porter.

128. It is love, not reason, that is stronger than death. THOMAS MANN, *The Magic Mountain* (1924), 6.7, tr. H. T. Lowe-Porter.

129. We don't love qualities, we love persons; sometimes by reason of their defects as well as of their qualities. JACQUES MARITAIN, *Reflections on America* (1958), 3.

130. Who ever loved, that loved not at first sight? CHRISTOPHER MARLOWE, "Hero and Leander" (1598), 1.

131. It takes two to make a love affair and a man's meat is too often a woman's poison. W. SOMERSET MAUGHAM, *The Summing Up* (1938), 52.

132. We are not the same persons this year as last; nor are those we love. It is a happy chance if we, changing, continue to love a changed person. W. SOMERSET MAUGHAM, *The Summing Up* (1938), 77.

133. Love is not always blind and there are few things that cause greater wretchedness than to love with all your heart someone who you know is unworthy of love. W. SOMERSET MAUGHAM, *The Summing Up* (1938), 77.

134. Human love is often but the encounter of two weaknesses. FRANÇOIS MAURIAC, "All Soul's Day," *Cain, Where Is Your Brother?* (1962).

135. The most disgusting cad in the world is the man who, on grounds of decorum and morality, avoids the game of love. He is one who puts his own ease and security above the most laudable of philanthropies. H. L. MENCKEN, *Prejudices: Second Series* (1920), 10.

136. Prepare, / You lovers, to know Love a thing of moods: / Not like hard life, of laws. GEORGE MEREDITH, *Modern Love* (1862), 10.

137. He that would eat of love must eat it where it hangs. EDNA ST. VINCENT MILLAY, "Never May the Fruit Be Plucked," *The Harp-Weaver* (1923).

138. Love is not all: it is not meat nor drink / Nor slumber nor a roof against the rain; / Nor yet a floating spar to men that sink. EDNA ST. VINCENT MILLAY, *Fatal Interview* (1931), 30.

139. Can one ever remember love? It's like trying to summon up the smell of roses in a cellar. You might see a rose, but never the perfume. ARTHUR MILLER, *After the Fall* (1964).

140. Love refines / The thoughts, and heart enlarges, hath his seat / In reason, and is judicious, is the scale / By which to heavenly love thou mayest ascend. MILTON, *Paradise Lost* (1667), 8.589.

141. There is something inexpressibly charming in falling in love and, surely, the whole pleasure lies in the fact that love isn't lasting. MOLIÈRE, *Don Juan* (1665), 1, tr. John Wood.

142. In love, 'tis no other than frantic desire for that which flies from us. MONTAIGNE, "Of friendship," *Essays* (1580–88), tr. Charles Cotton and W. C. Hazlitt.

143. There's nothing half so sweet in life / As love's young dream. THOMAS MOORE, "Love's Young Dream," *Irish Melodies* (1807–35).

144. Alas! how light a cause may move / Dissension between hearts that love! THOMAS MOORE, "The Light of the Harem," *Lalla Rookh* (1817).

145. To love, that's the point—what matters whom? / What does the bottle matter provided we can be drunk? ALFRED DE MUSSET, "La Coupe et les lèvres," *Premières poésies* (1829–35).

146. The only victory in love is flight. NAPOLEON I, *Maxims* (1804–15).

147. Love is the emotion that a woman feels always for a poodle dog and sometimes for a man. GEORGE JEAN NATHAN, "General Conclusions about the Coarse Sex," *The Theatre, the Drama, the Girls* (1921).

148. A broken heart is a monument to a love that will never die; fulfillment is a monument to a love that is already on its deathbed. GEORGE JEAN NATHAN, "Attitude toward Love and Marriage," *The Autobiography of an Attitude* (1925).

149. Love is an emotion experienced by the many and enjoyed by the few. GEORGE JEAN NATHAN, "Attitude toward Love and Marriage," *The Autobiography of an Attitude* (1925).

150. A man reserves his true and deepest love not for the species of woman in whose company he finds himself electrified and enkindled, but for that one in whose company he may feel tenderly drowsy. GEORGE JEAN NATHAN, "The Ultimately Desirable Woman," *The Theatre Book of the Year, 1949–1950*.

151. Love is more afraid of change than destruction. NIETZSCHE, *Miscellaneous Maxims and Opinions* (1879), 280, tr. Paul V. Cohn.

152. There is always some madness in love. But there is also always some reason in madness. NIETZSCHE, "On Reading and Writing," *Thus Spoke Zarathustra* (1883–92), 1, tr. Walter Kaufmann.

153. When a man is in love he endures more than at other times; he submits to everything. NIETZSCHE, *The Antichrist* (1888), 23, tr. Anthony M. Ludovici.

154. I am the least difficult of men. All I want is boundless love. FRANK O'HARA, title poem, *Meditations in an Emergency* (1967).

155. [Love:] A game of secret, cunning stratagems, in which only the fools who are fated to lose reveal their true aims or motives—even to themselves. EUGENE O'NEILL, *More Stately Mansions* (1964), 2.1.

156. If you'd be loved, be worthy to be loved. OVID, *The Art of Love* (c. A.D. 8), 2, tr. J. Lewis May.

157. Love's dominion, like a king's, admits of no partition. OVID, *The Art of Love* (c. A.D. 8), 3, tr. J. Lewis May.

158. Love is a driver, bitter and fierce if you fight and resist him, / Easy-going enough once you acknowledge his power. OVID, *The Loves* (c. A.D. 8), 1.2, tr. Rolfe Humphries.

159. Love is a naked child: do you think he has pockets for money? OVID, *The Loves* (c. A.D. 8), 1.10, tr. Rolfe Humphries.

160. Love fed fat soon turns to boredom. OVID, *The Loves* (c. A.D. 8), 2.19, tr. Rolfe Humphries.

161. Every love's the love before / In a

duller dress. DOROTHY PARKER, "Summary," *Death and Taxes* (1931).

162. We conceal it from ourselves in vain —we must always love something. In those matters seemingly removed from love, the feeling is secretly to be found, and man cannot possibly live for a moment without it. PASCAL, *Discours sur les passions de l'amour* (1653).

163. We never, then, love a person, but only qualities. PASCAL, *Pensées* (1670), 323, tr. W. F. Trotter.

164. In one sense, the opposite of fear is courage, but in the dynamic sense the opposite of fear is love, whether this be love of man or love of justice. ALAN PATON, "The Challenge of Fear," *Saturday Review*, Sept. 9, 1967.

165. 'Tis never for their wisdom that one loves the wisest, or for their wit that one loves the wittiest; 'tis for benevolence and virtue and honest fondness one loves people. HESTER LYNCH PIOZZI, letter to Fanny Burney, 1781.

166. [Love is] the joy of the good, the wonder of the wise, the amazement of the gods; desired by those who have no part in him, and precious to those who have the better part in him. PLATO, *The Symposium* (4th c. B.C.), tr. Benjamin Jowett.

167. The greatest love is a mother's; then comes a dog's; then comes a sweetheart's. POLISH PROVERB.

168. Love, free as air at sight of human ties, / Spreads his light wings, and in a moment flies. ALEXANDER POPE, "Eloisa to Abelard" (1717), 74.

169. Cupid is naked and does not like artifices contrived by beauty. PROPERTIUS, *Elegies* (c. 28–c. 16 B.C.), 1.2.8.

170. We are ordinarily so indifferent to people that when we have invested one of them with the possibility of giving us joy, or suffering, it seems as if he must belong to some other universe, he is imbued with poetry. MARCEL PROUST, *Remembrance of Things Past: Swann's Way* (1913–27).

171. There can be no peace of mind in love, since the advantage one has secured is never anything but a fresh starting-point for further desires. MARCEL PROUST, *Remembrance of Things Past: Within a Budding Grove* (1913–27), tr. C. K. Scott-Moncrieff.

172. Those whose suffering is due to love -e, as we say of certain invalids, their own physicians. MARCEL PROUST, *Remembrance of Things Past: Within a Budding Grove* (1913–27), tr. C. K. Scott-Moncrieff.

173. Indeed, among the lesser auxiliaries to success in love, an absence, the declining of an invitation to dinner, an unintentional, unconscious harshness are of more service than all the cosmetics and fine clothes in the world. MARCEL PROUST, *Remembrance of Things Past: The Guermantes Way* (1913–27), tr. C. K. Scott-Moncrieff.

174. A god could hardly love and be wise. PUBLILIUS SYRUS, *Moral Sayings* (1st c. B.C.), 25, tr. Darius Lyman.

175. Love, like a tear, rises in the eye and falls upon the breast. PUBLILIUS SYRUS, *Moral Sayings* (1st c. B.C.), 42, tr. Darius Lyman.

176. When you are in love you are not wise; or, when you are wise you are not in love. PUBLILIUS SYRUS, *Moral Sayings* (1st c. B.C.), 816, tr. Darius Lyman.

177. None love, but they who wish to love. RACINE, *Britannicus* (1669), 3, tr. Paul Landis and Robert Henderson.

178. Love is not dumb. The heart speaks many ways. RACINE, *Britannicus* (1669), 3, tr. Paul Landis and Robert Henderson.

179. There is need of variety in sex, but not in love. THEODOR REIK, *Of Love and Lust* (1957), 1.1.5.

180. The man who has never made a fool of himself in love will never be wise in love. THEODOR REIK, *Of Love and Lust* (1957), 1.3.14.

181. Beyond the wounds of the child and the scars of the man, there is something in the heart of love itself that makes love pathetic. PHILIP RIEFF, "Sexuality and Domination," *Freud: The Mind of the Moralist* (1959).

182. Love consists in this, that two solitudes protect and border and salute each other. RAINER MARIA RILKE, *Letters to a Young Poet*, May 14, 1904, tr. M. D. Herter Norton.

183. For one human being to love another: that is perhaps the most difficult of all our tasks, the ultimate, the last test and proof, the work for which all other work is but preparation. RAINER MARIA RILKE, *Letters to a Young Poet*, May 14, 1904, tr. M. D. Herter Norton.

184. To be loved means to be consumed. To love is to give light with inexhaustible

oil. To be loved is to pass away, to love is to endure. RAINER MARIA RILKE, *The Notebooks of Malte Laurids Brigge* (1910), tr. M. D. Herter Norton.

185. Those who are loved live poorly and in danger. Ah, that they might surmount themselves and become lovers. Around those who love is sheer security. No one casts suspicion on them any more, and they themselves are not in a position to betray themselves. RAINER MARIA RILKE, *The Notebooks of Malte Laurids Brigge* (1910), tr. M. D. Herter Norton.

186. Love is not love until love's vulnerable. THEODORE ROETHKE, "The Dream," *The Collected Verse of Theodore Roethke* (1961).

187. Love is a mystery which, when solved, evaporates. The same holds for music. NED ROREM, "Random Notes from a Diary," *Music from Inside Out* (1967).

188. To love is to choose. JOSEPH ROUX, *Meditations of a Parish Priest* (1886), 9.1, tr. Isabel F. Hapgood.

189. As long as we love, we lend to the beloved object qualities of mind and heart which we deprive him of when the day of misunderstanding arrives. JOSEPH ROUX, *Meditations of a Parish Priest* (1886), 9.25, tr. Isabel F. Hapgood.

190. Love is something far more than desire for sexual intercourse; it is the principal means of escape from the loneliness which afflicts most men and women throughout the greater part of their lives. BERTRAND RUSSELL, "The Place of Love in Human Life," *Marriage and Morals* (1929).

191. Love should be a tree whose roots are deep in the earth, but whose branches extend into heaven. BERTRAND RUSSELL, "Sex and Individual Well-Being," *Marriage and Morals* (1929).

192. Life has taught us that love does not consist in gazing at each other but in looking outward together in the same direction. SAINT-EXUPÉRY, *Wind, Sand, and Stars* (1939), 9.6, tr. Lewis Galantière.

193. The invisible path of gravity liberates the stone. The invisible slope of love liberates man. SAINT-EXUPÉRY, *Flight to Arras* (1942), 23, tr. Lewis Galantière.

194. If you tame me, then we shall need each other. To me, you will be unique in all the world. To you, I shall be unique in all the world. SAINT-EXUPÉRY, *The Little Prince* (1943), 21, tr. Katherine Woods.

195. Love does not cause suffering: what causes it is the sense of ownership, which is love's opposite. SAINT-EXUPÉRY, *The Wisdom of the Sands* (1948), 49, tr. Stuart Gilbert.

196. There is a warning love sends and the cost of it is never written till long afterward. CARL SANDBURG, "Explanations of Love," *Complete Poems* (1950).

197. Love, whether sexual, parental, or fraternal, is essentially sacrificial, and prompts a man to give his life for his friends. GEORGE SANTAYANA, *The Life of Reason: Reason in Religion* (1905–06), 14.

198. Not to believe in love is a great sign of dulness. There are some people so indirect and lumbering that they think all real affection must rest on circumstantial evidence. GEORGE SANTAYANA, *The Life of Reason: Reason in Society* (1905–06), 1.

199. When we love animals and children too much, we love them at the expense of men. JEAN-PAUL SARTRE, *The Words* (1964), 1.

200. Love rules the court, the camp, the grove, / And men below, and saints above; / For love is heaven, and heaven is love. SIR WALTER SCOTT, *The Lay of the Last Minstrel* (1805), 3.2.

201. True love's the gift which God has given / To man alone beneath the heaven. SIR WALTER SCOTT, *The Lay of the Last Minstrel* (1805), 5.8.

202. You can end love more easily than you can moderate it. SENECA THE ELDER, *Controversiae* (1st c.), 2.

203. Love is a spirit all compact of fire. SHAKESPEARE, *Venus and Adonis* (1593), 149.

204. They do not love that do not show their love. SHAKESPEARE, *The Two Gentlemen of Verona* (1594–95), 1.2.31.

205. The course of true love never did run smooth. SHAKESPEARE, *A Midsummer Night's Dream* (1595–96), 1.1.134.

206. Love looks not with the eyes, but with the mind; / And therefore is winged Cupid painted blind. SHAKESPEARE, *A Midsummer Night's Dream* (1595–96), 1.1.234.

207. Love's best habit is a soothing tongue. SHAKESPEARE, *The Passionate Pilgrim* (1599), 1.11.

208. If thou rememb'rest not the slightest folly / That ever love did make thee run

into, / Thou hast not loved. SHAKESPEARE, *As You Like It* (1599–1600), 2.4.33.

209. I may command where I adore. SHAKESPEARE, *Twelfth Night* (1599–1600), 2.5.115.

210. Love sought is good, but given unsought, is better. SHAKESPEARE, *Twelfth Night* (1599–1600), 3.1.168.

211. Base men being in love have then a nobility in their natures more than is native to them. SHAKESPEARE, *Othello* (1604–05), 2.1.218.

212. There's beggary in the love that can be reckoned. SHAKESPEARE, *Antony and Cleopatra* (1606–07), 1.1.15.

213. All love is sweet, / Given or returned. Common as light is love, / And its familiar voice wearies not ever. SHELLEY, *Prometheus Unbound* (1818–19), 2.5.

214. One word / Frees us of all the weight and pain of life: / That word is love. SOPHOCLES, *Oedipus at Colonus* (401 B.C.), tr. Robert Fitzgerald.

215. Where there is love, there is pain. SPANISH PROVERB.

216. Love is like war: you begin when you like and leave off when you can. SPANISH PROVERB.

217. We cease loving ourselves if no one loves us. MME DE STAËL, quoted by Sainte-Beuve in *Portraits de femmes* (1832–48).

218. A very small degree of hope is sufficient to cause the birth of love. STENDHAL, *On Love* (1822), 3, tr. H. B. V., under direction of C. K. Scott-Moncrieff.

219. If one is sure of a woman's love one asks one's self if she is more or less beautiful; if one is in doubt as to her feelings one has no time to think of her appearance. STENDHAL, *On Love* (1822), 17, tr. H. B. V., under direction of C. K. Scott-Moncrieff.

220. To be loved at first sight, a man should have at the same time something to respect and something to pity in his face. STENDHAL, *On Love* (1822), 21, tr. H. B. V., under direction of C. K. Scott-Moncrieff.

221. Is it not by love alone that we succeed in penetrating to the very essence of a being? IGOR STRAVINSKY, *An Autobiography* (1936), 5.

222. Let the dead have the immortality of fame, but the living the immortality of love. RABINDRANATH TAGORE, *Stray Birds* (1916), 279.

223. Love is an endless mystery, / for it has nothing else to explain it. RABINDRANATH TAGORE, *Fireflies* (1928).

224. Love remains a secret even when spoken, / for only a lover truly knows that he is loved. RABINDRANATH TAGORE, *Fireflies* (1928).

225. Love's gift cannot be given, / it waits to be accepted. RABINDRANATH TAGORE, *Fireflies* (1928).

226. The loving are the daring. BAYARD TAYLOR, *The Song of the Camp*.

227. O, beauty, are you not enough? / Why am I crying after love? SARA TEASDALE, "Spring Night," *Rivers to the Sea* (1915).

228. Take love when love is given, / But never think to find it / A sure escape from sorrow / Or a complete repose. SARA TEASDALE, "Day's Ending," *Dark of the Moon* (1926).

229. He that shuts Love out, in turn shall be / Shut out from Love, and on her threshold lie / Howling in the outer darkness. ALFRED, LORD TENNYSON, "To—" (1832).

230. 'Tis better to have loved and lost / Than never to have loved at all. ALFRED, LORD TENNYSON, "In Memoriam A. H. H." (1850), 27.

231. Love is the only gold. ALFRED, LORD TENNYSON, *Becket* (1884), 4.1.

232. For you to ask advice on the rules of love is no better than to ask advice on the rules of madness. TERENCE, *The Eunuch* (161 B.C.), tr. Robert Graves.

233. Love is a great thing, a great good in every wise; it alone maketh light every heavy thing and beareth evenly every uneven thing. THOMAS À KEMPIS, *The Imitation of Christ* (1426), 2.6.

234. There is no remedy for love but to love more. THOREAU, *Journal*, July 25, 1839.

235. The Love-god inflames / more fiercely / those he sees are reluctant to surrender. TIBULLUS, *Elegies* (1st c. B.C.), 1.8, tr. Hubert Creekmore.

236. One cannot be strong without love. For love is not an irrelevant emotion; it is the blood of life, the power of reunion of the separated. PAUL TILLICH, *The Eternal Now* (1963), 3.13.2.

237. If so many men, so many minds, certainly so many hearts, so many kinds of love. LEO TOLSTOY, *Anna Karenina* (1873–76), 2.7, tr. Constance Garnett.

238. Love is like those shabby hotels in

which all the luxury is in the lobby. PAUL JEAN TOULET, *Le Carnet de M. du Paur, homme public* (1898).

239. The absolute value of love makes life worth while, and so makes Man's strange and difficult situation acceptable. Love cannot save life from death; but it can fulfill life's purpose. ARNOLD J. TOYNBEE, "Why and How I Work," *Saturday Review*, April 5, 1969.

240. Love is the child of illusion and the parent of disillusion. MIGUEL DE UNAMUNO, "Love, Suffering, Pity and Personality," *Tragic Sense of Life* (1913), tr. J. E. Crawford Flitch.

241. Love is an act of endless forgiveness, a tender look which becomes a habit. PETER USTINOV, *Christian Science Monitor*, Dec. 9, 1958.

242. Love has various lodgings; the same word does not always signify the same thing. VOLTAIRE, "Abuse of Words," *Philosophical Dictionary* (1764).

243. Love has features which pierce all hearts, he wears a bandage which conceals the faults of those beloved. He has wings, he comes quickly and flies away the same. VOLTAIRE, "Fable," *Philosophical Dictionary* (1764).

244. Whatever pains disease may bring / Are but the tangy seasoning / To Love's delicious fare. RICHARD WILBUR, "Pangloss's Song: A Comic-Opera Lyric," *Advice to a Prophet* (1961).

245. When one is in love one begins by deceiving one's self. And one ends by deceiving others. That is what the world calls a romance. OSCAR WILDE, *A Woman of No Importance* (1893), 3.

246. Each man kills the thing he loves, / By each let this be heard, / Some do it with a bitter look, / Some with a flattering word. / The coward does it with a kiss, / The brave man with a sword! OSCAR WILDE, *The Ballad of Reading Gaol* (1898), 1.7.

247. Love is an energy which exists of itself. It is its own value. THORNTON WILDER, *Time*, Feb. 3, 1958.

248. The biggest of all differences in this world is between the ones that had or have pleasure in love and those that haven't and hadn't any pleasure in love, but just watched with sick envy. TENNESSEE WILLIAMS, *Sweet Bird of Youth* (1959), 1.2.

249. Love is / unworldly / and nothing / comes of it but love. WILLIAM CARLOS WILLIAMS, "Rain," *Selected Poems* (1949).

250. You must love him, ere to you / He will seem worthy of your love. WILLIAM WORDSWORTH, "A Poet's Epitaph" (1799).

251. A pity beyond all telling / Is in the heart of love. WILLIAM BUTLER YEATS, "The Pity of Love" (1893).

252. Love is sweet, but tastes best with bread. *Yiddish Proverbs* (1949), ed. Hanan J. Ayalti.

## 549. LOVE, LOSS OF

**See also 299. Estrangement; 470. Infidelity; 547. Loss; 550. Love, Unrequited; 786. Rejection**

1. It is obviously quite difficult to be no longer loved when we are still in love, but it is incomparably more painful to be loved when we ourselves no longer love. GEORGES COURTELINE, *La Philosophie de G. Courteline* (1917).

2. Hunger stops love, or, if not hunger, Time. CRATES (4th c. B.C.), quoted in Diogenes Laertius' *Lives and Opinions of Eminent Philosophers* (3rd. c. A.D.), tr. R. D. Hicks.

3. The loss of love is a terrible thing; / They lie who say that death is worse. COUNTEE CULLEN, "Variations on a Theme (The Loss of Love)," *On These I Stand* (1947).

4. We are never so defenceless against suffering as when we love, never so helplessly unhappy as when we have lost our loved object or its love. SIGMUND FREUD, *Civilization and Its Discontents* (1930), 2, tr. James Strachey.

5. In love, the one who is cured first is cured the best. LA ROCHEFOUCAULD, *Maxims* (1665), tr. Kenneth Pratt.

6. It is impossible to love a second time what we have really ceased to love. LA ROCHEFOUCAULD, *Maxims* (1665), tr. Kenneth Pratt.

7. There are scarcely any who are not ashamed of being beloved, when they love no more themselves. LA ROCHEFOUCAULD, *Maxims* (1665), tr. Kenneth Pratt.

8. A girl (and perhaps the same thing applies to a boy) would find life less broken apart after a misguided love affair if she could feel that she had been sinful rather than a fool. PHYLLIS MC GINLEY, "In De-

fense of Sin," *The Province of the Heart* (1959).

9. Women's hearts are like old china, none the worse for a break or two. W. SOMERSET MAUGHAM, *Lady Frederick* (1907), 1.

10. The great tragedy of life is not that men perish, but that they cease to love. W. SOMERSET MAUGHAM, *The Summing Up* (1938), 77.

11. After all, my erstwhile dear, / My no longer cherished, / Need we say it was no love, / Just because it perished? EDNA ST. VINCENT MILLAY, "Passer Mortuus Est," *Second April* (1921).

12. 'Tis not love's going hurts my days, / But that it went in little ways. EDNA ST. VINCENT MILLAY, "The Spring and the Fall," *The Harp-Weaver* (1923).

13. A broken hand works, but not a broken heart. PERSIAN PROVERB.

14. It is not because other people are dead that our affection for them grows faint, it is because we ourself are dying. MARCEL PROUST, *Remembrance of Things Past: The Sweet Cheat Gone* (1913–27), tr. C. K. Scott-Moncrieff.

15. The heart that can no longer / Love passionately, must with fury hate. RACINE, *Andromache* (1667), 1, tr. Robert Henderson.

16. Where love fails we espy all faults. JOHN RAY, *English Proverbs* (1670).

17. When love begins to sicken and decay / It useth an enforced ceremony. / There are no tricks in plain and simple faith. SHAKESPEARE, *Julius Caesar* (1599–1600), 4.2.20.

18. Love is not love / Which alters when it alteration finds. SHAKESPEARE, *Sonnets* (1609), 116.2.

## 550. LOVE, UNREQUITED
**See also 786. Rejection**

1. A mighty pain to love it is, / And 'tis a pain that pain to miss; / But of all pains, the greatest pain / It is to love, but love in vain. ABRAHAM COWLEY, "Gold," *From Anacreon* (1656).

2. It is the missed opportunity that counts, and in a love that vainly yearns from behind prison bars you have perchance the love supreme. SAINT-EXUPÉRY, *The Wisdom of the Sands* (1948), 45, tr. Stuart Gilbert.

## 551. LOVE AND HATE
**See also 410. Hatred; 548. Love**

1. Every one has conscience enough to hate; few have religion enough to love. HENRY WARD BEECHER, *Proverbs from Plymouth Pulpit* (1887).

2. Better is a dinner of herbs where love is, than a stalled ox and hatred therewith. *Bible*, Proverbs 15:17.

3. When I love most, Love is disguised / In Hate; and when Hate is surprised / In Love, then I hate most. ROBERT BROWNING, "Noon," *Pippa Passes* (1841).

4. When Love is suppressed Hate takes its place. HAVELOCK ELLIS, *On Life and Sex: Essays of Love and Virtue* (1937), 1.

5. Hatred is blind, as well as love. THOMAS FULLER, M.D., *Gnomologia* (1732), 1805.

6. Love that is ignorant and hatred have almost the same ends. BEN JONSON, "Explorata," *Timber* (1640).

7. Hatred paralyzes life; love releases it. Hatred confuses life; love harmonizes it. Hatred darkens life; love illumines it. MARTIN LUTHER KING, JR., *Strength to Love* (1963), 14.3.

8. If we judge of love by its usual effects, it resembles hatred more than friendship. LA ROCHEFOUCAULD, *Maxims* (1665), tr. Kenneth Pratt.

9. As the best wine doth make the sharpest vinegar, so the deepest love turneth to the deadliest hate. JOHN LYLY, *Euphues: The Anatomy of Wit* (1579).

10. Oh, I have loved him too much to feel no hate for him. RACINE, *Andromache* (1667), 2.1.

11. We love without reason, and without reason we hate. JEAN-FRANÇOIS REGNARD, *Les Folies amoureuses* (1704), 2.2.

12. Hatred, as well as love, renders its votaries credulous. ROUSSEAU, *Confessions* (1766–70), 5.

13. Hatred which is entirely conquered by love passes into love, and love on that account is greater than if it had not been preceded by hatred. SPINOZA, *Ethics* (1677), 3, tr. Andrew Boyle.

14. As love, if love be perfect, casts out fear, / So hate, if hate be perfect, casts out fear. ALFRED, LORD TENNYSON, "Merlin and Vivien," *Idylls of the King* (1859).

## 552. LOVERS

See also 548. Love; 549. Love, Loss of; 550. Love, Unrequited; 551. Love and Hate

1. Pity the selfishness of lovers: it is brief, a forlorn hope; it is impossible. ELIZABETH BOWEN, *The Death of the Heart* (1938), 2.4.

2. Everything disturbs an absent lover. CERVANTES, *Don Quixote* (1605–15), 1.2.6, tr. Peter Motteux and John Ozell.

3. Lovers are commonly industrious to make themselves uneasy. CERVANTES, *Don Quixote* (1605–15), 1.3.10, tr. Peter Motteux and John Ozell.

4. The lover is made happier by his love than the object of his affection. EMERSON, *Journals*, 1832.

5. All mankind love a lover. EMERSON, "Love," *Essays: First Series* (1841).

6. There is desire / in those who love to hear about their loved ones' pains. EURIPIDES, *Helen* (412 B.C.), tr. Richmond Lattimore.

7. Lovers who love truly do not write down their happiness. ANATOLE FRANCE, *The Crime of Sylvestre Bonnard* (1881), 1, tr. Lafcadio Hearn.

8. When a love relationship is at its height there is no room left for any interest in the environment; a pair of lovers are sufficient to themselves. SIGMUND FREUD, *Civilization and Its Discontents* (1930), 5, tr. James Strachey.

9. A lover without indiscretion is no lover at all. THOMAS HARDY, *The Hand of Ethelberta* (1876).

10. Wisely a woman prefers to a lover a man who neglects her. / This one may love her some day, some day the lover will not. JOHN HAY, "Distichs" (1871?), 1.

11. The reason why lovers are never weary of one another is this: they are always talking of themselves. LA ROCHEFOUCAULD, *Maxims* (1665).

12. Scratch a lover, and find a foe! DOROTHY PARKER, "Ballade of Great Weariness," *Enough Rope* (1926), 2.

13. Of all affliction taught a lover yet, / 'Tis sure the hardest science to forget. ALEXANDER POPE, "Eloisa to Abelard" (1717).

14. An angry lover tells himself many lies. PUBLILIUS SYRUS, *Moral Sayings* (1st c. B.C.), 19, tr. Darius Lyman.

15. Lovers know what they want, but not what they need. PUBLILIUS SYRUS, *Moral Sayings* (1st c. B.C.), 21, tr. Darius Lyman.

16. The lover is a monotheist who knows that other people worship different gods but cannot himself imagine that there could be other gods. THEODOR REIK, *Of Love and Lust* (1957), 1.3.1.

17. The lover knows much more about absolute good and universal beauty than any logician or theologian, unless the latter, too, be lovers in disguise. GEORGE SANTAYANA, *The Life of Reason: Reason in Society* (1905–06), 1.

18. They say all lovers swear more performance than they are able and yet reserve an ability that they never perform, vowing more than the perfection of ten and discharging less than the tenth part of one. SHAKESPEARE, *Troilus and Cressida* (1601–02), 3.2.91.

19. The anger of lovers renews their love. TERENCE, *The Woman of Andros* (166 B.C.).

## LOWER CLASS

See 675. The People

## 553. LOYALTY

See also 178. Constancy and Inconstancy; 489. Integrity

1. Loyalty is still the same, / Whether it win or lose the game; / True as a dial to the sun, / Although it be not shined upon. SAMUEL BUTLER (d. 1680), *Hudibras* (1663), 3.2.

2. When young we are faithful to individuals, when older we grow more loyal to situations and to types. CYRIL CONNOLLY, *The Unquiet Grave* (1945), 2.

3. An ounce of loyalty is worth a pound of cleverness. ELBERT HUBBARD, *The Note Book* (1927).

## LUCK

See 358. Fortune

## 554. LUXURY

See also 310. Excess; 322. Extravagance; 744. Prosperity

1. Minds, like bodies, will often fall into a pimpled, ill-conditioned state from mere ex-

cess of comfort. CHARLES DICKENS, *Barnaby Rudge* (1841), 7.

2. Our expense is almost all for conformity. It is for cake that we all run in debt. EMERSON, *Journals*, 1840.

3. The lust for comfort, that stealthy thing that enters the house a guest, and then becomes a host, and then a master. KAHLIL GIBRAN, "On Houses," *The Prophet* (1923).

4. Even luxury finds a zest in change. HORACE, *Odes* (23–c. 15 B.C.), 3.29.

5. Luxury . . . is a way of / being ignorant, comfortable / An approach to the open market / of least information. Where theories / Can thrive, under heavy tarpaulins / without being cracked by ideas. LE ROI JONES, "Political Poem," *The Dead Lecturer* (1964).

6. They must know but little of mankind who can imagine that, after they have been once seduced by luxury, they can ever renounce it. ROUSSEAU, *A Discourse on Political Economy* (1758), tr. G. D. H. Cole.

7. Luxury either comes of riches or makes them necessary; it corrupts at once rich and poor, the rich by possession and the poor by covetousness. ROUSSEAU, *The Social Contract* (1762), 3.4, tr. G. D. H. Cole.

8. What nature requires is obtainable, and within easy reach. It's for the superfluous we sweat. SENECA, *Letters to Lucilius* (1st c.), 4.11, tr. E. Phillips Barker.

9. Men first feel necessity, then look for utility, next attend to comfort, still later amuse themselves with pleasure, thence grow dissolute in luxury, and finally go mad and waste their substance. GIAMBATTISTA VICO, *The New Science* (1725–44), 1.2.

10. Give me the luxuries of life and I will willingly do without the necessities. FRANK LLOYD WRIGHT, quoted in his obituary, April 9, 1959.

## LYING

See 329. Falsehood

# M

## MACHINES

See 960. Technology

## 555. MADNESS

See also 620. Neurosis; 836. Sanity

1. We are all born mad. Some remain so. SAMUEL BECKETT, *Waiting for Godot* (1952), 2.

2. "Mad" is a term we use to describe a man who is obsessed with one idea and nothing else. UGO BETTI, *Struggle Till Dawn* (1949), 1, tr. G. H. McWilliam.

3. All of us are mad. If it weren't for the fact every one of us is slightly abnormal, there wouldn't be any point in giving each person a separate name. UGO BETTI, *The Fugitive* (1953), 2, tr. G. H. McWilliam.

4. Each of us keeps, battened down inside himself, a sort of lunatic giant—impossible socially, but full-scale—and it's the knockings and batterings we sometimes hear in each other that keep our intercourse from utter banality. ELIZABETH BOWEN, *The Death of the Heart* (1938), 3.6.

5. If a sane dog fights a mad dog, it's the sane dog's ear that is bitten off. *Burmese Proverbs* (1962), 436, ed. Hla Pe.

6. The wily lunatic is lost if through the narrowest crack he allows a sane eye to peer into his locked universe and thus profane it. COLETTE, "Freedom," *Earthly Paradise* (1966), 2, ed. Robert Phelps.

7. There is less harm to be suffered in being mad among madmen than in being sane all by oneself. DENIS DIDEROT, *Supplement to Bougainville's "Voyage"* (1796).

8. There is a pleasure sure / In being mad which none but madmen know. JOHN DRYDEN, *The Spanish Friar* (1681), 2.1.

9. Sanity is very rare: every man almost, and every woman, has a dash of madness. EMERSON, *Journals*, 1836.

10. What is madness / To those who only observe, is often wisdom / To those to whom it happens. CHRISTOPHER FRY, *A Phoenix Too Frequent* (1950).

11. The world is so full of simpletons and madmen, that one need not seek them in a madhouse. GOETHE, quoted in Johann Peter Eckermann's *Conversations with Goethe*, March 17, 1830.

12. Better mad with the rest of the world than wise alone. BALTASAR GRACIÁN, *The Art of Worldly Wisdom* (1647), 133, tr. Joseph Jacobs.

13. Everyone is more or less mad on one point. RUDYARD KIPLING, "On the Strength of a Likeness," *Plain Tales from the Hills* (1888).

14. Sometimes accidents happen in life from which we have need of a little madness to extricate ourselves successfully. LA ROCHEFOUCAULD, *Maxims* (1665), tr. Kenneth Pratt.

15. Here's an object more of dread / Than aught the grave contains—/ A human form with reason fled, / While wretched life remains. ABRAHAM LINCOLN, letter to Andrew Johnson, Sept. 6, 1846.

16. The great proof of madness is the disproportion of one's designs to one's means. NAPOLEON I, *Maxims* (1804–15).

17. Men are so necessarily mad, that not to be mad would amount to another form of madness. PASCAL, *Pensées* (1670), 414, tr. W. F. Trotter.

18. The madman thinks the rest of the world crazy. PUBLILIUS SYRUS, *Moral Sayings* (1st c. B.C.), 386, tr. Darius Lyman.

19. Whom Fortune wishes to destroy she first makes mad. PUBLILIUS SYRUS, *Moral Sayings* (1st c. B.C.), 911, tr. Darius Lyman.

20. Our occasional madness is less wonderful than our occasional sanity. GEORGE SANTAYANA, *Interpretations of Poetry and Religion* (1900).

21. A body seriously out of equilibrium, either with itself or with its environment, perishes outright. Not so a mind. Madness and suffering can set themselves no limit. GEORGE SANTAYANA, *The Life of Reason: Reason in Common Sense* (1905–06), 2.

22. The lunatic, the lover, and the poet / Are of imagination all compact. SHAKESPEARE, *A Midsummer Night's Dream* (1595–96), 5.1.7.

23. When we remember that we are all mad, the mysteries disappear and life stands explained. MARK TWAIN, *Notebook* (1935).

24. What is madness? To have erroneous perceptions and to reason correctly from them. VOLTAIRE, "Madness," *Philosophical Dictionary* (1764).

## 556. MAILMEN

See also 532. Letters

1. Neither snow, nor rain, nor heat, nor gloom of night stays these couriers from the swift completion of their appointed rounds. Inscription on the General Post Office, New York City, adapted from Herodotus' *The Histories* (5th c. B.C.).

## 557. MALICE

See also 293. Envy; 898. Slander

1. A truth that's told with bad intent / Beats all the Lies you can invent. WILLIAM BLAKE, "Auguries of Innocence" (1800–10).

2. I am convinced that we have a degree of delight, and that no small one, in the real misfortunes and pains of others. EDMUND BURKE, *A Philosophical Inquiry into the Origin of Our Ideas of the Sublime and Beautiful* (1756), 1.14.

3. I don't think we injye other people's sufferin', Hinnissy. It isn't acshally injyement. But we feel betther f'r it. FINLEY PETER DUNNE, "Enjoyment," *Observations by Mr. Dooley* (1902).

4. He that scattereth thorns must not go barefoot. THOMAS FULLER, M.D., *Gnomologia* (1732), 2289.

5. Man's life is a warfare against the malice of men. BALTASAR GRACIÁN, *The Art of Worldly Wisdom* (1647), 13, tr. Joseph Jacobs.

6. Malice often takes the garb of truth. WILLIAM HAZLITT, "On Depth and Superficiality," *The Plain Speaker* (1826).

7. The malicious have a dark happiness. VICTOR HUGO, "Fantine," *Les Misérables* (1862), 5.9, tr. Charles E. Wilbour.

8. In the misfortune of our best friends we always discover something not unpleasing to us. LA ROCHEFOUCAULD, *Maxims* (1665), tr. Kenneth Pratt.

9. Man loves malice, but not against one-eyed men nor the unfortunate, but against the fortunate and proud. MARTIAL, *Epigrams* (A.D. 86).

10. Malicious tongues spread their poison abroad and nothing here below is proof against them. MOLIÈRE, *Tartuffe* (1664), 5, tr. John Wood.

11. Do not trust a malicious man because you have long been intimate with him. A serpent will still bite, though it may have been kept and tended a long time. *Panchatantra* (c. 5th c.), 1, tr. Franklin Edgerton.

12. When malice has reason on its side it becomes proud, and parades reason in all its splendour. PASCAL, *Pensées* (1670), 407, tr. W. F. Trotter.

13. Often on earth the gentlest heart is fain / To feed and banquet on another's woe. PETRARCH, "Laura Dead," *Canzoniere* (1360), 294.

14. Malice swallows the greater part of its own venom. PUBLILIUS SYRUS, *Moral Sayings* (1st c. B.C.), 1030, tr. Darius Lyman.

15. If there were in the world today any large number of people who desired their own happiness more than they desired the unhappiness of others, we could have a paradise in a few years. BERTRAND RUSSELL, *The New York Times*, May 18, 1961.

16. The cat always leaves her mark upon her friend. SPANISH PROVERB.

17. One likes people much better when they're battered down by a prodigious siege of misfortune than when they triumph. VIRGINIA WOOLF, *A Writer's Diary*, Aug. 13, 1921.

## MAN, AGES OF

See 537. Life, Stages of

## MANAGEMENT

See 13. Administration; 313. Executives

## 558. MANKIND

See also 431. Human Nature; 536. Life

1. Man *becomes* man only by the intelligence, but he *is* man only by the heart. HENRI FRÉDÉRIC AMIEL, *Journal*, April 7, 1851, tr. Mrs. Humphry Ward.

2. Man is a passion which brings a will into play, which works an intelligence. HENRI FRÉDÉRIC AMIEL, *Journal*, Dec. 28, 1880, tr. Mrs. Humphry Ward.

3. Man, when perfected, is the best of animals, but, when separated from law and justice, he is the worst of all. ARISTOTLE, *Politics* (4th c. B.C.), 1.2, tr. Benjamin Jowett.

4. Know, man hath all which Nature hath, but more, / And in that *more* lie all his hopes of good. MATTHEW ARNOLD, "To an Independent Preacher" (1849).

5. Man is a creature adapted for life under circumstances which are very narrowly limited. A few degrees of temperature more or less, a slight variation in the composition of air, the precise suitability of food, make all the difference between health and sickness, between life and death. SIR ROBERT S. BALL, *The Story of the Heavens* (1885).

6. Is a man a salvage at heart, skinned o'er with fragile Manners? Or is salvagery but a faint taint in the natural man's gentility, which erupts now and again like pimples on an angel's arse? JOHN BARTH, *The Sot-Weed Factor* (1960), 3.12.

7. We drink without thirst and we make love anytime, madame; only this distinguishes us from the other animals. BEAUMARCHAIS, *The Marriage of Figaro* (1784), 2.21.

8. Man is at the bottom an animal, midway a citizen, and at the top divine. But the climate of this world is such that few ripen at the top. HENRY WARD BEECHER, *Proverbs from Plymouth Pulpit* (1887).

9. So God created man in his own image, in the image of God created he him; male and female created he them. *Bible*, Genesis 1:27.

10. Man, n. An animal so lost in rapturous contemplation of what he thinks he is as to overlook what he indubitably ought to be. AMBROSE BIERCE, *The Devil's Dictionary* (1881–1911).

11. O man! thou feeble tenant of an hour, / Debased by slavery, or corrupt by power, / Who knows thee well must quit thee with disgust, / Degraded mass of animated dust! / Thy love is lust, thy friendship all a cheat, / Thy smiles hypocrisy, thy word deceit! / By nature vile, ennobled but by name, / Each kindred brute might bid thee blush for shame. BYRON, "On the Monument of a Newfoundland Dog" (1808).

12. What characterizes man is the richness and subtlety, the variety and versatility of his nature. ERNST CASSIRER, "The Crisis in Man's Knowledge of Himself," *An Essay on Man* (1944).

13. Man is an exception, whatever else he is. If he is not the image of God, then he is a disease of the dust. G. K. CHESTERTON, "Wine When It Is Red," *All Things Considered* (1908).

14. A wonderful fact to reflect upon, that every human creature is constituted to be

that profound secret and mystery to every other. CHARLES DICKENS, *A Tale of Two Cities* (1859), 1.3.

15. What is man, when you come to think upon him, but a minutely set, ingenious machine for turning, with infinite artfulness, the red wine of Shiraz into urine? ISAK DINESEN, "The Dreamers," *Seven Gothic Tales* (1934).

16. Man is not only a contributary creature, but a total creature; he does not only make one, but he is all; he is not a piece of the world, but the world itself; and next to the glory of God, the reason why there is a world. JOHN DONNE, *Sermons*, No. 35, 1625.

17. Men are but children of a larger growth. JOHN DRYDEN, *All for Love* (1678), 4.1.

18. The majority of mankind is lazy-minded, incurious, absorbed in vanities, and tepid in emotion, and is therefore incapable of either much doubt or much faith. T. S. ELIOT, introduction to Pascal's *Pensées* (1931).

19. Man is physically as well as metaphysically a thing of shreds and patches, borrowed unequally from good and bad ancestors, and a misfit from the start. EMERSON, "Beauty," *The Conduct of Life* (1860).

20. It were no slight attainment could we merely fulfil what the nature of man implies. EPICTETUS, *Discourses* (2nd c.), 2.9, tr. Thomas W. Higginson.

21. Man is Nature's sole mistake! W. S. GILBERT, *Princess Ida* (1884), 2.

22. Human beings are like timid punctuation marks sprinkled among the incomprehensible sentences of life. JEAN GIRAUDOUX, *Siegfried* (1928), 2, tr. Phyllis La Farge with Peter H. Judd.

23. It is because nations tend to stupidity and baseness that mankind moves so slowly; it is because individuals have a capacity for better things that it moves at all. GEORGE GISSING, "Spring," *The Private Papers of Henry Ryecroft* (1903).

24. Man is a simple being. And however rich, varied, and unfathomable he may be, the cycle of his situations is soon run through. GOETHE, quoted in Johann Peter Eckermann's *Conversations with Goethe*, May 1, 1825.

25. Mankind are earthen jugs with spirits in them. NATHANIEL HAWTHORNE, *American Note-Books*, 1842.

26. Each man carries the vestiges of his birth – the slime and eggshells of his primeval past – with him to the end of his days. Some never become human, remaining frog, lizard, ant. Some are human above the waist, fish below. HERMANN HESSE, prologue to *Demian* (1919), tr. Michael Roloff and Michael Lebeck.

27. I am a human being: Do not fold, spindle or mutilate. Hippy button slogan.

28. Among all creatures that breathe on earth and crawl on it / there is not anywhere a thing more dismal than man is. HOMER, *Iliad* (9th c. B.C.), 17.446, tr. Richmond Lattimore.

29. Man as we know him is a poor creature; but he is half-way between an ape and a god, and he is travelling in the right direction. WILLIAM RALPH INGE, "Confessio Fidei," *Outspoken Essays: Second Series* (1922).

30. The Family of Man is more than three billion strong. It lives in more than one hundred nations. Most of its members are not white. Most of them are not Christians. Most of them know nothing about free enterprise, or due process of law or the Australian ballot. JOHN F. KENNEDY, address, Protestant Council of New York City, Nov. 8, 1963.

31. [Man] is the only one in whom the instinct of life falters long enough to enable it to ask the question "Why?" JOSEPH WOOD KRUTCH, "The Genesis of a Mood," *The Modern Temper* (1929).

32. Man would be *other*wise. That is the essence of the specifically human. ANTONIO MACHADO, *Juan de Mairena* (1943), 44, tr. Ben Belitt.

33. Whatever profits man, that is the truth. In him all nature is comprehended, in all nature only he is created, and all nature only for him. He is the measure of all things, and his welfare is the sole and single criterion of truth. THOMAS MANN, *The Magic Mountain* (1924), 6.3, tr. H. T. Lowe-Porter.

34. i suppose the human race / is doing the best it can / but hells bells thats / only an explanation / its not an excuse. DON MARQUIS, "archy says," *Archy Does His Part* (1935).

35. Man, in the ideal, is so noble and so sparkling, such a grand and glowing creature, that over any ignominious blemish in him all his fellows should run to throw their

costliest robes. HERMAN MELVILLE, *Moby Dick* (1851), 26.

36. Man is a beautiful machine that works very badly. He is like a watch of which the most that can be said is that its cosmetic effect is good. H. L. MENCKEN, *Minority Report* (1956), 20.

37. Man, in good earnest, is a marvelous vain, fickle, and unstable subject, and on whom it is very hard to form any certain and uniform judgment. MONTAIGNE, "That men by various ways arrive at the same end," *Essays* (1580–88), tr. Charles Cotton and W. C. Hazlitt.

38. Every man carries the entire form of human condition. MONTAIGNE, "Of repentance," *Essays* (1580–88), tr. Charles Cotton and W. C. Hazlitt.

39. I have never seen greater monster or miracle in the world than myself. MONTAIGNE, "Of cripples," *Essays* (1580–88), tr. Charles Cotton and W. C. Hazlitt.

40. Alas for this mad melancholy beast man! What phantasies invade it, what paroxysms of perversity, hysterical senselessness, and mental bestiality break out immediately, at the very slightest check on its being the beast of action. NIETZSCHE, *The Genealogy of Morals* (1887), 2.22, tr. Horace B. Samuel.

41. For in fact what is man in nature? A Nothing in comparison with the Infinite, an All in comparison with Nothing, a mean between nothing and everything. PASCAL, *Pensées* (1670), 72, tr. W. F. Trotter.

42. What a chimera then is man! What a novelty! What a monster, what a chaos, what a contradiction, what a prodigy! Judge of all things, imbecile worm of the earth; depository of truth, a sink of uncertainty and error; the pride and refuse of the universe! PASCAL, *Pensées* (1670), 434, tr. W. F. Trotter.

43. There are three classes of men – lovers of wisdom, lovers of honor, lovers of gain. PLATO, *The Republic* (4th c. B.C.), 9, tr. Benjamin Jowett.

44. It is exciting and emancipating to believe we are one of nature's latest experiments, but what if the experiment is unsuccessful? V. S. PRITCHETT, "The Scientific Romances," *The Living Novel & Later Appreciations* (1964).

45. A man has many parts, he is virtually everything, and you are free to select in him that part which pleases you. SAINT-EXUPÉRY, *The Wisdom of the Sands* (1948), 96, tr. Stuart Gilbert.

46. The mass of mankind is divided into two classes, the Sancho Panzas who have a sense for reality, but no ideals, and the Don Quixotes with a sense for ideals, but mad. GEORGE SANTAYANA, preface to *Interpretations of Poetry and Religion* (1900).

47. The world could get along very well without literature; it could get along even better without man. JEAN-PAUL SARTRE, "Qu'est-ce que la littérature?" *Situations* (1947–49), v. 2.

48. Lord, what fools these mortals be! SHAKESPEARE, *A Midsummer Night's Dream* (1595–96), 3.2.115.

49. What a piece of work is man! how noble in reason! how infinite in faculties! in form and moving how express and admirable! in action how like an angel! in apprehension how like a god! the beauty of the world! the paragon of animals! SHAKESPEARE, *Hamlet* (1600), 2.2.315.

50. A creed is a rod, / And a crown is of night; / But this thing is God, / To be man with thy might. ALGERNON CHARLES SWINBURNE, "Hertha," *Songs Before Sunrise* (1871).

51. The fish in the water is silent, the animal on the earth is noisy, the bird in the air is singing. / But Man has in him the silence of the sea, the noise of the earth and the music of the air. RABINDRANATH TAGORE, *Stray Birds* (1916), 43.

52. I am a man; I consider nothing human alien to me. TERENCE, *The Self-Tormentor* (163 B.C.).

53. Man has gone long enough, or even too long, without being man enough to face the simple truth that the trouble with man is Man. JAMES THURBER, "The Trouble with Man is Man," *Lanterns and Lances* (1961).

54. The noblest work of God? Man. Who found it out? Man. MARK TWAIN, *Autobiography* (1924), v. 2, ed. A. B. Paine.

55. We should expect the best and the worst from mankind, as from the weather. VAUVENARGUES, *Reflections and Maxims* (1746), 102, tr. F. G. Stevens.

56. We're all of us guinea pigs in the laboratory of God. Humanity is just a work in progress. TENNESSEE WILLIAMS, *Camino Real* (1953), 12.

## 559. MANNERS

**See also 112. Ceremony; 194. Courtesy; 210. Custom; 376. Gentlemen; 389. Good Breeding; 406. Handshake; 743. Propriety; 907. Society, Polite; 955. Tact**

1. Manners are the hypocrisy of a nation. BALZAC, quoted in André Gide's *Journals*, 1911, tr. Justin O'Brien.

2. Manners maketh man. Yes, but they make woman still more. SAMUEL BUTLER (d. 1902), "Higgledy-Piggledy," *Note-Books* (1912).

3. Society is smoothed to that excess, / That manners hardly differ more than dress. BYRON, *Don Juan* (1819–24), 13.94.

4. Manners must adorn knowledge and smooth its way through the world. LORD CHESTERFIELD, *Letters*, July 1, 1748.

5. Good manners are the settled medium of social, as specie is of commercial, life; returns are equally expected for both. LORD CHESTERFIELD, *Letters to His Son*, Dec. 25, 1753.

6. We are justified in enforcing good morals, for they belong to all mankind; but we are not justified in enforcing good manners, for good manners always mean our own manners. G. K. CHESTERTON, "Limericks and Counsels of Perfection," *All Things Considered* (1908).

7. There is nothing settled in manners, but the laws of behavior yield to the energy of the individual. EMERSON, "Manners," *Essays: Second Series* (1844).

8. Manners are the happy ways of doing things; each once a stroke of genius or of love, now repeated and hardened into usage. EMERSON, "Behavior," *The Conduct of Life* (1860).

9. Manners make the fortune of the ambitious youth. EMERSON, "Behavior," *The Conduct of Life* (1860).

10. Fine manners need the support of fine manners in others. EMERSON, "Behavior," *The Conduct of Life* (1860).

11. Manners require time, as nothing is more vulgar than haste. EMERSON, "Behavior," *The Conduct of Life* (1860).

12. A man without ceremony had need of great merit in its place. THOMAS FULLER, M.D., *Gnomologia* (1732), 315.

13. A bad manner spoils everything, even reason and justice; a good one supplies everything, gilds a No, sweetens truth, and adds a touch of beauty to old age itself. BALTASAR GRACIÁN, *The Art of Worldly Wisdom* (1647), 14, tr. Joseph Jacobs.

14. Neither affect nor despise etiquette: he cannot be great who is great at such little things. BALTASAR GRACIÁN, *The Art of Worldly Wisdom* (1647), 184, tr. Joseph Jacobs.

15. Under bad manners, as under graver faults, lies very commonly an overestimate of our special individuality, as distinguished from our generic humanity. OLIVER WENDELL HOLMES, SR., *The Professor at the Breakfast Table* (1860), 6.

16. It is certain that our manners and customs go for more in life than our qualities. The price that we pay for civilization is the fine yet impassable differentiation of these. WILLIAM DEAN HOWELLS, *The Rise of Silas Lapham* (1885), 27.

17. Etiquette is what you are doing and saying when people are looking and listening. What you are thinking is your business. VIRGINIA CARY HUDSON, *O Ye Jigs & Juleps!* (1962).

18. O, Manners! That this age should bring forth such creatures! BEN JONSON, *Every Man in His Humour* (1598), 4.7.

19. Etiquette can be at the same time a means of approaching people and of staying clear of them. DAVID RIESMAN, "A Jury of Their Peers," *The Lonely Crowd* (1950).

20. Manners are not idle, but the fruit / Of loyal nature and of noble mind. ALFRED, LORD TENNYSON, "Guinevere," *Idylls of the King* (1859).

21. Nothing seems at first sight less important than the outward form of human actions, yet there is nothing upon which men set more store: they grow used to everything except to living in a society which has not their own manners. ALEXIS DE TOCQUEVILLE, *Democracy in America* (1835–39), 2.3.14.

22. To the real artist in humanity, what are called bad manners are often the most picturesque and significant of all. WALT WHITMAN, "Emerson's Books," *Notes Left Over* (1881).

## MARCH

**See 848. Seasons**

### 560. MARRIAGE

See also 65. Bachelors; 121. Children; 195. Courtship; 260. Divorce; 332. Family; 470. Infidelity; 497. Intimacy; 663. Parenthood; 885. Sex; 1044. Weddings

1. When a match has equal partners / then I fear not. AESCHYLUS, *Prometheus Bound* (c. 478 B.C.), tr. David Grene.

2. Married love between / man and woman is bigger than oaths guarded by right of nature. AESCHYLUS, *The Eumenides* (458 B.C.), tr. Richmond Lattimore.

3. Wives are young men's mistresses, companions for middle age, and old men's nurses. FRANCIS BACON, "Of Marriage and Single Life," *Essays* (1625).

4. Well-married, a man is winged—ill-matched, he is shackled. HENRY WARD BEECHER, *Proverbs from Plymouth Pulpit* (1887).

5. A long association—prolonged human contact, when a man and woman live together—this ends up producing a sort of rot, a poison. UGO BETTI, *The Inquiry* (1944–45), 1.10, ed. Gino Rizzo.

6. Whoso findeth a wife findeth a good thing. *Bible*, Proverbs 18:22.

7. It is better to dwell in a corner of the housetop, than with a brawling woman in a wide house. *Bible*, Proverbs 21:9 and 25:24.

8. Can two walk together, except they be agreed? *Bible*, Amos 3:3.

9. That is partly why women marry—to keep up the fiction of being in the hub of things. ELIZABETH BOWEN, *The House in Paris* (1935), 2.2.

10. If two lives join, there is oft a scar, / They are one and one, with a shadowy third; / One near one is too far. ROBERT BROWNING, "By the Fire-side," *Men and Women* (1855), 46.

11. The bitterest creature under heaven is the wife who discovers that her husband's bravery is only bravado, that his strength is only a uniform, that his power is but a gun in the hands of a fool. PEARL S. BUCK, "Love and Marriage," *To My Daughters, With Love* (1967).

12. One was never married, and that's his hell; another is, and that's his plague. ROBERT BURTON, *The Anatomy of Melancholy* (1621), 2.4.2.1.

13. In matrimony, to hesitate is sometimes to be saved. SAMUEL BUTLER (d. 1902), "Higgledy-Piggledy," *Note-Books* (1912).

14. Though women are angels, yet wedlock's the devil. BYRON, "To Eliza," *Hours of Idleness* (1806), 4.

15. Marriage from Love, like vinegar from wine— / A sad, sour, sober beverage—by Time / Is sharpened from its high celestial flavour / Down to a very homely household savour. BYRON, *Don Juan* (1819–24), 3.5.

16. To marry a woman you love and who loves you is to lay a wager with her as to who will stop loving the other first. ALFRED CAPUS, *Notes et pensées* (1926).

17. Oh! how many torments lie in the small circle of a wedding-ring! COLLEY CIBBER, *The Double Gallant* (1707), 1.2.

18. Show me one couple unhappy merely on account of their limited circumstances, and I will show you ten who are wretched from other causes. SAMUEL TAYLOR COLERIDGE, *Table Talk*, June 10, 1824.

19. Marriage is a feast where the grace is sometimes better than the dinner. CHARLES CALEB COLTON, *Lacon* (1825), 2.47.

20. Marriage indeed may qualify the fury of his passion, but it very rarely mends a man's manners. WILLIAM CONGREVE, *Love for Love* (1695), 1.1.

21. The dread of loneliness is greater than the fear of bondage, so we get married. CYRIL CONNOLLY, *The Unquiet Grave* (1945), 1.

22. Most of the beauty of women evaporates when they achieve domestic happiness at the price of their independence. CYRIL CONNOLLY, *The Unquiet Grave* (1945), 2.

23. Every woman should marry—and no man. BENJAMIN DISRAELI, *Lothair* (1870), 30.

24. The chains of marriage are so heavy that it takes two to bear them, sometimes three. ALEXANDRE DUMAS FILS, quoted in L. Treich's *L'Esprit d'Alexandre Dumas*.

25. Manny a man that cud rule a hundherd millyon sthrangers with an ir'n hand is careful to take off his shoes in th' front hallway whin he comes home late at night. FINLEY PETER DUNNE, "Famous Men," *Mr. Dooley On Making a Will* (1919).

26. Having once embarked on your marital voyage, it is impossible not to be aware that you make no way and that the sea is not within sight—that, in fact, you are exploring an enclosed basin. GEORGE ELIOT, *Middlemarch* (1871–72), 20.

27. A man's wife has more power over him than the state has. EMERSON, *Journals*, 1836.

28. Marriage is the perfection which love aimed at, ignorant of what it sought. EMERSON, *Journals*, 1850.

29. Wedlock, a padlock. ENGLISH PROVERB.

30. Man's best possession is a sympathetic wife. EURIPIDES, *Antigone* (5th c. B.C.), 164, tr. M. H. Morgan.

31. It's not beauty but / Fine qualities, my girl, that keep a husband. EURIPIDES, *Andromache* (c. 426 B.C.), tr. John F. Nims.

32. A woman, even when married to a cad, / Ought to be deferential, not a squabbler. EURIPIDES, *Andromache* (c. 426 B.C.), tr. John F. Nims.

33. All other woes a woman bears are minor / But lose her husband!—might as well be dead. EURIPIDES, *Andromache* (c. 426 B.C.), tr. John F. Nims.

34. One man should love and honor one: / A bride-bed / Theirs alone till life's done. EURIPIDES, *Andromache* (c. 426 B.C.), tr. John F. Nims.

35. Marry, and with luck / it may go well. But when a marriage fails, / then those who marry live at home in hell. EURIPIDES, *Orestes* (408 B.C.), tr. William Arrowsmith.

36. A rare spoil for a man / Is the winning of a good wife; very / Plentiful are the worthless women. EURIPIDES, *Iphigenia in Aulis* (c. 405 B.C.), tr. Charles R. Walker.

37. Keep your eyes wide open before marriage, half shut afterwards. BENJAMIN FRANKLIN, *Poor Richard's Almanack* (1732–57).

38. You can bear your own faults, and why not a fault in your wife? BENJAMIN FRANKLIN, *Poor Richard's Almanack* (1732–57).

39. He knows little who will tell his wife all he knows. THOMAS FULLER, D.D., "The Good Husband," *The Holy State and the Profane State* (1642).

40. A man's best fortune, or his worst, is his wife. THOMAS FULLER, M.D., *Gnomologia* (1732), 306.

41. Choose a wife rather by your ear than your eye. THOMAS FULLER, M.D., *Gnomologia* (1732), 1107.

42. More belongs to marriage than four legs in a bed. THOMAS FULLER, M.D., *Gnomologia* (1732), 3450.

43. The comfortable estate of widowhood, is the only hope that keeps up a wife's spirits. JOHN GAY, *The Beggar's Opera* (1728), 1.8, air 10.

44. The bachelor is a peacock, the engaged man a lion, and the married man a jackass. GERMAN PROVERB.

45. When an old man marries, death laughs. GERMAN PROVERB.

46. Half the human race can change its name and sometimes its nation without suffering—at least half! All women! JEAN GIRAUDOUX, *Siegfried* (1928), 3, tr. Phyllis La Farge with Peter H. Judd.

47. A wife loves out of duty, and duty leads to constraint, and constraint kills desire. JEAN GIRAUDOUX, *Amphitryon 38* (1929), 1, tr. Phyllis La Farge with Peter H. Judd.

48. The sum which two married people owe to one another defies calculation. It is an infinite debt, which can only be discharged through all eternity. GOETHE, *Elective Affinities* (1809), 9.

49. When a woman gets married it's like jumping into a hole in the ice in the middle of winter: you do it once, and you remember it the rest of your days. MAXIM GORKY, *The Lower Depths* (1903), 1, tr. Alexander Bakshy.

50. Marriage is the only evil that men pray for. GREEK PROVERB.

51. Maidens! why should you worry in choosing whom you shall marry? / Choose whom you may, you will find you have got somebody else. JOHN HAY, "Distichs" (1871?), 10.

52. Two days are the best of a man's wedded life, / The days when he marries and buries his wife. HIPPONAX (6th c. B.C.).

53. There is nothing nobler or more admirable than when two people who see eye to eye keep house as man and wife, confounding their enemies and delighting their friends. HOMER, *Odyssey* (9th c. B.C.), 6, tr. E. V. Rieu.

54. For every quarrel a man and wife have before others, they have a hundred when alone. EDGAR WATSON HOWE, *Coun-*

*try Town Sayings* (1911).

55. Marriage is a good deal like a circus: there is not as much in it as is represented in the advertising. EDGAR WATSON HOWE, *Country Town Sayings* (1911).

56. A man should be taller, older, heavier, uglier, and hoarser than his wife. EDGAR WATSON HOWE, *Country Town Sayings* (1911).

57. The silken texture of the marriage tie bears a daily strain of wrong and insult to which no other human relation can be subjected without lesion. WILLIAM DEAN HOWELLS, *The Rise of Silas Lapham* (1885), 4.

58. There are six requisites in every happy marriage. The first is Faith and the remaining five are Confidence. ELBERT HUBBARD, *The Note Book* (1927).

59. A man who marries a woman to educate her falls a victim to the same fallacy as the woman who marries a man to reform him. ELBERT HUBBARD, *The Note Book* (1927).

60. Those men are most apt to be obsequious and conciliating abroad who are under the discipline of shrews at home. WASHINGTON IRVING, "Rip Van Winkle," *The Sketch Book of Geoffrey Crayon, Gent.* (1819–20).

61. No man knows what the wife of his bosom is until he has gone with her through the fiery trials of this world. WASHINGTON IRVING, "The Wife," *The Sketch Book of Geoffrey Crayon, Gent.* (1819–20).

62. It is not from reason and prudence that people marry, but from inclination. SAMUEL JOHNSON, quoted in Boswell's *Life of Samuel Johnson*, Oct. 26, 1769.

63. A gentleman who had been very unhappy in marriage, married immediately after his wife died: Johnson said, it was the triumph of hope over experience. SAMUEL JOHNSON, quoted in Boswell's *Life of Samuel Johnson*, 1770.

64. It is so far from being natural for a man and woman to live in a state of marriage, that we find all the motives which they have for remaining in that connection, and the restraints which civilised society imposes to prevent separation, are hardly sufficient to keep them together. SAMUEL JOHNSON, quoted in Boswell's *Life of Samuel Johnson*, March 31, 1772.

65. I would advise no man to marry who is not likely to propagate understanding. SAMUEL JOHNSON, quoted in Birkbeck Hill's *Johnsonian Miscellanies* (1897), v. 1.

66. Always see a fellow's weak point in his wife. JAMES JOYCE, *Ulysses* (1922).

67. Marrying a man is like buying something you've been admiring for a long time in a shop window. You may love it when you get it home, but it doesn't always go with everything else in the house. JEAN KERR, "The Ten Worst Things About a Man," *The Snake Has All the Lines* (1960).

68. There are few wives so perfect as not to give their husbands at least once a day good reason to repent of every having married, or at least of envying those who are unmarried. LA BRUYÈRE, *Characters* (1688), 3.78, tr. Henri Van Laun.

69. Nothing is to me more distasteful than that entire complacency and satisfaction which beam in the countenances of a new-married couple,—in that of the lady particularly; it tells you that her lot is disposed of in this world; that *you* can have no hopes of her. CHARLES LAMB, "A Bachelor's Complaint of the Behaviour of Married People," *Essays of Elia* (1823).

70. There are some good marriages, but no delightful ones. LA ROCHEFOUCAULD, *Maxims* (1665), tr. Kenneth Pratt.

71. The men that women marry, / And why they marry them, will always be / A marvel and a mystery to the world. LONGFELLOW, *Michael Angelo* (1883), 1.6.

72. It's a capital thing for a woman to wed, / But a shocking bad thing for a man. E. V. LUCAS, *Reading, Writing, and Remembering* (1932), 3.

73. There is no more lovely, friendly and charming relationship, communion or company than a good marriage. MARTIN LUTHER, *Table Talk* (1569).

74. The wives who are not deserted, but who have to feed and clothe and comfort and scold and advise, are the true objects of commiseration; wives whose existence is given over to a ceaseless vigil of cantankerous affection. WILLIAM MC FEE, "Knights and Turcopoliers," *Harbours of Memory* (1921).

75. Marriage is a lot of things—an alliance, a sacrament, a comedy, or a mistake; but it is definitely not a partnership because that implies equal gain. And every right-thinking woman knows the profit in mat-

rimony is by all odds hers. PHYLLIS MC GINLEY, "How to Get Along with Men," *The Province of the Heart* (1959).

76. Marriage was all a woman's idea, and for man's acceptance of the pretty yoke it becomes us to be grateful. PHYLLIS MC GINLEY, "How to Get Along with Men," *The Province of the Heart* (1959).

77. The wife in curlpapers is replaced by the wife who puts on lipstick before she wakens her husband. MARGARET MEAD, *Look*, Oct. 16, 1956.

78. The fundamental trouble with marriage is that it shakes a man's confidence in himself, and so greatly diminishes his general competence and effectiveness. His habit of mind becomes that of a commander who has lost a decisive and calamitous battle. He never quite trusts himself thereafter. H. L. MENCKEN, *Prejudices: Second Series* (1920), 10.

79. Hail, wedded love, mysterious law, true source / Of human offspring. MILTON, *Paradise Lost* (1667), 4.750.

80. Nothing lovelier can be found / In woman, than to study household good, / And good works in her husband to promote. MILTON, *Paradise Lost* (1667), 9.232.

81. Marriage is three parts love and seven parts forgiveness of sins. LANGDON MITCHELL, *The New York Idea* (1907), 2.

82. The modern American marriage is like a wire fence. The woman's the wire—the posts are the husbands. LANGDON MITCHELL, *The New York Idea* (1907), 3.

83. Wives rarely fuss about their beauty / To guarantee their mate's affection. MOLIÈRE, *The School for Wives* (1662), 3.2, tr. Donald M. Frame.

84. A good husband be the best sort of plaster for to cure a young woman's ailments. MOLIÈRE, *A Doctor in Spite of Himself* (1666), 2, tr. John Wood.

85. [Marriage] can be compared to a cage: birds outside it despair to enter, and birds within, to escape. MONTAIGNE, "Upon some verses of Virgil," *Essays* (1580–88).

86. Men are monopolists / of "stars, garters, buttons / and other shining baubles"– / unfit to be the guardians / of another person's happiness. MARIANNE MOORE, "Marriage," *Collected Poems* (1951).

87. A husband is a man who two minutes after his head / touches the pillow is snoring like an overloaded / omnibus. OGDEN NASH, "The Trouble with Women Is Men," *Marriage Lines* (1964).

88. Marriage is based on the theory that when a man discovers a particular brand of beer exactly to his taste he should at once throw up his job and go to work in the brewery. GEORGE JEAN NATHAN, "General Conclusions about the Coarse Sex," *The Theatre, the Drama, the Girls* (1921).

89. If married couples did not live together, happy marriages would be more frequent. NIETZSCHE, *Human, All Too Human* (1878), 393, tr. Helen Zimmern.

90. When marrying, one should ask oneself this question: Do you believe that you will be able to converse well with this woman into your old age? NIETZSCHE, *Human, All Too Human* (1878), 406, in *The Portable Nietzsche*, tr. Walter Kaufmann.

91. Man is for woman a means: the end is always the child. NIETZSCHE, "On Little Old and Young Women," *Thus Spoke Zarathustra* (1883–92), 1, tr. Walter Kaufmann.

92. Quarrels are the dowry which married folk bring one another. OVID, *The Art of Love* (c. A.D. 8), 2, tr. J. Lewis May.

93. What makes men indifferent to their wives is that they can see them when they please. OVID, *The Art of Love* (c. A.D. 8), 3, tr. J. Lewis May.

94. Never marry but for love; but see that thou lovest what is lovely. WILLIAM PENN, *Some Fruits of Solitude* (1693), 1.79.

95. In marriage do thou be wise: prefer the person before money, virtue before beauty, the mind before the body; then thou hast a wife, a friend, a companion, a second self. WILLIAM PENN, *Some Fruits of Solitude* (1693), 1.92.

96. Between a man and his wife nothing ought to rule but love. Authority is for children and servants, yet not without sweetness. WILLIAM PENN, *Some Fruits of Solitude* (1693), 1.100.

97. Strange to say what delight we married people have to see these poor fools decoyed into our condition. SAMUEL PEPYS, *Diary*, Dec. 25, 1665.

98. A good marriage is that in which each appoints the other guardian of his solitude. RAINER MARIA RILKE, *Letters* (1892–1910; 1910–26), tr. Jane Barnard Greene and M. D. Herter Norton.

99. Romance calls for "the faraway love" of the troubadours; marriage for love of

"one's neighbor." DENIS DE ROUGEMONT, *Love in the Western World* (1939), 7.7, tr. Montgomery Belgion.

100. Marriage is for women the commonest mode of livelihood, and the total amount of undesired sex endured by women is probably greater in marriage than in prostitution. BERTRAND RUSSELL, "Prostitution," *Marriage and Morals* (1929).

101. When love dies in the odour of sanctity, people venerate his relics. GEORGE SANTAYANA, *The Life of Reason: Reason in Society* (1905–06), 1.

102. It takes patience to appreciate domestic bliss; volatile spirits prefer unhappiness. GEORGE SANTAYANA, *The Life of Reason: Reason in Society* (1905–06), 2.

103. What is wedlock forced but a hell, / An age of discord and continual strife? Whereas the contrary bringeth bliss / And is a pattern of celestial peace. SHAKESPEARE, *1 Henry VI* (1591–92), 5.5.62.

104. A light wife doth make a heavy husband. SHAKESPEARE, *The Merchant of Venice* (1596–97), 5.1.130.

105. I could not endure a husband with a beard on his face. I had rather lie in the woollen! SHAKESPEARE, *Much Ado About Nothing* (1598–99), 2.1.31.

106. Men are April when they woo, December when they wed. Maids are May when they are maids, but the sky changes when they are wives. SHAKESPEARE, *As You Like It* (1599–1600), 4.1.147.

107. It is a woman's business to get married as soon as possible, and a man's to keep unmarried as long as he can. GEORGE BERNARD SHAW, *Man and Superman* (1903), 2.

108. Marriage is popular because it combines the maximum of temptation with the maximum of opportunity. GEORGE BERNARD SHAW, "Maxims for Revolutionists," *Man and Superman* (1903).

109. Marriage is tolerable enough in its way if youre easygoing and dont expect too much from it. But it doesnt bear thinking about. GEORGE BERNARD SHAW, *Getting Married* (1911).

110. 'Tis safest in matrimony to begin with a little aversion. RICHARD BRINSLEY SHERIDAN, *The Rivals* (1775), 1.2.

111. It is a matter of life and death for married people to interrupt each other's stories; for if they did not, they would burst. LOGAN PEARSALL SMITH, *Afterthoughts* (1931), 3.

112. Marriage resembles a pair of shears, so joined that they cannot be separated; often moving in opposite directions, yet always punishing anyone who comes between them. SYDNEY SMITH, quoted in Lady S. Holland's *Memoir* (1855), v. 1.11.

113. Woe to the house where the hen crows and the rooster keeps still. SPANISH PROVERB.

114. The married state, with and without the affection suitable to it, is the compleatest image of heaven and hell we are capable of receiving in this life. RICHARD STEELE, *The Spectator* (1711–12), 479.

115. Marriage is like life in this—that it is a field of battle, and not a bed of roses. ROBERT LOUIS STEVENSON, title essay, 1, *Virginibus Puerisque* (1881).

116. Marriage is one long conversation, checkered by disputes. ROBERT LOUIS STEVENSON, "Talk and Talkers" (1882), 2.

117. The reason why so few marriages are happy, is, because young ladies spend their time in making nets, not in making cages. JONATHAN SWIFT, *Thoughts on Various Subjects* (1711).

118. We study ourselves three weeks, we love each other three months, we squabble three years, we tolerate each other thirty years, and then the children start all over again. HIPPOLYTE TAINE, *Vie et opinions de Thomas Graingorge* (1867).

119. An ideal wife is any woman who has an ideal husband. BOOTH TARKINGTON, *Looking Forward to the Great Adventure* (1926).

120. In true marriage lies / Nor equal, nor unequal. Each fulfils / Defect in each, and always thought in thought, / Purpose in purpose, will in will, they grow, / The single pure and perfect animal, / The two-celled heart beating, with one full strike, / Life. ALFRED, LORD TENNYSON, "The Princess; A Medley" (1851), 7.

121. Both marriage and death ought to be welcome: the one promises happiness, doubtless the other assures it. MARK TWAIN, letter to Will Bowen, Nov. 4, 1888.

122. Love seems the swiftest, but it is the slowest of all growths. No man or woman really knows what perfect love is until they have been married a quarter of a century. MARK TWAIN, *Notebook* (1935).

123. It is true, that all married men have their own way, but the trouble is they don't all have their own way of having it! AR-

TEMUS WARD, "Market Morning," *Artemus Ward in London* (1872).

124. There isn't a wife in the world who has not taken the exact measure of her husband, weighed him and settled him in her own mind, and knows him as well as if she had ordered him after designs and specifications of her own. CHARLES DUDLEY WARNER, "Third Study," *Backlog Studies* (1873).

125. The one charm of marriage is that it makes a life of deception absolutely necessary for both parties. OSCAR WILDE, *The Picture of Dorian Gray* (1891), 1.

126. When a woman marries again it is because she detested her first husband. When a man marries again, it is because he adored his first wife. Women try their luck; men risk theirs. OSCAR WILDE, *The Picture of Dorian Gray* (1891), 15.

127. How marriage ruins a man. It's as demoralizing as cigarettes, and far more expensive. OSCAR WILDE, *Lady Windermere's Fan* (1892), 3.

128. Twenty years of romance makes a woman look like a ruin; but twenty years of marriage make her something like a public building. OSCAR WILDE, *A Woman of No Importance* (1893), 1.

129. [Married men] are horribly tedious when they are good husbands, and abominably conceited when they are not. OSCAR WILDE, *A Woman of No Importance* (1893), 2.

130. Men marry because they are tired; women because they are curious. Both are disappointed. OSCAR WILDE, *A Woman of No Importance* (1893), 3.

131. In married life three is company and two is none. OSCAR WILDE, *The Importance of Being Earnest* (1895), 1.

132. Marriage is a bribe to make a housekeeper think she's a householder. THORNTON WILDER, *The Matchmaker* (1955), 1.

133. At thirty years old they [women] got no more use for the letto matrimoniale, no. The big bed goes to the basement! They get little beds from Sears Roebuck and sleep on their bellies. TENNESSEE WILLIAMS, *The Rose Tattoo* (1951), 2.1.

## 561. MARTYRS AND MARTYRDOM

**See also 123. Christianity; 790. Religion; 831. Sacrifice; 834. Saints and Sainthood; 841. Scapegoat**

1. It is often pleasant to stone a martyr, no matter how much we may admire him. JOHN BARTH, *The Floating Opera* (1956).

2. To die for a religion is easier than to live it absolutely. JORGE LUIS BORGES, "Deutsches Requiem," *Labyrinthes* (1962).

3. Martyrs, my friend, have to choose between being forgotten, mocked or used. As for being understood—never. ALBERT CAMUS, *The Fall* (1956).

4. The martyr endured tortures to affirm his belief in truth but he never asserted his disbelief in torture. G. K. CHESTERTON, "About Impenitence," *As I Was Saying* (1936).

5. Opposition may become sweet to a man when he has christened it persecution. GEORGE ELIOT, *Janet's Repentance* (1857), 8.

6. He that will not live a saint can never die a martyr. THOMAS FULLER, M.D., *Gnomologia* (1732), 2352.

7. The few of understanding, vision rare, / Who veiled not from the herd their hearts, but tried, / Poor generous fools, to lay their feelings bare, / Them have men always burnt and crucified. GOETHE, "Night," *Faust: Part I* (1808), tr. Philip Wayne.

8. Perhaps there is no happiness in life so perfect as the martyr's. O. HENRY, "The Country of Elusion," *The Trimmed Lamp* (1907).

9. Everyone hates a martyr; it's no wonder martyrs were burned at the stake. EDGAR WATSON HOWE, *Country Town Sayings* (1911).

10. Our admiration is so given to dead martyrs that we have little time for living heroes. ELBERT HUBBARD, *The Note Book* (1927).

11. To die in agony upon a cross / Does not create a martyr; he must first / Will his own execution. HENRIK IBSEN, *Brand* (1866), 3.

12. If a man is in doubt whether it would be better for him to expose himself to martyrdom or not, he should not do it. He must be convinced that he has a delegation from heaven. SAMUEL JOHNSON, quoted in Boswell's *Life of Samuel Johnson*, April–May 1773.

13. It is not the least of a martyr's scourges to be canonized by the persons who burned him. MURRAY KEMPTON, "The Dry Bones," *Part of Our Time* (1955).

14. It is the cause and not the death that makes the martyr. NAPOLEON I, *Maxims* (1804–15).

15. Men die only for that by which they live. SAINT-EXUPÉRY, *Flight to Arras* (1942), 23, tr. Lewis Galantière.

16. Must then a Christ perish in torment in every age to save those that have no imagination? GEORGE BERNARD SHAW, epilogue to *Saint Joan* (1923).

17. It is truer to say that martyrs make faith than that faith makes martyrs. MIGUEL DE UNAMUNO, "Faith, Hope, and Charity," *Tragic Sense of Life* (1913), tr. J. E. Crawford Flitch.

18. A thing is not necessarily true because a man dies for it. OSCAR WILDE, *Sebastian Melmoth* (1904).

## 562. MASCULINITY AND FEMININITY

**See also 576. Men and Women**

1. As vivacity is the gift of women, gravity is that of men. JOSEPH ADDISON, *The Spectator* (1711–12), 128.

2. The finest people marry the two sexes in their own person. EMERSON, *Journals*, 1843.

3. The wholly manly man lacks the wit necessary to give objective form to his soaring and secret dreams, and the wholly womanly woman is apt to be too cynical a creature to dream at all. H. L. MENCKEN, "The Feminine Mind," *In Defense of Women* (1922).

4. Neither sex, without some fertilization of the complementary characters of the other, is capable of the highest reaches of human endeavor. H. L. MENCKEN, "The Feminine Mind," *In Defense of Women* (1922).

5. In our civilization, men are afraid that they will not be men enough and women are afraid that they might be considered only women. THEODOR REIK, *Esquire*, November 1958.

6. What is most beautiful in virile men is something feminine; what is most beautiful in feminine women is something masculine. SUSAN SONTAG, "Notes on Camp," *Against Interpretation* (1961).

## MASKS

**See 45. Appearance; 162. Concealment; 681. Personality, Dual; 726. Pretension**

## MASOCHISM

**See 866. Self-injury**

## THE MASSES

**See 675. The People**

## 563. MASS MEDIA

**See also 290. Entertainment; 362. Free Speech; 604. Movies; 623. Newspapers; 725. Press, Freedom of the; 758. Publishing**

1. What the mass media offer is not popular art, but entertainment which is intended to be consumed like food, forgotten, and replaced by a new dish. W. H. AUDEN, "The Poet and the City," *The Dyer's Hand* (1962).

2. Some television programs are so much chewing gum for the eyes. JOHN MASON BROWN, interview, July 28, 1955.

3. It [television] is a medium of entertainment which permits millions of people to listen to the same joke at the same time, and yet remain lonesome. T. S. ELIOT, *New York Post*, Sept. 22, 1963.

4. When he [man] ceased any longer to heed the words of the seers and prophets, Science lovingly brought forth the Radio Commentator. JEAN GIRAUDOUX, *The Enchanted* (1933), 3, adapted by Maurice Valency.

5. The hand that rules the press, the radio, the screen and the far-spread magazine, rules the country. LEARNED HAND, memorial address for Justice Brandeis, Dec. 21, 1942.

6. In an automobile civilization, which was one of constant motion and activity, there was almost no time to think; in a television one, there is small desire. LOUIS KRONENBERGER, *Company Manners* (1954), 1.3.

7. When distant and unfamiliar and complex things are communicated to great masses of people, the truth suffers a considerable and often a radical distortion. The complex is made over into the simple, the hypothetical into the dogmatic, and the relative into an absolute. WALTER LIPPMANN, *The Public Philosophy* (1955), 2.3.

8. Each day a few more lies eat into the seed with which we are born, little institu-

tional lies from the print of newspapers, the shock waves of televison, and the sentimental cheats of the movie screen. NORMAN MAILER, "First Advertisement for Myself," *Advertisements for Myself* (1959).

9. It is not enough to show people how to *live* better: there is a mandate for any group with enormous powers of communication to show people how to *be* better. MARYA MANNES, "A Word to the Wizards," *But Will It Sell?* (1955–64).

10. It is television's primary damage that it provides ten million children with the same fantasy, ready-made and on a platter. MARYA MANNES, *More in Anger* (1958), 3.1.

11. Television was not intended to make human beings vacuous, but it is an emanation of their vacuity. MALCOLM MUGGERIDGE, "I Like Dwight," *The Most of Malcolm Muggeridge* (1966).

12. Already we Viewers, when not viewing, have begun to whisper to one another that the more we elaborate our means of communication, the less we communicate. J. B. PRIESTLEY, "Televiewing," *Thoughts in the Wilderness* (1957).

13. There is now a vast crowd that is a permanent audience waiting to be amused, cash customers screaming for their money's worth, all fixed in a consumer's attitude. They look on at more and more, and join in less and less. J. B. PRIESTLEY, "The Writer in a Changing Society," *Thoughts in the Wilderness* (1957).

14. The mass media are the wholesalers; the peer-groups, the retailers of the communications industry. DAVID RIESMAN, "Storytellers as Tutors," *The Lonely Crowd* (1950).

15. There are days when any electrical appliance in the house, including the vacuum cleaner, seems to offer more entertainment possibilities than the TV set. HARRIET VAN HORNE, *New York World-Telegram and Sun*, June 7, 1957.

16. I hate television. I hate it as much as peanuts. But I can't stop eating peanuts. ORSON WELLES, *New York Herald Tribune*, Oct. 12, 1956.

## 564. MASS MOVEMENTS

**See also 109. Causes; 230. Demagoguery; 350. Following; 443. Ideology; 813. Revolution**

1. A mass movement attracts and holds a following not because it can satisfy the desire for self-advancement, but because it can satisfy the passion for self-renunciation. ERIC HOFFER, *The True Believer* (1951), 1.2.7.

2. Mass movements can rise and spread without belief in a God, but never without belief in a devil. ERIC HOFFER, *The True Believer* (1951), 3.14.65.

3. There is nothing more explosive than a skilled population condemned to inaction. Such a population is likely to become a hotbed of extremism and intolerance, and be receptive to any proselytizing ideology, however absurd and vicious, which promises vast action. ERIC HOFFER, "Automation, Leisure, and the Masses," *The Temper of Our Time* (1967), 2.

4. Reason may be the lever, but sentiment gives you the fulcrum and the place to stand on if you want to move the world. OLIVER WENDELL HOLMES, SR., *The Poet at the Breakfast Table* (1872), 5.

5. Social movements are at once the symptoms and the instruments of progress. Ignore them and statesmanship is irrelevant; fail to use them and it is weak. WALTER LIPPMANN, "Revolution and Culture," *A Preface to Politics* (1914).

## 565. MATERIALISM

**See also 638. Objects; 920. Spirituality**

1. Materialism is decadent and degenerate only if the spirit of the nation has withered and if individual people are so unimaginative that they wallow in it. BROOKS ATKINSON, "January 22," *Once Around the Sun* (1951).

2. We live in a world of things, and our only connection with them is that we know how to manipulate or to consume them. ERICH FROMM, *The Sane Society* (1955), 5.

3. High thinking is inconsistent with complicated material life based on high speed imposed on us by Mammon worship. MOHANDAS K. GANDHI, *Non-Violence in Peace and War* (1948), 2.121.

4. Acquisition means life to miserable mortals. HESIOD, *Works and Days* (8th c. B.C.), 686, tr. Richmond Lattimore.

5. Those who live by bread alone will-

submit, for the sake of it, to the vilest abuse, like a hungry dog. JAMI, "The Dog and the Loaf of Bread," *Baharistan* (15th c.).

6. The materialistic idealism that governs American life, that on the one hand makes a chariot of every grocery wagon, and on the other a mere hitching post of every star, lets every man lead a very enticing double life. LOUIS KRONENBERGER, *Company Manners* (1954), 3.3.

7. What is at the heart of all our national problems? It is that we have seen the hand of material interest sometimes about to close upon our dearest rights and possessions. WOODROW WILSON, speech, Oct. 27, 1913.

## 566. MATHEMATICS

1. If a man's wit be wandering, let him study the mathematics. FRANCIS BACON, "Of Studies," *Essays* (1625).

2. Here, where we reach the sphere of mathematics, we are among processes which seem to some the most inhuman of all human activities and the most remote from poetry. Yet it is here that the artist has the fullest scope of his imagination. HAVELOCK ELLIS, *The Dance of Life* (1923), 2.

3. There is no royal road to geometry. EUCLID (300 B.C.), quoted in Proclus' *Commentaria in Euclidem* (5th c. A.D.), 2.4.

4. One has to be able to count if only so that at fifty one doesn't marry a girl of twenty. MAXIM GORKY, *The Zykovs* (1914), 2.

5. Mathematicians who are only mathematicians have exact minds, provided all things are explained to them by means of definitions and axioms; otherwise they are inaccurate and insufferable, for they are only right when the principles are quite clear. PASCAL, *Pensées* (1670), 1, tr. W. F. Trotter.

6. Mathematics may be defined as the subject in which we never know what we are talking about, nor whether what we are saying is true. BERTRAND RUSSELL, "Mathematics and the Metaphysicians," *Mysticism and Logic* (1917).

7. The true spirit of delight, the exaltation, the sense of being more than Man, which is the touchstone of the highest excellence, is to be found in mathematics as surely as in poetry. BERTRAND RUSSELL, *Mysticism and Logic* (1917).

8. Arithmetic is where the answer is right and everything is nice and you can look out of the window and see the blue sky —or the answer is wrong and you have to start all over and try again and see how it comes out this time. CARL SANDBURG, "Arithmetic," *Complete Poems* (1950).

9. What would life be without arithmetic, but a scene of horrors? SYDNEY SMITH, letter to Miss —, July 22, 1835.

10. A man has one hundred dollars and you leave him with two dollars, that's subtraction. MAE WEST, in *My Little Chickadee* (1940).

11. Mathematics is thought moving in the sphere of complete abstraction from any particular instance of what it is talking about. ALFRED NORTH WHITEHEAD, *Science and the Modern World* (1925), 2.

## 567. MATURITY

**See also 402. Growth and Development; 450. Immaturity; 580. Middle Age; 646. Old Age; 1064. Youth**

1. When I was a child, I spake as a child, I understood as a child, I thought as a child: but when I became a man, I put away childish things. *Bible*, 1 Corinthians 13:11.

2. Strong meat belongeth to them that are of full age. *Bible*, Hebrews 5:14.

3. Rashness is the error of youth, timid caution of age. Manhood is . . . the ripe and fertile season of action, when alone we can hope to find the head to contrive, united with the hand to execute. CHARLES CALEB COLTON, *Lacon* (1825), 1.363.

4. Mature man needs to be needed, and maturity needs guidance as well as encouragement from what has been produced and must be taken care of. ERIK H. ERIKSON, *Childhood and Society* (1950), 7.

5. Grown up, and that is a terribly hard thing to do. It is much easier to skip it and go from one childhood to another. F. SCOTT FITZGERALD, "Note-Books," *The Crack-Up* (1945).

6. Where id was, there shall ego be. SIGMUND FREUD, *New Introductory Lectures on Psychoanalysis* (1932), tr. W. J. H. Sprott.

7. How do you know that the fruit is

ripe? Simply because it leaves the branch. ANDRÉ GIDE, "Portraits and Aphorisms," *Pretexts* (1903), tr. Angelo P. Bertocci and others.

8. We have not passed that subtle line between childhood and adulthood until we move from the passive voice to the active voice – that is, until we have stopped saying "It got lost," and say, "I lost it." SYDNEY J. HARRIS, *On the Contrary* (1962), 7.

9. It is unjust to claim the privileges of age, and retain the playthings of childhood. SAMUEL JOHNSON, *The Rambler* (1750–52), 50.

10. The turning point in the process of growing up is when you discover the core of strength within you that survives all hurt. MAX LERNER, "Faubus and Little Rock," *The Unfinished Country* (1959), 4.

11. Better one bite, at forty, of Truth's bitter rind, / Than the hot wine that gushed from the vintage of twenty! JAMES RUSSELL LOWELL, "Two Scenes from the Life of Blondel, Autumn, 1963," *Under the Willows and Other Poems* (1868), 2.4.

12. The process of maturing is an art to be learned, an effort to be sustained. By the age of fifty you have made yourself what you are, and if it is good, it is better than your youth. MARYA MANNES, *More in Anger* (1958), 1.3.

13. To be grown up is to sit at the table with people who have died, who neither listen nor speak; / Who do not drink their tea, though they always said / Tea was such a comfort. EDNA ST. VINCENT MILLAY, "Childhood Is the Kingdom Where Nobody Dies," *Wine from These Grapes* (1934).

14. A man's maturity consists in having found again the seriousness one had as a child, at play. NIETZSCHE, *Beyond Good and Evil* (1886), 94, tr. Walter Kaufmann.

15. To be adult is to be alone. JEAN ROSTAND, *Pensées d'un biologiste* (1939).

16. Nature, in denying us perennial youth, has at least invited us to become unselfish and noble. GEORGE SANTAYANA, *The Life of Reason: Reason in Religion* (1905–06), 14.

17. 'Tis but an hour ago since it was nine, / And after one hour more 'twill be eleven; / And so, from hour to hour, we ripe and ripe, / And then, from hour to hour, we rot and rot; / And thereby hangs a tale. SHAKESPEARE, *As You Like It* (1599–1600), 2.7.24.

18. The latter part of a wise man's life is taken up in curing the follies, prejudices, and false opinions he had contracted in the former. JONATHAN SWIFT, *Thoughts on Various Subjects* (1711).

19. When we rejoice in our fullness, then we can part with our fruits with joy. RABINDRANATH TAGORE, *Stray Birds* (1916), 159.

20. When I can look Life in the eyes, / Grown calm and very coldly wise, / Life will have given me the Truth, / And taken in exchange – my youth. SARA TEASDALE, "Wisdom," *Dark of the Moon* (1926).

21. To live with fear and not be afraid is the final test of maturity. EDWARD WEEKS, "A Quarter Century: Its Retreats," *Look*, July 18, 1961.

22. One of the signs of passing youth is the birth of a sense of fellowship with other human beings as we take our place among them. VIRGINIA WOOLF, "Hours in a Library," *Times Literary Supplement*, Nov. 30, 1916.

## 568. MAXIMS

See also 294. Epigrams; 767. Quotations

1. A proverb is the child of experience. ENGLISH PROVERB.

2. Solomon made a book of proverbs, but a book of proverbs never made a Solomon. ENGLISH PROVERB.

3. The maxims of men disclose their hearts. FRENCH PROVERB.

4. Nothing ever becomes real till it is experienced – Even a proverb is no proverb to you till your life has illustrated it. JOHN KEATS, letter to George and Georgiana Keats, Feb. 14–May 3, 1819.

5. The proverbist knows nothing of the two sides of a question. He knows only the roundness of answers. KARL SHAPIRO, *The Bourgeois Poet* (1964), 1.19.

6. A short saying oft contains much wisdom. SOPHOCLES, *Aletes* (5th c. B.C.), 99, tr. M. H. Morgan.

7. It is more trouble to make a maxim than it is to do right. MARK TWAIN, "Pudd'nhead Wilson's New Calendar," *Following the Equator* (1897), 1.3.

## MAY

See 848. Seasons

### 569. MEANING

See also 3. The Absurd; 952. Symbols; 1057. Words

1. There is no meaning to life except the meaning man gives his life by the unfolding of his powers, by living productively. ERICH FROMM, *Man for Himself* (1947), 3.

2. We must each find our separate meaning / In the persuasion of our days / Until we meet in the meaning of the world. CHRISTOPHER FRY, *The Firstborn* (1946), 3.2.

3. A thing in itself never expresses anything. It is the relation between things that gives meaning to them and that formulates a thought. A thought functions only as a fragmentary part in the formulation of an idea. HANS HOFMANN, *Search for the Real* (1967).

4. If we have our own *why* of life, we shall get along with almost any *how*. NIETZSCHE, "Maxims and Missiles," 12, *Twilight of the Idols* (1888), tr. Walter Kaufmann.

5. Meanings change amazingly. When people get accustomed to horrors, these form the foundation for good style. BORIS PASTERNAK, *Safe Conduct* (1931), 2.16, tr. Beatrice Scott.

6. The meaning of things lies not in the things themselves but in our attitude towards them. SAINT-EXUPÉRY, *The Wisdom of the Sands* (1948), 5, tr. Stuart Gilbert.

### MEANNESS

See 686. Pettiness; 929. Stinginess

### 570. MEANS AND ENDS

See also 317. Expediency; 579. Method

1. When we deliberate it is about means and not ends. ARISTOTLE, *Nicomachean Ethics* (4th c. B.C.), 3.3, tr. J. A. K. Thomson.

2. The first sign of corruption in a society that is still alive is that the end justifies the means. GEORGES BERNANOS, "Why Freedom?" *The Last Essays of Georges Bernanos* (1955), tr. Joan and Barry Ulanov.

3. Most of the great results of history are brought about by discreditable means. EMERSON, "Considerations by the Way," *The Conduct of Life* (1860).

4. We should be careful as to the play, but indifferent to the ball. EPICTETUS, *Discourses* (2nd c.), 2.5, tr. Thomas W. Higginson.

5. It is not enough to take steps which may some day lead to a goal; each step must be itself a goal and a step likewise. GOETHE, quoted in Johann Peter Eckermann's *Conversations with Goethe*, Sept. 18, 1823.

6. The means prepare the end, and the end is what the means have made it. JOHN MORLEY, "Carlyle," *Critical Miscellanies* (1871–1908).

7. When the journey from means to end is not too long, the means themselves are enjoyed if the end is ardently desired. BERTRAND RUSSELL, "Technique and Human Nature," *Authority and the Individual* (1949).

8. A good man would prefer to be defeated than to defeat injustice by evil means. SALLUST, *Jugurthine War* (1st c. B.C.), 42.

### 571. MEDDLING

See also 392. Gossip

1. Study to be quiet, and to do your own business. *Bible*, 1 Thessalonians 4:11.

2. "If everybody minded their own business," the Duchess said in a hoarse growl, "the world would go round a deal faster than it does." LEWIS CARROLL, *Alice's Adventures in Wonderland* (1865), 6.

3. Don't scald your tongue in other people's broth. ENGLISH PROVERB.

4. Those who in quarrels interpose, / Must often wipe a bloody nose. JOHN GAY, "The Mastiffs," *Fables* (1727–38).

5. A man is likely to mind his own business when it is worth minding. ERIC HOFFER, *The True Believer* (1951), 1.2.10.

6. For prying into any human affairs, none are equal to those whom it does not concern. VICTOR HUGO, "Fantine," *Les Misérables* (1862), 5.8, tr. Charles E. Wilbour.

7. A person should be free to do as he likes in his own concerns; but he ought not to be free to do as he likes in acting for another, under the pretext that the affairs of the other are his own affairs. JOHN STUART MILL, *On Liberty* (1859), 5.

8. Have you so much time to spare from your own affairs that you can attend to

another man's with which you have no concern? TERENCE, *The Self-Tormentor* (163 B.C.).

## 572. MEDICINE

**See also 241. Diagnosis; 261. Doctors; 411. Health; 751. Psychiatry; 791. Remedies; 889. Sickness**

1. Oh, the powers of nature! She knows what we need, and the doctors know nothing. BENVENUTO CELLINI, *Autobiography* (1558–66), tr. George Bull.

2. The time is comin' whin not more thin half iv us'll be rale, an' th' rest'll be rubber. FINLEY PETER DUNNE, "Christian Science," *Mr. Dooley's Opinions* (1901).

3. If th' Christyan Scientists had some science an' th' doctors more Christyanity, it wudden't make anny diff'rence which ye called in—if ye had a good nurse. FINLEY PETER DUNNE, "Christian Science," *Mr. Dooley's Opinions* (1901).

4. Patience is the best medicine. JOHN FLORIO, *First Frutes* (1578).

5. Study sickness while you are well. THOMAS FULLER, M.D., *Gnomologia* (1732), 4269.

6. Keep a watch also on the faults of the patients, which often make them lie about the taking of things prescribed. HIPPOCRATES, *Decorum* (c. 400 B.C.), 14, tr. W. H. S. Jones.

7. All interest in disease and death is only another expression of interest in life. THOMAS MANN, *The Magic Mountain* (1924), 6.7, tr. H. T. Lowe-Porter.

8. The general order of things that takes care of fleas and moles also takes care of men, if they will have the same patience that fleas and moles have, to leave it to itself. MONTAIGNE, "Of the resemblance of children to their fathers," *Essays* (1580–88), tr. Charles Cotton and W. C. Hazlitt.

9. Medicine being a compendium of the successive and contradictory mistakes of medical practitioners, when we summon the wisest of them to our aid, the chances are that we may be relying on a scientific truth the error of which will be recognized in a few years' time. MARCEL PROUST, *Remembrance of Things Past: The Guermantes Way* (1913–27), C. K. Scott-Moncrieff.

10. It is medicine, not scenery, for which a sick man must go searching. SENECA, *Letters to Lucilius* (1st c.), 104.18.

11. By medicine life may be prolonged, yet death / Will seize the doctor too. SHAKESPEARE, *Cymbeline* (1609–10), 5.5.29.

12. I doubt not that in due time, when the arts are brought to perfection, some means will be found to give a sound head to a man who has none at all. VOLTAIRE, "Serpents," *Philosophical Dictionary* (1764).

## 573. MEDIOCRITY

**See also 309. Excellence**

1. There is always a heavy demand for fresh mediocrity. In every generation the least cultivated taste has the largest appetite. THOMAS BAILEY ALDRICH, "Leaves from a Notebook," *Ponkapog Papers* (1903).

2. When half-gods go, / The gods arrive. EMERSON, "Give All to Love," *Poems* (1847).

3. Mediocrity has no greater consolation than in the thought that genius is not immortal. GOETHE, *Elective Affinities* (1809), 23.

4. The way to get on in the world is to be neither more nor less wise, neither better nor worse than your neighbours. WILLIAM HAZLITT, "On Knowledge of the World," *Sketches and Essays* (1839).

5. As a rule, the man who can do all things equally well is a very mediocre individual. ELBERT HUBBARD, *The Philistine* (1895–1915).

6. In the republic of mediocrity genius is dangerous. ROBERT G. INGERSOLL, *Prose-Poems and Selections* (1884).

7. When small men attempt great enterprises, they always end by reducing them to the level of their mediocrity. NAPOLEON I, *Maxims* (1804–15).

## MEDITATION

**See 180. Contemplation; 812. Reverie; 968. Thought**

## MEEKNESS

**See 433. Humility; 973. Timidity**

## MEETINGS

See 229. Deliberation

## 574. MEMORY

See also 631. Nostalgia

1. We forget because we must / And not because we will. MATTHEW ARNOLD, "Switzerland," 6, *Empedocles on Etna, and Other Poems* (1852).

2. Not the power to remember, but its very opposite, the power to forget, is a necessary condition for our existence. SHOLEM ASCH, *The Nazarene* (1939), 1.

3. Memories are like stones, time and distance erode them like acid. UGO BETTI, *Goat Island* (1946), 1.4, ed. Gino Rizzo.

4. How strange are the tricks of memory, which, often hazy as a dream about the most important events of a man's life, religiously preserve the merest trifles. SIR RICHARD BURTON, *Sind Revisited* (1851), v. 1.

5. Oblivion is the dark page, whereon Memory writes her light-beam characters, and makes them legible; were it all light, nothing could be read there, any more than if it were all darkness. THOMAS CARLYLE, "On History Again" (1833).

6. Memory is the thing you forget with. ALEXANDER CHASE, *Perspectives* (1966).

7. Memory is often the attribute of stupidity; it generally belongs to heavy spirits whom it makes even heavier by the baggage it loads them down with. CHATEAUBRIAND, *Mémoires d'outre-tombe* (1848–50), 1.

8. Our memories are card-indexes consulted, and then put back in disorder by authorities whom we do not control. CYRIL CONNOLLY, *The Unquiet Grave* (1945), 3.

9. We have all forgot more than we remember. THOMAS FULLER, M.D., *Gnomologia* (1732), 5442.

10. The things we remember best are those better forgotten. BALTASAR GRACIÁN, *The Art of Worldly Wisdom* (1647), 262, tr. Joseph Jacobs.

11. Memory is a net; one finds it full of fish when he takes it from the brook; but a dozen miles of water have run through it without sticking. OLIVER WENDELL HOLMES, SR., *The Autocrat of the Breakfast Table* (1858), 12.

12. A retentive memory may be a good thing, but the ability to forget is the true token of greatness. ELBERT HUBBARD, *The Note Book* (1927).

13. It would add much to human happiness, if an art could be taught of forgetting all of which the remembrance is at once useless and afflictive . . . that the mind might perform its functions without incumbrance, and the past might no longer encroach upon the present. SAMUEL JOHNSON, *The Idler* (1758–60), 72.

14. Memory is like all other human powers, with which no man can be satisfied who measures them by what he can conceive, or by what he can desire. SAMUEL JOHNSON, *The Idler* (1758–60), 74.

15. To be able to enjoy one's past life is to live twice. MARTIAL, *Epigrams* (A.D. 86), 10.23.7.

16. The memory represents to us not what we choose but what it pleases. MONTAIGNE, "Apology for Raimond de Sebonde," *Essays* (1580–88), tr. Charles Cotton and W. C. Hazlitt.

17. A strong memory is commonly coupled with infirm judgment. MONTAIGNE, "Of liars," *Essays* (1580–88), tr. Charles Cotton and W. C. Hazlitt.

18. Bliss in possession will not last; / Remembered joys are never past. JAMES MONTGOMERY, "The Little Cloud" (1825).

19. Memories may escape the action of the will, may sleep a long time, but when stirred by the right influence, though that influence be light as a shadow, they flash into full stature and life with everything in place. JOHN MUIR, *A Thousand-Mile Walk to the Gulf* (1916), 6.

20. The sweetest memory is that which involves something which one should not have done; the bitterest, that which involves something which one should not have done, and which one did not do. GEORGE JEAN NATHAN, "General Conclusions about the Coarse Sex," *The Theatre, the Drama, the Girls* (1921).

21. A great memory does not make a philosopher, any more than a dictionary can be called a grammar. JOHN HENRY NEWMAN, *The Idea of a University* (1853–58), 1.6.5.

22. What beastly incidents our memories insist on cherishing—the ugly and disgust-

ing—the beautiful things we have to keep diaries to remember. EUGENE O'NEILL, *Strange Interlude* (1928), 2.

23. Women and elephants never forget. DOROTHY PARKER, "Ballade of Unfortunate Mammals," *Death and Taxes* (1931).

24. We do not remember days, we remember moments. CESARE PAVESE, *The Burning Brand* (1961).

25. Forgetfulness transforms every occurrence into a non-occurrence. PLUTARCH, "Contentment," *Moralia* (c. A.D. 100), tr. Moses Hadas.

26. If you wish to forget anything on the spot, make a note that this thing is to be remembered. EDGAR ALLAN POE, *Marginalia* (1844–49), 1.

27. What was hard to bear is sweet to remember. PORTUGUESE PROVERB.

28. Memory is not so brilliant as hope, but it is more beautiful, and a thousand times as true. GEORGE DENNISON PRENTICE, *Prenticeana* (1860).

29. We may with advantage at times forget what we know. PUBLILIUS SYRUS, *Moral Sayings* (1st c. B.C.), 234, tr. Darius Lyman.

30. Better by far you should forget and smile / Than that you should remember and be sad. CHRISTINA ROSSETTI, "Remember" (1862).

31. It is a curious fact that in bad days we can very vividly recall the good time that is now no more; but that in good days we have only a very cold and imperfect memory of the bad. SCHOPENHAUER, "Further Psychological Observations," *Parerga and Paralipomena* (1851), tr. T. Bailey Saunders.

32. Reminiscences make one feel so deliciously aged and sad. GEORGE BERNARD SHAW, *The Irrational Knot* (1885–87), 14.

33. Music, when soft voices die, / Vibrates in the memory; / Odours, when sweet violets sicken, / Live within the sense they quicken. SHELLEY, "To —, Music, When Soft Voices Die" (1821).

34. Our memories are independent of our wills. It is not so easy to forget. RICHARD BRINSLEY SHERIDAN, *The Rivals* (1775), 1.2.

35. A man's real possession is his memory. In nothing else is he rich, in nothing else is he poor. ALEXANDER SMITH, "Of Death and the Fear of Dying," *Dreamthorp* (1863).

36. Memory, like women, is usually unfaithful. SPANISH PROVERB.

37. Memory, the priestess, / kills the present / and offers its heart to the shrine of the dead past. RABINDRANATH TAGORE, *Fireflies* (1928).

38. Oh better than the minting / Of a gold-crowned king / Is the safe-kept memory / Of a lovely thing. SARA TEASDALE, "The Coin," *Flame and Shadow* (1920).

39. We seem but to linger in manhood to tell the dreams of our childhood, and they vanish out of memory ere we learn the language. THOREAU, *Journal*, Feb. 19, 1841.

40. Memory has the singular characteristic of recalling in a friend absent, as in a journey long past, only that which is agreeable. CHARLES DUDLEY WARNER, "Fifth Study," *Backlog Studies* (1873).

41. Memory is the diary that we all carry about with us. OSCAR WILDE, *The Importance of Being Earnest* (1895), 1.

42. In memory everything seems to happen to music. TENNESSEE WILLIAMS, *The Glass Menagerie* (1945), 1.

43. Life is all memory, except for the one present moment that goes by you so quick you hardly catch it going. TENNESSEE WILLIAMS, *The Milk Train Doesn't Stop Here Anymore* (1963), 3.

44. What's memory but the ash / That chokes our fires that have begun to sink? WILLIAM BUTLER YEATS, *The Countess Cathleen* (1892), 2.

## 575. MEN

**See also 65. Bachelors; 376. Gentlemen; 562. Masculinity and Femininity; 576. Men and Women; 1055. Women**

1. Poor little men! Poor little strutting peacocks! They spread out their tails as conquerors almost as soon as they are able to walk. JEAN ANOUILH, *Cécile* (1949), tr. Luce and Arthur Klein.

2. What a life we men lead! Either bachelors or cuckolds—what a choice! HENRY BECQUE, *Woman of Paris* (1885), 2, tr. Jacques Barzun.

3. Male, n. A member of the unconsidered, or negligible sex. The male of the human race is commonly known (to the female) as Mere Man. The genus has two varieties: good providers and bad providers. AMBROSE BIERCE, *The Devil's Dictionary* (1881–1911).

4. A romantic man often feels more uplifted with two women than with one: his love seems to hit the ideal mark somewhere between two different faces. ELIZABETH BOWEN, *The Death of the Heart* (1938), 1.7.

5. Men build bridges and throw railroads across deserts, and yet they contend successfully that the job of sewing on a button is beyond them. Accordingly, they don't have to sew buttons. HEYWOOD BROUN, "Holding a Baby," *Seeing Things at Night* (1921).

6. Men's men: gentle or simple, they're much of a muchness. GEORGE ELIOT, *Daniel Deronda* (1874–76), 4.31.

7. There's nothing so stubborn as a man when you want him to do something. JEAN GIRAUDOUX, *The Madwoman of Chaillot* (1945), 2, adapted by Maurice Valency.

8. History is bright and fiction dull with homely men who have charmed women. O. HENRY, "Next to Reading Matter," *Roads of Destiny* (1909).

9. A man is a means; / What, amputated, leaves a widow. RANDALL JARRELL, "Hope," *The Lost World* (1965).

10. The beauty of stature is the only beauty of men. MONTAIGNE, "Of presumption," *Essays* (1580–88), tr. Charles Cotton and W. C. Hazlitt.

11. Men should not care too much for good looks; neglect is becoming. OVID, *The Art of Love* (c. A.D. 8), 1, tr. Rolfe Humphries.

12. There was, I think, never any reason to believe in any innate superiority of the male, except his superior muscle. BERTRAND RUSSELL, "Ideas That Have Harmed Mankind," *Unpopular Essays* (1950).

13. A man who has no office to go to—I don't care who he is—is a trial of which you can have no conception. GEORGE BERNARD SHAW, *The Irrational Knot* (1885–87), 18.

14. A man is like a phonograph with half-a-dozen records. You soon get tired of them all; and yet you have to sit at table whilst he reels them off to every new visitor. GEORGE BERNARD SHAW, *Getting Married* (1911).

15. A handsome man is not quite poor. SPANISH PROVERB.

16. A man in the house is worth two in the street. MAE WEST, in *Belle of the Nineties* (1934).

17. Nowadays, all the married men live like bachelors, and all the bachelors like married men. OSCAR WILDE, *A Woman of No Importance* (1893), 2.

18. No man has ever lived that had enough, / Of children's gratitude or woman's love. WILLIAM BUTLER YEATS, "Vacillation," *Words for Music Perhaps* (1932).

## 576. MEN AND WOMEN

**See also 562. Masculinity and Femininity; 575. Men; 1055. Women**

1. Women like silent men. They think they're listening. MARCEL ACHARD, *Quote*, Nov. 4, 1956.

2. The woman who is known only through a man is known wrong. HENRY ADAMS, *The Education of Henry Adams* (1907), 23.

3. Men know so little about us [women]. We've a weakness, it is true, for those who charm us, but we always come back to those who love us. HENRY BECQUE, *Woman of Paris* (1885), 3, tr. Jacques Barzun.

4. Verily, men do foolish things thoughtlessly, knowing not why; but no woman doeth aught without a reason. GELETT BURGESS, *The Maxims of Methuselah* (1907), 2.

5. Most women have all other women as adversaries; most men have all other men as their allies. GELETT BURGESS, "The Gentleman's Code," *The Romance of the Commonplace* (1916).

6. Man's love is of man's life a thing apart, / 'Tis a Woman's whole existence. BYRON, *Don Juan* (1819–24), 1.194.

7. The average woman is at the head of something with which she can do as she likes; the average man has to obey orders and do nothing else. G. K. CHESTERTON, "Woman," *All Things Considered* (1908).

8. In the sex-war thoughtlessness is the weapon of the male, vindictiveness of the female. CYRIL CONNOLLY, *The Unquiet Grave* (1945), 1.

9. The last thing a woman will consent to discover in a man whom she loves, or on whom she simply depends, is want of courage. JOSEPH CONRAD, *Victory* (1915), 2.5.

10. Every man is made of clay and daimon, and no woman can nourish both. LAWRENCE DURRELL, *Justine* (1957), 1.

11. I'm not denyin' the women are foolish: God Almighty made 'em to match the

men. GEORGE ELIOT, *Adam Bede* (1859), 53.

12. Men live by forgetting—women live on memories. T. S. ELIOT, *The Elder Statesman* (1958), 2.

13. When man and woman die, as poets sung, / His heart's the last part moves, her last, the tongue. BENJAMIN FRANKLIN, *Poor Richard's Almanack* (1732–57).

14. If the heart of a man is depressed with cares, / The mist is dispelled when a woman appears. JOHN GAY, *The Beggar's Opera* (1728), 2.3, air 21.

15. The man who discovers a woman's weakness is like the huntsman in the heat of the day who finds a cool spring. He wallows in it. JEAN GIRAUDOUX, *Tiger at the Gates* (1935), 1, tr. Christopher Fry.

16. Strange difference of sex, that time and circumstance, which enlarge the views of most men, narrow the views of women almost invariably. THOMAS HARDY, *Jude the Obscure* (1895), 6.10.

17. Man is a wretch without woman; but woman is a monster—and thank Heaven, an almost impossible and hitherto imaginary monster—without man, as her acknowledged principal! NATHANIEL HAWTHORNE, *The Blithedale Romance* (1852), 14.

18. It takes a man a lifetime to find out about one particular woman; but if he puts in, say, ten years, industrious and curious, he can acquire the general rudiments of the sex. O. HENRY, "Cupid à la Carte," *Heart of the West* (1907).

19. I should like to see any kind of a man, distinguishable from a gorilla, that some good and even pretty woman could not shape a husband out of. OLIVER WENDELL HOLMES, SR., *The Professor at the Breakfast Table* (1860), 7.

20. The average woman sees only the weak points in a strong man, and the good points in a weak one. ELBERT HUBBARD, *The Note Book* (1927).

21. The consequence of a very free commerce between the sexes, and of their living much together, will often terminate in intrigues and gallantry. DAVID HUME, *A Dialogue.*

22. Women speak because they wish to speak, whereas a man speaks only when driven to speech by something outside himself—like, for instance, he can't find any clean socks. JEAN KERR, "How to Talk to a Man," *The Snake Has All the Lines* (1960).

23. A woman's guess is much more accurate than a man's certainty. RUDYARD KIPLING, "Three and—an Extra," *Plain Tales from the Hills* (1888).

24. Women become attached to men by the favors they grant them; men are cured by these same favors. LA BRUYÈRE, *Characters* (1688), 3.16.

25. Men are the reason that women do not love one another. LA BRUYÈRE, *Characters* (1688), 3.55, tr. Henri Van Laun.

26. Nowadays beautiful women are counted among the talents of their husbands. GEORG CHRISTOPH LICHTENBERG, *Aphorisms* (1764–99), tr. F. H. Mautner and H. Hatfield.

27. As unto the bow the cord is, / So unto the man is woman; / Though she bends him, she obeys him, / Though she draws him, yet she follows; / Useless each without the other. LONGFELLOW, "The Song of Hiawatha" (1855), 10.

28. Though women have small force to overcome men by reason, yet have they good fortune to undermine them by policy [stratagem]. JOHN LYLY, *Euphues: The Anatomy of Wit* (1579).

29. The worldly relations of men and women often form an equation that cancels out without warning when some insignificant factor has been added to either side. WILLIAM MC FEE, *Casuals of the Sea* (1916), 1.1.14.

30. Women are not men's equals in anything except responsibility. We are not their inferiors, either, or even their superiors. We are quite simply different races. PHYLLIS MC GINLEY, "The Honor of Being a Woman," *The Province of the Heart* (1959).

31. When a man's in love, he at once makes a pedestal of the Ten Commandments and stands on the top of them with his arms akimbo. When a woman's in love she doesn't care two straws for Thou Shalt and Thou Shalt Not. W. SOMERSET MAUGHAM, *Lady Frederick* (1907), 2.

32. A woman can forgive a man for the harm he does her, but she can never forgive him for the sacrifices he makes on her account. W. SOMERSET MAUGHAM, *The Moon and Sixpence* (1919), 41.

33. Women want mediocre men, and men are working hard to be as mediocre as possible. MARGARET MEAD, *Quote*, May 15, 1958.

34. The allurement that women hold out to men is precisely the allurement that Cape Hatteras holds out to sailors: they are enormously dangerous and hence enormously fascinating. H. L. MENCKEN, "The Incomparable Buzz-Saw," *The Smart Set*, May 1919.

35. In argument with men a woman ever / Goes by the worse, whatever be her cause. MILTON, *Samson Agonistes* (1671), 903.

36. Disguise our bondage as we will, / 'Tis woman, woman, rules us still. THOMAS MOORE (1779–1852), "Sovereign Woman."

37. Women, as they grow older, rely more and more on cosmetics. Men, as they grow older, rely more and more on a sense of humor. GEORGE JEAN NATHAN, "Cosmetics vs. Humor," *American Mercury*, July 1925.

38. The happiness of man is: I will. The happiness of woman is: he wills. NIETZSCHE, "On Little Old and Young Women," *Thus Spoke Zarathustra* (1883–92), 1, tr. Walter Kaufmann.

39. Woman understands children better than man does, but man is more childlike than woman. NIETZSCHE, "On Little Old and Young Women," *Thus Spoke Zarathustra* (1883–92), 1, tr. Walter Kaufmann.

40. Only he who is man enough will release the woman in woman. NIETZSCHE, "On Virtue That Makes Small," *Thus Spoke Zarathustra* (1883–92), 3, tr. Walter Kaufmann.

41. Woman wants monogamy; / Man delights in novelty. DOROTHY PARKER, "General Review of the Sex Situation," *Enough Rope* (1926), 2.

42. Woman's life must be wrapped up in a man, and the cleverest woman on earth is the biggest fool with a man. DOROTHY PARKER, quoted in obituary, *The New York Times*, June 8, 1967.

43. Women have many faults, but the worst of them all is that they are too pleased with themselves and take too little pains to please the men. PLAUTUS, *The Little Carthaginian* (2nd c. B.C.), 5.4.1203.

44. No woman ever hates a man for being in love with her, but many a woman hates a man for being a friend to her. ALEXANDER POPE, *Thoughts on Various Subjects* (1727).

45. If she is pleasing to one man, a girl is taken care of. PROPERTIUS, *Elegies* (c. 28–c. 16 B.C.), 1.2.26.

46. Even the wisest men make fools of themselves about women, and even the most foolish women are wise about men. THEODOR REIK, *The Need to Be Loved* (1963).

47. In their hearts women think that it is men's business to earn money and theirs to spend it. SCHOPENHAUER, "On Women," *Parerga and Paralipomena* (1851), tr. T. Bailey Saunders.

48. Women upset everything. When you let them into your life, you find that the woman is driving at one thing and you're driving at another. GEORGE BERNARD SHAW, *Pygmalion* (1913), 2.

49. Man is the hunter; woman is his game. / The sleek and shining creatures of the chase, / We hunt them for the beauty of their skins; / They love us for it, and we ride them down. ALFRED, LORD TENNYSON, "The Princess; A Medley" (1851), 5.

50. Men at most differ as heaven and earth, / But women, worst and best, as heaven and hell. ALFRED, LORD TENNYSON, "Merlin and Vivien," *Idylls of the King* (1859).

51. There is trouble with a wife, but it's even worse with a woman who is not a wife. LEO TOLSTOY, *Anna Karenina* (1873–76), 5.33.

52. God created man and, finding him not sufficiently alone, gave him a companion to make him feel his solitude more keenly. PAUL VALÉRY, *Tel quel* (1943).

53. Woman is man's confusion. VINCENT OF BEAUVAIS, *Speculum Majus* (13th c.), 346.

54. There is nothing that disgusts a man like getting beaten at chess by a woman. CHARLES DUDLEY WARNER, "Third Study," *Backlog Studies* (1873).

55. Women are not so sentimental as men, and are not so easily touched with the unspoken poetry of nature; being less poetical, and having less imagination, they are more fitted for practical affairs, and would make less failures in business. CHARLES DUDLEY WARNER, "Ninth Study," *Backlog Studies* (1873).

56. Women are as old as they feel—and men are old when they lose their feelings. MAE WEST, in *Klondike Annie* (1936).

57. If a woman wants to hold a man, she has merely to appeal to what is worst in him. We make gods of men, and they leave

us. Others make brutes of them and they fawn and are faithful. OSCAR WILDE, *Lady Windermere's Fan* (1892), 3.

58. Men always want to be a woman's first love. That is their clumsy vanity. We women have a more subtle instinct about things. What we like is to be a man's last romance. OSCAR WILDE, *A Woman of No Importance* (1893), 2.

59. There's nothing like mixing with woman to bring out all the foolishness in a man of sense. THORNTON WILDER, *The Matchmaker* (1955), 1.

60. Hysteria is a natural phenomenon, the common denominator of the female nature. It's the big female weapon, and the test of a man is his ability to cope with it. TENNESSEE WILLIAMS, *The Night of the Iguana* (1961), 1.

## MENTAL HEATH

See 555. Madness; 836. Sanity

## 577. MERCY

See also 357. Forgiveness; 531. Leniency; 692. Pity

1. Where Mercy, Love, and Pity dwell / There God is dwelling too. WILLIAM BLAKE, "The Divine Image," *Songs of Innocence* (1789).

2. We hand folks over to God's mercy, and show none ourselves. GEORGE ELIOT, *Adam Bede* (1859), 42.

3. Pour not water on a drowning mouse. THOMAS FULLER, M.D., *Gnomologia* (1732), 3915.

4. Teach me to feel another's woe, / To hide the fault I see; / That mercy I to others show, / That mercy show to me. ALEXANDER POPE, "The Universal Prayer" (1738), 10.

5. Clemency is the support of justice. RUSSIAN PROVERB.

6. Sweet mercy is nobility's true badge. SHAKESPEARE, *Titus Andronicus* (1592–93), 1.1.119.

7. The quality of mercy is not strained; / It droppeth as the gentle rain from heaven / Upon the place beneath. It is twice blessed – / It blesseth him that gives, and him that takes. SHAKESPEARE, *The Merchant of Venice* (1596–97), 4.1.184.

8. Nothing emboldens sin so much as mercy. SHAKESPEARE, *Timon of Athens* (1607–08), 3.5.3.

## 578. MERIT

See also 309. Excellence; 330. Fame; 716. Praise; 798. Reputation; 945. Superiority

1. Merit and knowledge will not gain hearts, though they will secure them when gained. LORD CHESTERFIELD, *Letters to His Son*, Nov. 24, 1749.

2. In a noble soul / Merit alone should light the flame of love. CORNEILLE, *The Cid* (1636), 1.2, tr. Paul Landis.

3. The assumption of merit is easier, less embarrassing, and more effectual than the actual attainment of it. WILLIAM HAZLITT, *Characteristics* (1823), 21.

4. The world more often rewards the appearances of merit than merit itself. LA ROCHEFOUCAULD, *Maxims* (1665), tr. Kenneth Pratt.

5. The erection of a monument is superfluous; our memory will endure if our lives have deserved it. PLINY THE YOUNGER, *Letters* (c. 97–110), 9.19.3.

6. Charms strike the sight, but merit wins the soul. ALEXANDER POPE, *The Rape of the Lock* (1712), 5.34.

7. Let none presume / To wear an undeservèd dignity. / O that estates, degrees, and offices / Were not derived corruptly, and that clear honour / Were purchased by the merit of the wearer! SHAKESPEARE, *The Merchant of Venice* (1596–97), 2.9.39.

## 579. METHOD

See also 278. Efficiency; 570. Means and Ends; 654. Order; 670. Patience; 696. Plans; 715. Practice; 731. Problems; 826. Rules; 896. Single-mindedness; 932. Strategy

1. Little by little does the trick. AESOP, "The Crow and the Pitcher," *Fables* (6th c. B.C.?), tr. Joseph Jacobs.

2. Better one safe way than a hundred on which you cannot reckon. AESOP, "The Fox and the Cat," *Fables* (6th c. B.C.?), tr. Joseph Jacobs.

3. If there are obstacles, the shortest line between two points may be the crooked

line. BERTOLT BRECHT, *Galileo* (1938; 1947), 13, tr. Charles Laughton.

4. All I know about method is that when I am not working I sometimes think I know something, but when I am working, it is quite clear I know nothing. JOHN CAGE, "Lecture on Nothing," *Silence* (1961).

5. There is time enough for everything in the course of the day if you do but one thing at once; but there is not time enough in the year if you will do two things at a time. LORD CHESTERFIELD, *Letters to His Son*, April 14, 1747.

6. There is always a best way of doing everything, if it be to boil an egg. EMERSON, "Behavior," *The Conduct of Life* (1860).

7. It is not always by plugging away at a difficulty and sticking at it that one overcomes it; but, rather, often by working on the one next to it. Certain people and certain things require to be approached on an angle. ANDRÉ GIDE, *Journals*, Oct. 26, 1924, tr. Justin O'Brien.

8. Attempt easy tasks as if they were difficult, and difficult as if they were easy: in the one case that confidence may not fall asleep, in the other that it may not be dismayed. BALTASAR GRACIÁN, *The Art of Worldly Wisdom* (1647), 204, tr. Joseph Jacobs.

9. While Honey lies in Every Flower, no doubt, / It takes a Bee to get the Honey out. ARTHUR GUITERMAN, *A Poet's Proverbs* (1924).

10. We often get in quicker by the back door than by the front. NAPOLEON I, *Maxims* (1804–15).

11. The past is the *terra firma* of methods, of the roads which we believe we have under our feet. JOSÉ ORTEGA Y GASSET, "In Search of Goethe from Within, Letter to a German," *Partisan Review*, December 1949, tr. Willard R. Trask.

12. To do two things at once is to do neither. PUBLILIUS SYRUS, *Moral Sayings* (1st c. B.C.), 7, tr. Darius Lyman.

13. Look for a tough wedge for a tough log. PUBLILIUS SYRUS, *Moral Sayings* (1st c. B.C.), 723, tr. Darius Lyman.

14. What sets us against one another is not our aims—they all come to the same thing—but our methods, which are the fruit of our varied reasoning. SAINT-EXUPÉRY, *Wind, Sand, and Stars* (1939), 9.6, tr. Lewis Galantière.

15. One arrow does not bring down two birds. TURKISH PROVERB.

## 580. MIDDLE AGE

**See also 537. Life, Stages of; 567. Maturity; 646. Old Age; 1064. Youth**

1. Age, we find, is a time for hurry to get a lot of things done that youth should have accomplished but postponed doing; of despair; and of confidence that whatever is, is more than a stone's throw from the best. FRANKLIN P. ADAMS, *Half a Loaf* (1927).

2. Years ago we discovered the exact point, the dead center of middle age. It occurs when you are too young to take up golf and too old to rush up to the net. FRANKLIN P. ADAMS, *Nods and Becks* (1944).

3. The Indian Summer of life should be a little sunny and a little sad, like the season, and infinite in wealth and depth of tone—but never hustled. HENRY ADAMS, *The Education of Henry Adams* (1907), 35.

4. Men of age object too much, consult too long, adventure too little, repent too soon, and seldom drive business home to the full period, but content themselves with a mediocrity of success. FRANCIS BACON, "Of Fortune," *Essays* (1625).

5. Youth is cause, effect is age; so with the thickening of the neck we get data. DJUNA BARNES, *Nightwood* (1937).

6. In middle life politics are not a mental acquisition; they are a temperament. FRANK MOORE COLBY, "Notes and Comments," *The Colby Essays* (1926), v. 2.

7. When a middle-aged man says in a moment of weariness that he is half dead, he is telling the literal truth. ELMER DAVIS, "On Not Being Dead, As Reported," *By Elmer Davis* (1964).

8. The years between fifty and seventy are the hardest. You are always being asked to do things, and yet you are not decrepit enough to turn them down. T. S. ELIOT, *Time*, Oct. 23, 1950.

9. After thirty, a man wakes up sad every morning, excepting perhaps five or six, until the day of his death. EMERSON, *Journals*, 1834.

10. Whoever, in middle age, attempts to realize the wishes and hopes of his early youth, invariably deceives himself. Each ten years of a man's life has its own fortunes, its own hopes, its own desires. GOETHE, *Elective Affinities* (1809), 30.

11. As you got older, and felt yourself to be at the centre of your time, and not at a point in its circumference, as you felt when you were little, you were seized with a sort of shuddering. THOMAS HARDY, *Jude the Obscure* (1895), 1.2.

12. Men, like peaches and pears, grow sweet a little while before they begin to decay. OLIVER WENDELL HOLMES, SR., *The Autocrat of the Breakfast Table* (1858), 4.

13. Middle age is when your age starts to show around the middle. BOB HOPE, news summaries, Feb. 15, 1954.

14. Whenever a man's friends begin to compliment him about looking young, he may be sure that they think he is growing old. WASHINGTON IRVING, "Bachelors," *Bracebridge Hall* (1822).

15. The blush that flies at seventeen / Is fixed at forty-nine. RUDYARD KIPLING, "My Rival," *Departmental Ditties* (1886).

16. By the time a man notices that he is no longer young, his youth has long since left him. FRANÇOIS MAURIAC, "The Age of Success," *Second Thoughts* (1961), tr. Adrienne Foulke.

17. Middle age is when you've met so many / people that every new person you / meet reminds you of someone else. OGDEN NASH, "Let's Not Climb the Washington Monument Tonight," *Versus* (1949).

18. From forty to fifty a man is at heart either a stoic or a satyr. SIR ARTHUR WING PINERO, *The Second Mrs. Tanqueray* (1893), 1.

19. There is more felicity on the far side of baldness than young men can possibly imagine. LOGAN PEARSALL SMITH, *Afterthoughts* (1931), 2.

20. In a man's middle years there is scarcely a part of the body he would hesitate to turn over to the proper authorities. E. B. WHITE, "A Weekend with the Angels," *The Second Tree from the Corner* (1954).

## 581. MIDDLE CLASS

See also 52. Aristocracy; 133. Class; 675. The People; 773. Rank; 906. Society; 926. Status

1. I call bourgeois anyone who says no to himself, who gives up struggle and renounces love in favor of his security. I call bourgeois anyone who places anything above feeling. LÉON-PAUL FARGUE, "Banalité," *Sous la lampe* (1921).

2. [The bourgeois] prefers comfort to pleasure, convenience to liberty, and a pleasant temperature to that deathly inner consuming fire. HERMANN HESSE, "Treatise on the Steppenwolf," *Der Steppenwolf* (1927), tr. Basil Creighton, rev. Walter Sorell.

3. Who is it that exercises social power to-day? Who imposes the forms of his own mind on the period? Without a doubt, the man of the middle class. JOSÉ ORTEGA Y GASSET, "The Barbarism of 'Specialization,'" *The Revolt of the Masses* (1930).

4. A moderately honest man with a moderately faithful wife, moderate drinkers both, in a moderately healthy house: that is the true middle class unit. GEORGE BERNARD SHAW, "Maxims for Revolutionists," *Man and Superman* (1905).

5. I have to live for others and not for myself; that's middle class morality. GEORGE BERNARD SHAW, *Pygmalion* (1913), 5.

## 582. THE MILITARY

See also 932. Strategy; 1035. War; 1042. Weapons

1. Lucky are soldiers who strive in a just war; / for them it is an easy entry into heaven. *Bhagavadgita*, 2, tr. P. Lal.

2. A good soldier has his heart and soul in it. When he receives an order, he gets a hard-on, and when he sends his lance into the enemy's guts, he comes. BERTOLT BRECHT, *The Caucasian Chalk Circle* (1944–45), 1.2, tr. Eric Bentley and Maja Apelman.

3. Raw in the fields the rude militia swarms, / Mouth without hands; maintained at vast expense, / In peace a charge, in war a weak defence. JOHN DRYDEN, *Cymon and Iphigenia* (1699).

4. A sojer's life is on'y gloryous in times iv peace. Thin he can wear his good clothes with th' goold lace on thim, an' sthrut in scarlet an' blue through th' sthreets. FINLEY PETER DUNNE, "On Past Glories," *Mr. Dooley On Making a Will* (1919).

5. It is characteristic of the military mentality that non-human factors . . . are held essential, while the human being, his desires and thoughts—in short, the psychological

factors—are considered as unimportant and secondary. EINSTEIN, *Out of My Later Life* (1950), 36.

6. He who loves the bristle of bayonets, only sees in their glitter what beforehand he feels in his heart. EMERSON, "War," *Miscellanies* (1884).

7. When the public sets a war memorial up / Do those who really sweated get the credit? / Oh no! Some general wangles the prestige. EURIPIDES, *Andromache* (c. 426 B.C.), tr. John F. Nims.

8. It is essential to persuade the soldier that those he is being urged to massacre are bandits who do not deserve to live; before killing other good, decent fellows like himself, his gun would fall from his hands. ANDRÉ GIDE, *Journals*, Feb. 10, 1943, tr. Justin O'Brien.

9. I am the very model of a modern Major-General, / I've information vegetable, animal, and mineral, / I know the kings of England, and I quote the fights historical, / From Marathon to Waterloo, in order categorical. W. S. GILBERT, *The Pirates of Penzance* (1879), 1.

10. Our business in the field of fight / Is not to question, but to prove our might. HOMER, *Iliad* (9th c. B.C.), 20.304, tr. Alexander Pope.

11. It is the blood of the soldier that makes the general great. ITALIAN PROVERB.

12. The sound of the drum drives out thought; for that very reason it is the most military of instruments. JOSEPH JOUBERT, *Pensées* (1842), 12.5, tr. Katharine Lyttelton.

13. The soldier, above all other people, prays for peace, for he must suffer and bear the deepest wounds and scars of war. DOUGLAS MAC ARTHUR, address, U. S. Military Academy, West Point, N.Y., May 12, 1962.

14. The military caste did not originate as a party of patriots, but as a party of bandits. H. L. MENCKEN, *Minority Report* (1956), 317.

15. A cause breaks or exalts a soldier's strength; unless that cause is just, shame will make him throw his weapons away. PROPERTIUS, *Elegies* (c. 28–c. 16 B.C.), 4.6.51.

16. You cannot organize civilization around the core of militarism and at the same time expect reason to control human destinies. FRANKLIN D. ROOSEVELT, radio address, Oct. 26, 1938.

17. A man who is good enough to shed his blood for his country is good enough to be given a square deal afterwards. THEODORE ROOSEVELT, speech, Springfield, Ill., July 4, 1903.

18. The soldier's body becomes a stock of accessories that are no longer his property. SAINT-EXUPÉRY, *Flight to Arras* (1942), 9, tr. Lewis Galantière.

19. It is as a soldier that you make love and as a lover that you make war. SAINT-EXUPÉRY, *The Wisdom of the Sands* (1948), 45, tr. Stuart Gilbert.

20. Theirs not to make reply, / Theirs not to reason why, / Theirs but to do and die. ALFRED, LORD TENNYSON, "The Charge of the Light Brigade" (1854).

21.The pitifulest thing out is a mob; that's what an army is—a mob; they don't fight with courage that's born in them, but with courage that's borrowed from their mass, and from their officers. MARK TWAIN, *The Adventures of Huckleberry Finn* (1884), 22.

22. The army is a nation within the nation; it is a vice of our time. ALFRED DE VIGNY, *Servitude et grandeur militaires* (1835), 1.2.

23. We want to get rid of the militarist not simply because he hurts and kills, but because he is an intolerable thick-voiced blockhead who stands hectoring and blustering in our way to achievement. H. G. WELLS, *The Outline of History* (1920, 1921), 40.4.

## 583. MIND

**See also 448. Imagination; 490. Intellectuals and Intellectualism; 491. Intelligence; 584. Mind and Body; 812. Reverie; 968. Thought; 999. Unconsciousness; 1000. Understanding**

1. Mind is a light which the Gods mock us with, / To lead those false who trust it. MATTHEW ARNOLD, *Empedocles on Etna* (1852), 1.2.

2. The grand thing about the human mind is that it can turn its own tables and see meaninglessness as ultimate meaning. JOHN CAGE, "Where Are We Going? And What Are We Doing?" *Silence* (1961).

3. The mind covers more ground than the heart but goes less far. CHINESE PROVERB.

4. Mind is a most delicate evidence. / Not a soul has seen it yet. RICHARD EBERHART, "On the Fragility of Mind," *Selected Poems 1930–1965* (1965).

5. We should take care not to make the intellect our god; it has, of course, powerful muscles, but no personality. EINSTEIN, *Out of My Later Life* (1950), 51.

6. Outside, among your fellows, among strangers, you must preserve appearances, a hundred things you cannot do; but inside, the terrible freedom! EMERSON, *Journals*, 1832.

7. It is the mind which creates the world about us, and even though we stand side by side in the same meadow, my eyes will never see what is beheld by yours, my heart will never stir to the emotions with which yours is touched. GEORGE GISSING, "Summer," *The Private Papers of Henry Ryecroft* (1903).

8. A mind has still some strength, so long as it has strength to bewail its feebleness. JOSEPH JOUBERT, *Pensées* (1842), 3.8, tr. Katharine Lyttelton.

9. The direction of the mind is more important than its progress. JOSEPH JOUBERT, *Pensées* (1842), 18.13, tr. Katharine Lyttelton.

10. The understanding, like the eye, whilst it makes us see and perceive all things, takes no notice of itself; and it requires art and pains to set it at a distance and make it its own subject. JOHN LOCKE, *An Essay Concerning Human Understanding* (1690), 1.1.1.

11. The mind is its own place, and in itself / Can make a heaven of hell, a hell of heaven. MILTON, *Paradise Lost* (1667), 1.254.

12. The mind has great influence over the body, and maladies often have their origin there. MOLIÈRE, *Love's the Best Doctor* (1665), 3, tr. John Wood.

13. The mind is a dangerous weapon, even to the possessor, if he knows not discreetly how to use it. MONTAIGNE, "Apology for Raimond de Sebonde," *Essays* (1580–88), tr. Charles Cotton and W. C. Hazlitt.

14. Order and reason, beauty and benevolence, are characteristics and conceptions which we find solely associated with the mind of man. KARL PEARSON, quoted in Henry Adams' *The Education of Henry Adams* (1907), 31.

15. In the life of the spirit there are no facts, but only life, as it appears to us in one form or another. LUIGI PIRANDELLO, *To Clothe the Naked* (1922), 3, tr. William Murray.

16. We are less justified in saying that the thinking life of humanity is a miraculous perfectioning of animal and physical life than that it is an imperfection in the organization of spiritual life as rudimentary as the communal existence of protozoa in colonies. MARCEL PROUST, *Remembrance of Things Past: The Past Recaptured* (1913–27), tr. Stephen Hudson.

17. Men are not prisoners of fate, but only prisoners of their own minds. FRANKLIN D. ROOSEVELT, Pan American Day address, April 15, 1939.

18. The mind of men is a mystery; and, like the plant, each one of us naturally appropriates and assimilates that about him which responds to that which is within him. JOSEPH ROUX, "Prelude," *Meditations of a Parish Priest* (1886), tr. Isabel F. Hapgood.

19. The mind is a strange machine which can combine the materials offered to it in the most astonishing ways. BERTRAND RUSSELL, *The Conquest of Happiness* (1930), 11.

20. The mind is the expression of the soul, which belongs to God and must be let alone by government. ADLAI STEVENSON, speech, Salt Lake City, Utah, Oct. 14, 1952.

21. How few things can a man measure with the tape of his understanding! How many greater things might he be seeing in the meanwhile. THOREAU, *Journal*, Feb. 14, 1851.

22. Mind has transformed the world, and the world is repaying it with interest. It has led man where he had no idea how to go. PAUL VALÉRY, "Our Destiny and Literature," *Reflections on the World Today* (1931), tr. Francis Scarfe.

23. The mind of man is more intuitive than logical, and comprehends more than it can coordinate. VAUVENARGUES, *Reflections and Maxims* (1746), 2, tr. F. G. Stevens.

24. Minds differ still more than faces. VOLTAIRE, "Wit, Spirit, Intellect," *Philosophical Dictionary* (1764).

25. Strongest minds / Are often those of whom the noisy world / Hears least. WILLIAM WORDSWORTH, *The Excursion* (1814), 1.

### 584. MIND AND BODY

**See also 88. Body; 411. Health; 583. Mind; 875. Senses; 920. Spirituality**

1. The soul is that which denies the body. For example, that which refuses to run when the body trembles, to strike when the body is angry, to drink when the body is thirsty. ALAIN, *Definitions* (1953).

2. So much are our minds influenced by the accidents of our bodies, that every man is more the man of the day than a regular and consequential character. LORD CHESTERFIELD, *Letters to His Son*, Aug. 30, 1748.

3. The flesh endures the storms of the present alone, the mind those of the past and future as well as the present. EPICURUS, (4th–3rd c. B.C.), quoted in Diogenes Laertius' *Lives and Opinions of Eminent Philosophers* (3rd c. A.D.), tr. R. D. Hicks.

4. The flesh believes that pleasure is limitless and that it requires unlimited time; but the mind, understanding the end and limit of the flesh and ridding itself of fears of the future, secures a complete life and has no longer any need for unlimited time. EPICURUS, "Principal Doctrines" (3rd c. B.C.), 20, in *Letters, Principal Doctrines, and Vatican Sayings*, tr. Russel M. Geer.

5. Man is a mind betrayed, not served, by his organs. EDMOND and JULES DE GONCOURT, *Journal*, July 30, 1861, tr. Robert Baldick.

6. What we think and feel and are is to a great extent determined by the state of our ductless glands and our viscera. ALDOUS HUXLEY, "Meditation on El Greco," *Music at Night* (1931).

7. If the mind, which rules the body, ever forgets itself so far as to trample upon its slave, the slave is never generous enough to forgive the injury; but will rise and smite its oppressor. LONGFELLOW, *Hyperion* (1839), 1.7.

8. However broken down is the spirit's shrine, the spirit is there all the same. NIGERIAN PROVERB.

9. Man is to himself the most wonderful object in nature; for he cannot conceive what the body is, still less what the mind is, and least of all how a body should be united to a mind. PASCAL, *Pensées* (1670), 72, tr. W. F. Trotter.

10. Our soul is cast into a body, where it finds number, time, dimension. Thereupon it reasons, and calls this nature necessity, and can believe nothing else. PASCAL, *Pensées* (1670), 233, tr. W. F. Trotter.

11. All the soarings of my mind begin in my blood. RAINER MARIA RILKE, letter to a young girl, July 1921, in *Wartime Letters*, tr. M. D. Herter Norton.

12. Nothing can so pierce the soul as the uttermost sigh of the body. GEORGE SANTAYANA, *The Life of Reason: Reason in Art* (1905–06), 6.

13. The soul is the voice of the body's interests. GEORGE SANTAYANA, *The Life of Reason: Reason in Common Sense* (1905–06), 9.

14. The lusts and greeds of the Body scandalize the Soul; but it has to come to heel. LOGAN PEARSALL SMITH, *Afterthoughts* (1931), 1.

15. Body and spirit are twins: God only knows which is which: / The soul squats down in the flesh, like a tinker drunk in a ditch. ALGERNON CHARLES SWINBURNE, "The Higher Pantheism in a Nutshell," *The Heptalogia* (1880).

16. I have said that the soul is not more than the body, / And I have said that the body is not more than the soul, / And nothing, not God, is greater to one than one's self is. WALT WHITMAN, "Song of Myself," 48, *Leaves of Grass* (1855–92).

17. Nothing can cure the soul but the senses, just as nothing can cure the senses but the soul. OSCAR WILDE, *The Picture of Dorian Gray* (1891), 2.

18. The human body is the best picture of the human soul. LUDWIG WITTGENSTEIN, *Philosophical Investigations* (1953), 2.4, tr. G. E. M. Anscombe.

### 585. MINORITIES

**See also 83. Blacks; 769. Racial Prejudice**

1. Because half a dozen grasshoppers under a fern make the field ring with their importunate chink . . . do not imagine that those who make the noise are the only inhabitants of the field. EDMUND BURKE, *Reflections on the Revolution in France* (1790).

2. Ten persons who speak make more noise than ten thousand who are silent. NAPOLEON I, *Maxims* (1804–15).

3. A resolute minority has usually pre-

vailed over an easygoing or wobbly majority whose prime purpose was to be left alone. JAMES RESTON, *Sketches in the Sand* (1967).

4. No democracy can long survive which does not accept as fundamental to its very existence the recognition of the rights of minorities. FRANKLIN D. ROOSEVELT, letter to the National Association for the Advancement of Colored People, June 25, 1938.

## 586. MIRACLES

**See also 946. Supernatural**

1. True miracles are created by men when they use the courage and intelligence that God gave them. JEAN ANOUILH, *The Lark* (1955), 2, adapted by Lillian Hellman.

2. There is in every miracle a silent chiding of the world, and a tacit reprehension of them who require, or who need miracles. JOHN DONNE, *Sermons*, No. 47, 1627.

3. Miracles enable us to judge of doctrine, and doctrine enables us to judge of miracles. PASCAL, *Pensées* (1670), 802, tr. W. F. Trotter.

4. Religion seems to have grown an infant with age, and requires miracles to nurse it, as it had in its infancy. JONATHAN SWIFT, *Thoughts on Various Subjects* (1711).

5. Men talk about Bible miracles because there is no miracle in their lives. Cease to gnaw that crust. There is ripe fruit over your head. THOREAU, *Journal*, June 1850.

## 587. MIRRORS

**See also 442. Identity**

1. Every man carries with him through life a mirror, as unique and impossible to get rid of as his shadow. W. H. AUDEN, "Hic et Ille," *The Dyer's Hand* (1962).

2. Th' wurruld has held a lookin'-glass in front iv ye fr'm th' day ye were born an' compelled ye to make faces in it. FINLEY PETER DUNNE, "Things Spiritual," *Mr. Dooley Says* (1910).

3. The best mirror is an old friend. GERMAN PROVERB.

4. The mirror usually reflects only the way others see us, the way we are expected to behave, forced to behave—hardly ever what we really are. LUIGI PIRANDELLO, *The Rules of the Game* (1918), 1, tr. William Murray.

5. You, my Lady, certainly don't dye your hair to deceive the others, nor even yourself; but only to cheat your own image a little before the looking-glass. LUIGI PIRANDELLO, *Henry IV* (1922), 1, tr. Edward Storer.

6. Almost always it is the fear of being ourselves that brings us to the mirror. ANTONIO PORCHIA, *Voces* (1968), tr. W. S. Merwin.

7. [Mirrors] are there when we are and yet they never give anything back to us but our own image. Never, never shall we know what they are when they are alone or what is behind them. ERICH MARIA REMARQUE, *The Black Obelisk* (1957), 6, tr. Denver Lindley.

8. There was never yet fair woman but she made mouths in a glass. SHAKESPEARE, *King Lear* (1605–06), 3.2.35.

9. All mirrors are magical mirrors, and we never see our faces in them. LOGAN PEARSALL SMITH, *Afterthoughts* (1931), 1.

## 588. MISANTHROPY

**See also 253. Dislike; 410. Hatred; 430. Humanitarianism**

1. I do not want people to be very agreeable, as it saves me the trouble of liking them a great deal. JANE AUSTEN, letter to her sister Cassandra, Dec. 24, 1798.

2. True misanthropes are not found in solitude, but in the world: because it is practical experience of the world and not philosophy that makes men hate. GIACOMO LEOPARDI, *Pensieri* (1834–37), 89, tr. William Fense Weaver.

3. Any man who hates dogs and babies can't be all bad. LEO ROSTEN, speaking of W. C. Fields at a banquet for the latter given by the Masquers' Club in Hollywood, Feb. 16, 1939.

4. I love mankind—it's people I can't stand. CHARLES M. SCHULZ, *Go Fly a Kite, Charlie Brown* (1963).

## 589. MISERS

**See also 401. Greed; 929. Stinginess**

1. Misers take care of property as if it belonged to them, but derive no more benefit

from it than if it belonged to others. BION (2nd c. B.C.?), quoted in Diogenes Laertius' *Lives and Opinions of Eminent Philosophers* (3rd c. A.D.), tr. R. D. Hicks.

2. The miser is the man who starves himself, and everybody else, in order to worship wealth in its dead form, as distinct from its living form. G. K. CHESTERTON, "About Bad Comparisons," *As I Was Saying* (1936).

3. He [the miser] falls down and worships the god of this world, but will have neither its pomps, its vanities nor its pleasures for his trouble. CHARLES CALEB COLTON, *Lacon* (1825), 1.24.

4. If the prodigal quits life in debt to others, the miser quits it still deeper in debt to himself. CHARLES CALEB COLTON, *Lacon* (1825), 2.131.

5. The miser and the pig are of no use until dead. FRENCH PROVERB.

6. Misers put their back and their belly into their pocket. THOMAS FULLER, M.D., *Gnomologia* (1732), 3418.

7. The prodigal robs his heir, the miser himself. THOMAS FULLER, M.D., *Gnomologia* (1732), 4722.

8. The miser puts his gold pieces into a coffer; but as soon as the coffer is closed, it is as if it were empty. ANDRÉ GIDE, "Concerning Influence in Literature," *Pretexts* (1903), tr. Angelo P. Bertocci and others.

9. Water will not slip through the miser's grasp. MALAY PROVERB.

10. What greater evil could you wish a miser, than long life? PUBLILIUS SYRUS, *Moral Sayings* (1st c. B.C.), 68, tr. Darius Lyman.

11. The money of the miser is coming out of the earth when he is himself going into it. SA'DI, *Gulistan* (1258), 7.21, tr. James Ross.

## MISERY

**See 939. Suffering; 1004. Unhappiness**

## MISFORTUNE

**See 17. Adversity; 358. Fortune**

## 590. MISSIONARIES

**See also 835. Salvation**

1. Go ye into all the world, and preach the gospel to every creature. He that believeth and is baptized shall be saved; but he that believeth not shall be damned. *Bible*, Mark 16:15–16.

2. If he have faith, the believer cannot be restrained. He betrays himself. He breaks out. He confesses and teaches this gospel to the people at the risk of life itself. MARTIN LUTHER, preface to his translation of the *New Testament* (1522).

3. A difference of opinion is what makes horse racing and Missionaries. WILL ROGERS, *The Autobiography of Will Rogers* (1949), 18.

## MISTAKES

**See 86. Blunder; 297. Error**

## MISTRUST

**See 257. Distrust**

## 591. MOB

**See also 205. Crowds; 675. The People**

1. The best university that can be recommended to a man of ideas is the gauntlet of the mob. EMERSON, *Society and Solitude* (1870).

2. The mob gets out of hand, runs wild, worse / than raging fire, while the man who stands apart / is called a coward. EURIPIDES, *Hecuba* (c. 425 B.C.), tr. William Arrowsmith.

3. Mobs in their emotions are much like children, / subject to the same tantrums and fits of fury. EURIPIDES, *Orestes* (408 B.C.), tr. William Arrowsmith.

4. In the hands of vicious men, / a mob will do anything. But under good leaders / it's quite a different story. EURIPIDES, *Orestes* (408 B.C.), tr. William Arrowsmith.

5. The mob has many heads but no brains. THOMAS FULLER, M.D., *Gnomologia* (1732), 4653.

6. Every mob, in its ignorance and blindness and bewilderment, is a League of Frightened Men that seeks reassurance in collective action. MAX LERNER, "The Chivalry," *The Unfinished Country* (1959), 4.

7. There is no grievance that is a fit object of redress by mob law. ABRAHAM LINCOLN, speech, Springfield, Ill., Jan. 27, 1838.

8. The nose of a mob is its imagination.

By this, at any time, it can be quietly led. EDGAR ALLAN POE, *Marginalia* (1844–49), 13.

## MODEL

See 308. Example

## 592. MODERATION

See also 310. Excess; 492. Intemperance; 742. Proportion; 749. Prudence; 940. Sufficiency; 963. Temperance

1. Ask the gods nothing excessive. AESCHYLUS, *The Suppliant Maidens* (463 B.C.), tr. Seth G. Bernardete.

2. Give me more love or more disdain; / The torrid or the frozen zone / Bring equal ease unto my pain; / The temperate affords me none. THOMAS CAREW, "Mediocrity in Love Rejected," *Poems* (1640).

3. This only grant me, that my means may lie / Too low for envy, for contempt too high. ABRAHAM COWLEY, "Of Myself" (17th c.).

4. Butter spoils no meat and moderation no cause. DANISH PROVERB.

5. Moderation is the silken string running through the pearl chain of all virtues. JOSEPH HALL, introduction to *Christian Moderation* (1601).

6. Moderation, after all, is only the belief that you will be a better man tomorrow than you were yesterday. MURRAY KEMPTON, "The Last Hurrah," *America Comes of Middle Age* (1963).

7. Is not moderation an old refrain / Ringing in our ears? from which we all refrain. LA FONTAINE, "Moderation," *Fables* (1668–94), tr. Marianne Moore.

8. The moderate are not usually the most sincere, for the same circumspection which makes them moderate makes them likewise retentive of what could give offense. WALTER SAVAGE LANDOR, "Diogenes and Plato," *Imaginary Conversations* (1824–53).

9. Moderation has been created a virtue to limit the ambition of great men, and to console undistinguished people for their want of fortune and their lack of merit. LA ROCHEFOUCAULD, *Maxims* (1665), tr. Kenneth Pratt.

10. Moderation is the languor and indolence of the soul, as ambition is its ardour and activity. LA ROCHEFOUCAULD, *Maxims* (1665), tr. Kenneth Pratt.

11. Ah, men do not know how much strength is in poise, / That he goes the farthest who goes far enough. JAMES RUSSELL LOWELL, *A Fable for Critics* (1848).

12. It is circumstance and proper measure that give an action its character, and make it either good or bad. PLUTARCH, "Life of Agesilaus II," *Parallel Lives* (1st–2nd c. A.D.), tr. John Dryden.

13. The heart is great which shows moderation in the midst of prosperity. SENECA THE ELDER, *Suasoriae* (1st c.), 1.

14. Nothing in excess. SOLON (7th–6th c. B.C.), quoted in Diogenes Laertius' *Lives and Opinions of Eminent Philosophers* (3rd c. A.D.), tr. R. D. Hicks.

## 593. MODERNITY

See also 181. Contemporaneousness

1. A seventeenth-century painting can be "modern" because the living eye finds it fresh and new. A "modern" painting can be outdated because it was a product of the moment and not of time. MARYA MANNES, *More in Anger* (1958), 3.2.

2. It is only the modern that ever becomes old-fashioned. OSCAR WILDE, "The Decay of Lying," *Intentions* (1891).

## 594. MODESTY

See also 433. Humility

1. A just and reasonable modesty does not only recommend eloquence, but sets off every great talent which a man can be possessed of. JOSEPH ADDISON, *The Spectator* (1711–12), 231.

2. Nothing is more amiable than true modesty, and nothing more contemptible than the false. The one guards virtue, the other betrays it. JOSEPH ADDISON, *The Spectator* (1711–12), 458.

3. Modesty is the only sure bait when you angle for praise. LORD CHESTERFIELD, *Letters to His Son*, May 17, 1750.

4. Pocket all your knowledge with your watch, and never pull it out in company unless desired. LORD CHESTERFIELD, *Letters to His Son*, Nov. 1, 1750.

5. He who speaks without modesty will

find it difficult to make his words good. CONFUCIUS, *Analects* (6th c. B.C.), 14.21, tr. James Legge.

6. Loquacity storms the ear, but modesty takes the heart. THOMAS FULLER, M.D., *Gnomologia* (1732), 3276.

7. There speaks the man of truly noble ways, / Who will not listen to the words of praise. / In modesty averse, and with deaf ears, / He acts as though the others were his peers. GOETHE, "On the Lower Peneus," *Faust: Part II* (1832), tr. Philip Wayne.

8. The sage never seems to know his own merits, for only by not noticing them can you call others' attention to them. BALTASAR GRACIÁN, *The Art of Worldly Wisdom* (1647), 123, tr. Joseph Jacobs.

9. True modesty does not consist in an ignorance of our merits, but in a due estimate of them. JULIUS CHARLES HARE and AUGUSTUS WILLIAM HARE, *Guesses at Truth* (1827).

10. Who would succeed in the world should be wise in the use of his pronouns. / Utter the You twenty times, where you once utter the I. JOHN HAY, "Distichs" (1871?), 13.

11. A modest man is usually admired—if people ever hear of him. EDGAR WATSON HOWE, *Ventures in Common Sense* (1919), 4.7.

12. Modesty and diffidence make a man unfit for public affairs; they also make him unfit for brothels. WALTER SAVAGE LANDOR, "Diogenes and Plato," *Imaginary Conversations* (1824–53).

13. To speak less of one's self than what one really is, is folly, not modesty; and to take that for current pay which is under a man's value, is pusillanimity and cowardice. MONTAIGNE, "Use makes perfect," *Essays* (1580–88), tr. Charles Cotton and W. C. Hazlitt.

14. With people of only moderate ability modesty is a mere honesty; but with those who possess great talent it is hypocrisy. SCHOPENHAUER, "Further Psychological Observations," *Parerga and Paralipomena* (1851), tr. T. Bailey Saunders.

15. Modesty—is a quality in a lover more praised by women than liked. RICHARD BRINSLEY SHERIDAN, *The Rivals* (1775), 2.2.

16. It is the duty of a great person so to demean himself, as that whatever endowments he may have, he may appear to value himself upon no qualities but such as any man may arrive at. RICHARD STEELE, *The Spectator* (1711–12), 340.

## 595. MONASTICISM

**See also 120. Chastity; 136. Clergy; 180. Contemplation; 834. Saints and Sainthood; 859. Self-denial; 920. Spirituality**

1. It is easy to become a monk in one's old age. ETHIOPIAN PROVERB.

2. Monastic incarceration is castration. VICTOR HUGO, "Cosette," *Les Misérables* (1862), 7.3, tr. Charles E. Wilbour.

3. The convent is supreme egotism resulting in supreme self-denial. VICTOR HUGO, "Cosette," *Les Misérables* (1862), 7.7, tr. Charles E. Wilbour.

4. I cannot praise a fugitive and cloistered virtue, unexercised and unbreathed, that never sallies out and sees her adversary, but slinks out of the race where that immortal garland is to be run for, not without dust and heat. MILTON, *Areopagitica* (1644).

## 596. MONEY

**See also 8. Acquisition; 68. Banking; 102. Business and Commerce; 501. Investment; 673. Payment; 744. Prosperity; 970. Thrift; 1041. Wealth; 1051. Wills and Inheritance**

1. It seems to be a law of American life that whatever enriches us anywhere except in the wallet inevitably becomes uneconomic. RUSSELL BAKER, "Observer," *The New York Times*, March 24, 1968.

2. Money, it turned out, was exactly like sex, you thought of nothing else if you didn't have it and thought of other things if you did. JAMES BALDWIN, "The Black Boy Looks at the White Boy," *Nobody Knows My Name* (1961).

3. If you would know what the Lord God thinks of money, you have only to look at those to whom he gives it. MAURICE BARING, quoted by Dorothy Parker in *Writers at Work: First Series* (1958).

4. Every one, even the richest and most munificent of men, pays more by cheque more light-heartedly than he pays little in specie. MAX BEERBOHM, "Hosts and Guests," *And Even Now* (1920).

5. The love of money is the root of all evil. *Bible*, 1 Timothy 6:10.

6. Money, n. A blessing that is of no advantage to us excepting when we part with it. AMBROSE BIERCE, *The Devil's Dictionary* (1881–1911).

7. One must choose, in life, between making money and spending it. There's no time to do both. EDOUARD BOURDET, *Les Temps difficiles* (1934), 4.

8. Life is short and so is money. BERTOLT BRECHT, *The Threepenny Opera* (1928), 3.3, tr. Desmond Vesey and Eric Bentley.

9. Money has a power above / The stars and fate, to manage love: / Whose arrows, learned poets hold, / That never miss, are tipped with gold. SAMUEL BUTLER (d. 1680), *Hudibras* (1663), 3.3.

10. What makes all doctrines plain and clear? / About two hundred pounds a year. / And that which was proved true before, / Prove false again? Two hundred more. SAMUEL BUTLER (d. 1680), *Hudibras* (1663), 3.1.

11. Ready money is Aladdin's lamp. BYRON, *Don Juan* (1819–24), 12.12.

12. Money you know will hide many faults. CERVANTES, *Don Quixote* (1605–15), 2.3.19, tr. Peter Motteux and John Ozell.

13. A moderate addiction to money may not always be hurtful; but when taken in excess it is nearly always bad for the health. CLARENCE DAY, "Improving the Lives of the Rich," *The Crow's Nest* (1921).

14. Money is coined liberty, and so it is ten times dearer to a man who is deprived of freedom. If money is jingling in his pocket, he is half consoled, even though he cannot spend it. DOSTOEVSKY, *The House of the Dead* (1862), 1.1, tr. Constance Garnett.

15. If a man is wise, he gets rich an' if he gets rich, he gets foolish, or his wife does. That's what keeps th' money movin' around. FINLEY PETER DUNNE, "Newport," *Observations by Mr. Dooley* (1902).

16. The value of a dollar is social, as it is created by society. EMERSON, "Wealth," *The Conduct of Life* (1860).

17. An ass loaded with gold climbs to the top of a castle. ENGLISH PROVERB.

18. Money is the sinew of love as well as of war. ENGLISH PROVERB.

19. Money's the wise man's religion. EURIPIDES, *The Cyclops* (c. 425 B.C.), tr. William Arrowsmith.

20. Never ask of money spent / Where the spender thinks it went. / Nobody was ever meant / To remember or invent / What he did with every cent. ROBERT FROST, "The Hardship of Accounting," *A Further Range* (1936).

21. Be the business never so painful, you may have it done for money. THOMAS FULLER, M.D., *Gnomologia* (1732), 857.

22. Help me to money and I'll help myself to friends. THOMAS FULLER, M.D., *Gnomologia* (1732), 1030.

23. God makes, and apparel shapes: but it's money that finishes the man. THOMAS FULLER, M.D., *Gnomologia* (1732), 1680.

24. Money, like dung, does no good till 'tis spread. THOMAS FULLER, M.D., *Gnomologia* (1732), 3444.

25. To have money is to be virtuous, honest, beautiful and witty. And to be without is to be ugly and boring and stupid and useless. JEAN GIRAUDOUX, *The Madwoman of Chaillot* (1945), 2, adapted by Maurice Valency.

26. Money is time. With money I buy for cheerful use the hours which otherwise would not in any sense be mine; nay, which would make me their miserable bondsman. GEORGE GISSING, "Winter," *The Private Papers of Henry Ryecroft* (1903).

27. With his own money a person can live as he likes—a ruble that's your own is dearer than a brother. MAXIM GORKY, *The Zykovs* (1914), 4.

28. To learn the value of money, it is not necessary to know the nice things it can get for you, you have to have experienced the trouble of getting it. PHILIPPE HÉRIAT, *La Famille Boussardel* (1946), 17.

29. If a man has money, it is usually a sign, too, that he knows how to take care of it; don't imagine his money is easy to get simply because he has plenty of it. EDGAR WATSON HOWE, *Country Town Sayings* (1911).

30. Go into the street, and give one man a lecture on morality, and another a shilling, and see which will respect you most. SAMUEL JOHNSON, quoted in Boswell's *Life of Samuel Johnson*, July 20, 1763.

31. Some men make money not for the sake of living, but ache / In the blindness of greed and live just for their fortune's sake. JUVENAL, *Satires* (c. 100), 12.49, tr. Hubert Creekmore.

32. In our culture we make heroes of the men who sit on top of a heap of money, and we pay attention not only to what they say in their field of competence, but to their wisdom on every other question in the world. MAX LERNER, "The Epic of Model T," *Actions and Passions* (1949).

33. Moral principle is a looser bond than pecuniary interest. ABRAHAM LINCOLN, speech, October 1856.

34. It is extraordinary how many emotional storms one may weather in safety if one is ballasted with ever so little gold. WILLIAM MC FEE, *Casuals of the Sea* (1916), 1.1.10.

35. Money is not an aphrodisiac: the desire it may kindle in the female eye is more for the cash than the carrier. MARYA MANNES, "A Plea for Flirtation," *But Will It Sell?* (1955–64).

36. Money is the alienated essence of man's work and existence; this essence dominates him and he worships it. KARL MARX, "The capacity of the present-day Jews and Christians to become free" (1884), *Early Writings*, ed. T. B. Bottomore.

37. Money is like a sixth sense without which you cannot make a complete use of the other five. W. SOMERSET MAUGHAM, *Of Human Bondage* (1915), 51.

38. Much work is merely a way to make money; much leisure is merely a way to spend it. C. WRIGHT MILLS, "Diagnosis of Our Moral Uneasiness," *Power, Politics and People* (1963).

39. Gold is the key, whatever else we try; / And that sweet metal aids the conqueror / In every case, in love as well as war. MOLIÈRE, *The School for Wives* (1662), 1.4, tr. Donald M. Frame.

40. Cultivated people should be superior to any consideration so sordid as a mercenary interest. MOLIÈRE, *The Would-be Gentleman* (1670), 1, tr. John Wood.

41. Gold will buy the highest honours; and gold will purchase love. OVID, *The Art of Love* (c. A.D. 8), 2, tr. J. Lewis May.

42. He that has a penny in his purse, is worth a penny: Have and you shall be esteemed. PETRONIUS, *Satyricon* (1st c.), tr. William Burnaby.

43. Even genius is tied to profit. PINDAR, *Odes* (5th c. B.C.), Pythia 3, tr. Richmond Lattimore.

44. You, O money, are the cause of a restless life! Because of you we journey toward a premature death; you provide cruel nourishment for the evils of men; the seed of our cares sprouts from your head. PROPERTIUS, *Elegies* (c. 28–c. 16 B.C.), 3.7.1.

45. When reason rules, money is a blessing. PUBLILIUS SYRUS, *Moral Sayings* (1st c. B.C.), 50, tr. Darius Lyman.

46. When Gold argues the cause, eloquence is impotent. PUBLILIUS SYRUS, *Moral Sayings* (1st c. B.C.), 65, tr. Darius Lyman.

47. Money alone sets all the world in motion. PUBLILIUS SYRUS, *Moral Sayings* (1st c. B.C.), 656, tr. Darius Lyman.

48. I finally know what distinguishes man from the other beasts: financial worries. JULES RENARD, *Journal* (1887–1910).

49. The force of the guinea you have in your pocket depends wholly on the default of a guinea in your neighbour's pocket. If he did not want it, it would be of no use to you. JOHN RUSKIN, *Unto This Last* (1862), 2.27.

50. When money speaks, the truth keeps silent. RUSSIAN PROVERB.

51. Money is the power of impotence. LEON SAMSON, *The New Humanism* (1930), 12.

52. Money is power, freedom, a cushion, the root of all evil, the sum of blessings. CARL SANDBURG, *The People, Yes* (1936).

53. Nothing comes amiss, so money comes withal. SHAKESPEARE, *The Taming of the Shrew* (1593–94), 1.2.82.

54. Money is indeed the most important thing in the world; and all sound and successful personal and national morality should have this fact for its basis. GEORGE BERNARD SHAW, preface, *The Irrational Knot* (1885–87).

55. Money is the counter that enables life to be lived socially: it is life as truly as sovereigns and banknotes are money. GEORGE BERNARD SHAW, preface, *Major Barbara* (1905).

56. My life is a bubble; but how much solid cash it costs to keep that bubble floating! LOGAN PEARSALL SMITH, *Afterthoughts* (1931), 6.

57. There was a time when a fool and his money were soon parted, but now it happens to everybody. ADLAI STEVENSON, *The Stevenson Wit* (1966).

58. The jingling of the guinea helps the

hurt that Honor feels. ALFRED, LORD TENNYSON, "Locksley Hall" (1842).

59. Almost any man knows how to earn money, but not one in a million knows how to spend it. If he had known so much as this, he would never have earned it. THOREAU, *Journal*, 1841.

60. Some men worship rank, some worship heroes, some worship power, some worship God, and over these ideals they dispute—but they all worship money. MARK TWAIN, *Notebook* (1935).

61. Most men's hearts is located ruther closter to their britchis pockets than they are to their breast pockets. EDWARD NOYES WESTCOTT, *David Harum* (1898), 26.

62. The difference between a little money and no money at all is enormous—and can shatter the world. And the difference between a little money and an enormous amount of money is very slight—and that, also, can shatter the world. THORNTON WILDER, *The Matchmaker* (1955), 4.

63. With money in your pocket, you are wise and you are handsome and you sing well too. *Yiddish Proverbs* (1949), ed. Hanan J. Ayalti.

## MOODS

**See 282. Emotions; 962. Temperament**

## 597. MOON

**See also 413. The Heavens; 914. Space**

1. So there he is at last. Man on the moon. The poor magnificent bungler! He can't even get to the office without undergoing the agonies of the damned, but give him a little metal, a few chemicals, some wire and twenty or thirty billion dollars and, vroom! there he is, up on a rock a quarter of a million miles up in the sky. RUSSELL BAKER in *The New York Times*, July 21, 1969.

2. There is something haunting in the light of the moon; it has all the dispassionateness of a disembodied soul, and something of its inconceivable mystery. JOSEPH CONRAD, *Lord Jim* (1900), 24.

3. Treading the soil of the moon, palpitating its pebbles, tasting the panic and splendor of the event, feeling in the pit of one's stomach the separation from terra—these form the most romantic sensation an explorer has ever known. VLADIMIR NABOKOV in *The New York Times*, July 21, 1969.

4. The moon is a friend for the lonesome to talk to. CARL SANDBURG, "Moonlight and Maggots," *Complete Poems* (1950).

5. Moon, worn thin to the width of a quill, / In the dawn clouds flying, / How good to go, light into light, and still / Giving light, dying. SARA TEASDALE, "Moon's Ending," *Strange Victory* (1933).

## 598. MORALITY

**See also 75. Behavior; 171. Conscience; 391. Goodness; 489. Integrity; 1025. Virtue**

1. Morality is a private and costly luxury. HENRY ADAMS, *The Education of Henry Adams* (1907), 22.

2. The only immorality is to not do what one has to do when one has to do it. JEAN ANOUILH, *Becket* (1959), 2.

3. Decalogue, n. A series of commandments, ten in number—just enough to permit an intelligent selection for observance, but not enough to embarrass the choice. AMBROSE BIERCE, *The Devil's Dictionary* (1881–1911).

4. Moral, adj. Conforming to a local and mutable standard of right. Having the quality of general expediency. AMBROSE BIERCE, *The Devil's Dictionary* (1881–1911).

5. Morality's *not* practical. Morality's a gesture. A complicated gesture learned from books. ROBERT BOLT, *A Man for All Seasons* (1962), 2.

6. You may proclaim, good sirs, your fine philosophy / But till you feed us, right and wrong can wait! BERTOLT BRECHT, *The Threepenny Opera* (1928), 2.3, tr. Desmond Vesey and Eric Bentley.

7. Morality, thou deadly bane, / Thy tens o' thousands thou hast slain! / Vain is his hope, whose stay an' trust is / In moral mercy, truth, and justice! ROBERT BURNS, "A Dedication to Gavin Hamilton, Esq." (1786).

8. The only absolute morality is absolute stagnation. SAMUEL BUTLER (d. 1902), "Cash and Credit," *Note-Books* (1912).

9. Morality turns on whether the pleasure precedes or follows the pain. SAMUEL BUTLER (d. 1902), "Elementary Morality," *Note-Books* (1912).

10. Morality is the custom of one's coun-

try and the current feeling of one's peers. SAMUEL BUTLER (d. 1902), "Elementary Morality," *Note-Books* (1912).

11. Everything's got a moral, if only you can find it. LEWIS CARROLL, *Alice's Adventures in Wonderland* (1865), 9.

12. If there is one thing worse than the modern weakening of major morals it is the modern strengthening of minor morals. G. K. CHESTERTON, "On Lying in Bed," *Tremendous Trifles* (1909).

13. Distaste sounds more emphatic when expressed as moral disapproval. With most of us the moral counterblast is nothing more than the angry rendering of a yawn. FRANK MOORE COLBY, "Pleasures of Anxiety," *The Margin of Hesitation* (1921).

14. A man may not transgress the bounds of major morals, but may make errors in minor morals. CONFUCIUS, *Analects* (6th c. B.C.), 19.11, tr. Ch'u Chai and Winberg Chai.

15. Too many moralists begin with a dislike of reality. CLARENCE DAY, *This Simian World* (1920), 13.

16. Every man takes care that his neighbor shall not cheat him. But a day comes when he begins to care that he do not cheat his neighbor. Then all goes well. EMERSON, "Worship," *The Conduct of Life* (1860).

17. How can we be scrupulous / In a life which, from birth onwards, is so determined / To wring us dry of any serenity at all? CHRISTOPHER FRY, *The Firstborn* (1946), 3.1.

18. The success of any great moral enterprise does not depend upon numbers. WILLIAM LLOYD GARRISON, *Life* (1885–89), v. 3.

19. He who defines his conduct by ethics imprisons his song-bird in a cage. KAHLIL GIBRAN, "On Religion," *The Prophet* (1923).

20. What is moral is what you feel good after and what is immoral is what you feel bad after. ERNEST HEMINGWAY, *Death in the Afternoon* (1932), 1.

21. Our system of morality is a body of imperfect social generalizations expressed in terms of emotion. OLIVER WENDELL HOLMES, JR., "Ideals and Doubts," *Illinois Law Review* (1915), v. 10.

22. Morality is largely a matter of geography. ELBERT HUBBARD, *The Philistine* (1895–1915).

23. Morality is the thing upon which your friends smile, and immorality is the thing on which they frown. ELBERT HUBBARD, *The Philistine* (1895–1915).

24. There can be no final truth in ethics any more than in physics, until the last man has had his experience and said his say. WILLIAM JAMES, "The Moral Philosopher and the Moral Life," *The Will to Believe* (1896).

25. Be not too hasty to trust or to admire the teachers of morality: they discourse like angels, but they live like men. SAMUEL JOHNSON, *Rasselas* (1759), 18.

26. Rhetoric takes no real account of the art in literature and morality takes no account of the art in life. JOSEPH WOOD KRUTCH, "Life, Art, and Peace," *The Modern Temper* (1929).

27. Morality is either a social contract or you have to pay cash. STANISLAW LEC, *Unkempt Thoughts* (1962), tr. Jacek Galazka.

28. Every man has his moral backside too, which he doesn't expose unnecessarily but keeps covered as long as possible by the trousers of decorum. GEORG CHRISTOPH LICHTENBERG, *Aphorisms* (1764–99), tr. F. H. Mautner and H. Hatfield.

29. There is nothing so bad but it can masquerade as moral. WALTER LIPPMANN, "Some Necessary Iconoclasm," *A Preface to Politics* (1914).

30. The whole speculation about morality is an effort to find a way of living which men who live it will instinctively feel is good. WALTER LIPPMANN, "Some Necessary Iconoclasm," *A Preface to Politics* (1914).

31. There cannot any one moral rule be proposed whereof a man may not justly demand a reason. JOHN LOCKE, *An Essay Concerning Human Understanding* (1690), 1.3.4.

32. Uncle Sam has no conscience. They don't know what morals are. They don't try and eliminate an evil because it's evil, or because it's illegal, or because it's immoral; they eliminate it only when it threatens their existence. MALCOLM X, *Malcolm X Speaks* (1965), 3.

33. The difference between a moral man and a man of honor is that the latter regrets a discreditable act, even when it has worked and he has not been caught. H. L. MENCKEN, *Prejudices: Fourth Series* (1924), 11.

34. Sometimes I feel something akin to rage / At the corrupted morals of this age!

MOLIÈRE, *The School for Husbands* (1661), 1.3, tr. Donald M. Frame.

35. The essence of morality is the subjugation of nature in obedience to social needs. JOHN MORLEY, "Carlyle," *Critical Miscellanies* (1871–1908).

36. There are no moral phenomena at all, but only a moral interpretation of phenomena. NIETZSCHE, *Beyond Good and Evil* (1886), 108, tr. Walter Kaufmann.

37. Physical science will not console me for the ignorance of morality in the time of affliction. But the science of ethics will always console me for the ignorance of the physical sciences. PASCAL, *Pensées* (1670), 67, tr. W. F. Trotter.

38. When reason and instinct are reconciled, there will be no higher appeal. JEAN-PHILIPPE RAMEAU, *Observations sur notre instinct pour la musique et sur son principe* (1734).

39. Ethics is in origin the art of recommending to others the sacrifices required for co-operation with oneself. BERTRAND RUSSELL, "On Scientific Method in Philosophy," *Mysticism and Logic* (1917).

40. Without civic morality communities perish; without personal morality their survival has no value. BERTRAND RUSSELL, "Individual and Social Ethics," *Authority and the Individual* (1949).

41. Our virtues / Lie in th' interpretation of the time. SHAKESPEARE, *Coriolanus* (1607–08), 4.7.49.

42. Morality consists of suspecting other people of not being legally married. GEORGE BERNARD SHAW, *The Doctor's Dilemma* (1913), 3.

43. The great secret of morals is love. SHELLEY, *A Defence of Poetry* (1821).

44. We must never delude ourselves into thinking that physical power is a substitute for moral power, which is the true sign of national greatness. ADLAI STEVENSON, speech, Hartford, Conn., Sept. 18, 1952.

45. If your morals make you dreary, depend upon it, they are wrong. ROBERT LOUIS STEVENSON, *Across the Plains* (1892), 12.

46. To make our morality centre on forbidden acts is to defile the imagination and to introduce into our judgments of our fellow-men a secret element of gusto. ROBERT LOUIS STEVENSON, *Across the Plains* (1892), 12.

47. Our whole life is startlingly moral. There is never an instant's truce between virtue and vice. THOREAU, "Higher Laws," *Walden* (1854).

48. Morals are an acquirement—like music, like a foreign language, like piety, poker, paralysis—no man is born with them. MARK TWAIN, "Seventieth Birthday" (1910).

49. It is not best that we use our morals week days; it gets them out of repair for Sundays. MARK TWAIN, *Notebook* (1935).

50. The moral sense enables one to perceive morality—and avoid it. The immoral sense enables one to perceive immorality and enjoy it. MARK TWAIN, *Notebook* (1935).

51. Our errors and our controversies, in the sphere of morality, arise sometimes from looking on men as though they could be altogether bad, or altogether good. VAUVENARGUES, *Reflections and Maxims* (1746), 31, tr. F. G. Stevens.

52. All sects differ, because they come from men; morality is everywhere the same, because it comes from God. VOLTAIRE, "Theism," *Philosophical Dictionary* (1764).

53. As society is now constituted, a literal adherence to the moral precepts scattered throughout the Gospels would mean sudden death. ALFRED NORTH WHITEHEAD, *Adventures in Ideas* (1933), 2.

54. A man who moralizes is usually a hypocrite, and a woman who moralizes is invariably plain. OSCAR WILDE, *Lady Windermere's Fan* (1892), 3.

55. Morality is simply the attitude we adopt towards people whom we personally dislike. OSCAR WILDE, *An Ideal Husband* (1895), 2.

## 599. MORNING

**See also 71. Bed; 626. Night; 899. Sleep**

1. It is only your habitual late riser who takes in the full flavor of Nature at those rare intervals when he gets up to go a-fishing. He brings virginal emotions and unsatiated eyes to the sparkling freshness of earth and stream and sky. THOMAS BAILEY ALDRICH, "Asides: Writers and Talkers," *Ponkapog Papers* (1903).

2. Oft when the white, still dawn / Lifted the skies and pushed the hills apart, / I have

felt it like a glory in my heart. EDWIN MARKHAM, "Joy of the Morning" (1899).

3. The morning is wiser than the evening. RUSSIAN PROVERB.

4. For the mind disturbed, the still beauty of dawn is nature's finest balm. EDWIN WAY TEALE, "April 21," *Circle of the Seasons* (1953).

5. It is true, I never assisted the sun materially in his rising, but doubt not, it was of the last importance only to be present at it. THOREAU, "Economy," *Walden* (1854).

6. Only dull people are brilliant at breakfast. OSCAR WILDE, *An Ideal Husband* (1895), 1.

7. For what human ill does not dawn seem to be an alleviation? THORNTON WILDER, *The Bridge of San Luis Rey* (1927), 3.

## 600. MORTALITY

See also 218. Death; 452. Immortality; 983. Transience

1. Most men eddy about / Here and there—eat and drink, / Chatter and love and hate, / Gather and squander, are raised / Aloft, are hurled in the dust, / Striving blindly, achieving / Nothing; and then they die— / Perish;—and no one asks / Who or what they have been. MATTHEW ARNOLD, "Rugby Chapel," *New Poems* (1867).

2. To live, to have so much ambition, to suffer, to cry, to fight and, at the end, forgetfulness . . . as if I had never existed. MARIE BASHKIRTSEV, preface to *Journal* (1887).

3. Let us eat and drink; for tomorrow we shall die. *Bible*, Isaiah 22:13.

4. All flesh is grass, and all the goodliness thereof is as the flower of the field. *Bible*, Isaiah 40:6.

5. The gay will laugh / When thou art gone, the solemn brood of care / Plod on, and each one as before will chase / His favourite phantom; yet all these shall leave / Their mirth and their employments, and shall come, / And make their bed with thee. WILLIAM CULLEN BRYANT, "Thanatopsis" (1811).

6. To venerate the simple days / Which lead the seasons by, / Needs but to remember / That from you or I / They may take the trifle / Termed mortality! EMILY DICKINSON, poem (c. 1858).

7. The fall of a leaf is a whisper to the living. ENGLISH PROVERB.

8. There is one expense no mortal can recover: / A human life. For money, there are ways. EURIPIDES, *The Suppliant Women* (c. 421 B.C.), tr. Frank W. Jones.

9. Mortality / Creeps on the dung of earth, and cannot reach / The riddles which are purposed by the gods. JOHN FORD, *The Broken Heart* (1633), 1.2.

10. Such is the frailty of man that even where he makes the truest and most forcible impression—in the memory, in the heart of his beloved—, there also he must perish. GOETHE, *The Sorrows of Young Werther* (1774), 2, Oct. 26, 1772, tr. Victor Lange.

11. Come, for the House of Hope is built on sand: bring wine, for the fabric of life is as weak as the wind. HĀFIZ, ghazals from the *Divan* (14th c.), 12, tr. Justin Huntly McCarthy.

12. Our brains are seventy-year clocks. The Angel of Life winds them up once for all, then closes the case, and gives the key into the hand of the Angel of the Resurrection. OLIVER WENDELL HOLMES, SR., *The Autocrat of the Breakfast Table* (1858), 8.

13. Art is long, and Time is fleeting, / And our hearts, though stout and brave, / Still, like muffled drums, are beating / Funeral marches to the grave. LONGFELLOW, "A Psalm of Life" (1839), 4.

14. One thing is certain and the rest is Lies; / The Flower that once has blown for ever dies. OMAR KHAYYÁM, *Rubáiyát* (11th–12th c.), tr. Edward FitzGerald, 4th ed., 63.

15. Mortality has its compensations: one is that all evils are transitory, another that better times may come. GEORGE SANTAYANA, *The Life of Reason: Reason in Common Sense* (1905–06), 12.

16. Our life's a moment and less than a moment, but even this mite nature has mockingly humored with some appearance of a longer span. SENECA, *Letters to Lucilius* (1st c.), 49.3, tr. E. Phillips Barker.

17. We are such stuff / As dreams are made on, and our little life / Is rounded with a sleep. SHAKESPEARE, *The Tempest* (1611–12), 4.1.156.

18. Old and young, we are all on our last cruise. ROBERT LOUIS STEVENSON,

"Crabbed Age and Youth," *Virginibus Puerisque* (1881).

19. For all the compasses in the world, there's only one direction, and time is its only measure. TOM STOPPARD, *Rosencrantz & Guildenstern Are Dead* (1967), 2.

20. We thank with brief thanksgiving / Whatever gods may be / That no life lives for ever; / That dead men rise up never; / That even the weariest river / Winds somewhere safe to sea. ALGERNON CHARLES SWINBURNE, "The Garden of Proserpine," *Poems and Ballads: First Series* (1866).

21. Man comes and tills the field and lies beneath, / And after many a summer dies the swan. ALFRED, LORD TENNYSON, "Tithonus" (1860).

22. What fools men are to weep the dead and gone! / Unwept, youth drops its petals one by one. THEOGNIS (6th c. B.C.).

23. When I catch myself resenting not being immortal, I pull myself up short by asking whether I should really like the prospect of having to make out an annual income-tax return for an infinite number of years ahead. ARNOLD J. TOYNBEE, "Why and How I Work," *Saturday Review*, April 5, 1969.

## MOTHERS

See 663. Parenthood

## 601. MOTIVES

See also 284. Ends; 765. Purpose

1. All that we do is done with an eye to something else. ARISTOTLE, *Nicomachean Ethics* (4th c. B.C.), 3.3, tr. J. A. K. Thomson.

2. 'Tis e'er the wont of simple folk to prize the deed and o'erlook the motive, and of learned folk to discount the deed and lay open the soul of the doer. JOHN BARTH, *The Sot-Weed Factor* (1960), 3.9.

3. The true motives of our actions, like the real pipes of an organ, are usually concealed. But the gilded and the hollow pretext is pompously placed in the front for show. CHARLES CALEB COLTON, *Lacon* (1825), 1.97.

4. We are not more ingenious in searching out bad motives for good actions when performed by others, than good motives for bad actions when performed by ourselves. CHARLES CALEB COLTON, *Lacon* (1825), 2.1.

5. A good intention clothes itself with sudden power. When a god wishes to ride, any chip or pebble will bud and shoot out winged feet, and serve him for a horse. EMERSON, "Fate," *The Conduct of Life* (1860).

6. We should often feel ashamed of our best actions if the world could see all of the motives which produced them. LA ROCHEFOUCAULD, *Maxims* (1665), tr. Kenneth Pratt.

7. Men can be stimulated by hope or driven by fear, but the hope and the fear must be vivid and immediate if they are to be effective without producing weariness. BERTRAND RUSSELL, "Technique and Human Nature," *Authority and the Individual* (1949).

8. The Light of Lights / Looks always on the motive, not the deed, / The Shadow of Shadows on the deed alone. WILLIAM BUTLER YEATS, *The Countess Cathleen* (1892), 5.

## 602. MOUNTAINS

1. The influence of fine scenery, the presence of mountains, appeases our irritations and elevates our friendships. EMERSON, "Culture," *The Conduct of Life* (1860).

2. Mountains are the beginning and the end of all natural scenery. JOHN RUSKIN, *Modern Painters* (1843–60), v. 4, 5.20.1.

3. Hills are the earth's gesture of despair / for the unreachable. RABINDRANATH TAGORE, *Fireflies* (1928).

4. The mountain remains unmoved / at its seeming defeat by the mist. RABINDRANATH TAGORE, *Fireflies* (1928).

## 603. MOURNING

See also 101. Burial; 365. Funerals; 911. Sorrow; 1045. Weeping

1. It is better to go to the house of mourning, than to go to the house of feasting: for that is the end of all men; and the living will lay it to his heart. *Bible*, Ecclesiastes 7:2.

2. Ah! surely Nothing dies but Something mourns! BYRON, *Don Juan* (1819–24), 3.108.

3. Let mourning stop when one's grief is fully expressed. CONFUCIUS, *Analects* (6th c. B.C.), 19.14, tr. Ch'u Chai and Winberg Chai.

4. The vastest earthly Day / Is shrunken small / By one Defaulting Face / Behind a Pall. EMILY DICKINSON, poem (c. 1874).

5. The dead sleep in their moonless night; my business is with the living. EMERSON, *Journals*, 1825.

6. Lament not the dead but the living. THOMAS FULLER, M.D., *Gnomologia* (1732), 3144.

7. To weep excessively for the dead is to affront the living. THOMAS FULLER, M.D., *Gnomologia* (1732), 5251.

8. We who are left how shall we look again / Happily on the sun or feel the rain / Without remembering how they who went / Ungrudgingly and spent / Their lives for us loved, too, the sun and rain? WILFRED WILSON GIBSON, "Lament" (1917?).

9. The house of mourning is decorously darkened to the world, but within itself it is also the house of laughing. WILLIAM DEAN HOWELLS, *The Rise of Silas Lapham* (1885), 24.

10. The sorrow for the dead is the only sorrow from which we refuse to be divorced. WASHINGTON IRVING, "Rural Funerals," *The Sketch Book of Geoffrey Crayon, Gent.* (1819–20).

11. When we lose one we love, our bitterest tears are called forth by the memory of hours when we loved not enough. MAURICE MAETERLINCK, *Wisdom and Destiny* (1898), 44, tr. Alfred Sutro.

12. What we call mourning for our dead is perhaps not so much grief at not being able to call them back as it is grief at not being able to want to do so. THOMAS MANN, *The Magic Mountain* (1924), 7.8, tr. H. T. Lowe-Porter.

13. Not louder shrieks to pitying heaven are cast, / When husbands, or when lapdogs breathe their last. ALEXANDER POPE, *The Rape of the Lock* (1712), 3.157.

14. Now let the weeping cease; / Let no one mourn again. / These things are in the hands of God. SOPHOCLES, *Oedipus at Colonus* (401 B.C.), tr. Robert Fitzgerald.

15. None mourn more ostentatiously than those who most rejoice at it [a death]. TACITUS, *Annals* (A.D. 115–117?), 2.78, tr. Alfred J. Church and William J. Brodribb.

## 604. MOVIES

**See also 419. Hollywood; 563. Mass Media**

1. A film is a petrified fountain of thought. JEAN COCTEAU, *Esquire*, February 1961.

2. American motion pictures are written by the half-educated for the half-witted. ST. JOHN ERVINE, *New York Mirror*, June 6, 1963.

3. A wide screen just makes a bad film twice as bad. SAMUEL GOLDWYN, *Quote*, Sept. 9, 1956.

4. The stultifying effect of the movies is *not* that the children see them but that their parents do, as if Hollywood provided a plausible adult recreation to grow up into. PAUL GOODMAN, *Growing Up Absurd* (1960), 4.4.

5. At the drive-in cinemas nature itself in all the glory of Technicolor and Vista-Vision is available for the motorist and his mate. What more pleasant setting for sweetly deodorized bodies to meet, unzip, and commune? MALCOLM MUGGERIDGE, "Women of America," *The Most of Malcolm Muggeridge* (1966).

6. There is only one thing that can kill the Movies, and that is education. WILL ROGERS, *The Autobiography of Will Rogers* (1949), 6.

7. A film is a boat which is always on the point of sinking—it always tends to break up as you go along and drag you under with it. FRANÇOIS TRUFFAUT, interview in Peter Graham's *The New Wave* (1968).

## 605. THE MUNDANE

**See also 331. Familiarity; 989. Trifles; 1005. Unimportance**

1. Nothing is poetical if plain daylight is not poetical; and no monster should amaze us if the normal man does not amaze. G. K. CHESTERTON, "On Experience," *All Is Grist* (1931).

2. Every day cannot be a feast of lanterns. CHINESE PROVERB.

3. Many eyes go through the meadow, but few see the flowers in it. EMERSON, *Journals*, 1834.

4. There is health in table talk and nursery play. We must wear old shoes and have aunts and cousins. EMERSON, *Journals*, 1836.

5. That which one cannot experience in

daily life is not true for oneself. D. H. LAWRENCE, *The Rainbow* (1915), 11.

6. Not to know at large of things remote / From use, obscure and subtle, but to know / That which before us lies in daily life, / Is the prime wisdom. MILTON, *Paradise Lost* (1667), 8.191.

7. 'Tis the taste of effeminacy that disrelishes ordinary and accustomed things. MONTAIGNE, "Of experience," *Essays* (1580–88), tr. Charles Cotton and W. C. Hazlitt.

8. A mind too proud to unbend over the small ridiculosa of life is as painful as a library with no trash in it. CHRISTOPHER MORLEY, *Inward Ho!* (1923), 14.

9. Commonplaces are the tramways of intellectual transportation. JOSÉ ORTEGA Y GASSET, *The Revolt of the Masses* (1930), 14.

10. Objects which are usually the motives of our travels by land and by sea are often overlooked and neglected if they lie under our eye. PLINY THE YOUNGER, *Letters* (c. 97–110), 8.20.1, tr. William Melmoth.

11. If your daily life seems poor, do not blame it; blame yourself, tell yourself that you are not poet enough to call forth its riches. RAINER MARIA RILKE, *Letters to a Young Poet*, Feb. 17, 1903, tr. M. D. Herter Norton.

12. Familiar things happen, and mankind does not bother about them. It requires a very unusual mind to undertake the analysis of the obvious. ALFRED NORTH WHITEHEAD, *Science and the Modern World* (1925), 1.

13. The commonest thing is delightful if one only hides it. OSCAR WILDE, *The Picture of Dorian Gray* (1891), 1.

14. Most people become bankrupt through having invested too heavily in the prose of life. OSCAR WILDE, *The Picture of Dorian Gray* (1891), 4.

## MURDER
See 516. Killing

## 606. MUSEUMS

1. Each living art object, taken out of its native habitat so we can conveniently gaze at it, is like an animal in a zoo. Something about it has died in the removal. DANIEL J. BOORSTIN, *The Image* (1962), 3.4.

2. I seldom . . . go into a natural history museum without feeling as if I were attending a funeral. JOHN BURROUGHS, *Indoor Studies* (1889).

3. The Museum is not meant either for the wanderer to see by accident or for the pilgrim to see with awe. It is meant for the mere slave of a routine of self-education to stuff himself with every sort of incongruous intellectual food in one indigestible meal. G. K. CHESTERTON, "On Sightseeing," *All Is Grist* (1931).

## 607. MUSIC
See also 608. Musical Instruments; 648. Opera; 895. Singing; 912. Sound

1. Nothing is capable of being well set to music that is not nonsense. JOSEPH ADDISON, *The Spectator*, March 21, 1711.

2. The most exciting rhythms seem unexpected and complex, the most beautiful melodies simple and inevitable. W. H. AUDEN, "Notes on Music and Opera," *The Dyer's Hand* (1962).

3. A verbal art like poetry is reflective; it stops to think. Music is immediate, it goes on to become. W. H. AUDEN, "Notes on Music and Opera," *The Dyer's Hand* (1962).

4. Whether the angels play only Bach in praising God I am not quite sure; I am sure, however, that *en famille* they play Mozart. KARL BARTH, quoted in his obituary, *The New York Times*, Dec. 11, 1968.

5. Composers should write tunes that chauffeurs and errand boys can whistle. SIR THOMAS BEECHAM, *The New York Times*, March 9, 1961.

6. Music is a part of us, and either ennobles or degrades our behavior. BOETHIUS, *De Institutione Musica* (6th c. A.D.).

7. Who hears music, feels his solitude / Peopled at once. ROBERT BROWNING, *Balaustion's Adventure* (1871).

8. Many men are melancholy by hearing music, but it is a pleasing melancholy that it causeth; and therefore to such as are discontent, in woe, fear, sorrow, or dejected, it is a most present remedy. ROBERT BURTON, *The Anatomy of Melancholy* (1621).

9. To know whether you are enjoying a piece of music or not you must see whether you find yourself looking at the advertisements of Pear's soap at the end of the pro-

gram. SAMUEL BUTLER (d. 1902), "Unprofessional Sermons," *Note-Books* (1912).

10. New music: new listening. Not an attempt to understand something that is being said, for, if something were being said, the sounds would be given the shapes of words. Just an attention to the activity of sounds. JOHN CAGE, "Experimental Music," *Silence* (1961).

11. Music is edifying, for from time to time it sets the soul in operation. JOHN CAGE, "Forerunners of Modern Music," *Silence* (1961).

12. Let no one imagine that in owning a recording he has the music. The very practice of music is a celebration that we own nothing. JOHN CAGE, "Lecture on Something," *Silence* (1961).

13. Who is there that, in logical words, can express the effect music has on us? A kind of inarticulate unfathomable speech, which leads us to the edge of the Infinite, and lets us for moments gaze into that! THOMAS CARLYLE, *On Heroes, Hero-Worship and the Heroic in History* (1841), 3.

14. Music is well said to be the speech of angels; in fact, nothing among the utterances allowed to man is felt to be so divine. It brings us near to the Infinite. THOMAS CARLYLE, "The Opera" (1852).

15. Where there's music there can be no evil. CERVANTES, *Don Quixote* (1605–15), 2.4.34.

16. Music has charms to soothe a savage breast—but not the unmusical one. ALEXANDER CHASE, *Perspectives* (1966).

17. Music with dinner is an insult both to the cook and violinist. G. K. CHESTERTON, quoted in *The New York Times*, Nov. 16, 1967.

18. Music has charms to soothe a savage breast, / To soften rocks, or bend a knotted oak. WILLIAM CONGREVE, *The Mourning Bride* (1697), 1.1.

19. As poetry is the harmony of words, so music is that of notes. JOHN DRYDEN, Dedication to Purcell's *The Prophetess* (1690).

20. Music was invented to confirm human loneliness. LAWRENCE DURRELL, *Clea* (1960), 1.3.

21. [Music ] takes us out of the actual and whispers to us dim secrets that startle our wonder as to who we are, and for what, whence, and whereto. EMERSON, *Journals*, 1836.

22. Music is nothing else but wild sounds civilized into time and tune. THOMAS FULLER, D.D., *Worthies of England* (1662), 10.

23. A nation creates music—the composer only arranges it. MIKHAIL GLINKA, quoted in *Theatre Arts*, June 1958.

24. Take a music-bath once or twice a week for a few seasons, and you will find that it is to the soul what the water-bath is to the body. OLIVER WENDELL HOLMES, SR., *Over the Teacups* (1891), 5.

25. Music can be translated only by music. Just so far as it suggests worded thought, it falls short of its highest office. OLIVER WENDELL HOLMES, SR., *Over the Teacups* (1891), 5.

26. When people hear good music, it makes them homesick for something they never had, and never will have. EDGAR WATSON HOWE, *Country Town Sayings* (1911).

27. And the night shall be filled with music, / And the cares that infest the day, / Shall fold their tents, like the Arabs, / And as silently steal away. LONGFELLOW, "The Day Is Done" (1844), 11.

28. Music quickens time, she quickens us to the finest enjoyment of time. THOMAS MANN, *The Magic Mountain* (1924), 4.4, tr. H. T. Lowe-Porter.

29. It's not that music is too imprecise for words, but too precise. FELIX MENDELSSOHN, (1809–47), quoted by Ned Rorem in "Theme," *Music from Inside Out* (1967).

30. Music is a beautiful opiate, if you don't take it too seriously. HENRY MILLER, "With Edgar Varèse in the Gobi Desert," *The Air-Conditioned Nightmare* (1945).

31. Without music, life would be an error. The German imagines even God singing songs. NIETZSCHE, "Maxims and Missiles," 33, *Twilight of the Idols* (1888), tr. Walter Kaufmann.

32. To produce music is also in a sense to produce children. NIETZSCHE, *The Will to Power* (1888), 800, tr. Anthony M. Ludovici.

33. Jazz may be thought of as a current that bubbled forth from a spring in the slums of New Orleans to become the main spring of the twentieth century. HENRY PLEASANTS, news summaries, Dec. 30, 1955.

34. We must have recourse to the rules [of music] only when our genius and our ear seem to deny what we are seeking. JEAN-PHILIPPE RAMEAU, *Le nouveau système de musique théorique* (1726).

35. What strange impulse is it which induces otherwise truthful people to say they like music when they do not, and thus expose themselves to hours of boredom? AGNES REPPLIER, "The Idolatrous Dog," *Under Dispute* (1924).

36. [Of music]. Thou speakest to me of things which in all my endless life I have not found and shall not find. JEAN PAUL RICHTER, quoted in Emerson's "Love," *Essays: First Series* (1841).

37. If music could be translated into human speech, it would no longer need to exist. NED ROREM, "Composer and Performance," *Music from Inside Out* (1967).

38. Why, after all, must everyone like music? That they are missing something is just the lover's opinion. NED ROREM, "Listening and Hearing," *Music from Inside Out* (1967).

39. The sound of music—as opposed to rustling leaves or words of love—is sensual only secondarily. First it must make sense. NED ROREM, "Music for the Eye and the Mind," *Music from Inside Out* (1967).

40. Music exists—not on canvas nor yet on the staff—only in motion. The good listener will hear it as the present prolonged. NED ROREM, "Pictures and Pieces," *Music from Inside Out* (1967).

41. Music lasts by itself and cares not who composed it; nor can music recall the thousand anonymous fingers and mouths which tamper with it, beautifully or badly. NED ROREM, "Song and Singer," *Music from Inside Out* (1967).

42. Music is essentially useless, as life is. GEORGE SANTAYANA, *The Life of Reason: Reason in Art* (1905–06), 4.

43. Music is a means of giving form to our inner feelings without attaching them to events or objects in the world. GEORGE SANTAYANA, *Little Essays* (1920), 54, ed. Logan Pearsall Smith.

44. The notes I handle no better than many pianists. But the pauses between the notes—ah, that is where the art resides! ARTUR SCHNABEL, *Chicago Daily News*, June 11, 1958.

45. The man that hath no music in himself, / Nor is not moved with concord of sweet sounds, / Is fit for treasons, stratagems, and spoils; / The motions of his spirit are dull as night, / And his affections dark as Erebus. / Let no such man be trusted. SHAKESPEARE, *The Merchant of Venice* (1596–97), 5.1.83.

46. Music revives the recollections it would appease. MME DE STAËL, *Corinne* (1807), 9.2.

47. When a man is not disposed to hear music, there is not a more disagreeable sound in harmony than that of the violin. RICHARD STEELE, *The Tatler*, April 1, 1710.

48. Music is the sole domain in which man realizes the present. IGOR STRAVINSKY, *An Autobiography* (1936), 4.

49. If, as is nearly always the case, music appears to express something, this is only an illusion and not a reality. IGOR STRAVINSKY, *An Autobiography* (1936), 4.

50. The trouble with music appreciation in general is that people are taught to have too much respect for music; they should be taught to love it instead. IGOR STRAVINSKY, *The New York Times Magazine*, Sept. 27, 1964.

51. The one true comment on a piece of music is another piece of music. IGOR STRAVINSKY, "Stravinsky on the Musical Scene and Other Matters," *The New York Review of Books* (May 12, 1966).

52. The performance of performance has developed to such an extent in recent years that it challenges the music itself and will soon threaten it with relegation. IGOR STRAVINSKY, "Stravinsky on the Musical Scene and Other Matters," *The New York Review of Books* (May 12, 1966).

53. Conductors must give unmistakable and suggestive signals to the orchestra—not choreography to the audience. GEORGE SZELL, *Newsweek*, Jan. 28, 1963.

54. Men profess to be lovers of music, but for the most part they give no evidence in their opinions and lives that they have heard it. It would not leave them narrow-minded and bigoted. THOREAU, *Journal*, Aug. 5, 1851.

55. The harmony of a concert, to which you listen with delight, must have on certain classes of minute animals the effect of terrible thunder; perhaps it kills them. VOLTAIRE, "Appearance," *Philosophical Dictionary* (1764).

## 608. MUSICAL INSTRUMENTS

**See also 607. Music**

1. Accordion, n. An instrument in harmony with the sentiments of an assassin. AMBROSE BIERCE, *The Devil's Dictionary* (1881–1911).

2. Clarionet, n. An instrument of torture operated by a person with cotton in his ears. There are two instruments that are worse than a clarionet—two clarionets. AMBROSE BIERCE, *The Devil's Dictionary* (1881–1911).

3. The cello is like a beautiful woman who has not grown older, but younger with time, more slender, more supple, more graceful. PABLO CASALS, *Time*, April 29, 1957.

4. Violins are the lively, forward, importunate wits, that distinguish themselves by the flourishes of imagination, sharpness of repartee, glances of satire, and bear away the upper part in every consort. RICHARD STEELE, *The Tatler*, April 1, 1710.

## 609. MYSTICISM

**See also 276. Ecstasy; 920. Spirituality**

1. Without mysticism man can achieve nothing great. ANDRÉ GIDE, *The Counterfeiters* (1925), 2.5, tr. Dorothy Bussy.

2. Mysticism is, in essence, little more than a certain intensity and depth of feeling in regard to what is believed about the universe. BERTRAND RUSSELL, title essay, *Mysticism and Logic* (1917).

3. The mystic can live happy in the droning consciousness of his own heartbeats and those of the universe. GEORGE SANTAYANA, *Winds of Doctrine* (1913).

4. Mystics always hope that science will some day overtake them. BOOTH TARKINGTON, *Looking Forward to the Great Adventure* (1926).

## 610. MYTH

**See also 447. Illusion**

1. The anatomy of any myth is the anatomy of the men who believed in it and suffered by it. MURRAY KEMPTON, "A Prelude," *Part of Our Time* (1955).

2. The great enemy of the truth is very often not the lie—deliberate, contrived and dishonest—but the myth—persistent, persuasive and unrealistic. JOHN F. KENNEDY, commencement address, Yale University, New Haven, Conn., June 11, 1962.

3. When myth meets myth, the collision is very real. STANISLAW LEC, *Unkempt Thoughts* (1962), tr. Jacek Galazka.

4. Myths are not believed in, they are conceived and understood. GEORGE SANTAYANA, *Little Essays* (1920), 23, ed. Logan Pearsall Smith.

5. Mythology is what grown-ups believe, folklore is what they tell the children, and religion is both. CEDRIC WHITMAN, letter to Edward Tripp, Feb. 28, 1969.

# N

## 611. NAÏVETÉ

**See also 199. Credulity; 445. Ignorance; 476. Innocence**

1. The greenhorn is the ultimate victor in everything; it is he that gets the most out of life. G. K. CHESTERTON, "The Fairy Pickwick," *A Shilling for My Thoughts* (1916).

2. He who does not open his eyes must open his purse. GERMAN PROVERB.

3. The ignorance of the world leaves one at the mercy of its malice. WILLIAM HAZLITT, "On the Disadvantages of Intellectual Superiority," *Table Talk* (1821–22).

4. Naïve you are / if you believe / life favors those / who aren't naïve. PIET HEIN, "Naïve," *Grooks* (1966).

5. I like peasants—they are not sophisticated enough to reason speciously. MONTESQUIEU, *Variétés*.

## NAKEDNESS

**See 634. Nudity**

## 612. NAMES

**See also 442. Identity**

1. For every man there is something in the vocabulary that would stick to him like a second skin. His enemies have only to find it. AMBROSE BIERCE, "Oleaginous,"

*The Devil's Dictionary* (1881–1911).

2. Don't take action because of a name! A name is an uncertain thing, you can't count on it! BERTOLT BRECHT, *A Man's a Man* (1927), 10, adapted by Eric Bentley.

3. Names are but noise and smoke, / Obscuring heavenly light. GOETHE, "Martha's Garden," *Faust: Part I* (1808), tr. Philip Wayne.

4. Of all eloquence a nickname is the most concise; of all arguments the most unanswerable. WILLIAM HAZLITT, "On Nicknames," *Sketches and Essays* (1839).

5. Great names abase, instead of elevating, those who do not know how to bear them. LA ROCHEFOUCAULD, *Maxims* (1665), tr. Kenneth Pratt.

6. The name of a man is a numbing blow from which he never recovers. MARSHALL MC LUHAN, *Understanding Media* (1964), 2.

7. Titles are but nicknames, and every nickname is a title. THOMAS PAINE, *The Rights of Man* (1791), 1.

8. What's in a name? That which we call a rose / By any other name would smell as sweet. SHAKESPEARE, *Romeo and Juliet* (1594–95), 2.2.43.

9. Our names are the light that glows on the sea waves at night and then dies without leaving its signature. RABINDRANATH TAGORE, *Stray Birds* (1916), 229.

**NARCISSISM**

**See 869. Self-love**

## 613. NARROWNESS

**See also 333. Fanaticism; 498. Intolerance; 647. Open-mindedness; 720. Prejudices; 896. Single-mindedness**

1. Beware of the man of one book. ST. THOMAS AQUINAS, quoted in Isaac D'Israeli's *Curiosities of Literature* (1791–93).

2. The most fatal illusion is the settled point of view. Since life is growth and motion, a fixed point of view kills anybody who has one. BROOKS ATKINSON, "April 29," *Once Around the Sun* (1951).

3. It is as though nature must needs make men narrow in order to give them force. W. E. B. DU BOIS, *The Souls of Black Folk* (1903), 3.

4. There is no more certain sign of a narrow mind, of stupidity, and of arrogance, than to stand aloof from those who think differently from us. WALTER SAVAGE LANDOR, "Marcus Tullius and Quinctus Cicero," *Imaginary Conversations* (1824–53).

5. He who knows only his own side of the case, knows little of that. JOHN STUART MILL, *On Liberty* (1859), 2.

6. The poverty of goods is easily cured; the poverty of the soul is irreparable. MONTAIGNE, "Of managing the will," *Essays* (1580–88), tr. Charles Cotton and W. C. Hazlitt.

7. Blessed is the satirist; and blessed the ironist; blessed the witty scoffer, and blessed the sentimentalist; for each, having seen one spoke of the wheel, thinks to have seen all, and is content. CHRISTOPHER MORLEY, *Inward Ho!* (1923), 1.

8. It is with narrow-souled people as with narrow-necked bottles: the less they have in them, the more noise they make in pouring it out. ALEXANDER POPE, *Thoughts on Various Subjects* (1727).

9. If we think of this existence of the individual as a larger or smaller room, it appears evident that most people learn to know only a corner of their room, a place by the window, a strip of floor on which they walk up and down. RAINER MARIA RILKE, *Letters to a Young Poet*, Aug. 12, 1904, tr. M. D. Herter Norton.

10. All living souls welcome whatsoever they are ready to cope with; all else they ignore, or pronounce to be monstrous and wrong, or deny to be possible. GEORGE SANTAYANA, *Dialogues in Limbo* (1925), 4.

11. Narrow / The heart that loves, the brain that contemplates, / The life that wears, the spirit that creates / One object, and one form, and builds thereby / A sepulchre for its eternity. SHELLEY, *Epipsychidion* (1821).

12. Most people grow old within a small circle of ideas, which they have not discovered for themselves. There are perhaps less wrong-minded people than thoughtless. VAUVENARGUES, *Reflections and Maxims* (1746), 238, tr. F. G. Stevens.

13. Minds that have nothing to confer / Find little to perceive. WILLIAM WORDSWORTH, "Yes! Thou Art Fair, Yet Be Not Moved" (1845).

## 614. NATION

**See also 451. Immigration; 615. Nationalism; 671. Patriotism; 923. State**

1. The ruin of a nation begins in the homes of its people. ASHANTI PROVERB.

2. A nation will not count the sacrifice it makes, if it supposes it is engaged in a struggle for its fame, its influence and its existence. BENJAMIN DISRAELI, speech, "Prosecution of War," May 24, 1855.

3. There is a genius of a nation, which is not to be found in the numerical citizens, but which characterizes the society. EMERSON, "Nominalist and Realist," *Essays: Second Series* (1844).

4. The quality of the thought differences the Egyptian and the Roman, the Austrian and the American. EMERSON, "Fate," *The Conduct of Life* (1860).

5. Nations, like men, die by imperceptible disorders. We recognize a doomed people by the way they sneeze or pare their nails. JEAN GIRAUDOUX, *Tiger at the Gates* (1935), 2, tr. Christopher Fry.

6. The spirit of a nation is what counts—the look in its eyes. JEAN GIRAUDOUX, *Electra* (1937), 2, tr. Phyllis La Farge with Peter H. Judd.

7. Nothing is good for a nation but that which arises from its own core and its own general wants, without apish imitation of another. GOETHE, quoted in Johann Peter Eckermann's *Conversations with Goethe*, Jan. 24, 1824.

8. Men may be linked in friendship. Nations are linked only by interests. ROLF HOCHHUTH, *The Soldiers* (1967).

9. A nation without dregs and malcontents, is orderly, decent, peaceful and pleasant, but perhaps without the seed of things to come. ERIC HOFFER, *The True Believer* (1951), 2.4.18.

10. Size is not grandeur, and territory does not make a nation. THOMAS HENRY HUXLEY, "On University Education" (1876).

11. If our house be on fire, without inquiring whether it was fired from within or without, we must try to extinguish it. THOMAS JEFFERSON, letter to James Lewis, Jr., May 9, 1798.

12. Every country should realize that its turn at world domination, domination because its rights coincided more or less with the character or progress of the epoch, must terminate with the change brought about by this progress. JUAN RAMÓN JIMÉNEZ, "Heroic Reason," *Selected Writings* (1957), tr. H. R. Hays.

13. In this age when there can be no losers in peace and no victors in war—we must recognize the obligation to match national strength with national restraint. LYNDON B. JOHNSON, address to Congress, Nov. 27, 1963.

14. We must recognize that every nation determines its policies in terms of its own interests. JOHN F. KENNEDY, address, Mormon Tabernacle, Salt Lake City, Utah, Sept. 26, 1963.

15. A nation reveals itself not only by the men it produces but also by the men it honors, the men it remembers. JOHN F. KENNEDY, address, Amherst College, Mass., Oct. 26, 1963.

16. A nation can be no stronger abroad than she is at home. Only an America which practices what it preaches about equal rights and social justice will be respected by those whose choice affects our future. JOHN F. KENNEDY, undelivered address, Dallas, Texas, Nov. 22, 1963.

17. The very definition of a great power is that not only its actions but the cases in which it declines to act have major consequences. IRVING KRISTOL, quoted in a speech, "The Path to Vietnam," by William P. Bundy, Aug. 15, 1967.

18. A nation may be said to consist of its territory, its people, and its laws. The territory is the only part which is of certain durability. ABRAHAM LINCOLN, message to Congress, Dec. 1, 1862.

19. Borders are scratched across the hearts of men / By strangers with a calm, judicial pen, / And when the borders bleed we watch with dread / The lines of ink along the map turn red. MARYA MANNES, "Gaza Strip," *Subverse: Rhymes for Our Times* (1959).

20. It is in times of difficulty that great nations, like great men, display the whole energy of their character and become an object of admiration to posterity. NAPOLEON I, *Maxims* (1804–15).

21. A nation usually renews its youth on a political sick-bed, and there finds again the spirit which it had gradually lost in seeking

and maintaining power. NIETZSCHE, *Human, All Too Human* (1878), 464, tr. Helen Zimmern.

22. Nations, like individuals, have to limit their objectives, or take the consequences. JAMES RESTON, *Sketches in the Sand* (1967).

23. The driving force of a nation lies in its spiritual purpose, made effective by free, tolerant but unremitting national will. FRANKLIN D. ROOSEVELT, message to Congress, April 14, 1938.

24. Nations, like men, have their infancy. HENRY ST. JOHN, *Letters on the Study of History* (1752), 4.

25. Every nation thinks its own madness normal and requisite; more passion and more fancy it calls folly, less it calls imbecility. GEORGE SANTAYANA, *Dialogues in Limbo* (1925), 3.

26. Growing nations should remember that, in nature, no tree, though placed in the best conditions of light, soil, and plot, can continue to grow and spread indefinitely. PAUL VALÉRY, "Greatness and Decadence of Europe," *Reflections on the World Today* (1931), tr. Francis Scarfe.

27. Energy in a nation is like sap in a tree; it rises from bottom up. WOODROW WILSON, speech, Oct. 28, 1912.

28. We can afford to exercise the self-restraint of a really great nation which realizes its own strength and scorns to misuse it. WOODROW WILSON, message to Congress, Aug. 27, 1913.

## 615. NATIONALISM

**See also 496. International Relations; 614. Nation; 671. Patriotism**

1. Patriotism is a lively sense of responsibility. Nationalism is a silly cock crowing on its own dunghill. RICHARD ALDINGTON, *The Colonel's Daughter* (1931).

2. Nationalism is our form of incest, is our idolatry, is our insanity. "Patriotism" is its cult. ERICH FROMM, *The Sane Society* (1955), 3.

3. The nationalist has a broad hatred and a narrow love. He cannot stifle a predilection for dead cities. ANDRÉ GIDE, *Journals*, 1918, tr. Justin O'Brien.

4. Altogether, national hatred is something peculiar. You will always find it strongest and most violent where there is the lowest degree of culture. GOETHE, quoted in Johann Peter Eckermann's *Conversations with Goethe*, March 14, 1830.

5. The efficiency of the truly national leader consists primarily in preventing the division of the attention of a people, and always in concentrating it on a single enemy. ADOLF HITLER, *Mein Kampf* (1924), 1.3.

6. The landscape should belong to the people who see it all the time. LE ROI JONES, "The Legacy of Malcolm X," *Home* (1966).

7. All nations have present, or past, or future reasons for thinking themselves incomparable. PAUL VALÉRY, "Extraneous Remarks," *Selected Writings* (1964).

8. To wish the greatness of our own country is often to wish evil to our neighbors. He who could bring himself to wish that his country should always remain as it is, would be a citizen of the universe. VOLTAIRE, "Country," *Philosophical Dictionary* (1764).

9. Nationalism has two fatal charms for its devotees: it presupposes local self-sufficiency, which is a pleasant and desirable condition, and it suggests, very subtly, a certain personal superiority by reason of one's belonging to a place which is definable and familiar, as against a place which is strange, remote. E. B. WHITE, "Intimations," *One Man's Meat* (1944).

## 616. NATURE

**See also 174. Conservation; 270. Earth; 306. Evolution; 349. Flowers; 413. The Heavens; 431. Human Nature; 479. Insects; 484. Instinct; 597. Moon; 602. Mountains; 818. Rivers; 847. Sea; 848. Seasons; 904. Snow; 943. Sun; 988. Trees; 1039. Water; 1043. Weather; 1052. Wind**

1. Nature, with equal mind, / Sees all her sons at play; / Sees man control the wind, / The wind sweep man away; / Allows the proudly-riding and the foundering bark. MATTHEW ARNOLD, *Empedocles on Etna* (1852), 1.2.

2. The cult of nature is a form of patronage by people who have declared their materialistic independence from nature and do not have to struggle with nature every day of their lives. BROOKS ATKINSON,

"July 3," *Once Around the Sun* (1951).

3. Nature, to be commanded, must be obeyed. FRANCIS BACON, *Novum Organum* (1620).

4. Nature is often hidden, sometimes overcome, seldom extinguished. FRANCIS BACON, "Of Nature in Men," *Essays* (1625).

5. The three great elemental sounds in nature are the sound of rain, the sound of wind in a primeval wood, and the sound of outer ocean on a beach. HENRY BESTON, "The Headlong Wave," *The Outermost House* (1928).

6. Into every empty corner, into all forgotten things and nooks, Nature struggles to pour life, pouring life into the dead, life into life itself. HENRY BESTON, "Lantern on the Beach," *The Outermost House* (1928).

7. There is no forgiveness in nature. UGO BETTI, *Goat Island* (1946), 1.4, ed. Gino Rizzo.

8. To see a World in a Grain of Sand / And a Heaven in a Wild Flower, / Hold Infinity in the palm of your hand / And Eternity in an hour. WILLIAM BLAKE, "Auguries of Innocence" (1800–10).

9. Man is wise and constantly in quest of more wisdom; but the ultimate wisdom, which deals with beginnings, remains locked in a seed. There it lies, the simplest fact of the universe and at the same time the one which calls forth faith rather than reason. HAL BORLAND, "The Certainty—April 5," *Sundial of the Seasons* (1964).

10. You can't be suspicious of a tree, or accuse a bird or a squirrel of subversion or challenge the ideology of a violet. HAL BORLAND, "Spring Is for Laughter—April 13," *Sundial of the Seasons* (1964).

11. Man masters nature not by force but by understanding. JACOB BRONOWSKI, "The Creative Mind," *Science and Human Values* (1956).

12. To him who in the love of Nature holds / Communion with her visible forms, she speaks / A various language. WILLIAM CULLEN BRYANT, "Thanatopsis" (1811).

13. Gie me ae spark o' Nature's fire, / That's a' the learning I desire. ROBERT BURNS, "Epistle to John Lapraik No. 1" (1786).

14. There is a pleasure in the pathless woods, / There is a rapture on the lonely shore / There is society, where none intrudes, / By the deep Sea, and Music in its roar: / I love not Man the less, but Nature more. BYRON, *Childe Harold's Pilgrimage* (1812–18), 4.178.

15. The only words that ever satisfied me as describing Nature are the terms used in fairy books, "charm," "spell," "enchantment." They express the arbitrariness of the fact and its mystery. G. K. CHESTERTON, "The Logic of Elfland," *Orthodoxy* (1908).

16. Modern nature-worship is all upside down. Trees and fields ought to be the ordinary things; terraces and temples ought to be extraordinary. I am on the side of the man who lives in the country and wants to go to London. G. K. CHESTERTON, "The Surrender of a Cockney," *Alarms and Discursions* (1910).

17. I long for scenes, where man hath never trod, / A place where woman never smiled or wept— / There to abide with my Creator, God, / And Sleep as I in childhood sweetly slept, / Untroubling, and untroubled where I lie, / The grass below—above the vaulted sky. JOHN CLARE, "I Am" (1845).

18. We receive but what we give, / And in our life alone does Nature live: / Ours is her wedding garment, ours her shroud! SAMUEL TAYLOR COLERIDGE, "Dejection: An Ode" (1802).

19. Nature is the art of God. DANTE, *On World Government* (c. 1313), 1.3.

20. We talk of our mastery of nature, which sounds very grand; but the fact is we respectfully adapt ourselves, first, to her ways. CLARENCE DAY, *This Simian World* (1920), 8.

21. The peace of nature and of the innocent creatures of God seems to be secure and deep, only so long as the presence of man and his restless and unquiet spirit are not there to trouble its sanctity. THOMAS DE QUINCEY, "Preliminary Confessions," *Confessions of an English Opium-Eater* (1821–56).

22. Nature as a whole is a progressive realization of purpose strictly comparable to the realization of purpose in any single plant or animal. JOHN DEWEY, "The Influence of Darwinism on Philosophy" (1909).

23. Nature is a mutable cloud which is always and never the same. EMERSON, "History," *Essays: First Series* (1841).

24. When a man says to me, "I have the intensest love of nature," at once I know

that he has none. EMERSON, *Journals*, 1857.

25. Nature is reckless of the individual. When she has points to carry, she carries them. EMERSON, "Culture," *The Conduct of Life* (1860).

26. Nature is no spendthrift, but takes the shortest way to her ends. EMERSON, "Fate," *The Conduct of Life* (1860).

27. Why should we fear to be crushed by savage elements, we who are made up of the same elements? EMERSON, "Fate," *The Conduct of Life* (1860).

28. How cunningly nature hides every wrinkle of her inconceivable antiquity under roses and violets and morning dew! EMERSON, "The Progress of Culture," *Letters and Social Aims* (1876).

29. "Sail!" quoth the king; "Hold!" saith the wind. ENGLISH PROVERB.

30. How nature loves the incomplete. She knows / If she drew a conclusion it would finish her. CHRISTOPHER FRY, *Venus Observed* (1950), 2.2.

31. Forget not that the earth delights to feel your bare feet and the winds long to play with your hair. KAHLIL GIBRAN, "On Clothes," *The Prophet* (1923).

32. The true return to nature is the definitive return to the elements—death. ANDRÉ GIDE, "The Limits of Art," *Pretexts* (1903), tr. Angelo P. Bertocci and others.

33. A plant is like a self-willed man, out of whom we can obtain all which we desire, if we will only treat him his own way. GOETHE, *Elective Affinities* (1809), 27.

34. Nature goes her own way, and all that to us seems an exception is really according to order. GOETHE, quoted in Johann Peter Eckermann's *Conversations with Goethe*, Dec. 9, 1824.

35. Bring out your social remedies! They will fail, they will fail, every one, until each man has his feet somewhere upon the soil. DAVID GRAYSON, *Adventures in Contentment* (1907), 6.

36. We do not see nature with our eyes, but with our understandings and our hearts. WILLIAM HAZLITT, "On Taste," *Sketches and Essays* (1839).

37. The natural world is dynamic. From the expanding universe to the hair on a baby's head, nothing is the same from now to the next moment. HELEN HOOVER, "The Waiting Hills," *The Long-Shadowed Forest* (1963).

38. The chess-board is the world; the pieces are the phenomena of the universe; the rules of the game are what we call laws of Nature. THOMAS HENRY HUXLEY, "A Liberal Education" (1868).

39. Deviation from Nature is deviation from happiness. SAMUEL JOHNSON, *Rasselas* (1759), 22.

40. Never does nature say one thing and wisdom another. JUVENAL, *Satires* (c. 100), 14.21.

41. The roaring of the wind is my wife and the stars through the window pane are my children. JOHN KEATS, letter to George and Georgiana Keats, Oct. 14, 1818.

42. Nature, in her blind thirst for life, has filled every possible cranny of the rotting earth with some sort of fantastic creature. JOSEPH WOOD KRUTCH, "The Genesis of a Mood," *The Modern Temper* (1929).

43. Nature takes no account of even the most reasonable of human excuses. JOSEPH WOOD KRUTCH, "The Paradox of Humanism," *The Modern Temper* (1929).

44. Only those within whose own consciousness the suns rise and set, the leaves burgeon and wither, can be said to be aware of what living is. JOSEPH WOOD KRUTCH, "March," *The Twelve Seasons* (1949).

45. The God who planned the well-working machines which function as atom and solar system seems to have had no part in arranging the curiously inefficient society of plants and animals in which everything works against everything else. JOSEPH WOOD KRUTCH, "May," *The Twelve Seasons* (1949).

46. The reason for the sublime simplicity in the works of nature lies all too often in the sublime shortsightedness in the observer. GEORG CHRISTOPH LICHTENBERG, *Aphorisms* (1764–99), tr. J. P. Stern.

47. The visible marks of extraordinary wisdom and power appear so plainly in all the works of creation that a rational creature who will but seriously reflect on them cannot miss the discovery of a deity. JOHN LOCKE, *An Essay Concerning Human Understanding* (1690), 1.4.9.

48. There is not so contemptible a plant or animal that does not confound the most enlarged understanding. JOHN LOCKE, *An Essay Concerning Human Understanding* (1690), 3.6.9.

49. The child of civilization, remote from wild nature and all her ways, is more susceptible to her grandeur than is her untutored son who has looked at her and lived close to her from childhood up, on terms of prosaic familiarity. THOMAS MANN, *The Magic Mountain* (1924), 6.7, tr. H. T. Lowe-Porter.

50. God, I can push the grass apart / And lay my finger on Thy heart! EDNA ST. VINCENT MILLAY, title poem, *Renascence* (1917).

51. Accuse not Nature! she hath done her part; / Do thou but thine! MILTON, *Paradise Lost* (1667), 8.561.

52. Nature is a gentle guide, but not more sweet and gentle than prudent and just. MONTAIGNE, "Of experience," *Essays* (1580–88), tr. Charles Cotton and W. C. Hazlitt.

53. Nature, in her most dazzling aspects or stupendous parts, is but the background and theatre of the tragedy of man. JOHN MORLEY, "Byron," *Critical Miscellanies* (1871–1908).

54. Let children walk with Nature, let them see the beautiful blendings and communions of death and life, their joyous inseparable unity, . . . and they will learn that death is stingless indeed, and as beautiful as life, and that the grave has no victory, for it never fights. JOHN MUIR, *A Thousand-Mile Walk to the Gulf* (1916), 4.

55. Those honour Nature well, who teach that she can speak on everything, even on theology. PASCAL, *Pensées* (1670), 29, tr. W. F. Trotter.

56. Nature has some perfections to show that she is the image of God, and some defects to show that she is only His image. PASCAL, *Pensées* (1670), 579, tr. W. F. Trotter.

57. It were happy if we studied nature more in natural things, and acted according to nature, whose rules are few, plain, and most reasonable. WILLIAM PENN, *Some Fruits of Solitude* (1693), 1.9.

58. The day, water, sun, moon, night—I do not have to purchase these things with money. PLAUTUS, *The Comedy of Asses* (3rd c. B.C.).

59. All nature is but art, unknown to thee; / All chance, direction, which thou canst not see; / All discord, harmony not understood; / All partial evil, universal good. ALEXANDER POPE, *An Essay on Man* (1733–34), 1.289.

60. Nature's instructions are always slow, those of men are generally premature. ROUSSEAU, *Émile* (1762), 4.

61. The works of nature first acquire a meaning in the commentaries they provoke. GEORGE SANTAYANA, *Little Essays* (1920), 1, ed. Logan Pearsall Smith.

62. Nature is like a beautiful woman that may be as delightfully and as truly known at a certain distance as upon a closer view; as to knowing her through and through, that is nonsense in both cases, and might not reward our pains. GEORGE SANTAYANA, *Character and Opinion in the United States* (1921), 1.

63. True wisdom consists in not departing from nature and in molding our conduct according to her laws and model. SENECA, "On a Happy Life," *Moral Essays* (1st c.), tr. Aubrey Stewart.

64. In nature, there is less death and destruction than death and transmutation. EDWIN WAY TEALE, "July 5," *Circle of the Seasons* (1953).

65. Commonly we stride through the out-of-doors too swiftly to see more than the most obvious and prominent things. For observing nature, the best pace is a snail's pace. EDWIN WAY TEALE, "July 14," *Circle of the Seasons* (1953).

66. Nature is one with rapine, a harm no preacher can heal; / The Mayfly is torn by the swallow, the sparrow speared by the shrike, / And the whole little wood where I sit is a world of plunder and prey. ALFRED, LORD TENNYSON, "Maud; A Monodrama" (1856), 4.4.

67. Who can paint / Like Nature? Can imagination boast, / Amid its gay creation, hues like hers? JAMES THOMSON, "Spring," *The Seasons* (1726–30), 405.

68. Nature will bear the closest inspection. She invites us to lay our eye level with her smallest leaf, and take an insect view of its plain. THOREAU, *Journal*, Oct. 22, 1839.

69. Nature refuses to sympathize with our sorrow. She seems not to have provided for, but by a thousand contrivances against, it. THOREAU, *Journal*, July 27, 1840.

70. It is the marriage of the soul with Nature that makes the intellect fruitful, and gives birth to imagination. THOREAU, *Journal*, Aug. 21, 1851.

71. We soon get through with Nature. She excites an expectation which she cannot satisfy. The merest child which has rambled into a copsewood dreams of a wildness so wild and strange and inexhaustible as Nature can never show him. THOREAU, *Journal*, May 23, 1854.

72. Nature cares nothing for logic, our human logic: she has her own, which we do not recognize and do not acknowledge until we are crushed under its wheel. IVAN TURGENEV, *Smoke* (1867), 20.

73. Nature is entirely indifferent to any reform. She perpetuates a fault as persistently as a virtue. CHARLES DUDLEY WARNER, "Fifth Study," *Backlog Studies* (1873).

74. Nature is, in fact, a suggester of uneasiness, a promoter of pilgrimages and of excursions of the fancy which never come to any satisfactory haven. CHARLES DUDLEY WARNER, "Ninth Study," *Backlog Studies* (1873).

75. I hate Nature / this passionless spectator this unbreakable ice-berg-face / that can bear everything. PETER WEISS, *Marat / Sade* (1964), 1.12, tr. Geoffrey Skelton and Adrian Mitchell.

76. It is only now and then, in a jungle, or amidst the towering white menace of a burnt or burning Australian forest, that Nature strips the moral veils from vegetation and we apprehend its stark ferocity. H. G. WELLS, *The Happy Turning* (1946), 33–34.

77. The eye is pleased when nature stoops to art. RICHARD WILBUR, "A Courtyard Thaw," *Ceremony* (1950).

78. A vacuum is a hell of a lot better than some of the stuff that nature replaces it with. TENNESSEE WILLIAMS, *Cat on a Hot Tin Roof* (1955), 2.

79. Nature never did betray / The heart that loved her. WILLIAM WORDSWORTH, "Lines Composed a Few Miles Above Tintern Abbey" (1798).

80. I have learned / To look on nature, not as in the hour / Of thoughtless youth; but hearing oftentimes / The still, sad music of humanity. WILLIAM WORDSWORTH, "Lines Composed a Few Miles Above Tintern Abbey" (1798).

81. Come forth into the light of things, / Let Nature be your teacher. WILLIAM WORDSWORTH, "The Tables Turned" (1798).

## 617. NECESSITY

**See also 127. Circumstance; 238. Destiny; 337. Fate; 358. Fortune; 618. Need**

1. Against necessity, / against its strength, no one can fight and win. AESCHYLUS, *Prometheus Bound* (c. 478 B.C.), tr. David Grene.

2. Hold it wise . . . / To make a virtue of necessity. CHAUCER, "The Knight's Tale," *The Canterbury Tales* (c. 1387–1400), tr. Nevill Coghill.

3. Necessity is an evil; but there is no necessity for continuing to live subject to necessity. EPICURUS, "Vatican Sayings" (3rd c. B.C.), 9, in *Letters, Principal Doctrines, and Vatican Sayings*, tr. Russel M. Geer.

4. How base a thing it is / when a man will struggle with necessity! / We have to die. EURIPIDES, *Heracles* (c. 422 B.C.), tr. William Arrowsmith.

5. Nothing has more strength than dire necessity. EURIPIDES, *Helen* (412 B.C.), tr. Richmond Lattimore.

6. Necessity never made a good bargain. BENJAMIN FRANKLIN, *Poor Richard's Almanack* (1732–57).

7. Necessity dispenseth with decorum. THOMAS FULLER, M.D., *Gnomologia* (1732), 3515.

8. Necessity is the theme and the inventress, the eternal curb and law of nature. LEONARDO DA VINCI, *Notebooks* (c. 1500), tr. Jean Paul Richter.

9. There is no good in arguing with the inevitable. The only argument available with an east wind is to put on your overcoat. JAMES RUSSELL LOWELL, "Democracy," *Democracy and Other Addresses* (1887).

10. Necessity is not an established fact, but an interpretation. NIETZSCHE, *The Will to Power* (1888), 552, tr. Anthony M. Ludovici.

11. Necessity turns lion into fox. PERSIAN PROVERB.

12. Necessity is the argument of tyrants, it is the creed of slaves. WILLIAM PITT THE YOUNGER, speech on the India Bill, November 1783.

13. The true creator is necessity, who is the mother of our invention. PLATO, *The Republic* (4th c. B.C.), 2, tr. Benjamin Jowett.

14. Necessity can turn any weapon to advantage. PUBLILIUS SYRUS, *Moral Sayings* (1st c. B.C.), 539, tr. Darius Lyman.

15. A wise man never refuses anything to necessity. PUBLILIUS SYRUS, *Moral Sayings* (1st c. B.C.), 540, tr. Darius Lyman.

16. We give to necessity the praise of virtue. QUINTILIAN, *Institutio Oratoria* (c. A.D. 95), 1.8.14.

17. What is necessary is never a risk. CARDINAL DE RETZ, *Mémoires* (1718).

18. Where necessity speaks it demands. RUSSIAN PROVERB.

19. Necessity knows no laws. SPANISH PROVERB.

20. Necessity relieves us from the embarrassment of choice. VAUVENARGUES, *Reflections and Maxims* (1746), 592, tr. F. G. Stevens.

## 618. NEED

See also 234. Deprivation; 617. Necessity; 712. Poverty

1. The finest poems of the world have been expedients to get bread. EMERSON, *Journals*, 1834.

2. No living being is held by anything so strongly as by its own needs. Whatever therefore appears a hindrance to these, be it brother, or father, or child, or mistress, or friend, is hated, abhorred, execrated. EPICTETUS, *Discourses* (2nd c.), 2.22, tr. Thomas W. Higginson.

3. Want gave tongue, and, at her howl, / Sin awakened with a growl. JAMES RUSSELL LOWELL, "The Ghost Seer" (1845).

4. The constant demands of the heart and the belly can allow man only an incidental indulgence in the pleasures of the eye and the understanding. GEORGE SANTAYANA, *Little Essays* (1920), 49, ed. Logan Pearsall Smith.

5. The greater part of humanity is too much harassed and fatigued by the struggle with want, to rally itself for a new and sterner struggle with error. SCHILLER, *On the Aesthetic Education of Man* (1795), 8, tr. Reginald Snell.

6. Understanding human needs is half the job of meeting them. ADLAI STEVENSON, speech, Columbus, Ohio, Oct. 3, 1952.

## NEGOTIATION

See 987. Treaties

## NEGROES

See 83. Blacks

## 619. NEIGHBORS

1. Every man is the architect of his own fortunes, but the neighbors superintend the construction. GEORGE ADE, "The Rise and Flight of the Winged Insect," *Hand-Made Fables* (1920).

2. Thou shalt love thy neighbor as thyself. *Bible*, Leviticus 19:18.

3. Your next-door neighbour . . . is not a man; he is an environment. He is the barking of a dog; he is the noise of a pianola; he is a dispute about a party wall; he is drains that are worse than yours, or roses that are better than yours. G. K. CHESTERTON, "The Irishman," *The Uses of Diversity* (1920).

4. Every man's neighbor is his looking-glass. ENGLISH PROVERB.

5. The correlative to loving our neighbors as ourselves is hating ourselves as we hate our neighbors. OLIVER WENDELL HOLMES, SR., *The Professor at the Breakfast Table* (1860), 11.

6. People have discovered that they can fool the Devil; but they can't fool the neighbors. EDGAR WATSON HOWE, *Ventures in Common Sense* (1919), 3.34.

7. The good neighbor looks beyond the external accidents and discerns those inner qualities that make all men human and, therefore, brothers. MARTIN LUTHER KING, JR., *Strength to Love* (1963), 3.1.

8. Happiness puts on as many shapes as discontent, and there is nothing odder than the satisfactions of one's neighbor. PHYLLIS MC GINLEY, "Pipeline and Sinker," *The Province of the Heart* (1959).

9. Of the good things given / between man and man, I say that a neighbor, / true and loving in heart, to neighbor is a joy beyond / all things else. PINDAR, *Odes* (5th c. B.C.), Nemea 7, tr. Richmond Lattimore.

10. Each man is afraid of his neighbor's disapproval—a thing which, to the general run of the race, is more dreaded than

wounds and death. MARK TWAIN, "The United States of Lyncherdom"(1923).

11. Mix with the neighbors, and you learn what's doing in your own house. *Yiddish Proverbs* (1949), ed. Hanan J. Ayalti.

## NERVOUSNESS

See 43. Anxiety; 340. Fear; 620. Neurosis

## 620. NEUROSIS

See also 43. Anxiety; 161. Compulsiveness; 555. Madness; 643. Obsession; 751. Psychiatry; 752. Psychoanalysis; 836. Sanity; 866. Self-injury

1. Everybody in the world has the sensation of being tied down hand and foot– Everyone has his own private bloodsucker. UGO BETTI, *The Fugitive* (1953), 1, tr. G. D. McWilliam.

2. What a curious creature is man! With what a variety of powers and faculties is he endued! Yet how easily is he disturbed and put out of order! JAMES BOSWELL, *London Journal*, March 22, 1763.

3. The mistake which is commonly made about neurotics is to suppose that they are interesting. It is not interesting to be always unhappy, engrossed with oneself, ungrateful and malignant, and never quite in touch with reality. CYRIL CONNOLLY, *The Unquiet Grave* (1945), 2.

4. Oh the nerves, the nerves; the mysteries of this machine called man! Oh the little that unhinges it: poor creatures that we are! CHARLES DICKENS, "Third Quarter," *The Chimes* (1844).

5. There are characters which are continually creating collisions and nodes for themselves in dramas which nobody is prepared to act with them. GEORGE ELIOT, *Middlemarch* (1871–72), 19.

6. As every man is hunted by his own daemon, vexed by his own disease, this checks all his activity. EMERSON, "Fate," *The Conduct of Life* (1860).

7. The multitude of the sick shall not make us deny the existence of health. EMERSON, "Worship," *The Conduct of Life* (1860).

8. We may say that hysteria is a caricature of an artistic creation, a compulsion neurosis a caricature of a religion, and a paranoiac delusion a caricature of a philosophic system. SIGMUND FREUD, *Totem and Taboo* (1918), tr. A. A. Brill.

9. If you be sick, your own thoughts make you sick. BEN JONSON, *Every Man in His Humour* (1598), 4.8.

10. Has there ever been an age so rife with neurotic sensibility, with that state of near shudders, or near hysteria, or near nausea, much of it induced by trifles, which used to belong to people who were at once ill-adjusted and overcivilized? LOUIS KRONENBERGER, "The Spirit of the Age," *Company Manners* (1954).

11. Modern neurosis began with the discoveries of Copernicus. Science made man feel small by showing him that the earth was not the center of the universe. MARY MC CARTHY, "Tyranny of the Orgasm," *On the Contrary* (1961).

12. The "sensibility" claimed by neurotics is matched by their egotism; they cannot abide the flaunting by others of the sufferings to which they pay an ever increasing attention in themselves. MARCEL PROUST, *Remembrance of Things Past: The Guermantes Way* (1913–27), tr. C. K. Scott-Moncrieff.

13. The bow too tensely strung is easily broken. PUBLILIUS SYRUS, *Moral Sayings* (1st c. B.C.), 388, tr. Darius Lyman.

14. We are all prone to the malady of the introvert, who, with the manifold spectacle of the world spread out before him, turns away and gazes only upon the emptiness within. But let us not imagine that there is anything grand about the introvert's unhappiness. BERTRAND RUSSELL, *The Conquest of Happiness* (1930), 11.

## NEUTRALITY

See 453. Impartiality: 496. International Relations

## 621. NEW ENGLAND

1. How condescending to descend / And be of Buttercups the friend / In a New England Town–. EMILY DICKINSON, poem (c. 1873).

2. The most serious charge which can be brought against New England is not Puritanism but February. JOSEPH WOOD

KRUTCH, "February," *The Twelve Seasons* (1949).

3. There is a sumptuous variety about the New England weather that compels the stranger's admiration—and regret. . . . In the spring I have counted one hundred and thirty-six different kinds of weather inside of four-and-twenty hours. MARK TWAIN, speech, New York City, Dec. 22, 1876.

## NEWNESS

See 477. Innovation; 632. Novelty

## 622. NEWS

See also 623. Newspapers

1. What's wan man's news is another man's throubles. FINLEY PETER DUNNE, "The News of a Week," *Observations by Mr. Dooley* (1902).

2. News is history shot on the wing. The huntsmen from the Fourth Estate seek to bag only the peacock or the eagle of the swifting day. GENE FOWLER, *Skyline* (1961).

3. Nowadays truth is the greatest news. THOMAS FULLER, M.D., *Gnomologia* (1732), 3689.

4. Evil report carries farther than any applause. BALTASAR GRACIÁN, *The Art of Worldly Wisdom* (1647), 169, tr. Joseph Jacobs.

5. A great calamity is as old as the trilobites an hour after it has happened. OLIVER WENDELL HOLMES, SR., *The Autocrat of the Breakfast Table* (1858), 2.

6. Evil news rides post, while good news baits [delays]. MILTON, *Samson Agonistes* (1671), 1538.

7. A reporter is always concerned with tomorrow. There's nothing tangible of yesterday. All I can say I've done is agitate the air ten or fifteen minutes and then boom—it's gone. EDWARD R. MURROW, news summaries, Dec. 31, 1955.

8. If it's far away, it's news, but if it's close at home, it's sociology. JAMES RESTON, *Wall Street Journal*, May 27, 1963.

9. Give to a gracious message / An host of tongues, but let ill tidings tell / Themselves when they be felt. SHAKESPEARE, *Antony and Cleopatra* (1606–07), 2.5.86.

10. Nobody likes the bringer of bad news. SOPHOCLES, *Antigone* (442–41 B.C.), tr. Elizabeth Wyckoff.

## 623. NEWSPAPERS

See also 362. Free Speech; 563. Mass Media; 622. News; 725. Press, Freedom of the; 758. Publishing

1. Have you noticed that life, real honest-to-goodness life, with murders and catastrophes and fabulous inheritances, happens almost exclusively in the newspapers? JEAN ANOUILH, *The Rehearsal* (1950), 2, tr. Lucienne Hill.

2. The evil that men do lives on the front pages of greedy newspapers, but the good is oft interred apathetically inside. BROOKS ATKINSON, "December 11," *Once Around the Sun* (1951).

3. Nowhere else can one find so miscellaneous, so various, an amount of knowledge as is contained in a good newspaper. HENRY WARD BEECHER, *Proverbs from Plymouth Pulpit* (1887).

4. There was a time when the reader of an unexciting newspaper would remark, "How dull is the world today!" Nowadays he says, "What a dull newspaper!" DANIEL J. BOORSTIN, *The Image* (1962), 1.

5. Journalism is popular, but it is popular mainly as fiction. Life is one world, and life seen in the newspapers another. G. K. CHESTERTON, "On the Cryptic and the Elliptic," *All Things Considered* (1908).

6. A serious and profitable occupation, reading the papers. It removes everything abnormal from your make-up, everything that doesn't conform to accepted ideas. It teaches you to reason as well as the next person. It gives you irrefutable and generally admitted opinions on all events. MICHEL DE GHELDERODE, *Pantagleize* (1929), 1, tr. George Hauger.

7. That ephemeral sheet of paper, the newspaper, is the natural enemy of the book, as the whore is of the decent woman. EDMOND and JULES DE GONCOURT, *Journal*, July 1858, tr. Robert Baldick.

8. Were it left to me to decide whether we should have a government without newspapers, or newspapers without a government, I should not hesitate a moment to prefer the latter. THOMAS JEFFERSON, letter to Col. Edward Carrington, Jan. 16, 1787.

9. The man who never looks into a newspaper is better informed than he who reads

them; inasmuch as he who knows nothing is nearer to truth than he whose mind is filled with falsehood and errors. THOMAS JEFFERSON, letter to John Norvell, June 11, 1807.

10. It is the gossip columnist's business to write about what is none of his business. LOUIS KRONENBERGER, "Fashions in Vulgarity," *The Cart and the Horse* (1964), 2.

11. Newspapers always excite curiosity. No one ever lays one down without a feeling of disappointment. CHARLES LAMB, "Detached Thoughts on Books and Reading," *Last Essays of Elia* (1833).

12. The window to the world can be covered by a newspaper. STANISLAW LEC, *Unkempt Thoughts* (1962), tr. Jacek Galazka.

13. A politician wouldn't dream of being allowed to call a columnist the things a columnist is allowed to call a politician. MAX LERNER, "Love and Hate in Politics," *Actions and Passions* (1949).

14. People everywhere confuse / What they read in newspapers with news. A. J. LIEBLING, "A Talkative Something or Other," *The New Yorker*, April 7, 1956.

15. Society page they never die. / Girl gets asked. Girl gets married. / Girl gets photographed in night club. / Girl gets older. Girl gets off. / Never catch them dead on Society. ARCHIBALD MAC LEISH, *JB* (1958), 4.

16. A good newspaper, I suppose, is a nation talking to itself. ARTHUR MILLER, *The Observer*, Nov. 26, 1961.

17. One of the most valuable philosophical features of journalism is that it realizes that truth is not a solid but a fluid. CHRISTOPHER MORLEY, *Inward Ho!* (1923), 4.

18. Surely the glory of journalism is its transience. MALCOLM MUGGERIDGE, introduction to *The Most of Malcolm Muggeridge* (1966).

19. Four hostile newspapers are more to be feared than a thousand bayonets. NAPOLEON I, *Maxims* (1804–15).

20. We live under a government of men and morning newspapers. WENDELL PHILLIPS, speech, Jan. 28, 1852.

21. One reads the papers as one wants to with a bandage over one's eyes without trying to understand the facts, listening to the soothing words of the editor as to the words of one's mistress. MARCEL PROUST, *Remembrance of Things Past: The Past Recaptured* (1913–27), tr. Stephen Hudson.

22. A newspaper column, like a fish, should be consumed when fresh; otherwise it is not only undigestible but unspeakable. JAMES RESTON, *Sketches in the Sand* (1967).

23. The trouble with daily journalism is that you get so involved with "Who hit John?" that you never really know why John had his chin out in the first place. CHALMERS ROBERTS, *Newsweek*, Jan. 6, 1958.

24. In America journalism is apt to be regarded as an extension of history: in Britain, as an extension of conversation. ANTHONY SAMPSON, *Anatomy of Britain* (1962).

25. A newspaper, not having to act on its descriptions and reports, but only to sell them to idly curious people, has nothing but honor to lose by inaccuracy and unveracity. GEORGE BERNARD SHAW, *The Doctor's Dilemma* (1913), 4.

26. We [journalists] tell the public which way the cat is jumping. The public will take care of the cat. ARTHUR HAYS SULZBERGER, *Time*, May 8, 1950.

27. The First Duty of a newspaper is to be Accurate. If it be Accurate, it follows that it is Fair. HERBERT BAYARD SWOPE, letter to *New York Herald Tribune*, March 16, 1958.

28. Don't forget that the only two things people read in a [news] story are the first and last sentences. Give them blood in the eye on the first one. HERBERT BAYARD SWOPE, statement recalled in obituaries after his death on June 20, 1958.

29. How many beautiful trees gave their lives that today's scandal should, without delay, reach a million readers! EDWIN WAY TEALE, "March 13," *Circle of the Seasons* (1953).

30. Journalism—an ability to meet the challenge of filling the space. REBECCA WEST, *New York Herald Tribune*, April 22, 1956.

## 624. THE NEW YEAR

1. Drop the last year into the silent limbo of the past. Let it go, for it was imperfect, and thank God that it can go. BROOKS ATKINSON, "December 31," *Once Around the Sun* (1951).

2. Year's end is neither an end nor a be-

ginning but a going on, with all the wisdom that experience can instill in us. HAL BORLAND, "The Tomorrows—December 30," *Sundial of the Seasons* (1964).

3. Time has no divisions to mark its passage, there is never a thunder-storm or blare of trumpets to announce the beginning of a new month or year. Even when a new century begins it is only we mortals who ring bells and fire off pistols. THOMAS MANN, *The Magic Mountain* (1924), 5.4, tr. H. T. Lowe-Porter.

4. Now the New Year reviving old Desires, / The thoughtful Soul to Solitude retires. OMAR KHAYYÁM, *Rubáiyát* (11th–12th c.), tr. Edward FitzGerald, 4th ed., 4.

5. Looking forward into an empty year strikes one with a certain awe, because one finds therein no recognition. The years behind have a friendly aspect, and they are warmed by the fires we have kindled, and all their echoes are the echoes of our own voices. ALEXANDER SMITH, "Christmas," *Dreamthorp* (1863).

6. Ring out the old, ring in the new, / Ring, happy bells, across the snow: / The year is going, let him go; / Ring out the false, ring in the true. ALFRED, LORD TENNYSON, "In Memoriam A. H. H." (1850), 106.

## 625. NEW YORK
### See also 129. Cities

1. New Yorkers are inclined to assume it will never rain, and certainly not on New Yorkers. BROOKS ATKINSON, "June 25," *Once Around the Sun* (1951).

2. The only real advantage of New York is that all its inhabitants ascend to heaven right after their deaths, having served their full term in hell right on Manhattan Island. *Barnard Bulletin* (Barnard College newspaper), Sept. 22, 1967.

3. Nearly all th' most foolish people in th' country an' manny iv th' wisest goes to Noo York. Th' wise people ar-re there because th' foolish wint first. That's th' way th' wise men make a livin'. FINLEY PETER DUNNE, "Some Political Observations," *Mr. Dooley's Opinions* (1901).

4. Melting pot Harlem—Harlem of honey and chocolate and caramel and rum and vinegar and lemon and lime and gall. Dusky dream Harlem rumbling into a nightmare tunnel where the subway from the Bronx keeps right on downtown. LANGSTON HUGHES, "In Love with Harlem," *Freedomways*, Summer 1963.

5. The faces in New York remind me of people who played a game and lost. MURRAY KEMPTON, quoting Lane Adams' daughter, "Is This All?" *America Comes of Middle Age* (1963).

6. It is one of the sublime provincialities of New York that its inhabitants lap up trivial gossip about essential nobodies they've never set eyes on, while continuing to boast that they could live somewhere for twenty years without so much as exchanging pleasantries with their neighbors across the hall. LOUIS KRONENBERGER, *Company Manners* (1954), 2.2.

7. [New York] is the place where all the aspirations of the Western World meet to form one vast master aspiration, as powerful as the suction of a steam dredge. It is the icing on the pie called Christian civilization. H. L. MENCKEN, *Prejudices: Sixth Series* (1927), 9.

8. In New York City, the common bats fly only at twilight. Brick-bats fly at all hours. GEORGE DENNISON PRENTICE, *Prenticeana* (1860).

## NICKNAMES
### See 612. Names

## 626. NIGHT
### See also 214. Darkness; 599. Morning; 899. Sleep

1. This dead of midnight is the noon of thought. / And Wisdom mounts her zenith with the stars. ANNA LETITIA BARBAULD, "A Summer's Evening Meditation" (1826).

2. Monarch is night / Of all eldest things, / Pain and affright, / Rapturous wings. WILLIAM ROSE BENÉT, "Night," *The Falconer of God* (1914).

3. We of the age of the machines, having delivered ourselves of nocturnal enemies, now have a dislike of night itself. With lights and ever more lights, we drive the holiness and beauty of night back to the forests and the sea. HENRY BESTON, "Night on the Great Beach," *The Outermost House* (1928).

4. Learn to reverence night and to put away the vulgar fear of it, for, with the banishment of night from the experience of man, there vanishes as well a religious emotion, a poetic mood, which gives depth to the adventure of humanity. HENRY BESTON, "Night on the Great Beach," *The Outermost House* (1928).

5. The night / Shows stars and women in a better light. BYRON, *Don Juan* (1819–24), 2.152.

6. To make ourselves invisible to creditors or to the envious, and even to our own worries, we can take advantage here on earth of a great democratic institution—in fact, democracy's only success—the night. JEAN GIRAUDOUX, *Amphitryon 38* (1929), 1, tr. Phyllis La Farge with Peter H. Judd.

7. Night is the mother of counsels. GEORGE HERBERT, *Jacula Prudentum* (1651).

8. The day is done, and the darkness / Falls from the wings of Night, / As a feather is wafted downward / From an eagle in his flight. LONGFELLOW, "The Day Is Done" (1844), 1.

9. At night there is no such thing as an ugly woman. OVID, *The Art of Love* (c. A.D. 8), 1, tr. J. Lewis May.

10. Night, when words fade and things come alive. When the destructive analysis of day is done, and all that is truly important becomes whole and sound again. When man reassembles his fragmentary self and grows with the calm of a tree. SAINT-EXUPÉRY, *Flight to Arras* (1942), 1, tr. Lewis Galantière.

11. Night brings our troubles to the light, rather than banishes them. SENECA, *Letters to Lucilius* (1st c.), 56.6

## 627. NIHILISM

1. To think is to say no. ALAIN, *Le Citoyen contre les pouvoirs* (1925).

2. The Stars are setting and the Caravan / Starts for the Dawn of Nothing—Oh, make haste! OMAR KHAYYÁM, *Rubáiyát* (11th–12th c.), tr. Edward FitzGerald, 1st ed., 38.

## 628. NOBILITY

**See also 489. Integrity; 945. Superiority**

1. The nobler a man, the harder it is for him to suspect inferiority in others. CICERO, *Ad Quintum Fratrem* (1st c. B.C.), 1.

2. Virtue is the only true nobility. THOMAS FULLER, M.D., *Gnomologia* (1732), 5383.

3. All that is noble is in itself of a quiet nature, and appears to sleep until it is aroused and summoned forth by contrast. GOETHE, quoted in Johann Peter Eckermann's *Conversations with Goethe*, April 1, 1827.

4. Be noble! and the nobleness that lies / In other men, sleeping, but never dead, / Will rise in majesty to meet thine own. JAMES RUSSELL LOWELL, "Sonnet 4" (1840).

5. Not the intensity but the duration of high feelings makes high men. NIETZSCHE, *Beyond Good and Evil* (1886), 72, tr. Walter Kaufmann.

6. To be nobly wrong is more manly than to be meanly right. THOMAS PAINE, *The American Crisis* (1776–83), 10.

7. True nobility is exempt from fear. SHAKESPEARE, *2 Henry VI* (1590–91), 4.1.129.

8. Put more trust in nobility of character than in an oath. SOLON (7th–6th c. B.C.), quoted in Diogenes Laertius' *Lives and Opinions of Eminent Philosophers* (3rd c. A.D.), tr. R. D. Hicks.

9. Let a man nobly live or nobly die. SOPHOCLES, *Ajax* (c. 447 B.C.), tr. John Moore.

## 629. NOISE

1. Much outcry, little outcome. AESOP, "The Mountains in Labor," *Fables* (6th c. B.C.?), tr. Joseph Jacobs.

2. Noise is the most impertinent of all forms of interruption. SCHOPENHAUER, "On Noise," *Parerga and Paralipomena* (1851), tr. T. Bailey Saunders.

3. I have often lamented that we cannot close our ears with as much ease as we can our eyes. RICHARD STEELE, *The Spectator* (1711–12), 148.

4. Noise is evolving not only the endurers of noise but the needers of noise. EDWIN WAY TEALE, *Journey into Summer* (1960), 3.

5. Nowadays most men lead lives of noisy desperation. JAMES THURBER, "The Grizzly and the Gadgets," *Further Fables for Our Time* (1956).

## NONCONFORMITY

See 89. Bohemians; 256. Dissent; 466. Individualism; 467. Individuality

## NONSENSE

See 874. Sense and Nonsense

## NONVIOLENCE

See 658. Pacifism

## 630. NORMALITY

See also 168. Conformity

1. The normal is what you find but rarely. The normal is an ideal. It is a picture that one fabricates of the average characteristics of men, and to find them all in a single man is hardly to be expected. W. SOMERSET MAUGHAM, *The Summing Up* (1938), 20.

## NOSE

See 324. Face

## 631. NOSTALGIA

See also 547. Loss; 574. Memory; 669. Past

1. The next day is never so good as the day before. PUBLILIUS SYRUS, *Moral Sayings* (1st c. B.C.), 815, tr. Darius Lyman.

2. Praising what is lost / Makes the remembrance dear. SHAKESPEARE, *All's Well That Ends Well* (1602–03), 5.3.19.

## NOVELS

See 341. Fiction

## 632. NOVELTY

See also 115. Change; 335. Fashion; 477. Innovation; 500. Invention

1. There is nothing new except that which has become antiquated. MLLE BERTIN, remark, c. 1785.

2. There is no new thing under the sun. *Bible*, Ecclesiastes 1:9.

3. Novelties *please* less than they *impress*. BYRON, *Don Juan* (1819–24), 12.69.

4. Only God and some few rare geniuses can keep forging ahead into novelty. DENIS DIDEROT, *Rameau's Nephew* (1762), tr. Jacques Barzun and Ralph H. Bowen.

5. A brand new mediocrity is thought more of than accustomed excellence. BALTASAR GRACIÁN, *The Art of Worldly Wisdom* (1647), 269, tr. Joseph Jacobs.

6. We have learned so well how to absorb novelty that receptivity itself has turned into a kind of tradition—"the tradition of the new." Yesterday's avant-garde experiment is today's chic and tomorrow's cliché. RICHARD HOFSTADTER, *Anti-Intellectualism in American Life* (1963), 6.15.

7. It is always the latest song that an audience applauds the most. HOMER, *Odyssey* (9th c. B.C.), 1, tr. E. V. Rieu.

8. As soon as we are shown the existence of something old in a new thing, we are pacified. NIETZSCHE, *The Will to Power* (1888), 551, tr. Anthony M. Ludovici.

9. Homer is new this morning, and perhaps nothing is as old as today's newspaper. CHARLES PÉGUY, "Note sur M. Bergson," *Les Cahiers de la quinzaine*, April 8–26, 1914.

## NOVEMBER

See 848. Seasons

## 633. NUCLEAR POWER

See also 949. Survival; 960. Technology; 1042. Weapons

1. I don't know what will be the most important weapon in the next war, but I know what will be the most important weapon in the war after that—the bow and arrow. Anonymous World War II witticism quoted in JOSEPH WOOD KRUTCH's *The Measure of Man* (1954), 1.

2. It is ironical that in an age when we have prided ourselves on our progress in the intelligent care and teaching of children we have at the same time put them at the mercy of new and most terrible weapons of destruction. PEARL S. BUCK, *What America Means to Me* (1943), 12.

3. Gods are born and die, but the atom endures. ALEXANDER CHASE, *Perspectives* (1966).

4. No country without an atom bomb could properly consider itself independent. CHARLES DE GAULLE, quoted in *The New York Times Magazine*, May 12, 1968.

5. The content of physics is the concern of physicists, its effect the concern of all men. FRIEDRICH DÜRRENMATT, "21 Points," *The Physicists* (1962), tr. James Kirkup.

6. After the great destructions / Everyone will prove that he was innocent. GÜNTER EICH, "Think of This" (1955), tr. Vernon Watkins.

7. The new and terrible dangers which man has created can only be controlled by man. JOHN F. KENNEDY, address, University of California, Los Angeles, Nov. 2, 1959.

8. We will not act prematurely or unnecessarily risk the costs of world-wide nuclear war in which even the fruits of victory would be ashes in our mouth. But neither will we shrink from that risk at any time it must be faced. JOHN F. KENNEDY, television address, Oct. 22, 1962.

9. We have genuflected before the god of science only to find that it has given us the atomic bomb, producing fears and anxieties that science can never mitigate. MARTIN LUTHER KING, JR., *Strength to Love* (1963), 13.3

10. It is impossible, except for theologians, to conceive of a world-wide scandal or a universe-wide scandal; the proof of this is the way people have settled down to living with nuclear fission, radiation poisoning, hydrogen bombs, satellites, and space rockets. MARY MC CARTHY, "The Fact in Fiction," *On the Contrary* (1961).

11. There's argument about how much can hurt, / How high or low the threshold of our harm, / And while we argue, the slow-falling dirt, / Invisible and soundless, sounds alarm. MARYA MANNES, "Testing," *Subverse: Rhymes for Our Times* (1959).

12. We are, to put it mildly, in a mess, and there is a strong chance that we shall have exterminated ourselves by the end of the century. Our only consolation will have to be that, as a species, we have had an exciting term of office. DESMOND MORRIS, *The Naked Ape* (1967), 5.

13. Man has wrested from nature the power to make the world a desert or to make the deserts bloom. There is no evil in the atom; only in men's souls. ADLAI STEVENSON, speech, Hartford, Conn., Sept. 18, 1952.

14. The terror of the atom age is not the violence of the new power but the speed of man's adjustment to it—the speed of his acceptance. Already bombproofing is on approximately the same level as mothproofing. E. B. WHITE, "Notes on Our Time," *The Second Tree from the Corner* (1954).

15. The H-bomb rather favors small nations that don't as yet possess it; they feel slightly more free to jostle other nations, having discovered that a country can stick its tongue out quite far these days without provoking war, so horrible are war's consequences. E. B. WHITE, "Letter from the East," *The Points of My Compass* (1956).

## 634. NUDITY

**See also 743. Propriety; 750. Prudery; 886. Shame**

1. The undressed is vulgar—the nude is pure. ROBERT G. INGERSOLL, *Prose-Poems and Selections* (1884).

2. Man is the sole animal whose nudities offend his own companions, and the only one who, in his natural actions, withdraws and hides himself from his own kind. MONTAIGNE, "Apology for Raimond de Sebonde," *Essays* (1580–88), tr. Charles Cotton and W. C. Hazlitt.

# O

## 635. OATHS

**See also 737. Promises**

1. It is not the oath that makes us believe the man, but the man the oath. AESCHYLUS, *Fragments* (525–456 B.C.), 385, tr. M. H. Morgan.

2. When a man takes an oath . . . he's holding his own self in his own hands. Like water. And if he opens his fingers *then*—he needn't hope to find himself again. ROBERT BOLT, *A Man for All Seasons* (1962), 2.

3. Oaths are but words, and words but

wind, / Too feeble implements to bind. SAMUEL BUTLER (d. 1680), *Hudibras* (1663), 2.2.

4. The spirit of Oath is one who runs beside crooked judgments. HESIOD, *Works and Days* (8th c. B.C.), 219, tr. Richmond Lattimore.

## 636. OBEDIENCE

**See also 61. Authority; 254. Disobedience; 350. Following; 528. Leadership**

1. This free will business is a bit terrifying anyway. It's almost pleasanter to obey, and make the most of it. UGO BETTI, *Struggle Till Dawn* (1949), 2, tr. G. H. McWilliam.

2. The height of ability in the least able consists in knowing how to submit to the good leadership of others. LA ROCHEFOUCAULD, *Maxims* (1665), tr. Kenneth Pratt.

3. It is right that what is just should be obeyed; it is necessary that what is strongest should be obeyed. PASCAL, *Pensées* (1670), 298, tr. W. F. Trotter.

4. He who yields a prudent obedience, exercises a partial control. PUBLILIUS SYRUS, *Moral Sayings* (1st c. B.C.), 752, tr. Darius Lyman.

5. The man who obeys is nearly always better than the man who commands. ERNEST RENAN, "Certitudes," *Dialogues et fragments philosophiques* (1876).

6. The man who does something under orders is not unhappy; he is unhappy who does something against his will. SENECA, *Letters to Lucilius* (1st c.), 61.3.

7. Obedience, / Bane of all genius, virtue, freedom, truth, / Makes slaves of men, and, of the human frame, / A mechanized automaton. SHELLEY, *Queen Mab* (1813), 3.

8. Learn to obey before you command. SOLON (7th–6th c. B.C.), quoted in Diogenes Laertius' *Lives and Opinions of Eminent Philosophers* (3rd c. A.D.), tr. R. D. Hicks.

## 637. OBESITY

1. A fat paunch never bred a subtle mind. Anonymous Greek writer.

2. Count no matron happy until she hath passed thirty, and hath not waxed fat. GELETT BURGESS, *The Maxims of Methuselah* (1907), 10.

3. The one way to get thin is to re-establish a purpose in life. CYRIL CONNOLLY, *The Unquiet Grave* (1945), 1.

4. Imprisoned in every fat man a thin one is wildly signalling to be let out. CYRIL CONNOLLY, *The Unquiet Grave* (1945), 2.

5. More die in the United States of too much food than of too little. JOHN KENNETH GALBRAITH, *The Affluent Society* (1958), 9.2.

6. Women, melons, and cheese should be chosen by weight. SPANISH PROVERB.

## OBJECTIVITY

**See 453. Impartiality**

## 638. OBJECTS

**See also 565. Materialism**

1. The goal of all inanimate objects is to resist man and ultimately to defeat him. RUSSELL BAKER, "Observer," *The New York Times*, June 18, 1968.

2. Inanimate objects are classified scientifically into three major categories—those that don't work, those that break down and those that get lost. RUSSELL BAKER, "Observer," *The New York Times*, June 18, 1968.

3. After inside upheavals, it is important to fix on imperturbable *things*. Their imperturbableness, their air that nothing has happened renews our guarantee. ELIZABETH BOWEN, *The Death of the Heart* (1938), 2.6.

4. Things have their laws as well as men, and things refuse to be trifled with. EMERSON, "Politics," *Essays: Second Series* (1844).

5. We are the slaves of objects around us, and appear little or important according as these contract or give us room to expand. GOETHE, quoted in Johann Peter Eckermann's *Conversations with Goethe*, Sept. 11, 1828.

6. Life is a struggle with things to maintain itself among them. Concepts are the strategic plan we form in answer to the attack. JOSÉ ORTEGA Y GASSET, *The Revolt of the Masses* (1930), 14.

7. A coin, sleeve-button or a collar-button dropped in a bedroom will hide itself and be hard to find. A handkerchief in bed *can't* be found. MARK TWAIN, *Notebook* (1935).

8. The superior gratification derived from the use and contemplation of costly and

supposedly beautiful products is, commonly, in great measure a gratification of our sense of costliness masquerading under the name of beauty. THORSTEIN VEBLEN, *The Theory of the Leisure Class* (1899), 6.

9. All men feel an habitual gratitude, and something of an honourable bigotry, for the objects which have long continued to please them. WILLIAM WORDSWORTH, preface to 2nd edition of *Lyrical Ballads* (1800).

9. Benefits received are a delight to us as long as we think we can requite them; when that possibility is far exceeded, they are repaid with hatred instead of gratitude. TACITUS, *Annals* (A.D. 115–117?), 4.18, tr. Alfred J. Church and William J. Brodribb.

10. The soil in return for her service / keeps the tree tied to her, / the sky asks nothing and leaves it free. RABINDRANATH TAGORE, *Fireflies* (1928).

## 639. OBLIGATION

**See also 219. Debt; 269. Duty; 382. Gifts and Giving; 397. Gratitude; 473. Ingratitude; 780. Receiving**

1. We cannot render benefits to those from whom we receive them, or only seldom. But the benefits we receive must be rendered again line for line, deed for deed to somebody. EMERSON, *Journals*, 1836.

2. There are minds so impatient of inferiority that their gratitude is a species of revenge, and they return benefits, not because recompense is a pleasure, but because obligation is a pain. SAMUEL JOHNSON, *The Rambler*, Jan. 15, 1751.

3. Too great an eagerness to discharge an obligation is a species of ingratitude. LA ROCHEFOUCAULD, *Maxims* (1665), tr. Kenneth Pratt.

4. We are nearer loving those who hate us than those who owe us more than we wish. LA ROCHEFOUCAULD, *Maxims* (1665), tr. Kenneth Pratt.

5. Pride does not wish to owe, and self-love does not wish to pay. LA ROCHEFOUCAULD, *Maxims* (1665), tr. Kenneth Pratt.

6. A refined nature is vexed by knowing that some one owes it thanks, a coarse nature by knowing that it owes thanks to some one. NIETZSCHE, *Human, All Too Human* (1878), 330, tr. Helen Zimmern.

7. Great indebtedness does not make men grateful, but vengeful. NIETZSCHE, "On the Pitying," *Thus Spoke Zarathustra* (1883–92), 2, tr. Walter Kaufmann.

8. It is safer to offend certain men than it is to oblige them; for as proof that they owe nothing they seek recourse in hatred. SENECA, "On Peace of Mind," *Moral Essays* (1st c.).

## 640. OBSCURANTISM

**See also 148. Communication**

1. Untruth being unacceptable to the mind of man, there is no other defence left for absurdity but obscurity. JOHN LOCKE, *An Essay Concerning Human Understanding* (1690), 3.10.9.

2. You cannot write in the chimney with charcoal. RUSSIAN PROVERB.

3. Sanity, soundness, and sincerity, of which gleams and strains can still be found in the human brain under powerful microscopes, flourish only in a culture of clarification, which is now becoming harder and harder to detect with the naked eye. JAMES THURBER, "The New Vocabularianism," *Lanterns and Lances* (1961).

4. Where misunderstanding serves others as an advantage, one is helpless to make oneself understood. LIONEL TRILLING, "Art and Fortune," *The Liberal Imagination* (1950).

5. Obscurity is the realm of error. VAUVENARGUES, *Reflections and Maxims* (1746), 5, tr. F. G. Stevens.

## 641. OBSCURITY

**See also 398. Great and Small; 901. Smallness; 1005. Unimportance**

1. Obscurity often brings safety. AESOP, "The Tree and the Reed," *Fables* (6th c. B.C.?), tr. Joseph Jacobs.

2. When the oak-tree is felled, the whole forest echoes with it; but a hundred acorns are planted silently by some unnoticed breeze. THOMAS CARLYLE, "On History" (1830).

3. That which comes into the world to disturb nothing deserves neither respect nor patience. RENÉ CHAR, "To the Health of

the Serpent," *Le Poème pulvérisé* in *Hypnos Waking* (1956), tr. Jackson Mathews and others.

4. Full many a flower is born to blush unseen, / And waste its sweetness on the desert air. THOMAS GRAY, "Elegy Written in a Country Churchyard" (1742?–50), 14.

5. Obscurity is the refuge of incompetence. ROBERT A. HEINLEIN, *Stranger in a Strange Land* (1961), 33.

6. To be forgotten is to sleep in peace with the undisturbed myriads, no longer subject to the chills and heats, the blasts, the sleet, the dust, which assail in endless succession that shadow of a man which we call his reputation. OLIVER WENDELL HOLMES, SR., *The Poet at the Breakfast Table* (1872), 6.

7. He is happiest of whom the world says least, good or bad. THOMAS JEFFERSON, letter to John Adams, 1786.

8. One must choose between Obscurity with Efficiency, and Fame with its inevitable collateral of Bluff. WILLIAM MC FEE, "On a Balcony," *Harbours of Memory* (1921).

9. Not a day passes over the earth, but men and women of no note do great deeds, speak great words and suffer noble sorrows. CHARLES READE, *The Cloister and the Hearth* (1861), 1.

10. Obscurity and a competence—that is the life that is best worth living. MARK TWAIN, *Notebook* (1935).

11. It is better to be looked over than overlooked. MAE WEST, *Belle of the Nineties* (1934).

## 642. OBSERVATION

**See also 59. Audience; 216. Deadness, Spiritual; 464. Indifference; 676. Perception; 890. Sight**

1. Every onlooker is either a coward or a traitor. FRANTZ FANON, "The Pitfalls of National Consciousness," *The Wretched of the Earth* (1961), tr. Constance Farrington.

2. Cultivated men and women who do not skim the cream of life, and are attached to the duties, yet escape the harsher blows, make acute and balanced observers. GEORGE MEREDITH, *An Essay on Comedy* (1897).

3. A stander-by may sometimes, perhaps, see more of the game than he that plays it. JONATHAN SWIFT, *A Tritical Essay Upon the Faculties of the Mind* (1707).

4. Observation is an old man's memory. JONATHAN SWIFT, *Thoughts on Various Subjects* (1711).

5. To become the spectator of one's own life is to escape the suffering of life. OSCAR WILDE, *The Picture of Dorian Gray* (1891), 9.

## 643. OBSESSION

**See also 161. Compulsiveness; 620. Neurosis**

1. There's nothing worse than taking something into your head: it turns into a revolving wheel that you can't control. UGO BETTI, *Struggle Till Dawn* (1949), 1, tr. G. H. McWilliam.

## 644. OBSTINACY

**See also 262. Dogmatism; 347. Flexibility**

1. Obstinacy / standing alone is the weakest of all things / in one whose mind is not possessed by wisdom. AESCHYLUS, *Prometheus Bound* (c. 478 B.C.), tr. David Grene.

2. No man is good for anything who has not some particle of obstinacy to use upon occasion. HENRY WARD BEECHER, *Proverbs from Plymouth Pulpit* (1887).

3. An obstinacy's ne'er so stiff, / As when 'tis in a wrong belief. SAMUEL BUTLER (d. 1680), *Hudibras* (1663), 3.2.

4. The obstinacy of human beings is exceeded only by the obstinacy of inanimate objects. ALEXANDER CHASE, *Perspectives* (1966).

5. A man will do more for his stubbornness than for his religion or his country. EDGAR WATSON HOWE, *Country Town Sayings* (1911).

6. There are some men who turn a deaf ear to reason and good advice, and wilfully go wrong for fear of being controlled. LA BRUYÈRE, *Characters* (1688), 4.71, tr. Henri Van Laun.

7. Smallness of mind is the cause of stubbornness, and we do not credit readily what is beyond our view. LA ROCHEFOUCAULD, *Maxims* (1665), tr. Kenneth Pratt.

8. Obstinacy is the sister of constancy, at least in vigor and stability. MONTAIGNE,

"Defense of Seneca and Plutarch," *Essays* (1580–88), tr. Charles Cotton and W. C. Hazlitt.

9. Obstinacy and dogmatism are the surest signs of stupidity. Is there anything more confident, resolute, disdainful, grave and serious than an ass? MONTAIGNE, "Of the art of conference," *Essays* (1580–88).

10. Stubbornness and stupidity are twins. SOPHOCLES, *Antigone* (442–41 B.C.), tr. Elizabeth Wyckoff.

11. He can never be good that is not obstinate. THOMAS WILSON, *Maxims of Piety and Christianity* (c. 1781).

12. Time has a way of demonstrating / the most stubborn are the most intelligent. YEVGENY YEVTUSHENKO, "A Career," *The New Russian Poets: 1953 to 1966* (1966), tr. George Reavey.

## OCEAN

See 847. Sea

## OCTOBER

See 848. Seasons

## OFFENSE

See 474. Injury

## 645. OFFICIALISM

See also 100. Bureaucracy; 705. Politics and Politicians; 755. Public Office; 826. Rules

1. What is official / Is incontestable. It undercuts / The problematical world and sells us life / At a discount. CHRISTOPHER FRY, *The Lady's Not for Burning* (1949), 1.

## 646. OLD AGE

See also 223. Decline; 372. Generations; 537. Life, Stages of; 545. Longevity; 567. Maturity; 580. Middle Age; 807. Retirement; 1065. Youth and Age

1. Beyond age, leaf / withered, man goes three footed / no stronger than a child is, / a dream that falters in daylight. AESCHYLUS, *Agamemnon* (458 B.C.), tr. Richmond Lattimore.

2. Old men are always young enough to learn, with profit. AESCHYLUS, *Agamemnon* (458 B.C.), tr. Richmond Lattimore.

3. All the best sands of my life are somehow getting into the wrong end of the hourglass. If I could only reverse it! Were it in my power to do so, would I? THOMAS BAILEY ALDRICH, "Leaves from a Notebook," *Ponkapog Papers* (1903).

4. To keep the heart unwrinkled, to be hopeful, kindly, cheerful, reverent—that is to triumph over old age. THOMAS BAILEY ALDRICH, "Leaves from a Notebook," *Ponkapog Papers* (1903).

5. When you're forty, half of you belongs to the past—and when you are seventy, nearly all of you. JEAN ANOUILH, *Time Remembered* (1939), 2.2, tr. Patricia Moyes.

6. Age has a good mind and sorry shanks. PIETRO ARETINO, letter to Bernardo Tasso, 1537, tr. Samuel Putnam.

7. It is—last stage of all— / When we are frozen up within, and quite / The phantom of ourselves, / To hear the world applaud the hollow ghost / Which blamed the living man. MATTHEW ARNOLD, "Growing Old," *New Poems* (1867).

8. To me, old age is always fifteen years older than I am. BERNARD BARUCH, news reports, Aug. 20, 1955.

9. Old people are great braggarts. But it's never true they were happy and loved. UGO BETTI, *The Inquiry* (1944–45), 1.12, ed. Gino Rizzo.

10. With the ancient is wisdom; and in length of days understanding. *Bible*, Job 12:12.

11. We ought not to heap reproaches on old age, seeing that we all hope to reach it. BION (2nd c. B.C.?), quoted in Diogenes Laertius' *Lives and Opinions of Eminent Philosophers* (3rd c. A.D.), tr. R. D. Hicks.

12. Age doth not rectify, but incurvate our natures, turning bad dispositions into worser habits. SIR THOMAS BROWNE, *Religio Medici* (1642), 1.

13. Grow old along with me! / The best is yet to be, / The last of life, for which the first was made: / Our times are in His hand / Who saith "A whole I planned, / Youth shows but half; trust God: see all nor be afraid!" ROBERT BROWNING, "Rabbi Ben Ezra," *Dramatis Personae* (1864), 1.

14. What is the worst of woes that wait on Age? / What stamps the wrinkle deeper on

the brow? / To view each loved one blotted from Life's page, / And be alone on earth, as I am now. BYRON, *Childe Harold's Pilgrimage* (1812–18), 2.98.

15. Years steal / Fire from the mind as vigour from the limb; / And Life's enchanted cup but sparkles near the brim. BYRON, *Childe Harold's Pilgrimage* (1812–18), 3.8.

16. The heart never grows better by age; I fear rather worse, always harder. LORD CHESTERFIELD, *Letters to His Son*, May 17, 1750.

17. No one is so old that he does not think he could live another year. CICERO, *De Senectute* (44 B.C.).

18. Regrets are the natural property of grey hairs. CHARLES DICKENS, *Martin Chuzzlewit* (1844), 10.

19. As we grow old we slowly come to believe that everything will turn out badly for us, and that failure is in the nature of things; but then we do not much mind what happens to us one way or the other. ISAK DINESEN, "The Deluge at Norderney," *Seven Gothic Tales* (1934).

20. When a man fell into his anecdotage it was a sign for him to retire from the world. BENJAMIN DISRAELI, *Lothair* (1870), 28.

21. No spring, nor summer beauty hath such grace, / As I have seen in one autumnal face. JOHN DONNE, Elegy 9, "The Autumnal" (1635).

22. Old fellows like ye'ersilf an' me make a bluff about th' advantages iv age. But we know there's nawthin' in it. We have wisdom, but we wud rather have hair. We have expeeryence, but we wud thrade all iv its lessons f'r hope an' teeth. FINLEY PETER DUNNE, "Books," *Mr. Dooley Says* (1910).

23. Whin a man gets to be over siventy he boasts iv his age. Whin he passes eighty he's very lible to lie about it. An' whin he's ninety he will throw his wig in th' face iv anny man who insinyates that he ain't th' oldest man in th' wurruld. FINLEY PETER DUNNE, "On Old Age," *Mr. Dooley On Making a Will* (1919).

24. I grow old . . . I grow old . . . / I shall wear the bottoms of my trousers rolled. T. S. ELIOT, "The Love Song of J. Alfred Prufrock" (1915).

25. We do not count a man's years until he has nothing else to count. EMERSON, *Journals*, 1840.

26. As we grow old, . . . the beauty steals inward. EMERSON, *Journals*, 1845.

27. Within, I do not find wrinkles and used heart, but unspent youth. EMERSON, *Journals*, 1864.

28. Age is a bad traveling companion. ENGLISH PROVERB.

29. Old men's prayers for death are lying prayers, in which they abuse old age and long extent of life. But when death draws near, not one is willing to die, and age no longer is a burden to them. EURIPIDES, *Alcestis* (438 B.C.), 669, tr. M. H. Morgan.

30. Oftener than not the old are uncontrollable; / Their tempers make them difficult to deal with. EURIPIDES, *Andromache* (c. 426 B.C.), tr. John F. Nims.

31. Alas, how right the ancient saying is: / We, who are old, are nothing else but noise / And shape. Like mimicries of dreams we go, / And have no wits, although we think us wise. EURIPIDES, *Aeolus* (before 423 B.C.).

32. Old age is not / a total misery. Experience helps. EURIPIDES, *The Phoenician Women* (c. 411–409 B.C.), tr. Elizabeth Wyckoff.

33. The power of love itself weakens and gradually becomes lost with age, like all the other energies of man. ANATOLE FRANCE, *The Crime of Sylvestre Bonnard* (1881), 2, tr. Lafcadio Hearn.

34. An old goat is never the more reverend for his beard. THOMAS FULLER, M.D., *Gnomologia* (1732), 646.

35. Old age is not so fiery as youth, but when once provoked cannot be appeased. THOMAS FULLER, M.D., *Gnomologia* (1732), 3704.

36. 'Tis late e'er an old man comes to know he is old. THOMAS FULLER, M.D., *Gnomologia* (1732), 5089.

37. Let others hail the rising sun: / I bow to that whose course is run. DAVID GARRICK, "An Ode on the Death of Mr. Pelham" (1754).

38. An old man loved is winter with flowers. GERMAN PROVERB.

39. It is not becoming to lay to virtue the weariness of old age. ANDRÉ GIDE, *Journals*, July 25, 1934, tr. Justin O'Brien.

40. It's not that age brings childhood back again, / Age merely shows what children we remain. GOETHE, "Prelude in the Theatre," *Faust: Part I* (1808), tr. Philip Wayne.

41. We must not take the faults of our youth into our old age, for old age brings with it its own defects. GOETHE, quoted in Johann Peter Eckermann's *Conversations with Goethe*, August 16, 1824.

42. People always fancy that we must become old to become wise; but, in truth, as years advance, it is hard to keep ourselves as wise as we were. GOETHE, quoted in Johann Peter Eckermann's *Conversations with Goethe*, Feb. 17, 1831.

43. I love everything that's old: old friends, old times, old manners, old books, old wines. OLIVER GOLDSMITH, *She Stoops to Conquer* (1773), 1.

44. To an old man any place that's warm is homeland. MAXIM GORKY, *The Lower Depths* (1903), 1, tr. Alexander Bakshy.

45. Time goes by: reputation increases, ability declines. DAG HAMMARSKJÖLD, "1945–1949: Towards new shores—?" *Markings* (1964), tr. Leif Sjoberg and W. H. Auden.

46. Unto each man comes a day when his favorite sins all forsake him, / And he complacently thinks he has forsaken his sins. JOHN HAY, "Distichs" (1871?), 11.

47. As we grow old, our sense of the value of time becomes vivid. Nothing else, indeed, seems of any consequence. WILLIAM HAZLITT, "On the Feeling of Immortality in Youth," *Literary Remains* (1836).

48. We do not die wholly at our deaths: we have mouldered away gradually long before. Faculty after faculty, interest after interest, attachment after attachment disappear: we are torn from ourselves while living. WILLIAM HAZLITT, "On the Feeling of Immortality in Youth," *Literary Remains* (1836).

49. It may be made a question whether men grow wiser as they grow older, any more than they grow stronger or healthier or honester. WILLIAM HAZLITT, "On Knowledge of the World," *Sketches and Essays* (1839).

50. Old age is like an opium-dream. Nothing seems real except what is unreal. OLIVER WENDELL HOLMES, SR., *Over the Teacups* (1891), 2.

51. Envy not the old man the tranquillity of his existence, nor yet blame him if it sometimes looks like apathy. Time, the inexorable, does not threaten him with the scythe so often as with the sand-bag. He does not cut, but he stuns and stupefies. OLIVER WENDELL HOLMES, SR., *Over the Teacups* (1891), 2.

52. Our years / Glide silently away. No tears, / No loving orisons repair / The wrinkled cheek, the whitening hair / That drop forgotten to the tomb. HORACE, *Odes* (23–c. 15 B.C.), 2.14.

53. The real dread of men is not the devil, but old age. EDGAR WATSON HOWE, *Country Town Sayings* (1911).

54. How good we all are, in theory, to the old; and how in fact we wish them to wander off like old dogs, die without bothering us, and bury themselves. EDGAR WATSON HOWE, *Ventures in Common Sense* (1919), 18.2.

55. When grace is joined with wrinkles, it is adorable. There is an unspeakable dawn in happy old age. VICTOR HUGO, "Jean Valjean," *Les Misérables* (1862), 5.2, tr. Charles E. Wilbour.

56. The misery of a child is interesting to a mother, the misery of a young man is interesting to a young woman, the misery of an old man is interesting to nobody. VICTOR HUGO, "Saint Denis," *Les Misérables* (1862), 9.3, tr. Charles E. Wilbour.

57. The aging man of the middle twentieth century lives, not in the public world of atomic physics and conflicting ideologies, of welfare states and supersonic speed, but in his strictly private universe of physical weakness and mental decay. ALDOUS HUXLEY, "Variations on a Philosopher," *Themes and Variations* (1950).

58. Age is rarely despised but when it is contemptible. SAMUEL JOHNSON, *The Rambler* (1750–52), 50.

59. Life is a country that the old have seen, and lived in. Those who have to travel through it can only learn the way from them. JOSEPH JOUBERT, *Pensées* (1842), 6.32, tr. Katharine Lyttelton.

60. Old age deprives the intelligent man only of qualities useless to wisdom. JOSEPH JOUBERT, *Pensées* (1842), 7.35.

61. The brief span of our poor unhappy life to its final hour / Is hastening on; and while we drink and call for gay wreaths, / Perfumes, and young girls, old age creeps upon us, unperceived. JUVENAL, *Satires* (c. 100), 9.126, tr. Hubert Creekmore.

62. I warmed both hands before the fire

of life; / It sinks, and I am ready to depart. WALTER SAVAGE LANDOR, "Dying Speech of an Old Philosopher" (1849).

63. Few people know how to be old. LA ROCHEFOUCAULD, *Maxims* (1665), tr. Kenneth Pratt.

64. Old age is a tyrant who forbids, upon pain of death, all the pleasures of youth. LA ROCHEFOUCAULD, *Maxims* (1665), tr. Kenneth Pratt.

65. Old men like to give good advice in order to console themselves for not being any longer able to set bad examples. LA ROCHEFOUCAULD, *Maxims* (1665), tr. Kenneth Pratt.

66. Nature, with her customary beneficence, has ordained that man shall not learn how to live until the reasons for living are stolen from him, that he shall find no enjoyment until he has become incapable of vivid pleasure. GIACOMO LEOPARDI, *Pensieri* (1834–37), 79, tr. William Fense Weaver.

67. Age is opportunity no less / Than youth itself, though in another dress, / And as the evening twilight fades away / The sky is filled with stars, invisible by day. LONGFELLOW, *Morituri Salutamus* (1874).

68. Old age has its pleasures, which, though different, are not less than the pleasures of youth. W. SOMERSET MAUGHAM, *The Summing Up* (1938), 73.

69. Growing old is no more than a bad habit which a busy man has no time to form. ANDRÉ MAUROIS, quoted in *The Aging American* (1961).

70. Old age is always wakeful; as if, the longer linked with life, the less man has to do with aught that looks like death. HERMAN MELVILLE, *Moby Dick* (1851), 29.

71. Wiser in relish, if sedate, / Come graybeards to their roses late. HERMAN MELVILLE, "L'Envoi," *Weeds and Wildings Chiefly: with a Rose or Two* (1924).

72. Here's a song was never sung: / Growing old is dying young. EDNA ST. VINCENT MILLAY, "To a Poet That Died Young," *Second April* (1921).

73. 'Tis well for old age that it is always accompanied with want of perception, ignorance, and a facility of being deceived. For should we see how we are used and would not acquiesce, what would become of us? MONTAIGNE, "Of the affections of fathers to their children," *Essays* (1580–88), tr. Charles Cotton and W. C. Hazlitt.

74. Age imprints more wrinkles in the mind than it does on the face. MONTAIGNE, "Of repentance," *Essays* (1580–88), tr. Charles Cotton and W. C. Hazlitt.

75. The old men know when an old man dies. OGDEN NASH, "Old Men," *Verses from 1929 On* (1959).

76. Senescence begins / And middle age ends / The day your descendents / Outnumber your friends. OGDEN NASH, "Crossing the Boarder," *Marriage Lines* (1964).

77. The old – like children – talk to themselves, for they have reached that hopeless wisdom of experience which knows that though one were to cry it in the streets to multitudes, or whisper it in the kiss to one's beloved, the only ears that can ever hear one's secret are one's own! EUGENE O'NEILL, *Lazarus Laughed* (1927), 4.1.

78. Age's terms of peace, after the long interlude of war with life, have still to be concluded – Youth must keep decently away – so many old wounds may have to be unbound, and old scars pointed to with pride, to prove to ourselves we have been brave and noble. EUGENE O'NEILL, *Strange Interlude* (1928), 9.

79. When the roses are gone, nothing is left but the thorn. OVID, *The Art of Love* (c. A.D. 8), 2, tr. Rolfe Humphries.

80. Old age has a great sense of calm and freedom; when the passions relax their hold, then . . . we are freed from the grasp not of one mad master only, but of many. PLATO, *The Republic* (4th c. B.C.), 1, tr. Benjamin Jowett.

81. Old men, for the most part, are like old chronicles that give you dull but true accounts of times past, and are worth knowing only on that score. ALEXANDER POPE, *Thoughts on Various Subjects* (1727).

82. I began my comedy as its only actor and I come to the end of it as its only spectator. ANTONIO PORCHIA, *Voces* (1968), tr. W. S. Merwin.

83. Some old women and men grow bitter with age. The more their teeth drop out the more biting they get. GEORGE DENNISON PRENTICE, *Prenticeana* (1860).

84. He has existed only, not lived, who lacks wisdom in old age. PUBLILIUS SYRUS, *Moral Sayings* (1st c. B.C.), 55, tr. Darius Lyman.

85. Death laughs when old women frolic.

PUBLILIUS SYRUS, *Moral Sayings* (1st c. B.C.), 56, tr. Darius Lyman.

86. Old men grasp more at life than babies, and leave it with a much worse grace than young people. It is because all their labours having been for this life, they perceive at last their trouble lost. ROUSSEAU, *Reveries of a Solitary Walker* (1782), 3.

87. Before you contradict an old man, my fair friend, you should endeavour to understand him. GEORGE SANTAYANA, *Dialogues in Limbo* (1925), 1.

88. Old places and old persons in their turn, when spirit dwells in them, have an intrinsic vitality of which youth is incapable; precisely the balance and wisdom that comes from long perspectives and broad foundations. GEORGE SANTAYANA, *Persons and Places: My Host the World* (1953), 7.

89. No one's so old that he mayn't with decency hope for one more day. SENECA, *Letters to Lucilius* (1st c.), 12.6, tr. E. Phillips Barker.

90. What [Time] hath scanted men in hair, he hath given them in wit. SHAKESPEARE, *The Comedy of Errors* (1592–93), 2.2.81.

91. I wasted time, and now doth time waste me. SHAKESPEARE, *Richard II* (1595–96), 5.5.49.

92. When the age is in, the wit is out. SHAKESPEARE, *Much Ado About Nothing* (1598–99), 3.5.38.

93. Last scene of all, / That ends this strange eventful history, / Is second childishness and mere oblivion, / Sans teeth, sans eyes, sans taste, sans everything. SHAKESPEARE, *As You Like It* (1599–1600), 2.7.163.

94. Growing old is not a gradual decline, but a series of drops, full of sorrow, from one ledge to another below it. LOGAN PEARSALL SMITH, *Afterthoughts* (1931), 2.

95. There are people who are beautiful in dilapidation, like old houses that were hideous when new. LOGAN PEARSALL SMITH, *Afterthoughts* (1931), 2.

96. The denunciation of the young is a necessary part of the hygiene of older people, and greatly assists the circulation of the blood. LOGAN PEARSALL SMITH, *Afterthoughts* (1931), 2.

97. The mere process of growing old together will make our slightest acquaintances seem like bosom-friends. LOGAN PEARSALL SMITH, *Afterthoughts* (1931), 2.

98. Nobody loves life like an old man. SOPHOCLES, *Acrisius* (5th c. B.C.), 63, tr. M. H. Morgan.

99. Age in a virtuous person, of either sex, carries in it an authority which makes it preferable to all the pleasures of youth. RICHARD STEELE, *The Spectator* (1711–12), 153.

100. If a man lives to any considerable age, it can not be denied that he laments his imprudences, but I notice he often laments his youth a deal more bitterly and with a more genuine intonation. ROBERT LOUIS STEVENSON, "Crabbed Age and Youth," *Virginibus Puerisque* (1881).

101. Old men and comets have been reverenced for the same reason: their long beards, and pretences to foretell events. JONATHAN SWIFT, *Thoughts on Various Subjects* (1711).

102. The sad wisdom of age / Wells up without sound. SARA TEASDALE, "Age," *Strange Victory* (1933).

103. It is the common vice of all, in old age, to be too intent upon our interests. TERENCE, *The Brothers* (160 B.C.), 5.8.30, tr. Henry Thomas Riley.

104. The seas are quiet when the winds give o'er; / So, calm are we when passions are no more! EDMUND WALLER, "On the Foregoing Poems" (1645).

105. An aged man is but a paltry thing, / A tattered coat upon a stick, unless / Soul clap its hands and sing, and louder sing / For every tatter in its mortal dress. WILLIAM BUTLER YEATS, "Sailing to Byzantium" (1928), 2.

106. Dying while young is a boon in old age. *Yiddish Proverbs* (1949), ed. Hanan J. Ayalti.

## 647. OPEN-MINDEDNESS

**See also 115. Change; 347. Flexibility; 402. Growth and Development; 613. Narrowness; 894. Sincerity**

1. Oh, would that my mind could let fall its dead ideas, as the tree does its withered leaves! And without too many regrets, if possible! Those from which the sap has withdrawn. But, good Lord, what beautiful colors! ANDRÉ GIDE, *Journals*, 1947, tr. Justin O'Brien.

2. To get others to come into our ways of thinking, we must go over to theirs; and it is necessary to follow, in order to lead. WILLIAM HAZLITT, "A Farewell to Essay-Writing," *Winterslow: Essays and Characters* (1850).

3. The only means of strengthening one's intellect is to make up one's mind about nothing—to let the mind be a thoroughfare for all thoughts. JOHN KEATS, letter to George and Georgiana Keats, Sept. 17–27, 1819.

4. Where there is an open mind, there will always be a frontier. CHARLES F. KETTERING, quoted in *Profile of America* (1954), ed. E. Davie.

5. Ah, snug lie those that slumber / Beneath Conviction's roof. / Their floors are sturdy lumber, / Their windows weather-proof. / But I sleep cold forever / And cold sleep all my kind, / For I was born to shiver / In the draft from an open mind. PHYLLIS MC GINLEY, "Lament for a Wavering Viewpoint," *A Pocketful of Wry* (1940).

6. The beautiful souls are they that are universal, open, and ready for all things. MONTAIGNE, "Of presumption," *Essays* (1580–88), tr. Charles Cotton and W. C. Hazlitt.

## 648. OPERA

**See also 895. Singing**

1. An opera may be allowed to be extravagantly lavish in its decorations, as its only design is to gratify the senses and keep up an indolent attention in the audience. JOSEPH ADDISON, *The Spectator*, March 6, 1711.

2. No good opera plot can be sensible, for people do not sing when they are feeling sensible. W. H. AUDEN, *Time*, Dec. 29, 1961.

3. Opera, n. A play representing life in another world, whose inhabitants have no speech but song, no motions but gestures and no postures but attitudes. AMBROSE BIERCE, *The Devil's Dictionary* (1881–1911).

4. Whenever I go to an opera, I leave my sense and reason at the door with my half-guinea, and deliver myself up to my eyes and my ears. LORD CHESTERFIELD, *Letters to His Son*, Jan. 23, 1752.

5. The genuine music-lover may accept the carnal husk of opera to get at the kernel of actual music within, but that is no sign that he approves the carnal husk or enjoys gnawing through it. H. L. MENCKEN, *Prejudices: Second Series* (1920), 7.

6. Tenors are noble, pure and heroic and get the soprano, if she has not tragically expired before the final curtain. But baritones are born villains in opera. LEONARD WARREN, *New York World-Telegram and Sun*, March 13, 1957.

## 649. OPINION

**See also 51. Argument; 250. Discord; 347. Flexibility; 441. Ideas; 585. Minorities; 756. Public Opinion**

1. Some men are just as sure of the truth of their opinions as are others of what they know. ARISTOTLE, *Nicomachean Ethics* (4th c. B.C.), 7.3, tr. J. A. K. Thomson.

2. We tolerate differences of opinion in people who are familiar to us. But differences of opinion in people we do not know sound like heresy or plots. BROOKS ATKINSON, "February 4," *Once Around the Sun* (1951).

3. I could never divide myself from any man upon the difference of an opinion, or be angry with his judgment for not agreeing with me in that from which perhaps within a few days I should dissent myself. SIR THOMAS BROWNE, *Religio Medici* (1642), 1.

4. Men get opinions as boys learn to spell, / By reiteration chiefly. ELIZABETH BARRETT BROWNING, *Aurora Leigh* (1856), 6.6.

5. The more unpopular an opinion is, the more necessary is it that the holder should be somewhat punctilious in his observance of conventionalities generally. SAMUEL BUTLER (d. 1902), "The Position of a Homo Unius Libri," *Note-Books* (1912).

6. We are of different opinions at different hours, but we always may be said to be at heart on the side of truth. EMERSON, "Worship," *The Conduct of Life* (1860).

7. If all men saw the fair and wise the same / men would not have debaters' double strife. EURIPIDES, *The Phoenician Women* (c. 411–409 B.C.), tr. Elizabeth Wyckoff.

8. An opinion, though it is original, does not necessarily differ from the accepted opinion; the important thing is that it does

not try to conform to it. ANDRÉ GIDE, *Journals*, Feb. 6, 1929, tr. Justin O'Brien.

9. Everything is good or everything is bad according to the votes they gain. BALTASAR GRACIÁN, *The Art of Worldly Wisdom* (1647), 101, tr. Joseph Jacobs.

10. A man's opinions are generally of much more value than his arguments. OLIVER WENDELL HOLMES, SR., *The Professor at the Breakfast Table* (1860), 5.

11. With effervescing opinions, as with the not yet forgotten champagne, the quickest way to let them go flat is to let them get exposed to the air. OLIVER WENDELL HOLMES, JR., opinion, U. S. Supreme Court (1920).

12. When half the people believe one thing, and the other half another, it is usually safe to accept either opinion. EDGAR WATSON HOWE, *Ventures in Common Sense* (1919), 3.9.

13. It is often easier as well as more advantageous to conform to other men's opinions than to bring them over to ours. LA BRUYÈRE, *Characters* (1688), 5.48, tr. Henri Van Laun.

14. We listen to those whom we know to be of the same opinion as ourselves, and we call them wise for being of it; but we avoid such as differ from us. WALTER SAVAGE LANDOR, "Demosthenes and Eubulides," *Imaginary Conversations* (1824–53).

15. We credit scarcely any persons with good sense except those who are of our opinion. LA ROCHEFOUCAULD, *Maxims* (1665), tr. Kenneth Pratt.

16. One must judge men not by their opinions, but by what their opinions have made of them. GEORG CHRISTOPH LICHTENBERG, *Aphorisms* (1764–99), tr. F. H. Mautner and H. Hatfield.

17. New opinions are always suspected, and usually opposed, without any other reason but because they are not already common. JOHN LOCKE, "The Epistle Dedicatory," *An Essay Concerning Human Understanding* (1690).

18. In the human mind, one-sidedness has always been the rule, and many-sidedness the exception. Hence, even in revolutions of opinion, one part of the truth usually sets while another rises. JOHN STUART MILL, *On Liberty* (1859), 2.

19. Where there is much desire to learn, there of necessity will be much arguing, much writing, many opinions; for opinion in good men is but knowledge in the making. MILTON, *Areopagitica* (1644).

20. Every opinion is of force enough to cause itself to be espoused at the expense of life. MONTAIGNE, "That the relish of good and evil depends in a great measure upon the opinion we have of them," *Essays* (1580–88), tr. Charles Cotton and W. C. Hazlitt.

21. Opinion is a powerful party, bold, and without measure. MONTAIGNE, "That the relish of good and evil depends in a great measure upon the opinion we have of them," *Essays* (1580–88), tr. Charles Cotton and W. C. Hazlitt.

22. Our opinions are less important than the spirit and temper with which they possess us, and even good opinions are worth very little unless we hold them in a broad, intelligent, and spacious way. JOHN MORLEY, "Robespierre," *Critical Miscellanies* (1871–1908).

23. One often contradicts an opinion when it is really only the tone in which it has been presented that is unsympathetic. NIETZSCHE, *Human, All Too Human* (1878), 303, in *The Portable Nietzsche*, tr. Walter Kaufmann.

24. It is safer to learn than teach; and who conceals his opinion has nothing to answer for. WILLIAM PENN, *Some Fruits of Solitude* (1693), 2.118.

25. Truth is one forever absolute, but opinion is truth filtered through the moods, the blood, the disposition of the spectator. WENDELL PHILLIPS, lecture, "Idols," Boston, Oct. 4, 1859.

26. Refusing to have an opinion is a way of having one, isn't it? LUIGI PIRANDELLO, *Each in His Own Way* (1924), 1, tr. Arthur Livingston.

27. To observations which ourselves we make, / We grow more partial for th' observer's sake. ALEXANDER POPE, *Moral Essays* (1731–35), 1.11.

28. To reign by opinion, begin by trampling it under your feet. ROUSSEAU, *Émile* (1762), 3.

29. The sentiments of an adult are compounded of a kernal of instinct surrounded by a vast husk of education. BERTRAND RUSSELL, *Sceptical Essays* (1928).

30. Opinion is like a pendulum and obeys the same law. If it goes past the cen-

tre of gravity on one side, it must go a like distance on the other; and it is only after a certain time that it finds the sure point at which it can remain at rest. SCHOPENHAUER, "Further Psychological Observations," *Parerga and Paralipomena* (1851), tr. T. Bailey Saunders.

31. If a man would register all his opinions upon love, politics, religion, learning, etc., beginning from his youth, and so go to old age, what a bundle of inconsistencies and contradictions would appear at last! JONATHAN SWIFT, *Thoughts on Various Subjects* (1711).

32. Men seldom take the opinion of their equal, or of a man like themselves, upon trust. ALEXIS DE TOCQUEVILLE, *Democracy in America* (1835–39), 2.3.21.

33. It were not best that we should all think alike; it is difference of opinion that makes horse-races. MARK TWAIN, "Pudd'nhead Wilson's Calendar," *Pudd'nhead Wilson* (1894), 19.

34. Opinion is called the queen of the world; it is so, for when reason opposes it, it is condemned to death. It must rise twenty times from its ashes to gradually drive away the usurper. VOLTAIRE, "Opinion," *Philosophical Dictionary* (1764).

35. The chief effect of talk on any subject is to strengthen one's own opinions, and, in fact, one never knows exactly what he does believe until he is warmed into conviction by the heat of attack and defence. CHARLES DUDLEY WARNER, "Sixth Study," *Backlog Studies* (1873).

36. It is only about things that do not interest one that one can give a really unbiased opinion, which is no doubt the reason why an unbiased opinion is always absolutely valueless. OSCAR WILDE, "The Critic as Artist," *Intentions* (1891).

## 650. OPPORTUNITY

See also 711. Potential

1. A wise man will make more opportunities than he finds. FRANCIS BACON, "Of Ceremonies and Respects," *Essays* (1625).

2. A door that seems to stand open must be of a man's size, or it is not the door that Providence means for him. HENRY WARD BEECHER, *Proverbs from Plymouth Pulpit* (1887).

3. Opporchunity knocks at ivry man's dure wanst. On some men's dures it hammers till it breaks down th' dure an' thin it goes in an' wakes him up if he's asleep, an' iver aftherward it wurruks f'r him as a night-watchman. FINLEY PETER DUNNE, "Mr. Carnegie's Gift," *Mr. Dooley's Opinions* (1901).

4. Remember that you ought to behave in life as you would at a banquet. As something is being passed around, it comes to you; stretch out your hand, take a portion of it politely. It passes on; do not detain it. Or it has not come to you yet; do not project your desire to meet it, but wait until it comes in front of you. EPICTETUS, *Enchiridion* (2nd c.), 15, tr. Thomas W. Higginson.

5. In great affairs we ought to apply ourselves less to creating chances than to profiting from those that offer. LA ROCHEFOUCAULD, *Maxims* (1665), tr. Kenneth Pratt.

6. There is no security on this earth; there is only opportunity. DOUGLAS MACARTHUR, quoted in *MacArthur: His Rendezvous with History* (1955) by Courtney Whitney.

7. Know thine opportunity. PITTACUS (7th–6th c. B.C.), quoted in Diogenes Laertius' *Lives and Opinions of Eminent Philosophers* (3rd c. A.D.), tr. R. D. Hicks.

8. While we stop to think, we often miss our opportunity. PUBLILIUS SYRUS, *Moral Sayings* (1st c. B.C.), 185, tr. Darius Lyman.

9. The opportunity that God sends does not wake up him who is asleep. SENEGALESE PROVERB.

10. There is a tide in the affairs of men / Which, taken at the flood, leads on to fortune; / Omitted, all the voyage of their life / Is bound in shallows and in miseries. SHAKESPEARE, *Julius Caesar* (1599–1600), 4.3.218.

## OPPOSITES

See 184. Contrast

## 651. OPPOSITION

See also 250. Discord; 256. Dissent; 747. Protest; 779. Rebellion; 813. Revolution; 1024. Violence

1. Many a man's strength is in opposition, and when that faileth, he groweth out of

use. FRANCIS BACON, "Of Faction," *Essays* (1625).

2. Opposition, n. In politics the party that prevents the Government from running amuck by hamstringing it. AMBROSE BIERCE, *The Devil's Dictionary* (1881–1911).

3. He that wrestles with us strengthens our nerves and sharpens our skill. Our antagonist is our helper. EDMUND BURKE, *Reflections on the Revolution in France* (1790).

4. I respect only those who resist me, but I cannot tolerate them. CHARLES DE GAULLE, quoted in *The New York Times Magazine*, May 12, 1968.

5. No government can be long secure without formidable opposition. BENJAMIN DISRAELI, *Coningsby* (1844), 2.1.

6. The wise man always throws himself on the side of his assailants. It is more his interest than it is theirs to find his weak point. EMERSON, "Compensation," *Essays: First Series* (1841).

7. The fish, by struggling in the net, hampers itself the more. THOMAS FULLER, M.D., *Gnomologia* (1732), 4534.

8. Opposition brings concord. Out of discord comes the fairest harmony. HERACLITUS, *Fragments* (c. 500 B.C.), 98, tr. Philip Wheelwright.

9. What country can preserve its liberties, if its rulers are not warned from time to time, that this people preserve the spirit of resistance? THOMAS JEFFERSON, letter to Col. William S. Smith, Nov. 13, 1787.

10. Men naturally despise those who court them, but respect those who do not give way to them. THUCYDIDES, *The Peloponnesian War* (c. 400 B.C.), 3.39, tr. Benjamin Jowett.

11. The man who is swimming against the stream knows the strength of it. WOODROW WILSON, speech, "The New Freedom" (1913).

## OPPRESSION

See 882. Servitude; 995. Tyranny

## 652. OPTIMISM

See also 653. Optimism and Pessimism; 685. Pessimism

1. Any time things appear to be going better, you have overlooked something. Anonymous.

2. Optimism approves of everything, submits to everything, believes everything; it is the virtue above all of the taxpayer. GEORGES BERNANOS, "France Before the World of Tomorrow," *The Last Essays of Georges Bernanos* (1955), tr. Joan and Barry Ulanov.

3. Optimism, n. The doctrine or belief that everything is beautiful, including what is ugly, everything good, especially the bad, and everything right that is wrong. AMBROSE BIERCE, *The Devil's Dictionary* (1881–1911).

4. The essence of optimism is that it takes no account of the present, but it is a source of inspiration, of vitality and hope where others have resigned; it enables a man to hold his head high, to claim the future for himself and not to abandon it to his enemy. DIETRICH BONHOEFFER, "After Ten Years," *Letters and Papers from Prison* (1953), tr. Eberhard Bethge.

5. The year's at the spring / And day's at the morn; / Morning's at seven; / The hillside's dew-pearled; / The lark's on the wing; / The snail's on the thorn: / God's in his heaven—/ All's right with the world! ROBERT BROWNING, "Morning," *Pippa Passes* (1841).

6. Optimism is the content of small men in high places. F. SCOTT FITZGERALD, "Note-Books," *The Crack-Up* (1945).

7. Everybody, my friend, everybody lives for something better to come. That's why we want to be considerate of every man—Who knows what's in him, why he was born and what he can do? MAXIM GORKY, *The Lower Depths* (1903), 4, tr. Alexander Bakshy.

8. Optimism is a kind of heart stimulant—the digitalis of failure. ELBERT HUBBARD, *A Thousand and One Epigrams* (1911).

9. a optimist is a guy / that has never had / much experience. DON MARQUIS, "certain maxims of archy," *Archy and Mehitabel* (1927).

10. There is an optimism which nobly anticipates the eventual triumph of great moral laws, and there is an optimism which cheerfully tolerates unworthiness. AGNES REPPLIER, "Are Americans Timid?" *Under Dispute* (1924).

11. One day everything will be well, that is our hope: / Everything's fine today, that is our illusion. VOLTAIRE, *Poème sur le désastre de Lisbonne* (1756).

12. [Optimism] is the mania of maintaining that everything is well when we are wretched. VOLTAIRE, *Candide* (1759), 19.

13. If you pretend to be good, the world takes you very seriously. If you pretend to be bad, it doesn't. Such is the astounding stupidity of optimism. OSCAR WILDE, *Lady Windermere's Fan* (1892), 1.

### 653. OPTIMISM AND PESSIMISM

See also 652. Optimism; 685. Pessimism

1. Our notion of an optimist is a man who, knowing that each year was worse than the preceding, thinks next year will be better. And a pessimist is a man who knows the next year can't be any worse than the last one. FRANKLIN P. ADAMS, *Nods and Becks* (1944).

2. The optimist proclaims that we live in the best of all possible worlds; and the pessimist fears this is true. JAMES BRANCH CABELL, *The Silver Stallion* (1926).

3. O, merry is the Optimist, / With the troops of courage leaguing. / But a dour trend / In any friend / Is somehow less fatiguing. PHYLLIS MC GINLEY, "Song Against Sweetness and Light," *A Pocketful of Wry* (1940).

4. The man who is a pessimist before forty-eight knows too much; if he is an optimist after it, he knows too little. MARK TWAIN, *Notebook* (1935).

5. It is not usually our ideas that make us optimists or pessimists, but it is our optimism or our pessimism, of physiological or perhaps pathological origin, as much the one as the other, that makes our ideas. MIGUEL DE UNAMUNO, "Man of Flesh and Bone," *The Tragic Sense of Life* (1913), tr. J. E. Crawford Flitch.

### ORATORY

See 757. Public Speaking

### 654. ORDER

See also 255. Disorder; 408. Harmony; 526. Law and Order; 579. Method; 696. Plans; 822. Routine; 954. Systems

1. Some people like to make a little garden out of life and walk down a path. JEAN ANOUILH, *The Lark* (1955), 2, adapted by Lillian Hellman.

2. Let all things be done decently and in order. *Bible*, 1 Corinthians 14:40.

3. Order is the shape upon which beauty depends. PEARL S. BUCK, "The Homemaker," *To My Daughters, With Love* (1967).

4. Good order is the foundation of all things. EDMUND BURKE, *Reflections on the Revolution in France* (1790).

5. Structure without life is dead. But life without structure is un-seen. JOHN CAGE, "Lecture on Nothing," *Silence* (1961).

6. It is meritorious to insist on forms; religion and all else naturally clothes itself in forms. Everywhere the formed world is the only habitable one. THOMAS CARLYLE, *On Heroes, Hero-Worship and the Heroic in History* (1841), 6.

7. "Begin at the beginning," the King said, gravely, "and go till you come to the end; then stop." LEWIS CARROLL, *Alice's Adventures in Wonderland* (1865), 12.

8. Watch out for the fellow who talks about putting things in order! Putting things in order always means getting other people under your control. DENIS DIDEROT, *Supplement to Bougainville's "Voyage"* (1796).

9. It is best to do things systematically, / since we are only human, and disorder is our worst enemy. HESIOD, *Works and Days* (8th c. B.C.), 471, tr. Richmond Lattimore.

10. Symmetry is ennui, and ennui is the very essence of grief and melancholy. Despair yawns. VICTOR HUGO, "Cosette," *Les Misérables* (1862), 4.1, tr. Charles E. Wilbour.

11. The virtue of the soul does not consist in flying high, but in walking orderly. MONTAIGNE, "Of repentance," *Essays* (1580–88), tr. Charles Cotton and W. C. Hazlitt.

12. Order marches with weighty and measured strides; disorder is always in a hurry. NAPOLEON I, *Maxims* (1804–15).

13. Peace is present when man can see the face that is composed of things that have meaning and are in their place. Peace is present when things form part of a whole greater than their sum, as the diverse minerals in the ground collect to become the tree. SAINT-EXUPÉRY, *Flight to Arras* (1942), 13, tr. Lewis Galantière.

14. Order always weighs on the individual. Disorder makes him wish for the police or for death. These are two extreme

circumstances in which human nature is not at ease. PAUL VALÉRY, preface to Montesquieu's *Persian Letters* (1926).

## 655. ORIGINALITY

See also 274. Eccentricity; 466. Individualism; 467. Individuality; 1007. Uniqueness

1. The merit of originality is not novelty; it is sincerity. The believing man is the original man; whatsoever he believes, he believes it for himself, not for another. THOMAS CARLYLE, *On Heroes, Hero-Worship and the Heroic in History* (1841), 4.

2. He is great who is what he is from nature and who never reminds us of others. EMERSON, "Uses of Great Men," *Representative Men* (1850).

3. Where do we now meet an original nature? and where is the man who has the strength to be true, and to show himself as he is? GOETHE, quoted in Johann Peter Eckermann's *Conversations with Goethe*, Jan. 2, 1824.

4. When people are free to do as they please, they usually imitate each other. Originality is deliberate and forced, and partakes of the nature of a protest. ERIC HOFFER, *The Passionate State of Mind* (1954), 33.

5. It is perfectly easy to be original by violating the laws of decency and the canons of good taste. OLIVER WENDELL HOLMES, SR., *Over the Teacups* (1891), 5.

6. All good things which exist are the fruits of originality. JOHN STUART MILL, *On Liberty* (1859), 3.

7. Originality is the one thing which unoriginal minds cannot feel the use of. JOHN STUART MILL, *On Liberty* (1859), 3.

8. A technique or a style for saying something original does not exist *a priori*, it is created by the original saying itself. IGOR STRAVINSKY, *Conversations with Igor Stravinsky* (1959).

9. Nothing is said now that has not been said before. TERENCE, prologue to *The Eunuch* (161 B.C.), 41, tr. Henry Thomas Riley.

10. It is easier to say original things than to reconcile with one another things already said. VAUVENARGUES, *Reflections and Maxims* (1746), 1, tr. F. G. Stevens.

## 656. OTHERS

See also 513. Judging Others; 787. Relationships, Human; 1001. Understanding Others

1. We are better able to study our neighbors than ourselves, and their actions than our own. ARISTOTLE, *Nicomachean Ethics* (4th c. B.C.), 9.9, tr. J. A. K. Thomson.

2. People are made alarming by one's dread of their unremitting, purposeful continuity. ELIZABETH BOWEN, *The Death of the Heart* (1938), 2.4.

3. It is when we try to grapple with another man's intimate need that we perceive how incomprehensible, wavering, and misty are the beings that share with us the sight of the stars and the warmth of the sun. JOSEPH CONRAD, *Lord Jim* (1900), 16.

4. We cannot forgive another for not being ourselves. EMERSON, *Journals*, 1841.

5. None knows the weight of another's burden. THOMAS FULLER, M.D., *Gnomologia* (1732), 3655.

6. Most often it happens that one attributes to others only the feelings of which one is capable oneself. ANDRÉ GIDE, *Journals*, Jan. 11, 1932, tr. Justin O'Brien.

7. At last you are no longer searching for yourself, but for another—you are saved. JEAN GIRAUDOUX, *Siegfried* (1928), 4, tr. Phyllis La Farge with Peter H. Judd.

8. Just as much as we see in others we have in ourselves. WILLIAM HAZLITT, "Commonplaces," *The Round Table* (1817), 14.

9. The longer we live, the more we find we are like other persons. OLIVER WENDELL HOLMES, SR., *Over the Teacups* (1891), 1.

10. A person doesn't only love himself in others; he also hates himself in others. GEORG CHRISTOPH LICHTENBERG, *Aphorisms* (1764–99), tr. F. H. Mautner and H. Hatfield.

11. Others are to us like the "characters" in fiction, eternal and incorrigible; the surprises they give us turn out in the end to have been predictable—unexpected varia-

tions on the theme of being themselves. MARY MC CARTHY, "Characters in Fiction," *On the Contrary* (1961).

12. We are never the same with others as when we are alone; we are different, even, when we are in the dark with them. MAURICE MAETERLINCK, "The Pre-Destined," *The Treasure of the Humble* (1896), tr. Alfred Sutro.

13. I often marvel how it is that though each man loves himself beyond all else, he should yet value his own opinion of himself less than that of others. MARCUS AURELIUS, *Meditations* (2nd c.), 12.4, tr. Maxwell Staniforth.

14. It is the tragedy of other people that they are to us merely showcases for the very perishable collections of our own mind. MARCEL PROUST, *Remembrance of Things Past: The Sweet Cheat Gone* (1913–27), tr. C. K. Scott-Moncrieff.

15. Other people are quite dreadful. The only possible society is one's self. OSCAR WILDE, *An Ideal Husband* (1895), 3.

## 657. OVERCONFIDENCE

See also 854. Self-confidence

1. Let him that thinketh he standeth take heed lest he fall. *Bible*, 1 Corinthians 10:12.

2. Danger breeds best on too much confidence. CORNEILLE, *The Cid* (1636), 2.6, tr. Paul Landis.

3. Good swimmers are oftenest drowned. THOMAS FULLER, M.D., *Gnomologia* (1732), 1729.

4. How fortune brings to earth the oversure! PETRARCH, "Laura Dead," *Canzoniere* (1360), 270.

## OVERPOPULATION

See 82. Birth Control; 707. Population

## OWNERSHIP

See 710. Possession; 740. Property

# P

## 658. PACIFISM

See also 354. Force; 474. Injury; 674. Peace

1. Whosoever shall smite thee on thy right cheek, turn to him the other also. *Bible*, Matthew 5:39.

2. To Pacifists the proper course / Of conduct is to sit on Force. / For, in their dreams, Force can't resist / The well-intentioned Pacifists. CLARENCE DAY, "Thoughts on Joys and Triumphs," *Thoughts Without Words* (1928).

3. The peace of the man who has forsworn the use of the bullet seems to me not quite peace, but a canting impotence. EMERSON, *Journals*, 1839.

4. If you have a nation of men who have risen to that height of moral cultivation that they will not declare war or carry arms, for they have not so much madness left in their brains, you have a nation of lovers, of benefactors, of true, great, and able men. EMERSON, "War," *Miscellanies* (1884).

5. Non-violence is not a garment to be put on and off at will. Its seat is in the heart, and it must be an inseparable part of our very being. MOHANDAS K. GANDHI, *Non-Violence in Peace and War* (1948), 1.61.

6. It is open to a war resister to judge between the combatants and wish success to the one who has justice on his side. By so judging he is more likely to bring peace between the two than by remaining a mere spectator. MOHANDAS K. GANDHI, *Non-Violence in Peace and War* (1948), 1.241.

7. Mental violence has no potency and injures only the person whose thoughts are violent. It is otherwise with mental non-violence. It has potency which the world does not yet know. MOHANDAS K. GANDHI, *Non-Violence in Peace and War* (1948), 1.256.

8. The noble art of losing face / may one day save the human race / and turn into eternal merit / what weaker minds would call disgrace. PIET HEIN, "Losing Face," *Grooks* (1966).

9. If a donkey bray at you, don't bray at him. GEORGE HERBERT, *Jacula Prudentum* (1651).

10. The distant Trojans never injured me. HOMER, *Iliad* (9th c. B.C.), 1.200, tr. Alexander Pope.

11. Instead of loving your enemy, treat your friend a little better. EDGAR WATSON HOWE, *Ventures in Common Sense* (1919), 24.2

12. Rendering oneself unarmed when one had been the best-armed, out of a height of feeling—that is the means to real peace, which must always rest on a peace of mind. NIETZSCHE, *The Wanderer and His Shadow* (1880), 284, in *The Portable Nietzsche*, tr. Walter Kaufmann.

13. Sometime they'll give a war and nobody will come. CARL SANDBURG, *The People, Yes* (1936).

14. Beware of the man who does not return your blow: he neither forgives you nor allows you to forgive yourself. GEORGE BERNARD SHAW, "Maxims for Revolutionists," *Man and Superman* (1903).

15. One ought not to return injustice, nor do evil to anybody in the world, no matter what one may have suffered from them. SOCRATES, in Plato's *Crito* (4th c. B.C.), tr. Lane Cooper.

16. When fire and water are at war, it is the fire that loses. SPANISH PROVERB.

17. There is such a thing as man being too proud to fight. There is such a thing as a nation being so right that it does not need to convince others by force that it is right. WOODROW WILSON, address, Philadelphia, May 10, 1915.

## PAIN

See 939. Suffering

## 659. PAINTING

See also 53. Art and Artists; 142. Color

1. In painting, the most brilliant colors, spread at random and without design, will give far less pleasure than the simplest outline of a figure. ARISTOTLE, *Poetics* (4th c. B.C.), 2.3, tr. Thomas Twining.

2. Painting, n. The art of protecting flat surfaces from the weather and exposing them to the critic. AMBROSE BIERCE, *The Devil's Dictionary* (1881–1911).

3. There are only two styles of portrait painting: the serious and the smirk. CHARLES DICKENS, *Nicholas Nickleby* (1838–39), 10.

4. The picture waits for my verdict; it is not to command me, but I am to settle its claim to praise. EMERSON, "Self-Reliance," *Essays: First Series* (1841).

5. That which probably hears more stupidities than anything else in the world is a painting in a museum. EDMOND and JULES DE GONCOURT, *Idées et sensations* (1866).

6. One picture in ten thousand, perhaps, ought to live in the applause of mankind, from generation to generation until the colors fade and blacken out of sight or the canvas rot entirely away. NATHANIEL HAWTHORNE, *The Marble Faun* (1860).

7. I would rather see the portrait of a dog that I know, than all the allegorical paintings they can shew me in the world. SAMUEL JOHNSON, quoted in Birkbeck Hill's *Johnsonian Miscellanies* (1897), v. 2.

8. The painter who draws by practise and judgment of the eye without the use of reason is like the mirror which reproduces within itself all the objects which are set opposite to it without knowledge of the same. LEONARDO DA VINCI, *Notebooks* (c. 1500).

9. How vain painting is—we admire the realistic depiction of objects which in their original state we don't admire at all. PASCAL, *Pensées* (1670), 134.

10. For me, painting is a way to forget life. It is a cry in the night, a strangled laugh. GEORGES ROUAULT, *Look*, April 15, 1958.

11. A little amateur painting in water-colour shows the innocent and quiet mind. ROBERT LOUIS STEVENSON, title essay, *Virginibus Puerisque* (1881).

12. The obsequious brush curtails truth / in deference to the canvas which is narrow. RABINDRANATH TAGORE, *Fireflies* (1928).

13. Every portrait that is painted with feeling is a portrait of the artist, not of the sitter. OSCAR WILDE, *The Picture of Dorian Gray* (1891), 1.

## 660. PARADES

1. Parades should be classed as a Nuisance and participants should be subject to a term in prison. They stop more work, inconvenience more People, stop more traffic, cause more accidents, entail more expense, and commit and cause I don't remember the other hundred misdemeanors. WILL ROGERS, "Let's Treat Our Presidents Like Human Beings," *The Illiterate Digest* (1924).

## 661. PARADOXES

1. Paradoxes are useful to attract attention to ideas. MANDELL CREIGHTON, *Life and Letters* (1904).

2. He who confronts the paradoxical exposes himself to reality. FRIEDRICH DÜRRENMATT, "21 Points," *The Physicists* (1962), tr. James Kirkup.

3. Life is a paradox. Every truth has its counterpart which contradicts it; and every philosopher supplies the logic for his own undoing. ELBERT HUBBARD, *The Note Book* (1927).

4. A paradox is what adults tell. When a kid does it, it's called a big lie. ART LINKLETTER, *A Child's Garden of Misinformation* (1965), 3.

## 662. PARASITES

1. Great fleas have little fleas upon their backs to bite 'em, / And little fleas have lesser fleas, and so on *ad infinitum*. AUGUSTUS DE MORGAN, *A Budget of Paradoxes* (c. 1850).

2. All the wise world is little else, in nature, / But parasites or subparasites. BEN JONSON, *Volpone* (1605), 3.1.

3. The parasites live where the great have little secret sores. NIETZSCHE, "On Old and New Tablets," *Thus Spoke Zarathustra* (1883–92), 3, tr. Walter Kaufmann.

## PARDON

See 357. Forgiveness

## 663. PARENTHOOD

See also 64. Babies; 95. Boys; 121. Children; 215. Daughters; 332. Family; 383. Girls; 415. Heredity; 909. Sons; 981. Training

1. We are the buffoons of our children. PIETRO ARETINO, letter to Sebastiano the Painter, June 15, 1537, tr. Samuel Putnam.

2. This is the reason why mothers are more devoted to their children than fathers: it is that they suffer more in giving them birth and are more certain that they are their own. ARISTOTLE, *Nicomachean Ethics* (4th c. B.C.), 9.7, tr. J. E. C. Welldon.

3. The joys of parents are secret, and so are their griefs and fears: they cannot utter the one, nor they will not utter the other. FRANCIS BACON, "Of Parents and Children," *Essays* (1625).

4. Children sweeten labours, but they make misfortunes more bitter; they increase the cares of life, but they mitigate the remembrance of death. FRANCIS BACON, "Of Parents and Children," *Essays* (1625).

5. There is no slave out of heaven like a loving woman; and, of all loving women, there is no such slave as a mother. HENRY WARD BEECHER, *Proverbs from Plymouth Pulpit* (1887).

6. What the mother sings to the cradle goes all the way down to the coffin. HENRY WARD BEECHER, *Proverbs from Plymouth Pulpit* (1887).

7. We never know the love of our parents for us till we have become parents. HENRY WARD BEECHER, *Proverbs from Plymouth Pulpit* (1887).

8. When a woman is twenty, a child deforms her; when she is thirty, he preserves her; and when forty, he makes her young again. LÉON BLUM, *Du Mariage* (1907), 6.

9. Some are kissing mothers and some are scolding mothers, but it is love just the same, and most mothers kiss and scold together. PEARL S. BUCK, "To You on Your First Birthday," *To My Daughters, With Love* (1967).

10. As the salt-cellar whose cover cometh off in the soup, so is the matron who extolleth her babes. GELETT BURGESS, *The Maxims of Methuselah* (1907), 9.

11. In the mind of a woman, to give birth to a child is the short cut to omniscience. GELETT BURGESS, *The Maxims of Methuselah* (1907), 10.

12. How often do we not see children ruined through the virtues, real or supposed, of their parents? SAMUEL BUTLER (d. 1902), "Elementary Morality," *Note-Books* (1912).

13. One of the most visible effects of a child's presence in the household is to turn the worthy parents into complete idiots when, without him, they would perhaps have remained mere imbeciles. GEORGES COURTELINE, *La Philosophie de G. Courteline* (1917).

14. A rich child often sits in a poor mother's lap. DANISH PROVERB.

15. The new-come stepmother hates the children born / to a first wife. EURIPIDES, *Alcestis* (438 B.C.), tr. Richmond Lattimore.

16. All men know their children / Mean more than life. If childless people sneer— / Well, they've less sorrow. But what lonesome luck! EURIPIDES, *Andromache* (c. 426 B.C.), tr. John F. Nims.

17. Here all mankind is equal: / rich and poor alike, they love their children. EURIPIDES, *Heracles* (c. 422 B.C.), tr. William Arrowsmith.

18. Lucky that man / whose children make his happiness in life / and not his grief, the anguished disappointment of his hopes. EURIPIDES, *Orestes* (408 B.C.), tr. William Arrowsmith.

19. Oh, what a power is motherhood, possessing / A potent spell. All women alike / Fight fiercely for a child. EURIPIDES, *Iphigenia in Aulis* (c. 405 B.C.), tr. Charles R. Walker.

20. A father is a banker provided by nature. FRENCH PROVERB.

21. The mother-child relationship is paradoxical and, in a sense, tragic. It requires the most intense love on the mother's side, yet this very love must help the child grow away from the mother, and to become fully independent. ERICH FROMM, *The Sane Society* (1955), 3.

22. You don't have to deserve your mother's love. You have to deserve your father's. He's more particular. ROBERT FROST, interview, *Writers at Work: Second Series* (1963).

23. The character and history of each child may be a new and poetic experience to the parent, if he will let it. MARGARET FULLER, *Summer on the Lakes* (1844), 7.

24. There is not so much comfort in the having of children as there is sorrow in parting with them. THOMAS FULLER, M.D., *Gnomologia* (1732), 4932.

25. Where yet was ever found a mother, / Who'd give her booby [baby] for another? JOHN GAY, "The Mother, the Nurse, and the Fairy," *Fables* (1727–38).

26. You may give them [your children] your love but not your thoughts, / For they have their own thoughts. / You may house their bodies but not their souls, / For their souls dwell in the house of tomorrow, which you cannot visit, not even in your dreams. KAHLIL GIBRAN, "On Children," *The Prophet* (1923).

27. Where parents do too much for their children, the children will not do much for themselves. ELBERT HUBBARD, *The Note Book* (1927).

28. The most ferocious animals are disarmed by caresses to their young. VICTOR HUGO, "Fantine," *Les Misérables* (1862), 4.1, tr. Charles E. Wilbour.

29. I perceive affection makes a fool / Of any man too much the father. BEN JONSON, *Every Man in His Humour* (1598), 1.2.

30. The greatest reverence is due to a child! If you are contemplating a disgraceful act, despise not your child's tender years. JUVENAL, *Satires* (c. 100), 14.47.

31. The real menace in dealing with a five-year-old is that in no time at all you begin to sound like a five-year-old. JEAN KERR, "How to Get the Best of Your Children," *Please Don't Eat the Daisies* (1957).

32. It is . . . sometimes easier to head an institute for the study of child guidance than it is to turn one brat into a decent human being. JOSEPH WOOD KRUTCH, "Whom Do We Picket Tonight?" *If You Don't Mind My Saying So* (1964).

33. There are some extraordinary fathers, who seem, during the whole course of their lives, to be giving their children reasons for being consoled at their death. LA BRUYÈRE, *Characters* (1688), 11.17, tr. Henri Van Laun.

34. Our [women's] bodies are shaped to bear children, and our lives are a working-out of the processes of creation. All our ambitions and intelligence are beside that great elemental point. PHYLLIS MC GINLEY, "The Honor of Being a Woman," *The Province of the Heart* (1959).

35. A father is very miserable who has no other hold on his children's affection than the need they have of his assistance, if that can be called affection. MONTAIGNE, "Of the affections of fathers to their children," *Essays* (1580–88), tr. Charles Cotton and W. C. Hazlitt.

36. Every beetle is a gazelle in the eyes of its mother. MOORISH PROVERB.

37. Through the survival of their children, happy parents are able to think calmly, and with a very practical affection, of a world in which they are to have no direct share. WALTER PATER, *Marius the Epicurean* (1885), 25.

38. Men are generally more careful of the breed of their horses and dogs than of their

children. WILLIAM PENN, *Some Fruits of Solitude* (1693), 1.85.

39. An angry father is most cruel toward himself. PUBLILIUS SYRUS, *Moral Sayings* (1st c. B.C.), 638, tr. Darius Lyman.

40. Romance fails us and so do friendships, but the relationship of parent and child, less noisy than all others, remains indelible and indestructible, the strongest relationship on earth. THEODOR REIK, *Of Love and Lust* (1957), 1.3.10.

41. I opine . . . "Judicious mothers will always keep in mind, that they are the first book read, and the last put aside, in every child's library." C. LENOX REMOND, *The Mind of the Negro As Reflected in Letters Written During the Crisis, 1800–1860* (1926), ed. Carter G. Woodson.

42. Parents today are the stage managers for the meetings of three- and four-year-olds, just as, in earlier eras, the adults managed marriages. DAVID RIESMAN, "A Jury of Their Peers," *The Lonely Crowd* (1950).

43. The fundamental defect of fathers is that they want their children to be a credit to them. BERTRAND RUSSELL, *The New York Times*, June 9, 1963.

44. Parents lend children their experience and a vicarious memory; children endow their parents with a vicarious immortality. GEORGE SANTAYANA, *The Life of Reason: Reason in Society* (1905–06), 2.

45. The ideal mother, like the ideal marriage, is a fiction. MILTON R. SAPIRSTEIN, *Paradoxes of Everyday Life* (1955), 3.

46. It is not enough for parents to understand children. They must accord children the privilege of understanding them. MILTON R. SAPIRSTEIN, *Paradoxes of Everyday Life* (1955), 3.

47. It is impossible for any woman to love her children twenty-four hours a day. MILTON R. SAPIRSTEIN, *Paradoxes of Everyday Life* (1955), 3.

48. We never make sport of religion, politics, race, or mothers. A mother never gets hit with a custard pie. Mothers-in-law—yes. But mothers—never. MACK SENNETT, *The New York Times*, Nov. 6, 1960.

49. It is a wise father that knows his own child. SHAKESPEARE, *The Merchant of Venice* (1596–97), 2.2.80.

50. To make the child in your own image is a capital crime, for your image is not worth repeating. The child knows this and you know it. Consequently you hate each other. KARL SHAPIRO, *The Bourgeois Poet* (1964), 3.72.

51. Parentage is a very important profession; but no test of fitness for it is ever imposed in the interest of the children. GEORGE BERNARD SHAW, *Everybody's Political What's What* (1944), 9.

52. I have found the best way to give advice to your children is to find out what they want and then advise them to do it. HARRY S. TRUMAN, television interview, May 27, 1955.

53. Schoolmasters and parents exist to be grown out of. JOHN WOLFENDEN, *Sunday Times*, London, July 13, 1958.

54. The mealy look of men today is the result of momism and so is the pinched and baffled fury in the eyes of womankind. PHILIP WYLIE, *Generation of Vipers* (1942), 11.

## 664. PARIS

See also 359. France and Frenchmen

1. Trade is art, and art's philosophy, / In Paris. ELIZABETH BARRETT BROWNING, *Aurora Leigh* (1856), 6.96.

2. If you are lucky enough to have lived in Paris as a young man, then wherever you go for the rest of your life, it stays with you, for Paris is a moveable feast. ERNEST HEMINGWAY, epigraph to *A Moveable Feast* (1964).

3. To err is human. To loaf is Parisian. VICTOR HUGO, "Marius," *Les Misérables* (1862), 4.1, tr. Charles E. Wilbour.

4. Lunch kills half of Paris, supper the other half. MONTESQUIEU, *Variétés*.

## 665. PARTIES

1. The cocktail party has the form of friendship without the warmth and devotion. It is a device either for getting rid of social obligations hurriedly en masse, or for making overtures towards more serious social relationships, as in the etiquette of whoring. BROOKS ATKINSON, "November 29," *Once Around the Sun* (1951).

2. The real business of a ball is either to look out for a wife, to look after a wife, or to

look after somebody else's wife. ROBERT SMITH SURTEES, *Mr. Facey Romford's Hounds* (1865), 56.

3. I love such mirth as does not make friends ashamed to look upon one another next morning. IZAAK WALTON, *The Compleat Angler* (1653), 1.5.

## 666. PARTING
**See also 2. Absence**

1. Good-byes breed a sort of distaste for whomever you say good-bye to; this hurts, you feel, this must not happen again. ELIZABETH BOWEN, *The House in Paris* (1935), 2.7.

2. Going away: I can generally bear the separation, but I don't like the leave-taking. SAMUEL BUTLER (d. 1902), "Higgledy-Piggledy," *Note-Books* (1912).

3. There's a kind of release / And a kind of torment in every goodbye for every man. C. DAY-LEWIS, "Departure in the Dark," *Short Is the Time* (1943).

4. Ever has it been that love knows not its own depth until the hour of separation. KAHLIL GIBRAN, "The Coming of the Ship," *The Prophet* (1923).

5. To leave is to die a little; / It is to die to what one loves. / One leaves behind a little of oneself / At any hour, any place. EDMOND HARAUCOURT, "Rondel de l'adieu," *Choix de poésies* (1891).

6. The return makes one love the farewell. ALFRED DE MUSSET, "À mon frère revenant d'Italie," *Poésies nouvelles* (1836–52).

7. Every parting gives a foretaste of death; every coming together again a foretaste of the resurrection. This is why even people who were indifferent to each other rejoice so much if they come together again after twenty or thirty years' separation. SCHOPENHAUER, "Further Psychological Observations," *Parerga and Paralipomena* (1851), tr. T. Bailey Saunders.

## 667. PARTISANSHIP
**See also 109. Causes; 333. Fanaticism; 453. Impartiality; 704. Political Parties**

1. A sect or party is an elegant incognito devised to save a man from the vexation of thinking. EMERSON, *Journals*, 1831.

2. He who is as faithful to his principles as he is to himself is the true partisan. WILLIAM HAZLITT, "On the Spirit of Partisanship," *Sketches and Essays* (1839).

3. Party loyalty lowers the greatest men to the petty level of the masses. LA BRUYÈRE, *Characters* (1688), 11.63.

4. No new sect ever had humor; no disciples either, even the disciples of Christ. ANNE MORROW LINDBERGH, "Theodore," *Dearly Beloved* (1962).

5. The beating of drums, which delights young writers who serve a party, sounds to him who does not belong to the party like a rattling of chains, and excites sympathy rather than admiration. NIETZSCHE, *Miscellaneous Maxims and Opinions* (1879), 308, tr. Paul V. Cohn.

6. The less reasonable a cult is, the more men seek to establish it by force. ROUSSEAU, *Correspondance à Monseigneur l'Archevêque de Paris.*

7. A man doesn't save a century, or a civilization, but a militant party wedded to a principle can. ADLAI STEVENSON, address, Democratic National Convention, July 21, 1952.

8. Party is the madness of many for the gain of a few. JONATHAN SWIFT, *Thoughts on Various Subjects* (1711).

9. The sectarian thinks / that he has the sea / ladled into his private pond. RABINDRANATH TAGORE, *Fireflies* (1928).

10. There is no greater hindrance to the progress of thought than an attitude of irritated party-spirit. ALFRED NORTH WHITEHEAD, *Adventures in Ideas* (1933), 8.

## PARTY, POLITICAL
**See 704. Political Parties**

## 668. PASSION
**See also 236. Desires; 282. Emotions; 548. Love**

1. Without passion man is a mere latent force and possibility, like the flint which awaits the shock of the iron before it can give forth its spark. HENRI FRÉDÉRIC AMIEL, *Journal*, Dec. 17, 1856, tr. Mrs. Humphry Ward.

2. The way to avoid evil is not by maim-

ing our passions, but by compelling them to yield their vigor to our moral nature. HENRY WARD BEECHER, *Proverbs from Plymouth Pulpit* (1887).

3. We are minor in everything but our passions. ELIZABETH BOWEN, *The Death of the Heart* (1938), 1.2.

4. Passion in a lover's glorious, / But in a husband is pronounced uxorious. BYRON, *Don Juan* (1819–24), 3.6.

5. Vanity plays lurid tricks with our memory, and the truth of every passion wants some pretence to make it live. JOSEPH CONRAD, *Lord Jim* (1900), 41.

6. One declaims endlessly against the passions; one imputes all of man's suffering to them. One forgets that they are also the source of all his pleasures. DENIS DIDEROT, *Pensées philosophiques* (1746), 1.

7. Only passions, great passions, can elevate the soul to great things. DENIS DIDEROT, *Pensées philosophiques* (1746), 1.

8. Passions destroy more prejudices than philosophy does. DENIS DIDEROT, *Discours sur la poésie dramatique* (1773–78).

9. It is by no means self-evident that human beings are most real when most violently excited; violent physical passions do not in themselves differentiate men from each other, but rather tend to reduce them to the same state. T. S. ELIOT, "After Strange Gods" (1934).

10. Passion, though a bad regulator, is a powerful spring. EMERSON, "Considerations by the Way," *The Conduct of Life* (1860).

11. Our passions are ourselves. ANATOLE FRANCE, *The Crime of Sylvestre Bonnard* (1881), 2, tr. Lafcadio Hearn.

12. Serving one's own passions is the greatest slavery. THOMAS FULLER, M.D., *Gnomologia* (1732), 4103.

13. Nothing great in the world has been accomplished without passion. HEGEL, introduction to *Philosophy of History* (1832), tr. John Sibree.

14. Passions are spiritual rebels and raise sedition against the understanding. BEN JONSON, "Explorata," *Timber* (1640).

15. The passions are the only orators which always persuade. LA ROCHEFOUCAULD, *Maxims* (1665).

16. If we resist our passions, it is more on account of their weakness than of our own strength. LA ROCHEFOUCAULD, *Maxims* (1665), tr. Kenneth Pratt.

17. The duration of our passions is no more dependent on ourselves than the duration of our lives. LA ROCHEFOUCAULD, *Maxims* (1665), tr. Kenneth Pratt.

18. Those who have had great passions find themselves all their lives both happy and unhappy at being cured of them. LA ROCHEFOUCAULD, *Maxims* (1665), tr. Kenneth Pratt.

19. In the human heart there is a ceaseless birth of passions, so that the destruction of one is almost always the establishment of another. LA ROCHEFOUCAULD, *Maxims* (1665), tr. Kenneth Pratt.

20. Take heed lest passion sway / Thy judgement to do aught, which else free will / Would not admit. MILTON, *Paradise Lost* (1667), 8.635.

21. All passions that suffer themselves to be relished and digested are but moderate. MONTAIGNE, "Of sorrow," *Essays* (1580–88), tr. Charles Cotton and W. C. Hazlitt.

22. When the passions become masters, they are vices. PASCAL, *Pensées* (1670), 502, tr. W. F. Trotter.

23. The ruling passion, be it what it will, / The ruling passion conquers reason still. ALEXANDER POPE, *Moral Essays* (1731–35), 3.153.

24. Passion is like genius: a miracle. ROMAIN ROLLAND, "Le Buisson ardent," *Jean Christophe* (1904–12), 2.

25. We must act out passion before we can feel it. JEAN-PAUL SARTRE, *The Words* (1964), 1.

26. Give me that man / That is not passion's slave, and I will wear him / In my heart's core. SHAKESPEARE, *Hamlet* (1600), 3.2.76.

27. What to ourselves in passion we propose, / The passion ending, doth the purpose lose. SHAKESPEARE, *Hamlet* (1600), 3.2.204.

28. The mind is the soul's eye, not its source of power. That lies in the heart, in other words, in the passions. VAUVENARGUES, *Reflections and Maxims* (1746), 149, tr. F. G. Stevens.

**PASSIVITY**

**See 216. Deadness, Spiritual; 233. Dependence; 457. Impotence; 464. Indifference; 642. Observation**

## 669. PAST

**See also 42. Antiquity; 296. Era; 366. Future; 417. History and Historians; 505. Irrevocableness; 631. Nostalgia; 723. Present; 979. Tradition**

1. Nothing is improbable until it moves into the past tense. GEORGE ADE, "The Polite Poison Counter," *Hand-Made Fables* (1920).

2. This only is denied even to God: the power to undo the past. AGATHON, quoted in Aristotle's *Nicomachean Ethics* (4th c. B.C.), 6.2.

3. Obligations, hatreds, injuries—What did I expect memories to be? And I was forgetting remorse. I have a complete past now. JEAN ANOUILH, *Traveler Without Luggage* (1936), 2.1, tr. Lucienne Hill.

4. Man is a history-making creature who can neither repeat his past nor leave it behind. W. H. AUDEN, "D. H. Lawrence," *The Dyer's Hand* (1962).

5. While it is still Before, Afterwards has no power, but afterwards its is the kingdom, the power and the glory. You do not ask yourself, what am I doing? You know. What you do ask yourself, what have I done? you will never know. ELIZABETH BOWEN, *The House in Paris* (1935), 2.9.

6. One may return to the place of his birth, / He cannot go back to his youth. JOHN BURROUGHS, "The Return," *Bird and Bough* (1906).

7. The Past is such a curious Creature / To look her in the Face / A Transport may receipt us / Or a Disgrace—. EMILY DICKINSON, poem (c. 1871).

8. The Things that never can come back, are several— / Childhood—some forms of Hope—the Dead— / Though Joys—like Men—may sometimes make a Journey— / And still abide—. EMILY DICKINSON, poem (c. 1881).

9. We have to do with the past only as we can make it useful to the present and the future. FREDERICK DOUGLASS, *The Life and Writings of Frederick Douglass* (1950), v. 2, ed. Philip S. Foner.

10. We are not free to use today, or to promise tomorrow, because we are already mortgaged to yesterday. EMERSON, *Journals*, 1858.

11. It is sadder to find the past again and find it inadequate to the present than it is to have it elude you and remain forever a harmonious conception of memory. F. SCOTT FITZGERALD, "Show Mr. and Mrs. F. to Number —," *The Crack-Up* (1945).

12. Time and words can't be recalled. THOMAS FULLER, M.D., *Gnomologia* (1732), 5050.

13. To what a degree the same past can leave different marks—and especially admit of different interpretations. ANDRÉ GIDE, *Journals*, September 1931, tr. Justin O'Brien.

14. In the carriages of the past you can't go anywhere. MAXIM GORKY, *The Lower Depths* (1903), 4, tr. Alexander Bakshy.

15. There is nothing like the dead cold hand of the Past to take down our tumid egotism and lead us into the solemn flow of the life of our race. OLIVER WENDELL HOLMES, SR., "Iris, Her Book," *The Professor at the Breakfast Table* (1860).

16. Respect the past in the full measure of its deserts, but do not make the mistake of confusing it with the present nor seek in it the ideals of the future. JOSÉ INGENIEROS, *Proposiciones relativas al porvenir de la Filosofía* (1918).

17. Nothing impresses the mind with a deeper feeling of loneliness than to tread the silent and deserted scene of former throng and pageant. WASHINGTON IRVING, "Westminster Abbey," *The Sketch Book of Geoffrey Crayon, Gent.* (1819–20).

18. Why doesn't the past decently bury itself, instead of sitting waiting to be admired by the present? D. H. LAWRENCE, *St. Mawr* (1925).

19. Look not mournfully into the Past. It comes not back again. Wisely improve the Present. It is thine. Go forth to meet the shadowy Future, without fear, and with a manly heart. LONGFELLOW, *Hyperion* (1839), 4.7.

20. The passing minute is every man's equal possession, but what has once gone by is not ours. MARCUS AURELIUS, *Meditations* (2nd c.), 2.14, tr. Maxwell Staniforth.

21. The past is the present, isn't it? It's the future, too. We all try to lie out of that but life won't let us. EUGENE O'NEILL, *Long Day's Journey into Night* (1956), 2.2.

22. To excel the past we must not allow ourselves to lose contact with it; on the con-

trary, we must feel it under our feet because we raised ourselves upon it. JOSÉ ORTEGA Y GASSET, "In Search of Goethe from Within, Letter to a German," *Partisan Review*, December 1949, tr. Willard R. Trask.

23. The past not merely is not fugitive, it remains present. MARCEL PROUST, *Remembrance of Things Past: The Guermantes Way* (1913–27), tr. C. K. Scott-Moncrieff.

24. Mad is the man who is forever gritting his teeth against that granite block, complete and changeless, of the past. SAINT-EXUPÉRY, *The Wisdom of the Sands* (1948), 50, tr. Stuart Gilbert.

25. I tell you the past is a bucket of ashes. CARL SANDBURG, "Prairie," *Complete Poems* (1950).

26. Those who do not remember the past are condemned to relive it. GEORGE SANTAYANA, *The Life of Reason* (1905–06).

27. All things are taken from us, and become / Portions and parcels of the dreadful past. ALFRED, LORD TENNYSON, "The Lotos-Eaters" (1842), 4.

28. All the past is here, present to be tried; let it approve itself if it can. THOREAU, *Journal*, Nov. 5, 1839.

29. I said there was but one solitary thing about the past worth remembering and that was the fact that it is past—can't be restored. MARK TWAIN, letter to William Dean Howells, Sept. 19, 1877.

30. We live in reference to past experience and not to future events, however inevitable. H. G. WELLS, *Mind at the End of Its Tether* (1946), 2.

31. How the past perishes is how the future becomes. ALFRED NORTH WHITEHEAD, *Adventures in Ideas* (1933), 15.

32. It's futile to talk too much about the past—something like trying to make birth control retroactive. CHARLES EDWARD WILSON, news summaries, May 22, 1955.

## 670. PATIENCE

**See also 454. Impatience; 579. Method; 1033. Waiting**

1. Sad patience, too near neighbor to despair. MATTHEW ARNOLD, "The Scholar-Gipsy," *Poems* (1853).

2. Patience, n. A minor form of despair, disguised as a virtue. AMBROSE BIERCE, *The Devil's Dictionary* (1881–1911).

3. Our patience will achieve more than our force. EDMUND BURKE, *Reflections on the Revolution in France* (1790).

4. Patience, and the mulberry leaf becomes a silk gown. CHINESE PROVERB.

5. Beware the fury of a patient man. JOHN DRYDEN, *Absalom and Achitophel* (1681), 1.1005.

6. Patience is the virtue of asses. FRENCH PROVERB.

7. All commend patience, but none can endure to suffer. THOMAS FULLER, M.D., *Gnomologia* (1732), 508.

8. Abused patience turns to fury. THOMAS FULLER, M.D., *Gnomologia* (1732), 757.

9. Patience is a bitter plant but it has sweet fruit. GERMAN PROVERB.

10. Let him that hath no power of patience retire within himself, though even there he will have to put up with himself. BALTASAR GRACIÁN, *The Art of Worldly Wisdom* (1647), 159, tr. Joseph Jacobs.

11. Patience, that blending of moral courage with physical timidity. THOMAS HARDY, *Tess of the D'Urbervilles* (1891), 43.

12. Patience makes lighter / What sorrow may not heal. HORACE, *Odes* (23– c. 15 B.C.), 1.24.

13. You can't set a hen in one morning and have chicken salad for lunch. GEORGE HUMPHREY, *Time*, Jan. 26, 1953.

14. If you wait, there will come nectar-like fair weather. JAPANESE PROVERB.

15. We shall sooner have the fowl by hatching the egg than by smashing it. ABRAHAM LINCOLN, speech, April 11, 1865.

16. Only with winter-patience can we bring / The deep-desired, long-awaited spring. ANNE MORROW LINDBERGH, "Autumn 1939," *The Unicorn and Other Poems, 1935–1955* (1956).

17. Patience and diligence, like faith, remove mountains. WILLIAM PENN, *Some Fruits of Solitude* (1693), 1.234.

18. He who has patience may accomplish anything. RABELAIS, *Gargantua and Pantagruel* (1532–64), 4.48.

19. Whoever has no patience has no wisdom. SA'DI, *Gulistan* (1258), 3.1, tr. James Ross.

20. Patience accomplishes its object, while hurry speeds to its ruin. SA'DI, *Gulistan* (1258), 8.37, tr. James Ross.

21. Though patience be a tired mare, yet she will plod. SHAKESPEARE, *Henry V* (1598–99), 2.1.26.

22. A wise man does not try to hurry history. Many wars have been avoided by patience and many have been precipitated by reckless haste. ADLAI STEVENSON, speech, San Francisco, Sept. 5, 1952.

23. Patience is the art of hoping. VAUVENARGUES, *Reflections and Maxims* (1746), 251.

## PATIENTS

See 261. Doctors

## 671. PATRIOTISM

See also 421. Homeland; 615. Nationalism

1. Patriotism is in political life what faith is in religion. LORD ACTON, "Nationality," *The Home and Foreign Review*, July 1862.

2. What a pity is it / That we can die but once to save our country! JOSEPH ADDISON, *Cato* (1713), 1.4.

3. When I am abroad, I always make it a rule never to criticize or attack the government of my own country. I make up for lost time when I come home. SIR WINSTON CHURCHILL, speech, House of Commons, April 1947.

4. When a whole nation is roaring Patriotism at the top of its voice, I am fain to explore the cleanness of its hands and purity of its heart. EMERSON, *Journals*, 1824.

5. He who loves not his home and country which he has seen, how shall he love humanity in general which he has not seen? WILLIAM RALPH INGE, "Patriotism," *Outspoken Essays: First Series* (1919).

6. I think patriotism is like charity—it begins at home. HENRY JAMES, *The Portrait of a Lady* (1881), 10.

7. Patriotism is the last refuge of a scoundrel. SAMUEL JOHNSON, quoted in Boswell's *Life of Samuel Johnson*, April 7, 1775.

8. There are things a man must not do even to save a nation. MURRAY KEMPTON, "To Save a Nation," *America Comes of Middle Age* (1963).

9. Ask not what your country can do for you: Ask what you can do for your country. JOHN F. KENNEDY, Inaugural Address, Jan. 20, 1961.

10. With a good conscience our only sure reward, with history the final judge of our deeds, let us go forth to lead the land we love, asking His blessing and His help, but knowing that here on earth God's work must truly be our own. JOHN F. KENNEDY, Inaugural Address, Jan. 20, 1961.

11. When a nation is filled with strife, then do patriots flourish. LAOTSE, *The Simple Way* (6th c. B.C.).

12. You're not supposed to be so blind with patriotism that you can't face reality. Wrong is wrong, no matter who does it or who says it. MALCOLM X, *Malcolm X Speaks* (1965), 12.

13. The love of Americans for their country is not an indulgent, it is an exacting and chastising love; they cannot tolerate its defects. JACQUES MARITAIN, *Reflections on America* (1958), 5.

14. Patriotism is a kind of religion; it is the egg from which wars are hatched. GUY DE MAUPASSANT, *My Uncle Sosthenes*.

15. Not for the flag / Of any land because myself was born there / Will I give up my life. / But I will love that land where man is free, / And that will I defend. EDNA ST. VINCENT MILLAY, "Not for a Nation," *Mine the Harvest* (1954).

16. Who saves his country violates no law. NAPOLEON I, *Maxims* (1804–15).

17. There can be no fifty-fifty Americanism in this country. There is room here for only hundred per cent Americanism. THEODORE ROOSEVELT, speech, Saratoga, N.Y., July 19, 1918.

18. Do we wish men to be virtuous? Then let us begin by making them love their country. ROUSSEAU, *A Discourse on Political Economy* (1758), tr. G. D. H. Cole.

19. No one loves his country for its size or eminence, but because it's his own. SENECA, *Letters to Lucilius* (1st c.), tr. E. Phillips Barker.

20. To strike freedom of the mind with the fist of patriotism is an old and ugly subtlety. ADLAI STEVENSON, speech, New York City, Aug. 27, 1952.

21. Patriotism is not a short and frenzied outburst of emotion but the tranquil and steady dedication of a lifetime. ADLAI STEVENSON, address to American Legion Convention, Aug. 30, 1952.

22. The song that nerves a nation's heart / Is in itself a deed. ALFRED, LORD TENNY-

SON, "The Charge of the Heavy Brigade" (1885).

23. My kind of loyalty was loyalty to one's country, not to its institutions or its office-holders. MARK TWAIN, *A Connecticut Yankee at King Arthur's Court* (1889).

24. Talking of patriotism, what humbug it is; it is a word which always commemorates a robbery. There isn't a foot of land in the world which doesn't represent the ousting and re-ousting of a long line of successive owners. MARK TWAIN, *Notebook* (1935).

25. In the beginning of a change, the patriot is a scarce man, and brave, and hated and scorned. When his cause succeeds, the timid join him, for then it costs nothing to be a patriot. MARK TWAIN, *Notebook* (1935).

26. The things that the flag stands for were created by the experiences of a great people. Everything that it stands for was written by their lives. The flag is the embodiment, not of sentiment, but of history. WOODROW WILSON, speech, June 14, 1915.

## 672. PATRONAGE

1. Is not a patron one who looks with unconcern on a man struggling for life in the water, and, when he has reached ground, encumbers him with help? SAMUEL JOHNSON, letter to Lord Chesterfield, Feb. 7, 1755, quoted in Boswell's *Life of Samuel Johnson.*

## 673. PAYMENT

**See also 639. Obligation; 782. Recompense**

1. In nature nothing can be given, all things are sold. EMERSON, "Compensation," *Essays: First Series* (1841).

2. Always pay; for first or last you must pay your entire debt. EMERSON, "Compensation," *Essays: First Series* (1841).

3. He who pays the piper may call the tune. ENGLISH PROVERB.

4. Nothing is to be had for nothing. EPICTETUS, *Discourses* (2nd c.), 4.10, tr. Thomas W. Higginson.

5. In every work / a reward added makes the pleasure twice as great. EURIPIDES, *Rhesus* (c. 455–441 B.C.), tr. Richmond Lattimore.

6. He that payeth beforehand shall have his work ill done. THOMAS FULLER, M.D., *Gnomologia* (1732), 2245.

## 674. PEACE

**See also 164. Conciliation; 170. Conquest; 225. Defeat; 658. Pacifism; 982. Tranquility; 1035. War**

1. Better beans and bacon in peace than cakes and ale in fear. AESOP, "The Town Mouse and the Country Mouse," *Fables* (6th c. B.C.?), tr. Joseph Jacobs.

2. Perhaps there is nothing in the whole of creation that knows the meaning of peace. For is not the soil restless by comparison with the unyielding rock? UGO BETTI, *The Fugitive* (1953), 3, tr. G. H. McWilliam.

3. He knows peace who has forgotten desire. *Bhagavadgita*, 2, tr. Swami Prabhavananda and Christopher Isherwood.

4. The name of peace is sweet and the thing itself good, but between peace and slavery there is the greatest difference. CICERO, *Philippics* (44–43 B.C.), 2.

5. Peace is liberty in tranquillity. CICERO, *Philippics* (44–43 B.C.), 2.44.

6. I take it that what all men are really after is some form or perhaps only some formula of peace. JOSEPH CONRAD, prologue to Part 1, *Under Western Eyes* (1911).

7. Though peace be made, yet it is interest that keeps peace. OLIVER CROMWELL, speech in Parliament, Sept. 4, 1654.

8. No one can have peace longer than his neighbor pleases. DUTCH PROVERB.

9. Better a lean peace than a fat victory. THOMAS FULLER, M.D., *Gnomologia* (1732), 864.

10. On all the peaks lies peace. GOETHE, "Wanderers Nachtlied."

11. War makes rattling good history; but Peace is poor reading. THOMAS HARDY, *The Dynasts* (1904–08), 2.5.

12. Mankind has grown strong in eternal struggles and it will only perish through eternal peace. ADOLF HITLER, *Mein Kampf* (1924), 1.4.

13. The passions that incline men to peace are fear of death, desire of such things as are necessary to commodious liv-

ing, and a hope by their industry to obtain them. THOMAS HOBBES, *Leviathan* (1651), 1.13.

14. The only condition of peace in this world is to have no ideas, or, at least, not to express them. OLIVER WENDELL HOLMES, SR., *The Professor at the Breakfast Table* (1860), 4.

15. Mutual cowardice keeps us in peace. SAMUEL JOHNSON, quoted in Boswell's *Life of Samuel Johnson*, April 28, 1778.

16. Now we suffer the woes of long peace. Luxury, more savage / Than war, has smothered us, avenging the world we ravage. JUVENAL, *Satires* (c. 100), 6.292, tr. Hubert Creekmore.

17. Arms alone are not enough to keep the peace. It must be kept by men. JOHN F. KENNEDY, State of the Union Message, Jan. 11, 1962.

18. The mere absence of war is not peace. JOHN F. KENNEDY, State of the Union Message, Jan. 14, 1963.

19. Peace is a daily, a weekly, a monthly process, gradually changing opinions, slowly eroding old barriers, quietly building new structures. JOHN F. KENNEDY, address to United Nations General Assembly, Sept. 20, 1963.

20. You may call for peace as loudly as you wish, but where there is no brotherhood there can in the end be no peace. MAX LERNER, "The Gifts of the Magi," *Actions and Passions* (1949).

21. Certain peace is better and safer than anticipated victory. LIVY, *Ab Urbe Condita* (c. 29 B.C.), 30.30.

22. Peace / Is the temporary beautiful ignorance that War / Somewhere progresses. EDNA ST. VINCENT MILLAY, untitled poem, *Make Bright the Arrows* (1940).

23. If there is to be any peace it will come through being, not having. HENRY MILLER, "The Wisdom of the Heart," *The Wisdom of the Heart* (1941).

24. Peace hath her victories no less renowned than war. MILTON, Sonnet 16 (1652).

25. There is no way to peace. Peace is the way. A. J. MUSTE, quoted in an editorial in *The New York Times*, Nov. 16, 1967.

26. Fair peace is becoming to men; fierce anger belongs to beasts. OVID, *The Art of Love* (c. A.D. 8), 3.502.

27. It is better to have a war for justice than peace in injustice. CHARLES PÉGUY, "The Rights of Man," *Basic Verities* (1943), tr. Ann and Julian Green.

28. Peace, like charity, begins at home. FRANKLIN D. ROOSEVELT, speech, Chautauqua, N.Y., Aug. 14, 1936.

29. Peace, like war, can succeed only where there is a will to enforce it, and where there is available power to enforce it. FRANKLIN D. ROOSEVELT, speech at the Foreign Policy Association, New York City, Oct. 21, 1944.

30. The peace we now see / will run / till the next war begins / whereupon peace / will be ushered in / at the end of the next war. CARL SANDBURG, "Peace Between Wars," *Complete Poems* (1950).

31. Peace is when time doesn't matter as it passes by. MARIA SCHELL, *Time*, March 3, 1958.

32. It is expedient for the victor to wish for peace restored; for the vanquished it is necessary. SENECA, *Hercules Furens* (1st c.), 369.

33. A peace is of the nature of a conquest; / For then both parties nobly are subdued, / And neither party loser. SHAKESPEARE, 2 *Henry IV* (1597–98), 4.2.89.

34. Since wars begin in the minds of men, it is in the minds of men that the defenses of peace must be constructed. UNESCO constitution (1945).

35. Peace is a virtual, mute, sustained victory of potential powers against probable greeds. PAUL VALÉRY, "Greatness and Decadence of Europe," *Reflections on the World Today* (1931), tr. Francis Scarfe.

36. There could be real peace only if everyone were satisfied. That means there is not often a real peace. There are only actual states of peace which, like wars, are mere expedients. PAUL VALÉRY, "Greatness and Decadence of Europe," *Reflections on the World Today* (1931), tr. Francis Scarfe.

37. What we dignify with the name of peace is really only a short truce, in accordance with which the weaker party renounces his claims, whether just or unjust, until such time as he can find an opportunity of asserting them with the sword. VAUVENARGUES, *Reflections and Maxims* (1746), 413, tr. F. G. Stevens.

38. The deliberate aim at Peace very easily passes into its bastard substitute, Anaesthesia. ALFRED NORTH WHITEHEAD,

*Adventures of Ideas* (1935).

39. Peace hath higher tests of manhood / Than battle ever knew. JOHN GREENLEAF WHITTIER, "The Hero" (1853), 19.

40. There is a price which is too great to pay for peace, and that price can be put in one word. One cannot pay the price of self-respect. WOODROW WILSON, speech, Des Moines, Iowa, Feb. 1, 1916.

41. Only a peace between equals can last. WOODROW WILSON, address to U.S. Senate, 1917.

## PEDANTRY

**See 520. Knowledge; 842. Scholars and Scholarship**

## 675. THE PEOPLE

**See also 52. Aristocracy; 133. Class; 205. Crowds; 231. Democracy; 581. Middle Class; 591. Mob; 906. Society**

1. Civilization exists precisely so that there may be no masses but rather men alert enough never to constitute masses. GEORGES BERNANOS, "Why Freedom?" *The Last Essays of Georges Bernanos* (1955), tr. Joan and Barry Ulanov.

2. People on the whole are very simple-minded, in whatever country one finds them. They are so simple as to take literally, more often than no, the things their leaders tell them. PEARL S. BUCK, *What America Means to Me* (1943), 5.

3. The populace drag down the gods to their own level. EMERSON, *Journals*, 1858.

4. The instinct of the people is right. EMERSON, "Power," *The Conduct of Life* (1860).

5. The public always prefers to be reassured. There are those whose job this is. There are only too many. ANDRÉ GIDE, *Journal of "The Counterfeiters,"* Second Notebook, Mar. 29, 1925, tr. Justin O'Brien.

6. The people like neither the true nor the simple; they like novels and charlatans. EDMOND and JULES DE GONCOURT, *Journal*, Mar. 31, 1861.

7. Who builds on the mob builds on sand. ITALIAN PROVERB.

8. We hold the view that the people make the best judgment in the long run. JOHN F. KENNEDY, campaign remarks, rally, Greensboro, N. C., Sept. 17, 1960.

9. The efforts of governments alone will never be enough. In the end, the people must choose and the people must help themselves. JOHN F. KENNEDY, at reception for Latin-American diplomats, Washington, D.C., March 13, 1961.

10. Who can endure the crassness of the common herd! / Are folk not presumptuous, warped, and absurd: / Putting barriers between self and the thing they should see, / Self measuring by self the whole community! LA FONTAINE, "The Two Dogs and the Dead Ass," *Fables* (1668–94), tr. Marianne Moore.

11. While the people retain their virtue and vigilance, no administration, by any extreme of wickedness or folly, can very seriously injure the government in the short space of four years. ABRAHAM LINCOLN, first Inaugural Address, March 4, 1861.

12. Why should there not be a patient confidence in the ultimate justice of the people? Is there any better or equal hope in the world? ABRAHAM LINCOLN, first Inaugural Address, March 4, 1861.

13. The people, and the people alone, are the motive force in the making of world history. MAO TSE-TUNG, *Quotations from Chairman Mao Tse-tung* (1966), 11.

14. I am the people—the mob—the crowd—the mass. / Do you know that all the great work of the world is done through me? CARL SANDBURG, "I Am the People, the Mob," *Complete Poems* (1950).

15. An habitation giddy and unsure / Hath he that buildeth on the vulgar heart. SHAKESPEARE, 2 *Henry IV* (1597–98), 1.3.89.

16. Every country is renewed out of the unknown ranks and not out of the ranks of those already famous and powerful and in control. WOODROW WILSON, speech, Chester, Pa., Oct. 28, 1912.

## 676. PERCEPTION

**See also 85. Blindness, Spiritual; 323. Eyes; 499. Intuition; 682. Perspective; 875. Senses; 876. Sensibility; 890. Sight; 1000. Understanding; 1027. Vision**

1. A fool sees not the same tree that a wise man sees. WILLIAM BLAKE, "Proverbs

of Hell," *The Marriage of Heaven and Hell* (1790).

2. The Eye altering alters all. WILLIAM BLAKE, "The Mental Traveller" (1800–10).

3. No object is mysterious. The mystery is your eye. ELIZABETH BOWEN, *The House in Paris* (1935), 2.6.

4. If man did not, from time to time, *sovereignly* close his eyes, he would finally be unable to see anything worth looking at. RENÉ CHAR, *Leaves of Hypnos*, 59, in *Hypnos Waking* (1956), tr. Jackson Mathews and others.

5. Women see better than men. Men see lazily, if they do not expect to act. Women see quite without any wish to act. EMERSON, *Journals*, 1839.

6. People only see what they are prepared to see. EMERSON, *Journals*, 1863.

7. The searcher's eye / Not seldom finds more than he wished to find. GOTTHOLD EPHRAIM LESSING, *Nathan the Wise* (1779), 2.7, tr. Bayard Quincy Morgan.

8. Some eyes want spectacles to see things clearly and distinctly: but let not those that use them therefore say nobody can see clearly without them. JOHN LOCKE, *An Essay Concerning Human Understanding* (1690), 4.17.4.

9. To see things as they are, the eyes must be open; to see things as other than they are, they must open even wider; to see things as better than they are, they must be open to the full. ANTONIO MACHADO, *Juan de Mairena* (1943), 14, tr. Ben Belitt.

10. Resemblances are the shadows of differences. Different people see different similarities and similar differences. VLADIMIR NABOKOV, "Commentary," *Pale Fire* (1962), 894.

11. The man who sees little always sees less than there is to see; the man who hears badly always hears something more than there is to hear. NIETZSCHE, *Human, All Too Human* (1878), 544, tr. Helen Zimmern.

12. One must always tell what one sees. Above all, which is more difficult, one must always see what one sees. CHARLES PÉGUY, "The Honest People," *Basic Verities* (1943), tr. Ann and Julian Green.

13. Not only is there but one way of doing things rightly, but there is only one way of seeing them, and that is, seeing the whole of them. JOHN RUSKIN, *The Two Paths* (1859), 2.

## 677. PERFECTION

**See also 297. Error; 339. Faults; 455. Imperfection**

1. Not a having and a resting, but a growing and a becoming, is the character of perfection as culture conceives it. MATTHEW ARNOLD, "Sweetness and Light," *Culture and Anarchy* (1869).

2. When a man says that he is perfect already, there is only one of two places for him, and that is heaven or the lunatic asylum. HENRY WARD BEECHER, *Proverbs from Plymouth Pulpit* (1887).

3. All mankind / Is born for perfection / And each shall attain it / Will he but follow / His nature's duty. *Bhagavadgita*, 18, tr. Swami Prabhavananda and Christopher Isherwood.

4. If thou wilt be perfect, go and sell that thou hast, and give to the poor, and thou shalt have treasure in heaven. *Bible*, Matthew 19:21.

5. The maxim "Nothing avails but perfection" may be spelled, "Paralysis." SIR WINSTON CHURCHILL, "The Man," *The Churchill Wit* (1965), ed. Bill Adler.

6. Total freedom from error is what none of us will allow to our neighbors; however we may be inclined to flirt a little with such spotless perfection ourselves. CHARLES CALEB COLTON, *Lacon* (1825), 1.17.

7. Of what small spots pure white complains. JOHN DONNE, "Elegy on the Lady Marckham" (1609).

8. The wise man, the true friend, the finished character, we seek everywhere, and only find in fragments. EMERSON, *Journals*, 1833.

9. People who have no weaknesses are terrible; there is no way of taking advantage of them. ANATOLE FRANCE, *The Crime of Sylvestre Bonnard* (1881), 2.4, tr. Lafcadio Hearn.

10. We shall never have friends, if we expect to find them without fault. THOMAS FULLER, M.D., *Gnomologia* (1732), 5456.

11. Could everything be done twice everything would be done better. GERMAN PROVERB.

12. Trifles make perfection, but perfection is no trifle. ITALIAN PROVERB.

13. In small proportions we just beauties see, / And in short measures life may perfect be. BEN JONSON, "To the Immortal

Memory of Sir Lucius Cary and Sir Henry Morison," *Underwoods* (1640), 3.

14. Perfection has one grave defect: it is apt to be dull. W. SOMERSET MAUGHAM, *The Summing Up* (1938), 10.

15. Whoever thinks a faultless piece to see, / Thinks what ne'er was, nor is, nor shall be. ALEXANDER POPE, *An Essay on Criticism* (1711), 2.53.

16. Perfection is no more a requisite to art than to heroes. Frigidaires are perfect. Beauty limps. My frigidaire has had to be replaced. NED ROREM, "Random Notes from a Diary," *Music from Inside Out* (1967).

17. In anything at all, perfection is finally attained not when there is no longer anything to add, but when there is no longer anything to take away. SAINT-EXUPÉRY, *Wind, Sand, and Stars* (1939), 3, tr. Lewis Galantière.

18. There is tragedy in perfection, because the universe in which perfection arises is itself imperfect. GEORGE SANTAYANA, *The Life of Reason: Reason in Science* (1905–06), 9.

19. Striving to better, oft we mar what's well. SHAKESPEARE, *King Lear* (1605–06), 1.4.369.

20. The indefatigable pursuit of an unattainable Perfection, even though it consist in nothing more than the pounding of an old piano, alone gives a meaning to our life on this unavailing star. LOGAN PEARSALL SMITH, *Afterthoughts* (1931), 5.

21. The abuse of grace is affectation, as the abuse of the sublime is absurdity; all perfection is nearly a fault. VOLTAIRE, "Grace," *Philosophical Dictionary* (1764).

22. It is through Art, and through Art only, that we can realise our perfection. OSCAR WILDE, "The Critic as Artist," *Intentions* (1891).

## 678. PERFUME

**See also 189. Cosmetics**

1. To smell, though well, is to stink. MONTAIGNE, "Of smells," *Essays* (1580–88), tr. Charles Cotton and W. C. Hazlitt.

2. A woman smells well when she smells of nothing. PLAUTUS, *Mostellaria* (3rd c. B.C.).

## PERMANENCE

**See 116. Changelessness**

## 679. PERSEVERANCE

**See also 279. Effort; 285. Endurance; 579. Method**

1. Perseverance, n. A lowly virtue whereby mediocrity achieves an inglorious success. AMBROSE BIERCE, *The Devil's Dictionary* (1881–1911).

2. All work of man is as the swimmer's: a waste [vast] ocean threatens to devour him; if he front it not bravely, it will keep its word. THOMAS CARLYLE, *Past and Present* (1843).

3. The person who makes a success of living is the one who sees his goal steadily and aims for it unswervingly. That is dedication. CECIL B. DE MILLE, *Sunshine and Shadow* (1955).

4. To persevere, trusting in what hopes he has, / is courage in a man. The coward despairs. EURIPIDES, *Heracles* (c. 422 B.C.), tr. William Arrowsmith.

5. Somehow life doesn't always pay off to those who are most insistent. MAX LERNER, "The Postponed Generation," *Actions and Passions* (1949).

6. Perseverance can lend the appearance of dignity and grandeur to many actions, just as silence in company affords wisdom and apparent intelligence to a stupid person. GEORG CHRISTOPH LICHTENBERG, *Aphorisms* (1764–99), tr. F. H. Mautner and H. Hatfield.

7. Many strokes overthrow the tallest oaks. JOHN LYLY, *Euphues: The Anatomy of Wit* (1579).

8. Perseverance is more prevailing than violence; and many things which cannot be overcome when they are together, yield themselves up when taken little by little. PLUTARCH, "Life of Sertorius," *Parallel Lives* (1st–2nd c. A.D.), tr. John Dryden.

9. The wind-footed steed is broken down in his speed, whilst the camel-driver jogs on with his beast to the end of his journey. SA'DI, *Gulistan* (1258), 8.37, tr. James Ross.

10. Even after a bad harvest there must be sowing. SENECA, *Letters to Lucilius* (1st c.), 81.1, tr. E. Phillips Barker.

## 680. PERSONALITY

**See also 117. Character; 681. Personality, Dual; 962. Temperament**

1. Few men are of one plain, decided color; most are mixed, shaded, and blended; and vary as much, from different situations, as changeable silks do from different lights. LORD CHESTERFIELD, *Letters to His Son,* April 30, 1752.

2. A man is like a bit of Labrador spar, which has no lustre as you turn it in your hand, until you come to a particular angle; then it shows deep and beautiful colors. EMERSON, "Experience," *Essays: Second Series* (1844).

3. There is an invisible garment woven around us from our earliest years; it is made of the way we eat, the way we walk, the way we greet people, woven of tastes and colors and perfumes which our senses spin in childhood. JEAN GIRAUDOUX, *Siegfried* (1928), 3, tr. Phyllis La Farge with Peter H. Judd.

## 681. PERSONALITY, DUAL

**See also 438. Hypocrisy; 442. Identity; 680. Personality**

1. The image of myself which I try to create in my own mind in order that I may love myself is very different from the image which I try to create in the minds of others in order that they may love me. W. H. AUDEN, "Hic et Ille," *The Dyer's Hand* (1962).

2. God be thanked, the meanest of his creatures / Boasts two soul-sides, one to face the world with, / One to show a woman when he loves her! ROBERT BROWNING, "One Word More," *Men and Women* (1855), 17.

3. There are two sides to ivry man. Wan side is commercyal, an' th' other is sintimintal. Some men keep thim apart in private an' throt thim out together in public. Others niver let thim appear together where annywan can see thim. FINLEY PETER DUNNE, "On Past Glories," *Mr. Dooley On Making a Will* (1919).

4. A man must ride alternately on the horses of his private and his public nature. EMERSON, "Fate," *The Conduct of Life* (1860).

5. There is no one so bound to his own face that he does not cherish the hope of presenting another to the world. ANTONIO MACHADO, *Juan de Mairena* (1943), 17, tr. Ben Belitt.

## 682. PERSPECTIVE

**See also 58. Attitude; 331. Familiarity; 676. Perception; 788. Relativeness**

1. 'Tis distance lends enchantment to the view, / And robes the mountain in its azure hue. THOMAS CAMPBELL, *Pleasures of Hope* (1799), 1.7.

2. What you see, yet can not see over, is as good as infinite. THOMAS CARLYLE, *Sartor Resartus* (1833–34), 2.1.

3. He that is placed at a great distance from an object is a bad judge of the relative space that separates other objects from it. CHARLES CALEB COLTON, *Lacon* (1825), 1.583.

4. The field cannot well be seen from within the field. EMERSON, "Circles," *Essays: First Series* (1841).

5. It is the eye which makes the horizon. EMERSON, "Experience," *Essays: Second Series* (1844).

6. Distance has the same effect on the mind as on the eye. SAMUEL JOHNSON, *Rasselas* (1759), 35.

7. Every man takes the limits of his own field of vision for the limits of the world. SCHOPENHAUER, "Further Psychological Observations," *Parerga and Paralipomena* (1851), tr. T. Bailey Saunders.

## 683. PERSUASION

**See also 51. Argument; 157. Compliance; 281. Eloquence; 739. Propaganda**

1. To please people is a great step towards persuading them. LORD CHESTERFIELD, *Letters to His Son,* Nov. 1, 1739.

2. Most people have ears, but few have judgment; tickle those ears, and, depend upon it, you will catch their judgments, such as they are. LORD CHESTERFIELD, *Letters to His Son,* Dec. 9, 1749.

3. He who wants to persuade should put his trust not in the right argument, but in the right word. The power of sound has always been greater than the power of sense.

JOSEPH CONRAD, "A Familiar Preface," *A Personal Record* (1912).

4. Too much zeal offends / where indirection works. EURIPIDES, *Orestes* (408 B.C.), tr. William Arrowsmith.

5. Charming women can true converts make, / We love the precepts for the teacher's sake. GEORGE FARQUHAR, *The Constant Couple* (1699), 5.3.

6. Would you persuade, speak of interest, not of reason. BENJAMIN FRANKLIN, *Poor Richard's Almanack* (1732–57).

7. Soft words are hard arguments. THOMAS FULLER, M.D., *Gnomologia* (1732), 4203.

8. The persuasion of a friend is a strong thing. HOMER, *Iliad* (9th c. B.C.), 15.404, tr. Richmond Lattimore.

9. If the horn cannot be twisted, the ear can. MALAY PROVERB.

10. People are generally better persuaded by the reasons which they have themselves discovered than by those which have come into the mind of others. PASCAL, *Pensées* (1670), 10, tr. W. F. Trotter.

11. I see / that everywhere among the race of men / it is the tongue that wins and not the deed. SOPHOCLES, *Philoctetes* (409 B.C.), tr. David Grene.

## 684. PERVERSENESS

**See also 167. Conflict, Inner; 866. Self-injury**

1. Man never knows what he wants; he aspires to penetrate mysteries and as soon as he has, wants to re-establish them. Ignorance irritates him and knowledge cloys. HENRI FRÉDÉRIC AMIEL, *Journal* (1882–84).

2. There is in the human race some dark spirit of recalcitrance, always pulling us in the direction contrary to that in which we are reasonably expected to go. MAX BEERBOHM, "Some Damnable Errors About Christmas," *A Christmas Garland* (1895).

3. The good that I would I do not; but the evil which I would not, that I do. *Bible*, Romans 7:19.

4. What rapture, oh, it is to know / A good thing when you see it / And having seen a good thing, oh, / What rapture 'tis to flee it. BERTOLT BRECHT, *The Good Woman of Setzuan* (1938–40), 10, tr. Eric Bentley and Maja Apelman.

5. We trifle with, make sport of, and despise those who are attached to us, and follow those that fly from us. WILLIAM HAZLITT, "On the Conduct of Life," *Literary Remains* (1836).

6. Look round the habitable world: how few / Know their own good, or knowing it, pursue. JUVENAL, *Satires* (c. 100), 10, tr. John Dryden.

7. Few people want the pleasures they are free to take. OVID, *The Loves* (c. A.D. 8), 3.4, tr. J. Lewis May.

8. Man is neither angel nor beast, and the misfortune is that he who would act the angel acts the beast. PASCAL, *Pensées* (1670), 358.

9. Just as we are often moved to merriment for no other reason than that the occasion calls for seriousness, so we are correspondingly serious when invited too freely to be amused. AGNES REPPLIER, "The American Laughs," *Under Dispute* (1924).

10. Such is the blindness, nay, the insanity of mankind, that some men are driven to death by the fear of it. SENECA, *Letters to Lucilius* (1st c.), 24.23, tr. E. Phillips Barker.

11. The heart *prefers* to move against the grain of circumstance; perversity is the soul's very life. JOHN UPDIKE, "More Love in the Western World," *Assorted Prose* (1965).

12. The instinct of a man is to pursue everything that flies from him, and to fly from all that pursue him. VOLTAIRE, "Enchantment," *Philosophical Dictionary* (1764).

## 685. PESSIMISM

**See also 652. Optimism; 653. Optimism and Pessimism**

1. Pessimism does win us great happy moments. MAX BEERBOHM, "Hosts and Guests," *And Even Now* (1920).

2. To a profound pessimist about life, being in danger is not depressing. F. SCOTT FITZGERALD, quoted in Andrew Turnbull's *Scott Fitzgerald* (1962), 6.

3. He that hopes no good fears no ill. THOMAS FULLER, M.D., *Gnomologia* (1732), 2166.

4. A pessimist is a man who has been compelled to live with an optimist. ELBERT HUBBARD, *The Note Book* (1927).

5. Logic and sermons never convince, /

The damp of the night drives deeper into my soul. WALT WHITMAN, "Song of Myself," 30, *Leaves of Grass* (1855–92).

## 686. PETTINESS

**See also 522. Largeness; 573. Mediocrity; 989. Trifles; 1005. Unimportance**

1. No sadder proof can be given by a man of his own littleness than disbelief in great men. THOMAS CARLYLE, *On Heroes, Hero-Worship and the Heroic in History* (1841), 1.

2. To the mean eye all things are trivial, as certainly as to the jaundiced they are yellow. THOMAS CARLYLE, *On Heroes, Hero-Worship and the Heroic in History* (1841), 3.

3. That is the consolation of a little mind; you have the fun of changing it without impeding the progress of mankind. FRANK MOORE COLBY, "Simple Simon," *The Colby Essays* (1926), v.1.

4. Looking at small advantages prevents great affairs from being accomplished. CONFUCIUS, *Analects* (6th c. B.C.), 13.17, tr. James Legge.

5. When we play the part of a great man too much, we seem very small. PHILIPPE DESTOUCHES, *Le Glorieux* (1732), 3.5.

6. The pettiness of a mind can be measured by the pettiness of its adoration or its blasphemy. ANDRÉ GIDE, *Journals*, January 1902, tr. Justin O'Brien.

7. Poor fool! in whose petty estimation all things are little. GOETHE, *The Sorrows of Young Werther* (1774), 1, Aug. 18, 1771, tr. Victor Lange.

8. Small minds are much distressed by little things. Great minds see them all but are not upset by them. LA ROCHEFOUCAULD, *Maxims* (1665), tr. Kenneth Pratt.

9. A bucket full of water does not splash about, only a bucket half-full splashes. MALAY PROVERB.

10. But me, the fool, save / From waxing so grave, / As, reduced to skimmed milk, to slander / The cream. HERMAN MELVILLE, "Old Age in His Ailing," *At the Hostelry* (1925).

11. To the mean all becomes mean. NIETZSCHE, "On Old and New Tablets," *Thus Spoke Zarathustra* (1883–92), 3, tr. Walter Kaufmann.

12. Small things make base men proud. SHAKESPEARE, *2 Henry VI* (1590–91), 4.1.106.

13. We cannot be kind to each other here for an hour; / We whisper, and hint, and chuckle, and grin at a brother's shame; / However we brave it out, we men are a little breed. ALFRED, LORD TENNYSON, "Maud; A Monodrama" (1856), 4.5.

## 687. PHANTASY

**See also 264. Dreams; 381. Ghosts; 447. Illusion; 448. Imagination; 812. Reverie**

1. Imagination consists in expelling from reality several incomplete persons, and then using the magic and subversive powers of desire to bring them back in the form of one entirely satisfying presence. RENÉ CHAR, *The Formal Share*, 1, in *Hypnos Waking* (1956), tr. Jackson Mathews and others.

2. To believe in one's dreams is to spend all of one's life asleep. CHINESE PROVERB.

3. Dreams are the subtle Dower / That make us rich an Hour— / Then fling us poor / Out of the purple door. EMILY DICKINSON, poem (c. 1876).

4. Few have greater riches than the joy / That comes to us in visions, / In dreams which nobody can take away. EURIPIDES, *Iphigenia in Tauris* (c. 414–12 B.C.), tr. Witter Bynner.

5. Only the dreamer shall understand realities, though in truth his dreaming must be not out of proportion to his waking. MARGARET FULLER, *Summer on the Lakes* (1844), 5.

6. He who passes not his days in the realm of dreams is the slave of the days. KAHLIL GIBRAN, "The Goddess of Fantasy," *Thoughts and Meditations* (1960), tr. Anthony R. Ferris.

7. On men intoxicated with dreams women's tears act like smelling salts—they sober them up. MAXIM GORKY, *Enemies* (1906), 1.

8. Let us acknowledge it wiser, if not more sagacious, to follow out one's daydream to its natural consummation, although if the vision have been worth the having, it is certain never to be consummated otherwise than by a failure. NATHANIEL HAWTHORNE, *The Blithedale Romance* (1852), 2.

9. We do not really feel grateful toward those who make our dreams come true; they ruin our dreams. ERIC HOFFER, *The Passionate State of Mind* (1954), 232.

10. A fantasy can be equivalent to a paradise and if the fantasy passes, better yet, because eternal paradise would be very boring. JUAN RAMÓN JIMÉNEZ, "To Burn Completely," *Selected Writings* (1957), tr. H. R. Hays.

11. No man will be found in whose mind airy notions do not sometime tyrannize, and force him to hope or fear beyond the limits of sober probability. SAMUEL JOHNSON, *Rasselas* (1759), 44.

12. Ever let the Fancy roam, / Pleasure never is at home. JOHN KEATS, "Fancy" (1818).

13. Where all is but dream, reasoning and arguments are of no use, truth and knowledge nothing. JOHN LOCKE, *An Essay Concerning Human Understanding* (1690), 4.2.14.

14. Round about what is, lies a whole mysterious world of might be, a psychological romance of possibilities and things that do not happen. LONGFELLOW, "Table-Talk," *Driftwood* (1857).

15. Safe upon the solid rock the ugly houses stand: / Come and see my shining palace built upon the sand! EDNA ST. VINCENT MILLAY, "Second Fig," *A Few Figs from Thistles* (1921).

16. The lie of a pipe dream is what gives life to the whole misbegotten mad lot of us, drunk or sober. EUGENE O'NEILL, *The Iceman Cometh* (1946), 1.

17. A dreamer lives forever, / And a toiler dies in a day. JOHN BOYLE O'REILLY, "The Cry of the Dreamer," *Works* (1891).

18. Life is full of internal dramas, instantaneous and sensational, played to an audience of one. ANTHONY POWELL, *The New York Times*, July 22, 1958.

19. A dream is always simmering below the conventional surface of speech and reflection. GEORGE SANTAYANA, *The Life of Reason: Reason in Common Sense* (1905–06), 2.

20. The dreamer can know no truth, not even about his dream, except by awaking out of it. GEORGE SANTAYANA, *Dialogues in Limbo* (1925), 2.

21. How many of our daydreams would darken into nightmares if there seemed any danger of their coming true! LOGAN PEARSALL SMITH, *Afterthoughts* (1931), 1.

22. Our truest life is when we are in dreams awake. THOREAU, "The Inward Morning," *A Week on the Concord and Merrimack Rivers* (1849).

23. It is in our idleness, in our dreams, that the submerged truth sometimes comes to the top. VIRGINIA WOOLF, *A Room of One's Own* (1929), 2.

24. Life moves out of a red flare of dreams / Into a common light of common hours, / Until old age brings the red flare again. WILLIAM BUTLER YEATS, *The Land of Heart's Desire* (1894).

## PHILANTHROPY

See 430. Humanitarianism

## 688. PHILOSOPHERS AND PHILOSOPHY

See also 315. Existentialism; 429. Humanism; 569. Meaning; 627. Nihilism; 778. Reason; 897. Skepticism; 930. Stoicism; 954. Systems; 967. Theory; 968. Thought; 1012. The Unknown

1. A little philosophy inclineth man's mind to atheism, but depth in philosophy bringeth men's minds about to religion. FRANCIS BACON, "Of Atheism," *Essays* (1625).

2. All philosophies, if you ride them home, are nonsense; but some are greater nonsense than others. SAMUEL BUTLER (d. 1902), "First Principles," *Note-Books* (1912).

3. The presence of desire, like that of the god, ignores the philosopher. The philosopher's revenge is to chasten. RENÉ CHAR, *Leaves of Hypnos*, 202, in *Hypnos Waking* (1956), tr. Jackson Mathews and others.

4. There is nothing so strange and so unbelievable that it has not been said by one philosopher or another. DESCARTES, *Discourse on Method* (1639), 2.

5. Posterity for the philosopher is what the other world is for the religious man. DENIS DIDEROT, *lettre à Falconet*, 1765.

6. What is it to be a philosopher? Is it not to be prepared against events? EPICTETUS, *Discourses* (2nd c.), 3.10, tr. Thomas W. Higginson.

7. Let no young man delay the study of philosophy, and let no old man become weary of it; for it is never too early nor too late to care for the well-being of the soul. EPICURUS, Letter to Menoeceus (3rd c. B.C.), in *Letters, Principal Doctrines, and Vatican Sayings*, tr. Russel M. Geer.

8. You can't do without philosophy, since everything has its hidden meaning which we must know. MAXIM GORKY, *The Zykovs* (1914), 2.

9. The difference between gossip and philosophy lies only in one's way of taking a fact. OLIVER WENDELL HOLMES, JR., "The Bar as a Profession," *Youth's Companion*, 1896.

10. One of the main reasons for the existence of philosophy is not that it enables you to find truth (it can never do that) but that it does provide you a refuge for definitions. THOMAS ERNEST HULME, "Romanticism and Classicism," *Speculations* (1923).

11. The object of studying philosophy is to know one's own mind, not other people's. WILLIAM RALPH INGE, "Confessio Fidei," *Outspoken Essays: Second Series* (1922).

12. Pretend what we may, the whole man within us is at work when we form our philosophical opinions. WILLIAM JAMES, "The Sentiment of Rationality," *The Will to Believe* (1896).

13. Philosophy will clip an Angel's wings, / Conquer all mysteries by rule and line, / Empty the haunted air, and gnomed mine— / Unweave a rainbow. JOHN KEATS, "Lamia" (1819), 2.

14. Do not all charms fly / At the mere touch of cold philosophy? JOHN KEATS, "Lamia" (1819), 2.

15. All schools of philosophy, and almost all authors, are rather to be frequented for exercise than for freight. WALTER SAVAGE LANDOR, "Epicurus, Leontion, and Ternissa," *Imaginary Conversations* (1824–53).

16. A philosophy is characterized more by the formulation of its problems than by its solution of them. SUSANNE K. LANGER, *Philosophy in a New Key* (1942).

17. The constancy of philosophers is nothing but the art of concealing their disquietude in their hearts. LA ROCHEFOUCAULD, *Maxims* (1665), tr. Kenneth Pratt.

18. Oh! speculators on things, boast not of knowing the things that nature ordinarily brings about; but rejoice if you know the end of those things which you yourself devise. LEONARDO DA VINCI, *Notebooks* (c. 1500), tr. Jean Paul Richter.

19. When philosophers try to be politicians they generally cease to be philosophers. WALTER LIPPMANN, "The Changing Focus," *A Preface to Politics* (1914).

20. The great philosophers are poets who believe in the reality of their poems. ANTONIO MACHADO, *Juan de Mairena* (1943), 22, tr. Ben Belitt.

21. It has been said that metaphysics is the finding of bad reasons for what we believe upon instinct. W. SOMERSET MAUGHAM, *The Summing Up* (1938), 15.

22. Metaphysics is almost always an attempt to prove the incredible by an appeal to the unintelligible. H. L. MENCKEN, *Minority Report* (1956), 357.

23. Wonder is the foundation of all philosophy, inquiry the progress, ignorance the end. MONTAIGNE, "Of cripples," *Essays* (1580–88).

24. Philosophy is such an impertinently litigious lady that a man had as good be engaged in lawsuits as have to do with her. ISAAC NEWTON, letter to Edmund Halley, June 20, 1687.

25. Every philosophy is the philosophy of some stage of life. NIETZSCHE, *Mixed Opinions and Maxims* (1879), 271, in *The Portable Nietzsche*, tr. Walter Kaufmann.

26. A married philosopher belongs to comedy. NIETZSCHE, *The Genealogy of Morals* (1887), 3.7, tr. Horace B. Samuel.

27. Inertia rides and riddles me; / The which is called Philosophy. DOROTHY PARKER, "The Veteran," *Enough Rope* (1926), 2.

28. To make light of philosophy is to be a true philosopher. PASCAL, *Pensées* (1670), 4, tr. W. F. Trotter.

29. Philosophers.—We are full of things which take us out of ourselves. PASCAL, *Pensées* (1670), 464, tr. W. F. Trotter.

30. A great philosophy is not a flawless philosophy, but a fearless one. CHARLES PÉGUY, *Note sur M. Bergson et la philosophie bergsonienne* (1914).

31. A man of business may talk of philosophy; a man who has none may practise it. ALEXANDER POPE, *Thoughts on Various Subjects* (1727).

32. It is a proof of philosophical mediocrity, today, to look for a philosophy. PIERRE-JOSEPH PROUDHON, *La Révolution sociale* (1852).

33. The philosopher spends in becoming a man the time which the ambitious man spends in becoming a personage. JOSEPH ROUX, *Meditations of a Parish Priest* (1886), 4.94, tr. Isabel F. Hapgood.

34. Ethical metaphysics is fundamentally an attempt, however disguised, to give legislative force to our own wishes. BERTRAND RUSSELL, "On Scientific Method in Philosophy," *Mysticism and Logic* (1917).

35. For the learning of every virtue there is an appropriate discipline, and for the learning of suspended judgment the best discipline is philosophy. BERTRAND RUSSELL, "Philosophy for Laymen," *Unpopular Essays* (1950).

36. Philosophers, for the most part, are constitutionally timid, and dislike the unexpected. Few of them would be genuinely happy as pirates or burglars. Accordingly they invent systems which make the future calculable, at least in its main outlines. BERTRAND RUSSELL, "Philosophy's Ulterior Motives," *Unpopular Essays* (1950).

37. At best, the true philosopher can fulfil his mission very imperfectly, which is to pilot himself, or at most a few voluntary companions who may find themselves in the same boat. GEORGE SANTAYANA, *Character and Opinion in the United States* (1921), 2.

38. Philosophers are as jealous as women; each wants a monopoly of praise. GEORGE SANTAYANA, *Dialogues in Limbo* (1925), 2.

39. Philosophy has a fine saying for everything.—For Death it has an entire set. LAURENCE STERNE, *Tristram Shandy* (1759–67), 5.3.

40. A Chinaman of the T'ang Dynasty—and, by which definition, a philosopher—dreamed he was a butterfly, and from that moment he was never quite sure that he was not a butterfly dreaming it was a Chinese philosopher. TOM STOPPARD, *Rosencrantz & Guildenstern Are Dead* (1967), 2.

41. That's why I love philosophy: no one wins. DAISETZ TEITARO SUZUKI, quoted in John Cage's "Composition as Process," *Silence* (1961), 2.

42. The various opinions of philosophers have scattered through the world as many plagues of the mind as Pandora's box did those of the body; only with this difference, that they have not left hope at the bottom. JONATHAN SWIFT, *A Tritical Essay Upon the Faculties of the Mind* (1707).

43. To be a philosopher is not merely to have subtle thoughts, nor even to found a school, but so to love wisdom as to live according to its dictates, a life of simplicity, independence, magnanimity, and trust. THOREAU, *Walden* (1854).

44. If a philosopher is not a man, he is anything but a philosopher; he is above all a pedant, and a pedant is a caricature of a man. MIGUEL DE UNAMUNO, "The Man of Flesh and Bone," *Tragic Sense of Life* (1913), tr. J. E. Crawford Flitch.

45. When one man speaks to another man who doesn't understand him, and when the man who's speaking no longer understands, it's metaphysics. VOLTAIRE, *Candide* (1759).

46. All the persecutors declare against each other mortal war, while the philosopher, oppressed by them all, contents himself with pitying them. VOLTAIRE, "Philosopher," *Philosophical Dictionary* (1764).

47. Every philosophy is tinged with the colouring of some secret imaginative background, which never emerges explicitly into its trains of reasoning. ALFRED NORTH WHITEHEAD, *Science and the Modern World* (1925), 1.

48. Philosophy begins in wonder. And, at the end, when philosophic thought has done its best, the wonder remains. ALFRED NORTH WHITEHEAD, *Modes of Thought* (1938).

## 689. PHOTOGRAPHY

1. The virtue of the camera is not the power it has to transform the photographer into an artist, but the impulse it gives him to keep on looking. BROOKS ATKINSON, "August 28," *Once Around the Sun* (1951).

2. Photography records the gamut of feelings written on the human face, the beauty of the earth and skies that man has inherited, and the wealth and confusion man has created. It is a major force in explaining man to man. EDWARD STEICHEN, *Time*, April 7, 1961.

## 690. PHYSICAL FITNESS

See also 922. Sports; 1034. Walking

1. Bodily exercise profiteth little; but godliness is profitable unto all things. *Bible*, 1 Timothy 4:8.

2. Oh, the wild joys of living! the leaping from rock up to rock, / The strong rending of boughs from the fir-tree, the cool silver shock / Of the plunge in a pool's living water. ROBERT BROWNING, "Saul," *Men and Women* (1855), 9.

3. We are under-exercised as a nation. We look instead of play. We ride instead of walk. Our existence deprives us of the minimum of physical activity essential for healthy living. JOHN F. KENNEDY, address, National Football Foundation, New York City, Dec. 5, 1961.

4. There is nothing, I think, more unfortunate than to have soft, chubby, fat-looking children who go to watch their school play basketball every Saturday and regard that as their week's exercise. JOHN F. KENNEDY, address at U.S. Children's Bureau, Washington, D.C., April 9, 1962.

5. Bodily exercises are to be done discreetly; not to be taken evenly and alike by all men. THOMAS À KEMPIS, *The Imitation of Christ* (1426), 1.19.

6. Regimen is superior to medicine, especially as, from time immemorial, out of every hundred physicians, ninety-eight are charlatans. VOLTAIRE, "Physicians," *Philosophical Dictionary* (1764).

7. In all important respects, the man who has nothing but his physical power to sell has nothing to sell which it is worth anyone's money to buy. NORBERT WIENER, *The Human Use of Human Beings* (1954), 9.

## PHYSICIANS

See 261. Doctors

## PHYSICS

See 843. Science

## 691. PIETY

See also 391. Goodness; 504. Irreverence; 717. Prayer

1. The strength of a man consists in finding out the way in which God is going, and going in that way too. HENRY WARD BEECHER, *Proverbs from Plymouth Pulpit* (1887).

2. Set your affections on things above, not on things on the earth. *Bible*, Colossians 3:2.

3. Fear God, and where you go men shall think they walk in hallowed cathedrals. EMERSON, "Worship," *The Conduct of Life* (1860).

4. The best way to see divine light is to put out thy own candle. THOMAS FULLER, M.D., *Gnomologia* (1732), 4421.

5. Piety, like nobility, has its aristocracy. GOETHE, quoted in Johann Peter Eckermann's *Conversations with Goethe*, Feb. 25, 1824.

6. Love of God is not always the same as love of good. HERMANN HESSE, *Narcissus and Goldmund* (1930), 3, tr. Ursule Molinaro.

7. Piety with some people, but especially with women, is either a passion, or an infirmity of age, or a fashion which must be followed. LA BRUYÈRE, *Characters* (1688), 3.16, tr. Henri Van Laun.

8. A devout man is he who would be an atheist if the king were. LA BRUYÈRE, *Characters* (1688), 13.21.

9. Piety's hard enough to take / Among the poor who *have* to practice it. / A rich man's piety stinks. It's insufferable. ARCHIBALD MAC LEISH, *JB* (1958), 2.

10. Experience makes us see an enormous difference between piety and goodness. PASCAL, *Pensées* (1670), 496, tr. W. F. Trotter.

11. It is rash to intrude upon the piety of others: both the depth and the grace of it elude the stranger. GEORGE SANTAYANA, *Dialogues in Limbo* (1925), 4.

12. Religion in its humility restores man to his only dignity, the courage to live by grace. GEORGE SANTAYANA, *Dialogues in Limbo* (1925), 4.

13. Live with men as if God saw you: speak to God as if men heard you. SENECA, *Letters to Lucilius* (1st c.), 10.5, tr. E. Phillips Barker.

14. When the devil prays he is out to deceive you. SPANISH PROVERB.

## 692. PITY

See also 577. Mercy; 870. Self-pity; 953. Sympathy; 1001. Understanding Others

1. One cannot weep for the entire world. It is beyond human strength. One must choose. JEAN ANOUILH, *Cécile* (1949), tr. Luce and Arthur Klein.

2. The response man has the greatest difficulty in tolerating is pity, especially when he warrants it. Hatred is a tonic, it makes one live, it inspires vengeance, but pity kills, it makes our weakness weaker. BALZAC, *La Peau de chagrin* (1831), 3.

3. Pity would be no more / If we did not make somebody Poor; / And Mercy no more could be / If all were as happy as we. WILLIAM BLAKE, "The Human Abstract," *Songs of Experience* (1794).

4. There are a few things that'll move people to pity, a few, but the trouble is, when they've been used several times, they no longer work. BERTOLT BRECHT, *The Threepenny Opera* (1928), 1.1, tr. Desmond Vesey and Eric Bentley.

5. By compassion we make others' misery our own, and so, by relieving them, we relieve ourselves also. SIR THOMAS BROWNE, *Religio Medici* (1642), 2.

6. A tear dries quickly, especially when it is shed for the troubles of others. CICERO, *Partitiones Oratoriae* (c. 55 B.C.).

7. Most of our misfortunes are more supportable than the comments of our friends upon them. CHARLES CALEB COLTON, *Lacon* (1825), 1.517.

8. No man limps because another is hurt. DANISH PROVERB.

9. Endow the Living – with the Tears – / You squander on the Dead. EMILY DICKINSON, poem (c. 1862).

10. Pity melts the mind to love. JOHN DRYDEN, "Alexander's Feast" (1687), 96.

11. You may regret calamities if you can thereby help the sufferer, but if you cannot, mind your own business. EMERSON, *Journals*, 1836.

12. Sacrifice not thy heart upon every altar. THOMAS FULLER, M.D., *Gnomologia* (1732), 4062.

13. We may have uneasy feelings for seeing a creature in distress without pity; for we have not pity unless we wish to relieve them. SAMUEL JOHNSON, quoted in Boswell's *Life of Samuel Johnson*, July 20, 1763.

14. We all have enough strength to bear the misfortunes of others. LA ROCHEFOUCAULD, *Maxims* (1665), tr. Kenneth Pratt.

15. Compassion for the friend should conceal itself under a hard shell. NIETZSCHE, "On the Friend," *Thus Spoke Zarathustra* (1883-92), 1, tr. Walter Kaufmann.

16. Verily, I do not like them, the merciful who feel blessed in their pity: they are lacking too much in shame. If I must pity, at least I do not want it known; and if I do pity, it is preferably from a distance. NIETZSCHE, "On the Pitying," *Thus Spoke Zarathustra* (1883–92), 2, tr. Walter Kaufmann.

17. Who cries for another's / pain hasnt enough of his own. JOEL OPPENHEIMER, "The Couple," quoted in Paris Leary and Robert Kelly's *A Controversy of Poets* (1965).

18. What value has compassion that does not take its object in its arms? SAINT-EXUPÉRY, *The Wisdom of the Sands* (1948), 26, tr. Stuart Gilbert.

19. Piety to mankind must be three-fourths pity. GEORGE SANTAYANA, *The Life of Reason: Reason in Religion* (1905–06), 10.

20. The entire world would perish, if pity were not to limit anger. SENECA THE ELDER, *Controversiae* (1st c. A.D.), 1.

21. Compassion is the property of the privileged classes / When the pitier lowers himself / to give to a beggar / he throbs with contempt. PETER WEISS, *Marat/Sade* (1964), 1.12, tr. Geoffrey Skelton and Adrian Mitchell.

22. Compassionate understanding too often buys a long-range peace with a small-change gesture – like giving a quarter to a beggar. ROSS WETZSTEON, *Village Voice*, Nov. 28, 1968.

23. Worse than idle is compassion / If it end in tears and sighs. WILLIAM WORDSWORTH, "The Armenian Lady's Love" (1830), 4.

## 693. PLACE

See also 985. Travel

1. All places are distant from heaven alike. ROBERT BURTON, *The Anatomy of Melancholy* (1621), 2.2.4.

2. To be happy on earth one must be

born in Soo Chow. CHINESE PROVERB.

3. One always begins to forgive a place as soon as it's left behind. CHARLES DICKENS, *Little Dorrit* (1857–58), 1.2.

4. The difference between landscape and landscape is small, but there is a great difference in the beholders. EMERSON, "Nature," *Essays: Second Series* (1844).

5. The axis of the earth sticks out visibly through the centre of each and every town or city. OLIVER WENDELL HOLMES, SR., *The Autocrat of the Breakfast Table* (1858), 6.

6. A blade of grass is always a blade of grass, whether in one country or another. SAMUEL JOHNSON, quoted in Hester Lynch Piozzi's *Anecdotes of Samuel Johnson* (1786).

7. God gives all men all earth to love, / But, since man's heart is small, / Ordains for each one spot shall prove / Beloved over all. RUDYARD KIPLING, "Sussex" (1902).

8. A place is nothing, not even space, / Unless at its heart a figure stands. AMY LOWELL, "Thorn Piece," *A Shard of Silence* (1957).

9. All places are alike, / And every earth is fit for burial. CHRISTOPHER MARLOWE, *Edward II* (c. 1593), 5.2.

10. One place is everywhere, everywhere is nowhere. PERSIAN PROVERB.

## 694. PLAGIARISM

**See also 449. Imitation**

1. If we steal thoughts from the moderns, it will be cried down as plagiarism; if from the ancients, it will be cried up as erudition. CHARLES CALEB COLTON, *Lacon* (1825), 1.546.

2. Begin with another's to end with your own. BALTASAR GRACIÁN, *The Art of Worldly Wisdom* (1647), 144, tr. Joseph Jacobs.

3. We are all of us richer than we think we are; but we are taught to borrow and to beg, and brought up more to make use of what is another's than of our own. MONTAIGNE, "Of physiognomy," *Essays* (1580–88), tr. Charles Cotton and W. C. Hazlitt.

4. The human plagiarism which is most difficult to avoid, for individuals (and even for nations which persevere in their faults and continue to aggravate them) is the plagiarism of oneself. MARCEL PROUST, *Remembrance of Things Past: The Sweet Cheat Gone* (1913–27), tr. C. K. Scott-Moncrieff.

5. Immature artists imitate. Mature artists steal. LIONEL TRILLING, *Esquire*, September 1962.

## PLAIN DEALING

**See 360. Frankness; 423. Honesty; 894. Sincerity**

## 695. PLAIN LIVING

**See also 183. Contentment; 970. Thrift**

1. Give me neither poverty nor riches; feed me with food convenient for me. *Bible*, Proverbs 30:8.

2. When every blessed thing you hold / Is made of silver, or of gold, / You long for simple pewter. / When you have nothing else to wear / But cloth of gold and satins rare, / For cloth of gold you cease to care — / Up goes the price of shoddy. W. S. GILBERT, *The Gondoliers* (1889), 2.

3. Were a man to order his life by the rules of true reason, a frugal substance joined to a contented mind is for him great riches; for never is there any lack of a little. LUCRETIUS, *On the Nature of Things* (1st c. B.C.), 5, tr. H. A. J. Munro.

4. Plain living is nothing but voluntary poverty. SENECA, *Letters to Lucilius* (1st c.), 17.5, tr. E. Phillips Barker.

5. Four things impair the strength of man: sin, journeying, fasting, and royalty. Haggadah, *Palestinian Talmud* (4th c.).

6. Reduce the complexity of life by eliminating the needless wants of life, and the labors of life reduce themselves. EDWIN WAY TEALE, "February 4," *Circle of the Seasons* (1953).

7. An elegant sufficiency, content, / Retirement, rural quiet, friendship, books. JAMES THOMSON, "Spring," *The Seasons* (1726–30), 1156.

8. Plain living and high thinking are no more: / The homely beauty of the good old cause / Is gone; our peace, our fearful innocence, / And pure religion breathing household laws. WILLIAM WORDSWORTH, "O Friend! I Know Not Which Way I Must Look" (1802).

### 696. PLANS

**See also 579. Method; 654. Order; 932. Strategy**

1. Make no little plans: they have no magic to stir men's blood. DANIEL H. BURNHAM, motto of city planners, quoted in Charles Moore's *Daniel H. Burnham* (1921), 2.25.

2. The best-laid schemes o' mice an' men / Gang aft agley, / An' lea'e us nought but grief an' pain, / For promis'd joy! ROBERT BURNS, "To a Mouse" (1785), 7.

3. The more human beings proceed by plan the more effectively they may be hit by accident. FRIEDRICH DÜRRENMATT, "21 Points," *The Physicists* (1962), tr. James Kirkup.

4. Do not plan for ventures before finishing what's at hand. EURIPIDES, *Rhesus* (c. 455–441 B.C.), tr. Richmond Lattimore.

5. Amid a multitude of projects, no plan is devised. PUBLILIUS SYRUS, *Moral Sayings* (1st c. B.C.), 319, tr. Darius Lyman.

6. It is a bad plan that admits of no modification. PUBLILIUS SYRUS, *Moral Sayings* (1st c. B.C.), 469, tr. Darius Lyman.

7. Plans get you into things but you got to work your way out. WILL ROGERS, *The Autobiography of Will Rogers* (1949), 16.

8. Nobody ever drew up his plans for life so well but what the facts, and the years, and experience always introduce some modification. TERENCE, *The Brothers* (160 B.C.), tr. William A. Oldfather.

### PLANTS

**See 334. Farms and Farming; 349. Flowers; 369. Gardening; 616. Nature; 988. Trees**

### 697. PLAY

**See also 530. Leisure; 922. Sports**

1. Play so that you may be serious. ANACHARSIS (c. 600 B.C.), quoted in Aristotle's *Nicomachean Ethics* (4th c. B.C.), 10.6, tr. J. A. K. Thomson.

2. Play is the exultation of the possible. MARTIN BUBER, "Brother Body," *Pointing the Way* (1957).

3. The true object of all human life is play. Earth is a task garden; heaven is a playground. G. K. CHESTERTON, "Oxford from Without," *All Things Considered* (1908).

4. Game, noun: any unserious occupation designed for the relaxation of busy people and the distraction of idle ones; it's used to take people to whom we have nothing to say off our hands, and sometimes even ourselves. ETIENNE BONNOT, ABBÉ DE CONDILLAC, *Dictionnaire des synonymes*, *Oeuvres Philosophique* (1947–51), v. 3.

5. It is a happy talent to know how to play. EMERSON, *Journals*, 1834.

6. There are toys for all ages. ENGLISH PROVERB.

7. Our minds need relaxation, and give way / Unless we mix with work a little play. MOLIÈRE, *The School for Husbands* (1661), 1.3, tr. Donald M. Frame.

8. In our play we reveal what kind of people we are. OVID, *The Art of Love* (c. A.D. 8), 3, tr. Rolfe Humphries.

9. To condemn spontaneous and delightful occupations because they are useless for self-preservation shows an uncritical prizing of life irrespective of its content. GEORGE SANTAYANA, *The Sense of Beauty* (1896), 4.

10. To the art of working well a civilized race would add the art of playing well. GEORGE SANTAYANA, *Little Essays* (1920), 61, ed. Logan Pearsall Smith.

### PLAYS

**See 965. Theater**

### 698. PLEASURE

**See also 407. Happiness; 511. Joie de vivre; 699. Pleasure and Pain; 700. Pleasure-seeking; 733. Profligacy**

1. It is not abstinence from pleasures that is best, but mastery over them without being worsted. ARISTIPPUS (5th–4th c. B.C.), quoted in Diogenes Laertius' *Lives and Opinions of Eminent Philosophers* (3rd c. A.D.), tr. R. D. Hicks.

2. When Pleasure is at the bar the jury is not impartial. ARISTOTLE, *Nicomachean Ethics* (4th c. B.C.), 2.9, tr. J. A. K. Thomson.

3. One half of the world cannot understand the pleasures of the other. JANE AUSTEN, *Emma* (1816), 9.

4. People seem to enjoy things more when they know a lot of other people have been left out on the pleasure. RUSSELL

BAKER, "Observer," *The New York Times*, Nov. 2, 1967.

5. 'Twere too absurd to slight / For the hereafter the today's delight! ROBERT BROWNING, *Sordello* (1840), 6.

6. Pleasures are like poppies spread: You seize the flow'r, its bloom is shed. ROBERT BURNS, "Tam O' Shanter" (1793).

7. Though sages may pour out their wisdom's treasure, / There is no sterner moralist than Pleasure. BYRON, *Don Juan* (1819–24), 3.65.

8. Enjoying things which are pleasant; that is not the evil: it is the reducing of our moral self to slavery by them that is. THOMAS CARLYLE, *On Heroes, Hero-Worship and the Heroic in History* (1841), 2.

9. Enjoy pleasures, but let them be your own, and then you will taste them. LORD CHESTERFIELD, *Letters to His Son*, May 8, 1750.

10. It is often a mistake to combine two pleasures, because pleasures, like pains, can act as counter-irritants to each other. G. K. CHESTERTON, "On Misunderstanding," *Generally Speaking* (1928).

11. We may lay in a stock of pleasures, as we would lay in a stock of wine; but if we defer tasting them too long, we shall find that both are soured by age. CHARLES CALEB COLTON, *Lacon* (1825), 1.81.

12. After pleasant scratching comes unpleasant smarting. DANISH PROVERB.

13. Pleasure is none, if not diversified. JOHN DONNE, Elegy 19, "Variety" (1635).

14. The pleasure of life is according to the man who lives it, and not according to the work or the place. EMERSON, "Fate," *The Conduct of Life* (1860).

15. Enjoyment is *not* a goal, it is a feeling that accompanies important ongoing activity. PAUL GOODMAN, *Growing Up Absurd* (1960), 11.12.

16. Mankind is safer when men seek pleasure than when they seek the power and the glory. GEOFFREY GORER, *The New York Times Magazine*, Nov. 27, 1966.

17. We have more days to live through than pleasures. Be slow in enjoyment, quick at work, for men see work ended with pleasure, pleasure ended with regret. BALTASAR GRACIÁN, *The Art of Worldly Wisdom* (1647), 174, tr. Joseph Jacobs.

18. In all pleasure hope is a considerable part. SAMUEL JOHNSON, quoted in Boswell's *Life of Samuel Johnson*, April 7, 1779.

19. No man is a hypocrite in his pleasures. SAMUEL JOHNSON, quoted in Boswell's *Life of Samuel Johnson*, June 1784.

20. A bookworm in bed with a new novel and a good reading lamp is as much prepared for pleasure as a pretty girl at a college dance. PHYLLIS MC GINLEY, "You Take the High Road," *The Province of the Heart* (1959).

21. The spirit is often most free when the body is satiated with pleasure; indeed, sometimes the stars shine more brightly seen from the gutter than from the hilltop. W. SOMERSET MAUGHAM, *The Summing Up* (1938), 15.

22. Even pleasure and good fortune are not relished without vigor and understanding. MONTAIGNE, "Of the inequality among us," *Essays* (1580–88), tr. Charles Cotton and W. C. Hazlitt.

23. Enjoyment and innocence are the most bashful things: both do not want to be sought. NIETZSCHE, "On Old and New Tablets," *Thus Spoke Zarathustra* (1883–92), 3, tr. Walter Kaufmann.

24. Better be jocund with the fruitful Grape / Than sadden after none, or bitter, Fruit. OMAR KHAYYÁM, *Rubáiyát* (11th–12th c.), tr. Edward FitzGerald, 4th ed., 54.

25. The pleasure that is granted to me from a sense of duty ceases to be a pleasure at all. OVID, *The Art of Love* (c. A.D. 8 ), 2, tr. J. Lewis May.

26. A safe pleasure is a tame pleasure. OVID, *The Art of Love* (c. A.D. 8), 3, tr. J. Lewis May.

27. Too much pleasure disagrees with us. Too many concords are annoying in music; too many benefits irritate us; we wish to have the wherewithal to over-pay our debts. PASCAL, *Pensées* (1670), 72, tr. W. F. Trotter.

28. Music and women I cannot but give way to, whatever my business is. SAMUEL PEPYS, *Diary*, March 9, 1666.

29. Man's pleasure is a short time growing / And it falls to the ground / As quickly. PINDAR, *Odes* (5th c. B.C.), Pythia 8.88.

30. A child shows his toy; a man hides his. ANTONIO PORCHIA, *Voces* (1968), tr. W. S. Merwin.

31. No pleasure endures unseasoned by variety. PUBLILIUS SYRUS, *Moral Sayings*

(1st c. B.C.), 406, tr. Darius Lyman.

32. There is more of fear than delight in a secret pleasure. PUBLILIUS SYRUS, *Moral Sayings* (1st c. B.C.), 990, tr. Darius Lyman.

33. Pleasure once tasted satisfies less than the desire experienced for its torments. JOSEPH ROUX, *Meditations of a Parish Priest* (1886), 5.21, tr. Isabel F. Hapgood.

34. Vain is the hope of finding pleasure in that which one has hitherto disdained; as when the warrior hopes to find pleasure in the joys of the sedentaries. SAINT-EXUPÉRY, *The Wisdom of the Sands* (1948), 29, tr. Stuart Gilbert.

35. Pleasure dies at the very moment when it charms us most. SENECA, "On a Happy Life," *Moral Essays* (1st c.), tr. Aubrey Stewart.

36. No profit grows where is no pleasure ta'en. SHAKESPEARE, *The Taming of the Shrew* (1593–94), 1.1.39.

37. The daintiest last, to make the end most sweet. SHAKESPEARE, *Richard II* (1595–96), 1.3.68.

38. There are two things to aim at in life: first, to get what you want; and, after that, to enjoy it. Only the wisest of mankind achieve the second. LOGAN PEARSALL SMITH, *Afterthoughts* (1931), 1.

39. A man advanced in years that thinks fit to look back upon his former life, and calls that only life which was passed with satisfaction and enjoyment, excluding all parts which were not pleasant to him, will find himself very young, if not in infancy. RICHARD STEELE, *The Spectator* (1711–12), 100.

40. Pleasure is the object, the duty, and the goal of all rational creatures. VOLTAIRE, *Épître à Madame de G.* (1716).

41. I take it as a prime cause of the present confusion of society that it is too sickly and too doubtful frankly to use pleasure as a test of value. REBECCA WEST, in *I Believe* (1939), ed. Clifton Fadiman.

## 699. PLEASURE AND PAIN

**See also 698. Pleasure; 939. Suffering**

1. There is no gathering the rose without being pricked by the thorns. "The Two Travellers," *Fables of Bidpai* (c. 750).

2. Sweet is pleasure after pain. JOHN DRYDEN, "Alexander's Feast" (1687), 58.

3. No pleasure is evil in itself; but the means by which certain pleasures are gained bring pains many times greater than the pleasures. EPICURUS, "Principal Doctrines (3rd c. B.C.), 8, in *Letters, Principal Doctrines, and Vatican Sayings*, tr. Russel M. Geer.

4. Ay, in the very temple of Delight / Veiled Melancholy has her sovran shrine. JOHN KEATS, "Ode on Melancholy" (1819).

5. Few pleasures there are indeed without an aftertouch of pain, but that is the preservation which keeps them sweet. HELEN KELLER, *Helen Keller's Journal* (1938).

6. The heart can ne'er a transport know / That never feels a pain. GEORGE LYTTLETON, "Song."

7. I conceive that pleasures are to be avoided if greater pains be the consequence, and pains to be coveted that will terminate in greater pleasures. MONTAIGNE, "The story of Spurina," *Essays* (1580–88), tr. Charles Cotton and W. C. Hazlitt.

8. Where, pray, can be found happiness in enjoyments without something to spoil it? *Panchatantra* (c. 5th c.), 1, tr. Franklin Edgerton.

9. The most intolerable pain is produced by prolonging the keenest pleasure. GEORGE BERNARD SHAW, "Maxims for Revolutionists," *Man and Superman* (1903).

10. Marred pleasure's best, shadow makes the sun strong. STEVIE SMITH, "The Queen and the Young Princess," *Selected Poems* (1964).

11. All fits of pleasure are balanced by an equal degree of pain or langour; 'tis like spending this year part of the next year's revenue. JONATHAN SWIFT, *Thoughts on Various Subjects* (1711).

12. There is a pleasure in not being pleased. VOLTAIRE, *Candide* (1759), 25.

## 700. PLEASURE-SEEKING

**See also 698. Pleasure; 733. Profligacy**

1. Day after day, night after night, / My life at home is far from bright, / But even home has more variety / Than I find in cafe society. FRANKLIN P. ADAMS, *Nods and Becks* (1944).

2. One cannot both feast and become rich. ASHANTI PROVERB.

3. All pleasures have this way: those who enjoy them they drive on with stings. BOETHIUS, *The Consolation of Philosophy* (A.D. 524), 3, tr. W. V. Cooper.

4. Let us have Wine and Woman, Mirth and Laughter, / Sermons and soda-water the day after. BYRON, *Don Juan* (1819–24), 2.178.

5. The man of pleasure, by a vain attempt to be more happy than any man can be, is often more miserable than most men are. CHARLES CALEB COLTON, *Lacon* (1825), 1.177.

6. Many seek good nights and lose good days. DUTCH PROVERB.

7. Gather ye rosebuds while ye may, / Old Time is still a-flying, / And this same flower that smiles to-day / To-morrow will be dying. ROBERT HERRICK, "To the Virgins to make much of Time," *Hesperides* (1648).

8. By comparison with a night-club, churches are positively gay. ALDOUS HUXLEY, *Do What You Will* (1929).

9. Actual happiness always looks pretty squalid in comparison with the over-compensations for misery. ALDOUS HUXLEY, *Brave New World* (1932).

10. We torment ourselves rather to make it appear that we are happy than to become so. LA ROCHEFOUCAULD, *Maxims* (1665), tr. Kenneth Pratt.

11. The fly that prefers sweetness to a long life may drown in honey. GEORGE SANTAYANA, *Dialogues in Limbo* (1925), 3.

12. Pleasure seizes the whole man who addicts himself to it, and will not give him leisure for any good office in life which contradicts the gayety of the present hour. RICHARD STEELE, *The Spectator* (1711–12), 151.

13. Life would be very pleasant if it were not for its enjoyments. ROBERT SMITH SURTEES, *Mr. Facey Romford's Hounds* (1865), 32.

## 701. PLUMBERS

**See also 884. Sewers**

1. Anybody who has any doubt about the ingenuity or the resourcefulness of a plumber never got a bill from one. GEORGE MEANY, CBS-TV, Jan. 8, 1954.

## 702. POETRY AND POETS

**See also 198. Creation and Creativity; 521. Language; 1062. Writing and Writers**

1. Poetry is a whim of Nature in her lighter moods; it requires nothing but its own madness and, lacking that, it becomes a soundless cymbal, a belfry without a bell. PIETRO ARETINO, letter to Nicolò Franco, June 25, 1537, tr. Samuel Putnam.

2. Poetry makes nothing happen: it survives / In the valley of its saying. W. H. AUDEN, "In Memory of W. B. Yeats," *Another Time* (1940).

3. A poet is, before anything else, a person who is passionately in love with language. W. H. AUDEN, *The New York Times*, Oct. 9, 1960.

4. Not philosophy, after all, not humanity, just sheer joyous power of song, is the primal thing in poetry. MAX BEERBOHM, "No. 2, The Pines," *And Even Now* (1920).

5. Poetry is the impish attempt to paint the color of the wind. MAXWELL BODENHEIM, quoted in Ben Hecht's play *Winkelberg* (1958).

6. All poetry is difficult to read, / —The sense of it is, anyhow. ROBERT BROWNING, *The Ring and the Book* (1868–69), 7.

7. The verse will halt if the tongue's too true. *Burmese Proverbs* (1962), 419, ed. Hla Pe.

8. Who forgives the Senior's ceaseless verse, / Whose hairs grow hoary as his rhymes grow worse? BYRON, *English Bards and Scotch Reviewers* (1809).

9. Nothing so difficult as a beginning / In poesy, unless perhaps the end. BYRON, *Don Juan* (1819–24), 4.1.

10. I have nothing to say and I am saying it and that is poetry. JOHN CAGE, "45′ for a Speaker," *Silence* (1961).

11. Wise poets that wrapt Truth in tales, / Knew her themselves through all her veils. THOMAS CAREW, "Ingrateful Beauty Threatened," *Poems* (1640).

12. How does the poet speak to men with power, but by being still more a man than they? THOMAS CARLYLE, "Burns," *Edinburgh Review*, 1828.

13. Would you be a poet / Before you've been to school? / Ah, well! I hardly thought

you / So absolute a fool. LEWIS CARROLL, "Poeta Fit, Non Nascitur" (1869).

14. When you are describing / A shape, or sound, or tint; / Don't state the matter plainly, / But put it in a hint; / And learn to look at all things / With a sort of mental squint. LEWIS CARROLL, "Poeta Fit, Non Nascitur" (1869).

15. To be a poet is to have an appetite for a certain anxiety which, when tasted among the swirling sum of things existent or forefelt, causes, as the taste dies, joy. RENÉ CHAR, *The Formal Share*, 42, in *Hypnos Waking* (1956), tr. Jackson Mathews and others.

16. Lyricism cannot exist without rules, and it is essential that they should be strict. Otherwise there is only a faculty for lyricism, and that exists everywhere. CHARLES ALBERT CINGRIA, quoted in Igor Stravinsky's *An Autobiography* (1936).

17. Prose,—words in their best order; poetry,—the best words in their best order. SAMUEL TAYLOR COLERIDGE, *Table Talk* (1835).

18. To a poet, silence is an acceptable response, even a flattering one. COLETTE, "The Occupation," *Earthly Paradise* (1966), 6, ed. Robert Phelps.

19. Poetry does not necessarily have to be beautiful to stick in the depths of our memory, there to occupy most mischievously the place doomed to invasion by certain melodies which, however blameworthy, can never be expunged. COLETTE, "Under the Blue Lantern," *Earthly Paradise* (1966), 6, ed. Robert Phelps.

20. All poets pretend to write for immortality, but the whole tribe have no objection to present pay and present praise. CHARLES CALEB COLTON, *Lacon* (1825), 1.23.

21. Poets arguing about modern poetry: jackals snarling over a dried-up well. CYRIL CONNOLLY, *The Unquiet Grave* (1945), 1.

22. There is a pleasure in poetic pains / Which only poets know. WILLIAM COWPER, "The Timepiece," *The Task* (1785), 285.

23. The poets of each generation seldom sing a new song. They turn to themes men always have loved, and sing them in the mode of their times. CLARENCE DAY, "Humpty-Dumpty and Adam," *The Crow's Nest* (1921).

24. Poetry's unnat'ral; no man ever talked poetry 'cept a beadle on boxin' day. CHARLES DICKENS, *Pickwick Papers* (1836–37), 33.

25. Poetry is a counterfeit creation, and makes things that are not, as though they were. JOHN DONNE, *Sermons*, No. 13, 1622.

26. All good poetry is forged slowly and patiently, link by link, with sweat and blood and tears. LORD ALFRED DOUGLAS, introduction to *Collected Poems* (1919).

27. The poet's mind is in fact a receptacle for seizing and storing up numberless feelings, phrases, images, which remain there until all the particles which can unite to form a new compound are present together. T. S. ELIOT, "Tradition and the Individual Talent" (1919).

28. The business of the poet is not to find new emotions, but to use the ordinary ones and, in working them up into poetry, to express feelings which are not in actual emotions at all. T. S. ELIOT, "Tradition and the Individual Talent" (1919).

29. All great poetry gives the illusion of a view of life. T. S. ELIOT, "Shakespeare and the Stoicism of Seneca" (1927).

30. The majority of poems one outgrows and outlives, as one outgrows and outlives the majority of human passions. T. S. ELIOT, "Dante" (1929).

31. Maturing as a poet means maturing as the whole man, experiencing new emotions appropriate to one's age, and with the same intensity as the emotions of youth. T. S. ELIOT, "Yeats" (1940).

32. A poem is made up of thoughts, each of which filled the whole sky of the poet in its turn. EMERSON, *Journals*, 1834.

33. Poetry makes its own pertinence, and a single stanza outweighs a book of prose. EMERSON, *Journals*, 1839.

34. The people fancy they hate poetry, and they are all poets and mystics. EMERSON, "The Poet," *Essays: Second Series* (1844).

35. When a man does not write his poetry, it escapes by other vents through him. EMERSON, "Behavior," *The Conduct of Life* (1860).

36. A poem is true if it hangs together. Information points to something else. A poem points to nothing but itself. E. M.

FORSTER, "Anonymity: An Enquiry," *Two Cheers for Democracy* (1951).

37. A true sonnet goes eight lines and then takes a turn for better or worse and goes six or eight lines more. ROBERT FROST, news summaries, March 29, 1954.

38. I have never started a poem yet whose end I knew. Writing a poem is discovering. ROBERT FROST, *The New York Times*, Nov. 7, 1955.

39. Poetry is the language in which man explores his own amazement. CHRISTOPHER FRY, *Time*, April 3, 1950.

40. A very good or very bad poet is remarkable; but a middling one who can bear? THOMAS FULLER, M.D., *Gnomologia* (1732), 448.

41. The poet is a bird of strange moods. He descends from his lofty domain to tarry among us, singing; if we do not honor him he will unfold his wings and fly back to his dwelling place. KAHLIL GIBRAN, "The Poet from Baalbek," *Thoughts and Meditations* (1960), tr. Anthony R. Ferris.

42. The world is so great and rich, and life so full of variety, that you can never lack occasions for poems. GOETHE, quoted in Johann Peter Eckermann's *Conversations with Goethe*, Sept. 18, 1823.

43. The poet should seize the Particular, and he should, if there be anything sound in it, thus represent the Universal. GOETHE, quoted in Johann Peter Eckermann's *Conversations with Goethe*, June 11, 1825.

44. Poetry is the universal possession of mankind, revealing itself everywhere, and at all times, in hundreds and hundreds of men. GOETHE, quoted in Johann Peter Eckermann's *Conversations with Goethe*, Jan. 31, 1827.

45. At bottom, no real object is unpoetical, if the poet knows how to use it properly. GOETHE, quoted in Johann Peter Eckermann's *Conversations with Goethe*, July 5, 1827.

46. If a poet would work politically, he must give himself up to a party; and so soon as he does that, he is lost as a poet. GOETHE, quoted in Johann Peter Eckermann's *Conversations with Goethe*, March 1832.

47. A fine thought, to become poetry, must be seasoned in the upper warm garrets of the mind for long and long, then it must be brought down and slowly carved into words, shaped with emotion, polished with love. DAVID GRAYSON, *Adventures in Contentment* (1907), 5.

48. A verse may find him who a sermon flies, / And turn delight into sacrifice. GEORGE HERBERT, "The Church Porch," 1, *The Temple* (1633).

49. An artist who works in marble or colors has them all to himself and his tribe, but the man who moulds his thought in verse has to employ the materials vulgarized by everybody's use, and glorify them by his handling. OLIVER WENDELL HOLMES, SR., *The Poet at the Breakfast Table* (1872), 4.

50. When you write in prose you say what you mean. When you write in rhyme you say what you must. OLIVER WENDELL HOLMES, SR., *Over the Teacups* (1891), 2.

51. True poetry, the best of it, is but the ashes of a burnt-out passion. OLIVER WENDELL HOLMES, SR., *Over the Teacups* (1891), 4.

52. It is not enough for poems to be fine; they must charm, and draw the mind of the listener at will. HORACE, *Ars Poetica* (13–8 B.C.).

53. Poetry is like painting: one piece takes your fancy if you stand close to it, another if you keep at some distance. HORACE, *Ars Poetica* (13–8 B.C.).

54. The poet camouflages, in the expression of joy, his despair at not having found its reality. MAX JACOB, *La Défense de Tartuffe* (1919).

55. Literature is a state of culture, poetry a state of grace, before and after culture. JUAN RAMÓN JIMÉNEZ, "Poetry and Literature," *Selected Writings* (1957), tr. H. R. Hays.

56. A good poet's made as well as born. BEN JONSON, "To the Memory of Shakespeare" (1616).

57. All good verses are like impromptus made at leisure. JOSEPH JOUBERT, *Pensées* (1842).

58. A drainless shower / Of light is poesy; 'tis the supreme of power; / 'Tis might half slumb'ring on its own right arm. JOHN KEATS, "Sleep and Poetry" (1816).

59. Poetry should be great and unobtrusive, a thing which enters into one's soul, and does not startle it or amaze it with itself but with its subject. JOHN KEATS, letter to John Hamilton Reynolds, Feb. 3, 1818.

60. If Poetry comes not as naturally as the leaves to a tree it had better not come at all.

JOHN KEATS, letter to John Taylor, Feb. 27, 1818.

61. When power leads man toward arrogance, poetry reminds him of his limitations. When power narrows the areas of man's concern, poetry reminds him of the richness and diversity of his existence. When power corrupts, poetry cleanses. JOHN F. KENNEDY, address, Amherst College, Mass., Oct. 26, 1963.

62. The vain poet is of the opinion that nothing of his can be too much: he sends to you basketful after basketful of juiceless fruit, covered with scentless flowers. WALTER SAVAGE LANDOR, "Archdeacon Hare and Walter Landor," *Imaginary Conversations* (1824–53).

63. Prose on certain occasions can bear a great deal of poetry; on the other hand, poetry sinks and swoons under a moderate weight of prose. WALTER SAVAGE LANDOR, "Archdeacon Hare and Walter Landor," *Imaginary Conversations* (1824–53).

64. As to the pure mind all things are pure, so to the poetic mind all things are poetical. LONGFELLOW, "Twice-Told Tales," *Driftwood* (1857).

65. The true poet is a friendly man. He takes to his arms even cold and inanimate things, and rejoices in his heart. LONGFELLOW, "Twice-Told Tales," *Driftwood* (1857).

66. He who would be the tongue of this wide land / Must string his harp with chords of sturdy iron / And strike it with a toil-imbrowned hand. JAMES RUSSELL LOWELL, "Ode" (1841), 3.

67. A poem should not mean / But be. ARCHIBALD MAC LEISH, "Ars Poetica," *Streets in the Moon* (1926).

68. The crown of literature is poetry. It is its end and aim. It is the sublimest activity of the human mind. It is the achievement of beauty and delicacy. The writer of prose can only step aside when the poet passes. W. SOMERSET MAUGHAM, *Saturday Review*, July 20, 1957.

69. The arrogance of poets is only a defense; doubt gnaws the greatest among them; they need our testimony to escape despair. FRANÇOIS MAURIAC, "L'Orgueil des poètes," *Journal* (1936–53), v. 2.

70. The poem is the dream made flesh, in a two-fold sense: as work of art, and as life, which is a work of art. HENRY MILLER, "Creative Death," *The Wisdom of the Heart* (1941).

71. The courage of the poet is to keep ajar the door that leads into madness. CHRISTOPHER MORLEY, *Inward Ho!* (1923), 2.

72. The world, in its sheer exuberance of kindness, will try to bury the poet with warm and lovely human trivialities. It will even ask him to autograph books. CHRISTOPHER MORLEY, *Inward Ho!* (1923), 8.

73. A poet, any real poet, is simply an alchemist who transmutes his cynicism regarding human beings into an optimism regarding the moon, the stars, the heavens, and the flowers, to say nothing of Spring, love, and dogs. GEORGE JEAN NATHAN, "Poet," *Monks Are Monks* (1929).

74. The poet presents his thoughts festively, on the carriage of rhythm: usually because they could not walk. NIETZSCHE, *Human, All Too Human* (1878), 189, in *The Portable Nietzsche*, tr. Walter Kaufmann.

75. The spirit of the poet craves spectators—even if only buffaloes. NIETZSCHE, "On Poets," *Thus Spoke Zarathustra* (1883–92), 2, tr. Walter Kaufmann.

76. The great poet draws his creations only from out of his own reality. NIETZSCHE, *Ecce Homo* (1888), tr. Anthony M. Ludovici.

77. The poet begins where the man ends. The man's lot is to live his human life, the poet's to invent what is nonexistent. JOSÉ ORTEGA Y GASSET, *The Dehumanization of Art* (1925).

78. Poetry is adolescence fermented and thus preserved. JOSÉ ORTEGA Y GASSET, "In Search of Goethe from Within, Letter to a German," *Partisan Review*, December 1949, tr. Willard R. Trask.

79. A poet is not an author, but—the subject of a lyric, facing the world in the first person. BORIS PASTERNAK, *Safe Conduct* (1931), 3.4, tr. Beatrice Scott.

80. Poetry is the revelation of a feeling that the poet believes to be interior and personal [but] which the reader recognizes as his own. SALVATORE QUASIMODO, *The New York Times*, May 14, 1960.

81. The void yields up nothing. You have to be a great poet to make it ring. JULES RENARD, *Journal*, December 1906, ed. and tr. Louise Bogan and Elizabeth Roget.

82. Science is for those who learn; poetry, for those who know. JOSEPH ROUX, *Medita-*

tions of a Parish Priest (1886), 1.71, tr. Isabel F. Hapgood.

83. Poetry is the opening and closing of a door, leaving those who look through to guess about what is seen during a moment. CARL SANDBURG, "Tentative (First Model) Definitions of Poetry," *Complete Poems* (1950).

84. If artists and poets are unhappy, it is after all because happiness does not interest them. GEORGE SANTAYANA, *The Sense of Beauty* (1896).

85. Popular poets are the parish priests of the Muse, retailing her ancient divinations to a long since converted public. GEORGE SANTAYANA, *The Life of Reason: Reason in Art* (1905–06), 6.

86. Ne'er / Was flattery lost on poet's ear; / A simple race! they waste their toil / For the vain tribute of a smile. SIR WALTER SCOTT, *The Lay of the Last Minstrel* (1805), 4, conclusion.

87. The forms of things unknown, the poet's pen / Turns them to shapes, and gives to airy nothing / A local habitation and a name. SHAKESPEARE, *A Midsummer Night's Dream* (1595–96), 5.1.15.

88. Most wretched men / Are cradled into poetry by wrong. / They learn in suffering what they teach in song. SHELLEY, "Julian and Maddalo" (1818–19).

89. A poet is a nightingale, who sits in darkness and sings to cheer its own solitude with sweet sounds. SHELLEY, *A Defence of Poetry* (1821).

90. Poetry lifts the veil from the hidden beauty of the world, and makes familiar objects be as if they were not familiar. SHELLEY, *A Defence of Poetry* (1821).

91. Poets are the hierophants of an unapprehended inspiration; the mirrors of the gigantic shadows which futurity casts upon the present. SHELLEY, *A Defence of Poetry* (1821).

92. Poets are the unacknowledged legislators of the world. SHELLEY, *A Defence of Poetry* (1821).

93. Not by wisdom do they [poets] make what they compose, but by a gift of nature and an inspiration similar to that of the diviners and the oracles. SOCRATES, in Plato's *Apology* (4th c. B.C.), tr. Lane Cooper.

94. The poet is the priest of the invisible. WALLACE STEVENS, "Adagia," *Opus Posthumous* (1957).

95. In poetry, you must love the words, the ideas and the images and rhythms with all your capacity to love anything at all. WALLACE STEVENS, "Adagia," *Opus Posthumous* (1957).

96. With my singing I can make / A refuge for my spirit's sake, / A house of shining words, to be / My fragile immortality. SARA TEASDALE, "Interlude," 7, *Love Songs* (1917).

97. It is my heart that makes my songs, not I. SARA TEASDALE, "What Do I Care?" *Flame and Shadow* (1920).

98. Ah God! the petty fools of rhyme / That shriek and sweat in pigmy wars. ALFRED, LORD TENNYSON, "Literary Squabbles" (1846).

99. I do but sing because I must, / And pipe but as the linnets sing. ALFRED, LORD TENNYSON, "In Memoriam A. H. H." (1850), 21.

100. Poetry is what in a poem makes you laugh, cry, prickle, be silent, makes your toenails twinkle, makes you want to do this or that or nothing, makes you know that you are alone in the unknown world, that your bliss and suffering is forever shared and forever all your own. DYLAN THOMAS, introductory remarks to a reading given at Massachusetts Institute of Technology, July 3, 1952.

101. A good poem is a contribution to reality. The world is never the same once a good poem has been added to it. A good poem helps to change the shape and significance of the universe, helps to extend everyone's knowledge of himself and the world around him. DYLAN THOMAS, "On Poetry," *Quite Early One Morning* (1960).

102. The best poem is that whose worked-upon unmagical passages come closest, in texture and intensity, to those moments of magical accident. DYLAN THOMAS, "On Poetry," *Quite Early One Morning* (1960).

103. The best poets, after all, exhibit only a tame and civil side of nature. They have not seen the west side of any mountain. THOREAU, *Journal*, Aug. 18, 1841.

104. The poet is he that hath fat enough, like bears and marmots, to suck his claws all winter. THOREAU, "Sunday," *A Week on the Concord and Merrimack Rivers* (1849).

105. Color, which is the poet's wealth, is so expensive that most take to mere outline

sketches and become men of science. THOREAU, *Journal*, Feb. 13, 1851.

106. The poem—that prolonged hesitation between sound and sense. PAUL VALÉRY, *Tel quel* (1943).

107. Feeble verses are those which sin not against rules, but against genius. VOLTAIRE, "Style," *Philosophical Dictionary* (1764).

108. The world is full of poetry as the earth is of pay-dirt; one only needs to know how to strike it. CHARLES DUDLEY WARNER, "Third Study," *Backlog Studies* (1873).

109. Song is not Truth, not Wisdom, but the rose / Upon Truth's lips, the light in Wisdom's eyes. SIR WILLIAM WATSON, "Ode to J. C. Collins," *Collected Poems* (1905).

110. A poem gives the world back to the maker of the poem, in all its original strangeness, the shock of its first surprise. JOHN HALL WHEELOCK, "A True Poem Is a Way of Knowing," *What Is Poetry?* (1963).

111. All poets who, when reading from their own works, experience a choked feeling, are major. E. B. WHITE, "How to Tell a Major Poet," *Quo Vadimus?* (1939).

112. A poet's pleasure is to withhold a little of his meaning, to intensify by mystification. He unzips the veil from beauty, but does not remove it. E. B. WHITE, "Poetry," *One Man's Meat* (1944).

113. Of all mankind the great poet is the equable man. Not in him but off from him things are grotesque or eccentric or fail of their sanity. WALT WHITMAN, preface to *Leaves of Grass* (1855).

114. A great poet, a really great poet, is the most unpoetical of all creatures. But inferior poets are absolutely fascinating. OSCAR WILDE. *The Picture of Dorian Gray* (1891), 4.

115. It is difficult / to get the news from poems / yet men die miserably every day / for lack / of what is found there. WILLIAM CARLOS WILLIAMS, "Asphodel, That Greeny Flower," *Pictures from Brueghel* (1962), 1.

116. The Poet, gentle creature as he is, / Hath, like the Lover, his unruly times; / His fits when he is neither sick nor well, / Though no distress be near him but his own / Unmanageable thoughts. WILLIAM WORDSWORTH, *The Prelude* (1799–1805), 1.

117. Poetry is the spontaneous overflow of powerful feelings: it takes its origin from emotion recollected in tranquillity. WILLIAM WORDSWORTH, preface to 2nd edition of *Lyrical Ballads* (1800).

118. We Poets in our youth begin in gladness; / But thereof come in the end despondency and madness. WILLIAM WORDSWORTH, "Resolution and Independence" (1802), 7.

## 703. POLICE

**See also 526. Law and Order**

1. A vague uneasiness: the police. It's like when you suddenly understand you have to undress in front of the doctor. UGO BETTI, *The Inquiry* (1944–45), 1.10, ed. Gino Rizzo.

2. Detection is, or ought to be, an exact science, and should be treated in the same cold and unemotional manner. SIR ARTHUR CONAN DOYLE, *The Sign of Four* (1889).

3. A polisman goes afther vice as an officer iv th' law an' comes away as a philosopher. FINLEY PETER DUNNE, "The Crusade Against Vice," *Mr. Dooley's Opinions* (1901).

4. There's more joy over wan sinner rayturned to th' station thin f'r ninety an' nine that've rayformed. FINLEY PETER DUNNE, "The Crusade Against Vice," *Mr. Dooley's Opinions* (1901).

5. When constabulary duty's to be done, / The policeman's lot is not a happy one! W. S. GILBERT, *The Pirates of Penzance* (1879), 2.

6. There is a sleeping cop in all of us. He must be killed. Graffito written during French student revolt, May 1968.

7. For the middle class, the police protect property, give directions, and help old ladies. For the urban poor, the police are those who arrest you. MICHAEL HARRINGTON, *The Other America* (1962), 1.2.

8. Every society gets the kind of criminal it deserves. What is equally true is that every community gets the kind of law enforcement it insists on. ROBERT F. KENNEDY, "Free Enterprise in Organized Crime," *The Pursuit of Justice* (1964).

9. Policemen are soldiers who act alone; soldiers are policemen who act in unison. HERBERT SPENCER, *Social Statics* (1851), 3.21.8.

### POLITENESS

See 194. Courtesy; 559. Manners

### 704. POLITICAL PARTIES

See also 175. Conservatism; 533. Liberalism; 667. Partisanship; 705. Politics and Politicians; 770. Radicalism

1. All political parties die at last of swallowing their own lies. JOHN ARBUTHNOT, quoted in Richard Garnett's *Life of Emerson* (1887).

2. Those who think that all virtue is to be found in their own party principles push matters to extremes; they do not consider that disproportion destroys a state. ARISTOTLE, *Politics* (4th c. B.C.), 5.9, tr. Benjamin Jowett.

3. Whin a man gets to be my age, he ducks pol-itical meetin's, an' r-reads th' papers an' weighs th' ividence an' th' argymints,—pro-argymints an' con-argymints, —an' makes up his mind ca'mly, an' votes th' Dimmycratic ticket. FINLEY PETER DUNNE, "On the Hero in Politics," *Mr. Dooley in Peace and in War* (1898).

4. I often think it's comical / How Nature always does contrive / That every boy and every gal, / That's born into the world alive, / Is either a little Liberal, / Or else a little Conservative! W. S. GILBERT, *Iolanthe* (1882), 2.

5. If your heart is on the left, don't carry your portfolio on the right. Graffito written during French student revolt, May 1968.

6. He serves his party best who serves the country best. RUTHERFORD B. HAYES, Inaugural Address, March 5, 1877.

7. Let us not seek the Republican answer or the Democratic answer, but the right answer. Let us not seek to fix the blame for the past. Let us accept our own responsibility for the future. JOHN F. KENNEDY, address, Loyola College Alumni Banquet, Baltimore, Md., Feb. 18, 1958.

8. Under democracy one party always devotes its chief energies to trying to prove that the other party is unfit to rule—and both commonly succeed, and are right. H. L. MENCKEN, *Minority Report* (1956), 330.

9. The amount of effort put into a campaign by a worker expands in proportion to the personal benefits that he will derive from his party's victory. MILTON RAKOVE, *The Virginia Quarterly Review*, Summer 1965.

10. The more you read and observe about this Politics thing, you got to admit that each party is worse than the other. The one that's out always looks the best. WILL ROGERS, "Breaking into the Writing Game," *The Illiterate Digest* (1924).

11. There is a hundred things to single you out for promotion in party politics besides ability. WILL ROGERS, *The Autobiography of Will Rogers* (1949), 13.

12. Every Harvard class should have one Democrat to rescue it from oblivion. WILL ROGERS, *The Autobiography of Will Rogers* (1949), 19.

13. Even more important than winning the election is governing the nation. That is the test of a political party—the acid, final test. ADLAI STEVENSON, acceptance speech, Democratic National Convention, July 26, 1952.

14. An independent is the guy who wants to take the politics out of politics. ADLAI STEVENSON, "The Art of Politics," *The Stevenson Wit* (1966).

15. The elephant has a thick skin, a head full of ivory, and as everyone who has seen a circus parade knows, proceeds best by grasping the tail of his predecessor. ADLAI STEVENSON, "The Art of Politics," *The Stevenson Wit* (1966).

16. Every prince who puts himself at the head of a party, and succeeds, is sure of being praised to all eternity, if the party lasts that long. VOLTAIRE, "Theodosius," *Philosophical Dictionary* (1764).

### 705. POLITICS AND POLITICIANS

See also 130. Citizens; 169. Congress; 230. Demagoguery; 393. Government; 496. International Relations; 614. Nation; 645. Officialism; 704. Political Parties; 724. Presidency; 755. Public Office; 923. State; 924. Statesmen and Statesmanship; 1030. Voting

1. When the political columnists say "Every thinking man" they mean themselves, and when the candidates appeal to "Every intelligent voter" they mean everybody

who is going to vote for them. FRANKLIN P. ADAMS, *Nods and Becks* (1944).

2. The trouble with this country is that there are too many politicians who believe, with a conviction based on experience, that you can fool all of the people all of the time. FRANKLIN P. ADAMS, *Nods and Becks* (1944).

3. Politics, as a practice, whatever its professions, has always been the systematic organization of hatreds. HENRY ADAMS, *The Education of Henry Adams* (1907), 1.

4. Knowledge of human nature is the beginning and end of political education. HENRY ADAMS, *The Education of Henry Adams* (1907), 12.

5. Modern politics is, at bottom, a struggle not of men but of forces. The men become every year more and more creatures of force, massed about central powerhouses. HENRY ADAMS, *The Education of Henry Adams* (1907), 28.

6. As a man of politics, I cannot afford the doctrine of man's individual magnificence. JEAN ANOUILH, *The Lark* (1955), 1, adapted by Lillian Hellman.

7. It is evident that the state is a creation of nature, and that man is by nature a political animal. ARISTOTLE, *Politics* (4th c. B.C.), 1.2, tr. Benjamin Jowett.

8. The politician is an acrobat. He keeps his balance by saying the opposite of what he does. MAURICE BARRÈS, *Mes cahiers* (1896–1923), 12.

9. A political leader must keep looking over his shoulder all the time to see if the boys are still there. If they aren't still there, he's no longer a political leader. BERNARD M. BARUCH, quoted in obituary, *The New York Times*, June 21, 1965.

10. Public sentiment is to public officers what water is to the wheel of the mill. HENRY WARD BEECHER, *Proverbs from Plymouth Pulpit* (1887).

11. Delegation, n. In American politics, an article of merchandise that comes in sets. AMBROSE BIERCE, *The Devil's Dictionary* (1881–1911).

12. Politics, n. A strife of interests masquerading as a contest of principles. AMBROSE BIERCE, *The Devil's Dictionary* (1881–1911).

13. Nowhere are prejudices more mistaken for truth, passion for reason, and invective for documentation than in politics. That is a realm, peopled only by villains or heroes, in which everything is black or white and gray is a forbidden color. JOHN MASON BROWN, *Through These Men* (1956).

14. Magnanimity in politics is not seldom the truest wisdom; and a great empire and little minds go ill together. EDMUND BURKE, speech, "On Conciliation with the American Colonies," March 22, 1775.

15. Politics, and the fate of mankind, are shaped by men without ideals and without greatness. ALBERT CAMUS, *Notebooks 1935–1942* (1962), 2, tr. Philip Thody.

16. Half a truth is better than no politics. G. K. CHESTERTON, "The Boy," *All Things Considered* (1908).

17. A heavy and cautious responsibility of speech is the easiest thing in the world; anybody can do it. That is why so many tired, elderly, and wealthy men go in for politics. G. K. CHESTERTON, "The Case for the Ephemeral," *All Things Considered* (1908).

18. Politics are almost as exciting as war, and quite as dangerous. In war, you can only be killed once, but in politics many times. SIR WINSTON CHURCHILL, "Politics," *The Churchill Wit* (1965), ed. Bill Adler.

19. It would be a great reform in politics if wisdom could be made to spread as easily and as rapidly as folly. SIR WINSTON CHURCHILL, "Politics," *The Churchill Wit* (1965), ed. Bill Adler.

20. [Political skill] is the ability to foretell what is going to happen tomorrow, next week, next month, and next year. And to have the ability afterwards to explain why it didn't happen. SIR WINSTON CHURCHILL, "Politics," *The Churchill Wit* (1965), ed. Bill Adler.

21. Persistence in one opinion has never been considered a merit in political leaders. CICERO, *Ad Familiares* (1st c. B.C.), 1.

22. Politics is a place of humble hopes and strangely modest requirements, where all are good who are not criminal and all are wise who are not ridiculously otherwise. FRANK MOORE COLBY, "On Seeing Ten Bad Plays," *The Colby Essays* (1926), v. 1.

23. In politics as in religion, it so happens that we have less charity for those who believe the half of our creed, than for those that deny the whole of it. CHARLES CALEB COLTON, *Lacon* (1825), 1.27.

24. The political is replacing the meta-

physical as the characteristic mode of grasping reality. HARVEY COX, *The Secular City* (1966), 11.

25. Since a politician never believes what he says, he is surprised when others believe him. CHARLES DE GAULLE, *Newsweek*, Oct. 1, 1962.

26. Some things that look like lies to me to-day will seem all r-right in th' prisidential year. FINLEY PETER DUNNE, "On Lying," *Mr. Dooley's Opinions* (1901).

27. Rayformers, Hinnissy, is in favor iv suppressin' ivrything, but rale pollyticians believes in suppressin' nawthin' but ividince. FINLEY PETER DUNNE, "Some Political Observations," *Mr. Dooley's Opinions* (1901).

28. A man ought to be honest to start with an' afther that he ought to be crafty. A pollytician who's on'y honest is jus' th' same as bein' out in a winther storm without anny clothes on. FINLEY PETER DUNNE, "Reform Administration," *Observations by Mr. Dooley* (1902).

29. Spare me the sight / of this thankless breed, these politicians / who cringe for favors from a screaming mob / and do not care what harm they do their friends, / providing they can please a crowd! EURIPIDES, *Hecuba* (c. 425 B.C.), tr. William Arrowsmith.

30. Politics is not the art of the possible. It consists in choosing between the disastrous and the unpalatable. JOHN KENNETH GALBRAITH, *Ambassador's Journal* (1969).

31. I could not be leading a religious life unless I identified myself with the whole of mankind, and that I could not do unless I took part in politics. MOHANDAS K. GANDHI, *Non-Violence in Peace and War* (1948), 1.170.

32. Probably the most distinctive characteristic of the successful politician is selective cowardice. RICHARD HARRIS, "Annals of Legislation," *The New Yorker*, Dec. 14, 1968.

33. When we get sick, we want an uncommon doctor. If we have a construction job, we want an uncommon engineer. When we get into a war, we dreadfully want an uncommon admiral and an uncommon general. Only when we get into politics are we content with the common man. HERBERT HOOVER, quoted in his obituary notice in *The New York Times*, Oct. 21, 1964.

34. The greatest superstition now entertained by public men is that hypocrisy is the royal road to success. ROBERT G. INGERSOLL, speech, Dec. 13, 1886.

35. The tragedy of all political action is that some problems have no solution; none of the alternatives are intellectually consistent or morally uncompromising; and whatever decision is taken will harm somebody. JAMES JOLL, *Three Intellectuals in Politics* (1960).

36. Popular men, / They must create strange monsters, and then quell them, / To make their arts seem something. BEN JONSON, *Catiline His Conspiracy* (1611), 3.1.

37. A political convention is just not a place from which you can come away with any trace of faith in human nature. MURRAY KEMPTON, "All in Favor Say Aye," *America Comes of Middle Age* (1963).

38. Political action is the highest responsibility of a citizen. JOHN F. KENNEDY, campaign remarks, Pat Clancy Dinner, Astor Hotel, New York City, Oct. 20, 1960.

39. Politicians are the same all over. They promise to build a bridge even where there is no river. NIKITA KHRUSHCHEV, comment to reporters, Glen Cove, N.Y., October 1960.

40. In argument, truth always prevails finally; in politics, falsehood always. WALTER SAVAGE LANDOR, "Galileo, Milton, and a Dominican," *Imaginary Conversations* (1824–53).

41. We demand of our political life greater certainty and greater perfection than we demand of our personal life. MAX LERNER, "Politics and the Connective Tissue," *Actions and Passions* (1949).

42. There comes a time when even the reformer is compelled to face the fairly widespread suspicion of the average man that politics is an exhibition in which there is much ado about nothing. WALTER LIPPMANN, introduction, *A Preface to Politics* (1914).

43. Politicians tend to live "in character," and many a public figure has come to imitate the journalism which describes him. WALTER LIPPMANN, "The Changing Focus," *A Preface to Politics* (1914).

44. The man who raises new issues has always been distasteful to politicians. He

musses up what had been so tidily arranged. WALTER LIPPMANN, "The Red Herring," *A Preface to Politics* (1914).

45. Successful democratic politicians are insecure and intimidated men. They advance politically only as they placate, appease, bribe, seduce, bamboozle, or otherwise manage to manipulate the demanding and threatening elements in their constituencies. WALTER LIPPMANN, *The Public Philosophy* (1955), 2.4.

46. Toward caution all his lifetime bent, / Straddler and compromiser, he [politician] / Becomes a Public Monument / Through sheer longevity. PHYLLIS MC GINLEY, "The Old Politician," *The Love Letters of Phyllis McGinley* (1954).

47. Politics is the hard dealing of hard men over properties; their strength is in dealing and their virility. NORMAN MAILER, *Miami and the Siege of Chicago* (1968), 2.6.

48. The friend of humanity cannot recognize a distinction between what is political and what is not. There is nothing that is not political. THOMAS MANN, *The Magic Mountain* (1924), 6.8, tr. H. T. Lowe-Porter.

49. A candidate for office can have no greater advantage than muddled syntax; no greater liability than a command of language. MARYA MANNES, *More in Anger* (1958), 1.1

50. Political power grows out of the barrel of a gun. MAO TSE-TUNG, *Quotations from Chairman Mao Tse-tung* (1966), 5.

51. Politics is war without bloodshed while war is politics with bloodshed. MAO TSE-TUNG, *Quotations from Chairman Mao Tse-tung* (1966), 5.

52. did you ever / notice that when / a politician / does get an idea / he usually / gets it all wrong. DON MARQUIS, "archygrams," *Archy's Life of Mehitabel* (1933).

53. If experience teaches us anything at all, it teaches us this: that a good politician, under democracy, is quite as unthinkable as an honest burglar. H. L. MENCKEN, *Prejudices: Fourth Series* (1924), 6.

54. Politics, as hopeful men practise it in the world, consists mainly of the delusion that a change in form is a change in substance. H. L. MENCKEN, *Prejudices: Fourth Series* (1924), 13.

55. The public weal requires that men should betray, and lie, and massacre. MONTAIGNE, "Of profit and honesty," *Essays* (1580–88), tr. Charles Cotton and W. C. Hazlitt.

56. In politics, as in womanizing, failure is decisive. It sheds its retrospective gloom on earlier endeavor which at the time seemed full of promise. MALCOLM MUGGERIDGE, "Boring for England," *The Most of Malcolm Muggeridge* (1966).

57. Politics is the diversion of trivial men who, when they succeed at it, become important in the eyes of more trivial men. GEORGE JEAN NATHAN, news summaries, July 9, 1954.

58. There are men who desire power simply for the sake of the happiness it will bring; these belong chiefly to political parties. NIETZSCHE, *The Will to Power* (1888), 721, tr. Anthony M. Ludovici.

59. Political language—and with variations this is true of all political parties, from Conservatives to Anarchists—is designed to make lies sound truthful and murder respectable, and to give an appearance of solidity to pure wind. GEORGE ORWELL, "Politics and the English Language," *Shooting an Elephant* (1950).

60. In our time, political speech and writing are largely the defense of the indefensible. GEORGE ORWELL, "Politics and the English Language," *Shooting an Elephant* (1950).

61. The time has arrived when we must not poke fun at politicians. They can be rough with us but we must not be rough with them. They are the sacred white elephants of our era. J. B. PRIESTLEY, "Sacred White Elephants," *Thoughts in the Wilderness* (1957).

62. All politics are based on the indifference of the majority. JAMES RESTON, "New York," *The New York Times*, June 12, 1968.

63. If you ever injected truth into politics you have no politics. WILL ROGERS, *The Autobiography of Will Rogers* (1949), 8.

64. Politicians, after all, are not over a year behind Public Opinion. WILL ROGERS, *The Autobiography of Will Rogers* (1949), 8.

65. A Lobbyist is a person that is supposed to help a Politician to make up his mind, not only help him but pay him. WILL ROGERS, *The Autobiography of Will Rogers* (1949), 14.

66. The future lies with those wise political leaders who realize that the great public is interested more in government than in politics. FRANKLIN D. ROOSEVELT, speech, Washington, D.C., Jan. 8, 1940.

67. Our great democracies still tend to think that a stupid man is more likely to be honest than a clever man, and our politicians take advantage of this prejudice by pretending to be even more stupid than nature made them. BERTRAND RUSSELL, *New Hopes for a Changing World* (1951).

68. Experience suggests that the first rule of politics is never to say never. The ingenious human capacity for maneuver and compromise may make acceptable tomorrow what seems outrageous or impossible today. WILLIAM V. SHANNON, "Vietnam: America's Dreyfus Case," *The New York Times*, March 3, 1968.

69. The politician who once had to learn to flatter Kings has now to learn how to fascinate, amuse, coax, humbug, frighten, or otherwise strike the fancy of the electorate. GEORGE BERNARD SHAW, "The Revolutionist's Handbook," *Man and Superman* (1903).

70. He knows nothing and he thinks he knows everything. That points clearly to a political career. GEORGE BERNARD SHAW, *Major Barbara* (1905), 3.

71. Why is it that when political ammunition runs low, inevitably the rusty artillery of abuse is always wheeled into action? ADLAI STEVENSON, speech, New York City, Sept. 22, 1952.

72. The brain of our species is, as we know, made up largely of potassium, phosphorus, propaganda and politics with the result that how not to understand what should be clearer is becoming easier and easier for all of us. JAMES THURBER, "The New Vocabularianism," *Lanterns and Lances* (1961).

73. Unless we insist that politics is imagination and mind, we will learn that imagination and mind are politics, and of a kind we will not like. LIONEL TRILLING, "The Function of the Little Magazine," *The Liberal Imagination* (1950).

74. A politician is a man who understands government, and it takes a politician to run a government. A statesman is a politician who's been dead 10 or 15 years. HARRY S. TRUMAN, *New York World Telegram & Sun*, April 12, 1958.

75. As the master politician navigates the ship of state, he both creates and responds to public opinion. Adept at tacking with the wind, he also succeeds, at times, in generating breezes of his own. STEWART L. UDALL, *The Quiet Crisis* (1963), 11.

76. Politics is the art of preventing people from taking part in affairs which properly concern them. PAUL VALÉRY, *Tel quel* (1943).

77. Prosperity is necessarily the first theme of a political campaign. WOODROW WILSON, address, Sept. 4, 1912.

## POOR

See 712. Poverty

## 706. POPULARITY

See also 49. Approval; 472. Ingratiation

1. He that has many friends, has no friends. AESOP, "The Hare with Many Friends," *Fables* (6th c. B.C.?), tr. Joseph Jacobs.

2. The man with a host of friends who slaps on the back everybody he meets is regarded as the friend of nobody. ARISTOTLE, *Nicomachean Ethics* (4th c. B.C.), 9.10, tr. J. A. K. Thomson.

3. Woe unto you, when all men shall speak well of you! *Bible*, Luke 6:26.

4. When a man is familiar with many people he must expect many disagreeable familiarities. JAMES BOSWELL, *London Journal*, Feb. 17, 1763.

5. What most people in our culture mean by being lovable is essentially a mixture between being popular and having sex appeal. ERICH FROMM, *The Art of Loving* (1956), 1.

6. There must be something good in a thing that pleases so many; even if it cannot be explained, it is certainly enjoyed. BALTASAR GRACIÁN, *The Art of Worldly Wisdom* (1647), 270, tr. Joseph Jacobs.

7. A dish around which I see too many people doesn't tempt me. JULIEN GREEN, *Journal* (1938).

8. What is popular is not necessarily vulgar; and that which we try to rescue from fatal obscurity had in general much better

remain where it is. WILLIAM HAZLITT, "On Taste," *Sketches and Essays* (1839).

9. Popularity? Three-penny fame. VICTOR HUGO, *Ruy Blas* (1838), 3.5.

10. It is an unhappy lot which finds no enemies. PUBLILIUS SYRUS, *Moral Sayings* (1st c. B.C.), 499, tr. Darius Lyman.

11. Popularity is a crime from the moment it is sought; it is only a virtue where men have it whether they will or no. SIR GEORGE SAVILE, *Moral Thoughts and Reflections* (1750).

12. The more one pleases everybody, the less one pleases profoundly. STENDHAL, "Miscellaneous Fragments," *On Love* (1822).

13. The most popular persons in society are those who take the world as it is, find the least fault, and have [ride] no hobbies. CHARLES DUDLEY WARNER, "Fifth Study," *Backlog Studies* (1873).

## 707. POPULATION

See also 82. Birth Control; 205. Crowds; 796. Reproduction

1. All that tread / The globe are but a handful to the tribes / That slumber in its bosom. WILLIAM CULLEN BRYANT, "Thanatopsis" (1811).

2. Over-population is a phenomenon connected with the survival of the unfit, and it is a mechanism which has created conditions favourable to the survival of the unfit and the elimination of the fit. WILLIAM RALPH INGE, "The Dilemma of Civilisation," *Outspoken Essays: Second Series* (1922).

3. Creation destroys as it goes, throws down one tree for the rise of another. But ideal mankind would abolish death, multiply itself million upon million, rear up city upon city, save every parasite alive, until the accumulation of mere existence is swollen to a horror. D. H. LAWRENCE, *St. Mawr* (1925).

4. If people waited to know one another before they married, the world wouldn't be so grossly over-populated as it is now. W. SOMERSET MAUGHAM, *Mrs. Dot* (1912), 2.

5. Instead of needing lots of children, we need high-quality children. MARGARET MEAD, *The New York Times*, Oct. 30, 1966.

6. And fear not lest Existence closing your / Account, and mine, should know the like no more; / The Eternal Sákí from that Bowl has poured / Millions of Bubbles like us, and will pour. OMAR KHAYYÁM, *Rubáiyát* (11th–12th c.), tr. Edward FitzGerald, 4th ed., 46.

7. We have been God-like in our planned breeding of our domesticated plants and animals, but we have been rabbit-like in our unplanned breeding of ourselves. ARNOLD TOYNBEE, *National Observer*, June 10, 1963.

8. It is obvious that the best qualities in man must atrophy in a standing-room-only environment. STEWART L. UDALL, *The Quiet Crisis* (1963), 13.

## 708. PORNOGRAPHY

1. The value difference between pornographic playing cards when you're a kid, and pornographic playing cards when you're older. It's that when you're a kid you use cards as a substitute for a real experience, and when you're older you use real experience as a substitute for the fantasy. EDWARD ALBEE, *Zoo Story* (1958).

2. A taste for dirty stories may be said to be inherent in the human animal. GEORGE MOORE, *Confessions of a Young Man* (1888), 9.

3. Nine-tenths of the appeal of pornography is due to the indecent feelings concerning sex which moralists inculcate in the young; the other tenth is physiological, and will occur in one way or another whatever the state of the law may be. BERTRAND RUSSELL, "The Taboo on Sex Knowledge," *Marriage and Morals* (1929).

## 709. PORTENT

See also 304. Evidence; 749. Prudence

1. One swallow does not make a summer; neither does one fine day. ARISTOTLE, *Nicomachean Ethics* (4th c. B.C.), 1.7, tr. J. A. K. Thomson.

2. Every cloud engenders not a storm. SHAKESPEARE, *3 Henry VI* (1590–91), 5.3.13.

## POSITION
See 773. Rank

## 710. POSSESSION
See also 8. Acquisition; 106. Capitalism; 740. Property

1. What a man has honestly acquired is absolutely his own, which he may freely give, but cannot be taken from him without his consent. SAMUEL ADAMS, Massachusetts circular letter, Feb. 11, 1768.

2. There is, of course, a difference between what one seizes and what one really possesses. PEARL S. BUCK, *What America Means to Me* (1943), 2.

3. To keep demands as much skill as to win. CHAUCER, *Troilus and Cressida* (c. 1385), 3.234, tr. George Phillip Krapp.

4. Fie on possession, / But if a man be vertuous withal. CHAUCER, "The Squire's Tale," *The Canterbury Tales* (1387–1400), 686, ed. Thomas Tyrwhitt.

5. To possess, is past the instant / We achieve the Joy— / Immortality contented / Were Anomaly. EMILY DICKINSON, poem (c. 1865).

6. Our life on earth is, and ought to be, material and carnal. But we have not yet learned to manage our materialism and carnality properly; they are still entangled with the desire for ownership. E. M. FORSTER, "My Wood," *Abinger Harvest* (1936).

7. How sweet an emotion is possession! What charm is inherent in ownership! What a foundation for vanity, even for the greater quality of self-respect, lies in a little property! DAVID GRAYSON, *Adventures in Contentment* (1907), 3.

8. There is radicalism in all getting, and conservatism in all keeping. Lovemaking is radical, while marriage is conservative. ERIC HOFFER, *The Passionate State of Mind* (1954), 21.

9. Nothing can be so perfect while we possess it as it will seem when remembered. OLIVER WENDELL HOLMES, SR., *The Poet at the Breakfast Table* (1872), 12.

10. It is disastrous to own more of anything than you can possess, and it is one of the most fundamental laws of human nature that our power actually to possess is limited. JOSEPH WOOD KRUTCH, "The Miracle of Grass," *If You Don't Mind My Saying So* (1964).

11. He who possesses most must be most afraid of loss. LEONARDO DA VINCI, *Notebooks* (c. 1500), tr. Jean Paul Richter.

12. Vinegar in hand is better than halvah to come. PERSIAN PROVERB.

13. An object in possession seldom retains the same charm that it had in pursuit. PLINY THE YOUNGER, *Letters* (c. 97–110), 2.15.1, tr. William Melmoth.

14. It is as unjust to possess a woman exclusively as to possess slaves. MARQUIS DE SADE, *La Philosophie dans le boudoir* (1795), tr. Paul Dinnage.

15. An ill-favoured thing, sir, but mine own. SHAKESPEARE, *As You Like It* (1599–1600), 5.4.60.

16. When we desire or solicit any thing, our minds run wholly on the good side or circumstances of it; when it is obtained, our minds run wholly on the bad ones. JONATHAN SWIFT, *Thoughts on Various Subjects* (1711).

17. By touching you may kill, by keeping away you may possess. RABINDRANATH TAGORE, *Stray Birds* (1916), 197.

18. No one worth possessing / Can be quite possessed. SARA TEASDALE, "Advice to a Girl," *Strange Victory* (1933).

19. The want of a thing is perplexing enough, but the possession of it is intolerable. SIR JOHN VANBRUGH, *The Confederacy* (1705), 1.2.

## POSSIBILITIES
See 650. Opportunity; 711. Potential

## POSTPONEMENT
See 228. Delay

## 711. POTENTIAL
See also 650. Opportunity; 1003. Unfulfillment

1. All things are possible until they are proved impossible—and even the impossible may only be so, as of now. PEARL S. BUCK, *A Bridge for Passing* (1962), 3.

2. The important thing is this: to be able at any moment to sacrifice what we are for what we could become. CHARLES DU BOS, *Approximations* (1922–37), 3.

3. Where much is expected from an in-

dividual, he may rise to the level of events and make the dream come true. ELBERT HUBBARD, *The Note Book* (1927).

4. Nothing is unthinkable, nothing impossible to the balanced person, provided it arises out of the needs of life and is dedicated to life's further developments. LEWIS MUMFORD, "The Way and the Life," *The Conduct of Life* (1951).

5. Man is as full of potentiality as he is of impotence. GEORGE SANTAYANA, *The Life of Reason: Reason in Common Sense* (1905–06), 9.

6. Man is not the sum of what he has already, but rather the sum of what he does not yet have, of what he could have. JEAN-PAUL SARTRE, "Temporalité," *Situations* (1947–49), v. 1.

7. So many worlds, so much to do, / So little done, such things to be. ALFRED, LORD TENNYSON, "In Memoriam A. H. H." (1850), 73.

8. The world which credits what is done / Is cold to all that might have been. ALFRED, LORD TENNYSON, "In Memoriam A. H. H." (1850), 75.

## 712. POVERTY

**See also 17. Adversity; 72. Beggars; 234. Deprivation; 435. Hunger; 596. Money; 618. Need; 740. Property; 1002. Unemployment; 1041. Wealth**

1. The possession of gold has ruined fewer men than the lack of it. What noble enterprises have been checked and what fine souls have been blighted in the gloom of poverty the world will never know. THOMAS BAILEY ALDRICH, "Leaves from a Notebook," *Ponkapog Papers* (1903).

2. Poverty is the parent of revolution and crime. ARISTOTLE, *Politics* (4th c. B.C.), 2.6, tr. Benjamin Jowett.

3. Poverty is very good in poems, but it is very bad in a house. It is very good in maxims and in sermons, but it is very bad in practical life. HENRY WARD BEECHER, *Proverbs from Plymouth Pulpit* (1887).

4. A poor man with nothing in his belly needs hope, illusion, more than bread. GEORGES BERNANOS, *The Diary of a Country Priest* (1936), 2, tr. Pamela Morris.

5. The poor man's wisdom is despised, and his words are not heard. *Bible*, Ecclesiastes 9:16.

6. Poverty is taking your children to the hospital and spending the whole day waiting with no one even taking your name—and then coming back the next day, and the next, until they finally get around to you. MRS. JANICE BRADSHAW, quoted by Sargent Shriver in April 12, 1965 hearing of the House Committee on Education and Labor.

7. Poverty makes you sad as well as wise. BERTOLT BRECHT, *The Threepenny Opera* (1928), 2.3, tr. Desmond Vesey and Eric Bentley.

8. Unhappiness doesn't grow on the chest like leprosy. Poverty won't fall off the roof like a loose tile, no: poverty and unhappiness are man's doing. BERTOLT BRECHT, *The Measures Taken* (1930), 6, tr. Eric Bentley.

9. For the poor of this world, two major ways of expiring are available: either by the absolute indifference of your fellow-men in peace-time, or by the homicidal passion of these same when war breaks out. LOUIS-FERDINAND CÉLINE, *Voyage au bout de la nuit* (1932).

10. The rich man may never get into heaven, but the pauper is already serving his term in hell. ALEXANDER CHASE, *Perspectives* (1966).

11. The honest poor can sometimes forget poverty. The honest rich can never forget it. G. K. CHESTERTON, "Cockneys and Their Jokes," *All Things Considered* (1908).

12. Is there not yet oppression in the country? A starving of men and pampering of dogs? JOHN DONNE, *Sermons*, No. 68, 1630.

13. To be a poor man is hard, but to be a poor race in a land of dollars is the very bottom of hardships. W. E. B. DU BOIS, *The Souls of Black Folk* (1903), 1.

14. Those who have not, and live in want, are a menace, / Ridden with envy and fooled by demagogues. EURIPIDES, *The Suppliant Women* (c. 421 B.C.), tr. Frank W. Jones.

15. There is no scandal like rags, nor any crime so shameful as poverty. GEORGE FARQUHAR, *The Beaux' Strategem* (1707), 1.1.

16. An empty purse frightens away friends. THOMAS FULLER, M.D., *Gnomologia* (1732), 597.

17. He that is poor, all his kindred scorn him; he that is rich, all are kind to him.

THOMAS FULLER, M.D., *Gnomologia* (1732), 2189.

18. Poor men's reasons are not heard. THOMAS FULLER, M.D., *Gnomologia* (1732), 3897.

19. For every talent that poverty has stimulated it has blighted a hundred. JOHN W. GARDNER, *Excellence* (1961).

20. Beauty and myths are perennial masks of poverty. MICHAEL HARRINGTON, *The Other America* (1962), 1.1.

21. America has the best-dressed poverty the world has ever known. MICHAEL HARRINGTON, *The Other America* (1962), 1.1.

22. People who are much too sensitive to demand of cripples that they run races ask of the poor that they get up and act just like everyone else in the society. MICHAEL HARRINGTON, *The Other America* (1962), 7.5.

23. The poor on the borderline of starvation live purposeful lives. To be engaged in a desperate struggle for food and shelter is to be wholly free from a sense of futility. ERIC HOFFER, *The True Believer* (1951), 2.5.21.

24. Poverty comes pleading, not for charity, for the most part, but imploring us to find a purchaser for its unmarketable wares. OLIVER WENDELL HOLMES, SR., *Over the Teacups* (1891), 6.

25. There is always more misery among the lower classes than there is humanity in the higher. VICTOR HUGO, "Fantine," *Les Misérables* (1862), 1.2, tr. Charles E. Wilbour.

26. It is not poverty so much as pretense that harasses a ruined man—the struggle between a proud mind and an empty purse—the keeping up of a hollow show that must soon come to an end. WASHINGTON IRVING, "The Wife," *The Sketch Book of Geoffrey Crayon, Gent.* (1819–20).

27. It is easy enough to say that poverty is no crime. No; if it were men wouldn't be ashamed of it. It's a blunder, though, and is punished as such. JEROME K. JEROME, "On Being Hard Up," *The Idle Thoughts of an Idle Fellow* (1889).

28. Poverty has many roots, but the tap root is ignorance. LYNDON B. JOHNSON, message to Congress, Jan. 12, 1965.

29. Slow rises worth by poverty depressed. SAMUEL JOHNSON, *London* (1738).

30. Poverty has, in large cities, very different appearances; it is often concealed in splendour, and often in extravagance. SAMUEL JOHNSON, *Rasselas* (1759), 25.

31. All the arguments which are brought to represent poverty as no evil, show it to be evidently a great evil. You never find people laboring to convince you that you may live very happily upon a plentiful fortune. SAMUEL JOHNSON, quoted in Boswell's *Life of Samuel Johnson*, July 20, 1763.

32. Poverty is a great enemy to human happiness; it certainly destroys liberty, and it makes some virtues impracticable and others extremely difficult. SAMUEL JOHNSON, quoted in Boswell's *Life of Samuel Johnson*, Dec. 7, 1782.

33. Of the woes / Of unhappy poverty, none is more difficult to bear / Than that it heaps men with ridicule. JUVENAL, *Satires* (c. 100), 3.152, tr. Hubert Creekmore.

34. Seldom do people discern / Eloquence under a threadbare cloak. JUVENAL, *Satires* (c. 100), 7.145, tr. Hubert Creekmore.

35. A man who has nothing can whistle in a robber's face. JUVENAL, *Satires* (c. 100), 10.22, tr. Hubert Creekmore.

36. Love in a hut, with water and a crust, / Is—Love, forgive us!—cinders, ashes, dust. JOHN KEATS, "Lamia" (1819), 2.

37. If a free society cannot help the many who are poor, it cannot save the few who are rich. JOHN F. KENNEDY, Inaugural Address, Jan. 20, 1961.

38. Political sovereignty is but a mockery without the means of meeting poverty and illiteracy and disease. Self-determination is but a slogan if the future holds no hope. JOHN F. KENNEDY, address to United Nations General Assembly, Sept. 25, 1961.

39. If thy wealth waste, thy wit will give but small warmth. JOHN LYLY, *Euphues: The Anatomy of Wit* (1579).

40. Three were the fates—gaunt Poverty that chains, / Gray Drudgery that grinds the hope away, / And gaping Ignorance that starves the soul. EDWIN MARKHAM, "Young Lincoln" (1909).

41. We have two American flags always; one for the rich and one for the poor. When the rich fly it it means that things are under control; when the poor fly it it means danger, revolution, anarchy. HENRY MILLER, "Good News! God Is Love!" *The Air-Conditioned Nightmare* (1945).

42. Short of genius, a rich man cannot imagine poverty. CHARLES PÉGUY, "Socialism and the Modern World," *Basic Verities* (1943), tr. Ann and Julian Green.

43. In a change of government, the poor change nothing beyond the change of their master. PHAEDRUS, "The Ass and the Old Shepherd," *Fables* (1st c.), tr. Thomas James.

44. The more humanity owes him [the poor man], the more society denies him. Every door is shut against him, even when he has a right to its being opened: and if he ever obtains justice, it is with much greater difficulty than others obtain favours. ROUSSEAU, *A Discourse on Political Economy* (1758), tr. G. D. H. Cole.

45. The rich would have to eat money, but luckily the poor provide food. RUSSIAN PROVERB.

46. The poor don't know that their function in life is to exercise our generosity. JEAN-PAUL SARTRE, *The Words* (1964), 1.

47. Poverty with joy isn't poverty at all. The poor man is not one who has little, but one who hankers after more. SENECA, *Letters to Lucilius* (1st c.), 2, tr. E. Phillips Barker.

48. Security, the chief pretence of civilization, cannot exist where the worst of dangers, the danger of poverty, hangs over everyone's head. GEORGE BERNARD SHAW, preface, *Major Barbara* (1905).

49. Poverty is no disgrace to a man, but it is confoundedly inconvenient. SYDNEY SMITH, *Wit and Wisdom* (1900).

50. Poverty is not perversity. SPANISH PROVERB.

51. We who are liberal and progressive know that the poor are our equals in every sense except that of being equal to us. LIONEL TRILLING, "The Princess Casamassima," *The Liberal Imagination* (1950).

52. He who has no bread has no authority. TURKISH PROVERB.

53. Forgive us for pretending to care for the poor, when we do not like poor people and do not want them in our homes. UNITED PRESBYTERIAN CHURCH, *Litany for Holy Communion* (1968).

54. Empty pockets make empty heads. WILLIAM CARLOS WILLIAMS, "Raleigh Was Right," *Selected Poems* (1949).

55. The poor must be wisely visited and liberally cared for, so that mendicity shall not be tempted into mendacity, nor want exasperated into crime. ROBERT C. WINTHROP, Yorktown Oration, 1881.

56. Poverty is no disgrace, but no honor either. *Yiddish Proverbs* (1949), ed. Hanan J. Ayalti.

## 713. POWER

**See also 61. Authority; 457. Impotence; 933. Strength; 995. Tyranny**

1. Power tends to corrupt and absolute power corrupts absolutely. LORD ACTON, letter to Mandell Creighton, April 5, 1887.

2. A friend in power is a friend lost. HENRY ADAMS, *The Education of Henry Adams* (1907), 7.

3. Power when wielded by abnormal energy is the most serious of facts. HENRY ADAMS, *The Education of Henry Adams* (1907), 28.

4. For the mighty even to give way is grace. AESCHYLUS, *Agamemnon* (458 B.C.), tr. Richmond Lattimore.

5. The possession of unlimited power will make a despot of almost any man. There is a possible Nero in the gentlest human creature that walks. THOMAS BAILEY ALDRICH, "Leaves from a Notebook," *Ponkapog Papers* (1903).

6. Power can corrupt, but absolute power is absolutely delightful. Anonymous.

7. Give me where to stand, and I will move the earth. ARCHIMEDES (3rd c. B.C.), quoted in Pappus' *Collection* (c. 300 A.D.), 8.10.11.

8. We thought, because we had power, we had wisdom. STEPHEN VINCENT BENÉT, *Litany for Dictatorships* (1935).

9. The greater the power, the more dangerous the abuse. EDMUND BURKE, speech, "On the Middlesex Election," 1771.

10. God is usually on the side of big squadrons against little ones. ROGER DE BUSSY-RABUTIN, letter to the Comte de Limoges, Oct. 18, 1667.

11. We can't do without dominating others or being served. . . . Even the man on the bottom rung still has his wife, or his child. If he's a bachelor, his dog. The essential thing, in sum, is being able to get angry without the other person being able to answer back. ALBERT CAMUS, *The Fall* (1956).

12. To know the pains of power, we must go to those who have it; to know its pleas-

ures, we must go to those who are seeking it. CHARLES CALEB COLTON, *Lacon* (1825), 1.427.

13. No man is wise enough nor good enough to be trusted with unlimited power. CHARLES CALEB COLTON, *Lacon* (1825), 1.522.

14. To be a great autocrat you must be a great barbarian. JOSEPH CONRAD, *The Mirror of the Sea* (1906), 29.

15. Omnipotence is bought with ceaseless fear. CORNEILLE, *Cinna* (1639), 4.1, tr. Paul Landis.

16. You shall have joy, or you shall have power, said God; you shall not have both. EMERSON, *Journals*, 1842.

17. Life is a search after power; and this is an element with which the world is so saturated,—there is no chink or crevice in which it is not lodged,—that no honest seeking goes unrewarded. EMERSON, "Power," *The Conduct of Life* (1860).

18. All power is of one kind, a sharing of the nature of the world. The mind that is parallel with the laws of nature will be in the current of events, and strong with their strength. EMERSON, "Power," *The Conduct of Life* (1860).

19. Power gives no purchase / to the hand, it will not hold, soon perishes, / and greatness goes. EURIPIDES, *Hecuba* (c. 425 B.C.), tr. William Arrowsmith.

20. Oh, it is vile for a man, if he be noble, / And when he has won to the heights of power, / To put on new manners for old and change / His countenance. EURIPIDES, *Iphigenia in Aulis* (c. 405 B.C.), tr. Charles R. Walker.

21. The sole advantage of power is that you can do more good. BALTASAR GRACIÁN, *The Art of Worldly Wisdom* (1647), 286, tr. Joseph Jacobs.

22. Power is pleasure; and pleasure sweetens pain. WILLIAM HAZLITT, "On Application to Study," *The Plain Speaker* (1826).

23. It is when power is wedded to chronic fear that it becomes formidable. ERIC HOFFER, *The Passionate State of Mind* (1954), 43.

24. Our sense of power is more vivid when we break a man's spirit than when we win his heart. ERIC HOFFER, *The Passionate State of Mind* (1954), 90.

25. Power, whether exercised over matter or over man, is partial to simplification. ERIC HOFFER, *The Ordeal of Change* (1964), 15.4.

26. Power is always charged with the impulse to eliminate human nature, the human variable, from the equation of action. Dictators do it by terror or by the inculcation of blind faith; the military do it by iron discipline; and the industrial masters think they can do it by automation. ERIC HOFFER, "Automation, Leisure, and the Masses," *The Temper of Our Time* (1967), 2.

27. The only prize much cared for by the powerful is power. The prize of the general is not a bigger tent, but command. OLIVER WENDELL HOLMES, JR., speech, Harvard Law School Association of New York, Feb. 15, 1913.

28. An honest man can feel no pleasure in the exercise of power over his fellow citizens. THOMAS JEFFERSON, letter to John Melish, Jan. 13, 1813.

29. The problem of power is how to achieve its responsible use rather than its irresponsible and indulgent use—of how to get men of power to live *for* the public rather than *off* the public. ROBERT F. KENNEDY, "I Remember, I Believe," *The Pursuit of Justice* (1964).

30. The wise become as the unwise in the enchanted chambers of Power, whose lamps make every face of the same color. WALTER SAVAGE LANDOR, "Demosthenes and Eubulides," *Imaginary Conversations* (1824–53).

31. Immoderate power, like other intemperence, leaves the progeny weaker and weaker, until Nature, as in compassion, covers it with her mantle and it is seen no more. WALTER SAVAGE LANDOR, "Pericles and Sophocles," *Imaginary Conversations* (1824–53).

32. The first principle of a civilized state is that power is legitimate only when it is under contract. WALTER LIPPMANN, *The Public Philosophy* (1955), 11.3.

33. Deny a strong man his due, and he will take all he can get. LUCAN, *On the Civil War* (1st c.), tr. Robert Graves.

34. To ask for power is forcing uphill a stone which after all rolls back again from the summit and seeks in headlong haste the levels of the plain. LUCRETIUS, *On the Nature of Things* (1st c. B.C.), 3, tr. H. A. J. Munro.

35. Power never takes a back step—only in the face of more power. MALCOLM X, *Malcolm X Speaks* (1965), 12.

36. Every high degree of power always involves a corresponding degree of freedom from good and evil. NIETZSCHE, *The Will to Power* (1888), tr. Anthony M. Ludovici.

37. There is a universal need to exercise some kind of power, or to create for one's self the appearance of some power, if only temporarily, in the form of intoxication. NIETZSCHE, *The Will to Power* (1888), 721, tr. Anthony M. Ludovici.

38. Power-worship blurs political judgment because it leads, almost unavoidably, to the belief that present trends will continue. Whoever is winning at the moment will always seem to be invincible. GEORGE ORWELL, "Second Thoughts on James Burnham," *Shooting an Elephant* (1950).

39. The property of power is to protect. PASCAL, *Pensées* (1670), 310, tr. W. F. Trotter.

40. A cock has great influence on his own dunghill. PUBLILIUS SYRUS, *Moral Sayings* (1st c. B.C.), 357, tr. Darius Lyman.

41. Hares can gambol over the body of a dead lion. PUBLILIUS SYRUS, *Moral Sayings* (1st c. B.C.), 420, tr. Darius Lyman.

42. There is a homely adage which runs: "Speak softly and carry a big stick; you will go far." THEODORE ROOSEVELT, speech, Minnesota State Fair, Sept. 2, 1901.

43. The strongest is never strong enough to be always the master, unless he transforms strength into right, and obedience into duty. ROUSSEAU, *The Social Contract* (1762), 1.3, tr. G. D. H. Cole.

44. The eagle suffers little birds to sing. SHAKESPEARE, *Titus Andronicus* (1592–93), 4.4.83.

45. O, it is excellent / To have a giant's strength; but it is tyrannous / To use it like a giant. SHAKESPEARE, *Measure for Measure* (1604–05), 2.2.107.

46. Power, like a desolating pestilence, / Pollutes whate'er it touches. SHELLEY, *Queen Mab* (1813), 3.

47. It is better to be the head of a mouse than the tail of a lion. SPANISH PROVERB.

48. Legions and fleets are not such sure bulwarks of imperial power as a numerous family. TACITUS, *Histories* (A.D. 104–109), 4.52, tr. Alfred J. Church and William J. Brodribb.

49. Power said to the world, "You are mine." / The world kept it prisoner on her throne. / Love said to the world, "I am thine." / The world gave it the freedom of her house. RABINDRANATH TAGORE, *Stray Birds* (1916), 93.

50. Power takes as ingratitude the writhing of its victims. RABINDRANATH TAGORE, *Stray Birds* (1916), 158.

51. The clumsiness of power spoils the key, / and uses the pickaxe. RABINDRANATH TAGORE, *Fireflies* (1928).

52. When the reality of power has been surrendered, it's playing a dangerous game to seek to retain the appearance of it; the external aspect of vigor can sometimes support a debilitated body, but most often it manages to deal it the final blow. ALEXIS DE TOCQUEVILLE, *État social et politique de la France* (1834), 1.

53. If you would be powerful, pretend to be powerful. HORNE TOOKE (1736–1812), quoted in Emerson's *The Conduct of Life* (1860), 7.

54. We have, I fear, confused power with greatness. STEWART L. UDALL, commencement address, Dartmouth College, June 13, 1965.

55. True power and true politeness are above vanity. VOLTAIRE, "Ceremonies," *Philosophical Dictionary* (1764).

56. There is no need to fear the strong. All one needs is to know the method of overcoming them. There is a special jujitsu for every strong man. YEVGENY YEVTUSHENKO, *A Precocious Autobiography* (1963), tr. Andrew R. MacAndrew.

## POWERLESSNESS

**See 457. Impotence**

## 714. PRACTICALITY

**See also 147. Common Sense; 317. Expediency; 749. Prudence; 778. Reason; 1016. Usefulness**

1. I like a man who likes to see a fine barn as well as a good tragedy. EMERSON, *Journals*, 1828.

2. The Arab who built himself a hut with marbles from the temple of Palmyra is more philosophical than all the curators of the museums of London, Paris and Munich.

ANATOLE FRANCE, *The Crime of Sylvestre Bonnard* (1881), 2.

3. A mariner must have his eye upon rocks and sands, as well as upon the North Star. THOMAS FULLER, M.D., *Gnomologia* (1732), 319.

4. I had rather ride on an ass that carries me than a horse that throws me. GEORGE HERBERT, *Jacula Prudentum* (1651).

5. Admire a little ship, but put your cargo in a big one. HESIOD, *Works and Days* (8th c. B.C.), 643, tr. Richmond Lattimore.

6. Without oars you cannot cross in a boat. JAPANESE PROVERB.

7. A rational man acting in the real world may be defined as one who decides where he will strike a balance between what he desires and what can be done. WALTER LIPPMANN, *The Public Philosophy* (1955), 4.2.

## 715. PRACTICE

See also 529. Learning; 579. Method

1. The barber learns his trade on the orphan's chin. ARABIC PROVERB.

2. Practice is nine-tenths. EMERSON, "Power," *The Conduct of Life* (1860).

3. However much thou art read in theory, if thou hast no practice thou art ignorant. SA'DI, *Gulistan* (1258), 8.3, tr. James Ross.

## 716. PRAISE

See also 47. Appreciation; 49. Approval; 578. Merit

1. A man who does not love praise is not a full man. HENRY WARD BEECHER, *Proverbs from Plymouth Pulpit* (1887).

2. Praise out of season, or tactlessly bestowed, can freeze the heart as much as blame. PEARL S. BUCK, "First Meeting," *To My Daughters, With Love* (1967).

3. The advantage of doing one's praising to oneself is that one can lay it on so thick and exactly in the right places. SAMUEL BUTLER (d. 1902), *The Way of All Flesh* (1903), 34.

4. Praise, though it be our due, is not like a bank-bill, to be paid upon demand; to be valuable, it must be voluntary. COLLEY CIBBER, *An Apology for the Life of Mr. Colley Cibber* (1740), v. 2.

5. Expect not praise without envy until you are dead. CHARLES CALEB COLTON, *Lacon* (1825), 1.245.

6. Applause is the spur of noble minds, the end and aim of weak ones. CHARLES CALEB COLTON, *Lacon* (1825), 1.424.

7. I scorn men's curses, but I dread applause! PAUL LAURENCE DUNBAR, "The Crisis," *The Complete Poems* (1962).

8. Praise to the undeserving is severe satire. BENJAMIN FRANKLIN, *Poor Richard's Almanack* (1732–57).

9. Praise makes good men better and bad men worse. THOMAS FULLER, M.D., *Gnomologia* (1732), 3918.

10. Praises from an enemy imply real merit. THOMAS FULLER, M.D., *Gnomologia* (1732), 3924.

11. Praises from wicked men are reproaches. THOMAS FULLER, M.D., *Gnomologia* (1732), 3925.

12. To speak highly of one with whom we are intimate is a species of egotism. Our modesty as well as our jealousy teaches us caution on this subject. WILLIAM HAZLITT, *Characteristics* (1823), 3.

13. The safest kind of praise is to foretell that another will become great in some particular way. It has the greatest show of magnanimity, and the least of it in reality. WILLIAM HAZLITT, *Characteristics* (1823), 415.

14. Unmerited abuse wounds, while unmerited praise has not the power to heal. THOMAS JEFFERSON, letter to Edward Rutledge, Dec. 27, 1796.

15. Praise, like gold and diamonds, owes its value only to its scarcity. SAMUEL JOHNSON, *The Rambler*, June 6, 1751.

16. The applause of a single human being is of great consequence. SAMUEL JOHNSON, quoted in Boswell's *Life of Samuel Johnson*, 1781.

17. An ingenuous mind feels in unmerited praise the bitterest reproof. WALTER SAVAGE LANDOR, "Bossuet and the Duchess de Fontanges," *Imaginary Conversations* (1824–53).

18. We cannot at once catch the applauses of the vulgar and expect the approbation of the wise. WALTER SAVAGE LANDOR, "Lucullus and Caesar," *Imaginary Conversations* (1824–53).

19. The deafest man can hear praise, and is slow to think any an excess. WALTER SAV-

AGE LANDOR, "Milton and Marvel," *Imaginary Conversations* (1824–53).

20. Generally we praise only to be praised. LA ROCHEFOUCAULD, *Maxims* (1665), tr. Kenneth Pratt.

21. There are reproaches which praise, and praises which defame. LA ROCHEFOUCAULD, *Maxims* (1665), tr. Kenneth Pratt.

22. Refusal of praise is a desire to be praised twice. LA ROCHEFOUCAULD, *Maxims* (1665), tr. Kenneth Pratt.

23. There's no praise to beat the sort you can put in your pocket. MOLIÈRE, *The Would-be Gentleman* (1670), 1, tr. John Wood.

24. Praise is always pleasing, let it come from whom, or upon what account it will. MONTAIGNE, "Of vanity," *Essays* (1580–88), tr. Charles Cotton and W. C. Hazlitt.

25. Enjoying praise is in some people merely a courtesy of the heart—and just the opposite of vanity of the spirit. NIETZSCHE, *Beyond Good and Evil* (1886), 122, tr. Walter Kaufmann.

26. Praise is more obtrusive than a reproach. NIETZSCHE, *Beyond Good and Evil* (1886), 170, tr. Walter Kaufmann.

27. Envy bestrides praise. PINDAR, *Odes* (5th c. B.C.), Olympia 2, tr. Richmond Lattimore.

28. Every artist loves applause. The praise of his contemporaries is the most valuable part of his recompense. ROUSSEAU, *A Discourse on the Moral Effects of the Arts and Sciences* (1750), 2, tr. G. D. H. Cole.

29. Persons of delicate taste endure stupid criticism better than they do stupid praise. JOSEPH ROUX, *Meditations of a Parish Priest* (1886), 1.26, tr. Isabel F. Hapgood.

30. True praise comes often even to the lowly; false praise only to the strong. SENECA, *Thyestes* (1st c.), 211.

31 Praise is the best diet for us, after all. SYDNEY SMITH, quoted in Lady S. Holland's *Memoir* (1855), v. 1.9.

32. The praise of an ignorant man is only good-will, and you should receive his kindness as he is a good neighbour in society, and not as a good judge of your actions in point of fame and reputation. RICHARD STEELE, *The Spectator* (1711–12), 188.

33. All panegyrics are mingled with an infusion of poppy. JONATHAN SWIFT, *Thoughts on Various Subjects* (1711).

34. Praise shames me, for I secretly beg for it. RABINDRANATH TAGORE, *Stray Birds* (1916), 207.

35. We begin to praise when we begin to see a thing needs our assistance. THOREAU, *Journal*, June 20, 1840.

36. Mankind are tolerant of the praises of others so long as each hearer thinks he can do as well or nearly well himself. THUCYDIDES, *The Peloponnesian War* (c. 400 B.C.), 2.35, tr. Benjamin Jowett.

37. It is a great sign of mediocrity to praise always moderately. VAUVENARGUES, *Reflections and Maxims* (1746), 12.

38. Men sometimes feel injured by praise because it assigns a limit to their merit. VAUVENARGUES, *Reflections and Maxims* (1746), 66, tr. F. G. Stevens.

39. If thou wouldst have praise, die. WELSH PROVERB.

40. He who loves praise loves temptation. THOMAS WILSON, *Maxims of Piety and Christianity* (c. 1781).

## 717. PRAYER

**See also 180. Contemplation; 1061. Worship**

1. It is in vain to expect our prayers to be heard, if we do not strive as well as pray. AESOP, "Hercules and the Waggoner," *Fables* (6th c. B.C.?), tr. Thomas James.

2. It is not well for a man to pray cream and live skim milk. HENRY WARD BEECHER, *Proverbs from Plymouth Pulpit* (1887).

3. The wish to pray is a prayer in itself. GEORGES BERNANOS, *The Diary of a Country Priest* (1936), 4, tr. Pamela Morris.

4. When a man prays, do you know what he's doing? / What? / He's saying to himself: "Keep calm, everything's all right; it's all right." UGO BETTI, *Struggle Till Dawn* (1949), 1, tr. G. H. McWilliam.

5. Pray, v. To ask that the laws of the universe be annulled in behalf of a single petitioner confessedly unworthy. AMBROSE BIERCE, *The Devil's Dictionary* (1881–1911).

6. Prayers are to men as dolls are to children. They are not without use and comfort, but it is not easy to take them very seriously. SAMUEL BUTLER (d. 1902), "Unprofessional Sermons," *Note-Books* (1912).

7. We little know the things for which we pray. CHAUCER, "The Knight's Tale," *The Canterbury Tales* (c. 1387–1400), tr. Nevill Coghill.

8. He prayeth best, who loveth best / All things both great and small; / For the dear God who loveth us, / He made and loveth all. SAMUEL TAYLOR COLERIDGE, *The Rime of the Ancient Mariner* (1798), 7.23.

9. A prayer may chance to rise / From one whose heart lives in the grace of God. / A prayer from any other is unheeded. DANTE, "Purgatorio," *The Divine Comedy* (c. 1300–21), tr. Lawrence Grant White.

10. Prayer is the little implement / Through which Men reach / Where Presence—is denied them. EMILY DICKINSON, poem (c. 1862).

11. Prayer is the contemplation of the facts of life from the highest point of view. EMERSON, "Self-Reliance," *Essays: First Series* (1841).

12. Prayer as a means to effect a private end is theft and meanness. EMERSON, "Self-Reliance," *Essays: First Series* (1841).

13. None can pray well but he that lives well. THOMAS FULLER, M.D., *Gnomologia* (1732), 3647.

14. Prayer should be the key of the day and the lock of the night. THOMAS FULLER, M.D., *Gnomologia* (1732), 3927.

15. Prayer is not an old woman's idle amusement. Properly understood and applied, it is the most potent instrument of action. MOHANDAS K. GANDHI, *Non-Violence in Peace and War* (1948), 2.77.

16. Your cravings as a human animal do not become a prayer just because it is God whom you must ask to attend to them. DAG HAMMARSKJÖLD, "1941–1942: The middle years," *Markings* (1964), tr. Leif Sjoberg and W. H. Auden.

17. We all have our prayer-wheels which we set up on the steppes. The indifferent winds come and carry most of them away to gasp out their little lives in the desert, for few reach heaven. LEARNED HAND, address, Bryn Mawr College, June 2, 1927.

18. Certain thoughts are prayers. There are moments when, whatever be the attitude of the body, the soul is on its knees. VICTOR HUGO, "Saint Denis," *Les Misérables* (1862), 5.4, tr. Charles E. Wilbour.

19. How ready is heaven to those that pray! BEN JONSON, *Volpone* (1605), 5.12.

20. Affliction teacheth a wicked person sometime to pray; prosperity never. BEN JONSON, "Random Notes," *Timber* (1640).

21. Do not pray for easy lives. Pray to be stronger men. JOHN F. KENNEDY, address, prayer breakfast, Washington, D.C., Feb. 7, 1963.

22. Prayer is a strong wall and fortress of the church; it is a goodly Christian's weapon. MARTIN LUTHER, *Table Talk* (1569).

23. Who rises from prayer a better man, his prayer is answered. GEORGE MEREDITH, *The Ordeal of Richard Feverel* (1859), 12.

24. There are few men who durst publish to the world the prayers they make to Almighty God. MONTAIGNE, "Of prayers," *Essays* (1580–88), Charles Cotton and W. C. Hazlitt.

25. Today any successful and competent businessman will employ the latest and best-tested methods in production, distribution, and administration, and many are discovering that one of the greatest of all efficiency methods is prayer power. NORMAN VINCENT PEALE, *The Power of Positive Thinking* (1952), 4.

26. In his prayers he says, thy will be done: but means his own, at least acts so. WILLIAM PENN, *Some Fruits of Solitude* (1693), 1.26.

27. Pray to God but continue to row to the shore. RUSSIAN PROVERB.

28. Prayer, among sane people, has never superseded practical efforts to secure the desired end. GEORGE SANTAYANA, *The Life of Reason: Reason in Religion* (1905–06), 4.

29. My words fly up, my thoughts remain below. / Words without thoughts never to heaven go. SHAKESPEARE, *Hamlet* (1600), 3.3.97.

30. Complaint is the largest tribute Heaven receives, and the sincerest part of our devotion. JONATHAN SWIFT, *Thoughts on Various Subjects* (1711).

31. More things are wrought by prayer / Than this world dreams of. ALFRED, LORD TENNYSON, "The Passing of Arthur," *Idylls of the King* (1869).

32. What are men better than sheep or goats / That nourish a blind life within the brain, / If knowing God, they lift not hands of prayer / Both for themselves and those who call them friend? ALFRED, LORD TENNYSON, "The Passing of Arthur," *Idylls of the King* (1869).

33. You can't pray a lie. MARK TWAIN, *The Adventures of Huckleberry Finn* (1884), 31.

34. In prayer we call ourselves "worms of the dust," but it is only on a sort of tacit understanding that the remark shall not be taken at par. MARK TWAIN, "Does the Race of Man Love a Lord?" *North American Review*, April 1902.

35. We offer up prayers to God only because we have made Him after our own image. We treat Him like a pasha, or a sultan, who is capable of being exasperated and appeased. VOLTAIRE, "Prayer," *Philosophical Dictionary* (1764).

## 718. PREACHING AND PREACHERS

**See also 126. Churchgoing; 136. Clergy**

1. He that does not know how wisely to meddle with public affairs in preaching the gospel, does not know how to preach the gospel. HENRY WARD BEECHER, *Proverbs from Plymouth Pulpit* (1887).

2. He preaches well that lives well. CERVANTES, *Don Quixote* (1605–15), 2.3.20, tr. Peter Motteux and John Ozell.

3. Sermons remain one of the last forms of public discourse where it is culturally forbidden to talk back. HARVEY COX, *The Secular City* (1966), 10.

4. The sermon which I write inquisitive of truth is good a year after, but that which is written because a sermon must be writ is musty the next day. EMERSON, *Journals*, 1832.

5. Go into one of our cool churches, and begin to count the words that might be spared, and in most places the entire sermon will go. EMERSON, *Journals*, 1834.

6. Among provocatives, the next best thing to good preaching is bad preaching. EMERSON, *Journals*, 1836.

7. There are many preachers who don't hear themselves. GERMAN PROVERB.

8. What do our clergy lose by reading their sermons? They lose preaching, the preaching of the voice in many cases, the preaching of the eye almost always. JULIUS CHARLES HARE and AUGUSTUS WILLIAM HARE, *Guesses at Truth* (1827).

9. The preacher's garment is cut according to the pattern of that of the hearers, for the most part. OLIVER WENDELL HOLMES, SR., *Over the Teacups* (1891), 10.

10. A woman's preaching is like a dog's walking on his hind legs. It is not done well, but you are surprised to find it done at all. SAMUEL JOHNSON, quoted in Boswell's *Life of Samuel Johnson*, July 31, 1763.

11. He that has but one word of God before him, and out of that word cannot make a sermon, can never be a preacher. MARTIN LUTHER, *Table Talk* (1569), 10.

12. Preaching has become a by-word for a long and dull conversation of any kind; and whoever wishes to imply, in any piece of writing, the absence of everything agreeable and inviting, calls it a sermon. SYDNEY SMITH, quoted in Lady S. Holland's *Memoir* (1855), v. 1.3.

13. The preaching of divines helps to preserve well-inclined men in the course of virtue, but seldom or never reclaims the vicious. JONATHAN SWIFT, *Thoughts on Various Subjects* (1711).

## PREDICTION

**See 366. Future; 709. Portent; 741. Prophecies; 1027. Vision**

## 719. PREFERENCE

**See also 122. Choice; 957. Taste**

1. The Soul selects her own Society— / Then—shuts the Door— / To her divine Majority— / Present no more—. EMILY DICKINSON, poem (c. 1862).

2. There is no banquet but some dislike something in it. THOMAS FULLER, M.D., *Gnomologia* (1732), 4904.

3. There are as many preferences as there are men. HORACE, *Satires* (35–30 B.C.), 2.1.

4. I don't care anything about reasons, but I know what I like. HENRY JAMES, *The Portrait of a Lady* (1881), 24.

5. Esteem must be founded on some sort of preference. Bestow it on everybody and it ceases to have any meaning at all. MOLIÈRE, *The Misanthrope* (1666), 1, tr. John Wood.

6. Let us prefer, let us not exclude. JOSEPH ROUX, *Meditations of a Parish Priest* (1886), 5.5, tr. Isabel F. Hapgood.

7. I know of no redeeming qualities in myself but a sincere love for some things, and when I am reproved I fall back on to this ground. THOREAU, "Sunday," *A Week on the Concord and Merrimack Rivers* (1849).

### PREJUDICE, RACIAL

See 769. Racial Prejudice

## 720. PREJUDICES

See also 262. Dogmatism; 498. Intolerance; 613. Narrowness

1. Prejudice, n. A vagrant opinion without visible means of support. AMBROSE BIERCE, *The Devil's Dictionary* (1881–1911).

2. Our prejudices are our mistresses; reason is at best our wife, very often heard indeed, but seldom minded. LORD CHESTERFIELD, *Letters to His Son*, April 13, 1752.

3. We hate some persons because we do not know them; and we will not know them because we hate them. CHARLES CALEB COLTON, *Lacon* (1825), 1.103.

4. As in political so in literary action a man wins friends for himself mostly by the passion of his prejudices and by the consistent narrowness of his outlook. JOSEPH CONRAD, "A Familiar Preface," *A Personal Record* (1912).

5. There is no prejudice so strong as that which arises from a fancied exemption from all prejudice. WILLIAM HAZLITT, "On the Tendency of Sects," *The Round Table* (1817).

6. Prejudice is the child of ignorance. WILLIAM HAZLITT, "On Prejudice," *Sketches and Essays* (1839).

7. Prejudice is never easy unless it can pass itself off for reason. WILLIAM HAZLITT, "On Prejudice," *Sketches and Essays* (1839).

8. Dogs bark at a person whom they do not know. HERACLITUS, *Fragments* (c. 500 B.C.), 90, tr. Philip Wheelwright.

9. The world is like a map of antipathies, almost of hates, in which everyone picks the symbolic color of his difference. JUAN RAMÓN JIMÉNEZ, "Heroic Reason," *Selected Writings* (1957), tr. H. R. Hays.

10. The tendency of the casual mind is to pick out or stumble upon a sample which supports or defies its prejudices, and then to make it the representative of a whole class. WALTER LIPPMANN, *Public Opinion* (1929), 3.10.

11. Order a purge for your brain, it will there be much better employed than upon your stomach. MONTAIGNE, "Of the resemblance of children to their fathers," *Essays* (1580–88), tr. Charles Cotton and W. C. Hazlitt.

12. Knowledge humanizes mankind, and reason inclines to mildness; but prejudices eradicate every tender disposition. MONTESQUIEU, *L'Esprit des lois* (1748), 15.3.

13. Everyone is a prisoner of his own experiences. No one can eliminate prejudices —just recognize them. EDWARD R. MURROW, Dec. 31, 1955.

14. No man is prejudiced in favor of a thing knowing it to be wrong. He is attached to it on the belief of its being right. THOMAS PAINE, *The Rights of Man* (1791), 2.

15. Some men, under the notion of weeding out prejudices, eradicate virtue, honesty, and religion. JONATHAN SWIFT, *Thoughts on Various Subjects* (1711).

16. We are chameleons, and our partialities and prejudices change places with an easy and blessed facility. MARK TWAIN, "When in Doubt, Tell the Truth," *Speeches* (1923), ed. A. B. Paine.

## 721. PREMATURENESS

See also 228. Delay; 972. Timeliness

1. Boast not thyself of tomorrow; for thou knowest not what a day may bring forth. *Bible*, Proverbs 27:1.

2. Do not climb the hill until you get to it. ENGLISH PROVERB.

3. Praise not the day before night. THOMAS FULLER, M.D., *Gnomologia* (1732), 3919.

4. Sell not the bear's skin before you have caught him. THOMAS FULLER, M.D., *Gnomologia* (1732), 4095.

5. The wise at nightfall praise the day, / The wife when she has passed away, / The ice when it is crossed, the bride / When tumbled, and the horse when tried. VLADIMIR NABOKOV, "Commentary," *Pale Fire* (1962), 79.

6. Count no mortal happy till / he has passed the final limit of his life secure from pain. SOPHOCLES, *Oedipus the King* (c. 430 B.C.), tr. David Grene.

## 722. PREPAREDNESS
See also 356. Forethought

1. We are all, it seems, saving ourselves for the Senior Prom. But many of us forget that somewhere along the way we must learn to dance. ALAN HARRINGTON, *Life in the Crystal Palace* (1959).

2. For all your days prepare, / And meet them all alike: / When you are the anvil, bear – / When you are the hammer, strike. EDWIN MARKHAM, "Preparedness" (1918).

3. A forewarned man is worth two. SPANISH PROVERB.

4. Shape your heart to front the hour, but dream not that the hour will last. ALFRED, LORD TENNYSON, "Locksley Hall Sixty Years After" (1886), 106.

## 723. PRESENT
See also 366. Future; 669. Past

1. All our yesterdays are summarized in our now, and all the tomorrows are ours to shape. HAL BORLAND, "The Tomorrows – December 30," *Sundial of the Seasons* (1964).

2. The Will-be and the Has-been touch us more nearly than the Is. So we are more tender towards children and old people than to those who are in the prime of life. SAMUEL BUTLER (d. 1902), "Higgledy-Piggledy," *Note-Books* (1912).

3. Real generosity toward the future lies in giving all to the present. ALBERT CAMUS, "Beyond Nihilism," *The Rebel* (1951), tr. Anthony Bower.

4. The present time has one advantage over every other – it is our own. CHARLES CALEB COLTON, *Lacon* (1825), 1.81.

5. I would not fear nor wish my fate, / But boldly say each night, / To-morrow let my sun his beams display, / Or in clouds hide them; I have lived today. ABRAHAM COWLEY, "Of Myself" (17th c.).

6. It is the fashion to style the present moment an extraordinary crisis. BENJAMIN DISRAELI, speech, High Wycombe, Dec. 16, 1834.

7. Happy the man, and happy he alone, / He who can call to-day his own; / He who, secure within, can say, / To-morrow, do thy worst, for I have lived to-day. JOHN DRYDEN, *Imitation of Horace* (1697), 3.29.65.

8. The vanishing, volatile froth of the Present which any shadow will alter, any thought blow away, any event annihilate, is every moment converted into the Adamantine Record of the Past. EMERSON, *Journals*, 1832.

9. With the Past, as past, I have nothing to do; nor with the Future as future. I live now, and will verify all past history in my own moments. EMERSON, *Journals*, 1839.

10. We can see well into the past; we can guess shrewdly into the future; but that which is rolled up and muffled in impenetrable folds is today. EMERSON, *Journals*, 1854.

11. We live between two dense clouds – the forgetting of what was and the uncertainty of what will be. ANATOLE FRANCE, *Sur la pierre blanche* (1903), 2.

12. If we could wake each morning with no memory / Of living before we went to sleep, we might / Arrive at a faultless day, once in a great many. CHRISTOPHER FRY, *The Dark Is Light Enough* (1954), 2.

13. Today is yesterday's pupil. THOMAS FULLER, M.D., *Gnomologia* (1732), 5153.

14. Every situation – nay, every moment – is of infinite worth; for it is the representative of a whole eternity. GOETHE, quoted in Johann Peter Eckermann's *Conversations with Goethe*, Nov. 3, 1823.

15. No mind is much employed upon the present; recollection and anticipation fill up almost all our moments. SAMUEL JOHNSON, *Rasselas* (1759), 30.

16. The present, like a note in music, is nothing but as it appertains to what is past and what is to come. WALTER SAVAGE LANDOR, "Aesop and Rhodope," *Imaginary Conversations* (1824–53).

17. Each day the world is born anew / For him who takes it rightly. JAMES RUSSELL LOWELL, "Gold Egg: A Dream-Fantasy," *Under the Willows and Other Poems* (1868).

18. To disdain to-day is to prove that yesterday has been misunderstood. MAURICE MAETERLINCK, *Wisdom and Destiny* (1898), 94, tr. Alfred Sutro.

19. Remember that the sole life which a man can lose is that which he is living at the moment. MARCUS AURELIUS, *Meditations* (2nd c.), 2.14, tr. Maxwell Staniforth.

20. It is not the weight of the future or

the past that is pressing upon you, but ever that of the present alone. Even this burden, too, can be lessened if you confine it strictly to its own limits. MARCUS AURELIUS, *Meditations* (2nd c.), 8.36, tr. Maxwell Staniforth.

21. Each day provides its own gifts. MARTIAL, *Epigrams* (A.D. 86), 8.78, tr. Walter C. A. Ker.

22. The passing moment is all we can be sure of; it is only common sense to extract its utmost value from it; the future will one day be the present and will seem as unimportant as the present does now. W. SOMERSET MAUGHAM, *The Summing Up* (1938), 15.

23. The word "now" is like a bomb through the window, and it ticks. ARTHUR MILLER, *After the Fall* (1964).

24. Ah, take the Cash, and let the Credit go, / Nor heed the rumble of a distant Drum! OMAR KHAYYÁM, *Rubáiyát* (11th–12th c.), tr. Edward FitzGerald, 4th ed., 13.

25. The only living life is in the past and future—the present is an interlude—strange interlude in which we call on past and future to bear witness we are living. EUGENE O'NEILL, *Strange Interlude* (1928), 8.

26. The present offers itself to our touch for only an instant of time and then eludes the senses. PLUTARCH, "Contentment," *Moralia* (c. A.D. 100), tr. Moses Hadas.

27. Past, and to come, seems best; things present, worst. SHAKESPEARE, *2 Henry IV* (1597–98), 1.3.108.

28. I am in the present. I cannot know what tomorrow will bring forth. I can know only what the truth is for me today. That is what I am called upon to serve, and I serve it in all lucidity. IGOR STRAVINSKY, *An Autobiography* (1936), 10.

29. Do not say, "It is morning," and dismiss it with a name of yesterday. See it for the first time as a new-born child that has no name. RABINDRANATH TAGORE, *Stray Birds* (1916), 233.

30. Today's egg is better than tomorrow's hen. TURKISH PROVERB.

## 724. PRESIDENCY

**See also 393. Government; 755. Public Office**

1. Presidency, n. The greased pig in the field game of American politics. AMBROSE BIERCE, *The Devil's Dictionary* (1881–1911).

2. Th' prisidincy is th' highest office in th' gift iv th' people. Th' vice-prisidincy is th' next highest an' the lowest. It isn't a crime exactly. Ye can't be sint to jail f'r it, but it's a kind iv a disgrace. FINLEY PETER DUNNE, "The Vice-President," *Dissertations by Mr. Dooley* (1906).

3. No *easy* problems ever come to the President of the United States. If they are easy to solve, somebody else has solved them. DWIGHT D. EISENHOWER, quoted by John F. Kennedy, *Parade*, April 8, 1962.

4. The second office of this government is honorable and easy, the first is but a splendid misery. THOMAS JEFFERSON, letter to Elbridge Gerry, May 13, 1797.

5. Extremism in the pursuit of the Presidency is an unpardonable vice. Moderation in the affairs of the nation is the highest virtue. LYNDON B. JOHNSON, speech, New York City, Oct. 31, 1964.

6. A President's hardest task is not to do what is right, but to know what is right. LYNDON B. JOHNSON, State of the Union Message, Jan. 4, 1965.

7. The function and responsibility of the President is to set before the American people the unfinished business, the things we must do if we are going to succeed as a nation. JOHN F. KENNEDY, campaign remarks, Crestwood, Mo., Oct. 22, 1960.

8. When we got into office, the thing that surprised me most was to find that things were just as bad as we'd been saying they were. JOHN F. KENNEDY, address, dinner honoring his 44th birthday, Washington, D.C., May 27, 1961.

9. I know that when things don't go well they like to blame the Presidents, and that is one of the things which Presidents are paid for. JOHN F. KENNEDY, news conference, June 14, 1962.

10. In the White House, the future rapidly becomes the past; and delay is itself a decision. THEODORE SORENSEN, *Nation's Business*, June 1963.

11. You know how it is in an election year. They pick a president and then for four years they pick on him. ADLAI STEVENSON, speech, Aug. 28, 1952.

12. In America any boy may become President and I suppose it's just one of the risks he takes. ADLAI STEVENSON, speech, Indianapolis, Ind., Sept. 26, 1952.

13. The President is the representative of

the whole nation and he's the only lobbyist that all the 160 million people in this country have. HARRY S. TRUMAN, lecture, Columbia University, April 27, 1959.

14. The American Presidency, it occurs to us, is merely a way station en route to the blessed condition of being an ex-President. JOHN UPDIKE, "Eisenhower's Eloquence," *Assorted Prose* (1965).

## 725. PRESS, FREEDOM OF THE

**See also 111. Censorship; 256. Dissent; 362. Free Speech; 623. Newspapers; 758. Publishing; 817. Rights**

1. Freedom of the press is not an end in itself but a means to the end of a free society. FELIX FRANKFURTER. *The New York Times*, Nov. 28, 1954.

2. The liberty of the press is most generally approved when it takes liberties with the other fellow, and leaves us alone. EDGAR WATSON HOWE, *Country Town Sayings* (1911).

3. I du believe with all my soul / In the gret Press's freedom, / To pint the people to the goal / An' in the traces lead 'em. JAMES RUSSELL LOWELL, *The Biglow Papers: First Series* (1848), 6.

4. The freedom of the press is one of the great bulwarks of liberty, and can never be restrained but by despotic government. GEORGE MASON, Virginia Bill of Rights, June 12, 1776.

5. A free press stands as one of the great interpreters between the government and the people. To allow it to be fettered is to be fettered ourselves. JUSTICE GEORGE SUTHERLAND, *Grosjean v. American Press Co.* (1935).

6. In America, the majority raises formidable barriers around the liberty of opinion: within these barriers, an author may write what he pleases; but woe to him if he goes beyond them. ALEXIS DE TOCQUEVILLE, *Democracy in America* (1835–39), 1.15.

7. We write frankly and freely but then we "modify" before we print. MARK TWAIN, *Life on the Mississippi* (1883).

## PRETENSE

**See 162. Concealment; 221. Deception; 438. Hypocrisy; 448. Imagination; 726. Pretension**

## 726. PRETENSION

**See also 45. Appearance; 449. Imitation; 482. Insincerity; 819. Role-playing; 1020. Vanity**

1. The frog tried to look as big as the elephant, and burst. AFRICAN PROVERB.

2. Excusations, cessions, modesty itself well governed, are but arts of ostentation. FRANCIS BACON, "Of Vain-Glory," *Essays* (1625).

3. Affectation is a greater enemy to the face than small-pox. ENGLISH PROVERB.

4. Nothing is lasting that is feigned. ENGLISH PROVERB.

5. All human beings have gray little souls—and they all want to rouge them up. MAXIM GORKY, *The Lower Depths* (1903), 3, tr. Alexander Bakshy.

6. Some degree of affectation is as necessary to the mind as dress is to the body; we must overact our part in some measure, in order to produce any effect at all. WILLIAM HAZLITT, "On Cant and Hypocrisy," *Sketches and Essays* (1839).

7. We all wear some disguise, make some professions, use some artifice, to set ourselves off as being better than we are; and yet it is not denied that we have some good intentions and praiseworthy qualities at bottom. WILLIAM HAZLITT, "On Cant and Hypocrisy," *Sketches and Essays* (1839).

8. Hypocrisy is the necessary burden of villainy, affectation part of the chosen trappings of folly; the one completes a villain, the other only finishes a fop. SAMUEL JOHNSON, *The Rambler* (1750–52), 20

9. Almost every man wastes part of his life in attempts to display qualities which he does not possess, and to gain applause which he cannot keep. SAMUEL JOHNSON, *The Rambler* (1750–52), 189.

10. Coyness is a rather comically pathetic fault, a miscalculation in which, by trying to veil the ego, we let it appear stark naked. LOUIS KRONENBERGER, "Reflections and Complaints of Late Middle Age," *The Cart and the Horse* (1964), 3.

11. The qualities we have do not make us so ridiculous as those which we affect. LA ROCHEFOUCAULD, *Maxims* (1665), tr. Kenneth Pratt.

12. Nothing prevents our being natural so much as the desire to appear so. LA ROCHEFOUCAULD, *Maxims* (1665).

13. Affectation is an awkward and forced imitation of what should be genuine and easy, wanting the beauty that accompanies what is natural. JOHN LOCKE, *Some Thoughts Concerning Education* (1693), 66.

14. It is in vain that we get upon stilts, for, once on them, it is still with our legs that we must walk. And on the highest throne in the world we are still sitting on our own ass. MONTAIGNE, "Of experience," *Essays* (1580–88).

15. Pretending is a virtue. If you can't pretend, you can't be king. LUIGI PIRANDELLO, *Liolà* (1916), 1, tr. Eric Bentley and Gerardo Guerrieri.

16. Those who wish to seem learned to fools, seem fools to the learned. QUINTILIAN, *Institutio Oratoria* (c. A.D. 95), 10.7, tr. Clyde Murley.

17. All-glorious within us are our gay pretensions, but when they escape from our lips, how are they bereft of their glory! LOGAN PEARSALL SMITH, *Afterthoughts* (1931), 1.

## 727. PRIDE

**See also 87. Boasting; 155. Complacency; 163. Conceit; 433. Humility; 862. Self-esteem; 865. Self-importance; 869. Self-love; 903. Snobbery; 1020. Vanity**

1. There are two sorts of pride: one in which we approve ourselves, the other in which we cannot accept ourselves. HENRI FRÉDÉRIC AMIEL, *Journal*, Oct. 27, 1853.

2. Vanity is a static thing. It puts its faith in what it has, and is easily wounded. Pride is active, and satisfied only with what it can do, hence accustomed not to feel small stings. JACQUES BARZUN, *The House of Intellect* (1959), 3.

3. It's a fine thing to rise above pride, but you must have pride in order to do so. GEORGES BERNANOS, *The Diary of a Country Priest* (1936), 7, tr. Pamela Morris.

4. Pride goeth before destruction, and an haughty spirit before a fall. *Bible*, Proverbs 16:18.

5. Pride, like the magnet, constantly points to one object, self; but, unlike the magnet, it has no attractive pole, but at all points repels. CHARLES CALEB COLTON, *Lacon* (1825), 1.111.

6. The proud man places himself at a distance from other men; seen through that distance, others perhaps appear little to him; but he forgets that this very distance causes him to appear equally little to others. CHARLES CALEB COLTON, *Lacon* (1825), 1.150.

7. There is a paradox in pride—it makes some men ridiculous, but prevents others from becoming so. CHARLES CALEB COLTON, *Lacon* (1825), 1.207.

8. Pride, avarice, and envy are the tongues men know and heed, a Babel of despair. DANTE, "Inferno," 6, *The Divine Comedy* (c. 1300–21), tr. John Ciardi.

9. When a proud man hears another praised, he thinks himself injured. ENGLISH PROVERB.

10. Pride is said to be the last vice the good man gets clear of. BENJAMIN FRANKLIN, *Poor Richard's Almanack* (1732–57).

11. Pride that dines on vanity sups on contempt. BENJAMIN FRANKLIN, "The Way to Wealth" (July 7, 1757).

12. Pride, perceiving humility honourable, often borrows her cloak. THOMAS FULLER, M.D., *Gnomologia* (1732), 3948.

13. A proud man is satisfied with his own good opinion, and does not seek to make converts to it. WILLIAM HAZLITT, *Characteristics* (1823), 98.

14. The truly proud man knows neither superiors nor inferiors. The first he does not admit of—the last he does not concern himself about. WILLIAM HAZLITT, *Characteristics* (1823), 112.

15. Pride is the mask of one's own faults. HEBREW PROVERB.

16. Pride is seldom delicate; it will please itself with very mean advantages. SAMUEL JOHNSON, *Rasselas* (1759), 9.

17. It is as proper to have pride in oneself as it is ridiculous to show it to others. LA ROCHEFOUCAULD, *Maxims* (1665), tr. Kenneth Pratt.

18. Pride dwells in the thought; the tongue can have but a very little share in it. MONTAIGNE, "Use makes perfect," *Essays* (1580–88), tr. Charles Cotton and W. C. Hazlitt.

19. While you are still beautiful and Life still woos, it is such a fine gesture of disdainful pride to jilt it. EUGENE O'NEILL, *More Stately Mansions* (1964), 1.1.

20. The hurricane does not uproot grasses, which are pliant and bow low before it on every side. It is only the lofty trees that it attacks. *Panchatantra* (c. 5th c.), 1, tr. Franklin Edgerton.

21. There is but a step between a proud man's glory and his disgrace. PUBLILIUS SYRUS, *Moral Sayings* (1st c. B.C.), 138, tr. Darius Lyman.

22. I do not believe that any peacock envies another peacock his tail, because every peacock is persuaded that his own tail is the finest in the world. The consequence of this is that peacocks are peaceable birds. BERTRAND RUSSELL, *The Conquest of Happiness* (1930), 6.

23. All men who would surpass the other animals should do their best not to pass through life silently like the beasts whom nature made prone, obedient to their bellies. SALLUST, *Conspiracy of Catiline* (1st c. B.C.), 1.

24. He that is proud eats up himself. Pride is his own glass, his own trumpet, his own chronicle; and whatever praises itself but in the deed, devours the deed in the praise. SHAKESPEARE, *Troilus and Cressida* (1601–02), 2.3.164.

25. Pride is over-estimation of oneself by reason of self-love. SPINOZA, *Ethics* (1677), 3, tr. Andrew Boyle.

26. None are more taken in by flattery than the proud, who wish to be the first and are not. SPINOZA, *Ethics* (1677), 4, tr. Andrew Boyle.

27. Pride destroys all symmetry and grace, and affectation is a more terrible enemy to fine faces than the small-pox. RICHARD STEELE, *The Spectator* (1711–12), 33.

28. Dust are our frames; and, gilded dust, our pride / Looks only for a moment whole and sound. ALFRED, LORD TENNYSON, "Aylmer's Field" (1864).

29. Don't let that chip on your shoulder be your only reason for walking erect. JAMES THURBER, "Midnight at Tim's Place," *Lanterns and Lances* (1961).

## PRIESTS

See 136. Clergy

## 728. PRINCIPLE

See also 489. Integrity; 816. Right

1. Principle never forgives and its logic is to kill. JACQUES BARZUN, *The House of Intellect* (1959), 6.

2. Expedients are for the hour, but principles are for the ages. HENRY WARD BEECHER, *Proverbs from Plymouth Pulpit* (1887).

3. We speak of being anchored to our principles. But if the weather turns nasty you up with an anchor and let it down where there's less wind, and the fishing's better. ROBERT BOLT, *A Man for All Seasons* (1962), 1.

4. Men of principle are sure to be bold, but those who are bold may not always be men of principle. CONFUCIUS, *Analects* (6th c. B.C.), 14.5, tr. James Legge.

5. General principles are not the less true or important because from their nature they elude immediate observation; they are like the air, which is not the less necessary because we neither see nor feel it. WILLIAM HAZLITT, "Edmund Burke," *The Eloquence of the British Senate* (1807).

6. Amid the pressure of great events, a general principle gives no help. HEGEL, introduction to *Philosophy of History* (1832), tr. John Sibree.

7. Everywhere the basis of principle is tradition. OLIVER WENDELL HOLMES, JR., speech, Boston, Jan. 8, 1897.

8. A man is usually more careful of his money than he is of his principles. EDGAR WATSON HOWE, *Ventures in Common Sense* (1919), 30.4.

9. A man may be very sincere in good principles, without having good practice. SAMUEL JOHNSON, quoted in Boswell's *Journal of a Tour to the Hebrides with Samuel Johnson*, Oct. 25, 1773.

10. Principles—and I have in mind such principles as states' rights or national sovereignty or the free market or pacifism—have a way of drying up while the sap of life goes flowing in another direction. MAX LERNER, "Politics and the Connective Tissue," *Actions and Passions* (1949).

11. A marciful Providunce fashioned us holler / O' purpose thet we might our princerples swaller. JAMES RUSSELL LOWELL, *The Biglow Papers: First Series* (1848), 4.

12. Manners with fortunes, humours turn with climes, / Tenets with books, and principles with times. ALEXANDER POPE, *Moral Essays* (1731–35), 1.172.

13. The fate of America cannot depend on any one man. The greatness of America is grounded in principles and not on any single personality. FRANKLIN D. ROOSE-

VELT, speech, New York City, Nov. 5, 1932.

14. Ideas and principles that do harm are, as a rule, though not always, cloaks for evil passions. BERTRAND RUSSELL, "Ideas That Have Harmed Mankind," *Unpopular Essays* (1950).

15. It is often easier to fight for principles than to live up to them. ADLAI STEVENSON, speech, New York City, Aug. 27, 1952.

16. One of the most ordinary weaknesses of the human intellect is to seek to reconcile contrary principles, and to purchase peace at the expense of logic. ALEXIS DE TOCQUEVILLE, *Democracy in America* (1835–39), 2.1.6.

17. Prosperity is the best protector of principle. MARK TWAIN, "Pudd'nhead Wilson's New Calendar," *Following the Equator* (1897), 2.2.

18. There comes a time when it is good for a nation to know that it must sacrifice if need be everything that it has to vindicate the principles which it possesses. WOODROW WILSON, address, Washington, D.C., June 5, 1917.

## PRINTING

See 758. Publishing

## 729. PRISON

See also 107. Captivity

1. All prisons are brimming over with innocence. It is those who cram their fellows into them, in the name of empty ideas, who are the only guilty ones. JEAN ANOUILH, *Catch as Catch Can* (1960), tr. Lucienne Hill.

2. In prison, those things withheld from and denied to the prisoner become precisely what he wants most of all. ELDRIDGE CLEAVER, "On Becoming," *Soul on Ice* (1968).

3. Wherever any one is against his will, that is to him a prison. EPICTETUS, *Discourses* (2nd c.), 1.7, tr. Thomas W. Higginson.

4. A prison is a house of care, a place where none can thrive; / A touchstone true to try a friend, a grave for one alive. / Sometimes a place of right, sometimes a place of wrong, / Sometimes a place of rogues and thieves and honest men among. Inscription on Edinburgh's old Tolbooth prison (demolished in 1817).

5. Stone walls do not a prison make, / Nor iron bars a cage; / Minds innocent and quiet take / That for an hermitage. RICHARD LOVELACE, "To Althea from Prison" (1649), 4.

6. Prison is not a mere physical horror. It is using a pickaxe to no purpose that makes a prison. SAINT-EXUPÉRY, *Wind, Sand, and Stars* (1939), 9.6, tr. Lewis Galantière.

7. I know not whether Laws be right, / Or whether Laws be wrong; / All that we know who lie in gaol / Is that the wall is strong; / And that each day is like a year, / A year whose days are long. OSCAR WILDE, *The Ballad of Reading Gaol* (1898), 5.1.

8. Every prison that men build / Is built with bricks of shame, / And bound with bars lest Christ should see / How men their brothers maim. OSCAR WILDE, *The Ballad of Reading Gaol* (1898), 5.3.

9. The vilest deeds like poison weeds / Bloom well in prison-air: / It is only what is good in Man / That wastes and withers there: / Pale Anguish keeps the heavy gate, / And the warder is Despair. OSCAR WILDE, *The Ballad of Reading Gaol* (1898), 5.5.

## 730. PRIVACY

See also 754. Publicity; 908. Solitude

1. The saint and poet seek privacy to ends the most public and universal. EMERSON, "Culture," *The Conduct of Life* (1860).

2. A hedge between keeps friendship green. GERMAN PROVERB.

3. The human animal needs a freedom seldom mentioned, freedom from intrusion. He needs a little privacy quite as much as he wants understanding or vitamins or exercise or praise. PHYLLIS MC GINLEY, "A Lost Privilege," *The Province of the Heart* (1959).

4. In a crowd, on a journey, at a banquet even, a line of thought can itself provide its own seclusion. QUINTILIAN, *Institutio Oratoria* (c. A.D. 95), 10.3, tr. Clyde Murley.

5. In large Victorian houses with many rooms and heavy doors, the occupants could be mysterious and exciting to one another in a way that those who live in rackety developments can never hope to be. Not even the lust of a Lord Byron could survive

the fact of Levittown. GORE VIDAL, "On Pornography," *New York Review of Books*, March 31, 1966.

### PRIVILEGE
See 15. Advantage

### 731. PROBLEMS
See also 579. Method

1. What concerns everyone can only be resolved by everyone. FRIEDRICH DÜRRENMATT, "21 Points," *The Physicists* (1962), tr. James Kirkup.

2. Everything has two handles, one by which it may be borne, another by which it cannot. EPICTETUS, *Enchiridion* (2nd c.), 43, tr. Thomas W. Higginson.

3. Problems worthy / of attack / prove their worth / by hitting back. PIET HEIN, "Problems," *Grooks* (1966).

4. Problems are only opportunities in work clothes. HENRY J. KAISER (1882–1967), maxim.

5. Our problems are man-made, therefore they may be solved by man. And man can be as big as he wants. No problem of human destiny is beyond human beings. JOHN F. KENNEDY, address, The American University, Washington, D.C., June 10, 1963.

### PROCRASTINATION
ee 228. Delay

### PROFANITY
See 950. Swearing

### PROFESSIONS
See 1029. Vocations

### 732. PROFITEERING
See also 102. Business and Commerce; 103. Buying and Selling

1. When a man sells eleven ounces for twelve, he makes a compact with the devil, and sells himself for the value of an ounce. HENRY WARD BEECHER, *Proverbs from Plymouth Pulpit* (1887).

2. He that maketh haste to be rich shall not be innocent. *Bible*, Proverbs 28:20.

3. Prefer a loss to a dishonest gain: the one brings pain at the moment, the other for all time. CHILON (6th c. B.C.), quoted in Diogenes Laertius' *Lives and Opinions of Eminent Philosophers* (3rd c. A.D.), tr. R. D. Hicks.

4. What is a man if he is not a thief who openly charges as much as he can for the goods he sells? MOHANDAS K. GANDHI, *Non-Violence in Peace and War* (1948), 2.124.

5. Gain not base gains; base gains are the same as losses. HESIOD, *Works and Days* (8th c. B.C.), 353, tr. J. Banks.

6. The smell of profit is clean / And sweet, whatever the source. JUVENAL, *Satires* (c. 100), 14.204, tr. Hubert Creekmore.

7. He who wishes to be rich in a day will be hanged in a year. LEONARDO DA VINCI, *Notebooks* (c. 1500), tr. Jean Paul Richter.

8. Beware of that profound enemy of the free enterprise system who pays lip-service to free competition—but also labels every anti-trust prosecution as a "persecution." FRANKLIN D. ROOSEVELT, speech, Chicago, Oct. 28, 1944.

9. More men come to doom / through dirty profits than are kept by them. SOPHOCLES, *Antigone* (442–41 B.C.), tr. Elizabeth Wyckoff.

10. Not even a collapsing world looks dark to a man who is about to make his fortune. E. B. WHITE, "Intimations," *One Man's Meat* (1944).

### 733. PROFLIGACY
See also 492. Intemperance; 700. Pleasure-seeking

1. It is the hour to be drunken! To escape being the martyred slaves of time, be ceaselessly drunken. On wine, on poetry, or on virtue, as you wish. CHARLES BAUDELAIRE, "Enivrez-vous," *Paris Spleen* (1869).

2. An unrestricted satisfaction of every need presents itself as the most enticing method of conducting one's life, but it means putting enjoyment before caution, and soon brings its own punishment. SIGMUND FREUD, *Civilization and Its Discontents* (1930), 2, tr. James Strachey.

3. A libertine life is not a life of liberty.

THOMAS FULLER, M.D., *Gnomologia* (1732), 239.

4. The fly that sips treacle is lost in the sweets, / So he that tastes woman, woman, woman, / He that tastes woman, ruin meets. JOHN GAY, *The Beggar's Opera* (1728), 2.8, air 26.

5. Debauchery is perhaps an act of despair in the face of infinity. EDMOND and JULES DE GONCOURT, *Journal*, July 30, 1861, tr. Robert Baldick.

6. Where does the ant die except in sugar? MALAY PROVERB.

7. An orgy looks particularly alluring seen through the mists of righteous indignation. MALCOLM MUGGERIDGE, "Dolce Vita in a Cold Climate," *The Most of Malcolm Muggeridge* (1966).

8. Not joy but joylessness is the mother of debauchery. NIETZSCHE, *Miscellaneous Maxims and Opinions* (1879), 71, tr. Paul V. Cohn.

9. Violent pleasures which reach the soul through the body are generally of this sort—they are reliefs of pain. PLATO, *The Republic* (4th c. B.C.), 9, tr. Benjamin Jowett.

## 734. PROFUNDITY

See also 879. Seriousness; 944. Superficiality; 1053. Wisdom

1. Mystery is not profoundness. CHARLES CALEB COLTON, *Lacon* (1825), 2.57.

2. The profound thinker always suspects that he is superficial. BENJAMIN DISRAELI, *Contarini Fleming* (1832), 4.5.

3. Errors, like straws, upon the surface flow; / He who would search for pearls must dive below. JOHN DRYDEN, prologue to *All for Love* (1678).

4. There's no one so transparent as the person who thinks he's devilish deep. W. SOMERSET MAUGHAM, *Lady Frederick* (1907), 1.

5. Smooth runs the water where the brook is deep. SHAKESPEARE, *2 Henry VI* (1590–91), 3.1.53.

## 735. PROGRESS

See also 306. Evolution

1. A thousand things advance; nine hundred and ninety-nine retreat: that is progress. HENRI FRÉDÉRIC AMIEL, *Journal* (1882–84).

2. Progress, man's distinctive mark alone, / Not God's, and not the beasts': God is, they are; / Man partly is, and wholly hopes to be. ROBERT BROWNING, "A Death in the Desert," *Dramatis Personae* (1864).

3. All progress is based upon a universal innate desire on the part of every organism to live beyond its income. SAMUEL BUTLER (d. 1902), "Lord, What Is Man?" *Note-Books* (1912).

4. The fatal metaphor of progress, which means leaving things behind us, has utterly obscured the real idea of growth, which means leaving things inside us. G. K. CHESTERTON, "The Romance of Rhyme," *Fancies Versus Fads* (1923).

5. The distance from nothing to a little, is ten thousand times more, than from it to the highest degree in this life. JOHN DONNE, *Sermons*, No. 5, 1619.

6. [Progress] is like a merry-go-round. We get up on a speckled wooden horse an' th' mechanical pianny plays a chune an' away we go, hollerin'. We think we're thravellin' like th' divvle but th' man that doesn't care about merry-go-rounds knows that we will come back where we were. FINLEY PETER DUNNE, "Machinery," *Observations by Mr. Dooley* (1902).

7. All that is human must retrograde if it do not advance. EDWARD GIBBON, *Decline and Fall of the Roman Empire* (1776), 71.

8. The world owes all its onward impulses to men ill at ease. The happy man inevitably confines himself within ancient limits. NATHANIEL HAWTHORNE, *The House of the Seven Gables* (1851), 20.

9. In human affairs, the best stimulus for running ahead is to have something we must run from. ERIC HOFFER, *The Ordeal of Change* (1964), 9.

10. The greatest obstacle to progress is not man's inherited pugnacity, but his incorrigible tendency to parasitism. WILLIAM RALPH INGE, "Patriotism," *Outspoken Essays: First Series* (1919).

11. The natural progress of the works of men is from rudeness to convenience, from convenience to elegance, and from elegance to nicety. SAMUEL JOHNSON, *The Idler* (1758–60), 63.

12. The best road to progress is freedom's

road. JOHN F. KENNEDY, message to Congress, March 14, 1961.

13. There can be no progress if people have no faith in tomorrow. JOHN F. KENNEDY, address, Inter-American Press Association, Miami Beach, Fla., Nov. 18, 1963.

14. If freedom makes social progress possible, so social progress strengthens and enlarges freedom. The two are inseparable partners in the great adventure of humanity. ROBERT F. KENNEDY, "Berlin East and West," *The Pursuit of Justice* (1964).

15. All progress is precarious, and the solution of one problem brings us face to face with another problem. MARTIN LUTHER KING, JR., *Strength to Love* (1963), 8.3.

16. Is it progress if a cannibal uses knife and fork? STANISLAW LEC, *Unkempt Thoughts* (1962), tr. Jacek Galazka.

17. Human progress is furthered, not by conformity, but by aberration. H. L. MENCKEN, *Prejudices: Third Series* (1922), 18.

18. Progress—progress is the dirtiest word in the language—who ever told us— / And made us believe it—that to take a step forward was necessarily, was always / A good idea? EDNA ST. VINCENT MILLAY, untitled poem, *Make Bright the Arrows* (1940).

19. Whatever there be of progress in life comes not through adaptation but through daring, through obeying the blind urge. HENRY MILLER, "Reflections on Writing," *The Wisdom of the Heart* (1941).

20. The magnitude of a "progress" is gauged by the greatness of the sacrifice that it requires. NIETZSCHE, *The Genealogy of Morals* (1887), 2.12, tr. Horace B. Samuel.

21. Every step of progress the world has made has been from scaffold to scaffold, and from stake to stake. WENDELL PHILLIPS, speech, Oct. 15, 1851.

22. The desire to understand the world and the desire to reform it are the two great engines of progress, without which human society would stand still or retrogress. BERTRAND RUSSELL, "The Place of Sex Among Human Values," *Marriage and Morals* (1929).

23. The reasonable man adapts himself to the world: the unreasonable one persists in trying to adapt the world to himself. Therefore all progress depends on the unreasonable man. GEORGE BERNARD SHAW, "Maxims for Revolutionists," *Man and Superman* (1903).

24. Nothing is ever done in this world until men are prepared to kill one another if it is not done. GEORGE BERNARD SHAW, *Major Barbara* (1905), 4.

25. All progress means war with Society. GEORGE BERNARD SHAW, *Getting Married* (1911).

26. Let's talk sense to the American people. Let's tell them the truth, that there are no gains without pains. ADLAI STEVENSON, acceptance speech, Democratic National Convention, July 26, 1952.

27. I doubt not through the ages one increasing purpose runs, / And the thoughts of men are widened with the process of the suns. ALFRED, LORD TENNYSON, "Locksley Hall" (1842).

28. We have our arts, the ancients had theirs.... We cannot raise obelisks a hundred feet high in a single piece, but our meridians are more exact. VOLTAIRE, "Antiquity," *Philosophical Dictionary* (1764).

29. The policy of man consists, at first, in endeavoring to arrive at a state equal to that of animals, whom nature has furnished with food, clothing, and shelter. VOLTAIRE, "Policy," *Philosophical Dictionary* (1764).

30. In the past human life was lived in a bullock cart; in the future it will be lived in an aeroplane; and the change of speed amounts to a difference in quality. ALFRED NORTH WHITEHEAD, *Science and the Modern World* (1925), 6.

31. The simple faith in progress is not a conviction belonging to strength, but one belonging to acquiescence and hence to weakness. NORBERT WIENER, *The Human Use of Human Beings* (1954), 2.

32. Progress imposes not only new possibilities for the future but new restrictions. NORBERT WIENER, *The Human Use of Human Beings* (1954), 2.

## 736. PROMISCUITY

**See also 470. Infidelity; 851. Seduction; 885. Sex**

1. Like the bee its sting, the promiscuous leave behind them in each encounter something of themselves by which they are made

to suffer. CYRIL CONNOLLY, *The Unquiet Grave* (1945), 2.

2. Give but a grain of the heart's rich seed, / Confine some under cover, / And when love goes, bid him God-speed. / And find another lover. COUNTEE CULLEN, "Song in Spite of Myself," *On These I Stand* (1947).

3. A friend to all is a friend to none. THOMAS FULLER, M.D., *Gnomologia* (1732), 120.

4. Loving everybody is polygamy. I care for no friend who loves his enemy equally well. EDGAR WATSON HOWE, *Ventures in Common Sense* (1919), 15.5.

5. Accursed from birth they be / Who seek to find monogamy, / Pursuing it from bed to bed— / I think they would be better dead. DOROTHY PARKER, "Reuben's Children," *Sunset Gun* (1928).

## 737. PROMISES

See also 635. Oaths

1. Promises are not to be kept, if the keeping of them would prove harmful to those to whom you have made them. CICERO, *De Officiis* (44 B.C.), 1.10.32.

2. A promise is binding in the inverse ratio of the numbers to whom it is made. THOMAS DE QUINCEY, appendix, *Confessions of an English Opium-Eater* (1821–56).

3. Who breaks his faith, no faith is held with him. SEIGNEUR DU BARTAS, *Divine Weekes and Workes* (1578), 2.4.2.

4. Vows made in storms are forgot in calms. ENGLISH PROVERB.

5. Better break your word than do worse in keeping it. THOMAS FULLER, M.D., *Gnomologia* (1732), 883.

6. He that promises too much means nothing. THOMAS FULLER, M.D., *Gnomologia* (1732), 2253.

7. Who promises much and does little, dines a fool on hope. GERMAN PROVERB.

8. Neither promise wax to the saint, nor cakes to the child. GREEK PROVERB.

9. We promise according to our hopes, and perform according to our fears. LA ROCHEFOUCAULD, *Maxims* (1665), tr. Kenneth Pratt.

10. Ease would recant / Vows made in pain, as violent and void. MILTON, *Paradise Lost* (1667), 4.96.

11. The best way to keep one's word is not to give it. NAPOLEON I, *Maxims* (1804–15).

12. Everyone's a millionaire where promises are concerned. OVID, *The Art of Love* (c. A.D. 8), 1, tr. J. Lewis May.

13. A promise made is a debt unpaid. ROBERT W. SERVICE, "The Cremation of Sam McGee," *The Spell of the Yukon* (1907).

14. Promises and pie-crust are made to be broken. JONATHAN SWIFT, *Polite Conversation* (1738), 1.

15. The vow that binds too strictly snaps itself. ALFRED, LORD TENNYSON, "The Last Tournament," *Idylls of the King* (1871).

16. To promise not to do a thing is the surest way in the world to make a body want to go and do that very thing. MARK TWAIN, *The Adventures of Tom Sawyer* (1876), 22.

17. We promise much to avoid giving little. VAUVENARGUES, *Reflections and Maxims* (1746), 436.

18. To make a vow for life is to make oneself a slave. VOLTAIRE, "Vows," *Philosophical Dictionary* (1764).

## PROMPTNESS

See 972. Timeliness

## 738. PROOF

See also 304. Evidence; 778. Reason

1. We can prove whatever we want to, and the real difficulty is to know what we want to prove. ALAIN, *Système des beaux-arts* (1920).

2. He that, in the ordinary affairs of life, would admit of nothing but direct plain demonstration would be sure of nothing in this world but of perishing quickly. JOHN LOCKE, *An Essay Concerning Human Understanding* (1690), 4.11.10.

3. That which needs to be proved cannot be worth much. NIETZSCHE, "The Problem of Socrates," 5, *Twilight of the Idols* (1888), tr. Anthony M. Ludovici.

4. All beliefs are demonstrably true. All men are demonstrably in the right. Anything can be demonstrated by logic. SAINT-

EXUPÉRY, *Wind, Sand, and Stars* (1939), 9.6, tr. Lewis Galantière.

## 739. PROPAGANDA

**See also 18. Advertising; 754. Publicity**

1. Propaganda is a soft weapon: hold it in your hands too long, and it will move about like a snake, and strike the other way. JEAN ANOUILH, *The Lark* (1955), 1, adapted by Lillian Hellman.

2. Like the effect of advertising upon the customer, the methods of political propaganda tend to increase the feeling of insignificance of the individual voter. ERICH FROMM, *Escape from Freedom* (1941), 4.

3. Public-relations specialists make flower arrangements of the facts, placing them so that the wilted and less attractive petals are hidden by sturdy blooms. ALAN HARRINGTON, "Public Relations," *Life in the Crystal Palace* (1959).

4. The greatest triumphs of propaganda have been accomplished, not by doing something, but by refraining from doing. Great is truth, but still greater, from a practical point of view, is silence about truth. ALDOUS HUXLEY, foreword, *Brave New World* (1932).

5. The propagandist's purpose is to make one set of people forget that certain other sets of people are human. ALDOUS HUXLEY, *The Olive Tree* (1937).

6. I give you bitter pills in sugar coating. The pills are harmless; the poison is in the sugar. STANISLAW LEC, *Unkempt Thoughts* (1962), tr. Jacek Galazka.

7. Every method is used to prove to men that in given political, economic and social situations they are bound to be happy, and those who are unhappy are mad or criminals or monsters. ALBERTO MORAVIA, title essay, *Man As an End* (1964), tr. Bernard Wall.

8. Why is propaganda so much more successful when it stirs up hatred than when it tries to stir up friendly feeling? BERTRAND RUSSELL, *The Conquest of Happiness* (1930), 6.

9. There is no nonsense so arrant that it cannot be made the creed of the vast majority by adequate governmental action. BERTRAND RUSSELL, "An Outline of Intellectual Rubbish," *Unpopular Essays* (1950).

## 740. PROPERTY

**See also 8. Acquisition; 106. Capitalism; 428. Houses; 596. Money; 710. Possession; 712. Poverty; 1041. Wealth**

1. It is not the possessions but the desires of mankind which require to be equalized. ARISTOTLE, *Politics* (4th c. B.C.), 2.7, tr. Benjamin Jowett.

2. Where all of the man is what property he owns, it does not take long to annihilate him. HENRY WARD BEECHER, *Proverbs from Plymouth Pulpit* (1887).

3. Where your treasure is, there will your heart be also. *Bible*, Matthew 6:21.

4. Property is in its nature timid and seeks protection, and nothing is more gratifying to government than to become a protector. JOHN C. CALHOUN, speech, March 21, 1834.

5. If a man own land, the land owns him. Now let him leave home, if he dare. EMERSON, "Wealth," *The Conduct of Life* (1860).

6. A pig that has two owners is sure to die of hunger. ENGLISH PROVERB.

7. Men honor property above all else; / it has the greatest power in human life. EURIPIDES, *The Phoenician Women* (c. 411–409 B.C.), tr. Elizabeth Wyckoff.

8. He that hath nothing is frightened at nothing. THOMAS FULLER, M.D., *Gnomologia* (1732), 2150.

9. It is because property exists that there are wars, riots, and injustices. Graffito written during French student revolt, May 1968.

10. Of all obstacles to that complete democracy of which we dream, is there a greater than property? DAVID GRAYSON, *Adventures in Contentment* (1907), 3.

11. What we call real estate—the solic ground to build a house on—is the broac foundation on which nearly all the guilt o this world rests. NATHANIEL HAWTHORNE *The House of the Seven Gables* (1851), 17.

12. There is a desire of property in th sanest and best men, which Nature seems t have implanted as conservative of he works, and which is necessary to encourag and keep alive the arts. WALTER SAVAC LANDOR, "Aristoteles and Callisthenes *Imaginary Conversations* (1824–53).

13. In our rich consumers' civilization v

spin cocoons around ourselves and get possessed by our possessions. MAX LERNER, "What Shall I Save?" *The Unfinished Country* (1959), 1.

14. Where there is no property there is no injustice. JOHN LOCKE, *An Essay Concerning Human Understanding* (1690), 4.3.18.

15. An acre in Middlesex is better than a principality in Utopia. THOMAS BABINGTON MACAULAY, "Lord Bacon" (1837).

16. No man divulges his revenue, or at least which way it comes in: but every one publishes his acquisitions. MONTAIGNE, "Of the education of children," *Essays* (1580–88), tr. Charles Cotton and W. C. Hazlitt.

17. "This dog is mine," said those poor children; "that is my place in the sun." Here is the beginning and the image of the usurpation of all the earth. PASCAL, *Pensées* (1670), 295, tr. W. F. Trotter.

18. Property is theft. PIERRE-JOSEPH PROUDHON, *Qu'est-ce que la propriété?* (1840).

19. The first man to fence in a piece of land, saying "This is mine," and who found people simple enough to believe him, was the real founder of civil society. ROUSSEAU, *Discourse on the Origin and Bases of Inequality among Men* (1754).

20. It should be remembered that the foundation of the social contract is property; and its first condition, that every one should be maintained in the peaceful possession of what belongs to him. ROUSSEAU, *A Discourse on Political Economy* (1758), tr. G. D. H. Cole.

21. The newer people, of this modern age, are more eager to amass than to realize. RABINDRANATH TAGORE, introduction to *The Cycle of Spring* (1915).

22. So soon as the possession of property becomes the basis of popular esteem, therefore, it becomes also a requisite to that complacency which we call self-respect. THORSTEIN VEBLEN, *The Theory of the Leisure Class* (1899), 2.

23. The spirit of property doubles a man's strength. VOLTAIRE, "Property," *Philosophical Dictionary* (1764).

24. Broad acres are a patent of nobility; and no man but feels more of a man in the world if he have a bit of ground that he can call his own. However small it is on the surface, it is four thousand miles deep; and that is a very handsome property. CHARLES DUDLEY WARNER, "Preliminary," *My Summer in a Garden* (1871).

## 741. PROPHECIES

1. Study prophecies when they are become histories. SIR THOMAS BROWNE, *Christian Morals* (1716), 3.

2. I always avoid prophesying beforehand, because it is a much better policy to prophesy after the event has already taken place. SIR WINSTON CHURCHILL, press conference, Cairo, Feb. 1, 1943.

3. Prophecy is the most gratuitous form of error. GEORGE ELIOT, *Middlemarch* (1871–72), 10.

4. He that would know what shall be must consider what hath been. THOMAS FULLER, M.D., *Gnomologia* (1732), 2367.

5. Prognostics do not always prove prophecies,—at least the wisest prophets make sure of the event first. HORACE WALPOLE, letter to Thomas Walpole, Feb. 19, 1785.

## 742. PROPORTION

See also 322. Extravagance; 408. Harmony; 592. Moderation

1. Proportion is almost impossible to human beings. There is no one who does not exaggerate. EMERSON, "Nominalist and Realist," *Essays: Second Series* (1844).

2. Without a sense of proportion there can be neither good taste nor genuine intelligence, nor perhaps moral integrity. ERIC HOFFER, *The Passionate State of Mind* (1954), 233.

3. How sour sweet music is / When time is broke and no proportion kept! / So is it in the music of men's lives. SHAKESPEARE, *Richard II* (1595–96), 5.5.42.

## 743. PROPRIETY

See also 112. Ceremony; 194. Courtesy; 389. Good Breeding; 559. Manners; 634. Nudity; 750. Prudery; 803. Respectability

1. A prig always finds a last refuge in responsibility. JEAN COCTEAU, preface to *The*

*Wedding on the Eiffel Tower* (1921), tr. Michael Benedikt.

2. Propriety is the least of all laws, and the most observed. LA ROCHEFOUCAULD, *Maxims* (1665), tr. Kenneth Pratt.

3. Ceremony forbids us to express by words things that are lawful and natural, and we obey it; reason forbids us to do things unlawful and ill, and nobody obeys it. MONTAIGNE, "Of presumption," *Essays* (1580–88), tr. Charles Cotton and W. C. Hazlitt.

4. Politeness requires this thing; decorum that; ceremony has its forms, and fashion its laws, and these we must always follow, never the promptings of our own nature. ROUSSEAU, *A Discourse on the Moral Effects of the Arts and Sciences* (1750), 1, tr. G. D. H. Cole.

5. There are few things that so touch us with instinctive revulsion as a breach of decorum. THORSTEIN VEBLEN, *The Theory of the Leisure Class* (1899), 3.

## 744. PROSPERITY

See also 17. Adversity; 554. Luxury; 745. Prosperity and Adversity; 938. Success; 1041. Wealth

1. They who prosper take on airs of vanity. AESCHYLUS, *Agamemnon* (458 B.C.), tr. Richmond Lattimore.

2. Happiness seems to require a modicum of external prosperity. ARISTOTLE, *Nicomachean Ethics* (4th c. B.C.), 1.8, tr. J. A. K. Thomson.

3. If prosperity is regarded as the reward of virtue it will be regarded as the symptom of virtue. G. K. CHESTERTON, "The Book of Job," *G. K. C. as M. C.* (1929).

4. Prosperity is only an instrument to be used, not a deity to be worshiped. CALVIN COOLIDGE, speech, June 11, 1928.

5. A full cup must be carried steadily. ENGLISH PROVERB.

6. Prosperity is like a tender mother, but blind, who spoils her children. ENGLISH PROVERB.

7. Some men never find prosperity, / For all their voyaging, / While others find it with no voyaging. EURIPIDES, *Iphigenia in Tauris* (c. 414–12 B.C.), tr. Witter Bynner.

8. Hardship is vanishing, but so is style, and the two are more closely connected than the present generation supposes. E. M. FORSTER, "Cambridge," *Two Cheers for Democracy* (1951).

9. There never was a banquet so sumptuous but someone dined poorly at it. FRENCH PROVERB.

10. He whose belly is full believes not him whose is empty. THOMAS FULLER, M.D., *Gnomologia* (1732), 2399.

11. Prosperity has everything cheap. THOMAS FULLER, M.D., *Gnomologia* (1732), 3964.

12. The human race has had long experience and a fine tradition in surviving adversity. But we now face a task for which we have little experience, the task of surviving prosperity. ALAN GREGG, *The New York Times*, Nov. 4, 1956.

13. It is the curse of prosperity that it takes work away from us, and shuts that door to hope and health of spirit. WILLIAM DEAN HOWELLS, *The Rise of Silas Lapham* (1885), 17.

14. Social prosperity means man happy, the citizen free, the nation great. VICTOR HUGO, "Saint Denis," *Les Misérables* (1862), 1.4, tr. Charles E. Wilbour.

15. I should like to bring a case to trial: / Prosperity versus Beauty, / Cash registers teetering in a balance against the comfort of the soul. AMY LOWELL, "Charleston, South Carolina," *What's O'Clock* (1925).

16. When all is well who cannot be wise? *Panchatantra* (c. 5th c.), 1, tr. Franklin Edgerton.

17. We have produced a world of contented bodies and discontented minds. ADAM CLAYTON POWELL, "The Temptations of Modernity," *Keep the Faith, Baby!* (1967).

18. Prosperity's the very bond of love, / Whose fresh complexion and whose heart together / Affliction alters. SHAKESPEARE, *The Winter's Tale* (1610–11), 4.4.584.

19. The taste for well-being is the prominent and indelible feature of democratic times. ALEXIS DE TOCQUEVILLE, *Democracy in America* (1835–39), 2.1.5.

20. Few of us can stand prosperity. Another man's, I mean. MARK TWAIN, "Pudd'nhead Wilson's New Calendar," *Following the Equator* (1897), 2.4.

21. When you ascend the hill of prosperity, may you not meet a friend. MAR

TWAIN, "Pudd'nhead Wilson's New Calendar," *Following the Equator* (1897), 2.5.

22. Prosperity doth bewitch men, seeming clear; / But seas do laugh, show white, when rocks are near. JOHN WEBSTER, *The White Devil* (1612), 5.6.

## 745. PROSPERITY AND ADVERSITY

See also 17. Adversity; 358. Fortune; 744. Prosperity

1. In the day of prosperity, adversity is forgotten and in the day of adversity, prosperity is not remembered. *Apocrypha*, Ecclesiasticus 11:25.

2. They merit more praise who know how to suffer misery than those who temper themselves in contentment. PIETRO ARETINO, letter to the King of France, April 24, 1525, tr. Samuel Putnam.

3. The virtue of prosperity is temperance; the virtue of adversity is fortitude. FRANCIS BACON, "Of Adversity," *Essays* (1625).

4. In the day of prosperity be joyful, but in the day of adversity consider. *Bible*, Ecclesiastes 7:14.

5. Those who have risen from a banquet are loquacious / Before the hungry about the good times to come. BERTOLT BRECHT, "Those Who Deprive the Table of Meat," *Modern European Poetry* (1966), ed. Willis Barnstone.

6. Adversity is sometimes hard upon a man; but for one man who can stand prosperity, there are a hundred that will stand adversity. THOMAS CARLYLE, *On Heroes, Hero-Worship and the Heroic in History* (1841), 5.

7. In prosperity friends do not leave you unless desired, whereas in adversity they stay away of their own accord. DEMETRIUS (4th–3rd c. B.C.), quoted in Diogenes Laertius' *Lives and Opinions of Eminent Philosophers* (3rd c. A.D.), tr. R. D. Hicks.

8. Misfortunes tell us what fortune is. THOMAS FULLER, M.D., *Gnomologia* (1732), 3420.

9. One who was abhorred by all in prosperity is adored by all in adversity. BALTASAR GRACIÁN, *The Art of Worldly Wisdom* (1647), 163, tr. Joseph Jacobs.

10. Prosperity is a great teacher; adversity is a greater. WILLIAM HAZLITT, "On the Conversation of Lords," *Sketches and Essays* (1839).

11. Prosperity has no power over adversity. PUBLILIUS SYRUS, *Moral Sayings* (1st c. B.C.), 692, tr. Darius Lyman.

12. Prosperity makes friends, adversity tries them. PUBLILIUS SYRUS, *Moral Sayings* (1st c. B.C.), 872, tr. Darius Lyman.

13. A man is insensible to the relish of prosperity till he has tasted adversity. SA'DI, *Gulistan* (1258), 5.10, tr. James Ross.

14. In victory even the cowardly like to boast, while in adverse times even the brave are discredited. SALLUST, *Jugurthine War* (1st c. B.C.), 53.

15. The good things which belong to prosperity are to be wished, but the good things that belong to adversity are to be admired. SENECA (1st c.), quoted in Francis Bacon's "Of Adversity," *Essays* (1625).

16. Mankind apparently find it easier to drive away adversity than to retain prosperity. THUCYDIDES, *The Peloponnesian War* (c. 400 B.C.), 3.39, tr. Benjamin Jowett.

17. From fortune to misfortune is but a step; from misfortune to fortune is a long way. *Yiddish Proverbs* (1949), ed. Hanan J. Ayalti.

## 746. PROSTITUTION

1. Men will pay large sums to whores / For telling them they are not bores. W. H. AUDEN, "New Year Letter" (1940), 2.

2. Prisons are built with stones of law, brothels with bricks of religion. WILLIAM BLAKE, "Proverbs of Hell," *The Marriage of Heaven and Hell* (1790).

## 747. PROTEST

See also 256. Dissent; 651. Opposition; 779. Rebellion

1. Sometimes a scream is better than a thesis. EMERSON, *Journals*, 1836.

2. I want every American free to stand up for his rights, even if sometimes he has to sit down for them. JOHN F. KENNEDY, campaign address, Convention Hall, Philadelphia, Oct. 31, 1960.

## PROTESTANTISM

See 123. Christianity

## PROVERBS
See 568. Maxims

## 748. PROVIDENCE
See also 238. Destiny; 337. Fate; 385. God; 873. Self-sufficiency

1. There is a Power whose care / Teaches thy way along that pathless coast,— / The desert and illimitable air,— / Lone wandering, but not lost. WILLIAM CULLEN BRYANT, "To a Waterfowl" (1818).

2. To put one's trust in God is only a longer way of saying that one will chance it. SAMUEL BUTLER (d. 1902), "Higgledy-Piggledy," *Note-Books* (1912).

3. The Infinite Goodness has such wide arms that it takes whatever turns to it. DANTE, "Purgatorio," 3, *The Divine Comedy* (c. 1300–21), tr. Charles Eliot Norton.

4. We degrade Providence too much by attributing our ideas to it out of annoyance at being unable to understand it. DOSTOEVSKY, *The Idiot* (1868), 3.7, tr. David Magarshack.

5. God gives the milk but not the pail. ENGLISH PROVERB.

6. God tempers the wind to the shorn lamb. ENGLISH PROVERB.

7. How dark are all the ways of god to man! EURIPIDES, *Heracles* (c. 422 B.C.), tr. William Arrowsmith.

8. The man whom heaven helps / has friends enough. EURIPIDES, *Orestes* (408 B.C.), tr. William Arrowsmith.

9. God gives, but man must open his hand. GERMAN PROVERB.

10. God never sends the mouth but he sendeth meat. JOHN HEYWOOD, *Proverbs* (1546), 1.4.

11. The gods give to mortals not everything at the same time. HOMER, *Iliad* (9th c. B.C.), 4.320, tr. Richmond Lattimore.

12. Know from the bounteous heaven all riches flow; / And what man gives, the gods by man bestow. HOMER, *Odyssey* (9th c. B.C.), 18.26, tr. Alexander Pope.

13. The wisdom of providence is as much revealed in the rarity of genius, as in the circumstance that not everyone is deaf or blind. GEORG CHRISTOPH LICHTENBERG, *Aphorisms* (1764–99), tr. F. H. Mautner and H. Hatfield.

14. Whoever falls from God's right hand / Is caught into his left. EDWIN MARKHAM, "The Divine Strategy" (1920).

15. Men almost universally have acknowledged a Providence, but that fact has had no force to destroy natural aversions and fears in the presence of events. GEORGE SANTAYANA, *The Life of Reason: Reason in Religion* (1905–06), 4.

16. The superior man is quiet and calm, waiting for the appointments of Heaven, while the mean man walks in dangerous paths, looking for lucky occurrences. TZE-SZE, *The Doctrine of the Mean* (5th c. B.C.), 15.4, tr. James Legge.

17. I know not where His islands lift / Their fronded palms in air; / I only know I cannot drift / Beyond His love and care. JOHN GREENLEAF WHITTIER, "The Eternal Goodness" (1867), 20.

18. God will provide—if only God would provide until he provides. *Yiddish Proverbs* (1949), ed. Hanan J. Ayalti.

## 749. PRUDENCE
See also 110. Cautiousness; 147. Common Sense; 351. Folly; 592. Moderation; 714. Practicality; 742. Proportion; 774. Rashness; 1053. Wisdom

1. No one tests the depth of a river with both feet. ASHANTI PROVERB.

2. I would rather worry without need than live without heed. BEAUMARCHAIS, *The Barber of Seville* (1775), 2, tr. Albert Bermel.

3. Prudence is a rich, ugly old maid courted by Incapacity. WILLIAM BLAKE, "Proverbs of Hell," *The Marriage of Heaven and Hell* (1790).

4. Though you would like to beat the dog, you have to consider its master's face as well. *Burmese Proverbs* (1962), 439, ed. Hla Pe.

5. 'Tis the part of a wise man to keep himself today for tomorrow, and not venture all his eggs in one basket. CERVANTES, *Don Quixote* (1605–15), 1.3.9, tr. Peter Motteux and John Ozell.

6. Judgment is not upon all occasions required, but discretion always is. LORD CHESTERFIELD, *Letters to His Godson*, 1766?

7. In order to try whether a vessel be leaky, we first prove it with water before we trust it with wine. CHARLES CALEB COLTON, *Lacon* (1825), 1.46.

8. Act so in the valley that you need not fear those who stand on the hill. DANISH PROVERB.

9. The eye of prudence may never shut. EMERSON, "Prudence," *Essays: First Series* (1841).

10. If thou canst not see the bottom, wade not. ENGLISH PROVERB.

11. Don't try to fly before you have wings. FRENCH PROVERB.

12. If thy heart fails thee, climb not at all. THOMAS FULLER, D.D., *Worthies of England* (1662), v. 1.

13. A dram of discretion is worth a pound of wisdom. GERMAN PROVERB.

14. When you have nothing to say, or to hide, there is no need to be prudent. ANDRÉ GIDE, *Journals*, 1922, tr. Justin O'Brien.

15. My advice to you, if you should ever be in a hold-up, is to line up with the cowards and save your bravery for an occasion when it may be of some benefit to you. O. HENRY, "Holding Up a Train," *Sixes and Sevens* (1911).

16. Prudence is but experience, which equal time equally bestows on all men, in those things they equally apply themselves unto. THOMAS HOBBES, *Leviathan* (1651), 1.13.

17. A prudent man does not make the goat his gardener. HUNGARIAN PROVERB.

18. Tell not all you know, believe not all you hear, do not all you are able. ITALIAN PROVERB.

19. Although it rain, cast not away the watering pot. MALAY PROVERB.

20. Don't borrow from a *nouveau riche;* don't visit the newly wed. MALAY PROVERB.

21. Sincerity is glass, discretion is diamond. ANDRÉ MAUROIS, *Conseils à une jeune fille qui dit tout ce qu'elle pense* (1947).

22. He who is not a bird should not build his nest over abysses. NIETZSCHE, "On the Famous Wise Men," *Thus Spoke Zarathustra* (1883–92), 2, tr. Walter Kaufmann.

23. If thou thinkest twice before thou speakest once, thou wilt speak twice the better for it. WILLIAM PENN, *Some Fruits of Solitude* (1693), 1.131.

24. Be moderate in prosperity, prudent in adversity. PERIANDER (d. 585 B.C.), quoted in Diogenes Laertius' *Lives and Opinions of Eminent Philosophers* (3rd c. A.D.), tr. R. D. Hicks.

25. He who wants a rose must respect the thorn. PERSIAN PROVERB.

26. Consider the little mouse, how sagacious an animal it is which never entrusts its life to one hole only. PLAUTUS, *Truculentus* (c. 191–186 B.C.), 4.4.15, tr. Henry Thomas Riley.

27. It is well to moor your bark with two anchors. PUBLILIUS SYRUS, *Moral Sayings* (1st c. B.C.), 119, tr. Darius Lyman.

28. Never exceed your rights, and they will soon become unlimited. ROUSSEAU, *A Discourse on Political Economy* (1758), tr. G. D. H. Cole.

29. Reveal not every secret you have to a friend, for how can you tell but that friend may hereafter become an enemy. And bring not all the mischief you are able to do upon an enemy, for he may one day become your friend. SA'DI, *Gulistan* (1258), 8.10, tr. James Ross.

30. We are prudent people. We are afraid to let go of our petty reality in order to grasp at a great shadow. SAINT-EXUPÉRY, *Wind, Sand, and Stars* (1939), 9.5, tr. Lewis Galantière.

31. Better eat gray bread in your youth than in your age. SCOTTISH PROVERB.

32. The better part of valour is discretion. SHAKESPEARE, *1 Henry IV* (1597–98), 5.4.121.

33. If you are out of trouble, watch for danger. / And when you live well, then consider the most / your life, lest ruin take it unawares. SOPHOCLES, *Philoctetes* (409 B.C.), tr. David Grene.

34. So soon as prudence has begun to grow up in the brain, like a dismal fungus, it finds its first expression in a paralysis of generous acts. ROBERT LOUIS STEVENSON, "Aes Triplex," *Virginibus Puerisque* (1881).

35. Prudence is sometimes stretched too far, until it blocks the road of progress. TEHYI HSIEH, *Chinese Epigrams Inside Out and Proverbs* (1948), 261.

36. No wise man stands behind an ass when he kicks. TERENCE, *The Eunuch* (161 B.C.), tr. Robert Graves.

37. The prudent man does himself good; the virtuous one does it to other men. VOL-

TAIRE, "Virtue," *Philosophical Dictionary* (1764).

### 750. PRUDERY

**See also 634. Nudity; 743. Propriety; 763. Puritans and Puritanism**

1. A private sin is not so prejudicial in this world as a public indecency. CERVANTES, *Don Quixote* (1605–15), 2.3.22, tr. Peter Motteux and John Ozell.

2. The peculiarity of prudery is to multiply sentinels, in proportion as the fortress is less threatened. VICTOR HUGO, "Marius," *Les Misérables* (1862), 2.8, tr. Charles E. Wilbour.

3. Decency, not to dare to do that in public which it is decent enough to do in private. MONTAIGNE, "Apology for Raimond de Sebonde," *Essays* (1580–88), tr. Charles Cotton and W. C. Hazlitt.

4. Prudery is a kind of avarice, the worst of all. STENDHAL, "Miscellaneous Fragments," *On Love* (1822), tr. H. B. V., under direction of C. K. Scott-Moncrieff.

5. Nature knows no indecencies; man invents them. MARK TWAIN, *Notebook* (1935).

### PRYING

**See 571. Meddling**

### 751. PSYCHIATRY

**See also 620. Neurosis; 752. Psychoanalysis; 753. Psychology**

1. A neurotic is the man who builds a castle in the air. A psychotic is the man who lives in it. And a psychiatrist is the man who collects the rent. Author unidentified.

2. Psychiatry's chief contribution to philosophy is the discovery that the toilet is the seat of the soul. ALEXANDER CHASE, *Perspectives* (1966).

3. Canst thou not minister to a mind diseased, / Pluck from the memory a rooted sorrow, / Raze out the written troubles of the brain, / And with some sweet oblivious antidote / Cleanse the stuffed bosom of that perilous stuff / Which weighs upon the heart? SHAKESPEARE, *Macbeth* (1605–06), 5.3.40.

### 752. PSYCHOANALYSIS

**See also 43. Anxiety; 620. Neurosis; 751. Psychiatry; 753. Psychology; 868. Self-knowledge**

1. Do you not know, Prometheus, that words are healers of the sick temper? AESCHYLUS, *Prometheus Bound* (c. 478 B.C.), tr. David Grene.

2. A psychoanalyst is one who pretends he doesn't know everything. Anonymous.

3. Once read thy own breast right, / And thou hast done with fears. MATTHEW ARNOLD, *Empedocles on Etna* (1852), 1.2.

4. In today's highly complex society it takes years of training in rationalization, accommodation and compromise to qualify for the good jobs with the really big payoffs you need to retain a first-rate psychiatrist in today's world. RUSSELL BAKER, "Observer," *The New York Times*, March 21, 1968.

5. The greatest happiness is to know the source of unhappiness. DOSTOEVSKY, *A Diary of a Writer* (1876), 4, July–August.

6. All cases are unique, and very similar to others. T. S. ELIOT, *The Cocktail Party* (1949), 2.

7. It might be said of psychoanalysis that if you give it your little finger it will soon have your whole hand. SIGMUND FREUD, *Introductory Lectures on Psychoanalysis* (1917), tr. Joan Riviere.

8. Look into the depths of your own soul and learn first to know yourself, then you will understand why this illness was bound to come upon you and perhaps you will thenceforth avoid falling ill. SIGMUND FREUD, "One of the Difficulties of Psychoanalysis," *Collected Papers* (1924–50), tr. Joan Riviere.

9. The examined life has always been pretty well confined to a privileged class. EDGAR Z. FRIEDENBERG, "The Impact of the School," *The Vanishing Adolescent* (1959).

10. The man who once cursed his fate, now curses himself—and pays his psychoanalyst. JOHN W. GARDNER, *No Easy Victories* (1968), 1.

11. To have known how to change the past into a few saddened smiles—is this not to master the future? MAURICE MAETERLINCK, "The Star," *The Treasure of the Humble* (1896), tr. Alfred Sutro.

12. All the art of analysis consists in saying a truth only when the other person is ready for it, has been prepared for it by an organic process of gradation and evolution. ANAÏS NIN, *The Diary of Anaïs Nin*, April 1932.

13. Every life is, more or less, a ruin among whose debris we have to discover what the person ought to have been. JOSÉ ORTEGA Y GASSET, "In Search of Goethe from Within, Letter to a German," *Partisan Review*, December 1949, tr. Willard R. Trask.

14. Man is tied to the weight of his own past, and even by a great therapeutic labor little more can be accomplished than a shifting of the burden. PHILIP RIEFF, preface to *Freud: The Mind of the Moralist* (1959).

15. To understand oneself is the classic form of consolation; to elude oneself is the romantic. GEORGE SANTAYANA, *Winds of Doctrine* (1913).

16. Let us not seek our disease out of ourselves; 'tis in us, and planted in our bowels; and the mere fact that we do not perceive ourselves to be sick, renders us more hard to be cured. SENECA, *Letters to Lucilius* (1st c.).

17. The unexamined life is not worth living. SOCRATES, in Plato's *Apology* (4th c. B.C.), tr. Lane Cooper.

18. Until a man can quit talking loudly to himself in order to shout down the memories of blunderings and gropings, he is in no shape for the painstaking examination of distress. JAMES THURBER, "A Note at the End," *The Thurber Carnival* (1945).

## 753. PSYCHOLOGY

**See also 583. Mind; 620. Neurosis; 751. Psychiatry; 752. Psychoanalysis**

1. Man *qua* thinker may delight in the intricacies of psychology, but man *qua* lover has not learned to feel in its terms. JOSEPH WOOD KRUTCH, "The Genesis of a Mood," *The Modern Temper* (1929).

2. There are almost no limits to the discoveries of how the human brain operates—in illness and health, in sleep and waking and dreaming, in calm and under tension. The question is how far man can put these discoveries to use without using them not for cure but for power. MAX LERNER, "Manipulating Life," in the *New York Post*, Jan. 24, 1968.

3. Psychology which explains everything / explains nothing, / and we are still in doubt. MARIANNE MOORE, "Marriage," *Collected Poems* (1951).

4. Idleness is the parent of all psychology. NIETZSCHE, "Maxims and Missiles," 1, *Twilight of the Idols* (1888), tr. Anthony M. Ludovici.

5. The object of psychology is to give us a totally different idea of the things we know best. PAUL VALÉRY, *Tel quel* (1943).

## THE PUBLIC

**See 675. The People**

## 754. PUBLICITY

**See also 18. Advertising; 730. Privacy; 739. Propaganda**

1. Formerly, a public man needed a *private* secretary for a barrier between himself and the public. Nowadays he has a *press* secretary, to keep him properly in the public eye. DANIEL J. BOORSTIN, *The Image* (1962), 2.4.

2. There is a photographer in every bush, going about like a roaring lion seeking whom he may devour. SAMUEL BUTLER (d. 1902), "Unprofessional Sermons," *Note-Books* (1912).

3. We march through life an' behind us marches th' phottygrafter an' th' rayporther. There are no such things as private citizens. FINLEY PETER DUNNE, "Newspaper Publicity," *Observations by Mr. Dooley* (1902).

4. The very minute a thought is threatened with publicity it seems to shrink towards mediocrity. OLIVER WENDELL HOLMES, SR., *The Poet at the Breakfast Table* (1872), 12.

## PUBLIC LIFE

**See 330. Fame; 755. Public Office**

## 755. PUBLIC OFFICE

**See also 169. Congress; 393. Government; 645. Officialism;**

**705. Politics and Politicians; 724. Presidency; 756. Public Opinion**

1. Nowadays, for the sake of the advantage which is to be gained from the public revenues and from office, men want to be always in office. ARISTOTLE, *Politics* (4th c. B.C.), 3.6, tr. Benjamin Jowett.

2. It is not easy for a person to do any great harm when his tenure of office is short, whereas long possession begets tyranny. ARISTOTLE, *Politics* (4th c. B.C.), 5.8, tr. Benjamin Jowett.

3. Nominee, n. A modest gentleman shrinking from the distinction of private life and diligently seeking the honorable obscurity of public office. AMBROSE BIERCE, *The Devil's Dictionary* (1881–1911).

4. The very essence of a free government consists in considering offices as public trusts, bestowed for the good of the country, and not for the benefit of an individual or a party. JOHN C. CALHOUN, speech, Feb. 13, 1835.

5. It is an easy and a vulgar thing to please the mob, and not a very arduous task to astonish them; but essentially to benefit and improve them is a work fraught with difficulty and teeming with danger. CHARLES CALEB COLTON, *Lacon* (1825), 1.453.

6. A man ain't got no right to be a public man, unless he meets the public views. CHARLES DICKENS, *Martin Chuzzlewit* (1844), 34.

7. The conduct and opinions of public men at different periods of their careers must not be curiously contrasted in a free and aspiring society. BENJAMIN DISRAELI, speech, High Wycombe, Dec. 16, 1834.

8. He that puts on a public gown must put off a private person. THOMAS FULLER, M.D., *Gnomologia* (1732), 2257.

9. The public official must pick his way nicely, must learn to placate though not to yield too much, to have the art of honeyed words but not to seem neutral, and above all to keep constantly audible, visible, likable, even kissable. LEARNED HAND, speech, Washington, D.C., March 8, 1932.

10. A situation in a public office is secure, but laborious and mechanical, and without the two great springs of life, Hope and Fear. WILLIAM HAZLITT, "On the Conduct of Life," *Literary Remains* (1836).

11. Offices are as acceptable here as elsewhere, and whenever a man has cast a longing eye on them, a rottenness begins in his conduct. THOMAS JEFFERSON, letter to Tench Coxe, May 21, 1799.

12. When a man assumes a public trust, he should consider himself as public property. THOMAS JEFFERSON, remark to Baron von Humboldt, 1807.

13. The best servants of the people, like the best valets, must whisper unpleasant truths in the master's ear. It is the court fool, not the foolish courtier, whom the king can least afford to lose. WALTER LIPPMANN, "Some Necessary Iconoclasm," *A Preface to Politics* (1914).

14. In government offices which are sensitive to the vehemence and passion of mass sentiment public men have no sure tenure. They are in effect perpetual office seekers, always on trial for their political lives, always required to court their restless constituents. WALTER LIPPMANN, *The Public Philosophy* (1955), 2.4.

15. Shrewdness in Public Life all over the World is always honored, while honesty in Public Men is generally attributed to Dumbness and is seldom rewarded. WILL ROGERS, *The Autobiography of Will Rogers* (1949), 9.

16. In our democracy officers of the government are the servants, and never the masters of the people. FRANKLIN D. ROOSEVELT, speech, Hollywood, Calif., Feb. 27, 1941.

17. As soon as public service ceases to be the chief business of the citizens, and they would rather serve with their money than with their persons, the State is not far from its fall. ROUSSEAU, *The Social Contract* (1762), 3.15, tr. G. D. H. Cole.

18. Your public servants serve you right; indeed often they serve you better than your apathy and indifference deserve. ADLAI STEVENSON, speech, Los Angeles, Sept. 11, 1952.

## 756. PUBLIC OPINION

**See also 649. Opinion**

1. There is nothing that makes more cowards and feeble men than public opinion. HENRY WARD BEECHER, *Proverbs from Plymouth Pulpit* (1887).

2. Your representative owes you, not his

industry only, but his judgment; and he betrays instead of serving you if he sacrifices it to your opinion. EDMUND BURKE, speech to the Electors of Bristol, Nov. 3, 1774.

3. The public buys its opinions as it buys its meat, or takes in its milk, on the principle that it is cheaper to do this than to keep a cow. So it is, but the milk is more likely to be watered. SAMUEL BUTLER (d. 1902), "Material for a Projected Sequel to *Alps and Sanctuaries*," *Note-Books* (1912).

4. Nothing is more dangerous in wartime than to live in the temperamental atmosphere of a Gallup Poll, always feeling one's pulse and taking one's temperature. SIR WINSTON CHURCHILL, speech, House of Commons, Sept. 30, 1941.

5. When the multitude detests a man, inquiry is necessary; when the multitude likes a man, inquiry is equally necessary. CONFUCIUS, *Analects* (6th c. B.C.), 15.27, tr. Ch'u Chai and Winberg Chai.

6. What we call public opinion is generally public sentiment. BENJAMIN DISRAELI, speech, Aug. 3, 1880.

7. It is far more difficult to change the mentality of the people than it is to change a country's political order or even its economy. ILYA EHRENBURG, "What I Have Learned," *Saturday Review*, Sept. 30, 1967.

8. The idea of what the public will think prevents the public from ever thinking at all, and acts as a spell on the exercise of private judgment. WILLIAM HAZLITT, "On Living to One's-self," *Table Talk* (1821–22).

9. A straw vote only shows which way the hot air blows. O. HENRY, "A Ruler of Men," *Rolling Stones* (1912).

10. We are ruled by Public Opinion, not by Statute-law. ELBERT HUBBARD, *The Note Book* (1927).

11. Public opinion, a vulgar, impertinent, anonymous tyrant who deliberately makes life unpleasant for anyone who is not content to be the average man. WILLIAM RALPH INGE, "Our Present Discontents," *Outspoken Essays: First Series* (1919).

12. About things on which the public thinks long it commonly attains to think right. SAMUEL JOHNSON, *Lives of the Poets: Addison* (1779–81).

13. A universal feeling, whether well or ill founded, cannot be safely disregarded. ABRAHAM LINCOLN, speech, Peoria, Ill., Oct. 16, 1854.

14. With public sentiment, nothing can fail; without it, nothing can succeed. Consequently he who molds public sentiment goes deeper than he who enacts statutes or pronounces decisions. ABRAHAM LINCOLN, speech, Ottawa, Ill., July 31, 1858.

15. Public opinion is the thermometer a monarch should constantly consult. NAPOLEON I, *Maxims* (1804–15).

16. All becomes easy when we follow the current of opinion; it is the ruler of the world. NAPOLEON I, *Maxims* (1804–15).

17. Today's public opinion, though it may appear as light as air, may become tomorrow's legislation—for better or for worse. EARL NEWSOM, American Petroleum Institute newsletter, Winter 1963.

18. There is no group in America that can withstand the force of an aroused public opinion. FRANKLIN D. ROOSEVELT, statement on signing the National Industrial Recovery Act, June 16, 1933.

19. A government can be no better than the public opinion which sustains it. FRANKLIN D. ROOSEVELT, speech, Washington, D.C., Jan. 8, 1936.

20. One should respect public opinion in so far as is necessary to avoid starvation and to keep out of prison, but anything that goes beyond this is voluntary submission to an unnecessary tyranny. BERTRAND RUSSELL, *The Conquest of Happiness* (1930), 9.

21. A man must know how to brave public opinion, a woman how to submit to it. MME DE STAËL, *Delphine* (1802).

22. Public opinion is stronger than the legislature, and nearly as strong as the ten commandments. CHARLES DUDLEY WARNER, "Sixteenth Week," *My Summer in a Garden* (1871).

## PUBLIC RELATIONS

**See 18. Advertising; 739. Propaganda; 754. Publicity**

## 757. PUBLIC SPEAKING

**See also 230. Demagoguery; 281. Eloquence; 916. Speaking**

1. Great orators who are not also great writers become very indistinct shadows to the generations following them. The spell vanishes with the voice. THOMAS BAILEY

ALDRICH, "Leaves from a Notebook," *Ponkapog Papers* (1903).

2. Lecturer, n. One with his hand in your pocket, his tongue in your ear and his faith in your patience. AMBROSE BIERCE, *The Devil's Dictionary* (1881–1911).

3. Nothing is so unbelievable that oratory cannot make it acceptable. CICERO, *Paradoxa Stoicorum* (46 B.C.).

4. Eloquence is the language of nature, and cannot be learned in the schools; but rhetoric is the creature of art, which he who feels least will most excel in. CHARLES CALEB COLTON, *Lacon* (1825), 1.435.

5. Ivry gr-reat orator ought to be accompanied by an orchesthry or, at worst, a pianist who wud play trills while th' artist was refreshin' himsilf with a glass iv ice wather. FINLEY PETER DUNNE, "On the Gift of Oratory," *Mr. Dooley On Making a Will* (1919).

6. All the great speakers were bad speakers at first. EMERSON, "Power," *The Conduct of Life* (1860).

7. An orator can hardly get beyond commonplaces: if he does, he gets beyond his hearers. WILLIAM HAZLITT, "On the Difference Between Writing and Speaking," *The Plain Speaker* (1826).

8. Speeches measured by the hour die with the hour. THOMAS JEFFERSON, letter to David Harding, April 20, 1824.

9. What orators lack in depth they make up to you in length. MONTESQUIEU, *Letters* (1767).

10. All that is necessary to raise imbecility into what the mob regards as profundity is to lift it off the floor and put it on a platform. GEORGE JEAN NATHAN, "Profundity," *American Mercury*, September 1929.

11. Oratory is just like prostitution: you must have little tricks. VITTORIO EMANUELE ORLANDO, *Time*, Dec. 8, 1952.

12. It is a difficult task, O citizens, to make speeches to the belly, which has no ears. PLUTARCH, "Life of Marcus Cato," *Parallel Lives* (1st–2nd c.), tr. John Dryden.

13. When orators and auditors have the same prejudices, those prejudices run a great risk of being made to stand for incontestable truths. JOSEPH ROUX, *Meditations of a Parish Priest* (1886), 2.35, tr. Isabel F. Hapgood.

14. It is terrible to speak well and be wrong. SOPHOCLES, *Electra* (c. 418–14 B.C.), tr. David Grene.

15. The relationship of the toastmaster to the speaker should be the same as that of the fan to the fan dancer. It should call attention to the subject without making any particular effort to cover it. ADLAI STEVENSON, *The Stevenson Wit* (1966).

16. In oratory the greatest art is to hide art. JONATHAN SWIFT, *A Tritical Essay Upon the Faculties of the Mind* (1707).

## 758. PUBLISHING

**See also 362. Free Speech; 563. Mass Media; 623. Newspapers; 725. Press, Freedom of the**

1. The printing-press is either the greatest blessing or the greatest curse of modern times, one sometimes forgets which. J. M. BARRIE, *Sentimental Tommy* (1896).

2. Things evidently false are not only printed, but many things of truth most falsely set forth. SIR THOMAS BROWNE, "To the Reader," *Religio Medici* (1642).

3. 'Tis pleasant, sure, to see one's name in print; / A Book's a Book, altho' there's nothing in't. BYRON, *English Bards and Scotch Reviewers* (1809).

4. Th' printin'-press isn't wondherful. What's wondherful is that annybody shud want it to go on doin' what it does. FINLEY PETER DUNNE, "On the Midway," *Mr. Dooley's Opinions* (1901).

5. Great editors do not discover nor produce great authors; great authors create and produce great publishers. JOHN FARRAR, *What Happens in Book Publishing* (1957).

6. Madame, we are the press. You know our power. We fix all values. We set all standards. Your entire future depends on us. JEAN GIRAUDOUX, *The Madwoman of Chaillot* (1945), 2, adapted by Maurice Valency.

7. What are the publications that succeed? Those that pretend to teach the public that the persons they have been accustomed unwittingly to look up to as the lights of the earth are no better than themselves. WILLIAM HAZLITT, "On Reading New Books," *Sketches and Essays* (1839).

8. Publishers are usually not very intelligent, or they might be intelligent, but it's usually hard to tell. Publishers don't publish a lot of fine books they should publish. LE ROI JONES, "Black Writing," *Home* (1966).

9. A presentation copy, reader,—if haply

you are yet innocent of such favours—is a copy of a book which does not sell, sent you by the author. CHARLES LAMB, "Popular Fallacies, 11," *Last Essays of Elia* (1833).

10. Since the discovery of printing, knowledge has been called to power, and power has been used to make knowledge a slave. NAPOLEON I, *Maxims* (1804–15).

11. Editing is the same as quarreling with writers—same thing exactly. HAROLD ROSS, *Time*, March 6, 1950.

12. An editor is one who separates the wheat from the chaff and prints the chaff. ADLAI STEVENSON, *The Stevenson Wit* (1966).

13. A copy of verses kept in the cabinet, and only shown to a few friends, is like a virgin much sought after and admired; but when printed and published, is like a common whore, whom anybody may purchase for half-a-crown. JONATHAN SWIFT, *Thoughts on Various Subjects* (1711).

14. Editing is the most companionable form of education. EDWARD WEEKS, *In Friendly Candor* (1959).

## 759. PUNCTUALITY

See also 228. Delay

1. We are not saints, but we have kept our appointment. How many people can boast as much? SAMUEL BECKETT, *Waiting for Godot* (1952), 2.

2. Better late than before anybody has invited you. AMBROSE BIERCE, "Saw," *The Devil's Dictionary* (1881–1911).

3. Men count up the faults of those who keep them waiting. FRENCH PROVERB.

4. Few things tend more to alienate friendship than a want of punctuality in our engagements. WILLIAM HAZLITT, "On the Spirit of Obligations," *The Plain Speaker* (1826).

5. Better three hours too soon than a minute too late. SHAKESPEARE, *The Merry Wives of Windsor* (1597), 2.2.327.

## PUNCTUATION

See 935. Style

## 760. PUNISHMENT

See also 248. Discipline; 729. Prison; 761. Punishment, Capital; 809. Retribution; 883. Severity

1. All punishment is mischief. All punishment in itself is evil. JEREMY BENTHAM, *Introduction to Principles of Morals and Legislation* (1789), 15.

2. He that spareth his rod hateth his son. *Bible*, Proverbs 13:24.

3. Punishment without judgment is bearable. Besides, it has a name which guarantees our innocence: misfortune. ALBERT CAMUS, *The Fall* (1956).

4. Speak roughly to your little boy, / And beat him when he sneezes: / He only does it to annoy, / Because he knows it teases. LEWIS CARROLL, *Alice's Adventures in Wonderland* (1865), 6.

5. Beat your child once a day. If you don't know why, he does. CHINESE PROVERB.

6. Crime and punishment grow out of one stem. EMERSON, "Compensation," *Essays: First Series* (1841).

7. A whipping never hurts so much as the thought that you are being whipped. EDGAR WATSON HOWE, *Country Town Sayings* (1911).

8. Many punishments sometimes, and in some cases, as much discredit a prince as many funerals a physician. BEN JONSON, "Of Statecraft," *Timber* (1640).

9. many a man spanks his / children for / things his own / father should have / spanked out of him. DON MARQUIS, "certain maxims of archy," *Archy and Mehitabel* (1927).

10. I have never observed other effects of whipping than to render boys more cowardly, or more willfully obstinate. MONTAIGNE, "Of the affections of fathers to their children," *Essays* (1580–88), tr. Charles Cotton and W. C. Hazlitt.

11. Speaking generally, punishment hardens and numbs, it produces concentration, it sharpens the consciousness of alienation, it strengthens the power of resistance. NIETZSCHE, *The Genealogy of Morals* (1887), 2.14, tr. Horace B. Samuel.

12. The first of all laws is to respect the laws: the severity of penalties is only a vain resource, invented by little minds in order to substitute terror for that respect which they have no means of obtaining. ROUSSEAU, *A Discourse on Political Economy* (1758), tr. G. D. H. Cole.

13. Whipping and abuse are like laudanum; you have to double the dose as the sensibilities decline. HARRIET BEECHER STOWE, *Uncle Tom's Cabin* (1852), 20.

14. He only may chastise who loves. RABINDRANATH TAGORE, "The Judge," *The Crescent Moon* (1913).

## 761. PUNISHMENT, CAPITAL

**See also 760. Punishment**

1. It is fairly obvious that those who are in favor of the death penalty have more affinity with assassins than those who are not. RÉMY DE GOURMONT, *Pensees inedites* (1924?).

2. The scaffold is a sort of monster created by the judge and the workman, a spectre which seems to live with a kind of unspeakable life, drawn from all the death which it has wrought. VICTOR HUGO, "Fantine," *Les Misérables* (1862), 1.4, tr. Charles E. Wilbour.

3. When a man knows he is to be hanged in a fortnight, it concentrates his mind wonderfully. SAMUEL JOHNSON, quoted in Boswell's *Life of Samuel Johnson*, Sept. 19, 1777.

4. The compensation for a death sentence is knowledge of the exact hour when one is to die. A great luxury, but one that is well earned. VLADIMIR NABOKOV, *Invitation to a Beheading* (1934), 1.

5. It is far more ignominious to die by justice than by an unjust sedition. PASCAL, *Pensées* (1670), 789, tr. W. F. Trotter.

6. No one is hanged who has money in his pocket. RUSSIAN PROVERB.

7. There is no great difficulty to separate the soul from the body, but it is not so easy to restore life to the dead. SA'DI, *Gulistan* (1258), 8.56, tr. James Ross.

## 762. PUNS

**See also 1054. Wit**

1. There is no kind of false wit which has been so recommended by the practice of all ages, as that which consists in a jingle of words, and is comprehended under the general name of *Punning*. JOSEPH ADDISON, *The Spectator* (1711–12), 61.

2. Who makes a pun will pick a pocket. ENGLISH PROVERB.

3. The goodness of the true pun is in the direct ratio of its intolerability. EDGAR ALLAN POE, *Marginalia* (1844–49), 1.

## 763. PURITANS AND PURITANISM

**See also 750. Prudery**

1. Puritanism—The haunting fear that someone, somewhere, may be happy. H. L. MENCKEN, "Sententiae," *A Book of Burlesques* (1920).

2. We are decendid from the Puritins, who nobly fled from a land of despitism to a land of freedim, where they could not only enjoy their own religion, but prevent everybody else from enjoyin' *his*. ARTEMUS WARD, "Is Introduced at the Club," *Artemus Ward in London* (1872).

## 764. PURITY

**See also 57. Association; 476. Innocence**

1. The sun, though it passes through dirty places, yet remains as pure as before. FRANCIS BACON, *The Advancement of Learning* (1605), 2, ed. John Dewey.

2. No one is more dangerous than he who imagines himself pure in heart: for his purity, by definition, is unassailable. JAMES BALDWIN, "The Black Boy Looks at the White Boy," *Nobody Knows My Name* (1961).

3. When he has no lust, no hatred, / A man walks safely among the things of lust and hatred. *Bhagavadgita*, 2, tr. Swami Prabhavananda and Christopher Isherwood.

4. Unto the pure all things are pure. *Bible*, Titus 1:15.

5. In an ermine spots are soon discovered. THOMAS FULLER, M.D., *Gnomologia* (1732), 2814.

6. Whoso doth no evil is apt to suspect none. THOMAS FULLER, M.D., *Gnomologia* (1732), 5727.

7. Purity / Is obscurity. OGDEN NASH, "Reflection on a Wicked World," *Verses from 1929 On* (1959).

8. My strength is as the strength of ten, / Because my heart is pure. ALFRED, LORD TENNYSON, "Sir Galahad" (1842), 3.

## 765. PURPOSE

**See also 222. Decision; 284. Ends; 463. Indecision; 601. Motives; 801. Resolution; 860. Self-determination; 1049. Will; 1050. Willingness**

1. A man should have any number of little aims about which he should be conscious and for which he should have names, but he should have neither name for, nor consciousness concerning, the main aim of his life. SAMUEL BUTLER (d. 1902), "Unprofessional Sermons," *Note-Books* (1912).

2. A windmill is eternally at work to accomplish one end, although it shifts with every variation of the weathercock, and assumes ten different positions in a day. CHARLES CALEB COLTON, *Lacon* (1825), 2.63.

3. The secret of success is constancy to purpose. BENJAMIN DISRAELI, speech, June 24, 1870.

4. The idea of life having a purpose stands and falls with the religious system. SIGMUND FREUD, *Civilization and Its Discontents* (1930), 2, tr. James Strachey.

5. Good purposes should be the directors of good actions, not the apology for bad. THOMAS FULLER, M.D., *Gnomologia* (1732), 1728.

6. Many persons have a wrong idea of what constitutes true happiness. It is not attained through self-gratification but through fidelity to a worthy purpose. HELEN KELLER, *Helen Keller's Journal* (1938).

7. Men, like nails, lose their usefulness when they lose direction and begin to bend. WALTER SAVAGE LANDOR, "Cromwell and Walter Noble," *Imaginary Conversations* (1824–53).

8. Obstacles cannot crush me / Every obstacle yields to stern resolve / He who is fixed to a star does not change his mind. LEONARDO DA VINCI, *Notebooks* (c. 1500), tr. Jean Paul Richter.

9. He who would make serious use of his life must always act as though he had a long time to live and must schedule his time as though he were about to die. ÉMILE LITTRÉ, *Dictionnaire de la langue française* (1877), 3.

10. The great and glorious masterpiece of man is to know how to live to purpose. MONTAIGNE, "Of experience," *Essays* (1580–88), tr. Charles Cotton and W. C. Hazlitt.

11. The soul that has no established aim loses itself. MONTAIGNE, "Of idleness," *Essays* (1580–88), tr. Charles Cotton and W. C. Hazlitt.

12. There is one quality more important than "know-how" and we cannot accuse the United States of any undue amount of it. This is "know-what" by which we determine not only how to accomplish our purposes, but what our purposes are to be. NORBERT WIENER, *The Human Use of Human Beings* (1954), 10.

# Q

## 766. QUARRELING

**See also 51. Argument; 250. Discord; 342. Fighting**

1. The quarrels of friends are the opportunities of foes. AESOP, "The Lions and the Bulls," *Fables* (6th c. B.C.?), tr. Thomas James.

2. Little quarrels often prove / To be but new recruits of love. SAMUEL BUTLER (d. 1680), *Hudibras* (1663), 3.1.

3. Looking at God instantly reduces our disposition to dissent from our brother. EMERSON, *Journals*, 1831.

4. When we quarrel, how we wish we had been blameless. EMERSON, *Journals*, 1863.

5. Never fall out with your bread and butter. ENGLISH PROVERB.

6. The last sound on the worthless earth will be two human beings trying to launch a homemade space ship and already quarreling about where they are going next. WILLIAM FAULKNER, address, Denver, Colo., Oct. 2, 1959.

7. Most quarrels amplify a misunderstanding. ANDRÉ GIDE, *Journals*, 1920, tr. Justin O'Brien.

8. You can make up a quarrel, but it will always show where it was patched. EDGAR WATSON HOWE, *Country Town Sayings* (1911).

9. It takes in reality only one to make a quarrel. It is useless for the sheep to pass resolutions in favour of vegetarianism, while the wolf remains of a different opinion. WILLIAM RALPH INGE, "Patriotism," *Outspoken Essays: First Series* (1919).

10. An association of men who will not quarrel with one another is a thing which never yet existed, from the greatest confederacy of nations down to a town-meeting or a vestry. THOMAS JEFFERSON, letter to John Taylor, 1798.

11. Quarrels would not last long if the fault was only on one side. LA ROCHEFOUCAULD, *Maxims* (1665), tr. Kenneth Pratt.

12. Friendships ought to be immortal, hostilities mortal. LIVY, *Ab Urbe Condita* (c. 29 B.C.), 40.46.

13. The same reason that makes us wrangle with a neighbor, causes a war between princes. MONTAIGNE, "Apology for Raimond de Sebonde," *Essays* (1580–88), tr. Charles Cotton and W. C. Hazlitt.

14. I say, when there are spats, kiss and make up before the day is done and live to fight another day. RANDOLPH RAY, *New York World-Telegram & Sun*, June 30, 1956.

15. Beware / Of entrance to a quarrel; but being in, / Bear't that th' opposed may be beware of thee. SHAKESPEARE, *Hamlet* (1600), 1.3.65.

16. For souls in growth, great quarrels are great emancipations. LOGAN PEARSALL SMITH, *Afterthoughts* (1931), 1.

17. It is in disputes as in armies, where the weaker side sets up false lights, and makes a great noise, to make the enemy believe them more numerous and strong than they really are. JONATHAN SWIFT, *Thoughts on Various Subjects* (1711).

18. Weakness on both sides is, as we know, the motto of all quarrels. VOLTAIRE, "Weakness on Both Sides," *Philosophical Dictionary* (1764).

19. Make sure to be in with your equals if you're going to fall out with your superiors. *Yiddish Proverbs* (1949), ed. Hanan J. Ayalti.

### QUESTIONS

See 478. Inquiry

### QUICKNESS

See 409. Haste; 919. Speed

### 767. QUOTATIONS

See also 294. Epigrams; 568. Maxims

1. The majority of those who put together collections of verses or epigrams resemble those who eat cherries or oysters: they begin by choosing the best and end by eating everything. CHAMFORT, *Maxims et pensées* (1805), 1.

2. I hate quotations. Tell me what you know. EMERSON, *Journals*, 1849.

3. Classical quotation is the parole of literary men all over the world. SAMUEL JOHNSON, quoted in Boswell's *Life of Samuel Johnson*, May 8, 1781.

4. Though old the thought and oft exprest, / 'Tis his at last who says it best. JAMES RUSSELL LOWELL, "For an Autograph," *Under the Willows and Other Poems* (1868).

5. Most men are rich in borrowed sufficiency: a man may very well say a good thing, give a good answer, cite a good sentence, without at all seeing the force of either the one or the other. MONTAIGNE, "Of the art of conference," *Essays* (1580–88), tr. Charles Cotton and W. C. Hazlitt.

6. A good aphorism is too hard for the tooth of time, and is not worn away by all the centuries, although it serves as food for every epoch. NIETZSCHE, *Miscellaneous Maxims and Opinions* (1879), 168, tr. Paul V. Cohn.

7. A fine quotation is a diamond on the finger of a man of wit, and a pebble in the hand of a fool. JOSEPH ROUX, *Meditations of a Parish Priest* (1886), 1.74, tr. Isabel F. Hapgood.

8. What a good thing Adam had—when he said a good thing he knew nobody had said it before. MARK TWAIN, *Notebook* (1935).

## R

### 768. RACE

See also 40. Anglo-Saxons; 83. Blacks; 769. Racial Prejudice; 1047. Whites

1. It is not races but individuals that are noble and courageous or ignoble and craven or considerate or persistent or philosophical or reasonable. The race gets credit when the percentage of noble individuals is high. EDWIN WAY TEALE, "January 9," *Circle of the Seasons* (1953).

## 769. RACIAL PREJUDICE

See also 83. Blacks; 768. Race; 1047. Whites

1. Sometimes, it's [racial prejudice] like a hair across your cheek. You can't see it, you can't find it with your fingers, but you keep brushing at it because the feel of it is irritating. MARIAN ANDERSON, *Ladies' Home Journal*, September 1960.

2. Race prejudice is not only a shadow over the colored—it is a shadow over all of us, and the shadow is darkest over those who feel it least and allow its evil effects to go on. PEARL S. BUCK, *What America Means to Me* (1943), 1.

3. Cannot the nation that has absorbed ten million foreigners into its political life without catastrophe absorb ten million Negro Americans into that same political life at less cost than their unjust and illegal exclusion will involve? W. E. B. DU BOIS, "No Cowards or Trucklers," *In Their Own Words: 1865–1916*, v. 2, ed. Milton Meltzer.

4. Race prejudice decreases values both real estate and human; crime, ignorance and filth decrease values. W. E. B. DU BOIS, "What Would You Do?" *In Their Own Words: 1916–1966*, v. 3, ed. Milton Meltzer.

5. The problem of the Twentieth Century is the problem of the color-line. W. E. B. DU BOIS, *The Souls of Black Folk* (1903), 2.

6. Who makes and keeps the Jew or the Negro base, who but you, who exclude them from the rights which others enjoy? EMERSON, *Journals*, 1867.

7. To live anywhere in the world today and be against equality because of race or color, is like living in Alaska and being against snow. WILLIAM FAULKNER, "On Fear: Deep South in Labor: Mississippi," *Essays, Speeches & Public Letters* (1965).

8. The American economy, the American society, the American unconscious are all racist. MICHAEL HARRINGTON, *The Other America* (1962), 4.3.

9. There is a tendency to judge a race, a nation or any distinct group by its least worthy members. ERIC HOFFER, *The True Believer* (1951), 1.3.18.

10. There are no "white" or "colored" signs on the foxholes or graveyards of battle. JOHN F. KENNEDY, message to U.S. Congress on civil rights, June 19, 1963.

11. I have a dream that my four little children will one day live in a nation where they will not be judged by the color of their skin but by the content of their character. MARTIN LUTHER KING, JR., speech, Washington, D.C., June 15, 1963.

12. Segregation is on its deathbed—the question now is, how costly will the segregationists make the funeral? MARTIN LUTHER KING, JR., address, Villanova University, Jan. 20, 1965.

13. In the end, as any successful teacher will tell you, you can only teach the things that you are. If we practice racism then it is racism that we teach. MAX LERNER, "We Teach What We Are," *Actions and Passions* (1949).

14. A segregated school system produces children who, when they graduate, graduate with crippled minds. MALCOLM X, *Malcolm X Speaks* (1965), 3.

15. "Segregation" is such an active word that it suggests someone is trying to segregate somebody else. So the word "apartheid" was introduced. Now it has such a stench in the nostrils of the world, they are referring to "autogeneous development." ALAN PATON, *The New York Times*, Oct. 24, 1960.

16. Shame on the cant and hypocrisy of those who can teach virtue, preach righteousness, and pray blessings for those only with skins colored like their own. C. LENOX REMOND, *The Mind of the Negro As Reflected in Letters Written During the Crisis, 1800–1860* (1926), ed. Carter G. Woodson.

17. Forgive us for not wanting to recognize our relatives in Your family who are black or red or yellow or white, whose children's children may be our grandchildren; for accepting people we like, but rejecting those we do not like because they are not of our class or color. UNITED PRESBYTERIAN CHURCH, *Litany for Holy Communion* (1968).

## 770. RADICALISM

See also 175. Conservatism; 533. Liberalism; 704. Political Parties

1. The spirit of our American radicalism is destructive and aimless: it is not loving, it has no ulterior and divine ends; but is destructive only out of hatred and selfishness.

EMERSON, "Politics," *Essays: Second Series* (1844).

2. I never dared to be radical when young / For fear it would make me conservative when old. ROBERT FROST, "Ten Mills," *A Further Range* (1936).

3. Radicalism itself ceases to be radical when absorbed mainly in preserving its control over a society or an economy. ERIC HOFFER, *The Passionate State of Mind* (1954), 21a.

4. A Radical is a man with both feet firmly planted—in the air. FRANKLIN D. ROOSEVELT, radio address, Oct. 26, 1939.

5. You sometimes find something good in the lunatic fringe. In fact, we have got as part of our social and economic government today a whole lot of things which in my boyhood were considered lunatic fringe, and yet they are now part of everyday life. FRANKLIN D. ROOSEVELT, press conference, May 30, 1944.

6. The radical of one century is the conservative of the next. MARK TWAIN, *Notebook* (1935).

## RADIO
See 563. Mass Media

## 771. RAIN
See also 772. Rainbows; 848. Seasons; 1043. Weather

1. Rain! whose soft architectural hands have power to cut stones, and chisel to shapes of grandeur the very mountains. HENRY WARD BEECHER, *Proverbs from Plymouth Pulpit* (1887).

2. The thirsty earth soaks up the rain, / And drinks, and gapes for drink again. / The plants suck in the earth, and are / With constant drinking fresh and fair. ABRAHAM COWLEY, "Drinking," *From Anacreon* (1656).

3. The good rain, like a bad preacher, does not know when to leave off. EMERSON, *Journals*, 1834.

4. Rain is good for vegetables, and for the animals who eat those vegetables, and for the animals who eat those animals. SAMUEL JOHNSON, quoted in Boswell's *Life of Samuel Johnson*, July 6, 1763.

## 772. RAINBOWS
See also 771. Rain

1. After a debauch of thunder-shower, the weather takes the pledge and signs it with a rainbow. THOMAS BAILEY ALDRICH, "Leaves from a Notebook," *Ponkapog Papers* (1903).

2. One can enjoy a rainbow without necessarily forgetting the forces that made it. MARK TWAIN, "Queen Victoria's Jubilee" (1897).

3. My heart leaps up when I behold / A rainbow in the sky: / So was it when my life began; / So is it now I am a man; / So be it when I shall grow old, / Or let me die! WILLIAM WORDSWORTH, "My Heart Leaps Up When I Behold" (1802).

## 773. RANK
See also 52. Aristocracy; 133. Class; 641. Obscurity; 662. Parasites; 903. Snobbery; 926. Status; 1005. Unimportance

1. Surely men of low degree are vanity, and men of high degree are a lie. *Bible*, Psalms 62:9.

2. The defeats and victories of the fellows at the top aren't always defeats and victories for the fellows at the bottom. BERTOLT BRECHT, *Mother Courage* (1939), 3, tr. Eric Bentley.

3. Detestation of the high is the involuntary homage of the low. CHARLES DICKENS, *A Tale of Two Cities* (1859), 2.9.

4. Even workhouses have their aristocracy. ENGLISH PROVERB.

5. The greatest monarch on the proudest throne / is obliged to sit upon his own arse. BENJAMIN FRANKLIN, *Poor Richard's Almanack* (1732–57).

6. The higher an ape mounts, the more he shows his breech. THOMAS FULLER, M.D., *Gnomologia* (1732), 4591.

7. Better in the dust than crawl near the throne. GERMAN PROVERB.

8. When everyone is somebodee, / Then no one's anybody. W. S. GILBERT, *The Gondoliers* (1889), 2.

9. A man's name, title, and rank are artificial and impermanent; they do nothing to

reveal what he really is, even to himself. JEAN GIRAUDOUX, *Siegfried* (1928), 2, tr. Phyllis La Farge with Peter H. Judd.

10. The man who occupies the first place seldom plays the principal part. GOETHE, *The Sorrows of Young Werther* (1774), 2, Jan. 8, 1772, tr. Victor Lange.

11. A cat may look on a king. JOHN HEYWOOD, *Proverbs* (1546), 2.5.

12. It is a very curious fact that, with all our boasted "free and equal" superiority over the communities of the Old World, our people [Americans] have the most enormous appetite for Old World titles of distinction. OLIVER WENDELL HOLMES, SR., *Over the Teacups* (1891), 9.

13. A fly, Sir, may sting a stately horse and make him wince; but one is but an insect, and the other is a horse still. SAMUEL JOHNSON, quoted in Boswell's *Life of Samuel Johnson*, footnote on Warburton, 1754.

14. Subordination tends greatly to human happiness. Were we all upon an equality, we should have no other enjoyment than mere animal pleasure. SAMUEL JOHNSON, quoted in Boswell's *Life of Samuel Johnson*, July 20, 1763.

15. There is merit without rank, but there is no rank without some merit. LA ROCHEFOUCAULD, *Maxims* (1665), tr. Kenneth Pratt.

16. When fortune surprises us by giving us an important position, without having led us to it by degrees, or without our being elevated to it by our hopes, it is almost impossible for us to maintain ourselves suitably in it, and appear worthy of possessing it. LA ROCHEFOUCAULD, *Maxims* (1665), tr. Kenneth Pratt.

17. Bottom is bottom, even if it is turned upside down. STANISLAW LEC, *Unkempt Thoughts* (1962), tr. Jacek Galazka.

18. The good Lord sees your heart, not the braid on your jacket, before Him we are all in our birthday suits, generals and common men alike. THOMAS MANN, *The Magic Mountain* (1924), 6.8, tr. H. T. Lowe-Porter.

19. A throne is only a bench covered with velvet. NAPOLEON I, *Maxims* (1804–15).

20. There may be as much nobility in being last as in being first, because the two positions are equally necessary in the world, the one to complement the other. JOSÉ ORTEGA Y GASSET, "Preliminary Meditation," *Meditations on Quixote* (1914).

21. To call a king "Prince" is pleasing, because it diminishes his rank. PASCAL, *Pensées* (1670), 42, tr. W. F. Trotter.

22. That in the captain's but a choleric word / Which in the soldier is flat blasphemy. SHAKESPEARE, *Measure for Measure* (1604–05), 2.2.130.

23. Titles distinguish the mediocre, embarrass the superior, and are disgraced by the inferior. GEORGE BERNARD SHAW, "Maxims for Revolutionists," *Man and Superman* (1903).

24. It is a maxim, that those to whom everybody allows the second place, have an undoubted title to the first. JONATHAN SWIFT, dedication, *The Tale of a Tub* (1704).

25. The sparrow is sorry for the peacock at the burden of its tail. RABINDRANATH TAGORE, *Stray Birds* (1916), 58.

26. No man is safe above but he that will gladly be beneath. THOMAS À KEMPIS, *The Imitation of Christ* (1426), 1.20.

27. It is an interesting question how far men would retain their relative rank if they were divested of their clothes. THOREAU, "Economy," *Walden* (1854).

28. Emperors, kings, artisans, peasants, big people, little people—at bottom we are all alike and all the same; all just alike on the inside, and when our clothes are off, nobody can tell which of us is which. MARK TWAIN, "Does the Race of Man Love a Lord?" *North American Review*, April 1902.

29. Look down if you would know how high you stand. *Yiddish Proverbs* (1949), ed. Hanan J. Ayalti.

## 774. RASHNESS

**See also 110. Cautiousness; 351. Folly; 749. Prudence**

1. If you leap into a well, Providence is not bound to fetch you out. THOMAS FULLER, M.D., *Gnomologia* (1732), 2795.

2. Rashness succeeds often, still more often fails. NAPOLEON I, *Maxims* (1804–15).

## 775. RATIONALIZATION

See also 312. Excuses; 320. Explanation

1. The fox condemns the trap, not himself. WILLIAM BLAKE, "Proverbs of Hell," *The Marriage of Heaven and Hell* (1790).

2. We do what we can, and then make a theory to prove our performance the best. EMERSON, *Journals*, 1834.

3. To give a reason for anything is to breed a doubt of it. WILLIAM HAZLITT, "On the Difference Between Writing and Speaking," *The Plain Speaker* (1826).

4. In the conduct of life we make use of deliberation to justify ourselves in doing what we want to do. W. SOMERSET MAUGHAM, *The Summing Up* (1938), 15.

5. There's nothing people can't contrive to praise or condemn and find justification for doing so, according to their age and their inclinations. MOLIÈRE, *The Misanthrope* (1666), 3, tr. John Wood.

## READING

See 91. Books and Reading

## 776. REALISM

See also 302. Evasion; 714. Practicality; 777. Reality

1. I would be bold and bear / To look into the swarthiest face of things, / For God's sake who has made them. ELIZABETH BARRETT BROWNING, *Aurora Leigh* (1856), 6.147.

2. Realists do not fear the results of their study. DOSTOEVSKY, "The Latest Literary Phenomenon," *Polnoye Sobraniye Sochinyeni* (*Complete Collected Works*, 1895), v. 9.

3. Let us replace sentimentalism by realism, and dare to uncover those simple and terrible laws which, be they seen or unseen, pervade and govern. EMERSON, "Worship," *The Conduct of Life* (1860).

4. It is only by knowing how little life has in store for us that we are able to look on the bright side and avoid disappointment. ELLEN GLASGOW, *The Sheltered Life* (1932).

5. Our safety is not in blindness, but in facing our dangers. SCHILLER, "The Sublime" (1793?).

## 777. REALITY

See also 326. Facts; 447. Illusion; 776. Realism

1. I like reality. It tastes of bread. JEAN ANOUILH, *Catch as Catch Can* (1960), tr. Lucienne Hill.

2. We take our shape, it is true, within and against that cage of reality bequeathed us at our birth; and yet it is precisely through our dependence on this reality that we are most endlessly betrayed. JAMES BALDWIN, "Everybody's Protest Novel" (1949), *Notes of a Native Son* (1955).

3. If it were possible to talk to the unborn, one could never explain to them how it feels to be alive, for life is washed in the speechless real. JACQUES BARZUN, *The House of Intellect* (1959), 6.

4. Facts as facts do not always create a spirit of reality, because reality is a spirit. G. K. CHESTERTON, "On the Classics," *Come to Think of It* (1930).

5. Everything is a dangerous drug except reality, which is unendurable. CYRIL CONNOLLY, *The Unquiet Grave* (1945), 1.

6. The sky is not less blue because the blind man does not see it. DANISH PROVERB.

7. The real world is not easy to live in. It is rough; it is slippery. Without the most clear-eyed adjustments we fall and get crushed. A man must stay sober: not always, but most of the time. CLARENCE DAY, "In His Baby Blue Ship," *The Crow's Nest* (1921).

8. What is actual is actual only for one time / And only for one place. T. S. ELIOT, "Ash Wednesday" (1930), 1.

9. There is no reality except the one contained within us. That is why so many people live such an unreal life. They take the images outside them for reality and never allow the world within to assert itself. HERMANN HESSE, *Demian* (1919), 6, tr. Michael Roloff and Michael Lebeck.

10. All our separate fictions add up to joint reality. STANISLAW LEC, *Unkempt Thoughts* (1962), tr. Jacek Galazka.

11. To mention a loved object, a person, or a place to someone else is to invest that object with reality. ANNE MORROW LINDBERGH, "Baker Lake," *North to the Orient* (1935).

12. What was once called the objective world is a sort of Rorschach ink blot, into which each culture, each system of science and religion, each type of personality, reads a meaning only remotely derived from the shape and color of the blot itself. LEWIS MUMFORD, "Orientation to Life," *The Conduct of Life* (1951).

13. Reality is a staircase going neither up nor down, we don't move, today is today, always is today. OCTAVIO PAZ, "The Endless Instant," *Modern European Poetry* (1966), ed. Willis Barnstone.

14. Each one of us has his own reality to be respected before God, even when it is harmful to one's very self. LUIGI PIRANDELLO, *Six Characters in Search of an Author* (1921), 1, tr. Edward Storer.

15. You too must not count overmuch on your reality as you feel it today, since, like that of yesterday, it may prove an illusion for you tomorrow. LUIGI PIRANDELLO, *Six Characters in Search of an Author* (1921), 3, tr. Edward Storer.

16. More wisdom is latent in things-as-they-are than in all the words men use. SAINT-EXUPÉRY, *The Wisdom of the Sands* (1948), 22, tr. Stuart Gilbert.

17. In the American metaphysic, reality is always material reality, hard, resistant, unformed, impenetrable, and unpleasant. LIONEL TRILLING, "Reality in America," *The Liberal Imagination* (1950).

## 778. REASON

**See also 51. Argument; 491. Intelligence; 738. Proof; 954. Systems; 967. Theory; 968. Thought; 1013. Unreason**

1. The mind resorts to reason for want of training. HENRY ADAMS, *The Education of Henry Adams* (1907), 24.

2. Analysis kills spontaneity. The grain once ground into flour springs and germinates no more. HENRI FRÉDÉRIC AMIEL, *Journal*, Nov. 7, 1878, tr. Mrs. Humphry Ward.

3. Logic, n. The art of thinking and reasoning in strict accordance with the limitations and incapacities of the human misunderstanding. AMBROSE BIERCE, *The Devil's Dictionary* (1881–1911).

4. The world was made to be inhabited by beasts, but studied and contemplated by man: 'tis the debt of our reason we owe unto God, and the homage we pay for not being beasts. SIR THOMAS BROWNE, *Religio Medici* (1642), 1.

5. Logic is like the sword—those who appeal to it shall perish by it. SAMUEL BUTLER (d. 1902), "First Principles," *Note-Books* (1912).

6. No man observes the law of God but in applying his reason to it, by aid from above, through his faculty of thought. SARA COLERIDGE, "On Rationalism," quoted in Samuel Taylor Coleridge's *Aids to Reflection* (1825).

7. Peace rules the day, where reason rules the mind. WILLIAM COLLINS, *Persian Eclogues* (1742), 2.

8. Reason flies / When following the senses, on clipped wings. DANTE, "Paradiso," 2, *The Divine Comedy* (c. 1300–21), tr. Lawrence Grant White.

9. The difference between the reason of man and the instinct of the beast is this, that the beast does but know, but the man knows that he knows. JOHN DONNE, *Sermons*, No. 57, 1628.

10. Man has such a predilection for systems and abstract deductions that he is ready to distort the truth intentionally, he is ready to deny the evidence of his senses only to justify his logic. DOSTOEVSKY, *Notes from Underground* (1864), 1.7, tr. Constance Garnett.

11. To a reasonable creature, that alone is insupportable which is unreasonable; but everything reasonable may be supported. EPICTETUS, *Discourses* (2nd c.), 1.2, tr. Thomas W. Higginson.

12. Reason can wrestle / And overthrow terror. EURIPIDES, *Iphigenia in Aulis* (c. 405 B.C.), tr. Charles R. Walker.

13. 'Tis in vain to speak reason where 'twill not be heard. THOMAS FULLER, M.D., *Gnomologia* (1732), 5088.

14. Reason, ruling alone, is a force confining; and passion, unattended, is a flame that burns to its own destruction. KAHLIL GIBRAN, "On Reason and Passion," *The Prophet* (1923).

15. The want of logic annoys. Too much logic bores. Life eludes logic, and everything that logic alone constructs remains artificial and forced. ANDRÉ GIDE, *Journals*, May 12, 1927, tr. Justin O'Brien.

16. What eludes logic is the most precious element in us, and one can draw nothing

from a syllogism that the mind has not put there in advance. ANDRÉ GIDE, *Journals*, June 1927, tr. Justin O'Brien.

17. Logic is not satisfied with assertion. It cares nothing for the opinions of the great—nothing for the prejudices of the many, and least of all for the superstitions of the dead. ROBERT G. INGERSOLL, *Prose-Poems and Selections* (1884).

18. We may take Fancy for a companion, but must follow Reason as our guide. SAMUEL JOHNSON, letter to James Boswell, c. March 15, 1774, quoted in Boswell's *Life of Samuel Johnson*.

19. Logic is the art of making truth prevail. LA BRUYÈRE, *Characters* (1688), 1.55, tr. Henry Van Laun.

20. At the very smallest wheel of our reasoning it is possible for a handful of questions to break the bank of our answers. ANTONIO MACHADO, *Juan de Mairena* (1943), 43, tr. Ben Belitt.

21. Human reason needs only to will more strongly than fate, and she *is* fate! THOMAS MANN, *The Magic Mountain* (1924), 6.2, tr. H. T. Lowe-Porter.

22. Reason also is choice. MILTON, *Paradise Lost* (1667), 3.108.

23. Rational thought is interpretation according to a scheme which we cannot escape. NIETZSCHE, "Notes" (1887), 522, in *The Portable Nietzsche*, tr. Walter Kaufmann.

24. The last function of reason is to recognize that there are an infinity of things which surpass it. PASCAL, *Pensées* (1670), 267.

25. Reason commands us far more imperiously than a master; in disobeying the latter we are made unhappy, in disobeying the former, fools. PASCAL, *Pensées* (1670), 345.

26. Logic is one thing, the human animal another. You can quite easily propose a logical solution to something and at the same time hope in your heart of hearts it won't work out. LUIGI PIRANDELLO, *The Pleasure of Honesty* (1917), 2, tr. William Murray.

27. Say first, of God above or man below, / What can we reason but from what we know? ALEXANDER POPE, *An Essay on Man* (1733–34), 1.17.

28. Reason cannot save us, nothing can; but reason can mitigate the cruelty of living. PHILIP RIEFF, preface to *Freud: The Mind of the Moralist* (1959).

29. Reason? That dreary shed, that hutch for grubby schoolboys. THEODORE ROETHKE, "I Cry, Love! Love!" *The Collected Verse of Theodore Roethke* (1961).

30. We distrust our heart too much, and our head not enough. JOSEPH ROUX, *Meditations of a Parish Priest* (1886), 9.4, tr. Isabel F. Hapgood.

31. Pure logic is the ruin of the spirit. SAINT-EXUPÉRY, *Flight to Arras* (1942), 2, tr. Lewis Galantière.

32. The seed haunted by the sun never fails to find its way between the stones in the ground. And the pure logician, if no sun draws him forth, remains entangled in his logic. SAINT-EXUPÉRY, *Flight to Arras* (1942), 22, tr. Lewis Galantière.

33. Reason and happiness are like other flowers—they wither when plucked. GEORGE SANTAYANA, *The Life of Reason: Reason and Religion* (1905–06), 10.

34. Reason in my philosophy is only a harmony among irrational impulses. GEORGE SANTAYANA, *Persons and Places: The Middle Span* (1945), 4.

35. Reason deserves to be called a prophet; for in showing us the consequence and effect of our actions in the present, does it not tell us what the future will be? SCHOPENHAUER, "Further Psychological Observations," *Parerga and Paralipomena* (1851), tr. T. Bailey Saunders.

36. In these anxious times many of us are less astonished that reason is ever suspended than that it should ever prevail, even during the briefest of intervals. MORTON IRVING SEIDEN, *The Paradox of Hate: A Study in Ritual Murder* (1967), 1.

37. The man who listens to Reason is lost: Reason enslaves all whose minds are not strong enough to master her. GEORGE BERNARD SHAW, "Maxims for Revolutionists," *Man and Superman* (1903).

38. A mind all logic is like a knife all blade. It makes the hand bleed that uses it. RABINDRANATH TAGORE, *Stray Birds* (1916), 193.

39. The supreme triumph of reason, the analytical . . . faculty, is to cast doubt upon its own validity. MIGUEL DE UNAMUNO, "The Rationalist Dissolution," *Tragic Sense of Life* (1913), tr. J. E. Crawford Flitch.

40. All that is vital is irrational, and all that is rational is anti-vital, for reason is essentially skeptical. MIGUEL DE UNAMUNO,

"The Rationalist Dissolution," *Tragic Sense of Life* (1913), tr. J. E. Crawford Flitch.

41. Reason deceives us more often than does nature. VAUVENARGUES, *Reflections and Maxims* (1746), 123.

## 779. REBELLION

See also 254. Disobedience; 256. Dissent; 651. Opposition; 813. Revolution; 1024. Violence

1. Rebel, n. A proponent of a new misrule who has failed to establish it. AMBROSE BIERCE, *The Devil's Dictionary* (1881–1911).

2. No one can go on being a rebel too long without turning into an autocrat. LAWRENCE DURRELL, *Balthazar* (1958), 2.6.

3. Who draws his sword against the prince must throw away the scabbard. ENGLISH PROVERB.

4. A little rebellion, now and then, is a good thing, and as necessary in the political world as storms in the physical. THOMAS JEFFERSON, letter to James Madison, Jan. 30, 1787.

5. As a dimension of man, rebellion actually defines him. ROBERT LINDNER, "The Instinct of Rebellion," *Must You Conform?* (1956).

6. When I refuse to obey an unjust law, I do not contest the right of the majority to command, but I simply appeal from the sovereignty of the people to the sovereignty of mankind. ALEXIS DE TOCQUEVILLE, *Democracy in America* (1835–39), 1.15.

## 780. RECEIVING

See also 382. Gifts and Giving; 397. Gratitude; 473. Ingratitude; 639. Obligation; 782. Recompense

1. Nothing costs so much as what is given us. THOMAS FULLER, M.D., *Gnomologia* (1732), 3660.

2. The art of acceptance is the art of making someone who has just done you a small favor wish that he might have done you a greater one. RUSSELL LYNES, *Reader's Digest*, December 1961.

3. Should not the giver be thankful that the receiver received? Is not giving a need? Is not receiving mercy? NIETZSCHE, "On the Great Longing," *Thus Spoke Zarathustra* (1883–92), 3, tr. Walter Kaufmann.

4. Only those who have, receive. JOSEPH ROUX, *Meditations of a Parish Priest* (1886), 4.110, tr. Isabel F. Hapgood.

## 781. RECIPROCITY

1. If you do good, good will be done to you; but if you do evil, the same will be measured back to you again. "Dabschelim and Bidpai," *Fables of Bidpai* (c. 750).

2. The sort of thing you say is the thing that will be said to you. HOMER, *Iliad* (9th c. B.C.), 20.250, tr. Richmond Lattimore.

3. Men seldom give pleasure when they are not pleased themselves. SAMUEL JOHNSON, *The Rambler* (1750–52), 74.

4. He who loves others is constantly loved by them. He who respects others is constantly respected by them. MENCIUS, *Works* (4th–3rd c. B.C.), 4, tr. Charles A. Wong.

5. Evidence of trust begets trust, and love is reciprocated by love. PLUTARCH, "Marriage Counsel," *Moralia* (c. A.D. 100), tr. Moses Hadas.

## RECKLESSNESS

See 90. Boldness; 213. Danger; 774. Rashness

## RECOGNITION

See 47. Appreciation

## 782. RECOMPENSE

See also 474. Injury; 673. Payment; 811. Revenge

1. By paying our other debts, we are equal with all mankind; but in refusing to pay a debt of revenge, we are superior. CHARLES CALEB COLTON, *Lacon* (1825), 1.232.

2. Recompense injury with justice, and recompense kindness with kindness. CONFUCIUS, *Analects* (6th c. B.C.), 14.36, tr. James Legge.

3. Men are more prone to revenge injuries than to requite kindnesses. THOMAS FULLER, M.D., *Gnomologia* (1732), 3389.

## 783. REFORM

See also 430. Humanitarianism; 440. Idealism; 458. Improvement; 475. Injustice; 1018. Utopia

1. In uplifting, get underneath. GEORGE ADE, "The Good Fairy with the Lorgnette," *Fables in Slang* (1899).

2. If you kick a man he kicks you back again. Therefore never be too eager to combat injustice. BERTOLT BRECHT, *The Threepenny Opera* (1928), 3.3, tr. Desmond Vesey and Eric Bentley.

3. Nobody expects to find comfort and companionability in reformers. HEYWOOD BROUN, "Whims," *New York World*, Feb. 6, 1928.

4. Many . . . have too rashly charged the troops of error, and remain as trophies unto the enemies of truth. SIR THOMAS BROWNE, *Religio Medici* (1642), 1.

5. Men reform a thing by removing the reality from it, and then do not know what to do with the unreality that is left. G. K. CHESTERTON, "On Domestic Servants," *Generally Speaking* (1928).

6. Attempts at reform, when they fail, strengthen despotism, as he that struggles tightens those cords he does not succeed in breaking. CHARLES CALEB COLTON, *Lacon* (1825), 1.440.

7. Experience has two things to teach: the first is that we must correct a great deal; the second, that we must not correct too much. DELACROIX, *lettre à Philarète Chasles*, March 8, 1860.

8. A man that'd expict to thrain lobsters to fly in a year is called a loonytic; but a man that thinks men can be tur-rned into angels be an iliction is called a rayformer an' remains at large. FINLEY PETER DUNNE, "Casual Observations," *Mr. Dooley's Philosophy* (1900).

9. [Th' rayformer] don't undherstand that people wud rather be wrong an' comfortable thin right in jail. FINLEY PETER DUNNE, "Reform Administration," *Observations by Mr. Dooley* (1902).

10. Every reform was once a private opinion, and when it shall be a private opinion again, it will solve the problem of the age. EMERSON, "History," *Essays: First Series* (1841).

11. The religions are obsolete when the reforms do not proceed from them. EMERSON, *Journals*, 1872.

12. Those who have given themselves the most concern about the happiness of peoples have made their neighbours very miserable. ANATOLE FRANCE, *The Crime of Sylvestre Bonnard* (1881), 2, tr. Lafcadio Hearn.

13. In battling evil, excess is good; for he who is moderate in announcing the truth is presenting half-truth. He conceals the other half out of fear of the people's wrath. KAHLIL GIBRAN, "Narcotics and Dissecting Knives," *Thoughts and Meditations* (1960), tr. Anthony R. Ferris.

14. All the evil in the world is the fault of the self-styled pure in heart, a result of their eagerness to unearth secrets and expose them to the light of the sun. JEAN GIRAUDOUX, *Electra* (1937), 2, tr. Phyllis La Farge with Peter H. Judd.

15. All reformism is characterized by utopian strategy and tactical opportunism. Graffito written during French student revolt, May 1968.

16. Those who are fond of setting things to rights, have no great objection to seeing them wrong. WILLIAM HAZLITT, *Characteristics* (1823).

17. Men, said the Devil, / are good to their brothers: / they don't want to mend / their own ways but each other's. PIET HEIN, "Mankind," *Grooks* (1966).

18. Every man is a reformer until reform tramps on his toes. EDGAR WATSON HOWE, *Country Town Sayings* (1911).

19. As soon as the people fix one Shame of the World, another turns up. EDGAR WATSON HOWE, *Ventures in Common Sense* (1919), 2.24.

20. Long customs are not easily broken: he that attempts to change the course of his own life very often labours in vain: and how shall we do that for others, which we are seldom able to do for ourselves? SAMUEL JOHNSON, *Rasselas* (1759), 29.

21. You've tried to reform what will not learn. / Shut doors on traits that you wish were dead; / They will open a window and return. LA FONTAINE, "The Cat Changed to a Woman," *Fables* (1668–94), tr. Marianne Moore.

22. The only ideals that count are those which express the possible development of an existing force. Reformers must never forget that three legs are a Quixotic ideal; two good legs a genuine one. WALTER LIPPMANN, "The Golden Rule and After," A

*Preface to Politics* (1914).

23. Unless the reformer can invent something which substitutes attractive virtues for attractive vices, he will fail. WALTER LIPPMANN, "The Taboo," *A Preface to Politics* (1914).

24. If you try to cleanse others, you will waste away in the process, like soap. MADAGASCAN PROVERB.

25. The urge to save humanity is almost always only a false-face for the urge to rule it. H. L. MENCKEN, *Minority Report* (1956), 369.

26. The spirit of improvement is not always a spirit of liberty, for it may aim at forcing improvements on an unwilling people. JOHN STUART MILL, *On Liberty* (1859), 3.

27. The man who is forever disturbed about the condition of humanity either has no problems of his own or has refused to face them. HENRY MILLER, *Sunday after the War* (1944).

28. It is a folly second to none, / To try to improve the world. MOLIÈRE, *The Misanthrope* (1666), 1.1.

29. All reformers are bachelors. GEORGE MOORE, *The Bending of the Bough* (1900), 1.

30. The men who have changed the universe have never accomplished it by changing officials but always by inspiring the people. NAPOLEON I, *Maxims* (1804–15).

31. Whoever fights monsters should see to it that in the process he does not become a monster. NIETZSCHE, *Beyond Good and Evil* (1886), 146, tr. Walter Kaufmann.

32. A long habit of not thinking a thing wrong, gives it a superficial appearance of being right, and raises at first a formidable outcry in defense of custom. THOMAS PAINE, introduction to *Common Sense* (1776).

33. To give up the task of reforming society is to give up one's responsibility as a free man. ALAN PATON, "The Challenge of Fear," *Saturday Review*, Sept. 9, 1967.

34. The men with the muck-rake are often indispensable to the well-being of society, but only if they know when to stop raking the muck. THEODORE ROOSEVELT, address, Washington, D.C., April 14, 1906.

35. The superannuated bawd feels no hesitation in forswearing fornication, nor the displaced police magistrate in foregoing oppression. SA'DI, *Gulistan* (1258), 8.120, tr. James Ross.

36. It is one of the consolations of middle-aged reformers that the good they inculcate must live after them if it is to live at all. SAKI, "The Byzantine Omelette," *Beasts and Super-Beasts* (1914).

37. Think of [your contemporaries] as they ought to be when you have to influence them, but think of them as they are when you are tempted to act on their behalf. SCHILLER, *On the Aesthetic Education of Man* (1795), 9, tr. Reginald Snell.

38. If anything ail a man, so that he does not perform his functions, if he have a pain in his bowels even,— for that is the seat of sympathy,—he forthwith sets about reforming the world. THOREAU, "Economy," *Walden* (1854).

39. There are a thousand hacking at the branches of evil to one who is striking at the root. THOREAU, "Economy," *Walden* (1854).

40. Nothing so needs reforming as other people's habits. MARK TWAIN, "Pudd'nhead Wilson's Calendar," *Pudd'nhead Wilson* (1894), 15.

41. Every abuse ought to be reformed, unless the reform is more dangerous than the abuse itself. VOLTAIRE, *Philosophical Dictionary* (1764).

## 784. REFUSAL

**See also 799. Request**

1. A soft refusal is not always taken, but a rude one is immediately believed. ALEXANDER CHASE, *Perspectives* (1966).

2. Better deny at once than promise long. DANISH PROVERB.

3. He who awaits the call, but sees the need, / Already sets his spirit to refuse it. DANTE, "Purgatorio," 17, *The Divine Comedy* (c. 1300–21), tr. Lawrence Grant White.

4. A civil denial is better than a rude grant. THOMAS FULLER, M.D., *Gnomologia* (1732), 38.

5. Better a friendly denial than unwilling compliance. GERMAN PROVERB.

6. The prompter the refusal, the less the disappointment. PUBLILIUS SYRUS, *Moral Sayings* (1st c. B.C.), 492, tr. Darius Lyman.

7. He who never says "no" is no true man.

SAINT-EXUPÉRY, *The Wisdom of the Sands* (1948), 29, tr. Stuart Gilbert.

8. No is no negative in a woman's mouth. SIR PHILIP SIDNEY, *Arcadia* (1590), 3.

9. In refusing benefits caution must be used lest we seem to despise or to refuse them for fear of having to repay them in kind. SPINOZA, *Ethics* (1677), 4, tr. Andrew Boyle.

## 785. REGRET

**See also 44. Apology; 793. Repentance**

1. We as often repent the good we have done as the ill. WILLIAM HAZLITT, *Characteristics* (1823).

2. Opportunities flit by while we sit regretting the chances we have lost, and the happiness that comes to us we heed not, because of the happiness that is gone. JEROME K. JEROME, "On Memory," *The Idle Thoughts of an Idle Fellow* (1889).

3. Ah, in this world, where every guiding thread / Ends suddenly in the one sure centre, death, / The visionary hand of Might-have-been / Alone can fill Desire's cup to the brim! JAMES RUSSELL LOWELL, "On the Death of a Friend's Child" (1844).

4. I have loved badly, loved the great / Too soon, withdrawn my words too late; / And eaten in an echoing hall / Alone and from a chipped plate / The words that I withdrew too late. EDNA ST. VINCENT MILLAY, "Theme and Variations," *Huntsman, What Quarry?* (1939).

5. Let us not burden our remembrance with / A heaviness that's gone. SHAKESPEARE, *The Tempest* (1611–12), 5.1.199.

6. To regret deeply is to live afresh. THOREAU, *Journal*, Nov. 13, 1839.

## 786. REJECTION

**See also 549. Love, Loss of; 550. Love, Unrequited**

1. Heaven has no rage like love to hatred turned, / Nor hell a fury like a woman scorned. WILLIAM CONGREVE, *The Mourning Bride* (1697), 3.8.

2. Spurn not the nobly-born / With love affected, / Nor treat with virtuous scorn / The well-connected. W. S. GILBERT, *Iolanthe* (1882), 1.

3. To find oneself jilted is a blow to one's pride. One must do one's best to forget it and if one doesn't succeed, at least one must pretend to. MOLIÈRE, *Tartuffe* (1664), 2, tr. John Wood.

4. No woman need be a dragon of vindictiveness. A snub coolly and discreetly given is, I think, sufficiently effective in rebuffing advances. MOLIÈRE, *Tartuffe* (1664), 4, tr. John Wood.

5. Oh, seek, my love, your newer way; / I'll not be left in sorrow. / So long as I have yesterday, / Go take your damned to-morrow! DOROTHY PARKER, "Godspeed," *Enough Rope* (1926), 2.

## 787. RELATIONSHIPS, HUMAN

**See also 497. Intimacy; 656. Others; 1001. Understanding Others**

1. Almost all of our relationships begin and most of them continue as forms of mutual exploitation, a mental or physical barter, to be terminated when one or both parties run out of goods. W. H. AUDEN, "Hic et Ille," *The Dyer's Hand* (1962).

2. Persons are fine things, but they cost so much! for thee I must pay me. EMERSON, *Journals*, 1843.

3. Without wearing any mask we are conscious of, we have a special face for each friend. OLIVER WENDELL HOLMES, SR., *The Professor at the Breakfast Table* (1860), 8.

4. The first thing to learn in intercourse with others is non-interference with their own peculiar ways of being happy, provided those ways do not assume to interfere by violence with ours. WILLIAM JAMES, "What Makes a Life Significant?" *Talks to Teachers and to Students* (1899).

5. To really know someone is to have loved and hated him in turn. MARCEL JOUHANDEAU, "Erotologie," *Défense de l'enfer* (1935).

6. Existence warps too much. It sets us so we can only receive certain kinds of opposite numbers. But in the abstract, in essence, any two human beings can find warmth together. NORMAN MAILER, *Barbary Shore* (1951), 19.

7. I present myself to you in a form suitable to the relationship I wish to achieve with you. LUIGI PIRANDELLO, *The Pleasure of Honesty* (1917), 1, tr. William Murray.

8. The opinions which we hold of one another, our relations with friends and kinsfolk are in no sense permanent, save in appearance, but are as eternally fluid as the sea itself. MARCEL PROUST, *Remembrance of Things Past: The Guermantes Way* (1913–27), tr. C. K. Scott-Moncrieff.

9. The bonds that unite another person to ourself exist only in our mind. MARCEL PROUST, *Remembrance of Things Past: The Sweet Cheat Gone* (1913-27), tr. C. K. Scott-Moncrieff.

10. There is no hope of joy except in human relations. SAINT-EXUPÉRY, *Wind, Sand, and Stars* (1939), 2.1, tr. Lewis Galantière.

11. Man is a knot, a web, a mesh into which relationships are tied. Only those relationships matter. SAINT-EXUPÉRY, *Flight to Arras* (1942), 19, tr. Lewis Galantière.

12. According as the man is, so must you humour him. TERENCE, *The Brothers* (160 B.C.), 3.3.61, tr. Henry Thomas Riley.

13. Those whom we can love, we can hate; to others we are indifferent. THOREAU, *Journal*, Feb. 24, 1857.

## 788. RELATIVENESS

**See also 152. Comparison**

1. In the country of the blind, the one-eyed man is king. MICHAEL APOSTOLIUS, *Proverbs* (15th c.).

2. In this unbelievable universe in which we live, there are no absolutes. Even parallel lines, reaching into infinity, meet somewhere yonder. PEARL S. BUCK, *A Bridge for Passing* (1962), 1.

3. When the moon is not full, the stars shine more brightly. BUGANDA PROVERB.

4. If we say that a thing is great or small by its own standard of great or small, then there is nothing in all creation which is not great, nothing which is not small. CHUANG TZU, *Works* (4th–3rd c. B.C.), 2.2, tr. Lin Yutang.

5. Bad is never good until worse happens. DANISH PROVERB.

6. When a man sits with a pretty girl for an hour, it seems like a minute. But let him sit on a hot stove for a minute—and it's longer than any hour. That's relativity. EINSTEIN, quoted in his obituary, *The New York Times*, April 19, 1955.

7. He is a giant who has many dwarfs about him. *Yiddish Proverbs* (1949), ed. Hanan J. Ayalti.

## 789. RELATIVES

**See also 332. Family; 787. Relationships, Human**

1. It is a melancholy truth that even great men have their poor relations. CHARLES DICKENS, *Bleak House* (1852), 28.

2. Blood's thicker than water, and when one's in trouble / Best to seek out a relative's open arms. EURIPIDES, *Andromache* (c. 426 B.C.), tr. John F. Nims.

3. There is no greater bugbear than a strong-willed relative in the circle of his own connections. NATHANIEL HAWTHORNE, *The House of the Seven Gables* (1851), 11.

4. A poor relation—is the most irrelevant thing in nature,—a piece of impertinent correspondency,—an odious approximation,—a haunting conscience,—a preposterous shadow, lengthening in the noontide of our prosperity. CHARLES LAMB, "Poor Relations," *Last Essays of Elia* (1833).

5. When our relatives are at home, we have to think of all their good points or it would be impossible to endure them. GEORGE BERNARD SHAW, *Heartbreak House* (1929), 1.

## 790. RELIGION

**See also 76. Belief; 78. Bible; 123. Christianity; 124. Church; 125. Church and State; 126. Churchgoing; 136. Clergy; 262. Dogmatism; 263. Doubt, Religious; 328. Faith; 561. Martyrs and Martyrdom; 590. Missionaries; 595. Monasticism; 609. Mysticism; 691. Piety; 717. Prayer; 718. Preaching and Preachers; 763. Puritans and Puritanism; 810. Revelation, Divine; 829. Sabbath; 834. Saints and Sainthood; 835. Salvation; 844. Science and Religion; 966. Theology; 1061. Worship**

1. One's religion is whatever he is most interested in. J. M. BARRIE, *The Twelve-Pound Look* (1910).

2. Pure religion and undefiled before God and the Father is this, To visit the fatherless and widows in their affliction, and to keep himself unspotted from the world. *Bible*, James 1:27.

3. Religion, n. A daughter of Hope and Fear, explaining to Ignorance the nature of the Unknowable. AMBROSE BIERCE, *The Devil's Dictionary* (1881–1911).

4. It may be that religion is dead, and if it is, we had better know it and set ourselves to try to discover other sources of moral strength before it is too late. PEARL S. BUCK, *What America Means to Me* (1947), 11.

5. Nothing is so fatal to religion as indifference. EDMUND BURKE, letter to William Smith, Jan. 29, 1795.

6. The true laws of God are the laws of our own well-being. SAMUEL BUTLER (d. 1902), "Elementary Morality," *Note-Books* (1912).

7. More and more people care about religious tolerance as fewer and fewer care about religion. ALEXANDER CHASE, *Perspectives* (1966).

8. The old religionist cried out for his God. The new religionist cries out for some god to be his. G. K. CHESTERTON, "Spiritualism," *All Things Considered* (1908).

9. A cosmic philosophy is not constructed to fit a man; a cosmic philosophy is constructed to fit a cosmos. A man can no more possess a private religion than he can possess a private sun and moon. G. K. CHESTERTON, "The Book of Job," *G. K. C. as M. C.* (1929).

10. Men will wrangle for religion, write for it, fight for it, die for it; anything but live for it. CHARLES CALEB COLTON, *Lacon* (1825), 1.25.

11. Where true religion has prevented one crime, false religions have afforded a pretext for a thousand. CHARLES CALEB COLTON, *Lacon* (1825), 1.189.

12. Religion has treated knowledge sometimes as an enemy, sometimes as an hostage; often as a captive and more often as a child; but knowledge has become of age, and religion must either renounce her acquaintance, or introduce her as a companion and respect her as a friend. CHARLES CALEB COLTON, *Lacon* (1825), 2.141.

13. In my religion there would be no exclusive doctrine; all would be love, poetry and doubt. CYRIL CONNOLLY, *The Unquiet Grave* (1945), 1.

14. Persecution, religious pride, the love of contradiction, are the food of what the world commonly calls religion. MICHEL GUILLAUME JEAN DE CRÈVECOEUR, *Letters from an American Farmer* (1782), 3.

15. Intellectually, religious emotions are not creative but conservative. They attach themselves readily to the current view of the world and consecrate it. JOHN DEWEY, "The Influence of Darwinism on Philosophy" (1909).

16. The cosmic religious experience is the strongest and the noblest driving force behind scientific research. EINSTEIN, quoted in his obituary, April 19, 1955.

17. The test of a religion or philosophy is the number of things it can explain. EMERSON, *Journals*, 1836.

18. God enters by a private door into every individual. EMERSON, "Intellect," *Essays: First Series* (1841).

19. The religions of the world are the ejaculations of a few imaginative men. EMERSON, "The Poet," *Essays: Second Series* (1844).

20. For a great nature, it is a happiness to escape a religious training,—religion of character is so apt to be invaded. EMERSON, "Worship," *The Conduct of Life* (1860).

21. No man's religion ever survived his morals. ENGLISH PROVERB.

22. One who recovers from sickness forgets about God. ETHIOPIAN PROVERB.

23. Men make their choice: one man honors one God, / and one another. EURIPIDES, *Hippolytus* (428 B.C.), tr. David Grene.

24. What is god, what is not god, what is between man / and god, who shall say? EURIPIDES, *Helen* (412 B.C.), tr. Richmond Lattimore.

25. Nature teaches us to love our friends, but religion our enemies. THOMAS FULLER, M.D., *Gnomologia* (1732), 3508.

26. Religion is the best armour in the world, but the worst cloak. THOMAS FULLER, M.D., *Gnomologia* (1732), 4011.

27. The founders of the great world religions, Gautama Buddha, Jesus, Lao-Tzu, Mohammed, all seem to have striven for a worldwide brotherhood of man; but none of them could develop institutions which would include the enemy, the unbeliever. GEOFFREY GORER, *The New York Times Magazine*, Nov. 27, 1966.

28. Religion either makes men wise and virtuous, or it makes them set up false pretences to both. WILLIAM HAZLITT, "On Religious Hypocrisy," *The Round Table* (1817).

29. The garb of religion is the best cloak for power. WILLIAM HAZLITT, "On the Clerical Character," *Political Essays* (1819).

30. All religions are ancient monuments to superstition, ignorance, ferocity; and modern religions are only ancient follies rejuvenated. BARON D'HOLBACH, *Le bon sens, ou Idées naturelles opposées aux idées surnaturelles* (1772), 120.

31. The great end of being is to harmonize man with the order of things, and the church has been a good pitch-pipe, and may be so still. OLIVER WENDELL HOLMES, SR., *The Professor at the Breakfast Table* (1860), 1.

32. It is well that the stately synagogue should lift its walls by the side of the aspiring cathedral, a perpetual reminder that there are many mansions in Father's earthly house as well as in the heavenly ones. OLIVER WENDELL HOLMES, SR., *Over the Teacups* (1891), 8.

33. Nobody can have the consolations of religion or philosophy unless he has first experienced their desolations. ALDOUS HUXLEY, "Variations on a Baroque Tomb," *Themes and Variations* (1950).

34. Religion is always a patron of the arts, but its taste is by no means impeccable. ALDOUS HUXLEY, "Faith, Taste, and History," *Tomorrow and Tomorrow and Tomorrow* (1956).

35. To hate man and worship God seems to be the sum of all creeds. ROBERT G. INGERSOLL, *Some Mistakes of Moses* (1879).

36. No man with any sense of humor ever founded a religion. ROBERT G. INGERSOLL, *Prose-Poems and Selections* (1884).

37. There can be but little liberty on earth while men worship a tyrant in heaven. ROBERT G. INGERSOLL, *Prose-Poems and Selections* (1884).

38. In prosperity no altars smoke. ITALIAN PROVERB.

39. He who steadily observes those moral precepts in which all religions concur, will never be questioned at the gates of heaven as to the dogmas in which they all differ. THOMAS JEFFERSON, letter to William Canby, Sept. 18, 1813.

40. One man finds in religion his literature and his science, another finds in it his joy and his duty. JOSEPH JOUBERT, *Pensées* (1842), 1.30, tr. Katharine Lyttelton.

41. Men have torn up the roads which led to Heaven, and which all the world followed; now we have to make our own ladders. JOSEPH JOUBERT, *Pensées* (1842), 17.5, tr. Katharine Lyttelton.

42. What church I go to on Sunday, what dogma of the Catholic Church I believe in, is my business, and whatever faith any other American has is his business. JOHN F. KENNEDY, address, Washington, D.C., 1960.

43. Even the weakest disputant is made so conceited by what he calls religion, as to think himself wiser than the wisest who thinks differently from him. WALTER SAVAGE LANDOR, "Melancthon and Calvin," *Imaginary Conversations* (1824–53).

44. A religion which has lost its basic conviction about the interconnection of men with men in their common struggles for the human, will never command belief in the realm of the superhuman. MAX LERNER, "Laissez-Faire in Social Justice," *Actions and Passions* (1949).

45. I count religion but a childish toy,
And hold there is no sin but ignorance.
CHRISTOPHER MARLOWE, *The Jew of Malta* (c. 1589), 1.

46. Religion is the sign of the oppressed creature, the sentiment of a heartless world, and the soul of soulless conditions. It is the opium of the people. KARL MARX, introduction to "Contribution to the Critique of Hegel's Philosophy of Right" (1884), *Early Writings*, ed. T. B. Bottomore.

47. In religion above all things the only thing of use is an objective truth. The only God that is of use is a being who is personal, supreme and good, and whose existence is as certain as that two and two make four. W. SOMERSET MAUGHAM, *The Summing Up* (1938), 69.

48. We must respect the other fellow's religion, but only in the sense and to the extent that we respect his theory that his wife is beautiful and his children smart. H. L. MENCKEN, *Minority Report* (1956), 1.

49. Man is certainly stark mad; he cannot make a flea, and yet he will be making gods by dozens. MONTAIGNE, "Apology for Raimond de Sebonde," *Essays* (1580–88), tr. Charles Cotton and W. C. Hazlitt.

50. Religion is a candle inside a multicolored lantern. Everyone looks through a particular color, but the candle is always there. MOHAMMED NAGUIB, news summaries, Dec. 31, 1953.

51. Knowledge and history are the enemies of religion. NAPOLEON I, *Maxims* (1804–15).

52. Man's uneasiness is such, that the vagueness and the mystery which religion presents are absolutely necessary to him. NAPOLEON I, *Maxims* (1804–15).

53. Religion indeed enlightens, terrifies, subdues; it gives faith, it inflicts remorse, it inspires resolutions, it draws tears, it inflames devotion, but only for the occasion. JOHN HENRY NEWMAN, *The Idea of a University* (1853–58), 1.8.3.

54. True religion is slow in growth, and, when once planted, is difficult of dislodgement; but its intellectual counterfeit has no root in itself: it springs up suddenly, it suddenly withers. JOHN HENRY NEWMAN, *The Idea of a University* (1853–58), 1.8.8.

55. Wherever on earth the religious neurosis has appeared we find it tied to three dangerous dietary demands: solitude, fasting, and sexual abstinence. NIETZSCHE, *Beyond Good and Evil* (1886), 47, tr. Walter Kaufmann.

56. Men despise religion; they hate it, and fear it is true. PASCAL, *Pensées* (1670), 187, tr. W. F. Trotter.

57. That a religion may be true, it must have knowledge of our nature. PASCAL, *Pensées* (1670), 433, tr. W. F. Trotter.

58. Religion is so great a thing that it is right that those who will not take the trouble to seek it, if it be obscure, should be deprived of it. PASCAL, *Pensées* (1670), 573, tr. W. F. Trotter.

59. You corrupt religion either in favour of your friends, or against your enemies. PASCAL, *Pensées* (1670), 854, tr. W. F. Trotter.

60. To be furious in religion is to be irreligiously religious. WILLIAM PENN, *Some Fruits of Solitude* (1693), 1.533.

61. Religion blushing, veils her sacred fires, / And unawares Morality expires. ALEXANDER POPE, *The Dunciad* (1743), 4.642.

62. Religion may have been the original cure; Freud reminds us that it was also the original disease. PHILIP RIEFF, "The Religion of the Fathers," *Freud: The Mind of the Moralist* (1959).

63. Religion is something infinitely simple, ingenuous. It is not knowledge, not content of feeling, . . . it is not duty and not renunciation, it is not restriction: but in the infinite extent of the universe it is a direction of the heart. RAINER MARIA RILKE, letter to Ilse Blumenthal-Weiss, Dec. 28, 1921, in *Wartime Letters*, tr. M. D. Herter Norton.

64. Fanatical religion driven to a certain point is almost as bad as none at all, but not quite. WILL ROGERS, *There's Not a Bathing Suit in Russia* (1927), 8.

65. Religions which have any very strong hold over men's actions have generally some instinctive basis. BERTRAND RUSSELL, "Where Fatherhood Is Unknown," *Marriage and Morals* (1929).

66. Matters of religion should never be matters of controversy. We neither argue with a lover about his taste, nor condemn him, if we are just, for knowing so human a passion. GEORGE SANTAYANA, *The Life of Reason: Reason in Religion* (1905–06), 6.

67. Religion is the love of life in the consciousness of impotence. GEORGE SANTAYANA, *Winds of Doctrine* (1913).

68. Religion should be disentangled as much as possible from history and authority and metaphysics, and made to rest honestly on one's fine feelings, on one's indomitable optimism and trust in life. GEORGE SANTAYANA, *Character and Opinion in the United States* (1921), 1.

69. Religion is indeed a convention which a man must be bred in to endure with any patience; and yet religion, for all its poetic motley, comes closer than work-a-day opinion to the heart of things. GEORGE SANTAYANA, *Dialogues in Limbo* (1925), 4.

70. Each religion, by the help of more or less myth which it takes more or less seriously, proposes some method of fortifying the human soul and enabling it to make its peace with its destiny. GEORGE SANTAYANA, *Persons and Places: My Host the World* (1953), 1.

71. Men say they are of the same religion for quietness' sake; but if the matter were well examined, you would scarce find three anywhere of the same religion in all points. JOHN SELDEN, "Religion," *Table Talk* (1689).

72. There is only one religion, though there are a hundred versions of it. GEORGE BERNARD SHAW, preface, *Arms and the Man* (1894).

73. Without their fictions the truths of

religion would for the multitude be neither intelligible nor even apprehensible; and the prophets would prophesy and the teachers teach in vain. GEORGE BERNARD SHAW, preface, *Back to Methuselah* (1921).

74. Religion pervades intensely the whole frame of society, and is according to the temper of the mind which it inhabits, a passion, a persuasion, an excuse, a refuge; never a check. SHELLEY, preface, *The Cenci* (1819).

75. Extreme happiness invites religion almost as much as extreme misery. DODIE SMITH, *I Capture the Castle* (1948), 13.

76. If things are going well, religion and legislation are beneficial; if not, they are of no avail. SOLON (7th–6th c. B.C.), quoted in Diogenes Laertius' *Lives and Opinions of Eminent Philosophers* (3rd c. A.D.), tr. R. D. Hicks.

77. Religion has nothing more to fear than not being sufficiently understood. STANISLAUS I OF POLAND, *Maxims* (c. 18th c.), 36.

78. We have just religion enough to make us hate, but not enough to make us love one another. JONATHAN SWIFT, *Thoughts on Various Subjects* (1711).

79. The spirit of death is one, / the spirit of life is many. / When God is dead religion becomes one. RABINDRANATH TAGORE, *Fireflies* (1928).

80. We are self-uncertain creatures, and we may / Yea, even when we know not, mix our spites / And private hates with our defence of Heaven. ALFRED, LORD TENNYSON, *Becket* (1884), 5.2.

81. Religion is the substance of culture, and culture the form of religion. PAUL TILLICH, *Time*, Oct. 20, 1952.

82. Religions are such stuff as dreams are made of. H. G. WELLS, *The Happy Turning* (1946).

83. Religion is the reaction of human nature to its search for God. ALFRED NORTH WHITEHEAD, *Science and the Modern World* (1925), 12.

84. The fact of the religious vision, and its history of persistent expansion, is our one ground for optimism. Apart from it, human life is a flash of occasional enjoyments lighting up a mass of pain and misery, a bagatelle of transient experience. ALFRED NORTH WHITEHEAD, *Science and the Modern World* (1925), 12.

85. No religion can be considered in abstraction from its followers, or even from its various types of followers. ALFRED NORTH WHITEHEAD, *Adventures in Ideas* (1933), 2.

## 791. REMEDIES

**See also 177. Consolations; 241. Diagnosis; 572. Medicine**

1. What destroys one man preserves another. CORNEILLE, *Cinna* (1639), 2.1, tr. Paul Landis.

2. It's a pity to shoot the pianist when the piano is out of tune. RENÉ COTY, quoted in *Time*, Jan. 4, 1957.

3. The remedy for all blunders, the cure of blindness, the cure of crime, is love. EMERSON, "Worship," *The Conduct of Life* (1860).

4. Life as we find it is too hard for us; it entails too much pain, too many disappointments, impossible tasks. We cannot do without palliative remedies. SIGMUND FREUD, *Civilization and Its Discontents* (1930), tr. Joan Riviere.

5. Burn not your house to fright away the mice. THOMAS FULLER, M.D., *Gnomologia* (1732), 1024.

6. Extreme remedies are very appropriate for extreme diseases. HIPPOCRATES, *Aphorisms* (c. 400 B.C.), 1.6.

7. Most men die of their remedies, not of their diseases. MOLIÈRE, *The Imaginary Invalid* (1673), 3, tr. John Wood.

8. A thousand ills require a thousand cures. OVID, *Love's Cure* (c. A.D. 8), tr. J. Lewis May.

9. Gout is not relieved by a fine shoe nor a hangnail by a costly ring nor migraine by a tiara. PLUTARCH, "Contentment," *Moralia* (c. A.D. 100), tr. Moses Hadas.

10. There are some remedies worse than the disease. PUBLILIUS SYRUS, *Moral Sayings* (1st c. B.C.), 301, tr. Darius Lyman.

11. Better use medicines at the outset than at the last moment. PUBLILIUS SYRUS, *Moral Sayings* (1st c. B.C.), 866, tr. Darius Lyman.

12. Diseases desperate grown / By desperate appliances are relieved, / Or not at all. SHAKESPEARE, *Hamlet* (1600), 4.3.9.

13. Our remedies oft in ourselves do lie, / Which we ascribe to heaven. SHAKESPEARE, *All's Well That Ends Well* (1602–03), 1.1.231.

### REMINISCENCES
See 574. Memory

### REMORSE
See 793. Repentance

### 792. RENUNCIATION
See also 800. Resignation

1. The Heart asks Pleasure – first – / And then – Excuse from Pain – / And then – those little Anodynes / That deaden suffering –. EMILY DICKINSON, poem (c. 1862).

2. Renunciation – is a piercing Virtue – / The letting go / A Presence – for an Expectation –. EMILY DICKINSON, poem (c. 1863).

3. How seek the way which leadeth to our wishes? By renouncing our wishes. The crown of excellence is renunciation. HĀFIZ, ghazals from the *Divan* (14th c.), 15, tr. Justin Huntly McCarthy.

### REPAYMENT
See 782. Recompense

### 793. REPENTANCE
See 44. Apology; 785. Regret; 893. Sin

1. The sinning is the best part of repentance. ARABIC PROVERB.

2. Be grateful to the man who cares nothing for your remorse. You are his equal. RENÉ CHAR, "To the Health of the Serpent," *Le Poème pulvérisé* in *Hypnos Waking* (1956), tr. Jackson Mathews and others.

3. Revenge is a fever in our own blood, to be cured only by letting the blood of another; but the remedy too often produces a relapse, which is remorse – a malady far more dreadful than the first disease, because it is incurable. CHARLES CALEB COLTON, *Lacon* (1825), 1.361.

4. The seeds of repentance are sown in youth by pleasure, but the harvest is reaped in age by pain. CHARLES CALEB COLTON, *Lacon* (1825), 1.454.

5. Amendment is repentance. THOMAS FULLER, M.D., *Gnomologia* (1732), 789.

6. You cannot lay remorse upon the innocent nor lift it from the heart of the guilty. Unbidden shall it call in the night, that men may wake and gaze upon themselves. KAHLIL GIBRAN, "On Crime and Punishment," *The Prophet* (1923).

7. If you have behaved badly, repent, make what amends you can and address yourself to the task of behaving better next time. On no account brood over your wrongdoing. Rolling in the muck is not the best way of getting clean. ALDOUS HUXLEY, foreword, *Brave New World* (1932).

8. All criminals turn preachers when they are under the gallows. ITALIAN PROVERB.

9. Our repentance is not so much regret for the evil we have done as a fear of what may happen to us because of it. LA ROCHEFOUCAULD, *Maxims* (1665), tr. Kenneth Pratt.

10. Remorse is impotence; it will sin again. Only repentance is strong; it can end everything. HENRY MILLER, "Seraphita," *The Wisdom of the Heart* (1941).

11. There are people who are very resourceful / At being remorseful, / And who apparently feel that the best way to make friends / Is to do something terrible and then make amends. OGDEN NASH, "Hearts of Gold," *Many Long Years Ago* (1945).

12. He punishes himself who repents of his deeds. PUBLILIUS SYRUS, *Moral Sayings* (1st c. B.C.), 889, tr. Darius Lyman.

13. American People like to have you repent; then they are generous. WILL ROGERS, "One Oil Lawyer per Barrel," *The Illiterate Digest* (1924).

14. Remorse sleeps during prosperity but awakes to bitter consciousness during adversity. ROUSSEAU, *Confessions* (1766–70), 2.

15. He that lacks time to mourn, lacks time to mend. SIR HENRY TAYLOR, *Philip Van Artevelde* (1834), 1.1.5.

16. The repentant say never a brave word. Their resolves should be mumbled in silence. THOREAU, *Journal*, Feb. 28, 1842.

17. The repentance of man is accepted by God as virtue. VOLTAIRE, "Expiation," *Philosophical Dictionary* (1764).

### 794. REPETITION

1. There is repetition everywhere, and nothing is found only once in the world. GOETHE, quoted in Johann Peter Ecker-

mann's *Conversations with Goethe*, Oct. 29, 1823.

2. What if one does say the same things,—of course in a little different form each time,—over and over? If he has anything to say worth saying, that is just what he ought to do. OLIVER WENDELL HOLMES, SR., *Over the Teacups* (1891), 1.

3. What so tedious as a twice-told tale? HOMER, *Odyssey* (9th c. B.C.), 12.538, tr. Alexander Pope.

4. Repetition is the only form of permanence that nature can achieve. GEORGE SANTAYANA, "Aversion from Platonism," *Soliloquies in England* (1922).

5. After people have repeated a phrase a great number of times, they begin to realize it has meaning and may even be true. H. G. WELLS, *The Happy Turning* (1946), 3-4.

### REPRESENTATIVE ASSEMBLY

**See 169. Congress**

### 795. REPRESSION

**See also 107. Captivity; 354. Force; 995. Tyranny**

1. A poorly extinguished fire is quickly re-ignited. CORNEILLE, *Sertorius* (1637), 1.3.

2. The barricade closes the street but opens the way. Graffito written during French student revolt, May 1968.

3. Prison, blood, death, create enthusiasts and martyrs, and bring forth courage and desperate resolution. NAPOLEON I, *Maxims* (1804–15).

4. A little fire is quickly trodden out, / Which, being suffered, rivers cannot quench. SHAKESPEARE, *3 Henry VI* (1590–91), 4.8.7.

### REPROACH

**See 797. Reproof**

### 796. REPRODUCTION

**See also 82. Birth Control; 415. Heredity; 707. Population**

1. The love of posterity is the consequence of the necessity of death. If a man were sure of living forever here, he would not care about his offspring. NATHANIEL HAWTHORNE, *American Note-Books* (1868).

2. Nature is always magnificent when dealing with the privileges and prerogatives of love. She becomes miserly only when doling out the organs and instruments of labor. MAURICE MAETERLINCK, *The Life of the Bee* (1901), tr. Alfred Sutro.

3. Monks, nuns, long-term spinsters and bachelors and permanent homosexuals are all, in a reproductive sense, aberrant. Society has bred them, but they have failed to return the compliment. DESMOND MORRIS, *The Naked Ape* (1967), 2.

4. The turtle lives 'twixt plated decks / Which practically conceal its sex. / I think it clever of the turtle / In such a fix to be so fertile. OGDEN NASH, "The Turtle," *Many Long Years Ago* (1945).

### 797. REPROOF

**See also 203. Criticism; 339. Faults; 513. Judging Others**

1. There is no defence against reproach, but obscurity; it is a kind of concomitant to greatness. JOSEPH ADDISON, *The Spectator* (1711–12), 101.

2. The best preservative to keep the mind in health is the faithful admonition of a friend. FRANCIS BACON, "Of Friendship," *Essays* (1625).

3. Reprove not a scorner, lest he hate thee: rebuke a wise man, and he will love thee. *Bible*, Proverbs 9:8.

4. No man can justly censure or condemn another, because indeed no man truly knows another. SIR THOMAS BROWNE, *Religio Medici* (1642), 2.

5. He that sharply chides is the most ready to pardon. THOMAS FULLER, M.D., *Gnomologia* (1732), 2298.

6. The sting of a reproach is the truth of it. THOMAS FULLER, M.D., *Gnomologia* (1732), 4769.

7. The man who acts the least, upbraids the most. HOMER, *Iliad* (9th c. B.C.), 2.311, tr. Alexander Pope.

8. I wonder how anyone can have the face to condemn others when he reflects upon his own thoughts. W. SOMERSET MAUGHAM, *The Summing Up* (1938), 16.

9. Rash and incessant scolding runs into custom and renders itself despised. MON-

TAIGNE, "Of anger," *Essays* (1580–88), tr. Charles Cotton and W. C. Hazlitt.

10. Fear not the anger of the wise to raise; / Those best can bear reproof who merit praise. ALEXANDER POPE, *An Essay on Criticism* (1711), 3.23.

11. Better a little chiding than a great deal of heartbreak. SHAKESPEARE, *The Merry Wives of Windsor* (1597), 5.3.10.

12. The correction of silence is what kills; when you know you have transgressed, and your friend says nothing and avoids your eye. ROBERT LOUIS STEVENSON, "Talk and Talkers" (1882), 2.

13. Be thou, in rebuking evil, / Conscious of thine own. JOHN GREENLEAF WHITTIER, "What the Voice Said" (1847), 15.

## REPUBLICANS

See 704. Political Parties

## 798. REPUTATION

See also 57. Association; 578. Merit; 898. Slander

1. Have regard for your name, since it will remain for you longer than a great store of gold. *Apocrypha*, Ecclesiasticus 41:12.

2. A reputation for good judgment, for fair dealing, for truth, and for rectitude, is itself a fortune. HENRY WARD BEECHER, *Proverbs from Plymouth Pulpit* (1887).

3. A good name is rather to be chosen than great riches. *Bible*, Proverbs 22:1.

4. Shall I be remembered after death? I sometimes think and hope so. But I trust I may not be found out before my death. SAMUEL BUTLER (d. 1902), "The Life of the World to Come," *Note-Books* (1912).

5. Men are much more unwilling to have their weaknesses and their imperfections known than their crimes. LORD CHESTERFIELD, *Letters to His Son*, Sept. 5, 1748.

6. I have never hurried to meet a public expectation without leaving myself behind. FRANK MOORE COLBY, "Simple Simon," *The Colby Essays* (1926), v.1.

7. There are two modes of establishing our reputation; to be praised by honest men, and to be abused by rogues. CHARLES CALEB COLTON, *Lacon* (1825), 1.218.

8. There are many who dare not kill themselves for fear of what the neighbors will say. CYRIL CONNOLLY, *The Unquiet Grave* (1945), 2.

9. A man's real life is that accorded to him in the thoughts of other men by reason of respect or natural love. JOSEPH CONRAD, *Under Western Eyes* (1911), 1.1.

10. What shall I do to be for ever known, / And make the age to come my own? ABRAHAM COWLEY, "The Motto" (17th c.).

11. When the man is at home, his standing in society is well known and quietly taken; but when he is abroad, it is problematical, and is dependent on the success of his manners. EMERSON, *Journals*, 1827.

12. If you would not be known to do anything, never do it. EMERSON, "Spiritual Laws," *Essays: First Series* (1841).

13. A good name keeps its lustre in the dark. ENGLISH PROVERB.

14. Reputation is often got without merit and lost without fault. ENGLISH PROVERB.

15. Reputation is commonly measured by the acre. THOMAS FULLER, M.D., *Gnomologia* (1732), 4023.

16. There is no reputation so clear but a slander may stain it. THOMAS FULLER, M.D., *Gnomologia* (1732), 4920.

17. If your name is to live at all, it is so much more to have it live in people's hearts than only in their brains! OLIVER WENDELL HOLMES, SR., *The Poet at the Breakfast Table* (1872), 4.

18. What people say behind your back is your standing in the community in which you live. EDGAR WATSON HOWE, *Country Town Sayings* (1911).

19. Be it true or false, what is said about men often has as much influence upon their lives, and especially upon their destinies, as what they do. VICTOR HUGO, "Fantine," *Les Misérables* (1862), 1.1, tr. Charles E. Wilbour.

20. Those who are well assured of their own standing are least apt to trespass on that of others. WASHINGTON IRVING, "The Country Church," *The Sketch Book of Geoffrey Crayon, Gent.* (1819–20).

21. Life is for one generation; a good name is forever. JAPANESE PROVERB.

22. The Englishman wants to be recognized as a gentleman, or as some other suitable species of human being; the American wants to be considered a good guy. LOUIS KRONENBERGER, *Company Manners* (1954), 3.3.

23. When we are dead we are praised by those who survive us, though we frequently have no other merit than that of being no longer alive. LA BRUYÈRE, *Characters* (1688), 12.78, tr. Henri Van Laun.

24. Some men seem remarkable to the world in whom neither their wives nor their valets saw anything extraordinary. Few men have been admired by their servants. MONTAIGNE, "Of repentance," *Essays* (1580–88).

25. A great reputation is a great noise, the more there is of it, the further does it swell. Land, monuments, nations, all fall, but the noise remains, and will reach to other generations. NAPOLEON I, *Maxims* (1804–15).

26. Who has not, for the sake of his good reputation—sacrificed himself once? NIETZSCHE, *Beyond Good and Evil* (1886), 92, tr. Walter Kaufmann.

27. We do not content ourselves with the life we have in ourselves and in our own being; we desire to live an imaginary life in the mind of others, and for this purpose we endeavour to shine. PASCAL, *Pensées* (1670), 147, tr. W. F. Trotter.

28. It is generally much more shameful to lose a good reputation than never to have acquired it. PLINY THE YOUNGER, *Letters* (c. 97–110), 8.24, tr. Alfred P. Dorjahn.

29. It is easier to add to a great reputation than to get it. PUBLILIUS SYRUS, *Moral Sayings* (1st c. B.C.), 250, tr. Darius Lyman.

30. The purest treasure mortal times afford / Is spotless reputation. SHAKESPEARE, *Richard II* (1595–96), 1.1.177.

31. Reputation is an idle and most false imposition; oft got without merit and lost without deserving. SHAKESPEARE, *Othello* (1604–05), 2.3.268.

32. One can survive everything nowadays, except death, and live down anything except a good reputation. OSCAR WILDE, *A Woman of No Importance* (1893), 1.

33. He who is known for an early riser may lie abed till noon. *Yiddish Proverbs* (1949), ed. Hanan J. Ayalti.

## 799. REQUEST
See also 784. Refusal

1. To be happy with human beings, we should not ask them for what they cannot give. TRISTAN BERNARD, *L'Enfant prodigue du Vésinet* (1921).

2. The pitcher that goes too often to the well leaves behind either the handle or the spout. CERVANTES, *Don Quixote* (1605–15).

3. Not to ask is not to be denied. JOHN DRYDEN, *The Hind and the Panther* (1687), 1.1536.

4. The highest price we can pay for anything, is to ask it. WALTER SAVAGE LANDOR, "Eschines and Phocion," *Imaginary Conversations* (1824–53).

5. Even the gods are moved by the voice of entreaty. OVID, *The Art of Love* (c. A.D. 8), 1, tr. J. Lewis May.

6. Never ask of him who has, but of him who wishes you well. SPANISH PROVERB.

## RESERVE
See 31. Aloofness; 141. Coldness

## 800. RESIGNATION
See also 285. Endurance;
505. Irrevocableness; 617. Necessity;
792. Renunciation; 930. Stoicism

1. We must like what we have when we don't have what we like. ROGER DE BUSSY-RABUTIN, letter to Mme. de Sévigné, May 23, 1667.

2. Resignation, not mystic, not detached, but resignation open-eyed, conscious, and informed by love, is the only one of our feelings for which it is impossible to become a sham. JOSEPH CONRAD, "A Familiar Preface," *A Personal Record* (1912).

3. Teach us to care and not to care / Teach us to sit still. T. S. ELIOT, "Ash Wednesday" (1930), 1.

4. The doctrine of Necessity or Destiny is the doctrine of Toleration. EMERSON, *Journals*, 1841.

5. What cannot be altered must be borne, not blamed. THOMAS FULLER, M.D., *Gnomologia* (1732), 5481.

6. The mind which renounces, once and for ever, a futile hope, has its compensation in ever-growing calm. GEORGE GISSING, "Spring," *The Private Papers of Henry Ryecroft* (1903).

7. Mankind are more disposed to suffer, while evils are sufferable, than to right

themselves by abolishing the forms to which they are accustomed. THOMAS JEFFERSON, *Declaration of Independence*, July 4, 1776.

8. We often believe we are constant under misfortunes when we are only dejected; and we suffer them without daring to look on them, like cowards who allow themselves to be killed through fear of defending themselves. LA ROCHEFOUCAULD, *Maxims* (1665), tr. Kenneth Pratt.

9. Happy he who learns to bear what he cannot change! SCHILLER, "The Sublime" (1793?).

10. It's the great soul that surrenders itself to fate, but a puny degenerate thing that struggles. SENECA, *Letters to Lucilius* (1st c.), 107.12, tr. E. Phillips Barker.

11. A calm despair, without angry convulsions or reproaches directed at heaven, is the essence of wisdom. ALFRED DE VIGNY, *Journal d'un poète* (1832).

## RESISTANCE

**See 651. Opposition; 779. Rebellion**

## 801. RESOLUTION

**See also 222. Decision; 765. Purpose; 860. Self-determination; 1049. Will**

1. Resolve to perform what you ought. Perform without fail what you resolve. BENJAMIN FRANKLIN, *Autobiography* (1791), 2.

2. A resolution to avoid an evil is seldom framed till the evil is so far advanced as to make avoidance impossible. THOMAS HARDY, *Far From the Madding Crowd* (1874), 18.

3. Sudden resolutions, like the sudden rise of the mercury in the barometer, indicate little else than the changeableness of the weather. JULIUS CHARLES HARE and AUGUSTUS WILLIAM HARE, *Guesses at Truth* (1827).

4. We have more ability than will power, and it is often an excuse to ourselves that we imagine that things are impossible. LA ROCHEFOUCAULD, *Maxims* (1665), tr. Kenneth Pratt.

5. Good resolutions are useless attempts to interfere with scientific laws. OSCAR WILDE, *The Picture of Dorian Gray* (1891), 8.

## 802. RESPECT

**See also 14. Admiration; 424. Honors; 1061. Worship**

1. Reverence is a good thing, and part of its value is that the more we revere a man, the more sharply are we struck by anything in him (and there is always much) that is incongruous with his greatness. MAX BEERBOHM, "Laughter," *And Even Now* (1920).

2. Without feelings of respect, what is there to distinguish men from beasts? CONFUCIUS, *Analects* (6th c. B.C.), 2.7, tr. Ch'u Chai and Winberg Chai.

3. I don't want anny man's rayspict. It manes I don't count. FINLEY PETER DUNNE, "Youth and Age," *Mr. Dooley's Opinions* (1901).

4. If you have some respect for people as they are, you can be more effective in helping them to become better than they are. JOHN W. GARDNER, *No Easy Victories* (1968), 26.

5. The Porcupine, whom one must Handle, gloved, / May be respected, but is never Loved. ARTHUR GUITERMAN, *A Poet's Proverbs* (1924).

6. Man is still a savage to the extent that he has little respect for anything that cannot hurt him. EDGAR WATSON HOWE, *Ventures in Common Sense* (1919), 4.16.

7. It is difficult to like those whom we do not esteem; but it is no less so to like those whom we esteem more than ourselves. LA ROCHEFOUCAULD, *Maxims* (1665), tr. Kenneth Pratt.

8. We can always make ourselves liked provided we act likable, but we cannot always make ourselves esteemed, no matter what our merits are. NICOLAS MALEBRANCHE, *Traité de la morale* (1867), 11.

9. If you have any shame, forbear to pluck the beard of a dead lion. MARTIAL, *Epigrams* (A.D. 86), 10.90, tr. Walter C. A. Ker.

10. The honor we receive from those that fear us, is not honor; those respects are paid to royalty and not to me. MONTAIGNE, "Of the inequality among us," *Essays* (1580–88), tr. Charles Cotton and W. C. Hazlitt.

11. Concerning great things one should either be silent or speak loftily. NIETZSCHE, *The Will to Power* (1888), tr. Anthony M. Ludovici.

## 803. RESPECTABILITY

See also 743. Propriety

1. Respectability, n. The offspring of a liaison between a bald head and a bank account. AMBROSE BIERCE, *The Devil's Dictionary* (1881–1911).

2. What, in the devil's name, is the use of respectability, with never so many gigs and silver spoons, if thou inwardly art the pitifulest of all men? THOMAS CARLYLE, "Count Cagliostro" (1833).

3. Respectability is the dickey on the bosom of civilization. ELBERT HUBBARD, *The Note Book* (1927).

4. The world of shabby gentility is like no other; its sacrifices have less logic, its standards are harsher, its relation to reality is dimmer than comfortable property or plain poverty can understand. MURRAY KEMPTON, "The Sheltered Life," *Part of Our Time* (1955).

5. The genteel is a mighty catafalque of service-with-a-smile and flattering solicitude smothering every spontaneous movement of thought or feeling. MARSHALL MC LUHAN, "L'il Abner," *The Mechanical Bride* (1951).

6. The more things a man is ashamed of, the more respectable he is. GEORGE BERNARD SHAW, *Man and Superman* (1903), 1.

## 804. RESPONSIBILITY

See also 269. Duty

1. That which is common to the greatest number has the least care bestowed upon it. ARISTOTLE, *Politics* (4th C. B.C.), 2.3, tr. Benjamin Jowett.

2. Unto whomsoever much is given, of him shall much be required. *Bible*, Luke 12:48.

3. Responsibility, n. A detachable burden easily shifted to the shoulders of God, Fate, Fortune, Luck or one's neighbor. In the days of astrology it was customary to unload it upon a star. AMBROSE BIERCE, *The Devil's Dictionary* (1881–1911).

4. Responsibility is to oneself; and the highest form of it is irresponsibility to oneself which is to say the calm acceptance of whatever responsibility to others and things comes a-long. JOHN CAGE, "Lecture on Something," *Silence* (1961).

5. One can pass on responsibility, but not the discretion that goes with it. BENVENUTO CELLINI, *Autobiography* (1558–66), tr. George Bull.

6. Man must now assume the responsibility for his world. He can no longer shove it off on religious power. HARVEY COX, *The Secular City* (1966), 10.

7. Everybody's business is nobody's business. ENGLISH PROVERB.

8. Man's responsibility increases as that of the gods decreases. ANDRÉ GIDE, *Journals*, Sept. 27, 1940, tr. Justin O'Brien.

9. Though the wisdom or virtue of one can very rarely make many happy, the folly or vice of one man often make many miserable. SAMUEL JOHNSON, *Rasselas* (1759), 26.

10. Our privileges can be no greater than our obligations. The protection of our rights can endure no longer than the performance of our responsibilities. JOHN F. KENNEDY, address, Vanderbilt University, Nashville, Tenn., May 18, 1963.

11. Responsibility's like a string we can only see the middle of. Both ends are out of sight. WILLIAM MC FEE, *Casuals of the Sea* (1916), 2.1.6.

12. To be a man is, precisely, to be responsible. SAINT-EXUPÉRY, *Wind, Sand, and Stars* (1939), 2.2, tr. Lewis Galantière.

13. The fault, dear Brutus, is not in our stars, / But in ourselves, that we are underlings. SHAKESPEARE, *Julius Caesar* (1599–1600), 1.2.140.

14. A burden in the bush is worth two on your hands. JAMES THURBER, "The Hunter and the Elephant," *Fables for Our Time* (1943).

## 805. REST

See also 444. Idleness; 530. Leisure; 807. Retirement

1. We combat obstacles in order to get repose, and, when got, the repose is insupportable. HENRY ADAMS, *The Education of Henry Adams* (1907), 29.

2. One cannot rest except after steady practice. GEORGE ADE, "The Man Who Was Going to Retire," *Forty Modern Fables* (1901).

3. Too much rest itself becomes a pain. HOMER, *Odyssey* (9th c. B.C.), 15.429, tr. William Broome.

4. Nothing gives rest but the sincere search for truth. PASCAL, *Pensées* (1670), 907, tr. W. F. Trotter.

5. In all things rest is sweet; there is surfeit / even in honey, even in Aphrodite's lovely flowers. PINDAR, *Odes* (5th c. B.C.), Nemea 7, tr. Richmond Lattimore.

6. Rest is the sauce of labor. PLUTARCH, "The Education of Children," *Moralia* (c. A.D. 100), tr. Moses Hadas.

7. Rest is not a word of free peoples— / Rest is a monarchial word. CARL SANDBURG, "Is There Any Easy Road to Freedom?" *Complete Poems* (1950).

8. Restfulness is a quality for cattle; the virtues are all active, life is alert. ROBERT LOUIS STEVENSON, "Talk and Talkers" (1882), 2.

## 806. RESTLESSNESS

**See also 10. Activity; 454. Impatience; 1033. Waiting**

1. A wanderer is man from his birth. / He was born in a ship / On the breast of the river of Time. MATTHEW ARNOLD, "The Future" (1852).

2. The soul is restless and furious, it wants to tear itself apart, and cure itself of being human. UGO BETTI, *Goat Island* (1946), 1.4, ed. Gino Rizzo.

3. Never have I been able to settle in life. Always seated askew, as if on the arm of a chair; ready to get up, to leave. ANDRÉ GIDE, *Journals*, July 14, 1930, tr. Justin O'Brien.

4. Unrest of spirit is a mark of life. KARL MENNINGER, *This Week*, Oct. 16, 1958.

## RESTRAINT

**See 592. Moderation; 940. Sufficiency**

## 807. RETIREMENT

**See also 444. Idleness; 530. Leisure; 805. Rest**

1. Cessation of work is not accompanied by cessation of expenses. CATO THE ELDER, *De Agri Cultura* (2nd c. B.C.).

2. It is very grand to "die in harness," but it is very pleasant to have the tight straps unbuckled and the heavy collar lifted from the neck and shoulders. OLIVER WENDELL HOLMES, SR., *Over the Teacups* (1891), 2.

3. Dismiss the old horse in good time, lest he fail in the lists and the spectators laugh. HORACE, *Epistles* (20–c. 8 B.C. ), 1.1.8.

4. I am Retired Leisure. I am to be met with in trim gardens. I am already come to be known by my vacant face and careless gesture, perambulating at no fixed pace nor with any settled purpose. I walk about; not to and from. CHARLES LAMB, "The Superannuated Man," *Last Essays of Elia* (1833).

5. Few men of action have been able to make a graceful exit at the appropriate time. MALCOLM MUGGERIDGE, "Twilight of Greatness," *The Most of Malcolm Muggeridge* (1966).

## 808. RETREAT

**See also 298. Escape**

1. To withdraw is not to run away, and to stay is no wise action, when there's more reason to fear than to hope. CERVANTES, *Don Quixote* (1605–15), 1.3.9, tr. Peter Motteux and John Ozell.

2. Better to turn back than to lose your way. RUSSIAN PROVERB.

## 809. RETRIBUTION

**See also 108. Cause and Effect; 173. Consequence; 760. Punishment; 782. Recompense; 811. Revenge**

1. Our fathers and ourselves sowed dragon's teeth. / Our children know and suffer the armed men. STEPHEN VINCENT BENÉT, *Litany for Dictatorships* (1935).

2. And if any mischief follow, then thou shalt give life for life, / Eye for eye, tooth for tooth, hand for hand, foot for foot, / Burning for burning, wound for wound, stripe for stripe. *Bible*, Exodus 21:23–25.

3. Whatsoever a man soweth, that shall he also reap. *Bible*, Galatians 6:7.

4. He that plants thorns must never expect to gather roses. "The Ignorant Physician," *Fables of Bidpai* (c. 750).

5. He who makes his law a curse, / By his own law shall surely die. WILLIAM BLAKE, "To the Jews," *Jerusalem* (1804–20).

6. There's no need to hang about waiting for the Last Judgement—it takes place every day. ALBERT CAMUS, *The Fall* (1956).

7. Who more impious than he that sorrows at God's judgement? DANTE, "Inferno," 20, *The Divine Comedy* (c. 1300–21), tr. J. A. Carlyle and P. H. Wicksteed.

8. God gives each his due at the time allotted. EURIPIDES, *Electra* (413 B. C.), tr. Moses Hadas and John McLean.

9. The gods visit the sins of the fathers upon the children. EURIPIDES, *Phrixus* (c. 412 B. C.), 970, tr. M. H. Morgan.

10. As he brews, so shall he drink. BEN JONSON, *Every Man in His Humour* (1598), 2.2.

11. Though the mills of God grind slowly, yet they grind exceeding small; / Though with patience He stands waiting, with exactness grinds He all. FRIEDRICH VON LOGAU, *Retribution* (1654).

12. Justice divine / Mends not her slowest pace for prayers or cries. MILTON, *Paradise Lost* (1667), 10.858.

13. The laws of changeless justice bind / Oppressor and oppressed; / And, close as sin and suffering joined, / We march to Fate abreast. JOHN GREENLEAF WHITTIER, "At Port Royal" (1862).

14. Jupiter is slow looking into his notebook, but he always looks. ZENOBIUS, *Sententiae* (2nd c.), 4.11.

## REVELATION

**See 810. Revelation; Divine; 871. Self-revelation**

## 810. REVELATION, DIVINE

**See also 385. God**

1. My own mind is the direct revelation which I have from God and far least liable to mistake in telling his will of any revelation. EMERSON, *Journals*, 1831.

2. There is a sort of transcendental ventriloquy through which men can be made to believe that something which was said on earth came from heaven. GEORG CHRISTOPH LICHTENBERG, *Aphorisms* (1764–99), tr. F. H. Mautner and H. Hatfield.

3. Instead of complaining that God had hidden Himself, you will give Him thanks for having revealed so much of Himself. PASCAL, *Pensées* (1670), 288, tr. W. F. Trotter.

## 811. REVENGE

**See also 474. Injury; 782. Recompense; 809. Retribution**

1. May you not hurt your enemy, when he struck first? AESCHYLUS, *The Libation Bearers* (458 B.C.), tr. Richmond Lattimore.

2. Men regard it as their right to return evil for evil—and, if they cannot, feel they have lost their liberty. ARISTOTLE, *Nicomachean Ethics* (4th c. B. C.), 5.5, tr. J. A. K. Thomson.

3. In taking revenge, a man is but even with his enemy; but in passing it over, he is superior. FRANCIS BACON, "Of Revenge," *Essays* (1625).

4. A man that studieth revenge keeps his own wounds green, which otherwise would heal and do well. FRANCIS BACON, "Of Revenge," *Essays* (1625).

5. Since women do most delight in revenge, it may seem but feminine manhood to be vindictive. SIR THOMAS BROWNE, *Christian Morals* (1716), 3.

6. Sweet is revenge—especially to women. BYRON, *Don Juan* (1819–24), 1.124.

7. An act by which we make one friend and one enemy is a losing game; because revenge is a much stronger principle than gratitude. CHARLES CALEB COLTON, *Lacon* (1825), 1.98.

8. Revenge is a much more punctual paymaster than gratitude. CHARLES CALEB COLTON, *Lacon* (1825), 2.11.

9. Just vengeance does not call for punishment. CORNEILLE, *The Cid* (1636), 2.8, tr. Paul Landis.

10. Revenge is a dish that should be eaten cold. ENGLISH PROVERB.

11. This is sweet: to see your foe / perish and pay to justice all he owes. EURIPIDES, *Heracles* (c. 422 B.C.), tr. William Arrowsmith.

12. Revenge proves its own executioner. JOHN FORD, *The Broken Heart* (1633), 5.3.

13. Revenge is a luscious fruit which you must leave to ripen. ÉMILE GABORIAU, *File 113* (1867), 10.

14. It is difficult to fight against anger; for a man will buy revenge with his soul. HERACLITUS (c. 500 B.C.), quoted in Aris-

totle's *Politics* (4th c. B.C.), 5.11, tr. Benjamin Jowett.

15. Revenge is always the joy of narrow, / Sick, and petty minds. JUVENAL, *Satires* (c. 100), 13.189, tr. Hubert Creekmore.

16. Revenge, at first though sweet, / Bitter ere long back on itself recoils. MILTON, *Paradise Lost* (1667), 9.171.

17. Blood cannot be washed out with blood. PERSIAN PROVERB.

18. It is folly to punish your neighbor by fire when you live next door. PUBLILIUS SYRUS, *Moral Sayings* (1st c. B.C.), 910, tr. Darius Lyman.

19. Heat not a furnace for your foe so hot / That it do singe yourself. SHAKESPEARE, *Henry VIII* (1612–13), 1.1.140.

20. God will not punish the man / Who makes return for an injury. SOPHOCLES, *Oedipus at Colonus* (401 B.C.), tr. Robert Fitzgerald.

21. No revenge is more honorable than the one not taken. SPANISH PROVERB.

## REVERENCE

**See 802. Respect; 1061. Worship**

## 812. REVERIE

**See also 448. Imagination; 687. Phantasy; 968. Thought**

1. To make a prairie it takes a clover and one bee, / One clover, and a bee, / And revery, / The revery alone will do, / If bees are few. EMILY DICKINSON, *Poems* (c. 1862–86).

2. Thought is the labour of the intellect, reverie is its pleasure. VICTOR HUGO, "Saint Denis," *Les Misérables* (1862), 2.1, tr. Charles E. Wilbour.

3. We love to chew the cud of a foregone vision; to collect the scattered rays of a brighter phantasm, or act over again, with firmer nerves, the sadder nocturnal tragedies. CHARLES LAMB, "Popular Fallacies, 14," *Last Essays of Elia* (1833).

4. Reverie is the groundwork of creative imagination; it is the privilege of the artist that with him it is not as with other men an escape from reality, but the means by which he accedes to it. W. SOMERSET MAUGHAM, *The Summing Up* (1938), 23.

5. What a wee little part of a person's life are his acts and his words! His real life is led in his head, and is known to none but himself. MARK TWAIN, *Autobiography* (1924), v. 1, ed. A. B. Paine.

6. Let us leave every man at liberty to seek into himself and to lose himself in his ideas. VOLTAIRE, "Soul," *Philosophical Dictionary* (1764).

## REVIEWS

**See 204. Criticism, Professional**

## 813. REVOLUTION

**See also 256. Dissent; 439. Iconoclasm; 564. Mass Movements; 651. Opposition; 779. Rebellion; 795. Repression; 995. Tyranny; 1024. Violence**

1. Inferiors revolt in order that they may be equal, and equals that they may be superior. ARISTOTLE, *Politics* (4th c. B.C.), 5.2, tr. Benjamin Jowett.

2. Thinkers prepare the revolution; bandits carry it out. MARIANO AZUELA, *The Flies* (1918), tr. Lesley Byrd Simpson.

3. If there be fuel prepared, it is hard to tell whence the spark shall come that shall set it on fire. FRANCIS BACON, "Of Seditions and Troubles," *Essays* (1625).

4. All oppressed people are authorized, whenever they can, to rise and break their fetters. HENRY CLAY, speech, U. S. House of Representatives, March 24, 1818.

5. If we trace the history of most revolutions, we shall find that the first inroads upon the laws have been made by the governors, as often as by the governed. CHARLES CALEB COLTON, *Lacon* (1825), 1.528.

6. The revolutionary spirit is mighty convenient in this, that it frees one from all scruples as regards ideas. JOSEPH CONRAD, "A Familiar Preface," *A Personal Record* (1912).

7. Plots, true or false, are necessary things, / To raise up commonwealths, and ruin kings. JOHN DRYDEN, *Absalom and Achitophel* (1681), 1.83.

8. The overwhelming pressure of mediocrity, sluggish and indomitable as a glacier, will mitigate the most violent, and depress the most exalted revolution. T. S. ELIOT, "The Idea of a Christian Society" (1939).

9. Every revolution was first a thought in one man's mind; and when the same

thought occurs to another man, it is the key to that era. EMERSON, "History," *Essays: First Series* (1841).

10. The world is always childish, and with each new gewgaw of a revolution or new constitution that it finds, thinks it shall never cry any more. EMERSON, *Journals*, 1847.

11. The successful revolutionary is a statesman, the unsuccessful one a criminal. ERICH FROMM, *Escape from Freedom* (1941), 7.

12. A non-violent revolution is not a program of seizure of power. It is a program of transformation of relationships, ending in a peaceful transfer of power. MOHANDAS K. GANDHI, *Non-Violence in Peace and War* (1948), 2.8.

13. In troublesome times, nothing is more common than the alliance of audacious vice and turbulent virtue. PIERRE GAXOTTE, "Thème et variations," *Propos sur la liberté*.

14. Though a revolution may call itself "national," it always marks the victory of a single party. ANDRÉ GIDE, *Journals*, Oct. 17, 1941, tr. Justin O'Brien.

15. A great revolution is never the fault of the people, but of the government. GOETHE, quoted in Johann Peter Eckermann's *Conversations with Goethe*, Jan. 4, 1824.

16. Everywhere revolutions are painful yet fruitful gestations of a people: they shed blood but create light, they eliminate men but elaborate ideas. MANUEL GONZÁLEZ PRADA, *Horas de lucha* (1908).

17. A successful revolution establishes a new community. A missed revolution makes irrelevant the community that persists. And a compromised revolution tends to shatter the community that was, without an adequate substitute. PAUL GOODMAN, *Growing Up Absurd* (1960), 11.1.

18. There can be revolution only where there is a conscience. Graffito written during French student revolt, May 1968.

19. The Revolution must take place in men before it can be manifest in things. Graffito written during French student revolt, May 1968.

20. To be a revolutionary is first of all to make sure of permanence and of one's good reception. After which intellectual masturbation is permitted. Graffito written during French student revolt, May 1968.

21. When hopes and dreams are loose in the streets, it is well for the timid to lock doors, shutter windows and lie low until the wrath has passed. ERIC HOFFER, *The True Believer* (1951), 1.1.5.

22. Not actual suffering but the hope of better things incites people to revolt. ERIC HOFFER, *The Ordeal of Change* (1964), 10.

23. We used to think that revolutions are the cause of change. Actually it is the other way around: change prepares the ground for revolution. ERIC HOFFER, "A Time of Juveniles," *The Temper of Our Time* (1967), 1.

24. The wind of revolutions is not tractable. VICTOR HUGO, "Saint Denis," *Les Misérables* (1862), 10.4, tr. Charles E. Wilbour.

25. One should never put on one's best trousers to go out to battle for freedom and truth. HENRIK IBSEN, *An Enemy of the People* (1882), 5.

26. If there is one safe generalisation in human affairs, it is that revolutions always destroy themselves. How often have fanatics proclaimed "the year one"! WILLIAM RALPH INGE, "Our Present Discontents," *Outspoken Essays: First Series* (1919).

27. The tree of liberty must be refreshed from time to time, with the blood of patriots and tyrants. It is its natural manure. THOMAS JEFFERSON, letter to Col. William S. Smith, Nov. 13, 1787.

28. If the abuse be enormous, nature will rise up, and claiming her original rights, overturn a corrupt political system. SAMUEL JOHNSON, quoted in Boswell's *Life of Samuel Johnson*, July 6, 1763.

29. Every social war is a battle between the very few on both sides who care and who fire their shots across a crowd of spectators. MURRAY KEMPTON, "Father and Sons," *Part of Our Time* (1955).

30. A revolution requires of its leaders a record of unbroken infallibility; if they do not possess it, they are expected to invent it. MURRAY KEMPTON, "It's Time to Go, I Heard Them Say," *Part of Our Time* (1955).

31. We live in a hemisphere whose own revolution has given birth to the most powerful force of the modern age—the search for the freedom and self-fulfillment of man. JOHN F. KENNEDY, message to the Inter-American Economic and Social Conference, Punta del Este, Uruguay, Aug. 5, 1961.

32. If you feed the people just with revo-

lutionary slogans they will listen today, they will listen tomorrow, they will listen the day after tomorrow, but on the fourth day they will say, "To hell with you." NIKITA KHRUSHCHEV, quoted in "Ideas and Men," *The New York Times*, Oct. 4, 1964.

33. It is a quality of revolutions not to go by old lines or old laws; but to break up both, and make new ones. ABRAHAM LINCOLN, speech, House of Representatives, Jan. 12, 1848.

34. Women hate revolutions and revolutionists. They like men who are docile, and well-regarded at the bank, and never late at meals. H. L. MENCKEN, *Prejudices: Fourth Series* (1924), 5.

35. If obedience is the result of the instinct of the masses, revolt is the result of their thought. NAPOLEON I, *Maxims* (1804–15).

36. In revolutions there are only two sorts of men, those who cause them and those who profit by them. NAPOLEON I, *Maxims* (1804–15).

37. Revolutions are not made: they come. A revolution is as natural a growth as an oak. It comes out of the past. Its foundations are laid far back. WENDELL PHILLIPS, speech, Boston, Jan. 28, 1852.

38. Revolution is a transfer of property from class to class. LEON SAMSON, *The New Humanism* (1930), 16.

39. Revolutions have never lightened the burden of tyranny: they have only shifted it to another shoulder. GEORGE BERNARD SHAW, preface, "The Revolutionist's Handbook," *Man and Superman* (1903).

40. In most cases, when the lion, weary of obeying its master, has torn and devoured him, its nerves are pacified and it looks round for another master before whom to grovel. PAUL VALÉRY, "Fluctuations on Liberty," *Reflections on the World Today* (1931), tr. Francis Scarfe.

## RICHES

**See 1041. Wealth**

## 814. RIDICULE

**See also 4. Absurdity; 432. Humiliation; 434. Humor; 523. Laughter; 886. Shame**

1. The talent of turning men into ridicule, and exposing to laughter those one converses with, is the qualification of little ungenerous tempers. JOSEPH ADDISON, *The Spectator* (1711–12), 249.

2. To make fun of a person to his face is a brutal way of amusing one's self; be delicate and cunning, and keep your laugh in your sleeve, lest you frighten away your game. GELETT BURGESS, "The Use of Fools," *The Romance of the Commonplace* (1916).

3. Mockery is often the result of a poverty of wit. LA BRUYÈRE, *Characters* (1688), 5.57.

4. Ridicule dishonours more than dishonour. LA ROCHEFOUCAULD, *Maxims* (1665), tr. Kenneth Pratt.

5. The most effective way of attacking vice is to expose it to public ridicule. People can put up with rebukes but they cannot bear being laughed at: they are prepared to be wicked but they dislike appearing ridiculous. MOLIÈRE, preface to *Tartuffe* (1664), tr. John Wood.

6. The blind man is laughing at the baldhead. PERSIAN PROVERB.

7. There is no character, howsoever good and fine, but it can be destroyed by ridicule, howsoever poor and witless. MARK TWAIN, "Pudd'nhead Wilson's Calendar: A Whisper to the Reader," *Pudd'nhead Wilson* (1894).

8. The greatest height of heroism to which an individual, like a people, can attain is to know how to face ridicule. MIGUEL DE UNAMUNO, "Don Quixote Today," *Tragic Sense of Life* (1913), tr. J. E. Crawford Flitch.

## 815. RIDING

1. A canter is the cure for every evil. BENJAMIN DISRAELI, *The Young Duke* (1831), 2.11.

2. If you ride a horse, sit close and tight, / If you ride a man, sit easy and light. BENJAMIN FRANKLIN, *Poor Richard's Almanack* (1732–57).

3. There is no secret so close as that between a rider and his horse. ROBERT SMITH SURTEES, *Mr. Sponge's Sporting Tour* (1853), 31.

## 816. RIGHT

**See also 171. Conscience; 224. Deeds; 297. Error; 317. Expediency; 391. Goodness; 728. Principle; 1025. Virtue; 1063. Wrongdoing**

1. The fear of doing right is the grand treason in times of danger. HENRY WARD BEECHER, *Proverbs from Plymouth Pulpit* (1887).

2. How forcible are right words. *Bible*, Job 6:25.

3. Right is its own defense. BERTOLT BRECHT, *Roundheads and Peakheads* (1933), 4, tr. N. Goold-Verschoyle.

4. The humblest citizen of all the land, when clad in the armor of a righteous cause, is stronger than all the hosts of error. WILLIAM JENNINGS BRYAN, speech, Democratic National Convention, Chicago, July 8, 1896.

5. You cannot make yourself feel something you do not feel, but you can make yourself do right in spite of your feelings. PEARL S. BUCK, "My Neighbor's Son," *To My Daughters, With Love* (1967).

6. From a worldly point of view there is no mistake so great as that of being always right. SAMUEL BUTLER (d. 1902), "Higgledy-Piggledy," *Note-Books* (1912).

7. Might and right do differ frightfully from hour to hour; but give them centuries to try it in, they are found to be identical. THOMAS CARLYLE, *Chartism* (1839), 8.

8. Be always sure you are right—then go ahead. DAVID CROCKETT, *Autobiography* (1834).

9. Good and bad are but names very readily transferable to that or this; the only right is what is after my constitution; the only wrong what is against it. EMERSON, "Self-Reliance," *Essays: First Series* (1841).

10. What is the freedom of the most free? To do what is right! GOETHE, *Egmont* (1788), tr. Michael Hamburger.

11. We uniformly applaud what is right and condemn what is wrong, when it costs us nothing but the sentiment. WILLIAM HAZLITT, *Characteristics* (1823).

12. Right is right only when entire. VICTOR HUGO, "Marius," *Les Misérables* (1862), 4.4, tr. Charles E. Wilbour.

13. Those who believe that they are exclusively in the right are generally those who achieve something. ALDOUS HUXLEY, *Proper Studies* (1927).

14. The assailant is often in the right; the assailed is always. WALTER SAVAGE LANDOR, "John of Gaunt and Joanna of Kent," *Imaginary Conversations* (1824–53).

15. They are slaves who dare not be / In the right with two or three. JAMES RUSSELL LOWELL, "Stanzas on Freedom" (1843), 4.

16. I'm armed with more than complete steel— / The justice of my quarrel. *Lust's Dominion* (1657), 4.3, attributed to CHRISTOPHER MARLOWE.

17. May God prevent us from becoming "right-thinking men"—that is to say men who agree perfectly with their own police. THOMAS MERTON, quoted in his obituary, *The New York Times*, Dec. 11, 1968.

18. Few sometimes may know, when thousands err. MILTON, *Paradise Lost* (1667), 6.148.

19. I will follow the right side even to the fire, but excluding the fire if I can. MONTAIGNE, "Of profit and honesty," *Essays* (1580–88), tr. Charles Cotton and W. C. Hazlitt.

20. He who practices right, but in the hope of acquiring great renown, is very near to vice. NAPOLEON I, *Maxims* (1804–15).

21. To do a great right, do a little wrong. SHAKESPEARE, *The Merchant of Venice* (1596–97), 4.1.216.

22. One's belief that one is sincere is not so dangerous as one's conviction that one is right. We all feel we are right; but we felt the same way twenty years ago and today we know we weren't always right. IGOR STRAVINSKY, *Conversations with Igor Stravinsky* (1959).

23. Because right is right, to follow right / Were wisdom in the scorn of consequence. ALFRED, LORD TENNYSON, "Oenone" (1842).

24. It is not desirable to cultivate a respect for the law, so much as for the right. THOREAU, *Civil Disobedience* (1849).

25. The Moral Sense teaches us what is right, and how to avoid it—when unpopular. MARK TWAIN, "The United States of Lyncherdom" (1923).

26. The right is more precious than peace. WOODROW WILSON, address to Congress, April 2, 1917.

27. Protest long enough that you are right, and you will be wrong. *Yiddish Proverbs* (1949), ed. Hanan J. Ayalti.

## 817. RIGHTS

**See also 295. Equality; 362. Free Speech; 534. Liberty; 725. Press, Freedom of the**

1. It is fair to judge peoples by the rights they will sacrifice most for. CLARENCE DAY, *This Simian World* (1920), 6.

2. Rights that do not flow from duty well performed are not worth having. MOHANDAS K. GANDHI, *Non-Violence in Peace and War* (1948), 2.269.

3. Wherever there is a human being, I see God-given rights inherent in that being, whatever may be the sex or complexion. WILLIAM LLOYD GARRISON, *Life* (1885–89), v. 3.

4. Liberty is the right to silence. Graffito written during French student revolt, May 1968.

5. I am the inferior of any man whose rights I trample under foot. ROBERT G. INGERSOLL, *Prose-Poems and Selections* (1884).

6. All, too, will bear in mind this sacred principle, that though the will of the majority is in all cases to prevail, that will to be rightful must be reasonable; that the minority possess their equal rights, which equal law must protect, and to violate would be oppression. THOMAS JEFFERSON, first Inaugural Address, March 4, 1801.

7. I am not so much concerned with the right of everyone to say anything he pleases as I am about our need as a self-governing people to hear everything relevant. JOHN F. KENNEDY, address, National Civil Liberties Conference, Washington, D.C., April 16, 1959.

8. In giving rights to others which belong to them, we give rights to ourselves and to our country. JOHN F. KENNEDY, message on 100th annivesary of Emancipation Proclamation, Washington, D.C., Sept. 22, 1962.

9. This nation was founded by men of many nations and backgrounds. It was founded on the principle that all men are created equal, and that the rights of every man are diminished when the rights of one man are threatened. JOHN F. KENNEDY, television address, June 11, 1963.

10. Let us have faith that right makes might, and in that faith let us to the end do our duty as we understand it. ABRAHAM LINCOLN, speech, New York City, Feb. 27, 1860.

11. They have rights who dare maintain them. JAMES RUSSELL LOWELL, "The Present Crisis" (1844).

12. The suppression of civil liberties is to many less a matter for horror than the curtailment of the freedom to profit. MARYA MANNES, "A Time for Change," *But Will It Sell?* (1955–64).

13. What men value in this world is not rights but privileges. H. L. MENCKEN, *Minority Report* (1956), 36.

14. Nobody talks more passionately of his rights than he who, in the depths of his soul, is doubtful about them. NIETZSCHE, *Human, All Too Human* (1878), 597, tr. Helen Zimmern.

15. The rights which a man arrogates to himself are relative to the duties which he sets himself, and to the tasks which he feels capable of performing. NIETZSCHE, *The Will to Power* (1888), 872, tr. Anthony M. Ludovici.

16. Government laws are needed to give us civil rights, and God is needed to make us civil. RALPH W. SOCKMAN, sermon, Riverside Church, New York City, Dec. 13, 1964.

17. The greatest achievement of the civil-rights movement is that it has restored the dignity of indignation. FREDERIC WERTHAM, *A Sign for Cain: An Exploration in Human Violence* (1966).

18. A right is worth fighting for only when it can be put into operation. WOODROW WILSON, address, Chattanooga, Tenn., Aug. 31, 1910.

## RISING

**See 71. Bed; 599. Morning**

## RITUAL

**See 112. Ceremony**

## RIVALRY

**See 154. Competition**

## 818. RIVERS

**See also 847. Sea; 1039. Water**

1. If the voice of the brook was not the first song of celebration, it must have been at least an obbligato for that event. HAL

BORLAND, "The Song of the Brook—March 25," *Sundial of the Seasons* (1964).

2. I do not know much about gods; but I think that the river / Is a strong brown god. T. S. ELIOT, "Dry Salvages," *Four Quartets* (1941), 1.

3. Rivers are roads which move, and which carry us whither we desire to go. PASCAL, *Pensées* (1670), 17, tr. W. F. Trotter.

4. I chatter, chatter, as I flow, / To join the brimming river, / For men may come and men may go, / But I go on forever. ALFRED, LORD TENNYSON, "The Brook" (1887).

5. The Hudson River is like old October and tawny Indians in their camping places long ago; it is like long pipes and old tobacco; it is like cool depths and opulence; it is like the shimmer of liquid green on summer days. THOMAS WOLFE, *Of Time and the River* (1935), 58.

## ROBBERY
See 927. Stealing

## 819. ROLE-PLAYING
See also 45. Appearance; 726. Pretension

1. Play out the game, act well your part, and if the gods have blundered, we will not. EMERSON, *Journals*, 1856.

2. We accept every person in the world as that for which he gives himself out, only he must give himself out for something. We can put up with the unpleasant more easily than we can endure the insignificant. GOETHE, *Elective Affinities* (1809), 23.

3. In civilized life, where the happiness, and indeed almost the existence, of man depends so much upon the opinion of his fellowmen, he is constantly acting a studied part. WASHINGTON IRVING, "Philip of Pakanoket," *The Sketch Book of Geoffrey Crayon, Gent.* (1819–20).

4. Perhaps one never seems so much at one's ease as when one has to play a part. OSCAR WILDE, *The Picture of Dorian Gray* (1891), 15.

## 820. ROMANCE
See also 195. Courtship; 821. Romanticism

1. Romance, like alcohol, should be enjoyed but must not be allowed to become necessary. EDGAR Z. FRIEDENBERG, "Emotional Development in Adolescence," *The Vanishing Adolescent* (1959).

2. No one deserves to be called a man whose life is filled only with romance, but neither does he whose life was never touched by it. THEODOR REIK, *Of Love and Lust* (1957), 1.3.14.

3. Nothing spoils a romance so much as a sense of humour in the woman. OSCAR WILDE, *A Woman of No Importance* (1893), 1.

## 821. ROMANTICISM

1. It is not irregular hours or irregular diet that make the romantic life. EMERSON, *Journals*, 1840.

2. It may be that, while we plodding realists go on, for ever preoccupied with our daily chores, abstracting a microscopic pleasure from each microscopic duty, your true romantic has the truer vision, and beholds, afar off, in all its lurid splendour and terrible proportions, the piquant adventure we call life. WILLIAM MC FEE, "The Crusaders," *Harbours of Memory* (1921).

3. Men may be allowed romanticism; women, who can create life in their own bodies, dare not indulge in it. PHYLLIS MC GINLEY, "The Honor of Being a Woman," *The Province of the Heart* (1959).

4. Is not this the true romantic feeling—not to desire to escape life, but to prevent life from escaping you? THOMAS WOLFE, quoted in Andrew Turnbull's *Thomas Wolfe* (1968).

## 822. ROUTINE
See also 404. Habit; 654. Order

1. Men fall into a routine when they are tired and slack: it has all the appearance of activity with few of its burdens. WALTER LIPPMANN, "Revolution and Culture," *A Preface to Politics* (1914).

2. It is the leisured, I have noticed, who rebel the most at an interruption of routine. PHYLLIS MC GINLEY, "A Garland of Kindness," *The Province of the Heart* (1959).

3. Forms are for mediocrity, and it is fortunate that mediocrity can act only according to routine. Ability takes its flight unhindered. NAPOLEON I, *Maxims* (1804–15).

4. After you've done a thing the same way for two years, look it over carefully. After five years, look at it with suspicion. And after ten years, throw it away and start all over. ALFRED EDWARD PERLMAN, *The New York Times*, July 3, 1958.

5. Routine is the god of every social system; it is the seventh heaven of business, the essential component in the success of every factory, the ideal of every statesman. The social machine should run like clockwork. ALFRED NORTH WHITEHEAD, *Adventures in Ideas* (1933), 6.

6. If the human being is condemned and restricted to perform the same functions over and over again, he will not even be a good ant, not to mention a good human being. NORBERT WIENER, *The Human Use of Human Beings* (1954), 3.

## 823. ROYALTY

See also 193. Court, Royal; 518. Kings

1. Royalty does good and is badly spoken of. ANTISTHENES (5th–4th c. B.C.), quoted in Diogenes Laertius' *Lives and Opinions of Eminent Philosophers* (3rd c. A.D.), tr. R. D. Hicks.

2. A prince is a gr-reat man in th' ol' counthry, but he niver is as gr-reat over there as he is here [in America]. FINLEY PETER DUNNE, "Prince Henry's Reception," *Observations by Mr. Dooley* (1902).

## 824. RUDENESS

See also 194. Courtesy; 486. Insult; 955. Tact

1. An ungracious man is like a story told at the wrong time. *Apocrypha*, Ecclesiasticus 20:19.

2. He who says what he likes shall hear what he does not like. ENGLISH PROVERB.

3. Except in streetcars one should never be unnecessarily rude to a lady. O. HENRY, "The Gold That Glittered," *Strictly Business* (1910).

4. Rudeness is the weak man's imitation of strength. ERIC HOFFER, *The Passionate State of Mind* (1954), 241.

5. Folly often goes beyond her bounds, but impudence knows none. BEN JONSON, "Explorata," *Timber* (1640).

6. A man must have very eminent qualities to hold his own without being polite. LA BRUYÈRE, *Characters* (1688), 5.32, tr. Henri Van Laun.

7. Spiritual strength and passion, when accompanied by bad manners, only provoke loathing. NIETZSCHE, *The Will to Power* (1888), tr. Anthony M. Ludovici.

8. It is undoubtedly true that some people mistake sycophancy for good nature, but it is equally true that many more mistake impertinence for sincerity. GEORGE DENNISON PRENTICE, *Prenticeana* (1860).

## RUINS

See 42. Antiquity

## 825. RULERS

See also 61. Authority; 393. Government; 518. Kings; 528. Leadership; 724. Presidency

1. Every ruler is harsh whose rule is new. AESCHYLUS, *Prometheus Bound* (c. 478 B.C.), tr. David Grene.

2. If men think that a ruler is religious and has a reverence for the Gods, they are less afraid of suffering injustice at his hands. ARISTOTLE, *Politics* (4th c. B.C.), 5.11, tr. Benjamin Jowett.

3. Princes are like heavenly bodies, which cause good or evil times, and which have much veneration, but no rest. FRANCIS BACON, "Of Empire," *Essays* (1625).

4. Those who lead the State over a precipice / Call governing too onerous / For the plain man. BERTOLT BRECHT, "Those Who Deprive the Table of Meat," *Modern European Poetry* (1966), ed. Willis Barnstone.

5. Only with a new ruler do you realize the value of the old. BURMESE PROVERBS (1962), 350, ed. Hla Pe.

6. Those who see and observe kings, heroes, and statesmen, discover that they have headaches, indigestion, humors and passions, just like other people; every one of

which in their turns determine their wills in defiance of their reason. LORD CHESTERFIELD, *Letters to His Son*, Dec. 5, 1749.

7. Power educates the potentate. EMERSON, "Power," *The Conduct of Life* (1860).

8. The subject's love is the king's best guard. THOMAS FULLER, M.D., *Gnomologia* (1732), 4773.

9. He who would rule must hear and be deaf, see and be blind. GERMAN PROVERB.

10. To appear at church every Sunday; to look down upon, and let himself be looked at for an hour by the congregation, is the best means of becoming popular which can be recommended to a young sovereign. GOETHE, quoted in Johann Peter Eckermann's *Conversations with Goethe*, April 2, 1829.

11. The art of governing is a great *métier*, requiring the whole man, and it is therefore not well for a ruler to have too strong tendencies for other affairs. GOETHE, quoted in Johann Peter Eckermann's *Conversations with Goethe*, Feb. 18, 1831.

12. We will have a good master as soon as every person is his own. Graffito written during French student revolt, May 1968.

13. Whom hatred frights, / Let him not dream on sovereignty. BEN JONSON, *Sejanus His Fall* (1603), 2.2.

14. He that would govern others, first should be / The master of himself. PHILIP MASSINGER, *The Bondman* (c. 1624), 1.3.

15. We owe subjection and obedience to all our kings, whether good or bad, alike, for that has respect unto their office; but as to esteem and affection, these are only due to their virtue. MONTAIGNE, "That our affections carry themselves beyond us," *Essays* (1580–88), tr. Charles Cotton and W. C. Hazlitt.

16. Rigorous authority and justice are the kindness of kings. NAPOLEON I, *Maxims* (1804–15).

17. To rule is not so much a question of the heavy hand as the firm seat. JOSÉ ORTEGA Y GASSET, *The Revolt of the Masses* (1930), 14.

18. Better have as king a vulture advised by swans than a swan advised by vultures. *Panchatantra* (c. 5th c.), 1, tr. Arthur W. Ryder.

19. The power of kings is founded on the reason and on the folly of the people, and specially on their folly. PASCAL, *Pensées* (1670), 330, tr. W. F. Trotter.

20. Where princes are concerned, a man who is able to do good is as dangerous and almost as criminal as a man who intends to do evil. CARDINAL DE RETZ, *Mémoires* (1718).

21. Not the least of the qualities that go into the making of a great ruler is the ability of letting others serve him. CARDINAL RICHELIEU, *Political Testament* (1687), 1.4.

22. If you have but a single ruler, you lie at the discretion of a master who has no reason to love you: and if you have several, you must bear at once their tyranny and their divisions. ROUSSEAU, *A Discourse on Political Economy* (1758), tr. G. D. H. Cole.

23. One can't reign and be innocent. LOUIS ANTOINE LÉON DE SAINT-JUST, *Discours à la convention*, Nov. 13, 1792.

24. Within the hollow crown / That rounds the mortal temples of a king / Keeps Death his court. SHAKESPEARE, *Richard II* (1595–96), 3.2.160.

25. Uneasy lies the head that wears a crown. SHAKESPEARE, *2 Henry IV* (1597–98), 3.1.31.

26. To know nor faith, nor love, nor law; to be / Omnipotent but friendless is to reign. SHELLEY, *Prometheus Unbound* (1818–19), 2.4.

27. Ill can he rule the great that cannot reach the small. EDMUND SPENSER, *The Faerie Queene* (1596), 5.2.43.

28. A doubtful throne is ice on summer seas. ALFRED, LORD TENNYSON, "The Coming of Arthur," *Idylls of the King* (1869).

## 826. RULES

See also 579. Method

1. A technical objection is the first refuge of a scoundrel. HEYWOOD BROUN, " 'Jam-Tomorrow' Progressives," *New Republic*, Dec. 15, 1937.

2. No rule is so general, which admits not some exception. ROBERT BURTON, *The Anatomy of Melancholy* (1621), 1.2.2.3.

3. There is no useful rule without an exception. THOMAS FULLER, M.D., *Gnomologia* (1732), 4925.

4. In reading and writing, you cannot lay down rules until you have learnt to obey

them. Much more so in life. MARCUS AURELIUS, *Meditations* (2nd c.), 11.29, tr. Maxwell Staniforth.

5. You cannot put the same shoe on every foot. PUBLILIUS SYRUS, *Moral Sayings* (1st c. B.C.), 596, tr. Darius Lyman.

6. Any fool can make a rule / And every fool will mind it. THOREAU, *Journal*, Feb. 3, 1860.

## 827. RUMORS

See also 392. Gossip; 840. Scandal

1. Rumor travels Faster, but it don't stay put as long as Truth. WILL ROGERS, "Politics Getting Ready to Jell," *The Illiterate Digest* (1924).

2. Rumour is a pipe / Blown by surmises, jealousies, conjectures. SHAKESPEARE, induction to *2 Henry IV* (1597–98), 15.

3. Rumour doth double, like the voice and echo, / The numbers of the feared. SHAKESPEARE, *2 Henry IV* (1597–98), 3.1.97.

4. Rumor goes forth at once, Rumor than whom / No other speedier evil thing exists; / She thrives by rapid movement, and acquires / Strength as she goes; small at the first from fear, / She presently uplifts herself aloft, / And stalks upon the ground and hides her head / Among the clouds. VERGIL, *Aeneid* (30–19 B.C.), 4.173, tr. T. H. Delabere-May.

## 828. RUSSIA AND RUSSIANS

1. I cannot forecast to you the action of Russia. It is a riddle wrapped in a mystery inside an enigma. SIR WINSTON CHURCHILL, radio broadcast, Oct. 1, 1939.

2. Don't you forget what's divine in the Russian soul–and that's resignation. JOSEPH CONRAD, *Under Western Eyes* (1911), 1.1.

3. The Russians train; they do not dare educate. MAX LERNER, "Four Fallacies of Our Schools," *The Unfinished Country* (1959), 2.

4. Ideas in modern Russia are machine-cut blocks coming in solid colors; the nuance is outlawed, the interval walled up, the curve grossly stepped. VLADIMIR NABOKOV, "Commentary," *Pale Fire* (1962), 681.

# S

## 829. SABBATH

1. God blessed the seventh day, and sanctified it: because that in it he had rested from all his work which God created and made. *Bible*, Genesis 2:3.

2. Remember the sabbath day, to keep it holy. Six days shalt thou labour, and do all thy work: But the seventh day is the sabbath of the Lord thy God: in it thou shalt not do any work. *Bible*, Exodus 20:8–10.

3. Sabbath, n. A weekly festival having its origin in the fact that God made the world in six days and was arrested on the seventh. AMBROSE BIERCE, *The Devil's Dictionary* (1881–1911).

## 830. SACRAMENT

See also 952. Symbols

1. I mean by this word Sacrament an outward and visible sign of an inward and spiritual grace. Offices of Instruction, *The Book of Common Prayer* (1549, 1789, 1928).

## 831. SACRIFICE

See also 561. Martyrs and Martyrdom; 881. Services

1. Greater love hath no man than this, that a man lay down his life for his friends. *Bible*, John 15:13.

2. Sacrificers are not the ones to pity. The ones to pity are those they sacrifice. ELIZABETH BOWEN, *The Death of the Heart* (1938), 1.6.

3. Those who are certain to gain by the offering / Demand a spirit of sacrifice. BERTOLT BRECHT, "Those Who Deprive the Table of Meat," *Modern European Poetry* (1966), ed. Willis Barnstone.

4. Drown not thyself to save a drowning man. THOMAS FULLER, M.D., *Gnomologia* (1732), 1340.

5. The very act of sacrifice magnifies the one who sacrifices himself to the point where his sacrifice is much more costly to humanity than would have been the loss of those for whom he is sacrificing himself. But

in his abnegation lies the secret of his grandeur. ANDRÉ GIDE, *Journals*, June 23, 1931, tr. Justin O'Brien.

6. Sacrifice may be a flower that virtue will pluck on its road, but it was not to gather this flower that virtue set forth on its travels. MAURICE MAETERLINCK, *Wisdom and Destiny* (1898), 65, tr. Alfred Sutro.

7. For the sake of a family an individual may be sacrificed; for the sake of a village a family may be sacrificed; for the sake of a nation a village may be sacrificed; for the sake of one's self the world may be sacrificed. *Panchatantra* (c. 5th c.), 1, tr. Franklin Edgerton.

8. Only he can understand what a farm is, what a country is, who shall have sacrificed part of himself to his farm or country. SAINT-EXUPÉRY, *Flight to Arras* (1942), 23, tr. Lewis Galantière.

9. Nothing so much enhances a good as to make sacrifices for it. GEORGE SANTAYANA, *The Sense of Beauty* (1896), 26.

10. Self-sacrifice enables us to sacrifice other people without blushing. GEORGE BERNARD SHAW, "Maxims for Revolutionists," *Man and Superman* (1903).

11. Too long a sacrifice / Can make a stone of the heart. WILLIAM BUTLER YEATS, "Easter 1916" (1916).

## 832. SADISM

**See also 206. Cruelty**

1. We know well enough when we're being unjust and despicable. But we don't restrain ourselves because we experience a certain pleasure, a primitive sort of satisfaction in moments like that. UGO BETTI, *Landslide* (1936), 2, tr. G. H. McWilliam.

2. Pleasure is sweetest when 'tis paid for by another's pain. OVID, *The Art of Love* (c. A.D. 8), 1, tr. J. Lewis May.

3. Tears gratify a savage nature, they do not melt it. PUBLILIUS SYRUS, *Moral Sayings* (1st c. B.C.), 163, tr. Darius Lyman.

## SADNESS

**See 1004. Unhappiness**

## SAFETY

**See 850. Security**

## 833. SAILING

**See also 888. Ships and Boats**

1. Land was created to provide a place for steamers to visit. BROOKS ATKINSON, "January 20," *Once Around the Sun* (1951).

2. Ports are necessities, like postage stamps or soap, / but they seldom seem to care what impressions they make. ELIZABETH BISHOP, "Arrival at Santos," *Questions of Travel* (1965).

3. How holy people look when they are sea-sick! SAMUEL BUTLER (d. 1902), "Written Sketches," *Note-Books* (1912).

4. There is nothing more enticing, disenchanting, and enslaving than the life at sea. JOSEPH CONRAD, *Lord Jim* (1900), 2.

5. Nowhere else than upon the sea do the days, weeks, and months fall away quicker into the past. They seem to be left astern as easily as the light air-bubbles in the swirls of the ship's wake. JOSEPH CONRAD, *The Mirror of the Sea* (1906), 2.

6. The happiest hour a sailor sees / Is when he's down / At an inland town, / With his Nancy on his knees, yo ho! / And his arm around her waist! W. S. GILBERT, *The Mikado* (1885), 1.

7. Being in a ship is being in a jail, with the chance of being drowned. SAMUEL JOHNSON, quoted in Boswell's *Life of Samuel Johnson*, March 16, 1759.

## 834. SAINTS AND SAINTHOOD

**See also 561. Martyrs and Martyrdom; 920. Spirituality**

1. Saintliness is also a temptation. JEAN ANOUILH, *Becket* (1959), 3.

2. Saint, n. A dead sinner revised and edited. AMBROSE BIERCE, *The Devil's Dictionary* (1881–1911).

3. Can one be a saint without God? This is the only problem I know of today. ALBERT CAMUS, *La Peste* (1947).

4. Many of the insights of the saint stem from his experience as a sinner. ERIC HOFFER, *The Passionate State of Mind* (1954), 9.

5. We are content to place a statue of Francis of Assisi in the middle of a bird bath and let the whole business of the Saints go

at that. C. KILMER MYERS, *The New York Times*, March 19, 1962.

6. No doubt alcohol, tobacco, and so forth, are things that a saint must avoid, but sainthood is also a thing that human beings must avoid. GEORGE ORWELL, "Reflections on Gandhi," *Shooting an Elephant* (1950).

7. Many people genuinely do not wish to be saints, and it is probable that some who achieve or aspire to sainthood have never felt much temptation to be human beings. GEORGE ORWELL, "Reflections on Gandhi," *Shooting an Elephant* (1950).

8. Saints should always be judged guilty until they are proved innocent. GEORGE ORWELL, "Reflections on Gandhi," *Shooting an Elephant* (1950).

9. Grace is indeed needed to turn a man into a saint; and he who doubts it does not know what a saint or a man is. PASCAL, *Pensées* (1670), 508, tr. W. F. Trotter.

10. The saints indulge in subtleties in order to think themselves criminals, and impeach their better actions. PASCAL, *Pensées* (1670), 920, tr. W. F. Trotter.

11. It is easier to make a saint out of a libertine than out of a prig. GEORGE SANTAYANA, *The Life of Reason: Reason in Religion* (1905–06), 11.

12. Sanctity and genius are as rebellious as vice. GEORGE SANTAYANA, *Little Essays* (1920), 49, ed. Logan Pearsall Smith.

13. It's the bad that's in the best of us / Leaves the saint so like the rest of us. ARTHUR STRINGER, "Humanity."

14. The only difference between the saint and the sinner is that every saint has a past, and every sinner has a future. OSCAR WILDE, *A Woman of No Importance* (1893), 3.

## 835. SALVATION

**See also 590. Missionaries; 893. Sin**

1. Strait is the gate, and narrow is the way, which leadeth unto life, and few there be that find it. *Bible*, Matthew 7:14.

2. Souls are not saved in bundles. EMERSON, "Worship," *The Conduct of Life* (1860).

3. What is most contrary to salvation is not sin but habit. CHARLES PÉGUY, "Sinners and Saints," *Basic Verities* (1943), tr. Ann and Julian Green.

4. There is no expeditious road / To pack and label men for God, / And save them by the barrel-load. FRANCIS THOMPSON, epilogue to "A Judgment in Heaven" (1893).

## 836. SANITY

**See also 411. Health; 555. Madness; 620. Neurosis**

1. Our health is our sound relation to external objects; our sympathy with external being. EMERSON, *Journals*, 1836.

2. The criterion of mental health is not one of individual adjustment to a given social order, but a universal one, valid for all men, of giving a satisfactory answer to the problem of human existence. ERICH FROMM, *The Sane Society* (1955), 2.

3. Sanity is a madness put to good uses; waking life is a dream controlled. GEORGE SANTAYANA, *Interpretations of Poetry and Religion* (1900).

## 837. SARCASM

**See also 1054. Wit**

1. Sarcasm: the last refuge of modest and chaste-souled people when the privacy of their soul is coarsely and intrusively invaded. DOSTOEVSKY, *Notes from Underground* (1864), 2.4, tr. Constance Garnett.

## 838. SATIRE

**See also 1054. Wit**

1. One man's pointlessness is another's barbed satire. FRANKLIN P. ADAMS, *Nods and Becks* (1944).

2. That is the grave omission of the usual satirist, the omission of himself. FRANK MOORE COLBY, "Satire and Teeth," *The Colby Essays* (1926), v. 1.

3. By rights, satire is a lonely and introspective occupation, for nobody can describe a fool to the life without much patient self-inspection. FRANK MOORE COLBY, "Simple Simon," *The Colby Essays* (1926), v. 1.

4. Satirists gain the applause of others through fear, not through love. WILLIAM HAZLITT, *Characteristics* (1823), 72.

5. Satire should, like a polished razor

keen, / Wound with a touch that's scarcely felt or seen. LADY MARY WORTLEY MONTAGU, "To the Imitator of the First Satire of Horace, Book ii" (1733).

6. Satire's my weapon, but I'm too discreet / To run amuck, and tilt at all I meet. ALEXANDER POPE, *Imitations of Horace* (1733–38), 2.1.69.

7. Satire is a sort of glass, wherein beholders do generally discover everybody's face but their own. JONATHAN SWIFT, preface to *The Battle of the Books* (1704).

## 839. SATISFACTION

See also 183. Contentment; 236. Desires; 940. Sufficiency

1. He is rich that is satisfied. THOMAS FULLER, M.D., *Gnomologia* (1732), 1943.

2. From the satisfaction of desire there may arise, accompanying joy and as it were sheltering behind it, something not unlike despair. ANDRÉ GIDE, *The Counterfeiters* (1925), 1.7, tr. Dorothy Bussy.

3. The sovereign source of melancholy is repletion. Need and struggle are what excite and inspire us; our hour of triumph is what brings the void. WILLIAM JAMES, "Is Life Worth Living?" *The Will to Believe* (1896).

4. When we reside in an attic we enjoy a supper of fried fish and stout. When we occupy the first floor it takes an elaborate dinner at the Continental to give us the same amount of satisfaction. JEROME K. JEROME, "On Furnished Apartments," *The Idle Thoughts of an Idle Fellow* (1889).

5. He is well paid that is well satisfied. SHAKESPEARE, *The Merchant of Venice* (1596–97), 4.1.415.

6. In the world there are only two tragedies. One is not getting what one wants, and the other is getting it. OSCAR WILDE, *Lady Windermere's Fan* (1892), 3.

## SAVAGERY

See 69. Barbarism

## 840. SCANDAL

See also 392. Gossip; 827. Rumors

1. Love and scandal are the best sweeteners of tea. HENRY FIELDING, *Love in Several Masques* (1728), 2.11.

2. A lie has no leg, but a scandal has wings. THOMAS FULLER, M.D., *Gnomologia* (1732), 263.

3. Greatest scandal waits on greatest state. SHAKESPEARE, *The Rape of Lucrece* (1594), 1006.

4. There never was a scandalous tale without some foundation. RICHARD BRINSLEY SHERIDAN, *The School for Scandal* (1777), 2.2.

## 841. SCAPEGOAT

See also 403. Guilt; 561. Martyrs and Martyrdom

1. The scapegoat has always had the mysterious power of unleashing man's ferocious pleasure in torturing, corrupting, and befouling. FRANÇOIS MAURIAC, "Child Martyrs," *Second Thoughts* (1961), tr. Adrienne Foulke.

## 842. SCHOLARS AND SCHOLARSHIP

See also 277. Education; 520. Knowledge; 529. Learning; 917. Specialists; 959. Teaching

1. Learning is the property of those who fear to do disagreeable things. PIETRO ARETINO, letter to the Cardinal of Ravenna, Aug. 29, 1537, tr. Samuel Putnam.

2. To spend too much time in studies is sloth; to use them too much for ornament is affectation; to make judgment wholly by their rules is the humor of a scholar. FRANCIS BACON, "Of Studies," *Essays* (1625).

3. Erudition, n. Dust shaken out of a book into an empty skull. AMBROSE BIERCE, *The Devil's Dictionary* (1881–1911).

4. Things take indeed a wondrous turn / When learned men do stoop to learn. BERTOLT BRECHT, *Galileo* (1938; 1947), 5, tr. Charles Laughton.

5. We want a Society for the Suppression of Erudite Research and the Decent Burial of the Past. The ghosts of the dead past want quite as much laying as raising. SAMUEL BUTLER (d. 1902), "Cash and Credit," *Note-Books* (1912).

6. One learns little more about a man from the feats of his literary memory than from the feats of his alimentary canal.

FRANK MOORE COLBY, "Quotation and Allusion," *The Colby Essays* (1926), v. 1.

7. Pedantry crams our heads with learned lumber and takes out our brains to make room for it. CHARLES CALEB COLTON, *Lacon* (1825), 2.20.

8. When nature exceeds culture, we have the rustic. When culture exceeds nature, we have the pedant. CONFUCIUS, *Analects* (6th c. B.C.), 6.16, tr. Ch'u Chai and Winberg Chai.

9. A great man will find a great subject, or which is the same thing, make any subject great. EMERSON, *Journals*, 1833.

10. The office of the scholar is to cheer, to raise, and to guide men by showing them facts amidst appearances. EMERSON, *The American Scholar* (1837).

11. How we hate this solemn Ego that accompanies the learned, like a double, wherever he goes. EMERSON, *Journals*, 1839.

12. A scholar is a man with this inconvenience, that, when you ask him his opinion of any matter, he must go home and look up his manuscripts to know. EMERSON, *Journals*, 1855.

13. In truth man is made rather to eat ices than to pore over old texts. ANATOLE FRANCE, *The Crime of Sylvestre Bonnard* (1881), 1, tr. Lafcadio Hearn.

14. Tim was so learned that he could name a horse in nine languages: so ignorant that he bought a cow to ride on. BENJAMIN FRANKLIN, *Poor Richard's Almanack* (1732–57).

15. The world would perish were all men learned. THOMAS FULLER, M.D., *Gnomologia* (1732), 4846.

16. There is much more learning than knowing in the world. THOMAS FULLER, M.D., *Gnomologia* (1732), 4901.

17. The scholar seeks, the artist finds. ANDRÉ GIDE, *The Counterfeiters* (1925), 3.20, tr. Dorothy Bussy.

18. A scholar is like a book written in a dead language: it is not every one that can read in it. WILLIAM HAZLITT, "Commonplaces," *The Round Table* (1817), 13.

19. Learning is the knowledge of that which none but the learned know. WILLIAM HAZLITT, "On the Ignorance of the Learned," *Table Talk* (1821–22).

20. The humblest painter is a true scholar; and the best of scholars—the scholar of nature. WILLIAM HAZLITT, "On the Pleasure of Painting," *Table Talk* (1821–22).

21. It is the vice of scholars to suppose that there is no knowledge in the world but that of books. WILLIAM HAZLITT, "On the Conduct of Life," *Literary Remains* (1836).

22. The world's great men have not commonly been great scholars, nor its great scholars great men. OLIVER WENDELL HOLMES, SR., *The Autocrat of the Breakfast Table* (1858), 6.

23. Pedantry is the dotage of knowledge. HOLBROOK JACKSON, *The Anatomy of Bibliomania* (1930–31).

24. Life is surely given us for higher purposes than to gather what our ancestors have wisely thrown away, and to learn what is of no value but because it has been forgotten. SAMUEL JOHNSON, *The Rambler* (1750–52), 121.

25. Two evils, of almost equal weight, may befall the man of erudition: never to be listened to, and to be listened to always. WALTER SAVAGE LANDOR, "Epicurus, Leontion, and Ternissa," *Imaginary Conversations* (1824–53).

26. The ordinary man is ruined by the flesh lusting against the spirit; the scholar by the spirit lusting too much against the flesh. GEORG CHRISTOPH LICHTENBERG, *Aphorisms* (1764–99), tr. F. H. Mautner and H. Hatfield.

27. The mind of the scholar, if you would have it large and liberal, should come in contact with other minds. It is better that his armor should be somewhat bruised by rude encounters even, than hang for ever rusting on the wall. LONGFELLOW, *Hyperion* (1839), 1.8.

28. Every rostrum has its passing pedant. ANTONIO MACHADO, *Juan de Mairena* (1943), 14, tr. Ben Belitt.

29. Don't appear so scholarly, pray. Humanize your talk, and speak to be understood. Do you think a Greek name gives more weight to your reasons? MOLIÈRE, *The Critique of the School for Wives* (1663), 6, tr. Donald M. Frame.

30. Everything that's prose isn't verse and everything that isn't verse is prose. Now you see what it is to be a scholar! MOLIÈRE, *The Would-be Gentleman* (1670), 3, tr. John Wood.

31. Difficulty is a coin the learned make use of like jugglers, to conceal the inanity of

their art. MONTAIGNE, "Apology for Raimond de Sebonde," *Essays* (1580–88), tr. Charles Cotton and W. C. Hazlitt.

32. This is ever the test of the scholar: whether he allows intellectual fastidiousness to stand between him and the great issues of his time. JOHN MORLEY, "Emerson," *Critical Miscellanies* (1871–1908).

33. A fool is only troublesome, a pedant insupportable. NAPOLEON I, *Maxims* (1804–15).

34. Scholarship is polite argument. PHILIP RIEFF, *New York Herald Tribune*, Jan. 1, 1961.

35. The scholar is early acquainted with every department of the impossible. JOHN RUSKIN, review of Lord Lindsay's *Sketches of the History of Christian Art.*

36. A scholar without diligence is a lover without money. SA'DI, *Gulistan* (1258), 8.82, tr. James Ross.

37. Small have continual plodders ever won / Save base authority from others' books. SHAKESPEARE, *Love's Labour's Lost* (1594–95), 1.1.86.

38. A learned man is an idler who kills time with study. GEORGE BERNARD SHAW, "Maxims for Revolutionists," *Man and Superman* (1903).

39. This is the great vice of academicism, that it is concerned with ideas rather than with thinking. LIONEL TRILLING, "The Sense of the Past," *The Liberal Imagination* (1950).

## 843. SCIENCE

**See also 633. Nuclear Power; 844. Science and Religion; 914. Space; 960. Technology; 967. Theory**

1. The quick harvest of applied science is the usable process, the medicine, the machine. The shy fruit of pure science is Understanding. LINCOLN BARNETT, *Life*, Jan. 9, 1950.

2. Observatory, n. A place where astronomers conjecture away the guesses of their predecessors. AMBROSE BIERCE, *The Devil's Dictionary* (1881–1911).

3. The ordinary scientific man is strictly a sentimentalist. He is a sentimentalist in this essential sense, that he is soaked and swept away by mere associations. G. K. CHESTERTON, "The Logic of Elfland," *Orthodoxy* (1908).

4. Science has given to this generation the means of unlimited disaster or of unlimited progress. There will remain the greater task of directing knowledge lastingly towards the purpose of peace and human good. SIR WINSTON CHURCHILL, speech, New Delhi, Jan. 3, 1944.

5. There's always wan encouragin' thing about th' sad scientific facts that come out ivry week in th' pa-apers. They're usually not thrue. FINLEY PETER DUNNE, "On the Descent of Man," *Mr. Dooley On Making a Will* (1919).

6. The whole of science is nothing more than a refinement of everyday thinking. EINSTEIN, *Out of My Later Years* (1950), 13.1.

7. Science is the attempt to make the chaotic diversity of our sense-experience correspond to a logically uniform system of thought. EINSTEIN, *Out of My Later Years* (1950), 14.

8. 'Tis a short sight to limit our faith in laws to those of gravity, of chemistry, of botany, and so forth. EMERSON, "Worship," *The Conduct of Life* (1860).

9. Scientist alone is true poet he gives us the moon / he promises the stars he'll make us a new universe if it comes to that. ALLEN GINSBERG, "Poem Rocket," *Kaddish and Other Poems* (1961).

10. As soon as any one belongs to a narrow creed in science, every unprejudiced and true perception is gone. GOETHE, quoted in Johann Peter Eckermann's *Conversations with Goethe*, May 18, 1824.

11. Science is the knowledge of consequences, and dependence of one fact upon another. THOMAS HOBBES, *Leviathan* (1651), 1.5.

12. Science is a first-rate piece of furniture for a man's upper chamber, if he has common sense on the ground-floor. OLIVER WENDELL HOLMES, SR., *The Poet at the Breakfast Table* (1872), 5.

13. Astronomers work always with the past; because light takes time to move from one place to another, they see things as they were, not as they are. NEALE E. HOWARD, *The Telescope Handbook and Star Atlas* (1967), 3.

14. The great tragedy of Science—the slaying of a beautiful hypothesis by an ugly

fact. THOMAS HENRY HUXLEY, "Biogenesis and Abiogenesis" (1870).

15. Science is nothing but trained and organized common sense. THOMAS HENRY HUXLEY, "The Method of Zadig" (1878).

16. Science herself consults her heart when she lays it down that the infinite ascertainment of fact and correction of false belief are the supreme goods for man. WILLIAM JAMES, title essay, *The Will to Believe* (1896).

17. How many learned men are working at the forge of science—laborious, ardent, tireless Cyclopes, but one-eyed! JOSEPH JOUBERT, *Pensées* (1842), 17.32, tr. Katharine Lyttelton.

18. I am sorry to say that there is too much point to the wisecrack that life is extinct on other planets because their scientists were more advanced than ours. JOHN F. KENNEDY, address, Washington, D.C., Dec. 11, 1959.

19. Let both sides seek to invoke the wonders of science instead of its terrors. Together let us explore the stars, conquer the deserts, eradicate disease, tap the ocean depths, and encourage the arts and commerce. JOHN F. KENNEDY, Inaugural Address, Jan. 20, 1961.

20. If scientific discovery has not been an unalloyed blessing, if it has conferred on mankind the power not only to create but also to annihilate, it has at the same time provided humanity with a supreme challenge and a supreme testing. JOHN F. KENNEDY, address, National Academy of Sciences, Washington, D.C., Oct. 22, 1963.

21. The means by which we live have outdistanced the ends for which we live. Our scientific power has outrun our spiritual power. We have guided missiles and misguided men. MARTIN LUTHER KING, JR., *Strength to Love* (1963), 7.3.

22. Nominally a great age of scientific inquiry, ours has actually become an age of superstition about the infallibility of science; of almost mystical faith in its nonmystical methods; above all . . . of external verities; of traffic-cop morality and rabbit-test truth. LOUIS KRONENBERGER, *Company Manners* (1954), 1.4.

23. Science has always promised two things not necessarily related—an increase first in our powers, second in our happiness or wisdom, and we have come to realize that it is the first and less important of the two promises which it has kept most abundantly. JOSEPH WOOD KRUTCH, "The Disillusion with the Laboratory," *The Modern Temper* (1929).

24. Though many have tried, no one has ever yet explained away the decisive fact that science, which can do so much, cannot decide what it ought to do. JOSEPH WOOD KRUTCH, "The Loss of Confidence," *The Measure of Man* (1954).

25. Science itself is a humanist in the sense that it doesn't discriminate between human beings, but it is also morally neutral. It is no better or worse than the ethos with and for which it is used. MAX LERNER, "Manipulating Life," in the *New York Post*, Jan. 24, 1968.

26. In science, all facts, no matter how trivial or banal, enjoy democratic equality. MARY MC CARTHY, "The Fact in Fiction," *On the Contrary* (1961).

27. The physicists have known sin; and this is a knowledge which they cannot lose. J. ROBERT OPPENHEIMER, lecture, Massachusetts Institute of Technology, 1947.

28. Science is built of facts the way a house is built of bricks; but an accumulation of facts is no more science than a pile of bricks is a house. HENRI POINCARÉ, *La Science et l'hypothèse* (1902).

29. The simplest schoolboy is now familiar with truths for which Archimedes would have sacrificed his life. ERNEST RENAN, *Souvenirs d'enfance et de jeunesse* (1883).

30. In art nothing worth doing can be done without genius; in science even a very moderate capacity can contribute to a supreme achievement. BERTRAND RUSSELL, "Science and Culture," *Mysticism and Logic* (1917).

31. Science, by itself, cannot supply us with an ethic. It can show us how to achieve a given end, and it may show us that some ends cannot be achieved. BERTRAND RUSSELL, "The Science to Save Us from Science," *The New York Times Magazine*, March 19, 1950.

32. People must understand that science is inherently neither a potential for good nor for evil. It is a potential to be harnessed by man to do his bidding. GLENN T. SEABORG, Associated Press interview with Alton Blakeslee, Sept. 29, 1964.

33. The true scientist never loses the

faculty of amazement. It is the essence of his being. HANS SELYE, *Newsweek*, March 31, 1958.

34. Science is always simple and always profound. It is only the half-truths that are dangerous. GEORGE BERNARD SHAW, *The Doctor's Dilemma* (1913), 1.

35. Science is the great antidote to the poison of enthusiasm and superstition. ADAM SMITH, *The Wealth of Nations* (1776), 5.3.

36. The truth is, that those who have never entered upon scientific pursuits know not a tithe of the poetry by which they are surrounded. HERBERT SPENCER, *Education: Intellectual, Moral and Physical* (1861).

37. Science when well digested is nothing but good sense and reason. STANISLAUS I OF POLAND, *Maxims* (c. 18th c.), 43.

38. Science is the most intimate school of resignation and humility, for it teaches us to bow before the seemingly most insignificant of facts. MIGUEL DE UNAMUNO, "Faith, Hope, and Charity," *Tragic Sense of Life* (1913), tr. J. E. Crawford Flitch.

39. Modern science has imposed on humanity the necessity for wandering. ALFRED NORTH WHITEHEAD, *Science and the Modern World* (1925), 13.

40. Scientific discovery consists in the interpretation for our own convenience of a system of existence which has been made with no eye to our convenience at all. NORBERT WIENER, *The Human Use of Human Beings* (1954), 7.

41. Sweet is the lore which Nature brings; / Our meddling intellect / Mis-shapes the beauteous forms of things:— / We murder to dissect. WILLIAM WORDSWORTH, "The Tables Turned" (1798).

## 844. SCIENCE AND RELIGION

**See also 790. Religion; 843. Science**

1. Science and religion, religion and science, put it as I may, they are two sides of the same glass, through which we see darkly until these two, focusing together, reveal the truth. PEARL S. BUCK, *A Bridge for Passing* (1962), 3.

2. If they [scientists] are worthy of the name, they are indeed about God's path and about his bed and spying out all his ways. SAMUEL BUTLER, "Higgledy-Piggledy," *Note-Books* (1912).

3. "Faith" is a fine invention / When Gentlemen can *see*— / But *Microscopes* are prudent / In an Emergency. EMILY DICKINSON, poem (c. 1860).

4. Science without religion is lame, religion without science is blind. EINSTEIN, "Science and Religion," *Out of My Later Years* (1950).

5. The religion that is afraid of science dishonors God and commits suicide. EMERSON, *Journals*, 1831.

6. Don't set out to teach theism from your natural history. . . . You spoil both. EMERSON, *Journals*, 1857.

7. Science investigates; religion interprets. Science gives man knowledge which is power; religion gives man wisdom which is control. MARTIN LUTHER KING, JR., *Strength to Love* (1963), 1.1.

8. The effort to reconcile science and religion is almost always made, not by theologians, but by scientists unable to shake off altogether the piety absorbed with their mother's milk. H. L. MENCKEN, *Minority Report* (1956), 232.

9. Every formula which expresses a law of nature is a hymn of praise to God. MARIA MITCHELL (1818–89), inscription beneath her bust in the Hall of Fame for Great Americans, New York University, New York City.

10. Increasing knowledge of science without a corresponding growth of religious wisdom only increases our fear of death. SIR SARVEPALLI RADHAKRISHNAN, *The Philosophy of Sarvepalli Radhakrishnan* (1952), ed. Paul Arthur Schilpp.

11. Religion will not regain its old power until it can face change in the same spirit as does science. Its principles may be eternal, but the expression of those principles requires continual development. ALFRED NORTH WHITEHEAD, *Science and the Modern World* (1925), 12.

12. Religions die when they are proved to be true. Science is the record of dead religions. OSCAR WILDE, "Phrases and Philosophies for the Use of the Young" (1891).

13. An undevout astronomer is mad. EDWARD YOUNG, *Night Thoughts* (1742–46), 9.771.

## SCORN

**See 182. Contempt**

## 845. SCOTSMEN

1. A Scotchman must be a very sturdy moralist who does not love Scotland better than truth. SAMUEL JOHNSON, *Journey to the Hebrides* (1775).

2. It requires a surgical operation to get a joke well into a Scotch understanding. SYDNEY SMITH, quoted in Lady S. Holland's *Memoir* (1855), v. 1.2.

## 846. SCRATCHING

1. The itch is a mean, unconfessable, ridiculous malady; one can pity someone who is suffering; someone who wants to scratch himself makes one laugh. ANDRÉ GIDE, *Journals*, March 18, 1931, tr. Justin O'Brien.

2. Scratching is one of nature's sweetest gratifications, and nearest at hand. MONTAIGNE, "Of experience," *Essays* (1580–88), tr. Charles Cotton and W. C. Hazlitt.

3. One bliss for which / There is no match / Is when you itch / To up and scratch. OGDEN NASH, "Taboo to Boot," *Verses From 1929 On* (1959).

4. If you are with the quality, or at a funeral, or trying to go to sleep when you ain't sleepy—if you are anywheres where it won't do for you to scratch, why you will itch all over in upwards of a thousand places. MARK TWAIN, *The Adventures of Huckleberry Finn* (1884), 2.

## 847. SEA

**See also 344. Fish; 818. Rivers; 833. Sailing; 888. Ships and Boats; 1039. Water**

1. The seas are the heart's blood of the earth. Plucked up and kneaded by the sun and the moon, the tides are systole and diastole of earth's veins. HENRY BESTON, "The Headlong Wave," *The Outermost House* (1928).

2. All the rivers run into the sea; yet the sea is not full; unto the place from whence the rivers come, thither they return again. *Bible*, Ecclesiastes 1:7.

3. Little islands are all large prisons: one cannot look at the sea without wishing for the wings of a swallow. SIR RICHARD BURTON, *Wanderings in West Africa* (1863).

4. Roll on, thou deep and dark blue Ocean—roll! / Ten thousand fleets sweep over thee in vain; / Man marks the earth with ruin—his control / Stops with the shore. BYRON, *Childe Harold's Pilgrimage* (1812–18), 4.179.

5. It is a curious situation that the sea, from which life first arose, should now be threatened by the activities of one form of that life. But the sea, though changed in a sinister way, will continue to exist; the threat is rather to life itself. RACHEL CARSON, preface to revised edition of *The Sea Around Us* (1950).

6. Some of us, regarding the ocean with understanding and affection, have seen it looking old, as if the immemorial ages had been stirred up from the undisturbed bottom of ooze. For it is a gale of wind that makes the sea look old. JOSEPH CONRAD, *The Mirror of the Sea* (1906), 22.

7. For all that has been said of the love that certain natures (on shore) have professed to feel for it, for all the celebrations it has been the object of in prose and song, the sea has never been friendly to man. At most it has been the accomplice of human restlessness. JOSEPH CONRAD, *The Mirror of the Sea* (1906), 35.

8. The sea—this truth must be confessed—has no generosity. No display of manly qualities—courage, hardihood, endurance, faithfulness—has ever been known to touch its irresponsible consciousness of power. JOSEPH CONRAD, *The Mirror of the Sea* (1906), 36.

9. The Sea is Woman, the Sea is Wonder—/ Her other name is Fate! EDWIN MARKHAM, "Virgilia" (1905).

10. Implacable I, the implacable Sea; / Implacable most when most I smile serene— / Pleased, not appeased, by myriad wrecks in me. HERMAN MELVILLE, "Pebbles," *John Marr and Other Sailors* (1888).

11. Consider the sea's listless chime: / Time's self it is, made audible. DANTE GABRIEL ROSSETTI, "The Sea Limits" (1850).

12. The sea speaks a language polite people never repeat. It is a colossal scavenger slang and has no respect. CARL SANDBURG, "Two Nocturnes," *Complete Poems* (1950).

13. The freedom of the seas is the *sine qua non* of peace, equality and co-operation.

WOODROW WILSON, address to U.S. Senate, Jan. 22, 1917.

14. 'Tis said, fantastic ocean doth enfold / The likeness of whate'er on land is seen. WILLIAM WORDSWORTH, "Fish-Women.—On Landing at Calais" (1821).

## 848. SEASONS

**See also 771. Rain; 904. Snow; 1043. Weather**

1. Let us love winter, for it is the spring of genius. PIETRO ARETINO, letter to Agostino Ricchi, July 10, 1537, tr. Samuel Putnam.

2. The quality of life, which in the ardour of spring was personal and sexual, becomes social in midsummer. HENRY BESTON, "The Year at High Tide," *The Outermost House* (1928).

3. Here comes February, a little girl with her first valentine, a red bow in her wind-blown hair, a kiss waiting on her lips, a tantrum just back of her laughter. HAL BORLAND, "February—February 1," *Sundial of the Seasons* (1964).

4. March is a tomboy with tousled hair, a mischievous smile, mud on her shoes and a laugh in her voice. HAL BORLAND, "March—March 1," *Sundial of the Seasons* (1964).

5. No Winter lasts forever, no Spring skips its turn. April is a promise that May is bound to keep, and we know it. HAL BORLAND, "A Promise—April 29," *Sundial of the Seasons* (1964).

6. Summer ends, and Autumn comes, and he who would have it otherwise would have high tide always and a full moon every night. HAL BORLAND, "Autumn on the Doorstep—September 13," *Sundial of the Seasons* (1964).

7. October is the fallen leaf, but it is also a wider horizon more clearly seen. It is the distant hills once more in sight, and the enduring constellations above them once again. HAL BORLAND, "Autumn Is for Understanding—October 25," *Sundial of the Seasons* (1964).

8. It is in this unearthly first hour of spring twilight that earth's almost agonized livingness is most felt. This hour is so dreadful to some people that they hurry indoors and turn on the lights. ELIZABETH BOWEN, *The Death of the Heart* (1938), 2.1.

9. Autumn arrives in the early morning, but spring at the close of a winter day. ELIZABETH BOWEN, *The Death of the Heart* (1938), 2.1.

10. The lonely season in lonely lands, when fled / Are half the birds, and mists lie low, and the sun / Is rarely seen, nor strayeth far from his bed; / The short days pass unwelcomed one by one. ROBERT BRIDGES, "November," *New Poems* (1899).

11. Autumn wins you best by this, its mute / Appeal to sympathy for its decay. ROBERT BROWNING, *Paracelsus* (1835), 1.

12. The melancholy days are come, the saddest of the year, / Of wailing winds, and naked woods, and meadows brown and sere. WILLIAM CULLEN BRYANT, "The Death of the Flowers" (1825).

13. Long stormy spring-time, wet contentious April, winter chilling the lap of very May; but at length the season of summer does come. THOMAS CARLYLE, *Chartism* (1839), 8.

14. Hard is the heart that loveth nought / In May. CHAUCER, *The Romaunt of the Rose* (c. 1370).

15. Spring never is Spring unless it comes too soon. G. K. CHESTERTON, "The Gardener and the Guinea," *A Miscellany of Men* (1912).

16. April is the cruellest month, breeding / Lilacs out of the dead land, mixing / Memory and desire, stirring / Dull roots with spring rain. T. S. ELIOT, "The Waste Land" (1922), 1.

17. I should like to enjoy this summer flower by flower, as if it were to be the last one for me. ANDRÉ GIDE, *Journals*, May 18, 1930, tr. Justin O'Brien.

18. Honest winter, snow-clad and with the frosted beard, I can welcome not uncordially; but that long deferment of the calendar's promise, that weeping gloom of March and April, that bitter blast outraging the honour of May—how often has it robbed me of heart and hope. GEORGE GISSING, "Spring," *The Private Papers of Henry Ryecroft* (1903).

19. There is no season when such pleasant and sunny spots may be lighted on, and produce so pleasant an effect on the feelings, as now in October. NATHANIEL HAWTHORNE, *American Note-Books*, Oct. 7, 1841.

20. In May Nature holds up at us a chiding finger, bidding us remember that we

are not gods, but overconceited members of her own great family. O. HENRY, "The Marry Month of May," *Whirligigs* (1910).

21. Sweet spring, full of sweet days and roses, / A box where sweets compacted lie. GEORGE HERBERT, "Virtue," 3, *The Temple* (1633).

22. Every mile is two in winter. GEORGE HERBERT, *Jacula Prudentum* (1651).

23. The changing year's successive plan / Proclaims mortality to man. HORACE, *Odes* (23–c. 15 B.C. ), 4.7.

24. Winter changes into stone the water of heaven and the heart of man. VICTOR HUGO, "Fantine," *Les Misérables* (1862), 5.10, tr. Charles E. Wilbour.

25. Season of mists and mellow fruitfulness, / Close bosom-friend of the maturing sun. JOHN KEATS, "To Autumn" (1819).

26. In our hearts those of us who know anything worth knowing know that in March a new year begins, and if we plan any new leaves, it will be when the rest of Nature is planning them too. JOSEPH WOOD KRUTCH, "March," *The Twelve Seasons* (1949).

27. August creates as she slumbers, replete and satisfied. JOSEPH WOOD KRUTCH, "August," *The Twelve Seasons* (1949).

28. [Autumn] comes like a warrior, with the stain of blood upon his brazen mail. His crimson scarf is rent. His scarlet banner drips with gore. His step is like a flail upon the threshing floor. LONGFELLOW, "Autumn," *The Blank-Book of a Country Schoolmaster* (1857).

29. What is so rare as a day in June? / Then, if ever, come perfect days; / Then Heaven tries the earth if it be in tune, / And over it softly her warm ear lays. JAMES RUSSELL LOWELL, prelude to part 1, "The Vision of Sir Launfal" (1848).

30. No price is set on the lavish summer; / June may be had by the poorest comer. JAMES RUSSELL LOWELL, prelude to part 1, "The Vision of Sir Launfal" (1848).

31. May is a pious fraud of the almanac, / A ghastly parody of real Spring / Shaped out of snow and breathed with eastern wind. JAMES RUSSELL LOWELL, title poem, *Under the Willows and Other Poems* (1868).

32. Wag the world how it will, / Leaves must be green in Spring. HERMAN MELVILLE, "Malvern Hill," *Battlepieces and Aspects of the War* (1866).

33. April / Comes like an idiot, babbling and strewing flowers. EDNA ST. VINCENT MILLAY, "Spring," *Second April* (1921).

34. Winter is cold-hearted, / Spring is yea and nay, / Autumn is a weather-cock / Blown every way. / Summer days for me / When every leaf is on its tree. CHRISTINA ROSSETTI, "Summer" (1862).

35. November's sky is chill and drear, / November's leaf is red and sear. SIR WALTER SCOTT, *Marmion* (1808), 1, introduction.

36. Rough winds do shake the darling buds of May, / And summer's lease hath all too short a date. SHAKESPEARE, *Sonnets* (1609), 18.3.

37. Sing a song of seasons! / Something bright in all! / Flowers in the Summer, / Fires in the Fall. ROBERT LOUIS STEVENSON, "Autumn Fires" (1885).

38. The world's favorite season is the spring. All things seem possible in May. EDWIN WAY TEALE, *North with the Spring* (1951), 3.

39. How sad would be November if we had no knowledge of the spring! EDWIN WAY TEALE, "November 21," *Circle of the Seasons* (1953).

40. For man, autumn is a time of harvest, of gathering together. For nature, it is a time of sowing, of scattering abroad. EDWIN WAY TEALE, *Autumn Across America* (1956), 14.

41. A hush is over everything— / Silent as women wait for love, / The world is waiting for the spring. SARA TEASDALE, "Central Park at Dusk," *Helen of Troy* (1911).

42. In the spring a young man's fancy lightly turns to thoughts of love. ALFRED, LORD TENNYSON, "Locksley Hall" (1842).

43. Summer set lip to earth's bosom bare, / And left the flushed print in a poppy there. FRANCIS THOMPSON, "The Poppy" (1891).

44. Spring is come home with her world-wandering feet, / And all things are made young with young desires. FRANCIS THOMPSON, "From the Night of Forebeing" (1897).

45. Come, gentle Spring! ethereal Mildness! come. JAMES THOMSON, "Spring," *The Seasons* (1726–30), 1.

46. Autumn, nodding o'er the yellow plain, / Comes jovial on. JAMES THOMSON, "Autumn," *The Seasons* (1726–30), 2.

47. See, Winter comes to rule the varied

year, / Sullen and sad. JAMES THOMSON, "Winter," *The Seasons* (1726–30), 2.

48. April, April, / Laugh thy girlish laughter; / Then, the moment after, / Weep thy girlish tears! SIR WILLIAM WATSON, "April," *Collected Poems* (1905).

49. The first day of spring was once the time for taking the young virgins into the fields, there in dalliance to set an example in fertility for Nature to follow. Now we just set the clock an hour ahead and change the oil in the crankcase. E. B. WHITE, "Hot Weather," *One Man's Meat* (1944).

50. Caught Summer is always an imagined time. / Time gave it, yes, but time out of any mind. / There must be prime / In the heart to beget that season, to reach past rain and find / Riding the palest days / Its perfect blaze. RICHARD WILBUR, "My Father Paints the Summer," *The Beautiful Changes* (1947).

51. Hot summer has exhausted her intent / To the last rose and roundelay and seed. / No leaf has changed, and yet these leaves now read / Like a love-letter that's no longer meant. RICHARD WILBUR, "Two Quatrains for First Frost," *Advice to a Prophet* (1961).

52. Spring, the cruelest and fairest of the seasons, will come again. And the strange and buried men will come again, in flower and leaf the strange and buried men will come again, and death and the dust will never come again, for death and the dust will die. THOMAS WOLFE, *Look Homeward, Angel* (1929), 37.

53. All things on earth point home in old October: sailors to sea, travellers to walls and fences, hunters to field and hollow and the long voice of the hounds, the lover to the love he has forsaken. THOMAS WOLFE, *Of Time and the River* (1935), 39.

## 849. SECRETS
See also 166. Confidences

1. To know that one has a secret is to know half the secret itself. HENRY WARD BEECHER, *Proverbs from Plymouth Pulpit* (1887).

2. Little secrets are commonly told again, but great ones generally kept. LORD CHESTERFIELD, *Letters to His Son*, Sept. 13, 1748.

3. A woman only obliges a man to secrecy, that she may have the pleasure of telling herself. WILLIAM CONGREVE, *Love for Love* (1695), 1.1.

4. In the mind and nature of a man a secret is an ugly thing, like a hidden physical defect. ISAK DINESEN, "Of Hidden Thoughts and of Heaven," *Last Tales* (1957).

5. Nothing is so burdensome as a secret. FRENCH PROVERB.

6. Would you know secrets? Look for them in grief or pleasure. THOMAS FULLER, M.D., *Gnomologia* (1732), 5828.

7. He that communicates his secret to another makes himself that other's slave. BALTASAR GRACIÁN, *The Art of Worldly Wisdom* (1647), 237, tr. Joseph Jacobs.

8. Many a deep secret that cannot be pried out by curiosity can be drawn out by indifference. SYDNEY J. HARRIS, *On the Contrary* (1962), 7.

9. At no time are people so sedulously careful to keep their trifling appointments, attend to their ordinary occupations, and thus put a commonplace aspect on life, as when conscious of some secret that if suspected would make them look monstrous in the general eye. NATHANIEL HAWTHORNE, *The Marble Faun* (1860), 20.

10. Do not speak of secret matters in a field that is full of little hills. HEBREW PROVERB.

11. We don't know each other's secrets quite so well as we flatter ourselves we do. We don't always know our own secrets as well as we might. OLIVER WENDELL HOLMES, SR., *The Poet at the Breakfast Table* (1872), 6.

12. Another person's secret is like another person's money: you are not so careful with it as you are of your own. EDGAR WATSON HOWE, *Country Town Sayings* (1911).

13. The man who can keep a secret may be wise, but he is not half as wise as the man with no secrets to keep. EDGAR WATSON HOWE, *Country Town Sayings* (1911).

14. I do not know how it is that clergymen and physicians keep from telling their wives the secrets confided to them; perhaps they can trust their wives to find them out for themselves whenever they wish. WILLIAM DEAN HOWELLS, *The Rise of Silas Lapham* (1885), 27.

15. No one ever keeps a secret so well as a child. VICTOR HUGO, "Cosette," *Les Misérables* (1862), 8.8, tr. Charles E. Wilbour.

16. How can we expect another to keep our secret if we have been unable to keep it ourselves? LA ROCHEFOUCAULD, *Maxims* (1665), tr. Kenneth Pratt.

17. A good many men and women want to get possession of secrets just as spendthrifts want to get money—for circulation. GEORGE DENNISON PRENTICE, *Prenticeana* (1860).

18. None can be so true to your secret as yourself. SA'DI, *Gulistan* (1258), 8.10, tr. James Ross.

19. There are no secrets except the secrets that keep themselves. GEORGE BERNARD SHAW, *Back to Methuselah* (1921), 3.

20. The dead keep their secrets, and in a while we shall be as wise as they—and as taciturn. ALEXANDER SMITH, "Of Death and the Fear of Dying," *Dreamthorp* (1863).

21. Love, pain, and money cannot be kept secret. They soon betray themselves. SPANISH PROVERB.

## SECT

See 667. Partisanship

## 850. SECURITY

See also 113. Certainty; 226. Defense; 480. Insecurity

1. The eternal God is thy refuge, and underneath are the everlasting arms. *Bible*, Deuteronomy 33:27.

2. Uncertainty and expectation are the joys of life. Security is an insipid thing, and the overtaking and possessing of a wish, discovers the folly of the chase. WILLIAM CONGREVE, *Love for Love* (1695), 4.3.

3. It is folly to bolt a door with a boiled carrot. ENGLISH PROVERB.

4. Nothing's as good as holding on to safety. EURIPIDES, *The Phoenician Women* (c. 411–409 B.C.), tr. Elizabeth Wyckoff.

5. They that can give up essential liberty to obtain a little temporary safety deserve neither liberty nor safety. BENJAMIN FRANKLIN (attrib.), *An Historical Review of Pennsylvania* (1759).

6. The most beaten paths are certainly the surest; but do not hope to scare up much game on them. ANDRÉ GIDE, *Journals*, May 1930, tr. Justin O'Brien.

7. The protected man doesn't need luck; therefore it seldom visits him. ALAN HARRINGTON, "It's Cold Out There," *Life in the Crystal Palace* (1959).

8. God Himself is not secure, having given man dominion over His works. HELEN KELLER, *Let Us Have Faith* (1940).

9. Security depends not so much upon how much you have, as upon how much you can do without. JOSEPH WOOD KRUTCH, "If You Don't Mind My Saying So," *The American Scholar* (Summer 1967).

10. Only in growth, reform, and change, paradoxically enough, is true security to be found. ANNE MORROW LINDBERGH, *The Wave of the Future* (1940).

11. Most people want security in this world, not liberty. H. L. MENCKEN, *Minority Report* (1956), 170.

12. The man who looks for security, even in the mind, is like a man who would chop off his limbs in order to have artificial ones which will give him no pain or trouble. HENRY MILLER, *Sunday after the War* (1944).

13. Not a gift of a cow, nor a gift of land, nor yet a gift of food, is so important as the gift of safety, which is declared to be the great gift among all gifts in this world. *Panchatantra* (c. 5th c.), 1, tr. Franklin Edgerton.

14. People wish to learn to swim and at the same time to keep one foot on the ground. MARCEL PROUST, *Remembrance of Things Past: The Sweet Cheat Gone* (1913–27), tr. C. K. Scott-Moncrieff.

15. Happy he whoe'er, content with the common lot, with safe breeze hugs the shore, and, fearing to trust his skiff to the wider sea, with unambitious oar keeps close to the land. SENECA, *Agamemnon* (1st c.), 102, tr. Frank Justus Miller.

16. To keep oneself safe does not mean to bury oneself. SENECA, "On Peace of Mind," *Moral Essays* (1st c.), tr. Aubrey Stewart.

17. Security is when I'm very much in love with somebody extraordinary who loves me back. SHELLEY WINTERS, news summaries, July 9, 1954.

18. A lock is meant only for honest men. *Yiddish Proverbs* (1949), ed. Hanan J. Ayalti.

## 851. SEDUCTION

**See also 195. Courtship; 348. Flirtation; 548. Love; 736. Promiscuity; 885. Sex**

1. Brisk Confidence still best with woman copes: / Pique her and soothe in turn—soon Passion crowns thy hopes. BYRON, *Childe Harold's Pilgrimage* (1812–18), 2.34.

2. Once a woman parts with her virtue, she loses the esteem even of the man whose vows and tears won her to abandon it. CERVANTES, *Don Quixote* (1605–15), 1.4.7, tr. Peter Motteux and John Ozell.

3. Every man is to be had one way or another, and every woman almost any way. LORD CHESTERFIELD, *Letters to His Son*, June 5, 1750.

4. Every maiden's weak and willin' / When she meets the proper villain. CLARENCE DAY, "Thoughts on the Itch," *Thoughts Without Words* (1928).

5. A woman that loves to be at the window is a bunch of grapes on the highway. ENGLISH PROVERB.

6. To win a woman in the first place one must please her, then undress her, and then somehow get her clothes back on her. Finally, so that she will allow you to leave her, you've got to annoy her. JEAN GIRAUDOUX, *Amphitryon 38* (1929), 1, tr. Phyllis La Farge with Peter H. Judd.

7. A man can deceive a woman by his sham attachment to her provided he does not have a real attachment elsewhere. LA BRUYÈRE, *Characters* (1688), 3.69.

8. All really great lovers are articulate, and verbal seduction is the surest road to actual seduction. MARYA MANNES, *More in Anger* (1958), 4.3.

9. Had we but world enough, and time, / This coyness, lady, were no crime. ANDREW MARVELL, "To His Coy Mistress" (1650).

10. Women can always be caught; that's the first rule of the game. OVID, *The Art of Love* (c. A.D. 8), 1, tr. Rolfe Humphries.

11. What they [women] like to give, they love to be robbed of. OVID, *The Art of Love* (c. A.D. 8), 1, tr. J. Lewis May.

12. Venus yields to caresses, not to compulsion. PUBLILIUS SYRUS, *Moral Sayings* (1st c. B.C.), 101, tr. Darius Lyman.

13. Women sometimes forgive those who force an opportunity, never those who miss it. Attributed to TALLEYRAND.

14. Don't fear to pledge. By winds the perjuries of love / Are blown, null and void, across the land and farthest seas. TIBULLUS, *Elegies* (1st c. B.C.), 1.4, tr. Hubert Creekmore.

15. It is not enough to conquer; one must know how to seduce. VOLTAIRE, *Mérope* (1743), 1.4.

## SEEING

**See 890. Sight**

## SEGREGATION

**See 769. Racial Prejudice**

## 852. SELF

**See also 45. Appearance; 442. Identity; 467. Individuality; 587. Mirrors**

1. Our entire life, with our fine moral code and our precious freedom, consists ultimately in accepting ourselves as we are. JEAN ANOUILH, *Traveler Without Luggage* (1936), 2.1, tr. Lucienne Hill.

2. When I say "I," I mean a thing absolutely unique, not to be confused with any other. UGO BETTI, *The Inquiry* (1944–45), 2.2, ed. Gino Rizzo.

3. We carry with us the wonders we seek without us. SIR THOMAS BROWNE, *Religio Medici* (1642), 1.

4. My care is for myself; / Myself am whole and sole reality. ROBERT BROWNING, "Mr. Sludge, The Medium," *Dramatis Personae* (1864).

5. Inside myself is a place where I live all alone and that's where you renew your springs that never dry up. PEARL S. BUCK, *New York Post*, April 26, 1959.

6. The ideal is in thyself, the impediment too is in thyself. THOMAS CARLYLE, *Sartor Resartus* (1833–34), 2.9.

7. One may understand the cosmos, but never the ego; the self is more distant than any star. G. K. CHESTERTON, "The Logic of Elfland," *Orthodoxy* (1908).

8. The spirit is the true self, not that physical figure which can be pointed out by your finger. CICERO, *De Re Publica* (c. 51 B.C.), 6.

9. We are all serving a life-sentence in the dungeon of self. CYRIL CONNOLLY, *The Unquiet Grave* (1945), 2.

10. So much of our time is preparation, so

much is routine, and so much retrospect, that the pith of each man's genius contracts itself to a very few hours. EMERSON, "Experience," *Essays: Second Series* (1844).

11. Man can be defined as the animal that can say "I," that can be aware of himself as a separate entity. ERICH FROMM, *The Sane Society* (1955), 3.

12. Beware of no man more than thyself. THOMAS FULLER, M.D., *Gnomologia* (1732), 977.

13. Any man who does not see everything in terms of self, that is to say who wants to be something in respect of other men, to do good to them or simply give them something to do, is unhappy, disconsolate, and accursed. EDMOND and JULES DE GONCOURT, *Journal*, July 30, 1861, tr. Robert Baldick.

14. What other dungeon is so dark as one's own heart! What jailer so inexorable as one's self! NATHANIEL HAWTHORNE, *The House of the Seven Gables* (1851), 11.

15. No man would, I think, exchange his existence with any other man, however fortunate. We had as lief not be, as not be ourselves. WILLIAM HAZLITT, "On the Fear of Death," *Table Talk* (1821–22).

16. The remarkable thing is that we really love our neighbor as ourselves: we do unto others as we do unto ourselves. We hate others when we hate ourselves. We are tolerant toward others when we tolerate ourselves. ERIC HOFFER, *The Passionate State of Mind* (1954), 100.

17. Be rich for yourself and poor to your friends. JUVENAL, *Satires* (c. 100), 5.113, tr. Hubert Creekmore.

18. The self-evident truth which makes men invincible is that inalienably they are inviolable persons. WALTER LIPPMANN, *The Good Society* (1943), 4.17.

19. Not in the clamour of the crowded street, / Not in the shouts and plaudits of the throng, / But in ourselves, are triumph and defeat. LONGFELLOW, "The Poets" (1876).

20. To ourselves, we all seem coeval with creation. HERMAN MELVILLE, *Mardi and a Voyage Thither* (1849), 3.

21. There is as much difference between us and ourselves as between us and others. MONTAIGNE, "Of the inconstancy of our actions," *Essays* (1580–88), tr. Charles Cotton and W. C. Hazlitt.

22. Each one is all in all to himself; for being dead, all is dead to him. PASCAL, *Pensées* (1670), 457, tr. W. F. Trotter.

23. Man is the creature that cannot emerge from himself, that knows his fellows only in himself; when he asserts the contrary, he is lying. MARCEL PROUST, *Remembrance of Things Past: The Sweet Cheat Gone* (1913–27), tr. C. K. Scott-Moncrieff.

24. Self-reverence, self-knowledge, self-control, / These three alone lead life to sovereign power. ALFRED, LORD TENNYSON, "Oenone" (1842).

25. But ceremony never did conceal, / Save to the silly eye, which all allows, / How much we are the woods we wander in. RICHARD WILBUR, title poem, *Ceremony* (1950).

## 853. SELF-ASSERTION
**See also 90. Boldness**

1. The perfection preached in the Gospels never yet built an empire. Every man of action has a strong dose of egotism, pride, hardness, and cunning. CHARLES DE GAULLE, quoted in *The New York Times Magazine*, May 12, 1968.

2. Take the place and attitude to which you see your unquestionable right, and all men acquiesce. EMERSON, *Journals*, 1836.

3. There is always room for a man of force, and he makes room for many. EMERSON, "Power," *The Conduct of Life* (1860).

4. You must either conquer and rule or serve and lose, suffer or triumph, be the anvil or the hammer. GOETHE, *Der Gross-Cophta* (1792), 2.

5. Nobody can give you freedom. Nobody can give you equality or justice or anything. If you're a man, you take it. MALCOLM X, *Malcolm X Speaks* (1965), 9.

6. You dont learn to hold your own in the world by standing on guard, but by attacking, and getting well-hammered yourself. GEORGE BERNARD SHAW, *Getting Married* (1911).

## 854. SELF-CONFIDENCE
**See also 657. Overconfidence; 861. Self-doubt**

1. Self-trust is the essence of heroism. EMERSON, "Heroism," *Essays: First Series* (1841).

2. As is our confidence, so is our capacity. WILLIAM HAZLITT, *Characteristics* (1823), 89.

3. If you think you can win, you can win. Faith is necessary to victory. WILLIAM HAZLITT, "On Great and Little Things," *Literary Remains* (1836).

4. It generally happens that assurance keeps an even pace with ability. SAMUEL JOHNSON, *The Rambler* (1750–52), 159.

5. Assurance is contemptible and fatal unless it is self-knowledge. GEORGE SANTAYANA, *Character and Opinion in the United States* (1921), 3.

6. There's one blessing only, the source and cornerstone of beatitude—confidence in self. SENECA, *Letters to Lucilius* (1st c.), 31.3, tr. E. Phillips Barker.

7. They can do all because they think they can. VERGIL, *Aeneid* (30–19 B.C.), 5.231, tr. T. H. Delabere-May.

## 855. SELF-CONSCIOUSNESS

See also 886. Shame

1. If you happen to have a wart on your nose or forehead, you cannot help imagining that no one in the world has anything else to do but stare at your wart, laugh at it, and condemn you for it, even though you have discovered America. DOSTOEVSKY, *The Idiot* (1868), 3.1, tr. David Magarshack.

2. Those people who are uncomfortable in themselves are disagreeable to others. WILLIAM HAZLITT, "On Disagreeable People," *Sketches and Essays* (1839).

## 856. SELF-CONTROL

See also 248. Discipline

1. I am, / indeed, / a king, because I know how to rule myself. PIETRO ARETINO, letter to Agostino Ricchi, May 10, 1537, tr. Samuel Putnam.

2. What it lies in our power to do, it lies in our power not to do. ARISTOTLE, *Nicomachean Ethics* (4th c. B.C.), 3.4, tr. J. A. K. Thomson.

3. Freedom is not procured by a full enjoyment of what is desired, but by controlling the desire. EPICTETUS, *Discourses* (2nd c.), 4.1, tr. Thomas W. Higginson.

4. A wise reserve seasons the aims and matures the means. BALTASAR GRACIÁN, *The Art of Worldly Wisdom* (1647), 55, tr. Joseph Jacobs.

5. We learn to curb our will and keep our overt actions within the bounds of humanity, long before we can subdue our sentiments and imaginations to the same mild tone. WILLIAM HAZLITT, "On the Pleasure of Hating," *The Plain Speaker* (1826).

6. For better or worse, man is the tool-using animal, and as such he has become the lord of creation. When he is lord also of himself, he will deserve his self-chosen title of *homo sapiens*. WILLIAM RALPH INGE, "The Dilemma of Civilisation," *Outspoken Essays: Second Series* (1922).

7. He that would be superior to external influences must first become superior to his own passions. SAMUEL JOHNSON, *The Idler* (1758–60), 52.

8. There is a raging tiger inside every man whom God put on this earth. Every man worthy of the respect of his children spends his life building inside himself a cage to pen that tiger in. MURRAY KEMPTON, "Snapping the Leash," *America Comes of Middle Age* (1963).

9. He who conquers others is strong; / He who conquers himself is mighty. LAOTSE, *The Character of Tao* (6th c. B.C.), 33, tr. Lin Yutang.

10. Self-restraint may be alien to the human temperament, but humanity without restraint will dig its own grave. MARYA MANNES, "The Singular Woman," *But Will It Sell?* (1955–64).

11. Not being able to govern events, I govern myself, and apply myself to them, if they will not apply themselves to me. MONTAIGNE, "Of presumption," *Essays* (1580–88), tr. Charles Cotton and W. C. Hazlitt.

12. The strong man is the one who is able to intercept at will the communication between the senses and the mind. NAPOLEON I, *Maxims* (1804–15).

13. How shall I be able to rule over others, that have not full power and command of myself? RABELAIS, *Gargantua and Pantagruel* (1532-64), 1.52.

14. It is a new road to happiness, if you have strength enough to castigate a little the various impulses that sway you in turn. GEORGE SANTAYANA, *Winds of Doctrine* (1913).

15. Man who man would be, / Must rule

the empire of himself. SHELLEY, "Political Greatness" (1821).

16. A man who is master of himself can end a sorrow as easily as he can invent a pleasure. OSCAR WILDE, *The Picture of Dorian Gray* (1891), 9.

## 857. SELF-CRITICISM

**See also 861. Self-doubt; 864. Self-hatred**

1. How shall we expect charity towards others, when we are uncharitable to ourselves? SIR THOMAS BROWNE, *Religio Medici* (1642), 2.

2. What is this self inside us, this silent observer, / Severe and speechless critic, who can terrorize us / And urge us on to futile activity, / And in the end, judge us still more severely / For the errors into which his own reproaches drove us? T. S. ELIOT, *The Elder Statesman* (1958), 2.

3. He who makes great demands upon himself is naturally inclined to make great demands on others. ANDRÉ GIDE, *Journals*, Feb. 1, 1938, tr. Justin O'Brien.

4. I believe that it is harder still to be just toward oneself than toward others. ANDRÉ GIDE, *Journals*, Sept. 9, 1940, tr. Justin O'Brien.

5. He is a man whom it is impossible to please, because he is never pleased with himself. GOETHE, *The Sorrows of Young Werther* (1774), 2, Dec. 24, 1771, tr. Victor Lange.

6. Any one is to be pitied who has just sense enough to perceive his deficiencies. WILLIAM HAZLITT, *Characteristics* (1823), 213.

7. All censure of a man's self is oblique praise. It is in order to show how much he can spare. SAMUEL JOHNSON, quoted in Boswell's *Life of Samuel Johnson*, April 25, 1778.

8. There is a luxury in self-dispraise; / And inward self-disparagement affords / To meditative spleen a grateful feast. WILLIAM WORDSWORTH, *The Excursion* (1814), 4.

## 858. SELF-DECEPTION

**See also 869. Self-love; 1020. Vanity**

1. Never can true courage dwell with them, / Who, playing tricks with conscience, dare not look / At their own vices. SAMUEL TAYLOR COLERIDGE, *Fears in Solitude* (1798).

2. Lying to ourselves is more deeply ingrained than lying to others. DOSTOEVSKY, "Little Pictures on the Road," *Polnoye Sobraniye Sochinyeni (Complete Collected Works*, 1895), v. 9.

3. We lie loudest when we lie to ourselves. ERIC HOFFER, *The Passionate State of Mind* (1954), 70.

4. No estimate is more in danger of erroneous calculations than those by which a man computes the force of his own genius. SAMUEL JOHNSON, *The Rambler* (1750–52), 154.

5. The greatest deception men suffer is from their own opinions. LEONARDO DA VINCI, *Notebooks* (c. 1500), tr. Jean Paul Richter.

6. The most common sort of lie is the one uttered to one's self. NIETZSCHE, *The Antichrist* (1888), 55, tr. Anthony M. Ludovici.

7. We are only falsehood, duplicity, contradiction; we both conceal and disguise ourselves from ourselves. PASCAL, *Pensées* (1670), 377, tr. W. F. Trotter.

8. Nature never deceives us; it is we who deceive ourselves. ROUSSEAU, *Émile* (1762), 3.

## 859. SELF-DENIAL

**See also 120. Chastity; 595. Monasticism**

1. The abstinent run away from what they desire / But carry their desires with them. *Bhagavadgita*, 2, tr. Swami Prabhavananda and Christopher Isherwood.

2. Abstainer, n. A weak person who yields to the temptation of denying himself a pleasure. AMBROSE BIERCE, *The Devil's Dictionary* (1881–1911).

3. To refuse the sweets of life because they once must leave us, is as preposterous as to wish to have been born old, because we one day must be old. WILLIAM CONGREVE, *The Way of the World* (1700), 2.1.

4. True mortifications are those which are not known. LA ROCHEFOUCAULD, *Maxims* (1665), tr. Kenneth Pratt.

5. Look not thou on beauty's charming, / Sit thou still while kings are arming, / Taste not when the wine-cup glistens, / Speak not when the people listens, / Stop thine ear against the singer, / From the red gold keep

thy finger; / Vacant heart and hand, and eye, / Easy live and quiet die. SIR WALTER SCOTT, *The Bride of Lammermoor* (1819), 3.

6. Refrain to-night, / And that shall lend a kind of easiness / To the next abstinence; the next more easy; / For use almost can change the stamp of nature. SHAKESPEARE, *Hamlet* (1600), 3.4.165.

7. Self-denial is not a virtue: it is only the effect of prudence on rascality. GEORGE BERNARD SHAW, "Maxims for Revolutionists," *Man and Superman* (1903).

8. Self-denial is simply a method by which man arrests his progress, and self-sacrifice a survival of the mutilation of the savage. OSCAR WILDE, "The Critic as Artist," *Intentions* (1891).

## SELF-DESTRUCTION

See 866. Self-injury

## 860. SELF-DETERMINATION

See also 442. Identity; 765. Purpose; 801. Resolution; 873. Self-sufficiency; 1049. Will

1. I have discovered that we may be in some degree whatever character we choose. Besides, practice forms a man to anything. JAMES BOSWELL, *London Journal*, Nov. 21, 1762.

2. Every man is the son of his own works. CERVANTES, *Don Quixote* (1605–15), 1.1.4, tr. Peter Motteux and John Ozell.

3. If we must accept Fate, we are not less compelled to affirm liberty, the significance of the individual, the grandeur of duty, the power of character. EMERSON, "Fate," *The Conduct of Life* (1860).

4. In the history of the individual is always an account of his condition, and he knows himself to be a party to his present estate. EMERSON, "Fate," *The Conduct of Life* (1860).

5. Every spirit makes its house; but afterwards the house confines the spirit. EMERSON, "Fate," *The Conduct of Life* (1860).

6. You will fetter my leg, but not Zeus himself can get the better of my free will. EPICTETUS, *Discourses* (2nd c.), 1.1, tr. Thomas W. Higginson.

7. The wisest men follow their own direction. EURIPIDES, *Iphigenia in Tauris* (c. 414–12 B.C.), tr. Witter Bynner.

8. It is enough that we set out to mold the motley stuff of life into some form of our own choosing; when we do the performance is itself the wage. LEARNED HAND, speech, New York City, Jan. 27, 1952.

9. Some minds seem almost to create themselves, springing up under every disadvantage and working their solitary but irresistible way through a thousand obstacles. WASHINGTON IRVING, "Roscoe," *The Sketch Book of Geoffrey Crayon, Gent.* (1819–20).

10. Life is what our character makes it. We fashion it, as a snail does its shell. A man can say: "I never made a fortune because it is not in my character to be rich." JULES RENARD, *Journal*, February 1908, ed. and tr. Louise Bogan and Elizabeth Roget.

11. Every man is the architect of his own fortune. SALLUST, speech to Caesar on the state (1st c. B.C.), 1.

12. We can't reach old age by another man's road. MARK TWAIN, "Seventieth Birthday" (1910).

13. The tissue of Life to be / We weave with colors all our own, / And in the field of Destiny / We reap as we have sown. JOHN GREENLEAF WHITTIER, "Raphael" (1842), 16.

## 861. SELF-DOUBT

See also 43. Anxiety; 480. Insecurity; 854. Self-confidence; 857. Self-criticism; 862. Self-esteem

1. The fearful Unbelief is unbelief in yourself. THOMAS CARLYLE, *Sartor Resartus* (1833–34), 2.7.

2. Any work looks wonderful to me except the one which I can do. EMERSON, *Journals*, 1836.

3. He that listens after what people say of him shall never have peace. THOMAS FULLER, M.D., *Gnomologia* (1732), 2218.

4. He who undervalues himself is justly undervalued by others. WILLIAM HAZLITT, "On the Knowledge of Character," *Table Talk* (1821–22).

5. A man is a kind of inverted thermometer, the bulb uppermost, and the column of self-valuation is all the time going up and down. OLIVER WENDELL HOLMES, SR., *Over the Teacups* (1891), 5.

6. No one can make you feel inferior without your consent. ELEANOR ROOSEVELT, *Catholic Digest*, August 1960.

7. It is easy—terribly easy—to shake a man's faith in himself. To take advantage of that to break a man's spirit is devil's work. GEORGE BERNARD SHAW, *Candida* (1903), 1.

8. We are offended and resent it when people do not respect us; and yet no man, deep down in the privacy of his heart, has any considerable respect for himself. MARK TWAIN, *Notebook* (1935).

## 862. SELF-ESTEEM

**See also 727. Pride; 861. Self-doubt; 864. Self-hatred; 869. Self-love**

1. Behold within thee the long train of thy trophies, not without thee. SIR THOMAS BROWNE, *Christian Morals* (1716), 1.

2. It is easy to live for others; everybody does. I call on you to live for yourselves. EMERSON, *Journals*, 1845.

3. Be a friend to thyself, and others will be so too. THOMAS FULLER, M.D., *Gnomologia* (1732), 847.

4. Respect yourself if you would have others respect you. BALTASAR GRACIÁN, *The Art of Worldly Wisdom* (1647), 284, tr. Joseph Jacobs.

5. Let a man's talents or virtues be what they may, we only feel satisfaction in his society as he is satisfied in himself. WILLIAM HAZLITT, *Characteristics* (1823), 40.

6. Our reverence is good for nothing if it does not begin with self-respect. OLIVER WENDELL HOLMES, SR., *The Poet at the Breakfast Table* (1872), 10.

7. It is difficult to make a man miserable while he feels worthy of himself and claims kindred to the great God who made him. ABRAHAM LINCOLN, speech, Washington, D.C., Sept. 14, 1862.

8. If you love yourself meanly, childishly, timidly, even so shall you love your neighbor. MAURICE MAETERLINCK, *Wisdom and Destiny* (1898), 67, tr. Alfred Sutro.

9. Oft times nothing profits more / Than self-esteem, grounded on just and right / Well-managed. MILTON, *Paradise Lost* (1667), 8.571.

10. So much is a man worth as he esteems himself. RABELAIS, *Gargantua and Pantagruel* (1532–64), 2.29.

11. Self-respect will keep a man from being abject when he is in the power of enemies, and will enable him to feel that he may be in the right when the world is against him. BERTRAND RUSSELL, "Technique and Human Nature," *Authority and the Individual* (1949).

12. A man cannot be comfortable without his own approval. MARK TWAIN, "What Is Man?" (1906).

13. Only individuals with an aberrant temperament can in the long run retain their self-esteem in the face of the disesteem of their fellows. THORSTEIN VEBLEN, *The Theory of the Leisure Class* (1899), 2.

## 863. SELF-EXPRESSION

**See also 198. Creation and Creativity**

1. The man is only half himself, the other half is his expression. EMERSON, "The Poet," *Essays: Second Series* (1844).

## SELF-FORGETFULNESS

**See 921. Spontaneity**

## SELF-GOVERNMENT

**See 856. Self-control**

## 864. SELF-HATRED

**See also 857. Self-criticism; 861. Self-doubt; 862. Self-esteem; 866. Self-injury**

1. The self-despisers are less intent on their own increase than on the diminution of others. Where self-esteem is unobtainable, envy takes the place of greed. ERIC HOFFER, *The Passionate State of Mind* (1954), 114.

2. A man must first despise himself, and then others will despise him. MENCIUS, *Works* (4th–3rd c. B.C.), 4, tr. Charles A. Wong.

## 865. SELF-IMPORTANCE

**See also 163. Conceit; 869. Self-love; 1020. Vanity**

1. Man errs not that he deems / His welfare his true aim, / He errs because he

dreams / The world does but exist that welfare to bestow. MATTHEW ARNOLD, *Empedocles on Etna* (1852), 1.2.

2. Man desires to be free and he desires to feel important. This places him in a dilemma, for the more he emancipates himself from necessity the less important he feels. W. H. AUDEN, "Postscript: The Frivolous and the Earnest," *The Dyer's Hand* (1962).

3. Half of the harm that is done in this world / Is due to people who want to feel important. T. S. ELIOT, *The Cocktail Party* (1949), 2.

4. We all wish to be of importance in one way or another. The child coughs with might and main, since it has no other claim on the company. EMERSON, *Journals*, 1836.

5. When they came to shoe the horses, the beetle stretched out his leg. ENGLISH PROVERB.

6. What, will the world be quite overturned when you die? EPICTETUS, *Discourses* (2nd c.), 3.10, tr. Thomas W. Higginson.

7. Every cock is proud on his own dunghill. THOMAS FULLER, M.D., *Gnomologia* (1732), 1412.

8. Everyone thinks that all the bells echo his own thoughts. GERMAN PROVERB.

9. A sick man that gets talking about himself, a woman that gets talking about her baby, and an author that begins reading out of his own book, never know when to stop. OLIVER WENDELL HOLMES, SR., *The Poet at the Breakfast Table* (1872), 11.

10. We would rather speak badly of ourselves than not talk about ourselves at all. LA ROCHEFOUCAULD, *Maxims* (1665).

11. The extreme pleasure we take in speaking of ourselves should make us apprehensive that it gives hardly any to those who listen to us. LA ROCHEFOUCAULD, *Maxims* (1665), tr. Kenneth Pratt.

12. Egotism is the anesthetic that dulls the pain of stupidity. FRANK LEAHY, *Look*, Jan. 10, 1955.

13. The turtle lays thousands of eggs without anyone knowing, but when the hen lays an egg, the whole country is informed. MALAY PROVERB.

14. there is something to be said / for the lyric and imperial / attitude / that everything is for / you until you discover / that you are for it. DON MARQUIS, "the robin and the worm," *Archy and Mehitabel* (1927).

15. Glory consists of two parts: the one in setting too great a value upon ourselves, and the other in setting too little a value upon others. MONTAIGNE, "Of presumption," *Essays* (1580–88), tr. Charles Cotton and W. C. Hazlitt.

16. The big drum only sounds well from afar. PERSIAN PROVERB.

17. If you do not raise your eyes you will think that you are the highest point. ANTONIO PORCHIA, *Voces* (1968), tr. W. S. Merwin.

18. It astounds us to come upon other egoists, as though we alone had the right to be selfish, and be filled with eagerness to live. JULES RENARD, *Journal*, Nov. 18, 1887, ed. and tr. Louise Bogan and Elizabeth Roget.

## SELF-IMPROVEMENT

See 458. Improvement

## SELF-INDULGENCE

See 468. Indulgence

## 866. SELF-INJURY

See also 684. Perverseness; 864. Self-hatred; 941. Suicide

1. We often give our enemies the means for our own destruction. AESOP, "The Eagle and the Arrow," *Fables* (6th c. B.C.?), tr. Joseph Jacobs.

2. Truly, man is always at enmity with himself—a secret sly kind of hostility. Tares, scattered no matter where, will almost certainly take root. Whereas the smallest seed of good needs more than ordinary good fortune, needs prodigious luck, not to be stifled. GEORGES BERNANOS, *The Diary of a Country Priest* (1936), 4, tr. Pamela Morris.

3. Our greatest foes, and whom we must chiefly combat, are within. CERVANTES, *Don Quixote* (1605–15), 2.3.8, tr. Peter Motteux and John Ozell.

4. He invites future injuries who rewards past ones. THOMAS FULLER, M.D., *Gnomologia* (1732), 1905.

5. He that's cheated twice by the same man is an accomplice with the cheater.

THOMAS FULLER, M.D., *Gnomologia* (1732), 2281.

6. To seek out in a world full of joy the one thing that is certain to give you pain, and hug that to your bosom with all your strength—that's the greatest human happiness. JEAN GIRAUDOUX, *Ondine* (1939), 3, adapted by Maurice Valency.

7. If he has no other burden, he'll take up a load of stones. MALAY PROVERB.

8. I, who have never willfully pained another, have no business to pain myself. MARCUS AURELIUS, *Meditations* (2nd c.), 8.42, tr. Maxwell Staniforth.

9. A hair shirt does not always render those chaste who wear it. MONTAIGNE, "The story of Spurina," *Essays* (1580–88), tr. Charles Cotton and W. C. Hazlitt.

10. Troubles hurt the most / when they prove self-inflicted. SOPHOCLES, *Oedipus the King* (c. 430 B.C.), tr. David Grene.

11. Why, since we are always complaining of our ills, are we constantly employed in redoubling them? VOLTAIRE, "Whys," *Philosophical Dictionary* (1764).

12. A man's worst enemy can't wish him what he thinks up for himself. *Yiddish Proverbs* (1949), ed. Hanan J. Ayalti.

## SELF-INTEREST

**See 493. Interest; 867. Selfishness; 869. Self-love**

## 867. SELFISHNESS

**See also 493. Interest; 869. Self-love; 929. Stinginess**

1. No man is more cheated than the selfish man. HENRY WARD BEECHER, *Proverbs from Plymouth Pulpit* (1887).

2. Human history is the sad result of each one looking out for himself. JULIO CORTÁZAR, *The Winners* (1960), 17, tr. Elaine Kerrigan.

3. Selfish persons are incapable of loving others, but they are not capable of loving themselves either. ERICH FROMM, *Man for Himself* (1947), 4.

4. i have noticed / that when / chickens quit / quarreling over their / food they often / find that there is / enough for all of them / i wonder if / it might not / be the same way / with the / human race. DON MARQUIS, "random thoughts by archy," *Archy's Life of Mehitabel* (1933).

5. He who lives only for himself is truly dead to others. PUBLILIUS SYRUS, *Moral Sayings* (1st c. B.C.), 771, tr. Darius Lyman.

6. Selfishness is not living as one wishes to live, it is asking others to live as one wishes to live. OSCAR WILDE, *The Soul of Man Under Socialism* (1891).

## 868. SELF-KNOWLEDGE

**See also 180. Contemplation; 442. Identity; 752. Psychoanalysis; 852. Self**

1. Sink in thyself! there ask what ails thee, at that shrine! MATTHEW ARNOLD, *Empedocles on Etna* (1852), 1.2.

2. The questions which one asks oneself begin, at last, to illuminate the world, and become one's key to the experience of others. JAMES BALDWIN, introduction, *Nobody Knows My Name* (1961).

3. There is no purifier like knowledge in this world: / time makes man find himself in his heart. *Bhagavadgita*, 4, tr. P. Lal.

4. O wad some Power the giftie gie us / To see oursels as ithers see us! / It wad frae monie a blunder free us, / An' foolish notion. ROBERT BURNS, "To a Louse" (1786).

5. To know oneself, one should assert oneself. ALBERT CAMUS, *Notebooks 1935–1942* (1962), 1, tr. Philip Thody.

6. Full wise is he that can himselven knowe. CHAUCER, "The Monk's Tale," *The Canterbury Tales* (1387–1400), 3329, ed. Thomas Tyrwhitt.

7. He that knows himself knows others. CHARLES CALEB COLTON, *Lacon* (1825), 1.520.

8. The test of a civilized person is first self-awareness, and then depth after depth of sincerity in self-confrontation. CLARENCE DAY, "A Wild Polish Hero," *The Crow's Nest* (1921).

9. It is not enough to understand what we ought to be, unless we know what we are; and we do not understand what we are, unless we know what we ought to be. T. S. ELIOT, "Religion and Literature" (1935).

10. Wherever we go, whatever we do, self is the sole subject we study and learn. EMERSON, *Journals*, 1833.

11. It is doubtless a vice to turn one's eyes inward too much, but I am my own comedy

and tragedy. EMERSON, *Journals*, 1833.

12. Know thyself! A maxim as pernicious as it is ugly. Whoever observes himself arrests his own development. A caterpillar who wanted to know itself well would never become a butterfly. ANDRÉ GIDE, *Les Nouvelles Nourritures* (1935).

13. Self-reflection is the school of wisdom. BALTASAR GRACIÁN, *The Art of Worldly Wisdom* (1647), 69, tr. Joseph Jacobs.

14. Let a man once see himself as others see him, and all enthusiasm vanishes from his heart. ELBERT HUBBARD, *The Note Book* (1927).

15. He who knows others is learned; / He who knows himself is wise. LAOTSE, *The Character of Tao* (6th c. B.C.), 33, tr. Lin Yutang.

16. When one is a stranger to oneself then one is estranged from others too. ANNE MORROW LINDBERGH, "Moon Shell," *Gift from the Sea* (1955).

17. No man can produce great things who is not thoroughly sincere in dealing with himself. JAMES RUSSELL LOWELL, *Rousseau and the Sentimentalists* (1870).

18. In moments of despair, we look on ourselves leadenly as objects; we see ourselves, our lives, as someone else might see them and may even be driven to kill ourselves if the separation, the "knowledge," seems sufficiently final. MARY MC CARTHY, "Characters in Fiction," *On the Contrary* (1961).

19. It is far more important that one's life should be perceived than that it should be transformed; for no sooner has it been perceived, than it transforms itself of its own accord. MAURICE MAETERLINCK, "The Deeper Life," *The Treasure of the Humble* (1896), tr. Alfred Sutro.

20. Knowledge of the soul would unfailingly make us melancholy if the pleasures of expression did not keep us alert and of good cheer. THOMAS MANN, "Tonio Kröger" (1903), *Death in Venice*, tr. H. T. Lowe-Porter.

21. We are nearer neighbors to ourselves than the whiteness of snow or the weight of stones are to us: if man does not know himself, how should he know his functions and powers? MONTAIGNE, "Apology for Raimond de Sebonde," *Essays* (1580–88), tr. Charles Cotton and W. C. Hazlitt.

22. If men knew themselves, God would heal and pardon them. PASCAL, *Pensées* (1670), 778, tr. W. F. Trotter.

23. Learn what you are and be such. PINDAR, *Odes* (5th c. B.C.), Pythia 2, tr. Richmond Lattimore.

24. Know then thyself, presume not God to scan; / The proper study of mankind is man. ALEXANDER POPE, *An Essay on Man* (1733–34), 2.1.

25. We may fail of our happiness, strive we ever so bravely; but we are less likely to fail if we measure with judgment our chances and our capabilities. AGNES REPPLIER, "The Spinster," *Compromises* (1904).

26. To "know thyself" is to be known by another. PHILIP RIEFF, "The Hidden Self," *Freud: The Mind of the Moralist* (1959).

27. Who's not sat tense before his own heart's curtain? RAINER MARIA RILKE, "The Fourth Elegy," *Duino Elegies* (1923), tr. J. B. Leishman and Stephen Spender.

28. Each man must look to himself to teach him the meaning of life. It is not something discovered: it is something moulded. SAINT-EXUPÉRY, *Wind, Sand, and Stars* (1939), 2.1, tr. Lewis Galantière.

29. If a man really knew himself he would utterly despise the ignorant notions others might form on a subject in which he had such matchless opportunities for observation. GEORGE SANTAYANA, *The Life of Reason: Reason in Society* (1905–06), 6.

30. A man may call to mind the face of his friend, but not his own. Here, then, is an initial difficulty in the way of applying the maxim, *Know Thyself*. SCHOPENHAUER, "Further Psychological Observations," *Parerga and Paralipomena* (1851), tr. T. Bailey Saunders.

31. Go to your bosom; / Knock there, and ask your heart what it doth know. SHAKESPEARE, *Measure for Measure* (1604–05), 2.2.136.

32. Self-knowledge is a dangerous thing, tending to make man shallow or insane. KARL SHAPIRO, *The Bourgeois Poet* (1964), 3.74.

33. Explore thyself. Herein are demanded the eye and the nerve. THOREAU, "Conclusions," *Walden* (1854).

34. All men should strive to learn before they die what they are running from, and to, and why. JAMES THURBER, "The Shore

and the Sea," *Further Fables for Our Time* (1956).

35. Search thine own heart. What paineth thee / In others in thyself may be. JOHN GREENLEAF WHITTIER, "The Chapel of the Hermits" (1853), 11.

## SELFLESSNESS

See 433. Humility; 880. Service; 1014. Unselfishness

## 869. SELF-LOVE

See also 163. Conceit; 727. Pride; 858. Self-deception; 862. Self-esteem; 867. Selfishness; 1020. Vanity

1. In another's, yes, but in his own eye he sees no dirt. *Burmese Proverbs* (1962), 69, ed. Hla Pe.

2. Our own self-love draws a thick veil between us and our faults. LORD CHESTERFIELD, *Letters to His Son*, June 21, 1748.

3. Narcissus never wrote well nor was a friend. EDWARD DAHLBERG, "On Writers and Writing," *Reasons of the Heart* (1965).

4. What is an obstacle in our loving men is the love they have for themselves, which is touchy, exclusive, inordinate, tragic. We could never love them as much as that. PAUL GÉRALDY, *L'Homme et l'amour* (1951).

5. We prefer ourselves to others, only because we have a more intimate consciousness and confirmed opinion of our own claims and merits than of any other person's. WILLIAM HAZLITT, *Characteristics* (1823), 25.

6. Everyone gives himself credit for more brains than he has and less money. ITALIAN PROVERB.

7. Self-love is the greatest of all flatterers. LA ROCHEFOUCAULD, *Maxims* (1665), tr. Kenneth Pratt.

8. We feel good and ill only in proportion to our self-love. LA ROCHEFOUCAULD, *Maxims* (1665), tr. Kenneth Pratt.

9. He who is in love with himself has at least this advantage—he won't encounter many rivals. GEORG CHRISTOPH LICHTENBERG, *Aphorisms* (1764–99), tr. F. H. Mautner and H. Hatfield.

10. Simple narcissism gives the power of beasts to politicians, professional wrestlers and female movie stars. NORMAN MAILER, *Miami and the Siege of Chicago* (1968), 2.24.

11. One must learn to love oneself . . . with a wholesome and healthy love, so that one can bear to be with oneself and need not roam. NIETZSCHE, "On the Spirit of Gravity," *Thus Spoke Zarathustra* (1883–92), 3, tr. Walter Kaufmann.

12. No person loving or admiring himself is alone. THEODOR REIK, *Of Love and Lust* (1957), 1.1.6.

13. We believe, first and foremost, what makes us feel that we are fine fellows. BERTRAND RUSSELL, "An Outline of Intellectual Rubbish," *Unpopular Essays* (1950).

14. Self-love, my liege, is not so vile a sin / As self-neglecting. SHAKESPEARE, *Henry V* (1598–99), 2.4.75.

15. My teeth are closer to me than my relatives. SPANISH PROVERB.

16. Self-love is the instrument of our preservation; it resembles the provision for the perpetuity of mankind; it is necessary, it is dear to us, it gives us pleasure, and we must conceal it. VOLTAIRE, "Self-Love," *Philosophical Dictionary* (1764).

17. It is not love we should have painted as blind, but self-love. VOLTAIRE, *Correspondance, à M. Damilaville*, May 11, 1764.

18. I dote on myself, there is that lot of me and all so luscious. WALT WHITMAN, "Song of Myself," 24, *Leaves of Grass* (1855–92).

19. I find no sweeter fat than sticks to my own bones. WALT WHITMAN, "Song of Myself," *Leaves of Grass* (1855–92).

20. To love oneself is the beginning of a life-long romance. OSCAR WILDE, *An Ideal Husband* (1895), 3.

## 870. SELF-PITY

See also 692. Pity

1. The dangerous ones are those who stop you every time you want to turn around, who instead of patting your hand, insist that you feel their guts. And the more they suffer, the more they make you suffer, the happier they are. JEAN ANOUILH, *Mademoiselle Colombe* (1950), 2.2, tr. Louis Kronenberger.

2. God put self-pity by the side of despair like the cure by the side of the disease. ALBERT CAMUS, *Notebooks 1935–1942* (1962), 1, tr. Philip Thody.

3. Every man supposes himself not to be fully understood or appreciated. EMERSON, *Journals*, 1840.

4. Every horse thinks his own pack heaviest. THOMAS FULLER, M.D., *Gnomologia* (1732), 1420.

5. Life, I fancy, would very often be insupportable, but for the luxury of self-compassion. GEORGE GISSING, "Spring," *The Private Papers of Henry Ryecroft* (1903).

6. Self-pity comes so naturally to all of us, that the most solid happiness can be shaken by the compassion of a fool. ANDRÉ MAUROIS, *Ariel* (1924), 16, tr. Ella D'Arcy.

7. Shall a man go and hang himself because he belongs to the race of pygmies, and not be the biggest pygmy that he can? THOREAU, "Conclusion," *Walden* (1854).

### SELF-PRESERVATION
**See 226. Defense; 949. Survival**

### SELF-RELIANCE
**See 860. Self-determination; 873. Self-sufficiency**

### SELF-RESPECT
**See 862. Self-esteem; 869. Self-love**

### 871. SELF-REVELATION
**See also 166. Confidences**

1. His Cheek is his Biographer— / As long as he can blush. EMILY DICKINSON, poem (c. 1879).

2. When I speak to you about myself, I am speaking to you about yourself. How is it you don't see that? VICTOR HUGO, quoted in John Hall Wheelock's "The Poem in the Nuclear Age," *What Is Poetry?* (1963).

3. Adults discover themselves, consciously and unconsciously, to the very young as they never do to other adults. W. SOMERSET MAUGHAM, *The Summing Up* (1938), 43.

4. The most difficult secret for a man to keep is his own opinion of himself. MARCEL PAGNOL, news summaries, March 15, 1954.

### 872. SELF-RIGHTEOUSNESS
**See also 262. Dogmatism; 333. Fanaticism**

1. Why beholdest thou the mote that is in thy brother's eye, but considerest not the beam that is in thine own eye? *Bible*, Matthew 7:3.

2. The righteous one has no sense of humor. BERTOLT BRECHT, *Baal* (1926), 9, tr. Eric Bentley and Martin Esslin.

3. Self-righteousness is a loud din raised to drown the voice of guilt within us. ERIC HOFFER, *The True Believer* (1951), 3.14.69.

4. Men never do evil so completely and cheerfully as when they do it from a religious conviction. PASCAL, *Pensées* (1670), 894, tr. W. F. Trotter.

5. Forgive us for cheering legislators who promise low taxes, but deny homes and schools and help to those in need; for self-righteousness that blames the poor for their poverty or the oppressed for their oppression. UNITED PRESBYTERIAN CHURCH, *Litany for Holy Communion* (1968).

### SELF-SACRIFICE
**See 831. Sacrifice**

### SELF-SEEKING
**See 493. Interest; 867. Selfishness; 869. Self-love**

### 873. SELF-SUFFICIENCY
**See also 233. Dependence; 289. Enterprise; 860. Self-determination**

1. The foundations which we would dig about and find are within us, like the Kingdom of Heaven, rather than without. SAMUEL BUTLER (d. 1902), "Elementary Morality," *Note-Books* (1912).

2. We carry our homes within us which enables us to fly. JOHN CAGE, "45′ for a Speaker," *Silence* (1961).

3. Who to himself is law no law doth need, / Offends no law, and is a king indeed. GEORGE CHAPMAN, *Bussy D'Ambois* (c. 1604), 2.1.

4. Be thine own palace, or the world's thy jail. JOHN DONNE, "To Sir Henry Wotton" (1633).

5. We must be our own before we can be another's. EMERSON, "Friendship," *Essays: First Series* (1841).

6. The great man is he who in the midst of the crowd keeps with perfect sweetness the independence of solitude. EMERSON, "Self-Reliance," *Essays: First Series* (1841).

7. It is folly for a man to pray to the gods for that which he has the power to obtain for himself. EPICURUS, "Vatican Sayings" (3rd c. B.C.), 65, in *Letters, Principal Doctrines, and Vatican Sayings*, tr. Russel M. Geer.

8. Every tub must stand upon its own bottom. THOMAS FULLER, M.D., *Gnomologia* (1732), 1472.

9. He that was all in all to himself carried all with him when he carried himself. BALTASAR GRACIÁN, *The Art of Worldly Wisdom* (1647), 137, tr. Joseph Jacobs.

10. Independence is the first condition of dialogue between men. Graffito written during French student revolt, May 1968.

11. Every man for himself and God for us all. JOHN HEYWOOD, *Proverbs* (1546), 1.9.

12. Be yourself and think for yourself; and while your conclusions may not be infallible they will be nearer right than the conclusions forced upon you by those who have a personal interest in keeping you in ignorance. ELBERT HUBBARD, *The Note Book* (1927).

13. A great maxim of personal responsibility and mature achievement—Do It Yourself—is now the enthroned cliché for being occupied with nonessentials. LOUIS KRONENBERGER, "Unbrave New World," *The Cart and the Horse* (1964), 2.

14. Who / cannot resolve upon a moment's notice / To live his own life, he forever lives / A slave to others. GOTTHOLD EPHRAIM LESSING, *Nathan the Wise* (1779), 2.9, tr. Bayard Quincy Morgan.

15. How much time he gains who does not look to see what his neighbour says or does or thinks, but only at what he does himself, to make it just and holy. MARCUS AURELIUS, *Meditations* (2nd c.), 4.18, tr. Morris Hickey Morgan.

16. I care not so much what I am in the opinion of others, as what I am in my own; I would be rich of myself, and not by borrowing. MONTAIGNE, "Of glory," *Essays* (1580–88), tr. Charles Cotton and W. C. Hazlitt.

17. A learned man is not learned in all things; but a sufficient man is sufficient throughout, even to ignorance itself. MONTAIGNE, "Of repentance," *Essays* (1580–88), tr. Charles Cotton and W. C. Hazlitt.

18. A wise man never loses anything if he have himself. MONTAIGNE, "Of solitude," *Essays* (1580–88), tr. Charles Cotton and W. C. Hazlitt.

19. If you want a thing done well, do it yourself. NAPOLEON I, *Maxims* (1804–1815).

20. Independence is for the very few; it is a privilege of the strong. NIETZSCHE, *Beyond Good and Evil* (1886), 29, tr. Walter Kaufmann.

21. Now I know the things I know, / And do the things I do; / And if you do not like me so, / To hell, my love, with you! DOROTHY PARKER, "Indian Summer," *Enough Rope* (1926), 2.

22. Men are made stronger on realization that the helping hand they need is at the end of their own right arm. SIDNEY J. PHILLIPS, address, July 1953.

23. Any man who is really a man must learn to be alone in the midst of others, to think alone for others, and, if necessary, against others. ROMAIN ROLLAND, introduction, *Clérambault* (1919).

24. We never reflect how pleasant it is to ask for nothing. SENECA, *Letters to Lucilius* (1st c.), 15.9, tr. E. Phillips Barker.

25. If you want good service, serve yourself. SPANISH PROVERB.

26. The most affluent man is he that confronts all the shows he sees by equivalents out of the stronger wealth of himself. WALT WHITMAN, preface to *Leaves of Grass* (1855).

## SELLING

See 103. Buying and Selling

## 874. SENSE AND NONSENSE

1. To appreciate nonsense requires a serious interest in life. GELETT BURGESS, "The Sense of Humor," *The Romance of the Commonplace* (1916).

2. True wisdom knows / it must comprise / some nonsense / as a compromise, / lest fools should fail / to find it wise. PIET HEIN, "Lest Fools Should Fail," *Grooks* (1966).

3. Even God has been defended with nonsense. WALTER LIPPMANN, "The

Golden Rule and After," *A Preface to Politics* (1914).

4. Nonsense is good only because common sense is so limited. GEORGE SANTAYANA, "The Comic," *The Sense of Beauty* (1896).

5. A man talking sense to himself is no madder than a man talking nonsense not to himself. TOM STOPPARD, *Rosencrantz & Guildenstern Are Dead* (1967), 2.

## 875. SENSES

See also 217. Deafness; 323. Eyes; 324. Face; 584. Mind and Body; 676. Perception; 877. Sensuality; 890. Sight

1. The ear tends to be lazy, craves the familiar, and is shocked by the unexpected: the eye, on the other hand, tends to be impatient, craves the novel and is bored by repetition. W. H. AUDEN, "Hic et Ille," *The Dyer's Hand* (1962).

2. Happily, the senses are not easy to trick —or to trick often. They fix, and fix us with them, on what is possessable. ELIZABETH BOWEN, *The Death of the Heart* (1938), 2.2.

3. The soul may be a mere pretense, / the mind makes very little sense. / So let us value the appeal / of that which we can taste and feel. PIET HEIN, "A Toast," *Grooks* (1966).

4. Men trust their ears less than their eyes. HERODOTUS, *The Histories* (5th c. B.C.), 1.8, tr. A. D. Godley.

5. Nothing awakens a reminiscence like an odour. VICTOR HUGO, "Jean Valjean," *Les Misérables* (1862), 9.4, tr. Charles E. Wilbour.

6. What can give us surer knowledge than our senses? With what else can we better distinguish the true from the false? LUCRETIUS, *On the Nature of Things* (1st c. B.C.), 1.

7. The modern nose, like the modern eye, has developed a sort of microscopic, intercellular intensity which makes our human contacts painful and revolting. MARSHALL MC LUHAN, "How Not to Offend," *The Mechanical Bride* (1951).

8. We don't trust our five senses; we rely on our critics and educators, all of whom are failures in the realm of creation. HENRY MILLER, "With Edgar Varèse in the Gobi Desert," *The Air-Conditioned Nightmare* (1945).

9. All credibility, all good conscience, all evidence of truth come only from the senses. NIETZSCHE, *Beyond Good and Evil* (1886), 134, tr. Walter Kaufmann.

10. The loss of a sense adds as much beauty to the world as its acquisition. MARCEL PROUST, *Remembrance of Things Past: The Guermantes Way* (1913–27), tr. C. K. Scott-Moncrieff.

11. We are astonished at thought, but sensation is equally wonderful. VOLTAIRE, "Sensation," *Philosophical Dictionary* (1764).

12. Seeing, hearing, feeling, are miracles, and each part and tag of me is a miracle. WALT WHITMAN, "Song of Myself," 24, *Leaves of Grass* (1855–92).

13. Devils can be driven out of the heart by the touch of a hand on a hand, or a mouth on a mouth. TENNESSEE WILLIAMS, *The Milk Train Doesn't Stop Here Anymore* (1963), 5.

## 876. SENSIBILITY

See also 172. Consciousness; 282. Emotions; 481. Insensitivity; 499. Intuition; 676. Perception

1. It is axiomatic that we should all think of ourselves as being more sensitive than other people because, when we are insensitive in our dealings with others, we cannot be aware of it at the time: conscious insensitivity is a self-contradiction. W. H. AUDEN, foreword to Dag Hammarskjöld's *Markings* (1964).

2. Chords that vibrate sweetest pleasure / Thrill the deepest notes of woe. ROBERT BURNS, "On Sensibility" (1791).

3. If we had keen vision and feeling of all ordinary human life, it would be like hearing the grass grow and the squirrel's heart beat, and we should die of that roar which lies on the other side of silence. GEORGE ELIOT, *Middlemarch* (1871–72), 20.

4. The great man, that is, the man most imbued with the spirit of the time, is the impressionable man. EMERSON, "Fate," *The Conduct of Life* (1860).

5. Laughter and tears are meant to turn the wheels of the same machinery of sensibility; one is wind-power, and the other

water-power; that is all. OLIVER WENDELL HOLMES, SR., *The Autocrat of the Breakfast Table* (1858), 4.

6. Nothing is little to him that feels it with great sensibility. SAMUEL JOHNSON, letter to Joseph Baretti, July 20, 1762, quoted in Boswell's *Life of Samuel Johnson.*

7. The heart that is soonest awake to the flowers / Is always the first to be touched by the thorns. THOMAS MOORE, "Oh, Think Not My Spirits Are Always as Light," *Irish Melodies* (1807–35).

8. The sensibility of man to trifles, and his insensibility to great things, indicates a strange inversion. PASCAL, *Pensées* (1670), 198, tr. W. F. Trotter.

9. Any sensibility which can be crammed into the mold of a system, or handled with the rough tools of proof, is no longer a sensibility at all. It has hardened into an idea. SUSAN SONTAG, "Notes on Camp," *Against Interpretation* (1961).

10. The two pioneering forces of modern sensibility are Jewish moral seriousness and homosexual aestheticism and irony. SUSAN SONTAG, "Notes on Camp," *Against Interpretation* (1961).

## SENSITIVITY
See 876. Sensibility

## 877. SENSUALITY
See also 875. Senses

1. Moral qualities rule the world, but at short distances the senses are despotic. EMERSON, "Manners," *Essays: Second Series* (1844).

2. Great eaters and great sleepers are incapable of anything else that is great. HENRY IV OF FRANCE (1553–1610), epigram.

3. They never taste who always drink. MATTHEW PRIOR, "Upon a Passage in the Scaligerana" (1697).

4. Sensuality, too, which used to show itself coarse, smiling, unmasked, and unmistakable, is now serious, analytic, and so burdened with a sense of its responsibilities that it passes muster half the time as a new type of asceticism. AGNES REPPLIER, "Fiction in the Pulpit," *Points of View* (1891).

## 878. SENTIMENTALITY

1. Sentimentality, the ostentatious parading of excessive and spurious emotion, is the mark of dishonesty, the inability to feel. JAMES BALDWIN, "Everybody's Protest Novel" (1949), *Notes of a Native Son* (1955).

2. To the modern spirit, disillusioned, or at least unillusioned, the great evil to be avoided is sentimentality. IRWIN EDMAN, "How to be Sweet Though Sophisticated," *Adam, the Baby, and the Man from Mars* (1929).

3. Sentimentality is the emotional promiscuity of those who have no sentiment. NORMAN MAILER, "Lambs," *Cannibals and Christians* (1966).

4. Sentimentality is only sentiment that rubs you up the wrong way. W. SOMERSET MAUGHAM, *A Writer's Notebook*, 1941.

5. The sentimental people fiddle harmonics on the string of sensualism. GEORGE MEREDITH, *Diana of the Crossways* (1885), 1.

6. I hope my tongue in prune juice smothers / If I belittle dogs and mothers. OGDEN NASH, "Compliments of a Friend," *Versus* (1949).

7. Sentimentality is a failure of feeling. WALLACE STEVENS, "Adagia," *Opus Posthumous* (1957).

8. A sentimentalist is a man who sees an absurd value in everything and doesn't know the market price of any single thing. OSCAR WILDE, *Lady Windermere's Fan* (1892), 3.

9. There is no more subtle dissolvent of morals than sentimentality. WOODROW WILSON, address, Princeton University, June 7, 1908.

## SEPARATION
See 666. Parting

## SERENITY
See 982. Tranquility

## 879. SERIOUSNESS
See also 734. Profundity

1. Earnest people are often people who habitually look on the serious side of things

that have no serious side. VAN WYCK BROOKS, *From a Writer's Notebook* (1958).

2. Every man is grave alone. EMERSON, *Journals*, 1824.

3. There is ever a slight suspicion of the burlesque about earnest, good men. EMERSON, *Journals*, 1840.

4. Taking fun / as simply fun / and earnestness / in earnest / shows how thoroughly / thou none / of the two / discernest. PIET HEIN, "The Eternal Twins," *Grooks* (1966).

5. There are people who think that everything one does with a serious face is sensible. GEORG CHRISTOPH LICHTENBERG, *Aphorisms* (1764–99), tr. F. H. Mautner and H. Hatfield.

6. Solemnity is the shield of idiots. MONTESQUIEU, *Pensées et jugements* (1899).

7. Almost everything serious is difficult, and everything is serious. RAINER MARIA RILKE, *Letters to a Young Poet*, July 16, 1903, tr. M. D. Herter Norton.

8. You have to have a serious streak in you or you can't see the funny side in the other fellow. WILL ROGERS, "What We Need Is More Fred Stones," *The Illiterate Digest* (1924).

9. Taking sides is the beginning of sincerity, and earnestness follows shortly afterwards, and the human being becomes a bore. OSCAR WILDE, *A Woman of No Importance* (1893), 1.

## SERMONS

See 718. Preaching and Preachers

## 880. SERVICE

See also 56. Assistance; 224. Deeds; 430. Humanitarianism; 1016. Usefulness

1. All service ranks the same with God— / With God, whose puppets, best and worst, / Are we: there is no last nor first. ROBERT BROWNING, "Night," *Pippa Passes* (1841).

2. To serve is beautiful, but only if it is done with joy and a whole heart and a free mind. PEARL S. BUCK, "Men and Women," *To My Daughters, With Love* (1967).

3. Pressed into service means pressed out of shape. ROBERT FROST, "The Self-Seeker," *North of Boston* (1914).

4. The noblest service comes from nameless hands, / And the best servant does his work unseen. OLIVER WENDELL HOLMES, SR., *The Poet at the Breakfast Table* (1872), 5.

5. Human service is the highest form of self-interest for the person who serves. ELBERT HUBBARD, *The Note Book* (1927).

6. "Let me light my lamp," / says the star, / "And never debate / if it will help to remove the darkness." RABINDRANATH TAGORE, *Fireflies* (1928).

7. There is something better, if possible, that a man can give than his life. That is his living spirit to a service that is not easy, to resist counsels that are hard to resist, to stand against purposes that are difficult to stand against. WOODROW WILSON, speech, May 30, 1919.

## 881. SERVICES

See also 224. Deeds; 382. Gifts and Giving; 430. Humanitarianism; 831. Sacrifice

1. The man who confers a favour would rather not be repaid in the same coin. ARISTOTLE, *Nicomachean Ethics* (4th c. B.C.), 4.1, tr. J. A. K. Thomson.

2. We should render a service to a friend to bind him closer to us, and to an enemy in order to make a friend of him. CLEOBULUS (6th c. B.C.), quoted in Diogenes Laertius' *Lives and Opinions of Eminent Philosophers* (3rd c. A.D.), tr. R. D. Hicks.

3. He merits no thanks that does a kindness for his own end. THOMAS FULLER, M.D., *Gnomologia* (1732), 1989.

4. He that doth a good turn looketh for a good turn. THOMAS FULLER, M.D., *Gnomologia* (1732), 2087.

5. Verily the kindness that gazes upon itself in a mirror turns to stone, / And a good deed that calls itself by tender names becomes the parent to a curse. KAHLIL GIBRAN, "The Farewell," *The Prophet* (1923).

6. To oblige persons often costs little and helps much. BALTASAR GRACIÁN, *The Art of Worldly Wisdom* (1647), 226, tr. Joseph Jacobs.

7. The pleasure we derive from doing favors is partly in the feeling it gives us that we are not altogether worthless. ERIC

HOFFER, *The Passionate State of Mind* (1954), 113.

8. The charity that is a trifle to us can be precious to others. HOMER, *Odyssey* (9th c. B.C.), 6, tr. E. V. Rieu.

9. Men become attached to us not by reason of the services we render them, but by reason of the services they render us. EUGÈNE LABICHE, *Le Voyage de M. Perrichon* (1860), 4.8.

10. He who boasts of a favor bestowed, would like it back again. PUBLILIUS SYRUS, *Moral Sayings* (1st c. B.C.), 91, tr. Darius Lyman.

11. A favour well bestowed is almost as great an honour to him who confers it as to him who receives it. RICHARD STEELE, *The Spectator* (1711–12), 497.

## 882. SERVITUDE

**See also 107. Captivity; 534. Liberty; 995. Tyranny**

1. He who is by nature not his own but another's man, is by nature a slave. ARISTOTLE, *Politics* (4th c. B.C.), 1.4, tr. Benjamin Jowett.

2. You rebel—and yet you want them: those obligations, those penalties, those debts!—Man wants to serve! UGO BETTI, *The Fugitive* (1953), 3, tr. G. H. McWilliam.

3. Virtue cannot dwell with slaves, nor reign / O'er those who cower to take a tyrant's yoke. WILLIAM CULLEN BRYANT, "The Ages" (1821).

4. Men would rather be starving and free than fed in bonds. PEARL S. BUCK, *What America Means to Me* (1943), 10.

5. Slavery they can have anywhere. It is a weed that grows in every soil. EDMUND BURKE, speech, "On Conciliation with the American Colonies," March 22, 1775.

6. I didn't know I was a slave until I found out I couldn't do the things I wanted. FREDERICK DOUGLASS, *Narrative of the Life of Frederick Douglass* (1845).

7. This is what it means / to be a slave: to be abused and bear it, / compelled by violence to suffer wrong. EURIPIDES, *Hecuba* (c. 425 B.C.), tr. William Arrowsmith.

8. Whatever day / Makes man a slave, takes half his worth away. HOMER, *Odyssey* (9th c. B.C.), 17.392, tr. Alexander Pope.

9. Freedom is indivisible, and when one man is enslaved, all are not free. JOHN F. KENNEDY, address, West Berlin, June 26, 1963.

10. This is a world of compensation; and he who would be no slave must consent to have no slave. Those who deny freedom to others deserve it not for themselves, and, under a just God, cannot long retain it. ABRAHAM LINCOLN, letter to H. L. Pierce and others, April 6, 1859.

11. —antoninus the emperor / and epictetus the slave / arrived at the same / philosophy of life / that there is neither mastery / nor slavery / except as it exists / in the attitude of the soul / toward the world. DON MARQUIS, "archy turns highbrow for a minute," *Archy's Life of Mehitabel* (1933).

12. This is servitude, / To serve the unwise. MILTON, *Paradise Lost* (1667), 6.178.

13. Art thou less a slave by being loved and favoured by thy master? Thou art indeed well off, slave. Thy master favours thee; he will soon beat thee. PASCAL, *Pensées* (1670), 209, tr. W. F. Trotter.

14. Coercion created slavery, the cowardice of the slaves perpetuated it. ROUSSEAU, *The Social Contract* (1762), 1.2.

15. Slaves lose everything in their chains, even the desire of escaping from them. ROUSSEAU, *The Social Contract* (1762), 1.2, tr. G. D. H. Cole.

16. Slavery holds few men fast; the greater number hold fast their slavery. SENECA, *Letters to Lucilius* (1st c.), 22.11, tr. E. Phillips Barker.

17. No man is good enough to be another man's master. GEORGE BERNARD SHAW, *Major Barbara* (1905), 3.

18. All spirits are enslaved which serve things evil. SHELLEY, *Prometheus Unbound* (1818–19), 2.4.

19. Servitude debases men to the point where they end up liking it. VAUVENARGUES, *Reflections and Maxims* (1746), 22.

## 883. SEVERITY

**See also 531. Leniency; 760. Punishment**

1. If you hit a pony over the nose at the outset of your acquaintance, he may not love you, but he will take a deep interest in your movements ever afterwards. RUDYARD

KIPLING, "False Dawn," *Plain Tales from the Hills* (1888).

2. If you love your children, you will slap them sometimes; if you love your wife, you will leave her sometimes. MALAY PROVERB.

3. Excess of severity is not the path to order. On the contrary, it is the path to the bomb. JOHN MORLEY, *Recollections* (1917), 2.5.4.

4. Excessive severity misses its own aim. PUBLILIUS SYRUS, *Moral Sayings* (1st c. B.C.), 62, tr. Darius Lyman.

5. Be not so severe as to cause shyness, nor so clement as to encourage boldness. SA'DI, *Gulistan* (1258), 8.19, tr. James Ross.

6. Nothing comes of severity if there be no leanings towards a change of heart. And if there be natural leanings towards a change of heart, what need for severity? SAINT-EXUPÉRY, *The Wisdom of the Sands* (1948), 43, tr. Stuart Gilbert.

7. I must be cruel, only to be kind. SHAKESPEARE, *Hamlet* (1600), 3.4.178.

## 884. SEWERS

**See also 701. Plumbers**

1. A sewer is a cynic. It tells all. VICTOR HUGO, "Jean Valjean," *Les Misérables* (1862), 2.2, tr. Charles E. Wilbour.

## 885. SEX

**See also 120. Chastity; 348. Flirtation; 422. Homosexuality; 519. Kissing; 548. Love; 562. Masculinity and Femininity; 708. Pornography; 736. Promiscuity; 746. Prostitution; 851. Seduction; 877. Sensuality**

1. Desire is poison at lunch and wormwood at dinner; your bed is a stone, friendship is hateful and your fancy is always fixed on one thing. PIETRO ARETINO, letter to Count di San Secondo, June 24, 1537, tr. Samuel Putnam.

2. Sexuality is the lyricism of the masses. CHARLES BAUDELAIRE, *Intimate Journals* (1887), 93, tr. Christopher Isherwood.

3. When you put a man and woman together, there are some things they simply have to do. They embrace. They warm each other. All the rest is dead and empty. UGO BETTI, *The Inquiry* (1944–45), 1.10, ed. Gino Rizzo.

4. If venereal delight and the power of propagating the species were permitted only to the virtuous, it would make the world very good. JAMES BOSWELL, *London Journal*, March 26, 1763.

5. If our elaborate and dominating bodies are given us to be denied at every turn, if our nature is always wrong and wicked, how ineffectual we are—like fishes not meant to swim. CYRIL CONNOLLY, *The Unquiet Grave* (1945), 1.

6. Sex is the great amateur art. The professional, male or female, is frowned on; he or she misses the whole point and spoils the show. DAVID CORT, *Social Astonishments* (1963).

7. What most men desire is a virgin who is a whore. EDWARD DAHLBERG, "On Lust," *Reasons of the Heart* (1965).

8. Love's mysteries in souls do grow, / But yet the body is his book. JOHN DONNE, "The Ecstasy," *Songs and Sonnets* (1633).

9. Whoever loves, if he do not propose / The right true end of love, he's one that goes / To sea for nothing but to make him sick. JOHN DONNE, Elegy 18, "Love's Progress" (1661).

10. The sexual embrace can only be compared with music and with prayer. HAVELOCK ELLIS, *On Life and Sex: Essays of Love and Virtue* (1937), 1.

11. If your life at night is good, you think you have / Everything; but, if in that quarter things go wrong, / You will consider your best and truest interests / Most hateful. EURIPIDES, *Medea* (431 B.C.), tr. Rex Warner.

12. You know women as well as I do. They are only willing when you compel them, but after that they're as enthusiastic as you are. JEAN GIRAUDOUX, *Tiger at the Gates* (1935), 1, tr. Christopher Fry.

13. Women are silver dishes into which we put golden apples. GOETHE, quoted in Johann Peter Eckermann's *Conversations with Goethe*, Oct. 22, 1828.

14. My own view, for what it's worth, is that sexuality is lovely, there cannot be too much of it, it is self-limiting if it is satisfactory, and satisfaction diminishes tension and clears the mind for attention and learning. PAUL GOODMAN, *Compulsory Mis-education* (1964).

15. If a woman hasn't got a tiny streak of a harlot in her, she's a dry stick as a rule. D. H.

LAWRENCE, *Pornography and Obscenity* (1930).

16. The old man, especially if he is in society, in the privacy of his thoughts, though he may protest the opposite, never stops believing that, through some singular exception of the universal rule, he can in some unknown and inexplicable way still make an impression on women. GIACOMO LEOPARDI, *Pensieri* (1834–37), 54, tr. William Fense Weaver.

17. The body searches for that which has injured the mind with love. LUCRETIUS, *On the Nature of Things* (1st c. B.C.), 4.

18. The truly erotic sensibility, in evoking the image of woman, never omits to clothe it. The robing and disrobing: that is the true traffic of love. ANTONIO MACHADO, *Juan de Mairena* (1943), 46, tr. Ben Belitt.

19. To the mind of the modern girl, legs, like busts, are power points which she has been taught to tailor, but as parts of the success kit rather than erotically or sensuously. MARSHALL MC LUHAN, title essay, *The Mechanical Bride* (1951).

20. Most creatures have a vague belief that a very precarious hazard, a kind of transparent membrane, divides death from love; and that the profound idea of nature demands that the giver of life should die at the moment of giving. MAURICE MAETERLINCK, *The Life of the Bee* (1901), tr. Alfred Sutro.

21. The orgasm has replaced the Cross as the focus of longing and the image of fulfillment. MALCOLM MUGGERIDGE, "Down with Sex," *The Most of Malcolm Muggeridge* (1966).

22. When a lady's erotic life is vexed / God knows what God is coming next. OGDEN NASH, "The Seven Spiritual Ages of Mrs. Marmaduke Moore," *Verses from 1929 On* (1959).

23. Like hatred, sex must articulated or, like hatred, it will produce a disturbing internal malaise. GEORGE JEAN NATHAN, "Mens Sana in Corpore Sano," *Passing Judgments* (1935).

24. The degree and kind of a man's sexuality reach up into the ultimate pinnacle of his spirit. NIETZSCHE, *Beyond Good and Evil* (1886), 75, tr. Walter Kaufmann.

25. Christianity gave Eros poison to drink: he did not die of it but degenerated—into vice. NIETZSCHE, *Beyond Good and Evil* (1886), 168, tr. Walter Kaufmann.

26. I hate a woman who offers herself because she ought to do so, and, cold and dry, thinks of her sewing when she's making love. OVID, *The Art of Love* (c. A.D. 8), 2, tr. J. Lewis May.

27. I'd call it love if love / didn't take so many years / but lust too is a jewel. ADRIENNE RICH, "Two Songs," *Necessities of Life* (1966).

28. Some have held the Eye to be / The instrument of lechery, / More furtive than the Hand in low / And vicious venery—Not so! / Its rape is gentle, never more / Violent than a metaphor. THEODORE ROETHKE, "Prayer," *The Collected Verse of Theodore Roethke* (1961).

29. Civilized people cannot fully satisfy their sexual instinct without love. BERTRAND RUSSELL, "The Place of Love in Human Life," *Marriage and Morals* (1929).

30. Much contention and strife will arise in that house where the wife shall get up dissatisfied with her husband. SA'DI, *Gulistan* (1258), 6.2, tr. James Ross.

31. Is it not strange that desire should so many years outlive performance? SHAKESPEARE, *2 Henry IV* (1597–98), 2.4.283.

32. Certainly nothing is unnatural that is not physically impossible. RICHARD BRINSLEY SHERIDAN, *The Critic* (1779), 2.1.

33. Desire looks clear from the eyes of a lovely bride: / power as strong as the founded world. SOPHOCLES, *Antigone* (442–41 B.C.), tr. Elizabeth Wyckoff.

34. The eyes of men love to pluck / the blossoms; from the faded flowers they turn away. SOPHOCLES, *The Women of Trachis* (c. 413 B.C.), tr. Michael Jameson.

35. The sex instinct is one of the three or four prime movers of all that we do and are and dream, both individually and collectively. PHILIP WYLIE, *Generation of Vipers* (1942), 6.

## 886. SHAME

**See also 403. Guilt; 432. Humiliation; 814. Ridicule; 855. Self-consciousness**

1. If we have anything kind to say, any tender sentiment to express, we feel a sense of shame. UGO BETTI, *Landslide* (1936), 2, tr. G. H. McWilliam.

2. Blushing is the color of virtue. DIOG-

ENES THE CYNIC (4th c. B.C.), quoted in Diogenes Laertius' *Lives and Opinions of Eminent Philosophers* (3rd c. A.D.), tr. R. D. Hicks.

3. He that is shameless is graceless. THOMAS FULLER, M.D., *Gnomologia* (1732), 2192.

4. One of the misfortunes of our time is that in getting rid of false shame we have killed off so much real shame as well. LOUIS KRONENBERGER, *Company Manners* (1954), 2.1.

5. We never forgive those who make us blush. JEAN-FRANÇOIS DE LA HARPE, *Mélanie* (1770), 3.1.

6. The only shame is to have none. PASCAL, *Pensées* (1670), 194, tr. W. F. Trotter.

7. Better a red face than a black heart. PORTUGUESE PROVERB.

8. Give your friend cause to blush, and you will be likely to lose him. PUBLILIUS SYRUS, *Moral Sayings* (1st c. B.C.), 848, tr. Darius Lyman.

9. I never wonder to see men wicked, but I often wonder to see them not ashamed. JONATHAN SWIFT, *Thoughts on Various Subjects* (1711).

10. Man is the only animal that blushes. Or needs to. MARK TWAIN, "Pudd'nhead Wilson's New Calendar," *Following the Equator* (1897), 1.27.

11. The man that blushes is not quite a brute. EDWARD YOUNG, *Night Thoughts* (1742–46), 7.496.

## 887. SHARING

See also 382. Gifts and Giving

1. The ass that is common property is always the worst saddled. ENGLISH PROVERB.

2. The Holy Supper is kept, indeed, / In whatso we share with another's need; / Not what we give, but what we share. / For the gift without the giver is bare. JAMES RUSSELL LOWELL, "The Vision of Sir Launfal" (1848), 2.8.

3. If wisdom were offered me with the proviso that I should keep it shut up and refrain from declaring it, I should refuse. There's no delight in owning anything unshared. SENECA, *Letters to Lucilius* (1st c.), 6.4, tr. E. Phillips Barker.

4. He who divides gets the worst share. SPANISH PROVERB.

5. Grief can take care of itself, but to get the full value of joy you must have somebody to divide it with. MARK TWAIN, *Notebook* (1935).

## 888. SHIPS AND BOATS

See also 833. Sailing

1. A modern fleet of ships does not so much make use of the sea as exploit a highway. JOSEPH CONRAD, *The Mirror of the Sea* (1906), 22.

2. A ship in dock, surrounded by quays and the walls of warehouses, has the appearance of a prisoner meditating upon freedom in the sadness of a free spirit put under restraint. JOSEPH CONRAD, *The Mirror of the Sea* (1906), 33.

3. Believe me, my young friend, there is *nothing*—absolutely nothing—half so much worth doing as simply messing about• in boats. KENNETH GRAHAME, *The Wind in the Willows* (1908), 1.

## SHYNESS

See 973. Timidity

## 889. SICKNESS

See also 380. Germs; 411. Health; 437. Hypochondria; 572. Medicine

1. Diseases crucify the soul of man, attenuate our bodies, dry them, wither them, shrivel them up like old apples, make them so many anatomies. ROBERT BURTON, *The Anatomy of Melancholy* (1621), 1.

2. I reckon being ill as one of the great pleasures of life, provided one is not too ill and is not obliged to work till one is better. SAMUEL BUTLER (d. 1902), *The Way of All Flesh* (1903), 80.

3. Can there be worse sickness, than to know / that we are never well, nor can be so? JOHN DONNE, *An Anatomy of the World; The First Anniversary* (1612).

4. Ivry sick man is a hero, if not to th' wurruld or aven to th' fam'ly, at laste to himsilf. FINLEY PETER DUNNE, "Going to See the Doctor," *Mr. Dooley On Making a Will* (1919).

5. Sickness comes on horseback and departs on foot. DUTCH PROVERB.

6. We forget ourselves and our destinies in health, and the chief use of temporary sickness is to remind us of these concerns. EMERSON, *Journals*, 1821.

7. All diseases run into one, old age. EMERSON, *Journals*, 1840.

8. There is one topic peremptorily forbidden to all well-bred, to all rational mortals, namely, their distempers. If you have not slept, or if you have slept, or if you have headache, or sciatica, or leprosy, or thunder-stroke, I beseech you, by all angels, to hold your peace, and not pollute the morning. EMERSON, "Behavior," *The Conduct of Life* (1860).

9. Sleep to the sick is half health. GERMAN PROVERB.

10. Those who have never been ill are incapable of real sympathy for a great many misfortunes. ANDRÉ GIDE, *Journals*, July 25, 1930, tr. Justin O'Brien.

11. A human being sheds its leaves like a tree. Sickness prunes it down; and it no longer offers the same silhouette to the eyes which loved it, to the people to whom it afforded shade and comfort. EDMOND and JULES DE GONCOURT, *Journal*, July 22, 1862, tr. Robert Baldick.

12. Sickness sensitizes man for observation, like a photographic plate. EDMOND and JULES DE GONCOURT, *Journal*, March 27, 1865, tr. Robert Baldick.

13. A bodily disease, which we look upon as whole and entire within itself, may, after all, be but a symptom of some ailment in the spiritual part. NATHANIEL HAWTHORNE, *The Scarlet Letter* (1850), 10.

14. Every invalid is a physician. IRISH PROVERB.

15. One of the most difficult things to contend with in a hospital is the assumption on the part of the staff that because you have lost your gall bladder you have also lost your mind. JEAN KERR, "Operation Operation," *Please Don't Eat the Daisies* (1957).

16. How sickness enlarges the dimensions of a man's self to himself! he is his own exclusive object. Supreme selfishness is inculcated upon him as his only duty. CHARLES LAMB, "The Convalescent," *Last Essays of Elia* (1833).

17. How convalescence shrinks a man back to his pristine stature! where is now the space, which he occupied so lately, in his own, in the family's eye? CHARLES LAMB, "The Convalescent," *Last Essays of Elia* (1833).

18. Disease makes men more physical, it leaves them nothing but body. THOMAS MANN, *The Magic Mountain* (1924), 4.10, tr. H. T. Lowe-Porter.

19. Let us a little permit Nature to take her own way; she better understands her own affairs than we. MONTAIGNE, "Of experience," *Essays* (1580–88), tr. Charles Cotton and W. C. Hazlitt.

20. A cough is something that you yourself can't help, but everybody else does on purpose just to torment you. OGDEN NASH, "Can I Get You a Glass of Water? Or Please Close the Glottis After You," *You Can't Get There from Here* (1957).

21. The sick woman especially: no one surpasses her in refinements for ruling, oppressing, tyrannising. NIETZSCHE, *The Genealogy of Morals* (1887), 3.14, tr. Horace B. Samuel.

22. When a man is ill his very goodness is sickly. NIETZSCHE, *The Will to Power* (1888), tr. Anthony M. Ludovici.

23. Show him death, and he'll be content with fever. PERSIAN PROVERB.

24. The diseases which destroy a man are no less natural than the instincts which preserve him. GEORGE SANTAYANA, *Dialogues in Limbo* (1925), 3.

25. There was never yet philosopher / That could endure the toothache patiently. SHAKESPEARE, *Much Ado About Nothing* (1598–99), 5.1.35.

26. I enjoy convalescence. It is the part that makes the illness worth while. GEORGE BERNARD SHAW, *Back to Methuselah* (1921), 2.

27. The sleep of a sick man has keen eyes. / It is a sleep unsleeping. SOPHOCLES, *Philoctetes* (409 B.C.), tr. David Grene.

28. An ailing woman lives forever. SPANISH PROVERB.

29. We are so fond of one another, because our ailments are the same. JONATHAN SWIFT, *Journal to Stella*, Feb. 1, 1711.

## 890. SIGHT

**See also 84. Blindness, Physical; 323. Eyes; 676. Perception; 875. Senses; 1027. Vision**

1. Our sight is the most perfect and most delightful of all our senses. It fills the mind

with the largest variety of ideas, converses with its objects at the greatest distance, and continues the longest in action without being tired or satiated with its proper enjoyments. JOSEPH ADDISON, *The Spectator* (1711–12), 411.

2. The hunger of the eye is not to be despised; and they are to be pitied who have starvation of the eye. HENRY WARD BEECHER, *Proverbs from Plymouth Pulpit* (1887).

3. The eye obeys exactly the action of the mind. EMERSON, "Behavior," *The Conduct of Life* (1860).

4. Eyes are more accurate witnesses than ears. HERACLITUS, *Fragments* (c. 500 B.C.), 12, tr. Philip Wheelwright.

5. True vision is always twofold. It involves emotional comprehension as well as physical perception. Yet how rarely we have either. We generally only glance at an object long enough to tag it with a name. ROSS PARMENTER, "The Pothook," *The Plant in My Window* (1949).

6. I am chained to the earth to pay for the freedom of my eyes. ANTONIO PORCHIA, *Voces* (1968), tr. W. S. Merwin.

7. Things seen are mightier than things heard. ALFRED, LORD TENNYSON, "Enoch Arden" (1864).

## SIGNS

See 304. Evidence; 709. Portent

## 891. SILENCE

See also 916. Speaking

1. Silences have a climax, when you have got to speak. ELIZABETH BOWEN, *The House in Paris* (1935), 2.5.

2. There is no such thing as an empty space or an empty time. There is always something to see, something to hear. In fact, try as we may to make a silence, we cannot. JOHN CAGE, "Experimental Music," *Silence* (1961).

3. Speech is of time, silence is of eternity. THOMAS CARLYLE, *Sartor Resartus* (1833–34), 3.3.

4. The words the happy say / Are paltry melody / But those the silent feel / Are beautiful—. EMILY DICKINSON, *Poems* (c. 1862–86).

5. Silence is all we dread. / There's Ransom in a Voice— / But Silence is Infinity. EMILY DICKINSON, poem (1873).

6. Nothing is often a good thing to say, and always a clever thing to say. WILL DURANT, *New York World-Telegram & Sun*, June 6, 1958.

7. Better say nothing than nothing to the purpose. ENGLISH PROVERB.

8. The stillest tongue can be the truest friend. EURIPIDES, *Iphigenia in Tauris* (c. 414–12 B.C.), tr. Witter Bynner.

9. Silence is wisdom, when speaking is folly. THOMAS FULLER, M.D., *Gnomologia* (1732), 4169.

10. 'Tis easier to know how to speak than how to be silent. THOMAS FULLER, M.D., *Gnomologia* (1732), 5075.

11. The silent dog is the first to bite. GERMAN PROVERB.

12. Elected Silence, sing to me / And beat upon my whorlèd ear, / Pipe me to pastures still and be / The music that I care to hear. GERARD MANLEY HOPKINS, "The Habit of Perfection" (c. 1866).

13. Silence is as full of potential wisdom and wit as the unhewn marble of great sculpture. ALDOUS HUXLEY, *Point Counter Point* (1928), 1.

14. Your highest female grace is silence. BEN JONSON, *Volpone* (1605), 3.4.

15. Three Silences there are: the first of speech, / The second of desire, the third of thought. LONGFELLOW, "The Three Silences of Molinos" (1877).

16. Silence is sorrow's best food. JAMES RUSSELL LOWELL, *A Fable for Critics* (1848).

17. Sticks and stones are hard on bones. / Aimed with angry art, / Words can sting like anything. / But silence breaks the heart. PHYLLIS MC GINLEY, "Ballade of Lost Objects," *The Love Letters of Phyllis McGinley* (1954).

18. Silence is the element in which great things fashion themselves together, that at length they may emerge, full-formed and majestic, into the daylight of Life, which they are henceforth to rule. MAURICE MAETERLINCK, "Silence," *The Treasure of the Humble* (1896), tr. Alfred Sutro.

19. Do not the most moving moments of our lives find us all without words? MARCEL MARCEAU, *Reader's Digest*, June 1958.

20. There is the silence of age, / Too full

of wisdom for the tongue to utter it / In words intelligible to those who have not lived / The great range of life. EDGAR LEE MASTERS, "Silence," *Songs and Satires* (1916).

21. We need a reason to speak, but none to keep silent. PIERRE NICOLE, *De la paix avec les hommes*, 2.1.

22. Do you wish people to believe good of you? Don't speak. PASCAL, *Pensées* (1670), 44, tr. W. F. Trotter.

23. Many a time the thing left silent makes for happiness. PINDAR, *Odes* (5th c. B.C.), Isthmia 1, tr. Richmond Lattimore.

24. A sage thing is timely silence, and better than any speech. PLUTARCH, "The Education of Children," *Moralia* (c. A.D. 100), tr. Moses Hadas.

25. Let a fool hold his tongue and he will pass for a sage. PUBLILIUS SYRUS, *Moral Sayings* (1st c. B.C.), 914, tr. Darius Lyman.

26. I have often regretted my speech, never my silence. PUBLILIUS SYRUS, *Moral Sayings* (1st c. B.C.), 1070, tr. Darius Lyman.

27. Intelligence is silence, truth being invisible. But what a racket I make in declaring this. NED ROREM, "Random Notes from a Diary," *Music from Inside Out* (1967).

28. An absolute silence leads to sadness: it is the image of death. ROUSSEAU, *Reveries of a Solitary Walker* (1782), 5.

29. What, O wise man, is the tongue in the mouth? It is a key to the casket of the intellectual treasurer; so long as the lid remains shut how can any person say whether he be a dealer in gems or in pedlery? SA'DI, introduction, *Gulistan* (1258), tr. James Ross.

30. In silence alone does a man's truth bind itself together and strike root. SAINT-EXUPÉRY, *The Wisdom of the Sands* (1948), 10, tr. Stuart Gilbert.

31. I do know of these / That therefore only are reputed wise / For saying nothing. SHAKESPEARE, *The Merchant of Venice* (1596–97), 1.1.95.

32. The silence often of pure innocence / Persuades when speaking fails. SHAKESPEARE, *The Winter's Tale* (1610–11), 2.2.41.

33. Silence will save me from being wrong (and foolish), but it will also deprive me of the possibility of being right. IGOR STRAVINSKY, "Contingencies," *Themes and Episodes* (1966).

34. In human intercourse the tragedy begins, not when there is misunderstanding about words, but when silence is not understood. THOREAU, "The Atlantides," *A Week on the Concord and Merrimack Rivers* (1849).

35. The right word may be effective, but no word was ever as effective as a rightly timed pause. MARK TWAIN, introduction, *Speeches* (1923), ed. A. B. Paine.

## 892. SIMPLICITY

**See also 476. Innocence; 695. Plain Living**

1. Simplicity is the most deceitful mistress that ever betrayed man. HENRY ADAMS, *The Education of Henry Adams* (1907), 30.

2. Less is more. ROBERT BROWNING, "Andrea Del Sarto," *Men and Women* (1855), 78. Maxim of Ludwig Mies van der Rohe.

3. To be simple is the best thing in the world; to be modest is the next best thing. I am not so sure about being quiet. G. K. CHESTERTON, "The Worship of the Wealthy," *All Things Considered* (1908).

4. It is proof of high culture to say the greatest matters in the simplest way. EMERSON, "Beauty," *The Conduct of Life* (1860).

5. The greatest truths are the simplest: and so are the greatest men. JULIUS CHARLES HARE and AUGUSTUS WILLIAM HARE, *Guesses at Truth* (1827).

6. There is / one art, / no more, / no less: / to do / all things / with art- / lessness. PIET HEIN, "Ars Brevis," *Grooks* (1966).

7. The ability to simplify means to eliminate the unnecessary so that the necessary may speak. HANS HOFMANN, *Search for the Real* (1967).

8. Give me a look, give me a face, / That makes simplicity a grace; / Robes loosely flowing, hair as free, / Such sweet neglect more taketh me / Than all the adulteries of art: / They strike mine eyes, but not my heart. BEN JONSON, *Epicene, or The Silent Woman* (1609), 1.1.

9. Teach us Delight in simple things, / And Mirth that has no bitter springs. RUDYARD KIPLING, "The Children's Song," *Puck of Pook's Hill* (1906).

10. Thou canst not adorn simplicity. What is naked or defective is susceptible of decoration: what is decorated is simplicity no longer. WALTER SAVAGE LANDOR, "Epic-

tetus and Seneca," *Imaginary Conversations* (1824–53).

11. Affected simplicity is an elegant imposture. LA ROCHEFOUCAULD, *Maxims* (1665), tr. Kenneth Pratt.

12. Perfect simplicity is unconsciously audacious. GEORGE MEREDITH, *The Ordeal of Richard Feverel* (1859), 1.

13. And all the loveliest things there be / Come simply, so, it seems to me. EDNA ST. VINCENT MILLAY, "The Goose-Girl," *The Harp-Weaver* (1923).

14. Simplicity of character is no hindrance to subtlety of intellect. JOHN MORLEY, *Life of Gladstone* (1903).

15. Beauty of style and harmony and grace and good rhythm depend on simplicity. PLATO, *The Republic* (4th c. B.C. ), 3, tr. Benjamin Jowett.

16. Simplicity is the mean between ostentation and rusticity. ALEXANDER POPE, preface to the *Iliad* (1715–20).

17. Simplicity, simplicity, simplicity! I say, let your affairs be as two or three, and not a hundred or a thousand; instead of a million count half a dozen, and keep your accounts on your thumb-nail. THOREAU, "Where I Lived, and What I Lived For," *Walden* (1854).

18. The art of art, the glory of expression and the sunshine of the light of letters, is simplicity. WALT WHITMAN, preface to *Leaves of Grass* (1855–92).

## 893. SIN

**See also 305. Evil; 446. Illegality; 793. Repentance; 835. Salvation; 964. Temptation; 1048. Wickedness; 1063. Wrongdoing**

1. Be sure your sin will find you out. *Bible*, Numbers 32:23.

2. Earth reserves no blessing / For the unblessed of Heaven! EMILY BRONTË, "A.E." (1845).

3. Pleasure's a sin, and sometimes Sin's a pleasure. BYRON, *Don Juan* (1819–24), 1.133.

4. Without the spice of guilt, sin cannot be fully savored. ALEXANDER CHASE, *Perspectives* (1966).

5. Sin in this country [America] has been always said to be rather calculating than impulsive. FRANK MOORE COLBY, "The Two Alleged Generations," *The Colby Essays* (1926), v. 1.

6. Between these two, the denying of sins, which we have done, and the bragging of sins, which we have not done, what a space, what a compass is there, for millions of millions of sins! JOHN DONNE, *Sermons*, No. 2, 1618.

7. In best understandings, sin began, / Angels sinned first, then Devils, and then Man. JOHN DONNE, "To Sir Henry Wotton," *Letters to Several Personages* (1651).

8. It's harder to confess the sin that no one believes in / Than the crime that everyone can appreciate. / For the crime is in relation to the law / And the sin is in relation to the sinner. T. S. ELIOT, *The Elder Statesman* (1958), 3.

9. Oh, Lord, it is not the sins I have committed that I regret, but those which I have had no opportunity to commit. GHALIB, *Prayer* (c. 1800).

10. We do ourselves wrong, and too meanly estimate the holiness above us, when we deem that any act or enjoyment good in itself, is not good to do religiously. NATHANIEL HAWTHORNE, *The Marble Faun* (1860).

11. We are punished by our sins, not for them. ELBERT HUBBARD, *The Note Book* (1927).

12. Really to sin you have to be serious about it. HENRIK IBSEN, *Peer Gynt* (1867), 5.

13. The mind sins, not the body; if there is no intention, there is no blame. LIVY, *Ab Urbe Condita* (c. 29 B.C.), 1.58.

14. People are no longer sinful, they are only immature or underprivileged or frightened or, more particularly, sick. PHYLLIS MC GINLEY, "In Defense of Sin," *The Province of the Heart* (1959).

15. A man does not sin by commission only, but often by omission. MARCUS AURELIUS, *Meditations* (2nd c.), 9.5, tr. Maxwell Staniforth.

16. Sin is a dangerous toy in the hands of the virtuous. It should be left to the congenitally sinful, who know when to play with it and when to let it alone. H. L. MENCKEN, "A Good Man Gone Wrong," *The American Mercury*, February 1929.

17. The public scandal is what constitutes the offence: sins sinned in secret are no sins at all. MOLIÈRE, *Tartuffe* (1664), 4, tr. John Wood.

18. The only people who should really sin / Are the people who can sin with a grin. OGDEN NASH, "Inter-Office Memorandum," *I'm a Stranger Here Myself* (1938).

19. How many are there who do not sin from lack of desire or lack of occasion? JOSEPH ROUX, *Meditations of a Parish Priest* (1886), 4.83, tr. Isabel F. Hapgood.

20. The twin conceptions of sin and vindictive punishment seem to be at the root of much that is most vigorous, both in religion and politics. BERTRAND RUSSELL, "Ideas That Have Harmed Mankind," *Unpopular Essays* (1950).

21. Sin recognised—but that—may keep us humble, / But oh, it keeps us nasty. STEVIE SMITH, "Recognition Not Enough," *Selected Poems* (1964).

22. Sins cannot be undone, only forgiven. IGOR STRAVINSKY, *Conversations with Igor Stravinsky* (1959).

23. We cannot well do without our sins; they are the highway of our virtue. THOREAU, *Journal*, March 22, 1842.

24. There is a charm about the forbidden that makes it unspeakably desirable. MARK TWAIN, *Notebook* (1935).

25. Sin travels faster than they that ride in chariots. CHARLES DUDLEY WARNER, "Fifteenth Week," *My Summer in a Garden* (1871).

## 894. SINCERITY

See also 360. Frankness; 423. Honesty; 438. Hypocrisy; 482. Insincerity; 489. Integrity; 993. Truthfulness

1. No one means all he says, and yet very few say all they mean. HENRY ADAMS, *The Education of Henry Adams* (1907), 31.

2. Men are always sincere. They change sincerities, that's all. TRISTAN BERNARD, *Ce que l'on dit aux femmes* (1923).

3. The spontaneity of slaps is sincerity, whereas the ceremonial of caresses is largely convention. UGO BETTI, *The Gambler* (1950), 2.3, ed. Gino Rizzo.

4. I should say sincerity, a deep, great, genuine sincerity, is the first characteristic of all men in any way heroic. THOMAS CARLYLE, *On Heroes, Hero-Worship and the Heroic in History* (1841), 2.

5. Sincerity is not a spontaneous flower, nor is modesty either. COLETTE, "La Chevalière," *Earthly Paradise* (1966), 5, ed. Robert Phelps.

6. Sincerity is the highest compliment you can pay. EMERSON, *Journals*, 1836.

7. A friend is a person with whom I may be sincere. Before him I may think aloud. EMERSON, "Friendship," *Essays: First Series* (1841).

8. Nature forever puts a premium on reality. What is done for effect is seen to be done for effect; what is done for love is felt to be done for love. A man inspires affection and honor because he was not lying in wait for these. EMERSON, "Behavior," *The Conduct of Life* (1860).

9. Be as you would seem to be. THOMAS FULLER, M.D., *Gnomologia* (1732), 849.

10. What is uttered from the heart alone / Will win the hearts of others to your own. GOETHE, "Night," *Faust: Part I* (1808), tr. Philip Wayne.

11. Civility is not a sign of weakness, and sincerity is always subject to proof. JOHN F. KENNEDY, Inaugural Address, Jan. 20, 1961.

12. Sincerity is an opening of the heart; we find it in very few persons; and that which we see ordinarily is only a cunning deceit to attract the confidence of others. LA ROCHEFOUCAULD, *Maxims* (1665), tr. Kenneth Pratt.

13. Weak people cannot be sincere. LA ROCHEFOUCAULD, *Maxims* (1665), tr. Kenneth Pratt.

14. It's never what you say, but how / You make it sound sincere. MARYA MANNES, "Controverse," *But Will It Sell?* (1955–64).

15. having something / to say is the thing being sincere / counts for more than forms of expression. DON MARQUIS, "the stuff of literature," *Archy's Life of Mehitabel* (1933).

16. Never has there been one possessed of complete sincerity who did not move others. Never has there been one who had not sincerity who was able to move others. MENCIUS, *Works* (4th–3rd c. B.C.), 4, tr. Charles A. Wong.

17. A man must not always tell all, for that were folly: but what a man says should be what he thinks. MONTAIGNE, "Of presumption," *Essays* (1580–88), tr. Charles Cotton and W. C. Hazlitt.

18. We are in the presence of the contradiction of a style of living which cultivates sincerity and is at the same time a fraud.

There is truth only in an existence which feels its acts as irrevocably necessary. JOSÉ ORTEGA Y GASSET, *The Revolt of the Masses* (1930), 14.

19. The primary condition for being sincere is the same as for being humble: not to boast of it, and probably not even to be aware of it. HENRI PEYRE, *Literature and Sincerity* (1963).

20. The way I see it, it doesn't matter what you believe just so you're sincere. CHARLES M. SCHULZ, *Go Fly a Kite, Charlie Brown* (1963).

21. Suit the action to the word, the word to the action. SHAKESPEARE, *Hamlet* (1600), 3.2.19.

22. I only desire sincere relations with the worthiest of my acquaintance, that they may give me an opportunity once in a year to speak the truth. THOREAU, *Journal*, Aug. 24, 1851.

23. A little sincerity is a dangerous thing, and a great deal of it is absolutely fatal. OSCAR WILDE, *The Critic as Artist* (1891), 2.

## 895. SINGING

**See also 607. Music; 648. Opera**

1. If a thing isn't worth saying, you sing it. BEAUMARCHAIS, *The Barber of Seville* (1775), 1, tr. Albert Bermel.

2. It is the best of all trades, to make songs, and the second best to sing them. HILAIRE BELLOC, "On Song," *On Everything* (1909).

3. There is a fault common to all singers. When they're among friends and are asked to sing they don't want to, and when they're not asked to sing they never stop. HORACE, *Satires* (35–30 B.C.), 1.3.

4. There is delight in singing, tho' none hear / Beside the singer. WALTER SAVAGE LANDOR, "To Robert Browning" (1846).

## 896. SINGLE-MINDEDNESS

**See also 613. Narrowness**

1. While the work or play is on, it is a lot of fun if while you are doing one you don't constantly feel that you ought to be doing the other. FRANKLIN P. ADAMS, *Nods and Becks* (1944).

2. One should always think of what one is about; when one is learning, one should not think of play; and when one is at play, one should not think of one's learning. LORD CHESTERFIELD, *Letters to His Son*, July 24, 1739.

3. A straight path never leads anywhere except to the objective. ANDRÉ GIDE, *Journals*, 1922, tr. Justin O'Brien.

4. It is in self-limitation that a master first shows himself. GOETHE, *Natur und Kunst*.

5. As any action or posture, long continued, will distort and disfigure the limbs, so the mind likewise is crippled and contracted by perpetual application to the same set of ideas. SAMUEL JOHNSON, *The Rambler* (1750–52), 173.

6. When you are at sea, keep clear of the land. PUBLILIUS SYRUS, *Moral Sayings* (1st c. B.C.), 480, tr. Darius Lyman.

7. The field of consciousness is tiny. It accepts only one problem at a time. Get into a fist fight, put your mind on the strategy of the fight, and you will not feel the other fellow's punches. SAINT-EXUPÉRY, *Flight to Arras* (1942), 7, tr. Lewis Galantière.

8. There's some end at last for the man who follows a path: mere rambling is interminable. SENECA, *Letters to Lucilius* (1st c.), 16.9, tr. E. Phillips Barker.

## 897. SKEPTICISM

**See also 263. Doubt, Religious; 997. Unbelief**

1. Doubt is not below knowledge, but above it. ALAIN, *Libres-propos* (1908–14).

2. The crying need of today is—to detach ourselves. And all you require is a sense of elegance: to regard the general situation with a modicum of scepticism. UGO BETTI, *The Fugitive* (1953), 1, tr. G. H. McWilliam.

3. Doubt is the vestibule which all must pass, before they can enter into the temple of truth. CHARLES CALEB COLTON, *Lacon* (1825), 1.251.

4. What has not been examined impartially has not been well examined. Skepticism is therefore the first step toward truth. DENIS DIDEROT, *Pensées philosophiques* (1746), 31.

5. Doubt is an element of criticism, and the tendency of criticism is necessarily skeptical. BENJAMIN DISRAELI, "Church Policy," Nov. 25, 1864.

6. Man's most valuable trait / is a judicious sense of what not to believe. EURIPIDES, *Helen* (412 B.C.), tr. Richmond Lattimore.

7. Superstition renders a man a fool, and skepticism makes him mad. THOMAS FULLER, M.D., *Gnomologia* (1732), 4287.

8. A wise skepticism is the first attribute of a good critic. JAMES RUSSELL LOWELL, "Shakespeare Once More," *Among My Books* (1870).

9. Let the greatest part of the news thou hearest be the least part of what thou believest, lest the greater part of what thou believest be the least part of what is true. FRANCIS QUARLES, *Enchiridion* (1640), 2.50.

10. When all beliefs are challenged together, the just and necessary ones have a chance to step forward and to re-establish themselves alone. GEORGE SANTAYANA, *The Life of Reason: Reason in Science* (1905–06), 11.

11. Modest doubt is called / The beacon of the wise, the tent that searches / To th' bottom of the worst. SHAKESPEARE, *Troilus and Cressida* (1601–02), 2.2.15.

12. The skeptic does not mean him who doubts, but him who investigates or researches, as opposed to him who asserts and thinks that he has found. MIGUEL DE UNAMUNO, "My Religion," *Essays and Soliloquies* (1924), tr. J. E. Crawford Flitch.

## SKILL

See 1. Ability

## 898. SLANDER

See also 5. Accusation; 392. Gossip; 798. Reputation; 840. Scandal

1. There is nothing that more betrays a base ungenerous spirit than the giving of secret stabs to a man's reputation. Lampoons and satires, that are written with wit and spirit, are like poisoned darts, which not only inflict a wound, but make it incurable. JOSEPH ADDISON, *The Spectator* (1711–12), 23.

2. He that flings dirt at another dirtieth himself most. THOMAS FULLER, M.D., *Gnomologia* (1732), 2107.

3. There is no sufficient recompense for an unjust slander. THOMAS FULLER, M.D., *Gnomologia* (1732), 4923.

4. Every one in a crowd has the power to throw dirt: nine out of ten have the inclination. WILLIAM HAZLITT, "On Reading New Books," *Sketches and Essays* (1839).

5. Into the space of one little hour sins enough may be conjured up by evil tongues to blast the fame of a whole life of virtue. WASHINGTON IRVING, "The Widow's Ordeal," *Wolfert's Roost* (1855).

6. If a man could say nothing against a character but what he can prove, history could not be written. SAMUEL JOHNSON, quoted in Boswell's *Life of Samuel Johnson*, April 3, 1776.

7. Calumnies are answered best with silence. BEN JONSON, *Volpone* (1605), 2.2.

8. People are more slanderous from vanity than from malice. LA ROCHEFOUCAULD, *Maxims* (1665), tr. Kenneth Pratt.

9. Folk whose own behaviour is most ridiculous are always to the fore in slandering others. MOLIÈRE, *Tartuffe* (1664), 1, tr. John Wood.

10. There are different ways of assassinating a man—by pistol, sword, poison, or moral assassination. They are the same in their results except that the last is more cruel. NAPOLEON I, *Maxims* (1804–15).

11. Calumny ever pursues the great, even as the winds hurl themselves on high places. OVID, *Love's Cure* (c. A.D. 8), tr. J. Lewis May.

12. Whole surfaces are carried away even from a mountain when undermined by a gentle flow of water; how much more the soft hearts of men by clever persons who attack them with slander! *Panchatantra* (c. 5th c.), 1, tr. Franklin Edgerton.

13. What is slander? A verdict of "guilty" pronounced in the absence of the accused, with closed doors, without defence or appeal, by an interested and prejudiced judge. JOSEPH ROUX, *Meditations of a Parish Priest* (1886), 4.67, tr. Isabel F. Hapgood.

14. Slander, like coal, will either dirty your hand or burn it. RUSSIAN PROVERB.

15. Slander lives upon succession, / For ever housed where it gets possession. SHAKESPEARE, *The Comedy of Errors* (1592–93), 3.1.105.

16. Be thou as chaste as ice, as pure as snow, thou shalt not escape calumny. SHAKESPEARE, *Hamlet* (1600), 3.1.140.

17. Slander, / Whose edge is sharper than the sword, whose tongue /Outvenoms all the worms of Nile, whose breath / Rides on the posting winds and doth belie / All corners of the world. SHAKESPEARE, *Cymbeline* (1609–10), 3.4.35.

18. Strike at a great man, and you will not miss. SOPHOCLES, *Ajax* (c. 447 B.C.), tr. John Moore.

19. It takes your enemy and your friend, working together, to hurt you to the heart; the one to slander you and the other to get the news to you. MARK TWAIN, "Pudd'nhead Wilson's New Calendar," *Following the Equator* (1897), 2.9.

SLANG
See 521. Language

SLAVERY
See 882. Servitude

## 899. SLEEP

See also 71. Bed; 264. Dreams; 599. Morning; 626. Night

1. Care-charming Sleep, thou easer of all woes, / Brother to Death. BEAUMONT and FLETCHER, *Valentinian* (1647), 5.2.

2. You know, sleep and confidence are almost the same thing; they both come together. UGO BETTI, *Struggle Till Dawn* (1949), 3, tr. G. H. McWilliam.

3. The sleep of a labouring man is sweet, whether he eat little or much: but the abundance of the rich will not suffer him to sleep. *Bible*, Ecclesiastes 5:12.

4. Sleep hath its own world, / And a wide realm of wild reality, / And dreams in their development have breath, / And tears, and tortures, and the touch of Joy. BYRON, "The Dream" (1816), 1.

5. Now blessings light on him that first invented this same sleep. It covers a man all over, thoughts and all, like a cloak. CERVANTES, *Don Quixote* (1605–15), 2.4.68, tr. Peter Motteux and John Ozell.

6. Oh sleep! it is a gentle thing, / Beloved from pole to pole! SAMUEL TAYLOR COLERIDGE, *The Rime of the Ancient Mariner* (1798), 5.1.

7. Sleep is pain's easiest salve, and doth fulfill / All offices of death, except to kill. JOHN DONNE, "The Storm: to Mr. Christopher Brooke," *Letters to Several Personages* (1651).

8. The pillow is a silent Sibyl, and it is better to sleep on things beforehand than lie awake about them afterwards. BALTASAR GRACIÁN, *The Art of Worldly Wisdom* (1647), 151, tr. Joseph Jacobs.

9. Even sleepers are workers and collaborators in what goes on in the universe. HERACLITUS, *Fragments* (c. 500 B.C.), 124, tr. Philip Wheelwright.

10. Even where sleep is concerned, too much is a bad thing. HOMER, *Odyssey* (9th c. B.C.), 15, tr. E. V. Rieu.

11. That we are not much sicker and much madder than we are is due exclusively to that most blessed and blessing of all natural graces, sleep. ALDOUS HUXLEY, "Variations on a Philosopher," *Themes and Variations* (1950).

12. You can't sleep until noon with the proper élan unless you have some legitimate reason for staying up until three (parties don't count). JEAN KERR, introduction, *Please Don't Eat the Daisies* (1957).

13. For sleep, one needs endless depths of blackness to sink into; daylight is too shallow, it will not cover one. ANNE MORROW LINDBERGH, "Dark," *North to the Orient* (1935).

14. Cut if you will, with Sleep's dull knife, / Each day to half its length, my friend,— / The years that Time takes off *my* life, / He'll take off the other end! EDNA ST. VINCENT MILLAY, "Midnight Oil," *A Few Figs from Thistles* (1920).

15. Sleeping is no mean art: for its sake one must stay awake all day. NIETZSCHE, "On the Teachers of Virtue," *Thus Spoke Zarathustra* (1883–92), 1, tr. Walter Kaufmann.

16. He sleeps well who knows not that he sleeps ill. PUBLILIUS SYRUS, *Moral Sayings* (1st c. B.C.), 77, tr. Darius Lyman.

17. Sleep does make us all equal, it seems to me, like his big brother—Death. ARTHUR SCHNITZLER, *La Ronde* (1900), 10.

18. Sleep that knits up the ravelled sleave of care, / The death of each day's life, sore labour's bath, / Balm of hurt minds, great nature's second course, / Chief nourisher in life's feast. SHAKESPEARE, *Macbeth* (1605–06), 2.2.37.

19. Weariness / Can snore upon the flint when resty sloth / Finds the down pillow hard. SHAKESPEARE, *Cymbeline* (1609–10), 3.6.33.

20. There ain't no way to find out why a snorer can't hear himself snore. MARK TWAIN, *Tom Sawyer Abroad* (1894), 10.

21. In Sleep we lie all naked and alone, in Sleep we are united at the heart of night and darkness, and we are strange and beautiful asleep; for we are dying in the darkness, and we know no death. THOMAS WOLFE, "Death the Proud Brother," *From Death to Morning* (1935).

## 900. SLOWNESS

See also 228. Delay; 409. Haste; 919. Speed

1. Slowness of movement in a quick-thinking person makes you feel some complication of thought or feeling behind anything that is done. ELIZABETH BOWEN, *The House in Paris* (1935), 2.5.

2. If you go slowly, / Time will walk behind you / Like a submissive ox. JUAN RAMÓN JIMÉNEZ, "To Miss Rápida," *Selected Writings* (1957), tr. H. R. Hays.

3. There is a slowness in affairs which ripens them, and a slowness which rots them. JOSEPH ROUX, *Meditations of a Parish Priest* (1886), 4.93, tr. Isabel F. Hapgood.

## SLYNESS

See 197. Craftiness

## 901. SMALLNESS

See also 398. Great and Small; 522. Largeness; 641. Obscurity; 686. Pettiness; 989. Trifles; 1005. Unimportance

1. Many a smale maketh a grate. CHAUCER, "The Parson's Tale," *The Canterbury Tales* (1387–1400), 361, ed. Thomas Tyrwhitt.

2. A big man knows he don't have to fight, but whin a man is little an' knows he's little an' is thinkin' all th' time he's little an' feels that ivrybody else is thinkin' he's little, look out f'r him. FINLEY PETER DUNNE, "The Japanese Scare," *Mr. Dooley Says* (1910).

3. In the ant's house the dew is a flood. PERSIAN PROVERB.

## SMELLING

See 875. Senses

## SMILING

See 523. Laughter

## SMOKING

See 975. Tobacco

## 902. SMUGNESS

See also 155. Complacency

1. Of all the horrid, hideous notes of woe, / Sadder than owl-songs or the midnight blast, / Is that portentous phrase, "I told you so," / Uttered by friends, those prophets of the *past.* BYRON, *Don Juan* (1819–24), 14.50.

2. People who have what they want are very fond of telling people / who haven't what they want that they really don't want it. OGDEN NASH, "The Terrible People," *Verses from 1929 On* (1959).

## 903. SNOBBERY

See also 133. Class; 719. Preference; 727. Pride; 773. Rank; 907. Society, Polite

1. Men hate the haughty of heart who will not be / the friend of every man. EURIPIDES, *Hippolytus* (428 B.C.), tr. David Grene.

2. We must exclude someone from our gathering, or we shall be left with nothing. E. M. FORSTER, *A Passage to India* (1924), 1.4.

3. Levellers wish to level *down* as far as themselves; but they cannot bear levelling *up* to themselves. SAMUEL JOHNSON, quoted in Boswell's *Life of Samuel Johnson*, July 21, 1763.

4. All the people like us are We, / And every one else is They. RUDYARD KIPLING, "We and They" (1926).

5. The true snob never rests; there is always a higher goal to attain, and there are, by the same token, always more and more people to look down upon. RUSSELL LYNES, "The New Snobbism," *Harper's Magazine*, November 1950.

6. In men this blunder still you find,— /

All think their little set mankind. HANNAH MORE, *Florio* (1786), 1.

7. The worst cliques are those which consist of one man. GEORGE BERNARD SHAW, *Back to Methuselah* (1921), 5.

8. Snobbery, being an aspiring failing, is sometimes the prophecy of better things. CHARLES DUDLEY WARNER, "Second Study," *Backlog Studies* (1873).

## 904. SNOW
See also 848. Seasons

1. A snowdrift is a beautiful thing—if it doesn't lie across the path you have to shovel or block the road that leads to your destination. HAL BORLAND, "Snowdrifts—January 26," *Sundial of the Seasons* (1964).

2. The snow itself is lonely or, if you prefer, self-sufficient. There is no other time when the whole world seems composed of one thing and one thing only. JOSEPH WOOD KRUTCH, "December," *The Twelve Seasons* (1949).

3. Snow is all right while it is snowing; / It is like inebriation because it is very pleasing when it is coming, but very unpleasing when it is going. OGDEN NASH, "Jangle Bells," *I'm a Stranger Here Myself* (1938).

4. Snow is what you are up to your neck in when people / send you post cards from Florida saying they wish / you were there. OGDEN NASH, "Jangle Bells," *I'm a Stranger Here Myself* (1938).

## 905. SOCIALISM
See also 149. Communism; 393. Government

1. Socialism without liberty is the barracks. Graffito written during French student revolt, May 1968.

2. There is the fundamental paradox of the welfare state: that it is not built for the desperate, but for those who are already capable of helping themselves. MICHAEL HARRINGTON, *The Other America* (1962), 9.1.

3. The fact is that life has become a sweepstake. Millions of people who have lost the sense of being able to make anything of the collective effort of shaping their economic society, now expect fortune to descend like pie from the sky. MAX LERNER, "I'm Dreaming of a Bright Sweepstake," *Actions and Passions* (1949).

4. What the collectivist age wants, allows, and approves is the perpetual holiday from the self. THOMAS MANN, "Europe, Beware," *The Thomas Mann Reader* (1950), tr. H. T. Lowe-Porter.

5. Socialism must come down from the brain and reach the heart. JULES RENARD, *Journal*, August 1905, ed. and tr. Louise Bogan and Elizabeth Roget.

## SOCIAL WORK
See 430. Humanitarianism

## 906. SOCIETY
See also 36. Anarchy; 52. Aristocracy; 131. Civilization; 133. Class; 393. Government; 485. Institutions; 581. Middle Class; 675. The People; 923. State

1. Society is immoral and immortal; it can afford to commit any kind of folly, and indulge in any sort of vice; it cannot be killed, and the fragments that survive can always laugh at the dead. HENRY ADAMS, *The Education of Henry Adams* (1907), 18.

2. No scheme for a change of society can be made to appear immediately palatable, except by falsehood, until society has become so desperate that it will accept any change. T. S. ELIOT, "The Idea of a Christian Society" (1939).

3. Society acquires new arts and loses old instincts. EMERSON, "Self-Reliance," *Essays: First Series* (1841).

4. The power that keeps cities of men together / Is noble preservation of law. EURIPIDES, *The Suppliant Women* (c. 421 B.C.), tr. Frank W. Jones.

5. Human life in common is only made possible when a majority comes together which is stronger than any separate individual and which remains united against all separate individuals. SIGMUND FREUD, *Civilization and Its Discontents* (1930), 3, tr. James Strachey.

6. In the mouth of Society are many diseased teeth, decayed to the bones of the jaws. But Society makes no effort to have them extracted and be rid of the affliction.

It contents itself with gold fillings. KAHLIL GIBRAN, "Decayed Teeth," *Thoughts and Meditations* (1960), tr. Anthony R. Ferris.

7. One cannot raise the bottom of a society without benefiting everyone above. MICHAEL HARRINGTON, *The Other America* (1962), 9.1.

8. Society is always trying in some way or other to grind us down to a single flat surface. OLIVER WENDELL HOLMES, SR., *The Professor at the Breakfast Table* (1860), 2.

9. The great society is a place where men are more concerned with the quality of their goals than the quantity of their goods. LYNDON B. JOHNSON, speech, University of Michigan, May 22, 1964.

10. In civilized society we all depend upon each other, and our happiness is very much owing to the good opinion of mankind. SAMUEL JOHNSON, quoted in Boswell's *Life of Samuel Johnson*, July 20, 1763.

11. The principles of the good society call for a concern with an order of being—which cannot be proved existentially to the sense organs—where it matters supremely that the human person is inviolable, that reason shall regulate the will, that truth shall prevail over error. WALTER LIPPMANN, *The Public Philosophy* (1955), 11.4.

12. In civilized communities men's idiosyncrasies are mitigated by the necessity of conforming to certain rules of behaviour. Culture is a mask that hides their faces. W. SOMERSET MAUGHAM, *The Summing Up* (1938), 53.

13. Necessity reconciles and brings men together; and this accidental connection afterward forms itself into laws. MONTAIGNE, "Of vanity," *Essays* (1580–88), tr. Charles Cotton and W. C. Hazlitt.

14. A decrepit society shuns humor as a decrepit individual shuns drafts. MALCOLM MUGGERIDGE, "Tread Softly for You Tread on My Jokes," *The Most of Malcolm Muggeridge* (1966).

15. Man did not enter into society to become worse than he was before, nor to have fewer rights than he had before, but to have those rights better secured. THOMAS PAINE, *The Rights of Man* (1791), 1.

16. Every society to which you remain bound robs you of a part of your essence, and replaces it with a speck of the gigantic personality which is its own. JOSÉ RODÓ, *Motivos de Proteo* (1941).

17. What man loses by the social contract is his natural liberty and an unlimited right to everything he tries to get and succeeds in getting; what he gains is civil liberty and the proprietorship of all he possesses. ROUSSEAU, *The Social Contract* (1762), 1.8, tr. G. D. H. Cole.

18. Society itself is an accident to the spirit, and if society in any of its forms is to be justified morally it must be justified at the bar of the individual conscience. GEORGE SANTAYANA, *Dialogues in Limbo* (1925), 6.

19. Society is a kind of parent to its members. If it, and they, are to thrive, its values must be clear, coherent and generally acceptable. MILTON R. SAPIRSTEIN, *Paradoxes of Everyday Life* (1955), 8.

20. Nature holds no brief for the human experiment: it must stand or fall by its results. GEORGE BERNARD SHAW, preface to *Back to Methuselah* (1921).

21. Cursed be the social lies that warp us from the living truth. ALFRED, LORD TENNYSON, "Locksley Hall" (1842).

22. Every social system is more or less against nature, and at every moment nature is at work to reclaim her rights. PAUL VALÉRY, "The Idea of Dictatorship," *Reflections on the World Today* (1931), tr. Francis Scarfe.

23. We live in society; there is therefore nothing truly good for us that which does good to society. VOLTAIRE, "Virtue," *Philosophical Dictionary* (1764).

24. A great society is a society in which its men of business think greatly of their functions. ALFRED NORTH WHITEHEAD, *Adventures in Ideas* (1933), 6.

25. The chaos of our society is the product of the dishevelment of our ideas. PHILIP WYLIE, *Generation of Vipers* (1942), 6.

## 907. SOCIETY, POLITE

See also 151. Company; 599. Manners; 665. Parties; 903. Snobbery

1. The secret of success in society is a certain heartiness and sympathy. EMERSON, "Manners," *Essays: Second Series* (1844).

2. Society is a masked ball, where every

one hides his real character, and reveals it in hiding. EMERSON, "Worship," *The Conduct of Life* (1860).

3. If all your clothes are worn to the same state, it means you go out too much. F. SCOTT FITZGERALD, "Note-Books," *The Crack-Up* (1945).

4. Society is a more level surface than we imagine. Wise men or absolute fools are hard to be met with, as there are few giants or dwarfs. WILLIAM HAZLITT, *Characteristics* (1823), 52.

5. There are people whom one should like very well to drop, but would not wish to be dropped by. SAMUEL JOHNSON, quoted in Boswell's *Life of Samuel Johnson*, March 26, 1781.

6. Men would not live in society long if they were not each other's dupes. LA ROCHEFOUCAULD, *Maxims* (1665).

7. A commercial society whose members are essentially ascetic and indifferent in social ritual has to be provided with blueprints and specifications for evoking the right tone for every occasion. MARSHALL MC LUHAN, "Emily Post," *The Mechanical Bride* (1951).

8. Human society is founded on mutual deceit; few friendships would endure if each knew what his friend said of him in his absence. PASCAL, *Pensées* (1670), 100, tr. W. F. Trotter.

9. Teas, / Where small talk dies in agonies. SHELLEY, "Peter Bell the Third" (1819), 3.12.

10. There is a toad in every social dish, however well they cook it. LOGAN PEARSALL SMITH, *Afterthoughts* (1931), 6.

11. The path of social advancement is, and must be, strewn with broken friendships. H. G. WELLS, *Kipps* (1905), 2.5.

12. To get into the best society nowadays, one has either to feed people, amuse people, or shock people. OSCAR WILDE, *A Woman of No Importance* (1893), 3.

13. To be in it [society] is merely a bore. But to be out of it simply a tragedy. OSCAR WILDE, *A Woman of No Importance* (1893), 3.

14. You are ushered in according to your dress; shown out according to your brains. *Yiddish Proverbs* (1949), ed. Hannan J. Ayalti.

## SOLACE

See 177. Consolations; 953. Sympathy

## SOLDIERS

See 582. The Military

## SOLEMNITY

See 879. Seriousness

## 908. SOLITUDE

See also 30. Alienation; 31. Aloofness; 544. Loneliness; 730. Privacy

1. The earth is a beehive; we all enter by the same door but live in different cells. AFRICAN PROVERB.

2. He who is unable to live in society, or who has no need because he is sufficient for himself, must be either a beast or a god. ARISTOTLE, *Politics* (4th c. B.C.), 1.2, tr. Benjamin Jowett.

3. Yes! in the sea of life enisled, / With echoing straits between us thrown, / Dotting the shoreless watery wild, / We mortal millions live *alone*. MATTHEW ARNOLD, "Switzerland," 5, *Empedocles on Etna, and Other Poems* (1852).

4. Little do men perceive what solitude is, and how far it extendeth. For a crowd is not company, and faces are but a gallery of pictures, and talk but a tinkling cymbal, where there is no love. FRANCIS BACON, "Of Friendship," *Essays* (1625).

5. Those that want [lack] friends to open themselves unto are cannibals of their own hearts. FRANCIS BACON, "Of Friendship," *Essays* (1625).

6. He never is alone that is accompanied with noble thoughts. BEAUMONT and FLETCHER, *Love's Cure* (1647), 3.3.

7. Perhaps even one's feelings get tired, when one is alone with oneself. UGO BETTI, *Goat Island* (1946), 1.4, ed. Gino Rizzo.

8. The person who tries to live alone will not succeed as a human being. His heart withers if it does not answer another heart. His mind shrinks away if he hears only the echoes of his own thoughts and finds no other inspiration. PEARL S. BUCK, "To You on Your First Birthday," *To My Daughters, With Love* (1967).

9. To fly from, need not be to hate, mankind: / All are not fit with them to stir and toil, / Nor is it discontent to keep the mind / Deep in its fountain. BYRON, *Childe Harold's Pilgrimage* (1812–18), 3.69.

10. If from society we learn to live, / 'Tis Solitude should teach us how to die; / It hath no flatterers. BYRON, *Childe Harold's Pilgrimage* (1812–18), 4.33.

11. Solitary trees, if they grow at all, grow strong. SIR WINSTON CHURCHILL, quoted in Randolph S. Churchill's *Winston S. Churchill* (1966), v. 1.

12. In spite of the large population of this planet men and women remain today the most inaccessible things on it. FRANK MOORE COLBY, untitled essay, *The Colby Essays* (1926), v. 2.

13. There are days when solitude is a heady wine that intoxicates you with freedom, others when it is a bitter tonic, and still others when it is a poison that makes you beat your head against the wall. COLETTE, "Freedom," *Earthly Paradise* (1966), 2, ed. Robert Phelps.

14. To dare to live alone is the rarest courage; since there are many who had rather meet their bitterest enemy in the field, than their own hearts in their closet. CHARLES CALEB COLTON, *Lacon* (1825), 1.445.

15. We never touch but at points. EMERSON, *Journals*, 1836.

16. Isolation must precede true society. EMERSON, "Self-Reliance," *Essays: First Series* (1841).

17. When you have shut your doors and darkened your room, remember, never to say that you are alone; for you are not alone, but God is within, and your genius is within. EPICTETUS, *Discourses* (2nd c.), 1.14, tr. Thomas W. Higginson.

18. Better be alone than in bad company. THOMAS FULLER, M.D., *Gnomologia* (1732), 872.

19. Solitude is bearable only with God. ANDRÉ GIDE, *Journals*, Sept. 1, 1942, tr. Justin O'Brien.

20. To every man it is decreed: Thou shalt live alone. Happy they who imagine that they have escaped the common lot; happy, whilst they imagine it. GEORGE GISSING, "Spring," *The Private Papers of Henry Ryecroft* (1903).

21. He that can live alone resembles the brute beast in nothing, the sage in much, and God in everything. BALTASAR GRACIÁN, *The Art of Worldly Wisdom* (1647), 137, tr. Joseph Jacobs.

22. We are all of us calling and calling across the incalculable gulfs which separate us even from our nearest friends. DAVID GRAYSON, *Adventures in Contentment* (1907), 8.

23. One would not be alone even in Paradise. ITALIAN PROVERB.

24. You find in solitude only what you take to it. JUAN RAMÓN JIMÉNEZ, *Selected Writings* (1957), 8, tr. H. R. Hays.

25. The fates have a way of demanding of a man that he suffer his greatest moments all by himself; being alone seems as often attendant upon reality as being in company is attendant upon the flight from reality. MURRAY KEMPTON, "The Shadow Line," *Part of Our Time* (1955).

26. A solitude is the audience-chamber of God. WALTER SAVAGE LANDOR, "Lord Brooke and Sir Philip Sidney," *Imaginary Conversations* (1824–53).

27. What a commentary on our civilization, when being alone is considered suspect; when one has to apologize for it, make excuses, hide the fact that one practices it—like a secret vice! ANNE MORROW LINDBERGH, "Moon Shell," *Gift from the Sea* (1955).

28. It is in solitude that the works of hand, heart and mind are always conceived, and in solitude that individuality must be affirmed. ROBERT LINDNER, "The Mutiny of the Young," *Must You Conform?* (1956).

29. Ships that pass in the night, and speak each other in passing, / Only a signal shown and a distant voice in the darkness; / So on the ocean of life, we pass and speak one another, / Only a look and a voice, then darkness again and a silence. LONGFELLOW, "Elizabeth," 4, *Tales of a Wayside Inn* (1863).

30. The nurse of full-grown souls is solitude. JAMES RUSSELL LOWELL, "Columbus" (1844).

31. Solitude is as needful to the imagination as society is wholesome for the character. JAMES RUSSELL LOWELL, "Dryden," *Among My Books* (1870).

32. It's always strange the heart is: only / It's the skin we ever know. ARCHIBALD MAC LEISH, *JB* (1958), 8.

33. Solitude gives birth to the original in us, to beauty unfamiliar and perilous—to poetry. But also, it gives birth to the opposite: to the perverse, the illicit, the absurd. THOMAS MANN, title story (1913), *Death in Venice*, tr. H. T. Lowe-Porter.

34. Solitude sometimes is best society, / And short retirement urges sweet return. MILTON, *Paradise Lost* (1667), 9.249.

35. Nature has presented us with a large faculty of entertaining ourselves alone; and often calls us to it, to teach us that we owe ourselves in part to society, but chiefly and mostly to ourselves. MONTAIGNE, "On giving the lie," *Essays* (1580–88), tr. Charles Cotton and W. C. Hazlitt.

36. Solitude is the playfield of Satan. VLADIMIR NABOKOV, "Commentary," *Pale Fire* (1962), 62.

37. Life is for each man a solitary cell whose walls are mirrors. EUGENE O'NEILL, *Lazarus Laughed* (1927), 2.1.

38. We are fools to depend upon the society of our fellow-men. Wretched as we are, powerless as we are, they will not aid us; we shall die alone. PASCAL, *Pensées* (1670), 211, tr. W. F. Trotter.

39. Solitude is the profoundest fact of the human condition. Man is the only being who knows he is alone. OCTAVIO PAZ, *The Labyrinth of Solitude* (1950).

40. If you shut yourself up disdainfully in your ivory tower and insist that you have your own conscience and are satisfied with its approval, it is because you know that everybody is criticizing you, condemning you, or laughing at you. LUIGI PIRANDELLO, *Each in His Own Way* (1924), 1, tr. Arthur Livingston.

41. There are some solitary wretches who seem to have left the rest of mankind, only, as Eve left Adam, to meet the devil in private. ALEXANDER POPE, *Thoughts on Various Subjects* (1727).

42. Solitude is the mother of anxieties. PUBLILIUS SYRUS, *Moral Sayings* (1st c. B.C.), 222, tr. Darius Lyman.

43. He who lives in solitude may make his own laws. PUBLILIUS SYRUS, *Moral Sayings* (1st c. B.C.), 432, tr. Darius Lyman.

44. There are places and moments in which one is so completely alone that one sees the world entire. JULES RENARD, *Journal*, December 1900, ed. and tr. Louise Bogan and Elizabeth Roget.

45. We *are* solitary. We may delude ourselves and act as though this were not so. That is all. RAINER MARIA RILKE, *Letters to a Young Poet*, Aug. 12, 1904, tr. M. D. Herter Norton.

46. Solitude vivifies; isolation kills. JOSEPH ROUX, *Meditations of a Parish Priest* (1886), 5.60, tr. Isabel F. Hapgood.

47. You and I possess manifold ideal bonds in the interests we share; but each of us has his poor body and his irremediable, incommunicable dreams. GEORGE SANTAYANA, *The Life of Reason: Reason in Science* (1905–06), 9.

48. Life without a friend is death without a witness. SPANISH PROVERB.

49. One can acquire everything in solitude except character. STENDHAL, "Miscellaneous Fragments," *On Love* (1822).

50. The man who goes alone can start today; but he who travels with another must wait till that other is ready, and it may be a long time before they get off. THOREAU, "Economy," *Walden* (1854).

51. You may live a long while with some people, and be on friendly terms with them, and never once speak openly with them from your soul. IVAN TURGENEV, "The District Doctor," *A Sportsman's Sketches* (1852), v. 1, tr. Constance Garnett.

52. Only in solitude do we find ourselves; and in finding ourselves, we find in ourselves all our brothers in solitude. MIGUEL DE UNAMUNO, "Solitude," *Essays and Soliloquies* (1924), tr. J. E. Crawford Flitch.

53. We are rarely proud when we are alone. VOLTAIRE, "Laughter," *Philosophical Dictionary* (1764).

54. Isolation breeds conceit. CHARLES DUDLEY WARNER, "Sixth Study," *Backlog Studies* (1873).

55. We're all of us sentenced to solitary confinement inside our own skins, for life. TENNESSEE WILLIAMS, *Orpheus Descending* (1957), 2.1.

56. Which of us has known his brother? Which of us has looked into his father's heart? Which of us has not remained forever prison-pent? Which of us is not forever a stranger and alone? THOMAS WOLFE, flyleaf, *Look Homeward, Angel* (1929).

### 909. SONS

See also 95. Boys; 663. Parenthood

1. The ungrateful son is a wart on his father's face; to leave it is a blemish, to cut it off is pain. AFGHANISTAN PROVERB.

2. A wise son maketh a glad father: but a foolish son is the heaviness of his mother. *Bible*, Proverbs 10:1.

3. A motherless son is a fish in low water. *Burmese Proverbs* (1962), 240, ed. Hla Pe.

4. Everyone calls his son his son, whether he has talents or has not talents. CONFUCIUS, *Analects* (6th c. B.C.), 11.7, tr. James Legge.

5. In order to get as much fame as one's father one has to be much more able than he. DENIS DIDEROT, *Rameau's Nephew* (1762), tr. Jacques Barzun and Ralph H. Bowen.

6. Few sons, indeed, are like their fathers. Generally they are worse; but just a few are better. HOMER, *Odyssey* (9th c. B.C.), 2, tr. E. V. Rieu.

7. Sons have always a rebellious wish to be disillusioned by that which charmed their fathers. ALDOUS HUXLEY, "Vulgarity in Literature," *Music at Night* (1931).

8. There must always be a struggle between a father and son, while one aims at power and the other at independence. SAMUEL JOHNSON, quoted in Boswell's *Life of Samuel Johnson*, July 14, 1763.

9. Greatness of name in the father oftentimes overwhelms the son; they stand too near one another. The shadow kills the growth. BEN JONSON, *Timber* (1640).

10. Sons do not need you. They are always out of your reach, / Walking strange waters. PHYLLIS MC GINLEY, "The Old Woman with Four Sons," *A Pocketful of Wry* (1940).

11. How easily a father's tenderness is recalled, and how quickly a son's offenses vanish at the slightest word of repentance! MOLIÈRE, *Don Juan* (1665), 5.1, tr. Donald M. Frame.

12. Any father whose son raises his hand against him is guilty: of having produced a son who raised his hand against him. CHARLES PÉGUY, *Les Cahiers de la quinzaine*, Dec. 2, 1906.

13. You don't raise heroes, you raise sons. And if you treat them like sons, they'll turn out to be heroes, even if it's just in your own eyes. WALTER SCHIRRA, SR., *This Week*, Feb. 3, 1963.

14. 'Tis a happy thing / To be the father unto many sons. SHAKESPEARE, *3 Henry VI* (1590–91), 3.2.104.

15. To a hoarding father succeeds an extravagant son. SPANISH PROVERB.

16. This is what a father ought to be about: helping his son to form the habit of doing right on his own initiative, rather than because he's afraid of some serious consequence. TERENCE, *The Brothers* (160 B.C.), tr. William A. Oldfather.

17. The time not to become a father is eighteen years before a world war. E. B. WHITE, "Answers to Hard Questions," *The Second Tree from the Corner* (1954).

### 910. SOPHISTICATION

See also 190. Cosmopolitanism; 319. Experience

1. The finished man of the world must eat of every apple once. EMERSON, "Culture," *The Conduct of Life* (1860).

2. The mark of the man of the world is absence of pretension. EMERSON, "Culture," *The Conduct of Life* (1860).

3. Worldly people rarely learn anything new because it befits them to possess a great number of ready-made, acceptable opinions on the greatest number of topics. PIERRE MILLE, *Le bel art d'apprendre* (1924), 4.

4. Be wisely worldly, be not worldly wise. FRANCIS QUARLES, *Emblems* (1635), 2.2.

### 911. SORROW

See also 603. Mourning; 939. Suffering; 1004. Unhappiness; 1045. Weeping

1. Grief drives men into habits of serious reflection, sharpens the understanding and softens the heart. JOHN ADAMS, letter to Thomas Jefferson, May 6, 1816.

2. A man's sorrow runs uphill; true it is difficult for him to bear, but it is also difficult for him to keep. DJUNA BARNES, *Nightwood* (1937).

3. Sorrow is better than laughter: for by the sadness of the countenance the heart is made better. *Bible*, Ecclesiastes 7:3.

4. Joys impregnate. Sorrows bring forth.

WILLIAM BLAKE, "Proverbs of Hell," *The Marriage of Heaven and Hell* (1790).

5. There is no doubt that sorrow brings one down in the world. The aristocratic privilege of silence belongs, you soon find out, to only the happy state—or, at least, to the state when pain keeps within bounds. ELIZABETH BOWEN, *The Death of the Heart* (1938), 3.3.

6. The finer the nature, and the higher the level at which it seeks to live, the lower in grief it not only sinks but dives: it goes to weep with beggars and mountebanks, for these make the shame of being unhappy less. ELIZABETH BOWEN, *The Death of the Heart* (1938), 3.3.

7. Grief should be the Instructor of the wise; / Sorrow is Knowledge. BYRON, *Manfred* (1817) 1.1.

8. Grief is not in the nature of things, but in opinion. CICERO, *Tusculan Disputations* (44 B.C.), 3.

9. There is something pleasurable in calm remembrance of a past sorrow. CICERO, *Ad Familiares* (1st c. B.C.), 5.

10. Melancholy and remorse form the deep leaden keel which enables us to sail into the wind of reality. CYRIL CONNOLLY, *The Unquiet Grave* (1945), 3.

11. Grief even in a child hates the light and shrinks from human eyes. THOMAS DE QUINCEY, "The Affliction of Childhood," *Suspiria de Profundis* (1845).

12. I measure every Grief I meet / With narrow, probing Eyes— / I wonder if It weighs like Mine— / Or has an Easier size. EMILY DICKINSON, poem (c. 1862).

13. There are some men above grief and some men below it. EMERSON, *Journals*, 1836.

14. Sorrow makes us all children again. EMERSON, *Journals*, 1842.

15. Man sheds grief as his skin sheds rain. EMERSON, *Journals*, 1843.

16. There is a sort of pleasure in indulging of grief. THOMAS FULLER, M.D., *Gnomologia* (1732), 4883.

17. Sadness flies on the wings of the morning and out of the heart of darkness comes the light. JEAN GIRAUDOUX, *The Madwoman of Chaillot* (1945), 2, adapted by Maurice Valency.

18. It is better to drink of deep griefs than to taste shallow pleasures. WILLIAM HAZLITT, *Characteristics* (1823), 306.

19. Learn weeping, and thou shalt gain laughing. GEORGE HERBERT, *Jacula Prudentum* (1651).

20. There is not / any advantage to be won from grim lamentation. HOMER, *Iliad* (9th c. B.C.), 24.523, tr. Richmond Lattimore.

21. Great grief is a divine and terrible radiance which transfigures the wretched. VICTOR HUGO, "Fantine," *Les Misérables* (1862), 5.13, tr. Charles E. Wilbour.

22. When a man or woman loves to brood over a sorrow and takes care to keep it green in their memory, you may be sure it is no longer a pain to them. JEROME K. JEROME, "On Being in the Blues," *The Idle Thoughts of an Idle Fellow* (1889).

23. Grief is a species of idleness. SAMUEL JOHNSON, letter to Mrs. Henry Thrale, March 17, 1773.

24. While grief is fresh, every attempt to divert only irritates. SAMUEL JOHNSON, quoted in Boswell's *Life of Samuel Johnson*, April 10, 1776.

25. Real sorrow is incompatible with hope. No matter how great that sorrow may be, hope raises it one hundred cubits higher. COMTE DE LAUTRÉAMONT, *Poésies* (1870), 1.

26. Grief can't be shared. Everyone carries it alone, his own burden, his own way. ANNE MORROW LINDBERGH, "Theodore," *Dearly Beloved* (1962).

27. Take this sorrow to thy heart, and make it a part of thee, and it shall nourish thee till thou art strong again. LONGFELLOW, *Hyperion* (1839), 4.2.

28. The first pressure of sorrow crushes out from our hearts the best wine; afterwards the constant weight of it brings forth bitterness, the taste and stain from the lees of the vat. LONGFELLOW, "Table-Talk," *Driftwood* (1857).

29. Rapture's self is three parts sorrow. AMY LOWELL, "Happiness," *Sword Blades and Poppy Seeds* (1914).

30. There is far too much talk of love and grief benumbing the faculties, turning the hair gray, and destroying a man's interest in his work. Grief has made many a man look younger. WILLIAM MC FEE, "On a Balcony," *Harbours of Memory* (1921).

31. What man is there that does not laboriously, though all unconsciously, himself fashion the sorrow that is to be the pivot of his life! MAURICE MAETERLINCK, "The

Star," *The Treasure of the Humble* (1896), tr. Alfred Sutro.

32. Physical suffering apart, not a single sorrow exists that can touch us except through our thoughts. MAURICE MAETERLINCK, *Wisdom and Destiny* (1898), 39, tr. Alfred Sutro.

33. He truly sorrows who sorrows unseen. MARTIAL, *Epigrams* (A.D. 86), 1.33, tr. Walter C. A. Ker.

34. Why not leave their private sorrows to people? Is sorrow not, one asks, the only thing in the world people really possess? VLADIMIR NABOKOV, *Pnin* (1957), 2.5.

35. Hope is incredible to the slave of grief. PETRARCH, "Laura Living," *Canzoniere* (1360), 117.

36. It is our human lot, it is heaven's will, that sorrow follow joy. PLAUTUS, *Amphitryon* (3rd c. B.C.).

37. Sorrows remembered sweeten present joy. ROBERT POLLOK, *The Course of Time* (1827), 1.464.

38. There is in this world in which everything wears out, everything perishes, one thing that crumbles into dust, that destroys itself still more completely, leaving behind still fewer traces of itself than Beauty: namely Grief. MARCEL PROUST, *Remembrance of Things Past: The Sweet Cheat Gone* (1913–27), tr. C. K. Scott-Moncrieff.

39. Happiness is beneficial for the body, but it is grief that develops the powers of the mind. MARCEL PROUST, *Remembrance of Things Past: The Past Recaptured* (1913–27).

40. We wasters of sorrows! / How we stare away into sad endurance beyond them, / trying to foresee their end! Whereas they are nothing else / than our winter foliage, our sombre evergreen, *one* / of the seasons of our interior year. RAINER MARIA RILKE, "The Tenth Elegy," *Duino Elegies* (1923), tr. J. B. Leishman and Stephen Spender.

41. Great joys weep, great sorrows laugh. JOSEPH ROUX, *Meditations of a Parish Priest* (1886), 5.3, tr. Isabel F. Hapgood.

42. That sorrow which is the harbinger of joy is preferable to the joy which is followed by sorrow. SA'DI, *Gulistan* (1258), 8.107, tr. James Ross.

43. Sorrow is one of the vibrations that prove the fact of living. SAINT-EXUPÉRY, *Wind, Sand, and Stars* (1939), 8, tr. Lewis Galantière.

44. It is sweet to mingle tears with tears; / Griefs, where they wound in solitude, / Wound more deeply. SENECA, *Agamemnon* (1st c.), 664.

45. No emotion falls into dislike so readily as sorrow. SENECA, *Letters to Lucilius* (1st c.), 63.3. tr. E. Phillips Barker.

46. Sorrow breaks seasons and reposing hours, / Makes the night morning and the noontide night. SHAKESPEARE, *Richard III* (1592–93), 1.4.76.

47. Gnarling sorrow hath less power to bite / The man that mocks at it and sets it light. SHAKESPEARE, *Richard II* (1595–96), 1.3.292.

48. I will instruct my sorrows to be proud; / For grief is proud, and makes his owner stoop. SHAKESPEARE, *King John* (1596–97), 3.1.68.

49. Every one can master a grief but he that has it. SHAKESPEARE, *Much Ado About Nothing* (1598–99), 3.2.28.

50. When sorrows come, they come not single spies, / But in battalions! SHAKESPEARE, *Hamlet* (1600), 4.5.78.

51. Give sorrow words. The grief that does not speak / Whispers the o'erfraught heart and bids it break. SHAKESPEARE, *Macbeth* (1605–06), 4.3.209.

52. Winter is come and gone, / But grief returns with the revolving year. SHELLEY, *Adonais* (1821), 18.

53. When people fall in deep distress, their native sense departs. SOPHOCLES, *Antigone* (442–41 B.C.), tr. Elizabeth Wyckoff.

54. Do not rejoice at my grief, for when mine is old, yours will be new. SPANISH PROVERB.

55. It is a very melancholy reflection that men are usually so weak that it is absolutely necessary for them to know sorrow and pain to be in their right senses. RICHARD STEELE, *The Spectator* (1711–12), 312.

56. A sorrow's crown of sorrow is remembering happier things. ALFRED, LORD TENNYSON, "Locksley Hall" (1842).

57. He that conceals his grief finds no remedy for it. TURKISH PROVERB.

58. Where there is sorrow there is holy ground. OSCAR WILDE, *De Profundis* (1905).

59. A deep distress hath humanised my Soul. WILLIAM WORDSWORTH, "Elegiac Stanzas" (1805).

60. In heaven above, / And earth below, they best can serve true gladness / Who

meet most feelingly the calls of sadness. WILLIAM WORDSWORTH, " 'Tis He Whose Yester-Evening's High Disdain" (1838).

## SOUL
See 920. Spirituality

## 912. SOUND
See also 607. Music; 629. Noise; 875. Senses

1. A time that's just time will let sounds be just sounds and if they are folk tunes, unresolved ninth chords, or knives and forks, just folk tunes, unresolved ninth chords, or knives and forks. JOHN CAGE "Erik Satie," *Silence* (1961).

## 913. SOUR GRAPES
See also 182. Contempt; 247. Disappointment

1. It is easy to despise what you cannot get. AESOP, "The Fox and the Grapes," *Fables* (6th c. B.C.?), tr. Joseph Jacobs.

2. Believe not much them that seem to despise riches, for they despise them that despair of them. FRANCIS BACON, "Of Riches," *Essays* (1625).

3. Sour grapes can ne'er make sweet wine. THOMAS FULLER, M.D., *Gnomologia* (1732), 4233.

4. He whose mouth is out of taste says the wine is flat. MONTAIGNE, "Apology for Raimond de Sebonde," *Essays* (1580–88), tr. Charles Cotton and W. C. Hazlitt.

## 914. SPACE
See also 413. The Heavens; 597. Moon; 1010. Universe

1. Walking in space, man has never looked more puny or more significant. ALEXANDER CHASE, *Perspectives* (1966).

2. Space is the stature of God. JOSEPH JOUBERT, *Pensées* (1842).

3. Space flights are merely an escape, a fleeing away from oneself, because it is easier to go to Mars or to the moon than it is to penetrate one's own being. CARL GUSTAV JUNG, quoted in Miguel Serrano's "The Farewell," *C. G. Jung and Hermann Hesse* (1966), tr. Frank MacShane.

4. Peace in space will help us nought once peace on earth is gone. JOHN F. KENNEDY, State of the Union Message, Jan. 11, 1962.

5. We believe that when men reach beyond this planet, they should leave their national differences behind them. JOHN F. KENNEDY, news conference, Washington, D.C., Feb. 21, 1962.

6. The eternal silence of these infinite spaces frightens me. PASCAL, *Pensées* (1670), 206, tr. W. F. Trotter.

7. Everything in space obeys the laws of physics. If you know these laws, and obey them, space will treat you kindly. And don't tell me man doesn't belong out there. Man belongs wherever he wants to go—and he'll do plenty well when he gets there. WERNHER VON BRAUN, *Time*, Feb. 17, 1958.

## 915. SPAIN AND SPANIARDS

1. In Spain, the dead are more alive than the dead of any other country in the world. FEDERICO GARCÍA LORCA, "The Duende: Theory and Divertissement," *Poet in New York* (1940), appendix 6, tr. Ben Belitt.

2. Three Spaniards, four opinions. SPANISH PROVERB.

## 916. SPEAKING
See also 96. Brevity; 132. Clarity; 148. Communication; 185. Conversation; 281. Eloquence; 521. Language; 540. Listening; 757. Public Speaking; 891. Silence; 955. Tact; 1057. Words

1. The most difficult thing in the world is to say thinkingly what everybody says without thinking. ALAIN, *Histoire de mes pensées* (1936).

2. A man is hid under his tongue. ALI IBN-ABI-TALIB, *Sentences* (7th c.), 83, tr. Simon Ockley.

3. To speak agreeably to him with whom we deal is more than to speak in good words or in good order. FRANCIS BACON, "Of Discourse," *Essays* (1625).

4. The voice is a second face. GÉRARD BAUËR, *Carnets inédits*.

5. None love to speak so much, when the mood of speaking comes, as they who are naturally taciturn. HENRY WARD BEECHER,

*Proverbs from Plymouth Pulpit* (1887).

6. A fool uttereth all his mind. *Bible*, Proverbs 29:11.

7. Let your speech be alway with grace, seasoned with salt. *Bible*, Colossians 4:6.

8. Loquacity, n. A disorder which renders the sufferer unable to curb his tongue when you wish to talk. AMBROSE BIERCE, *The Devil's Dictionary* (1881–1911).

9. Mouth, n. In man, the gateway to the soul; in woman, the outlet of the heart. AMBROSE BIERCE, *The Devil's Dictionary* (1881–1911).

10. Too much talk will include errors. *Burmese Proverbs* (1962), 461, ed. Hla Pe.

11. Speech is too often not the art of concealing thought, but of quite stifling and suspending thought, so that there is none to conceal. THOMAS CARLYLE, *Sartor Resartus* (1833–34), 3.3.

12. Little said is soon amended. CERVANTES, *Don Quixote* (1605–15), 1.3.11, tr. Peter Motteux and John Ozell.

13. Talk does not cook rice. CHINESE PROVERB.

14. A dog is not considered good because of his barking, and a man is not considered clever because of his ability to talk. CHUANG TZU, *Works* (4th–3rd c. B.C.), 32.1, tr. Lin Yutang.

15. One never repents of having spoken too little, but often of having spoken too much. PHILIPPE DE COMMYNES, *Mémoires* (1524), 1.14.

16. Oh, who would not lose his speech, upon condition to have joys above it? WILLIAM CONGREVE, *The Double-Dealer* (1694), 4.5.

17. Let thy speech be better than silence, or be silent. DIONYSIUS THE ELDER, extant fragment (4th c. B.C.).

18. Do not say things. What you are stands over you the while and thunders so that I cannot hear what you say to the contrary. EMERSON, *Journals*, 1840.

19. Must we always talk for victory, and never once for truth, for comfort, and joy? EMERSON, *Journals*, 1856.

20. First learn the meaning of what you say, and then speak. EPICTETUS, *Discourses* (2nd c.), 3.23, tr. Thomas W. Higginson.

21. When you speak to a man, look on his eyes; when he speaks to you, look on his mouth. BENJAMIN FRANKLIN, *Poor Richard's Almanack* (1732–57).

22. In much of your talking, thinking is half murdered. / For thought is a bird of space, that in a cage of words may indeed unfold its wings but cannot fly. KAHLIL GIBRAN, "On Talking," *The Prophet* (1923).

23. Is there any place where there is no traffic in empty talk? Is there on this earth one who does not worship himself talking? KAHLIL GIBRAN, "Mister Gabber," *Thoughts and Meditations* (1960), tr. Anthony R. Ferris.

24. The true use of speech is not so much to express our wants as to conceal them. OLIVER GOLDSMITH, *The Bee*, Oct. 20, 1759.

25. There is always time to add a word, never to withdraw one. BALTASAR GRACIÁN, *The Art of Worldly Wisdom* (1647), 160, tr. Joseph Jacobs.

26. People do not seem to talk for the sake of expressing their opinions, but to maintain an opinion for the sake of talking. WILLIAM HAZLITT, "On Coffee-House Politicians," *Table Talk* (1821–22).

27. If no thought / your mind does visit, / make your speech / not too explicit. PIET HEIN, "The Case for Obscurity," *Grooks* (1966).

28. Talking is like playing on the harp; there is as much in laying the hand on the strings to stop their vibrations as in twanging them to bring out their music. OLIVER WENDELL HOLMES, SR., *The Autocrat of the Breakfast Table* (1858), 1.

29. Nobody talks much that doesn't say unwise things—things he did not mean to say; as no person plays much without striking a false note sometimes. OLIVER WENDELL HOLMES, SR., *The Professor at the Breakfast Table* (1860), 1.

30. Many people would be more truthful were it not for their uncontrollable desire to talk. EDGAR WATSON HOWE, *Country Town Sayings* (1911).

31. From listening comes wisdom, and from speaking repentance. ITALIAN PROVERB.

32. The tongue is more to be feared than the sword. JAPANESE PROVERB.

33. No glass renders a man's form or likeness so true as his speech. BEN JONSON, "Of Language in Oratory," *Timber* (1640).

34. Whom the disease of talking still once possesseth, he can never hold his peace. BEN JONSON, "Of Talking Overmuch," *Timber* (1640).

35. The trumpet does not more stun you by its loudness, than a whisper teases you by its provoking inaudibility. CHARLES LAMB, "The Old and the New Schoolmaster," *Essays of Elia* (1823).

36. We oftener say things because we can say them well, than because they are sound and reasonable. WALTER SAVAGE LANDOR, "Marcus Tullius and Quinctus Cicero," *Imaginary Conversations* (1824–53).

37. He who talks more is sooner exhausted. LAOTSE, *The Character of Tao* (6th c. B.C.), 5, tr. Ch'u Ta-Kao.

38. We talk little when vanity does not make us. LA ROCHEFOUCAULD, *Maxims* (1665), tr. Kenneth Pratt.

39. It is never more difficult to speak well than when we are ashamed of keeping silent. LA ROCHEFOUCAULD, *Maxims* (1665), tr. Kenneth Pratt.

40. What is uttered is finished and done with. THOMAS MANN, "Tonio Kröger" (1903), *Death in Venice*, tr. H. T. Lowe-Porter.

41. Speech is civilization itself. The word, even the most contradictious word, preserves contact – it is silence which isolates. THOMAS MANN, *The Magic Mountain* (1924), 6.8, tr. H. T. Lowe-Porter.

42. Every man may speak truly, but to speak methodically, prudently, and fully is a talent that few men have. MONTAIGNE, "Of the art of conference," *Essays* (1580–88), tr. Charles Cotton and W. C. Hazlitt.

43. The unluckiest insolvent in the world is the man whose expenditure of speech is too great for his income of ideas. CHRISTOPHER MORLEY, *Inward Ho!* (1923), 9.

44. Speaking is a beautiful folly: with that man dances over all things. NIETZSCHE, "The Convalescent," *Thus Spoke Zarathustra* (1883–92), 3, tr. Walter Kaufmann.

45. Pleasant words are the food of love. OVID, *The Art of Love* (c. A.D. 8), 2, tr. J. Lewis May.

46. One who speaks aright never says his say at an unsuitable place or time, nor before one of immature faculties or without excellence. This is why his words are not spoken in vain. *Panchatantra* (c. 5th c.), 1, tr. Franklin Edgerton.

47. There are some who speak well and write badly. For the place and the audience warm them, and draw from their minds more than they think of without that warmth. PASCAL, *Pensées* (1670), 47, tr. W. F. Trotter.

48. It is easy to utter what has been kept silent, but impossible to recall what has been uttered. PLUTARCH, "The Education of Children," *Moralia* (c. A.D. 100), tr. Moses Hadas.

49. They always talk who never think. MATTHEW PRIOR, "Upon a Passage in the Scaligerana" (1697).

50. Speech is a mirror of the soul: as a man speaks, so is he. PUBLILIUS SYRUS, *Moral Sayings* (1st c. B.C.), 1073, tr. Darius Lyman.

51. Whenever I have talked to anyone at too great length, I am like a man who has drunk too much, and, ashamed, doesn't know where to put himself. JULES RENARD, *Journal*, December 1893, ed. and tr. Louise Bogan and Elizabeth Roget.

52. In the faculty of speech man excels the brute; but if thou utterest what is improper, the brute is thy superior. SA'DI, introduction, *Gulistan* (1258), tr. James Ross.

53. When I think over what I have said, I envy dumb people. SENECA, "On a Happy Life," *Moral Essays* (1st c.), tr. Aubrey Stewart.

54. Talkers are no good doers. SHAKESPEARE, *Richard III* (1592–93), 1.3.351.

55. Her voice was ever soft, / Gentle, and low – an excellent thing in woman. SHAKESPEARE, *King Lear* (1605–06), 5.3.272.

56. Speech is the mirror of action. SOLON (7th–6th c. B.C.), quoted in Diogenes Laertius' *Lives and Opinions of Eminent Philosophers* (3rd c. A.D.), tr. R. D. Hicks.

57. Surely human affairs would be far happier if the power in men to be silent were the same as that to speak. But experience more than sufficiently teaches that men govern nothing with more difficulty than their tongues, and can moderate their desires more easily than their words. SPINOZA, *Ethics* (1677), 3, tr. Andrew Boyle.

58. There can be no fairer ambition than to excel in talk; to be affable, gay, ready, clear, and welcome. ROBERT LOUIS STEVENSON, "Talk and Talkers" (1882), 1.

59. Nature, which gave us two eyes to see, and two ears to hear, has given us but one tongue to speak. JONATHAN SWIFT, *A Tritical Essay Upon the Faculties of the Mind* (1707).

60. No man speaketh safely but he that is glad to hold his peace. THOMAS À KEMPIS, *The Imitation of Christ* (1426), 1.20.

61. It is the man determines what is said, not the words. THOREAU, *Journal*, July 11, 1840.

## 917. SPECIALISTS

**See also 842. Scholars and Scholarship; 1029. Vocations**

1. A poet on Pegasus, reciting his own verses, is hardly more to be dreaded than a mounted specialist. OLIVER WENDELL HOLMES, SR., *Over the Teacups* (1891), 7.

2. Do not be bullied out of your common sense by the specialist; two to one, he is a pedant. OLIVER WENDELL HOLMES, SR., *Over the Teacups* (1891), 7.

3. I know of no teachers so powerful and persuasive as the little army of specialists. They carry no banners, they beat no drums; but where they are men learn that bustle and push are not the equals of quiet genius and serene mastery. OLIVER WENDELL HOLMES, JR., speech, Harvard Law School Association, Nov. 5, 1886.

4. Specialized meaninglessness has come to be regarded, in certain circles, as a kind of hall mark of true science. ALDOUS HUXLEY, "Beliefs," *Ends and Means* (1937).

5. The essence of the expert is that his field shall be very special and narrow: one of the ways in which he inspires confidence is to rigidly limit himself to the little toe; he would scarcely venture an off-the-record opinion on an infected little finger. LOUIS KRONENBERGER, *Company Manners* (1954), 1.4.

6. Wherever learning breeds specialists, the sum of human culture is enhanced thereby. That is the illusion and consolation of specialists. ANTONIO MACHADO, *Juan de Mairena* (1943), 1, tr. Ben Belitt.

## 918. SPECTACLES

1. Wearing spectacles makes men conceited, because spectacles raise them to a degree of sensual perfection which is far above the power of their own nature. JOHANN PETER ECKERMANN, *Conversations with Goethe*, April 5, 1830.

2. Men seldom make passes / At girls who wear glasses. DOROTHY PARKER, "News Item."

## SPECTATORS

**See 59. Audience; 642. Observation**

## SPEECH

**See 185. Conversation; 362. Free Speech; 757. Public Speaking; 916. Speaking**

## 919. SPEED

**See also 409. Haste; 900. Slowness**

1. There is no secrecy comparable to celerity. FRANCIS BACON, "Of Delay," *Essays* (1625).

2. In skating over thin ice our safety is in our speed. EMERSON, "Prudence," *Essays: First Series* (1841).

3. Celerity is the mother of good fortune. He has done much who leaves nothing over till to-morrow. BALTASAR GRACIÁN, *The Art of Worldly Wisdom* (1647), 53, tr. Joseph Jacobs.

4. Celerity is never more admired / Than by the negligent. SHAKESPEARE, *Antony and Cleopatra* (1606–07), 3.7.25.

## SPIRIT

**See 583. Mind; 920. Spirituality**

## 920. SPIRITUALITY

**See also 180. Contemplation; 488. The Intangible; 565. Materialism; 584. Mind and Body; 595. Monasticism; 609. Mysticism; 834. Saints and Sainthood**

1. I am certainly convinced that it is one of the greatest impulses of mankind to arrive at something higher than a natural state. JAMES BALDWIN, "The Male Prison," *Nobody Knows My Name* (1961).

2. Give unto us this day the daily manna / Without which, in this desert where we dwell, / He must go backward who would most advance. DANTE, "Purgatorio," 11, *The Divine Comedy* (c. 1300–21), tr. Lawrence Grant White.

3. To the poet, to the philosopher, to the

saint, all things are friendly and sacred, all events profitable, all days holy, all men divine. EMERSON, "History," *Essays: First Series* (1841).

4. There is one spectacle grander than the sea, that is the sky; there is one spectacle grander than the sky, that is the interior of the soul. VICTOR HUGO, "Fantine," *Les Misérables* (1862), 7.3, tr. Charles E. Wilbour.

5. Physical strength can never permanently withstand the impact of spiritual force. FRANKLIN D. ROOSEVELT, speech, Staunton, Va., May 4, 1941.

6. All spiritual interests are supported by animal life. GEORGE SANTAYANA, *The Life of Reason: Reason in Society* (1905–06), 1.

7. [Man's] soul longs for beauty, for the absolute, the transcendental. When he attains it, he has no use for it; it oppresses him. MAURICE VALENCY, introduction to *Jean Giraudoux: Four Plays* (1958).

8. Teach me, like you, to drink creation whole / And, casting out my self, become a soul. RICHARD WILBUR, "The Aspen and the Stream," *Advice to a Prophet* (1961).

9. Nuns fret not at their convent's narrow room; / And hermits are contented with their cells. WILLIAM WORDSWORTH, "Nuns Fret Not at Their Convent's Narrow Room" (1807).

## 921. SPONTANEITY

**See also 291. Enthusiasm; 459. Impulsiveness; 1028. Vitality; 1046. Whim**

1. Improvisation is the essence of good talk. Heaven defend us from the talker who doles out things prepared for us! But let heaven not less defend us from the beautifully spontaneous writer who puts his trust in the inspiration of the moment! MAX BEERBOHM, "Lytton Strachey," *Mainly On the Air* (1946).

2. The individual never asserts himself more than when he forgets himself. ANDRÉ GIDE, "Portraits and Aphorisms," *Pretexts* (1903), tr. Angelo P. Bertocci and others.

3. We never do anything well till we cease to think about the manner of doing it. This is the reason why it is so difficult for any but natives to speak a language correctly or idiomatically. WILLIAM HAZLITT, "On Prejudice," *Sketches and Essays* (1839).

4. Too much improvisation leaves the mind stupidly void. Running beer gathers no foam. VICTOR HUGO, "Fantine," *Les Misérables* (1862), 3.7, tr. Charles E. Wilbour.

## 922. SPORTS

**See also 345. Fishing; 436. Hunting; 690. Physical Fitness; 697. Play; 815. Riding; 1034. Walking**

1. In America, it is sport that is the opiate of the masses. RUSSELL BAKER, "Observer," *The New York Times*, Oct. 3, 1967.

2. Pro football is like nuclear warfare. There are no winners, only survivors. FRANK GIFFORD, *Sports Illustrated*, July 4, 1960.

3. A golf course is the epitome of all that is purely transitory in the universe, a space not to dwell in, but to get over as quickly as possible. JEAN GIRAUDOUX, *The Enchanted* (1933), 1, adapted by Maurice Valency.

4. Every one knows that horse-racing is carried on mainly for the delight and profit of fools, ruffians, and thieves. GEORGE GISSING, "Spring," *The Private Papers of Henry Ryecroft* (1903).

5. The human spirit sublimates / the impulses it thwarts; / a healthy sex life mitigates / the lust for other sports. PIET HEIN, "Hint and Suggestion," *Grooks* (1966).

6. We are inclined to think that if we watch a football game or a baseball game, we have taken part in it. JOHN F. KENNEDY, interview with Dave Garroway, Jan. 31, 1961.

7. Rodeoing is about the only sport you can't fix. You'd have to talk to the bulls and horses, and they wouldn't understand you. BILL LINDERMAN, news summaries, March 8, 1954.

8. Serious sport has nothing to do with fair play. It is bound up with hatred, jealousy, boastfulness, disregard of all rules and sadistic pleasure in witnessing violence: in other words it is war minus the shooting. GEORGE ORWELL, "The Sporting Spirit," *Shooting an Elephant* (1950).

9. Most sorts of diversion in men, children, and other animals, are an imitation of

fighting. JONATHAN SWIFT, *Thoughts on Various Subjects* (1711).

10. Ideally, the umpire should combine the integrity of a Supreme Court justice, the physical agility of an acrobat, the endurance of Job and the imperturbability of Buddha. "The Villains in Blue," *Time*, Aug. 25, 1961.

**SPRING**
See 848. Seasons

**STARS**
See 413. The Heavens

**STARTING**
See 73. Beginning

## 923. STATE

See also 125. Church and State; 130. Citizens; 393. Government; 614. Nation; 906. Society

1. We weed out the darnel from the corn and the unfit in war, but do not excuse evil men from the service of the state. ANTISTHENES (5th–4th c. B.C.), quoted in Diogenes Laertius' *Lives and Opinions of Eminent Philosophers* (3rd c. A.D.), tr. R. D. Hicks.

2. The state exists for the sake of a good life, and not for the sake of life only. ARISTOTLE, *Politics* (4th c. B.C.), 3.9, tr. Benjamin Jowett.

3. Nothing doth more hurt in a state than that cunning men pass for wise. FRANCIS BACON, "Of Cunning," *Essays* (1625).

4. The modern state no longer has anything but rights; it does not recognize duties any more. GEORGES BERNANOS, "Why Freedom?" *The Last Essays of Georges Bernanos* (1955), tr. Joan and Barry Ulanov.

5. A state without some means of change is without the means of its conservation. EDMUND BURKE, *Reflections on the Revolution in France* (1790).

6. A thousand years scarce serve to form a state; / An hour may lay it in the dust. BYRON, *Childe Harold's Pilgrimage* (1812–18), 2.84.

7. A state worthy of the name has no friends – only interests. CHARLES DE GAULLE, quoted in *The New York Times Magazine*, May 12, 1968.

8. The State is made for man, not man for the State. EINSTEIN, "The Disarmament Conference of 1932," *The World As I See It* (1934), tr. Alan Harris.

9. When fear enters the heart of a man at hearing the names of candidates and the reading of laws that are proposed, then is the State safe, but when these things are heard without regard, as above or below us, then is the Commonwealth sick or dead. EMERSON, *Journals*, 1836.

10. The State is our neighbors; our neighbors are the State. EMERSON, *Journals*, 1845.

11. The State is a poor, good beast who means the best: it means friendly. EMERSON, *Journals*, 1846.

12. The state is the servant of the citizen, and not his master. JOHN F. KENNEDY, State of the Union Message, Jan. 11, 1962.

13. The State not seldom tolerates a comparatively great evil to keep out millions of lesser ills and inconveniences which otherwise would be inevitable and without remedy. LA' BRUYÈRE, *Characters* (1688), 10.7, tr. Henri Van Laun.

14. States, like men, have their growth, their manhood, their decrepitude, their decay. WALTER SAVAGE LANDOR, "Leonora di Este and Panigarola," *Imaginary Conversations* (1824–53).

15. While the state exists there is no freedom; when there is freedom there will be no state. LENIN, *The State and Revolution* (1917).

16. Thou, too, sail on, O Ship of State! / Sail on, O Union, strong and great! / Humanity with all its fears, / With all the hopes of future years, / Is hanging breathless on thy fate! LONGFELLOW, "The Building of the Ship" (1849).

17. As great edifices collapse of their own weight, so Heaven sets a similar limit to the growth of prosperous states. LUCAN, *On the Civil War* (1st c.), tr. Robert Graves.

18. The true wealth of a state consists in the number of its inhabitants, in their toil and industry. NAPOLEON I, *Maxims* (1804–15).

19. Each State can have for enemies only other States, and not men; for between things disparate in nature there can be no real relation. ROUSSEAU, *The Social Contract* (1762), 1.4, tr. G. D. H. Cole.

20. The responsibility of great states is to serve and not to dominate the world. HARRY S. TRUMAN, message to Congress, April 16, 1945.

## 924. STATESMEN AND STATESMANSHIP

See also 245. Diplomats and Diplomacy; 705. Politics and Politicians

1. I know no South, no North, no East, no West, to which I owe any allegiance. The Union, sir, is my country. HENRY CLAY, speech, U.S. Senate, 1848.

2. It is seldom that statesmen have the option of choosing between a good and an evil. CHARLES CALEB COLTON, *Lacon* (1825), 1.73.

3. The difference between being an elder statesman / And posing successfully as an elder statesman / Is practically negligible. T. S. ELIOT, *The Elder Statesman* (1958), 2.

4. A politician becomes a statesman after he is elected. EDGAR WATSON HOWE, *Country Town Sayings* (1911).

5. The minds of some of our statesmen, like the pupil of the human eye, contract themselves the more, the stronger light there is shed upon them. THOMAS MOORE, preface to *Corruption and Intolerance* (1808).

6. The heart of a statesman should be in his head. NAPOLEON I, *Maxims* (1804–15).

7. In statesmanship there are predicaments from which it is impossible to escape without some wrongdoing. NAPOLEON I, *Maxims* (1804–15).

8. You can always get the truth from an American statesman after he has turned seventy, or given up all hope of the Presidency. WENDELL PHILLIPS, speech, Nov. 7, 1860.

9. There are some whom the applause of the multitude has deluded into the belief that they are really statesmen. PLATO, *The Republic* (4th c. B.C.), 4, tr. Benjamin Jowett.

10. Statesmen are not only liable to give an account of what they say or do in public, but there is a busy inquiry made into their very meals, beds, marriages, and every other sportive or serious action. PLUTARCH, "Political Precepts," *Moralia* (c. A.D. 100).

11. In statesmanship get formalities right, never mind about the moralities. MARK TWAIN, "Pudd'nhead Wilson's New Calendar," *Following the Equator* (1897), 2.29.

## 925. STATISTICS

1. You and I are forever at the mercy of the census-taker and the census-maker. That impertinent fellow who goes from house to house is one of the real masters of the statistical situation. The other is the man who organizes the results. WALTER LIPPMANN, "The Golden Rule and After," *A Preface to Politics* (1914).

2. There are three kinds of lies—lies, damned lies and statistics. MARK TWAIN, *Autobiography* (1924), v. 1, ed. A. B. Paine.

## 926. STATUS

See also 168. Conformity; 773. Rank

1. The prestige you acquire by being able to tell your friends that you know famous men proves only that you are yourself of small account. W. SOMERSET MAUGHAM, *The Summing Up* (1938), 2.

2. The poor man is ruined as soon as he begins to ape the rich. PUBLILIUS SYRUS, *Moral Sayings* (1st c. B.C.), 941, tr. Darius Lyman.

3. In Boston they ask, How much does he know? In New York, How much is he worth? In Philadelphia, Who were his parents? MARK TWAIN, "What Paul Bourget Thinks of Us," *North American Review*, January 1895.

## 927. STEALING

See also 188. Corruption; 201. Crime

1. Pickpockets and beggars are the best practical physiognomists. CHARLES CALEB COLTON, *Lacon* (1825), 1.437.

2. All stealing is comparative. If you come to absolutes, pray who does not steal? EMERSON, "Experience," *Essays: Second Series* (1844).

3. Opportunity makes the thief. ENGLISH PROVERB.

4. A thief passes for a gentleman when stealing has made him rich. THOMAS FULLER, M.D., *Gnomologia* (1732), 431.

5. Old burglars never die, they just steal away. GLEN GILBREATH, on facing his thir-

teenth robbery charge, *Chicago Sun-Times*, April 26, 1958.

6. A thief believes everybody steals. EDGAR WATSON HOWE, *Country Town Sayings* (1911).

7. If you dip your arm into the pickle-pot, let it be up to the elbow. MALAY PROVERB.

8. An egg-thief becomes a camel-thief. PERSIAN PROVERB.

9. The stolen ox sometimes puts his head out of the stall. PUBLILIUS SYRUS, *Moral Sayings* (1st c. B.C.), 918, tr. Darius Lyman.

10. The faults of the burglar are the qualities of the financier. GEORGE BERNARD SHAW, preface, *Major Barbara* (1905).

## 928. STEREOTYPES

See also 168. Conformity

1. There's nothing the world loves more than a ready-made description which they can hang on to a man, and so save themselves all trouble in future. W. SOMERSET MAUGHAM, *Mrs. Dot* (1912), 2.

2. Labels are devices for saving talkative persons the trouble of thinking. JOHN MORLEY, "Carlyle," *Critical Miscellanies* (1871–1908).

3. Every society has a tendency to reduce its opponents to caricatures. NIETZSCHE, *The Will to Power* (1888), tr. Anthony M. Ludovici.

## 929. STINGINESS

See also 382. Gifts and Giving; 589. Misers

1. Man hoards himself when he has nothing to give away. EDWARD DAHLBERG, "On Love and Friendship," *Reasons of the Heart* (1965).

2. Who will not feed the cats, must feed the mice and rats. GERMAN PROVERB.

3. Meanness is more in half-doing than in omitting acts of generosity. ELBERT HUBBARD, *The Note Book* (1927).

4. We often excuse our own want of philanthropy by giving the name of fanaticism to the more ardent zeal of others. LONGFELLOW, "Table-Talk," *Driftwood* (1857).

5. He who cannot give anything away cannot feel anything either. NIETZSCHE, *The Will to Power* (1888), 801, tr. Anthony M. Ludovici.

## STOCK MARKET

See 501. Investment

## 930. STOICISM

See also 285. Endurance; 800. Resignation

1. He who has calmly reconciled his life to fate, and set proud death beneath his feet, can look fortune in the face, unbending both to good and bad: his countenance unconquered he can shew. BOETHIUS, *The Consolation of Philosophy* (A.D. 524), 1, tr. W. V. Cooper.

2. To accept whatever comes re-gardless of the consequences is to be unafraid or to be full of that love which comes from a sense of at-one-ness with whatever. JOHN CAGE, "Lecture on Something," *Silence* (1961).

3. He who despises life is his life's master. CORNEILLE, *Cinna* (1639), 1.2, tr. Paul Landis.

4. Let a man accept his destiny, / No pity and no tears. EURIPIDES, *Iphigenia in Tauris* (c. 414–12 B.C.), tr. Witter Bynner.

5. We cannot conquer fate and necessity, yet we can yield to them in such a manner as to be greater than if we could. WALTER SAVAGE LANDOR, "Marcus Tullius and Quinctus Cicero," *Imaginary Conversations* (1824–53).

6. Here is a rule to remember in future, when anything tempts you to feel bitter: not, "This is a misfortune," but "To bear this worthily is good fortune." MARCUS AURELIUS, *Meditations* (2nd c.), 4.49, tr. Maxwell Staniforth.

7. Be content with what you are, and wish not change; nor dread your last day, nor long for it. MARTIAL, *Epigrams* (A.D. 86), 10.47, tr. Walter C. A. Ker.

8. Whoever has nothing to hope, let him despair of nothing. SENECA, *Medea* (1st c.), 163, tr. Frank Justus Miller.

9. Why, courage then! What cannot be avoided / 'Twere childish weakness to lament or fear. SHAKESPEARE, 3 *Henry VI* (1590–91), 5.4.37.

10. The stoical scheme of supplying our wants by lopping off our desires, is like cutting off our feet, when we want shoes. JONATHAN SWIFT, *Thoughts on Various Subjects* (1711).

## 931. STORYTELLING

See also 341. Fiction; 1062. Writing and Writers

1. A story has been thought to its conclusion when it has taken its worst possible turn. FRIEDRICH DÜRRENMATT, "21 Points," *The Physicists* (1962), tr. James Kirkup.

2. There is pleasure in hardship heard about. EURIPIDES, *Helen* (412 B.C.), tr. Richmond Lattimore.

3. There is much good sleep in an old story. GERMAN PROVERB.

4. A story with a moral appended is like the bill of a mosquito. It bores you, and then injects a stinging drop to irritate your conscience. O. HENRY, "The Gold That Glittered," *Strictly Business* (1910).

5. A touch of science, even bogus science, gives an edge to the superstitious tale. V. S. PRITCHETT, "An Irish Ghost," *The Living Novel & Later Appreciations* (1964).

6. An honest tale speeds best being plainly told. SHAKESPEARE, *Richard III* (1592–93), 4.4.358.

7. There are several kinds of stories, but only one difficult kind—the humorous. MARK TWAIN, "How to Tell a Story" (1895).

## STRANGERS

See 355. Foreigners and Foreignness

## 932. STRATEGY

See also 579. Method

1. Unhappy the general who comes on the field of battle with a system. NAPOLEON I, *Maxims* (1804–15).

2. The mightiest rivers lose their force when split up into several streams. OVID, *Love's Cure* (c. A.D. 8), tr. J. Lewis May.

3. Those oft are stratagems which errors seem, / Nor is it Homer nods, but we that dream. ALEXANDER POPE, *An Essay on Criticism* (1711), 1.177.

4. Divide the fire, and you will the sooner put it out. PUBLILIUS SYRUS, *Moral Sayings* (1st c. B.C.), 201, tr. Darius Lyman.

5. In baiting a mouse-trap with cheese, always leave room for the mouse. SAKI, "The Infernal Parliament," *The Square Egg* (1924).

## 933. STRENGTH

See also 192. Courage; 1040. Weakness

1. The high strength of men / knows no content with limitation. AESCHYLUS, *Agamemnon* (458 B.C.), tr. Richmond Lattimore.

2. Nobody can honestly think of himself as a strong character because, however successful he may be in overcoming them, he is necessarily aware of the doubts and temptations that accompany every important choice. W. H. AUDEN, foreword to Dag Hammarskjöld's *Markings* (1964).

3. When is man strong until he feels alone? ROBERT BROWNING, *Colombe's Birthday* (1844), 3.

4. The awareness of our own strength makes us modest. PAUL CÉZANNE, *Letters* (1937), ed. John Rewald.

5. When strong, be merciful, if you would have the respect, not the fear of your neighbors. CHILON (6th c. B.C.), quoted in Diogenes Laertius' *Lives and Opinions of Eminent Philosophers* (3rd c. A.D.), tr. R. D. Hicks.

6. It is as easy for the strong man to be strong, as it is for the weak to be weak. EMERSON, "Self-Reliance," *Essays: First Series* (1841).

7. If you're strong enough, there *are* no precedents. F. SCOTT FITZGERALD, "Note-Books," *The Crack-Up* (1945).

8. A weak man is just by accident. A strong but non-violent man is unjust by accident. MOHANDAS K. GANDHI, *Non-Violence in Peace and War* (1948), 1.354.

9. Like strength is felt from hope, and from despair. HOMER, *Iliad* (9th c. B.C.), 15.852, tr. Alexander Pope.

10. Strength and strength's will are the supreme ethic. All else are dreams from hospital beds, the sly, crawling goodness of sneaking souls. ELBERT HUBBARD, *The Philistine* (1895–1915).

11. Strong men can always afford to be gentle. Only the weak are intent on "giving as good as they get." ELBERT HUBBARD, *The Note Book* (1927).

12. The strongest man on earth is he who stands most alone. HENRIK IBSEN, *An Enemy of the People* (1882), 5.

13. Neither smiles nor frowns, neither good intentions nor harsh words, are a substitute for strength. JOHN F. KENNEDY, campaign address, Alexandria, Va., Aug. 24, 1960.

14. If we are strong, our character will speak for itself. If we are weak, words will be of no help. JOHN F. KENNEDY, undelivered address, Dallas, Texas, Nov. 22, 1963.

15. So long as some are strong and some are weak, the weak will be driven to the wall. W. SOMERSET MAUGHAM, *The Summing Up* (1938), 73.

16. What is strength without a double share / Of wisdom? MILTON, *Samson Agonistes* (1671), 53.

17. An inability to take seriously for any length of time their enemies, their disasters, their misdeeds—that is the sign of the full strong natures. NIETZSCHE, *The Genealogy of Morals* (1887), 1.10, tr. Horace B. Samuel.

18. The strongest iron, hardened in the fire, / most often ends in scraps and shatterings. SOPHOCLES, *Antigone* (442–41 B.C.), tr. Elizabeth Wyckoff.

### STRIFE
**See 250. Discord**

### STRIKES
**See 1006. Unions**

### STUBBORNNESS
**See 644. Obstinacy**

### STUDY
**See 529. Learning**

## 934. STUPIDITY
**See also 268. Dullness; 351. Folly; 353. Fools; 445. Ignorance; 491. Intelligence**

1. Idiot, n. A member of a large and powerful tribe whose influence in human affairs has always been dominant and controlling. AMBROSE BIERCE, *The Devil's Dictionary* (1881–1911).

2. There must always be some who're brighter and some who're stupider. The latter make up for it by being better workers. BERTOLT BRECHT, *Baal* (1926), 10, tr. Eric Bentley and Martin Esslin.

3. With stupidity and sound digestion man may front much. THOMAS CARLYLE, *Sartor Resartus* (1833–34), 2.7.

4. When a finger points at the moon, the imbecile looks at the finger. CHINESE PROVERB.

5. An ass may bray a good while before he shakes the stars down. GEORGE ELIOT, *Romola* (1863), 3.50.

6. He that hath a head of wax must not walk in the sun. ENGLISH PROVERB.

7. A learned blockhead is a greater blockhead than an ignorant one. BENJAMIN FRANKLIN, *Poor Richard's Almanack* (1732–57).

8. He that makes himself an ass must not take it ill if men ride him. THOMAS FULLER, M.D., *Gnomologia* (1732), 2232.

9. Persons of slender intellectual stamina dread competition, as dwarfs are afraid of being run over in the street. WILLIAM HAZLITT, *Characteristics* (1823), 30.

10. The hardest thing to cope with is not selfishness or vanity or deceitfulness, but sheer stupidity. ERIC HOFFER, *The Passionate State of Mind* (1954), 210.

11. Stupidity often saves a man from going mad. OLIVER WENDELL HOLMES, SR., *The Autocrat of the Breakfast Table* (1858), 2.

12. An ox remains an ox, even if driven to Vienna. HUNGARIAN PROVERB.

13. It is so pleasant to come across people more stupid than ourselves. We love them at once for being so. JEROME K. JEROME, "On Cats and Dogs," *The Idle Thoughts of an Idle Fellow* (1889).

14. He that reads and grows no wiser seldom suspects his own deficiency, but complains of hard words and obscure sentences, and asks why books are written which cannot be understood. SAMUEL JOHNSON, *The Idler* (1758–60), 70.

15. If poverty is the mother of all crimes, lack of intelligence is their father. LA BRUYÈRE, *Characters* (1688), 11.13, tr. Henri Van Laun.

16. The empty vessel giveth a greater sound than the full barrel. JOHN LYLY, *Euphues: The Anatomy of Wit* (1579).

17. To serve an unintelligent man is like crying in the wilderness, massaging the

body of a dead man, planting water-lilies on dry land, whispering in the ear of the deaf. *Panchatantra* (c. 5th c.), 1, tr. Franklin Edgerton.

18. Nothing sways the stupid more than arguments they can't understand. CARDINAL DE RETZ, *Mémoires* (1718).

19. Against stupidity the very gods / Themselves contend in vain. SCHILLER, *The Maid of Orleans* (1801), 3.6.

20. He who deals with a blockhead will need much brain. SPANISH PROVERB.

21. One great mistake made by intelligent people is to refuse to believe that the world is as stupid as it is. MME DE TENCIN, quoted in Chamfort's *Caractères et anecdotes* (1771).

22. Whenever a man does a thoroughly stupid thing it is always from the noblest motive. OSCAR WILDE, *The Picture of Dorian Gray* (1891).

## 935. STYLE

**See also 280. Elegance; 396. Grammar; 1062. Writing and Writers**

1. The style is the man himself. GEORGES BUFFON, discourse on his reception into the French Academy, 1750.

2. Epithets, like pepper, / Give zest to what you write; / And if you strew them sparely, / They whet the appetite: / But if you lay them on too thick, / You spoil the matter quite! LEWIS CARROLL, "Poeta Fit, Non Nascitur" (1869).

3. Style is the dress of thoughts; and let them be ever so just, if your style is homely, coarse, and vulgar, they will appear to as much disadvantage. LORD CHESTERFIELD, *Letters to His Son*, Nov. 24, 1749.

4. Manner is all in all, whate'er is writ, / The substitute for genius, sense, and wit. WILLIAM COWPER, *Table Talk* (1782), 542.

5. Style is the perfection of a point of view. RICHARD EBERHART, "Meditation Two," *Selected Poems 1930–1965* (1965).

6. The great writer finds style as the mystic finds God, in his own soul. HAVELOCK ELLIS, *The Dance of Life* (1923), 4.

7. All progress in literary style lies in the heroic resolve to cast aside accretions and exuberances, all the conventions of a past age that were once beautiful because alive and are now false because dead. HAVELOCK ELLIS, *The Dance of Life* (1923), 4.

8. If any man wish to write a clear style, let him be first clear in his thoughts; and if any would write in a noble style, let him first possess a noble soul. GOETHE, quoted in Johann Peter Eckermann's *Conversations with Goethe*, April 14, 1824.

9. I might say that what amateurs call a style is usually only the unavoidable awkwardness in first trying to make something that has not heretofore been made. ERNEST HEMINGWAY, interview, *Writers at Work: Second Series* (1963).

10. One has to dismount from an idea, and get into the saddle again, at every parenthesis. OLIVER WENDELL HOLMES, SR., *The Autocrat of the Breakfast Table* (1858), 8.

11. Read over your compositions, and wherever you meet with a passage which you think is particularly fine, strike it out. SAMUEL JOHNSON, quoting a college tutor, in Boswell's *Life of Samuel Johnson*, April 30, 1773.

12. In all pointed sentences, some degree of accuracy must be sacrificed to conciseness. SAMUEL JOHNSON, "On the Bravery of the English Common Soldier," *Works* (1787), v. 10.

13. The most important things must be said simply, for they are spoiled by bombast; whereas trivial things must be described grandly, for they are supported only by aptness of expression, tone and manner. LA BRUYÈRE, *Characters* (1688), 5.77.

14. A period is to let the writer know he has finished his thought and he should stop there if he will only take the hint. ART LINKLETTER, *A Child's Garden of Misinformation* (1965), 3.

15. A good style should show no sign of effort. What is written should seem a happy accident. W. SOMERSET MAUGHAM, *The Summing Up* (1938), 13.

16. Style is the hallmark of a temperament stamped upon the material at hand. ANDRÉ MAUROIS, *The Art of Writing* (1960).

17. When we see a natural style, we are astonished and delighted; for we expected to see an author, and we find a man. PASCAL, *Pensées* (1670), 29, tr. W. F. Trotter.

18. Mere elegance of language can produce at best but an empty renown. PETRARCH, *Letter to Posterity* (1367–72).

19. Many writers profess great exactness

in punctuation, who never yet made a point. GEORGE DENNISON PRENTICE, *Prenticeana* (1860).

20. Style is a magic wand, and turns everything to gold that it touches. LOGAN PEARSALL SMITH, *Afterthoughts* (1931), 5.

21. In composing, as a general rule, run your pen through every other word you have written; you have no idea what vigor it will give your style. SYDNEY SMITH, quoted in Lady S. Holland's *Memoir* (1855), v. 1.11.

22. Proper words in proper places, make the true definition of a style. JONATHAN SWIFT, letter to a young clergyman, Jan. 9, 1720.

23. Style, like the human body, is specially beautiful when the veins are not prominent and the bones cannot be counted. TACITUS, *A Dialogue on Oratory* (c. A.D. 81), 21, tr. Alfred J. Church and William J. Brodribb.

24. As to the adjective: when in doubt, strike it out. MARK TWAIN, "Pudd'nhead Wilson's Calendar," *Pudd'nhead Wilson* (1894), 11.

25. A man's style is intrinsic and private with him like his voice or his gesture, partly a matter of inheritance, partly of cultivation. It is more than a pattern of expression. It is the pattern of the soul. MAURICE VALENCY, introduction to *Jean Giraudoux: Four Plays* (1958).

26. He most honors my style who learns under it to destroy the teacher. WALT WHITMAN, "Song of Myself," 47, *Leaves of Grass* (1855–92).

27. In matters of grave importance, style, not sincerity, is the vital thing. OSCAR WILDE, *The Importance of Being Earnest* (1895), 3.

## 936. SUBTLETY

**See also 137. Cleverness; 197. Craftiness**

1. I like to have a thing suggested rather than told in full. When every detail is given, the mind rests satisfied, and the imagination loses the desire to use its own wings. THOMAS BAILEY ALDRICH, "Leaves from a Notebook," *Ponkapog Papers* (1903).

2. There be many wise men that have secret hearts and transparent countenances. FRANCIS BACON, "Of Cunning," *Essays* (1625).

3. Be ye therefore wise as serpents, and harmless as doves. *Bible*, Matthew 10:16.

4. The most subtle, the strongest and deepest art—supreme art—is the one that does not at first allow itself to be recognized. ANDRÉ GIDE, *Journals*, 1921, tr. Justin O'Brien.

5. If you are not respected as subtle, you will be regarded as sure. BALTASAR GRACIÁN, *The Art of Worldly Wisdom* (1647), 271, tr. Joseph Jacobs.

6. Some people take more care to hide their wisdom than their folly. JONATHAN SWIFT, *Thoughts on Various Subjects* (1711).

## 937. SUBURBS

**See also 129. Cities; 191. The Country**

1. Slums may well be breeding-grounds of crime, but middle-class suburbs are incubators of apathy and delirium. CYRIL CONNOLLY, *The Unquiet Grave* (1945), 1.

2. Conformity may not always reign in the prosperous bourgeois suburb, but it ultimately always governs. LOUIS KRONENBERGER, *Company Manners* (1954), 3.3.

3. Suburbs are things to come into the city from. ART LINKLETTER, *A Child's Garden of Misinformation* (1965), 13.

4. The suburbs are merely vast dormitories, where a man may sleep in comparatively pure air while his office is being washed. WILLIAM MC FEE, *Casuals of the Sea* (1916), 1.1.14.

5. A commuter is one who never knows / how a show comes out because he / has to leave early to catch a train / to get him back to the country in / time to catch a train to bring him / back to the city. OGDEN NASH, "The Banker's Special," *Versus* (1949).

## 938. SUCCESS

**See also 6. Achievement; 33. Ambition; 170. Conquest; 327. Failure; 744. Prosperity**

1. The ability to convert ideas to things is the secret of outward success. HENRY WARD BEECHER, *Proverbs from Plymouth Pulpit* (1887).

2. The toughest thing about success is that you've got to keep on being a success. IRVING BERLIN, *Theatre Arts*, February 1958.

3. A minute's success pays the failure of years. ROBERT BROWNING, "Apollo and the Fates" (1886).

4. Constant success shows us but one side of the world. For as it surrounds us with friends who will tell us only our merits, so it silences those enemies from whom alone we can learn our defects. CHARLES CALEB COLTON, *Lacon* (1825), 1.513.

5. Success seems to be that which forms the distinction between confidence and conceit. CHARLES CALEB COLTON, *Lacon* (1825), 1.75.

6. To win without risk is to triumph without glory. CORNEILLE, *The Cid* (1636), 2.2.

7. Success is counted sweetest / By those who ne'er succeed. EMILY DICKINSON, poem (c. 1859).

8. Success is relative: It is what we can make of the mess we have made of things. T. S. ELIOT, *The Family Reunion* (1939), 2.3.

9. He who would climb the ladder must begin at the bottom. ENGLISH PROVERB.

10. According to success do we gain a reputation for judgment. EURIPIDES, *Hippolytus* (428 B.C.), tr. Moses Hadas and John McLean.

11. Success is feminine and like a woman; if you cringe before her, she will override you. So the way to treat her is to show her the back of your hand. Then maybe she will do the crawling. WILLIAM FAULKNER, interview, *Writers at Work: First Series* (1958).

12. The compensation of a very early success is a conviction that life is a romantic matter. In the best sense one stays young. F. SCOTT FITZGERALD, "Early Success," *The Crack-Up* (1945).

13. Nothing is more humiliating than to see idiots succeed in enterprises we have failed in. FLAUBERT, *Sentimental Education* (1869), 5.

14. A successful man loses no reputation. THOMAS FULLER, M.D., *Gnomologia* (1732), 426.

15. The way to secure success is to be more anxious about obtaining than about deserving it. WILLIAM HAZLITT, "On the Qualifications Necessary to Success in Life," *The Plain Speaker* (1826).

16. A successful man cannot realize how hard an unsuccessful man finds life. EDGAR WATSON HOWE, *Country Town Sayings* (1911).

17. When a man gets up in the world, people want to down him; when he gets down in the world, people want to help him. EDGAR WATSON HOWE, *Country Town Sayings* (1911).

18. Pray that success will not come any faster than you are able to endure it. ELBERT HUBBARD, *The Note Book* (1927).

19. Some men succeed by what they know; some by what they do; and a few by what they are. ELBERT HUBBARD, *The Note Book* (1927).

20. The way to rise is to obey and please. BEN JONSON, *Sejanus His Fall* (1603), 3.3.

21. The technique of winning is so shoddy, the terms of winning are so ignoble, the tenure of winning is so brief; and the specter of the has-been—a shameful rather than a pitiable sight today—brings a sudden chill even to our sunlit moments. LOUIS KRONENBERGER, "The Spirit of the Age," *Company Manners* (1954).

22. Succeed we must, at all cost—even if it means being a *dead* millionaire at fifty. LOUIS KRONENBERGER, "Our Unhappy Happy Endings," *The Cart and the Horse* (1964), 2.

23. There are two ways of rising in the world, either by your own industry or by the folly of others. LA BRUYÈRE, *Characters* (1688), 6.52, tr. Henri Van Laun.

24. It is almost as easy to be enervated by triumph as by defeat. MAX LERNER, "The Consequences of the Atom," *Actions and Passions* (1949).

25. Success makes men rigid and they tend to exalt stability over all the other virtues; tired of the effort of willing they become fanatics about conservatism. WALTER LIPPMANN, "Routineer and Inventor," *A Preface to Politics* (1914).

26. Nothing fails like success; nothing is so defeated as yesterday's triumphant Cause. PHYLLIS MC GINLEY, "How to Get Along with Men," *The Province of the Heart* (1959).

27. Failure makes people bitter and cruel. Success improves the character of the man. W. SOMERSET MAUGHAM, *The Summing Up* (1938), 48.

28. The success of most things depends upon knowing how long it will take to succeed. MONTESQUIEU, *Pensées diverses* (1750).

29. There is only one success—to be able to spend your life in your own way. CHRISTOPHER MORLEY, *Where the Blue Begins* (1922).

30. If a man be self-controlled, truthful, wise, and resolute, is there aught that can stay out of the reach of such a man? *Panchatantra* (c. 5th c.), 3, tr. Franklin Edgerton.

31. Most men that do thrive in the world do forget to take pleasure during the time that they are getting their estate, but reserve that till they have got one, and then it is too late for them to enjoy it. SAMUEL PEPYS, *Diary*, March 10, 1666.

32. Success abides longer among men / when it is planted by the hand of God. PINDAR, *Odes* (5th c. B.C.), Nemea 8, tr. Richmond Lattimore.

33. Success / for the striver washes away the effort of striving. PINDAR, *Odes* (5th c. B.C.), Olympia 2, tr. Richmond Lattimore.

34. When men succeed, even their neighbors think them wise. PINDAR, *Odes* (5th c. B.C.), Olympia 5, tr. Richmond Lattimore.

35. Success causes us to be more praised than known. JOSEPH ROUX, *Meditations of a Parish Priest* (1886), 4.46, tr. Isabel F. Hapgood.

36. Unless a man has been taught what to do with success after getting it, the achievement of it must inevitably leave him a prey to boredom. BERTRAND RUSSELL, *The Conquest of Happiness* (1930), 3.

37. Success is not greedy, as people think, but insignificant. That's why it satisfies nobody. SENECA, *Letters to Lucilius* (1st c.), 118.6, tr. E. Phillips Barker.

38. Lowliness is young ambition's ladder, / Whereto the climber-upward turns his face; / But when he once attains the upmost round, / He then unto the ladder turns his back, / Looks in the clouds, scorning the base degrees / By which he did ascend. SHAKESPEARE, *Julius Caesar* (1599–1600), 2.1.22.

39. There is no success without hardship. SOPHOCLES, *Electra* (c. 418–14 B.C.), tr. David Grene.

40. Is there anything in life so disenchanting as attainment? ROBERT LOUIS STEVENSON, "The Adventure of the Hansom Cab," *New Arabian Nights* (1882).

41. The key to success isn't much good until one discovers the right lock to insert it in. TEHYI HSIEH, *Chinese Epigrams Inside Out and Proverbs* (1948), 7.

42. A man who raises himself by degrees to wealth and power, contracts, in the course of this protracted labor, habits of prudence and restraint which he cannot afterwards shake off. A man cannot gradually enlarge his mind as he does his house. ALEXIS DE TOCQUEVILLE, *Democracy in America* (1835-39), 2.3.19.

43. I know that unremitting attention to business is the price of success, but I don't know what success is. CHARLES DUDLEY WARNER, "First Study," *Backlog Studies* (1873).

## 939. SUFFERING

**See also 17. Adversity; 474. Injury; 698. Pleasure; 699. Pleasure and Pain; 870. Self-pity; 911. Sorrow; 1004. Unhappiness; 1045. Weeping**

1. For sufferers it is sweet to know beforehand clearly the pain that still remains for them. AESCHYLUS, *Prometheus Bound* (c. 478 B.C.), tr. David Grene.

2. Who, except the gods, / can live time through forever without any pain? AESCHYLUS, *Agamemnon* (458 B.C.), tr. Richmond Lattimore.

3. Nothing is more dear to them [men] than their own suffering— They are afraid that they will lose it— They feel it, like a whip cracking over their heads, striking them and yet befriending them; it wounds them, but it also reassures them. UGO BETTI, *Landslide* (1936), 3, tr. G. H. McWilliam.

4. It is infinitely easier to suffer in obedience to a human command than to accept suffering as free, responsible men. DIETRICH BONHOEFFER, "After Ten Years," *Letters and Papers from Prison* (1953), tr. Eberhard Bethge.

5. There is no point in being overwhelmed by the appalling total of human suffering; such a total does not exist. Neither poverty nor pain is accumulable. JORGE LUIS BORGES, "A New Refutation of Time," *Other Inquisitions* (1952), 1, tr. R. L. Simms.

6. The suffering man ought really to consume his own smoke; there is no good in emitting smoke till you have made it into fire. THOMAS CARLYLE, *On Heroes, Hero-Worship and the Heroic in History* (1841), 5.

7. We cannot live, sorrow or die for somebody else, for suffering is too precious to be shared. EDWARD DAHLBERG, *Because I Was Flesh* (1963).

8. Either the human being must suffer and struggle as the price of a more searching vision, or his gaze must be shallow and without intellectual revelation. THOMAS DE QUINCEY, "Vision of Life," *Suspiria de Profundis* (1845).

9. A *Wounded* Deer—leaps highest. EMILY DICKINSON, poem (c. 1860).

10. Pain—has an Element of Blank— / It cannot recollect / When it begun—or if there were / A time when it was not—. EMILY DICKINSON, poem (c. 1862).

11. Suffering is the sole origin of consciousness. DOSTOEVSKY, *Notes from Underground* (1864), 1.9, tr. Constance Garnett.

12. Pain and death are a part of life. To reject them is to reject life itself. HAVELOCK ELLIS, *On Life and Sex: Essays of Love and Virtue* (1937), 2.5.

13. Pain, indolence, sterility, endless ennui have also their lesson for you, if you are great. EMERSON, *Journals*, 1845.

14. An hour of pain is as long as a day of pleasure. ENGLISH PROVERB.

15. Much of your pain is self-chosen. / It is the bitter potion by which the physician within you heals your sick self. KAHLIL GIBRAN, "On Pain," *The Prophet* (1923).

16. Forget your personal tragedy. We are all bitched from the start and you especially have to be hurt like hell before you can write seriously. But when you get the damned hurt use it—don't cheat with it. ERNEST HEMINGWAY, quoted in Andrew Turnbull's *Scott Fitzgerald* (1962), 14.

17. All the reasoning in the world, all the proof-texts in old manuscripts, cannot reconcile this supposition of a world of sleepless and endless torment with the declaration that "God is love." OLIVER WENDELL HOLMES, SR., *Over the Teacups* (1891), 10.

18. Each one of us must suffer long to himself before he can learn that he is but one in a great community of wretchedness which has been pitilessly repeating itself from the foundation of the world. WILLIAM DEAN HOWELLS, *The Rise of Silas Lapham* (1885), 17.

19. God will not look you over for medals, degrees or diplomas, but for scars! ELBERT HUBBARD, *The Note Book* (1927).

20. Pleasure is oft a visitant; but pain / Clings cruelly to us. JOHN KEATS, *Endymion* (1817), 1.

21. Although the world is full of suffering, it is full also of the overcoming of it. HELEN KELLER, *Optimism* (1903), 1.

22. Beauty cannot disguise nor music melt / A pain undiagnosable but felt. ANNE MORROW LINDBERGH, "The Stone," *The Unicorn and Other Poems, 1935–1955* (1956).

23. Know how sublime a thing it is / To suffer and be strong. LONGFELLOW, "The Light of the Stars," *Voices of the Night* (1839).

24. Even pain / Pricks to livelier living. AMY LOWELL, "Happiness," *Sword Blades and Poppy Seeds* (1914).

25. To be good we must needs have suffered; but perhaps it is necessary to have caused suffering before we can become better. MAURICE MAETERLINCK, "The Invisible Goodness," *The Treasure of the Humble* (1896), tr. Alfred Sutro.

26. If you are distressed by anything external, the pain is not due to the thing itself but to your own estimate of it; and this you have the power to revoke at any moment. MARCUS AURELIUS, *Meditations* (2nd c.), 8.47, tr. Maxwell Staniforth.

27. It is not true that suffering ennobles the character; happiness does that sometimes, but suffering, for the most part, makes men petty and vindictive. W. SOMERSET MAUGHAM, *The Moon and Sixpence* (1919), 17.

28. Suffering for truth's sake / Is fortitude to highest victory, / And to the faithful death the gate of life. MILTON, *Paradise Lost* (1667), 12.569.

29. He who fears he shall suffer, already suffers what he fears. MONTAIGNE, "Of experience," *Essays* (1580–88), tr. Charles Cotton and W. C. Hazlitt.

30. We are more sensible of one little touch of a surgeon's lancet than of twenty wounds with a sword in the heat of fight. MONTAIGNE, "That the relish of good and evil depends in a great measure upon the opinion we have of them," *Essays* (1580–88), tr. Charles Cotton and W. C. Hazlitt.

31. What really raises one's indignation against suffering is not suffering intrinsi-

cally, but the senselessness of suffering. NIETZSCHE, *The Genealogy of Morals* (1887), 2.7, tr. Horace B. Samuel.

32. This is Daddy's bedtime secret for today: Man is born broken. He lives by mending. The grace of God is glue. EUGENE O'NEILL, *The Great God Brown* (1926).

33. Most people get a fair amount of fun out of their lives, but on balance life is suffering, and only the very young or the very foolish imagine otherwise. GEORGE ORWELL, "Lear, Tolstoy and the Fool," *Shooting an Elephant* (1950).

34. Man's grandeur stems from his knowledge of his own misery. A tree does not know itself to be miserable. PASCAL, *Pensées* (1670), 397.

35. Pain makes man think. Thought makes man wise. Wisdom makes life endurable. JOHN PATRICK, *The Teahouse of the August Moon* (1953).

36. Man never reasons so much and becomes so introspective as when he suffers; since he is anxious to get at the cause of his sufferings, to learn who has produced them, and whether it is just or unjust that he should have to bear them. LUIGI PIRANDELLO, *Six Characters in Search of an Author* (1921), 3, tr. Edward Storer.

37. Suffering is above, not below. And everyone thinks that suffering is below. And everyone wants to rise. ANTONIO PORCHIA, *Voces* (1968), tr. W. S. Merwin.

38. Who breathes must suffer, and who thinks must mourn; / And he alone is blessed who ne'er was born. MATTHEW PRIOR, *Solomon on the Vanity of the World* (1718), 3.

39. To a great extent, suffering is a sort of need felt by the organism to make itself familiar with a new state, which makes it uneasy, to adapt its sensibility to that state. MARCEL PROUST, *Remembrance of Things Past: The Guermantes Way* (1913–27), tr. C. K. Scott-Moncrieff.

40. We are healed of a suffering only by experiencing it to the full. MARCEL PROUST, *Remembrance of Things Past: The Sweet Cheat Gone* (1913–27), tr. C. K. Scott-Moncrieff.

41. Pain will force even the truthful to speak falsely. PUBLILIUS SYRUS, *Moral Sayings* (1st c. B.C.), 232, tr. Darius Lyman.

42. Pain is unjust, and all the arguments / That cannot soothe it only rouse suspicion. RACINE, *Britannicus* (1669), 1, tr. Paul Landis and Robert Henderson.

43. If pain could have cured us we should long ago have been saved. GEORGE SANTAYANA, *The Life of Reason: Reason in Common Sense* (1905–06), 9.

44. A man who suffers before it is necessary, suffers more than is necessary. SENECA, *Letters to Lucilius* (1st c.), 98, tr. E. Phillips Barker.

45. One fire burns out another's burning; / One pain is lessened by another's anguish. SHAKESPEARE, *Romeo and Juliet* (1594–95), 1.2.46.

46. Oh, lift me as a wave, a leaf, a cloud! / I fall upon the thorns of life! I bleed! SHELLEY, "Ode to the West Wind" (1819), 4.

47. The history of a soldier's wound beguiles the pain of it. LAURENCE STERNE, *Tristram Shandy* (1759–67), 1.25.

48. How vivid is the suffering of the few when the people are few and how the suffering of nameless millions in two world wars is blurred over by numbers. EDWIN WAY TEALE, *Autumn Across America* (1956), 19.

49. We feel and weigh soon enough what we suffer from others: but how much others suffer from us, of this we take no heed. THOMAS À KEMPIS, *The Imitation of Christ* (1426), 2.5.

50. Nothing begins and nothing ends / That is not paid with moan; / For we are born in other's pain, / And perish in our own. FRANCIS THOMPSON, "Daisy" (1890).

51. Hearts live by being wounded. OSCAR WILDE, *A Woman of No Importance* (1893), 3.

52. Suffering is one very long moment. We can not divide it by seasons. We can only record its moods and chronicle their return. OSCAR WILDE, *De Profundis* (1905).

53. Clergymen and people who use phrases without wisdom sometimes talk of suffering as a mystery. It is really a revelation. OSCAR WILDE, *De Profundis* (1905).

54. Suffering is permanent, obscure and dark, / And shares the nature of infinity. WILLIAM WORDSWORTH, *The Borderers* (1795–96).

55. Nothing can be sole or whole / That has not been rent. WILLIAM BUTLER YEATS, "Crazy Jane Talks with the Bishop," *Words for Music Perhaps* (1932).

## 940. SUFFICIENCY

**See also 310. Excess; 592. Moderation; 839. Satisfaction**

1. You never know what is enough unless you know what is more than enough. WILLIAM BLAKE, "Proverbs of Hell," *The Marriage of Heaven and Hell* (1790).

2. Sufficiency's enough for men of sense. EURIPIDES, *The Phoenician Women* (c. 411–409 B.C.), tr. Elizabeth Wyckoff.

3. Enough is as good as a feast. JOHN HEYWOOD, *Proverbs* (1546), 1.11.

4. There is satiety in all things, in sleep, and love-making, / in the loveliness of singing and the innocent dance. HOMER, *Iliad* (9th c. B.C.), 13.636, tr. Richmond Lattimore.

## 941. SUICIDE

**See also 866. Self-injury**

1. To run away from trouble is a form of cowardice and, while it is true that the suicide braves death, he does it not for some noble object but to escape some ill. ARISTOTLE, *Nicomachean Ethics* (4th c. B.C.), 3.7, tr. J. A. K. Thomson.

2. There is but one truly serious philosophical problem, and that is suicide. Judging whether life is or is not worth living amounts to answering the fundamental question of philosophy. ALBERT CAMUS, "An Absurd Reasoning," *The Myth of Sisyphus* (1942), tr. Justin O'Brien.

3. As soon as one does not kill oneself, one must keep silent about life. ALBERT CAMUS, *Notebooks 1935–1942* (1962), 1, tr. Philip Thody.

4. To attempt suicide is a criminal offense. Any man who, of his own will, tries to escape the treadmill to which the rest of us feel chained incites our envy, and therefore our fury. We do not suffer him to go unpunished. ALEXANDER CHASE, *Perspectives* (1966).

5. When even despair ceases to serve any creative purpose, then surely we are justified in suicide. CYRIL CONNOLLY, *The Unquiet Grave* (1945), 1.

6. The question is whether [suicide] is the way *out*, or the way *in*. EMERSON, *Journals*, 1839.

7. He who saves a man against his will as good as murders him. HORACE, *Ars Poetica* (13–8 B.C.).

8. When all the blandishments of life are gone, / The coward sneaks to death, the brave live on. MARTIAL, *Epigrams* (A.D. 86), 11.56, tr. Sewell.

9. Why dost thou complain of this world? It detains thee not; thy own cowardice is the cause, if thou livest in pain. MONTAIGNE, "A custom of the Isle of Cea," *Essays* (1580–88), tr. Charles Cotton and W. C. Hazlitt.

10. Razors pain you; / Rivers are damp; / Acids stain you; / And drugs cause cramp. / Guns aren't lawful; / Nooses give; / Gas smells awful; / You might as well live. DOROTHY PARKER, "Résumé," *Enough Rope* (1926), 2.

11. Amid the sufferings of life on earth, suicide is God's best gift to man. PLINY THE ELDER, *Natural History* (1st c.), 2.

12. We cannot tear out a single page from our life, but we can throw the whole book into the fire. GEORGE SAND, *Mauprat* (1837).

13. Is it sin / To rush into the secret house of death / Ere death dare come to us? SHAKESPEARE, *Antony and Cleopatra* (1606–07), 4.15.80.

14. It is great / To do that thing that ends all other deeds, / Which shackles accidents and bolts up change. SHAKESPEARE, *Antony and Cleopatra* (1606–07), 5.2.4.

15. Whatever crazy sorrow saith, / No life that breathes with human breath / Has ever truly longed for death. ALFRED, LORD TENNYSON, "The Two Voices" (1842).

16. The man who, in a fit of melancholy, kills himself today, would have wished to live had he waited a week. VOLTAIRE, "Cato," *Philosophical Dictionary* (1764).

## 942. SUITABILITY

**See also 972. Timeliness**

1. Send not for a hatchet to break open an egg with. THOMAS FULLER, M.D., *Gnomologia* (1732), 4097.

2. Servants and ornaments are to be used only in their proper places. For a man does not fasten a crest-gem on his foot simply because he has the power to do so. *Panchatantra* (c. 5th c.), 1, tr. Franklin Edgerton.

3. With our mortal minds we should seek from the gods that which becomes us. PINDAR, *Odes* (5th c. B.C.), Pythia 3, tr. Richmond Lattimore.

4. The officer and the office, the doer and the thing done, seldom fit so exactly that we can say they were almost made for each other. SYDNEY SMITH, *Sketches of Moral Philosophy* (1804–06), 9.

5. Every beauty, when out of its place, is a beauty no longer. VOLTAIRE, "Wit, Spirit, Intellect," *Philosophical Dictionary* (1764).

## SUMMER

**See 848. Seasons**

## 943. SUN

**See also 138. Climate; 413. The Heavens**

1. The adventure of the sun is the great natural drama by which we live, and not to have joy in it and awe of it, not to share in it, is to close a dull door on nature's sustaining and poetic spirit. HENRY BESTON, "Midwinter," *The Outermost House* (1928).

2. Goodness comes out of people who bask in the sun, as it does out of a sweet apple roasted before the fire. CHARLES DUDLEY WARNER, "Seventeenth Week," *My Summer in a Garden* (1871).

## 944. SUPERFICIALITY

**See also 54. Artificiality; 734. Profundity**

1. We are the hollow men / We are the stuffed men / Leaning together. T. S. ELIOT, "The Hollow Men" (1925), 1.

2. God will have life to be real; we will be damned, but it shall be theatrical. EMERSON, *Journals*, 1843.

3. The moral deteriorations attendant on a false and shallow life, without strength enough to keep itself sweet, are among the most pitiable wrongs that mortals suffer. NATHANIEL HAWTHORNE, *The Blithedale Romance* (1852), 12.

4. Do not turn your back on anyone. You may be painted on one side only. STANISLAW LEC, *Unkempt Thoughts* (1962), tr. Jacek Galazka.

5. Anyone who has looked deeply into the world may guess how much wisdom lies in the superficiality of men. The instinct that preserves them teaches them to be flighty, light, and false. NIETZSCHE, *Beyond Good and Evil* (1886), 59, tr. Walter Kaufmann.

6. Light boats sail swift, though greater hulks draw deep. SHAKESPEARE, *Troilus and Cressida* (1601–02), 2.3.277.

7. Only the shallow know themselves. OSCAR WILDE, "Phrases and Philosophies for the Use of the Young" (1891).

## 945. SUPERIORITY

**See also 309. Excellence; 578. Merit; 628. Nobility**

1. He who ascends to mountain tops, shall find / The loftiest peaks most wrapt in clouds and snow; / He who surpasses or subdues mankind, / Must look down on the hate of those below. BYRON, *Childe Harold's Pilgrimage* (1812–18), 3.45.

2. What the superior man seeks is in himself. What the mean man seeks is in others. CONFUCIUS, *Analects* (6th c. B.C.), 15.20, tr. James Legge.

3. Be more than man, or thou'rt less than an ant. JOHN DONNE, *An Anatomy of the World; The First Anniversary* (1612).

4. To me one man is worth ten thousand if he is first-rate. HERACLITUS, *Fragments* (c. 500 B.C.), 84, tr. Philip Wheelwright.

5. There is nothing noble about being superior to some other man. The true nobility is in being superior to your previous self. HINDUSTANI PROVERB.

6. Whoever rises above those who once pleased themselves with equality, will have many malevolent gazers at his eminence. SAMUEL JOHNSON, *The Rambler* (1750–52), 172.

7. The highest summits and those elevated above the level of other things are mostly blasted by envy as by a thunderbolt. LUCRETIUS, *On the Nature of Things* (1st c. B.C.), 5, tr. H. A. J. Munro.

8. In our society to admit inferiority is to be a fool, and to admit superiority is to be an outcast. Those who are in reality superior in intelligence can be accepted by their fellows only if they pretend they are not. MARYA MANNES, *More in Anger* (1958), 1.1.

9. we parted each feeling / superior to the other / and is not that / feeling after all one

of the great / desiderata of social intercourse. DON MARQUIS, "the merry flea," *Archy and Mehitabel* (1927).

10. We are wrong to fear superiority of mind and soul; this superiority is very moral, for understanding everything makes a person tolerant and the capacity to feel deeply inspires great goodness. MME DE STAËL, *Corinne* (1807), 18.5.

11. Superiority and inferiority are individual, not racial or national. PHILIP WYLIE, *Generation of Vipers* (1942), 1.

## 946. SUPERNATURAL

**See also 381. Ghosts; 586. Miracles**

1. Religion has made an honest woman of the supernatural, / And we won't have it kicking over the traces again. CHRISTOPHER FRY, *The Lady's Not for Burning* (1949), 1.

2. The supernatural is the natural not yet understood. ELBERT HUBBARD, *The Note Book* (1927).

3. Faith in the supernatural is a desperate wager made by man at the lowest ebb of his fortunes. GEORGE SANTAYANA, *The Life of Reason: Reason in Science* (1905–06), 10.

4. There are more things in heaven and earth, Horatio, / Than are dreamt of in your philosophy. SHAKESPEARE, *Hamlet* (1600), 1.5.166.

## 947. SUPERSTITION

**See also 76. Belief**

1. In all superstition wise men follow fools. FRANCIS BACON, "Of Superstition," *Essays* (1625).

2. All people have their blind side—their superstitions. CHARLES LAMB, "Mrs. Battle's Opinions on Whist," *Essays of Elia* (1823).

3. The superstition in which we grew up, / Though we may recognize it, does not lose / Its power over us.—Not all are free / Who make mock of their chains. GOTTHOLD EPHRAIM LESSING, *Nathan the Wise* (1779), 4.4, tr. Bayard Quincy Morgan.

4. Men become superstitious, not because they have too much imagination, but because they are not aware that they have any. GEORGE SANTAYANA, *Little Essays* (1920), 25, ed. Logan Pearsall Smith.

5. Superstition sets the whole world in flames; philosophy extinguishes them. VOLTAIRE, "Superstition," *Philosophical Dictionary* (1764).

## SURFEIT

**See 310. Excess**

## 948. SURPRISE

**See also 199. Credulity; 1056. Wonder**

1. A man surprised is half beaten. THOMAS FULLER, M.D., *Gnomologia* (1732), 310.

2. Stupefaction, when it persists, becomes stupidity. JOSÉ ORTEGA Y GASSET, "In Search of Goethe from Within, Letter to a German," *Partisan Review*, December 1949, tr. Willard R. Trask.

3. Surprise is the greatest gift which life can grant us. BORIS PASTERNAK, "On Modesty and Boldness," speech at the Writers' Plenum, Minsk, February 1936.

4. Life is very singularly made to surprise us (where it does not utterly appall us). RAINER MARIA RILKE, letter to Major-General von Sedlakowitz, Dec. 9, 1920, in *Wartime Letters*, tr. M. D. Herter Norton.

5. Unfamiliarity lends weight to misfortune, and there was never a man whose grief was not heightened by surprise. SENECA, *Letters to Lucilius* (1st c.), 91.3, tr. E. Phillips Barker.

## 949. SURVIVAL

**See also 226. Defense; 285. Endurance; 633. Nuclear Power; 1042. Weapons**

1. It isn't important to come out on top, what matters is to be the one who comes out alive. BERTOLT BRECHT, *Jungle of Cities* (1924), 10, tr. Anselm Hollo.

2. Self-preservation is the first principle of our nature. ALEXANDER HAMILTON, *A Full Vindication. . . ,* Dec. 15, 1774.

3. Irrational barriers and ancient prejudices fall quickly when the question of survival itself is at stake. JOHN F. KENNEDY, address, United Negro College Fund Convocation, Indianapolis, Ind., April 12, 1959.

4. Whether science—and indeed civilization in general—can long survive depends upon psychology, that is to say, it depends

upon what human beings desire. BERTRAND RUSSELL, "The Science to Save Us from Science," *The New York Times Magazine*, March 19, 1950.

5. Nature is indifferent to the survival of the human species, including Americans. ADLAI STEVENSON, speech, radio and television, Sept. 29, 1952.

## SUSPICION

See 257. Distrust

## 950. SWEARING

See also 209. Cursing; 635. Oaths

1. Th' best thing about a little judicyous swearin' is that it keeps th' temper. 'Twas intinded as a compromise between runnin' away an' fightin'. FINLEY PETER DUNNE, "Swearing," *Observations by Mr. Dooley* (1902).

2. When you're lying awake with a dismal headache, and repose is tabooed by anxiety, / I conceive you may use any language you choose to indulge in without impropriety. W. S. GILBERT, *Iolanthe* (1882), 2.

3. Let us swear while we may, for in heaven it will not be allowed. MARK TWAIN, *Notebook* (1935).

## 951. SWITZERLAND

1. I look upon Switzerland as an inferior sort of Scotland. SYDNEY SMITH, letter to Lord Holland, 1815.

## 952. SYMBOLS

See also 569. Meaning; 830. Sacrament

1. A person gets from a symbol the meaning he puts into it, and what is one man's comfort and inspiration is another's jest and scorn. JUSTICE ROBERT JACKSON, *West Virginia State Board v. Barnette* (1943).

## 953. SYMPATHY

See also 166. Confidences; 692. Pity; 1001. Understanding Others

1. There is no consoler, no confidant that half the instinct does not want to reject. The spilling over, the burst of tears and words, the ejaculation of the private personal grief accomplishes itself, like a convulsion, in circumstances that one would never choose. ELIZABETH BOWEN, *The Death of the Heart* (1938), 3.3.

2. Unto a broken heart / No other one may go / Without the high prerogative / Itself hath suffered too. EMILY DICKINSON, *Poems* (c. 1862–86).

3. Sympathy is a supporting atmosphere, and in it we unfold easily and well. EMERSON, *Journals*, 1836.

4. A sympathetic person is placed in the dilemma of a swimmer among drowning men, who all catch at him, and if he gives so much as a leg or a finger, they will drown him. EMERSON, "Experience," *Essays: Second Series* (1844).

5. Search not a wound too deep lest thou make a new one. THOMAS FULLER, M.D., *Gnomologia* (1732), 4084.

6. Our sympathy is cold to the relation of distant misery. EDWARD GIBBON, *Decline and Fall of the Roman Empire* (1776), 49.

7. When you are in trouble, people who call to sympathize are really looking for the particulars. EDGAR WATSON HOWE, *Country Town Sayings* (1911).

8. Wisdom must go with Sympathy, else the emotions will become maudlin and pity may be wasted on a poodle instead of a child—on a field-mouse instead of a human soul. ELBERT HUBBARD, *The Note Book* (1927).

9. The comforter's head never aches. ITALIAN PROVERB.

10. Pity may represent little more than the impersonal concern which prompts the mailing of a check, but true sympathy is the personal concern which demands the giving of one's soul. MARTIN LUTHER KING, JR., *Strength to Love* (1963), 3.3.

11. Of all cruelties those are the most intolerable that come under the name of condolence and consolation. WALTER SAVAGE LANDOR, letter to Robert Southey, 1816.

12. No one is so accursed by fate, / No one so utterly desolate, / But some heart, though unknown, / Responds unto his own. LONGFELLOW, "Endymion" (1842), 8.

13. When you live next to the cemetery, you cannot weep for everyone. RUSSIAN PROVERB.

14. Pathos is the sense of distance. SAINT-

EXUPÉRY, *Flight to Arras* (1942), 12, tr. Lewis Galantière.

15. There is nothing sweeter than to be sympathized with. GEORGE SANTAYANA, *The Life of Reason: Reason in Common Sense* (1905–06), 6.

16. Before an affliction is digested, consolation ever comes too soon; and after it is digested, it comes too late. LAURENCE STERNE, *Tristram Shandy* (1759–67), 3.29.

## 954. SYSTEMS

**See also 485. Institutions; 654. Order; 688. Philosophers and Philosophy; 778. Reason; 967. Theory**

1. Our systems, perhaps, are nothing more than an unconscious apology for our faults—a gigantic scaffolding whose object is to hide from us our favorite sin. HENRI FRÉDÉRIC AMIEL, *Journal*, Aug. 13, 1865, tr. Mrs. Humphry Ward.

2. I must create a system or be enslaved by another man's. WILLIAM BLAKE, motto, *Jerusalem* (1804–20).

3. A system is nothing more than the subordination of all aspects of the universe to any one such aspect. JORGE LUIS BORGES, "Tlon, Uqbar, Orbis Tertius," *Labyrinths* (1962).

4. I distrust all systematisers, and avoid them. The will to a system shows a lack of honesty. NIETZSCHE, "Maxims and Missiles," 26, *Twilight of the Idols* (1888), tr. Anthony M. Ludovici.

# T

## 955. TACT

**See also 824. Rudeness**

1. You never know till you try to reach them how accessible men are; but you must approach each man by the right door. HENRY WARD BEECHER, *Proverbs from Plymouth Pulpit* (1887).

2. Silence is not always tact and it is tact that is golden, not silence. SAMUEL BUTLER (d. 1902), "Higgledy-Piggledy," *Note-Books* (1912).

3. A tactless man is like an axe on an embroidery frame. MALAY PROVERB.

4. Some people mistake weakness for tact. If they are silent when they ought to speak and so feign an agreement they do not feel, they call it being tactful. Cowardice would be a much better name. SIR FRANK MEDLICOTT, *Reader's Digest*, July 1958.

5. Talk to every woman as if you loved her, and to every man as if he bored you, and at the end of your first season you will have the reputation of possessing the most perfect social tact. OSCAR WILDE, *A Woman of No Importance* (1893), 3.

## 956. TALENT

**See also 1. Ability; 309. Excellence; 375. Genius vs. Talent**

1. Talent is like a faucet; while it is open, one must write. Inspiration is a farce that poets have invented to give themselves importance. JEAN ANOUILH, *The New York Times*, Oct. 2, 1960.

2. It takes little talent to see clearly what lies under one's nose, a good deal of it to know in what direction to point that organ. W. H. AUDEN, "Writing," *The Dyer's Hand* (1962).

3. The handsome gifts that fate and nature lend us / Most often are the very ones that end us. CHAUCER, "Words of the Host to the Physician and to the Pardoner," *The Canterbury Tales* (c. 1387–1400), tr. Nevill Coghill.

4. There is hardly anybody good for everything, and there is scarcely anybody who is absolutely good for nothing. LORD CHESTERFIELD, *Letters to His Son*, Jan. 2, 1748.

5. Mediocrity knows nothing higher than itself, but talent instantly recognizes genius. SIR ARTHUR CONAN DOYLE, *The Valley of Fear* (1915).

6. A forte always makes a foible. EMERSON, *Journals*, 1859.

7. The most gifted natures are perhaps also the most trembling. ANDRÉ GIDE, *Journals*, 1907, tr. Justin O'Brien.

8. Talent, I say, is what an actor needs. And talent is faith in oneself, one's own powers. MAXIM GORKY, *The Lower Depths* (1903), 1, tr. Alexander Bakshy.

9. Nothing is so frequent as to mistake an ordinary human gift for a special and extraordinary endowment. OLIVER WENDELL

HOLMES, SR., *The Poet at the Breakfast Table* (1872), 6.

10. Never to be cast away are the gifts of the gods, magnificent, / which they give of their own will, no man could have them for wanting them. HOMER, *Iliad* (9th c. B.C.), 3.65, tr. Richmond Lattimore.

11. There is no so wretched and coarse a soul wherein some particular faculty is not seen to shine. MONTAIGNE, "Of presumption," *Essays* (1580–88), tr. Charles Cotton and W. C. Hazlitt.

12. What a man *is* begins to betray itself when his talent decreases—when he stops showing what he *can do*. Talent, too, is finery; finery, too, is a hiding place. NIETZSCHE, *Beyond Good and Evil* (1886), 130, tr. Walter Kaufmann.

13. Behind a remarkable scholar one finds, not infrequently, a mediocre man, and behind a mediocre artist quite often—a very remarkable man. NIETZSCHE, *Beyond Good and Evil* (1886), 137, tr. Walter Kaufmann.

14. Talent is a question of quantity. Talent does not write one page: it writes three hundred. JULES RENARD, *Journal*, 1887, ed. and tr. Louise Bogan and Elizabeth Roget.

15. It is a very rare thing for a man of talent to succeed by his talent. JOSEPH ROUX, *Meditations of a Parish Priest* (1886), 4.88, tr. Isabel F. Hapgood.

16. Be equal to your talent, not your age. / At times let the gap between them be embarrassing. YEVGENY YEVTUSHENKO, "Others May Judge You," *The Poetry of Yevgeny Yevtushenko: 1953–1965* (1965), tr. George Reavey.

## TALKING

See 916. Speaking

## 957. TASTE

See also 280. Elegance; 719. Preference

1. Every one carries his own inch-rule of taste, and amuses himself by applying it, triumphantly, wherever he travels. HENRY ADAMS, *The Education of Henry Adams* (1907), 12.

2. One man's poison ivy is another man's spinach. GEORGE ADE, "The Brand That Was Plucked," *Hand-Made Fables* (1920).

3. Between friends differences in taste or opinion are irritating in direct proportion to their triviality. W. H. AUDEN, "Hic et Ille," *The Dyer's Hand* (1962).

4. People care more about being thought to have taste than about being thought either good, clever, or amiable. SAMUEL BUTLER (d. 1902), *Note-Books* (1912).

5. We have no laws against bad taste, perhaps because in a democracy the majority of the people who make the laws dont recognise bad taste when they see it, or perhaps because in our democracy bad taste has been converted into a marketable and therefore taxable and therefore lobbyable commodity. WILLIAM FAULKNER, "On Privacy," *Essays, Speeches & Public Letters* (1965).

6. The diffusion of taste is not the same thing as the improvement of taste. WILLIAM HAZLITT, "Why the Arts Are Not Progressive," *Round Table* (1817).

7. Those who are pleased with the fewest things know the least, as those who are pleased with everything know nothing. WILLIAM HAZLITT, "On Taste," *Sketches and Essays* (1839).

8. Taste is the literary conscience of the soul. JOSEPH JOUBERT, *Pensées* (1842).

9. One of the surest signs of the Philistine is his reverence for the superior tastes of those who put him down. PAULINE KAEL, "Zeitgeist and Poltergeist," *I Lost It at the Movies* (1965).

10. Tastes in young people are changed by natural impetuosity, and in the aged are preserved by habit. LA ROCHEFOUCAULD, *Maxims* (1665), tr. Kenneth Pratt.

11. Taste is the fundamental quality which sums up all other qualities. It is the ne plus ultra of the intelligence. COMTE DE LAUTRÉAMONT, *Poésies* (1870), 1.

12. In literature as in love, we are astonished at what is chosen by others. ANDRÉ MAUROIS, *The New York Times*, April 14, 1963.

13. A person's taste is as much his own peculiar concern as his opinion or his purse. JOHN STUART MILL, *On Liberty* (1859), 4.

14. All of life is a dispute over taste and tasting. NIETZSCHE, "On Those Who Are Sublime," *Thus Spoke Zarathustra* (1883–92), 2, tr. Walter Kaufmann.

15. Taste is the enemy of creativeness. PABLO PICASSO, *Quote*, March 24, 1957.

16. "Good taste" is a virtue of the keepers of museums. If you scorn bad taste, you will have neither painting nor dancing, neither palaces nor gardens. SAINT-EXUPÉRY, *The Wisdom of the Sands* (1948), 9, tr. Stuart Gilbert.

17. Beautiful things, when taste is formed, are obviously and unaccountably beautiful. GEORGE SANTAYANA, *The Life of Reason: Reason in Society* (1905–06), 1.

18. Taste has no system and no proofs. SUSAN SONTAG, "Notes on Camp," *Against Interpretation* (1961).

19. There is nobody but eats and drinks. But they are few who can distinguish flavours. TZE-SZE, *The Doctrine of the Mean* (5th c. B.C.), 4.2, tr. James Legge.

20. "Loud" dress becomes offensive to people of taste, as evincing an undue desire to reach and impress the untrained sensibilities of the vulgar. THORSTEIN VEBLEN, *The Theory of the Leisure Class* (1899), 7.

## 958. TAXES

**See also 99. Budget; 275. Economics**

1. Houseless, adj. Having paid all taxes on household goods. AMBROSE BIERCE, *The Devil's Dictionary* (1881–1911).

2. To tax and to please, no more than to love and be wise, is not given to men. EDMUND BURKE, speech, "On American Taxation," April 19, 1774.

3. There is one difference between a tax collector and a taxidermist—the taxidermist leaves the hide. MORTIMER CAPLAN, *Time*, Feb. 1, 1963.

4. The art of taxation consists in so plucking the goose as to obtain the largest possible amount of feathers with the smallest possible amount of hissing. Attributed to JEAN BAPTISTE COLBERT (c. 1665).

5. The point to remember is that what the government gives it must first take away. JOHN S. COLEMAN, address to the Detroit Chamber of Commerce.

6. It is inseparably essential to the freedom of a people that no taxes be imposed on them but with their own consent, given personally or by their representatives. Attributed to JOHN DICKINSON, Resolutions of the Stamp Act Congress, Oct. 19, 1765.

7. Man is not like other animals in the ways that are really significant: animals have instincts, we have taxes. ERVING GOFFMAN, interview, *The New York Times*, Feb. 12, 1969.

8. The wisdom of man never yet contrived a system of taxation that would operate with perfect equality. ANDREW JACKSON, Proclamation to the People of South Carolina, Dec. 10, 1832.

9. The Income Tax has made more Liars out of the American people than golf has. WILL ROGERS, "Helping the Girls with Their Income Taxes," *The Illiterate Digest* (1924).

10. When everybody has got money they cut taxes, and when they're broke they raise 'em. That's statesmanship of the highest order. WILL ROGERS, *The Autobiography of Will Rogers* (1949), 17.

11. Noah must have taken into the Ark two taxes, one male and one female, and did they multiply bountifully! Next to guinea pigs, taxes must have been the most prolific animals. WILL ROGERS, *The Autobiography of Will Rogers* (1949), 19.

12. Taxes, after all, are the dues that we pay for the privileges of membership in an organized society. FRANKLIN D. ROOSEVELT, speech, Worcester, Mass., Oct. 21, 1936.

13. It is the part of a good shepherd to shear his flock, not to flay it. TIBERIUS, quoted in Suetonius' *Lives of the Caesars: Tiberius* (2nd c. A.D.), 32.2.

## 959. TEACHING

**See also 277. Education; 529. Learning**

1. A teacher affects eternity; he can never tell where his influence stops. HENRY ADAMS, *The Education of Henry Adams* (1907), 20.

2. Nothing is more tiresome than a superannuated pedagogue. HENRY ADAMS, *The Education of Henry Adams* (1907), 23.

3. Teachers, who educate children, deserve more honor than parents, who merely gave them birth; for the latter provided mere life, while the former ensure a good life. ARISTOTLE (4th c. B.C.), quoted in Diogenes Laertius' *Lives and Opinions of Eminent Philosophers* (3rd c. A.D.), tr. R. D. Hicks.

4. The dons are too busy educating the

young men to be able to teach them anything. SAMUEL BUTLER (d. 1902), "Higgledy-Piggledy," *Note-Books* (1912).

5. First he wrought, and afterwards he taught. CHAUCER, "Prologue," *The Canterbury Tales* (1387–1400), 496, ed. Thomas Tyrwhitt.

6. If a man keeps cherishing his old knowledge, so as continually to be acquiring new, he may be a teacher of others. CONFUCIUS, *Analects* (6th c. B.C.), 2.11, tr. James Legge.

7. The whole secret of the teacher's force lies in the conviction that men are convertible. EMERSON, *Journals*, 1834.

8. I pay the schoolmaster, but 'tis the schoolboys that educate my son. EMERSON, *Journals*, 1849.

9. The whole art of teaching is only the art of awakening the natural curiosity of young minds for the purpose of satisfying it afterwards. ANATOLE FRANCE, *The Crime of Sylvestre Bonnard* (1881), 2, tr. Lafcadio Hearn.

10. A teacher is better than two books. GERMAN PROVERB.

11. No man can reveal to you aught but that which already lies half asleep in the dawning of your knowledge. KAHLIL GIBRAN, "On Teaching," *The Prophet* (1923).

12. A teacher who can arouse a feeling for one single good action, for one single good poem, accomplishes more than he who fills our memory with rows and rows of natural objects, classified with name and form. GOETHE, *Elective Affinities* (1809), 25.

13. He that teaches us anything which we knew not before is undoubtedly to be reverenced as a master. SAMUEL JOHNSON, *The Idler* (1758–60), 85.

14. To teach is to learn twice over. JOSEPH JOUBERT, *Pensées* (1842), 18.18, tr. Katharine Lyttelton.

15. He [the schoolmaster] is awkward, and out of place, in the society of his equals. He comes like Gulliver from among his little people, and he cannot fit the stature of his understanding to yours. CHARLES LAMB, "The Old and the New Schoolmaster," *Essays of Elia* (1823).

16. Men universally are ungrateful toward him who instructs them, unless, in the hours or in the intervals of instruction, he presents a sweet cake to their self-love. WALTER SAVAGE LANDOR, "Aristoteles and Callisthenes," *Imaginary Conversations* (1824–53).

17. The greater part of the people we assign to educate our sons we know for certain are not educated. Yet we do not doubt that they can give what they have not received, a thing which cannot be otherwise acquired. GIACOMO LEOPARDI, *Pensieri* (1834–37), 10, tr. William Fense Weaver.

18. It is easier for a tutor to command than to teach. JOHN LOCKE, *Some Thoughts Concerning Education* (1693), 50.

19. A man who knows a subject thoroughly, a man so soaked in it that he eats it, sleeps it and dreams it—this man can always teach it with success, no matter how little he knows of technical pedagogy. H. L. MENCKEN, *Prejudices: Third Series* (1922), 13.

20. I maintain, in truth, / That with a smile we should instruct our youth, / Be very gentle when we have to blame, / And not put them in fear of virtue's name. MOLIÈRE, *The School for Husbands* (1661), 1.2, tr. Donald M. Frame.

21. An educator never says what he himself thinks, but only that which he thinks it is good for those whom he is educating to hear. NIETZSCHE, *The Will to Power* (1888), 980, tr. Anthony M. Ludovici.

22. He who wishes to teach us a truth should not tell it to us, but simply suggest it with a brief gesture, a gesture which starts an ideal trajectory in the air along which we glide until we find ourselves at the feet of the new truth. JOSÉ ORTEGA Y GASSET, "Preliminary Meditation," *Meditations on Quixote* (1914).

23. Men must be taught as if you taught them not, / And things unknown proposed as things forgot. ALEXANDER POPE, *An Essay on Criticism* (1711), 3.15.

24. Too much rigidity on the part of teachers should be followed by a brisk spirit of insubordination on the part of the taught. AGNES REPPLIER, "Literary Shibboleths," *Points of View* (1891).

25. The severity of the master is more useful than the indulgence of the father. SA'DI, *Gulistan* (1258), 7.4, tr. James Ross.

26. My joy in learning is partly that it enables me to teach. SENECA, *Letters to Lucilius* (1st c.), 6.4, tr. E. Phillips Barker.

27. He who can, does. He who cannot, teaches. GEORGE BERNARD SHAW, "Maxims

for Revolutionists," *Man and Superman* (1903).

28. Delightful task! to rear the tender thought, / To teach the young idea how to shoot. JAMES THOMSON, "Spring," *The Seasons* (1726–30), 1149.

29. The first duty of a lecturer—to hand you after an hour's discourse a nugget of pure truth to wrap up between the pages of your notebooks and keep on the mantelpiece for ever. VIRGINIA WOOLF, *A Room of One's Own* (1929), 1.

30. One good teacher in a lifetime may sometimes change a delinquent into a solid citizen. PHILIP WYLIE, *Generation of Vipers* (1942), 7.

## 960. TECHNOLOGY

**See also 500. Invention; 633. Nuclear Power; 843. Science; 994. Twentieth Century**

1. If the human race wants to go to hell in a basket, technology can help it get there by jet. It won't change the desire or the direction, but it can greatly speed the passage. CHARLES M. ALLEN, "Unity in a University," speech at Wake Forest University, Winston-Salem, N. C., April 25, 1967.

2. When a machine begins to run without human aid, it is time to scrap it—whether it be a factory or a government. ALEXANDER CHASE, *Perspectives* (1966).

3. Take the socalled standardofliving. What do mostpeople mean by "living"? They don't mean living. They mean the latest and closest plural approximation to singular prenatal passivity which science, in its finite but unbounded wisdom, has succeeded in selling their wives. E. E. CUMMINGS, introduction to *New Poems* in *Poems (1923–1954)* (1954).

4. Only science can hope to keep technology in some sort of moral order. EDGAR Z. FRIEDENBERG, "The Impact of the School," *The Vanishing Adolescent* (1959).

5. The danger of the past was that men became slaves. The danger of the future is that men may become robots. ERICH FROMM, *The Sane Society* (1955), 9.

6. The moment man cast off his age-long belief in magic, Science bestowed upon him the blessings of the Electric Current. JEAN GIRAUDOUX, *The Enchanted* (1933), 3, adapted by Maurice Valency.

7. If there is technological advance without social advance, there is, almost automatically, an increase in human misery. MICHAEL HARRINGTON, appendix to *The Other America* (1962).

8. Is it a fact—or have I dreamt it—that, by means of electricity, the world of matter has become a great nerve, vibrating thousands of miles in a breathless point of time? NATHANIEL HAWTHORNE, *The House of the Seven Gables* (1851), 17.

9. Where there is the necessary technical skill to move mountains, there is no need for the faith that moves mountains. ERIC HOFFER, *The Passionate State of Mind* (1954), 12.

10. Applied Science is a conjuror, whose bottomless hat yields impartially the softest of Angora rabbits and the most petrifying of Medusas. ALDOUS HUXLEY, *Tomorrow and Tomorrow and Tomorrow* (1956).

11. Man is still the most extraordinary computer of all. JOHN F. KENNEDY, May 21, 1963.

12. We have forgotten the beast and the flower not in order to remember either ourselves or God, but in order to forget everything except the machine. JOSEPH WOOD KRUTCH, "March," *The Twelve Seasons* (1949).

13. Electronic calculators can solve problems which the man who made them cannot solve; but no government-subsidized commission of engineers and physicists could create a worm. JOSEPH WOOD KRUTCH, "March," *The Twelve Seasons* (1949).

14. Technology made large populations possible; large populations now make technology indispensable. JOSEPH WOOD KRUTCH, "The Nemesis of Power," *Human Nature and the Human Condition* (1959).

15. A world technology means either a world government or world suicide. MAX LERNER, "The Imagination of H. G. Wells," *Actions and Passions* (1949).

16. Man must be at once more humble and more confident—more humble in the face of the destructive potentials of what he can achieve, more confident of his own humanity as against computers and robots which are only engines to simulate him. MAX LERNER, "Manipulating Life," in the *New York Post*, Jan. 24, 1968.

17. You cannot endow even the best machine with initiative; the jolliest steam-

roller will not plant flowers. WALTER LIPPMANN, "Routineer and Inventor," *A Preface to Politics* (1914).

18. A computer with as many vacuum tubes as a man has neurons in his head would require the Pentagon to house it, Niagara's power to run it, and Niagara's waters to cool it. WARREN S. MC CULLOCH, quoted in Robert Lindner's *Must You Conform?* (1956).

19. It is critical vision alone which can mitigate the unimpeded operation of the automatic. MARSHALL MC LUHAN, "Magic That Changes Mood," *The Mechanical Bride* (1951).

20. Everywhere in the world the industrial regime tends to make the unorganized or unorganizable individual, the pauper, into the victim of a kind of human sacrifice offered to the gods of civilization. JACQUES MARITAIN, *Reflections on America* (1958), 19.2.

21. By his very success in inventing labor-saving devices, modern man has manufactured an abyss of boredom that only the privileged classes in earlier civilizations have ever fathomed. LEWIS MUMFORD, "The Challenge to Renewal," *The Conduct of Life* (1951).

22. One has to look out for engineers—they begin with sewing machines and end up with the atomic bomb. MARCEL PAGNOL, *Critique des critiques* (1949), 3.

23. We cannot get grace from gadgets. In the bakelite house of the future, the dishes may not break, but the heart can. Even a man with ten shower baths may find life flat, stale and unprofitable. J. B. PRIESTLEY, news summaries, April 1, 1956.

24. Sometimes you might think the machines we worship make all the chief appointments, promoting the human beings who seem closest to them. J. B. PRIESTLEY, "Candles Burning Low," *Thoughts in the Wilderness* (1957).

25. The machine does not isolate man from the great problems of nature but plunges him more deeply into them. SAINT-EXUPÉRY, *Wind, Sand, and Stars* (1939), 3, tr. Lewis Galantière.

26. The machine yes the machine / never wastes anybody's time / never watches the foreman / never talks back. CARL SANDBURG, *The People, Yes* (1936).

27. It is said that one machine can do the work of fifty ordinary men. No machine, however, can do the work of one extraordinary man. TEHYI HSIEH, *Chinese Epigrams Inside Out and Proverbs* (1948), 470.

28. If it [automation] keeps up, man will atrophy all his limbs but the push-button finger. FRANK LLOYD WRIGHT, *The New York Times*, Nov. 27, 1955.

## TEEN-AGERS
See 1064. Youth

## TELEVISION
See 563. Mass Media

## 961. TEMPER, BAD
See also 39. Anger; 390. Good Nature; 962. Temperament

1. All music jars when the soul's out of tune. CERVANTES, *Don Quixote* (1605–15), 2.4.44, tr. Peter Motteux and John Ozell.

2. A tart temper never mellows with age, and a sharp tongue is the only edged tool that grows keener with constant use. WASHINGTON IRVING, "Rip Van Winkle," *The Sketch Book of Geoffrey Crayon, Gent.* (1819–20).

3. He who is of a calm and happy nature will hardly feel the pressure of age, but to him who is of an opposite disposition youth and age are equally a burden. PLATO, *The Republic* (4th c. B.C.), 1, tr. Benjamin Jowett.

## 962. TEMPERAMENT
See also 282. Emotions; 390. Good Nature; 680. Personality; 961. Temper, Bad

1. There is no harbor of peace / From the changing waves of joy and despair. EURIPIDES, *Ion* (c. 421–08 B.C.), tr. Ronald F. Willetts.

2. Temperament, like liberty, is important despite how many crimes are committed in its name. LOUIS KRONENBERGER, *Company Manners* (1954), 1.2.

3. The tranquility or agitation of our temper does not depend so much on the big things which happen to us in life, as on the pleasant or unpleasant arrangements of the

little things which happen daily. LA ROCHEFOUCAULD, *Maxims* (1665), tr. Kenneth Pratt.

4. The happiness and unhappiness of men depend as much on their turn of mind as on fortune. LA ROCHEFOUCAULD, *Maxims* (1665), tr. Kenneth Pratt.

5. A human being tends to believe that the mood of the moment, be it troubled or blithe, peaceful or stormy, is the true, native, and permanent tenor of his existence . . . whereas the truth is that he is condemned to improvisation and morally lives from hand to mouth all the time. THOMAS MANN, "A Man and His Dog" (1918), *Death in Venice*, tr. H. T. Lowe-Porter.

6. If health and a fair day smile upon me, I am a very good fellow; if a corn trouble my toe, I am sullen, out of humor, and inaccessible. MONTAIGNE, "Apology for Raimond de Sebonde," *Essays* (1580–88), tr. Charles Cotton and W. C. Hazlitt.

7. Certainly there are good and bad times, but our mood changes more often than our fortune. JULES RENARD, *Journal*, January 1905, ed. and tr. Louise Bogan and Elizabeth Roget.

## 963. TEMPERANCE

See also 266. Drinking; 492. Intemperance; 592. Moderation

1. Subdue your appetites, my dears, and you've conquered human natur. CHARLES DICKENS, *Nicholas Nickleby* (1838–39), 5.

2. Sobriety is love of health, or inability to eat much. LA ROCHEFOUCAULD, *Maxims* (1665), tr. Kenneth Pratt.

3. Temperance is the acknowledged ruler of the pleasures and desires, and no pleasure ever masters Love; he is their master and they are his servants; and if he conquers them he must be temperate indeed. PLATO, *The Symposium* (4th c. B.C.), tr. Benjamin Jowett.

4. Intemperate temperance injures the cause of temperance, while temperate temperance helps it in its fight against intemperate intemperance. MARK TWAIN, *Notebook* (1935).

## 964. TEMPTATION

See also 97. Bribery; 188. Corruption; 893. Sin

1. It is good to be without vices, but it is not good to be without temptations. WALTER BAGEHOT, *Biographical Studies* (1881).

2. All men are tempted. There is no man that lives that can't be broken down, provided it is the right temptation, put in the right spot. HENRY WARD BEECHER, *Proverbs from Plymouth Pulpit* (1887).

3. Why comes temptation but for man to meet / And master and make crouch beneath his foot, / And so be pedestaled in triumph? ROBERT BROWNING, "The Pope," *The Ring and the Book* (1868–69).

4. When temptations march monotonously in regiments, one waits for them to pass. FRANK MOORE COLBY, "Some of the Difficulties of Frollicking," *The Colby Essays* (1926), v. 1.

5. No temptation can ever be measured by the value of its object. COLETTE, "Human Nature," *Earthly Paradise* (1966), 4, ed. Robert Phelps.

6. Though the bird may fly over your head, let it not make its nest in your hair. DANISH PROVERB.

7. There is a certain degree of temptation which will overcome any virtue. Now, in so far as you approach temptation to a man, you do him an injury; and, if he is overcome, you share his guilt. SAMUEL JOHNSON, quoted in Boswell's *Life of Samuel Johnson*, April 3, 1778.

8. Who will not judge him worthy to be robbed / That sets his doors wide open to a thief, / And shows the felon where his treasure lies? BEN JONSON, *Every Man in His Humour* (1598), 3.3.

9. I have a simple principle for the conduct of life—never to resist an adequate temptation. MAX LERNER, "The Law of Austere Hedonism," *The Unfinished Country* (1959), 1.

10. Blessed is he who has never been tempted; for he knows not the frailty of his rectitude. CHRISTOPHER MORLEY, *Inward Ho!* (1923), 1.

11. There are several good protections against temptations, but the surest is cowardice. MARK TWAIN, "Pudd'nhead Wilson's New Calendar," *Following the Equator* (1897), 1.36.

12. I generally avoid temptation unless I can't resist it. MAE WEST, in *My Little Chickadee* (1940).

13. The only way to get rid of a temptation is to yield to it. Resist it, and your soul grows sick with longing for the things it has forbidden to itself. OSCAR WILDE, *The Picture of Dorian Gray* (1891), 2.

14. I can resist everything except temptation. OSCAR WILDE, *Lady Windermere's Fan* (1892), 1.

## THANKS

See 397. Gratitude

## THANKSGIVING DAY

See 418. Holidays

## 965. THEATER

See also 11. Actors; 143. Comedians; 144. Comedy; 212. Dancing; 604. Movies; 648. Opera; 980. Tragedy

1. There is as much difference between the stage and the films as between a piano and a violin. Normally you can't become a virtuoso in both. ETHEL BARRYMORE, *New York Post*, June 7, 1956.

2. Plays, gentlemen, are to their authors what children are to women: they cost more pain than they give pleasure. BEAUMARCHAIS, preface to *The Barber of Seville* (1775), tr. Joyce Bermel.

3. Theatre takes place all the time wherever one is and art simply facilitates persuading one this is the case. JOHN CAGE, "45′ for a Speaker," *Silence* (1961).

4. In London, theatregoers expect to laugh; in Paris, they wait grimly for proof that they should. ROBERT DHÉRY, *Look*, March 4, 1958.

5. A play should give you something to think about. When I see a play and understand it the first time, then I know it can't be much good. T. S. ELIOT, *New York Post*, Sept. 22, 1963.

6. Like hungry guests, a sitting audience looks: / Plays are like suppers; poets are the cooks. / The founder's you: the table is this place: / The carvers we: the prologue is the grace. / Each act a course, each scene, a different dish. GEORGE FARQUHAR, prologue to *The Inconstant* (1702).

7. In my plays I want to look at life—at the commonplace of existence—as if we had just turned a corner and run into it for the first time. CHRISTOPHER FRY, *Time*, Nov. 20, 1950.

8. The stage-play is a trial, not a deed of violence. The soul is opened, like the combination of a safe, by means of a word. You don't require an acetylene torch. JEAN GIRAUDOUX, quoted in introduction to *Jean Giraudoux: Four Plays* (1958), adapted by Maurice Valency.

9. One's roused by this, another finds that fit: / Each loves the play for what he brings to it. GOETHE, "Prelude in the Theatre," *Faust: Part I* (1808), tr. Philip Wayne.

10. You need three things in the theatre—the play, the actors and the audience, and each must give something. KENNETH HAIGH, *Theatre Arts*, July 1958.

11. The stage but echoes back the public voice. / The drama's laws the drama's patrons give, / For we that live to please, must please to live. SAMUEL JOHNSON, *Prologue at the Opening of the Drury Lane Theatre* (1747).

12. In New York people don't go to the theatre—they go to see hits. Attributed to LOUIS JOURDAN.

13. We do not go [to the theatre], like our ancestors, to escape from the pressure of reality, so much as to confirm our experience of it. CHARLES LAMB, "On the Artificial Comedy of the Last Century," *Essays of Elia* (1823).

14. I wear my shackles more contentedly for having respired the breath of an imaginary freedom. CHARLES LAMB, "On the Artificial Comedy of the Last Century," *Essays of Elia* (1823).

15. Words can be deceitful, but pantomime necessarily is simple, clear and direct. MARCEL MARCEAU, *Theatre Arts*, March 1958.

16. If the audience never understands the plot, it can be counted on to be attentive to the very end. BENEDETTO MARCELLO, *Il teatro alla moda* (1720).

17. The inclination to digress is human. But the dramatist must avoid it even more strenuously than the saint must avoid sin, for while sin may be venial, digression is mortal. W. SOMERSET MAUGHAM, *The Summing Up* (1938), 35.

18. The drama is make-believe. It does not deal with truth but with effect. W. SOMERSET MAUGHAM, *The Summing Up* (1938), 39.

19. The theater, when all is said and done, is not life in miniature, but life enormously magnified, life hideously exaggerated. H. L. MENCKEN, *Prejudices: First Series* (1919), 17.

20. The structure of a play is always the story of how the birds came home to roost. ARTHUR MILLER, "The Shadows of the Gods: A Critical View of the American Theatre," *Harper's Magazine*, August 1958.

21. Great drama is the souvenir of the adventure of a master among the pieces of his own soul. GEORGE JEAN NATHAN, "Great Drama," *The World in Falseface* (1923).

22. Men go to the theatre to forget; women, to remember. GEORGE JEAN NATHAN, "The Theatre," *American Mercury*, July 1926.

23. In the theatre, a hero is one who believes that all women are ladies, a villain one who believes that all ladies are women. GEORGE JEAN NATHAN, *The New York Times*, Nov. 5, 1950.

24. What is the stage? It's a place, baby, you know, where people play at being serious, a place where they act comedies. LUIGI PIRANDELLO, *Six Characters in Search of an Author* (1921), 2, tr. Edward Storer.

25. Drama is action, sir, action and not confounded philosophy. LUIGI PIRANDELLO, *Six Characters in Search of an Author* (1921), 3, tr. Edward Storer.

26. A novelist may lose his readers for a few pages; a playwright never dares lose his audience for a minute. TERENCE RATTIGAN, in *New York Journal-American*, Oct. 29, 1956.

27. Not to go to the theatre is like making one's toilet without a mirror. SCHOPENHAUER, "Further Psychological Observations," *Parerga and Paralipomena* (1851), tr. T. Bailey Saunders.

28. The Happening operates by creating an asymmetrical network of surprises, without climax or consummation; this is the alogic of dreams rather than the logic of most art. SUSAN SONTAG, "Happenings: An Art of Radical Juxtaposition," *Against Interpretation* (1961).

29. A happening is a composition, at least in retrospect. IGOR STRAVINSKY, "Stravinsky on the Musical Scene and Other Matters," *The New York Review of Books* (May 12, 1966).

30. I see the playwright as a lay preacher peddling the ideas of his time in popular form. AUGUST STRINDBERG, preface to *Miss Julie* (1888), tr. Elizabeth Sprigge.

31. It is the destiny of the theater nearly everywhere and in every period to struggle even when it is flourishing. HOWARD TAUBMAN, *The New York Times*, Aug. 4, 1964.

32. A good many inconveniences attend playgoing in any large city, but the greatest of them is usually the play itself. KENNETH TYNAN, *New York Herald Tribune*, Feb. 17, 1957.

33. A talent for drama is not a talent for writing, but is an ability to articulate human relationships. GORE VIDAL, *The New York Times*, June 17, 1956.

34. On the stage it is always *now;* the personages are standing on that razor-edge, between the past and the future, which is the essential character of conscious being. THORNTON WILDER, interview, *Writers at Work: First Series* (1958).

35. A dramatist is one who from his earliest years has found that sheer gazing at the shocks and countershocks among people is quite sufficiently engrossing without having to encase it in comment. THORNTON WILDER, interview, *Writers at Work: First Series* (1958).

36. We live in what is, but we find a thousand ways not to face it. Great theater strengthens our faculty to face it. THORNTON WILDER, interview, *Writers at Work: First Series* (1958).

37. The unencumbered stage encourages the truth operative in everyone. The less seen, the more heard. The eye is the enemy of the ear in real drama. THORNTON WILDER, *The New York Times*, Nov. 6, 1961.

38. Some mystery should be left in the revelation of character in a play, just as a great deal of mystery is always left in the revelation of character in life, even in one's own character to himself. TENNESSEE WILLIAMS, stage directions, *Cat on a Hot Tin Roof* (1955).

39. Every now and then, when you're on stage, you hear the best sound a player can hear. It's a sound you can't get in movies or in television. It is the sound of a wonderful, deep silence that means you've hit them where they live. SHELLEY WINTERS, *Theatre Arts*, June 1956.

### THEFT
See 927. Stealing

### 966. THEOLOGY
See also 385. God; 790. Religion

1. The theologian who has no joy in his work is not a theologian at all. Sulky faces, morose thoughts and boring ways of speaking are intolerable in this science. KARL BARTH, quoted in his obituary, *The New York Times*, Dec. 11, 1968.

2. Doctrine is nothing but the skin of truth set up and stuffed. HENRY WARD BEECHER, *Proverbs from Plymouth Pulpit* (1887).

3. The most tedious of all discourses are on the subject of the Supreme Being. EMERSON, *Journals*, 1836.

4. The cure for false theology is motherwit. Forget your books and traditions, and obey your moral perceptions at this hour. EMERSON, "Worship," *The Conduct of Life* (1860).

5. Unloose the cords of thine heart, and consider not the sky's secret; for the thought of no geometrician hath ever untied that knot. HĀFIZ, ghazals from the *Divan* (14th c.), 135, tr. Justin Huntly McCarthy.

6. Theology is an attempt to explain a subject by men who do not understand it. The intent is not to tell the truth but to satisfy the questioner. ELBERT HUBBARD, *The Philistine* (1895–1915).

7. Theology in religion is what poisons are in food. NAPOLEON I, *Maxims* (1804–15).

8. Theology moves back and forth between two poles, the eternal truth of its foundations and the temporal situation in which the eternal truth must be received. PAUL TILLICH, *Systematic Theology* (1951), v. 1.

9. Theological religion is the source of all imaginable follies and disturbances; it is the parent of fanaticism and civil discord; it is the enemy of mankind. VOLTAIRE, "Religion," *Philosophical Dictionary* (1764).

### 967. THEORY
See also 9. Action; 326. Facts; 688. Philosophers and Philosophy; 843. Science; 954. Systems

1. Professors in every branch of the sciences prefer their own theories to truth; the reason is that their theories are private property, but truth is common stock. CHARLES CALEB COLTON, *Lacon* (1825), 1.378.

2. It is a capital mistake to theorize before one has data. SIR ARTHUR CONAN DOYLE, "Scandal in Bohemia," *The Adventures of Sherlock Holmes* (1891).

3. The astonishment of life is the absence of any appearances of reconciliation between the theory and the practice of life. EMERSON, *Journals*, 1844.

4. In theory, there is nothing to hinder our following what we are taught, but in life there are many things to draw us aside. EPICTETUS, *Discourses* (2nd c.), 1.26, tr. Thomas W. Higginson.

5. No theory is good except on condition that one use it to go beyond. ANDRÉ GIDE, *Journals*, 1918, tr. Justin O'Brien.

6. On carelessly made or insufficient observations how many fine theories are built up which do not bear examination! ANDRÉ GIDE, *Journals*, Aug. 5, 1931, tr. Justin O'Brien.

7. To be sure, theory is useful. But without warmth of heart and without love it bruises the very ones it claims to save. ANDRÉ GIDE, *Journals*, 1937, tr. Justin O'Brien.

8. Hypotheses are only the pieces of scaffolding which are erected round a building during the course of construction, and which are taken away as soon as the edifice is completed. GOETHE (1749–1832), quoted in Anthony M. Ludovici's introduction to Nietzsche's *The Will to Power*.

9. All theory, my friend, is grey, / But green is life's glad golden tree. GOETHE, "Night," *Faust: Part I* (1808), tr. Philip Wayne.

10. It is so much easier to talk of poverty than to think of the poor, to argue the rights of capital than to see its results. Pretty soon we come to think of the theories and abstract ideas as things in themselves. WALTER LIPPMANN, "Some Necessary Iconoclasm," *A Preface to Politics* (1914).

11. It is only theory that makes men completely incautious. BERTRAND RUSSELL, "Ideas That Have Harmed Mankind," *Unpopular Essays* (1950).

12. A theorist without practice is a tree without fruit; and a devotee without learning is a house without an entrance. SA'DI, *Gulistan* (1258), 8.82, tr. James Ross.

13. Theory helps us to bear our ignorance of facts. GEORGE SANTAYANA, "The Average Modified in the Direction of Pleasure," *The Sense of Beauty* (1896).

14. It is the nature of an hypothesis, when once a man has conceived it, that it assimilates every thing to itself as proper nourishment, and, from the first moment of your begetting it, it generally grows the stronger by every thing you see, hear, read, or understand. LAURENCE STERNE, *Tristram Shandy* (1759–67), 2.19.

15. It is better to emit a scream in the shape of a theory than to be entirely insensible to the jars and incongruities of life and take everything as it comes in a forlorn stupidity. ROBERT LOUIS STEVENSON, "Crabbed Age and Youth," *Virginibus Puerisque* (1881).

16. Let us work without theorizing . . . 'tis the only way to make life endurable. VOLTAIRE, *Candide* (1759), 30.

17. The utmost abstractions are the true weapons with which to control our thought of concrete fact. ALFRED NORTH WHITEHEAD, *Science and the Modern World* (1925), 2.

## THIEF

**See 927. Stealing**

## THINGS

**See 638. Objects**

## THINKING

**See 968. Thought**

## 968. THOUGHT

**See also 24. Afterthought; 441. Ideas; 490. Intellectuals and Intellectualism; 491. Intelligence; 583. Mind; 688. Philosophers and Philosophy; 778. Reason; 812. Reverie**

1. Since it is seldom clear whether intellectual activity denotes a superior mode of being or a vital deficiency, opinion swings between considering intellect a privilege and seeing it as a handicap. JACQUES BARZUN, *The House of Intellect* (1959), 2.

2. Deliberation, n. The act of examining one's bread to determine which side it is buttered on. AMBROSE BIERCE, *The Devil's Dictionary* (1881–1911).

3. One thought fills immensity. WILLIAM BLAKE, "Proverbs of Hell," *The Marriage of Heaven and Hell* (1790).

4. One must live the way one thinks or end up thinking the way one has lived. PAUL BOURGET, "Conclusion," *Le Démon de midi* (1914).

5. In itself, a thought, / A slumbering thought, is capable of years, / And curdles a long life into one hour. BYRON, "The Dream" (1816), 1.

6. The highest possible stage in moral culture is when we recognize that we ought to control our thoughts. CHARLES DARWIN, *The Descent of Man* (1871), 4.

7. I think, therefore I am. DESCARTES, *Discourse on Method* (1639), 4.

8. Miditation is a gift confined to unknown philosophers an' cows. Others don't begin to think till they begin to talk or write. FINLEY PETER DUNNE, "Casual Observations," *Mr. Dooley's Philosophy* (1900).

9. What was once thought can never be unthought. FRIEDRICH DÜRRENMATT, *The Physicists* (1962), 2, tr. James Kirkup.

10. If a man sits down to think, he is immediately asked if he has the headache. EMERSON, *Journals*, 1833.

11. What is the hardest task in the world? To think. EMERSON, *Journals*, 1836.

12. To think is to act. EMERSON, "Spiritual Laws," *Essays: First Series* (1841).

13. Thought makes every thing fit for use. EMERSON, "The Poet," *Essays: Second Series* (1844).

14. Intellect annuls fate. So far as a man thinks, he is free. EMERSON, "Fate," *The Conduct of Life* (1860).

15. All thought is a feat of association: having what's in front of you bring up something in your mind that you almost didn't know you knew. ROBERT FROST, interview, *Writers at Work: Second Series* (1963).

16. We must dare to think about "unthinkable things," because when things become "unthinkable," thinking stops and action becomes mindless. J. WILLIAM

FULBRIGHT, speech, U.S. Senate, March 25, 1964.

17. Those that think must govern those that toil. OLIVER GOLDSMITH, *The Traveller* (1765), 372.

18. Thinking is hard work. One can't bear burdens and ideas at the same time. RÉMY DE GOURMONT, *Promenades philosophiques* (1905–09).

19. The secret thoughts of a man run over all things, holy, profane, clean, obscene, grave, and light, without shame or blame. THOMAS HOBBES, *Leviathan* (1651), 1.7.

20. A thought is often original, though you have uttered it a hundred times. It has come to you over a new route, by a new and express train of associations. OLIVER WENDELL HOLMES, SR., *The Autocrat of the Breakfast Table* (1858), 1.

21. Every real thought on every real subject knocks the wind out of somebody or other. OLIVER WENDELL HOLMES, SR., *The Autocrat of the Breakfast Table* (1858), 5.

22. There is one disadvantage which the man of philosophical habits of mind suffers, as compared with the man of action. While he is taking an enlarged and rational view of the matter before him, he lets his chance slip through his fingers. OLIVER WENDELL HOLMES, SR., *The Professor at the Breakfast Table* (1860), 11.

23. We find it hard to get and to keep any private property in thought. Other people are all the time saying the same things we are hoarding to say when we get ready. OLIVER WENDELL HOLMES, SR., *The Poet at the Breakfast Table* (1872), 11.

24. To think great thoughts you must be heroes as well as idealists. OLIVER WENDELL HOLMES, JR., lecture, Harvard University, Feb. 17, 1886.

25. To meditate is to labour; to think is to act. VICTOR HUGO, "Cosette," *Les Misérables* (1862), 7.8, tr. Charles E. Wilbour.

26. You may derive thoughts from others; your way of thinking, the mould in which your thoughts are cast, must be your own. CHARLES LAMB, "The Old and the New Schoolmaster," *Essays of Elia* (1823).

27. My thoughts are my company; I can bring them together, select them, detain them, dismiss them. WALTER SAVAGE LANDOR, "Diogenes and Plato," *Imaginary Conversations* (1824–53).

28. Thoughts, like fleas, jump from man to man. But they don't bite everybody. STANISLAW LEC, *Unkempt Thoughts* (1962), tr. Jacek Galazka.

29. The thoughts that come often unsought, and, as it were, drop into the mind, are commonly the most valuable of any we have. JOHN LOCKE, letter to Samuel Bold, May 16, 1699.

30. To think is to meander from highway to byway, and from byway to alleyway, till we come to a dead end. Stopped dead in our alley, we think what a feat it would be to get out. That is when we look for the gate to the meadows beyond. ANTONIO MACHADO, *Juan de Mairena* (1943), 18, tr. Ben Belitt.

31. Our life is what our thoughts make it. MARCUS AURELIUS, *Meditations* (2nd c.), 4.3, tr. Morris Hickey Morgan.

32. All deep, earnest thinking is but the intrepid effort of the soul to keep the open independence of her sea, while the wildest winds of heaven and earth conspire to cast her on the treacherous, slavish shore. HERMAN MELVILLE, *Moby Dick* (1851), 23.

33. Thinking is, or ought to be, a coolness and a calmness; and our poor hearts throb, and our poor brains beat too much for that. HERMAN MELVILLE, *Moby Dick* (1851), 135.

34. Most thinkers write badly, because they communicate not only their thoughts, but also the thinking of them. NIETZSCHE, *Human, All Too Human* (1878), 188, tr. Helen Zimmern.

35. Profundity of thought belongs to youth, clarity of thought to old age. NIETZSCHE, *Miscellaneous Maxims and Opinions* (1879), 289, tr. Paul V. Cohn.

36. Thinking is the endeavor to capture reality by means of ideas. JOSÉ ORTEGA Y GASSET, *The Dehumanization of Art* (1925).

37. We do not live to think, but, on the contrary, we think in order that we may succeed in surviving. JOSÉ ORTEGA Y GASSET, "In Search of Goethe from Within, Letter to a German," *Partisan Review*, December 1949, tr. Willard R. Trask.

38. Thought is not a gift to man but a laborious, precarious and volatile acquisition. JOSÉ ORTEGA Y GASSET, "In Search of Goethe from Within, Letter to a German," *Partisan Review*, December 1949, tr. Willard R. Trask.

39. Man is obviously made to think. It is

his whole dignity and his whole merit. PASCAL, *Pensées* (1670), 146, tr. W. F. Trotter.

40. Man is but a reed, the feeblest thing in nature; but he is a thinking reed. PASCAL, *Pensées* (1670), 347.

41. By space the universe encompasses and swallows me up like an atom; by thought I comprehend the world. PASCAL, *Pensées* (1670), 348, tr. W. F. Trotter.

42. Human thought, like God, makes the world in its own image. ADAM CLAYTON POWELL, "What We Must Do About Africa," *Keep the Faith, Baby!* (1967).

43. All the mind's activity is easy if it is not subjected to reality. MARCEL PROUST, *Remembrance of Things Past: Cities of the Plain* (1913–27).

44. Thought is essentially practical in the sense that but for thought no motion would be an action, no change a progress. GEORGE SANTAYANA, *The Life of Reason: Reason in Common Sense* (1905–06), 9.

45. Nimble thought can jump both sea and land. SHAKESPEARE, *Sonnets* (1609), 44.7.

46. The body always ends by being a bore. Nothing remains beautiful and interesting except thought, because the thought is the life. GEORGE BERNARD SHAW, *Back to Methuselah* (1921), 5.

47. What happens in life is mere litter; but from this waste-paper of perishable events Thought can unpack priceless and imperishable meanings. LOGAN PEARSALL SMITH, *Afterthoughts* (1931), 1.

48. I have no riches but my thoughts, / Yet these are wealth enough for me. SARA TEASDALE, "Riches," *Love Songs* (1917).

49. When a thought is too weak to be expressed simply, it should be rejected. VAUVENARGUES, *Reflections and Maxims* (1746), 3.

50. Great thoughts come from the heart. VAUVENARGUES, *Reflections and Maxims* (1746), 127, tr. F. G. Stevens.

51. I have thought too much to deign to act. VILLIERS DE L'ISLE-ADAM, *Axel* (1890), 4.2.

52. Those who think are excessively few; and those few do not set themselves to disturb the world. VOLTAIRE, "Soul," *Philosophical Dictionary* (1764).

53. Thought depends absolutely on the stomach, but in spite of that, those who have the best stomachs are not the best thinkers. VOLTAIRE, letter to d'Alembert, Aug. 20, 1770.

54. Mind is the great lever of all things; human thought is the process by which human ends are ultimately answered. DANIEL WEBSTER, address on laying the cornerstone of the Bunker Hill Monument, Boston, Mass., June 17, 1825.

55. There's nothing of so infinite vexation / As man's own thoughts. JOHN WEBSTER, *The White Devil* (1612), 5.6.

56. The importance of an individual thinker owes something to chance. For it depends upon the fate of his ideas in the minds of his successors. ALFRED NORTH WHITEHEAD, *Science and the Modern World* (1925), 2.

57. It belongs to the self-respect of intellect to pursue every tangle of thought to its final unravelment. ALFRED NORTH WHITEHEAD, *Science and the Modern World* (1925), 12.

58. Thinking is the most unhealthy thing in the world, and people die of it just as they die of any other disease. OSCAR WILDE, "The Decay of Lying," *Intentions* (1891).

59. Uncompromising thought is the luxury of the closeted recluse. Untrammeled reasoning is the indulgence of the philosopher, of the dreamer of sweet dreams. WOODROW WILSON, address, University of Tennessee, June 17, 1890.

60. A man's thinking goes on within his consciousness in a seclusion in comparison with which any physical seclusion is an exhibition to public view. LUDWIG WITTGENSTEIN, *Philosophical Investigations* (1953), 2.2, tr. G. E. M. Anscombe.

61. Things thought too long can be no longer thought, / For beauty dies of beauty, worth of worth, / And ancient lineaments are blotted out. WILLIAM BUTLER YEATS, "The Gyres," *New Poems* (1938).

## 969. THREAT

See also 213. Danger

1. Threatened folks live long. THOMAS FULLER, M.D., *Gnomologia* (1732), 5036.

2. The rattling thunderbolt hath but his clap, the lightning but his flash, and as they both come in a moment, so do they both end in a minute. JOHN LYLY, *Euphues: The Anatomy of Wit* (1579).

3. The dog's bark is not might, but fright. MADAGASCAN PROVERB.

4. If you can't bite, don't show your teeth. *Yiddish Proverbs* (1949), ed. Hanan J. Ayalti.

## 970. THRIFT

See also 322. Extravagance

1. Men are divided between those who are as thrifty as if they would live forever, and those who are as extravagant as if they were going to die the next day. ARISTOTLE (4th c. B.C.), quoted in Diogenes Laertius' *Lives and Opinions of Eminent Philosophers* (3rd c. A.D.), tr. R. D. Hicks.

2. A penny saved is a penny to squander. AMBROSE BIERCE, "Saw," *The Devil's Dictionary* (1881–1911).

3. Frugality is the sure guardian of our virtues. BRAHMAN PROVERB.

4. Expense, and great expense, may be an essential part of true economy. EDMUND BURKE, *Letter to a Noble Lord* (1796).

5. Economy is a distributive virtue, and consists not in saving but in selection. EDMUND BURKE, *Letter to a Noble Lord* (1796).

6. I once knew a very covetous, sordid fellow, who used to say, "Take care of the pence, for the pounds will take care of themselves." LORD CHESTERFIELD, *Letters to His Son*, Nov. 6, 1747.

7. Men do not realize how great an income thrift is. CICERO, *Paradoxa Stoicorum* (46 B.C.).

8. Annual income twenty pounds, annual expenditure nineteen nineteen six, result happiness. Annual income twenty pounds, annual expenditure twenty pounds ought and six, result misery. CHARLES DICKENS, *David Copperfield* (1849–50), 12.

9. There are two halves to ivry dollar. Wan is knowin' how to make it an' th' other is not knowin' how to spend it comfortably. FINLEY PETER DUNNE, "The Big Fine," *Mr. Dooley Says* (1910).

10. A man often pays dear for a small frugality. EMERSON, "Compensation," *Essays: First Series* (1841).

11. Economy, in the estimation of common minds, often means the absence of all taste and comfort. SYDNEY SMITH, quoted in Lady S. Holland's *Memoir* (1855), v. 1.8.

12. Anyone who lives within his means suffers from a lack of imagination. LIONEL STANDER, quoted in Helen Lawrenson's "Lionel Stander," *Playboy*, December 1967.

13. Let us all be happy, and live within our means, even if we have to borrer money to do it with. ARTEMUS WARD, "Science and Natural History," *Artemus Ward in London* (1872).

## 971. TIME

See also 300. Eternity; 537. Life, Stages of; 983. Transience

1. Time in its aging course teaches all things. AESCHYLUS, *Prometheus Bound* (c. 478 B.C.), tr. David Grene.

2. Time in his aging overtakes all things alike. AESCHYLUS, *The Eumenides* (458 B.C.), tr. Richmond Lattimore.

3. Time brings all things to pass. AESCHYLUS, *The Libation Bearers* (458 B.C.), tr. Richmond Lattimore.

4. Time and space are fragments of the infinite for the use of finite creatures. HENRI FRÉDÉRIC AMIEL, *Journal*, Nov. 16, 1864, tr. Mrs. Humphry Ward.

5. Time is a great conference planning our end, and youth is only the past putting a leg forward. DJUNA BARNES, *Nightwood* (1937).

6. Killing time is the chief end of our society. UGO BETTI, *The Fugitive* (1953), 1, tr. G. H. McWilliam.

7. The ruins of Time build mansions in Eternity. WILLIAM BLAKE, letter to William Hayley, May 6, 1800.

8. Time lost is time when we have not lived a full human life, time unenriched by experience, creative endeavor, enjoyment and suffering. DIETRICH BONHOEFFER, "After Ten Years," *Letters and Papers from Prison* (1953), tr. Eberhard Bethge.

9. Time is the only true purgatory. SAMUEL BUTLER (d. 1902), "Higgledy-Piggledy," *Note-Books* (1912).

10. Time! the Corrector where our judgments err, / The test of Truth, Love—sole philosopher, / For all beside are sophists. BYRON, *Childe Harold's Pilgrimage* (1812–18), 4.130.

11. Time ripens all things. No man's born wise. CERVANTES, *Don Quixote* (1605–15),

2.4.33, tr. Peter Motteux and John Ozell.

12. Time is born in the eyes, everybody knows that. JULIO CORTÁZAR, *The Winners* (1960), 17, tr. Elaine Kerrigan.

13. Time is a Test of Trouble— / But not a Remedy— / If such it prove, it prove too / There was no Malady—. EMILY DICKINSON, poem (c. 1863).

14. Scales and clocks ar-re not to be thrusted to decide annything that's worth deciding. Who tells time be a clock? Ivry hour is th' same to a clock an' ivry hour is diff'rent to me. Wan long, wan short. FINLEY PETER DUNNE, "Things Spiritual," *Mr. Dooley Says* (1910).

15. The days come and go like muffled and veiled figures sent from a distant friendly party, but they say nothing, and if we do not use the gifts they bring, they carry them as silently away. EMERSON, *Journals*, 1847.

16. Time is a file that wears and makes no noise. ENGLISH PROVERB.

17. Time is a fluid condition which has no existence except in the momentary avatars of individual people. WILLIAM FAULKNER, interview, *Writers at Work: First Series* (1958).

18. Time deals gently only with those who take it gently. ANATOLE FRANCE, *The Crime of Sylvestre Bonnard* (1881), 2, tr. Lafcadio Hearn.

19. Dost thou love life, then do not squander time, for that's the stuff life is made of. BENJAMIN FRANKLIN, "The Way to Wealth" (July 7, 1757).

20. Modern man thinks he loses something—time—when he does not do things quickly; yet he does not know what to do with the time he gains—except kill it. ERICH FROMM, *The Art of Loving* (1956), 4.

21. As good have no time as make no good use of it. THOMAS FULLER, M.D., *Gnomologia* (1732), 686.

22. What reason and endeavor cannot bring about, often time will. THOMAS FULLER, M.D., *Gnomologia* (1732), 5504.

23. It is familiarity with life that makes time speed quickly. When every day is a step in the unknown, as for children, the days are long with gathering of experience. GEORGE GISSING, "Winter," *The Private Papers of Henry Ryecroft* (1903).

24. Time cures one of everything—even of living. EDMOND and JULES DE GONCOURT, *Journal*, Oct. 14, 1856, tr. Robert Baldick.

25. God Himself chasteneth not with a rod but with time. BALTASAR GRACIÁN, *The Art of Worldly Wisdom* (1647), 55, tr. Joseph Jacobs.

26. Time flies over us, but leaves its shadow behind. NATHANIEL HAWTHORNE, *The Marble Faun* (1860), 24.

27. Most of the methods for measuring the lapse of time have, I believe, been the contrivance of monks and religious recluses, who, finding time hang heavy on their hands, were at some pains to see how they got rid of it. WILLIAM HAZLITT, "On a Sundial," *Sketches and Essays* (1839).

28. Time is the rider that breaks youth. GEORGE HERBERT, *Jacula Prudentum* (1651).

29. The most intractable of our experiences is the experience of Time—the intuition of duration, combined with the thought of perpetual perishing. ALDOUS HUXLEY, *Tomorrow and Tomorrow and Tomorrow* (1956).

30. Time is but the shadow of the world upon the background of Eternity. JEROME K. JEROME, "Clocks," *The Idle Thoughts of an Idle Fellow* (1889).

31. Those who make the worst use of their time are the first to complain of its brevity. LA BRUYÈRE, *Characters* (1688), 12.101, tr. Henri Van Laun.

32. For tribal man space was the uncontrollable mystery. For technological man it is time that occupies the same role. MARSHALL MC LUHAN, "Magic That Changes Mood," *The Mechanical Bride* (1951).

33. When one day is like all the others, then they are all like one; complete uniformity would make the longest life seem short, and as though it had stolen away from us unawares. THOMAS MANN, *The Magic Mountain* (1924), 4.2, tr. H. T. Lowe-Porter.

34. But at my back I always hear / Time's wingèd chariot hurrying near. ANDREW MARVELL, "To His Coy Mistress" (1650).

35. Time is a great legalizer, even in the field of morals. H. L. MENCKEN, *A Book of Prefaces* (1917), 4.6.

36. There is one kind of robber whom the law does not strike at, and who steals what is most precious to men: time. NAPOLEON I, *Maxims* (1804–15).

37. Age and time are but timidities of thought. EUGENE O'NEILL, *Lazarus Laughed* (1927), 4.1.

38. Time flies apace—we would fain believe that everything flies forward with it. NIETZSCHE, *The Will to Power* (1888), tr. Anthony M. Ludovici.

39. Time makes more converts than reason. THOMAS PAINE, introduction to *Common Sense* (1776).

40. Time heals griefs and quarrels, for we change and are no longer the same persons. PASCAL, *Pensées* (1670), 122, tr. W. F. Trotter.

41. Life hurries on, a frantic refugee, / And Death, with great forced marches, follows fast; / And all the present leagues with all the past / And all the future to make war on me. PETRARCH, "Laura Dead," *Canzoniere* (1360), 231.

42. Years following years steal something every day; / At last they steal us from ourselves away. ALEXANDER POPE, *Imitations of Horace* (1733–38), 2.2.72.

43. It seems no more than right that men should seize time by the forelock, for the rude old fellow, sooner or later, pulls all their hair out. GEORGE DENNISON PRENTICE, *Prenticeana* (1860).

44. In theory one is aware that the earth revolves, but in practice one does not perceive it, the ground upon which one treads seems not to move, and one can live undisturbed. So it is with Time in one's life. MARCEL PROUST, *Remembrance of Things Past: Within a Budding Grove* (1913–27), tr. C. K. Scott-Moncrieff.

45. Time, which changes people, does not alter the image we have retained of them. MARCEL PROUST, *Remembrance of Things Past: The Past Recaptured* (1913–27).

46. Half our life is spent trying to find something to do with the time we have rushed through life trying to save. WILL ROGERS, *The Autobiography of Will Rogers* (1949), 15.

47. Both in thought and in feeling, even though time be real, to realise the unimportance of time is the gate of wisdom. BERTRAND RUSSELL, title essay, *Mysticism and Logic* (1917).

48. "Time is blind; man stupid." / Thus one of the cynics. / "Time is relentless; man shrewd." / Thus one of the hopefuls. CARL SANDBURG, *The People, Yes* (1936).

49. Time is like an enterprising manager always bent on staging some new and surprising production, without knowing very well what it will be. GEORGE SANTAYANA, "Tipperary," *Soliloquies in England* (1922).

50. Time is that in which all things pass away. SCHOPENHAUER, "The Vanity of Existence," *Parerga and Paralipomena* (1851), tr. T. Bailey Saunders.

51. Time heals what reason cannot. SENECA, *Agamemnon* (1st c.).

52. Time's glory is to calm contending kings, / To unmask falsehood and bring truth to light. SHAKESPEARE, *The Rape of Lucrece* (1594), 939.

53. The whirligig of time brings in his revenges. SHAKESPEARE, *Twelfth Night* (1599–1600), 5.1.384.

54. Come what come may, / Time and the hour runs through the roughest day. SHAKESPEARE, *Macbeth* (1605–06), 1.3.146.

55. Great Time makes all things dim. SOPHOCLES, *Ajax* (c. 447 B.C.), tr. John Moore.

56. Time is a kindly God. SOPHOCLES, *Electra* (c. 418–14 B.C.), tr. David Grene.

57. The lowest of jewelry thieves is the robber of that precious jewel of another's time. ADLAI STEVENSON, *The Stevenson Wit* (1966).

58. No preacher is listened to but Time, which gives us the same train and turn of thought that elder people have in vain tried to put into our heads before. JONATHAN SWIFT, *Thoughts on Various Subjects* (1711).

59. Time turns the old days to derision, / Our loves into corpses or wives. ALGERNON CHARLES SWINBURNE, "Dolores" (1866).

60. Time is a wealth of change, but the clock in its parody makes it mere change and no wealth. RABINDRANATH TAGORE, *Stray Birds* (1916), 139.

61. The butterfly counts not months but moments, / and has time enough. RABINDRANATH TAGORE, *Fireflies* (1928).

62. We lack not rhymes and reasons, / As on this whirligig of Time / We circle with the seasons. ALFRED, LORD TENNYSON, "Will Waterproof's Lyrical Monologue" (1842).

63. Our costliest expenditure is time. THEOPHRASTUS (c. 370–287 B.C.), quoted in Diogenes Laertius' *Lives and Opinions of*

*Eminent Philosophers* (3rd c. A.D.), tr. R. D. Hicks.

64. We must expect everything and fear everything from time and from men. VAUVENARGUES, *Reflections and Maxims* (1746), 102.

65. Time bears away all things, even the mind. VERGIL, *Eclogues* (37 B.C.), 9.51, tr. T. F. Royds.

66. Time is the longest distance between two places. TENNESSEE WILLIAMS, *The Glass Menagerie* (1945), 1.

67. I think time is a merciless thing. I think life is a process of burning oneself out and time is the fire that burns you. But I think the spirit of man is a good adversary. TENNESSEE WILLIAMS, *New York Post*, April 30, 1958.

68. The years like great black oxen tread the world, / And God the herdsman goads them on behind, / And I am broken by their passing feet. WILLIAM BUTLER YEATS, *The Countess Cathleen* (1892), 5.

69. We take no note of time / But from its loss. EDWARD YOUNG, *Night Thoughts* (1742–46), 1.55.

## 972. TIMELINESS

See also 228. Delay; 721. Prematureness; 759. Punctuality; 942. Suitability

1. A word spoken in due season, how good is it! *Bible*, Proverbs 15:23.

2. To every thing there is a season, and a time to every purpose under the heaven. *Bible*, Ecclesiastes 3:1.

3. If you trap the moment before it's ripe, / The tears of repentence you'll certainly wipe; / But if once you let the ripe moment go / You can never wipe off the tears of woe. WILLIAM BLAKE, "The Marriage Ring" (1793–99).

4. There are times when sense may be unseasonable, as well as truth. WILLIAM CONGREVE, *The Double-Dealer* (1694), 1.1.

5. I hate it in friends when they come too late to help. EURIPIDES, *Rhesus* (c. 455–41 B.C.), tr. Richmond Lattimore.

6. Timeliness is best in all matters. HESIOD, *Works and Days* (8th c. B.C.), 694, tr. Richmond Lattimore.

7. A stone thrown at the right time is better than gold given at the wrong time. PERSIAN PROVERB.

8. To each thing belongs / its measure. Occasion is best to know. PINDAR, *Odes* (5th c. B.C.), Olympia 13, tr. Richmond Lattimore.

9. That which is virtue in season is madness out of season, as when an old man makes love. GEORGE SANTAYANA, *Dialogues in Limbo* (1925), 3.

10. How many things by season seasoned are / To their right praise and true perfection! SHAKESPEARE, *The Merchant of Venice* (1596–97), 5.1.107.

11. In season, all is good. SOPHOCLES, *Oedipus the King* (c. 430 B.C.), tr. David Grene.

## THE TIMES

See 296. Era

## 973. TIMIDITY

See also 90. Boldness; 110. Cautiousness; 302. Evasion; 340. Fear; 433. Humility

1. There is that destroyeth his own soul through bashfulness. *Apocrypha*, Ecclesiasticus 20:22.

2. There are men whose language is strong and defying enough, yet their eyes and their actions ask leave of other men to live. EMERSON, *Journals*, 1832.

3. Do not be too timid and squeamish about your actions. All life is an experiment. EMERSON, *Journals*, 1842.

4. He who is afraid of every nettle should not piss in the grass. THOMAS FULLER, M.D., *Gnomologia* (1732).

5. He that handles a nettle tenderly is soonest stung. THOMAS FULLER, M.D., *Gnomologia* (1732), 2126.

6. He will never have true friends who is afraid of making enemies. WILLIAM HAZLITT, *Characteristics* (1823), 401.

7. It is easy to frighten a bull from the window. ITALIAN PROVERB.

8. If you are reluctant to ask the way, you will be lost. MALAY PROVERB.

9. Happiness hates the timid! So does Science! EUGENE O'NEILL, *Strange Interlude* (1928), 4.

10. What is more mortifying than to feel that you have missed the plum for want of courage to shake the tree? LOGAN PEARSALL SMITH, *Afterthoughts* (1931), 1.

## 974. TIPPING

1. Whin I give a tip 'tis not because I want

to but because' I'm afraid iv what th' waiter'll think. FINLEY PETER DUNNE, "Casual Observations," *Mr. Dooley's Philosophy* (1900).

### TIREDNESS

See 338. Fatigue

### TITLES

See 612. Names

### 975. TOBACCO

1. He who doth not smoke hath either known no great griefs, or refuseth himself the softest consolation, next to that which comes from heaven. BULWER-LYTTON, *What Will He Do with It?* (1859), 1.6.

2. To the average cigarette smoker the world is his ashtray. ALEXANDER CHASE, *Perspectives* (1966).

3. Smokers, male and female, inject and excuse idleness in their lives every time they light a cigarette. COLETTE, "Freedom," *Earthly Paradise* (1966), 2, ed. Robert Phelps.

4. The believing we do something when we do nothing is the first illusion of tobacco. EMERSON, *Journals*, 1859.

5. A man of no conversation should smoke. EMERSON, *Journals*, 1866.

6. A custom [smoking] loathsome to the eye, harmful to the brain, dangerous to the lungs, and in the black stinking fume thereof, nearest resembling the horrible Stygian smoke of the pit that is bottomless. JAMES I OF ENGLAND, *Counterblaste to Tobacco* (1604).

7. A woman is only a woman, but a good cigar is a smoke. RUDYARD KIPLING, "The Betrothed," *Departmental Ditties* (1886).

8. It is now proved beyond doubt that smoking is one of the leading causes of statistics. FLETCHER KNEBEL, *Reader's Digest*, December 1961.

9. For thy sake, tobacco, I / Would do anything but die. CHARLES LAMB, *A Farewell to Tobacco* (1805).

10. This very night I am going to leave off tobacco! Surely there must be some other world in which this unconquerable purpose shall be realized. CHARLES LAMB, letter to Thomas Manning, Dec. 26, 1815.

11. Some things are better eschewed than chewed; tobacco is one of them. GEORGE DENNISON PRENTICE, *Prenticeana* (1860).

### TODAY

See 723. Present

### 976. TOGETHERNESS

See also 31. Aloofness; 150. Community; 151. Company; 497. Intimacy

1. Something there is that doesn't love a wall, / That wants it down. ROBERT FROST, "Mending Wall," *North of Boston* (1914).

2. We go right enough, darling, if we go wrong together! GEORGE SANTAYANA, *Persons and Places: My Host the World* (1953), 2.

3. Togetherness is a substitute sense of community, a counterfeit communion. GABRIEL VAHANIAN, *The Death of God* (1962), 1.

4. We're left alone with each other. We have to creep close to each other and give those gentle little nudges with our paws and our muzzles before we can slip into sleep and rest for the next day's playtime . . . and the next day's mysteries. TENNESSEE WILLIAMS, *The Milk Train Doesn't Stop Here Anymore* (1963), 5.

### 977. TOLERANCE

See also 118. Charity; 498. Intolerance; 517. Kindness

1. The peak of tolerance is most readily achieved by those who are not burdened with convictions. ALEXANDER CHASE, *Perspectives* (1966).

2. If you will please people, you must please them in their own way; and as you cannot make them what they should be, you must take them as they are. LORD CHESTERFIELD, *Letters to His Son*, Dec. 5, 1749.

3. Persecution was at least a sign of personal interest. Tolerance is composed of nine parts of apathy to one of brotherly love. FRANK MOORE COLBY, "Trials of an Encyclopedist," *The Colby Essays* (1926), v. 1.

4. True goodness is not without that germ of greatness that can bear with patience the mistakes of the ignorant. CHARLES CALEB COLTON, *Lacon* (1825), 2.39.

5. Laws alone cannot secure freedom of expression; in order that every man present his views without penalty there must be a spirit of tolerance in the entire population. EINSTEIN, *Out of My Later Years* (1950), 6.

6. [Tolerance] is just a makeshift, suitable for an overcrowded and overheated planet. It carries on when love gives out, and love generally gives out as soon as we move away from our home and our friends. E. M. FORSTER, "Tolerance," *Two Cheers for Democracy* (1951).

7. We are all tolerant enough of those who do not agree with us, provided only they are sufficiently miserable. DAVID GRAYSON, *Adventures in Contentment* (1907), 10.

8. People tolerate those they fear further than those they love. EDGAR WATSON HOWE, *Country Town Sayings* (1911).

9. It does me no injury for my neighbor to say there are twenty gods, or no God. THOMAS JEFFERSON, *Notes on the State of Virginia* (1784–85).

10. The highest result of education is tolerance. HELEN KELLER, *Optimism* (1903), 2.

11. Tolerance implies no lack of commitment to one's own beliefs. Rather it condemns the oppression or persecution of others. JOHN F. KENNEDY, letter to National Conference of Christians and Jews, Washington, D.C., Oct. 10, 1960.

12. If we cannot end our differences, at least we can help make the world safe for diversity. JOHN F. KENNEDY, commencement address, American University, Washington, D.C., June 10, 1963.

13. Those wearing Tolerance for a label / Call other views intolerable. PHYLLIS MCGINLEY, "In Praise of Diversity," *The Love Letters of Phyllis McGinley* (1954).

14. Mankind are greater gainers by suffering each other to live as seems good to themselves, than by compelling each to live as seems good to the rest. JOHN STUART MILL, *On Liberty* (1859), 1.

15. Sometimes with secret pride I sigh / To think how tolerant am I; / Then wonder which is really mine: / Tolerance, or a rubber spine? OGDEN NASH, "Yes and No," *I'm a Stranger Here Myself* (1938).

16. It is a good thing to demand liberty for ourselves and for those who agree with us, but it is a better thing and a rarer thing to give liberty to others who do not agree with us. FRANKLIN D. ROOSEVELT, radio address, Nov. 22, 1933.

17. So long as a man rides his hobbyhorse peaceably and quietly along the King's highway, and neither compels you or me to get up behind him,—pray, Sir, what have either you or I to do with it? LAURENCE STERNE, *Tristram Shandy* (1759–67), 1.7.

## 978. TOTALITARIANISM

See also 393. Government; 995. Tyranny

1. So efficient are the available instruments of slavery—fingerprints, lie detectors, brainwashings, gas chambers—that we shiver at the thought of political change which might put these instruments in the hands of men of hate. BERNARD M. BARUCH, *A Philosophy for Our Time* (1954), 1.

2. I suspect that in our loathing of totalitarianism, there is infused a good deal of admiration for its efficiency. T. S. ELIOT, "The Idea of a Christian Society" (1939).

3. Totalitarianism spells simplification: an enormous reduction in the variety of aims, motives, interests, human types, and, above all, in the categories and units of power. ERIC HOFFER, *The Ordeal of Change* (1964), 12.

4. Nothing more exactly identifies the totalitarian or closed society than the rigid and, more often than not, brutish direction of labor at all levels. JOHN F. KENNEDY, State of the Union Message, Jan. 14, 1963.

5. You have not converted a man because you have silenced him. JOHN MORLEY, *On Compromise* (1874).

## TOUCH

See 875. Senses

## TOURISM

See 985. Travel

## TRADE

See 102. Business and Commerce; 1029. Vocations

## 979. TRADITION

**See also 42. Antiquity; 134. Classics; 210. Custom; 439. Iconoclasm; 669. Past**

1. They that reverence too much old times are but a scorn to the new. FRANCIS BACON, "Of Innovations," *Essays* (1625).

2. It is pure illusion to think that an opinion which passes down from century to century, from generation to generation, may not be entirely false. PIERRE BAYLE, *Thoughts on the Comet* (1682).

3. Remove not the ancient landmark, which the fathers have set. *Bible*, Proverbs 22:28.

4. Hardened round us, encasing wholly every notion we form, is a wrappage of traditions, hearsays, mere words. THOMAS CARLYLE, *On Heroes, Hero-Worship and the Heroic in History* (1841), 1.

5. A love for tradition has never weakened a nation, indeed it has strengthened nations in their hour of peril; but the new view must come, the world must roll forward. SIR WINSTON CHURCHILL, speech, House of Commons, Nov. 29, 1944.

6. The dead govern the living. AUGUSTE COMTE, *Catéchisme positiviste* (1852).

7. Tradition, thou art for suckling children, / Thou art the enlivening milk for babes, / But no meat for men is in thee. STEPHEN CRANE, *The Black Riders and Other Lines* (1896), 45.

8. A precedent embalms a principle. BENJAMIN DISRAELI, speech, Feb. 22, 1848.

9. A tradition without intelligence is not worth having. T. S. ELIOT, "After Strange Gods" (1934).

10. Much of this world's wisdom is still acquired by necromancy,—by consulting the oracular dead. JULIUS CHARLES HARE and AUGUSTUS WILLIAM HARE, *Guesses at Truth* (1827).

11. To rest upon a formula is a slumber that, prolonged, means death. OLIVER WENDELL HOLMES, JR., "Ideals and Doubts," *Illinois Law Review* (1915), v. 10.

12. Old ways will always remain unless some one invents a new way and then lives and dies for it. ELBERT HUBBARD, *The Note Book* (1927).

13. Few people have ever seriously wished to be exclusively rational. The good life which most desire is a life warmed by passions and touched with that ceremonial grace which is impossible without some affectionate loyalty to traditional forms and ceremonies. JOSEPH WOOD KRUTCH, "Ignoble Utopias," *The Measure of Man* (1954).

14. Worshippers of light ancestral make the present light a crime. JAMES RUSSELL LOWELL, "The Present Crisis" (1844).

15. Tradition is a guide and not a jailer. W. SOMERSET MAUGHAM, *The Summing Up* (1938), 60.

16. The less men are fettered by tradition, the greater becomes the inward activity of their motives; the greater, again, in proportion thereto, the outward restlessness, the confused flux of mankind, the polyphony of strivings. NIETZSCHE, *Human, All Too Human* (1878), 23, tr. Helen Zimmern.

17. Every tradition grows continually more venerable, and the more remote its origin, the more this is lost sight of. The veneration paid the tradition accumulates from generation to generation, until it at last becomes holy and excites awe. NIETZSCHE, *Human, All Too Human* (1878), 96.

18. Continuity does not rule out fresh approaches to fresh situations. DEAN RUSK, *Time*, Dec. 6, 1963.

19. People are what they are / because they have come out of what was. / Therefore they should bow down before what was / and take it and say it's good—or should they? CARL SANDBURG, *The People, Yes* (1936).

20. No way of thinking or doing, however ancient, can be trusted without proof. THOREAU, "Economy," *Walden* (1854).

21. Loyalty to petrified opinion never yet broke a chain or freed a human soul. MARK TWAIN, inscribed beneath his bust in the Hall of Fame for Great Americans, New York University.

22. We're all so clogged with dead ideas / passed from generation to generation / that even the best of us / don't know the way out. PETER WEISS, *Marat / Sade* (1964), 1.15, tr. Geoffrey Skelton and Adrian Mitchell.

## 980. TRAGEDY

**See also 144. Comedy; 965. Theater**

1. Tragedy is restful; and the reason is that hope, that foul, deceitful thing, has no part

in it. JEAN ANOUILH, *Antigone* (1942), tr. Lewis Galantière.

2. Why is it that man desires to be made sad, beholding doleful and tragical things, which yet himself would by no means suffer? ST. AUGUSTINE, *Confessions* (5th c.), 3, tr. E. B. Pusey.

3. Only a great mind overthrown yields tragedy. JACQUES BARZUN, *The House of Intellect* (1959), 2.

4. One cannot balance tragedy in the scales / Unless one weighs it with the tragic heart. STEPHEN VINCENT BENÉT, *John Brown's Body* (1928), 4.

5. In nature, the most violent passions are silent; in Tragedy they must speak, and speak with dignity too. LORD CHESTERFIELD, *Letters to His Son*, Jan. 23, 1752.

6. A tragedy means always a man's struggle with that which is stronger than man. G. K. CHESTERTON, "The Bluff of the Big Shops," *Outline of Sanity* (1926).

7. In tragedy every moment is eternity; in comedy, eternity is a moment. CHRISTOPHER FRY, *Time*, Nov. 20, 1950.

8. Tragedy and comedy are simply questions of value; a little misfit in life makes us laugh; a great one is tragedy and cause for expression of grief. ELBERT HUBBARD, *The Note Book* (1927).

9. A tragic writer does not have to believe in God, but he must believe in man. JOSEPH WOOD KRUTCH, "The Tragic Fallacy," *The Modern Temper* (1929).

10. Ours is essentially a tragic age, so we refuse to take it tragically. D. H. LAWRENCE, *Lady Chatterley's Lover* (1928), 1.

11. In tragedy great men are more truly great than in history. We see them only in the crises which unfold them. NAPOLEON I, *Maxims* (1804–15).

12. Men play at tragedy because they do not believe in the reality of the tragedy which is actually being staged in the civilised world. JOSÉ ORTEGA Y GASSET, *The Revolt of the Masses* (1930), 11.

13. A tragic situation exists precisely when virtue does *not* triumph but when it is still felt that man is nobler than the forces which destroy him. GEORGE ORWELL, "Lear, Tolstoy and the Fool," *Shooting an Elephant* (1950).

14. Writers of comedy have outlook, whereas writers of tragedy have, according to them, insight. JAMES THURBER, "The Case for Comedy," *Lanterns and Lances* (1961).

15. The essence of dramatic tragedy is not unhappiness. It resides in the solemnity of the remorseless working of things. ALFRED NORTH WHITEHEAD, *Science and the Modern World* (1925), 1.

## 981. TRAINING

**See also 248. Discipline; 277. Education; 402. Growth and Development**

1. Train up a child in the way he should go: and when he is old he will not depart from it. *Bible*, Proverbs 22:6.

2. A young branch takes on all the bends that one gives it. CHINESE PROVERB.

3. Give a man a fish, and you feed him for a day. Teach a man to fish, and you feed him for a lifetime. CHINESE PROVERB.

4. Train up a fig-tree in the way it should go, and when you are old sit under the shade of it. CHARLES DICKENS, *Dombey and Son* (1848), 19.

5. Art is long, life short; judgment difficult, opportunity transient. GOETHE, *Wilhelm Meister's Apprenticeship* (1795–96), 7.9.

6. Life is short and the art long. HIPPOCRATES, *Aphorisms* (c. 400 B.C.), 1.1.

7. It is no hard matter to get children; but after they are born, then begins the trouble, solicitude, and care rightly to train, principle, and bring them up. MONTAIGNE, "Of the education of children," *Essays* (1580–88), tr. Charles Cotton and W. C. Hazlitt.

8. Man is the only one that knows nothing, that can learn nothing without being taught. He can neither speak nor walk nor eat, and in short he can do nothing at the prompting of nature only, but weep. PLINY THE ELDER, *Natural History* (1st c.), 7.4, tr. J. Bostock and H. T. Riley.

9. 'Tis education forms the common mind, / Just as the twig is bent the tree's inclined. ALEXANDER POPE, *Moral Essays* (1731–35), 1.149.

10. Children should be led into the right paths, not by severity, but by persuasion. TERENCE, *The Brothers* (160 B.C.).

11. A man can seldom—very, very, seldom—fight a winning fight against his training: the odds are too heavy. MARK TWAIN, "As Regards Patriotism" (1923).

**TRAITORS**
See 986. Treason

## 982. TRANQUILITY

See also 159. Composure; 183. Contentment; 674. Peace

1. Calm's not life's crown, though calm is well. MATTHEW ARNOLD, "Youth and Calm," *Empedocles on Etna, and Other Poems* (1852).

2. There's nought, no doubt, so much the spirit calms / As rum and true religion. BYRON, *Don Juan* (1819–24), 2.34.

3. Tranquillity! thou better name / Than all the family of Fame. SAMUEL TAYLOR COLERIDGE, "Ode to Tranquillity" (1801).

4. No one can achieve Serenity until the glare of passion is past the meridian. CYRIL CONNOLLY, *The Unquiet Grave* (1945), 1.

5. Back of tranquility lies always conquered unhappiness. DAVID GRAYSON, quoted in *The Autobiography of Eleanor Roosevelt* (1961).

6. By trading in our impatience for peace of mind we have sold out not to the devil but to the still, sad music of Muzak. ALAN HARRINGTON, "The Middle Depths," *Life in the Crystal Palace* (1959).

7. My experience in government is that when things are noncontroversial, beautifully coordinated and all the rest, it must be that there is not much going on. JOHN F. KENNEDY, quoted in Bill Adler's *The Kennedy Wit* (1964).

8. When we are unable to find tranquillity within ourselves, it is useless to seek it elsewhere. LA ROCHEFOUCAULD, *Maxims* (1665), tr. Kenneth Pratt.

9. We are used to the actions of human beings, not to their stillness. V. S. PRITCHETT, "The Hypocrite," *The Living Novel & Later Appreciations* (1964).

10. There is no joy but calm. ALFRED, LORD TENNYSON, "The Lotos-Eaters" (1842), 2.

11. If you want inner peace find it in solitude, not speed, and if you would find yourself, look to the land from which you came and to which you go. STEWART L. UDALL, *The Quiet Crisis* (1963), 14.

12. Nothing but stillness can remain when hearts are full / Of their own sweetness, bodies of their loveliness. WILLIAM BUTLER YEATS, "Meditations in Time of Civil War" (1923), 7.

## 983. TRANSIENCE

See also 115. Change; 300. Eternity; 600. Mortality; 971. Time

1. The entire most beautiful order of things that are very good, when their measures have been accomplished, is to pass away. ST. AUGUSTINE, *Confessions* (5th c.), 13, tr. John K. Ryan.

2. How is it possible for the brand of justice to be indelibly imprinted, and upon what, when we and all the things connected with us shall be transmuted and destroyed? UGO BETTI, *Struggle Till Dawn* (1949), 3, tr. G. H. McWilliam.

3. We are but of yesterday, and know nothing, because our days upon earth are a shadow. *Bible*, Job 8:9.

4. As for man, his days are as grass: as a flower of the field, so he flourisheth. *Bible*, Psalms 103:15.

5. Loveliest of lovely things are they, / On earth, that soonest pass away. WILLIAM CULLEN BRYANT, "A Scene on the Bank of the Hudson" (1827).

6. Ambition is a meteor-gleam; / Fame a restless airy dream; / Pleasures, insects on the wing / Round Peace, th' tend'rest flow'r of spring. ROBERT BURNS, "Written in Friars Carse Hermitage" (1793).

7. Our lives . . . are but a little while, / so let them run as sweetly as you can, / and give no thought to grief from day to day. / For time is not concerned to keep our hopes, / but hurries on its business, and is gone. EURIPIDES, *Heracles* (c. 422 B.C.), tr. William Arrowsmith.

8. What a day may bring a day may take away. THOMAS FULLER, M.D., *Gnomologia* (1732), 5475.

9. All of us are pilgrims on this earth. I've even heard people say that the earth itself is a pilgrim in the heavens. MAXIM GORKY, *The Lower Depths* (1903), 1, tr. Alexander Bakshy.

10. A permanent state of transition is man's most noble condition. JUAN RAMÓN JIMÉNEZ, "Heroic Reason," *Selected Writings* (1957), tr. H. R. Hays.

11. Life is but a day; / A fragile dew-drop on its perilous way / From a tree's summit. JOHN KEATS, "Sleep and Poetry" (1816).

12. The world is fleeting; all things pass away; / Or is it we that pass and they that stay? LUCIAN (c. 120–200).

13. All is ephemeral,—fame and the famous as well. MARCUS AURELIUS, *Meditations* (2nd c.), 4.35, tr. Morris Hickey Morgan.

14. The Worldly Hope men set their Hearts upon / Turns Ashes—or it prospers; and anon, / Like Snow upon the Desert's dusty Face, / Lighting a little hour or two—is gone. OMAR KHAYYÁM, *Rubáiyát* (11th–12th c.), tr. Edward FitzGerald, 4th ed., 16.

15. Chastity, as everybody knows, triumphs over Love, Death over Chastity, Fame over Death, and Time over Fame—to be conquered only by Eternity. ERWIN PANOFSKY, *Studies in Iconology* (1939), 3.

16. Nothing mortal is enduring, and there is nothing sweet which does not presently end in bitterness. PETRARCH, *Letter to Posterity* (1367–72).

17. We are things of a day. What are we? What are we not? The shadow of a dream / is man, no more. PINDAR, *Odes* (5th c. B.C.), Pythia 8, tr. Richmond Lattimore.

18. Joy and sorrow, beauty and deformity, equally pass away. SA'DI, *Gulistan* (1258), 1.30, tr. James Ross.

19. No reliance can be placed on the friendship of kings, nor vain hope put in the melodious voice of boys; for that passes away like a vision, and this vanishes like a dream. SA'DI, *Gulistan* (1258), 8.9, tr. James Ross.

20. Worlds on worlds are rolling ever / From creation to decay, / Like the bubbles on a river / Sparkling, bursting, borne away. SHELLEY, *Hellas* (1821).

21. We are not sure of sorrow, / And joy was never sure; / Today will die tomorrow; / Time stoops to no man's lure. ALGERNON CHARLES SWINBURNE, "The Garden of Proserpine," *Poems and Ballads: First Series* (1866).

22. Would that life were like the shadow cast by a wall or a tree, but it is like the shadow of a bird in flight. Haggadah, *Palestinian Talmud* (4th c.).

23. Our little systems have their day; / They have their day and cease to be; / They are but broken lights of thee, / And thou, O Lord, art more than they. ALFRED, LORD TENNYSON, "In Memoriam A. H. H." (1850).

24. The fairest things have fleetest end, / Their scent survives their close: / But the rose's scent is bitterness / To him that loved the rose. FRANCIS THOMPSON, "Daisy" (1890).

25. Fame is a vapor, popularity an accident; the only earthly certainty is oblivion. MARK TWAIN, *Notebook* (1935).

26. As generations come and go, / Their arts, their customs, ebb and flow; / Fate, fortune, sweep strong powers away, / And feeble, of themselves, decay. WILLIAM WORDSWORTH, "The Highland Broach" (1831).

## TRANSLATION

See 521. Language

## 984. TRANSPORTATION

See also 28. Airplanes; 63. Automobiles

1. Consider the wheelbarrow. It may lack the grace of an airplane, the speed of an automobile, the initial capacity of a freight car, but its humble wheel marked out the path of what civilization we still have. HAL BORLAND, "The Wheelbarrow—June 11," *Sundial of the Seasons* (1964).

2. In the space age, man will be able to go around the world in two hours—one hour for flying and the other to get to the airport. NEIL MC ELROY, *Look*, Feb. 18, 1958.

## 985. TRAVEL

See also 28. Airplanes; 63. Automobiles; 427. Hotels; 693. Place; 833. Sailing; 984. Transportation

1. The less a tourist knows, the fewer mistakes he need make, for he will not expect himself to explain ignorance. HENRY ADAMS, *The Education of Henry Adams* (1907), 27.

2. The time to enjoy a European trip is about three weeks after unpacking. GEORGE ADE, "The Hungry Man from Bird Center," *Forty Modern Fables* (1901).

3. No matter how many miles a man may travel, he will never get ahead of himself.

GEORGE ADE, "The Man Who Wanted His Europe," *Hand-Made Fables* (1920).

4. When I am here [at Milan], I do not fast on the Sabbath; when I am at Rome, I do fast on the Sabbath. ST. AMBROSE, *Letters to Augustine* (4th c.), 36.14. (The saying "When in Rome, do as the Romans do" probably originated in this piece of advice.)

5. Many shall run to and fro, and knowledge shall be increased. *Bible*, Daniel 12:4.

6. Road, n. A strip of land along which one may pass from where it is too tiresome to be to where it is futile to go. AMBROSE BIERCE, *The Devil's Dictionary* (1881–1911).

7. The traveler was active; he went strenuously in search of people, of adventure, of experience. The tourist is passive; he expects interesting things to happen to him. He goes "sight-seeing." DANIEL J. BOORSTIN, *The Image* (1962), 3.2.

8. Travellers, like poets, are mostly an angry race. SIR RICHARD BURTON, "Narrative of a Trip to Harar," *Royal Geographical Society Journal* (1855), 25.

9. What affects men sharply about a foreign nation is not so much finding or not finding familiar things; it is rather not finding them in the familiar place. G. K. CHESTERTON, "On Flags," *Generally Speaking* (1928).

10. How much a dunce that has been sent to roam / Excels a dunce that has been kept at home! WILLIAM COWPER, *The Progress of Error* (1782), 415.

11. To roam / Giddily, and be everywhere but at home, / Such freedom doth a banishment become. JOHN DONNE, "To Mr. Rowland Woodward," *Letters to Several Personages* (1651).

12. Trees often transplanted seldom prosper. DUTCH PROVERB.

13. No man should travel until he has learned the language of the country he visits. Otherwise he voluntarily makes himself a great baby,—so helpless and so ridiculous. EMERSON, *Journals*, 1833.

14. Travelling is a fool's paradise. We owe to our first journeys the discovery that place is nothing. EMERSON, "Self-Reliance," *Essays: First Series* (1841).

15. Men run away to other countries because they are not good in their own, and run back to their own because they pass for nothing in the new places. EMERSON, "Culture," *The Conduct of Life* (1860).

16. The world is his who has money to go over it. EMERSON, "Wealth," *The Conduct of Life* (1860).

17. The heaviest baggage for a traveler is an empty purse. ENGLISH PROVERB.

18. The crow went traveling abroad and came home just as black. ENGLISH PROVERB.

19. As a member of an escorted tour, you don't even have to know the Matterhorn isn't a tuba. TEMPLE FIELDING, *Fielding's Guide to Europe*, 1963.

20. He that travels much knows much. THOMAS FULLER, M.D., *Gnomologia* (1732), 2335.

21. If an ass goes traveling, he'll not come home a horse. THOMAS FULLER, M.D., *Gnomologia* (1732), 2668.

22. Each traveler should know what he has to see, and what properly belongs to him, on a journey. GOETHE, quoted in Johann Peter Eckermann's *Conversations with Goethe*, Nov. 3, 1823.

23. They change their climate, not their soul, who rush across the sea. HORACE. *Epistles* (20–c. 8 B.C.), 1.10.

24. One travels more usefully when alone, because he reflects more. THOMAS JEFFERSON, letter to J. Bannister, Jr., June 19, 1787.

25. Travelling. This makes men wiser, but less happy. THOMAS JEFFERSON, letter to Peter Carr, Aug. 10, 1787.

26. In traveling: a man must carry knowledge with him, if he would bring home knowledge. SAMUEL JOHNSON, quoted in Boswell's *Life of Samuel Johnson*, April 17, 1778.

27. The use of travelling is to regulate imagination by reality, and instead of thinking how things may be, to see them as they are. SAMUEL JOHNSON, quoted in Hester Lynch Piozzi's *Anecdotes of Samuel Johnson* (1786).

28. My heart is warm with the friends I make, / And better friends I'll not be knowing; / Yet there isn't a train I wouldn't take, / No matter where it's going. EDNA ST. VINCENT MILLAY, "Travel," *Second April* (1921).

29. We cannot learn to love other tourists, —the laws of nature forbid it,—but, meditating soberly on the impossibility of their loving us, we may reach some common platform of tolerance, some common exchange of recognition and amenity. AGNES REP-

PLIER, "The Tourist," *Compromises* (1904).

30. There are tourists incapable of looking at a masterpiece for its own sake. They bow into a camera, snap experiences never had, then rush home and develop these celluloid events so as to see where they've been. NED ROREM, "Listening and Hearing," *Music from Inside and Out* (1967).

31. Roam abroad in the world, and take thy fill of its enjoyments before the day shall come when thou must quit it for good. SA'DI, *Gulistan* (1258), 3.28, tr. James Ross.

32. A traveller without knowledge is a bird without wings. SA'DI, *Gulistan* (1258), 8.82, tr. James Ross.

33. He who would travel happily must travel light. SAINT-EXUPÉRY, *Wind, Sand, and Stars* (1939), 8, tr. Lewis Galantière.

34. The traveller must be somebody and come from somewhere, so that his definite character and moral traditions may supply an organ and a point of comparison for his observations. GEORGE SANTAYANA, *Persons and Places: My Host the World* (1953), 3.

35. Those who pass their lives in foreign travel find they contract many ties of hospitality, but form no friendships. SENECA, *Letters to Lucilius* (1st c.), 2, tr. E. Phillips Barker.

36. When I was at home, I was in a better place; but travellers must be content. SHAKESPEARE, *As You Like It* (1599–1600), 2.4.17.

37. For my part, I travel not to go anywhere, but to go. I travel for travel's sake. The great affair is to move. ROBERT LOUIS STEVENSON, "Cheylard and Luc," *Travels with a Donkey* (1879).

38. Wealth I ask not, hope nor love, / Nor a friend to know me; / All I seek, the heaven above / And the road below me. ROBERT LOUIS STEVENSON, "The Vagabond," *Songs of Travel* (1886).

39. To forget pain is to be painless; to forget care is to be rid of it; to go abroad is to accomplish both. MARK TWAIN, *Autobiography* (1924), v. 2, ed. A. B. Paine.

40. To go abroad has something of the same sense that death brings. I am no longer of ye—what ye say of me is now of no consequence. MARK TWAIN, *Notebook* (1935).

41. Most of / the beauties of travel are due to / the strange hours we keep to see them. WILLIAM CARLOS WILLIAMS, "January Morning," *Selected Poems* (1949), 1.

42. I travelled among unknown men, / In lands beyond the sea; / Nor, England! did I know till then / What love I bore to thee. WILLIAM WORDSWORTH, "I Travelled Among Unknown Men" (1801).

## 986. TREASON

**See also 77. Betrayal**

1. The treason pleases, but the traitors are odious. CERVANTES, *Don Quixote* (1605–15), 1.4.12, tr. Peter Motteux and John Ozell.

2. Treason doth never prosper: what's the reason? / For if it prosper, none dare call it treason. SIR JOHN HARINGTON, "Of Treason," *Epigrams* (1615).

3. Treason in our time is a proof of genius. SAINT-EXUPÉRY, *Flight to Arras* (1942), 13, tr. Lewis Galantière.

4. Traters, I will here remark, are a onfortnit class of peple. If they wasn't, they wouldn't be traters. They conspire to bust up a country—they fail, and they're traters. They bust her, and they become statesmen and heroes. ARTEMUS WARD, "The Tower of London," *Artemus Ward in London* (1872).

## 987. TREATIES

**See also 46. Appeasement; 160. Compromise; 164. Conciliation; 496. International Relations**

1. Treaties are like roses and young girls. They last while they last. CHARLES DE GAULLE, *Time*, July 12, 1963.

2. "Let us agree not to step on each other's feet," said the cock to the horse. ENGLISH PROVERB.

3. Let us never negotiate out of fear. But let us never fear to negotiate. JOHN F. KENNEDY, Inaugural Address, Jan. 20, 1961.

4. Peace does not rest in charters and covenants alone. It lies in the hearts and minds of the people. JOHN F. KENNEDY, address, United Nations General Assembly, Sept. 20, 1963.

5. Treaties are observed as long as they are in harmony with interests. NAPOLEON I, *Maxims* (1804–15).

6. The hand that signed the treaty bred a fever, / And famine grew, and locusts came; / Great is the hand that holds dominion over / Man by a scribbled name. DYLAN

THOMAS, "The Hand That Signed the Paper," *Collected Poems* (1953).

7. The only treaties that ought to count are those which would effect a settlement between ulterior motives. PAUL VALÉRY, "Greatness and Decadence of Europe," *Reflections on the World Today* (1931), tr. Francis Scarfe.

8. There is nothing more likely to start disagreement among people or countries than an agreement. E. B. WHITE,"My Day," *One Man's Meat* (1944).

## 988. TREES

1. No town can fail of beauty, though its walks were gutters and its houses hovels, if venerable trees make magnificent colonnades along its streets. HENRY WARD BEECHER, *Proverbs from Plymouth Pulpit* (1887).

2. A woodland in full color is awesome as a forest fire, in magnitude at least; but a single tree is like a dancing tongue of flame to warm the heart. HAL BORLAND, "Autumn in Your Hand," *Sundial of the Seasons* (1964).

3. He that plants trees loves others besides himself. ENGLISH PROVERB.

4. The forest is the poor man's overcoat. NEW ENGLAND PROVERB.

5. Trees are the earth's endless effort to speak to the listening heaven. RABINDRANATH TAGORE, *Fireflies* (1928).

6. Any fine morning a power saw can fell a tree that took a thousand years to grow. EDWIN WAY TEALE, *Autumn Across America* (1956), 29.

## TRICKERY

**See 197. Craftiness; 221. Deception; 932. Strategy**

## 989. TRIFLES

**See also 398. Great and Small; 605. The Mundane; 686. Pettiness; 901. Smallness; 1005. Unimportance**

1. Little things seem nothing, but they give peace, like those meadow flowers which individually seem odorless but all together perfume the air. GEORGES BERNANOS, *The Diary of a Country Priest* (1936), 6.

2. It has long been an axiom of mine that the little things are infinitely the most important. SIR ARTHUR CONAN DOYLE, "A Case of Identity," *The Adventures of Sherlock Holmes* (1891).

3. The displacement of a little sand can change occasionally the course of deep rivers. MANUEL GONZÁLEZ PRADA, *Horas de lucha* (1908).

4. A little thing can be everything; but one must be able to see it, and sometimes to be content with it. Graffito written during French student revolt, May 1968.

5. Men trip not on mountains, they stumble on stones. HINDUSTANI PROVERB.

6. Those who apply themselves too much to little things usually become incapable of great ones. LA ROCHEFOUCAULD, *Maxims* (1665), tr. Kenneth Pratt.

7. In life's small things be resolute and great / To keep thy muscle trained. JAMES RUSSELL LOWELL, "Epigram" (1888).

8. It's the people who're comfortable who have time to worry over little trivial things. WILLIAM MC FEE, *Casuals of the Sea* (1916), 2.1.6.

9. Trifles make the sum of human things, / And half our misery from our foibles springs. HANNAH MORE, *Sensibility* (1783).

10. A toothache will cost a battle, a drizzle cancel an insurrection. VLADIMIR NABOKOV, *The Eye* (1930).

11. For the person for whom small things do not exist, the great is not great. JOSÉ ORTEGA Y GASSET, "To the Reader," *Meditations on Quixote* (1914).

12. A mere trifle consoles us, for a mere trifle distresses us. PASCAL, *Pensées* (1670), 136, tr. W. F. Trotter.

13. What dire offence from amorous causes springs! / What mighty contests rise from trivial things! ALEXANDER POPE, *The Rape of the Lock* (1712), 1.1.

14. Even a single hair casts its shadow. PUBLILIUS SYRUS, *Moral Sayings* (1st c. B.C.), 228, tr. Darius Lyman.

15. Trifles make up the happiness or the misery of human life. ALEXANDER SMITH, "Men of Letters," *Dreamthorp* (1863).

16. Small causes are sufficient to make a man uneasy, when great ones are not in the way: for want of a block he will stumble at a straw. JONATHAN SWIFT, *Thoughts on Various Subjects* (1711).

17. Think naught a trifle, though it small appear; / Small sands the mountain, moments make the year, / And trifles life. EDWARD YOUNG, *Love of Fame* (1728), 6.208.

## TRIVIALITY

See 67. Banality; 989. Trifles

## TROUBLE

See 17. Adversity

## 990. TRUST

See also 77. Betrayal; 257. Distrust

1. Thrust ivrybody—but cut th' ca-ards. FINLEY PETER DUNNE, "Casual Observations," *Mr. Dooley's Philosophy* (1900).

2. The essence of friendship is entireness, a total magnanimity and trust. EMERSON, "Friendship," *Essays: First Series* (1841).

3. Trust men and they will be true to you; treat them greatly and they will show themselves great. EMERSON, "Prudence," *Essays: First Series* (1841).

4. Trust thyself only, and another shall not betray thee. THOMAS FULLER, M.D., *Gnomologia* (1732).

5. No man ever quite believes in any other man. One may believe in an idea absolutely, but not in a man. H. L. MENCKEN, "The Skeptic," *The Smart Set*, May 1919.

6. As contagion / of sickness makes sickness, / contagion of trust makes trust. MARIANNE MOORE, "In Distrust of Merits," *Collected Poems* (1951).

7. Various are the uses of friends, beyond all else / in difficulty, but joy also looks for trust that is clear / in the eyes. PINDAR, *Odes* (5th c. B.C.), Nemea 8, tr. Richmond Lattimore.

8. Confidence is the only bond of friendship. PUBLILIUS SYRUS, *Moral Sayings* (1st c. B.C.), 34, tr. Darius Lyman.

9. A man who doesn't trust himself can never really trust anyone else. CARDINAL DE RETZ, *Mémoires* (1718).

10. It's a vice to trust all, and equally a vice to trust none. SENECA, *Letters to Lucilius* (1st c.), 3.4, tr. E. Phillips Barker.

11. Love all, trust a few. SHAKESPEARE, *All's Well That Ends Well* (1602–03), 1.1.74.

## 991. TRUTH

See also 297. Error; 329. Falsehood; 661. Paradoxes; 992. Truth and Falsehood; 993. Truthfulness

1. Too much *Truth* / Is uncouth. FRANKLIN P. ADAMS, *Nods and Becks* (1944).

2. Every truth has two sides; it is well to look at both, before we commit ourselves to either. AESOP, "The Mule," *Fables* (6th c. B.C.?), tr. Thomas James.

3. Great is truth and strongest of all. *Apocrypha*, 1 Esdras 4:22.

4. It would be wrong to put friendship before the truth. ARISTOTLE, *Nicomachean Ethics* (4th c. B.C.), 1.6, tr. J. A. K. Thomson.

5. Truth sits upon the lips of dying men. MATTHEW ARNOLD, "Sohrab and Rustum," *Poems* (1853).

6. Pushing any truth out very far, you are met by a counter-truth. HENRY WARD BEECHER, *Proverbs from Plymouth Pulpit* (1887).

7. The truth shall make you free. *Bible*, John 8:32.

8. A man may be in as just possession of truth as of a city, and yet be forced to surrender; 'tis therefore far better to enjoy her with peace, than to hazard her on a battle. SIR THOMAS BROWNE, *Religio Medici* (1642), 1.

9. So absolutely good is truth, truth never hurts / The teller. ROBERT BROWNING, *Fifine at the Fair* (1872), 32.

10. Look on this beautiful world, and read the truth / In her fair page. WILLIAM CULLEN BRYANT, "The Ages" (1821).

11. A truth's prosperity is like a jest's; it lies in the ear of him that hears it. SAMUEL BUTLER (d. 1902), "The Germs of *Erewhon* and of *Life and Habit*," *Note-Books* (1912).

12. Some men love truth so much that they seem to be in continual fear lest she should catch cold on over-exposure. SAMUEL BUTLER (d. 1902), "Truth and Convenience," *Note-Books* (1912).

13. There is no permanent absolute unchangeable truth; what we should pursue is the most convenient arrangement of our ideas. SAMUEL BUTLER (d. 1902), "Truth and Convenience," *Note-Books* (1912).

14. Truth's fountains may be clear—her streams are muddy, / And cut through such canals of contradiction, / That she must

often navigate o'er fiction. BYRON, *Don Juan* (1819–24), 15.88.

15. How could sincerity be a condition of friendship? A taste for truth at any cost is a passion which spares nothing. ALBERT CAMUS, *The Fall* (1956).

16. We call first truths those we discover after all the others. ALBERT CAMUS, *The Fall* (1956).

17. To know, to get into the truth of anything, is ever a mystic act, of which the best logics can but babble on the surface. THOMAS CARLYLE, *On Heroes, Hero-Worship and the Heroic in History* (1841), 2.

18. The form of truth will bear exposure, as well as that of beauty herself. SAMUEL TAYLOR COLERIDGE, "Preliminary Observations," *Aids to Reflection* (1825).

19. Pure truth, like pure gold, has been found unfit for circulation, because men have discovered that it is far more convenient to adulterate the truth than to refine themselves. CHARLES CALEB COLTON, *Lacon* (1825), 2.108.

20. They who know the truth are not equal to those who love it, and they who love it are not equal to those who delight in it. CONFUCIUS, *Analects* (6th c. B.C.), 6.18, tr. James Legge.

21. The superior man is anxious lest he should not get truth; he is not anxious lest poverty should come upon him. CONFUCIUS, *Analects* (6th c. B.C.), 15.31, tr. James Legge.

22. Truth is a river that is always splitting up into arms that reunite. Islanded between the arms the inhabitants argue for a lifetime as to which is the main river. CYRIL CONNOLLY, *The Unquiet Grave* (1945), 3.

23. As time goes on, new and remoter aspects of truth are discovered, which can seldom or never be fitted into creeds that are changeless. CLARENCE DAY, *This Simian World* (1920), 17.

24. The Truth must dazzle gradually / Or every man be blind—. EMILY DICKINSON, poem (c. 1868).

25. Opinion is a flitting thing, / But Truth, outlasts the Sun— / If then we cannot own them both— / Possess the oldest one—. EMILY DICKINSON, poem (c. 1879).

26. Truth, like time, is an idea arising from, and dependent upon, human intercourse. ISAK DINESEN, "The Roads Round Pisa," 1, *Seven Gothic Tales* (1934).

27. On a huge hill, / Cragged and steep, Truth stands, and he that will / Reach her, about must, and about must go. JOHN DONNE, Satire 3 (1635).

28. How often have I said to you that when you have eliminated the impossible, whatever remains, however improbable, must be the truth? SIR ARTHUR CONAN DOYLE, *The Sign of Four* (1889).

29. The Truth has such a face and such a mien, / As to be loved needs only to be seen. JOHN DRYDEN, *The Hind and the Panther* (1687), 11.33.

30. Truth is what most contradicts itself. LAWRENCE DURRELL, *Balthazar* (1958), 1.5.

31. Truth is a matter of direct apprehension—you can't climb a ladder of mental concepts to it. LAWRENCE DURRELL, *Balthazar* (1958), 2.6.

32. Truth disappears with the telling of it. LAWRENCE DURRELL, *Clea* (1960), 2.2.

33. Ethical axioms are found and tested not very differently from the axioms of science. Truth is what stands the test of experience. EINSTEIN, *Out of My Later Years* (1950), 16.

34. All necessary truth is its own evidence. EMERSON, *Journals*, 1833.

35. Truth has already ceased to be itself if polemically said. EMERSON, *Journals*, 1836.

36. God offers to every mind its choice between truth and repose. EMERSON, "Intellect," *Essays: First Series* (1841).

37. No man has a right perception of any truth, who has not been reacted on by it, so as to be ready to be its martyr. EMERSON, "Fate," *The Conduct of Life* (1860).

38. Time trieth truth. ENGLISH PROVERB.

39. The soul is unwillingly deprived of truth. EPICTETUS, *Discourses* (2nd c.), 1.28, tr. Thomas W. Higginson.

40. Truth—that long clean clear simple undeviable unchallengeable straight and shining line, on one side of which black is black and on the other white is white, has now become an angle, a point of view. WILLIAM FAULKNER, "On Privacy," *Essays, Speeches & Public Letters* (1965).

41. Truth is child of Time. JOHN FORD, *The Broken Heart* (1633), 4.3.

42. Truth is a flower in whose neighbourhood others must wither. E. M. FORSTER, "Joseph Conrad: A Note," *Abinger Harvest* (1936).

43. Truth fears no trial. THOMAS FULLER, M.D., *Gnomologia* (1732), 5297.

44. Truth may sometimes come out of the Devil's mouth. THOMAS FULLER, M.D., *Gnomologia* (1732), 5308.

45. Truth has a handsome countenance but torn garments. GERMAN PROVERB.

46. Say not, "I have found the truth," but rather, "I have found a truth." KAHLIL GIBRAN, "On Self-Knowledge," *The Prophet* (1923).

47. We no longer admit any other truth than that which is expedient; for there is no worse error than the truth that may weaken the arm that is fighting. ANDRÉ GIDE, "Reflections on Germany," *Pretexts* (1903), tr. Angelo P. Bertocci and others.

48. To love the truth is to refuse to let oneself be saddened by it. ANDRÉ GIDE, *Journals*, Oct. 14, 1940, tr. Justin O'Brien.

49. The truths of life are not discovered by us. At moments unforeseen, some gracious influence descends upon the soul, touching it to an emotion which, we know not how, the mind transmutes into thought. GEORGE GISSING, "Autumn," *The Private Papers of Henry Ryecroft* (1903).

50. The brilliant passes, like the dew at morn; / The true endures, for ages yet unborn. GOETHE, "Prelude in the Theatre," *Faust: Part I* (1808), tr. Philip Wayne.

51. The very truths which concern us most can only be half spoken, but with attention we can grasp the whole meaning. BALTASAR GRACIÁN, *The Art of Worldly Wisdom* (1647), 25, tr. Joseph Jacobs.

52. Truth always lags last, limping along on the arm of Time. BALTASAR GRACIÁN, *The Art of Worldly Wisdom* (1647), 146, tr. Joseph Jacobs.

53. Political truth is a libel—religious truth blasphemy. WILLIAM HAZLITT, "Commonplaces," *The Round Table* (1817), 42.

54. One truth discovered, one pang of regret at not being able to express it, is better than all the fluency and flippancy in the world. WILLIAM HAZLITT, "My First Acquaintance with Poets," *The Plain Speaker* (1826).

55. Truth is a torch which gleams in the fog but does not dispel it. CLAUDE-ADRIEN HELVÉTIUS, preface to *De l'esprit* (1758).

56. Unless you expect the unexpected you will never find [truth], for it is hard to discover and hard to attain. HERACLITUS, *Fragments* (c. 500 B.C.), 19, tr. Philip Wheelwright.

57. Such truth as opposeth no man's profit nor pleasure is to all men welcome. THOMAS HOBBES, "A Review and Conclusion," *Leviathan* (1651).

58. Add a few drops of venom to a half truth and you have an absolute truth. ERIC HOFFER, *The Passionate State of Mind* (1954), 216.

59. As with the pursuit of happiness, the pursuit of truth is itself gratifying whereas the consummation often turns out to be elusive. RICHARD HOFSTADTER, *Anti-Intellectualism in American Life* (1963), 1.2.

60. Truth is tough. It will not break, like a bubble, at a touch; nay, you may kick it about all day like a football, and it will be round and full at evening. OLIVER WENDELL HOLMES, SR., *The Professor at the Breakfast Table* (1860), 5.

61. Our test of truth is a reference to either a present or imagined future majority in favor of our view. OLIVER WENDELL HOLMES, JR., "Natural Law," *Harvard Law Review* (1918), v. 32.

62. I used to say, when I was young, that truth was the majority vote of that nation that could lick all others. OLIVER WENDELL HOLMES, JR., "Natural Law," *Harvard Law Review* (1918), v. 32.

63. It is the customary fate of new truths to begin as heresies and to end as superstitions. THOMAS HENRY HUXLEY, "The Coming of Age of *The Origin of Species*" (1880).

64. One point is certain, that truth is one and immutable; until the jurors all agree, they cannot all be right. WASHINGTON IRVING, "The Widow's Ordeal," *Wolfert's Roost* (1855).

65. It is dangerous for mortal beauty, or terrestrial virtue, to be examined by too strong a light. The torch of Truth shows much that we cannot, and all that we would not, see. SAMUEL JOHNSON, *The Rambler* (1750–52), 10.

66. In order that all men may be taught to speak truth, it is necessary that all likewise should learn to hear it. SAMUEL JOHNSON, *The Rambler* (1750–52), 96.

67. The dignity of truth is lost / With much protesting. BEN JONSON, *Catiline His Conspiracy* (1611), 3.2.

68. Truth is man's proper good, and the

only immortal thing was given to our mortality to use. BEN JONSON, "Explorata," *Timber* (1640).

69. It profits not me to have any man fence or fight for me, to flourish or take a side. Stand for truth and 'tis enough. BEN JONSON, "Of Liberal Studies," *Timber* (1640).

70. What the imagination seizes as beauty must be truth. JOHN KEATS, letter to Benjamin Bailey, Nov. 22, 1817.

71. Men speak the truth as they understand it, and women as they think men would like to understand it. RUDYARD KIPLING, "Bitters Neat," *Plain Tales from the Hills* (1888).

72. Truth is a point, the subtlest and finest; harder than adamant; never to be broken, worn away, or blunted. Its only bad quality is, that it is sure to hurt those who touch it; and likely to draw blood, perhaps the life blood, of those who press earnestly upon it. WALTER SAVAGE LANDOR, "Diogenes and Plato," *Imaginary Conversations* (1824–53).

73. Truth, like the juice of the poppy, in small quantities, calms men; in larger, heats and irritates them, and is attended by fatal consequences in its excess. WALTER SAVAGE LANDOR, "Middleton and Magliabecchi," *Imaginary Conversations* (1824–53).

74. Truth does not lie beyond humanity, but is one of the products of the human mind and feeling. D. H. LAWRENCE, *The Rainbow* (1915), 12.

75. Duration is not a test of true or false. ANNE MORROW LINDBERGH, "Double-Sunrise," *Gift from the Sea* (1955).

76. We say that the truth will make us free. Yes, but that truth is a thousand truths which grow and change. WALTER LIPPMANN, "The Golden Rule and After," *A Preface to Politics* (1914).

77. Truth, like gold, is not less so for being newly brought out of the mine. JOHN LOCKE, "The Epistle Dedicatory," *An Essay Concerning Human Understanding* (1690).

78. To love truth for truth's sake is the principal part of human perfection in this world, and the seed-plot of all other virtues. JOHN LOCKE, letter to Anthony Collins, Oct. 29, 1703.

79. Truth forever on the scaffold, Wrong forever on the throne,— / Yet that scaffold sways the future. JAMES RUSSELL LOWELL, "The Present Crisis" (1844).

80. Man's passion for truth is such that he will welcome the bitterest of all postulates so long as it strikes him as true. ANTONIO MACHADO, *Juan de Mairena* (1943), 1, tr. Ben Belitt.

81. But it is not enough to possess a truth; it is essential that the truth should possess us. MAURICE MAETERLINCK, "The Deeper Life," *The Treasure of the Humble* (1896), tr. Alfred Sutro.

82. I search after truth, by which man never yet was harmed. MARCUS AURELIUS, *Meditations* (2nd c.), 6.21, tr. Morris Hickey Morgan.

83. If truth is a value it is because it is true and not because it is brave to speak it. W. SOMERSET MAUGHAM, *The Summing Up* (1938), 75.

84. To be mistaken is a misfortune to be pitied; but to know the truth and not to conform one's actions to it is a crime which Heaven and Earth condemn. GIUSEPPE MAZZINI, *The Duties of Man and Other Essays* (1910).

85. The smallest atom of truth represents some man's bitter toil and agony; for every ponderable chuck of it there is a brave truth-seeker's grave upon some lonely ash-dump and a soul roasting in hell. H. L. MENCKEN, *Prejudices: Third Series* (1922), 14.

86. The real advantage which truth has, consists in this, that when an opinion is true, it may be extinguished once, twice, or many times, but in the course of ages there will generally be found persons to rediscover it. JOHN STUART MILL, *On Liberty* (1859), 2.

87. Indeed, the dictum that truth always triumphs over persecution, is one of those pleasant falsehoods which men repeat after one another till they pass into commonplaces, but which all experience refutes. JOHN STUART MILL, *On Liberty* (1859), 2.

88. The truth of these days is not that which really is, but what every man persuades another man to believe. MONTAIGNE, "On giving the lie," *Essays* (1580–88), tr. Charles Cotton and W. C. Hazlitt.

89. There is an innate decorum in man, and it is not fair to thrust Truth upon people when they don't expect it. Only the very generous are ready for Truth impromptu.

CHRISTOPHER MORLEY, *Inward Ho!* (1923), 1.

90. Here is the end of the Eternal Verities, when one lets them bulk so big in his eyes as to shut out that perishable speck, the human race. JOHN MORLEY, "Carlyle," *Critical Miscellanies* (1871–1908).

91. The love of truth has its reward in heaven and even on earth. NIETZSCHE, *Beyond Good and Evil* (1886), 45, tr. Walter Kaufmann.

92. There are many kind of eyes. Even the Sphinx has eyes—therefore there must be many kinds of "truths," and consequently there can be no truth. NIETZSCHE, *The Will to Power* (1888), 540, tr. Anthony M. Ludovici.

93. The will to truth is merely the longing for a stable world. NIETZSCHE, *The Will to Power* (1888), 585, tr. Anthony M. Ludovici.

94. To me the truth is something which cannot be told in a few words, and those who simplify the universe only reduce the expansion of its meaning. ANAÏS NIN, *The Diary of Anaïs Nin*, Winter 1931–32.

95. Such is the irresistible nature of truth that all it asks, and all it wants, is the liberty of appearing. THOMAS PAINE, *The Rights of Man* (1791), 2.

96. We have an idea of truth, invincible to all scepticism. PASCAL, *Pensées* (1670), 395, tr. W. F. Trotter.

97. There would be too great darkness, if truth had not visible signs. PASCAL, *Pensées* (1670), 856, tr. W. F. Trotter.

98. We know the truth, not only by the reason, but also by the heart. PASCAL, *Pensées* (1670), 10.1, tr. O. W. Wight.

99. He who does not bellow the truth when he knows the truth makes himself the accomplice of liars and forgers. CHARLES PÉGUY, "The Honest People," *Basic Verities* (1943), tr. Ann and Julian Green.

100. Truth often suffers more by the heat of its defenders than from the arguments of its opposers. WILLIAM PENN, *Some Fruits of Solitude* (1693), 1.142.

101. They all want the truth—*a* truth that is: Something specific; something concrete! They don't care what it is. All they want is something categorical, something that speaks plainly! LUIGI PIRANDELLO, *It Is So! (If You Think So)* (1917), 3, tr. Arthur Livingston.

102. The greater amount of truth is impulsively uttered; thus the greater amount is spoken, not written. EDGAR ALLAN POE, *Marginalia* (1844–49), 1.

103. Why do we not hear the truth? Because we do not speak it. PUBLILIUS SYRUS, *Moral Sayings* (1st c. B.C.), 963, tr. Darius Lyman.

104. Nothing makes a man or body of men as mad as the truth. If there is no truth in it they laugh it off. WILL ROGERS, *The Autobiography of Will Rogers* (1949), 16.

105. The truths of the past are the clichés of the present. NED ROREM, "Listening and Hearing," *Music from Inside Out* (1967).

106. Truth is no road to fortune. ROUSSEAU, *The Social Contract* (1762), 2.2, tr. G. D. H. Cole.

107. Truth, for any man, is that which makes him a man. SAINT-EXUPÉRY, *Wind, Sand, and Stars* (1939), 9.6, tr. Lewis Galantière.

108. Truth is not that which is demonstrable but that which is ineluctable. SAINT-EXUPÉRY, *Wind, Sand, and Stars* (1939), 9.6, tr. Lewis Galantière.

109. Truths may clash without contradicting each other. SAINT-EXUPÉRY, *The Wisdom of the Sands* (1948), 22, tr. Stuart Gilbert.

110. No truth is proved, no truth achieved, by argument, and the ready-made truths men offer you are mere conveniences or drugs to make you sleep. SAINT-EXUPÉRY, *The Wisdom of the Sands* (1948), 44, tr. Stuart Gilbert.

111. The truth is cruel, but it can be loved, and it makes free those who have loved it. GEORGE SANTAYANA, *Little Essays* (1920), 44, ed. Logan Pearsall Smith.

112. Even under the most favourable circumstances no mortal can be asked to seize the truth in its wholeness or at its centre. GEORGE SANTAYANA, *Character and Opinion in the United States* (1921), 1.

113. The truth, my friends, is not eloquent, except unspoken; its vast shadow lends eloquence to our sparks of thought as they die into it. GEORGE SANTAYANA, *Dialogues in Limbo* (1925), 3.

114. Truth is a dream unless my dream is true. GEORGE SANTAYANA, *Persons and Places: My Host the World* (1953), 2.

115. Truth lives on in the midst of deception. SCHILLER, *On the Aesthetic Education of Man* (1795), 9, tr. Reginald Snell.

116. Truth's open to everyone, and the claims aren't all staked yet. SENECA, *Letters to Lucilius* (1st c.), 33.11, tr. E. Phillips Barker.

117. Truth hath a quiet breast. SHAKESPEARE, *Richard II* (1595–96), 1.3.96.

118. Truth is truth / To th' end of reck'ning. SHAKESPEARE, *Measure for Measure* (1604–05), 5.1.45.

119. Deep truth is imageless. SHELLEY, *Prometheus Unbound* (1818–19), 2.4.

120. The truth is always the strongest argument. SOPHOCLES, *Phaedra* (c. 435–29 B.C.), tr. M. H. Morgan.

121. Truth and oil always come to the surface. SPANISH PROVERB.

122. You will find that the truth is often unpopular and the contest between agreeable fancy and disagreeable fact is unequal. For, in the vernacular, we Americans are suckers for good news. ADLAI STEVENSON, *The New York Times*, June 9, 1958.

123. All your life you live so close to truth, it becomes a permanent blur in the corner of your eye, and when something nudges it into outline it is like being ambushed by a grotesque. TOM STOPPARD, *Rosencrantz & Guildenstern Are Dead* (1967), 1.

124. Everything has to be taken on trust; truth is only that which is taken to be true. It's the currency of living. There may be nothing behind it, but it doesn't make any difference so long as it is honored. TOM STOPPARD, *Rosencrantz & Guildenstern Are Dead* (1967), 2.

125. Truth looks tawdry when she is overdressed. RABINDRANATH TAGORE, introduction to *The Cycle of Spring* (1915).

126. Truth in her dress finds facts too tight. / In fiction she moves with ease. RABINDRANATH TAGORE, *Stray Birds* (1916), 140.

127. The water in a vessel is sparkling; the water in the sea is dark. / The small truth has words that are clear; the great truth has great silence. RABINDRANATH TAGORE, *Stray Birds* (1916), 176.

128. Truth seems to come with its final word; and the final word gives birth to its next. RABINDRANATH TAGORE, *Stray Birds* (1916), 294.

129. You can prove almost anything with the evidence of a small enough segment of time. How often, in any search for truth, the answer of the minute is positive, the answer of the hour qualified, the answers of the year contradictory! EDWIN WAY TEALE, "January 6," *Circle of the Seasons* (1953).

130. It is morally as bad not to care whether a thing is true or not, so long as it makes you feel good, as it is not to care how you got your money so long as you have got it. EDWIN WAY TEALE, "February 18," *Circle of the Seasons* (1953).

131. Nowadays flattery wins friends, truth hatred. TERENCE, *The Woman of Andros* (166 B.C.).

132. Between whom there is hearty truth there is love. THOREAU, "The Atlantides," *A Week on the Concord and Merrimack Rivers* (1849).

133. Rather than love, than money, than fame, give me truth. THOREAU, "Conclusion," *Walden* (1854).

134. So little trouble do men take in the search after truth; so readily do they accept whatever comes first to hand. THUCYDIDES, *The Peloponnesian War* (c. 400 B.C.), 1.20, tr. Benjamin Jowett.

135. Truth is mighty and will prevail. There is nothing the matter with this, except that it ain't so. MARK TWAIN, *Notebook* (1935).

136. Truth is more of a stranger than fiction. MARK TWAIN, *Notebook* (1935).

137. Knowledge for the sake of knowledge! Truth for truth's sake! This is inhuman. MIGUEL DE UNAMUNO, "The Starting-Point," *Tragic Sense of Life* (1913), tr. J. E. Crawford Flitch.

138. The only truths which are universal are those gross enough to be. PAUL VALÉRY, *Mauvaises pensées* (1941).

139. Truth is not so threadbare as speech, because fewer people can make use of it. VAUVENARGUES, *Reflections and Maxims* (1746), 468, tr. F. G. Stevens.

140. There is nothing so powerful as truth,—and often nothing so strange. DANIEL WEBSTER, argument on the murder of Captain White, April 6, 1830.

141. The only truths we can point to / are the ever-changing truths of our own experience. PETER WEISS, *Marat / Sade* (1964), 1.15, tr. Geoffrey Skelton and Adrian Mitchell.

142. Heaven knows what seeming nonsense may not tomorrow be demonstrated truth. ALFRED NORTH WHITEHEAD, *Science and the Modern World* (1925), 7.

143. Whatever satisfies the soul is truth. WALT WHITMAN, preface to *Leaves of Grass* (1855–92).

144. The truth is rarely pure and never simple. OSCAR WILDE, *The Importance of Being Earnest* (1895), 1.

145. Every thing to be true must become a religion. OSCAR WILDE, *De Profundis* (1905).

146. Truth cannot be escaped within, any more than it can be escaped without. PHILIP WYLIE, *Generation of Vipers* (1942), 1.

147. Truth is on the march; nothing can stop it now. ÉMILE ZOLA, "J'accuse," *Aurore* (1898).

## 992. TRUTH AND FALSEHOOD

**See also 297. Error; 329. Falsehood; 991. Truth; 993. Truthfulness**

1. Truth exists. Only lies are invented. GEORGES BRAQUE, *Pensées sur l'art.*

2. It is only a good, sound, truthful person who can lie to any good purpose; if a man is not habitually truthful his very lies will be false to him and betray him. SAMUEL BUTLER (d. 1902), "Truth and Convenience," *Note-Books* (1912).

3. Would that I could discover truth as easily as I can uncover falsehood. CICERO, *De Natura Deorum* (44 B.C.), 1.

4. Though truth and falsehood be / Near twins, yet truth a little elder is. JOHN DONNE, Satire 3 (1635).

5. If a man fasten his attention on a single aspect of truth and apply himself to that alone for a long time, the truth becomes distorted and not itself but falsehood. EMERSON, "Intellect," *Essays: First Series* (1841).

6. Lies are the religion of slaves and bosses. Truth is the god of the free man. MAXIM GORKY, *The Lower Depths* (1903), 4, tr. Alexander Bakshy.

7. The truth cannot be erased. Neither can lies. Graffito written during French student revolt, May 1968.

8. Irrationally held truths may be more harmful than reasoned errors. THOMAS HENRY HUXLEY, "The Coming of Age of *The Origin of Species*" (1880).

9. It is error alone which needs the support of government. Truth can stand by itself. THOMAS JEFFERSON, *Notes on the State of Virginia* (1784–85), 17.

10. Lies are as communicative as fleas; and truth is as difficult to lay hold upon as air. WALTER SAVAGE LANDOR, "Diogenes and Plato," *Imaginary Conversations* (1824–53).

11. Truth does not do as much good in the world as its imitations do harm. LA ROCHEFOUCAULD, *Maxims* (1665), tr. Kenneth Pratt.

12. Truth gains more even by the errors of one who, with due study and preparation, thinks for himself, than by the true opinions of those who only hold them because they do not suffer themselves to think. JOHN STUART MILL, *On Liberty* (1859), 2.

13. What kind of truth is it which has these mountains as its boundary and is a lie beyond them? MONTAIGNE, "Apology for Raimond de Sebonde," *Essays* (1580–88).

14. Truth is always twins; for every truth is accompanied by its facsimile error—which is the application of that by literal-minded people. CHRISTOPHER MORLEY, *Inward Ho!* (1923), 1.

15. A Hair perhaps divides the False and True. OMAR KHAYYÁM, *Rubáiyát* (11th–12th c.), tr. Edward FitzGerald, 4th ed., 49.

16. We perceive an image of truth, and possess only a lie. PASCAL, *Pensées* (1670), 434, tr. W. F. Trotter.

17. A peace-mingling falsehood is preferable to a mischief-stirring truth. SA'DI, *Gulistan* (1258), 1.1, tr. James Ross.

18. The truth is balance, but the opposite of truth, which is unbalance, may not be a lie. SUSAN SONTAG, "Simon Weil," *Against Interpretation* (1961).

19. The history of our race, and each individual's experience, are sown thick with evidence that a truth is not hard to kill and that a lie told well is immortal. MARK TWAIN, "Advice to Youth" (1923).

## 993. TRUTHFULNESS

**See also 329. Falsehood; 360. Frankness; 423. Honesty; 894. Sincerity; 991. Truth; 992. Truth and Falsehood**

1. I love you and, because I love you, I would sooner have you hate me for telling you the truth than adore me for telling you lies. PIETRO ARETINO, letter to Giovanni Pollastra, Aug. 28, 1537, tr. Samuel Putnam.

2. The highest compact we can make with our fellow is, "Let there be truth between us two for evermore." EMERSON, "Behavior," *The Conduct of Life* (1860).

3. Whatever games are played with us, we must play no games with ourselves, but deal in our privacy with the last honesty and truth. EMERSON, "Illusions," *The Conduct of Life* (1860).

4. All truth is not to be told at all times. THOMAS FULLER, M.D., *Gnomologia* (1732), 567.

5. He that does not speak truth to me does not believe me when I speak truth. THOMAS FULLER, M.D., *Gnomologia* (1732), 2084.

6. To be modest in speaking truth is hypocrisy. KAHLIL GIBRAN, "Narcotics and Dissecting Knives," *Thoughts and Meditations* (1960), tr. Anthony R. Ferris.

7. To be wiser than other men is to be honester than they; and strength of mind is only courage to see and speak the truth. WILLIAM HAZLITT, "On Knowledge of the World," *Sketches and Essays* (1839).

8. Dare to be true: nothing can need a lie; / A fault which needs it most, grows two thereby. GEORGE HERBERT, "The Church Porch," 13, *The Temple* (1633).

9. Veracity is the heart of morality. THOMAS HENRY HUXLEY, "Universities, Actual and Ideal" (1874).

10. It is always the best policy to speak the truth, unless of course you are an exceptionally good liar. JEROME K. JEROME, *The Idler*, February 1892.

11. A man's word / Is believed just to the extent of the wealth in his coffers stored. JUVENAL, *Satires* (c. 100), 3.143, tr. Hubert Creekmore.

12. Who speaks the truth stabs Falsehood to the heart. JAMES RUSSELL LOWELL, "L'Envoi" (1843).

13. On the one hand, we may tell the truth, regardless of consequences, and on the other hand we may mellow it and sophisticate it to make it humane and tolerable. H. L. MENCKEN, "The Art Eternal," *The New York Evening Mail*, 1918.

14. I speak truth, not so much as I would, but as much as I dare; and I dare a little the more, as I grow older. MONTAIGNE, "Of repentance," *Essays* (1580–88), tr. Charles Cotton and W. C. Hazlitt.

15. To be believed, make the truth unbelievable. NAPOLEON I, *Maxims* (1804–15).

16. All truths that are kept silent become poisonous. NIETZSCHE, "On Self-Overcoming," *Thus Spoke Zarathustra* (1883–92), 2, tr. Walter Kaufmann.

17. The inability to lie is far from the love of truth. NIETZSCHE, "On the Higher Man," *Thus Spoke Zarathustra* (1883–92), 4, tr. Walter Kaufmann.

18. They deem him their worst enemy who tells them the truth. PLATO, *The Republic* (4th c. B.C.), 4, tr. Benjamin Jowett.

19. There are few nudities so objectionable as the naked truth. AGNES REPPLIER, "The Gayety of Life," *Compromises* (1904).

20. O, while you live, tell truth and shame the devil! SHAKESPEARE, *1 Henry IV* (1597–98), 3.1.62.

21. If you want to be thought a liar, always tell the truth. LOGAN PEARSALL SMITH, *Afterthoughts* (1931), 4.

22. Truth is the most valuable thing we have. Let us economize it. MARK TWAIN, "Pudd'nhead Wilson's New Calendar," *Following the Equator* (1897), 1.7.

23. Often, the surest way to convey misinformation is to tell the strict truth. MARK TWAIN, "Pudd'nhead Wilson's New Calendar," *Following the Equator* (1897), 2.23.

24. If you tell the truth you don't have to remember anything. MARK TWAIN, *Notebook* (1935).

## TRYING
See 279. Effort

## TURN
See 32. Alternation

## 994. TWENTIETH CENTURY
See also 3. The Absurd; 296. Era; 633. Nuclear Power; 960. Technology; 1060. World

1. At its mid-afternoon the twentieth century seems afflicted by a gigantic and progressive power failure. Powerlessness and the sense of powerlessness may be the environmental disease of the age. RUSSELL BAKER, "Observer," *The New York Times*, May 1, 1969.

2. If civilization has risen from the Stone

Age, it can rise again from the Wastepaper Age. JACQUES BARZUN, *The House of Intellect* (1959), 9.

3. The trouble with the age we live in is that it lacks consistence. People start reasoning things out, and as soon as they begin to get anywhere they drop everything and run. UGO BETTI, *Struggle Till Dawn* (1949), 2, tr. G. H. McWilliam.

4. Let nothing be called natural / In an age of bloody confusion / Ordered disorder, planned caprice, / And dehumanized humanity, lest all things / Be held unalterable! BERTOLT BRECHT, prologue, *The Exception and the Rule* (1937), tr. Eric Bentley.

5. It is easy enough to praise men for the courage of their convictions. I wish I could teach the sad young of this mealy generation the courage of their confusions. JOHN CIARDI, *Saturday Review*, June 2, 1962.

6. This is a crazy culture. Absolutely nutty. You see it reflected everywhere you look, this desperate search—who are we, what are we, can we ever make it in the hip world? On the scene, on the go, in the know. JUDY COLLINS, interview, *Life*, May 2, 1969.

7. It takes a kind of shabby arrogance to survive in our time, and a fairly romantic nature to want to. EDGAR Z. FRIEDENBERG, "The Vanishing Adolescent," *The Vanishing Adolescent* (1959).

8. We have the power to make this the best generation of mankind in the history of the world—or to make it the last. JOHN F. KENNEDY, address, United Nations General Assembly, Sept. 20, 1963.

9. The trouble with our age is that it is all signpost and no destination. LOUIS KRONENBERGER, "The Spirit of the Age," *Company Manners* (1954).

10. "Real life" often appears, at least, to be an imitation of art. Today, it is poster art. MARSHALL MC LUHAN, "Cokes and Cheesecake," *The Mechanical Bride* (1951).

11. Modern man—whether in the womb of the masses, or with his workmates, or with his family, or alone—can never for one moment forget that he is living in a world in which he is a means and whose end is not his business. ALBERTO MORAVIA, title essay, *Man As an End* (1964), tr. Bernard Wall.

12. We have created an industrial order geared to automatism, where feeble-mindedness, native or acquired, is necessary for docile productivity in the factory; and where a pervasive neurosis is the final gift of the meaningless life that issues forth at the other end. LEWIS MUMFORD, "The Fulfillment of Man," *The Conduct of Life* (1951).

13. Whoever has not felt the danger of our times palpitating under his hand, has not really penetrated to the vitals of destiny, he has merely pricked its surface. JOSÉ ORTEGA Y GASSET, *The Revolt of the Masses* (1930), 2.

14. The atom bombs are piling up in the factories, the police are prowling through the cities, the lies are streaming from the loudspeakers, but the earth is still going round the sun. GEORGE ORWELL, "Thoughts on the Common Toad," *Shooting an Elephant* (1950).

15. In these times you have to be an optimist to open your eyes when you awake in the morning. CARL SANDBURG, *New York Post*, Sept. 9, 1960.

16. Artists have no less talents than ever; their taste, their vision, their sentiment are often interesting; they are mighty in their independence and feeble only in their works. GEORGE SANTAYANA, *Winds of Doctrine* (1913).

17. In the twentieth century what astonishes many of us is not so much that human nature is fundamentally corrupt; we are astonished rather that it does not behave more wickedly than it obviously does. MORTON IRVING SEIDEN, *The Paradox of Hate: A Study in Ritual Murder* (1967), 1.

18. Time and space—time to be alone, space to move about—these may well become the great scarcities of tomorrow. EDWIN WAY TEALE, *Autumn Across America* (1956), 33.

## 995. TYRANNY

**See also 354. Force; 456. Imperialism; 713. Power; 795. Repression; 813. Revolution; 882. Servitude; 978. Totalitarianism**

1. This is a sickness rooted and inherent / in the nature of a tyranny: / that he that holds it does not trust his friends. AESCHYLUS, *Prometheus Bound* (c. 478 B.C.), tr. David Grene.

2. Death is a softer thing by far than tyranny. AESCHYLUS, *Agamemnon* (458 B.C.), tr. Richmond Lattimore.

3. Any excuse will serve a tyrant. AESOP, "The Wolf and the Lamb," *Fables* (6th c. B.C.?), tr. Joseph Jacobs.

4. Make men large and strong, and tyranny will bankrupt itself in making shackles for them. HENRY WARD BEECHER, *Proverbs from Plymouth Pulpit* (1887).

5. The slave begins by demanding justice and ends by wanting to wear a crown. He must dominate in his turn. ALBERT CAMUS, "Metaphysical Rebellion," *The Rebel* (1951), tr. Anthony Bower.

6. The laws can't be enforced against the man who is the laws' master. BENVENUTO CELLINI, *Autobiography* (1558–66), tr. George Bull.

7. The dictator, in all his pride, is held in the grip of his party machine. He can go forward; he cannot go back. He must blood his hounds and show them sport, or else, like Actaeon of old, be devoured by them. All-strong without, he is all-weak within. SIR WINSTON CHURCHILL, radio address to the United States, Oct. 16, 1938.

8. When a nation has allowed itself to fall under a tyrannical regime, it cannot be absolved from the faults due to the guilt of that regime. SIR WINSTON CHURCHILL, message after visit to Italy, July 28, 1944.

9. The people may be made to follow a path of action, but they may not be made to understand it. CONFUCIUS, *Analects* (6th c. B.C.), 8.9, tr. James Legge.

10. Of all the tyrannies on humankind, / The worst is that which persecutes the mind. JOHN DRYDEN, *The Hind and the Panther* (1687), 11.239.

11. He who despises his own life is soon master of another's. ENGLISH PROVERB.

12. Dictators ride to and fro upon tigers from which they dare not dismount. HINDUSTANI PROVERB, quoted in Sir Winston Churchill's *While England Slept* (1936).

13. The benevolent despot who sees himself as a shepherd of the people still demands from others the submissiveness of sheep. ERIC HOFFER, *The Ordeal of Change* (1964), 15.2.

14. So long as men worship the Caesars and Napoleons, Caesars and Napoleons will duly rise and make them miserable. ALDOUS HUXLEY, *Ends and Means* (1937).

15. Resistance to tyrants is obedience to God. THOMAS JEFFERSON, motto found among his papers.

16. If a sovereign oppresses his people to a great degree, they will rise and cut off his head. There is a remedy in human nature against tyranny that will keep us safe under every form of government. SAMUEL JOHNSON, quoted in Boswell's *Life of Samuel Johnson*, March 31, 1772.

17. A police state finds it cannot command the grain to grow. JOHN F. KENNEDY, State of the Union Message, Jan. 14, 1963.

18. Tyrants never perish from tyranny, but always from folly, — when their fantasies have built up a palace for which the earth has no foundation. WALTER SAVAGE LANDOR, "Anacreon and Polycrates," *Imaginary Conversations* (1824–53).

19. When the white man governs himself, that is self-government; but when he governs himself and also governs another man, that is more than self-government–that is despotism. ABRAHAM LINCOLN, speech, Peoria, Ill., Oct. 16, 1854.

20. Tyrants are but the spawn of Ignorance, / Begotten by the slaves they trample on. JAMES RUSSELL LOWELL, "Prometheus" (1843).

21. I believe there are more instances of the abridgment of the freedom of the people by gradual and silent encroachments of those in power than by violent and sudden usurpations. JAMES MADISON, speech, Virginia Convention, June 16, 1788.

22. Time is on the side of the oppressed today, it's against the oppressor. Truth is on the side of the oppressed today, it's against the oppressor. You don't need anything else. MALCOLM X, *Malcolm X Speaks* (1965), 6.

23. Beware the People weeping / When they bare the iron hand. HERMAN MELVILLE, "The Martyr," *Battlepieces and Aspects of the War* (1866).

24. The most insupportable of tyrannies is that of inferiors. NAPOLEON I, *Maxims* (1804–15).

25. Among those who dislike oppression are many who like to oppress. NAPOLEON I, *Maxims* (1804–15).

26. He whom many fear, has himself many to fear. PUBLILIUS SYRUS, *Moral Sayings* (1st c. B.C.), 522, tr. Darius Lyman.

27. The face of tyranny / Is always mild at

first. RACINE, *Britannicus* (1669), 1, tr. Paul Landis and Robert Henderson.

28. There is a cowardly propensity in the human heart that delights in oppressing somebody else, and in the gratification of this base desire we always select a victim that can be outraged with safety. JAMES T. RAPIER, *Congressional Globe*, 1873.

29. I never could believe that Providence had sent a few men into the world, ready booted and spurred to ride, and millions ready saddled and bridled to be ridden. RICHARD RUMBOLD, on the scaffold, quoted in Macaulay's *History of England* (1685), 5.

30. To pardon the oppressor is to deal harshly with the oppressed. SA'DI, *Gulistan* (1258), 8.8, tr. James Ross.

31. True, it is evil that a single man should crush the herd, but see not there the worst form of slavery, which is when the herd crushes out the man. SAINT-EXUPÉRY, *The Wisdom of the Sands* (1948), 11, tr. Stuart Gilbert.

32. The tyrant claims freedom to kill freedom / and yet to keep it for himself. RABINDRANATH TAGORE, *Fireflies* (1928).

33. To succeed in chaining the multitude you must seem to wear the same fetters. VOLTAIRE, "Christianity," *Philosophical Dictionary* (1764).

# U

## 996. UGLINESS

**See also 70. Beauty**

1. I cannot tell by what logic we call a toad, a bear, or an elephant ugly; they being created in those outward shapes and figures which best express the actions of their inward forms. SIR THOMAS BROWNE, *Religio Medici* (1642), 1.

2. The secret of ugliness consists not in irregularity, but in being uninteresting. EMERSON, "Beauty," *The Conduct of Life* (1860).

3. Since our persons are not of our own making, when they are such as appear defective or uncomely, it is, methinks, an honest and laudable fortitude to dare to be ugly. RICHARD STEELE, *The Spectator* (1711–12), 17.

4. I don't mind plain women being Puritans. It is the only excuse they have for being plain. OSCAR WILDE, *A Woman of No Importance* (1893), 1.

## 997. UNBELIEF

**See also 76. Belief; 263. Doubt, Religious; 328. Faith; 790. Religion; 897. Skepticism**

1. Atheism is rather in the lip than in the heart of man. FRANCIS BACON, "Of Atheism," *Essays* (1625).

2. The fool hath said in his heart, There is no God. *Bible*, Psalms 14:1 and 53:1.

3. There is no proselyter half so energetic as the hard-shelled atheist. HEYWOOD BROUN, "A New Preface to an Old Story," *Broun's Nutmeg*, Aug. 19, 1939.

4. All we have gained then by our unbelief / Is a life of doubt diversified by faith, / For one of faith diversified by doubt: / We called the chess-board white,—we call it black. ROBERT BROWNING, "Bishop Blougram's Apology," *Men and Women* (1855).

5. The writers against religion, whilst they oppose every system, are wisely careful never to set up any of their own. EDMUND BURKE, preface to *A Vindication of Natural Society* (1756).

6. An atheist's laugh's a poor exchange / For Deity offended. ROBERT BURNS, "Epistle to a Young Friend" (1786).

7. The three great apostles of practical atheism, that make converts without persecuting and retain them without preaching, are Wealth, Health, and Power. CHARLES CALEB COLTON, *Lacon* (1825), 2.158.

8. To lose one's faith—surpass / The loss of an Estate— / Because Estates can be / Replenished—faith cannot—. EMILY DICKINSON, poem (c. 1862).

9. The unbelief of the age is attested by the loud condemnation of trifles. EMERSON, *Journals*, 1836.

10. If there are none [no gods], / All our toil is without meaning. EURIPIDES, *Iphigenia in Aulis* (c. 405 B.C.), tr. Charles R. Walker.

11. Atheism. There is not a single exalting and emancipating influence that does not in turn become inhibitory. ANDRÉ GIDE, *Journals*, Jan. 13, 1929, tr. Justin O'Brien.

12. When incredulity becomes a faith, it is less rational than a religion. EDMOND and JULES DE GONCOURT, *Journal*, March 1, 1862.

13. If there is a God, atheism must strike Him as less of an insult than religion. EDMOND and JULES DE GONCOURT, *Journal*, Jan. 24, 1868, tr. Robert Baldick.

14. Anti-clericalism and non-belief, have their bigots just as orthodoxy does. JULIEN GREEN, *Journal*, July 23, 1945.

15. There seems to be a terrible misunderstanding on the part of a great many people to the effect that when you cease to believe you may cease to behave. LOUIS KRONENBERGER, "The Spirit of the Age," *Company Manners* (1954).

16. In ages not of faith, there will always be multitudinous troops of people crying for the moon. JOHN MORLEY, "Carlyle," *Critical Miscellanies* (1871–1908).

17. Atheists put on a false courage and alacrity in the midst of their darkness and apprehensions, like children who, when they fear to go in the dark, will sing for fear. ALEXANDER POPE, *Thoughts on Various Subjects* (1727).

18. When faith burns itself out, 'tis God who dies and thenceforth proves unavailing. SAINT-EXUPÉRY, *The Wisdom of the Sands* (1948), 11, tr. Stuart Gilbert.

19. If faith can move mountains, disbelief can deny their existence. And faith is impotent against such impotence. ARNOLD SCHOENBERG, preface to Anton Webern's "Six Bagatelles for String Quartet" (1908).

20. By night an atheist half believes a God. EDWARD YOUNG, *Night Thoughts* (1742–46), 5.177.

## 998. UNCERTAINTY

**See also 113. Certainty; 463. Indecision; 480. Insecurity; 897. Skepticism**

1. Doubt of the reality of love ends by making us doubt everything. HENRI FRÉDÉRIC AMIEL, *Journal*, Dec. 26, 1868, tr. Mrs. Humphry Ward.

2. We are not certain, we are never certain. If we were, we could reach some conclusions, and we could, at last, make others take us seriously. ALBERT CAMUS, *The Fall* (1956).

3. Diffidence is the better part of knowledge. CHARLES CALEB COLTON, preface, *Lacon* (1825).

4. Oft from new truths, and new phrase, new doubts grow, / As strange attire aliens the men we know. JOHN DONNE, "To the Countess of Bedford," *Letters to Several Personages* (1651).

5. The quest for certainty blocks the search for meaning. Uncertainty is the very condition to impel man to unfold his powers. ERICH FROMM, *Man for Himself* (1947), 3.

6. Uncertainty is the worst of all evils until the moment when reality makes us regret uncertainty. ALPHONSE KARR, *L'Esprit d'A. Karr* (1877).

7. Doubt and mistrust are the mere panic of timid imagination, which the steadfast heart will conquer, and the large mind transcend. HELEN KELLER, *Optimism* (1903), 1.

8. All uncertainty is fruitful . . . so long as it is accompanied by the wish to understand. ANTONIO MACHADO, *Juan de Mairena* (1943), 43, tr. Ben Belitt.

9. We sail within a vast sphere, ever drifting in uncertainty, driven from end to end. PASCAL, *Pensées* (1670), 72, tr. W. F. Trotter.

10. The only limit to our realization of tomorrow will be our doubts of today. FRANKLIN D. ROOSEVELT, message for Jefferson Day, April 13, 1945.

11. Our doubts are traitors / And make us lose the good we oft might win / By fearing to attempt. SHAKESPEARE, *Measure for Measure* (1604–05), 1.4.77.

## 999. UNCONSCIOUSNESS

**See also 172. Consciousness; 583. Mind; 1013. Unreason**

1. It is our less conscious thoughts and our less conscious actions which mainly mould our lives and the lives of those who spring from us. SAMUEL BUTLER (d. 1902), *The Way of All Flesh* (1903), 5.

2. The waking mind is the least serviceable in the arts. HENRY MILLER, interview, *Writers at Work: Second Series* (1963).

3. How should men know what is coming to pass within them, when there are no words to grasp it? How could the drops of water know themselves to be a river? Yet the river flows on. SAINT-EXUPÉRY, *The*

*Wisdom of the Sands* (1948), 43, tr. Stuart Gilbert.

4. Our unconscious is like a vast subterranean factory with intricate machinery that is never idle, where work goes on day and night from the time we are born until the moment of our death. MILTON R. SAPIRSTEIN, *Paradoxes of Everyday Life* (1955), 8.

## 1000. UNDERSTANDING

**See also 491. Intelligence; 499. Intuition; 520. Knowledge; 583. Mind; 676. Perception; 876. Sensibility; 953. Sympathy; 1001. Understanding Others; 1012. The Unknown; 1053. Wisdom**

1. Light; or, failing that, lightning: the world can take its choice. THOMAS CARLYLE, *On Heroes, Hero-Worship and the Heroic in History* (1841), 5.

2. One who understands much displays a greater simplicity of character than one who understands little. ALEXANDER CHASE, *Perspectives* (1966).

3. Things and men have always a certain sense, a certain side by which they must be got hold of if one wants to obtain a solid grasp and a perfect command. JOSEPH CONRAD, *Under Western Eyes* (1911), 4.1.

4. It takes a long time to understand nothing. EDWARD DAHLBERG, "On Wisdom and Folly," *Reasons of the Heart* (1965).

5. Between / Our birth and death we may touch understanding / As a moth brushes a window with its wing. CHRISTOPHER FRY, *The Boy with a Cart* (1945).

6. Understanding is the beginning of approving. ANDRÉ GIDE, *Journals*, 1902, tr. Justin O'Brien.

7. In what we really understand, we reason but little. WILLIAM HAZLITT, "On the Conduct of Life," *Literary Remains* (1836).

8. A moment's insight is sometimes worth a life's experience. OLIVER WENDELL HOLMES, SR., "Iris, Her Book," *The Professor at the Breakfast Table* (1860).

9. Perfect understanding will sometimes almost extinguish pleasure. A. E. HOUSMAN, *The Name and Nature of Poetry* (1933).

10. It is less dishonour to hear imperfectly than to speak imperfectly. The ears are excused: the understanding is not. BEN JONSON, "Of Flatterers," *Timber* (1640).

11. Nothing can be loved or hated unless it is first known. LEONARDO DA VINCI, *Notebooks* (c. 1500), tr. Jean Paul Richter.

12. There is no way of seeing things without first taking leave of them. ANTONIO MACHADO, *Juan de Mairena* (1943), 28, tr. Ben Belitt.

13. All the glory of greatness has no lustre for people who are in search of understanding. PASCAL, *Pensées* (1670), 792, tr. W. F. Trotter.

14. Time which diminishes all things increases understanding for the aging. PLUTARCH, "The Education of Children," *Moralia* (c. A.D. 100), tr. Moses Hadas.

## 1001. UNDERSTANDING OTHERS

**See also 66. Background; 656. Others; 676. Perception; 692. Pity; 953. Sympathy; 1000. Understanding**

1. It takes longer for man to find out man than any other creature that is made. HENRY WARD BEECHER, *Proverbs from Plymouth Pulpit* (1887).

2. To understand is to forgive, even oneself. ALEXANDER CHASE, *Perspectives* (1966).

3. If you do not understand a man you cannot crush him. And if you do understand him, very probably you will not. G. K. CHESTERTON, "Humanitarianism and Strength," *All Things Considered* (1908).

4. Insight—the titillating knack for hurting! COLETTE, "The Pure and the Impure," *Earthly Paradise* (1966), 5, ed. Robert Phelps.

5. Grieve not that men do not know you; grieve that you do not know men. CONFUCIUS, *Analects* (6th c. B.C.), 1.16, tr. Ch'u Chai and Winberg Chai.

6. Herein lies the tragedy of the age: not that men are poor,—all men know something of poverty; not that men are wicked,—who is good? not that men are ignorant,—what is truth? Nay, but that men know so little of men. W. E. B. DU BOIS, *The Souls of Black Folk* (1903), 12.

7. It is impossible for one person to know another so well that he can dispense with belief. FRIEDRICH DÜRRENMATT, *The Marriage of Mr. Mississippi* (1952), 2, tr. Michael Bullock.

8. All persons are puzzles until at last we find in some word or act the key to the man,

to the woman; straightway all their past words and actions lie in light before us. EMERSON, *Journals*, 1842.

9. God grant me to contend with those that understand me. THOMAS FULLER, M.D., *Gnomologia* (1732), 1673.

10. Each of us really understands in others only those feelings he is capable of producing himself. ANDRÉ GIDE, *Journal of "The Counterfeiters,"* Second Notebook, August 1921, tr. Justin O'Brien.

11. It is profound philosophy to sound the depths of feeling and distinguish traits of character. Men must be studied as deeply as books. BALTASAR GRACIÁN, *The Art of Worldly Wisdom* (1647), 157, tr. Joseph Jacobs.

12. No one can understand unless, holding to his own nature, he respects the free nature of others. Graffito written during French student revolt, May 1968.

13. We can see through others only when we see through ourselves. ERIC HOFFER, *The Passionate State of Mind* (1954), 158.

14. It is easier to know (and understand) men in general than one man in particular. LA ROCHEFOUCAULD, *Maxims* (1665), tr. Kenneth Pratt.

15. We like to read others but we do not like to be read. LA ROCHEFOUCAULD, *Maxims* (1665), tr. Kenneth Pratt.

16. The deep sea can be fathomed, but who knows the hearts of men? MALAY PROVERB.

17. Until we know what motivates the hearts and minds of men we can understand nothing outside ourselves, nor will we ever reach fulfillment as that greatest miracle of all, the human being. MARYA MANNES, *More in Anger* (1958), 2.2.

18. A man, to be greatly good, must imagine intensely and comprehensively; he must put himself in the place of another and of many others; the pains and pleasures of his species must become his own. SHELLEY, *A Defence of Poetry* (1821).

19. One learns peoples through the heart, not the eyes or the intellect. MARK TWAIN, "What Paul Bourget Thinks of Us," *North American Review*, January 1895.

20. I don't ask for your pity, but just your understanding—not even that—no. Just for your recognition of me in you, and the enemy, time, in us all. TENNESSEE WILLIAMS, *Sweet Bird of Youth* (1959), 3.

21. Ten lands are sooner known than one man. *Yiddish Proverbs* (1949), ed. Hanan J. Ayalti.

## 1002. UNEMPLOYMENT

1. A man willing to work, and unable to find work, is perhaps the saddest sight that fortune's inequality exhibits under this sun. THOMAS CARLYLE, *Chartism* (1839), 4.

2. We believe that if men have the talent to invent new machines that put men out of work, they have the talent to put those men back to work. JOHN F. KENNEDY, address, Wheeling, W. Va., Sept. 27, 1962.

3. No one gains from a fair employment practice bill if there is no employment to be had. JOHN F. KENNEDY, State of the Union Message, Jan. 14, 1963.

## UNFAIRNESS

**See 475. Injustice**

## 1003. UNFULFILLMENT

**See also 364. Frustration; 711. Potential**

1. Meetings that do not come off keep a character of their own. They stay as they were projected. ELIZABETH BOWEN, *The House in Paris* (1935), 2.1.

2. What we have never had, remains; / It is the things we have that go. SARA TEASDALE, "Wisdom," *Dark of the Moon* (1926).

## 1004. UNHAPPINESS

**See also 249. Discontent; 407. Happiness; 911. Sorrow; 913. Sour Grapes; 939. Suffering; 1045. Weeping**

1. A man should always consider how much he has more than he wants, and how much more unhappy he might be than he really is. JOSEPH ADDISON, *The Spectator* (1711–12; 1714), 574.

2. Nothing is miserable unless you think it so. BOETHIUS, *The Consolation of Philosophy* (A.D. 524), 2.

3. Melancholy cannot be clearly proved to others, so it is better to be silent about it. JAMES BOSWELL, *London Journal*, May 17, 1763.

4. Nobody believes in his own misery, my boy. If you've got the stomach-ache and say so, it only sounds disgusting. BERTOLT BRECHT, *The Threepenny Opera* (1928), 1.1, tr. Desmond Vesey and Eric Bentley.

5. Naught so sweet as melancholy. ROBERT BURTON, "Author's Abstract," *The Anatomy of Melancholy* (1621).

6. For the unhappy man death is the commutation of a sentence of life imprisonment. ALEXANDER CHASE, *Perspectives* (1966).

7. The Morning after Woe— / 'Tis frequently the Way— / Surpasses all that rose before— / For utter Jubilee—. EMILY DICKINSON, poem (c. 1862).

8. All artists today are expected to cultivate a little fashionable unhappiness. LAWRENCE DURRELL, *Justine* (1957), 2.

9. Where there are two, one cannot be wretched, and one not. EURIPIDES, *Helen* (412 B.C.), tr. Richmond Lattimore.

10. Fate finds for every man / His share of misery. EURIPIDES, *Iphigenia in Aulis* (c. 405 B.C.), tr. Charles R. Walker.

11. Unhappiness does make people look stupid. ANATOLE FRANCE, *The Crime of Sylvestre Bonnard* (1881), 2, tr. Lafcadio Hearn.

12. Is there anything men take more pains about than to render themselves unhappy? BENJAMIN FRANKLIN, *Poor Richard's Almanack* (1732–57).

13. One cloud is enough to eclipse all the sun. THOMAS FULLER, M.D., *Gnomologia* (1732), 3743.

14. Sadness is almost never anything but a form of fatigue. ANDRÉ GIDE, *Journals*, 1922, tr. Justin O'Brien.

15. Man can only endure a certain degree of unhappiness; what is beyond that either annihilates him or passes by him and leaves him apathetic. GOETHE, *Elective Affinities* (1809), 22.

16. For fate has wove the thread of life with pain, / And twins ev'n from the birth are misery and man! HOMER, *Odyssey* (9th c. B.C.), 7.263, tr. Alexander Pope.

17. The world will never be long without some good reason to hate the unhappy; their real faults are immediately detected; and if those are not sufficient to sink them into infamy, an additional weight of calumny will be superadded. SAMUEL JOHNSON, *The Adventurer* (1753), 99.

18. True melancholy breeds your perfect, fine wit, sir. BEN JONSON, *Every Man in His Humour* (1598), 3.1.

19. When the melancholy fit shall fall / Sudden from heaven like a weeping cloud, / That fosters the droop-headed flowers all, / And hides the green hill in an April shroud; / Then glut thy sorrow on a morning rose. JOHN KEATS, "Ode on Melancholy" (1819).

20. Into each life some rain must fall, / Some days must be dark and dreary. LONGFELLOW, "The Rainy Day" (1842).

21. The value of ourselves is but the value of our melancholy and our disquiet. MAURICE MAETERLINCK, "The Star," *The Treasure of the Humble* (1896), tr. Alfred Sutro.

22. What makes man most unhappy is to be deprived not of that which he had, but of that which he did not have, and did not really know. JACQUES MARITAIN, *Reflections on America* (1958), 16.

23. Life is a well of joy; but for those out of whom an upset stomach speaks, which is the father of melancholy, all wells are poisoned. NIETZSCHE, "On Old and New Tablets," *Thus Spoke Zarathustra* (1883–92), 3, tr. Walter Kaufmann.

24. I have discovered that all man's unhappiness derives from only one source—not being able to sit quietly in a room. PASCAL, *Pensées* (1670), 139.

25. How quick the old woe follows a little bliss! PETRARCH, "Laura Living," *Canzoniere* (1360), 166.

26. The wretched reflect either too much or too little. PUBLILIUS SYRUS, *Moral Sayings* (1st c. B.C.), 225, tr. Darius Lyman.

27. Life is so full of miseries, minor and major; they press so close upon us at every step of the way, that it is hardly worth while to call one another's attention to their presence. AGNES REPPLIER, "The Gayety of Life," *Compromises* (1904).

28. Only those sadnesses are dangerous and bad which one carries about among people in order to drown them out. RAINER MARIA RILKE, *Letters to a Young Poet*, Aug. 12, 1904, tr. M. D. Herter Norton.

29. Since unhappiness excites interest, many, in order to render themselves interesting, feign unhappiness. JOSEPH ROUX, *Meditations of a Parish Priest* (1886), 5.24, tr. Isabel F. Hapgood.

30. When we sing everybody hears us; when we sigh, nobody hears us. RUSSIAN PROVERB.

31. It would hardly be possible to exaggerate man's wretchedness if it were not so easy to overestimate his sensibility. GEORGE SANTAYANA, *The Life of Reason: Reason in Religion* (1905–06), 10.

32. Our aches and pains conform to opinion. A man's as miserable as he thinks he is. SENECA, *Letters to Lucilius* (1st c.), 78.13, tr. E. Phillips Barker.

33. Noble deeds and hot baths are the best cures for depression. DODIE SMITH, *I Capture the Castle* (1948), 3.

34. When a man has lost all happiness, / he's not alive. Call him a breathing corpse. SOPHOCLES, *Antigone* (442–41 B.C.), tr. Elizabeth Wyckoff.

35. Is anyone in all the world / Safe from unhappiness? SOPHOCLES, *Oedipus at Colonus* (401 B.C.), tr. Robert Fitzgerald.

36. If misery loves company, misery has company enough. THOREAU, *Journal*, Sept. 1, 1851.

37. If you are bitter at heart, sugar in the mouth will not help you. *Yiddish Proverbs* (1949), ed. Hanan J. Ayalti.

## 1005. UNIMPORTANCE

See also 318. Expendability; 398. Great and Small; 467. Individuality; 605. The Mundane; 641. Obscurity; 686. Pettiness; 901. Smallness; 989. Trifles

1. Our insignificance is often the cause of our safety. AESOP, "The Great and the Little Fishes," *Fables* (6th c. B.C.?), tr. Thomas James.

2. Rightly viewed no meanest object is insignificant; all objects are as windows, through which the philosophic eye looks into infinitude itself. THOMAS CARLYLE, *Sartor Resartus* (1833–34), 1.11.

3. A man can look upon his life and accept it as good or evil; it is far, far harder for him to confess that it has been unimportant in the sum of things. MURRAY KEMPTON, "O'er Moor and Fen," *Part of Our Time* (1955).

4. mans feet have grown / so big that he / forgets his littleness. DON MARQUIS, "archy turns revolutionist," *Archy's Life of Mehitabel* (1933).

5. Strange how few, / After all's said and done, the things that are / Of moment. EDNA ST. VINCENT MILLAY, "Interim," *Renascence* (1917).

## 1006. UNIONS

See also 1059. Workers

1. There is no right to strike against the public safety by anybody, anywhere, any time. CALVIN COOLIDGE, telegram to Samuel Gompers, Sept. 14, 1919.

2. With all their faults, trade-unions have done more for humanity than any other organization of men that ever existed. They have done more for decency, for honesty, for education, for the betterment of the race, for the developing of character in man, than any other association of men. CLARENCE S. DARROW, in *The Railroad Trainman*, November 1909.

3. Sthrikes are a great evil f'r th' wurrukin' man, but so are picnics an' he acts th' same at both. FINLEY PETER DUNNE, "Work," *Mr. Dooley Says* (1910).

4. I am glad to see that a system of labor prevails in New England under which laborers can strike when they want to, where they are not obliged to work under all circumstances and are not tied down and obliged to labor whether you pay them or not. ABRAHAM LINCOLN, speech, New Haven, Conn., March 6, 1860.

5. Unionism seldom, if ever, uses such power as it has to insure better work; almost always it devotes a large part of that power to safeguarding bad work. H. L. MENCKEN, *Prejudices: Third Series* (1922), 4.

6. It is one of the characteristics of a free and democratic modern nation that it have free and independent labor unions. FRANKLIN D. ROOSEVELT, address before the Teamsters' Union convention, Washington, D.C., Sept. 11, 1940.

## 1007. UNIQUENESS

See also 258. Diversity; 467. Individuality; 655. Originality

1. There never were, since the creation of the world, two cases exactly parallel. LORD CHESTERFIELD, *Letters to His Son*, Feb. 22, 1748.

2. The poetry of art is in beholding the single tower; the poetry of nature in seeing

the single tree; the poetry of love in following the single woman; the poetry of religion in worshipping the single star. G. K. CHESTERTON, "The Advantages of Having One Leg," *Tremendous Trifles* (1909).

3. Nothing is repeated, and everything is unparalleled. EDMOND and JULES DE GONCOURT, *Journal*, April 15, 1867, tr. Robert Baldick.

4. Every man is more than just himself; he also represents the unique, the very special and always significant and remarkable point at which the world's phenomena intersect, only once in this way and never again. HERMANN HESSE, prologue to *Demian* (1919), tr. Michael Roloff and Michael Lebeck.

## 1008. UNITED NATIONS

**See also 496. International Relations**

1. Until all the powerful are just, the weak will be secure only in the strength of this [United Nations] Assembly. JOHN F. KENNEDY, address to United Nations General Assembly, Sept. 25, 1961.

2. Our instrument and our hope is the United Nations, and I see little merit in the impatience of those who would abandon this imperfect world instrument because they dislike our imperfect world. JOHN F. KENNEDY, State of the Union Message, Jan. 11, 1962.

3. This 122-nation body, United Nations, is far from being a Parliament of Man, but it is a kind of mirror of our world, warts and all. Editorial, "U.N. Assembly at 22," *The New York Times*, Sept. 19, 1967.

## 1009. UNITY

**See also 98. Brotherhood; 150. Community; 187. Cooperation; 258. Diversity**

1. A common danger unites even the bitterest enemies. ARISTOTLE, *Politics* (4th c. B.C.), 5.5, tr. Benjamin Jowett.

2. Behold, how good and how pleasant it is for brethren to dwell together in unity! *Bible*, Psalms 133:1.

3. When spider webs unite, they can tie up a lion. ETHIOPIAN PROVERB.

4. We must all hang together, or assuredly we shall all hang separately. BENJAMIN FRANKLIN, at signing of the Declaration of Independence, July 4, 1776.

5. It is always possible to bind together a considerable number of people in love, so long as there are other people left over to receive the manifestations of their aggressiveness. SIGMUND FREUD, *Civilization and Its Discontents* (1930), 5, tr. James Strachey.

6. Not vain the weakest, if their force unite. HOMER, *Iliad* (9th c. B.C.), 13.311, tr. Alexander Pope.

7. A single arrow is easily broken, but not ten in a bundle. JAPANESE PROVERB.

8. With malice toward none, with charity for all, with firmness in the right as God gives us to see the right, let us strive on to finish the work we are in, to bind up the nation's wounds. ABRAHAM LINCOLN, second Inaugural Address, March 4, 1865.

9. There are only two forces that unite men—fear and interest. NAPOLEON I, *Maxims* (1804–15).

10. Plurality which is not reduced to unity is confusion; unity which does not depend on plurality is tyranny. PASCAL, *Pensées* (1670), 870, tr. W. F. Trotter.

11. Horror causes men to clench their fists, and in horror men join together. SAINT-EXUPÉRY, *Wind, Sand, and Stars* (1939), 9.3, tr. Lewis Galantière.

## 1010. UNIVERSE

**See also 413. The Heavens; 914. Space; 1060. World**

1. The universe is but a kaleidoscope which turns within the mind of the so-called thinking being, who is himself a curiosity without a cause, an accident conscious of the great accident around him, and who amuses himself with it so long as the phenomenon of his vision lasts. HENRI FRÉDÉRIC AMIEL, *Journal*, March 19, 1868, tr. Mrs. Humphry Ward.

2. The universe does not jest with us, but is in earnest. EMERSON, *Journals*, 1841.

3. I do not wonder at a snowflake, a shell, a summer landscape, or the glory of the stars; but at the necessity of beauty under which the universe lies. EMERSON, "Fate," *The Conduct of Life* (1860).

4. Law rules throughout existence, a Law which is not intelligent but Intelligence. EMERSON, "Fate," *The Conduct of Life* (1860).

5. Nature, it seems, is the popular name / for milliards and milliards and milliards / of particles playing their infinite game / of billiards and billiards and billiards. PIET HEIN, "Atomyriades," *Grooks* (1966).

6. The universe is not hostile, nor yet is it friendly. It is simply indifferent. JOHN HAYNES HOLMES, *The Sensible Man's View of Religion* (1933).

7. Nothing puzzles me more than time and space; and yet nothing troubles me less. CHARLES LAMB, letter to Thomas Manning, Jan. 2, 1810.

8. The cosmos is a gigantic fly-wheel making 10,000 revolutions a minute. Man is a sick fly taking a dizzy ride on it. Religion is the theory that the wheel was designed and set spinning to give him the ride. H. L. MENCKEN, *Prejudices: Third Series* (1922), 5.

9. The whole visible world is only an imperceptible atom in the ample bosom of nature. No idea approaches it. PASCAL, *Pensées* (1670), 72, tr. W. F. Trotter.

10. All are but parts of one stupendous whole, / Whose body Nature is, and God the soul. ALEXANDER POPE, *An Essay on Man* (1733–34), 1.267.

11. To be happy in this world, especially when youth is past, it is necessary to feel oneself not merely an isolated individual whose day will soon be over, but part of the stream of life flowing on from the first germ to the remote and unknown future. BERTRAND RUSSELL, *The Conquest of Happiness* (1930), 13.

12. Thou canst not stir a flower / Without troubling of a star. FRANCIS THOMPSON, "The Mistress of Vision" (1897).

13. I do not value any view of the universe into which man and the institutions of man enter very largely and absorb much of the attention. Man is but the place where I stand, and the prospect hence is infinite. THOREAU, *Journal*, April 2, 1852.

## 1011. UNKINDNESS

**See also 206. Cruelty; 517. Kindness**

1. It is less dangerous to treat most men badly than to treat them too well. LA ROCHEFOUCAULD, *Maxims* (1665).

2. Now that another is suffering pain at thy hand, trust not that thy heart shall be exempt from affliction. SA'DI, *Gulistan* (1258), 3.28, tr. James Ross.

3. O! many a shaft, at random sent / Finds mark the archer little meant! SIR WALTER SCOTT, *The Lord of the Isles* (1815), 5.18.

## 1012. THE UNKNOWN

**See also 520. Knowledge; 1000. Understanding**

1. 'Tis very puzzling on the brink / Of what is called Eternity to stare, / And know no more of what is *here*, than *there*. BYRON, *Don Juan* (1819–24), 10.20.

2. The fairest thing we can experience is the mysterious. It is the fundamental emotion which stands at the cradle of true art and true science. EINSTEIN, title essay, *The World As I See It* (1934), tr. Alan Harris.

3. Between the idea / And the reality / Between the motion / And the act / Falls the Shadow. T. S. ELIOT, "The Hollow Men" (1925), 5.

4. All is riddle, and the key to a riddle is another riddle. EMERSON, "Illusions," *The Conduct of Life* (1860).

5. Whoever starts out toward the unknown must consent to venture alone. ANDRÉ GIDE, *Journals*, May 12, 1927, tr. Justin O'Brien.

6. Grieve not, because thou understandest not life's mystery; behind the veil is concealed many a delight. HĀFIZ, ghazals from the *Divan* (14th c.), 18, tr. Justin Huntly McCarthy.

7. Behind the dim unknown, / Standeth God within the shadow, keeping watch above his own. JAMES RUSSELL LOWELL, "The Present Crisis" (1844), 8.

8. Penetrating so many secrets, we cease to believe in the unknowable. But there it sits nevertheless, calmly licking its chops. H. L. MENCKEN, *Minority Report* (1956), 364.

9. Would there be this eternal seeking if the found existed? ANTONIO PORCHIA, *Voces* (1968), tr. W. S. Merwin.

10. We are ignorant of the Beyond because this ignorance is the condition *sine qua non* of our own life. Just as ice cannot know fire except by melting, by vanishing. JULES RENARD, *Journal*, September 1890, ed. and tr. Louise Bogan and Elizabeth Roget.

11. Our dream dashes itself against the great mystery like a wasp against a window pane. Less merciful than man, God never opens the window. JULES RENARD, *Journal*, August 1906, ed. and tr. Louise Bogan and Elizabeth Roget.

12. Once men are caught up in an event they cease to be afraid. Only the unknown frightens men. SAINT-EXUPÉRY, *Wind, Sand, and Stars* (1939), 2.2, tr. Lewis Galantière.

13. The unknown always passes for the marvellous. TACITUS, *Agricola* (c. A.D. 98), 30, tr. Alfred J. Church and William J. Brodribb.

14. However much you knock at nature's door, she will never answer you in comprehensible words. IVAN TURGENEV, *On the Eve* (1860), 1, tr. Constance Garnett.

## 1013. UNREASON

**See also 778. Reason; 999. Unconsciousness**

1. A life based on reason will always require to be balanced by an occasional bout of violent and irrational emotion, for the instinctual drives must be satisfied. CYRIL CONNOLLY, *The Unquiet Grave* (1945), 1.

2. Philosophy may describe unreason, as it may describe force; it cannot hope to refute them. GEORGE SANTAYANA, *The Life of Reason: Reason in Religion* (1905–06), 6.

## 1014. UNSELFISHNESS

**See also 373. Generosity; 430. Humanitarianism; 867. Selfishness; 880. Service**

1. To reach perfection, we must all pass, one by one, through the death of self-effacement. DAG HAMMARSKJÖLD, "1945–1949: Towards new shores—?" *Markings* (1964), tr. Leif Sjoberg and W. H. Auden.

2. The small share of happiness attainable by man exists only insofar as he is able to cease to think of himself. THEODOR REIK, author's note, *Of Love and Lust* (1957).

3. There's nothing in Christianity or Buddhism that quite matches the sympathetic unselfishness of an oyster. SAKI, "The Match-Maker," *The Chronicles of Clovis* (1912).

4. In every part and corner of our life, to lose oneself is to be gainer; to forget oneself is to be happy. ROBERT LOUIS STEVENSON, "Old Mortality" (1884), 2.

5. The only thing that saves the world is the little handful of disinterested men that are in it. WOODROW WILSON, address, Washington, D.C., May 15, 1916.

## 1015. UNWILLINGNESS

**See also 1050. Willingness**

1. There is nothing so easy but that it becomes difficult when you do it with reluctance. TERENCE, *The Self-Tormentor* (163 B.C.), 4.6.1, tr. Henry Thomas Riley.

## 1016. USEFULNESS

**See also 714. Practicality; 880. Service; 1017. Uselessness**

1. We often despise what is most useful to us. AESOP, "The Hart and the Hunter," *Fables* (6th c. B.C.?), tr. Joseph Jacobs.

2. It is a great misfortune to be of use to nobody; scarcely less to be of use to everybody. BALTASAR GRACIÁN, *The Art of Worldly Wisdom* (1647), 85, tr. Joseph Jacobs.

3. Keep a thing for seven years and you'll find use for it. IRISH PROVERB.

4. A cloak is not made for a single shower of rain. ITALIAN PROVERB.

5. A man cannot sleep in his cradle: whatever is useful must in the nature of life become useless. WALTER LIPPMANN, "The Taboo," *A Preface to Politics* (1914).

6. Success can corrupt; usefulness can only exalt. DMITRI MITROPOULOS, *Hi-Fi Music at Home*, May-June 1956.

7. Utility is the great idol of the age, to which all powers must do service and all talents swear allegiance. SCHILLER, *On the Aesthetic Education of Man* (1795), 2, tr. Reginald Snell.

8. I have known some men possessed of good qualities which were very serviceable to others, but useless to themselves; like a sun-dial on the front of a house, to inform the neighbours and passengers, but not the owner within. JONATHAN SWIFT, *Thoughts on Various Subjects* (1711).

9. The difference between utility and

utility plus beauty is the difference between telephone wires and the spider's web. EDWIN WAY TEALE, "September 18," *Circle of the Seasons* (1953).

10. The sure way of knowing nothing about life is to try to make oneself useful. OSCAR WILDE, "The Critic as Artist," *Intentions* (1891).

## 1017. USELESSNESS

**See also 1016. Usefulness**

1. A scarecrow in a garden of cucumbers keepeth nothing. *Apocrypha*, Baruch 6:70.

2. A good edge is good for nothing, if it has nothing to cut. THOMAS FULLER, M.D., *Gnomologia* (1732), 145.

3. To be employed in useless things is half to be idle. THOMAS FULLER, M.D., *Gnomologia* (1732), 5134.

4. A useless life is early death. GOETHE, *Iphigenia in Tauris* (1787), 1, tr. Charles E. Passage.

5. Uselessness is a fatal accusation to bring against any act which is done for its presumed utility, but those which are done for their own sake are their own justification. GEORGE SANTAYANA, *The Sense of Beauty* (1896), 4.

## UTILITY

**See 1016. Usefulness**

## 1018. UTOPIA

**See also 440. Idealism; 783. Reform**

1. The most awful tyranny is that of the proximate Utopia where the last sins are currently being eliminated and where, tomorrow, there will be no more sins because all the sinners will have been wiped out. THOMAS MERTON, introduction to selected texts from Mohandas K. Gandhi's *Non-Violence in Peace and War* (1948).

2. Every one who has ever built anywhere a "new heaven" first found the power thereto in his own hell. NIETZSCHE, *The Genealogy of Morals* (1887), 3.10, tr. Horace B. Samuel.

3. Ah, Love! could thou and I with Fate conspire / To grasp this sorry Scheme of Things entire, / Would not we shatter it to bits—and then / Re-mould it nearer to the Heart's Desire! OMAR KHAYYÁM, *Rubáiyát* (11th–12th c.), tr. Edward FitzGerald, 1st ed., 73.

4. Ideal society is a drama enacted exclusively in the imagination. GEORGE SANTAYANA, *The Life of Reason: Reason in Society* (1905–06), 6.

# V

## VALOR

**See 192. Courage**

## 1019. VALUE

**See also 47. Appreciation**

1. *Nothing* is intrinsically valuable; the value of everything is attributed to it, assigned to it from outside the thing itself, by people. JOHN BARTH, *The Floating Opera* (1956).

2. To live is, in itself, a value judgment. To breathe is to judge. ALBERT CAMUS, introduction to *The Rebel* (1951), tr. Anthony Bower.

3. The world is an old woman, and mistakes any gilt farthing for a gold coin; whereby being often cheated, she will thenceforth trust nothing but the common copper. THOMAS CARLYLE, *Sartor Resartus* (1833–34), 2.4.

4. That which cost little is less valued. CERVANTES, *Don Quixote* (1605–15), 1.4.7, tr. Peter Motteux and John Ozell.

5. Let him go where he will, he can only find so much beauty or worth as he carries. EMERSON, "Culture," *The Conduct of Life* (1860).

6. The world is always curious, and people become valuable merely for their inaccessibility. F. SCOTT FITZGERALD, "Note-Books," *The Crack-Up* (1945).

7. What we must decide is perhaps how we are valuable rather than how valuable we are. EDGAR Z. FRIEDENBERG, "The Impact of the School," *The Vanishing Adolescent* (1959).

8. We never know the worth of water till the well is dry. THOMAS FULLER, M.D., *Gnomologia* (1732), 5451.

9. We cannot be sure that we have some-

thing worth living for unless we are ready to die for it. ERIC HOFFER, *The True Believer* (1951), 1.2.13.

10. Every time a value is born, existence takes on a new meaning; every time one dies, some part of that meaning passes away. JOSEPH WOOD KRUTCH, "Love—or the Life and Death of a Value," *The Modern Temper* (1929).

11. Those things are dearest to us that have cost us most. MONTAIGNE, "Of the affections of fathers to their children," *Essays* (1580–88), tr. Charles Cotton and W. C. Hazlitt.

12. The value of a man can only be measured with regard to other men. NIETZSCHE, *The Will to Power* (1888), 878, tr. Anthony M. Ludovici.

13. What we obtain too cheap, we esteem too lightly; it is dearness [expensiveness] only that gives everything its value. THOMAS PAINE, *The American Crisis* (1776–83), 1.

14. Men understand the worth of blessings only when they have lost them. PLAUTUS, *The Captives* (3rd c. B.C.).

15. Everything is worth what its purchaser will pay for it. PUBLILIUS SYRUS, *Moral Sayings* (1st c. B.C.), 847, tr. Darius Lyman.

16. If a piece of worthless stone can bruise a cup of gold, its worth is not increased, nor that of the gold diminished. SA'DI, *Gulistan* (1258), 8.57, tr. James Ross.

17. What is false in the science of facts may be true in the science of values. GEORGE SANTAYANA, *Interpretations of Poetry and Religion* (1900).

18. The real price of everything, what everything really costs to the man who wants to acquire it, is the toil and trouble of acquiring it. ADAM SMITH, *The Wealth of Nations* (1776), 1.5.

19. The timid man yearns for full value and demands a tenth. The bold man strikes for double value and compromises on par. MARK TWAIN, "Pudd'nhead Wilson's New Calendar," *Following the Equator* (1897), 1.13.

20. There is no such thing as absolute value in this world. You can only estimate what a thing is worth to *you*. CHARLES DUDLEY WARNER, "Sixteenth Week," *My Summer in a Garden* (1871).

21. There is something between the gross specialized values of the mere practical man, and the thin specialized values of the mere scholar. Both types have missed something; and if you add together the two sets of values, you do not obtain the missing elements. ALFRED NORTH WHITEHEAD, *Science and the Modern World* (1925), 13.

## 1020. VANITY

**See also 163. Conceit; 726. Pretension; 727. Pride; 858. Self-deception; 862. Self-esteem; 865. Self-importance; 869. Self-love**

1. A desire to be observed, considered, esteemed, praised, beloved, and admired by his fellows is one of the earliest as well as the keenest dispositions discovered in the heart of man. JOHN ADAMS, *Discourses on Davila* (1789), 1.

2. Fools take to themselves the respect that is given to their office. AESOP, "The Jackass in Office," *Fables* (6th c. B.C.?), tr. Thomas James.

3. There is no such flatterer as is a man's self. FRANCIS BACON, "Of Friendship," *Essays* (1625).

4. Nobody can be kinder than the narcissist while you react to life in his own terms. ELIZABETH BOWEN, *The Death of the Heart* (1938), 3.3.

5. None of us are so much praised or censured as we think. CHARLES CALEB COLTON, *Lacon* (1825), 1.506.

6. It's always our touches of vanity / That manage to betray us. CHRISTOPHER FRY, *The Lady's Not for Burning* (1949), 1.

7. Every ass loves to hear himself bray. THOMAS FULLER, M.D., *Gnomologia* (1732), 1404.

8. The anxiety we have for the figure we cut, for our personage, is constantly cropping out. We are showing off and are often more concerned with making a display than with living. Whoever feels observed observes himself. ANDRÉ GIDE, *Journals*, March 12, 1938, tr. Justin O'Brien.

9. Until the Donkey tried to clear / The Fence, he thought himself a Deer. ARTHUR GUITERMAN, *A Poet's Proverbs* (1924).

10. Vanity is truly the motive-power that moves humanity, and it is flattery that

greases the wheels. JEROME K. JEROME, "On Vanity and Vanities," *The Idle Thoughts of an Idle Fellow* (1889).

11. What renders other people's vanity insufferable is that it wounds our own. LA ROCHEFOUCAULD, *Maxims* (1665), tr. Kenneth Pratt.

12. The most violent passions sometimes leave us at rest, but vanity agitates us constantly. LA ROCHEFOUCAULD, *Maxims* (1665), tr. Kenneth Pratt.

13. He who denies his own vanity usually possesses it in so brutal a form that he instinctively shuts his eyes to avoid the necessity of despising himself. NIETZSCHE, *Miscellaneous Maxims and Opinions* (1879), 38, tr. Paul V. Cohn.

14. The most vulnerable and yet most unconquerable of things is human vanity; nay, through being wounded its strength increases and can grow to giant proportions. NIETZSCHE, *Miscellaneous Maxims and Opinions* (1879), 46, tr. Paul V. Cohn.

15. We crave support in vanity, as we do in religion, and never forgive contradictions in that sphere. GEORGE SANTAYANA, *The Life of Reason: Reason in Society* (1905–06), 6.

16. It is not vain-glory for a man and his glass to confer in his own chamber. SHAKESPEARE, *Cymbeline* (1609–10), 4.1.8.

17. A vain man may become proud and imagine himself pleasing to all when he is in reality a universal nuisance. SPINOZA, *Ethics* (1677), 3, tr. Andrew Boyle.

18. Such is the weakness of our nature, that when men are a little exalted in their condition they immediately conceive they have additional senses, and their capacities enlarged not only above other men, but above human comprehension itself. RICHARD STEELE, *The Spectator* (1711–12), 193.

19. There are no grades of vanity, there are only grades of ability in concealing it. MARK TWAIN, *Notebook* (1935).

20. Man habitually sacrifices his life to his purse, but he sacrifices his purse to his vanity. MIGUEL DE UNAMUNO, "The Hunger of Immortality," *Tragic Sense of Life* (1913), tr. J. E. Crawford Flitch.

21. Few people are modest enough to be content to be estimated at their true worth. VAUVENARGUES, *Reflections and Maxims* (1746), 66, tr. F. G. Stevens.

## 1021. VEGETARIANISM

See also 352. Food

1. Most vigitaryans I iver see looked enough like their food to be classed as cannybals. FINLEY PETER DUNNE, "Casual Observations," *Mr. Dooley's Philosophy* (1900).

2. I have no doubt that it is a part of the destiny of the human race, in its gradual improvement, to leave off eating animals, as surely as the savage tribes have left off eating each other when they came in contact with the more civilized. THOREAU, "Higher Laws," *Walden* (1854).

## VENGEANCE

See 809. Retribution; 811. Revenge

## 1022. VENICE

See also 507. Italy

1. Venice is like eating an entire box of chocolate liqueurs in one go. TRUMAN CAPOTE, news summaries, Nov. 26, 1961.

## 1023. VICE

See also 201. Crime; 893. Sin; 1025. Virtue; 1026. Virtue and Vice; 1048. Wickedness; 1063. Wrongdoing

1. Vices are their own punishment. AESOP, "Avaricious and Envious," *Fables* (6th c. B.C.?), tr. Joseph Jacobs.

2. We make a ladder of our vices, if we trample those same vices underfoot. ST. AUGUSTINE, "De Ascensione," *Sermons* (5th c.).

3. The vices we scoff at in others laugh at us within ourselves. SIR THOMAS BROWNE, *Christian Morals* (1716), 3.

4. Half the vices which the world condemns most loudly have seeds of good in them and require moderate use rather than total abstinence. SAMUEL BUTLER (d. 1902), *The Way of All Flesh* (1903), 52.

5. It is the function of vice to keep virtue within reasonable bounds. SAMUEL BUTLER (d. 1902), *Note-Books* (1912).

6. Let them show me a cottage where there are not the same vices of which they

accuse courts. LORD CHESTERFIELD, *Letters to His Son*, June 6, 1751.

7. We are more apt to catch the vices of others than their virtues, as disease is far more contagious than health. CHARLES CALEB COLTON, *Lacon* (1825), 1.247.

8. When all run by common consent into vice, none appear to do so. CHARLES CALEB COLTON, *Lacon* (1825), 2.61.

9. Vice is a creature of such heejous mien, as Hogan says, that th' more ye see it th' betther ye like it. FINLEY PETER DUNNE, "The Crusade Against Vice," *Mr. Dooley's Opinions* (1901).

10. Vice goes a long way tow'rd makin' life bearable. A little vice now an' thin is relished be th' best iv men. FINLEY PETER DUNNE, "The Crusade Against Vice," *Mr. Dooley's Opinions* (1901).

11. Every vice is only an exaggeration of a necessary and virtuous function. EMERSON, *Journals*, 1836.

12. What maintains one vice would bring up two children. ENGLISH PROVERB.

13. Vice knows she's ugly, so puts on her mask. BENJAMIN FRANKLIN, *Poor Richard's Almanack* (1732–57).

14. Vice often rides triumphant in virtue's chariot. THOMAS FULLER, M.D., *Gnomologia* (1732), 5538.

15. Many a man's vices have at first been nothing worse than good qualities run wild. JULIUS CHARLES HARE and AUGUSTUS WILLIAM HARE, *Guesses at Truth* (1827).

16. This is the danger, when vice becomes a precedent. BEN JONSON, "Of the Diversity of Wits," *Timber* (1640).

17. Everybody likes to see somebody else get caught for the vices practiced by themselves. MARYA MANNES, *More in Anger* (1958), 2.3.

18. He who hates vices hates men. JOHN MORLEY, "Robespierre," *Critical Miscellanies* (1871–1908).

19. Men are more easily governed through their vices than through their virtues. NAPOLEON I, *Maxims* (1804–15).

20. Jupiter has loaded us with a couple of wallets: the one, filled with our own vices, he has placed at our backs; the other, heavy with those of others, he has hung before. PHAEDRUS, *Fables* (1st c.) 4.10.1, tr. H. T. Riley.

21. For lawless joys a bitter ending waits. PINDAR, *Odes* (5th c. B.C.), Isthmia 7.23.

22. Vice is a monster of so frightful mien, / As to be hated needs but to be seen; / Yet seen too oft, familiar with her face, / We first endure, then pity, then embrace. ALEXANDER POPE, *An Essay on Man* (1733–34), 2.217.

23. We tolerate without rebuke the vices with which we have grown familiar. PUBLILIUS SYRUS, *Moral Sayings* (1st c. B.C.), 150, tr. Darius Lyman.

24. Every vice has its excuse ready. PUBLILIUS SYRUS, *Moral Sayings* (1st c. B.C.), 986, tr. Darius Lyman.

25. The little vices of the great must needs be accounted very great. PUBLILIUS SYRUS, *Moral Sayings* (1st c. B.C.), 1004, tr. Darius Lyman.

26. Vice, like virtue, / Grows in small steps, and no true innocence / Can ever fall at once to deepest guilt. RACINE, *Phaedra* (1677), 4, tr. Robert Henderson.

27. Astronomy was born of superstition; eloquence of ambition, hatred, falsehood, and flattery; geometry of avarice; physics of an idle curiosity; and even moral philosophy of human pride. Thus the arts and sciences owe their birth to our vices. ROUSSEAU, *A Discourse on the Moral Effects of the Arts and Sciences* (1750), 2, tr. G. D. H. Cole.

28. There is no vice so simple but assumes / Some mark of virtue on his outward parts. SHAKESPEARE, *The Merchant of Venice* (1596–97), 3.2.81.

29. Through tattered clothes small vices do appear; / Robes and furred gowns hide all. Plate sin with gold, / And the strong lance of justice hurtless breaks; / Arm it in rags, a pygmy's straw does pierce it. SHAKESPEARE, *King Lear* (1605–06), 4.6.168.

30. The gods are just, and of our pleasant vices / Make instruments to scourge us. SHAKESPEARE, *King Lear* (1605–06), 5.3.170.

31. If you wish to save men from any particular vice, set up a tremendous cry of warning about some other, and they will all give their special efforts to the one to which attention is called. CHARLES DUDLEY WARNER, "Tenth Week," *My Summer in a Garden* (1871).

32. Nurse one vice in your bosom. Give it the attention it deserves and let your virtues spring up modestly around it. Then you'll

have the miser who's no liar; and the drunkard who's the benefactor of a whole city. THORNTON WILDER, *The Matchmaker* (1955), 3.

### VICE-PRESIDENCY

See 724. Presidency

### VICTORY

See 170. Conquest

### VIEWPOINT

See 58. Attitude; 682. Perspective

### 1024. VIOLENCE

See also 26. Aggression; 354. Force; 516. Killing; 779. Rebellion; 1035. War

1. Violence is just where kindness is vain. CORNEILLE, *Héraclius* (1647), 1.

2. God hates violence. He has ordained that all men / fairly possess their property, not seize it. EURIPIDES, *Helen* (412 B.C.), tr. Richmond Lattimore.

3. Most Americans would say that they disapproved of violence. But what they really mean is that they believe it should be the monopoly of the state. EDGAR Z. FRIEDENBERG, *New York Review of Books*, Oct. 20, 1966.

4. Not only do most people accept violence if it is perpetuated by legitimate authority, they also regard violence against certain kinds of people as inherently legitimate, no matter who commits it. EDGAR Z. FRIEDENBERG, *New York Review of Books*, Oct. 20, 1966.

5. It is better to be violent, if there is violence in our hearts, than to put on the cloak of non-violence to cover impotence. MOHANDAS K. GANDHI, *Non-Violence in Peace and War* (1948), 1.240.

6. Liberty and democracy become unholy when their hands are dyed red with innocent blood. MOHANDAS K. GANDHI, *Non-Violence in Peace and War* (1948), 1.357.

7. The most heterogeneous ideas are yoked by violence together. SAMUEL JOHNSON, *Lives of the Poets: Cowley* (1779–81).

8. In violence, we forget who we are, just as we forget who we are when we are engaged in sheer perception. MARY MC CARTHY, "Characters in Fiction," *On the Contrary* (1961).

9. Be peaceful, be courteous, obey the law, respect everyone; but if someone puts his hand on you, send him to the cemetery. MALCOLM X, *Malcolm X Speaks* (1965), 1.

10. Violence is essentially wordless, and it can begin only where thought and rational communication have broken down. THOMAS MERTON, introduction to selected texts from Mohandas K. Gandhi's *Non-Violence in Peace and War* (1948).

11. To-day violence is the rhetoric of the period. JOSÉ ORTEGA Y GASSET, *The Revolt of the Masses* (1930), 11.

12. Wherever a people has grown savage in arms so that human laws have no longer any place among it, the only powerful means of reducing it is religion. GIAMBATTISTA VICO, *The New Science* (1725–44), 1.2.

### 1025. VIRTUE

See also 391. Goodness; 489. Integrity; 598. Morality; 816. Right; 1023. Vice; 1026. Virtue and Vice

1. All sober inquirers after truth, ancient and modern, pagan and Christian, have declared that the happiness of man, as well as his dignity, consists in virtue. JOHN ADAMS, *Thoughts on Government* (1776).

2. Public virtue cannot exist in a nation without private, and public virtue is the only foundation of republics. JOHN ADAMS, letter to Mercy Warren, April 16, 1776.

3. A state of temperance, sobriety and justice without devotion is a cold, lifeless, insipid condition of virtue, and is rather to be styled philosophy than religion. JOSEPH ADDISON, *The Spectator* (1711–12), 201.

4. Virtue is more clearly shown in the performance of fine actions than in the nonperformance of base ones. ARISTOTLE, *Nicomachean Ethics* (4th C. B.C.), 4.1, tr. J. A. K. Thomson.

5. Virtue is like precious odours,—most fragrant when they are incensed or crushed. FRANCIS BACON, "Of Adversity," *Essays* (1625).

6. Whenever there are great virtues, it's a sure sign something's wrong. BERTOLT

BRECHT, *Mother Courage* (1939), 2, tr. Eric Bentley.

7. Make not the consequences of virtue the ends thereof. SIR THOMAS BROWNE, *A Letter to a Friend* (1690).

8. A virtue to be serviceable must, like gold, be alloyed with some commoner but more durable metal. SAMUEL BUTLER (d. 1902), *The Way of All Flesh* (1903), 19.

9. Abstract qualities begin / With capitals alway: / The True, the Good, the Beautiful— / Those are the things that pay! LEWIS CARROLL, "Poeta Fit, Non Nascitur" (1869).

10. Virtue can be afforded only by the poor, who have nothing to lose. ALEXANDER CHASE, *Perspectives* (1966).

11. Virtue is not the absence of vices or the avoidance of moral dangers; virtue is a vivid and separate thing, like pain or a particular smell. G. K. CHESTERTON, "A Piece of Chalk," *Tremendous Trifles* (1909).

12. The existence of virtue depends entirely upon its use. CICERO, *De Re Publica* (c. 51 B.C.), 1.

13. Cruel men are the greatest lovers of mercy—avaricious men of generosity—and proud men of humility,—that is to say, in others, not in themselves. CHARLES CALEB COLTON, *Lacon* (1825), 1.477.

14. The good opinion of our fellow men is the strongest, though not the purest motive to virtue. CHARLES CALEB COLTON, *Lacon* (1825), 2.104.

15. If a superior man abandon virtue, how can he fulfil the requirements of that name? CONFUCIUS, *Analects* (6th c. B.C.), 4.5, tr. James Legge.

16. Seldom indeed does human virtue rise / From trunk to branch. DANTE, "Purgatorio," 7, *The Divine Comedy* (c. 1300–21), tr. Lawrence Grant White.

17. Virtue is praised, but hated. People run away from it, for it is ice-cold and in this world you must keep your feet warm. DENIS DIDEROT, *Rameau's Nephew* (1762), tr. Jacques Barzun and Ralph H. Bowen.

18. Who knows his virtue's name or place, hath none. JOHN DONNE, "A Letter to the Lady Carey, and Mrs. Essex Riche, from Amyens," *Letters to Several Personages* (1651).

19. Virtue, though in rags, will keep me warm. JOHN DRYDEN, *Imitation of Horace* (1697), 3.29.87.

20. The order of things consents to virtue. EMERSON, *Journals*, 1834.

21. The essence of greatness is the perception that virtue is enough. EMERSON, "Heroism," *Essays: First Series* (1841).

22. The highest virtue is always against the law. EMERSON, "Worship," *The Conduct of Life* (1860).

23. Silver and gold are not the only coin; virtue too passes current all over the world. EURIPIDES, *Oedipus* (5th c. B.C.), 546, tr. M. H. Morgan.

24. He hath no mean portion of virtue that loveth it in another. THOMAS FULLER, M.D., *Gnomologia* (1732), 1894.

25. Virtue brings honour, and honour vanity. THOMAS FULLER, M.D., *Gnomologia* (1732), 5367.

26. Virtue is despised if it be seen in a threadbare cloak. THOMAS FULLER, M.D., *Gnomologia* (1732), 5374.

27. That virtue which requires to be ever guarded is scarce worth the sentinel. OLIVER GOLDSMITH, *The Vicar of Wakefield* (1766), 5.

28. The measure of any man's virtue is what he would do, if he had neither the laws nor public opinion, nor even his own prejudices, to control him. WILLIAM HAZLITT, *Characteristics* (1823), 128.

29. I don't believe the Devil would give half as much for the services of a sinner as he would for those of one of these folks that are always doing virtuous acts in a way to make them unpleasing. OLIVER WENDELL HOLMES, SR., *The Professor at the Breakfast Table* (1860), 4.

30. Even virtue followed beyond reason's rule / May stamp the just man knave, the sage a fool. HORACE, *Epistles* (20–c. 8 B.C.), 1.6.

31. Of all the pleasures I know, I know of none comparable to that of feeling capable of virtue. EUGENIO MARÍA DE HOSTOS, "Hombres e ideas," *Obras* (1939–54), 14.

32. Every man prefers virtue, when there is not some strong incitement to transgress its precepts. SAMUEL JOHNSON, quoted in Boswell's *Life of Samuel Johnson*, July 21, 1763.

33. There are people who are virtuous only in a piece-meal way; virtue is a fabric from which they never make themselves a whole garment. JOSEPH JOUBERT, *Pensées* (1842), 9.37.

34. If it be usual to be strongly impressed by things that are scarce, why are we so little impressed by virtue? LA BRUYÈRE, *Characters* (1688), 2.20, tr. Henri Van Laun.

35. Virtue would not go to such lengths if vanity did not keep her company. LA ROCHEFOUCAULD, *Maxims* (1665), tr. Kenneth Pratt.

36. He is a truly virtuous man who wishes always to be open to the observation of honest men. LA ROCHEFOUCAULD, *Maxims* (1665), tr. Kenneth Pratt.

37. Happiness cannot be the reward of virtue; it must be the intelligible consequence of it. WALTER LIPPMANN, *A Preface to Morals* (1929), 1.7.7.

38. Virtue is an angel, but she is a blind one, and must ask of Knowledge to show her the pathway that leads to her goal. HORACE MANN, lecture, "Thoughts for a Young Man," 1859.

39. Love Virtue, she alone is free, / She can teach ye how to climb / Higher than the sphery chime; / Or, if Virtue feeble were, / Heav'n itself would stoop to her. MILTON, *Comus* (1634), 1019.

40. Most men admire / Virtue who follow not her lore. MILTON, *Paradise Regained* (1671), 1.482.

41. Virtue cannot be followed but for herself, and if one sometimes borrows her mask to some other purpose, she presently pulls it away again. MONTAIGNE, "Of the inconstancy of our actions," *Essays* (1580–88), tr. Charles Cotton and W. C. Hazlitt.

42. Every virtue has its privileges; for example, that of contributing its own little faggot to the scaffold of every condemned man. NIETZSCHE, *Human, All Too Human* (1878), 67, tr. Helen Zimmern.

43. It is a distinction to have many virtues, but a hard lot. NIETZSCHE, "On Enjoying and Suffering the Passions," *Thus Spoke Zarathustra* (1883–92), 1, tr. Walter Kaufmann.

44. Only a modest virtue gets along with contentment. NIETZSCHE, "On Virtue That Makes Small," *Thus Spoke Zarathustra* (1883–92), 3, tr. Walter Kaufmann.

45. When we are planning for posterity, we ought to remember that virtue is not hereditary. THOMAS PAINE, "Of the Present Ability of America," *Common Sense* (1776).

46. Virtues are virtues only to those who can appreciate them. *Panchatantra* (c. 5th c.), 1, tr. Franklin Edgerton.

47. The strength of a man's virtue must not be measured by his efforts, but by his ordinary life. PASCAL, *Pensées* (1670), 352, tr. W. F. Trotter.

48. There may be guilt when there is too much virtue. RACINE, *Andromache* (1667), 3, tr. Robert Henderson.

49. The chief cause of our misery is less the violence of our passions than the feebleness of our virtues. JOSEPH ROUX, *Meditations of a Parish Priest* (1886), 5.25, tr. Isabel F. Hapgood.

50. The glory that goes with wealth and beauty is fleeting and fragile; virtue is a possession glorious and eternal. SALLUST, *Conspiracy of Catiline* (1st c. B.C.), 4.

51. Virtue is bold, and goodness never fearful. SHAKESPEARE, *Measure for Measure* (1604–05), 3.1.215.

52. Virtue herself is her own fairest reward. SILIUS ITALICUS, *Punica* (1st c.), 13.663.

53. When men grow virtuous in their old age, they only make a sacrifice to God of the devil's leavings. JONATHAN SWIFT, *Thoughts on Various Subjects* (1711).

54. Virtue must shape itself in deed. ALFRED, LORD TENNYSON, "Tiresias" (1885).

55. Forgive us for bypassing political duties; for condemning civil disobedience when we will not obey You; for reducing Your holy law to average virtues, by trying to be no better or worse than most men. UNITED PRESBYTERIAN CHURCH, *Litany for Holy Communion* (1968).

56. If virtue were its own reward, it would no longer be a human quality, but supernatural. VAUVENARGUES, *Reflections and Maxims* (1746), 587, tr. F. G. Stevens.

57. I have seen men incapable of the sciences, but never any incapable of virtue. VOLTAIRE, "Philosopher," *Philosophical Dictionary* (1764).

58. Virtue between men is a commerce of good actions: he who has no part in this commerce must not be reckoned. VOLTAIRE, "Virtue," *Philosophical Dictionary* (1764).

59. Virtue is the roughest way, / But proves at night a bed of down. SIR HENRY WOTTON, "Upon the Sudden Restraint of the Earl of Somerset," *Poems* (1842).

## 1026. VIRTUE AND VICE

See also 1023. Vice; 1025. Virtue

1. Show me a community or a country where all the minor vices are discouraged and I will show you one bereft of major virtues. HEYWOOD BROUN, "Saratoga Fades," *New York World Telegram*, Aug. 19, 1939.

2. They that endeavour to abolish vice, destroy also virtue; for contraries, though they destroy one another, are yet the life of one another. SIR THOMAS BROWNE, *Religio Medici* (1642), 2.

3. The extremes of vice and virtue are alike detestable; absolute virtue is as sure to kill a man as absolute vice is. SAMUEL BUTLER (d. 1902), "Elementary Morality," *Note-Books* (1912).

4. Vice has more martyrs than virtue; and it often happens that men suffer more to be lost than to be saved. CHARLES CALEB COLTON, *Lacon* (1825), 1.170.

5. This is the tax a man must pay to his virtues—they hold up a torch to his vices, and render those frailties notorious in him which would have passed without observation in another. CHARLES CALEB COLTON, *Lacon* (1825), 1.237.

6. There is a capacity of virtue in us, and there is a capacity of vice to make your blood creep. EMERSON, *Journals*, 1831.

7. Men imagine that they communicate their virtue or vice only by overt actions, and do not see that virtue or vice emit a breath every moment. EMERSON, "Self-Reliance," *Essays: First Series* (1841).

8. Search others for their virtues, thy self for thy vices. BENJAMIN FRANKLIN, *Poor Richard's Almanack* (1732–57).

9. As virtue is its own reward, so vice is its own punishment. THOMAS FULLER, M.D., *Gnomologia* (1732), 743.

10. Our virtues would be proud if our vices whipped them not. THOMAS FULLER, M.D., *Gnomologia* (1732), 3829.

11. It takes a vice to check a vice, and virtue is the byproduct of a stalemate between opposite vices. ERIC HOFFER, *The Ordeal of Change* (1964), 12.

12. No vice exists which does not pretend to be more or less like some virtue and which does not take advantage of this assumed resemblance. LA BRUYÈRE, *Characters* (1688), 4.72, tr. Henri Van Laun.

13. It is convention and arbitrary rewards which make all the merit and demerit of what we call vice and virtue. JULIEN OFFROY DE LA METTRIE, *Anti-Sénèque ou Discours sur le bonheur*.

14. Our virtues are most frequently but vices disguised. LA ROCHEFOUCAULD, *Maxims* (1665).

15. Vices are ingredients of virtues just as poisons are ingredients of remedies. Prudence mixes and tempers them and uses them effectively against life's ills. LA ROCHEFOUCAULD, *Maxims* (1665).

16. The absence of vices adds so little to the sum of one's virtues. ANTONIO MACHADO, *Juan de Mairena* (1943), 28, tr. Ben Belitt.

17. If virtue cannot shine bright, but by the conflict of contrary appetites, shall we then say that she cannot subsist without the assistance of vice, and that it is from her that she derives her reputation and honor? MONTAIGNE, "Of cruelty," *Essays* (1580–88), tr. Charles Cotton and W. C. Hazlitt.

18. When I religiously confess myself to myself, I find that the best virtue I have has in it some tincture of vice. MONTAIGNE, "That we taste nothing pure," *Essays* (1580–88), tr. Charles Cotton and W. C. Hazlitt.

19. When virtue has slept, she will get up more refreshed. NIETZSCHE, *Human, All Too Human* (1878), 83, in *The Portable Nietzsche*, tr. Walter Kaufmann.

20. Virtue and vice, evil and good, are siblings, or next-door neighbors, / Easy to make mistakes, hard to tell them apart. OVID, *The Remedies for Love* (c. A.D. 8), tr. Rolfe Humphries.

21. Who does not sufficiently hate vice, / Does not sufficiently love virtue. JEAN-BAPTISTE ROUSSEAU, *Fables*, *Oeuvres* (1743).

22. Virtue itself turns vice, being misapplied, / And vice sometime's by action dignified. SHAKESPEARE, *Romeo and Juliet* (1594–95), 2.3.21.

23. Some rise by sin, and some by virtue fall. SHAKESPEARE, *Measure for Measure* (1604–05), 2.1.38.

24. More people are flattered into virtue than bullied out of vice. ROBERT SMITH SURTEES, *The Analysis of the Hunting Field* (1846), 1.

25. I never was so rapid in my virtue but my vice kept up with me. THOREAU, *Journal*, Feb. 8, 1841.

26. If a man has no vices, he's in great

danger of making vices about his virtues, and there's a spectacle. THORNTON WILDER, *The Matchmaker* (1955), 3.

### 1027. VISION

**See also 356. Forethought; 676. Perception; 890. Sight**

1. No man sees far; the most see no farther than their noses. THOMAS CARLYLE, "Count Cagliostro" (1833).

2. He who plants a walnut tree expects not to eat of the fruit. ENGLISH PROVERB.

3. A great mind is one that can forget or look beyond itself. WILLIAM HAZLITT, "Commonplaces," *The Round Table* (1817), 67.

4. Visionary people are visionary partly because of the very great many things they don't see. BERKELEY RICE, *The New York Times Magazine*, March 17, 1968.

5. The fellow that can only see a week ahead is always the popular fellow, for he is looking with the crowd. But the one that can see years ahead, he has a telescope but he cant make anybody believe he has it. WILL ROGERS, *The Autobiography of Will Rogers* (1949), 14.

6. Hundreds of people can talk for one who can think, but thousands can think for one who can see. To see clearly is poetry, prophecy, and religion—all in one. JOHN RUSKIN, *Modern Painters* (1843–60), v. 3, 4.16.28.

7. A rock pile ceases to be a rock pile the moment a single man contemplates it, bearing within him the image of a cathedral. SAINT-EXUPÉRY, *Flight to Arras* (1942), 22, tr. Lewis Galantière.

8. Vision is the art of seeing things invisible. JONATHAN SWIFT, *Thoughts on Various Subjects* (1711).

### VISITING

**See 426. Hospitality**

### 1028. VITALITY

**See also 291. Enthusiasm; 511. Joie de vivre; 921. Spontaneity**

1. Vitality shows in not only the ability to persist but the ability to start over. F. SCOTT FITZGERALD, "Note-Books," *The Crack-Up* (1945).

2. When vitality runs high, death takes men by surprise. But if they close their eyes to this possibility, what they gain in peace they lose in sensibility and significance. LEWIS MUMFORD, "Cosmos and Person," *The Conduct of Life* (1951).

3. Human vitality is so exuberant that in the sorriest desert it still finds a pretext for glowing and trembling. JOSÉ ORTEGA Y GASSET, *Notes on the Novel* (1925).

4. Nature drives with a loose rein and vitality of any sort can blunder through many a predicament in which reason would despair. GEORGE SANTAYANA, *The Sense of Beauty* (1896).

### 1029. VOCATIONS

**See also 1. Ability; 309. Excellence; 981. Training; 1058. Work**

1. The price one pays for pursuing any profession, or calling, is an intimate knowledge of its ugly side. JAMES BALDWIN, "The Black Boy Looks at the White Boy," *Nobody Knows My Name* (1961).

2. Vocations which we wanted to pursue, but didn't, bleed, like colors, on the whole of our existence. BALZAC, "Scènes de la vie parisienne," *La Maison Nucingen* (1838), v. 3.

3. Blessed is he who has found his work; let him ask no other blessedness. THOMAS CARLYLE, *Past and Present* (1843), 3.11.

4. Every man has his own vocation. The talent is the call. EMERSON, "Spiritual Laws," *Essays: First Series* (1841).

5. In every age and clime we see / Two of a trade can never agree. JOHN GAY, "The Rat-catcher and Cats," *Fables* (1727–38).

6. The player envies only the player, the poet envies only the poet. WILLIAM HAZLITT, "Envy," *Sketches and Essays* (1839).

7. Every calling is great when greatly pursued. OLIVER WENDELL HOLMES, JR., speech, Suffolk Bar Association, Feb. 5, 1885.

8. The artisan or scientist or the follower of whatever discipline who has the habit of comparing himself not with other followers but with the discipline itself will have a lower opinion of himself, the more excellent he is. GIACOMO LEOPARDI, *Pensieri* (1834–37), 64, tr. William Fense Weaver.

9. Every science has for its basis a system of principles as fixed and unalterable as those by which the universe is regulated and governed. Man cannot make principles; he can only discover them. THOMAS PAINE, *The Age of Reason* (1794, 1796), 1.

10. When men are rightly occupied, their amusement grows out of their work, as the colour-petals out of a fruitful flower. JOHN RUSKIN, *Sesame and Lilies* (1865), 1.39.

11. All professions are conspiracies against the laity. GEORGE BERNARD SHAW, *The Doctor's Dilemma* (1913), 1.

12. The test of a vocation is the love of the drudgery it involves. LOGAN PEARSALL SMITH, *Afterthoughts* (1931), 5.

13. Every man who does not teach his son a trade, it is as though he teaches him to rob. Haggadah, *Palestinian Talmud* (4th c.).

## 1030. VOTING

**See also 130. Citizens; 231. Democracy; 393. Government; 705. Politics and Politicians**

1. Elections are won by men and women chiefly because most people vote against somebody, rather than for somebody. FRANKLIN P. ADAMS, *Nods and Becks* (1944).

2. Where the annual elections end, there slavery begins. JOHN ADAMS, *Thoughts on Government* (1776).

3. Vote for the man who promises least; he'll be the least disappointing. BERNARD BARUCH, quoted in Meyer Berger's *New York* (1960).

4. A man without a vote is in this land like a man without a hand. HENRY WARD BEECHER, *Proverbs from Plymouth Pulpit* (1887).

5. At the bottom of all the tributes paid to democracy is the little man, walking into the little booth, with a little pencil, making a little cross on a little bit of paper—no amount of rhetoric or voluminous discussion can possibly diminish the overwhelming importance of the point. SIR WINSTON CHURCHILL, speech, House of Commons, Oct. 31, 1944.

6. Disfranchisement is the deliberate theft and robbery of the only protection of poor against rich and black against white. W. E. B. DU BOIS, "We Return—Fighting," *In Their Own Words: 1916–1966*, v. 3.

7. Those who stay away from the election think that one vote will do no good: 'Tis but one step more to think one vote will do no harm. EMERSON, *Journals*, 1854.

8. Referendum: to vote for one's own ball and chain. Graffito written during French student revolt, May 1968.

9. The apathy of the modern voter is the confusion of the modern reformer. LEARNED HAND, speech, Washington, D.C., March 8, 1932.

10. The vote is the most powerful instrument ever devised by man for breaking down injustice and destroying the terrible walls which imprison men because they are different from other men. LYNDON B. JOHNSON, address on signing the voting-rights bill, Washington, D.C., Aug. 6, 1965.

11. The ignorance of one voter in a democracy impairs the security of all. JOHN F. KENNEDY, address, Vanderbilt University, Nashville, Tenn., May 18, 1963.

12. Ballots are the rightful and peaceful successors to bullets. ABRAHAM LINCOLN, message to Congress, July 7, 1861.

13. Football strategy does not originate in a scrimmage: it is useless to expect solutions in a political campaign. WALTER LIPPMANN, "The Changing Focus," *A Preface to Politics* (1914).

14. No candidate too pallid, / No issue too remote, / But it can snare / A questionnaire / To analyze our vote. PHYLLIS MC GINLEY, "Ballad of the Preelection Vote," *A Pocketful of Wry* (1940).

15. Voting is simply a way of determining which side is the stronger without putting it to the test of fighting. H. L. MENCKEN, *Minority Report* (1956), 312.

16. More men have been elected between Sundown and Sunup than ever were elected between Sunup and Sundown. WILL ROGERS, "Mr. Ford and Other Political Self-Starters," *The Illiterate Digest* (1924).

17. No Voter in the World ever voted for nothing; in some way he has been convinced that he is to get something for that vote. His vote is all that our Constitution gives him, and it goes to the highest bidder. WILL ROGERS, *The Autobiography of Will Rogers* (1949), 14.

18. Let us never forget that government is

*ourselves* and not an alien power over us. The ultimate rulers of our democracy are not a President and senators and congressmen and government officials, but the voters of this country. FRANKLIN D. ROOSEVELT, speech, Marietta, Ohio, July 8, 1938.

19. Nobody will ever deprive the American people of the right to vote except the American people themselves—and the only way they could do that is by not voting. FRANKLIN D. ROOSEVELT, radio address, Oct. 5, 1944.

20. An election is a moral horror, as bad as a battle except for the blood: a mud bath for every soul concerned in it. GEORGE BERNARD SHAW, *Back to Methuselah* (1921), 2.

21. The idea that you can merchandise candidates for high office like breakfast cereal—that you can gather votes like box tops—is, I think, the ultimate indignity to the democratic process. ADLAI STEVENSON, acceptance speech, Democratic National Convention, Aug. 18, 1956.

### VOWS
**See 737. Promises**

### 1031. VULGARITY
**See also 139. Coarseness**

1. The vulgar man is always the most distinguished, for the very desire to be distinguished is vulgar. G. K. CHESTERTON, "The Boy," *All Things Considered* (1908).

2. It is disgusting to pick your teeth; what is vulgar is to use a gold toothpick. LOUIS KRONENBERGER, "Fashions in Vulgarity," *The Cart and the Horse* (1964), 2.

3. The old-style dandy hated vulgarity. The new-style dandy, the lover of Camp, appreciates vulgarity. SUSAN SONTAG, "Notes on Camp," *Against Interpretation* (1961).

### 1032. VULNERABILITY
**See also 1040. Weakness**

1. One always knocks oneself on the sore place. FRENCH PROVERB.

## W

### 1033. WAITING
**See also 316. Expectation; 425. Hope; 454. Impatience; 670. Patience**

1. Serene, I fold my hands and wait, / Nor care for wind, nor tide, nor sea; / I rave no more 'gainst time or fate, / For lo! my own shall come to me. JOHN BURROUGHS, "Waiting" (1862).

2. Everything comes if a man will only wait. BENJAMIN DISRAELI, *Tancred* (1847).

3. How much of human life is lost in waiting! EMERSON, "Prudence," *Essays: First Series* (1841).

4. The philosophy of waiting is sustained by all the oracles of the universe. EMERSON, *Journals*, 1847.

5. They also serve who only stand and wait. MILTON, Sonnet 19 (1655).

6. Half the agony of living is waiting. ALEXANDER ROSE, *Memoirs of a Heterosexual* (1968).

7. Long ailments wear out pain, and long hopes, joy. STANISLAUS I OF POLAND, *Maxims* (c. 18th c.)

8. It's good to hope, it's the waiting that spoils it. *Yiddish Proverbs* (1949), ed. Hanan J. Ayalti.

### 1034. WALKING
**See also 690. Physical Fitness; 922. Sports**

1. People seem to think there is something inherently noble and virtuous in the desire to go for a walk. MAX BEERBOHM, "Going Out for a Walk," *And Even Now* (1920).

2. When you stroll you never hurry back, because if you had anything to do, you wouldn't be strolling in the first place. VIRGINIA CARY HUDSON, *O Ye Jigs & Juleps!* (1962).

3. A sedentary life is the real sin against the Holy Spirit. Only those thoughts that come by walking have any value. NIETZSCHE, "Maxims and Missiles," 34, *Twilight of the Idols* (1888), tr. Anthony M. Ludovici.

### WANDERING
**See 806. Restlessness; 985. Travel**

### WANTS

See 236. Desires; 618. Need

### 1035. WAR

See also 170. Conquest; 225. Defeat; 226. Defense; 250. Discord; 342. Fighting; 516. Killing; 582. The Military; 633. Nuclear Power; 658. Pacifism; 674. Peace; 932. Strategy; 1024. Violence; 1036. War, Civil; 1042. Weapons

1. The art of war is like the art of the courtesan—indeed, they might be called sisters, since both are the slaves of desperation. PIETRO ARETINO, letter to Ambrogio Eusebio, Nov. 28, 1537, tr. Samuel Putnam.

2. After each war there is a little less democracy to save. BROOKS ATKINSON, "January 7," *Once Around the Sun* (1951).

3. A just fear of an imminent danger, though there be no blow given, is a lawful cause of war. FRANCIS BACON, "Of Empire," *Essays* (1625).

4. Youth is the first victim of war; the first fruit of peace. It takes twenty years or more of peace to make a man; it takes only twenty seconds of war to destroy him. BAUDOUIN I OF BELGIUM, address to joint session of U.S. Congress, May 12, 1959.

5. It is not merely cruelty that leads men to love war, it is excitement. HENRY WARD BEECHER, *Proverbs from Plymouth Pulpit* (1887).

6. A general and a bit of shooting makes you forget your troubles . . . it takes your mind off the cost of living. BRENDAN BEHAN, *The Hostage* (1958), 3.

7. We do not fight for the real but for shadows we make. / A flag is a piece of cloth and a word is a sound, / But we make them something neither cloth nor a sound, / Totems of love and hate, black sorcery-stones. STEPHEN VINCENT BENÉT, *John Brown's Body* (1928), 4.

8. Make war on the men—the ladies have too-long memories. STEPHEN VINCENT BENÉT, *John Brown's Body* (1928), 4.

9. Battle, n. A method of untying with the teeth a political knot that would not yield to the tongue. AMBROSE BIERCE, *The Devil's Dictionary* (1881–1911).

10. War is like love, it always finds a way. BERTOLT BRECHT, *Mother Courage* (1939), 6, tr. Eric Bentley.

11. We used to wonder where war lived, what it was that made it so vile. And now we realize that we know where it lives, that it is inside ourselves. ALBERT CAMUS, *Notebooks 1935–1942* (1962), 3, tr. Philip Thody.

12. Clear undeniable right, clear undeniable might: either of these once ascertained puts an end to battle. All battle is a confused experiment to ascertain one and both of these. THOMAS CARLYLE, *Chartism* (1839), 1.

13. There is nothing so subject to the inconstancy of fortune as war. CERVANTES, *Don Quixote* (1605–15), 1.1.8, tr. Peter Motteux and John Ozell.

14. There is no working middle course in wartime. SIR WINSTON CHURCHILL, speech, House of Commons, July 2, 1942.

15. Boys are the cash of war. Whoever said / we're not free-spenders doesn't know our likes. JOHN CIARDI, "New Year's Eve," *This Strangest Everything* (1966).

16. Laws are silent in time of war. CICERO, *Pro Milone* (52 B.C.).

17. War is a continuation of policy by other means. It is not merely a political act but a real political instrument. KARL VON CLAUSEWITZ, *War, Politics & Power* (1962), 1, tr. Edward M. Collins.

18. War is nothing but a duel on a larger scale. KARL VON CLAUSEWITZ, *War, Politics & Power* (1962), 1, tr. Edward M. Collins.

19. War is the province of chance. In no other sphere of human activity must such a margin be left for this intruder. It increases the uncertainty of every circumstance and deranges the course of events. KARL VON CLAUSEWITZ, *War, Politics & Power* (1962), 3, tr. Edward M. Collins.

20. All the gods are dead except the god of war. ELDRIDGE CLEAVER, "Four Vignettes," *Soul on Ice* (1968).

21. As wounded men may limp through life, so our war minds may not regain the balance of their thoughts for decades. FRANK MOORE COLBY, "War Minds," *The Colby Essays* (1926), v. 2.

22. Boys and girls, / And women, that would groan to see a child / Pull off an insect's leg, all read of war, / The best amusement for our morning meal. SAMUEL TAYLOR COLERIDGE, *Fears in Solitude* (1798).

23. War is a game in which princes seldom win, the people never. CHARLES CALEB COLTON, *Lacon* (1825), 1.534.

24. For what are the triumphs of war, planned by ambition, executed by violence, and consummated by devastation? The means are the sacrifice of many, the end, the bloated aggrandizement of the few. CHARLES CALEB COLTON, *Lacon* (1825), 2.283.

25. To lead an uninstructed people to war is to throw them away. CONFUCIUS, *Analects* (6th c. B.C.), 13.30, tr. James Legge.

26. The disasters of the world are due to its inhabitants not being able to grow old simultaneously. There is always a raw and intolerant nation eager to destroy the tolerant and mellow. CYRIL CONNOLLY, *The Unquiet Grave* (1945), 2.

27. War's a game which were their subjects wise / Kings would not play at. WILLIAM COWPER, "The Winter Morning Walk," *The Task* (1785), 187.

28. As peace is of all goodness, so war is an emblem, a hieroglyphic, of all misery. JOHN DONNE, *Sermons*, No. 12, 1622.

29. All delays are dangerous in war. JOHN DRYDEN, *Tyrannic Love* (1669), 1.1.

30. A war expert is a man ye niver heerd iv befure. If ye can think iv annywan whose face is onfamilyar to ye an' ye don't raymimber his name, an' he's got a job on a pa-aper ye didn't know was published, he's a war expert. FINLEY PETER DUNNE, "The War Expert," *Mr. Dooley's Philosophy* (1900).

31. I have come to hate war not only because it kills off the flower of every nation, but because it destroys spiritual as well as material values. ILYA EHRENBURG, "What I Have Learned," *Saturday Review*, Sept. 30, 1967.

32. In the final choice a soldier's pack is not so heavy a burden as a prisoner's chains. DWIGHT D. EISENHOWER, first Inaugural Address, Jan. 20, 1953.

33. War educates the senses, calls into action the will, perfects the physical constitution, brings men into such swift and close collision in critical moments that man measures man. EMERSON, "War," *Miscellanies* (1884).

34. The most disadvantageous peace is better than the most just war. ERASMUS, *Adagia* (1500).

35. In guerilla warfare the struggle no longer concerns the place where you are, but the place where you are going. Each fighter carries his warring country between his toes. FRANTZ FANON, "Spontaneity: Its Strength and Weakness," *The Wretched of the Earth* (1961), tr. Constance Farrington.

36. Men love war because it allows them to look serious. Because it is the one thing that stops women laughing at them. JOHN FOWLES, *The Magus* (1965), 52.

37. There never was a good war or a bad peace. BENJAMIN FRANKLIN, letter to Josiah Quincy, Sept. 11, 1773.

38. Morality is contraband in war. MOHANDAS K. GANDHI, *Non-Violence in Peace and War* (1948), 1.268.

39. War is an unmitigated evil. But it certainly does one good thing. It drives away fear and brings bravery to the surface. MOHANDAS K. GANDHI, *Non-Violence in Peace and War* (1948), 1.270.

40. What difference does it make to the dead, the orphans and the homeless, whether the mad destruction is wrought under the name of totalitarianism or the holy name of liberty or democracy? MOHANDAS K. GANDHI, *Non-Violence in Peace and War* (1948), 1.357.

41. In time of war the devil makes more room in hell. GERMAN PROVERB.

42. It is easier to lead men to combat and to stir up their passions than to temper them and urge them to the patient labors of peace. ANDRÉ GIDE, *Journals*, Sept. 13, 1938, tr. Justin O'Brien.

43. Who would prefer peace to the glory of hunger and thirst, of wading through mud, and dying in the service of one's country? JEAN GIRAUDOUX, *Amphitryon 38* (1929), 1, tr. Phyllis La Farge with Peter H. Judd.

44. During war we imprison the rights of man. JEAN GIRAUDOUX, *Tiger at the Gates* (1935), 2, tr. Christopher Fry.

45. Everyone, when there's war in the air, learns to live in a new element: falsehood. JEAN GIRAUDOUX, *Tiger at the Gates* (1935), 2, tr. Christopher Fry.

46. There's a kind of permission for war which can be given only by the world's mood and atmosphere, the feel of its pulse. It would be madness to undertake a war without that permission. JEAN GIRAUDOUX,

*Tiger at the Gates* (1935), 2, tr. Christopher Fry.

47. Man is preceded by forest, followed by desert. Graffito written during French student revolt, May 1968.

48. She, Ruin, is strong and sound on her feet, and therefore / far outruns all Prayers, and wins into every country / to force men astray; and the Prayers follow as healers after her. HOMER, *Iliad* (9th c. B.C.), 9.505, tr. Richmond Lattimore.

49. Older men declare war. But it is youth that must fight and die. HERBERT HOOVER, speech, Republican National Convention, Chicago, June 27, 1944.

50. The most shocking fact about war is that its victims and its instruments are individual human beings, and that these individual beings are condemned by the monstrous conventions of politics to murder or be murdered in quarrels not their own. ALDOUS HUXLEY, *The Olive Tree* (1937).

51. The only monuments to this war [Vietnam] will be the dead, the maimed, the despairing and the forlorn. Letter to President Johnson from the International Voluntary Services Agency, cited by Bernard Weinraub in *The New York Times*, Sept. 20, 1967.

52. It is but seldom that any one overt act produces hostilities between two nations; there exists, more commonly, a previous jealousy and ill will, a predisposition to take offense. WASHINGTON IRVING, "English Writers on America," *The Sketch Book of Geoffrey Crayon, Gent.* (1819–20).

53. Mankind must put an end to war or war will put an end to mankind. JOHN F. KENNEDY, address, United Nations General Assembly, Sept. 25, 1961.

54. No man who witnessed the tragedies of the last war, no man who can imagine the unimaginable possibilities of the next war can advocate war out of irritability or frustration or impatience. JOHN F. KENNEDY, Veterans Day Address, Arlington National Cemetery, Nov. 11, 1961.

55. [Man] is, perhaps, no more prone to war than he used to be and no more inclined to commit other evil deeds. But a given amount of ill will or folly will go further than it used to. JOSEPH WOOD KRUTCH, "The Loss of Confidence," *The Measure of Man* (1954).

56. The slaying of multitudes should be mourned with sorrow. / A victory should be celebrated with the funeral rite. LAOTSE, *The Character of Tao* (6th c. B.C.), 31, tr. Lin Yutang.

57. The way to prevent war is to bend every energy toward preventing it, not to proceed by the dubious indirection of preparing for it. MAX LERNER, "On Peacetime Military Training," *Actions and Passions* (1949).

58. This is war: / Boys flung into a breach / Like shoveled earth; / And old men, / Broken, / Driving rapidly before crowds of people / In a glitter of silly decorations. / Behind the boys / And the old men, / Life weeps, / And shreds her garments / To the blowing winds. AMY LOWELL, "In the Stadium," *A Shard of Silence* (1957).

59. Abstract war is horrid, / I sign to thet with all my heart,— / But civlyzation doos git forrid / Sometimes upon a powder-cart. JAMES RUSSELL LOWELL, *The Biglow Papers: First Series* (1848), 7.

60. It is fatal to enter any war without the will to win it. DOUGLAS MAC ARTHUR, speech, Republican National Convention, July 7, 1952.

61. When elephants fight, the mousedeer between them is killed. MALAY PROVERB.

62. One believes in the coming of war if one does not sufficiently abhor it. THOMAS MANN, *The Magic Mountain* (1924), 6.2, tr. H. T. Lowe-Porter.

63. War can only be abolished through war, and in order to get rid of the gun it is necessary to take up the gun. MAO TSE-TUNG, *Quotations from Chairman Mao Tse-tung* (1966), 5.

64. Blood is the god of war's rich livery. CHRISTOPHER MARLOWE, *Tamburlaine the Great* (c. 1587), 2.3.2.

65. All wars are boyish, and are fought by boys. HERMAN MELVILLE, "The March into Virginia," *Battlepieces and Aspects of the War* (1866).

66. War may make a fool of man, but it by no means degrades him; on the contrary, it tends to exalt him, and its net effects are much like those of motherhood on women. H. L. MENCKEN, *Minority Report* (1956), 17.

67. We think—although of course, now, we very seldom / Clearly think— / That the other side of War is Peace. EDNA ST. VINCENT MILLAY, untitled poem, *Make Bright the Arrows* (1940).

68. We kill because we're afraid of our own shadow, afraid that if we used a little common sense we'd have to admit that our glorious principles were wrong. HENRY MILLER, "The Alcoholic Veteran with the Washboard Cranium," *The Wisdom of the Heart* (1941).

69. How different the new order would be if we could consult the veteran instead of the politician. HENRY MILLER, "The Alcoholic Veteran with the Washboard Cranium," *The Wisdom of the Heart* (1941).

70. War is both the product of an earlier corruption and a producer of new corruptions. LEWIS MUMFORD, "The Challenge to Renewal," *The Conduct of Life* (1951).

71. Against war it may be said that it makes the victor stupid and the vanquished revengeful. NIETZSCHE, *Human, All Too Human* (1878), 444, tr. Helen Zimmern.

72. How good bad music and bad reasons sound when one marches against an enemy! NIETZSCHE, *The Dawn* (1881), 557, in *The Portable Nietzsche*, tr. Walter Kaufmann.

73. The quickest way of ending a war is to lose it. GEORGE ORWELL, "Second Thoughts on James Burnham," *Shooting an Elephant* (1950).

74. He who is the author of a war lets loose the whole contagion of hell and opens a vein that bleeds a nation to death. THOMAS PAINE, *The American Crisis* (1776–83), 5.

75. War involves in its progress such a train of unforeseen and unsupposed circumstances that no human wisdom can calculate the end. It has but one thing certain, and that is to increase taxes. THOMAS PAINE, *Prospects on the Rubicon* (1787).

76. War is the faro table of governments, and nations the dupes of the games. THOMAS PAINE, *The Rights of Man* (1791), 2.

77. Life and fame and wealth – all these must, I say, be defended by fighting. Death in battle is the most glorious for men. Who lives under the sway of his foe – it is he that is dead. *Panchatantra* (c. 5th c.), 1, tr. Franklin Edgerton.

78. Can anything be more ridiculous than that a man should have the right to kill me because he lives on the other side of the water, and because his ruler has a quarrel with mine, though I have none with him? PASCAL, *Pensées* (1670), 294, tr. W. F. Trotter.

79. The cause of some going to war, and of others avoiding it, is the same desire in both, attended with different views. PASCAL, *Pensées* (1670), 425, tr. W. F. Trotter.

80. The grim fact is that we prepare for war like precocious giants and for peace like retarded pygmies. LESTER PEARSON, news summaries, March 15, 1955.

81. Diplomats are just as essential to starting a war as Soldiers are for finishing it. You take Diplomacy out of war and the thing would fall flat in a week. WILL ROGERS, *The Autobiography of Will Rogers* (1949), 12.

82. I find war detestable but those who praise it without participating in it even more so. ROMAIN ROLLAND, *Inter arma Caritas, Journal de Genève*, Oct. 30, 1914.

83. I have seen children starving. I have seen the agony of mothers and wives. I hate war. FRANKLIN D. ROOSEVELT, speech, Chautauqua, N.Y., Aug. 14, 1936.

84. The motto of war is: "Let the strong survive; let the weak die." The motto of peace is: "Let the strong help the weak to survive." FRANKLIN D. ROOSEVELT, address before the Congress and Supreme Court of Brazil, Rio de Janeiro, Nov. 27, 1936.

85. When the whole world turns clown, and paints itself red with its own heart's blood instead of vermilion, it is something else than comic. JOHN RUSKIN, *The Crown of Wild Olive* (1866), 2.59.

86. People who are vigorous and brutal often find war enjoyable, provided that it is a victorious war and that there is not too much interference with rape and plunder. This is a great help in persuading people that wars are righteous. BERTRAND RUSSELL, "Ideas That Have Harmed Mankind," *Unpopular Essays* (1950).

87. It is the savor of bread broken with comrades that makes us accept the values of war. SAINT-EXUPÉRY, *Wind, Sand, and Stars* (1939), 9.6, tr. Lewis Galantière.

88. War is not an adventure. It is a disease. It is like typhus. SAINT-EXUPÉRY, *Flight to Arras* (1942), 8, tr. Lewis Galantière.

89. To call war the soil of courage and virtue is like calling debauchery the soil of love. GEORGE SANTAYANA, *The Life of Reason: Reason in Society* (1905–06), 3.

90. To delight in war is a merit in the soldier, a dangerous quality in the captain,

and a positive crime in the statesman. GEORGE SANTAYANA, *The Life of Reason: Reason in Society* (1905–06), 3.

91. Of war men ask the outcome, not the cause. SENECA, *Hercules Furens* (1st c.), 407, tr. Frank Justus Miller.

92. Every war is its own excuse. That's why they're all surrounded with ideals. That's why they're all crusades. KARL SHAPIRO, *The Bourgeois Poet* (1964), 1.6.

93. War is cruelty, and you cannot refine it. WILLIAM T. SHERMAN, *Memoirs* (1875), v. 1.

94. War. There is no solution for it. There is never a conqueror. The winner generates such hatred that he is ultimately defeated. MICHEL SIMON, quoted in *The New York Times*, March 17, 1968.

95. Let him who does not know what war is go to war. SPANISH PROVERB.

96. War, hunting, and love have a thousand pains for one pleasure. SPANISH PROVERB.

97. They make a desert and call it peace. TACITUS, *Agricola* (c. A.D. 98), 30.

98. What madness is this, inviting sable Death by warfare? / It always hovers close and comes unforeseen on silent steps. TIBULLUS, *Elegies* (1st c. B.C.), 1.10, tr. Hubert Creekmore.

99. The butter to be sacrificed because of the war always turns out to be the margarine of the poor. JAMES TOBIN, speech, Social Sciences Association, Washington, D.C., Dec. 27, 1967.

100. Vice foments war; it is virtue which actually fights. If there were no virtue, we would live in peace forever. VAUVENARGUES, *Reflections and Maxims* (1746), 225.

101. Men appear to prefer ruining one another's fortunes, and cutting each other's throats about a few paltry villages, to extending the grand means of human happiness. VOLTAIRE, "Roads," *Philosophical Dictionary* (1764).

102. It is said that God is always on the side of the heaviest battalions. VOLTAIRE, letter to M. le Riche, Feb. 6, 1770.

103. How many wars have been caused by fits of indigestion, and how many more dynasties have been upset by the love of woman than by the hate of man. CHARLES DUDLEY WARNER, "Eighteenth Week," *My Summer in a Garden* (1871).

104. Once we thought a few hundred corpses would be enough / then we saw thousands were still too few / and today we can't even count all the dead / Everywhere you look. PETER WEISS, *Marat / Sade* (1964), 1.8, tr. Geoffrey Skelton and Adrian Mitchell.

105. Nothing except a battle lost can be half so melancholy as a battle won. DUKE OF WELLINGTON, dispatch, 1815.

106. As long as war is regarded as wicked, it will always have its fascination. When it is looked upon as vulgar, it will cease to be popular. OSCAR WILDE, "The Critic as Artist," *Intentions* (1891).

## 1036. WAR, CIVIL
See also 1035. War

1. If a house be divided against itself, that house cannot stand. *Bible*, Mark 3:25.

2. In a civil war the firing line is invisible; it passes through the hearts of men. SAINT-EXUPÉRY, *Wind, Sand, and Stars* (1939), 9.1, tr. Lewis Galantière.

## 1037. WASHINGTON, D.C.

1. The more I observed Washington, the more frequently I visited it, and the more people I interviewed there, the more I understood how prophetic L'Enfant was when he laid it out as a city that goes around in circles. JOHN MASON BROWN, *Through These Men*, 1956.

2. Washington is a city of Southern efficiency and Northern charm. JOHN F. KENNEDY, quoted in William Manchester's *Portrait of a President* (1962).

3. New York has total depth in every area. Washington has only politics; after that, the second biggest thing is white marble. JOHN V. LINDSAY, *Vogue*, Aug. 1, 1963.

4. People only leave [Washington] by way of the box–ballot or coffin. CLAIBORNE PELL, *Vogue*, Aug. 1, 1963.

## 1038. WASTEFULNESS
See also 322. Extravagance

1. See a pin and let it lie, you'll want a pin before you die. FRENCH PROVERB.

2. Waste is not grandeur. WILLIAM MASON, *The English Garden* (1772–81), 2.

### 1039. WATER

See also 771. Rain; 818. Rivers; 847. Sea

1. Water, gentlemen, is the one substance from which the earth can conceal nothing. It sucks out its innermost secrets and brings them to our very lips. JEAN GIRAUDOUX, *The Madwoman of Chaillot* (1945), 1, adapted by Maurice Valency.

2. Water, thou hast no taste, no color, no odor; canst not be defined, art relished while ever mysterious. Not necessary to life, but rather life itself, thou fillest us with a gratification that exceeds the delight of the senses. SAINT-EXUPÉRY, *Wind, Sand, and Stars* (1939), 8, tr. Lewis Galantière.

### 1040. WEAKNESS

See also 339. Faults; 457. Impotence; 539. Limitations; 933. Strength; 973. Timidity; 1032. Vulnerability

1. The spirit indeed is willing, but the flesh is weak. *Bible*, Matthew 26:41.

2. Man's biological weakness is the condition of human culture. ERICH FROMM, *Escape from Freedom* (1941), 2.

3. The weakest and most timorous are the most revengeful and implacable. THOMAS FULLER, M.D., *Gnomologia* (1732), 4822.

4. He is a fool who tries to match his strength with the stronger. / He will lose his battle, and with the shame will be hurt also. HESIOD, *Works and Days* (8th c. B.C.), 210, tr. Richmond Lattimore.

5. We cannot win the weak by sharing our wealth with them. They feel our generosity as oppression. ERIC HOFFER, *The Ordeal of Change* (1964), 2.

6. It is to escape the responsibility for failure that the weak so eagerly throw themselves into grandiose undertakings. ERIC HOFFER, *The Ordeal of Change* (1964), 15.5.

7. Whenever the weak make an alliance with the strong, they are the strong's dependents. WALTER SAVAGE LANDOR, "Milton and Marvel," *Imaginary Conversations* (1824–53).

8. Often we are firm from weakness, and audacious from timidity. LA ROCHEFOUCAULD, *Maxims* (1665), tr. Kenneth Pratt.

9. To be weak is miserable, / Doing or suffering. MILTON, *Paradise Lost* (1667), 1.157.

10. There is nothing so imperious as feebleness which feels itself supported by force. NAPOLEON I, *Maxims* (1804–15).

11. I have often laughed at the weaklings who thought themselves good because they had no claws. NIETZSCHE, "On Those Who Are Sublime," *Thus Spoke Zarathustra* (1883–92), 2, tr. Walter Kaufmann.

12. The sick are the greatest danger for the healthy; it is not from the strongest that harm comes to the strong, but from the weakest. NIETZSCHE, *The Genealogy of Morals* (1887), 3.14, tr. Horace B. Samuel.

13. The weak can be terrible / because they try furiously to appear strong. RABINDRANATH TAGORE, *Fireflies* (1928).

14. Oh, you weak, beautiful people who give up with such grace. What you need is someone to take hold of you — gently, with love, and hand your life back to you. TENNESSEE WILLIAMS, *Cat on a Hot Tin Roof* (1955), 3.

### 1041. WEALTH

See also 8. Acquisition; 401. Greed; 554. Luxury; 596. Money; 712. Poverty; 740. Property; 744. Prosperity

1. Riches attract the attention, consideration, and congratulations of mankind. JOHN ADAMS, *Discourses on Davila* (1789), 2.

2. Let there be / wealth without tears; enough for / the wise man who will ask no further. AESCHYLUS, *Agamemnon* (458 B.C.), tr. Richmond Lattimore.

3. Wealth unused might as well not exist. AESOP, "The Miser and His Gold," *Fables* (6th c. B.C.?), tr. Joseph Jacobs.

4. Be not penny-wise: riches have wings, and sometimes they fly away of themselves; sometimes they must be set flying to bring in more. FRANCIS BACON, "Of Riches," *Essays* (1625).

5. Wealth maketh many friends. *Bible*, Proverbs 19:4.

6. Riches certainly make themselves wings; they fly away as an eagle toward heaven. *Bible*, Proverbs 23:5.

7. It is easier for a camel to go through the eye of a needle, than for a rich man to enter

the kingdom of God. *Bible*, Matthew 19:24.

8. If a man who is born to a fortune cannot make himself easier and freer than those who are not, he gains nothing. JAMES BOSWELL, *London Journal*, Feb. 25, 1763.

9. In big houses in which things are done properly, there is always the religious element. The diurnal cycle is observed with more feeling when there are servants to do the work. ELIZABETH BOWEN, *The Death of the Heart* (1938), 1.6.

10. He is rich who hath enough to be charitable. SIR THOMAS BROWNE, *Religio Medici* (1642), 2.

11. The rich are more envied by those who have a little, than by those who have nothing. CHARLES CALEB COLTON, *Lacon* (1825), 1.181.

12. It is only when the rich are sick that they fully feel the impotence of wealth. CHARLES CALEB COLTON, *Lacon* (1825), 1.538.

13. To be poor without murmuring is difficult. To be rich without being proud is easy. CONFUCIUS, *Analects* (6th c. B.C.), 14.11, tr. James Legge.

14. All heiresses are beautiful. JOHN DRYDEN, *King Arthur* (1691), 1.1.

15. 'Tis as hard f'r a rich man to enther th' kingdom iv Hiven as it is f'r a poor man to get out iv Purgatory. FINLEY PETER DUNNE, "Casual Observations," *Mr. Dooley's Philosophy* (1900).

16. It's aisier to ampytate a millyonaire's leg thin his bank roll, an' manny a man goes hopefully to th' op'ratin' table who's afraid he'll bleed to death if he pays th' bill. FINLEY PETER DUNNE, "Going to See the Doctor," *Mr. Dooley On Making a Will* (1919).

17. There is a time when a man distinguishes the idea of felicity from the idea of wealth; it is the beginning of wisdom. EMERSON, *Journals*, 1830.

18. Without the rich heart, wealth is an ugly beggar. EMERSON, "Manners," *Essays: Second Series* (1844).

19. It requires a great deal of boldness and a great deal of caution to make a great fortune, and when you have got it, it requires ten times as much wit to keep it. EMERSON, "Power," *The Conduct of Life* (1860).

20. Poor men seek meat for their stomach, rich men stomach for their meat. ENGLISH PROVERB.

21. Riches serve a wise man but command a fool. ENGLISH PROVERB.

22. Natural wealth is limited and easily obtained; the wealth defined by vain fancies is always beyond reach. EPICURUS, "Principal Doctrines" (3rd c. B.C.), 15, in *Letters, Principal Doctrines, and Vatican Sayings*, tr. Russel M. Geer.

23. If some appalling disaster befalls, there's / Always a way for the rich. EURIPIDES, *Andromache* (c. 426 B.C.), tr. John F. Nims.

24. That glittering hope is immemorial / And beckons many men / To their undoing. EURIPIDES, *Iphigenia in Tauris* (c. 414–12 B.C.), tr. Witter Bynner.

25. Wealth stays with us a little moment if at all; / only our characters are steadfast, not our gold. EURIPIDES, *Electra* (413 B.C.), tr. Emily Townsend Vermeule.

26. He is not fit for riches who is afraid to use them. THOMAS FULLER, M.D., *Gnomologia* (1732), 1934.

27. Not possession, but use, is the only riches. THOMAS FULLER, M.D., *Gnomologia* (1732), 3681.

28. Rich men feel misfortunes that fly over poor men's heads. THOMAS FULLER, M.D., *Gnomologia* (1732), 4035.

29. Riches rather enlarge than satisfy appetites. THOMAS FULLER, M.D., *Gnomologia* (1732), 4048.

30. The ass loaded with gold still eats thistles. GERMAN PROVERB.

31. All else – valor, a good name, glory, everything in heaven and earth – is secondary to the charm of riches. HORACE, *Satires* (35–30 B.C.), 2.3.

32. Let me smile with the wise, and feed with the rich. SAMUEL JOHNSON, quoted in Boswell's *Life of Samuel Johnson*, Oct. 6, 1769.

33. It is better to live rich than to die rich. SAMUEL JOHNSON, quoted in Boswell's *Life of Samuel Johnson*, April 17, 1778.

34. Majestic mighty Wealth is the holiest of our gods. JUVENAL, *Satires* (c. 100), 1.112, tr. Hubert Creekmore.

35. Wealth is the means, and people are the ends. All our material riches will avail us little if we do not use them to expand the opportunities of our people. JOHN F. KENNEDY, State of the Union Message, Jan. 11, 1962.

36. It is in vain to ridicule a rich fool, for

the laughers will be on his side. LA BRUYÈRE, *Characters* (1688), 6.10, tr. Henri Van Laun.

37. Wherever there is excessive wealth, there is also in the train of it excessive poverty; as, where the sun is brightest, the shade is deepest. WALTER SAVAGE LANDOR, "Aristoteles and Callisthenes," *Imaginary Conversations* (1824–53).

38. The most valuable of all human possessions, next to a superior and disdainful air, is the reputation of being well to do. Nothing else so neatly eases one's way through life, especially in democratic countries. H. L. MENCKEN, *Prejudices: Third Series* (1922), 18.

39. Let none admire that riches grow in hell; that soil may best / Deserve the precious bane. MILTON, *Paradise Lost* (1667), 1.690.

40. Riches do not consist in the possession of treasures, but in the use made of them. NAPOLEON I, *Maxims* (1804–15).

41. Every man who is worth thirty millions and is not wedded to them, is dangerous to the government. NAPOLEON I, *Maxims* (1804–15).

42. Get wealth when you have it not; guard what you have got; increase what you have guarded; and bestow on worthy persons what you have increased. *Panchatantra* (c. 5th c.), 1, tr. Franklin Edgerton.

43. The larger a man's roof, the more snow it collects. PERSIAN PROVERB.

44. The makers of fortunes have a second love of money as a creation of their own, resembling the affection of authors for their own poems, or of parents for their children, besides that natural love of it for the sake of use and profit. PLATO, *The Republic* (4th c. B.C.), 1, tr. Benjamin Jowett.

45. Wealth is well known to be a great comforter. PLATO, *The Republic* (4th c. B.C.), 1, tr. Benjamin Jowett.

46. We may see the small value God has for riches by the people he gives them to. ALEXANDER POPE, *Thoughts on Various Subjects* (1727).

47. Get place and wealth, if possible, with grace; / If not, by any means get wealth and place. ALEXANDER POPE, *Epilogue to the Satires* (1738), 1.1.103.

48. There are men who gain from their wealth only the fear of losing it. ANTOINE RIVAROLI, *L'Esprit de Rivarol* (1808).

49. True wealth is not a static thing. It is a living thing made out of the disposition of men to create and to distribute the good things of life with rising standards of living. FRANKLIN D. ROOSEVELT, speech, Washington, D.C., Oct. 24, 1934.

50. It is an unfortunate human failing that a full pocketbook often groans more loudly than an empty stomach. FRANKLIN D. ROOSEVELT, speech, Brooklyn, N.Y., Nov. 1, 1940.

51. As long as there are rich people in the world, they will be desirous of distinguishing themselves from the poor. ROUSSEAU, *A Discourse on Political Economy* (1758), tr. G. D. H. Cole.

52. Riches are intended for the comfort of life, and not life for the purpose of hoarding riches. SA'DI, *Gulistan* (1258), 8.1, tr. James Ross.

53. The rich man is everywhere expected and at home. SA'DI (12th–13th c.), quoted in Emerson's "Wealth," *The Conduct of Life* (1860).

54. When the rich wage war it's the poor who die. JEAN-PAUL SARTRE, *The Devil and the Good Lord* (1951), 1, first tableau.

55. A great fortune is a great slavery. SENECA, *Ad Polybium de Consolatione* (1st c.).

56. Many a man has found the acquisition of wealth only a change, not an end of miseries. SENECA, *Letters to Lucilius* (1st c.), 17.11, tr. E. Phillips Barker.

57. O, what a world of vile ill-favoured faults / Looks handsome in three hundred pounds a year! SHAKESPEARE, *The Merry Wives of Windsor* (1597), 3.4.32.

58. In an ugly and unhappy world the richest man can purchase nothing but ugliness and unhappiness. GEORGE BERNARD SHAW, "Maxims for Revolutionists," *Man and Superman* (1903).

59. Every man is rich or poor according to the degree in which he can afford to enjoy the necessaries, conveniences, and amusements of human life. ADAM SMITH, *The Wealth of Nations* (1776), 1.5.

60. Solvency is entirely a matter of temperament and not of income. LOGAN PEARSALL SMITH, *Afterthoughts* (1931), 1.

61. Wealth breeds satiety, satiety outrage. SOLON (7th–6th c. B.C.), quoted in Diogenes Laertius' *Lives and Opinions of Eminent Philosophers* (3rd c. A.D.), tr. R. D. Hicks.

62. Just as war is waged with the blood of others, fortunes are made with other people's money. ANDRÉ SUARÈS, *Voici l'homme* (1906).

63. Superfluous wealth can buy superfluities only. THOREAU, "Conclusion," *Walden* (1854).

64. Men living in democratic times have many passions, but most of their passions either end in the love of riches, or proceed from it. ALEXIS DE TOCQUEVILLE, *Democracy in America* (1835–39), 2.3.17.

65. I wish to become rich, so that I can instruct the people and glorify honest poverty a little, like those kind-hearted, fat, benevolent people do. MARK TWAIN, in the San Francisco *Alta California*, July 21, 1867.

66. In order to stand well in the eyes of the community, it is necessary to come up to a certain, somewhat indefinite, conventional standard of wealth. THORSTEIN VEBLEN, *The Theory of the Leisure Class* (1899), 2.

67. Pearls around the neck—stones upon the heart. *Yiddish Proverbs* (1949), ed. Hanan J. Ayalti.

## 1042. WEAPONS

**See also 226. Defense; 633. Nuclear Power; 949. Survival; 1035. War**

1. [In war] the latest refinements of science are linked with the cruelties of the Stone Age. SIR WINSTON CHURCHILL, speech, London, March 26, 1942.

2. We can do without butter, but, despite all our love of peace, not without arms. One cannot shoot with butter but with guns. PAUL JOSEPH GOEBBELS, speech, Berlin, Jan. 17, 1936.

3. You may be obliged to wage war, but not to use poisoned arrows. BALTASAR GRACIÁN, *The Art of Worldly Wisdom* (1647), 164, tr. Joseph Jacobs.

4. Only technology has permitted us to put a city to the sword without quite realizing what we are doing. JOSEPH WOOD KRUTCH, "If You Don't Mind My Saying So," *The American Scholar* (Summer 1967).

5. He has made his weapons his gods. / When his weapons win he is defeated himself. RABINDRANATH TAGORE, *Stray Birds* (1916), 45.

6. A weapon is an enemy even to its owner. TURKISH PROVERB.

## 1043. WEATHER

**See also 138. Climate; 771. Rain; 848. Seasons; 904. Snow; 943. Sun; 1052. Wind**

1. A cloudy day, or a little sunshine, have as great an influence on many constitutions as the most real blessings or misfortunes. JOSEPH ADDISON, *The Spectator* (1711–12), 162.

2. There it is, fog, atmospheric moisture still uncertain in destination, not quite weather and not altogether mood, yet partaking of both. HAL BORLAND, "Fog—September 27," *Sundial of the Seasons* (1964).

3. For the man sound in body and serene of mind there is no such thing as bad weather; every sky has its beauty, and storms which whip the blood do but make it pulse more vigorously. GEORGE GISSING, "Winter," *The Private Papers of Henry Ryecroft* (1903).

4. We shall never be content until each man makes his own weather and keeps it to himself. JEROME K. JEROME, "On the Weather," *The Idle Thoughts of an Idle Fellow* (1889).

5. Weather in towns is like a skylark in a counting-house—out of place and in the way. JEROME K. JEROME, "On the Weather," *The Idle Thoughts of an Idle Fellow* (1889).

6. Who knows whither the clouds have fled? / In the unscarred heaven they leave no wake; / And the eyes forget the tears they have shed, / The heart forgets its sorrow and ache. JAMES RUSSELL LOWELL, prelude to part 1, "The Vision of Sir Launfal" (1848).

7. The fog comes / on little cat feet. / It sits looking / over the harbor and city / on silent haunches / and then moves on. CARL SANDBURG, "Fog" (1916).

8. There is nothing more universally commended than a fine day; the reason is, that people can commend it without envy. WILLIAM SHENSTONE, *Essays on Men and Manners* (1764).

9. The mist, like love, plays upon the heart of the hills and brings out surprises of

beauty. RABINDRANATH TAGORE, *Stray Birds* (1916), 73.

10. Extreme cold when it first arrives seems to generate cheerfulness and sociability. For a few hours all life's dubious problems are dropped in favor of the clear and congenial task of keeping alive. E. B. WHITE, "Cold Weather," *One Man's Meat* (1944).

## 1044. WEDDINGS

See also 560. Marriage

1. If it were not for the presents, an elopement would be preferable. GEORGE ADE, "The General Manager of the Love Affair," *Forty Modern Fables* (1901).

2. Bride, n. A woman with a fine prospect of happiness behind her. AMBROSE BIERCE, *The Devil's Dictionary* (1881–1911).

3. Girls usually have a papier mâché face on their wedding day. COLETTE, "Wedding Day," *Earthly Paradise* (1966), 2, ed. Robert Phelps.

4. I guess walking slow getting married is because it gives you time to maybe change your mind. VIRGINIA CARY HUDSON, *O Ye Jigs & Juleps!* (1962).

5. Holy is the wife; revered the mother; galliptious is the summer girl—but the bride is the certified check among the wedding presents that the gods send in when man is married to mortality. O. HENRY, "Sisters of the Golden Circle," *The Four Million* (1906).

## 1045. WEEPING

See also 523. Laughter; 524. Laughter and Tears; 603. Mourning; 911. Sorrow; 939. Suffering; 1004. Unhappiness

1. Weeping may endure for a night, but joy cometh in the morning. *Bible*, Psalms 30:5.

2. There's no seeing one's way through tears. ENGLISH PROVERB.

3. Waste not fresh tears over old griefs. EURIPIDES, *Alexander* (c. 415 B.C.), 44, tr. M. H. Morgan.

4. They who are sad find somehow sweetness in tears. EURIPIDES, *The Trojan Women* (415 B.C.), tr. Richmond Lattimore.

5. Nothing dries sooner than a tear. GERMAN PROVERB.

6. Who would recognize the unhappy if grief had no language? PUBLILIUS SYRUS, *Moral Sayings* (1st c. B.C.), 791, tr. Darius Lyman.

7. Cries of despair, misery, sobbing grief are a kind of wealth. SAINT-EXUPÉRY, *Wind, Sand, and Stars* (1939), 8, tr. Lewis Galantière.

8. Let tears flow of their own accord: their flowing is not inconsistent with inward peace and harmony. SENECA, *Letters to Lucilius* (1st c.), 99.20, tr. E. Phillips Barker.

9. To weep is to make less the depth of grief. SHAKESPEARE, *3 Henry VI* (1590–91), 2.1.85.

10. How much better is it to weep at joy than to joy at weeping! SHAKESPEARE, *Much Ado About Nothing* (1598–99), 1.1.28.

## WEST

See 271. East and West

## 1046. WHIM

See also 459. Impulsiveness; 921. Spontaneity

1. The pleasure of gratifying whim is very great. It is known only by those who are whimsical. JAMES BOSWELL, *London Journal*, Dec. 12, 1762.

2. Where I cannot satisfy my reason, I love to humour my fancy. SIR THOMAS BROWNE, *Religio Medici* (1642), 1.

3. The only difference between a caprice and a lifelong passion is that the caprice lasts a little longer. OSCAR WILDE, *The Picture of Dorian Gray* (1891), 2.

## 1047. WHITES

See also 83. Blacks; 769. Racial Prejudice

1. This world is white no longer, and it will never be white again. JAMES BALDWIN, "Stranger in the Village" (1953), *Notes of a Native Son* (1955).

2. There can be no whiter whiteness than this one: / An insurance man's shirt on its morning run. GWENDOLYN E. BROOKS, "Mrs. Small," *The Bean Eaters* (1960).

3. White people who insist on their su-

periority because of the color of the skin they were born with—can there be so empty and false a superiority as this? Who is injured the most by that foolish assumption, the colored or the white? In his soul it is the white man. PEARL S. BUCK, *What America Means to Me* (1943), 1.

4. God is white. JEAN GENET, *The Blacks* (1958), tr. Bernard Frechtman.

5. There are many humorous things in the world, among them the white man's notion that he is less savage than the other savages. MARK TWAIN, "The White Man's Notion," *Following the Equator* (1897).

## 1048. WICKEDNESS

**See also 188. Corruption; 305. Evil; 893. Sin; 964. Temptation; 1023. Vice; 1063. Wrongdoing**

1. It takes a certain courage and a certain greatness even to be truly base. JEAN ANOUILH, *Ardèle* (1948), 1, tr. Lucienne Hill.

2. There is a method in man's wickedness,— / It grows up by degrees. BEAUMONT and FLETCHER, *A King and No King* (1619), 5.4.

3. There is no peace, saith the Lord, unto the wicked. *Bible*, Isaiah 48:22.

4. The wickedness of the world is so great you have to run your legs off to avoid having them stolen from under you. BERTOLT BRECHT, *The Threepenny Opera* (1928), 1.3, tr. Desmond Vesey and Eric Bentley.

5. As for an authentic villain, the real thing, the absolute, the artist, one rarely meets him even once in a lifetime. The ordinary bad hat is always in part a decent fellow. COLETTE, "The South of France," *Earthly Paradise* (1966), 4, ed. Robert Phelps.

6. A belief in a supernatural source of evil is not necessary; men alone are quite capable of every wickedness. JOSEPH CONRAD, *Under Western Eyes* (1911), 2.4.

7. Wicked is not much worse than indiscreet. JOHN DONNE, *An Anatomy of the World; The First Anniversary* (1612).

8. It is an esoteric doctrine of society, that a little wickedness is good to make muscle; as if conscience were not good for hands and legs. EMERSON, "Power," *The Conduct of Life* (1860).

9. The unrighteous are never really fortunate. EURIPIDES, *Helen* (412 B.C.), tr. Richmond Lattimore.

10. Wickedness is always easier than virtue, for it takes the short cut to everything. SAMUEL JOHNSON, quoted in Boswell's *Journal of a Tour to the Hebrides with Samuel Johnson*, Sept. 17, 1773.

11. No man ever became extremely wicked all at once. JUVENAL, *Satires* (c. 100), 2.83.

12. One man's wickedness may easily become all men's curse. PUBLILIUS SYRUS, *Moral Sayings* (1st c. B.C.), 463, tr. Darius Lyman.

13. Man is not born wicked; he becomes so, as he becomes sick. VOLTAIRE, "Wicked," *Philosophical Dictionary* (1764).

14. Wickedness is a myth invented by good people to account for the curious attractiveness of others. OSCAR WILDE, "Phrases and Philosophies for the Use of the Young" (1891).

## 1049. WILL

**See also 122. Choice; 765. Purpose; 801. Resolution; 860. Self-determination; 1050. Willingness**

1. The will is never free—it is always attached to an object, a purpose. It is simply the engine in the car—it can't steer. JOYCE CARY, interview, *Writers at Work: First Series* (1958).

2. Be there a will, and wisdom finds a way. GEORGE CRABBE, *The Birth of Flattery* (1823).

3. Will cannot be quenched against its will. DANTE, "Paradiso," 4, *The Divine Comedy* (c. 1300–21), tr. Lawrence Grant White.

4. Will and Wisdom are both mighty leaders. Our times worship Will. CLARENCE DAY, "Humpty-Dumpty and Adam," *The Crow's Nest* (1921).

5. The good or ill of man lies within his own will. EPICTETUS, *Discourses* (2nd c.), 1.25, tr. Thomas W. Higginson.

6. A fat kitchen, a lean will. BENJAMIN FRANKLIN, *Poor Richard's Almanack* (1732–57).

7. I wish it, I command it. Let my will take the place of a reason. JUVENAL, *Satires* (c. 100), 6.223.

8. Man's will creates the things that paralyze his brain and brutalize his heart. MAX LERNER, "The Human Heart and the Human Will," *Actions and Passions* (1949).

9. Will springs from the two elements of moral sense and self-interest. ABRAHAM LINCOLN, speech, Springfield, Ill., June 26, 1857.

10. Our wills and fates do so contrary run / That our devices still are overthrown; / Our thoughts are ours, their ends none of our own. SHAKESPEARE, *Hamlet* (1600), 3.2.221.

11. If we cannot do what we will, we must will what we can. *Yiddish Proverbs* (1949), ed. Hanan J. Ayalti.

## 1050. WILLINGNESS

**See also 765. Purpose; 1015. Unwillingness; 1049. Will**

1. When a man's / Willing and eager, god joins in. AESCHYLUS, *The Persians* (472 B.C.), tr. Seth G. Bernardete.

2. All lay load on the willing horse. ENGLISH PROVERB.

3. He that hath love in his breast hath spurs in his sides. ENGLISH PROVERB.

4. A willing mind makes a light foot. THOMAS FULLER, M.D., *Gnomologia* (1732), 467.

5. Nothing is impossible to a willing heart. JOHN HEYWOOD, *Proverbs* (1546), 1.4.

6. Nothing is troublesome that we do willingly. THOMAS JEFFERSON, letter to Thomas Jefferson Smith, Feb. 21, 1825.

## 1051. WILLS AND INHERITANCE

**See also 1041. Wealth**

1. Before I die, I shall leave a will, because if you want something done, sentimentality is effective. JOHN CAGE, "45′ for a Speaker," *Silence* (1961).

2. Posthumous charities are the very essence of selfishness when bequeathed by those who, when alive, would part with nothing. CHARLES CALEB COLTON, *Lacon* (1825), 1.341.

3. When it comes to divide an estate, the politest men quarrel. EMERSON, *Journals*, 1863.

4. They that marry ancient people, merely in expectation to bury them, hang themselves in hope that one will come and cut the halter. THOMAS FULLER, D.D., "Of Marriage," *The Holy State and the Profane State* (1642).

5. He who inherits a penny is expected to spend a dollar. GERMAN PROVERB.

6. The art of will-making chiefly consists in baffling the importunity of expectation. WILLIAM HAZLITT, "On Will-Making," *Table Talk* (1821–22).

7. There is nothing earthly that lasts so well, on the whole, as money. A man's learning dies with him; even his virtues fade out of remembrance; but the dividends on the stocks he bequeaths to his children live and keep his memory green. OLIVER WENDELL HOLMES, SR., *The Professor at the Breakfast Table* (1860), 6.

8. A son can bear with composure the death of his father, but the loss of his inheritance might drive him to despair. MACHIAVELLI, *The Prince* (1517), 17.

9. I've often had to notice that a man'll sometimes do the foolishist thing or the meanest thing in his hull life after he's dead. EDWARD NOYES WESTCOTT, *David Harum* (1898), 35.

## 1052. WIND

**See also 848. Seasons**

1. The wind goeth toward the south, and turneth about unto the north; it whirleth about continually, and the wind returneth again according to his circuits. *Bible*, Ecclesiastes 1:6.

2. The Westerly Wind asserting his sway from the south-west quarter is often like a monarch gone mad, driving forth with wild imprecations the most faithful of his courtiers to shipwreck, disaster, and death. JOSEPH CONRAD, *The Mirror of the Sea* (1906), 26.

3. The East Wind, an interloper in the dominions of Westerly Weather, is an impassive-faced tyrant with a sharp poniard held behind his back for a treacherous stab. JOSEPH CONRAD, *The Mirror of the Sea* (1906), 28.

4. The substance of the winds is too thin for human eyes, their written language is

too difficult for human minds, and their spoken language mostly too faint for the ears. JOHN MUIR, *A Thousand-Mile Walk to the Gulf* (1916), 8.

5. Who has seen the wind? / Neither you nor I: / But when the trees bow down their heads / The wind is passing by. CHRISTINA ROSSETTI, "Sing-Song" (1872).

6. The wind in the grain is the caress to the spouse, it is the hand of peace stroking her hair. SAINT-EXUPÉRY, *Flight to Arras* (1942), 22, tr. Lewis Galantière.

7. O wild West Wind, thou breath of Autumn's being, / Thou, from whose unseen presence the leaves dead / Are driven, like ghosts from an enchanter fleeing, / Yellow, and black, and pale, and hectic red, / Pestilence-stricken multitudes. SHELLEY, "Ode to the West Wind" (1819), 1.

8. O wind, a-blowing all day long, / O wind, that sings so loud a song! ROBERT LOUIS STEVENSON, "The Wind" (1885).

### WINE
**See 226. Drinking**

### WINNERS
**See 15. Advantage; 938. Success**

### WINTER
**See 848. Seasons**

### 1053. WISDOM
**See also 491. Intelligence; 520. Knowledge; 734. Profundity; 749. Prudence; 1000. Understanding**

1. Wisdom / comes alone through suffering. AESCHYLUS, *Agamemnon* (458 B.C.), tr. Richmond Lattimore.

2. The tongue of a wise man lieth behind his heart. ALI IBN-ABI-TALIB, *Sentences* (7th c.), 95, tr. Simon Ockley.

3. The height of heaven, the breadth of the earth, the abyss, and wisdom—who can search them out? *Apocrypha*, Ecclesiasticus 1:3.

4. Knowing what is right does not make a sagacious man. ARISTOTLE, *Nicomachean Ethics* (4th c. B.C.), 7.10, tr. J. A. K. Thomson.

5. To wisdom belongs the intellectual apprehension of eternal things; to knowledge, the rational knowledge of temporal things. ST. AUGUSTINE, *On the Trinity* (5th c.), 12.

6. The price of wisdom is above rubies. *Bible*, Job 28:18.

7. The fear of the Lord is the beginning of wisdom. *Bible*, Psalms 111:10 and Proverbs 9:10.

8. Wisdom is the principal thing; therefore get wisdom; and with all thy getting get understanding. *Bible*, Proverbs 4:7.

9. It may be a mistake to mix different wines, but old and new wisdom mix admirably. BERTOLT BRECHT, prologue, *The Caucasian Chalk Circle* (1944–45), tr. Eric Bentley and Maja Apelman.

10. The heart of the wise man lies quiet like limpid water. CAMEROONIAN PROVERB.

11. The function of wisdom is to discriminate between good and evil. CICERO, *De Officiis* (44 B.C.), 3.17.71.

12. There is this difference between happiness and wisdom: he that thinks himself the happiest man, really is so; but he that thinks himself the wisest, is generally the greatest fool. CHARLES CALEB COLTON, *Lacon* (1825), 1.326.

13. It is better to have wisdom without learning, than to have learning without wisdom; just as it is better to be rich without being the possessor of a mine, than to be the possessor of a mine without being rich. CHARLES CALEB COLTON, *Lacon* (1825), 2.26.

14. If one is too lazy to think, too vain to do a thing badly, too cowardly to admit it, one will never attain wisdom. CYRIL CONNOLLY, *The Unquiet Grave* (1945), 1.

15. Knowledge is proud that he has learned so much; / Wisdom is humble that he knows no more. WILLIAM COWPER, "Winter Walk at Noon," *The Task* (1785), 95.

16. Life is a festival only to the wise. EMERSON, "Heroism," *Essays: First Series* (1841).

17. Wisdom has its root in goodness, and not goodness its root in wisdom. EMERSON, *Journals*, 1857.

18. Wise men are not wise at all times. EMERSON, "Wealth," *The Conduct of Life* (1860).

19. He is not wise that is not wise for himself. ENGLISH PROVERB.

20. He that's a wise man by day is no fool by night. ENGLISH PROVERB.

21. Fortune seldom troubles the wise man. Reason has controlled his greatest and most important affairs, controls them throughout his life, and will continue to control them. EPICURUS, "Principal Doctrines" (3rd c. B.C.), 16, in *Letters, Principal Doctrines, and Vatican Sayings*, tr. Russel M. Geer.

22. Those who are held / Wise among men and who search the reasons of things / Are those who bring the most sorrow on themselves. EURIPIDES, *Medea* (431 B.C.), tr. Rex Warner.

23. The heart of a fool is in his mouth, but the mouth of a wise man is in his heart. BENJAMIN FRANKLIN, *Poor Richard's Almanack* (1732–57).

24. He is no wise man that cannot play the fool upon occasion. THOMAS FULLER, M.D., *Gnomologia* (1732), 1929.

25. Wisdom rises upon the ruins of folly. THOMAS FULLER, M.D., *Gnomologia* (1732), 5770.

26. The sage has one advantage: he is immortal. If this is not his century, many others will be. BALTASAR GRACIÁN, *The Art of Worldly Wisdom* (1647), 20, tr. Joseph Jacobs.

27. The wise are always impatient, for he that increases knowledge increases impatience of folly. BALTASAR GRACIÁN, *The Art of Worldly Wisdom* (1647), 159, tr. Joseph Jacobs.

28. Knowledge is the parent of love; wisdom, love itself. JULIUS CHARLES HARE and AUGUSTUS WILLIAM HARE, *Guesses at Truth* (1827).

29. The seat of knowledge is in the head; of wisdom, in the heart. We are sure to judge wrong if we do not feel right. WILLIAM HAZLITT, *Characteristics* (1823), 380.

30. The road to wisdom? — Well, it's plain / and simple to express: / Err / and err / and err again / but less / and less / and less. PIET HEIN, "The Road to Wisdom," *Grooks* (1966).

31. Men who love wisdom should acquaint themselves with a great many particulars. HERACLITUS, *Fragments* (c. 500 B.C.), 3, tr. Philip Wheelwright.

32. Knowledge can be communicated, but not wisdom. One can find it, live it, be fortified by it, do wonders through it, but one cannot communicate and teach it. HERMANN HESSE, "Govinda," *Siddhartha* (1923), tr. Hilda Rosner.

33. Such is the nature of men, that howsoever they may acknowledge many others to be more witty, or more eloquent, or more learned, yet they will hardly believe there be many so wise as themselves. THOMAS HOBBES, *Leviathan* (1651), 1.13.

34. It is the province of knowledge to speak and it is the privilege of wisdom to listen. OLIVER WENDELL HOLMES, SR., *The Poet at the Breakfast Table* (1872), 10.

35. How prone to doubt, how cautious are the wise! HOMER, *Odyssey* (9th c. B.C.), 13.375, tr. Alexander Pope.

36. Wisdom is an affair of values, and of value judgments. It is intelligent conduct of human affairs. SIDNEY HOOK, "Does Philosophy Have a Future?" *Saturday Review*, Nov. 11, 1967.

37. Wisdom consists not so much in knowing what to do in the ultimate as in knowing what to do next. HERBERT HOOVER, *Reader's Digest*, July 1958.

38. Wisdom, I know, is social. She seeks her fellows, but Beauty is jealous, and illy bears the presence of a rival. THOMAS JEFFERSON, letter to Abigail Adams, Sept. 25, 1785.

39. Common sense suits itself to the ways of the world. Wisdom tries to conform to the ways of Heaven. JOSEPH JOUBERT, *Pensées* (1842), 8.6, tr. Katharine Lyttelton.

40. If it be true that a man is rich who wants nothing, a wise man is a very rich man. LA BRUYÈRE, *Characters* (1688), 6.49, tr. Henri Van Laun.

41. They who are jealous of power are so from a consciousness of strength; they who are jealous of wisdom are so from a consciousness of wanting [lacking] it. WALTER SAVAGE LANDOR, "Aristoteles and Callisthenes," *Imaginary Conversations* (1824–53).

42. It is very foolish to wish to be exclusively wise. LA ROCHEFOUCAULD, *Maxims* (1665), tr. Kenneth Pratt.

43. It is easier to be wise on behalf of others than to be so for ourselves. LA ROCHEFOUCAULD, *Maxims* (1665), tr. Kenneth Pratt.

44. In the world we live in, one fool makes many fools, but one sage only a few sages. GEORG CHRISTOPH LICHTENBERG,

*Aphorisms* (1764–99), tr. F. H. Mautner and H. Hatfield.

45. It requires wisdom to understand wisdom; the music is nothing if the audience is deaf. WALTER LIPPMANN, *A Preface to Morals* (1929), 3.15.2.

46. The true sage is not he who sees, but he who, seeing the furthest, has the deepest love for mankind. MAURICE MAETERLINCK, *Wisdom and Destiny* (1898), 13, tr. Alfred Sutro.

47. Wisdom requires no form; her beauty must vary, as varies the beauty of flame. She is no motionless goddess, for ever couched on her throne. MAURICE MAETERLINCK, *Wisdom and Destiny* (1898), 24, tr. Alfred Sutro.

48. Wisdom enough to leech us of our ill / Is daily spun; but there exists no loom / To weave it into fabric. EDNA ST. VINCENT MILLAY, *Sonnets* (1941), 137.

49. Wisdom is a solid and entire building, of which every piece keeps its place and bears its mark. MONTAIGNE, "Of experience," *Essays* (1580–88), tr. Charles Cotton and W. C. Hazlitt.

50. The growth of wisdom may be gauged exactly by the diminution of ill-temper. NIETZSCHE, *The Wanderer and His Shadow* (1880), 348, tr. Paul V. Cohn.

51. A wise man, to accomplish his end, may even carry his foe on his shoulder. *Panchatantra* (c. 5th c.), 3, tr. Franklin Edgerton.

52. Wisdom is always an overmatch for strength. PHAEDRUS, *Fables* (1st c.), 1.13.13, tr. Henry Thomas Riley.

53. Not by years but by disposition is wisdom acquired. PLAUTUS, *The Three-Penny Day* (c. 194 B.C.), 2.2.48, tr. Henry Thomas Riley.

54. Wisdom had rather be buffeted than not listened to. PUBLILIUS SYRUS, *Moral Sayings* (1st c. B.C.), 152, tr. Darius Lyman.

55. He bids fair to grow wise who has discovered that he is not so. PUBLILIUS SYRUS, *Moral Sayings* (1st c. B.C.), 598, tr. Darius Lyman.

56. Nine-tenths of wisdom is being wise in time. THEODORE ROOSEVELT, speech, Lincoln, Neb., June 14, 1917.

57. Youth is the time to study wisdom; old age is the time to practice it. ROUSSEAU, *Reveries of a Solitary Walker* (1782), 3.

58. A short wise man is preferable to a tall blockhead. SA'DI, *Gulistan* (1258), 1.3, tr. James Ross.

59. The fool doth think he is wise, but the wise man knows himself to be a fool. SHAKESPEARE, *As You Like It* (1599–1600), 5.1.34.

60. To be wise and love / Exceeds man's might: that dwells with gods above. SHAKESPEARE, *Troilus and Cressida* (1601–02), 3.2.163.

61. Wisdom brings back the basic beliefs of eighteen. KARL SHAPIRO, *The Bourgeois Poet* (1964), 1.30.

62. How terrible is wisdom when / it brings no profit to the man that's wise! SOPHOCLES, *Oedipus the King* (c. 430 B.C.), tr. David Grene.

63. Sciences may be learned by rote, but wisdom not. LAURENCE STERNE, *Tristram Shandy* (1759–67), 5.32.

64. Knowledge comes, but wisdom lingers, and he bears a laden breast, / Full of sad experience, moving toward the stillness of his rest. ALFRED, LORD TENNYSON, "Locksley Hall" (1842).

65. Not by constraint or severity shall you have access to true wisdom, but by abandonment, and childlike mirthfulness. If you would know aught, be gay before it. THOREAU, *Journal*, June 23, 1840.

66. It is a characteristic of wisdom not to do desperate things. THOREAU, "Economy," *Walden* (1854).

67. Of the demonstrably wise there are but two; those who commit suicide, and those who keep their reasoning faculties atrophied with drink. MARK TWAIN, *Notebook* (1935).

68. The well-bred contradict other people. The wise contradict themselves. OSCAR WILDE, "Phrases and Philosophies for the Use of the Young" (1891).

69. To be free is not necessarily to be wise. Wisdom comes with counsel, with the frank and free conference of untrammeled men united in the common interest. WOODROW WILSON, acceptance speech, Democratic National Convention, July 7, 1912.

70. Wisdom is ofttimes nearer when we stoop / Than when we soar. WILLIAM WORDSWORTH, *The Excursion* (1814), 3.

71. It takes a wise man to recognize a wise man. XENOPHANES (6th–5th c. B.C.), quoted in Diogenes Laertius' *Lives and*

*Opinions of Eminent Philosophers* (3rd c. A.D.), tr. R. D. Hicks.

72. A wise man hears one word and understands two. *Yiddish Proverbs* (1949), ed. Hanan J. Ayalti.

## WISHES

See 236. Desires

## 1054. WIT

See also 137. Cleverness; 144. Comedy; 434. Humor; 523. Laughter; 762. Puns; 837. Sarcasm; 838. Satire

1. The more wit we have, the less satisfied we are with it. JEAN LE ROND D'ALEMBERT, "Essai sur les gens de lettres," *Oeuvres philosophique* (1805), v. 3.

2. The mere wit is only a human bauble. He is to life what bells are to horses—not expected to draw the load, but only to jingle while the horses draw. HENRY WARD BEECHER, *Proverbs from Plymouth Pulpit* (1887).

3. Wit is a treacherous dart. It is perhaps the only weapon with which it is possible to stab oneself in one's own back. GEOFFREY BOCCA, *The Woman Who Would Be Queen* (1954).

4. Humorous persons have pleasant mouths turned up at the corners. . . . But the mouth of a merely witty man is hard and sour until the moment of its discharge. CHARLES S. BROOKS, "On the Difference Between Wit and Humor," in *I Was Just Thinking* (1959), ed. Elinor Parker.

5. A man must have a good share of wit himself to endure a great share in another. LORD CHESTERFIELD, *Letters to His Godson*, Dec. 18, 1765.

6. Wit is so shining a quality that everybody admires it; most people aim at it, all people fear it, and few love it unless in themselves. LORD CHESTERFIELD, *Letters to His Godson*, Dec. 18, 1765.

7. Wit makes its own welcome and levels all distinctions. EMERSON, "The Comic," *Letters and Social Aims* (1876).

8. Men never think their fortune too great, nor their wit too little. THOMAS FULLER, M.D., *Gnomologia* (1732), 3400.

9. A delicate wit is a corruption which a nation takes a long time to acquire. It is only worn-out nations that possess it. EDMOND and JULES DE GONCOURT, *Journal*, May 2, 1858, tr. Robert Baldick.

10. Many get the repute of being witty, but thereby lose the credit of being sensible. Jest has its little hour, seriousness should have all the rest. BALTASAR GRACIÁN, *The Art of Worldly Wisdom* (1647), 75, tr. Joseph Jacobs.

11. The wit we wish we had spoils the wit we have. JEAN BAPTISTE LOUIS GRESSET, *Le Méchant* (1745), 4.7.

12. Wit is the salt of conversation, not the food. WILLIAM HAZLITT, "On Wit and Humour," *Lectures on the English Comic Writers* (1819).

13. Wit's an unruly engine, wildly striking / Sometimes a friend, sometimes the engineer. GEORGE HERBERT, "The Church Porch," 41, *The Temple* (1633).

14. The wit knows that his place is at the tail of a procession. OLIVER WENDELL HOLMES, SR., *The Autocrat of the Breakfast Table* (1858), 3.

15. Wit and coin are always doubted with a threadbare coat. WASHINGTON IRVING, "The Club of Queer Fellows," *Tales of a Traveller* (1824).

16. Impertinent wits are a kind of insect which are in everybody's way and plentiful in all countries. LA BRUYÈRE, *Characters* (1688), 5.3, tr. Henri Van Laun.

17. True wit, to every man, is that which falls on another. WALTER SAVAGE LANDOR, "Alexander and the Priest of Hammon," *Imaginary Conversations* (1824–53).

18. What is perfectly true is imperfectly witty. WALTER SAVAGE LANDOR, "Diogenes and Plato," *Imaginary Conversations* (1824–53).

19. The greatest fault of a penetrating wit is to go beyond the mark. LA ROCHEFOUCAULD, *Maxims* (1665).

20. A wit would often be embarrassed without the company of fools. LA ROCHEFOUCAULD, *Maxims* (1665), tr. Kenneth Pratt.

21. In the midst of the fountain of wit there arises something bitter, which stings in the very flowers. LUCRETIUS, *On the Nature of Things* (1st c. B.C.), 4.1133.

22. I have ever thought so superstitiously of wit, that I fear I have committed idolatry against wisdom. JOHN LYLY, *Euphues: The Anatomy of Wit* (1579).

23. Wit has a deadly aim and it is possible to prick a large pretense with a small pin. MARYA MANNES, "Controverse," *But Will It Sell?* (1955–64).

24. Impropriety is the soul of wit. W. SOMERSET MAUGHAM, *The Moon and Sixpence* (1919), 4.

25. It is not enough to possess wit. One must have enough of it to avoid having too much. ANDRÉ MAUROIS, *De la conversation* (1921).

26. Wit is the epitaph of an emotion. NIETZSCHE, *Miscellaneous Maxims and Opinions* (1879), 202, tr. Paul V. Cohn.

27. Wit has truth in it; wisecracking is simply calisthenics with words. DOROTHY PARKER, interview, *Writers at Work: First Series* (1958).

28. True wit is Nature to advantage dressed, / What oft was thought, but ne'er so well expressed. ALEXANDER POPE, *An Essay on Criticism* (1711), 2.97.

29. The greatest advantage I know of being thought a wit by the world is, that it gives one the greater freedom of playing the fool. ALEXANDER POPE, *Thoughts on Various Subjects* (1727).

30. Wit is as infinite as love, and a deal more lasting in its qualities. AGNES REPPLIER, "A Plea for Humor," *Points of View* (1891).

31. To be over much facetious is the accomplishment of courtiers and blemish of the wise. SA'DI, *Gulistan* (1258), 1.15, tr. James Ross.

32. The quality of wit inspires more admiration than confidence. GEORGE SANTAYANA, "Wit," *The Sense of Beauty* (1896).

33. Brevity is the soul of wit. SHAKESPEARE, *Hamlet* (1600), 2.2.90.

34. There is hardly that person to be found who is not more concerned for the reputation of wit and sense, than honesty and virtue. RICHARD STEELE, *The Spectator* (1711–12), 6.

35. Wit is the sudden marriage of ideas which before their union were not perceived to have any relation. MARK TWAIN, *Notebook* (1935).

36. He who cannot shine by thought, seeks to bring himself into notice by a witticism. VOLTAIRE, "Wit, Spirit, Intellect," *Philosophical Dictionary* (1764).

## 1055. WOMEN

**See also 119. Charm; 189. Cosmetics; 265. Dress; 335. Fashion; 562. Masculinity and Femininity; 576. Men and Women; 587. Mirrors; 678. Perfume**

1. Women have, commonly, a very positive moral sense; that which they will is right; that which they reject is wrong; and their will, in most cases, ends by settling the moral. HENRY ADAMS, *The Education of Henry Adams* (1907), 6.

2. Forgetting is woman's first and greatest art. RICHARD ALDINGTON, *The Colonel's Daughter* (1931).

3. Women wish to be loved without a why or a wherefore; not because they are pretty, or good, or well-bred, or graceful, or intelligent, but because they are themselves. HENRI FRÉDÉRIC AMIEL, *Journal*, March 17, 1868.

4. These impossible women! How they do get around us! / The poet was right: can't live with them, or without them. ARISTOPHANES, *Lysistrata* (411 B.C.), tr. Dudley Fitts.

5. With women, the heart argues, not the mind. MATTHEW ARNOLD, *Merope* (1858).

6. A lady's imagination is very rapid; it jumps from admiration to love, from love to matrimony in a moment. JANE AUSTEN, *Pride and Prejudice* (1813), 6.

7. A woman can be anything that the man who loves her would have her be. J. M. BARRIE, *Tommy and Grizel* (1900).

8. There is no other purgatory but a woman. BEAUMONT and FLETCHER, *The Scornful Lady* (c. 1614), 3.1.

9. When a man makes her laugh, a woman feels protected. UGO BETTI, *Goat Island* (1946), 1.3, ed. Gino Rizzo.

10. As a jewel of gold in a swine's snout, so is a fair woman which is without discretion. *Bible*, Proverbs 11:22.

11. Here's to woman! Would that we could fall into her arms without falling into her hands. AMBROSE BIERCE, quoted in C. H. Grattan's *Bitter Bierce* (1929).

12. Women have no wilderness in them, / They are provident instead, / Content in the tight hot cell of their hearts / To eat dusty bread. LOUISE BOGAN, "Women," *Collected Poems* (1923–53).

13. Intimacies between women often go backwards, beginning in revelations and ending up in small talk without loss of es-

teem. ELIZABETH BOWEN, *The Death of the Heart* (1938), 2.1.

14. The rivalry of women is visited upon their children to their third and fourth generation. GELETT BURGESS, *The Maxims of Methuselah* (1907), 15.

15. As the cat lapses into savagery by night, and barbarously explores the dark, so primal and titanic is a woman with the love-madness. GELETT BURGESS, "The Gentleman's Code," *The Romance of the Commonplace* (1916).

16. Alas! the love of Women! it is known / To be a lovely and a fearful thing. BYRON, *Don Juan* (1819–24), 2.199.

17. Now what I love in women is, they won't / Or can't do otherwise than lie, but do it / So well, the very truth seems falsehood to it. BYRON, *Don Juan* (1819–24), 11.36.

18. What a woman says to an eager lover, / write it on running water, write it on air. CATULLUS, *Poems* (1st c. B.C.), 70, tr. Gilbert Highet.

19. That's the nature of women, not to love when we love them, and to love when we love them not. CERVANTES, *Don Quixote* (1605–15), 1.3.6, tr. Peter Motteux and John Ozell.

20. Old, that's an affront no woman can well bear. CERVANTES, *Don Quixote* (1605–15), 2.3.31, tr. Peter Motteux and John Ozell.

21. Women who are either indisputably beautiful, or indisputably ugly, are best flattered upon the score of their understandings. LORD CHESTERFIELD, *Letters to His Son*, Sept. 5, 1748.

22. Variability is one of the virtues of a woman. It avoids the crude requirement of polygamy. So long as you have one good wife you are sure to have a spiritual harem. G. K. CHESTERTON, "The Glory of Grey," *Alarms and Discursions* (1910).

23. Women singly do a good deal of harm. Women in bulk are chastening. FRANK MOORE COLBY, "Some of the Difficulties of Frollicking," *The Colby Essays* (1926), v. 1.

24. Women generally consider consequences in love, seldom in resentment. CHARLES CALEB COLTON, *Lacon* (1825), 1.517.

25. Most females will forgive a liberty rather than a slight. CHARLES CALEB COLTON, *Lacon* (1825), 1.557.

26. Women, like flames, have a destroying power, / Ne'er to be quenched till they themselves devour. WILLIAM CONGREVE, *The Double-Dealer* (1694), 4.5.

27. Women are like tricks by sleight of hand, / Which, to admire, we should not understand. WILLIAM CONGREVE, *Love for Love* (1695), 4.3.

28. There is no fury like a woman searching for a new lover. CYRIL CONNOLLY, *The Unquiet Grave* (1945), 1.

29. A woman's desire for revenge outlasts all her other emotions. CYRIL CONNOLLY, *The Unquiet Grave* (1945), 1.

30. A woman never sees what we do for her, she only sees what we don't do. GEORGES COURTELINE, *La Paix chez soi* (1903), 4.

31. Women are better than they are reputed to be: they don't mock the tears men shed unless they themselves are responsible for them. GEORGES COURTELINE, *La Philosophie de G. Courteline* (1917).

32. What is woman?—only one of Nature's agreeable blunders. HANNAH COWLEY, *Who's the Dupe?* (1779), 2.

33. Women are never stronger than when they arm themselves with their weaknesses. MARQUISE DU DEFFAND, *Letters to Voltaire* (1759–75).

34. Women never use their intelligence—except when they need to prop up their intuition. JACQUES DEVAL, news summaries, May 10, 1954.

35. The entire being of a woman is a secret which should be kept. ISAK DINESEN, "Of Hidden Thoughts and of Heaven," *Last Tales* (1957).

36. Women are most fascinating between the age of thirty-five and forty after they have won a few races and know how to pace themselves. Since few women ever pass forty, maximum fascination can continue indefinitely. CHRISTIAN DIOR, *Collier's*, June 10, 1955.

37. Women are like the arts, forced unto none, / Open to all searchers, unprized, if unknown. JOHN DONNE, Elegy 3, "Change" (1635).

38. What does a woman want iv rights whin she has priv'leges? FINLEY PETER DUNNE, "Rights and Privileges of Women," *Observations by Mr. Dooley* (1902).

39. There are only three things to be done with a woman. You can love her, suffer for her, or turn her into literature. LAWRENCE DURRELL, *Justine* (1957), 1.

40. The happiest women, like the happiest nations, have no history. GEORGE ELIOT, *The Mill on the Floss* (1860), 6.3.

41. A woman's hopes are woven of sunbeams; a shadow annihilates them. GEORGE ELIOT, *Felix Holt* (1866), 1.

42. Half the sorrows of women would be averted if they could repress the speech they know to be useless—nay, the speech they have resolved not to utter. GEORGE ELIOT, *Felix Holt* (1866), 2.

43. A woman's strength is the unresistible might of weakness. EMERSON, *Journals*, 1836.

44. A woman should always challenge our respect, and never move our compassion. EMERSON, *Journals*, 1836.

45. A beautiful woman is a practical poet. EMERSON, "Beauty," *The Conduct of Life* (1860).

46. All are good maids, but whence come the bad wives? ENGLISH PROVERB.

47. What else goes wrong for a woman—except her marriage? EURIPIDES, *Andromache* (c. 426 B.C.), tr. John F. Nims.

48. Love's all in all to women. EURIPIDES, *Andromache* (c. 426 B.C.), tr. John F. Nims.

49. Neither earth nor ocean / produces a creature as savage and monstrous / as woman. EURIPIDES, *Hecuba* (c. 425 B.C.), tr. William Arrowsmith.

50. There seems to be some pleasure / for women in sick talk of one another. EURIPIDES, *The Phoenician Women* (c. 411–409 B.C.), tr. Elizabeth Wyckoff.

51. Woman is woman's natural ally. EURIPIDES, *Alope* (5th c. B.C.), 109, tr. M. H. Morgan.

52. How a little love and good company improves a woman! GEORGE FARQUHAR, *The Beaux' Strategem* (1707), 4.1.

53. To most women art is a form of scandal. F. SCOTT FITZGERALD, "The Note-Books," *The Crack-Up* (1945).

54. Ugly women may be naturally quite as capricious as pretty ones; but as they are never petted and spoiled, and as no allowances are made for them, they soon find themselves obliged either to suppress their whims or to hide them. ANATOLE FRANCE, *The Crime of Sylvestre Bonnard* (1881), 1, tr. Lafcadio Hearn.

55. Women are equal because they are not different any more. ERICH FROMM, *The Art of Loving* (1956), 2.

56. A woman scoffs at evidence. Show her the sun, tell her it is daylight, at once she will close her eyes and say to you, "No, it is night." ÉMILE GABORIAU, *Monsieur Lecoq* (1869), 10.

57. Women never confess; even when they seemingly resign themselves to such a course, they are never sincere. ÉMILE GABORIAU, *Monsieur Lecoq* (1869), 10.

58. In all the woes that curse our race / There is a lady in the case. W. S. GILBERT, *Fallen Fairies* (1909), 2.

59. A woman is a creature who has discovered her own nature. JEAN GIRAUDOUX, *Judith* (1931), 2, tr. John K. Savacool.

60. I have been a woman for fifty years, and I've never yet been able to discover precisely what it is I am. JEAN GIRAUDOUX, *Tiger at the Gates* (1935), 1, tr. Christopher Fry.

61. A pretty woman has the right to be ignorant of everything, provided she knows when to keep still. JEAN GIRAUDOUX, *Ondine* (1939), 2, adapted by Maurice Valency.

62. Women have no sense of the abstract—a woman admiring the sky is a woman caressing the sky. In a woman's mind beauty is something she needs to touch. JEAN GIRAUDOUX, *The Apollo of Bellac* (1942), adapted by Maurice Valency.

63. Only the woman of the world is a woman; the rest are females. EDMOND and JULES DE GONCOURT, *Journal*, Oct. 13, 1855, tr. Robert Baldick.

64. A woman prefers a man without money to money without a man. GREEK PROVERB.

65. Women never reason, and therefore they are (comparatively) seldom wrong. WILLIAM HAZLITT, *Characteristics* (1823).

66. A woman's vanity is interested in making the object of her choice the God of her idolatry. WILLIAM HAZLITT, "On the Spirit of Obligations," *The Plain Speaker* (1826).

67. If men knew how women pass the time when they are alone, they'd never marry. O. HENRY, "Memoirs of a Yellow Dog," *The Four Million* (1906).

68. What a woman wants is what you're out of. She wants more of a thing when it's scarce. O. HENRY, "Cupid à la Carte," *Heart of the West* (1907).

69. Nothing agreeth worse / Than a lady's

heart and a beggar's purse. JOHN HEYWOOD, *Proverbs* (1546), 1.10.

70. A woman never forgets her sex. She would rather talk with a man than an angel, any day. OLIVER WENDELL HOLMES, SR., *The Poet at the Breakfast Table* (1872), 4.

71. When a man holds his tongue it does not signify much. But when a woman dispenses with the office of that mighty member, when she sheathes her natural weapon at a trying moment, it means that she trusts to still more formidable enginery; to tears it may be. OLIVER WENDELL HOLMES, SR., *The Poet at the Breakfast Table* (1872), 11.

72. Oh woman, woman! when to ill thy mind / Is bent, all hell contains no fouler fiend. HOMER, *Odyssey* (9th C. B.C.), 11.531, tr. Alexander Pope.

73. A woman is as old as she looks before breakfast. EDGAR WATSON HOWE, *Country Town Sayings* (1911).

74. A woman does not spend all her time in buying things; she spends part of it in taking them back. EDGAR WATSON HOWE, *Country Town Sayings* (1911).

75. At first a woman doesn't want anything but a husband, but just as soon as she gets one, she wants everything else in the world. EDGAR WATSON HOWE, *Country Town Sayings* (1911).

76. A woman will doubt everything you say except it be compliments to herself. ELBERT HUBBARD, *The Note Book* (1927).

77. One of the magnanimities of woman is to yield. VICTOR HUGO, "Saint Denis," *Les Misérables* (1862), 8.1, tr. Charles E. Wilbour.

78. A woman's whole life is a history of the affections. WASHINGTON IRVING, "The Broken Heart," *The Sketch Book of Geoffrey Crayon, Gent.* (1819–20).

79. There is in every true woman's heart a spark of heavenly fire, which lies dormant in the broad daylight of prosperity, but which kindles up and beams and blazes in the dark hour of adversity. WASHINGTON IRVING, "The Wife," *The Sketch Book of Geoffrey Crayon, Gent.* (1819–20).

80. When female minds are embittered by age or solitude, their malignity is generally exerted in a rigorous and spiteful superintendence of domestic trifles. SAMUEL JOHNSON, *The Rambler* (1750–52), 113.

81. A woman, the more curious [careful] she is about her face, is commonly the more careless about her house. BEN JONSON, "Random Thoughts," *Timber* (1640).

82. There's no effrontery like that of a woman caught in the act; her very guilt inspires her with wrath and insolence. JUVENAL, *Satires* (c. 100), 6.284.

83. Never praise a sister to a sister, in the hope of your compliments reaching the proper ears. RUDYARD KIPLING, "The False Dawn," *Plain Tales from the Hills* (1888).

84. The female of the species is more deadly than the male. RUDYARD KIPLING, "The Female of the Species" (1911).

85. If a handsome woman allows that another woman is beautiful, we may safely conclude she excels her. LA BRUYÈRE, *Characters* (1688), 12.8, tr. Henri Van Laun.

86. God made the rose out of what was left of woman at the creation. The great difference is, we feel the rose's thorns when we gather it; and the other's when we have had it some time. WALTER SAVAGE LANDOR, "Mahomet and Sergius," *Imaginary Conversations* (1824–53).

87. In their first passion women love their lovers, in all the others they love love. LA ROCHEFOUCAULD, *Maxims* (1665).

88. One must choose between loving women and knowing them. Attributed to NINON DE LENCLOS (1620–1705).

89. The pleasure of talking is the inextinguishable passion of a woman, coeval with the act of breathing. ALAIN-RENÉ LESAGE, *Histoire de Gil Blas de Santillane* (1715–35), 7.7.

90. Woman's normal occupations in general run counter to creative life, or contemplative life, or saintly life. ANNE MORROW LINDBERGH, "Channelled Whelk," *Gift from the Sea* (1955).

91. Women, like princes, find few real friends. GEORGE LYTTLETON, "Advice to a Lady" (1733).

92. [Women] dwell always in the Palace of Unpalatable Truth and never by any chance is there a magic talisman to save them from their destiny. Speech is their ultimate need. We [men] exist for them only in so far as we can be described. WILLIAM MC FEE, "Knights and Turcopoliers," *Harbours of Memory* (1921).

93. Women like other women fine. The more feminine she is, the more comfortable a woman feels with her own sex. It is only the occasional and therefore noticeable ad-

venturess who refuses to make friends with us. PHYLLIS MC GINLEY, "Some of My Best Friends . . . ," *The Province of the Heart* (1959).

94. the females of all species are most / dangerous when they appear to retreat. DON MARQUIS, "a farewell," *Archy Does His Part* (1935).

95. Women are poets by just being women. JOSÉ MARTÍ, *Granos de oro: pensamientos seleccionados en las Obras de José Martí* (1942).

96. A woman will always sacrifice herself if you give her the opportunity. It is her favourite form of self-indulgence. W. SOMERSET MAUGHAM, *The Circle* (1921), 3.

97. We don't love a woman for what she says, we like what she says because we love her. ANDRÉ MAUROIS, *De la conversation* (1921).

98. There are many wild beasts on land and in the sea, but the beastliest of all is woman. MENANDER, *The Changeling* (4th–3rd c. B.C .), 488.

99. Women have simple tastes. They can get pleasure out of the conversation of children in arms and men in love. H. L. MENCKEN, "Sententiae," *A Book of Burlesques* (1920).

100. When women kiss it always reminds one of prizefighters shaking hands. H. L. MENCKEN, "Sententiae," *A Book of Burlesques* (1920).

101. Woman's reason is in the milk of her breasts. GEORGE MEREDITH, *The Ordeal of Richard Feveral* (1859), 43.

102. There is no such thing as an old woman. Any woman of any age, if she loves, if she is good, gives a man a sense of the infinite. JULES MICHELET, *L'Amour* (1859), v. 4.

103. To inspire love is a woman's greatest ambition, believe me. It's the one thing women care about and there's no woman so proud that she doesn't rejoice at heart in her conquests. MOLIÈRE, *The Sicilian* (1666), 1, tr. John Wood.

104. It costs an unreasonable woman no more to pass over one reason than another; they cherish themselves most where they are most wrong. MONTAIGNE, "Of the affections of fathers to their children," *Essays* (1580–88), tr. Charles Cotton and W. C. Hazlitt.

105. American Women: How they mortify the flesh in order to make it appetizing! Their beauty is a vast industry, their enduring allure a discipline which nuns or athletes might find excessive. MALCOLM MUGGERIDGE, "Women of America," *The Most of Malcolm Muggeridge* (1966).

106. Women would rather be right than reasonable. OGDEN NASH, "Frailty, Thy Name Is a Misnomer," *Marriage Lines* (1964).

107. Let man fear woman when she loves: then she makes any sacrifice, and everything else seems without value to her. NIETZSCHE, "On Little Old and Young Women," *Thus Spoke Zarathustra* (1883–92), 1, tr. Walter Kaufmann.

108. Women themselves always still have in the background of all personal vanity an impersonal contempt for "woman." NIETZSCHE, *Beyond Good and Evil* (1886), 86, tr. Walter Kaufmann.

109. Where neither love nor hatred is in the game, a woman's game is mediocre. NIETZSCHE, *Beyond Good and Evil* (1886), 115, tr. Walter Kaufmann.

110. Woman was God's second mistake. NIETZSCHE, *The Antichrist* (1888), 48, tr. Anthony M. Ludovici.

111. Every woman thinks herself attractive; even the plainest is satisfied with the charms she deems that she possesses. OVID, *The Art of Love* (c. A.D. 8), 1, tr. J. Lewis May.

112. Many women long for what eludes them, and like not what is offered them. OVID, *The Art of Love* (c. A.D. 8), 1, tr. J. Lewis May.

113. Women's words are as light as the doomed leaves whirling in autumn, / Easily swept by the wind, easily drowned by the wave. OVID, *The Loves* (c. A.D. 8), 2.16, tr. Rolfe Humphries.

114. What one beholds of a woman is the least part of her. OVID, *Love's Cure* (c. A.D. 8), tr. J. Lewis May.

115. Kings, women, and creeping vines as a rule embrace whatever is beside them. *Panchatantra* (c. 5th c.), 1, tr. Franklin Edgerton.

116. Most good women are hidden treasures who are only safe because nobody looks for them. DOROTHY PARKER, quoted in obituary, *The New York Times*, June 8, 1967.

117. Women are one and all a set of vul-

tures. PETRONIUS, *Satyricon* (1st c.), 42.

118. Regret is a woman's natural food—she thrives upon it. SIR ARTHUR WING PINERO, *Sweet Lavender* (1888), 3.

119. Women are like dreams—they are never the way you would like to have them. LUIGI PIRANDELLO, *Each in His Own Way* (1924), 1, tr. Arthur Livingston.

120. Woman is certainly the daughter of Delay personified! PLAUTUS, *The Braggart Warrior* (c. 205 B.C.), 4.7.1292, tr. Paul Nixon.

121. There's no such thing, you know, as picking out the best woman: it's only a question of comparative badness, brother. PLAUTUS, *The Pot of Gold* (c. 200 B.C.), 2.1.139, tr. Paul Nixon.

122. It is a high distinction for a homely woman to be loved for her character rather than for beauty. PLUTARCH, "Marriage Counsel," *Moralia* (c. A.D. 100), tr. Moses Hadas.

123. Women, as they are like riddles in being unintelligible, so generally resemble them in this, that they please us no longer once we know them. ALEXANDER POPE, *Thoughts on Various Subjects* (1727).

124. Women are quite unlike men. Women have higher voices, longer hair, smaller waistlines, daintier feet and prettier hands. They also invariably have the upper hand. STEPHEN POTTER, advertisement of *Ladies' Home Journal*, Sept. 17, 1957.

125. Woman loves or hates: she knows no middle course. PUBLILIUS SYRUS, *Moral Sayings* (1st c. B.C.), 66, tr. Darius Lyman.

126. She wavers, she hesitates: in a word, she is a woman. RACINE, *Athaliah* (1691), 3.3.

127. Women see through each other, but they rarely look into themselves. THEODOR REIK, *Of Love and Lust* (1957), 4.48.

128. [Woman] is quick to revere genius, but in her secret soul she seldom loves it. AGNES REPPLIER, "English Love-Songs," *Points of View* (1891).

129. The whole thing about the women is, they lust to be misunderstood. WILL ROGERS, *The Autobiography of Will Rogers* (1949), 18.

130. Women and elephants never forget an injury. SAKI, "Reginald on Besetting Sins," *Reginald* (1904).

131. Kindness in women, not their beauteous looks, / Shall win my love. SHAKESPEARE, *The Taming of the Shrew* (1593–94), 4.2.41.

132. A woman moved is like a fountain troubled, / Muddy, ill-seeming, thick, bereft of beauty. SHAKESPEARE, *The Taming of the Shrew* (1593–94), 5.2.142.

133. Do you not know I am a woman? When I think, I must speak. SHAKESPEARE, *As You Like It* (1599–1600), 3.2.263.

134. Women are as roses, whose fair flower, / Being once displayed, doth fall that very hour. SHAKESPEARE, *Twelfth Night* (1599–1600), 2.4.39.

135. A woman is a dish for the gods, if the devil dress her not. SHAKESPEARE, *Antony and Cleopatra* (1606–07), 5.2.275.

136. What will not woman, gentle woman dare, / When strong affection stirs her spirit up? ROBERT SOUTHEY, *Madoc in Wales* (1805), 2.2.

137. The nightingale will run out of songs before a woman runs out of conversation. SPANISH PROVERB.

138. Woman and calendars are good only for a year. SPANISH PROVERB.

139. No woman can be handsome by the force of features alone, any more than she can be witty only by the help of speech. RICHARD STEELE, *The Spectator* (1711–12), 33.

140. Women are always eagerly on the lookout for any emotion. STENDHAL, *On Love* (1822), 7, tr. H. B. V., under direction of C. K. Scott-Moncrieff.

141. Women prefer poverty with love to luxury without it. Haggadah, *Palestinian Talmud* (4th c.).

142. The woman is so hard / Upon the woman. ALFRED, LORD TENNYSON, "The Princess; A Medley" (1851), 6.

143. I know the disposition of women: when you will, they won't; when you won't, they set their hearts upon you of their own inclination. TERENCE, *The Eunuch* (161 B.C.), 4.7.42, tr. Henry Thomas Riley.

144. Most women have small waists the world throughout, / But their desires are thousand miles about. CYRIL TOURNEUR, *The Revenger's Tragedy* (1607), 5.

145. A thoroughly beautiful woman and a thoroughly homely woman are creations which I love to gaze upon, and which I cannot tire of gazing upon, for each is perfect in her own line. MARK TWAIN, *Autobiography* (1924), v. 1, ed. A. B. Paine.

146. A woman springs a sudden reproach upon you which provokes a hot retort—and then she will presently ask you to apologize. MARK TWAIN, *Notebook* (1935).

147. Womankind / Is ever a fickle and a changeful thing. VERGIL, *Aeneid* (30–19 B.C.), 4.569, tr. T. H. Delabere-May.

148. Woman is perpetual revolution, and is that element in the world which continually destroys and re-creates. CHARLES DUDLEY WARNER, "Ninth Study," *Backlog Studies* (1873).

149. Women are a decorative sex. They never have anything to say, but they say it charmingly. OSCAR WILDE, *The Picture of Dorian Gray* (1891), 4.

150. The only way to behave to a woman is to make love to her, if she is pretty, and to someone else if she is plain. OSCAR WILDE, *The Importance of Being Earnest* (1895), 1.

151. No woman should ever be quite accurate about her age. It looks so calculating. OSCAR WILDE, *The Importance of Being Earnest* (1895), 3.

152. A witch and a bitch always dress up for each other, because otherwise the witch would upstage the bitch, or the bitch would upstage the witch, and the result would be havoc. TENNESSEE WILLIAMS, *The Milk Train Doesn't Stop Here Anymore* (1963), 3.

153. All women are not Helen . . . but have Helen in their hearts. WILLIAM CARLOS WILLIAMS, "Asphodel, That Greeny Flower," *Pictures from Brueghel* (1962), 1.

154. If woman had no existence save in the fiction written by men, one would imagine her a person of the utmost importance; very various; heroic and mean; splendid and sordid; infinitely beautiful and hideous in the extreme; as great as a man, some think even greater. VIRGINIA WOOLF, *A Room of One's Own* (1929), 3.

## 1056. WONDER

See also 948. Surprise

1. Wonder is the basis of worship. THOMAS CARLYLE, *Sartor Resartus* (1833–34), 1.10.

2. Men love to wonder, and that is the seed of our science. EMERSON, "Works and Days," *Society and Solitude* (1870).

3. To be surprised, to wonder, is to begin to understand. JOSÉ ORTEGA Y GASSET, *The Revolt of the Masses* (1930), 1.

## 1057. WORDS

See also 91. Books and Reading; 132. Clarity; 227. Definition; 242. Dictionaries; 396. Grammar; 521. Language; 541. Literalness; 569. Meaning; 916. Speaking; 1062. Writing and Writers

1. Words may be deeds. AESOP, "The Trumpeter Taken Prisoner," *Fables* (6th c. B.C.?), tr. Joseph Jacobs.

2. All words are pegs to hang ideas on. HENRY WARD BEECHER, *Proverbs from Plymouth Pulpit* (1887).

3. Thought itself needs words. It runs on them like a long wire. And if it loses the habit of words, little by little it becomes shapeless, somber. UGO BETTI, *Goat Island* (1946), 1.4, ed. Gino Rizzo.

4. It is extremely natural for us to desire to see such our thoughts put into the dress of words, without which indeed we can scarce have a clear and distinct idea of them our selves. EUSTACE BUDGELL in *The Spectator* (1711–12), 379.

5. Words are like money; there is nothing so useless, unless when in actual use. SAMUEL BUTLER (d. 1902), "On the Making of Music, Pictures and Books," *Note-Books* (1912).

6. A word carries far—very far—deals destruction through time as the bullets go flying through space. JOSEPH CONRAD, *Lord Jim* (1900), 15.

7. Words, as is well known, are the great foes of reality. JOSEPH CONRAD, prologue to Part 1, *Under Western Eyes* (1911).

8. A word is dead / When it is said, / Some say. / I say it just / Begins to live / That day. EMILY DICKINSON, poem (1872?).

9. It's strange that words are so inadequate. / Yet, like the asthmatic struggling for breath, / So the lover must struggle for words. T. S. ELIOT, *The Elder Statesman* (1958), 3.

10. You can stroke people with words. F. SCOTT FITZGERALD, "The Note-Books," *The Crack-Up* (1945).

11. If a people have no word for something, either it does not matter to them or it matters too much to talk about. EDGAR Z. FRIEDENBERG, "Adolescence," *The Vanishing Adolescent* (1959).

12. Articulate words are a harsh clamor and dissonance. When man arrives at his highest perfection, he will again be dumb! NATHANIEL HAWTHORNE, *American Note-Books*, April 1841.

13. Words are really a mask. They rarely express the true meaning; in fact they tend to hide it. HERMANN HESSE, quoted in Miguel Serrano's *C. G. Jung and Hermann Hesse* (1966), tr. Frank MacShane.

14. Words are wise men's counters, they do but reckon by them; but they are the money of fools. THOMAS HOBBES, *Leviathan* (1651), 1.4.

15. Action can give us the feeling of being useful, but only words can give us a sense of weight and purpose. ERIC HOFFER, *The Passionate State of Mind* (1954), 98.

16. We must think things not words, or at least we must constantly translate our words into the facts for which they stand, if we are to keep the real and the true. OLIVER WENDELL HOLMES, JR., address, New York State Bar Association, Jan. 17, 1889.

17. Words form the thread on which we string our experiences. ALDOUS HUXLEY, *The Olive Tree* (1937).

18. Words have users, but as well, users have words. And it is the users that establish the world's realities. LE ROI JONES, "Expressive Language," *Home* (1966).

19. Words, like glass, obscure when they do not aid vision. JOSEPH JOUBERT, *Pensées* (1842), 21.15, tr. Katharine Lyttelton.

20. Any euphemism ceases to be euphemistic after a time and the true meaning begins to show through. It's a losing game, but we keep on trying. JOSEPH WOOD KRUTCH, title essay, 1, *If You Don't Mind My Saying So* (1964).

21. I hate false words, and seek with care, difficulty, and moroseness, those that fit the thing. WALTER SAVAGE LANDOR, "Bishop Burnet and Humphrey Hardcastle," *Imaginary Conversations* (1824–53).

22. Words, in their primary or immediate signification, stand for nothing but the ideas in the mind of him who uses them. JOHN LOCKE, *An Essay Concerning Human Understanding* (1690), 3.2.2.

23. We should have a great many fewer disputes in the world if words were taken for what they are, the signs of our ideas only, and not for things themselves. JOHN LOCKE, *An Essay Concerning Human Understanding* (1690), 3.10.

24. How strangely do we diminish a thing as soon as we try to express it in words. MAURICE MAETERLINCK, "Mystic Morality," *The Treasure of the Humble* (1896), tr. Alfred Sutro.

25. Buffaloes are held by cords, man by his words. MALAY PROVERB.

26. Words have weight, sound and appearance; it is only by considering these that you can write a sentence that is good to look at and good to listen to. W. SOMERSET MAUGHAM, *The Summing Up* (1938), 13.

27. It's when the thing itself is missing that you have to supply the word. HENRY DE MONTHERLANT, *Queen After Death* (1942), 2.1.

28. Those things for which we find words, are things we have already overcome. NIETZSCHE, "Skirmishes in a War with the Age," 26, *Twilight of the Idols* (1888), tr. Anthony M. Ludovici.

29. Meanings receive their dignity from words instead of giving it to them. PASCAL, *Pensées* (1670), 50, tr. W. F. Trotter.

30. Everything's been said, no doubt. If words hadn't changed meaning, and meaning, words. JEAN PAULHAN, *Clef de la poésie* (1944).

31. A word is not the same with one writer as with another. One tears it from his guts. The other pulls it out of his overcoat pocket. CHARLES PÉGUY, "The Honest People," *Basic Verities* (1943), tr. Ann and Julian Green.

32. Isn't everyone consoled when faced with a trouble or fact he doesn't understand, by a word, some simple word, which tells us nothing and yet calms us? LUIGI PIRANDELLO, *Six Characters in Search of an Author* (1921), 1, tr. Edward Storer.

33. All our life is crushed by the weight of words: the weight of the dead. LUIGI PIRANDELLO, *Henry IV* (1922), 2, tr. Edward Storer.

34. Words are like leaves; and where they most abound, / Much fruit of sense beneath is rarely found. ALEXANDER POPE, *An Essay on Criticism* (1711), 2.109.

35. Words are the small change of thought. JULES RENARD, *Journal*, November 1888, ed. and tr. Louise Bogan and Elizabeth Roget.

36. How describe the delicate thing that happens when a brilliant insect alights on a

flower? Words, with their weight, fall upon the picture like birds of prey. JULES RENARD, *Journal*, September 1893, ed. and tr. Louise Bogan and Elizabeth Roget.

37. Words not only affect us temporarily; they change us, they socialize or unsocialize us. DAVID RIESMAN, "Storytellers as Tutors," *The Lonely Crowd* (1950).

38. Man does not live by words alone, despite the fact that sometimes he has to eat them. ADLAI STEVENSON, speech, Denver, Colo., Sept. 5, 1952.

39. Man is a creature who lives not upon bread alone, but principally by catchwords. ROBERT LOUIS STEVENSON, title essay, 2, *Virginibus Puerisque* (1881).

40. Words, like Nature, half reveal / And half conceal the Soul within. ALFRED, LORD TENNYSON, "In Memoriam A. H. H." (1850), 5.

41. Words should be an intense pleasure just as leather should be to a shoemaker. EVELYN WAUGH, *The New York Times*, Nov. 19, 1950.

42. Words should be weighed and not counted. *Yiddish Proverbs* (1949), ed. Hanan J. Ayalti.

## 1058. WORK

**See also 279. Effort; 461. Incompetence; 673. Payment; 805. Rest; 807. Retirement; 917. Specialists; 1002. Unemployment; 1006. Unions; 1029. Vocations; 1059. Workers**

1. Most men in a brazen prison live, / Where, in the sun's hot eye, / With heads bent o'er their toil, they languidly / Their lives to some unmeaning taskwork give, / Dreaming of nought beyond their prison-wall. MATTHEW ARNOLD, "A Summer Night," *Empedocles on Etna, and Other Poems* (1852).

2. Don't condescend to unskilled labor. Try it for half a day first. BROOKS ATKINSON, "March 27," *Once Around the Sun* (1951).

3. It is necessary to work, if not from inclination, at least from despair. Everything considered, work is less boring than amusing oneself. CHARLES BAUDELAIRE, *Mon coeur mis à nu* (1887), 18.

4. Work is not the curse, but drudgery is. HENRY WARD BEECHER, *Proverbs from Plymouth Pulpit* (1887).

5. No fine work can be done without concentration and self-sacrifice and toil and doubt. MAX BEERBOHM, "Books Within Books," *And Even Now* (1920).

6. A man's work is rather the needful supplement to himself than the outcome of it. MAX BEERBOHM, "Hethway Speaking," *Mainly On the Air* (1946).

7. To work is to pray. ST. BENEDICT OF NURSIA (480?–?543), motto.

8. What is work? and what is not work? are questions that perplex the wisest of men. *Bhagavadgita*, 4, tr. P. Lal.

9. In the sweat of thy face shalt thou eat bread, till thou return unto the ground; for out of it wast thou taken. *Bible*, Genesis 3:16.

10. Whether our work is art or science or the daily work of society, it is only the form in which we explore our experience which is different. JACOB BRONOWSKI, "The Sense of Human Dignity," *Science and Human Values* (1956).

11. Most people spend most of their days doing what they do not want to do in order to earn the right, at times, to do what they may desire. JOHN MASON BROWN, *Esquire*, April 1960.

12. Everything under the sun is work. Sweat, even in our sleep. GEORG BÜCHNER, *Woyzeck* (1836), 6, tr. Theodore Hoffman.

13. He that will not work according to his faculty, let him perish according to his necessity: there is no law juster than that. THOMAS CARLYLE, *Chartism* (1839), 3.

14. He that can work is a born king of something. THOMAS CARLYLE, *Chartism* (1839), 3.

15. He who considers his work beneath him will be above doing it well. ALEXANDER CHASE, *Perspectives* (1966).

16. The ant is knowing and wise; but he doesn't know enough to take a vacation. CLARENCE DAY, *This Simian World* (1920), 5.

17. Honest labour bears a lovely face. THOMAS DEKKER, *Patient Grissell* (1603), 1.1.

18. To crush, to annihilate a man utterly, to inflict on him the most terrible of punishments so that the most ferocious murderer would shudder at it and dread it beforehand, one need only give him work of an absolutely, completely useless and irrational character. DOSTOEVSKY, *The House of the*

*Dead* (1862), 1.2, tr. Constance Garnett.

19. Originality and the feeling of one's own dignity are achieved only through work and struggle. DOSTOEVSKY, *A Diary of a Writer* (1873), 3.

20. Wurruk is wurruk if ye're paid to do it an' it's pleasure if ye pay to be allowed to do it. FINLEY PETER DUNNE, "Work and Sport," *Observations by Mr. Dooley* (1902).

21. Where there is most labour there is not always most life. HAVELOCK ELLIS, preface, *The Dance of Life* (1923).

22. We put our love where we have put our labor. EMERSON, *Journals*, 1836.

23. The life of labor does not make men, but drudges. EMERSON, *Journals*, 1843.

24. It is the privilege of any human work which is well done to invest the doer with a certain haughtiness. EMERSON, "Wealth," *The Conduct of Life* (1860).

25. Every man's task is his life-preserver. EMERSON, "Worship," *The Conduct of Life* (1860).

26. Toil, says the proverb, is the sire of fame. EURIPIDES, *Licymnius* (c. 450 B.C.), 477, tr. M. H. Morgan.

27. If the building of a bridge does not enrich the awareness of those who work on it, then that bridge ought not to be built. FRANTZ FANON, "The Pitfalls of National Consciousness," *The Wretched of the Earth* (1961), tr. Constance Farrington.

28. One of the saddest things is that the only thing a man can do for eight hours a day, day after day, is work. You can't eat eight hours a day nor drink for eight hours a day nor make love for eight hours. WILLIAM FAULKNER, interview, *Writers at Work: First Series* (1958).

29. Day's work is still to do, / Whatever the day's doom. CHRISTOPHER FRY, *Thor, with Angels* (1948).

30. Men for the sake of getting a living forget to live. MARGARET FULLER, *Summer on the Lakes* (1844), 7.

31. All work is empty save when there is love. KAHLIL GIBRAN, "On Work," *The Prophet* (1923).

32. Most people work the greater part of their time for a mere living; and the little freedom which remains to them so troubles them that they use every means of getting rid of it. GOETHE, *The Sorrows of Young Werther* (1774), 1, May 17, 1771, tr. Victor Lange.

33. The hand that has the week-day broom to ply, / On Sunday gives the pleasantest caresses. GOETHE, "Night," *Faust: Part I* (1808), tr. Philip Wayne.

34. When work is a pleasure, life is a joy! When work is a duty, life is slavery. MAXIM GORKY, *The Lower Depths* (1903), 1, tr. Alexander Bakshy.

35. Human happiness is the true odour of growth, the sweet exhalation of work. DAVID GRAYSON, *Adventures in Contentment* (1907), 6.

36. He who does nothing renders himself incapable of doing any thing; but while we are executing any work, we are preparing and qualifying ourselves to undertake another. WILLIAM HAZLITT, "On Application to Study," *The Plain Speaker* (1826).

37. Serious occupation is labor that has reference to some want. HEGEL, *Philosophy of History* (1832), 1.2.1, tr. John Sibree.

38. It is weariness to keep toiling at the same things so that one becomes ruled by them. HERACLITUS, *Fragments* (c. 500 B.C.), 89, tr. Philip Wheelwright.

39. To labour is the lot of man below; / And when Jove gave us life, he gave us woe. HOMER, *Iliad* (9th c. B.C.), 10.78, tr. Alexander Pope.

40. There is only one thing for a man to do who is married to a woman who enjoys spending money, and that is to enjoy earning it. EDGAR WATSON HOWE, *Country Town Sayings* (1911).

41. The best preparation for good work tomorrow is to do good work today. ELBERT HUBBARD, *The Note Book* (1927).

42. Do your work with your whole heart and you will succeed—there is so little competition! ELBERT HUBBARD, *The Note Book* (1927).

43. A man is not idle because he is absorbed in thought. There is a visible labour and there is an invisible labour. VICTOR HUGO, "Cosette," *Les Misérables* (1862), 7.8, tr. Charles E. Wilbour.

44. Work is prayer. Work is also stink. Therefore stink is prayer. ALDOUS HUXLEY, *Jesting Pilate* (1926), 1.

45. It is a poor art that maintains not the artisan. ITALIAN PROVERB.

46. I like work: it fascinates me. I can sit and look at it for hours. I love to keep it by me: the idea of getting rid of it nearly

breaks my heart. JEROME K. JEROME, *Three Men in a Boat* (1889), 15.

47. The world is sown with good; but unless I turn my glad thoughts into practical living and till my own field, I cannot reap a kernel of the good. HELEN KELLER, *Optimism* (1903), 1.

48. Who first invented work and bound the free / And holiday-rejoicing spirit down? CHARLES LAMB, "Work" (1819).

49. Thou, O God, dost sell us all good things at the price of labor. LEONARDO DA VINCI, *Notebooks* (c. 1500), tr. Jean Paul Richter.

50. Where there is no desire, there will be no industry. JOHN LOCKE, *Some Thoughts Concerning Education* (1693), 126.

51. No man is born into the world whose work / Is not born with him; there is always work, / And tools to work withal, for those who will. JAMES RUSSELL LOWELL, "A Glance Behind the Curtain" (1843).

52. a great many people / who spend their time mourning / over the brevity of life / could make it seem longer / if they did a little more work. DON MARQUIS, "archy on this and that," *Archy Does His Part* (1935).

53. Constant labor of one uniform kind destroys the intensity and flow of a man's animal spirits, which find recreation and delight in mere change of activity. KARL MARX, *Capital* (1867–94), 2.9, tr. Stephen L. Trask.

54. How Sunday into Monday melts! OGDEN NASH, "Time Marches On," *I'm a Stranger Here Myself* (1938).

55. God does not want men to overtax themselves. He wants men to be happy. WASLAW NIJINSKY, quoted in Henry Miller's "The Enormous Womb," *The Wisdom of the Heart* (1941).

56. Work expands to fill the time available for its completion. C. NORTHCOTE PARKINSON, *Parkinson's Law* (1962).

57. Love labor: for if thou dost not want it for food, thou mayest for physic. It is wholesome for thy body and good for thy mind. WILLIAM PENN, *Some Fruits of Solitude* (1693), 1.57.

58. If you direct your whole thought to work itself, none of the things which invade eyes or ears will reach the mind. QUINTILIAN, *Institutio Oratoria* (c. A.D. 95), 10.3, tr. Clyde Murley.

59. Far and away the best prize that life offers is the chance to work hard at work worth doing. THEODORE ROOSEVELT, Labor Day address, Syracuse, N. Y., 1903.

60. It is only by labour that thought can be made healthy, and only by thought that labour can be made happy, and the two cannot be separated with impunity. JOHN RUSKIN, "The Nature of Gothic," *The Stones of Venice* (1851–53), v. 2.6.

61. Labour without joy is base. Labour without sorrow is base. Sorrow without labour is base. Joy without labour is base. JOHN RUSKIN, *Time and Tide* (1867), 5.

62. My nature is subdued / To what it works in, like the dyer's hand. SHAKESPEARE, *Sonnets* (1609), 111.6.

63. Greater is he who enjoys the fruits of his labor than he who fears heaven. Haggadah, *Palestinian Talmud* (4th c.).

64. All things have rest: why should we toil alone, / We only toil, who are the first of things, / And make perpetual moan. ALFRED, LORD TENNYSON, "The Lotos-Eaters" (1842), 2.

65. Death is the end of life; ah, why / Should life all labor be? ALFRED, LORD TENNYSON, "The Lotos-Eaters" (1842), 4.

66. If thou be not busy for thyself now, who shall be busy for thee in time to come? THOMAS À KEMPIS, *The Imitation of Christ* (1426), 1.23.

67. Those who work much do not work hard. THOREAU, *Journal*, March 31, 1841.

68. Let us be grateful to Adam our benefactor. He cut us out of the "blessing" of idleness and won for us the "curse" of labor. MARK TWAIN, "Pudd'nhead Wilson's New Calendar," *Following the Equator* (1897), 1.33.

69. Work spares us from three great evils: boredom, vice, and need. VOLTAIRE, *Candide* (1759), 30.

70. No race can prosper till it learns there is as much dignity in tilling a field as in writing a poem. BOOKER T. WASHINGTON, address, Atlanta Exposition, Sept. 18, 1895.

71. No task, rightly done, is truly private. It is part of the world's work. WOODROW WILSON, address, Princeton University, Nov. 1, 1902.

### 1059. WORKERS
**See also 313. Executives; 1002. Unemployment; 1006. Unions; 1058. Work**

1. A good horse should be seldom spurred. THOMAS FULLER, M.D., *Gnomologia* (1732), 156.

2. If the servant grows rich and the master grows poor, they are both good for nothing. GERMAN PROVERB.

3. I tell you, sir, the only safeguard of order and discipline in the modern world is a standardized worker with interchangeable parts. That would solve the entire problem of management. JEAN GIRAUDOUX, *The Madwoman of Chaillot* (1945), 1, adapted by Maurice Valency.

4. His brow is wet with honest sweat, / He earns whate'er he can, / And looks the whole world in the face, / For he owes not any man. LONGFELLOW, "The Village Blacksmith" (1839), 2.

5. Slave of the wheel of labor, what to him / Are Plato and the swing of Pleiades? EDWIN MARKHAM, "The Man with the Hoe" (1899).

6. When white-collar people get jobs, they sell not only their time and energy, but their personalities as well. They sell by the week, or month, their smiles and their kindly gestures, and they must practice that prompt repression of resentment and aggression. C. WRIGHT MILLS, *White Collar* (1956).

7. The really efficient laborer will be found not to crowd his day with work, but will saunter to his task surrounded by a wide halo of ease and leisure. THOREAU, *Journal*, March 31, 1841.

8. If you do things by the job, you are perpetually driven: the hours are scourges. If you work by the hour, you gently sail on the stream of Time, which is always bearing you on to the haven of Pay, whether you make any effort, or not. CHARLES DUDLEY WARNER, "Eleventh Week," *My Summer in a Garden* (1871).

### 1060. WORLD
**See also 270. Earth; 536. Life; 994. Twentieth Century; 1010. Universe**

1. Ah, love, let us be true / To one another! for the world, which seems / To lie before us like a land of dreams, / So various, so beautiful, so new, / Hath really neither joy, nor love, nor light, / Nor certitude, nor peace, nor help for pain. MATTHEW ARNOLD, "Dover Beach," *New Poems* (1867).

2. For the world, I count it not an inn, but an hospital; and a place not to live, but to die in. SIR THOMAS BROWNE, *Religio Medici* (1642), 2.

3. The world is a gambling-table so arranged that all who enter the casino must play and all must lose more or less heavily in the long run, though they win occasionally by the way. SAMUEL BUTLER (d. 1902), "Lord, What Is Man?" *Note-Books* (1912).

4. I have not loved the World, nor the World me; / I have not flattered its rank breath, nor bowed / To its idolatries a patient knee, / Nor coined my cheek to smiles,—nor cried aloud / In worship of an echo. BYRON, *Childe Harold's Pilgrimage* (1812–18), 3.113.

5. The world is a bundle of hay, / Mankind are the asses who pull; / Each tugs it a different way,— / And the greatest of all is John Bull! BYRON, "Epigram" (1821).

6. This world, after all our science and sciences, is still a miracle; wonderful, inscrutable, magical and more, to whosoever will think of it. THOMAS CARLYLE, *On Heroes, Hero-Worship and the Heroic in History* (1841), 1.

7. The world is a great volume, and man the index of that book; even in the body of man, you may turn to the whole world. JOHN DONNE, *Sermons*, No. 42, 1626.

8. The world is bad, but not hopeless; it only becomes hopeless when measured by absolute standards. FRIEDRICH DÜRRENMATT, *The Marriage of Mr. Mississippi* (1952), 1, tr. Michael Bullock.

9. The most incomprehensible thing about the world is that it is comprehensible. EINSTEIN, quoted in his obituary, April 19, 1955.

10. This is the way the world ends / Not with a bang but a whimper. T. S. ELIOT, "The Hollow Men" (1925), 5.

11. What's wrong with this world is, it's not finished yet. It is not completed to that point where man can put his final signature to the job and say, "It is finished. We made it, and it works." WILLIAM FAULKNER address, Wellesley, Mass., June 8, 1953.

12. The world only exists in your eyes—your conception of it. You can make it as big or as small as you want to. F. SCOTT FITZGERALD, "The Crack-Up" *The Crack-Up* (1945).

13. It is not man, but the world that has become abnormal. Graffito written during French student revolt, May 1968.

14. The world is a bride of surpassing beauty—but remember that this maiden is never bound to anyone. HĀFIZ, ghazals from the *Divan* (14th c.), 34, tr. Justin Huntly McCarthy.

15. That cold accretion called the world, so terrible in the mass, is so unformidable, even pitiable, in its units. THOMAS HARDY, *Tess of the D'Urbervilles* (1891), 13.

16. Books are a world in themselves, it is true; but they are not the only world. The world itself is a volume larger than all the libraries in it. WILLIAM HAZLITT, "On the Conversation of Authors," *The Plain Speaker* (1826).

17. To him who looks upon the world rationally, the world in its turn presents a rational aspect. HEGEL, introduction to *Philosophy of History* (1832), tr. John Sibree.

18. The world is a fine place and worth the fighting for and I hate very much to leave it. ERNEST HEMINGWAY, *For Whom the Bell Tolls* (1940), 43.

19. The unrest which keeps the never stopping clock of metaphysics going is the thought that the nonexistence of this world is just as possible as its existence. WILLIAM JAMES, "The Problem of Being," *Some Problems of Philosophy* (1911).

20. The world has narrowed to a neighborhood before it has broadened to brotherhood. LYNDON B. JOHNSON, address, New York City, Dec. 17, 1963.

21. Huge though the world is, I always miss when I hit at it. MALAY PROVERB.

22. The world in all doth but two nations bear, / The good, the bad; and these mixed everywhere. ANDREW MARVELL, "The Loyal Scot" (1650).

23. Set the foot down with distrust upon the crust of the world–it is thin. EDNA ST. VINCENT MILLAY, "Underground System," *Huntsman, What Quarry?* (1939).

24. The world goes on because a few men in every generation believe in it utterly, accept it unquestioningly; they underwrite it with their lives. HENRY MILLER, "With Edgar Varèse in the Gobi Desert," *The Air-Conditioned Nightmare* (1945).

25. For in and out, above, about, below, / 'Tis nothing but a Magic Shadow-show, / Played in a Box whose Candle is the Sun, / Round which we Phantom Figures come and go. OMAR KHAYYÁM, *Rubáiyát* (11th–12th c.), tr. Edward FitzGerald, 1st ed., 46.

26. The world is a thing we must of necessity either laugh at or be angry at; if we laugh at it, they say we are proud; if we are angry at it, they say we are ill-natured. ALEXANDER POPE, *Thoughts on Various Subjects* (1727).

27. All the world's a stage, / And all the men and women merely players. / They have their exits and their entrances, / And one man in his time plays many parts. SHAKESPEARE, *As You Like It* (1599–1600), 2.7.139.

28. The world is so full of a number of things, / I'm sure we should all be as happy as kings. ROBERT LOUIS STEVENSON, "Happy Thought," *A Child's Garden of Verses* (1885).

29. We read the world wrong and say that it deceives us. RABINDRANATH TAGORE, *Stray Birds* (1916), 75.

30. We live in the world when we love it. RABINDRANATH TAGORE, *Stray Birds* (1916), 278.

31. The world is hard to love, though we must love it because we have no other, and to fail to love it is not to exist at all. MARK VAN DOREN, *Autobiography of Mark Van Doren* (1958).

32. "To what end was this world formed?" said Candide. "To infuriate us," replied Martin. VOLTAIRE, *Candide* (1759), 21.

33. The world is a comedy to those that think; a tragedy to those that feel. HORACE WALPOLE, letter to Horace Mann, Dec. 31, 1769.

34. We milk the cow of the world, and as we do / We whisper in her ear, "You are not true." RICHARD WILBUR, "Epistemology," *Ceremony* (1950).

35. The beauty of the world which is so soon to perish, has two edges, one of laughter, one of anguish, cutting the heart asunder. VIRGINIA WOOLF, *A Room of One's Own* (1929), 1.

## WORLDLINESS

See 910. Sophistication

## WORRY

See 43. Anxiety

## 1061. WORSHIP

See also 14. Admiration; 350. Following; 439. Iconoclasm; 504. Irreverence; 717. Prayer; 790. Religion

1. Heathen, n. A benighted creature who has the folly to worship something that he can see and feel. AMBROSE BIERCE, *The Devil's Dictionary* (1881–1911).

2. Does not every true man feel that he is himself made higher by doing reverence to what is really above him? THOMAS CARLYLE, *On Heroes, Hero-Worship and the Heroic in History* (1841), 1.

3. Men are idolaters, and want something to look at and kiss and hug, or throw themselves down before; they always did, they always will; and if you don't make it of wood, you must make it of words. OLIVER WENDELL HOLMES, SR., *The Poet at the Breakfast Table* (1872), 5.

4. Man is a venerating animal. He venerates as easily as he purges himself. When they take away from him the gods of his fathers, he looks for others abroad. MAX JACOB, "Hamletism," *Art poétique* (1922), tr. Wallace Fowlie.

5. Where it is a duty to worship the sun, it is pretty sure to be a crime to examine the laws of heat. JOHN MORLEY, *Voltaire* (1872).

6. He worships God who knows him. SENECA, *Letters to Lucilius* (1st c.), 95.47, tr. E. Phillips Barker.

7. God waits to win back his own flowers as gifts from man's hands. RABINDRANATH TAGORE, *Stray Birds* (1916), 215.

8. God prefers bad verses recited with a pure heart, to the finest verses possible chanted by the wicked. VOLTAIRE, "Prayer," *Philosophical Dictionary* (1764).

9. We adore, we invoke, we seek to appease, only that which we fear. VOLTAIRE, "Religion," *Philosophical Dictionary* (1764).

10. The worship of God is not a rule of safety–it is an adventure of the spirit, a flight after the unattainable. ALFRED NORTH WHITEHEAD, *Science and the Modern World* (1925), 12.

## WORTH

See 1019. Value

## 1062. WRITING AND WRITERS

See also 62. Autobiography; 79. Biography; 91. Books and Reading; 132. Clarity; 198. Creation and Creativity; 341. Fiction; 396. Grammar; 521. Language; 542. Literature; 702. Poetry and Poets; 931. Storytelling; 935. Style; 1057. Words

1. Having imagination, it takes you an hour to write a paragraph that, if you were unimaginative, would take you only a minute. Or you might not write the paragraph at all. FRANKLIN P. ADAMS, *Half a Loaf* (1927).

2. The universal object and idol of men of letters is reputation. JOHN ADAMS, *Discourses on Davila* (1789), 2.

3. Among all kinds of writing, there is none in which authors are more apt to miscarry than in works of humour, as there is none in which they are more ambitious to excel. JOSEPH ADDISON, *The Spectator* (1711–12), 35.

4. Between the reputation of the author living and the reputation of the same author dead there is ever a wide discrepancy. THOMAS BAILEY ALDRICH, "Leaves from a Notebook," *Ponkapog Papers* (1903).

5. For the creation of a master-work of literature two powers must concur, the power of the man and the power of the moment. MATTHEW ARNOLD, "The Function of Criticism" (1864).

6. Writing comes more easily if you have something to say. SHOLEM ASCH, *New York Herald Tribune*, Nov. 6, 1955.

7. Nothing a man writes can please him as profoundly as something he does with his back, shoulders and hands. For writing is an artificial activity. It is a lonely and private substitute for conversation. BROOKS ATKINSON, "June 13," *Once Around the Sun* (1951).

8. In relation to a writer, most readers believe in the Double Standard: they may be unfaithful to him as often as they like, but

he must never, never be unfaithful to them. W. H. AUDEN, "Reading," *The Dyer's Hand* (1962).

9. No poet or novelist wishes he were the only one who ever lived, but most of them wish they were the only one alive, and quite a number fondly believe their wish has been granted. W. H. AUDEN, "Writing," *The Dyer's Hand* (1962).

10. Reading maketh a full man, conference a ready man, and writing an exact man. FRANCIS BACON, "Of Studies," *Essays* (1625).

11. The writer's greed is appalling. He wants, or seems to want, everything and practically everybody; in another sense, and at the same time, he needs no one at all. JAMES BALDWIN, "Alas, Poor Richard," *Nobody Knows My Name* (1961).

12. The pen is the tongue of the hand – a silent utterer of words for the eye. HENRY WARD BEECHER, *Proverbs from Plymouth Pulpit* (1887).

13. No one who cannot limit himself has ever been able to write. NICOLAS BOILEAU, *L'Art poétique* (1674), 1.63.

14. When a man can observe himself suffering and is able, later, to describe what he's gone through, it means he was born for literature. EDOUARD BOURDET, *Vient de paraître* (1927), 4.

15. Poets are sultans, if they had their will; / For every author would his brother kill. ROGER BOYLE, *Prologues* (c. 17th c.).

16. Many a fervid man / Writes books as cold and flat as graveyard stones. ELIZABETH BARRETT BROWNING, *Aurora Leigh* (1856), 5.359.

17. The pen is mightier than the sword. BULWER-LYTTON, *Richelieu* (1838), 2.2.

18. One hates an author that's *all author* – fellows / In foolscap uniforms turned up with ink, / So very anxious, clever, fine, and jealous, / One don't know what to say to them, or think, / Unless to puff them with a pair of bellows. BYRON, *Beppo* (1818), 75.

19. I think you must remember that a writer is a simple-minded person to begin with and go on that basis. He's not a great mind, he's not a great thinker, he's not a great philosopher, he's a story-teller. ERSKINE CALDWELL, *The Atlantic Monthly*, July 1958.

20. To write is to become disinterested. There is a certain renunciation in art. ALBERT CAMUS, *Notebooks 1935–1942* (1962), 1, tr. Philip Thody.

21. Writing has laws of perspective, of light and shade, just as painting does, or music. If you are born knowing them, fine. If not, learn them. Then rearrange the rules to suit yourself. TRUMAN CAPOTE, interview, *Writers at Work: First Series* (1958).

22. Considering the multitude of mortals that handle the pen in these days, and can mostly spell, and write without glaring violations of grammar, the question naturally arises: How is it, then, that no work proceeds from them, bearing any stamp of authenticity and permanence; of worth for more than one day? THOMAS CARLYLE "Biography" (1832).

23. If a book come from the heart, it will contrive to reach other hearts; all art and authorcraft are of small amount to that. THOMAS CARLYLE, *On Heroes, Hero-Worship and the Heroic in History* (1841), 2.

24. There ought to be some sign in a book about Man, that the writer knows thoroughly one man at least. FRANK MOORE COLBY, "Simple Simon," *The Colby Essays* (1926), v. 1.

25. The writer who loses his self-doubt, who gives way as he grows old to a sudden euphoria, to prolixity, should stop writing immediately: the time has come for him to lay aside his pen. COLETTE, "Lady of Letters," *Earthly Paradise* (1966), 4, ed. Robert Phelps.

26. Our admiration of fine writing will always be in proportion to its real difficulty and its apparent ease. CHARLES CALEB COLTON, *Lacon* (1825), 2.143.

27. In plucking the fruit of memory one runs the risk of spoiling its bloom, especially if it has got to be carried into the marketplace. JOSEPH CONRAD, "Author's Note," *The Arrow of Gold* (1919).

28. In America only the successful writer is important, in France all writers are important, in England no writer is important, and in Australia you have to explain what a writer is. GEOFFREY COTTERELL, *New York Journal-American*, Sept. 22, 1961.

29. Authors are sometimes like tomcats: they distrust all the other toms, but they are kind to kittens. MALCOLM COWLEY, introduction to *Writers at Work: First Series* (1958).

30. No one, not even a pretty woman who wakes up to find a pimple on her nose, feels so vexed as an author who threatens to survive his own reputation. DENIS DIDEROT, *Rameau's Nephew* (1762), tr. Jacques Barzun and Ralph H. Bowen.

31. An author who speaks about his own books is almost as bad as a mother who talks about her own children. BENJAMIN DISRAELI, speech, Glasgow, Nov. 19, 1873.

32. In good writing, words become one with things. EMERSON, *Journals*, 1831.

33. The maker of a sentence launches out into the infinite and builds a road into Chaos and old Night, and is followed by those who hear him with something of wild, creative delight. EMERSON, *Journals*, 1834.

34. A poem, a sentence, causes us to see ourselves. I be, and I see my being, at the same time. EMERSON, *Journals*, 1836.

35. He that writes to himself writes to an eternal public. EMERSON, "Spiritual Laws," *Essays: First Series* (1841).

36. If you would be a reader, read; if a writer, write. EPICTETUS, *Discourses* (2nd c.), 2.18, tr. Thomas W. Higginson.

37. No man can write who is not first a humanitarian. WILLIAM FAULKNER, *Time*, Feb. 25, 1957.

38. A writer needs three things, experience, observation, and imagination, any two of which, at times any one of which, can supply the lack of the others. WILLIAM FAULKNER, interview, *Writers at Work: First Series* (1958).

39. You don't write because you want to say something; you write because you've got something to say. F. SCOTT FITZGERALD, "The Note-Books," *The Crack-Up* (1945).

40. To one who has enjoyed the full life of any scene, of any hour, what thoughts can be recorded about it seem like the commas and semicolons in the paragraph—mere stops. MARGARET FULLER, *Summer on the Lakes* (1844), 1.

41. The most beautiful things are those that madness prompts and reason writes. ANDRÉ GIDE, *Journals*, 1894, tr. Justin O'Brien.

42. Enduring fame is promised only to those writers who can offer to successive generations a substance constantly renewed; for every generation arrives upon the scene with its own particular hunger. ANDRÉ GIDE, "Baudelaire and M. Faguet," *Pretexts* (1903), tr. Angelo P. Bertocci and others.

43. Great authors are admirable in this respect: in every generation they make for disagreement. Through them we become aware of our differences. ANDRÉ GIDE, "Third Imaginary Interview," *Pretexts* (1903), tr. Angelo P. Bertocci and others.

44. He who does not expect a million readers should not write a line. GOETHE, quoted in Johann Peter Eckermann's *Conversations with Goethe*, May 12, 1825.

45. Even monarchs have need of authors, and fear their pens more than ugly women the painter's pencil. BALTASAR GRACIÁN, *The Art of Worldly Wisdom* (1647), 281, tr. Joseph Jacobs.

46. Thought flies and words go on foot. Therein lies all the drama of a writer. JULIEN GREEN, *Journal*, May 4, 1943.

47. The only impeccable writers are those who never wrote. WILLIAM HAZLITT, "On the Aristocracy of Letters," *Table Talk* (1821–22).

48. They're fancy talkers about themselves, writers. If I had to give young writers advice, I would say don't listen to writers talking about writing or themselves. LILLIAN HELLMAN, *The New York Times*, Feb. 21, 1960.

49. Writing, at its best, is a lonely life. Organizations for writers palliate the writer's loneliness, but I doubt if they improve his writing. ERNEST HEMINGWAY, acceptance speech for the Nobel Prize, Dec. 10, 1954.

50. An old author is constantly rediscovering himself in the more or less fossilized productions of his earlier years. OLIVER WENDELL HOLMES, SR., *Over the Teacups* (1891), 12.

51. The secret of all good writing is sound judgment. HORACE, *Ars Poetica* (13–8 B.C.).

52. A writer and nothing else: a man alone in a room with the English language, trying to get human feelings right. JOHN K. HUTCHENS, *New York Herald Tribune*, Sept. 10, 1961.

53. The fact that many people should be shocked by what he writes practically imposes it as a duty upon the writer to go on shocking them. ALDOUS HUXLEY, "Vulgarity in Literature," *Music at Night* (1931).

54. A man may write at any time, if he will set himself doggedly to it. SAMUEL JOHNSON, quoted in Boswell's *Journal of a*

*Tour to the Hebrides with Samuel Johnson*, Aug. 16, 1773.

55. No man but a blockhead ever wrote except for money. SAMUEL JOHNSON, quoted in Boswell's *Life of Samuel Johnson*, April 5, 1776.

56. What is written without effort is in general read without pleasure. SAMUEL JOHNSON, quoted in Birkbeck Hill's *Johnsonian Miscellanies* (1897), v. 2.

57. An inveterate and incurable itch for writing besets many and grows old with their sick hearts. JUVENAL, *Satires* (c. 100), 7.51.

58. In a very real sense, the writer writes in order to teach himself, to understand himself, to satisfy himself; the publishing of his ideas, though it brings gratifications, is a curious anticlimax. ALFRED KAZIN, *Think*, February 1963.

59. To make a book is as much a trade as to make a clock; something more than intelligence is required to become an author. LA BRUYÈRE, *Characters* (1688), 1.3, tr. Henri Van Laun.

60. A mediocre mind thinks it writes divinely; a good mind thinks it writes reasonably. LA BRUYÈRE, *Characters* (1688), 1.18.

61. The same common sense which makes an author write good things, makes him dread they are not good enough to deserve reading. LA BRUYÈRE, *Characters* (1688), 1.18, tr. Henri Van Laun.

62. It is the glory and the merit of some men to write well, and of others not to write at all. LA BRUYÈRE, *Characters* (1688), 1.59, tr. Henri Van Laun.

63. Authors are like cattle going to a fair: those of the same field can never move on without butting one another. WALTER SAVAGE LANDOR, "Archdeacon Hare and Walter Landor," *Imaginary Conversations* (1824–53).

64. Every great writer is a writer of history, let him treat on almost what subject he may. He carries with him for thousands of years a portion of his times. WALTER SAVAGE LANDOR, "Diogenes and Plato," *Imaginary Conversations* (1824–53).

65. Clear writers, like fountains, do not seem so deep as they are; the turbid look the most profound. WALTER SAVAGE LANDOR, "Southey and Porson," *Imaginary Conversations* (1824–53).

66. If you once understand an author's character, the comprehension of his writings becomes easy. LONGFELLOW, *Hyperion* (1839), 1.5.

67. The unpublished manuscript is like an unconfessed sin that festers in the soul, corrupting and contaminating it. ANTONIO MACHADO, *Juan de Mairena* (1943), 48, tr. Ben Belitt.

68. It is one test of a fully developed writer that he reminds us of no one but himself. MELVIN MADDOCKS, *Christian Science Monitor*, May 2, 1963.

69. If you have one strong idea, you can't help repeating it and embroidering it. Sometimes I think that authors should write one novel and then be put in a gas chamber. JOHN P. MARQUAND, *New York Herald Tribune*, Oct. 5, 1958.

70. i never think at all when i write / nobody can do two things at the same time / and do them both well. DON MARQUIS, "archy on the radio," *Archy's Life of Mehitabel* (1933).

71. 'Tis easy to write epigrams nicely, but to write a book is hard. MARTIAL, *Epigrams* (A.D. 86), 7.85, tr. Walter C. A. Ker.

72. The writer is more concerned to know than to judge. W. SOMERSET MAUGHAM, *The Moon and Sixpence* (1919), 41.

73. It has been said that good prose should resemble the conversation of a well-bred man. W. SOMERSET MAUGHAM, *The Summing Up* (1938), 12.

74. A writer is essentially a man who does not resign himself to loneliness. FRANÇOIS MAURIAC, *Dieu et Mammon* (1929), 5.

75. Sin is the writer's element. FRANÇOIS MAURIAC, "Literature and Sin," *Second Thoughts* (1961), tr. Adrienne Foulke.

76. No man would set a word down on paper if he had the courage to live out what he believed in. HENRY MILLER, *Sunday after the War* (1944).

77. I always do the first line well, but I have trouble doing the others. MOLIÈRE, *The Ridiculous Précieuses* (1659), 11, tr. Donald M. Frame.

78. The only people who can be excused for letting a bad book loose on the world are the poor devils who have to write for a living! MOLIÈRE, *The Misanthrope* (1666), 1, tr. John Wood.

79. He who commits his decrepitude to the press plays the fool if he thinks to

squeeze anything out thence that does not relish of dreaming, dotage and driveling. MONTAIGNE, "Of physiognomy," *Essays* (1580–88), tr. Charles Cotton and W. C. Hazlitt.

80. All the world knows me in my book, and my book in me. MONTAIGNE, "Upon some verses of Virgil," *Essays* (1580–88), tr. Charles Cotton and W. C. Hazlitt.

81. A writer is unfair to himself when he is unable to be hard on himself. MARIANNE MOORE, interview, *Writers at Work: Second Series* (1963).

82. When writing is good, everything is symbolic, but symbolic writing is seldom good. WRIGHT MORRIS, *A Bill of Rites, A Bill of Wrongs, A Bill of Goods* (1967), 6.

83. The last thing one settles in writing a book is what one should put in first. PASCAL, *Pensées* (1670), 19, tr. W. F. Trotter.

84. The writer is the Faust of modern society, the only surviving individualist in a mass age. To his orthodox contemporaries he seems a semi-madman. BORIS PASTERNAK, *The Observer*, Dec. 20, 1959.

85. There is no lighter burden, nor more agreeable, than a pen. PETRARCH, *Letter to Posterity* (1367–72).

86. An essayist is a lucky person who has found a way to discourse without being interrupted. CHARLES POORE, *The New York Times*, May 31, 1962.

87. True ease in writing comes from art, not chance, / As those move easiest who have learned to dance. ALEXANDER POPE, *An Essay on Criticism* (1711), 2.162.

88. Most people won't realize that writing is a craft. You have to take your apprenticeship in it like anything else. KATHERINE ANNE PORTER, *Saturday Review*, March 31, 1962.

89. The pen is a formidable weapon, but a man can kill himself with it a great deal more easily than he can other people. GEORGE DENNISON PRENTICE, *Prenticeana* (1860).

90. The businessman who is a novelist is able to drop in on literature and feel no suicidal loss of esteem if the lady is not at home, and he can spend his life preparing without fuss for the awful interview. V. S. PRITCHETT, "An Amateur," *The Living Novel & Later Appreciations* (1964).

91. Our passions shape our books, repose writes them in the intervals. MARCEL PROUST, *Remembrance of Things Past: The Past Recaptured* (1913–27), tr. Stephen Hudson.

92. From writing rapidly it does not result that one writes well, but from writing well it results that one writes rapidly. QUINTILIAN, *Institutio Oratoria* (c. A.D. 95), 10.3, tr. Clyde Murley.

93. In literature, there are only oxen. The biggest ones are the geniuses—the ones who toil eighteen hours a day without tiring. JULES RENARD, *Journal*, 1887, ed. and tr. Louise Bogan and Elizabeth Roget.

94. A writer lives, at best, in a state of astonishment. Beneath any feeling he has of the good or evil of the world lies a deeper one of wonder at it all. To transmit that feeling, he writes. WILLIAM SANSOM, *Blue Skies, Brown Studies* (1961).

95. No one can ever write about anything that happened to him after he was twelve years old. IGNAZIO SILONE, quoted in Murray Kempton's *America Comes of Middle Age* (1963).

96. Writing is not a profession but a vocation of unhappiness. GEORGES SIMENON, interview, *Writers at Work: First Series* (1958).

97. Every author, however modest, keeps a most outrageous vanity chained like a madman in the padded cell of his breast. LOGAN PEARSALL SMITH, *Afterthoughts* (1931), 5.

98. Why does my Muse only speak when she is unhappy? / She does not, I only listen when I am unhappy / When I am happy I live and despise writing / For my Muse this cannot but be dispiriting. STEVIE SMITH, "My Muse," *Selected Poems* (1964).

99. Some men have only one book in them; others, a library. SYDNEY SMITH, quoted in Lady S. Holland's *Memoir* (1855), v. 1.11.

100. For the modern consciousness, the artist (replacing the saint) is the exemplary sufferer. And among artists, the writer, the man of words, is the person to whom we look to be able best to express his suffering. SUSAN SONTAG, "The Artist as Exemplary Sufferer," *Against Interpretation* (1961).

101. The profession of book writing makes horse racing seem like a solid, stable business. JOHN STEINBECK, *Newsweek*, Dec. 24, 1962.

102. The difficulty of literature is not to

write, but to write what you mean. ROBERT LOUIS STEVENSON, title essay, 4, *Virginibus Puerisque* (1881).

103. The good writing of any age has always been the product of *someone's* neurosis, and we'd have a mighty dull literature if all the writers that came along were a bunch of happy chuckleheads. WILLIAM STYRON, interview, *Writers at Work: First Series* (1958).

104. Nothing goes by luck in composition. It allows of no tricks. The best you can write will be the best you are. THOREAU, *Journal*, Feb. 28, 1841.

105. There are two classes of authors: the one write the history of their times, the other their biography. THOREAU, *Journal*, April 22, 1841.

106. Ideally, the writer needs no audience other than the few who understand. It is immodest and greedy to want more. GORE VIDAL, "French Letters: Theories of the New Novel," *Encounter*, December 1967.

107. Your business as a writer is not to illustrate virtue but to show how a fellow may move toward it or away from it. ROBERT PENN WARREN, *Paris Review*, Spring-Summer 1957.

108. There is no royal path to good writing; and such paths as exist do not lead through neat critical gardens, various as they are, but through the jungles of self, the world, and of craft. JESSAMYN WEST, *Saturday Review*, Sept. 21, 1957.

109. To speak in literature with the perfect rectitude and insouciance of the movements of animals and the unimpeachableness of the sentiment of trees in the woods and grass by the roadside is the flawless triumph of art. WALT WHITMAN, preface to *Leaves of Grass* (1855).

110. Literature is strewn with the wreckage of men who have minded beyond reason the opinion of others. VIRGINIA WOOLF, *A Room of One's Own* (1929), 3.

111. Every great and original writer, in proportion as he is great and original, must himself create the taste by which he is to be relished. WILLIAM WORDSWORTH, preface to 2nd edition of *Lyrical Ballads* (1800).

## WRONG

**See 297. Error; 474. Injury; 475. Injustice; 1063. Wrongdoing**

## 1063. WRONGDOING

**See also 171. Conscience; 188. Corruption; 201. Crime; 224. Deeds; 305. Evil; 809. Retribution; 893. Sin; 1023. Vice; 1048. Wickedness**

1. The act of evil / breeds others to follow, / young sins in its own likeness. AESCHYLUS, *Agamemnon* (458 B.C.), tr. Richmond Lattimore.

2. A bad man can do a million times more harm than a beast. ARISTOTLE, *Nicomachean Ethics* (4th c. B.C.), 7.6, tr. J. A. K. Thomson.

3. Whoso diggeth a pit shall fall therein. *Bible*, Proverbs 26:27.

4. If once a man indulges himself in murder, very soon he comes to think little of robbing; and from robbing he comes next to drinking and Sabbath-breaking, and from that to incivility and procrastination. THOMAS DE QUINCEY, "On Murder Considered as One of the Fine Arts" (1827–54).

5. Throughout our life, our worst weaknesses and meannesses are usually committed for the sake of the people whom we most despise. CHARLES DICKENS, *Great Expectations* (1860–61), 27.

6. The flea, though he kill none, he does all the harm he can. JOHN DONNE, *Devotions* (1624), 12.

7. You cannot do wrong without suffering wrong. EMERSON, "Compensation," *Essays: First Series* (1841).

8. For a wrongdoer to be undetected is difficult; and for him to have confidence that his concealment will continue is impossible. EPICURUS, "Vatican Sayings" (3rd c. B.C.), 7, in *Letters, Principal Doctrines, and Vatican Sayings*, tr. Russel M. Geer.

9. If one must do a wrong, it's best to do it / pursuing power—otherwise, let's have virtue. EURIPIDES, *The Phoenician Women* (c. 411–409 B.C.), tr. Elizabeth Wyckoff.

10. A small demerit extinguishes a long service. THOMAS FULLER, M.D., *Gnomologia* (1732), 404.

11. As a single leaf turns not yellow but with the silent knowledge of the whole tree, so the wrong-doer cannot do wrong without the hidden will of you all. KAHLIL GIBRAN, "On Crime and Punishment," *The Prophet* (1923).

12. A good man can be stupid and still be good. But a bad man must have brains—absolutely. MAXIM GORKY, *The Lower Depths* (1903), 4, tr. Alexander Bakshy.

13. Most vices may be committed very genteelly: a man may debauch his friend's wife genteelly: he may cheat at cards genteelly. SAMUEL JOHNSON, quoted in Boswell's *Life of Samuel Johnson*, April 6, 1775.

14. Many might go to heaven with half the labour they go to hell, if they would venture their industry the right way. BEN JONSON, "Random Thoughts," *Timber* (1640).

15. There is scarcely any man sufficiently clever to appreciate all the evil he does. LA ROCHEFOUCAULD, *Maxims* (1665), tr. Kenneth Pratt.

16. Those who are once found to be bad are presumed to be so forever. LATIN PROVERB.

17. Violence and wrong enclose all who commit them in their meshes and do mostly recoil on him from whom they begin. LUCRETIUS, *On the Nature of Things* (1st c. B.C.), 5, tr. H. A. J. Munro.

18. The sinner sins against himself; the wrongdoer wrongs himself, becoming the worse by his own action. MARCUS AURELIUS, *Meditations* (2nd c.), 9.4, tr. Maxwell Staniforth.

19. Men of most renowned virtue have sometimes by transgressing most truly kept the law. MILTON, *Tetrachordon* (1645).

20. There is no shame in the accidents of chance, but only in the consequence of our own misdeeds. PHAEDRUS, "The Cripple and the Bully," *Fables* (1st c.), tr. Thomas James.

21. He who is bent on doing evil can never want [lack] occasion. PUBLILIUS SYRUS, *Moral Sayings* (1st c. B.C.), 459, tr. Darius Lyman.

22. It is so often on the *name* of a misdeed that a life goes to pieces, not the nameless and personal action itself, which was perhaps a perfectly definite necessity of that life and would have been absorbed by it without effort. RAINER MARIA RILKE, *Letters to a Young Poet*, Aug. 12, 1904, tr. M. D. Herter Norton.

23. How oft the sight of means to do ill deeds / Make deeds ill done! SHAKESPEARE, *King John* (1596–97), 4.2.219.

24. Men whose wit has been mother of villainy once / have learned from it to be evil in all things. SOPHOCLES, *Philoctetes* (409 B.C.), tr. David Grene.

# Y

## YANKEES

**See 34. America and Americans**

## 1064. YOUTH

**See also 95. Boys; 121. Children; 383. Girls; 537. Life, Stages of; 1065. Youth and Age**

1. Young men have a passion for regarding their elders as senile. HENRY ADAMS, *The Education of Henry Adams* (1907), 11.

2. Those who tell you that youth needs an ideal are idiots. It has one already, which is youth itself and the wondrous diversity of life—private life, the only real one. JEAN ANOUILH, *Catch as Catch Can* (1960), tr. Lucienne Hill.

3. The young are permanently in a state resembling intoxication; for youth is sweet and they are growing. ARISTOTLE, *Nicomachean Ethics* (4th c. B.C.), 7.14, tr. J. A. K. Thomson.

4. Young men are fitter to invent than to judge, fitter for execution than for counsel, fitter for new projects than for settled business. FRANCIS BACON, "Of Youth and Age," *Essays* (1625).

5. Americans began by loving youth, and now, out of adult self-pity, they worship it. JACQUES BARZUN, *The House of Intellect* (1959), 4.

6. Can love and peace live in the same heart? Youth is unhappy because it is faced with this terrible choice: love without peace, or peace without love. BEAUMARCHAIS, *The Barber of Seville* (1775), 2, tr. Albert Bermel.

7. Money is sullen / And wisdom is sly, / But youth is the pollen / That blows through the sky / And does not ask why. STEPHEN VINCENT BENÉT, *John Brown's Body* (1928), 1.

8. Our youth we can have but to-day, / We may always find time to grow old. GEORGE BERKELEY, *Can Love Be Controlled by Advice?*

9. What a cunning mixture of sentiment, pity, tenderness, irony surrounds adolescence, what knowing watchfulness! Young birds on their first flight are hardly so hovered around. GEORGES BERNANOS, *The Diary of a Country Priest* (1936), 4, tr. Pamela Morris.

10. Very young people are true but not resounding instruments. ELIZABETH BOWEN, *The Death of the Heart* (1938), 2.1.

11. The excesses of our youths are drafts upon our old age, payable with interest, about thirty years after date. CHARLES CALEB COLTON, *Lacon* (1825), 1.76.

12. A youth is to be regarded with respect. How do you know that his future will not be equal to our present? CONFUCIUS, *Analects* (6th c. B.C.), 9.22, tr. James Legge.

13. It is better to waste one's youth than to do nothing with it at all. GEORGES COURTELINE, *La Philosophie de G. Courteline* (1917).

14. All young people want to kick up their heels and defy convention; most of them would prefer to do it at a not too heavy cost. ELMER DAVIS, "On the Eve: Reminiscences of 1913," *By Elmer Davis* (1964).

15. While we are young the idea of death or failure is intolerable to us; even the possibility of ridicule we cannot bear. ISAK DINESEN, "The Deluge at Norderney," *Seven Gothic Tales* (1934).

16. The youth of a nation are the trustees of posterity. BENJAMIN DISRAELI, *Sybil* (1845), 6.13.

17. If youth is the season of hope, it is often so only in the sense that our elders are hopeful about us; for no age is so apt as youth to think its emotions, partings and resolves are the last of their kind. GEORGE ELIOT, *Middlemarch* (1871–72), 55.

18. In youth, we clothe ourselves with rainbows, and go as brave as the zodiac. EMERSON, "Fate," *The Conduct of Life* (1860).

19. Those who love the young best stay young longest. EDGAR Z. FRIEDENBERG, "Adult Imagery and Feeling," *The Vanishing Adolescent* (1959).

20. The "teen-ager" seems to have replaced the Communist as the appropriate target for public controversy and foreboding. EDGAR Z. FRIEDENBERG, "Adult Imagery and Feeling," *The Vanishing Adolescent* (1959).

21. Adolescents tend to be passionate people, and passion is no less real because it is directed toward a hot-rod, a commercialized popular singer, or the leader of a black-jacketed gang. EDGAR Z. FRIEDENBERG, "Emotional Development in Adolescence," *The Vanishing Adolescent* (1959).

22. I go to school to youth to learn the future. ROBERT FROST, "What Fifty Said," *West Running Brook* (1928).

23. A wild colt may become a sober horse. THOMAS FULLER, M.D., *Gnomologia* (1732), 463.

24. Youth's the season made for joys, / Love is then our duty. JOHN GAY, *The Beggar's Opera* (1728), 2.4, air 22.

25. Give me those days with heart in riot, / The depths of bliss that touched on pain, / The force of hate, and love's disquiet— / Ah, give me back my youth again! GOETHE, "Prelude in the Theatre," *Faust: Part I* (1808), tr. Philip Wayne.

26. Every one believes in his youth that the world really began with him, and that all merely exists for his sake. GOETHE, quoted in Johann Peter Eckermann's *Conversations with Goethe*, Dec. 6, 1829.

27. No young man believes he shall ever die. WILLIAM HAZLITT, "On the Feeling of Immortality in Youth," *Literary Remains* (1836).

28. Young people are thoughtless as a rule. HOMER, *Odyssey* (9th c. B.C.), 7, tr. E. V. Rieu.

29. Youth, even in its sorrows, always has a brilliancy of its own. VICTOR HUGO, "Saint Denis," *Les Misérables* (1862), 3.8, tr. Charles E. Wilbour.

30. A majority of young people seem to develop mental arteriosclerosis forty years before they get the physical kind. ALDOUS HUXLEY, interview, *Writers at Work: Second Series* (1963).

31. A riotous youth; / There's little hope of him. / That fault his age / Will, as it grows, correct. BEN JONSON, *Sejanus His Fall* (1603), 1.1.

32. The imagination of a boy is healthy, and the mature imagination of a man is healthy; but there is a space of life between, in which the soul is in a ferment, the character undecided, the way of life uncertain, the ambition thicksighted. JOHN

KEATS, preface, *Endymion* (1818).

33. It is not possible for civilization to flow backward while there is youth in the world. Youth may be headstrong, but it will advance its allotted length. HELEN KELLER, *Midstream* (1930).

34. Fond youth flatters itself that all must heed its prayer. LA FONTAINE, "The Old Cat and the Young Mouse," *Fables* (1668–94), tr. Marianne Moore.

35. Not childhood alone, but the young man till thirty, never feels practically that he is mortal. CHARLES LAMB, "New Year's Eve," *Essays of Elia* (1823).

36. We were happier when we were poorer, but we were also younger. CHARLES LAMB, "Old China," *Last Essays of Elia* (1833).

37. Youth is perpetual intoxication; it is a fever of the mind. LA ROCHEFOUCAULD, *Maxims* (1665), tr. Kenneth Pratt.

38. How beautiful is youth! how bright it gleams / With its illusions, aspirations, dreams! LONGFELLOW, *Morituri Salutamus* (1874).

39. It is an illusion that youth is happy, an illusion of those who have lost it. W. SOMERSET MAUGHAM, *Of Human Bondage* (1915), 29.

40. The young are themselves only with timidity. W. SOMERSET MAUGHAM, *The Summing Up* (1938), 46.

41. It is, indeed, one of the capital tragedies of youth—and youth is the time of real tragedy—that the young are thrown mainly with adults they do not quite respect. H. L. MENCKEN, "Travail," *The Baltimore Evening Sun*, Oct. 8, 1928.

42. The American ideal is youth—handsome, empty youth. HENRY MILLER, "Raimu," *The Wisdom of the Heart* (1941).

43. You never see the old austerity / That was the essence of civility; / Young people hereabouts, unbridled, now / Just want. MOLIÈRE, *The School for Husbands* (1661), 1.3, tr. Donald M. Frame.

44. Immature is the love of the youth, and immature his hatred of man and earth. His mind and the wings of his spirit are still tied down and heavy. NIETZSCHE, "On Free Death," *Thus Spoke Zarathustra* (1883–92), 1, tr. Walter Kaufmann.

45. When one is young, one venerates and despises without that art of nuances which constitutes the best gain of life. NIETZSCHE, *Beyond Good and Evil* (1886), 31, tr. Walter Kaufmann.

46. Alas, that Spring should vanish with the Rose! / That Youth's sweet-scented Manuscript should close! OMAR KHAYYÁM, *Rubáiyát* (11th–12th c.), tr. Edward FitzGerald, 1st ed., 72.

47. Youth does not require reasons for living, it only needs pretexts. JOSÉ ORTEGA Y GASSET, *The Revolt of the Masses* (1930), 14.

48. The old Happiness is unreturning. / Boy's griefs are not so grievous as youth's yearning, / Boys have no sadness sadder than our hope. WILFRED OWEN, "Happiness," *Collected Poems* (1920).

49. The ripeness of adolescence is prodigal in pleasures, skittish, and in need of a bridle. PLUTARCH, "The Education of Children," *Moralia* (c. A.D. 100), tr. Moses Hadas.

50. So much of adolescence is an ill-defined dying, / An intolerable waiting, / A longing for another place and time, / Another condition. THEODORE ROETHKE, "I'm Here," *The Collected Verse of Theodore Roethke* (1961).

51. As a result of all his education, from everything he hears and sees around him, the child absorbs such a lot of lies and foolish nonsense, mixed in with essential truths, that the first duty of the adolescent who wants to be a healthy man is to disgorge it all. ROMAIN ROLLAND, *Jean Christophe* (1904–12).

52. We cannot always build the future for our youth, but we can build our youth for the future. FRANKLIN D. ROOSEVELT, speech, University of Pennsylvania, Philadelphia, Sept. 20, 1940.

53. In early youth, as we contemplate our coming life, we are like children in a theatre before the curtain is raised, sitting there in high spirits and eagerly waiting for the play to begin. SCHOPENHAUER, "On the Sufferings of the World," *Parerga and Paralipomena* (1851), tr. T. Bailey Saunders.

54. Don't laugh at a youth for his affectations; he is only trying on one face after another to find a face of his own. LOGAN PEARSALL SMITH, *Afterthoughts* (1931), 2.

55. The right way to begin is to pay attention to the young, and make them just as good as possible. SOCRATES, in Plato's *Euthyphro* (4th–3rd c. B.C.), tr. Lane Cooper.

56. Youth is the time to go flashing from one end of the world to the other, both in

mind and body. ROBERT LOUIS STEVENSON, "Crabbed Age and Youth," *Virginibus Puerisque* (1881).

57. The boy who expects every morning to open into a new world finds that to-day is like yesterday, but he believes to-morrow will be different. CHARLES DUDLEY WARNER, "First Study," *Backlog Studies* (1873).

58. Youth smiles without any reason. It is one of its chiefest charms. OSCAR WILDE, *The Picture of Dorian Gray* (1891), 14.

59. A young man is so strong, so mad, so certain, and so lost. He has everything and he is able to use nothing. THOMAS WOLFE, *Of Time and the River* (1935), 51.

60. Heaven lies about us in our infancy! / Shades of the prison-house begin to close / Upon the growing boy. WILLIAM WORDSWORTH, "Intimations of Immortality" (1803), 5.

61. For youthful faults ripe virtues shall atone. WILLIAM WORDSWORTH, "Artegal and Elidure" (1815).

## 1065. YOUTH AND AGE

**See also 537. Life, Stages of; 646. Old Age; 1064. Youth**

1. Believe me, all evil comes from the old. They grow fat on ideas and young men die of them. JEAN ANOUILH, *Catch as Catch Can* (1960), tr. Lucienne Hill.

2. If age, which is certainly / Just as wicked as youth, look any wiser, / It is only that youth is still able to believe / It will get away with anything, while age / Knows only too well that it has got away with nothing. W. H. AUDEN, "The Sea and the Mirror," *Collected Poetry* (1945), 1.

3. The old repeat themselves and the young have nothing to say. The boredom is mutual. JACQUES BAINVILLE, "Charme de la conversation," *Lectures* (1937).

4. Young men think old men are fools; but old men know young men are fools. GEORGE CHAPMAN, *All Fools* (c. 1599), 5.1.

5. A youth without fire is followed by an old age without experience. CHARLES CALEB COLTON, *Lacon* (1825), 1.89.

6. The young fancy that their follies are mistaken by the old for happiness. The old fancy that their gravity is mistaken by the young for wisdom. CHARLES CALEB COLTON, *Lacon* (1825), 2.92.

7. Man is like palm-wine: when young, sweet but without strength; in old age, strong but harsh. CONGOLESE PROVERB.

8. In youth the life of reason is not in itself sufficient; afterwards the life of emotion, except for short periods, becomes unbearable. CYRIL CONNOLLY, *The Unquiet Grave* (1945), 1.

9. Pollytics and bankin' is th' on'y two games where age has th' best iv it. Youth has betther things to attind to, an' more iv thim. FINLEY PETER DUNNE, "Avarice and Generosity," *Observations by Mr. Dooley* (1902).

10. Young folk, silly folk; old folk, cold folk. DUTCH PROVERB.

11. Old hands soil, it seems, what they caress; but they too have their beauty when they are joined in prayer. Young hands are made for caresses and the sheathing of love; it is a pity to make them join too soon. ANDRÉ GIDE, *Journals*, Jan. 21, 1929, tr. Justin O'Brien.

12. When a man is young he is so wild he is insufferable. When he is old he plays the saint and becomes insufferable again. NIKOLAI GOGOL, *Gamblers* (1842).

13. Old people are a kind of monsters to little folks; mild manifestations of the terrible, it may be, but still, with their white locks and ridged and grooved features, which those horrid little eyes exhaust of their details like so many microscopes, not exactly what human beings ought to be. OLIVER WENDELL HOLMES, SR., *The Poet at the Breakfast Table* (1872), 1.

14. He that would pass the latter part of life with honour and decency must, when he is young, consider that he shall one day be old; and remember, when he is old, that he has once been young. SAMUEL JOHNSON, *The Rambler* (1750–52), 50.

15. In youth, it is common to measure right and wrong by the opinion of the world, and in age, to act without any measure but interest, and to lose shame without substituting virtue. SAMUEL JOHNSON, *The Rambler* (1750–52), 197.

16. Age looks with anger on the temerity of youth, and youth with contempt on the scrupulosity of age. SAMUEL JOHNSON, *Rasselas* (1759), 26.

17. Now we are all fallen, youth from

their fear, / And age from that which bred it, good example. BEN JONSON, *Every Man in His Humour* (1598), 2.5.

18. The passions of the young are vices in the old. JOSEPH JOUBERT, *Pensées* (1842), 7.13.

19. Most men spend the first half of their lives making the second half miserable. LA BRUYÈRE, *Characters* (1688), 11.102.

20. Youth is incautious. / Wisdom learns to tread softly, / Valuing moments. AMY LOWELL, "The Anniversary," *What's O'Clock* (1925).

21. If you will be cherished when you are old, be courteous while you be young. JOHN LYLY, *Euphues: The Anatomy of Wit* (1579).

22. Youth is immortal; / 'Tis the elderly only grow old! HERMAN MELVILLE, "The Wise Virgins to Madam Mirror," *At the Hostelry* (1925).

23. What though youth gave love and roses, / Age still leaves us friends and wine. THOMAS MOORE, "Spring and Autumn," *National Airs* (1815).

24. The aged love what is practical, while impetuous youth longs only for what is dazzling. PETRARCH, *Letter to Posterity* (1367–72).

25. In youth one has tears without grief; in age, griefs without tears. JOSEPH ROUX, *Meditations of a Parish Priest* (1886), 5.55, tr. Isabel F. Hapgood.

26. The young man who has not wept is a savage, and the older man who will not laugh is a fool. GEORGE SANTAYANA, *Dialogues in Limbo* (1925).

27. Crabbed age and youth cannot live together: / Youth is full of pleasance, age is full of care. SHAKESPEARE, *The Passionate Pilgrim* (1599), 12.1.

28. Youth, which is forgiven everything, forgives itself nothing: age, which forgives itself everything, is forgiven nothing. GEORGE BERNARD SHAW, "Maxims for Revolutionists," *Man and Superman* (1903).

29. It's all that the young can do for the old, to shock them and keep them up to date. GEORGE BERNARD SHAW, "Induction," *Fanny's First Play* (1912).

30. All sorts of allowances are made for the illusions of youth; and none, or almost none, for the disenchantments of age. ROBERT LOUIS STEVENSON, "Crabbed Age and Youth," *Virginibus Puerisque* (1881).

31. To the old our mouths are always partly closed; we must swallow our obvious retorts and listen. They sit above our heads, on life's raised dais, and appeal at once to our respect and pity. ROBERT LOUIS STEVENSON, "Talk and Talkers" (1882), 2.

32. Dignity, high station, or great riches, are in some sort necessary to old men, in order to keep the younger at a distance, who are otherwise too apt to insult them upon the score of their age. JONATHAN SWIFT, *Thoughts on Various Subjects* (1711).

33. Age is no better, hardly so well, qualified for an instructor as youth, for it has not profited so much as it has lost. THOREAU, "Economy," *Walden* (1854).

34. Consider well the proportions of things. It is better to be a young June-bug than an old bird of paradise. MARK TWAIN, "Pudd'nhead Wilson's Calendar," *Pudd'nhead Wilson* (1894), 8.

35. Life should begin with age and its privileges and accumulations, and end with youth and its capacity to splendidly enjoy such advantages. MARK TWAIN, letter to Edward L. Dimmit, July 19, 1901.

36. The young suffer less from their own errors than from the cautiousness of the old. VAUVENARGUES, *Reflections and Maxims* (1746), 158.

37. The old believe everything, the middle-aged suspect everything, the young know everything. OSCAR WILDE, "Phrases and Philosophies for the Use of the Young" (1891).

38. I really believe that more harm is done by old men who cling to their influence than by young men who anticipate it. OWEN D. YOUNG, *New York Herald Tribune*, July 12, 1962.

# Z

## 1066. ZEAL

See also 291. Enthusiasm; 333. Fanaticism

1. Whenever we find ourselves more inclined to persecute than to persuade, we may then be certain that our zeal has more of pride in it than of charity. CHARLES CALEB COLTON, *Lacon* (1825), 1.17.

2. Zeal without knowledge is fire without

light. THOMAS FULLER, M.D., *Gnomologia* (1732), 6069.

3. Zeal will do more than knowledge. WILLIAM HAZLITT, "On the Difference Between Writing and Speaking," *The Plain Speaker* (1826).

4. Let a man in a garret but burn with enough intensity and he will set fire to the world. SAINT-EXUPÉRY, *Wind, Sand, and Stars* (1939), 9.1, tr. Lewis Galantière.

## 1067. ZEN

See also 790. Religion

1. Zen is a way of liberation, concerned not with discovering what is good or bad or advantageous, but what is. ALAN WATTS, *Life*, April 21, 1961.

# INDEX OF AUTHORS AND SOURCES

# INDEX OF AUTHORS AND SOURCES

This index contains brief identifications of all persons quoted and of works that cannot be ascribed to an author. The numbers in the entries refer not to pages but to individual quotations. That part of the number before the period indicates the category; the second part indicates the quotation within the category. Numbers and titles of categories appear at the tops of the text pages so that the user can readily find the quotation he is looking for.

A very large block of numbers after an author's name would be too formidable for practical use. Therefore, when more than 75 quotations have been selected from a single author or source, the quotation numbers have been omitted. Such entries are preceded by an asterisk.

## A

Achard, Marcel (1899– ). French playwright. 576.1

Acton, Lord (Sir John Emerich Edward Dalberg-Acton, 1st Baron Acton) (1834–1902). English historian. 117.1; 330.1; 388.1; 417.1; 534.1; 534.2; 671.1; 713.1

Adams, Franklin P. (1881–1960). American journalist and humorist. 111.1; 260.1; 322.1; 393.1; 462.1; 580.1; 580.2; 653.1; 700.1; 705.1; 705.2; 838.1; 896.1; 991.1; 1030.1; 1062.1

Adams, Henry [Brooks] (1838–1918). American historian, scholar, man of letters. 95.1; 114.1; 255.1; 277.1; 291.1; 299.1; 317.1; 363.1; 363.2; 363.3; 417.2; 417.3; 529.1; 576.2; 580.3; 598.1; 705.3; 705.4; 705.5; 713.2; 713.3; 778.1; 805.1; 892.1; 894.1; 906.1; 957.1; 959.1; 959.2; 985.1; 1055.1; 1064.1

Adams, John (1735–1826). Second President of the United States (1797–1801). 137.1; 277.2; 374.1; 393.2; 393.3; 393.4; 911.1; 1020.1; 1025.1; 1025.2; 1030.2; 1041.1; 1062.2

Adams, Samuel (1722–1803). American pamphleteer, member of Continental Congress. 710.1

Addison, Joseph (1672–1719). English essayist, critic, poet. 14.1; 19.1; 41.1; 49.1; 91.1; 142.1; 178.1; 185.1; 195.1; 206.1; 218.1; 223.1; 330.2; 348.1; 377.1; 389.1; 390.1; 405.1; 407.1; 454.1; 486.1; 508.1; 508.2; 562.1; 594.1; 594.2; 607.1; 648.1; 671.2; 762.1; 797.1; 814.1; 890.1; 898.1; 1004.1; 1025.3; 1043.1; 1062.3

Ade, George (1866–1944). American humorist and playwright. 185.2; 331.1; 386.1; 420.1; 424.1; 545.1; 619.1; 669.1; 783.1; 805.2; 957.2; 985.2; 985.3; 1044.1

Adler, Renata. Contemporary American film critic. 372.1

Aeschylus (525–456 B.C.). Greek tragic playwright. 17.1; 19.2; 137.2; 156.1; 218.2; 266.1; 293.1; 293.2; 340.1; 340.2; 340.3; 353.1; 355.1; 366.1; 385.1; 426.1; 438.1; 517.1; 517.2; 525.1; 560.1; 560.2; 592.1; 617.1; 635.1; 644.1; 646.1; 646.2; 713.4; 744.1; 752.1; 811.1; 825.1; 933.1; 939.1; 939.2; 971.1; 971.2; 971.3; 995.1; 995.2; 1041.2; 1050.1; 1053.1; 1063.1

Aesop (c. 620–c. 560 B.C.). Greek fabulist. 17.2; 19.3; 19.4; 22.1; 33.1; 45.1; 46.1; 57.1; 60.1; 163.1; 183.1; 192.1; 236.1; 236.2; 249.1; 250.1; 286.1; 286.2; 305.1; 308.1; 321.1; 329.1; 353.2; 356.1; 361.1; 363.4; 398.1; 434.1; 442.1; 447.1; 472.1; 474.1; 481.1; 506.1; 517.3; 579.1; 579.2; 629.1; 641.1; 674.1; 706.1; 717.1; 766.1; 866.1; 913.1; 991.2; 995.3; 1005.1; 1016.1; 1020.2; 1023.1; 1041.3; 1057.1

Agathon (second half of 5th c. B.C.). Athenian tragic poet. 53.1; 669.2

Alain. Pen name of Emile [Auguste] Chartier (1868–1951). French philosopher, essayist, teacher. 441.1; 584.1; 627.1; 738.1; 897.1; 916.1

Albee, Edward [Franklin] (1928– ). American playwright. 708.1

Alcmaeon of Crotona (fl. c. 500 B.C.). Greek physician and Pythagorean philosopher. 74.1

Aldington, Richard (1892–1962). English poet, novelist, biographer, translator. 615.1; 1055.2

Aldrich, Thomas Bailey (1836–1907). American poet, editor, novelist, playwright. 53.2; 71.1; 91.2; 93.1; 131.1; 134.1; 434.2; 482.1; 498.1; 521.1; 573.1; 599.1; 646.3; 646.4; 712.1; 713.5; 757.1; 772.1; 936.1; 1062.4

Alembert, Jean Le Rond d' (1717–1783). French mathematician and skeptical philosopher. 1054.1

Ali ibn-abi-Talib (c. 600–661). Cousin and son-in-law of Mohammed; fourth caliph of the Moslems. 75.1; 181.1; 238.1; 286.3; 363.5; 391.1; 401.1; 916.2; 1053.2

Allen, Charles M. (1918– ). American educator. 63.1; 960.1

Allen, Fred. Real name, John F. Sullivan (1894–1956). American comedian. 143.1; 330.3

Altrincham, Lord. *See* Grigg, John.

Ambrose, St. Latin name, Aurelius Ambrosius (c. A.D. 333–397). Bishop of Milan, one of the Fathers of the Latin church. 985.4

Ames, Fisher (1758–1808). American statesman and essayist. 393.5

Amiel, Henri Frédéric (1821–1881). Swiss philosopher and poet. 119.1; 121.1; 222.1; 231.1; 238.2; 257.1; 269.1; 283.1; 375.1; 404.1; 438.2; 485.1; 489.1; 558.1; 558.2; 668.1; 684.1; 727.1; 735.1; 778.2; 954.1; 971.4; 998.1; 1010.1; 1055.3

Amory, Cleveland (1917– ). American writer and social critic. 326.1

Amphis (4th c. B.C.). Greek playwright. 53.3

Anacharsis (fl. c. 600 B.C.). Scythian philosopher. 266.2; 697.1

Anaxagoras (c. 500–c. 428 B.C.). Greek philosopher and scientist. 218.3

Anderson, Marian (1902– ). American contralto. 769.1

Anouilh, Jean (1910– ). French playwright and screen writer. 9.1; 43.1; 53.4; 70.1; 70.2; 70.3; 192.2; 218.5; 218.6; 237.1; 340.4; 359.1; 382.1; 385.2; 502.1; 525.2; 536.1; 536.2; 537.1; 539.1; 548.1; 548.2; 548.3; 548.4; 575.1; 586.1; 598.2; 623.1; 646.5; 654.1; 669.3; 692.1; 705.6; 729.1; 739.1; 777.1; 834.1; 852.1; 870.1; 956.1; 980.1; 1048.1; 1064.2; 1065.1

Antisthenes (c. 445–365 B.C.). Greek philosopher, founder of the Cynic school. 286.4; 293.3; 332.1; 823.1; 923.1

*Apocrypha*. A part of the sacred literature of the Alexandrian Jews. 43.2; 57.2; 96.1; 162.1; 203.1; 213.1; 218.7; 239.1; 282.1; 284.1; 300.1; 353.3; 363.6; 363.7; 385.3; 407.2; 508.3; 745.1; 798.1; 824.1; 973.1; 991.3; 1017.1; 1053.3

Apostolius, Michael (1422–1480). Greek scholar in Italy during Renaissance. 788.1

Aquinas, St. Thomas (c. 1225–1274). Italian theologian and philosopher. 613.1

Aragon, Louis (1897– ). French novelist, poet, essayist. 374.2

Arbuthnot, John (1667–1735). Scottish writer and physician. 704.1

Archimedes (c. 287–212 B.C.). Syracusan mathematician, astronomer, inventor. 713.7

Aretino, Pietro (1492–1556). Italian Renaissance satirist. 17.3; 39.1; 39.2; 81.1; 330.4; 346.1; 363.8; 489.2; 514.1; 527.1; 536.3; 646.6; 663.1; 702.1; 745.2; 842.1; 848.1; 856.1; 885.1; 993.1; 1035.1

Ariosto, Lodovico (1474–1533). Italian poet. 206.2

Aristippus (fl. c. 435–c. 356 B.C.). Greek philosopher, founder of Cyrenaic School. 698.1

Aristophanes (c. 445–380 B.C.). Greek comic playwright. 420.2; 1055.4

*Aristotle (384–322 B.C.). Greek philosopher.

Arnold, Matthew (1822–1888). English critic, essayist, poet. 7.1; 75.2; 114.3; 115.1; 207.1; 224.2; 236.3; 237.2; 247.1; 365.1; 385.4; 442.2; 442.3; 502.2; 558.4; 574.1; 583.1; 600.1; 616.1; 646.7; 670.1; 677.1; 752.3; 806.1; 865.1; 868.1; 908.3; 982.1; 991.5; 1055.5; 1058.1; 1060.1; 1062.5

Aron, Raymond [Claude Ferdinand] (1905– ). French educator and writer. 359.2

Asch, Sholem (1880–1957). Polish-born American novelist. 574.2; 1062.6

Athenagoras I (1886– ). Archbishop and ecumenical patriarch of Constantinople. 124.1

Athenodorus [Cananites] (c. 74 B.C.–A.D. 8). Greek Stoic philosopher. 545.2

Atkinson, [Justin] Brooks (1894– ). American dramatic critic and essayist. 34.1; 53.6; 80.1; 100.1; 100.2; 106.1; 124.2; 199.1; 204.2; 277.5; 296.1; 393.7; 403.1; 418.1; 441.2; 502.3; 536.5; 539.2; 565.1; 613.2; 616.2; 623.2; 624.1; 625.1; 649.2; 665.1; 689.1; 833.1; 1035.2; 1058.2; 1062.7

Attlee, Clement [Richard], 1st Earl (1883–1967). British political leader. Prime Minister of Great Britain (1945–1951). 231.4; 287.1

Auden, W[ystan] H[ugh] (1907– ). English-born American poet and playwright. 20.1; 34.2; 91.3; 204.3; 205.1; 328.1; 374.4; 391.3; 467.1; 546.1; 548.5; 563.1; 587.1; 607.2; 607.3; 648.2; 669.4; 681.1; 702.2; 702.3; 746.1; 787.1; 865.2; 875.1; 876.1; 933.2; 956.2; 957.3; 1062.8; 1062.9; 1065.2

Augustine, St. Latin name, Aurelius Augustinus (A.D. 354–430). Early Christian church father and philosopher. 55.1; 120.1; 328.2; 407.6; 980.2; 983.1; 1023.2; 1053.5

Austen, Jane (1775–1817). English novelist. 65.1; 191.1; 290.1; 363.13; 588.1; 698.3; 1055.6

Azuela, Mariano (1873–1952). Mexican novelist. 813.2

## B

Bacchylides (c. 505–c. 450 B.C.). Greek lyric poet. 218.8

Bacon, Francis (1561–1626). English philosopher, statesman, essayist. 1.1; 8.1; 19.5; 39.4; 85.1; 91.4; 91.5; 102.2; 129.3; 166.1; 192.4; 198.1; 204.4; 210.1; 213.2; 218.9; 218.10; 257.2; 293.4; 297.1; 319.2; 329.3; 330.5; 332.4; 351.1; 358.1; 363.14; 363.15; 399.1; 426.2; 474.2; 477.1; 478.1; 512.2; 520.1; 548.6; 560.3; 566.1; 580.4; 616.3; 616.4; 650.1; 651.1; 663.3; 663.4; 688.1; 726.2; 745.3; 764.1; 797.2; 811.3; 811.4; 813.3; 825.3; 842.2; 908.4; 908.5; 913.2; 916.3; 919.1; 923.3; 936.2; 947.1; 979.1; 997.1; 1020.3; 1025.5; 1035.3; 1041.4; 1062.10; 1064.4

Bagehot, Walter (1826–1877). English economist and critic. 964.1

Bainville, Jacques (1879–1936). French historian, journalist, essayist. 1065.3

Baker, Ray Stannard. *See* Grayson, David.

Baker, Russell [Wayne] (1925– ). American journalist. 352.1; 368.1; 457.1; 596.1; 597.1; 638.1; 638.2; 698.4; 752.4; 922.1; 994.1

Baldwin, James (1924– ). American novelist and essayist. 34.3; 39.5; 53.7; 83.1; 83.2; 83.3; 85.2; 121.3; 129.4; 201.1; 233.1; 301.1; 361.2; 366.2; 417.5; 596.2; 764.2; 777.2; 868.2; 878.1; 920.1; 1029.1; 1047.1; 1062.11

Ball, Sir Robert S[tawell] (1840–1913). Irish astronomer, educator, writer. 558.5

Balzac [Honoré de] (1799–1850). French novelist. 534.3; 559.1; 692.2; 1029.2

Banning, Margaret Culkin (1891– ). American novelist and political writer. 341.1

Barbauld, Anna Letitia, née Aikin (1743–1825). English writer. 626.1

Barbey d'Aurevilly, Jules (1808–1889). French novelist and critic. 53.8; 92.1; 131.2; 407.7

Baring, Maurice (1874–1945). English novelist, essayist, poet, playwright. 596.3

Barnes, Djuna (1892– ). American novelist, short-story writer, playwright. 42.1; 282.2; 399.2; 442.5; 536.6; 548.7; 580.5; 911.2; 971.5

Barnett, Lincoln [Kinnear] (1909– ). American writer. 843.1

Barr, A[lfred] H[amilton], Jr. (1902– ). American art historian and museum director. 63.2

Barrès, [Augustin-] Maurice (1862–1923). French novelist, journalist, politician. 705.8

Barrie, Sir J[ames] M[atthew] (1860–1937). Scottish dramatist and novelist. 119.2; 192.5; 286.5; 330.6; 536.7; 758.1; 790.1; 1055.7

Barron, Frank. Contemporary American educator and writer. 198.2

Barrymore, Ethel (1879–1959). American actress. 11.1; 965.1

Barth, John [Simmons] (1930– ). American novelist. 417.6; 476.1; 558.6; 561.1; 601.2; 1019.1

Barth, Karl (1886–1968). Swiss Protestant Reformed theologian and educator. 329.4; 607.4; 966.1

Barthélémy, Auguste [Marseille] (1796–1867). French poet and satirist. 115.2

Bartók, Béla (1881–1945). Hungarian composer, pianist, collector of folk songs. 154.1

Baruch, Bernard M[annes] (1870–1965). American businessman and statesman. 393.8; 646.8; 705.9; 978.1; 1030.3

Barzun, Jacques [Martin] 1907– ). French-born American critic and educator. 53.9; 115.3; 250.2; 277.6; 295.4; 440.1; 490.1; 520.2; 727.2; 728.1; 777.3; 968.1; 980.3; 994.2; 1064.5

Bashkirtsev, Marie (1860–1884). Russian painter and diarist. 600.2

Baudelaire, Charles [Pierre] (1821–1867). French poet. 27.1; 102.3; 733.1; 885.2; 1058.3

Baudouin I (1930– ). King of Belgium. (1951– ). 1035.4

Bauër, Gérard (1888– ). French writer. 916.4

Baxter, Richard (1615–1691). English divine. 118.1

Bayle, Pierre (1647–1706). French philosopher. 979.2

Bazin, Hervé (1917– ). French novelist. 410.1

Beaumarchais, Pierre Augustin Caron de (1732–1799). French playwright, courtier, watchmaker to Louis XV. 558.7; 749.2; 895.1; 965.2; 1064.6

Beaumont, Francis (c. 1584–1616). English playwright. *See* Beaumont and Fletcher.

Beaumont and Fletcher. 17.5; 335.1; 899.1; 908.6; 1048.2; 1055.8

Beauvoir, Simone de (1908– ). French existentialist novelist and essayist. 361.3

Beckett, Samuel (1906– ). Irish-born French novelist and playwright. 555.1; 759.1

Becque, Henry [François] (1837–1899). French playwright. 102.4; 222.2; 508.4; 575.2; 576.3

Beecham, Sir Thomas (1879–1961). English conductor. 287.2; 607.5

*Beecher, Henry Ward (1813–1887). American clergyman, editor, writer.

Beerbohm, Sir Max (1872–1956). English essayist and caricaturist. 14.2; 129.5; 163.3; 189.1; 204.5; 224.3; 287.3; 327.1; 330.8; 339.1; 382.2; 399.3; 416.1; 426.3; 426.4; 426.5; 428.1; 515.2; 521.2; 596.4; 684.2; 685.1; 702.4; 802.1; 921.1; 1034.1; 1058.5; 1058.6

Behan, Brendan (1923–1964). Irish playwright and wit. 1035.6

Belloc, [Joseph] Hilaire [Pierre] (1870–1953). English writer. 41.3; 113.1; 363.16; 895.2

Bellow, Saul (1915– ). American novelist and playwright. 122.1; 391.5; 391.6

Benedict of Nursia, St. (480?–?543). Monk, founder of the Benedictine order. 1058.7

Benét, Stephen Vincent (1898–1943). American poet and short-story writer. 34.4; 264.1; 305.3;

441.3; 713.8; 809.1; 980.4; 1035.7; 1035.8; 1064.7

Benét, William Rose (1886–1950). American poet, critic, editor. 626.2

Benn, Anthony [Neil] Wedgwood (1925– ). English politician; renounced title of Lord Stansgate, 1963. 287.4

Benn, Gottfried (1886–1956). German poet, short-story writer, essayist. 10.2

Bentham, Jeremy (1748–1832). English philosopher. 407.9; 760.1

Bentley, Eric (1916– ). English-born American drama critic, teacher, editor. 54.1; 144.1; 335.2; 407.10

Berenson, Bernard (1865–1959). Lithuanian-born American art connoisseur. 53.10

Bergson, Henri (1859–1941). French philosopher. 441.4; 491.1

Berkeley, George (1685–1753). Irish-born English bishop and philosopher. 1064.8

Berle, Milton. Real name, Milton Berlinger (1908– ). American actor and comedian. 146.1

Berlin, Irving. Real name, Israel Baline (1888– ). Russian-born American composer. 938.2

Berlioz, [Louis] Hector (1803–1869). French composer. 210.3; 374.5

Bernanos, Georges (1888–1948). French novelist and political writer. 9.3; 62.1; 114.4; 414.1; 425.2; 570.2; 652.2; 675.1; 712.4; 717.3; 727.3; 866.2; 923.4; 989.1; 1064.9

Bernard, Tristan. Pen name of Paul Bernard (1866–1947). French playwright and novelist. 407.11; 799.1; 894.2

Berry, John (1915– ). American poet and fiction writer. 407.12

Bertin, Mlle (18th c.). Milliner to Marie Antoinette. 632.1

Beston, Henry [Sheahan] (1888–1968). American writer. 41.4; 54.2; 88.1; 174.1; 174.2; 270.1; 292.1; 616.5; 616.6; 626.3; 626.4; 847.1; 848.2; 943.1

Betti, Ugo (1892–1953). Italian playwright. 6.2; 17.6; 76.1; 101.1; 114.5; 121.5; 218.11; 218.12; 255.2; 269.3; 314.1; 332.5; 332.6; 340.5; 363.17; 441.5; 442.6; 464.1; 480.1; 515.3; 515.4; 516.2; 536.8; 536.9; 536.10; 548.8; 555.2; 555.3; 560.5; 574.3; 616.7; 620.1; 636.1; 643.1; 646.9; 674.2; 703.1; 717.4; 806.2; 832.1; 852.2; 882.2; 885.3; 886.1; 894.3; 897.2; 899.2; 908.7; 939.3; 971.6; 983.2; 994.3; 1055.9; 1057.3

Beyle, Marie Henri. *See* Stendhal.

*Bhagavadgita* (Sanskrit, *The Song of God*). 9.4; 9.5; 10.3; 328.3; 414.2; 445.2; 471.1; 520.4; 582.1; 674.3; 677.3; 764.3; 859.1; 868.3; 1058.8

Bias (fl. middle of 6th c. B.C.). Greek philosopher, one of the Seven Sages of Greece. 363.18

*Bible. The Authorized King James Version (1611).

*Bidpai* [also *Bidpay, Pilpay*], *Fables of* (c. 750). An Arabic version of a collection of Indian fables. 699.1; 781.1; 809.4

*Bierce, Ambrose [Gwinett] (1842–?1914). American journalist, short-story writer, poet.

Bion (probably 2nd c. B.C.). Greek poet. 17.9; 589.1; 646.11

Bird, [Cyril] Kenneth. Pseudonym, Fougasse (1887– ). English illustrator, cartoonist, editor. 434.4

Bishop, Elizabeth (1911– ). American poet. 833.2

Bishop, Jim [James Alonzo] (1907– ). American writer, editor, newspaperman. 204.6; 366.5; 417.8

Bismarck-Schönhausen, Otto Eduard Leopold von (1815–1898). Prussian statesman and first chancellor of the German Empire; "the Iron Chancellor." 379.1

Black, Hugo L[aFayette] (1886– ). American jurist. 362.1

Blake, William (1757–1827). English poet, engraver, painter, mystic. 33.3; 39.9; 76.2; 123.1; 197.1; 236.5; 262.2; 297.2; 310.1; 328.7; 351.2; 353.6; 357.3; 407.16; 433.2; 444.2; 458.1; 476.2; 491.2; 511.1; 524.1; 557.1; 577.1; 616.8; 676.1; 676.2; 692.3; 746.2; 749.3; 775.1; 809.5; 911.4; 940.1; 954.2; 968.3; 971.7; 972.3

Blondel, Maurice (1861–1949). French philosopher. 53.11

Blum, Léon (1872–1950). French statesman and critic. 663.8

Bocca, Geoffrey. Contemporary American writer. 1054.3

Bodenheim, Maxwell (1893–1954). American poet and novelist. 702.5

Boethius, Anicius Manlius Severinus (c. 480–525). Roman philosopher. 17.10; 407.17; 548.11; 607.6; 700.3; 930.1; 1004.2

Bogan, Louise (1897–1970). American poet and critic. 1055.12

Bohlen, Charles E[ustis] (1904– ). American diplomat. 149.1

Boileau [-Despréaux], Nicolas (1636–1711). French poet and critic. 132.1; 183.3; 296.2; 445.5; 489.4; 1062.13

Bolingbroke, Viscount. *See* St. John, Henry.

Bolt, Robert (1924– ). English playwright. 168.2; 218.15; 525.9; 598.5; 635.2; 728.3

Bonhoeffer, Dietrich (1906–1945). German theologian, imprisoned and executed by Nazis. 9.6; 120.2; 123.2; 218.16; 222.4; 385.8; 652.4; 939.4; 971.8

Bonnot, Étienne. *See* Condillac, Étienne Bonnot, Abbé de.

*The Book of Common Prayer* (1549, 1789, 1928). Prayer book of the Church of England and of the Protestant Episcopal Church in the U.S.A. 538.1; 830.1

Boorstin, Daniel J. (1914– ). American educator and writer. 18.2; 34.5; 34.6; 53.12; 91.9; 330.9; 385.9; 416.2; 447.2; 606.1; 623.4; 754.1; 985.7

816.5; 844.1; 852.5; 880.2; 882.4; 908.8; 1047.3

Budgell, Eustace (1686–1737). English essayist and man of letters. 51.5; 170.1; 363.23; 1057.4

Buffon, Comte Georges Louis Leclerc de (1707–1788). French naturalist and writer. 374.6; 935.1

Bulwer-Lytton, Edward George Earle Lytton, 1st Baron Lytton (1803–1873). English novelist and playwright. 975.1; 1062.17

Burgess, Anthony (1917– ). English novelist. 91.11; 91.12; 261.1

Burgess, [Frank] Gelett (1866–1951). American humorist and illustrator. 154.2; 214.1; 307.1; 363.24; 376.1; 392.2; 448.3; 576.4; 576.5; 637.2; 663.10; 663.11; 814.2; 874.1; 1055.14; 1055.15

Burke, Edmund (1729–1797). English statesman, orator, writer. 17.13; 160.2; 210.4; 213.3; 327.6; 340.6; 354.3; 366.6; 393.12; 496.2; 557.2; 585.1; 651.3; 654.4; 670.3; 705.14; 713.9; 756.2; 790.5; 882.5; 923.5; 958.2; 970.4; 970.5; 997.5

Burnham, Daniel H[udson] (1846–1912). American architect. 696.1

Burns, Robert (1756–1796). Scottish poet. 118.2; 151.4; 206.3; 332.8; 425.4; 598.7; 616.13; 696.2; 698.6; 868.4; 876.2; 983.6; 997.6

Burroughs, John (1837–1921). American naturalist, essayist, poet. 91.13; 409.1; 606.2; 669.6; 1033.1

Burton, Sir Richard Francis (1821–1890). English explorer and writer of travel books. 574.4; 847.3; 985.8

Burton, Robert (1577–1640). English clergyman and writer. 19.8; 186.2; 188.2; 335.4; 433.3; 560.12; 607.8; 693.1; 826.2; 889.1; 1004.5

Bussy-Rabutin, Roger de (1618–1693). French soldier and writer. 713.10; 800.1

Butler, Samuel (1612–1680). English poet and satirist. 96.3; 157.1; 196.1; 224.5; 298.2; 337.3; 340.7; 553.1; 596.9; 596.10; 635.3; 644.3; 766.2

*Butler, Samuel (1835–1902). English novelist, scholar, translator.

Byrd, William (1540?–1623). English composer. 331.3

Byron, George Gordon [Noel], 6th Baron Byron of Rochdale. Called Lord Byron (1788–1824). English poet. 9.11; 17.15; 31.1; 92.2; 120.3; 123.3; 129.7; 136.3; 138.1; 141.1; 144.2; 204.8; 204.9; 204.10; 218.27; 218.28; 266.4; 272.6; 287.6; 296.5; 329.11; 351.3; 363.26; 407.20; 410.3; 417.13; 447.4; 487.3; 508.7; 517.6; 524.2; 525.11; 534.7; 545.3; 548.23; 558.11; 559.3; 560.14; 560.15; 576.6; 596.11; 603.2; 616.14; 626.5; 632.3; 646.14; 646.15; 668.4; 698.7; 700.4; 702.8; 702.9; 758.3; 811.6; 847.4; 851.1; 893.3; 899.4; 902.1; 908.9; 908.10; 911.7; 923.6; 945.1; 968.5; 971.10; 982.2; 991.14; 1012.1; 1055.16; 1055.17; 1060.4; 1060.5; 1062.18

## C

Cabell, James Branch (1879–1958). American novelist and essayist. 653.2

Caesar, [Caius] Julius (100–44 B.C.). Roman general and statesman. 43.3; 250.4; 525.12

Cage, John (1912– ). American composer. 53.18; 53.19; 53.20; 70.8; 114.6; 249.3; 297.8; 327.7; 352.3; 536.17; 579.4; 583.2; 607.10; 607.11; 607.12; 654.5; 702.10; 804.4; 873.2; 891.2; 912.1; 930.2; 965.3; 1051.1

Caldwell, Erskine [Preston] (1903– ). American novelist and short-story writer. 1062.19

Calhoun, John C[aldwell] (1782–1850). American statesman, Vice President of the United States under John Q. Adams and Andrew Jackson (1825–1832). 34.8; 115.7; 740.4; 755.4

Campbell, Thomas (1777–1844). Scottish poet. 195.2; 285.2; 407.21; 452.1; 548.24; 682.1

Camus, Albert (1913–1960). French philosopher, novelist, playwright, journalist. 3.2; 3.3; 51.7; 53.21; 53.22; 70.9; 117.4; 145.1; 166.2; 172.1; 173.3; 182.2; 218.29; 218.30; 269.5; 319.5; 341.2; 361.4; 363.27; 366.7; 385.16; 399.7; 403.3; 403.4; 407.22; 407.23; 413.2; 430.5; 476.3; 490.2; 491.3; 536.18; 538.3; 561.3; 705.15; 713.11; 723.3; 760.3; 809.6; 834.3; 868.5; 870.2; 941.2; 941.3; 991.15; 991.16; 995.5; 998.2; 1019.2; 1035.11; 1062.20

Canning, George (1740–1827). English statesman. 360.2

Caplan, Mortimer M[axwell] (1916– ). American lawyer and public official. 958.3

Capote, Truman (1924– ). American novelist and short-story writer. 1022.1; 1062.21

Capus, Alfred (1858–1922). French journalist and playwright. 269.6; 508.8; 560.16

Cardarelli, Vincenzo (1887– ). Italian poet and critic. 450.2

Carew, Thomas (c. 1598–c. 1639). English poet. 384.2; 548.25; 592.2; 702.11

*Carlyle, Thomas (1795–1881). Scottish-born English prose writer.

Carroll, Lewis. Pen name of Charles Lutwidge Dodgson (1832–1898). English writer and mathematician. 91.15; 311.2; 571.2; 598.11; 654.7; 702.13; 702.14; 760.4; 935.2; 1025.9

Carson, Rachel [Louise] (1907–1964). American writer and scientist. 847.5

Cary, Joyce (1888–1957). Anglo-Irish novelist. 198.6; 1049.1

Casals, Pablo (1876– ). Spanish cellist and conductor. 608.3

Cassirer, Ernst (1874–1945). German philosopher. 558.12

Cato the Elder. Full name, Marcus Porcius, Cato. Also known as Cato the Censor (234–149 B.C.). Roman statesman. 334.2; 807.1

Catullus. Full Latin name, Gaius Valerius Catullus (c. 84– c. 54 B.C.). Roman poet. 167.2; 1055.18

philosopher. 549.2

Cratinus (c. 520–c. 423 B.C.). Greek playwright. 266.7

Cravens, Kathryn. Contemporary American journalist, writer, and radio news commentator. 346.7

Crébillon, Prosper Jolyot. Pen name of Prosper Jolyot, sieur de Crais-Billon (1674–1762). French playwright. 518.1

Creeley, Robert [White] (1926– ). American poet, editor, novelist. 397.2

Creighton, Mandell (1843–1901). English prelate and historian. 661.1

Crèvecoeur, Michel Guillaume Jean de. Pen name, J. Hector St. John (1735–1813). French writer, agronomist, traveler, settler in America. 292.2; 790.14

Crockett, David (1786–1836). American frontiersman, soldier, public official. 816.8

Cromwell, Oliver (1599–1658). English Puritan leader. Lord Protector of the Realm (1653–1658). 674.7

Cruse, Heloise. Contemporary American writer. 135.3

Cullen, Countee (1903–1946). American poet. 228.3; 538.4; 548.37; 549.3; 736.2

Cumberland, Richard (1632–1718). English bishop. 10.5

Cummings, E[dward] E[stlin] (1894–1962). American poet. 269.9; 297.12; 442.9; 445.9; 519.1; 960.3

Curran, John Philpot (1750–1817). Irish orator and magistrate. 534.9

Curtis, Charles P. (1891–1959). American lawyer, educator, writer. 354.4

# D

Dahlberg, Edward (1900– ). American novelist and critic. 21.2; 30.3; 56.2; 114.9; 117.6; 233.3; 286.8; 297.13; 339.5; 494.1; 515.7; 536.24; 869.3; 885.7; 929.1; 939.7; 1000.4

Daniels, Jonathan [Worth] (1902– ). American newspaperman, writer, public official. 91.23

Dankevich, Konstantin. Contemporary Russian composer. 204.12

Dante. Full name, Dante Alighieri (1265–1321). Italian poet. 164.4; 173.4; 236.7; 238.5; 305.9; 327.9; 330.15; 330.16; 356.2; 385.22; 413.3; 448.9; 514.3; 515.8; 548.38; 548.39; 616.19; 717.9; 727.8; 748.3; 778.8; 784.3; 809.7; 920.2; 1025.16; 1049.3

Dargent, Joseph. Contemporary French vintner. 245.3

Darrow, Clarence S. (1857–1938). American lawyer, lecturer, reformer, writer. 1006.2

Darwin, Charles [Robert] (1809–1882). English naturalist. 306.2; 968.6

Davies, W[illiam] H[enry] (1871–1940). Welsh-born English poet. 530.3

da Vinci, Leonardo. *See* Leonardo da Vinci.

Davis, David (1815–1886). American jurist. Associate Justice of the U.S. Supreme Court (1862–1877). 179.1

Davis, Elmer [Holmes] (1890–1958). American journalist and radio commentator. 580.7; 1064.14

Day, Clarence [Shepard], Jr. (1874–1935). American writer. 10.6; 41.7; 41.8; 42.4; 53.29; 64.3; 64.4; 81.3; 208.3; 240.3; 291.4; 297.14; 306.3; 363.35; 374.8; 436.1; 479.1; 520.13; 520.14; 596.13; 598.15; 616.20; 658.2; 702.23; 777.7; 817.1; 851.4; 868.8; 991.23; 1049.4; 1058.16

Day-Lewis, C[ecil] (1904– ). Irish-born English poet laureate and writer of detective stories. 666.3

Debs, Eugene V[ictor] (1855–1926). American socialist leader. 98.2

Deffand [Marie de Vichy-Chamrond], Marquise du. Also called Mme. du Deffand (1697–1780). French noblewoman, leader in social, literary and philosophical circles. 1055.33

Defoe, Daniel (1660–1731), born Daniel Foe. English novelist, pamphleteer, journalist, political agent. 515.9

de Gaulle, Charles [André Joseph Marie] (1890–1970). French general and statesman. President of the Fifth Republic of France (1958–1969). 245.4; 359.3; 528.5; 633.4; 651.4; 705.25; 853.1; 923.7; 987.1

Dekker, Thomas (1572?–1632). English playwright. 1058.17

de Kooning, Willem (1904– ). Dutch painter. 53.30

Delacroix [Ferdinand Victor Eugène] (1799–1863). French painter; leader of the romantic school of painting. 783.7

Dement, William (1928– ). American psychiatrist. 264.3

Demetrius of Phalerum (c. 345–c. 280 B.C.). Greek orator and statesman. 281.1; 324.3; 745.7

De Mille, Agnes [George] (1905– ). American dancer, choreographer, writer. 212.1; 212.2

De Mille, Cecil B[lount] (1881–1959). American motion-picture producer and director. 679.3

Democritus (c. 460–c. 370 B.C.). Thracian philosopher. 183.6; 467.3

De Morgan, Augustus (1806–1871). English mathematician and logician. 662.1

De Quincey, Thomas (1785–1859). English essayist and critic. 162.4; 171.3; 616.21; 737.2; 911.11; 939.8; 1063.4

Descartes, René (1596–1650). French philosopher and mathematician. 91.24; 147.2; 399.14; 407.30; 491.5; 688.4; 968.7

Destouches, Louis-Ferdinand. *See* Céline, Louis-Ferdinand.

Destouches, Philippe. Pen name of Philippe Néricault (1680–1754). French playwright. 204.13; 686.5
Deval, Jacques (1894– ). French playwright. 1055.34
de Valois, Dame Ninette (1898– ). Irish-born English ballet director. 374.9
Dewey, John (1859–1952). American teacher, philosopher, educational reformer. 115.10; 441.8; 616.22; 790.15
Dhéry, Robert (1921– ). French actor, director, writer. 965.4
Dibdin, Charles (1745–1814). English playwright and lyricist. 266.9
Dickens, Charles (1812–1870). English novelist. 41.9; 64.5; 102.11; 121.10; 151.6; 258.1; 265.3; 265.4; 265.5; 332.14; 361.7; 420.7; 436.2; 441.9; 487.4; 505.4; 525.17; 554.1; 558.14; 620.4; 646.18; 659.3; 693.3; 702.24; 755.6; 773.3; 789.1; 963.1; 970.8; 981.4; 1063.5
Dickinson, Emily [Elizabeth] (1830–1886). American poet. 17.18; 39.14; 41.10; 70.11; 80.5; 91.25; 148.2; 172.2; 184.1; 218.34; 218.35; 218.36; 218.37; 237.5; 256.3; 276.1; 314.2; 328.11; 330.17; 330.18; 337.6; 340.11; 349.2; 358.6; 384.5; 385.23; 407.31; 420.8; 425.6; 448.10; 479.2; 480.2; 501.2; 517.8; 523.6; 548.40; 548.41; 548.42; 600.6; 603.4; 621.1; 669.7; 669.8; 687.3; 692.9; 710.5; 717.10; 719.1; 792.1; 792.2; 812.1; 844.3; 871.1; 891.4; 891.5; 911.12; 938.7; 939.9; 939.10; 953.2; 971.13; 991.24; 991.25; 997.8; 1004.7; 1057.8
Dickinson, John. Pen name, Fabius (1732–1808), American lawyer and pamphleteer. 958.6
Diderot, Denis (1713–1784). French encyclopedist, materialistic philosopher, novelist, satirist, playwright, art critic. 57.7; 430.10; 525.18; 555.7; 632.4; 654.8; 668.6; 668.7; 668.8; 688.5; 897.4; 909.5; 1025.17; 1062.30
Dimnet, Ernest (1866–1954). French abbé and writer. 91.26; 91.27; 277.12; 277.13; 319.14; 374.10; 514.4
Dinesen, Isak. pen name of Baroness Karen Blixen, née Dinesen (1885–1962). Danish short-story writer. 208.4; 548.43; 558.15; 646.19; 849.4; 991.26; 1055.35; 1064.15
Diogenes the Cynic (c. 400–c. 325 B.C.). Greek philosopher. 57.8; 190.2; 201.2; 886.2
Dionysius the Elder (c. 430–367 B.C.). Tyrant of Syracuse, politician, militarist. 916.17
Dior, Christian (1905–1957). French fashion designer. 511.2; 1055.36
Dirksen, Everett M[cKinley] (1896–1969.). American political leader. 115.11
Disraeli, Benjamin, 1st Earl of Beaconsfield (1804–1881). English statesman and novelist. 25.1; 44.1; 51.9; 79.4; 127.2; 131.8; 133.1; 175.4; 203.9; 204.14; 320.1; 374.11; 445.10; 485.2; 485.3; 516.4; 520.15; 537.5; 560.23; 614.2; 646.20; 651.5; 723.6; 734.2; 755.7; 756.6; 765.3; 815.1; 897.5; 979.8; 1033.2; 1062.31; 1064.16
Doddridge, Philip (1702–1751). English nonconformist clergyman. 511.3
Dodgson, Charles Lutwidge. *See* Carroll, Lewis.
Donne, John (1572?–1631). English metaphysical poet and divine. 2.4; 70.12; 101.3; 120.5; 123.5; 143.2; 150.3; 151.7; 151.8; 171.4; 180.1; 192.10; 218.38; 218.39; 328.12; 332.15; 339.6; 385.24; 391.12; 407.32; 430.11; 452.3; 464.2; 512.4; 532.1; 538.5; 548.44; 548.45; 548.46; 548.47; 548.48; 548.49; 548.50; 558.16; 586.2; 646.21; 677.7; 698.13; 702.25; 712.12; 735.5; 778.9; 873.4; 885.8; 885.9; 889.3; 893.6; 893.7; 899.7; 945.3; 985.11; 991.27; 992.4; 998.4; 1025.18; 1035.28; 1048.7; 1055.37; 1060.7; 1063.6
Dooley, Mr. *See* Dunne, Finley Peter.
Dorn, Edward (1929– ). American poet. 201.3
Dostoevsky, Fyodor Mikhailovich (1821–1881). Russian novelist. 4.1; 58.2; 109.4; 122.2; 148.3; 172.3; 203.10; 237.6; 249.4; 407.33; 430.12; 431.5; 477.3; 520.16; 523.7; 548.51; 548.52; 548.53; 596.14; 748.4; 752.5; 776.2; 778.10; 837.1; 855.1; 858.2; 939.11; 1058.18; 1058.19
Douglas, Lord Alfred [Bruce] (1870–1945). English poet. 702.26
Douglas, Kirk (1918– ). American actor. 536.25
Douglass, Frederick (1817?–1895). American abolitionist, orator, journalist. 83.7; 669.9; 882.6
Doyle, Sir Arthur Conan (1859–1930). English physician and detective-story writer. 191.5; 201.4; 520.17; 543.1; 703.2; 956.5; 967.2; 989.2; 991.28
Dryden, John (1631–1700). English poet, dramatist, critic. 33.8; 192.11; 218.40; 218.41; 231.9; 238.6; 260.4; 357.5; 357.6; 399.15; 407.34; 508.11; 536.26; 548.54; 548.55; 548.56; 555.8; 558.17; 582.3; 607.19; 670.5; 692.10; 699.2; 723.7; 734.3; 799.3; 813.7; 991.29; 995.10; 1025.19; 1035.29; 1041.14
du Bartas, Seigneur, Guillaume de Salluste (1544–1590). French poet and soldier. 309.1; 479.3; 737.3
Du Bois, W[illiam] E[dward] B[urghardt] (1868–1963). American writer, editor, teacher, lecturer. 34.11; 201.5; 277.14; 613.3; 712.13; 769.3; 769.4; 769.5; 1001.6; 1030.6
Du Bos, Charles (1882–1939). French critic. 469.1; 711.2
Duhamel, Georges. Pen name Denis Thévenin (1884–1966). French playwright, novelist, critic, poet. 297.15
Dumas, Alexandre. Known as Dumas fils (1824–1895). French playwright, illegitimate son of Alexandre Dumas, the novelist. 277.15; 560.24
Dunbar, Paul Laurence (1872–1906). American poet. 319.15; 414.4; 536.27; 716.7

*Dunne, Finley Peter (1867–1936). American journalist and humorist, creator of "Mr. Dooley."
Durant, Will[iam James] (1885– ). American teacher, philosopher, historian. 891.6
Durrell, Lawrence [George] (1912– ). Anglo-Irish novelist, poet, playwright. 17.19; 53.31; 53.32; 53.33; 53.34; 166.3; 198.9; 403.7; 448.11; 508.12; 548.58; 576.10; 607.20; 779.2; 991.30; 991.31; 991.32; 1004.8; 1055.39
Dürrenmatt, Friedrich (1921– ). Swiss novelist, playwright, short-story writer, writing in German. 429.1; 515.12; 633.5; 661.2; 696.3; 731.1; 931.1; 968.9; 1001.7; 1060.8

## E

Eberhart, Richard (1904– ). American poet and teacher. 538.6; 583.4; 935.5
Echeverría, Esteban (1809–1851). Argentine poet and political leader. 489.6
Eckermann, Johann Peter (1792–1854). German writer, friend and literary assistant to Goethe. 918.1
Edman, Irwin (1896–1954). American philosopher and educator. 305.10; 878.2
Ehrenburg, Ilya [Grigoryevich] (1891–1967). Russian novelist, poet, journalist. 53.35; 53.36; 53.37; 277.19; 297.17; 756.7; 1035.31
Eich, Günter (1907– ). German poet. 633.6
Einstein, Albert (1879–1955). German-Swiss-American physicist. 30.4; 149.3; 191.6; 279.3; 326.4; 361.8; 393.19; 404.6; 459.1; 464.3; 582.5; 583.5; 788.6; 790.16; 843.6; 843.7; 844.4; 923.8; 977.5; 991.33; 1012.2; 1060.9
Eisenhower, Dwight D[avid] (1890–1969). American general and thirty-fourth President of the United States (1953–1961). 34.13; 99.1; 289.2; 334.3; 342.2; 384.6; 417.19; 724.3; 1035.32
Eliot, George. Pen name of Mary Ann or Marian Evans (1819–1880). English novelist. 15.2; 41.11; 163.6; 224.8; 257.4; 316.2; 363.36; 402.5; 434.10; 490.4; 521.5; 560.26; 561.5; 575.6; 576.11; 577.2; 620.5; 741.3; 876.3; 934.5; 1055.40; 1055.41; 1055.42; 1064.17
Eliot, T[homas] S[tearns] (1888–1965). American-born English poet, critic, editor, playwright. 9.17; 12.2; 53.38; 53.39; 78.3; 91.28; 109.6; 115.12; 204.15; 207.2; 216.2; 218.42; 222.5; 252.1; 293.8; 303.2; 332.16; 338.2; 361.9; 363.37; 374.12; 411.3; 414.5; 417.20; 471.3; 493.1; 504.2; 521.6; 536.28; 542.2; 548.59; 558.18; 563.3; 576.12; 580.8; 646.24; 668.9; 702.27; 702.28; 702.29; 702.30; 702.31; 752.6; 777.8; 800.3; 813.8; 818.2; 848.16; 857.2; 865.3; 868.9; 893.8; 906.2; 924.3; 938.8; 944.1; 965.5; 978.2; 979.9; 1012.3; 1057.9; 1060.10
Elliott, Ebenezer (1781–1849). English poet, called the Corn-Law Rhymer. 149.4
Ellis, [Henry] Havelock (1859–1939). English psychologist, essayist, art critic. 53.40; 115.13; 131.10; 212.3; 213.6; 248.2; 328.13; 508.13; 536.29; 551.4; 566.2; 885.10; 935.6; 935.7; 939.12; 1058.21
Ellison, Ralph [Waldo] (1914– ). American writer and educator. 34.14; 53.41; 341.4; 341.5
*Emerson, Ralph Waldo (1803–1882). American poet, essayist, philosopher.
Epictetus (fl. A.D. 100). Greek philosopher. 9.21; 55.6; 61.1; 122.4; 163.7; 218.45; 243.4; 265.6; 277.24; 340.13; 356.3; 361.14; 371.2; 391.17; 399.21; 539.7; 558.20; 570.4; 618.2; 650.4; 673.4; 688.6; 729.3; 731.2; 778.11; 856.3; 860.6; 865.6; 908.17; 916.20; 967.4; 991.39; 1049.5; 1062.36
Epicurus (341–270 B.C.). Greek philosopher. 9.22; 17.22; 51.10; 117.11; 183.7; 218.46; 218.47; 236.9; 340.14; 361.15; 363.43; 366.9; 366.10; 407.36; 424.4; 492.3; 515.13; 538.7; 584.3; 584.4; 617.3; 688.7; 699.3; 873.7; 1041.22; 1053.21; 1063.8
Erasmus, Desiderius (1466–1536). Dutch scholar and philosopher. 227.3; 1035.34
Erikson, Erik H[omburger] (1902– ). German-born American psychoanalyst and educator. 34.16; 156.3; 171.8; 361.16; 538.8; 567.4
Ervine, St. John [Greer] (1883–1971). Irish playwright and novelist. 604.2
Euclid (fl. 300 B.C.). Greek mathematician. 566.3
*Euripides (480–405 B.C.). Greek tragic playwright
Evans, Bergen (1904– ). American educator and writer. 528.7
Evans, Mary Ann or Marian. *See* Eliot, George.
Evans, Richard L[ouis] (1906– ). American writer and radio commentator. 251.1
Evenus [of Paros] (5th c. B.C.). Greek elegist and sophist. 404.7

## F

Faber, Harold. Contemporary American newspaperman and editor. 525.24
Fabius. *See* Dickinson, John.
Fadiman, Clifton (1904– ). American critic, lecturer, radio entertainer, editor. 352.4; 396.2
Fanon, Frantz (1925–1961). French psychiatrist and writer. 130.4; 207.6; 372.2; 642.1; 1035.35; 1058.27
Fargue, Léon-Paul (1876–1947). French poet. 581.1
Farouk or Faruk I (1920–1965). King of Egypt, 1936–1952. 518.3
Farquhar, George (1678–1707). English playwright. 683.5; 712.15; 965.6; 1055.52
Farrar, John [Chipman] (1896– ). American editor, publisher, poet. 758.5

Farrell, James T[homas] (1904– ). American novelist. 34.17

Faulkner, William (1897–1962). American novelist and short-story writer. 53.45; 53.46; 53.47; 123.10; 204.19; 766.6; 769.7; 938.11; 957.5; 971.17; 991.40; 1058.28; 1060.11; 1062.37; 1062.38

Fénelon [François de Salignac de la Mothe-] (1651–1715). French prelate and writer. 467.7; 548.66

Ferguson, Homer (1889– ). American politician. 490.6

Ferlinghetti, Lawrence (1919– ). American poet and publisher. 385.31

Fielding, Henry (1707–1754). English novelist. 136.4; 204.20; 218.51; 261.5; 293.10; 327.10; 397.5; 407.39; 840.1

Fielding, Temple [Hornaday] (1913– ). American writer, foreign correspondent, travel writer. 985.19

Fitch, James Marston (1909– ). American educator. 63.4

Fitzgerald, F[rancis] Scott [Key] (1896–1940). American novelist and short-story writer. 229.2; 237.7; 251.2; 357.7; 363.49; 374.16; 374.17; 384.7; 416.5; 422.2; 423.3; 491.8; 519.2; 567.5; 652.6; 669.11; 685.2; 907.3; 933.7; 938.12; 1019.6; 1028.1; 1055.53; 1057.10; 1060.12; 1062.39

Fitz-Gibbon, Bernice (1897?– ). American advertising executive and businesswoman. 198.11

Flaubert, Gustave (1821–1880). French novelist. 204.21; 511.4; 938.13

Flers, Robert [Pellevé de La Motte-Ango, marquis de] (1872–1927). French playwright. 231.11

Fletcher, John (1579–1625). English playwright. *See also* Beaumont and Fletcher; Fletcher and Massinger. 224.10

Fletcher and Massinger. 266.15; 266.16

Florian, Jean Pierre Claris de (1755–1794). French novelist, playwright, fabulist. 548.67

Florio, John (1553–1625). English lexicographer and translator. 572.4

Fontenelle, Bernard le Bovier de (1657–1757). French man of letters. 407.40

Ford, John (1586–c. 1640). English playwright. 285.4; 361.17; 489.8; 505.6; 548.68; 600.9; 811.12; 991.41

Forster, E[dward] M[organ] (1879–1970). English novelist, short-story writer, essayist. 53.48; 77.2; 90.3; 91.37; 111.2; 198.12; 200.1; 231.12; 282.13; 287.10; 295.5; 328.16; 337.11; 341.9; 399.23; 416.6; 417.23; 441.10; 499.3; 534.10; 538.11; 542.3; 548.69; 702.36; 710.6; 744.8; 903.2; 977.6; 991.42

Fouché, Joseph, Duc d'Otrante (1763–1820). French statesman and Minister of Police. 86.3

Fougasse. *See* Bird, [Cyril] Kenneth.

Fowler, Gene [Eugene Devlan] (1890–1960). American editor and writer. 493.3; 622.2

Fowles, John (1926– ). English-born American novelist. 269.11; 478.8; 539.8; 1035.36

France, Anatole. Pen name of Jacques Anatole François Thibault (1844–1924). French novelist, poet, critic. 53.49; 98.4; 115.16; 121.16; 204.22; 210.9; 277.26; 282.14; 329.17; 520.21; 536.35; 552.7; 646.33; 668.11; 677.9; 714.2; 723.11; 783.12; 842.13; 959.9; 971.18; 1004.11; 1055.54

Frankfurter, Felix (1882–1965). American jurist and teacher. 117.12; 467.8; 525.25; 534.11; 725.1

Franklin, Benjamin (1706–1790). American statesman, writer, inventor, printer, scientist. 58.3; 71.4; 103.6; 154.5; 185.11; 192.16; 219.5; 236.10; 247.3; 261.6; 339.11; 353.12; 393.21; 407.41; 417.24; 418.4; 425.9; 444.5; 470.5; 482.3; 520.22; 525.26; 525.27; 527.3; 560.37; 560.38; 576.13; 617.6; 683.6; 716.8; 727.10; 727.11; 773.5; 801.1; 815.2; 842.14; 850.5; 916.21; 934.7; 971.19; 1004.12; 1009.4; 1023.13; 1026.8; 1035.37; 1049.6; 1053.23

Freud, Anna (1895– ). Austrian psychoanalyst, daughter of Sigmund Freud. 198.13

Freud, Sigmund (1856–1939). Austrian psychologist and originator of psychoanalysis. 21.4; 35.2; 55.8; 121.17; 184.2; 407.42; 538.12; 549.4; 552.8; 567.6; 620.8; 733.2; 752.7; 752.8; 765.4; 791.4; 906.5; 1009.5

Friedenberg, Edgar Z[odiag] (1921– ). American sociologist. 1.7; 34.18; 34.19; 34.20; 121.18; 201.7; 365.6; 442.10; 752.9; 820.1; 960.4; 994.7; 1019.7; 1024.3; 1024.4; 1057.11; 1064.19; 1064.20; 1064.21

Fromm, Erich (1900– ). German-born American psychoanalyst and philosopher. 31.4; 92.3; 102.14; 103.7; 178.4; 198.14; 198.15; 216.3; 218.52; 218.53; 236.11; 295.6; 314.4; 401.9; 402.7; 407.43; 412.3; 417.25; 465.2; 467.9; 491.9; 502.10; 536.38; 548.72; 548.73; 548.74; 548.75; 548.76; 565.2; 569.1; 615.2; 663.21; 706.5; 739.2; 813.11; 836.2; 852.11; 867.3; 960.5; 971.20; 998.5; 1040.2; 1055.55

Frost, Robert (1874–1963). American poet. 31.5; 115.17; 151.10; 218.54; 277.27; 277.28; 298.4; 332.17; 407.44; 413.5; 420.12; 502.11; 596.20; 663.22; 702.37; 702.38; 770.2; 880.3; 968.15; 976.1; 1064.22

Fry, Christopher (1907– ). English playwright. 12.3; 144.4; 218.55; 225.2; 239.5; 250.6; 295.7; 385.32; 467.10; 468.2; 480.5; 538.13; 555.10; 569.2; 598.17; 616.30; 645.1; 702.39; 723.12; 946.1; 965.7; 980.7; 1000.5; 1020.6; 1058.29

Fulbright, J[ames] William (1905– ). American political leader. 27.4; 968.16

Fuller, [Sara] Margaret. Marchesa Ossoli (1810–1850). American editor, essayist, poet, teacher. 126.3; 131.12; 181.3; 236.12; 399.24; 399.25; 478.9; 489.9; 548.77; 663.23; 687.5;

1058.30; 1062.40

Fuller, Thomas, D.D. (1608–1661). English clergyman and writer. 39.17; 50.6; 91.38; 330.21; 560.39; 607.22; 749.12; 1051.4

*Fuller, Thomas, M.D. (1654–1734). English physician, writer, compiler.

## G

Gaboriau, Émile (1835–1873). French writer of detective stories. 811.13; 1055.56; 1055.57

Galbraith, John Kenneth (1908– ). Canadian-born American economist, diplomat, writer. 102.17; 103.9; 303.5; 637.5; 705.30

Gallico, Paul [William] (1897– ) American journalist, novelist, short-story writer. 486.2

Galsworthy, John (1867–1933). English novelist and playwright. 55.10; 525.30

Gandhi, Mohandas K[aramchand], called Mahatma (1869–1948). Hindu nationalist leader. 98.5; 102.18; 109.11; 231.13; 272.12; 305.16; 361.18; 385.33; 509.1; 525.31; 534.13; 565.3; 658.5; 658.6; 658.7; 705.31; 717.15; 732.4; 813.12; 817.2; 933.8; 1024.5; 1024.6; 1035.38; 1035.39; 1035.40

García Lorca, Federico (1898–1936). Spanish poet and playwright. 915.1

Gardner, John W. (1912– ). American foundation executive and public official. 333.6; 391.20; 417.26; 712.19; 752.10; 802.4

Garrick, David (1717–1779). English actor and theater manager. 22.3; 646.37

Garrison, William Lloyd (1805–1879). American abolitionist. 98.6; 231.14; 492.4; 598.18; 817.3

Gary, Romain (1914– ). Russian-born French novelist and diplomat. 434.12; 542.4

Gaxotte, Pierre (1895– ). French historian. 813.13

Gay, John (1685–1732). English poet and playwright. 3.6; 31.6; 221.6; 266.20; 293.13; 348.2; 560.43; 571.4; 576.14; 663.25; 733.4; 1029.5; 1064.24

Genet, Jean (1910– ). French playwright, novelist, poet, essayist. 1047.4

Géraldy, Paul. Pen name of Paul Le Fèvre (1885– ). French poet and playwright. 548.80; 548.81; 869.4

Ghalib (Asad Allah Khan) (1796–1869). Turkish poet. 893.9

Ghelderode, Michel de (1898–1962). Belgian playwright. 623.6

Gibbon, Edward (1737–1794). English historian. 1.9; 397.6; 735.7; 953.6

Gibran, Kahlil (1883–1931). Syrian-American mystic, poet, painter. 2.7; 121.20; 171.11; 361.19; 382.15; 385.34; 388.7; 407.47; 548.83; 554.3; 598.19; 616.31; 663.26; 666.4; 687.6; 702.41; 778.14; 783.13; 793.6; 881.5; 906.6; 916.22; 916.23; 939.15; 959.11; 991.46; 993.6; 1058.31; 1063.11

Gibson, Wilfred Wilson (1878–1962). English poet. 603.8

*Gide, André (1869–1951). French novelist, critic, essayist, editor, translator.

Gifford, Frank (1930– ). Sports announcer and professional football player. 922.2

Gilbert, Sir W[illiam] S[chwenck] (1836–1911). English dramatist, librettist, writer of humorous verse. 37.5; 42.5; 45.9; 87.3; 183.11; 201.10; 207.7; 218.58; 277.30; 306.5; 337.12; 398.8; 512.6; 536.40; 536.41; 558.21; 582.9; 695.2; 703.5; 704.4; 773.8; 786.2; 833.6; 950.2; 1055.58

Gilbreath, Glen (1886– ). Contemporary American thief. 927.5

Gill, Brendan (1914– ). American film and drama critic. 144.5

Ginsberg, Allen (1926– ). American poet. 843.9

Ginsberg, Louis (1896– ). American poet, father of Allen Ginsberg. 548.84

Giraldi, Giglio Gregorio. *See* Gyraldus, Lilius Gregorius.

Giraudoux, [Hippolyte] Jean (1882–1944). French dramatist, novelist, essayist, diplomat. 25.2; 85.7; 100.4; 136.6; 178.5; 178.6; 188.4; 218.59; 218.60; 238.9; 258.2; 269.12; 277.31; 329.18; 329.19; 339.14; 348.3; 349.3; 383.3; 385.36; 399.29; 416.7; 452.4; 524.3; 525.33; 525.34; 538.16; 548.85; 558.22; 560.46; 560.47; 563.4; 575.7; 576.15; 596.25; 614.5; 614.6; 626.6; 656.7; 680.3; 758.6; 773.9; 783.14; 851.6; 866.6; 885.12; 911.17; 922.3; 960.6; 965.8; 1035.43; 1035.44; 1035.45; 1035.46; 1039.1; 1055.59; 1055.60; 1055.61; 1055.62; 1059.3

Gissing, George [Robert] (1857–1903). English novelist, critic, essayist. 91.40; 129.18; 407.49; 558.23; 583.7; 596.26; 800.6; 848.18; 870.5; 908.20; 922.4; 971.23; 991.49; 1043.3

Glasgow, Ellen [Anderson Gholson] (1874–1945). American novelist. 776.4

Glinka, Mikhail [Ivanovich] (1804–1857). Russian composer. 607.23

Goebbels, Paul Joseph (1897–1945). German Nazi propagandist. 1042.2

*Goethe [Johann Wolfgang von] (1749–1832). German poet, playwright, novelist.

Goffman, Erving (1922– ). American anthropologist and educator. 323.2; 958.7

Gogol, Nikolai Vasilyevich (1809–1852). Russian novelist, playwright, short-story writer. 367.5; 1065.12

Goheen, Robert [Francis] (1919– ). American educator. 277.33

Goldsmith, Oliver (1730?–1774). Irish-born English poet, playwright, novelist. 102.20; 171.12; 316.4; 525.35; 548.87; 646.43; 916.24; 968.17; 1025.27

Goldwater, Barry [Morris] (1909– ). American political leader. 333.7; 393.22

Goldwyn, Samuel (1882– ). Polish-born American motion-picture producer. 604.3

Goncourt, Edmond [Louis Antoine Huot] de (1822–1896) and Jules [Alfred Huot] de (1830–1870). French writers and collaborators, known as the Brothers Goncourt. 42.6; 69.3; 102.21; 185.12; 204.23; 296.12; 305.17; 341.10; 417.27; 441.11; 584.5; 623.7; 659.5; 675.6; 733.5; 852.13; 889.11; 889.12; 971.24; 997.12; 997.13; 1007.3; 1054.9; 1055.63

González Prada, Manuel (1848–1918). Peruvian politician and writer. 813.16; 989.3

Goodman, Paul (1911– ). American writer, educator, psychoanalyst. 34.21; 34.22; 89.2; 102.22; 111.3; 198.16; 277.34; 277.35; 399.31; 502.12; 530.5; 604.4; 698.15; 813.17; 885.14

Gorer, Geoffrey (1905– ). English psychologist and historian. 41.12; 698.16; 790.27

Gorky, Maxim. Pen name of Aleksei Maximovich Peshkov (1868–1936). Russian writer. 287.11; 366.13; 391.21; 407.50; 435.4; 516.5; 516.6; 525.36; 526.1; 548.88; 560.49; 566.4; 596.27; 646.44; 652.7; 669.14; 687.7; 688.8; 726.5; 956.8; 983.9; 992.6; 1058.34; 1063.12

Gourmont, Rémy de (1858–1915). French literary critic and novelist. 130.5; 761.1; 968.18

*Gracián, Baltasar (1601–1658). Spanish prose writer and Jesuit priest.

Grahame, Kenneth (1859–1932). English essayist and writer of children's books. 888.3

Grant, Ulysses S[impson] (1822–1885). American soldier and eighteenth President of the United States (1869–1877). 525.37

Graves, Robert [Ranke] (1895– ). English poet, novelist, critic. 218.61; 548.90

Gray, Thomas (1716–1771). English poet. 384.10; 445.15; 641.4

Grayson, David. Pen name of Ray Stannard Baker (1870–1946). American journalist, biographer, essayist. 40.2; 91.41; 91.42; 103.11; 115.19; 129.19; 270.4; 352.5; 363.57; 391.22; 616.35; 702.47; 710.7; 740.10; 908.22; 977.7; 982.5; 1058.35

*Greek Anthology* (7th c. B.C.–A.D. 10th c.). A collection of several thousand poems, songs, epigrams and epitaphs by numerous Greek writers, known and unknown. 189.2; 261.7; 266.23; 266.24; 360.6

Green, Julien (1900– ). French novelist of American parentage. 177.1; 706.7; 997.14; 1062.46

Greene, Graham (1904– ). English novelist, short-story writer, playwright. 116.3; 149.6; 237.8; 328.17

Gregg, Alan (1890–1957). American physician and foundation official. 744.12

Gregory, Dick (1932– ). American comedian and civil rights activist. 34.23; 83.8

Gresset, Jean Baptiste Louis (1709–1777). French poet and playwright. 1054.11

Grigg, John [Edward Poynder] (1924– ). English political journalist; renounced the title of Lord Altrincham in 1963. 62.3

Griswold, [Alfred] Whitney (1909–1963). American educator. 441.12

Guiterman, Arthur (1871–1943). American poet. 204.24; 579.9; 802.5; 1020.9

Guitry, Sacha (1885–1957). French actor and playwright. 445.16; 470.6

Gunn, Thom[son] (1929– ). English poet. 154.6

Gutman, Walter Knowleton (1903– ). American economist and writer. 501.5

Gyraldus, Lilius Gregorius. Also known as Giglio Gregorio Giraldi (1479–1552). Italian scholar and poet. 294.2

## H

Haberman, Phillip W., Jr. Contemporary American writer. 272.13

Hāfiz. Pen name of Shams-ud-din Muhammad (c. 1300–1388). Persian poet. 114.12; 183.13; 289.3; 385.37; 425.14; 538.17; 548.91; 600.11; 792.3; 966.5; 1012.6; 1060.14

Haigh, Kenneth. Contemporary English actor. 965.10

Hailsham, 2nd Viscount (Quintin McGarel Hogg) (1907– ). British government official. 51.13

Hall, Joseph (1574–1656). English clergyman and satirist. 218.62; 592.5

Hamilton, Alexander (1757–1804). American statesman. 220.1; 295.8; 393.23; 949.2

Hammarskjöld, Dag (1905–1961). Swedish statesman. United Nations Secretary-General (1953–1961). 9.25; 192.17; 218.63; 238.11; 244.3; 357.10; 433.7; 440.5; 450.4; 646.45; 717.16; 1014.1

Hammurabi. King of Babylon (2067–2025 B.C.) 515.19

Hand, Learned (1872–1961). American jurist. 9.26; 115.20; 231.15; 257.7; 333.8; 361.23; 525.38; 534.15; 534.16; 563.5; 717.17; 755.9; 860.8; 1030.9

Haraucourt, Edmond (1856–1941). French novelist, poet, playwright. 666.5

Hardwicke, Sir Cedric [Webster] (1893–1964). English actor. 11.3

Hardy, Thomas (1840–1928). English novelist and poet. 37.7; 131.13; 206.8; 270.5; 358.18; 385.38; 458.4; 536.42; 545.4; 552.9; 576.16; 580.11; 670.11; 674.11; 801.2; 1060.15

Hare, Augustus William. *See* Hare, Julius Charles.

Hare, Julius Charles (1795–1855) and his brother Augustus William Hare (1792–1834). English clergyman, joint authors of *Guesses at Truth*. 4.2; 44.2; 74.6; 91.43; 194.9; 204.25; 236.16; 305.19; 328.18; 329.21; 363.58; 391.23; 442.12;

463.2; 468.3; 473.4; 538.18; 594.9; 718.8; 801.3; 892.5; 979.10; 1023.15; 1053.28

Harington or Harrington, Sir John (1561–1612). English satirist and miscellaneous writer. 91.44; 162.6; 358.19; 986.2

Harkness, Richard [Long] (1907– ). American radio and television commentator and journalist. 146.3

Harriman, W[illiam] Averell (1891– ). American businessman, politician, diplomat. 496.4

Harrington, Alan (1919– ). American social critic and writer. 722.1; 739.3; 850.7; 982.6

Harrington, Michael (1928– ). American writer and social critic. 34.24; 55.11; 83.9; 150.4; 703.7; 712.20; 712.21; 712.22; 769.8; 905.2; 906.7; 960.7

Harris, Richard. Contemporary American journalist. 705.32

Harris, Sydney J[ustin] (1917– ). English-born American newspaper columnist. 211.1; 373.5; 478.12; 567.8; 849.8

Hawthorne, Nathaniel (1804–1864). American novelist and short-story writer. 48.4; 53.57; 101.6; 120.8; 141.3; 162.7; 191.7; 195.5; 272.14; 360.7; 373.6; 374.18; 388.9; 399.32; 416.8; 416.9; 431.7; 452.6; 521.8; 536.43; 558.25; 576.17; 659.6; 687.8; 735.8; 740.11; 789.3; 796.1; 848.19; 849.9; 852.14; 889.13; 893.10; 944.3; 960.8; 971.26; 1057.12

Hay, John [Milton] (1838–1905). American statesman and man of letters. 168.7; 245.5; 266.25; 349.4; 363.59; 367.6; 392.5; 548.92; 552.10; 560.51; 594.10; 646.46

Hayes, Rutherford B[irchard] (1822–1893). Nineteenth President of the United States, (1877–1881). 704.6

Hays, Brooks (1898– ). American lawyer, educator, presidential aide, congressman. 6.11

*Hazlitt, William (1778–1830). English essayist and critic.

Hegel, Georg Friedrich Wilhelm (1770–1831). German philosopher. 203.13; 361.25; 417.28; 536.46; 668.13; 728.6; 1058.37; 1060.17

Hein, Piet (1905– ). Dutch inventor and poet. 6.12; 136.7; 226.4; 226.5; 520.25; 536.47; 611.4; 658.8; 731.3; 783.17; 874.2; 875.3; 879.4; 892.6; 916.27; 922.5; 1010.5; 1053.30

Heine, Heinrich (1797–1856). German poet, satirist, journalist. 296.14

Heinlein, Robert A. Pen name, Anson MacDonald (1907– ). American novelist and science fiction writer. 388.10; 548.93; 641.5

Hellman, Lillian (1905– ). American playwright. 1062.48

Helvétius, Claude-Adrien (1715–1771). French encyclopedist and materialist philosopher. 991.55

Hemingway, Ernest [Miller] (1899–1961). American novelist and short-story writer. 196.7; 598.20; 664.2; 935.9; 939.16; 1060.18; 1062.49

Henry IV of France. Also Henry of Navarre (1553–1610). King of France (1589–1610). 877.2

Henry, O. Pen name of William Sydney Porter (1862–1910). American short-story writer. 89.3; 129.20; 423.5; 435.5; 536.48; 536.49; 561.8; 575.8; 576.18; 749.15; 756.9; 824.3; 848.20; 931.4; 1044.5; 1055.67; 1055.68

Henry, Patrick (1736–1799). American statesman and orator. 319.26; 425.17; 534.17

Heraclitus (fl. c. 500 B.C.). Greek philosopher. 17.29; 85.8; 115.21; 115.22; 117.14; 184.3; 236.19; 236.20; 259.5; 261.8; 262.8; 264.8; 266.26; 277.38; 385.39; 408.2; 525.39; 651.8; 720.8; 811.14; 890.4; 899.9; 945.4; 991.56; 1053.31; 1058.38

Herbert, Edward, 1st Baron Herbert of Cherbury (1583–1648). English philosopher, diplomat, historian, poet. Brother of George Herbert. 470.7

Herbert, George (1593–1633). English clergyman and metaphysical poet. 1.11; 103.13; 103.14; 160.4; 221.9; 226.6; 233.5; 266.27; 323.3; 357.11; 379.2; 391.24; 505.9; 547.3; 548.94; 626.7; 658.9; 702.48; 714.4; 848.21; 848.22; 911.19; 971.28; 993.8; 1054.13

Hériat, Philippe. Pen name of Raymond-Gérard Payelle (1898– ). French actor and writer. 596.28

Hermant, Abel (1862–1950). French novelist and essayist. 360.8; 416.10; 423.6

Herodotus (c. 480–c. 425 B.C.). Greek historian. 293.16; 457.2; 875.4

Herrick, Robert (1591–1674). English poet. 700.7

Hersey, John [Richard] (1914– ). American novelist and journalist. 341.11

Hershey, Lewis B[laine] (1893– ). American general. Former director of Selective Service. 95.4

Herzog, Emile. *See* Maurois, André.

Hesiod (8th century B.C.). Greek poet, known as the father of Greek didactic poetry. 154.7; 195.6; 286.15; 305.20; 319.27; 332.19; 363.62; 391.25; 392.7; 392.8; 565.4; 635.4; 654.9; 714.5; 732.5; 972.6; 1040.4

Hesse, Hermann (1877–1962). German novelist. 192.18; 207.9; 218.67; 410.10; 440.6; 525.40; 558.26; 581.2; 691.6; 777.9; 1007.4; 1053.32; 1057.13

Heywood, John (1497?–?1580). English poet. 27.5; 74.7; 90.5; 295.10; 353.15; 407.51; 748.10; 773.11; 873.11; 940.3; 1050.5; 1055.69

Higginson, Thomas Wentworth (1823–1911). American clergyman, editor, writer. 190.3

Hill, Aaron (1685–1750). English playwright and poet. 90.6

Hill, Sir Rowland (1795–1879). English postal authority, originator of "penny postage." 240.6

Hippocrates (460?–?377 B.C.). Greek physician, the father of medicine. 261.9; 261.10; 572.6; 791.6; 981.6

Hipponax (fl. c. 540 B.C.). Greek poet. 560.52

Hutchens, John K[ennedy] (1905– ). American journalist and editor. 1062.52

Hutcheson, Francis (1694–1746). Scottish philosopher and professor. 430.16

Hutchins, Robert M[aynard] (1899– ). American educator, foundation executive, writer. 530.7

Huxley, Aldous [Leonard] (1894–1963). English novelist, essayist, satirist. 12.6; 91.49; 98.9; 112.4; 121.23; 125.3; 155.6; 176.2; 207.10; 218.73; 239.7; 267.3; 272.16; 319.28; 319.29; 326.10; 333.11; 363.67; 393.25; 402.8; 407.55; 417.30; 440.8; 548.97; 584.6; 646.57; 700.8; 700.9; 739.4; 739.5; 790.33; 790.34; 793.7; 816.13; 891.13; 899.11; 909.7; 917.4; 960.10; 971.29; 995.14; 1035.50; 1057.17; 1058.44; 1062.53; 1064.30

Huxley, Thomas Henry (1825–1895). English biologist, teacher, writer. 9.30; 173.8; 277.41; 306.6; 327.15; 393.26; 431.11; 467.15; 520.28; 614.10; 616.38; 843.14; 843.15; 991.63; 992.8; 993.9

## I

Ibarruri, Dolores. Called La Pasionaria (1895– ). Spanish Communist leader. 361.30

Ibsen, Henrik [Johan] (1828–1906). Norwegian playwright and poet. 363.68; 381.2; 440.9; 447.10; 467.16; 561.11; 813.25; 893.12; 933.12

Inge, Dean William Ralph (1860–1954). English prelate and writer. 34.26; 41.14; 129.23; 131.15; 231.17; 249.7; 272.17; 354.9; 355.3; 372.5; 393.27; 431.12; 456.2; 485.6; 518.5; 520.29; 542.6; 558.29; 671.5; 688.11; 707.2; 735.10; 756.11; 766.9; 813.26; 856.6

Ingenieros, José (1877–1925). Argentine psychiatrist, educator, politician. 669.16

Ingersoll, Robert G[reen] (1833–1899). American lawyer, public official, agnostic. 16.3; 125.4; 277.42; 354.10; 385.42; 412.6; 433.10; 453.4; 515.23; 515.24; 573.6; 634.1; 705.34; 778.17; 790.35; 790.36; 790.37; 817.5

Irving, Washington (1783–1859). American essayist, biographer, historian. 53.62; 65.3; 115.24; 195.8; 204.29; 287.13; 348.4; 444.9; 452.7; 501.6; 542.7; 542.8; 560.60; 560.61; 580.14; 603.10; 669.17; 712.26; 798.20; 819.3; 860.9; 898.5; 961.2; 991.64; 1035.52; 1054.15; 1055.78; 1055.79

## J

Jackson, Andrew (1767–1845). Seventh President of the United States (1829–1837). 393.28; 958.8

Jackson, Holbrook (1874–1948). English literary scholar and editor. 842.23

Jackson, Robert [Houghwout] (1892–1954). American jurist. Justice of the U.S. Supreme Court (1941–1954). 256.6; 952.1

Jacob, Max (1876–1944). French poet, prose writer, painter. 53.63; 416.13; 702.54; 1061.4

Jacobs, Jane (1916– ). American social critic and writer. 129.24

James I of England (1566–1625). King of Great Britain (1603–1625); also ruled as James VI of Scotland (1567–1625). 975.6

James, Henry [Jr.] (1843–1916). American novelist, short-story writer, man of letters. 287.14; 502.15; 671.6; 719.4

James, William (1842–1910). American philosopher, physiologist, psychologist, teacher. 76.9; 200.3; 326.11; 449.6; 463.3; 598.24; 688.12; 787.4; 839.3; 843.16; 1060.19

Jami. Pen name of Nur ud-din 'Abd-ur-rahman ibn Ahmad (1414–1492). Persian poet, mystic, short-story writer. 147.8; 565.5

Jarrell, Randall (1914–1965). American poet, novelist, critic. 575.9

Jefferson, Thomas (1743–1826). American statesman, third President of the United States (1801–1809). 10.13; 34.27; 43.5; 50.9; 52.1; 102.23; 103.17; 111.5; 111.6; 175.11; 179.2; 179.3; 194.11; 228.9; 231.18; 231.19; 263.4; 269.16; 270.6; 277.43; 295.13; 297.21; 393.29; 407.56; 445.18; 491.16; 525.44; 536.57; 614.11; 623.8; 623.9; 641.7; 651.9; 713.28; 716.14; 724.4; 755.11; 755.12; 757.8; 766.10; 779.4; 790.39; 800.7; 813.27; 817.6; 977.9; 985.24; 985.25; 992.9; 995.15; 1050.6; 1053.38

Jerome, Jerome K[lapka] (11859–1927). English novelist and playwright. 33.14; 98.10; 137.7; 163.10; 183.15; 183.16; 186.5; 266.34; 339.19; 374.24; 444.10; 548.99; 548.100; 712.27; 785.2; 839.4; 911.22; 934.13; 971.30; 993.10; 1020.10; 1043.4; 1043.5; 1058.46

Jerrold, Douglas (1803–1857). English playwright and humorist. 546.4

Jiménez, Juan Ramón (1881–1958). Spanish poet. 66.1; 129.25; 409.8; 536.58; 614.12; 687.10; 702.55; 720.9; 900.2; 908.24; 983.10

Johnson, Georgia Douglas (1886– ). American poet and playwright. 72.1

Johnson, Lyndon B[aines] (1908– ). Thirty-sixth President of the United States (1963–1969). 34.28; 98.11; 226.7; 362.7; 366.17; 393.30; 614.13; 712.28; 724.5; 724.6; 906.9; 1030.10; 1060.20

*Johnson, Samuel. Also known as Dr. Johnson (1709–1784). English lexicographer, essayist, poet.

Johnston, Eric [Allen] (1896–1963). American business association official and motion picture industry executive. 310.4

Joll, James (1918– ). American political analyst. 705.35

Jolyot, Prosper. *See* Crébillon, Prosper Jolyot.

## K

## L

armies. 269.21

Lenclos, Ninon. Pen name of Anne Lenclos (1620–1705). French wit and lady of fashion. 1055.88

Lenin, Nikolai. Pseudonym of Vladimir Ilyich Ulyanov (1870–1924). Russian Communist leader. 231.25; 923.15

Leonardo da Vinci (1452–1519). Italian artist, inventor, scientist. 51.18; 80.6; 138.3; 151.14; 319.34; 340.21; 358.28; 428.4; 520.40; 529.10; 538.22; 617.8; 659.8; 688.18; 710.11; 732.7; 765.8; 858.5; 1000.11; 1058.49

Leopardi, Count Giacomo (1798–1837). Italian poet and essayist. 93.5; 151.15; 162.14; 203.16; 588.2; 646.66; 885.16; 959.17; 1029.8

Leopold, Aldo (1886–1948). American forester and conservationist. 174.4

Leopold, Nathan [Freudenthal] (1904– ). Principal in Leopold-Loeb case, paroled in 1958. 536.63

Lerner, Max (1902– ). Russian-born American teacher, editor, journalist. 34.34; 34.35; 71.7; 98.16; 106.3; 111.7; 131.18; 199.7; 226.11; 231.26; 239.9; 267.4; 275.4; 279.15; 305.25; 305.26; 321.3; 355.4; 385.45; 474.13; 493.7; 496.8; 520.41; 567.10; 591.6; 596.32; 623.13; 674.20; 679.5; 705.41; 728.10; 740.13; 753.2; 769.13; 790.44; 828.3; 843.25; 905.3; 938.24; 960.15; 960.16; 964.9; 1035.57; 1049.8

Lesage, Alain-René (1668–1747). French playwright and novelist. 407.69; 1055.89

Lessing, Gotthold Ephraim (1729–1781). German playwright, aesthetician, critic. 57.15; 391.32; 416.15; 448.18; 676.7; 873.14; 947.3

Lewis, Cecil Day. *See* Day-Lewis, C.

Lewis, [Harry] Sinclair (1885–1951). American novelist. 313.4

Lichtenberg, Georg Christoph (1742–1799). German physicist and writer. 76.10; 91.58; 91.59; 151.16; 361.36; 374.26; 399.43; 402.10; 426.19; 464.5; 576.26; 598.28; 616.46; 649.16; 656.10; 679.6; 748.13; 810.2; 842.26; 869.9; 879.5; 1053.44

Liebling, A[bbott] J[oseph] (1904–1963). American journalist and satirist. 623.14

Lincoln, Abraham (1809–1865). Sixteenth President of the United States (1861–1865). 8.5; 34.36; 107.6; 176.3; 231.27; 239.10; 372.8; 374.27; 393.37; 393.38; 534.23; 555.15; 591.7; 596.33; 614.18; 670.15; 675.11; 675.12; 756.13; 756.14; 813.33; 817.10; 862.7; 882.10; 995.19; 1006.4; 1009.8; 1030.12; 1049.9

Lindbergh, Anne Morrow (1906– ). American writer. 8.6; 34.37; 59.3; 148.9; 482.4; 490.9; 548.119; 548.120; 667.4; 670.16; 777.11; 850.10; 868.16; 899.13; 908.27; 911.26; 939.22; 991.75; 1055.90

Linderman, Bill (1922?–1961). American rodeo performer. 922.7

Lindner, Robert [Mitchell] (1914–1956). American psychoanalyst and writer. 12.9; 61.5; 109.14; 149.12; 168.11; 168.12; 205.6; 277.47; 466.4; 779.5; 908.28

Lindsay, John V[liet] (1921– ). American political leader. Mayor of New York City (1966– ). 1037.3

Ling Po. Chinese philosopher. 319.35

Linkletter, Art (1912– ). Canadian-born American radio and television personality. 8.7; 88.3; 146.4; 283.2; 378.3; 537.10; 661.4; 935.14; 937.3

Lippmann, Walter (1889– ). American teacher, editor, journalist. 53.72; 61.6; 69.4; 117.16; 171.14; 198.23; 231.28; 231.29; 231.30; 236.29; 236.30; 236.31; 240.7; 328.21; 333.14; 366.19; 393.39; 393.40; 393.41; 429.3; 433.13; 440.10; 441.18; 451.2; 489.16; 525.49; 528.11; 563.7; 564.5; 598.29; 598.30; 688.19; 705.42; 705.43; 705.44; 705.45; 713.32; 714.7; 720.10; 755.13; 755.14; 783.22; 783.23; 822.1; 852.18; 874.3; 906.11; 925.1; 938.25; 960.17; 967.10; 991.76; 1016.5; 1025.37; 1030.13; 1053.45

Lithgow, William (1582–c. 1645). Scottish traveler and writer. 272.22

Littré, [Maximilien Paul] Émile (1801–1881). French scholar and lexicographer. 765.9

Livy. Full name, Titus Livius (59 B.C.–A.D.17). Roman historian. 90.10; 205.7; 244.4; 473.6; 525.50; 674.21; 766.12; 893.13

Locke, John (1632–1704). English philosopher. 9.32; 91.60; 210.14; 221.13; 297.23; 297.24; 319.36; 331.11; 411.11; 440.11; 478.15; 514.13; 525.51; 539.13; 583.10; 598.31; 616.47; 616.48; 640.1; 649.17; 676.8; 687.13; 726.13; 738.2; 740.14; 959.18; 968.29; 991.77; 991.78; 1057.22; 1057.23; 1058.50

Lodge, Henry Cabot, Jr. (1902– ). American politician and diplomat. 34.38; 435.7

Logau, Baron Friedrich von (1604–1655). German poet and epigrammatist. 809.11

Longfellow, Henry Wadsworth (1807–1882). American poet and translator. 6.15; 6.16; 21.6; 33.21; 55.14; 74.10; 91.62; 95.7; 121.29; 129.30; 129.31; 141.4; 163.11; 191.12; 277.48; 285.6; 286.18; 297.25; 323.4; 399.44; 420.15; 425.25; 438.19; 444.12; 529.11; 560.71; 576.27; 584.7; 600.13; 607.27; 626.8; 646.67; 669.19; 687.14; 702.64; 702.65; 842.27; 848.28; 852.19; 891.15; 908.29; 911.27; 911.28; 923.16; 929.4; 939.23; 953.12; 1004.20; 1059.4; 1062.66; 1064.38

Lorca, Federico García. *See* Gracía Lorca, Federico.

Lorenz, Konrad Z. (1903– ). Viennese-born zoologist and writer. 41.19

Lovelace, Richard (1618–1658). English poet. 266.39; 489.17; 729.5

Lowell, Amy [Lawrence] (1874–1925). American poet, critic, biographer. 34.39; 91.63; 129.32; 200.6; 314.7; 384.12; 407.70; 407.71; 522.1; 693.8; 744.15; 911.29; 939.24; 1035.58; 1065.20

Lowell, James Russell (1819–1891). American

poet, critic, editor, diplomat. 17.36; 55.15; 70.26; 70.27; 94.5; 111.8; 121.30; 129.33; 134.5; 151.17; 192.25; 198.24; 204.32; 218.77; 224.16; 236.32; 269.22; 285.7; 319.37; 357.14; 358.29; 361.37; 369.2; 375.9; 382.25; 385.46; 410.15; 417.32; 431.15; 475.9; 520.42; 534.24; 544.4; 548.121; 548.122; 567.11; 592.11; 617.9; 618.3; 628.4; 702.66; 723.17; 725.3; 728.11; 767.4; 785.3; 816.15; 817.11; 848.29; 848.30; 848.31; 868.17; 887.2; 891.16; 897.8; 908.30; 908.31; 979.14; 989.7; 991.79; 993.12; 995.20; 1012.7; 1035.59; 1043.6; 1058.51

Lucan (full name, Marcus Annaeus Lucanus) (A.D. 39–65). Roman poet and prose writer. 90.11; 399.45; 401.17; 546.5; 713.33; 923.17

Lucas, E[dward ] V[errall] (1868–1938). English novelist, poet, essayist, man of letters. 194.12; 277.49; 341.12; 374.28; 560.72

Lucian (c. 120–200). Greek satirist. 983.12

Lucretius. Full name, Titus Lucretius Carus (98?–55 B.C.). Roman poet and natural philosopher. 108.4; 115.29; 213.14; 218.78; 372.9; 506.3; 695.3; 713.34; 875.6; 885.17; 945.7; 1054.21; 1063.17

Luther, Martin (1483–1546). German theologian and founder of the Protestant Reformation. 38.1; 282.22; 328.22; 560.73; 590.2; 717.22; 718.11

Lyly, John (1554?–1606). English prose writer, poet, playwright. 51.19; 58.4; 266.40; 319.38; 390.6; 438.20; 448.19; 467.17; 548.123; 551.9; 576.28; 679.7; 712.39; 934.16; 969.2; 1054.22; 1065.21

Lynd, Robert (1879–1949). Anglo-Irish essayist and journalist. 478.16

Lynes, [Joseph] Russell [Jr.] (1910– ). American editor, critic, writer. 780.2; 903.5

Lyttleton, George. 1st Baron Lyttleton of Frankley (1709–1773). English statesman, patron, writer. 699.6; 1055.91

## M

MacArthur, Douglas (1880–1964). American general. 582.13; 650.6; 1035.60

Macaulay, Thomas Babington, 1st Baron Macaulay of Rothley (1800–1859). English statesman, poet, historian, essayist, biographer. 78.4; 198.25; 210.15; 740.15

McCarthy, Mary (1912- ). American novelist, short-story writer, critic. 34.40; 34.41; 34.42; 102.25; 103.21; 169.3; 224.17; 296.17; 301.3; 417.33; 475.10; 536.64; 620.11; 633.10; 656.11; 843.26; 868.18; 1024.8

McCulloch, Warren S[turgis] (1898– ). American neurophysiologist. 960.18

McDonagh, Edward C[harles] (1915– ). Canadian-born American sociologist. 63.5

MacDonald, Anson. *See* Heinlein, Robert A.

McElroy, Neil H. (1904– ). American business executive and public official. 984.2

McFee, William [Morley Punshon] (1881–1966). English-born American novelist and essayist. 17.37; 43.8; 53.73; 53.74; 81.5; 166.5; 287.15; 291.6; 337.14; 441.19; 441.20; 470.8; 474.14; 560.74; 576.29; 596.34; 641.8; 804.11; 821.2; 911.30; 937.4; 989.8; 1055.92

McGinley, Phyllis (1905– ). American essayist and writer of light verse and books for children. 19.25; 93.6; 151.18; 160.7; 339.25; 506.4; 548.124; 549.8; 560.75; 560.76; 576.30; 619.8; 647.5; 653.3; 663.34; 698.20; 705.46; 730.3; 821.3; 822.2; 891.17; 893.14; 909.10; 938.26; 977.13; 1030.14; 1055.93

Machado [y Ruiz], Antonio (1875–1939). Spanish poet. 76.11; 319.39; 414.6; 477.6; 504.3; 521.15; 558.32; 676.9; 681.5; 688.20; 778.20; 842.28; 885.18; 917.6; 968.30; 991.80; 998.8; 1000.12; 1026.16; 1062.67

Machiavelli, Niccolò (1469–1527). Florentine statesman and political philosopher. 1051.8

MacLeish, Archibald (1892– ). American poet. 106.4; 121.31; 218.79; 327.19; 385.47; 403.12; 403.13; 536.65; 623.15; 691.9; 702.67; 908.32

McLuhan, [Herbert] Marshall (1911– ). Canadian educator, author, media expert. 12.10; 18.8; 34.43; 63.6; 103.22; 226.12; 277.50; 281.7; 287.16; 360.10; 612.6; 803.5; 875.7; 885.19; 907.7; 960.19; 971.32; 994.10

Macmillan, [Maurice] Harold (1894– ). Prime Minister of Great Britain (1957–1963). 203.17; 213.15

Mac Orlan, Pierre [Dumarchey] (1883–1970). French writer. 16.5

Maddocks, Melvin. Contemporary American writer. 1062.68

Maddox, Lester G[arfield] (1916– ). American politician. 469.3

Madison, James (1751–1836). Fourth President of the United States (1809–1817). 995.21

Maeterlinck, Count Maurice (1862–1949). Belgian poet, dramatist, essayist. 218.80; 238.12; 303.7; 305.27; 366.20; 391.33; 407.72; 407.73; 416.16; 515.29; 548.125; 603.11; 656.12; 723.18; 752.11; 796.2; 831.6; 862.8; 868.19; 885.20; 891.18; 911.31; 911.32; 939.25; 991.81; 1004.21; 1053.46; 1053.47; 1057.24

Magee, Bishop William Connor (1821–1891). Irish prelate, archbishop of York. 86.8

Mailer, Norman (1923– ). American novelist and essayist. 53.75; 89.4; 333.15; 401.18; 422.3; 548.126; 563.8; 705.47; 787.6; 869.10; 878.3

Maine, Sir Henry James [Sumner] (1822–1888). English jurist. 400.2

Malcolm X. Original name, Malcolm Little (1925–1965). American civil-rights activist and orator. 23.2; 34.44; 39.23; 106.5; 275.5; 361.38; 456.3; 598.32; 671.12; 713.35; 769.14; 853.5; 995.22; 1024.9

Malebranche, Nicolas (1638–1715). French

philosopher and theologian. 441.21; 448.20; 802.8

Mallarmé, Stéphane (1842–1898). French poet. 288.2

Malraux, André (1901– ). French novelist and critic. 53.76; 342.4

Mann, Horace (1796–1859). American educator. 277.51; 1025.38

Mann, Thomas (1875–1955). German novelist and essayist. 53.77; 53.78; 122.5; 171.15; 181.6; 198.26; 218.82; 282.23; 365.9; 404.11; 429.4; 441.22; 548.127; 548.128; 558.33; 572.7; 603.12; 607.28; 616.49; 624.3; 705.48; 773.18; 778.21; 868.20; 889.18; 905.4; 908.33; 916.40; 916.41; 962.5; 971.33; 1035.62

Mannes, Marya (1904– ). American essayist and journalist. 8.8; 34.45; 34.46; 53.79; 63.7; 123.18; 174.5; 175.12; 348.6; 387.7; 390.7; 407.74; 489.18; 491.19; 496.9; 514.14; 528.12; 530.9; 563.9; 563.10; 567.12; 593.1; 596.35; 614.19; 633.11; 705.49; 817.12; 851.8; 856.10; 894.14; 945.8; 1001.17; 1023.17; 1054.23

Mao Tse-tung (1893– ). Chairman of the Central Committee of the Chinese Communist Party. 133.2; 149.13; 155.8; 175.13; 675.13; 705.50; 705.51; 1035.63

Marceau, Marcel (1923– ). French actor and pantomimist. 891.19; 965.15

Marcello, Benedetto (1686–1739). Italian composer. 965.16

Marcus Aurelius. Full name, Marcus Aurelius Antoninus (121–180). Roman emperor and Stoic philosopher. 33.23; 70.28; 98.17; 150.6; 180.2; 206.11; 216.7; 224.18; 238.14; 261.12; 339.26; 366.21; 391.34; 391.35; 407.75; 449.9; 474.15; 536.66; 536.67; 545.6; 547.5; 656.13; 669.20; 723.19; 723.20; 826.4; 866.8; 873.15; 893.15; 930.6; 939.26; 968.31; 983.13; 991.82; 1063.18

Maritain, Jacques (1882– ). French philosopher and man of letters. 34.47; 34.48; 202.6; 231.31; 296.18; 397.9; 441.23; 548.129; 671.13; 960.20; 1004.22

Markham, Edwin (1852–1940). American poet. 98.18; 131.19; 269.24; 466.5; 599.2; 712.40; 722.2; 748.14; 847.9; 1059.5

Marlowe, Christopher (1564–1593). English dramatist and poet. 414.7; 518.6; 548.130; 693.9; 790.45; 816.16; 1035.64

Marquand, John P[hillips] (1893–1960). American novelist. 1062.69

Marquis, Don[ald Robert Perry] (1878–1937). American newspaperman and humorist. 8.9; 17.38; 17.39; 26.4; 70.29; 201.12; 228.10; 266.41; 275.6; 317.4; 358.30; 393.42; 407.76; 423.11; 425.26; 479.5; 506.5; 529.12; 558.34; 652.9; 705.52; 760.9; 865.14; 867.4; 882.11; 894.15; 945.9; 1005.4; 1055.94; 1058.52; 1062.70

Marshall, John (1755–1835). American jurist. Chief Justice of the U.S. Supreme Court (1801–1835). 102.26

Martí, José [Julian] (1853–1895). Cuban patriot, poet, essayist. 119.5; 361.39; 399.47; 404.12; 1055.95

Martial. Full name, Marcus Valarius Martialis (A.D. 42?–?102). Latin epigrammatist born in Spain. 45.15; 201.13; 294.3; 382.26; 384.13; 411.12; 416.17; 442.14; 511.5; 536.68; 557.9; 574.15; 723.21; 802.9; 911.33; 930.7; 941.8; 1062.71

Martin-Chauffier, Louis (1894– ). French writer. 218.83

Marvell, Andrew (1621–1678). English poet. 218.84; 851.9; 971.34; 1060.22

Marx, Karl (1818–1883). German philosopher and socialist. 106.6; 510.2; 596.36; 790.46; 1058.53

Mason, George (1725–1792). American statesman, author of the Virginia Constitution and Bill of Rights, on which were modeled the Federal Constitution and Bill of Rights. 725.4

Mason, William (1725–1797). English poet, playwright, clergyman. 1038.2

Massinger, Philip (1583–1640). English playwright. *See also* Fletcher and Massinger. 33.24; 218.85; 825.14

Masters, Edgar Lee (1868–1950). American poet and novelist. 536.69; 891.20

*Maugham, W[illiam] Somerset (1874–1965). English novelist and playwright.

Maupassant, [Henri René Albert] Guy de (1850–1893). French short-story writer and novelist. 671.14

Mauriac, François (1885–1970). French novelist, essayist, playwright. 53.84; 79.7; 101.8; 196.11; 204.33; 234.2; 548.134; 580.16; 702.69; 841.1; 1062.74; 1062.75

Maurois, André. Pen name of Emile Herzog (1885–1967). French biographer, novelist, essayist. 21.8; 207.15; 497.5; 646.69; 749.21; 870.6; 935.16; 957.12; 1054.25; 1055.97

Mazzini, Giuseppe (1805–1872). Italian patriot and writer. 991.84

Mead, Margaret (1901– ). American anthropologist and psychologist. 89.6; 560.77; 576.33; 707.5

Meany, George (1894– ). American labor leader. 701.1

Medlicott, Sir Frank (1903– ). English solicitor. 955.4

Melville, Herman (1819–1891). American novelist, short-story writer, poet. 159.3; 216.8; 224.19; 328.23; 328.24; 349.5; 453.5; 474.16; 496.10; 523.16; 558.35; 646.70; 646.71; 686.10; 847.10; 848.32; 852.20; 968.32; 968.33; 995.23; 1035.65; 1065.22

Menander (342–?292 B.C.). Greek comic playwright. 319.40; 319.41; 1055.98

Mencius (372–289 B.C.). Chinese philosopher. 117.18; 354.12; 393.44; 476.6; 781.4; 864.2; 894.16

Mencken, H[enry] L[ouis] (1880–1956). American newspaperman, editor, writer. 34.49; 50.10; 102.27; 113.10; 123.19; 135.5; 149.14; 170.12; 171.17; 188.7; 204.34; 207.16; 231.32; 231.33; 260.6; 269.25; 277.52; 328.25; 328.26; 329.30; 330.30; 332.20; 363.79; 385.48; 385.49; 416.18; 420.16; 430.20; 430.21; 440.12; 440.13; 470.9; 515.31; 523.17; 536.71; 548.135; 558.36; 560.78; 562.3; 562.4; 576.34; 582.14; 598.33; 625.7; 648.5; 688.22; 704.8; 705.53; 705.54; 735.17; 763.1; 783.25; 790.48; 813.34; 817.13; 844.8; 850.11; 893.16; 959.19; 965.19; 971.35; 990.5; 991.85; 993.13; 1006.5; 1010.8; 1012.8; 1030.15; 1035.66; 1041.38; 1055.99; 1055.100; 1064.41

Mendelssohn [-Bartholdy], [Jakob Ludwig] Felix (1809–1847). German composer, conductor, pianist. 607.29

Menninger, Karl [Augustus] (1893– ). American psychiatrist. 806.4

Menon, V. K. Krishna. *See* Krishna Menon, V. K.

Meredith, George (1828–1909). English novelist, poet, critic. 207.17; 519.4; 548.136; 642.2; 717.23; 878.5; 892.12; 1055.101

Merton, Thomas (1915–1968). French-born poet, writer, Trappist monk. 816.17; 1018.1; 1024.10

Michaux, Henri (1899– ). Belgian poet and artist. 39.24

Michelet, Jules (1798–1874). French historian. 1055.102

Mill, John Stuart (1806–1873). English philosopher and economist. 15.7; 210.16; 210.17; 274.2; 277.53; 361.40; 362.8; 374.29; 407.77; 407.78; 431.16; 571.7; 613.5; 649.18; 655.6; 655.7; 783.26; 957.13; 977.14; 991.86; 991.87; 992.12

Millay, Edna St. Vincent (1892–1950). American poet. 2.11; 70.32; 71.8; 101.9; 121.32; 137.9; 178.12; 178.13; 218.86; 266.42; 277.54; 282.24; 305.29; 328.27; 361.41; 404.13; 415.3; 464.6; 481.2; 511.6; 534.25; 536.72; 544.5; 548.137; 548.138; 549.11; 549.12; 567.13; 616.50; 646.72; 671.15; 674.22; 687.15; 735.18; 785.4; 848.33; 892.13; 899.14; 985.28; 1005.5; 1035.67; 1053.48; 1060.23

Mille, Pierre (1864–1941). French journalist and writer of fiction. 910.3

Miller, Arthur (1915– ). American playwright and novelist. 77.3; 548.139; 623.16; 723.23; 965.20

Miller, Henry (1891– ). American writer. 3.8; 34.50; 34.51; 34.52; 53.85; 53.86; 53.87; 185.25; 188.8; 201.14; 228.11; 231.34; 255.3; 272.23; 286.19; 287.18; 295.16; 352.7; 354.13; 359.5; 402.11; 417.34; 441.24; 477.7; 502.18; 515.32; 516.9; 520.44; 520.45; 528.13; 528.14; 536.73; 538.23; 607.30; 674.23; 702.70; 712.41; 735.19; 783.27; 793.10; 850.12; 875.8; 999.2; 1035.68; 1035.69; 1060.24; 1062.76; 1064.42

Mills, C[harles] Wright (1916–1962). American sociologist. 277.55; 290.2; 292.3; 337.15; 596.38; 1059.6

Milton, John (1608–1674). English poet and prose writer. 70.33; 70.34; 91.66; 91.67; 126.5; 188.9; 216.9; 224.20; 226.13; 240.8; 309.8; 328.28; 328.29; 330.31; 354.14; 385.50; 385.51; 391.37; 391.38; 397.10; 407.79; 414.8; 520.46; 536.74; 548.140; 560.79; 560.80; 576.35; 583.11; 595.4; 605.6; 616.51; 622.6; 649.19; 668.20; 674.24; 737.10; 778.22; 809.12; 811.16; 816.18; 862.9; 882.12; 908.34; 933.16; 939.28; 1025.39; 1025.40; 1033.5; 1040.9; 1041.39; 1063.19

Mimnermus (7th c. B.C.). Greek elegiac poet. 330.32

Mistinguett. Stage name of Jeanne Bourgeois (1874?–1956). French dancer and singer. 519.5

Mitchell, Langdon [Elwyn] (1862–1935). American playwright and poet. 34.53; 394.6; 560.81; 560.82

Mitchell, Maria (1818–1889). American astronomer and educator. 844.9

Mitropoulos, Dmitri (1896–1960). Greek-born American conductor. 1016.6

Moineaux, Georges. *See* Courteline, Georges.

Molière. Pen name of Jean Baptiste Poquelin (1622–1673). French comic playwright. 37.9; 168.14; 199.8; 203.20; 204.35; 204.36; 218.87; 224.21; 261.13; 262.13; 265.12; 277.56; 339.27; 353.21; 359.6; 387.8; 407.80; 431.17; 438.21; 486.3; 520.47; 536.75; 548.141; 557.10; 560.83; 560.84; 583.12; 596.39; 596.40; 598.34; 697.7; 716.23; 719.5; 775.5; 783.28; 786.3; 786.4; 791.7; 814.5; 842.29; 842.30; 893.17; 898.9; 909.11; 959.20; 1055.103; 1062.77; 1062.78; 1064.43

Montagu, Lady Mary Wortley (1689–1762). English letter writer and poet. 838.5

*Montaigne, Michel [Eyquem] de (1533–1592). French moralist and essayist.

Montale, Eugenio (1896– ). Italian poet. 418.5

Montesquieu [Charles de Secondat, Baron de la Brède et de] (1689–1755). French philosopher, man of letters, lawyer. 81.6; 91.71; 123.21; 188.11; 210.20; 224.23; 363.82; 385.52; 525.52; 534.26; 611.5; 664.4; 720.12; 757.9; 879.6; 938.28

Montgomery, James (1771–1854). English poet and editor. 538.25; 574.18

Montherlant, Henry [Millon] de (1896– ). French playwright, novelist, poet, essayist. 21.9; 218.91; 441.25; 1057.27

Moore, George (1852–1933). Irish novelist, playwright, poet, critic. 122.6; 708.2; 783.29

Moore, John [Cecil] (1907– ). English novelist and nonfiction writer. 521.16

Moore, Marianne [Craig] (1887– ). American poet. 70.35; 76.13; 454.2; 463.6; 560.86; 753.3; 990.6; 1062.81

Moore, Thomas (1779–1852). Irish poet. 195.10;

328.30; 359.7; 412.8; 470.10; 548.143; 548.144; 576.36; 876.7; 924.5; 1065.23

Mora, José María Luis (1794–1850). Mexican historian. 534.27

Moravia, Alberto. Pen name of Alberto Pincherle (1907– ). Italian novelist, short-story writer, essayist. 739.7; 994.11

More, Hannah (1745–1833). English writer and philanthropist. 903.6; 989.9

Morley, Christopher [Darlington] (1890–1957). American novelist, journalist, essayist. 26.5; 34.54; 70.36; 124.9; 210.21; 250.9; 294.4; 605.8; 613.7; 623.17; 702.71; 702.72; 916.43; 938.29; 964.10; 991.89; 992.14

Morley, John, Viscount Morley of Blackburn (1838–1923). English statesman and man of letters. 117.19; 204.39; 296.19; 333.16; 399.49; 430.22; 441.26; 536.77; 570.6; 598.35; 616.53; 649.22; 842.32; 883.3; 892.14; 928.2; 978.5; 991.90; 997.16; 1023.18; 1061.5

Morris, Desmond (1928– ). English zoologist and writer. 207.18; 633.12; 796.3

Morris, Wright (1910– ). American novelist. 466.6; 1062.82

Muggeridge, Malcolm (1903– ). English editor and writer. 34.55; 277.59; 287.19; 434.20; 563.11; 604.5; 623.18; 705.56; 733.7; 807.5; 885.21; 906.14; 1055.105

Muir, John (1838–1914). Scottish-born American naturalist and writer. 135.6; 349.6; 574.19; 616.54; 1052.4

Mumford, Lewis (1895– ). American writer, philosopher, historian, teacher. 63.8; 172.4; 319.42; 372.10; 536.78; 711.4; 777.12; 960.21; 994.12; 1028.2; 1035.70

Munro, H. H. *See* Saki.

Murrow, Edward R[oscoe] (1908–1965). American news commentator. 622.7; 720.13

Musset, Alfred de (1810–1857). French poet, novelist, playwright. 548.145; 666.6

Muste, A[braham] J[ohannes] (1885–1967). American clergyman and pacifist. 674.25

Myers, C. Kilmer. Episcopalian bishop of California (1916– ). 834.5

## N

Nabokov, Vladimir (1899– ). Russian-born American novelist, poet, critic. 452.9; 536.79; 538.26; 597.3; 676.10; 721.5; 761.4; 828.4; 908.36; 911.34; 989.10

Naguib, Mohammed (1901– ). Egyptian political leader. 790.50

*Napoleon I (Napoleon Bonaparte) (1769–1821). Emperor of France (1804–1815).

Nash, Ogden (1902–1971). American writer of light verse. 17.42; 17.43; 18.9; 27.7; 41.20; 41.21; 63.9; 68.3; 135.7; 137.10; 171.19; 203.22; 265.14; 266.43; 319.43; 332.22; 392.11; 418.6; 461.4; 479.7; 527.7; 536.81; 560.87; 580.17; 646.75; 646.76; 764.7; 793.11; 796.4; 846.3; 878.6; 885.22; 889.20; 893.18; 902.2; 904.3; 904.4; 937.5; 977.15; 1055.106; 1058.54

Nathan, George Jean (1882–1958). American drama and social critic, editor, memoirist. 53.88; 65.5; 144.8; 204.40; 211.2; 265.15; 363.83; 447.13; 465.4; 548.147; 548.148; 548.149; 548.150; 560.88; 574.20; 576.37; 702.73; 705.57; 757.10; 885.23; 965.21; 965.22; 965.23

Nehru, Jawaharlal (1889–1964). Hindu political leader. Prime Minister of India (1947–1964). 231.36

Newman, Barnett (1905–1970). American painter. 20.4

Newman, John Henry, Cardinal (1801–1890). English churchman and writer. 263.5; 376.4; 402.12; 520.48; 574.21; 790.53; 790.54

Newsom, [Edwin] Earl (1897– ). American public relations counsel. 756.17

Newton, Isaac (1642–1727). English physicist and mathematician. 688.24

Nicole, Pierre (1625–1695). French essayist and teacher. 891.21

Niebuhr, Reinhold (1892–1971). American theologian. 98.19; 475.11

*Nietzsche, Friedrich [Wilhelm] (1844–1900). German philosopher.

Nijinsky, Waslaw (1890–1950). Russian ballet dancer. 1058.55

Nin, Anaïs (1914– ). French-born American novelist, short-story writer, dancer. 402.14; 502.21; 752.12; 991.94

## O

O'Casey, Sean (1884–1964). Irish playwright. 382.29; 441.27

Ochs, Adolph S[imon] (1858–1935). American publisher and editor. 18.10

O'Faolain, Sean (1900– ). Irish novelist, short-story writer, biographer, playwright, teacher. 341.14

O'Hara, Frank (1926–1966). American poet and art critic. 45.16; 548.154

Olmedo, José Joaquín (1780–1847). Ecuadorian poet and statesman. 33.25

Omar Khayyám (d. 1123). Persian astronomer and poet. 218.94; 218.95; 223.7; 238.16; 266.44; 266.45; 328.31; 337.16; 412.10; 600.14; 624.4; 627.2; 698.24; 707.6; 723.24; 983.14; 992.15; 1018.3; 1060.25; 1064.46

O'Neill, Eugene [Gladstone] (1888–1953). American playwright. 127.5; 183.18; 381.3; 385.55; 447.14; 536.83; 536.84; 544.8; 548.155; 574.22; 646.77; 646.78; 669.21; 687.16; 723.25; 727.19; 908.37; 939.32; 971.37; 973.9

Oppenheimer, Joel (1930– ). American poet. 692.17

## P

Pound, Roscoe (1870–1964). American jurist, educator, writer. 525.55
Powell, Adam Clayton (1908– ). American politician, clergyman, writer. 76.16; 83.16; 295.19; 526.2; 744.17; 968.42
Powell, Anthony [Dymoke] (1905– ). English novelist. 687.18
Prentice, George Dennison (1802–1870). American newspaperman and editor. 19.29; 159.4; 402.17; 411.15; 430.27; 472.5; 492.6; 574.28; 625.8; 646.83; 824.8; 849.17; 935.19; 971.43; 975.11; 1062.89
Priest, Ivy Baker (1905– ). American politician. 74.11
Priestley, J[ohn] B[oynton] (1894– ). English novelist, playwright, essayist. 103.23; 104.1; 374.36; 496.12; 563.12; 563.13; 705.61; 960.23; 960.24
Prior, Matthew (1664–1721). English poet and diplomat. 53.99; 445.26; 877.3; 916.49; 939.38
Pritchett, V[ictor] S[awdon] (1900– ). English novelist, short-story writer, literary critic. 327.21; 341.16; 434.22; 558.44; 931.5; 982.9; 1062.90
Propertius. Full name, Sextus Propertius (50-48 B.C.–before A.D. 2). Roman poet. 483.2; 548.169; 576.45; 582.15; 596.44
Proudhon, Pierre-Joseph (1809–1865). French libertarian and socialist. 688.32; 740.18
Proust, Marcel (1871–1922). French novelist. 53.100; 53.101; 76.17; 151.20; 222.7; 224.30; 236.34; 319.49; 324.6; 324.7; 374.37; 404.15; 430.28; 452.12; 548.170; 548.171; 548.172; 548.173; 549.14; 572.9; 583.16; 620.12; 623.21; 656.14; 669.23; 694.4; 787.8; 787.9; 850.14; 852.23; 875.10; 911.38; 911.39; 939.39; 939.40; 968.43; 971.44; 971.45; 1062.91
Provence, Marcel. *See* Jouhandeau, Marcel.
Proverb, Afghanistan. 909.1
Proverbs, African. *See also* proverbs for specific African nations, tribes, and languages. 23.1; 516.1; 726.1; 908.1
Proverb, American. *See also* New England and Pennsylvania Dutch proverbs. 505.1
Proverb, American Indian. 513.1
Proverbs, Arabic. 30.2; 56.1; 57.3; 94.1; 102.1; 156.2; 188.1; 209.1; 354.1; 384.1; 715.1; 793.1
Proverbs, Ashanti. 266.3; 319.1; 329.2; 442.4; 614.1; 700.2; 749.1
Proverb, Babylonian. 345.1
Proverb, Brahman. 970.3
Proverb, Buganda. 788.3
Proverbs, Burmese. 33.4; 48.2; 236.6; 272.3; 330.10; 389.2; 426.7; 449.1; 548.22; 555.5; 702.7; 749.4; 825.5; 869.1; 909.3; 916.10
Proverbs, Cameroonian. 150.1; 478.2; 1053.10
Proverbs, Chinese. 10.4; 33.5; 37.2; 73.1; 102.9; 103.5; 112.2; 269.7; 277.11; 319.10; 330.12; 332.11; 399.10; 407.25; 430.7; 501.1; 539.5; 583.3; 605.2; 670.4; 687.2; 693.2; 760.5; 916.13; 934.4; 981.2; 981.3
Proverbs, Congolese. 116.1; 390.3; 1065.7
Proverbs, Danish. 19.11; 19.12; 33.7; 95.3; 121.9; 218.33; 219.3; 266.8; 293.7; 353.8; 398.4; 426.9; 478.5; 525.16; 592.4; 663.14; 692.8; 698.12; 749.8; 777.6; 784.2; 788.5; 964.6
Proverbs, Dutch. 85.4; 109.5; 236.8; 279.2; 318.1; 461.2; 674.8; 700.6; 889.5; 985.12; 1065.10
Proverbs, Egyptian. 73.2; 297.16; 364.2
*Proverbs, English.
Proverbs, Ethiopian. 162.5; 305.13; 595.1; 790.22; 1009.3
Proverbs, French. 64.7; 124.7; 266.17; 266.18; 272.10; 286.12; 293.11; 312.1; 319.21; 384.8; 394.2; 395.1; 401.7; 401.8; 425.10; 444.6; 445.11; 463.1; 536.36; 536.37; 548.70; 548.71; 568.3; 589.5; 663.20; 670.6; 744.9; 749.11; 759.3; 849.5; 1032.1; 1038.1
Proverbs, German. 6.10; 10.9; 19.15; 37.4; 39.19; 106.2; 107.2; 124.8; 158.1; 183.10; 201.9; 221.7; 266.21; 319.23; 354.5; 382.14; 445.14; 455.2; 460.1; 478.11; 508.14; 525.32; 548.82; 560.44; 560.45; 587.3; 611.2; 646.38; 670.9; 677.11; 718.7; 730.2; 737.7; 748.9; 749.13; 773.7; 784.5; 825.9; 865.8; 889.9; 891.11; 929.2; 931.3; 959.10; 991.45; 1035.41; 1041.30; 1045.5; 1051.5; 1059.2
Proverbs, Greek. 9.24; 39.20; 103.12; 183.12; 264.5; 309.4; 513.4; 560.50; 737.8; 1055.64
Proverbs, Hebrew. 519.3; 727.15; 849.10
Proverb, Hindu. 17.30
Proverbs, Hindustani. 50.8; 148.8; 308.5; 453.3; 945.5; 989.5; 995.12
Proverbs, Hungarian. 749.17; 934.12
Proverbs, Irish. 889.14; 1016.3
Proverbs, Italian. 6.14; 12.7; 17.32; 19.19; 37.8; 56.6; 70.22; 74.8; 85.10; 96.8; 103.16; 107.3; 160.5; 162.9; 188.6; 196.8; 218.74; 228.8; 278.1; 298.8; 319.30; 401.15; 434.15; 474.10; 515.25; 548.98; 582.11; 675.7; 677.12; 749.18; 790.38; 793.8; 869.6; 908.23; 916.31; 953.9; 973.7; 1016.4; 1058.45
Proverbs, Japanese. 56.7; 90.9; 183.14; 285.5; 398.10; 449.7; 489.11; 505.10; 520.30; 670.14; 714.6; 798.21; 916.32; 1009.7
Proverb, Jewish. 87.4
Proverbs, Kenyan. 243.10; 520.38
Proverbs, Latin. 2.10; 5.4; 48.7; 54.3; 57.14; 192.24; 335.20; 1063.16
Proverb, Latin American. *See also* Spanish proverbs. 107.5
Proverbs, Madagascan. 463.4; 783.24; 969.3
Proverb, Malagasy. 19.26
Proverbs, Malay. 33.22; 45.14; 56.8; 86.9; 87.6; 107.7; 110.5; 117.17; 168.13; 187.3; 201.11; 203.18; 218.81; 229.3; 233.8; 238.13; 245.7; 269.23; 312.3; 388.15; 398.12; 398.13; 399.46; 421.5; 433.14; 455.4; 502.17; 513.6; 515.30; 537.11; 589.9; 683.9; 686.9; 733.6; 749.19; 749.20; 865.13; 866.7; 883.2; 927.7; 955.3; 973.8; 1001.16; 1035.61; 1057.25; 1060.21

Proverb, Moorish. 663.36
Proverb, New England. 988.4
Proverbs, Nigerian. 90.14; 233.9; 363.86; 445.24; 584.8
Proverbs, Pennsylvania Dutch. 289.6; 356.8
Proverbs, Persian. 17.45; 17.46; 85.12; 152.4; 163.12; 218.100; 223.9; 237.10; 257.14; 289.7; 319.47; 358.33; 402.15; 420.18; 475.12; 505.11; 549.13; 617.11; 693.10; 710.12; 749.25; 811.17; 814.6; 865.16; 889.23; 901.3; 927.8; 972.7; 1041.43
Proverbs, Polish. 426.20; 548.167
Proverbs, Portugese. 226.15; 354.18; 495.4; 574.27; 886.7
Proverb, Rhodesian. 539.15
Proverbs, Russian. 45.17; 102.31; 221.19; 261.17; 266.53; 289.8; 342.5; 355.8; 392.13; 435.9; 440.19; 442.18; 489.22; 517.18; 577.5; 596.50; 599.3; 617.18; 640.2; 712.45; 717.27; 761.6; 808.2; 898.14; 953.13; 1004.30
Proverb, Sanskrit. 529.16
Proverbs, Scottish. 243.14; 749.31
Proverbs, Senegalese. 166.7; 398.18; 650.9
Proverbs, Spanish. *See also* Latin American proverb. 12.11; 17.60; 37.12; 57.21; 58.6; 65.6; 103.25; 113.13; 117.26; 120.10; 120.11; 149.17; 166.8; 215.4; 223.12; 226.18; 239.11; 261.19; 266.59; 319.56; 331.14; 332.26; 332.27; 347.4; 363.106; 391.51; 392.14; 403.20; 411.18; 432.2; 435.11; 453.8; 461.5; 471.10; 474.23; 486.4; 548.215; 548.216; 557.16; 560.113; 574.36; 575.15; 617.19; 637.6; 658.16; 691.14; 712.50; 713.47; 722.3; 799.6; 811.21; 849.21; 869.15; 873.25; 887.4; 889.28; 908.48; 909.15; 911.54; 915.2; 934.20; 991.121; 1035.95; 1035.96; 1055.137; 1055.138
Proverb, Swahili. 409.15
Proverb, Tongan. 363.110
Proverbs, Turkish. 57.23; 110.7; 140.3; 156.6; 286.27; 332.32; 444.17; 463.8; 579.15; 712.52; 723.30; 911.57; 1042.6
Proverbs, Welsh. 94.8; 353.30; 716.39
Proverbs, Yiddish. 27.10; 43.15; 137.14; 203.33; 208.11; 223.14; 266.64; 282.41; 285.11; 327.26; 351.23; 401.29; 430.36; 433.30; 437.2; 444.19; 461.6; 491.29; 527.10; 536.138; 546.7; 548.252; 596.63; 619.11; 646.106; 712.56; 745.17; 748.18; 766.19; 773.29; 788.7; 798.33; 816.27; 850.18; 866.12; 907.14; 969.4; 1001.21; 1004.37; 1033.8; 1041.67; 1049.11; 1053.72; 1057.42
*Publilius Syrus (fl. 1st century B.C.). Latin writer of mimes.

## Q

Quarles, Francis (1592–1644). English metaphysical poet. 897.9; 910.4
Quasimodo, Salvatore (1901– ). Italian poet and critic. 702.80
Quintilian. Full name, Marcus Fabius Quintilianus (c. 35–c. 99). Roman rhetorician. 33.31; 329.34; 617.16; 726.16; 730.4; 1058.58; 1062.92

## R

Rabelais, François (1494?–1553). French scholar, humanist, physician, writer. 520.57; 523.21; 670.18; 856.13; 862.10
Racine, Jean [Baptiste] (1639–1699). French playwright. 201.16; 298.10; 489.21; 515.39; 548.177; 548.178; 549.15; 551.10; 939.42; 995.27; 1023.26; 1025.48; 1055.126
Radford, Arthur William (1896– ). American admiral and business consultant. 313.5
Radhakrishnan, Sir Sarvepalli (1888– ). Indian educator, philosopher, statesman. 844.10
Radiguet, Raymond (1903–1923). French novelist and poet. 404.16
Rakove, Milton. Contemporary American educator and political adviser. 130.7; 704.9
Ramadier, Paul (1888–1961). French political leader. 99.3
Rameau, Jean-Philippe (1683–1764). French composer and musical theorist. 598.38; 607.34
Randall, Clarence B[elden] (1891– ). American industrialist. 528.19
Rapier, James T[homas] (1837–1883). American lawyer, journalist, congressman. 995.28
Rattigan, Terence [Mervyn] (1911– ). English playwright. 965.26
Ray, John (1627–1705). English naturalist. 121.34; 121.35; 273.1; 549.16
Ray, Randolph (1886–1963). American clergyman and writer. 766.14
Reade, Charles (1814–1884). English novelist. 641.9
Redfield, William (1927– ). American actor and writer. 464.7
Regnard, Jean-François (1655–1709). French playwright. 551.11
Reid, Alastair (1926– ). American poet and writer. 121.36
Reik, Theodor (1888–1969). Austrian-born American psychologist and writer. 548.179; 548.180; 552.16; 562.5; 576.46; 663.40; 820.2; 869.12; 1014.2; 1055.127
Reiland, Karl. Contemporary American Episcopalian clergyman. 56.10
Remarque, Erich Maria (1898–1970). German journalist and novelist. 587.7
Remond, C. Lenox (1810–1873). American antislavery lecturer and orator. 663.41; 769.16
Renan, [Joseph] Ernest (1823–1892). French writer, critic, scholar. 76.18; 263.6; 390.11; 416.19; 417.40; 536.95; 636.5; 843.29
Renard, Jules (1864–1910). French novelist and

playwright. 4.6; 19.31; 132.5; 172.5; 263.7; 314.9; 330.40; 339.31; 385.62; 407.88; 440.16; 441.30; 459.3; 515.40; 517.16; 523.22; 527.8; 536.96; 537.13; 596.48; 702.81; 860.10; 865.18; 905.5; 908.44; 916.51; 956.14; 962.7; 1012.10; 1012.11; 1057.35; 1057.36; 1062.93

Repplier, Agnes (1855–1950). American essayist, biographer, historian, poet. 17.50; 41.22; 41.23; 53.102; 185.29; 203.27; 210.25; 266.52; 390.12; 493.10; 496.13; 511.7; 523.23; 540.3; 607.35; 652.10; 684.9; 868.25; 877.4; 959.24; 985.29; 993.19; 1004.27; 1054.30; 1055.128

Reston, James [Barrett] (1909– ). Scottish-born American journalist and editor. 245.9; 496.14; 496.15; 585.3; 614.22; 622.8; 623.22; 705.62

Retz [Jean François-Paul de Gondi], Cardinal de (1614–1679). French prelate and writer. 201.17; 257.16; 297.28; 312.4; 340.25; 617.17; 825.20; 934.18; 990.9

Rexroth, Kenneth (1905– ). American poet. 41.24

Rice, Berkeley (1937– ). Contemporary American writer. 1027.4

Rice, Robert (1916– ). American criminologist. 201.18

Rich, Adrienne (1929– ). American poet. 885.27

Richelieu, Armand-Jean du Plessis, duc de. Known as Cardinal Richelieu (1585–1642). French statesman and prelate. 393.53; 825.21

Richter, Jean Paul [Friedrich] (1763–1825). German novelist and aesthetician. 184.4; 523.24; 607.36

Rieff, Philip (1922– ). American sociologist and writer. 319.50; 548.181; 752.14; 778.28; 790.62; 842.34; 868.26

Riesman, David (1909– ). American sociologist, writer, lecturer. 103.24; 133.3; 168.15; 559.19; 563.14; 663.42; 1057.37

Rilke, Rainer Maria (1875–1926). German poet. 53.103; 53.104; 56.11; 91.79; 192.32; 204.44; 243.13; 282.29; 324.8; 330.41; 356.10; 366.27; 402.19; 522.2; 536.97; 548.182; 548.183; 548.184; 548.185; 560.98; 584.11; 605.11; 613.9; 790.63; 868.27; 879.7; 908.45; 911.40; 948.4; 1004.28; 1063.22

Rivarol, Comte de. *See* Rivaroli, Antoine.

Rivaroli, Antoine. Known as Comte de Rivarol (1753–1801). French journalist of Italian parentage. 1041.48

Roberts, Chalmers [McGeagh] (1910– ). American writer. 623.23

Robsjohn-Gibbings, T[erence] H[arold] (1905– ). English interior decorator and writer. 428.5

Rochefoucauld, François, Duc de la. *See* La Rochefoucauld, François, Duc de.

Rodman, Frances. Contemporary American writer. 192.33

Rodó, José [Enrique] (1872–1917). Uruguayan critic and philosopher. 906.16

Roethke, Theodore (1908–1963). American poet. 548.186; 778.29; 885.28; 1064.50

Rogers, Will[iam Penn Adair] (1879–1935). American actor and humorist. 18.11; 34.56; 62.4; 62.5; 63.10; 99.4; 102.30; 131.22; 149.16; 169.5; 169.6; 181.7; 219.12; 219.13; 231.41; 245.10; 245.11; 261.16; 277.65; 295.20; 412.12; 416.20; 434.23; 501.7; 518.7; 534.34; 534.35; 590.3; 604.6; 660.1; 696.7; 704.10; 704.11; 704.12; 705.63; 705.64; 705.65; 755.15; 790.64; 793.13; 827.1; 879.8; 958.9; 958.10; 958.11; 971.46; 991.104; 1027.5; 1030.16; 1030.17; 1035.81; 1055.129

Roland, Jeanne Manon Phlipon. Known as Madame Roland (1754–1793). During the French Revolution her salon was the meeting place for the Girondists. 534.36

Rolland, Romain (1866–1944). French novelist, playwright, essayist, musicologist. 416.21; 668.24; 873.23; 1035.82; 1064.51

Romains, Jules. Pen name of Louis Farigoule (1885– ). French novelist, playwright, essayist, poet. 363.92

Ronan, Thomas P. Contemporary journalist; London correspondent of the *New York Times*. 168.16

Roosevelt, [Anna] Eleanor (1884–1962). American humanitarian, columnist, lecturer, wife of President Franklin D. Roosevelt. 861.6

Roosevelt, Franklin D[elano] (1882–1945). Thirty-second President of the United States (1933–1945). 34.57; 34.58; 46.4; 169.7; 174.6; 175.14; 175.15; 175.16; 202.7; 220.3; 226.16; 226.17; 231.42; 231.43; 295.21; 329.35; 340.26; 354.19; 361.43; 393.54; 418.7; 485.7; 496.16; 517.17; 520.58; 529.15; 533.3; 534.37; 534.38; 582.16; 583.17; 585.4; 614.23; 674.28; 674.29; 705.66; 728.13; 732.8; 755.16; 756.18; 756.19; 770.4; 770.5; 920.5; 958.12; 977.16; 998.10; 1006.6; 1030.18; 1030.19; 1035.83; 1035.84; 1041.49; 1041.50; 1064.52

Roosevelt, Theodore (1858–1919). Twenty-sixth President of the United States (1901–1909). 34.59; 46.5; 130.8; 525.56; 582.17; 671.17; 713.42; 783.34; 1053.56; 1058.59

Rorem, Ned (1923– ). American composer and writer. 53.105; 53.106; 53.107; 62.6; 204.45; 290.4; 363.93; 372.13; 399.54; 399.55; 483.3; 483.4; 521.20; 548.187; 607.37; 607.38; 607.39; 607.40; 607.41; 677.16; 891.27; 985.30; 991.105

Rose, Alexander (1901– ). American writer. 1033.6

Ross, Harold [Wallace] (1892–1951). American editor, founder of *The New Yorker*. 758.11

Ross, Leonard Q. *See* Rosten, Leo Calvin.

Rossetti, Christina [Georgina] (1830–1894). English poet. 191.13; 536.98; 538.31; 574.30; 848.34; 1052.5

Rossetti, Dante Gabriel. Full name, Gabriel

Charles Dante Rossetti (1828–1882). English poet and painter. 847.11

Rostand, Edmond (1868–1918). French poet and playwright. 324.9; 519.6

Rostand, Jean (1894– ). French biologist and writer. 516.11; 567.15

Rosten, Leo [Calvin]. Pen name, Leonard Q. Ross (1908– ). Polish-born American writer and political scientist. 588.3

Roth, Philip (1933– ). American novelist and short-story writer. 510.3

Rouault, Georges (1871–1958). French painter and printmaker. 659.10

Rougemont, Denis de (1906– ). Swiss writer, writing in French. 407.89; 560.99

Rousseau, Jean-Baptiste (1671–1741). French poet. 1026.21

Rousseau, Jean-Jacques (1712–1778). Swiss-born French philosopher, novelist, political theorist. 107.8; 111.9; 123.23; 131.23; 165.5; 170.15; 174.7; 213.16; 231.44; 233.10; 234.3; 277.66; 305.32; 387.11; 387.12; 393.55; 407.90; 441.31; 474.19; 476.11; 513.9; 525.57; 534.39; 536.99; 545.9; 551.12; 554.6; 554.7; 616.60; 646.86; 649.28; 667.6; 671.18; 712.44; 713.43; 716.28; 740.19; 740.20; 743.4; 749.28; 755.17; 760.12; 793.14; 825.22; 858.8; 882.14; 882.15; 891.28; 906.17; 923.19; 991.106; 1023.27; 1041.51; 1053.57

Roux, Joseph (1834–1905). French priest and writer. 122.7; 129.35; 224.32; 236.35; 269.27; 277.67; 282.30; 282.31; 297.29; 319.51; 351.13; 363.94; 407.91; 417.41; 425.34; 433.21; 447.15; 448.24; 449.11; 474.20; 515.41; 515.42; 542.10; 548.188; 548.189; 583.18; 688.33; 698.33; 702.82; 716.29; 719.6; 757.13; 767.7; 778.30; 780.4; 893.19; 898.13; 900.3; 908.46; 911.41; 938.35; 956.15; 1004.29; 1025.49; 1065.25

Rowan, Carl [Thomas] (1925– ). American journalist and diplomat. 245.12; 478.17

Rubinstein, Artur (1886– ). Polish-born American concert pianist. 407.92

Rudin, Stanley. Contemporary Canadian psychologist. 34.60

Rumbold, Richard (1622?–1685). English conspirator and soldier. 995.29

Rusk, [David] Dean (1909– ). U.S. Secretary of State (1961–1969). 115.32; 979.18

Ruskin, John (1819–1900). English writer and critic. 50.12; 50.13; 50.14; 50.15; 53.108; 53.109; 53.110; 53.111; 53.112; 61.9; 70.40; 70.41; 91.80; 121.37; 131.24; 142.3; 163.13; 268.2; 277.68; 283.3; 344.2; 393.56; 423.17; 433.22; 455.5; 471.8; 536.100; 596.49; 602.2; 676.13; 842.35; 1027.6; 1029.10; 1035.85; 1058.60; 1058.61

*Russell, Bertrand [Arthur William], 3rd Earl Russell (1872–1970). English philosopher, mathematician, social reformer.

Russell, Rosalind (1911– ). American actress. 327.22

## S

Saarinen, [Gottlieb] Eliel (1873–1950). Finnish-American architect. 235.1

Sade, Comte Donatien Alphonse François de. Known as Marquis de Sade (1740–1814). French soldier, writer. 710.14

*Sa'di. Pen name of Musharrif-uddin (born Muslih-uddin; c. 1184–1291). Persian poet.

Sagan, Françoise. Pen name of Françoise Quoirez (1935– ). French novelist. 53.113; 508.21; 542.11

St. Augustine. *See* Augustine, St.

St. Benedict of Nursia. *See* Benedict of Nursia, St.

Saint-Évremond, seigneur de (Charles de Marguetel de Saint-Denis) (1613–1703). French wit and man of letters. 473.7

*Saint-Éxupéry, Antoine de (1900–1944). French novelist, essayist, aviator.

St. John, Henry, 1st Viscount Bolingbroke (1678–1751). English statesman, orator, man of letters. 297.30; 614.24

St. John, J. Hector. *See* Crèvecoeur, Michel Guillaume Jean de.

Saint-Just, Louis Antoine Léon de (1767–1794). French revolutionary leader, intimate of Robespierre. 416.23; 825.23

St. Thomas Aquinas. *See* Aquinas, St. Thomas.

Saki. Pen name of Hector Hugh Munro (1870–1916). Scottish novelist and short-story writer. 783.36; 932.5; 1014.3; 1055.130

Salacrou, Armand (1899– ). French playwright. 385.63

Sallust. Full name, Gaius Valerius Sallustius Crispus (86–35 B.C.). Roman historian. 363.95; 570.8; 727.23; 745.14; 860.11; 1025.50

Sampson, Anthony (1926– ). English journalist and biographer. 623.24

Samson, Leon. Contemporary writer. 596.51; 813.38

Sand, George. Pen name of Amandine Lucie Aurore Dupin, Baronne Dudevant (1804–1876). French writer. 941.12

Sandburg, Carl (1878–1967). American poet. 10.17; 192.34; 197.9; 218.106; 231.47; 284.4; 329.37; 329.38; 351.15; 353.25; 361.45; 414.10; 417.42; 425.36; 521.22; 526.3; 548.196; 566.8; 596.52; 597.4; 658.13; 669.25; 674.30; 675.14; 702.83; 805.7; 847.12; 960.26; 971.48; 979.19; 994.15; 1043.7

Sanger, Margaret [Higgins] (1883–1966). American birth-control leader. 82.2

Sansom, William (1912– ). English novelist and short-story writer. 1062.94

*Santayana, George (1863–1952). Spanish-born American philosopher, poet, novelist, critic.

Sapirstein, Milton R. (1914– ). American psychiatrist and writer. 70.45; 121.41; 277.71; 332.24; 333.20; 663.45; 663.46; 663.47; 906.19; 999.4

361.49; 362.10; 366.32; 372.14; 393.60; 404.18; 417.43; 435.12; 472.6; 520.64; 534.44; 545.12; 583.20; 596.57; 598.44; 618.6; 633.13; 667.7; 670.22; 671.20; 671.21; 704.13; 704.14; 704.15; 705.71; 724.11; 724.12; 728.15; 735.26; 755.18; 757.15; 758.12; 949.5; 971.57; 991.122; 1030.21; 1057.38

Stevenson, Robert Louis [Balfour] (1850–1894). Scottish novelist, poet, essayist. 2.12; 37.13; 41.27; 55.21; 91.85; 102.34; 121.45; 176.4; 269.33; 279.22; 289.9; 297.32; 319.57; 328.36; 329.44; 341.17; 351.20; 407.105; 444.15; 457.3; 536.121; 538.38; 542.14; 544.10; 560.115; 560.116; 598.45; 598.46; 600.18; 646.100; 659.11; 749.34; 797.12; 805.8; 848.37; 916.58; 938.40; 967.15; 985.37; 985.38; 1014.4; 1052.8; 1057.39; 1060.28; 1062.102; 1064.56; 1065.30; 1065.31

Stinnett, Caskie (1911– ). American writer. 245.13

Stone, I[sidor] F[einstein] (1907– ). American journalist and social commentator; editor and publisher of *I. F. Stone's Weekly*. 226.19

Stoppard, Tom (1937– ). English playwright and novelist. 74.12; 218.123; 300.4; 457.4; 536.122; 600.19; 688.40; 874.5; 991.123; 991.124

Stowe, Harriet [Elizabeth] Beecher (1811–1896). American novelist. 760.13

Stravinsky, Igor Feodorovitch (1882–1971). Russian-born American composer. 53.128; 59.7; 198.39; 330.46; 335.28; 372.15; 399.62; 483.5; 529.19; 548.221; 607.48; 607.49; 607.50; 607.51; 607.52; 655.8; 723.28; 816.22; 891.33; 893.22; 965.29

Strindberg, [Johan] August (1849–1912). Swedish playwright, novelist, poet. 332.28; 332.29; 407.106; 965.30

Stringer, Arthur [John Arbuthnott] (1874–1950). American novelist and poet. 70.49; 252.5; 834.13

Styron, William [Clark, Jr.] (1925– ). American novelist. 91.86; 1062.103

Suarès, André (1868–1948). French poet, critic, essayist. 143.3; 256.10; 1041.62

Suckling, Sir John (1609–1642). English poet. 178.17; 316.12

Sulzberger, Arthur Hays (1891–1968). American newspaper publisher. 623.26

Sulzberger, C[yrus] L[eo] (1912– ). American newspaperman and political writer. 359.9

Surtees, Robert Smith (1803–1864). English novelist and sports writer. 191.17; 265.23; 665.2; 700.13; 815.3; 1026.24

Sutherland, George (1862–1942). American jurist. Associate Justice of the U.S. Supreme Court (1922–1938). 725.5

Suzuki, Daisetz Teitaro (1870–1966). Japanese Zen Buddhist scholar and writer. 688.41

Swerling, Jo (1897– ). Russian-born playwright and scenarist. 78.8

Swift, Jonathan (1667–1745). English satirist. 15.9; 31.9; 33.32; 57.22; 65.7; 71.9; 178.18; 193.3; 203.31; 204.55; 261.21; 262.15; 297.33; 297.34; 320.4; 336.2; 346.21; 351.21; 355.11; 358.43; 358.44; 374.40; 390.14; 403.21; 412.14; 536.123; 545.13; 546.6; 560.117; 567.18; 586.4; 642.3; 642.4; 646.101; 649.31; 667.8; 688.42; 699.11; 710.16; 716.33; 717.30; 718.13; 720.15; 737.14; 757.16; 758.13; 766.17; 773.24; 790.78; 838.7; 886.9; 889.29; 916.59; 922.9; 930.10; 935.22; 936.6; 971.58; 989.16; 1016.8; 1025.53; 1027.8; 1065.32

Swinburne, Algernon Charles (1837–1909). English poet and man of letters. 218.124; 263.8; 328.37; 509.2; 558.50; 584.15; 600.20; 971.59; 983.21

Swope, Herbert Bayard (1882–1958). American newspaperman, editor, public official. 623.27; 623.28

Syrus, Publilius. *See* Publilius Syrus.

Szell, George (1897–1970). Hungarian-born American conductor, composer, pianist. 607.53

## T

Tacitus, Cornelius (55?–117). Roman historian. 2.13; 33.33; 170.18; 281.12; 317.7; 339.35; 374.41; 384.21; 388.25; 474.24; 489.28; 603.15; 639.9; 713.48; 935.23; 1012.13; 1035.97

Taft, William Howard (1857–1930). Twenty-seventh President of the United States (1909–1913). 179.6

*Tagore, [Sir] Rabindranath (1861–1941). Bengali poet, novelist, essayist, composer.

Taine, Hippolyte [Adolphe] (1828–1893). French philosopher, critic, historian. 353.28; 560.118

Talleyrand-Périgord, Charles-Maurice de, prince de Bénévent. Commonly known as Talleyrand (1754–1838). French statesman. 851.13

Talmud, Palestinian (4th c.). 219.15; 260.7; 277.74; 433.27; 489.29; 695.5; 983.22; 1029.13; 1055.141; 1058.63

Tarkington, [Newton] Booth (1869–1946). American novelist and playwright. 51.27; 407.107; 560.119; 609.4

Taubman, [Hyman] Howard (1907– ). American journalist and essayist. 965.31

Taylor, Bayard (1825–1878). American poet, journalist, novelist. 548.226

Taylor, Sir Henry (1800–1886). English playwright. 793.15

Taylor, Jeremy (1613–1667). English clergyman and writer. 261.22; 332.30

Teale, Edwin Way (1899– ). American teacher, editor, writer, naturalist. 41.28; 129.37; 174.8; 291.7; 413.9; 530.10; 536.126; 599.4; 616.64; 616.65; 623.29; 629.4; 695.6;

768.1; 848.38; 848.39; 848.40; 939.48; 988.6; 991.129; 991.130; 994.18; 1016.9

Teasdale, Sara (1884–1933). American poet. 20.6; 70.52; 70.53; 70.54; 70.55; 127.10; 319.58; 470.13; 519.7; 536.127; 536.128; 548.227; 548.228; 567.20; 574.38; 597.5; 646.102; 702.96; 702.97; 710.18; 848.41; 968.48; 1003.2

Tehyi Hsieh (1884– ). Chinese educator, writer, diplomat. 9.37; 49.2; 233.12; 271.3; 277.75; 363.107; 402.25; 408.5; 445.31; 534.45; 749.35; 938.41; 960.27

Temple, Sir William (1628–1699). English diplomat, statesman, essayist. 91.87

Tencin [Claudine-Alexandrine Guérin] Mme de (1682–1749). French letter writer, novelist, and leader in Parisian intellectual circles. 934.21

*Tennyson, Alfred, 1st Baron Tennyson. Commonly called Alfred, Lord Tennyson (1809–1892). English poet.

Terence. Full name, Publius Terentius Afer (195?–159 B.C.). Roman playwright. 164.7; 210.28; 319.61; 358.45; 411.20; 467.21; 525.64; 548.232; 552.19; 558.52; 571.8; 646.103; 655.9; 696.8; 749.36; 787.12; 909.16; 981.10; 991.131; 1015.1; 1055.143

Tertullian. Full name, Quintus Septimius Florens Tertullianus (160? – ?230). Latin ecclesiastical writer; a father of the church. 298.12; 385.73

Thackeray, William Makepeace (1811–1863). English novelist. 341.18

Theobald, Lewis (1688–1744). English essayist, playwright, Shakespearian critic. 467.22

Theocritus (fl. c. 270 B.C.). Greek pastoral poet. 382.39

Theognis (6th c. B.C.). Greek elegiac and gnomic poet. 218.127; 266.60; 600.22

Theophrastus (c. 370–287 B.C.). Greek philosopher and man of letters. 971.63

Thévenin, Denis. *See* Duhamel, Georges.

Thomas, Dylan [Marlais] (1914–1953). Welsh poet and prose writer. 218.128; 702.100; 702.101; 702.102; 987.6

Thomas à Kempis. More properly Thomas Hamerken von Kempen (c. 1380–1471). German monk and writer. 6.20; 17.61; 171.31; 180.3; 210.29; 218.129; 339.36; 433.28; 442.22; 458.6; 514.23; 520.65; 545.14; 548.233; 690.5; 773.26; 916.60; 939.49; 1058.66

Thomas Aquinas, St. *See* Aquinas, St. Thomas.

Thompson, Francis (1859–1907). English poet. 385.74; 538.40; 835.4; 848.43; 848.44; 939.50; 983.24; 1010.12

Thomson, James (1700–1748). Scottish-born English poet. 70.57; 411.21; 616.67; 695.7; 848.45; 848.46; 848.47; 959.28

*Thoreau, Henry David (1817–1862). American essayist, naturalist, poet.

Thrale, Mrs. *See* Piozzi, Hester Lynch.

Thucydides (c. 460–c. 400 B.C.). Greek historian. 192.39; 213.21; 231.52; 330.48; 400.3; 651.10; 716.36; 745.16; 991.134

Thurber, James [Grover] (1894–1961). American essayist, short-story writer, humorist. 10.21; 33.34; 34.65; 71.10; 84.3; 144.10; 144.11; 144.12; 148.15; 221.22; 244.6; 256.12; 269.34; 272.31; 401.27; 431.26; 434.27; 434.28; 444.16; 463.7; 478.18; 520.66; 521.25; 558.53; 629.5; 640.3; 705.72; 727.29; 752.18; 804.14; 868.34; 980.14

Tiberius. Full Latin name Tiberius Claudius Nero (42 B.C.–A.D. 37). Roman emperor, called a cruel tyrant and a sound administrator. 958.13

Tibullus, Albius (c. 48–19 B.C.). Roman elegiac poet. 407.109; 548.235; 851.14; 1035.98

Tillich, Paul (1886–1965). German-born American philosopher and theologian. 6.21; 218.130; 328.40; 328.41; 351.22; 357.17; 388.28; 548.236; 790.81; 966.8

Tillotson, John (1630–1694). English writer and prelate. 385.75

Tobin, James (1918– ). American educator. 1035.99

Tobin, John (1770–1804). English playwright. 265.25

Tocqueville, Count Alexis [Charles Henri Maurice Clérel] de (1805–1859). French political leader, historian, writer. 34.66; 34.67; 102.35; 176.5; 231.53; 231.54; 231.55; 295.24; 295.25; 372.16; 393.62; 469.4; 559.21; 649.32; 713.52; 725.6; 728.16; 744.19; 779.6; 938.42; 1041.64

Toffler, Alvin (1928– ). American social commentator, editor, writer. 207.19

Tolkien, J[ohn] R[onald] R[enel] (1892– ). English scholar and writer. 208.10; 283.4

Tolstoy, Count Leo [or Lev] Nikolayevich. Also Tolstoi (1828–1910). Russian novelist and moral philosopher. 12.12; 92.9; 332.31; 438.26; 548.237; 576.51

Tooke, [John] Horne (1736–1812). English radical politician and writer. 713.53

Toulet, Paul Jean (1867–1920). French poet and novelist. 548.238

Tourneur, Cyril (c. 1575–1626). English playwright. 1055.144

Toynbee, Arnold J[oseph] (1889– ). English historian. 34.68; 43.13; 131.29; 548.239; 600.23; 707.7

Trilling, Lionel (1905– ). American critic, short-story writer, educator, novelist. 53.130; 133.4; 443.4; 542.15; 640.4; 694.5; 705.73; 712.51; 777.17; 842.39

Truffaut, François (1932– ). French film director and critic. 604.7

Truman, Harry S. (1884– ). Thirty-third President of the United States (1945–1953). 393.63; 663.52; 705.74; 724.13; 923.20

Tsang Sin (5th c. B.C.). Disciple of Confucius. 528.23

Turgenev, Ivan Sergeyevich (1818–1883). Rus-

sian novelist. 218.131; 407.110; 616.72; 908.51; 1012.14

*Twain, Mark. Pen name of Samuel Langhorne Clemens (1835–1910). American writer and humorist.

Tynan, Kenneth [Peacock] (1927– ). English drama critic. 204.56; 965.32

Tze-sze (5th c. B.C.). Grandson of Confucius. 517.24; 529.20; 748.16; 957.19

## U

Udall, Stewart L[ee] (1920– ). American political leader. U.S. Secretary of the Interior (1961–1969). 174.9; 705.75; 707.8; 713.54; 982.11

Unamuno [y Jugo], Miguel de (1864–1936). Spanish philosopher, poet, novelist. 124.13; 175.18; 185.34; 263.10; 328.43; 385.76; 407.112; 441.35; 538.45; 548.240; 561.17; 653.5; 688.44; 778.39; 778.40; 814.8; 843.38; 897.12; 908.52; 991.137; 1020.20

United Presbyterian Church, *Litany for Holy Communion* (1968). 103.26; 126.8; 129.38; 712.53; 769.17; 872.5; 1025.55

Updike, John [Hoyer] (1932– ). American novelist, short-story writer, poet. 34.72; 53.131; 53.132; 53.133; 54.4; 93.7; 121.47; 121.48; 684.11; 724.14

Ustinov, Peter [Alexander] (1921– ). English actor, producer, playwright. 548.241

## V

Vahanian, Gabriel [Antoine] (1927– ). American educator and writer. 123.26; 123.27; 263.11; 315.2; 976.3

Valency, Maurice (1903– ). American educator, playwright, translator. 441.36; 920.7; 935.25

Valéry, [Ambroise] Paul [Toussaint Jules] (1871–1945). French poet and critic. 3.12; 76.24; 379.5; 399.63; 417.46; 534.48; 576.52; 583.22; 614.26; 615.7; 654.14; 674.35; 674.36; 702.106; 705.76; 753.5; 813.40; 906.22; 987.7; 991.138

Vanbrugh, Sir John (1664–1726). English playwright. 470.14; 710.19

Van Doren, Mark (1894– ). American poet, critic, educator, novelist, short-story writer, editor. 520.67; 1060.31

Van Horne, Harriet (1920– ). American newspaper columnist and critic. 186.11; 563.15

Van Loon, Hendrik Willem (1882–1944). Dutch-born American journalist and historian. 131.31; 294.5

Van Slyke, Helen [Lenore Vogt] (1919– ). American businesswoman, prominent in cosmetics industry. 265.26

Vauvenargues, marquis de Luc de Clapiers, (1715–1747). French moralist. 6.22; 19.37; 33.35; 221.23; 252.7; 282.38; 291.8; 297.38; 330.49; 339.38; 373.9; 373.10; 425.41; 462.5; 520.68; 527.9; 536.131; 558.55; 583.23; 598.51; 613.12; 617.20; 640.5; 655.10; 668.28; 670.23; 674.37; 716.37; 716.38; 737.17; 778.41; 882.19; 968.49; 968.50; 971.64; 991.139; 1020.21; 1025.56; 1035.100; 1065.36

Veblen, Thorstein [Bunde] (1857–1929). American economist and social philosopher. 103.27; 265.27; 265.28; 275.8; 335.31; 455.10; 521.26; 530.12; 638.8; 740.22; 743.5; 862.13; 957.20; 1041.66

Vergil. Full name, Publius Vergilius Maro (70–19 B.C.). Roman poet. 8.12; 56.14; 225.5; 257.19; 285.10; 340.33; 358.46; 827.4; 854.7; 971.65; 1055.147

Vico, Giambattista or Giovanni Battista (1668–1744). Italian philosopher and jurist. 448.30; 525.67; 554.9; 1024.12

Vidal, Gore (1925– ). American novelist and playwright. 100.6; 292.6; 326.19; 730.5; 965.33; 1062.106

Vigny, Alfred [Victor] de (1797–1863). French poet, playwright, novelist. 69.7; 536.132; 582.22; 800.11

Villiers de l'Isle-Adam [Comte Jean Marie Mathias Philippe Auguste de] (1838–1889). French writer of fiction and drama. 968.51

Vincent of Beauvais (fl. 13th c.). Dominican monk and scholar. 576.53

Vinci, Leonardo da. *See* Leonardo da Vinci.

Vinokurov, Yevgeniy [Mikhaylovich] (1925– ). Russian poet. 442.23

Virgil. *See* Vergil.

*Voltaire. Pen name of François Marie Arouet (1694–1778). French satirist, essayist, dramatist, philosopher, historian.

Von Braun, Wernher (1912– ). German-born American rocket engineer. 914.7

Voznesensky, Andrey (1934– ). Russian poet. 198.40; 511.9

Vreeland, Diana. Contemporary French-born American fashion editor. 280.2

## W

Wakoski, Diane (1937– ). American poet. 515.51

Walker, David (1785–1830). American abolitionist. 83.17

Waller, Edmund (1606–1687). English poet. 412.15; 458.7; 646.104

Walpole, Horace, 4th Earl of Orford (1717–1797). English writer and historian. 287.29; 741.5; 1060.33

Walsh, William (1663–1708). English critic and

poet. 293.29
Walton, Izaak (1593–1683). English writer and lover of fishing. 151.28; 345.4; 345.5; 411.22; 474.26; 547.12; 665.3
Ward, Artemus. Pen name of Charles Farrar Browne (1834–1867). American humorist, newspaperman, editor, lecturer. 17.64; 65.8; 374.42; 396.5; 396.6; 560.123; 763.2; 970.13; 986.4
Ward, Barbara [Lady (Robert) Jackson] (1914– ). English economist and writer. 330.51
Warner, Charles Dudley (1829–1900). American essayist, editor, novelist. 51.28; 54.5; 55.23; 56.15; 91.91; 121.49; 126.9; 129.39; 168.17; 185.36; 186.13; 186.14; 201.22; 218.133; 221.24; 246.1; 296.24; 316.13; 334.6; 334.7; 341.20; 352.9; 369.3; 369.4; 372.17; 382.40; 410.25; 417.47; 455.11; 539.18; 560.124; 574.40; 576.54; 576.55; 616.73; 616.74; 649.35; 702.108; 706.13; 740.24; 756.22; 893.25; 903.8; 908.54; 938.43; 943.2; 1019.20; 1023.31; 1035.103; 1055.148; 1059.8; 1064.57
Warren, Earl (1891– ). American jurist. Chief Justice of U. S. Supreme Court (1953–1968). 130.11
Warren, Leonard (1911–1960). American baritone. 648.6
Warren, Robert Penn (1905– ). American poet, novelist, educator. 417.48; 1062.107
Washington, Booker T[aliaferro] (1856–1915). American Negro educator and writer. 1058.70
Washington, George (1732–1799). First President of the United States (1789–1797). 226.20; 423.19
Watson, Sir William (1858–1935). English poet. 529.21; 702.109; 848.48
Watts, Alan [Wilson] (1915– ). English-born American philosopher and writer, exponent of Zen Buddhism. 1067.1
Watts, Isaac (1674–1748). English theologian and hymn writer. 41.30; 265.29; 414.13; 479.9
Waugh, Evelyn [Arthur St. John] (1903–1966). English novelist. 1057.41
Webster, Daniel (1782–1852). American statesman and orator. 130.12; 334.8; 515.52; 520.70; 520.71; 534.50; 968.54; 991.140
Webster, John (1580?–1625). English playwright. 261.24; 358.47; 358.48; 384.22; 412.16; 744.22; 968.55
Weeks, Edward [Augustus], Jr. (1898– ). American editor, lecturer, essayist. 567.21; 758.14
Weil, Simone (1909–1943). French philosophical writer. 207.20
Weiler, A. H. Contemporary American editor and newspaperman. 313.6
Weiss, Peter (1916– ). German-born painter, film director, novelist, playwright. 9.39; 58.8; 88.9; 218.134; 224.39; 448.31; 477.11; 538.46; 616.75; 692.21; 979.22; 991.141; 1035.104
Welles, [George] Orson (1915– ). American actor, producer, film director. 11.8; 17.65; 563.16
Wellington, 1st Duke of (Arthur Wellesley) (1769–1852). English general and statesman. 1035.105
Wells, H[erbert] G[eorge] (1866–1946). English novelist and journalist. 12.13; 98.22; 417.49; 582.23; 616.76; 669.30; 790.82; 794.5; 907.11
Wertham, Frederic (1895– ). German-born American psychiatrist, writer, teacher. 817.17
West, Jessamyn (1907– ). American novelist and short-story writer. 1062.108
West, Mae (1892– ). American actress. 62.8; 305.40; 525.70; 566.10; 575.16; 576.56; 641.11; 964.12
West, Rebecca. Pen name of Mrs. Cicily Maxwell Andrews, born Fairfield. (1892– ). English novelist, critic, essayist. 79.9; 623.30; 698.41
Westcott, Edward Noyes (1846–1898). American banker and novelist. 41.31; 386.5; 431.28; 596.61; 1051.9
Wetzsteon, Ross (1932– ). American writer. 692.22
Wheelock, John Hall (1886– ). American poet. 521.27; 702.110
White, E[lwyn] B[rooks] (1899– ). American humorist and essayist. 34.73; 63.11; 98.23; 102.36; 106.7; 108.7; 129.40; 245.14; 334.9; 358.49; 374.43; 396.7; 434.31; 534.51; 580.20; 615.9; 633.14; 633.15; 702.111; 702.112; 732.10; 848.49; 909.17; 987.8; 1043.10
Whitehead, Alfred North (1861–1947). English philosopher and mathematician. 9.40; 16.8; 51.29; 53.134; 115.38; 210.31; 282.39; 296.25; 319.63; 372.18; 385.79; 393.66; 441.37; 520.72; 525.71; 542.16; 566.11; 598.53; 605.12; 667.10; 669.31; 674.38; 688.47; 688.48; 735.30; 790.83; 790.84; 790.85; 822.5; 843.39; 844.11; 906.24; 967.17; 968.56; 968.57; 980.15; 991.142; 1019.21; 1061.10
Whitman, Cedric (1916– ). American educator and classical scholar. 610.5
Whitman, Walt[er] (1819–1892). American poet, journalist, essayist. 34.74; 41.32; 59.8; 88.10; 118.11; 129.41; 168.18; 218.135; 360.14; 382.41; 393.67; 417.50; 445.33; 462.6; 534.52; 536.133; 559.22; 584.16; 685.5; 702.113; 869.18; 869.19; 873.26; 875.12; 892.18; 935.26; 991.143; 1062.109
Whittier, John Greenleaf (1807–1892). American poet and editor. 37.14; 269.35; 489.30; 505.13; 674.39; 748.17; 797.13; 809.13; 860.13; 868.35
Wicker, Tom (1926– ). American newspaperman. 393.68
Wiener, Norbert (1894–1964). American mathematician and educator. 34.75; 97.6; 174.10; 520.73; 690.7; 735.31; 735.32; 765.12; 822.6; 843.40
Wilbur, Richard (1921– ). American poet. 80.8; 132.6; 309.12; 548.244; 616.77; 848.50;

## X



## Y



## Z

# INDEX OF KEY WORDS

# INDEX OF KEY WORDS

This index is intended primarily to help the user in finding a quotation that he only half recalls. One or more key words—that is, important words most likely to be remembered—are given here, surrounded by related words. These word-clusters form brief synopses of the quotations by which they can be readily identified.

The numbers that follow the precis refer not to pages but to individual quotations. That part of the number before the period indicates the category; the second part locates the quotation within the category. The numbers and titles of the categories appear at the tops of text pages so that the user can readily find the quotation he is looking for.

Because key words may often be the subjects of their quotations, this index can supplement category headings. However, a user who is looking for quotations on a subject, rather than a specific saying, should also turn to the Index of Categories for an overview of the subject headings and cross references.

## A

**abandon:** it is madder never to a. one's self than often to be infatuated 548.77
**abdomen:** a. is why man does not take self for god 88.5
**abecedarian:** what a contemptible thing is an old a. 277.58
**abilities:** natural a. need pruning by study 1.1
**ability:** a. takes its flight unhindered 822.3
assurance keeps even pace with a. 854.4
God obligeth no man to more than his a. 269.19
great a. in knowing how to conceal a. 197.5
height of a. in the least able is knowing how to submit to good leadership 636.2
reputation increases, a. declines 646.45
**abject:** those believed a., usually ambitious 433.25
**abnormal:** every one of us is slightly a. 555.3
it is not man, but the world that is a. 1060.13
to be independent is to be a. 168.1
**above:** all we know of a. is that they happy are 412.15
no man is safe a. but he that will gladly be beneath 773.26
**abridgment:** every a. of a good book is a stupid a. 91.69
**abroad:** crow went a., came home just as black 985.18
man's standing a. is problematical 798.11
to go a. has same sense death brings 985.40
to go a. is to forget pain, care 985.39
**absence:** a. lessens small passions, augments great 2.9
a. sharpens love 2.6
a. tries how long this love will be 2.4
hours in a. have crutches 2.2
love reckons every a. an age 548.56
senses know that a. blots people out 2.1
what you love most in friend may be clearer in his a. 2.7
**absences:** a. are a good influence in love 2.12
**absent:** a. shall not be made heir 2.10
after death, the a. take on a firmer outline 2.3
greater things are believed of those a. 2.13
those who are a. are always wrong 2.5
**absents:** presents, I often say, endear a. 382.22
**absolute:** man's soul longs for the a. 920.7
no such thing as a. value in this world 1019.20
**absolutes:** in this universe, there are no a. 788.2
**abstainer:** a.: weak person who yields to temptation of denying himself a pleasure 859.2

**abstinence:** mastery of pleasures better than a. 698.1
refrain to-night, a will be more easy 859.6
vices require moderate use, not total a. 1023.4
**abstinent:** the a. carry their desires with them 859.1
**abstract:** a. qualities all have capitals: Good, True 1025.9
women have no sense of the a. 1055.62
**abstracting:** a. an idea, one may lose its humanity 441.33
**abstractions:** a. are weapons to control fact 967.17
**absurd:** a. is born of confrontation between human call, unreasonable silence of world 3.2
a. man is he who never changes 115.2
a. mind judges consequences calmly 173.3
if life is a., death is insupportable 3.11
the a. is sin without God 3.3
**absurdities:** life is full of infinite a. 4.5
**absurdity:** no defence for a. but obscurity 640.1
privilege of a. accorded to none but man 4.3
**abuse:** a. man unjustly: make friends for him 475.7
a. to be reformed, unless reform worse 783.41
if persons a. us, ask what characters they admire 203.8
men let you a., if you make them laugh 434.3
unmerited a. wounds 716.14
who live by bread alone submit to a. 565.5
**abysses:** only a bird should build nest over a. 749.22
**academicism:** a. is concerned with ideas, not thinking 842.39
**academies:** great men formed independent of a. 399.64
they teach in a. much that is useless 277.32
**accept:** to a. whatever comes is to be unafraid 930.2
**acceptance:** art of a. of favors 780.2
**accepted:** not right to shun a. ways from spite 168.14
**accepting:** a. what we are inhibits what we ought to be 539.8
life consists in a. ourselves as we are 852.1
**accessible:** each man is a. by the right door 955.1
**accident:** a. counts for much in companionship 114.1
a. is greatest of all inventors 500.2
proceed by plan, be hit by a. 696.3
what reason of the ant drags into a heap, wind of a. collects in a breath 114.16
**accidents:** a. will happen in best-regulated families 332.14
ambush is everywhere from the army of a. 114.12
many a. discompose the well-off 15.9
no shame in the a. of chance 1063.20
there is person who runs into another's a. 358.30
**acclaimed:** greatest reward is to have one's work a. 204.35
**accomplice:** who's cheated twice by same man is a. 866.5
**accomplish:** he who has patience may a. anything 670.18
to a. end, wise man may carry his foe 1053.51
**accomplishes:** nobody a. all he feels he can do 539.18
who begins too much a. little 6.10
**accomplishments:** knowledge gives weight, a. give lustre 1.2
no a. to be envied as those rudely hindered by circumstances 455.11
**accordion:** a.: instrument in harmony with sentiments of an assassin 608.1
**accounts:** keep your a. on your thumb-nail 892.17
**accusation:** guilty man justifies himself before a. 403.8
**accusations:** even doubtful a. leave a stain 5.3
**accused:** it is honorable to be a. by those who deserve to be a. 5.4
**accusing:** a. is proving, with Malice as judge 5.2
**accustomed:** no conditions to which man can't grow a. 12.12
unpleasant to miss things we are a. to 404.9
**ache:** no deadlier a. than striving to be oneself 442.23
**aches:** comforter's head never a. 953.9
**achieve:** to a. great things, live as if never to die 6.22
**achievement:** a. death of endeavor, birth of disgust 6.4
behind each a. is surprised mother-in-law 6.11
happiness lies in the a. of it 407.33
**achievements:** awareness of the ambiguity of one's a. 6.21
**aching:** better a tooth out than always a. 260.5
**acknowledged:** do not expect to be a. for what you are 47.3
**acquaintance:** a. I would have 363.34
a.: person we know well enough to borrow from but not well enough to lend to 7.2
**acquaintances:** how casually we make our most valued a. 7.3
we like new a. in hope of more admiration 7.6
**acquiescence:** no peace from a. in wrong 46.6
**acquired:** what man has honestly a. is his own 710.1

**acquiring:** price of everything is trouble of a. it 1019.18
**acquisition:** a. means life to miserable mortals 565.4
**acquisitions:** every man publishes his a. 740.16
**act:** a. done for its own sake is its own justification 1017.5
a. only on maxim you can will to be universal law 9.31
a. quickly, think slowly 9.24
a. so in valley that you need not fear those who stand on the hill 749.8
a. well your part, there all honour lies 489.20
I have thought too much to deign to a. 968.51
in your a. you exist, not in your body 224.33
last a. tragic however happy the rest 218.99
man who knows when not to a. is wise 356.4
our passivity would be an a. 9.35
people who can a. are never preachers 9.19
play out the game, a. well your part 819.1
to think is to a. 968.12
what a. proved all its thought had been 9.9
worst pain: know much, be impotent to a. 457.2
**acting:** between a. dreadful thing and first motion, all the interim is a hideous dream 201.20
in civilized life, man is a. a part 819.3
**action:** a. can give us feeling of being useful 1057.15
a. is the proper fruit of knowledge 9.23
a. is thought tempered by illusion 9.29
a. is transitory—a step, a blow 9.41
a. not from thought is nothing at all 9.3
a. should culminate in wisdom 9.4
a. springs from readiness for responsibility 9.6
a. started because one must do something 9.17
a. the great business of mankind 9.32
a. will remove doubt theory cannot solve 9.37
against nature's silence I use a. 9.39
all sentiments weigh less than lovely a. 224.16
artist is a man of a. 53.28
but for thought no motion would be an a. 968.44
circumstance gives an a. its character 592.12
do good a. stealthily, have it found out 224.14
drama is a. and not philosophy 965.25
every great a. is extreme when undertaken 224.37
few men of a. make graceful exit 807.5
great end of life is a., not knowledge 9.30
I must mix with a., or wither by despair 9.38
in a. be primitive 9.15
in arena of life, honours fall to those who show their good qualities in a. 9.2
in each a. we must look beyond the a. 173.10
life made up of constant calls to a. 9.26
man of a. has strong dose of egotism 853.1
materials of a. variable, their use constant 9.21
men of a. are generally fools 491.11
men of a. too busy to see beyond day's work 9.10
no human a. which custom has not at one time justified and at another condemned 210.13
one knows bad a. in flash of regret 224.17
our a. only fitfully guided by thought 9.40
profit on good a. is to have done it 224.34
speech is the mirror of a. 916.56
suit a. to word, the word to a. 894.21
test of any man lies in a. 9.34
the road to holiness passes through world of a. 9.25
to dispose a soul to a. we must upset its equilibrium 9.28
unreal is a. without discipline 9.5
**actions:** a. are our epochs 9.11
do not be too timid about your a. 973.3
easier to dream than do good a. 391.32
good purposes directors of good a. 765.5
great a. not sons of great resolutions 224.5
human a. are second causes 224.19
life's decisive a. are often unconsidered 224.13
lust and force source of all a. 9.33
man's most open a. have secret side 9.16
not always a. show the man 224.29
only a. of the just smell sweet 224.35
our less conscious thoughts, a., mold lives 999.1
stellar universe not so difficult to comprehend as the a. of other people 224.30
we are use to a., not stillness, of humans 982.9
we learn to curb a. long before sentiments 856.5
we must judge men by present a. 224.24
we search out good motives for our bad a. 601.4
**active:** virtues are all a.; life is alert 805.8
**activity:** men, inactive within, need external a. 10.18
self urges us on to futile a. 857.2
**actor:** a. believes bad things printed about him 11.8
a. remembers briefest notice into old age 11.5
by the time an a. knows how to act any part he is too old to act any but a few 11.6
movie a. is a god in captivity 11.2
talent is what an a. needs 956.8
**actors:** a. should be overheard, not listened to 59.1
good a. tell without talking 11.3
**actress:** for an a. to be a success 11.1
**acts:** a. and words are wee part of a life 812.5
familiar a. are beautiful through love 331.13
make morality center on forbidden a. 598.46

man who a least, upbraids most 797.7
nameless, unremembered a. of kindness 517.25
our a. are our angels that walk with us 224.10
our own a. are mightier powers than chance 224.2
**actual:** music takes us out of the a. 607.21
what is a. is a. only for one time 777.8
**ad:** one a. worth more than forty editorials 18.11
today models of eloquence are a. agencies 281.7
**Adam:** A. and Eve escaped teething 64.8
A. won for us the curse of labor 1058.68
we owe deep debt of gratitude to A. 538.41
when A. said a good thing he knew nobody had said it before 767.8
**Adam's:** all A. children, but silk distinguishes 469.2
**adapt:** a. or perish is nature's imperative 12.13
a. to the environment that is your lot 98.17
**adequate:** who ever is a. 539.3
**adjective:** a. is banana peel of parts of speech 396.2
when in doubt, strike out a. 935.24
**adjustment:** a. is the theme of our swan song 12.9
every new a. is crisis in self-esteem 12.4
for young people things move so fast there's no problem of a. 115.28
our goal is not fulfillment but a. 12.8
**administration:** a. does not create; it carries on 13.1
a. receives kicks due the president 393.11
bad a. can destroy good policy 13.2
no government matters as much as the a. 393.42
while people retain vigilance, no a. can injure government in four years 675.11
**administrative:** geniuses ordered by a. types 374.36
**administrators:** a. of justice like cat protecting cheese 512.10
**admiration:** a. involves obliquity of vision 14.2
a. is a short-lived passion 14.1
a.: our recognition of another's resemblance to ourselves 14.3
familiarity takes off the edge of a. 331.8
modern world not given to uncritical a. 330.51
'tis much to gain universal a. 548.89
**admirations:** some molded by a., others hostilities 402.1
**admire:** fools a., men of sense approve 14.5
we do not always like those whom we a. 14.4
**admired:** desire to be a. early disposition of man 1020.1
he who goes unenvied shall not be a. 293.2
**admirer:** it's the a. and watcher who provoke us to all the insanities we commit 59.6
**admirers:** woman with staff of a. 348.3
**adolescence:** chaste a. makes for a dissolute old age 120.6
ripeness of a. is in need of a bridle 1064.49
so much of a. is an ill-defined dying 1064.50
what knowing watchfulness surrounds a. 1064.9
**adolescents:** a. tend to be passionate people 1064.21
**adore:** I may command where I a. 548.209
**adorn:** know who you are; a. self accordingly 265.6
**adorned:** she's a. that in husband's eye is lovely 265.25
when unadorned, loveliness is most a. 70.57
**ads:** he watched the a., not the road 63.9
**adult:** boy is a. before parents think so 95.4
sentiments of a: instinct and education 649.29
to be a. is to be alone 567.15
**adultery:** a. is an evil inasmuch as it is a theft 470.15
a. is more common where climate's sultry 138.1
a. is the application of democracy to love 470.9
**adulthood:** we pass into a. when we stop saying, It got lost, and say I lost it 567.8
**adults:** a. discover themselves to the very young 871.3
**advance:** not to go back is to a. 402.16
**advances:** snub is sufficient to rebuff a. 786.4
**advantage:** every a. has its tax 15.3
no way to take a. of those with no weaknesses 677.9
them as take a. get a. i' this world 15.2
**advantages:** little a. produce felicity 407.41
many accidents discompose, but few please, men with a. of life 15.9
**adventure:** a.: an inconvenience rightly considered 16.1
a. exists in minds of men who pursue it 16.5
every a. wears the shape of our thoughts 303.7
it is only in a. that some people succeed in knowing themselves 16.2
life is either daring a. or nothing 16.4
life without a. is unsatisfying 16.7
without a. civilisation is in decay 16.8
**adversaries:** law a. strive mightily, eat as friends 154.13
**adversary:** easy to confute if I don't answer an a. 51.15
right to hear advice of a., not follow it 19.32
**adverse:** in a. times even brave are discredited 745.14
**adversity:** a. is greater teacher than prosperity 745.10
a. is more supportable than prosperity 17.14
a. is the first path to truth 17.15
be prudent in a. 749.24

education is a refuge in a. 277.3
fire is test of gold, a. of strong men 17.53
firmest friendships are formed in a. 363.31
good things of a. are to be admired 745.15
in a., bitter to remember happiness 17.10
in prosperity be joyful, in a. consider 745.4
in the day of prosperity, a. is forgotten 745.1
knows not own strength who hasn't met a. 17.34
man insensible to prosperity till has a. 745.13
many can bear a., few contempt 182.3
many who are struggling with a. are happy 388.25
no comfort in a. more sweet than art 53.3
none can smile in face of a. and mean it 17.31
one abhorred in prosperity is adored in a. 745.9
prosperity has no power over a. 745.11
prosperity makes friends, a. tries them 745.12
sweet are the uses of a. 17.54
virtue of a. is fortitude 745.3
we can learn to endure another man's a. 17.62
who has not suffered extreme a. knows not extent of his depravation 17.16

**advertisement:** promise, large promise, is soul of a. 18.5

**advertisements:** a. get attention by magnificent promises 18.4
a. have more knowledge concerning the community 18.1

**advertiser:** a. is court jester at democratic court 18.7

**advertising:** a. and salesmanship create needs 103.23
a. in final analysis should be news 18.10
business without a. is like winking at a girl in the dark 18.3
forgive us for a. the unnecessary 103.26
we want to be deceived in a. 18.2

**advice:** a. after injury is medicine after death 19.11
a. is stranger: if welcome he stays night 19.26
a. of elders to young apt to be unreal 19.17
a. should help, not please 19.34
a.: the smallest current coin 19.7
best way to give a. to your children 663.52
cheated if we take a. given gratis 19.29
counsels lost on one who cannot take a. 19.27
distrust interested a. 19.4
easy for one outside calamity to give a. 19.2
give a. and buy a foe 19.25
good scare is worth more than good a. 340.17
he who builds to every man's a. will have a crooked house 19.12
many receive a., few profit by it 19.30
men ignore good a., fear being controlled 644.6
never trust a. of man in difficulties 19.3
no enemy is worse than bad a. 19.36
teeth before the tongue give good a. 19.19
we ask a., but mean approbation 19.9
we censure, but cannot endure a. 203.24
we give nothing so freely as a. 19.22
we receive nothing so reluctantly as a. 19.1
when man asks a., he usually tells you how to decide 19.18
when we desire to thrust a. on others 19.10
when well, all have a. for the ill 411.20
woman's a. is no great thing 19.14
wrong to follow a. of adversary 19.32

**advise:** we are so happy to a. others 19.31

**aeon:** altar cloth of one a. is doormat of next 296.23

**aesthetics:** a. is for artists as ornithology for birds 20.4
a. make life lovely and wonderful 20.7

**affability:** a. has not hatred but contempt for men 390.8

**affairs:** a. are easier of entrance than exit 356.1
every man's a. important to himself 493.4
have you time to spare from your own a. that you can attend to another man's 571.8
in great a. profit from chances offered 650.5
let your a. be as two or three 892.17
one can't manage too many a.: like pumpkins in water, one pops up while other down 10.4
slowness in a. ripens them or rots them 900.3
there is a tide in the a. of men 650.10

**affect:** qualities we have do not make us so ridiculous as those which we a. 726.11

**affectation:** a. as necessary to mind as dress to body 726.6
a.: imitation of what should be natural 726.13
a. is greater enemy to face than small-pox 726.3
a. is more enemy to faces than small-pox 727.27
a. only finishes a fop 726.8

**affectations:** by a. youth is seeking a face of his own 1064.54

**affection:** a. dwells with danger 192.7
a. is created by habit 21.7
a. makes fool of man too much the father 663.29
a. most precious reward man can win 21.11
a. never was wasted 21.6
child hasn't grown-up's appetite for a. 121.42
human nature gives a. most readily to those who seem least to demand it 21.10
love may light cozy fire of a. 548.100
measure a. by constancy, not ardor 178.2
mix admiration, pity as sure recipe for a. 21.8
most would rather get than give a. 21.1
natural a. is a prejudice 332.18

some think a. rests on circumstantial evidence 548.198
speech is one symptom of a. 148.2
trial not fair where a. is judge 515.17
what woman dares, when a. stirs her 1055.136

**affectionate:** we are uneasy with an a. man 21.2

**affections:** a. left untouched diminish imperceptibly 21.4
a. must be breakable chains 548.64
it's often interest, vanity that cause a. 21.5
most a. are habits we lack courage to end 21.9
set a. on things above, not on the earth 691.2
the a. cannot keep their youth 21.3

**affinities:** profoundest a. are most readily felt 22.4

**affirmations:** our a. are mere matters of chronology 181.9

**affliction:** a. smarts most in the most happy state 17.11
a. sometime teacheth wicked to pray 717.20
before a. digested, consolation comes too soon 953.16

**afflictions:** a. refine some, consume others 17.27
one can't shed light on a. he's never had 319.39

**affluence:** many amid great a. are utterly miserable 388.25

**affluent:** a. man confronts all he sees by equivalents out of stronger wealth of self 873.26

**affronts:** young men soon give and soon forget a. 486.1

**afraid:** a. of nettles, do not piss in grass 973.4
they who are a. somehow feel guilty 403.9
who possesses most is most a. of loss 710.11

**African:** A. race is an india-rubber ball 23.1

**afterthought:** a. makes first resolve a liar 24.2

**afterwards:** while it is still before, a. has no power 669.5

**against:** men not a. you; merely for themselves 493.3

**age:** a. and wedlock bring man to nightcap 71.5
a. has a good mind and sorry shanks 646.6
a. in the virtuous carries an authority 646.99
a. is a bad traveling companion 646.28
a. is a time of hurry, despair 580.1
a. is despised but when it is contemptible 646.58
a. is opportunity no less than youth 646.67
a. knows it has got away with nothing 1065.2
a. looks with anger on temerity of youth 1065.16
a. not as qualified to instruct as youth 1065.33
a. of anxiety: along with what weighs on our minds is what grates on our nerves 43.6
a. prints more wrinkles on mind than face 646.74
a. shows what children we remain 646.40
a. still leaves us friends and wine 1065.23
a., time, are but timidities of thought 971.37
almost no allowances are made for the disenchantments of a. 1065.30
be equal to your talent, not your a. 956.16
better eat gray bread in youth than in a. 749.31
beyond a., man no stronger than child is 646.1
connected with our own a. if we recognize ourselves in relation to events 181.5
crabbed a. and youth cannot live together 1065.27
each a. has choice of death it will die 296.24
each a. selects philosophy apt for it 296.19
every a. beheld too close is ill-discerned 296.4
every a. has eye pasted to a keyhole 296.17
every a. has its pleasures, wit, and ways 296.2
every a. is fed on illusions 447.7
every a. thinks its battle most important 296.14
fear of a. is prime cause of infidelity 470.2
golden a. was never the present a. 296.8
golden a., when gold did not reign 296.13
happy man will not feel pressure of a. 961.3
harvest of repentance reaped in a. 793.4
heart grows not better but worse with a. 646.16
in a. one has griefs without tears 1065.25
in every a., "good old days" were a myth 296.1
in pollytics and bankin' a. has th' best iv it 1065.9
it is unjust to claim the privileges of a. and retain playthings of childhood 567.9
knowledge is shelter in advanced a. 520.8
let a., not envy, wrinkle thy cheeks 293.5
let me stand in my a. 181.3
life should begin with a., end with youth 1065.35
love weakens with a. like all human energies 646.33
men of a. object, consult too much 580.4
middle a. is too young for golf 580.2
middle a. is when a. shows around middle 580.13
middle a., when you've met so many people 580.17
no woman should ever be accurate about her a. 1055.151
now a. is fallen from good example 1065.17
our a. is all signpost, no destination 994.9
our bad taste is the bad taste of our a. 181.9
ours is essentially a tragic a. 980.10
ours is the a. of substitutes 54.1
over siventy, a man boasts iv his a. 646.23
riotous youth, growing a. will correct 1064.31
sad wisdom of a. wells up without sound 646.102

silence of a. is full of wisdom 891.20
that this a. should bring forth such creatures 559.18
the a.: a few profound and active men 296.7
timid caution is the error of a. 567.3
'tis hard to find a whole a. to imitate 296.3
we must place ourselves on the level of our a. before we can rise above it 181.11
what is the worst of woes that wait on a. 646.14
when the a. is in, the wit is out 646.92
woe to those with no appetite for dish of their a. 181.4
youth is cause, effect is a. 580.5
**age's:** a. peace terms with life are yet to be made 646.78
**aged:** a. man is but a paltry thing 646.105
the a. love what is practical 1065.24
**aggressiveness:** possible to bind people in love if others are left to receive their a. 1009.5
**aggressors:** if a. wrong above, are right here below 26.6
**aging:** a. man of twentieth century lives in private universe of weakness and decay 646.57
time increases understanding for the a. 1000.14
**agnostic:** most satisfying faith is purely a. 328.25
**agony:** safe despair raves—a. is frugal 237.5
**agree:** by universal misunderstanding, all a. 27.1
if brothers a., no fortress so strong 332.1
we tolerate those who do not a. with us 977.7
**agreeable:** conversation passing for a. is made up of civility and falsehood 438.23
custom determines what is a. 210.23
few men shine, but most can be a. 390.14
gentle-breeding lies in wish to be a. 389.7
people not a. save me trouble of liking them 588.1
**agreed:** can two walk together except they be a. 560.8
men are not a. about any one thing 27.6
**agreement:** a. is never reached in love 548.85
a. made more precious by disagreement 27.8
nothing starts disagreement like an a. 987.8
too much a. kills a chat 185.5
**agrees:** nobody a. with anybody; infants show it 27.7
**agriculture:** blessed be a. if one doesn't have too much 334.6
**ahead:** passion to get a. is sometimes born of fear lest we be left behind 289.4
**aid:** in a., proper to omit gratitude 496.9
only a. we can give is incidental 56.3
**ail:** if anything a. a man, he sets about reforming the world 783.38
**ailing:** a. woman lives forever 889.28
**ailment:** imaginary a. is worse than a disease 437.2
**ailments:** fond of each other because a. the same 889.29
long a. wear out pain, and long hopes, joy 1033.7
**aim:** despair: price for setting impossible a. 237.8
if you would hit the mark, a. above it 55.14
it is not enough to a., you must hit 6.14
men hit only what they a. at 55.22
name little aims, but neither name nor be conscious of main a. of your life 765.1
not failure, but low a., is crime 55.15
**aims:** our methods, not our a., set us at odds 579.14
wise reserve seasons the a. 856.4
**air:** lovers of a. travel hang poised between illusion of immortality, fact of death 28.1
opening my lips and receiving bad a. 29.1
**airplane:** a. has unveiled true face of the earth 28.2
**airport:** in space age men will circle world in two hours: one to fly, one to get to a. 984.2
**alarming:** people are made a. by their continuity 656.2
**alcohol:** use of a., tobacco, test of civilization 131.10
**alien:** everyone's quick to blame the a. 355.1
nothing that is real is a. to me 448.25
**alienated:** when you're all a., you're not lonely 30.1
**alienation:** a. ends where yours begins 30.6
**alike:** before the Lord we're all a. 773.18
**alimony:** a.: the ransom the happy pay to the devil 260.6
**alive:** one only stays a. for fear of death 538.28
to be a. at all involves some risk 213.15
to be a. is power 314.2
to preserve a man a. is a miracle 261.22
what matters is to come out a., not on top 949.1
you die because you're a. 538.34
**all:** each one is a. in a. to himself 852.22
we a. breathe same air, are mortal 98.13
**allegiance:** no South, North, to which I owe a. 924.1
**allegory:** a man's life is a continual a. 536.60
**alliance:** a.: union of two thieves who cannot separately plunder a third 496.1
from a. of men are great things born 187.4
lofty words cannot construct an a. 245.6
**ally:** a. need not own the land he helps 496.3
**alms:** I am not poor enough to give a. 430.24
not a soul who does not have to beg a. 233.3
on a. given from pity beggar would starve 430.23
when thou doest a., let not thy left hand know what thy right doeth 430.2
**alone:** a. with oneself, feelings get tired 908.7
a., you are your own master 151.14

basest pattern of relatedness better than being a. 502.10
better be a. than in bad company 908.18
decreed to every man: thou shalt live a. 908.20
every man is grave a. 879.2
in our civilization, being a. is suspect 908.27
in the most important things, we are a. 56.11
in the sea of life we millions live a. 908.3
inside myself is place where I live a. 852.5
live a.: you won't succeed as human being 908.8
man is the only being who knows he's a. 908.39
man suffers greatest moments by himself; being a. seems attendant on reality 908.25
man who goes a. can start today 908.50
man who walks a. soon trailed by F.B.I. 466.6
mob only refuge: I fear to find myself a. 205.9
never same with others as when a. 656.12
no man can labor for himself a. 98.10
no person loving himself is a. 869.12
none goes his way a. 98.18
not a. if accompanied by noble thoughts 908.6
one would not be a. even in Paradise 908.23
power to be a. and vote with God 466.5
strongest man is he who stands most a. 933.12
there are places, moments, in which one is so a. one sees the world entire 908.44
to be adult is to be a. 567.15
to dare to live a. is the rarest courage 908.14
true man must learn to be a. 873.23
we shall die a. 908.38
we're left a. with each other 976.4
when is man strong until he feels a. 933.3
which of us is not forever a stranger, a. 908.56
who can live a. resembles sage and God 908.21
who does not fill world with phantoms is a. 381.5
woe to him that is a. when he falleth 327.2
you are not a.; God and your genius within 908.17

**altar:** acolyte knows what boys do behind a. 319.56
**altars:** in prosperity no a. smoke 790.38
**alter:** old dog can't a. his way of barking 404.8
**altered:** what cannot be a. must be borne 800.5
**alternatives:** a. grow only on imaginary trees 122.1
**altruism:** a. grounded on fact that it is uncomfortable to have unhappy people about one 430.20
a. which is not egoism is sterile 430.28
**amass:** modern age more eager to a. than realize 740.21
**amateur:** a. is a man of enthusiasm 204.2
**amazement:** true scientist never loses faculty of a. 843.33
**ambassador:** a. is an honest man sent abroad to lie 245.15
**ambassadors:** a. of peace shall weep bitterly 245.1
**ambiguity:** character of human life is a. 388.28
**ambition:** a. does not see earth she treads on 33.18
a. is a meteor-gleam 983.6
a. is only vanity ennobled 33.14
a. is the excrement of glory 330.4
a. makes more trusty slaves than need 33.15
a. often the mother of virtues 33.31
a. prefers fortune's ice to virtue's land 33.8
a. puts men doing meanest offices 33.32
generosity is often only disguised a. 33.20
greatest evil: small talents, great a. 33.35
no fairer a. than to excel in talk 916.58
nothing so arouses a. as another's fame 33.11
sense of inferiority, called a. 33.27
to succeed, vein a. with humanity 33.5
we hardly ever return from a. to love 33.19
wise man is cured of a. by a. itself 33.16
**ambition's:** lowliness is young a. ladder 938.38
**ambitions:** all a. lawful but those based on misery 33.6
man's worth no greater than worth of a. 33.23
most people would succeed in small things, if not troubled by great a. 33.21
**ambitious:** a. man has as many masters as there are people useful in bettering his position 33.17
a. man spends time becoming a personage 688.33
a. men most liable to fortune's blasts 33.28
those believed abject, usually a. 433.25
**amended:** little said is soon a. 916.12
**amendment:** a. is repentance 793.5
**America:** A., bizarre breaker of moulds 34.39
A. can seduce God 456.3
A. died from delusion that she had moral leadership 34.56
A. diminished daily by pollution, blight 174.9
A. established to maintain liberty 34.80
A. hardly stops to enjoy the present with her appetite for the future 34.37
A. has always gone for the loud laugh 34.65
A. has best-dressed poverty in world 712.21
A. is a passionate idea or it is nothing 34.34
A. is government of, for, by the naïve 34.54
A. is large, friendly dog in small room 34.68
A. is so vast that almost all said about it is true; opposite is also true 34.17
A. is the greatest of opportunities and the worst of influences 34.61
A. lives among cars, soap, not by them 102.25
A. purrs at every stranger's praise 34.25

A. shudders at anything alien 355.4
A. stands for sovereignty of people 34.81
art in A. is not organic 34.31
ask not what A. will do for you 534.19
being in A. doesn't make you an American 34.44
discussion in A. means dissent 256.12
Europe is the unfinished negative of A. 301.3
fate of A. in its principles, not in one man 728.13
freedom in A.; not silencing brand of idea 111.7
future A. to match its military strength with moral restraint, power with purpose 34.30
I cannot look upon A. as young 34.50
I don't see A. as a mainland, but as a sea 202.6
I feel that A. is against the artist 53.87
in A. everybody is of opinion he has no social superiors 295.22
in A., ivry man's as good as ivry other man 34.12
in A. Journalism governs for ever and ever 34.76
in A., majority bars liberty of opinion 725.6
in A. man presoomed guilty ontil proved so 515.11
in A. nature is autocratic 34.16
in A. only successful writer is important 1062.28
in A. parents obey their children 34.82
in A. poetry has turned to advertising 18.6
in A., sport is the opiate of the masses 922.1
in A. there are no ladies except salesladies 34.53
in A., with all its faults, you can still reach through the forest and see the sun 34.23
little of beauty has A. given the world 34.11
not healthy when nation lives within a nation, as colored are living within A. 83.5
second payment, not politics, worries A. 219.12
sin in A. is said to be calculating 893.5
strength of A.: A. is the American people 34.48
what A. hopes to bring to pass in world must come to pass first in A.'s heart 34.13
youth of A. is their oldest tradition 34.77
**America's:** A. adventure: absorption of peoples 451.2
supermarket is A. temple 34.63
**American:** A., by nature, is optimistic 34.29
A. character looks as if it had bad haircut 34.41
A. citizen tries to perpetuate youth 34.55
A. confined to own affairs would be robbed of one half of his existence 34.66
A. economy, society, unconscious, are all racist 769.8
A. feels rich in free expression 361.16
A. has dwindled into an Odd Fellow 151.25
A. has nothing to fear but truth 34.45
A. ideal is youth, handsome and empty 1064.42
A. likes you to repent, then is generous 793.13
A. man is trustworthy, loyal, helpful, friendly, courteous, kind, obedient 34.72
A. marriage is like wire fence 560.82
A. motion pictures written for half-wits 604.2
A. muse, you are as various as your land 34.4
A. people deprived of vote by not voting 1030.19
A. people: the most timorous mob of serfs 34.49
A. production for profit, not for use 102.22
A. social life is evasion of talking 151.13
A. society a system of semi-monopolies, unenlightened electorate 34.22
A. society contains those of talent, driven to prefer poverty to abundance 34.24
A. tradition: self-help, self-control 34.58
A. vice reduces everything unique 295.16
A. wants to be considered a good guy 798.22
A. Way is to carry common sense itself almost to point of madness 34.32
A. way is to seduce a man by bribery 188.8
A. women mortify the flesh 1055.105
action, swiftness, violence, power: native, homegrown A. qualities 34.35
all changes are alike in A. society 34.67
clothes, money and new fear constitute differences between A. and Attila's men 131.32
each A. sure he has a sense of humor 34.73
every A. free to stand up for his rights, even if he must sit down for them 747.2
frustrate an A., he will get drunk, kill 34.60
I am waiting for them to prove God is A. 385.31
if A. dream is for Americans only 34.78
if A. men are obsessed with money, A. women are obsessed with weight 34.46
in nothing is there more evolution than the A. mind 34.74
in the A. metaphysic, reality is always material reality 777.17
inside polling booth every A. equal 295.21
it isn't oceans which cut us off from the world —it's the A. way of looking at things 34.52
it's complicated, being an A. 34.62
law of A. life: what enriches other than wallet is uneconomic 596.1
learning to be an A. is learning not to let individuality become a nuisance 34.19
life for the A. is a hazard 536.64
mass production of distraction a part of the A. way of life 290.2
materialistic idealism of A. life 565.6
no characteristic can be labeled A. 34.69
no crime in cynical A. calendar more humiliating than to be a sucker 199.7

part of A. dream: live long, die young 365.6
part of A. greatness: discrimination 469.3
spirit of A. radicalism is destructive 770.1
the making of an A. begins when he rejects all other ties, any other history 34.3
two A. flags; one for the rich and one for the poor 712.41
typical A. believes no necessity of soul is free and few cannot be bought 34.33
when A. life most A. it is theatrical 34.14
**Americanism:** room only for hundred per cent A. 671.17
**Americanized:** we go to Europe to be A. 301.2
**Americans:** A. are suckers for good news 326.18
A. are the lavishest people on earth 34.70
A. began by loving youth, now worship it 1064.5
A. believe violence is monopoly of state 1024.3
A. burn incense before democracy 34.26
A. can eat garbage 272.23
A. cheerfully assume love conquers all 34.1
A. detest all lies except lies spoken in public or printed lies 329.26
A. don't understand studied insult 486.2
A. expect more than world can offer 34.5
A. expect to eat and stay thin 34.6
A. have a sense of life's possibilities 301.1
A. have an appetite for Old World titles 773.12
A. have ardor for gain, passion for rights 34.79
A. have combined practical and ideal 34.59
A. have sense of humor, proportion 34.57
A. pick president, then pick on him 724.11
A. seem to believe a thinker is a bore 34.47
A. think they are huge rescue squad 34.10
A. worship the dollar 34.71
art for most A. is a very queer fish 53.70
for A., progress is fact and principle 34.75
in modern world, A. are old inhabitants 34.21
love of A. for their country is exacting 671.13
morality of A. is a team morality 34.18
nature is indifferent to survival of A. 949.5
nothing wrong with A. except ideals 34.9
serious leisure not genius of A. 530.5
tax has made more liars of A. than golf 958.9
we A. suffer primarily from illusions 447.2
**amity:** a. maintained only by reciprocal respect 496.10
**amnesty:** a.: act by which sovereigns pardon injustices committed by themselves 357.9
**Amor:** nothing heals while A. remembers wrong 474.16
**amorous:** what dire offence from a. causes springs 989.13
**amusement:** men rightly occupied derive a. from work 1029.10
**analogies:** make one feel more at home 35.2
**analogy:** a. is the least misleading thing we have 35.1
perception of truth is detection of a. 35.4
**analysis:** a. kills spontaneity 778.2
art of a. consists in saying a truth only when other is ready for it 752.12
**analyze:** when a man is happy he doesn't a. it 407.84
**anarchy:** a. and competition are the laws of death 393.56
a. is the stepping stone to absolute power 36.3
it is not honest inquiry that makes a. 36.1
**ancestors:** atop tree of a. sits Probably Arboreal 37.13
to forget a. is to be a tree without a root 37.2
we can call our a. barbarous 372.17
**ancestors':** good birth fine, but merit is a. 37.10
**ancestral:** worshippers of light a. make the present light a crime 979.14
**ancestry:** I can trace a. to protoplasmal globule 37.5
man who prides himself on a. 37.12
pride of a. is an imposing superstructure 37.3
**anchors:** it is well to moor your bark with two a. 749.27
**ancient:** praise of a. authors proceeds from mutual envy of the living 134.4
with the a. is wisdom 646.10
**ancients:** speak of a. without idolatry 134.2
we have our arts, the a. had theirs 735.28
**anecdotage:** a. was sign for man to retire from world 646.20
**anecdote:** a. will pitch talk off track 185.36
**angel:** a. is a spiritual creature 38.1
each sees a. in his future self 458.3
he who would act the a. acts the beast 684.8
**angels:** better to be improvement on monkey thin such a fallin' off fr'm th' a. 306.4
*en famille* the a. play Mozart 607.4
fools rush in where a. fear to tread 353.23
it is not known precisely where a. dwell 38.2
**anger:** a.: a power when great mind moved by it 39.1
a. as soon as fed is dead 39.14
a. due to a cause will be appeased 410.18
a. is one of the sinews of the soul 39.17
a. may be foolish and absurd 39.21
a. of lovers renews their love 552.19
a. wishes its judgment to seem just 514.22
a. without power is folly 39.19
a. would inflict punishment on another; meanwhile, it tortures itself 39.30
bare recollection of a. kindles a. 39.28

fear not the a. of the wise to raise 797.10
fierce a. belongs to beasts 674.26
hell has three gates: lust, a., greed 414.2
it is difficult to fight against a. 811.14
jealousy, a., and anxiety shorten life 43.2
more violent the love, more violent the a. 548.22
no old age for a man's a., only death 39.32
to tear out foe's brain washes away a. 286.24
who doesn't know a. doesn't know anything 39.24
who is slow to a. is better than mighty 39.7
world would perish did pity not limit a. 692.20

**angle:** certain people and certain things require to be approached on an a. 579.7
from right a., man shows depth, beauty 680.2

**angler:** no man is born an a. 345.4

**angling:** a. like mathematics: never fully learnt 345.5

**Anglo-Saxon:** A.: German who forgot who was his parents 40.1

**Anglo-Saxons:** most A. tremble before a tear 40.2

**angry:** a. men are blind and foolish 39.2
always shun whatever may make you a. 39.29
essential thing is being able to get a. 713.11
feeling a. without anybody to be a. at 39.11
he who has been a. becomes cool again 39.20
no man is a. that feels not himself hurt 39.4
not easy to be a. with right person, to right extent, at right time 39.3
people when a. bring about a change 39.23
shun a. man a moment—enemy forever 286.23
tall man is never his own man till a. 39.22
to be a. is to revenge the fault of others upon ourselves 39.27
when a., count four; when very a., swear 39.33
who cannot be a. cannot be good 39.6

**anguish:** beauty of world is of laughter and a. 1060.35
mirth is the mail of a. 523.6
no man without some manner of a. 17.61

**animal:** a. confounds the understanding 616.48
a. would depict Devil in human form 41.14
be a good a., true to your a. instincts 484.2
love of a. parent violent while it lasts 41.1
man is worse than an a. when he's an a. 206.16
spiritual interests supported by a. life 920.6
who forgets man is a. is made less humane 431.14

**animals:** a. are disarmed by caresses to their young 663.28
a. are such agreeable friends 41.11
a. caught with ourselves in life and time 41.4
a. have endless patience for enduring 41.15
best about a. is they don't talk much 41.33
destiny of human race to stop eating a. 1021.2
excessive love of a. at expense of men 548.199
higher a. follow from war of nature 306.2
inefficient society of plants and a. 616.45
man tries to equal a. 735.29
rain is good for the a. who eat a. 771.4
those who respect natures of wild a. 41.28

**annihilate:** to a. a man, give him useless work 1058.18

**annuities:** persons living on a. are longer lived 487.3

**annuity:** a. makes your life interesting to yourself 487.4

**anonymity:** a. represents a liberating phenomenon 31.3

**another:** true wit is that which falls on a. 1054.17
we cannot forgive a. for not being ourselves 656.4

**another's:** begin with a. to end with your own 694.2
don't measure a. coat on your body 513.6
we must be our own before a. 873.5

**answer:** a. is always a form of death 478.8
a. of the minute is positive 991.129
not every question deserves a. 478.10
soft a. turneth away wrath 164.1

**answers:** better to ask questions than know all a. 478.18
many people today don't want honest a. 302.3
more trouble caused by indiscreet a. 478.12
who asks questions cannot avoid the a. 478.2

**ant:** a. hole may collapse an embankment 398.10
go to the a., thou sluggard 527.2
where does the a. die except in sugar 733.6

**ant's:** in a. house dew is a flood 901.3

**antagonism:** real a. based on love not yet recognized 286.19

**antagonist:** our a. is our helper 651.3

**anticipating:** wise man avoids evil by a. it 356.9

**anticipation:** pleasures and trouble greatest in a. 316.7
recollection and a. fill our moments 723.15

**antiquated:** nothing new except what has become a. 632.1

**antique:** precious pleasure to meet an a. book 91.25

**antiquity:** a. full of praises of a more remote a. 42.8
a. provides professors with bread 42.6
if we look backwards to a., it should be as those that are winning a race 42.3

**antitrust:** enemy of free enterprise system labels every a. prosecution as "persecution" 732.8

**ants:** a. and savages put strangers to death 355.7
a. place group interest first 479.1
**anvil:** either suffer or triumph, be a. or hammer 853.4
if you're the a., bear; if hammer, strike 722.2
**anxieties:** solitude is the mother of a. 908.42
**anxiety:** a. and conscience are powerful dynamos 43.13
a. is normal course of man's existence 43.7
age of a.: along with what weighs on our minds is what grates on our nerves 43.6
American defends against a. by learning not to become involved 34.20
character forms at first pinch of a. 117.28
jealousy, anger, and a. shorten life 43.2
people want soft answer that turneth away a. 302.3
stupidity is without a. 43.4
**anxious:** tenterhooks are upholstery of a. seat 43.12
**apartheid:** a. is a stench in world's nostrils 769.15
**apathy:** science has found no cure for a. 216.6
**ape:** a. mounts high, shows his breech 773.6
**aphorism:** good a. too hard for tooth of time 767.6
**Apollo:** words of Mercury harsh after songs of A. 269.31
**apologies:** a. only account for what they don't alter 44.1
**apology:** a. is egotism wrong side out 44.3
**apparel:** a. shapes, but money finishes, the man 596.23
the a. oft proclaims the man 265.19
**appearance:** a.: looking the best you can for the money 45.11
insinuating a. seldom linked with virtue 45.3
man looketh on the outward a. 45.2
**appearances:** always scorn a. and you always may 45.4
publicly you must preserve a. 583.6
shallow people do not judge by a. 45.19
**appeasement:** no a. with ruthlessness 46.4
**appeaser:** a. feeds crocodile so he's eaten last 46.2
**appetite:** a.: solution to labor question 435.1
health and a. impart sweetness to food 411.4
nothing so incontinent as man's a. 401.13
**appetites:** others' a. appear excessive if unshared 236.13
riches more enlarge than satisfy a. 1041.29
subdue your a., you conquer human nature 963.1
**applauds:** audience always a. latest song most 632.7
**applause:** a. of single human is of great consequence 716.16
a.: spur of noble mind, aim of weak one 716.6
every artist loves a. 716.28
evil report carries farther than a. 622.4
he only is great man who can neglect a. 49.1
I scorn men's curses, but I dread a. 716.7
**apple:** finished man of world eats of every a. 910.1
**appointment:** we aren't saints, but we have kept our a. 759.1
**appreciate:** rather a. things I can not have than have things I am not able to a. 47.2
**appreciated:** each supposes himself not fully a. 870.3
**appreciation:** greatest humiliation: not to get a. 48.5
**apprehension:** grief has limits, a. none 43.9
**apprehensions:** my a. come in crowds 43.14
**approval:** lean on a. and it becomes bed of thorns 49.2
man isn't comfortable without his own a. 862.12
**approve:** fools admire, men of sense a. 14.5
**approving:** understanding is the beginning of a. 1000.6
**April:** A., A., laugh thy girlish laughter 848.48
A. a promise that May is bound to keep 848.5
A. comes like an idiot, babbling 848.33
A. is the cruellest month 848.16
first day of A. reminds us of what we always are 418.9
weeping gloom of March and A. 848.18
**aptitude:** most do violence to their natural a. 1.10
**arch:** a. never sleeps 50.8
**archeologist:** an a. is the best husband 42.2
**archer:** a. that shoots over, misses as much as he that falls short 310.7
**Archimedes:** simplest schoolboy knows truths for which A. would have given his life 843.29
**architect:** a.: drafts plan of house, plans draft of your money 50.1
if not a sculptor or painter, can't be a. 50.15
life's brevity makes a.'s trade sad 50.5
**architects:** a., like clients, want to show off 428.5
**architecture:** a. is inhabited sculpture 50.2
a. is oratory of power by means of forms 50.11
genius of a. has shed maledictions over land 50.9
I call a. petrified music 50.7
no a. is so haughty as the simple 50.14
promise and ruin seen in Gothic a. 50.16
**are:** as we a., so we do 238.8
what you a. drowns out what you say 916.18
what you a. must displease, if you would attain to what you a. not 55.1
you a., when all is done, just what you a. 442.11
**arguing:** a. of shadow, we forgo the substance 51.19

all a. is at once surface and symbol 53.136
apply to a. as much discrimination as to work 53.6
basic unit of contemporary a.: analysis of and extension of sensations 53.126
beginnings of a. acquire a greater celebrity than a. in perfection 477.10
being impressed in a. often stands in the way of emotion 53.54
connoisseurs in a. reveal its beauty 204.23
criticism is easy, a. is difficult 204.13
criticism is the windows of a. 204.40
delight in a. is growth of taste, knowledge 53.58
difficult for man to realize his life an a. 536.29
does a. have higher function than to make one enjoy natural objects 53.10
eye is pleased when nature stoops to a. 616.77
fashion: to realize a. in living forms 335.17
for the best we must have recourse to a. 53.56
great a. is expression of great men 53.109
great works of a. do not begin by giving us all their best 53.100
if a. were to redeem man, it could do so only by restoring him to boyishness 53.92
illusions are a. and by a. we live 447.3
in a., as in love, instinct is enough 53.49
in a. nothing can be done without genius 843.30
in a., there are tears that do often lie too deep for thoughts 53.71
in fine a., hand, head, heart go together 53.112
interpretation is revenge of intellect on a. 204.51
it is through a. that we realise our perfection 677.22
it's the aim of a. to give life form 53.4
life imitates a. more than a., life 536.134
life is an imitation of poster a. 994.10
life is short and the a. long 981.6
man apt to be moved by a. of his period 53.37
man who would emancipate a. from discipline 53.118
man works to recover, through a., images that first gained access to his heart 53.22
minimal a., maximum explanation 53.69
mirror reflects your face, a. your soul 53.123
mood means more than object in a. 53.42
morality takes no account of the a. in life 598.26
more inexpressible than all else is a. 53.103
no better deliverance from world than a. 53.55
no comfort in adversity sweeter than a. 53.3
no generation interested in a. in same way 53.39
not strength, but a., obtains prize 137.6
one may do whate'er one likes in a. 53.15
perfection not requisite to a. 677.16
poor a. that maintains not artisan 1058.45
prig, philistine, Ph.D., C.P.A. hate a. 207.12
problem in a. is one of translation 53.21
real a. has capacity to make us nervous 204.52
science, a., often a kind of dope 267.3
supreme a. is one that does not at first allow itself to be recognized 936.4
thanks to a., many worlds are at our disposal 53.101
there is a certain renunciation in a. 1062.20
there is no progress in a. 53.35
there is one a.: to do all artlessly 892.6
to follow a. for sake of being great is surest way of ending in total extinction 53.108
to make us feel small is a function of a. 53.48
to most women a. is a form of scandal 1055.53
to reveal a., conceal artist, is a.'s aim 53.137
to whiten ivory with dye is to spoil nature by a. 54.3
trend toward pure a. shows modesty 53.93
true a. selects and paraphrases 53.2
under-tow of time can't drag true a. back 53.27
when we separate music from life we get a. 53.18
without a. reality is unbearable 53.124
without innovation, a. is a corpse 53.25
work of a. is the exaggeration of an idea 53.51
works of a. are of an infinite loneliness 204.44
youth of an a. is its most interesting period 53.17
**art's:** absolute completion marks a. decline 53.110
**arteriosclerosis:** young people develop mental a. 1064.30
**articulate:** a. voice distracts more than mere noise 148.14
**artifice:** customary use of a. is sign of small mind 162.13
**artifices:** Cupid is naked and does not like a. 548.169
**artificial:** first duty in life is to be a. 54.6
natural beauty is temporary; hence impression of obscene mockery a. flowers give 54.4
to know only a. night is absurd 54.2
**artisan:** poor art that maintains not the a. 1058.45
**artist:** a. cannot get along without a public 53.52
a. cannot speak about his art 53.26
a. excavates accessible areas and shows people what can be done with themselves 53.34
a. finds greater pleasure in painting 198.36
a. functions in afterglow of divine fires 483.4
a. has conversation with public 53.24
a. has need to share joy with others 53.128
a. has never been a dictator 53.14

a. in teens who is happy is a charlatan 53.73
a. is a creature driven by demons 53.47
a. is a cut above the critic 204.19
a. is a man of action 53.28
a. is as dissatisfied as revolutionary 53.59
a. is one who has faith in himself 53.86
a. is the exemplary sufferer 1062.100
a. isn't keen on getting a thing done 53.74
a. like everyone else, only more so 53.106
a. limits vision to his own ego 53.79
a.: lover of nature, her slave and master 53.129
a. moves in a direction and hopes he arrives before death overtakes him 53.19
a. must blow trumpet of defiance 53.75
a. must perfect work so that it may become attractively disinteresting 53.20
a.: one who creates something not here before with tools of human spirit 53.45
a. produces for the liberation of his soul 198.27
a. should be fit for best society 53.111
a. to keep awake sense of wonder 53.23
a. works on next composition because he was not satisfied with his previous one 198.38
aim of a. is to arrest motion 53.46
beauty ends where the a. begins 70.8
behind mediocre a. find remarkable man 956.13
being an a. means ceasing to take seriously person we are when we are not an a. 53.91
cheat for sake of beauty, you're an a. 53.63
every a. loves applause 716.28
every a. writes his own autobiography 53.40
every master knows material teaches the a. 53.36
first prerogative of a. in any medium is to make a fool of himself 53.64
I, an a., am here to live out loud 53.141
I feel that America is against the a. 53.87
life lived *in potentia* until a. deploys it 53.31
no a. has his complete meaning alone 53.38
no a. sees things as they really are 53.135
no fate more distressing for an a. than to have to show his work to fools 204.36
no longing sweeter to a. than longing after bliss of the commonplace 53.77
nobody ought to look at pictures who cannot find more in them than a. expressed 53.57
scholar seeks, a. finds 842.17
society must let a. follow vision anywhere 53.66
that a. puts order into nature is absurd 53.30
the a. has power to shape the material of pain we all have 53.130
this is the a., then—life's hungry man 53.139
to the a. communication is a by-product 53.81
true a. will let his wife starve 53.122
when critics disagree, the a. is in accord with himself 204.57
with an a. no sane man quarrels 204.47
woe to a. if he is disciple of his time 53.120
**artist's:** a. egoism is outrageous 53.82
a. joy: thought and feeling merged 53.78
a. morality: truth, force of description 53.8
a. work constitutes the only relationship he can have with fellow men 53.33
**artistic:** a. impulse seems not to wish to produce finished work 53.29
**artists:** a. are by definition children 53.107
a. don't steal, but borrow 53.105
a. have no less talents than ever 994.16
a., poets uninterested in happiness 702.84
a. today expected to cultivate unhappiness 1004.8
a. whom love inspires have light of fame 53.98
all men are creative but few are a. 198.16
competitions are for horses, not a. 154.1
for a. waits the compromise through art 53.32
good a. exist in what they make 53.138
immature a. imitate; mature a. steal 694.5
refusal to rest content distinguishes a. from entertainers 53.133
**artlessness:** a.: women attain it by long study 482.2
**arts:** a. and sciences owe birth to our vices 1023.27
a. must study their occasions 53.115
a. will one day give headless man head 572.12
hardest of a. to speak of is music 204.45
lover of a. imposes rapture on himself 204.30
religion always a patron of the a. 790.34
society acquires new a. and loses old instincts 906.3
waking mind is least serviceable in the a. 999.2
**ashamed:** I often wonder to see men not a. 886.9
more a man a. of, more respectable he is 803.6
**ashes:** man when he burns leaves handful of a. 218.136
**asides:** character comes out best in a. 117.25
**ask:** a. not what America will do for you 534.19
a. of him who wishes you well 799.6
better a. twice than lose your way once 478.5
how pleasant it is to a. for nothing 873.24
if reluctant to a. way, you will be lost 973.8
not to a. is not to be denied 799.3
we should not a. people for what they cannot give 799.1
**aspiration:** a. is a joy for ever 55.21
I drink wine of a. and am never dull 55.10
path made clear, a. of everyone 113.4
takes certain level of a. before one can take advantage of opportunities 55.11
whole of satisfaction not from single a. 55.8

**aspirations**: life's a. come in the guise of children 121.46
**aspire**: if you a. to the highest place 55.4
**aspired**: what I a. to be, and was not, comforts me 327.5
**ass**: a. loaded with gold climbs to the top 596.17
a. loaded with gold still eats thistles 1041.30
a. may bray long before he shakes stars 934.5
a. that is common property is always the worst saddled 887.1
every a. loves to hear himself bray. 1020.7
hay is more acceptable to an a. than gold 48.7
hood a. with purple, he shall pass for cathedral doctor 136.12
rather ride on a. that carries me 714.4
traveling a. will not come home a horse 985.21
who makes himself an a., men will ride 934.8
wise do not stand behind kicking a. 749.36
**assailant**: a. often in the right; assailed, always 816.14
**assailants**: wise man takes the side of his a. 651.6
**assassination**: a. has never changed history of the world 516.4
a. the extreme form of censorship 111.10
moral a. more cruel than pistol a. 898.10
**assent**: a., and you are sane 256.3
**assert**: to know oneself, a. oneself 868.5
**asserts**: individual never a. himself more than when he forgets himself 921.2
**assimilates**: one completely overcomes only what one a. 170.7
**associating**: a. with men, one acquires their virtues, vices 57.16
wise man a. with vicious becomes idiot 57.3
**association**: all thought is a feat of a. 968.15
long a. ends up producing a sort of rot 560.5
unquarreling a. of men never existed 766.10
**assurance**: a. contemptible unless self-knowledge 854.5
a. keeps even pace with ability 854.4
nothing gives more a. than a mask 162.3
**astonishment**: writer lives in a state of a. 1062.94
**astray**: some go a. because no right path for them 122.5
**astronomer**: undevout a. is mad 844.13
**astronomers**: a. work always with the past 843.13
**atheism**: a. must insult God less than religion 997.13
a. rampant in community without blasphemy 504.3
a. rather in lip than heart of man 997.1
a.: there's not a single emancipating influence that doesn't become inhibitory 997.11
apostles of a.: wealth, health, power 997.7
little philosophy inclineth to a. 688.1
to put faith in lies and hate is true a. 410.15
**atheist**: by night an a. half believes a God 997.20
fight between theist, a. is whether God shall be called God or some other name 385.15
no proselyter so energetic as a. 997.3
**atheist's**: a. laugh's a poor exchange for Deity offended 997.6
**atheists**: a. put on a false courage and alacrity 997.17
**atom**: a. bombs pile up, but earth still goes round the sun 994.14
an a. tossed in a chaos made of yeasting worlds; whence have I come 314.7
gods are born and die; the a. endures 633.3
no country without a. bomb independent 633.4
no evil in a., only in men's souls 633.13
terror of a. age: man's adjustment to it 633.14
**atomic**: god of science gave us a. bomb 633.9
**attached**: men are a. to us for services they render 881.9
**attack**: a. is the reaction 26.2
isn't the best defense always a good a. 226.14
**attacking**: you learn to hold your own by a. 853.6
**attainable**: let me strive for a. things 55.17
**attainment**: is anything in life disenchanting as a. 938.40
**attempted**: nothing ever a., if all objections must first be overcome 289.5
something a. has earned night's repose 6.15
**attention**: a. is narrow-mouthed vessel; fill with care 59.2
we despise no source paying us pleasing a. 346.22
**attic**: in an a. we enjoy supper of fried fish 839.4
**attitude**: meaning lies in our a. toward things 569.6
**attorney**: a.'s duty to lie, conceal, distort 525.34
**attractions**: men by sympathetic a. lead human race 528.6
**auctioneer**: a.: proclaims with hammer that he has picked a pocket with his tongue 103.4
**audacious**: often we are a. from timidity 1040.8
perfect simplicity is unconsciously a. 892.12
**audacity**: a. augments courage; hesitation, fear 90.15
fly should be used as symbol of a. 479.8
tact in a. is knowing how far to go 90.1
with a. one can undertake anything 90.12
**audience**: a. an abstraction, it has no taste 59.7
a. is a very curious animal 59.4
a. is fifty percent of performance 59.1
a. is not least important actor in the play 59.5

if a. never understands plot, it will be very attentive 965.16
one can't exchange thoughts with an a. 59.3
permanent a. waiting to be amused 563.13
solitude is a.-chamber of God 908.26
writer needs no a. other than the few 1062.106
**audiences:** to have great poets, must have great a. 59.8
**August:** A. creates as she slumbers 848.27
**author:** a. needs more than intelligence 1062.59
a. reading his own book can't stop 865.9
a. who speaks about his books as bad as mother about children 1062.31
a. who threatens to survive reputation 1062.30
every a. keeps an outrageous vanity 1062.97
every a. would his brother kill 1062.15
every production must resemble its a. 198.7
fill an a. with fame and you burst him 330.14
I never met an a. who admitted people did not buy his book because it was dull 268.1
obscure a. does not think clearly 91.18
old a. rediscovers himself in fossilized production of earlier years 1062.50
one hates an a. that's all a. 1062.18
same common sense makes a. write good things, dread they are not good enough 1062.61
we expected to see a., we find a man 935.17
when characters are alive before their a. 341.15
who first praises book, next in merit to a. 204.31
wide discrepancy between reputation of a. living and dead 1062.4
**author's:** a. work furnishes critics with food 204.27
understand a. character, comprehension of his writings becomes easy 1062.66
**authority:** a. forgets a dying king 223.13
a. has every reason to fear the skeptic 61.5
a. is for children and servants 560.96
a. is never without hate 61.3
a. seldom resisted when well employed 61.4
a. we are given now is a trinity: the grin, the generality, and God 528.12
age has an a. making it preferable to youth 646.99
anyone who in discussion relies on a. 51.18
base a. from others' books 842.37
he who has no bread has no a. 712.52
most men after freedom prefer a. 61.6
new faces have more a. than old 61.2
proud man, dressed in a little brief a. 61.10
rigorous a., justice: kindness of kings 825.16
we have to hate our immediate predecessors to get free of their a. 372.7
**authors:** a. are like cattle going to a fair 1062.63
a. are sometimes like tomcats 1062.29
a. should write one novel, then be gassed 1062.69
bad a. write with reference to an inner context the reader cannot know 53.21
even monarchs have need of a. 1062.45
great a. make for disagreement 1062.43
great a. produce great publishers 758.5
of a. there is great scarcity 204.37
one class of a. write history of their times; the other, biography 1062.105
**authors':** some judge of a. names, not works 204.43
**autobiography:** a. is now as common as adultery 62.3
every artist writes his own a. 53.40
**autocrat:** to be great a., must be great barbarian 713.14
**automatic:** critical vision can mitigate a. operation 960.19
**automation:** a., industrialists, and the human variable 713.26
if a. keeps up, man will atrophy all limbs but the push-button finger 960.28
**automatism:** we have created an industrial order geared to a. 994.12
**automobile:** a. has dissolved living tissue of city 63.4
a. is more sophisticated than bundling board, but motives in use often the same 63.1
except the American woman, nothing interests eye of American man more than a. 63.2
in a. society, no time to think 563.6
**autonomy:** men lose individual a. seeking to be alike 168.15
**autumn:** a. arrives in the early morning 848.9
a. comes like a warrior 848.28
a., nodding o'er yellow plain, comes on 848.46
a.: season of mists, friend of sun 848.25
a. time for gathering, scattering 848.40
a. wins you by mute appeal to sympathy 848.11
summer ends, and a. comes 848.6
**autumn's:** wild west wind, breath of a. being 1052.7
**autumnal:** grace I have seen in one a. face 646.21
**avant gardes:** conformism hot on heels of a. 335.28
**avarice:** a. hoards itself poor 382.14
a. is a cursed vice 401.17
a. is a fine, absorbin' passion 401.4
a. is as destitute as poverty 401.23
a. makes man too timorous to be wealthy 401.21
extreme a. misapprehends itself always 401.16
miser's a. is sepulchre of other passions 401.3
pride, a., envy are tongues men heed 727.8

prudery is the worst kind of a. 750.4
to hazard much for much is a., not wisdom 401.22
when other sins are old, a. is young 401.8
**avaricious:** men hate the a.; nothing gained from him 401.28
**average:** a. man rich enough when he has more 249.7
**averageness:** a. is a quality we must put up with 131.5
**avoided:** weakness to lament what cannot be a. 930.9
**aware:** to live means to be divinely a. 536.73
**awareness:** if building a bridge does not enrich a. of builders, don't build 1058.27
**awful:** anything a. makes me laugh 523.14
**awkwardness:** a. has no forgiveness in heaven or earth 370.1

## B

**babies:** b. expect far too much of existence 64.3
man who hates dogs and b. can't be all bad 588.3
**baby:** b. is angel whose wings decrease 64.7
cradle is rocked but b. is pinched 269.23
each b. is a finer one than the last 64.5
152 ways of holding a b. 64.1
**baby's:** men profess inability to wash b. face 64.2
**Bacchus:** B. hath drowned more men than Neptune 266.19
**bachelor:** b. don't die at all—sort of rots away 65.8
b. is peacock, married man a jackass 560.44
no character harder to play well than old b. 65.3
**bachelor's:** b. admired freedom is often a yoke 65.5
b. fare is bread, cheese, kisses 65.7
**bachelors:** all reformers are b. 783.29
all the married men live like b. 575.17
**back:** better turn b. than lose your way 808.2
do not turn your b. on anyone 944.4
**background:** b. reveals the true being of man or thing 66.1
every philosophy tinged with secret imaginative b. 688.47
**bad:** b. in best of us leaves saint like rest of us 834.13
b. is never good until worse happens 788.5
b. man can do more harm than a beast 1063.2
b. man must have brains 1063.12
better fare hard with good men than feast with b. 57.13
good and b. is helping or hurting 388.5
good and b. may not be dissevered 388.6
good is good doctor, b. sometimes better 305.12
good so good that b. when b. can't be b. 387.8
he that can't endure b. won't see good 285.11
man not good or b. for one action 224.11
no benefit in gifts of a b. man 382.10
nothing good, b. but thinking makes it so 387.14
nothing good for him for whom nothing b. 388.8
nothing is good or b. but by comparison 152.2
nothing so b. but can masquerade as moral 598.29
one knows b. action in flash of regret 224.17
surprised to find things as b. as we'd said 724.8
the b. often let you see how b. they are 162.19
the good suffers while the b. prevails 388.11
those found b. are presumed so forever 1063.16
when the b. imitate the good, there is no knowing what mischief is intended 449.10
who spares the b. injures the good 531.1
world bears two nations: good and b. 1060.22
**badly:** less dangerous to treat men b. than well 1011.1
**badness:** b. is accidental, like disease 305.24
good people make b. very important 391.56
**balance:** false b. is an abomination 103.3
fortune holds even, scrupulous b. 114.8
truth is b., but unbalance not a lie 992.18
**balanced:** nothing is unthinkable to the b. person 711.4
**bald:** b. head is soon shaven 325.1
**baldhead:** blind man is laughing at the b. 814.6
**baldness:** more felicity on the far side of b. 580.19
**ball:** at a b. we look for a wife, look after a wife or after sombody else's wife 665.2
be careful about play, indifferent to b. 570.4
**ballots:** b. rightful successors to bullets 1030.12
**banality:** great minds tend toward b. 399.28
**bang:** world ends not with a b. but a whimper 1060.10
**bank:** b. lends money if you don't need it 68.2
**banker:** father is a b. provided by nature 663.20
**bankers:** b. just like anybody else except richer 68.3
**bankrupt:** people become b. having invested too heavily in the prose of life 605.14
**banquet:** never a b. where one didn't dine poorly 744.9
some dislike something in every b. 719.2
those who have risen from a b. 745.5
**barbarian:** man born b., raises self by culture 207.8

to be great autocrat, must be great b. 713.14
**barbarians:** men have been b. much longer than civilized 69.4
**barbarism:** b. is not appreciating what is excellent 69.2
b. is the condition of past customs 210.9
b.: lack of standards to which to appeal 69.5
b. naturally has its apologists 69.6
civilization is b. in lamb's skin 131.1
soldier is grievous vestige of b. 69.7
**barber:** b. learns his trade on orphan's chin 715.1
one b. shaves not so close but another finds work 154.3
**bard:** wine to gifted b. is mount that races 266.7
**barefoot:** who scattereth thorns must not go b. 557.4
**bargain:** life greatest b.; we get it for nothing 536.138
unpleasant to get more than you b. for 310.9
**bargains:** rule for b.: do others, they would do you 102.11
someone always cheated in b. 103.11
**baritones:** b. are born villains in opera 648.6
**barn:** I like a man who likes to see a fine b. 714.1
it's your barn a woman's after 195.6
**barracks:** socialism without liberty is the b. 905.1
**barricade:** b. closes the street but opens the way 795.2
**base:** b. men in love gain a nobility 548.211
it takes courage, greatness, even to be b. 1048.1
small things make b. men proud 686.12
what b. things fear makes men do 340.20
**baseness:** two infinities: God above, human b. below 305.17
**bashfulness:** there is that destroyeth his soul by b. 973.1
**bat:** the b. is dun, with wrinkled wings 41.10
**bath:** I test my b. before I sit 135.7
**bathrooms:** nation of b. with humanist in each tub 34.40
**battalions:** God is always on the side of heaviest b. 1035.102
**battle:** all b. is a confused experiment to ascertain clear undeniable might or right 1035.12
b.: untying with teeth a political knot 1035.9
nothing except a b. lost can be half so melancholy as a b. won 1035.105
peace hath higher tests than b. 674.39
toothache will cost a b. 989.10
unhappy the general who comes on field of b. with a system 932.1
**bayonets:** lover of b. sees in glitter what he feels 582.6
man may build, but not sit on, throne of b. 354.9
**be:** b. as you would seem to b. 894.9
b. what you are 442.12
b. what you wish to be thought to b. 384.20
b. yourself and think for yourself 873.12
every moment, one is what one will b. 442.24
tell yourself what you would b. 55.6
to know what shall b., consider the past 741.4
what thou art, that thou art; that God knoweth thee to b. 442.22
**bear:** who learns to b. what he cannot change 800.9
**beard:** b. does not make philosopher 405.3
I could not endure a husband with a b. 560.105
old goat not more reverend for b. 646.34
**bearded:** there are b. fools 353.10
**bearing:** we may be masters of our lot by b. it 285.10
**beast:** he who would act the angel acts the b. 684.8
we ride through life on the b. within us 431.20
when human being says b. in him aroused 431.26
**beasts:** men not to live silently like b. 727.23
who will pity any who go near wild b. 213.1
world is full of nothing but b. of prey 26.1
**beat:** all b. the man whom fortune buffets 206.7
b. your child once a day 760.5
out to b. dog, you're sure to find stick 203.33
though you would like to b. the dog 749.4
you can't b. anybody for nothing 526.1
**beaten:** man surprised is half b. 948.1
**Beats:** B. act out critique of organized system 89.2
**beautician's:** at b. you buy hair, complexion, lips 189.2
**beauties:** all b. to be honored, only one embraced 70.44
statesmen, b., rarely sense own decay 223.2
**beautifier:** no b. like wish to scatter joy 517.9
**beautiful:** b. derives its beauty from itself 70.28
b. rests on foundations of the necessary 70.14
b. souls are they that are open and ready 647.6
b. things, when taste is formed 957.17
it's easy to be b., hard to appear so 45.16
man makes b. what he loves 76.18
most b. things are those that madness prompts and reason writes 1062.41
most b. things in world are most useless 70.41
no woman can be b. who can be false 470.12
some people are b. in dilapidation 646.95
things are b. if you love them 70.1
things not b. until they speak to the imagina-

tion 70.16
we find things b. because we recognize them 70.31

**beauty**: a b. you notice; a charmer notices you 119.7
a little b. is preferable to much wealth 70.42
as we grow old, b. steals inward 646.26
ask a toad what is b.—a female toad 70.59
b. a greater recommendation than any letter of introduction 70.5
b., after offense returning, regains love 70.34
b. and deformity equally pass away 983.18
b. corrodes, corrupts all it touches 70.19
b. deprived of adjuncts ceases to be b. 70.40
b. dies of b., worth dies of worth 968.61
b. draws us with a single hair 405.4
b. ends where the artist begins 70.8
b. fades, leaves record upon face as to what became of it 324.5
b., find self in love, not thy mirror 70.50
b. gets the best of it in this world 70.29
b., good, knowledge are three sisters 387.15
b. hath no true glass, but loving eyes 70.26
b., invisible, has visible reflection 70.20
b. is an ecstasy; it's as simple as hunger 70.30
b. is everlasting; dust is for a time 70.35
b. is feared more than death 70.62
b. is its own excuse for being 70.18
b. is joint force and full result of all 70.39
b. is not for sharing 70.21
b. is not immortal 70.49
b. is one of the rare things that do not lead to doubt of God 70.3
b. is the promise of happiness 70.48
b. is truth, truth b. 70.24
b. is unbearable, drives us to despair 70.9
b. is wherever there is a soul to admire 70.58
b. more than bitterness breaks the heart 70.52
b. must not be hoarded 70.33
b. of American women is vast industry 1055.105
b. of world is of laughter and anguish 1060.35
b. persuades eyes of men without orator 70.46
b.: power by which woman charms lover and terrifies husband 70.6
b. provoketh thieves sooner than gold 70.47
b. sums up the secret aims of nature 70.7
b.: truth's smile beholding her own face 70.51
b. without expression tires 70.15
better to be happy and burned up with b. 407.76
cannot hope for b. in all things 70.32
chase b. and it ceases 70.11
cheat for sake of b., you're an artist 53.63
culture opens the sense of b. 207.3
every b., out of place, is a b. no longer 942.5
extraordinary b. involves a moral charm 70.17
exuberance is b. 511.1
forever seek for b; she fights death 70.54
frigidaires perfect, b. limps 677.16
from b. we draw conception of divine life 408.3
genius lasts longer than b. 277.79
glory of b. is fleeting; virtue, eternal 1025.50
is b. not enough, why do I cry for love 548.227
judgment of b. can err with wine, dark 70.38
justice balances the b. in the world 515.51
little of b. has America given the world 34.11
looking for b. makes us see shortcomings 455.7
love built on b., soon as b., dies 548.49
man's soul longs for b. 920.7
mightiest of Puritans who first insisted b. is only skin deep 70.25
narrow souls dare not to admire true b. 70.10
natural b. is temporary and sad 54.4
no b. like that spoiled by an accident 455.11
not b. but fine qualities keep a husband 560.31
not enough to see and know b. of a work 70.60
one finds only so much b. as one carries 1019.5
order is the shape upon which b. depends 654.3
outstanding b. tends to hamper happiness 70.45
personal b. requires that one be tall 70.4
poet unzips veil of b., doesn't remove it 702.112
prosperity versus b.; cash against soul 744.15
real b. is something very grave 70.2
she who is born a b. is born betrothed 70.22
thing of b. is a joy forever 70.23
thou seest no b. save thou make it first 70.27
to keep b. in place makes all beautiful 70.43
to the elect, beautiful things mean b. 70.61
truth will bear exposure as well as b. 991.18
universe lies under necessity of b. 1010.3
we fly to b. from terrors of the finite 70.13
what imagination seizes as b. is truth 991.70
who can set the bounds of b. 20.6
wisdom is social, b. is jealous 1053.38
without grace b. is an unbaited hook 394.2
zest is the secret of all b. 511.2

**become**: man needs only to b. 8.11
sacrifice what we are for what we could b. 711.2
we b. what we are by radical refusal 442.20

**bed**: at thirty, women send big b. to basement 560.133
bride b.: theirs alone till life's done 560.34
handkerchief in b. can't be found 638.7
in b., I prefer beauty before goodness 185.26

lying in b. late you learn to distinguish first things from trivia 71.7
man's b. his cradle; woman's her rack 71.10
marriage more than four legs in b. 560.42
very warm weather when one's in b. 71.9
we go to b. with reluctance 71.3
**bedfellows:** misery acquaints a man with strange b. 17.56
**bee:** honey in every flower, takes b. to get it 579.9
how doth the little busy b. improve each shining hour 479.9
not good for swarm, not good for b. 150.6
**beehive:** earth is a b.; we live in different cells 908.1
**beer:** running b. gathers no foam 921.4
what's more inseparable than b., Britannia 287.27
**bees:** b. sip honey and hum their thanks 397.12
is any polity better ordered than that of b. 479.6
what state excels b. for government 479.3
**beetle:** when they came to shoe the horses, the b. stretched out his leg 865.5
**before:** while it is still b., afterwards has no power 669.5
**beg:** not a soul who does not have to b. alms 233.3
**beggar:** pitier gives to b., throbs with contempt 692.21
poor command respect; b. excites anger 72.2
the strong prevail; the b. is a fool 72.1
**beggar's:** lady's heart doesn't agree with a b. purse 1055.69
**beggars:** b. should be abolished entirely 72.3
pickpockets, b., are best physiognomists 927.1
**begging:** people are averse to b. pardon 44.2
**begin:** b. at beginning, go on to end; then stop 654.7
better to b. in evening than not at all 73.4
in creating, only hard thing's to b. 198.24
you b. well only in what you end well 74.4
**beginner:** merit goes to b. if successor does better 73.2
**beginning:** all great deeds have a ridiculous b. 399.7
art of ending greater than that of b. 74.10
b. of anything and end are alike touching 74.9
bad b. makes a bad ending 173.6
good b. makes a good ending 74.3
hard b. maketh a good ending 74.7
men perish because they cannot join b. with end 74.1
world is round: end may be b. 74.11
**beginnings:** most men are bundles of b. 73.3
we should have our eyes intent on b. 73.6
**begins:** who b. many things finishes but few 74.8
who b. too much accomplishes little 6.10
**begun:** once task b., half work is done 73.5
**behave:** b. in life as if at a banquet 650.4
cease to believe, you may cease to b. 997.15
in great matters men b. as expected 75.4
men who b. well may be creatures of habit 75.8
**behavior:** b.: conduct determined by breeding 75.3
b. is the index of the man 75.1
b.: mirror where one displays his image 75.7
beautiful b. better than beautiful form 75.5
call bad b. righteous indignation 239.7
explanation of human b. must end in simplification 75.11
laws of b. yield to energy of individual 559.7
test of a creed is in daily b. 200.5
**beholders:** less difference in landscapes than in b. 693.4
**being:** b. is the great explainer 314.12
each must form himself as a particular b. 467.14
every life is its own excuse for b. 314.6
man needs to die in fullness of b. 8.11
peace will come through b. 674.23
sanctity hangs about sources of our b. 314.10
**belief:** b. which allows me best use of my strength 76.6
eloquent man is drunk with a certain b. 281.2
firm b. attracts facts 76.3
it is desire that engenders b. 76.17
not free until captive of supreme b. 76.13
widespread b. is likely to be foolish 76.19
**beliefs:** all b. are demonstrable by logic 738.4
no fury like that against one who may succeed in making us disloyal to our b. 333.8
there is a multitude of individual b. 76.5
when all b. are challenged together 897.10
**believe:** b. in something for another world 412.12
b. not all you hear 749.18
b. that life is worth living 76.9
cease to b., you may cease to behave 997.15
childish to expect men to b. like fathers 372.3
faith is to b. what you do not yet see 328.2
first we b. everything, then nothing, then everything again 76.10
he does not b. who does not so live 76.4
he's a fool who tries to make blockhead b. 328.7
hundreds b., but each has to b. by himself 328.1
it doesn't matter what you b., just so you're sincere 894.20
man as big as number who b. in him 399.65
man is credulous and must b. something 76.20

no man ready to b. all he is told does well 102.29
reason should make you b. 328.32
to b., begin with doubting 76.23
to b. in something you have to b. in everything necessary for belief 76.1
under all that we think, lives all we b. 76.11
valuable trait is sense of what not to b. 897.6
we b. the most incredible things 76.7
we b. what makes us feel fine fellows 869.13
what will make us b. in what we must do 440.2
when half b. one thing, half another, safe to accept either opinion 649.12
**believed:** everything b. is an image of truth 76.2
nothing so b., as what we least know 76.12
that b. by all has every chance of being false 76.24
to be b., make truth unbelievable 993.15
**believer:** b. cannot be restrained 590.2
b. undisturbed that others do not yet see 328.14
**believes:** each b. what he fears or desires 199.5
more a man dreams, less he b. 113.10
no man ever quite b. in any other man 990.5
**believest:** let greatest part of what thou hearest be the least part of what thou b. 897.9
**believing:** b. man is the original man 655.1
loving is half of b. 76.8
people enjoy b. things they know untrue 199.1
**bell:** never send to know for whom the b. tolls 218.39
**bells:** everyone thinks b. echo his thoughts 865.8
**belly:** b. is ungrateful 435.9
b. overreaches the head 401.7
constant demands of heart and b. 618.4
difficult to make speeches to the b. 757.12
whose b. is full believes not him whose b. is empty 744.10
**belongs:** man b. wherever he wants to go 914.7
**beloved:** ashamed of being b. when we no longer love 549.7
everyone is seeking after the B. 385.37
**beneath:** nothing is b. you if it is in direction of your life 433.5
**benefactor:** every evil not yielded to is a b. 305.11
**beneficent:** be b., but defend your rights 226.3
**benefits:** b. we receive must be rendered again 639.1
in refusing b. caution should be used 784.9
more pleased seeing those on whom we confer b. than those from whom we receive b. 382.24
unrequitable b. repaid with hatred 639.9
who talk of b. do them to talk of them 430.18
**benevolence:** b. not in the prosperous pitying others 430.35
great exercise of b.: loving relatives 517.24
**best:** each entitled to be valued by b. moment 513.3
there is always b. way to do everything 579.6
**best seller:** b. is celebrity among books 91.9
b. is gilded tomb of mediocre talent 91.81
**best sellers:** procrastinated rape is rule of all b. 341.16
**bestiality:** any check on human action brings mental b. 558.40
**betray:** all a man can b. is his conscience 77.1
I hope I should have the guts to b. country 77.2
to b. you must first belong 77.4
to take refuge with inferior is to b. self 57.18
trust thyself, no other shall b. thee 990.4
**betrayal:** distrust is our only defense against b. 257.20
why is b. the only truth that sticks 77.3
**betrayed:** those that are b. feel treason sharply 77.5
**better:** be what you are: first step to being b. 442.12
everybody lives for something b. to come 652.7
have zeal first to b. thyself 458.6
striving to b., oft we mar what's well 677.19
way to the b. exacts a look at the worst 458.4
when things seem b., something's overlooked 652.1
who rises from prayer a b. man 717.23
**beware:** b. of no man more than thyself 852.12
**bewilderment:** b. cause of much unhappiness 148.3
**bewitched:** to be b. is not to be saved 276.2
**beyond:** ignorance of B. *sine qua non* of life 1012.10
**Bible:** B. admired over grave of Christianity 78.3
B. twice as accurate as scratch sheet 78.8
Christian's B. is a drug store 78.9
English B. shows power of the language 78.4
**big:** a man as b. as number who believe in him 399.65
b. drum only sounds well from afar 865.16
b. mouthfuls often choke 401.15
don't make self b., you're not so small 87.4
frog tried to look as b. as elephant 726.1
you take b. paces, you leave b. spaces 33.4
**bigness:** overabundance of b. not good 310.4
**bigot:** b.: one with opinion you don't entertain 262.1
one who has thought thoroughly called a b. 262.4
**bigotry:** b. holds truth with a grip that kills it 262.16

b. is the sacred disease 262.8
religion is destroyed by b. 262.7
**bigots:** anti-clericalism, non-belief, have their b. 997.14
**billboard:** I shall never see b. as lovely as tree 18.9
**binding:** better the book, less it demands from b. 91.56
**biographies:** b. are but clothes and buttons of a man 79.8
history is the essence of innumerable b. 417.14
**biography:** b. allows us to live a thousand lives 79.5
how difficult it is to write b. 79.9
I can find my b. in every fable I read 341.8
in b., fact, fiction shouldn't be mixed 79.1
read no history: read only b. 79.4
there is no history, only b. 417.21
**bird:** b. can roost but on one branch 539.5
b. of paradise alights on ungrasping hand 407.12
b. thinks it kindness to give fish a lift 56.13
don't let b. make its nest in your hair 964.6
if you can't catch a b. of paradise 160.6
it's hard to tell the purpose of a b. 80.8
no b. soars too high, with his own wings 33.3
no ladder needs the b. but skies 80.5
one beats bush, another catches the b. 106.2
only a b. should build nest over abysses 749.22
**birds:** only admirable event is migration of b. 80.1
**birth:** at b., death stands but a little aside 218.15
b., copulation, death: all the facts 536.28
b. is nothing without virtue 37.9
day of b. is step towards death 81.4
death borders upon our b. 218.62
each man carries vestiges of his b. 558.26
good b. fine, but merit is ancestors' 37.10
high b. is a poor dish at table 37.8
man's task is to give b. to himself 198.14
mourn not death of men, but b. 81.6
need chaos to give b. to dancing star 198.28
only cure for b., death, is to enjoy interval 536.105
our b. is nothing but our death begun 81.9
to give b. is short-cut to omniscience 663.11
we rejoice at a b. because we are not the person involved 538.42
**bishop:** how can a b. flirt 136.16
**bitch:** witch, b. always dress up for each other 1055.152
**bite:** if you can't b., don't show your teeth 969.4
**bitten:** b. by snake, fears piece of string 319.47
**bitter:** b. and sweet come from outside 279.3
no fruit not b. before it is ripe 402.18
nothing so b. a patient mind can't find solace for it 177.3
sugar won't help the b. at heart 1004.37
**bitterness:** nothing sweet which does not end in b. 983.16
**black:** b. boy's badness is badness 83.15
b. man is striding freedom road 83.16
if you are b. only roads into American life are through subservience 83.11
they are of the color of night, b. 138.3
**blade:** each b. of grass has spot on earth 421.1
**blame:** if there is no intention, there is no b. 893.13
keep alive justice, much b. will pass you by 515.14
**blamed:** what cannot be altered must not be b. 800.5
**blameless:** when we quarrel, we wish we had been b. 766.4
**blames:** one must learn to live before one b. others 203.10
one unable to dance b. uneven floor 312.3
**blasphemies:** all great truths begin as b. 504.4
**blasphemy:** b. is a product of partial belief 504.2
where b. does not exist, atheism rampant 504.3
**blessing:** earth has no b. for unblessed of Heaven 893.2
one b. only: confidence in self 854.6
**blessings:** good government greatest of human b. 393.27
how b. brighten as they take their flight 547.13
men slower to recognize b. than evils 473.6
men value b. only when they lose them 1019.14
**blind:** all have their b. side—superstitions 947.2
b. lead b., it's democratic way 231.34
b. man is laughing at the baldhead 814.6
b. man who sees is better than seeing man who is b. 85.12
b. man will not thank for looking-glass 85.6
consolation enjoyed only by the b. 84.3
he has the greatest b. side who thinks he has none 85.4
if b. lead b. both shall fall into ditch 445.3
in land of the b., one-eyed man is king 788.1
it is we that are b., not Fortune 85.3
none so b. as they that won't see 85.5
sky is not less blue because the b. man does not see it 777.6
sounds are things b. see 84.2
the b. esteem it be enough estate to see 184.1
**blindness:** there is a triple sight in b. keen 84.1
**bliss:** how quick old woe follows a little b. 1004.25
joy is b. without otherworldliness 407.10
one moment may with b. repay hours of pain 407.21

**blockhead:** a b. makes a b. of his companion 57.9
learned b. worse than ignorant b. 934.7
who deals with a b. needs much brain 934.20
**blood:** all soarings of my mind begin in my b. 584.11
b. cannot be washed out with b. 811.17
b. is heavy; who sheds it can't run away 516.1
b. is the god of war's rich livery 1035.64
noble and common b. are same color 37.4
ounce of b. worth more than pound of friendship 332.26
prison, b., death create enthusiasts 795.3
there is no sure foundation set on b. 516.13
**blood's:** b. thicker than water 789.2
**bloodsucker:** everyone has his own private b. 620.1
**blossoms:** b. of the heart no wind can touch 282.20
eyes of men love to pluck the b. 885.34
**blow:** to b., swallow at once isn't easy 221.17
**blunder:** worse than a crime, it is a b. 86.3
**blunders:** great b. made of multitude of fibres 86.6
pain of our b. never passes away 86.11
**blush:** b. that flies at seventeen is fixed at forty-nine 580.15
give friend cause to b.: likely lose him 886.8
his cheek is his biographer, as long as he can b. 871.1
we never forgive those who make us b. 886.5
**blushes:** man is only animal that b.—or needs to 886.10
man that b. is not quite a brute 886.11
whoever b. is already guilty 476.11
**blushing:** b. is the color of virtue 886.2
**boast:** b. not thyself of tomorrow 721.1
**boastful:** created after flea, man cannot be b. 433.27
**boat:** who take devil into b. must carry him 57.10
without oars you cannot cross in a b. 714.6
**boatmen:** too many b. will run boat up mountain 56.7
**boats:** light b. sail swift 944.6
nothing so worth doing as messing in b. 888.3
**bodies:** this is a world of b. 88.9
we have a world of contented b. 744.17
what is more important than our b. 88.7
**body:** b. always ends by being a bore 968.46
b. am I entirely, and nothing else 88.4
b. and spirit are twins 584.15
b. is a house of windows 544.10
b. is love's book 885.8
b. is not more than the soul 584.16
b. never forgives injury by mind 584.7
b. seeks what injured the mind with love 885.17
death reveals what a nothing the b. is 88.2
happiness is spirit fulfilled through b. 407.28
human b. is best picture of human soul 584.18
if any thing sacred the b. is sacred 88.10
in middle years scarcely a part of b. man would hesitate to turn over to authorities 580.20
lusts and greeds of b. scandalize soul 584.14
mind sins, not the b. 893.13
nature the b., God the soul 1010.10
poor b., time taught you use of clothes 88.1
pray for a sane mind in a sound b. 411.9
sound mind in sound b. is a happy state 411.11
though disfigured, to whom is b. not dear 88.6
trouble with preserving health of b. is to do it without destroying mind 411.2
we are ashamed of our own b. 431.5
**body's:** he is slave of many masters who is his b. slave 88.8
nothing so pierces soul as b. sigh 584.12
soul is the voice of the b. interests 584.13
**Bohemia:** B. is state of mind: scoffing at babbitts 89.7
B.: little country in which you do not live 89.3
**bold:** b. are helpless without cleverness 137.5
b. are not always men of principle 728.4
b. man does best, at home or abroad 90.8
b. man strikes for double value and compromises on par 1019.19
folly is always b. 351.8
Venus favors the b. 348.8
**boldest:** when hope is feeble, b. plans are safest 90.10
**boldness:** b. in business is the first thing 102.15
b. without propriety is insubordination 90.2
be not so clement as to encourage b. 883.5
decent b. ever meets with friends 90.7
**bolt:** it's folly to b. door with boiled carrot 850.3
**bomb:** excessive severity is the path to the b. 883.3
god of science has given us the atomic b. 633.9
H-b. favors small nations 633.15
no country without atom b. independent 633.4
no reasoning with an incendiary b. 46.4
**bombs:** Atom b. pile up 994.14
guns and b. are witness to human folly 226.7
people have settled down to living with b. 633.10
**bondage:** corrupt nations love b. more than liberty 188.9
familiarize yourself with chains of b. 107.6
**bonds:** b. that unite us exist only in our mind 787.9

they do most by b. who could do much without them 529.5
today's b. seem to be written in one day 91.16
true university is a collection of b. 535.1
we are too civil to b. 91.32
world of b. is delightful if you enter it as an adventurer 91.42
**bookworm:** b. with new novel is prepared for pleasure 698.20
b. wraps himself in web of generalities 91.45
**borders:** b. scratched across hearts of men 614.19
**bore:** b. consumes each year one and a half times his own weight in others' patience 93.7
b. is one who talks to you about himself 185.19
b. is the last to find himself out 93.4
b.: person who talks when you wish him to listen 93.2
secret of being b. is to tell everything 93.8
**bored:** better to be happy for moment than long b. 407.76
man only animal that can be b. 92.3
**boredom:** b. can become the sublimest of emotions 92.7
b.: the desire for desires 92.9
modern man has manufactured an abyss of b. 960.21
neglect more from b. than from interest 92.5
one must choose between b. and torment 92.8
passions are less mischievous than b. 92.1
prospect of being pleased tomorrow never consoles me for the b. of today 92.4
**bores:** b. we have with us even to the end 93.6
society is formed of b. and the bored 92.2
**born:** being b. is undeniably a start 81.5
he alone is blessed who ne'er was b. 939.38
man always dies before he is fully b. 402.7
man should be b., and b., die at once 81.1
we are b. crying, live complaining 536.39
**borne:** what cannot be altered must be b. 800.5
**borrow:** don't b. from a *nouveau riche* 749.20
have own horse and you may b. another's 94.8
human species made of men who b., lend 94.4
**borrowed:** b. cloak does not keep one warm 94.1
most men are rich in b. sufficiency 767.5
**borrower:** b. is servant to the lender 94.2
neither a b. nor a lender be 94.6
**borrowers:** b. of books, mutilators of collections 535.7
**boss:** Americans ruled by the B., the Trust 34.26
**Boston:** in B. they ask, how much does he know 926.3
**botany:** laws of gravity, chemistry, b. 843.8
**bottle:** it's only the first b. that's expensive 266.18
over the b. many a friend is found 266.64
**bottom:** b. is b., even if turned upside down 773.17
if thou canst not see the b., wade not 749.10
victories of fellows at the top aren't always victories for fellows at the b. 773.2
who cannot swim must go to the b. 461.5
who would climb must begin at the b. 938.9
**boundary:** b.: imaginary line between two nations 378.1
**boundless:** in b. universe, b. better, b. worse 388.26
**bounty:** b. receives value from manner of bestowal 382.21
**bourgeois:** b.: one who places anything above feeling 581.1
b. prefers convenience to liberty 581.2
**bow:** b. tensely strung is easily broken 620.13
stretch a b. very full, you will wish you had stopped in time 226.10
**boy:** b. is a piece of existence quite separate 95.2
b. is adult before parents think so 95.4
imagination of a b. is healthy 1064.32
prison-house shades close on growing b. 1064.60
speak roughly to your little b. 760.4
**boy's:** b. will is the wind's will 95.7
white b. badness is animal spirits; black b. badness is badness 83.15
**boyhood:** our b. is what any boy in our environment would have had 121.48
**boys:** acolyte knows what b. do behind altar 319.56
b. are the cash of war 1035.15
b. are unwholesome companions for grown people 95.6
b. have no sadness sadder than our hope 1064.48
b. look on all force as an enemy 95.1
b. spirited but not tender as daughter 215.1
no hope be put in melodious voice of b. 983.19
truly passionate are little b. 95.5
**brag:** I b. of not knowing something 520.19
**brain:** a man should keep his b. attic stocked with usable furniture 520.17
almost no limits to the discoveries of how the human b. operates 753.2
half a b. is enough if one says little 96.8
where the heart lies, let the b. lie also 282.7
who deals with a blockhead needs much b. 934.20
**brains:** each is satisfied with his own b. 155.2
everyone credits himself for more b., less money 869.6
long whiskers cannot take place of b. 45.17

many complain of looks, none of their b. 491.29
mob has many heads but no b. 591.5
our b. are seventy-year clocks 600.12
we can't all combine good looks, b. 539.12
you are shown out according to your b. 907.14
**brandy:** b. is lead in the morning, gold at night 266.21
who aspires to be a hero must drink b. 266.36
**brave:** all are b. on observing one who despairs 192.28
b. creature is part coward 192.40
b. man thinks no one his superior who does him an injury 474.18
b. men can make any danger spot tenable 213.13
b. or fortunate man can bear envy 293.25
coward calls b. rash; rash calls b. coward 192.3
coward shuns but b. chooses danger 192.15
coward sneaks to death, the b. live on 941.8
easy to be b. from a safe distance 192.1
fortune favors the b. 358.45
in misfortune even b. are discredited 745.14
man not b. who is afraid to be a coward 192.31
none but the b. deserves the fair 192.11
we become b. by performing b. actions 224.1
**bravery:** all b. stands upon comparisons 192.4
b. is forethought 356.4
b. is knowledge of cowardice in the enemy 192.19
**bravest:** b. spirits do not shrink from danger 192.39
**bray:** every ass loves to hear himself b. 1020.7
**bread:** better loaf wet with tears than unsalted b. 502.22
cast thy b. upon the waters 373.1
eaten b. is forgotten 473.3
finest poems are expedients to get b. 618.1
he who has no b. has no authority 712.52
in sweat of thy face shalt thou eat b. 1058.9
it's hard to pay for b. that's eaten 219.3
love is sweet, but tastes best with b. 548.252
man lives not by b. but by catchwords 1057.39
never fall out with you b. and butter 766.5
who live by b. alone submit to abuse 565.5
you can travel fifty thousand miles in America without once tasting good b. 352.7
**breakfast:** only dull people are brilliant at b. 599.6
pleasantest prospect indoors: b. table 272.14
**breaking:** b. and building go hand in hand 239.5
**breaks:** he that b. a thing to find out what it is 208.10
**breath:** one possession outvalues others: last b. 536.130
**breed:** men are more careful of the b. of their dogs, horses, than of their children 663.38
**breeding:** gentle-b. lies in wish to be agreeable 389.7
good b.: concealing how much we think of ourselves, how little of others 389.9
good b. finds favor at first sight 389.3
good b. is man's substitute for good nature 389.1
good b.: union of kindness, independence 389.6
lay aside good b., intimacy degenerates into coarse familiarity 497.1
scholar without good b. is a pedant 389.4
test of b. how one acts in quarrel 389.8
we are rabbit-like in our unplanned b. 707.7
with fowls, the pedigree; with men, b. 389.2
**brethren:** as ye have done it unto one of the least of my b., ye have done it unto me 430.3
souls of b. hovering, craving caress 548.125
**brevity:** b. good when we are or aren't understood 96.3
b. is the soul of wit 1054.33
life's b. makes architect's trade sad 50.5
**brewer:** best b. sometimes makes bad beer 455.2
**brews:** as he b., so shall he drink 809.10
**bribe:** refuses the b. but puts forth a hand 97.2
**bribery:** American way is to seduce a man by b. 188.8
**brickbats:** in New York City b. fly at all hours 625.8
**bride:** b. is certified check among wedding gifts 1044.5
b.: woman with fine prospect of happiness behind her 1044.2
desire in eyes of b. is a strong power 885.33
**bride-bed:** b: theirs alone till life's done 560.34
**bridge:** it's a bad b. that's shorter than stream 460.1
**brief:** honest b. has its own eloquence 525.23
to be b. is almost to be inspired 96.9
**brilliant:** only dull people are b. at breakfast 599.6
the b. passes; the true endures 991.50
**Britain:** B. may be more honored for way she disposed of empire than way she acquired it 287.20
in B. journalism is apt to be regarded as an extension of conversation 623.24
**Britannia:** what's more inseparable than beer and B. 287.27
**British:** B. have distinction of putting new wine in old bottles without bursting them 287.1
maxim of B. people: "business as usual" 287.7
no one can be as calculatedly rude as B. 486.2
**broken:** b. hand works, but not b. heart 549.13

unto a b. heart no other one may go 953.2
**bronze:** b. is the mirror of form; wine, of heart 266.1
**brook:** voice of b. an obbligato of creation 818.1
**broom:** hand that plies b. gives caresses 1058.33
new b. is good for three days 278.1
**brothels:** b. are built with bricks of religion 746.2
modesty, diffidence make man unfit for public affairs, b. 594.12
**brother:** sympathetic friend can be dear as b. 363.64
when you deal with your b., be pleasant, but get a witness 332.19
which of us has known his b. 908.56
**brother's:** primal eldest curse on a b. murder 516.14
why beholdest the mote in thy b. eye 872.1
**brotherhood:** b. of man precious—what there is of it 98.21
low capacity for getting along with those near goes with receptivity to idea of b. 98.7
theirs alone is b. who work together 198.34
where no b. there can be no peace 674.20
world is a neighborhood before becoming b. 1060.20
**brothers:** because men are unequal they need to be b. 469.1
between b., two witnesses and a notary 332.27
cruel is the strife of b. 332.3
freedom is to share chains our b. wear 361.37
good neighbor sees what makes men b. 619.7
if b. agree, no fortress so strong 332.1
live like b., do business like strangers 102.1
men are b., their pockets not sisters 332.32
men live like b. or die like beasts 98.16
there is a destiny which makes us b. 98.18
**brute:** man that blushes is not quite a b. 886.11
**brutes:** b. show wisdom in enjoying the present 41.26
**bucket:** only a b. half-full splashes 686.9
**budget:** b. is a mythical bean bag 99.4
federal b. reflects need of the people 99.2
**buffoons:** we are the b. of our children 663.1
**build:** Americans b. best when called on to b. greatly 34.29
to b. is to be robbed 198.19
too low they b., who b. beneath the stars 55.25
when we b., let us think we b. for ever 50.13
why b. cities, if man unbuilded goes 131.19
**building:** breaking and b. go hand in hand 239.5
he that, b., stays at one floor 198.20
if design of b. bad, antiquity is its only virtue 50.12
light is a principal beauty in a b. 50.6
**buildings:** we shape b.; thereafter they shape us 50.3
**builds:** man rejoices only in what he b. up 198.35
when one b. and another tears down, what do they gain but toil 239.1
**bull:** b. does not enjoy fame in two herds 539.15
it's easy to frighten a b. from a window 973.7
**bullet:** man who has forsworn b. is impotent 658.3
**bullets:** ballots rightful successors to b. 1030.12
**bundling:** motives in use of car, b. board, often the same 63.1
**burden:** b. in bush worth two on your hands 804.14
lacking b. he'll take up load of stones 866.7
none knows weight of another's b. 656.5
same b. weighs more heavily on some 196.11
to bear b. of others' faults worst 339.10
we shall bear any b. for liberty 534.20
**burdensome:** nothing is so b. as a secret 849.5
**bureaucracy:** b. comes to regard the public as enemy 100.2
**bureaucrat:** perfect b. manages to make no decisions 100.1
something about a b. doesn't like a poem 100.6
**burglar:** faults of b. are qualities of financier 927.10
**burglars:** old b. never die; just steal away 927.5
**burial:** after sixty, b. service becomes personal 365.7
all places alike, every earth fit for b. 693.9
**buried:** small difference to dead if b. in luxury 101.4
**burlesque:** something of b. in earnest, good men 879.3
**burn:** b. not house to fright away mice 791.5
let a man b. with intensity, he will set fire to the world 1066.4
little fire to warm, a great one to b. 183.9
**burnt:** b. child can't wait to get back at fire 319.43
who has b. his mouth blows his soup 319.23
**bush:** one beats b., another catches the bird 106.2
**bushel:** whole b. is made of single grains 467.11
**business:** attention to b. is price of success 938.43
b. of America is b. 102.10
b.: something goes through, something doesn't 102.4
big b. dangerous because of privileges 102.38
boldness in b. is the first thing 102.15

bonus is one great give-away in b. 102.36
build b. up big enough, it's respectable 102.30
crime is extension of behavior in b. 201.18
dinner lubricates b. 272.28
dispatch is the soul of b. 102.8
everybody's b. is nobody's b. 804.7
if everybody minded their own b., the world would go round faster 571.2
it's better to be at ease than at b. 530.6
live like brothers, do b. like strangers 102.1
man in b. puts up affronts if he loves quiet 102.28
man minds his b., if it's worth minding 571.5
man of b. may talk of philosophy, man who has none may practise it 688.31
maxim of British people: "b. as usual" 287.7
perpetual devotion to b. is sustained by neglect of many other things 102.34
study to be quiet and to do your own b. 571.1
time is the measure of b. 102.2
we must keep b. separate from life 102.19
without dissimulation no b. possible 221.2
**businessman:** b. who is novelist drops in on literature 1062.90
no b. who believes all he is told does well 102.29
**busy:** aging is a habit b. man hasn't time for 646.69
b. life is nearest to a purposeful life 10.10
b. person never knows how much he weighs 10.11
being b. is proof of happiness 10.19
if thou be not b. for thyself now, who shall be b. for thee in time to come 1058.66
if you want work well done, select b. man 10.12
**busyness:** b., travelling to and from 10.2
**butter:** one cannot shoot with b. but with guns 1042.2
**buttercups:** condescending to be of b. the friend 621.1
**butterfly:** b. counts moments and has time enough 971.61
b. is sure flowers owe thanks to him 397.12
consider ways of b. and get wise 322.1
**buy:** friend you b. will be bought from you 97.4
he that speaks ill of the mare will b. her 103.6
he who findeth fault meaneth to b. 103.8
if you don't want prosperity to falter, b. 103.20
**buyer:** b. needs hundred eyes, seller not one 103.13
**buying:** forgive us for frantic b. and selling 103.26
man's happiness consists in b. all he can 407.43
**by-and-by:** b. is easily said 228.12

# C

**Caesar:** render to C. the things that are C.'s 125.1
**cafe:** home has more variety than c. society 700.1
**cage:** he yearns for c. if conceived in c. 107.9
narrower the c., sweeter the liberty 107.2
**Cain:** he who bears brand of C. shall rule 516.16
**cake:** we praise when c., not ours, is divided 438.17
**calamities:** c. of two kinds: misfortune to ourselves and good fortune to others 17.8
high heart ought to bear c. and not flee 17.3
regret c. only if it helps the sufferer 692.11
**calamity:** c. is man's true touchstone 17.5
easy for one outside c. to give advice 19.2
every c. is a spur and valuable hint 17.20
great c. is old an hour after happening 622.5
in another's c., see what ills to avoid 17.49
public c. is a mighty leveller 17.13
**calculus:** I'm very good at differential c. 277.30
**California:** C., advance post of our civilisation 104.1
**call:** he who awaits the c., but sees the need, already sets his spirit to refuse it 784.3
**calling:** every c. great when greatly pursued 1029.7
we are c. across incalculable gulfs 908.22
**calls:** c. and the theater propagate platitudes 185.34
**calm:** any can hold helm when sea is c. 528.18
calm's not life's crown, though c. is well 982.1
mind which renounces hope grows c. 800.6
there is no joy but c. 982.10
to bear truths with c. is sovereignty 159.2
**calmness:** c. is always Godlike 159.1
nothing is so aggravating as c. 159.5
**calumnies:** c. are answered best with silence 898.7
**calumny:** be chaste as ice, thou shan't escape c. 898.16
c. ever pursues the great 898.11
mysterious power of flattery and c. 199.4
**camel:** c.-driver jogs on to end of journey 679.9
easier for c. to go through eye of needle than rich man to enter kingdom of God 1041.7
if c. once get his nose in the tent 188.1
**camera:** c. encourages photographer to keep on looking 689.1
**camp:** c.: vision of the world in terms of style 307.6
lover of C. appreciates vulgarity 1031.3
**campaign:** effort put into c. by worker 704.9
prosperity first theme of political c. 705.77
solutions not expected in political c. 1030.13

**campus:** three administrative problems on c. 277.46
**Canada:** geography made America and C. neighbors 105.1
**candid:** save me from the c. friend 360.2
**candidate:** c. for office can have no greater advantage than muddled syntax 705.49
**candidates:** merchandise c. like breakfast cereal 1030.21
to c., "every intelligent voter" means those who will vote for them 705.1
**candle:** better to light a c. than curse darkness 430.7
how far that little c. throws his beams 430.31
my c. burns at both ends 511.6
unnecessary to light a c. to the sun 56.4
**candles:** all c. out, all cats gray 295.10
**candor:** faults forgiven of man of perfect c. 360.14
world of vested interests doesn't want c. 493.10
**candy:** c is dandy but liquor is quicker 266.43
**cant:** c. of criticism is the most tormenting 204.54
**canter:** c. is cure for every evil 815.1
**cap:** once you have the c. and gown whatever nonsense you talk becomes wisdom 277.56
**capacities:** we magnify man's rights, minimize his c. 231.24
**capacity:** as is our confidence, so is our c. 854.2
**capital:** much cant of common interests of c., labor 106.1
**capitalism:** c. is the exploitation of man by man; communism is the reverse 149.7
**capitalist:** if being a c. is a crime 275.5
show me c., I'll show you bloodsucker 106.5
**caprice:** c. lasts longer than lifelong passion 1046.3
**captain's:** c. choleric word is blasphemy in soldier 773.22
**car:** c. has become secular sanctuary 63.5
c. is dress without which we are unclad 63.6
everything in life is somewhere else, and you get there in a c. 63.11
**caravan:** dogs bark, but the c. moves on 156.2
**card:** man's idee in a c. game is war 367.2
**cards:** all men are equal—at c. 367.5
c. are war, in disguise of sport 367.8
game iv c. may start among frinds, but I niver see frinds in a game iv c. 367.3
I complain c. ill shuffled till my hand is good 358.43
sorry I have not learnt to play at c. 367.7
true luck consists not in holding best c. 367.6
**care:** c. and diligence bring luck 279.8
c. corrosive for things not remedied 43.11
not to c. is never to be born 464.7
teach us to c. and not to c. 800.3
we don't c. at all 464.1
**cares:** c. fold tents like Arabs, steal away 607.27
if desires are endless, c. will be so 401.11
those with no c. fear next life 412.4
**caresses:** ceremonial of c. is convention 894.3
**cargo:** admire little ship; put c. in big one 714.5
**caricatures:** each society reduces its opponents to c. 928.3
**carnal:** our life ought to be material and c. 710.6
**carpenter:** the house praises the c. 6.7
the worse the c., the more the chips 461.2
you may scold c. who has made bad table 203.15
**carried:** who is c. does not realize how far the town is 233.9
**cars:** people in c. look worse 63.7
**case:** who can't mend own c. will impair other's 293.4
**cases:** all c. are unique, and similar to others 752.6
great c. like hard c. make bad law 525.42
**cash:** ah, take the c. and let the credit go 723.24
if a little doesn't go, much c. will not come 501.1
life is a bubble floated by solid c. 596.56
**cask:** every c. smells of wine it contains 117.26
**caste:** ideas are fatal to c. 441.10
**castration:** monastic incarceration is c. 595.2
**cat:** c. in gloves catches no mice 377.4
c. leaves her mark upon her friend 557.16
c. may look on a king 773.11
c. pent up becomes a lion 107.3
c.: to be kicked when things go wrong 41.5
to cross man with c. would improve man, deteriorate c. 41.29
trouble with a kitten is it becomes a c. 41.21
what comes of a c. will catch mice 415.1
when I play with c., who makes more sport 290.3
**catastrophes:** c. come when dominant institution crumbles at the touch of what seems an idea 485.10
**catch:** wolves can't c. what dogs don't expose 162.11
**catching:** with c. end pleasures of chase 8.5
**catchwords:** man lives not upon bread, but by c. 1057.39
**cathedral:** Gothic c. is a blossoming in stone 50.4
synagogue lifts its walls by side of c. 790.32
who bears in his heart a c. 55.18
**Catholic:** being C. is like working within a sonnet 123.17
C. must adopt the decision handed him 123.23
**cats:** all candles out, all c. gray 295.10
c. are delicate but never suffer insomnia 41.17
c., like men, are flatterers 41.18
c. seem to think it never harms to ask 41.16

scalded c. fear even cold water 319.22
who play with c. will be scratched 213.4
who won't feed c. must feed mice, rats 929.2
**cause:** best c. requires a good pleader 109.5
c. breaks or exalts soldier's strength 582.15
faith in c. substitute for faith in self 109.12
faith in holy c. must be extravagant 109.13
First C. worked automatically 385.38
God is indwelling c. of all things 385.70
good c. makes stout heart, strong arm 109.9
good c., yet money must carry it 109.8
he who hath worst c. makes most noise 109.10
if a c. be good, attack will not injure it so much as injudicious defense 109.3
in a just c. the weak beat the strong 109.15
just c. needs no interpreting 525.22
just c. never lacks good arguments 109.7
just c. not ruined by a few mistakes 109.4
nothing can be lower than c. of all things 385.65
nothing so defeated as yesterday's c. 938.26
our least deed wends its way to sea of c. and effect 108.6
strong men believe in c. and effect 108.3
take away c. and effect ceases 108.1
truth never damages a c. that is just 109.11
who serve greater c. make c. serve them 109.6
**causes:** small c. can make a man uneasy 989.16
**cautious:** if you cannot be chaste, be c. 120.10
look beyond each action, be very c. 173.10
when a man feels the difficulty of doing, can he be other than c. 110.2
**celebrated:** we imagine works of c. men are commonly admired because their names are 330.23
**celebrity:** c.: I picture myself as a bust with legs 330.13
c. in politics or trade gains esteem for intellectual taste or skill 490.5
c.: known by those who don't know you 330.11
c. works to be known, then shields face 330.3
c.'s name is worth more than services 330.9
the c. is created by the media 416.2
we have made God the biggest c. 385.9
**celerity:** c. is the mother of good fortune 919.3
c. never more admired than by negligent 919.4
no secrecy comparable to c. 919.1
**celestial:** one c. father gives to all 385.50
**celibacy:** marriage has pains, c. no pleasures 65.4
**cello:** c. is like woman grown younger 608.3
**cemetery:** c.: only place we do not meet dead again 101.8
if anyone puts hand on you, send him to c. 1024.9
when live next to c., cannot weep for all 953.13
**censoriousness:** hating leaves to virtue nothing but c. 410.9
**censors:** no government ought to be without c. 111.5
respectable minority useful as c. 111.6
**censorship:** assassination is extreme form of c. 111.10
c. a stupid giant traffic policeman 111.1
c. may preserve, but not restore, morality 111.9
we get nervous about freedom and admit c. 111.2
where official c., speech is serious 111.3
**censure:** c. is tax paid for being eminent 203.31
c. of man's self is oblique praise 857.7
folly to c. him whom all the world adores 203.26
he has right to c. who has heart to help 203.25
let such c. freely who have written well 204.42
no man can justly c., condemn another, for no man truly knows another 797.4
take each man's c., but reserve judgment 203.30
**censured:** none are so much praised, c., as we think 1020.5
**censuring:** we are pert at c., cannot endure advice 203.24
**census:** we are at mercy of c.-taker and c.-maker 925.1
**century:** problem of twentieth c. is color-line 769.5
twentieth c. afflicted by power failure 994.1
**ceremonies:** surround friendship with c. and respects 112.3
**ceremony:** c. devised to set gloss on faint deeds 112.6
c. forbids, we obey; reason forbids, nobody obeys 743.3
c. is the smoke of friendship 112.2
man without c. needs great merit 559.12
**certain:** it is c. that nothing is c. 113.2
there is little about which one can be c. 113.9
we are c. about things we do not understand 113.5
we are not c., we are never c. 998.2
when we are c., we're impervious to fear 340.16
**certainties:** c. are arrived at only on foot 113.12
**certainty:** belief in divine mission a form of c. 333.18
c. generally is illusion 113.6
one unchangeable c. is nothing is certain 113.8
only earthly c. is oblivion 983.25

quest for c. blocks the search for meaning 998.5
reasonable probability is only c. 113.7
woman's guess is more accurate than man's c. 576.23
**chaining:** in c. multitude, seem to wear same fetters 995.33
**chains:** if any in c., all freedom endangered 107.4
intelligence in c. loses in lucidity 491.3
**challenge:** measure of a man: his stand in time of c. 250.8
**chameleons:** we are c., and our prejudices change 720.16
**champagne:** no government could survive without c. 245.3
**chance:** be a football to time and c. 502.8
c. gives and removes thoughts 114.15
c. makes a football of man's life 114.18
c. provides leap out of reach of oneself 114.6
call life today your own, rest belongs to c. 114.10
does random c., change, control the world 263.2
great actions often are result only of c. 224.15
no shame in the accidents of c. 1063.20
we are ruled by c. 114.9
we cannot bear to regard ourselves as playthings of blind c. 114.5
we lean on thought c. will bring us through 224.2
who await no gifts from c., conquer fate 114.3
why need man fear since c. is all in all 114.19
wise man turns c. to good fortune 114.11
**chances:** life is full of c. and changes 114.2
there are no c. against God 114.4
**change:** accept past till need for c. cries out 115.20
all is c.; all yields place and goes 115.14
be content with what you are; wish not c. 930.7
c. as c. is flux, and insults intelligence 115.10
c. due to truths in and out of favor 115.17
c. is death of that which was 115.29
c. is scientific, progress is ethical 115.33
c. is the basic law 115.4
c. is the law of life 115.26
c. prepares the ground for revolution 813.23
displacement of a little sand can c. the course of deep rivers 989.3
even luxury finds zest in c. 554.4
for happiness, man needs hope and c. 407.93
from c. to c. men's being rolls 115.1
habit will reconcile us to all but c. 404.4
happy who learns to bear what he cannot c. 800.9
in c. unhappiness remembers happiness 115.15
in worst of fortune is best chance for c. 358.11
loss is c. and c. is nature's delight 547.5
love fears c. more than destruction 548.151
man delights in mere c. of activity 1058.53
men seldom c.; hearts remain the same 116.4
more things c., more they remain same 115.25
nothing is permanent but c. 115.22
only in c. is true security to be found 850.10
progress is a nice word but c. is its motivator 115.27
state without c. is without means of conservation 923.5
there's relief in c.—even bad to worse 115.24
time works c. for better or worse 115.31
to remain young one must c. 115.8
we only c. our fancies 450.6
when the man you like switches, he has courage to c. his mind 462.1
who tries to c. his life tries in vain 783.20
**changeableness:** sudden resolutions indicate little but c. 801.3
**changed:** universe c. by inspiring people 783.30
we c. with the times 181.7
**changelessness:** happiness is never so welcome as c. 116.3
**changes:** absurd man is he who never c. 115.2
all c. are alike in American society 34.67
c. are melancholy; part of us is left behind 115.16
cultural c. begin in affectation 115.3
life is full of chances and c. 114.2
the world's a scene of c. 115.9
weep not that the world c. 115.6
wise man c. his mind, fool never 347.4
**changing:** it's a happy chance if we, c., continue to love a changed person 548.132
**chaos:** c. often breeds life; order, habit 255.1
c. stamped with a seal becomes order 255.2
need c. to give birth to dancing star 198.28
**character:** all c. can be destroyed by ridicule 814.7
between selves and real natures we put our c. 117.16
c. forms at first pinch of anxiety 117.28
c. is inured habit 117.22
c. much easier kept than recovered 117.21
c. not developed in ease and quiet 117.15
c. tested by sentiments more than conduct 117.1
conceit is to c. what salt is to ocean 163.9
conscience is the frame of c. 171.1
events expand with the c. 303.3
genius formed in quiet; c., in life stream 117.13
gnarled nodosities of c. move liking 117.24
good, evil lie close; no unity in c. 388.1
happiness is not the end of life: c. is 117.2
his own c. is arbiter of one's fortune 117.23
I can't smell c. unless it stinks 117.6
if strong, our c. will speak for itself 933.14

judge your c. by your dreams 264.4
knowledge has outstripped c. development 277.19
life is what our c. makes it 860.10
look at eye: how can man conceal c. 117.18
loss of c. spells ruin 117.17
man that makes a c. makes foes 117.29
man's c. is his guardian divinity 117.14
man's real c. comes out in asides 117.25
more peculiarly his own a man's c. is, the better it fits him 117.5
mystery should be left in c. 965.38
no man can climb out beyond the limitations of his own c. 117.19
no public c. ever stood revelation of private utterance, correspondence 330.1
nobody can think himself a strong c. 933.2
one can acquire all in solitude but c. 908.49
opinion of world is confession of c. 117.10
people betray c. in what they laugh at 523.10
people with courage, c., seem sinister 192.18
religion of c. apt to be invaded by religious training 790.20
society: masked ball where all hide c. 907.2
space of life in which c. is undecided 1064.32
trust c. more than an oath 628.8
value of culture is its effect on c. 207.14
we find the finished c. only in fragments 677.8
we may be whatever c. we choose 860.1
we need someone on whom to mould our c. 308.6
what a man is depends on his c. 127.9
when person lacks c., needs method 117.4
who plays deep must lose money or c. 367.1
you show c. when you act, sit, or sleep 117.7
**character's:** when c. right, looks are greater delight 117.20
**characters:** as if our own handiwork, we value our c. 117.11
others are to us like c. in fiction 656.11
wealth with us a moment; only our c. steadfast 1041.25
when c. are alive before their author 341.15
**charcoal:** you can't write in the chimney with c. 640.2
**charitable:** he is rich who hath enough to be c. 1041.10
**charities:** posthumous c. are selfish made by those who, when alive, would part with nothing 1051.2
**charity:** all mankind's concern is c. 118.8
c. gives itself rich 382.14
c., personal force are the only worthwhile investments 118.11
c. should not end at home 118.5
c. that is trifle to us can be precious to others 881.8
did universal c. prevail, earth would be a heaven, hell a fable 118.3
generosity relinquished to practice c. 430.5
he that has no c. deserves no mercy 118.4
how shall we expect c. towards others, when we are uncharitable to ourselves 857.1
I little fear God will damn man with c. 118.7
if c. cost no money, world would be full of philanthropists 430.36
in all things, c. 118.1
silver ore of c. an expensive article 118.10
unreal is c. without sympathy 9.5
with malice toward none, c. for all 1009.8
**charm:** c. is a product of the unexpected 119.5
c. is a sort of bloom on a woman 119.2
c. is glow that casts light on others 119.3
c.: that quality in others of making us more satisfied with ourselves 119.1
**charmer:** a beauty you notice; a c. notices you 119.7
**charming:** all c. people, I fancy, are spoiled 119.9
c. people live up to edge of charm 119.6
people are either c. or tedious 119.8
**charms:** c. strike the sight, but merit wins soul 578.6
corporeal c. may gain admirers, but there must be mental c. to retain them 119.4
do not all c. fly at touch of philosophy 688.14
**chase:** I flee who chases me and c. who flees me 195.11
with catching end pleasures of c. 8.5
**chaste:** be warm, but pure; be amorous, but be c. 120.3
if you cannot be c., be cautious 120.10
only c. woman is one not asked 120.11
twenty lascivious turtles found ere c. man 120.9
**chastise:** he only may c. who loves 760.14
**chastity:** c. in old man: disability to be unchaste 120.5
c. is orientation of life towards goal 120.2
c. often the effect of lack of appetite 120.7
c. triumphs over love, death over c. 983.15
c.: wealth coming from abundance of love 120.12
filth and old age are wardens upon c. 120.4
give me c., but not just now 120.1
woman's c., like onion, is series of coats 120.8
**chatter:** I c., c., as I flow 818.4
**cheap:** c. coat makes a c. man 265.27
never buy what you do not want because it is c.; it will be costly to you 103.17
prosperity has everything c. 744.11
what we obtain too c., we esteem lightly 1019.13
**cheat:** c. me in price, not in goods 103.25
man must be careful not to c. neighbor 598.16
**cheated:** no man is more c. than the selfish man 867.1
when c., wife or husband feels same 470.4

who's c. twice by same man is accomplice 866.5
**cheating:** better fail with honor than win by c. 327.23
usual trade is c. by consent 102.16
**check:** every one pays light-heartedly by c. 596.4
**cheek:** where's the c. that doth not fade 331.9
whoever shall smite thee, turn other c. 658.1
**cheer:** what is good c. if death threats disrupt 407.65
**cheerfulness:** c. is a habit of mind; mirth, an act 390.1
c. is proper to the cock 80.6
the more c. is spent, the more remains 390.5
**cheese:** c.—milk's leap toward immortality 352.4
can't govern country with 246 kinds of c. 359.3
**chemistry:** laws of gravity, c., botany 843.8
**chess:** man hates to be beaten at c. by woman 576.54
**chickens:** you can't hatch c. from fried eggs 356.8
**chides:** who sharply c. most readily pardons 797.5
**chiding:** c. is better than heartbreak 797.11
**chief:** c. assumes responsibility 528.20
**chiefs:** multiple c. disappear for lack of unity 528.16
**child:** all women fight fiercely for a c. 663.19
beat your c. once a day; he knows why 760.5
burnt c. can't wait to get back at fire 319.43
c. does not fear thought of aging 121.39
c. fussed over gets feeling of destiny 121.44
c. hasn't grown-up's appetite for affection 121.42
c. is father of the man 402.27
c. is hungry and curious all over 121.49
c. not smiled on by mother is not worthy of the gods 121.16
c. should always say what's true 121.45
c. shows his toy; man hides his 698.30
depend on c.: blindness in one eye 233.8
each c. may be new, poetic experience 663.23
easier to head institute for c. guidance than make brat into decent human 663.32
energy which makes c. hard to manage is energy which later makes him manage life 121.4
everyone thinks own c. handsome 163.14
give little love to c., get great deal 121.37
greatest reverence is due to a c. 663.30
hard words bruise the heart of a c. 121.29
making terms with reality is a full-time business for the c. 121.41
more to be learned from questions of c. 478.15
mother-c. relation is paradoxical 663.21
mother glad to get loveliest c. asleep 121.11
no one keeps a secret so well as a c. 849.15
presence of c. turns parents into idiots 663.13
rich c. often sits in poor mother's lap 663.14
sharper than serpent's tooth: thankless c. 473.9
sweet c. is the sweetest thing in nature 121.27
to become as c. one must overcome youth 476.7
to make c. in your own image a capital crime; your image not worth repeating 663.50
train up a c. in the way he should go 981.1
what should a simple c. know of death 121.51
when a woman is twenty, a c. deforms her; at forty, he makes her her young again 663.8
when c. has left room, toys are affecting 121.12
when I was a c., I spake as a c. 567.1
who takes c. by hand takes mother by heart 121.9
wise father knows his own c. 663.49
wretched c. does not return parents' care 473.2
**child's:** c. liberty concealed from him 361.3
c. nature too serious to be regarded as a mere appendage to another being 121.26
great man is he who does not lose c. heart 476.6
**childhood:** c. brings heaven to our rough earthliness 121.1
c. is the kingdom where nobody dies 121.32
c. weaves invisible garment around us 680.3
our c. is what we alone have had 121.48
pleasure of c. is in mysteries 121.21
we do not have c., maturity, old age 537.13
**childishness:** last scene of all is second c., oblivion 646.93
**childless:** noblest works come from c. men 198.1
**childlike:** c. man not one whose development has been arrested 402.8
**children:** after c. born begins the trouble, care 981.7
age shows what c. we remain 646.40
all men know their c. mean more than life 663.16
artists are by definition c. 53.107
best way to advise your c. 663.52
c. are always cruel 206.9
c. are anchors that hold a mother to life 121.43
c. are completely egoistic 121.17
c. are God's apostles of love and hope 121.30
c. are natural mythologists 121.40
c. are poor men's riches 121.14
c. are ruined through virtues of parents 663.12
c. are the true connoisseurs 121.25
c. discern true law of life 536.129
c. endow parents with immortality 663.44
c. entitled to otherness, as anyone is 121.36
c. fed with mouthfuls of pap 420.2

c. have intelligence, ardor, clarity 121.23
c. have never failed to imitate elders 121.3
c. have reverted to being little devils 121.38
c. have to be educated and educate selves 277.12
c. know grace of God better than most 121.31
c. need models rather than critics 121.24
c. pick up words as pigeons peas 121.35
c. rarely forgive their parents 121.50
c. should be led by persuasion 981.10
c. sweeten labours but make misfortunes more bitter 663.4
c. when little make parents fools 121.34
c. will not fear life if their elders do not fear death 538.8
capable men are c. more than once a day 450.5
delicate skin, sweet breath of c. 121.15
excessive love of c. at expense of men 548.199
gods visit sins of fathers on the c. 809.9
hypocrisy deceives men; c. recognize it 438.26
if you love your c., you will slap them 883.2
impossible to love one's c. all day long 663.47
in age of progress in care of c., c. put at mercy of terrible weapons 633.2
in America parents obey their c. 34.82
in survival of c., parents can think of world in which they will have no share 663.37
in world of c. injustice is finely felt 121.10
less comfort having c. than sorrow in parting with them 663.24
let c. walk with nature, and they will learn that death is stingless 616.54
life of c. is wholly governed by desires 121.2
life's aspirations come in the guise of c. 121.46
love, c., work are sources of contact 502.23
man lucky if c. make his happiness 663.18
men are but c. of a larger growth 558.17
men more careful of breed of dogs than c. 663.38
men not on speaking terms with c. cease to be men, become machines 121.47
mothers more devoted to c. than fathers 663.2
no end to violations by c. on c. 121.6
no greater pain for mortals than seeing their c. dead 218.49
no test for parentage in interest of c. 663.51
one hopes things turn out better for c. 121.5
our c. know, suffer the armed men 809.1
parents must allow c. to understand them 663.46
rich and poor alike love their c. 663.17
some seem as if they were never c. 402.17
sorrow makes us all c. again 911.14
stars through window pane are my c. 616.41
to produce music is also to produce c. 607.32
unfortunate for chubby c. to watch basketball, regard it as their exercise 690.4
we are more taken with the games of our c. than with their complete actions 121.33
we are the buffoons of our c. 663.1
we delight in beauty, happiness of c. 121.13
we need high-quality c., not just c. 707.5
what c. hear at home is soon abroad 121.19
where parents do too much for c. 663.27
who loves not c. broods nest of sorrows 332.30
wife and c. hostages to fortune 332.4
you may give your c. your love but not your thoughts 663.26
your c. are sons and daughters of life's longing for itself 121.20
**children's:** no man has had enough of c. gratitude 575.18
**chimera:** what a c. then is man 558.42
**chimney:** you can't write in the c. with charcoal 640.2
**chip:** c. on shoulder reason for walking erect 727.29
**chivalries:** by c. the seeds of smiles are planted 517.8
**choice:** c. compels c. 122.4
difficulty in life is the c. 122.6
door of c. is not open to thee or me 183.13
doubts and temptations accompany every important c. 933.2
life's terrible c. is between good, bad 388.3
necessity relieves us from c. 617.20
principle of growth lies in human c. 402.5
reason also is c. 778.22
there's small c. in rotten apples 305.36
very few live by c. 358.22
what man wants is independent c. 122.2
who does anything by custom makes no c. 210.17
**choices:** men have thousand desires to bushel of c. 236.4
**choke:** big mouthfuls often c. 401.15
**choose:** we cannot wisely c. unless we know both good and evil 388.13
**chooseth:** as a man c. so is he 122.3
**Christ:** C. beats his drum, but does not press men 123.5
fashion parade on Fifth Avenue measures denial of C. 418.1
how but by broken heart may C. enter in 123.28
must then a C. perish in every age 561.16
**Christ's:** no kingdom suffered as many wars as C. 123.21
**Christian:** C. believes New Testament book admirably suited to spiritual needs of his neighbor 78.2
C. is theorizing Jew 510.2
C. religion attended with miracles 123.16
C. traditions have lost their hold by maturing of general mind 123.9
in Christendom where is the C. 123.7
no man a C. who cheats his fellows 123.18
to Jew, C. is daring man 510.1

true C. a pilgrim and a stranger 123.24
**Christian's:** prayer is a goodly C. weapon 717.22
**Christian Scientists:** if C.S. had science, doctors Christianity 572.3
**Christianity:** C. a treasure-chamber of consolations 123.22
C. begins by making people unhappy 123.11
C. does not absorb; it repulses 123.12
C. has sunk into religiosity 123.27
C. supplies hell for people who disagree, heaven for friends 123.15
Eros poisoned by C. degenerated to vice 885.25
glory of C. is to conquer by forgiveness 123.1
idealistic C. is attacked by idealists 123.8
modern C. has reduced man to gossiping about God 123.26
most sects of C. pervert its essence 123.13
no one is without C. 123.10
truth is only a horse for C. 123.6
**Christians:** C. have burnt each other, persuaded that Apostles would have done as they did 123.3
C. want something for nothing 510.5
C. who lose faith keep sense of sin 123.4
C. who stand with one leg on earth also stand with only one leg in heaven 123.2
in visible church true C. are invisible 124.8
Jew struck by anonymity, not virtues, of C. 123.25
Occident is part of world inhabited by C. 438.3
own dealing teaches C. to suspect others 257.18
what makes good C. makes good citizens 130.12
**church:** beautiful to have c. always open 126.1
c. and state are indispensable Molochs 125.3
c. must be the conscience of the state 125.5
c. must issue common money of love 124.1
disputation will prove scab of c. 124.14
end of being is to harmonize man with order; c. has been a good pitch-pipe 790.31
go to funeral, not c., to be uplifted 365.9
holy man without learning: enemy of c. 125.6
how often we go to c. only to see company 151.8
in c. false sentiment is frequent 124.5
in c., true Christians are invisible 124.8
many bring clothes to c., not selves 126.4
my own mind is my own c. 124.10
perhaps c. is trying to lock the stable door after the Messiah has been stolen 124.9
what c. I go to is my business 790.42
who builds c. to God, not to fame 433.19
who is near the c. is often far from God 124.7
**churches:** forgive us for turning c. into clubs 126.8
no objection to c. so long as they do not interfere with God's work 124.2
**cigar:** good c. is a smoke 975.7
**cigarette:** smokers inject idleness with every c. 975.3
**cinema:** at drive-in c., nature is available 604.5
**circumstance:** c. gives an action its character 592.12
endurance of friendship depends upon c. 363.37
I am myself plus my c. 127.6
the c. is nature, what you may do 127.3
we give joy to the c. 127.4
**circumstances:** c. are the creatures of man, not man of c. 127.2
it is futile to rail at c. 127.1
some look for c., or make them 127.8
what a man does depends on his c. 127.9
**circus:** c.: where horses see men acting the fool 128.1
**citadel:** man, like spider, may spin his own c. 448.15
man's estate is as a c. 361.44
**cities:** c. are, by definition, full of strangers 129.24
c. degrade us by magnifying trifles 129.14
c. produce corrupt, ferocious men 129.22
c. rob men of eyes and hands and feet 129.33
in c. men are like stones in a bag 129.34
in c. poverty has different appearances 712.30
in great c. men are more callous 129.10
mountains are a feeling; hum of c., torture 129.7
neglecting our c., we neglect the nation 129.27
sweetest souls soon canker in c. 129.29
**citizen:** c. is influenced by principle 130.7
c. is to man as alley-cat to jungle cat 130.5
c. wiser than fathers of country 130.3
humblest c., with righteous cause, stronger than all the hosts of error 816.4
I am a c. of the world 190.2
not same to be good man and good c. 130.1
political action highest responsibility of c. 705.38
requisite of good c. is to pull weight 130.8
state is servant, not master, of the c. 923.12
**citizens:** ants are good c. 479.1
before man made us c. nature made us men 431.15
c. equally free, not equally powerful 130.10
in America there must be only c. 130.6
no such things as private c. 754.3
what makes good Christians makes good c. 130.12
**citizenship:** c.: the right to have rights 130.11
c. won by immigrants equal to c. by birth 179.4

**city:** c.: aggregate of incongruous materials 129.15
c. has a face; country, a soul 191.11
c. man knows nothing of midnight 129.37
commuters give c. its restlessness; natives give it solidity; settlers give it passion 129.40
confusion, epitome of what c. is herself 129.42
God made the first garden, Cain, first c. 129.12
great c.—great solitude 129.16
great c. has greatest men and women 129.41
great c. is not the same as populous one 129.1
I have an affection for a great c. 129.31
illness of American c. is voicelessness 129.13
in the big c. a man will disappear suddenly 129.20
men, not houses, make the c. 129.17
no c. should be too large for a man to walk out of in a morning 129.11
quiet c. is a contradiction in terms 129.5
sample of the country does the c. good 129.35
the c. is squalid and sinister 129.32
thing generally raised on c. land: taxes 129.39
to know and be not known, live in a c. 129.9
to one long in c. pent 191.9
very populous c. is rarely well governed 129.2
we don't get life in the c. 129.19
what is the c. but the people 129.36
**civic:** without c. morality communities perish 598.40
**civil:** c. denial better than rude grant 784.4
c. dissension is a viperous worm 250.13
c.-rights movement has restored dignity of indignation 817.17
c. service a fortress of forms, red tape 100.5
forgive us for condemning c. disobedience 1025.55
government laws are needed to give us c. rights; God is needed to make us c. 817.16
no creature perfectly c. but a husband 389.5
**civility:** c. not sign of weakness 894.11
**civilization:** c. advances; each war they kill a new way 131.22
c. built on what is required of men 131.28
c. can rise again from the Wastepaper Age 994.2
c. exists so there may be no masses 675.1
c. favors mind at expense of body 131.20
c. is a movement, not a condition 131.29
c. is barbarism in lamb's skin 131.1
c. is condition of present customs 210.9
c. is the making of civil persons 131.24
c. of one epoch becomes manure of next 131.7
can't make c. around core of militarism 582.16
child of c. susceptible to nature 616.49
combustion of present with past forms c. 131.6
consumption of alcohol sure test of c. 131.10
crimes of c. worse than those of barbarism 131.2
every advance in c. has been denounced as unnatural while recent 131.25
farmers are founders of human c. 334.8
good c., a tree; bad c., an umbrella 131.4
men march toward c. in column formation 131.5
nation advances in c. by increasing in wealth and accessories 131.15
provision for poor is true test of c. 430.17
savagery is necessary antidote to c. 69.3
shall we confer our c. on peoples that sit in darkness 456.5
social moulds c. fits us into 131.13
speech is c. itself 916.41
strong c. fills man to the brim 131.27
survival of c. depends on what man desires 949.4
test of c. is kind of man it turns out 131.11
there is no high c. without ample leisure 530.1
triumph of c.: taming of human male 131.18
without adventure c. is in decay 16.8
**civilizations:** c. die from philosophical calm 131.16
**civilized:** anybody can gain a reputation for being c. 265.30
c. get more out of life than uncivilized 502.7
c. man: free, talking of what he may do 131.3
c. man is a larger mind but more imperfect nature than the savage 131.12
c. man's pastime: croolty to other c. man 131.9
c. race would add art of playing well 697.10
in c. life, man is acting a studied part 819.3
men have been barbarians longer than c. 69.4
nature is rarely allowed into c. society 131.31
test of a c. person is self-awareness 868.8
we cut our nails to appear c. 131.21
**clapping:** c. with right hand only won't produce noise 187.3
**clarification:** sanity, soundness, flourish in culture of c. 640.3
**clarinet:** c.: instrument of torture operated by a person with cotton in his ears 608.2
**clarity:** c. is politeness of man of letters 132.5
**class:** diminution of reality of c. lessens our ability to see difference, specialness 133.4
in c. society, thinking branded by its c. 133.2
independence: that's middle class c. blasphemy 233.11
live for others: middle c. morality 581.5
middle c. exercises social power 581.3
middle c. unit: couple living moderately 581.4

**classic:** c.: a book people praise and don't read 134.7
c.: man one can praise without reading 134.3
everybody wants to have read c. 134.8
only way to save c.: stop revering him 134.6
**classical:** c. artist recognized by his sincerity 53.96
c. quotation is parole of literary men 767.3
**classics:** c. get more praise than perusal 134.1
public swallow their c. whole 134.9
**clean:** c. glove often hides dirty hand 221.5
God looks at c. hands, not full ones 423.16
**cleanliness:** c. is not next to godliness nowadays 135.1
what separates people most is sense of c. 135.8
**cleanse:** try to c. others, you will waste away 783.24
**clear:** error would die if given c. expression 297.38
matter becomes c., ceases to concern us 132.4
there is a poignancy in all things c. 132.6
**clearer:** how not to understand what should be c. is becoming easier 705.72
**clearly:** what is conceived well is expressed c. 132.1
**clearness:** c. produces despair, despair produces c. 237.11
**clemency:** c. is the support of justice 577.5
**clement:** be not so c. as to encourage boldness 883.5
**clergy:** c. are men as well as other folks 136.4
c. would have us believe them against our own reason 136.15
ounce of mother wit worth pound of c. 137.1
**clergyman:** c. the father of too large a family 136.11
c. undertakes management of our spiritual affairs to better his temporal ones 136.1
man good enough to go to heaven is good enough to be c. 136.10
we expect c. to be a kind of human Sunday 136.2
**clergymen:** I do not know how it is that c. keep from their wives the secrets confided to them 849.14
there are three sexes—men, women and c. 136.17
**clerk:** sub-c. equal of conqueror 172.1
**clever:** all c. men are birds of prey 137.4
be good, and let who will be c. 391.29
c. people seem not to feel bewilderment 478.3
desire to appear c. prevents us being so 137.8
good rule of thumb: too c. is dumb 137.10
if good people were c., c. people good 137.13
if just they are better than c. 515.49
progress in cunning: not to seem too c. 197.4
world must be rough place for c. people 137.7
**cleverness:** bold are helpless without c. 137.5
ounce of loyalty is worth pound of c. 553.3
when luck joins game, c. scores double 137.14
**clichés:** truths of past are c. of present 991.105
**climate:** lands favoured in c. not always happiest 12.2
who rush across sea change c., not soul 985.23
**climb:** do not c. the hill until you get to it 721.2
if thy heart fails thee, c. not at all 749.12
to live is to c. the Andes 536.53
when you feel how slowly you c. 6.12
who would c. must begin at the bottom 938.9
who would have fruit must c. tree 279.9
**climbed:** who never c. high never fell low 33.10
**climber:** c. scorns degrees by which he did ascend 938.38
**climbing:** c. performed in creeping posture 33.32
**cliques:** worst c. consist of one man 903.7
**cloak:** c. is not made for a single shower 1016.4
**clock:** c. makes time mere change and no wealth 971.60
**clocks:** scales an' c. ar-re not to be thrusted 971.14
**closer:** c. is He than breathing 385.72
**clothes:** beware enterprises that require new c. 265.24
c., manners, greatly improve appearance 265.1
fine c. are good only as they supply the want of other means of procuring respect 265.10
fine c. may disguise a fool 353.2
good c. open all doors 265.7
if your c. are worn to the same state, it means you go out too much 907.3
in c. as well as speech, the man of sense shuns extremes 265.12
many bring c. to church, not themselves 126.4
poor body, time taught you use of c. 88.1
women makes herself fit her c. 265.8
would men retain rank without their c. 773.27
**cloud:** every c. engenders not a storm 709.2
one c. is enough to eclipse the sun 1004.13
**clouds:** he that regardeth the c. shall not reap 110.1
who knows whither the c. have fled 1043.6
**cloudy:** c. day has influence on constitutions 1043.1
**clown:** art of the c.: comic mirror of tragedy, tragic mirror of comedy 143.3
**cloy:** best of things, beyond their measure, c. 310.3
**clubs:** c. produce words, not thought 185.7
**coarse:** those lacking c. streak possess cruel one 139.2
**coat:** don't measure another's c. on your body 513.6

man with good c. meets better reception 265.9
**cock:** c. has great influence on own dunghill 713.40
cheerfulness is proper to the c. 80.6
every c. is proud on his own dunghill 865.7
let us not step on each other's feet, said the c. to the horse 987.2
when the c. is drunk, he forgets the hawk 266.3
**cockroach:** c. and bird were here long before we were 368.2
**cocks:** crow in the company of c. 168.13
**coffee:** c. should be black as hell 140.3
c., which makes the politician wise 140.2
morning cup of c. has an exhilaration 140.1
**coffin:** he who is not in c. has enough 536.133
**cold:** c. in clime are c. in blood 141.1
c. is agreeable that we may get warm 115.30
first extreme c. generates sociability 1043.10
we call a man c., when he's only sad 141.4
**collections:** who assemble c. are like cherry eaters 767.1
**collectivist:** c. age wants perpetual holiday from self 905.4
**collector:** c. sees nothing but the prize 8.6
first-rate c. can collect his wits 159.4
**college:** aim of c. is to eliminate need for c. 277.55
takes five years to recover from c. education 277.5
**colleges:** c.: where pebbles polished, diamonds dimmed 277.42
meek young men grow up slaves in c. 277.21
**color:** c. is the poet's wealth 702.105
forgive us for rejecting because of c. 769.17
I have a dream that my children will one day not be judged by c. of their skin 769.11
problem of twentieth century is c.- line 769.5
purest and thoughtful minds love c. most 142.3
regardless of c. all need same nourishment 295.20
**colored:** no "white" or "c." signs on foxholes 769.10
not healthy when nation lives within a nation, as the c. live inside America 83.5
**colors:** c. speak all languages 142.1
**colt:** wild c. may become a sober horse 1064.23
**columnists:** to political c., "every thinking man" means themselves 705.1
**columnist's:** gossip c. business not his business 623.10
**combat:** easier to lead men to c. than peace 1035.42
**combative:** c. instinct is a savage prompting 154.11
**comedian:** all c. has to show is echo of laughter 143.1
test of a real c. is whether you laugh at him before he opens his mouth 144.8
**comedies:** stage is place where people act c. 965.24
**comedy:** c.: an experience of underinvolvement 144.9
c. is escape from despair into faith 144.4
c. naturally wears itself out 144.6
c. no longer challenge to mental processes 144.11
I am my own c. and tragedy 868.11
I began my c. as its only actor 646.82
in black c. you murder your grandmother 144.5
in c. eternity is a moment 980.7
judge c. by how long it lasts 169.5
rules of c. those of taste; limitations, of libel 144.10
tragedy, c., are simply questions of value 980.8
tribute to c.: tendency of eyes to fill 144.12
world is a c. to those that think 1060.33
writers of c. have outlook 980.14
**comets:** c. are the nearest thing to nothing 413.6
old men and c. reverenced for same reason 646.101
**comfort:** bourgeois perfers c. to pleasure 581.2
c.: state of mind produced by contemplation of neighbor's uneasiness 155.1
lust for c. enters the house a guest 554.3
no c. in adversity more sweet than art 53.3
society in shipwreck is a c. to all 151.22
**comfortable:** c. people worry over trivial things 989.8
man cannot be c. without own approval 862.12
you canna expect to be baith grand and c. 330.6
**comforter's:** c. head never aches 953.9
**comic:** the c., when human, takes face of pain 144.3
**coming:** 'tis sweet to know eye will mark our c. 548.23
**command:** c. wisely, be obeyed cheerfully 528.8
do not c. what you cannot enforce 528.22
harder to c. great things than to do them 528.17
how shall I rule others without c. of myself 856.13
I c. it; let my will replace a reason 1049.7
I may c. where I adore 548.209
learn to obey before you c. 636.8
only one in c. in home or state 393.20
**commander:** who has not learned to obey cannot be c. 528.1
**commandments:** decalogue: enough c. to permit selection 598.3
easier to keep holidays than c. 418.4
**commands:** man who c. must have obeyed in

the past 528.3
men not important; what counts is who c. 528.5
who obeys is usually better than who c. 636.5
**commentaries:** every place swarms with c. 204.37
works of nature acquire meaning by c. 616.61
**commentator:** science brought forth radio c. 563.4
**commerce:** c. exploits need and desire 102.21
c. is led by the strong, works against weak 102.6
honour sinks where c. long prevails 102.20
in democracies, nothing is greater than c. 102.35
**commercial:** c. society needs blueprints for every occasion 907.7
failure is lovable and c. 327.21
singing c.: America's litany 34.63
two sides to ivry man: c. an' sintimintal 681.3
**commercials:** Red Riding Hood reared on singing c. 18.8
**commitment:** beauty of strong c. often best understood by a man incapable of it 145.3
**commitments:** something must happen: explains c. 145.1
**committee:** c. is group of unwilling, picked from unfit, to do unnecessary 146.3
c. keeps the minutes and loses hours 146.1
we carry out by c. anything in which one of us would be too reasonable to persist 146.2
**committees:** c. homogenize everybody's thinking 146.4
**commodity:** human being as c. is disease of our age 321.3
man feels himself to be a c. 103.7
**common:** c. man may have no soul, but he consumes 103.19
life in c. only possible when majority stronger than any separate individual 906.5
noble and c. blood are same color 37.4
only in politics are we content with c. man 705.33
sweets grown c. lose their dear delight 331.12
that held most in c. gets least care 804.1
who can endure crassness of the c. herd 675.10
**commonest:** c. thing is delightful if one hides it 605.13
**commonplace:** men are c. on supreme occasions 67.1
no longing sweeter to artist than longing after bliss of the c. 53.77
nothing so c. as wish to be remarkable 33.13
**commonplaces:** c.: tramways of intellectual transportation 605.9
**communicating:** c. of self to friend doubles joys 363.15
**communication:** any group with powers of c. has mandate to show people how to be better 563.9
good c. is stimulating as black coffee 148.9
more we elaborate means of c., less we communicate 563.12
perfectest c. is heard of none 148.2
precision of c. more important than ever 148.15
to the artist c. is a by-product 53.81
**communications:** mass media are wholesalers of c. industry 563.14
**communism:** beware of those who want to apply c. coldly 149.5
c. is corruption of dream of justice 149.18
c. is like Prohibition 149.16
c. is not a classless society 149.11
c. succeeded as scavenger, never as leader 149.10
capitaltsm is the exploitation of man by man; c. is the reverse 149.7
success of c. is much that of religion 149.12
**communist:** c. one who hath yearnings for equal division of unequal earnings 149.4
c. system has some character of religion 149.3
if being a c. is a crime 275.5
objection to c.: he is not a gentleman 149.14
**communists:** c. are seeds and the people, soil 149.13
c. committed crimes but didn't stand aside 149.6
c. have done less to damage our society than those who defend us 149.9
c. take away sense of sin 149.8
with c., what is secret is serious and what is public is propaganda 149.1
**communities:** without civic morality c. perish 598.40
**community:** life is lived in common, but not in c. 150.4
standing in c. requires wealth 1041.66
**commuter:** c. never knows how a show comes out 937.5
**commuters:** c. give city its tidal restlessness 129.40
**compact:** highest c. with fellow is for truth 993.2
**companion:** agreeable c. on journey is as good as a carriage 151.21
c. loves man's qualities; friend, the man 363.21
God gave man c. to make him feel solitude 576.52
man knows his c. in a long journey 497.2
no man pleased with c. who does not increase fondness of himself 151.11
with one c., you are half your own 151.14
**companionship:** accident counts for much in c. 114.1
profounder need for devotion than for c. 145.4
**company:** bad c. is as instructive as debauchery 57.7

better be alone than in bad c. 908.18
did you expect justice from a c. 102.33
every man is like the c. he keeps 57.11
good c., discourse, are sinews of virtue 151.28
how often we go to church only to see c. 151.8
if misery loves c., misery has c. enough 1004.36
ill c. is like a dog, who dirts most those he loves 57.22
learning makes man fit c. for himself 277.29
man known by the c. he organizes 57.5
man loves c. even if only a small candle 151.16
man may do well with little knowledge in c. 185.21
tell me thy c. and I'll tell thee what thou art 57.6
that c. we leave feeling most satisfied with ourselves, we leave most bored 93.5
to have good c. man's entry is a grave 151.7
we do not mind not arriving so much as not having c. on the way 151.5
we may not choose our c. 151.2
who must have c. must have at times bad c. 151.3
**comparative:** all human excellence is c. 309.7
**comparison:** c. makes men happy or wretched 152.1
nothing is good or bad but by c. 152.2
**comparisons:** all bravery stands upon c. 192.4
**compassion:** by c. we make others' misery our own 692.5
c. for friend should conceal itself 692.15
c. is property of the privileged classes 692.21
what value has c. that does not embrace its object 692.18
woman should never move our c. 1055.44
worse than idle is c. if ends in tears 692.23
**compassionate:** c. understanding buys long peace 692.22
**compensation:** this is a world of c. 882.10
**competence:** obscurity and a c.—the best life 641.10
**competition:** men of small intellectual stamina dread c. 934.9
**competitions:** c. are for horses, not artists 154.1
**complacency:** c. is enemy of study 155.8
**complain:** people who cease to c., cease to think 156.5
**complaint:** c. is the largest tribute to heaven 717.30
**completion:** c., to artist, is an incident 53.74
**compliance:** better friendly denial than unwilling c. 784.5
much c., much craft 157.2
**complicated:** no limit to how c. things can get 108.7
**complies:** he that c. against his will, is of his own opinion still 157.1
**compliment:** c. is like a kiss through a veil 158.2
if you cannot get a c., pay yourself one 158.5
sincerity is highest c. you can pay 894.6
there is nothing you can say to a c. 158.4
to say a c. well is high art few possess 158.3
**compliments:** c. are the only things we can pay 158.6
c. cost nothing, yet many pay for them 158.1
woman will doubt everything except c. 1055.76
**compose:** if two c. one song, the muse fans wrath 154.4
**composer:** nation creates music; c. arranges it 607.23
**composers:** c. should write tunes chauffeurs can whistle 607.5
**composition:** happening is a c., in retrospect 965.29
nothing goes by luck in c. 1062.104
things are much finer in c. than alone 408.1
**compositions:** read over c., strike out passage which you think particularly fine 935.11
**compromise:** c., if not spice of life, is its solidity 160.7
c. may make the outrageous acceptable 705.68
c.: when each feels deprived of just due 160.1
every human benefit is founded on c. 160.2
lean c. better than fat lawsuit 160.4
life is a long second-best, perpetual c. 536.101
**compulsion:** c. neurosis is a caricature of a religion 620.8
**computer:** c. with as many vacuum tubes as a man has neurons would require Pentagon to house it 960.18
man is still the most extraordinary c. 960.11
**comrades:** bread broken with c. makes us accept values of war 1035.87
**comradeship:** in c. is danger countered best 213.11
**conceal:** ability in knowing how to c. ability 197.5
have an open face, but c. your thoughts 162.9
we c. ourselves from ourselves 858.7
**concealed:** man trying to escape never sufficiently c. 298.7
**concealment:** c. is equated with individuality 162.18
commit a crime and there is no c. 201.6
**conceals:** who c. his disease cannot be cured 162.5
**conceit:** business of philosophy: to part with self-c. 163.7
c. is the finest armour a man can wear 163.10
c. is to character what salt is to ocean 163.9

c. is vanity forced to appeal to itself 163.8
c. may puff man up, but never prop him up 163.13
chief c. concerns ancestry 37.1
hole in mind plastered over with c. 163.11
isolation breeds c. 908.54
smaller the mind, the greater the c. 163.1
**conceited:** c. people carry their comfort with them 163.6
effect on himself satisfies c. man 163.3
**concentrates:** knowing one is to be hanged c. the mind 761.3
**concept:** every c. is in itself an exaggeration 307.5
**concepts:** life a struggle to maintain life among things; c.: the plan in answer to the attack 638.6
**concerns:** what c. everyone can only be resolved by everyone 731.1
**concert:** c. must have on minute animals the effect of terrible thunder 607.55
**concessions:** rational institution suffers not by c. 485.9
**conciliation:** c. alone dispels darkness born of enmity 164.5
**conciseness:** pointed sentences sacrifice accuracy to c. 935.12
**conclusions:** empiricism has sworn never to draw c. 319.52
**concrete:** c. cloverleaf our national flower 63.8
**condemn:** I wonder how anyone can c. others when he reflects upon his own thoughts 797.8
justice will not c. even Devil wrongfully 515.15
there is something to c. in everything 357.15
**condemns:** fox c. the trap, not himself 775.1
**condiments:** c. are like old friends 186.6
**condition:** every man carries entire human c. 558.38
man seldom willing to exchange his c. 156.4
**conditioning:** c. aims to make us like our destiny 12.6
**conditions:** no c. to which man can't grow accustomed 12.12
**condolence:** worst cruelties come under the name of c. 953.11
**conduct:** c. is largest concern of life 75.2
fine c. is always spontaneous 75.12
our c. is true mirror of our doctrine 75.9
right c. is never promoted by ignorance 75.10
we may give advice, but can't inspire c. 19.23
**conductor:** audience depends on c. for its taste 59.7
**conductors:** c. not to give choreography to audience 607.53
**conference:** c. maketh a ready man 1062.10
no grand idea was ever born in a c. 229.2
**conferences:** c. at top level are always courteous 496.4
**confess:** ridiculous things hardest to c. 165.5
to deny all is to c. all 403.20
**confesses:** he that jokes c. 434.15
**confession:** c. of faults is next to innocence 165.4
c. of one man humbles all 165.3
generous c. disarms slander 165.1
**confidant:** no c. that half the instinct does not want to reject 953.1
**confide:** we rarely c. in those better than we 166.2
**confidence:** as is our c., so is our capacity 854.2
brisk c. still best with woman copes 851.1
c. is a slow-growing plant in aged 113.11
c. is the only bond of friendship 990.8
danger breeds best on too much c. 657.2
no c. in man whose faults you can't see 339.5
one blessing only: c. in self 854.6
public c. is basis of effective government 393.36
skill, c., are an unconquered army 1.11
sleep and c. are almost the same thing 899.2
we need the c. of friends' help in need 363.43
**confident:** man must be at once more humble, c. 960.16
**conform:** public opinion or fear makes all c. 168.5
**conformism:** c. hot on heels of avant gardes 335.28
**conformist:** c. keeps worried eye on what is in wind 466.3
intelligence lends itself to c. error 168.12
**conformists:** quality of nonconformists same as c. 89.6
**conformity:** adjustment is modern synonyn for c. 12.9
c. is jailer of freedom, enemy of growth 168.8
c. is the ape of harmony 168.3
c. is to pay our fares to paradise 168.11
c. ultimately governs the suburb 937.2
our expense is almost all for c. 554.2
saddest thing about c. is the ghastly sort of non-conformity it breeds 168.10
we are half ruined by c. 168.17
**confusion:** c., epitome of what the city is herself 129.42
c.: invented word for order not understood 255.3
call nothing natural in age of bloody c. 994.4
guilt ever at a loss, and c. waits upon it 403.6
**confusions:** teach the young the courage of their c. 994.5

**confuted:** one may be c. and yet not convinced 51.12
**Congress:** C. has turned out comedies 169.5
C.: illiterate hacks spotted with gravy 169.3
no American criminal class except C. 169.8
privilege of C. to dispose 169.7
**Congressman:** C. is never any better than his roads 169.6
**connoisseurs:** children are the true c. 121.25
real c. in art reveal its beauty 204.23
**conquer:** to c. with arms is temporary conquest 170.19
you must c. and rule or serve and lose 853.4
**conqueror:** only one way of fighting: to be the c. 342.4
there is never a c. in war 1035.94
**conquerors:** men, poor strutting peacocks, spread their tails as c. as soon as they can walk 575.1
**conquers:** who c. others is strong; c. self, mighty 856.9
**conquest:** right of c. is right of strongest 170.15
**conscience:** all a man can betray is his c. 77.1
all have c. to hate; few, religion to love 551.1
anxiety and c. are powerful dynamos 43.13
bite of c. teaches men to bite 171.21
c. and cowardice are the same things 171.33
c. bought once will be bought twice 97.6
c. does make cowards of us all 171.28
c.: guardian of rules of the community 171.16
c. hasn't to do with gallantry or politics 348.11
c. is a coward 171.12
c. is a just but a weak judge 171.11
c. is a warning that someone may be looking 171.17
c. is good for hands and legs 1048.8
c. is not vessel of eternal verities 171.14
c. is nothing but other people inside you 171.22
c. is the frame of character 171.1
c. is well-bred: stops talking if one wishes 171.2
c. often more expensive than wife, carriage 171.3
even when there is no law, there is c. 171.24
everyone carries heavy burden on c. 403.1
evil c. is often quiet, but never secure 171.25
friends, books, sleepy c. is ideal life 183.23
glory of good men is in their c. 171.31
good c. is the best divinity 171.10
guilty c. needs no accuser 171.6
human c. remains partially infantile for life 171.8
humanness consists in what we call c. 171.23
if you insist you have your own c. 908.40
laws of c. proceed from custom 171.18
my c. hath a thousand tongues 171.27
one thing stands brunt of life: quiet c. 171.9
only happiness: a clear c. or none 171.19
peace above earthly dignities, a still c. 171.29
policy sits above c. 317.5
quiet c. sleeps in thunder 171.7
state of c. is higher than of innocence 171.15
strongest feelings assigned to the c. express physical antipathies 171.26
there is no evil unless c. says there is 305.18
there's revolution only where there's c. 813.18
Uncle Sam has no c. 598.32
value health next to a good c. 411.22
we invent c. and prey on ourselves 171.13
wild liberty breeds iron c. 361.13
**conscientious:** c. men are less encouraged than tolerated 269.27
nothing as dangerous as c. stupidity 445.20
**conscious:** gift of c. life is a sense of mystery 172.4
our less c. thoughts, actions, mold lives 999.1
to be too c. is an illness 172.3
**consciousness:** c. accepts only one problem at a time 896.7
c. makes clerk and conqueror equal 172.1
c. of a fact is not knowing it 326.17
I do not know man so bold he dare face c. 172.2
suffering is the sole origin of c. 939.11
**consensus:** c. as reconciliation is a fine thing 27.4
**consent:** c. of people is foundation of government 393.2
essence of republican governnment is c. 231.51
none good enough to govern without c. 393.37
**consequences:** c. indifferent to our improvement 173.9
**conservatism:** c. drives the children into radicalism 175.6
success makes men rigid, fanatics about c. 938.25
there is c. in all keeping 710.8
**conservative:** c. government is organised hypocrisy 175.4
c. has two good legs, can't walk forward 175.15
c.: statesman enamored of existing evils 175.2
c. takes thought against day of reckoning 175.14
every boy and gal is liberal or c. 704.4
I never dared to be radical when young, for fear that it would make me c. when old 770.2
radical invents views, c. adopts 175.17
radical of one century is c. of next 770.6
the c. is a tame man 525.66
when nation's young men are c., its funeral bell is already rung 175.1
**conservatives:** all c. are such from personal defects 175.5
c. know institutions conserved by adjusting 485.7
in history of mankind, baseness makes c. 417.27

**considerateness:** c.: not to wound feelings of fellows 515.5
**consistence:** trouble with age we live in is lack of c. 994.3
**consistency:** c. is simply a confession of failures 178.19
foolish c. is hobgoblin of little minds 176.1
lawyer's truth is not truth but c. 525.65
to stick in a rut is called c. 176.6
**consistent:** c. thinker may be a monomaniac 176.2
can't remain c. with world save by growing inconsistent with our past selves 115.13
who mean to be true contradict selves less than those who try to be c. 462.4
**consolation:** before affliction digested, c. comes too soon 953.16
classic form of c. is to understand oneself; to elude oneself is the romantic 752.15
it's over, can't be helped: one c. 505.4
worst cruelties come under the name of c. 953.11
**consoled:** isn't everyone c. by a simple word 1057.32
**constancy:** c. in love is a perpetual inconstancy 178.10
fickleness of women I love equaled by c. of women who love me 470.11
foolish to experiment on c. of friend 178.8
measure affection by c. 178.2
obstinacy in bad cause is but c. in a good 109.1
two sorts of c. in love 178.9
**constant:** often believe we're c. when only dejected 800.8
there is nothing c. but inconstancy 178.18
to be c. in nature were inconstancy 115.9
were man c., he were perfect 178.14
**Constitution:** basis of C.: all are equal as citizens 179.4
C. is a law for rulers, people; in war, peace 179.1
**constitutions:** c. are checks on hasty action of majority 179.6
c. good if progress made under them 179.5
society's blessings depend on c. 393.3
some deem c. too sacred to be touched 179.3
written c. furnish text to rally people 179.2
**constraint:** need freedom and c. to be yourself 442.19
**construct:** those who cannot c. take to pieces 204.17
**consul:** c.: given office on condition that he leave the country 245.2
**consume:** afflictions refine some, c. others 17.27
urge to c. is fathered by value system 103.9
**consumer:** c. is victim of the manufacturer 103.21
**consumers:** future of moppets is to be skilled c. 103.24
**consumes:** thank God, the common man c. 103.19
**consumption:** conspicuous c. is a means of reputability 103.27
**contemplates:** rock pile ceases to be rock pile when man c. it 1027.7
**contemporaries:** man lives the life of his c. 181.6
think of c. as they ought to be when you have to influence them 783.37
**contempt:** c.: feeling for enemy too formidable safely to be opposed 182.1
c. for anything shows we feel level with it 182.4
everything can be borne except c. 182.12
many can bear adversity, few c. 182.3
may my means lie too high for c. 592.3
moral c. is greater insult than any crime 182.8
pride that dines on vanity sups on c. 727.11
to be low, but above c., may be high enough to be happy 183.4
**contend:** never c. with man who has nothing to lose 342.3
**contends:** whoever c. with great sheds own blood 342.6
**content:** be c. to seem what you really are 45.15
be c. with what you are, wish not change 930.7
be c. with your lot 183.1
c. may dwell in all stations 183.4
happy who, c. with common lot, hugs shore 850.15
he is poor who does not feel c. 183.14
in whatsoever state I am, to be c. 183.2
my crown is called c. 183.21
nothing will c. him who is not c. with a little 183.12
poor and c. is rich, and rich enough 183.22
who is c. with nothing possesses all 183.3
**contented:** all fortune belongs to him with c. mind 183.19
he who is c. is rich 183.17
if foolish enough be c., don't show it 183.16
no word against c. people who keep quiet 183.15
world of c. bodies, discontented minds 744.17
**contention:** spread the table and c. will cease 272.7
**contentment:** butterfly preaches c. to toad under harrow 19.21
c. is a warm sty for eaters, sleepers 183.18
c. preserves one even from catching cold 265.16
familiarity breeds c. 331.1
if thou covetest riches, ask but for c. 183.20
only modest virtue gets along with c. 1025.44
seat of c. is in the head 155.2

to know c., let your deeds be few 183.6
true c. is as active as agriculture 183.5
**continence:** give me c., but not just now 120.1
**continuity:** c. does not rule out fresh approaches 979.18
c. in everything is unpleasant 115.30
people are made alarming by their c. 656.2
**contradict:** before you c. old man, understand him 646.87
I may c. tomorrow what I think today 462.2
men c. themselves every day of lives 297.34
speak what you think tomorrow, though it c. what you said today 462.3
**contradicting:** accused of c. myself, I reply: wrong once, I do not aspire to be always wrong 462.5
**contradiction:** c. is first step in evolution of knowledge 51.29
what a c. is man 558.42
**contrast:** we derive intense enjoyment only from c. 184.2
**contrasts:** we live a life of c. and patchwork 536.31
**control:** he who yields a prudent obedience exercises a partial c. 636.4
**controlled:** some wilfully go wrong for fear of being c. 644.6
**controversial:** all who reflect on c. matters should be free from hatred, friendship, anger, pity 250.4
**controversies:** most savage c. are those to which there is no good evidence either way 51.23
**controversy:** who shows better temper scores most in c. 51.6
**convalescence:** c. makes illness worth while 889.26
c. shrinks man back to pristine stature 889.17
**convenience:** bourgeois prefers c. to liberty 581.2
**convenient:** danger comes when we choose the c. paths 279.16
**convent:** c. is supreme egotism 595.3
**convention:** there is nothing sacred about c. 210.26
**conversation:** art of c. is a certain self-control 185.8
art of c. is hearing as well as being heard 185.16
c.: display of minor mental commodities 185.3
c. enriches us by elation that comes of contact with currents of thought 185.29
c. is an aristocratic art 281.11
c. is an endeavour at effect 185.18
c. is art where all are competitors 185.10
c.: one of the greatest pleasures in life 185.24
c. which passes for agreeable is made up of civility and falsehood 438.23
c. with wise man better than books 277.48
confidence gives more to c. than wit 185.23
free c. will not bear a dictator 185.4
happiest c. is calm quiet interchange 185.17
in c. consider whether man has inclination to hear you or that you hear him 185.31
in c. discretion is more important than eloquence 185.14
it is a fault in c. for one man to take up all the discourse 185.33
listen closely, reply well is art of c. 185.22
man of no c. should smoke 975.5
marriage is one long c. 560.116
mingle c. with instruction 529.8
more the pleasures of the body fade, greater is the pleasure of c. 185.27
nightingale runs out of songs before woman runs out of c. 1055.137
private, accidental c. breeds thought 185.7
repose as necessary in c. as in picture 185.15
success in c.: bringing out wit in others 185.20
the best of life is c. 185.9
wit in c. is a quick conception and an easy delivery 185.28
wit is salt of c., not the food 1054.12
writing is lonely substitute for c. 1062.7
**conversationalist:** c.: one who talks to you about yourself 185.19
**converse:** many c. by giving history of their pains 185.32
**converted:** man not c. because he is silenced 978.5
**convertible:** teacher's conviction that men are c. 959.7
**converts:** charming women can true c. make 683.5
time makes more c. than reason 971.39
**conviction:** it is your own c. that compels you 122.4
mix c. with a man and something happens 76.16
**conviction's:** snug lie those slumbering beneath c. roof 647.5
**convictions:** c. are worse enemies of truth than lies 76.14
easy to praise men for courage of c. 994.5
painless c. are worthless 76.22
tolerance best achieved by those without c. 977.1
**convince:** to c., seem open to conviction 51.8
**convinced:** men c. of your sincerity only by your death 218.30
one may be confuted and yet not c. 51.12
**conviviality:** what is the odds when the fire of soul is kindled at thel taper of c. 151.6
**cook:** God is great; the c. is his prophet 186.5
good c. is a certain slow poisoner 186.12
good c. is the peculiar gift of the gods 186.7
ill c. should have a good cleaver 186.4
men c. food to show they aren't beasts 186.8

**cookery:** c. is now noble science; cook, a gentleman 186.2
kissing don't last: c. do 519.4
**cooking:** c. should be entered into with abandon 186.11
**cooks:** bad c. have delayed human development 186.9
God sends meat, the Devil sends c. 186.3
**cool:** world belongs to enthusiast who keeps c. 291.6
**coolly:** to do anything c. is to do it genteelly 159.3
**cop:** sleeping c. in all of us must be killed 703.6
**cope:** all living welcome what they can c. with 613.10
**copulation:** birth, c., death: that's all the facts 536.28
**coquetry:** love's greatest miracle is curing of c. 348.5
**coquette:** he who keeps undisputed sway over heart of a c. is indeed a hero 348.4
life is too short for all tricks of a c. 348.1
**corn:** c. is the child of song 186.14
**coronets:** kind hearts are more than c. 517.23
**corporation:** c.: device for individual profit without individual responsibility 102.7
c. is an artificial being 102.26
**correct:** it is easier to be critical than to be c. 203.9
we must c. a great deal, but not too much 783.7
when we wish to c. with advantage 51.20
**correction:** c. of silence is what kills 797.12
**corrupt:** nature will overturn c. political system 813.28
power tends to c. 713.1
**corrupted:** I feel rage at c. morals of this age 598.34
**corruption:** c. is like a ball of snow 188.3
c. made up of contribution of individuals 188.10
c. of government begins with principles 188.11
c. sees everything stained, impure 188.12
c. wins not more than honesty 188.14
sign of c. when end justifies means 570.2
**corruptions:** war is a producer of new c. 1035.70
**corset:** in economics, c. is a mutilation 265.28
**cosmic:** no object can't be looked at from c. view 58.2
our impotence in the face of c. forces 131.26
**cosmopolitan:** nearly all bad men are c. 190.1
truly c. man is at home even in own country 190.3
**cosmopolite:** best c. loves his native country best 190.5
**cost:** c. of living not bad if you don't pay it 275.6
persons c. much; for thee I must pay me 787.2
that which c. little is less valued 1019.4
**costliness:** c. masquerades as beauty 638.8
**costs:** nothing c. so much as what is given 780.1
we condemn wrong when it c. us nothing 816.11
**cottage:** c. has same vices as courts 1023.6
**cough:** c. is something you can't help 889.20
love, itch, and c. cannot be hid 548.78
**counsel:** all know good c. except one who needs it 19.15
another's c. gives purer light than own 19.5
friendly c. cuts off many foes 19.33
taking c. rounds men to one mind 229.3
three may keep c., if two be away 27.5
what takes place after dinner must never be taken as c. 229.1
where's the man who c. can bestow 19.28
who cannot give good c.; 'tis cheap 19.8
**counselors:** books will speak plain when c. blanch 91.4
in the multitude of c. there is safety 19.6
**counsels:** c. lost on one who can't take advice 19.27
c. of old age give light without heat 19.37
**count:** one must be able to c. 566.4
**countenance:** man's heart changes his c. 282.1
**countenances:** many wise men have transparent c. 936.2
**countries:** c. are like fruit, worms are inside 188.4
little c. apologize when they do wrong 496.17
men in hot c. love the night 138.3
not good in own c., men run to others 985.15
**country:** a pity we can die but once to save our c. 671.2
ask not what your c. can do for you 671.9
best c. is the one which has most 539.17
best cosmopolite loves his native c. 190.5
c. belongs to people who inhabit it 231.27
c. has its charms—cheapness for one 191.17
c. renewed by unknown, not powerful 675.16
city has a face: c., a soul 191.11
flat c. gives the sky a chance 191.15
God made the c. and man made the town 191.4
good thing about the c. is no bad weather 191.10
he serves party best who serves c. best 704.6
he who could wish his c. to remain as it is, would be a citizen of the universe 615.8
I don't like the c., it's a healthy grave 191.16
I tremble for my c., for God is just 34.27
in c. quiet life stimulates creative mind 191.6
in c. we forget town; in town, despise c. 191.8
in love of home, love of c. has rise 420.7
it is right to prefer own c. to others 421.6

man good enough to shed blood for c. should be given a square deal afterwards 582.17
man must be quiet, happy to endure c. 191.12
man's feet should be planted in own c. 190.4
my c. is world; countrymen, mankind 98.6
my loyalty was to c., not office-holders 671.23
no sweeter sight than one's own c. 421.3
one day in c. is worth month in town 191.13
one loves his c. because it's his own 671.19
only in c. we get to know person or book 191.2
sacrifice to c. teaches what c. is 831.8
sample of the city does the c. good 129.35
self-important fathers of their c. think they're above the people 130.3
to make men virtuous, make them love their c. 671.18
what is good for c. is good for General Motors, and vice versa 102.37
when in Rome you long for the c. 249.6
who loves not his c., how shall he love humanity 671.5
who saves his c. violates no law 671.16

**countryside:** as much sin in smiling c. as in vile London alleys 191.5

**couple:** c. is unhappy not merely from limited means 560.18

**courage:** beware ready-made ideas about cowardice, c. 196.11
c. does not always march to a bugle 192.33
c. for the strange, the inexplicable 192.32
c. imperils life, fear protects it 340.21
c. is a kind of salvation 192.30
c. is the thing; all goes if c. goes 192.5
c. is to bear fate unflinchingly 192.14
c. mounteth with occasion 192.37
c. must have hope for nourishment 192.27
c. not in those who won't look at own vices 858.1
c. of all one really knows comes late 489.19
c. of convictions, confusions 994.5
c. raises the blood to crimson splendor 192.38
c. resistance to fear—not its absence 192.40
even to live sometimes act of c. 192.36
every man has his own c. 192.12
great crises produce great deeds of c. 202.3
last thing woman will consent to discover in man she loves is want of c. 576.9
life without c. for death is slavery 192.35
many would be cowards if they had the c. 196.6
men often bear little grievances with less c. than they do large misfortunes 506.1
miss plum for want of c. to shake tree 973.10
much of c. is c. of doing thing before 192.13
narrow souls dare not to admire true c. 70.10
no man would set a word down on paper if he had c. to live what he believed in 1062.76
no one can answer for his c. when he has never been in danger 192.22
paradox of c.: man must be a little careless of life even in order to keep it 192.9
people with c., character, seem sinister 192.18
perfect c., utter cowardice rarely occur 196.10
plenty of c. among us for the abstract 192.20
to persevere is c. in a man 679.4
until day of death, no man sure of c. 192.2
weak in c. is strong in cunning 197.1
where guilt is, rage and c. abound 403.10
will of God to be borne with c. 238.20
will to jump after drowning man doubles in presence of people lacking c. 56.9
without justice, c. is weak 192.16

**couriers:** neither snow nor rain stays these c. 556.1

**course:** I bow to that whose c. is run 646.37

**court:** art of c., as hard to leave as keep 193.2
th' supreme c. follows iliction returns 525.19
two maxims of great man at c. are to keep countenance, never keep word 193.3

**courted:** better c. and jilted than never c. 195.2

**courteous:** if c. when young, then cherished when old 1065.21

**courtesan:** war and c. are slaves of desperation 1035.1

**courtesies:** no man gains credit for cowardly c. 196.5

**courtesy:** all doors open to c. 194.6
c. is politic witchery of the great 194.8
c. is the due of man to man 194.2
c. wins woman as well as valor 195.14
gratitude is most exquisite form of c. 397.9
greater man, the greater c. 194.15
knowledge of c. is a necessary study 194.13
no defense like elaborate c. 194.12
there is a c. of the heart 194.7
truth is always first point of c. 194.4
use c. and guide elephant with a hair 377.5

**courtiers:** ability to stand is meritorious among c. 193.1

**courts:** cottages have same vices as c. 1023.6

**courtship:** best marriages are preceded by long c. 195.1
c. is a witty prologue to a dull play 195.4

**coverage:** few have c. of what they really know 192.29

**covetous:** c. man fares worse than poor man 401.19
c. man's penny is a stone 401.1

**covetousness:** c. has made few rich men 401.12

**cow:** c. crunching surpasses any statue 41.32
c. of many: well milked, badly fed 149.17

**coward:** brave creature is part c. 192.40
c. calls the brave man rash 192.3
c., outfaced in this life, fears another 414.4
c. sneaks to death, the brave live on 941.8
man not brave who is afraid to be a c. 192.31

man who stands apart from mob called c. 591.2
**coward's:** hatred is the c. revenge 410.24
**cowardice:** between c. and despair valour is born 192.10
beware ready-made ideas about c., courage 196.11
c. is inability to suspend imagination 196.7
c. is incorrigible which love of power cannot overcome 196.3
c.: surest protection against temptation 964.11
conscience and c. are the same things 171.33
hidden valor is as bad as c. 192.24
I hold it c. to rest mistrustful 257.17
if thou livest in pain, c. is the cause 941.9
mortifying infirmity in human nature is c. 196.9
mutual c. keeps us in peace 674.15
optimism and self-pity are poles of c. 196.4
perfect courage, utter c. rarely occur 196.10
to run away from trouble is a form of c. 941.1
**cowardly:** in victory even c. like to boast 745.14
no man gains credit for c. courtesies 196.5
**cowards:** between two c., he has the advantage who first detects the other 196.8
c. die many times before their deaths 196.12
c. never use might, but against such as will not fight 196.1
human race is race of c. 196.13
many would be c. if they had the courage 196.6
**coyness:** c. a comically pathetic fault baring ego 726.10
had we time, c. would be no crime 851.9
**crab:** c. instructs young: walk straight ahead 308.5
**crabgrass:** lie down and listen to the c. grow 530.9
**cradle:** c. is rocked but the baby is pinched 269.23
mother's song to c. is carried to coffin 663.6
**craft:** much compliance, much c. 157.2
**crank:** c. insists on laying down law to others 274.1
**cranks:** c. take up unfashionable errors 274.3
**craves:** he is poor that c. much 401.10
what the eye sees not, the heart c. not 236.8
**crazy:** madman thinks rest of world c. 555.18
to do certain c. things 459.3
**create:** impulse to destroy as ancient as to c. 239.8
long and hard and painful to c. life 516.15
men must live and c. 536.18
to c. there must be a dynamic force 198.39
who knows not how to c. should not know 198.33
**created:** no great thing is c. suddenly 399.21
**creates:** man is, above all, he who c. 198.34
man, like Deity, c. in his own image 198.18
**creating:** in c., the only hard thing's to begin 198.24
**creation:** art of c. is older than art of killing 198.40
artist's c. must become multitude's desire 53.114
c. destroys as it goes 707.3
c. is the great redemption from suffering 198.29
destruction is new c. on a wider scale 239.2
if I bind my will I strangle c. 198.37
in our time, man believes he's capable of c. 198.30
man unites with world in process of c. 198.15
rational being will discover deity in c. 616.47
teach me, like you, to drink c. whole 920.8
to ourselves, we seem coeval with c. 852.20
women's lives work out processes of c. 663.34
**creation's:** speak before you think is c. motto 198.12
**creative:** all men are c. but few are artists 198.16
being c. is having something to sell 321.2
c. minds known to survive bad training 198.13
c. person is more primitive and cultivated than average person 198.2
gifted members of the human species are at c. best when they cannot have their way 198.17
man is a free c. spirit 198.6
passion for destruction is a c. joy 239.6
**creativeness:** taste is the enemy of c. 957.15
**creativity:** c. varies inversely with number of cooks 198.11
**creator:** man thinks of himself as c. 174.3
one must die to life to be a c. 198.26
spirit of c. not evoked by opium or wine 267.2
**creature:** nature has filled each cranny with fantastic c. 616.42
**creatures:** highest c. take longest to mature 402.22
we love c. with two, four legs, but not six 479.4
we treat wild c. as outlaws 436.1
**credit:** who has enough c. to pay for mistakes 297.13
**creditor:** c. worse than master; c. has your dignity 219.9
**creditors:** c. are great observers of set days 219.5
nobody loves c. and dead men 536.8
we are either debtors or c. 219.8
**credulity:** c. greatest about things we know least 199.4
c. is man's weakness, child's strength 199.6
youth is the season of c. 113.11
**credulous:** imaginative people are the most c. 199.2
man is c. and must believe something 76.20
most positive men are the most c. 262.15

**creed:** at back of every c. lies something hard 200.1
c. is an ossified metaphor 200.2
embrace unsullied c., be in right 200.7
I know a c. is the shell of a lie 200.6
no nonsense that cannot be made c. 739.9
our c. tested only in emergencies of life 200.3
we have less charity for those who believe half our c. 705.23
when one belongs to narrow c. in science 843.10
**creeds:** art raises its head where c. relax 53.89
hate man, worship God seems sum of all c. 790.35
**cries:** c. of despair are a kind of wealth 1045.7
he that falls by himself never c. 156.6
**crime:** c. and punishment grow out of one stem 760.6
c. is extension of behavior in business 201.18
c. leaves trail like water-beetle 201.11
cause of idleness, c. is deferring hopes 425.7
commit a c. and there is no concealment 201.6
commonplace c. difficult to solve 201.4
for one c. expiated in prison ten thousand committed by those who condemn 515.32
harder to confess sin no one believes in than c. everyone can appreciate 893.8
number of malefactors no excuse for c. 201.8
poverty is parent of revolution and c. 712.2
problem of community cursed with c. is preventing the young from training in c. 201.5
punishment of c. is fear 201.21
study of c. begins with knowledge of self 201.14
successful, fortunate c. called virtue 201.19
there is no absolute c. 475.8
want should not be exasperated into c. 712.55
worse than a c., it is a blunder 86.3
**crimes:** baseness of c. requires wise not only to be angry but to go insane 305.35
c. of civilization worse than those of barbarism 131.2
collective c. incriminate no one 201.15
fantastic c. imputed to the degraded 201.1
great c. linked to sins that went before 201.16
lack of intelligence is father of all c. 934.15
men incapable of c. don't suspect others 476.5
men more willing to have c. known than weaknesses 798.5
most men only commit great c. because of their scruples about petty ones 201.17
**criminal:** c. acts are not more unnatural than virtues 431.16
every society gets kind of c. it deserves 703.8
judge condemned when c. is acquitted 515.37
no American c. class except Congress 169.8
society forgives c., never the dreamer 448.32
**criminals:** c. turn preachers under the gallows 793.8
**cripple:** if live with c., you will learn to limp 57.17
**crises:** c. frighten weak, inspire strong 496.15
great c. produce great men, great deeds 202.3
nationwide planning will prevent c. 202.7
**crisis:** c. means danger and opportunity 202.4
present moment an extraordinary c. 723.6
**critic:** accuse c. who destroys too many illusions 204.18
artist is a cut above the c. 204.19
c. knows the way but can't drive the car 204.56
c. must get into the mind of artist 204.34
c.: sorcerer who makes hidden spring gush 204.33
c. who justly admires many things simultaneously cannot love any of them 204.5
drama c. leaves no turn unstoned 204.48
dramatic c. comes out after dark, up to no good 204.58
good c. is the man who describes his adventures among masterpieces 204.22
good writer is not per se good book c. 204.6
man is a c. when he cannot be an artist 204.21
wise skepticism is attribute of good c. 897.8
**critical:** author furnishes c. larvae with food 204.27
c. vision can mitigate automatic operation 960.19
every nation has own c. turn of mind 204.15
it is easier to be c. than to be correct 203.9
pleasure is least fallible c. guide 20.1
the c. spirit creates 198.41
**criticism:** art can hardly be reached with c. 204.44
c. is easy, art is difficult 204.13
c. is like champagne 204.11
c. is never inhibited by ignorance 203.17
c. is the windows and chandeliers of art 204.40
c. should not be querulous but guiding 203.11
c. that overlays text with windy sermon 204.39
cant of c. is the most tormenting 204.54
I do not resent c. 203.6
judgments of fact, not of value, a sign of pedantic c. 204.46
no effective c. until a man provoked 203.32
people ask for c., but only want praise 203.19
rain of c. makes garden of music flourish 204.12
should be a dash of the amateur in c. 204.2
stupid c. versus stupid praise 716.29
to love without c. is to be betrayed 548.7

tomes of c. hang on moments of delight 20.5
**criticism's:** think before you speak is c. motto 198.12
**criticized:** one can be c. only by a greater man 204.16
**critics:** c. all are ready made 204.8
c. are like brushers of nobles' clothes 204.4
c., like insects, desire blood, not pain 204.41
c.: men who have failed in literature, art 204.14
if c. were as clear-sighted as malignant 204.49
seek roses in December before you trust c. 204.9
stones c. hurl man may use for monument 204.24
we don't trust our senses, we rely on c. 875.8
we have paid too great a compliment to c. 204.20
when c. disagree, the artist is in accord with himself 204.57
**Cross:** orgasm has replaced the C. 885.21
**crow:** c. that mimics cormorant gets drowned 449.7
c. went abroad, came home just as black 985.18
**crowd:** c. has a generalized stink 205.1
c. is not company without love 908.4
everyone in c. has power to throw dirt 898.4
hating the c., I love society 151.17
I am the people, the mob, c., mass 675.14
I live in c. of jollity to shun myself 151.12
in a c. now go one way then another 205.8
in the c. a mass-mind operates 205.6
man goes into a c. to drown own silence 205.10
no human happier for being lost in a c. 205.3
nothing so unpredictable as feelings of c. 205.7
we may better join the foolish c. 168.14
**crowded:** I'd rather sit alone on a pumpkin than be c. on a velvet cushion 205.11
**crowds:** as c. increase we build forts of inattention 205.4
**crown:** c. of roses makes the prettier appearance 61.1
uneasy lies the head that wears a c. 825.25
within c. of king keeps Death his court 825.24
**crucified:** men of rare vision are always c. 561.7
**crudity:** certain c. makes people interesting 139.1
**cruel:** c. describe themselves as frank 360.15
I must be c., only to be kind 883.7
man adds to grief by being c. to man 206.1
those lacking coarse streak have c. one 139.2
**cruelest:** man is the c. animal 206.13
**cruelties:** worst c. come under name of condolence 953.11
**cruelty:** c., excitement, lead men to love war 1035.5
c. is a tyrant always attended by fear 206.6
c. is law pervading nature, society 206.8
c. stems from vile mind, cowardly heart 206.2
c. to other civilized man 131.9
fear is one of the main sources of c. 340.27
intellectual c. is the worst kind of c. 206.4
love compels c. 548.59
one's c. is one's power 206.5
opinions which justify c. are inspired by cruel impulses 206.14
there is in man a specific lust for c. 206.15
**cruise:** old and young, all on last c. 600.18
**crusades:** psychopathic element rises to top of c. 109.14
**crutch:** love is a c. 548.126
nothing more frightening than to be divested of a c. 233.1
sometimes good c. better than bad foot 233.12
**cubs:** must enter tiger's den to take c. 90.9
**cucumber:** c. should be seasoned, then thrown out 352.6
**cult:** less reasonable a c. is, more men seek to establish it by force 667.6
**cultivated:** c. man is end to which nature works 207.5
c. man make acute, balanced observers 642.2
c. people need not speak at all 207.13
c. people should be superior to mercenary interest 596.40
**cultural:** c. changes begin in affectation 115.3
**culture:** biological weakness is condition of c. 1040.2
c.: acquainting ourselves with best known, thus with history of human spirit 207.1
c. can't be deliberately aimed at 207.2
c. is a mask that hides men's faces 906.12
c. is an atmosphere and a heritage 207.16
c. is an instrument wielded by professors to manufacture professors 207.20
c. is half-way to heaven 207.17
c. is how one lives and is connected to history by habit 207.11
c. is the form of religion 790.81
c. opens the sense of beauty 207.3
c., to say great things in simplest way 892.4
cheerful, intelligent face is end of c. 207.4
custom is the deterioration of c. 207.6
if you're anxious to be a man of c., you must get transcendental terms 207.7
man born barbarian, raises self by c. 207.8
this is a crazy c.—absolutely nutty 994.6
value of c. is its effect on character 207.14
what we call education and c. is nothing but substitution of literature for life 277.72
wider any c. is spread, thinner it gets 207.19
**cunning:** greatest c. is to have none at all 197.9
knowledge without justice is c. 520.55
progress in c.: not to seem too clever 197.4

state hurt when c. pass for wise 923.3
they who cannot be wise are c. 197.3
weak in courage is strong in c. 197.1
**cup:** many a slip 'twixt c. and lip 114.14
**Cupid:** C. is naked and does not like artifices 548.169
**cure:** canter is c. for every evil 815.1
we labour against our own c., for death is the c. of all diseases 218.19
**cured:** disease known is half c. 241.1
**cures:** thousand ills require thousand c. 791.8
**curiosity:** c. is free-wheeling intelligence 208.2
c. is permanent trait of vigorous intellect 208.7
creatures whose mainspring is c. enjoy accumulating facts 208.3
glory and c. are two scourges of the soul 208.9
man should live if only to satisfy c. 208.11
newspapers always excite c. 623.11
there are various sorts of c.; one is from interest, and the other from pride 208.8
we have no c. about sun which warms us 478.6
**curious:** child is c. all over 121.49
**curriculum:** only one c.: basics of human experience 277.34
world's c. doesn't include Latin and Greek 277.49
**curry:** when c. good, rice is half-cooked 455.4
**cursed:** none so c. but Eternal Love may return 548.38
**curses:** I scorn men's c., but dread applause 716.7
thousand c. never tore a shirt 209.1
**custom:** an old c. is so sacred when it is bad 210.3
bad c. is like a good cake, better broken than kept 210.8
c. adapts itself to expediency 317.7
c. can't conquer nature, she's unconquered 431.3
c. creates the whole of equity 210.22
c. determines what is agreeable 210.23
c., fashion are blind to what is to come 210.6
c. is principal magistrate of life 210.1
c. is second nature and no less powerful 210.19
c. is the deterioration of culture 207.6
c. is the guide of the ignorant 210.7
c. makes all things easy 210.10
c. reconciles us to everything 210.4
habit raises outcry in defense of c. 783.32
innumerable are the illusions of c. 210.5
laws of conscience proceed from c. 171.18
lest one good c. should corrupt the world 115.37
morality is the c. of one's country 598.10
no human action which c. has not at one time justified and at another condemned 210.13
old c. is hard to break 210.29
old c. without truth is but old error 210.11
that monster, c. 210.27
things both just, unjust sanctioned by c. 210.28
universality of a c.: pledge of its worth 210.25
we are more sensible of what is done against c. than against nature 210.24
what humanity abhors, c. recommends 210.14
who does anything by c. makes no choice 210.17
**customer:** c. is an object to be manipulated 102.14
**customs:** c. are made for customary circumstances 210.16
c. go for more in life than qualities 559.16
c. represent the experience of mankind 210.2
don't change laws to change c. 210.20
long c. are not easily broken 783.20
new c., though ridiculous, are followed 335.25
**cut:** measure a thousand times and c. once 110.7
**cynic:** c. is prematurely disappointed in future 211.1
c. knows the price of everything 211.4
c. lives by denying civilisation 211.3
**cynicism:** only the c. born of success is valid 211.2
**cynics:** time blind, man stupid: thus say c. 971.48

# D

**daintiest:** d. last, to make the end most sweet 698.37
**dalliance:** first spring day was once time of d. 848.49
**dance:** d. is only art wherein we are stuff of which it is made 212.5
either d. well or quit the ballroom 309.4
girl who can't d. says band can't play 461.6
I d. to the tune that is played 12.11
men must walk before they d. 402.16
one unable to d. blames uneven floor 312.3
**danced:** consider day lost on which we have not d. 407.82
**dancer:** good education usually harmful to a d. 212.1
**dancers:** modern d. give sinister portent to times 212.2
**dancing:** d. is attempt to get into life's rhythm 212.4
d. loftiest, most beautiful of the arts 212.3
**dandelion's:** d. pallid tube astonishes the grass 349.2
**dandelions:** you fight d., and there they are thriving 369.1

**Dane:** once you have paid the D.-geld you never get rid of the D. 46.3
**danger:** affection dwells with d. 192.7
any d. spot is tenable – by brave men 213.13
avoiding d. no safer than exposure to it 110.4
common d. unites even enemies 1009.1
d. and delight grown on one stalk 213.8
d. breeds best on too much confidence 657.2
d. comes when we pick convenient paths 279.16
d. foreseen is half avoided 356.5
d. past, God is forgotten 213.10
delay breeds d. 228.1
if not in trouble, watch for d. 749.33
in comradeship is d. countered best 213.11
in d there are various ways of winning 317.6
life of d. moderates dread of death 9.27
mystery magnifies d. as fog the sun 213.5
out of d., man forgets his fears 213.9
the path is smooth that leadeth on to d. 155.10
to pessimist d. is not depressing 685.2
whoever has not felt the d. of our times 994.13
wise man prays not for safety from d. 213.7
**dangerous:** all fame is d. 330.22
we're d. till fears grow thoughtful 340.9
**dangers:** d., by being despised, grow great 213.3
only man can control new d. man created 633.7
who won't sail till d. are over sails not 110.3
**D. A. R.:** D. A. R. vetoes all revolutions 175.12
**dare:** not to d. is to dwindle 53.132
**dares:** fortune sides with him who d. 358.46
**daring:** best mask for demoralization is d. 90.11
progress in life comes through d. 735.19
the loving are the d. 548.226
**dark:** much easier to tell intimate things in d. 166.5
**darkness:** better to light candle than to curse d. 430.7
in d., shameful deed brings no disgrace 214.2
none who passed door of d. return to tell 218.95
there is no such thing as absolute d. 214.1
**darknesses:** we move between two d. 538.11
**Darwinian:** D. man is only a monkey shaved 306.5
**data:** mistake to theorize without d. 967.2
**daughter:** d. am I in my mother's house 420.14
to old father, nothing sweeter than d. 215.1
**daughters:** he who has d. is always a shepherd 215.4
**daughters':** trust not d. minds by what they act 215.2
**dawn:** darkness of d., like peace, is silent 214.3
I have felt d. like a glory in my heart 599.2
still beauty of d. is nature's balm 599.4
what human ill not alleviated by d. 599.7
**day:** cloudy d. has influence on constitutions 1043.1
d. is done, and the darkness falls 626.8
each d. provides its own gifts 723.21
every d. cannot be a feast of lanterns 605.2
God blessed the seventh d. 829.1
if one d. like all, all are like one 971.33
life loses in a d. what many years amassed 547.6
next d. is never so good as d. before 631.1
nothing more commended than fine d. 1043.8
praise not the d. before night 721.3
prayer should be the key of the d. 717.14
sufficient unto the d. is the evil thereof 305.4
thou knowest not what a d. may bring forth 721.1
time and hour runs through roughest d. 971.54
what a d. may bring a d. may take away 983.8
what d. fails to reveal some theft 455.3
**daydream:** follow d. to its natural consummation 687.8
**daydreaming:** average man must take to d. 292.6
**daydreams:** how many of our d. would be nightmares 687.21
**days:** aren't d. long when nothing goes wrong 183.11
d. come and go like veiled figures 971.15
I do not cut my life up into d. 536.58
one of these d. is none of these d. 228.5
upon the sea d. fall away quicker 833.5
we've more d. to live than pleasures 698.17
**dead:** a living man of the slightest pretensions is stronger than d. man's memory 538.27
d. are all holy, even they that were base 218.31
d. govern the living 979.6
d. keep their secrets 849.20
d. men have no victory 170.6
distance the d. have gone does not at first appear 218.35
earth belongs to living, not to d. 536.57
few wholly d.: blow embers, flame starts 218.61
for the d. there are no more toils 218.122
in Spain d. more alive than d. elsewhere 915.1
it takes many years to learn that one is d. 216.2
lament not the d. but the living 603.6
let the d. bury the d.: no word of Christ has been more ignored by the Christians 101.5
let the d. have fame, but the living love 548.222
living dog is better than a d. lion 536.11

man'll do meanest thing after he's d. 1051.9
nobody loves creditors and d. men 536.8
not easy to restore life to the d. 761.7
one being d., all is d. to him 852.22
one cannot live with the d. 218.83
one is better off seated than standing, asleep than awake, d. than alive 30.2
only two topics of interest: sex, the d. 520.75
our affection for the d. grows faint because we ourself are dying 549.14
pity is for the living, envy for the d. 538.43
praised when d., we often have no other merit than that of being no longer alive 798.23
small difference to d. if buried in luxury 101.4
sorrow for the d. is only one from which we refuse to be divorced 603.10
the d. sleep in their moonless night 603.5
those most like d. are most loath to die 218.75
those who fear life are three parts d. 216.10
to ashes of d. glory comes too late 384.13
to mourn d. unduly affronts the living 603.7
to the d. rugs are no richer than thorns 218.127
today we can't even count all the d. 1035.104
we are more fair toward the d. 218.29
we aren't honest, we embalm our d. 101.1
we rob selves when we make presents to d. 365.10
you never find the d. making any complaint against the doctor who killed them 261.13

**deadly:** female of species more d. than male 1055.84

**deaf:** it is folly to sing twice to a d. man 48.3
music is nothing if the audience is d. 1053.45
none so d. as he who will not hear 217.1

**deal:** to d. only with honest men, stop dealing 423.4

**dealing:** nothing astonishes men like plain d. 147.4
plain d. is a jewel out of fashion 360.5
plain d. is kicked out of doors 346.9

**dearest:** those things d. that have cost us most 1019.11

**death:** action, danger moderate dread of d. 9.27
Adam brought d. into the world 538.41
all our life is but a going out to d. 538.5
ants and savages put strangers to d. 355.7
any man's d. diminishes me 218.39
as men, we are all equal in presence of d. 218.102
as to d., we live in city without walls 218.47
at birth, d. stands but a little aside 218.15
beauty is feared more than d. 70.62
belief in hell never prevented people from behaving as though d. were a rumor 218.73
better a quiet d. than public misfortune 432.2
children will not fear life if their elders do not fear d. 538.8
compensation for a d. sentence 761.4
d. a stake put up to play game of life 538.16
d. always comes too early or too late 218.44
d. avenges wrongs of the friendless 218.22
d. be not proud 452.3
d. borders upon our birth 218.62
d. but an instant, life a long torment 538.32
d. by justice is ignominious 761.5
d. cancels everything but truth 218.4
d. cuts in marble what would sink to dust 218.86
d. does not blow a trumpet 218.33
d. drowns in the indifference of nature 218.134
d. eats up all, both lamb and old sheep 218.32
d. either destroys or unhusks us 218.107
d. guide of life, no goal but d. 218.80
d. has no sting, but life has 538.44
d. has one terror: it has no tomorrow 218.70
d. hath a thousand doors to let out life 218.85
d. in battle is the most glorious for men 1035.77
d. is a rearrangement of the world 218.103
d. is a thing which makes men weep 218.28
d. is camel that lies down at every door 218.100
d. is given in a kiss 538.38
d. is greatest evil, for it cuts off hope 425.16
d. is like a fisherman 218.131
d. is never sweet 218.52
d. is not the greatest misfortune 536.80
d. is nothing; we fear what we know not 218.40
d. is of no concern to us 218.46
d. is one moment, life so many of them 538.47
d. is perpetual retirement without pay 218.60
d. is premium we pay for benefit derived from so many having lived, died before us 218.26
d. is stingless, grave never fights 616.54
d. is supreme festival on the road to freedom 218.16
d. is the absence of presence 218.123
d. is the cure of all diseases 218.19
d. is the supple suitor that wins at last 218.36
d. is the veil those who live call life 452.16
d. is ultimate horror of life 218.59
d. laughs when old women frolic 646.85
d. lays his icy hands on kings 337.19
d. makes life live, gives it significance 218.20
d. must be, like the rest, a mockery 218.116
d. must be waiting at end of ride before you see earth, feel heart, love world 218.5
d. must not be taken too seriously 3.1
d. reveals what a nothing the body is 88.2
d. softer thing by far than tyranny 995.2
d. stronger than all governments 218.106
d. surprises us amidst our hopes 218.56
d. takes away commonplace of life 218.119
d. takes us piecemeal, not at a gulp 218.108
d. wanted when auguish of living too great 538.9

d. will not see me flinch 218.96
d. will take us all at last 218.23
day of birth is a step towards d. 81.4
dignity of d. or undertakers 101.7
do not fear d., but the inadequate life 502.4
do not seek d.; d. will find you 218.63
each age has choice of d. it will die 296.24
end of all is d. 218.129
even Rome can't grant dispensation from d. 218.87
even the bold fly when d. draws close 218.121
fear of d. or pain is to be dreaded 340.13
for the unhappy man d. is end of life imprisonment 1004.6
give me liberty or give me d. 534.17
good life fears not life nor d. 538.15
hardest of deaths is d. one sees ahead 218.8
he who has set d. beneath his feet 930.1
honorable d. man's immortality 452.13
how little room do we take up in d. 218.118
how shall man know d., which he hath not seen 538.2
however long you live, d. awaits you 218.78
I have asked for d. 218.79
I have hope there is something after d. 452.11
I hope not found out before d. 798.4
I know least this d. I cannot escape 218.98
I postpone d. by living, risking, losing 502.21
ideal mankind would abolish d. 707.3
if life is absurd, d. is insupportable 3.11
in great measure d. is past already 538.33
in the midst of life we are in d. 538.1
instinct serves end of bringing about d. 538.12
interest in d. is interest in life 572.7
inviting sable d. by warfare 1035.98
is it sin to rush into d. ere d. come 941.13
is life a boon? If so, d. is too soon 218.58
life a great surprise; d. even greater one 538.26
life and d. is cat and dog 538.13
life, d., appear ours, yet are hardly so 538.21
life hurries on, and d. follows fast 971.41
life is a coquetry of d. 538.40
life levels all men; d. reveals eminent 218.115
life, the permission to know d. 536.6
life without courage for d. is slavery 192.35
liquor, d., ways out of system we live in 329.49
long life, and short, are by d. made one 538.24
love of posterity caused by d. 796.1
man has given a false importance to d. 538.46
man is only animal that doubts d. 218.68
man sorry for himself doubles d. 218.50
marriage promises happiness, d. assures it 560.121
men convinced of your sincerity only by your d. 218.30
men fear d. as children fear dark 218.9
men's natural sentiment in face of d. 452.15
nearest friends can go with anyone to d. 218.54
no certain life achieved by others' d. 516.13
no life that breathes has longed for d. 941.15
no preaching has made d. other than d. 218.77
nobody knows what d. is, yet we fear it 218.120
nothing after d., and d. itself nothing 218.109
obloquy is more painful than d. 203.28
old men's prayers for d. are lying prayers 646.29
one can survive everything except d. 798.32
one is the silence of d. 538.31
one only stays alive for fear of d. 538.28
only cure for birth, d., is to enjoy interval 536.105
only way to be prepared for d.: be sated 218.91
origin of evils not d., but the fear of d. 218.45
our birth is nothing but our d. begun 81.9
our life is made by the d. of others 538.22
philosophy has a set of sayings for d. 688.39
prison, blood, d. create enthusiasts 795.3
prolonged rest on a formula means d. 979.11
rejoice not over anyone's d. 218.7
repugnance to d. is proportionate to our consciousness of having lived in vain 218.65
rich and poor alike move toward d. 218.101
science without religion increases fear of d. 844.10
shown d., he'll be content with fever 889.23
some driven to d. by fear of it 684.10
some think d. the only reality in life 538.18
spare me the ceremonious air of gloom—which makes d. a hideous show 365.1
spring will come, d. and dust will die 848.52
sun and d. cannot be looked at steadily 218.76
suspense is hostiler than d. 480.2
sweet to hold common scorn of d. 328.38
the sense of d. is most in apprehension 218.112
the weariest and most loathed worldly life is a paradise to what we fear of d. 538.36
there is no God stronger than d. 218.124
this sergeant, d., is strict in arrest 218.111
those who favor d. penalty have more affinity with assassins than those who don't 761.1
time promises time in every d. 218.55
to cure fear of d. set just value on life 538.19
to defeat d. man obliged to defeat life 538.23
to have the universe bear one company would be a great consolation in d. 151.23
to live a life half dead, a living d. 216.9
to reject pain, d., is to reject life 939.12
to the faithful d. is the gate of life 939.28
true return to nature is d. 616.32
useless life is early d. 1017.4

we dread d. as the close of hope 218.64
we face facts of sex but not of d. 326.12
we fear d. as we fear a short summer 218.43
we find in d. not meaning, but an end 538.29
weakest arm can take away life, but the strongest cannot deprive us of d. 218.18
what is good cheer if d. threats disrupt 407.65
what is this d.—a quiet of the heart 218.27
what lives is granted breath by d. 538.4
what should a simple child know of d. 121.51
when vitality runs high, d. takes men by surprise 1028.2
while young, idea of d., failure, intolerable 1064.15
work of life is to lay foundation of d. 218.90

**death's:** d. dark way must be trodden once 218.71
d. stamp gives value to the coin of life 538.39

**deaths:** he must die more d. than one 438.28

**debate:** let no one think that d. means division 362.7
let us not be afraid of d. or dissent 256.8

**debaters':** if all saw fair, wise, the same, no d. strife 649.7

**debauchee:** d.: has pursued pleasure and overtaken it 492.2

**debauchery:** d. is despair in face of infinity 733.5
joylessness, not joy, is mother of d. 733.8

**debt:** d. is the worst poverty 219.7
first or last you must pay entire d. 673.2
national d. if not excessive is a blessing 220.1
national d. is a national bond 220.2
national d. owed by and to nation 220.3
no nation ought to be without a d. 220.2
poor man's d. makes a great noise 219.6
promise made is d. unpaid 737.13
two ways of paying d. 219.2
we've a war, an' a d., an' a flag 534.24

**debtor:** if a d. prove insolvent, don't ruin him 219.10

**debtors:** we are either d. or creditors 219.8

**debts:** forgive us our d. 357.1
he that dies pays all d. 218.114
paying d., we are equal with all men 782.1
say nothing of my d. or pay them 219.4
we shall have to pay d. to world when it may be inconvenient for survival 174.10
words pay no d. 219.14

**decay:** all human things are subject to d. 218.41
men, like fruit, grow sweet before d. 580.12
statesmen, beauties, rarely sense own decay 223.2

**deceit:** fooled with hope, men favor life's d. 536.26
human society founded on mutual d. 907.8
in love d. goes further than mistrust 548.116
one d. needs many others 221.8

**deceive:** d. not thy physician, confessor, lawyer 221.9
man can d. a woman by sham attachment 851.7
nature never deceives us; we d. ourselves 858.8

**deceived:** happier d. than undeceived in love 548.117
life is art of being well d. 447.9
more tolerable to be refused than d. 221.18
we're most easily d. deceiving others 221.12
who will not be d. must have many eyes 221.7

**deceives:** faithful woman d. with a good book 178.5
hope d. more men than cunning does 425.41
reason d. us more often than does nature 778.41
that which d. and does harm also undeceives and does good 474.20
we read world wrong and say it d. us 1060.29

**deceiving:** vain to find fault with arts of d. 221.13

**December:** thoughts suitable to 25th of D. 418.6

**decency:** as simians we have done well as to d. 306.3
d.: not to dare do in public what is decent enough in private 750.3

**decent:** if we cannot be d., let us be graceful 394.6

**decently:** man lives d. as discipline saves his life 248.4

**deception:** men suffer d. from their own opinions 858.5
people always overdo it in attempting d. 221.24
truth lives on in the midst of d. 991.115

**decide:** d.: to succumb to preponderance of one set of influences over another set 222.3
nothing more difficult than ability to d. 222.6

**decision:** d. is action taken when incomplete information does not suggest answer 313.5
delay is itself a d. 724.10
strong man advances issues, makes a d. 222.4

**decisions:** impelled by a state of mind destined not to last, we make our irrevocable d. 222.7
in minute, time for d. that minute reverses 222.5

**decisive:** life's d. actions are often unconsidered 224.13

**decisiveness:** d. is often the art of timely cruelty 222.2

**decorum:** breach of d. causes revulsion 743.5
follow d., never promptings of nature 743.4
man keeps moral backside covered by d. 598.28
necessity dispenseth with d. 617.7

**decree:** hot temper leaps o'er a cold d. 39.31

**decrepitude:** who commits his d. to press plays fool 1062.79

**deed**: among men, the tongue wins, not the d. 683.11
good d. shines in a naughty world 430.31
I do not judge men by d., but impression 513.10
man makes no noise over a good d. 224.18
one good d. dying tongueless 48.9
our least d. wends its way to sea of cause and effect 108.6
Shadow of Shadows looks on d. alone 601.8
virtue must shape itself in d. 1025.54
**deeds**: d. determine us as we determine our d. 224.8
gentle mind by gentle d. is known 376.6
great d. have ridiculous beginning 399.7
great to do that which ends all other d. 941.14
means to do ill d. makes d. ill done 1063.23
men alike in promises, differ in d. 224.21
noble d. most estimable when hidden 224.28
only concrete d. can maintain an alliance 245.6
to know contentment, let your d. be few 183.6
ugly d. are taught by ugly d. 224.36
we kill everybody with our d. 516.6
words may be d. 1057.1
**deep**: smooth runs water where the brook is d. 734.5
**deer**: d. with chain of gold will eat grass 107.7
**defaulting**: vastest day is shrunken by one d. face 603.4
**defeat**: as easy to be enervated by triumph as d. 938.24
d. is above all a thing of futility 225.4
d. is school in which truth grows strong 225.1
d. preferable to defeating injustice by evil 570.8
if the idea is good it will survive d. 441.3
in ourselves are triumph and d. 852.19
**defeats**: there are d. more triumphant than victories 225.3
who can see any difference between our victories and d. 225.2
**defect**: easier to confess d. than claim a quality 339.1
one shining quality hides glaring d. 309.5
**defects**: a man must thank his d. 339.7
when d. of others perceived clearly 339.31
**defense**: d. is faith in institutions defended 226.17
diplomacy, d. not substitutes for each other 226.9
isn't the best d. always a good attack 226.14
no d. like elaborate courtesy 194.12
right is its own d. 816.3
the only d. is that there is no d. 226.5
what boots it at one gate to make d. 226.13
**defenses**: what's to defend us against our own d. 226.4
**defer**: d. not till to-morrow to be wise 228.2
**defiance**: artist must blow trumpet of d. 53.75
**deficiencies**: pity one whose only sense is to see his d. 857.6
**deficiency**: easier to see a d. than import or value 203.13
**defiled**: sun visits cesspools and is not d. 57.8
whoever touches pitch will be d. 57.2
**define**: d., d., well-educated infant 227.4
**definition**: d.: wilderness of idea within wall of words 227.2
every d. is dangerous 227.3
**definitions**: d., like scratching, make sore spot sorer 227.1
philosophy provides a refuge for d. 688.10
**deformity**: beauty and d. equally pass away 983.18
no d. but saves us from a dream 455.12
**degenerates**: everything d. in the hands of man 174.7
**degree**: men of low d. are vanity, of high d. a lie 773.1
**degrees**: d. is good things; they livils all ranks 277.16
**dehumanization**: d. of Negro indivisible from d. of ourselves 83.3
**deity**: rational being discovers d. in creation 616.47
**delay**: d. breeds danger 228.1
d. is itself a decision 724.10
d. is preferable to error 228.9
woman is the daughter of d. 1055.120
**delays**: all d. are dangerous in war 1035.29
**delegation**: d.: merchandise that comes in sets 705.11
**deliberation**: d.: examining one's bread to determine which side it is buttered on 968.2
we use d. to justify doing what we want 775.4
**delight**: absurd to slight today's d. for the hereafter 698.5
danger and d. grow on one stalk 213.8
in temple of d. melancholy has shrine 699.4
some d. smiles on us even in melancholy 407.81
teach us d. in simple things 892.9
tomes of criticism hang on moments of d. 20.5
**delinquency**: juvenile d. provides adults with fantasies 201.7
**delinquent**: teacher may change d. into solid citizen 959.30
**deliverance**: liberation is not d. 534.18
**delusion**: ignorance prevents wisdom; d. is result 445.2
**demagogues**: the people are capable of good judgment when they do not listen to d. 230.2
where laws are not supreme, d. arise 230.1
**demagogy**: d.: when equality becomes identity 230.3
**demands**: who makes great d. upon himself is inclined to make great d. on others 857.3

**demean:** it is duty of great man to d. himself 594.16
**demerit:** small d. extinguishes long service 1063.10
**democracies:** great d. tend to think stupid man is more likely to be honest than clever man 705.67
in d., nothing is greater than commerce 102.35
**democracy:** after each war there's less d. to save 1035.2
Americans burn incense before d. 34.26
armed forces cannot protect our d. 226.11
at bottom of d. is little man making a little cross on a little bit of paper 1030.5
d. admits variety and permits criticism 231.12
d. best, for it respects man as reasonable 231.20
d.: covenant among men to respect rights 231.43
d. effective only if people can stop talking 231.4
d.: election by incompetent many 231.49
d. furthered when minorities cancel each other out 231.6
d.: government less bad than others 231.17
d. is a charming form of government 231.40
d. is good, for other systems are worse 231.36
d. is the theory that the common people know what they want and deserve to get it 231.32
d. is worst form of government except all other forms 231.7
d. last flowering of human experience 231.21
d.: name for the people when we need them 231.11
d. needs a party that will separate the good in it from evils that beset it 231.33
d. never a final achievement 231.23
d. not static but an everlasting march 231.42
d. represents disbelief in all great men 231.37
d.: subjection of minority to majority 231.25
envy is the basis of d. 231.45
evil of d., to put up with man you elect 231.41
fight to save wild beauty is d. at its best 174.8
government should use aristocracy under form of d. 52.3
if offered d. or a bag of grain 231.46
in a d., administration is by many, not few 231.52
in a d. the free are rulers 231.2
in d. officers of government are servants 755.16
justice delayed is d. denied 515.28
liberty in d. when all share government 231.3
masses are the material of d. 231.1
modern democracies do not yet effect d. 231.31
no difference in destruction wrought under name of totalitarianism or d. 1035.40
nothing will make d. of illiterate people 231.29
obstacle to d. is property 740.10
rulers of d. are the voters 1030.18
self-criticism is secret weapon of d. 231.50
taste of d. bitter when full d. denied 231.26
though reconciled to d., I can't be sanguine 231.8
under d. the weakest should have the same opportunity as the strongest 231.13
what chance has d. if it requires a whole population of capable voters 231.48
world must be made safe for d. 231.57
**democracy's:** d. only success—the night 626.6
**Democrat:** every Harvard class should have one D. 704.12
**democratic:** amongst d. nations, each new generation is a new people 372.16
at my age, man ducks pol-itical meetin's, an' votes th' D. ticket 704.3
blind lead blind, it's the d. way 231.34
d. American idea is not one level for all but liberty for each to be what he is 231.5
d. disease reduces everything unique 295.16
d. government too perfect for mere men 231.44
d. institutions give men lofty notion of their country, themselves 231.55
d. movement loves crowd, fears individuals 231.30
d. nation has independent labor unions 1006.6
d. nations are haunted by what will be 231.54
freemen have d. feeling which will not submit to arrogance, servility 231.16
let us not seek D. answer, but right answer 704.7
man of d. principles must overcome physical repugnances 98.9
passions of men in d. times end in love of riches, or proceed from it 1041.64
taste for well-being is feature of d. times 744.19
that a peasant may become king does not render the kingdom d. 231.56
**democrats:** d. think they should be equal in all 295.2
**demon:** every man is hunted by his own d. 620.6
**demonstration:** he who admits only d. can be sure only of perishing quickly 738.2
**demoralization:** best mask for d. is daring 90.11
**denial:** better d. than unwilling compliance 784.5
civil d. better than rude grant 784.4
**denied:** not to ask is not to be d. 799.3
**dentist:** d.: puts metal in your mouth, pulls coins out of your pocket 232.1

**deny:** better d. at once than promise long 784.2
to d. all is to confess all 403.20
**depart:** fire of life sinks and I am ready to d. 646.62
**departure:** time for d. even when no place to go 115.39
**depend:** in civilized society we d. on each other 906.10
remember you cannot d. upon yourself 247.3
to d. on child is blindness in one eye 233.8
we put up with most from those on whom we most d. 233.4
**depressed:** if didn't live venturously, never be d. 16.9
**depression:** noble deeds, hot baths, best cures for d. 1004.33
**deprived:** jealousy is the fact of being d. 508.4
men cannot bear being d. even of fears 234.1
unhappy man d. of what he did not have 1004.22
we know well only what we are d. of 234.2
**depth:** no one tests d. of river with both feet 749.1
**deputies:** God has delegated a million d. 171.5
**deride:** men learn more quickly what they d. 182.5
**describe:** how d. delicate thing that happens when brilliant insect alights on flower 1057.36
**describing:** when d. don't state the matter plainly 702.14
**description:** world loves a ready-made d. to hang on a man 928.1
**desert:** d. speaks of man's insignificance 413.9
I scare myself with my own d. places 413.5
man: preceded by forest, followed by d. 1035.47
they make a d. and call it peace 1035.97
use every man after his d. 515.43
**deserted:** wives invariably flourish when d. 470.8
wives not d.: objects of commiseration 560.74
**deserting:** d. male often ends in disaster 470.8
**design:** color without d. less pleasing than simple outline 659.1
d. a thing by considering it in next larger context 235.1
things difficult to d. easy to perform 243.8
**designers:** interior d., like clients, want to show off 428.5
**desire:** all envy is proportionate to d. 293.18
boredom: the d. for desires 92.9
d. for imaginary benefits often involves loss of present blessings 236.1
d. in eyes of bride is a strong power 885.33
d. is poison at lunch, wormwood at dinner 885.1
d. outlives performance many years 885.31
first d. easier to extinguish than successors 236.27
freedom won by controlling d. 856.3
from satisfaction of d. may arise despair 839.2
great d. obtains little 236.6
he knows peace who has forgotten d. 674.3
if we imagine anyone to d. what we d. 471.11
if you d. many things, they will seem few 236.10
it is d. that engenders belief 76.17
it is hard to fight against impulsive d. 236.19
make us, not fly to dreams, but moderate d. 236.3
most men d. a virgin who is a whore 885.7
pleasure tasted satisfies less than d. 698.33
possible to harness d. to many interests 236.30
presence of d. ignores the philosopher 688.3
some d. necessary to keep life in motion 236.23
some, from dread of losing what they ardently d., leave nothing undone to lose it 236.25
to d. is in some sense to enjoy 236.18
tragedies: to lose heart's d., to gain it 236.39
we d. only objects we're capable of desiring 236.31
we do not d. only through reason 236.26
we do not succeed in changing things to our d.; gradually our d. changes 236.34
we'd scarcely d. things if we knew them 236.28
when d. dies, fear is born 236.15
when we d. or solicit any thing, our minds run wholly on the good side of it 710.16
where no d., no industry 1058.50
**desire's:** only might-have-been can fill d. cup 785.3
**desired:** no object could be what whole soul d. 252.3
**desires:** can't abolish by law or axe d. of men 236.29
d., realized, haunt us less readily 236.12
each believes what he fears or d. 199.5
heaven of each is but what each d. 412.8
if d. are endless, cares will be so 401.11
ignore a man's d.: ignore source of power 525.49
men have thousand d. to bushel of choices 236.4
New Year reviving d., soul retires to solitude 624.4
not possessions, but d., need equalizing 740.1
supplying wants by lopping off d. is like cutting off feet 930.10
the abstinent carry their d. with them 859.1
those d. that do not bring pain if they are not satisfied are not necessary 236.9
who d. but acts not, breeds pestilence 236.5
**desiring:** don't spoil what you have by d. more 183.7

**despair:** after d., one is almost happy 237.1
between cowardice and d. valour is born 192.10
calm d. is the essence of wisdom 800.11
clearness produces d. 237.11
cries of d. are a kind of wealth 1045.7
ennui makes more suicides than d. 288.1
d.: price for setting an impossible aim 237.8
debauchery is d. in face of infinity 733.5
difference between d. and fear 340.11
from satisfaction of desire may arise d. 839.2
God put self-pity by the side of d. 870.2
I can endure my d., not another's hope 293.29
in d. are intense enjoyments 237.6
in d. we look on ourselves as objects 868.18
like strength is felt from hope, d. 933.9
no peace in changing waves of joy, d. 962.1
poet hides d. in expression of joy 702.54
sad patience, neighbor to d. 670.1
safe d. raves—agony is frugal 237.5
suicide justified if no purpose to d. 941.5
who has never hoped can never d. 464.9
who has nothing to hope should d. of nothing 930.8
**desperate:** wisdom does not do d. things 1053.66
**desperation:** d. a grandiose form of funk 237.3
men lead lives of quiet d. 237.13
nowadays most lead lives of noisy d. 629.5
**despise:** despising the past, we teach others to d. us 439.2
it is easy to d. what you cannot get 913.1
man must d. himself, then others will 864.2
men d. those who court them 651.10
those whom men have injured they d. 474.22
**despisers:** great d. are the great reverers 182.7
**despot:** benevolent d. demands from others the submissiveness of sheep 995.13
**despotism:** d. does great things illegally 534.3
failure of reform strengthens d. 783.6
man about the same with d. or freedom 393.67
when white man governs another man, that is d. 995.19
**destination:** our age is all signpost and no d. 994.9
**destinies:** greater dooms win greater d. 17.29
our d. are decided by nothings, accident 238.2
**destiny:** 'tis all a chequer-board of nights, days where d. with men for pieces plays 238.16
conditioning aims to make us like our d. 12.6
d. grants our wishes, but in its own way 238.10
d. is relentless logic of each day 238.9
d.: tyrant's authority for crime and fool's excuse for failure 238.3
efforts to escape d. lead us into it 298.3
how easy it is, when d. is kind 238.6
in field of d., we reap as we've sown 860.13
let a man accept his d. 930.4
love only that which is woven in your d. 238.14
man's d.: half within self, half without 238.21
no problem of human d. is beyond human beings 731.5
one link of chain of d. at a time 238.4
our d. rules over us 238.15
reversion to d. is called eternity 300.2
sometimes better to abandon one's self to d. 110.6
to go in search of d. is to seek sorrows 238.12
we are not permitted to choose our d. 238.11
where d. blunders, prudence will not avail 238.18
who glories in luck may be overthrown by d. 358.10
whoever has not felt the danger of our times has not penetrated to vitals of d. 994.13
**destroy:** fortune, to d., first makes mad 555.19
if a man d. another's eye, d. his eye 515.19
impulse to d. as ancient as to create 239.8
minute can d. what an age must rebuild 239.3
short, easy to d. life others have made 516.15
to be able to d. with good conscience 239.7
**destroys:** what d. one man preserves another 791.1
**destruction:** d. is new creation on a wider scale 239.2
if d. be our lot we must be its author 34.36
passion for d. is a creative joy 239.6
**destructions:** after the great d. everyone will prove he was innocent 633.6
**detach:** crying need of today is to d. ourselves 897.2
**detachment:** d. excludes ability to experience happiness 31.4
**detail:** if every d. given, imagination loses desire 936.1
**detection:** d. is an exact science 703.2
**detective:** life is rotten writer of d. stories 536.63
**detest:** men love in haste, but they d. at leisure 410.3
**detractions:** happy they that put their d. to mending 458.5
**detractor:** next to joy of egotist is joy of d. 203.27
**developed:** do not seek so anxiously to be d. 433.29
**devil:** animal would depict d. in human form 41.14
apology for the d.: we hear only one side of case; God has written all the books 240.2
arch of religion is hardly firm without d. 240.5
d. always insists on having the last word 240.4

d. can cite Scripture for his purpose 137.12; 329.39
d. gets to belfry by vicar's skirts 305.15
d. himself is good when he is pleased 391.19
d. seeks slaves and claims obedience 240.10
God is good, there is no d. but fear 340.18
God without the d. is dead, being alone 385.13
idle men tempt the d. 444.17
mass movements need belief in a d. 564.2
men give d. the form of a snake 240.3
modern town-dweller has no God, no D. 129.23
sometimes the d. is a gentleman 240.9
they must needs go whom the d. drives 161.1
when d. prays he's out to deceive you 691.14
where God hath a temple, d. hath a chapel 188.2
who takes d. into boat must carry him 57.10
why should d. have all the good tunes 240.6
with pious action we sugar o'er the d. 438.24
your adversary, the d., walketh about 240.1

**devil's:** truth may come from the d. mouth 991.44

**devils:** d. driven from heart by touch of hand 875.13

**devotion:** need for d. to something outside ourselves 145.4
temperance, justice without d. is cold virtue 1025.3

**devotion's:** with d. visage we sugar o'er the devil 438.24

**devour:** men would d. men but for power of hiding 162.2

**devout:** d. man would be an atheist if king were 691.8
if man is d., we accuse him of hypocrisy 203.5

**dialect:** d. with slang admirable medium for those with nothing to say 521.1

**dialogue:** independence is first condition of d. 873.10

**diary:** d.: daily record of what one can relate to oneself without blushing 62.2
keep a d. and someday it'll keep you 62.8

**dice:** best throw of d.: throw them away 367.4

**dictator:** artist has never been a d. 53.14
d. held in grip of party machine 995.7
free conversation will not bear a d. 185.4

**dictators:** d. ride on tigers they dare not dismount 995.12

**dictatorship:** efficient government is a d. 393.63

**dictionaries:** d. like watches: worst better than none 242.5

**dictionary:** neither is a d. a bad book to read 242.2
to read poetry I take down my d. 242.3

**die:** a pity we can d. but once to save country 671.2
anxiety of having to d. is anxiety of being eternally forgotten 218.130
as natural to d. as to be born 218.10
base to fight necessity; we have to d. 617.4
cannot love to live if cannot bear to d. 538.30
could the Devil make me believe I could never d., I would not outlive that thought 218.17
d. proudly when one cannot live proudly 218.93
d. to life to be a creator 198.26
easy live and quiet d. 859.5
except a corn of wheat d. 198.4
greatest good luck: to d. at right time 399.36
he who hath lived ill cannot d. well 218.57
if thou wouldst have praise, d. 716.39
it is better to d. on your feet than to live on your knees 361.30
it is very grand to d. in harness 807.2
knowledge of hour when one is to d. 761.4
longest-lived, shortest-lived lose same thing when they d. 545.6
man should be born, and born, d. at once 81.1
man thinks he was not made to d. 452.18
men are convinced an interval of time will be allowed them before they d. 452.12
men d. only for that by which they live 561.15
men eddy about, achieving nothing; then d. 600.1
must spend all one's life learning to d. 538.35
no young man believes he shall ever d. 1064.27
nothing to d.; frightful not to live 216.5
old men must d., or the world would only breed the past again 218.125
only benefit of old age: to d. by degrees 218.88
other men d.; I'm not another; I'll not d. 452.9
people can d. of mere imagination 448.4
theirs but to do and d. 582.20
there are two respectable ways to d. 218.72
those most like dead are most loath to d. 218.75
'tis solitude should teach us how to d. 908.10
to d. completely, one must be forgotten 218.25
to d. is different from what anyone supposed 218.135
to d. is to go into the Collective Unconscious 218.67
to d. is to stop dying and finally do it 218.24
to d. with glory is still pain for dier 218.48
to d. without having lived is unbearable 218.53
to live in hearts we leave is not to d. 452.1
to work, live, d. hard and go to hell 414.10
we can't be sure of something worth living for

unless we are ready to d. for it 1019.9
we d. disappointed 536.39
we have mouldered away long before we d. 646.48
we must d. to one life to enter another 115.16
we must needs d., and are as water spilt 218.14
we shall d. alone 908.38
when man and woman d., his heart's the last part to move 576.13
where does the ant d. except in sugar 733.6
who's learned to d. has unlearned to serve 218.89
will world be overturned when you d. 865.6
you d. because you're alive 538.34
you'll find it when you try to d. the easier to let go 218.34
**died:** can't know a man's life until he has d. 536.119
most persons have d. before they expire 216.4
**dies:** after many a summer d. the swan 600.21
flower that once has blown for ever d. 600.14
he that d. pays all debts 218.114
it matters not how a man d. 538.20
man always d. before he is fully born 402.7
man d. when he wants, as he wants 218.6
man d. whether he's done nothing or much 6.13
surely nothing d. but something mourns 603.2
**diet:** anxiety about d. no better than disease 411.15
every d. teaches french fries are out 272.20
**differ:** freedom to d. is not limited 256.6
we hate for points on which we d. 27.3
**differed:** we owe our knowledge to those who have d. 256.2
**difference:** as much d. between us and ourselves as between us and others 852.21
**differences:** if we cannot end our d., we can make world safe for diversity 977.12
resemblances are shadows of d. 676.10
**different:** anybody who is any good is d. from others 467.8
d. men seek happiness in d. ways 407.5
men are born equal and d. 467.9
men are created d. 168.15
them of other naturs think d. 258.1
we must be d. in order to love each other 548.81
**difficult:** all things are d. before they are easy 243.5
attempt d. tasks as if they were easy 579.8
easy is d. when done with reluctance 1015.1
history has made life d. for us all 243.9
in the d. are the friendly forces 243.13
things d. to design easy to perform 243.8
**difficulties:** d. are things that show what men are 243.4
he who accounts all things easy will have many d. 325.2
never trust advice of man in d. 19.3
ten thousand d. do not make one doubt 263.5
**difficulty:** d.: coin used by learned to conceal inanity 842.31
d. gives all things their estimation 243.12
have courage to face d. lest it kick you 243.15
plugging away at a d. 579.7
**diffidence:** d. is the better part of knowledge 998.3
**digestion:** d. exists for health 411.1
with sound d. man may front much 934.3
**digestions:** few radicals have good d. 175.3
**dignity:** d.: a matter which concerns only mankind 244.4
d. achieved only through struggle 1058.19
d.: heart, mind lifted by perception, grace 244.6
d. is genuine which is not diminished by the indifference of others 244.3
d.: not in what we do, but understand 244.5
let none wear an undeserved d. 578.7
let not a man guard his d. 244.2
man's d. reduced by largesse 430.30
what is d. without honesty 244.1
**digression:** sin may be venial, d. is mortal 965.17
**dilapidation:** some people are beautiful in d. 646.95
**dilemma:** there is an epigram for every d. 294.5
**diligence:** care and d. bring luck 279.8
few things impossible to d. and skill 279.11
patience, d., like faith, remove mountains 670.17
scholar without d.: lover without money 842.36
what is the use of such terrible d. 269.18
**dilly-dalliers:** d. never where they were supposed to get 228.3
**dined:** many are d. out of their religion, politics 97.1
one cannot think well, love well, sleep well if one has not d. well 272.32
**dining:** the art of d. well is no slight art 272.24
**dinner:** d. lubricates business 272.28
good d., feasting reconciles everybody 272.25
in France everything is a pretext for d. 359.1
man thinks more earnestly of d. than anything 272.18
music with d. is an insult both to the cook and violinist 607.17
people must have d. table laid as usual 210.21
the tocsin of the soul—the d.-bell 272.6
what takes place after d. must never be taken as counsel 229.1
**dinosaur's:** d. lesson: overabundance of bigness 310.4
**diplomacy:** d., defense not substitutes for each other 226.9

d. is the lowest form of politeness 245.14
d. is the police in grand costume 245.8
real d. when diplomat deceives his own people 245.11
**diplomat:** d. is one who says go to hell so that you look forward to trip 245.13
d. should be yielding, supple as liana 245.7
my advice to d. is to have kids and dog 245.12
**diplomats:** d. are essential to starting a war 1035.81
d. are useful only in fair weather 245.4
d., women, crabs seem coming when going 245.5
d. write notes because they lack nerve 245.10
**direction:** if all pulled in one d., world would keel over 27.10
nothing below you if in d. of your life 433.5
only one d. in world, time its measure 600.19
we have no sense of d., only impetus 481.2
**directness:** the weak and confused worship brutal d. 360.10
**dirt:** everyone in crowd has power to throw d. 898.4
he sees d. in other's eye, but not in own 869.1
he that flings d. dirtieth himself 898.2
slow-falling d. sounds alarm 633.11
**dirty:** clean glove often hides d. hand 221.5
only man, civilized animals become d. 135.6
so long as we are d., we are pure 246.1
taste for d. stories inherent in humans 708.2
**disagreeable:** those uncomfortable in themselves are d. to others 855.2
**disagreement:** agreement made more precious by d. 27.8
**disappoint:** are you angry that others d. you 247.3
**disappointed:** he who expects nothing shall never be d. 316.9
we are d. because we expect that for which we have not provided 316.13
we look for reward and are d. 457.3
**disappointment:** d. tears the bearable film of life 247.2
look on bright side and avoid d. 776.4
prompter the refusal, the less d. 784.6
**disappoints:** man appoints and God d. 385.19
**disapproval:** each man is afraid of neighbor's d. 619.10
**disaster:** d. crushes one now, afterward another 17.23
man does better to run from d. than be caught 298.6
**disastrous:** no events so d. adroit men don't advance 303.6
**disavowed:** least said is soonest d. 96.2
**disbelief:** if faith can move mountains, d. can deny their existence 997.19
**disciple:** every master has but one d. 350.3
**disciples:** having d. is like having children 350.2
**discipline:** life a d. for lower animals as for men 248.2
man lives decently, as d. saves his life 248.4
who compares self with the d., not followers of the d., has lower opinion of self 1029.8
**discontent:** d. first step in progress of man, nation 249.10
nor is it d. to keep the mind deep in its fountain 908.9
**discontented:** d. one place, seldom happy in another 249.1
**discord:** d. gives a relish for concord 250.11
harmony needs background of d. 408.5
out of d. comes the fairest harmony 651.8
**discourage:** don't let life d. you; man who got where he is had to begin where he was 251.1
**discouragement:** trouble has no connection with d. 251.2
**discourse:** d. is index of a man's understanding 75.1
d. makes a clear man 185.11
good company, d., are sinews of virtue 151.28
**discourses:** most tedious d. those on Supreme Being 966.3
**discoverers:** ill d. think there's no land when they see only sea 85.1
**discovery:** scientific d.: interpretation for our own convenience 843.40
scientific d. is not unalloyed blessing 843.20
**discretion:** d. is on all occasions required 749.6
dram of d. is worth a pound of wisdom 749.13
one can pass on responsibility, not d. 804.5
sincerity is glass, d. is diamond 749.21
the better part of valor is d. 749.32
**discrimination:** that's part of American greatness, d. 469.3
**discussion:** aim of d. should be progress, not victory 51.16
anyone who in d. relies on authority 51.18
d. in America means dissent 256.12
**disease:** bodily d. may be symptom of spiritual d. 889.13
d. known is half cured 241.1
d. makes men more physical 889.18
every physician has his favourite d. 261.5
imaginary ailment is worse than a d. 437.2
interest in d. is interest in life 572.7
it is by d. that health is pleasant 184.3
life is an incurable d. 536.23
some remedies worse than the d. 791.10
who conceals his d. cannot be cured 162.5
**diseased:** canst thou not minister to a mind d. 751.3
**diseases:** all d. run into one, old age 889.7
d. crucify the soul of man 889.1
d. desperate grown by desperate appliances are relieved, or not at all 791.12
d. which destroy a man are natural 889.24

extreme remedies appropriate to extreme d. 791.6
**disenchanting:** is anything so d. as attainment 938.40
**disfranchisement:** d. robs poor of only protection against rich 1030.6
**disgrace:** in darkness shameful deed brings no d. 214.2
**disguise:** accustomed to d. ourselves to others, we become disguised to ourselves 162.12
man is practised in d. 221.6
to go naked is the best d. 221.4
we all wear some d. 726.7
we d. ourselves from ourselves 858.7
**dish:** d. around which I see too many people doesn't tempt me 706.7
high birth is a poor d. at table 37.8
**dishonesty:** d. is the raw material of dupes 221.1
hatred of d. is from fear of being deceived 221.23
honesty is less profitable than d. 423.14
no clear boundary separates honesty, d. 423.5
**dishonor:** do no d. to the earth 174.2
**disillusion:** d. can become illusion if we rest in it 252.1
hope is only good thing d. respects 252.7
**disintegration:** endless part of d.: it will build again 538.6
**disinterested:** world saved by handful of d. men 1014.5
**dislike:** dark are the minds of those who d. us 253.2
some d. something in every banquet 719.2
sorrow falls readily into d. 911.45
**dismal:** nothing on earth more d. than man 558.28
**disobedience:** d. is man's original virtue 254.2
d. is seldom distinguished from neglect 254.1
forgive us for condemning civil d. 1025.55
**disorder:** d. immediately defeats itself 310.10
d. is always in a hurry 654.12
d. is our worst enemy 654.9
d. makes one wish for police or death 654.14
**dispatch:** d. is the soul of business 102.8
**disposition:** best part of health is fine d. 390.4
good d. is virtue in itself and is lasting 390.9
**disputant:** d. no more cares for truth than sportsman for the hare 51.21
**disputants:** d. like sportsmen; delight in pursuit 51.22
**disputation:** itch of d. will prove scab of Church 124.14
**dispute:** in philosophical d., defeated gains most 51.10
**disputes:** in d., so much as there is of passion, so much there is of nothing to the purpose 51.3
**dissatisfied:** we are less d. when we lack many things 236.21
**dissect:** we murder to d. 843.41
**dissension:** civil d. is a viperous worm 250.13
d. may divide even the true-hearted 250.10
**dissent:** discussion in America means d. 256.12
let us not be afraid of debate or d. 256.8
looking at God reduces our disposition to human d. 766.3
**dissimulation:** without d. no business possible 221.2
world is so full of d. that words are empty 346.19
**dissolute:** if their pleasures drove away the fears of the d., we'd find no fault in them 492.3
**distance:** d. has same effect on mind as on eye 682.6
d. lends enchantment to the view 682.1
greatest d. is from nothing to little 735.5
if a man makes me keep my d., the comfort is, he keeps his as well 31.9
one at d. from object is bad judge of space separating it from other objects 682.3
**distant:** d. Trojans never injured me 658.10
superiority of the d. over the present 236.36
**distaste:** d. expressed as moral disapproval 598.13
**distempers:** one topic, their d., forbidden to all well-bred mortals 889.8
**distinction:** envy is tax d. must pay 293.9
how many wounds are given to win a d. 51.4
**distress:** deep d. hath humanised my soul 911.59
in deep d. native sense departs 911.53
until man stops shouting down his blunderings, he's not in shape to examine d. 752.18
what end served by running to meet d. 316.10
**distressed:** knowing sorrow I learn to succor the d. 56.14
**distrust:** better traitors escape than have spirit of d. 257.7
d. is our only defense against betrayal 257.20
our d. justifies the deceit of others 257.12
set the foot down with d. 1060.23
what loneliness is more lonely than d. 257.4
**disturb:** what comes into the world to d. nothing deserves neither respect nor patience 641.3
**diverse:** d. elements joined in heart of man 258.2
**diversion:** most sorts of d. an imitation of fighting 922.9
**diversity:** the most universal quality is d. 258.3
we can make world safe for d. 977.12
**divide:** d. the fire, and you will put it out 932.4
**divided:** house d. against itself cannot stand 1036.1
we praise when cake, not ours, is d. 438.17

**divides:** he who d. gets the worst share 887.4
**divine:** belief in d. mission a form of certainty 333.18
from beauty we draw conception of d. life 408.3
only domain where d. visible: art 53.76
pretenders to d. knowledge are possessed with the sin of pride 333.14
to see d. light put out thy candle 691.4
what is d. escapes men's notice 259.5
**divinity:** good conscience is the best d. 171.10
I will work out d. busy within my mind 198.32
indwelling ideal lends all gods their d. 259.7
there is surely a piece of d. in us 259.1
there's a d. that shapes our ends 238.19
**division:** let no one think that debate means d. 362.7
**divorce:** marriage some weeks more ancient than d. 260.8
read about d., can't see why two people can't have harmony 260.1
**divorced:** four minds in bed of d. man who marries d. woman 260.7
**do:** all seek to d. what they please 361.14
as we are, so we d. 238.8
boast not of what thou would'st have done: d. 224.20
can d. all because they think they can 854.7
can't d. what we will: will what we can 1049.11
d. and have done; the former is easiest 74.6
d. it yourself—now enthroned cliché for being occupied with nonessentials 873.13
d. not all you are able 749.18
d. unto the other feller the way he'd like to d. unto you 386.5
d. unto yourself as neighbors d. 386.1
d. what you have to d. 55.6
don't d. to others as you would they d. to you 386.4
hideous to assume we can d. something for others 56.2
if to d. were as easy as to know what were good to d. 391.48
if you would not be known to d. anything, never d. it 798.12
man can d. what he cannot imagine 3.4
man may d. or know but little 9.18
our dignity not in what we d. 244.5
people always neglect something they can d. trying to d. something they can't 55.12
people who d. things exceed endurance 33.26
somebody must make us d. what we can 471.5
theirs but to d. and die 582.20
to d. nothing is most difficult thing 444.18
to promise not to d. a thing 737.16
want thing done well, d. it yourself 873.19
we d. all with an eye to something else 601.1
we d. nothing well till we cease to think about the manner of doing it 921.3
we d. what we can, then make a theory 775.2
we d. what we must 317.2
what I must d. is all that concerns me 224.9
what it lies in our power to d., it lies in our power not to d. 856.2
what men daily d. not knowing what they d. 481.3
what to d. is shadow of what we want to d. 224.39
what ye would men d. to you, d. to them 386.2
what you d. not want done to yourself, d. not to others 386.3
whatsoever thy hand findeth to d. 224.4
who has much to d. will d. something wrong 86.7
**docility:** d. is the observable half of reason 347.3
**doctor:** d. and patient are employer and employee 261.18
D. Marcus went to see statue of Zeus 261.7
death will seize the d. too 572.11
God heals, the d. takes the fees 261.6
hood ass with purple, he shall pass for cathedral d. 136.12
only a fool will make a d. his heir 261.17
**doctors:** best d. are Diet, Quiet, Merryman 261.21
d. torture the sick and demand a fee 261.8
if d. had more Christianity 572.3
nature knows needs; d. know nothing 572.1
there are more old drunkards than old d. 266.17
**doctrine:** d. enables us to judge of miracles 586.3
d. is the skin of truth set up and stuffed 966.2
no d. does good where nature is wanting 200.4
**doctrines:** what makes all d. clear? two hundred pounds a year 596.10
**doers:** talkers are no good d. 916.54
**does:** what man would do, not d., exalts him 55.3
**dog:** d. is a lion in his own house 420.18
d., pampered by mistress, is lamentable 41.23
d. reasons the way he sniffs 484.4
d. was created specially for children 41.2
d. will never forget crumb thou gavest 41.25
if a sane d. fights a mad d. 555.5
make d. prosperous, he will not bite you 473.10
no faith never broken save that of a d. 41.19
pleasure of a d. is that you may make a fool of yourself with him 41.6
reasonable amount of fleas is good for d. 41.31

silent d. is the first to bite 891.11
**dog's:** d. best friend is his illiteracy 41.20
**dogma:** d.: the pleasure of answering questions 478.16
danger lies in the uncompromisingness with which d. is held, not in the d. 262.3
**dogmas:** he who observes moral precepts of religions won't be questioned in heaven as to d. 790.39
**dogmatic:** profound ignorance makes a man d. 262.12
unconscious dogmatists most d. 262.5
**dogmatism:** obstinacy, d., surest signs of stupidity 644.9
**dogmatize:** no man should d. except on theology 262.11
**dogs:** d. bark at a person they do not know 720.8
d. bark, but the caravan moves on 156.2
d. have more love than integrity 41.7
d. live with man as courtiers 41.27
if I belittle d. or mothers 878.6
let d. delight to bark and bite 41.30
'orses and d. are wittles and drink to me 41.9
our d. will love the meanest of us 41.22
who hates d. and babies can't be all bad 588.3
who lies with d. shall rise with fleas 57.14
**doing:** anything worth d. has been done 224.3
between saying, d., many shoes worn out 228.8
d. is overrated 327.8
no d. till thing to be done is recognized 9.14
saying is one thing and d. is another 224.22
step from knowing to d. rarely taken 9.20
we spend days d. what we don't want 1058.11
what is worth d. is worth trouble of asking somebody to do it 313.1
**dollar:** Americans worship the d. 34.71
there are two halves to every d. 970.9
value of a d. is social 596.16
**dollars:** solid scholars get degrees, jobs, d. 277.73
**domestic:** d. as a plate, I retire half-past eight 71.8
female malignity exerted in d. trifles 1055.80
gaining d. happiness, women lose beauty 560.22
it takes patience to appreciate d. bliss 560.102
**dominate:** slave must d. in his turn 995.5
**dominating:** we can't do without d. others 713.11
**domination:** country's turn at world d. ends with change 614.12
**done:** he that has d. nothing has known nothing 9.12
what is well d. is d. soon enough 309.1
what may be d. any time is d. no time 228.6
what's d. is d.; spend not time in tears 505.6
**donkey:** if a d. bray at you, don't bray at him 658.9
until the d. tried to clear fence, he thought himself a deer 1020.9
**Don Quixotes:** mankind either Sancho Panzas or D.Q. 558.46
**doom:** he deposes d. who hath suffered him 17.18
**dooms:** greater d. win greater destinies 17.29
**door:** each man is accessible by right d. 955.1
open d. must be of a man's size 650.2
our interests are those of the open d. 496.18
we often get in quicker by back d. 579.10
**doors:** all d. open to courtesy 194.6
**doubt:** authority rarely survives in face of d. 61.5
cleave to the sunnier side of d. 328.39
d. is an element of criticism 897.5
d. is faith: but faith is d. 263.8
d. is not below knowledge, but above it 897.1
d. is the vestibule of temple of truth 897.3
d., mistrust: panic of timid imagination 998.7
d. of reality of love makes us d. all 998.1
faith embraces itself and d. 328.41
faith had dissociated itself from d. 263.11
implacableness is directed against inner d. 262.10
let us never d. what nobody is sure about 113.1
majority of mankind incapable of d., faith 558.18
man with humility will acquire in his beliefs the saving d. of his certainty 433.13
modest d. called the beacon of the wise 897.11
more of d., the stronger faith 263.1
ten thousand difficulties do not make one d. 263.5
there lives more faith in honest d. 263.9
to give reason for anything breeds d. of it 775.3
when in d., win the trick 170.11
wilt Thou not take d. of Thy children 263.3
**doubtful:** d. friend is worse than certain enemy 363.4
**doubting:** to believe with certainty, begin with d. 76.23
**doubts:** d. make us lose good we oft might win 998.11
from new truths, new phrase, new d. grow 998.4
he who knows nothing d. nothing 113.13
the skeptic does not mean him who d. 897.12
**dour:** d. friend is less fatiguing than optimist 653.3
**dove:** oh that I had wings like a d. 298.1
who is wholly a d., without a grain of serpent, often discredits his best actions 377.1
**doves:** be ye therefore harmless as d. 936.3
**down:** look d. to know how high you stand 773.29

when fountain has gone up, it comes d. 358.33
when man is up, people want to d. him 938.17

**dragon's:** our fathers and ourselves sowed d. teeth 809.1

**drama:** d. deals not with truth, but with effect 965.18
d. is action and not philosophy 965.25
eye is the enemy of ear in real d. 965.37
great d. is the souvenir of the adventure of a master among pieces of his own soul 965.21
talent for d. is not talent for writing 965.33

**drama's:** d. laws the d. patrons give 965.11

**dramas:** life is full of internal d. 687.18
some always create parts for selves in d. which nobody is prepared to act with them 620.5

**dramatist:** d. finds watching shocks among men engrossing enough without comment 965.35
d. must avoid digression more than a saint does sin 965.17

**dreaded:** he is to be d. who dreads poverty 33.30

**dream:** because thou must not d., thou need'st not despair 237.2
characteristic of a d.: nothing surprises us 264.2
d. is always below the surface of speech 687.19
lie of pipe d. is what gives us life 687.16
life is a bad d. between two awakenings 536.83
man that is born falls into d. 447.6
no deformity but saves us from a d. 455.12
nothing happens unless first a d. 231.47
our d. dashes against the great mystery 1012.11
shadow of a d. is man, no more 983.17
sleep that allows me to d. 264.11
there's nothing like d. to create future 366.16
truth is a d. unless my d. is true 991.114
we need men who can d., not skeptics 448.17
we wake from one d. into another d. 447.8
where all is d., reasoning is useless 687.13

**dreamer:** d. can know no truth but by awaking 687.20
d. lives forever; toiler dies in a day 687.17
only d. shall understand realities 687.5
society forgives criminal, never the d. 448.32

**dreaming:** d. men are haunted men 264.1
d. permits us to be insane every night 264.3

**dreams:** believe in d., spend life asleep 687.2
d. are dower that make us rich an hour 687.3
d. are interpreters of our inclinations 264.9
d. are the children of an idle brain 264.13
d. are true while they last 264.15
d. have breath, tears, and the touch of joy 899.4
d. live deaf amid cries of real world 264.12
each busy brain creates its own d. 264.10
each of us has his irremediable d. 908.47
easier to swoon in d. than do good 391.32
he who passes not his days in d. is slave of the days 687.6
in manhood we tell d. of childhood 574.39
in our d. submerged truth comes to top 687.23
in the mind, d. build nest with fragments 264.14
joy of d. which none can take away 687.4
judge your character by your d. 264.4
make us, not fly to d., but moderate desire 236.3
old age brings red flare of d. again 687.24
religions such stuff as d. are made of 790.82
truest life is when we are in d. awake 687.22
we are not really grateful to those who make our d. come true 687.9
we are such stuff as d. are made on 600.17
we forget our d. so speedily 264.7
when hopes and d. are loose in streets 813.21
women's tears sober up men intoxicated with d. 687.7

**dress:** loud d. offends people of taste 957.20
man can't d. without clothing his ideas 265.22
you are ushered in according to your d. 907.14

**dressed:** any may be in good spirits when well d. 265.4
d. fine as I will, flies exceed me still 265.29
lady wants to be d. like everybody else 265.14

**driftwood:** like d. spars which meet, man meets man 7.1

**drink:** as he brews, so shall he d. 809.10
d., for you know not whence you came, nor why 266.44
d. has caused ladies to be loved that otherwise might've died single 266.10
d. niver made a man betther 266.11
d. not the third glass 266.27
d.: there is one Hades for all men 266.23
d. today, and drown all sorrow 266.15
earth drinks, and gapes for d. again 771.2
every man should eat and d. 272.1
lechery d. provokes, and unprovokes 266.57
let us eat and d., for tomorrow we die 600.3
they never taste who always d. 877.3
we d. each other's healths, spoil our own 266.34
where people d., they spill 511.9

**drinker:** under a bad cloak there's often a good d. 266.5

**drinkers:** old stomach reforms more d. than new resolve 266.41

**drinketh:** he that d. well sleepeth well 272.22

**drinking:** d. man never less himself than when sober 266.38
d. man wants to forget he isn't still young 266.63

man begins d. in youth, is credited with fine qualities 266.52
there are two reasons for d. 266.49
there's nothing like d. so pleasant 266.9

**drinks:** I fear the man who d. water 266.24

**drive:** cannot d. straight on twisting lane 489.22

**driven:** we sail, ever d. in uncertainty 998.9

**drop:** there are people one should like to d. 907.5

**drown:** d. not thyself to save a drowning man 831.4
it is folly to d. on dry land 351.6

**drowning:** d. man is not troubled by rain 17.45
I was further out than you thought, not waving but d. 237.12
pour not water on a d. mouse 577.3

**drudgery:** test of vocation is love of its d. 1029.12
three fates: poverty, d., ignorance 712.40
work is not the curse, but d. is 1058.4

**drudges:** life of labor makes d., not men 1058.23

**drug:** everything is a dangerous d. but reality 777.5

**drum:** big d. beats fast, does not realize its hollowness 87.6
big d. only sounds well from afar 865.16
d. drives out thought, is military instrument 582.12
noisiest d. has nothing in it but air 87.2
take cash, nor heed rumble of distant d. 723.24

**drummer:** because he hears a different d. 466.8

**drums:** beating d. sound like rattling chains 667.5

**drunk:** demand for the superlative attained by getting d. 266.28
good d. is not always a good bartender 204.6
man, being reasonable, must get d. 266.4
when the cock is d., he forgets the hawk 266.3
wise man stays home when d. 266.14

**drunkard:** to dispute d. is to debate empty house 266.51

**drunkards:** there are more old d. than old doctors 266.17

**drunken:** be d., on wine, poetry, virtue, as you wish 733.1
d. man's happiness blind; has no motive 266.46
sober man's secret is d. man's speech 266.53
what the sober man has in his heart, the d. man has on his lips 266.8

**drunkenness:** d. doesn't create vices 266.54
d. insulates us in thought 266.13
d. is never anything but a substitute for happiness 266.22
d. neither keeps a secret nor observes a promise 266.6
what does d. not accomplish 266.31

**dull:** d. man is always sure, sure man always d. 113.10
I drink wine of aspiration, thus am not d. 55.10
to the d. mind all nature is leaden 491.6

**dullness:** d. is the coming of age of seriousness 268.3
d. makes life supportable, welcome 216.1
gentle d. ever loves a joke 434.21
there is no law which consecrates d. 268.2

**dumbness:** d. in the speech of men more agonizing than d. in the eyes of animals 148.8

**dunce:** there is no d. like a mature d. 445.29

**dung:** money and d. are no good till spread 596.24

**duped:** who fears being d. cannot be magnanimous 257.1

**dupes:** dishonesty is the raw material of d. 221.1
most mistrustful are often greatest d. 257.16

**durable:** people are too d. 285.1

**duration:** d. is not a test of true or false 991.75
that formed for long d. matures slowly 402.9

**dust:** beauty is everlasting; d. is for a time 70.35
better in d. than crawl near throne 773.7
d. are our frames 727.28
d. into d., and under d. to lie 218.94
d. thou art, and unto d. shalt return 218.13

**duties:** modern state has only rights, no d. 923.4
new occasions teach new d. 269.22
to be righteous is the first of all d. 489.14
when habit has strengthened sense of d., they leave us no time for other things 269.16

**duty:** always some who think they know your d. 269.10
d. as legitimate as any experience 269.5
d., honor; we make these say what we want 269.6
d. is the sublimest word in our language 269.21
d. is what one expects from others 269.36
d. leads to constraint, kills desire 560.47
d. lies in the thing nearby 269.7
d.: pretending that trivial is critical 269.11
d. toward others is a way of attaching our drowning selves to a passing raft 269.15
do your d. and leave the rest to the gods 269.8
he gives worthless gold who gives from d. 382.25
I've done my d., and I've done no more 397.5
it is not hard to do one's d. if one knows it 269.4
last pleasure in life is discharging our d. 269.14
no d. so underrated as being happy 269.33
paths of d. may not get you anywhere 269.34

rights that do not flow from d. are not worth having 817.2
sense of d. enables man to do prodigies 269.25
sense of d. offensive in personal relations 269.28
there is element of d. in love 269.12
there's life in d., rest in striving 269.35
to the honest, an honor to do d. 269.26
what is your d.; what the day demands 269.13
when d. comes a-knocking, welcome him in 269.24
when d. grows thy law, enjoyment fades 269.30
when stupid man does thing he is ashamed of, he declares that it is his d. 269.32
without d., life is soft and boneless 269.17

**dwarf:** d. on a giant's shoulders sees farther 233.5

**dwarfs:** he is a giant who has many d. about him 788.7

**dying:** arts of living well and d. well are one 538.7
d. is as natural as living 538.14
d. is more the survivors' affair 218.82
d. while young is a boon in old age 646.106
every part of us cries against idea of d. 218.11
growing old is d. young 646.72
it is not death but d. which is terrible 218.51
reason for living also reason for d. 538.3
the tongues of d. men enforce attention 218.110
to our real, naked selves there is nothing on earth or heaven worth d. for 218.69
truth sits upon the lips of d. men 991.5
your d. breath barely tarnishes the air 218.12

**dynamic:** natural world is d. 616.37

# E

**eager:** when a man's willing and e., god joins in 1050.1

**eagle:** e. clasps the crag with crooked hands 80.7
e. never lost so much time as when he submitted to learn of the crow 433.2
the e. suffers little birds to sing 713.44

**ear:** e. is shocked by the unexpected 875.1
eye is the painter and e. the singer 20.2
give every man thine e., few thy voice 540.4
if horn cannot be twisted, e. can 683.9
we consult e. because heart wanting 540.2

**early:** fate of worm shows danger of e. rising 71.1
genius always finds itself a century e. 374.14
who is known as e. riser may sleep late 798.33

**earnest:** e. men have no time to patch naked truth 111.8
e. people habitually look on serious side of things that have no serious side 879.1
something of burlesque in e., good men 879.3

**earnestness:** taking fun as fun and e. in earnest 879.4

**ears:** eyes are more accurate witnesses than e. 890.4
hungry stomach has no e. 435.6
men trust their e. less than their eyes 875.4
most have e., few have judgment 683.2
two e., one mouth: listen more, talk less 540.5
we cannot close our e. easily as eyes 629.3

**earth:** ambition does not see e. she treads on 33.18
axis of e. through center of every town 693.5
do no dishonour to the e. 174.2
e. being so good, would Heaven seem best 270.2
e. delights to feel your bare feet 616.31
e. is a pilgrim in the heavens 983.9
e. is beehive; we live in different cells 908.1
e. is given as a common stock 270.6
e. like woman's breasts: useful, pleasing 270.8
e. we abuse will take revenge 174.5
e., with her thousand voices, praises God 270.3
give me where to stand, I will move the e. 713.7
God gives all men all e. to love 693.7
let me enjoy the e. no less 270.5
more things in heaven, e., than dreamt of 946.4
our days upon e. are a shadow 983.3
that sky is brighter than e. means little unless e. is appreciated and enjoyed 270.7
thirsty e. soaks up the rain 771.2
touch, love, and honour the e. 270.1
we are so often ashamed of the e. 270.4
we've settled on e., forgotten heaven 429.6

**earth's:** e. crammed with heaven 259.2

**earthquake:** e. achieves equality of all men 17.57

**ease:** e. would recant vows made in pain 737.10

**East:** E. is E., West is West, never the twain shall meet 271.2
E. must eventually show West how to live 271.3
E., West barrier: whites won't give up superiority, colored won't endure inferiority 271.1
there is neither E. nor West, when two strong men stand face to face 98.15

**easy:** all things are difficult before e. 243.5
attempt e. tasks as if difficult 579.8
do not pray for e. lives 717.21
for e. things men set little store 325.3

he who accounts all things e. will have many difficulties 325.2
nothing is e. to the unwilling 243.6
**eat:** every man should e. and drink 272.1
let us e. and drink, for tomorrow we die 600.3
nature a conjugation of the verb to e. 272.17
tell what you e., I will tell who you are 272.2
to e. well is no whoredom 272.11
to e. without hope is still to starve 237.4
**eaten:** e. bread is forgotten 473.3
**eaters:** great e. are incapable of all else great 877.2
**eateth:** he that e. well drinketh well 272.22
**eating:** all e. is a kind of proselytising 272.5
destiny of human race to stop e. animals 1021.2
e. is believing 272.31
**eats:** man e. the big fish, mud e. man 26.4
**eccentric:** e. is a man who is a law unto himself 274.1
**eccentricity:** e. abounds when character abounds 274.2
**echo:** I have not cried aloud in worship of an e. 1060.4
**economic:** e. growth without social progress lets majority of people remain in poverty 275.3
emulation is strong e. motive 275.8
**economy:** American e.: jungle of eat or be eaten 34.35
e. consists not in saving but in selection 970.5
e. in common minds means no taste, comfort 970.11
expense may be essential part of true e. 970.4
**ecstasy:** take all away from me, but leave me e. 276.1
**ecumenical:** e. crisis is between traditional and experimental forms of church life 124.4
**Eden:** E. is that house we dwell in every day 407.31
**edge:** finest e. is made with blunt whetstone 319.38
good e. no good if nothing to cut 1017.2
**editing:** e. is most companionable form of education 758.14
e. is same as quarreling with writers 758.11
**editor:** e. separates wheat from chaff, prints chaff 758.12
**editorial:** advertisements have more knowledge concerning the community than e. columns 18.1
**editorials:** one ad is worth more than forty e. 18.11
**educate:** children have to be educated and e. selves 277.12
people that e. aren't always educated 959.17
schoolboys, not schoolmaster, e. my son 959.8
**educated:** define, define, well-e. infant 227.4
e. people speak the same languages 207.13
higher than God's tribunal—the e. man's 277.9
only the e. are free 277.24
there is nothing so stupid as an e. man 277.65
**educates:** power e. the potentate 825.7
**educating:** dons are too busy e. to be able to teach 959.4
**education:** by nature men alike; by e., very different 277.11
e. accumulates ignorance in inert facts 277.1
e.: balance wheel of the social machinery 277.51
e. consists in what we have unlearned 277.78
e. determines a man's future life 277.61
e.: discloses to wise and disguises from foolish their lack of understanding 277.7
e. doesn't change life much 277.28
e. in a technological world is neuter 277.50
e. instills nonsense, unifies people 277.69
e. is an admirable thing 520.74
e. is an endless process, not a product 277.44
e. is an ornament in prosperity 277.3
e. is leading souls to what is best 277.68
e. is listening without losing temper 277.27
e. is that which teaches discernment 277.67
e. is what you learn in books 277.40
e.: learning how to make facts live 277.39
e., like neurosis, begins at home 277.71
e. makes a people easy to govern, but impossible to enslave 277.8
e. makes greater difference between man and man 277.2
e. makes straight ditch of free brook 277.76
e. makes us more stupid than brutes 277.31
e. produces and erases intuitions 277.60
e. that fails to cultivate will depraves mind 277.26
experience, travel an e. in themselves 319.20
first duty of adolescent is to disgorge all his e. 1064.51
goal of e. is advancement of knowledge and dissemination of truth 277.45
great difficulty in e. 277.70
higher e. is booming in the U.S. 277.59
highest result of e. is tolerance 977.10
history a race between e., catastrophe 417.49
how is it children are intelligent, men stupid; it must be e. that does it 277.15
it is only the ignorant who despise e. 277.64
making children honest is beginning of e. 423.17
man must pull e. out iv hole be th' hair 277.17
nature has always had more power than e. 431.27
philosophic aim of e. to get one out of isolated class into humanity 277.35
roots of e. are bitter, fruit is sweet 277.4
soap and e. are deadly in the long run 131.30

takes five years to recover from college e. 277.5
test and use of a man's e. 277.6
things taught in schools are not an e. 277.20
'tis e. forms the common mind 981.9
what we call e. and culture is nothing but substitution of literature for life 277.72
what we do not call e. is more precious than what we call e. 277.23
**educator:** e. says what he thinks pupils should hear 959.21
**effect:** best e. of fine persons felt afterward 471.4
take away cause and e. ceases 108.1
what is done for e. is seen to be done for e. 894.8
**effective:** e. action is always unjust 9.1
**effeminacy:** 'tis e. that disrelishes ordinary things 605.7
**efficiency:** greatest e. method is prayer power 717.25
**efficient:** e. laborer will not crowd day with work 1059.7
superlatively e. government is anti-human 393.25
**effort:** e. is only e. when it begins to hurt 279.17
law of human life is e. 455.5
men moved not by goal, but by the e. 279.15
much e., much prosperity 279.7
**efforts:** man's virtue not measured by his e. 1025.47
**effrontery:** no e. like that of woman caught in act 1055.82
**egg:** e. source of all, everyone's ancestral hall 81.3
send not for a hatchet to break open an e. 942.1
sooner have fowl by hatching the e. 670.15
to make omelet you have to break e. 239.11
today's e. is better than tomorrow's hen 723.30
**egghead:** e. is one who stands on both feet in mid-air on both sides of an issue 490.6
**eggs:** wise do not venture all e. in one basket 749.5
you can't unscramble scrambled e. 505.1
**ego:** solemn e. accompanies the learned 842.11
where id was, there shall e. be 567.6
**egoism:** altruism which is not e. is sterile 430.28
artist's e. is outrageous 53.82
our e. leads us to judge people by their relations to ourselves 513.8
**egoistic:** children are completely e. 121.17
**egoists:** it astounds us to come upon other e. 865.18
**egotism:** apology is e. wrong side out 44.3
e.: anesthetic dulling pain of stupidity 865.12
to speak highly of an intimate is e. 716.12
**egotist:** next to joy of e. is joy of detractor 203.27
**elbow:** e. grease is the best polish 279.4
**elders:** advice of e. apt to be unreal 19.17
**elected:** more men e. between sundown and sunup 1030.16
**election:** democracy is e. by incompetent many 231.49
e. is a moral horror 1030.20
more important than winning e. is governing nation 704.13
supreme court follows e. returns 525.19
**elections:** in e. people vote against, not for 1030.1
where annual e. end, slavery begins 1030.2
**electric:** when man cast off magic, science bestowed upon him the e. current 960.6
**electricity:** by e. matter became great vibrating nerve 960.8
**elegance:** e. is good taste plus dash of daring 280.1
mere e. of language produces empty renown 935.18
only real e. is in the mind 280.2
**elemental:** world to-day: sick for lack of e. things 174.1
**elements:** why fear savage e. that we are made of 616.27
**elephant:** a frog will kick an e. in trouble 17.30
e. has thick skin, head full of ivory 704.15
frog tried to look as big as e. 726.1
he is unconscious of e. on his nose 203.18
**elephants:** e. fight, mousedeer between is killed 1035.61
e. suffer from too much patience 41.8
trumpet in a herd of e. 168.13
**elopement:** if not for presents, e. preferable 1044.1
**eloquence:** continous e. wearies 281.9
e. is a republican art 281.11
e. is the language of nature 757.4
e. lies in voice and eyes as much as words 281.6
e. requires the pleasant and the real 281.8
e. wins fame from enemies as from friends 281.12
honest brief has its own e. 525.23
in conversation discretion more important than e. 185.14
seldom discern e. under threadbare cloak 712.34
today models of e. are ad agencies 281.7
true e. makes light of e. 60.2
true e. says all to be said and that only 281.5
we can't all combine good looks and e. 539.12
when gold argues cause, e. impotent 596.46
**eloquent:** e. man is drunk with a certain belief 281.2
**emancipation:** e. from the soil is no freedom for a tree 361.51

**emancipator:** every e. is apprentice as a crank 333.1
**embalm:** nature is honest, we aren't; we e. dead 101.1
**embarrassing:** no e. questions; just e. answers 478.17
**embrace:** kings, women, vines e. what is nearest 1055.115
**emergencies:** in e. we fall back on our gods 200.3
**eminence:** a plague on e. 330.46
false praise says e. comes from nobility 330.36
men of e. get as much flattery as censure 330.2
whoever rises will have many malevolent gazers at his e. 945.6
**eminent:** censure is tax paid for being e. 203.31
**emotion:** after youth life of e. becomes unbearable 1065.8
being impressed in art often stands in the way of e. 53.54
e. has taught mankind to reason 282.38
e. is always new, the word has served 282.19
e. is primarily about nothing 282.36
life is the enjoyment of e. 282.39
life of reason balanced by irrational e. 1013.1
mental processes make good through e. 282.35
never have an e. that is unbecoming 282.40
no e. or wave can long retain its form 282.3
poetry: e. recollected in tranquillity 702.117
women are eagerly on lookout for any e. 1055.140
**emotions:** e. are pure which gather and lift you up 282.29
intelligent able to control e. 491.19
nothing vivifies and kills like the e. 282.31
the e. may be endless 282.13
to experience only one's own e. would be a sorry limitation 282.16
**emphatic:** difficult to be e. when other side is not 51.28
**empire:** great e., little minds, go ill together 705.14
perfection of Gospels never built e. 853.1
to e. builders, men are instruments 456.4
who man would be, must rule e. of himself 856.15
who seek e. have no alternative between success and downfall 33.33
why look at land; they were e. builders 106.4
**empiricism:** e. has sworn never to draw conclusions 319.52
**employed:** he is idle who might be better e. 444.7
to be e. in useless things is to be idle 1017.3
**employment:** none gain from fair e. bill if no e. exists 1002.3
**emptiness:** greatest pretenses built up to hide e. 162.8
**empty:** better an e. purse than an e. head 445.14
cannot scare me with their e. spaces 413.5
e. of grain, ear grows taller and taller 433.14
e. pockets make e. heads 712.54
e. stomach won't listen to anything 435.11
e. vessel giveth a greater sound 934.16
**emulate:** sparrows who e. peacocks may break thigh 449.1
**emulation:** e. is strong economic motive 275.8
**enchanter:** spell of true e. operates upon imagination and heart 53.62
**encounter:** people do not heed the things they e. 85.8
**end:** beginning and e. are alike touching 74.9
better the e. of a thing than beginning 74.2
e. is what the means have made it 570.6
let the end try the man 6.19
little earth, that is the e. 218.99
look to the e. in whatever you consider 356.13
means are enjoyed if e. is desired 570.7
men perish because they cannot join beginning with e. 74.1
no man can see what e. waits for him 366.31
not every e. is the goal 284.3
remember the e., thou shalt never do amiss 284.1
world is round: e. may be beginning 74.11
you begin well only in what you e. well 74.4
**endeavor:** what e. cannot bring about, time may 971.22
where no hope there can be no e. 237.9
**endeavors:** success not inevitable result of e. 279.19
**ended:** nothing is ever e., all is only begun 536.128
**ending:** art of e. greater than that of beginning 74.10
bad beginning makes a bad e. 173.6
good beginning makes a good e. 74.3
hard beginning maketh a good e. 74.7
**ends:** great to do that which e. all other deeds 941.14
more e. in world than anything else 284.4
there's a divinity that shapes our e. 238.19
**endurance:** e. is crowning quality of great hearts 285.7
patient e. is godlike 285.6
**endure:** art of life: how to enjoy and e. 536.44
to e. unendurable is true endurance 285.5
**enemies:** common danger unites even e. 1009.1
e. are first to discover your mistakes 286.4
for ten jokes thou hast an hundred e. 434.26
friends provoked become bitterest e. 363.56
from e. alone we can learn our defects 938.4
if we read secret history of e., we should find

sorrow enough to disarm 286.18
it is unhappy lot which finds no e. 706.10
life'd not be worth livin' without our e. 286.9
trust friends of today as if e. tomorrow 257.6
we often give e. means for our own ruin 866.1
who fears making e. will have no friends 973.6
wise man gets more from his e. than a fool from his friends 286.14
you only injure yourself if you take notice of despicable e. 286.1

**enemies'**: e. promises were made to be broken 286.2

**enemy**: be thine e. an ant, see him as elephant 286.27
bound to forgive e., not trust him 286.13
bring not all mischief on an e. 749.29
concentrating attention of people on e. 615.5
e. becomes friend when underground 286.11
e. can't wish what man thinks up for self 866.12
hate e. as if he might again be friend 286.25
have nothing to do with your e. 286.15
how good bad music and bad reasons sound when one marches against an e. 1035.72
I owe to my e. not to be revenged 474.4
if thine e. hunger, feed him 286.6
instead of loving e., treat friend better 658.11
kisses of an e. are deceitful 363.19
may you not hurt your e., when he struck first 811.1
men put e. in mouths to steal away brains 266.55
no safety in regaining favor of e. 286.22
nothing like sight of e. down on his luck 286.10
one active e. is worth two friends 286.16
praises from an e. imply real merit 716.10
prove to e. that he did you some good 286.21
real e. can always be met and conquered 286.19
their worst e.: who tells them the truth 993.18
there is no little e. 286.12
to befriend e. is essence of true religion 98.5
weapon is an e. even to its owner 1042.6
who has one e. shall meet him everywhere 286.3
who is in prison or chains still an e. 170.9
who lives by fighting e. has interest in preserving e.'s life 286.20
whoever has foe at his mercy and does not kill is his own e. 531.3

**enemy's**: e. gift is ruinous and no gift 382.36
never soar aloft on an e. pinions 33.1

**energy**: e. in nation like sap in a tree 614.27
e. which makes child hard to manage is e. which later makes him manager of life 121.4
our e. is in proportion to resistance met 243.7
repeated shocks exhaust the e. of strongest souls 115.1
too much work and e. kill a man 310.5
worshipper of e. is too energetic 10.6

**enforce**: do not command what you cannot e. 528.22

**engaged**: e. man is lion, married man a jackass 560.44

**engineers**: e. cannot create a worm 960.13
one has to look out for e. 960.22

**England**: E. is the paradise of individuality 287.22
in E. stables centre of household 287.25
to ensure summer in E., have it framed 287.29

**English**: correct E.: slang of prigs writing essays 521.5
E. are most awkward in the pulpit 287.26
E. are serious only about humor 287.19
E. Bible shows power of E. language 78.4
E. don't like music, but love its noise 287.2
E. gentleman galloping after a fox 436.5
E. have a way of calling the French light 287.5
E. home – haunt of ancient peace 287.28
E. is a magnificent vehicle for poetry 521.2
E. make light of great griefs 287.3
E. orthography is conspicuous waste 521.26
E. usage more than education – it's luck 396.7
E. winter ends in July to begin in August 287.6
look to standard man for standard E. 521.24

**Englishman**: "bad taste" most formidable term to E. 287.9
E. apt to neglect present good in preparing against possible evil 287.13
E. does everything on principle 287.24
E. is afraid to feel 287.10
E. is content to say nothing, when he has nothing to say 359.4
E. is natural when holding his tongue 287.14
E. never takes collar off when writing 287.15
E. seldom resorts to violence 287.18
E. thinks everything not English is wrong 287.12
E. thinks he is moral when he is only uncomfortable 287.23
E. walks before the law like a trained horse 287.11
E. wants to be recognized as gentleman 798.22
E. will fight before he reasons or reason before he fights 287.8
guard against E. who speaks French perfectly 287.17

**Englishmen**: E. laugh and jeer at everything strange 287.21
E. think they have sense of humor 287.16

**enigma:** Russia a riddle wrapped in mystery inside e. 828.1
**enjoy:** art of life: how to e. and endure 536.44
people e. things more knowing others have been left out 698.4
two aims: to get what you want and e. it 698.38
**enjoyed:** things chased with more spirit than e. 247.5
**enjoying:** e. things is not evil 698.8
**enjoyment:** e. before caution soon brings punishment 733.2
e.: feeling accompanying ongoing activity 698.15
e. good in itself is good religiously 893.10
e. is bashful, does not want to be sought 698.23
life is not a progress from e. to e. 236.24
no e. for man until incapable of pleasure 646.66
we derive intense e. only from contrast 184.2
**enjoyments:** in despair there are intense e. 237.6
**enmity:** to eye of e. virtue seems ugliest blemish 410.22
**ennui:** e. has made more gamblers than avarice 288.1
symmetry is e., the essence of grief 654.10
**enough:** e. is as good as a feast 940.3
you never know what is e. unless you know what is more than e. 940.1
**enriches:** what e. other than wallet is uneconomic 596.1
**enslaved:** all spirits e. which serve evil 882.18
**enterprise:** enemy of free e. system 732.8
for happiness, man needs e. and change 407.93
on young man no gem so gracious as e. 289.3
**entertaining:** man who can be e. for a full day 494.1
**entertainment:** art is response to demand for e. 53.116
e. confirms rather than challenges 290.4
mass media offer e. to be consumed 563.1
**enthusiasm:** e.: a distemper of youth 291.3
man never rises to great truths without e. 291.8
measure e. between interesting events 291.7
nothing great was ever done without e. 291.5
science is antidote to poison of e. 843.35
**enthusiast:** world belongs to e. who keeps cool 291.6
**entreaty:** even the gods are moved by voice of e. 799.5
**entry:** every exit is an e. somewhere else 74.12
**envied:** man will do all things to get himself e. 293.28
much better to be e. than to be pitied 293.16
**envies:** no peacock e. another peacock his tail 727.22
player e. only player, poet only poet 1029.6
**envious:** e. consumed by their own passion 293.3
e. die as oft as envied win applause 293.14
e. man grows lean as neighbor fattens 293.17
not even success softens heart of e. 293.23
those believed humble, usually e. 433.25
**environment:** adapt to the e. that is your lot 98.17
adaptation between man and e. 12.2
Americans the masters of their e. 34.5
grateful e. is substitute for happiness 292.5
individual's desire to dominate his e. 292.6
over-all e. diminished daily by pollution 174.9
qualities atrophy in standing-room-only e. 707.8
**envy:** all e. is proportionate to desire 293.18
brave or fortunate man can bear e. 293.25
e. a sharper spur than pay 293.13
e. bestrides praise 716.27
e. blasts things elevated above rest 945.7
e. is a littleness of soul 293.15
e. is destroyed by true friendship 293.21
e. is everywhere 293.8
e. is more irreconcilable than hatred 293.20
e. is the basis of democracy 231.45
e. is the tax distinction must pay 293.9
e. lasts longer than happiness of envied 293.22
e.: see things only in their relations 293.26
expect not praise without e. until death 716.5
great are spoken against from e. 293.19
great power incites e., destruction 424.8
if e. were fever, all world would be ill 293.7
let age, not e., wrinkle thy cheeks 293.5
may my means lie too low for e. 592.3
men e. those who fare well 431.25
no passion so strong in the heart as e. 293.27
nothing sharpens sight like e. 293.12
our nature holds much e. and malice 293.24
people commend fine day without e. 1043.8
pity is for the living, e. for the dead 538.43
pride, avarice, e. are tongues men heed 727.8
show of e. is an insult to oneself 293.30
**ephemeral:** all is e.—even fame and the famous 983.13
**epic:** e. vanished with age of personal heroism 416.19
**epicure:** e. says, fate cannot harm me, I've dined 272.29
**epigram:** e. requires wit, occasion, good luck 294.4
force of e. is in the conclusion 294.2
there is an e. for every dilemma 294.5
what is an e.? a dwarfish whole 294.1
**epigrams:** e. need no crier 294.3
easy to write e., but hard to write book 1062.71

**epitaph:** e.: inscription showing that virtues acquired by death have retroactive effect 101.2
**epithets:** e., like pepper, give zest to your writing 935.2
**epoch:** at each e., world was lost, saved 296.18
every e. has character determined by way population react to material events 296.25
every e. has deified its peculiar errors 296.22
man lives the life of his e. 181.6
to make an e. in the world, good head and great inheritance are essential 399.30
**equal:** all have e. right to government protection 295.8
all men are created e. 295.13
all men are e.—at cards 367.5
as men, we are all e. in presence of death 218.102
contemplation of God created e. men 295.23
democrats think they should be e. in all 295.2
in company of e., fortune must decline 57.19
in polling booth every American e. 295.21
men are born e. but also born different 467.9
men seldom trust the opinion of their e. 649.32
quarrels arise when those who are e. have not got e. shares, or vice versa 295.1
who cares not for your remorse is your e. 793.2
**equality:** can be friends only on terms of e. 363.114
demagogy: when e. becomes identity 230.3
e. in democracy when all share rule 231.3
e. is a mortuary word 295.7
e. is treating similar men alike 295.3
e. lowers flight of imagination 295.25
earthquake achieves e. of all men 17.57
I am proud up to the point of e. 295.9
intellect respects e. as a convention 295.4
nobody can give you e. 853.5
on e. we would have only animal pleasure 773.14
perfect e. affords no temptation 295.18
some unhappy is better than none happy, which would be the case in a state of e. 295.14
standardization of man is called e. 295.6
to be against e. today like living in Alaska and being against snow 769.7
unless man believes all mankind his brothers, he labors vainly in vineyards of e. 295.19
we clamor for e. in matters in which we cannot hope to obtain excellence 295.11
**equals:** e. revolt to be superior 813.1
falling out with superiors, be in with e. 766.19
friendship seldom lasting but between e. 363.69
little friendship in world; least between e. 363.14
**equity:** custom creates the whole of e. 210.22
there is no real e. 475.8
**ermine:** in an e. spots are soon discovered 764.5
**erotic:** truly e. sensibility in evoking the image of woman never omits to clothe it 885.18
when a lady's e. life is vexed 885.22
**err:** experience does not e. 319.34
few sometimes know, when thousands e. 816.18
road to wisdom: e. and e., less and less 1053.30
striving, man must e. 297.19
the most may e. as grossly as the few 231.9
to e. is human, to forgive divine 357.16
**errands:** pleasure we treasure is to run e. for the Ministers of State 398.8
**erroneous:** e. ideas would perish if clearly expressed 297.38
**error:** all liable to e.; most tempted to it 297.24
beware barking close to heels of an e. 297.10
cause of e. is war of senses, reason 297.27
delay is preferable to e. 228.9
e. alone needs support of government 992.9
e. flies from mouth to mouth, pen to pen 297.40
e. is always in haste 297.18
e. is failure to adjust from preconception 297.8
e. is the rule; truth, accident of e. 297.15
e.: scribbled sheet we must first erase 297.11
e. states current truth is incomplete 297.32
e., wounded, writhes in pain and dies 297.4
humanity too harassed by want to struggle with e. 618.5
I postpone death by suffering, e. 502.21
ignorance preferable to e. 445.18
in practice e. and truth do not consort 9.13
intelligence lends itself to conformist e. 168.12
love truth, but pardon e. 297.39
man who can own up to his e. is greater than he who merely avoids making it 297.28
many have rashly charged troops of e. 783.4
no e. is such as pursuit of absolute truth 297.6
no worse e. than truth 991.47
obscurity is the realm of e. 640.5
old custom without truth is but old e. 210.11
progress of rivers to ocean is not so rapid as that of man to e. 297.41
prophecy is most gratuitous form of e. 741.3
to show e. is not to give truth 297.23
truth lies within compass, e. is immense 297.30
we don't allow freedom from e. to our neighbors 677.6
were half power, wealth given to redeem mind from e., no need of arsenals 297.25
**errors:** cranks take up unfashionable e. 274.3
e. of young men are ruin of business 297.1

e. on surface flow, for pearls dive below 734.3
every age confutes old e., begets new 296.10
every epoch has deified its peculiar e. 296.22
general, abstract ideas: source of e. 441.31
if door shut to all e., truth shut out 297.35
justice, custodian of the world's e. 515.4
life's e. cry for harmony with the whole 297.37
make your rule the e. of a wise man 297.2
men positive in e. out of zeal to truth 297.34
those oft are stratagems which e. seem 932.3
too much talk will include e. 916.10

**errs:** to show another that he e. 51.20

**erudition:** e.: dust shaken from book into empty skull 842.3
if we steal thoughts from ancients, it's e. 694.1
two evils for man of e.: never be listened to, and be listened to always 842.25

**escape:** man trying to e. never concealed enough 298.7
non-attachment is e. from pain, love 31.8
space flights are an e. from oneself 914.3

**Eskimos:** always find some E. ready to instruct Congolese on heat waves 19.24

**essayist:** e. can discourse without interruption 1062.86

**establish:** to e. himself, a man appears established 45.13

**estate:** politest men quarrel at division of e. 1051.3
real e. is foundation of world's guilt 740.11

**esteem:** difficult to like those whom we don't e. 802.7
e. must be founded on preference 719.5

**esteemed:** have, and you shall be e. 596.42
we cannot always make ourselves e. 802.8

**estimation:** hold in vile e. what is most dear 221.10

**estrangement:** e. of opinions: for two to speak ironically and neither to feel the irony 299.4

**eternal:** past is e., the sea will wash it up again 116.5
we feel and know that we are e. 452.17

**eternity:** e. is terrible thought 300.4
every moment the representative of an e. 723.14
hold e. in an hour 616.8
I am not e., but a man 539.7
reversion to destiny is called e. 300.2
'tis puzzling on the brink of e. to know no more of what is here than there 1012.1
toward e., without reprieve 457.4
who can count rain drops or days of e. 300.1

**eternity's:** he who kisses joy as it flies lives in e. sun rise 407.16

**ethic:** science, by itself, cannot supply an e. 843.31
strength and strength's will are supreme e. 933.10

**ethical:** e. axioms are like axioms of science 991.33

**ethics:** do not confuse vested interests with e. 493.7
e. is recommending to others sacrifices required for co-operation with oneself 598.39
e. make existence possible 20.7
no final truth in e. 598.24
science of e. consoles me for ignorance of physical sciences 598.37
who defines his conduct by e. imprisons his song-bird in cage 598.19

**Ethiopian:** can E. change skin, or leopard, spots 442.7

**etiquette:** e. is what you do, say, when others looking 559.17
e.: means of approaching, avoiding people 559.19
neither affect nor despise e. 559.14

**euphemism:** e. ceases to be euphemistic after a time 1057.20

**Europe:** E. has a sense of tragedy 301.1
E. is the unfinished negative of America 301.3
E. nothin' but a great big auction 301.4
we go to E. to be Americanized 301.2

**European:** E. character has all too professional air 34.41
life for the E. is a career 536.64

**evasion:** without health, courage, take refuge in e. 302.1

**evening:** in e. man walks only with his legs 338.3
morning is wiser than the e. 599.3

**event:** an e. is only actualization of thoughts 303.4
do we not all spend lives under shadow of e. not yet come 366.20
no man before the e. can see 366.31
person makes e. and e. person 108.2

**events:** e. expand with the character 303.3
enemy of wisdom is the march of e. 303.5
greatest e. are our stillest hours 303.8
in pressure of e., principle is no help 728.6
most e. are inexpressible 53.103
old e. have modern meanings 417.32
one thing to be moved by e., another to be mastered by them 303.9
people to whom nothing has happened cannot understand unimportance of e. 303.2
spirits of great e. stride on before the e. 303.1
to be philosopher is to be prepared against e. 688.6

**eventually:** e.: has the soothing effect of a promise 228.7

**everybody:** everything happens to e. in time 319.54

**everybody's:** e. business is nobody's business 804.7
**everyday:** e. life is order and haphazardry 536.121
**everything:** e. happens to everybody in time 319.54
little thing can be e. 989.4
**everywhere:** he that is e. is nowhere 10.8
one place is e., e. is nowhere 693.10
some want to be e. but get nowhere 10.17
**evidence:** all necessary truth is its own e. 991.34
circumstantial e. is very strong 304.2
**evil:** a thousand hack at branches of e. 783.39
act of e. breeds others to follow 1063.1
all are spirits enslaved which serve e. 882.18
all e. comes from the old 1065.1
all e. is universal good 616.59
always fair sailing if you escape e. 298.11
among those who think no e., e. flourishes 305.39
be good and let people speak e. of thee 391.46
belief in supernatural e. unnecessary 1048.6
canter is cure for every e. 815.1
defeat preferable to victory by e. means 570.8
destroy seed of e. lest it grow 305.1
e. alone has oil for every wheel 305.29
e. attracts the weak by promise of power 305.21
e. communications corrupt good manners 471.2
e. condoned if compensated by good 388.16
e. done to another is e. done to oneself 305.20
e. enters like needle, spreads like oak 305.13
e., fault of self-styled pure in heart 783.14
e. in us is intolerant of e. in others 305.27
e. is a necessary part of the universe 305.28
e. is uncertain in same degree as good 340.19
e. men by their nature cannot ever prosper 305.14
e. men not excused from service of state 923.1
e. not yielded to is a benefactor 305.11
e. one form of a desire, not its nature 236.30
e. report carries farther than applause 622.4
e. tongues may blast a whole life of virtue 898.5
e. which I would not, that I do 684.3
every e. hath its good 153.1
good and e. lie close together 388.1
good preventing greater good is e. 388.24
great epochs come when we rechristen e. as what is best in us 305.30
harmful ideas are cloaks for e. passions 728.14
he who accepts e. is involved in it 305.23
he who does e. that good may come 305.19
if we saw all e. that may spring from good 388.19
if you do e., e. will be done to you 781.1
in battling e., excess is good 783.13
in rebuking e. be conscious of own 797.13
instruments of e. believe what they do is not e. but honorable 305.26
it by e. that good is pleasant 184.3
judge should have learned to know e. 512.8
life's a field for good and e. 536.110
love of money is root of all e. 596.5
marriage is the only e. men pray for 560.50
men do e. from religious conviction 872.4
men think it a right to return e. for e. 811.2
men's e. manners live in brass 305.38
must I do all the e. I can before I shun it? 305.16
no e. in atom, only in men's souls 633.13
no man appreciates all the e. he does 1063.15
no notice is taken of a little e. 305.2
no resolve for good or e. until execution 388.9
not all those to whom we do e. hate us 224.32
oldest e. more supportable than the new 17.41
omission of good is no less reprehensible than commission of e. 388.20
one ought not to return e. to anybody 658.15
overcome e. with good 391.7
real e. is to cringe to the evils 305.34
resolution is too late to avoid e. 801.2
some men wish e. and accomplish it 305.3
state tolerates e. to keep out lesser ills 923.13
submit to present e. lest greater befall 305.31
sufficient unto the day is the e. thereof 305.4
the e. that men do lives after them 388.23
there is no e. unless conscience says so 305.18
there is some goodness in things e. 305.37
those who would extirpate e. from world 305.5
to a good man there can come no e. 391.49
to avoid e. utilize passions, not maim them 668.2
where there's music there's no e. 607.15
who doth no e. is apt to suspect none 764.6
who is bent on e. never wants occasion 1063.21
who returns good for e. wins victory 224.12
wise avoid e. by anticipating it 356.9
worst e.: give up living before one dies 216.11
**evils:** all e. are equal when they are extreme 305.8
between two e., pick the one never tried 305.40
cause of e. inability to apply principles 371.2
e., like hills, appear great at distance 305.7
how much pain have cost us the e. which have never happened 43.5
lesser of two e. is still an evil 305.25
mankind are disposed to suffer e. 800.7
men slower to recognize blessings than e. 473.6
most important e. are those men inflict upon each other 305.33

our greatest e. flow from ourselves 305.32
real e. deliver us from petty despotism of imaginary e. 305.6
to great e. we submit; we resent little provocations 506.2
**evolution:** e. does not signify increased perfection 306.6
in nothing is there more e. than the American mind 34.74
tide of e. carries everything before it 306.7
**exaggerate:** proportion almost impossible: all e. 742.1
to e. is to begin to invent 307.3
to e. is to weaken 307.4
**exaggeration:** e., inseparable companion of greatness 307.7
e. is prodigality of judgment 307.2
**exalted:** men a little e. conceive their capacities enlarged above human comprehension 1020.18
**examinations:** e. are formidable even to best prepared 478.4
**examined:** e. life confined to privileged class 752.9
**example:** e. is better than following it 308.2
e. is the best precept 308.1
e. of good men is visible philosophy 308.3
few things harder to endure than good e. 308.7
now age is fallen from good e. 1065.17
**exasperation:** men live lives of quiet e. 506.4
**excel:** men of genius labour because they e. 309.6
**excellence:** all e. is equally difficult 309.13
all human e. is comparative 309.7
e. nothing without consent of God 309.2
great or bright infers not e. 309.8
less excellent the man, more he claims e. for nation, religion, race 333.9
our pride to imagine e., try to make it 309.12
**excellency:** we measure e. in others by e. in self 309.10
**excellent:** barbarism is not appreciating what is e. 69.2
man's heart doesn't tolerate absence of the e. 309.9
none so e. but he is excelled 309.3
**exception:** man is an e., whatever else he is 558.13
no rule is so general which admits no e. 826.2
no useful rule without an e. 826.3
**exceptional:** we are all e. cases 403.4
**excess:** e. on occasion is exhilarating 310.6
good carried to e. ceases to be good 387.17
in battling evil, e. is good 783.13
nothing in e. 592.14
quality carried to e. defeats itself 41.8
road of e. leads to the palace of wisdom 310.1
**excesses:** e. accomplish nothing 310.10
**excitement:** cruelty, e., lead men to love war 1035.5
**exclude:** every individual strives to grow and e. 467.6
let us prefer, let us not e. 719.6
we must e. someone from our gathering 903.2
**excuse:** any e. will serve a tyrant 995.3
every vice has its e. ready 1023.24
man looks for an e. before a remedy 312.4
without "E. me" I would not have known there was anything amiss 44.4
**excuses:** bad e. are worse than none 312.2
nature takes no account of human e. 616.43
**excusing:** e. of a fault doth make the fault worse 312.5
**executive:** e. officers not made out of saints 317.3
**executives:** damn great e., men of measured merriment 313.4
**exercise:** bodily e. profiteth little 690.1
e. is the vital principle of health 411.21
philosophy for e. rather than freight 688.15
unfortunate for chubby children to watch basketball, regard it as their e. 690.4
**exercises:** bodily e. are to be done discreetly 690.5
**exist:** at a given moment I open my eyes and e. 314.1
you e. in your act, not in your body 224.33
**existence:** e. of individual like a room 613.9
falsehood lies deep in necessities of e. 329.14
human e. is not a tragedy, but a bore 536.71
man is only animal for whom e. is a problem 314.4
problem of e.: we should love, do not 98.19
true tenor of e. is improvisation 962.5
**existentialism:** e. is possible only in world where God and Christianity are dead 315.2
first principle of e.: man is nothing but what he makes of himself 315.1
**exit:** affairs are easier of entrance than of e. 356.1
every e. is an entry somewhere else 74.12
**expect:** we e. more of ourselves than we should 539.11
we must e., fear, everything from time, men 971.64
**expectation:** I have never hurried to meet a public e. without leaving myself behind 798.6
oft e. fails where most it promises 316.11
'tis e. makes a blessing dear 316.12
uncertainty and e. are the joys of life 850.2
**expectations:** for people who live on e., to face realisation is an ordeal 316.1
**expected:** where much is e., individual may rise 711.3
**expects:** who e. nothing shall not be disappointed 316.9

**expediency:** alloy of e. improves the gold of morality 317.4
custom adapts itself to e. 317.7
**expedients:** e. are for an hour; principles, for ages 728.2
**expenditure:** our costliest e. is time 971.63
**expense:** e. may be essential part of true economy 970.4
our e. is almost all for conformity 554.2
**expenses:** cessation of work not accompanied by cessation of e. 807.1
**experience:** all e. is an arch 319.59
art helps nature, and e. art 53.50
better to borrow e. than to buy it 319.12
drink e. or die in desert of ignorance 319.35
e. and travel are an education 319.20
e. and understanding are our god-figures 207.18
e.: comb nature gives us when we're bald 319.10
e. differentiates piety, goodness 691.10
e. does not err 319.34
e. has two things to teach 783.7
e.: illusions lost, not wisdom acquired 447.15
e. in fingers, head, not heart 319.62
e. is hardly e. until it repeats itself 319.3
e. is hut made from ruins of illusions 319.51
e. is like the stern lights of a ship 319.11
e. is the banker of hope 425.5
e. is the name everyone gives to mistakes 319.64
e. is the only teacher 319.17
e. now claimed exclusively by young 319.9
e. of any human soul is real knowledge 319.6
e. seems to lead to conclusions 319.52
e. teaches only the good observer 319.24
e.: what you do with what happens to you 319.28
ever-changing truths of our own e. 991.141
information is thin stuff without e. 520.14
innocence is full, e. is empty 476.8
man deaf to that to which e. has given him no access 529.13
measure life by e., not length 545.4
men wise in proportion to capacity for e. 319.53
moderns ask what can we e. 319.63
most of worth is what own e. preaches 319.60
my feet are guided by lamp of e. 319.26
no man's knowledge can go beyond his e. 319.36
not data but purposes constitute human e. 319.42
nothing so unfair as man without e. 319.61
old age not total misery; e. helps 646.32
people know little beyond their own e. 319.32
proverb is the child of e. 568.1
prudence is but e. 749.16
questions asked self are key to others' e. 868.2
studies should be bounded in by e. 1.1
that which one cannot e. in daily life is not true for oneself 605.5
thorn of e. worth a wilderness of warning 319.37
to get e. out of ideas 277.70
unreliability of e. has led to nausea 115.35
we live in reference to past e. 669.30
when you have really exhausted an e., you always reverence and love it 319.8
whether our work is art, science, only the form in which we explore e. is different 1058.10
who learns only by e. is too dull to learn by e. 529.12
you cannot create e.; you must undergo it 319.5
**experienced:** nothing becomes real till it is e. 568.4
**experiences:** everyone is prisoner of own e. 720.13
knowledge hangs on regularity of e. 319.48
only the simplest e. open to all 207.10
single right idea saves labor of e. 441.23
strong man digests his e. 319.46
to regret e. is to arrest development 319.65
**experiment:** all life is an e. 973.3
exciting to think we are nature's latest e. 558.44
**expert:** e. limits himself to the little toe 917.5
**explain:** never e. 320.3
**explains:** innocent is person who e. nothing 476.3
**explanations:** no waste of time in life like making e. 320.1
**exploitation:** relationships are forms of e. 787.1
**explore:** e. thyself 868.33
**explorer:** most romantic sensation an e. has known 597.3
**expose:** wolves can't catch what dogs don't e. 162.11
**expressed:** what is conceived well is e. clearly 132.1
**expression:** beauty without e. tires 70.15
e. is only altered by a man of genius 374.12
glory of e. is simplicity 892.18
great e. furnishes its own standards 399.24
he whose genius seems truest excels in e. 374.18
man is half himself, other half is his e. 863.1
pleasures of e. keep us alert 868.20
we must institute conventional forms of e. or pretend nothing to express 148.12
**expressionist:** e. is simply a desperate man 53.104
**extraordinary:** for an e. situation, e. measures 202.2
**extravagance:** poverty often concealed in e. 712.30

**extravagant:** some e. as if they would die tomorrow 970.1
to hoarding father succeeds e. son 909.15
**extreme:** every great action is e. when undertaken 224.37
nothing so e. that's not allowed by some 210.18
**extremism:** e. in pursuit of presidency is a vice 724.5
e. in the defense of liberty is no vice 333.7
political e. involves two ingredients 333.6
**extremists:** evil of e. is that they are intolerant 333.13
**extremities:** manlike to bear e., godlike to forgive 285.4
**exuberance:** e. is beauty 511.1
e. is better than taste 511.4
**eye:** among men, wet e. manes dhry heart 438.6
beautiful e. luminous, not sparkling 323.4
e. altering alters all 676.2
e. is bored by repetition 875.1
e. is the painter and ear the singer 20.2
e. obeys exactly action of the mind 890.3
e. of the master fattens the steed 58.6
he who has one e. is prince among those with none 15.4
hunger of the e. is not to be despised 890.2
if a man destroy another's e., destroy his 515.19
if e. too near, opal's hues not seen 331.6
it is the e. which makes the horizon 682.5
listen to man's words and look at his e. 117.18
no object mysterious; mystery is your e. 676.3
some held e. to be instrument of lechery 885.28
thou shalt give e. for e. 809.2
to know e. will mark our coming is sweet 548.23
what e. ne'er sees, heart ne'er rues 108.1
what e. sees not, heart craves not 236.8
what makes impression on heart seems lovely in the e. 282.33
**eyebrows:** e. can darken life by scorn expressed 324.3
**eyes:** e. are more accurate witnesses than ears 890.4
e. are the great intruders 323.2
e. have one language everywhere 323.3
e. indicate the antiquity of the soul 323.1
e. not responsible when mind does seeing 448.23
fear has the largest e. of all 340.22
I am earth-bound to pay for freedom of e. 890.6
men are born with two e., one tongue 96.5
men of cold passions have quick e. 141.3
men trust their ears less than their e. 875.4
one may have good e. and see nothing 85.10
practised man trusts e. more than tongue 148.4
when you speak to man, look on his e. 916.21
who does not open his e. opens his purse 611.2

## F

**fable:** f.: recital of facts presented as fiction 341.19
**face:** beauty leaves record on f. as to what became of it 324.5
better a red f. than a black heart 886.7
cheerful, intelligent f. is end of culture 207.4
f. shows family traits, history, wants 324.4
God gave you one f., you make another 189.3
happy the man who never puts on a f. 426.10
have open f., but conceal thoughts 162.9
losing f. may one day save human race 658.8
lovely f. is the solace of wounded hearts 324.10
man remembers friend's f., not his own 868.30
mask tells us more than a f. 162.21
no one can wear one f. to self, one to multitude and not forget which is true 162.7
none so bound to his own f. that he doesn't hope of presenting another to world 681.5
often noble f. hides filthy ways 438.10
the voice is a second f. 916.4
we have a special f. for each friend 787.3
woman careful about her f. is careless about her house 1055.81
**faces:** looking at f., take advice of the day 70.37
minds differ still more than f. 583.24
more f. than humans; each has several 324.8
our f. carry in them motto of our souls 324.1
we never see our f. in mirrors 587.9
we remain same when our f. fall to pieces 442.8
**facetious:** to be f. is accomplishment of courtiers 1054.31
**fact:** a f. is like a sack which won't stand when it is empty 326.14
abstractions are weapons to control f. 967.17
all f. collectors are one-story men 491.14
consciousness of a f. is not knowing it 326.17
never any such thing as a bare f. 326.2
new f. enhances constant f. of life 326.7
no one has banished mystery of f. 326.11
rejected f. will always return 326.6
science makes ascertainment of f., correction of false belief the supreme goods 843.16
spirit of the age to believe any f. superior to any imaginative exercise 326.19
wise man bows to authority of f. 326.9
**facts:** accumulation of f. is not science 843.28
conclusive f. are separated from inclusive only by head that already understands 326.3

education: learning to make f. live 277.39
f. are all accidents 326.16
f. are like an unlit oil-lamp 326.15
f. as f. do not create reality 777.4
f.: brute beasts of intellectual domain 326.8
f. of life are very stubborn things 326.1
firm belief attracts f. 76.3
historian who seeks truth falsifies f. 417.3
in science, all f. enjoy democratic equality 843.26
same f. that make one laugh make one weep 524.4
theory helps us to bear ignorance of f. 967.13
time dissipates the angularity of f. 326.5
to state f. is not to despair for future 423.9
we are all imprisoned by f. 326.13
we must translate words into f. 1057.16
what is false in science of f. may be true in science of values 1019.17

**faculties:** he is rich who can use all men's f. 313.3

**fade:** where's the cheek that doth not f. 331.9

**faded:** eyes of men turn from f. flowers 885.34

**fail:** books succeed, lives f. 91.10
f. I alone—all men strive, who succeeds 327.4
I'd sooner f. than not be of greatest 399.41
no freedom without freedom to f. 361.27
to f. is something too awful to think of 327.17
when we f., pride supports us 6.6

**failing:** aware of own f., won't find fault with others' 339.32
scarcely a man lacks some f. that diminishes his family's regret at his loss 339.20

**failings:** expose not the secret f. of mankind 203.29
f. bind us together as closely as virtue 339.38

**fails:** everything I start f. with a boldness 327.7

**failure:** as we grow old we believe that f. is in the nature of things 646.19
f. is allotted to men by their stars 337.11
f. is lovable and commercial 327.21
f. makes people bitter and cruel 938.27
f. more interesting than success 327.1
f. not only punishment for laziness 527.8
fine line between f. and success 327.14
kicking against the goads is way to f. 285.8
no f. except in no longer trying 327.13
no fiercer hell than f. in great object 327.16
not f., but low aim, is crime 55.15
optimism is the digitalis of f. 652.8
success is undesirable, f. more so 327.8
the f. is a stranger in his own house 327.12
the good have come to wisdom through f. 391.47
to avoid occasion for virtues is worse f. than to push pluckily and fall 289.9
while young, idea of death, f., intolerable 1064.15

**failures:** awareness of the ambiguity of one's f. 6.21
benefit in making a few f. early in life 327.15
f. arise from pulling in horse as he leaps 463.2
women adore f. 327.25

**faint-hearted:** fortune is not on side of the f. 358.41

**fair:** each speaks of f. as his market has gone 58.7
f. and softly goes far 377.3
he injures f. lady who beholds her not 464.4
none but the brave deserves the f. 192.11
our problem is not to fancy what were f. 539.4

**fairies:** f.: nature's attempt to get rid of soft boys by sterilizing them 422.2

**fairness:** f. with one's own enables one to do justice in the state 515.47

**fairyland:** f. the sunny country of common sense 448.6

**faith:** American's f. is his business 790.42
Christians who lose f. keep sense of sin 123.4
cling to f. beyond the forms of f. 328.39
doubt has become immune to f. 263.11
doubt is f.: but f. is doubt 263.8
easy to shake a man's f. in himself 861.7
f.: belief without evidence in what is told by one who speaks without knowledge 328.6
f. can move mountains; disbelief can deny their existence 997.19
f. counts on failure 328.36
f. embraces contradictory truths 328.34
f. embraces itself and doubt 328.41
f.: illogical belief in the improbable 328.26
f. implies disbelief of a lesser fact 328.19
f. in a cause is a substitute for f. in selves 109.12
f. in a holy cause has to be extravagant 109.13
f. in supernatural is desperate wager 946.3
f. is a fine invention when gentlemen can see 844.3
f. is a stiffening process 328.16
f. is believing what seems false 328.44
f. is believing what you know ain't so 328.42
f. is but a kind of betting, speculation 328.9
f. is necessary to victory 854.3
f. is not a formula agreed to if evidence favors it 328.21
f. is the evidence of things not seen 328.4
f. is the pierless bridge 328.11
f. is to believe what you do not yet see 328.2
f. is wishing that God may exist 328.43
f., like a jackal, feeds among the tombs 328.23
f., not truth, keeps the world alive 328.27
f. opposed to experience, learning, investigation is not worth expression 328.20
f. speaks when hope dissembles 328.37
f.: state of being ultimately concerned 328.40
f. that sets bounds to itself is none 328.18
f., wed to falsehood, hugs it to the last 328.30

f. which does not doubt is a dead f. 263.10
f. without works is dead 328.5
give me stormy thought, not dead calm of f. 16.3
he wears his f. as fashion of his hat 178.15
how sweet to have a common f. 328.38
if one f. abandoned, don't abandon all f. 328.17
in ages not of f., there will always be people crying for the moon 997.16
it is truer that martyrs make f. than f. makes martyrs 561.17
let none seek cause to approve their f. 328.29
majority of mankind incapable of doubt, f. 558.18
man consists of the f. that is in him 328.3
man would die a thousand deaths for f. 328.22
more of doubt, the stronger f. 263.1
most satisfying f. is purely agnostic 328.25
never believe on f., see for yourself 529.3
no f. never broken save that of a dog 41.19
no f. our own that we have not arduously won 328.13
only f. comprehends mysteries of religion 123.20
relation of f. between subject and object is unique in every case 328.1
talent is f. in one's own powers 956.8
terrors of truth, death are vain to f. 328.24
there lives more f. in honest doubt 263.9
to believe only possibilities is not f. 328.8
to lose one's f. surpass loss of estate 997.8
we need the f. to go a path untrod 466.5
what is f., love, virtue alone 328.28
when f. burns out, 'tis God who dies 997.18
when f. lost, honor dies, man is dead 489.30
where technical skill, no need for f. 960.9
who breaks his f., no f. is held with him 737.3
you can do little with f., nothing without it 328.10

**faithful:** f. know the trivial side of love 470.16
f. woman deceives with a good book 178.5
he who is f. in little is f. in much 489.3
person who has faith in himself can be f. to others 178.4
violence we do ourselves to remain f. is hardly better than an infidelity 178.11
young men want to be f., and are not 470.17

**faithfulness:** f. is simply a confession of failures 178.19

**faithless:** f. know love's tragedies 470.16

**fall:** flowers and buds f., and old and ripe f. 218.81
haughty spirit goeth before a f. 727.4
he that lies on the ground cannot f. 327.26
if a man f., all will tread on him 546.3
if the sky f., hold up your hands 226.18
never f. out with your bread and butter 766.5
soar not too high to f.; stoop to rise 33.24
stumble may prevent a f. 86.4
who thinks he stands beware lest he f. 657.1
why do ye f. at such a little wind 327.9

**falls:** he that f. by himself never cries 156.6
when dead tree f., woodpeckers share death 398.13

**false:** f. balance is an abomination 103.3
f. friend, shadow, attend while sun shines 482.3
f. words infect the soul with evil 329.41
hair perhaps divides the f. and true 992.15
how often are we angry against truth, being moved under a f. cause 39.25
in church f. sentiment is frequent 124.5
no woman can be beautiful who can be f. 470.12

**falsehood:** cannot turn over old f. without scattering horrid population dwelling under it 329.24
f. is a dead thing but often moves about 329.12
f. is like a sabre cut: the scar remains 329.36
f. is the jockey of misfortune 329.18
f. lies deep in necessities of existence 329.14
f., rocked by truth, outgrows her cradle 329.13
in politics, f. always prevails 705.40
long attention to single aspect of truth leads to f. 992.5
man cannot make truth f. 329.4
O, what a goodly outside f. hath 329.40
one f. spoils a thousand truths 329.2
peace-mingling f. preferable to mischievous truth 992.17
truth and f. be near twins 992.4
we are only f., duplicity 858.7
when war in air everyone learns f. 1035.45
who speaks truth stabs f. to the heart 993.12
without f., there would be no knowledge 329.29

**fame:** all f. is dangerous 330.22
all is ephemeral—even f. and the famous 983.13
blessed is he whose f. does not outshine his truth 330.47
book against f. bears author's name 438.8
bull does not enjoy f. in two herds 539.15
charm of f. is so great 330.37
do good by stealth and blush to find it f. 391.42
drawback of f. pleasing other men 330.45
drying up a single tear has more of honest f. than shedding seas of gore 517.6
f. but an inscription on a grave 330.43
f. drowns things weighty and solid 330.5
f. has often created something of nothing 330.21
f. is a bee 330.18
f. is a constant effort 330.40
f. is a magnifying glass 330.19
f. is a vapor, popularity an accident 983.25

f. is conquered only by eternity 983.15
f. is the stepmother of death 330.4
f.: public destruction of one in process of becoming 330.41
f. raises the spirit to scorn delights 330.31
f. usually comes to those who are thinking about something else 330.24
fill an author with f., you burst him 330.14
folly loves the martyrdom of f. 351.3
he lives in f. who died in virtue's cause 330.42
he who seeks f. by the practice of virtue 330.49
men have a solicitude about f. 330.26
nothing so arouses ambition as another's f. 33.11
nothing so troublesome as pursuit of f. 330.28
O grant an honest f., or grant me none 330.38
one must choose between obscurity and f. 641.8
to get as much f. as one's father 909.5
toil is the sire of f. 1058.26
who builds church to God, not to f. 433.19
**familiar:** f. acts are beautiful through love 331.13
f. use of things cures not ignorance 331.11
man f. with many must expect familiarities 706.4
men do not bother about the f. 605.12
poetry makes f. be as if not f. 702.90
**familiarity:** coarse f. productive of contempt 497.1
f. breeds contempt—and children 331.15
f. breeds contentment 331.1
f. confounds all traits of distinction 514.9
f. takes off the edge of admiration 331.8
**families:** f. break up when people take hints you don't intend 332.17
f. should have parliament within doors 332.15
**family:** bringing up a f. should be an adventure 332.24
chief conceit is about f. 37.1
f. is chief source of unhappiness 332.9
f. is the home of all social evils 332.28
f. is where most ridiculous things go on 332.5
f. is where self-respect is smothered 332.29
f. of man more than three billion strong 558.30
f. often a commonwealth of malignants 332.23
flesh perishes, the f. face lives on 37.7
govern f. as you would cook fish—gently 332.11
happy the f. that can eat onions together 352.9
less trouble governing f. than kingdom 332.21
my f. pride is inconceivable 37.5
nature set up f. to supply man's wants 332.2
no vocabulary for love within a f. 332.16
numerous f. is bulwark of power 713.48
small f. is soon provided for 82.1
the f. is the test of freedom 332.10
unhappy f. is unhappy in its own way 332.31
**famine:** all's good in a f. 435.3
**famous:** prestige you acquire by knowing f. men 926.1
we are clever at envying a f. man while alive, at praising him when he's dead 330.32
whole earth is the sepulchre of f. men 330.48
whole segments of population wake up f. 330.27
**fanatic:** f. can't change mind, won't change subject 333.2
f. does what Lord would if He knew facts 333.3
f. is a leader just entering room 333.1
there is nobody as enslaved as the f. 333.20
**fanatic's:** no place in f. head for reason 333.17
**fanatical:** f. religion is not quite as bad as none 790.64
**fanaticism:** f. consists in redoubling effort when you have forgotten aim 333.19
strong performance needs f. in performer 333.5
we give name of f. to zeal of others 929.4
**fanatics:** f. have dreams, weave paradise for sect 333.12
to make f., persuade before you instruct 333.21
**fancy:** ever let the f. roam 687.12
f. is a balloon that soars at wind's will 448.3
impediments to f. are motives of more f. 236.38
to give reason for f. were to weigh fire 448.19
we may take f. for a companion 778.18
where I cannot satisfy my reason, I love to humour my f. 1046.2
**fantasy:** childish f. like sheath over bud 121.7
f. can be equivalent to a paradise 687.10
**far:** fair and softly goes f. 377.3
**farce:** f. appeals to the collective belly 144.7
**farces:** like dreams, f. show fulfillment of wishes 144.1
**farewell:** the return makes one love the f. 666.6
**farm:** remote though your f. may be 334.4
sacrifice to f. teaches what a f. is 831.8
**farmer:** good f. is handy man with sense of humus 334.9
only the f. buys retail, sells wholesale 334.5
**farmers:** f. are founders of human civilization 334.8
f. worry only during the growing season 129.21
**farming:** f. looks easy when your plow is a pencil 334.3
f. not really a business; an occupation 334.10
in f., do one thing late, you will be late in everything 334.2
**farms:** destroy f. and grass will grow in cities 334.1
**farthest:** he goes f. who goes far enough 592.11

**fascinating:** evening with f. person leaves vivid memories; with interesting person, bouquet 494.4
**fashion:** Adam and Eve started the world of f. 335.30
as good be out of world as out of f. 335.8
custom, f. are blind to what is to come 210.6
even knowledge has to be in f. 335.13
f. condemns us to many follies 335.21
f.: despot whom wise ridicule and obey 335.3
f. elevates bad to level of good 335.2
f. has brought all into vogue but virtue 335.10
f. is gentility running from vulgarity 335.14
f. is issue of ostentation, egotism 335.15
f. is made to become unfashionable 335.5
f. is more powerful than any tyrant 335.20
f. produces beautiful things that become ugly with time 335.9
f.: to realize art in living forms 335.17
f. wears out more apparel than the man 335.24
he is fantastical who is not in f. 335.4
I can't keep track of all vagaries of f. 335.22
if not in f., you are nobody 335.7
ladies of f. starve love to feed pride 335.11
no new f. worth salt is ever wearable 265.20
nothing is so hideous as an obsolete f. 335.27
present f. is always handsome 335.12
there's never a new f. but it's old 335.6
**fashionable:** f. idea is an adulterated one 441.16
**fashions:** every generation laughs at the old f. 335.29
f. are only induced epidemics 335.26
fancy, not taste, produces many new f. 335.32
in perspective f. are grotesque 335.31
**fast:** they stumble that run f. 409.13
**fastidious:** to be f. is troublesome and slavish 336.1
**fat:** f. hens lay few eggs 183.10
f. paunch never bred subtle mind 637.1
imprisoned in every f. man a thin one is wildly signalling to be let out 637.4
let me have men about me that are f. 57.20
sweetest f. sticks to my own bones 869.19
**fate:** a part of f. is freedom of man 361.12
book of nature is book of f. 505.5
by the side of f., set up resistance to f. 337.4
difficulty of f. lies in complexity 536.97
f. can be surmounted by scorn 182.2
f. falls on men unless they act 337.5
f. finds for every man his share of misery 1004.10
f., fortune, sweep strong powers away 983.26
f. has terrible power none can avoid 337.20
f. has to do with the unintended results of innumerable men 337.15
f. hath but one law for small and great 337.13
f. is at your elbow 391.34
f. leads the willing 337.17
f. loves the fearless 192.25
f.: name for unpenetrated causes 337.9
f. not an eagle, it creeps like a rat 337.1
f. shaped by men without greatness 705.15
great soul surrenders itself to f. 800.10
I would not fear nor wish my f. 723.5
if f. means you to lose, give a fight 337.14
if reason wills f., she is f. 778.21
if we accept f., we must affirm liberty 860.3
intellect annuls f. 968.14
it is f. of coconut husk to float 238.13
man once cursed his f., now curses himself 752.10
men are not prisoners of f. 583.17
necessity is harsh; f. has no reprieve 337.10
superiority to f. is difficult to gain 337.6
there is no armor against f. 337.19
to be wise in misfortune is to conquer f. 17.50
to bear is to conquer our f. 285.2
we can't conquer f., yet we can yield in a way as to be greater than if we could 930.5
we march to f. abreast 809.13
we stand against f. as children stand against wall to mark their height 337.8
whatever limits us we call f. 337.7
whatever we perpetrate we're steered by f. 337.3
when f. summons, monarchs must obey 218.41
who await no gifts from chance, conquer f. 114.3
who fights against his f. is a fool 285.3
who has calmly reconciled his life to f. 930.1
**fate's:** granting our wish: f. saddest joke 236.32
**fates:** F. seldom allow a single line to stand perfect 455.8
our wills and f. do contrary run 1049.10
see how the f. their gifts allot 337.12
three f.: poverty, drudgery, ignorance 712.40
what f. impose men must needs abide 337.18
**father:** affection makes fool of man too much the f. 663.29
angry f. is most cruel toward himself 663.39
child is f. of the man 402.27
f. is a banker provided by nature 663.20
f. miserable who holds children's affection because they need his assistance 663.35
f. should help son form habit of doing right on his own initiative 909.16
f. whose son raises his hand to him is guilty 909.12
greatness in f. often overwhelms son 909.9
have we not all one f. 98.1
it is a wise f. that knows his own child 663.49
must be struggle between f. and son 909.8
one celestial f. gives to all 385.50
son can bear death of his f. 1051.8
time not to become a f. is eighteen years before a war 909.17
'tis happy thing to be f. unto many sons 909.14

to be famous as one's f.: be more able 909.5
to old f. nothing sweeter than daughter 215.1
wise son maketh a glad f. 909.2
**father's**: f. nature lives anew in infant 415.2
how easily a f. tenderness is recalled 909.11
you have to deserve your f. love 663.22
**fathers**: childish to expect men to believe like f. 372.3
fundamental defect of f. 663.43
happy the man who recalls his f. with joy 37.6
men more like own time than like f. 181.1
our f. and ourselves sowed dragon's teeth 809.1
some f. never stop giving their children reasons for being consoled at their death 663.33
sons are generally worse than their f. 909.6
we do things because our f. have done them 210.12
**fatigue**: sadness is almost always a form of f. 1004.14
**fattens**: what does not poison, f. 319.30
**fault**: excusing of a f. doth make the f. worse 312.5
f. is not in our stars, but in ourselves 804.13
he who findeth f. meaneth to buy 103.8
one without f. would not have a friend 339.17
real f.: to have faults, not amend them 339.4
we desire to make other men perfect but we will not amend our own f. 339.36
we find f. with perfection itself 203.23
we won't have friends if we expect no f. 677.10
who think they're generous to a f. 373.5
why not bear a f. in your wife 560.38
**faultless**: he is lifeless that is f. 339.8
whoever thinks a f. piece to see 677.15
**faults**: benevolent man should allow f. in himself 339.11
best men are moulded out of f. 339.34
confession of f. next to innocence 165.4
each day our f. are stifled under forgetfulness, death and justice 339.14
f. forgiven man of perfect candor 360.14
f. look handsome in three hundred pounds 1041.57
f. of those who keep men waiting 759.3
f. shared are comfortable as slippers 339.25
faultfinder will find f. in paradise 339.37
for youthful f. ripe virtues shall atone 1064.61
forget our f. if they're known to us only 339.24
greatest of f. is to be conscious of none 339.2
in f. we touch one another, find sympathy 339.19
man whose f. you cannot see 339.5
man without f. is a mountain without crevasses 339.3
money will hide many f. 596.12
more f. committed while obliging 339.35
must not take f. of youth into old age 646.41
no one is born without f. 339.18
our f. are not seen, but past us 339.6
our f. more pardonable than the shifts we make to hide them 339.23
people impatient if have to lay f. aside 339.15
pride is the mask of one's own f. 727.15
rich men's f. are covered with money 339.9
self-love veils our f. from us 869.2
small f. indulged let in greater 339.12
telling man his f. helps, if with love 203.2
they see only f. who seek nothing else 339.13
to bear burden of others' f. worst 339.10
to suffer from one's own f. is the sting of life 339.40
truly an evil to be full of f. 339.29
we acknowledge our f. to repair the damage they've done us in others' eyes 165.2
we can't stand other people having our f. 339.39
we only admit to minor f. 339.21
when a man laughs he shows all his f. 523.8
when f. seen in others, we behold our own 339.33
where love fails we espy all f. 549.16
whoe'er tells my f., I hate him mortally 339.30
without our own f. we wouldn't enjoy seeing them in others 339.22
**favor**: easier to get than keep f. from fortune 358.37
f. well bestowed is almost as great an honour to the giver as to the receiver 881.11
man who confers f. would rather not be repaid in same coin 881.1
we appreciate the motive rather than the f. 382.16
who boasts of f. bestowed, wants it back 881.10
**favors**: art of acceptance of f. 780.2
pleasure we derive doing f. is in the feeling that we are not worthless 881.7
pretty woman likes to be asked for her f. 348.9
to confer f. with grace 382.6
**fear**: as love casts out f., hate casts out f. 551.14
behind all we feel, there is sense of f. 340.5
better beans and bacon in peace than cakes and ale in f. 674.1
better hazard once than remain in f. 90.4
courage imperils life, f. protects it 340.21
cruelty is a tyrant attended by f. 206.6
death is nothing; we f. what we know not 218.40
difference between despair and f. 340.11
excessive f. is always powerless 340.2
expect, f., everything from time and men 971.64

f. betrays unworthy souls 340.33
f., born of stern matron Responsibility 43.8
f. comes from uncertainty 340.16
f. could never make virtue 340.34
f. created gods; audacity, kings 518.1
f. first brought gods into the world 385.59
f. has the largest eyes of all 340.22
f. is an instructor of great sagacity 340.12
f. is herald of all revolutions 340.12
f. is sharp-sighted 340.8
f. is stronger than arms 340.1
f. is the main source of superstition 340.27
f. not clouds will always lour 425.4
f. of death or pain is to be dreaded 340.13
f. of doing right is treason when in danger 816.1
f. succeeds crime, is its punishment 201.21
f. to let fall a drop, you spill a lot 110.5
God is good, there is no devil but f. 340.18
hate is the consequence of f. 410.6
he whom many f., has himself many to f. 995.26
hope, f., must be vivid to be effective 601.7
hope should no more be a virtue than f. 425.42
how does one kill f., I wonder 340.10
how vain and vile a passion is this f. 340.20
I f. Greeks even when they bring gifts 257.19
man thinks as a coward till he have f. under his feet 196.2
maturity: to live with f., not be afraid 567.21
never negotiate out of f. 987.3
none act humanely under influence of f. 340.28
nothing robs the mind of its powers as f. 340.6
of all passions, f. weakens judgment most 340.25
one may attribute petty actions to f. 224.25
only f. and interest unite men 1009.9
only thing we have to f. is f. itself 340.26
opposite of f. is love 548.164
ought not to f. with too much dejection 340.19
people tolerate those they f. 977.8
perfect love casteth out f. 548.10
scalded cats f. even cold water 319.22
some driven to death by f. of it 684.10
there are situations in which hope and f. run together and destroy one another 425.12
there are times when f. is good 340.3
to stay is no wise action when there's more reason to f. than to hope 808.1
true nobility is exempt from f. 628.7
we adore, invoke, seek to appease what we f. 1061.9
we are in deadly f. of life 361.23
we poison our lives with f. of burglary 43.1
weakness to f. what cannot be avoided 930.9
what frees one from f. of others is good 340.14
what we f. comes to pass more speedily than what we hope 340.24
when desire dies, f. is born 236.15
when men ruled by f., they strive to prevent the very changes that will abate it 340.23
where f. is, happiness is not 340.30
who shrinks from knowledge of calamities aggravates his f. 302.4
wise man prays for deliverance from f. 213.7

**feareth:** he who killeth a lion when absent f. a mouse when present 87.1

**fearful:** f. are caught as often as the bold 110.4

**fearless:** fate loves the f. 192.25

**fears:** belief in providence has not allayed f. 748.15
each believes what he f. or desires 199.5
f. should not keep us from pursuing hopes 425.22
if desires are endless, f. will be so 401.11
men cannot bear to be deprived even of f. 234.1
out of danger, man forgets his f. 213.9
present f. are less than imaginings 340.32
read thy own breast right, and thou hast done with f. 752.3
we perform according to our f. 737.9
we're dangerous till f. grow thoughtful 340.9
who f. from near at hand f. less 340.31
who f. he shall suffer, suffers what he f. 939.29
who f. you present will hate you absent 340.15

**feast:** enough is as good as a f. 940.3
every day cannot be a f. of lanterns 605.2
he of a merry heart hath a continual f. 407.13
one cannot both f. and become rich 700.2

**feasting:** better to go to house of mourning than f. 603.1

**feasts:** true f. are solemn and rare 112.4

**features:** the f. of our face are gestures which have become permanent 324.6

**February:** here comes F., a kiss waiting on her lips 848.3
most serious charge against New England is F. 621.2

**feeble:** f. man can see only farms already built 33.9
'tis not enough to help the f. up 56.12

**feebleness:** supported by force, f. is imperious 1040.10

**feed:** till you f. us, philosophy can wait 598.6
who won't f. cats must f. mice, rats 929.2

**feel:** behind all we f., there is sense of fear 340.5
can't make yourself f. what you don't f. 816.5
let us value that which we can taste, f. 875.3
thinking when we ought to f. 86.1
we know too much and f. too little 282.32
what we think, f., determined by glands 584.6
who cannot give away cannot f. anything 929.5

**feeling:** bourgeois: one who places anything above f. 581.1
direct speech of f. cannot be replaced 282.27
Englishman taught that f. is bad form 287.10
f. merged with thought, artist's joy 53.78
next pleasantest f. to bein' perfectly happy is bein' perfectly cross 39.15
universal f. cannot be disregarded 756.13
**feeling's:** seeing's believing, but f. the truth 282.15
**feelings:** everyone's f. have a front and side door 282.18
often one attributes to others only f. of which one is capable oneself 656.6
understand in others f. we're capable of 1001.10
**feet:** man's f. grown so big he forgets littleness 1005.4
until I met a man who had no f. 152.4
**feigned:** nothing is lasting that is f. 726.4
**felicity:** human f. is produced by little advantages 407.41
one cannot but mistrust a prospect of f. 407.80
seldom that f. not tempered by sorrow 407.24
there is no virtue in f. 407.26
**fell:** who never climbed high never f. low 33.10
**fellow:** f.-feeling makes one wondrous kind 22.3
how comfortable to know our f. creature 79.3
who love not f.-beings live unfruitfully 98.20
**fellowship:** good f. is commonly but the virtue of pigs in a litter 151.26
good-f. prime requisite for success 390.7
more f. among snakes than among mankind 206.10
sign of passing youth: birth of f. 567.22
that which becks our minds to f. divine 407.61
**felon's:** f. capacity for innocent enjoyment is just as great as any honest man's 201.10
**female:** f. malignity exerted in domestic trifles 1055.80
f. of species more deadly than male 1055.84
highest f. grace is silence 891.14
hysteria is phenomenon of f. nature 576.60
**females:** f. most dangerous when appear to retreat 1055.94
f. will forgive a liberty, not a slight 1055.25
**feminine:** f. woman feels comfortable with women 1055.93
**festival:** life is a f. only to the wise 1053.16
**fetters:** f. of gold are still f. 107.1
**fever:** shown death, he'll be content with f. 889.23
**few:** f. sometimes know, when thousands err 816.18
**fiancé:** brothers make fun of f. stealing sister 332.12
**fickle:** womankind ever f. and changeful thing 1055.147
**fickleness:** f. of women I love equaled by constancy of women who love me 470.11
**fiction:** f. gives opportunity to live history 341.11
f. is a kind of magic and trickery 341.21
f. is imagining based on facts 341.1
f. is like a spider's web 341.22
f. to man what play is to child 341.17
good f. made of that which is real 341.5
truth dressed in f. moves with ease 991.126
truth is more of a stranger than f. 991.136
**fictions:** our separate f. add up to joint reality 777.10
**fidelity:** faithful women think only of f. 178.6
**field:** f. not well seen from within 682.4
**fifty:** years between f. and seventy are hardest 580.8
**fig-tree:** train up f. in way it should go; when you are old sit under the shade of it 981.4
**fight:** fine thing to f. for another's freedom 534.47
he who flees will f. again 298.12
in f. our business is to prove our might 582.10
in f. rich man saves face; poor man, coat 342.5
kiss and make up: live to f. another day 766.14
people seem to f. about things very unsuitable for fighting 342.1
there is such a thing as a nation being too right to f. 658.17
those that fly may f. again 298.2
'tis man's to f., heaven's to give success 170.10
to f. is a radical instinct 342.7
we do not f. for the real 1035.7
what counts is size of f. in dog 342.2
**fighting:** defend life, fame, wealth by f. 1035.77
diversions an imitation of f. 922.9
man is a f. animal 441.32
only one way of f.: to be the conqueror 342.4
**film:** f.: boat always on the point of sinking 604.7
f. is petrified fountain of thought 604.1
wide screen makes bad f. twice as bad 604.3
**films:** you can't be virtuoso in stage and f. 965.1
**finance:** f. was once a trade, today it is an art 542.10
minister of f. is authorized pickpocket 99.3
**financial:** f. worries distinguishes man from beast 596.48
**financier:** faults of burglar are qualities of f. 927.10
**fine:** best effect of f. persons felt afterward 471.4
**finest:** f. edge is made with blunt whetstone 319.38
**finger:** moving f. writes and having writ moves on 337.16

**finish:** God alone can f. 283.3
job never started takes longest to f. 283.4
**finished:** f. product has already seen better days 283.2
one must be thrust out of f. cycle in life 402.14
**finishes:** who begins many things f. but few 74.8
**finishing:** plan nothing new before f. present task 696.4
**fire:** a little f. is quickly trodden out 795.4
by labor f. is got out of a stone 279.2
can a man take f. in his bosom 57.4
divide the f., and you will put it out 932.4
f. is the most tolerable third party 343.1
heap coals of f. on enemy's head 286.6
house is on f.—let us warm ourselves 12.7
how great a matter a little f. kindleth 173.2
if house on f., we must extinguish it 614.11
I'll follow the right side even to the f. 816.19
it may be a f.—tomorrow, ashes 384.1
let a man burn with intensity, he will set f. to the world 1066.4
little f. warms, a great one burns 183.9
one f. burns out another's burning 939.45
people's sympathies are with the f. 311.1
poorly extinguished f. quickly re-ignited 795.1
we all live in house on f., locked in it 457.7
when f. and water at war, f. loses 658.16
**fireside:** to make a happy f. clime to weans, wife 332.8
you are a king by your own f. 420.5
**firm:** often we are f. from weakness 1040.8
**firmness:** f. without intellect is perverseness 491.24
**first:** it is the f. shower that wets 17.32
one cannot be f. in everything 183.1
who has f. place seldom has principal part 773.10
**first-rate:** one man is worth ten thousand if f. 945.4
**fish:** f. die belly-upward and fall to the surface 344.1
f. struggling in net hampers itself 651.7
fuel not sold in forest, nor f. on lake 102.9
net of the sleeper catches f. 264.5
no human being was ever so free as a f. 344.2
sensible f. swims downstream 527.7
teach man to f., feed him for life 981.3
**fishes:** he f. on who catches one 425.10
**fishing:** float f.: worm at one end, fool at other 345.3
gods do not deduct hours spent in f. 345.1
who is not lucky, let him not go f. 358.13
**fit:** officer and office, doer and thing done, seldom f. 942.4
**five:** menace in dealing with a f.-year-old 663.31
**flag:** American f. is the gaudiest ever seen 34.70
f. is embodiment of history, not sentiment 671.26
not for f. of birthplace will I give life 671.15
we've a war, an' a debt, an' a f. 534.24
**flame:** mighty f. followeth a tiny spark 173.4
**flat:** f. country gives the sky a chance 191.15
**flatter:** he who can f. can also slander 346.18
**flattered:** beautiful women f. for understandings 1055.21
**flatterer:** every f. lives at flattered listener's cost 346.14
f., unlike physician, must administer strongest dose to the weakest patient 346.6
no such f. as is a man's self 1020.3
of all tame beasts, preserve me from f. 346.13
**flattering:** we don't hate flattery, but manner of f. 346.17
**flattery:** f. is a coin current only through vanity 346.15
f. is a juggler, no kin unto sincerity 346.4
f. is all right—if you don't inhale 346.20
f. may turn one's stomach 346.10
f. of posterity is not worth more than contemporary f. 346.3
f. pleases very generally 346.12
f. sits in the parlour 346.9
greater the love, the less room for f. 203.20
if we did not flatter ourselves, the f. of others would not hurt us 346.16
imitation is the sincerest f. 449.3
love of f. stems from mean opinion men have of selves 346.21
mysterious power of f. and calumny 199.4
ne'er was f. lost on poet's ear 702.86
necessary that f. be accommodated to circumstances or characters 346.11
none more taken in by f. than proud 727.26
nowadays f. wins friends 991.131
some profess to despise all f. 346.5
some whom gold would not seduce, f. would 346.2
too much f. never lost a gentleman 346.7
vanity moves humanity; f. greases wheels 1020.10
we love f. even when not deceived 346.8
**flavors:** all eat, few can distinguish f. 957.19
**flea:** f. kills none but does all harm he can 1063.6
**fleas:** f. do not know whether they are upon giant 48.6
great f. have little f. upon their backs 662.1
haste in nothing but catching f. 409.6
reasonable amount of f. is good for dog 41.31
who lies with dogs shall rise with f. 57.14
**flee:** I f. who chases me and chase who flees me 195.11
what we f. from flees from us 238.7
**flees:** he who f. will fight again 298.12
**fleeting:** world is f., all things pass—or do we 983.12

**flesh:** all f. is grass 600.4
f. must bear only storms of present 584.2
spirit is willing but the f. is weak 1040.1
the f. is sad, and I've read all books 288.2
**flight:** f. is lawful, when one flies from tyrants 298.10
**flirtation:** f.: expression of considered desire 348.6
**flood:** in the ant's house the dew is a f. 901.3
**flops:** f. are a part of life's menu 327.22
**flower:** canst not stir f. without troubling star 1010.12
f. in the crannied wall 349.7
f. is the poetry of reproduction 349.3
f. may at time control braggart lords 349.6
f. that once has blown for ever dies 600.14
f. you single out is rejection of all others 467.19
full many a f. is born to blush unseen 641.4
meanest f. can give thoughts that often lie too deep for tears 349.8
our national f. is concrete cloverleaf 63.8
weed is no more than a f. in disguise 369.2
**flowers:** God waits for his own f. as man's gifts 1061.7
many look at meadow, few see the f. 605.3
**fluency:** one truth discovered is better than all f. 991.54
**fly:** don't try to f. before you have wings 749.11
f. may sting horse and make him wince 773.13
f. ought to be used as symbol of audacity 479.8
God made f., forgot to tell us why 479.7
one cannot f. into flying 402.13
shell must break before bird can f. 402.26
then would I f. away and be at rest 298.1
those that f. may fight again 298.2
**foe:** he makes no friend who never made a f. 286.26
heat not a furnace so hot for your f. 811:19
strong f. better than weak friend 286.8
sweet to see your f. perish 811.11
**foe's:** tear out thy f. brain 286.24
**foes:** our greatest f. are within 866.3
who makes a character makes f. 117.29
you shall judge a man by friends, f. 286.7
**fog:** f. comes on little cat feet 1043.7
f.: not weather and not mood, yet both 1043.2
**foible:** forte always makes a f. 956.6
most powerful f.: love of living 536.75
**fold:** do not f., spindle, or mutilate 558.27
**folklore:** f. is what they tell the children 610.5
**follies:** others' f. teach us not 319.60
what is life but a series of inspired f. 351.18
**follow:** necessary to f. in order to lead 647.2
people, like sheep, tend to f. leader 350.1
we f. those that fly from us 684.5
**followers:** every man with idea has two or three f. 441.2
great man's f. put out eyes that they may better sing his praise 350.4
**following:** most lives spent in seeming and f. 168.4
**follows:** in affairs consider what precedes and f. 356.3
**folly:** be fool without shame, learn from f. 351.15
f. is perennial, yet human race survives 351.14
f. loves the martyrdom of fame 351.3
f. of one can make many miserable 804.9
f. of one man is fortune of another 351.1
f. of the world confounds its wisdom 351.9
f. often goes beyond her bounds 824.5
f. pursues us at all periods of our lives 351.12
f. to censure him whom world adores 203.26
if thou rememberest not the f. of love 548.208
it is f. to drown on dry land 351.6
it is f. to sing twice to a deaf man 48.3
it's f. to bolt door with boiled carrot 850.3
kings' power founded on f. of people 825.19
living without f. not so wise as believed 351.11
men content to be laughed at for wit, but not for f. 351.21
riches forsake a man, we discover his f. 223.5
what use is wisdom when f. reigns 351.23
who realize their f. are not true fools 351.5
wisdom at times is found in f. 351.10
wisdom rises upon the ruins of f. 1053.25
**fond:** f. of each other because ailments same 889.29
one f. of us not necessarily a friend 363.99
**food:** Americans eat f., aware of poison added to improve its appearance 352.3
I hate man who swallows f., affecting not to know what he is eating 272.21
men cook f. to show they aren't beasts 186.8
more die in U. S. of much f. than of little 637.5
nothing to which men with f. and drink cannot reconcile themselves 272.27
to him stinted of f. a boiled turnip will be relished like a roast fowl 435.10
who savors f. is no glutton 272.30
**fool:** answer a f. according to his folly 353.5
any f. can make a rule, every f. minds it 826.6
dullness of f. is whetstone of wits 353.27
every man hath a f. in his sleeve 353.13
f. can ask more than wisest can answer 478.4
f. cannot enter Heaven, be he ever so holy 353.6
f. doesn't know to cash in on foolishness 353.17
f. hath said there is no G. 997.2
f. is always satisfied with himself 353.22
f. is only troublesome, pedant insupportable 842.33
f. knows after he's suffered 319.27
f. matches strength with stronger 1040.4
f. must follow his natural bent 353.19

f. publishes the triumph of the deceiver 353.7
f., reduced to skim milk, slanders cream 686.10
f. sees not the same tree a wise man sees 676.1
f. uttereth all his mind 916.6
f. who holdeth his peace counted wise 353.4
fine clothes may disguise, but foolish words will disclose a f. 353.2
give me the young man who has brains enough to make a f. of himself 351.20
heart of a f. is in his mouth 1053.23
how ill white hairs become a f., jester 353.26
if every f. wore a crown, we should all be kings 353.30
learned f. sillier than an ignorant one 353.21
let f. hold tongue, he will pass for sage 891.25
life of the f. is worse than death 353.3
misfortune of wise better than prosperity of f. 17.22
need very clever woman to manage a f. 353.18
no creature smarts so little as a f. 353.24
nobody can describe a f. without much self-inspection 838.3
one f. makes many 1053.44
people can f. Devil, but not neighbors 619.6
prosperous f. is a grievous burden 353.1
riches serve wise man but command f. 1041.21
sometimes wisdom to seem a f. 353.14
talk sense to f., he calls you foolish 353.11
tell him to be a f. every so often 351.15
the f. doth think he is wise 1053.59
there's no need to fasten a bell to a f. 353.8
to never see f. smash looking-glass 353.25
too many politicians believe you can f. all the people all the time 705.2
who fights against his fate is a f. 285.3
who has not made a f. of himself in love 548.180
wise man by day is no f. by night 1053.20
wise man can play the f. on occasion 1053.24
wise man changes mind, f. never will 347.4
you can f. too many too much of the time 221.22
**fool's:** f. bolt is soon shot 353.15
f. head never whitens 353.9
**fooled:** superior man may be imposed upon, not f. 491.4
**foolish:** if others had not been f., we should be 351.2
if we're not f. young, we're f. old 351.4
profitable if one is wise to seem f. 137.2
**foolishness:** f. revenges self by excommunicating world 351.16
how foolish, seen at wisdom's side, is f. 351.7
my seeming f. may be in fool's eye 351.19
**fools:** absolute f. are hard to be met with 907.4
better to weep with wise men than laugh with f. 57.21
f. admire, men of sense approve 14.5
f. rush in, for folly is always bold 351.8
f. rush in where angels fear to tread 353.23
I am two f., for loving and saying so 548.48
if f. do not control world, it isn't because they are not in majority 353.16
learning begets arrogance in f. 520.51
let us be thankful for the f. 353.29
Lord, what f. these mortals be 558.48
old f. are more foolish than young 353.20
only f. strain at high C all their lives 55.23
out of the mouths of f. and cheats we may get our truest lessons 351.9
there are bearded f. 353.10
there are two f. in every market 102.31
things people make f. of themselves for 351.17
we think fathers f., sons think us so 372.12
who are a little wise, the best f. be 143.2
who realize their folly are not true f. 351.5
who seem learned to f. seem f. to learned 726.16
wise man ridiculous in company of f. 57.12
young think the old f. 1065.4
**foot:** willing mind makes a light f. 1050.4
**football:** be a f. to time and chance 502.8
in pro f. as in nuclear warfare, no winners 922.2
**footman:** I have seen the eternal f. hold my coat 218.42
**forbearance:** who shows f. scores most in controversy 51.6
**forbidden:** there is a charm about the f. 893.24
to make idea of morality center on f. acts 598.46
**force:** accomplish by kindness what you can't by f. 517.15
accusing is proving, with f. as judge 5.2
against naked f. only defense is naked f. 354.19
as if nature makes men narrow to give f. 613.3
boys look on all f. as an enemy 95.1
easiest victor over reason: terror, f. 354.7
f. may subdue for a moment 354.3
f. overcomes but half the foe 354.14
f. without justice is tyranny 354.16
f. without reason falls of own weight 354.8
f. works on servile natures, not free 354.11
in their dreams f. can't resist the pacifists 658.2
knowledge is more than f. 520.31
lust and f. source of all actions 9.33
not take another's house by f. 98.3
submission to exterior f. rots me 354.6
there is always room for a man of f. 853.3
there is no real f. without justice 354.15

what has to be maintained by f. is doomed 354.13
when fact can be demonstrated, f. is unnecessary; when it cannot, f. is infamous 354.10
**forcible:** f. ways do not end evil, but leave hatred 354.2
how f. are right words 816.2
**foreign:** everything f. is respected 355.2
f. affairs will not conform to whim 496.14
f. relations endless, like human relations 245.9
humor first to perish in foreign tongue 434.32
international incidents should not govern f. policy 496.11
nation needs f. stock to thrive well 451.1
what affects men about f. nation is not finding things in the familiar place 985.9
**foreigner:** America shuts its mind against man's ideas by calling him a f. 355.4
**foreigners:** admiration for ourselves too often measured by our contempt for f. 355.3
**foresight:** in action be primitive; in f. a strategist 9.15
**forest:** f. is the poor man's overcoat 988.4
man: preceded by f., followed by desert 1035.47
**forethought:** bravery is f. 356.4
f. and ready wit both prosper in peace 356.7
**forewarned:** f. man is worth two 722.3
**forget:** ability to f. is true token of greatness 574.12
advantage at times to f. what we know 574.29
better f. and smile than remember, be sad 574.30
eyes f. the tears they have shed 1043.6
it is not so easy to f. 574.34
memory is the thing you f. with 574.6
'tis sure the hardest science to f. 552.13
to f. anything, make a note to remember 574.26
to f. is a necessary condition of life 574.2
to f. oneself is to be happy 1014.4
we f. because we must, not because we will 574.1
**forgetfulness:** f. transforms occurrence to nonoccurrence 574.25
to live, to suffer, and at the end—f. 600.2
**forgetting:** f. a wrong is a mild revenge 474.7
f. is woman's first and greatest art 1055.2
it would add to happiness if art of f. could be taught 574.13
men live by f.—women live on memories 576.12
we live between clouds of f., uncertainty 723.11
**forgive:** bound to f. enemy, not to trust him 286.13
did man e'er live saw priest, woman f. 357.14
f. us our debts 357.1
how unhappy is he who cannot f. himself 403.16
it is easier to f. an enemy than a friend 357.3
manlike to bear extremities, godlike to f. 285.4
men offend where they find goodness to f. 474.5
to err is human, to f. divine 357.16
to understand is to f., even oneself 1001.2
we f. a place as soon as it's left behind 693.3
we love best those who make it most easy for us to f. them 357.4
we never f. those who make us blush 886.5
who does you ill will not f. you 474.6
worst men are those who do not f. 357.8
**forgiven:** forgotten is f. 357.7
injuries may be f., but not forgotten 474.1
**forgiveness:** f. is the answer to the child's dream 357.10
f. to the injured does belong 357.5
glory of Christianity is to conquer by f. 123.1
love is an act of endless f. 548.241
there is no f. in nature 616.7
what power has love but f. 357.18
**forgives:** man who does not return your blow neither f. you nor allows you to forgive self 658.14
**forgiving:** be tenderhearted, f. one another 357.2
f. presupposes remembering 357.17
joy of f. might well arouse envy of gods 357.12
to be social is to be f. 151.10
**forgot:** we have all f. more than we remember 574.9
**forgotten:** celebrities wake to find themselves f. 330.27
f. is forgiven 357.7
he who is not f. is not dead 218.25
to be f. is to sleep in peace 641.6
what I fear is not being enough f. 79.7
**fork:** he is better with a rake than a f. 401.6
**form:** f. is heart of humor, salvation of comedy 434.28
government defines man by printed f. 100.4
pay attention to f.; emotion will come 20.3
picture, sculpture are festivities of f. 53.43
**formalities:** superstition to put hope in f. 112.5
**forms:** f. are for mediocrity 822.3
it is meritorious to insist on f. 654.6
**formula:** f. expressing law of nature praises God 844.9
new f. is virtually old at appearance 441.13
to rest on a f. is a slumber 979.11
**fornication:** old bawd hesitates not to forswear f. 783.35
**forte:** f. always makes a foible 956.6
**forties:** in f. we know friends won't save us 363.49
**fortitude:** heaven has space for all modes of f. 412.2

**fortunate:** be f., and you will be thought great 358.21
brave or f. man can bear envy 293.25
f. persons hardly ever amend their ways 358.27
no events so f. that the imprudent cannot turn to their own prejudice 303.6
'tis better to be f. than wise 358.48
unrighteous are never really f. 1048.9
**fortune:** all beat the man whom f. buffets 206.7
ambitious men most liable to blasts of f. 33.28
behind, f. is bald 358.28
boldness, caution, make f.; wit keeps it 1041.19
celerity is mother of good f. 919.3
every man is architect of his own f. 860.11
f. and humour govern the world 114.13
f. belongs to him with contented mind 183.19
f. blind to those she does no good 358.26
f. brings in boats that are not steered 358.40
f. confers aura of worth, unworthily 358.9
f. favors the bold and the young 358.16
f. favors the brave 358.45
f. gives advantage to those she favours. 15.6
f. gives much to many, never enough to any 358.19
f. had no deity if men had wisdom 358.23
f. holds even, scrupulous balance 114.8
f. is not on side of faint-hearted 358.41
f. like market where price may fall 358.1
f. makes a fool of him whom she favors too much 358.35
f. never takes her favorite unawares 358.32
f. seldom troubles the wise man 1053.21
f. sides with him who dares 358.46
f. soon tires of carrying any one long 358.17
f., to destroy, first makes mad 555.19
f., what god is more cruel than thou 358.20
folly of one man is f. of another 351.1
from f. to misfortune is but a step 745.17
good f. leads one to the highest glory, but to renounce it calls for equal courage 358.5
good or bad f. usually comes to those who have more of one than the other 358.25
great f. is a great slavery 1041.55
how f. brings to earth the oversure 657.4
how many cards f. has up her sleeve 358.3
if f. turns against you, even jelly breaks your tooth 17.46
ill f. never crushed that man whom good f. deceived not 358.24
in worst of f. is best chance for change 358.11
it is f. with nature that makes heroes 416.14
it is we that are blind, not f. 85.3
man's best or worst f. is his wife 560.40
men balance between good and bad f. 358.42
men never think their f. too great 1054.8
misfortunes tell us what f. is 745.8
must master good f. or it will master us 358.34
near-missing of happiness looks like insult of f. 407.39
none can hold f. still and make it last 358.12
not even a collapsing world looks dark to a man about to make his f. 732.10
our mood changes more than our f. 962.7
own character the arbiter of one's f. 117.23
power of f. confessed only by the miserable 358.44
truth is no road to f. 991.106
war is subject to inconstancy of f. 1035.13
when f. flatters, she does it to betray 358.36
when f. on our side, popular favor also 15.8
when f. surprises us with a position, it is almost impossible to maintain it 773.16
who is born to a f. must be freer than those who are not, or he gains nothing 1041.8
wise man turns chance to good f. 114.11
**fortune's:** f. a right whore 358.47
f. expensive smile is earned 358.6
f. not content with knocking a man down 358.38
f. slave has one foot in gravy, one in grave 33.34
industry is f. right hand 358.14
some live just for their f. sake 596.31
yield not thy neck to f. yoke 90.16
**fortunes:** every man architect of own f., but neighbors superintend construction 619.1
f. are made with other people's money 1041.62
man's f. are fruit of his character 117.8
those who had no share in good f. of the mighty often share their misfortunes 546.2
**forty:** better one bite, at f., of truth's rind 567.11
man of f. to fifty is stoic or satyr 580.18
to hold same views at f. as at twenty 176.4
when f., half of you belongs to the past 646.5
**foundations:** loftiest edifices need deepest f. 399.57
our f. are within us, not without 873.1
**founds:** he who f. a line is honored 37.14
**fountain:** what f. sends forth returns to f. 21.6
when f. has gone up, it comes down 358.33
**fox:** English gentleman galloping after a f. 436.5
f. condemns the trap, not himself 775.1
f. is followed for the pleasure of it 436.4
f. knows many tricks 197.7
lion is ashamed when he hunts with f. 57.15
with foxes we must play the f. 197.2
**foxholes:** no "white" or "colored" signs on f. 769.10
**fragrance:** rose too often smelled loses f. 331.14
unless incense is burnt, it emits no f. 502.17
**France:** F. has neither winter, summer, nor morals 359.10
in F. everything is a pretext for dinner 359.1
political thought in F. is nostalgic or utopian 359.2

who cannot love F., which taught us 685 ways to dress eggs 359.7
**frank:** how can I be f.; I don't dare know myself 360.4
**frankness:** cruel describe selves as paragons of f. 360.15
lies kill love: what about f. 360.8
**fraternity:** a. f. is the antithesis of f. 98.23
great perils bring out the f. of strangers 213.12
**fraud:** f. is homage force pays to reason 354.4
pious f. begets need for going on 221.14
whoever has become notorious by f. 221.15
**frauds:** some f. are so well conducted 221.3
**free:** American feels rich in f. expression 361.16
basis of f. society: cohesive sentiment 534.11
better starve f. than be a fat slave 361.1
enemy of f. enterprise system 732.8
essence of f. government 755.4
f. government consists in control of rivalries 393.4
f. mind must have policeman, Irony 434.14
f. way of life does not prescribe means 361.34
for a people to be f., the governed must be sages 534.28
force works on servile natures, not f. 354.11
him I love, I wish to be f. even from me 548.119
history of f. men written by choice 417.19
hungry man is not a f. man 435.12
I only ask to be f.; butterflies are f. 361.7
I will love, defend land where man is f. 671.15
if you cannot be f., be as f. as you can 361.10
live f. and uncommitted 361.52
lord of one green lizard—and f. 334.4
man believes he acts as a f. being 361.36
man desires to be f. and feel important 865.2
man f. to do as likes only in own concerns 571.7
man is born f., is everywhere in chains 107.8
man's belief that he is f. causes remorse 171.20
men would rather be starving and f. than fed in bonds 882.4
modesty is a virtue of f. men 231.16
most powerful force in world today is man's desire to be f. and independent 361.33
nation has character only when it is f. 534.43
no human being was ever so f. as a fish 344.2
no man can be just who is not f. 515.53
no man f.; slaves of money or necessity 168.5
nobody really favors f. speech 362.3
not all are f. who mock their chains 947.3
not f. until captive of supreme belief 76.13
only the educated are f. 277.24
renew pledge to man, his right to be f. 361.41
so far as a man thinks, he is f. 968.14
strive to live f., caught in own toils 361.17
the f. have part in National Palaver 169.2
this f. will business is a bit terrifying 636.1
to be f. is not necessarily to be wise 1053.69
truth shall make you f. 991.7
virtue of f. man equally great in refusing difficulties, overcoming them 361.48
we have confused f. with f. and easy 361.49
what you get f. costs too much 382.1
while a soul is in prison, I am not f. 98.2
who would be f. themselves must act 534.7
who would keep land f. must be martyred 534.25
**freedom:** a part of fate is f. of man 361.12
abridgment of f. by gradual encroachments 995.21
absolute f. mocks at justice 361.4
bachelor's admired f. is often a yoke 65.5
black man is striding f. road 83.16
carelessness about our f. is dangerous 534.44
civilized men impose own restraint against abuse of f. 534.38
dagger plunged in name of f. is plunged into the breast of f. 361.39
death is supreme festival on road to f. 218.16
don't wear best trousers to battle for f. 813.25
everything great is created by the individual who can labor in f. 361.8
f. and slavery are mental states 361.18
f. baffling: known only when gone 361.45
f. can't be bestowed, it must be achieved 534.37
f. can't be bought for nothing 361.46
f. depends on self-discipline of the free 534.21
f. from self-imposed limitation 361.29
f. has thousand charms slaves never know 361.6
f. in America: not silencing brand of idea 111.7
f. is a condition of mind 361.28
f. is greatest fruit of self-sufficiency 361.15
f. is indivisible 882.9
f. is not something anybody can be given 361.2
f. is to share chains our brothers wear 361.37
f. means, above all, f. from lies 361.35
f. never relied on uniformity of opinion 250.7
f. of press a bulwark of liberty 725.4
f. of press a means, not end 725.1
f. of speech means you shall not do something to people for their views 362.1
f. of the most free: to do what is right 816.10
f. praised when she is tucked away in past 111.2
f. suppressed, regained bites with keener fangs than f. never endangered 361.5
f. to differ is not limited 256.6
f. to learn the first part of being free 529.15
f. when it loses fetters becomes fetter of a greater f. 361.19
f.: will to be responsible to ourselves 361.42
f. won by controlling desire 856.3

fine thing to fight for another man's f. 534.47
gain f. when price paid for right to live 361.50
genius can only breathe in atmosphere of f. 374.29
he earns f. who daily conquers it anew 361.21
highest pleasure to be got of f. is labor 530.11
history: progress of consciousness of f. 361.25
I am earth-bound to pay for f. of my eyes 890.6
if any in chains anywhere, f. endangered everywhere 107.4
if world knew how to use f. 534.45
in f. people take care of government 393.70
inside, the terrible f. 583.6
laws alone cannot secure f. of expression 977.5
man about the same with despotism or f. 393.67
me this unchartered f. tires 116.6
men lose social f. seeking to become alike 168.15
more joy hollering for f. than getting it 534.35
most men after f. prefer authority 61.6
need f. and constraint to be oneself 442.19
no one can be at peace unless he has f. 361.38
no real f. without economic security 361.43
nobody can give you f. 853.5
peace and f. walk together 129.28
people demand f. when they have no power 534.29
people use every means to get rid of f. 1058.32
real evil is to surrender f. 305.34
search for f. greatest force of modern age 813.31
social progress strengthens f. 735.14
there can be no f. without f. to fail 361.27
there can't be any apprenticeship for f. 361.32
thing is to know what to do with f. 361.20
those always free can't understand power of hope of f. to those who are not free 534.6
those who deny f. deserve it not 882.10
to march to f., men must deal with political as with scientific questions 393.26
to obey God is f. 385.67
to reap blessings of f., men must undergo fatigue of supporting it 534.30
to strike f. of the mind with fist of patriotism is old, ugly subtlety 671.20
tyranny is always better organized than f. 534.32
tyrant claims f. to kill f. and yet to keep it for himself 995.32
unless a man has talents to make something of himself, f. is an irksome burden 361.26
we have f. of speech and conscience, and prudence never to practice them 534.46
we love goodness, but also f. 361.11
we prate of f.; we are in fear of life 361.23
we stand for f.: that is our only commitment to others 534.22
when man gains f., he loses being 361.44
when there is f. there will be no state 923.15

**freedom's:** best road to progress is f. road 735.12

**freedoms:** four sandwiches vs. four f. 435.7

**freight:** philosophy for exercise rather than f. 688.15

**French:** English have a way of calling the F. light 287.5
F. complain of everything, always 359.8
the F. are individualistic, ungovernable 359.9

**Frenchman:** F. is first and foremost a man 359.5
F. must always be talking, informed or not 359.4
F. thinks everything right that is French 287.12

**Frenchmen:** F. have unlimited capacity for gallantry 359.6

**friend:** a f. to all is a f. to none 736.3
a true f. is the greatest of all blessings 363.75
admonition of f. best preservative of mind's health 797.2
be a f. to thyself, others will be too 862.3
best f. can show and accept kindness 517.21
best mirror is an old f. 587.3
better lose a jest than a f. 434.11
communicating self to f. doubles joys 363.15
compassion for f. should conceal itself 692.15
do f. good as if he might yet be foe 286.25
doubtful f. is worse than certain enemy 363.4
f. in power is a f. lost 713.2
f. is person with whom I may be sincere 894.7
f. knows all about you, still likes you 363.65
f. loves whole man; companion, his qualities 363.21
f. may be reckoned masterpiece of nature 363.40
f. often chosen to flatter our self-love 363.60
f. should bear his friend's infirmities 363.102
f. should guess and keep still 363.85
f. that you buy will be bought from you 97.4
f. to everybody and nobody is same thing 453.8
faithful are the wounds of a f. 363.19
false f., shadow, attend while sun shines 482.3
few will endure a true f. 363.51
foolish to experiment on constancy of f. 178.8
forsake not an old f. 363.6
give f. cause to blush: likely lose him 886.8
good f. is my nearest relation 363.50
he makes no f. who never made a foe 286.26
he that wrongs f. wrongs self more 474.25
he's a f. that speaks well behind back 392.4
hold a true f. with both your hands 363.86

I care for no f. who loves his enemy equally well 736.4
I loathe f. who shares no grief 363.45
I would prefer as f. a good man ignorant 363.46
if each knew what his f. said of him 907.8
if f. is equal to brother, don't wrong him 363.62
in misfortune what f. remains a f. 17.25
instead of loving enemy, treat f. better 658.11
invite your f. to dinner 286.15
life without f. is death without witness 908.48
longest journey is search for a sincere f. 363.5
must eat peck of salt with f. to know him 363.28
my best f. wishes me well for my sake 363.11
Narcissus never wrote well nor was a f. 869.3
new f. is like new wine 363.7
no love for f. whose love is words 363.104
no man can be happy without a f. 407.46
not f. if cannot open honest mind 423.2
nothing openeth the heart but a f. 166.1
office of a f. is to side with you when you are wrong 363.112
on meeting old f., first temptation is to look the other way 363.17
one afraid of laughing at f. lacks love 363.58
one f. in a lifetime is much; two are many 363.3
one f. worth ten thousand relatives 363.48
one fond of us not necessarily a f. 363.99
one function of f. is to suffer punishments meant for our enemies 363.67
only way to have f. is to be one 363.41
over the bottle many a f. is found 266.64
persuasion of a f. is a strong thing 683.8
reveal not every secret to a f. 749.29
save me from the candid f. 360.2
stillest tongue can be truest f. 891.8
stranger has no f.; unless a stranger 355.9
strong foe better than a weak f. 286.8
successful man can satisfy one f. 363.109
sympathetic f. can be dear as brother 363.64
to throw away honest f. is to throw your life away 363.105
we die as often as we lose a f. 363.90
we find the true f. only in fragments 677.8
we have a special face for each f. 787.3
what you love most in f. may be clearer in his absence 2.7
what you share with f. you save from heir 382.19
when you find out a f. is a liar 329.19
who keepeth God a f. loseth nothing 547.2
**friendless:** no one would choose f. life on condition of having all other things 544.1
**friendly:** social, f. man fulfills nature's plan 151.4
**friends:** all's dear that comes from f. 382.39
best loved man would perish if he heard all his f. say in a dav 392.5
between f., differences in taste 957.3
between f. there is no need of justice 363.9
can be f. only on terms of equality 363.114
count not him among f. who will retail your privacies to the world 392.12
delight to make f. with someone despised 363.30
don't be honest with f. who ask it 363.27
empty purse frightens away f. 712.16
f. are born, not made 363.1
f. are generally of the same sex 27.9
f. are the sunshine of life 363.59
f. are to be feared for what they keep us from doing 363.68
f. provoked become bitterest enemies 363.56
f. show love in times of trouble 363.47
God save me from my f. 363.88
good to have f., even in hell 363.106
hateful in f. to help too late 972.5
have f., 'tis a second existence 363.53
he that is neither one thing nor the other has no f. 442.1
help me to money and I'll have f. 596.22
I keep my f. as misers do their treasure 363.8
if f. are one-eyed, look at them in profile 363.71
in adversity f. stay away of own accord 745.7
in the thirties we want f. 363.49
life is partly made by f. we choose 363.107
love f. as if they might become your enemies 363.18
make your f. your teachers 529.8
man with host of f. who slaps everyone on back is regarded as friend of nobody 706.2
man's growth seen in succession of f. 402.6
more shameful to mistrust one's f. than to be deceived by them 257.11
most f. are those of circumstances 363.54
not on number, but the choice of f. 363.34
old f. are best, we say, when disillusionment shakes faith in new comrade 363.24
one active enemy is worth two f. 286.16
one can be stupid with old f. 363.38
one uses early f. to mark progress 363.63
ornament of house is f. who frequent it 420.11
procure yourself critical f. 445.5
scarcity of friendship but not of f. 7.4
those that lack f. to open themselves unto are cannibals of own hearts 908.5
true f. are punctilious equals 496.10
trust f. of today as if enemies tomorrow 257.6
various are the uses of f. 990.7
we have really no absent f. 2.1
we know our f. by their defects 363.78
we need new f. 363.103
we often turn backs on actual f. 363.108
we regret loss of f. because of our needs 363.76

we won't have f. if we expect no fault 677.10
wealth maketh many f. 1041.5
who fears making enemies will have no f. 973.6
who has many f. has no f. 706.1
who has thousand f. hasn't one to spare 286.3
who treats f., foes the same lacks love, justice 453.4
whom heaven helps has f. enough 748.8
win f. by prejudices, narrowness 720.4
women, like princes, find few real f. 1055.91
yield to f. and you win victory 170.16
you shall judge a man by f., foes 286.7
you've heard all f. have to say 363.93

**friendship:** broken f. soldered is never sound 299.2
business may bring money, f. does rarely 363.13
can sincerity be condition of f. 991.15
ceremony is the smoke of f. 112.2
characteristic of f. to take without enquiry the unseen doings of our friends 363.98
confidence is the only bond of f. 990.8
endurance of f. depends upon circumstance 363.37
f. admits of difference of character 363.94
f. either finds or makes equals 363.89
f. ends in love; but love in f.—never 548.30
f.: inclination to promote other's good 363.23
f. increases in visiting friends 426.12
f. is a furrow in the sand 363.110
f. is a single soul in two bodies 363.12
f. is a slow-ripening fruit 363.10
f. is constant in all things save love 363.101
f. is disinterested commerce of equals 548.87
f. is like money, easier made than kept 363.25
f. is like sound health, valued when lost 363.32
f. is love without his wings 363.26
f. is marriage of the soul 363.113
f. is reciprocal conciliation of interests 363.73
f. is sole remedy against misfortune 363.55
f. is too time-consuming for busy men 530.4
f. lasts if not asked to lend money 363.111
f., like credit, highest where not used 363.66
f. makes prosperity more brilliant 363.29
f. may step in advance of truth 363.72
f. needs a parallelism of life 363.2
f. seldom lasting but between equals 363.69
f.: ship big enough for two in fair weather, but only one in foul 363.20
f. that can come to an end, never began 363.91
f. that flames goes out in a flash 363.52
f. union of parts of two minds 363.96
f. without the everyday becomes allegory 363.92
for women to preserve f. with men, slight physical antipathy helpful 363.84
great f. is never without anxiety 363.100
hedge between keeps f. green 730.2
high f. demands ability to do wtihout it 363.42
in f. is sympathy; in love, antipathy 548.29
in f. we render small services for big 363.82
it is wise to apply politeness to f. 194.3
it would be wrong to put f. before truth 991.4
lack of punctuality alienates f. 759.4
laughter is not a bad beginning for a f. 523.27
little f. in world; least between equals 363.14
love demands infinitely less than f. 363.83
love rarer than genius, f. rarer than love 363.87
man passes life in seeking f. 363.39
man should keep f. in constant repair 7.5
minds tend to change in hate and f. 178.16
no f. made without initial clashing 363.57
nobody chooses already unfortunate for f. 546.5
ounce of blood worth more than pound of f. 332.26
philanthropy and f. seldom exist together 430.27
proof of little f. not to see cooling 299.3
real f. shown in times of trouble 363.44
same likes, dislikes make solid f. 363.95
Satan's f. reaches to the prison door 57.23
scarcity of f. but not of friends 7.4
steady f. best proves strength of mind 178.7
surround f. with ceremonies and respects 112.3
that f. be lasting, virtue must be equal 363.70
the essence of f. is entireness 990.2
to cement a new f. a spark must fly 363.97
true f. is self-love at second-hand 363.61
true love is less rare than true f. 363.74
where true f., there needs no ceremony 112.6

**friendships:** f. begin with liking or gratitude 363.36
f. last when each friend wants nothing 363.33
f. of nations built on interests 496.13
f. ought to be immortal 766.12
firmest f. are formed in adversity 363.31
in close f. what one is not informed about one may not inquire about 166.4
it's no good trying to keep up old f. 363.77
man of active mind outwears f. 363.79
real f. among men are rare 363.35
what we call f. are only acquaintance 363.81

**fright:** dog's bark is not might but f. 969.3

**frighten:** it is easy to f. a bull from a window 973.7

**frightened:** he who hath nothing is f. at nothing 740.8
is there anything uglier than a f. man 340.4
we are more often f. than hurt 43.10

**frog:** f. would leap from throne of gold to puddle 48.8

**frolic:** dog was made for children, is god of f. 41.2
**frontier:** where there is open mind, there will be f. 647.4
**frugality:** f. is fortune's left hand 358.14
f. is guardian of virtues 970.3
man often pays dear for a small f. 970.10
**fruit:** how do you know that the f. is ripe 567.7
if it die, it bringeth forth much f. 198.4
no f. not bitter before it is ripe 402.18
people throw stones at tree loaded with f. 293.11
there are cases where the plant flowers, but no f. is produced 450.3
vine made to bear f. in spring dies soon 277.66
who would have f. must climb tree 279.9
**fruitfully:** joy at eventide if day spent f. 6.20
**fruits:** by their f. ye shall know them 6.3
**frustrate:** f. an American, he will get drunk, kill 34.60
**frustration:** f. is dangerous to run a world with 457.1
**frying-pan:** f. says to kettle: avaunt, black brows 203.12
**fuel:** f. not sold in forest, nor fish on lake 102.9
if f. prepared, hard to tell whence spark shall come 813.3
**fulfillment:** f. as human being is greatest miracle 1001.17
indulgences, not f., is what world permits 468.2
only peace, only security is in f. 502.18
seek the road which makes death a f. 218.63
**full:** bucket f. of water does not splash 686.9
f. cup must be carried steadily 744.5
f. gut supports moral precepts 272.3
**fuller:** the f. ear is of grain, the lower it bends 433.14
**fullness:** when we rejoice in our f., then we can part with our fruits with joy 567.19
**fun:** f. good when it spoils nothing better 434.24
taking f. as f., earnestness in earnest 879.4
to make f. of person to his face 814.2
**funeral:** chief mourner not always at f. 365.5
f.: pageant whereby we attest respect for dead by enriching undertaker 365.2
go to f., not church, to be uplifted 365.9
I misbehaved once at a f. 523.14
no American attends his f. without services of cosmeticians 365.6
'tis good thing f. sermons ar-re not composed in th' confissional 365.4
we grieve at a f. because we are not the person involved 538.42
who bequeath selves a pompous f. 365.3
**funerals:** f. are pretty compared to death 365.11
f. have more regard to vanity of the living 365.8
many f. discredit a physician 760.8
**funny:** everything's f. if it happens to others 434.23
life remains f. when people die 538.37
you need a serious streak to see f. side 879.8
**furnace:** heat not a f. so hot for your foe 811.19
**furniture:** no f. so charming as books 91.83
**fury:** abused patience turns to f. 670.8
beware the f. of a patient man 670.5
**futility:** a mortal breed most full of f. 33.29
f.: playing a harp before a buffalo 48.2
**future:** cynic is prematurely disappointed in f. 211.1
danger of f.: men may become robots 960.5
do not seek ideals of f. in the past 669.16
each sees angel in his f. self 458.3
f. cannot be repetition of past 366.19
f. enters us to transform itself 366.27
f. is an opaque mirror 366.5
f. is called "perhaps" 366.33
f. is like heaven 366.2
f. is neither ours nor wholly not ours 366.9
f. is past entered through another gate 366.25
f. makes laws for our to-day 238.15
f. overcomes past by swallowing it 366.24
f.: period when affairs prosper, friends are true and happiness is assured 366.4
f. struggles not to become the past 366.26
f. the only transcendental value 366.7
fear, desire, hope, push us on toward f. 366.22
generosity to f. is giving to present 723.3
he who fears not f. may enjoy present 366.12
how much man lives in the f. 366.8
how past perishes is how f. becomes 669.31
I go to school to youth to learn the f. 1064.22
if I bind the f. I bind my will 198.37
if we do not grasp f., others will 366.32
if we open a quarrel between the past and present, we shall lose the f. 505.3
in contempt of what is, some strain into f. 33.29
in f., life will be lived in aeroplane 735.30
meet f. without fear, with manly heart 669.19
never let the f. disturb you 366.21
no way of judging f. but by past 319.26
only mothers can think of the f. 366.13
only way to predict f. is to have power to shape f. 366.15
preoccupation with the f. prevents seeing the present, prompts rearranging of past 366.14
schools are the f. in miniature 277.75
there's nothing like dream to create the f. 366.16
to be part of the f. 1010.11
to change past into sad smiles is to master the f. 752.11
we are diminishing our f. 174.5
we can build our youth for the f. 1064.52
we can chart f. clearly only when we know

path which has led to present 417.43
you can never plan the f. by the past 366.6
you shall know f. when it has come 366.1
your task for the f. is to enable it 366.28
**futurity**: fate of man to seek consolations in f. 316.8

## G

**gadgets**: we cannot get grace from g. 960.23
**gaiety**: g. of life, like beauty, is saving grace 511.7
**gain**: Americans have a great ardor for g. 34.79
prefer loss to dishonest g. 732.3
sometimes better incur loss than make g. 547.7
**gainer**: to lose oneself is to be g. 1014.4
**gains**: base g. are the same as losses 732.5
light g. make heavy purses 102.13
there are no g. without pains 735.26
**Galilean**: thou hast conquered, O pale G. 509.2
**gallantry**: Frenchman have unlimited capacity for g. 359.6
g. is more common where climate's sultry 138.1
**gallows**: criminals turn preachers under the g. 793.8
**gambling**: g. is the great leveller 367.5
world is a g.-table 1060.3
**game**: g.: any unserious occupation 697.4
one vexed at losing g. by a single hole 327.11
play out the g., act well your part 819.1
stander-by may see more of g. than player 642.3
we think if we watch g. we have taken part 922.6
**game's**: genius loves play for own sake; the g. the thing 154.2
**games**: we are forced to participate in g. of life before we learn to use the options 319.50
we must play no g. with ourselves 993.3
**gaming**: man is g. animal, trying to get the better 154.8
**gangs**: we live in an earth of well-dressed g. 201.3
**garbage**: principal product of environment is g. 368.1
**garden**: God the first g. made 129.12
good g. may have some weeds 455.1
some make a g. of life, walk down a path 654.1
**gardening**: need in g.: cast-iron back with a hinge 369.4
**garment**: childhood weaves invisible g. around us 680.3
new g. ever fails wearer's expectation 265.5
our last g. is made without pockets 218.74
**garret**: g. has been the nursery of genius 374.24
**gate**: strait is the g., narrow the way 835.1
**gather**: g. thyself together, at least once a day 180.3
g. ye rosebuds while ye may 700.7
**general**: blood of the soldier makes the g. great 582.11
g. makes you forget your troubles 1035.6
g. statement like check drawn on bank 371.3
I am very model of modern major g. 582.9
prize of g. not tent, but command 713.27
some g. wangles prestige of war memorial 582.7
unhappy the g. who comes on field of battle with a system 932.1
**generalities**: bookworm wraps himself in web of g. 91.45
g. are intellectually necessary evils 326.10
g. in morals mean absolutely nothing 371.4
**generality**: for parlor use vague g. is a life-saver 185.2
**generalization**: g. necessary to advancement of knowledge 198.25
God is name for ultimate g. 385.26
**generalizations**: all g. are false, including this one 371.1
**generation**: dead ideas passed from g. to g. 979.22
each g. criticises assumptions of parent 372.18
each g. does not comprehend its own ignorance 372.17
each g. must discover its mission 372.2
each g. removes parents' household gods 372.5
each new g. is a new people 372.16
every g. laughs at the old fashions 335.29
every g. must be free to act for itself 372.11
every g. revolts against its fathers 372.10
every old man complains of the rising g. 372.6
immortality is attained only by g. 452.10
no g. interested in art in same way 53.39
self-defeating to pretend to style of younger g. than your own 372.1
strife hushed by passing of one g. 372.8
to decry younger g. dates a man 372.14
we can be best g. in history—or the last 994.8
who thinks only of own g. born for few 181.8
world is a whole g. older and wiser 372.3
**generations**: as g. come and go, their arts ebb, flow 983.26
g. pass like a snowstorm 372.13
g. quickly change, pass on torches of life 372.9
we feel closer to distant g. 372.15
**generosity**: function of poor to exercise our g. 712.46
g. gives assistance, rather than advice 373.10
g. is often only disguised ambition 33.20

g. is the flower of justice 373.6
g. relinquished to practice charity 430.5
lavishness is not g. 373.4
sea has no g. 847.8
the weak feel our g. as oppression 1040.5
**generous:** be just before you're g. 515.46
far fewer g. men than we think 473.7
if a man is g., we call his courage pride 203.5
impossible to be just if one is not g. 515.42
prodigal man cannot be truly g. 373.2
prudence engenders paralysis of g. acts 749.34
who think they're g. to a fault 373.5
**genius:** beware of notions like g., inspiration 374.32
bustle, push, not equal to quiet g. 917.3
coffee good for talent; g. needs prayer 375.2
concept of g. as akin to madness fostered by public's inferiority complex 374.35
crooked roads without improvement are roads of g. 458.1
danger of erroneous calculations when man computes force of his own g. 858.4
even g. is tied to profit 596.43
everyone is a g. at least once a year 374.26
flavor of g. in common person detestable 374.22
function of g. is to furnish cretins with ideas twenty years later 374.2
G stands for goat and also for g. 41.24
g. acts unconsciously 374.20
g. always finds itself a century early 374.14
g. and morality are often bitter enemies 374.42
g. belongs to individuals 375.8
g. can only breathe in atmosphere of freedom 374.29
g. depends upon the data within reach 374.10
g. is but greater aptitude for patience 374.6
g. is formed in quiet; character, in life stream 117.13
g. is man who does unique things 374.28
g. is power, talent applicability 375.5
g. is sacrificed to talent daily 375.3
g. is sorrow's child 374.1
g. is that in whose power a man is 375.9
g. lasts longer than beauty 277.79
g., like life, is known only by effects 374.7
g. loves play for its own sake 154.2
g. more often in cracked pot than whole 374.43
g. native to soil where it grows 374.19
g. never accepted without a measure of condonement 374.39
g. says things he has never heard 375.4
g. seems to consist in trueness of sight 374.13
g. should marry person of character 374.23
g.: to effect what's in your mind 374.16
g.: vitality expended in enrichment of life 374.21
g. will fight against oblivion 374.38
garret has been the nursery of g. 374.24
if men of g. never complained of critics 204.55
if men of g. only knew what love their works inspire 374.5
in republic of mediocrity g. is dangerous 573.6
lucky person passes for a g. 358.9
man's g. contracts itself to a few hours 852.10
men of g. are far more abundant 374.33
men of g. labour because they excel 309.6
men of g. regarded as fools 477.3
men who produce works of g. make use of their personality as of a mirror 374.37
no great g. without some madness 374.3
one type of g. begets, other gives birth 374.30
patience is a necessary ingredient of g. 374.11
persecution of g. fosters its influence 374.41
profound g. baffled by trivial questions 478.7
public forgives everything except g. 374.44
sanctity, g., are as rebellious as vice 834.12
sign of g.: dunces are against him 374.40
talent is to be envied, g. pitied 375.7
the g. is necessarily a squanderer 374.31
to do what is impossible for talent is g. 375.1
towering g. disdains beaten path 374.27
treason in our time is a proof of g. 986.3
true g. is mind of large general powers 374.25
true g. prefers silence to incompleteness 374.34
wisdom of providence seen in rarity of g. 748.13
with g., throes are in conception 198.8
woman seldom loves g. 1055.128
world does not know what to do with g. 375.6
world makes a g. lose his youth 374.8
you cannot create g.; only nurture it 374.9
young g. apologizes for his large feet 374.17
young man reveres men of g. 374.15
**geniuses:** biggest oxen are the g. 1062.93
g. ordered by administrative types 374.36
what g. must do is what they most want to 374.4
**genteel:** g.: catafalque smothering spontaneity 803.5
**genteelly:** to do anything coolly is to do it g. 159.3
**gentility:** world of shabby g. is like no other 803.4
**gentle:** g. mind by g. deeds is known 376.6
strong men can always afford to be g. 933.11
**gentleman:** g. is one who never inflicts pain 376.4
repose and cheerfulness are badge of g. 376.2
rich thief passes for a g. 927.4
sometimes the devil is a g. 240.9
to be a g. is to be oneself 376.3
you have to be a g. all the time 376.5
**gentleman's:** as dog becomes thoroughbred, so

is a man who accepts the g. code 376.1

**gentleness:** great mind knows the power of g. 377.2

nothing is so strong as g. 377.6

use g. and guide elephant with a hair 377.5

**gentlest:** possible Nero in g. human 713.5

the g. feeds on another's woe 557.13

**gently:** g. scan your brother man 118.2

**geography:** history is all explained by g. 417.48

morality is largely matter of g. 598.22

without geology no place to put g. 378.3

**geology:** without g. no place to put geography 378.3

**geometry:** there is no royal road to g. 566.3

**German:** virtues of G. people have created evils 379.5

when literary G. dives into a sentence 379.4

**German's:** G. wit is in his fingers 379.2

**Germans:** all ponderous styles are developed among G. 379.3

we G. fear God, but nothing else 379.1

**get:** easy to g. everything you want 8.3

it is easy to despise what you cannot g. 913.1

not to g. heart's desire bad as getting nothing 364.1

**gettings:** end to our g. is only end to our losses 8.10

**ghetto:** g. improved one way: out of existence 129.4

**ghost:** frozen within, we hear the world applaud the hollow g. which blamed the living man 646.7

g.: outward sign of an inward fear 381.1

**ghosts:** I think we are all g., every one of us 381.2

modern mansion has no place for g. 428.3

you can't live with g. or without them 381.3

**giant:** fleas do not know whether they are upon g. 48.6

he is a g. who has many dwarfs about him 788.7

tyrannous to use giant's strength like g. 713.45

**gift:** a g. deprives us of our liberty 382.13

enemy's g. is ruinous and no g. 382.36

every good g. is from above 382.4

excellence of g. is in appropriateness 382.40

g. in season is a double favor to needy 382.32

g., with kind countenance, is double 382.11

g. without the giver is bare 887.2

hasten to give while g. can be enjoyed 382.20

intention, not value, of g. is weighed 382.33

loving-kindness may go with a little g. 382.39

nothing so frequent as to mistake an ordinary human g. for a special endowment 956.9

only g. is a portion of thyself 382.9

painful to give g. to man of sensibility 382.7

surprise is greatest g. life can grant 948.3

**gifted:** most g. natures perhaps the most trembling 956.7

**gifts:** each day provides its own g. 723.21

g. are like hooks 382.26

g. fate and nature lend us often end us 956.3

gods themselves moved by g. 97.3

I fear Greeks even when they bring g. 257.19

if we do not use g. the days bring, they carry them silently away 971.15

never to be cast away are g. of the gods 956.10

no benefit in g. of a bad man 382.10

rich g. wax poor when givers prove unkind 382.34

**girl:** dear to heart of a g. is her beauty, charm 383.5

if pleasing to one man, g. is taken care of 576.45

little g. without doll as unfortunate as woman without children 121.22

nothing so difficult to support imperturbably as head of lovely g., except her grief 383.4

to modern g., legs parts of success kit 885.19

**girls:** there is no need to waste pity on young g. 383.2

young g. like excess of any quality 383.1

**give:** can't g. to everyone often the excuse to g. to no one 382.29

do not g. like hen that lays egg, cackles 430.1

g. all thou canst 382.42

it is more blessed to g. than to receive 382.3

man hoards self when has nothing to g. 929.1

we receive but what we g. 616.18

well to g. when asked, better unasked 382.15

when I g. I g. myself 382.41

who cannot g. away cannot feel anything 929.5

**given:** I know what I have g. you; I do not know what you have received 382.31

nothing costs so much as what is g. 780.1

to whom much is g., much is required 804.2

unto every one that hath shall be g. 15.1

you pay too dear for what's g. freely 382.35

**giver:** g. should be thankful receiver received 780.3

we do not quite forgive a g. 382.8

**givers:** rich gifts wax poor when g. prove unkind 382.34

**gives:** God g., but man must open his hand 748.9

he g. worthless gold who g. from duty 382.25

what man g., the gods by man bestow 748.12

who g. to be seen will not relieve man in the dark 382.12

**giving:** there is sublime thieving in all g. 382.18

to give, but not feel it: best way of g. 382.2

we promise much to avoid g. little 737.17

**glad:** one can bear grief, takes two to be g. 407.53

**gladness:** g. of heart is the life of man 407.2

they serve g. who meet calls of sadness 911.60

**glass:** it is not vain-glory for man and his g. to

confer 1020.16
**glasses:** seldom make passes at girls who wear g. 918.2
**glories:** g., like glow-worms, afar off shine 384.22
**glorious:** hour of g. life worth age without name 384.17
people who seem so g. are all show 330.20
**glory:** better live miserably than die in g. 538.10
desire of g. last infirmity, even of wise 384.21
g. and curiosity are two scourges of soul 208.9
g. and repose can't inhabit same place 384.15
g. comes from the din-din-din of one gift 384.7
g. consists of two parts 865.15
g. is largely a theatrical concept 384.11
g. is like a circle in the water 384.18
g. is that tragic thing that means dominion 384.5
g. melancholy blazon on coffin lid 330.43
g. should be a consequence, not a motive 384.16
good fortune leads one to the highest g. 358.5
hasty g. goes out in a snuff 384.9
paths of g. at least lead to grave 269.34
paths of g. lead but to the grave 384.10
pursuit of human g. yields only a grave 384.2
shortest way to g. is to be what you would be thought to be 384.20
shortest way to g. is to do that for conscience which we do for g. 384.14
sudden g. makes grimaces called laughter 523.11
take away writing, you take away g. 384.3
those most desirous of honour or g. cry out loudest of its abuse 424.10
to ashes of dead g. comes too late 384.13
to die with g. is still pain for dier 218.48
when g. comes, memory departs 384.8
**glove:** clean g. often hides dirty hand 221.5
**glutton:** g. can't sleep on empty or sated stomach 272.26
g. digs his grave with his teeth 272.8
who savors food is no g. 272.30
**gluttony:** g. makes drowsy without tranquility 527.6
**go:** more you let yourself g., less others will 468.4
**goal:** not every end is the g. 284.3
step must be g. and a step likewise 570.5
successful person sees g. and aims for it 679.3
**goat:** if you are a genius, learn from the g. 41.24
**goats:** bleat in a flock of g. 168.13
**God:** all service ranks the same with G. 880.1
Americans expect to revere G., be G. 34.6
an honest G. is the noblest work of man 385.42
before Kepler, heavens told glory of G. 413.7
behind the dim unknown standeth G. 1012.7
by night atheist half believes a G. 997.20
canst thou by searching find out G. 385.5
closer is G. than breathing 385.72
contemplating G., men became equal 295.23
damned by men, we are absolved by G. 385.73
danger past, G. is forgotten 213.10
do not ask G. the way to heaven 412.7
do not speak of G. much 385.25
do we seek G. or G.'s gifts 385.69
even G. has been defended with nonsense 874.3
every common bush afire with G. 259.2
every man for himself and G. for us all 873.11
every man thinks G. is on his side 385.2
excellence nothing without consent of G. 309.2
fear G., and where you are will be like a cathedral 691.3
fool hath said there is no G. 997.2
G. accomplishes all term to hopes 385.61
G. all mercy is a G. unjust 385.81
G. alone can finish 283.3
G. batters at sails of happiness 407.38
G. blessed the seventh day 829.1
G. builds temple in the heart 124.6
G. cannot bear we had rather with each other play 385.23
G. chastens not with rod but with time 971.25
G. complex and hard to predict 385.30
G. created man in his own image 558.9
G. creating man to run risk of hell 385.63
G. does not want men to overtax themselves 1058.55
G. enters by private door into each person 790.18
G. finds way for what none foresaw 366.11
G. for men, religion for women 385.21
G. fulfills himself in many ways 115.37
G. gives almonds to those with no teeth 17.60
G. gives, but man must open his hand 748.9
G. gives each his due at the time allotted 809.8
G. gives the milk but not the pail 748.5
G. giving meaning to life attractive 385.16
G. has been replaced with respectability and air conditioning 385.43
G. has delegated a million deputies 171.5
G., he whom everyone knows, by name 385.62
G. heals, the doctor takes the fees 261.6
G. Himself not secure 850.8
G., I can push the grass apart 616.50
G.: immemorial refuge of the incompetent 385.48
G. is day and night, satiety and want 385.39

G. is good, there is no devil but fear 340.18
G. is indwelling cause of all things 385.70
G. is name for ultimate generalization 385.26
G. is on the side of heaviest battalions 1035.102
G. is our refuge and strength 385.6
G. is seen G. in the star, stone, flesh 385.11
G. is the perfect poet 385.10
G. is thought making all straight crooked 385.53
G. is unthinkable if we are innocent 403.12
G. is usually on side of big squadrons 713.10
G. is what man finds divine in himself 385.45
G. is white 1047.4
G. knows what G. is coming next 885.22
G. looks at clean hands, not full ones 423.16
G. lost in Satan one of best lieutenants 240.7
G. made all from the void, but void shows 3.12
G. made only water, but man made wine 266.33
G. made rose of what was left of woman 1055.86
G. may be in his heaven, but all's not right 305.10
G. might seem made for benefit of men 385.75
G. needs immortality to vindicate his ways to man 388.16
G. never sends mouth without meat 748.10
G. obligeth no man to more than his ability 269.19
G. overtakes the flying eagle 385.61
G. plucks burden of sorrow from man 328.15
G. seeks comrades and claims love 240.10
G. seems to have had no part in arranging inefficient society of plants, animals 616.45
G. tempers the wind to the shorn lamb 748.6
G. the author learned Greek but not well 78.5
G. waits for his own flowers as man's gifts 1061.7
G. was satisfied with his work; that is fatal 198.5
G. who loveth us made and loveth all 717.8
G. will not help even trustful person 385.49
G. without the devil is dead, being alone 385.13
G. won't look for medals, but for scars 939.19
G.: word invented to explain the world 385.44
G. works wonders now and then 525.26
give G. thanks for revealing Himself 810.3
great man stands on G. 398.5
he loseth nothing who keepeth G. a friend 547.2
he that fears G. fears nothing else 328.12
he worships G. who knows him 1061.6
heart experiences G., not reason 385.57
heavens declare the glory of G. 413.1
how do you expect to search out G. 385.3
hymnbooks resound with cursing of G. 126.7
I am afraid I shall not find G. 263.7
I am full of hope, but end lies in G. 425.32
I found G. in the shining of the stars 259.8
I neglect G., angels, for noise of a fly 180.1
I suspect that G. is not rich 385.41
I'm waiting for them to prove G. American 385.31
idea of G. ends in a meeting-house 126.2
if G. created us in his own image, we have more than reciprocated 385.77
if G. did not exist, would be invented 385.78
if G. is Will, Will is well, what's ill 385.47
if I ascend to heaven, thou, G., art there 385.7
if men knew selves, G. would pardon 868.22
if one religion, G. would be manifest 385.58
if only G. would provide until he provides 748.18
in nineteenth century problem was G. is dead; in twentieth, problem is man is dead 216.3
is there no G., then, but an absentee G. 385.17
it does me no injury for my neighbor to say there are twenty gods or no G. 977.9
it is through us that G. is achieved 385.35
just are the ways of G. 385.51
just man walks humbly in presence of G. 489.15
let none mourn; these things are in the hands of G. 603.14
looking at G. reduces our disposition to human dissent 766.3
love of G. is not always love of good 691.6
malt justifies G. to man 266.32
man appoints and G. disappoints 385.19
man is G. by his faculty for 259.6
man wrong who thinks to swindle G. 221.16
man's strength is to find, follow way of G. 691.1
mills of G. grind slowly 809.11
modern town-dweller has no G., no Devil 129.23
nature is the art of G. 616.19
no expeditious road to label men for G. 835.4
no one has the capacity to judge G. 385.33
not even G. is waiting for humanity 3.9
one man has one G., and one another G. 790.23
perfections of nature show image of G. 616.56
personal G. must be a disappointing G. 385.20
poorest worm tells me there is a G. 385.24
Protestantism proves that G. is a bore 123.19
question even the existence of a G. 263.4
reason cannot reconcile this world of torment with the declaration G. is love 939.17
render to G. the things that are G.'s 125.1
respectable society believed in G. to avoid having to speak about him 385.66
solitude is audience-chamber of G. 908.26
solitude is bearable only with G. 908.19

speak to G. as if men heard you 691.13
terror of G. is the secret of religion 340.35
the eternal G. is thy refuge 850.1
the only money of G. is G. 385.27
the only useful G. is one whose existence is certain 790.47
theologies based on G. as senile delinquent 385.80
there are no chances against G. 114.4
there is no G. stronger than death 218.124
this is G.: to be man with thy might 558.50
'tis only G. may be had for the asking 385.46
to obey G. is freedom 385.67
to put trust in G. means one will chance it 748.2
true laws of G. are laws of our well-being 790.6
trust in G., but tie your camel 257.14
try first thyself, and after call in G. 279.6
we have made G. the biggest celebrity 385.9
we make G. accomplice to legalize our sins 438.2
we need G. to give a meaning to the Universe 385.76
we should find G. in what we know 385.8
we treat G. like a pasha, or a sultan 717.35
weigh gain, loss in wagering that G. is 385.56
what love begets, what rebellion creates, what freedom rears: all manifest G. 385.34
when faith burns out, G. dies 997.18
when G. is dead religion becomes one 790.79
when men make gods, there is no G. 385.55
where G. hath a temple, Devil hath chapel 188.2
where mercy, love, pity dwell, G. dwells 577.1
while G. waits for His temple to be built of love, men bring stones 124.12
who recovers from sickness forgets G. 790.22
who serve G. and Mammon lose faith in G. 495.5
who's near the Church is often far from G. 124.7
whom heart of man shuts out, G. takes in 544.4
whom man kills, G. restoreth to life 516.7
will of G. to be borne with courage 238.20
worship of G. is flight after unattainable 1061.10

**god:** as if some lesser g. had made the world 455.9
g. of cannibal will be a cannibal 385.28
how dark the ways of g. to man 748.7
if triangles had g., he'd have three sides 385.52
one's g. is not allowed to sin 385.54
though a g., I've learned to obey the times 296.21
to do all one would like: to be a g. 502.20
true g. is perfect, lacking nothing 385.29
when a man's willing and eager, g. joins in 1050.1
who shall say what is or is not g. 790.24

**God's:** all things are G. already 124.11
G. in his heaven—all's right with world 652.5
G. mercy more attractive than his justice 385.18
G. merits are so transcendent no wonder his faults are in reasonable proportion 385.14
G. nature is ground of rationality 385.79
I cannot drift beyond G. love and care 748.17
I would be bold, bear to look into swarthiest things for G. sake who has made them 776.1
it is G. giving if we laugh or weep 407.103
most impious sorrows at G. judgement 809.7
on earth G. work must truly be our own 671.10
one on G. side is a majority 385.60
whoever falls from G. right hand is caught into his left 748.14

**godliness:** g. is profitable unto all things 690.1

**gods:** all g. dead except god of war 1035.20
ask the g. nothing excessive 592.1
dead are all the g. 429.5
do we deceive ourselves that g. exist 263.2
fear created g.; audacity, kings 518.1
fear first brought g. into the world 385.59
g. give mortals not everything at once 748.11
I believe the g. are absent-minded 385.36
I do not know much about g. 818.2
if man obeys g., they listen to him also 385.40
if no g. all toil is without meaning 997.10
in emergencies we fall back on our g. 200.3
indwelling ideal lends g. divinity 259.7
injustice makes us doubt g. 475.4
man can't make flea, makes dozens of g. 790.49
man can't reach riddles purposed by g. 600.9
many roads to happiness if g. assent 407.83
never to be cast away are gifts of the g. 956.10
only g. can live forever without pain 939.2
populace drag down g. to their own level 675.3
should seek from g. that which becomes us 942.3
skirts of the g. drag in our mud 385.32
the g. kill us for their sport 385.68
we make g. to whom to impute the ills we ought to bear 385.4
we meet no g. if we harbor none 259.4
when g. taken away, man seeks others 1061.4
when half-gods go, the g. arrive 573.2

**going:** men must endure their g. and coming 218.113
we never know we go when we are g. 218.37

**gold:** ass loaded with g. climbs to the top 596.17
ass loaded with g. still eats thistles 1041.30

deer with chain of g. will eat grass 107.7
fetters of g. are still fetters 107.1
g. aids the conqueror in love and war 596.39
g. buys honours; g. will purchase love 596.41
g. has ruined fewer men than lack of it 712.1
g. is found in fields, river beds, pockets 8.7
g. pays for a slip of the tongue 86.9
greed for g., to what does thou drive man 8.12
hay is more acceptable to an ass than g. 48.7
I can't count the g.-digging ruses of women 401.20
if stone bruises g., worth undiminished 1019.16
love is the only g. 548.231
stone thrown at right time better than g. given at wrong time 972.7
weather emotional storms with g. ballast 596.34
when g. argues cause, eloquence impotent 596.46

**golden:** g. age was never the present age 296.8
g. age was one when gold did not reign 296.13

**golf:** g. course is epitome of the transitory 922.3
middle age is too young for g. 580.2

**gone:** the gay will laugh when thou art g. 600.5

**good:** advantage of power: you can do more g. 713.21
all evil is universal g. 616.59
all g. things will pass away 983.1
anybody who is any g. is different 467.8
apprehension of the g. gives but the greater feeling to the worse 388.22
as often as we do g. we sacrifice 430.13
be g. and let people speak evil of thee 391.46
be g., and let who will be clever 391.29
beauty, g., knowledge are three sisters 387.15
betrothed of g. is evil 388.15
better to fare hard with g. men 57.13
better ungrateful men than miss chance to do g. 430.10
can't endure bad, won't live to see g. 285.11
devil himself is g. when he is pleased 391.19
do g. action stealthily, have it found it out 224.14
do g. by stealth 391.42
do g. even to the wicked 430.29
do not argue what g. man should be 391.35
do not call painful what is g. for you 248.3
do not requite evil with g. 286.21
easier to swoon in dreams than do g. 391.32
easy to do g. action, but not as habit 391.2
enjoyment g. in itself is g. religiously 893.10
everyone has as much of g. as he can 387.16
everything g. or bad according to votes 649.9
example of g. men is visible philosophy 308.3
few appear as g. as they really are 391.23
finer wits say knowledge is the g. 520.54
God sells g. things at the price of labor 1058.49
g. and bad is simply helping or hurting 388.5
g. and bad may not be dissevered 388.6
g. and evil lie close together 388.1
g. befriend themselves 391.50
g. carried to excess is no longer g. 387.17
g., communicated, more abundant grows 391.38
g. deed shines in a naughty world 430.31
g. edge no g. if nothing to cut 1017.2
g. humor is a philosophic state of mind 390.11
g. is g. doctor, bad is sometimes better 305.12
g. is not g. unless a thousand it possess 391.12
g. is to forgive evil 391.43
g. man can be stupid and still be g. 1063.12
g. man in exclusive heaven would be in hell 412.5
g. man isn't g. for everything 391.20
g. man must rather sit with loss than rise unjust 547.4
g. man never looks for others' faults 339.26
g. man prefers defeat to using evil to win 570.8
g. man's pedigree is little hunted up 391.51
g. men are stars, illustrate the times 391.28
g. men join one g. act to another 391.4
g. men must not obey laws too well 391.16
g. nature is better in conversation than wit 185.1
g. nature is worth more than knowledge 390.2
g. not achieved when sought directly 387.13
g. people make badness very important 391.56
g. shall not compensate bad in man 388.3
g. so g. that bad when bad can't be bad 387.8
g. that I would I do not 684.3
g. things are fruits of originality 655.6
g. things of adversity are to be admired 745.15
g. things of life come with a mixture 387.6
g. things when short are twice as g. 387.5
g. to be tired by search for true g. 387.10
g. which prevents greater g. is evil 388.24
g. will be the final goal of ill 388.27
glory of g. men is in their conscience 171.31
great and g. are seldom the same man 399.26
hardly anybody g. for everything 956.4
he cannot be g. who is not obstinate 644.11
he is not g. who speaks well of all 453.2
he teaches me to be g. that does me g. 308.4
he that hopes no g. fears no ill 685.3

he too busy doing g. has no time to be g. 430.33
how few know their own g., or pursue it 684.6
I prefer as friend a g. man ignorant 363.46
if the g. were clever, the clever g. 137.13
if we saw all evil that may spring from g. 388.19
if you are happy you will be g. 391.45
if you do g., g. will be done to you 781.1
if you pretend to be g., the world takes you seriously 652.13
in every age "g. old days" were a myth 296.1
in g. days we've cold memory of bad times 574.31
it is by evil that g. is pleasant 184.3
it is hard to be simple enough to be g. 391.14
it must be a g. thing to be g. 391.13
it's wiser being g. than bad 388.2
jail doesn't teach anyone to do g. 391.21
life's a field for g. and evil 536.110
love of God is not always love of g. 691.6
man is only as g. as what he loves 391.6
man makes no noise over a g. deed 224.18
man not g. or bad for one action 224.11
man who insists he is as g. as anybody believes he is better 295.12
man's g. or ill lies in his own will 1049.5
may the g. God pardon all g. men 391.9
men are g. when free from passion, error 391.26
men become g. creatures, but so slow 391.10
men love g., but can't judge what is g. 387.12
men more capable of great actions than g. 224.23
moral g. is effect of physical evil 388.12
more hope in death of g. than in life of wicked 391.18
most g. women are hidden treasures 1055.116
most harmful harm is done by the g. 391.41
nature, not standing, makes g. man 391.44
no man can devise plan of extensive g. unadulterated with evil 388.4
no man g. enough to be another's master 882.17
no man so g. he wouldn't deserve hanging 391.39
no resolve for g. or evil until execution 388.9
no society can be kept up without g. nature 389.1
not all those to whom we do g. love us 224.32
not enough to do g. 430.22
nothing g., bad but thinking makes it so 387.14
nothing g. for all 387.4
nothing g. for him for whom nothing bad 388.8
nothing is g. or bad but by comparison 152.2
nothing is so g. as it seems beforehand 316.2
nothing so enhances a g. as sacrifices 831.9
often g. things have hurtful consequences 173.1
omission of g. is no less reprehensible than commission of evil 388.20
one g. deed dying tongueless 48.9
profit on g. action is to have done it 224.34
prudence does not always lead to g. 173.7
pure g. soon grows insipid 410.8
question of g. and evil remains in chaos 388.29
seek not g. from without, but from within 391.17
smallest seed of g. needs luck 866.2
some men have g. qualities useless to themselves 1016.8
the g. have come to wisdom through failure 391.47
the g. is landscape man advances through 387.9
the g. is oft interred with men's bones 388.23
the g. suffers while the bad prevails 388.11
there is so much g. in the worst of us 203.14
there must be g. in what pleases many 706.6
they're only truly great who are truly g. 391.11
to a g. man there can come no evil 391.49
to be g. we must needs have suffered 939.25
to be greatly g., a man must imagine intensely 1001.18
to become a g. man, one must have faithful friends or outright enemies 391.40
to know g. is to react against bad 387.7
to show others how to be g. is noble and no trouble 391.55
we as often repent g. we have done as ill 785.1
we do g. to accomplish evil with impunity 388.14
we do not always see our own g. 387.11
we know the g., can't achieve it 387.2
we look for g. but do not recognize it 387.3
we slight man whose g. will can't help 493.9
what falls in accordance with nature is g. 387.1
what rapture to know g. thing when you see it 684.4
when the bad imitate the g., there is no knowing what mischief is intended 449.10
who cannot be angry cannot be g. 39.6
who does g. comes to the temple gate, who loves reaches the shrine 391.52
who doth a g. turn looketh for a g. turn 881.4
who returns g. for evil wins victory 224.12
who spares the bad injures the g. 531.1
who wants to do g. knocks at gate; who loves finds it open 430.32
why care for grammar if we are g. 396.5
wise men see the g. in all 47.1
world bears two nations: g. and bad 1060.22

world is sown with g. 1058.47
youngster who does not know what he is g. at 1.7
**good-bye:** there's release and torment in every g. 666.3
**good-byes:** g. breed a sort of distaste 666.1
**good-humored:** man who thinks himself unequalled sure to be g. 155.5
**good-natured:** g. man has world to be happy in 390.10
**goodness:** capacity to feel deeply inspires g. 945.10
experience differentiates piety, g. 691.10
g. achieved in company of other men 391.5
g. can bear mistakes of the ignorant 977.4
g. comes out of people who bask in sun 943.2
g. is born of wisdom 391.33
g. is easier to recognize than to define 391.3
g. is only investment that never fails 391.54
g. is uneventful 391.22
g. makes men happy, happiness good 391.30
g. that preaches undoes itself 391.15
g. thinks no ill where no ill seems 391.37
g. without wisdom accomplishes evil 388.10
greatness and g. are not means, but ends 399.11
Infinite G. takes whatever turns to it 748.3
loving-kindness is the better part of g. 391.36
no odor so bad as that from g. tainted 188.15
no one can be good if g. is not in demand 391.8
nobody deserves to be praised for his g. if he has not power to be wicked 391.31
one good action after another: perfection of g. 391.1
profit smiles on g. when good profitable 391.53
there is some soul of g. in things evil 305.37
virtue is bold, g. never fearful 1025.51
we love g., but also freedom 361.11
when a man is ill, his very g. is sickly 889.22
wisdom has its root in g. 1053.17
**goodwill:** we are thankful for g. rather than services 382.16
**goose:** wild g.: epitome of wanderlust and dream 80.2
**gospel:** believer teaches g. at risk of life 590.2
go ye into the world and preach the g. 590.1
**gospels:** literal adherence to G. would mean death 598.53
**gossip:** civilized men fight with g. 392.9
difference between g. and philosophy 688.9
g. columnist's business not his business 623.10
g. is light to lift up, hard to put down 392.8
g. is one who talks to you about others 185.19
g. needs no carriage 392.13
g. within everybody's reach 392.11
whoever gossips to you will g. about you 392.14
**gossips:** who g. well has a reputation for being good company, a wit, but never a gossip 392.10
**Gothic:** G. cathedral is a blossoming in stone 50.4
G. is most logical, most beautiful form of visible otherworldliness 50.10
promise, ruin seen in G. architecture 50.16
**gourmet:** g. is glutton with brains 272.13
**gout:** g. is not relieved by a fine shoe 791.9
**govern:** can't g. country having 246 cheeses 359.3
dead g. the living 979.6
g. by counting, not breaking, heads 231.15
let the people think they g. 231.39
men have choice to g., or be governed 393.10
none good enough to g. without consent 393.37
not being able to g. events, I g. myself 856.11
nothing as dangerous for state as those who would g. with maxims found in books 393.53
to g. a nation you need specific talent 393.43
who would g. others should master self 825.14
**governed:** consent of g. safeguard against both ignorant tyrants and benevolent despots 231.28
nation perpetually conquered is not g. 354.3
very populous city is rarely well g. 129.2
**governing:** art of g.: not let men grow old in jobs 393.46
art of g. requires the whole man 825.11
g. too onerous for the plain man 825.4
pleasure of g. must certainly be exquisite 393.65
**government:** all are interested in struggle for better living conditions, not in form of g. 393.8
all g. is founded on compromise and barter 160.2
all know that g. never began anything 393.51
basis of g. is justice, not pity 393.69
compassionate g. is servant of people 393.30
consent of people is foundation of g. 393.2
conservative g. is organised hypocrisy 175.4
corruption of g. begins with principles 188.11
each man has equal right to protection of g. 295.8
easy to accuse g. of imperfection 393.45
effective g. based on public confidence 393.36
efficient g. is a dictatorship 393.63
essence of free g. is considering offices as public trusts 755.4
essence of republican g. is consent 231.51
even for neutrality you must have strong g. 393.23
every central g. worships uniformity 393.62
every g. is exact symbol of its people 393.13
every man who is not wedded to his millions is dangerous to the g. 1041.41

forms of g. arise from differences in men 407.5
free g. consists in control of rivalries 393.4
freedom when people take care of g. 393.70
g. a trust, officers of g. trustees 393.14
g. and co-operation are the laws of life 393.56
g. can easily exist without law 525.58
g. cannot be stronger than its people 393.60
g. consists in taking money from one part of citizens to give to the other 99.5
g. defines man by the printed form 100.4
g. expands to absorb revenue, then some 393.68
g. function to invent philosophies to explain demands 393.33
g. gratified to become a protector 740.4
g. is a contrivance of human wisdom 393.12
g. is not a representative of reason 393.58
g. is not an art but a fatality 393.59
g. is ourselves, not alien power 1030.18
g. is produced by our wickedness 393.48
g. is science of social happiness 393.3
g. no better than public opinion sustaining it 756.19
g. requires sufficient food, military equipment, confidence of people in ruler 393.15
g. that functions in pinches survives 393.34
g. that gives you all can take all away 393.22
good g. greatest human blessing 393.27
good laws, disobeyed, are not good g. 525.4
great revolution is the fault of the g. 813.15
guilt of g. is crime of whole country 393.49
I would not give half a guinea to live under one form of g. rather than another 393.31
if a g. blurs decency it is an evil g. 393.24
in change of g., poor only change masters 712.43
in g., justice means force, virtue 515.34
in g. offices sensitive to mass sentiment, no sure tenure 755.14
invisible g. is malign 393.40
liberty is limitation of g. power 534.53
mind, soul, must be let alone by g. 583.20
modhren idee iv g. is snub th' people, buy th' people, jaw th' people 393.18
next to anarchy, g. is the worst thing 393.9
no broader basis for g. than that which includes all people 231.14
no g. better than men who compose it 393.35
no g. could survive without champagne 245.3
no g. has provision for own termination 393.38
no g. matters as much as the administration 393.42
no g. ought to be without censors 111.5
no g. secure without opposition 651.5
object of g.: secure happiness to mass 393.29
officers of g. are servants 755.16
people are the safe depositories of g. 231.18
popular g. awakens spirit and energy 231.10
popular g. not proved to guarantee good g. 393.41
public interested more in g. than politics 705.66
purpose of g. to conserve rights of many 393.54
society a blessing, g. necessary evil 393.47
superlatively efficient g. is anti-human 393.25
that g. best which provides most 393.39
that g. is best which secures manhood 393.64
there are no necessary evils in g. 393.28
there can be g. without initiative 393.57
true policy of g. is to use aristocracy 52.3
virtue alone not sufficient for g. 393.44
we live under g. of men, newspapers 623.20
what g. gives it must first take away 958.5
when abroad I never criticize my own g. 671.3
when g. tries to handle our affairs, it costs more and the results are worse 393.17
when things are noncontroversial in g., not much is going on 982.7
where's the state that excels bees for g. 479.3
**governments:** death stronger than all g. 218.106
efforts of g. not enough without the people 675.9
g. arise out of people or over people 393.50
g. classified by considering who are the somebodies they endeavor to satisfy 393.66
g. exist to protect rights of minorities 393.52
most g. are usually inexpedient 393.61
nations may have fashioned their g. 393.16
**grace:** abuse of g. is affectation 677.21
deformed men ponder g. 184.1
g. is the absence of all that indicates pain, difficulty, hesitation, incongruity 394.4
g. needed to turn man into saint 834.9
highest female g. is silence 891.14
merit is not enough without g. 394.3
no spring, nor summer beauty hath such g. 646.21
religion restores courage to live by g. 691.12
to confer favors with g. 382.6
we cannot get g. from gadgets 960.23
when g. is joined with wrinkles 646.55
without g. beauty is an unbaited hook 394.2
**graceful:** if we cannot be decent, let us be g. 394.6
**gracefulness:** g. is to body what understanding is to mind 394.5
**graceless:** he that is shameless is g. 886.3
**graces:** g. which encourage imitation are inimitable 394.1
**gradually:** everything comes g. at its appointed hour 238.17
**graft:** first gold star child gets in school is its first lesson in g. 188.16
**grain:** police state cannot command g. to grow 995.17
**grains:** whole bushel is made of single g. 467.11

**grammar:** g. is common speech formulated 396.3
g.: system of pitfalls for feet of the self-made man 396.1
why care for g. as long as we are good 396.5
**grandeur:** if g. in you, you find it in all 259.4
waste is not g. 1038.2
**granted:** men have infinite capacity for taking things for g. 155.6
**grape:** better be jocund with the fruitful g. 698.24
**grasp:** man's reach should exceed his g. 55.2
people do not g. the things they learn 85.8
**grass:** all flesh is g. 600.4
as for man, his days are as g. 983.4
blade of g. is always a blade of g. 693.6
I can push g. apart, touch God's heart 616.50
**grateful:** g. mind by owing owes not 397.10
great indebtedness does not make men g. 639.7
people ar-re not g. because they niver feel they get half that they desarve 473.1
**gratefulness:** g. is the poor man's payment 397.4
**gratitude:** all men feel g. for pleasing objects 638.9
for some, g. is a species of revenge 639.2
g. almost as hard to bear as ingratitude 397.1
g. is a debt like blackmail 397.13
g. is most exquisite form of courtesy 397.9
g. is veiled desire for more benefaction 397.7
God give pardon from g., other servitude 397.2
happiness is a kind of g. 407.64
in aid, proper to omit g. 496.9
revenge is a more punctual paymaster than g. 811.8
revenge is a stronger principle than g. 811.7
revenge is profitable, g. is expensive 397.6
some have knack of putting upon you gifts of no value to engage substantial g. 382.23
you can't extract g. as you would a tooth 496.8
**grave:** every man is g. alone 879.2
good man's g. is his Sabbath 218.38
hearts beating funeral marches to g. 600.13
no pulpit sends voice far as g. 471.8
paths of glory lead but to the g. 384.10
sustained and soothed, approach thy g. 218.21
to have good company man's entry is a g. 151.7
who is not in g. has enough 536.133
**grave's:** g. a fine place, but none there embrace 218.84
**gravity:** laws of g., chemistry, botany 843.8
vivacity is gift of women, g. that of men 562.1
**gray:** g. a colour always on eve of change 142.2
**graybeards:** wiser, if sedate, come g. to roses late 646.71
**great:** a g. man profits by his good fortune 399.42
a g. man will find a g. subject 842.9
all have house-broken hearts except g. 399.2
banalities of g. man pass for wit 67.2
be g. in thyself, more than thou appearest 399.5
calumny ever pursues the g. 898.11
come nearest the g. when g. in humility 433.26
errors of g. men are more fruitful than truths of little men 297.26
every g. action is extreme when undertaken 224.37
everything g. is created by individual who can labor in freedom 361.8
few g. men could pass Personnel 399.31
first test of g. man is humility 433.22
for the person for whom small things don't exist, the g. is not g. 989.11
g. actions not always sons of g. resolutions 224.5
g. and good are seldom the same man 399.26
g. crises produce g. men, g. deeds 202.3
g. don't innovate, they fertilize 399.55
g. eaters incapable of all else g. 877.2
g. engines turn on small pivots 398.6
g. fleas have little fleas to bite 'em 662.1
g. ideas are not charitable 441.25
g. life is young idea lived by mature man 536.132
g. man doesn't lose his self-possession 399.52
g. man is ganglion in nerves of society 399.37
g. man is he who does not lose child's-heart 476.6
g. man is the impressionable man 876.4
g. man need not be virtuous 399.58
g. man resents partner in greatness 399.45
g. man stands on God 398.5
g. man's failures to understand define him 399.27
g. men are but life-sized 399.3
g. men, comets, are eccentric in courses 399.12
g. men hallow a whole people 399.61
g. men lose greatness by being near us 331.10
g. men must be lifted on world's shoulders 399.32
g. men toiling upward in the night 6.16
g. men too make many mistakes 399.43
g. men too often have greater faults than little men can find room for 398.11
g. men with g. truths seldom had support from their associates 399.67
g. mind can look beyond itself 1027.3
g. offices will have g. talents 399.13
g. society concerned with goals not goods 906.9
g. soul surrenders itself to fate 800.10
g. things accomplished by men who are not

conscious of the impotence of man 399.63
g. things are made of little things 398.3
g. welcome the herd out of vanity 398.15
he is g. who is what he is from nature 655.2
he only is g. man who can neglect applause 49.1
hearts of the g. can be changed 347.1
height from which the g. look down makes all the rest of mankind seem equal 398.9
I distrust g. men 399.23
I will be small in small things, g. in g. 398.16
if we play g. man too much, we seem small 686.5
in narrow sphere g. men are blunderers 399.50
in tragedy g. men are more truly great than in history 980.11
it is duty of g. man to demean himself 594.16
let him be g. and love shall follow him 399.18
little vices of g. must be accounted g. 1023.25
lives of g. men all remind us 399.44
low man seeks, does a little thing; high man seeks g. thing, dies ere he knows it 6.5
many a small maketh a g. 901.1
men in g. places are thrice servants 399.1
men more capable of g. actions than good 224.23
men of no note do g. deeds 641.9
men worship the shows of g. men 399.9
no g. thing is created suddenly 399.21
no man can produce g. things who is not sincere in dealing with himself 868.17
no man is g. enough for us to surrender our destiny to 528.13
no man was ever g. by imitation 399.39
no one can measure a g. man but upon bier 47.3
no really g. man ever thought himself so 399.35
none think the g. unhappy but the g. 399.68
nothing g. accomplished without passion 668.13
nothing g. ever done without enthusiasm 291.5
of g. things, be silent or speak loftily 802.11
only passions can raise soul to g. things 668.7
our g. men not commonly g. scholars 842.22
privilege of the g. is to see catastrophes from a terrace 399.29
strike at g. man, you will not miss 898.18
the g. man is often all of a piece 398.14
they're only truly g. who are truly good 391.11
'tis good sign when people acknowledge others are g. 399.16
to be g. is to be misunderstood 399.17
to know g. men dead is compensation for having to live with mediocre 399.38
treat men greatly and they will be g. 990.3
when a g. man dies no successor comes 399.19
when g. men don't know how g. they are 399.49
when house of a g. one collapses, many little ones are slain 398.2
whoever contends with g. sheds own blood 342.6
without mysticism man can do nothing g. 609.1
**greater:** g. dooms win g. destinies 17.29
g. man, the g. courtesy 194.15
**greatest:** g. man is man most in men's good thoughts 399.6
g. monarch sits on his own arse 773.5
g. spirits capable of g. vices and virtues 399.14
g. truths and men are the simplest 892.5
I would sooner fail than not be of g. 399.41
our g. men are as good as lost 399.8
**greatness:** all g. affects minds differently 399.25
desire of g. is a godlike sin 399.15
do not despise the bottom rungs in the ascent to g. 399.53
exaggeration inseparable companion of g. 307.7
g. and goodness are not means, but ends 399.11
g. brings no profit to people 399.22
g. confers intense happiness with insignificant gifts 399.51
g. has no lustre for those in search of understanding 1000.13
g. is perception that virtue is enough 1025.21
g. not effect of inspiration 399.54
g. of father often overwhelms son 909.9
in youth you want g. taken for granted 399.4
men win g. unawares working to other aim 284.2
must be humility to go on to g. 433.18
small man attains g. by vilifying great man 398.17
some achieve g., others have it pinned on 424.1
some have g. thrust upon them 399.60
some owe their g. to detecting needed strength in those they destine for tools 313.2
test of g. is the page of history 399.33
we have confused power with g. 713.54
who meets own idea of g. has low standard 399.34
**Greece:** spirit of G. animated universal nature 400.1
**greed:** for g. all nature is too little 401.25
g. for gold, to what does thou drive man 8.12
g. is a bottomless pit 401.9
hell has three gates: lust, anger, g. 414.2
some ache in the blindness of g. 596.31
**greed's:** g. worst point is its ingratitude 401.26

**greedy:** g. have extraordinary capacity for waste 401.18
g. man incontinent with world before him 401.24
there is something g. about trying to enjoy dinner, concert at same time 401.2
**Greek:** nothing which is not G. in origin 400.2
**Greeks:** G. love the beautiful, cultivate the mind 400.3
I fear G. even when they bring gifts 257.19
**greenhorn:** g. is the ultimate victor in everything 611.1
**gregariousness:** American is known by his organ of g. 151.25
**greybeard:** g. finds greybeard's tongue sweetest 22.2
**grief:** dark nights cost man less g. than false dawns 425.23
do not rejoice at my g. 911.54
every one can master g. but he that has it 911.49
g. can take care of itself 887.5
g. can't be shared; one carries it alone 911.26
g. drives men into serious reflection 911.1
g. has limits, apprehension none 43.9
g. has made many a man look younger 911.30
g. hates the light and shrinks from eyes 911.11
g. is a species of idleness 911.23
g. is always heightened by surprise 948.5
g. is in opinion, not in nature of things 911.8
g. is proud, and makes his owner stoop 911.48
g. returns with the revolving year 911.52
g. should be the instructor of the wise 911.7
g. that does not speak bids heart break 911.51
great g. transfigures the wretched 911.21
happiness benefits body, g. develops mind 911.39
heart free of g. over stranger's unhappiness 355.5
hope is incredible to the slave of g. 911.35
I loathe friend who will not voyage in g. 363.45
I measure g. with narrow, probing eyes 911.12
lighten g. with hopes of brighter morrow 316.6
look for secrets in g. or pleasure 849.6
man sheds g. as his skin does rain 911.15
one can bear g., takes two to be glad 407.53
one thing in this world that destroys itself more completely than beauty: g. 911.38
some are above and some below g. 911.13
stop mourning when g. is fully expressed 603.3
there is pleasure in indulging g. 911.16
to spare oneself from g. achieved only at price of total detachment 31.4
to weep is to make less the depth of g. 1045.9
what's past help should be past g. 505.12
when thirsty g. in wine we steep 266.39
while g. fresh, attempt to divert only irritates 911.24
who conceals g. finds no remedy for it 911.57
**griefs:** better deep g. than shallow pleasures 911.18
g. that wound in solitude wound deeply 911.44
no temple can still g. and strifes 126.3
of all g. most bitter is scornful jest 434.16
waste not fresh tears over old g. 1045.3
**grievance:** g. is most poignant when almost redressed 475.5
no g. fit for redress by mob law 591.7
to have a g. is to have a purpose in life 249.5
**grind:** mills of God g. slowly 809.11
**gripes:** a man must keep himself up by his own g. 156.3
**ground:** he that lies on the g. cannot fall 327.26
loftiest towers rise from the g. 399.10
man feels more a man if he has a bit of g. 740.24
never test g. before taking your next step 440.5
out of the g. wast thou taken 1058.9
there is life in the g. 334.7
**grounds:** we often do not know the g. on which we act 9.7
**grow:** every individual strives to g. and exclude 467.6
you are the one who must g. up 450.4
**growing:** g., becoming, is character of perfection 677.1
g. up: discovering inner core of strength 567.10
**grown:** g. up is to sit with people who have died 567.13
g. up, that is a hard thing to do 567.5
nurse of full-g. souls is solitude 908.30
wisest man is boy grieving that he's g. 450.2
**growth:** all g. is a leap in the dark 402.11
g. is the only evidence of life 402.12
g. itself contains the germ of happiness 402.2
g. means leaving things inside us 735.4
human happiness is true odour of g. 1058.35
life is cut to allow for g. 402.19
love dies only when g. stops 548.21
man is a born child with the power of g. 402.24
man's g. seen in succession of friends 402.6
only g. is in fulfilling obligations 269.29
only in g. is true security to be found 850.10
principle of g. lies in human choice 402.5
**guardians:** men unfit as g. of another's happiness 560.86
**guest:** equally offensive to speed a g. who'd like to stay as detain one who'd leave 426.15
g. never forgets kind host 426.14
g. sees more in hour than host in year 426.20

I will lecture for fifty dollars, but not be g. for less than a hundred 426.17
man should behave in own house as g. 420.9
to be an ideal g., stay at home 426.16
what is there more kindly than the feeling between host and g. 426.1
**guest's:** seven days is the length of a g. life 426.7
**guests:** fish and g. smell at three days old 426.9
humility is a virtue innate in g. 426.3
unbidden g. are welcomest when gone 426.21
where g. are well-acquainted, they eat more 272.15
**guides:** He who g. through boundless sky thy flight will lead my steps aright 385.12
**guilt:** g. ever at a loss, confusion waits on it 403.6
g. hurries towards punishment 403.7
g. spills itself in fearing to be spilt 403.19
real estate: foundation of world's g. 740.11
self-righteousness drowns our g. 872.3
sin, g., fruit of tree of knowledge 520.44
there may be g. if too much virtue 1025.48
where g. is, rage and courage abound 403.10
without g. what is man 403.13
without spice of g., sin can't be savored 893.4
**guilty:** better to save g. than condemn innocent 515.50
easy to compel sensitive being to feel g. 403.17
g. conscience needs no accuser 171.6
g. man justifies self before accusation 403.8
g. think all talk is of themselves 403.5
in America man presoomed g. ontil proved g. 515.11
in his own heart no g. man is acquitted 403.11
no g. persons, only responsible ones 403.3
they who feel g. are afraid 403.9
we have no choice but to be g. 403.12
whoever blushes is already g. 476.11
**guinea:** force of the g. you have depends on the default in your neighbor 596.49
jingling of the g. helps honor's hurt 596.58
**gulfs:** we all call across incalculable g. 908.22
**gun:** political power grows out of g. barrel 705.50
to get rid of g. necessary to take up g. 1035.63
**guns:** g. and bombs are witness to human folly 226.7
one cannot shoot with butter but with g. 1042.2
**gutter:** we are all in g., but some look at stars 55.24

# H

**habit:** chaos often breeds life; order breeds h. 255.1
character is inured h. 117.22
costly thy h. as thy purse can buy 265.18
evolution from happiness to h. is one of death's best weapons 404.5
h.: a shackle for the free 404.2
h. does not make the monk 45.8
h. is coaxed downstairs, not flung out 404.19
h. is practice that becomes man himself 404.7
h. is second nature, bars knowing first 404.15
h. is stronger than reason 404.17
h. not subjugation, but tender tie 404.3
h. will reconcile us to all but change 404.4
in h. we find the greatest pleasure 404.16
man's h. clings 404.13
one may attribute average actions to h. 224.25
progress has no greater enemy than h. 404.12
what is most contrary to salvation is h. 835.3
who behave well may be creatures of h. 75.8
**habits:** ill h. gather by unseen degrees 404.14
laws are never as effective as h. 404.18
life is but a tissue of h. 404.1
nothing so needs reforming as others' h. 783.40
wise living consists in acquiring as few h. as possible 404.10
**habituation:** h. a falling asleep of sense of time 404.11
**Hades:** descent to H. same from all starting places 218.3
there is one H. for all men 266.23
**hair:** don't let bird make its nest in your h. 964.6
even a single h. casts its shadow 989.14
every h. makes its shadow on ground 471.10
h. shirt doesn't render the wearer chaste 866.9
time hath scanted men in h. 646.90
time pulls men's h. out 971.43
you don't dye your h. to deceive yourself 587.5
**haircut:** h. is a metaphysical operation 405.2
**halo:** h. round priestly head is his horizon 136.7
**halvah:** vinegar in hand better than h. to come 710.12
**hammer:** either suffer or triumph, be anvil or h. 853.4
**hand:** h.: commonly thrust into somebody's pocket 8.2
h. that signed the treaty bred a fever 987.6
hard to close open h. because one loves 382.27
I hate giving of h. without whole man 406.1
let not left h. know what right doeth 430.2
what h. and brain went ever paired 9.9

**handles:** everything has two h. 731.2
**hands:** if we shake h. with icy fingers 319.55
old h. soil what they caress 1065.11
one head better than a hundred h. 491.10
**handshakes:** more history made by secret h. 417.6
**handsome:** h. man is not quite poor 575.15
no woman is h. by features alone 1055.139
**hand-wrought:** imperfections of h. goods accounted marks of superiority 455.10
**hang:** we must all h. together 1009.4
**hanged:** one with money is not h. 761.6
who knows he is to be h. concentrates well 761.3
**hangnail:** h. is not relieved by a costly ring 791.9
**happen:** no man can say, This shall not h. to me 319.40
something must h., even war 145.1
**happened:** nothing has h. to you unless you make much of it 319.41
**happening:** h. is a composition, in retrospect 965.29
h. operates by a network of surprises 965.28
**happier:** h. when we were poorer, but also younger 1064.36
**happiest:** h. is he who suffers the least pain 407.90
h. lives from day to day, asks no more 183.8
he is h. of whom world says least 641.7
he that thinks self h. really is so 1053.12
**happily:** live in ascending scale when we live h. 407.105
**happiness:** actual h. looks squalid in comparison with over-compensations for misery 700.9
all h. lost, man is a breathing corpse 1004.34
artists, poets uninterested in h. 702.84
bitter to see h. through another's eyes 407.100
different men seek h. in different ways 407.5
discovery of a new dish does more for man's h. than discovery of a star 186.1
dry h. is like dry bread 322.3
every h. lent by chance for uncertain time 114.17
extreme h., misery invite religion 790.75
flaw in h., to see beyond our bourn 249.8
for h. we need hope, enterprise, change 407.93
God gives man a glimpse of h., ruins him 356.13
goodness makes men happy, h. good 391.30
grateful environment a substitute for h. 292.5
greatest h. of greatest number is foundation of morals and legislation 407.9
growth itself contains the germ of h. 402.2
h. a sunbeam the least shadow intercepts 407.25
h. always looks small in your hands 407.50
h. attained when man ceases to think of self 1014.2
h. bound up in circumstances demands of life more than it has to give 127.7
h. cannot be the reward of virtue 1025.37
h. depends less on exteriors than supposed 407.29
h. depends on turn of mind 962.4
h. depends upon ourselves 407.4
h. enjoyed only in proportion as known 407.57
h. felt only if you don't set conditions 407.92
h. forgiven if you share it 407.23
h. hates the timid; so does science 973.9
h. is a Eurydice, vanishing when gazed on 407.89
h. is a kind of gratitude 407.64
h. is a thing of gravity 407.54
h. is attained by fidelity to purpose 765.6
h. is beneficial for the body 911.39
h. is brief and will not stay 407.38
h. is composed of misfortunes avoided 407.60
h. is fulfillment of spirit through body 407.28
h. is fun, food Kodachromed 407.74
h. is in the taste, and not the things 407.67
h. is knowing you don't require it 407.96
h. is never so welcome as changelessness 116.3
h. is never to be found 407.58
h. is not the end of life: character is 117.2
h. is owing to good opinion of mankind 906.10
h. is the only sanction of life 407.94
h. is to know source of unhappiness 752.5
h. lacking makes h. one has unbearable 407.91
h. leads none of us by the same route 407.27
h., like a flower, withers when plucked 778.33
h. makes up in height what it lacks in length 407.44
h. not achieved when sought directly 387.13
h. not in h. but achievement of it 407.33
h. of life is to be measured by the extent it has been free from suffering 407.97
h. of man consists in virtue 1025.1
h. of people is end of government 393.2
h. puts on as many shapes as discontent 619.8
h. requires a modicum of prosperity 744.2
h. resides in imaginative reflection 407.95
h.: satisfaction of dammed-up needs 407.42
h.: sensation arising from contemplating misery of another 407.15
h.: soul expressed in considered actions 407.3
h.: to look back on a life usefully and virtuously employed 502.16
h. to me is wine 407.71
h., to some, mere stagnation 407.70
h. was born a twin 407.20
happy men are grave; carry h. cautiously 407.7
human h. is true odour of growth 1058.35
I have the h. of the passing moment 407.49

if h. in self-content is placed, the wise are wretched, fools only blessed 155.3
if one door of h. closes, another opens 407.63
if we can't buy h., we musn't gaze on it 407.11
income 20 pounds, expenditure 19.19.6: h. 970.8
keep from telling h. to the unhappy 407.111
knowledge of possible is beginning of h. 539.16
life bursts in too cruelly for h. 53.73
love: h. of another essential to own h. 548.93
malicious have a dark h. 557.7
man feels h. is his indisputable right 407.62
man seeks weightiest in him, not h. 55.19
man's h. built on other's unhappiness 407.110
man's h. is I will; woman's h., he wills 576.38
man's h.: to do things proper to man 407.75
many roads to h. if gods assent 407.83
men unfit as guardians of another's h. 560.86
modern man's h. consists in buying all he can 407.43
near-missing of h. looks like insult of fortune 407.39
new road to h.: castigate impulses 856.14
nineteen-twentieths of mankind do without h. 407.77
no h. in life so perfect as martyr's 561.8
no right to consume h. without producing it 407.102
nothing so fatal to h. as remembrance of h. 407.48
obstacle to h.: to anticipate great h. 407.40
old h. is unreturning 1064.48
only h.: a clear conscience or none 171.19
our h. depends on wisdom always 407.104
outstanding beauty tends to hamper h. 70.45
present h. unheeded because of h. gone 785.2
pursuit of h. makes Americans try to perpetuate youth 34.55
right to h. is fundamental 407.18
rob man of illusion, rob him of his h. 447.10
search for h. is source of unhappiness 407.52
so long as we can lose h., we possess some 407.107
subordination tends greatly to h. 773.14
supreme h. is conviction we are loved 548.96
that action is best which procures greatest h. for greatest numbers 430.16
thing left silent often makes for h. 891.23
those most concerned about the h. of peoples have made their neighbours miserable 783.12
to be without some things you want is an indispensable part of h. 234.4
to beg daily h. from others 233.2
to fill the hour, – that is h. 407.35
to seek pain greatest h. 866.6
tranquility and occupation give h. 407.56
true h. is of a retired nature 407.1
universal h. keeps the wheels turning 407.55
we are less likely to fail of h. if we measure our chances and capabilities 868.25
we possess only the h. we understand 407.72
we seek h., find misery and death 364.3
where can be found h. in enjoyments without something to spoil it 699.8
where fear is, h. is not 340.30
wherein lies h. 407.61
whose h. is so established that he has no quarrel with his estate of life 407.17
with love one can live without h. 548.52

**happy**: A is h., B is not 337.12
after despair, one is almost h. 237.1
as you are helpful, you will be h. 56.10
ask if you are h. and you cease to be so 407.78
better to be h. for a moment 407.76
bitter to remember that one once was h. 17.10
count no mortal h. before he has died secure from pain 721.6
every method is used to prove to man he is h. 739.7
God wants men to be h. 1058.55
h. ending is America's national belief 34.42
h. families are all alike 332.31
h. is he that serveth not another's will 489.31
h. man seems thus to himself 407.87
h. man will not feel pressure of age 961.3
h. man's without a shirt 407.51
h. the man content in his own ground 420.19
h. the man who calls to-day his own 723.7
he is h. that knoweth not otherwise 407.45
I am h., content because I think I am 407.69
I were little h. if I could say how much 407.99
I'm sure we should all be as h. as kings 1060.28
if you are h. you will be good 391.45
it is not enough to be h. 407.88
make a h. fireside clime to weans, wife 332.8
man wishes to be h. even when his life is such as to make happiness impossible 407.6
man's life h. expecting it soon to be so 407.85
no duty we so underrate as being h. 269.33
no man h. who does not think himself so 407.86
noninterference with others' ways of being h. 787.4
of mortals there is none who is h. 407.37
others look at what I have and think me h. 236.35
peasant and philosopher not equally h. 407.59
poor man thinks rich man h. 152.5
that thou art h., owe to God 407.79
to be h. by means of the heart – have none 548.13
to be h., must not be too concerned with others 407.22
to be h. one must be born in Soo Chow 693.2

to be h., resign self to seeing others h. 150.7
to forget oneself is to be h. 1014.4
we appear h. rather than become so 700.10
we are always preparing to be h. 536.88
we must be doing something to be h. 527.4
we're never so h. or unhappy as we imagine 407.66
when man is h. he doesn't analyze it 407.84
wine is only sweet to h. men 266.37
**hard**: h. comes from within, from efforts 279.3
what was h. to bear is sweet to remember 574.27
what's too h. is worth looking into 243.10
**hardhearted**: what makes people h. is this, each has as much as he can bear in his own troubles 141.6
**hardship**: h. is vanishing, but so is style 744.8
there is no success without h. 938.39
there is pleasure in h. heard about 931.2
**hare**: I'll not run with h., hold with hound 438.20
**hares**: h. can gambol over body of dead lion 713.41
run after two h., you catch neither 495.3
**Harlem**: melting pot H.—H. of honey, chocolate 625.4
**harm**: flea kills none but does all h. he can 1063.6
h. done by people who want to feel important 865.3
most harmful h. is done by the good 391.41
**harmless**: be ye wise as serpents and h. as doves 936.3
**harmony**: conformity is the ape of h. 168.3
h. needs background of discord 408.5
hidden h. is better than the obvious 408.2
**harms**: wise men learn by others' h. 353.12
**harrow**: butterfly preaches contentment to toad under h. 19.21
**Harvard**: every H. class should have one Democrat 704.12
**harvest**: must be sowing even after bad h. 679.10
**has-been**: fear of becoming a h. keeps some people from becoming anything 335.16
**haste**: error is always in h. 297.18
greatest assassin of life is h. 409.8
nothing is more vulgar than h. 559.11
pernicious effect of h. is obscurity 409.9
stars setting and caravan starts, make h. 627.2
that produced in h. goes hastily to waste 409.12
**hastily**: do nothing h. but flea-catching 409.6
no werkman may both werken wel and h. 409.2
nothing done at once h., prudently 409.11
**hasty**: wise man will not dispute with h. one 51.24
**hat**: broad h. not always on venerable head 136.5
h. is difference between clothes and costume 265.21
none look so ungentlemanly as in a bad h. 265.23
power not as becoming as a new h. 265.26
**hatchet**: send not for a h. to break open an egg 942.1
**hate**: all men naturally h. one another 410.19
all victories breed h. 170.8
authority is never without h. 61.3
deepest love turneth to deadliest h. 551.9
everyone has conscience enough to h. 551.1
h., compressed in heart, burns fiercer 410.7
h. fears to be delivered of itself 410.1
h., if h. be perfect, casts out fear 551.14
h. is the consequence of fear 410.6
h. man, worship God seems sum of creeds 790.35
I h. and love, how I know not 167.2
I loved too much not to h. him 551.10
if we imagine anyone to h. what we h. 471.11
if you h. a person, you h. something in him that is part of yourself 410.10
it is human to h. those you've injured 474.24
minds tend to change in h., friendship 178.16
one does not h. as long as one despises 410.16
only one man need h. for h. to gain mankind 410.23
practical experience makes men h. 588.2
those whom we can love, we can h. 787.13
to put faith in h. is the true atheism 410.15
we h. for points on which we differ 27.3
we h. people because we don't know them 720.3
we love and h. without reason 551.11
when h. is surprised in love, I h. most 551.3
when love suppressed, h. takes its place 551.4
who fears you present will h. you absent 340.15
who harbours h., how shall another appease 410.18
you need to h. somebody 410.25
**hated**: good, evil deeds oppress man once h. 410.12
nothing can be h. unless it is known 1000.11
**hates**: he who h. vices h. men. 1023.18
heart that no longer loves, h. 549.15
who h. dogs and babies can't be all bad 588.3
**hath**: he is not poor that h. not much 401.10
unto every one that h. shall be given 15.1
**hating**: h. eats into the heart of religion 410.9
price of h. is loving oneself less 410.4
**hatred**: even h. of vileness distorts features 410.2
foremost art of kings is enduring h. 518.9
h. alone is immortal 410.8
h. can be concealed in countenance, kiss 410.20
h. conquered by love passes into love 551.13
h., ignorant love have same ends 551.6

h. is a tonic, it makes one live 692.2
h. is blind, as well as love 551.5
h. is by far the longest pleasure 410.3
h. is often felt, seldom avowed 410.5
h. is so lasting, stubborn that reconciliation on sickbed certainly forebodes death 410.13
h. is the coward's revenge 410.24
h. leads to the extinction of values 410.17
h., like love, renders votaries credulous 551.12
h. paralyzes life; love releases it 551.7
h. will not strive against self-interest 493.1
heart is more prone to h. 410.21
let us forget words like h., bitterness 361.41
national h. is the most violent where there is the lowest degree of culture 615.4
propaganda successful when it stirs h. 739.8
to wrong those we hate is to add fuel to h. 410.11
when h. too keen, we're below those hated 410.14
who has no h. is safe among things of h. 764.3
whom h. frights, let him dream not on sovereignty 825.13
**hatreds:** politics is the organization of h. 705.3
**haughtiness:** work well done invests doer with h. 1058.24
**haughty:** men hate h. who will not be friend 903.1
**have:** coat of H. not big enough to cover Want 401.5
h., and you shall be esteemed 596.42
miserable to say "I had" when I h. nothing 547.8
only those who h., receive 780.4
other folks h. what some would be glad of 293.10
**having:** peace comes through being, not h. 674.23
**hawk:** when the cock is drunk, he forgets the h. 266.3
**hazard:** better h. once than remain in fear 90.4
**H-bomb:** H. favors small nations 633.15
**head:** arts will one day give headless man h. 572.12
belly overreaches the h. 401.7
better empty purse than empty h. 445.14
better h. of mouse than tail of lion 713.47
bigger a man's h., the worse his headache 163.12
h. doesn't know how to play heart's part 282.21
he with h. of wax must not walk in sun 934.6
if you alone keep your h., you haven't grasped the situation 202.5
knowing h. is second blessing 491.16
no one dares to speak well of his h. 491.18
one h. better than a hundred hands 491.10
there's nothing worse than taking something into your h. 643.1
we distrust heart too much, h. not enough 778.30
what use good h. if legs won't carry it 527.10
when h. aches, all members share pain 150.2
**headache:** bigger a man's head, the worse his h. 163.12
when you're lying awake with a dismal h. 950.2
**headaches:** kings have h. like other people 825.6
**headdress:** nothing is so variable as a lady's h. 405.1
**heads:** empty pockets make empty h. 712.54
**healing:** wish for h. half of health 411.16
**health:** best part of h. is fine disposition 390.4
fear of women is basis of good h. 65.6
h. and appetite impart sweetness to food 411.4
h. in table talk and nursery play 605.4
h. is a blessing that money cannot buy 411.22
h. is sound relation to external objects 836.1
h. is the vital principle of bliss 411.21
h. merits that a man lay out his life to obtain it 411.14
h. shuts us off from certain truths 411.7
h., to be enjoyed, must be interrupted 184.4
if h. smile upon me, I'm a good fellow 962.6
if you would live in h., be old early 411.18
in h. we forget ourselves and destinies 889.6
in the decay of h., let us endeavour at such temper as may be our best support 411.19
it is by disease that h. is pleasant 184.3
life is not living, but living in h. 411.12
many sick do not make us deny h. exists 620.7
preserving h. by severe rule is a malady 411.10
sickness is felt, but h. not at all 411.6
the first wealth is h. 411.5
to keep well, think little about h. 411.8
use your h., to the point of wearing it out 411.17
what some call h. no better than disease 411.15
wish for healing half of h. 411.16
**healthy:** dignity of physician requires he look h. 261.10
h. ear can stand hearing sick words 166.7
**hear:** be swift to h., slow to speak 164.3
less dishonor to h. than speak imperfectly 1000.10
what children h. at home is soon abroad 121.19
**heard:** h. melodies are sweet 448.16
things seen are mightier than things h. 890.7
**hearest:** let greatest part of what thou h. be the least part of what thou believest 897.9
**hearing:** conversation is h. as well as being heard 185.16

h. ear is always close to speaking tongue 540.1
**hears:** who h. badly h. more than there is 676.11
**heart:** adhering to life with last muscle: h. 282.2
all can acquire my knowledge, but not my h. 282.17
among men, wet eye manes dhry h. 438.6
better a red face than a black h. 886.7
blossoms of the h. no wind can touch 282.20
broken h.: monument to never-dying love 548.148
broken hand works, but not broken h. 549.13
constant demands of h. and belly 618.4
diverse elements joined in h. of man 258.2
every man has a house-broken h. except the great man 399.2
give him key of thy h. who hath lock of his 363.22
give me those days with h. in riot 1064.25
go to your bosom, ask h. what it knows 868.31
God builds temple in the h. 124.6
h. asks pleasure first and then excuse from pain 792.1
h. errs like the head, no less fatally 282.14
h. experiences God, not reason 385.57
h. grows not better but worse with age 646.16
h. has its reasons 282.26
h. influences the understanding 282.9
h. is forever inexperienced 282.37
h. is half a prophet 282.41
h. is more prone to hatred 410.21
h. must break or become as bronze 536.19
h. of the wise man lies quiet like water 1053.10
h. prefers to move against circumstance 684.11
h. sees before the head can see 499.1
h. soon wearies of what it loved awhile 178.12
h. speaks many ways 548.178
h. that is soonest awake to flowers is always first to be touched by thorns 876.7
honest h. first blessing 491.16
how but by broken h. may Christ enter in 123.28
human h. is like a ship on a stormy sea 282.22
if maiden's h. stolen, she steals after it 195.10
if thy h. fails thee, climb not at all 749.12
in a full h. there is room for everything 282.28
it is one thing to lack a h. 514.21
it's always strange the h. is 908.32
let go of h., one loses control of head 282.25
let h. be wise; it is gods' best gift 282.12
Lord looketh on the h. 45.2
Lord sees your h., not jacket braid 773.18
man is man only by the h. 558.1
man's h. changes his countenance 282.1
mind goes less far than h. 583.3
my h. leaps up when I behold a rainbow 772.3
narrow h. that loves one object 613.11
no harvest for h.; love must be resown 548.120
not to get what you have set your h. on 364.1
one learns peoples through the h. 1001.19
only with the h. can one see rightly 282.34
pity me that the h. is slow to learn 282.24
put self on bosom of one whose h. you'd eat 438.16
sacrifice not thy h. upon every altar 692.12
search thine own h. 868.35
shape your h. to front the hour 722.4
soul's power lies in the h. 668.28
strange how often h. must be broken before the years can make it wise 319.58
teeth are smiling, but is the h. 390.3
tender h. our noblest quality 517.14
the h. is inexperienced 319.62
to be happy by means of the h.—have none 548.13
unloose the cords of thine h. 966.5
unto a broken h. no other one may go 953.2
we consult ear because h. is wanting 540.2
we distrust h. too much, head not enough 778.30
we know truth by reason and by the h. 991.98
what dungeon is so dark as one's own h. 852.14
what eye ne'er sees, h. ne'er rues 108.1
what h. alike conceived and dared 9.9
what is uttered from h. alone wins hearts 894.10
what makes impression on h. seems lovely 282.33
where the h. lies, let the brain lie also 282.7
where your treasure is your h. will be 740.3
who gives h. will not deny money 430.14
whom the h. of man shuts out, God takes in 544.4
with vacant h., eye: easy live, quiet die 859.5
without hopes the h. would break 425.11
without rich h. wealth is an ugly beggar 1041.18
you cannot plumb depths of human h. 385.3
**heart's:** give but a grain of the h. rich seed 736.2
who's not sat tense before own h. curtain 868.27
**hearts:** all are oftener led by h. than by understandings 282.10
h. live by being wounded 939.51
h. of the great can be changed 347.1
home-keeping h. are happiest 420.15
many wise men have secret h. 936.2
maxims of men disclose their h. 568.3
men's h. close to britches pockets 596.61

merit and knowledge do not gain h. 578.1
sea can be fathomed; who knows h. of men 1001.16
so many h., so many kinds of love 548.237
we do not see nature with eyes, but h. 616.36
we have h. within: warm, live, indecent 282.6
would that men's h. were truer 470.1
**heathen:** h.: has folly to worship something he can see and feel 1061.1
**heaven:** all I seek is h. above, the road below 985.38
all places are distant from h. alike 693.1
complaint is largest tribute to h. 717.30
culture is half-way to h. 207.17
earth being so good, would h. seem best 270.2
for modern man h. is big department store 412.3
from the bounteous h. all riches flow 748.12
God will show you the hardest way to h. 412.7
good man in exclusive h. would be in hell 412.5
h. always bears proportion to earth 385.28
h. barely glances at earth's miseries 412.6
h. equally distant everywhere 412.11
h.-gates not so highly arched as palaces 412.16
h. has space for all modes of love 412.2
h. lies about us in our infancy 1064.60
h. of each is but what each desires 412.8
h. rejects the lore of less or more 382.42
h. were not h. if we knew what it were 316.12
how ready is h. to those that pray 717.19
in h., what they do not do is marry 412.14
many might go to h. with half labour they go to hell 1063.14
men are admitted to h. for cultivating their understandings, not curbing passions 491.2
men conceived h. only to find it insipid 412.13
men tore up roads to h.; now make ladders 790.41
more things in h., earth, than dreamt of 946.4
see h. in a wild flower 616.8
short arm man needs to reach to h. 385.74
there is no humor in h. 434.29
'tis h. alone that is given away 385.46
'tis sweet to look into open face of h. 191.9
we mix our spites and hates with our defence of h. 790.80
we've settled on earth, forgotten h. 429.6
who bears sword of h. should be holy 512.9
who built new h. took power from own hell 1018.2
whom h. helps has friends enough 748.8
**heaven's:** h. help better than early rising 358.4
h. joys do not satisfy cravings of nature 431.8
**heavens:** before Kepler, h. told glory of Lord 413.7
h. call; your eye gazes only to earth 413.3
h. declare the glory of God 413.1
**heaviest:** every horse thinks his own pack h. 870.4
**hedge:** h. between keeps friendship green 730.2
**hedgehog's:** h. one trick is best of all 197.7
**heights:** warmer on h. than those in valley suppose 490.10
**heir:** absent shall not be made h. 2.10
only a fool will make a doctor his h. 261.17
what you share with friend you save from h. 382.19
**heiresses:** all h. are beautiful 1041.14
**heirs:** nor honored less than he who h. 37.14
**Helen:** all women not H. but have H. in hearts 1055.153
**hell:** belief in h. distorts judgement on life 414.3
God creating man to run risk of h. 385.63
good to have friends, even in h. 363.106
h. has three gates: lust, anger, greed 414.2
h. hath no limits; where we are is h. 414.7
h. is others 414.11
h. is the bloodcurdling mansion of time 414.6
h., madame, is to love no longer 414.1
h. populous, smoky city much like London 414.12
many might go to heaven with half labour they go to h. 1063.14
men conceived h. only to find it ridiculous 412.13
no fiercer h. than failure 327.16
pauper is already serving his term in h. 712.10
there is a dreadful h. 414.13
to work, live, die hard and go to h. 414.10
what is h.? h. is oneself 414.5
which way I fly is h.; myself am h. 414.8
who built heaven took power from own h. 1018.2
**hellbent:** the h. get where they are going 10.21
**help:** hate friends who come too late to h. 972.5
he has right to censure who has heart to h. 203.25
love is only way each can h. other 548.65
none can h. another without helping self 56.15
often we can h. most by leaving alone 56.5
'tis not enough to h. the feeble up 56.12
we need the confidence of friends' h. 363.43
what's past h. should be past grief 505.12
when man is down, people want to h. 938.17
when man must h. himself, he says he lacks liberty and justice 233.6
**helpful:** as you are h., you will be happy 56.10
**helping:** good and bad is simply h. or hurting 388.5

h. hand is at the end of man's own arm 873.22
**hen:** when h. lays egg, whole country informed 865.13
woe to house where h. crows 560.113
you can't set a h. in one morning and have chicken salad for lunch 670.13
**hens:** fat h. lay few eggs 183.10
**herd:** h. seek out the great for their influence 398.15
who can endure crassness of common h. 675.10
**hereafter:** absurd to slight for the h. today's delight 698.5
**heredity:** dollar a worthier god than H. Privilege 34.71
**heresies:** in a dead religion there are no more h. 256.10
**heresy:** h. of one age becomes orthodoxy of next 256.7
h. springs only from system in full vigor 256.5
those misliking private opinion call it h. 256.4
**heretic:** essence of a h.: he clings to his ideas 256.1
**hermits:** h. are contented with their cells 920.9
**hero:** better not be a h. than work oneself into heroism by shouting lies 416.24
every h. becomes a bore at last 416.3
every h. is a Samson 416.25
h. believes that all women are ladies 965.23
h. cannot be h. unless in heroic world 416.8
h. he who, without death, can win praise 416.17
h. is a man who does what he can 416.21
h. is suffered to be himself 416.4
if deficient in humanity, thou art no h. 416.22
in war-time a man is called a h. 416.7
no man is a h. to his undertaker 331.5
posterity attributes to h. deeds of the unknown 416.13
show me a h. and I'll write you a tragedy 416.5
the h. created himself 416.2
to be h., main thing is know when to die 416.20
we expect smallest h. to act as demigod 416.15
**heroes:** admiration given to dead martyrs rather than living h. 561.10
chief business of nation: setting up h. 416.18
deeds of heroism offered to those who have been h. in obscurity 416.16
efficiency regime can't be run without h. 416.6
it is fortune with nature that makes h. 416.14
misfortunes, poverty have their h. 416.12
most h. are easily touched by praise 416.1
we make h. of men sitting on money heap 596.32
you don't raise h., you raise sons 909.13
**heroic:** anyone can be h. from time to time 376.5
h. man does not pose 416.11
sincerity is first quality of h. men 894.4
when a man bears with composure one mischance after another, he is of h. temper 17.4
**heroism:** epic vanished with age of personal h. 416.19
h. does not require spiritual maturity 416.10
h. has no model 416.23
h.: to know how to face ridicule 814.8
obstacle to h.: fear of proving self fool 416.9
self-trust is the essence of h. 854.1
you cannot throw away a word like h. 489.18
**hesitate:** it's all right to h. if you then go ahead 9.8
**hesitates:** he who h. is sometimes saved 463.7
**hesitating:** he became an infidel h. between two mosques 463.8
**hesitation:** audacity augments courage; h., fear 90.15
**heterogeneous:** h. ideas yoked by violence together 1024.7
**hid:** man is h. under his tongue 916.2
**hide:** h. nothing from confessor, lawyer, doctor 162.6
hardest thing to h. is what's not there 162.8
**hides:** I detest man who h. one thing in his heart, and speaks forth another 438.13
**hiding:** men would devour men but for power of h. 162.2
**high:** detestation of h. is homage of the low 773.3
duration of h. feelings makes h. men 628.5
h. people, sir, are the best 52.2
look down to know how h. you stand 773.29
they that stand h. have blasts shake them 399.59
**highest:** h. are blasted by envy 945.7
if you aspire to the h. place 55.4
if you do not raise your eyes you will think that you are the h. point 865.17
**hill:** do not climb the h. until you get to it 721.2
I walk firmer up h. than down 243.11
**hills:** h.: earth's despair for the unreachable 602.3
**himself:** every man for h. and God for us all 873.11
who lives only for h. truly dead to others 867.5
**hip:** can we ever make it in the h. world 994.6
h. is sophistication of wise primitive 89.4
**hippies:** h. usurp children's prerogatives 89.1
**historian:** h. must not try to know truth 417.3

**historians:** h. creates true ensemble from half-true 417.40
h. relate what they would have believed 417.24
the middle sort of h. spoil all 417.35
**historic:** h. picks up individual and deposits him in trend 417.33
**historical:** h. sense is perception of past 417.20
**histories:** if h. properly told romances unneeded 417.50
**history:** at each epoch of h. world was lost, saved 296.18
educate the masses: make h. personal 130.4
every great writer writes h. 1062.64
fiction gives opportunity to live h. 341.11
game of h. is played by the best and worst over the heads of the majority 417.29
good writer of h. is suspicious 417.8
h.: account mostly false of events mostly unimportant 417.7
h.: action, reaction of nature, thought 417.22
h. always enunciates new truths 417.36
h. concerned with arranging good entrances for people 417.11
h. has made life difficult for us all 243.9
h. is a hill, high point of vantage 417.15
h. is a novel which did take place 341.10
h. is a tangled skein 417.2
h. is all explained by geography 417.48
h. is attractive to the timid 417.23
h. is essence of innumerable biographies 417.14
h. is facts which become lies in the end 417.17
h. is one long regret 417.47
h. is record of weakness of public opinion 417.12
h. justifies whatever we want it to 417.46
h. makes all ages contemporary, all peoples fellows 417.41
h. never looks like h. when being lived 417.26
h. of free men is written by choice 417.19
h. of world is the h. of privileged few 417.34
h.: progress of consciousness of freedom 361.25
h. provides neither compensation for suffering nor penalties for wrong 417.1
h.: race between education, catastrophe 417.49
h.: recital of facts represented as true 341.19
h. sacrifices totality for continuity 417.31
h.: sad result of each looking out for self 867.2
h. says excuse, won't happen again 417.42
h. unpainful, memory doesn't cloud it 417.9
h., with all her volumes, hath but one page 417.13
human life worthless unless woven into that of ancestors by h. 417.16
if a man said only what was proven, h. could not be written 898.6
in an individual's h. is an account of his condition 860.4
ink in which h. written: fluid prejudice 417.45
it is impossible to write modern h. 417.38
language is the archives of h. 521.7
man hasn't learned from h. 417.4
more h. made by secret handshakes 417.6
need h. to see if we can escape from it 417.37
no wise or brave man lies on tracks of h. 289.2
our h. is every human h. 417.51
people are trapped in h. and h. in them 417.5
peoples, governments never learn from h. 417.28
read no h.: read only biography 79.4
shape of h. seldom clear to men who live it 296.16
test of greatness is the page of h. 399.33
that men do not learn from h. is the most important lesson of h. 417.30
the more we know h., the less we esteem subjects of it 417.18
there is no h. of mankind 417.39
there is no h., only biography 417.21
wise man does not try to hurry h. 670.22
world h. made by the people alone 675.13
world h. would be different if humanity did more sitting on its rear 417.10
**hit:** if you h. pony on nose at outset 883.1
it is not enough to aim, you must h. 6.14
**hoards:** man h. himself when has nothing to give 929.1
**hobbies:** popular persons ride no h. 706.13
**hobby:** he that rides h. gently must cede to him that rides his h. hard 333.4
**hobbyhorse:** as long as a man rides his h. peaceably 977.17
**hold-up:** in a h., line up with the cowards 749.15
**hole:** who digs h. for other may fall in himself 221.19
**holidays:** easier to keep h. than commandments 418.4
h. have no pity 418.5
if year all h., sport as tedious as work 418.8
**holiness:** the road to h. passes through the world of action 9.25
**hollow:** we are the h. men leaning together 944.1
**hollowness:** big drum beats fast, does not realize h. 87.6
**Hollywood:** H. is place where no definition of your worth earlier than your last picture 419.1
H. money is congealed snow 419.2
**holy:** faith in a h. cause has to be extravagant 109.13
h. cannot rise beyond highest in you 388.7

h. man without learning: enemy of church 125.6
how h. people look when sea-sick 833.3
man makes h. what he believes 76.18
remember the sabbath, to keep it h. 829.2
they are not all saints who use h. water 45.5
**home:** dunce sent to roam excels dunce kept h. 985.10
essence of a h. lies in its permanence 420.16
for man of sluggish mind, no place like h. 420.20
h. has more variety than cafe society 700.1
h. is where they must take you in 420.12
h.-keeping hearts are happiest 420.15
h.-keeping youth have ever homely wits 420.21
hotel is refuge from h. life 427.1
in love of h., love of country has rise 420.7
make wherever we're lost in look like h. 12.3
man who rules sthrangers with ir'n hand takes off shoes whin he comes h. late 560.25
man's h. is his wife's castle 420.6
men are merriest when they are from h. 420.22
no place like h. for wearing what you like 420.1
O thrice unhappy h. 461.4
only one in command in h. or state 393.20
sentiments build the necessary h. 282.4
though it rain daggers and spears, it is better to be at h. 421.5
to know the familiar after absence is h. 420.4
we shall be judged more by what we do at h. than what we preach abroad 496.5
when at h., I was in a better place 985.36
where thou art, that is h. 420.8
who makes young happy at h. benefits public 420.3
whose welfare is assured at h. is fortunate 420.13
**Homer:** Achilles exists only by the grace of H. 384.3
H. is new, nothing's so old as newspaper 632.9
**homes:** ruin of a nation begins in its h. 614.1
we carry our h. within us 873.2
**homosexual:** h. aestheticism and irony 876.10
**homosexuality:** h. a sickness as is baby-rape 422.1
probably no sensitive heterosexual alive not preoccupied with his latent h. 422.3
**honest:** don't be h. with friends who ask it 363.27
friendly, h. man fulfills nature's plan 151.4
h. brief has its own eloquence 525.23
h. man's the noblest work of God 423.15
h. man's word is as good as his bond 423.1
happy he whose armour is h. thought 489.31
life of h. man is perpetual infidelity 423.13
lock is meant only for h. men 850.18
mind of an h. man is terrifying 423.6
most enviable of all titles: an h. man 423.19
no such thing as man willing to be h. 423.3
praised by h. men, abused by rogues 798.7
rogue in limelight acts like h. man 330.35
surest way to remain poor, be h. 423.12
to deal only with h. men, stop dealing 423.4
**honesty:** for merchant, h. is financial speculation 102.3
h., delightful pastime at other's expense 360.7
h. in public men attributed to dumbness 755.15
h. is a good thing if kept under control 423.11
h. is beginning of education 423.17
h. is incompatible with amassing fortune 102.18
h. is knowing dishonesty is a mistake 423.7
h. is less profitable than dishonesty 423.14
no clear boundary separates h., dishonesty 423.5
no legacy is so rich as h. 423.18
show of h. is the surest way to riches 423.10
we must deal in privacy with h. and truth 993.3
what is dignity without h. 244.1
workmanship instinct will take care of h. 198.23
**honesty's:** h. praised, then left to freeze 423.8
**honey:** h. in every flower, takes a bee to get it 579.9
**honor:** act well your part, there all the h. lies 489.20
better fail with h. than win by cheating 327.23
difference between moral man, man of h. 598.33
duty, h.; we make these say what we want 269.6
few have ethical energy enough for more than one inflexible point of h. 489.26
great people face war rather than purchase prosperity at price of national h. 46.5
h. confirms men's opinion of themselves 163.2
h. is a steep island without a shore 489.4
h. makes enemies as it condemns opposite 489.28
h. received from those who fear us is not h. 802.10
h. regulates man's acts as public man 489.6
h. sinks where commerce long prevails 102.20
h. travels in a narrow strait 489.25
he has h. if he holds himself to an ideal of conduct 489.16
hold it great wrong to prefer life to h. 489.13
how we fight weakness to preserve h. 489.8
I could not love, loved I not h. more 489.17
jingling of the guinea helps h.'s hurt 596.58
man of h. should not forget what he is 489.10

man who permits his h. to be taken, permits his life to be taken 489.2
many men set high the show of h. 438.1
O that h. were purchased by merit 578.7
prophet is without h. in his own country 424.2
those most desirous of h. or glory cry out loudest of its abuse 424.10
virtue brings h., and h., vanity 1025.25
when faith lost, h. dies, man is dead 489.30
without money, h. is a malady 489.21
would that public and private h. might become identical 489.9
you cannot throw away a word like h. 489.18
**honor's**: quarrel at a straw when h. is at stake 489.24
**honors**: great h. are great burdens 424.7
great power drowns some men in h. 424.8
high h. sweet but they stand close to grief 424.5
nation reveals itself by men it h. 614.15
**hope**: around-the-corner h. prompts action 425.18
come, for house of h. is built on sand 600.11
courage must have h. for nourishment 192.27
death is end, not of enjoyment, but of h. 218.64
death is greatest evil, for it cuts off h. 425.16
faith speaks when h. dissembles 328.37
first we h. too much, later, not enough 425.34
fooled with h., men favor life's deceit 536.26
glittering h. beckons many to undoing 1041.24
good to h., it's waiting that spoils it 1033.8
h. an echo, ties itself yonder 425.36
h. beyond reason shows desire, not judgment 425.30
h. deceives more men than cunning does 425.41
h. deferred maketh the heart sick 425.3
h., fear, must be vivid to be effective 601.7
h. has as many lives as cat, king 425.25
h. is a great falsifier of truth 425.13
h. is a risk that must be run 425.2
h. is a strange invention 425.6
h. is a waking dream 425.1
h. is brightest when it dawns from fears 425.37
h. is incredible to the slave of grief 911.35
h. is necessary in every condition 425.21
h. is only good thing disillusion respects 252.7
h. is the best possession 425.15
h. is worst evil, it prolongs torments 425.28
h. leads us agreeably to end of our lives 425.24
h. looks for unqualified success 328.36
h. makes meaner creatures kings 425.38
h. more brilliant than memory, less true 574.28
h. not sunshine every hour 425.4
h. prodigal heir, experience his banker 425.5
h. should no more be a virtue than fear 425.42
h. springs eternal in the human breast 425.33
h. stimulates life more than realised joy 425.29
he that lives upon h. will die fasting 425.9
humans not caught without nibble of h. 425.31
I am full of h. but end lies in God 425.32
I can endure my despair, not other's h. 293.29
if h. is feeble, boldest plans are safest 90.10
in all pleasure h. is considerable part 698.18
leader is a dealer in h. 528.15
like strength is felt from h., despair 933.9
Lord save us from a h. tree that has lost the faculty of putting out blossoms 237.14
love lives on h., dies when h. is dead 548.36
mind which renounces h. grows calm 800.6
natural to indulge in illusions of h. 425.17
not suffering but h. incites revolt 813.22
poor man needs h. more than bread 712.4
prisons with h. cost man less grief than Promised Lands 425.23
real sorrow is incompatible with h. 911.25
small h. sufficient for birth of love 548.218
the miserable have no medicine but h. 425.39
there are situations in which h. and fear run together and destroy one another 425.12
to eat bread without h. is to starve 237.4
to keep h. in world, change population 425.26
we expect something for nothing and call it h. 425.20
what a valiant faculty is h. 425.27
what we fear comes to pass more speedily than what we h. 340.24
where no h. there can be no endeavour 237.9
whoever has nothing to h., let him despair of nothing 930.8
worldly h. turns ashes or prospers, is gone 983.14
**hoped**: who has never h. can never despair 464.9
**hopefuls**: h. say: time relentless, man shrewd 971.48
**hopes**: all have h., most of which go awry 425.8
cause of idleness, crime is deferring h. 425.7
death surprises us amidst our h. 218.56
extreme h. are born of extreme misery 425.35
fears should not keep us from pursuing h. 425.22
he that h. no good fears no ill 685.3
long ailments wear out pain; long h., joy 1033.7
short life forbids far-reaching h. 425.19
when h. and dreams are loose in streets 813.21
without h. the heart would break 425.11

woman's h. are woven of sunbeams 1055.41
**horizon:** it is the eye which makes the h. 682.5
who keeps his eye fixed on the h. will find the right road 440.5
**horn:** if h. cannot be twisted, ear can 683.9
**horror:** death is ultimate h. of life 218.59
h. causes men to clench fists, unite 1009.11
**horse:** difference of opinion makes h.-races 649.33
dismiss old h. in good time 807.3
every h. thinks his own pack heaviest 870.4
good h. should be seldom spurred 1059.1
h. fastest when has others to outpace 154.10
h.-racing for delight and profit of fools 922.4
if you ride h., sit close and tight 815.2
never join friend in abuse of h. or wife 203.7
no secret so close as between rider, h. 815.3
**horses:** h. and dorgs are wittles and drink to me 41.9
not best to swap h. crossing river 176.3
people on h. look better 63.7
**hospitable:** h. instinct is not wholly altruistic 426.5
**hospital:** h. staff assumes if you lose gall bladder you also lose your mind 889.15
**hospitality:** when h. becomes an art, it loses its soul 426.4
**host:** guest never forgets kind h. 426.14
what is there more kindly than the feeling between h. and guest 426.1
**hostilities:** h. should be mortal; friendships, immortal 766.12
one act seldom produces h. in nations 1035.52
some molded by admirations, others h. 402.1
**hostility:** h. lurks at the heart of our relations 151.20
**hotel:** h. is a refuge from home life 427.1
saints can do miracles, few can keep a h. 427.2
**hotels:** love is like shabby h. 548.238
**hound:** I'll not run with hare, hold with h. 438.20
**hour:** from h. to h., we ripe and ripe 567.17
shape your heart to front the h. 722.4
**hours:** h. in love have wings 2.2
**house:** burn not h. to fright away mice 791.5
dog is lion in his own h. 420.18
every spirit makes its h. 860.5
except Lord build h., labour is in vain 124.3
h. divided against itself cannot stand 1036.1
h. draws visitors, possessor detains them 426.8
h. is on fire—let us warm ourselves 12.7
if h. on fire, we must extinguish it 614.11
let not houseless pull down other's h. 239.10
man builds h.; now he has master for life 428.2
man should behave in own h. as guest 420.9
man's h. is his castle 420.17
man's h. is his stage 428.7
on finishing h., we realize we have learned what we needed to know before start 319.45
ornament of h. is friends who frequent it 420.11
the h. praises the carpenter 6.7
when the h. of a great one collapses, many little ones are slain 398.2
woman careful with face, careless with h. 1055.81
**householders:** surroundings h. crave are glorified, ghost-written autobiographies 428.5
**housekeeping:** h. in common is for women the acid test 497.5
**houseless:** h.: when taxes all paid on household goods 958.1
**houses:** graveyards full of women whose h. were spotless 135.3
in big h. always religious element 1041.9
in Victorian h. occupants could be mysterious and exciting to one another 730.5
men, not h., make the city 129.17
more want to break out of h. than in 420.23
old h. mended cost little less than new 458.2
our h. are such unwieldy property 428.8
some women marry h.; it's another skin 428.6
**Hudson:** H. River is like old October 818.5
**human:** about as much h. nature in some folks as in others, if not more 431.28
any two h. beings can find warmth together 787.6
astonishing what h. beings have achieved 131.26
character of h. life is ambiguity 388.28
could we perfect h. nature 431.6
each h. is profound secret to every other 558.14
every man carries the entire h. condition 558.38
fulfillment as h. being is greatest miracle 1001.17
h. actions are second causes 224.19
h. being doing same thing over and over 822.6
h. being sheds its leaves like a tree 889.11
h. beings are like punctuation marks 558.22
h. nature is not a machine but a tree 277.53
h. nature is the same everywhere 431.2
h. nature loves more readily than hates 431.7
h. nature so constituted that we are reassured as foolishly as we are alarmed 480.6
h. nature to stand in middle of a thing 463.6
h. race is a race of cowards 196.13
h. race is doing the best it can 558.34
h. species made of men who borrow, lend 94.4
I am a man; nothing h. is alien to me 558.52
I am h.: don't fold, spindle, mutilate 558.27
in a different time, place, some other side of our h. nature has been developing 431.1

it's a burden to us even to be h. beings 431.5
logic is one thing, h. animal another 778.26
man would be otherwise, essence of the h. 558.32
man's goal: be h., defend against nature 431.9
nature holds no brief for the h. experiment 906.20
no h. characteristic can be labeled American 34.69
no problem of h. destiny is beyond h. beings 731.5
O h. race! Born to ascend on wings 327.9
only hope of joy is in h. relations 787.10
our history is every h. history 417.51
political education: knowledge of h. nature 705.4
scenery is fine—but h. nature is finer 431.13
some men never become h. 558.26
soul wants to cure itself of being h. 806.2
spirit of recalcitrance in h. race 684.2
to be h. is not to seek perfection 431.19
to flea, h. being is something good to eat 479.5
to step aside is h. 118.2
what astonishes us is that h. nature doesn't behave more wickedly than it does 994.17
what is h. must retrograde if not advance 735.7
when h. being says beast in him aroused 431.26
who would extirpate all evil know little of h. nature 305.5

**humane:** life should be a h. undertaking 154.6
who forgets man is animal is made less h. 431.14

**humanely:** none act h. under influence of fear 340.28

**humanism:** in all h. there is an element of weakness 429.4

**humanist:** nation of bathrooms with h. in each tub 34.40
unless the h. tradition survives, there can be no civilization 429.2

**humanists:** men no longer theists must become h. 429.3

**humanitarian:** h. wishes to be prime mover 430.25
no man can write who is not first a h. 1062.37

**humanitarians:** h. constantly overestimate suffering 430.21

**humanity:** h. is just a work in progress 558.56
I look on nature, hearing sad music of h. 616.80
if deficient in h., thou art no hero 416.22
in abstract love of h. one loves oneself 430.12
man forever disturbed about condition of h. has no problems of his own 783.27
man of h. is one who, in seeking to establish self, finds a foothold for others 430.8
more misery among lower classes than h. in the higher 712.25
now h. does not know where to go 3.9
religion of h. has no faith in humans 231.30
when you say you are in love with h. 430.26
who loves not his home, how shall he love h. 671.5

**humanness:** h. consists in what we call conscience 171.23

**humble:** condition for being h.: not to boast of it 894.19
if a man is h., we call this weakness 203.5
if not h. as dust, men are less than men 433.23
man must be at once more h., confident 960.16
many wish to be devout, no one to be h. 433.11
one may be h. out of pride 433.15
those believed h., usually envious 433.25
too h. is half proud 433.30

**humbleth:** he that h. himself wishes to be exalted 433.16

**humiliate:** nothing ought more to h. great men than their care to boast of little things 87.5

**humiliating:** h. to see idiots succeed 938.13

**humiliation:** greatest h.: not to get appreciation 48.5
there is no h. for humility 433.21

**humility:** come nearest the great when great in h. 433.26
first test of a great man is his h. 433.22
h. begins in awareness of unworthiness 433.4
h. has the toughest hide 433.17
h. is a virtue innate in guests 426.3
h. is first of virtues—for other people 433.9
h. is often only feigned submission which people use to render others submissive 433.12
h. is the opposite of self-abasement 433.7
h. is the virtue all preach, none practice 433.24
h. must be portion of any man whose acclaim is earned in the blood of his followers 384.6
h. neither falls far, nor heavily 433.20
h. reveals the heavenly lights 433.29
h.: substitution of one pride for another 433.8
man with h. will acquire in his beliefs the saving doubt of his certainty 433.13
must be h. to go to greatness 433.18
pride often borrows cloak of h. 727.12
proud men love h.—in others 1025.13
there is no humiliation for h. 433.21
they are proud in h. 433.3

**humor:** as the man is, so must you h. him 787.12
decrepit society shuns h. 906.14

each American sure he has sense of h. 34.73
English are serious only about h. 287.19
form is heart of h., salvation of comedy 434.28
fortune and h. govern the world 114.13
good h. is a philosophic state of mind 390.11
good h. is dress to appear in when we meet 390.13
good taste, h.: contradiction in terms 434.20
h. first to perish in foreign tongue 434.32
h. is a delicate shrub 434.2
h. is an affirmation of dignity 434.12
h. is chaos remembered in tranquility 434.27
h. is falling downstairs while warning your wife not to 434.4
h. simultaneously wounds and heals 434.17
h. teaches tolerance 523.15
man with h. never founded a religion 790.36
men confess to murder, but not lack of h. 434.8
no new sect or its disciples ever had h. 667.4
no writing is more apt to miscarry than h. 1062.3
righteous one has no sense of h. 872.2
secret source of h. not joy but sorrow 434.29
sense of h. keeps man from nearly all sins 434.5
world treats h. patronizingly 434.31

**humorist:** h. has a good eye for humbug, not saint 434.19

**humorous:** h. man realizes perfection is beyond man 539.2
h. persons have pleasant turned-up mouths 1054.4
h. writers are responsive to the hopeless concatenations of life 434.22
one difficult kind of story, the h. 931.7

**hunger:** all vile acts are done to satisfy h. 435.4
good meal ought to begin with h. 272.10
h. breeds madness, not reform 435.13
h. is the teacher of arts 435.8
love is stopped by h. or by time 549.2
no sauce in world like h. 435.2
what h. is to food, zest is to life 511.8
world needs redemption from h., oppression 429.1

**hungry:** h. do not care about liberty 534.10
h. man is more interested in four sandwiches than in four freedoms 435.7
h. man is not a free man 435.12
h. people: stuff of which dictatorships made 361.43
h. stomach has no ears 435.6
those who are loquacious before the h. 745.5

**hunter:** man is the h.; woman his game 576.49

**hunting:** h. has thousand pains, one pleasure 1035.96
it is strange that we call h. a pleasure 436.3
passion for h. implanted in human breast 436.2

**hurricane:** h. attacks only the lofty trees 727.20

**hurry:** great disadvantage of h.: takes time 409.4
h., h. has no blessing 409.15
h. speeds to its ruin 670.20
one is in a h., leaving things behind 409.10
people in a h. cannot think, grow, decay 409.7
we cannot outrun the demon of h. 409.1
whoever is in a h. is doing a thing too big for him 409.3

**hurt:** it takes enemy and friend working together to h. you to the heart 898.19
no man is angry that feels not himself h. 39.4
no man limps because another is h. 692.8
to deaden self against h. is to deaden self also against the h. of others 474.13

**hurting:** good and bad is simply helping or h. 388.5

**husband:** an archeologist is the best h. 42.2
h. is best plaster for woman's ailments 560.84
h.: man who snores like overloaded bus 560.87
I could not endure a h. with a beard 560.105
I should like to see a man some good woman could not shape a h. out of 576.19
if woman loses h.—might as well be dead 560.33
light wife doth make a heavy h. 560.104
no creature perfectly civil but a h. 389.5
not beauty but fine qualities keep a h. 560.31
passion in a h. is pronounced uxorious 668.4
strife where wife is dissatisfied with h. 885.30
when cheated, wife and h. feel same 470.4
wife takes exact measure of her h. 560.124
woman naturally angry if h. strays 470.3

**husband's:** she's adorned that in h. eye is lovely 265.25

**husbands:** h. to be patted, put in good tempers 420.2
married men are tedious when good h. 560.129
no shrieks cast louder to heaven than when h. or lap-dogs die 603.13

**husk:** by the h. you may guess at the nut 45.7

**hygiene:** h. is corruption of medicine by morality 135.5

**hymnbooks:** h. resound with cursing of God 126.7

**hypochondriacs:** h. squander time seeking nostrums 437.1

**hypocrisy:** h. completes a villain 726.8
h. deceives men; children recognize it 438.26
h. is a fashionable vice 438.21
h. is royal road to success 705.34
h. is the homage vice pays to virtue 438.18
manners are the h. of a nation 559.1
on entrance of second person, h. begins 438.7
there is very little h. in the world 438.15

to be modest in speaking truth is h. 993.6
who pretends to be what he's not and hides what he is knows h. 438.5
**hypocrite:** h. always playing same part stops being h. 438.22
he is h. who professes what he does not believe 438.12
man who moralizes is usually a h. 598.54
no man is a h. in his pleasures 698.19
true h. lies with sincerity 438.11
**hypocrites:** we are not h. in our sleep 264.6
**hypotheses:** h. are pieces of scaffolding 967.8
**hypothesis:** h. assimilates every thing to itself 967.14
**hysteria:** h. common denominator of female nature 576.60
h. is a caricature of an artistic creation 620.8

## I

**I:** I am large, I contain multitudes 462.6
I am myself plus my circumstance 127.6
I am part of all that I have met 150.10
"I" means a thing absolutely unique 852.2
**ice cream:** first i. is soul-stirring surprise 352.2
**iconoclasm:** i.—the only way to get at truth 439.3
**id:** where i. was, there shall ego be 567.6
**idea:** between i. and reality falls the shadow 1012.3
dangerous commitment to constricting i. 333.10
dismount from an i., and get into the saddle again, at every parenthesis 935.10
every man with an i. has followers 441.2
fashionable i. is an adulterated one 441.16
historical peoples export i. by war 443.1
i. does not pass from one language to another without change 441.35
i., if right, saves labor of experiences 441.23
i. is a putting truth in checkmate 441.28
i. is old age of spirit, disease of mind 441.11
if the i. is good, it will survive defeat 441.3
if you have one strong i., you repeat it 1062.69
in abstracting i., one may lose its humanity 441.33
is there a dead i. that does not live on 441.15
nations rise and fall, but an i. lives on 441.17
new i. is delicate 441.6
no grand i. ever born in a conference 229.2
no man can establish title to an i. 441.36
nothing is more dangerous than an i., when it is the only i. 441.1
one may believe in an i., but not a man 990.5
originator of i. always called a crank 441.14
possessed by i., you even smell it 441.22
sensibility crammed into a system is an i. 876.9
there is no i. that cannot be vulgarized 4.1
worst squabbling is between those who accepted i. yesterday, those who will tomorrow 250.9
you can't put rope around neck of i. 441.27
**ideal:** Americans combined practical, i. 34.59
don't make a will before dying for an i. 440.4
i. is in thyself, the impediment, too 852.6
i. man is noble and sparkling 558.35
i. society is an imaginary drama 1018.4
straining towards an i. expresses i. 440.20
**idealism:** chief curse of the world is i. 440.13
i. and a politician's will to power 440.8
i. springs from deep feelings 440.1
**idealist:** i. can make ideal out of heaven or hell 440.15
i. notices a rose smells better than a cabbage, concludes it will make better soup 440.12
that at core of i. reigns demon of cruelty is not universal law 440.7
**idealists:** i. obtain what they have struggled for in a form which destroys their ideals 440.18
idealistic Christianity attacked by i. 123.8
**ideals:** bitterest wine drained from crushed i. 252.5
don't use "i."; use native word "lies" 440.9
i. are understanding of that which is desirable in that which is possible 440.10
i. that count express possible development of an existing force 783.22
in marriage with world our i. bear fruit 440.17
men do the incredible if i. threatened 440.6
**ideas:** all great i. are dangerous 441.38
chaos of society due to dishevelment of i. 906.25
essence of heretic: he clings to his i. 256.1
general, abstract i. source of errors 441.31
great i. are not charitable 441.25
hang i.; they are tramps, vagabonds 441.7
harmful i. are cloaks for evil passions 728.14
heterogeneous i. yoked by violence 1024.7
i. are fatal to caste 441.10
i. in Russia are machine-cut blocks 828.4
i. least our own are most easily expressed 441.4
in matters of i. he who meditates is lost 441.20
man's i. get clothed when he dresses 265.22
men are mortal; but i. are immortal 441.18
mind crippled by same set of i. 896.5
minds need i. to conceive 441.21
old i. are habits, ingrained attitudes 441.8
one part of world is slow to adopt valuable i. of another part 441.34
one should operate by dissociation of i. 441.30
one thing to study i. historically 441.26
only condition of peace is to have no i. 674.14
only weapon against bad i. is better i. 441.12

optimism or pessimism makes our i. 653.5
paradoxes useful to attract attention to i. 661.1
revolutionary spirit frees one from scruples as regards i. 813.6
secret of success: to convert i. to things 938.1
that my mind could let fall its dead i. 647.1
to get experience out of i. 277.70
unpleasant to ponder i. that nobody suspects you of having 441.5
we should pursue best arrangement of our i. 991.13
we're all so clogged with dead i. 979.22
words stand for i. in mind of user 1057.22
young man must let his i. grow 441.19

**identity**: demagogy: when equality becomes i. 230.3
faculty for idleness implies sense of i. 444.15
opiate: unlocked door in prison of i. 267.1
strong sense of i. gives man idea he can do no wrong; too little does same 442.5

**ideology**: i. is the habit of showing respect for certain formulas 443.4
religion is now called an i. 443.3

**idiosyncrasies**: i. are mitigated by necessity of conforming 906.12

**idiot**: i.: member of tribe whose influence has always been dominant and controlling 934.1
only i. persists in his error 297.9

**idiots**: God first made i., then school boards 277.77
solemnity is the shield of i. 879.6

**idle**: determine never to be i. 10.13
hardest work is to go i. 444.19
he is i. who might be better employed 444.7
i. men tempt the devil 444.17
if you are i., be not solitary 444.11
man not i. because absorbed in thought 1058.43
useless employment is to be i. 1017.3

**idleness**: dignifies itself by appearance of business 10.14
faculty for i. implies catholic appetite 444.15
i. and pride tax with heavy hand 444.5
i. has a son, robbery 444.8
i. is the parent of all psychology 753.4
i., like kisses, to be sweet must be stolen 444.10
love is born of i. and fostered by it 444.13
reason of i., crime is deferring hopes 425.7

**idler**: no man so methodical as complete i. 444.9

**idol**: i. shattered to prove God's dust greater 385.71
no one is unhappier than superannuated i. 223.1

**idolaters**: men are i.; want something to kiss, hug 1061.3

**idolence**: i. is delightful but distressing state 527.4

**idols**: civilized man bows to flesh-and-blood i. 416.26
we must not smash other people's i. 439.4

**if**: with an i. you might bottle Paris 312.1
your i. is the only peacemaker 164.6

**ignominies**: no pursuit more elegant than collecting and showing the i. of our nature 62.7

**ignoramus**: i.: person unacquainted with knowledge familiar to yourself 445.4

**ignorance**: a man is ignorant with i. of his time 181.10
all i. toboggans into know 445.9
as our knowledge increases, our i. unfolds 520.36
criticism is never inhibited by i. 203.17
drink experience or die in desert of i. 319.35
expanding knowledge we but increase i. 520.45
familiar use of things cures not i. 331.11
from i. our comfort flows 445.26
genuine victories are those over i. 445.23
great pleasure of i. is asking questions 478.16
i.: a blank sheet on which we may write 297.11
i. delivers judgments on all things 445.32
i., incuriosity two very soft pillows 445.11
i. irritates man, knowledge cloys 684.1
i. is always ready to admire itself 445.5
i. is not bliss—it is oblivion 445.34
i. is not innocence but sin 445.6
i. is the womb of monsters 445.1
i. of Beyond *sine qua non* of our life 1012.10
i. of one voter impairs security of all 1030.11
i. of world puts one at mercy of its malice 611.3
i. preferable to error 445.18
if i. bliss, it's low grade of article 445.31
little I know, I owe to my i. 445.16
man must have intelligent i. to succeed 445.19
no generation comprehends its own i. 372.17
nothing is more dangerous than sincere i. 445.20
poverty has many roots; tap root is i. 712.28
prejudice is the child of i. 720.6
pride and i. mutually beget each other 445.8
profound i. makes a man dogmatic 262.12
there is no sin but i. 790.45
three fates: poverty, drudgery, i. 712.40
to hide our i. is hard to do over wine 266.26
tyrants are but the spawn of i. 995.20
where i. is bliss, 'tis folly to be wise 445.15
who displays his knowledge shows his i. 185.30
who would be cured of i. must confess it 445.21

**ignorant**: better be i. than half know matter 445.27
conscious you're i. is first step to knowledge 445.10

custom is the guide of the i. 210.7
goodness can bear mistakes of the i. 977.4
I would prefer as friend a good man i. 363.46
i. don't value good till it's gone 48.10
i. man insignificant and contemptible 445.7
if thou hast no practice thou art i. 715.3
it is only the i. who despise education 277.64
learned conversation: affectation of i. 185.37
let wise beware: i. hungry for action 471.1
luxury is a way of being i. 554.5
millions live, die, i. of selves, of world 445.25
nothing so good for i. man as silence 445.28
praise from i. man is only good-will 716.32
pretty woman has right to be i. 1055.61

**ill:** being i. is a great pleasure, provided one is not too i. and does not have to work 889.2
given amount of i. will goes further now 1035.55
good will be the final goal of i. 388.27
he that hopes no good fears no i. 685.3
means to do i. deeds makes deeds i. done 1063.23
to be unable to bear i. is great i. 17.9
what human i. not alleviated by dawn 599.7
when a man is i., his goodness is sickly 889.22
when well, all have advice for the i. 411.20
who does you i. will not forgive you 474.6
who have never been i. are incapable of real sympathy for many misfortunes 889.10

**ill-favoured:** an i. thing, but my own 710.15

**ill-luck:** some are so fond of i. they run to it 546.4

**illiteracy:** dog's best friend is his i. 41.20

**illiterate:** indescribable freshness about an i. person 445.33
nothing will make democracy of i. people 231.29

**illness:** convalescence makes i. worth while 889.26
i. shuts us off from certain truths 411.7
know self and you'll understand this i. 752.8

**ills:** in i., we look at intention 474.19
see in other's calamity i. to avoid 17.49
thousand i. require thousand cures 791.8
why are we constantly redoubling our i. 866.11

**illusion:** action is thought tempered by i. 9.29
disillusion can become i. if we rest in it 252.1
everything's fine today, that is our i. 652.11
I drink drug of i. and am never dull 55.10
love is the child of i. 548.240
poor man needs i. more than bread 712.4
rob man of life i., rob his happiness 447.10
to be happy, we select i. and embrace it 447.5
today's reality may prove an i. tomorrow 777.15
young girls will recover their i. 383.2

**illusions:** accuse critic who destroys too many i. 204.18
Americans suffer primarily from i. 447.2
as man gets older, old i. supplanted by new 447.13
best part of our lives takes place in i. 447.11
every age is fed on i. 447.7
flowers of life are but i. 252.2
i. are art and by art we live 447.3
if you prefer i. to realities 447.16
time strips our i. of their hue 447.4

**image:** i. of myself in my own mind 681.1
our culture impedes definition of self-i. 442.10
you dye your hair to cheat your own i. 587.5

**imageless:** deep truth is i. 991.119

**imaginary:** i. ailment is worse than a disease 437.2

**imagination:** cannot gratify i. and senses together 448.12
having i., it takes longer to write 1062.1
I have i.; nothing real is alien to me 448.25
i. and mind are politics 705.73
i. grows by exercise 448.21
i. is expelling several persons from reality, bringing them back as one presence 687.1
i. is potentially infinite 448.26
i. is the liquid solution in which art develops the snapshots of reality 448.7
i. is the mad boarder 448.20
i. is the marrow of civilization 448.1
i. like lofty building reared to meet sky 448.3
i. respects the similitudes of things 448.28
i. robust in proportion as reasoning weak 448.30
i. so abstracts us that we are not aware 448.9
i. supreme master of art, life 448.8
i., that deceitful part in man 448.22
i.: warehouse of facts with poet and liar in joint ownership 448.2
instant all we have unless i. startle us 448.33
marriage of soul with nature gives birth to i. 616.70
memorable days vibrate to i. 448.13
men are not aware they have any i. 947.4
people can die of mere i. 448.4
power enabling man to entertain good impulse same as one to make good gun: i. 448.5
principle of equality lowers flight of i. 295.25
solitude is needful to the i. 908.31
such tricks hath strong i. 448.27
the i. imitates 198.41
the possible's slow fuse is lit by i. 448.10
things not beautiful until they speak to the i. 70.16
were it not for i., a man would be happy in arms of chambermaid 448.14
who lives within means suffers lack of i. 970.12
woe to him who tries to stretch the i. 448.31
you can't depend on judgment when i. is out of focus 448.29

**imaginative:** i. people are the most credulous 199.2
**imagine:** I i., therefore I belong and am free 448.11
man is able to do what he is unable to i. 3.4
more we i., more we must think we see 448.18
nothing in the world can one i. beforehand 356.10
**imaginings:** present fears are less than horrible i. 340.32
**imbecile:** i. looks at finger pointing to moon 934.4
**imbeciles:** of four types of men, i. are happiest 353.28
**imbecility:** to raise i. to profundity, put it on a platform 757.10
**imitate:** free to do as we please, we i. 449.4
when people are free, they i. each other 655.4
**imitated:** no one so low as not to be i. by somebody 449.6
**imitation:** absurdity of conduct arises from the i. of those whom we cannot resemble 449.8
act of i. breeds resentment 449.5
i. is a necessity of nature 449.11
i. is the sincerest flattery 449.3
men often applaud i. and hiss real thing 60.1
no man was ever great by i. 399.39
to refrain from i. is the best revenge 449.9
we are what we are mainly by i. 449.2
**immature:** i. is love and hatred of the youth 1064.44
**immaturity:** highest creatures helpless during i. 402.22
**immigrants:** citizenship won by i. 179.4
**immoral:** what is i. is what you feel bad after 598.20
**immoralists:** i. see value of action in unintentional 224.26
**immorality:** i. is thing upon which your friends frown 598.23
i.: not doing what one must when one must 598.2
immoral sense enables one to perceive i. and enjoy it 598.50
**immortal:** aspire not to i. life; exhaust the possible 539.14
man has only one way of being i. 452.4
mortal nature is seeking to be i. 452.10
people I respect behave as if they were i. 90.3
truth only i. thing given us to use 991.68
when I resent not being i. 600.23
would not have lovely days, hearts to enjoy them, unless we were meant to be i. 452.6
**immortality:** all the doctrines about i. 452.15
if belief in soul's i. is mere delusion, it is a pleasing one 452.2
let him who believes in i. enjoy his happiness in silence 452.5
life is short; honorable death man's i. 452.13
love is i. 548.40
ne'er crowned with i. who fears to follow where airy voices lead 399.40
thing well said walks in i. 281.10
to occupy inch of dusty shelf is i. 452.7
**impartiality:** i. may simply mean indifference 453.1
justice is i. 515.45
**impatience:** i. is the mark of independence 454.2
trading in our i. for peace of mind 982.6
**impatient:** wise are always i. 1053.27
**impediment:** ideal is in thyself, the i., too 852.6
**imperfect:** United Nations: i. instrument in i. world 1008.2
universe in which perfection arises is i. 677.18
**imperfections:** i. make hand-made goods superior 455.10
things better for divinely appointed i. 455.5
**imperial:** something to be said for the i. attitude 865.14
**imperialism:** in i. nothing fails like success 456.2
**impertinence:** many people mistake i. for sincerity 824.8
**impertinent:** i. wits are a kind of universal insect 1054.16
**impiety:** i.: your irreverence toward my deity 504.1
**impious:** most i. sorrows at God's judgement 809.7
**implacable:** i. stand is directed against inner doubt 262.10
**importance:** we all wish to be of i. in some way 865.4
**important:** harm done by people who want to feel i. 865.3
man desires to be free and feel i. 865.2
say i. things simply; bombast spoils them 935.13
**impossible:** dwelling-place of i.: dreams of impotent 457.5
few things are of themselves i. 279.13
few things i. to diligence and skill 279.11
man can believe the i. 76.25
nothing is i. for the man who doesn't have to do it himself 313.6
nothing is i. to a willing heart 1050.5
**impostors:** made wary by i., men look for wrong 257.13
**impotence:** man is as full of potentiality as of i. 711.5
man who has forsworn bullet has i. 658.3
money is the power of i. 596.51
religion: love of life, conscious of i. 790.67

**impotent**: dwelling-place of impossible: dreams of i. 457.5
**impression**: I do not judge men by deed, but by i. 513.10
**impressionable**: the great man is the i. man 876.4
**improbable**: man can never believe the i. 76.25
nothing i. until it's past tense 669.1
**impropriety**: i. is the soul of wit 1054.24
**improve**: none will i. your lot if you do not 289.1
**improvement**: he who reads for i. is beyond hope of i. 91.23
i. makes straight roads 458.1
spirit of i. not always spirit of liberty 783.26
**improvisation**: human being is condemned to i. 962.5
i. is the essence of good talk 921.1
too much i. leaves mind void 921.4
**imprudences**: man laments i., but his youth more 646.100
**impudence**: i. knows no bounds 824.5
**impulse**: to its own i. every creature stirs 442.2
**impulses**: new road to happiness: castigate i. 856.14
**impulsive**: it is hard to fight against i. desire 236.19
**inaccessibility**: people become valuable merely for their i. 1019.6
**inaccessible**: men and women are most i. things 908.12
**inaccuracy**: I do not mind lying, but hate i. 297.7
**inaction**: population condemned to i. is explosive 564.3
**inanimate**: goal of i. objects is to resist, defeat man 638.1
obstinacy of i. objects 644.4
three scientific classes of i. objects: those that don't work, break down, get lost 638.2
**incautious**: theory makes men i. 967.11
**incense**: unless i. burnt, it emits no fragrance 502.17
**inclinations**: argument seldom convinces against i. 51.11
**income**: solvency a matter of temperament, not i. 1041.60
**incommunicable**: distrust the i.; it is source of violence 148.13
we have bonds, but each has i. dreams 908.47
**incompetence**: obscurity is the refuge of i. 641.5
**incomplete**: nature loves the i. 616.30
**incomprehensible**: how i. are beings who share with us sight of stars, warmth of sun 656.3
**inconsistency**: to climb out of a rut is called i. 176.6
**inconstancy**: i. no sin will prove 470.7
there is nothing constant but i. 178.18
world sees nothing so contemptible as i. 178.1
**incontinent**: greedy man i. with whole world before him 401.24
impulses of i. man carry him in opposite direction from that aimed at 492.1
nothing so i. as man's appetite 401.13
**inconvenience**: i.: an adventure wrongly considered 16.1
**incredulity**: i. as faith is less rational than religion 997.12
**incuriosity**: ignorance, i. are two very soft pillows 445.11
**indebtedness**: great i. makes men vengeful, not grateful 639.7
**indecencies**: nature knows no i.; man invents them 750.5
**indecency**: private sin not so prejudicial as public i. 750.1
**indecision**: he is most miserable whose only habit is i. 463.3
i. is like the stepchild 463.4
**independence**: i. is a privilege of the strong 873.20
i. is the first condition of dialogue 873.10
i.: that's middle class blasphemy 233.11
impatience is the mark of i. 454.2
in crowd, great man keeps i. of solitude 873.6
thinking is effort of soul to keep i. 968.32
**independent**: i.: guy who wants politics out of politics 704.14
to be i. is to be abnormal 168.1
war, debt, flag: ain't this to be i. 534.24
what man wants is i. choice 122.2
**Indian**: I. summer of life should never be hustled 580.3
**indictment**: I do not know the method of drawing up an i. against a whole people 496.2
**indifference**: i. a mode of bearing ills of life 17.17
i. is the mark of deprivation 387.7
in the vast i. I invent a meaning 9.39
price of eternal vigilance is i. 226.12
secret can be drawn out by i. 849.8
**indifferent**: communists have not been i. 149.6
if all experiences i., duty is also 269.5
we are so i. to people 548.170
worst sin to be i. to others 464.8
**indigestion**: how many wars have been caused by i. 1035.103
**indignant**: no one lies as much as the i. do 465.5
**indignation**: a good i. brings out one's powers 465.1
call bad behavior righteous i. 239.7
civil-rights movement has restored dignity of i. 817.17
i. is no good unless backed with a club 465.3

i. is the seducer of thought 465.4
moral i. permits envy and hate 465.2
no more sovereign eloquence than truth in i. 281.4
**indirection:** too much zeal offends where i. works 683.4
**indiscreet:** more trouble is caused by i. answers 478.12
wicked is not much worse than i. 1048.7
**indiscretion:** lover without i. is no lover at all 552.9
**individual:** every i. is a repelling orb 467.4
every i. strives to grow and exclude 467.6
go from i. to i. to gain totality of race 467.20
i. man in his freedom can mature the world 467.10
i. man tries to escape the race 467.12
liberty of i. must be limited 361.40
men speaking in i. manner are interesting 494.2
nature is reckless of the i. 616.25
the general preys upon the i. mind 129.33
**individualism:** i. is like innocence 466.2
**individualists:** i. tend to be unobservant 466.3
**individuality:** concealment is equated with i. 162.18
defects are necessary for existence of i. 339.16
England is the paradise of i. 287.22
i. must be affirmed in solitude 908.28
learning to be an American is learning not to let your i. become a nuisance 34.19
without i. society doesn't advance 467.15
**individualizes:** man whom God wills to slay he first i. 467.16
**individuals:** not races but i. that are noble 768.1
we think men i.; so are pumpkins 467.5
**indivisibility:** supreme reality is our i. as God's children 98.14
**indolent:** man is by nature i. 404.6
**indulgence:** excessive i. is only self-i. 468.3
i. is what the world permits us 468.2
severity is more useful than i. 959.25
**industrial:** pauper a human sacrifice in i. regime 960.20
**industry:** i. is fortune's right hand 358.14
rising in life by own i., others' folly 938.23
where no desire, no i. 1058.50
**ineffectual:** if bodies are to be denied, nature wicked, we are i.—fishes not meant to swim 885.5
**inequality:** individuals seek an i. to their advantage 469.4
**inertia:** men oppose progress, for they love i. 175.10
**inevitable:** there is no good in arguing with the i. 617.9
**inexperienced:** heart is forever i. 282.37
**infancy:** heaven lies about us in our i. 1064.60
i. conforms to none, but all to it 64.6
**infant:** happy to be the trustful i. 476.12
what am I: an i. crying in the night 457.6
**infant's:** father's nature lives anew in i. breast 415.2
**infants:** nobody agrees with anybody; i. show it 27.7
**infected:** all seems i. that the i. spy 58.5
**inferior:** no one can make you feel i. without your consent 861.6
to take refuge with i. is to betray self 57.18
**inferiority:** sense of i., called ambition 33.27
superiority and i. are individual 945.11
to admit i. is to be a fool 945.8
**inferiors:** i. revolt to be equal 813.1
most insupportable of tyrannies is that of i. 995.24
what man dislikes in superiors, let him not display in treatment of his i. 528.23
**infidel:** he became an i. between two mosques 463.8
**infidelity:** i., that infallible rejuvenator 470.2
life of honest man is perpetual i. 423.13
only i.: for man to vote himself dead 216.8
**infinite:** eternal silence of these i. spaces 914.6
what you see, yet can not see over, is as good as i. 682.2
**infinities:** two i.: God above, human baseness below 305.17
**infinity:** hold i. in the palm of your hand 616.8
suffering shares the nature of i. 939.54
**influence:** cock has great i. on his own dunghill 713.40
harm done by old men who cling to i. 1065.38
i. is neither good nor bad absolutely 471.6
**influenced:** unconscious selection exercised in being i. 471.3
**information:** i. is thin stuff without experience 520.14
live effectively: live with adequate i. 520.73
we live by i., not by sight 520.24
**informer:** man is i. when he cannot be a soldier 204.21
**ingenuous:** i. mind feels reproof in unmerited praise 716.17
**ingratitude:** greed's worst point is its i. 401.26
man apt to complain of i. of those who have risen far above him 473.5
too great an eagerness to discharge an obligation is a species of i. 639.3
we'd hear little of i., if we did not exaggerate the worth of our own deeds 473.4
wind, thou art not so unkind as man's i. 473.8
**inheritance:** loss of i. might drive son to despair 1051.8
**inherits:** he who i. a penny is expected to spend a dollar 1051.5
**inhuman:** take care not to feel i. towards i. men 206.11

**inhumanity:** man's i. to man makes thousands mourn 206.3
nature has imprinted in man instinct of i. 206.12
**initiative:** no fruitful i. without government 393.57
you cannot endow machine with i. 960.17
**injure:** to i., then beg forgiveness, shows power 474.17
**injured:** he threatens many that hath i. one 474.11
it is human to hate those you have i. 474.24
those whom men have i. they despise 474.22
**injures:** he i. fair lady who beholds her not 464.4
**injuries:** he invites i. who rewards past ones 866.4
i. may be forgiven, but not forgotten 474.1
men more prone to revenge i. 782.3
**injury:** advice after i. is medicine after death 19.11
brave man thinks no one his superior who does him an i. 474.18
God will not punish return for an i. 811.20
hard to keep secret, employ leisure, bear i. 243.1
i. sooner forgotten than insult 474.3
reject your sense of i. and i. disappears 474.15
women, elephants never forget an i. 1055.130
**injustice:** defeat preferable to defeating i. by evil 570.8
feeling of i. is insupportable to men 475.3
i. all around is justice 475.12
i. feared less if ruler is religious 825.2
i. is not something comparative 475.15
i. sweeps the earth and tramples mankind 475.6
i. three centuries old is an accomplished fact of life 475.16
i.: whatever prevents my doing what I like 475.1
if i. prevails we must doubt gods 475.4
in children's world i. is finely felt 121.10
justice can't subsist without mixture of i. 515.33
justice discreet; i. makes big noise 515.40
mankind censure i., fearing they may be victims of it 475.13
never be too eager to combat i. 783.2
no man at bottom means i. 475.2
one ought not to return i. to anybody 658.15
rigid justice is the greatest i. 515.16
rigorous law is often rigorous i. 525.64
source of justice was fear of i. 515.21
unrectified i. has way of lingering 475.10
war for justice better than peaceful i. 674.27
where no property, no i. 740.14
**innocence:** all prisons are brimming over with i. 729.1
childish fantasy protects world from power of i. 121.7
confession of faults next to i. 165.4
i. and truth are always ready for expression 403.6
i. dwells with wisdom, never with ignorance 476.2
i. is bashful, does not want to be sought 698.23
i. is full, experience is empty 476.8
loss of i. brings loss of prejudice 57.7
man should keep his hair and his i. 476.4
silence of i. often persuades 891.32
through our recovered i. we discern i. of neighbors 476.13
true i. never falls at once to deep guilt 1023.26
when i. trembles, it condemns the judge 475.14
who blushes is guilty; true i. not ashamed 476.11
**innocent:** after the great destructions everyone will prove he was i. 633.6
better to save guilty man than condemn i. 515.50
each man insists on being i. 403.4
every man is i. in his own eyes 515.9
God is unthinkable if we are i. 403.12
he's armed without that's i. within 476.9
i. is person who explains nothing 476.3
lot of i. in world to fly to the wolf for succor from the lion 476.1
one can't reign and be i. 825.23
somebody's responsible and somebody's i. 515.3
who hastes to be rich shall not be i. 732.2
**innocently:** if you would live i., seek solitude 476.10
**innovate:** great don't i., they fertilize 399.55
**innovation:** be not over-anxious to encourage i. 477.2
without i., art is a corpse 53.25
**innovations:** of ten i. attempted, nine end in silliness 477.6
**innovator:** time is the greatest i. 477.1
**inquire:** i. not what boils in another's pot 208.6
**inquiry:** no i. is forbidden to man to pursue 478.9
**inquisitive:** one shouldn't be too i. in life about God or one's wife 208.1
**inquisitor:** true i. is a creature of policy 333.16
**insensible:** better to emit scream than to be i. 967.15
useless to attack the i. 481.1
**insensitivity:** conscious i. is a self-contradiction 876.1
**insight:** i. of any human soul is real knowledge 319.6
i.–the titillating knack for hurting 1001.4
moment's i. is sometimes worth a life's experience 1000.8
**insignificance:** our i. is often the cause of our safety 1005.1

**insignificant:** easier to bear the unpleasant than the i. 819.2
no meanest object is i. 1005.2
**insincere:** most exhausting thing in life is being i. 482.4
**insincerity:** by i. we can multiply our personalities 482.5
great enemy of clear language is i. 521.18
**insistent:** life doesn't pay off to those most i. 679.5
**inspiration:** as appetite by eating, i. comes by work 483.5
beware of notions like genius and i. 374.32
defend us from the i. of the moment 921.1
greatness not effect of i. 399.54
i.: inhaling the memory of an act never experienced 483.3
i. is a farce that poets have invented 956.1
**inspired:** to be brief is almost to be i. 96.9
**instant:** i., trivial as it is, is all we have 448.33
**instinct:** combative i. is a savage prompting 154.11
i. is enough in art, as in love 53.49
i. is to forget lunch as house burns, but to eat it later in the ashes 484.3
i. serves end of bringing about death 538.12
justice substituted for i. in civil state 131.23
none of us can estimate what we do from i. 484.5
the i. of the people is right 675.4
trust i. though you cannot explain why 484.1
we lack intelligence, have forgotten i. 137.9
well-bred i. meets reason half-way 484.6
when reason and i. are reconciled 598.38
**instincts:** be true to your animal i. 484.2
does not matter what men say in words if activities controlled by i. 210.31
if men surrender to their i. 459.1
society acquires new arts, loses old i. 906.3
**institution:** every i. prepares way for its rival 485.6
i. is lengthened shadow of one man 485.5
rational i. suffers not by concessions 485.9
**institutions:** i. alone can create a nation 485.2
i. hand in hand with progress of mind 525.44
we fall into i. already made 485.4
**instruct:** with a smile we should i. our youth 959.20
**instruction:** man seldom has so much knowledge of another as necessary to make i. useful 19.20
men ungrateful to him who gives them i. 959.16
tigers of wrath are wiser than horses of i. 39.9
**instructions:** nature's i. slow, those of men premature 616.60
**insult:** Americans don't understand studied i. 486.2
injury sooner forgotten than i. 474.3
**insults:** best reply to i.: patience, moderation 486.3
i. should be avenged or endured 486.4
**insurance:** God, for a man that solicits i. 33.26
i.: a modern game of chance 487.1
when praying does no good, i. does help 487.2
**integrity:** i. without knowledge is weak 489.12
nothing sacred but i. of our own mind 489.7
simple i. baffles one full of duplicity 489.5
**intellect:** at twenty, will rules; at thirty, i. 537.7
everyone thinks own i. perfect 163.14
greater i. one has, more originality one finds in men 491.23
human i. functions to solve problems which the man's inner destiny sets it 491.21
i. annuls fate 968.14
i. mis-shapes the beauteous things 843.41
i. respects equality as a convention 295.4
i. should pursue thought to unravelment 968.57
i. without firmness is craft, chicanery 491.24
marriage of soul with nature makes i. fruitful 616.70
means of strengthening i. is to make up one's mind about nothing 647.3
not clear if i. is privilege or handicap 968.1
take care not to make the i. our god 583.5
thought is the labor of the i. 812.2
weakness of the human i.: seeks to reconcile contrary principles 728.16
wrath plunders all the riches of the i. 39.2
**intellectual:** commonplaces: tramways of i. transportation 605.9
i. betrayed by own vanity, assuming he can express everything in words 490.9
i. is someone whose mind watches itself 490.2
it is the task of the i. to "think otherwise" 490.3
men of slender i. stamina dread competition 934.9
our credulity as to i. powers of others 199.3
the i. is pledged, committed, enlisted 490.8
those who know supremacy of i. life 490.4
to do nothing is the most i. thing 444.18
tongue is a key to the i. treasure 891.29
**intellectualism:** i. is often the sole piety of the skeptic 490.7
**intellectuals:** i. suppose previous ages less sick 296.15
**intellectuals':** i. cause of anguish is other i. works 490.1
**intelligence:** first mark of i. is not to start things 491.22
greatest i. suffers most from own limits 491.12
i. has an incomprehension of life 491.1
i. in chains loses in lucidity 491.3
i. is man's ability to manipulate world with help of thought 491.9
i. is not to make no mistakes 297.3

i. is quickness in seeing things as they are 491.26
i. is silence, truth being invisible 891.27
i. is the ability to hold two opposed ideas in the mind 491.8
I. rules throughout existence 1010.4
lack of i. is father of all crimes 934.15
man becomes man only by the i. 558.1
we lack i., and have forgotten instinct 137.9
**intelligent:** cheerful, i. face is end of culture 207.4
high price for being i.; wisdom hurts 491.7
i. man flourishes within a dullard and holds a lunatic in leash 491.25
i. people able to control emotions 491.19
i. people are generally paralytics 491.11
kings need the company of the i. 518.8
man must have i. ignorance to succeed 445.19
time shows most stubborn are most i. 644.12
**intemperance:** i. is the only vulgarity 266.12
i. is the physician's provider 492.7
i. is the plague of sensuality 492.5
no tyrant like i. 492.4
**intemperate:** blush of an i. man painted by liquor 492.6
life of i. is wholly governed by desires 121.2
**intention:** good i. clothes itself with sudden power 601.5
half the results of a good i. are evil 173.11
if there is no i., there is no blame 893.13
in ills, we look more at i. than effect 474.19
**intentions:** good i. useless without common sense 147.8
**interest:** I don't believe in principle; I do in i. 94.5
i. does not tie nations together 496.19
i. even plays part of disinterestedness 493.6
i. gnaws at a man's substance 219.1
in danger, none blamed looking to own i. 213.21
it is i. that keeps peace 674.7
only fear and i. unite men 1009.9
we talk on principle, act on i. 493.5
would you persuade, speak of i., not reason 683.6
**interested:** to know when one is i. is the first condition of interesting other people 494.5
**interesting:** evening with fascinating person leaves vivid memories; with i. person, bouquet 494.4
life's perplexity: too many i. things 495.2
men speaking in individual manner are i. 494.2
test of i. people is that subject matter doesn't matter 494.3
to render themselves i., many feign unhappiness 1004.29
**interests:** do not confuse vested i. with ethics 493.7
man fights harder for i. than rights 493.8
nation's policies determined by its i. 614.14
nations linked by i., not friendship 614.8
world of vested i. doesn't want candour 493.10
**interludes:** our lives are merely strange dark i. 536.84
**international:** all good men are i. 190.1
frightened, indifferent, people behold the tragi-comedy on the i. stage 464.3
i. crises frighten weak, inspire strong 496.15
i. incidents should not govern foreign policy 496.11
**interpretation:** i. is the revenge of intellect upon art 204.51
our virtues lie in the i. of the time 598.41
**interpretations:** more ado to interpret i. than things 204.38
**interruption:** noise is most impertinent form of i. 629.2
**intimacies:** i. between women often go backwards 1055.13
**intimate:** much easier to tell i. things in the dark 166.5
to speak highly of an i. is egotism 716.12
**intolerance:** i. is a "Do Not Touch" sign 498.2
i.: to oppose death penalty but electrocute those who disagree 498.1
no destruction has deprived man of so many noble lives as i. 498.3
**intoxication:** man must get drunk: best of life is i. 266.4
one creates power for self by way of i. 713.37
**introspective:** man becomes i. when he suffers 939.36
**introvert:** i. gazes only upon the emptiness within 620.14
**intruders:** eyes are the great i. 323.2
**intuition:** i. attracts those who wish to be spiritual without any bother 499.3
women use intelligence to prop up i. 1055.34
**intuitions:** i. produced and erased by education 277.60
**intuitive:** mind of man is more i. than logical 583.23
**invalid:** every i. is a physician 889.14
**invalids:** when elderly i. with same ailment converse, life is delicious 22.5
**invent:** to exaggerate is to begin to i. 307.3
we can i. only with memory 198.21
**invention:** hunger is the bestower of i. 435.8
necessity, the mother of our i. 617.13
**inventions:** our i. mirror our secret wishes 198.9
**inventor:** i.: makes arrangement of wheels, levers and springs, and believes it civilization 500.1
**inventors:** greatest of i.: accident 500.2
i. almost always regarded as fools 477.3
i. of the mechanical arts have been much more useful than i. of syllogisms 500.3

**investment:** goodness is the only i. that never fails 391.54
**investments:** charity, personal force only worthwhile i. 118.11
**invincible:** men are i. because inviolable 852.18
**invisible:** i. government is malign 393.40
poet is the priest of the i. 702.94
to make ourselves i. to creditors 626.6
**involved:** American defends against anxiety by not becoming i. 34.20
**Irish:** I. never speak well of each other 503.1
where there are I. there's loving and fighting 503.2
**Irishman:** I. fights before he reasons 287.8
**iron:** strong i. often ends in shatterings 933.18
**irony:** free mind must have one policeman, I. 434.14
i. and pity are two good counselors 536.35
**irrational:** one can't legislate against the i. 525.59
to explain behavior, especially the i. 75.11
**irregular:** romantic life not made by i. hours, diet 821.1
**irreverence:** i. is the champion of liberty 504.5
**irritating:** it's i. to think about being somewhere else 249.3
**irritations:** fine scenery appeases our i. 602.1
**island:** no man is an i., entire of itself 150.3
**islands:** little i. are all large prisons 847.3
**isolated:** i. individual does not exist 150.9
**isolation:** i. breeds conceit 908.54
i. must precede true society 908.16
solitude vivifies; i. kills 908.46
**Italy:** man who has not been in I. is inferior 507.1
**itch:** bliss: when you i., to up and scratch 846.3
i. is a ridiculous malady 846.1
if you are anywheres where it won't do to scratch, you will i. all over 846.4
love, i., and cough cannot be hid 548.78

# J

**jail:** be thine own palace, or world's thy j. 873.4
in j. each day is like a year 729.7
j. doesn't teach anyone to do good 391.21
need ways to keep people out of j. 201.22
**jargon:** instead of language, we have j. 54.1
**jaundiced:** all looks yellow to the j. eye 58.5
**jazz:** j. is main spring of twentieth century 607.33
**jealous:** art is a j. mistress 53.44
j. ear hears all things 508.3
j. man fares worse than cuckold 401.19
j. man is quick in application 508.2
j. trouble others, but torment selves 508.20
philosophers are as j. as women 688.38
tramp is j. of tramp 154.7
trifles are to the j. strong proofs 508.22
**jealousy:** in j. there is more self-love than love 508.16
it is not love that is blind, but j. 508.12
j., anger, and anxiety shorten life 43.2
j. dislikes the world to know it 508.7
j. exacts hard service, pays bitter wages 508.10
j. feeds on suspicion, ends with certainty 508.15
j. is beautiful only on a young face 508.8
j. is born with love, doesn't die with it 508.17
j. is cruel as the grave 508.5
j. is just the fact of being deprived 508.4
j. is not low, but it catches us humbled 508.9
j. is pain from fear of not being equally loved 508.1
j. is the greatest of all evils 508.18
j. no more than feeling alone against smiling enemies 508.6
j. slays love under pretense of keeping it alive 508.13
love that is fed by j. dies hard 508.19
nothing more frightful to j. than laughter 508.21
where there is no j. there is no love 508.14
**jealousy's:** j. a proof of love, but can't cure it 508.11
**jest:** better lose a j. than a friend 434.11
j. often more effectual than seriousness 434.13
of all griefs most bitter is scornful j. 434.16
**jest's:** j. prosperity lies in the ear of hearer 434.25
**jesting:** clumsy j. is no joke 434.1
**Jesus:** J., in sacrifice, became ransom of the world 509.1
**Jew:** hath not a J. eyes, hands, organs 510.4
he makes J. base who denies him rights 769.6
J. fascinated by anonymity of Christians 123.25
J. is practical Christian 510.2
to Christian, J. is obdurate man 510.1
**Jewish:** J. man with parents alive is a fifteen-year-old boy 510.3
J. moral seriousness 876.10
**Jews:** J. generally give value 510.5
**jilted:** better be courted and j. than never courted 195.2
one must forget being j. or pretend to 786.3
**job:** j. never started takes longest to finish 283.4
**jobs:** when white-collar people get j. 1059.6
**join:** if two lives j., there is oft a scar 560.10
**joined:** what God hath j. let not man put asunder 260.2
**joint:** j. undertakings must benefit both sides 187.2

**joke**: clumsy jesting is no j. 434.1
gentle dullness ever loves a j. 434.21
las' man that makes a j. owns it 434.9
surgery needed to get j. into Scotch mind 845.2
vulgar j.: a subtle and spiritual idea 434.7
**jokes**: differing taste in j. strains affections 434.10
for ten j. thou hast an hundred enemies 434.26
he that j. confesses 434.15
**journalism**: glory of j. is its transience 623.18
in America j. governs for ever and ever 34.76
in Britain j. extension of conversation 623.24
j. allows readers to witness history 341.11
j. is meeting challenge of filling space 623.30
j. is popular mainly as fiction 623.5
j. realizes truth is fluid, not solid 623.17
trouble with daily j. 623.23
**journalists**: j. tell public which way cat is jumping 623.26
**journey**: agreeable companion on a j. is as good as a carriage 151.21
count every step, you make j. long 6.9
j. of thousand miles begins with step 73.1
man knows his companion in a long j. 497.2
**joy**: all who j. would win must share it 407.20
better to weep at j. than j. at weeping 1045.10
excess of j. weeps; of sorrow, laughs 524.1
God grants j. or power, not both 713.16
heaven wills that sorrow follow j. 911.36
illusory j. worth more than real sorrow 407.30
inch of j. surmounts a span of grief 523.21
j. and sorrow equally pass away 983.18
j. at eventide if day spent fruitfully 6.20
j. cometh in the morning 1045.1
j. consists in forgetting life 502.14
j. is hard for being pure and delicate 407.10
j. of life is to put out one's power 502.13
j. seems normal course of life in nature 43.7
j. that is dead weighs heavy 407.73
j. without labour is base 1058.61
my j. of living is in the battles of life 407.106
no beautifier like wish to scatter j. 517.9
no peace in changing waves of j., despair 962.1
Oh who can tell the range of j. 20.6
only hope of j. is in human relations 787.10
silence is the perfectest herald of j. 407.99
sorrow before j. better than after it 911.42
sorrows remembered sweeten present j. 911.37
temper j. in fear of changed fortune 316.6
the world, so various, hath neither j. nor love 1060.1
there is no j. but calm 982.10
thing of beauty is a j. forever 70.23
to get full value of j. you must divide it 887.5
to possess is past the instant we achieve the j. 710.5
to win j. through struggle is better than to yield to melancholy 279.10
tomorrow's j. is possible only if today's makes way for it 115.18
true j. is the earnest we have of heaven 407.32
we give j. to the circumstance 127.4
well of j. is poisoned for those out of whom an upset stomach speaks 1004.23
what's a j. to one is nightmare to other 407.19
when you jump for j., beware that no one moves the ground from beneath your feet 407.68
who binds j. to self destroys winged life 407.16
wise man sings his j. in his heart 407.109
world hath failed to impart j. 247.1
your j. is your sorrow unmasked 407.47
**joy's**: j. smile is closer to tears than laughter 407.54
**joylessness**: j., not joy, is the mother of debauchery 733.8
**joys**: bitter ending awaits lawless j. 1023.21
great j. weep, great sorrows laugh 911.41
j. are often tender shadows of sorrows 407.8
j. impregnate; sorrows bring forth 911.4
j. may make a journey and still abide 669.8
live life as it were spoil, pluck the j. 511.5
man fond of counting troubles, not j. 249.4
oh, the wild j. of living 690.2
present j. are more to flesh and blood 407.34
remembered j. are never past 574.18
undeserved j. are they that sing 407.108
**judge**: do not j., and you will never be mistaken 513.9
don't hear one and j. two 513.4
don't j. man until you walk in his moccasins 513.1
j. is condemned when criminal acquitted 515.37
j. men by what their opinions made of them 649.16
j. not, that ye be not judged 203.3
j. should not be young 512.8
men j. men by their fashion and fortune 335.18
no one should be j. in his own cause 515.38
there is a tendency to j. a race, nation, group, by its least worthy members 769.9
to an incompetent j. I may be silent 512.4
to j. a man, ask about concept of humanity if he were its sole representative 513.5
to j., get away from what one is judging 514.7
we j. others by an image we have formed of ourselves 513.7
we j. wrong if we do not feel right 1053.29
we must j. men by present actions 224.24
when innocence trembles, it condemns the j. 475.14

you shall j. a man by friends, foes 286.7
**judges:** j. are elderly men likely to hate analysis 512.7
j. must also be performers 204.1
j. must beware of hard constructions 512.2
robes of all good j. that ever lived could not cover iniquity of one corrupt judge 512.3
**judgest:** thou j. another, condemnest thyself 203.4
**judgeth:** as a man is inwardly so he j. outwardly 514.23
**judging:** interest, prejudice take away power of j. 514.9
without informing himself to utmost, one can't acquit himself of j. amiss 514.13
**judgment:** an advantage in j. we yield to none 514.16
at twenty, will rules; at forty, j. 537.7
don't wait for last j.; it's every day 809.6
everyone complains of memory, none of j. 514.11
for learning suspended j., best discipline is philosophy 688.35
for right j., it's essential to see good qualities before pronouncing on bad 514.2
good j. not to rely wholly on oneself 514.6
hasty j. first step to recantation 514.20
in j. be ye not too confident 514.3
in success we gain reputation for j. 938.10
j. is not always required 749.6
j. is the extent of mind's illumination 514.12
knowledge is treasure, j. the treasurer 514.18
most have ears, but few have j. 683.2
most people suspend j. 514.4
nothing of greater value than power of j. 514.1
of all passions, fear weakens j. most 340.25
rightness of j. is bitterness to the heart 514.5
the j. is proper for all, has oar in all 514.15
the people make best j. in long run 675.8
to live, in itself, a value j. 1019.2
too much anxiety about j. is fatal 514.10
ultimate cynicism is to suspend j. so you are not judged 514.14
we praise or blame, whichever exhibits j. 514.17
you can't depend on j. when imagination is out of focus 448.29
**judgments:** ignorance delivers j. on all things 445.32
j. as watches, each believes his own 514.19
our j. vary according to the time we think is left us to live 514.8
spirit of Oath runs beside crooked j. 635.4
**judiciary:** j. is a fine lot of cross, indignant men 512.5
**jujitsu:** special j. to overcome every strong man 713.56
**June:** J. may be had by the poorest comer 848.30
what is so rare as a day in J. 848.29
**jungle:** j. is a place where everything grows 23.2
**Jupiter:** J. is slow looking into his notebook 809.14
**jurisdiction:** j. given not for judge but litigant 61.8
**jury:** j. may in the sworn twelve have a thief 515.44
**just:** be j. before you're generous 515.46
be j. in views: move among sword-points 453.5
if j. they are better than clever 515.49
impossible to be j. if one not generous 515.42
in a j. cause the weak beat the strong 109.15
it's harder to be j. toward oneself 857.4
j. and unjust things sanctioned by custom 210.28
j. are the ways of God 385.51
j. cause is not ruined by a few mistakes 109.4
j. cause needs no interpreting 525.22
j. cause never lacks good arguments 109.7
j. man walks humbly in presence of God 489.15
men are too unstable to be j. 515.7
no man can be j. who is not free 515.53
only actions of the j. smell sweet 224.35
right that j. should be obeyed 636.3
to possess eyes and a j. imagination 514.21
we become j. by performing j. actions 224.1
when you cannot be j. through virtue, be so through pride 515.22
**justice:** absolute j. denies freedom 361.4
administrators of j. are like a cat set to take care of a cheese 512.10
armed with more than steel: j. of quarrel 816.16
at times even j. brings harm with it 515.48
basis of government is j., not pity 393.69
between friends there is no need of j. 363.9
brand of j. can't be indelibly imprinted 983.2
clemency is the support of j. 577.5
death by j. is ignominious 761.5
difficult to do j. to others 515.20
do not expect j. where might is right 354.17
each loves j. in the affairs of another 515.25
even, j. is as the sun on a flat plain 515.30
extreme j. is often unjust 515.39
fairness with one's own enables one to do j. in the state 515.47
generosity is the flower of j. 373.6
in government, j. means force, virtue 515.34
injustice all around is j. 475.12
injustice easy to bear; what stings is j. 515.31
it is from reason that j. springs 391.33
it is not j. that holds a balance 114.8
j. balances the beauty in the world 515.51
j. comes not without council to the bow 515.8
j. condemns not even Devil wrongfully 515.15

j., custodian of the world's errors 515.4
j. delayed is democracy denied 515.28
j. discreet; injustice makes noise 515.40
j. divine mends not slow pace for cries 809.12
j., injustice change with climate 515.35
j. is blind an' deef an' has wooden leg 515.10
j. is impartiality 515.45
j. is last concern of universe 515.29
j. is not a mincing-machine but a compromise 515.12
j. is the great interest of man on earth 515.52
j. is the right of the weakest 515.26
j. is truth in action 515.27
j. is violent to the party offending 515.9
j. like a train that's nearly always late 515.54
j.: my being allowed to do whatever I like 475.1
j.: not to do wrong to fellow men 515.5
j. should remove her bandage to distinguish between vicious and unfortunate 515.23
j. substituted for instinct in civil state 131.23
j. without force is impotent 354.16
keep alive j., much blame will pass you by 515.14
knowledge without j. is cunning 520.55
laws of j. bind oppressor and oppressed 809.13
liberty plucks j. by the nose 534.41
many set high show of honor yet break j. 438.1
most may be done by impartial j. 515.18
no such thing as j. in the abstract 515.13
nobody can give you j. 853.5
our sense of j. sleeps till others have been aroused by sense of injustice 515.2
rigid j. is the greatest injustice 515.16
rigorous authority, j.: kindness of kings 825.16
source of j. was fear of injustice 515.21
the more laws, the less j. 525.32
there is no real force without j. 354.15
there is one principle of j.: the interest of the stronger 515.36
triumph of j. is the only peace 515.24
we love j. greatly, and just men little 515.41
we will not be satisfied until j. rolls down like waters 83.14
where might is master, j. is servant 354.5
why not confidence in j. of the people 675.12
without j., courage is weak 192.16
**justifiable:** all bad precedents began as j. measures 525.12
**justification:** people can praise anything and find j. 775.5
**justifies:** guilty man j. himself before accusation 403.8
**justify:** he who must j. his existence by own efforts is in eternal bondage to himself 314.5
**juvenile:** j. appraisals of other juveniles make up in clarity what they lack in charity 121.18
j. delinquency provides adults with fantasies 201.7

## K

**keep:** k. it for seven years, you'll find use for it 1016.3
to k. demands as much skill as to win 710.3
**kept:** strongly spent is synonymous with k. 502.11
**kettle:** pan says to k.: avaunt, black brows 203.12
**keyhole:** every age has k. to which eye is pasted 296.17
**kick:** if you k. a man he kicks you back again 783.2
**kill:** k. oneself or keep silent about life 941.3
must we k. to prevent any wicked 516.10
not by wrath does one k. but by laughter 523.18
nothing is done until men are prepared to k. one another if it is not done 735.24
ridiculous to k. for rulers' quarrel 1035.78
touching may k., keeping away may possess 710.17
we k. because we're afraid of our shadow 1035.68
we k. everybody with our deeds 516.6
**killer's:** sword is but a tool in k. hand 516.12
**killing:** art of creation is older than art of k. 198.40
to live without k. could electrify world 516.9
what can you do by k. 516.5
**kills:** each man k. the thing he loves 548.246
man who k. himself today, would have wished to live had he waited a week 941.16
one k. a man, one is an assassin; one k. everybody, one is a god 516.11
whom man k., God restoreth to life 516.7
**kin:** less danger from wiles of stranger if one's own k., kith were more fun to be with 332.22
one touch of nature makes whole world k. 431.23
**kind:** be ye k. one to another 357.2
do not ask me to be k. 517.16
everyone k. to those weaker than themselves 517.2
fellow-feeling makes one wondrous k. 22.3
gift, with k. countenance, is double 382.11
having anything k. to say, we feel shame 886.1
I must be cruel, only to be k. 883.7
k. hearts are more than coronets 517.23
men are cruel, but man is k. 517.22
not necessarily natural that fondness for own k. lead to subjection of others 456.1

we can't be k. to each other for an hour 686.13
who does a kindness is not always k. 224.29
**kind-hearted:** majority of men are secretly k. 206.17
**kindness:** accomplish by k. what you can't by force 517.15
best friend knows how to show, accept k. 517.21
bird thinks it a k. to take fish in air 56.13
hated hand makes k. odious 517.7
k.: brief preface to volumes of exaction 517.5
k. brings forth k. always 517.20
k. can become its own motive 517.12
k. effects more than severity 517.3
k. for selfish end merits no thanks 881.3
k. imagines others' joys, suffering as own 517.11
k. that gazes in a mirror turns to stone 881.5
nameless, unremembered acts of k. 517.25
set a high value on spontaneous k. 517.13
unseasonable k. gets no thanks 517.10
violence is just where k. is vain 1024.1
word of k. is better than a fat pie 517.18
**kindnesses:** dearest k. are fatal 538.38
men not prone to requite k. 782.3
**kindred:** him that is poor all his k. scorn 712.17
**king:** authority forgets a dying k. 223.13
better have as k. vulture advised by swans 825.18
cat may look on a k. 773.11
first who was k. was a fortunate soldier 518.15
I am a k. since I know how to rule myself 856.1
if you can't pretend, you can't be k. 726.15
it is no bad thing to be a k. 518.4
k. can't last if people start thinking 518.7
k. is a hitchin' post f'r pollyticians 518.2
k. is he who has laid fear aside 518.10
k. without clemency is enemy of state 125.6
not all the water can wash balm off k. 518.11
sail, quoth the k.; hold, saith the wind 616.29
to call k. "Prince" is pleasing 773.21
within crown of k. keeps Death his court 825.24
you are a k. by your own fire-side 420.5
**king's:** k. power founded on people's folly 825.19
subject's love is k. best guard 825.8
**kingdom:** good mind possesses a k. 491.27
**kingly:** k. office is entitled to no respect 518.14
**kings:** a crown it is that seldom k. enjoy 183.21
all k. is mostly rapscallions 518.13
fear created gods; audacity created k. 518.1
foremost art of k. is to endure hatred 518.9
if men are shrewd, they may serve k. 197.6
k. have headaches like other people 825.6
k. have worship of world, but no repose 518.12
k. need company of the intelligent 518.8
k., women, vines embrace what is nearest 1055.115
no reliance placed on friendship of k. 983.19
priests put crowns on thieves, called k. 125.4
soon only five k. in world—king of England and four k. in pack of cards 518.3
we owe obedience to our k.; but esteem, affection are due only to their virtue 825.15
what are k., when regiment is gone 518.6
**kiss:** death is given in a k. 538.38
hatred can be concealed in countenance, k. 410.20
k. can be a comma, a question mark 519.5
k., make up: live to fight another day 766.14
k. originated when first male reptile licked first female 519.2
k. was not so wonderful as dreams I had 519.7
k., when all is said, what is it 519.6
when women k. it always reminds one of prizefighters shaking hands 1055.100
**kisses:** k. are a better fate than wisdom 519.1
k. of an enemy are deceitful 363.19
when a rogue k. you, count your teeth 519.3
**kissing:** k. don't last: cookery do 519.4
**kitchen:** fat k., lean will 1049.6
**kitten:** trouble with k. is that it becomes a cat 41.21
**knew:** if a man k. himself he would despise the ignorant notions others might form 868.29
if men k. themselves, God would pardon 868.22
**knock:** few sounds exceed interest of k. at door 426.18
to k. a thing down is a delight 26.7
**knocks:** one k. oneself on the sore place 1032.1
**know:** advantage at times to forget what we k. 574.29
all ignorance toboggans into k. 445.9
beast does but k., man knows he knows 778.9
better be ignorant than half k. matter 445.27
difficulty of maxim "k. thyself": man remembers face of his friend, but not his own 868.30
dogs bark at a person they do not k. 720.8
each thinks he must k. best about himself 19.16
full wise is he that can himselven k. 868.6
grieve not that men do not k. you 1001.5
I k. by my own pot how others boil 319.21
I'd like to k. what this show's about 536.47
if man does not k. himself, how should he know his functions and powers 868.21
if you would k. aught, be gay before it 1053.65
impossible for one person to k. another so well he can dispense with belief 1001.7
k. self and perhaps you'll avoid illness 752.8
k. thine opportunity 650.7
k. thyself: maxim as pernicious as ugly 868.12
k.-what more important than k.-how 765.12
k. who you are; adorn self accordingly 265.6
little I k., I owe to my ignorance 445.16

man may do or k. but little 9.18
more crucial than what we k. is what we do not want to k. 445.17
more I read, more I am able to affirm that I k. nothing 520.69
not to wish to k. worse than not to k. 445.24
nothing I would not rather k. than not 520.33
O might man k. day's end ere it come 366.29
rather k. nothing than half-k. much 520.49
right to k. is like right to live 520.62
things we k. best haven't been taught us 520.68
thirst to k., understand, is excellent 529.21
those who k. the least of others think the highest of themselves 163.5
to each belongs its measure, best to k. 972.8
to k. a little often brings ridicule 520.7
to k. a man is to have loved, hated him 787.5
to k. is to accede to vision 76.21
to k. is to grasp end realized through changes 115.10
to k. little makes man suspect much 257.2
to k. oneself, assert oneself 868.5
to k. others is learned; k. self, wise 868.15
to k. thyself is to be known by another 868.26
to k. what none k., read things year later 520.18
we hate people because we don't k. them 720.3
we k. little, but have presentiment of much 448.24
we k. ourselves chiefly by hearsay 442.13
we k. too much and feel too little 282.32
we k. well only what we are deprived of 234.2
we k. what we are, not what we may be 366.30
we ought to k. a little about everything 520.53
what can we reason but from what we k. 778.27
who does not k. one thing knows another 520.38
wisest professed to k. he knew nothing 520.46
**know-how:** know-what more important than k. 765.12
**knowing:** I brag of not k. something 520.19
k. what is useful makes a wise man 520.23
k. what thou knowest not is omniscience 520.25
more learning than k. in world 842.16
nothing worth k. can be taught 520.74
speculators, boast not of k. things 688.18
step from k. to doing rarely taken 9.20
**knowledge:** action is the proper fruit of k. 9.23
all can acquire my k., but not my heart 282.17
all k. is of itself of some value 520.33
any k. I acquire today 520.67
any kind of k. is its own reward 520.48
as our k. increases, our ignorance unfolds 520.36
beauty, good, and k. are three sisters 387.15
conscious you're ignorant is first step to k. 445.10
contradiction is first step in evolution of k. 51.29
conversation is not a search after k. 185.18
desire for k. increases with acquisition 520.63
desire of k. natural feeling of mankind 520.32
diffidence is the better part of k. 998.3
doubt is not below k., but above it 897.1
even k. has to be in fashion 335.13
expanding k. we but increase ignorance 520.45
experience of anybody is real k. 319.6
extensive k. needful to thinking people 520.35
finer wits say k. is the good 520.54
fruit of tree of k. always drives man from paradise 520.29
if little k. dangerous, who's out of danger 520.28
if we value k., we must be free 520.64
ignorance irritates man, k. cloys 684.1
it is the province of k. to speak 1053.34
k. accompanied by emotion, purpose 520.72
k. acquired under compulsion 277.62
k. can be communicated, but not wisdom 1053.32
k. comes, but wisdom lingers 1053.64
k. digested is k. swallowed with appetite 520.21
k. equalizes social condition of man 520.15
k. for the sake of k.! this is inhuman 991.137
k. hangs on regularity of experiences 319.48
k. has come of age, and religion must respect her as a friend 790.12
k. has outstripped character development 277.19
k. humanizes mankind 720.12
k. is in the head; wisdom, in the heart 1053.29
k. is not an abstract homogeneous good 520.2
k. is of two kinds 520.34
k. is power 520.1
k. is power; dupes of this saying will read until their initiative is stunned 520.13
k. is proud that he has learned so much 1053.15
k. is recognition of something absent 520.60
k. is shelter in advanced age 520.8
k. is the fountain of human liberty 520.71
k. is the great sun in the firmament 520.70
k. is the parent of love 1053.28
k. is treasure, judgment the treasurer 514.18
k. is true organ of sight, not the eyes 520.52
k. is two-fold 520.10
k. may give weight 1.2
k. of the world acquired in world 319.7

k. the best protection against prejudice 520.58
k., timber not to be used till seasoned 520.26
k.: to hold to what you know, admit when you do not know 520.12
k. which stops at what it does not know is highest k. 520.9
k. without integrity is dangerous 489.12
k. without justice is cunning 520.55
leisure and curiosity might make advances in k. 530.8
man can reveal to you only what already lies in dawning of your k. 959.11
man is not weak, k. is more than force 520.31
man may do well with little k. in company 185.21
man seldom has so much k. of another as necessary to make instruction useful 19.20
manners must adorn k. 559.4
many men are stored full of unused k. 520.3
many will run to and fro, k. will grow 985.5
merit and k. will not gain hearts 578.1
no man's k. can go beyond his experience 319.36
no purifier like k. in this world 868.3
nowhere is k. as varied as in a newspaper 623.3
our k. is always superficial and imperfect 520.39
pedantry is the dotage of k. 842.23
pocket all your k. with your watch 594.4
power is used to make k. a slave 758.10
raft of k. ferries worst sinner to safety 520.4
sin, guilt, neurosis: fruit of tree of k. 520.44
special k. required to describe picture, fix car 520.43
step by which men add to their k. is step also by which they can control other men 520.41
to be fond of learning is to be near k. 529.20
to be proud of k. is to be blind with light 520.22
to conceal limits of k. don't overstep them 162.14
to k. belongs rational k. of temporal things 1053.5
to master any branch of k. you must master those next to it 520.27
traveler without k. is bird without wings 985.32
we are least open to precise k. concerning things we are most vehement about 262.9
we owe our k. to those who have differed 256.2
what harm in getting k. from a sot, pot 520.57
who acquires k. and doesn't practise it 520.59
who displays his k. shows his ignorance 185.30
who increaseth k. increaseth sorrow 520.5
why do we make so much of k. 520.20
wisdom sets bounds even to k. 520.50
without k., life but the shadow of death 520.47
zeal will do more than k. 1066.3
zeal without k. is fire without light 1066.2

**known:** he that has done nothing has k. nothing 9.12
if k. by everybody you know nobody 330.39
not to be k. to do anything, never do it 798.12
nothing can be loved, hated, unless k. 1000.11
ten lands are sooner k. than one man 1001.21
what shall I do to be forever k. 798.10

**knows:** courage of all one really k. comes late 489.19
he k. little who will tell his wife all 560.39
he k. nothing and thinks he k. everything 705.70
he that k. himself k. others 868.7
he that k. least presumes most 445.12
he that k. little often repeats it 445.13
he that travels much k. much 985.20
he who k. nothing doubts nothing 113.13
no man can justly censure, condemn another, for no man truly k. another 797.4
sea can be fathomed; who k. heart of man 1001.16
what man k. is at war with what he wants 167.4
who k. only his side of the case, k. little of that 613.5

# L

**labels:** l. save the trouble of thinking 928.2

**labor:** Adam won for us the curse of l. 1058.68
by l. fire is got out of a stone 279.2
direction of l. rigid in totalitarian society 978.4
don't condescend to unskilled l. 1058.2
free nation has independent l. unions 1006.6
God sells good things at the price of l. 1058.49
great is he who enjoys fruits of his l. 1058.63
honest l. bears a lovely face 1058.17
l. of one kind destroys man's spirits 1058.53
l.-saving devices have brought boredom 960.21
l. that has reference to a want 1058.37
l. without joy and sorrow is base 1058.61
life of l. makes drudges, not men 1058.23
love l.: if not for food, then for physic 1058.57
much cant of common interests of capital, l. 106.1
obliged to l. whether paid or not 1006.4
only by l. can thought be made healthy 1058.60
pleasure to be got out of freedom is l. 530.11
rest is the sauce of l. 805.6
slave of l. wheel, what to him is Plato 1059.5
there is visible l. and invisible l. 1058.43

to l. is the lot of man 1058.39
true success is to l. 279.22
we put love where we have put l. 1058.22
where there's l. there's not always life 1058.21
why should life all l. be 1058.65
**Labor Day:** L. D. symbolizes determination to achieve economic freedom for average man 418.7
**laborer:** if l. complain, set him to do nothing 444.14
**laboring:** sleep of a l. man is sweet 899.3
**labors:** eliminate needless wants, and l. will reduce themselves 695.6
may share l. of great but not spoil 398.1
**lack:** we are less dissatisfied when we l. many things 236.21
**ladder:** kick away l., one's feet left dangling 56.8
who would climb l. must begin at bottom 938.9
**ladies:** in America there are no l. except salesladies 34.53
l. of fashion starve love to feed pride 335.11
take a hundred l. of quality 52.2
**lady:** he injures fair l. who beholds her not 464.4
in all woes there is a l. 1055.58
l. wants to be dressed like everybody else 265.14
**lady's:** l. heart doesn't agree with beggar's purse 1055.69
l. imagination is very rapid 1055.6
nothing so variable as a l. headdress 405.1
when a l. erotic life is vexed 885.22
**laity:** professions are conspiracies against l. 1029.11
**lamb:** no absolute will make lion lie down with l. 26.3
**lament:** l. not the dead but the living 603.6
l., to win tear from audience, is worthwhile 156.1
**lamentation:** no advantage to be won from grim l. 911.20
**lamp:** Thy word is a l. unto my feet 78.1
when l. shattered, light lies dead 218.117
**land:** first man to fence in l. 740.19
he who would be the tongue of this wide l. 702.66
if a man own l., the l. owns him 740.5
if you would find yourself, look to the l. 982.11
it was prices to them, never looked at l. 106.4
l. abused when seen as commodity we own 174.4
l. created as place for steamers to visit 833.1
man is rooted to the l. 421.1
this is my own, my native l. 421.7
**landlords:** l. love to reap where they never sowed 106.6
**landmark:** remove not the ancient l. 979.3
**landmarks:** these are brave, free days of destroyed l. 439.1
**landscape:** difference between l. and l. is small 693.4
l. should belong to the people who see it 615.6
**lane:** it is a long l. that has no turning 116.2
**language:** a dog we know is better company than a man whose l. we do not understand 151.19
as difficult to be inconsistent in l. as consistent in conduct 176.5
do not travel before learning l. 985.13
enemy of clear l. is insincerity 521.18
eyes have one l. everywhere 323.3
hardest to translate tempo of style from one l. to another 521.17
idea does not pass from one l. to another without change 441.35
if l. be not in accordance with the truth, affairs cannot be carried to success 521.3
l. is by nature communal 521.11
l. is little better than croak of fowls 521.8
l. is the archives of history 521.7
l., not desires, sets men at variance 250.12
l. veils ideas, but softens, refines them 521.9
mere elegance of l. produces empty renown 935.18
next to him who violates the laws of his country is he who violates the l. 521.13
no l. expresses all human comprehension 521.19
only living l.: one in which we think 521.15
ours is a precarious l. 521.25
pleasing by flattery makes a l. soft; fear of offending by truth, circuitous 521.14
poet is in love with l. 702.3
those ideas which are least our own are most easily expressed in l. 441.4
to speak without speaking a particular l. 148.11
transfuse from one l. into another the creations of a poet 521.23
use any l., you say only what you are 148.5
we use l. of past to grasp present 521.21
who would recognize the unhappy if grief had no l. 1045.6
**languages:** colors speak all l. 142.1
l. are the pedigree of nations 521.12
to teacher of l. world but place of words 521.4
**lapidary:** in l. inscriptions a man is not on oath 424.6
**large:** I am l., I contain multitudes 462.6
**larger:** l. a roof, more snow it collects 1041.43
**largesse:** man reduced to vassalage by l. 430.30
**lascivious:** twenty l. turtles found ere chaste man 120.9
**last:** old and young, all on l. cruise 600.18
somebody has to have the l. word 51.7

there may be nobility in being l. 773.20
**lasting:** nothing is l. that is feigned 726.4
**late:** better hours too soon than minute too l. 759.5
better l. than before anybody has invited you 759.2
hate friends who come too l. to help 972.5
he that riseth l. must trot all day 71.4
only habitual l. riser, up early, takes in full flavor of nature 599.1
**latest:** audience always applauds l. song most 632.7
**laugh:** absurdities have crumbled before a l. 523.23
all of those I love make me l. 548.5
America has always gone for the loud l. 34.65
anything awful makes me l. 523.14
better to l. at life than lament over it 536.111
call truth false if not accompanied by l. 407.82
horse-l. worth ten thousand syllogisms 523.17
I durst not l. for fear of taking bad air 29.1
if I l., 'tis that I may not weep 524.2
it is God's giving if we l. or weep 407.103
l., and the world laughs with you 524.6
man makes her l., woman feels protected 1055.9
man who cannot l. is fit for treasons 523.3
men let you abuse, if you make them l. 434.3
one can know a man from his l. 523.7
people betray character in what they l. at 523.10
same facts that make one l. make one weep 524.4
to l. is proper to the man 523.21
we are in the world to l. 523.22
we l., cry—then feebler l., then die 524.5
we must l. before we are happy 523.13
**laugh's:** l. wisest answer to all that's queer 523.16
**laughed:** he is not l. at who laughs at self first 523.9
wasted day is one in which we haven't l. 523.5
who has once l. cannot be altogether bad 523.4
world became afraid of man when he l. 523.26
**laughing:** few worth loving who are not worth l. at 4.2
house of mourning is also house of l. 603.9
learn weeping and gain l. 911.19
one afraid of l. at friend lacks love 363.58
**laughs:** he who l. best to-day also l. last 523.20
no one laughable who l. at himself 4.7
no one more sad than he who l. too much 523.24
when a man l. he shows all his faults 523.8
**laughter:** all comedian has to show is echo of l. 143.1
beauty of world is of l. and anguish 1060.35
even in l. the heart is sorrowful 523.1
in l. evil is absolved by its own bliss 523.19
l.: interior convulsion producing distortion of features and inarticulate noises 523.2
l. is higher than all pain 523.12
l. is not a bad beginning for friendship 523.27
l., tears, turn wheel of same sensibility 876.5
not by wrath does one kill but by l. 523.18
only l., love are worth wear of winning 363.16
our sincerest l. with pain is fraught 523.25
sudden glory maketh grimaces called l. 523.11
unextinguished l. shakes the skies 3.7
**laundress:** l. washeth her own smock first 493.2
**laurel:** I find the l. also bears a thorn 424.9
**laurels:** do we want l. or that no one else shall have any 384.12
**lavishness:** l. is not generosity 373.4
**law:** by transgressing men have kept the l. 1063.19
can't abolish by l. or axe desires of men 236.29
cultivate respect not for l. but right 816.24
defiance of l. is surest road to tyranny 525.46
even when no l., there is conscience 171.24
every community gets kind of l. enforcement it insists on 703.8
every new time will give its l. 525.36
great cases make bad l. 525.42
highest virtue is always against the l. 1025.22
if there isn't a l., there will be 525.24
in l., what plea so tainted and corrupt 525.61
it takes a hundred years to make a l., then a hundred years to get rid of it 525.6
l. and reason only things between us and tyranny 525.25
l. cannot exist without government 525.58
l. cannot persuade where cannot punish 525.28
l., introduced without reason, has become reasonable 525.53
l. is a causeway on which a citizen may walk safely 525.9
l. is an edifice sheltering all of us 525.30
l. is experience developed by reason 525.55
l. is good, if a man use it lawfully 525.7
l. is made to exploit those who do not understand it 525.10
l. is passionless 525.3
l. is the last result of human wisdom 525.45
l. is the witness of our moral life 525.41
l. is true embodiment of everything that's excellent 512.6
l. rules throughout existence 1010.4
language of l. must not be foreign 525.38
man for whom l. exists is a tame man 525.66
man observes l. of God by applying reason 778.6
no grievance fit for redress by mob l. 591.7
no l. quite appropriate for all 525.50
no man above l. or below it 525.56
nobody has a more sacred obligation to obey

the l. that those who make the l. 525.2
none can enforce l. not supported by people 525.43
opinion of all lawyers, unanimous cry of nation, good of state are l. 525.69
order and l. have a cost 526.3
our bodies can be mobilized by l. 440.2
people say l. but they mean wealth 525.20
people should fight for their l. 525.39
power that keeps cities together is l. 906.4
respect for l. related to size of paycheck 526.2
rigorous l. is often rigorous injustice 525.64
there's l. and order in everything 526.1
unjust l. is itself a species of violence 525.31
victim to too severe a l. is considered martyr 515.6
we must not make a scarecrow of the l. 525.62
when I refuse to obey an unjust l. 779.6
wherever l. ends, tyranny begins 525.51
who makes his l. a curse dies by his l. 809.5
who saves his country violates no l. 671.16
who takes it upon himself to break bad l. 525.18
who to himself is l. no l. doth need 873.3
**lawless:** bitter ending awaits l. joys 1023.21
**laws:** brain may devise l. for the blood 39.31
certitude of l. is an obscurity of judgment backed by authority 525.67
don't change l. to change customs 210.20
first of all l. is to respect the l. 760.12
good l., disobeyed, not good government 525.4
good l. lead to better; bad l. to worse 525.57
good l. teach men to trample bad l. 525.54
good men must not obey l. too well 391.16
I know not whether l. be right 729.7
if soul cannot breathe, l. are too tight 534.4
it ain't no sin if you crack a few l. 525.70
l. alone cannot secure freedom of expression 977.5
l. are like spider's webs 525.63
l. are never as effective as habits 404.18
l. are silent in time of war 1035.16
l. can't be enforced against master 995.6
l. cannot carry themselves into practice 393.44
l. grind the poor, rich men rule law 525.35
l. hand in hand with progress of mind 525.44
l. of gravity, chemistry, botany 843.8
l. that only threaten are soon scorned 525.13
l. too gentle are seldom obeyed 525.27
many l. make bad men, bad men many l. 525.48
necessity knows no l. 617.19
no worse torture than torture of l. 512.2
run against the grain of a nation's genius and see where you get with your l. 525.49
some sense their own l. within them 525.40
strict execution best way to repeal bad l. 525.37
the more l., the less justice 525.32
the more l., the more offenders 525.29
things have l. as well as men 638.4
to interpret l. is to corrupt them 525.68
unwritten l. more fixed than the written 525.60
useless l. weaken necessary ones 525.52
we get good people to restrain bad l. 525.14
where l. are not supreme, demagogues arise 230.1
who lives in solitude may make own l. 908.43
**lawsuit:** lean compromise better than fat l. 160.4
**lawyer:** behold a l., an honest man 525.26
deceive not thy physician, confessor, l. 221.9
hide nothing from confessor, l., doctor 162.6
poet never interpreted nature as freely as l. interprets truth 525.33
**lawyer's:** l. truth is not truth but consistency 525.65
**lawyers:** if no bad people there would be no good l. 525.17
l., painters, can change white to black 525.16
**laziness:** don't yield to that alluring witch, l. 527.5
doom of l. to be inactive without ease 527.6
failure not our only punishment for l. 527.8
flee l., it ends in sorrow of repentance 527.1
l. travels slowly, poverty overtakes him 527.3
**lazy:** l. are always wanting to do something 527.9
l. boy, warm bed are difficult to part 95.3
**lead:** men by sympathetic attractions l. nations 528.6
necessary to follow in order to l. 647.2
**leader:** efficiency of the national l. 615.5
l. is a dealer in hope 528.15
l. is in common mass of matter lost 528.9
l. leaves in others the will to carry on 528.11
l. must know, must know he knows 528.19
people, like sheep, tend to follow l. 350.1
real l. is content to point the way 528.14
weaknesses of the many make l. possible 528.10
**leaders:** most l. merely follow in front 528.7
who can look up to l. with ears to ground 528.2
**leaf:** fall of a l. is a whisper to the living 600.7
**leak:** small l. will sink a great ship 398.7
**leaky:** to try whether a vessel be l., we prove it with water before wine 749.7
**lean:** yond Cassius has a l. and hungry look 57.20
**leap:** who would l. high must take a long run 33.7
**learn:** freedom to l. first part of being free 529.15
it is safer to l. than teach 649.24
l. as if you'd never be able to master it 529.6
l. what you are and be such 868.23

men l. only what their passions allow 319.29
no dishonor to l. from others 19.35
old men still young enough to l. 646.2
some will never l. anything because they understand everything too soon 137.11
to l. is a pleasure common to all men 529.2
we l. geology morning after earthquake 202.1
we l. not for life but for the debating-room 154.12
we l. only from those we love 529.7
we l. to-day what our better advanced judgements will unteach us to-morrow 319.4
what you yourself don't l., you don't know 529.3
where there is desire to l., there is arguing 649.19
who can l. only by personal experience is too dull to l. anything important 529.12
worldly people rarely l. anything new 910.3

**learned:** I l. from my students more than from all 277.74
I've l. by mistakes, false assumptions 529.19
l. blockhead is worse than ignorant one 934.7
l. conversation: affectation of ignorant 185.37
l. discount deed, open soul of doer 601.2
l. fool is sillier than ignorant one 353.21
l. man: idler who kills time with study 842.38
l. man so ignorant he bought cow to ride 842.14
no profit to have l. well, if you neglect to do well 224.31
solemn ego accompanies the l. 842.11
to master torrent of life, l. man meditates 536.86
when l. men do stoop to learn 842.4
who seem l. to fools seem fools to l. 726.16
world would perish were all men l. 842.15

**learning:** devotee without l. is house without entrance 967.12
it is better to have wisdom without l. 1053.13
joy in l.: it enables me to teach 959.26
l. acquired in youth helps old age 520.40
l.: an ignorance distinguishing the studious 520.6
l. apart from nature is fractional 277.63
l. begets arrogance in fools 520.51
l. gained most on books by which printer lost 91.38
l. is but an adjunct to ourself 520.61
l. is for those fearing disagreeable action 842.1
l. is its own exceeding great reward 529.9
l.: knowledge of what none but learned know 842.19
l. makes man fit company for himself 277.29
l. nothing without cultivated manners 207.15
l. without liberty is always in vain 520.37
l. without thought is labour lost 520.11
little l. is a dangerous thing 520.56
make l. of books your own wisdom 529.16
more l. than knowing in the world 842.16
much l. does not teach understanding 277.38
my pleasure comes from l. something 407.106
nature's fire is all the l. I desire 616.13
no national frontiers to l. 520.30
to be fond of l. is to be near knowledge 529.20
what one has been long l. unwillingly, he unlearns with eagerness, haste 277.37
when l. one should not think of play 896.2
whoso neglects l. in his youth, loses the past and is dead for the future 277.25
wise man not ashamed of l. more 529.18
wisest men set in order results of l. 535.4

**learns:** youths know enough who know how to l. 529.1

**learnt:** to have l. feels like losing something 529.17

**leave:** to l. is to die a little 666.5

**lechery:** l. drink provokes, and unprovokes 266.57
some held eye to be instrument of l. 885.28

**lecturer:** duty of l.: give nugget of pure truth 959.29
l.: has hand in your pocket, tongue in your ear and faith in your patience 757.2

**left:** if your heart is on the l., don't carry your portfolio on the right 704.5

**leg:** man without l. does not value shoes 382.5

**legacies:** eras die, l. are left to strange police 42.4

**legal:** l. broom's a moral chimney-sweeper 525.11

**legends:** l. are lies which become history 417.17

**legislate:** one can't l. against the irrational itself 525.59

**legislation:** if all is well, l. is beneficial 790.76
in l. as in medicine, it's easier to show what does harm than what does good 525.15
public opinion may become l. 756.17

**legislative:** large l. bodies resolve into coteries 169.4

**legislators:** poets are unacknowledged l. of world 702.92

**legislature:** public opinion is stronger than the l. 756.22

**legs:** to modern girl, l. parts of success kit 885.19
what use good head if l. won't carry it 527.10

**leisure:** Beats a pilot study in use of l. 89.2
hard to keep secret, employ l., bear injury 243.1
I am Retired L. 807.4
increased means, l., two civilisers of man 131.8
life of l. is beautiful and ennobling 530.12
much l. merely a way to spend money 596.38
no high civilization exists without ample l. 530.1

serious l. not genius of Americans 530.5
when a man's busy, l. strikes him as pleasure 530.2
**leisured:** l. rebel most at interruption of routine 822.2
**lend:** friendship lasts if not asked to l. money 363.111
human species made of men who borrow, l. 94.4
**lender:** borrower is servant to the l. 94.2
neither a borrower nor a l. be 94.6
**leopard:** can Ethiopian change skin, or l., spots 442.7
**leopard's:** rain beats l. skin, does not wash out the spots 442.4
**less:** l. is more 892.2
**lesson:** pain, sterility, ennui teach l. 939.13
**lessons:** life is a succession of l. 319.18
**letter:** l. killeth, but spirit giveth life 541.1
**letters:** more than kisses, l. mingle souls 532.1
we destroy l., a beautiful breath of life 532.2
**lettuce:** l., like talk, needs oil to avoid friction 186.13
**levelers:** l. wish to level down 903.3
**lexicographer:** l.: does what he can to arrest, stiffen, and mechanize language 242.1
l.: writer of dictionaries, harmless drudge 242.4
**liar:** best l. makes the least lying go farthest 329.8
each lie is a sort of suicide in the l. 329.16
l. denies truth to others, not self 440.14
l. goes in fine clothes, rags 329.38
l. not believed even when he speaks truth 329.1
l. should have a good memory 329.34
miser and l. bargain quickly 103.12
to be thought a l., always tell the truth 993.21
when you find out a friend is a l. 329.19
**liars:** mischievous l.: those on verge of truth 329.21
**liberal:** essence of the l. outlook lies in how opinions are held 533.4
every boy and gal is l. or conservative 704.4
l. institutions stop being l. the moment they are soundly established 533.2
l. tells others what to do with their money 533.1
l. uses legs, hands at command of his head 533.3
l. wishes to replace existing evils with others 175.2
mellowing rigorist is pleasanter than tightening l. 175.8
that man has had a l. education whose body is the servant of his will 277.41
**liberality:** hand of l. stronger than arm of power 373.8
**liberals:** we l. know the poor are our equals in every sense except being equal to us 712.51
**liberation:** l. is not deliverance 534.18
**liberties:** country preserves l. if rulers warned that people preserve spirit of resistance 651.9
suppression of civil l. less horrifying than curtailment of freedom to profit 817.12
**libertine:** easier to make a saint out of a l. 834.11
l. life is not life of liberty 733.3
**liberty:** a gift deprives us of our l. 382.13
America established to maintain l. 34.80
American majority bar l. of opinion 725.6
as child, man's l. is concealed from him 361.3
by social contract man gains civil l. 906.17
corrupt nations love bondage more than l. 188.9
eternal vigilance is the price of l. 534.9
freedom of press a bulwark of l. 725.4
give l. to those not agreeing with us 977.16
give me l. or give me death 534.17
he that would make own l. secure must guard even enemy from oppression 534.31
hungry do not care about l. 534.10
if we must accept fate we must also affirm l. 860.3
in chains, laurels, l. knows only victory 534.33
in doubtful things, l. 118.1
irreverence is the champion of l. 504.5
knowledge is the fountain of human l. 520.71
l. a mockery if price is the destruction of those who are to enjoy l. 534.13
l. and democracy become unholy when dyed with innocent blood 1024.6
l. doesn't even do small things legally 534.3
l. exists in proportion to restraint 534.50
l. in democracy when all share rule 231.3
l. is a different kind of pain from prison 361.9
l. is hardest test inflicted on a people 534.48
l. is independence maintained by force 534.49
l. is its own reward 534.54
l. is itself the highest political end 534.2
l. is latitude the powerful accord to weak 534.15
l. is limitation of government power 534.53
l. is necessity's conscience 534.14
l. is the only true riches 361.24
l. is the right to do what laws permit 534.26
l. is the right to silence 817.4
l. is the soul's right to breathe 534.4
l. may do no more than stir up civil wars 534.8
l. means freedom to improve 534.57
l. means responsibility 534.42
l., motive for good, pretext for crime 534.1
l. never out of bounds or off limits 534.51
l. not as good in practice as in speech 534.34
l. of others extends mine to infinity 361.22
l. of the individual must be limited 361.40

l. plucks justice by the nose 534.41
l.: precious possession of imagination 534.5
l.: translation of declarations into action 534.56
l. without learning is always in peril 520.37
lean l. is better than fat slavery 534.12
libertine life is not life of l. 733.3
little l. on earth while tyrant in heaven 790.37
money is coined l. 596.14
most people want security, not l. 850.11
narrower the cage, sweeter the l. 107.2
observance of law is safeguard of l. 525.46
oh l., what crimes are done in your name 534.36
religions united with government inimical to l. 125.2
spirit of improvement not always of l. 783.26
spirit of l. not too sure it is right 534.16
they that give up l. to obtain safety 850.5
to renounce l. is to renounce being a man 534.39
to whom you tell your secrets you resign your l. 166.8
too little l. brings stagnation, and too much brings chaos 534.40
tree of l. refreshed by patriots' blood 813.27
we shall pay any price for survival of l. 534.20
wild l. breeds iron conscience 361.13
wise see in l. the potent Law of Laws 534.52
wolf says shepherd is destroyer of l. 534.23
word l. has served for destruction of l. 534.27
you cannot tear up ancient rootages and safely plant tree of l. 534.55

**libraries:** l.: first volume of book I want is out 535.5

**library:** a man's l. is a sort of harem 535.3
public l. shows vanity of human hopes 535.6
th' first thing to have in l. is a shelf 535.2

**lie:** fool can tell truth: sense is needed to l. 329.9
I know a creed is the shell of a l. 200.6
inability to l. is far from love of truth 993.17
l. always needs truth for a handle 329.5
l. faces God and shrinks from man 329.3
l. has no leg, but scandal has wings 840.2
l. is a very present help in trouble 329.43
l. is but the truth in masquerade 329.11
l. is handle that fits all sin's tools 329.25
l. needs great many more to make it good 329.42
l. of pipe dream is what gives us life 687.16
l. told well is immortal 992.19
l. which is half a truth is blackest l. 329.45
man who can't tell a l. thinks he is the best judge of one 329.48
masses will fall victims to a big l. 329.23
most common l.: one uttered to one's self 858.6
most striking difference between cat and l. is cat has only nine lives 329.47
never to l. is to have no lock to door 329.6
not one of us can l. or pretend 442.16
only a truthful man can l. to any purpose 992.2
paradox is a l. when told by kids 661.4
people l. because they don't remember 329.37
purposeful l.: worst an' mos' profitable 329.15
repetition doesn't transform l. into truth 329.35
single l. destroys whole reputation 329.20
there's a real love of a l. 329.7
we admit superiority of man we l. to 329.10
we l. loudest when we l. to ourselves 858.3
we perceive image of truth, possess a l. 992.16
when I l. down 71.2
who serves two masters has to l. to one 495.4
women l. so well that truth seems false to it 1055.17
you can't pray a l. 717.33

**lies:** Americans detest all l. except l. spoken in public or printed l. 329.26
art of living: knowing how to believe l. 536.90
cruellest l. told in silence 329.44
cursed be the social l. 906.21
don't use "ideals," use native word "l." 440.9
each day more l. eat into seed with which we are born 563.8
freedom means freedom from l. 361.35
if we live under l., it's difficult to see anything not having to do with these l. 329.28
l. are as communicative as fleas 992.10
l. are the religion of slaves 992.6
life is a system of half-truths and l. 329.27
man had rather a hundred l. told of him 162.10
no mask like truth to cover l. 221.4
no one l. as much as the indignant do 465.5
of l., false modesty is the most decent 438.4
one l. in words, gets bad reputation 329.46
sooner hate for truth than adore for l. 993.1
that l. are necessary to life is part of questionable character of existence 329.33
there are l., damned l., and statistics 925.2
to put faith in l. is the true atheism 410.15
truth cannot be erased; neither can l. 992.7
truth exists; only l. are invented 992.1
without l., man dies of despair, boredom 329.17

**life:** a man's l. is a continual allegory 536.60
aim of l. is to live 536.73
all l. is an experiment 973.3
all l.: the struggle, effort to be itself 314.8
all our l. is but a going out to death 538.5
all we do passes into great machine of l. 224.40
any man wants to be left alone with his l. 361.31
art is long, l. short 981.5
art, like l., should be free 53.117

art of l.: how to enjoy and endure 536.44
art teaches the significance of l. 53.85
behave in l. as if at a banquet 650.4
believe l. is worth living 76.9
believe more in l., fling less to moment 459.2
best sands of my l. getting into wrong end of hour-glass 646.3
best way to prepare for l. is to live 536.55
betrothed of l. is death 388.15
better a moment of l. than epoch-long unconsciousness of a stone 536.126
better to laugh at l. than lament over it 536.111
brief span of l. is hastening on 646.61
call l. you live today your own 114.10
cannot evaluate man's l. till he is dead 536.119
character of human l. is ambiguity 388.28
complete l. includes old age 537.12
death has no sting, but l. has 538.44
death is an instant, l. a long torment 538.32
death is ultimate horror of l. 218.59
death takes away commonplace of l. 218.119
death's stamp gives value to coin of l. 538.39
deem not l. a thing of consequence 536.66
determine quality of l. by its activities 10.1
difficult for man to realize his l. an art 536.29
do not fear death, but the inadequate l. 502.4
dost thou love l., do not squander time 971.19
dullness makes l. supportable 216.1
each ten years of man's l. has own hopes 580.10
end of man's l. is like end of a good play 218.1
every l. is its own excuse for being 314.6
every l. is, more or less, a ruin 752.13
every man lives to give a meaning to l. 536.92
every man passes l. in seeking friendship 363.39
everyday l. is order and haphazardry 536.121
familiarity with l. makes time speed 971.23
flowers of l. are but illusions 252.2
full l. cannot be recorded 1062.40
giver of l. should die at moment of giving 885.20
God will have l. to be real 944.2
good friends, books and a sleepy conscience: this is the ideal l. 183.23
good l. fears not l. nor death 538.15
great l. is young idea lived by mature man 536.132
growth is the only evidence of l. 402.12
happiness is the only sanction of l. 407.94
hard for man to confess his l. was unimportant 1005.3
having tasted l. in this world, one has no wish to begin as a new boy in another 452.14
he who despises l. is his l.'s master 930.3
hold it wrong to prefer l. to honor 489.13
hour which gives us l. begins to take it 81.8
how much of human l. lost in waiting 1033.3
however mean your l. is, live it 502.26
I don't understand l., but God may 536.96
I fall upon thorns of l.; I bleed 939.46
I warmed both hands before fire of l. 646.62
if daily l. seems poor, you are not poet 605.11
if I were to begin l. again 172.5
if l. is absurd, death is insupportable 3.11
if money can answer, wrong to endanger l. 213.17
if we had keen vision, feeling of l. 876.3
in morn of l. we are alert, we are heated in its noon, in its decline we repose 537.9
in short measures l. may perfect be 677.13
in the midst of l. we are in death 538.1
Indian summer of l. is not to be hustled 580.3
instinct of l. falters only in man 558.31
interest in death is interest in l. 572.7
is l. a boon? If so, death is too soon 218.58
is l. so wretched 450.4
it is the acme of l. to understand l. 536.104
it takes l. to love l. 536.69
joy of l. is to put out one's power 502.13
just conception of l. too large to grasp in short lifetime 536.42
kill oneself or keep silent about l. 941.3
knowing how little l. has in store for us 776.4
l. a petty thing unless moved by the indomitable urge to extend its boundaries 55.16
l. an end in itself 536.51
l. and death is cat and dog 538.13
l. as we find it is too hard for us 791.4
l. backs up l. 536.8
l. consists in accepting ourselves 852.1
l., death, appear ours, yet are hardly so 538.21
l. difficult because of its simplicity 536.97
l. driven forward by apprehension of notions too general for language 441.37
l. finds its wealth by claims of world 502.25
l. for the American is a hazard 536.64
l. force is vigorous 536.70
l.: full of stairs to go up and come down 233.7
l. given to us, we earn it by giving it 536.124
l. given us for higher purposes than to gather what ancestors have thrown away 842.24
l. greatest bargain; get it for nothing 536.138
l. has become a sweepstake 905.3
l. has meaning if bartered for something else 536.103
l. has to be given a meaning 3.8
l. has value when it has valuable object 536.46
l. hurries on, and death follows fast 971.41
l. imitates art more than art imitates l. 536.134
l. in itself is neither good nor evil 388.17
l. insupportable but for self-pity 870.5
l. is a bad dream between two awakenings 536.83

l. is a bubble floated by solid cash 596.56
l. is a child playing around your feet 537.1
l. is a coquetry of death 538.40
l. is a country the old have seen, lived in 646.59
l. is a diary in which man means to write one story, and writes another 536.7
l. is a discipline for all animals 248.2
l. is a disease 537.14
l. is a fatal, contagious complaint 536.50
l. is a festival only to the wise 1053.16
l. is a gamble, at terrible odds 536.122
l. is a Gordian knot, cut sooner or later 536.16
l. is a great surprise 538.26
l. is a jest 3.6
l. is a maze in which we take the wrong turning before we have learnt to walk 536.21
l. is a progress from want to want. 236.24
l. is a search after power 713.17
l. is a stuff to try soul's strength 536.12
l. is a succession of lessons 319.18
l. is a succession of lessons enforced by reward or chastisement 319.14
l. is a system of half-truths and lies 329.27
l. is a task to be done 536.106
l. is a toy made of glass 536.3
l. is a well of joy 1004.23
l. is amorphous, literature formal 542.11
l. is an imitation of poster art 994.10
l. is an incurable disease 536.23
l. is an irreversible process 366.19
l. is an unanswered question 536.136
l. is art of being well deceived 447.9
l. is art of drawing sufficient conclusions from insufficient premises 113.3
l. is as tedious as a twice-told tale 536.112
l. is baseless expectation of brighter tomorrow 536.95
l. is but a day; a fragile dew-drop 983.11
l. is but a series of inspired follies 351.18
l. is compromise between ideal, possible 536.101
l. is cut to allow for growth 402.19
l. is either daring adventure or nothing 16.4
l. is external text from which God speaks 536.85
l. is fleeting—and therefore endurable 536.20
l. is footnotes to unfinished masterpiece 536.79
l. is for most one long postponement 228.11
l. is frail moth caught in web of years 536.127
l. is full of internal dramas 687.18
l. is half spent before one knows l. 536.36
l. is like a B-picture script 536.25
l. is like a Japanese picture 536.52
l. is like an onion one peels crying 536.37
l. is like shadow of bird in flight 983.22
l. is little more than a loan shark 536.91
l. is made by the friends we choose 363.107
l. is made up of marble and mud 536.43
l. is made up of sobs, sniffles, smiles 536.48
l. is not a static thing 115.11
l. is not governed by will or intention 536.135
l. is not living, but living in health 411.12
l. is one damn thing over and over 536.72
l. is one damned thing after another 536.56
l. is one long process of getting tired 338.1
l. is one vast tangled conglomeration 536.9
l. is paradox; each truth has counterpart 661.3
l. is pill none can swallow without gilding 536.59
l. is rotten writer of detective stories 536.63
l. is short and the art long 981.6
l. is short, but its ills make it seem long 536.94
l. is solitary cell 908.37
l. is struggle to be, do, what we cannot 536.45
l. is suffering 939.33
l. is the agent of your sufferings 536.10
l. is the enjoyment of emotion 282.39
l. is the only reality in death 538.18
l. is thorny; youth is vain 39.13
l. is too short to take seriously 536.116
l. is tragedy: we're spectators, actors 536.123
l. is washed in the speechless real 777.3
l. is what a man thinks of all day 536.32
l. is what despairs in death 536.65
l. is what our character makes it 860.10
l. laughs shaking its rattle of death 536.125
l. levels all men 218.115
l. like after-dinner hour with cigar 536.22
l. looked at one way is cause for alarm 58.1
l. loses in a day what many years amassed 547.6
l. made up of constant calls to action 9.26
l. must always be full of risks 213.6
l.: not having been told floor just waxed 536.81
l. of man to shift from sorrow to sorrow 536.120
l. only art we practice without preparation 536.78
l. only avails, not the having lived 536.30
l. only demands the strength you possess 192.17
l. ought to be material and carnal 710.6
l. passeth away suddenly as a shadow 218.129
l. perceived transforms itself 868.19
l. pleasant without its enjoyments 700.13
l. protracted is protracted woe 545.5
l. reduced to hell when cultures overlap 207.9
l. remains funny when people die 538.37
l. seldom as unendurable as it logically ought to be 536.5
l. sets things in order; very tidy is l. 536.2
l. short; should try to make it smooth 536.33
l. should be a humane undertaking 154.6
l. should begin with age, end with youth 1065.35
l. stains the white radiance of eternity 300.3

l. stands on verge of single breath 536.102
l.: struggle to maintain l. among things 638.6
l. surprises where it does not appall us 948.4
l. the frailest thing in the world 536.89
l., the permission to know death 536.6
l. without absorbing occupation is hell 502.14
l. without adventure is unsatisfying 16.7
l. without courage for death: slavery 192.35
l. without structure is un-seen 654.5
l. wonderful to talk about, not to live 536.1
last of l. is best: youth shows but half 646.13
later l. flings itself along faster 404.11
leave l. blessing it rather than in love with it 218.92
leaves of l. keep falling one by one 223.7
living well, one must have pleasant l. 407.36
long and hard and painful to create l. 516.15
long quaffing maketh a short l. 266.40
love cannot save l. from death 548.239
man arrives as novice at each age of l. 537.3
man can muff l. as badly as his lines 327.19
man is adapted for l. in narrow limits 558.5
man lives the l. of his epoch 181.6
man must look to himself to learn meaning of l. 868.28
man wastes part of l. to display qualities he does not possess 726.9
man's l. accorded him in thoughts of others 798.9
man's l. happy expecting it soon to be so 407.85
man's l. is warfare against men's malice 557.5
man's virtue measured by his l. 1025.47
measure l. by experience, not length 545.4
men cling to l. even in misfortune 536.4
mental ease gives smoothness to rough edge of l. 390.12
minute to smile, hour to weep: that is l. 536.27
molding stuff of l. is the wage 860.8
moments make the year, and trifles l. 989.17
motto of modern l.: just as good as real 54.5
music is essentially useless, as l. is 607.42
must be thrust out of finished cycle in l. 402.14
new fact enhances constant fact of l. 326.7
no easy path out of l., few easy within 536.62
no man has tasted full flavor of l. until he has known poverty, love, and war 536.49
no man quick enough to enjoy l. 536.68
no one would accept l. as gift, if he had knowledge of it 536.109
nobody can write l. of a man but friends 79.6
none can help things l. has done to us 127.5
nor love l., nor hate; but live well 536.74
not easy to restore l. to the dead 761.7
nothing is unthinkable provided it arises out of the needs of l. 711.4
obscurity and a competence—the best l. 641.10
one expense no mortal can recover: l. 600.8
one is the silence of l. forlorn 538.31
one's real l. is led in his head 812.5
only in the microscope that l. looks big 536.107
our l. is made by the death of others 538.22
our l. is what our thoughts make it 968.31
our whole l. is startlingly moral 598.47
scenes of l. beautiful only from distance 536.108
shame on soul, to falter on road of l. 216.7
short l. forbids far-reaching hopes 425.19
shortness of l. cannot dissuade us from its pleasures, console us for its pains 536.131
so long as we do not blow brains out, l. is worth living 536.54
sole l. man loses is l. he is now living 723.19
some make a garden of l., walk down path 654.1
something better man can give than his l. 880.7
strait is the gate which leadeth to l. 835.1
thank gods that no l. lives for ever 600.20
that I exist is a surprise which is l. 314.11
the time of l. is short 536.113
theory and practice of l. not reconciled 967.3
there is l. in the ground 334.7
there is no wealth but l. 536.100
there is one meaning of l.: living itself 536.38
this mutability, l. in the making 115.19
thou shalt give l. for l. 809.2
though grieved at shortness of l., we wish every period of it at an end 454.1
three modes of bearing ills of l. 17.17
'tis certain the desire of l. prolongs it 545.3
to cure fear of death, set just value on l. 538.19
to defeat death man obliged to defeat l. 538.23
to fear love is to fear l. 216.10
to feel part of the stream of l. 1010.11
to know nothing about l., be useful 1016.10
tragedy of l. is that man almost wins 327.3
trifles make up happiness, misery of l. 989.15
truest l. is when we are in dreams awake 687.22
unexamined l. is not worth living 752.17
uniformity makes the longest l. short 971.33
unrest of spirit is a mark of l. 806.4
useless l. is early death 1017.4
vanity to want long l., heed not good l. 545.14
we are forced to participate in games of l. before we learn to use the options 319.50
we are in a l. that passes understanding 536.17
we are in deadly fear of l. 361.23
we cannot tear page from our l. but can throw whole book into fire 941.12

we cross the ocean of this world, each in his average cabin of a l. 536.13
we desire to live an imaginary l. 798.27
we face facts of sex but not of l. 326.12
we have one l., just one, our l. 6.2
we live l. of contrasts and patchwork 536.31
we love l. because we are used to loving 536.82
we spend lives talking of mystery: l. 314.9
web of l. is a mingled yarn 536.114
well-written l. is rare as well-spent one 79.2
what a miserable thing l. is 249.2
what am I if not a participant in l. 502.24
what happens in l. is mere litter 968.47
what is l. without time to stand, stare 530.3
when one realizes his l. is worthless 30.3
when work is a duty, l. is slavery 1058.34
where l. is more terrible than death, it is truest valour to dare to live 192.6
whether l. will be successful depends on power of accommodation to changes 12.1
while l. still woos, it is such a fine gesture to jilt it 727.19
who calls that only l. which was passed with enjoyment finds himself very young 698.39
who despises his l. is soon master of another's 995.11
who regards l. as meaningless is almost disqualified for l. 30.4
who would tread again the scene he trod through l. before 538.25
why should l. all labor be 1058.65
work of l. is to lay foundation of death 218.90

**life's:** all theory is grey, but green is l. tree 967.9
flops are a part of l. menu 327.22
in l. small things be resolute and great 989.7
l. a moment and less than a moment 600.16
l. a pudding full of plums 536.40
l. brevity makes architect's trade sad 50.5
l. business: be, do, do without, go 536.77
l. but a walking shadow 536.115
l. enchanted cup but sparkles near the brim 646.15
l. like a play 309.11
l. neither a good nor an evil 536.110
l. the only riddle we don't give up 536.41

**life-preserver:** every man's task is his l. 1058.25

**lifeless:** he is l. that is faultless 339.8

**light:** l. boats sail swift 944.6
l. is a principal beauty in a building 50.6
l. or, failing that, lightning 1000.1
man, like a picture, deserves advantage of good l. 194.5
no one is a l. unto himself 471.7
one flash of true l. within tavern caught better than in temple lost outright 328.31
out of heart of darkness comes l. 911.17
to see divine l. put out thy candle 691.4

**lightning:** l. hath but his flash 969.2
light, or, failing that, l. 1000.1

**lights:** with l. we drive night to forest and sea 626.3

**like:** all the people l. us are We 903.4
don't care about reasons, know what I l. 719.4
to l., dislike, same things makes a solid friendship 363.95
we must l. what we have when we don't have what we l. 800.1

**liked:** how I like to be l.; what I do to be l. 472.3
since I wronged you, I have never l. you 474.23
we can always make ourselves l. 802.8

**likeness:** little liking where there is no l. 22.1
no glass renders man's l. as his speech 916.33

**liking:** things that move l. in human beings 117.24

**likings:** man's road marked by graves of l. 402.23

**lilies:** consider l. of the field: they toil not 444.1
l. that fester smell worse than weeds 188.13

**limitation:** freedom from self-imposed l. 361.29

**limitations:** men cease to interest us when we find l. 539.6

**limits:** thing I am most aware of is my l. 539.10
we take l. of vision for l. of the world 682.7
whatever l. us we call fate 337.7

**limps:** he who l. is still walking 279.14
no man l. because another is hurt 692.8

**line:** I always do the first l. well 1062.77
queuemania is a compulsive urge to l. up 168.16
shortest l. may be crooked l. 579.3

**lion:** cat pent up becomes a l. 107.3
dog is a l. in his own house 420.18
forbear to pluck beard of a dead l. 802.9
hares can gambol over body of dead l. 713.41
l. is ashamed when he hunts with the fox 57.15
no absolute will make l. lie down with lamb 26.3
spider webs united can tie up l. 1009.3
who has cut claws of l. will not be secure till he has drawn teeth 170.4

**lip:** many a slip 'twixt cup and l. 114.14

**liquor:** blush of an intemperate man painted by l. 492.6
candy is dandy but l. is quicker 266.43
l., death, ways out of mendacity we live in 329.49
l. will end a contest quicker 266.58
men are disguised by sobriety, not by l. 162.4

**listen:** l. to crabgrass grow, faucet leak 530.9
two ears, one mouth: l. more, talk less 540.5

**listened:** two evils: never be l. to, always be l.

to 842.25
**listeners:** l. ne'er hear good of themselves 273.1
**listening:** from l. comes wisdom 916.31
only l. that counts is l. of the talker 540.3
**listens:** who l. for what people say has no peace 861.3
**literary:** in l. action a man wins friends by prejudices 720.4
l. sensibility geared to the timeless 542.12
l. world made of little confederacies 542.7
llama is like an unsuccessful l. man 41.3
one learns little more about man from his l. memory than from his alimentary canal 842.6
progress in l. style lies in the resolve to cast aside conventions of past 935.7
taste is the l. conscience of the soul 957.8
**literature:** by thought, l. becomes escape into living 91.22
difficulty of l.: to write what you mean 1062.102
for creation of l. two powers must concur 1062.5
great l. brings to birth in us the creative impulse 542.3
greatness of l. not determined by literary standards 542.2
in l. as in love, we are astonished at what is chosen by others 957.12
in l. the concrete outlook of humanity receives its expression 542.16
in l., there are only oxen 1062.93
l. flourishes when half trade, half art 542.6
l. is a state of culture 702.55
l. is an inspiration for reality 542.4
l. is fairy land at a distance 542.8
l. is human activity that takes the fullest account of possibility, difficulty 542.15
l. is orchestration of platitudes 542.17
l. strewn with wreckage of men minding others' opinion 1062.110
l. was once an art, today it is a trade 542.10
life is amorphous, l. is formal 542.11
perversity is the muse of modern l. 542.13
rhetoric takes no account of the art in l. 598.26
to speak in l. with perfect rectitude of movements of animals is triumph of art 1062.109
unusual is exactly what makes l. 542.1
we hear too much of scenery in l. 542.14
who can describe his suffering is meant for l. 1062.14
with noble sentiments bad l. gets written 542.5
world could get along well without l. 558.47
**litigant:** jurisdiction for l., not judge 61.8
l.: person about to give up skin for hope of retaining his bones 525.8
**little:** great fleas have l. fleas to bite 'em 662.1
if a l. tree grows in the shade of a larger, it will die small 398.18
in fool's petty estimate all things are l. 686.7
l. by l. does the trick 579.1
l. man is a bundle of contradictory elements 398.14
l. people may have charm, not beauty 70.4
l. thing can be everything 989.4
l. things are the most important 989.2
l. things go lessening till God comes behind them 398.3
l. things seem nothing, but give peace 989.1
never is there any lack of a l. 695.3
whin man knows he's l., look out f 'r him 901.2
who apply themselves too much to l. things become incapable of great ones 989.6
**littleness:** man's feet grown so big he forgets his l. 1005.4
no sadder proof by man of his own l. than disbelief in great men 686.1
**live:** act as if you had long time to l. 765.9
better l. wretched than die famous 538.10
better to die on your feet than l. on your knees 361.30
better to l. rich than to die rich 1041.33
cannot love to l. if cannot bear to die 538.30
even to l. sometimes act of courage 192.36
for the sake of a living men forget to l. 1058.30
he does not believe who does not so l. 76.4
I, an artist, am here to l. out loud 53.141
I call on you to l. for yourselves 862.2
I l. not in self, am part of that around me 129.7
it's nothing to die; frightful not to l. 216.5
l. all you can; it's a mistake not to 502.15
l. by thy light, and earth will l. by hers 442.2
l. enough befure thirty, ye won't care to l. afther fifty 319.16
l. life as it were spoil, pluck the joys 511.5
l. not as though you had a thousand years 391.34
l. with men as if God saw you 691.13
let us l. while we l. 511.3
let us l. within our means 970.13
let us so l. that when we die even the undertaker will be sorry 218.132
longer we l., more we find we are like others 656.9
man can't l. until reasons for living are stolen 646.66
man pines to l., can't endure days of life 536.24
man should l. if only to satisfy curiosity 208.11
mankind gain by suffering each other to l. 977.14
men are unconscious of their birth, suffer when they die, and neglect to l. 537.8
men die only for that by which they l. 561.15
men must l. to point of tears 536.18
men should learn to deserve to l. 536.99

must spend all one's life learning to l. 538.35
my trade and art is to l. 502.19
none takes thought to l. well, only to l. long 545.11
nooses give, you might as well l. 941.10
nor love life, nor hate; but l. well 536.74
nothing meaner than anxiety to l. on 545.10
one must l. the way one thinks 968.4
one must learn to l. before blaming others 203.10
right to know is like right to l. 520.62
they l. ill who expect to l. always 545.8
to l. a life half dead, a living death 216.9
to l., in itself, a value judgment 1019.2
to l. is like to love – reason is against it 536.15
to l. is to be slowly born 402.20
to l. is to climb the Andes 536.53
to l. is to feel oneself lost 30.7
to l.: to find ourselves in an atmosphere of definite possibilities 536.87
to l., to suffer, to fight, and to forget 600.2
to love a thing means wanting it to l. 548.31
to work, l., die hard and go to hell 414.10
we are always getting ready to l. 228.4
we l. complaining 536.39
we never l., but we hope to l. 536.88
what counts is not to l., but l. aright 536.118
who can l. alone resembles sage and God 908.21
who can't l. his own life lives a slave 873.14
whoever l. elsewhere in town from me, I think out of the world 355.11
you can learn to l. if you aren't happy 407.26
**lived:** boldly say each night, I have l. today 723.5
he who hath l. ill cannot die well 218.57
man of great sensibility has l. long 545.9
**lives:** all great l. have contained uninteresting stretches 399.56
he preaches well that l. well 718.2
he who l. more than one life 438.28
matters not how man dies but how he l. 538.20
men lead l. of quiet desperation 237.13
men live l. of quiet exasperation 506.4
men spend first half of their l. making second half miserable 1065.19
most people's l. but trails of debris 536.137
one l. in the hope of becoming a memory 536.93
only he can pray well who l. well 717.13
our l. are merely strange dark interludes 536.84
we pass best part of l. counting on future 316.5
what l. is granted breath by death 538.4
who l. within means lacks imagination 970.12
**living:** all l. welcome what they can cope with 613.10
art of l. is knowing how to believe lies 536.90
art of l. is like wrestling 536.67
arts of l. well and dying well are one 538.7
by l., people mean prenatal passivity science has succeeded in selling their wives 960.3
cost of l. not bad if you don't have to pay for it 275.6
dying is as as natural as l. 538.14
earth belongs to l., not to the dead 536.57
half the agony of l. is waiting 1033.6
how good is mere l. 536.14
I postpone death by l., risking 502.21
if we could wake with no memory of l. we might arrive at a faultless day 723.12
l. dog is better than a dead lion 536.11
l. is in the past, future – not in present 723.25
l. man stronger than dead man's memory 538.27
l. well, beautifully, justly, are one 536.117
lament not the dead but the l. 603.6
let the dead have fame, but the l. love 548.222
love of l. is the most powerful foible 536.75
my business is with the l. 603.5
my joy of l. is in battles of life 407.106
oh, the wild joys of l. 690.2
only those within whose consciousness the suns rise and set can be aware of what l. is 616.44
our style of l. has contradiction of cultivating sincerity and being a fraud 894.18
plain l. and high thinking are no more 695.8
reason for l. also reason for dying 538.3
reason mitigates the cruelty of l. 778.28
secret of l. is to find a pivot 441.29
to mourn dead unduly affronts the l. 603.7
we are sentenced to death for crime of l. 12.5
we cannot be sure we have something worth l. for unless we are ready to die for it 1019.9
worst evil to give up l. before one dies 216.11
**llama:** l. is like an unsuccessful literary man 41.3
**load:** all lay l. on the willing horse 1050.2
**loaf:** to err human; to l., Parisian 664.3
**loafed:** better to have l. and lost than never to have l. 444.16
**loan:** good man whom you favor with l. will feel indebted after he has paid you 94.7
l. oft loses both itself and friend 94.6
small l. makes debtor, great l. enemy 219.11
**lobbyist:** l. helps politician decide and pays him 705.65
president only l. of whole nation 724.13
**lock:** l. is meant only for honest men 850.18
**loftiest:** l. edifices need deepest foundations 399.57
l. towers rise from the ground 399.10
**lofty:** hurricane attacks only the l. trees 727.20
**logic:** all beliefs are demonstrable by l. 738.4
l. and sermons never convince 685.5
l.: art of reasoning in accordance with limitations of human misunderstanding 778.3

l. is like sword: appeal to it, perish by it 778.5
l. is not satisfied with assertion 778.17
l. is one thing, commonsense another 147.7
l. is one thing, human animal another 778.26
l. is the art of making truth prevail 778.19
men purchase peace at expense of l. 728.16
mind all l. is like knife all blade 778.38
nature cares nothing for human l. 616.72
pure l. is the ruin of the spirit 778.31
want of l. annoys; too much l. bores 778.15
what eludes l. is our most precious element 778.16
**logical:** l. consequences are the scarecrows of fools 173.8
mind of man is more intuitive than l. 583.23
**logician:** l. needs sun to draw him forth from his logic 778.32
**London:** hell a populous, smoky city much like L. 414.12
L., that cesspool into which the loungers of Empire are drained 543.1
there is in L. all life can afford 543.2
**London's:** nursed amid L. noise, crowds, smoke 543.3
**loneliness:** fearing l. more than bondage, we marry 560.21
l. is bred of a mind grown earthbound 544.9
love is principal means of escape from l. 548.190
man's l. is but his fear of life 544.8
music was invented to confirm human l. 607.20
no deeper l. than to tread silent, deserted scene of former throng 669.17
no l. is greater than l. of a failure 327.12
what l. is more lonely than distrust 257.4
who knows what true l. is 544.3
**lonely:** in house where one is l., one has solicitude for things 544.2
l. man is eaten up by himself 544.6
l. one offers his hand too quickly 544.7
we go l., side by side but not together 148.10
when you're all alienated, you're not l. 30.1
**long:** man wants to live l. but not be old 545.13
not how l. you stick around but what you put over 545.1
**look:** l. at all things with a mental squint 702.14
l. not thou on beauty's charming 859.5
only those at levers of control have chance to l. out for themselves 457.8
they l. at more, join in less 563.13
under-exercised, we l. instead of play 690.3
**looking-glass:** blind man will not thank for l. 85.6
every man's neighbor is his l. 619.4
th' wurruld has held a l. before ye fr'm birth 587.2
**looks:** if character's right, l. are a delight 117.20
many complain of l., none of brains 491.29
we can't all combine good l. and brains 539.12
we love good l., though they may destroy 45.12
**loquacity:** l.: renders sufferer unable to curb tongue when you wish to talk 916.8
l. storms the ear, modesty the heart 594.6
**Lord:** except L. build house, labour is in vain 124.3
O, L., if there is a L., save my soul 263.6
**Lords:** House of L. is British Outer Mongolia 287.4
**lose:** better to l. the saddle than the horse 160.5
better turn back than l. your way 808.2
if fate means you to l., give a fight 337.14
it is more necessary to l. than gain 198.31
never contend with man who has nothing to l. 342.3
no man can l. what he never had 547.12
to l. oneself is to be gainer 1014.4
whatever you can l., reckon of no account 547.10
when we l. one we love, bitterest tears are for hours we loved not enough 603.11
won't win him if words showed fear to l. 195.12
you must l. a fly to catch a trout 547.3
**loser's:** in life the l. score is always zero 546.1
**loses:** wise man never l. anything if he has self 873.18
**losing:** by l. himself man becomes something 502.12
one vexed at l. game by single hole 327.11
**loss:** good man must rather sit with l. than rise unjust 547.4
l. is nothing else but change 547.5
l. shapes image of lost treasures 547.1
l. which is unknown is no l. at all 547.9
prefer l. to dishonest gain 732.3
sometimes better incur l. than make gain 547.7
who possesses most is most afraid of l. 710.11
world so quickly readjusts after l. 218.133
**losses:** base gains are the same as l. 732.5
end to gettings is only end to l. 8.10
**lost:** if reluctant to ask way, you will be l. 973.8
make wherever we're l. in look like home 12.3
praising the l. makes remembrance dear 631.2
who does not hope to win has already l. 33.25
**lottery:** adventure all tickets in l., you lose 367.9
**louse:** he can see l. as far away as China 203.18
**lovable:** being l. is having popularity, sex appeal 706.5

failure is l. and what is l. is commercial 327.21

**love**: absence, an unconscious harshness, more helpful to success in l. than anything else 548.173
absence sharpens l. 2.6
absences a good influence in l. 2.12
advice on rules of l. like advice on rules of madness 548.232
against great advantages in another, no means of defending ourselves except l. 15.5
agreement is never reached in l. 548.85
alas! how light a cause may move dissension between hearts that l. 548.144
all I want is boundless l. 548.154
all is lawful in l., which is lawless 548.123
all l. is sweet, given or returned 548.213
all of those I l. make me laugh 548.5
all thoughts, passions are ministers of l. 548.27
all wurruld is l., soft, sweet an' sticky 548.57
always some madness in l. 548.152
around those who l. is sheer security 548.185
as gravity frees stone, l. frees man 548.193
as l. crowns so shall he crucify you 548.83
base men in l. gain a nobility 548.211
beggary in the l. that can be reckoned 548.212
begin l. when you like, stop when you can 548.216
best of a man's life, his acts of l. 517.25
betrothed of l. is divorce 388.15
better is a dinner of herbs where l. is 551.2
between whom there is truth there is l. 991.132
biggest of all differences: those who have had pleasure of l., those who haven't 548.248
body seeks what injured the mind with l. 885.17
broken heart: monument to never-dying l. 548.148
by l. alone we succeed in penetrating the very essence of a being 548.221
can one ever remember l. 548.139
cannot satisfy sexual instinct without l. 885.29
charm of falling in l.: l. isn't lasting 548.141
chastity triumphs over l. 983.15
course of true l. never did run smooth 548.205
deepest l. turneth to deadliest hate 551.9
defenceless against suffering when we l. 549.4
desire in those who l. to hear of lovers' pains 552.6
dogs live a longer life than l. does 178.13
doubting l., we end by doubting everything 998.1
embarrassed alone together when l. begins, dies 548.105
erotic l. begins with separateness, ends in oneness 548.72
eternal l. doth keep earth, air, deep 548.20
every l.'s the l. before in duller dress 548.161
evil l. makes crooked path seem straight 305.9
fabric of l. won't ravel unless I travel 2.11
familiar acts are beautiful through l. 331.13
far from lips we l., we make l. to lips near 470.10
few have religion enough to l. 551.1
fill a woman with l. of herself 195.3
first l. swings its object clear of the everyday 548.14
for one human to l. another is the most difficult of all tasks 548.183
give little l. to child, get great deal 121.37
give me more l. or more disdain 592.2
god could hardly l. and be wise 548.174
great secret of morals is l. 598.43
greater l. hath no man than this, that he lay down his life for his friends 831.1
greatest l. is a mother's; then comes a dog's; then comes a sweetheart's 548.167
greatest pain is to l. in vain 550.1
hail, wedded l. 560.79
half a l. is better than none 548.124
hard to know what those we l. really need 548.8
hardly any activity is started with such hopes, and fails so regularly, as l. 548.75
hatred conquered by l. passes into l. 551.13
hatred, ignorant l. have same ends 551.6
hatred is blind, as well as l. 551.5
hatred paralyzes life; l. releases it 551.7
he that shuts l. out, shall be shut out from l. 548.229
he who loves approach of l. never attains it 348.10
he whom l. touches not walks in darkness 53.98
heaven has no rage like l. turned to hate 786.1
hell, madame, is to l. no longer 414.1
hours in l. have wings 2.2
how great l. is, presence best trial 2.4
I am like to l. if it prove fair weather 178.17
I cannot drift beyond His l. and care 748.17
I could not l. thee, dear, so much 489.17
I hate and l., how I know not 167.2
I'd call it l. if l. didn't take years 885.27
if delight in l., 'tis when I see heart which others bleed for, bleed for me 548.33
if he do not propose right true end of l. 885.9
if thou rememberest not the folly of l. 548.208
if we imagine anyone to l. what we l. 471.11
if you l. yourself meanly, so shall you l. your neighbor 862.8
immature l. says: I l. you because I need you 548.76
impossible to l. again what we ceased to l. 549.6
in abstract l. of humanity one loves oneself 430.12

in friendship is sympathy; in l., antipathy 548.29
in l. not wise; when wise not in l. 548.176
in l. one begins by deceiving one's self 548.245
in l., who is cured first is cured best 549.5
is beauty not enough, why do I cry for l. 548.227
it is impossible to l. and be wise 548.6
it is not l. that is blind, but jealousy 508.12
it is possible to bind people in l. 1009.5
it takes two to make a l. affair 548.131
knowledge is the parent of l. 1053.28
l.: a tree with roots deep in earth 548.191
l.: advance payment for what is expected 330.52
l., all alike, no season knows, nor clime 548.47
l. all l. of other sights controls 548.45
l.: an emotion many experience, few enjoy 548.149
l. and scandal are best sweeteners of tea 840.1
l. based on good disposition endures 390.9
l. built on beauty soon as beauty dies 548.49
l. cannot save life from death 548.239
l. charms by display, not by merit 548.114
l., children, work: sources of contact 502.23
l. compels cruelty to those who do not understand l. 548.59
l. consists in two solitudes that protect, border, salute each other 548.182
l.: cure for blunders, blindness, crime 791.3
l. demands infinitely less than friendship 363.83
l.: desire for that which flies from us 548.142
l. dies only when growth stops 548.21
l. dies when it ceases to hope or fear 548.113
l. fears change more than destruction 548.151
l. fed fat soon turns to boredom 548.160
l. flies at sight of human ties 548.168
l. for one, from which springs not l. for all, is but worthless 548.122
l. frees us of weight and pain of life 548.214
l.: game in which only fools reveal motives 548.155
l.-god inflames more fiercely the reluctant 548.235
l. goes out gate which suspicion enters 257.5
l.: happiness of another essential to own 548.93
l. has features which pierce all hearts 548.243
l. has no language to be heard 548.32
l. has one archenemy—that is life 548.1
l. has thousand pains, one pleasure 1035.96
l. has various lodgings 548.242
l., if l. be perfect, casts our fear 551.14
l. in a hut is cinders, ashes, dust 712.36
l. in public affairs does not work 548.69
l. is a driver, bitter if you fight him 548.158
l. is a great good in every wise 548.233
l. is a migraine, blotting out reason 548.90
l. is a naked child 548.159
l. is a spirit all compact of fire 548.203
l. is a tender look that becomes a habit 548.241
l. is a thing of moods, not of law 548.136
l. is a tyrant, resisted 548.68
l. is a tyrant sparing none 548.35
l. is, above all, the gift of oneself 548.2
l. is admiring, cherishing the beloved, on condition you are object of their action 548.28
l. is all we have, only way to help 548.65
l. is an energy which exists of itself 548.247
l. is an excuse for its own faults 548.98
l. is born of and fostered by idleness 444.13
l. is desire of flattery by another 548.80
l. is done when l.'s begun 548.42
l. is emotion woman feels for a poodle 548.147
l. is essentially sacrificial 548.197
l. is growing or full constant light 548.46
l. is heaven, and heaven is l. 548.200
l. is immortality 548.40
l. is intercourse between tyrants, slaves 548.87
l. is like coconut: good while it's fresh 548.17
l. is like shabby hotels 548.238
l. is mystery which, solved, evaporates 548.187
l. is nature's second sun 548.26
l. is not all: it is not meat nor drink 548.138
l. is not always blind 548.133
l. is not dumb; heart speaks many ways 548.178
l. is not l. until l.'s vulnerable 548.186
l. is not l. which alters 549.18
l. is reciprocated by l. 781.5
l. is stopped by hunger or by time 549.2
l. is strong as death 508.5
l. is sweet, but tastes best with bread 548.252
l. is the bright foreigner 548.62
l. is the child of illusion and the parent of disillusion 548.240
l. is the irresistible desire to be desired irresistibly 548.84
l. is the joy of the good 548.166
l. is the only gold 548.231
l. is the slowest of all growths 560.122
l. is the true price of l. 548.94
l. is to gaze outward together 548.192
l. is too pure a light to burn long 548.100
l. is true seed of every merit in you 548.39
l. is union retaining separateness 548.73
l. is unto itself a higher law 548.11
l. is wisdom of the fool, folly of the wise 548.101
l. is woman's whole existence, not man's 576.6
l., itch, and cough cannot be hid 548.78
l. knows hidden paths 548.82
l. knows not own depth until separation 666.4

l., let us be true to one another 1060.1
l., like a tear, rises in the eye 548.175
l. lives on hope, dies when hope is dead 548.36
l. looks not with eyes, but with mind 548.206
l. makes for obligations 548.4
l. makes time pass; time makes l. pass 548.70
l.: means of escape from loneliness 548.190
l. must not touch marrow of soul 548.64
l.: mystery nothing else can explain 548.223
l. never ends in friendship 548.30
l., not reason, stronger than death 548.128
l. of women is lovely and fearful 1055.16
l. often but encounter of two weaknesses 548.134
l.: often nothing but a favorable exchange 548.74
l. only what is woven in your destiny 238.14
l. or perish not same as mingle or fail 151.18
l., pain, money can't be kept secret 849.21
l. rarer than genius, friendship more rare 363.87
l. reckons every absence an age 548.56
l. remains a secret even when spoken 548.224
l. resembles hatred more than friendship 551.8
l.: scale by which ascend to heavenly l. 548.140
l. should be practiced like Lent 548.118
l. simple to understand: it's a crutch 548.126
l. sought is good; given unsought, better 548.210
l. that is fed by jealousy dies hard 508.19
l. unworldly; nothing comes of it but l. 548.249
l. we give away is only l. we keep 548.95
l. weakens with age like all human energies 646.33
l. with its joy clears the vision 548.102
l., with very young, is heartless 548.43
l. without peace, or peace without l. 1064.6
l. yourself with wholesome, healthy l. 869.11
lasting l. best proves strength of mind 178.7
let him be great and l. shall follow him 399.18
let the dead have fame, but the living l. 548.222
lies kill l.: what about frankness 360.8
life finds its worth by the claims of l. 502.25
life less broken after l. affair if one can feel sinful rather than a fool 549.8
life without l.: mere magic-lantern show 548.86
loss of l. is a terrible thing 549.3
lover made happier by l. than loved one 552.4
man saves l. for woman with whom he may feel drowsy 548.150
man who, on grounds of decorum and morality, avoids game of l. is a cad 548.135
many waters cannot quench l. 548.9
marriage is the perfection l. aimed at 560.28
marriage without l., l. without marriage 470.5
mature l. says: I need you because I l. you 548.76
merit alone should light flame of l. 578.2
minds conquered by l., magnanimity 170.17
money has a power to manage l. 596.9
money is the sinew of l. and of war 596.18
more easy to end l. than moderate it 548.202
more violent the l., more violent the anger 548.22
much may be done by l. 515.18
need outward show to conclude inward l. 548.44
need we say it was no l. because it perished 549.11
never l. with all your heart 548.37
no disguise can hide l. or simulate it 548.110
no harvest for heart; l. must be resown 548.120
no l. for friend whose l. is words 363.104
no man dies for l., but on the stage 548.55
no oath secures l. against a higher l. 548.60
no redeeming qualities in me but sincere l. for some things 719.7
no remedy for l. but to l. more 548.234
no vocabulary for l. within a family 332.16
none l., but they who wish to l. 548.177
none so cursed but Eternal L. may return 548.38
not to believe in l. is sign of dullness 548.198
O lyric l., half angel and half bird 548.19
old l., old l., how can I be true 470.13
one cannot be strong without l. 548.236
one must eat of l. where it hangs 548.137
only l. of friends is worth wear of winning 363.16
only l. should rule between man and wife 560.96
only they conquer l. that run away 548.25
only victory in l. is flight 548.146
opposite of fear is l. 548.164
ownership, not l., causes suffering 548.195
pains of l. sweeter than all pleasures 548.54
perfect l. casteth out fear 548.10
perjuries of l. blown away by winds 851.14
pity beyond telling is in heart of l. 548.251
pity melts the mind to l. 692.10
pleasant words are the food of l. 916.45
pleasure of l. is in loving 548.109
pleasure of l. lasts but a moment, pain of l. lasts a lifetime 548.67
problem of existence is we do not l. 98.19
proof of l.: to be unsparing in criticism 203.20
prosperity's the very bond of l. 744.18
richest l. submits to arbitration of time 548.58
robing, disrobing, is true traffic of l. 885.18
sisterly l. is most abstract sentiment 332.6
small hope sufficient for birth of l. 548.218
so many hearts, so many kinds of l. 548.237

so primal is a woman with the l.-madness 1055.15
something in heart of l. is pathetic 548.181
take l. when l. is given 548.228
the satisfied, the happy, do not l. 407.112
there are always some whom one can l. 98.4
there can be no peace of mind in l. 548.171
there is a warning l. sends 548.196
there is element of duty in l. 269.12
they do not l. that do not show their l. 548.204
they l. too much that die for l. 548.63
things are beautiful if you l. them 70.1
this bane, the boon of all alive, is l. 548.41
those who l. not fellow-beings live unfruitful lives 98.20
those whom we can l., we can hate 787.13
those whose suffering is due to l. are their own physicians 548.172
though got by chance, l. is kept by art 548.50
time strengthens friendship, weakens l. 548.104
'tis much to gain universal admiration; more, universal l. 548.89
to be wise and l. exceeds man's might 1053.60
to compare l. is to liken it to a fever 548.115
to fall in l.: to create a religion that has a fallible god 548.12
to fear l. is to fear life 216.10
to hell, my l., with you 873.21
to inspire l. is woman's ambition 1055.103
to l. a thing means wanting it to live 548.31
to l. feebly is to languish 548.66
to l. is to choose 548.188
to l. is to endure 548.184
to l. nothing is not to live 548.66
to l. oneself is to begin a long romance 869.20
to l. simply, know how to show l. 548.53
to l., that's the point 548.145
to l. without criticism: to be betrayed 548.7
to live is like to l. — reason is against it 536.15
tragedy of life is that men cease to l. 549.10
true l. is but a humble, low-born thing 548.121
true l. like ghosts, talked of but unseen 548.107
try to reason about l., you'll lose reason 548.71
variety needed in sex, but not in l. 548.179
we all go through l. like measles, once 548.99
we cry on passers-by to l. us 544.10
we don't l. qualities, we l. persons 548.129
we l. and hate without reason 551.11
we l. animals, children at expense of men 548.199
we l. each other three months 560.118
we learn only from those we l. 529.7
we live in the world when we l. it 1060.30
we must always l. something 548.162
we must be different to l. each other 548.81
we never know the l. of our parents for us till we have become parents 663.7
we never l. a person, but qualities 548.163
we often pass from l. to ambition 33.19
we put l. where we have put labor 1058.22
we really l. our neighbor as ourselves 852.16
what bloom is to fruit, novelty is to l. 548.112
what force is more potent than l. 198.39
what is done for l. is felt to be done for l. 894.8
what is faith, l., virtue alone 328.28
what is first l. worth 548.92
what power has l. but forgiveness 357.18
whatever is done for l. always occurs beyond good and evil 224.27
when I l. most, l. is disguised in hate 551.3
when in l. a man submits to everything 548.153
when l. dies in the odour of sanctity 560.101
when l. sickens, it useth ceremony 549.17
when l. suppressed, hate takes its place 551.4
when we l., we doubt what we most believe 548.108
when we l. we lend qualities to beloved 548.189
when we lose one we l., bitterest tears are for hours we loved not enough 603.11
when you l., saved-up wishes come out 548.15
when you say you are in l. with humanity 430.26
where l. fails we espy all faults 549.16
where l. finds soul he neglects body 548.106
where mercy, l., pity dwell, God dwells 577.1
where there is l., there is pain 548.215
where there is no l. there is no sense 548.51
where there's no jealousy there's no l. 508.14
while God waits for His temple to be built of l., men bring stones 124.12
who cares not whom I l., loves not me 464.2
who has not made a fool of himself in l. 548.180
who hath l. in breast hath spurs in sides 1050.3
who is in l. with himself has few rivals 869.9
with l. one can live without happiness 548.52
women prefer l. to luxury 1055.141
word "l." bridges indifference 548.97
world kept power prisoner, gave l. freedom 713.49
you don't have to deserve your mother's l. 663.22
you make l. like a soldier 582.19
you must l. him, ere to you he seem worthy of your l. 548.250
**loved:** better to have l. and lost 548.230
I have l. badly, l. the great too soon 785.4
I l. him too much to feel no hate for him 551.10
if you'd be l., be worthy to be l. 548.156
is it so small a thing to have l. 502.2
l., because it was he, because it was I 363.80

nothing can be l. unless it is known 1000.11
painful to be l. when we no longer love 549.1
supreme happiness is conviction we are l. 548.96
those l. live poorly and in danger 548.185
to be l. at first sight 548.220
to be l. long 348.7
to be l. means to be consumed 548.184
to mention thing l.: to invest it with reality 777.11
who ever l., that l. not at first sight 548.130

**loveless:** better be left by dears than lie in l. bed 502.22

**loveliest:** l. are things that soonest pass away 983.5
l. things come simply 892.13

**loveliness:** l. is when unadorned adorned the most 70.57
spend all you have for l. 70.53
who l. within hath found, outward loathes 70.12

**lovely:** l. face is the solace of wounded hearts 324.10
look for l. thing and you will find it 70.55

**lover:** all mankind love a l. 552.5
an angry l. tells himself many lies 552.14
everything disturbs an absent l. 552.2
l. cannot feel in terms of psychology 753.1
l. is a monotheist 552.16
l. knows about absolute good and beauty 552.17
l. made happier by love than loved one 552.4
l., poet, are of imagination all compact 555.22
l. without indiscretion no l. at all 552.9
no fury like woman searching for new l. 1055.28
of all affliction taught a l. yet 552.13
only a l. truly knows that he is loved 548.224
scratch a l., and find a foe 552.12
who has not been l. is like unused cup 548.103
wish to lead out l. is tribal feeling 548.16
woman prefers to l. man who neglects her 552.10
write what woman says to l. on water 1055.18

**lovers:** all really great l. are articulate 851.8
anger of l. renews their love 552.19
l. are always talking of themselves 552.11
l. industrious to make selves uneasy 552.3
l. know what they want, not what they need 552.15
l. swear more performance than they are able 552.18
pair of l. are sufficient to themselves 552.8
pity the selfishness of l. 552.1
there are no ugly l. nor handsome prisons 58.3
true l. do not write of their happiness 552.7

**love's:** at l. height no interest in environment 552.8
l. all in all to women 1055.48
l. best habit is a soothing tongue 548.207
l. gift waits to be accepted 548.225
l. mysteries in souls do grow 885.8
l. of king's dominion admits of no partition 548.157
nothing half so sweet as l. young dream 548.143
pains are seasoning to l. delicious fare 548.244
the faithless know l. tragedies 470.16
'tis l. going in little ways that hurts 549.12
true l. the gift God gave to man alone 548.201

**loves:** each man kills the thing he l. 548.246
fear woman who l.; all else has no value 1055.107
half our standards come from first l. 471.9
hardest to close open hand because one l. 382.27
he only may chastise who l. 760.14
he who l. others is loved by them 781.4
he who l. the more is the inferior 548.127
heart that no longer l., hates 549.15
human nature l. more readily than hates 431.7
man is only as good as what he l. 391.6
no good comes of having two l. 178.3
one l. for his own pleasure 548.3
one l. people for benevolence and virtue 548.165
time turns l. into corpses or wives 971.59
type who says he l. his fellow men 98.8
when one l. somebody, everything is clear 548.88
who does good comes to the temple gate, who l. reaches the shrine 391.52
who wants to do good knocks at gate; who l. finds it open 430.32
whoso l. believes the impossible 548.18

**loveth:** he prayeth best who l. best 717.8
he that l. maketh his own the grandeur he loves 548.61

**loving:** beauty hath no true glass, but l. eyes 70.26
few worth l. who not worth laughing at 4.2
I am two fools, for l. and for saying so 548.48
l. everybody is polygamy 736.4
l. is half of believing 76.8
l. more pleasant than being loved 548.79
nearer l. those who hate us than owe us 639.4
no person l. himself is alone 869.12
object of l. is to end love 548.34
obstacle in our l. men is their self-love 869.4
restraints to refrain from l. often more cruel than severities of our beloved 548.111
selfish persons are not capable of l. 867.3
the l. are the daring 548.226
we cease l. ourselves if no one loves us 548.217

**loving-kindness:** l. is the better part of goodness 391.36
**low:** detestation of the high is homage of l. 773.3
**lowliness:** l. is young ambition's ladder 938.38
**loyal:** young l. to individuals, old to types 553.2
**loyalty:** l. the same if it win or lose the game 553.1
my l. to country, not office-holders 671.23
ounce of l. is worth pound of cleverness 553.3
**luck:** art is in love with l., and l. with art 53.1
care and diligence bring l. 279.8
don't envy men because they have run of l. 358.8
go and wake up your l. 289.7
great skill to guide l. while awaiting it 358.15
greatest good l.: to die at right time 399.36
have but l., you will have the rest 358.21
l. is not chance—it's toil 358.6
l. is the prerogative of valiant souls 358.29
l. isn't mentioned before self-made men 358.49
l. joins game, cleverness scores double 137.14
l. never made a man wise 358.39
none has so much l. he can play with it 358.50
pleasant to see enemy have ill l. 286.10
protected man doesn't need l. 850.7
shallow men believe in l. 108.3
some folk want their l. buttered 358.18
to believe in l. is skepticism 358.7
true l. consists not in holding best cards 367.6
who glories in l. may be overthrown 358.10
who has good l. is good 358.2
women try their l.; men risk theirs 560.126
**lucky:** l. person passes for a genius 358.9
not l., do not go a-fishing 358.13
**ludicrous:** any idea may be shown in l. light 4.1
**lunatic:** l. is lost if he allows a sane eye to peer into his locked universe 555.6
l., lover, are of imagination all compact 555.22
sometimes find something good in l. fringe 770.5
we keep inside ourselves a l. giant 555.4
**lunch:** man may be a pessimistic determinist before l. 272.16
**lust:** hell has three gates: l., anger, greed 414.2
I'd call it love but l. too is a jewel 885.27
l. and force source of all actions 9.33
who has no l. is safe among things of l. 764.3
**luxuries:** give me l.; will do without necessities 554.10
**luxury:** even l. finds zest in change 554.4
l. corrupts rich and poor 554.7
l. is a way of being ignorant 554.5
l., more savage than war 674.16
mankind seduced by l. cannot renounce it 554.6
men grow dissolute in l., then go mad 554.9
**lying:** I do myself the greater injury in l. 329.32
I do not mind l., but hate inaccuracy 297.7
in plain truth, l. is an accursed vice 329.31
l. is acknowledgment of force of truth 329.22
l. is necessary and unavoidable 329.30
l. to ourselves more ingrained than l. to others 858.2
**lyricism:** l. cannot exist without rules 702.16

# M

**machine:** m. never wastes anybody's time 960.26
m. plunges man more deeply into problems of nature 960.25
no m. can do work of extraordinary man 960.27
we have forgotten beast and flower in order to forget everything except the m. 960.12
when m. runs without human aid, scrap it 960.2
you cannot endow m. with initiative 960.17
**machines:** if men invent m. that put men out of work 1002.2
seems m. make all the chief appointments 960.24
**mad:** all of us are m. 555.3
better m. with the rest than wise alone 555.12
everyone is more or less m. on one point 555.13
fortune, to destroy, first makes m. 555.19
if a sane dog fights a m. dog 555.5
imagination is the m. boarder 448.20
less harm in being m. among madmen 555.7
man is m. who is obsessed with one idea 555.2
most men are m. when they act 9.22
pleasure in being m. none but madmen know 555.8
stupidity often saves a man from going m. 934.11
we are all born m.; some remain so 555.1
when we remember we are all m. 555.23
**made:** stick to the thing for which one was m. 1.12
**madman:** m. thinks the rest of the world crazy 555.18
**madmen:** world is full of simpletons and m. 555.11
**madness:** almost every man, woman has dash of m. 555.9
always m. in love but also reason in m. 548.152
be sure your m. corresponds to your era 330.50

in some accidents need m. to extricate us 555.14
m. is to reason correctly from erroneous perceptions 555.24
m. is wisdom to those to whom it happens 555.10
m., suffering can set themselves no limit 555.21
no great genius without some m. 374.3
not to be mad would be form of m. 555.17
our m. less wonderful than our sanity 555.20
proof of m. is disproportion of designs to means 555.16
sanity is a m. put to good uses 836.3
virtue in season is m. out of season 972.9
**magic:** when man cast off belief in m., science bestowed upon him the electric current 960.6
where we have buried the silent races we've buried much of m. of life 131.17
**magnanimity:** m. in politics is the truest wisdom 705.14
m. is the rarest virtue 373.7
m. will not consider prudence of its motives 373.9
minds conquered by love, m. 170.17
**magnanimous:** who fears being duped cannot be m. 257.1
**Mahomet:** M. founded a religion without an inferno 414.9
**maiden:** if heart of m. stolen, m. steals after it 195.10
**maiden's:** every m. willin' when she meets the proper villain 851.4
**maidens':** m. hearts are always soft 470.1
**maids:** all are good m.—whence come bad wives 1055.46
do as the m. do, say no and take it 438.9
m. are May when they are m. 560.106
**mail:** m. is the consolation of life 532.4
**majority:** all politics based on indifference of m. 705.62
m. best, yet opinion of least able 231.38
m. is always the best repartee 51.9
one on God's side is a m. 385.60
security of identification with the m. 168.9
will of m. in all cases to prevail 817.6
wobbly m. falls to resolute minority 585.3
**make-believe:** man lives not by truth but by m. 447.12
**maladies:** m. often have their origin in the mind 583.12
**maladjusted:** salvation lies in hands of creatively m. 198.22
**malcontents:** nation without m. is without seed of future 614.9
**male:** innate superiority of m. is in muscle 575.12
m.: member of the negligible sex 575.3
triumph of civilization: taming human m. 131.18
**malice:** accusing is proving, with m. as judge 5.2
m. often takes the garb of truth 557.6
m. swallows greater part of its own venom 557.14
man loves m. against the fortunate, proud 557.9
man's life is warfare against m. of men 557.5
meekness is the mask of m. 433.10
miseries spring from stupidity, m. 333.11
our nature holds much envy and m. 293.24
when m. has reason on its side 557.12
with m. toward none, charity for all 1009.8
world's ignorance exposes one to its m. 611.3
**malicious:** don't trust a m. man 557.11
m. have a dark happiness 557.7
nothing is proof against m. tongues 557.10
**malt:** m., more than Milton, justifies God to man 266.32
**Mammon:** who serve God and M. find there is no God 495.5
**man:** a m. has his personal scent 205.1
a m. is virtually everything 558.45
absence of pretension marks m. of world 910.2
alas for this mad melancholy beast m. 558.40
any m.'s truth is what makes him a m. 991.107
as an infant, m. is wrapped in mother's womb; grown up, in custom; dead, in earth 537.11
as for m., his days are as grass 983.4
at twenty m. is a peacock; at eighty, nothing 537.6
be more than m. or thou'rt less than ant 945.3
beneath the uniformity of fashions, m. remains an animal, hero, savage 431.12
buffaloes held by cords, m. by his words 1057.25
by losing himself m. becomes something 502.12
child is father of the m. 402.27
created after flea, m. cannot be boastful 433.27
Darwinian m. is only a monkey shaved 306.5
disappointed in monkey, God invented m. 306.9
diverse elements joined in heart of m. 258.2
each has day when he must accept he is a m. 539.1
every m. is a m. of the day 584.2
every m. is to be had some way 851.3
family of m. more than three billion strong 558.30
finished m. of world eats of each apple 910.1
from right angle, m. shows depth, beauty 680.2
God created m. in his own image 558.9
God made only water, but m. made wine 266.33
God makes, but money finishes, the m. 596.23
how dark the ways of god to m. 748.7

how easily m. is disturbed, put out of order 620.2
I am a m.; nothing human is alien 558.52
I am not eternity, but a m. 539.7
if a m. is vain, flatter him 346.7
if you ride m., sit easy and light 815.2
it is m. who has destroyed m. 239.9
it takes longer for m. to find out m. than any other creature 1001.1
like leaves on trees the race of m. is found 372.4
m.: a born child with the power of growth 402.24
m. an animal who lifts head to sky 440.16
m.: animal lost in contemplation of what he thinks he is 558.10
m. appoints and God disappoints 385.19
m.: beautiful machine that works badly 558.36
m. can be as big as he wants 731.5
m. can be best or worst of animals 558.3
m. can deceive a woman by sham attachment 851.7
m. cannot emerge from himself 852.23
m. ceases to be concerned with himself 150.8
m. consists of the faith that is in him 328.3
m. determines what is said, not words 916.61
m. drinks without thirst, makes love anytime 558.7
m. eats the big fish and mud eats m. 26.4
m. exists for his own sake 130.2
m. feels himself to be a commodity 103.7
m. half-way between ape and god 558.29
m. has in him water's silence, earth's noise, and bird's song 558.51
m. hath all which nature hath, but more 558.4
m. in the house worth two in the street 575.16
m., in the ideal, is noble and sparkling 558.35
m. is a fighting animal 441.32
m. is a free creative spirit 198.6
m. is a kind of inverted thermometer 861.5
m. is a masterpiece of creation 361.36
m. is a means; amputated, leaves widow 575.9
m. is a mind betrayed by his organs 584.5
m. is a misfit from the start 558.19
m. is a simple being 558.24
m. is a venerating animal 1061.4
m. is a wolf to those he does not know 355.6
m. is a wretch without woman 576.17
m. is adapted for life in narrow limits 558.5
m. is always at enmity with himself 866.2
m. is an exception, whatever else he is 558.13
m. is at bottom an animal, midway a citizen, at top divine 558.8
m. is born broken; lives by mending 939.32
m. is but a reed, a thinking reed 968.40
m. is but the place where I stand 1010.13
m. is by nature a political animal 705.7
m. is by nature indolent 404.6
m. is depressed until woman appears 576.14
m. is for woman a means to a child 560.91
m. is God by his faculty for thought 259.6
m. is like phonograph with few records 575.14
m. is m. only by the heart 558.1
m. is machine for turning wine into urine 558.15
m. is made of clay and daimon 576.10
m. is more childlike than woman 576.39
m. is more interesting than men 467.13
m. is nature's sole mistake 558.21
m. is neither angel nor beast 684.8
m. is not contributary but total creature 558.16
m. is obviously made to think 968.39
m. is only animal for whom existence is a problem 314.4
m. is only animal that blushes 886.10
m. is only animal that can remain on friendly terms with victims he intends to eat 272.4
m. is only animal that doubts death 218.68
m. is passion which brings will into play 558.2
m. is preceded by forest, followed by desert 1035.47
m. is rooted to the land 421.1
m. is the animal that can say "I" 852.11
m. is the cruelest animal 206.13
m. is the hunter; woman his game 576.49
m. is the measure of all things 558.33
m. is the most extraordinary computer 960.11
m. is the most important creation of human effort 417.25
m. is the sum of what he could have 711.6
m. knows nothing without being taught 981.8
m., like Deity, creates in own image 198.18
m., like spider, may spin his citadel 448.15
m. loves woman with whom he may feel drowsy 548.150
m. made to eat ices, not pore over texts 842.13
m. must be more humble and confident 960.16
m. of forty to fifty is stoic or satyr 580.18
m. only animal that can be bored 92.3
m. partly is, and wholly hopes to be 735.2
m. readier to feel than to think 282.8
m. speaks when he can't find clean socks 576.22
m., subject hard to form any judgment on 558.37
m. the only being who knows he's alone 908.39
m. thinks of self as creator, not user 174.3
m., thou feeble tenant of an hour 558.11
m., tool-using animal, is lord of creation 856.6

m. uses brains he has to get into trouble 17.38
m. wants what he is supposed to want 236.11
m. who is really a m. must learn to be alone 873.23
m. who m. would be must rule himself 856.15
m.: worse than animal when he's an animal 206.16
m.'s inhumanity to m. makes thousands mourn 206.3
m.'s misfortunes occasioned by m. 17.47
machine cannot do work of extraordinary m. 960.27
manly m. lacks wit to realize dreams 562.3
measure of a m.: his stand at time of challenge 250.8
measure value of m. only by other men 1019.12
men are cruel, but m. is kind 517.22
modern m. a means; end not his business 994.11
no m. worth having is true to his wife 470.14
no monster should amaze, if m. does not 605.1
no slight attainment to fulfill what nature of m. implies 558.20
noblest work of God: m.; who found it out: m. 558.54
nothing on earth more dismal than m. 558.28
nothing so fine as well to play the m. 536.76
oh the little that unhinges m. 620.4
one m. means as much as a multitude 467.3
only m. can control new dangers m. created 633.7
only m. works on self with inborne stings 171.4
pity is not natural to m. 206.9
principal difference between dog and m. 473.10
proper study of mankind is m. 868.24
put m. and woman together, they embrace 885.3
raging tiger inside every m. 856.8
rebellion is a dimension of m. 779.5
shadow of a dream is m., no more 983.17
shall m. hang self because he is pygmy 870.7
silliest woman can manage a clever m. 353.18
so many times is he a m. as he has languages, friends, arts, trades 1.4
stages of m.: infancy, childhood, adolescence, obsolescence 537.10
state made for m., not m. for state 923.8
talk to every m. as if he bored you 955.5
ten lands are sooner known than one m. 1001.21
test of m.: coping with female hysteria 576.60
that m. is wolf to m. is a libel on the wolf 41.12
this is God: to be m. with thy might 558.50
time blind, m. stupid, say cynics 971.48
to be a m. is to be responsible 804.12
to do all one able to do: to be a m. 502.20
to himself m. is most wonderful object 584.9
tragic writer must believe in m. 980.9
trouble with m. is m. 558.53
what a chimera then is m. 558.42
what a piece of work is m. 558.49
what characterizes m. is the richness, subtlety and versatility of his nature 558.12
what is m. in nature? nothing, all 558.41
when a m., I put away childish things 567.1
when m. burns he leaves handful of ashes 218.136
where there are no men, strive to be a m. 489.29
where's m. could ease heart like satin gown 265.17
while a m. exists there is need of him 314.3
who is m. enough releases woman in woman 576.40
why does m. wish to be made sad by seeing tragical things 980.2
world is a great volume, m. the index 1060.7

**man's:** m. grandeur: knowledge of his misery 939.34
m. main task is to give birth to himself 198.14
m. meat is often a woman's poison 548.131
m. women folk regard him as an ass 332.20
woman is m. confusion 576.53

**management:** m. problem solved by standardized worker 1059.3

**manhood:** in m. we tell dreams of childhood 574.39
m. and sagacity ripen of themselves 402.21
m. is the fertile season of action 567.3
that government is best which secures m. 393.64

**mankind:** all think their little set m. 903.6
expect best, worst from m. and weather 558.55
expose not the secret failings of m. 203.29
I am involved in m. 218.39
I love m.; it's people I can't stand 588.4
in solitude it is possible to love m. 26.8
know more of m., expect less of them 391.27
m. are disposed to suffer evils 800.7
m. are earthen jugs with spirits in them 558.25
m. either Sancho Panzas or Quixotes 558.46
m. has become so much one family 150.7
m. moves so slowly 558.23
m. will perish through eternal peace 674.12
more fellowship among snakes than m. 206.10
my country is world; countrymen, m. 98.6
our true nationality is m. 98.22
to be religious, identify with m. 705.31
to fly from, need not be to hate, m. 908.9
to think ill of m., and not wish m. ill, is perhaps highest wisdom, virtue 118.6

**mankind's:** all m. concern is charity 118.8

**manna:** without daily m., he must go backward who would most advance 920.2

**manner:** bad m. spoils everything; good one supplies everything 559.13
m. is substitute for genius, sense, wit 935.4
**manners:** bad m. often most picturesque of all 559.22
clothes, m., greatly improve appearance 265.1
evil communications corrupt good m. 471.2
fine m. need support of others' fine m. 559.10
good m. are the medium of social life 559.5
is man a savage with fragile m. 558.6
learning nothing without cultivated m. 207.15
m. are fruit of loyal nature, noble mind 559.20
m. are the happy ways of doing things 559.8
m. are the hypocrisy of a nation 559.1
m. go for more in life than qualities 559.16
m. hardly differ more than dress 559.3
m. make the fortune of ambitious youth 559.9
m. maketh man, but make woman still more 559.2
m. must adorn knowledge 559.4
m. require time 559.11
m.: that this age should bring forth such creatures 559.18
m. turn with fortunes 728.12
man in power puts on new m. 713.20
marriage very rarely mends a man's m. 560.20
men grow used to everything but living in society which has not their own m. 559.21
one lies in m., enjoys good reputation 329.46
spiritual passion and bad m. provoke loathing 824.7
sympathy of m. joins minds 75.6
there is nothing settled in m. 559.7
under bad m. lies overestimate of individuality 559.15
we are not justified in enforcing good m. 559.6
**manufacturer:** consumer is victim of the m. 103.21
**manuscript:** unpublished m. is like unconfessed sin 1062.67
**many:** cow of m.: well milked, badly fed 149.17
too m. boatmen will run boat up mountain 56.7
**March:** in M. a new year begins 848.26
M. is a tomboy with tousled hair 848.4
weeping gloom of M. and April 848.18
**mariner:** m. must have his eye upon rocks 714.3
smooth sea never made a skillful m. 243.2
**marital:** on m. voyage, you explore enclosed basin 560.26
**mark:** if you would hit the m., aim above it 55.14
one may miss m. by aiming too high 55.9
**market:** each speaks of fair as his m. has gone 58.7
fortune like m. where price may fall 358.1
there are two fools in every m. 102.31
**marks:** who cares about great m. left behind 6.2
**marksman:** good m. may miss 539.9
**marriage:** accident counts for much in m. 114.1
American m. is like a wire fence 560.82
birds outside m. despair to enter cage 560.85
chains of m. are so heavy 560.24
courtship to m. is a witty prologue to a dull play 195.4
far from natural to live in state of m. 560.64
ideal mother, like ideal m., is a fiction 663.45
if m. fails, those married live in hell 560.35
in good m. each appoints the other guardian of his solitude 560.98
in m. be wise: prefer virtue before beauty 560.95
in m. one can pass on visitors to wife 426.19
in true m. lies nor equal, nor unequal 560.120
keep your eyes wide open before m. 560.37
m. based on theory that man who likes a certain beer should work in the brewery 560.88
m. calls for love of one's neighbor 560.99
m. combines temptation and opportunity 560.108
m.: feast where grace better than dinner 560.19
m. field of battle, not bed of roses 560.115
m. from love, like vinegar from wine, is sharpened by time to a household savour 560.15
m. has pains, celibacy no pleasures 65.4
m. is a bribe to make a housekeeper think she's a householder 560.132
m. is as demoralizing as cigarettes 560.127
m. is one long conversation 560.116
m. is the only evil men pray for 560.50
m. is the perfection love aimed at 560.28
m. is three parts love and seven parts forgiveness of sins 560.81
m. is to morality as licensed liquor traffic is to sobriety 266.62
m. is tolerable if you're easygoing 560.109
m. makes a woman like a public building 560.128
m. makes life of deception necessary 560.125
m. may qualify the fury of man's passion 560.20
m. not a partnership, for gain is unequal 560.75
m. portion is elemental discord 548.85
m. promises happiness, death assures it 560.121
m. resembles a pair of shears 560.112
m. shakes a man's confidence in himself 560.78
m. tie bears a daily strain of wrong 560.57
m. was all a woman's idea 560.76
m. without love, love without m. 470.5
more to m. than four legs in bed 560.42

mother weeps at her daughter's m. 215.5
not as much in m. as is represented 560.55
our m. is dead when pleasure is fled 260.4
second m.: triumph of hope over experience 560.63
six requisites in happy m. 560.58
there's no lovelier relationship than good m. 560.73
tragedies end by death; comedies, by m. 144.2
what else goes wrong for woman but her m. 1055.47

**marriages:** best m. are preceded by long courtship 195.1
few m. are happy because ladies make nets, not cages 560.117
if couples lived apart m. would be happier 560.89
there are some good m., none delightful 560.70

**married:** all the bachelors live like m. men 575.17
bachelor is peacock, m. man a jackass 560.44
dread of loneliness is greater than the fear of bondage, so we get m. 560.21
I would be m. to a single life 65.2
in m. life three is company and two is none 560.131
m. love is bigger than oaths 560.2
m. man dies in good stile at home 65.8
m. men have their own way 560.123
m. people interrupt each other's stories 560.111
m. state is compleatest image of heaven and hell we can have in this life 560.114
nothing more distasteful than complacency of new-m. couple 560.69
one was never m., and that's his hell 560.12
strange delight we m. people have to see these fools decoyed to our condition 560.97
sum m. couple owe to each other infinite 560.48
walking slow getting m. gives you time to change your mind 1044.4
well-m., a man is winged; ill-matched, he is shackled 560.4
when a woman gets m. it's like jumping into a hole in the ice 560.49
when m. people don't get on they separate; if they're not m., it's impossible 497.4
woman's business to get m. soon as possible 560.107

**marries:** when an old man m., death laughs 560.45
who m. woman to educate her falls victim to fallacy of woman who m. to reform 560.59
woman m. again because she detested her first husband 560.126

**marry:** at fifty one doesn't m. a girl of twenty 566.4
every woman should m.—and no man 560.23
I would advise no man to m. who is not likely to propagate understanding 560.65
m. but for love, but love the lovely 560.94
maidens, why worry whom to m. 560.51
men m. because they are tired 560.130
men women m. will always be a marvel 560.71
people m. from inclination, not reason 560.62
they that m. old people hang themselves 1051.4
to m. a woman you love is to lay a wager as to who will stop loving first 560.16
women m. to be in hub of things 560.9

**marrying:** m. a man is like buying what you admired a long time in a shop window 560.67
m., ask if you can converse into old age 560.90
men always wooing goddesses, m. mortals 195.8

**martyr:** cause, not death, makes m. 561.14
everyone hates a m. 561.9
m. never asserted his disbelief in torture 561.4
often pleasant to stone a m. 561.1
to die a m., one must will own execution 561.11
who is not a saint cannot die a m. 561.6

**martyr's:** no happiness in life is so perfect as m. 561.8
not the least of m. scourges to be canonized by persons who burned him 561.13

**martyrdom:** for m., man must be convinced he has delegation from heaven 561.12

**martyred:** m. many times must be who would keep his country free 534.25

**martyrs:** m. forgotten, mocked or used 561.3
truer that m. make faith than faith makes m. 561.17
vice has more m. than virtue 1026.4

**marvelous:** unknown always passes for m. 1012.13

**mask:** m. tells us more than a face 162.21
nothing gives more assurance than a m. 162.3
vice knows she's ugly, so puts on m. 1023.13
woe to him who doesn't know how to wear his m. 162.17
words are really a m. 1057.13
you cannot unmask a m. 3.5

**mass:** m. media are wholesalers of communications 563.14
m.-mind of crowd, gang is uncivilized 205.6
m. movement holds a following because it can satisfy passion for self-renunciation 564.1
m. movements cannot rise without belief in a devil 564.2

**massacre:** each successful m. consecrated by Te Deum 438.2

**masses:** away with this hurrah of m. 205.5
civilization exists so men may not be m. 675.1

m. will fall victims to a big lie 329.23
obedience is result of instinct of the m. 813.35
sexuality is the lyricism of the m. 885.2
**master:** creditor is worse than a m. 219.9
every m. has but one disciple 350.3
eye of the m. fattens the steed 58.6
if the servant grows rich, the m. poor 1059.2
m. eventually wins all to his opinion 399.20
m. shows himself in self-limitation 896.4
man who is m. of himself can end sorrow 856.16
no man good enough to be another's m. 882.17
slave has but one m.; ambitious man, many 33.17
we'll have good m. when each is his own 825.12
when lion weary of obeying m. has devoured him, it looks for another m. 813.40
who despises his life is soon m. of another's 995.11
**masterpieces:** m. are not single and solitary births 399.66
nothing likely about m. 399.62
**masters:** half our standards come from our first m. 471.9
no man can serve two m. 495.1
we cannot all be m. 528.21
we may be m. of lot by bearing it 285.10
**mastery:** neither m. nor slavery except in attitude 882.11
**match:** I fear not m. of equal partners 560.1
**material:** high thinking inconsistent with m. life 565.3
m. interest about to close on our rights 565.7
our life ought to be m. and carnal 710.6
**materialism:** m. decadent only if nation's spirit withered 565.1
**materialistic:** m. idealism of American life 565.6
**mathematicians:** m. who are only m. have exact minds 566.5
**mathematics:** exaltation found in m. as in poetry 566.7
if a man's wit wanders, let him study m. 566.1
m. gives artist fullest scope of imagination 566.2
m. is thought moving in sphere of abstraction 566.11
m. the subject in which we never know what we are talking about 566.6
**matrimony:** in m., to hesitate may be to be saved 560.13
lady's imagination jumps to m. in a moment 1055.6
safest in m. to begin with some aversion 560.110
**matron:** as the salt-cellar whose cover cometh off in soup is m. who extolleth her babes 663.10
no m. happy till past thirty and not fat 637.2
**mature:** highest creatures take longest to m. 402.22
m. man needs to be needed 567.4
there is no dunce like a m. dunce 445.29
**maturing:** process of m. is an art to be learned 567.12
**maturity:** awareness of ambiguity of one's achievements and failures is a symptom of m. 6.21
m., to find seriousness of child at play 567.14
to live with fear is final test of m. 567.21
we do not have childhood, m., old age 537.13
whatever is formed for long duration arrives slowly to its m. 402.9
**maxim:** more trouble to make m. than do right 568.7
**maxims:** govern kingdoms with m. 393.53
m. of men disclose their hearts 568.3
**May:** all things seem possible in M. 848.38
April a promise M. is bound to keep 848.5
hard is heart that loveth nought in M. 848.14
in M. nature reminds us we are not gods 848.20
M. is a ghastly parody of real spring 848.31
must's a schoolroom in the month of M. 269.9
rough winds shake the darling buds of M. 848.36
**mayor:** m. who won't steal is a triumph 129.8
**meal:** good m. ought to begin with hunger 272.10
**mean:** m. man looks for lucky occurrences 748.16
none m. all they say, few say all they m. 894.1
to the m. all becomes m. 686.11
to the m. eye all things are trivial 686.2
what m. man seeks is in others, not self 945.2
**meaning:** each culture reads m. into objective world 777.12
every man lives to give a m. to life 536.92
God giving m. to life attractive 385.16
learn m. of what you say, then speak 916.20
life has to be given m. since it has no m. 3.8
m. lies in attitude toward things 569.6
man must look to himself to learn m. of life 868.28
pursuit of perfection gives m. to life 677.20
quest for certainty blocks search for m. 998.5
repeated phrase gains m. 794.5
there is no m. to life except the m. man gives by living productively 569.1
we find in death not m., but an end 538.29
we must find our separate m. 569.2
**meaninglessness:** human mind can see m. as ultimate meaning 583.2

specialized m. a hallmark of science 917.4
**meanings:** m. change amazingly 569.5
m. receive dignity from words 1057.29
words change m. and m., words 1057.30
**meanness:** m. is in half-doing 929.3
**means:** I will tend m. that are mine 198.32
increased m., leisure, two civilisers 131.8
let us live within our m. 970.13
m. are enjoyed if the end is desired 570.7
m. prepare the end 570.6
man is a m.; amputated, leaves a widow 575.9
we deliberate about m. and not ends 570.1
wise reserve matures the m. 856.4
**measure:** m. a thousand times and cut once 110.7
to each thing belongs its m. 972.8
whin they've got ye'er m. ye'er in danger 513.2
**meat:** God never sends mouth without m. 748.10
God sends m., the Devil sends cooks 186.3
strong m. belongeth to them of full age 567.2
**medal:** m. glitters, also casts a shadow 424.3
**media:** mass m. are wholesalers of communications 563.14
mass m. offer entertainment to be consumed, forgotten and replaced 563.1
**medicine:** by m. life may be prolonged 572.11
hygiene is corruption of m. by morality 135.5
m. a compendium of successive and contradictory mistakes of its practitioners 572.9
patience is the best m. 572.4
sick man must search for m., not scenery 572.10
**medicines:** better use m. at outset than last moment 791.11
**mediocre:** m. mind thinks it writes divinely 1062.60
who can do all things equally well is m. 573.5
women want m. men; men work to be m. 576.33
**mediocrity:** always heavy demand for fresh m. 573.1
consolation of m.: genius isn't immortal 573.3
forms are for m., m. acts by routine 822.3
in the republic of m. genius is dangerous 573.6
it is a pleasure to m. to have its superiors brought within range 204.28
m. knows nothing higher than itself 956.5
m. mitigates the most violent revolution 813.8
men of age content with m. of success 580.4
new m. thought more of than accustomed excellence 632.5
rapport between m. of author's and public's ideas 91.17
sign of m. to praise always moderately 716.37
**meditate:** to m. is to labor; to think is to act 968.25
**meditates:** in the matter of ideas he who m. is lost 441.20
**meditation:** m. is confined to philosophers an' cows 968.8
m. makes a profound man 185.11
**meek:** it's safer being m. than fierce 388.2
**meekness:** if thou have good things believe better things of others that thou may keep thy m. 433.28
m. is the mask of malice 433.10
m.: patience in planning revenge 433.1
**meeting:** m. people unlike oneself confirms one's idea that one is unique 467.2
**meetings:** length of m. rises with number present 229.4
m. that do not come off keep character of their own 1003.1
observe any m. of people 205.2
**meets:** man m. man – m. and quits again 7.1
**melancholy:** in temple of delight m. has her shrine 699.4
m. and remorse are our keel 911.10
m. cannot be proved to others, so be silent 1004.3
m. days are come, saddest of year 848.12
music causeth m., but it is pleasing m. 607.8
naught so sweet as m. 1004.5
sovereign source of m. is repletion 839.3
to win joy through struggle is better than to yield to m. 279.10
true m. breeds perfect, fine wit 1004.18
value of selves but value of our m. 1004.21
when the m. fit shall fall 1004.19
**mellowing:** m. rigorist is much pleasanter than a tightening liberal 175.8
**melodies:** heard m. are sweet, those unheard sweeter 448.16
most beautiful m. seem simple and inevitable 607.2
**memoirs:** m. is to put down good, leave out bad 62.4
nothing breaks up homes, country, like m. 62.5
**memorable:** m. days vibrate to imagination 448.13
**memorial:** in war m. general wangles the prestige 582.7
**memories:** m. like stones; time, distance erode them 574.3
m. may sleep a long time 574.19
men live by forgetting – women live on m. 576.12
our m. are disorderly card-indexes 574.8
our m. independent of our wills 574.34
our m. insist on cherishing the ugly 574.22
**memory:** better than minting of king is lovely m. 574.38

bitterest m. involves what one should not have done, and which one did not do 574.20
everyone complains of m., none of judgment 514.11
great m. does not make a philosopher 574.21
in good days we've cold m. of bad times 574.31
in m., dead more present than living 218.105
in m. everything seems to happen to music 574.42
liar should have a good m. 329.34
life all m. except for present moment 574.43
m. but ash choking sinking fires 574.44
m. is a net, full of fish but not water 574.11
m. is diary we all carry about with us 574.41
m. is often the attribute of stupidity 574.7
m. is the thing you forget with 574.6
m. kills present, offers its heart to past 574.37
m., like women, usually unfaithful 574.36
m. may be good, to forget is greatness 574.12
m. not brilliant as hope; more beautiful 574.28
m. of man is as old as misfortune 17.19
m. preserves the merest trifles 574.4
m. recalls agreeable traits of friend 574.40
man dies even in the m. of his beloved 600.10
man's real possession is his m. 574.35
no man can be satisfied with m. 574.14
oblivion is the page whereon m. writes 574.5
one lives in the hope of becoming a m. 536.93
our m. will endure if we deserve it 578.5
plucking fruit of m., one runs risk 1062.27
strong m. is coupled with infirm judgment 574.17
study without liking spoils the m. 529.10
the m. represents what it pleases 574.16
vanity plays lurid tricks with m. 668.5
we can invent only with m. 198.21
we labor to stuff m. and leave rest void 277.57
when glory comes, m. departs 384.8

**men:** all m. accessible by the right door 955.1
all m. be not cast in one mold 467.17
all m. naturally hate one another 410.19
as m. grow older, rely on sense of humor 576.37
as many m., so many minds 467.21
beautiful in m. is something feminine 562.6
by keeping m. off, you keep them on 31.6
by nature, m. are nearly alike 431.4
easier to know m. in general than one man 1001.14
expect, fear, everything from time and m. 971.64
few m. are of one plain color 680.1
four types of m. in the world 353.28
gravity is the gift of m. 562.1
he who hates vices hates m. 1023.18
history is bright and fiction dull with homely m. who have charmed women 575.8
if m. are shrewd, they may dally with women 197.6
if not humble, m. are less than m. 433.23
it disturbs me no more to find m. base than to see apes mischievous 431.17
it is not the whip that makes m. 248.5
m. all seek their satisfaction 236.33
m. always want to be woman's first love 576.58
m. and women agree only in conclusions 27.9
m. are afraid they won't be m. enough 562.5
m. are April when they woo 560.106
m. are born equal and different 467.9
m. are but children of a larger growth 558.17
m. are children more than once a day 450.5
m. are created different 168.15
m. are cured by women's favors 576.24
m. are inviolable persons 852.18
m. are like plants: fruit of their soil 292.2
m. are like stars: some make own light, others reflect brilliance they receive 399.47
m. are like trees: each puts forth own leaf 198.3
m. are most inaccessible things on planet 908.12
m. are my teachers 529.14
m. are necessarily mad 555.17
m. are of no importance 528.5
m. are what their mothers made them 117.9
m. contend sewing is beyond them 575.5
m. die – no one asks who, what they've been 600.1
m. differ as heaven and earth 576.50
m., like fruit, grow sweet before decay 580.12
m. lose usefulness when they lose direction 765.7
m. love flattery from low opinion of themselves 346.21
m. make new experience a ploughshare 319.44
m. may come and m. may go 818.4
m. must be studied as deeply as books 1001.11
m. must work and women must weep 536.61
m. not born wolves, have become wolves 26.9
m., not houses, make the city 129.17
m. not to live silently like beasts 727.23
m. of few words are the best m. 96.10
m. of low degree are vanity, and m. of high degree are a lie 773.1
m. profess they can't wash baby's face 64.2
m. see lazily when not expecting to act 676.5
m. shouldn't care too much for good looks 575.11
m. under discipline of shrews at home 560.60
m. woo goddesses, marry mortals 195.8
m.'s m.: they're much of a muchness 575.6
most m. have all other m. as allies 576.5

real friendships among m. are rare 363.35
relations of m. and women like equation 576.29
things and m. have always a certain sense 1000.3
three classes of m.—lovers of wisdom, lovers of honor, lovers of gain 558.43
to empire builders, m. are instruments 456.4
tragedy of age: m. know so little of m. 1001.6
type who says he loves his fellow m. 98.8
we m. are a little breed 686.13
we make gods of m. and they leave us 576.57
what a life m. lead! bachelors or cuckolds 575.2
what m. daily do not knowing what they do 481.3
women and m. are simply different races 576.30

**men's**: would that m. hearts were truer 470.1

**mend**: men want to m. others' ways, not own 783.17
who cannot m. own case will impair other's 293.4
who lacks time to mourn, lacks time to m. 793.15

**mendacity**: m. system we live in; liquor, death ways out 329.49

**mended**: old houses m. cost little less than new 458.2

**mental**: m. health not individual adjustment to society 836.2

**mentality**: difficult to change m. of the people 756.7

**merchant**: for m., honesty is financial speculation 102.3
whoever reigns, the m. reigns 102.5

**merchants**: m. have no country 102.23

**Mercury**: words of M. harsh after songs of Apollo 269.31

**mercy**: cruel men are lovers of m.—in others 1025.13
he that has no charity deserves no m. 118.4
law of human judgment is m. 455.5
m. blesses him that gives, him that takes 577.7
m. I to others show, that m. show to me 577.4
m. no more could be if all were as happy as we 692.3
nothing emboldens sin so much as m. 577.8
reason is law, but m. prerogative 357.6
sweet m. is nobility's true badge 577.6
we give folks to God's m. and show none 577.2
where m., love, pity dwell, God dwells 577.1

**merit**: assumption of m. easier than its attainment 578.3
charms strike the sight, but m. wins soul 578.6
how vain, without the m., is the name 330.25
in noble soul, only m. lights love's flame 578.2
m. and knowledge do not gain hearts 578.1
m. is not enough without grace 394.3
man without ceremony needs great m. 559.12
more reward the appearance of m. than m. 578.4
O that honour were purchased by m. 578.7
praises from an enemy imply real m. 716.10
we are hardly sensible of m. of others 515.20

**merits**: modesty consists in a due estimate of m. 594.9
sage never seems to know own m. 594.8

**merriest**: men are m. when they are from home 420.22

**merriment**: damn the men of measured m. 313.4

**merry**: he of a m. heart hath a continual feast 407.13
m. heart doeth good like medicine 407.14
m. heart goes all day, sad tires in mile 407.101

**mess**: we are, to put it mildly, in a m. 633.12

**message**: give to a gracious m. an host of tongues 622.9

**messes**: not tragedies that kill us, it's m. 86.10

**metaphor**: creed is an ossified m. 200.2
m.: its efficacy verges on magic 35.3

**metaphysics**: ethical m. is an attempt to give legislative force to our wishes 688.34
m.: attempt to prove the incredible by appeal to the unintelligible 688.22
m. is the finding of bad reasons for what we believe upon instinct 688.21
when speaker no longer understands, it's m. 688.45

**method**: all I know about m. is that when I am not working I think I know something 579.4
m. most important in dispatch 102.8
person lacking character needs m. 117.4

**methods**: our m., not our aims, set us at odds 579.14

**meting**: heart, hand become callous from m. out 382.28

**mice**: burn not house to fright away m. 791.5

**microbes**: m. is vigitable an' man like conservatory 380.1

**microscopes**: m. are prudent in an emergency 844.3

**middle**: human nature to stand in m. of a thing 463.6
in m. life, politics are a temperament 580.6
independence: that's m. class blasphemy 233.11
live for others: m. class morality 581.5
m. age is too young for golf 580.2
m. age is when age shows around m. 580.13
m. age, when you've met so many people 580.17
m. class exercises social power 581.3
m. class unit: couple living moderately 581.4
true way is the m. one 33.12

**middle-aged:** consolation of m. reformers 783.36
if m. man says he's half dead, it's true 580.7
m. suspect everything 1065.37
youth plans bridge to moon, m. man concludes to build a woodshed 252.6
**middleman:** m. bamboozles one party, plunders other 25.1
**Middlesex:** acre in M. better than realm in Utopia 740.15
**midnight:** there is a budding morrow in m. 84.1
this dead of m. is the noon of thought 626.1
**midsummer:** quality of life is social in m. 848.2
**might:** do not expect justice where m. is right 354.17
dog's bark is not m. but fright 969.3
m., right, over centuries found identical 816.7
right makes m. 817.10
saddest words: it m. have been 505.13
where m. is master, justice is servant 354.5
where there is no m. right loses itself 354.18
**might-have-been:** m. can fill desire's cup 785.3
**mighty:** for m. even to give way is grace 713.4
those who had no share in good fortune of the m. often share their misfortunes 546.2
**migraine:** m. not relieved by a tiara 791.9
**militarism:** can't make civilization around core of m. 582.16
**militarist:** we want to get rid of the m. 582.23
**military:** drum drives out thought, is m. instrument 582.12
in m. mentality, non-human factors essential, human being considered secondary 582.5
m. caste originated as party of bandits 582.14
**militia:** raw in the fields the rude m. swarms 582.3
**milk:** God gives the m. but not the pail 748.5
**milk's:** cheese: m. leap toward immortality 352.4
**mill:** m. can't grind with water that's past 505.9
**millionaire's:** aisier to ampytate m. leg thin bank roll 1041.16
**mills:** m. of God grind slowly 809.11
**mimics:** crow that m. cormorant gets drowned 449.7
**mind:** all soarings of my m. begin in my blood 584.11
base m. mounts no higher than bird soars 55.20
best preservative to keep m. in health 797.2
body never forgives injury by m. 584.7
canst thou not minister to a m. diseased 751.3
consolation of a little m.: changing it without impeding mankind 686.3
direction of m. more important than progress 583.9
educated man finds pleasure in his m. 277.6
eye obeys exactly the action of the m. 890.3
eyes not responsible when m. does seeing 448.23
for m. disturbed, dawn is balm 599.4
free m. not to be tethered on chain 520.64
good m. possesses a kingdom 491.27
great m. can look beyond itself 1027.3
Gross National M. is mounting in U.S. 277.59
happiness depends on turn of m. 962.4
he who is fixed does not change his m. 765.8
I shiver in the draft from an open m. 647.5
imagination and m. are politics 705.73
it is natural for m. to believe 76.15
lasting love best proves strength of m. 178.7
let m. be thoroughfare for all thoughts 647.3
m. all logic is like knife all blade 778.38
m. creates the world about us 583.7
m. crippled by same set of ideas 896.5
m. goes less far than heart 583.3
m. grows old as well as body 512.1
m. has strength if bewails own feebleness 583.8
m. has transformed the world 583.22
m. is a light the gods mock us with 583.1
m. is a most delicate evidence 583.4
m. is a mystery; we assimilate that which responds to what is within 583.18
m. is a strange machine 583.19
m. is dangerous if discreet use not known 583.13
m. is the great lever of all things 968.54
m. is the soul's eye 668.28
m. its own place, makes heaven of hell 583.11
m. leaps through immensities of space 480.7
m. must be let alone by government 583.20
m. must bear storms of past and future as well as of present 584.2
m. of an honest man is terrifying 423.6
m. of man is more intuitive than logical 583.23
m. quite vacant is a m. distressed 444.4
m. sins, not the body 893.13
m. too proud to unbend over ridiculosa 605.8
m., unlike flesh, secures complete life 584.4
man cannot gradually enlarge his m. 938.42
man is a m. betrayed by his organs 584.5
man known by company his m. keeps 91.2
man of active m. outwears friendships 363.79
mass-m. of crowd, gang is uncivilized 205.6
my m. is my direct revelation from God 810.1
my own m. is my own church 124.10
not enough to have good m. 491.5
nothing robs the m. of its powers as fear 340.6
of all tyrannies, worst persecutes m. 995.10
only a small m. traffics in scorn 182.10

order, reason, beauty are characteristics associated with the m. of man 583.14
pray for a sane m. in a sound body 411.9
processes of m. make good through emotion 282.35
sharp m. gives edge to pains, pleasures 491.20
small rooms discipline the m. 428.4
smaller the m., greater the conceit 163.1
sound m. in sound body is a happy state 411.11
strength of m.: courage to see, speak truth 993.7
strong m. can embrace great and small 491.17
study philosophy to know one's own m. 688.11
tendency of casual m. is to pick a sample which supports its prejudices 720.10
that m. draws me which I cannot read 208.5
time bears away all, even the m. 971.65
'tis strange the m. should let itself be snuffed out by an article 204.10
to illumined m. world burns with light 491.6
too much sitting, m. gets unhealthy 444.12
waking m. least serviceable in the arts 999.2
who can't open honest m. won't be friend 423.2
wise man changes m., fool never will 347.4
**mind's:** m. activity easy, if never meets reality 968.43
questions show the m. range 478.13
**minds:** as many men, so many m. 467.21
great m. are not upset by little things 686.8
I love to lose myself in other men's m. 91.55
m. conquered by love, magnanimity 170.17
m. differ still more than faces 583.24
m. do not act together in public 27.2
m. give way unless we mix work with play 697.7
m., like bodies, fall into ill-conditioned state from excess of comfort 554.1
m. need ideas in order to conceive 441.21
m. that have nothing to confer find little to perceive 613.13
our m. are influenced much by our bodies 584.2
some m. seem almost to create themselves 860.9
strongest m. are often those of whom noisy world hears least 583.25
sympathy of manners joins m. 75.6
uncultivated m. not full of wild flowers 445.30
wars begin in m. of men 674.34
we have a world of discontented m. 744.17
we must satisfy our own m. in what we do 489.27
**mine:** an ill-favoured thing, but m. own 710.15
this dog is m. 740.17
**mingle:** love or perish is not same as m. or fail 151.18
**minister:** m. is coming to level of useful citizen 136.9
**minorities:** governments exist to protect rights of m. 393.52
no democracy can survive without recognition of the rights of m. 585.4
**minority:** democracy: subjection of m. to majority 231.25
individual is a m. 341.4
respectable m. useful as censors 111.6
to violate m. rights would be oppression 817.6
wobbly majority falls to resolute m. 585.3
**minute:** in m., time for decisions which m. reverses 222.5
passing m. is every man's possession 669.20
**miracle:** in each m. is silent chiding of the world 586.2
this world is still a m. 1060.6
we never know m. wrought in our life 279.12
**miracles:** Christian religion attended with m. 123.16
m. enable us to judge of doctrine 586.3
men talk of Bible m. because there is no miracle in their lives 586.5
seeing, hearing, feeling, are m. 875.12
true m. are created by men when they use the courage God gave them 586.1
**miraculous:** m. by repetition ceases to be m. 210.5
**mirror:** best m. is an old friend 587.3
every man carries through life a m. 587.1
fear of being ourselves brings us to the m. 587.6
m. reflects the way others see us 587.4
**mirrors:** all m. are magical 587.9
m. never give anything back but our image 587.7
**mirth:** cheerfulness is habit; m., a transient act 390.1
end of m. is heaviness 523.1
I love m. as doesn't make friends ashamed 665.3
m. is the mail of anguish 523.6
m. resting on earnestness and sadness 434.6
teach us m. that has no bitter springs 892.9
**mirthful:** in m. tale we're content with less truth 434.18
**misanthropes:** true m. found not in solitude but in world 588.2
**mischance:** ride in triumph over all m. 90.16
take warning by the m. of others 17.51
**misdeed:** on name of a m. a life goes to pieces 1063.22
**miser:** m. and liar bargain quickly 103.12
m. and pig are no use until dead 589.5
m. quits life in debt to himself 589.4
m. worships god of this world 589.3
m. worships wealth in its dead form 589.2
prodigal robs heir, the m. himself 589.7
what greater evil for m. than long life 589.10
when coffer of m. closed, it's as if empty 589.8

**miser's**: m. money comes from earth as he goes in 589.11
water will not slip through m. grasp 589.9
**miserable**: difficult to make man m. while he feels worthy and claims kindred to God 862.7
man's as m. as he thinks he is 1004.32
men spend first half of their lives making second half m. 1065.19
most m. is he who enjoys least pleasure 407.90
nothing m. unless you think so 1004.2
the m. have no other medicine but hope 425.39
what a m. thing life is 249.2
**miseries**: heaven barely glances at earth's m. 412.6
life is so full of m. 1004.27
m. spring from idealism, dogmatism, zeal 333.11
**misers**: m. put back and belly into pocket 589.6
m. tend property but don't benefit from it 589.1
**misery**: actual happiness looks squalid in comparison with over-compensations for m. 700.9
cause of m. is feebleness of our virtues 1025.49
child's m. interesting to mother, young man's to young woman, old man's to nobody 646.56
extreme happiness, m. invite religion 790.75
extreme hopes are born of extreme m. 425.35
fate finds for every man his share of m. 1004.10
half our m. from our foibles springs 989.9
he who finds himself, loses his m. 442.3
if m. loves company, m. has enough 1004.36
income 20 pounds, expenditure 20.0.6: m. 970.8
m. acquaints man with strange bedfellows 17.56
m. must somewhere have a stop 17.24
man's grandeur: knowledge of his m. 939.34
merit praise who know how to suffer m. 745.2
more m. among lower classes than humanity in the higher 712.25
must be green isles in sea of m. 177.4
nobody believes in his own m. 1004.4
relieving others' m., we relieve ourselves 692.5
solace from company in m. is spiteful 177.2
sympathy is cold to relation of distant m. 953.6
technological advance without social advance usually increases human m. 960.7
there is no recourse to mention of pure m. 17.33
twins even from birth are m. and man 1004.16
we seek happiness, find m. and death 364.3
**misfit**: man is a m. from the start 558.19
**misfortune**: better a quiet death than public m. 432.2
doing what's right's no guarantee against m. 17.37
falsehood is the jockey of m. 329.18
friendship is sole remedy against m. 363.55
from m. to fortune is a long way 745.17
in friends' m. we find something pleasing 557.8
in m. what friend remains a friend 17.25
m. lights now upon one, now upon another 17.1
m.: name which guarantees innocence 760.3
men cling to life even in great m. 536.4
one likes people better when battered down with m. than when they triumph 557.17
the memory of man is as old as m. 17.19
to bear m. worthily is good fortune 930.6
world quickly bored by recital of m. 17.40
**misfortunes**: better be wise by m. of others 17.2
happiness is composed of m. avoided 407.60
if man talks of his m. there is something in them that is not disagreeable to him 17.33
ignorance of one's m. is clear gain 17.26
m. are battlefields which have heroes 416.12
m. hardest to bear: those which never come 17.36
m. more supportable than friends' comments 692.7
m. one can endure—they come from outside 339.40
m. tell us what fortune is 745.8
m. when asleep are not to be awakened 17.21
man bears another's m. like a Christian 17.48
more individual m., the better 17.63
rich men feel m. that miss the poor 1041.28
to be wise in m. is to conquer fate 17.50
we all have strength to bear others' m. 692.14
we delight in real m. and pains of others 557.2
with man, most m. are occasioned by man 17.47
**misinformation**: to convey m. tell the strict truth 993.23
**misrepresentation**: don't use m. to pamper bigotry, self-love 262.6
**miss**: good marksman may m. 539.9
one may m. mark by aiming too high 55.9
**missiles**: we have guided m. and misguided men 843.21
**missing**: one person m. can make world depopulated 2.8
**missionaries**: difference of opinion makes horse racing and m. 590.3
**mist**: m. plays on hills and brings out beauty 1043.9

**mistake:** every m. has a halfway moment 297.5
every m. must be paid for in full 297.14
greatest m. is fearing you will make one 297.20
no m. is so great as being always right 816.6
**mistaken:** do not judge, and you will never be m. 513.9
**mistakes:** any man can make m. 297.9
enemies are first to discover your m. 286.4
experience is name everyone gives to m. 319.64
great men too make m., many do it often 399.43
I've learned by m., false assumptions 529.19
intelligence is not to make no m. 297.3
just cause is not ruined by a few m. 109.4
m. arise from feeling when we ought to think, thinking when we ought to feel 86.1
m. live near truth, therefore delude us 297.36
making m. is more honorable than doing nothing 297.31
only things one never regrets are m. 147.12
people seldom learn from m. of others 297.17
who has enough credit to pay for his m. 297.13
who makes no m. does not make anything 86.8
**mistress:** daughter in my mother's house, m. in own 420.14
**mistrust:** doubt, m., are panic of timid imagination 998.7
more shameful to m. one's friends 257.11
**mistrustful:** I hold it cowardice to rest m. 257.17
most m. are often greatest dupes 257.16
**misunderstanding:** most quarrels amplify a m. 766.7
where m. serves others as advantage, one cannot make self understood 640.4
**misunderstands:** no one would talk much, if he knew how often he m. others 148.6
**misunderstood:** to be great is to be m. 399.17
women lust to be m. 1055.129
**mixture:** good things of life come to us with a m. 387.6
**mob:** best university for man of ideas: gauntlet of the m. 591.1
I am the people, the m., crowd, mass 675.14
I feel pity for man applauded by the m. 330.30
in hands of vicious, m. will do anything 591.4
it is easy to please the m. 755.5
m. has many heads but no brains 591.5
m. is League of Frightened Men 591.6
man who stands apart from m. called coward 591.2
no grievance fit for redress by m. law 591.7
nose of m. is its imagination 591.8
pitifulest thing is a m. 582.21
who builds on the m. builds on sand 675.7
**mobs:** m. in emotions are like children 591.3
**mockery:** m. is often the result of poverty of wit 814.3
**moderate:** be m. in prosperity 749.24
m. are not usually the most sincere 592.8
**moderately:** m. honest man with m. faithful wife 581.4
**moderation:** butter spoils no meat and m. no cause 592.4
excess prevents m. from acquiring the deadening effect of a habit 310.6
heart great which shows m. in prosperity 592.13
m.: belief you'll be better tomorrow 592.6
m. in national affairs is virtue 724.5
m. in the pursuit of justice is no virtue 333.7
m. is a refrain from which we all refrain 592.7
m. is the languor and indolence of soul 592.10
m. runs through all virtues 592.5
m. was created to limit and console men 592.9
**modern:** a m. painting can be outdated 593.1
in m. world, Americans are old inhabitants 34.21
m. age is sad: looks for truth in everything and finds it 296.12
m. age more eager to amass than realize 740.21
m. man a means; end not his business 994.11
m. man wants what he is supposed to want 236.11
m. mansion has no place for ghosts 428.3
m. nose and eye have developed intensity 875.7
motto of m. life: just as good as real 54.5
old events have m. meanings 417.32
only the m. ever becomes old-fashioned 593.2
**moderns:** m. ask what can we experience 319.63
speak of m. without contempt 134.2
**modest:** awareness of our strength makes us m. 933.4
few people are m. enough to be content to be estimated at their true worth 1020.21
m. man is usually admired–if people ever hear of him 594.11
to be simple is best, m. next best 892.3
**modesty:** as simians we have done well as to m. 306.3
for those of great talent m. is hypocrisy 594.14
he who speaks without m. will find it difficult to make his words good 594.5
loquacity storms ear, m. the heart 594.6
m. and reverence are virtues of freemen 231.16
m., diffidence make man unfit for public affairs, brothels 594.12

m. guards virtue; false m. betrays it 594.2
m. is not a spontaneous flower 894.5
m. more praised in lover than liked 594.15
m. sets off every great talent 594.1
m. the only sure bait for praise 594.3
of lies, false m. is the most decent 438.4
to speak less of oneself is folly, not m. 594.13
true m. consists in due estimate of merits 594.9

**modification:** bad plan admits of no m. 696.6

**mold:** all men be not cast in one m. 467.17

**moment:** believe more in life, fling less to m. 459.2
every situation, m., is of infinite worth 723.14
I have the happiness of the passing m. 407.49
if you let the ripe m. go, you can never wipe off tears of woe 972.3
life's a m. and less than a m. 600.16
passing m. is all we can be sure of 723.22
strange how few things of m. 1005.5

**moments:** m. make the year 989.17
we do not remember days, but m. 574.24

**momism:** mealy look of men is the result of m. 663.54

**monarch:** greatest m. sits on his own arse 773.5
m. represents his subjects better than elected assembly 518.5

**monarchy:** m. is a merchantman, may strike a rock 393.5
we have been born under a m. 385.67

**monastic:** m. incarceration is castration 595.2

**Monday:** how Sunday into M. melts 1058.54

**money:** all men worship m. 596.60
all morality should have m. as basis 596.54
American men are obsessed with m. 34.46
any man knows how to earn m., but few how to spend it 596.59
difference between little and no m. is enormous 596.62
do you think love has pockets for m. 548.159
everyone credits himself for more brains, less m. 869.6
excessive addiction to m. is hurtful 596.13
federal m. in large amounts looks like free m. 99.1
fortunes made with other people's m. 1041.62
friendship lasts if not asked to lend m. 363.111
good cause, yet m. must carry it 109.8
having m. and bad conscience 34.62
help me to m. and I'll have friends 596.22
heroes: men who sit on top of heap of m. 596.32
Hollywood m. is congealed snow 419.2
human race can't run fast enough to collect m. they owe themselves 8.9
if a man has m., he knows how to take care of it 596.29
if m. can answer, wrong to endanger life 213.17
in race for m. man comes last 8.8
it's m. that finishes the man 596.23
life is short and so is m. 596.8
love of m. is root of all evil 596.5
love, pain, m. cannot be secret 849.21
m.: alienated essence of man's existence 596.36
m. alone sets all the world in motion 596.47
m. and dung are no good till spread 596.24
m.: blessing of no advantage excepting when we part with it 596.6
m. enables life to be lived socially 596.55
m. in pocket, you are wise, handsome 596.63
m. is coined liberty 596.14
m. is like a sixth sense 596.37
m. is not an aphrodisiac 596.35
m. is root of evil, sum of blessings 596.52
m. is the power of impotence 596.51
m. is the sinew of love and of war 596.18
m. is time 596.26
m. not needed to buy day, water, sun 616.58
m., power to manage love 596.9
m. the cause of a restless life 596.44
m. was exactly like sex 596.2
m. will hide many faults 596.12
makers of fortunes love m. as their own creation 1041.44
man is more careful of m. than principles 728.8
man married to woman who enjoys spending m. must enjoy earning it 1058.40
men make m. not for the sake of living 596.31
miser's m. comes from earth as he goes in 589.11
morally bad not to care how you got m. 991.130
much work merely a way to make m. 596.38
never ask of m. spent where it went 596.20
nothing comes amiss, so m. comes withal 596.53
once fool, m. parted, now happens to all 596.57
one with m. is not hanged 761.6
only a blockhead ever wrote except for m. 1062.55
public m. like holy water—taken by all 188.6
put no trust in m., but m. in trust 68.1
ready m. is Aladdin's lamp 596.11
soul buried under dungheap or pile of m. 191.7
there is nothing that lasts so well as m. 1051.7
there's no time to both make and spend m. 596.7
timp'rature normal save whin I'm asked f'r m. 94.3
'tis m. that begets m. 501.4
to have m. is to be virtuous, honest, beautiful and witty 596.25
to know what God thinks of m., look at those to whom he gives it 596.3

to learn the value of m. 596.28
Washington reflex: throw m. at problem 393.32
when m. speaks, truth keeps silent 596.50
when reason rules, m. is a blessing 596.45
who gives heart will not deny m. 430.14
who plays deep must lose m. or character 367.1
with his own m. a person can live as he likes 596.27
without m., honor is a malady 489.21
woman prefers man without m. to m. alone 1055.64
women think it their business to spend m. 576.47
world is his who has m. to go over it 985.16
you may have painful thing done for m. 596.21

**money's:** m. the wise man's religion 596.19

**monk:** habit does not make the m. 45.8
it is easy to become a m. in old age 595.1
runaway m. never praises monastery 298.8

**monkey:** better to be improvement on m. thin such a fallin' off fr'm th' angels 306.4
disappointed in the m., God invented man 306.9

**monogamy:** accursed from birth those who seek m. 736.5
woman wants m.; man delights in novelty 576.41

**monopolists:** men are m. of stars, garters, buttons 560.86

**monotheist:** lover is a m. 552.16

**monsters:** who fights m. must beware of becoming one 783.31

**monument:** erection of a m. is superfluous 578.5
no man who needs m. ever should have one 101.6

**monuments:** when smashing m., save the pedestals 439.5

**mood:** m. means more than object in art 53.42
m. of moment believed permanent 962.5
no m. is unaltered through hours 282.23
our m. changes more often than fortune 962.7

**moon:** everyone is a m. and has a dark side 162.20
m. a friend for lonesome to talk to 597.4
m. worn thin to the width of a quill 597.5
something haunting in light of m. 597.2
there he is at last, man on the m. 597.1
treading the soil of the m. 597.3
when m. not full, stars shine brightly 788.3

**moral:** difference between m. man, man of honor 598.33
every man has his m. backside too 598.28
everything's got a m., if you can find it 598.11
full gut supports m. precepts 272.3
highest stage in m. culture: control of our thoughts 968.6
if we can't be m., we can avoid being vulgar 394.6
is there any m. shut in bosom of rose 70.56
law is the witness of our m. life 525.41
m.: conforming to local standard of right 598.4
m. contempt is greater insult than crime 182.8
m. deterioration of false, shallow life 944.3
m. good is effect of physical evil 388.12
m. indignation permits envy and hate 465.2
m. principle is a looser bond than pecuniary interest 596.33
m. qualities rule the world 877.1
m. sense teaches how to avoid the right 816.25
man may demand reason for every m. rule 598.31
national greatness is m. power 598.44
no m. phenomena, only m. interpretation 598.36
no such thing as a m. or immoral book 91.92
nothing so bad but can masquerade as m. 598.29
our whole life is startlingly m. 598.47
state a m. case to a ploughman 277.43
story with m. is like bill of a mosquito 931.4
success of any great m. enterprise does not depend upon numbers 598.18
what is m. is what you feel good after 598.20
with most, the m. counterblast is a yawn 598.13
women have a very positive m. sense 1055.1

**moralists:** m. suppose previous ages less sinful 296.15
many m. begin with a dislike of reality 598.15

**morality:** absolute m. is absolute stagnation 598.8
all m. should have money for basis 596.54
alloy of expediency improves gold of m. 317.4
artist's m.: truth, force of description 53.8
censorship may preserve, but not restore, m. 111.9
genius and m. are often bitter enemies 374.42
in name of m., saintly old people hinder removal of legal brutalities 525.71
live for others: middle class m. 581.5
m. cannot be legislated, but behavior can be regulated 525.47
m. consists of suspecting people of not being legally married 598.42
m. is a private and costly luxury 598.1
m. is body of imperfect generalizations 598.21
m. is contraband in war 1035.38
m. is either a social contract or you have to pay cash 598.27
m. is everywhere the same 598.52
m. is the attitude we adopt towards people we personally dislike 598.55

m. is the custom of one's country 598.10
m. is thing upon which your friends smile 598.23
m. largely matter of geography 598.22
m. of Americans is a team m. 34.18
m. regulates man's acts as private individual 489.6
m.: subjugation of nature to social needs 598.35
m. takes no account of the art in life 598.26
m., thy tens o' thousands thou hast slain 598.7
m. turns on whether pleasure precedes or follows pain 598.9
marriage is to m. as licensed liquor traffic is to sobriety 266.62
moral sense enables one to perceive m. and avoid it 598.50
our errors, controversies in sphere of m. arise from seeing men as all bad, all good 598.51
religion veils sacred fires, m. expires 790.61
speculation about m.: effort to find way of living which men feel is good 598.30
systems of m. judge by consequences 173.3
teachers of m. discourse like angels 598.25
to make idea of m. center on forbidden acts 598.46
traffic-cop m. and rabbit-test truth 843.22
true m. makes light of m. 60.2
veracity is the heart of m. 993.9
without civic m. communities perish 598.40

**morality's:** m. a gesture learned from books 598.5

**moralizes:** man who m. is usually a hypocrite 598.54

**morals:** generalities in m. mean absolutely nothing 371.4
great secret of m. is love 598.43
I feel rage at corrupted m. of this age 598.34
if your m. make you dreary, they're wrong 598.45
m. are an acquirement, like music 598.48
m. in art like legislature in sex 53.88
make errors in minor m., not major ones 598.14
not best that we use our m. weekdays 598.49
religion has never survived m. 790.21
sentimentality is dissolvent of m. 878.9
terror of society is the basis of m. 340.35
time is a great legalizer, even of m. 971.35
worse than weakening of major m. is strengthening of minor m. 598.12

**more:** less is m. 892.2

**morning:** healthy adult awakes in m. feeling terrible 71.6
in m. man walks with his whole body 338.3
m. is wiser than the evening 599.3
see m. as new-born child with no name 723.29

**morrow:** man least dependent on m. meets m. happily 366.10

**mortal:** all men think all men m. but themselves 452.19
m. nature is seeking to be immortal 452.10
we all breathe same air, are m. 98.13
young man never feels that he is m. 1064.35

**mortality:** changing year's plan proclaims m. to man 848.23
m. can't reach riddles purposed by gods 600.9
m. has its compensations 600.15
why alas; it's m. we experience 536.34

**mortals:** gods give to m. not everything at once 748.11
Lord, what fools these m. be 558.48

**mortifications:** true m. are those which are not known 859.4

**most:** I make the m. of all that comes 127.10

**mote:** why beholdest the m. in brother's eye 872.1

**mother:** children are anchors that hold m. to life 121.43
every beetle is a gazelle in eyes of its m. 663.36
foolish son is the heaviness of his m. 909.2
ideal m., like ideal marriage, is fiction 663.45
loving woman is a slave; none so much as m. 663.5
m.-child relation is paradoxical, tragic 663.21
m. glad to get loveliest child asleep 121.11
m. weeps at her daughter's marriage 215.5
no woman free unless she can choose whether to be a m. 82.2
was ever found a m. who'd give her baby for another 663.25
what m. sings to cradle carries to coffin 663.6
who takes child by hand takes m. by heart 121.9

**mother-in-law:** back of every achievement is surprised m. 6.11

**mother's:** tender are a m. dreams 64.4
you don't have to deserve your m. love 663.22

**motherhood:** oh, what a power is m. 663.19

**motherless:** m. son is a fish in low water 909.3

**motherly:** m. love begins with oneness, leads to separateness 548.72

**mothers:** if I belittle dogs or m. 878.6
m. are the first book read, last put aside 663.41
m. more devoted to children than fathers 663.2
men are what their m. made them 117.9
most m. kiss and scold together 663.9
only m. can think of the future 366.13
we never make sport of m. 663.48

**motion:** aim of artist is to arrest m. 53.46
music exists only in m. 607.40
our nature consists in m. 10.16
scoured to nothing with perpetual m. 10.20

**motive:** Light of Lights looks on m., not deed 601.8

stupid thing done from noblest m. 934.22
we are thankful for the m., not the favour 382.16
**motives:** feel ashamed of best actions if m. seen 601.6
never ascribe to foe meaner m. than yours 286.5
true m., like organ pipes, are concealed 601.3
we search out good m. for our bad actions 601.4
**mountain:** m. unmoved at its defeat by the mist 602.4
there are many paths to the m. top 330.12
**mountains:** high m. are a feeling, but cities torture 129.7
m.: beginning and end of natural scenery 602.2
m. interposed make enemies of nations 378.2
men trip not on m., but on stones 989.5
**mourn:** let none m.; these things are in the hands of God 603.14
none m. more ostentatiously than those who rejoice at a death 603.15
one must m. birth, not death 81.6
who lacks time to m., lacks time to mend 793.15
**mourner:** chief m. does not always attend funeral 365.5
**mourning:** all m. fears its end 410.1
house of m. is also house of laughing 603.9
it is better to go to the house of m. 603.1
m. is grief at not wanting back the dead 603.12
stop m. when grief is fully expressed 603.3
you do not see the river of m. because it lacks one tear of your own 141.5
**mourns:** surely nothing dies but something m. 603.2
**mouse:** if m. laughs at cat, there is hole nearby 90.14
m. can't drink more than fill from river 539.5
m. miracle enough to stagger infidels 41.32
m. never trusts its life to one hole 749.26
wily m. that breeds in a cat's ear 90.5
**mousetrap:** in baiting m., leave room for mouse 932.5
**mouth:** God never sends m. without meat 748.10
m.: in man, gateway to the soul 916.9
man overboard, a m. the less 318.1
two ears, one m.: listen more, talk less 540.5
when man speaks to you, look on his m. 916.21
**mouthfuls:** big m. often choke 401.15
**mouths:** men put enemy in m. to steal away brains 266.55
never fair woman but made m. in a glass 587.8
**move:** do we m. ourselves, or are moved by an unseen hand 327.24
give me where to stand, I will m. earth 713.7
the great affair is to m. 985.37
**movement:** m. of life has its rest in its own music 408.4
vitality of new m. gauged by fury aroused 477.9
**movements:** psychopathic element rises to top of m. 109.14
**movie:** m. actor is a god in captivity 11.2
sentimental cheats of the m. screen 563.8
**movies:** only thing that can kill m. is education 604.6
stultifying effect of m.: parents see them 604.4
**Mozart:** *en famille* the angels play M. 607.4
**muckrake:** men with m. often indispensable 783.34
**multitude:** if m. detests a man, inquiry is necessary 756.5
one man means as much to me as a m. 467.3
without fictions the truths of religion would not be intelligible to the m. 790.73
**multitudes:** I am large, I contain m. 462.6
**murder:** if man indulges in m., soon he thinks little of robbing 1063.4
no humane being will m. any creature 516.17
primal eldest curse on a brother's m. 516.14
we m. to dissect 843.41
**murderers:** m. are people who are consistent 516.2
m. punished who kill not in large companies and to the sound of trumpets 516.18
**muses:** no wide road leads to the m. 483.2
**museum:** I go into a natural history m. feeling as if I were attending a funeral 606.2
m. meant for slave of self-education 606.3
painting in m. hears most stupidities 659.5
**music:** all art aspires towards condition of m. 53.94
all m. jars when soul's out of tune 961.1
and the night shall be filled with m. 607.27
criticism makes m. flourish 204.12
English don't like m.—love its noise 287.2
good m. makes people homesick 607.26
hardest of arts to speak of is m. 204.45
if m. appears to express something, this is only an illusion 607.49
if m. translated into human speech, it would no longer need to exist 607.37
m. and women I cannot but give way to 698.28
m. can be translated only by m. 607.25
m. ennobles or degrades our behavior 607.6
m. exists only in motion 607.40
m. has charms to soothe a savage breast 607.18
m. has charms to soothe a savage breast—but

not the unmusical one 607.16
m. is a beautiful opiate 607.30
m. is a most present remedy 607.8
m. is celebration that we own nothing 607.12
m. is essentially useless, as life is 607.42
m. is immediate, it goes on to become 607.3
m. is mystery which, solved, evaporates 548.187
m. is the sole domain in which man realizes the present 607.48
m. is too precise for words 607.29
m. is well said to be speech of angels 607.14
m. is wild sounds civilized 607.22
m. lasts by itself 607.41
m. quickens us to enjoyment of time 607.28
m. revives memories it would appease 607.46
m. sets the soul in operation 607.11
m. speaks to me of things I have not found and shall not 607.36
m. takes us out of the actual 607.21
m. was invented to confirm human loneliness 607.20
m.: way of giving form to inner feelings 607.43
m., when soft voices die, vibrates in the memory 574.33
m. with dinner is an insult both to the cook and violinist 607.17
man without m. in him fit for treasons 607.45
men profess to be lovers of m. 607.54
nation creates m.; composer arranges it 607.23
new m., new listening 607.10
nothing can be well set to m. but nonsense 607.1
only in m. has Negro been able to tell his story 83.1
only true comment on m. is other m. 607.51
people say they like m. when they do not 607.35
people taught too much respect for m. 607.50
performance challenges m. itself 607.52
poetry is harmony of words; m., notes 607.19
sound of m. sensual only secondarily 607.39
sweet m. is sour when no proportion kept 742.3
take a m. bath once or twice a week 607.24
to know if you are enjoying m. see if you are looking at advertisements in program 607.9
to produce m. is also to produce children 607.32
we must have recourse to rules of m. 607.34
when we separate m. from life we get art 53.18
where there's m. there's no evil 607.15
who can express the effect m. has on us 607.13
who hears m., feels his solitude peopled 607.7
why, after all, must everyone like m. 607.38
without m., life would be an error 607.31

**must:** m.'s a schoolroom in month of May 269.9
we do what we m. 317.2

**mutability:** nought may endure but m. 115.34
what more enthralling to mind than m. 115.19

**myself:** I dote on m. 869.18
I live in crowd of jollity to shun m. 151.12
image of m. in my own mind 681.1
inside m. is place where I live alone 852.5
my care is for m.; m. am whole reality 852.4
never seen greater monster, miracle than m. 558.39
to be nobody-but-m. means to fight battle and never stop fighting 442.9
when I speak to you about m., I am speaking to you about yourself 871.2

**mysterious:** fairest we can experience is the m. 1012.2
no object m.; mystery is your eye 676.3

**mystery:** gift of conscious life is sense of m. 172.4
grieve not for not understanding life's m. 1012.6
m. is not profoundness 734.1
m. magnifies danger as fog the sun 213.5
m. of a person is divine to him that has a sense for the godlike 259.3
m. should be left in character 965.38
our dream dashes against the great m. 1012.11
we spend lives talking of m.: life 314.9

**mystic:** m. lives happy in his own consciousness 609.3
to get into the truth is a m. act 991.17

**mysticism:** m. is intensity of feeling about beliefs held of universe 609.2
without m. man can achieve nothing great 609.1

**mystics:** m. hope that science will overtake them 609.4

**mystique:** all starts as a m. and ends as politics 443.2

**myth:** anatomy of any m. is anatomy of men who believed in it and suffered by it 610.1
enemy of truth is often not lie but m. 610.2
when m. meets m., collision is very real 610.3

**mythologists:** children are natural m. 121.40

**mythology:** m. is what grown-ups believe 610.5

**myths:** m. are not believed in, but understood 610.4

## N

**naïve:** n. you are if you believe life favors those who aren't n. 611.4

**naked:** I'm n. under my shirt, whatever its

color 295.5
to go n. is the best disguise 221.4
**name:** don't take action because of a n. 612.2
good n. keeps its lustre in the dark 798.13
good n. rather to be chosen than riches 798.3
have regard for your n. 798.1
how vain, without the merit, is the n. 330.25
leave out my n., but keep my song 382.37
life for one generation; good n. forever 798.21
man's n.: blow he never recovers from 612.6
much more for your n. to live in people's hearts than in their brains 798.17
n., title, rank are artificial 773.9
on n. of misdeed a life collapses 1063.22
who hath not owned the magic of a n. 548.24
women can change n. and nation 560.46
**names:** great n. abase those unable to bear them 612.5
n. are but noise and smoke 612.3
n.: light that glows on sea at night, then dies without leaving its signature 612.9
scattering of our n. into many mouths, we call making them more great 330.33
some judge of authors' n., not works 204.43
**nap:** n. overtakes the old when they try to entertain unwelcome visitors 92.6
**narcissism:** n. gives the power of beasts 869.10
**narcissist:** nobody kinder than n. while you react to life in his terms 1020.4
**Narcissus:** N. never wrote well nor was a friend 869.3
**narrow:** as if nature makes men n. to give force 613.3
n. heart that loves one object 613.11
n.-souled people like narrow-necked bottles 613.8
**nasty:** nice man is a man of n. ideas 336.2
**nation:** chief business of n.: setting up heroes 416.18
driving force of n. is spiritual purpose 614.23
educate the n.: make history personal 130.4
energy in n. like sap in a tree 614.27
every n. determines policies in terms of its own interests 614.14
every n. thinks its own madness normal 614.25
genius of a n. characterizes the society 614.3
healthy n.: balance of people, government 393.19
impossible for n. to be politically internationalist, economically isolated 275.7
institutions alone can create a n. 485.2
moderation in the affairs of the n. 724.5
n. advances in civilisation by increasing in wealth and accessories 131.15
n. can be no stronger abroad than at home 614.16
n. consists of territory, people, laws 614.18
n. doesn't have to be cruel to be tough 517.17
n. has character only when it is free 534.43
n., if has anything to say, should say it 245.14
n. must sacrifice all for principles 728.18
n. needs foreign stock to thrive 451.1
n. renews youth on political sick-bed 614.21
n. revealed by men it honors, remembers 614.15
n. will not count sacrifices in struggle 614.2
n. without dregs, malcontents, is without the seed of things to come 614.9
nothing good for a n. but that which arises from its own core and general wants 614.7
ruin of a n. begins in its homes 614.1
spirit of n. is what counts 614.6
territory does not make a n. 614.10
there are things a man must not do even to save a n. 671.8
there is always a raw and intolerant n. eager to destroy the tolerant and mellow 1035.26
we are not a n., but a union 34.8
when n. is in strife, patriots flourish 671.11
women can change name and n. 560.46
**national:** match n. strength with n. restraint 614.13
n. debt a blessing if not excessive 220.1
n. debt is a n. bond 220.2
n. debt owed by and to nation 220.3
n. greatness moral, not physical, power 598.44
n. hatred is something peculiar 615.4
no n. frontiers to learning 520.30
the free have part in N. Palaver 169.2
when men reach beyond this planet, they should leave n. differences behind 914.5
**nationalism:** n.: a silly cock crowing on own dunghill 615.1
n. is our form of incest, insanity 615.2
n. supposes self-sufficiency, superiority 615.9
**nationalist:** moral powers of n. exhibit ferocity 333.15
n. has a broad hatred and a narrow love 615.3
**nationality:** our true n. is mankind 98.22
**nations:** all n. think they are incomparable 615.7
because n. tend to stupidity, baseness, mankind moves slowly 558.23
friendship links men; only interests link n. 614.8
friendships of n. built on interests 496.13
growing n. should remember that no tree can continue to grow indefinitely 614.26
in difficulty great n., like great men, display energy of character 614.20
interest does not tie n. together 496.19
languages are the pedigree of n. 521.12
mountains interposed make enemies of n. 378.2
n. die by imperceptible disorders 614.5
n. have to limit their objectives 614.22
n., like men, have their infancy 614.24

n. may have fashioned governments 393.16
n. meet politically to settle differences 496.12
one act seldom produces hostilities in n. 1035.52
world bears two n.: good and bad 1060.22
**nationwide:** n. thinking, planning, prevent n. crises 202.7
**native:** best cosmopolite loves his n. country 190.5
every man has a lurking wish to appear considerable in his n. place 421.4
no sorrow above loss of n. land 421.2
**natural:** call nothing n. in age of bloody confusion 994.4
n. world is dynamic 616.37
nothing prevents being n. as wish to be so 726.12
one of greatest impulses of mankind is to arrive at something higher than n. state 920.1
supernatural is n. not yet understood 946.2
to be n. is to be as immoral as nature 431.18
**nature:** accuse not n., she hath done her part 616.51
all n. is but art, unknown to thee 616.59
art helps n., and experience art 53.50
art imitates n. in this: not to dare is to dwindle 53.132
art is the right hand of n. 53.119
artist: lover of n., her slave and master 53.129
beauty sums up the secret aims of n. 70.7
before man made us citizens, n. made us men 431.15
book of n. is book of fate 505.5
child of civilization susceptible to n. 616.49
cult of n. a patronage by people who don't have to struggle with n. every day 616.2
cultivated man is goal of n. 207.5
custom can't conquer n., she's unconquered 431.3
custom is second n. and no less powerful 210.19
deviation from n. is deviation from happiness 616.39
drive n. away and she will return again 431.10
eye is pleased when n. stoops to art 616.77
for observing n., snail's pace best 616.65
formula expressing law of n. praises God 844.9
gifts fate and n. lend us often end us 956.3
he who claims deep love of n. has none 616.24
heaven's joys do not satisfy cravings of n. 431.8
I hate n., this passionless spectator 616.75
I look on n., hear sad music of humanity 616.80
I love not man the less, but n. more 616.14
in America n. is autocratic 34.16
in man all n. is comprehended 558.33
in n. nothing is given, all is sold 673.1
in n., there is death and transmutation 616.64
in our life alone does n. live 616.18
in remaking world we violate kinship of n. 292.4
in state of n., weakest go to the wall 131.14
joy seems normal course of life in n. 43.7
let n. be your teacher 616.81
let us permit n. to take her own way 889.19
little we see in n. that is ours 102.39
man learned pugnaciousness from n. 26.5
man masters n. not by force but by understanding 616.11
man's goal: be human, defend against n. 431.9
marriage of soul with n. 616.70
mind parallel with laws of n. will be strong with their strength 713.18
modern n.-worship is all upside down 616.16
my n. is subdued to what it works in 1058.62
n. a conjugation of the verb to eat 272.17
n. always has more power than education 431.27
n. can speak on everything 616.55
n. cares nothing for human logic 616.72
n. drives with a loose rein 1028.4
n. goes her own way 616.34
n. has filled every cranny of the earth 616.42
n. has given us two eyes, two ears, and one tongue 916.59
n. her custom holds 431.22
n. hides wrinkles of antiquity under rose 616.28
n. holds no brief for the human experiment 906.20
n. invented authors, contrived to make critics out of the chips left 204.26
n. is a guide, not more gentle than just 616.52
n. is a mutable cloud 616.23
n. is a rag merchant 198.10
n. is a suggester of uneasiness 616.74
n. is but theater of the tragedy of man 616.53
n. is entirely indifferent to any reform 616.73
n. is honest, we aren't; we embalm dead 101.1
n. is indifferent to survival of Americans 949.5
n. is like a beautiful woman 616.62
n. is one with rapine 616.66
n. is progressive realization of purpose 616.22
n. is rarely allowed into civilization 131.31
n. is reckless of the individual 616.25
n. is the art of God 616.19
n. is what you may do 127.3
n. knows no indecencies; man invents them 750.5
n. knows what we need 572.1
n. loves the incomplete 616.30
n. magnificent when dealing with love 796.2
n.: milliards of atoms playing billiards 1010.5
n. never betrayed heart that loved her 616.79
n. never deceives us 858.8

n. never says one thing, wisdom another 616.40
n., not standing, makes the good man 391.44
n. often hidden, sometimes overcome 616.4
n. pours life into dead, into life 616.6
n. refuses to sympathize with sorrow 616.69
n. scarcely ever gives us very best 53.56
n. seems so careless of the single life 306.8
n. speaks a various language 616.12
n. suits the man to his fortunes 117.8
n. takes no account of human excuses 616.43
n. takes shortest way to her ends 616.26
n. teaches us to love our friends 790.25
n., to be commanded, must be obeyed 616.3
n. will bear the closest inspection 616.68
n., with equal mind, sees her sons at play 616.1
n. without learning is blind 277.63
n. would watch unmoved if we destroyed entire human race 218.134
necessity is curb and law of n. 617.8
no doctrine does good where n. is wanting 200.4
one touch of n. makes whole world kin 431.23
only habitual late riser, up early, takes in full flavor of n. 599.1
our n. consists in motion 10.16
peace of n. secure so long as man not there 616.21
perfections of n. show image of God 616.56
reason deceives us more often than n. 778.41
reason demands man live in accord with his own n. 431.21
repetition: only permanence of n. 794.4
simplicity of n. lies in shortsightedness of observer 616.46
sounds in n.: rain, wind, ocean 616.5
sweet is the lore which n. brings 843.41
the rules of the game are laws of n. 616.38
there is no forgiveness in n. 616.7
thief and murderer follow n. just as much as the philanthropist 431.11
to be constant in n. were inconstancy 115.9
to do what misfits one's n. is disgust 431.24
to whiten ivory is to spoil n. with art 54.3
true religion must know our n. 790.57
true return to n. is death 616.32
true wisdom is not departing from n. 616.63
we adapt ourselves to n.; we don't master it 616.20
we do not see n. with eyes, but hearts 616.36
we should study n. more in natural things 616.57
we soon get through with n. 616.71
what falls in accordance with n. is good 387.1
what is man in n.? nothing, all 558.41
when n. strips veils from vegetation, we apprehend its ferocity 616.76
where n. does most, man does the least 138.2
who can paint as n., boast hues like hers 616.67
words describing n. found in fairy books 616.15
works of n. acquire meaning by commentary 616.61
world an atom in ample bosom of n. 1010.9

**nature's:** adapt or perish is n. imperative 12.13
against n. silence, action 9.39
exciting that we are n. latest experiment 558.44
honest man fulfills n. plan 151.4
man is n. sole mistake 558.21
n. answers are never comprehensible words 1012.14
n. fire is all the learning I desire 616.13
n. instructions are always slow 616.60

**natures:** them of other n. thinks different 258.1

**nausea:** unreliability of experience has led to n. 115.35

**navigation:** how can a man learn n. where there's no rudder 480.5

**navigators:** winds, waves are on the side of the ablest n. 1.9

**near:** if eye too n., hues of opal not seen 331.6
slight not what's n. aiming at what's far 55.7

**necessary:** beautiful rests on foundations of the n. 70.14
things as they are seems n. state 210.15
what is n. is never a risk 617.17

**necessities:** give me the luxuries; will do without n. 554.10

**necessity:** against n. no one can fight and win 617.1
doctrine of n. is that of toleration 800.4
how base to struggle with n. 617.4
men first feel n., then look for utility 554.9
n.: argument of tyrants, creed of slaves 617.12
n. can turn any weapon to advantage 617.14
n. dispenseth with decorum 617.7
n. is an interpretation, not fixed fact 617.10
n. is harsh; fate has no reprieve 337.10
n. is the theme and the inventress 617.8
n. knows no laws 617.19
n. never made a good bargain 617.6
n. prompts to do things at thought of which one would start at other times 224.6
n. reconciles men, forms itself into laws 906.13
n. relieves us of embarrassment of choice 617.20
n. turns lion into fox 617.11
nothing has more strength than dire n. 617.5
there is no n. to live subject to n. 617.3
true creator is n. 617.13
we give to n. the praise of virtue 617.16
where n. speaks it demands 617.18

wise man never refuses anything to n. 617.15
wise to make a virtue of n. 617.2
**necessity's:** liberty is n. conscience 534.14
**need:** ambition makes more trusty slaves than n. 33.15
hard to know what those we love really n. 548.8
he who awaits the call but sees the n. 784.3
if you tame me we shall n. each other 548.194
when we grapple with another man's n. 656.3
while a man exists there is n. of him 314.3
**needed:** mature man needs to be n. 567.4
**needs:** happiness: satisfaction of dammed-up n. 407.42
living being held most by own n. 618.2
understanding human n. is half the job of meeting them 618.6
**needy:** gift in season is a double favor to n. 382.32
**neglect:** such sweet n. more taketh me 892.8
**negligent:** celerity never more admired than by n. 919.4
**negotiate:** never n. out of fear, but never fear to n. 987.3
**Negro:** being N. doesn't make you expert on race 83.8
can't the nation that absorbed foreigners absorb N. Americans 769.3
dehumanization of N. is indivisible from dehumanization of ourselves 83.3
for N. in America, winning smallest things takes so long they become miracles 83.12
he makes N. base who denies him rights 769.6
N. is superior to the white race 83.4
N. revolt is aimed at winning freedom, not friends 83.6
only in case of N. has melting pot failed 83.13
only in music has N. been able to tell his story 83.1
to be N.: to participate in culture of poverty and fear 83.9
**Negroes:** having despised us N. it's not strange that Americans render us despicable 83.7
treat us N. like men; we'll live in peace 83.17
**neighbor:** as man draws nearer to the stars, why shouldn't he also draw nearer to his n. 98.11
every man's n. is his looking-glass 619.4
folly to punish n. by fire 811.18
good n. looks beyond external accidents 619.7
he gains time who does not watch his n. 873.15
n. true and loving is joy beyond all else 619.9
nothing odder than satisfactions of n. 619.8
pity for all means hardness to n. 453.7
we really love our n. as ourselves 852.16
your next-door n. is an environment 619.3
**neighbor's:** each man is afraid of n. disapproval 619.10
withdraw thy foot from thy n. house 426.6
your safety at stake if n. wall burns 150.5
**neighborhood:** n.: where, when you go out, you get beat up 129.26
**neighbors:** be no better nor worse than your n. 573.4
correlative to loving n. as ourselves is hating ourselves as we hate n. 619.5
do unto yourself as your n. do 386.1
mix with n.; learn what's doing at home 619.11
people can fool Devil, but not n. 619.6
the state is our n.; n. are the state 923.10
there are many who dare not kill themselves for fear of what the n. will say 798.8
thou shalt love thy n. as thyself 619.2
we can better study our n. than ourselves 656.1
we do things because our n. do them 210.12
we make sport for our n., laugh at them 290.1
when men succeed, even n. think them wise 938.34
**nerves:** life is a question of n. 536.135
n., the n., mysteries of this machine, man 620.4
**nettle:** tender-handed stroke a n. 90.6
who handles a n. tenderly is stung 973.5
**neurosis:** education, like n., begins at home 277.71
good writing is product of someone's n. 1062.103
n. began with discoveries of Copernicus 620.11
n. is final gift of industrial order 994.12
religious n. is tied to dietary demands 790.55
sin, n., fruit of tree of knowledge 520.44
**neurotic:** has there ever been an age so rife with n. sensibility 620.10
n. is man who builds castle in air 751.1
**neurotics:** "sensibility" claimed by n. matched by their egotism 620.12
mistake to suppose n. are interesting 620.3
**neutrality:** even for n. a government must be strong 393.23
n. has same weights, measures for each 453.6
there can be no positive n. 496.7
**new:** be not the first by whom the n. are tried 335.23
experience of the n. is rarely without foreboding 115.23
from n. truths, n. phrase, n. doubts grow 998.4
if we see old in n. thing we are pacified 632.8
let no one say I've said nothing n. 477.8

n. broom is good for three days 278.1
n. carries sense of sacrilege, violation 477.7
n. comes into being in the midst of clumsy deals 477.11
n. faces have more authority than old 61.2
n. occasions teach n. duties 269.22
no n. garment lives up to expectation 265.5
no subject too old for n. comment 520.16
nothing n. but what has become antiquated 632.1
nothing thought rare which is not n. 335.1
old deeds for old people, n. deeds for n. 224.39
old remains unless one lives, dies for n. 979.12
old tracks lost, n. country is revealed 115.36
only with n. ruler do you value the old 825.5
there is no n. thing under the sun 632.2
to discover n. lands, lose sight of shore 477.4

**New England:** most serious charge against N. E. is February 621.2
N. E. weather compels admiration, regret 621.3

**New Englander:** N. E. nearly worships an argument 51.1

**New York:** all foolish an' manny wise men go to N.Y. 625.3
faces in N.Y. remind me of people who played a game and lost 625.5
in N.Y. aspirations of Western world meet 625.7
in N.Y. City, brick-bats fly at all hours 625.8
in N.Y. they ask, how much is he worth 926.3
N.Y. has depth; Washington, politics 1037.3
N.Y. inhabitants boast about not knowing neighbors 625.6

**New Yorkers:** N.Y. assume it will never rain 625.1
N.Y. don't go to theatre, but to hits 965.12
N.Y. go straight to heaven 625.2

**news:** Americans are suckers for good n. 991.122
evil n. rides post, good n. delays 622.6
if far, it's n.; if close, it's sociology 622.8
n. is history shot on the wing 622.2
nobody likes the bringer of bad n. 622.10
nowadays truth is the greatest n. 622.3
wan man's n. is another man's throubles 622.1

**newspaper:** first duty of a n. is to be accurate 623.27
good n. is a nation talking to itself 623.16
Homer is new, and nothing's so old as n. 632.9
man who never looks into a n. is better informed than he who reads them 623.9
n. column, like fish, to be consumed fresh 623.22
n. has nothing but honor to lose 623.25
n. is the natural enemy of the book 623.7
nowhere is knowledge as varied as in a n. 623.3
reader of an unexciting n. 623.4
window to world can be covered by a n. 623.12

**newspapers:** evil that men do lives on front pages of n. 623.2
hostile n. more fearful than bayonets 623.19
I prefer n. without a government 623.8
lies from the print of n. 563.8
life one world, life seen in n. another 623.5
n. always excite curiosity 623.11
people confuse that read in n. with news 623.14
real life happens exclusively in the n. 623.1
serious, profitable occupation: reading n. 623.6
we live under government of men, n. 623.20

**nice:** n. man is a man of nasty ideas 336.2
to be n. is troublesome, slavish 336.1

**nicknames:** of all eloquence a n. is most concise 612.4
titles but n.; every n. a title 612.7

**night:** and the n. shall be filled with music 607.27
at n. there is no such thing as ugly woman 626.9
at n. words fade and things come alive 626.10
by n. an atheist half believes a God 997.20
damp of the n. drives deeper into my soul 685.5
darkness falls from the wings of n. 626.8
darkness of n., like pain, is dumb 214.3
democracy's only success—the n. 626.6
do not go gentle into that good n. 218.128
for a bad n., a mattress of wine 266.59
if life at n. good you think you have all 885.11
lamps defend man from age-old n. 129.37
learn to reverence n. 626.4
men in hot countries love the n. 138.3
monarch is n. of all eldest things 626.2
n. brings our troubles to the light 626.11
n. is the mother of counsels 626.7
n. shows stars and women in better light 626.5
praise not the day before n. 721.3
prayer should be the lock of the n. 717.14
to know only artificial n. is absurd 54.2
we now have a dislike of n. itself 626.3
when shall the n. be gone 71.2

**nightcap:** age and wedlock bring man to n. 71.5

**nightclub:** in comparison to n. churches are gay 700.8

**nightmare:** what's a joy to one is n. to the other 407.19

**nightmares:** how many of our daydreams would be n. 687.21

**nights:** many seek good n. and lose good days 700.6

**nimble:** n. sixpence better than slow shilling 501.3

**nineteenth:** n. century problem: God is dead 216.3
**no:** he who never says n. is n. true man 784.7
n. is n. negative in a woman's mouth 784.8
to think is to say n. 627.1
yes and n. are soon said 96.6
**nobility:** n.: being superior to your past self 945.5
there may be n. in being last 773.20
true n. is exempt from fear 628.7
virtue is the only true n. 628.2
you cannot throw away a word like n. 489.18
**noble:** baths, n. deeds, best for depression 1004.33
man of truly n. ways listens not to praise 594.7
men of no note suffer n. sorrows 641.9
n. and common blood are same color 37.4
n. deed most estimable hidden 224.28
nature has invited us to become n. 567.16
often n. face hides filthy ways 438.10
to write n. style, possess a n. soul 935.8
what is n. is in itself of a quiet nature 628.3
**nobleness:** n. in others will rise to meet thine own 628.4
**nobler:** n. a man, harder it is for him to suspect inferiority in others 628.1
**noblest:** honest man's the n. work of God 423.15
stupid thing done from n. motive 934.22
**nobly:** let a man n. live or n. die 628.9
spurn not the n.-born 786.2
**nobody's:** everybody's business is n. business 804.7
**noise:** clapping with right hand only won't make n. 187.3
he who hath worst cause makes most n. 109.10
n. is evolving endurers, needers of n. 629.4
n.: most impertinent form of interruption 629.2
ten who speak make more n. than ten thousand who are silent 585.2
who make the n. are not only inhabitants of field 585.1
**noisiest:** n. drum has nothing in it but air 87.2
**noisy:** most men lead lives of n. desperation 629.5
**nominee:** n.: gentleman shrinking from distinction of private life 755.3
**nonconformism:** n. is the major sin of our time 466.4
**nonconformists:** quality of n. same as of conformists 89.6
**noninterference:** n. with others' ways of being happy 787.4
**nonsense:** even God has been defended with n. 874.3
man talking sense to himself is no madder than man talking n. to others 874.5
n. good because common sense limited 874.4
n. may tomorrow be demonstrated truth 991.142
there is no n. that cannot be made creed 739.9
to appreciate n. requires serious interest in life 874.1
**nonviolence:** n. is not a garment to be put on at will 658.5
**nonviolent:** n. revolution not a seizure of power 813.12
strong, n. man is unjust by accident 933.8
**normal:** n. is an ideal 630.1
**north:** dark, true and tender is the n. 138.4
**nose:** any n. may ravage with impunity a rose 349.1
great n. indicates a great man 324.9
modern n. and eye have developed intensity 875.7
stupidity displayed in the n. 324.7
**noses:** when you're down and out, something always turns up; usually friends' n. 17.65
**note:** men of n. do great deeds 641.9
**nothing:** caravan starts for the dawn of n. 627.2
he who hath n. is frightened at n. 740.8
how pleasant it is to ask for n. 873.24
it takes a long time to understand n. 1000.4
many find n. within themselves 319.32
miserable to say "I had" when I have n. 547.8
n. can come of n. 279.21
n. comes from n. 108.4
n. is always a clever thing to say 891.6
n. is to be had for n. 673.4
people do not practise doing n. 444.3
we brought n. into world, carry n. out 81.2
while you can't resolve what you are, at last you will be n. 442.14
who does n. renders himself incapable 1058.36
who has n. can whistle in robber's face 712.35
**notions:** airy n. tyrannize in all men's minds 687.11
life driven forward by apprehension of n. too general for language 441.37
**nourishment:** regardless of color all require same n. 295.20
**novel:** don't write n. to establish a principle 341.7
final test for n. is affection for it 341.9
n. is conviction of fellow-men's existence 341.3
n. is history that could take place 341.10
n. reading is a passion for results 91.34
what, in fact, is a n. but a universe 341.2
**novelist:** n. businessman drops in on literature 1062.90
painter thinks with brush, n. with story 341.13
**novels:** have you any right to read n. 91.91

n. are about minorities: individuals 341.4
n. are sweets 341.18
readers of n. are a strange folk 341.12
to love n. is to prefer sentiment 341.6
**novelties:** n. please less than they impress 632.3
try n. for salesman's bait 103.10
**novelty:** had Greeks disdained n., what ancient work would now exist 42.7
only God and some few rare geniuses can keep forging ahead into n. 632.4
we have learned so well how to absorb n. 632.6
what bloom is to fruit, n. is to love 548.112
**November:** how sad N. if no knowledge of spring 848.39
N.: lonely season in lonely lands 848.10
**November's:** N. sky is chill and drear 848.35
**novice:** man arrives a n. at each age of his life 537.3
**novices:** we arrive at various stages of life as n. 319.33
**now:** I live n. 723.9
word "n." like a bomb, and it ticks 723.23
**nowhere:** he that is everywhere is n. 10.8
one place is everywhere, everywhere, n. 693.10
some want to be everywhere, get n. 10.17
**nuclear:** we will not unnecessarily risk n. war 633.8
**nude:** undressed is vulgar—n. pure 634.1
**nudism:** in world of moral n., wearing clothes suggests you have something to hide 265.11
**nudities:** man sole animal whose n. offend own kind 634.2
**nuisance:** vain man in reality a universal n. 1020.17
**number:** greatest happiness of greatest n. is foundation of morals and legislation 407.9
**numbers:** suffering of millions blurred by n. 939.48
**numerous:** if the sailors too n., the ship sinks 56.1
**nuns:** n. fret not at their narrow room 920.9
**nut:** by the husk you may guess at the n. 45.7
if don't crack shell, can't eat n. 289.8

## O

**oak:** when o. is felled, the forest echoes 641.2
**oaks:** many strokes overthrow the tallest o. 679.7
**oars:** without o. you cannot cross in boat 714.6
**oath:** no o. secures love against higher love 548.60
o. doesn't make us believe man, man the o. 635.1
spirit of o. runs beside crooked judgments 635.4
trust character more than an o. 628.8
who takes an o. holds himself in his hands 635.2
**oaths:** o. are but words, and words but wind 635.3
**obedience:** he who yields a prudent o., exercises a partial control 636.4
it is a bitter dose to be taught o. after you have learned to rule 432.1
o., bane of all genius, virtue, freedom 636.7
o. is result of instinct of the masses 813.35
**obedient:** men not to live like beasts, prone, o. 727.23
**obey:** it's almost pleasanter to o. 636.1
learn to o. before you command 636.8
way to rise is to o. and please 938.20
who has not learned to o. cannot command 528.1
**obeyed:** command wisely, be o. cheerfully 528.8
man who commands must have o. in the past 528.3
**obeys:** man who orders has more sense of difficulty than man who o. 61.9
who o. usually better than who commands 636.5
**object:** at bottom, no real o. is unpoetical 702.45
no meanest o. is insignificant 1005.2
**objection:** technical o. is refuge of scoundrel 826.1
**objective:** o. world is a sort of Rorschach ink blot 777.12
**objects:** goal of inanimate o. is to defeat man 638.1
men feel gratitude for pleasing o. 638.9
obstinacy of inanimate o. 644.4
we are the slaves of o. around us 638.5
**obligation:** none bound by o. unless freely accepted 269.3
**obligations:** only growth is in fulfillment of o. 269.29
you want them, those o. 882.2
**oblige:** safer to offend some men than to o. them 639.8
to o. costs little and helps much 881.6
**oblivion:** ignorance is not bliss—it is o. 445.34
o. is the page whereon memory writes 574.5
only earthly certainty is o. 983.25
**obloquy:** o. is, to most, more painful than death 203.28
**obscurity:** no defense for absurdity but o. 640.1
o. and a competence—the best life 641.10
o. is the realm of error 640.5
o. is the refuge of incompetence 641.5
o. often brings safety 641.1
one must choose between o. and fame 641.8
only defence against reproach is o. 797.1
pernicious effect of haste is o. 409.9
things in o. had better remain there 706.8

**observation:** o. is an old man's memory 642.4
**observations:** make o. of others we might make of self 203.21
to o. which ourselves we make, we grow more partial for observer's sake 649.27
**observatory:** o.: where astronomers conjecture away guesses of predecessors 843.2
**observed:** whoever feels o. observes himself 1020.8
**observers:** cultivated men make acute, balanced o. 642.2
**observeth:** he that o. the wind shall not sow 110.1
**obstacles:** best can exact motive power from o. 1.16
if there are o., shortest line between two points may be crooked line 579.3
o. cannot crush me 765.8
we combat o. to get repose 805.1
**obstinacy:** firmness without intellect is o. 491.24
no man is any good without some o. 644.2
o., dogmatism, surest signs of stupidity 644.9
o. in bad cause is but constancy in a good 109.1
o. is the sister of constancy 644.8
o. of human beings is exceeded only by the o. of inanimate objects 644.4
o. weakest of things in one without wisdom 644.1
**obstinacy's:** o. ne'er so stiff as in a wrong belief 644.3
**obstinate:** he cannot be good who is not o. 644.11
**obvious:** analysis of o. takes unusual mind 605.12
**occasions:** men are commonplace on supreme o. 67.1
new o. teach new duties 269.22
**Occident:** O.: part of world inhabited by Christians 438.3
**occupation:** future o. is to be skilled consumers 103.24
life without absorbing o. is hell 502.14
serious o. has reference to some want 1058.37
tranquility and o. give happiness 407.56
**occupations:** woman's o. run counter to creative life 1055.90
worse o. than feeling a woman's pulse 261.20
**ocean:** fantastic o. doth enfold the likeness of whate'er on land is seen 847.14
roll on, thou deep and dark blue o. 847.4
you cannot speak of o. to a well-frog 148.1
**October:** all things on earth point home in old O. 848.53
never such pleasant, sunny spots as in O. 848.19
O.: fallen leaf, and horizon seen clearly 848.7
**odor:** no o. so bad as from goodness tainted 188.15
nothing awakens a memory like an o. 875.5
**odors:** o., when sweet violets sicken, live within the sense they quicken 574.33
**offend:** men o. where they find goodness to forgive 474.5
safer to o. some men than to oblige them 639.8
**offended:** who is o. writes on marble 474.10
**offender:** o. never pardons 357.11
**offenders:** the more laws, the more o. 525.29
**offends:** O, it o. me to the soul 11.7
who o. writes on sand 474.10
**offense:** pardon one o. and encourage many 531.2
**offenses:** some o. not given but taken 474.26
**office:** fools take to selves respect given to o. 1020.2
man who has no o. to go to, a trial 575.13
men want public o. for its advantage 755.1
public o. is secure, but lacks hope, fear 755.10
when we got into o. things were bad 724.8
**offices:** great o. will have great talents 399.13
man casts eye on o., rottenness begins 755.11
**official:** o. must be audible, visible, kissable 755.9
what is o. is incontestable 645.1
**oil:** truth and o. always come to the surface 991.121
**old:** all diseases run into one, o. age 889.7
all evil comes from the o. 1065.1
as teeth drop out, the o. get more biting 646.83
as we grow o., beauty steals inward 646.26
as we grow o., it is hard to keep wise 646.42
as we grow o., value of time becomes vivid 646.47
as we grow o. we come to believe that everything will turn out badly for us 646.19
be not the last to lay the o. aside 335.23
before you contradict o. man, understand him 646.87
better to be young bug than o. bird 1065.34
chaste adolescence makes dissolute o. age 120.6
chastity is not chastity in an o. man 120.5
complete life includes o. age 537.12
counsels of o. age give light without heat 19.37
denunciation of young necessary to o. 646.96
dignity, riches necessary to o. men 1065.32
dismiss o. horse in time 807.3
dying young is boon in o. age 646.106
envy not the o. man his tranquillity 646.51
every o. man complains of rising generation 372.6
few people know how to be o. 646.63
good o. times.: all times when o. are good. 296.5
grow o. with me; the best is yet to be 646.13
growing o. is dying young 646.72
growing o. is no more than a bad habit 646.69

growing o. is not a gradual decline 646.94
harm done by o. men who cling to influence 1065.38
I grow o., I shall wear the bottoms of my trousers rolled 646.24
I love everything that's o. 646.43
if we see o. in new thing we are pacified 632.8
if we're not foolish young, we're foolish o. 351.4
if you would be tasted for o. wine, be in the mouth a pleasant grape 390.6
in o. age common to act from interest 1065.15
it is easy to become a monk in o. age 595.1
learning acquired in youth helps o. age 520.40
like children, the o. talk to themselves 646.77
man in o. age is strong but harsh 1065.7
man wants to live long but not be o. 545.13
mind grows o. as well as body 512.1
misery of o. man interesting to nobody 646.56
no subject too o. for new comment 520.16
nobody loves life like an o. man 646.98
none so o. he does not think he could live another year 646.17
none so o. that he may not hope for one more day 646.89
o. age brings out essential characteristics 117.12
o. age brings red flare of dreams again 687.24
o. age brings with it its own defects 646.41
o. age creeps upon us, unperceived 646.61
o. age deprives the intelligent man only of qualities useless to wisdom 646.60
o. age has great sense of calm, freedom 646.80
o. age has its pleasures 646.68
o. age has no precise boundary 537.4
o. age is a warden upon chastity 120.4
o. age is always wakeful 646.70
o. age is fifteen years older than I 646.8
o. age is forgiven nothing 1065.28
o. age is like an opium-dream 646.50
o. age is not so fiery as youth 646.35
o. age is tyrant who forbids pleasures 646.64
o. age not total misery; experience helps 646.32
o. age provoked can't be appeased. 646.35
o. age should burn and rave at close 218.128
o. age slow to give or forget affronts 486.1
o. age: too intent on our interests 646.103
o. age turns bad dispositions into worse habits 646.12
o. and the ripe fall 218.81
o. believe everything 1065.37
o. deeds for o. people, new deeds for new 224.38
o. dog can't alter his way of barking 404.8
o. events have modern meanings 417.32
o. feel tired at beginning of an action 338.2
o. fellows have wisdom but prefer hair 646.22
o. fools are more foolish than young 353.20
o. goat not more reverend for beard 646.34
o. hands soil what they caress 1065.11
o. man loved is winter with flowers 646.38
o. man never stops believing that he can still make an impression on women 885.16
o. man plays saint, is insufferable 1065.12
o. men and comets reverenced for same reason 646.101
o. men are like old chronicles 646.81
o. men give good advice to console selves 646.65
o. men grasp more at life than babies 646.86
o. men know when an o. man dies 646.75
o. men still young enough to learn 646.2
o. men want to be faithless, and cannot 470.17
o. men's prayers for death are lying ones 646.29
o. order changeth 115.37
o. people are great braggarts 646.9
o. people are monsters to little folk 1065.13
o. persons, places, have intrinsic vitality 646.88
o. remains unless one lives, dies for new 979.12
o., that's affront no woman can bear 1055.20
o. words die, new melodies break forth 115.36
oftener than not the o. are uncontrollable 646.30
one must, when o., remember one's youth 1065.14
only benefit of o. age: to die by degrees 218.88
passions of the young are vices in the o. 1065.18
people don't conform to instructions of us o. ones 19.16
real dread of men not devil but o. age 646.53
some o. in years have only age to prove they have lived long 545.2
the o. appeal to our respect and pity 1065.31
the o. fancy their gravity is mistaken by the young for wisdom 1065.6
the o. repeat themselves 1065.3
the o. sit on life's raised dais 1065.31
there is no such thing as an o. woman 1055.102
there is unspeakable dawn in happy o. age 646.55
they that reverence too much o. times are but a scorn to the new 979.1
those we grow o. with seem bosom-friends 646.97
'tis late when o. man knows he is o. 646.36
to an o. man any warm place is home 646.44
to be hopeful is to triumph over o. age 646.4
to lay to virtue the weariness of o. age 646.39
to live in health, be o. early 411.18
way through life must be learned from o. 646.59

we can't reach o. age by another's road 860.12
we do not have childhood, maturity, o. age; our lives have seasons 537.13
we may always find time to grow o. 1064.8
we should not reproach o. age. 646.11
we who are o. are but noise and shape 646.31
we wish the o. to wander off, die, and bury themselves 646.54
well that o. age accompanied by ignorance 646.73
when an o. man marries, death laughs 560.45
when friends compliment a man about looking young, they think he is growing o. 580.14
when snake is o., frog will tease him 223.9
who lacks wisdom in o. age has existed only 646.84
woman is as o. as she looks before breakfast 1055.73
women are as o. as they feel—men are o. when they lose their feelings 576.56
young can shock and keep o. up to date 1065.29
young folk silly, o. folk cold 1065.10
young think o. fools, o. know young are 1065.4
youth is a blunder; o. age a regret 537.5
youth must study wisdom, o. practice it 1053.57

**old-fashioned:** only the modern ever becomes o. 593.2

**older:** as men grow o., rely on a sense of humor 576.37
do men grow wiser as they grow o. 646.49
o. and at centre of your time 580.11
o. man who will not laugh is a fool 1065.26
young loyal to individuals, o. to types 553.2

**omelet:** to make an o. you have to break an egg 239.11

**omnipotence:** o. is bought with ceaseless fear 713.15

**omnipotent:** to be o. but friendless is to reign 825.26

**omniscience:** knowing what thou knowest not is o. 520.25

**one:** o. arrow does not bring down two birds 579.15
o. man should love and honor o. 560.34
only o. in command in home or state 393.20
the O. remains, the many change and pass 300.3

**one-eyed:** in land of the blind, the o. man is king 788.1

**oneself:** no ache more deadly than striving to be o. 442.23
writing of o. one should show no mercy 62.1

**onion:** life is like an o. one peels crying 536.37

**onions:** happy is family that can eat o. together 352.9
o. within the bowl animate the whole 186.10

**onlooker:** every o. is either coward or traitor 642.1

**onward:** world owes o. impulses to men ill at ease 735.8

**open:** have o. face but conceal thoughts 162.9
nothing won to admit men with o. door, and to receive them with shut countenance 426.2
our interests are those of the o. door 496.18

**openly:** you may live with people and not speak o. 908.51

**opera:** at the o. I leave reason at the door 648.4
baritones are born villains in o. 648.6
music-lover may accept o. for music in it 648.5
no o. plot can be sensible 648.2
o. may be allowed lavish decorations 648.1
o.: representation of life in another world 648.3

**opiate:** o.: unlocked door in prison of identity 267.1

**opinion:** all mankind not justified in silencing one person of contrary o. 362.8
American majority bar liberty of o. 725.6
current of o. is ruler of the world 756.16
difference of o. makes horse-races 649.33
difference of o. makes horse racing and missionaries 590.3
error of o. may be tolerated where reason is left free to combat it 297.21
every o. espoused at the expense of life 649.20
every reform was once a private o. 783.10
freedom never relied on uniformity of o. 250.7
government no better than public o. sustaining it 756.19
having no o. conducive to peace of mind 464.5
history is record of weakness of public o. 417.12
how many wounds have been given for the poor victory of an o. 51.4
I care not what I am in the o. of others 873.16
I could never divide myself from any man upon the difference of an o. 649.3
illusion to think ancient o. may not be false 979.2
loyalty to petrified o. never freed a soul 979.21
majority best, yet o. of least able 231.38
man must brave public o., woman submit 756.21
man values own o. of self less 656.13
men seldom trust the o. of their equal 649.32
more unpopular an o., more its holder should observe conventionalities 649.5
most difficult secret to keep: self-o. 871.4
my o. is a view I hold until I find out something that changes it 347.2
no group can withstand public o. 756.18

nothing makes more cowards than public o. 756.1
o. in good men is knowledge in the making 649.19
o. is a flitting thing 991.25
o. is a powerful party, without measure 649.21
o. is called the queen of the world 649.34
o. is like a pendulum and obeys same law 649.30
o. is truth filtered through moods 649.25
o. of world is confession of character 117.10
one often contradicts o. because of unsympathetic tone 649.23
original o. does not necessarily differ from the accepted o. 649.8
people maintain o. for sake of talking 916.26
proud man satisfied with his own good o. 727.13
public o. is generally public sentiment 756.6
public o. is stronger than legislature 756.22
public o. is the thermometer a monarch should constantly consult 756.15
public o. makes life unpleasant for one not content to be the average man 756.11
public o. may become legislation 756.17
refusing to have an o. is having one 649.26
respect public o. as far as necessary 756.20
scholar needs manuscripts to know his o. 842.12
they that approve private o. call it o. 256.4
to reign by o., begin by trampling it 649.28
unbiased o. is absolutely valueless 649.36
we are ruled by public o., not law 756.10
we avoid such as differ in o. from us 649.14
we tolerate differences of o. only in people familiar to us 649.2
who hides his o. has nothing to answer for 649.24
who never alters his o. is like standing water 262.2
youth measures right by world o. 1065.15

**opinions:** arguments confirm people in own o. 51.27
chief effect of talk: strengthens own o. 649.35
different hours, we are of different o. 649.6
easier to conform to o. than to sway o. 649.13
effervescing o., like champagne, get flat when exposed to the air 649.11
judge men by what their o. made of them 649.16
men get o. by reiteration chiefly 649.4
men suffer deception from their own o. 858.5
new o. are suspected because they are not already common 649.17
o. are of much more value than arguments 649.10
o. from youth to age are inconsistent and contradictory 649.31
our o. are less important than the spirit with which they possess us 649.22
our o. of others are not permanent 787.8
people oppose established o. from pride 256.9
public buys its o. as it buys meat, milk 756.3
some men are as sure of truth of their o. as others are of what they know 649.1
sound of tireless voices is price we pay to hear music of our own o. 362.10
there never were two o. alike 258.3

**opium:** religion is o. of the people 790.46
spirit of world not evoked by o. or wine 267.2

**opponent:** never ascribe to o. meaner motives than your own 286.5

**opportunities:** o. flit by while we regret chances lost 785.2
problems are only o. in work clothes 731.4
takes certain level of aspiration before one can take advantage of o. 55.11
wise man makes more o. than he finds 650.1

**opportunity:** all deserve equal o. to develop talents 295.15
it is the missed o. that counts 550.2
know thine o. 650.7
o. God sends does not wake sleeper 650.9
o. knocks wanst; on some dures it hammers 650.3
o. makes the thief 927.3
there is no security on earth, only o. 650.6
while we stop to think, we often miss o. 650.8

**opposites:** 'tis o. entice 184.1

**opposition:** many a man's strength is in o. 651.1
no government secure without o. 651.5
o. becomes sweet when called persecution 561.5
o. brings concord 651.8
o.: party that prevents government from running amuck by hamstringing it 651.2

**oppressed:** greatest consolation of the o. is to consider themselves superior to their tyrants 177.1
o. people authorized to break fetters 813.4
pardon oppressor is to deal harshly with o. 995.30
truth, time, on the side of the o. today 995.22

**oppressing:** we delight in o. somebody else 995.28

**oppression:** displaced police magistrate feels no hesitation in foregoing o. 783.35
many dislikers of o. like to oppress 995.25
world needs redemption from hunger and o. 429.1

**oppressor:** pardon o. is to deal harshly with oppressed 995.30

**optimism:** o. and self-pity are poles of cowardice 196.4
o. approves, submits, believes all 652.2
o.: belief that everything is beautiful, including the ugly 652.3

o.: content of small men in high places 652.6
o. is kind of heart stimulant 652.8
o. maintains all is well when wretched 652.12
o. takes no account of the present 652.4
our o. or our pessimism makes our ideas 653.5
there is o. which tolerates unworthiness 652.10

**optimist:** dour friend is less fatiguing than o. 653.3
must be o. to open your eyes in morning 994.15
o. after forty-eight knows too little 653.4
o. is guy that never had much experience 652.9
o. knows each year worse, thinks next year will be better 653.1
pessimist is a man who's lived with an o. 685.4

**Oracle:** I'm O., when I ope lips, let no dog bark 262.14

**orator:** no o. ever thought another better 163.4
o. can hardly get beyond commonplaces 757.7
o. should be accompanied by an orchesthry 757.5

**orators:** o. not also great writers are shadows to following generations 757.1
passions are only o. that always persuade 668.15
what o. lack in depth they make up to you in length 757.9

**oratory:** in o. greatest art is to hide art 757.16
nothing so unbelievable that o. cannot make it acceptable 757.3
o. is like prostitution; must have tricks 757.11

**order:** chaos often breeds life; o., habit 255.1
chaos stamped with a seal becomes o. 255.2
excessive severity is not the path to o. 883.3
good o. is the foundation of all things 654.4
if you beat someone, it's got to be for the sake of o. 526.1
let all things be done decently and in o. 654.2
life sets things in o.; very tidy is life 536.2
o. always weighs on the individual 654.14
o. and law have a cost 526.3
o. is shape upon which beauty depends 654.3
o. marches with measured strides 654.12
old o. changeth 115.37
putting things in o. 654.8
respect for o. related to size of paycheck 526.2
the o. of things consents to virtue 1025.20
the o. of things that takes care of fleas and moles also takes care of men 572.8
to put some o. into ourselves 53.30

**orders:** who does thing under o. is not unhappy 636.6

**ordinary:** o. men gain greatness by being near us 331.10
o. persons find no differences in men 491.23

**organization:** large o. is loose o. 100.3

**orgasm:** o. has replaced the Cross 885.21

**orgy:** o. made alluring by righteous indignation 733.7

**original:** easier to say o. things than to reconcile with one another things already said 655.10
it is easy to be o. by violating taste 655.5
style for saying the o. created by o. 655.8
thought often o., though often uttered 968.20
where do we now meet an o. nature 655.3

**originality:** all good things are fruits of o. 655.6
merit of o. is sincerity 655.1
o., dignity achieved only through struggle 1058.19
o. is deliberate, in nature of protest 655.4
o.: one thing unoriginal cannot feel use of 655.7
people are always talking about o. 168.6

**ornaments:** use servants, o., only in proper places 942.2

**orphan's:** barber learns his trade on o. chin 715.1

**orthodoxy:** heresy of one age becomes o. of the next 256.7
o. can't eliminate old idea or absorb new 175.9

**orthography:** English o. is conspicuous waste 521.26

**ostentation:** arts of o.: excusations, cessions, modesty 726.2

**other:** o. people are quite dreadful 656.15
o. people are showcases for our ideas 656.14

**others:** hell is o. 414.11
it is easy to live for o. 862.2
just as much as we see in o. is in us 656.8
o. are to us like characters in fiction 656.11
our life is made by the death of o. 538.22
person loves and hates himself in o. 656.10
those who know the least of o. 163.5
try to cleanse o., you will waste away 783.24
unhappiness of o. 557.15
what pains thee in o. in thyself may be 868.35
who knows himself knows o. 868.7

**ought:** we do not what we o., what we o. not, we do 224.2

**ours:** that which we have not been forced to decipher or personally clarify, is not o. 319.49

**ourselves:** everything intercepts us from o. 30.5
nothing befalls us not of nature of o. 303.7
our passions are o. 668.11
we cannot forgive another for not being o. 656.4
we had as lief not be, as not be o. 852.15
we know o. chiefly by hearsay 442.13

we owe o. to society, but chiefly to o. 908.35
we prefer o. to others 869.5
we see, read, acquire only o. 91.29
**out:** best way o. is through 298.4
it is easier to stay o. than get o. 502.27
**outcome:** much outcry, little o. 629.1
**outcry:** much o., little outcome 629.1
**outgrow:** as we o. trousers, we o. acquaintances 402.10
**outlive:** most I ever did for you was to o. you 544.5
**outraged:** man never o. unless at bottom right 39.21
**outspoken:** o.: easy if not waiting to speak truth 360.13
**overact:** we must o. to produce any effect at all 726.6
**overboard:** man o., a mouth the less 318.1
**overcomes:** one o. only what one assimilates 170.7
who o. by force o. but half the foe 354.14
**overlooked:** better to be looked over than o. 641.11
object often o. if it lies under our eye 605.10
**overpopulated:** if people waited to know one another before they married, world wouldn't be so o. 707.4
**overpopulation:** o. connected with survival of unfit 707.2
**oversure:** how fortune brings to earth the o. 657.4
**overwork:** o.: disorder affecting functionaries who want to go fishing 345.2
**owes:** he looks world in face, o. not any 1059.4
if man o. you money and cannot pay 219.15
**owing:** grateful mind by o. owes not 397.10
**owl:** o. is a question wrapped in insulation 80.3
**own:** ally need not o. the land he helps 496.3
an ill-favoured thing, but mine o. 710.15
begin with another's to end with your o. 694.2
I know by my o. pot how others boil 319.21
if a man o. land, the land owns him 740.5
o. a horse, and you may borrow another's 94.8
sweetest fat sticks to my o. bones 869.19
we must be our o. before another's 873.5
**owners:** pig with two o. dies of hunger 740.6
**ownership:** o., not love, causes suffering 548.195
**owning:** no delight in o. anything unshared 887.3
**ox:** long-horned o. will be accused of butting 45.14
o. remains an o., even if driven to Vienna 934.12
stolen o. puts head out of stall 927.9
when o. stumbles, all whet their knives 223.14
**oyster:** nothing in Christianity, Buddhism, matches unselfishness of o. 1014.3

# P

**pace:** if a man does not keep p. 466.8
**paces:** if you take big p. you leave big spaces 33.4
**pacifist:** moral powers of p. exhibit ferocity 333.15
**pacifists:** to p. course of conduct is to sit on force 658.2
**paid:** he is well p. that is well satisfied 839.5
**pain:** advantage in wisdom won from p. 340.3
another suffering p. at thy hand, thy heart not exempt from affliction 1011.2
ease would recant vows made in p. 737.10
even p. pricks to livelier living 939.24
fate has wove the thread of life with p. 1004.16
gentleman never inflicts p. 376.4
give no heart p. so long as can avoid it 517.19
greatest p. is to love in vain 550.1
heart can ne'er a transport know that never feels a p. 699.6
heart's bold that p. has made incapable of p. 218.96
history of soldier's wound beguiles its p. 939.47
hour of p. as long as a day of pleasure 939.14
I have no business to p. myself 866.8
if p. cured, we should have been saved 939.43
love, p., money can't be kept secret 849.21
men must know p. to be in right senses 911.55
much of your p. is self-chosen 939.15
neither poverty nor p. is accumulable 939.5
no p. in wound received in victory 170.14
nothing helps a p. undiagnosable but felt 939.22
nothing is got without p. but dirt and long nails 279.5
one moment may with bliss repay hours of p. 407.21
one p. is lessened by another's anguish 939.45
only gods can live forever without p. 939.2
p. cannot recollect when it began 939.10
p. forces even truthful to speak falsely 939.41
p. from anything external is due to your estimate of it 939.26
p. is deeper than all thought 523.12
p. is produced by prolonging pleasure 699.9
p. is unjust 939.42
p. keeps pleasures sweet 699.5
p. lays not its touch upon a corpse 218.2
p. makes man think 939.35
p. others give passes away 86.11
pleasure is a visitant; p. clings to us 939.20
pleasure sweetest if paid for by other's p. 832.2

sincerest laughter with p. is fraught 523.25
sweet is pleasure after p. 699.2
the comic, when human, takes face of p. 144.3
to reject p., death, is to reject life 939.12
to seek p. greatest happiness 866.6
we are born in other's p., perish in own 939.50
when head aches, all members share p. 150.2
where there is love, there is p. 548.215
who cries for other's p. hasn't enough own 692.17
you can learn from p., sterility, ennui 939.13
**painful:** do not consider p. what is good for you 248.3
you may have p. business done for money 596.21
**pains:** many converse by giving history of their p. 185.32
p. are seasoning to love's fare 548.244
p. of love sweeter than all pleasures 548.54
p. to be coveted that end in pleasures 699.7
there are no gains without p. 735.26
we delight in others' misfortunes and p. 557.2
**paint:** great is p. 204.18
**painter:** humblest p. is true scholar—of nature 842.20
p. who draws without use of reason 659.8
**painters:** lawyers, p., can change white to black 525.16
**painting:** a modern p. can be outdated 593.1
amateur p. in water-colour shows innocent and quiet mind 659.11
for me, p. is a way to forget life 659.10
p. in museum hears most stupidities 659.5
p. is measured by its reproduction 53.12
p.: protecting flat surfaces from weather 659.2
we admire realistic depiction in p. 659.9
**paintings:** I prefer dog portrait to all allegorical p. 659.7
**palace:** be thine own p. or the world's thy jail 873.4
come and see my shining p. built upon the sand 687.15
**palate:** the benefits of fortune require a fit p. 358.31
**palaver:** the free have part in National P. 169.2
**panegyrics:** all p. mingled with an infusion of poppy 716.33
**pantomime:** p. is simple, clear and direct 965.15
**papacy:** p. is the ghost of the Roman empire 123.14
**paper:** white wall is the fool's p. 395.1
**papers:** one reads the p. as one wants to with a bandage over one's eyes 623.21
**parades:** p. should be classed as a nuisance 660.1
**paradise:** fantasy can be equivalent to a p. 687.10
if you can't catch a bird of p. 160.6
p.: center whither all souls proceeding 412.9
**paradox:** life is a p.; every truth has counterpart 661.3
p. is a lie when told by kids 661.4
**paradoxes:** p. useful to attract attention to ideas 661.1
**paradoxical:** who confronts p. exposes self to reality 661.2
**parallel:** never two cases exactly p. 1007.1
none but himself can be his p. 467.22
**paralysis:** "nothing avails but perfection" spells "p." 677.5
**paranoiac:** p. delusion: caricature of a philosophic system 620.8
**parasites:** all the wise world is little else but p. 662.2
p. live where great have secret sores 662.3
**pardon:** if men knew selves, God would p. them 868.22
may the good God p. all good men 391.9
p. one offence and encourage many 531.2
people are averse to begging p. 44.2
they ne'er p. who have done the wrong 357.5
we are least ready to p. folly we ourselves might have committed 351.13
we p. as long as we love 357.13
who sharply chides most ready to p. 797.5
**pardons:** offender never p. 357.11
**parent:** each generation criticises assumptions of p. 372.18
p. and child: strongest relationship of all 663.40
**parentage:** no test of fitness for p. imposed 663.51
pride thyself on virtue, not on p. 37.11
**parents:** boy is adult before p. think so 95.4
children are ruined through virtues of p. 663.12
children rarely forgive their p. 121.50
children, when great, make p. mad 121.34
how p. love us is not known till we are p. 663.7
in America p. obey their children 34.82
in survival of children, p. can think of world in which they will have no share 663.37
joys of p. secret, as are griefs, fears 663.3
p. lend children experience and memory 663.44
p. must allow children to understand them 663.46
p. stage-manage meetings of four-year-olds 663.42
presence of child turns p. into idiots 663.13
schoolmasters, p., to be grown out of 663.53
teachers deserve more honor than p. 959.3
where p. do too much for children 663.27

**parents'**: must remember p. age for joy, anxiety 332.13
wretched child does not return p. care 473.2
**Paris**: in London theatregoers laugh; in P. they wait grimly for proof they should 965.4
lunch kills half of P., supper the rest 664.4
P. is a moveable feast 664.2
trade is art and art's philosophy in P. 664.1
with an "if" you might bottle P. 312.1
**Parisian**: to err human; to loaf, P. 664.3
**park**: silence of shut p. tense, confined 129.6
**parks**: p. are but pavement disguised with grass 129.18
**parsons**: p. as well as other folks must live 136.3
**part**: I am p. of all that I have met 150.10
**partialities**: our p. and prejudices change places 720.16
**partiality**: p. may simply mean mental activity 453.1
**participant**: what am I if not a p. in life 502.24
**particular**: each must form himself as a p. being 467.14
poet should seize the p. 702.43
**particularity**: p. necessary to creations of imagination 198.25
**particulars**: p. make for virtue and happiness 326.10
**parting**: every p. gives a foretaste of death 666.7
**partisan**: p. is anxious only to convince his hearers 51.26
true p. as true to principles as to self 667.2
**partner**: great man resents p. in greatness 399.45
**party**: acid test of political p. is governing 704.13
beating drums delight p. writers 667.5
cocktail p. has the form of friendship 665.1
he serves p. best who serves country best 704.6
in democracy each p. proves other unfit 704.8
p.: incognito to save man from thinking 667.1
p. is madness of many for gain of few 667.8
p. loyalty lowers great men to mass level 667.3
p.-spirit a hindrance to thought 667.10
p. wedded to principle can save century 667.7
political p. that's out looks the best 704.10
prince who puts self at head of p. 704.16
**pass**: all good things will p. away 983.1
all things p. away—or is it we who p. 983.12
**passage**: worse the p., more welcome the port 17.28
**passion**: caprice lasts longer than lifelong p. 1046.3
lover's p. is glorious; husband's uxorious 668.4
man in a p. rides a runaway horse 39.18
man is a p. which brings a will into play 558.2
nothing great accomplished without p. 668.13
p., a bad regulator, is powerful spring 668.10
p. is like genius: a miracle 668.24
p. must ever sway the heart of man 525.3
p. sways to what free will wouldn't admit 668.20
p., unattended, is flame that burns to its own destruction 778.14
ruling p. conquers reason still 668.23
strong p. for any object ensures success 236.17
tear a p. to tatters 11.7
truth of p. wants pretence to make it live 668.5
we must act out p. before we can feel it 668.25
what to ourselves in p. we propose 668.27
without p. man is a mere latent force 668.1
**passion's**: give me that man that is not p. slave 668.26
**passionate**: truly p. are little boys 95.5
**passions**: all p. relished and digested are moderate 668.21
calm are we when p. are no more 646.104
duration of our p. is not dependent on us 668.17
human heart has a ceaseless birth of p. 668.19
if we resist our p., the p. are weak 668.16
in nature, violent p. are silent 980.5
men of cold p. have quick eyes 141.3
one imputes all suffering to the p. forgetting p. are source of all pleasures 668.6
only p. can elevate soul to great things 668.7
our p. are ourselves 668.11
p. are less mischievous than boredom 92.1
p. are only orators that always persuade 668.15
p. kill more prejudices than philosophy 668.8
p. of the young are vices in the old 1065.18
p. raise sedition against understanding 668.14
p., when masters, become vices 668.22
serving one's own p. is greatest slavery 668.12
soul's power lies in the p. 668.28
those who have great p. are happy and unhappy at being cured of them 668.18
to avoid evil utilize p., not maim them 668.2
violent p. reduce men to the same state 668.9
we are minor in everything but our p. 668.3
who would be superior to external influences must become superior to his p. 856.7
**passivity**: were we mute as stones, our very p. would be an act 9.35
**past**: accept p. till need for change cries out 115.20
all the p. is here, to be tried 669.28
all things are taken from us, and become por-

tions of the dreadful p. 669.27
denied even to God: power to undo the p. 669.2
future overcomes p. by swallowing it 366.24
ghosts of the p. want both laying and raising 842.5
how p. perishes is how future becomes 669.31
in books lies the soul of the whole p. 91.14
in carriages of the p. you can't go anywhere 669.14
it is sadder to find the p. inadequate to the present than to have it elude you 669.11
it's futile to talk too much about p. 669.32
look not mournfully into the p. 669.19
mad is he who opposes the p. 669.24
man can't repeat p. or leave it behind 669.4
man is tied to the weight of his own p. 752.14
mill cannot grind with water that's p. 505.9
no way of judging future but by p. 319.26
nothing improbable until it's p. tense 669.1
obligations, hatreds, injuries, remorse: memories; I have a complete p. now 669.3
old men must die, or the world would only breed the p. again 218.125
one thing about the p. worth remembering is that it can't be restored 669.29
p., and to come, seems best 723.27
p. is a bucket of ashes 669.25
p. is not fugitive, but remains present 669.23
p. is such a curious creature 669.7
p. is the present and future too 669.21
p. is the terra firma of methods 579.11
p. takes down our egotism and leads us into life of race 669.15
respect p.; do not confuse with present 669.16
same p. can leave different marks 669.13
time flies, and what is p. is done 505.8
to change p. into sad smiles is to master the future 752.11
to enjoy p. life is to live twice 574.15
to excel p., mustn't lose contact with it 669.22
volatile present changes to adamantine p. 723.8
we have to do with the p. only as it is useful to the present and future 669.9
who do not remember p. must relive it 669.26
who look only to p. are sure to miss future 115.26
why doesn't p. decently bury itself 669.18
with the p. as p. I have nothing to do 723.9
you can never plan the future by the p. 366.6
**path:** end at last for man who follows p. 896.8
every p. has its puddle 243.3
no easy p. out of life, few easy within 536.62
p. made clear, aspiration of everyone 113.4
**pathos:** p. is the sense of distance 953.14
**paths:** most beaten p. are the surest 850.6
**patience:** abused p. turns to fury 670.8
all commend p., none can endure to suffer 670.7
genius is but greater aptitude for p. 374.6
he who has p. may accomplish anything 670.18
let him with no p. retire within himself 670.10
our p. will achieve more than our force 670.3
p. accomplishes its object 670.20
p., and mulberry leaf becomes silk gown 670.4
p. bitter plant but it has sweet fruit 670.9
p., diligence, like faith, remove mountains 670.17
p.: form of despair disguised as virtue 670.2
p. is a necessary ingredient of genius 374.11
p. is all the passion of great hearts 285.7
p. is the art of hoping 670.23
p. is the best medicine 572.4
p. is the virtue of asses 670.6
p. lightens what sorrow can't heal 670.12
p.: moral courage, physical timidity 670.11
p., neighbor to despair 670.1
though p. be a tired mare, she will plod 670.21
whoever has no p. has no wisdom 670.19
**patient:** beware the fury of a p. man 670.5
doctor and p. are employer and employee 261.18
nothing so bitter a p. mind can't find solace for it 177.3
p. like hero in hands of a story writer 261.3
**patients:** p. lie about taking of things prescribed 572.6
physicians puckering their brows over p. 261.12
**patriot:** when cause of a p. wins, the timid join 671.25
**patriotism:** don't be so blind with p. you can't face reality 671.12
hating makes p. an excuse for war 410.9
p. is a word which commemorates a robbery 671.24
p. is lively sense of responsibility 615.1
p. is steady dedication of a lifetime 671.21
p. is the egg from which wars are hatched 671.14
p. is the last refuge of a scoundrel 671.7
p. is to politics as faith to religion 671.1
p., like charity, begins at home 671.6
to strike freedom of the mind with fist of p. is an old, ugly subtlety 671.20
when a nation roars p., I question the cleanness of its hands 671.4
**patriots:** p. those who love America enough to see her as a model for mankind 34.64
when nation is in strife, p. flourish 671.11
**patron:** p. looks with unconcern on man struggling for life in the water 672.1
**paunch:** fat p. never bred subtle mind 637.1

**pauper:** p. is already serving his term in hell 712.10
p. is human sacrifice in industrial regime 960.20
**pause:** no word was ever as effective as a p. 891.35
**pauses:** pianist's art resides in p. 607.44
**pay:** first or last you must p. entire debt 673.2
it's hard to p. for bread that's eaten 219.3
you p. too dear for what's given freely 382.35
**paycheck:** respect for law related to size of p. 526.2
**payeth:** who p. beforehand has work ill done 673.6
**payment:** second p., not politics, worries America 219.12
**payments:** first p. made us think we were prosperous 219.13
**pays:** everyone p. light-heartedly by cheque 596.4
**peace:** all men after form or formula of p. 674.6
ambassadors of p. shall weep bitterly 245.1
better a lean p. than a fat victory 674.9
better beans and bacon in p. than cakes and ale in fear 674.1
better just war than unjust p. 674.27
certain p. better than anticipated victory 674.21
deliberate aim at p. passes into its bastard substitute, anaesthesia 674.38
disadvantageous p. better than just war 1035.34
easier to lead men to combat than p. 1035.42
fair p. is becoming to men 674.26
find inner p. in solitude, not speed 982.11
freedom of seas *sine qua non* of p. 847.13
greatest difference between p., slavery 674.4
having no opinion conducive to p. of mind 464.5
he knows p. who has forgotten desire 674.3
little things seem nothing but give p. 989.1
love without p., or p. without love 1064.6
mankind will perish through eternal p. 674.12
mere absence of war is not p. 674.18
motto of p.: let strong help weak to survive 1035.84
mutual cowardice keeps us in p. 674.15
never was a good war or a bad p. 1035.37
no one can have p. longer than his neighbor pleases 674.8
nothing in creation knows meaning of p. 674.2
now we suffer the woes of long p. 674.16
on all the peaks lies p. 674.10
only a p. between equals can last 674.41
only condition of p. is to have no ideas 674.14
only p., only security is in fulfillment 502.18
p. and freedom walk together 129.28
p. does not rest in charters, covenants 987.4
p. expedient for victor, necessary for vanquished 674.32
p. gives victory to both sides 170.5
p. hath her victories no less than war 674.24
p. hath higher tests than battle 674.39
p. in space no help once p. on earth gone 914.4
p. is an emblem of all goodness 1035.28
p. is daily, weekly, monthly process 674.19
p. is liberty in tranquillity 674.5
p. is of the nature of a conquest 674.33
p. is poor reading 674.11
p. is temporary beautiful ignorance 674.22
p. is victory against probable greeds 674.35
p., like charity, begins at home 674.28
p. must be kept by men, not by arms 674.17
p. of man who has forsworn bullet 658.3
p. requires a personal framework 30.8
p. rules day where reason rules mind 778.7
p. succeeds only with power to enforce it 674.29
p., the tenderest flower of spring 983.6
p.: when time doesn't matter passing by 674.31
p., when whole is greater than parts 654.13
p. will come through being, not having 674.23
p. will run till next war begins 674.30
p. with a cudgel in hand is war 226.15
passions toward p.: fear of death, desire for commodious living 674.13
preparedness for war best means of p. 226.20
real p. must always rest on p. of mind 658.12
resister of war can bring p. 658.6
right is more precious than p. 816.26
self-respect too great a price for p. 674.40
separation only p. for man and wife 260.3
since wars begin in minds of men, it is there defenses of p. must be constructed 674.34
soldier, above all others, prays for p. 582.13
states of p., like wars, are expedients 674.36
there can be no p. of mind in love 548.171
there is no p. unto the wicked 1048.3
there is no way to p.; p. is the way 674.25
there is p. in being what one is 442.6
there must be an organized p. 496.20
they make a desert and call it p. 1035.97
though p. be made, yet interest keeps p. 674.7
trading our impatience for p. of mind 982.6
triumph of justice is the only p. 515.24
we can secure p. only by preparing for war 226.8
we prepare for p. like retarded pygmies 1035.80
we think the other side of war is p. 1035.67
what we dignify as p. is only a short truce 674.37
where no brotherhood there can be no p. 674.20
who listens for what people say has no p. 861.3

who would prefer p. to glory of hunger, thirst and dying 1035.43
world p. requires mutual tolerance, not love 496.6
you can't separate p. from freedom 361.38
**peacemaker:** your If is the only p. 164.6
**peacemakers:** blessed are p.; they are freed from wrath 164.4
blessed are the p. 164.2
**peacock:** no p. envies another p. his tail 727.22
p. blushing at sight of his ugly feet 455.6
sparrow sorry for p. at burden of tail 773.25
**peacocks:** sparrows who emulate p. may break thigh 449.1
**peaks:** on all the p. lies peace 674.10
**pearl:** diver thinking of shark would not get p. 340.29
**pearls:** errors on surface flow, for p. dive below 734.3
neither cast ye p. before swine 48.1
p. around the neck: stones on the heart 1041.67
**peasant:** p. and philosopher equally satisfied 407.59
**peasants:** p. not sophisticated enough to reason speciously 611.5
**pecuniary:** moral principle is a looser bond than p. interest 596.33
**pedagogue:** nothing tiresome as superannuated p. 959.2
**pedant:** every rostrum has its passing p. 842.28
fool is only troublesome, p. insupportable 842.33
p. is a caricature of a man 688.44
when culture exceeds nature, we have the p. 842.8
**pedantic:** judgments of fact, not of value, a sign of p. criticism 204.46
**pedantry:** beyond significant knowledge, p. begins 520.2
p. crams our heads with learned lumber 842.7
p. is the dotage of knowledge 842.23
p. prides herself on being wrong by rules 147.1
**pedestrian:** p.: man with two cars driven by family 63.3
**pedigree:** good man's p. is little hunted up 391.51
with fowls, the p.; with men, breeding 389.2
**peer:** p. groups are retailers of communications 563.14
**peers:** morality is the feeling of one's p. 598.10
**pegs:** words are p. to hang ideas on 1057.2
**pen:** man can kill himself with p. more easily than others 1062.89
no lighter burden, nor more agreeable than p. 1062.85
p. is mightier than sword 1062.17
p. is the tongue of the hand 1062.12
slanders of the p. pierce to the heart 204.29
**penalties:** severity of p. is a vain resource 760.12
**pence:** care for p., pounds care for themselves 970.6
**penny:** p. saved is a p. to squander 970.2
who has a p. in his purse is worth a p. 596.42
**people:** America stands for sovereignty of p. 34.81
best servants of p. must whisper unpleasant truths in the master's ear 755.13
beware the p. weeping 995.23
difficult to change mentality of the p. 756.7
government cannot be stronger than p. 393.60
I am the p., the mob, crowd, mass 675.14
I love mankind; it's p. I can't stand 588.4
let the p. think they govern 231.39
observe any meetings of p. 205.2
other p. are quite dreadful 656.15
other p. are showcases for our ideas 656.14
p. and p. alone make world history 675.13
p. are government's safe depositories 231.18
p. are too durable 285.1
p. are what they are because of what was 979.19
p. like us are We, everyone else is They 903.4
p. will fall victims to a big lie 329.23
the instinct of the p. is right 675.4
the p. like novels and charlatans 675.6
the p. make best judgment in long run 675.8
the p. must help themselves 675.9
universe changed by inspiring the p. 783.30
we appreciate p. in small gathering 151.15
we are so indifferent to p. 548.170
wealth is the means, p. are the ends 1041.35
what is the city but the p. 129.36
when p. rule, they must be made happy 231.53
why not confidence in justice of the p. 675.12
you must take p. as they are 977.2
**peoples:** one learns p. through the heart 1001.19
**perceived:** life p. transforms itself 868.19
**perception:** why level downward to our dullest p. 147.11
**perfect:** could we p. human nature 431.6
everything is p. coming from Creator 174.7
Fates seldom allow single line to stand p. 455.8
if thou wilt be p., give to the poor 677.4
in short measures life may p. be 677.13
nothing so p. possessed as remembered 710.9
we desire to make other men p. 339.36
when a man says he is p. already, he belongs in heaven or in a lunatic asylum 677.2
**perfection:** all p. is nearly a fault 677.21
dance of the water sings pebbles into p. 354.20
growing and becoming is character of p. 677.1

humorous man realizes p. is beyond man 539.2
marriage is the p. love aimed at 560.28
"nothing avails but p." spells "paralysis" 677.5
one good action after another: p. of goodness 391.1
our sense misses the p. it demands 455.7
p. is apt to be dull 677.14
p. not a requisite to art 677.16
p. of Gospels never built an empire 853.1
p., when there is nothing to remove 677.17
pursuit of p. gives meaning to our life 677.20
there is tragedy in p. 677.18
things by season are seasoned to p. 972.10
to be human is not to seek p. 431.19
to reach p. we must pass through death of self-effacement 1014.1
trifles make p., but p. is no trifle 677.12
we find fault with p. itself 203.23
who follows his nature's duty attains p. 677.3

**perfections:** p. of nature show image of God 616.56

**perform:** resolve to p. what you ought 801.1

**performance:** p. of p. threatens music 607.52
strong p. needs fanaticism in performer 333.5
things difficult to design easy to p 243.8

**performers:** judges must also be p. 204.1

**perils:** great p. bring to light fraternity of strangers 213.12
p. ask to be paid in pleasures 213.2

**period:** all men of one p. are related 181.2
man apt to be moved by art of his p. 53.37

**perjuries:** p. of love blown away by winds 851.14

**permanent:** actions of nations must be p.; we can set up p. processes but not p. decisions 164.8
nothing is p. but change 115.22

**perpetrate:** whatsoe'er we p., we are steered by fate 337.3

**persecute:** when more inclined to p. than persuade 1066.1

**persecution:** opposition becomes sweet when called p. 561.5
p. was a sign of personal interest 977.3
truth does not always triumph over p. 991.87

**perseverance:** p. can lend actions appearance of dignity 679.6
p. is more prevailing than violence 679.8
p.: virtue whereby mediocrity achieves success 679.1

**persevere:** to p. is courage in a man 679.4

**person:** one p. missing can depopulate world 2.8
p. makes event and event p. 108.2

**personality:** men who produce works of genius make use of their p. as of a mirror 374.37

**personnel:** few great men could pass P. 399.31

**persons:** all p. are puzzles 1001.8

p. cost much; for thee I must pay me 787.2

**persuade:** law cannot p. where cannot punish 525.28

**persuaded:** people better p. by own reasons 683.10

**persuading:** to please is great step toward p. 683.1

**persuasion:** children should be led by p. 981.10
p. of a friend is a strong thing 683.8

**perversity:** p. is the muse of modern literature 542.13
p. is the soul's very life 684.11

**pessimism:** our optimism or our p. makes our ideas 653.5
p. does win us great happy moments 685.1

**pessimist:** optimist proclaims we live in best of worlds; p. fears this is true 653.2
p. before forty-eight knows too much 653.4
p. is a man who's lived with an optimist 685.4
p. knows next year can't be any worse than the last 653.1
to a profound p. danger is not depressing 685.2

**pettiness:** p. of a mind can be measured by the p. of its adoration or its blasphemy 686.6

**petty:** in fool's p. estimate all things are little 686.7

**pewter:** when everything you hold is made of gold, you long for simple p. 695.2

**phantoms:** p. are trifling disorders of the spirit 381.4
who does not fill his world with p. is alone 381.5

**Philadelphia:** in P. they ask, who were his parents 926.3

**philanthropists:** if charity cost no money, the world would be full of p. 430.36

**philanthropy:** economic injustice which makes p. necessary 430.19
p. and friendship seldom exist together 430.27
p. is almost only virtue appreciated 430.34
we excuse our lack of p. 929.4

**Philistine:** P. reveres superior tastes 957.9

**philosopher:** beard does not make p. 405.3
great memory does not make a p. 574.21
if p. isn't a man, he's anything but a p. 688.44
married p. belongs to comedy 688.26
never yet p. that could endure toothache 889.25
nothing so strange that it has not been said by one p. or another 688.4
p. contents self with pitying persecutors 688.46
p. dreamed he was a butterfly 688.40
p. fulfills his mission imperfectly 688.37
p. spends time becoming a man 688.33
p. without good breeding is a cynic 389.4
peasant and p. may be equally satisfied 407.59

posterity for the p. is what the other world is for the religious man 688.5
presence of desire ignores the p. 688.3
to be p. is not to have subtle thoughts 688.43
to be p. is to be prepared against events 688.6
to the p. all things are friendly and sacred 920.3
true p. makes light of philosophy 688.28
**philosophers:** constancy of p. conceals their disquietude 688.17
great p.: poets believing poems' reality 688.20
p. are as jealous as women 688.38
p. are timid and dislike the unexpected 688.36
p. cannot arise where is no prying beast 388.21
p. have scattered as many plagues as Pandora's box, but without hope at bottom 688.42
p. who try to be politicians no longer p. 688.19
say, Not so, and you will outcircle p. 256.11
we p. are full of things which take us out of ourselves 688.29
**philosophical:** Arab who built hut with ancient temple marbles is more p. than museum curators 714.2
in p. dispute, the defeated gains most 51.10
p. man lets his chance escape 968.22
whole man within us forms our p. opinions 688.12
**philosophies:** some p. are greater nonsense than others 688.2
**philosophy:** business of p.: to part with self-conceit 163.7
difference between gossip and p. 688.9
do not all charms fly at mere touch of p. 688.14
every p. is p. of some stage of life 688.25
every p. tinged with secret imaginative background 688.47
example of good men is visible p. 308.3
for learning of suspended judgment the best discipline is p. 688.35
great p. is not flawless but fearless 688.30
inertia rides me; the which is called p. 688.27
let no young man delay the study of p. 688.7
little p. inclineth to atheism 688.1
man of business may talk of p., man who has none may practise it 688.31
no consolations of religion or p. unless one experiences their desolations 790.33
p. a mode of bearing ills of life 17.17
p. begins in wonder and the wonder remains 688.48
p. doesn't triumph over the present evils 17.35
p. forms us for ourselves, not others 442.15
p. has a fine saying for everything 688.39
p. is characterized more by formulation of problems than by solution of them 688.16
p. is such a litigious lady 688.24
p. may describe unreason, not refute it 1013.2
p. provides a refuge for definitions 688.10
p. will clip an angel's wings 688.13
passions kill more prejudices than p. 668.8
proof today of philosophical mediocrity is to look for a p. 688.32
schools of p. frequented for exercise 688.15
study p. to know own mind, not others' 688.11
suicide only serious question of p. 941.2
test of p. is how much it explains 790.17
that's why I love p.: no one wins 688.41
till you feed us, p. can wait 598.6
wonder is foundation of all p. 688.23
you can't do without p. 688.8
**photographer:** p. is in every bush like lion seeking prey 754.2
**photography:** p.: major force in explaining man to man 689.2
**physical:** man with nothing but p. power to sell 690.7
nation deprived of essential p. activity 690.3
**physician:** as long as men die and desire to live, a p. will be made fun of but well paid 261.11
deceive not thy p., confessor, lawyer 221.9
dignity of p. requires he look healthy 261.10
every invalid is a p. 889.14
every p. has his favourite disease 261.5
hide nothing from confessor, lawyer, p. 162.6
p. has no power over sand in hourglass 261.15
p. must have at his command a ready wit 261.9
**physician's:** intemperance is the p. provider 492.7
**physicians:** I do not know how it is that p. keep from their wives the secrets confided to them 849.14
out of every hundred p., ninety-eight are charlatans 690.6
p. leave cure to nature, but take credit 261.1
p., like kings, brook no contradiction 261.24
p. must humour weaknesses of human mind 261.2
p. puckering their brows over patients 261.12
**physicians':** p. faults are covered with earth 339.9
**physicists:** p. have known sin 843.27
**physics:** the effect of p. is concern of all men 633.5
**pianists:** art of p. resides in pauses 607.44
**piano:** pity to shoot pianist when p. out of tune 791.2
**pickle:** if you dip into the p.-pot, let it be up to the elbow 927.7
**pickpockets:** p., beggars, are the best physiognomists 927.1
**picture:** one p. in 10,000 ought to live in applause 659.6
p. and sculpture are festivities of form 53.43

the p. awaits my verdict 659.4
**pictures**: American motion p. are for half-wits 604.2
**piety**: experience differentiates p., goodness 691.10
p., like nobility, has its aristocracy 691.5
p. of some is passion, infirmity, fashion 691.7
p. to mankind must be three-fourths pity 692.19
p.'s hard enough to take among the poor 691.9
rash to intrude upon the p. of others 691.11
**pig**: p. with two owners dies of hunger 740.6
**pigeons**: roasted p. will not fly into one's mouth 289.6
**pilgrims**: all of us are p. on this earth 983.9
**pillow**: p. is a silent Sibyl 899.8
**pills**: I give you bitter p. in sugar coating 739.6
**pimps**: p. have taken over the world 25.2
**pin**: see a p. and let it lie 1038.1
**pinches**: only wearer knows where the shoe p. 319.19
**pinnacle**: top of a p. now, fire-wood soon 330.10
**pious**: religion is rendered illustrious by the p. 485.8
with p. action we sugar o'er the devil 438.24
**piper**: he who pays the p. may call the tune 673.3
**pit**: whoso diggeth a p. shall fall therein 1063.3
**pitch**: whoever touches p. will be defiled 57.2
**pitcher**: p. that goes too often to the well leaves behind either the handle or spout 799.2
**pitied**: much better to be envied than to be p. 293.16
**pity**: a few things move people to p. 692.4
I do not like the merciful who feel blessed in their p. 692.16
irony and p. are two good counselors 536.35
men p. those who fare badly 431.25
p. beyond telling is in heart of love 548.251
p. for all means hardness to neighbor 453.7
p. is for the living, envy for the dead 538.43
p. is not natural to man 206.9
p. is often avowed, seldom felt 410.5
p. kills, it makes our weakness weaker 692.2
p. may represent impersonal concern 953.10
p. melts the mind to love 692.10
p. would be no more if we did not make somebody poor 692.3
piety to mankind must be three-fourths p. 692.19
we have not p. unless we wish to relieve distress 692.13
where mercy, love, p. dwell, God dwells 577.1
world would die did p. not limit anger 692.20
**pivot**: secret of living is to find a p. 441.29
**place**: first journeys teach that p. is nothing 985.14
get p. and wealth with grace 1041.47
God attributes to p. no sanctity 126.5
have a p. for everything, keep the thing somewhere else 255.4
in the world I fill up a p. 318.3
one forgives a p. soon as it's left behind 693.3
one p. is everywhere 693.10
p. is nothing unless at its heart a figure stands 693.8
those allowed second p. have undoubted title to first 773.24
**places**: all p. alike, every earth fit for burial 693.9
all p. are distant from heaven alike 693.1
**plagiarism**: if we steal thoughts from moderns, it's p. 694.1
p. most difficult to avoid is self-p. 694.4
**plain**: p. dealing is a jewel out of fashion 360.5
p. living nothing but voluntary poverty 695.4
p. speech breeds hate 360.6
**plan**: amid multitude of projects, no p. devised 696.5
bad p. admits of no modification 696.6
do not p. ahead before finishing present task 696.4
proceed by p., be hit by accident 696.3
**planet**: when men reach beyond this p., they should leave national differences behind 914.5
**plans**: make no little p.; won't stir men's blood 696.1
p. for life modified by facts, years, experience 696.8
p. get you into things, work gets you out 696.7
**plant**: a p. is like a self-willed man 616.33
p. confounds the understanding 616.48
to p. seeds is commonest delight 369.3
**plants**: inefficient society of p. and animals 616.45
**plasticity**: p. loves new moulds because it can fill them 420.20
**platform**: to raise imbecility to profundity, put it on a p. 757.10
**platitude**: good p. makes the whole world kin 67.3
**platitudes**: calls and the theater propagate p. 185.34
**play**: a p. is how birds came home to roost 965.20
at p. one should not think of learning 896.2
be careful about p., indifferent to ball 570.4
each loves the p. for what he brings to it 965.9
fiction to man what p. is to child 341.17
genius loves p. for its own sake 154.2
greatest inconvenience to playgoer is p. 965.32

sun strong 699.10
**pleasures**: better deep griefs than shallow p. 911.18
enjoy p., but let them be your own 698.9
few people want p. they are free to take 684.7
life exacts high interest rate for p. 536.91
mastery of p. better than abstinence 698.1
no man is a hypocrite in his p. 698.19
old age has its p. 646.68
one half of the world cannot understand the p. of the other 698.3
p. are like poppies spread 698.6
p. can act as counter-irritants 698.10
p. deferred are soured by age 698.11
p., insects on the wing 983.6
p. to be avoided if greater pains result 699.7
p., trouble, greatest in anticipation 316.7
pain keeps p. sweet 699.5
perils ask to be paid in p. 213.2
those who enjoy p., p. drive with stings 700.3
violent p. which reach soul through body 733.9
we've more days to live through than p. 698.17
**pledge**: don't fear to p. 851.14
**Pleiades**: when P. no longer part of human spirit, man lacks completeness and true humanity 292.1
**plenty**: men cannot escape responsibility for p. 275.4
**plodders**: small have continual p. ever won 842.37
**plots**: p.: no more exhausted than men are 341.20
p. raise up commonwealths, ruin kings 813.7
**plum**: miss p. for want of courage to shake tree 973.10
**plumber**: anybody who has doubt about resourcefulness of p. never got bill from one 701.1
**pocketbook**: full p. often groans more loudly than empty stomach 1041.50
**pockets**: empty p. make empty heads 712.54
men are brothers, their p. not sisters 332.32
our last garment is made without p. 218.74
**poem**: a p. makes us see ourselves 1062.34
best p. comes close to magical accident 702.102
bureaucrat does not like a p. 100.6
each thought of a p. filled poet's sky 702.32
good p. is a contribution to reality 702.101
great p., deep theorem, are reader's own experiences 529.4
I have never started p. whose end I knew 702.38
p. gives world back to maker of p. 702.110
p.—hesitation between sound, sense 702.106
p. is the dream made flesh 702.70
p. is true if it hangs together 702.36
p. should not mean but be 702.67
**poems**: difficult to get the news from p. 702.115
finest p. are expedients to get bread 618.1
it is not enough for p. to be fine 702.52
majority of p. one outgrows, outlives 702.30
world so rich: never lack occasions for p. 702.42
**poesy**: drainless shower of light is p. 702.58
nothing so difficult as a beginning in p. 702.9
**poet**: beautiful woman is a practical p. 1055.45
courage of the p. is to keep ajar the door that leads into madness 702.71
for vain p., nothing of his is too much 702.62
God is the perfect p. 385.10
good p. made as well as born 702.56
great p. draws creations from own reality 702.76
great p. is the most unpoetical creature 702.114
great p. makes the void ring 702.81
how does p. speak to men with power 702.12
lot of p.: to invent what's nonexistent 702.77
lover, p., are of imagination all compact 555.22
maturing as p. means maturing as whole man 702.31
no p. ever thought another better 163.4
of all mankind great p. is equable man 702.113
p. can earn more money writing about his art than he can practicing it 34.2
p. craves spectators, if only buffaloes 702.75
p. expresses feelings which are not in actual emotions 702.28
p. gives thoughts on carriage of rhythm 702.74
p. has appetite for a certain anxiety 702.15
p. hath, like lover, his unruly times 702.116
p. hides despair in expression of joy 702.54
p. is a bird of strange moods 702.41
p. is a nightingale 702.89
p. is he who hath fat enough, like bear, to suck his claws all winter 702.104
p. is in love with language 702.3
p. is the priest of the invisible 702.94
p. is the subject of a lyric 702.79
p. knows little, has presentiment of much 448.24
p. lost as p. if gives himself to a party 702.46
p. on Pegasus, reciting his own verses 917.1
p. should seize the particular 702.43
p. transmutes cynicism into optimism 702.73
p. wishes he were the only one alive 1062.9
saint and p. seek privacy to public ends 730.1
scientist alone is true p. 843.9
to master the torrent of life, p. quivers 536.86
to p. all things are friendly and sacred 920.3
to p., silence is an acceptable response 702.18
transfuse from one language to another the creations of a p. 521.23

true p. is a friendly man 702.65
who can bear a middling p. 702.40
world will try to bury p. with trivialities 702.72
would you be a p. before going to school 702.13

**poet's:** color is the p. wealth 702.105
ne'er was flattery lost on p. ear 702.86
p. mind receptacle for storing feelings 702.27
p. pen gives to airy nothing a habitation 702.87
p. pleasure is to withhold some meaning 702.112

**poetic:** to p. mind all things are poetical 702.64

**poetical:** nothing is p. if plain daylight is not p. 605.1

**poetry:** a thought, to be p., must be seasoned 702.47
English is a magnificent vehicle for p. 521.2
good p. forged with sweat, blood, tears 702.26
great p. gives illusion of a view of life 702.29
I have nothing to say and saying it is p. 702.10
if p. comes not naturally 702.60
in America p. has turned to advertising 18.6
in p. man explores his own amazement 702.39
in p. must love words with all capacity 702.95
most wretched cradled into p. by wrong 702.88
p., — best words in their best order 702.17
p. doesn't necessarily have to be beautiful 702.19
p.: emotion recollected in tranquillity 702.117
p. is a counterfeit creation 702.25
p. is a state of grace 702.55
p. is adolescence fermented and preserved 702.78
p. is attempt to paint color of wind 702.5
p. is but the ashes of burnt-out passion 702.51
p. is crown, end, aim of literature 702.68
p. is for those who know 702.82
p. is hard to read — its sense is, anyhow 702.6
p. is harmony of words; music, notes 607.19
p. is like painting 702.53
p. is opening and closing of a door 702.83
p. is reflective; it stops to think 607.3
p. is revelation of personal feeling the reader recognizes as his own 702.80
p. is whim of nature in her lighter moods 702.1
p. lifts veil from hidden beauty of world 702.90
p. makes its own pertinence 702.33
p. makes nothing happen 702.2
p. makes your toenails twinkle 702.100
p. of art: beholding single tower 1007.2
p. should be great and unobtrusive 702.59
p. should prevent language from changing too rapidly 521.6
p. sinks under moderate weight of prose 702.63
p. the universal possession of mankind 702.44
p.'s unnat'ral; no man ever talked p. 'cept a beadle on boxin' day 702.24
people fancy they hate p., and are poets 702.34
poets arguing about modern p.: jackals snarling over a dried-up well 702.21
song is the primal thing in p. 702.4
those who have never entered scientific pursuits know not p. surrounding them 843.36
to read p. I take down my dictionary 242.3
unwritten p. escapes by other vents 702.35
when power corrupts, p. cleanses 702.61
world full of p. as earth is of pay-dirt 702.108

**poets:** all p. who, when reading from own works, experience choked feeling, are major 702.111
arrogance of p. is only a defense 702.69
artists, p. uninterested in happiness 702.84
not by wisdom do p. make what they compose 702.93
p. are hierophants of unapprehended inspiration 702.91
p. are sultans, would kill their brothers 1062.15
p. creators and creations of their age 53.125
p. exhibit only civil side of nature 702.103
p. in youth begin in gladness 702.118
p. lose praise by what they discreetly blot 458.7
p. pretend to write for immortality 702.20
p. seldom sing a new song 702.23
p. unacknowledged legislators of world 702.92
p. wrap truth in tales, yet they know her 702.11
pleasure in poetic pains only p. know 702.22
popular p. are parish priests of the Muse 702.85
to have great p., there must be great audiences too 59.8
women are p. just by being women 1055.95

**pointlessness:** one man's p. is another's satire 838.1

**points:** when a man p. a finger at another 5.1

**poise:** men don't know how much strength in p. 592.11

**poison:** expect p. from standing water 444.2
one man's p. ivy is another's spinach 957.2
what does not p., fattens 319.30

**police:** for middle class, p. help old ladies; for urban poor, p. arrest you 703.7
men who agree perfectly with their p. 816.17
p. state cannot command the grain to grow 995.17
vague uneasiness, the p. 703.1

**policeman:** p. are soldiers who act alone 703.9
p. goes afther vice as law officer an' comes

away as philosopher 703.3
principle is not as powerful as a p. 423.7
**policeman's**: p. lot is not a happy one 703.5
**policies**: nation's p. determined by its interests 614.14
**policy**: bad administration can destroy good p. 13.2
p. sits above conscience 317.5
**polish**: elbow-grease is the best p. 279.4
**polite**: everyone has to think to be p. 194.10
only great man holds own without being p. 824.6
**politeness**: it is wise to apply p. to friendship 194.3
p. is artificial good humor 194.11
p. is the outward garment of goodwill 194.9
p. is to human nature as warmth is to wax 194.14
p. requires this thing; decorum that 743.4
p.: the most acceptable hypocrisy 194.1
true power and p. are above vanity 713.55
**politic**: body p. carries in itself causes of its destruction 393.55
**political**: forgive us for bypassing p. duties 1025.55
French p. thought: nostalgic or utopian 359.2
ignorance, conceit, point to p. career 705.70
knowledge of human nature the beginning and end of p. education 705.4
liberty is the highest p. end 534.2
man is by nature a p. animal 705.7
nature will overturn corrupt p. system 813.28
p. action is citizen's highest responsibility 705.38
p. convention not place you can come away from with any faith in human nature 705.37
p. extremism involves two ingredients 333.6
p. history is elevated to world history 417.39
p. is replacing metaphysical as mode of grasping reality 705.24
p. language makes lies sound true 705.59
p. leader must keep looking over his shoulder to see if the boys are still there 705.9
p. parties die of swallowing own lies 704.1
p. party members seek power for happiness 705.58
p. power grows out of barrel of gun 705.50
p. propaganda makes voter feel small 739.2
p. skill is ability to foretell what will happen and to explain later why it didn't 705.20
p. sovereignty a mockery without means to meet poverty, illiteracy, disease 712.38
p. speech defense of indefensible 705.60
p. truth is libel 991.53
persistence in one opinion never considered a merit in p. leaders 705.21
power-worship blurs p. judgment 713.38
solutions not expected in p. campaign 1030.13
some p. problems have no solution 705.35
test of p. institutions: condition of country whose future they regulate 485.3
there is nothing that is not p. 705.48
to master life, p. hero erects fortress 536.86
we demand more of p. life than personal 705.41
when p. ammunition low, artillery of abuse is wheeled into action 705.71
**politically**: educate masses p.: make history personal 130.4
nations meet p. to settle their differences 496.12
**politician**: coffee, which makes the p. wise 140.2
consult the veteran instead of the p. 1035.69
good p., under democracy, is unthinkable 705.53
idealism and a p.'s will to power 440.8
it takes a p. to run a government 705.74
lobbyist helps p. decide and pays him 705.65
most distinctive characteristic of successful p. is selective cowardice 705.32
one has to be a murderer to be a p. 441.24
p. becomes statesman after he is elected 924.4
p. can't call columnist the things columnist is allowed to call p. 623.13
p. is an acrobat 705.8
p. must learn to coax the electorate 705.69
p. never believes what he says 705.25
p. ought to be honest; afther that, crafty 705.28
p. tacks with wind, but also makes breezes 705.75
sheer longevity makes p. public monument 705.46
when p. gets an idea he gets it all wrong 705.52
**politicians**: p. are the sacred white elephants of our era 705.61
p. not over a year behind public opinion 705.64
p. promise bridge even where no river 705.39
p. tend to live "in character" 705.43
p. want power for happiness' sake 705.58
rale p. suppress nawthin' but ividince 705.27
spare me sight of thankless breed of p. 705.29
successful democratic p. insecure men 705.45
too many p. believe you can fool all the people all the time 705.2
who raises new issues is distasteful to p. 705.44
**politics**: all p. based on indifference of majority 705.62
all starts as a mystique and ends as p. 443.2
conscience hasn't to do with gallantry, p. 348.11
eloquence in p. can win what is won in war 281.1
first rule of p. is never to say never 705.68
half a truth is better than no p. 705.16

identify with mankind, take part in p. 705.31
in argument, truth always prevails finally; in p., falsehood always 705.40
in middle life, p. are a temperament 580.6
in p. failure is decisive 705.56
in p. gray is a forbidden color 705.13
in p. the out party looks the best 704.10
independent wants to take p. out of p. 704.14
inject truth into p., you have no p. 705.63
magnanimity in p. is the truest wisdom 705.14
man of p. cannot afford the doctrine of man's individual magnificence 705.6
modern p. a struggle of forces, not men 705.5
only in p. are we content with common man 705.33
p.: choice between the disastrous and the unpalatable 705.30
p. consists of the delusion that a change in form is a change in substance 705.54
p. is a place of modest requirements 705.22
p. is dealing of hard men over property 705.47
p. is imagination and mind 705.73
p. is the diversion of trivial men 705.57
p. is the systematic organization of hatreds 705.3
p. is war without bloodshed 705.51
p. keeps us out of affairs concerning us 705.76
p. shaped by men without ideals 705.15
p.: strife of interests masquerading as contest of principles 705.12
p. suspected to be much ado about nothing 705.42
p. would reform if wisdom spread like folly 705.19
promotion in party p. for things besides ability 704.11
public interested more in government than p. 705.66
sin a basic concept in religion and p. 893.20
"this department will be run without p." is our favorite soporific 393.1
tired, elderly men go in for p. 705.17
war can kill you but once; p., many times 705.18

**polling:** inside p. booth every American equal 295.21

**pollution:** America diminished daily by p., blight 174.9

**poor:** a p. race in a land of dollars 712.13
be rich for yourself, p. to friends 852.17
children are p. men's riches 121.14
easier to talk of poverty than think of p. 967.10
evermore thanks, the exchequer of the p. 397.11
forest is the p. man's overcoat 988.4
forgive us blaming p. for their poverty 872.5
forgive us for pretending to care for p. 712.53
function of p. to exercise our generosity 712.46
gratefulness is the p. man's payment 397.4
handsome man is not quite p. 575.15
he is p. that can promise nothing 145.2
he is p. that craves much 401.10
he is p. who does not feel content 183.14
him that is p. all kindred scorn 712.17
if free society cannot help the many who are p., it cannot save the few who are rich 712.37
in change of government, p. change masters 712.43
in fight rich man saves face; p. man, coat 342.5
man rich or p. according to whether he can afford necessaries, conveniences 1041.59
no being so p. who does not think there is somebody still poorer 182.6
one flag for the rich, one for the p. 712.41
p. and content is rich, and rich enough 183.22
p. command respect; beggar excites anger 72.2
p. die of indifference in peace-time, or by homicidal passion if war breaks out 712.9
p. man needs hope more than bread 712.4
p. man ruined as soon as he apes the rich 926.2
p. man's debt makes a great noise 219.6
p. man's roast is sniffed far off 401.29
p. man's wisdom is despised 712.5
p. men seek meat for their stomach 1041.20
p. men's reasons are not heard 712.18
p. must be wisely visited and cared for 712.55
p. on borderline of starvation live purposeful lives 712.23
p. provide food for the rich 712.45
p. see sky as an infinite grace 413.2
p. spirit poorer than p. purse 433.6
people don't demand cripples run races, yet ask p. to act like everyone else 712.22
provision for p. is test of civilization 430.17
rich child often sits in p. mother's lap 663.14
sell what thou hast, and give to the p. 677.4
surest way to remain p., be honest 423.12
the more humanity owes the p. man, more society denies him 712.44
to be p. without murmuring is hard 1041.13
virtue can be afforded only by the p. 1025.10
we liberals know the p. are our equals in every sense except being equal to us 712.51
what to the p. we give, to Jove is lent 430.15
when rich wage war it's p. who die 1041.54
with full stomach rich and p. are alike 272.9

**poorer:** happier when p., but were also younger 1064.36

**populace:** p. drag down gods to their own level 675.3

**popular:** being lovable is being p. 706.5
p. government awakens spirit and energy 231.10

p. government no guarantee of good government 393.41
p. men create monsters then quell them 705.36
p. persons: those who take world as it is 706.13
what is p. is not necessarily vulgar 706.8
when fortune is with us, p. favor is too 15.8
who sees only a week ahead is p. 1027.5
**popularity**: fame is a vapor, p. an accident 983.25
p. is a crime from moment it's sought 706.11
p.: three-penny fame 706.9
**population**: p. condemned to inaction is explosive 564.3
to keep hope in world, keep changing p. 425.26
**populations**: large p. make technology indispensable 960.14
**populous**: great city not same as p. one 129.1
very p. city is rarely well governed 129.2
**porcupine**: p. may be respected, but never loved 802.5
**pornographic**: when a kid you substitute p. cards for real experience 708.1
**pornography**: appeal of p. due to indecent feelings about sex which moralists inculcate in young 708.3
**port**: worse the passage, more welcome the p. 17.28
**portrait**: p. painted with feeling is p. of artist 659.13
two styles of p. painting: serious, smirk 659.3
**ports**: p. don't care what impressions they make 833.2
**positions**: easy to appear worthy of p. we don't have 1.13
**positive**: most p. men the most credulous 262.15
p.: mistaken at top of one's voice 51.2
**possess**: as unjust to p. woman as slaves 710.14
human nature limits our power to p. 710.10
not enough to p. truth; it must p. us 991.81
to p. is past the instant we achieve the joy 710.5
touching may kill, keeping away may p. 710.17
**possesses**: what one seizes, what one p.: different 710.2
who p. most is most afraid of loss 710.11
**possessing**: no one worth p. can be quite possessed 710.18
**possession**: bliss in p. will not last 574.18
every p. lent by chance for uncertain time 114.17
fie on p. but if a man be vertuous withal 710.4
hope is the best p. 425.15
how sweet an emotion is p. 710.7
man's real p. is his memory 574.35
not p. but use is the only riches 1041.27
object in p. seldom has charm it had in pursuit 710.13
one p. outvalues all others: last breath 536.130
prospect is often better than p. 316.3
want of thing perplexing, p. intolerable 710.19
**possessions**: not p., but desires, need equalizing 740.1
we get possessed by our p. 740.13
**possibilities**: round about what is, lies world of p. 687.14
**possibility**: each believes he has a greater p. 55.5
**possible**: all things p. until proved impossible 711.1
aspire not to immortality; exhaust the p. 539.14
knowing the p. is beginning of happiness 539.16
**possible's**: p. slow fuse is lit by imagination 448.10
**posterity**: let us transmit to p. a memorial 6.17
love of p. caused by death 796.1
p. attributes to hero deeds of unknown 416.13
p. is likely to be wrong 204.7
**postponement**: life is for most one long p. 228.11
**postscript**: woman seldom writes her mind but in p. 532.3
**pot**: enquire not what boils in another's p. 208.6
I know by my own p. how others boil 319.21
**potato**: French fried p.: inescapable horror 352.1
**potentiality**: man is as full of p. as of impotence 711.5
**potter**: p. is potter's enemy 154.7
**pounds**: care for pence, p. care for themselves 970.6
**poverty**: all arguments that p. is no evil, show it to be great evil 712.31
America has best-dressed p. in world 712.21
American society contains those of talent, driven to prefer p. to abundance 34.24
avarice is as destitute as p. 401.23
beauty and myths: perennial masks of p. 712.20
debt is the worst p. 219.7
easier to talk of p. than think of poor 967.10
for every talent that p. has stimulated it has blighted a hundred 712.19
give me neither p. nor riches 695.1
gold has ruined fewer men than p. 712.1
he is to be dreaded who dreads p. 33.30
honest rich can never forget p. 712.11
I wish to be rich to glorify honest p. 1041.65
in train of excessive wealth, excessive p. 1041.37
laziness travels slowly, p. overtakes him 527.3

neither p. nor pain is accumulable 939.5
p. comes imploring us to find a purchaser for its unmarketable wares 712.24
p. has many roots; tap root is ignorance 712.28
p. has very different appearances 712.30
p. heaps men with ridicule 712.33
p. is enemy to happiness, liberty, virtues 712.32
p. is good in poems, but bad in a house 712.3
p. is no crime, it's a blunder 712.27
p. is no disgrace, but it is inconvenient 712.49
p. is no disgrace, but no honor either 712.56
p. is not perversity 712.50
p. is parent of revolution and crime 712.2
p. is the indifference of hospitals 712.6
p. makes you sad as well as wise 712.7
p. of the soul is irreparable 613.6
p.-stricken man thinks rich man happy 152.5
p. the worst of dangers 712.48
p. with joy isn't p. at all 712.47
p. won't fall off roof; it is man's doing 712.8
plain living is voluntary p. 695.4
pretense, more than p., harasses ruined man 712.26
rich man cannot imagine p. 712.42
slow rises worth by p. depressed 712.29
there is no crime so shameful as p. 712.15
three fates: p., drudgery, ignorance 712.40
wealth, p.: parents of discontent 249.9

**power:** a P. teaches thy way along pathless coast 748.1
absolute p. is absolutely delightful 713.6
advantage of p.: you can do more good 713.21
anarchy is stepping stone to absolute p. 36.3
by promise of p., evil attracts the weak 305.21
cowardice is incorrigible which love of p. cannot overcome 196.3
definition of a great p. 614.17
friend in p. is a friend lost 713.2
garb of religion best cloak for p. 790.29
God grants joy or p., not both 713.16
great p. drowns some men in honors 424.8
greater the p., more dangerous the abuse 713.9
hand of liberality stronger than arm of p. 373.8
how to get men of p. to live for rather than off the public 713.29
idealism and a politician's will to p. 440.8
if one does wrong, best to do it pursuing p. 1063.9
immoderate p. leaves the progeny weaker 713.31
joy of life to put out p. in useful way 502.13
kings' p. founded on people's folly 825.19
knowledge is p. 520.1
life is a search after p. 713.17
man in p. puts on new manners 713.20
mankind is safer when men seek pleasure, not p. 698.16
national greatness is moral, not physical, p. 598.44
no man is wise nor good enough to be trusted with unlimited p. 713.13
no pleasure in p. over fellow citizens 713.28
no safe depository of p. but people 231.19
not balance of p., but community of p. 496.20
numerous family is bulwark of p. 713.48
one's cruelty is one's p. 206.5
p.: a sharing of the nature of the world 713.18
p. always charged with the impulse to eliminate human nature from action 713.26
p. corrupts and absolute p., absolutely 713.1
p. corrupts the few; weakness, the many 188.5
p. educates the potentate 825.7
p. gives no purchase to hand, will not hold 713.19
p. involves freedom from good and evil 713.36
p. is more vivid when we break a man's spirit than when we win his heart 713.24
p. is partial to simplification 713.25
p. is pleasure, and pleasure sweetens pain 713.22
p. is used to make knowledge a slave 758.10
p. legitimate only under contract 713.32
p. not as becoming as a new hat 265.26
p. of the unprivileged to extort 15.7
p. pollutes whate'er it touches 713.46
p. spoils the key, and uses the pickaxe 713.51
p. steps back only in face of more p. 713.35
p. takes as ingratitude the writhing of its victims 713.50
p. wedded to chronic fear is formidable 713.23
p. wielded by abnormal energy is serious fact 713.3
p.-worship blurs political judgment 713.38
people demand freedom when they lack p. 534.29
political p. grows out of barrel of gun 705.50
politicians want p. for happiness' sake 705.58
prize cared for by powerful is p. 713.27
property has greatest p. in life 740.7
property of p. is to protect 713.39
self-reverence, self-knowledge, self-control lead life to sovereign p. 852.24
to ask for p. is forcing uphill a stone which rolls back again 713.34
to be alive is p. 314.2
to know pains of p. go to him who has it 713.12
true p. and politeness are above vanity 713.55
universal need to exercise some kind of p. 713.37
unlimited p. makes any man a despot 713.5
we have confused p. with greatness 713.54
we thought since we had p. we had wisdom 713.8

when p. corrupts, poetry cleanses 702.61
when reality of p. has been surrendered 713.52
wise, unwise, same color in lamps of p. 713.30
without p. to awe them, men live at war 36.2
world kept p. prisoner, gave love freedom 713.49
**powerful**: if you would be p., pretend to be p. 713.53
liberty is latitude the p. accord weak 534.15
the p. can take your life 516.3
until the p. are just, the weak are secure only in strength of United Nations 1008.1
**powerlessness**: absolute p. frustrates absolutely 457.1
p. may be the disease of the age 994.1
**powers**: getting and spending we lay waste our p. 102.39
**practical**: Americans have combined p. and ideal 34.59
ignoring contradictions in principle makes the p. man 317.1
specialized values of mere p. man 1019.21
unless I turn thoughts into p. living, I cannot reap good 1058.47
**practice**: grand schoolmaster is p. 277.10
habit is p. that becomes man himself 404.7
if thou hast no p. thou art ignorant 715.3
in p. error and truth do not consort 9.13
man may be sincere in principles, not p. 728.9
p. aimless in absence of nature, learning 277.63
p. forms a man to anything 860.1
p. is nine-tenths 715.2
theorist without p. is tree without fruit 967.12
theory and p. of life not reconciled 967.3
**prairie**: to make a p. it takes a clover and one bee 812.1
**prairies**: these are gardens of the desert—the p. 34.7
**praise**: all motivated by desire for p. 384.4
censure of man's self is oblique p. 857.7
deafest man can hear p. 716.19
envy bestrides p. 716.27
expect not p. without envy until death 716.5
for some, enjoying p. is courtesy of heart 716.25
generally we p. only to be praised 716.20
he who loves p. loves temptation 716.40
if thou wouldst have p., die 716.39
ingenuous mind feels reproof in unmerited p. 716.17
man of truly noble ways listens not to p. 594.7
men feel injured by p.; limits merits 716.38
modesty the only sure bait for p. 594.3
never p. a sister to a sister 1055.83
no p. beats one you can put in your pocket 716.23
nothing is made worse or better by p. 70.28
p. from ignorant man is only good-will 716.32
p. is always pleasing 716.24
p. is more obtrusive than a reproach 716.26
p. is the best diet for us, after all 716.31
p., like gold, owes value to its scarcity 716.15
p. makes good men better, bad men worse 716.9
p. shames me, for I secretly beg for it 716.34
p., tactlessly given, can freeze a heart 716.2
p. to the undeserving is severe satire 716.8
people ask for criticism, but want p. 203.19
people swallow anything seasoned with p. 199.8
refusal of p. is desire for p. twice 716.22
safest p.: to foretell greatness for another 716.13
sign of mediocrity to p. moderately 716.37
stupid criticism versus stupid p. 716.29
to be valuable, p. must be voluntary 716.4
true p. comes even to the lowly 716.30
unmerited p. has not the power to heal 716.14
we p. when a thing needs our assistance 716.35
who does not love p. is not a full man 716.1
**praised**: none are so much p., censured, as we think 1020.5
p. by honest men, abused by rogues 798.7
when a proud man hears another p. 727.9
**praises**: p. from an enemy imply real merit 716.10
p. from wicked men are reproaches 716.11
there are p. which defame 716.21
we are tolerant of p. of others if we think we do as well 716.36
who first p. book next in merit to author 204.31
**praising**: good of p. self is one can lay it on thick 716.3
**pray**: affliction sometime teacheth wicked to p. 717.20
do not p. for easy lives 717.21
folly for a man to p. to gods for that which he has power to obtain for himself 873.7
how ready is heaven to those that p. 717.19
it is not well to p. cream, live skim milk 717.2
only he can p. well who lives well 717.13
p.: to ask laws of universe be annulled for petitioner confessedly unworthy 717.5
p. to God but continue to row to the shore 717.27
to work is to p. 1058.7
we little know the things for which we p. 717.7
what we p. to ourselves for is granted 303.4
you can't p. a lie 717.33
**prayer**: cravings do not become a p. 717.16
in p. we call ourselves "worms of dust" 717.34

more things are wrought by p. than this world dreams of 717.31
one great efficiency method is p. power 717.25
p. for private end is theft and meanness 717.12
p. from other than one whose heart lives in grace of God is unheeded 717.9
p. has never superseded practical efforts 717.28
p. is a goodly Christian's weapon 717.22
p. is contemplation of facts of life 717.11
p. is not an old woman's idle amusement 717.15
p. is the implement through which men reach where presence is denied them 717.10
p. should be the key of the day 717.14
we all have p.-wheels we set up on steppes 717.17
what are men better than sheep, if knowing God, they lift not hands of p. 717.32
who rises from p. a better man 717.23
wish to pray is a p. 717.3
work is p., stink is p. 1058.44
**prayers:** certain thoughts are p. 717.18
few men durst publish their p. to God 717.24
for p. to be heard we must also strive 717.1
in p. he says, thy will be done 717.26
p. are to men as dolls to children: comforting but hard to take seriously 717.6
ruin outruns all p., forces men astray 1035.48
we offer p. to God, treat Him like a pasha 717.35
**prayeth:** he p. best who loveth best 717.8
**praying:** when p. does no good, insurance does help 487.2
**prays:** when devil p. he's out to deceive 691.14
when man p., he's saying "Keep calm" 717.4
**preach:** go ye into the world and p. the gospel 590.1
judged more by what we do at home than what we p. abroad 496.5
who cannot wisely meddle with public affairs in preaching gospel, cannot p. 718.1
**preacher:** no p. listened to but time 971.58
rain and bad p. do not know when to stop 771.3
who has but one word of God before him, and cannot make a sermon, cannot be a p. 718.11
**preacher's:** p. garment is cut to pattern of hearers 718.9
**preachers:** people who can act are never p. 9.19
there are many p. who don't hear selves 718.7
**preaches:** goodness that p. undoes itself 391.15
he p. well that lives well 718.2
orator p. to get bishopric, an apostle to save souls; latter deserves bishopric 136.13
**preaching:** by reading sermons, clergy lose art of p. 718.8
next best thing to good p. is bad p. 718.6
no p. has made death other than death 218.77
p. helps preserve well-inclined men 718.13
p. is by-word for long, dull conversation 718.12
woman's p. like dog walking on hind legs 718.10
**precautions:** torment of p. often exceeds dangers 110.6
**precedent:** danger, when vice becomes a p. 1023.16
p. embalms a principle 979.8
**precedents:** bad p. began as justifiable measures 525.12
if you're strong enough, there are no p. 933.7
**precedes:** in affairs consider what p. and follows 356.3
**precept:** example is the best p. 308.1
**precipice:** we run carelessly to the p. 85.11
**prefer:** let us p., let us not exclude 719.6
**preference:** esteem must be founded on p. 719.5
**preferences:** there are as many p. as there are men 719.3
**prejudice:** ink in which history is written: fluid p. 417.45
knowledge the best protection against p. 520.58
loss of innocence brings loss of p. 57.7
natural affection is a p. 332.18
p. is the child of ignorance 720.6
p. uneasy unless it can pass for reason 720.7
p.: vagrant opinion without visible means of support 720.1
race p. decreases values 769.4
race p. is a shadow over all of us 769.2
racial p. is like hair across cheek 769.1
strongest p.: fancied exemption from all p. 720.5
**prejudiced:** no man p. for thing he knows is wrong 720.14
**prejudices:** ancient p. fall when survival is at stake 949.3
man wins friends by p., narrowness 720.4
one cannot eliminate p.—just recognize them 720.13
our p. are our mistresses 720.2
our partialities and p. change places 720.16
p. eradicate every tender disposition 720.12
passions kill more p. than philosophy 668.8
weeding out p., some eradicate virtue 720.15
when orators and auditors have same p., the p. run risk of standing for truths 757.13
**preparation:** life is only art we practice without p. 536.78
**prepare:** for all your days p. 722.2
**prepared:** to be philosopher is to be p. against events 688.6
**prescribed:** patients lie about taking of things p. 572.6

**prescription:** who saw a physician approve another's p. 261.14
**presence:** good p. is letters of recommendation 45.6
how great love is, p. best trial makes 2.4
p. strengthens love 2.6
**present:** brutes show wisdom in enjoying the p. 41.26
future lies in giving all to p. 723.3
golden age was never the p. age 296.8
he who bringeth p. findeth door open 97.5
he who fears not future may enjoy p. 366.12
I am in the p. 723.28
in music man realizes the p. 607.48
memory kills p., offers its heart to past 574.37
no mind much employed upon the p. 723.15
p. alone presses, not future or past 723.20
p. has one advantage – it is our own 723.4
p. is nothing but as it appertains to past and future 723.16
p. joys are more to flesh and blood 407.34
p. moment an extraordinary crisis 723.6
p. offers itself for only instant of time 723.26
superiority of the distant over the p. 236.36
the p. is a strange interlude 723.25
things p. seem worst 723.27
volatile p. converts to adamantine past 723.8
we constantly abuse p. age, which our children will praise 296.6
wisely improve the p.; it is thine 669.19
without health, courage, we can't face p. 302.1
**presents:** p., believe me, seduce both men and gods 382.30
p., I often say, endear absents 382.22
**preserve:** to p. a man alive is a miracle 261.22
to p., renew almost as noble as to create 261.23
**presidency:** extremism in pursuit of p. is a vice 724.5
p.: greased pig in game of American politics 724.1
p. is but splendid misery 724.4
p. is highest office in gift of people 724.2
p.: way station en route to blessed condition of being an ex-president 724.14
**president:** Americans pick p., then pick on him 724.11
any boy may become p., it's risk he takes 724.12
duty of P. to propose; Congress disposes 169.7
function of p. is to set unfinished business before the American people 724.7
no easy problems ever come to the p. 724.3
p. only lobbyist of whole nation 724.13
**president's:** p. hardest task is to know what is right 724.6
**presidential:** what seem lies will seem r-right in p. year 705.26
**presidents:** p. are paid to take blame 724.9
**press:** freedom of p. a bulwark of liberty 725.4
freedom of p. is means, not an end 725.1
hand that rules p. rules country 563.5
if p. free, no government lacks censors 111.5
liberty of p. is approved if it takes liberties with others 725.2
p. can't be restrained by government 725.4
p. has power, fixes all values 758.6
p. secretary to keep man in public eye 754.1
the p. and idols with feet of clay 330.51
to fetter p. is to fetter ourselves 725.5
who commits his decrepitude to the p. 1062.79
**press's:** I du believe in the p. freedom to pint the people to the goal 725.3
**pressed:** p. into service means p. out of shape 880.3
**presumes:** he that knows least p. most 445.12
**pretend:** not one of us can lie or p. 442.16
we p. to take each other seriously 464.1
**pretending:** p. is a virtue 726.15
**pretense:** p., more than poverty, harasses ruined man 712.26
possible to prick large p. with pin 1054.23
**pretenses:** greatest p. are built to hide emptiness 162.8
**pretension:** mark of man of world is absence of p. 910.2
**pretensions:** all-glorious within us are our gay p. 726.17
**prey:** if can't p. on others, we p. on ourselves 171.13
**price:** highest p. can pay for anything: to ask it 799.4
p. of everything is trouble acquiring it 1019.18
we shall pay any p. for liberty 534.20
**prices:** it was all p. to them 106.4
**pride:** gilded dust, our p. looks whole, sound 727.28
idleness and p. tax with heavy hand 444.5
it's a fine thing to rise above p. 727.3
one may be humble out of p. 433.15
p., avarice, envy are tongues men heed 727.8
p. destroys all symmetry and grace 727.27
p. doesn't wish to owe, self-love to pay 639.5
p. goeth before destruction 727.4
p., ignorance mutually beget each other 445.8
p. is active, does not feel small stings 727.2
p. is in thought; tongue has small share 727.18
p. is last vice good man sheds 727.10
p. is seldom delicate 727.16
p. is the mask of one's own faults 727.15
p. makes some men ridiculous 727.7
p. often borrows humility's cloak 727.12
p. over-estimation by self-love 727.25
p. that dines on vanity sups on contempt 727.11
p. thyself on virtue, not on parentage 37.11

people oppose established opinions from p. 256.9
proper to have p., ridiculous to show it 727.17
two sorts of p.: in one we approve ourselves, in other we cannot accept ourselves 727.1
unlike a magnet, p. at all points repels 727.5
unwillingness to submit to formalities is p. 112.5
when we fail, p. supports us 6.6
**priest:** p., delicate animal who scorns not hates 136.14
**priestly:** halo round p. head is his horizon 136.7
**priests:** in death and famine, reason is on the side of the p. 136.6
p. are no more necessary to religion than politicians to patriotism 136.8
p. put crowns on thieves, called kings 125.4
**prig:** p. finds last refuge in responsibility 743.1
**primitive:** hip is sophistication of the wise p. 89.4
**prince:** p. not as gr-reat in ol' counthry as here 823.2
p. who puts self at head of party 704.16
to call king "p." is pleasing 773.21
who draws his sword against the p. 779.3
**princes:** p. are like heavenly bodies 825.3
where p. are concerned, man able to do good is as dangerous as one who intends evil 825.20
**principal:** who has first place seldom plays p. part 773.10
**principle:** amid pressure of events, p. is no help 728.6
citizen is influenced by p. 130.7
contradictions in p. easily set aside 317.1
don't make a novel to establish a p. 341.7
Englishman does everything on p. 287.24
everywhere the basis of p. is tradition 728.7
I don't believe in p.; I do in interest 94.5
men of p. are sure to be bold 728.4
p. is not as powerful as a policeman 423.7
p. never forgives; its logic is to kill 728.1
party wedded to p. can save century 667.7
precedent embalms a p. 979.8
prosperity is the best protector of p. 728.17
to split the ranks, appeal to a p. 250.2
we talk on p., but we act on interest 493.5
**principles:** cause of evils inability to apply p. 371.2
corruption of government begins with p. 188.11
easier to fight for p. than live them 728.15
expedients are for an hour; p., for ages 728.2
fate of America is in its p. 728.13
general p., like air, are no less important because they elude observation 728.5
humours turn with climes, p. with times 728.12
man cannot make p.; only discover 1029.9
man is more careful of money than of p. 728.8
man may be sincere in p., not practice 728.9
marciful Providunce fashioned us holler o' purpose thet we might our p. swaller 728.11
nation must sacrifice all for p. 728.18
p. have a way of drying up 728.10
true partisan as true to p. as to self 667.2
we speak of being anchored to our p. 728.3
**print:** 'tis pleasant to see one's name in p. 758.3
we write frankly, "modify" before we p. 725.7
**printed:** things false not only are p., but things of truth most falsely set forth 758.2
**printing-press:** it's wondherful annybody wants p. to go on doin' what it does 758.4
p. greatest blessing or curse 758.1
**prison:** every p. is built with bricks of shame 729.8
liberty is different kind of pain from p. 361.9
most men in a brazen p. live 1058.1
p., blood, death create enthusiasts 795.3
p. is a house of care, where none thrive 729.4
pickaxe used to no purpose makes a p. 729.6
stone walls do not a p. make 729.5
vilest deeds bloom well in p. air 729.9
wherever one is against will is a p. 729.3
while there is soul in p., I am not free 98.2
**prisoner:** p. dashes for the open door 361.47
things denied are what p. wants most 729.2
**prisoner's:** soldier's pack not so heavy as p. chains 1035.32
**prisoners:** men not p. of fate, but p. of own minds 583.17
**prisons:** all p. are brimming over with innocence 729.1
no ugly lovers nor handsome p. 58.3
p. are built with stones of law 746.2
**privacies:** count not him among friends who will retail your p. to the world 392.12
**privacy:** human needs p. as much as understanding 730.3
**private:** man uses now p., now public, nature 681.4
public account of selves differs from p. 320.2
there are no such things as p. citizens 754.3
who dons public gown doffs p. person 755.8
**privations:** little p. are easily endured 234.3
**privilege:** dollar a worthier god than Heredity P. 34.71
**privileged:** comparing our lot, we are among the p. 152.3
concessions of the p. to the unprivileged 15.7
history of world is history of p. few 417.34
p. and the people formed two nations 133.1
**privileges:** our p. no greater than our obligations 804.10

what men value is not rights but p. 817.13
**prize:** p. cared for by powerful is power 713.27
**probability:** reasonable p. is the only certainty 113.7
**problem:** no p. of human destiny beyond human beings 731.5
solution to one p. brings us to another 735.15
Washington reflex: throw money at p. 393.32
**problems:** p. are opportunities in work clothes 731.4
p. prove their worth by hitting back 731.3
people are faced with new p. 297.17
some politicial p. have no solution 705.35
**procrastination:** p. is art of keeping up with yesterday 228.10
p. is the thief of time 228.13
**prodigal:** if man is p., he cannot be truly generous 373.2
it is fun to be p. 322.1
p. quits life in debt to others 589.4
p. robs his heir, the miser himself 589.7
**product:** finished p. has seen better days 283.2
**production:** America defends p. for profit, not for use 102.22
every p. must resemble its author 198.7
p. goes up and up 103.23
p. only fills void it has itself created 102.17
**profession:** price for pursuing any p. is intimate knowledge of its ugly side 1029.1
**professions:** all p. are conspiracies against the laity 1029.11
**professor:** p. led astray by artificial rules 277.43
**professors:** antiquity provides p. with bread, butter 42.6
culture wielded by p. to manufacture p. 207.20
p. guard the glory that was Greece 42.4
p. prefer own theories to truth 967.1
**profit:** even genius is tied to p. 596.43
no p. grows where is no pleasure ta'en 698.36
p. smiles on goodness when good profitable 391.53
p. system always unprofitable to most 106.7
smell of p. sweet, whatever the source 732.6
what p. to gain world and lose soul 33.2
**profits:** dirty p. ruin more than they keep 732.9
**profound:** p. thinker suspects that he is superficial 734.2
**profoundness:** mystery is not p. 734.1
**progress:** all p. is precarious 735.15
all p. means war with society 735.25
basis of p.: desire to live beyond income 735.3
best road to p. is freedom's road 735.12
change is scientific, p. is ethical 115.33
desire to understand, to reform the world, are the two great engines of p. 735.22
discontent is the first step in p. 249.10
greatest obstacle to p. is parasitism 735.10
human p. is furthered by aberration 735.17
is it p. if cannibal uses knife and fork 735.16
men oppose p., for they love inertia 175.10
natural p. is from rudeness to convenience, to elegance, to nicety 735.11
no p. without faith in tomorrow 735.13
p. as fact, ethical principle 34.75
p. depends on the unreasonable man 735.23
p. has been made through disobedience 254.2
p. has no greater enemy than habit 404.12
p. imposes new possibilities, restrictions 735.32
p. in life comes through daring 735.19
p. is a nice word but change is its motivator 115.27
p. is gauged by sacrifice it requires 735.20
p. is like a merry-go-round 735.6
p. is man's mark, not God's nor beasts' 735.2
p. is the dirtiest word in the language 735.18
p. is the law of life 306.1
p.: to learn questions lack meaning 3.10
prudence sometimes blocks road of p. 749.35
routine of most active lives precludes p. 10.7
simple faith in p. a weakness 735.31
social movements are symptoms of p. 564.5
social p. strengthens freedom 735.14
there is no p. in art 53.35
thousand things advance; nine hundred and ninety-nine retreat: that is p. 735.1
world's p. made from scaffold to scaffold 735.21
**prom:** all saving ourselves for senior p. 722.1
**prominent:** most p. men are hard to converse with 330.8
**promiscuous:** as bee its sting, p. leave behind something of selves by which they must suffer 736.1
**promise:** better deny at once than p. long 784.2
he is poor indeed that can p. nothing 145.2
p. binding in inverse ratio of the numbers to whom it is made 737.2
p. is most given when the least is said 96.4
p., large p., is soul of advertisement 18.5
p. made is a debt unpaid 737.13
p. not cakes to the child 737.8
to p. not to do a thing 737.16
we p. much to avoid giving little 737.17
**promises:** enemies' p. were made to be broken 286.2
everyone's a millionaire concerning p. 737.12
men are alike in their p. 224.21
out of danger, man may forget p. 213.9
p. and pie-crust made to be broken 737.14
p. not to be kept if harmful to those to whom you have made them 737.1
who p. much dines a fool on hope 737.7
who p. too much means nothing 737.6

**pronouns:** to succeed in world be wise using p. 594.10
**proof:** blockhead wants p. of what he can't see 328.7
no way of thinking or doing, however ancient, can be trusted without p. 979.20
**proofs:** p. looked for last by religious mind 328.35
**propaganda:** p. is a soft weapon 739.1
p. more successful when it stirs hatred 739.8
triumphs of p. accomplished not by doing, but by refraining from doing 739.4
**propagandist:** p. makes one set of people forget that other sets are human 739.5
**propagating:** if p. the species were permitted only to the virtuous, world would be very good 885.4
**properties:** politics is dealing of hard men over p. 705.47
**property:** all must fairly possess p., not seize it 1024.2
because p. exists there are wars, riots 740.9
desire of p. implanted by nature 740.12
foundation of the social contract is p. 740.20
hater of p. has deed recorded 438.8
he whose all is his p. is easily destroyed 740.2
men honor p. above all; has greatest power 740.7
obstacle to democracy is p. 740.10
p. is requisite to self-respect 740.22
p. is theft 740.18
p. is timid and seeks protection 740.4
revolution is a transfer of p. 813.38
spirit of p. doubles a man's strength 740.23
what foundation for vanity lies in p. 710.7
where no p., no injustice 740.14
**prophecies:** study p. when they are become histories 741.1
**prophecy:** p. is the most gratuitous form of error 741.3
**prophesy:** better to p. after event has taken place 741.2
**prophet:** best p. common sense, our native wit 147.6
heart is half a p. 282.41
p. is without honour in his own country 424.2
reason deserves to be called a p. 778.35
when God makes p., he doesn't unmake the man 440.11
**prophets:** wisest p. make sure of the event first 741.5
**proportion:** p. almost impossible; all exaggerate 742.1
without sense of p. there cannot be taste, intelligence, integrity 742.2
**propose:** woman might as well p. 195.7
**propriety:** p. is least of all laws and most observed 743.2
**prose:** good p. should resemble the conversation of a well-bred man 1062.73
one stanza outweighs book of p. 702.33
p. can bear a great deal of poetry 702.63
p.,—words in their best order 702.17
people become bankrupt having invested too heavily in the p. of life 605.14
when writing in p. you say what you mean 702.50
**proselyter:** no p. so energetic as atheist 997.3
**prospect:** p. is often better than possession 316.3
**prospects:** hours with happy p. in view more pleasing 316.4
**prosper:** those who p. take on airs of vanity 744.1
**prosperity:** adversity is greater teacher than p. 745.10
be moderate in p., prudent in adversity 749.24
curse of p.: it takes work away from us 744.13
easier to drive off adversity than keep p. 745.16
few of us can stand another man's p. 744.20
few respect p. without begrudging 293.1
for one man who can stand p., there are a hundred who can stand adversity 745.6
happiness requires a modicum of p. 744.2
heart great which shows moderation in p. 592.13
in p. be joyful, in adversity consider 745.4
in p. no altars smoke 790.38
in the day of p., adversity is forgotten 745.1
man insensible to p. till has adversity 745.13
much effort, much p. 279.7
one abhorred in p. is adored in adversity 745.9
p. doth bewitch men, seeming clear 744.22
p. first theme of political campaign 705.77
p. has everything cheap 744.11
p. has no power over adversity 745.11
p. is full of friends 363.44
p. is like a tender mother, but blind 744.6
p. is the best protector of principle 728.17
p. makes friends, adversity tries them 745.12
p. only an instrument, not a deity 744.4
p. regarded as symptom of virtue 744.3
p. versus beauty; cash against soul 744.15
p. won't falter if you buy, buy, buy 103.20
social p. means man happy, citizen free, nation great 744.14
some never find p. for all their voyaging 744.7
to insure own p., must insure p. of all 150.7
virtue of p. is temperance 745.3
we now face task of surviving p. 744.12
when you ascend hill of p., may you not meet a friend 744.21
**prosperity's:** p. the very bond of love 744.18
**prosperous:** p. need people to be kind to 517.4
**protect:** property of power is to p. 713.39

**protected:** p. man doesn't need luck 850.7
**Protestant:** P. must learn to decide for himself 123.23
**Protestantism:** P. proves that God is a bore 123.19
**protracted:** life p. is p. woe 545.5
**proud:** but a step between p. man's glory, disgrace 727.21
every cock is p. on his own dunghill 865.7
he that is p. eats up himself 727.24
I am p. up to the point of equality 295.9
mind too p. to unbend over ridiculosa 605.8
p. man knows no superiors, inferiors 727.14
p. man puts himself at a distance 727.6
p. man satisfied with his own good opinion 727.13
struggle between p. mind, empty purse 712.26
the p. taken in by flattery 727.26
they are p. in humility 433.3
too humble is half p. 433.30
we are rarely p. when we are alone 908.53
when a p. man hears another praised 727.9
**proudly:** die p. when one can no longer live p. 218.93
**prove:** p. anything with small segment of time 991.129
real difficulty is to know what to p. 738.1
**proved:** what needs to be p. cannot be worth much 738.3
**proverb:** p. is the child of experience 568.1
**proverbist:** p. knows only roundness of answers 568.5
**proverbs:** book of p. never made a Solomon 568.2
**provide:** if only God would p. until he provides 748.18
**providence:** belief in p. has not allayed fears 748.15
if you leap into a well, P. may not help 774.1
we degrade p. by imputing our ideas to it 748.4
wisdom of p. revealed in rarity of genius 748.13
**proving:** accusing is p., with Malice as judge 5.2
**provoked:** old age once p. cannot be appeased 646.35
**prudence:** misfortune attended with guilt and shame unqualifies man to act with p. 403.21
p. engenders paralysis of generous acts 749.34
p. is but experience 749.16
p. is ugly old maid courted by incapacity 749.3
p. sometimes blocks road of progress 749.35
self-made man acquires habit of p. 938.42
the eye of p. may never shut 749.9
where destiny blunders, p. will not avail 238.18
**prudent:** be p. in adversity 749.24
p. man does himself good 749.37
p. man doesn't make the goat gardener 749.17
p. person tries everything before arms 164.7
what is p. does not always lead to good 173.7
when you have nothing to say or hide, there is no need to be p. 749.14
**prudently:** nothing can be done at once hastily, p. 409.11
**prudery:** p. is the worst kind of avarice 750.4
p. multiplies sentinels 750.2
**pry:** who p. into sewer cannot have nice noses 111.4
**prying:** for p. into human affairs, none equal those whom it does not concern 571.6
**psychiatrist:** p. collects rent on castle in air 751.1
train years for jobs needed to retain p. 752.4
**psychiatry's:** p. chief contribution to philosophy 751.2
**psychoanalysis:** p.: give it little finger, takes whole hand 752.7
**psychoanalyst:** man who once cursed his fate, now curses himself and pays his p. 752.10
p. pretends he doesn't know everything 752.2
**psychology:** idleness is the parent of all p. 753.4
man qua thinker delights in p. 753.1
p. explains nothing; we are still in doubt 753.3
p. gives a different idea of what we know 753.5
**psychopathic:** p. element rises to top of all crusades 109.14
**psychotic:** p. is man who lives in castle in air 751.1
**public:** artist cannot get along without a p. 53.52
best p. measures are forced by the occasion 393.21
better a quiet death than p. misfortune 432.2
can't be p. man unless man meets p. views 755.6
conduct, opinions of p. men at different periods of career must not be contrasted 755.7
government no better than p. opinion sustaining it 756.19
he that writes to himself writes to an eternal p. 1062.35
history is a record of weakness of p. opinion 417.12
honesty in p. men attributed to dumbness 755.15
how dreary to be p. like a frog 330.17
love in p. affairs does not work 548.69
man assumes p. trust, he's p. property 755.12
man must brave p. opinion, woman submit 756.21
man uses now private, now p., nature 681.4
men want p. office for its advantage 755.1
minds do not act together in p. 27.2
modesty, diffidence make man unfit for p.

affairs 594.12
no group can withstand p. opinion 756.18
nothing makes more cowards than p. opinion 756.1
p. account of selves differs from private 320.2
p. always prefers to be reassured 675.5
p. buys opinions as it buys meat, milk 756.3
p. calamity is a mighty leveller 17.13
p. confidence is basis of effective government 393.36
p. forgives everything except genius 374.44
p. is odorless 205.1
p. men are bees working in a glass hive 330.7
p. men deem hypocrisy road to success 705.34
p. money like holy water—taken by all 188.6
p. office is secure, but lacks hope, fear 755.10
p. official must be visible, kissable 755.9
p. opinion is generally p. sentiment 756.6
p. opinion is stronger than legislature 756.22
p. opinion is the thermometer a monarch should constantly consult 756.15
p. opinion makes life unpleasant for one not content to be the average man 756.11
p. opinion may become legislation 756.17
p. sentiment is to p. officers what water is to the wheel of the mill 705.10
p. virtue is foundation of republics 1025.2
p. weal requires men betray, massacre 705.55
people before the p. live imagined life 330.44
press secretary to keep man in p. eye 754.1
respect p. opinion as far as necessary 756.20
the p. swallow their classics whole 134.9
we are ruled by p. opinion, not law 756.10
what p. will think prevents p. from thinking 756.8
what the p. wants is graphed in curves 103.22
when p. thinks long, it thinks right 756.12
who cannot wisely meddle with p. affairs in preaching gospel, cannot preach 718.1
who dons p. gown doffs private person 755.8
with p. sentiment nothing can fail 756.14
your p. servants serve you right 755.18
**public-relations:** p. men make flower arrangements of facts 739.3
**publications:** p. that succeed pretend that persons admired by public are no better than public 758.7
**publishers:** great authors produce great p. 758.5
p. are usually not very intelligent 758.8
**puddle:** every path has its p. 243.3
**pugnacious:** man learned habit of being p. from nature 26.5
**pulpit:** English are most awkward in the p. 287.26
**pulse:** feeling a woman's p. 261.20
**pumpkin:** every p. goes through all p. history 467.5
**pun:** goodness of p. in ratio of intolerability 762.3
who makes a p. will pick a pocket 762.2
**punctuality:** lack of p. alienates friendship 759.4
**punish:** folly to p. neighbor by fire 811.18
law cannot persuade where cannot p. 525.28
**punishment:** all p. is mischief 760.1
capital p. is vestige of barbarism 69.7
crime and p. grow out of one stem 760.6
p. basic concept in religion and politics 893.20
p. hardens, numbs, produces concentration 760.11
p. without judgment bearable 760.3
we are all sentenced to capital p. 12.5
**punishments:** many p. discredit a prince 760.8
**punning:** no false wit is so well practiced as p. 762.1
**purchase:** no need to p. day, water, sun, moon 616.58
**purchaser:** everything is worth what p. will pay 1019.15
**pure:** evil, fault of self-styled p. in heart 783.14
my strength is as the strength of ten, because my heart is p. 764.8
so long as we are dirty, we are p. 246.1
unto the p. all things are p. 764.4
who imagines himself p. in heart is dangerous 764.2
**purgatory:** as hard f'r rich to enther Hiven as f'r poor to get out iv P. 1041.15
there is no other p. but a woman 1055.8
time is the only true p. 971.9
**purge:** order a p. for your brain, not stomach 720.11
**Puritanism:** P.: the fear that someone may be happy 763.1
**Puritans:** I don't mind plain women being P. 996.4
mightiest of P. who first insisted that beauty is only skin deep 70.25
P. fled despotism to enjoy own religion 763.2
we are presarved fr'm th' P. 418.2
**purity:** p. is obscurity 764.7
**purpose:** happiness is attained by fidelity to p. 765.6
it's hard to tell the p. of a bird 80.8
life having p. based on religious system 765.4
masterpiece of man is knowing how to live to p. 765.10
nature is progressive realization of p. 616.22
secret of success is constancy to p. 765.3
the passion ending, doth the p. lose 668.27
through the ages one p. runs 735.27
to have a grievance is to have a p. 249.5
we all must have some p. in life 145.4
**purposeful:** busy life is nearest to a p. life 10.10

**purposes:** good p. directors of good actions 765.5
not data but p. constitute human experience 319.42
**purse:** better an empty p. than an empty head 445.14
empty p. frightens away friends 712.16
heaviest bag for traveler is empty p. 985.17
man sacrifices his life to his p. 1020.20
should be silver in p. or on tongue 281.3
who does not open his eyes opens his p. 611.2
**purses:** light gains make heavy p. 102.13
**pursue:** instinct of man to p. all that flies from him 684.12
thing we p. is often substitute for thing we really want 236.22
**puzzles:** all persons are p. 1001.8
**pygmy:** shall man hang self because he is a p. 870.7

## Q

**quacks:** dishonesty is the raw material of q. 221.1
**quaffing:** long q. maketh a short life 266.40
**qualities:** some men have useless good q. 1016.8
we don't love q., we love persons 548.129
we love q., not a person 548.163
**quality:** easier to confess defect than claim a q. 339.1
one shining q. lends lustre to another 309.5
take a hundred ladies of q. 52.2
**quarrel:** association of men will always q. 766.10
beware of entrance to a q. 766.15
for every q. man and wife have before others, they have a hundred alone 560.54
it takes only one to make a q. 766.9
justice of my q. 816.16
politest men q. at division of estate 1051.3
q. will always show where it was patched 766.8
test of breeding: how one acts in q. 389.8
we are losers when we q. with ourselves 167.3
when we q. we wish we had been blameless 766.4
**quarreling:** last sound on earth will be two human beings trying to launch space ship and q. 766.6
when chickens quit q., enough food for all 867.4
**quarrels:** great q. are great emancipations 766.16
most q. amplify a misunderstanding 766.7
q.: dowry married folk bring each other 560.92
q. of friends are opportunities of foes 766.1
q. often prove to be new recruits of love 766.2
q. wouldn't last if fault only on one side 766.11
those who interpose in q. often wipe a bloody nose 571.4
weakness on both sides is motto of all q. 766.18
**question:** not every q. deserves an answer 478.10
q. even the existence of a God 263.4
sudden q. may surprise man, lay him open 478.1
to q. a wise man is beginning of wisdom 478.11
**questions:** better to ask q. than to know all answers 478.18
chief relish of a life is to ask q. 478.3
great pleasure of ignorance is asking q. 478.16
it is possible for a handful of q. to break the bank of our answers 778.20
more to be learned from q. of child 478.15
no embarrassing q., just embarrassing answers 478.17
q. asked self are key to others' experience 868.2
q. shows the mind's range 478.13
who asks q. cannot avoid the answers 478.2
**quick:** no man q. enough to enjoy life 536.68
**quickly:** things done q. are not done thoroughly 409.5
**quiet:** heart of wise man lies q. like water 1053.10
I am not so sure about being q. 892.3
no retreat as q. as one's own soul 180.2
study to be q. and to do your business 571.1
whilst q., man in his house well guarded 420.17
**quotation:** classical q. is parole of literary men 767.3
fine q. is diamond on finger of a wit 767.7
**quotations:** I hate q.; tell me what you know 767.2

## R

**race:** a poor r. in a land of dollars 712.13
he may well win the r. that runs by himself 154.5
individual man tries to escape the r. 467.12
Negro is superior to the white r. 83.4
no r. can prosper till it learns dignity of tilling field 1058.70
r. prejudice decreases values 769.4
r. prejudice is a shadow over all of us 769.2
you have to go the rounds from individual to individual to gather totality of r. 467.20
**races:** not r. but individuals are noble 768.1

**racial:** r. prejudice is like hair across cheek 769.1
**racism:** if we practice r. then it is r. we teach 769.13
**racist:** American economy, society, unconscious, are all r. 769.8
**radical:** I never dared to be r. when young 770.2
r. has both feet firmly planted in air 770.4
r. invents views, conservative adopts 175.17
r. of one century is conservative of next 770.6
**radicalism:** conservatism drives the children into r. 175.6
r. ceases to be radical when absorbed in preserving control over a society 770.3
spirit of American r. is destructive 770.1
there is r. in all getting 710.8
**radicals:** few r. have good digestions 175.3
**radio:** hand that rules r. rules country 563.5
science brought forth r. commentator 563.4
**rage:** r. can never entirely be brought under the domination of the intelligence 39.5
where guilt is, r. and courage abound 403.10
**rain:** drowning man is not troubled by r. 17.45
into each life some r. must fall 1004.20
r., bad preacher, do not know when to stop 771.3
r. does not fall on one roof alone 150.1
r. has soft architectural hands 771.1
r. is good for vegetables 771.4
thirsty earth soaks up the r. 771.2
though it r., cast not away watering pot 749.19
who can count the drops of r. 300.1
**rainbow:** after debauch of shower, r. a pledge 772.1
my heart leaps up when I behold a r. 772.3
one can enjoy r. without forgetting forces that made it 772.2
**rainy:** preparing for r. day is sure to bring it on 103.20
**rake:** he is better with a r. than a fork 401.6
**rambling:** mere r. is interminable 896.8
**rank:** name, title, r. are artificial 773.9
there is no r. without some merit 773.15
would men retain r. without clothes 773.27
**rape:** procrastinated r. is rule of bestsellers 341.16
**rapine:** nature is one with r. 616.66
**rapture:** first fine careless r. 80.4
**rapture's:** r. self is three parts sorrow 911.29
**rare:** what is so r. as a day in June 848.29
**rash:** r. man calls the brave man a coward 192.3
**rashness:** r. succeeds often, more often fails 774.2
**rational:** all that is r. is anti-vital 778.40
few ever wished to be exclusively r. 979.13
r. being discovers deity in creation 616.47
r. man balances what he desires, what he can do 714.7
**rationally:** to him who looks upon the world r. 1060.17
**reach:** man's r. should exceed his grasp 55.2
**reactionaries:** all r. are paper tigers 175.13
r. are those at home in the present 175.18
**reactionary:** r. is a somnambulist walking backwards 175.16
**read:** better to be able neither to r., write than to be able to do nothing else 277.36
have you any right to r. novels 91.91
I'd swim to Boston soon as r. books in originals 91.35
man ought to r. as inclination leads 91.51
some r. to think; majority r. to talk 91.20
thousand new books to r., with time to r. a hundred 91.46
to r. a writer is to travel with him 91.39
to r. means to borrow 91.59
we like to r. others, don't like to be r. 1001.15
we r. things but never feel them until we've gone same steps as author 91.53
when we r. too fast or too slowly 91.74
**reader:** if you would be a r., read 1062.36
make r. laugh, he thinks you trivial 91.64
r. seldom peruses book with pleasure 'till he knows particulars about writer 91.1
**readers:** r. may be unfaithful to a writer 1062.8
r. of novels are a strange folk 341.12
**reading:** a r. machine, he mastered the worthless 520.42
he that I'm r. seems to have most force 91.68
many date new era in life from r. book 91.88
no distress that r. can't relieve 91.71
novel r. is a passion for results 91.34
people say that life is the thing, but I prefer r. 91.82
possession of book substitutes for r. 91.12
r. furnishes mind with materials of knowledge; thinking makes what we read ours 91.60
r. good books like talking with fine men 91.24
r. is but silent conversation 91.57
r.: killing time under dignified name 91.27
r. makes a full man 185.11
r. maketh a full man 1062.10
r. should be absorbing, voluptuous 91.85
there are favorable hours for r. 91.62
where some wisdom is, r. makes it more 91.44
**reads:** who r. and grows no wiser seldom suspects his own deficiency 934.14
who r. for improvement is beyond hope of it 91.23
**ready:** to be always r. man must be able to cut knot 222.1
**real:** God will have life to be r. 944.2
life is washed in the speechless r. 777.3
men often applaud imitation and hiss r. 60.1
nothing is r. until it is experienced 568.4

nothing that is r. is alien to me 448.25
r. estate is foundation of world's guilt 740.11
**realism:** let us replace sentimentalism by r. 776.3
r.: whatever is genuinely begotten by life 53.140
**realists:** r. do not fear results of study 776.2
**realities:** if you prefer illusions to r. 447.16
only dreamer shall understand r. 687.5
**reality:** between idea and r. falls the shadow 1012.3
comparison, not r., makes men happy or wretched 152.1
each has his r. to be respected before God 777.14
everything is a dangerous drug but r. 777.5
I like r.; it tastes of bread 777.1
in the American metaphysic, r. is always material r. 777.17
making terms with r. 121.41
melancholy and remorse form keel enabling us to sail into the wind of r. 911.10
mind's activity easy if r. is not met 968.43
moralists begin with a dislike of r. 598.15
no r. except the one within us 777.9
our separate fictions add up to joint r. 777.10
political is mode of grasping r. 705.24
r. is a spirit 777.4
r. is a staircase going neither up, down 777.13
r. is not an inspiration for literature 542.4
supreme r. of our time is common vulnerability of this planet 98.14
today's r. may be an illusion tomorrow 777.15
we are afraid to let go of petty r. to grasp great shadow 749.30
we take shape within and against that r. bequeathed us at birth 777.2
who confronts the paradoxical finds r. 661.2
who shut eyes to r. invite destruction 85.2
words are the great foes of r. 1057.7
**realization:** men can starve from a lack of self-r. 442.25
**realize:** modern age more eager to amass than r. 740.21
**reap:** in field of destiny, we r. as we've sown 860.13
they that sow in tears shall r. in joy 279.1
we shall r., if we faint not 430.4
whatever a man soweth, that shall he r. 809.3
**reason:** cause of error is war of senses, r. 297.27
docility is the observable half of r. 347.3
easiest victor over r.: terror, force 354.7
emotion has taught mankind to r. 282.38
force without r. falls of own weight 354.8
frugal substance is riches for a man of r. 695.3
God must approve of the homage of r. 263.4
government is not a representative of r. 393.58
habit is stronger than r. 404.17
heart experiences God, not r. 385.57
idle r. lessens weight of good ones 320.4
if r. wills fate, she is fate 778.21
in death and famine, r. is on the side of the priests 136.6
in what we understand, we r. but little 1000.7
in youth life of r. is not sufficient 1065.8
it is from r. that justice springs 391.33
law and r. only things between us and tyranny 525.25
life of r. balanced by irrational emotion 1013.1
love is a migraine, blotting out r. 548.90
love, not r., stronger than death 548.128
man observes law of God by applying r. 778.6
man who listens to r. is lost 778.37
men live but by intervals of r. 282.5
mind resorts to r. for want of training 778.1
no place in fanatic's head for r. 333.17
object of dread is human form with r. fled, while wretched life remains 555.15
peace rules the day, where r. rules mind 778.7
peasants not sophisticated enough to r. speciously 611.5
r.: a harmony among irrational impulses 778.34
r., alone, is a force confining 778.14
r. also is choice 778.22
r. can wrestle and overthrow terror 778.12
r. can't save us but can mitigate living 778.28
r. deceives us more often than nature 778.41
r. demands man live in accord with his own nature 431.21
r. deserves to be called a prophet 778.35
r.: faculty for grasping world by thought 491.9
r. flies, following senses, on clipped wings 778.8
r. for living is also r. for dying 538.3
r. guides but a small part of man 282.30
r. inclines to mildness 720.12
r. is essentially skeptical 778.40
r., like a flower, withers when plucked 778.33
r., like wife, is heard but not minded 720.2
r. may be lever, but sentiment is fulcrum 564.4
r. must keep rising to depose opinion 649.34
r. recognizes infinity of things which surpass it 778.24
r. respects the differences of things 448.28
r. rules more imperiously than a master 778.25
r., that hutch for grubby schoolboys 778.29
r. wishes judgment it gives be just 514.22
some men ignore r., fear being controlled 644.6
supreme triumph of r. is to cast doubt upon its own validity 778.39

takes r. to rule, mercy to forgive 357.6
theirs not to r. why 582.20
time makes more converts than r. 971.39
'tis vain to speak r. where not heard 778.13
to give r. for anything breeds doubt of it 775.3
try to r. about love, you'll lose your r. 548.71
untrammeled r. is indulgence of philosopher 968.59
we are less astonished that r. is suspended than it should ever prevail 778.36
we love without r., without r. we hate 551.11
we must follow r. as our guide 778.18
well-bred instinct meets r. half-way 484.6
what can we r. but from what we know 778.27
what r. cannot bring about, time may 971.22
when malice has r. on its side 557.12
when r. and instinct are reconciled 598.38
where I cannot satisfy my r., I love to humour my fancy 1046.2
woman's r. is in milk of her breasts 1055.101
women never r. and thus are seldom wrong 1055.65
would you persuade, speak of interest, not r. 683.6
your own r. should make you believe 328.32
**reasonable:** to r. man everything r. may be supported 778.11
**reasoning:** imagination robust in proportion as r. weak 448.30
where all is dream, r. is useless 687.13
**reasons:** dog r. the way he sniffs 484.4
I don't care about r., know what I like 719.4
those seeking r. bring sorrow on themselves 1053.22
**rebel:** no one can be r. too long and not turn into autocrat 779.2
r.: proponent of a new misrule who has failed to establish it 779.1
**rebellion:** as a dimension of man, r. defines him 779.5
little r., now and then, is good thing 779.4
progress has been made through r. 254.2
**rebuff:** welcome each r. 17.12
**recalcitrance:** in the human race is spirit of r. 684.2
**receive:** only those who have, r. 780.4
we r. but what we give 616.18
**receiver:** giver should be thankful r. received 780.3
**recognition:** I ask for r. of me in you, and r. of time 1001.20
**recollection:** r. and anticipation fill our moments 723.15
**recommendation:** good presence is letters of r. 45.6
**recompense:** no r. for an unjust slander 898.3
r. injury by justice; kindness by kindness 782.2
**reconciles:** good dinner, feasting r. everybody 272.25
**recording:** let no one imagine that in owning a r. he has the music 607.12
**red:** better a r. face than a black heart 886.7
leave the fear of r. to horned animals 149.15
**Redeemer:** tired by search after true good we stretch out arms to R. 387.10
**referendum:** r.: to vote for one's own ball and chain 1030.8
**refine:** afflictions r. some, consume others 17.27
**refinement:** in state of over-r. weak and strong go to the gutter 131.14
**reflection:** happiness resides in imaginative r. 407.95
**reform:** abuse to be reformed, unless r. worse 783.41
every r. was once a private opinion 783.10
men r. a thing by removing reality 783.5
nature is entirely indifferent to any r. 616.73
only in r. is true security to be found 850.10
r., if it fails, strengthens despotism 783.6
you've tried to r. what will not learn 783.21
**reformer:** apathy of voter is confusion of r. 1030.9
man a r. until reform tramps on his toes 783.18
r. don't see that people wud rather be wrong an' comfortable thin right in jail 783.9
r. must substitute attractive virtues for attractive vices or he will fail 783.23
r. thinks election turns men into angels 783.8
**reformers:** all r. are bachelors 783.29
consolation of middle-aged r. 783.36
nobody expects comfort from r. 783.3
**reforming:** give up r. society, give up responsibility 783.33
if anything ail a man, he sets about r. the world 783.38
nothing so needs r. as others' habits 783.40
**reformism:** r. characterized by utopian strategy 783.15
**reforms:** religions obsolete if they bring no r. 783.11
**refreshment:** to sit in shade on fine day is perfect r. 191.1
**refuge:** God is our r. and strength 385.6
the eternal God is thy r. 850.1
**refusal:** prompter the r., the less disappointment 784.6
soft r. not always taken 784.1
we become what we are by radical r. 442.20
**refused:** more tolerable to be r. than deceived 221.18
**refute:** who can r. a sneer 182.9
**regret:** history is one long r. 417.47
one knows bad action in flash of r. 224.17
r. calamities only if it helps sufferer 692.11
r. is woman's natural food 1055.118
to r. deeply is to live afresh 785.6
we often experience more r. over part left

than pleasure over part preferred 122.7
**regrets:** r. are natural property of grey hairs 646.18
**regularity:** knowledge hangs on r. of experiences 319.48
**reign:** one can't r. and be innocent 825.23
to be omnipotent but friendless is to r. 825.26
**reigns:** whoever r., the merchant r. 102.5
**rejection:** r. is a form of self-assertion 253.1
**rejoicing:** r. of a man is length of days 407.2
**relation:** good friend is my nearest r. 363.50
poor r. is most irrelevant thing in nature 789.4
r. between things gives meaning to them 569.3
**relations:** even great men have their poor r. 789.1
hostility lurks at the heart of our r. 151.20
renewal of broken r. is a nervous matter 299.1
**relationship:** I present myself to you in a form suitable to r. I wish to achieve with you 787.7
strongest r. on earth: parent and child 663.40
**relationships:** man is a knot into which r. are tied 787.11
r. are forms of exploitation 787.1
**relative:** in trouble best to seek out r. 789.2
no greater bugbear than strong-willed r. 789.3
**relatives:** great exercise of benevolence: loving r. 517.24
my teeth closer to me than my r. 869.15
one loyal friend worth ten thousand r. 363.48
when our r. are at home 789.5
**relativity:** that's r. 788.6
**reliance:** no man is worthy of unlimited r. 188.7
**religion:** all have conscience to hate; few, r. to love 551.1
atheism must insult God less than r. 997.13
cosmos is a fly-wheel; r. is theory that the wheel was designed to give man ride 1010.8
depth in philosophy inclineth to r. 688.1
effort to reconcile science and r. 844.8
every thing to be true must become a r. 991.145
extreme happiness, misery invite r. 790.75
false r. a pretext for thousand crimes 790.11
fanatical r. is not quite as bad as none 790.64
garb of r. is best cloak for power 790.29
God for men, r. for women 385.21
hating turns r. to spleen, bigotry 410.9
I know no r. that has moral claim on man 200.5
if all is well, r. is beneficial 790.76
if one r., God would be manifest 385.58
in a dead r. there are no more heresies 256.10
in my r. all would be love, poetry, doubt 790.13
in r. the only thing of use is an objective truth 790.47
knowledge, history are enemies of r. 790.51
Mahomet founded a r. without an inferno 414.9
man can no more possess a private r. than he can possess private sun, moon 790.9
man with sense of humor never founded a r. 790.36
man's uneasiness makes r. necessary 790.52
matters of r. should never be matters of controversy 790.66
men despise r. and fear it is true 790.56
men say they are of same r. for quietness' sake 790.71
men will die for r., but not live for it 790.10
money's the wise man's r. 596.19
need new source of moral strength if r. dead 790.4
no consolations of r. or philosophy unless one experiences their desolations 790.33
no r. can be considered in abstraction from its followers 790.85
no r. has given a picture of deity which men could imitate without immorality 385.64
nothing so fatal to r. as indifference 790.5
nought calms the spirit as rum and true r. 982.2
one man finds in r. his literature, science; another finds in it his joy, duty 790.40
only one r., though a hundred versions 790.72
persecution, religious pride, love of contradiction are the food of r. 790.14
pure r. and undefiled before God 790.2
pure r. breathing household laws 695.8
Puritans fled despotism to enjoy own r. 763.2
r. a childish toy; no sin but ignorance 790.45
r. a mode of bearing ills of life 17.17
r. comes closer to the heart of things 790.69
r.: daughter of Hope and Fear 790.3
r. easier to die for than live absolutely 561.2
r. enlightens, terrifies, subdues 790.53
r. has never survived morals 790.21
r. has only to fear not being understood 790.77
r. has treated knowledge as an enemy 790.12
r. is a direction of the heart 790.63
r. is always a patron of the arts 790.34
r. is both mythology and folklore 610.5
r. is candle in multicolored lantern 790.50
r. is destroyed by bigotry 262.7
r. is never a check 790.74
r. is now called an ideology 443.3
r. is opium of the people 790.46
r. is reaction of human nature to search for God 790.83
r. is rendered illustrious by the pious 485.8
r. is the best armour, the worst cloak 790.26
r. is the substance of culture 790.81
r. is whatever one is most interested in 790.1

r.: loving life, conscious of impotence 790.67
r. made an honest woman of supernatural 946.1
r. makes men wise and virtuous, or makes them set up false pretences to both 790.28
r. makes one think oneself wiser than wisest who thinks differently 790.43
r. of character apt to be invaded by religious training 790.20
r. only means of reducing people grown savage in arms 1024.12
r.: original cure and original disease 790.62
r. proposes method of fortifying soul 790.70
r. restores the courage to live by grace 691.12
r. seems grown an infant with age 586.4
r. should rest on one's fine feelings 790.68
r. teaches us to love our enemies 790.25
r. that fears science dishonors God 844.5
r. veils sacred fires, morality expires 790.61
r. which has lost conviction about men's struggles for the human 790.44
r. will not regain power until it can face change 844.11
r. without science is blind 844.4
science and r. are two sides of the same glass, through which we see darkly 844.1
science investigates; r. interprets 844.7
sin a basic concept in r. and politics 893.20
terror of God is the secret of r. 340.35
test of r. is how much it explains 790.17
theological r. is the enemy of mankind 966.9
theology in r. like poisons in food 966.7
to befriend enemy is essence of true r. 98.5
true r. must know our nature 790.57
true r. slow in growth, hard to dislodge 790.54
we crave support in vanity and r. 1020.15
we have r. enough to hate, not love 790.78
we must respect the other fellow's r. 790.48
when God is dead r. becomes one 790.79
who seek not r. should be deprived of it 790.58
without fictions the truths of r. would not be intelligible to the multitude 790.73
writers against r. never set up their own 997.5
you corrupt r. in favour of friends 790.59

**religionist:** new r. cries out for some god to be his 790.8

**religions:** all r. are monuments to superstition 790.30
founders of r. didn't include unbeliever 790.27
he who observes moral precepts of r. won't be questioned in heaven as to dogmas 790.39
r. are obsolete if they bring no reforms 783.11
r. die when they are proved to be true 844.12
r.: ejaculations of a few imaginative men 790.19
r. generally have some instinctive basis 790.65
r. such stuff as dreams are made of 790.82
r. united with government inimical to liberty 125.2

**religious:** in big houses always r. element 1041.9
injustice feared less if ruler is r. 825.2
life having purpose based on r. system 765.4
man can no longer shove responsibility off on r. power 804.6
men do evil from r. conviction 872.4
more and more care about r. tolerance 790.7
proofs looked for last by r. mind 328.35
r. emotions are conservative, not creative 790.15
r. experience is force behind scientific research 790.16
r. neurosis is tied to dietary demands 790.55
r. truth is blasphemy 991.53
r. vision is our one ground for optimism 790.84
science without r. wisdom increases fear of death 844.10
social evil sanctified by r. sentiment 475.11
to be furiously r. is irreligiously r. 790.60
to lead r. life, identify with mankind 705.31

**religiously:** any act good in itself is good to do r. 893.10

**reluctance:** easy is difficult when done with r. 1015.1

**remains:** what we never had r., things we have go 1003.2

**remark:** assified r. is often sanctified by use 210.30

**remarkable:** nothing so commonplace as wish to be r. 33.13

**remedies:** extreme r. appropriate to extreme diseases 791.6
most men die of r., not of diseases 791.7
our r. oft in ourselves do lie 791.13
social r. will fail 616.35
some r. worse than the disease 791.10
we cannot do without palliative r. 791.4

**remedy:** everyone suffers wrongs which have no r. 474.9
man looks for an excuse before a r. 312.4
r. for all blunders is love 791.3

**remember:** better forget and smile than r., be sad 574.30
we do not r. days, we r. moments 574.24
we have all forgot more than we r. 574.9
we r. best those things better forgotten 574.10
what was hard to bear is sweet to r. 574.27

**remembered:** nothing is so perfect possessed as r. 710.9

**remembering:** forgiving presupposes r. 357.17
how shall we look on sun and feel rain, r. those who loved sun and rain 603.8

**remembrance:** burden not r. with heaviness that's gone 785.5
praising what is lost makes the r. dear 631.2

**reminiscence:** nothing awakens a r. like an

odour 875.5
**reminiscences:** r. makes one feel aged, sad 574.32
**remorse:** melancholy and r. are our keel 911.10
r. is impotence; it will sin again 793.10
r. sleeps in prosperity, not adversity 793.14
revenge produces incurable r. 793.3
who cares not for your r. is your equal 793.2
you cannot lay r. upon innocent, nor lift it from heart of guilty 793.6
**remorseful:** some are very resourceful at being r. 793.11
**rend:** all we value we shall sometime r. 239.4
**renounce:** to work is better than to r. 10.3
**renown:** measure r. according to how it's acquired 330.29
r. is like hue of grass that comes, goes 330.15
to practice right in hope of r. is near to vice 816.20
worldly r. is but a breath of wind 330.16
**rent:** nothing whole that has not been r. 939.55
**renunciation:** crown of excellence is r. 792.3
r. is a piercing virtue 792.2
**repair:** time to r. roof is when sun is shining 356.6
**repartee:** majority is always best r. 51.9
**repay:** in refusing benefits caution to be used, lest we seem to fear having to r. them 784.9
**repeated:** nothing is r., everything is unparalleled 1007.3
r. phrase gains meaning 794.5
**repeateth:** he that r. a matter separateth friends 392.1
**repeats:** he that knows little often r. it 445.13
**repelling:** every man is an infinitely r. orb 467.4
**repent:** Americans like to have you r. 793.13
r., don't brood over your wrongdoing 793.7
we as often r. good we have done as ill 785.1
**repentance:** amendment is r. 793.5
only r. is strong; it can end everything 793.10
our r. is fear of what might happen 793.9
r. of man is accepted by God as virtue 793.17
seeds of r. sown in youth, reaped in age 793.4
sinning is the best part of r. 793.1
**repentant:** the r. say never a brave word 793.16
**repents:** he punishes self who r. of his deeds 793.12
**repetition:** r. everywhere: nothing found only once 794.1
r.: nature's only form of permanence 794.4
**repletion:** sovereign source of melancholy is r. 839.3
**report:** evil r. carries farther than applause 622.4
**reporter:** r. is concerned with tomorrow 622.7
**repose:** glory and r. can't inhabit same place 384.15
God offers choice between truth and r. 991.36
I long for r. that ever is the same 116.6
r. as necessary in conversation as in art 185.15
r. in energy is badge of gentleman 376.2
r. is not the destiny of man 113.6
something attempted, something done, has earned a night's r. 6.15
we combat obstacles to get r. 805.1
**representative:** r. assembly lets parties fight by petition 169.1
your r. betrays you if he sacrifices his judgment to your opinion 756.2
**reproach:** only defence against r. is obscurity 797.1
sting of a r. is its truth 797.6
**reproaches:** there are r. which praise 716.21
**reproduction:** flower is the poetry of r. 349.3
**reproductive:** monks, nuns, spinsters are not r. 796.3
**reproof:** ingenuous mind feels r. in unmerited praise 716.17
those best can bear r. who merit praise 797.10
**reprove:** r. not a scorner, lest he hate thee 797.3
**republic:** r. is a dream 231.47
r. is a raft, one's feet always in water 393.5
**Republican:** let us not seek R. answer, but right answer 704.7
r. despotism is fertile in tyranny 231.35
**republics:** public virtue is only foundation of r. 1025.2
**reputability:** conspicuous consumption is a means of r. 103.27
**reputation:** author who threatens to survive his r. 1062.30
easier to add to great r. than to get it 798.29
for sake of good r., all sacrifice selves 798.26
good r. is itself a fortune 798.2
great r. is a great noise 798.25
he who survives his r. lives like a man listening to his own reproach 223.8
how many worthy men have survived own r. 223.6
more shameful to lose good r. than never to have acquired it 798.28
one can live down anything except a good r. 798.32
one lies in words and gets bad r. 329.46
people care more for r. of wit than virtue 1054.34
purest treasure is spotless r. 798.30
r. got without merit, lost without fault 798.14
r. increases, ability declines 646.45
r. is an idle and most false imposition 798.31
r. is commonly measured by the acre 798.15
single lie destroys whole r. 329.20
slander may stain even clearest r. 798.16
successful man loses no r. 938.14

to secretly stab a r. betrays a base spirit 898.1
two modes of establishing r. 798.7
universal idol of men of letters is r. 1062.2
valuable possession: r. of being well to do 1041.38
**required:** to whom much is given, much is r. 804.2
**requires:** who r. much from himself 248.1
**resemblances:** r. are the shadows of differences 676.10
**resentment:** nothing consumes man more quickly than r. 39.26
who requires much of self, little of others, will not be the object of r. 248.1
**reserve:** r. is an artificial quality 31.7
suspect emptiness if man carries on r. to a third interview 31.2
wise r. seasons the aims 856.4
**resignation:** divine in Russian soul–r. 828.2
r., only feeling for which impossible to become sham 800.2
**resist:** I respect only those who r. me 651.4
**resistance:** country preserves liberties if rulers warned that people preserve spirit of r. 651.9
our energy is in proportion to r. met 243.7
**resolute:** men as r. appear with too much, as too little fear 340.7
**resolution:** r. to avoid evil is made too late 801.2
**resolutions:** good r. interfere with scientific laws 801.5
great actions not sons of great r. 224.5
sudden r. only indicate changeableness 801.3
**resolve:** afterthought makes first r. a liar 24.2
every obstacle yields to stern r. 765.8
perform without fail what you r. 801.1
**respect:** fools take to selves r. given to office 1020.2
give one man lecture, another shilling, and see which will r. you most 596.30
I don't want r.; it means I don't count 802.3
I r. only those who resist me 651.4
if you have r. for people as they are, you can help them to become better 802.4
men r. those who do not give way to them 651.10
no man has considerable r. for himself 861.8
people I r. behave as if they were immortal 90.3
r. self if you wish others to r. you 862.4
when we know all a man's views, we lose r. for him 331.2
without r. what distinguishes man, beast 802.2
woman should always challenge our r. 1055.44
**respectability:** r. is the dickey on bosom of civilization 803.3
r.: offspring of liaison between bald head and bank account 803.1
what is the use of r. to pitifulest man 803.2
**respectable:** build business up big enough, it's r. 102.30
more man ashamed of, more r. he is 803.6
**respects:** he who r. others is respected by them 781.4
**responds:** no one so accursed, desolate, but some heart r. unto his own 953.12
**responsibility:** action springs from readiness for r. 9.6
chief is a man who assumes r. 528.20
fear, born of the stern matron R. 43.8
highest form of r. is irresponsibility 804.4
liberty means r. 534.42
man must assume the r. for his world 804.6
man's r. increases as the gods' decreases 804.8
one can pass on r., not discretion 804.5
prig always finds a last refuge in r. 743.1
r.: detachable burden easily shifted to God, fate, fortune, luck or one's neighbor 804.3
**responsibility's:** r. like string we can only see middle of 804.11
**responsible:** freedom is will to be r. to ourselves 361.42
somebody's r. and sombody's innocent 515.3
there are r. persons, no guilty ones 403.3
to be a man is, precisely, to be r. 804.12
**rest:** absence of occupation is not r. 444.4
complete r. is death 10.16
in all things r. is sweet 805.5
most men in a coma when at r. 9.22
nothing gives r. but search for truth 805.4
one can r. only after steady practice 805.2
r. is not a word of free peoples 805.7
r. is the sauce of labor 805.6
too much r. itself becomes a pain 805.3
**restfulness:** r. is a quality for cattle 805.8
**restraint:** all seek to do what they please without r. 361.14
liberty exists in proportion to r. 534.50
**result:** everything we do has a r. 173.7
**results:** most great r. of history are brought about by discreditable means 570.3
**retirement:** death is perpetual r. without pay 218.60
elegant sufficiency, content, r. 695.7
r. accords with the tone of my mind 31.1
**retreat:** females most dangerous when appear to r. 1055.94
no r. as quiet as one's own soul 180.2
**return:** the r. makes one love the farewell 666.6
**returns:** arrow that has left bow never r. 505.11
**reveal:** do not r. your thoughts to everyone 162.1
**revelation:** my mind is direct r. from God 810.1
**revenge:** a man will buy r. with his soul 811.14
forgetting a wrong is a mild r. 474.7
in not paying debt of r., we're superior 782.1

in r. man but even with enemy 811.3
man that studieth r. keeps wounds green which otherwise heal 811.4
men more prone to r. injuries 782.3
no r. more honorable than one not taken 811.21
r. back on itself recoils 811.16
r. is a dish to be eaten cold 811.10
r. is a fever, cured by letting blood 793.3
r. is a much more punctual paymaster than gratitude 811.8
r. is a stronger principle than gratitude 811.7
r. is fruit which you must leave to ripen 811.13
r. is joy of narrow, sick, petty minds 811.15
r. is profitable, gratitude is expensive 397.6
r. proves its own executioner 811.12
rest not secure against r. 474.21
since women delight in r., it may seem but feminine manhood to be vindictive 811.5
sweet is r.—especially to women 811.6
to refrain from imitation is the best r. 449.9
woman's desire for r. outlasts emotions 1055.29
**revenged:** I will not be r., this I owe to my enemy 474.4
**revengeful:** weakest are the most r. 1040.3
**revenges:** whirligig of time brings in his r. 971.53
**revenue:** government expands to absorb r. 393.68
no man divulges which way his r. comes in 740.16
**revere:** more we r. a man, more we are struck by his flaws 802.1
**reverence:** does not man feel he is made higher by doing r. to what is above him 1061.2
r. is nothing without self-respect 862.6
**reverend:** old goat not more r. for beard 646.34
**reverie:** r. is the groundwork of creative imagination 812.4
to make a prairie, r. alone will do 812.1
**review:** one can't r. bad book without showing off 204.3
who would write and can't, can surely r. 204.32
**reviewing:** I never read a book before r. it 204.50
**reviews:** do not read the r. 204.16
**revolt:** inferiors r. to be equal 813.1
not suffering but hope incites men to r. 813.22
r. and terror pay a price 526.3
r. is result of thought of the masses 813.35
**revolution:** change prepares the ground for r. 813.23
childish world pleased with each new r. 813.10
compromised r. shatters community that was 813.17
every r. was first one man's thought 813.9
God gives r. as merchant gives a ball 385.41
great r. is the fault of the government 813.15
mediocrity mitigates the most violent r. 813.8
modern search for freedom, self-fulfillment born of r. in our hemisphere 813.31
poverty is parent of r. and crime 712.2
r. always marks victory of single party 813.14
r. is a transfer of property 813.38
r. must take place in men before things 813.19
r. requires leaders' infallibility 813.30
there's r. only where there's conscience 813.18
thinkers prepare r.; bandits carry it out 813.2
woman is perpetual r. 1055.148
**revolutionaries:** in history of mankind, envy makes r. 417.27
**revolutionary:** artist is as dissatisfied as r. 53.59
if you feed people just r. slogans 813.32
r. spirit frees one from scruples as regards ideas 813.6
successful r. is a statesman, unsuccessful one a criminal 813.11
to be a r. is first to make sure of permanence and one's good reception 813.20
**revolutions:** in r., first inroads upon laws often made by governors 813.5
in r. there are those who cause them and those who profit by them 813.36
quality of r. to make new lines, laws 813.33
r. always destroy themselves 813.26
r. are not made; they come 813.37
r. eliminate men but elaborate ideas 813.16
r. never lightened the burden of tyranny 813.39
wind of r. is not tractable 813.24
women hate r. and revolutionists 813.34
**reward:** r. doubles pleasure of every work 673.5
r. of thing well done is to have done it 6.8
virtue herself is her own fairest r. 1025.52
we look for r., are disappointed 457.3
**rewards:** who r. past injuries invites more 866.4
**rhetoric:** r. is the creature of art 757.4
r. takes no account of the art in literature 598.26
to-day violence is the r. of the period 1024.11
**rhyme:** fools of r. sweat in pigmy wars 702.98
r. of false sorrow as recognizable as ring of false coin 482.1
when writing in r. you say what you must 702.50
**rhymes:** his hairs grow hoary as his r. grow worse 702.8
we lack not r. and reasons 971.62
**rhythms:** most exciting r. seem unexpected and complex 607.2
**rice:** when r. good, curry is half-cooked 455.4

**rich:** abundance won't suffer the r. to sleep 899.3
average man r. enough when he has more 249.7
be r. for yourself, poor to friends 852.17
be r. in a day, be hanged in a year 732.7
better to live r. than to die r. 1041.33
craving of the r. for titles 52.4
easier for camel to go through eye of needle than r. man to enter kingdom of God 1041.7
for r. people, sky is just an extra 413.2
he is r. that is satisfied 839.1
he is r. who can use all men's faculties 313.3
he is r. who hath enough to be charitable 1041.10
he that is r., all are kind to him 712.17
he who is contented is r. 183.17
honest r. can never forget poverty 712.11
I don't think you can spend yourself r. 275.1
I wish to be r., glorify honest poverty 1041.65
in fight r. man saves face; poor man, coat 342.5
it is in vain to ridicule a r. fool 1041.36
laws grind the poor, r. men rule law 525.35
man r. or poor according to whether he can afford necessaries, conveniences 1041.59
one cannot both feast and become r. 700.2
poor and content is r. 183.22
poor man ruined as soon as he apes the r. 926.2
r. child often sits in poor mother's lap 663.14
r. envied by those who have a little 1041.11
r. man cannot imagine poverty 712.42
r. man is everywhere expected and at home 1041.53
r. man's death is sniffed far off 401.29
r. men are to bear infirmities of poor 269.2
r. men feel misfortunes that miss poor 1041.28
r. men seek stomach for their meat 1041.20
r. men's faults are covered with money 339.9
r., powerful know God is on their side 385.2
r. purchase heaven by their alms 430.11
r. will ever distinguish selves from poor 1041.51
r. would have to eat money 712.45
show of honesty is surest way to grow r. 423.10
smile with the wise, feed with the r. 1041.32
take no satisfaction in dying but living r. 502.5
the r., when sick, feel impotence of wealth 1041.12
there's always a way for the r. 1041.23
to be r. without being proud is easy 1041.13
troubles of r. are troubles money can't cure 17.43
when r. wage war it's poor who die 1041.54
who hastes to be r. will not be innocent 732.2
wise man gets r.; if r. he gets foolish 596.15
wise man is very r., wanting nothing 1053.40
with full stomach r. and poor are alike 272.9

**richer:** we are all of us r. than we think we are 694.3

**riches:** all else is secondary to charm of r. 1041.31
all r. but liberty make us masters, slaves 361.24
as r. forsake a man we discover his folly 223.5
believe not them that seem to despise r. 913.2
children are poor men's r. 121.14
give me neither poverty nor r. 695.1
he is not fit for r. who fears to use r. 1041.26
I have no r. but my thoughts 968.48
if r. increase, think it not enough to be liberal, but munificent 373.3
if thou covetest r., ask for contentment 183.20
let none admire that r. grow in hell 1041.39
not possession but use is the only r. 1041.27
passions of men in democratic times end in love of riches, or proceed from it 1041.64
r. are for comfort, not hoarding 1041.52
r. attract the attention of mankind 1041.1
r. certainly make themselves wings 1041.6
r. consist in use made of treasures 1041.40
r. have made more covetous men 401.12
r. have wings; sometimes they fly away 1041.4
r. more enlarge than satisfy appetites 1041.29
r. serve wise man but command a fool 1041.21
r., to be enjoyed, must be interrupted 184.4
r. without law are more dangerous than poverty without law 525.5
seek not proud r. 8.1
we may see the small value God has for r. by the people he gives them to 1041.46

**richest:** in ugly world r. can buy only ugliness 1041.58

**riddle:** all is r., and the key is another r. 1012.4
life's the only r. we don't give up 536.41
Russia a r. wrapped in mystery inside enigma 828.1

**riddles:** some have unconquerable love of r. 208.4
women are like r.; they please us no longer once we know them 1055.123

**ride:** few men to r., millions to be ridden 995.29
if you r. horse, sit close and tight 815.2
who makes himself an ass, men will r. 934.8

**rider:** no secret so close as between r., horse 815.3

**ridicule:** all character can be destroyed by r. 814.7
height of heroism: know how to face r. 814.8
public r. is best way to attack vice 814.5
r. dishonours more than dishonour 814.4

to r. is the talent of ungenerous tempers 814.1
**ridiculous:** but one step from sublime to r. 4.4
in r. world nothing can be ridiculed 3.5
look for r. in all, you'll find it 4.6
r. things are hardest to confess 165.5
three things render even a great man r. 185.35
**right:** be always sure you are r.—then go ahead 816.8
because r. is r., to follow r. is wisdom 816.23
cultivate respect not for law but for r. 816.24
do not expect justice where might is r. 354.17
do well and r., let world sink 391.24
doing what's r. no guarantee against misfortune 17.37
even r. does not receive consideration if it does not seem r. 45.10
freedom of the most free: to do what is r. 816.10
God may be in his heaven, but all's not r. 305.10
God prevent us from becoming r.-thinking 816.17
God's in his heaven—all's r. with world 652.5
I'll follow the r. side even to the fire 816.19
if everyone is wrong, everyone is r. 297.22
man contends for obscure, distorted r. 475.2
man never outraged unless at bottom r. 39.21
might, r., over centuries found identical 816.7
moral sense teaches how to avoid the r. 816.25
more trouble to make maxim than do r. 568.7
no mistake is so great as being always r. 816.6
nobly wrong more manly than meanly r. 628.6
only a practicable r. is worth fighting for 817.18
protest you're r.: you'll be wrong 816.27
r. conduct never promoted by ignorance 75.10
r. is its own defense 816.3
r. is more precious than peace 816.26
r. is r. only when entire 816.12
r. is what is after my constitution 816.9
r. makes might 817.10
r. to be heard is not r. to be heeded 362.6
slaves: who dare not be in r. with few 816.15
spirit of liberty not too sure it is r. 534.16
take the place which is your r. 853.2
those who believe they alone are r. succeed 816.13
to do a great r., do a little wrong 816.21
to practice r. in hope of renown is near to vice 816.20
to win argument, start by being r. 51.13
until jurors agree, they cannot all be r. 991.64
we applaud r. when it costs us nothing 816.11
we felt we were r. twenty years ago; today we know we weren't always r. 816.22
we go r. enough if we go wrong together 976.2
where there is no might r. loses itself 354.18
why run, if not on the r. road 10.9
you can do r. in spite of your feelings 816.5
**righteous:** call bad behavior r. indignation 239.7
hard to be r. if unrighteous have greater right 391.25
r. are bold as a lion 403.2
r. one has no sense of humor 872.2
to be r. is the first of all duties 489.14
**rights:** Americans have ardor for gain, passion for r. 34.79
be beneficent but defend your r. 226.3
citizenship: the right to have r. 130.11
civil-r. movement has restored dignity of indignation 817.17
during war we imprison r. of man 1035.44
every American free to stand up for his r., even if he must sit down for them 747.2
giving others their r., we give ourselves r. 817.8
it is fair to judge peoples by r. they will sacrifice most for 817.1
man entered society to secure his r. 906.15
man inferior to any whose r. he tramples 817.5
material interest closing on our r. 565.7
modern state has only r., no duties 923.4
need laws to give us civil r., God to make us civil 817.16
never exceed r.: r. will become unlimited 749.28
no broader basis for government than all people with r. in their hands 231.14
protection of our r. endures no longer than performance of our responsibilities 804.10
r. inherent, whatever sex, complexion 817.3
r. of all diminish if r. of one threatened 817.9
r. that do not flow from duty are not worth having 817.2
self-given r. are relative to self-imposed duties 817.15
they have r. who dare maintain them 817.11
we magnify man's r., minimize his capacities 231.24
what men value is not r. but privileges 817.13
who doubts his r. talks with most passion 817.14
**ring:** r. out the old, r. in the new 624.6
**riots:** because property exists, there are r. 740.9
**ripe:** from hour to hour, we r. and r. 567.17
if you trap the moment before it's r., tears of repentence you'll certainly wipe 972.3

old and the r. fall 218.81
**rise:** no longer clear which way is up, even if one wants to r. 133.3
way to r. is to obey and please 938.20
**rising:** r. in life by own industry, others' folly 938.23
**risk:** everything is sweetened by r. 213.20
man has right to r. own life to save it 213.16
to be alive at all involves some r. 213.15
what is necessary is never a r. 617.17
win without r., triumph without glory 938.6
**risks:** life must always be full of r. 213.6
**ritual:** unreal is r. without devotion 9.5
**ritualism:** r.: Dutch Garden of God, where He may walk in rectilinear freedom 112.1
**rival:** if you have a r., you must please 195.9
**rivalry:** r. of women visited on fourth generation 1055.14
**river:** Hudson R. is like old October 818.5
I think that the r. is a strong brown god 818.2
to join the brimming r. 818.4
weariest r. winds somewhere safe to sea 600.20
when you have crossed r., you can say crocodile has lump on his snout 319.1
who never saw r. thought his first a sea 445.22
you cannot step twice into the same r. 115.21
**rivers:** all the r. run into the sea 847.2
mighty r. easily leaped at their source 6.18
r. are roads which move 818.3
r. lose force when split into streams 932.2
**road:** all I seek: heaven above and r. below me 985.38
does r. wind up-hill all the way 536.98
he watched the ads, not the r. 63.9
man determined never to move out of beaten r. cannot lose his way 175.7
man's r. marked by graves of likings 402.23
no r. which does not lead to an end 538.17
r. not leading to other roads must be retraced 402.25
r.: where one passes from where it's tiresome to be to where it's futile to go 985.6
they say you are on wrong r., if it is yours 466.7
we can't reach old age by another's r. 860.12
why run, if not on the right r. 10.9
you know more of r. by having travelled it 319.25
**roads:** Congressman never any better than his r. 169.6
**roam:** dunce sent to r. excels dunce kept home 985.10
r. abroad in the world 985.31
to r. giddily and be everywhere but home 985.11
**robbed:** he that is r., not wanting what's stol'n 547.11
the r. that smiles steals from the thief 118.9
worthy to be r., who shows felon where his treasure lies 964.8
**robber:** nothing is worse than a naked r. 201.13
**robber's:** who has nothing can whistle in r. face 712.35
**robbery:** idleness has a son, r. 444.8
**robots:** danger of future: men may become r. 960.5
**rocks:** mariner must have his eye upon r. 714.3
**rod:** he that spareth his r. hateth his son 760.2
**rodeoing:** r. is about only sport you can't fix 922.7
**rogue:** in limelight, r. acts like honest man 330.35
when a r. kisses you, count your teeth 519.3
**romance:** no one a man who was never touched by r. 820.2
r. calls for faraway love of troubadours 560.99
r. is to deceive oneself, then others 548.245
shouldn't allow r. to become necessary 820.1
woman's sense of humour spoils r. 820.3
years of r. makes a woman look like a ruin 560.128
**romances:** if histories properly told r. unneeded 417.50
**romantic:** boys like r. tales 121.8
every ship is r. object save our own 331.7
it may be that r. has the truer vision 821.2
it takes a r. nature to want to survive 994.7
r. artist recognized by his insincerity 53.96
r. desires to prevent life from escaping 821.4
r. life not due to irregular hours, diet 821.1
r. man more uplifted by two women 575.4
**romanticism:** women dare not indulge in r. 821.3
**Rome:** when at R. I fast on the Sabbath 985.4
**roof:** every r., when lifted, reveals tragedy 420.10
larger a roof, more snow it collects 1041.43
repair r. when sun shines 356.6
**room:** how little r. do we take up in death 218.118
love makes one little r. an everywhere 548.45
**rooms:** small r. discipline the mind 428.4
**rooster:** woe to house where hen crows, r. still 560.113
**roosters:** with so many r. crowing, sun never rises 56.6
**rose:** break not the r., never feel a thorn 349.4
forbear to read rood to learn r. 277.54
God made r. of what was left of woman 1055.86
is there any moral shut in bosom of r. 70.56
no gathering the r. without thorn pricks 699.1
r. by any other name would smell as sweet 612.8
r. is a r. is a r. is a r. 442.21
r. too often smelled loses fragrance 331.14
r.'s scent is bitterness to one who loved r. 983.24

reign endless, r., for fair you are 349.5
where dies r., buds the new, another year 81.7
who wants a r. must respect the thorn 749.25
**rosebuds**: gather ye r. while ye may 700.7
**roses**: heap not on mound r. she cannot smell 101.9
when r. are gone, nothing left but thorn 646.79
who plants thorns must not expect r. 809.4
**rostrum**: every r. has its passing pedant 842.28
**rot**: from hour to hour, we r. and r. 567.17
**rote**: wisdom cannot be learned by r. 1053.63
**rotten**: there's small choice in r. apples 305.36
**roughness**: r. may turn one's humour 346.10
**routine**: leisured rebel most at interruption of r. 822.2
men fall into r. when slack and tired 822.1
r. is god of every social system 822.5
r. of active lives precludes progress 10.7
**rove**: where'er we r. we find something dear 470.10
**row**: everyone must r. with the oars he has 1.5
**royalty**: r. does good and is badly spoken of 823.1
**rubber**: soon half iv us'll be rale, th' rest r. 572.2
**rude**: civil denial better than r. grant 784.4
except in streetcars, never be r. 824.3
no one as r. as the British 486.2
r. refusal is immediately believed 784.1
**rudeness**: r. is weak man's imitation of strength 824.4
**ruin**: a r.: Time easing itself of endurance 42.1
each life a r. containing what person ought to have been 752.13
if prosperous, beware of sudden r. 749.33
r. outruns all prayers, forces men astray 1035.48
there's a frantic fascination in a r. 42.5
**ruined**: men are r. on the side of their natural propensities 327.6
**ruining**: men prefer r. one another's fortunes 1035.101
**rule**: he who bears brand of Cain shall r. 516.16
he who would r. must hear and be deaf 825.9
how shall I r. others without command of myself 856.13
I am a king since I know how to r. myself 856.1
ill can he r. that can't reach the small 825.27
no r. so general which admits no exception 826.2
no useful r. without an exception 826.3
that r. is better which is exercised over better subjects 393.6
to r. is not so much a question of the heavy hand as the firm seat 825.17
we need supermen to r. us; job is so vast 393.7
when people r., they must be made happy 231.53
**ruler**: every r. harsh whose rule is new 825.1
great r. able to let others serve him 825.21
if you have a single r., you lie at his discretion 825.22
injustice feared less if r. is religious 825.2
only with new r. do you value the old 825.5
r. shouldn't have tendency for other affairs 825.11
**rulers**: government degenerates when trusted to r. of people alone 231.18
**rules**: cannot make r. till you can obey them 826.4
professor led astray by artificial r. 277.43
**rum**: nought calms the spirit as r. and religion 982.2
**rumor**: no speedier evil thing than r. 827.4
r. don't stay put as long as truth 827.1
r. doth double the numbers of the feared 827.3
r. is pipe blown by surmises, jealousies 827.2
**run**: many shall r. to and fro 985.5
nothing in own country, men r. to others 985.15
r. after two hares, you catch neither 495.3
**runaway**: r. monk nevers speaks well of monastery 298.8
**rungs**: do not despise the bottom r. in the ascent to greatness 399.53
**running**: best stimulus for r. ahead is to have something we must run from 735.9
men should learn what they are r. to, from 868.34
r. from ourselves we either fall on our neighbor's shoulder or fly at his throat 298.5
what is the use of r. on wrong road 10.9
**runs**: man does better who r. from disaster 298.6
**rural**: r. sights with r. sounds restore spirit 191.3
**Russia**: ideas in R. are machine-cut blocks 828.4
R.: riddle wrapped in mystery in enigma 828.1
**Russian**: divine in R. soul–resignation 828.2
R. Bolshevik concepts first realized by ant 149.2
**Russians**: R. train; they do not dare educate 828.3
**rust**: better to be eaten to death with r. 10.20
it is better to wear out than r. out 10.5
r. wastes more than use 444.6
**rustic**: when nature exceeds culture, we have the r. 842.8
**rut**: to stick in a r. is called consistency 176.6

# S

**sákí:** eternal s. has poured millions of bubbles like us, and will pour 707.6
**Sabbath:** good man's grave is his S. 218.38
remember the s. day, to keep it holy 829.2
S.: festival originating in fact that God made world in six days, was arrested on seventh 829.3
when at Rome I fast on the S. 985.4
**sacrament:** s.: an outward sign of an inward grace 830.1
**sacrifice:** as often as we do good we s. 430.13
nation must s. all for principles 728.18
s. is favorite self-indulgence of woman 1055.96
s. magnifies the one who sacrifices 831.5
s. may be flower virtue will pluck 831.6
too long a s. can make stone of heart 831.11
who gain by the offering demand spirit of s. 831.3
you cannot throw away a word like s. 489.18
**sacrificed:** for sake of one's self, world may be s. 831.7
**sacrificers:** s. are not the ones to pity 831.2
**sacrifices:** for extraordinary situation, s. 202.2
nothing so enhances a good as s. 831.9
**sacrificial:** love is essentially s. 548.197
**sad:** merry heart goes all day, s. tires in mile 407.101
none more s. than he who laughs too much 523.24
s. find sweetness in tears 1045.4
the flesh is s., and I've read all books 288.2
when people s., they don't do anything 39.23
**saddest:** s. words are these: it might have been 505.13
**sadness:** boys have no s. sadder than our hope 1064.48
by s. of countenance, heart made better 911.3
s. flies on wings of morning 911.17
s. is almost always a form of fatigue 1004.14
they serve gladness who meet calls of s. 911.60
**sadnesses:** s. are dangerous which one carries among people to drown them out 1004.28
**safe:** better one s. way than hundred unreckonable 579.2
easy to be brave from s. distance 192.1
he that is too secure is not s. 155.4
to keep self s. is not to bury self 850.16
**safety:** gift of s. is great gift among gifts 850.13
insignificance is often the cause of s. 1005.1
nothing's as good as holding on to s. 850.4
obscurity often brings s. 641.1
one s. vanquished have: hope for none 225.5
s. not in blindness but in facing danger 776.5
s. will be the sturdy child of terror 226.1
they that can give up liberty to obtain s. 850.5
your s. at stake if neighbor's wall burns 150.5
**sagacious:** knowing what is right doesn't make s. man 1053.4
**sagacity:** manhood and s. ripen of themselves 402.21
no more s. is needed for business, medicine, law, than for operating taxicab 102.27
**sage:** let fool hold tongue, he will pass for s. 891.25
one fool makes many, but one s. few sages 1053.44
s. has one advantage: he is immortal 1053.26
s. never seems to know his own merits 594.8
s. sees furthest, has love for mankind 1053.46
**said:** least s. is soonest disavowed 96.2
little s. is soon amended 916.12
nothing's s. now that's not been s. before 655.9
promise is most given when the least is s. 96.4
thing well s. walks in immortality 281.10
what is s. about men has as much influence on their lives as what they do 798.19
what's s. is s. and goes upon its way 505.2
when I think over what I have s., I envy dumb people 916.53
**sail:** who won't s. till danger over sails not 110.3
**sailor:** best s. steers closest to wind 1.16
happiest hour a s. sees is when his Nancy is on his knees 833.6
s. should know the length of his line 539.13
**sailors:** if s. too numerous, the ship sinks 56.1
**saint:** bad in best of us leaves s. like rest of us 834.13
can one be a s. without God 834.3
easier to make a s. out of a libertine 834.11
every s. has a past 834.14
grace needed to turn man into s. 834.9
many insights of the s. stem from his experience as a sinner 834.4
s. and poet seek privacy to public ends 730.1
s.: dead sinner revised and edited 834.2
to s. all things are friendly and sacred 920.3
who is not a s. cannot die a martyr 561.6
**sainthood:** s. a thing human beings must avoid 834.6
**saintliness:** humility is a dazzled awareness of s. 433.4
s. is also a temptation 834.1
**saints:** executive officers not made from s. 317.3
s. can do miracles, few can keep a hotel 427.2
s. cannot arise where are no warriors 388.21
s. guilty until proved innocent 834.8

s. indulge in subtleties 834.10
some s. never wanted be human 834.7
statue in bird bath: let s. go at that 834.5
they are not all s. who use holy water 45.5
**salad:** good s. may be prologue to bad supper 247.4
**salesman's:** try novelties for s. bait 103.10
**salesmanship:** advertising and s. create needs 103.23
**salvation:** courage is a kind of s. 192.30
s. lies in hands of creatively maladjusted 198.22
what is most contrary to s. is habit 835.3
**same:** if all saw fair as s., no debaters' strife 649.7
king, artisan, peasant—we are all s. 773.28
more things change, more they remain s. 115.25
when two do s. thing it is not the s. 467.18
when you've done a thing the s. way for ten years, throw it away, start over 822.4
**sample:** by small s. may judge of whole piece 304.1
**Sancho Panzas:** mankind either S.P. or Don Quixotes 558.46
**sanctity:** God attributes to place no s. 126.5
s., genius, are as rebellious as vice 834.12
**sand:** who can count the s. of the sea 300.1
**sane:** assent, and you are s. 256.3
harm in being s. all by oneself 555.7
if a s. dog fights a mad dog 555.5
it's fitter being s. than mad 388.2
no man is s. who cannot be insane at times 291.2
pray for a s. mind in a sound body 411.9
**sanity:** our madness less wonderful than our s. 555.20
s. is a madness put to good uses 836.3
s. is very rare 555.9
**sans:** s. teeth, s. eyes, s. taste, s. everything 646.93
**sarcasm:** s. the last refuge of modest people 837.1
**Satan:** God lost in S. one of best lieutenants 240.7
S. is political head of human race 240.12
solitude is the playfield of S. 908.36
we can respect talents of S. 240.11
**Satan's:** S. friendship reaches to the prison door 57.23
**satellite:** it's easy to become a s. unawares 456.3
**satiety:** there is s. in all things 940.4
wealth breeds s., s. outrage 1041.61
**satin:** where's man could ease heart like s. gown 265.17
**satire:** one's pointlessness is another's s. 838.1
praise to the undeserving is severe s. 716.8
s. a glass wherein everybody's face but beholder's is discovered 838.7
s. is lonely, introspective occupation 838.3
s., like a polished razor keen 838.5
**satire's:** s. my weapon 838.6
**satires:** s. not only wound, but make wound incurable 898.1
**satirist:** blessed is the s. 613.7
grave omission of usual s. is himself 838.2
**satirists:** s. gain applause through fear, not love 838.4
**satisfaction:** men all seek their s. 236.33
whole of s. not from single aspiration 55.8
**satisfied:** he is rich that is s. 839.1
he is well paid that is well s. 839.5
the s. do not love; fall asleep in habit 407.112
we cannot be s. with things as they are 155.7
we only feel satisfaction in man's society as he is s. in himself 862.5
**sauce:** no s. in world like hunger 435.2
**savage:** civilized man is a larger mind but more imperfect nature than the s. 131.12
is a man a s. at heart 558.6
man is still a s.: he has little respect for anything that cannot hurt him 802.6
music has charms to soothe a s. breast 607.18
s. doesn't wear oncomf'rtable clothes 69.1
s.: slave talking about what he must do 131.3
white man's notion is that he is less s. 1047.5
**savagery:** s. necessary to bring world back to life 69.3
**savages:** ants and s. put strangers to death 355.7
**save:** drown not self to s. a drowning man 831.4
s. men by the barrel-load 835.4
urge to s. humanity is almost always a false-face for urge to rule it 783.25
**saved:** if pain cured, we should have been s. 939.43
penny s. is a penny to squander 970.2
searching for another, you are s. 656.7
to be bewitched is not to be s. 276.2
**saves:** who s. a man against his will as good as murders him 941.7
**saving:** we deny it is fun to be s. 322.1
**say:** a people able to s. everything becomes able to do everything 362.9
better s. nothing than nothing apropos 891.7
nothing is always a clever thing to s. 891.6
one does s. the same things if he has anything to s. worth saying 794.2
right to s. anything is of less concern than need of people to hear everything 817.7
s. a bad thing, you may soon hear worse of yourself 392.7
sort of thing you s. will be said to you 781.2
we oftener s. things because we s. them well 916.36
what people s. behind your back 798.18
what you are drowns out what you s. 916.18
wise men s. nothing in dangerous times 213.18

you cannot s. anything but what you are 148.5
**saying:** between s., doing, many shoes worn out 228.8
man does not know what he is s. until he knows what he is not s. 132.2
s. is one thing and doing is another 224.22
short s. oft contains much wisdom 568.6
**says:** half a brain is enough if one s. little 96.8
he who s. what he likes shall hear what he does not like 824.2
'tis his at last who s. it best 767.4
what a man s. should be what he thinks 894.17
**scaffold:** s. is monster created by judge, workman 761.2
**scald:** don't s. your tongue in others' broth 571.3
**scalded:** s. cats fear even cold water 319.22
**scales:** clocks ar-re habichool liars, so ar-re s. 488.1
**scandal:** greatest s. waits on greatest state 840.3
impossible to conceive of world-wide s. 633.10
lie has no leg, but s. has wings 840.2
love and s. are best sweeteners of tea 840.1
**scandalous:** never a s. tale without some foundation 840.4
**scapegoat:** s. unleashes man's ferocious pleasure 841.1
**scarcities:** time, space, may be s. of tomorrow 994.18
**scare:** cannot s. me with their empty spaces 413.5
good s. is worth more than good advice 340.17
**scarecrow:** s. in a cucumber garden keepeth nothing 1017.1
we must not make a s. of the law 525.62
**scars:** God won't look you over for medals, but s. 939.19
wounds heal and become s.; but s. grow 474.12
**scenery:** fine s. appeases our irritations 602.1
s. is fine—but human nature is finer 431.13
we hear too much of s. in literature 542.14
**scenes:** I long for s. where man hath never trod 616.17
**scheme:** to grasp this sorry s. of things entire 1018.3
**schemes:** best-laid s. of mice and men 696.2
**scholar:** all that's prose isn't verse, all that isn't verse is prose: see what it is to be a s. 842.30
behind remarkable s. find mediocre man 956.13
duty of s.: show facts amidst appearances 842.10
painter is best s.—s. of nature 842.20
s. is early acquainted with impossible 842.35
s. is like book written in dead language 842.18
s. needs manuscripts to know his opinion 842.12
s. ruined by spirit lusting against flesh 842.26
s. seeks, artist finds 842.17
s. should come in contact with other minds 842.27
s. without diligence: lover without money 842.36
s. without good breeding is a pedant 389.4
specialized values of mere s 1019.21
test of s.: if lets intellectual fastidiousness stand between him and his times 842.32
**scholarly:** don't appear so s., pray 842.29
**scholars:** our great s. not commonly our great men 842.22
solid s. get degrees, jobs, dollars 277.73
vice of s. is to suppose there is no knowledge in world but that of books 842.21
**scholarship:** s. is polite argument 842.34
**school:** God first made idiots, then s. boards 277.77
s. days are the unhappiest in all existence 277.52
s. does not prepare you for life 277.13
segregated s. produces crippled minds 769.14
**schoolboys:** s. have no fear of facing life 95.8
s., not schoolmaster, educate my son 959.8
**schoolmaster:** grand s. is practice 277.10
s. is awkward in society of his equals 959.15
**schoolmasters:** s., parents, exist to be grown out of 663.53
**schools:** s. are factories for manufacture of robots 277.47
s. are the future in miniature 277.75
we leave s. full of words, not knowledge 277.22
**science:** accumulation of facts is not s. 843.28
aim of s.: to cover great number of facts by small number of hypotheses 326.4
applied s. is a conjuror 960.10
art is meant to disturb; s. reassures 53.13
art, s. create balance to material life 53.60
every s. has fixed system of principles 1029.9
happiness hates the timid; so does s. 973.9
in s. a moderate capacity can contribute to a supreme achievement 843.30
in s., all facts enjoy democratic equality 843.26
in war, s. linked with Stone Age cruelties 1042.1
let both sides invoke wonders of s. instead of its terrors 843.19
men of s. are Cyclopes, ardent but one-eyed 843.17
only s. can keep technology in moral order 960.4
physical s. will not console me for ignorance of morality 598.37

religion that fears s. dishonors God 844.5
s. and religion are two sides of the same glass, through which we see darkly 844.1
s.: antidote to poison of enthusiasm 843.35
s., art often a superior kind of dope 267.3
s., by itself, cannot supply an ethic 843.31
s. can destroy but not enrich illusions 447.11
s. cannot decide what it ought to do 843.24
s. consults her heart when she lays down supreme goods for man 843.16
s. gives means of unlimited disaster, good 843.4
s. has found no cure for apathy 216.6
s. has imposed necessity to wander 843.39
s. has not destroyed the world 239.9
s. increases powers more than happiness 843.23
s. investigates; religion interprets 844.7
s. is a humanist, but morally neutral 843.25
s. is a refinement of everyday thinking 843.6
s. is always simple and profound 843.34
s. is for those who learn 702.82
s. is furniture for man's upper chamber 843.12
s. is inherently neither good nor evil 843.32
s. is nothing but good sense and reason 843.37
s. is the attempt to make our sense-experience correspond to a uniform system 843.7
s. is the knowledge of consequences 843.11
s. is the record of dead religions 844.12
s. is trained and organized common sense 843.15
s. made man feel small 620.11
s. says we must live, seeks means of life 538.45
s. teaches us to bow before the most insignificant of facts 843.38
s. without religion is lame 844.4
s. without religion increases fear of death 844.10
shy fruit of pure s. is understanding 843.1
specialized meaninglessness a hallmark of s. 917.4
superstition about infallibility of s. 843.22
tragedy of s.: slaying hypothesis by fact 843.14
we have genuflected before the god of s. 633.9
when one belongs to narrow creed in s. 843.10
wonder is the seed of our s. 1056.2
**sciences:** arts and s. owe birth to our vices 1023.27
**scientific:** I know the s. names of beings animalculous 277.30
it's encouragin' that s. facts in pa-apers are not usually thrue 843.5
religious experience is force behind s. research 790.16
s. discovery is not unalloyed blessing 843.20
s. man is strictly a sentimentalist 843.3
s. power has outrun spiritual power 843.21
those who have never entered s. pursuits know not poetry surrounding them 843.36
**scientist:** s. alone is true poet, he gives us the moon 843.9
true s. never loses faculty of amazement 843.33
**scientists:** life extinct on other planets because their s. were more advanced than ours 843.18
s. unable to shake off piety 844.8
s. worthy of the name are about God's path 844.2
**scolding:** s. runs into custom and is despised 797.9
**scorn:** eyebrows darken life by s. they express 324.3
fate can be surmounted by s. 182.2
only a small mind traffics in s. 182.10
silence is best expression of s. 182.11
**scorned:** hell has no fury like a woman s. 786.1
**scorner:** reprove not a s., lest he hate thee 797.3
**scornful:** of all griefs most bitter is s. jest 434.16
**Scotch:** surgery required to get joke into S. mind 845.2
**Scotchman:** S. must be a very sturdy moralist who does not love Scotland better than truth 845.1
S. reasons before he fights 287.8
**Scotland:** I see Switzerland as inferior sort of S. 951.1
**scrapes:** only those who get into s. with their eyes open can find safe way out 356.12
**scratch:** Bible twice as accurate as s. sheet 78.8
**scratching:** after pleasant s. comes smarting 698.12
s.: one of nature's sweetest gratifications 846.2
**scream:** better to emit s. than be insensible 967.15
sometimes s. is better than a thesis 747.1
**scripture:** devil can cite s. for his purpose 137.12; 329.3
s. in time of disputes is like an open town in wartime, serving both parties 78.6
**scrupulous:** how can we be s. in a life determined to wring us of serenity 598.17
**sculpture:** picture and s. are festivities of form 53.43
**sea:** at s. you wish for wings of swallow 847.3
gale of wind makes the s. look old 847.6
life at s.: enticing, disenchanting 833.4
modern fleet of ships does not so much make use of s. as it exploits highway 888.1
s. has never been friendly to man 847.7
s. has no generosity 847.8
s. is threatened by activities of man 847.5

s. is woman, wonder, fate 847.9
s. most implacable when smiles serene 847.10
s. speaks colossal scavenger slang 847.12
upon the s. days fall away quicker 833.5
when at s., keep clear of the land 896.6
yet the s. is not full 847.2

**sea's:** consider the s. listless chime 847.11

**search:** nothing gives rest but s. for truth 805.4

**searcher's:** s. eye often finds more than he wished 676.7

**searching:** s. for another, you are saved 656.7
we spend our lives s. for lost kingdom 447.14

**seas:** freedom of s. *sine qua non* of peace 847.13
s. are quiet when winds give o'er 646.104
s. are the heart's blood of the earth 847.1

**seasick:** how holy people look when they are s. 833.3

**season:** each new s. grows from leftovers of past 115.4
how many things by s. seasoned are 972.10
in s., all is good 972.11
to every thing there is a s. 972.2
virtue in s. is madness out of s. 972.9

**seasons:** simple days which lead the s. by 600.6
sing a song of s. 848.37
we circle with the s. 971.62

**seclusion:** in a crowd thought itself can provide s. 730.4

**second:** s. thoughts are ever wiser 24.1

**secrecy:** no s. comparable to celerity 919.1
woman obliges man to s. to have pleasure of telling 849.3

**secret:** another's s. is like another's money 849.12
can another keep our s. when even we can't 849.16
do not speak of s. matters in a field that is full of little hills 849.10
each human is profound s. to every other 558.14
hard to keep s., employ leisure, bear injury 243.1
he that communicates s. to another makes himself that other's slave 849.7
in a man, s. is ugly thing, like hidden defect 849.4
love, pain, money cannot be s. 849.21
man who can keep a s. may be wise 849.13
man's most open actions have s. side 9.16
more fear than delight in s. pleasure 698.32
most difficult s. to keep: self-opinion 871.4
no one keeps a s. so well as a child 849.15
none can be so true to your s. as yourself 849.18
nothing is so burdensome as a s. 849.5
people most careful to put commonplace aspect on life when concealing s. 849.9
s. that cannot be pried out by curiosity 849.8
sober man's s. is drunken man's speech 266.53
to know one has s. is to know half the s. 849.1

**secretary:** press s. to keep man in public eye 754.1

**secrets:** dead keep their s. 849.20
little s. retold, great ones kept 849.2
look for s. in grief or pleasure 849.6
many want possession of s. for circulation 849.17
there are no s. except those that keep themselves 849.19
to whom you tell your s. you resign your liberty 166.8
we don't know each other's s. so well 849.11

**sect:** every s. of Christianity is perversion 123.13

**sectarian:** s. thinks he has the sea in his pond 667.9

**sects:** all s. differ, as they come from men 598.52

**secure:** God Himself is not s. 850.8
he that is too s. is not safe 155.4
nothing is s., nothing keeps 480.4

**security:** bourgeois: one who renounces love for s. 581.1
carelessness about our s. is dangerous 534.44
looking for s. like chopping off limbs 850.12
most people want s., not liberty 850.11
only in change is true s. to be found 850.10
s.: being in love, being loved back 850.17
s. cannot exist with danger of poverty 712.48
s. depends on how much you can do without 850.9
s. is an insipid thing 850.2
s. not a matter of weapons alone 226.16
there is s. on earth, only opportunity 650.6

**sedentary:** s. life is real sin against Holy Spirit 1034.3

**seduce:** not enough to conquer, know how to s. 851.15

**seduction:** verbal s. surest road to actual s. 851.8

**see:** he does not weep who does not s. 85.9
if a man s. himself as others s. him 868.14
just as much as we s. in others is in us 656.8
man must close his eyes to s. anything worth looking at 676.4
many look at meadow, few s. the flowers 605.3
more we s., more must be able to imagine 448.18
most s. no farther than their noses 1027.1
none so blind as they that won't s. 85.5
not all eyes need spectacles to s. 676.8
one may have good eyes and s. nothing 85.10
one must always tell, s. what one sees 676.12
people s. things in their own fashion 262.13
people s. what they are prepared to s. 676.6

s. the whole world with fresh eyes 58.8
to s. is poetry, prophecy, religion 1027.6
to s. things as better, open eyes full 676.9
we can s. through others only when we s. through ourselves 1001.13
what is out of sight more disturbing than what men s. 43.3
women s. better than men 676.5
**see:** O wad some Power the giftie gie us to s. oursels as ithers s. us 868.4
**seed:** destroy s. of evil lest it grow 305.1
s. of cedar becomes cedar; s. of bramble can only become bramble 415.5
ultimate wisdom remains locked in a s. 616.9
**seeds:** to plant s. is commonest delight 369.3
**seeing:** no way of s. without first taking leave 1000.12
s. is deceiving; eating is believing 272.31
there is only one way of s.: s. the whole 676.13
**seeing's:** s. believing, but feeling's truth 282.15
**seek:** let each man s. into himself 812.6
thou wouldst not s. Me, if hadst not found 328.33
what we s. we shall find 238.7
**seeking:** be at rest from s. after thy lot of life 238.1
would eternal s. go on if the found existed 1012.9
**seem:** be as you would s. to be 894.9
be content to s. what you really are 45.15
things are seldom what they s. 45.9
**seemed:** every object must cease to be what it s. 252.3
**seeming:** most lives spent in s. and following 168.4
**seen:** field not well s. from within 682.4
things s. are mightier than things heard 890.7
what is not s. is as if it was not 45.10
**sees:** who s. little s. less than there is 676.11
who s. only a week ahead is popular 1027.5
**segregated:** eleven a.m., Sunday, the most s. hour 126.6
s. school system produces crippled minds 769.14
**segregation:** s. is on its deathbed 769.12
s. is such an active word 769.15
**seizes:** difference between what one s., possesses 710.2
**self:** censure of s. is oblique praise 857.7
for sake of s., world is sacrificed 831.7
he that was all in all to s. carried all with him when he carried s. 873.9
nothing is greater to one than one's s. 584.16
only possible society is one's s. 656.15
s. is sole subject we study and learn 868.10
speaking of s. gives us pleasure 865.11
talking about s. is means to conceal s. 162.16
the s. more distant than any star 852.7
to know s. is wise 868.15
to thine own s. be true 489.23
we serve life-sentence in dungeon of s. 852.9
what is this s. inside us 857.2
what jailer so inexorable as one's s. 852.14
who doesn't see things in terms of s. is unhappy, disconsolate, and accursed 852.13
**self-abasement:** humility is the opposite of s. 433.7
**self-assertion:** rejection is a form of s. 253.1
**self-awareness:** test of a civilized person is s. 868.8
**self-confidence:** s. recovered by snubbing the dead 417.23
**self-control:** art of conversation is a certain s. 185.8
self-reverence, self-knowledge, s. 852.24
**self-controlled:** can aught stay out of reach of s. man 938.30
**self-criticism:** s. is the secret weapon of democracy 231.50
**self-denial:** s. is man's method to arrest progress 859.8
s.: the effect of prudence on rascality 859.7
**self-determination:** s. but slogan if future holds no hope 712.38
**self-discipline:** s. of the free must match iron discipline 534.21
**self-dispraise:** there is a luxury in s. 857.8
**self-esteem:** every new adjustment is a crisis in s. 12.4
few can retain s. in face of disesteem of fellows 862.13
oft times nothing profits more than s. 862.9
where s. is unobtainable, envy takes the place of greed 864.1
**self-fulfillment:** search for s. greatest force of modern age 813.31
**self-governing:** s. people need to hear everything 817.7
**self-government:** s. requires self-denial and restraint 231.22
**self-interest:** hatred will not strive against s. 493.1
human service is highest form of s. 880.5
**self-knowledge:** assurance contemptible unless it is s. 854.5
s. is a dangerous thing 868.32
self-reverence, s., self-control 852.24
**self-limitation:** it is in s. a master first shows himself 896.4
**self-love:** feel good and ill in proportion to our s. 869.8
friend often chosen to flatter our s. 363.60
pride doesn't wish to owe, s. to pay 639.5
s. is preservation; and we must conceal it 869.16
s. is the greatest of all flatterers 869.7
s. not so vile a sin as self-neglecting 869.14
s. should be painted as blind 869.17
s. veils our faults from us 869.2

**self-made:** in presence of s. men don't mention luck 358.49
**self-opinion:** most difficult secret to keep: s. 871.4
**self-pity:** God put s. by the side of despair 870.2
life insupportable but for s. 870.5
optimism and s. are poles of cowardice 196.4
s. comes so naturally to us all 870.6
**self-possession:** great man doesn't lose s. when afflicted 399.52
**self-praise:** good of s.: one can lay it on thick 716.3
**self-preservation:** s. is the first principle of our nature 949.2
**self-realization:** men can starve from lack of s. 442.25
**self-reflection:** s. is the school of wisdom 868.13
**self-respect:** property is basis of s. 740.22
reverence is nothing without s. 862.6
s. too great a price to pay for peace 674.40
s. will keep man from being abject when in the power of enemies 862.11
**self-restraint:** nation can afford to use s. 614.28
without s. humanity digs own grave 856.10
**self-reverence:** s., self-knowledge, self-control 852.24
**self-righteousness:** s. is a din raised to drown our guilt 872.3
**self-sacrifice:** s. enables us to sacrifice other people 831.10
s. is a survival of mutilation of savage 859.8
**self-satisfied:** form most contradictory to life: s. man 155.9
**self-sufficiency:** freedom is the greatest fruit of s. 361.15
**self-sufficient:** no man is s., something's always missing 539.17
**self-trust:** s. is the essence of heroism 854.1
**selfish:** no man is more cheated than the s. man 867.1
s. persons are incapable of loving others 867.3
**selfishness:** pity the s. of lovers: it is impossible 552.1
s. and complaint cloud the mind 548.102
s. is asking others to live as one wishes 867.6
**sell:** being creative is having something to s. 321.2
don't imagine man trying to s. something is always so polite 103.15
he would s. even his share of the sun 103.16
s. not bear's skin before he is caught 721.4
to s. product, work like hell to s. self 103.18
what pretenses men that s. goods make 103.2
**seller:** buyer needs hundred eyes, s. not one 103.13
**selling:** forgive us for frantic buying and s. 103.26
**sells:** he is a thief who charges too much for goods he s. 732.4
man s. himself, feels self to be commodity 103.7
when man s. eleven ounces for twelve, he s. himself for the value of an ounce 732.1
**senescence:** s.: when descendents outnumber friends 646.76
**senile:** young men regard elders as s. 1064.1
**sensation:** life a spasm, history a whiz: that's s. 311.2
thought, s., equally wonderful 875.11
**sense:** best prophet is common s., our native wit 147.6
common s. and good taste – without originality or moral courage 147.10
common s. conforms to world 1053.39
common s. is as rare as genius 147.5
common s. is most fairly distributed 147.2
common s. is right without rules 147.1
common s. is the wick of the candle 483.1
commonest s. is s. of men asleep 147.11
fairyland the sunny country of common s. 448.6
fine s. not so useful as common s. 147.9
frost, famine, rain hold us to common s. 147.3
good intentions useless without common s. 147.8
in deep distress native s. departs 911.53
logic is one thing, common s. another 147.7
loss of a s. adds as much beauty to world as acquisition of one 875.10
man talking s. to himself is no madder than man talking nonsense to others 874.5
most people die of creeping common s. 147.12
nonsense good because common s. limited 874.4
nothing astonishes men like common s. 147.4
power of sound greater than of s. 683.3
s., not stature, gives a man advantage 491.28
science is trained common s. 843.15
talk s. to fool, he calls you foolish 353.11
there are times when s. is unseasonable 972.4
things and men have always a certain s. 1000.3
we credit only those of our opinion with s. 649.15
where there is no love there is no s. 548.51
**senses:** at short distances s. are despotic 877.1
cannot gratify imagination, s. together 448.12
cause of error is war of s., reason 297.27
credibility comes only from the s. 875.9
nothing can cure the soul but the s. 584.17
s. not easy to trick – or trick often 875.2
we don't trust our s., we rely on critics 875.8
what gives us surer knowledge than our s. 875.6
**sensibility:** any s. crammed into a system is an idea 876.9
easy to overestimate man's s. 1004.31

nothing little to him with great s. 876.6
s. alters from generation to generation 374.12
s. claimed by neurotics matched by their egotism 620.12
s. of man to trifles 876.8
two forces of modern s.: Jewish moral seriousness and homosexual aestheticism 876.10
who has had greatest s. has lived longest 545.9
**sensitive:** easy to compel a s. being to feel guilty 403.17
we think ourselves more s. than others 876.1
**sensuality:** intemperance is the plague of s. 492.5
s. passes as a new type of asceticism 877.4
**sentence:** the maker of a s. launches out into the infinite 1062.33
when literary German dives into a s. 379.4
**sentences:** for a few golden s. we read whole books 91.32
**sentiment:** as healthy to enjoy s. as jam 282.11
foundation of free society: cohesive s. 534.11
in church false s. is frequent 124.5
reason may be lever, but s. is fulcrum 564.4
with public s. nothing can fail 756.14
**sentimental:** s. people fiddle harmonics 878.5
two sides to ivry man: commercyal an' s. 681.3
**sentimentalism:** let us replace s. by realism 776.3
**sentimentalist:** blessed is the s. 613.7
s. sees an absurd value in everything 878.8
**sentimentality:** if you want something done, s. is effective 1051.1
s. is a failure of feeling 878.7
s. is emotional promiscuity 878.3
s. is subtle dissolvent of morals 878.9
s., parading of emotion, mark of dishonesty 878.1
s.: sentiment that rubs you the wrong way 878.4
to modern spirit, evil to be avoided is s. 878.2
**sentiments:** all s. weigh less than a lovely action 224.16
character is tested by true s. 117.1
our s. build the necessary home 282.4
s. of an adult: instinct and education 649.29
**separation:** I can bear s. but not leave-taking 666.2
love knows not its own depth until s. 666.4
s. only solid peace between man and wife 260.3
**sepulchre:** whole earth is the s. of famous men 330.48
**serenity:** achieve s. when glare of passion fades 982.4
how can we be scrupulous in a life determined to wring us of s. 598.17
**serious:** everything s. is difficult, everything is s. 879.7
invited too freely to be amused, we are s. 684.9
play so that you may be s. 697.1
some think everything done with s. face is sensible 879.5
**seriousness:** dullness is the coming of age of s. 268.3
**sermon:** a mandatory s. is musty the next day 718.4
count superfluous words, whole s. goes 718.5
s. implies absence of the inviting 718.12
who has one word of God before him, and cannot make a s., cannot be a preacher 718.11
**sermons:** have wine, woman, then s. and soda-water 700.4
logic and s. never convince 685.5
s. remain one last form of discourse where it is forbidden to talk back 718.3
**serpent:** the s., subtlest beast of all the field 240.8
**serpents:** be ye therefore wise as s. 936.3
**servant:** best s. does his work unseen 880.4
if the s. grows rich, the master poor 1059.2
**servants:** few men have been admired by their s. 798.24
men in great places are thrice s. 399.1
use s., ornaments, only in proper places 942.2
**serve:** man wants to s. 882.2
no man can s. two masters 495.1
they also s. who only stand and wait 1033.5
to s. is beautiful if done with whole heart 880.2
**serves:** he too s. who only stands, cheers 291.1
he who s. two masters has to lie to one 495.4
**service:** all s. ranks the same with God 880.1
civil s. a fortress of papers, red tape 100.5
human s. is highest form of self-interest 880.5
if you want good s., serve yourself 873.25
noblest s. comes from nameless hands 880.4
pressed into s.: pressed out of shape 880.3
should render s. to friend to bind him closer and to enemy to make him friend 881.2
small demerit extinguishes long s. 1063.10
when public s. ceases to be chief business of citizens, state not far from fall 755.17
**services:** men are attached to us for s. they render 881.9
**servile:** force works on s. natures, not free 354.11
**servingmen:** I keep six honest s. 478.14
**servitude:** s. debases men to point where they like it 882.19
this is s., to serve the unwise 882.12
**setting:** men shut their doors against a s. sun 223.11
**settle:** never have I been able to s. in life 806.3
**settled:** people wish to be s. 480.3

**seventh:** God blessed the s. day 829.1
**seventy:** when s., most of you belongs to the past 646.5
**severe:** be not so s. as to cause shyness 883.5
**severity:** children should not be led by s. 981.10
excess of s. is not path to order 883.3
excessive s. misses its own aim 883.4
kindness effects more than s. 517.3
much may be done by s. 515.18
s. is more useful than indulgence 959.25
s. is useless to force change of heart 883.6
**sewer:** s. is a cynic; it tells all 884.1
who pry into s. cannot have nice noses 111.4
**sewing:** men contend s. on button is beyond them 575.5
**sex:** amount of undesired s. endured by women 560.100
being lovable is having s. appeal 706.5
good s. mitigates lust for other sports 922.5
in s.-war thoughtlessness is weapon of male, vindictiveness of the female 576.8
like hatred, s. must be articulated 885.23
money was exactly like s. 596.2
neither s., without complementary characters of other, is capable of great endeavor 562.4
only two topics of interest: s., the dead 520.75
s. instinct one prime mover of all we do 885.35
s. is the great amateur art 885.6
variety needed in s., but not in love 548.179
we face facts of s. but not of death 326.12
**sexes:** finest people marry two s. in own person 562.2
free commerce between the s. 576.21
three s.: men, women, and clergymen 136.17
**sexual:** cannot satisfy s. instinct without love 885.29
s. embrace can be compared with music 885.10
**sexuality:** degree of man's s. reaches into spirit 885.24
s. is lovely 885.14
s. is the lyricism of the masses 885.2
**shackles:** I wear s. more contentedly for having respired breath of an imaginary freedom 965.14
**shade:** to sit in the s. on a fine day 191.1
**shadow:** arguing of s., we forgo the substance 51.19
between idea and reality falls the s. 1012.3
even a single hair casts its s. 989.14
every hair makes its s. on ground 471.10
life is like s. of bird in flight 983.22
our days upon earth are a s. 983.3
'tis nothing but a s.-show 1060.25
we are afraid to let go of petty reality to grasp great s. 749.30
you may lose substance by grasping at s. 447.1
**shaft:** many a s. at random sent finds mark the archer little meant 1011.3
**shake:** if we s. hands with icy fingers 319.55
**shallow:** only the s. know themselves 944.7
**shame:** as soon as the people fix one s. of the world, another turns up 783.19
avoid s., but do not seek glory 384.19
having anything kind to say, we feel s. 886.1
if you have any s., forbear to pluck the beard of a dead lion 802.9
in getting rid of false s. we have killed off much real s. as well 886.4
only s. is to have none 886.6
**shameful:** s. things are hardest to confess 165.5
**shameless:** he that is s. is graceless 886.3
**share:** happiness forgiven if you s. it 407.23
he who divides gets the worst s. 887.4
not what we give, but what we s. 887.2
**shared:** mankind, why do ye set your hearts on things that, of necessity, may not be s. 236.7
**shark:** diver thinking of s. would not get pearl 340.29
**sharp:** s. men, like s. needles, break easy 137.3
s. temper easier to handle than silence 39.16
**sharper:** s. than serpent's tooth is thankless child 473.9
**shell:** if you don't crack s., can't eat nut 289.8
s. must break before the bird can fly 402.26
**shepherd:** good s. should not flay his flock 958.13
he who has daughters is always a s. 215.4
**shield:** for impenetrable s., stand inside self 31.10
**shine:** few s., but most can be agreeable 390.14
no soul wherein some faculty doesn't s. 956.11
**ship:** admire little s.; put cargo in big one 714.5
being in a s. is being in a jail 833.7
every s. is romantic object save our own 331.7
our s. is moving through troubled waters 34.28
pleasure in being in storm-beaten s. 311.3
s. in dock has appearance of prisoner 888.2
small leak will sink a great s. 398.7
thou, too, sail on, O S. of State 923.16
**ships:** modern fleet of s. does not so much make use of sea as it exploits highway 888.1
s. that pass in the night 908.29
**shipwreck:** society in s. is a comfort to all 151.22
**shipwrecked:** who is s. twice cannot blame Neptune 86.2
**shlemiehl:** s. lands on his back, bruises his nose 546.7
**shock:** to some, emotional s. arouses soul's activity 474.14
**shocked:** most have seen worse in private than they pretend to be s. at in public 438.14

**shocking:** s. event ceases to be s. if it occurs daily 331.4
**shoe:** only wearer knows where the s. pinches 319.19
you can't put same s. on every foot 826.5
**shoes:** I murmured because I had no s. 152.4
man without leg does not value s. 382.5
**shoot:** pity to s. pianist when piano out of tune 791.2
**shooting:** s. takes your mind off cost of living 1035.6
**shop:** keep thy s., and thy s. will keep thee 102.12
man without smile must not open s. 103.5
**shopping:** men go s. just as men go out fishing 103.1
**short:** good things when s. are twice as good 387.5
let thy speech be s. 96.1
pleasantry should be s.; the serious also 96.11
s. wise man preferable to tall blockhead 1053.58
**shortcomings:** men fall from same s. that led to rise 327.18
our s. are eyes with which we see ideal 339.28
**show:** outside s. poor substitute for inner worth 45.1
people who seem glorious are all s. 330.20
**shower:** it is the first s. that wets 17.32
**shrewd:** if men are s. enough they may serve kings 197.6
**shrewdness:** s. in public life is always honored 755.15
**shun:** always s. whatever may make you angry 39.29
**shyness:** be not so severe as to cause s. 883.5
s. has laws 166.3
**sick:** healthy ear can stand hearing s. words 166.7
if s., your own thoughts make you s. 620.9
ivry s. man is a hero at laste to himsilf 889.4
man becomes wicked as he becomes s. 1048.13
many s. do not make us deny health exists 620.7
none surpass s. woman in ruling 889.21
not perceiving ourselves to be s. makes us harder to cure 752.16
people no longer sinful, only s. 893.14
s. man must go searching for medicine 572.10
s. man talking about himself can't stop 865.9
sleep of s. man has keen eyes 889.27
sleep to the s. is half health 889.9
the rich, when s., feel impotence of wealth 1041.12
the s. are greatest danger for the healthy 1040.12
**sickness:** aren't sensible to health as to least s. 411.13
s. brings out essential characteristics 117.12
s. comes on horseback, departs on foot 889.5
s. enlarges dimensions of a man's self 889.16
s. is felt, but health not at all 411.6
s. sensitizes man for observation 889.12
study s. while you are well 572.5
temporary s. reminds us of our destinies 889.6
who recovers from s. forgets God 790.22
worst s. is to know we can never be well 889.3
**side:** who knows only his s. knows little of that 613.5
**sides:** God's meanest creature boasts two soul-s. 681.2
**sigh:** one s. may set whole world into a flame 517.19
when we s., nobody hears us 1004.30
**sight:** genius consists in trueness of s. 374.13
knowledge is true organ of s., not eyes 520.52
nothing sharpens s. like envy 293.12
s. is the most perfect of all our senses 890.1
we live by information, not by s. 520.24
**silence:** best sound a player can hear is deep s. 965.39
calumnies are answered best with s. 898.7
correction of s. is what kills 797.12
cruellest lies told in s. 329.44
elected s., sing to me 891.12
eternal s. of these infinite spaces 914.6
highest female grace is s. 891.14
I have often regretted speech, never s. 891.26
in s. alone man's truth strikes root 891.30
in s. great things fashion themselves together 891.18
liberty is the right to s. 817.4
man goes into a crowd to drown his own s. 205.10
nothing so good for ignorant man as s. 445.28
one is s. of life forlorn, one s. of death 538.31
s. is best expression of scorn 182.11
s. is full of potential wisdom and wit 891.13
s. is not tact and tact is golden, not s. 955.2
s. is sorrow's best food 891.16
s. is the perfectest herald of joy 407.99
s. is wisdom when speaking is folly 891.9
s. leads to sadness: is the image of death 891.28
s. of a shut park tense, confined 129.6
s. of age is full of wisdom 891.20
s. often is wisest 360.12
s. saves me from being wrong or right 891.33
sorrow and s. are strong 285.6
speech is of time, s. of eternity 891.3
there's ransom in a voice but s. is infinity 891.5
timely s. is sage, and better than speech 891.24
tragedy begins when s. is not understood 891.34
try as we may to make a s., we cannot 891.2

word preserves contact, s. isolates 916.41
words can sting, but s. breaks the heart 891.17
**silences:** s. have climax, when you must speak 891.1
three s.: of speech, desire, thought 891.15
**silent:** cleverest among the s. are the transparent 162.15
easy to utter what's been kept s. 916.48
human affairs far happier if power to be s. were the same as that to speak 916.57
misfortune to lack judgment to keep s. 370.2
s. dog is the first to bite 891.11
thing left s. often makes for happiness 891.23
'tis easier to speak than to be s. 891.10
we need reason to speak, none to keep s. 891.21
women like s. men; think they listen 576.1
words the s. feel are beautiful 891.4
**silently:** a hundred acorns are planted s. 641.2
**silver:** should be s. in purse or on tongue 281.3
**simple:** it is hard to be s. enough to be good 391.14
man is a s. being 558.24
s. folk prize deed, overlook motive 601.2
teach us delight in s. things 892.9
the people do not like the s. 675.6
to be s. is best thing in the world 892.3
**simple-minded:** people on the whole are very s. 675.2
**simplest:** greatest truths are the s. 892.5
**simplicity:** affected s. is an elegant imposture 892.11
art of art is s. 892.18
beauty of style and grace depend on s. 892.15
give me a face that makes s. a grace 892.8
perfect s. is unconsciously audacious 892.12
s. is man's most deceitful mistress 892.1
s.: mean between ostentation and rusticity 892.16
s. of character is no hindrance to subtlety of intellect 892.14
s., s., s. 892.17
thou canst not adorn s. 892.10
who understands much displays greater s. 1000.2
**simplification:** power is partial to s. 713.25
**simplify:** to s.: eliminate unnecessary for necessary 892.7
**simply:** loveliest things come s. 892.13
**sin:** as much s. in smiling countryside as in vile London alleys 191.5
be sure your s. will find you out 893.1
Christians lose faith, keep sense of s. 123.4
harder to confess s. no one believes in 893.8
in best understandings, s. began 893.7
lie is handle that fits all s.'s tools 329.25
many do not s. for lack of desire, occasion 893.19
men s. by omission as well as commission 893.15
nonconformism is major s. of our time 466.4
nothing emboldens s. so much as mercy 577.8
only those who can s. with grin should s. 893.18
plate s. with gold, the lance of justice breaks 1023.29
pleasure's s. and sometimes s.'s a pleasure 893.3
private s. not so prejudicial as public indecency 750.1
really to s. you must be serious about it 893.12
s. basic concept in religion and politics 893.20
s. in America is said to be calculating 893.5
s. is dangerous in hands of the virtuous 893.16
s. is the writer's element 1062.75
s. recognised keeps us humble but nasty 893.21
s. travels faster than those in chariots 893.25
some rise by s., some by virtue fall 1026.23
the absurd is s. without God 3.3
want gave tongue and s. awakened 618.3
who forbids not s., commands it 531.4
without guilt's spice, s. can't be savored 893.4
worst s. to be indifferent to others 464.8
**sincere:** being s. is having something to say 894.15
child is s., and man alone if not writer 438.7
condition for being s.: not to boast of it 894.19
friend is person with whom I may be s. 894.7
I desire s. relations with worthiest acquaintances to speak the truth once a year 894.22
it doesn't matter what you believe, just so you're s. 894.20
it's never what you say, but how you make it sound s. 894.14
men are always s., but change sincerities 894.2
no man can produce great things who is not s. with himself 868.17
one's belief that one is s. not so dangerous as conviction that one is right 816.22
**sincerity:** a little s. is a dangerous thing 894.23
can s. be condition of friendship 991.15
many mistake impertinence for s. 824.8
merit of originality is s. 655.1
one of complete s. always moves others 894.16
s. always subject to proof 894.11
s.: first characteristic of heroic men 894.4
s. is an opening of heart we find in few 894.12
s. is glass, discretion is diamond 749.21
s. is highest compliment you can pay 894.6
s. is not a spontaneous flower 894.5

taking sides is the beginning of s. 879.9
**sinful**: people no longer s., only sick 893.14
**sing**: I do but s. because I must 702.99
if a thing isn't worth saying, you s. it 895.1
it is folly to s. twice to a deaf man 48.3
people don't s. when feeling sensible 648.2
when we s., everybody hears us 1004.30
**singers**: s. asked won't sing, unasked never stop 895.3
**singing**: delight in s., tho' only singer hear 895.4
in congregational s. you can join in 126.9
with s. I can make a refuge 702.96
**single**: I would be married to a s. life 65.2
nature seems so careless of the s. life 306.8
not the hurrah of masses, but the considerate vote of s. men 205.5
poetry of art: beholding s. tower 1007.2
s. arrow is easily broken 1009.7
s. man with fortune must need a wife 65.1
**singularity**: s. is dangerous in everything 467.7
to affect s., be very virtuous 466.1
**sinner**: every s. has a future 834.14
more joy over wan s. rayturned to station thin f'r ninety an' nine rayformed 703.4
s. sins against himself 1063.18
**sinneth**: he that sleepeth well s. not 272.22
**sinning**: s. is the best part of repentance 793.1
**sins**: between denying s. done and bragging of s. not done is space for millions of s. 893.6
comes a day when a man's s. forsake him 646.46
gods visit s. of fathers on the children 809.9
I regret s. I'd no opportunity to commit 893.9
s. are the highway of our virtue 893.23
s. cannot be undone, only forgiven 893.22
s. have origin in sense of inferiority 33.27
s. sinned in secret are no s. at all 893.17
sense of humor keeps man from most s. 434.5
we are punished by s., not for them 893.11
**sire**: with him as s., her as dam, what should I be but just what I am 415.3
**sister**: never praise a s. to a s. 1055.83
**sisterly**: s. love is most abstract of sentiments 332.6
**sisters**: big s. are crab grass in lawn of life 332.25
**sitting**: too much s., body becomes unhealthy 444.12
**situation**: every s., moment, is of infinite worth 723.14
**sixpence**: nimble s. better than slow shilling 501.3
**size**: s. is not grandeur 614.10
**skating**: in s. over thin ice safety is in speed 919.2
**skeptic**: authority has every reason to fear s. 61.5
intellectualism is sole piety of s. 490.7
s. means him who investigates 897.12
**skepticism**: good critic's first attribute is wise s. 897.8
idea of truth invincible of s. 991.96
s. is the first step toward truth 897.4
s. makes a man mad 897.7
to believe in luck is s. 358.7
**skill**: s., confidence, are unconquered army 1.11
s., not strength, governs a ship 1.8
we work for a s. not worth the effort 520.20
**skilled**: one man cannot be s. in everything 1.6
**skillful**: smooth sea never made a s. mariner 243.2
**skills**: s. vary with the man 1.15
**skin**: can the Ethiopian change his s. 442.7
it's only the s. we ever know 908.32
s.: wax paper to hold all in with no drip 88.3
**skins**: shame on those who preach, pray for those only with s. colored like their own 769.16
**sky**: flat country gives the s. a chance 191.15
for the rich, s. is just an extra 413.2
if the s. fall, hold up your hands 226.18
lift not your hands to s. for help 412.10
s. is all men's together 98.3
soil keeps tree tied, s. leaves it free 639.10
**sky's**: power that holds s. majesty wins worship 385.1
unloose thy heart, consider not s. secret 966.5
**slander**: generous confession disarms s. 165.1
he who can flatter can also s. 346.18
hearts of men are undermined by s. 898.12
no recompense for an unjust s. 898.3
s. is a verdict of guilty in the absence of the accused 898.13
s., like coal, will dirty hand or burn it 898.14
s. lives upon succession 898.15
s. may stain even clearest reputation 798.16
s., whose edge is sharper than the sword 898.17
**slandering**: ridiculous folk to the fore in s. others 898.9
**slanders**: s. of the pen pierce to the heart 204.29
**slang**: dialect with s. admirable medium for those with nothing to say 521.1
s. is poor man's poetry 521.16
s. spits on hands, goes to work 521.22
strongest s. of all is s. of poets 521.5
**slaps**: spontaneity of s. is sincerity 894.3
**slave**: art thou less a s., loved by master 882.13
better starve free than be a fat s. 361.1
day making man s. takes worth away 882.8
he is s. of many masters who is his body's s. 88.8
he who is not his own man is a s. 882.1

I didn't know I was a s. until I found out I couldn't do the things I wanted 882.6
loving woman is a s.; none so much as mother 663.5
s. first wants justice, then crown 995.5
to be s. means to be abused, bear it 882.7
who can't live his own life lives a s. 873.14
who would be no s. must have none 882.10
**slavery:** cowardice of slaves perpetuated s. 882.14
freedom and s. are mental states 361.18
great fortune is a great s. 1041.55
greatest difference between peace, s. 674.4
lean liberty is better than fat s. 534.12
neither mastery nor s. except in attitude 882.11
s. holds few fast; many hold their s. 882.16
s. is a weed that grows in every soil 882.5
serving one's own passions is greatest s. 668.12
so efficient are the instruments of s.: fingerprints, lie detectors 978.1
where annual elections end, s. begins 1030.2
worst s. is when herd crushes man 995.31
**slaves:** all are s. of money or necessity 168.5
ambition makes more trusty s. than need 33.15
freedom has thousand charms s. never know 361.6
necessity is the creed of s. 617.12
s. lose everything in their chains 882.15
virtue cannot dwell with s. 882.3
we are the s. of objects around us 638.5
who dare not be in right with few are s. 816.15
**sleep:** a third of life is spent in s. 218.28
better s. on things than lie awake after 899.8
care-charming s., thou brother to death 899.1
even where s. concerned, too much is bad 899.10
for s., one needs depths of blackness 899.13
in bed my real love has always been s. 264.11
in s. we lie all naked and alone 899.21
liberty is bestowed by s. 295.17
men s. and death's veil is lifted 452.16
most blessed of all natural graces, s. 899.11
our little life is rounded with a s. 600.17
s. and confidence almost the same thing 899.2
s. covers man, thoughts and all 899.5
s. cuts each day to half its length 899.14
s. hath its own world of wild reality 899.4
s. is pain's easiest salve 899.7
s., it is a gentle thing 899.6
s. makes us all equal – like death 899.17
s. of a labouring man is sweet 899.3
s. of a sick man has keen eyes 889.27
s. that knits up ravelled sleave of care 899.18
s., to be enjoyed, must be interrupted 184.4
s. to the sick is half health 889.9
there is much good s. in an old story 931.3
to be in bed and s. not 364.2
to s. until noon you need legitimate reason to stay up until three 899.12
we are not hypocrites in our s. 264.6
who is known as early riser may s. late 798.33
**sleeper:** net of the s. catches fish 264.5
**sleepers:** even s. are collaborators in what goes on in the universe 899.9
great s. are incapable of all else great 877.2
s. have each a private world of his own 264.8
**sleepeth:** he that s. well sinneth not 272.22
**sleepiness:** feeling of s. when not in bed is the meanest feeling in the world 338.4
**sleeping:** for sake of s. one stays awake all day 899.15
**sleeps:** arch never s. 50.8
he s. well who knows not that he s. ill 899.16
**slight:** we s. man whose good will cannot help us 493.9
**slip:** many a s. 'twixt the cup and the lip 114.14
**slippery:** who stands on s. place makes nice of no hold 213.19
**sloth:** s. finds the down pillow hard 899.19
**slow:** nimble sixpence better than s. shilling 501.3
wisely, and s.; they stumble that run fast 409.13
**slowly:** go s., time will walk behind you like ox 900.2
**slowness:** s. in affairs ripens them or rots them 900.3
s. of movement in quick-thinking person 900.1
**sluggard:** go to the ant, thou s. 527.2
**slumber:** all that tread globe are but a handful to the tribes that s. in its bosom 707.1
**small:** don't make self big, you're not so s. 87.4
great engines turn on s. pivots 398.6
I will be s. in s. things, great in great 398.16
if we play great man too much, we seem s. 686.5
in life's s. things be resolute and great 989.7
looking at s. advantages prevents great affairs from being accomplished 686.4
many a s. maketh a great 901.1
no man is so s. that he need never stoop 398.4
s. causes sufficient to make a man uneasy 989.16
s. man stands on a great man 398.5
s. men reduce great enterprises to level of their mediocrity 573.7
s. rooms discipline the mind 428.4
**smart:** no man is s. except by comparison 491.15
**smell:** to s., though well, is to stink 678.1
**smells:** woman s. well when she s. of nothing 678.2

**smile:** minute to s., hour to weep in 536.27
one may s., and s., and be a villain 221.21
**smiles:** by chivalries the seeds of s. are planted 517.8
**smiling:** man without s. face must not open shop 103.5
teeth are s., but is the heart 390.3
**smite:** whoever shall s. thee, turn other cheek 658.1
**smoke:** good cigar is a s. 975.7
man of no conversation should s. 975.5
who doth not s. hath known no griefs 975.1
**smoker:** to average s. the world is his ashtray 975.2
**smokers:** s. inject idleness with every cigarette 975.3
**smoking:** s.: a custom loathsome to the eye 975.6
s. is one of leading causes of statistics 975.8
**snake:** bitten by s., fears piece of string 319.47
when s. is old, frog will tease him 223.9
who will pity s. charmer bitten by a s. 213.1
**snare:** he avoids a s. who knows how to set one 197.8
**sneer:** who can refute a s. 182.9
**sneezes:** speak roughly to your little boy, and beat him when he s. 760.4
**sniffles:** life is sobs, s., smiles—s. predominate 536.48
**snob:** true s. never rests 903.5
**snobbery:** s. is sometimes prophecy of better things 903.8
**snorer:** there ain't no way to find out why a s. can't hear himself snore 899.20
**snores:** husband: man who s. like overloaded bus 560.87
**snow:** neither s. nor rain stays these couriers 556.1
s. is lonely, self-sufficient 904.2
s. is what you are up to your neck in 904.4
s. pleasant when coming, unpleasant going 904.3
**snowdrift:** s. beautiful if doesn't block your road 904.1
**snub:** s. is sufficient to rebuff advances 786.4
**soap:** man does not live by s. alone 135.2
s., education, are deadly in the long run 131.30
**soar:** s. not too high to fall; stoop to rise 33.24
**sob:** are you unable to recognize a s. unless it has the same sound as yours 141.2
**sober:** be s., be vigilant 240.1
he that will to bed go s. falls with leaf 266.16
man must stay s. 777.7
wild colt may become a s. horse 1064.23
**sobriety:** most men are disguised by s., not by liquor 162.4
s. is the inability to eat much 963.2
**sociable:** society is no comfort to one not s. 151.24
**social:** American does not admit he has no s. inferiors 295.22
American s. life: evasion of talking 151.13
by s. contract man gains civil liberty 906.17
cursed be the s. lies 906.21
economic growth without s. progress lets majority of people remain in poverty 275.3
every s. system is against nature 906.22
path of s. advancement strewn with broken friendships 907.11
s. evil sanctified by religious sentiment 475.11
s., friendly man fulfills nature's plan 151.4
s. moulds unrelated to actual shapes 131.13
s. movements are symptoms of progress 564.5
s. process requires standardization 295.6
s. progress strengthens freedom 735.14
s. remedies will fail 616.35
s. war always between the very few 813.29
s. work is a band-aid on society's wounds 430.6
society without s. ritual needs specifications 907.7
there is a toad in every s. dish 907.10
to be s. is to be forgiving 151.10
**socialism:** s. must come down from brain to heart 905.5
s. without liberty is the barracks 905.1
**socialist:** if being a s. is a crime 275.5
**society:** all progress means war with s. 735.25
chaos of s. due to dishevelment of ideas 906.25
decrepit s. shuns humor 906.14
each lie is a stab at health of human s. 329.16
each s. reduces opponents to caricatures 928.3
every s. gets the criminal it deserves 703.8
first to fence in land: founder of s. 740.19
fools to depend on s. of fellow-men 908.38
good for us is that which is good for s. 906.23
great s. concerned with goals not goods 906.9
great s. is one in which men of business think greatly of their functions 906.24
hating the crowd, I love s. 151.17
human s. founded on mutual deceit 907.8
ideal s. is drama enacted in imagination 1018.4
in civilized s. we depend on each other 906.10
in class s., thinking branded by class 133.2
isolation must precede true s. 908.16
lives arranged by what s. rules right 168.18
man entered s. to secure his rights 906.15
men would not live in s. long if they were not each other's dupes 907.6
mouth of s. has many diseased teeth 906.6
national genius characterizes a s. 614.3
no change of s. palatable until s. so desperate it will accept any change 906.2
one cannot have s. on one's own terms 151.9

only possible s. is one's self 656.15
prime cause of present confusion of s. 698.41
principles of the good s. call for concern with an order of being 906.11
raising bottom of s. benefits all above 906.7
s. acquires new arts, loses old instincts 906.3
s. corrupt if end justifies means 570.2
s. forgives the criminal, never dreamer 448.32
s. in every state is a blessing 393.47
s. is a more level surface than we imagine 907.4
s. is always trying to grind us down to a single flat surface 906.8
s. is an accident to the spirit 906.18
s. is commonly too cheap 151.27
s. is immoral and immortal 906.1
s. is no comfort to one not sociable 151.24
s. is now formed of the Bores and Bored 92.2
s. is produced by our wants 393.48
s.: masked ball where all hide character 907.2
s. page they never die 623.15
s. robs you of part of your essence 906.16
secret of success in s. is certain heartiness and sympathy 907.1
soul selects her own s. 719.1
terror of s. is the basis of morals 340.35
to be in s. is merely a bore 907.13
to get into the best s. one has to feed, amuse, or shock people 907.12
value of a dollar is created by s. 596.16
values of s. must be clear and acceptable 906.19
who lives out of s. must be either beast or god 908.2

**sociology**: if far, it's news; if close, it's s. 622.8

**sodawater**: let us have wine, woman, then sermons, s. 700.4

**softly**: fair and s. goes far 377.3
speak s. and carry a big stick 713.42

**soil**: nation that destroys s. destroys self 174.6
s. keeps tree tied, sky leaves it free 639.10

**solace**: s. from company in misery is spiteful 177.2

**sold**: pleasing ware is half s. 103.14

**soldier**: blood of the s. makes the general great 582.11
captain's choleric word is blasphemy in s. 773.22
essential to persuade s. that those he is to massacre don't deserve to live 582.8
first who was king was a fortunate s. 518.15
good s. has his heart and soul in it 582.2
s., above all others, prays for peace 582.13
s. is grievous vestige of barbarism 69.7

**soldier's**: s. body is no longer his property 582.18
s. life is on'y gloryous in times iv peace 582.4
s. pack not so heavy as prisoner's chains 1035.32
s. strength broken or exalted by a cause 582.15

**soldiers**: lucky are s. who strive in a just war 582.1
s. are policemen who act in unison 703.9

**solemnity**: s. is the shield of idiots 879.6

**solitary**: I love all waste and s. places 191.14
if you are idle, be not s. 444.11
life is a s. cell 908.37
s. trees, if grow at all, grow strong 908.11
some s. wretches seem to have left mankind to meet the devil in private 908.41
we are s. 908.45
we're all sentenced to s. confinement 908.55

**solitude**: find inner peace in s., not speed 982.11
God gave man companion to make him feel s. 576.52
great city—great s. 129.16
he who lives in s. may make own laws 908.43
if you would live innocently, seek s. 476.10
in s. it is possible to love mankind 26.8
in the crowd, great man keeps independence of s. 873.6
individuality must be affirmed in s. 908.28
little do men perceive what s. is 908.4
New Year reviving desires, soul retires to s. 624.4
nurse of full-grown souls is s. 908.30
one can acquire all in s. but character 908.49
only in s. do we find ourselves 908.52
s. gives birth to the original in us 908.33
s. is audience-chamber of God 908.26
s. is bearable only with God 908.19
s. is needful to the imagination 908.31
s. is the mother of anxieties 908.42
s. is the playfield of Satan 908.36
s. sometimes is best society 908.34
s. vivifies; isolation kills 908.46
some days s. a wine; other days, a poison 908.13
'tis s. should teach us how to die 908.10
who hears music, feels his s. peopled 607.7
you find in s. only what you take to it 908.24

**Solomon**: book of proverbs never made a S. 568.2

**solvency**: s. a matter of temperament, not income 1041.60

**somebody**: how dreary to be s. 330.17
when everyone is s., no one's anybody 773.8

**somewhere**: it is irritating to think about being s. else 249.3

**son**: always struggle between father and s. 909.8
every man is the s. of his own works 860.2
everyone calls his s. his s., whether he has talents or not 909.4
extravagant s. succeeds hoarding father 909.15
greatness in father often overwhelms s. 909.9

he that spareth his rod hateth his s. 760.2
motherless s. is a fish in low water 909.3
s. can bear death of his father 1051.8
ungrateful s. is a wart on father's face 909.1
wise s. maketh a glad father 909.2
**son's:** s. offenses vanish at word of repentance 909.11
**song:** grandeur of man lies in s., not thought 53.84
leave out my name, but keep my s. 382.37
must one swear to the truth of a s. 53.99
s. is the primal thing in poetry 702.4
s. is the rose upon truth's lips 702.109
s. that nerves a nation's heart 671.22
that s. is most esteemed with which our ears are most acquainted 331.3
what is s., when world lacks taste 48.4
**songs:** it is my heart that makes my s., not I 702.97
it is the best of all trades to make s. 895.2
some resemble s. which are sung for a while 335.19
**sonnet:** true s. goes eight lines; takes turn for better or worse 702.37
**sons:** s. are generally worse than fathers 909.6
s. do not need you 909.10
s. have rebellious wish to be disillusioned by what charmed their fathers 909.7
'tis happy thing to be father to many s. 909.14
you don't raise heroes, you raise s. 909.13
**soothing:** love's best habit is a s. tongue 548.207
**sore:** one knocks oneself on the s. place 1032.1
**sorrow:** belief in God ends burden of s. 328.15
crown of s.: remembering happier things 911.56
drink today, and drown all s. 266.15
excess of s. laughs, excess of joy weeps 524.1
first pressure of s. crushes out best wine from hearts 911.28
give s. words 911.51
glut thy s. on a morning rose 1004.19
heart forgets its s. and ache 1043.6
heaven wills that s. follow joy 911.36
illusory joy worth more than real s. 407.30
joy and s. equally pass away 983.18
knowing s. I learn to help distressed 56.14
life of man is to shift from s. to s. 536.120
loss of native land is greatest s. 421.2
man's s. runs uphill 911.2
men must know s. to be in right senses 911.55
nature refuses to sympathize with s. 616.69
patience lightens what s. can't heal 670.12
rapture's self is three parts s. 911.29
real s. is incompatible with hope 911.25
s. and silence are strong 285.6
s. before joy better than s. after joy 911.42
s. brings one down in the world 911.5
s. falls readily into dislike 911.45
s. for dead is only s. from which we refuse to be divorced 603.10
s. hath less power to bite man that mocks it 911.47
s. is better than laughter 911.3
s. is knowledge 911.7
s. is only thing people really possess 911.34
s. makes night morning, noontide night 911.46
s. makes us all children again 911.14
s. one broods over is no longer a pain 911.22
s. proves the fact of living 911.43
s. shall nourish thee till strong 911.27
s. touches us through our thoughts 911.32
s. without labour is base 1058.61
seldom felicity is not tempered by s. 407.24
something pleasurable in memory of past s. 911.9
to show unfelt s. false man does easy 438.25
we are not sure of s., joy never sure 983.21
what man does not fashion the s. that is to be the pivot of his life 911.31
when wine is plentiful, s. takes wing 266.47
where there is s. there is holy ground 911.58
who increaseth knowledge increaseth s. 520.5
who is master of himself can end s. 856.16
your joy is your s. unmasked 407.47
**sorrow's:** genius is s. child 374.1
silence is s. best food 891.16
**sorrowful:** even in laughter the heart is s. 523.1
**sorrows:** great joys weep, great s. laugh 911.41
he truly s. who s. unseen 911.33
heart has secret s. world knows not 141.4
joys are often tender shadows of s. 407.8
joys impregnate; s. bring forth 911.4
our cruelty to each other adds to our s. 206.1
s. are our winter foliage 911.40
s. come, not singly, but in battalions 911.50
s. remembered sweeten present joy 911.37
tell thy s. to him in whose countenance thou mayst be assured of consolation 166.6
**soul:** a man should have fine point of his s. taken off to become fit for this world 319.31
always three A.M. in dark night of s. 237.7
art is for fertilisation of the s. 53.134
deep distress hath humanised my s. 911.59
every subject's s. is his own 130.9
eyes indicate antiquity of the s. 323.1
God's meanest creature boasts two s.-sides 681.2
human body is best picture of human s. 584.18
knowledge of s. would make us melancholy 868.20
lusts and greeds of body scandalize s. 584.14
man's s. longs for beauty 920.7
nature the body, God the s. 1010.10
no retreat as quiet as one's own s. 180.2

nothing can cure the s. but the senses 584.17
nothing so pierces s. as body's sigh 584.12
O Lord, save my s., if I have a s. 263.6
s. beauty seen when man bears mischances 17.4
s. buried under furrow or pile of money 191.7
s. cast into body; it reasons 584.10
s. is not more than the body 584.16
s. is only a word for body 88.4
s. is restless and furious 806.2
s. is that which denies the body 584.1
s. is the voice of the body's interests 584.13
s. is unwillingly deprived of truth 991.39
s. must be let alone by government 583.20
s. selects her own society 719.1
s. with no established aim loses itself 765.11
shame on s. to falter when body perseveres 216.7
spectacle grander than sky is interior of the s. 920.4
teach me to cast out my self, become s. 920.8
typical American believes no necessity of s. is free and few cannot be bought 34.33
virtue of s. consists in walking orderly 654.11
what profit to gain world and lose s. 33.2

**soul's:** all music jars when s. out of tune 961.1
life is a stuff to try s. strength 536.12
s. power lies in the heart, not in the mind 668.28

**souls:** all human beings have gray little s. 726.5
nurse of full-grown s. is solitude 908.30
s. are not saved in bundles 835.2
these are the times that try men's s. 296.20

**sound:** power of s. greater than of sense 683.3

**sounds:** elemental s.: rain, wind in woods, ocean 616.5
few s. exceed interest of knock at door 426.18
s. are things blind see 84.2
time that's just time will let s. be s. 912.1

**soup:** worries go down better with s. 43.15

**sour:** s. grapes cannot make sweet wine 913.3

**south:** bright, fierce and fickle is the s. 138.4

**sovereign:** to appear at church is the best means of becoming popular for a young s. 825.10

**sovereignty:** to bear naked truths with calm is s. 159.2
when I refuse to obey unjust law I appeal from s. of people to s. of mankind 779.6
whom hatred frights, let him not dream on s. 825.13

**sow:** he that observeth the wind shall not s. 110.1
they that s. in tears shall reap in joy 279.1

**sower:** s. sows crooked; peas show crooked line 173.5

**soweth:** whatsoever a man s., that shall he reap 809.3

**sowing:** must be s. even after bad harvest 679.10

**space:** by s. the universe encompasses me 968.41
don't say man doesn't belong out in s. 914.7
nothing puzzles more, troubles less, than s. 1010.7
peace in s. no help without peace on earth 914.4
s. flights are an escape from oneself 914.3
s.. fragment of the infinite for finite use 971.4
s. is the stature of God 914.2
time, s.: scarcities of tomorrow 994.18
walking in s., man has never looked more puny or more significant 914.1

**spaces:** cannot scare me with their empty s. 413.5
if you take big paces, you leave big s. 33.4

**spacious:** be s. and wise 522.1

**spaciousness:** all s. is a question of proportion 522.2

**Spain:** in S. dead more alive than dead elsewhere 915.1

**Spaniards:** three S., four opinions 915.2

**spanks:** many a man s. children for things his father should have spanked out of him 760.9

**spark:** if fuel prepared, hard to tell whence s. shall come 813.3

**sparrow:** s. sorry for peacock's burden of tail 773.25

**sparrows:** s. who emulate peacocks may break a thigh 449.1

**speak:** be swift to hear, slow to s. 164.3
be yourself and s. your mind 360.9
difficult to s. when ashamed to be silent 916.39
don't s., people will believe good of you 891.22
every man may s. truly, but few s. fully 916.42
humanize your talk, s. to be understood 842.29
learn meaning of what you say, then s. 916.20
less dishonor to hear than s. imperfectly 1000.10
misfortune to lack wit to s. well 370.2
never s. of yourself to others 185.12
s. softly and carry a big stick 713.42
s. speech of world, think thoughts of few 168.7
s. what you think today 462.3
some s. well and write badly 916.47
ten who s. are noisier than ten thousand silent 585.2
terrible to s. well and be wrong 757.14
'tis easier to s. than be silent 891.10
to s. agreeably is more than to s. in good words or in good order 916.3
to s. without speaking a particular language 148.11

we care more that men s. of us than how 330.34
we need reason to s., none to be silent 891.21
we s. badly of ourselves than not at all 865.10
when a child begins to s., it learns what it knows 521.27
when you s. to man, look on his eyes 916.21
woe unto you, when all s. well of you 706.3
women wish to s.; men are driven to 576.22
you may live with people and not s. openly 908.51
**speakers:** all great s. were bad s. at first 757.6
**speakest:** think twice before thou s. once 749.23
**speaketh:** no man s. safely but he that is glad to hold peace 916.60
**speaking:** from s. comes repentance 916.31
hearing ear is always close to s. tongue 540.1
none love s. so much as the taciturn 916.5
open way of s. draws out discoveries 360.11
s. is a beautiful folly 916.44
s. of self gives us pleasure, others none 865.11
silence is wisdom when s. is folly 891.9
**speaks:** he is not good who s. well of all alike 453.2
I detest man who hides one thing in his heart, and s. forth another 438.13
who s. aright never s. at unsuitable time 916.46
**specialist:** do not be bullied by the s. 917.2
poet on Pegasus, reciting own verses, no more dreaded than mounted s. 917.1
**specialists:** illusion of s.: think they enhance culture 917.6
no teachers powerful as army of s. 917.3
**spectacles:** not all eyes need s. to see clearly 676.8
wearing s. makes men conceited 918.1
**spectator:** become s. of one's life, escape suffering 642.5
**spectre:** how do you shoot s. through heart 340.10
**speculate:** two times when man should not s. 501.8
**speculation:** s. is the romance of trade 501.6
**speculators:** s., boast not of knowing things 688.18
**speech:** almost nobody really favors free s. 362.3
direct s. of feeling cannot be replaced 282.27
dream is always below surface of s. 687.19
everyone is in favor of free s. 362.4
free s. shoved aside for things more vital 362.2
freedom of s. means don't do something to people for their views 362.1
have often regretted s., never silence 891.26
heavy, cautious s. is easy 705.17
in the faculty of s. man excels the brute 916.52
let s. be better than silence or be quiet 916.17
let thy s. be short 96.1
let your s. be alway with grace 916.7
make your s. not too explicit 916.27
man whose expenditure of s. is greater than his income of ideas 916.43
men employ s. to conceal their thoughts 438.27
no glass renders man's likeness as his s. 916.33
plain s. breeds hate 360.6
s.: art of stifling, suspending thought 916.11
s. is civilization itself 916.41
s. is of time, silence of eternity 891.3
s. is one symptom of affection 148.2
s. is the mirror of action 916.56
s. mirror of soul: as man speaks, so is he 916.50
true use of s. is to conceal our wants 916.24
we have freedom of s. and prudence not to practice it 534.46
where there is censorship. s. is serious 111.3
who would not lose s. upon condition to have joys above it 916.16
**speeches:** it is difficult to make s. to the belly 757.12
s. measured by hour, die with hour 757.8
**speed:** change of s. is a difference in quality 735.30
in skating over thin ice safety is in s. 919.2
wind-footed steed is broken in his s. 679.9
**spend:** I don't think you can s. yourself rich 275.1
**spent:** strongly s. is synonymous with kept 502.11
**spider:** s. as an artist has never been employed 479.2
when s. webs unite they can tie up lion 1009.3
**spill:** fear to let fall a drop, you s. a lot 110.5
**spinach:** one man's poison ivy is another's s. 957.2
**spirit:** body and s. are twins 584.15
every s. makes its house 860.5
happiness is s. fulfilled through body 407.28
home of s. is the realm of meaning 544.9
however broken s.'s shrine, s. remains 584.8
in the life of the s. there are no facts 583.15
letter killeth, but s. giveth life 541.1
poor s. poorer than poor purse 433.6
pure logic is the ruin of the s. 778.31
s. is most free when body is satiated with pleasure 698.21
s. is willing but the flesh is weak 1040.1
s. longs for inverted bowl over its head 480.7
s. of death one, s. of life many 790.79
s. of man is a good adversary 971.67
s. of nation is what counts 614.6
the s. is the true self 852.8
unrest of s. is a mark of life 806.4
**spirits:** we learn we are s., not animals 109.2
**spiritual:** physical strength can't withstand s.

force 920.5
s. interests supported by animal life 920.6
scientific power has outrun s. power 843.21
**splendor:** delight in s. is no more than happiness with little 322.2
God grant me love for things of s. 55.17
**spoil:** may share labours of great but not s. 398.1
**spoiled:** all charming people, I fancy, are s. 119.9
**spoken:** one never repents of having s. too little 916.15
**spontaneity:** analysis kills s. 778.2
**spontaneous:** fine conduct is always s. 75.12
to condemn s. acts because useless 697.9
**sport:** if year all holidays, s. would be dull 418.8
in America, s. is opiate of the masses 922.1
only s. you can't fix is rodeoing 922.7
serious s. contains no fair play 922.8
**sports:** good sex mitigates lust for other s. 922.5
**spots:** in an ermine s. are soon discovered 764.5
**spring:** after stormy s. summer comes 848.13
alas, that s. should vanish with the rose 1064.46
come, gentle s., ethereal mildness, come 848.45
first s. day was once time of dalliance 848.49
hush over everything – world awaits s. 848.41
if winter comes, can s. be far behind 425.40
in s. a young man's fancy lightly turns to thoughts of love 848.42
May is a ghastly parody of real s. 848.31
only winter-patience can bring the s. 670.16
quality of life is sexual in s. 848.2
s., a box where sweets compacted lie 848.21
s. arrives at close of winter day 848.9
s., cruel fair season, will come again 848.52
s. is come home with world-wandering feet 848.44
s. never s. unless it comes too soon 848.15
vine made to bear fruit in s. dies soon 277.66
wag world how it will, leaves green in s. 848.32
world's favorite season is the s. 848.38
**spurn:** s. not the nobly-born 786.2
**spurred:** good horse should be seldom s. 1059.1
**spurs:** no need of s. if the horse is running away 298.9
who hath love in breast hath s. in sides 1050.3
**stables:** in England s. centre of household 287.25
**stag:** chasing hare, men don't notice s. 85.7
**stage:** all the world's a s. 1060.27
no man dies for love, but on the s. 548.55
on the s. it is always now 965.34
s. but echoes back the public voice 965.11
s. is where people play at being serious 965.24
you can't be virtuoso in s. and films 965.1
**stairs:** life full of s. to go up and down 233.7
**stake:** death a s. put up to play game of life 538.16
**stand:** ability to s. is meritorious among courtiers 193.1
every tub must s. on its own bottom 873.8
give me where to s., I will move earth 713.7
what is life without time to s. and stare 530.3
**standard:** if a thing is judged great or small by its own s. 788.4
look to s. man for s. English 521.24
**standardization:** social process requires s. of man 295.6
**standards:** barbarism: lack of s. to which to appeal 69.5
great expression furnishes its own s. 399.24
half our s. come from our first masters 471.9
**stander-by:** s. may see more of game than player 642.3
**standing:** man's s. abroad depends on manners 798.11
nature, not s., makes the good man 391.44
those well assured of own s. least apt to trespass on that of others 798.20
what people say behind your back is your s. 798.18
**stands:** he who s. on tiptoe s. not firm 55.13
**star:** canst not stir flower without troubling s. 1010.12
follow thy s., canst not fail of heaven 238.5
let me light my lamp, says the s. 880.6
mariner's eye must be on rocks, North S. 714.3
toe of the s. gazer is often stubbed 440.19
**stare:** what is life without time to stand and s. 530.3
**stars:** as man draws nearer to s. he should draw nearer to his neighbors 98.11
fault is not in our s., but in ourselves 804.13
gazing on s., man at mercy of puddles 440.21
if we could count s., we should not weep 413.8
s. show men to be slight and evanescent 413.4
s. speak of man's insignificance 413.9
too low they build who build beneath the s. 55.25
we are all in gutter, but some look at s. 55.24
when moon is not full, s. shine brightly 788.3
**start:** nothing is more expensive than a s. 73.7
there is nothing like a s. 81.5
**starting:** anything may be s. point, termination 74.5
**starve:** can s. from lack of self-realization 442.25

to eat without hope is still to s. 237.4
to s. is no gentility 272.11
**starving:** love, art are shadows of words to s. man 435.5
s. of men, pampering of dogs 712.12
**state:** bungling in s. affairs produces mischief 86.5
church and s. are indispensable Molochs 125.3
church must be the conscience of the s. 125.5
disproportion destroys a s. 704.2
evil men not excused from service of s. 923.1
king without clemency is enemy of s. 125.6
man not just laborer for the s. 130.2
modern s. has only rights, no duties 923.4
only one in command in home or s. 393.20
s. exists for good life, not life only 923.2
s. has for enemy only other states, not men 923.19
s. has no friends – only interests 923.7
s. hurt when cunning pass for wise 923.3
s. is a creation of nature 705.7
s. is servant, not master, of the citizen 923.12
s. made for man, not man for s. 923.8
s. safe when men fear candidates, laws 923.9
s. tolerates evil to keep out lesser ills 923.13
s. without change is without means of conservation 923.5
the s. is a poor, good beast 923.11
the s. is neighbors; neighbors are s. 923.10
those who lead the s. over a precipice 825.4
thou, too, sail on, O Ship of S. 923.16
thousand years scarce serve to form a s. 923.6
true wealth of s., its inhabitants 923.18
while the s. exists there is no freedom 923.15
**statement:** general s. like check drawn on bank 371.3
s. let loose can't be caught by horses 505.10
**states:** limit is set to growth of prosperous s. 923.17
responsibility of great s.: serve world 923.20
s. have growth, manhood, decrepitude, decay 923.14
**statesman:** can get the truth from a s. after he's seventy 924.8
difference between being an elder s. and posing as one is negligible 924.3
heart of s. should be in his head 924.6
politician becomes s. after he's elected 924.4
s. is politician dead 10 or 15 years 705.74
to delight in war is crime in the s. 1035.90
**statesmanship:** in s. get formalities right 924.11
s. cannot always escape wrong-doing 924.7
**statesmen:** inquiry made into meals and beds of s. 924.10
minds of s. contract with the light 924.5
s. and beauties rarely sense their decay 223.2
s. seldom have choice between good, evil 924.2
some deluded into belief they are s. 924.9
**static:** life is not a s. thing 115.11
**statistics:** there are lies, damned lies, and s. 925.2
**stature:** beauty of s. is the only beauty of men 575.10
**statute:** s.: currency we stamp with our portrait 525.21
**steal:** artists don't s., but borrow 53.105
old burglars never die; just s. away 927.5
**stealing:** all s. comparative; who does not steal 927.2
**steamers:** land created as place for s. to visit 833.1
**steep:** set a stout heart to a s. hillside 243.14
**step:** count every s., you make journey long 6.9
each s. must be a goal and a s. likewise 570.5
thousand-mile journey begins with s. 73.1
**stepchild:** indecision is like the s. 463.4
**stepmother:** new-come s. hates children of first wife 663.15
**sterility:** pain, indolence, s., ennui teach lesson 939.13
**stew:** there may be things better than beef s. 352.5
**stick:** out to beat dog, you're sure to find s. 203.33
speak softly and carry a big s. 713.42
**stillest:** greatest events are s. not loudest hours 303.8
**stillness:** nothing but s. can remain when hearts are full of their own sweetness 982.12
we are use to actions, not s., of humans 982.9
**stock:** earth is given as a common s. 270.6
**stocks:** 'tis sweet to know that s. will stand 501.2
**stolen:** s. ox puts head out of stall 927.9
s. sweets are best 446.2
s. waters are sweet 446.1
**stomach:** empty s. won't listen to anything 435.11
healthy s. is nothing if not conservative 175.3
old s. reforms more drinkers than new resolve 266.41
with full s. rich and poor are alike 272.9
**stomachs:** those with best s. are not best thinkers 968.53
**stone:** continual dripping wears away a s. 506.3
if s. bruises gold, worth undiminished 1019.16
s. thrown at right time better than gold given at wrong time 972.7
word and s. cannot be called back 505.7
**stones:** pearls around the neck: s. on the heart 1041.67

people throw s. at tree loaded with fruit 293.11
**stools:** between two s. one sits on the ground 463.1
**stoop:** soar not too high to fall; s. to rise 33.24
**store:** for modern man heaven is a big department s. 412.3
**stories:** s., like whiskey, must mature in the cask 341.14
taste for dirty s. inherent in humans 708.2
**storm:** every cloud engenders not a s. 709.2
they sicken of the calm, who know the s. 16.6
**story:** one difficult kind of s., the humorous 931.7
only thing read in s. are the first and last sentences 623.28
s. has been thought to its conclusion when it has taken its worst possible turn 931.1
s. with moral is like bill of mosquito 931.4
there is much good sleep in an old s. 931.3
where men have lived there is a s. 417.44
**stout:** set a s. heart to a steep hillside 243.14
**straight:** s. path leads only to the objective 896.3
you cannot drive s. on a twisting lane 489.22
**straightforwardness:** s. without propriety is rudeness 360.3
**stranger:** he deals harshly with s. who's not been a s. 355.10
s. cannot torture a human soul 497.3
s. has no friend, unless it be a s. 355.9
to depend on s. is blindness 233.8
when s. to self, estranged from others too 868.16
which of us is not forever a s. 908.56
**strangers:** ants and savages put s. to death 355.7
cities are, by definition, full of s. 129.24
tears of s. are only water 355.8
**stratagem:** let sword decide after s. has failed 354.1
**stratagems:** those oft are s. which errors seem 932.3
**street:** city s., a river leading nowhere 129.32
**streetcars:** except in s. never be rude to a lady 824.3
**strength:** awareness of our own s. makes us modest 933.4
envy man who lays down life when s. spent 223.3
fool matches s. with stronger 1040.4
four things impair the s. of man 695.5
God is our refuge and s. 385.6
growing up: discovering inner core of s. 567.10
knows not own s. who hasn't met adversity 17.34
life only demands the s. you possess 192.17
like s. is felt from hope and despair 933.9
man's s. is to find God's way, follow it 691.1
match national s. with restraint 614.13
men's s. discontent with limitation 933.1
my s. is as the s. of ten 764.8
nation realizes s., scorns to misuse it 614.28
neither smiles nor frowns substitute for s. 933.13
nothing is so gentle as real s. 377.6
physical s. can't withstand spiritual force 920.5
s. and s.'s will are supreme ethic 933.10
skill, not s., governs a ship 1.8
to bear lightly the neck's yoke brings s. 285.8
tyrannous to use giant's s. like a giant 713.45
what's s. without double share of wisdom 933.16
wisdom is always an overmatch for s. 1053.52
woman's s. is might of weakness 1055.43
**stretch:** s. your foot to length of your blanket 402.15
**strife:** cruel is the s. of brothers 332.3
s. hushed by passing of one generation 372.8
where there is no talebearer, the s. ceases 250.3
worse to incite to s. than to take part 250.1
**strifes:** no temple can still griefs and s. 126.3
**strike:** no right to s. against public safety 1006.1
s. at a great man, you will not miss 898.18
system under which laborers can s. 1006.4
**strikes:** s. an' picnics are evils f'r wurrukin man 1006.3
**strive:** man must s., and striving he must err 297.19
we must s. by what is born in us 1.15
**striving:** success erases the effort of s. 938.33
there's life alone in duty, rest in s. 269.35
**stroll:** when you s. you never hurry back 1034.2
**strong:** adversity is the test of s. men 17.53
deny s. man his due and he'll take all 713.33
harm comes to s. from the weakest 1040.12
how shall one so weak become s. 450.6
if you're s., there are no precedents 933.7
it is easy the for s. to be s. 933.6
know how sublime to suffer and be s. 939.23
language of some men s., but their eyes and actions ask leave to live 973.2
no need to fear the s. 713.56
one cannot be s. without love 548.236
s. and weak cannot keep company 57.1
s. man advances issues, makes a decision 222.4
s. man can intercept the communication between the senses and the mind 856.12
s. man digests his experiences 319.46
s. man sees possible houses and farms 33.9
s. man succumbs to the weak 416.25
s. men can always afford to be gentle 933.11
s. nature cannot take enemies seriously 933.17
the s. prevail; the beggar is a fool 72.1

weak can be terrible trying to appear s. 1040.13
when is man s. until he feels alone 933.3
when s., be merciful to have respect 933.5
**stronger:** pray to be s. men 717.21
that which does not kill me makes me s. 17.44
**strongest:** necessary that s. should be obeyed 636.3
right of conquest is right of s. 170.15
s. have their moments of fatigue 338.5
s. iron most often ends in scraps 933.18
s. man is he who stands most alone 933.12
s. not strong enough to be always master 713.43
**structure:** s. without life is dead 654.5
**struggle:** s. alone pleases us, not victory 279.18
to win joy through s. is better than to yield to melancholy 279.10
**struggling:** fish s. in net hampers itself 651.7
**stubborn:** there's nothing so s. as a man 575.7
time shows most s. are most intelligent 644.12
**stubbornness:** man will do more for s. than for religion 644.5
s. and stupidity are twins 644.10
smallness of mind is the cause of s. 644.7
**students:** I learned from my s. more than from all 277.74
**studied:** men must be s. as deeply as books 1001.11
**studies:** change of s. will fire a dull brain 529.11
to spend too much time in s. is sloth 842.2
**study:** complacency is enemy of s. 155.8
much s. is a weariness of the flesh 91.8
must always s., not always go to school 277.58
natural abilities need pruning by s. 1.1
people that s. more to have knowledge than to live well bring forth little fruit 520.65
proper s. of mankind is man 868.24
realists do not fear results of s. 776.2
s. without liking spoils the memory 529.10
self is sole subject we s. and learn 868.10
**stumble:** men s. on stones, not mountains 989.5
s. may prevent a fall 86.4
**stumbles:** when ox s., all whet their knives 223.14
**stung:** who handles a nettle tenderly is s. 973.5
**stupefaction:** s., when it persists, becomes stupidity 948.2
**stupid:** good man can be s. and still be good 1063.12
mistake of intelligent: to refuse to believe the world as s. as it is 934.21
nothing so s. as an educated man 277.65
nothing sways the s. more than arguments they can't understand 934.18
one can be s. with old friends 363.38
pleasant to meet people more s. than we 934.13
s. thing done from noblest motive 934.22
those of delicate taste endure s. criticism better than s. praise 716.29
when s. man does thing he is ashamed of, he declares that it is his duty 269.32
**stupidity:** against s., even gods contend in vain 934.19
anesthetic for pain of s.: egotism 865.12
certain sign of s. to stand aloof from those who think differently from us 613.4
hardest thing to cope with is s. 934.10
memory is often the attribute of s. 574.7
miseries spring from human s., malice 333.11
nothing is more dangerous than conscientious s. 445.20
obstinacy, dogmatism, surest signs of s. 644.9
s. is without anxiety 43.4
s. often saves a man from going mad 934.11
stubbornness and s. are twins 644.10
when stupefaction persists it becomes s. 948.2
with s. man may front much 934.3
**style:** good s. should show no sign of effort 935.15
great writer finds s. in his soul 935.6
hardship is vanishing, but so is s. 744.8
horrors form the foundation for good s. 569.5
man's s. is intrinsic and private 935.25
progress in literary s. 935.7
proper words in proper places make s. 935.22
run your pen through every other word written, it will give your s. vigor 935.21
s. beautiful when veins not prominent 935.23
s. is temperament stamped upon material at hand 935.16
s. is the dress of thoughts 935.3
s. is the perfection of a point of view 935.5
s., not sincerity, is the vital thing 935.27
s. turns all it touches to gold 935.20
the s. is the man himself 935.1
we are delighted to see natural s. 935.17
what amateurs call s. is only awkwardness 935.9
**subject:** a great man will make any s. great 842.9
**subject's:** s. duty is king's, s. soul is his own 130.9
**subjunctive:** damn the s.: brings all writers to shame 396.4
**sublime:** abuse of the s. is absurdity 677.21
but one step from s. to ridiculous 4.4
**submission:** each act of s. to exterior force rots me 354.6
**submit:** men subdued by force do not s. in heart 354.12
we s. to great evils, resent small offenses 506.2
**subordination:** s. tends greatly to human happiness 773.14
**substance:** you may lose s. by grasping at

shadow 447.1
**substitutes:** ours is the age of s. 54.1
**subtle:** fat paunch never bred s. mind 637.1
not respected as s., you will be regarded as sure 936.5
**subtraction:** a man has one hundred dollars; you leave him with two; that's s. 566.10
**suburb:** conformity ultimately governs the s. 937.2
**suburbs:** s. are incubators of apathy and delirium 937.1
s. are things to come into the city from 937.3
s.: vast dormitories where a man sleeps 937.4
s., where lawns are clipped 129.38
**subversion:** communists have done less to damage us than those defending us against s. 149.9
**subway:** though reconciled to democracy, including people in s., I can't be sanguine 231.8
**succeed:** do work with whole heart and you will s. 1058.42
humiliating to see idiots s. 938.13
man cannot be said to s. in this life who does not satisfy one friend 363.109
s. we must even if means death at fifty 938.22
some s. by what they know, some by what they do, and a few by what they are 938.19
very rare for man of talent to s. by it 956.15
when men s., neighbors think them wise 938.34
when we s., pride betrays us 6.6
**succeeds:** fail I alone—all men strive and who s. 327.4
one s. because to fail is too awful 327.17
**success:** attention to business is price of s. 938.43
coming into port determines s. of voyage 6.1
compensation of early s. is a conviction that life is romantic 938.12
constant s. shows but one side of world 938.4
fine line between failure and s. 327.14
for s., aim unswervingly for goal 679.3
good-fellowship requisite for s. 390.7
hypocrisy is royal road to s. 705.34
in s. we gain reputation for judgment 938.10
key to s. no good until right lock found 938.41
minute's s. pays the failure of years 938.3
near approach to good aggravates ill s. 327.10
not even s. softens heart of envious 293.23
nothing fails like s. 938.26
only the cynicism born of s. is valid 211.2
pray s. won't come faster than you can endure 938.18
s. abides longer when planted by God 938.32
s. can corrupt; usefulness only exalt 1016.6
s. distinguishes confidence from conceit 938.5
s. erases effort of striving 938.33
s. improves the character of the man 938.27
s. is allotted to men by their stars 337.11
s. is counted sweetest by those who ne'er succeed 938.7
s. is feminine 938.11
s. is undesirable 327.8
s. makes men rigid; they exalt stability 938.25
s. makes us more praised than known 938.35
s. not greedy, but insignificant 938.37
s. not inevitable result of endeavors 279.19
s. of most things depends upon knowing how long it will take to succeed 938.28
s. of others punishment for laziness 527.8
s.: to spend your life in your own way 938.29
s.: what we can make of mess we have made 938.8
secret of s. is constancy to purpose 765.3
secret of s.: to convert ideas to things 938.1
strong passion for any object ensures s. 236.17
there are a thousand who hate our s. 293.6
there is no s. without hardship 938.39
'tis man's to fight, heaven's to give s. 170.10
to secure s., be more anxious about obtaining than about deserving it 938.15
toughest thing about s. is one must keep on being a s. 938.2
true s. is to labor 279.22
unless a man has been taught what to do with s. it leaves him a prey to boredom 938.36
what is responsible for s. of many works 91.17
**successes:** s. forgiven if you share them 407.23
**successful:** s. adults were first s. children 402.4
s. man cannot realize how hard an unsuccessful man finds life 938.16
s. man loses no reputation 938.14
**successor:** merit goes to beginner if s. does better 73.2
**succotash:** s. is vulgar 186.14
**sucker:** no crime more humiliating than to be a s. 199.7
**suddenly:** no great thing is created s. 399.21
**suffer:** because my mouth is wide with laughter, you do not think I s. 83.10
each must s. long before he knows he is but one in a community of wretchedness 939.18
how others s. from us we take no heed 939.49
human must s. as price of vision 939.8
know how sublime to s. and be strong 939.23
mankind are disposed to s. evils 800.7
more the dangerous ones s., more they make you s., happier they are 870.1
none can endure to s. 670.7
to s. in obedience to a command is easier than to accept suffering as a free man 939.4
who breathes must s. 939.38
who fears he shall s., suffers what he fears 939.29
**suffered:** fool knows after he's s. 319.27
**sufferers:** for s. sweet to know pain that re-

mains 939.1
**suffering:** although world is full of s., it is full also of the overcoming of it 939.21
become spectator of one's life, escape s. 642.5
creation is the great redemption from s. 198.29
defenceless against s. when we love 549.4
I postpone death by living, s. 502.21
it's not true that s. ennobles character 939.27
life is s. 939.33
life reduced to s. when two ages overlap 207.9
madness, s. can set themselves no limit 555.21
nothing more dear to men than their s. 939.3
only through s. can soul be strengthened 117.15
ownership, not love, causes s. 548.195
s. for truth is fortitude to victory 939.28
s. is above, not below, as everyone thinks 939.37
s. is need felt to familiarize and adapt sensibility to a new state 939.39
s. is not a mystery but a revelation 939.53
s. is one very long moment 939.52
s. is permanent, obscure and dark 939.54
s. is the sole origin of consciousness 939.11
s. is too precious to be shared 939.7
s. man ought to consume his own smoke 939.6
s. of millions blurred by numbers 939.48
senselessness of s. raises indignation 939.31
they learn in s. what they teach in song 702.88
we are healed of a s. by experiencing it to the full 939.40
we cause s. before we become better 939.25
we don't injye other people's s., but we feel betther f'r it 557.3
who can describe his s. is meant for literature 1062.14
wisdom comes alone through s. 1053.1
**sufferings:** life is the agent of your s. 536.10
**suffers:** man never reasons so much as when he s. 939.36
who s. before necessary, s. more than is necessary 939.44
**sufficiency:** elegant s., retirement, rural quiet 695.7
**sufficiency's:** s. enough for men of sense 940.2
**sufficient:** s. man is s., even to ignorance itself 873.17
**suggested:** I like things s., not told in full 936.1
**suicide:** if despair serves no purpose s. justified 941.5
is s. the way out or the way in 941.6
s. does not brave death for noble object 941.1
s. is a criminal offense 941.4
s. is God's best gift to man 941.11
s. the only philosophical problem 941.2
**suicides:** ennui has made as many s. as despair 288.1
**summer:** after many a s. dies the swan 600.21
after stormy spring-time, s. does come 848.13
caught s. is always an imagined time 848.50
flowers in the s., fires in the fall 848.37
hot s. has exhausted her intent 848.51
I am s. to your heart, not four seasons 464.6
I'd like to enjoy s. flower by flower 848.17
Indian s. of life should never be hustled 580.3
no price is set on the lavish s. 848.30
one swallow does not make a s. 709.1
s. days for me when every leaf is on its tree 848.34
s. ends, and autumn comes 848.6
s. set lip to earth's bosom bare 848.43
to ensure s. in England, have it framed 287.29
we fear death as we fear a short s. 218.43
**summer's:** s. lease hath all too short a date 848.36
**sun:** adventure of s.: drama by which we live 943.1
goodness comes from people who bask in s. 943.2
he with head of wax must not walk in s. 934.6
I never assisted the s. in his rising 599.5
is it so small a thing to enjoy the s. 502.2
no need to purchase s., water, moon 616.58
one cloud is enough to eclipse the s. 1004.13
s. is pure, though shines in dirty places 764.1
s. visits cesspools undefiled 57.8
unnecessary to light a candle to the s. 56.4
we have no curiosity about the s. 478.6
with many cocks crowing, s. never rises 56.6
**Sunday:** eleven a.m., S., most segregated hour 126.6
hand that plies weekday broom gives S. caresses 1058.33
how S. into Monday melts 1058.54
**sunset:** s. and evening star 218.126
**sunshine:** s. has influence on constitutions 1043.1
**superannuated:** no one is unhappier than s. idol 223.1
**superficiality:** wisdom lies in the s. of men 944.5
**superfluous:** I wish for the s., the useless 322.3
it's for the s. that we sweat 554.8
lop s. branches that bearing boughs may live 278.2
**superior:** court the society of a s. 57.19
if s. man abandons virtue, how can he be s. 1025.15
nobility: being s. to your past self 945.5

s. man anxious about truth, not poverty 991.21
s. man is easy to serve, hard to please 528.4
s. man waits for appointments of Heaven 748.16
we parted each feeling s. to the other 945.9
what the s. man seeks is in himself 945.2
**superiority:** s. and inferiority are individual 945.11
s. of mind and soul is very moral 945.10
to admit s. is to be an outcast 945.8
**superiors:** American thinks he has no social s. 295.22
falling out with s., be in with equals 766.19
what man dislikes in his s. 528.23
**superlative:** poor devil with no way of attaining s. gets drunk 266.28
**superman:** gods are dead: now we want s. to live 429.5
**supermarket:** s.: America's temple 34.63
**supermen:** we need s. to rule us 393.7
**supernatural:** belief in s. evil not necessary 1048.6
faith in the s. is a desperate wager 946.3
religion made an honest woman of the s. 946.1
s. is the natural not yet understood 946.2
**superstition:** fear is the main source of s. 340.27
in all s. wise men follow fools 947.1
s. renders a man a fool 897.7
s. sets the whole world in flames; philosophy extinguishes them 947.5
s. though recognized doesn't lose power 947.3
science is antidote to poison of s. 843.35
**superstitions:** all people have their blind side—s. 947.2
minds yield to s. of their age 181.10
**superstitious:** men become s. 947.4
touch of science gives edge to s. tale 931.5
**supper:** good salad may be prologue to bad s. 247.4
**support:** we have greater love for those we s. than those who s. us 382.17
**supreme:** man's heart doesn't tolerate absence of the s. 309.9
most tedious discourses on S. Being 966.3
**sure:** dull man always s., s. man always dull 113.10
not respected as subtle, you will be regarded as s. 936.5
s. things: death, taxes, and the bore 93.6
**surfeit:** there is s. even in honey 805.5
they that s. as sick as they that starve 310.8
**surgeon:** best s. hath been hacked himself 261.4
no better s. than one with many scars 261.19
**surgeon's:** more sensitive to s. cut than sword wounds 939.30
**surpasses:** who s., subdues mankind must look down on the hate of those below 945.1
**surprise:** grief is heightened by s. 948.5
life is made to s. us 948.4
s. is the greatest gift life can grant 948.3
that I exist: perpetual s. which is life 314.11
**surprised:** man s. is half beaten 948.1
to be s. is to begin to understand 1056.3
**survival:** prejudices fall quickly when s. at stake 949.3
s. will be twin brother of annihilation 226.1
**suspect:** to know little makes man s. much 257.2
who doth no evil is apt to s. none 764.6
**suspense:** s. is hostiler than death 480.2
**suspicion:** few people can entertain s. without letting hypothesis turn into fact 257.3
love goes out the gate which s. enters 257.5
s. always haunts the guilty mind 403.18
s. begets s. 257.15
s. on one side breeds s. on the other 257.10
**suspicions:** many low, mean s. are well founded 257.8
**suspicious:** when you grow s. of a person, you will find suspicions true 257.9
**swallow:** one s. does not make a summer 709.1
to blow, s. at once isn't easy 221.17
**swan:** after many a summer dies the s. 600.21
**swap:** not best to s. horses crossing river 176.3
**swear:** if angry, count four; if very angry, s. 39.33
let us s. while we may 950.3
**swearing:** little judicyous s. keeps th' temper 950.1
**sweat:** in s. of thy face shalt thou eat bread 1058.9
**sweep:** you can't s. others off their feet, if you can't be swept off your own 291.4
**sweepstake:** fact is that life has become a s. 905.3
**sweet:** bitter and s. come from outside 279.3
daintiest last, to make the end s. 698.37
every s. hath its sour 153.1
men, like fruit, grow s. before decay 580.12
nothing s. which does not end in bitterness 983.16
things s. prove in digestion sour 252.4
**sweetest:** apples taste s. when they're going 223.10
**sweetness:** fly that prefers s. to a long life 700.11
**sweets:** s. grown common lose their dear delight 331.12
stolen s. are best 446.2
to refuse the s. of life because they must leave us is preposterous 859.3
**swift:** to be s. is less than to be wise 137.6
too s. arrives as tardy as too slow 409.14
**swim:** people wish to learn to s. but keep one foot on ground 850.14
who cannot s. must go to the bottom 461.5

swimmers: good s. are oftenest drowned 657.3
swimming: man who is s. against the stream knows the strength of it 651.11
swindle: man wrong who to thinks to s. God 221.16
swine: neither cast ye pearls before s. 48.1
Switzerland: I see S. as an inferior sort of Scotland 951.1
sword: let s. decide after stratagem has failed 354.1
one s. keeps another in the sheath 226.6
overfaithful s. returns the user his heart's desire at price of blood 516.8
pen is mightier than s. 1062.17
s. is but a tool in killer's hand 516.12
tongue more to be feared than s. 916.32
who bears s. of heaven should be holy 512.9
who draws his s. against the prince 779.3
symbol: person gets from s. what he puts into it 952.1
symbolic: good writing is s.; s. writing is seldom good 1062.82
symmetry: s. is ennui, the essence of grief 654.10
sympathetic: s. man is like swimmer among drowning 953.4
sympathize: people who s. are really looking for the particulars 953.7
sympathized: nothing sweeter than to be s. with 953.15
sympathy: s. demands the giving of one's soul 953.10
s. is a supporting atmosphere 953.3
s. is cold to relation of distant misery 953.6
s. is sound relation with external being 836.1
who have never been ill incapable of s. 889.10
wisdom must go with s. 953.8
synagogue: s. lifts its walls by side of cathedral 790.32
system: create a s. or be enslaved by another's s. 954.2
old s. has two advantages over new 477.2
s.: all aspects subordinated to one aspect 954.3
test of every s. is the man it forms 485.1
systematically: it is best to do things s. 654.9
systematizers: I distrust all s. and avoid them 954.4
systems: man has predilection for s. 778.10
our s. have their day and cease to be 983.23
our s.: unconscious apology for our faults 954.1

# T

table: spread the t. and contention will cease 272.7
table-talk: for t., I prefer the witty to the grave 185.26
taciturn: none love to speak so much as the t. 916.5
tact: some people mistake weakness for t. 955.4
t. in audacity is knowing how far to go 90.1
t., not silence, is golden 955.2
tactless: t. man like an axe on embroidery frame 955.3
tail: better head of mouse than t. of lion 713.47
take: do as maids do: say no and t. it 438.9
taken: from him that hath not shall be t. 15.1
tale: honest t. speeds best plainly told 931.6
in mirthful t. we're content with less truth 434.18
science gives an edge to superstitious t. 931.5
temptation to vivify the t. hard to deny 307.1
what so tedious as twice-told t. 794.3
talebearer: where there is no t., the strife ceaseth 250.3
talent: be equal to your t., not your age 956.16
best-seller: gilded tomb of mediocre t. 91.81
coffee good for t.; genius needs prayer 375.2
for every t. poverty has stimulated, it has blighted a hundred 712.19
for those of great t. modesty is hypocrisy 594.14
genius is power, t. applicability 375.5
genius is sacrificed to t. daily 375.3
it is a happy t. to know how to play 697.5
it takes little t. to see what lies under one's nose 956.2
t. is a common family trait 375.8
t. is a question of quantity 956.14
t. is faucet; while open, one must write 956.1
t. is that which is in a man's power 375.9
t. is the call of vocation 1029.4
t. is to be envied, genius pitied 375.7
t. is what an actor needs 956.8
t. recognizes genius 956.5
t. says things he has heard only once 375.4
to do the difficult easily is mark of t. 375.1
very rare for man of t. to succeed by t. 956.15
what a man is betrays itself when his t. decreases 956.12
world receives t. with open arms 375.6
talents: all deserve equal opportunity to develop t. 295.15
great offices will have great t. 399.13
greatest evil: small t., great ambition 33.35
man must stand in terror of his t. 339.7
talk: anecdote will pitch t. off track 185.36
effect of t.: strengthens own opinions 649.35
fair ambition: to excel in t. 916.58
health in table t. and nursery play 605.4
hundreds can t. for one who can think 1027.6

if to t. to oneself is folly, it is unwise to listen to oneself in company 185.13
improvisation is the essence of good t. 921.1
man not clever for his ability to t. 916.14
many would be more truthful if not for uncontrollable desire to t. 916.30
more we t., easier it is to mean little 205.4
must we always t. for victory 916.19
no one would t. much, if he only knew how often he misunderstands others 148.6
t. does not cook rice 916.13
t. ought always to run obliquely 185.6
t. to every woman as if you loved her 955.5
they always t. who never think 916.49
too much t. will include errors 916.10
two ears, one mouth: listen more, t. less 540.5
we do not t.—we bludgeon one another 185.25
we t. little when vanity doesn't make us 916.38
when people t. about others they are dull 185.38
who t. of benefits do them to t. of them 430.18
women enjoy sick t. of one another 1055.50
**talked:** when I have t. at too great length 916.51
worse than to be t. about is not to be 392.15
**talkers:** t. are no good doers 916.54
**talking:** in t., thinking is half murdered 916.22
people maintain opinion for sake of t. 916.26
t. about self is means to conceal self 162.16
t. is like playing on the harp 916.28
t. is the passion of a woman 1055.89
who does not worship himself t. 916.23
whom t. possesseth, cannot hold his peace 916.34
**talks:** he who t. more is sooner exhausted 916.37
nobody t. that doesn't say unwise things 916.29
**tall:** beauty requires that one should be t. 70.4
no man so t. that he need never stretch 398.4
short wise man preferable to t. blockhead 1053.58
t. man is never his own man till angry 39.22
**tallest:** many strokes overthrow the t. oaks 679.7
**tame:** if you t. me we shall need each other 548.194
**task:** each man's t. is his life-preserver 1058.25
no t., rightly done, is truly private 1058.71
to think is hardest t. in world 968.11
**taste:** all life is dispute over t. and tasting 957.14
"bad t." most formidable term to the English 287.9
beautiful things, when t. is formed 957.17
between friends, differences in t. 957.3
common sense and good t.—without originality or moral courage 147.10
depraved t. likes what disgusts others 352.8
diffusion of t. not same as improvement 957.6
every one carries his own inch-rule of t. 957.1
exuberance is better than t. 511.4
good t., humor: contradiction in terms 434.20
good t. is virtue of museum keepers 957.16
least cultivated t. has largest appetite 573.1
let us value that which we can t., feel 875.3
loud dress offends people of t. 957.20
our bad t. is the bad t. of our age 181.9
people want to be known for t., not virtues 957.4
person's t. is his own peculiar concern 957.13
purity of t. is almost as rare as talent 514.24
t. has no system and no proofs 957.18
t. is enemy of creativeness 957.15
t. is the fundamental quality 957.11
t. is the literary conscience of the soul 957.8
they never t. who always drink 877.3
we have no laws against bad t. 957.5
what is song, when world lacks t. 48.4
whose mouth out of t. says wine is flat 913.4
**tastes:** Philistine reveres superior t. 957.9
t. in young people are changed by impetuosity; in the aged, preserved by habit 957.10
t. may not be the same 386.4
**taught:** first he wrought, and afterwards he t. 959.5
man knows, learns nothing without being t. 981.8
many things draw us from what we are t. 967.4
men must be t. as if you t. them not 959.23
nothing worth knowing can be t. 520.74
things we know best haven't been t. us 520.68
**tax:** difference between t. collector and taxidermist: taxidermist leaves the hide 958.3
every advantage has its t. 15.3
t. has made more liars than golf has 958.9
to do income t. for infinite years 600.23
to t. and to please is not given to men 958.2
**taxation:** no system of t. operates with equality 958.8
t.: plucking the goose for largest amount of feathers, with least hissing 958.4
**taxes:** animals have instincts, man has t. 958.7
forgive us for cheering legislators who promise low t. 872.5
no t. imposed without consent by people 958.6
Noah must have taken into the ark two t. 958.11
one thing certain in war: increased t. 1035.75
t.: dues paid for membership in society 958.12

thing generally raised on city land: t. 129.39
when everybody is broke, they raise t. 958.10
**taxpayer:** optimism is above all virtue of t. 652.2
**teach:** delightful task! to t., rear the young 959.28
dons are too busy educating to t. 959.4
easier for tutor to command than t. 959.18
it is safer to learn than t. 649.24
joy in learning: it enables me to t. 959.26
let such t. others who themselves excel 204.42
man who knows a subject well can t. it 959.19
none who cannot t. somebody something 309.3
others' follies t. us not 319.60
t. man to fish, you feed him for life 981.3
t. us to care and not to care 800.3
they t. in academies much that is useless 277.32
to t. is to learn twice over 959.14
who wishes to t. truth should suggest it 959.22
writer writes in order to t. himself 1062.58
**teacher:** a t. is better than two books 959.10
experience is the only t. 319.17
he honors my style who learns under it to destroy t. 935.26
if a man cherishes old knowledge and acquires new, he may be a t. 959.6
let nature be your t. 616.81
one good t. may change a delinquent into a solid citizen 959.30
t. affects eternity 959.1
t. arousing feeling for one good action better than he filling memory with objects 959.12
to t. of languages world but place of words 521.4
**teacher's:** t. conviction that men are convertible 959.7
**teachers:** make your friends your t. 529.8
men are my t. 529.14
rigidity in t. deserves insubordination 959.24
t. deserve more honor than parents 959.3
**teaches:** he who can, does; he who cannot, t. 959.27
who t. us anything we knew not is to be reverenced as a master 959.13
**teaching:** art of t. is art of awakening curiosity 959.9
**tear:** most of us tremble before a t. 40.2
nothing dries sooner than a t. 1045.5
t. dries quickly if for others' troubles 692.6
**tears:** endow the living with the t. you squander on the dead 692.9
it is sweet to mingle t. with t. 911.44
laughter, t., turn wheels of same sensibility 876.5
no t. for happenings that undeceive 319.15
sad find somehow sweetness in t. 1045.4
t. gratify savage nature, do not melt it 832.3
t. not inconsistent with inward peace 1045.8
t. of strangers are only water 355.8
t. show a tender heart 517.14
there's no seeing one's way through t. 1045.2
they that sow in t. shall reap in joy 279.1
thoughts that lie too deep for t. 349.8
waste not fresh t. over old griefs 1045.3
women's t. act like smelling salts 687.7
**teas:** t., where small talk dies in agonies 907.9
**technical:** where t. skill, no need for faith 960.9
**technicalities:** wrong must not win by t. 525.1
**technological:** education in a t. world is neuter 277.50
for t. man, time is uncontrollable mystery 971.32
t. advance without social advance almost automatically increases human misery 960.7
**technology:** only science can keep t. in moral order 960.4
t. can help human race go to hell by jet 960.1
t. has permitted us to put a city to the sword, not realizing what we are doing 1042.4
t. made large populations possible 960.14
world t.: world government or suicide 960.15
**tedious:** each reserves to himself right to be t. 93.3
people are either charming or t. 119.8
what so t. as twice-told tale 794.3
**tediousness:** man who suspects his own t. not yet born 93.1
**teen-ager:** t. has replaced the Communist as the target for public controversy 1064.20
**teeth:** as t. drop out, the old get more biting 646.83
God gives almonds to those with no t. 17.60
if you can't bite, don't show your t. 969.4
it is disgusting to pick your t. 1031.2
my t. closer to me than my relatives 869.15
sans t., sans eyes, sans taste 646.93
t. are smiling, but is the heart 390.3
**teething:** Adam and Eve escaped t. 64.8
**television:** I hate t. 563.16
in t. society, small desire to think 563.6
shock waves of t. 563.8
sometimes any electrical applicance seems to offer more entertainment than t. 563.15
t. is an emanation of human vacuity 563.11
t. lets us listen together, be lonesome 563.3
t. programs are chewing gum for eyes 563.2
**television's:** t. primary damage: it provides same fantasy for ten million children 563.10
**tell:** t. not all you know 749.18
**temper:** hot t. leaps o'er a cold decree 39.31
our t. depends on the daily, little things 962.3
tart t. never mellows with age 961.2
words are healers of the sick t. 752.1

**temperament:** t., like liberty, is important 962.2
**temperance:** intemperate t. injures the cause of t. 963.4
t. is the ruler of pleasures and desires 963.3
t. without devotion is a cold virtue 1025.3
**temperate:** we become t. by performing t. actions 224.1
**tempers:** many lose their t. seeing you keep yours 39.12
t. of old make them difficult 646.30
**temple:** chiefest sanctity of a t. is that men go there to weep in common 124.13
God builds t. in heart, on church ruins 124.6
no t. can still griefs and strifes 126.3
**temptation:** cowardice: surest protection against t. 964.11
degree of t. will overcome any virtue 964.7
he who loves praise loves t. 716.40
I avoid t. unless I can't resist it 964.12
I can resist everything except t. 964.14
never resist an adequate t. 964.9
no t. measurable by value of its object 964.5
saintliness is also a t. 834.1
t. comes but for man to meet and master 964.3
way to get rid of a t. is to yield to it 964.13
**temptations:** it's good to be without vices, but not t. 964.1
when t. march in regiments, one waits for them to pass 964.4
**tempted:** all men are t. by the right temptation 964.2
blessed is he who has never been t. 964.10
**tenable:** any danger spot t. if brave men make it so 213.13
**tender:** t. heart our noblest quality 517.14
we are more t. towards children and old people than to those in prime of life 723.2
**tenderly:** who handles a nettle t. is stung 973.5
**tenors:** t. are noble; baritones born villains 648.6
**tensely:** bow too t. strung is easily broken 620.13
**tenterhooks:** t. are upholstery of anxious seat 43.12
**tenure:** long t. of office begets tyranny 755.2
**territory:** t. does not make a nation 614.10
t. only durable part of nation 614.18
**terror:** easiest victor over reason: t., force 354.7
reason can wrestle and overthrow t. 778.12
revolt and t. pay a price 526.3
**terrors:** we fly to beauty from t. of the finite 70.13
**terse:** when I try to be t., I end being obscure 96.7
**test:** t. of any man lies in action 9.34
**text:** we pick a t. to make it serve our turn 78.7
**texts:** man made to eat ices, not pore over t. 842.13
**thanked:** when I'm not t. at all, I'm t. enough 397.5
**thankful:** be t. f'r what ye have not 397.3
**thanks:** evermore t., the exchequer of the poor 397.11
kindness for selfish end merits no t. 881.3
refined nature vexed when owed t. 639.6
**Thanksgiving:** we keep T. to give thanks we are presarved fr'm th' Puritans 418.2
**theater:** calls and t. propagate platitudes 185.34
great t. strengthens our faculty to face what is 965.36
men go to t. to forget; women to remember 965.22
New Yorkers go to see hits, not to the t. 965.12
not going to t.: dressing without mirror 965.27
t. is life hideously exaggerated 965.19
t. struggles even when it flourishes 965.31
t. takes place wherever one is 965.3
we go to t. to confirm experience of reality 965.13
you need three things in t.—play, actors, audience, each must give something 965.10
**theatergoers:** in London t. laugh; in Paris, they wait 965.4
**theatrical:** God will have life real; we make it t. 944.2
**theism:** t. taught by natural history spoils both 844.6
**theist:** fight between t., atheist is whether God shall be called God or some other name 385.15
**theists:** men no longer t. must become humanists 429.3
**theologian:** t. with no joy in his work is not a t. 966.1
**theologies:** t. based on God as senile delinquent 385.80
**theology:** nature can speak on everything, even t. 616.55
no man should dogmatize except on t. 262.11
t. in religion like poisons in food 966.7
t. is attempt to explain subject by men who do not understand it 966.6
t. moves between eternal truth and the temporal situation 966.8
the cure for false t. is mother-wit 966.4
**theorem:** great poem, deep t., are reader's own experiences 529.4
**theories:** fine t. are built which do not bear examination 967.6
t., abstract ideas, things in themselves 967.10
t. are private property; truth is common 967.1
**theorist:** t. without practice is tree without fruit 967.12
**theorize:** it is mistake to t. without data 967.2

**theorizing:** work without t. makes life endurable 967.16
**theory:** action will remove doubt t. cannot solve 9.37
all t. is grey, but green is life's tree 967.9
better to emit t. than be insensible 967.15
no t. is good unless used to go beyond 967.5
t. and practice of life not reconciled 967.3
t. helps us to bear ignorance of facts 967.13
t. makes men incautious 967.11
we do what we can, then make a t. 775.2
without love t. bruises the very ones it claims to save 967.7
**thesis:** sometimes a scream is better than a t. 747.1
**thief:** egg-t. becomes a camel-t. 927.8
he is a t. who charges too much for goods he sells 732.4
he who holds ladder is as bad as t. 201.9
opportunity makes the t. 927.3
rich t. passes for a gentleman 927.4
t. believes everybody steals 927.6
t. doth fear each bush an officer 403.18
**thieves:** beauty provoketh t. sooner than gold 70.47
great t. lead away the little thief 201.2
lowest of t. is robber of time 971.57
**thieving:** there is sublime t. in all giving 382.18
**thin:** to get t., re-establish purpose in life 637.3
**things:** after inside upheavals, fix on imperturbable t. 638.3
in house where one is lonely, one has solicitude for t. 544.2
t. and men have always a certain sense 1000.3
t. have their laws as well as men 638.4
we live in a world of t. 565.2
we must think t., not words 1057.16
**think:** act quickly, t. slowly 9.24
aim of our institutions is that we may t. what we like and say what we t. 362.5
be yourself and t. for yourself 873.12
can do all because they t. they can 854.7
feeling when we ought to t. 86.1
I am happy, content because I t. I am 407.69
I cannot sit and t.; books t. for me 91.55
I t., therefore I am 968.7
I wish to say what I t., feel today 462.2
if a man sits down to t., he is asked if he has a headache 968.10
in television society, small desire to t. 563.6
man is obviously made to t. 968.39
nothing miserable unless you t. so 1004.2
obscure author does not t. clearly 91.18
people who cease to complain, cease to t. 156.5
speak speech of world, t. thoughts of few 168.7
telling a man exactly what you t. of him 360.6
they always talk who never t. 916.49
those that t. must govern those that toil 968.17
thousands can t. for one who can see 1027.6
to meditate is to labor; to t., to act 968.25
to t. is hardest task in world 968.11
to t. is to act 968.12
to t. is to say no. 627.1
to t. justly, understand what others mean 148.7
to t.: meander to a dead end, seek exit 968.30
under all we t. lives all we believe 76.11
we must dare to t. unthinkable things 968.16
we t. in order that we may survive 968.37
what concerns me is what I must do, not what people t. 224.9
what we t., feel, is determined by glands 584.6
while we stop to t., we miss opportunity 650.8
who t. do not set selves to disturb world 968.52
**thinker:** importance of t. depends upon fate of his ideas in minds of his successors 968.56
t. dies, his thoughts are beyond reach 441.18
**thinkers:** most t. write badly 968.34
**thinkest:** if thou t. twice before speaking once 749.23
**thinketh:** as he t. in his heart, so is he 117.3
**thinking:** Americans believe t. is so damn serious 34.47
extensive knowledge needful to t. people 520.35
high t. inconsistent with material life 565.3
in talking, t. is half murdered 916.22
labels save the trouble of t. 928.2
life is what a man is t. of all day 536.32
man is but a reed; but he is a t. reed 968.40
most difficult thing is to say thinkingly what others say without t. 916.1
nothing good or bad but t. makes it so 387.14
others come to our t. if we go to theirs 647.2
plain living and high t. are no more 695.8
sect, party, saves man from vexation of t. 667.1
t. being is a curiosity without a cause 1010.1
t.: effort of soul to keep independence 968.32
t.: endeavor to capture reality with ideas 968.36
t. goes on in seclusion within 968.60
t. is hard work 968.18
t. is the most unhealthy thing in the world 968.58
t. life less a perfectioning of animal and physical life 583.16
t. ought to be a calmness 968.33
your way of t. must be your own 968.26
**thinks:** he t. too much; such men are dangerous 57.20
one must live the way one t. 968.4
**thirst:** I came upon no wine so wonderful as t. 266.42

**thirties:** it's in the t. that we want friends 363.49
**thirty:** after t. a man wakes up sad every morning 580.9
at t. women send big bed to basement 560.133
no matron happy till past t. and not fat 637.2
**thirty-five:** no one over t. is worth meeting who has not more to teach us than does a book 319.13
**thistle-down:** we are like t. blown by the wind 450.1
**thorn:** who wants a rose must respect the t. 749.25
**thorns:** I fall upon the t. of life; I bleed 939.46
no gathering roses without pricks of t. 699.1
who plants t. must not expect roses 809.4
who scatters t. must not go barefoot 557.4
**thought:** all t. is a feat of association 968.15
black the clouds and troubled the waters when Sea of T. gives up its dead 441.9
but for t. no motion would be an action 968.44
by t. I comprehend the world 968.41
delightful to rear tender t., young idea 959.28
every real t. knocks wind out of someone 968.21
every revolution was first one man's t. 813.9
from waste-paper of perishable events t. can derive imperishable meanings 968.47
give me stormy t., not calm of faith 16.3
human t. makes world in its own image 968.42
I have t. too much to deign to act 968.51
if no t. your mind does visit 916.27
if t. too weak to express simply, reject it 968.49
in a crowd t. can provide seclusion 730.4
indignation is the seducer of t. 465.4
intellect should pursue t. to end 968.57
it matters not what you are t. to be 442.17
it's hard to keep private property in t. 968.23
man is God by his faculty for t. 259.6
man not idle because absorbed in t. 1058.43
men use t. as authority for injustice 438.27
nimble t. can jump both sea and land 968.45
nothing remains beautiful except t. 968.46
one t. fills immensity 968.3
only by t. can labour be made happy 1058.60
our action only fitfully guided by t. 9.40
party-spirit a hindrance to t. 667.10
profundity of t. belongs to youth, clarity of t. to old age 968.35
quality of the t. makes nations differ 614.4
rational t. is to interpret by inescapable scheme 778.23
t. altereth the nature of the thing 58.4
t. depends absolutely on the stomach 968.53
t. functions as fragmentary part of idea 569.3
t. is not a gift, but an acquisition 968.38
t. is process by which ends are answered 968.54
t. is the labor of the intellect 812.2
t. itself needs words 1057.3
t. makes every thing fit for use 968.13
t. merged with feeling, artist's joy 53.78
t. often original, though often uttered 968.20
t. spans years, curdles a life into an hour 968.5
t. threatened with publicity shrinks towards mediocrity 754.4
t. without action is nothing much 9.3
t. without learning is perilous 520.11
things t. too long can be no longer t. 968.61
this dead of midnight is the noon of t. 626.1
train of t. never false 329.14
uncompromising t. is luxury of recluse 968.59
what was once t. can never be unthought 968.9
while t. exists, words are alive 91.22
words are the small change of t. 1057.35
**thoughtless:** there may be less wrong-minded men than t. 613.12
young people t. as a rule 1064.28
**thoughts:** all t. are always ready 296.19
all t. are ministers of love 548.27
certain t. are prayers 717.18
chance gives rise to and removes t. 114.15
do not reveal your t. to everyone 162.1
everyone thinks bells echo his own t. 865.8
great t. come from the heart 968.50
great t. have ridiculous beginning 399.7
have open face, but conceal your t. 162.9
I have no riches but my t. 968.48
if sick, your own t. make you sick 620.9
little-minded people's t. move in small circles 491.13
man's life accorded him in t. of others 798.9
man's secret t. run over all things 968.19
man's t. are his banners 441.32
my t. are my company 968.27
not alone if accompanied by noble t. 908.6
nothing's of such vexation as own t. 968.55
our less conscious t., actions, mold lives 999.1
our life is what our t. make it 968.31
our t. are unclear until put into words 1057.4
second t. are ever wiser 24.1
sorrow touches us through our t. 911.32
style is the dress of t. 935.3
t., like fleas, jump from man to man 968.28
t. of men widened by process of suns 735.27
t. that lie too deep for tears 349.8
to think great t. you must be heroes as well as idealists 968.24
to value own t. try their effects on others 148.7
unsought t.: commonly the most valuable 968.29
we ought to control our t. 968.6
you may derive t. from others 968.26
**threadbare:** seldom discern eloquence under t.

cloak 712.34
wit and coin are doubted with t. coat 1054.15
**threatened:** t. folks live long 969.1
**threatens:** he t. many that hath injured one 474.11
**three:** to be t. is to be in public, safe 151.1
**thrift:** men don't realize how great an income t. is 970.7
**thrifty:** some t. as if they would live forever 970.1
**throne:** better in dust than crawl near t. 773.7
doubtful t. is ice on summer seas 825.28
frog would leap from t. of gold to puddle 48.8
man cannot sit on t. he built of bayonets 354.9
on highest t. we still sit on our own ass 726.14
t. is only a bench covered with velvet 773.19
**through:** best way out is t. 298.4
**thrush:** wise t. sings each song twice over 80.4
**thunderbolt:** t. comes in a moment, ends in a minute 969.2
**thyself:** be a friend to t., others will be too 862.3
beware of no man more than t. 852.12
explore t. 868.33
sink in t.: there ask what ails thee 868.1
**ticker:** nothing like t. tape except a woman 501.5
**tide:** there is a t. in the affairs of men 650.10
**tides:** struggling t. of life are eddies of mighty stream rolling to its appointed end 337.2
t.: systole and diastole of earth's veins 847.1
**tidings:** let ill t. tell themselves 622.9
**tied:** everyone has feeling of being t. down 620.1
**tiger:** no man can tame a t. into a kitten 46.4
there is a raging t. inside every man 856.8
**tiger's:** must enter t. den to take cubs 90.9
**tigers:** all reactionaries are paper t. 175.13
**time:** age, t., are but timidities of thought 971.37
art is long and t. is fleeting 600.13
as good have no t. as no good use of it 971.21
as we grow old, value of t. becomes vivid 646.47
be a football to t. and chance 502.8
butterfly counts moments and has t. enough 971.61
dost thou love life, do not squander t. 971.19
earth revolves, but one lives undisturbed; so it is with t. in one's life 971.44
endless volumes prove intellectual climb, but come of having lots of t. 91.61
every new t. will give its law 525.36
everyone has t. if he likes 10.19
existence doth depend on t. 9.11
expect, fear, everything from t. and men 971.64
familiarity with life makes t. speed 971.23
for technological man, t. is the mystery 971.32
go slowly and t. will walk submissively 900.2
God chastens not with rod but with t. 971.25
great t. makes all things dim 971.55
habituation is a falling asleep of sense of t. 404.11
had we but world enough, and t. 851.9
half our life we try to fill t. we rushed through life trying to save 971.46
he gains t. who does not watch his neighbor 873.15
hell is t., where Satan winds a watch 414.6
I wasted t., and now doth t. waste me 646.91
in life of one man never same t. returns 115.12
killing t. is chief end of our society 971.6
late visitors should find t. in my face 426.11
love is stopped by hunger or by t. 549.2
love makes t. pass; t. makes love pass 548.70
lowest of thieves is robber of t. 971.57
men are convinced an interval of t. will be allowed them before they die 452.12
men more like own t. than like fathers 181.1
men should seize t. by the forelock 971.43
methods to measure t. contrived by monks 971.27
modern man doesn't know what to do with t. 971.20
more free t. means more t. to waste 530.7
most intractable of experiences is t. 971.29
music quickens us to enjoyment of t. 607.28
nine-tenths of wisdom: being wise in t. 1053.56
no preacher listened to but t. 971.58
none so scrupulous in measuring t. as he whose t. is worth nothing 444.9
nothing puzzles more, troubles less, than t. 1010.7
nothing really belongs to us but t. 530.6
on the whirligig of t. we circle 971.62
one direction in world, t. its measure 600.19
our costliest expenditure is t. 971.63
peace: when t. doesn't matter passing by 674.31
procrastination is the thief of t. 228.13
remember that things take t. 6.12
ruins of t. build mansions in eternity 971.7
t. a great conference planning our end 971.5
t. and circumstance enlarge views of men, narrow views of women 576.16
t. and hour runs through roughest day 971.54
t. and words can't be recalled 669.12
t. bears away all, even the mind 971.65
t. blind, man stupid, say cynics 971.48
t. brings all things to pass 971.3
t. cools, t. clarifies 282.23
t. cures one of everything – even living 971.24
t. deals gently only with gentle takers of t. 971.18

t. dissipates the angularity of facts 326.5
t. doesn't alter image we have of people 971.45
t. enough to do all, if one thing at a t. 579.5
t. flies, and what is past is done 505.8
t. flies apace; we would believe all flies forward with it 971.38
t. flies over us; leaves shadow behind 971.26
t.: fragment of the infinite for finite use 971.4
t. gives the promise of t. in every death 218.55
t. goes by: reputation increases, ability declines 646.45
t. has no divisions to mark its passage 624.3
t. heals griefs and quarrels 971.40
t. heals what reason cannot 971.51
t. in every century has a different face 296.11
t. in its aging course teaches all things 971.1
t. increases understanding for the aging 1000.14
t. is a file that wears, makes no noise 971.16
t. is a fluid condition 971.17
t. is a great legalizer, even of morals 971.35
t. is a kindly God 971.56
t. is a merciless thing 971.67
t. is a robber 971.36
t. is a wealth of change 971.60
t. is at fault; men become good, but so slow 391.10
t. is born in the eyes 971.12
t. is but shadow of world upon eternity 971.30
t. is idea arising from human intercourse 991.26
t. is on the side of the oppressed today 995.22
t. is sole philosopher; all others, sophists 971.10
t. is test of trouble, but not remedy 971.13
t. is that in which all things pass away 971.50
t. is the greatest innovator 477.1
t. is the measure of business 102.2
t. is the only true purgatory 971.9
t. is the rider that breaks youth 971.28
t. like manager staging new production 971.49
t.: longest distance between two places 971.66
t. lost is t. unenriched by experience 971.8
t. makes man find himself in his heart 868.3
t. makes more converts than reason 971.39
t. not concerned but hurries on 983.7
t. often justifies what seems unjustifiable 224.7
t. overtake all things alike 971.2
t. ripens all things; no man's born wise 971.11
t., space: scarcities of tomorrow 994.18
t. stoops to no man's lure 983.21
t. strengthens friendship, weakens l. 548.104
t. strips our illusions of their hue 447.4
t. that's just t. will let sounds be sounds 912.1
t. threatens with sand-bag, not scythe 646.51
t. to every purpose under the heaven 972.2
t. trieth truth 991.38
t. turns the old days to derision 971.59
t. works change for better or worse 115.31
the t. of life is short 536.113
to realize the unimportance of t. is the gate of wisdom 971.47
travel, trouble, kiss pass my t. 10.15
truth is child of t. 991.41
truth lags last, limping on arm of t. 991.52
use t. as though you were about to die 765.9
we can leave footprints on sands of t. 399.44
we take no note of t. but from it loss 971.69
what may be done any t. is done no t. 228.6
what reason cannot bring about, t. may 971.22
whirligig of t. brings in his revenges 971.53
who waste t. complain of its brevity 971.31
why trouble about t. when we cease to be 218.66
young man old in hours if no t. lost 319.2
**time's:** I hear t. wingèd chariot hurrying near 971.34
t. glory is to bring truth to light 971.52
**timeliness:** t. is best in all matters 972.6
**times:** accusing the t. is excusing ourselves 296.9
good men are stars, illustrate their t. 391.28
good old t.: all t. when old are good 296.5
the t.: a few profound and active men 296.7
these are the t. that try men's souls 296.20
they that reverence too much old t. are but a scorn to the new 979.1
though a god, I've learned to obey the t. 296.21
we changed with the t. 181.7
**timid:** do not be too t. about your actions 973.3
happiness hates the t.; so does science 973.9
t. yearn for full value, demand a tenth 1019.19
**tip:** I t., afraid of what the waiter'll think 974.1
**tired:** life is one long process of getting t. 338.1
**title:** name, t., rank are artificial 773.9
**titled:** craving of the t. for riches 52.4
**titles:** Americans have appetite for Old World t. 773.12
most enviable of all t.: an honest man 423.19
t. but nicknames; every nickname a title 612.7
t. distinguish the mediocre 773.23
**toad:** there is a t. in every social dish 907.10
**toastmaster:** t. should call attention to the subject without making an effort to cover it 757.15
**tobacco:** first illusion of t.: believing we do something when we do nothing 975.4
for thy sake, t., I'd do anything but die 975.9

other world must exist where I can quit t. 975.10
t. is better eschewed than chewed 975.11
use of alcohol, t., test of civilization 131.10
**today:** boldly say each night, I have lived t. 723.5
call the life you live t. your own 114.10
doubts of t. limit realization of tomorrow 998.10
in t. already walks tomorrow 303.1
mortgaged to yesterday, we cannot use t. 669.10
t. is like yesterday 1064.57
t. is muffled in impenetrable folds 723.10
t. is t., always is t. 777.13
t. is yesterday's pupil 723.13
t. will die tomorrow 983.21
they who lose t. may win tomorrow 114.7
to disdain t. is to misunderstand yesterday 723.18
to-morrow do thy worst, I have lived t. 723.7
watch tomorrow to be in touch with t. 115.32
**today's:** t. egg is better than tomorrow's hen 723.30
**together:** Americans don't get t., only do things t. 151.13
coming t. again: foretaste of resurrection 666.7
we must all hang t. 1009.4
**togetherness:** t. is a counterfeit communion 976.3
**toil:** if no gods, all t. meaningless 997.10
luck is not chance—it's t. 358.6
most men in a brazen prison live, with heads bent o'er their t. 1058.1
t. is the sire of fame 1058.26
those that think must govern those who t. 968.17
we only t. who are first of things 1058.64
**toiler:** dreamer lives forever; t. dies in a day 687.17
**toilet:** t. is the seat of the soul 751.2
**toiling:** great men t. upward in the night 6.16
it is weariness to keep t. at same things 1058.38
**told:** sad is the phrase: I t. you so 902.1
**tolerance:** after you've heard all friends have to say, then comes t. of love 363.93
highest result of education is t. 977.10
more and more care about religious t. 790.7
t. best achieved by those without convictions 977.1
t. is makeshift for an overcrowded planet 977.6
t. is nine parts apathy to one of love 977.3
t. is not lack of commitment to own beliefs 977.11
those wearing t. for label call other views intolerable 977.13
which is really mine: t. or rubber spine 977.15
world peace requires mutual t. 496.6
**tolerant:** evil in us is least t. of evil in others 305.27
we are t. of those who do not agree with us 977.7
we are t. when we tolerate ourselves 852.16
**tolerate:** if we had to t. in others what we permit in ourselves, life would be unbearable 468.1
people t. those they fear 977.8
we t. each other thirty years 560.118
**toleration:** doctrine of necessity is that of t. 800.4
**tomorrow:** boast not thyself of t. 721.1
boy believes t. will be different 1064.57
doubts of today are limit to realization of t. 998.10
go take your damned t. 786.5
in today already walks t. 303.1
it may be a fire—t. it will be ashes 384.1
keep sights on t. to be in touch today 115.32
no progress without faith in t. 735.13
t. do thy worst, for I have lived to-day 723.7
t. is ours to win or lose 366.17
t. will be wonderful—unless it is terrible 366.18
the day after t. is doubtful 366.23
they who lose today may win t. 114.7
we steal if we touch t.: it is God's 366.3
**tomorrow's:** today's egg is better than t. hen 723.30
**tomorrows:** all the t. are ours to shape 723.1
**tongue:** among men, the t. wins and not the deed 683.11
blow of the t. crushes bones 203.1
don't scald your t. in others' broth 571.3
Englishman is natural when holding t. 287.14
fluent t. only thing mother don't like her daughter to resemble her in 215.3
gold pays for slip of the t. 86.9
he who would be the t. of this wide land 702.66
let fool hold t., he will pass for sage 891.25
man is hid under his t. 916.2
men are born with two eyes, one t. 96.5
nature has given us two eyes, two ears, and one t. 916.59
practised man trusts eyes more than t. 148.4
rather trip with feet than with t. 86.12
sharp t. grows keener with use 961.2
should be silver in purse or on t. 281.3
stillest t. can be truest friend 891.8
t. is a key to the intellectual treasure 891.29
t. more to be feared than sword 916.32
t. of man is twisty, plenty of words 521.10
t. of wise man lieth behind his heart 1053.2
teeth before the t. give good advice 19.19
too free a t. makes for wrangle 392.3
use sweet t., guide elephant with a hair 377.5

**tongues:** men govern nothing with more difficulty than their t. 916.57
**tool:** bad workman never gets a good t. 461.3
man, t.-using animal, is lord of creation 856.6
**tooth:** better a t. out than always aching 260.5
**toothache:** man with t. thinks all without t. happy 152.5
never philosopher that could endure t. 889.25
t. will cost a battle 989.10
**top:** ass loaded with gold climbs to the t. 596.17
defeats of fellows at the t. aren't defeats for fellows at the bottom 773.2
many paths to the mountain t. 330.12
**torment:** more estimable the offender, greater the t. 171.32
one must choose between boredom and t. 92.8
**torture:** stranger cannot t. a human soul 497.3
**Tory:** timid man fears people, is T. by nature 175.11
**totalitarian:** direction of labor rigid in t. society 978.4
**totalitarianism:** in our loathing of t. there is admiration for its efficiency 978.2
t. spells simplification 978.3
**touch:** we never t. but at points 908.15
**tough:** look for a t. wedge for a t. log 579.13
**tour:** on escorted t. you don't even have to know the Matterhorn isn't a tuba 985.19
**tourist:** less a t. knows, the fewer mistakes he need make 985.1
t. expects things to happen to him 985.7
**tourists:** there are t. incapable of looking at masterpiece for its own sake 985.30
we cannot learn to love other t. 985.29
**town:** day in country is worth month in t. 191.13
earth's axis through center of every t. 693.5
God made the country and man made the t. 191.4
in country we forget t.; in t., despise country 191.8
in great t. friends are scattered 129.3
modern t.-dweller has no God, no Devil 129.23
no t. can fail of beauty with trees 988.1
t. life makes one tolerant, liberal 129.30
t. people worry the year 'round 129.21
when in country you praise distant t. 249.6
whoever live elsewhere in t. from me, I think out of the world 355.11
**toy:** child shows his t.; a man hides his 698.30
**toys:** there are t. for all ages 697.6
when child has left, t. become affecting 121.12
**trade:** it is not your t. to make tables 203.15
not to teach son a t. teaches him to rob 1029.13
people of same t. seldom meet but conversation ends in conspiracy 102.32
speculation is the romance of t. 501.6
t.-unions have done more for humanity 1006.2
two of a t. can never agree 1029.5
usual t. is cheating by consent 102.16
**tradition:** each t. grows continually more venerable 979.17
everywhere the basis of principle is t. 728.7
less fettered by t., greater becomes inward activity of men's motives 979.16
love for t. has never weakened a nation 979.5
t. is a guide and not a jailer 979.15
t. is milk for babes but no meat for men 979.7
t. without intelligence not worth having 979.9
without t., art is sheep without shepherd 53.25
**traditional:** good life impossible without t. forms 979.13
**traditions:** hardened round us is a wrappage of t. 979.4
**traffic:** only way to solve t. problems 63.10
**tragedies:** not t. that kill us, it's the messes 86.10
t.: to lose heart's desire, to gain it 236.39
there are two t., not getting what one wants, and getting it 839.6
**tragedy:** essence of dramatic t. not unhappiness 980.15
every roof, when lifted, reveals t. 420.10
forget your personal t. 939.16
I am my own comedy and t. 868.11
I like a man who likes to see a fine barn as well as a good t. 714.1
in t. every moment is eternity 980.7
in t. great men are more truly great than in history 980.11
in t., violent passions must speak 980.5
life is t.: we are spectators, actors 536.123
men play at t. because don't believe in reality of t. actually staged in world 980.12
nature is but theater of t. of man 616.53
only a great mind overthrown yields t. 980.3
show me a hero and I will write a t. 416.5
t.: an experience of hyperinvolvement 144.9
t., comedy, are simply questions of value 980.8
t. is restful: hope has no part in it 980.1
t.: man's struggle with stronger 980.6
t. of life is that man almost wins 327.3
t. of life is that men cease to love 549.10
t. of the age: men know so little of men 1001.6
to balance t., weigh it with tragic heart 980.4
world is a t. to those that feel 1060.33
writers of t. say they have insight 980.14
**tragic:** last act t. however happy the rest 218.99
t. situation exists when virtue does not triumph 980.13
t. writer must believe in man 980.9

we refuse to take our t. age tragically 980.10
**tragical:** why does man wish to be made sad by seeing t. things 980.2
**train:** t. up a child in the way he should go 981.1
there isn't a t. I wouldn't take 985.28
**training:** creative minds known to survive bad t. 198.13
man can seldom win fight against his t. 981.11
t. necessary for most experiences 207.10
t. which makes men happiest 277.68
**traitor:** t. stands in worse case of woe 77.5
**traitors:** better t. escape than have spirit of distrust 257.7
t. conspire, bust country, become heroes 986.4
treason pleases but t. are odious 986.1
**traits:** shut doors on t., they open windows, return 783.21
**tranquility:** back of t. lies conquered unhappiness 982.5
not finding t. within, don't go elsewhere 982.8
t. and occupation give happiness 407.56
t.! better name than all family of fame 982.3
**tranquilizers:** t. bring a packaged peace of mind 267.4
**transcendental:** future the only t. value 366.7
**transition:** in age of t. habitual dumb practice is passing, new complex of habit oncoming 115.38
period of t. always one of uncertainty 115.7
state of t.: man's most noble condition 983.10
**transitory:** golf course is the epitome of the t. 922.3
**translation:** art of t. lies in knowing own language 521.20
**transparent:** cleverest among the silent are the t. 162.15
none so t. as he who thinks he's deep 734.4
**transplanted:** trees often t. seldom prosper 985.12
**trap:** don't want cheese, want to get out of t. 107.5
**travel:** beauties of t. due to strange hours kept 985.41
do not t. before learning language 985.13
experience, t. an education in themselves 319.20
I t. not to go anywhere, but to go 985.37
man may t. many miles, never get ahead of himself 985.3
to t. happily, one must t. light 985.33
to t. hopefully better than to arrive 279.22
who pass their lives in foreign t. 985.35
**traveled:** I t. among unknown men 985.42
**traveler:** each t. should know what he has to see 985.22
heaviest baggage for a t. is empty purse 985.17
t. must come from somewhere 985.34
t. went in search of people, adventure 985.7
t. without knowledge is bird without wings 985.32
**travelers:** home better place, but t. must be content 985.36
t., like poets, are mostly an angry race 985.8
**traveling:** age is a bad t. companion 646.28
busyness, t. to and from 10.2
in t., carry knowledge to bring it home 985.26
t. ass will not come home a horse 985.21
t. is a fool's paradise 985.14
t. is to regulate imagination by reality 985.27
t. makes men wiser but less happy 985.25
**travels:** he that t. much knows much 985.20
man who t. alone can start today 908.50
one either commits suicide or t. 30.3
one t. more usefully alone 985.24
**treason:** fear of doing right is t. in time of danger 816.1
if t. prosper, none dare call it t. 986.2
t. in our time is a proof of genius 986.3
t. only waits for sufficient temptation 188.7
t. pleases but traitors are odious 986.1
**treasure:** thou shalt have t. in heaven 677.4
where your t. is, your heart will be 740.3
**treaties:** only t. that ought to count are those which would settle ulterior motives 987.7
t. last while they last 987.1
t. observed if in harmony with interests 987.5
**treaty:** hand that signed t. bred a fever 987.6
**tree:** as the twig is bent the t.'s inclined 981.9
dead t. falls, woodpeckers share in death 398.13
emancipation from soil: no freedom for t. 361.51
saw can fell t. of a thousand years 988.6
single t. like a dancing tongue of flame 988.2
t. casts shade even upon woodcutter 453.3
though t. grow high, falling leaves return to the root 399.46
you can't be suspicious of a t. 616.10
**trees:** how many t. gave lives that today's scandal should reach a million readers 623.29
men are like t.: each puts forth own leaf 198.3
no town can fail of beauty with t. 988.1
t.: earth's effort to speak to heaven 988.5
t. often transplanted seldom prosper 985.12
who plants t. loves others 988.3
**trembling:** what is this t. sensation 480.1
**trial:** t. not fair where affection judges 515.17
truth fears no t. 991.43
**trials:** pleasurable to watch great t. of another 213.14
**tribulation:** no man without some manner of t. 17.61
**trick:** we are bitter against those who t. us 221.11

when in doubt, win the t. 170.11
**tricks:** fox knows many t. 197.7
**tries:** no one knows what he can do till he t. 279.20
**trifle:** mere t. consoles us, distresses us 989.12
**trifles:** cities degrade us by magnifying t. 129.14
moments make the year, and t. life 989.17
sensibility of man to t. 876.8
she who t. with all is less likely to fall 348.2
t. make perfection, which is no trifle 677.12
t. make the sum of human things 989.9
t. make up happiness, misery of life 989.15
unbelief shown by condemnation of t. 997.9
**trip:** enjoy European t. after unpacking 985.2
rather t. with feet than with tongue 86.12
**triumph:** as easy to be enervated by t. as defeat 938.24
hour of t. is what brings the void 839.3
in ourselves are t. and defeat 852.19
t. cannot help being cruel 170.13
to win without risk is to t. without glory 938.6
**trivial:** comfortable people worry over t. things 989.8
t. things must be described grandly 935.13
to the mean eye all things are t. 686.2
what mighty contests rise from t. things 989.13
**Trojans:** distant T. never injured me 658.10
**trophies:** behold thy t. within thee, not without 862.1
**trouble:** a frog will kick an elephant in t. 17.30
bringing friends to t. is hard grief 17.59
comforting in time of t. when not our t. 17.39
education lifts t. to higher plane 277.28
friends show love in times of t. 363.47
if you must make t., make the sort expected 168.2
in t. best to seek out relative 789.2
in time of t. avert not face from hope 425.14
man born unto t., as sparks fly upward 17.7
man uses his brains to get into t. 17.38
painful to know you caused own t. 17.58
people could survive natural t. 17.42
pleasures, t., greatest in anticipation 316.7
t. amiably greeted soon goes away 17.64
t. has no connection with discouragement 251.2
time is test of t., but not remedy 971.13
**troubles:** each has as much as he can bear in his t. 141.6
light t. speak; weighty are struck dumb 17.52
man fond of counting t., not joys 249.4
night brings our t. to the light 626.11
one man's news is another man's t. 622.1
our t. arise often from fancy 43.10
t. half seen do torture all the more 302.4
t. hurt most when self-inflicted 866.10
t. of rich are t. money can't cure 17.43
**troublesome:** nothing t. that we do willingly 1050.6
**true:** be t.: this is highest maxim of art, life 489.1
dare to be t.; nothing can need a lie 993.8
every thing to be t. must become a religion 991.145
hair perhaps divides the false and t. 992.15
morally bad not to care if thing t. 991.130
no man worth having is t. to his wife 470.14
the brilliant passes; the t. endures 991.50
the people do not like the t. 675.6
thing isn't t. because a man dies for it 561.18
to thine own self be t. 489.23
where is man who has strength to be t. 655.3
**trumpet:** t. does not more stun than whisper teases 916.35
you must blow your own t. 87.3
**trust:** Americans ruled by the Boss, the T. 34.26
bound to forgive enemy, not t. him 286.13
contagion of t. makes t. 990.6
everything has to be taken on t. 991.124
evidence of t. begets t. 781.5
joy looks for t. clear in friends' eyes 990.7
love all, t. a few 990.11
put no t. in money, but money in t. 68.1
t. character more than an oath 628.8
t. in God, but tie your camel 257.14
t. ivrybody—but cut th' ca-ards 990.1
t. men and they will be true to you 990.3
t. not man without a conscience in everything 171.30
t. thyself, no other shall betray thee 990.4
vice to t. all, or to t. none 990.10
what can we t. in this uncertain life 480.4
who doesn't t. himself can't t. anyone 990.9
**truth:** add venom to a half t. and you have an absolute t. 991.58
adversity is the first path to t. 17.15
all men should learn to hear t. 991.66
all necessary t. is its own evidence 991.34
all t. is not to be told at all times 993.4
all t. wants is liberty of appearing 991.95
all your life you live so close to t. 991.123
any man's t. is what makes him a man 991.107
apt to shut eyes against painful t. 425.17
art not propaganda but a form of t. 53.67
at heart, we are always on side of t. 649.6
atom of t. represents some man's agony 991.85
beauty is t., t. beauty 70.24
between whom there is t. there is love 991.132
bigotry holds t. with grip that kills it 262.16
blessed is he whose fame does not outshine his t. 330.47
brush curtails t. in deference to the canvas which is narrow 659.12
call t. false if not accompanied by laugh 407.82

convictions worse enemies of t. than lies 76.14
death cancels everything but t. 218.4
deep t. is imageless 991.119
defeat is school in which t. grows strong 225.1
dignity of t. is lost with much protesting 991.67
disputant no more cares for t. than sportsman for the hare 51.21
don't wear best trousers to battle for t. 813.25
doubt is the vestibule of temple of t. 897.3
dreamer can know no t. but by awaking 687.20
earnest men have no time to patch t. 111.8
eliminate the impossible, the t. remains 991.28
enemies nearer t. in judging us than we 286.17
enemy of t. is often not lie but myth 610.2
error is the rule; t., accident of error 297.15
error states current t. is incomplete 297.32
every t. has two sides; look at both 991.2
everything believed is an image of t. 76.2
expect the unexpected, or never find t. 991.56
few nudities so objectionable as naked t. 993.19
friendship may step in advance of t. 363.72
God offers choice between t. and repose 991.36
great is t. and strongest of all 991.3
great is t., greater is silence about t. 739.4
greater amount of t. spoken, not written 991.102
half a t. is better than no politics 705.16
he who lies does not believe the t. 993.5
highest compact with our fellow is for t. 993.2
historian must not try to know t. 417.3
hope is a great falsifier of t. 425.13
I can know only what t. is for me today 723.28
I speak t. not as I would, but as I dare 993.14
I used to say t. majority vote of nation that could lick all others 991.62
iconoclasm—the only way to get at t. 439.3
idea is a putting t. in checkmate 441.28
idea of t. invincible to scepticism 991.96
if door shut to all errors, t. shut out 297.35
if you tell the t. you don't have to remember anything 993.24
in argument, t. always prevails finally 705.40
in idleness and dreams, t. comes to top 687.23
in imagination t. finds existence 448.8
in practice error and t. do not consort 9.13
in silence, man's t. strikes root 891.30
in wine there is t. 266.50
inability to lie is far from love of t. 993.17
intelligence is silence; t. invisible 891.27
it ain't so that t. is mighty, will prevail 991.135
it is not enough to possess a t. 991.81
it is wrong to put friendship before t. 991.4
journalism realizes that t. is a fluid 623.17
justice is t. in action 515.27
lawyer's t. is not t. but consistency 525.65
let us economize on t. 993.22
life is paradox: each t. has counterpart 661.3
long attention to single aspect of t. leads to distortion of t. 992.5
love of t. has reward in heaven, on earth 991.91
lying is acknowledgment of force of t. 329.22
malice often takes the garb of t. 557.6
man cannot make t. falsehood 329.4
man has right perception of a t. only if willing to be its martyr 991.37
man is ready to distort t. intentionally 778.10
man lives not by t. but by make-believe 447.12
man never yet harmed by t. 991.82
man's passion for t. is such he welcomes the bitterest of all postulates 991.80
men maintain errors from zeal for t. 297.34
men speak t. as they understand it 991.71
men take little trouble in search for t. 991.134
meridian decides the t. 515.35
modern age is sad: looks for t. in everything and finds it 296.12
new aspects of t. can seldom be fitted into creeds that are changeless 991.23
no error is such as pursuit of absolute t. 297.6
no final t. in ethics 598.24
no more sovereign eloquence than t. in indignation 281.4
no mortal can seize t. in its wholeness 991.112
no t. is proved by argument 991.110
nonsense may tomorrow be demonstrated t. 991.142
not every t. is better for showing face 360.12
nothing gives rest but search for t. 805.4
nothing makes a man as mad as the t. 991.104
nothing so powerful as t.—nor so strange 991.140
nowadays t. is the greatest news 622.3
nowadays t. wins hatred 991.131
old custom without t. is but old error 210.11
on a huge hill, cragged and steep, t. stands 991.27
one part of t. sets while another rises 649.18
one t. a man does not wish told 162.10
one t. discovered is better than all fluency 991.54
only the generous ready for t. impromptu 991.89
outspoken: easy if not waiting to speak t. 360.13
peace-mingling falsehood preferable to mischievous t. 992.17
perception of t. is detection of analogy 35.4

political t. is libel; religious t., blasphemy 991.53
pure t., gold, are unfit for circulation 991.19
pursuit of t. is gratifying 991.59
pushing a t. far, you meet a counter-t. 991.6
rather than love, money, fame, give me t. 991.133
read the t. in world's fair page 991.10
rumor don't stay put as long as t. 827.1
say not I have found the t., only a t. 991.46
simple t. his utmost skill 489.31
skepticism is the first step toward t. 897.4
small t. has words that are clear; great t. has great silence 991.127
so good is t., t. never hurts the teller 991.9
some love t. so much that they live in fear lest she catch cold on over-exposure 991.12
sooner hate me for t. than adore for lies 993.1
soul is unwillingly deprived of t. 991.39
speak the t. unless you're a good liar 993.10
stand for t. and 'tis enough 991.69
sting of a reproach is its t. 797.6
t. a passion which spares nothing 991.15
t., a totality sacrificed by history 417.31
t. and falsehood be near twins 992.4
t. and oil always come to the surface 991.121
t.: as difficult to lay hold upon as air 992.10
t. can stand by itself 992.9
t. cannot be erased; neither can lies 992.7
t. cannot be escaped within or without 991.146
t. cannot be told in a few words 991.94
t. comes with final word; and final word gives birth to its next 991.128
t.: compost in which beauty may germinate 70.36
t., crushed to earth, shall rise again 297.4
t. disappears with the telling of it 991.32
t. does less good than imitations do harm 992.11
t. does not always triumph over persecution 991.87
t. does not lie beyond humanity 991.74
t. exists; only lies are invented 992.1
t. fears no trial 991.43
t. for t.'s sake! this is inhuman 991.137
t. forever on scaffold, wrong on throne 991.79
t. gains more by errors of one who thinks than by true opinions of those who do not 992.12
t. has a handsome countenance 991.45
t. has advantage of being rediscovered 991.86
t. has become an angle, point of view 991.40
t. has visible signs 991.97
t. hath a quiet breast 991.117
t. hurts those who touch it 991.72
t. in small quantities calms men 991.73
t. is a dream unless my dream is true 991.114
t. is a flower that makes others wither 991.42
t. is a matter of direct apprehension 991.31
t. is a torch which gleams in the fog 991.55
t. is a value because it is true 991.83
t. is accompanied by its facsimile error 992.14
t. is always first point of courtesy 194.4
t. is always the strongest argument 991.120
t. is balance, but unbalance not a lie 992.18
t. is child of time 991.41
t. is common stock 967.1
t. is cruel, but frees those who love it 991.111
t. is good dog, but do not bark at error 297.10
t. is her dress finds facts too tight 991.126
t. is idea arising from human intercourse 991.26
t. is man's proper good 991.68
t. is more of a stranger than fiction 991.136
t. is no road to fortune 991.106
t. is not eloquent except unspoken 991.113
t. is not hard to kill 992.19
t. is not less so for being new 991.77
t. is not so threadbare as speech 991.139
t. is often unpopular 326.18
t. is on the march; nothing can stop it 991.147
t. is on the side of the oppressed today 995.22
t. is one and immutable 991.64
t. is one forever absolute 649.25
t. is only a horse for Christianity 123.6
t. is only that which is taken to be true 991.124
t. is rarely pure and never simple 991.144
t. is river split into arms that reunite 991.22
t. is t. to the end of reck'ning 991.118
t. is that which is ineluctable 991.108
t. is the god of the free man 992.6
t. is thousand truths which grow and change 991.76
t. is tough, won't break like a bubble 991.60
t. is what man persuades man to believe 991.88
t. is what most contradicts itself 991.30
t. is what stands the test of experience 991.33
t. lags last, limping on arm of time 991.52
t. lies within little, certain compass 297.30
t. lives on in the midst of deception 991.115
t. looks tawdry when overdressed 991.125
t. may come from the devil's mouth 991.44
t. must dazzle gradually or every man be blind 991.24
t. never damages a cause that is just 109.11
t. no longer t. if polemically said 991.35
t. opposing neither profit nor pleasure is welcome 991.57
t. outlasts the sun 991.25
t. shall make you free 991.7
t. sits upon the lips of dying men 991.5
t. suffers more from defenders than foes 991.100
t., to be loved, needs only be seen 991.29
t. told with bad intent beats all lies 557.1
t. will bear exposure as well as beauty 991.18
test of t.: reference to present or future majority in favor of our view 991.61

thank God that t. lies outside of books 91.7
their worst enemy: who tells them the t. 993.18
there are times when t. is unseasonable 972.4
there is no absolute unchangeable t. 991.13
they all want the t.—a t. that is 991.101
they who know the t. are not equal to those who love it 991.20
time trieth t. 991.38
time's glory is to bring t. to light 971.52
'tis better to enjoy t. with peace than to hazard her on a battle 991.8
to be believed, make t. unbelievable 993.15
to be modest in speaking t. is hypocrisy 993.6
to be thought a liar, always tell the t. 993.21
to convey misinformation tell the t. 993.23
to get into the t. is a mystic act 991.17
to know t. and not conform to it is crime 991.84
to love t. for t.'s sake is part of perfection 991.78
to love the t. is to refuse to let oneself be saddened by it 991.48
to show error is not to give t. 297.23
too much t. is uncouth 991.1
torch of t. shows much we cannot see 991.65
traffic-cop morality, rabbit-test t. 843.22
we admit no t. other than the expedient 991.47
we desire t., find uncertainty 364.3
we know t. by reason and by the heart 991.98
we may mellow t. to make it humane 993.13
we perceive image of t., possess a lie 992.16
what imagination seizes as beauty is t. 991.70
what kind of t. has mountains for boundary 992.13
whatever profits man is t. 558.33
whatever satisfies the soul is t. 991.143
when complex things are communicated to masses of people, t. suffers distortion 563.7
when I can look life in the eyes, it will have given me t. in exchange for youth 567.20
when money speaks, t. keeps silent 596.50
where all is dream, t. is nothing 687.13
while you live, tell t. and shame devil 993.20
who doesn't tell t. is liar's accomplice 991.99
who speaks t. stabs falsehood to heart 993.12
who wishes to teach t. should suggest it 959.22
why do we not hear the t. 991.103
why is betrayal the only t. that sticks 77.3
will to t. is longing for a stable world 991.93
would that I could discover t. as easily as I can uncover falsehood 992.3
young girls are chatelaines of t. 383.3
**truth's:** beauty: t. smile beholding her own face 70.51
better one bite, at forty, of t. rind 567.11
t. fountains are clear—t. streams, muddy 991.14
t. open to all, claims not all staked 991.116
t. prosperity lies in ear of the hearer 991.11
**truthful:** many would be more t. 916.30
only a t. man can lie to any purpose 992.2
**truths:** all great t. begin as blasphemies 504.4
change due to t. in and out of favor 115.17
ever-changing t. of our own experience 991.141
faith embraces contradictory t. 328.34
first t. those we discover last 991.16
greatest t. are the simplest 892.5
irrationally held t. may be more harmful than reasoned errors 992.8
man never rises to great t. without enthusiasm 291.8
many eyes means many t. and thus no truth 991.92
one falsehood spoils a thousand t. 329.2
ready-made t. are drugs 991.110
simplest schoolboy knows t. for which Archimedes would have given his life 843.29
t. begin as heresies, end as superstitions 991.63
t. may clash without contradicting 991.109
t. of life are not discovered by us 991.49
t. of past are clichés of present 991.105
t. that are kept silent become poisonous 993.16
t. which concern us most can only be half spoken 991.51
to bear t. with calm is sovereignty 159.2
universal t. are those gross enough to be 991.138
**try:** t. first thyself, then call in God 279.6
to t. may be to die 464.7
we are more ready to t. the untried when what we do is inconsequential 477.5
**trying:** no failure except in no longer t. 327.13
**tub:** ever t. must stand on its own bottom 873.8
**tune:** he who pays the piper may call the t. 673.3
I to the t. dance that is played 12.11
**turkey:** t. bur-rd's rale cause iv Thanksgivin' 418.3
**turn:** my t. today may be thine tomorrow 32.1
who doth a good t. looketh for a good t. 881.4
**turning:** it is a long lane that has no t. 116.2
**turtle:** t. lives 'twixt plated decks 796.4
**tutor:** easier for t. to command than teach 959.18
**twentieth:** t. century afflicted by power failure 994.1
t.-century problem: color-line 769.5
t.-century problem: man is dead 216.3
**twenty:** at t. man's a peacock; at eighty, nothing 537.6
**twice:** everything done t. would be done better 677.11

**twig:** as the t. is bent the tree's inclined 981.9
**twilight:** first hour of spring t. dreadful to some 848.8
**two:** between t. stools one sits on ground 463.1
don't hear one and judge t. 513.4
if t. make one song, muse fans wrath 154.4
to do t. things at once is to do neither 579.12
when t. do same thing, it is not the same 467.18
where t., one cannot be wretched, other not 1004.9
**tyrannical:** nation under t. regime can't be absolved of faults due to regime's guilt 995.8
**tyrannies:** most insupportable of t. is that of inferiors 995.24
of all t., worst persecutes the mind 995.10
**tyranny:** death softer thing by far than t. 995.2
defiance of law is road to t. 525.46
face of t. is always mild at first 995.27
he that holds t. does not trust friends 995.1
if men are strong, t. will bankrupt itself making shackles for them 995.4
long tenure of office begets t. 755.2
most awful t. is of the proximate Utopia 1018.1
remedy in human nature against t. 995.16
republican despotism is fertile in t. 231.35
revolutions never lighten burden of t. 813.39
t. is always better organized than freedom 534.32
t. would not exist if freedom not abused 534.45
unity without plurality is t. 1009.10
wherever law ends, t. begins 525.51
**tyrant:** any excuse will serve a t. 995.3
no t. like intemperance 492.4
of all wild beasts, preserve me from t. 346.13
t. claims freedom to kill freedom and yet to keep it for himself 995.32
**tyrants:** flight is lawful when one flies from t. 298.10
necessity is the argument of t. 617.12
people who are masters in their own house are never t. 61.7
resistance to t. is obedience to God 995.15
t. are but the spawn of ignorance 995.20
t. perish from folly, not tyranny 995.18

# U

**ugliness:** how ugly, seen near beauty's pride, is u. 351.7
secret of u. is in being uninteresting 996.2
**ugly:** by what logic do we call a toad u. 996.1
in u. world, rich can buy only ugliness 1041.58
it is laudable fortitude to dare to be u. 996.3
justice is reason for anything u. 515.51
many people live in u. wastelands 292.3
u. deeds are taught by u. deeds 224.36
wise man leaves in dark everything u. 302.2
**umpire:** u. must be justice, acrobat, Job, Buddha 922.10
**unbelief:** all we gain by our u. is doubt diversified by faith 997.4
fearful u. is u. in yourself 861.1
u. shown by condemnation of trifles 997.9
**unbeliever:** founders of religions didn't include u. 790.27
**unbiased:** u. opinion is absolutely valueless 649.36
**uncertain:** we are self-u. creatures 790.80
**uncertainty:** it is u. that lends life fascination 452.8
u. and expectation are the joys of life 850.2
u. evil till reality makes us regret it 998.6
u. fruitful if with a wish to understand 998.8
we desire truth, find u. 364.3
we live between clouds of forgetting, u. 723.11
we sail within a vast sphere, ever drifting in u. 998.9
**unchangeable:** one u. certainty is nothing is certain or u. 113.8
**Uncle Sam:** U. S. has no conscience 598.32
**Uncle Tom:** Aunt Jemima and U. T. are dead 83.2
**uncomfortable:** those u. in themselves are disagreeable to others 855.2
**uncommitted:** as long as possible live free and u. 361.52
**unconfessable:** every man knows what u. things pass within the secrecy of his own heart 403.15
**unconscious:** our u. is a vast factory going night, day 999.4
**unconventionality:** u. not difficult if convention of your set 89.5
**uncultivated:** u. minds are not full of wild flowers 445.30
**undeceive:** I have no tears for happenings that u. 319.15
**underground:** enemy becomes friend once he's u. 286.11
**understand:** dignity not in what we do, but u. 244.5
God let me contend with those who u. me 1001.9
if you don't u. a man you can't crush him; if you do u. him, you probably won't 1001.3
in what we really u., we reason little 1000.7
it is the acme of life to u. life 536.104
it takes a long time to u. nothing 1000.4
none can u. unless he respects the free nature of others 1001.12
people may be made to follow, but not u. 995.9
thirst to know and u. is excellent 529.21

to be surprised, to wonder: to begin to u. 1056.3
to u. is to forgive, even oneself 1001.2
to u. oneself: classic form of consolation 752.15
we are certain about things we do not u. 113.5
we do not u. what we are, unless we know what we ought to be 868.9
you give yourself to those who least u. 166.3
**understanding:** between birth and death, we may touch u. 1000.5
compassionate u. buys long peace 692.22
discourse is index of a man's u. 75.1
experience and u. are our god-figures 207.18
few things measured with tape of u. 583.21
greatest success of life is u. between sincere people 185.9
greatness has no lustre for those in search of u. 1000.13
heart has such influence over u. 282.9
in length of days is u. 646.10
much learning does not teach u. 277.38
passions raise sedition against the u. 668.14
perfect u. almost extinguishes pleasure 1000.9
plant and animal confound the u. 616.48
pleasure, fortune not relished without u. 698.22
shy fruit of pure science is u. 843.1
time increases u. for the aging 1000.14
u. everything makes a person tolerant 945.10
u. is the beginning of approving 1000.6
u. needs is half job of meeting them 618.6
u. takes no notice of itself 583.10
with all thy getting, get u. 1053.8
**understandings:** all are led more by hearts than by u. 282.10
flatter beautiful women for u. 1055.21
men are admitted to Heaven for cultivating u. 491.2
**understands:** who u. much displays greater simplicity 1000.2
wise man hears one word, u. two 1053.72
**understood:** each supposes himself not fully u. 870.3
every man speaks and writes to be u. 132.3
**undertaker:** may even the u. be sorry when we die 218.132
no man is a hero to his u. 331.5
**undertakers:** dignity of death or u. 101.7
**undertakings:** joint u. must benefit both sides 187.2
**undervalued:** who is u. by himself is justly u. by others 861.4
**underwear:** from cradle to coffin, u. comes first 265.2
**underworld:** it takes all sorts of people to make an u. 201.12
**undoing:** glittering hope calls many to u. 1041.24
**uneasy:** u. lies the head that wears a crown 825.25
we are u. with an affectionate man 21.2
**unenvied:** he who goes u. shall not be admired 293.2
**unequal:** because men are u. they need to be brothers 469.1
**unexamined:** u. life is not worth living 752.17
**unexpected:** expect the u., or never find truth 991.56
**unfair:** nothing so u. as man without experience 319.61
**unfavorable:** to create an u. impression, things need not be true, only said 392.6
**unfinished:** u. is nothing 283.1
**unforeseen:** man fears not death but the u. 218.104
**unfortunate:** nobody chooses already u. for friendship 546.5
u. need people who will be kind to them 517.4
**ungracious:** u. man is like story told at wrong time 824.1
**ungrateful:** belly is u. 435.9
better u. men than miss chance to do good 430.10
far fewer u. men than we believe 473.7
people are seldom u. if we are beneficial 397.8
u. son is a wart on his father's face 909.1
**unhappiness:** artists are expected to cultivate u. 1004.8
back of tranquility lies conquered u. 982.5
bewilderment the cause of much u. 148.3
happiness is to know source of u. 752.5
heart is free of grief over stranger's u. 355.5
is anyone in world safe from u. 1004.35
man can only endure certain degree of u. 1004.15
man's happiness is built on another's u. 407.110
own happiness vs. the u. of others 557.15
since u. excites interest, many feign u. 1004.29
u. isn't like leprosy; it is man's doing 712.8
u. makes people look stupid 1004.11
u.: not being able to sit quietly 1004.24
u. remembering happiness intolerable 115.15
volatile spirits prefer u. 560.102
**unhappy:** couple u. not merely from limited means 560.18
how much more u. a man might be than he is 1004.1
how u. is he who cannot forgive himself 403.16
I look at what I have not and think myself u. 236.35
I only listen to Muse when I am u. 1062.98
in u. world, rich buy only unhappiness 1041.58

men take pains to render themselves u. 1004.12
no one more u. than superannuated idol 223.1
that some are u. is better than none happy 295.14
u. is the man who doesn't consider himself supremely blest 407.98
u. man deprived of what he did not have 1004.22
who would recognize the u. if grief had no language 1045.6
world never without reason to hate the u. 1004.17
**uniform:** good u. must work its way with the women 265.3
man becomes the creature of his u. 265.13
**uniformity:** complete u. makes longest life short 971.33
every central government worships u. 393.62
freedom never relied on u. of pinion 250.7
**unimportant:** hard for man to confess sum of life u. 1005.3
**unintelligent:** to serve u. man like crying in wilderness 934.17
**unintentional:** immoralists see value of action in u. 224.26
**uninteresting:** secret of ugliness is in being u. 996.2
**union:** the U. is my country 924.1
we are not a nation, but a u. 34.8
**unionism:** u. uses its power to safeguard bad work 1006.5
**unions:** free nation has independent labor u. 1006.6
if capitalism the right of a few to make all decisions, u. threaten capitalism 106.3
trade-u. have done more for humanity 1006.2
**unique:** democratic disease reduces everything u. 295.16
every man represents the u. 1007.4
you will be u. to me and I to you 548.194
**uniqueness:** my sense of my own u. 467.1
**unite:** not vain the weakest if they u. 1009.6
only fear and interest u. men 1009.9
**United Nations:** only security of the weak is in U.N. 1008.1
our instrument, our hope, is the U.N. 1008.2
U.N. mirrors our world, warts and all 1008.3
**United States:** cannot accuse U.S. of undue amount of know-what 765.12
more die in U.S. of much food than of little 637.5
**unity:** how pleasant for brethren to dwell in u. 1009.2
in necessary things, u. 118.1
plurality without u. is confusion 1009.10
u. without plurality is tyranny 1009.10
**universal:** act only on maxim you can will to be u. law 9.31
I seek the u., that must be the best 181.3
u. feeling cannot be disregarded 756.13
**universe:** justice is the last concern of u. 515.29
the u. does not jest with us 1010.2
u. changed by inspiring people 783.30
u. is but a kaleidoscope turning in the mind 1010.1
u. is not hostile but simply indifferent 1010.6
**university:** best u. for man of ideas: gauntlet of mob 591.1
function of u.: to be organ of adjustment between real life, knowledge of life 277.14
if you feel both feet are on ground, u. has failed you 277.33
lade man to u., ye can't make him think 277.18
true u. is a collection of books 535.1
**unjust:** he who is u. in little is u. in much 489.3
just and u. things sanctioned by custom 210.28
nothing is absolutely u. 475.8
we know when we're being u., despicable 832.1
**unkind:** all the world appears u. 43.14
don't care how u. things people say about me 203.22
**unknowable:** we cease belief in u., but there it sits 1012.8
**unknown:** behind the dim u. standeth G. 1012.7
only the u. frightens men 1012.12
u. always passes for marvellous 1012.13
whoever starts toward the u. must consent to venture alone 1012.5
**unlike:** meeting people u. oneself confirms one's idea that one is unique 467.2
**unlucky:** u. person runs into another's accidents 358.30
**unnatural:** nothing u. that is not physically impossible 885.32
that a thing is u. does not make it blamable 431.16
**unpleasant:** seek for the salutary in the u. 388.18
**unprivileged:** concessions of the privileged to the u. 15.7
**unpublished:** u. manuscript is like an unconfessed sin 1062.67
**unreachable:** hills: earth's gesture of despair for u. 602.3
**unreason:** philosophy may describe u., not refute it 1013.2
**unreasonable:** all progress depends on the u. man 735.23
**unreservedly:** if we spoke u. there would be less sorrow 360.1
**unrest:** u. of spirit is a mark of life 806.4
**unrighteous:** u. are never really fortunate 1048.9
**unsaid:** u. things cause of much unhappiness 148.3

unseen: full many a flower is born to blush u. 641.4
unsettled: is not man the most u. of all creatures 480.1
there is hope for men when they are u. 480.3
unstable: men are too u. to be just 515.7
unthinkable: we must dare to think u. things 968.16
untruth: u. unacceptable to mind of man 640.1
unusual: u. is rare, except in literature 542.1
unwelcomed: short days pass u. one by one 848.10
unwilling: nothing is easy to the u. 243.6
up: I walk firmer u. hill than down 243.11
no longer clear which way is u. 133.3
we may stop ourselves when going u., never when coming down 327.20
when fountain has gone u., it comes down 358.33
when man is u., people want to down him 938.17
upbraids: the man who acts least, u. the most 797.7
uphill: does road wind u. all the way 536.98
uplifted: go to funeral, not church, to be u. 365.9
uplifting: in u. get underneath 783.1
upstart: u. is sparrow eager to be betrothed to a hornbill 33.22
upstream: game fish swims u., sensible fish down 527.7
urban: u. man is an uprooted tree 129.25
urn: well-wrought u. becomes great ashes 101.3
usage: English u. more than education—it's luck 396.7
use: if men u. you for your own purposes, they will u. you for theirs 321.1
it's a misfortune to be of u. to nobody 1016.2
not possession but u. is riches 1041.27
rust wastes more than u. 444.6
thought makes every thing fit for u. 968.13
u. almost can change the stamp of nature 859.6
useful: be u. according to powers, not desires 269.1
to know nothing about life, be u. 1016.10
u. knowledge makes a wise man 520.23
we often despise what is most u. 1016.1
whatever is u. must become useless 1016.5
usefulness: men lose u. when they lose direction, begin to bend 765.7
success can corrupt; u. can only exalt 1016.6
useless: to be employed in u. things is to be idle 1017.3
to condemn spontaneous acts because u. 697.9
whatever is useful must become u. 1016.5
utility: u. is the great idol of the age 1016.7
u. plus beauty is the spider's web 1016.9
Utopia: acre in Middlesex better than realm in U. 740.15
most awful tyranny is of the proximate U. 1018.1
"yes" is the password to u. 502.3
uttered: impossible to recall what has been u. 916.48
what is u. is finished and done with 916.40

# V

vacation: ant doesn't know enough to take a v. 1058.16
vacuum: v. better than some of what replaces it 616.78
vain: v. man may imagine himself pleasing, in reality is a nuisance 1020.17
v. man pleased with effect on others 163.3
vainglory: it is not v. for man and his glass to confer 1020.16
valiant: luck is the prerogative of v. souls 358.29
not enough for v. to wield broadsword, they must know against whom 90.13
the v. never taste of death but once 196.12
valor: between cowardice and despair v. is born 192.10
hidden v. is as bad as cowardice 192.24
love of fame, fear of disgrace are often at the root of the v. men esteem 192.21
perfect v. consists in doing without witnesses what we would do before everyone 192.23
the better part of v. is discretion 749.32
v. half way between rashness and cowheartedness 192.8
v. is a gift 192.34
v. is stability of courage and soul 192.26
valuable: decide how we're v. not how v. we are 1019.7
nothing is intrinsically v. 1019.1
people become v. for their inaccessibility 1019.6
value: all we v. we shall sometime rend 239.4
dearness gives everything its v. 1019.13
future the only transcendental v. 366.7
Jews generally give v. 510.5
life has v. when it has valuable object 536.46
measure v. of man only by other men 1019.12
no such thing as absolute v. 1019.20
too many creatures estimate own v. by amount of irritation caused others 506.5
v. of ourselves is v. of our melancholy 1004.21
with each v. born, life takes on new meaning 1019.10
valued: each entitled to be v. by best moment 513.3
that which cost little is less v. 1019.4
values: hatred leads to extinction of v. 410.17
what is false in science of facts may be true in science of v. 1019.17

**vanity**: every author keeps an outrageous v. 1062.97
human v. is vulnerable yet unconquerable 1020.14
man sacrifices his purse to his v. 1020.20
one may attribute extreme actions to v. 224.25
others' v. is insufferable; wounds our own 1020.11
our touches of v. betray us 1020.6
passions leave us at rest, v. agitates us 1020.12
people slander more from v. than malice 898.8
pompous funeral informs world that v. has survived body 365.3
pride that dines on v. sups on contempt 727.11
static v. puts its faith in what it has 727.2
there are no grades of v. 1020.19
those who prosper take on airs of v. 744.1
true power, politeness, are above v. 713.55
v. carries more weight than self-interest 382.17
v. is motive-power that moves humanity 1020.10
v. plays lurid tricks with memory 668.5
v. wants what we do best considered hard 1.14
virtue brings honour, and honour, v. 1025.25
we crave support in v. and religion 1020.15
who denies own v. is avoiding self-hate 1020.13
woman's v. makes object of choice her idol 1055.66
**vanquished**: one safety v. have: to hope for none 225.5
**variance**: language sets men at v. 250.12
**variety**: no pleasure endures unseasoned by v. 698.31
**vassalage**: man reduced to v. by largesse 430.30
**vegetarian**: moral powers of v. exhibit ferocity 333.15
**vegetarians**: I have known meat eaters more non-violent than v. 272.12
v. look enough like their food to be classed as cannybals 1021.1
**veil**: many is the gracious form covered with a v. 45.18
**venerable**: broad hat is not always on v. head 136.5
**venerating**: man is a v. animal 1061.4
**vengeance**: just v. does not call for punishment 811.9
**Venice**: V. like eating box of chocolate liqueurs 1022.1
**venom**: malice swallows great part of own v. 557.14
**ventriloquy**: through transcendental v. men believe that which was said on earth came from heaven 810.2
**venturously**: if didn't live v., never be depressed 16.9
**Venus**: V. favors the bold 348.8
V. yields to caresses, not compulsion 851.12
**veracity**: v. is the heart of morality 993.9
**verities**: eternal v. end if they bulk too big 991.90
**verse**: v. may find him who a sermon flies 702.48
v. will halt if the tongue's too true 702.7
who forgives the senior's ceaseless v. 702.8
who moulds his thought in v. employs materials vulgarized by everybody's use 702.49
**verses**: feeble v. sin against genius 702.107
God prefers bad v. recited with pure heart 1061.8
good v. are like impromptus made at leisure 702.57
v. kept in cabinet are like virgin 758.13
**veteran**: consult the v. instead of the politician 1035.69
**veterinarian**: v. is best doctor, can't ask what's wrong 261.16
**vicar's**: devil gets to belfry by v. skirts 305.15
**vice**: alliance of audacious v., turbulent virtue 813.13
army is a v. of our time 582.22
best virtue I have has some v. 1026.18
best way to attack v. is public ridicule 814.5
convention, rewards make v., virtue 1026.13
every v. has its excuse ready 1023.24
I never was so rapid in my virtue but my v. kept up with me 1026.25
it takes a v. to check a v. 1026.11
let your virtues spring up around one v. 1023.32
sanctity, genius, are as rebellious as v. 834.12
th' more ye see v. th' betther ye like it 1023.9
the danger, when v. becomes precedent 1023.16
there is a capacity of v. in us to make your blood creep 1026.6
to save men from v., warn against another v. 1023.31
v. assumes, exploits likeness to virtue 1026.12
v. assumes virtue's mark on outward parts 1023.28
v. function: to keep virtue within bounds 1023.5
v. goes long way to makin' life bearable 1023.10
v. has more martyrs than virtue 1026.4
v. is exaggeration of virtuous function 1023.11
v. is its own punishment 1026.9
v. knows she's ugly, so puts on mask 1023.13
v., like virtue, grows in small steps 1023.26
v. often rides in virtue's chariot 1023.14
v. seen too oft, we endure, pity, embrace 1023.22
v. to trust all, or to trust none 990.10

virtue and v. are siblings or neighbors 1026.20
virtue and v. emit a breath every moment 1026.7
virtue itself turns v., being misapplied 1026.22
what maintains one v. would bring up two children 1023.12
when all run into v., none seem to do so 1023.8
who doesn't hate v., doesn't love virtue 1026.21
who tries to abolish v., destroys virtue 1026.2

**vice-presidency:** v. isn't a crime; it's kind of disgrace 724.2

**vices:** absence of v. adds little to one's virtues 1026.16
all fashionable v. pass for virtues 438.21
cottages have same v. as courts 1023.6
courage not in those who won't look at own v. 858.1
everybody likes somebody else to get caught for v. practiced by themselves 1023.17
gods scourge us with our pleasant v. 1023.30
good to be without v., not temptations 964.1
great are capable of great v., virtues 399.14
he who hates v. hates men 1023.18
little v. of great must be accounted great 1023.25
man's virtues hold a torch to his v. 1026.5
many v. are only good qualities run wild 1023.15
men more easily governed through their v. than their virtues 1023.19
most v. may be committed very genteelly 1063.13
one can't shed light on v. he doesn't have 319.39
passions, when masters, become v. 668.22
search thy self for thy v. 1026.8
through tattered clothes small v. do appear 1023.29
v. are ingredients of virtues 1026.15
v. are their own punishment 1023.1
v. require moderate use, not abstinence 1023.4
v. we scoff at in others laugh at us within 1023.3
virtues proud if v. did not whip them 1026.10
we are loaded with wallets of v. 1023.20
we are more apt to catch v. than virtues 1023.7
we make a ladder of v., if trample them 1023.2
we tolerate v. with which we're familiar 1023.23
where minor v. are discouraged, major virtues are lacking 1026.1
who has no v. makes v. about his virtues 1026.26

**vicious:** preaching seldom reclaims the v. 718.13

**victories:** all v. breed hate 170.8
brave v. are never really won 536.128
genuine v. are those over ignorance 445.23
who can see any difference between our v. and defeats 225.2

**victorious:** who bears in his heart a cathedral to be built is v. 55.18

**victory:** better a lean peace than a fat v. 674.9
certain peace better than anticipated v. 674.21
dead men have no v. 170.6
do not push a v. too far 170.1
faith is necessary to v. 854.3
god of v. is one-handed 170.5
in v. even the cowardly like to boast 745.14
moral v. degrades both victor, vanquished 170.12
no pain in wound received in moment of v. 170.14
problems of v. are more agreeable than those of defeat, but no less difficult 170.3
struggle alone pleases us, not v. 279.18
v. at all costs, v. in spite of all terror 170.2
v. should be celebrated with funeral rite 1035.56
we seek not worldwide v. of one nation but worldwide v. of men 98.12
who returns good for evil wins v. 224.12
yield to friends and you win v. 170.16

**Vietnam:** monuments to V.: the dead, maimed, forlorn 1035.51

**view:** fatal illusion is settled point of v. 613.2

**views:** to hold same v. at forty as at twenty 176.4

**vigilance:** eternal v. is the price of liberty 534.9
price of eternal v. is indifference 226.12

**vigor:** pleasure, fortune not relished without v. 698.22

**vileness:** even hatred of v. distorts man's features 410.2

**village:** to be known and not know, vegetate in v. 129.9

**villain:** one may smile and be a v. 221.21
one rarely meets authentic v. in lifetime 1048.5
v. believes all ladies are women 965.23

**villain's:** I like not fair terms and a v. mind 221.20

**villainy:** one v. teaches men to be evil in all 1063.24

**vine:** v. bears grapes of pleasure, intoxication, and disgust 266.2

**vinegar:** v. in hand better than halvah to come 710.12

**vintners:** what do v. buy half so precious as stuff they sell 266.45

**violence:** Americans believe v. is monopoly of state 1024.3
forgive us when we deplore v. in our cities 129.38

God hates v. 1024.2
heterogeneous ideas yoked by v. 1024.7
in v., we forget who we are 1024.8
let house be safe from v. 239.10
mental v. injures only the person whose thoughts are violent 658.7
most regard v. against certain kinds of people as inherently legitimate 1024.4
perseverance is more prevailing than v. 679.8
the incommunicable is source of all v. 148.13
to-day v. is the rhetoric of the period 1024.11
unjust law is a species of v. 525.31
v. enmeshes him from whom it begins 1063.17
v. is essentially wordless 1024.10
v. is just where kindness is vain 1024.1

**violent:** it is better to be v. than put on the cloak of non-violence to cover impotence 1024.5

**violin:** when man is not disposed to music, no sound is more disagreeable than that of v. 607.47

**violins:** v. are lively, forward, importunate wits 608.4

**virgin:** most men desire a v. who is a whore 885.7

**virtue:** absolute v. kills as surely as absolute vice 1026.3
all v. is summed up in dealing justly 515.1
alliance of audacious vice and turbulent v. 813.13
alloy v., like gold, with more durable metal 1025.8
assume a v., if you have it not 210.27
best v. I have has some vice 1026.18
blushing is the color of v. 886.2
care more for reputation of wit than v. 1054.34
convention, rewards make vice, v. 1026.13
every man prefers v. 1025.32
evil tongues may blast a whole life of v. 898.5
existence of v. depends on its use 1025.12
fine words seldom associated with true v. 45.3
glory of wealth is fleeting; v., eternal 1025.50
good company, discourse, are sinews of v. 151.28
good opinion of fellow men is strongest motive to v. 1025.14
greatness: to perceive that v. is enough 1025.21
happiness must be intelligible consequence of v. 1025.37
happiness of man consists in v. 1025.1
he who seeks fame by practice of v. 330.49
highest v. is always against the law 1025.22
I cannot praise a cloistered v. 595.4
I never was so rapid in my v. but my vice kept up with me 1026.25
if no v., we would live in peace 1035.100
if v. can't shine bright but by conflict, can she subsist without vice 1026.17
if v. own reward, cannot be human quality 1025.56
impressed by rare things—why not by v. 1025.34
love v., she alone is free 1025.39
make not consequences of v. the ends of v. 1025.7
man's v. measured by his life 1025.47
measure man's v. by what he would do without laws, public opinion to control him 1025.28
men are flattered into v. 1026.24
modest v. gets along with contentment 1025.44
most men admire v. who follow her not 1025.40
of all pleasures, I know none comparable to that of feeling capable of v. 1025.31
once a woman parts with v. 851.2
philanthropy is almost the only v. appreciated 430.34
pride thyself on v., not parentage 37.11
privilege of v. to add faggot to scaffold of every condemned man 1025.42
public v. is foundation of republics 1025.2
seldom does v. rise from trunk to branch 1025.16
sins are the highway of our v. 893.23
some incapable of sciences, but not v. 1025.57
some never make whole coat of fabric of v. 1025.33
some rise by sin, some by v. fall 1026.23
successful and fortunate crime called v. 201.19
the order of things consents to v. 1025.20
the virtuous love v. in another 1025.24
there is a capacity of v. in us 1026.6
there may be guilt if too much v. 1025.48
to eye of enmity v. seems ugliest blemish 410.22
to have v. is distinction but a hard lot 1025.43
to lay to v. the weariness of old age 646.39
v. and vice emit a breath every moment 1026.7
v. and vice, evil and good, are siblings 1026.20
v. between men: commerce of good actions 1025.58
v. beyond reason makes the sage a fool 1025.30
v.: blind angel asking knowledge the way 1025.38
v. brings honour, and honour, vanity 1025.25
v. can be afforded only by the poor 1025.10
v. cannot be followed but for herself 1025.41
v. cannot dwell with slaves 882.3
v., having slept, gets up more refreshed 1026.19

v. herself is her own fairest reward 1025.52
v. in season is madness out of season 972.9
v. in threadbare cloak is despised 1025.26
v. is bold, goodness never fearful 1025.51
v. is ice-cold 1025.17
v. is most fragrant when incensed, crushed 1025.5
v. is not hereditary 1025.45
v. is roughest way—proves a bed of down 1025.59
v. is the only true nobility 628.2
v. its own reward, vice its own punishment 1026.9
v. itself turns vice, being misapplied 1026.22
v. makes enemies as it condemns opposite 489.28
v. more clearly shown in fine actions than in nonperformance of base ones 1025.4
v. must shape itself in deed 1025.54
v. passes as currency all over the world 1025.23
v. requiring guarding not worth sentinel 1025.27
v., though in rags, will keep me warm 1025.19
v. vivid, separate; like pain, smell 1025.11
v. wouldn't go to such lengths if vanity did not keep her company 1025.35
vice assumes, exploits likeness to v. 1026.12
weakness keeps us to duty, v. gets credit 269.20
what is faith, love, v. alone 328.28
who does not hate vice, does not love v. 1026.21
wickedness is always easier than v. 1048.10
wisdom and v. like two wheels of cart 489.11
wise to make a v. of necessity 617.2
writer is not to illustrate v. 1062.107

**virtue's:** he lives in fame who died in v. cause 330.42
vice often rides in v. chariot 1023.14
who knows his v. name, place, hath none 1025.18

**virtues:** absence of vices adds little to one's v. 1026.16
ambition is often the mother of v. 33.31
for youthful faults ripe v. shall atone 1064.61
frugality is guardian of v. 970.3
great are capable of great vices, v. 399.14
if men were true, what use would v. be 339.27
let your v. spring up around one vice 1023.32
man's v. hold up a torch to his vices 1026.5
men's v. we write in water 305.38
moderation runs through all v. 592.5
our v. are most often but vices disguised 1026.14
search others for their v. 1026.8
social v. are commonly but the virtue of pigs in a litter 151.26
to avoid an occasion for our v. 289.9
v. are all active; life is alert 805.8
v. are v. to those who appreciate them 1025.46
v. lie in interpretation of the time 598.41
v. proud if vices did not whip them 1026.10
we are more apt to catch vices than v. 1023.7
when there are great v., something's wrong 1025.6
where minor vices are discouraged, major v. are lacking 1026.1

**virtuous:** any side can accuse the other and feel v. 250.6
folks who do v. acts in unpleasing way 1025.29
great man need not be v. 399.58
if I am v., about whom should I not care 430.9
if you wish to be singular, be v. 466.1
men grown v. in old age make sacrifice to God of devil's leavings 1025.53
prudent do selves good; v. do to others 749.37
to make men v., make them love their country 671.18
v. man is open to honest men's observation 1025.36
wise are joyful, v., long-lived 502.6

**visible:** true mystery of the world is the v. 45.19

**vision:** human being must suffer as price of v. 939.8
if we had keen v., feeling of life 876.3
men of rare v. are always crucified 561.7
true v. is always twofold 890.5
v. is art of seeing the invisible 1027.8
we love to chew the cud of a foregone v. 812.3
we take limits of v. for limits of world 682.7
your hands are too small, v. muddied 450.4

**visionary:** v. denies truth to self, a liar to others 440.14
v. people are v. partly because of the great many things they don't see 1027.4

**visit:** don't v. the newly wed 749.20

**visiting:** friendship increases in v. friends 426.12

**visitors:** late v. should find time in my face 426.11

**vital:** all that is v. is irrational 778.40

**vitality:** in sorriest desert, human v. still glows 1028.3
v. blunders through predicaments 1028.4
v. shows in the ability to start over 1028.1
when v. runs high, death takes men by surprise 1028.2

**vivacity:** v. is gift of women, gravity that of men 562.1

**vocabulary:** for every man something in v. sticks to him like second skin 612.1

**vocation:** talent is the call of v. 1029.4
test of v. is love of its drudgery 1029.12

**vocations:** v. we wanted to pursue, but didn't, bleed 1029.2

voice: give every man thine ear, but few thy v. 540.4
the v. is a second face 916.4
there's ransom in a v. 891.5
v. soft, low: excellent thing in woman 916.55
void: God made all from the v., but v. shows 3.12
hour of triumph is what brings the v. 839.3
v. yields up nothing 702.81
vote: man without v. is like man without hand 1030.4
no candidate too pallid, issue too remote for questionnaire to analyze our v. 1030.14
straw v. shows which way the hot air blows 756.9
v. for man who promises least 1030.3
v. is most powerful instrument ever devised for breaking down injustice 1030.10
who think one v. does no good will soon think one v. will do no harm 1030.7
voter: apathy of v. is confusion of reformer 1030.9
ignorance of one v. impairs security of all 1030.11
no v. in the world ever voted for nothing 1030.17
political propaganda makes v. feel small 739.2
voters: rulers of democracy are the v. 1030.18
votes: everything good or bad according to v. 649.9
voting: American people deprived of vote by not v. 1030.19
v.: determines stronger side without fight 1030.15
vow: to make v. for life makes self slave 737.18
v. that binds too strictly snaps itself 737.15
vows: ease would recant v. made in pain 737.10
v. made in storms are forgot in calms 737.4
voyage: coming into port determines success of v. 6.1
voyaging: v. no help in finding prosperity 744.7
vulgar: if we can't be moral, we can avoid being v. 394.6
it is v. to use a gold toothpick 1031.2
loud dress worn to impress the v. 957.20
not at once applauses of v. and approbation of wise 716.18
to work upon the v. with fine sense is like trying to hew blocks with a razor 139.3
unsure habitation built on v. heart 675.15
v. man always the most distinguished 1031.1
vulgarity: intemperance is the only v. 266.12
old dandy hated v.; new one appreciates v. 1031.3
vulgarization: ours is an age not of vulgarity but of v. 102.24
vulgarized: there is no idea that cannot be v. 4.1

# W

wade: if thou canst not see bottom, w. not 749.10
wags: world decorates w. with Brussels sprouts 434.31
wait: everything comes if a man will only w. 1033.2
if you w., there will come fair weather 670.14
serene, I w., for my own shall come to me 1033.1
they also serve who only stand and w. 1033.5
waiting: faults of those who keep men w. 759.3
good to hope, it's w. that spoils it 1033.8
half the agony of living is w. 1033.6
how much of human life is lost in w. 1033.3
philosophy of w. upheld by all oracles 1033.4
waking: the w. have one world in common 264.8
walk: can two w. together except they be agreed 560.8
men must w. before they dance 402.16
people think desire to w. is noble 1034.1
walking: he who limps is still w. 279.14
wall: before I built a w. I'd ask what I was walling in or walling out 31.5
something there is that doesn't love a w. 976.1
white w. is the fool's paper 395.1
walls: stone w. do not a prison make 729.5
Wall Street: W. S. has nightmare, whole country has to help get them back in bed again 501.7
walnut: he who plants w. tree expects not to eat of the fruit 1027.2
wanderer: a w. is man from his birth 806.1
wandering: science has imposed necessity for w. 843.39
want: easy to get everything you w. 8.3
humanity too harassed by struggle with w. to struggle with error 618.5
life is a progress from w. to w. 236.24
people who have what they w. 902.2
those in w. are menace, ridden with envy 712.14
to w. for one who comes not 364.2
w. gave tongue and sin awakened 618.3
W. is a growing giant 401.5
w. of a thing is perplexing enough 710.19
we spend days doing what we don't w. 1058.11
what to do is shadow of what we w. to do 224.39
young people, unbridled, just w. 1064.43
wanted: every man w. and none w. much 318.2
wanting: one can refrain from w. what he has not 236.37
wants: eliminate the needless w. of life 695.6

few our real w.; how easy to satisfy them 236.16
he whose real w. are supplied must admit those of fancy 236.23
man should consider he has more than he w. 1004.1
man w. what he is supposed to want 236.11
supplying w. by lopping off desires is like cutting off feet 930.10
what man knows is at war with what he w. 167.4
war: abstract w. is horrid 1035.59
after each . less democracy to save 1035.2
all delays are dangerous in w. 1035.29
all gods dead except god of w. 1035.20
author of w. opens vein, bleeds nation 1035.74
begin w. when you like, stop when you can 548.216
better w. for justice than unjust peace 674.27
boys are the cash of w. 1035.15
bread broken with comrades makes us accept values of w. 1035.87
butter sacrificed because of w. 1035.99
cause of going to w. and avoiding it is same desire 1035.79
cruelty, excitement, lead men to love w. 1035.5
diplomats essential to starting a w. 1035.81
disadvantageous peace better than just w. 1035.34
during w., devil makes more room in hell 1035.41
during w. we imprison rights of man 1035.44
eloquence in politics wins what is won in w. 281.1
every w. is its own excuse 1035.92
fatal to enter w. without will to win 1035.60
great nation has not madness to make w. 658.4
great people face w. rather than purchase base prosperity at price of honor 46.5
historical peoples export idea by w. 443.1
I have seen children starving; I hate w. 1035.83
in civil w., firing line passes through men's hearts 1036.2
in civil w., triumphs are defeats 167.3
in every w. they kill you a new way 131.22
in w. memorial, general gets credit 582.7
in w., science linked with Stone Age cruelties 1042.1
in w.-time a man is called a hero 416.7
just fear of imminent danger is lawful cause of w. 1035.3
laws are silent in time of w. 1035.16
let him who doesn't know what w. is go to w. 1035.95
make w. on men; ladies have long memories 1035.8
man no more prone to w. than he once was 1035.55
mankind must end w. or w. will end mankind 1035.53
men ask outcome of w., not cause 1035.91
men love w. because it allows them to look serious 1035.36
mere absence of w. is not peace 674.18
money is the sinew of love and of w. 596.18
morality is contraband in w. 1035.38
motto of w.: let strong survive, weak die 1035.84
never was good w. or a bad peace 1035.37
no man who witnessed tragedies of last w. can advocate w. 1035.54
old men declare w., but youth must fight 1035.49
one believes in w. if one does not abhor it 1035.62
peace will run till next w. begins 674.30
peace with a cudgel in hand is w. 226.15
permission for w. given by world's mood 1035.46
preparedness for w. best means of peace 226.20
quickest way to end a w. is to lose 1035.73
regarded as wicked, w. has fascination 1035.106
resister of w. can bring peace 658.6
same reason that makes us wrangle with neighbor, causes w. between princes 766.13
sometime no one will come to w. 658.13
the means of w. are sacrifice of many 1035.24
those who praise w. are detestable 1035.82
to call w. the soil of courage 1035.89
to delight in w. is a merit in soldier 1035.90
to lead an uninstructed people to w. is to throw them away 1035.25
vice foments w.; virtue actually fights 1035.100
vigorous, brutal people find w. enjoyable 1035.86
w. affects men as motherhood does women 1035.66
w. and courtesan: slaves of desperation 1035.1
w.: best amusement for our morning meal 1035.22
w. destroys spiritual and material values 1035.31
w. drives away fear, brings bravery to surface 1035.39
w. educates senses, activates will 1035.33
w. expert is man ye niver heerd iv befure 1035.30
w.: game princes seldom win, people never 1035.23
w. has thousand pains, one pleasure 1035.96
w. increases taxes 1035.75
w. is abolished only through w. 1035.63
w. is an emblem of all misery 1035.28

w. is boys flung into a breach 1035.58
w. is but duel on a larger scale 1035.18
w. is cruelty; you cannot refine it 1035.93
w. is like love, it always finds a way 1035.10
w. is not an adventure but a disease 1035.88
w. is politics with bloodshed 705.51
w. is subject to inconstancy of fortune 1035.13
w. is the faro table of governments 1035.76
w. is the product of an earlier corruption 1035.70
w. is the province of chance 1035.19
w. lays open wounds of victorious party 170.18
w. lives inside ourselves 1035.11
w. makes rattling good history 674.11
w. makes victor stupid, loser revengeful 1035.71
w. minds may not regain their balance 1035.21
w. of every man against every man 36.2
w.: political act, political instrument 1035.17
w.: the winner is ultimately defeated 1035.94
w.'s a game which, were their subjects wise, kings would not play at 1035.27
w.'s victims and instruments are human beings 1035.50
way to prevent w. is not by preparing for it 1035.57
we can secure peace only by preparing for w. 226.8
we prepare for w. like precocious giants 1035.80
we think the other side of w. is peace 1035.67
we will not unnecessarily risk nuclear w. 633.8
we've a w., an' a debt, an' a flag 534.24
weapon of w. after next w.: bow and arrow 633.1
when fire and water at w., fire loses 658.16
when rich wage w. it's poor who die 1041.54
when w. in air all learn falsehood 1035.45
you make w. like a lover 582.19
you may be obliged to wage w., but not to use poisoned arrows 1042.3
**warfare:** in guerilla w., each fighter carries his warring country between his toes 1035.35
what madness this, inviting death by w. 1035.98
**warm:** better a little fire to w. us 183.9
cold is agreeable that we may get w. 115.30
halfway w. is better than freezing 548.124
**warmth:** any two human beings can find w. together 787.6
**warning:** take w. by mischance of others 17.51
thorn of experience worth wilderness of w. 319.37
**wars:** because property exists, there are w. 740.9
liberty may do no more than stir up civil w. 534.8
many w. avoided by patience 670.22
no kingdom suffered as many w. as Christ's 123.21
w. are boyish, and are fought by boys 1035.65
w. of opinion are most disgraceful 250.5
we are in an epoch of w. of religion 443.3
we want end of beginning to all w. 496.16
**wart:** if you have a w. on your nose 855.1
**wartime:** dangerous in w. to live as by Gallup Poll 756.4
no working middle course in w. 1035.14
**wash:** those who w. much talk down to those who w. little 135.4
**Washington:** people only leave W. by way of the box 1037.4
W. a city that goes around in circles 1037.1
W. has only politics—and white marble 1037.3
W. has Southern efficiency, Northern charm 1037.2
W. reflex is to throw money at a problem 393.32
W. should not do for the people what they can do for themselves 275.2
**waste:** greedy have extraordinary capacity for w. 401.18
national vice is w. 34.51
that produced in haste goes hastily to w. 409.12
w. is not grandeur 1038.2
**waste-paper:** every one should keep a mental w. basket 402.3
**wastelands:** many people live in ugly w. 292.3
**wastes:** rust w. more than use 444.6
**watch:** we think if we w. game we have taken part 922.6
**water:** earth can conceal nothing from w. 1039.1
expect poison from standing w. 444.2
I fear the man who drinks w. 266.24
smooth runs w. where the brook is deep 734.5
w., not life's need but life itself 1039.2
w. taken in moderation can't hurt anyone 266.61
w. will not slip through miser's grasp 589.9
we know worth of w. when well is dry 1019.8
when w. covers the head, a hundred fathoms are as one 237.10
**water-closet:** character, turn of mind connected with w. 117.27
**water-colour:** amateur painting in w. shows innocent and quiet mind 659.11
**watt:** unhappy home whose master doesn't know difference between w. and ohm 461.4
**way:** better turn back than lose your w. 808.2
strait is the gate, narrow the w. 835.1
there is always best w. to do everything 579.6

**weak:** always see man's w. point in his wife 560.66
evil attracts w. by promise of power 305.21
how shall one so w. become strong 450.6
in a just cause w. beat the strong 109.15
in alliance with strong, w. dependent 1040.7
only w. intent on giving as good as get 933.11
rudeness is w. man's imitation of strength 824.4
spirit is willing but the flesh is w. 1040.1
strong and w. cannot keep company 57.1
the w. feel our generosity as oppression 1040.5
the w. will be driven to the wall 933.15
the w. worship brutal directness 360.10
to be w. is miserable 1040.9
to escape responsibility for failure, the w. engage in grandiose undertakings 1040.6
w. can be terrible trying to appear strong 1040.13
w. man is just by accident 933.8
w. people cannot be sincere 894.13
you w. need someone to hand your life back 1040.14
**weaker:** w. side makes a great noise 766.17
**weakest:** harm comes to the strong from the w. 1040.12
not vain the w. if their force unite 1009.6
w. are the most revengeful 1040.3
**weaklings:** I laugh at w. who think themselves good 1040.11
**weakness:** biological w. is condition of culture 1040.2
man wallows in a woman's w. 576.15
power corrupts the few; w., the many 188.5
some people mistake w. for tact 955.4
who can carp at human w. is held divine 204.53
woman's strength is might of w. 1055.43
**weaknesses:** commit worst w. for those we most despise 1063.5
men more willing to have their crimes known than their w. 798.5
people with no w. are terrible 677.9
w. of many make leader possible 528.10
women strongest when armed with their w. 1055.33
**wealth:** a little beauty is preferable to much w. 70.42
get place and w. with grace 1041.47
get w. when you have it not 1041.42
glory of w. is fleeting; virtue, eternal 1025.50
I glory more in cunning purchase of w. 8.4
if w. waste, wit gives but small warmth 712.39
let there be w. without tears 1041.2
man discovers w. when God asks for gifts 382.38
man's word believed to extent of his w. 993.11
many find w. change, not end, of miseries 1041.56
mighty w. is holiest of our gods 1041.34
people say law but they mean w. 525.20
some gain from w. only fear of losing it 1041.48
standing in community requires w. 1041.66
superfluous w. buys superfluities only 1041.63
the first w. is health 411.5
there is no w. but life 536.100
thirst for w. grows as our fortunes grow 401.14
true w. is not a static thing 1041.49
w. breeds satiety, satiety outrage 1041.61
w. defined by fancies is beyond reach 1041.22
w. is known to be a great comforter 1041.45
w. is the means, people are the ends 1041.35
w. maketh many friends 1041.5
w., poverty: parents of discontent 249.9
w. unused might as well not exist 1041.3
w. with us a moment; only our characters steadfast 1041.25
wherever excessive w., excessive poverty 1041.37
wise man distinguishes felicity from w. 1041.17
with w. one may be lucky but not happy 407.37
without rich heart w. is ugly beggar 1041.18
**wealthy:** when none but the w. had watches they were all good ones 295.24
**weapon:** necessity can turn any w. to advantage 617.14
satire's my w. 838.6
w. is an enemy even to its owner 1042.6
w. of war after next war: bow and arrow 633.1
**weapons:** arm that wields w. must be strong 226.16
he has made his w. his gods 1042.5
new w. beget counterweapons 257.10
**wear:** it is better to w. out than to rust out 10.5
**weariness:** it is w. to keep toiling at same things 1058.38
w. can snore upon the flint 899.19
w. shortest way to equality, fraternity 295.17
**wearing:** no place like home for w. what you like 420.1
**wears:** continual dripping w. away a stone 506.3
**weary:** let us not be w. in well doing 430.4
**weather:** I am like to love if it prove fair w. 178.17
if you wait, there will come fair w. 670.14
many can brook w. that love not the wind 285.9
never content until each makes his own w. 1043.4
no bad w. at all in the country 191.10

there is no such thing as bad w. 1043.3
'tis very warm w. when one's in bed 71.9
w. in towns like skylark in counting-house 1043.5
w. takes pledge, signs it with rainbow 772.1
**wed:** shocking bad thing for a man to w. 560.72
**wedded:** two best days of man's w. life: days when he marries and buries his wife 560.52
w. love, true source of human offspring 560.79
**wedding:** girls have a papier mâché face on w. day 1044.3
many torments lie in circle of w. ring 560.17
**wedlock:** age and w. bring man to nightcap 71.5
w., a padlock 560.29
what is w. forced but a hell 560.103
**wedlock's:** women are angels, yet w. the devil 560.14
**weed:** w. is no more than a flower in disguise 369.2
**weeds:** good garden may have some w. 455.1
**weeks:** w. slide by like funeral procession 372.13
**weep:** better to w. at joy than joy at weeping 1045.10
finer nature goes to w. with beggars 911.6
he does not w. who does not see 85.9
if we could count stars, we should not w. 413.8
it is God's giving if we laugh or w. 407.103
man can do nothing untaught, but w. 981.8
men w. the dead but not passing of youth 600.22
minute to smile, hour to w. in 536.27
one cannot w. for the entire world 692.1
same facts that make one laugh make one w. 524.4
those who w. recover more quickly 524.3
to have me w., you must feel grief 53.61
to w. is to make less the depth of grief 1045.9
w., and you w. alone 524.6
you cannot w. for everyone 953.13
**weeping:** learn w. and gain laughing 911.19
w. may endure for a night 1045.1
**weighs:** busy person never knows how much he w. 10.11
**weight:** American women are obsessed with w. 34.46
just w. is the Lord's delight 103.3
none knows w. of another's burden 656.5
**welcome:** w. is the best cheer 426.13
**welfare:** man errs not that he deems his w. his true aim 865.1
w. state not built for the desperate, but those capable of helping themselves 905.2
we live in w. state which seeks to put floor below but builds no ceiling 34.38
**well:** let us not be weary in w. doing 430.4
study sickness while you are w. 572.5
want thing done w., do it yourself 873.19
we do nothing w. till we cease to think about manner of doing it 921.3
what is w. done is done soon enough 309.1
when things go w., they're still going poorly 17.6
when w., all have advice for the ill 411.20
**well-adjusted:** w. man has learned to hop into the meat-grinder 12.10
**well-being:** sense of w. with us when young 411.3
taste for w. is feature of democratic times 744.19
w. attained little by little 183.24
**well-bred:** w. contradict other people 1053.68
**West:** East is East, W. is W., never the twain shall meet 271.2
East, W. barrier: whites won't give up superiority, colored won't endure inferiority 271.1
W. can teach East how to get living 271.3
**whale:** however big the w., tiny harpoon can rob him of life 398.12
**wheat:** except a corn of w. fall into the ground 198.4
**wheel:** mill w. turns forever 115.5
**wheelbarrow:** w. has marked the path of civilization 984.1
**whim:** pleasure of gratifying w. is very great 1046.1
**whip:** it is not the w. that makes men 248.5
**whipping:** w. is like laudanum, dose must double 760.13
w. never hurts so much as thought of it 760.7
w. renders boys more cowardly or obstinate 760.10
who should scape w. 515.43
**whiskers:** long w. cannot take the place of brains 45.17
**whisper:** trumpet does not more stun than w. teases 916.35
**white:** God is w. 1047.4
how ill w. hairs become a fool and jester 353.26
Negro is superior to the w. race 83.4
no "w." or "colored" signs on foxholes 769.10
of what small spots pure w. complains 677.7
w. man's notion: that he is less savage 1047.5
w. who claim superiority based on skin color injured more than the colored 1047.3
when w. man governs another man, that is despotism 995.19
world is w. no longer, won't be w. again 1047.1
**white-collar:** when w. people get jobs 1059.6
**White House:** in W. H. delay is a decision 724.10
**whiteness:** w.: insurance man's shirt on morning run 1047.2
**whole:** nothing w. that has not been rent 939.55
only one way of seeing: seeing the w. 676.13

**whore:** most men desire a virgin who is a w. 885.7
**whores:** men pay large sums to w. 746.1
**why:** every w. hath a wherefore 108.5
if we have own w. of life, we shall get along with almost any how 569.4
instinct of life falters in man to ask w. 558.31
**wicked:** affliction sometime teacheth w. to pray 717.20
do good even to the w. 430.29
I never wonder to see men w. 886.9
killing to prevent w. makes w. 516.10
man not born w.; gets so, as gets sick 1048.13
more hope in death of good than in life of w. 391.18
no man became extremely w. all at once 1048.11
praises from w. men are reproaches 716.11
there is no peace unto the w. 1048.3
w. cannot fall lower than lowest in you 388.7
w. flee when no man pursueth 403.2
w. is not much worse than indiscreet 1048.7
**wickedness:** a little w. makes muscle 1048.8
man's w. grows by degrees 1048.2
men capable of every w. 1048.6
one's w. may become all men's curse 1048.12
w. is a myth invented by good people 1048.14
w. is always easier than virtue 1048.10
w. of the world is so great 1048.4
**widowhood:** w.: hope that keeps up wife's spirits 560.43
**wife:** always see man's weak point in his w. 560.66
best days of a man's wedded life: days he marries and buries his w. 560.52
bitterest creature: w. who discovers husband's bravery is only bravado 560.11
choose w. rather by ear than by eye 560.41
he knows little who will tell his w. all 560.39
ideal w. any woman with an ideal husband 560.119
if you love w., you will leave her sometimes 883.2
light w. doth make a heavy husband 560.104
man is better pleased with good dinner than when his w. talks Greek 272.19
man should be taller, older, heavier, uglier, and hoarser than his w. 560.56
man's best or worst fortune is his w. 560.40
man's best possession is a sympathetic w. 560.30
never join friend in abuse of horse or w. 203.7
no man knows w. until he has gone with her through fiery trials 560.61
no man worth having is true to his w. 470.14
nothing nobler than when two who see eye to eye keep house as man and w. 560.53
one good w. is a spiritual harem 1055.22
one shouldn't be too inquisitive about one's w. 208.1
only love should rule between man and w. 560.96
rare spoil for man is winning of good w. 560.36
roaring of wind is my w. 616.41
single man with fortune must need a w. 65.1
strife if w. is dissatisfied with husband 885.30
w. and children hostages to fortune 332.4
w. has more power than state over man 560.27
w. in curlpapers is replaced 560.77
w. loves out of duty 560.47
w. takes exact measure of her husband 560.124
when a man steals your w., no better revenge than to let him keep her 470.6
when cheated, w. and husband feel same 470.4
who loves not his w., feeds a lioness 332.30
whoso findeth a w. findeth a good thing 560.6
why not bear a fault in your w. 560.38
worse trouble with a woman who is not a w. 576.51
**wife's:** man's home is his w. castle 420.6
**wild:** fight to save w. beauty is democracy at its best 174.8
those who respect natures of w. animals 41.28
w. colt may become a sober horse 1064.23
w. things are not people 41.13
we treat w. creatures as outlaws 436.1
who will pity any who go near w. beasts 213.1
**will:** art of making a w. is baffling expectation 1051.6
at twenty, w. rules; at forty, judgment 537.7
be there a w., and wisdom finds a way 1049.2
don't make w. before dying for an ideal 440.4
fat kitchen, lean w. 1049.6
good or ill of man lies within his own w. 1049.5
happiness of man is: I w. 576.38
he does his own w. who has no need of another's arm to lengthen his own 233.10
he is unhappy who does thing against w. 636.6
he prays, thy w. be done: but means own w. 717.26
His w., that binds ours, is peace to us 385.22
if can't do what we w., w. what we can 1049.11
if I bind the future I bind my w. 198.37
ill w. goes further now 1035.55
it is natural for the w. to love 76.15
let my w. take the place of a reason 1049.7
man's w. creates the things that paralyze his brain, brutalize his heart 1049.8

not to cultivate the w. depraves the mind 277.26
not Zeus himself can get better of my free w. 860.6
our times worship w. 1049.4
our w. is always for own good 387.11
this free w. business is a bit terrifying 636.1
w. cannot be quenched against its w. 1049.3
w. is from moral sense, self-interest 1049.9
w. is never free, is attached to a purpose 1049.1
we have more ability than w. power 801.4
we learn to curb w. long before sentiments 856.5
wherever one is against w. is prison 729.3
**willing:** all lay load on the w. horse 1050.2
w. mind makes a light foot 1050.4
when a man's w. and eager, god joins in 1050.1
**willingly:** nothing troublesome that we do w. 1050.6
**wills:** our w. and fates do contrary run 1049.10
**wily:** w. mouse that breeds in a cat's ear 90.5
**win:** fatal to enter war without will to w. 1035.60
if you think you can w., you can w. 854.3
to keep demands as much skill as to w. 710.3
to w. a woman one must please her 851.6
when in doubt, w. the trick 170.11
who doesn't hope to w. has already lost 33.25
**wind:** blow, blow, thou winter w. 473.8
east w. an impassive-faced tyrant 1052.3
God tempers the w. to the shorn lamb 748.6
nature sees man control the w., the w. sweep man away 616.1
no w. serves him who voyages to no port 463.5
O w., a-blowing all day long 1052.8
sail, quoth the king; hold, saith the w. 616.29
w. in the grain is caress to spouse 1052.6
w. whirleth about continually 1052.1
westerly w. like monarch gone mad 1052.2
who has seen the w. 1052.5
wild west w., breath of autumn's being 1052.7
**windmill:** w. eternally works to accomplish one end 765.2
**window:** w. is to human being as frame is to painting 428.1
**winds:** substance of w. too thin for human eyes 1052.4
w. long to play with your hair 616.31
**Windsor:** can't make Duchess of W. into Rebecca of Sunnybrook Farm 326.1
**wine:** after w. who talks of war or poverty 266.30
bitterest w. drained from crushed ideals 252.5
bronze is the mirror of form; w., of heart 266.1
every cask smells of the w. it contains 117.26
for a bad night, a mattress of w. 266.59
from w. what sudden friendship springs 266.20
God made only water, but man made w. 266.33
good w. is a good creature well used 266.56
I came upon no w. so wonderful as thirst 266.42
in w. there is truth 266.50
it's hard to hide ignorance over w. 266.26
let us have w., woman, mirth and laughter 700.4
spirit of world not evoked by opium, w. 267.2
too much and too little w. 266.48
w. can make sage frolic, the serious smile 266.29
w. gives man neither knowledge nor wit 266.35
w. is like rain 266.25
w. is only sweet to happy men 266.37
w. is wont to show the mind of man 266.60
w. to gifted bard is mount that races 266.7
when thirsty grief in w. we steep 266.39
with plenty of w., sorrow takes wing 266.47
**wings:** oh that I had w. like a dove 298.1
**winning:** too light w. make the prize light 195.13
w. is shoddy, ignoble, brief 938.21
whoever is w. seems invincible 713.38
**wins:** tragedy of life is that man almost w. 327.3
**winter:** English w. ends in July to begin in August 287.6
every mile is two in w. 848.22
if w. comes, can spring be far behind 425.40
love w., for it is the spring of genius 848.1
only w.-patience can bring the long-awaited spring 670.16
w. changes into stone the water of heaven and the heart of man 848.24
w. comes to rule the year, sullen and sad 848.47
w. instantly becomes an infinite alas 349.2
w. is come and gone, but grief returns 911.52
**wisdom:** a man is wise with w. of his time only 181.10
action should culminate in w. 9.4
be there a will, and w. finds a way 1049.2
calm despair is the essence of w. 800.11
dram of discretion worth a pound of w. 749.13
enemy of w. is the march of events 303.5
fear of the Lord is the beginning of w. 1053.7
fortune had no deity if men had w. 358.23
function of w.: discriminate good, evil 1053.11
gauge growth of w. by loss of ill-temper 1053.50
goodness is born of w. 391.33
goodness without w. accomplishes evil 388.10
it is better to have w. without

learning 1053.13
it is the privilege of w. to listen 1053.34
it requires w. to understand w. 1053.45
kisses are a better fate than w. 519.1
knowledge comes, but w. lingers 1053.64
knowledge is in the head; w., in the heart 1053.29
make learning of books your own w. 529.16
men who love w. should acquaint themselves with many particulars 1053.31
much of w. still acquired by necromancy 979.10
nature never says one thing, w. another 616.40
nine-tenths of w. is being wise in time 1053.56
not by constraint shall you find w. 1053.65
one never loves wisest for their w. 548.165
our happiness depends on w. always 407.104
road to w.: err and err, less and less 1053.30
sad w. of age wells up without sound 646.102
sciences may be learned by rote, w. not 1053.63
self-reflection is school of w. 868.13
sense conforms to world, w. to Heaven 1053.39
short saying oft contains much w. 568.6
some take more care to hide w. than folly 936.6
sum of w. not contained in one language 521.19
terrible is w. that does not profit wise 1053.62
the good have come to w. through failure 391.47
the price of w. is above rubies 1053.6
there is advantage in w. won from pain 340.3
those jealous of w. are so from its lack 1053.41
'tis w. sometimes to seem a fool 353.14
to be a philosopher is to love w. 688.43
to question wise man is beginning of w. 478.11
to realize the unimportance of time is the gate of w. 971.47
to w. belongs intellectual apprehension of eternal things 1053.5
true w. is not departing from nature 616.63
ultimate w. remains locked in a seed 616.9
unlike wines, old and new w. mix admirably 1053.9
w. and virtue like two wheels of cart 489.11
w. appears in all works of creation 616.47
w. at times is found in folly 351.10
w. brings back beliefs of eighteen 1053.61
w. cannot be communicated 1053.32
w. comes alone through suffering 1053.1
w. consists in knowing what to do next 1053.37
w., delightful pastime at other's expense 360.7
w. does not do desperate things 1053.66
w. got not by years but by disposition 1053.53
w. has its root in goodness 1053.17
w. hurts 491.7
w. is a solid and entire building 1053.49
w. is always an overmatch for strength 1053.52
w. is an affair of values, value judgments 1053.36
w. is humble that he knows no more 1053.15
w. is latent in things-as-they-are 777.16
w. is love itself 1053.28
w. is principal thing; therefore get w. 1053.8
w. is social, beauty jealous 1053.38
w.: knowing what's before us in daily life 605.6
w. lost upon the unintelligent 19.27
w. loves the children of men 351.22
w. makes life endurable 939.35
w. must comprise some nonsense for fools 874.2
w. must go with sympathy 953.8
w. of one can rarely make many happy 804.9
w. ofttimes nearer when we stoop than when we soar 1053.70
w. rather buffeted than not listened to 1053.54
w. requires no form 1053.47
w. rises upon the ruins of folly 1053.25
w. seeks how to make us die well 538.45
w. sets bounds even to knowledge 520.50
w. to leech us of ill is daily spun 1053.48
w.: to live greatest number of good hours 502.9
w. treads softly, valuing moments 1065.20
we thought since we had power we had w. 713.8
what use is w. when folly reigns 351.23
who can search out w. 1053.3
who is too lazy to think never attains w. 1053.14
who lacks w. in old age has existed only 646.84
whoever has no patience has no w. 670.19
will and w. are both mighty leaders 1049.4
with the ancient is w. 646.10
youth must study w., old age practice it 1053.57

**wise:** all are w. for others, none for himself 19.13
as we grow old, it is hard to keep w. 646.42
be spacious and w. 522.1
be w. as serpents and harmless as doves 936.3
be wisely worldly, be not worldly w. 910.4
better mad with the rest than w. alone 555.12
better to weep with w. men than laugh with fools 57.21
conversation with w. man better than books 277.48
defer not till to-morrow to be w. 228.2
desire of glory last infirmity even of w. 384.21
fear not the anger of the w. to raise 797.10

fool sees not the same tree a w. man sees 676.1
fortune seldom troubles the w. man 1053.21
god could hardly love and be w. 548.174
he bids fair to grow w. who has discovered that he is not so 1053.55
he is not w. who is not w. for himself 1053.19
heart of the w. man lies quiet like water 1053.10
honor paid w. man good for those honoring 424.4
how prone to doubt, cautious, are the w. 1053.35
in love not w.; when w. not in love 548.176
it is foolish to wish to be exclusively w. 1053.42
it is impossible to love and be w. 548.6
it takes w. man to recognize w. man 1053.71
it's easier to be w. on behalf of others 1053.43
kingdom is embellished by the w. 485.8
latter part of w. man's life is taken up in curing follies of the first 567.18
let w. beware: ignorant hungry for action 471.1
life is a festival only to the w. 1053.16
luck never made a man w. 358.39
men believe none so w. as themselves 1053.33
misfortune of w. better than prosperity of fool 17.22
mouth of w. man is in his heart 1053.23
needs but one w. man and all are w. 57.9
not at once applauses of vulgar and approbation of w. 716.18
profitable if one is w. to seem foolish 137.2
rebuke a w. man, and he will love thee 797.3
riches serve w. man but command fool 1041.21
short w. man preferable to tall blockhead 1053.58
smile with the w., feed with the rich 1041.32
state hurt when cunning pass for w. 923.3
the only wretched are the w. 445.26
the w. commit suicide or drink 1053.67
these are reputed w. for saying nothing 891.31
they who cannot be w. are cunning 197.3
time ripens all things; no man's born w. 971.11
'tis better to be fortunate than w. 358.48
to be free is not necessarily to be w. 1053.69
to be swift is less than to be w. 137.6
to be w. and love exceeds man's might 1053.60
to know others is learned; know self, w. 868.15
tongue of w. man lieth behind his heart 1053.2
useful knowledge makes a w. man 520.23
w. among men bring most sorrow on selves 1053.22
w. are always impatient 1053.27
w. are joyful; virtuous, long-lived 502.6
w. at nightfall praise the day 721.5
w. avoid evil by anticipating it 356.9
w. contradict themselves 1053.68
w. do not stand behind kicking ass 749.36
w. do not venture all eggs in one basket 749.5
w. heart is gods' best gift 282.12
w. man by day is no fool by night 1053.20
w. man can play the fool on occasion 1053.24
w. man changes mind, fool never will 347.4
w. man doth know himself to be a fool 1053.59
w. man hears one word, understands two 1053.72
w. man is very rich, wanting nothing 1053.40
w. man lives as long as he ought, not can 545.7
w. man may be duped as well as a fool 353.7
w. man ridiculous in company of fools 57.12
w. man sings his joy in his heart 407.109
w. man takes the side of his assailants 651.6
w. man to accomplish end may carry foe 1053.51
w. man turns chance to good fortune 114.11
w. man will not dispute with hasty one 51.24
w. men appreciate all men 47.1
w. men are not w. at all times 1053.18
w. men are to bear mistakes of ignorant 269.2
w. men learn by others' harms 353.12
w. men say nothing in dangerous times 213.18
w. never refuse anything to necessity 617.15
we find the w. man only in fragments 677.8
we old have no wits but we think us w. 646.31
when all is well, who cannot be w. 744.16
when ignorance is bliss, 'tis folly to be w. 445.15
**wisecracking:** w. is simply calisthenics with words 1054.27
**wiser:** do men grow w. as they grow older 646.49
to be w. is to be honester 993.7
**wisest:** he that thinks self w. is greatest fool 1053.12
only w. can enjoy what they've got 698.38
w. man is boy grieving that he's grown 450.2
w. men follow own direction 860.7
w. men make fools of selves about women 576.46
w. professed to know he knew nothing 520.46
**wish:** granting our w.: fate's saddest joke 236.32
it would not be better if things happened to men just as they w. 236.20

overtaking a w. discovers folly 850.2
wishes: like shadows, w. lengthen as sun declines 223.15
never further from our w. than when we imagine we possess what we desired 236.14
our inventions mirror our secret w. 198.9
we would be sorry if w. were gratified 236.2
when you love, saved-up w. come out 548.15
wit: advantage of being a w.: gives one greater freedom of playing the fool 1054.29
banalities of a great man pass for w. 67.2
brevity is the soul of w. 1054.33
great fault of a w. is to go beyond mark 1054.19
I have thought so superstitiously of w. 1054.22
if wealth waste, w. gives small warmth 712.39
impropriety is the soul of w. 1054.24
in midst of w. something bitter arises 1054.21
man must have w. to endure it in others 1054.5
men content to be laughed at for w., not for folly 351.21
men never think their w. too little 1054.8
mockery is often result of poverty of w. 814.3
more w. we have, less satisfied with it 1054.1
mother w. worth more than clergy 137.1
one must have enough w. to avoid too much 1054.25
one never loves wittiest for their w. 548.165
people care more for reputation of w. 1054.34
physician must have a certain ready w. 261.9
quality of w. inspires more admiration than confidence 1054.32
true melancholy breeds perfect, fine w. 1004.18
true w. is that which falls on another 1054.17
w. and coin are doubted with threadbare coat 1054.15
w. has a deadly aim 1054.23
w. has truth in it 1054.27
w. in conversation is a quick conception and an easy delivery 185.28
w.: infinite as love, and more lasting 1054.30
w. is a shining quality that few love 1054.6
w. is a treacherous dart 1054.3
w. is salt of conversation, not the food 1054.12
w. is the epitaph of an emotion 1054.26
w. is the sudden marriage of ideas 1054.35
w. knows place is at tail of procession 1054.14
w. makes its own welcome 1054.7
w.: oft thought, ne'er so well expressed 1054.28
w. takes a nation a long time to acquire 1054.9
w. we wish we had spoils w. we have 1054.11
w. would be embarrassed without fools 1054.20
who is a mere w. is only a human bauble 1054.2
wine gives man not knowledge or w. 266.35
wit's: w. an unruly engine, wildly striking 1054.13
witch: w., bitch always dress up for each other 1055.152
within: can men know what is w. them 999.3
our greatest foes are w. 866.3
witnesses: eyes are more accurate w. than ears 890.4
wits: dullness of fool is whetstone of w. 353.27
first-rate collector can collect his w. 159.4
impertinent w. are a kind of universal insect 1054.16
witticism: he who cannot shine by thought, seeks to bring himself into notice by a w. 1054.36
witty: for repute of being w. many lose the credit of being sensible 1054.10
mouth of a w. man is hard until discharge 1054.4
no woman is w. only by the help of speech 1055.139
what is perfectly true is imperfectly w. 1054.18
wives: all are good maids—whence come bad w. 1055.46
few w. so perfect that husbands do not daily repent marriage 560.68
the sky changes when maids become w. 560.106
time turns our loves into corpses or w. 971.59
w. are young men's mistresses 560.3
w. invariably flourish when deserted 470.8
w. not deserted: objects of commiseration 560.74
w. rarely fuss about their beauty 560.83
what makes men indifferent to their w.: they can see them when they please 560.93
woe: how quick old w. follows a little bliss 1004.25
morning after w. surpasses all that rose before 1004.7
teach me to feel another's w. 577.4
the gentlest feeds on another's w. 557.13
when Jove gave us life, he gave us w. 1058.39
wolf: man is a w. to those he does not know 355.6
no matter how much you feed a w. he will always return to the forest 442.18
that man is a w. to man is a libel on the w. 41.12
w. loses teeth, not his inclinations 223.12
whelp of w. must prove a w. at last 415.4
wolves: men not born w., they have become w. 26.9
woman: a sort of bloom [charm] is all a w. needs to have 119.2
a w. moved is like a fountain troubled 1055.132
ailing w. lives forever 889.28
an unreasonable w. cherishes herself most when she is most wrong 1055.104

as a jewel of gold in a swine's snout, so is a fair w. without discretion 1055.10
as soon as w. gets husband, she wants everything else in the world 1055.75
as unjust to possess w. as slaves 710.14
as unto the bow the cord is, so unto man is w. 576.27
at night there is no such thing as ugly w. 626.9
average w. is at the head of something; the average man has to obey orders 576.7
beastliest beast of all is w. 1055.98
beautiful w. and homely w. are perfect 1055.145
beautiful w. is a practical poet 1055.45
better to dwell in corner of housetop than with brawling w. in wide house 560.7
cleverest w. is biggest fool with a man 576.42
confidence still best with w. copes 851.1
courtesy wins w. as well as valor 195.14
did man e'er live saw priest, w. forgive 357.14
distinction for a homely w. to be loved for her character 1055.122
entire being of a w. is a secret 1055.35
every w. is to be had almost any way 851.3
every w. thinks herself attractive 1055.111
fear w. who loves; all else has no value 1055.107
fill a w. with love of herself 195.3
God made rose of what was left of w. 1055.86
happiness of w. is: he wills 576.38
he that tastes w. ruin meets 733.4
hell has no fury like a w. scorned 786.1
how a little love, company improves a w. 1055.52
how many dynasties upset by love of w. 1035.103
I am a w.; when I think, I must speak 1055.133
I hate a w. who thinks of her sewing when she's making love 885.26
I have been a w. for fifty years 1055.60
if a handsome w. allows that another w. is beautiful, conclude she excels her 1055.85
if a w. wants a man, she has to appeal to what is worst in him 576.57
if w. had no existence save in the fiction written by men 1055.154
in argument with men a w. goes by worse 576.35
in new frock, faithful w. imagines a liaison 265.15
last thing w. will consent to discover in man she loves is want of courage 576.9
let no w. beguile your good sense 195.6
little girl without doll as unfortunate as w. without children 121.22
love is emotion w. feels for a poodle 548.147
loveliest in w.: study of household good 560.80
make love to a w. if she is pretty 1055.150
man can deceive a w. by sham attachment 851.7
man is depressed until w. appears 576.14
man is for w. a means to a child 560.91
man is the hunter; w. his game 576.49
man makes her laugh, w. feels protected 1055.9
man married to w. who enjoys spending money must enjoy earning it 1058.40
man must brave public opinion, w. submit 756.21
man takes lifetime to find out about one w. 576.18
man wants great deal here below, w. more 401.27
many a w. hates a man for being a friend to her 576.44
never fair w. but made mouths in a glass 587.8
nightingale runs out of songs before w. runs out of conversation 1055.137
no best w., only comparatively bad 1055.121
no creature so savage as w. 1055.49
no effrontery like that of w. 1055.82
no fouler fiend than w. with ill-bent mind 1055.72
no fury like w. searching for new lover 1055.28
no w. can nourish both clay, daimon in man 576.10
no w. doeth aught without a reason 576.4
no w. hates a man for being in love with her 576.44
no w. is beautiful who can be false 470.12
no w. is handsome by features alone 1055.139
none surpass sick w. in ruling 889.21
old, that's affront no w. can bear 1055.20
one of magnanimities of w. is to yield 1055.77
only chaste w. is one not asked 120.11
only the w. of the world is a w. 1055.63
pretty w. has right to be ignorant 1055.61
pretty w. likes to be asked for her favors 348.9
put man and w. together, they embrace 885.3
she wavers, hesitates: in short she is a w. 1055.126
silliest w. can manage a clever man 353.18
so primal is a w. with the love-madness 1055.15
talk to every w. as if you loved her 955.5
talking is the passion of a w. 1055.89
the w. known only through a man is known wrong 576.2
there is no other purgatory but a w. 1055.8
there is no such thing as an old w. 1055.102
'tis w., w., rules us still 576.36
to leave a w. one must annoy her 851.6
to lose husband worst woe for w. 560.33
to recapture companionship with child and man w. must follow them into world 332.7

tremble to win hand of w. unless win heart 195.5
variability is a virtue of a w. 1055.22
voice soft, low: excellent thing in w. 916.55
w. brings out foolishness in man of sense 576.59
w. can be anything lover would have her be 1055.7
w. cannot forgive man for sacrifices made on her account 576.32
w. careful with face, careless with house 1055.81
w. dish for gods if devil dress her not 1055.135
w. doesn't spend all her time buying things 1055.74
w. doubts everything except compliments 1055.76
w. is a monster without man as principal 576.17
w. is a w., but a good cigar is a smoke 975.7
w. is as old as she looks before breakfast 1055.73
w. is creature who has discovered her own nature 1055.59
w. is man's confusion 576.53
w. is revolution; she destroys and creates 1055.148
w. is so hard upon the w. 1055.142
w. is the daughter of Delay 1055.120
w. is woman's natural ally 1055.51
w. knows profit in matrimony is hers 560.75
w. loves or hates: no middle course 1055.125
w. makes herself fit her clothes 265.8
w. might as well propose 195.7
w., mouse carry tale wherever they go 392.2
w. naturally angry if husband strays 470.3
w. obliges man to secrecy, that she may have the pleasure of telling 849.3
w.: one of nature's agreeable blunders 1055.32
w. only sees what we don't do for her 1055.30
w. ought to be deferential 560.32
w. prefers man without money to money alone 1055.64
w. prefers to lover man who neglects her 552.10
w. scoffs at evidence 1055.56
w. sees only weak points in strong man 576.20
w. seldom loves genius 1055.128
w. seldom writes her mind but in postscript 532.3
w. should always challenge our respect 1055.44
w. smells well when smells of nothing 678.2
w. springs a sudden reproach upon you 1055.146
w. talking about her baby can't stop 865.9
w. that loves to be at the window 851.5
w. understands children better than man 576.39
w. was God's second mistake 1055.110
w. who moralizes is invariably plain 598.54
w. will sacrifice self, given opportunity 1055.96
w. with staff of admirers 348.3
w. without bit of harlot in her is dry stick 885.15
w. would rather talk to man than angel 1055.70
we don't love w. for what she says 1055.97
what a w. wants is what you're out of 1055.68
what but marriage goes wrong for w. 1055.47
what one beholds of w., least part of her 1055.114
what w. dares, when affection stirs her 1055.136
when a w. is twenty, a child deforms her; at forty, he makes her young again 663.8
when w. holds her tongue it means tears 1055.71
who is man enough releases w. in w. 576.40
why does w. want rights; w. has priv'leges 1055.38
with w.: you can love her, suffer for her, or turn her into literature 1055.39
womanly w. is too cynical to dream 562.3
would that we could fall into arms of w. without falling into her hands 1055.11
write what w. says to lover on water 1055.18
**woman's:** forgetting is w. first and greatest art 1055.2
if one is sure of a w. love 548.219
man wallows in a w. weakness 576.15
no is no negative in a w. mouth 784.8
no man has had enough of w. love 575.18
regret is w. natural food 1055.118
there is in every w. heart a spark of heavenly fire 1055.79
to inspire love is w. greatest ambition 1055.103
w. advice is no great thing 19.14
w. desire for revenge outlasts emotions 1055.29
w. game is mediocre where no love, hate 1055.109
w. guess is more accurate than a man's certainty 576.23
w. hopes are woven of sunbeams 1055.41
w. life is history of the affections 1055.78
w. occupations run counter to creative life 1055.90
w. preaching like dog on hind legs 718.10
w. reason is in milk of her breasts 1055.101
w. strength is might of weakness 1055.43
w. vanity makes object of choice her idol 1055.66
when a w. in love she doesn't care two straws for Thou Shalt and Thou Shalt Not 576.31
**womankind:** w. ever a fickle and changeful thing 1055.147

**women:** all w. have Helen in their hearts 1055.153
American w. mortify the flesh 1055.105
amount of undesired sex endured by w. 560.100
as w. grow older they rely on cosmetics 576.37
at first w. love lovers, then love love 1055.87
beautiful in w. is something masculine 562.6
beautiful or ugly w. best flattered for their understandings 1055.21
beautiful w. counted among talents of husbands 576.26
beauty of w. evaporates when they trade independence for domestic happiness 560.22
charming w. can true converts make 683.5
death laughs when old w. frolic 646.85
disposition of w.: when you will, they won't 1055.143
even most foolish w. are wise about men 576.46
fear of w. is basis of good health 65.6
first rule of game: w. can be caught 851.10
God for men, religion for w. 385.21
happiest w., like nations, have no history 1055.40
housekeeping in common is acid test for w. 497.5
I can't count the gold-digging ruses of w. 401.20
if men knew how w. pass the time when they are alone, they'd never marry 1055.67
intimacies between w. go backwards 1055.13
it's hard for w. to get away 420.2
kindness in w., not looks, shall win love 1055.131
kings, w., vines embrace what is nearest 1055.115
love of w. is lovely and fearful 1055.16
love's all in all to w. 1055.48
man's w. folk secretly regard him as an ass 332.20
many w. long for what eludes them 1055.112
men and w. agree only in conclusions 27.9
men are reason w. do not love one another 576.25
men live by forgetting—w. live on memories 576.12
men must work and w. must weep 536.61
most good w. are hidden treasures 1055.116
most w. have all other w. as adversaries 576.5
most w. have small waists, big desires 1055.144
music and w. I cannot but give way to 698.28
nature of w. not to love when we love 1055.19
one must choose loving or knowing w. 1055.88
piety in w. is passion, infirmity, fashion 691.7
relations of men and w. like an equation 576.29
rivalry of w. visited on fourth generation 1055.14
some w. marry houses; it's another skin 428.6
sorrows of w. would be averted could they repress speech they know is useless 1055.42
sweet is revenge—especially to w. 811.6
time, circumstance, narrow views of w. 576.16
to most w. art is a form of scandal 1055.53
ugly w. learn to suppress their whims 1055.54
vivacity is the gift of w. 562.1
w. adore failures 327.25
w. always return to those who love them 576.3
w. and elephants never forget 574.23
w. and men are simply different races 576.30
w. are a decorative sex 1055.149
w. are afraid to be considered only w. 562.5
w. are as roses 1055.134
w. are best index of the coming hour 499.2
w. are eagerly on lookout for any emotion 1055.140
w. are equal because they are not different 1055.55
w. are foolish: God made 'em to match men 576.11
w. are like dreams—never the way you would like to have them 1055.119
w. are like riddles; they please us no longer once we know them 1055.123
w. are like the arts, forced unto none 1055.37
w. are most fascinating between thirty-five and forty 1055.36
w. are one and all a set of vultures 1055.117
w. are poets just by being w. 1055.95
w. are quite unlike men 1055.124
w. are silver dishes into which we put golden apples 885.13
w. are to admire, not understand 1055.27
w. attached, men cured by w.'s favors 576.24
w., calendars good only for a year 1055.138
w. can change name and nation 560.46
w.: can't live with or without them 1055.4
w. consider consequences in love, seldom in resentment 1055.24
w., crabs seem to be coming when going 245.5
w. dare not indulge in romanticism 821.3
w. differ as heaven and hell 576.50
w. don't mock the tears men shed unless they themselves are responsible for them 1055.31
w. dwell in palace of unpalatable truth 1055.92
w., elephants never forget an injury 1055.130
w. enjoy sick talk of one another 1055.50
w. hate revolutionists and like docile men 813.34
w. have a very positive moral sense 1055.1

w. have contempt for woman 1055.108
w. have no sense of the abstract 1055.62
w. have no wilderness in them 1055.12
w. have simple tastes 1055.99
w. kissing resemble fighters shaking hands 1055.100
w., like Cape Hatteras, are enormously dangerous and hence enormously fascinating 576.34
w., like flames, have a destroying power 1055.26
w., like princes, find few real friends 1055.91
w. like silent men; think they listen 576.1
w. like to be a man's last romance 576.58
w. like w. fine 1055.93
w. love flattery from high opinion of themselves 346.21
w. lust to be misunderstood 1055.129
w. make new experience an ornament 319.44
w. marry to be in hub of things 560.9
w., melons, should be chosen by weight 637.6
w. never confess sincerely 1055.57
w. never forgive those who miss opportunity 851.13
w. never reason and thus are seldom wrong 1055.65
w. not so young as they are painted 189.1
w. only willing when you compel them 885.12
w. overcome men by policy, not reason 576.28
w. prefer love to luxury 1055.141
w. rarely look into themselves 1055.127
w. see without any wish to act 676.5
w. singly do a good deal of harm 1055.23
w. speak because they wish to 576.22
w. speak truth as they think men like to understand it 991.71
w. strongest when armed with their weaknesses 1055.33
w. take too little pains to please men 576.43
w. think it their business to spend money 576.47
w. upset everything 576.48
w. use intelligence to prop up intuition 1055.34
w. want mediocre men 576.33
w. wish to be loved simply for themselves 1055.3
w. won't or can't do otherwise than lie 1055.17
w. would make less failures in business 576.55
w. would rather be right than reasonable 1055.106
what w. like to give, they love to be robbed of 851.11
with w., the heart argues, not the mind 1055.5

**women's:** w. bodies shaped to bear children 663.34
w. hearts are like old china 549.9
w. words, light as doomed autumn leaves 1055.113

**wonder:** philosophy begins and ends in w. 688.48
to w. is to begin to understand 1056.3
w. is foundation of all philosophy 688.23
w. is the basis of worship 1056.1
w. is the seed of our science 1056.2

**wonders:** we carry with us the w. we seek without 852.3

**wood:** w. ten years in water will never become a crocodile 116.1

**woodland:** w. in color is awesome as a forest fire 988.2

**woods:** how much we are the w. we wander in 852.25

**word:** ashamed of my emptiness said w. to work 9.36
best way to keep w. is not to give it 737.11
break w. if you do worse to keep it 737.5
honest man's w. good as his bond 423.1
if people have no w. for something, either it doesn't matter or it matters too much 1057.11
isn't everyone consoled by a simple w. 1057.32
man is seldom better than his w. 117.1
man's w. believed to extent of wealth 993.11
no w. was ever as effective as a pause 891.35
one can add a w., never withdraw one 916.25
suit action to w., the w. to action 894.21
Thy w. is a lamp unto my feet 78.1
to persuade, trust w., not argument 683.3
truth comes with final w.; and final w. gives birth to its next 991.128
w. and stone cannot be called back 505.7
w. carries far, deals destruction 1057.6
w. is dead when it is said, some say 1057.8
w. isn't same with one writer as another 1057.31
w. preserves contact 916.41
w. spoken in due season, how good is it 972.1
when thing itself missing, must supply w. 1057.27
wise man hears one w., understands two 1053.72

**words:** acts and w. are wee part of a life 812.5
articulate w. are harsh clamor, dissonance 1057.12
buffaloes held by cords, man by his w. 1057.25
comprehending much in few w. 96.1
does not matter what men say in w. 210.31
false w. infect the soul with evil 329.41
gold does more with men than w. 97.3
hard w. bruise the heart of a child 121.29
house of shining w. to be my immortality 702.96

how forcible are right w. 816.2
I hate false w. and seek those that fit 1057.21
I have withdrawn my w. too late 785.4
in good writing w. and things are one 1062.32
it's strange that w. are so inadequate 1057.9
less disputes in world if w. taken for signs of ideas, not for things themselves 1057.23
lofty w. cannot construct an alliance 245.6
man determines what is said, not w. 916.61
man does not live by w. alone 1057.38
meanings receive dignity from w. 1057.29
men are ready to suffer anything but w. 203.16
men of few w. are the best men 96.10
men's w. hardly signify their thoughts 346.19
most moving moments find us without w. 891.19
oaths are but w., and w. but wind 635.3
only w. can give us a sense of purpose 1057.15
our life is crushed by the weight of w. 1057.33
our thoughts are unclear until put into w. 1057.4
perfumed and gallant w. make ears belch 346.1
pleasant w. are the food of love 916.45
proper w. in proper places make style 935.22
saddest w. are: it might have been 505.13
soft w. are hard arguments 683.7
soft w. like roses put in muskets 438.19
some things not totally expressible in w. 490.9
things diminished when expressed in w. 1057.24
thought flies, w. go on foot 1062.46
thought itself needs w. 1057.3
time and w. can't be recalled 669.12
to teacher of languages, world a place of w. 521.4
tongue of man is twisty, plenty of w. 521.10
w. are healers of the sick temper 752.1
w. are pegs to hang ideas on 1057.2
w. are really a mask 1057.13
w. are the great foes of reality 1057.7
w. are the small change of thought 1057.35
w. are the weak support of indifference 548.32
w. are thread to string our experiences 1057.17
w. are wise men's counters, fools' money 1057.14
w. calculated to catch everyone may catch no one 472.6
w. can sting but silence breaks the heart 891.17
w. change meanings and meanings, w. 1057.30
w. change us, socialize or unsocialize us 1057.37
w. fall on picture like birds of prey 1057.36
w. half reveal, conceal the soul within 1057.40
w. have no language for secrets of love 548.91
w. have users, but users have w. 1057.18
w. have weight, sound and appearance 1057.26
w., like money, are useless unless in use 1057.5
w. may be deeds 1057.1
w. obscure if they do not aid vision 1057.19
w. pay no debts 219.14
w. should be intense pleasure 1057.41
w. should be weighed and not counted 1057.42
w. stand for ideas in mind of user 1057.22
w. the happy say are paltry melody 891.4
w. without thoughts never to heaven go 717.29
we find w. for things already overcome 1057.28
we leave school filled only with w. 277.22
we must translate w. into facts 1057.16
where w. abound sense is rarely found 1057.34
worst sickness: w. that to be kind must lie 517.1
you can stroke people with w. 1057.10

**work:** all w. is empty save when there is love 1058.31
all w. of man is as the swimmer's 679.2
any w. looks wonderful except what I do 861.2
best preparation for good w. tomorrow is to do good w. today 1058.41
blessed is he who has found his w. 1029.3
cessation of w. not accompanied by cessation of expenses 807.1
day's w. is still to do 1058.29
efficient laborer will not crowd his day with w. 1059.7
every man's w. is a portrait of himself 53.16
everything under the sun is w. 1058.12
greatest reward is to have w. acclaimed 204.35
happiness is sweet exhalation of w. 1058.35
hardest w. is to go idle 444.19
he that can w. is king of something 1058.14
he who considers his w. beneath him will be above doing it well 1058.15
I like w., sit and look at it for hours 1058.46
if men can invent machines that put men out of w., men can put men back to w. 1002.2
if you w. by the job, hours are scourges 1059.8
if you want w. well done, select busy man 10.12
in w., reward added makes pleasure greater 673.5
it's necessary to w., even from despair 1058.3
life's best prize is chance to w. hard 1058.59
love, children, w.: sources of contact 502.23
man unable to find w. is saddest sight 1002.1
man's w. is supplement to himself 1058.6

many could make life seem longer with w. 1058.52
men must w. and women must weep 536.61
men rightly occupied derive amusement from w. 1029.10
minds give way unless we mix w. with play 697.7
much w. merely a way to make money 596.38
no fine w. without toil and doubt 1058.5
nothing seen, heard will reach mind concentrated on w. 1058.58
only thing that a man can do eight hours a day is w. 1058.28
people w. greater part of their time 1058.32
prosperity takes w. away from us 744.13
rightly done task is world's w. 1058.71
six days shalt thou do all thy w. 829.2
there is always w. for those who will 1058.51
those who w. much do not w. hard 1058.67
to crush a man give him useless w. 1058.18
to w. is better than to renounce 10.3
to w. is to pray 1058.7
to w., live, die hard and go to hell 414.10
too much w., energy kill a man 310.5
w. brings inspiration 483.5
w. expands to fill time available 1058.56
w. is not the curse, but drudgery is 1058.4
w. is prayer, also stink 1058.44
w. is w. if ye're paid to do it 1058.20
w. spares us evils: boredom, vice, need 1058.69
w. well done invests doer with a certain haughtiness 1058.24
w. with whole heart and you will succeed 1058.42
what is w.? what is not? perplexes wise 1058.8
when w. is a pleasure, life is a joy 1058.34
while at w. or play it's fun not to feel you should be doing other 896.1
while executing any w., we are preparing for another 1058.36
who invented w. and bound free spirit down 1058.48
who pays beforehand has w. ill done 673.6
who will not w. according to his faculty 1058.13
**worker:** standardized w. safeguard of order 1059.3
**workers:** the stupid make up for it by being better w. 934.2
**workhouses:** even w. have their aristocracy 773.4
**working:** when I am w. I know nothing 579.4
**workman:** bad w. never gets a good tool 461.3
bad w. quarrels with the man who calls him that 461.1
no w. may both work well and hastily 409.2
**workmanship:** instinct of w. will take care of honesty 198.23
**works:** all w. conceived in solitude 908.28
every man is son of his own w. 860.2
faith without w. is dead 328.5
my nature is subdued to what it w. in 1058.62
**world:** as if some lesser god had made the w. 455.9
busyness stamp of w. which does not see 10.2
chess-board is the w. 616.38
childish w. pleased with each new revolution or constitution 813.10
do well and right, let w. sink 391.24
feet in own country, but eyes survey w. 190.4
few persons with high aim and great powers could rule w. 440.3
foolishness excommunicates the w. 351.16
God: a word invented to explain the w. 385.44
had we but w. enough, and time 851.9
I am a citizen of the w. 190.2
I count w. not an inn, but an hospital 1060.2
I have not loved the w., nor the w. me 1060.4
I miss when I hit at the w. 1060.21
if all pulled one way, w. would keel over 27.10
in remaking w. we violate kinship of nature 292.4
in the morning we carry the w. like Atlas; at night it crushes us flat 537.2
in youth, one believes w. began with him 1064.26
it is a folly to try to improve the w. 783.28
knowledge of the w. acquired in w. 319.7
look on w., read truth in her fair page 991.10
many come into, go out of w., ignorant 445.25
mind creates the w. about us 583.7
mind has transformed the w. 583.22
more we get out of w., the less we leave 174.10
most incomprehensible thing about the w. is that it is comprehensible 1060.9
my country is w.; countrymen, mankind 98.6
no better deliverance from w. than art 53.55
nonexistence of w. as possible as existence 1060.19
once w. has used us ill, it continues with less ceremony, as men do a whore 546.6
real w. is not easy to live in 777.7
roam abroad in w. and take its enjoyments 985.31
see a w. in a grain of sand 616.8
see the whole w. with fresh eyes 58.8
step on thin crust of w. with distrust 1060.23
the w. is but a school of inquisition 154.9
there is the w. to live in 98.3
this is hard w. where mistakes paid for in full 297.14
this w. cannot explain its difficulties without assistance of another 412.1
this w. is still a miracle 1060.6
this w. was formed to infuriate us 1060.32
to him who looks on the w. rationally 1060.17

to succeed in w. be wise using pronouns 594.10
visible w. only an atom in nature 1010.9
w. a comedy if men think; tragedy, if feel 1060.33
w. a volume larger than libraries in it 1060.16
w. an existence between two nonentities 536.102
w. born anew for him who takes it rightly 723.17
w. credits what is done, is cold to all that might have been 711.8
w. ends not with a bang but a whimper 1060.10
w. exists in your eyes—your conception 1060.12
w. full of nothing but beasts of prey 26.1
w. goes on because some men believe in it 1060.24
w. is a bride, never bound to anyone 1060.14
w. is a bundle of hay 1060.5
w. is a fine place, worth fighting for 1060.18
w. is a great volume, man the index 1060.7
w. is a neighborhood before a brotherhood 1060.20
w. is a thing we must either laugh at or be angry at 1060.26
w. is an old woman 1019.3
w. is bad, but not hopeless 1060.8
w. is for beasts to inhabit, man to study 778.4
w. is full of simpletons and madmen 555.11
w. is gambling-table; all lose in long run 1060.3
w. is hard to love, but we must love it 1060.31
w. is his who has money to go over it 985.16
w. is like a map of antipathies 720.9
w. is right, but you have to be kicked about a little to convince you 319.57
w. is round: end may be beginning 74.11
w. is sick for lack of the elemental 174.1
w. is so full of a number of things 1060.28
w. is too much with us 102.39
w. is white no longer 1047.1
w. kept power prisoner, gave love freedom 713.49
w. loved man when he smiled; became afraid of him when he laughed 523.26
w. owes onward impulses to men ill at ease 735.8
w. saved by disinterested men in it 1014.5
w., terrible in mass, pitiable in units 1060.15
w. would perish were all men learned 842.15
we do not make w. of our own 485.4
we milk cow of the w. 1060.34
we read w. wrong and say it deceives us 1060.29
what's wrong with this w. is, it's not finished yet 1060.11
when w. clowns, something else than comic 1035.85
whole w. thinks and governs 393.51

**world's:** w. curriculum doesn't include Latin and Greek 277.49

**worldly:** be wisely w.; be not w. wise 910.4
w. people rarely learn anything new 910.3

**worlds:** so many w. are at our disposal 53.101
so many w., so much to do 711.7
w. on w. rolling from creation to decay 983.20

**worm:** engineers, physicists, cannot create a w. 960.13
fate of w. shows danger of early rising 71.1
w., your clan will pay me back 218.97

**worries:** freedom from w., surcease from strain, are illusions 530.10
w. go down better with soup than without 43.15

**worry:** rather w. without need 749.2

**worship:** all men w. money 596.60
no liberty on earth if men w. tyrant above 790.37
so long as men w. them, Caesars and Napoleons will rise, make them miserable 995.14
where it is a duty to w. the sun 1061.5
wonder is the basis of w. 1056.1

**worst:** there is so much good in the w. of us 203.14
to fear the w. oft cures the worse 356.11
w. is not so long can say "this the w." 17.55
way to the better exacts look at the w. 458.4

**worth:** beauty dies of beauty, w. dies of w. 968.61
everything is w. what purchaser will pay 1019.15
man's w. no greater than w. of ambitions 33.23
men understand w. of blessings when lost 1019.14
outside show poor substitute for inner w. 45.1
slow rises w. by poverty depressed 712.29
so much is a man w. as he esteems himself 862.10
we know w. of water when well is dry 1019.8
when fight begins within self, man has w. 167.1

**worthy:** difficult to make man miserable while he feels w. and claims kindred to God 862.7

**wound:** history of soldier's w. beguiles its pain 939.47
search not a w. too deep 953.5

**wounded:** w. deer leaps highest 939.9

**wounds:** w. cannot be cured without searching 474.2
w. heal and become scars; but scars grow 474.12
we unbind old w. to prove our past bravery 646.78

**wrath:** background of w. lies in every man 39.10
be swift to hear, slow to w. 164.3

let not the sun go down upon your w. 39.8
the soft answer turneth away w. 164.1
tigers of w. are wiser than horses of instruction 39.9
**wretched:** w. are fortunate: they yearn for happiness 236.18
w. reflect either too much or too little 1004.26
where two, one cannot be w., other not 1004.9
**wretchedness:** hardly possible to exaggerate man's w. 1004.31
**wrinkles:** w.: service stripes in campaign of life 324.2
when grace is joined with w. 646.55
within I find not w. but unspent youth 646.27
**write:** bad book as hard to w. as good book 91.49
better to be able neither to read, w. than to be able to do nothing else 277.36
difficulty of literature is not to w., but to w. what you mean 1062.102
having imagination, it takes longer to w. 1062.1
i never think at all when i w. 1062.70
it is the glory, merit of some men to w. well, and of others not to w. at all 1062.62
man may w. at any time 1062.54
man who can w. great works is still a man 399.48
multitude w.; why no work of worth 1062.22
no man can w. unless a humanitarian 1062.37
no one can w. about anything that happened to him after he was twelve 1062.95
no one who cannot limit himself can w. 1062.13
nobody can w. life of a man but friends 79.6
some speak well and w. badly 916.47
the best you w. will be best you are 1062.104
to w. clear style, be clear in thoughts 935.8
to w. is to become disinterested 1062.20
we w. frankly, "modify" before we print 725.7
when one can read, why write 91.19
who can't w. grammerly better shut up shop 396.6
who does not expect a million readers should not w. a line 1062.44
who would w. and can't w. can review 204.32
you have to be hurt before you can w. 939.16
you w. because you've got something to say 1062.39
**writer:** developed w. reminds us of no one 1062.68
duty of w. to shock 1062.53
every great w. is a w. of history 1062.64
every great w. must create the taste by which he is to be relished 1062.111
good w. is not per se good book critic 204.6
great w. finds style in his soul 935.6
if you would be a w., write 1062.36
in Australia one explains what a w. is 1062.28
period tells w. to stop 935.14
thought flies and words go on foot; therein lies all the drama of a w. 1062.46
tragic w. must believe in man 980.9
w. does not resign himself to loneliness 1062.74
w. is Faust of today; seems semi-mad 1062.84
w. is man alone with English language 1062.52
w. is more concerned to know than to judge 1062.72
w. is simple-minded, a storyteller 1062.19
w. lives in state of astonishment 1062.94
w. must never be unfaithful to readers 1062.8
w. needs experience, observation, imagination 1062.38
w. needs no audience other than the few 1062.106
w. ought to know thoroughly one man at least 1062.24
w. unfair to himself when unable to be hard on himself 1062.81
w. who loses self-doubt should stop 1062.25
w. writes in order to teach himself 1062.58
we think w. best able to express suffering 1062.100
word isn't the same with one w. as another 1057.31
your business as a w. is not to illustrate virtue 1062.107
**writer's:** sin is the w. element 1062.75
w. greed is appalling 1062.11
**writers:** clear w. do not seem so deep as they are 1062.65
don't listen to w. talking about writing 1062.48
fame is promised w. who can offer successive generations a renewed substance 1062.42
humorous w. are responsive to hopeless, uncouth concatenations of life 434.22
many w. punctuate exactly, have no point 935.19
only impeccable w.: those who never wrote 1062.47
subjunctive brings all w. to shame 396.4
w. wish not to be studied but read 91.50
**writes:** man tormented by his bad actions is type that most often w. about himself 403.14
mediocre mind thinks it w. divinely 1062.60
who w. to himself w. to eternal public 1062.35
**writing:** admiration of fine w. is in proportion to its real difficulty and apparent ease 1062.26
book w. makes horse racing look solid 1062.101
good w. is product of someone's neurosis 1062.103

in good w. words and things become one 1062.32
incurable itch for w. besets many 1062.57
last thing one settles in w. a book 1062.83
no w. is more apt to miscarry than humour 1062.3
people won't realize w. is craft 1062.88
secret of good w. is sound judgment 1062.51
take away w., you take away glory 384.3
there is no royal path to good w. 1062.108
to start w. about your life is to stop living it 62.6
true ease in w. comes from art not chance 1062.87
two w. the same book: each believes he gets all worries, half royalties 187.1
w., at its best, is a lonely life 1062.49
w. comes more easily with something to say 1062.6
w. has laws, just as painting does 1062.21
w. is a vocation of unhappiness 1062.96
w. lonely substitute for conversation 1062.7
w. maketh an exact man 1062.10
w. of oneself one should show no mercy 62.1
w. rapidly does not result in w. well 1062.92
when I am happy I live and despise w. 1062.98
when w. is good, everything is symbolic 1062.82

**written**: so much already w. about everything 520.66
what is w. without effort is in general read without pleasure 1062.56

**wrong**: better to suffer w. than do it 474.8
forgetting a w. is mild revenge 474.7
habit of not thinking a thing w. 783.32
he who is w. fights against himself 297.16
if everyone is w., everyone is right 297.22
if one does w., best to do it pursuing power 1063.9
man owning he has been in the w. is wiser to-day than he was yesterday 297.33
man should go strong agin w. in abstract 475.9
may I be w., for right are not young 297.12
men look for w. even in the righteous 257.13
no peace from acquiescence in w. 46.6
nobly w. more manly than meanly right 628.6
protest you're right: you'll be w. 816.27
terrible to speak well and be w. 757.14
they ne'er pardon who have done the w. 357.5
they say you are on w. road, if it is yours 466.7
those fond of setting things to rights have no objection to seeing them w. 783.16
those who are absent are always w. 2.5
to do a great right, do a little w. 816.21
to go beyond is as w. as to fall short 310.2
truth forever on scaffold, w. on throne 991.79
w. enmeshes him from whom it begins 1063.17
w. is deep, clear, and absolute 475.15
w. is that against my constitution 816.9
w. is w., no matter who does, says it 671.12
w. must not win by technicalities 525.1
we are conscious someone w. when w. concerns us 297.29
we condemn w. when it costs us nothing 816.11
we go right enough if we go w. together 976.2
what is divine purpose in putting us into conditions in which so many go w. 305.22
who has much to do will do something w. 86.7
you cannot do w. without suffering w. 1063.7

**wrongdoer**: for a w. to be undetected is difficult 1063.8
w. cannot do wrong without hidden will of all 1063.11
w. wrongs himself 1063.18

**wrongdoing**: repent, do not brood over your w. 793.7

**wronged**: since I w. you, I have never liked you 474.23

**wrongs**: everyone suffers w. which have no remedy 474.9
he that w. his friend w. himself more 474.25

**wrote**: Narcissus never w. well nor was a friend 869.3
only a blockhead ever w. except for money 1062.55

# Y

**Yankee**: Y., when set on a thing, will not let go 34.15

**year**: drop last y. into silent limbo of past 624.1
looking forward into an empty y. 624.5
moments make the y. 989.17
y. is going, let him go 624.6

**year's**: changing y. plan proclaims mortality to man 848.23
y. end is neither an end nor a beginning 624.2

**years**: count man's y. when nothing else to count 646.25
it is the life in your y. that counts 545.12
our y. glide silently away 646.52
passing y. steal one thing after another 223.4
y. between fifty and seventy hardest 580.8
y. following y. steal something every day 971.42
y. like great black oxen tread world 971.68

**yes:** to say y. you must sweat, roll up sleeves 502.1
y. and no are soon said 96.6
y. is the password to utopia 502.3
**yesterday:** man's y. may ne'er be like his morrow 115.34
mortgaged to y., we cannot use today 669.10
to disdain today is to misunderstand y. 723.18
today is like y. 1064.57
we are but of y. 983.3
y. is not ours to recover 366.17
**yesterday's:** today is y. pupil 723.13
**yesterdays:** all our y. are summarized in our now 723.1
**yield:** y. to all and you will soon have nothing to y. 46.1
**you:** y. are, when all is done, just what y. are 442.11
**young:** advice of elders to y. unreal 19.17
all things are made y. with y. desires 848.44
animals disarmed by caresses to their y. 663.28
better to be y. June-bug than old bird 1065.34
crab instructs y.: walk straight ahead 308.5
denunciation of y. necessary to old 646.96
errors of y. men are ruin of business 297.1
experience claimed exclusively by y. 319.9
for the y. things move so fast 115.28
growing old is dying y. 646.72
if we're not foolish y., we're foolish old 351.4
love, with the y., is heartless 548.43
man may be y. in years but old in hours 319.2
man when y. is sweet but without strength 1065.7
may I be wrong, for right are not y. 297.12
no y. man believes he shall ever die 1064.27
one must, when y., consider old age 1065.14
pay attention to y., make them good 1064.55
the y. fancy their follies are mistaken by the old for happiness 1065.6
the y. have nothing to say 1065.3
the y. man reveres men of genius 374.15
those who love the y. best stay y. longest 1064.19
to remain y. one must change 115.8
when a man notices he is no longer y. 580.16
while y., idea of death, failure, intolerable 1064.15
wish to teach sad y. generation the courage of their confusions 994.5
women are not so y. as they are painted 189.1
y. are themselves only with timidity 1064.40
y. branch takes on all bends it's given 981.2
y. can shock and keep old up to date 1065.29
y. climber up of knees 121.28
y. faithful to individuals; old, to types 553.2
y. feel tired at the end of an action 338.2
y. folk silly, old folk cold 1065.10
y. girls are chatelaines of truth 383.3
y. know everything 1065.37
y. man must let his ideas grow 441.19
y. man never feels that he is mortal 1064.35
y. man: so strong, mad, certain, and lost 1064.59
y. man so wild he is insufferable 1065.12
y. man who has not wept is savage 1065.26
y. men fitter to invent than to judge 1064.4
y. men regard elders as senile 1064.1
y. men soon give, soon forget, affronts 486.1
y. men want to be faithful, and are not 470.17
y. people get mental arteriosclerosis 1064.30
y. people thoughtless as a rule 1064.28
y. people, unbridled, now just want 1064.43
y. permanently in state like intoxication 1064.3
y. suffer from cautiousness of the old 1065.36
y. think old fools, old know y. are fools 1065.4
y. today given education, not upbringing 277.19
y. true, not resounding, instruments 1064.10
y. venerate and despise without nuances 1064.45
**younger:** happier when poorer, but were also y. 1064.36
to decry y. generation dates a man 372.14
**youngster:** y. who does not know what he is good at 1.7
**yourself:** be y. and think for y. 873.12
for impenetrable shield, stand inside y. 31.10
respect y. if you wish others to do so 862.4
**youth:** affected y. is seeking a face of his own 1064.54
age looks with anger on temerity of y. 1065.16
age not as qualified to instruct as y. 1065.33
allowances made for illusions of y. 1065.30
American ideal is y., handsome, empty 1064.42
American y. attributes importance to arriving at driver's-license age 34.43
Americans loved y., now they worship it 1064.5
Americans try to perpetuate y. 34.55
better eat gray bread in y. than in age 749.31
better waste y. than do nothing with it 1064.13
give me back my y. again 1064.25
how beautiful is y. 1064.38
I go to school to y. 1064.22
immature is the love and hatred of the y. 1064.44
impetuous y. longs only for the dazzling 1065.24
in early y. we are like children in a theatre 1064.53
in y., one believes world began with him 1064.26
in y. one has tears without grief 1065.25
in y. we clothe ourselves in rainbows 1064.18

it is an illusion that y. is happy 1064.39
life is thorny; y. is vain 39.13
life should begin with age, end with y. 1065.35
man laments y. more than imprudences 646.100
manners make fortune of ambitious y. 559.9
may return to birthplace, but not y. 669.6
must not take faults of y. into old age 646.41
nature, in denying us perennial y. 567.16
not possible for civilization to flow backward while there is y. in the world 1064.33
now y. are fallen from their fear 1065.17
our y. we can have but to-day 1064.8
rashness is the error of y. 567.3
recovering the spirit of y., one's indignation would be for what one has become 160.3
riotous y., growing age will correct 1064.31
seeds of repentance are sown in y. 793.4
sign of passing y.: birth of fellowship 567.22
thoughts of y. long, long thoughts 95.7
time is the rider that breaks y. 971.28
tragedy of y. is that the young are thrown with adults they do not respect 1064.41
unwept, y. drops its petals one by one 600.22
we can build our y. for the future 1064.52
what one knows is, in y., of little moment 529.1
with a smile we should instruct our y. 959.20
within I find not wrinkles but unspent y. 646.27
world fails to impart joy y. forbodes 247.1
y. believes it will get away with anything 1065.2
y. blows through sky, does not ask why 1064.7
y. even in sorrows has own brilliancy 1064.29
y. forgives itself nothing 1065.28
y. gets together materials to build a bridge to the moon 252.6
y. has an ideal – y. itself 1064.2
y. immortal; only elderly grow old 1065.22
y. is a blunder; old age a regret 537.5
y. is a fever of the mind 1064.37
y. is cause, effect is age 580.5
y. is first victim of war 1035.4
y. is full of pleasance; age, of care 1065.27
y. is incautious; wisdom treads softly 1065.20
y. is past putting a leg forward 971.5
y. is season of hope in the sense that our elders are hopeful about us 1064.17
y. is the season of credulity 113.11
y. is the time to flash across the world 1064.56
y. is to be regarded with respect 1064.12
y. measures right by world opinion 1065.15
y. needs pretexts, not reasons, for living 1064.47
y. of a nation are trustees of posterity 1064.16
y. of America is their oldest tradition 34.77
y. of an art is its most interesting period 53.17
y. smiles without reason 1064.58
y. thinks that all must heed its prayer 1064.34
y. want to defy at not too heavy cost 1064.14
y. without fire is followed by old age without experience 1065.5
**youth's:** alas, that y. manuscript should close 1064.46
y. the season made for joys 1064.24
**youths:** excesses of our y. are drafts on old age 1064.11

# Z

**zeal:** have z. to better thyself, then neighbour 458.6
too much z. offends where indirection works 683.4
z. has more pride than charity 1066.1
z. will do more than knowledge 1066.3
z. without knowledge is fire without light 1066.2
**Zen:** Z. is a way of liberation 1067.1
**zest:** what hunger is to food, z. is to life 511.8
z. is the secret of all beauty 511.2

# INDEX OF CATEGORIES

# INDEX OF CATEGORIES

With Cross-References